Microsoft WORD 2013

COMPREHENSIVE **ENHANCED EDITION**

Microsoft® WORD 2013

COMPREHENSIVE

ENHANCED EDITION

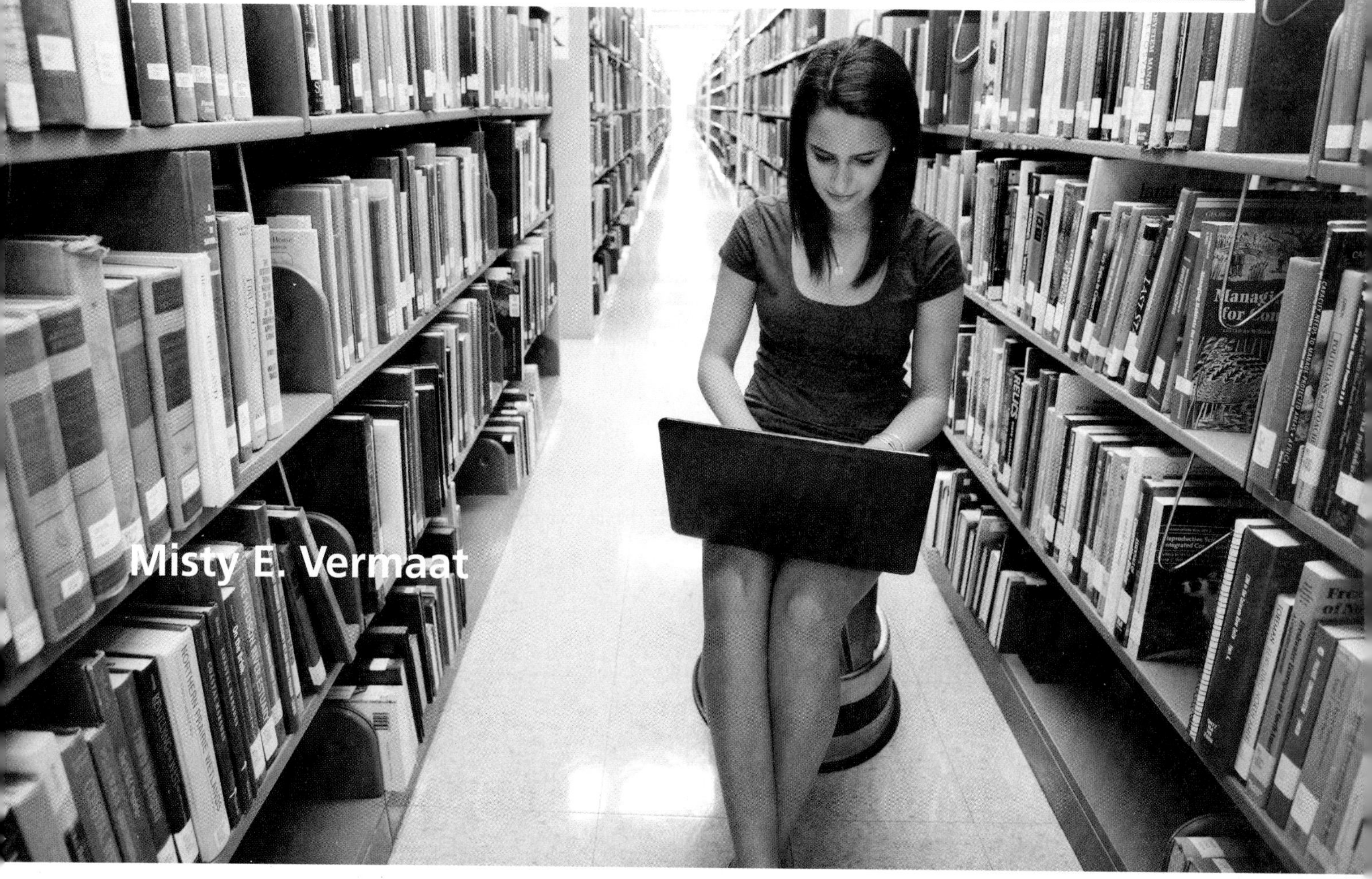

Misty E. Vermaat

Australia • Brazil • Japan • Korea • Mexico • Singapore • Spain • United Kingdom • United States

Microsoft® Word 2013: Comprehensive Enhanced Edition
Misty E. Vermaat

Product Director: Kathleen McMahon

Senior Director of Development: Marah Bellegarde

Senior Product Team Manager: Lauren Murphy

Product Team Manager: Brian Hyland

Product Development Manager: Leigh Hefferon

Content Developer: Jon Farnham

Associate Content Developer: Crystal Parenteau

Product Assistant: Brianna Vorce

Development Editors: Lyn Markowicz

Director of Production: Patty Stephan

Senior Content Project Manager: Matthew Hutchinson

Marketing Director: Michele McTighe

Marketing Manager: Kristie Clark

Manufacturing Planner: Julio Esperas

QA Manuscript Reviewers: Jeffrey Schwartz, John Freitas, Serge Palladino, Susan Pedicini, Danielle Shaw, Susan Whalen

Composition: Lumina Datamatics, Inc.

Art Director: Marissa Falco

Text Design: Joel Sadagursky

Cover Design: Lisa Kuhn, Curio Press, LCC

Cover Photo: Tom Kates Photography

Proofreader: Lumina Datamatics, Inc.

Library of Congress Control Number: 2015934772

ISBN-13: 978-1-305-50721-0
ISBN-10: 1-305-50721-5

Cengage Learning
20 Channel Center Street
Boston, MA 02210
USA

Cengage Learning is a leading provider of customized learning solutions with office locations around the globe, including Singapore, the United Kingdom, Australia, Mexico, Brazil, and Japan. Locate your local office at: **international.cengage.com/region**

Cengage Learning products are represented in Canada by Nelson Education, Ltd.

To learn more about Cengage Learning, visit **www.cengage.com**

Purchase any of our products at your local college bookstore or at our preferred online store at **www.cengagebrain.com**

We dedicate this book to the memory of Thomas J. Cashman (4/29/32 – 1/7/15). As one of the founders of the Shelly Cashman Series, Tom partnered with Gary Shelly to write and publish their first computer education textbook in 1969, revolutionizing the introductory computing course and changing the path of computing course materials. From 1969 through his retirement in 2008, Tom served as educator, author, leader, and inspiration to his fellow authors and Shelly Cashman Series team members. His mark on the series and the introductory computing market is indelible and he will be both remembered and missed.

Printed in the United States of America
Print Number: 1 Print Year: 2015

Microsoft® WORD 2013

COMPREHENSIVE **ENHANCED EDITION**

Contents

Microsoft Office 365

Office 365 Essentials

Microsoft Word 2013

CHAPTER ONE

Creating, Formatting, and Editing a Word Document with a Picture

CHAPTER TWO

Creating a Research Paper with References and Sources

CHAPTER THREE
Creating a Business Letter with a Letterhead and Table

CHAPTER FOUR
Creating a Document with a Title Page, Lists, Tables, and a Watermark

CHAPTER FIVE

Using a Template to Create a Resume and Sharing a Finished Document

CHAPTER SIX

Generating Form Letters, Mailing Labels, and a Directory

CHAPTER SEVEN

Creating a Newsletter with a Pull-Quote and Graphics

CHAPTER EIGHT

Using Document Collaboration, Integration, and Charting Tools

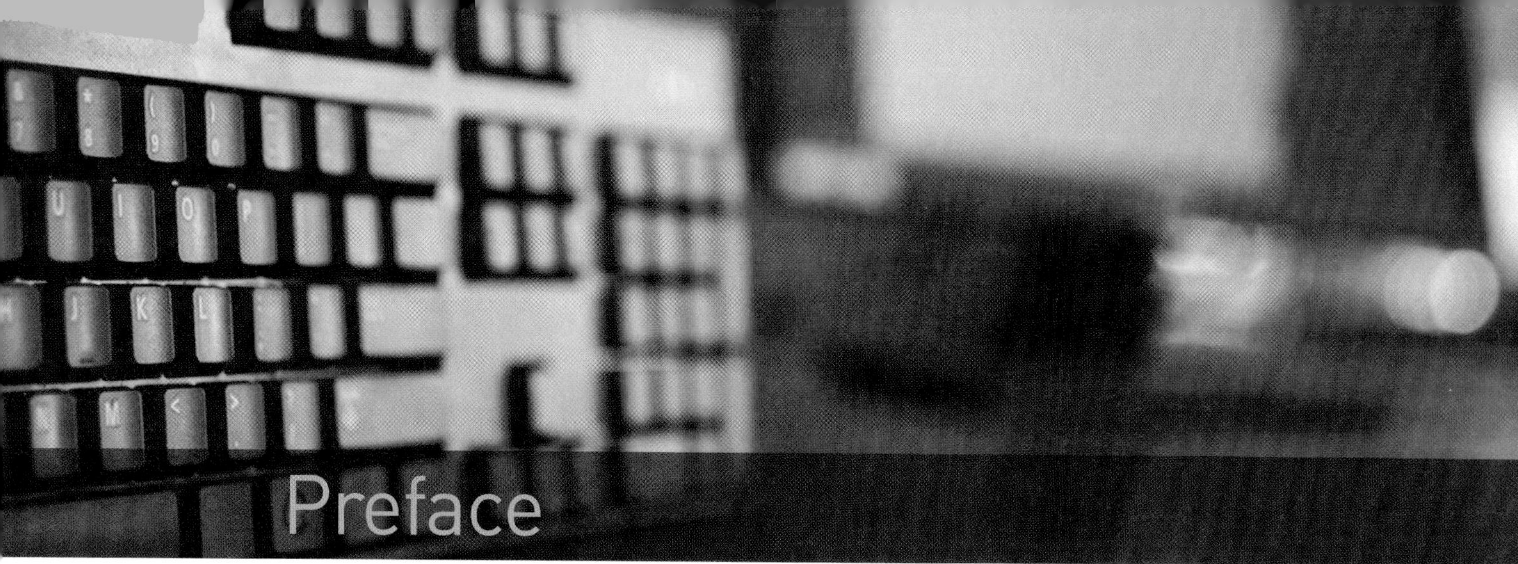

Preface

The Shelly Cashman Series® offers the finest textbooks in computer education. We are proud that since Mircosoft Office 4.3, our series of Microsoft Office textbooks have been the most widely used books in education. With each new edition of our Office books, we make significant improvements based on the software and comments made by instructors and students. For this Microsoft Word 2013 text, the Shelly Cashman Series development team carefully reviewed our pedagogy and analyzed its effectiveness in teaching today's Office student. Students today read less, but need to retain more. They need not only to be able to perform skills, but to retain those skills and know how to apply them to different settings. Today's students need to be continually engaged and challenged to retain what they're learning.

With this Microsoft Word 2013 text, we continue our commitment to focusing on the users and how they learn best.

Objectives of This Textbook

Microsoft Word 2013: Comprehensive is intended for a ten- to fifteen-week period in a course that teaches Word 2013 as the primary component. No experience with a computer is assumed, and no mathematics beyond the high school freshman level is required. The objectives of this book are:

- To offer a comprehensive presentation of Microsoft Word 2013
- To expose students to practical examples of the computer as a useful tool
- To acquaint students with the proper procedures to create documents suitable for coursework, professional purposes, and personal use
- To help students discover the underlying functionality of Word 2013 so they can become more productive
- To develop an exercise-oriented approach that allows learning by doing

The Shelly Cashman Approach

A Proven Pedagogy with an Emphasis on Project Planning

Each chapter presents a practical problem to be solved within a project planning framework. The project orientation is strengthened by the use of the Roadmap, which provides a visual framework for the project. Step-by-step instructions with supporting screens guide students through the steps. Instructional steps are supported by the Q&A, Experimental Step, and BTW features.

A Visually Engaging Book that Maintains Student Interest

The step-by-step tasks, with supporting figures, provide a rich visual experience for the student. Call-outs on the screens that present both explanatory and navigational information provide students with information they need when they need to know it.

Supporting Reference Materials (Quick Reference)

With the Quick Reference, students can quickly look up information about a single task, such as keyboard shortcuts, and find page references to where in the book the task is illustrated.

Integration of the World Wide Web

The World Wide Web is integrated into the Word 2013 learning experience with (1) BTW annotations; (2) BTW, Q&A, and Quick Reference Summary Web pages; and (3) the Learn Online resources for each chapter.

End-of-Chapter Student Activities

Extensive end-of-chapter activities provide a variety of reinforcement opportunities for students to apply and expand their skills through individual and group work. To complete some of these assignments, you will be required to use the Data Files for Students. Visit www.cengage.com/ct/studentdownload for detailed access instructions or contact your instructor for information about accessing the required files.

New to this Edition

Enhanced Coverage of Critical Thinking Skills

A new Consider This element poses thought-provoking questions throughout each chapter, providing an increased emphasis on critical thinking and problem-solving skills. Also, every task in the project now includes a reason *why* the students are performing the task and *why* the task is necessary.

Enhanced Retention and Transference

A new Roadmap element provides a visual framework for each project, showing students where they are in the process of creating each project, and reinforcing the context of smaller tasks by showing how they fit into the larger project.

Integration of Office with Cloud and Web Technologies

A new Lab focuses entirely on integrating cloud and web technologies with Word 2013, using technologies like Web Apps, online tools, and Google Docs.

More Personalization

Each chapter project includes an optional instruction for the student to personalize his or her solution, if required by an instructor, making each student's solution unique.

More Collaboration

A new Research and Collaboration project has been added to the Consider This: Your Turn assignment at the end of each chapter.

Instructor Resources

The Instructor Resources include both teaching and testing aids and can be accessed at www.cengage.com/login.

Instructor's Manual Includes lecture notes summarizing the chapter sections, figures and boxed elements found in every chapter, teacher tips, classroom activities, lab activities, and quick quizzes in Microsoft Word files.

Syllabus Easily customizable sample syllabi that cover policies, assignments, exams, and other course information.

Figure Files Illustrations for every figure in the textbook in electronic form.

Powerpoint Presentations A multimedia lecture presentation system that provides slides for each chapter. Presentations are based on chapter objectives.

Solutions to Exercises Includes solutions for all end-of-chapter and chapter reinforcement exercises.

Test Bank & Test Engine Test banks powered by Cognero include 112 questions for every chapter, featuring objective-based and critical thinking question types, and including page number references and figure references, when appropriate.

Data Files for Students Includes all the files that are required by students to complete the exercises.

Additional Activities for Students Consists of Chapter Reinforcement Exercises, which are true/false, multiple-choice, and short answer questions that help students gain confidence in the material learned.

Learn Online

Cengagebrain.com is the premier destination for purchasing or renting Cengage Learning textbooks, eBooks, eChapters, and study tools at a significant discount (eBooks up to 50% off Print). In addition, cengagebrain.com provides direct access to all digital products, including eBooks, eChapters, and digital solutions, such as MindTap and SAM, regardless of where purchased. The following are some examples of what is available for this product on www.cengagebrain.com.

SAM: Skills Assessment Manager Get your students workplace-ready with SAM, the market-leading proficiency-based assessment and training solution for Microsoft Office! SAM's active, hands-on environment helps students master Microsoft Office skills and computer concepts that are essential to academic and career success, delivering the most comprehensive online learning solution for your course!

Through skill-based assessments, interactive trainings, business-centric projects, and comprehensive remediation, SAM engages students in mastering the latest Microsoft Office programs on their own, giving instructors more time to focus on teaching. Computer concepts labs supplement instruction of important technology-related topics and issues through engaging simulations and interactive, auto-graded assessments. With enhancements including streamlined course setup, more robust grading and reporting features, and the integration of fully interactive MindTap Readers containing Cengage Learning's premier textbook content, SAM provides the best teaching and learning solution for your course.

MindLinks MindLinks is a new Cengage Learning Service designed to provide the best possible user experience and facilitate the highest levels of learning retention and outcomes, enabled through a deep integration of Cengage Learning's digital suite into an instructor's Learning Management System (LMS). MindLinks works on any LMS that supports the IMS Basic LTI open standard. Advanced features, including gradebook exchange, are the result of active, enhanced LTI collaborations with industry-leading LMS partners to drive the evolving technology standards forward.

CourseNotes

Cengage Learning's CourseNotes are six-panel quick reference cards that reinforce the most important and widely used features of a software application in a visual and user-friendly format. CourseNotes serve as a great reference tool during and after the course. CourseNotes are available for software applications, such as Microsoft Office 2013. There are also topic-based CourseNotes available, such as Best Practices in Social Networking, Hot Topics in Technology, and Web 2.0. Visit www.cengagebrain.com to learn more!

Certification Prep Tool

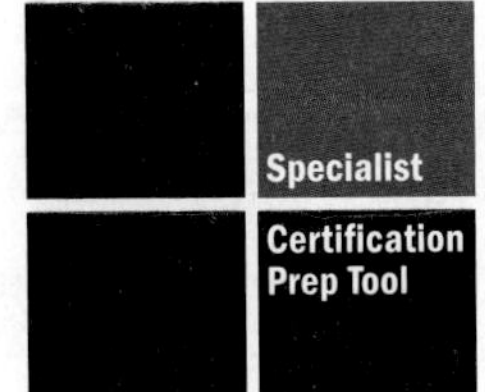

This textbook was developed to instruct on the Microsoft® Office 2013 certification objectives. Microsoft Corporation has developed a set of standardized, performance-based examinations that you can take to demonstrate your overall expertise with Microsoft Office 2013 programs. Microsoft Office 2013 certification provides a number of benefits for you:

- Differentiate yourself in the employment marketplace from those who are not Microsoft Office Specialist or Expert certified.
- Prove skills and expertise when using Microsoft Office 2013.
- Perform at a higher skill level in your job.
- Work at a higher professional level than those who are not certified.
- Broaden your employment opportunities and advance your career more rapidly.

For more information about Microsoft Office 2013 certification, including a complete list of certification objectives, visit the Microsoft website, http://www.microsoft.com/learning. To see which Microsoft Office 2013 certification objectives are addressed by the contents of this text and where each is included in the text, visit the Certification resource on the Student Companion Site located on www.cengagebrain.com. For detailed instructions about accessing available resources, visit www.cengage.com/ct/studentdownload or contact your instructor for information about accessing the required files.

About Our Covers

The Shelly Cashman Series is continually updating our approach and content to reflect the way today's students learn and experience new technology. This focus on student success is reflected on our covers, which feature real students from The University of Rhode Island using the Shelly Cashman Series in their courses, and reflect the varied ages and backgrounds of the students learning with our books. When you use the Shelly Cashman Series, you can be assured that you are learning computer skills using the most effective courseware available.

Textbook Walk-Through

The Shelly Cashman Series Pedagogy: Project-Based — Step-by-Step — Variety of Assessments

Roadmaps provide a visual framework for each project, showing the students where they are in the process of creating each project.

Step-by-step instructions provide a context beyond the point-and-click. Each step provides information on why students are performing each task and what will occur as a result.

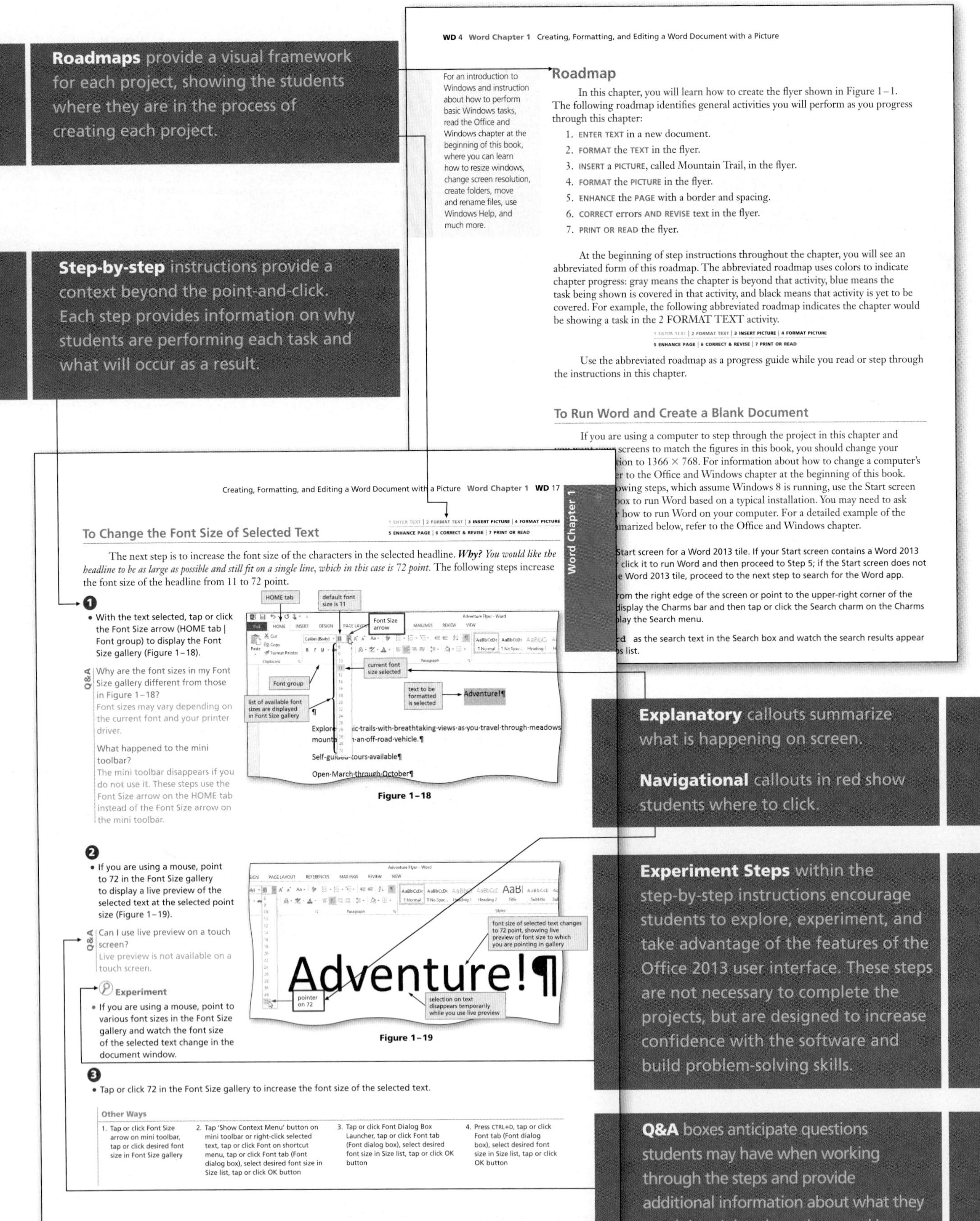

WD 4 Word Chapter 1 Creating, Formatting, and Editing a Word Document with a Picture

For an introduction to Windows and instruction about how to perform basic Windows tasks, read the Office and Windows chapter at the beginning of this book, where you can learn how to resize windows, change screen resolution, create folders, move and rename files, use Windows Help, and much more.

Roadmap

In this chapter, you will learn how to create the flyer shown in Figure 1–1. The following roadmap identifies general activities you will perform as you progress through this chapter:

1. ENTER TEXT in a new document.
2. FORMAT the TEXT in the flyer.
3. INSERT a PICTURE, called Mountain Trail, in the flyer.
4. FORMAT the PICTURE in the flyer.
5. ENHANCE the PAGE with a border and spacing.
6. CORRECT errors AND REVISE text in the flyer.
7. PRINT OR READ the flyer.

At the beginning of step instructions throughout the chapter, you will see an abbreviated form of this roadmap. The abbreviated roadmap uses colors to indicate chapter progress: gray means the chapter is beyond that activity, blue means the task being shown is covered in that activity, and black means that activity is yet to be covered. For example, the following abbreviated roadmap indicates the chapter would be showing a task in the 2 FORMAT TEXT activity.

1 ENTER TEXT | 2 FORMAT TEXT | 3 INSERT PICTURE | 4 FORMAT PICTURE
5 ENHANCE PAGE | 6 CORRECT & REVISE | 7 PRINT OR READ

Use the abbreviated roadmap as a progress guide while you read or step through the instructions in this chapter.

To Run Word and Create a Blank Document

If you are using a computer to step through the project in this chapter and ... screens to match the figures in this book, you should change your ...tion to 1366 × 768. For information about how to change a computer's ...r to the Office and Windows chapter at the beginning of this book. ...owing steps, which assume Windows 8 is running, use the Start screen ...ox to run Word based on a typical installation. You may need to ask ...r how to run Word on your computer. For a detailed example of the ...marized below, refer to the Office and Windows chapter.

...Start screen for a Word 2013 tile. If your Start screen contains a Word 2013 ...r click it to run Word and then proceed to Step 5; if the Start screen does not ...e Word 2013 tile, proceed to the next step to search for the Word app.

...rom the right edge of the screen or point to the upper-right corner of the ...display the Charms bar and then tap or click the Search charm on the Charms ...play the Search menu.

...rd as the search text in the Search box and watch the search results appear ...s list.

Creating, Formatting, and Editing a Word Document with a Picture Word Chapter 1 WD 17

Word Chapter 1

To Change the Font Size of Selected Text

1 ENTER TEXT | 2 FORMAT TEXT | 3 INSERT PICTURE | 4 FORMAT PICTURE
5 ENHANCE PAGE | 6 CORRECT & REVISE | 7 PRINT OR READ

The next step is to increase the font size of the characters in the selected headline. ***Why?** You would like the headline to be as large as possible and still fit on a single line, which in this case is 72 point.* The following steps increase the font size of the headline from 11 to 72 point.

1

- With the text selected, tap or click the Font Size arrow (HOME tab | Font group) to display the Font Size gallery (Figure 1–18).

Q&A Why are the font sizes in my Font Size gallery different from those in Figure 1–18?
Font sizes may vary depending on the current font and your printer driver.

What happened to the mini toolbar?
The mini toolbar disappears if you do not use it. These steps use the Font Size arrow on the HOME tab instead of the Font Size arrow on the mini toolbar.

Figure 1–18

2

- If you are using a mouse, point to 72 in the Font Size gallery to display a live preview of the selected text at the selected point size (Figure 1–19).

Q&A Can I use live preview on a touch screen?
Live preview is not available on a touch screen.

Experiment

- If you are using a mouse, point to various font sizes in the Font Size gallery and watch the font size of the selected text change in the document window.

Figure 1–19

3

- Tap or click 72 in the Font Size gallery to increase the font size of the selected text.

Other Ways

1. Tap or click Font Size arrow on mini toolbar, tap or click desired font size in Font Size gallery
2. Tap 'Show Context Menu' button on mini toolbar or right-click selected text, tap or click Font on shortcut menu, tap or click Font tab (Font dialog box), select desired font size in Size list, tap or click OK button
3. Tap or click Font Dialog Box Launcher, tap or click Font tab (Font dialog box), select desired font size in Size list, tap or click OK button
4. Press CTRL+D, tap or click Font tab (Font dialog box), select desired font size in Size list, tap or click OK button

Explanatory callouts summarize what is happening on screen.

Navigational callouts in red show students where to click.

Experiment Steps within the step-by-step instructions encourage students to explore, experiment, and take advantage of the features of the Office 2013 user interface. These steps are not necessary to complete the projects, but are designed to increase confidence with the software and build problem-solving skills.

Q&A boxes anticipate questions students may have when working through the steps and provide additional information about what they are doing right where they need it.

Consider This boxes pose thought-provoking questions with answers throughout each chapter, promoting critical thought along with immediate feedback.

Chapter Summary A listing of the tasks completed within the chapter, grouped into major task categories in an outline format.

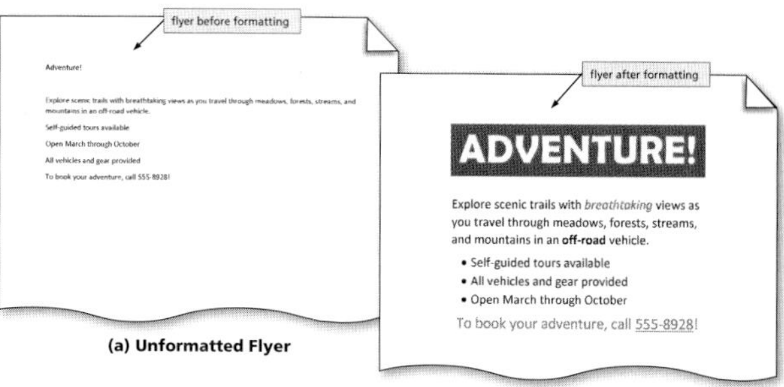
flyer before formatting
Adventure!
Explore scenic trails with breathtaking views as you travel through meadows, forests, streams, and mountains in an off-road vehicle.
Self-guided tours available
Open March through October
All vehicles and gear provided
To book your adventure, call 555-8928!
flyer after formatting
ADVENTURE!
Explore scenic trails with breathtaking views as you travel through meadows, forests, streams, and mountains in an off-road vehicle.
• Self-guided tours available
• All vehicles and gear provided
• Open March through October
To book your adventure, call 555-8928!

(a) Unformatted Flyer

(b) Formatted Flyer

Figure 1–13

Font, Font Sizes, and Themes

Characters that appear on the screen are a specific shape and size. The **font**, or typeface, defines the appearance and shape of the letters, numbers, and special characters. In Word, the default font usually is Calibri (shown in Figure 1–14 on page WD 15). You can leave characters in the default font or change them to a different font. **Font size** specifies the size of the characters and is determined by a measurement system called points. A single **point** is about 1/72 of one inch in height. The default font size in Word typically is 11 (Figure 1–14). Thus, a character with a font size of 11 is about 11/72 or a little less than 1/6 of one inch in height. You can increase or decrease the font size of characters in a document.

A document **theme** is a set of unified formats for fonts, colors, and graphics. Word includes a variety of document themes to assist you with coordinating these visual elements in a document. The default theme fonts are Calibri Light for headings and Calibri for body text. By changing the document theme, you quickly can give your document a new look. You also can define your own document themes.

BTW
Formatting Marks
With some fonts, the formatting marks will not be displayed properly on the screen. For example, the raised dot that signifies a blank space between words may be displayed behind a character instead of in the blank space, causing the characters to look incorrect.

CONSIDER THIS

How do I know which formats to use in a flyer?
In a flyer, consider the following formatting suggestions.

- **Increase the font size of characters.** Flyers usually are posted on a bulletin board or in a window. Thus, the font size should be as large as possible so that passersby easily can read the flyer. To give the headline more impact, its font size should be larger than the font size of the text in the body copy. If possible, make the font size of the signature line larger than the body copy but smaller than the headline.
- **Change the font of characters.** Use fonts that are easy to read. Try to use only two different fonts in a flyer; for example, use one for the headline and the other for all other text. Too many fonts can make the flyer visually confusing.
- **Change the paragraph alignment.** The default alignment for paragraphs in a document is **left-aligned**, that is, flush at the left margin of the document with uneven right edges. Consider changing the alignment of some of the paragraphs to add interest and variety to the flyer.
- **Highlight key paragraphs with bullets.** A bulleted paragraph is a paragraph that begins with a dot or other symbol. Use bulleted paragraphs to highlight important points in a flyer.
- **Emphasize important words.** To call attention to certain words or lines, you can underline them, italicize them, or bold them. Use these formats sparingly, however, because overuse will minimize their effect and make the flyer look too busy.
- **Use color.** Use colors that complement each other and convey the meaning of the flyer. Vary colors in terms of hue and brightness. Headline colors, for example, can be bold and bright. Signature lines should stand out more than body copy but less than headlines. Keep in mind that too many colors can detract from the flyer and make it difficult to read.

Chapter Summary

In this chapter, you have learned how to enter text in a document, forr
page border, adjust paragraph and page spacing, and print and read a d
all the new Word skills you have learned in this chapter, with the tasks

Enter and Edit Text
Type Text (WD 5)
Insert a Blank Line (WD 7)
Wordwrap Text as You Type (WD 9)
Check Spelling and Grammar as You Type (WD 10)
Insert Text in an Existing Document (WD 48)
Delete Text (WD 48)
Move Text (WD 49)

File Management
Run Word (WD 46)
Save a Document (WD 12)
Save an Existing Document with the Same File Name (WD 33)
Exit Word (WD 46)
Change Document Properties (WD 44)
Open a Document from Word (WD 47)
Print a Document (WD 51)

Format a Page
Change Theme Colors (WD 31)
Add a Page Border (WD 41)
Center Page Contents Vertically (WD 43)

Format Text
Center a Paragraph (WD 15)
Change the Font Size of Selected Text (WD 17)
Change the Font of Selected Text (WD 18)
Change the Case of Selected Text (WD 19)
Apply a Text Effect to Selected Text (WD 20)

Shade a Pa
Bullet a Li
Undo and
Italicize Te
Color Text
Use the M
Underline
Bold Text (
Change Sp
Paragra

Select Text
Select a Li
Select Mul
Select a G

Word Settings
Display Formatting Marks (WD 6)
Zoom Page Width (WD 7)
Zoom One Page (WD 30)
Zoom the Document (WD 35)
Zoom 100% (WD 37)
Switch to Read Mode (WD 52)
Switch to Print Layout View (WD 53)

Work with Graphics (Pictures)
Insert a Picture (WD 34)
Resize a Graphic (WD 36)
Apply a Picture Style (WD 38)
Apply Picture Effects (WD 39)

CONSIDER THIS

What decisions will you need to make when creating your next flyer?
Use these guidelines as you complete the assignments in this chapter and create your own flyers outside of this class.

1. Choose the text for the headline, body copy, and signature line—using as few words as possible to make a point.
2. Format various elements of the text.
   a) Select appropriate font sizes for text in the headline, body copy, and signature line.
   b) Select appropriate fonts for text in the headline, body copy, and signature line.
   c) Adjust paragraph alignment, as appropriate.
   d) Highlight key paragraphs with bullets.
   e) Emphasize important words.
   f) Use color to convey meaning and add appeal.
3. Find an eye-catching graphic(s) that conveys the overall message and meaning of the flyer.
4. Establish where to position and how to format the graphical image(s) so that the image grabs the attention of passersby and draws them into reading the flyer.
5. Determine whether the flyer needs enhancements such as a graphical, color-coordinated border or spacing adjustments to improve readability or overall appearance.
6. Correct errors and revise the document as necessary.
   a) Post the flyer on a wall and make sure all text and images are legible from a distance.
   b) Ask someone else to read the flyer and give you suggestions for improvements.
7. Determine the best method for distributing the document such as printing, sending via email, or posting on the web.

Consider This: Plan Ahead box presents a single master planning guide that students can use as they create documents on their own.

Textbook Walk-Through

Apply Your Knowledge This exercise usually requires students to open and manipulate a file that parallels the activities learned in the chapter.

How should you submit solutions to questions in the assignments identified with a symbol?
Every assignment in this book contains one or more questions identified with a symbol. These questions require you to think beyond the assigned document. Present your solutions to the questions in the format required by your instructor. Possible formats may include one or more of these options: write the answer; create a document that contains the answer; present your answer to the class; discuss your answer in a group; record the answer as audio or video using a webcam, smartphone, or portable media player; or post answers on a blog, wiki, or website.

CONSIDER THIS

STUDENT ASSIGNMENTS Word Chapter 1

Apply Your Knowledge

Reinforce the skills and apply the concepts you learned in this chapter.

Modifying Text and Formatting a Document

Note: To complete this assignment, you will be required to use the Data Files for Students. Visit www.cengage.com/ct/studentdownload for detailed instructions or contact your instructor for information about accessing the required files.

Instructions: Run Word. Open the document, Apply 1-1 County Park Flyer Unformatted, from the Data Files for Students. The document you open is an unformatted flyer. You are to modify text, format paragraphs and characters, and insert a picture in the flyer to create the flyer shown in Figure 1–74.

Perform the following tasks:

1. Delete the word, below, in the sentence below the headline.
2. Insert the word, Valley, between the words, Green County, in the second to last line of the flyer.
3. Change the period to an exclamation point in the last line so the text reads: Thank You!
4. If requested by your instructor, change the phone number in the flyer to your phone number.
5. Center the headline and the last two paragraphs of the flyer.
6. Select the third, fourth, and fifth paragraphs in the flyer and add bullets to the selected paragraphs.
7. Change the theme colors to the Red Orange color scheme.
8. Change the font and font size of the headline to 48-point Franklin Gothic Heavy, or a similar font. Change the case of the headline text to uppercase letters. Apply the text effect called Fill - Black, Text 1, Outline - Background 1, Hard Shadow - Background 1 to the headline. Change the font color of the headline text to Dark Red, Accent 6.

headline

PLEASE DO NOT FEED THE WILDLIFE!

Follow these guidelines to keep our wildlife healthy and our environment clean.

bulleted list

- Do not feed the wildlife.
- Never leave food unattended.
- Discard *all* trash in provided containers.

Questions? Call Green Valley County Park at 329-555-1020.

Thank You!

Courtesy of Misty Vermaat

Figure 1–74

Continued >

STUDENT ASSIGNMENTS

Apply Your Knowledge *continued*

9. Change the font size of the sentence below the h flyer to 26 point.
10. Use the mini toolbar to change the font size of t
11. Select the words, Follow these guidelines, in the p
12. Bold the word, not, in the first bulleted paragrap Dark Red, Accent 6.
13. Italicize the word, all, in the second bulleted iter
14. Switch the last two bulleted paragraphs. That is, and move it so that it is the second bulleted para
15. Bold the text, Thank You!, in the last line of the Accent 6, Darker 25%. If the font color does not change its color to White, Background 1.
16. Change the zoom so that the entire page is visib
17. Insert the picture of the squirrel eating the suck headline. The picture is called Squirrel and is ava the Soft Edge Oval picture style to the inserted picture.
18. Change the spacing before the first bulleted paragraph to 12 point and the spacing after the last bulleted paragraph to 24 point.
19. The entire flyer should fit on a single page. If it flows to two pages, resize the picture or decrease spacing before and after paragraphs until the entire flyer text fits on a single page.
20. Change the zoom to text width, then page width, then 100% and notice the differences.
21. If requested by your instructor, enter the text, Green Valley, as the keywords in the document properties. Change the other document properties, as specified by your instructor.
22. Click FILE on the ribbon and then click Save As. Save the document using the file name, Apply 1-1 County Park Flyer Formatted.
23. Print the document. Switch to Read Mode and browse pages through the document. Switch to Print Layout view.
24. Submit the revised document, shown in Figure 1–74, in the format specified by your instructor.
25. Exit Word.
26. If this flyer were announcing the park reopening instead of including a warning, which color scheme would you apply and why?

Extend Your Knowledge

Extend the skills you learned in this chapter and experiment with new skills. You may need to use Help to complete the assignment.

Modifying Text and Picture Formats and Adding Page Borders

Note: To complete this assignment, you will be required to use the Data Files for Students. Visit www.cengage.com/ct/studentdownload for detailed instructions or contact your instructor for information about accessing the required files.

Instructions: Run Word. Open the document, Extend 1-1 Baseball Tryouts Flyer Draft, from the Data Files for Students. You will enhance the look of the flyer shown in Figure 1–75.
Hint: Remember, if you make a mistake while formatting the picture, you can reset it by using the Reset Picture button or Reset Picture arrow (PICTURE TOOLS FORMAT tab | Adjust group).

Extend Your Knowledge projects at the end of each chapter allow students to extend and expand on the skills learned within the chapter. Students use critical thinking to experiment with new skills to complete each project.

Analyze, Correct, Improve projects call on the students to analyze a file, discover errors in it, fix the errors, and then improve upon the file using the skills they learned in the chapter.

12. If requested by your instructor, print a single mailing label for the letter and then a full page of mailing labels, each containing the address shown in Figure 3–78.
13. Answer the questions posed in #2 and #6. Why would you group objects? Which picture bullet did you use and why?

Analyze, Correct, Improve

Analyze a document, correct all errors, and improve it.

Formatting a Business Letter

Note: To complete this assignment, you will be required to use the Data Files for Students. Visit www.cengage.com/ct/studentdownload for detailed instructions or contact your instructor for information about accessing the required files.

Instructions: Run Word. Open the document, Analyze 3-1 Recommendation Letter Draft, located on the Data Files for Students. The document is a business letter that is missing elements and is formatted poorly or incorrectly (Figure 3–79). You are to change the color of the text, insert symbols, remove a hyperlink, change the letter style from block to modified block, insert and format clip art, and format the table.

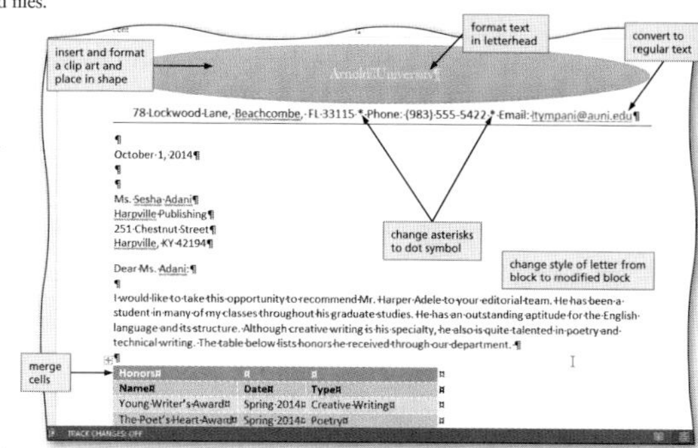

Figure 3–79

1. Correct In the letter, correct the following items:

a. Increase the font size of the text in the letterhead. Change the color of the text in the letterhead so that the text is readable.
b. Change the asterisks in the contact information to the dot symbol.
c. Convert the email address hyperlink to regular text.
d. The letter currently is the block letter style. It should be the modified block letter style. Format the appropriate paragraphs by setting custom tab stops and then positioning those paragraphs at the tab stops. Be sure to position the insertion point in the paragraph before setting the tab stop.
e. Merge the three cells in the first row of the table into one cell and then center the title in the cell. Center the entire table between the page margins.

2. Improve Enhance the letterhead by changing the theme to one you prefer. Then, locate and insert at least one appropriate clip art image in the letterhead. If necessary, resize the graphic(s). Change the text wrapping of the clip art to In Front of Text and move the graphic(s) into the shape. Change the color of the graphic to match the color of the text or shape. Adjust the brightness and contrast of the graphic. Format one color in the graphic as transparent. Change the picture border color. If requested by your instructor, change the name in the signature block to your name. Save the modified document with the file name, Analyze 3-1 Recommendation Letter Modified, and then submit it in the format specified by your instructor.

3. In this assignment, you located and inserted clip art. What image did you select and why?

In the Lab Three in-depth assignments in each chapter that require students to apply the chapter concepts and techniques to solve problems. One Lab is devoted entirely to Cloud and Web 2.0 integration.

In the Labs

Design and/or create a document using the guidelin
in this chapter. Labs 1 and 2, which increase in diffic
based on what you learned in the chapter; Lab 3 re
uses cloud and web technologies, by learning and i
general guidance.

Lab 1: Creating a Letter with a L

Problem: As office manager for a fitness club, you send r
One letter you prepare is shown in Figure 3–80.

shape style: Moderate Effect - Orange, Accent 1

centered

BUGBY'S FITNESS CLUB

35 Lake Street, Donner, OH 44772 • Phone: 677-555-9023 • Email: info@bugby.com

September 9, 2014

Mr. Timo Perez
404 Runway Road
Ponrolet, OH 44770

Dear Mr. Perez:

Your membership at Bugby's Fitness Club will expire at the end of next month. We hope you choose to continue to take advantage of our state-of-the-art fitness equipment and facilities.

The longer your term of renewal, the more you save! Current members can guarantee their membership rates as follows:

- Six-month renewal: $185
- One-year renewal: $350
- Two-year renewal: $675

You can renew your membership in one of three ways: online at www.bugby.com, by phone at 677-555-9023, or in person at the registration desk. We look forward to seeing you soon!

Sincerely,

Jonathon White
Office Manager

Figure 3–80

Textbook Walk-Through

5. Insert the picture called Bean Bag Toss, which is located on the Data Files for Students.
6. Use the features available in the Word Web App, along with the concepts and techniques presented in this chapter, to format this flyer. Be sure to change the font and font size of text, center a paragraph(s), italicize text, color text, underline text, and apply a picture style. Adjust spacing above and below paragraphs as necessary. Resize the picture, if necessary.
7. If requested by your instructor, replace the contact name in the flyer with your name.
8. Save the document again. Tap or click the button to open the document in the Word desktop app. If necessary, sign in to your Microsoft account when prompted. Notice how the document appears in the Word desktop app.
9. Using either the Word Web App or Word desktop app, submit the document in the format requested by your instructor. Exit the Word Web App (FILE tab | Exit). Sign out of your SkyDrive account. Sign out of the Microsoft account in Word.
10. What is the Word Web App? Which features that are covered in this chapter are not available in the Word Web App? Do you prefer using the Word Web App or the Word desktop app? Why?

Consider This: Your Turn

Apply your creative thinking and problem solving skills to design and implement a solution.

Note: To complete these assignments, you may be required to use the Data Files for Students. Visit www.cengage.com/ct/studentdownload for detailed instructions or contact your instructor for information about accessing the required files.

1: Design and Create a Photography Club Flyer

Personal

Part 1: As secretary of your school's Photography Club, you are responsible for creating and distributing flyers announcing the club. The flyer should contain two digital pictures appropriately resized; the Data Files for Students contains two pictures called Photography 1 and Photography 2, or you can use your own digital pictures if they are appropriate for the topic of the flyer. The flyer should contain the headline, Photography Club, and this signature line: Questions? Call Emily at (883) 555-0901. The body copy consists of the following text, in any order: Do you love photography? This is the club for you! All skill levels are welcome. Meetings every Tuesday at 5:00 p.m. in the Student Center (room 232). Bring your camera. We look forward to seeing you at our next meeting!

Use the concepts and techniques presented in this chapter to create and format this flyer. Be sure to check spelling and grammar. Submit your assignment and answers to the critical thinking questions in the format specified by your instructor.

Part 2: You made several decisions while creating the flyer in this assignment: where to place text, how to format the text (i.e., font, font size, paragraph alignment, bulleted paragraphs, underlines, italics, bold, color, etc.), which graphics to use, where to position the graphics, how to format the graphics, and which page enhancements to add (i.e., borders and spacing). What was the rationale behind each of these decisions? When you proofread the document, what further revisions did you make and why? How would you recommend distributing this flyer?

2: Design and Create a Hot Air Balloon Rides Flyer

Professional

Part 1: As a part-time employee at Galaxy Recreations, your boss has asked you to create and distribute flyers announcing hot air balloon rides. The flyer should contain two digital pictures appropriately resized; the Data Files for Students contains two pictures called Hot Air Balloon 1

Continued >

Consider This: Your Turn exercises call on students to apply creative thinking and problem solving skills to design and implement a solution.

Microsoft®
WORD 2013

COMPREHENSIVE **ENHANCED EDITION**

Student Success Guide

On the Path to Success

In this Student Success Guide, you explore tools, techniques, and skills essential to your success as a student. In particular, you focus on planning, time management, study tools, critical thinking, and problem solving. As you explore effective practices in these areas, you will also be introduced to Microsoft OneNote 2013, a free-form note-taking application in the Microsoft Office suite that lets you gather, organize, and share digital notes.

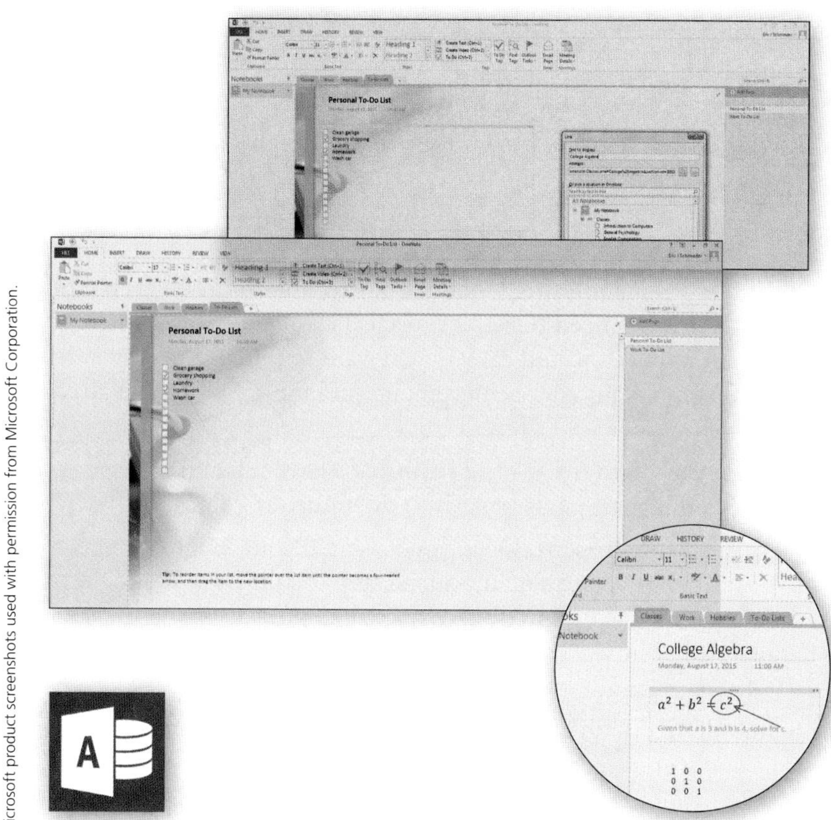

Objectives

You will have mastered the material in this chapter when you can:

- Use Microsoft OneNote to track tasks and organize ideas
- Set and achieve short-term and long-term goals
- Take notes during PowerPoint presentations
- Share OneNote content with others
- Apply critical-thinking strategies to evaluate information
- Follow a four-step process to solve problems

Planning Sets You Free

Benjamin Franklin once said, "If you fail to plan, you are planning to fail." When you set goals and manage time, your life does not just happen by chance. Instead, you design your life. Planning sets you free.

Without planning, you simply dig in and start writing or generating material you might use — but might not. You can actually be less productive and busier at the same time. Planning replaces this haphazard behavior with clearly defined outcomes and action steps.

Planning is a creative venture that continues for a lifetime. Following are planning suggestions that flow directly from this point of view and apply to any type of project or activity, from daily tasks to a multiyear career:

- **Schedule for flexibility and fun.** Be realistic. Expect the unexpected. Set aside time for essential tasks and errands, but don't forget to make room for fun.
- **Back up to view a bigger picture.** Consider your longer-range goals — what you want to accomplish in the next six months, the next year, the next five years, and beyond. Ask whether the activities you're about to schedule actually contribute to those goals.
- **Look boldly for things to change.** Don't accept the idea that you have to put up with substandard results in a certain area of your life. Staying open-minded about what is possible to achieve can lead to a future you never dreamed was possible.
- **Look for what's missing — and what to maintain.** Goals are often fueled by problems you need to resolve, projects you need to complete, relationships you want to develop, and careers you want to pursue. However, consider other goals that maintain your achievements and the activities you already perform effectively.
- **Think even further into the future.** To have fun and unleash your creativity while planning, set goals as far into the future as you can.
- **Return to the present.** Once you've stated your longest-range goals, work backward until you can define a next step to take now. Write down the shorter-term goals along the way. Leave some space in your schedule for unplanned events. Give yourself time to deal with obstacles before they derail you from realizing your dreams.
- **Schedule fixed blocks of time first.** When planning your week, start with class time and work time. Next, schedule essential daily activities such as sleeping and eating. In addition, schedule some time each week for actions that lead directly to one of your written goals.
- **Set clear starting and stopping times.** Set a timer and stick to it. Set aside a specific number of minutes or hours to spend on a certain task. Feeling rushed or sacrificing quality is not the goal here. The point is to push yourself and discover your actual time requirements.
- **Plan for changes in your workload.** To manage your workload over the length of a term or project, plan for a change of pace. Stay on top of your assignments right from the start. Whenever possible, work ahead.
- **Involve others when appropriate.** When you schedule a task that depends on another person's involvement, let that person know — the sooner, the better.

- **Start the day with your Most Important Task.** Review your to-do list and calendar first thing each morning. For an extra level of clarity, condense your to-do list to only one top-priority item — your Most Important Task. Do it as early in the day as possible, impeccably, and with total attention.
- **Plan in a way that works for you.** You can perform the kind of planning that sets you free with any set of tools. What matters above all is clear thinking and specific intentions. You can take any path that leads to your goal.

As you continue through this chapter, you will learn how to use Microsoft OneNote to plan, organize, and maintain the important information and ideas in your life. You will also explore methods for setting and achieving goals, improving study practices, and thinking critically to solve problems.

Quick Tour of Microsoft OneNote

Microsoft OneNote is part of the Microsoft Office suite and provides a single location for storing everything that is important to you, accessible from any device or on the web. Using OneNote, you store information in a **notebook**, a collection of electronic pages with text, graphics, and other content, including sound and video recordings. You organize the pages into tabbed sections as you would a tabbed ring binder. In your school notebook, for example, create a section for each of your courses, and then take notes during class on the pages within each section.

Exploring the OneNote Interface

As part of the Microsoft Office suite, the Microsoft OneNote 2013 desktop application contains a ribbon at the top of the window with seven default tabs: FILE, HOME, INSERT, DRAW, HISTORY, REVIEW, and VIEW. See Figure 1.

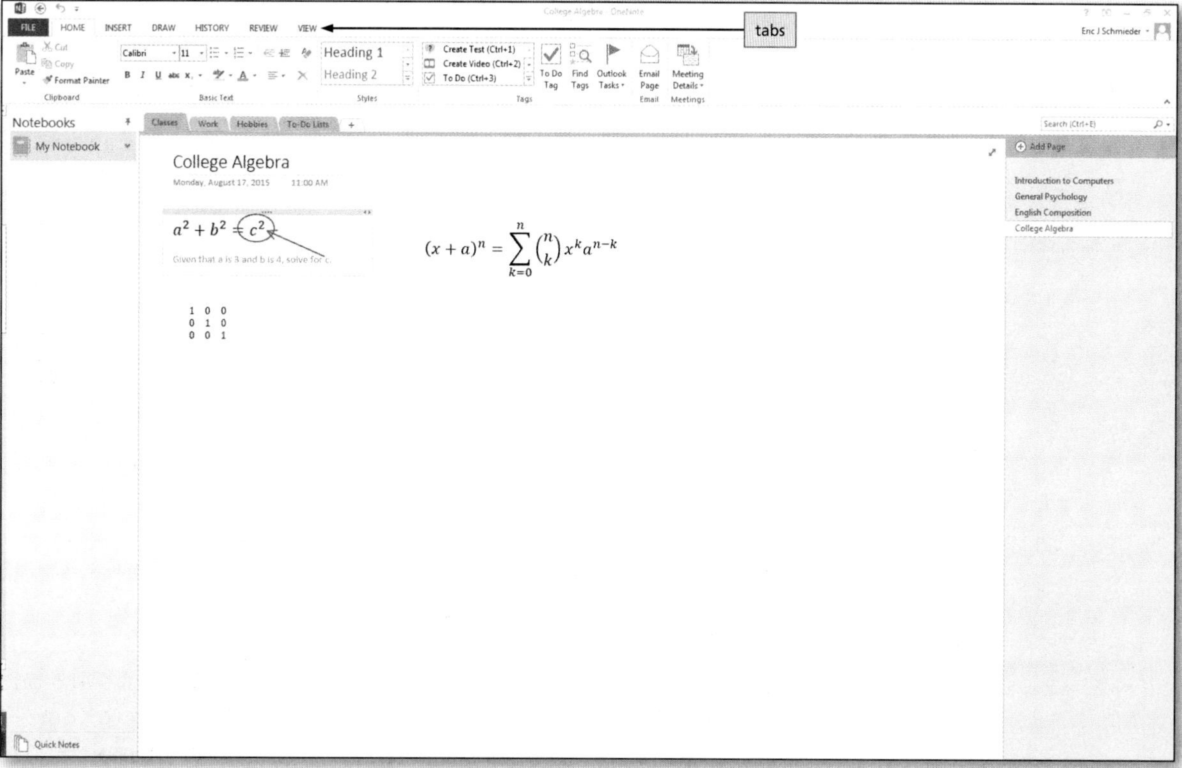

Figure 1 Microsoft OneNote 2013 ribbon

Each tab contains the following types of commands and features:

- **HOME tab**: This tab contains the most commonly used commands and features of Microsoft OneNote, which are divided into six groups: Clipboard, Basic Text, Styles, Tags, Email, and Meetings.
- **INSERT tab**: This tab includes commands for inserting tables, files, images, links, audio and video recordings, date/time stamps, page templates, and symbols.
- **DRAW tab**: This tab includes commands and tools for writing notes on pages, inserting shapes, arranging content, and converting handwritten notes to text or mathematical symbols.
- **HISTORY tab**: This tab includes tools for reviewing unread notes, managing multiple authors in a notebook, and reviewing pages and content in previous versions or pages and content that have been placed in the Notebook Recycle Bin.
- **REVIEW tab**: This tab provides research tools, including a spelling checker and thesaurus, language and translation tools, password-protection options, and links to other notebook sections and pages.
- **VIEW tab**: This tab contains page setup options, zoom tools, and application views, including docking options and the Send to OneNote tool.

Using Page Templates

To get started with OneNote and fill a blank page more quickly and easily, OneNote provides a collection of page templates. A **page template** is a design you apply to new pages in your notebook to provide an appealing background or to create a consistent layout. The OneNote page templates are organized into five categories: Academic, Blank, Business, Decorative, and Planners.

Additional templates are available on Office.com. After you define a standard way of organizing information, you can also create your own templates.

Time Management

When you say you don't have enough time, the problem might be that you are not spending the time you do have in the way you want. This section surveys ways to solve that time-management problem.

Time is an equal-opportunity resource. Everyone, regardless of gender, race, creed, or national origin, has exactly the same number of hours in a week. No matter how famous you are, no matter how rich or poor, you have 168 hours to spend each week — no more, no less.

As you explore time management in this section, you will learn how to set and achieve goals, how to apply the ABC method to writing a daily to-do list, and how to use technology for effective time management, with a special focus on using Microsoft OneNote to brainstorm ideas, set and achieve goals, and create to-do lists.

Setting and Achieving Goals

You can employ many useful methods for setting goals. One method is based on writing goals that relate to several periods and areas of your life. Writing down your goals greatly increases your chances of meeting them. Writing exposes incomplete information, undefined terms, unrealistic deadlines, and other symptoms of fuzzy thinking.

Write Specific Goals

State your written goals as observable actions or measurable results. Think in detail about what will be different when you attain your goals. List the changes in what you'll see, feel, touch, taste, hear, be, do, or have. Specific goals make clear what actions you need to take or what results you can expect. Figure 2 compares vague and specific goals.

Vague Goal	Specific Goal
Get a good education.	Graduate with BS degree in engineering, with honors, by 2017.
Get good grades.	Earn a 3.5 grade point average next semester.
Enhance my spiritual life.	Meditate for 15 minutes daily.
Improve my appearance.	Lose 6 pounds during the next 6 months.
Gain control of my money.	Transfer $100 to my savings account each month.

Figure 2 Vague and specific goals

Write Goals for Several Time Frames

To develop a comprehensive vision of your future, write down the following types of goals:

- **Long-term goals**: Long-term goals represent major targets in your life. They can include goals in education, careers, personal relationships, travel, financial security, and more — whatever is important to you.
- **Midterm goals**: Midterm goals are objectives you can accomplish in one to five years. They include goals such as completing a course of education, paying off a car loan, or achieving a specific career level. These goals usually support your long-term goals.
- **Short-term goals**: Short-term goals are the ones you can accomplish in a year or less. These goals are specific achievements that require action now or in the near future.

Write Goals in Several Areas of Life

People who set goals in only one area of life may find that their personal growth becomes one-sided. They might experience success at work while neglecting their health or relationships with family members and friends.

To avoid this outcome, set goals in a variety of categories, such as education, career, financial life, family life or relationships, social life, contribution (volunteer activities, community services), spiritual life, and level of health. Add goals in other areas as they occur to you.

Reflect on Your Goals

Each week, take a few minutes to think about your goals. You can perform the following spot checks:

- **Check in with your feelings.** Think about how it feels to set your goals. Consider the satisfaction you'll gain in attaining your objectives. If you don't feel a significant emotional connection with a written goal, consider letting it go or filing it away to review later.

- **Check for alignment.** Look for connections among your short-term to midterm goals and your midterm to long-term goals. Look for a fit between all of your goals and your purpose for taking part in higher education as well as your overall purpose in life.
- **Check for obstacles.** Complications can come between you and your goals, such as constraints on time and money. Anticipate obstacles and look for solutions.
- **Check for next steps.** Decide on a series of small, achievable steps you can take to accomplish your short-term goals. Write down these small steps on a daily to-do list. Note your progress and celebrate your successes.

Take Action Immediately

To increase your odds of success, take immediate action. Decrease the gap between stating a goal and starting to achieve it. If you slip and forget about the goal, you can get back on track at any time by *doing* something about it.

Using OneNote to Set Goals

The versatility of Microsoft OneNote allows you to write ideas anywhere on the page, identify notes with a variety of tags, and organize notes into pages and sections, making it a great tool for writing down your goals, organizing your thoughts and ideas, and building connections among them all.

Brainstorm with Quick Notes

Ideas often present themselves without order, structure, or clear fit in the organization of your existing content. Microsoft OneNote provides a feature called Quick Notes for such ideas. A **Quick Note** is a small window you can move anywhere on-screen and use to write reminders and other short notes. Getting the ideas on paper (or in your OneNote notebook) can be the first step in using them to define larger ideas and related goals. Quick Notes are initially unfiled within your notebook, but you can easily move or copy them to other sections. Think of an electronic Quick Note as you would a sticky note on your desk.

Organize Larger Ideas with Sections and Pages

For larger or more defined ideas, establish an organization system in your OneNote notebook so you can easily locate related information. OneNote provides multiple levels of organization within a notebook.

Most OneNote users store content on pages within sections. As your use of OneNote increases, you can organize related sections into groups or increase the detail of pages by creating subpages for better organization. See Figure 3.

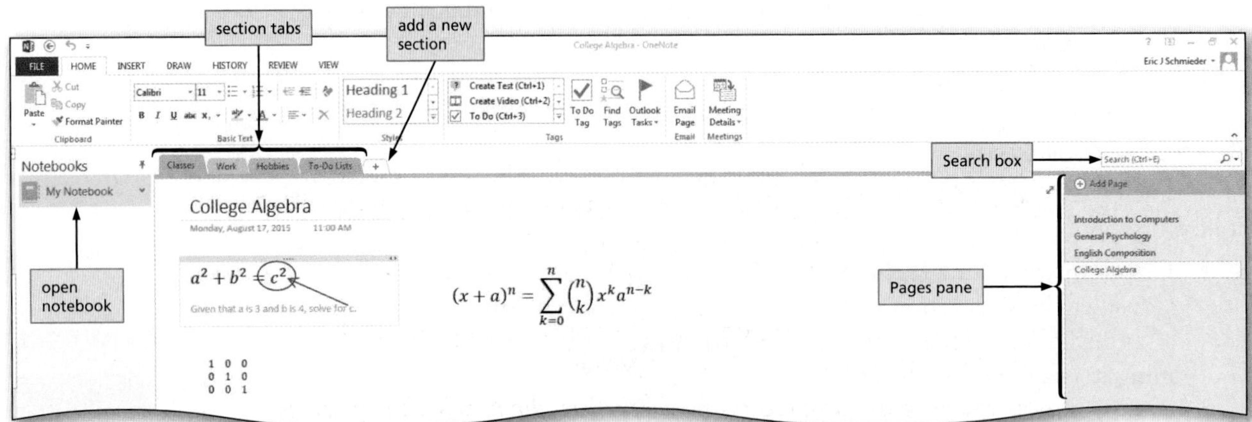

Figure 3 OneNote section tabs and Pages pane

Use Tags to Organize Content in OneNote

OneNote lets you mark notes and other content with tags — keywords that help you find important information — to set reminders, classify information, or set priorities, for example. OneNote provides the following tags by default: To Do, Important, Question, Remember for later, Definition, Highlight, Contact, Address, Phone number, website to visit, Idea, Password, Critical, Project A, Project B, Movie to see, Book to read, Music to listen to, Source for article, Remember for blog, Discuss with <Person A>, Discuss with <Person B>, Discuss with manager, Send in email, Schedule meeting, Call back, To Do priority 1, To Do priority 2, and Client request.

You assign a tag to page content by moving the insertion point to the text you want to tag and then selecting an item from the Tags gallery on the HOME tab of the ribbon. You can create custom tags to meet personal needs for organizing OneNote content in your notebooks.

Creating an ABC Daily To-Do List

One advantage to keeping a daily to-do list is that you don't have to remember what to do next. It's on the list. A typical day in the life of a student is full of separate, often unrelated tasks — reading, attending lectures, reviewing notes, working at a job, writing papers, researching special projects, and running errands. It's easy to forget an important task on a busy day. When that task is written down, you don't have to rely on your memory.

The following steps present the ABC method for creating and using to-do lists. This method involves ranking each item on your list according to three levels of importance: A, B, or C.

Step 1: Brainstorm Tasks

To get started, list all of the tasks you want to complete in a day. Each task will become an item on a to-do list. Don't worry about putting the entries in order or scheduling them yet. Just list everything you want to accomplish.

Step 2: Estimate Time

For each task you wrote down in Step 1, estimate how long it will take to complete the task. Estimating can be tricky. If you allow too little time, you end up feeling rushed. If you allow too much time, you become less productive. For now, use your best guess. If you are unsure, overestimate rather than underestimate how long you need for each task.

Add up the time you estimated to complete all your to-do items. Also add up the number of unscheduled hours in your day. Then compare the two totals. If you have more time assigned to tasks than unscheduled hours in the day, that's a potential problem. To solve it, proceed to Step 3.

Step 3: Rate Each Task by Priority

To prevent overscheduling, decide which to-do items are the most important given the time you have available. One suggestion for making this decision comes from the book *How to Get Control of Your Time and Your Life*, by Alan Lakein — simply label each task A, B, or C:

- The A tasks on your list are the most critical. They include assignments that are coming due or jobs that need to be done immediately.
- The B tasks on your list are important, but less so than the A tasks. They can be postponed, if necessary, for another day.

- The C tasks do not require immediate attention. C tasks are often small, easy jobs with no set deadline. They too can be postponed.

After labeling the items on your to-do list, schedule time for all of the A tasks.

Step 4: Cross off Tasks

Keep your to-do list with you at all times. Cross off, check, or otherwise mark activities when you finish them, and add new tasks when you think of them.

When using the ABC method, you might experience an ailment common to students: C fever. Symptoms include the uncontrollable urge to drop an A task and begin crossing off C items on your to-do list. The reason C fever is so common is that A tasks are usually more difficult or time consuming to achieve and have a higher risk of failure.

Use your to-do list to keep yourself on track, working on your A tasks. Don't panic or berate yourself when you realize that in the last six hours, you have completed nine Cs and not a single A. Just calmly return to the A tasks.

Step 5: Evaluate

At the end of the day, evaluate your performance. Look for A priorities you didn't complete. Look for items that repeatedly turn up as Bs or Cs on your list and never seem to get done. Consider changing them to A tasks or dropping them altogether. Similarly, you might consider lowering the priority of an A task you didn't complete to a B or C task.

When you're finished evaluating, start on tomorrow's to-do list. That way, you can wake up and start working on tasks productively without panicking about what to do.

Creating To-Do Lists in OneNote

The To Do tag in OneNote makes it easy to change any notebook item into a task. When you select an item and then assign the To Do tag to it, a check box appears next to the item. Insert a check mark in the box when you complete the task. You can also use the Planners subcategory of Page Templates in OneNote to generate Simple To Do Lists, Prioritized To Do Lists, and Project To Do Lists quickly and easily — leaving you to merely provide the action items. Figure 4 shows a to-do list based on the Simple To-Do List page template.

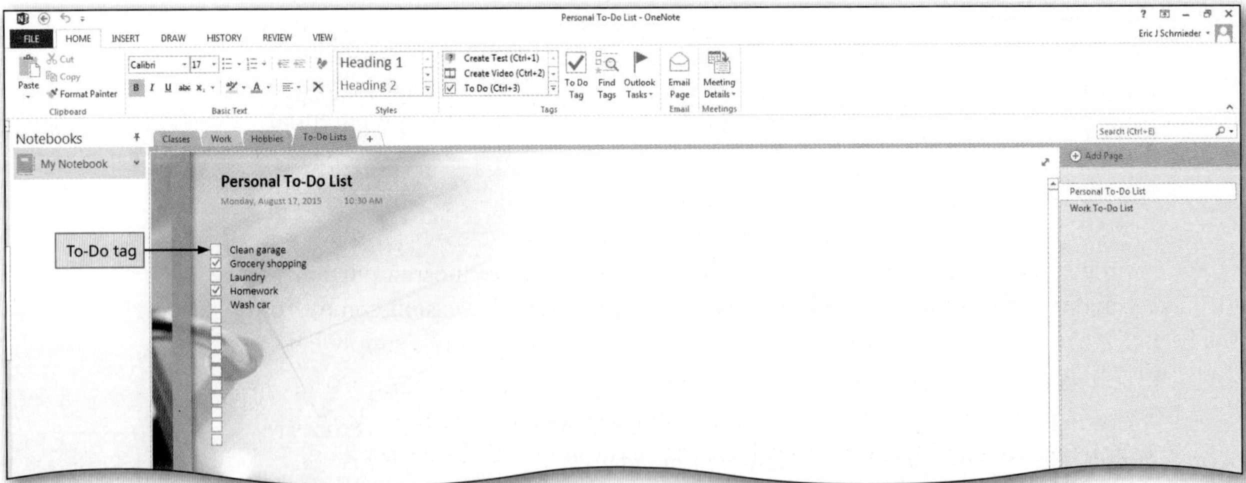

Figure 4 List based on the Simple To-Do List page template

Finding Time

Good news: You have enough time to accomplish the tasks you want to do. All it takes is thinking about the possibilities and making conscious choices.

Everything written about time management can be reduced to three main ideas:

1. Know exactly *what* you want. State your wants as clear, specific goals. Put them in writing.
2. Know *how* to get what you want. Take action to meet your goals. Determine what you'll do *today* to get what you want in the future. Put those actions in writing as well.
3. Strive for balance. When your life lacks balance, you spend most of your time responding to interruptions, last-minute projects, and emergencies. Life feels like a scramble just to survive. You're so busy achieving someone else's goals that you forget about getting what *you* want.

According to Stephen R. Covey, author of *The Seven Habits of Highly Effective People*, the purpose of planning is to carve out space in your life for tasks that are not urgent but are truly important. Examples are exercising regularly, reading, praying or meditating, spending quality time alone or with family members and friends, traveling, and cooking nutritious meals. Each of these tasks contributes directly to your personal goals for the future and to the overall quality of your life in the present.

Think of time management as time *investment*. Spend your most valuable resource in the way you choose.

Study Tools

In this section, you will learn ways to effectively use technology to promote positive study habits and successful results. Specifically, you explore ways to integrate Microsoft OneNote with PowerPoint presentations, web content, and **screen clippings**, also called screenshots, which are images of your screen that you capture using a OneNote tool. You will also learn techniques for interacting with e-books and for collaborating with others through the sharing features of OneNote and Office Online.

Turning PowerPoint Presentations into Powerful Notes

Some students stop taking notes during a PowerPoint presentation. This choice can be hazardous to your academic health for three major reasons:

- **PowerPoint presentations don't include everything.** Instructors and other speakers use PowerPoint to organize their presentations. Topics covered in the slides make up an outline of what your instructor considers important. Speakers create slides to flag the main points and signal transitions between topics. However, speakers usually enhance a presentation with examples and explanations that don't appear on the slides. In addition, slides will not contain any material from class discussion, including any answers that the instructor gives in response to questions.
- **You stop learning.** Taking notes forces you to capture ideas and information in your own words. The act of writing also helps you remember the material. If you stop writing and let your attention drift, you can quickly lose track of the presentation or topic.

- **You end up with major gaps in your notes.** When it's time to review your notes, you'll find that material from PowerPoint presentations is missing. This can be a major problem at exam time.

To create value from PowerPoint presentations, take notes directly on the slides. Continue to observe, record, and review. Use the presentation as a way to *guide* rather than to *replace* your own note taking.

Prepare Before the Presentation

Sometimes instructors make PowerPoint slides available before a lecture. Scan the slides, just as you would preview a reading assignment. Consider printing the slides and bringing them along to class. You can take notes directly on the printed pages.

If you use a laptop for taking notes during class, then you might not want to bother with printing. Open the PowerPoint presentation file and type your notes in the Notes pane, which appears below each slide.

Create OneNote Page Content from PowerPoint Slides

Use the File Printout button on the OneNote INSERT tab in the Files group to print PowerPoint slides directly to OneNote. You can store the slides where you keep your other notes and then take notes on the same page of your notebook as the slide content.

Take Notes During the Presentation

As you take notes during a presentation, be selective in what you write down. Determine what kind of material appears on each slide. Stay alert for new topics, main points, and important details. Taking too many notes makes it hard to keep up with a speaker and separate main points from minor details.

In any case, go *beyond* the slides. Record valuable questions and answers that come up during a discussion, even if they are not a planned part of the presentation.

Use Drawing Objects, Audio, and Video in Your Notes

On touch interface devices, OneNote makes it easy to handwrite your notes or draw symbols and shapes on the notebook pages. For mouse users, the OneNote DRAW tab contains predefined shapes and pen options for creating notes that are more than just text.

On devices that include microphones or webcams, you can use OneNote to capture audio and video recordings in your notebook pages, ensuring that every moment of an important lecture is captured for later review and study.

Review After the Presentation

If you printed out slides before class and took notes on those pages, then find a way to integrate them with the rest of your notes. For example, add references in your notebook to specific slides. Create summary notes that include the major topics and points from readings, class meetings, and PowerPoint presentations.

If you have a copy of the presentation, consider editing it. Cut slides that don't include information you want to remember. Rearrange slides so that the order makes more sense to you. Remember that you can open the original file later to see exactly what your instructor presented.

Add Links to Other Notebook Content

When creating summary note pages in your OneNote notebook, it is good practice to link text or content on the summary page to the detailed notes elsewhere in your notebook. To do so, select the content you want to use as the link, click the Link button in the Links group on the INSERT tab to open the Link dialog box (shown in Figure 5), and then select the location in the OneNote notebook with the detailed content.

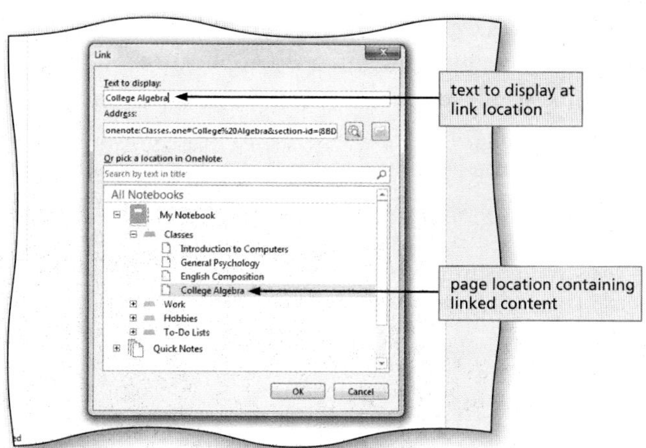

Figure 5 Link dialog box in OneNote 2013

Search Notes and Printouts

You can quickly locate content in your OneNote notebooks using the built-in search features of OneNote 2013. For basic text searches, you can limit the results to content on the current page, current section, current section group, current notebook, or all open notebooks.

After you apply tags to content within the notebook, use the Find Tags button in the Tags group on the HOME tab to locate and filter results based on tags.

Extending Reading to Webpages and E-Books

While reading, skilled readers focus on finding answers to their questions and flagging them in the text. E-books offer features that help with the following steps:

- **Access the table of contents.** For a bigger picture of the text, look for a table of contents that lists chapter headings and subheadings. Click a heading to expand the text for that part of the book.
- **Use navigation tools.** To flip electronic pages, look for Previous and Next buttons or arrows on the right and left borders of each page. Many e-books also offer a Go to Page feature that allows you to enter a specific page number to access the page.
- **Search the text.** Look for a search box that allows you to enter key words and find all the places in the text where those words are mentioned.
- **Follow links to definitions and related information.** Many e-books supply a definition to any word in the text. All you need to do is highlight a word and then click it.
- **Highlight and annotate.** E-books allow you to select words, sentences, or entire paragraphs and highlight them in a bright color. You can also annotate a book by entering your own notes on the pages.

Collect Web Content in OneNote

OneNote makes it easy to collect content with notations and links to the original source. When copying content from an electronic source, OneNote adds a reference to the original location below the pasted content. For web-based resources, OneNote inserts a hyperlink so you can access the source again later.

Insert Screen Clippings

In addition to copying content directly from websites, you can use the Screen Clipping tool to collect an image from any open application. To insert a screen clipping into a notebook, display the item you want to capture in another application, switch to OneNote, and then click the Screen Clipping button in the Images group on the INSERT tab. OneNote is minimized and the most recently used application is displayed with a transparent overlay. Draw a box around the area you want to capture to insert the screen clipping into the OneNote page as an image with details of when you collected the screen clipping. You can include additional notes and annotations using other text and drawing tools in OneNote.

Setting Limits on Screen Time

To get an accurate picture of your involvement in social networking and other online activity, monitor how much time you spend on them for one week. Make conscious choices about how much time you want to spend online and on the phone. Don't let social networking distract you from meeting personal and academic goals.

Using Technology to Collaborate

When planning group projects, look for tools that allow you to create, edit, and share documents, spreadsheets, drawings, presentations, and other files. You can find a growing list of applications for these purposes, including Office Online, which includes an online version of OneNote.

When using collaborative technology, your people skills are as important as your technology skills. Set up a process to make sure that everyone's voice is heard during a virtual meeting. People who are silenced will probably tune out.

Function as a professional whenever you're online. Team members might get to know you mainly through emails and instant messages. Consider the impression you're making with your online presence. Avoid slang, idioms, sarcastic humor, and other expressions that can create misunderstanding. A small dose of civility can make a big difference in the quality of your virtual team experience.

Use Office Online

Office Online is the free, online version of Microsoft Word, Microsoft Excel, Microsoft PowerPoint, and Microsoft OneNote available through Office 365, SharePoint Online, and OneDrive accounts. These tools provide basic functionality from the desktop applications directly in a web browser, giving you the ability to view and edit documents, workbooks, presentations, and notebooks from virtually any device with an Internet connection.

Supported by the cloud storage options associated with Office 365, SharePoint Online, and OneDrive, Office Online makes it easy to do real-time collaborative editing of shared files with classmates, friends, family, and colleagues.

SHARE CONTENT FROM ONENOTE

If you store OneNote notebooks on OneDrive or SharePoint, you can share pages, sections, or entire notebooks with others by using the commands in the Share group on the OneNote FILE tab. You can even share paragraphs of text on pages by right-clicking selected content and then clicking the Copy Link to Paragraph option on the shortcut menu. Export pages, sections, or entire notebooks from OneNote in various formats, including PDF and XPS, for sharing with users who don't have Microsoft OneNote.

Critical Thinking and Problem Solving

It has been said that human beings are rational creatures. Yet no one is born as an effective thinker. Critical thinking — the objective analysis and evaluation of an issue in order to form a judgment — is a learned skill. This is one reason that you study so many subjects in higher education. A broad base of courses helps you develop as a thinker, giving you a foundation for dealing with complex challenges in your career, your relationships, and your community.

Following a Process for Critical Thinking

Learning to think well matters. The rewards are many, and the stakes are high. Major decisions in life — from choosing a major to choosing a spouse — depend on your thinking skills.

Following are strategies that you can use to move freely through six levels of thinking: remembering, understanding, applying, analyzing, evaluating, and creating. The strategies fall into three major categories: check your attitudes, check for logic, and check for evidence.

CHECK YOUR ATTITUDES

The following suggestions help you understand and analyze information free from bias and other filters that cloud clear thinking:

- **Be willing to find various points of view on any issue.** People can have dozens of viewpoints on every important issue. In fact, few problems have any single, permanent solution. Begin seeking alternative views with an open mind. When talking to another person, be willing to walk away with a new point of view — even if it's similar to your original idea, supported with new evidence.
- **Practice tolerance.** One path to critical thinking is tolerance for a wide range of opinions. Taking a position on important issues is natural. Problems emerge, however, when people become so attached to their current viewpoints that they refuse to consider alternatives.
- **Understand before criticizing.** The six levels of thinking build on each other. Before you agree or disagree with an idea, make sure that you *remember* it accurately and truly *understand* it. Polished debaters make a habit of doing this. Often they can sum up their opponent's viewpoint better than anyone else can. This puts them in a much stronger position to *apply*, *analyze*, *evaluate*, and *create* ideas.
- **Watch for hot spots.** Many people have mental "hot spots" — topics that provoke strong opinions and feelings. To become more skilled at examining various points of view, notice your own particular hot spots. In addition, be sensitive to other people's hot spots. Demonstrate tolerance and respect before discussing personal issues.

- **Be willing to be uncertain.** Some of the most profound thinkers have practiced the art of thinking by using a magic sentence: "I'm not sure yet." It is courageous and unusual to take the time to pause, look, examine, be thoughtful, consider many points of view — and be unsure. Uncertainty calls for patience. Give yourself permission to experiment, practice, and learn from mistakes.

Check for Logic

Learning to think logically offers many benefits: When you think logically, you take your reading, writing, speaking, and listening skills to a higher level. You avoid costly mistakes in decision making. You can join discussions and debates with more confidence, cast your votes with a clear head, and become a better-informed citizen.

The following suggestions will help you work with the building blocks of logical thinking — terms, assertions, arguments, and assumptions:

- **Define key terms.** A *term* is a word or phrase that refers to a clearly defined concept. Terms with several different meanings are ambiguous — fuzzy, vague, and unclear. One common goal of critical thinking is to remove ambiguous terms or define them clearly.
- **Look for assertions.** An *assertion* is a complete sentence that contains one or more key terms. The purpose of an assertion is to define a term or to state relationships between terms. These relationships are the essence of what we mean by the term *knowledge*.
- **Look for arguments.** For specialists in logic, an *argument* is a series of related assertions. There are two major types of reasoning used in building arguments — deductive and inductive. *Deductive reasoning* builds arguments by starting with a general assertion and leading to a more specific one. With *inductive reasoning*, the chain of logic proceeds in the opposite direction — from specific to general.
- **Remember the power of assumptions.** Assumptions are beliefs that guide our thinking and behavior. Assumptions can be simple and ordinary. In other cases, assumptions are more complex and have larger effects. Despite the power to influence our speaking and actions, assumptions are often unstated. People can remain unaware of their most basic and far-reaching assumptions — the very ideas that shape their lives. Heated conflict and hard feelings often result when people argue on the level of opinions and forget that the real conflict lies at the level of their assumptions.
- **Look for stated assumptions.** Stated assumptions are literally a thinker's starting points. Critical thinkers produce logical arguments and evidence to support most of their assertions. However, they are also willing to take other assertions as "self-evident" — so obvious or fundamental that they do not need to be proved.
- **Look for unstated assumptions.** In many cases, speakers and writers do not state their assumptions or offer evidence for them. In addition, people often hold many assumptions at the same time, with some of those assumptions contradicting each other. This makes uncovering assumptions a feat worthy of the greatest detective. You can follow a two-step method for testing the validity of any argument. First, state the assumptions. Second, see whether you can find any exceptions to the assumptions. Uncovering assumptions and looking for exceptions can help you detect many errors in logic.

Check for Evidence

In addition to testing arguments with the tools of logic, look carefully at the evidence used to support those arguments. Evidence comes in several forms, including facts, comments from recognized experts in a field, and examples.

Thinking Critically About Information on the Internet

Sources of information on the Internet range from the reputable (such as the Library of Congress) to the flamboyant (such as the *National Enquirer*). People are free to post *anything* on the Internet, including outdated facts as well as intentional misinformation.

Taking a few simple precautions when you surf the Internet can keep you from crashing onto the rocky shore of misinformation.

Distinguish Between Ideas and Information

To think more powerfully about what you find on the Internet, remember the difference between information and ideas. *Information* refers to facts that can be verified by independent observers. *Ideas* are interpretations or opinions based on facts. Several people with the same information might adopt different ideas based on that information.

Don't assume that an idea is more current, reasonable, or accurate just because you find it on the Internet. Apply your critical thinking skills to all published material — print and online.

Look for Overall Quality

Examine the features of a website in general. Notice the effectiveness of the text and visuals as a whole. Also note how well the site is organized and whether you can navigate the site's features with ease. Look for the date that crucial information was posted, and determine how often the site is updated.

Next, get an overview of the site's content. Examine several of the site's pages, and look for consistency of facts, quality of information, and competency with grammar and spelling. Evaluate the site's links to related webpages. Look for links to pages of reputable organizations.

Look at the Source

Find a clear description of the person or organization responsible for the website. If a site asks you to subscribe or become a member, then find out what it does with the personal information that you provide. Look for a way to contact the site's publisher with questions and comments.

Look for Documentation

When you encounter an assertion on a webpage or another Internet resource, note the types and quality of the evidence offered. Look for credible examples, quotations from authorities in the field, documented statistics, or summaries of scientific studies.

Set an Example

In the midst of the Internet's chaotic growth, you can light a path of rationality. Whether you're sending a short email message or building a massive website, bring your own critical thinking skills into play. Every word and image that you send down the wires to the web can display the hallmarks of critical thinking: sound logic, credible evidence, and respect for your audience.

Using OneNote to Enhance Critical Thinking

Using Microsoft OneNote as a tool for collecting your thoughts and ideas into organized sections of information puts your broad base of knowledge in a single searchable location for retrieval, analysis, and connection. During the critical thinking process, you can create a new section or a new page in OneNote and use the techniques discussed earlier in this chapter to link information from multiple areas of your notebook and synthesize those concepts into a final product.

Completing Four Steps to Solve Problems

Think of problem solving as a process with four Ps: Define the *problem*, generate *possibilities*, create a *plan*, and *perform* your plan.

Define the Problem

To define a problem effectively, understand what a problem is: a mismatch between what you want and what you have. Problem solving is all about reducing the gap between these two factors. One simple and powerful strategy for defining problems is simply to put them in writing. When you do this, you might find that potential solutions appear as well.

Generate Possibilities

Now put on your creative thinking hat. Open up. Brainstorm as many possible solutions to the problem as you can. As you generate possibilities, gather relevant facts.

Create a Plan

After rereading your problem definition and list of possible solutions, choose the solution that seems most workable. Think about specific actions that will reduce the gap between what you have and what you want. Visualize the steps you will take to make this solution a reality, and arrange them in chronological order. To make your plan even more powerful, put it in writing.

Perform Your Plan

Ultimately, your skill in solving problems lies in how well you perform your plan. Through the quality of your actions, you become the architect of your own success.

Office 2013 and Windows 8: Essential Concepts and Skills

Objectives

You will have mastered the material in this chapter when you can:

- Use a touch screen
- Perform basic mouse operations
- Start Windows and sign in to an account
- Identify the objects in the Windows 8 desktop
- Identify the apps in and versions of Microsoft Office 2013
- Run an app
- Identify the components of the Microsoft Office ribbon
- Create folders
- Save files
- Change screen resolution
- Perform basic tasks in Microsoft Office apps
- Manage files
- Use Microsoft Office Help and Windows Help

Office 2013 and Windows 8: Essential Concepts and Skills

This introductory chapter uses Word 2013 to cover features and functions common to Office 2013 apps, as well as the basics of Windows 8.

Roadmap

In this chapter, you will learn how to perform basic tasks in Windows and Word. The following roadmap identifies general activities you will perform as you progress through this chapter:

1. SIGN IN to an account
2. USE WINDOWS
3. USE Features in Word that are Common across Office APPS
4. FILE and Folder MANAGEMENT
5. SWITCH between APPS
6. SAVE and Manage FILES
7. CHANGE SCREEN RESOLUTION
8. EXIT APPS
9. USE ADDITIONAL Office APP FEATURES
10. USE Office and Windows HELP

At the beginning of the step instructions throughout the chapter, you will see an abbreviated form of this roadmap. The abbreviated roadmap uses colors to indicate chapter progress: gray means the chapter is beyond that activity, blue means the task being shown is covered in that activity, and black means that activity is yet to be covered. For example, the following abbreviated roadmap indicates the chapter would be showing a task in the 2 USE APPS activity.

1 SIGN IN | 2 USE WINDOWS | 3 USE APPS | 4 FILE MANAGEMENT | 5 SWITCH APPS | 6 SAVE FILES
7 CHANGE SCREEN RESOLUTION | 8 EXIT APPS | 9 USE ADDITIONAL APP FEATURES | 10 USE HELP

Use the abbreviated roadmap as a progress guide while you read or step through the instructions in this chapter.

Introduction to the Windows 8 Operating System

Windows 8 is the newest version of Microsoft Windows, which is a popular and widely used operating system. An **operating system** is a computer program (set of computer instructions) that coordinates all the activities of computer hardware, such as memory, storage devices, and printers, and provides the capability for you to communicate with the computer.

The Windows operating system simplifies the process of working with documents and apps by organizing the manner in which you interact with the computer. Windows is used to run apps. An **app** (short for application) consists of programs designed to make users more productive and/or assist them with personal tasks, such as word processing or browsing the web.

The Windows 8 interface begins with the **Start screen**, which shows tiles (Figure 1). A **tile** is a shortcut to an app or other content. The tiles on the Start screen include installed apps that you use regularly. From the Start screen, you can choose which apps to run using a touch screen, mouse, or other input device.

Figure 1

Using a Touch Screen and a Mouse

Windows users who have computers or devices with touch screen capability can interact with the screen using gestures. A **gesture** is a motion you make on a touch screen with the tip of one or more fingers or your hand. Touch screens are convenient because they do not require a separate device for input. Table 1 on the next page presents common ways to interact with a touch screen.

If you are using your finger on a touch screen and are having difficulty completing the steps in this chapter, consider using a stylus. Many people find it easier to be precise with a stylus than with a finger. In addition, with a stylus you see the pointer. If you still are having trouble completing the steps with a stylus, try using a mouse.

Table 1 Touch Screen Gestures

Motion	Description	Common Uses
Tap	Quickly touch and release one finger one time.	Activate a link (built-in connection) Press a button Run a program or an app
Double-tap	Quickly touch and release one finger two times.	Run a program or an app Zoom in (show a smaller area on the screen, so that contents appear larger) at the location of the double-tap
Press and hold	Press and hold one finger to cause an action to occur, or until an action occurs.	Display a shortcut menu (immediate access to allowable actions) Activate a mode enabling you to move an item with one finger to a new location
Drag, or slide	Press and hold one finger on an object and then move the finger to the new location.	Move an item around the screen Scroll
Swipe	Press and hold one finger and then move the finger horizontally or vertically on the screen.	Select an object Swipe from edge to display a bar such as the Charms bar, Apps bar, and Navigation bar (all discussed later)
Stretch	Move two fingers apart.	Zoom in (show a smaller area on the screen, so that contents appear larger)
Pinch	Move two fingers together.	Zoom out (show a larger area on the screen, so that contents appear smaller)

BTW
BTWs
For a complete list of the BTWs found in the margins of this book, visit the BTW resource on the Student Companion Site located on www.cengagebrain.com. For detailed instructions about accessing available resources, visit www.cengage.com/ct/studentdownload or contact your instructor for information about accessing the required files.

BTW
Touch Screen Differences
The Office and Windows interfaces may vary if you are using a touch screen. For this reason, you might notice that the function or appearance of your touch screen differs slightly from this chapter's presentation.

CONSIDER THIS

Will your screen look different if you are using a touch screen?
The Windows and Microsoft Office interface varies slightly if you are using a touch screen. For this reason, you might notice that your Windows or Word screens look slightly different from the screens in this book.

Windows users who do not have touch screen capabilities typically work with a mouse that usually has at least two buttons. For a right-handed user, the left button usually is the primary mouse button, and the right mouse button is the secondary mouse button. Left-handed people, however, can reverse the function of these buttons.

Table 2 explains how to perform a variety of mouse operations. Some apps also use keys in combination with the mouse to perform certain actions. For example, when you hold down the CTRL key while rolling the mouse wheel, text on the screen may become larger or smaller based on the direction you roll the wheel. The function of the mouse buttons and the wheel varies depending on the app.

Table 2 Mouse Operations

Operation	Mouse Action	Example
Point	Move the mouse until the pointer on the desktop is positioned on the item of choice.	Position the pointer on the screen.
Click	Press and release the primary mouse button, which usually is the left mouse button.	Select or deselect items on the screen or run an app or app feature.
Right-click	Press and release the secondary mouse button, which usually is the right mouse button.	Display a shortcut menu.
Double-click	Quickly press and release the primary mouse button twice without moving the mouse.	Run an app or app feature.
Triple-click	Quickly press and release the primary mouse button three times without moving the mouse.	Select a paragraph.
Drag	Point to an item, hold down the primary mouse button, move the item to the desired location on the screen, and then release the mouse button.	Move an object from one location to another or draw pictures.
Right-drag	Point to an item, hold down the right mouse button, move the item to the desired location on the screen, and then release the right mouse button.	Display a shortcut menu after moving an object from one location to another.
Rotate wheel	Roll the wheel forward or backward.	Scroll vertically (up and down).
Free-spin wheel	Whirl the wheel forward or backward so that it spins freely on its own.	Scroll through many pages in seconds.
Press wheel	Press the wheel button while moving the mouse.	Scroll continuously.
Tilt wheel	Press the wheel toward the right or left.	Scroll horizontally (left and right).
Press thumb button	Press the button on the side of the mouse with your thumb.	Move forward or backward through webpages and/or control media, games, etc.

Scrolling

A **scroll bar** is a horizontal or vertical bar that appears when the contents of an area may not be visible completely on the screen (Figure 2). A scroll bar contains **scroll arrows** and a **scroll box** that enable you to view areas that currently cannot be seen on the screen. Tapping or clicking the up and down scroll arrows moves the screen content up or down one line. You also can tap or click above or below the scroll box to move up or down a section, or drag the scroll box up or down to move to a specific location.

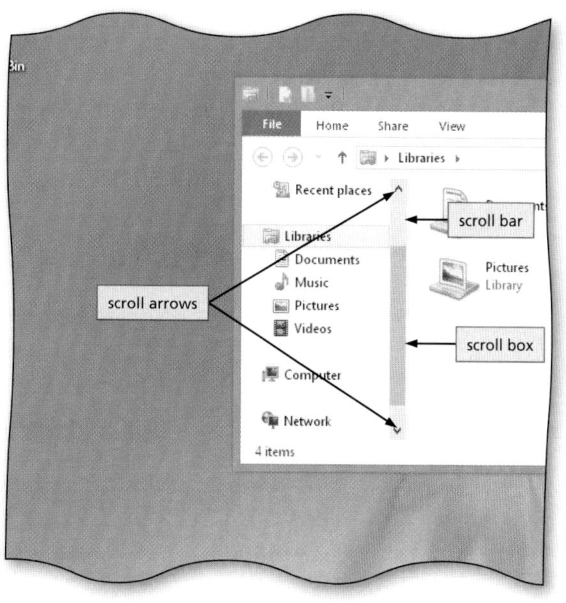

Figure 2

BTW

Pointer

If you are using a touch screen, the pointer may not appear on the screen as you perform touch gestures. The pointer will reappear when you begin using the mouse.

BTW

Minimize Wrist Injury

Computer users frequently switch between the keyboard and the mouse during a word processing session; such switching strains the wrist. To help prevent wrist injury, minimize switching. For instance, if your fingers already are on the keyboard, use keyboard keys to scroll. If your hand already is on the mouse, use the mouse to scroll. If your hand is on the touch screen, use touch gestures to scroll.

CONSIDER THIS

What should you do if you are running Windows 7 instead of Windows 8?

Although Windows 8 includes several user interface and feature enhancements, many of the steps in this book work in both Windows 7 and Windows 8. If you have any questions about differences between the two operating systems or how to perform tasks in an earlier version of Windows, contact your instructor.

Keyboard Shortcuts

In many cases, you can use the keyboard instead of the mouse to accomplish a task. To perform tasks using the keyboard, you press one or more keyboard keys, sometimes identified as a **keyboard shortcut**. Some keyboard shortcuts consist of a single key, such as the F1 key. For example, to obtain help in many apps, you can press the F1 key. Other keyboard shortcuts consist of multiple keys, in which case a plus sign separates the key names, such as CTRL+ESC. This notation means to press and hold down the first key listed, press one or more additional keys, and then release all keys. For example, to display the Start screen, press CTRL+ESC, that is, hold down the CTRL key, press the ESC key, and then release both keys.

Starting Windows

It is not unusual for multiple people to use the same computer in a work, educational, recreational, or home setting. Windows enables each user to establish a **user account**, which identifies to Windows the resources, such as apps and storage locations, a user can access when working with the computer.

Each user account has a user name and may have a password and an icon, as well. A **user name** is a unique combination of letters or numbers that identifies a specific user to Windows. A **password** is a private combination of letters, numbers, and special characters associated with the user name that allows access to a user's account resources. An icon is a small image that represents an object, thus a **user icon** is a picture associated with a user name.

When you turn on a computer, Windows starts and displays a **lock screen** consisting of the time and date (Figure 3a). To unlock the screen, swipe up or click the lock screen. Depending on your computer's settings, Windows may or may not display a sign-in screen that shows the user names and user icons for users who have accounts on the computer (Figure 3b). This **sign-in screen** enables you to sign in to your user account and makes the computer available for use. Tapping or clicking the user icon begins the process of signing in, also called logging on, to your user account.

At the bottom of the sign-in screen is the 'Ease of access' button and a Shut down button. Tapping or clicking the 'Ease of access' button displays the Ease of access menu, which provides tools to optimize a computer to accommodate the needs of the mobility, hearing, and vision impaired users. Tapping or clicking the Shut down

Figure 3a

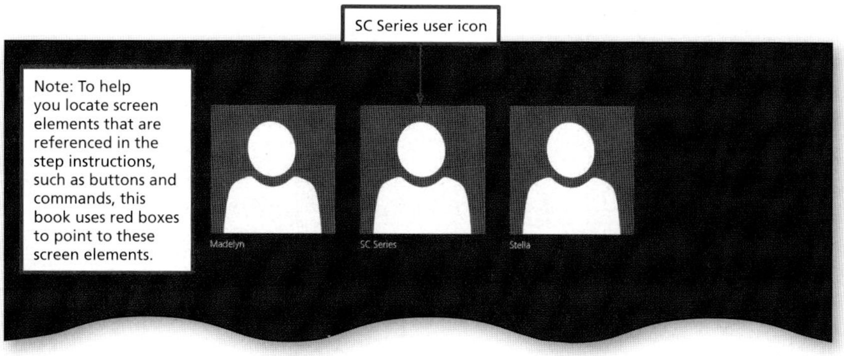

SC Series user icon

Note: To help you locate screen elements that are referenced in the step instructions, such as buttons and commands, this book uses red boxes to point to these screen elements.

Madelyn SC Series Stella

Figure 3b

button displays a menu containing commands related to restarting the computer, putting it in a low-power state, and shutting it down. The commands available on your computer may differ.

- The Sleep command saves your work, turns off the computer fans and hard disk, and places the computer in a lower-power state. To wake the computer from sleep mode, press the power button or lift a laptop's cover, and sign in to your account.
- The Shut down command exits running apps, shuts down Windows, and then turns off the computer.
- The Restart command exits running apps, shuts down Windows, and then restarts Windows.

BTW

Q&As

For a complete list of the Q&As found in many of the step-by-step sequences in this book, visit the Q&A resource on the Student Companion Site located on www.cengagebrain.com. For detailed instructions about accessing available resources, visit www.cengage.com/ct/studentdownload or contact your instructor for information about accessing the required files.

To Sign In to an Account

1 SIGN IN | 2 USE WINDOWS | 3 USE APPS | 4 FILE MANAGEMENT | 5 SWITCH APPS | 6 SAVE FILES
7 CHANGE SCREEN RESOLUTION | 8 EXIT APPS | 9 USE ADDITIONAL APP FEATURES | 10 USE HELP

The following steps, which use SC Series as the user name, sign in to an account based on a typical Windows installation. ***Why?*** *After starting Windows, you might be required to sign in to an account to access the computer's resources.* You may need to ask your instructor how to sign in to your account. If you are using Windows 7, skip these steps and instead perform the steps in the yellow box that immediately follows these Windows 8 steps.

- Swipe up or click the lock screen (shown in Figure 3a) to display a sign-in screen (shown in Figure 3b).
- Tap or click the user icon (for SC Series, in this case) on the sign-in screen, which depending on settings, either will display a second sign-in screen that contains a Password text box (Figure 4) or will display the Windows Start screen (shown in Figure 5 on the next page).

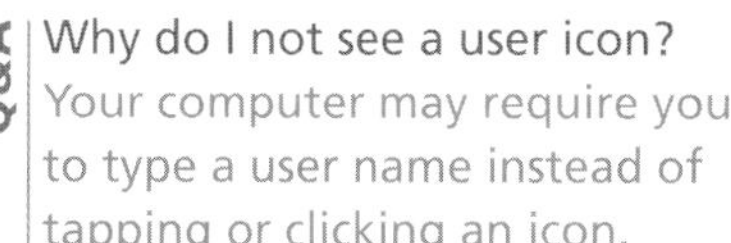

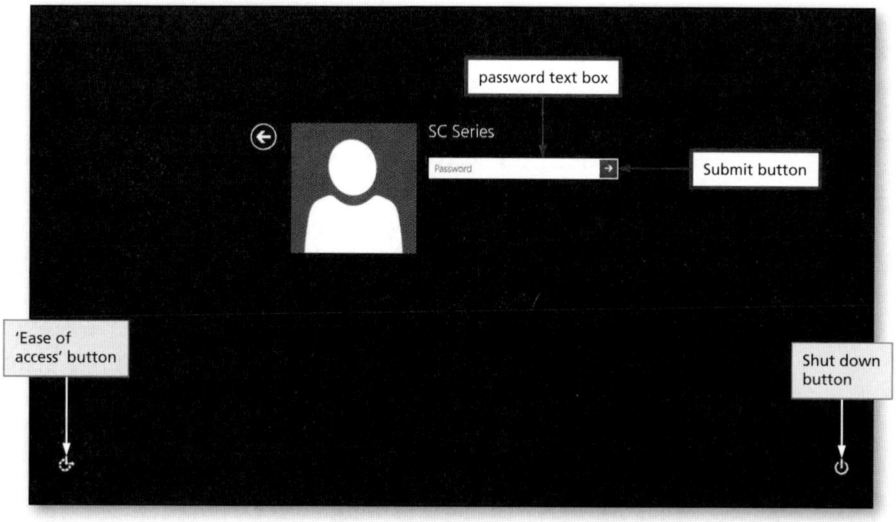

Q&A

Why do I not see a user icon?
Your computer may require you to type a user name instead of tapping or clicking an icon.

What is a text box?
A text box is a rectangular box in which you type text.

Why does my screen not show a Password text box?
Your account does not require a password.

password text box

SC Series

Password

Submit button

'Ease of access' button

Shut down button

Figure 4

- If Windows displays a sign-in screen with a Password text box, type your password in the text box.

2

- Tap or click the Submit button (shown in Figure 4 on the previous page) to sign in to your account and display the Windows Start screen (Figure 5).

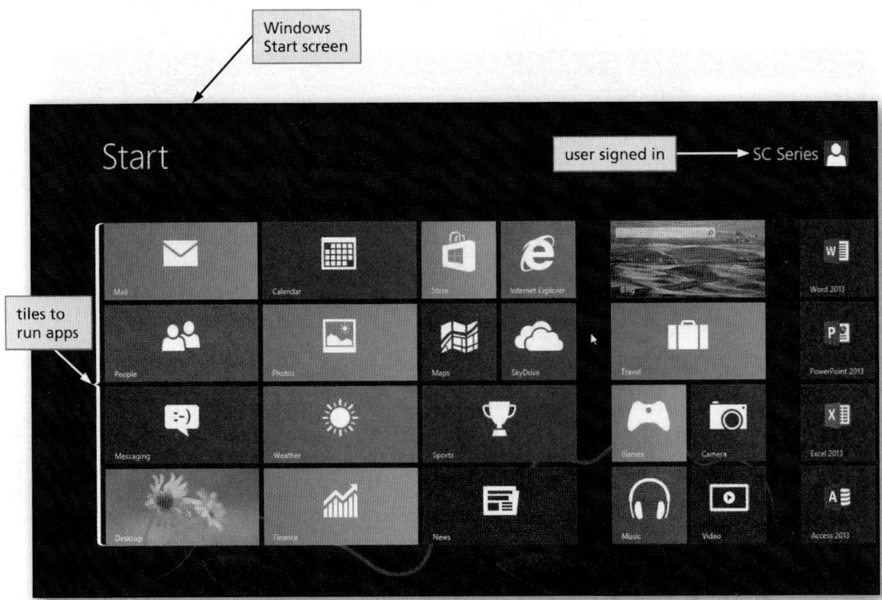

Figure 5

Q&A

Why does my Start screen look different from the one in Figure 5?
The Windows Start screen is customizable, and your school or employer may have modified the screen to meet its needs. Also, your screen resolution, which affects the size of the elements on the screen, may differ from the screen resolution used in this book. Later in this chapter, you learn how to change screen resolution.

How do I type if my tablet has no keyboard?
You can use your fingers to press keys on a keyboard that appears on the screen, called an on-screen keyboard, or you can purchase a separate physical keyboard that attaches to or wirelessly communicates with the tablet.

To Sign In to an Account Using Windows 7

If you are using Windows 7, perform these steps to sign in to an account instead of the previous steps that use Windows 8.

1. Click the user icon on the Welcome screen; depending on settings, this either will display a password text box or will sign in to the account and display the Windows 7 desktop.
2. If Windows 7 displays a password text box, type your password in the text box and then click the arrow button to sign in to the account and display the Windows 7 desktop.

The Windows Start Screen

BTW
Modern UI
The new Windows 8 user interface also is referred to as the Modern UI (user interface).

The Windows Start screen provides a scrollable space for you to access apps that have been pinned to the Start screen (shown in Figure 5). Pinned apps appear as tiles on the Start screen. In addition to running apps, you can perform tasks such as pinning apps (placing tiles) on the Start screen, moving the tiles around the Start screen, and unpinning apps (removing tiles) from the Start screen.

If you swipe up from the bottom of or right-click an open space on the Start screen, the App bar will appear. The **App bar** includes a button that enables you to display all of your apps. When working with tiles, the App bar also provides options for manipulating the tiles, such as resizing them.

CONSIDER THIS

How do you pin apps, move tiles, and unpin apps?

- To pin an app, swipe up from the bottom of the Start screen or right-click an open space on the Start screen to display the App bar, tap or click the All apps button on the App bar to display the Apps list, swipe down on or right-click the app you want to pin, and then tap or click the 'Pin to Start' button on the App bar. One way to return to the Start screen is to swipe up from the bottom or right-click an open space in the Apps list and then tap or click the All apps button again.
- To move a tile, drag the tile to the desired location.
- To unpin an app, swipe down on or right-click the app to display the App bar and then tap or click the 'Unpin from Start' button on the App bar.

Introduction to Microsoft Office 2013

Microsoft Office 2013 is the newest version of Microsoft Office, offering features that provide users with better functionality and easier ways to work with the various files they create. These features include enhanced design tools, such as improved picture formatting tools and new themes, shared notebooks for working in groups, mobile versions of Office apps, broadcast presentations for the web, and a digital notebook for managing and sharing multimedia information.

Microsoft Office 2013 Apps

Microsoft Office 2013 includes a wide variety of apps such as Word, PowerPoint, Excel, Access, Outlook, Publisher, OneNote, InfoPath, SharePoint Workspace, and Lync:

- **Microsoft Word 2013**, or Word, is a full-featured word processing app that allows you to create professional-looking documents and revise them easily.
- **Microsoft PowerPoint 2013**, or PowerPoint, is a complete presentation app that enables you to produce professional-looking presentations and then deliver them to an audience.
- **Microsoft Excel 2013**, or Excel, is a powerful spreadsheet app that allows you to organize data, complete calculations, make decisions, graph data, develop professional-looking reports, publish organized data to the web, and access real-time data from websites.
- **Microsoft Access 2013**, or Access, is a database management system that enables you to create a database; add, change, and delete data in the database; ask questions concerning the data in the database; and create forms and reports using the data in the database.
- **Microsoft Outlook 2013**, or Outlook, is a communications and scheduling app that allows you to manage email accounts, calendars, contacts, and access to other Internet content.
- **Microsoft Publisher 2013**, or Publisher, is a desktop publishing app that helps you create professional-quality publications and marketing materials that can be shared easily.
- **Microsoft OneNote 2013**, or OneNote, is a note taking app that allows you to store and share information in notebooks with other people.
- **Microsoft InfoPath Designer 2013**, or InfoPath, is a form development app that helps you create forms for use on the web and gather data from these forms.
- **Microsoft SharePoint Workspace 2013**, or SharePoint, is a collaboration app that allows you to access and revise files stored on your computer from other locations.
- **Microsoft Lync 2013** is a communications app that allows you to use various modes of communications such as instant messaging, videoconferencing, and sharing files and apps.

Microsoft Office 2013 Suites

A **suite** is a collection of individual apps available together as a unit. Microsoft offers a variety of Office suites, including a stand-alone desktop app (boxed software), Microsoft Office 365, and Microsoft Office Web Apps. **Microsoft Office 365**, or Office 365, provides plans that allow organizations to use Office in a mobile setting while also being able to communicate and share files, depending upon the type of plan selected by the organization. **Microsoft Office Web Apps**, or Web Apps, are apps that allow you to edit and share files on the web using the familiar Office interface. Table 3 on the next page outlines the differences among these Office suites.

Table 3 Office Suites

Apps/ Licenses	Office 365 Home Premium	Office 365 Small Business Premium	Office Home & Student	Office Home & Business	Office Professional
Word	✓	✓	✓	✓	✓
PowerPoint	✓	✓	✓	✓	✓
Excel	✓	✓	✓	✓	✓
Access	✓	✓			✓
Outlook	✓	✓		✓	✓
Publisher	✓	✓			✓
Lync		✓			
OneNote			✓	✓	✓
InfoPath		✓			
Licenses	5	5	1	1	1

During the Office 365 installation, you select a plan, and depending on your plan, you receive different apps and services. Office Web Apps do not require a local installation and are accessed through SkyDrive and your browser. **SkyDrive** is a cloud storage service that provides storage and other services, such as Office Web Apps, to computer users.

CONSIDER THIS

How do you sign up for a SkyDrive account?

- Use your browser to navigate to skydrive.live.com.
- Create a Microsoft account by tapping or clicking the 'Sign up now' link (or a similar link) and then entering your information to create the account.
- Sign in to SkyDrive using your new account or use it in Word to save your files on SkyDrive.

Apps in a suite, such as Microsoft Office, typically use a similar interface and share features. Once you are comfortable working with the elements and the interface and performing tasks in one app, the similarity can help you apply the knowledge and skills you have learned to another app(s) in the suite. For example, the process for saving a file in Word is the same in PowerPoint, Excel, and the other Office apps. While briefly showing how to use Word, this chapter illustrates some of the common functions across the Office apps and identifies the characteristics unique to Word.

Running and Using an App

To use an app, such as Word, you must instruct the operating system to run the app. Windows provides many different ways to run an app, one of which is presented in this section (other ways to run an app are presented throughout this chapter). After an app is running, you can use it to perform a variety of tasks. The following pages use Word to discuss some elements of the Office interface and to perform tasks that are common to other Office apps.

Word

Word is a full-featured word processing app that allows you to create many types of personal and business documents, including flyers, letters, memos, resumes, reports, fax cover sheets, mailing labels, and newsletters. Word also provides tools that enable you to create webpages and save these webpages directly on a web server. Word has many features designed to simplify the production of documents and add visual appeal. Using Word, you easily can change the shape, size, and color of text. You also can include borders, shading, tables, images, pictures, charts, and web addresses in documents.

To Run an App from the Start Screen

1 SIGN IN | 2 USE WINDOWS | 3 USE APPS | 4 FILE MANAGEMENT | 5 SWITCH APPS | 6 SAVE FILES
7 CHANGE SCREEN RESOLUTION | 8 EXIT APPS | 9 USE ADDITIONAL APP FEATURES | 10 USE HELP

The Start screen contains tiles that allow you to run apps, some of which may be stored on your computer. ***Why?*** *When you install an app, for example, tiles are added to the Start screen for the various Office apps included in the suite.*

The following steps, which assume Windows is running, use the Start screen to run Word based on a typical installation. You may need to ask your instructor how to run Word on your computer. Although the steps illustrate running the Word app, the steps to run any Office app are similar. If you are using Windows 7, skip these steps and instead perform the steps in the yellow box that immediately follows these Windows 8 steps.

- If necessary, scroll to display the Word tile on the Start screen (Figure 6).

Q&A Why does my Start screen look different?
It may look different because of your computer's configuration. The Start screen may be customized for several reasons, such as usage requirements or security restrictions.

What if the app I want to run is not on the Start screen?
You can display all installed apps by swiping up from the bottom of the Start screen or right-clicking an open space on the Start screen and then tapping or clicking the All apps button on the App bar.

How do I scroll on a touch screen?
Use the slide gesture; that is, press and hold your finger on the screen and then move your finger in the direction you wish to scroll.

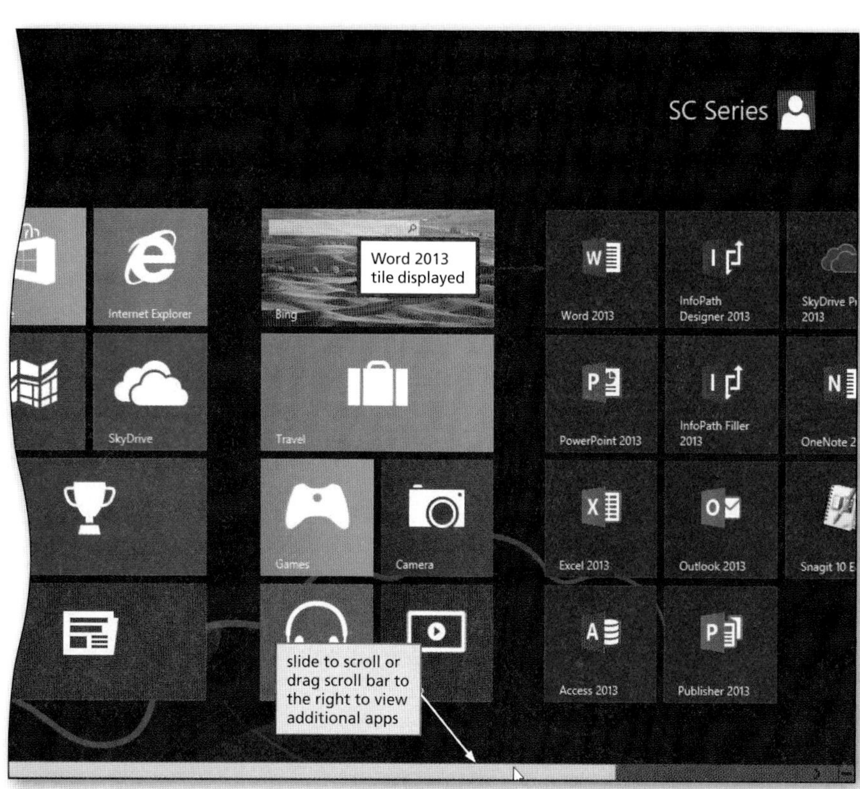

Figure 6

- Tap or click the Word 2013 tile to run the Word app and display the Word start screen (Figure 7).

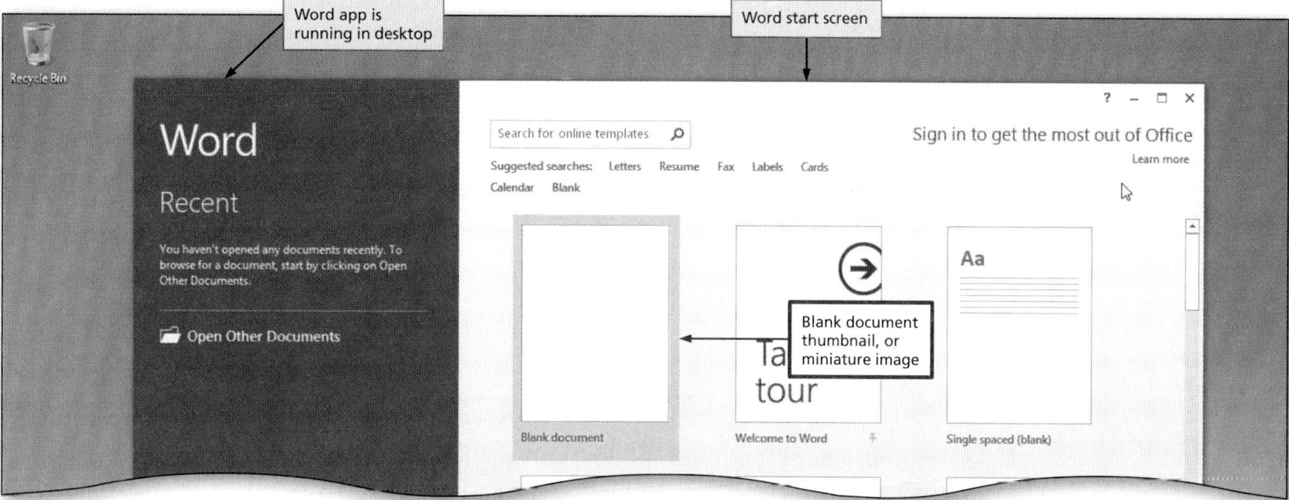

Figure 7

3

- Tap or click the Blank document thumbnail on the Word start screen to create a blank Word document in the Word window (Figure 8).

Q&A What happens when you run an app?
Some apps provide a means for you to create a blank document, as shown in Figure 7 on the previous page; others immediately display a blank document in an app window, such as the Word window shown in Figure 8. A **window** is a rectangular area that displays data and information. The top of a window has a **title bar**, which is a horizontal space that contains the window's name.

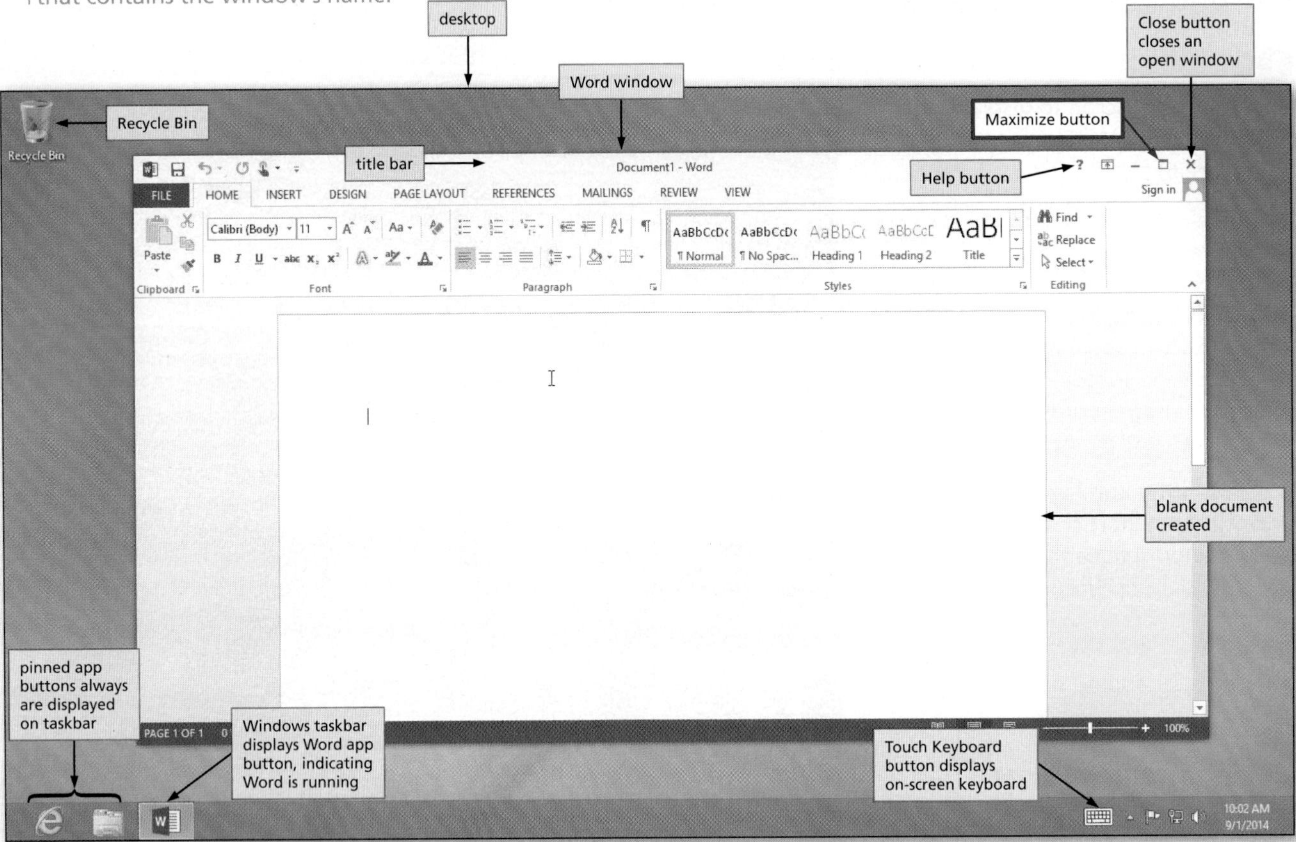

Figure 8

Other Ways

1. Tap or click Search charm on Charms bar, type app name in search box, tap or click app name in results list
2. Double-tap or double-click file created in app you want to run

BTW
Touch Keyboard
To display the on-screen touch keyboard, tap the Touch Keyboard button on the Windows taskbar. When finished using the touch keyboard, tap the X button on the touch keyboard to close the keyboard.

To Run an App Using the Start Menu in Windows 7

If you are using Windows 7, perform these steps to run Word using the Start menu instead of the previous steps that use Windows 8.

1. Click the Start button on the Windows 7 taskbar to display the Start menu.
2. Click All Programs at the bottom of the left pane on the Start menu to display the All Programs list.
3. If the Word app is located in a folder, click, or scroll to and then click, the folder in the All Programs list to display a list of the folder's contents.
4. Click, or scroll to and then click, the app name (Word, in this case) in the list to run the selected app.

Windows Desktop

When you run an app in Windows, it may appear in an on-screen work area app, called the **desktop** (shown in Figure 8). You can perform tasks such as placing objects in the desktop, moving the objects around the desktop, and removing items from the desktop.

Some icons also may be displayed in the desktop. For instance, the icon for the **Recycle Bin**, the location of files that have been deleted, appears in the desktop by default. A **file** is a named unit of storage. Files can contain text, images, audio, and video. You can customize your desktop so that icons representing apps and files you use often appear in the desktop.

To Switch between an App and the Start Screen

While working with an app, such as Word, or in the desktop, you easily can return to the Start screen. The following steps switch from the Word app to the Start screen. ***Why?*** *Returning to the Start screen allows you to run any of your other apps.* If you are using Windows 7, read these steps without performing them because Windows 7 does not have a Start screen.

- Swipe in from the left edge of the screen and then back to the left, or point to the lower-left corner of the desktop to display a thumbnail of the Start screen (Figure 9).

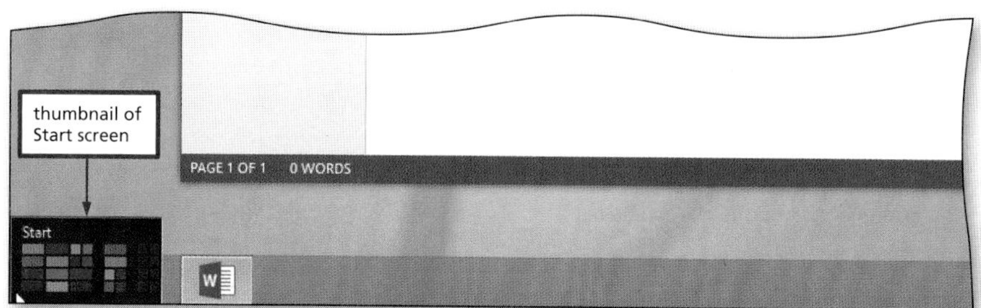

Figure 9

- Tap or click the thumbnail of the Start screen to display the Start screen (Figure 10).

- Tap or click the Desktop tile to redisplay the Word app in the desktop (shown in Figure 8).

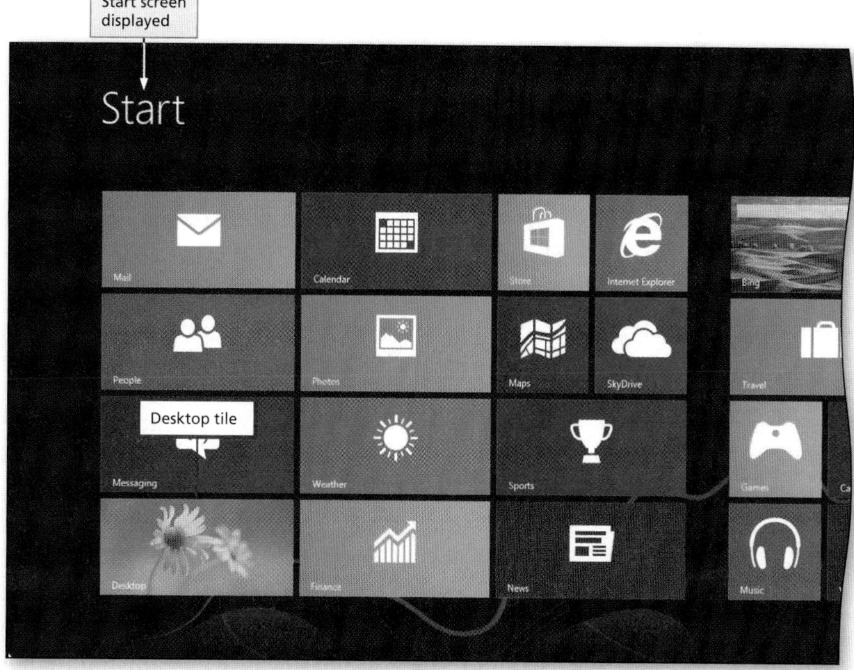

Figure 10

Other Ways

1. Press WINDOWS key to display Start screen

To Maximize a Window

Sometimes content is not visible completely in a window. One method of displaying the entire contents of a window is to **maximize** it, or enlarge the window so that it fills the entire screen. The following step maximizes the Word window; however, any Office app's window can be maximized using this step. ***Why?*** *A maximized window provides the most space available for using the app.*

- If the Word window is not maximized already, tap or click the Maximize button (shown in Figure 8 on page OFF 12) next to the Close button on the window's title bar to maximize the window (Figure 11).

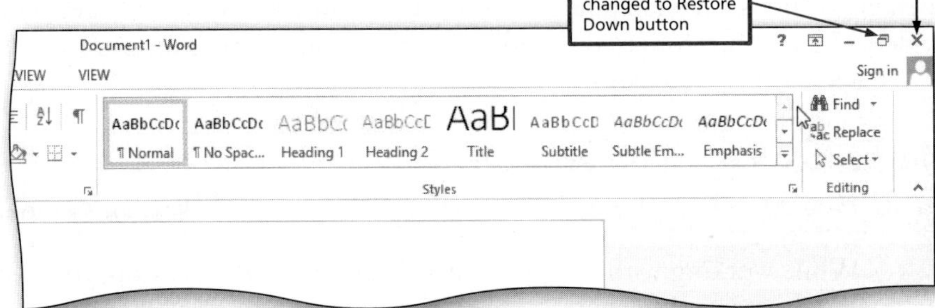

Figure 11

Q&A

What happened to the Maximize button?
It changed to a Restore Down button, which you can use to return a window to its size and location before you maximized it.

How do I know whether a window is maximized?
A window is maximized if it fills the entire display area and the Restore Down button is displayed on the title bar.

Other Ways

1. Double-tap or double-click title bar
2. Drag title bar to top of screen

Word Document Window, Ribbon, and Elements Common to Office Apps

The Word window consists of a variety of components to make your work more efficient and documents more professional. These include the document window, ribbon, mini toolbar, shortcut menus, Quick Access Toolbar, and Microsoft Account area. Most of these components are common to other Microsoft Office apps; others are unique to Word.

You view a portion of a document on the screen through a **document window** (Figure 12). The default (preset) view is **Print Layout view**, which shows the document on a mock sheet of paper in the document window.

Scroll Bars You use a scroll bar to display different portions of a document in the document window. At the right edge of the document window is a vertical scroll bar. If a document is too wide to fit in the document window, a horizontal scroll bar also appears at the bottom of the document window. On a scroll bar, the position of the scroll box reflects the location of the portion of the document that is displayed in the document window.

Status Bar The **status bar**, located at the bottom of the document window above the Windows taskbar, presents information about the document, the progress of current tasks, and the status of certain commands and keys; it also provides controls for viewing the document. As you type text or perform certain tasks, various indicators and buttons may appear on the status bar.

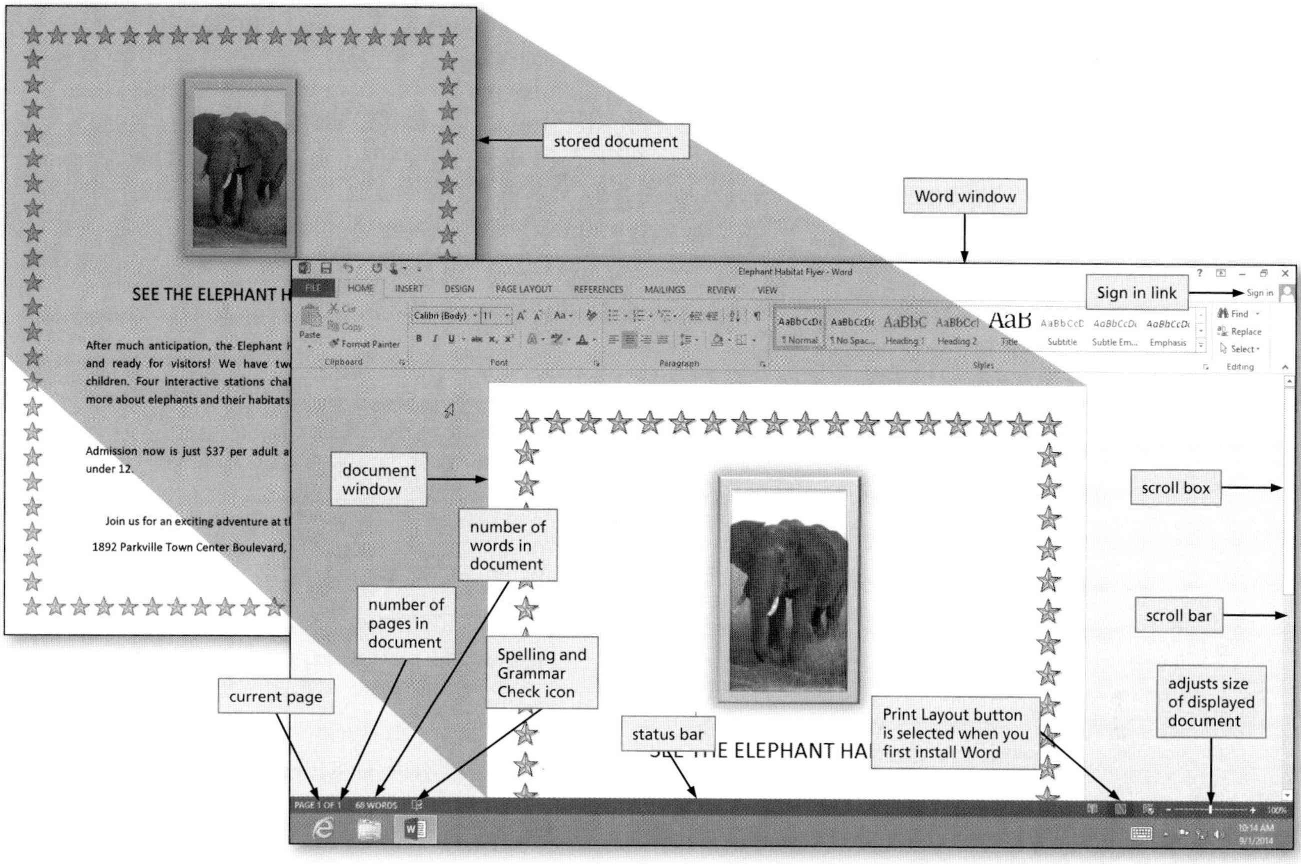

Figure 12

The left side of the status bar in Figure 12 shows the current page followed by the total number of pages in the document, the number of words in the document, and an icon to check spelling and grammar. The right side of the status bar includes buttons and controls you can use to change the view of a document and adjust the size of the displayed document.

Ribbon The ribbon, located near the top of the window below the title bar, is the control center in Word and other Office apps (Figure 13). The ribbon provides easy, central access to the tasks you perform while creating a document. The ribbon consists of tabs, groups, and commands. Each **tab** contains a collection of groups, and each **group** contains related commands. When you run an Office app, such as Word, it initially displays several main tabs, also called default or top-level tabs. All Office apps have a HOME tab, which contains the more frequently used commands.

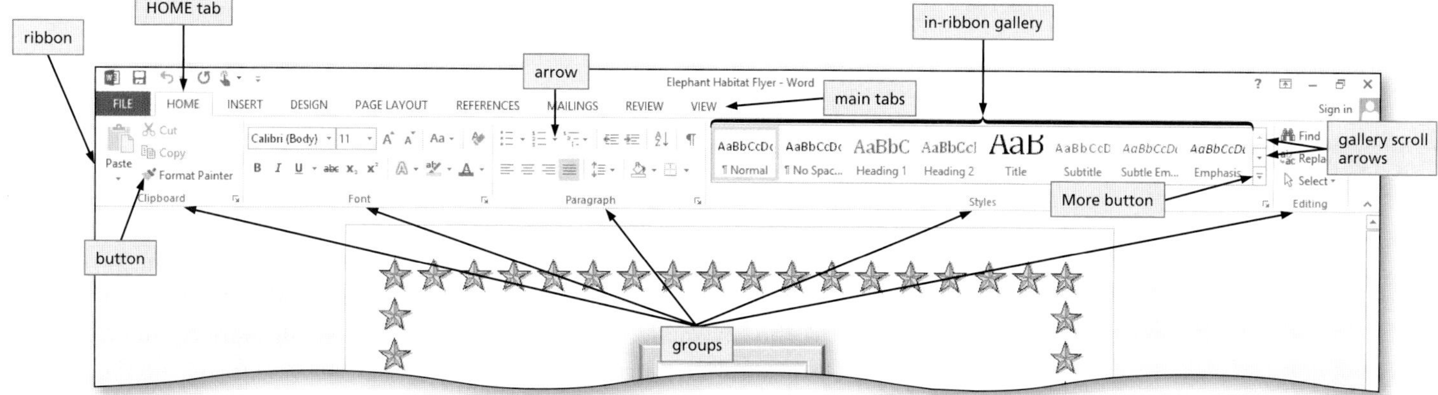

Figure 13

In addition to the main tabs, the Office apps display **tool tabs**, also called contextual tabs (Figure 14), when you perform certain tasks or work with objects such as pictures or tables. If you insert a picture in a Word document, for example, the PICTURE TOOLS tab and its related subordinate FORMAT tab appear, collectively referred to as the PICTURE TOOLS FORMAT tab. When you are finished working with the picture, the PICTURE TOOLS FORMAT tab disappears from the ribbon. Word and other Office apps determine when tool tabs should appear and disappear based on tasks you perform. Some tool tabs, such as the TABLE TOOLS tab, have more than one related subordinate tab.

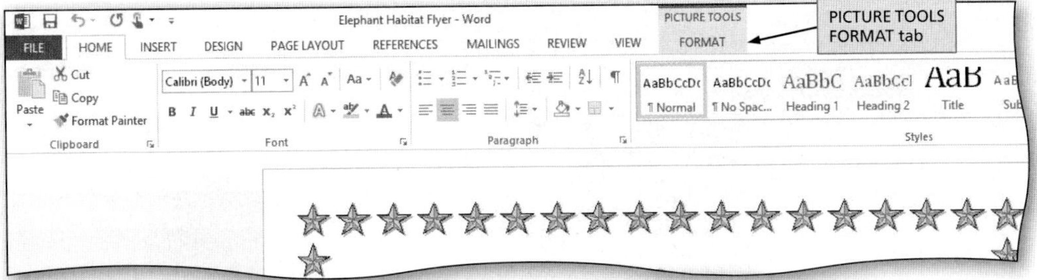

Figure 14

Figure 15

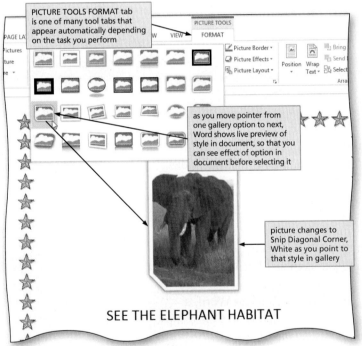

Items on the ribbon include buttons, boxes, and galleries (shown in Figure 13 on the previous page). A **gallery** is a set of choices, often graphical, arranged in a grid or in a list. You can scroll through choices in an in-ribbon gallery by tapping or clicking the gallery's scroll arrows. Or, you can tap or click a gallery's More button to view more gallery options on the screen at a time.

Some buttons and boxes have arrows that, when tapped or clicked, also display a gallery; others always cause a gallery to be displayed when tapped or clicked. Most galleries support **live preview**, which is a feature that allows you to point to a gallery choice and see its effect in the document — without actually selecting the choice (Figure 15). Live preview works only if you are using a mouse; if you are using a touch screen, you will not be able to view live previews.

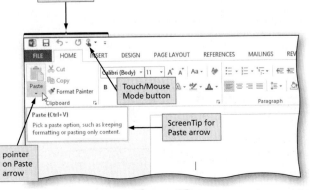

Figure 16

Some commands on the ribbon display an image to help you remember their function. When you point to a command on the ribbon, all or part of the command glows in a shade of blue, and a ScreenTip appears on the screen. A **ScreenTip** is an on-screen note that provides the name of the command, available keyboard shortcut(s), a description of the command, and sometimes instructions for how to obtain help about the command (Figure 16).

Some groups on the ribbon have a small arrow in the lower-right corner, called a **Dialog Box Launcher**, that when tapped or clicked, displays a dialog box or a task pane with additional options for the group (Figure 17). When presented with a dialog box, you make selections and must close the dialog box before returning to the document. A **task pane**, in contrast to a dialog box, is a window that can remain open and visible while you work in the document.

BTW

Touch Mode
The Office and Windows interfaces may vary if you are using Touch mode. For this reason, you might notice that the function or appearance of your touch screen in Word differs slightly from this book's presentation.

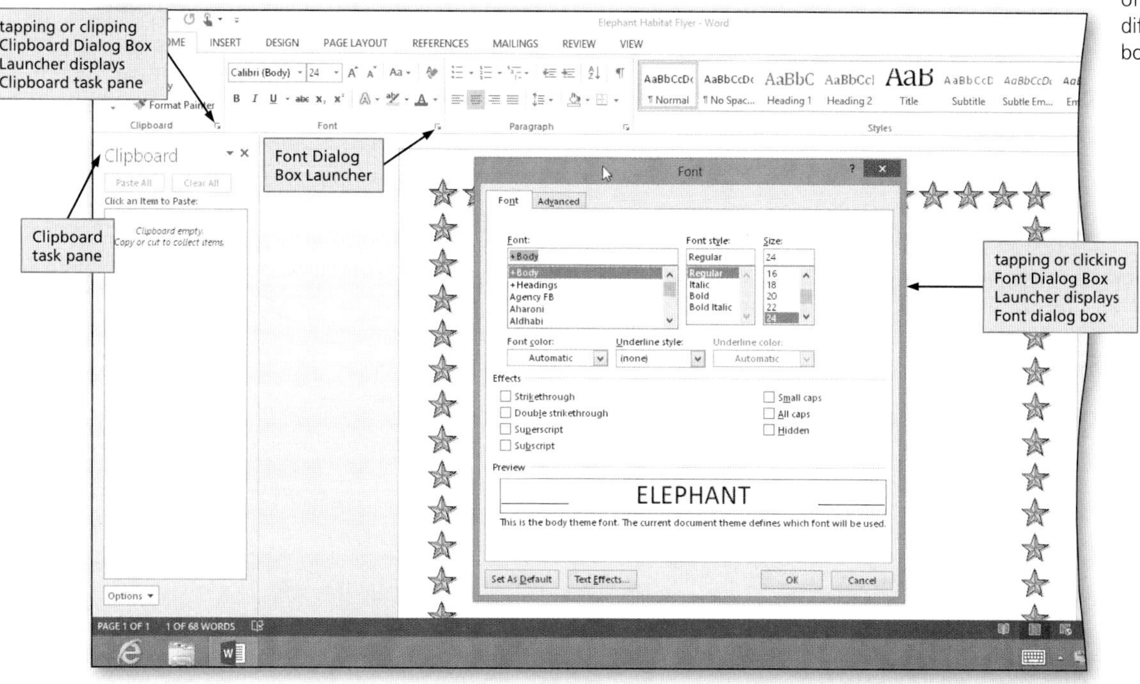

Figure 17

Mini Toolbar The **mini toolbar**, which appears automatically based on tasks you perform, contains commands related to changing the appearance of text in a document (Figure 18). If you do not use the mini toolbar, it disappears from the screen. The buttons, arrows, and boxes on the mini toolbar vary, depending on whether you are using Touch mode versus Mouse mode. If you press and hold or right-click an item in the document window, Word displays both the mini toolbar and a shortcut menu, which is discussed in a later section in this chapter.

All commands on the mini toolbar also exist on the ribbon. The purpose of the mini toolbar is to minimize hand or mouse movement.

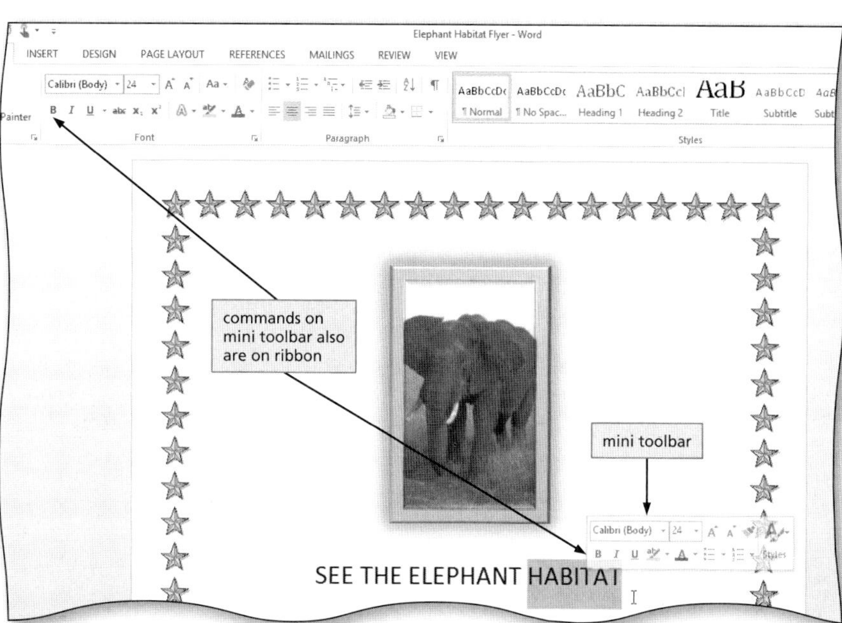

Figure 18

Quick Access Toolbar The **Quick Access Toolbar**, located initially (by default) above the ribbon at the left edge of the title bar, provides convenient, one-tap or one-click access to frequently used commands (shown in Figure 16). The commands on the Quick Access Toolbar always are available, regardless of the task you are performing. The Touch/Mouse Mode button on the Quick Access Toolbar allows you to switch between Touch mode and Mouse mode. If you primarily are using touch gestures, Touch mode will add more

BTW
Turning Off the Mini Toolbar
If you do not want the mini toolbar to appear, tap or click FILE on the ribbon to open the Backstage view, tap or click Options in the Backstage view, tap or click General (Options dialog box), remove the check mark from the 'Show Mini Toolbar on selection' check box, and then tap or click the OK button.

space between commands on menus and on the ribbon so that they are easier to tap. While touch gestures are convenient ways to interact with Office apps, not all features are supported when you are using Touch mode. If you are using a mouse, Mouse mode will not add the extra space between buttons and commands. The Quick Access Toolbar is discussed in more depth later in the chapter.

KeyTips If you prefer using the keyboard instead of the mouse, you can press the ALT key on the keyboard to display **KeyTips**, or keyboard code icons, for certain commands (Figure 19). To select a command using the keyboard, press the letter or number displayed in the KeyTip, which may cause additional KeyTips related to the selected command to appear. To remove KeyTips from the screen, press the ALT key or the ESC key until all KeyTips disappear, or tap or click anywhere in the app window.

Microsoft Account Area In this area, you can use the Sign in link to sign in to your Microsoft account. Once signed in, you will see your account information as well as a picture if you have included one in your Microsoft account.

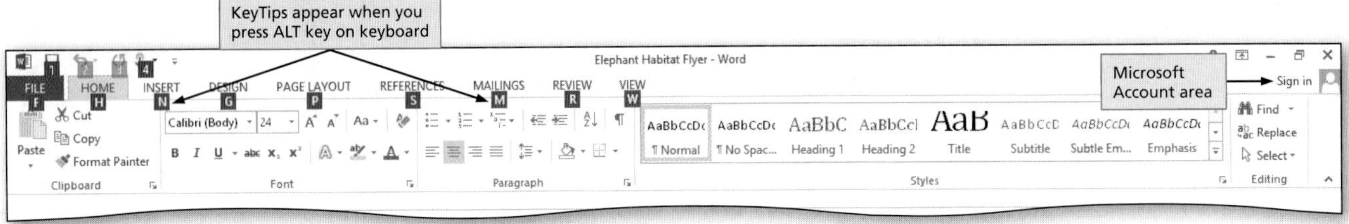

Figure 19

To Display a Different Tab on the Ribbon

1 SIGN IN | 2 USE WINDOWS | 3 USE APPS | 4 FILE MANAGEMENT | 5 SWITCH APPS | 6 SAVE FILES
7 CHANGE SCREEN RESOLUTION | 8 EXIT APPS | 9 USE ADDITIONAL APP FEATURES | 10 USE HELP

When you run Word, the ribbon displays nine main tabs: FILE, HOME, INSERT, DESIGN, PAGE LAYOUT, REFERENCES, MAILINGS, REVIEW, and VIEW. The tab currently displayed is called the **active tab**.

The following step displays the INSERT tab, that is, makes it the active tab. ***Why?*** *When working with an Office app, you may need to switch tabs to access other options for working with a document.*

- Tap or click INSERT on the ribbon to display the INSERT tab (Figure 20).

- Tap or click the other tabs on the ribbon to view their contents. When you are finished, tap or click INSERT on the ribbon to redisplay the INSERT tab.

Q&A If I am working in a different Office app, such as PowerPoint or Access, how do I display a different tab on the ribbon?
Follow this same procedure; that is, tap or click the desired tab on the ribbon.

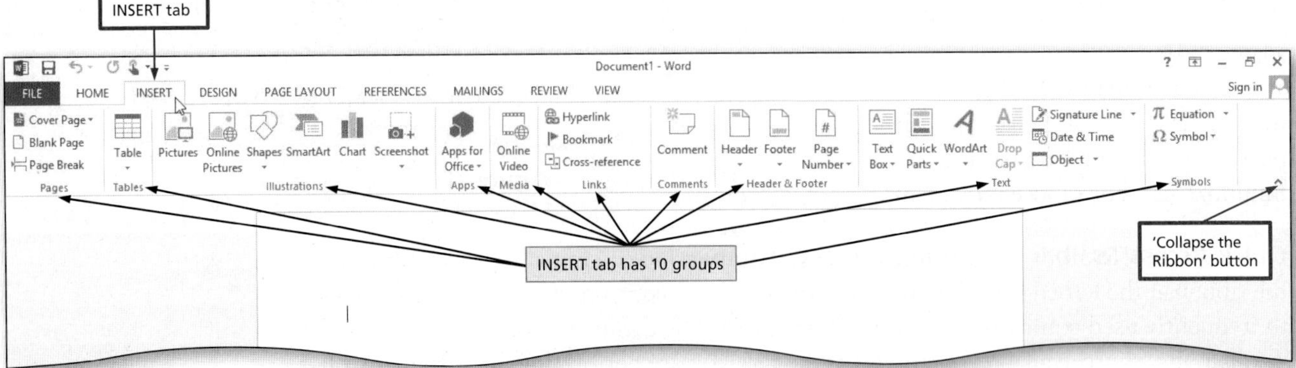

Figure 20

To Collapse and Expand the Ribbon and Use Full Screen Mode

To display more of a document or other item in the window of an Office app, some users prefer to collapse the ribbon, which hides the groups on the ribbon and displays only the main tabs, or to use **Full Screen mode**, which hides all the commands and just displays the document. Each time you run an Office app, such as Word, the ribbon appears the same way it did the last time you used that Office app. The chapters in this book, however, begin with the ribbon appearing as it did at the initial installation of Office or Word.

The following steps collapse, expand, and restore the ribbon in Word and then switch to Full Screen mode. ***Why?*** *If you need more space on the screen to work with your document, you may consider collapsing the ribbon or switching to Full Screen mode to gain additional workspace.*

- Tap or click the 'Collapse the Ribbon' button on the ribbon (shown in Figure 20) to collapse the ribbon (Figure 21).

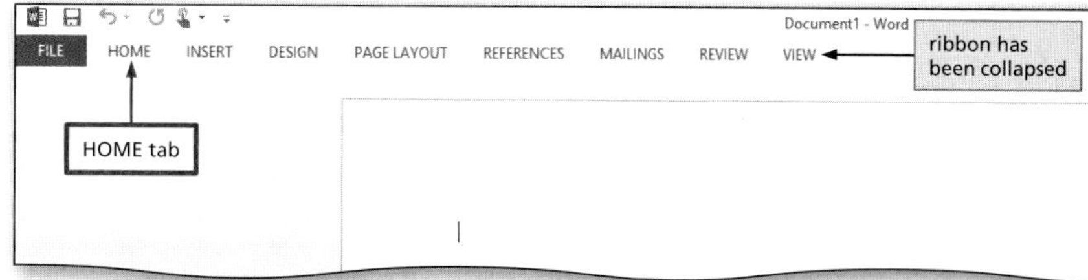

Figure 21

Q&A What happened to the groups on the ribbon?
When you collapse the ribbon, the groups disappear so that the ribbon does not take up as much space on the screen.

What happened to the 'Collapse the Ribbon' button?
The 'Pin the ribbon' button replaces the 'Collapse the Ribbon' button when the ribbon is collapsed. You will see the 'Pin the ribbon' button only when you expand a ribbon by tapping or clicking a tab.

- Tap or click HOME on the ribbon to expand the HOME tab (Figure 22).

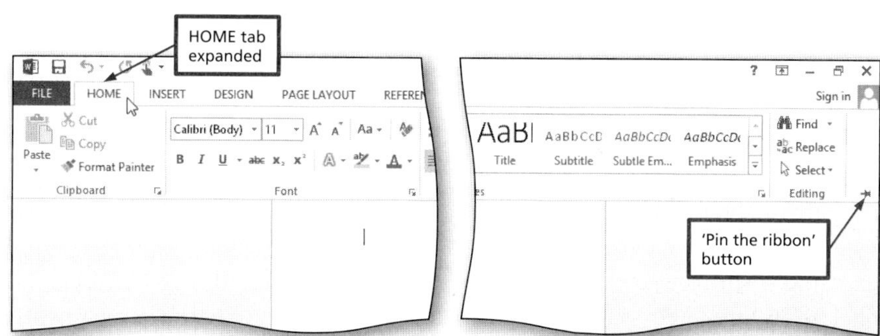

Figure 22

Q&A Why would I click the HOME tab?
If you want to use a command on a collapsed ribbon, tap or click the main tab to display the groups for that tab. After you select a command on the ribbon, the groups will be collapsed once again. If you decide not to use a command on the ribbon, you can collapse the groups by tapping or clicking the same main tab or tapping or clicking in the app window.

Experiment

- Tap or click HOME on the ribbon to collapse the groups again. Tap or click HOME on the ribbon to expand the HOME tab.

- Tap or click the 'Pin the ribbon' button on the expanded HOME tab to restore the ribbon.
- Tap or click the 'Ribbon Display Options' button to display the Ribbon Display Options menu (Figure 23).

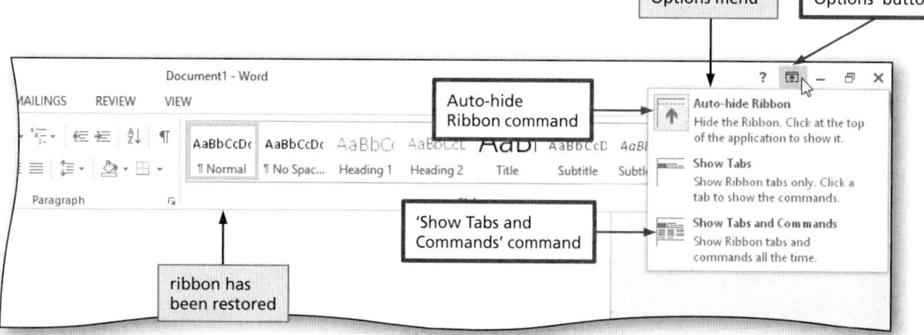

Figure 23

4

- Tap or click Auto-hide Ribbon to use Full Screen mode, which hides all the commands from the screen (Figure 24).
- Tap or click the ellipsis to display the ribbon temporarily.
- Tap or click the 'Ribbon Display Options' button to display the Ribbon Display Options menu (shown in Figure 23 on the previous page).
- Tap or click 'Show Tabs and Commands' to exit Full Screen mode.

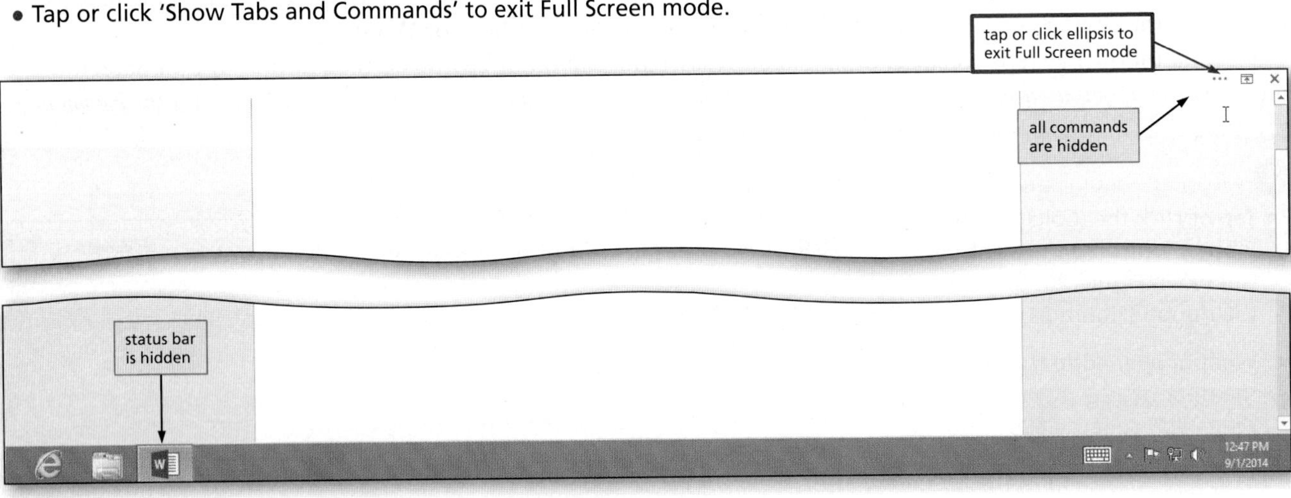

Figure 24

Other Ways

1. Double-tap or double-click a main tab on the ribbon
2. Press CTRL+F1

To Use a Shortcut Menu to Relocate the Quick Access Toolbar

1 SIGN IN | 2 USE WINDOWS | 3 USE APPS | 4 FILE MANAGEMENT | 5 SWITCH APPS | 6 SAVE FILES
7 CHANGE SCREEN RESOLUTION | 8 EXIT APPS | 9 USE ADDITIONAL APP FEATURES | 10 USE HELP

When you press and hold or right-click certain areas of the Word and other Office app windows, a shortcut menu will appear. A **shortcut menu** is a list of frequently used commands that relate to an object. ***Why?*** *You can use shortcut menus to access common commands quickly.* When you press and hold or right-click the status bar, for example, a shortcut menu appears with commands related to the status bar. When you press and hold or right-click the Quick Access Toolbar, a shortcut menu appears with commands related to the Quick Access Toolbar. The following steps use a shortcut menu to move the Quick Access Toolbar, which by default is located on the title bar.

1

- Press and hold or right-click the Quick Access Toolbar to display a shortcut menu that presents a list of commands related to the Quick Access Toolbar (Figure 25).

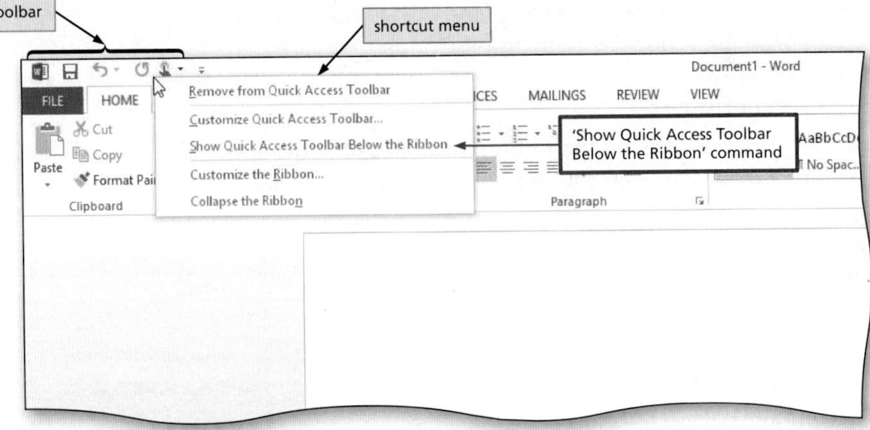

Figure 25

Q&A What if I cannot make the shortcut menu appear using the touch instruction?
When you use the press and hold technique, be sure to release your finger when the circle appears on the screen to display the shortcut menu. If the technique still does not work, you might need to add more space around objects on the screen, making it easier for you to press or tap them. Click the 'Customize Quick Access Toolbar' button and then click Touch/Mouse Mode on the menu. Another option is to use the stylus.

- Tap or click 'Show Quick Access Toolbar Below the Ribbon' on the shortcut menu to display the Quick Access Toolbar below the ribbon (Figure 26).

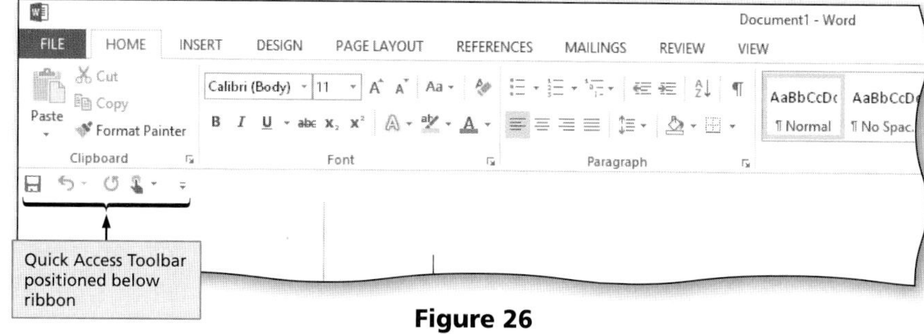

Figure 26

- Press and hold or right-click the Quick Access Toolbar to display a shortcut menu (Figure 27).

- Tap or click 'Show Quick Access Toolbar Above the Ribbon' on the shortcut menu to return the Quick Access Toolbar to its original position (shown in Figure 25).

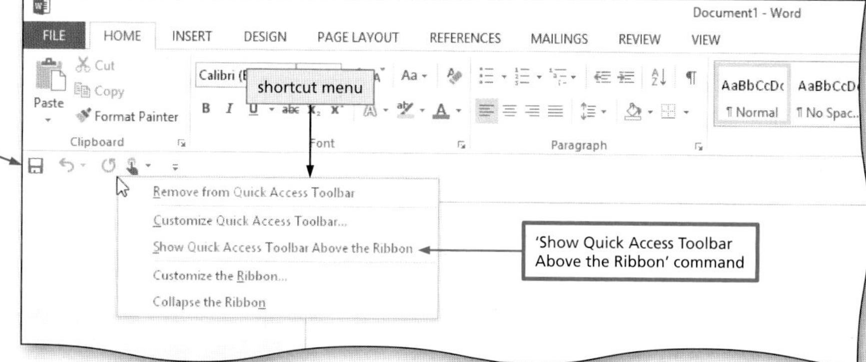

Figure 27

Other Ways

1. Tap or click 'Customize Quick Access Toolbar' button on Quick Access Toolbar, tap or click 'Show Below the Ribbon' or 'Show Above the Ribbon'

To Customize the Quick Access Toolbar

1 SIGN IN | 2 USE WINDOWS | 3 USE APPS | 4 FILE MANAGEMENT | 5 SWITCH APPS | 6 SAVE FILES
7 CHANGE SCREEN RESOLUTION | 8 EXIT APPS | 9 USE ADDITIONAL APP FEATURES | 10 USE HELP

The Quick Access Toolbar provides easy access to some of the more frequently used commands in the Office apps. By default, the Quick Access Toolbar contains buttons for the Save, Undo, and Redo commands. You can customize the Quick Access Toolbar by changing its location in the window, as shown in the previous steps, and by adding more buttons to reflect commands you would like to access easily. The following steps add the Quick Print button to the Quick Access Toolbar in the Word window. ***Why?*** *Adding the Quick Print button to the Quick Access Toolbar speeds up the process of printing.*

- Tap or click the 'Customize Quick Access Toolbar' button to display the Customize Quick Access Toolbar menu (Figure 28).

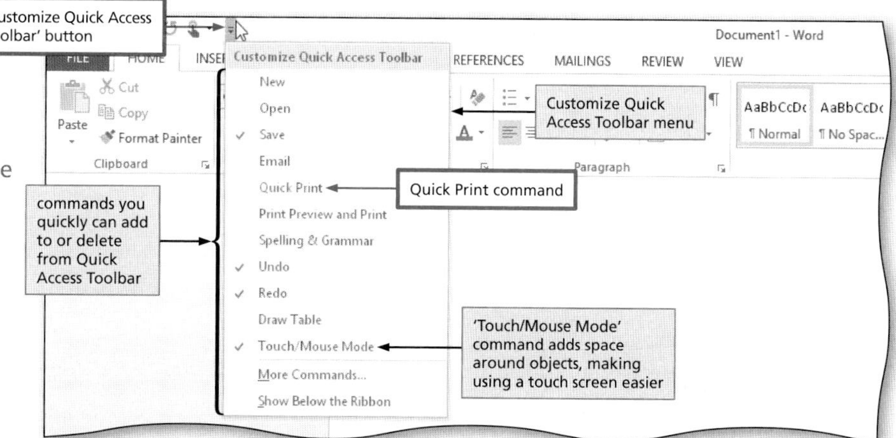

Figure 28

Q&A

Which commands are listed on the Customize Quick Access Toolbar menu?

It lists commands that commonly are added to the Quick Access Toolbar.

What do the check marks next to some commands signify?

Check marks appear next to commands that already are on the Quick Access Toolbar. When you add a button to the Quick Access Toolbar, a check mark will be displayed next to its command name.

2

- Tap or click Quick Print on the Customize Quick Access Toolbar menu to add the Quick Print button to the Quick Access Toolbar (Figure 29).

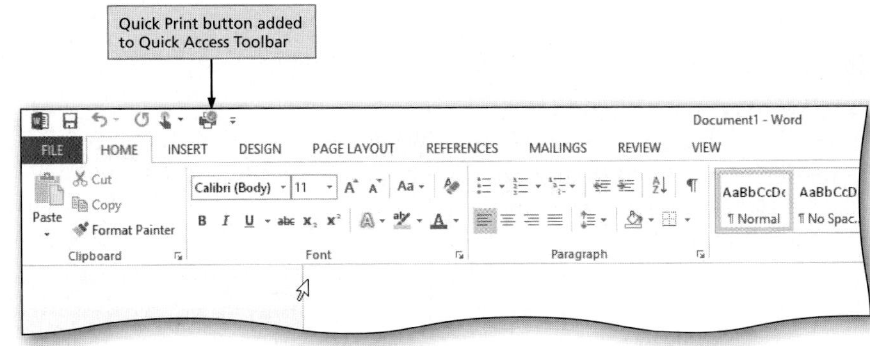

Figure 29

Q&A How would I remove a button from the Quick Access Toolbar?
You would press and hold or right-click the button you wish to remove and then tap or click 'Remove from Quick Access Toolbar' on the shortcut menu or tap or click the 'Customize Quick Access Toolbar' button on the Quick Access Toolbar and then click the button name in the Customize Quick Access Toolbar menu to remove the check mark.

To Enter Text in a Document

The first step in creating a document is to enter its text by typing on the keyboard. By default, Word positions text at the left margin as you type. The following steps type this first line of a flyer. ***Why?*** *To begin creating a flyer, for example, you type the headline in the document window.*

1

- Type **SEE THE ELEPHANT HABITAT** as the text (Figure 30).

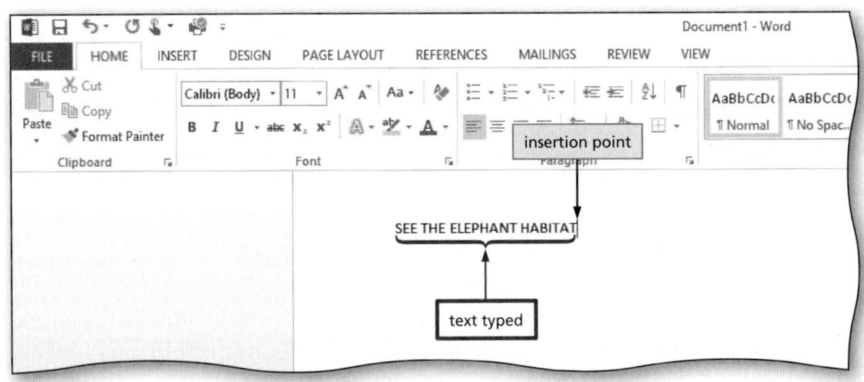

Figure 30

Q&A What is the blinking vertical bar to the right of the text?
The blinking bar is the insertion point, which indicates where text, graphics, and other items will be inserted in the document. As you type, the insertion point moves to the right, and when you reach the end of a line, it moves down to the beginning of the next line.

What if I make an error while typing?
You can press the BACKSPACE key until you have deleted the text in error and then retype the text correctly.

Why does a circle appear below the insertion point?
If you are using a touch screen, a selection handle (small circle) may appear below the text so that you can format the text easily.

2

- Press the ENTER key to move the insertion point to the beginning of the next line (Figure 31).

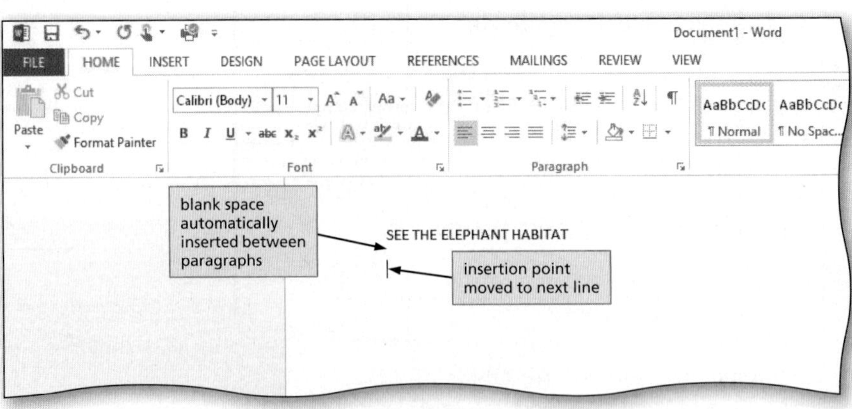

Figure 31

Q&A Why did blank space appear between the entered text and the insertion point?
Each time you press the ENTER key, Word creates a new paragraph and inserts blank space between the two paragraphs. Depending on your settings, Word may or may not insert a blank space between the two paragraphs.

Saving and Organizing Files

While you are creating a document, the computer stores it in memory. When you save a document, the computer places it on a storage medium such as a hard disk, solid-state drive (SSD), USB flash drive, or optical disc. The storage medium can be permanent in your computer, may be portable where you remove it from your computer, or may be on a web server you access through a network or the Internet.

A saved document is referred to as a file. A **file name** is the name assigned to a file when it is saved. When saving files, you should organize them so that you easily can find them later. Windows provides tools to help you organize files.

CONSIDER THIS

How often should you save a document?

It is important to save a document frequently for the following reasons:

- The document in memory might be lost if the computer is turned off or you lose electrical power while an app is running.
- If you run out of time before completing a project, you may finish it at a future time without starting over.

Organizing Files and Folders

A file contains data. This data can range from a research paper to an accounting spreadsheet to an electronic math quiz. You should organize and store files in folders to avoid misplacing a file and to help you find a file quickly.

If you are taking an introductory computer class (CIS 101, for example), you may want to design a series of folders for the different subjects covered in the class. To accomplish this, you can arrange the folders in a hierarchy for the class, as shown in Figure 32.

The hierarchy contains three levels. The first level contains the storage medium, such as a hard disk. The second level contains the class folder (CIS 101, in this case), and the third level contains seven folders, one each for a different Office app that will be covered in the class (Word, PowerPoint, Excel, Access, Outlook, Publisher, and OneNote).

When the hierarchy in Figure 32 is created, the storage medium is said to contain the CIS 101 folder, and the CIS 101 folder is said to contain the separate Office folders (i.e., Word, PowerPoint, Excel, etc.). In addition, this hierarchy easily can be expanded to include folders from other classes taken during additional semesters.

The vertical and horizontal lines in Figure 32 form a pathway that allows you to navigate to a drive or folder on a computer or network. A **path** consists of a drive letter (preceded by a drive name when necessary) and colon, to identify the storage device, and one or more folder names. A hard disk typically has a drive letter of C. Each drive or folder in the hierarchy has a corresponding path.

By default, Windows saves documents in the Documents library, music in the Music library, pictures in the Pictures library, and videos in the Videos library. A **library**

BTW

File Type

Depending on your Windows settings, the file type .docx may be displayed immediately to the right of the file name after you save the file. The file type .docx is a Word 2013 document.

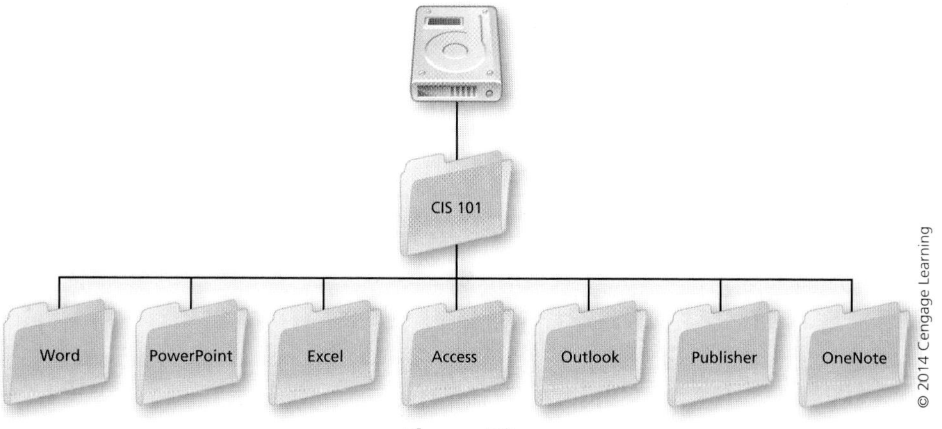

Figure 32

helps you manage multiple folders stored in various locations on a computer and devices. It does not store the folder contents; rather, it keeps track of their locations so that you can access the folders and their contents quickly. For example, you can save pictures from a digital camera in any folder on any storage location on a computer. Normally, this would make organizing the different folders difficult. If you add the folders to a library, however, you can access all the pictures from one location regardless of where they are stored.

The following pages illustrate the steps to organize the folders for this class and save a file in a folder:

1. Create the folder identifying your class.
2. Create the Word folder in the folder identifying your class.
3. Save a file in the Word folder.
4. Verify the location of the saved file.

To Create a Folder

When you create a folder, such as the CIS 101 folder shown in Figure 32 on the previous page, you must name the folder. A folder name should describe the folder and its contents. A folder name can contain spaces and any uppercase or lowercase characters, except a backslash (\), slash (/), colon (:), asterisk (*), question mark (?), quotation marks (“), less than symbol (<), greater than symbol (>), or vertical bar (|). Folder names cannot be CON, AUX, COM1, COM2, COM3, COM4, LPT1, LPT2, LPT3, PRN, or NUL. The same rules for naming folders also apply to naming files.

The following steps create a class folder (CIS 101, in this case) in the Documents library. ***Why?*** *When storing files, you should organize the files so that it will be easier to find them later.* If you are using Windows 7, skip these steps and instead perform the steps in the yellow box that immediately follows these Windows 8 steps.

- Tap or click the File Explorer app button on the taskbar to run the File Explorer app (Figure 33).

Q&A Why does the title bar say Libraries?
File Explorer, by default, displays the name of the selected library or folder on the title bar.

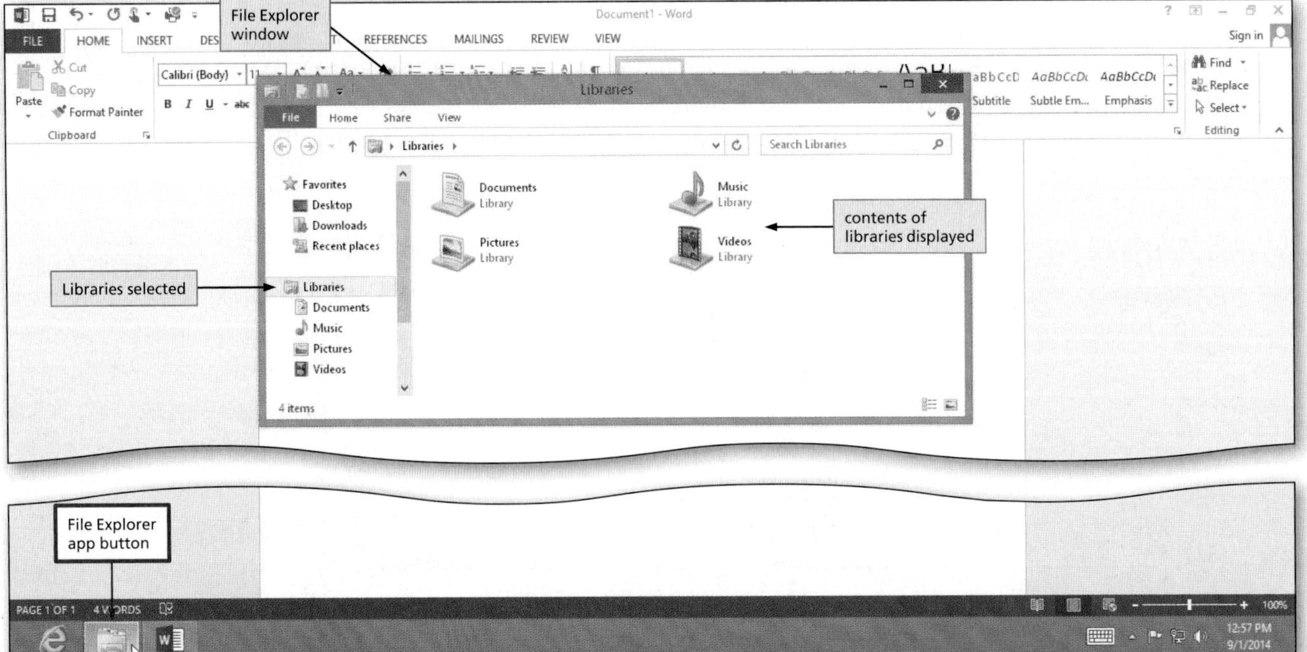

Figure 33

- Tap or click the Documents library in the navigation pane to display the contents of the Documents library in the file list (Figure 34).

Q&A What if my screen does not show the Documents, Music, Pictures, and Videos libraries?
Double-tap or double-click Libraries in the navigation pane to expand the list.

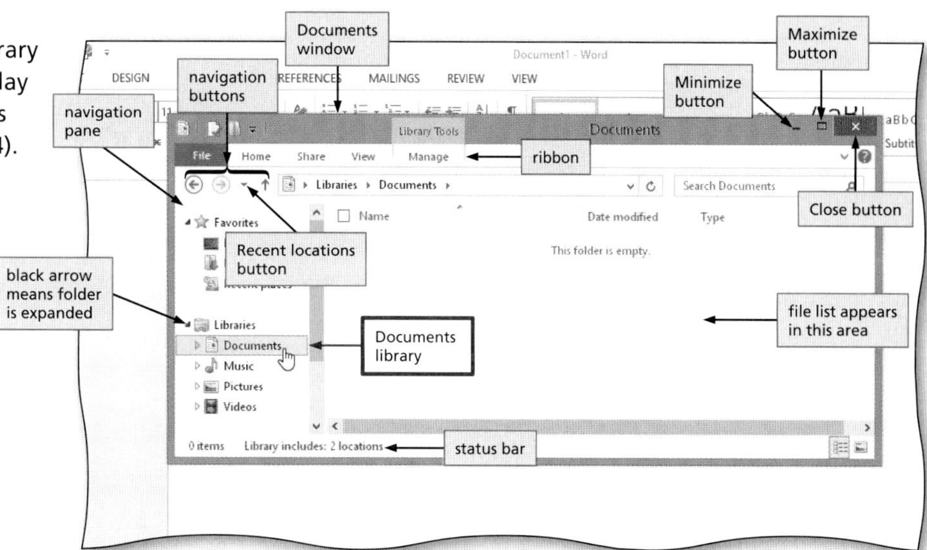

Figure 34

- Tap or click the New folder button on the Quick Access Toolbar to create a new folder with the name, New folder, selected in a text box (Figure 35).

Q&A Why is the folder icon displayed differently on my computer?
Windows might be configured to display contents differently on your computer.

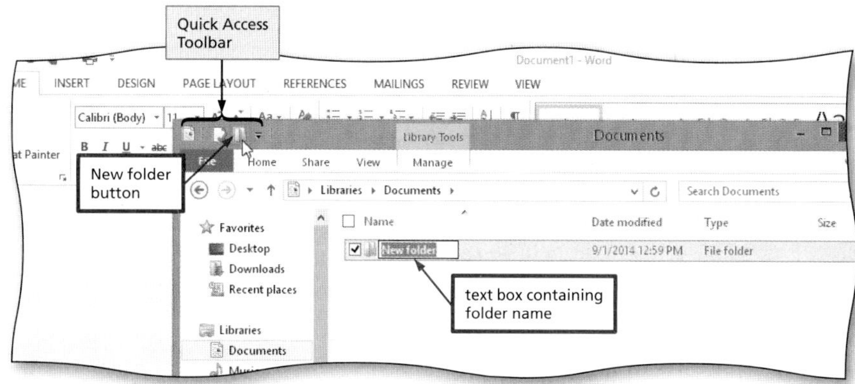

Figure 35

- Type `CIS 101` (or your class code) in the text box as the new folder name.
  If requested by your instructor, add your last name to the end of the folder name.
- Press the ENTER key to change the folder name from New folder to a folder name identifying your class (Figure 36).

Q&A What happens when I press the ENTER key?
The class folder (CIS 101, in this case) is displayed in the file list, which contains the folder name, date modified, type, and size.

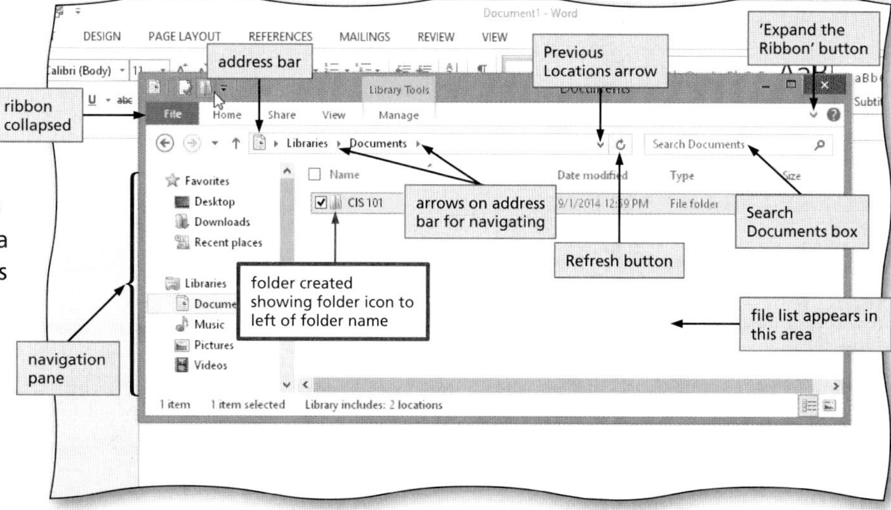

Figure 36

Other Ways

1. Press CTRL+SHIFT+N
2. Tap or click the New folder button (Home tab | New group)

To Create a Folder Using Windows 7

If you are using Windows 7, perform these steps to create a folder instead of the previous steps that use Windows 8.

1. Click the Windows Explorer button on the taskbar to run Windows Explorer.
2. Click the Documents library in the navigation pane to display the contents of the Documents library in the file list.
3. Click the New folder button on the toolbar to display a new folder icon with the name, New folder, selected in a text box.
4. Type `CIS 101` (or your class code) in the text box to name the folder.
5. Press the ENTER key to create the folder.

Folder Windows

The Documents window (shown in Figure 36 on the previous page) is called a folder window. Recall that a folder is a specific named location on a storage medium that contains related files. Most users rely on **folder windows** for finding, viewing, and managing information on their computers. Folder windows have common design elements, including the following (shown in Figure 36).

- The **address bar** provides quick navigation options. The arrows on the address bar allow you to visit different locations on the computer.
- The buttons to the left of the address bar allow you to navigate the contents of the navigation pane and view recent pages.
- The **Previous Locations arrow** displays the locations you have visited.
- The **Refresh button** on the right side of the address bar refreshes the contents of the folder list.
- The **search box** contains the dimmed words, Search Documents. You can type a term in the search box for a list of files, folders, shortcuts, and elements containing that term within the location you are searching. A **shortcut** is an icon on the desktop that provides a user with immediate access to an app or file.
- The **ribbon** contains five tabs used to accomplish various tasks on the computer related to organizing and managing the contents of the open window. This ribbon works similarly to the ribbon in the Office apps.
- The **navigation pane** on the left contains the Favorites area, Libraries area, Homegroup area, Computer area, and Network area.
- The **Favorites area** shows your favorite locations. By default, this list contains only links to your Desktop, Downloads, and Recent places.
- The **Libraries area** shows folders included in a library.

To Create a Folder within a Folder

With the class folder created, you can create folders that will store the files you create using Word. The following steps create a Word folder in the CIS 101 folder (or the folder identifying your class). ***Why?*** *To be able to organize your files, you should create a folder structure.* If you are using Windows 7, skip these steps and instead perform the steps in the yellow box that immediately follows these Windows 8 steps.

- Double-tap or double-click the icon or folder name for the CIS 101 folder (or the folder identifying your class) in the file list to open the folder (Figure 37).

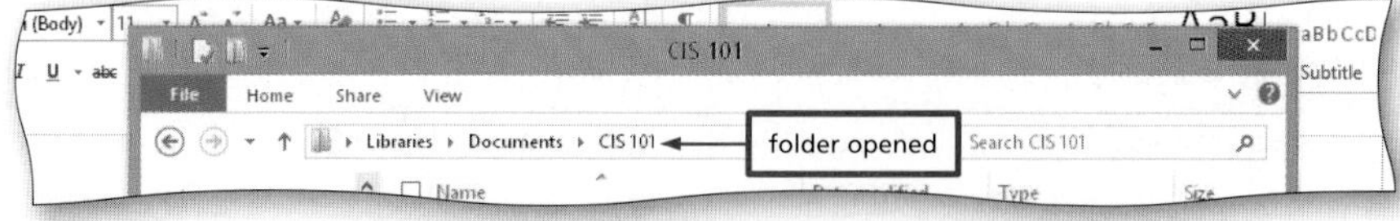

Figure 37

- Tap or click the New folder button on the Quick Access Toolbar to create a new folder with the name, New folder, selected in a text box folder.
- Type **Word** in the text box as the new folder name.
- Press the ENTER key to rename the folder (Figure 38).

Figure 38

Other Ways

1. Press CTRL+SHIFT+N
2. Tap or click the New folder button (Home tab | New group)

To Create a Folder within a Folder Using Windows 7

If you are using Windows 7, perform these steps to create a folder within a folder instead of the previous steps that use Windows 8.

1. Double-click the icon or folder name for the CIS 101 folder (or the folder identifying your class) in the file list to open the folder.
2. Click the New folder button on the toolbar to display a new folder icon and text box for the folder.
3. Type **Word** in the text box to name the folder.
4. Press the ENTER key to create the folder.

To Expand a Folder, Scroll through Folder Contents, and Collapse a Folder

Folder windows display the hierarchy of items and the contents of drives and folders in the file list. You might want to expand a library or folder in the navigation pane to view its contents, slide or scroll through its contents, and collapse it when you are finished viewing its contents. ***Why?*** *When a folder is expanded, you can see all the folders it contains. By contrast, a collapsed folder hides the folders it contains.* The following steps expand, slide or scroll through, and then collapse the folder identifying your class (CIS 101, in this case).

- Double-tap or double-click the Documents library in the navigation pane, which expands the library to display its contents and displays a black arrow to the left of the Documents library icon (Figure 39).

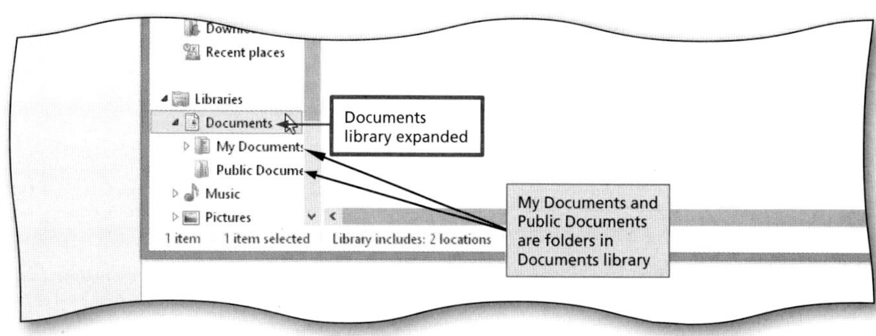

Figure 39

- Double-tap or double-click the My Documents folder, which expands the folder to display its contents and displays a black arrow to the left of the My Documents folder icon.

Q&A What is the My Documents folder?
When you save files on your hard disk, the My Documents folder is the default save location.

- Double-tap or double-click the CIS 101 folder, which expands the folder to display its contents and displays a black arrow to the left of the folder icon (Figure 40).

Experiment

- Slide the scroll bar down or click the down scroll arrow on the vertical scroll bar to display additional folders at the bottom of the navigation pane. Slide the scroll bar up or click the scroll bar above the scroll box to move the scroll box to the top of the navigation pane. Drag the scroll box down the scroll bar until the scroll box is halfway down the scroll bar.

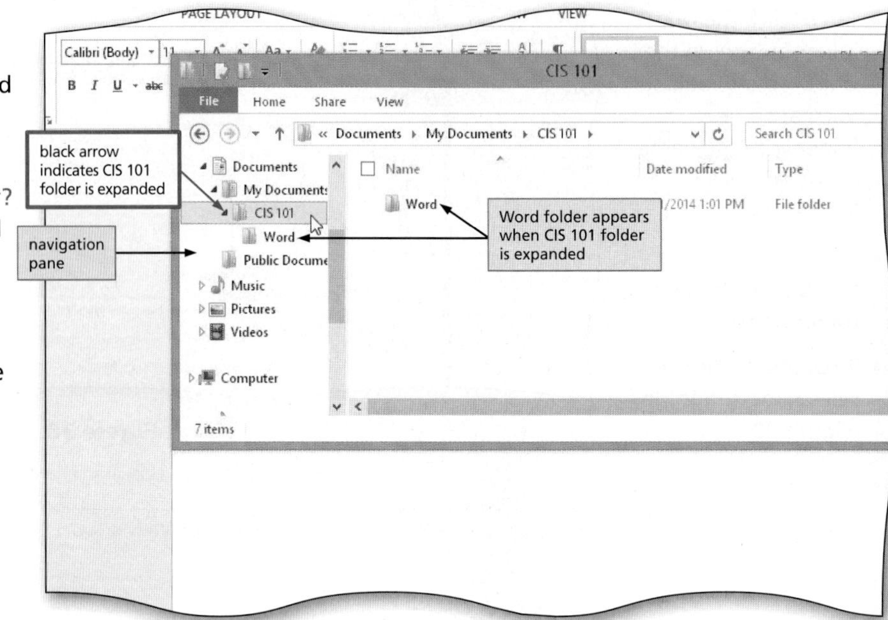

Figure 40

- Double-tap or double-click the folder identifying your class (CIS 101, in this case) to collapse the folder (Figure 41).

Q&A Why are some folders indented below others?
A folder contains the indented folders below it.

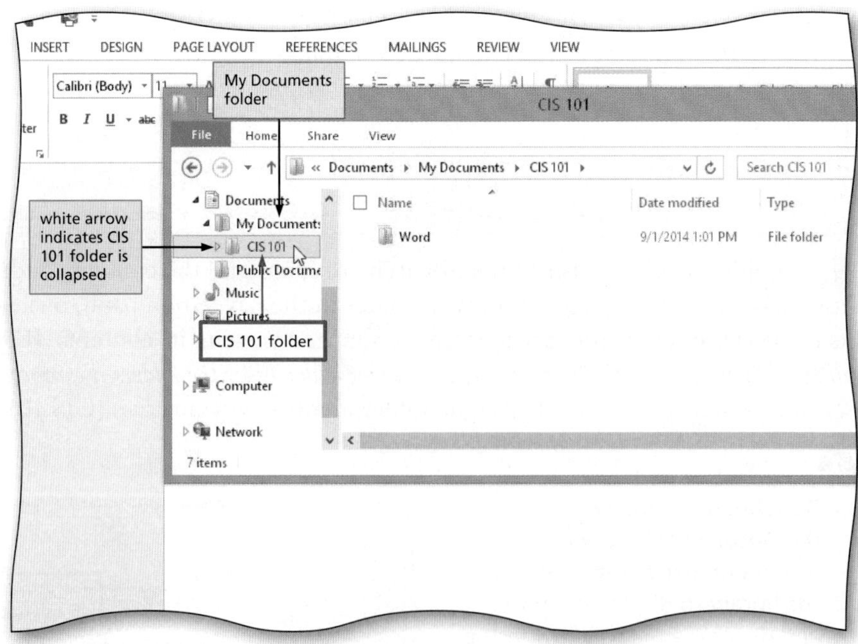

Figure 41

Other Ways

1. Point to display arrows in navigation pane, tap or click white arrow to expand or tap or click black arrow to collapse
2. Select folder to expand or collapse using arrow keys, press RIGHT ARROW to expand; press LEFT ARROW to collapse.

To Switch from One App to Another

The next step is to save the Word file containing the headline you typed earlier. Word, however, currently is not the active window. You can use the app button on the taskbar and live preview to switch to Word and then save the document in the Word document window.

Why? *By clicking the appropriate app button on the taskbar, you can switch to the open app you want to use.* The following steps switch to the Word window; however, the steps are the same for any active Office app currently displayed as an app button on the taskbar.

1

- If you are using a mouse, point to the Word app button on the taskbar to see a live preview of the open document(s) or the window title(s) of the open document(s), depending on your computer's configuration (Figure 42).

live preview

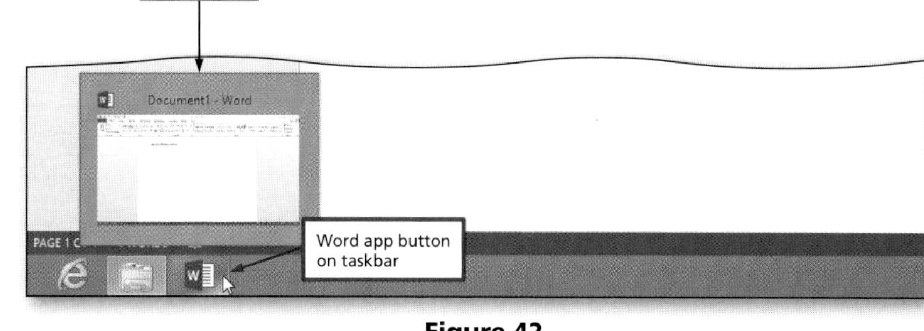

Figure 42

2

- Tap or click the Word app button or the live preview to make the app associated with the app button the active window (Figure 43).

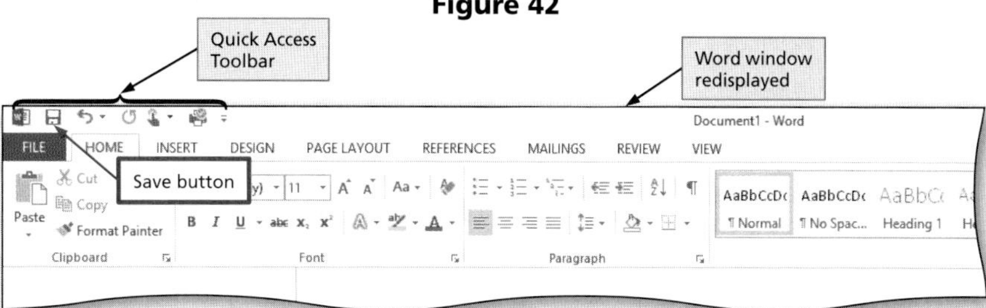

Figure 43

Q&A What if multiple documents are open in an app?
Tap or click the desired live preview to switch to the window you want to use.

To Save a File in a Folder

With the Word folder created, you can save the Word document shown in the document window in the Word folder. ***Why?*** *Without saving a file, you may lose all the work you have completed and will be unable to reuse or share it with others later.* The following steps save a file in the Word folder contained in your class folder (CIS 101, in this case) using the file name, Elephant Habitat.

1

- Tap or click the Save button (shown in Figure 43) on the Quick Access Toolbar, which depending on settings, will display either the Save As gallery in the Backstage view (Figure 44) or the Save As dialog box (Figure 45 on the next page).

Backstage view
Back button
Save As
Save As tab automatically selected
Computer selected
SkyDrive
Computer
Add a Place
Recent Folders
My Documents
Desktop
Browse
Browse button
right pane of Save As gallery automatically displays options related to saving on your computer
Save As gallery

Figure 44

Q&A What is the Backstage view?
The **Backstage view** contains a set of commands that enable you to manage documents and data about the documents.

What if the Save As gallery is not displayed in the Backstage view?
Tap or click the Save As tab to display the Save As gallery.

How do I close the Backstage view?
Tap or click the Back button in the upper-left corner of the Backstage view to return to the Word window.

2

- If your screen displays the Backstage view, tap or click Computer, if necessary, to display options in the right pane related to saving on your computer; if your screen already displays the Save As dialog box, proceed to Step 3.

Q&A What if I wanted to save on SkyDrive instead?
You would tap or click SkyDrive. Saving on SkyDrive is discussed in a later section in this chapter.

- Tap or click the Browse button in the right pane to display the Save As dialog box (Figure 45).

Q&A Why does a file name already appear in the File name box?
Word automatically suggests a file name the first time you save a document. The file name normally consists of the first few words contained in the document. Because the suggested file name is selected, you do not need to delete it; as soon as you begin typing, the new file name replaces the selected text.

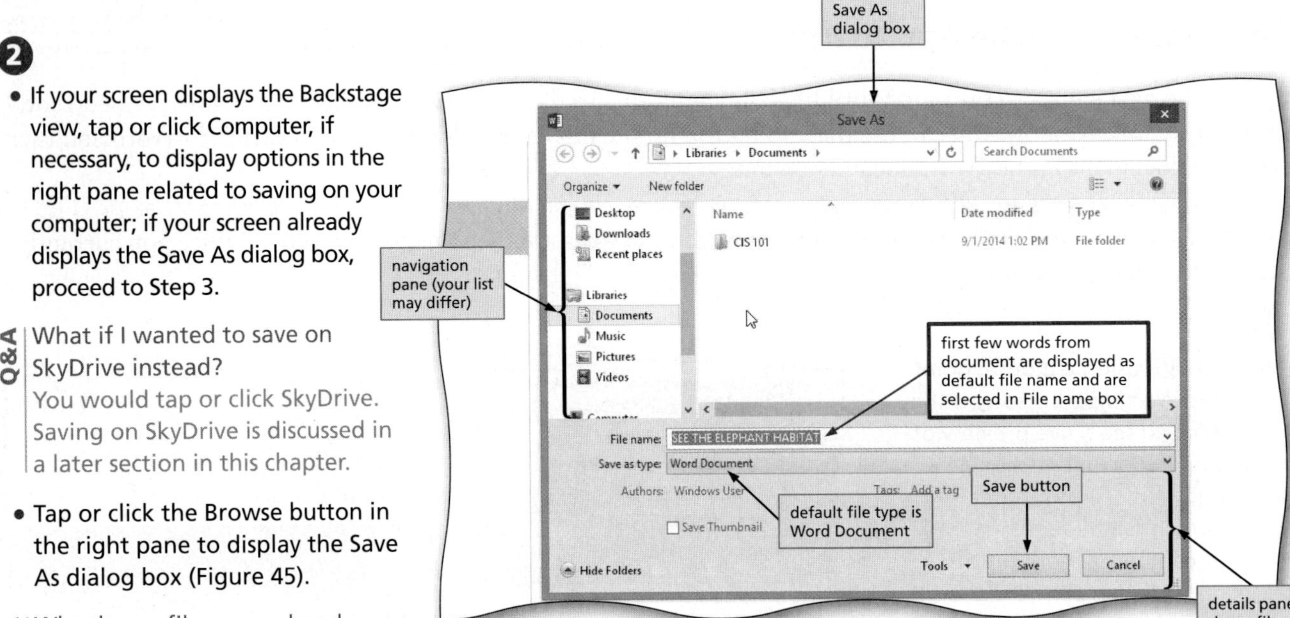

Figure 45

3

- Type **`Elephant Habitat`** in the File name box (Save As dialog box) to change the file name. Do not press the ENTER key after typing the file name because you do not want to close the dialog box at this time (Figure 46).

Q&A What characters can I use in a file name?
The only invalid characters are the backslash (\), slash (/), colon (:), asterisk (*), question mark (?), quotation mark ("), less than symbol (<), greater than symbol (>), and vertical bar (|).

Figure 46

4

- Navigate to the desired save location (in this case, the Word folder in the CIS 101 folder [or your class folder] in the My Documents folder in the Documents library) by performing the tasks in Steps 4a and 4b.

4a

- If the Documents library is not displayed in the navigation pane, slide to scroll or drag the scroll bar in the navigation pane until Documents appears.
- If the Documents library is not expanded in the navigation pane, double-tap or double-click Documents to display its folders in the navigation pane.
- If the My Documents folder is not expanded in the navigation pane, double-tap or double-click My Documents to display its folders in the navigation pane.
- If your class folder (CIS 101, in this case) is not expanded, double-tap or double-click the CIS 101 folder to select the folder and display its contents in the navigation pane (Figure 47).

Q&A What if I do not want to save in a folder?
Although storing files in folders is an effective technique for organizing files, some users prefer not to store files in folders. If you prefer not to save this file in a folder, select the storage device on which you wish to save the file and then proceed to Step 5.

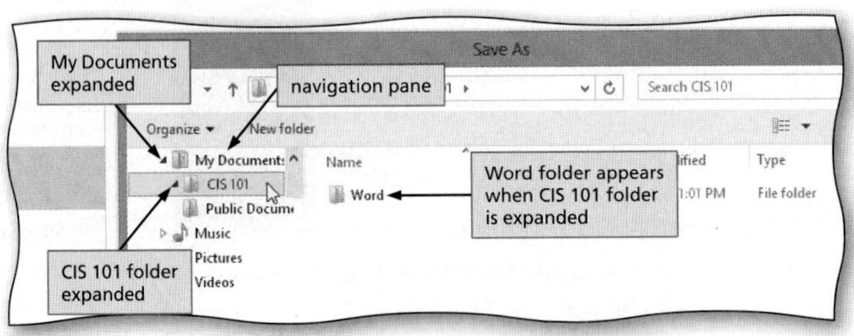

Figure 47

- Tap or click the Word folder in the navigation pane to select it as the new save location and display its contents in the file list (Figure 48).

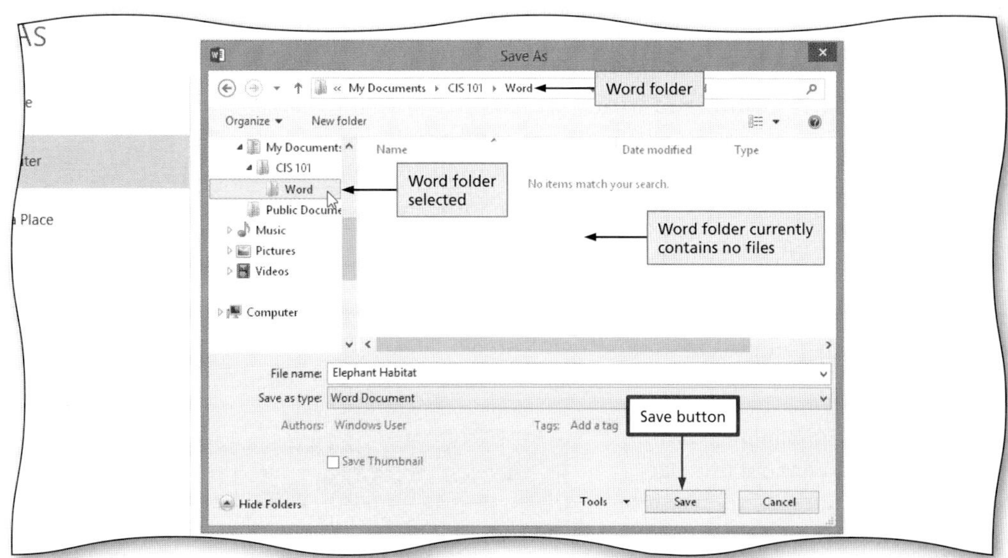

Figure 48

5

- Tap or click the Save button (Save As dialog box) to save the document in the selected folder in the selected location with the entered file name (Figure 49).

Figure 49

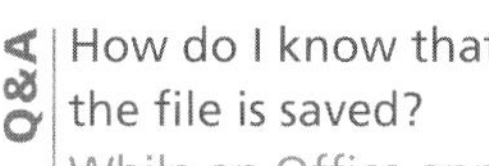

Q&A How do I know that the file is saved?

While an Office app such as Word is saving a file, it briefly displays a message on the status bar indicating the amount of the file saved. In addition, the file name appears on the title bar.

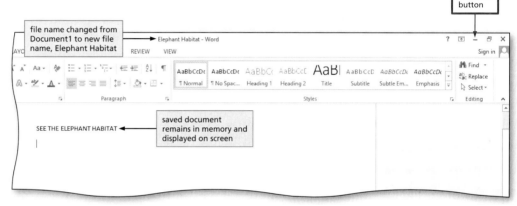

Other Ways

1. Tap or click FILE on ribbon, tap or click Save As in Backstage view, tap or click Computer, tap or click Browse button, type file name (Save As dialog box), navigate to desired save location, tap or click Save button
2. Press F12, type file name (Save As dialog box), navigate to desired save location, tap or click Save button

Navigating in Dialog Boxes

Navigating is the process of finding a location on a storage device. While saving the Elephant Habitat file, for example, Steps 4a and 4b in the previous set of steps navigated to the Word folder located in the CIS 101 folder in the My Documents folder in the Documents library. When performing certain functions in Windows apps, such as saving a file, opening a file, or inserting a picture in an existing document, you most likely will have to navigate to the location where you want to save the file or to the folder containing the file you want to open or insert. Most dialog boxes in Windows apps requiring navigation follow a similar procedure; that is, the way you navigate to a folder in one dialog box, such as the Save As dialog box, is similar to how you might navigate in another dialog box, such as the Open dialog box. If you chose to navigate to a specific location in a dialog box, you would follow the instructions in Steps 4a and 4b.

To Minimize and Restore a Window

Before continuing, you can verify that the Word file was saved properly. To do this, you will minimize the Word window and then open the CIS 101 window so that you can verify the file is stored in the CIS 101 folder on the hard disk. A **minimized window** is an open window that is hidden from view but can be displayed quickly by clicking the window's app button on the taskbar.

In the following example, Word is used to illustrate minimizing and restoring windows; however, you would follow the same steps regardless of the Office app you are using. ***Why?*** *Before closing an app, you should make sure your file saved correctly so that you can find it later.*

The following steps minimize the Word window, verify that the file is saved, and then restore the minimized window. If you are using Windows 7, skip these steps and instead perform the steps in the yellow box that immediately follows these Windows 8 steps.

1

- Tap or click the Minimize button on the Word window title bar (shown in Figure 49) to minimize the window (Figure 50).

Q&A Is the minimized window still available?
The minimized window, Word in this case, remains available but no longer is the active window. It is minimized as an app button on the taskbar.

- If the File Explorer window is not open on the screen, tap or click the File Explorer app button on the taskbar to make the File folder window the active window.

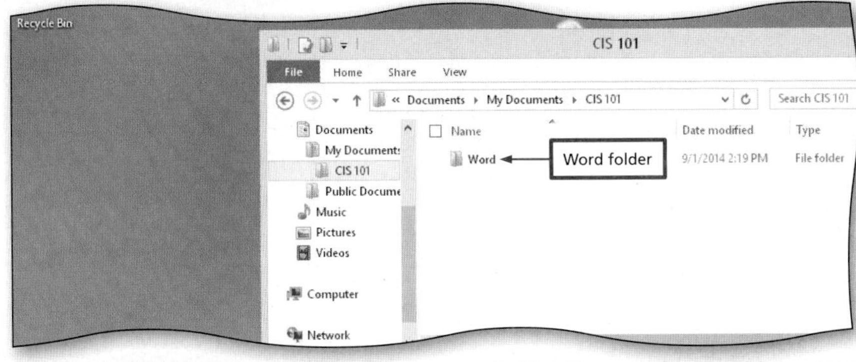

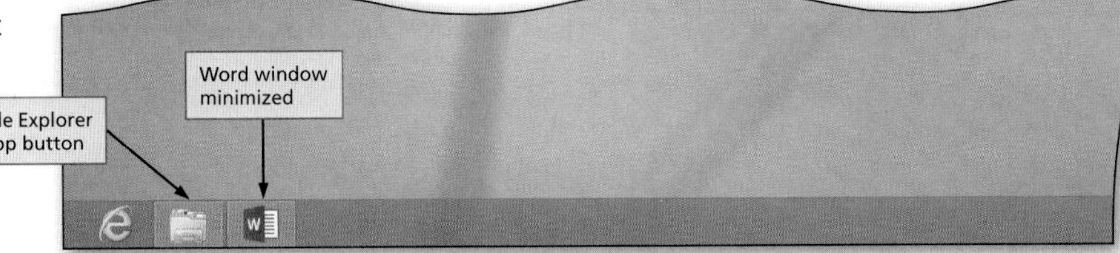

Figure 50

2

- Double-tap or double-click the Word folder in the file list to select the folder and display its contents (Figure 51).

Q&A Why does the File Explorer app button on the taskbar change?
A selected app button indicates that the app is active on the screen. When the button is not selected, the app is running but not active.

- After viewing the contents of the selected folder, tap or click the Word app button on the taskbar to restore the minimized window (as shown in Figure 49 on the previous page).

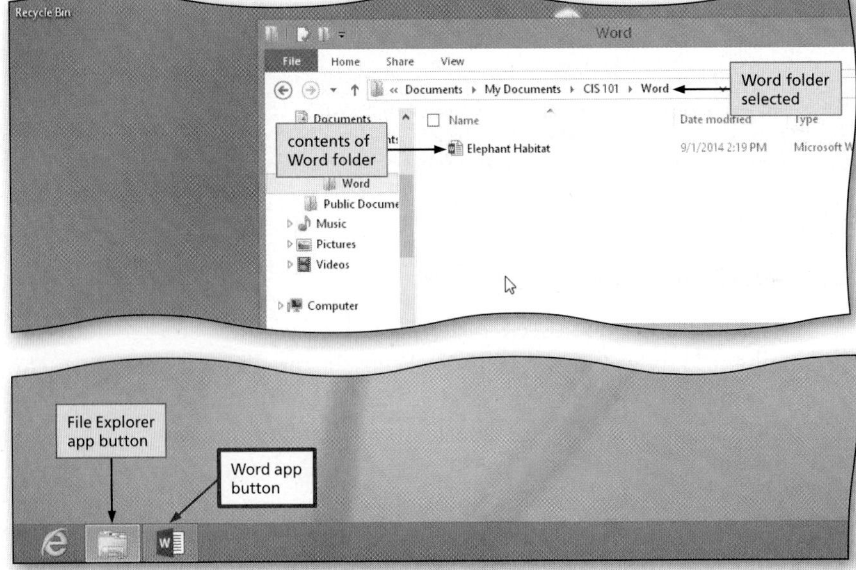

Figure 51

Other Ways

1. Press and hold or right-click title bar, tap or click Minimize on shortcut menu, tap or click taskbar button in taskbar button area
2. Press WINDOWS+M, press WINDOWS+SHIFT+M

To Minimize and Restore a Window Using Windows 7

If you are using Windows 7, perform these steps to minimize and restore a window instead of the previous steps that use Windows 8.

1. Click the Minimize button on the app's title bar to minimize the window.
2. If the Windows Explorer window is not open on the screen, click the Windows Explorer button on the taskbar to make the Windows Explorer window the active window.
3. Double-click the Word folder in the file list to select the folder and display its contents.
4. After viewing the contents of the selected folder, click the Word button on the taskbar to restore the minimized window.

To Save a File on SkyDrive

1 SIGN IN | 2 USE WINDOWS | 3 USE APPS | 4 FILE MANAGEMENT | 5 SWITCH APPS | 6 SAVE FILES
7 CHANGE SCREEN RESOLUTION | 8 EXIT APPS | 9 USE ADDITIONAL APP FEATURES | 10 USE HELP

One of the features of Office is the capability to save files on SkyDrive so that you can use the files on multiple computers without having to use external storage devices such as a USB flash drive. Storing files on SkyDrive also enables you to share files more efficiently with others, such as when using Office Web Apps and Office 365.

In the following example, Word is used to save a file to SkyDrive. ***Why?*** *Storing files on SkyDrive provides more portability options than are available from storing files in the Documents library.*

You can save files directly to SkyDrive from within Word, PowerPoint, and Excel. The following steps save the current Word file to the SkyDrive. These steps require you have a Microsoft account and an Internet connection.

- Tap or click FILE on the ribbon to open the Backstage view (Figure 52).

Q&A What is the purpose of the FILE tab?
The FILE tab opens the Backstage view for each Office app, including Word.

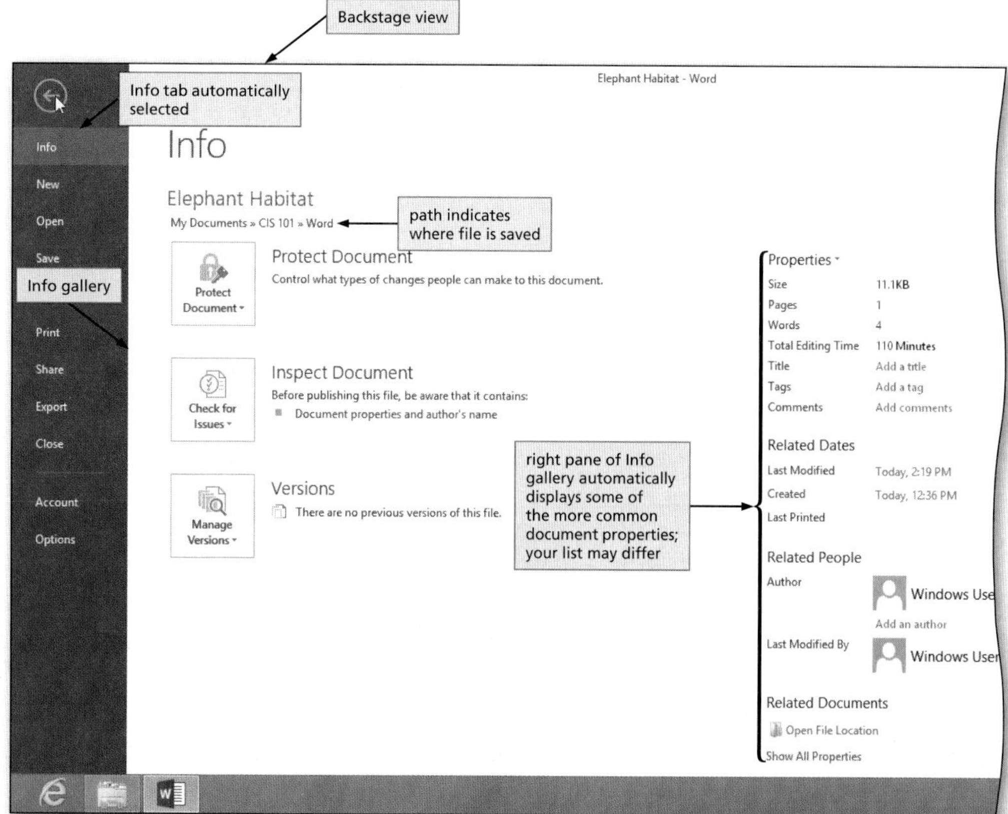

Figure 52

2

- Tap or click the Save As tab in the Backstage view to display the Save As gallery.
- Tap or click SkyDrive to display SkyDrive saving options or a Sign In button, if you are not signed in already to your Microsoft account (Figure 53).

Q&A What if my Save As gallery does not display SkyDrive as a save location?

Tap or click 'Add a Place' and proceed to Step 3.

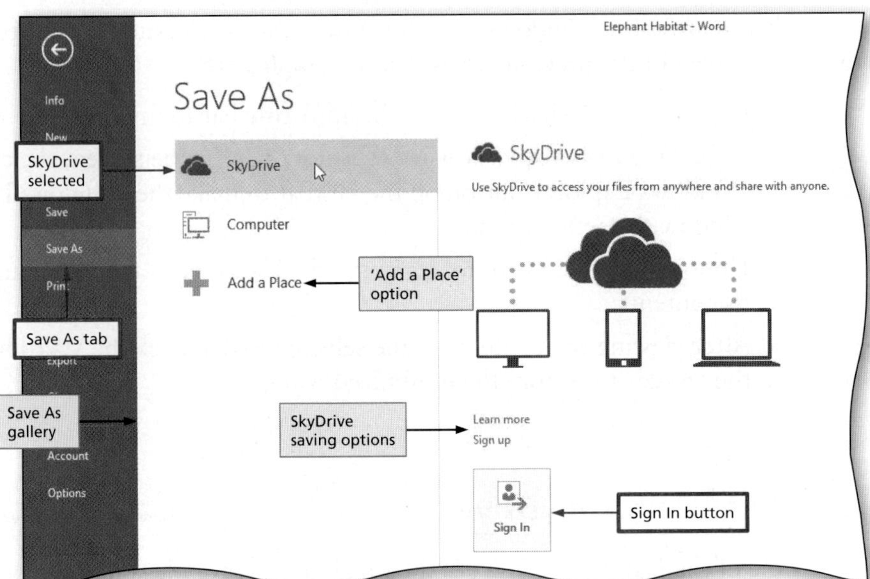

Figure 53

3

- If your screen displays a Sign In button, tap or click it to display the Sign in dialog box (Figure 54).

Q&A What if the Sign In button does not appear?

If you already are signed into your Microsoft account, the Sign In button will not be displayed. In this case, proceed to Step 5.

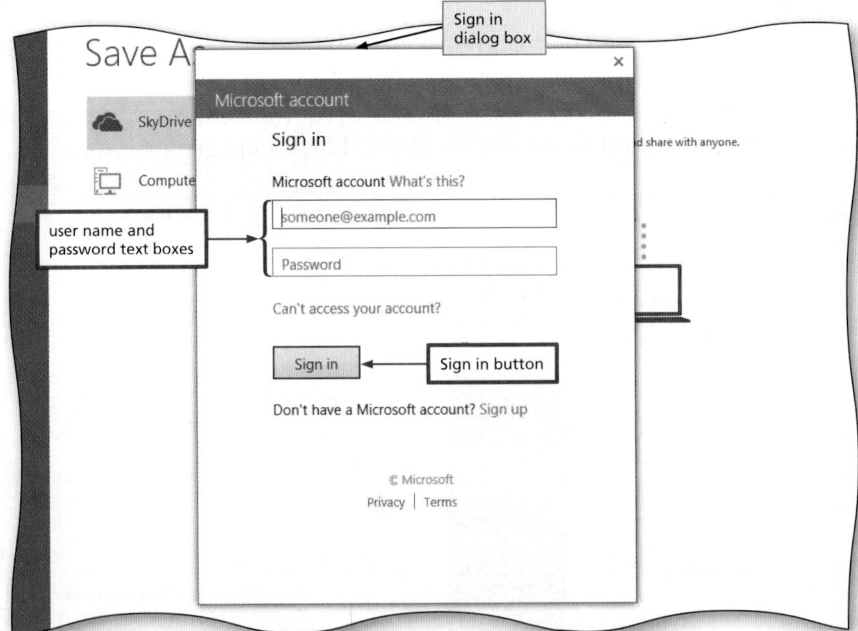

Figure 54

4

- Type your Microsoft account user name and password in the text boxes and then tap or click the Sign in button (Sign in dialog box) to sign in to SkyDrive.

5

- Tap or click your SkyDrive to select your SkyDrive as the storage location (Figure 55).

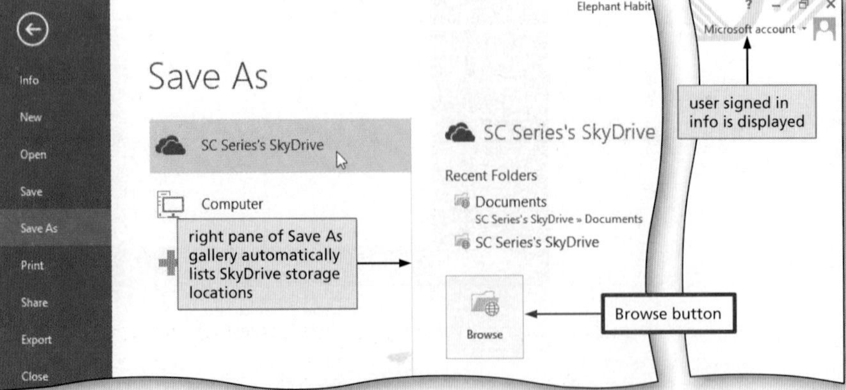

Figure 55

- Tap or click the Browse button to contact the SkyDrive server (which may take some time, depending on the speed of your Internet connection) and then display the Save As dialog box (Figure 56).

Q&A Why does the path in the address bar contain various letters and numbers?
The letters and numbers in the address bar uniquely identify the location of your SkyDrive files and folders.

7

- Tap or click the Save button (Save As dialog box) to save the file on SkyDrive.

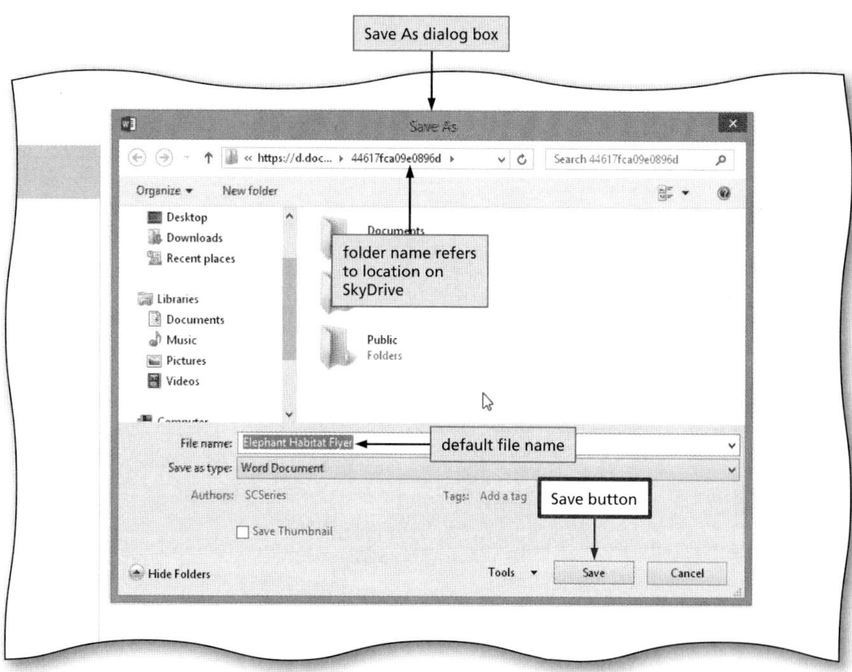

Figure 56

To Sign Out of a Microsoft Account

If you are using a public computer or otherwise wish to sign out of your Microsoft account, you should sign out of the account from the Accounts gallery in the Backstage view. Signing out of the account is the safest way to make sure that nobody else can access online files or settings stored in your Microsoft account. For security reasons, you should sign out of your Microsoft account when you are finished using a public or shared computer. Staying signed in to your Microsoft account might enable others to access your files.

The following steps sign out of a Microsoft account from Word. You would use the same steps in any Office app. If you do not wish to sign out of your Microsoft account, read these steps without performing them.

1. Tap or click FILE on the ribbon to open the Backstage view.
2. Tap or click the Account tab to display the Account gallery (Figure 57 on the next page).
3. Tap or click the Sign out link, which displays the Remove Account dialog box. If a Can't remove Windows accounts dialog box appears instead of the Remove Account dialog box, click the OK button and skip the remaining steps.

Q&A Why does a Can't remove Windows accounts dialog box appear?
If you signed in to Windows using your Microsoft account, then you also must sign out from Windows, rather than signing out from within Word. When you are finished using Windows, be sure to sign out at that time.

4. Tap or click the Yes button (Remove Account dialog box) to sign out of your Microsoft account on this computer.

Q&A Should I sign out of Windows after removing my Microsoft account?
When you are finished using the computer, you should sign out of Windows for maximum security.

5. Tap or click the Back button in the upper-left corner of the Backstage view to return to the document.

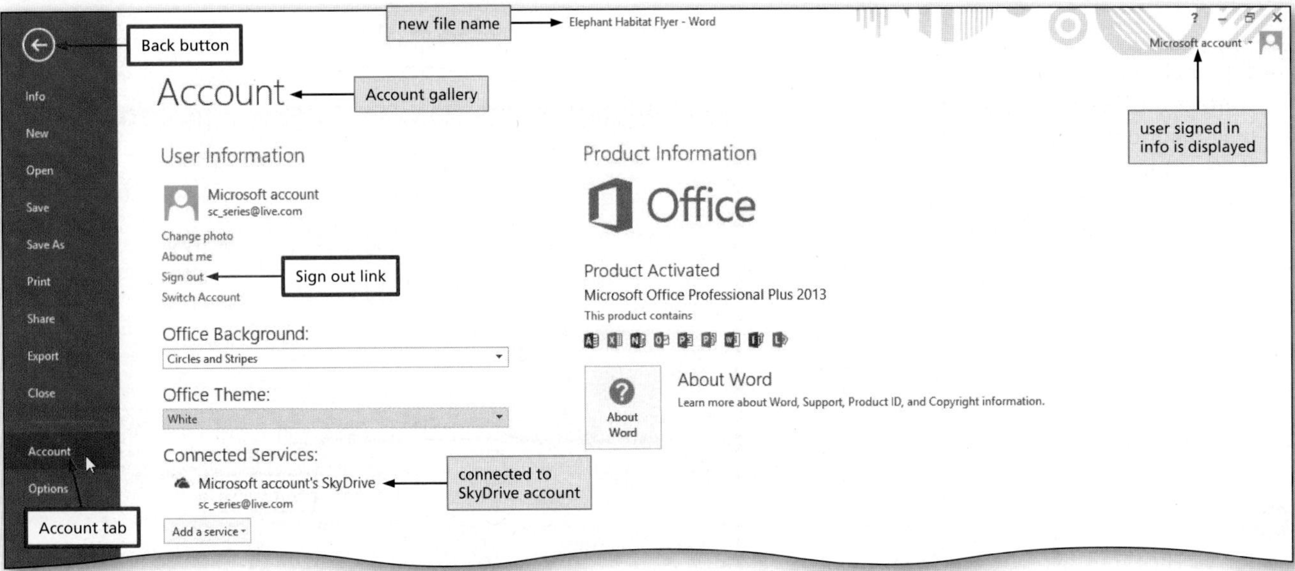

Figure 57

Screen Resolution

Screen resolution indicates the number of pixels (dots) that the computer uses to display the letters, numbers, graphics, and background you see on the screen. When you increase the screen resolution, Windows displays more information on the screen, but the information decreases in size. The reverse also is true: as you decrease the screen resolution, Windows displays less information on the screen, but the information increases in size.

Screen resolution usually is stated as the product of two numbers, such as 1366 × 768 (pronounced "thirteen sixty-six by seven sixty-eight"). A 1366 × 768 screen resolution results in a display of 1366 distinct pixels on each of 768 lines, or about 1,050,624 pixels. Changing the screen resolution affects how the ribbon appears in Office apps and some Windows dialog boxes. Figure 58, for example, shows the Word ribbon at screen resolutions of 1366 × 768 and 1024 × 768. All of the same commands are available regardless of screen resolution. The app (Word, in this case), however, makes changes to the groups and the buttons within the groups to accommodate the various screen resolutions. The result is that certain commands may need to be accessed differently depending on the resolution chosen. A command that is visible on the ribbon and available by tapping or clicking a button at one resolution may not be visible and may need to be accessed using its Dialog Box Launcher at a different resolution.

Comparing the two ribbons in Figure 58, notice the changes in content and layout of the groups and galleries. In some cases, the content of a group is the same in each resolution, but the layout of the group differs. For example, the same gallery and buttons appear in the Styles groups in the two resolutions, but the layouts differ. In other cases, the content and layout are the same across the resolution, but the level of detail differs with the resolution.

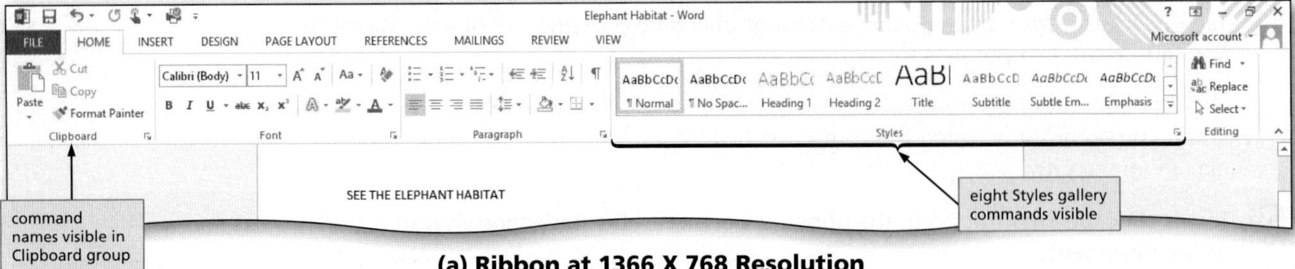

(a) Ribbon at 1366 X 768 Resolution

Figure 58 (continued)

not all command names visible in Clipboard group

four Styles gallery commands visible

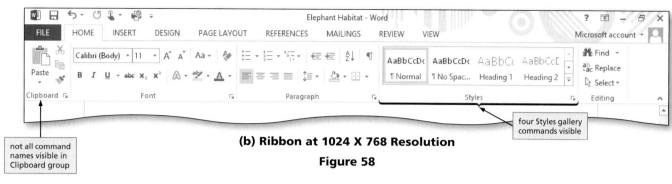

(b) Ribbon at 1024 X 768 Resolution

Figure 58

To Change the Screen Resolution

1 SIGN IN | 2 USE WINDOWS | 3 USE APPS | 4 FILE MANAGEMENT | 5 SWITCH APPS | 6 SAVE FILES
7 CHANGE SCREEN RESOLUTION | 8 EXIT APPS | 9 USE ADDITIONAL APP FEATURES | 10 USE HELP

If you are using a computer to step through the chapters in this book and you want your screen to match the figures, you may need to change your screen's resolution. ***Why?*** *The figures in this book use a screen resolution of 1366 × 768.* The following steps change the screen resolution to 1366 × 768. Your computer already may be set to 1366 × 768. Keep in mind that many computer labs prevent users from changing the screen resolution; in that case, read the following steps for illustration purposes.

- Tap or click the Show desktop button, which is located at the far-right edge of the taskbar, to display the Windows desktop.

Q&A I cannot see the Show desktop button. Why not?
When you point to the far-right edge of the taskbar, a small outline appears to mark the Show desktop button.

- Press and hold or right-click an empty area on the Windows desktop to display a shortcut menu that contains a list of commands related to the desktop (Figure 59).

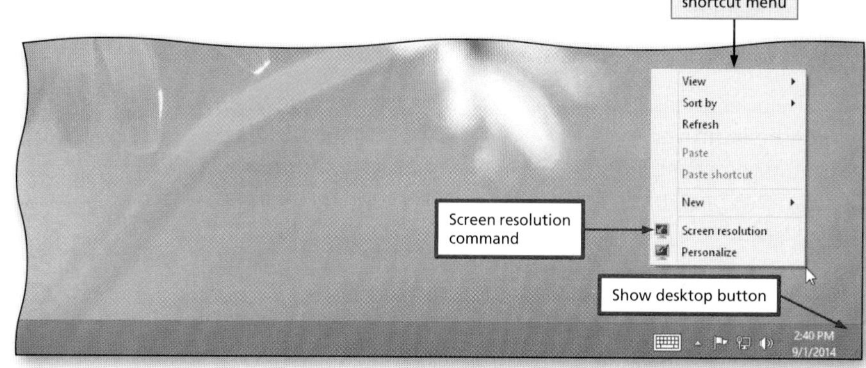

Figure 59

Q&A Why does my shortcut menu display different commands?
Depending on your computer's hardware and configuration, different commands might appear on the shortcut menu.

- Tap or click Screen resolution on the shortcut menu to open the Screen Resolution window (Figure 60).

- Tap or click the Resolution button in the Screen Resolution window to display the resolution slider.

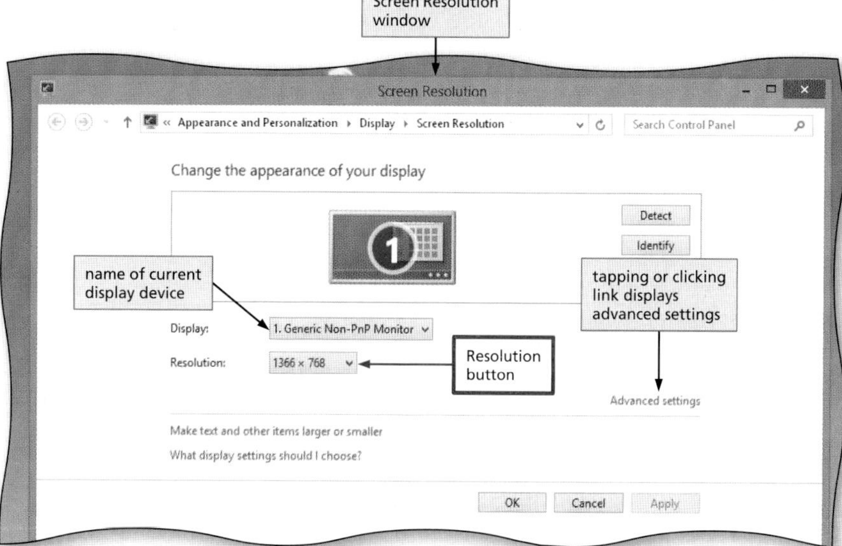

Figure 60

4

- If necessary, drag the resolution slider until the desired screen resolution (in this case, 1366 × 768) is selected (Figure 61).

Q&A What if my computer does not support the 1366 × 768 resolution?
Some computers do not support the 1366 ×768 resolution. In this case, select a resolution that is close to the 1366 × 768 resolution.

What is a slider?
A **slider** is an object that allows users to choose from multiple predetermined options. In most cases, these options represent some type of numeric value. In most cases, one end of the slider (usually the left or bottom) represents the lowest of available values, and the opposite end (usually the right or top) represents the highest available value.

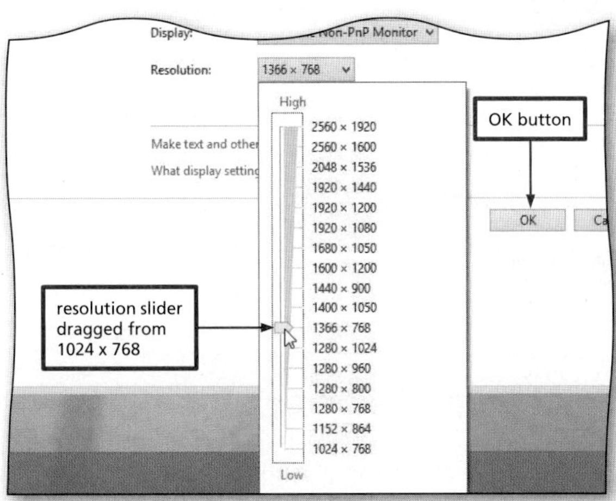

Figure 61

5

- Tap or click an empty area of the Screen Resolution window to close the resolution slider.
- Tap or click the OK button to change the screen resolution and display the Display Settings dialog box (Figure 62).
- Tap or click the Keep changes button (Display Settings dialog box) to accept the new screen resolution.

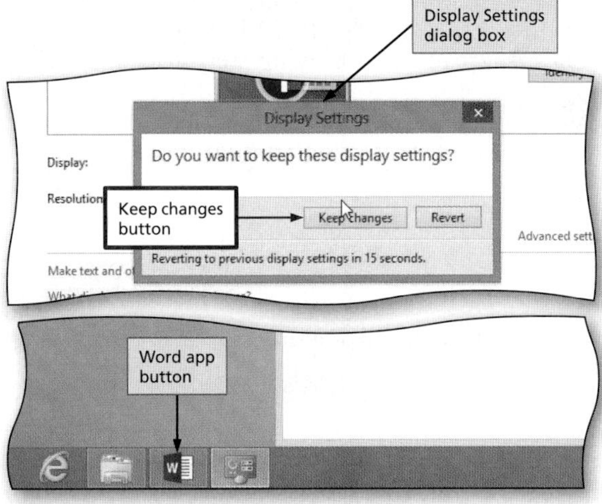

Figure 62

Q&A Why does a message display stating that the image quality can be improved?
Some computer monitors or screens are designed to display contents better at a certain screen resolution, sometimes referred to as an optimal resolution.

To Exit an App with One Document Open

1 SIGN IN | 2 USE WINDOWS | 3 USE APPS | 4 FILE MANAGEMENT | 5 SWITCH APPS | 6 SAVE FILES
7 CHANGE SCREEN RESOLUTION | **8 EXIT APPS** | **9 USE ADDITIONAL APP FEATURES** | **10 USE HELP**

When you exit an Office app, such as Word, if you have made changes to a file since the last time the file was saved, the app displays a dialog box asking if you want to save the changes you made to the file before it closes the app window. ***Why?*** *The dialog box contains three buttons with these resulting actions: the Save button saves the changes and then exits the Office app, the Don't Save button exits the Office app without saving changes, and the Cancel button closes the dialog box and redisplays the file without saving the changes.*

If no changes have been made to an open document since the last time the file was saved, the Office app will close the window without displaying a dialog box.

The following steps exit Word. You would follow similar steps in other Office apps.

1

- If necessary, tap or click the Word app button on the taskbar (shown in Figure 62) to display the Word window on the desktop.
- If you are using a mouse, point to the Close button on the right side of the Word window title bar (Figure 63).

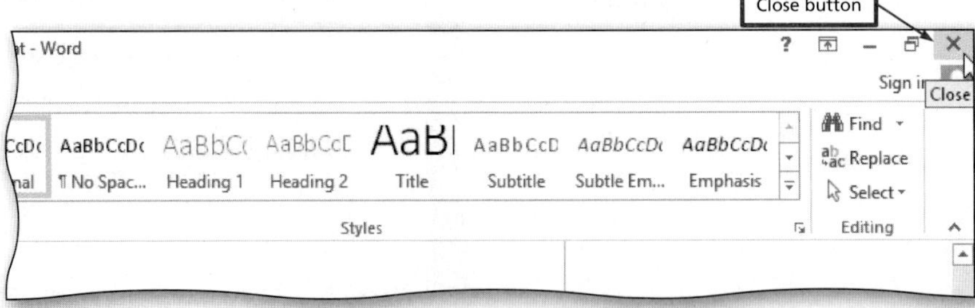

Figure 63

2

- Tap or click the Close button to close the document and exit Word.

Q&A What if I have more than one document open in Word?
You could click the Close button for each open document. When you click the last open document's Close button, you also exit Word. As an alternative that is more efficient, you could press and hold or right-click the Word app button on the taskbar and then tap or click 'Close all windows' on the shortcut menu to close all open documents and exit Word.

3

- If a Microsoft Word dialog box appears, tap or click the Save button to save any changes made to the document since the last save.

Other Ways

1. Press and hold or right-click the Word app button on Windows taskbar, click 'Close all windows' on shortcut menu
2. Press ALT+F4

To Copy a Folder to a USB Flash Drive

1 SIGN IN | 2 USE WINDOWS | 3 USE APPS | **4 FILE MANAGEMENT** | 5 SWITCH APPS | 6 SAVE FILES
7 CHANGE SCREEN RESOLUTION | 8 EXIT APPS | **9 USE ADDITIONAL APP FEATURES** | **10 USE HELP**

To store files and folders on a USB flash drive, you must connect the USB flash drive to an available USB port on a computer. The following steps copy your CIS 101 folder to a USB flash drive. ***Why?*** *It often is good practice to have a backup of your files. Besides SkyDrive, you can save files to a portable storage device, such as a USB flash drive.* If you are using Windows 7, skip these steps and instead perform the steps in the yellow box that immediately follows these Windows 8 steps.

1

- Insert a USB flash drive in an available USB port on the computer to connect the USB flash drive.

Q&A How can I ensure the USB flash drive is connected?
In File Explorer, you can use the navigation bar to find the USB flash drive. If it is not showing, then it is not connected properly.

2

- Tap or click the File Explorer app button on the taskbar to make the folder window the active window.
- If necessary, navigate to the CIS 101 folder in the File Explorer window (see Step 4a on page OFF 30 for instructions about navigating to a folder location).
- Press and hold or right-click the CIS 101 folder to display a shortcut menu (Figure 64).

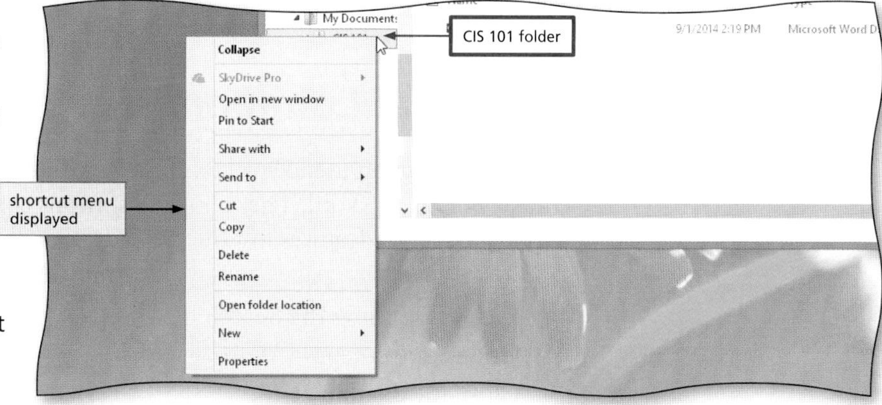

Figure 64

3

- Tap or point to Send to, which causes a submenu to appear (Figure 65).

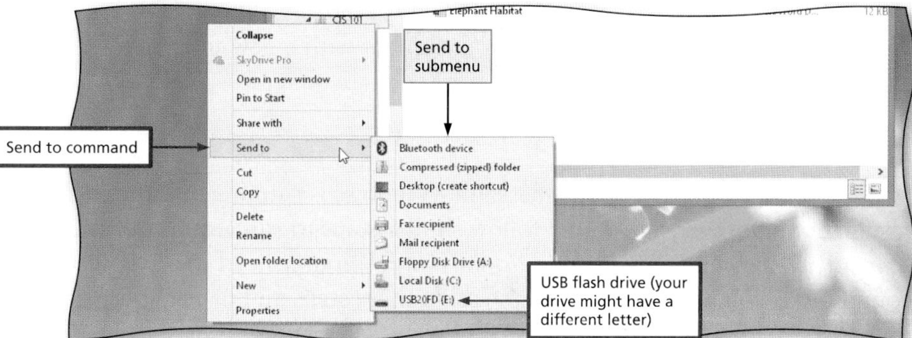

Figure 65

• Tap or click the USB flash drive to copy the folder to the USB flash drive (Figure 66).

Q&A Why does the drive letter of my USB flash drive differ?
Windows assigns the next available drive letter to your USB flash drive when you connect it. The next available drive letter may vary by computer, depending on the number of storage devices that currently are connected.

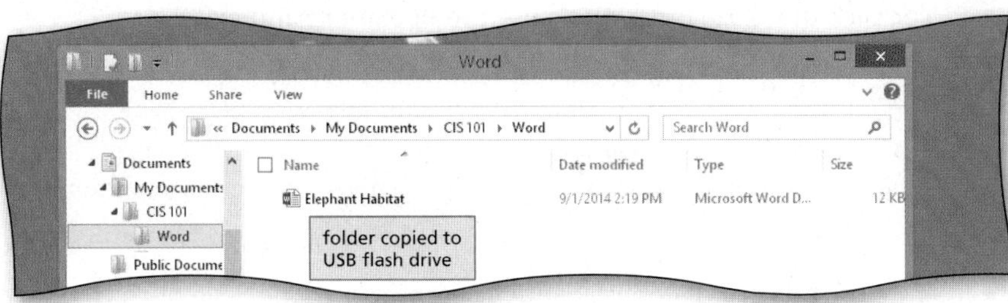

Figure 66

To Copy a Folder to a USB Flash Drive Using Windows 7

If you are using Windows 7, perform these steps to copy a folder to a USB flash drive instead of the previous steps that use Windows 8.

1. Insert a USB flash drive in an available USB port on the computer to open the AutoPlay window.
2. Click the 'Open folder to view files' link in the AutoPlay window to open the Windows Explorer window.
3. Navigate to the Documents library.
4. Right-click the CIS 101 folder to display a shortcut menu.
5. Point to Send to, which causes a submenu to appear.
6. Click the USB flash drive to copy the folder to the USB flash drive.

Break Point: If you wish to take a break, this is a good place to do so. To resume at a later time, continue to follow the steps from this location forward.

Additional Common Features of Office Apps

The previous section used Word to illustrate common features of Office and some basic elements unique to Word. The following sections continue to use Word to present additional common features of Office.

In the following pages, you will learn how to do the following:

1. Run Word using the Search box.
2. Open a document in Word.
3. Close the document.
4. Reopen the document just closed.
5. Create a blank Word document from Windows Explorer and then open the file.
6. Save a document with a new file name.

To Run an App Using the Search Box

1 SIGN IN | 2 USE WINDOWS | 3 USE APPS | 4 FILE MANAGEMENT | 5 SWITCH APPS | 6 SAVE FILES
7 CHANGE SCREEN RESOLUTION | 8 EXIT APPS | **9 USE ADDITIONAL APP FEATURES** | **10 USE HELP**

The following steps, which assume Windows is running, use the search box to run Word based on a typical installation; however, you would follow similar steps to run any app. ***Why?*** *Sometimes an app does not appear on the Start screen, so you can find it quickly by searching.* You may need to ask your instructor how to run apps for your computer. If you are using Windows 7, skip these steps and instead perform the steps in the yellow box that immediately follows these Windows 8 steps.

- Swipe in from the right edge of the screen or point to the upper-right corner of the screen to display the Charms bar (Figure 67).

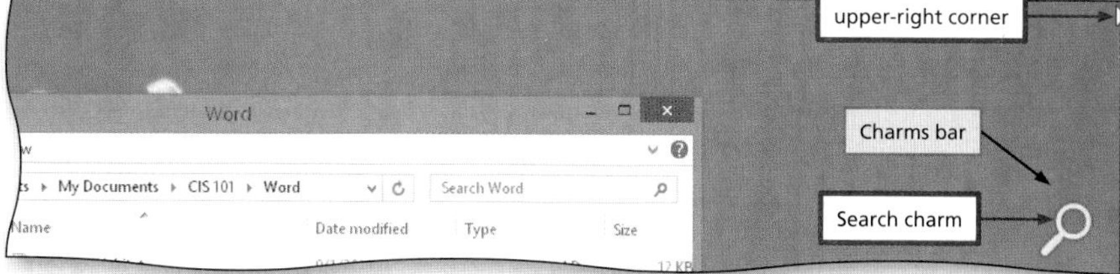

Figure 67

2

- Tap or click the Search charm on the Charms bar to display the Search menu (Figure 68).

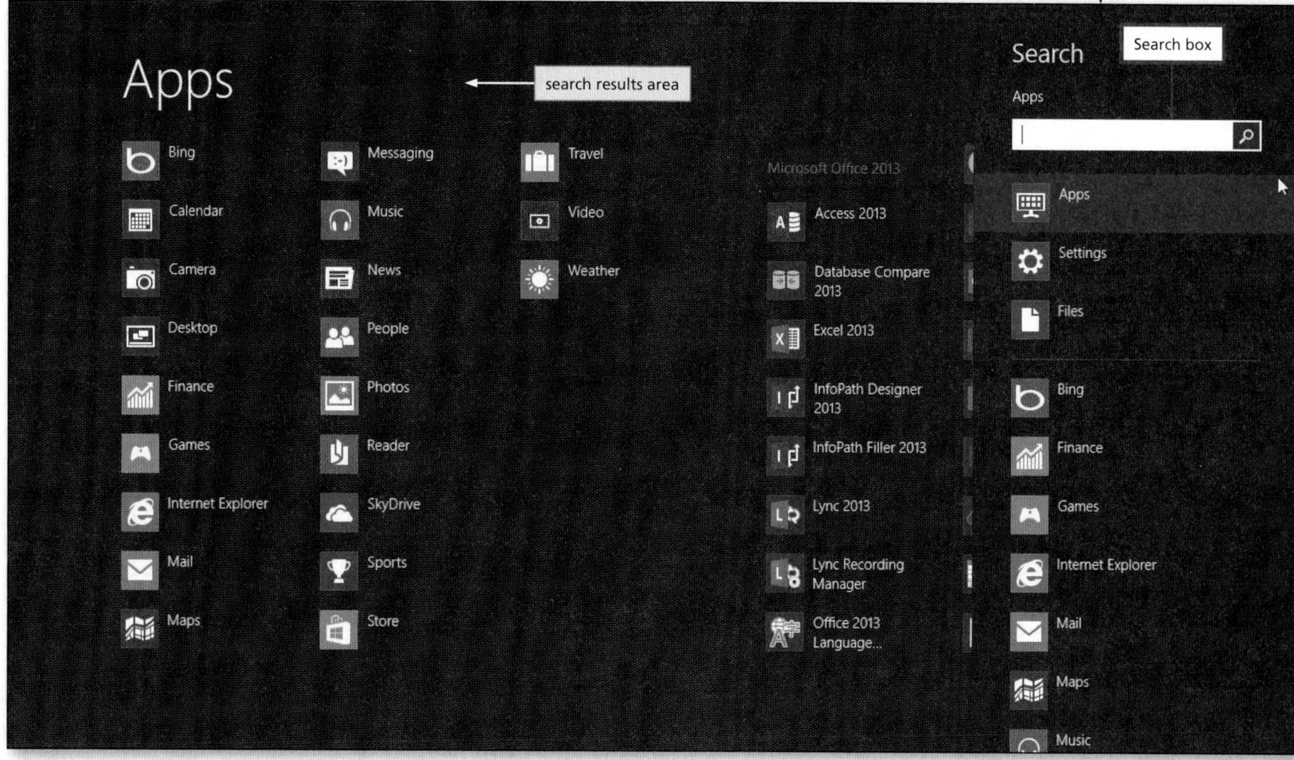

Figure 68

3

- Type **`Word 2013`** as the search text in the Search box and watch the search results appear in the Apps list (Figure 69).

Q&A Do I need to type the complete app name or use correct capitalization?

No, you need to type just enough characters of the app name for it to appear in the Apps list. For example, you may be able to type Word or word, instead of Word 2013.

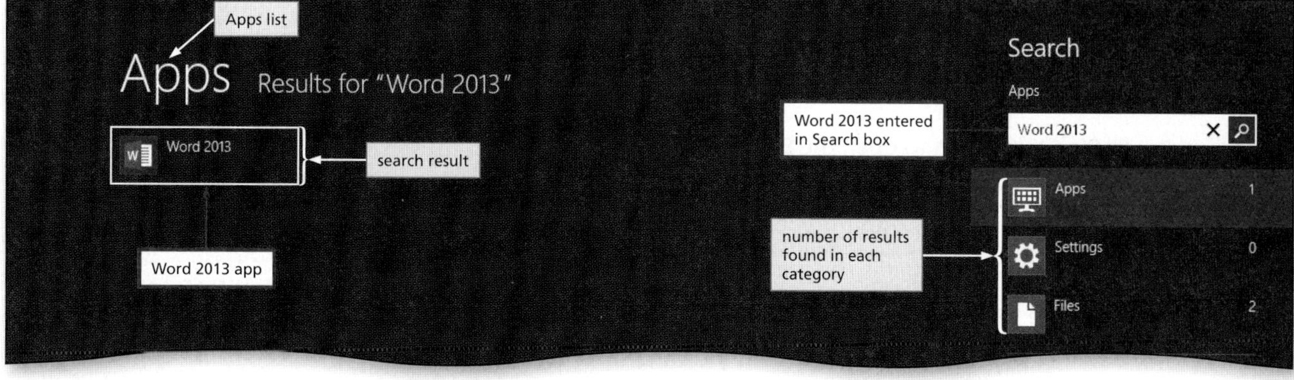

Figure 69

- Tap or click Word 2013 in the search results to run Word.
- Tap or click the Blank document thumbnail to create a blank document and display it in the Word window.
- If the Word window is not maximized, tap or click the Maximize button on its title bar to maximize the window (Figure 70).

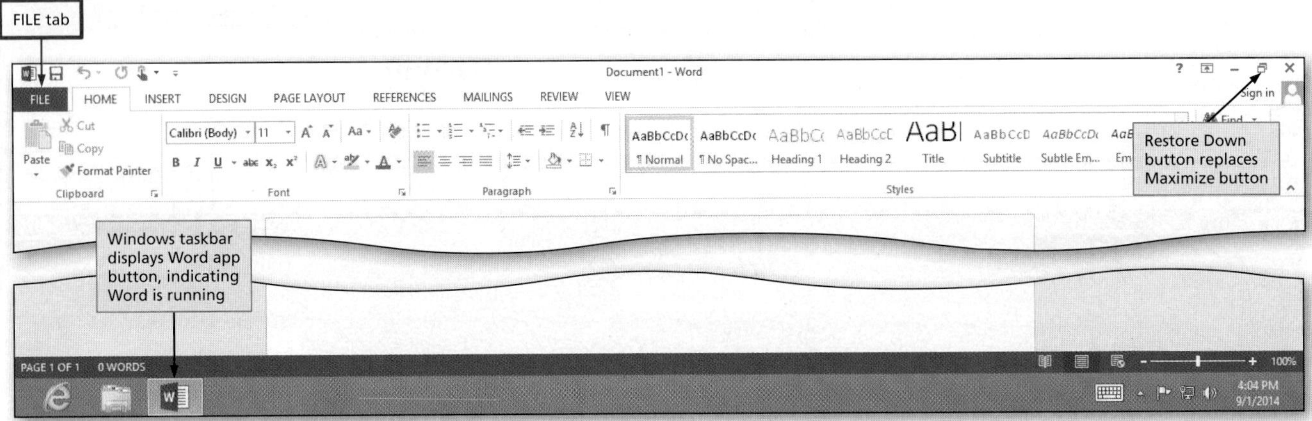

Figure 70

To Run an App Using the Search Box Using Windows 7

If you are using Windows 7, perform these steps to run an app using the search box instead of the previous steps that use Windows 8.

1. Click the Start button on the Windows 7 taskbar to display the Start menu.
2. Type `Word 2013` as the search text in the 'Search programs and files' text box and watch the search results appear on the Start menu.
3. Click Word 2013 in the search results on the Start menu to run Word.
4. Click the Blank document thumbnail to create a blank document and display it in the Word window.
5. If the Word window is not maximized, click the Maximize button on its title bar to maximize the window.

To Open an Existing File

As discussed earlier, the Backstage view contains a set of commands that enable you to manage documents and data about the documents. ***Why?*** *From the Backstage view in Word, for example, you can create, open, print, and save documents. You also can share documents, manage versions, set permissions, and modify document properties. In other Office 2013 apps, the Backstage view may contain features specific to those apps.* The following steps open a saved file, specifically the Elephant Habitat file, that recently was saved.

- Tap or click FILE on the ribbon to open the Backstage view and then tap or click Open in the Backstage view to display the Open gallery in the Backstage view.
- Tap or click Computer to display recent folders accessed on your computer.
- Tap or click the Browse button to display the Open dialog box.
- If necessary, navigate to the location of the file to open as described in Steps 4a and 4b on pages OFF 30–31.
- Tap or click the file to open, Elephant Habitat in this case, to select the file (Figure 71).

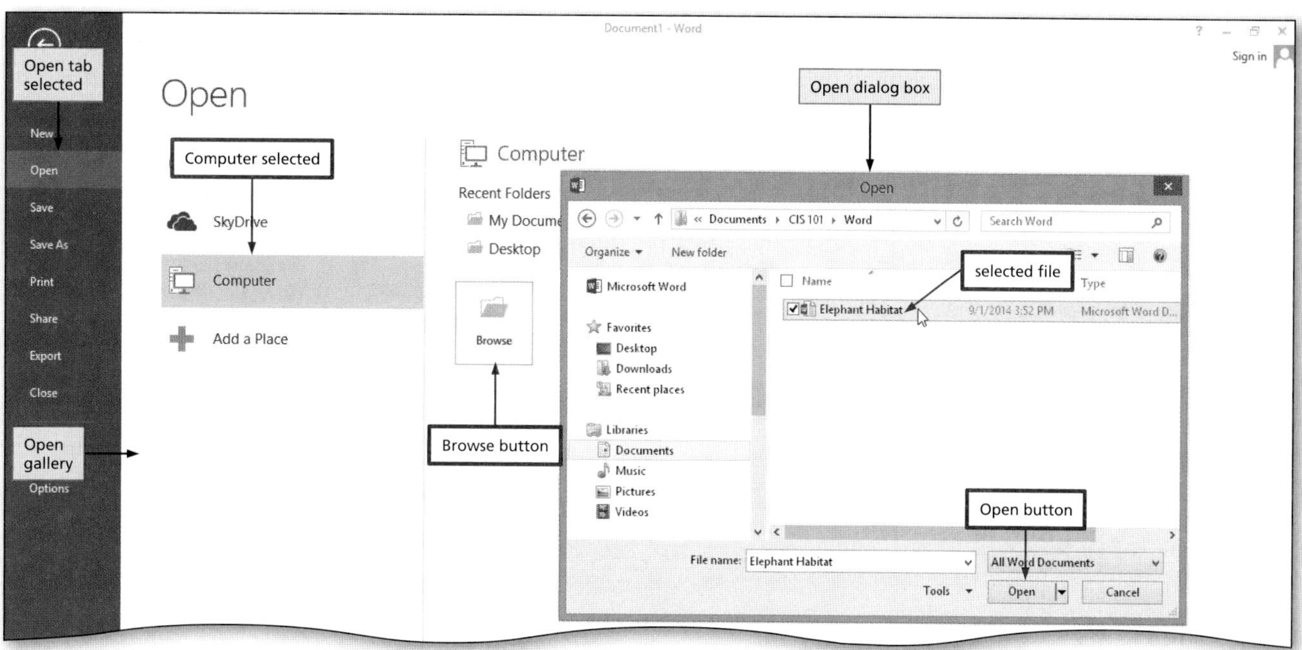

Figure 71

- Tap or click the Open button (Open dialog box) to open the file (shown in Figure 49 on page OFF 31).

Other Ways

1. Press CTRL+O 2. Navigate to file in File Explorer window, double-tap or double-click file

To Create a New Document from the Backstage View

1 SIGN IN | 2 USE WINDOWS | 3 USE APPS | 4 FILE MANAGEMENT | 5 SWITCH APPS | 6 SAVE FILES
7 CHANGE SCREEN RESOLUTION | 8 EXIT APPS | **9 USE ADDITIONAL APP FEATURES** | **10 USE HELP**

You can open multiple documents in an Office program, such as Word, so that you can work on the documents at the same time. The following steps create a file, a blank document in this case, from the Backstage view. ***Why?*** *You want to create a new document while keeping the current document open.*

1

- Tap or click FILE on the ribbon to open the Backstage view.
- Tap or click the New tab in the Backstage view to display the New gallery (Figure 72).

Q&A Can I create documents through the Backstage view in other Office apps?
Yes. If the Office app has a New tab in the Backstage view, the New gallery displays various options for creating a new file.

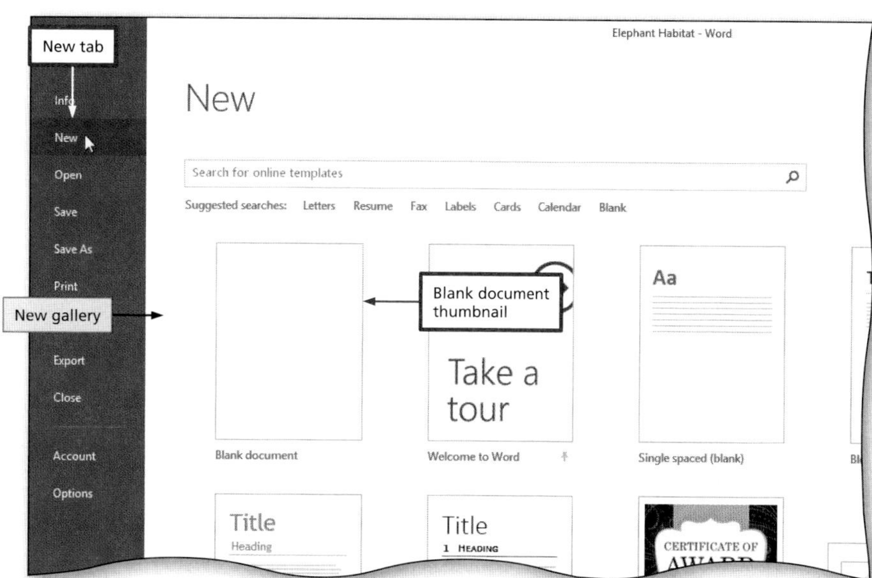

Figure 72

2

• Tap or click the Blank document thumbnail in the New gallery to create a new document (Figure 73).

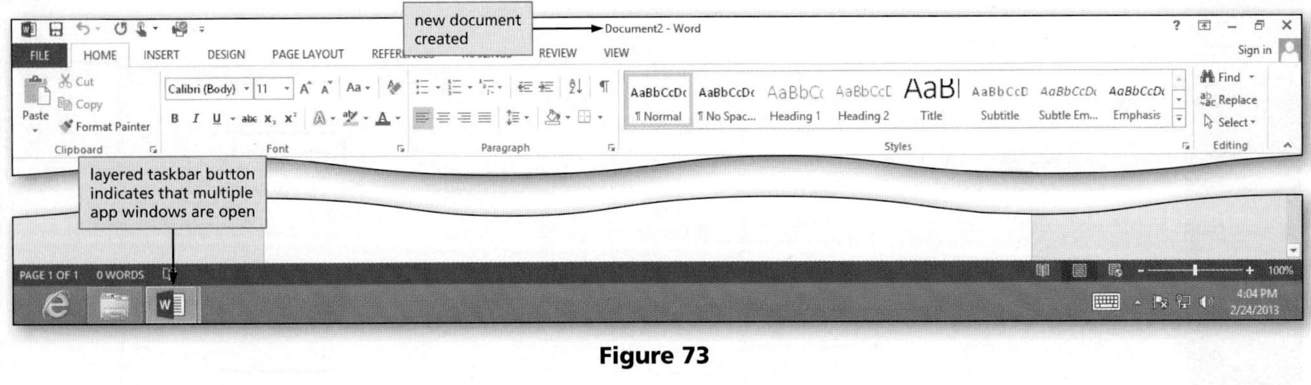

Figure 73

Other Ways

1. Press CTRL+N

To Enter Text in a Document

The next Word document identifies the names of the Elephant Habitat sponsors. The following step enters text in a document.

1 Type `List of Current Sponsors for the Elephant Habitat` and then press the ENTER key to move the insertion point to the beginning of the next line (Figure 74).

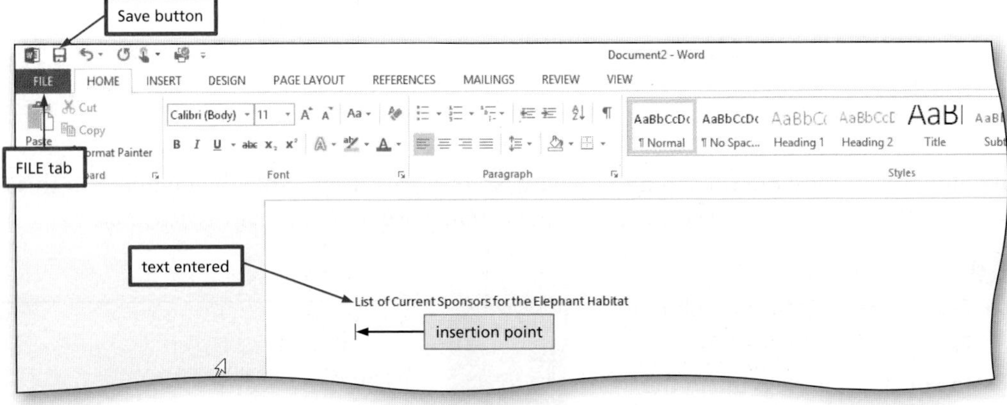

Figure 74

BTW
Customizing the Ribbon
In addition to customizing the Quick Access Toolbar, you can add items to and remove items from the ribbon. To customize the ribbon, click FILE on the ribbon to open the Backstage view, click Options in the Backstage view, and then click Customize Ribbon in the left pane of the Options dialog box. More information about customizing the ribbon is presented in a later chapter.

To Save a File in a Folder

The following steps save the second document in the Word folder in the class folder (CIS 101, in this case) in the My Documents folder in the Documents library using the file name, Elephant Habitat Sponsors.

1 Tap or click the Save button on the Quick Access Toolbar (shown in Figure 74), which depending on settings will display either the Save As gallery in the Backstage view or the Save As dialog box.

2 If your screen displays the Backstage view, tap or click Computer, if necessary, to display options in the right pane related to saving on your computer; if your screen already displays the Save As dialog box, proceed to Step 4.

3. Tap or click the Browse button in the right pane to display the Save As dialog box.

4. If necessary, type `Elephant Habitat Sponsors` in the File name box (Save As dialog box) to change the file name. Do not press the ENTER key after typing the file name because you do not want to close the dialog box at this time.

5. If necessary, navigate to the desired save location (in this case, the Word folder in the CIS 101 folder [or your class folder] in the My Documents folder in the Documents library). For specific instructions, perform the tasks in Steps 4a and 4b on pages OFF 30–31.

6. Tap or click the Save button (Save As dialog box) to save the document in the selected folder on the selected drive with the entered file name.

To Close a File Using the Backstage View

1 SIGN IN | 2 USE WINDOWS | 3 USE APPS | 4 FILE MANAGEMENT | 5 SWITCH APPS | 6 SAVE FILES
7 CHANGE SCREEN RESOLUTION | 8 EXIT APPS | **9 USE ADDITIONAL APP FEATURES** | **10 USE HELP**

Sometimes, you may want to close an Office file, such as a Word document, entirely and start over with a new file. ***Why else would I close a file?*** *You also may want to close a file when you are finished working with it so that you can begin a new file.* The following steps close the current active Word file, that is, the Elephant Habitat Sponsors document, without exiting Word.

- Tap or click FILE on the ribbon (shown in Figure 74) to open the Backstage view (Figure 75).

- Tap or click Close in the Backstage view to close the open file (Elephant Habitat Sponsors, in this case) without exiting the active app.

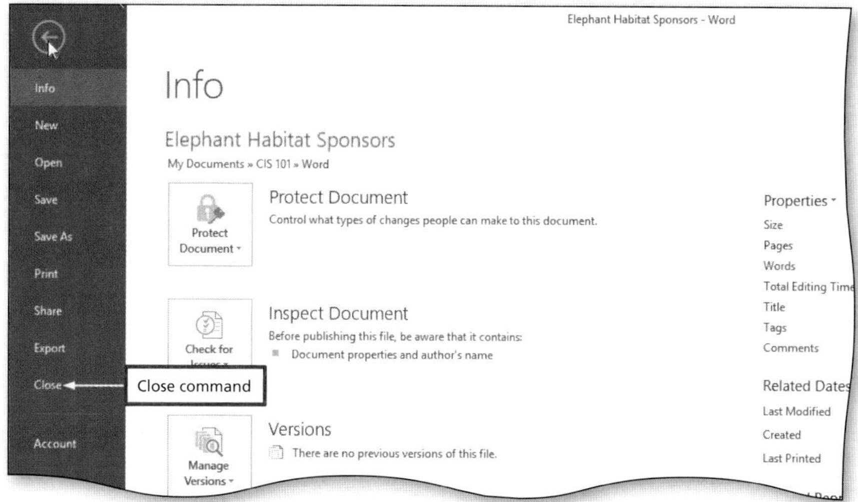

Figure 75

Q&A

What if Word displays a dialog box about saving?
Tap or click the Save button if you want to save the changes, tap or click the Don't Save button if you want to ignore the changes since the last time you saved, and tap or click the Cancel button if you do not want to close the document.

Can I use the Backstage view to close an open file in other Office apps, such as PowerPoint and Excel?
Yes.

Other Ways

1. Press CTRL+F4

To Open a Recent File Using the Backstage View

1 SIGN IN | 2 USE WINDOWS | 3 USE APPS | 4 FILE MANAGEMENT | 5 SWITCH APPS | 6 SAVE FILES
7 CHANGE SCREEN RESOLUTION | 8 EXIT APPS | **9 USE ADDITIONAL APP FEATURES** | **10 USE HELP**

You sometimes need to open a file that you recently modified. ***Why?*** *You may have more changes to make, such as adding more content or correcting errors.* The Backstage view allows you to access recent files easily. The steps on the next page reopen the Elephant Habitat Sponsors file just closed.

- Tap or click FILE on the ribbon to open the Backstage view.
- Tap or click the Open tab in the Backstage view to display the Open gallery (Figure 76).

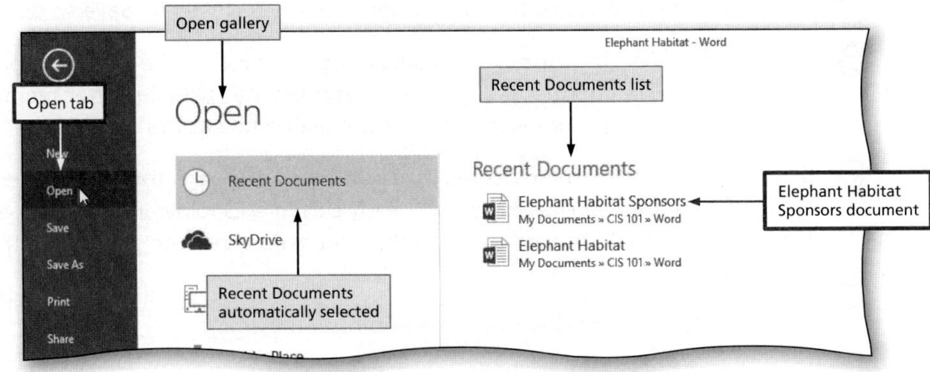

Figure 76

2

- Tap or click the desired file name in the Recent Documents list, Elephant Habitat Sponsors in this case, to open the file (shown in Figure 74 on page OFF 44).

Q&A Can I use the Backstage view to open a recent file in other Office apps, such as PowerPoint and Excel?
Yes, as long as the file name appears in the list of recent files.

Other Ways

1. Tap or click FILE on ribbon, tap or click Open in Backstage view, tap or click Computer, tap or click Browse, navigate to file (Open dialog box), tap or click Open button

To Create a New Blank Document from File Explorer

1 SIGN IN | 2 USE WINDOWS | 3 USE APPS | 4 FILE MANAGEMENT | 5 SWITCH APPS | 6 SAVE FILES
7 CHANGE SCREEN RESOLUTION | 8 EXIT APPS | 9 USE ADDITIONAL APP FEATURES | 10 USE HELP

File Explorer provides a means to create a blank Office document without running an Office app. The following steps use File Explorer to create a blank Word document. ***Why?*** *Sometimes you might need to create a blank document and then return to it later for editing.* If you are using Windows 7, skip these steps and instead perform the steps in the yellow box that immediately follows these Windows 8 steps.

- Tap or click the File Explorer app button on the taskbar to make the folder window the active window.
- If necessary, double-tap or double-click the Documents library in the navigation pane to expand the Documents library.
- If necessary, double-tap or double-click the My Documents folder in the navigation pane to expand the My Documents folder.
- If necessary, double-tap or double-click your class folder (CIS 101, in this case) in the navigation pane to expand the folder.
- Tap or click the Word folder in the navigation pane to display its contents in the file list.
- With the Word folder selected, press and hold or right-click an open area in the file list to display a shortcut menu.
- Tap or point to New on the shortcut menu to display the New submenu (Figure 77).

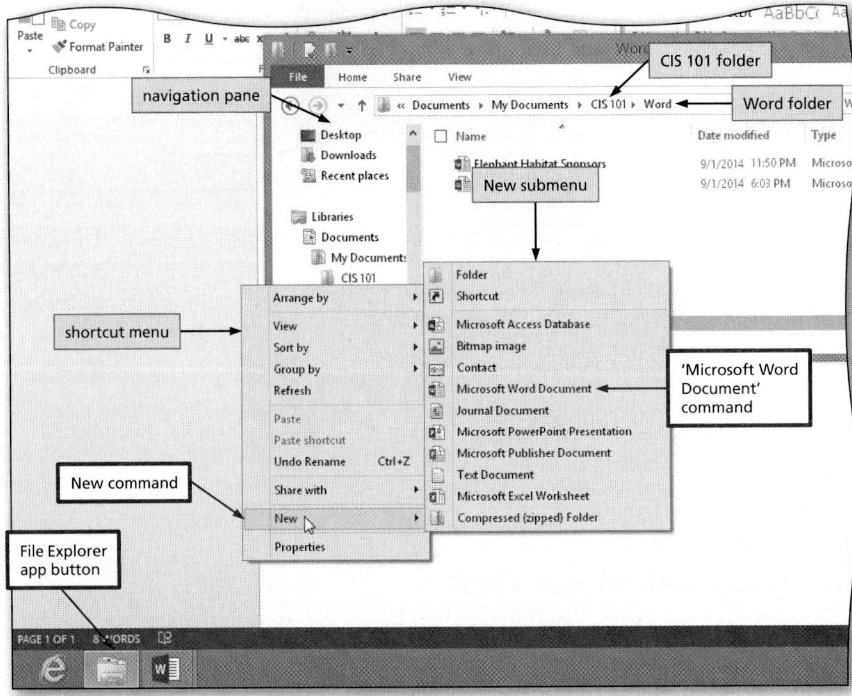

Figure 77

- Tap or click 'Microsoft Word Document' on the New submenu to display an icon and text box for a new file in the current folder window with the file name, New Microsoft Word Document, selected (Figure 78).

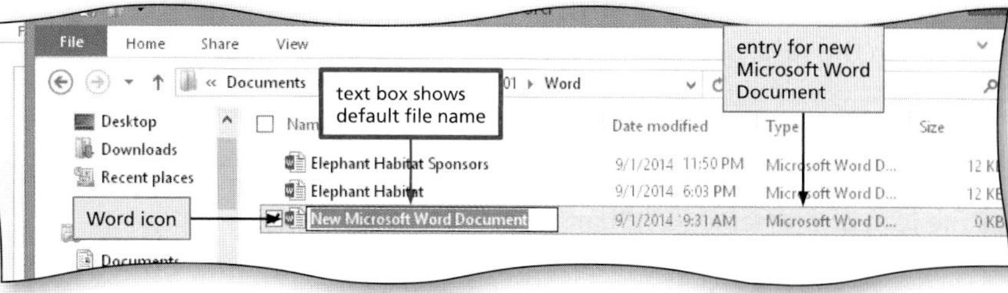

Figure 78

3

- Type **`Elephant Habitat Volunteers`** in the text box and then press the ENTER key to assign a new name to the new file in the current folder (Figure 79).

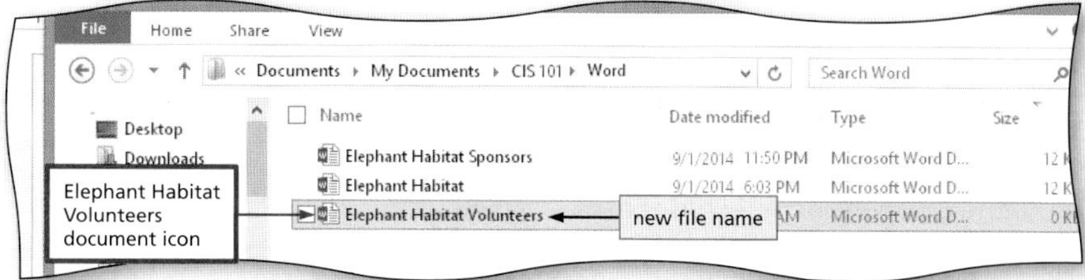

Figure 79

To Create a New Blank Document from Windows Explorer Using Windows 7

If you are using Windows 7, perform these steps to create a new blank Office document from Windows Explorer instead of the previous steps that use Windows 8.

1. If necessary, click the Windows Explorer button on the taskbar to make the folder window the active window.
2. If necessary, double-click the Documents library in the navigation pane to expand the Documents library.
3. If necessary, double-click the My Documents folder in the navigation pane to expand the My Documents folder.
4. If necessary, double-click your class folder (CIS 101, in this case) in the navigation pane to expand the folder.
5. Click the Word folder in the navigation pane to display its contents in the file list.
6. With the Word folder selected, right-click an open area in the file list to display a shortcut menu.
7. Point to New on the shortcut menu to display the New submenu.
8. Click 'Microsoft Word Document' on the New submenu to display an icon and text box for a new file in the current folder window with the name, New Microsoft Word Document, selected.
9. Type **`Elephant Habitat Volunteers`** in the text box and then press the ENTER key to assign a new name to the new file in the current folder.

To Run an App from File Explorer and Open a File

1 SIGN IN | 2 USE WINDOWS | 3 USE APPS | 4 FILE MANAGEMENT | 5 SWITCH APPS | 6 SAVE FILES
7 CHANGE SCREEN RESOLUTION | 8 EXIT APPS | 9 USE ADDITIONAL APP FEATURES | **10 USE HELP**

Previously, you learned how to run Word using the Start screen and the Search charm. The steps on the next page, which assume Windows is running, use File Explorer to run Word based on a typical installation. ***Why?*** *Another way to run an Office app is to open an existing file from File Explorer, which causes the app in which the file was created to run and then open the selected file.* You may need to ask your instructor how to run Word for your computer. If you are using Windows 7, follow the steps in the yellow box that immediately follows these Windows 8 steps.

1

- If necessary, display the file to open in the folder window in File Explorer (shown in Figure 79 on the previous page).
- Press and hold or right-click the file icon or file name (Elephant Habitat Volunteers, in this case) to display a shortcut menu (Figure 80).

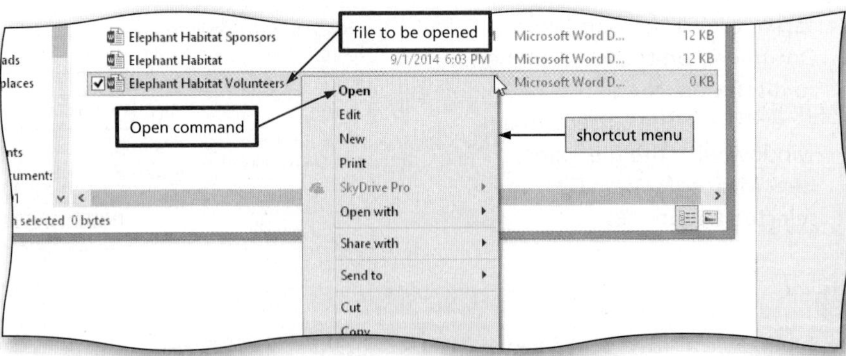

Figure 80

2

- Tap or click Open on the shortcut menu to open the selected file in the app used to create the file, Word in this case (Figure 81).
- If the Word window is not maximized, tap or click the Maximize button on the title bar to maximize the window.

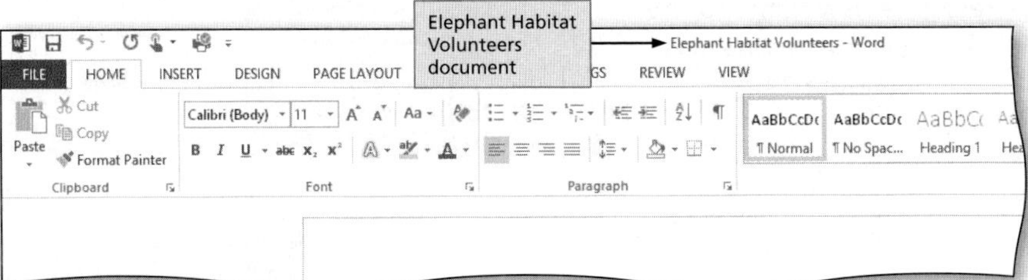

Figure 81

To Run an App from Windows Explorer and Open a File Using Windows 7

If you are using Windows 7, perform these steps to run an app from Windows Explorer and open a file instead of the previous steps that use Windows 8.

1. Display the file to open in the folder window in Windows Explorer.
2. Right-click the file icon or file name (Elephant Habitat Volunteers, in this case) to display a shortcut menu.
3. Click Open on the shortcut menu to open the selected file in the app used to create the file, Word in this case.
4. If the Word window is not maximized, click the Maximize button on the title bar to maximize the window.

To Enter Text in a Document

The next step is to enter text in this blank Word document. The following step enters a line of text.

1 Type `Elephant Habitat Staff and Volunteers` and then press the ENTER key to move the insertion point to the beginning of the next line (shown in Figure 82).

To Save an Existing File with the Same File Name

1 SIGN IN | 2 USE WINDOWS | 3 USE APPS | 4 FILE MANAGEMENT | 5 SWITCH APPS | 6 SAVE FILES
7 CHANGE SCREEN RESOLUTION | 8 EXIT APPS | 9 USE ADDITIONAL APP FEATURES | **10 USE HELP**

Saving frequently cannot be overemphasized. ***Why?*** *You have made modifications to the file (document) since you created it. Thus, you should save again. Similarly, you should continue saving files frequently so that you do not lose the changes you have made since the time you last saved the file.* You can use the same file name, such as Elephant Habitat Volunteers, to save the changes made to the document. The next step saves a file again with the same file name.

1

- Tap or click the Save button on the Quick Access Toolbar to overwrite the previously saved file (Elephant Habitat Volunteers, in this case) in the Word folder (Figure 82).

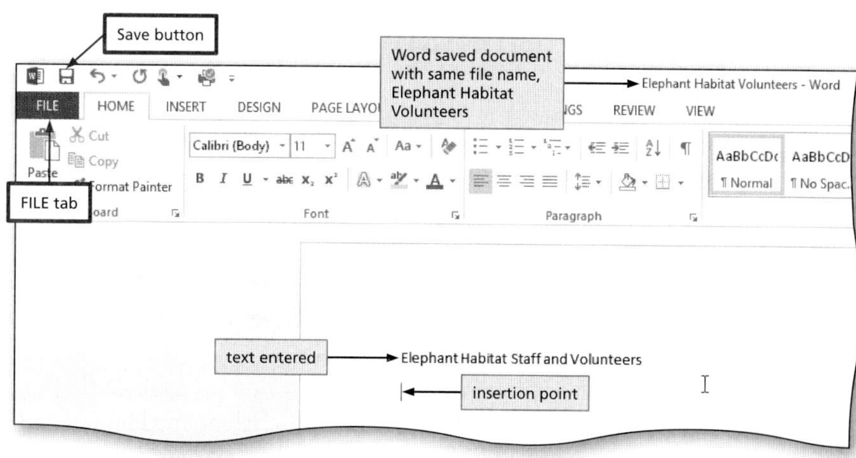

Figure 82

Other Ways

1. Press CTRL+S or press SHIFT+F12

To Save a File with a New File Name

You might want to save a file with a different name or to a different location. For example, you might start a homework assignment with a data file and then save it with a final file name for submission to your instructor, saving it to a location designated by your instructor. The following steps save a file with a different file name.

1. Tap or click the FILE tab to open the Backstage view.
2. Tap or click the Save As tab to display the Save As gallery.
3. If necessary, tap or click Computer to display options in the right pane related to saving on your computer.
4. Tap or click the Browse button in the right pane to display the Save As dialog box.
5. Type **`Elephant Habitat Staff and Volunteers`** in the File name box (Save As dialog box) to change the file name. Do not press the ENTER key after typing the file name because you do not want to close the dialog box at this time.
6. If necessary, navigate to the desired save location (in this case, the Word folder in the CIS 101 folder [or your class folder] in the My Documents folder in the Documents library). For specific instructions, perform the tasks in Steps 4a and 4b on pages OFF 30–31.
7. Tap or click the Save button (Save As dialog box) to save the document in the selected folder on the selected drive with the entered file name.

To Exit an Office App

You are finished using Word. The following steps exit Word. You would use similar steps to exit other Office apps.

1. Because you have multiple Word documents open, press and hold or right-click the app button on the taskbar and then tap or click 'Close all windows' on the shortcut menu to close all open documents and exit Word.
2. If a dialog box appears, tap or click the Save button to save any changes made to the file since the last save.

Renaming, Moving, and Deleting Files

Earlier in this chapter, you learned how to organize files in folders, which is part of a process known as **file management**. The following sections cover additional file management topics including renaming, moving, and deleting files.

To Rename a File

1 SIGN IN | 2 USE WINDOWS | 3 USE APPS | **4 FILE MANAGEMENT** | 5 SWITCH APPS | 6 SAVE FILES
7 CHANGE SCREEN RESOLUTION | 8 EXIT APPS | 9 USE ADDITIONAL APP FEATURES | **10 USE HELP**

In some circumstances, you may want to change the name of, or rename, a file or a folder. ***Why?*** *You may want to distinguish a file in one folder or drive from a copy of a similar file, or you may decide to rename a file to better identify its contents.* The Word folder shown in Figure 66 on page OFF 40 contains the Word document, Elephant Habitat. The following steps change the name of the Elephant Habitat file in the Word folder to Elephant Habitat Flyer. If you are using Windows 7, skip these steps and instead perform the steps in the yellow box that immediately follows these Windows 8 steps.

- If necessary, tap or click the File Explorer app button on the taskbar to make the folder window the active window.
- If necessary, navigate to the location of the file to be renamed (in this case, the Word folder in the CIS 101 [or your class folder] folder in the My Documents folder in the Documents library) to display the file(s) it contains in the file list.
- Press and hold or right-click the Elephant Habitat icon or file name in the file list to select the Elephant Habitat file and display a shortcut menu that presents a list of commands related to files (Figure 83).

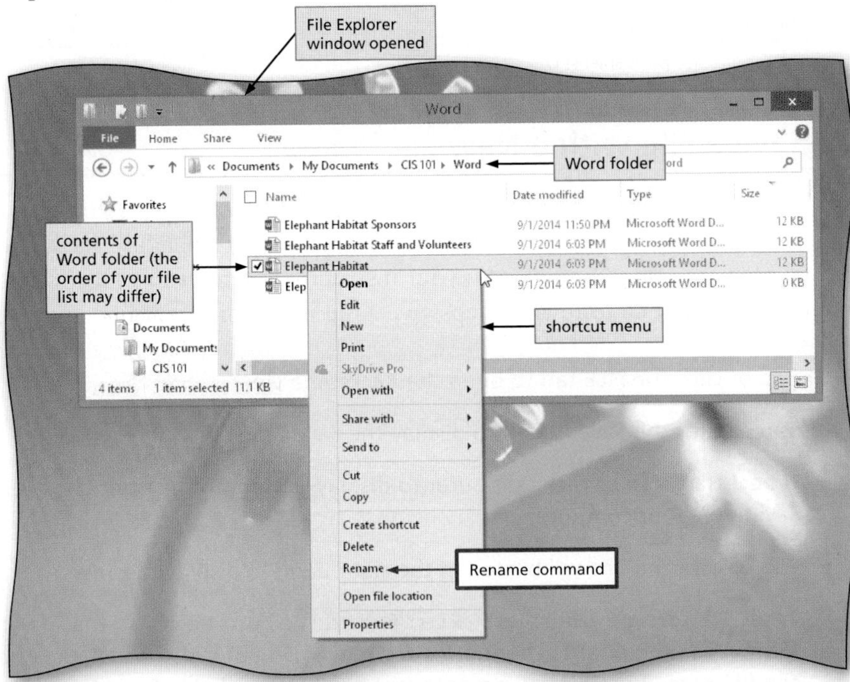

Figure 83

- Tap or click Rename on the shortcut menu to place the current file name in a text box.
- Type `Elephant Habitat Flyer` in the text box and then press the ENTER key (Figure 84).

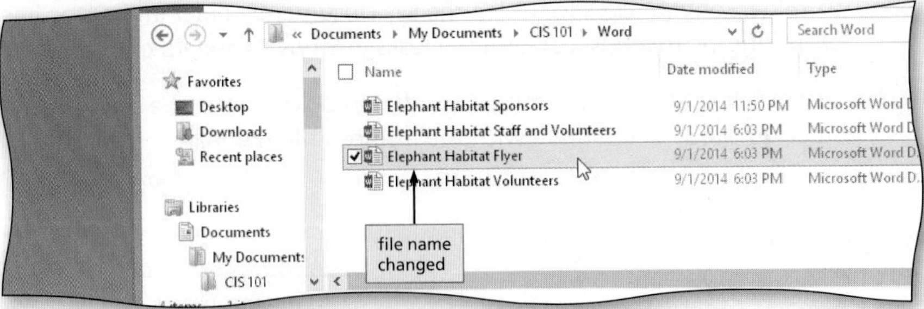

Figure 84

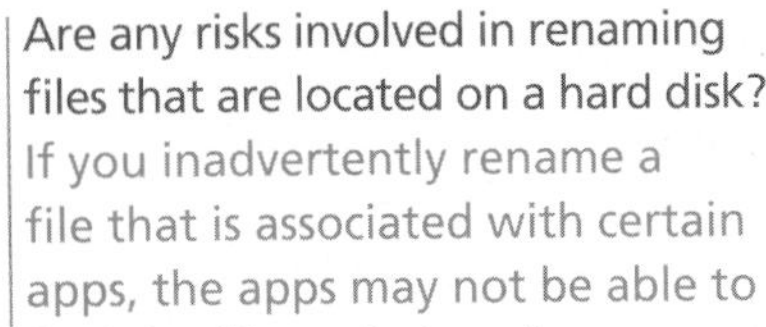

Q&A

Are any risks involved in renaming files that are located on a hard disk?
If you inadvertently rename a file that is associated with certain apps, the apps may not be able to find the file and, therefore, may not run properly. Always use caution when renaming files.

Can I rename a file when it is open?
No, a file must be closed to change the file name.

Other Ways

1. Select file, press F2, type new file name, press ENTER 2. Select file, tap or click Rename (Home tab | Organize group), type new file name, press ENTER

To Rename a File Using Windows 7

If you are using Windows 7, perform these steps to rename a file instead of the previous steps that use Windows 8.

1. If necessary, click the Windows Explorer app button on the taskbar to make the folder window the active window.
2. Navigate to the location of the file to be renamed (in this case, the Word folder in the CIS 101 [or your class folder] folder in the My Documents folder in the Documents library) to display the file(s) it contains in the file list.
3. Right-click the Elephant Habitat icon or file name in the file list to select the Elephant Habitat file and display a shortcut menu that presents a list of commands related to files.
4. Click Rename on the shortcut menu to place the current file name in a text box.
5. Type **Elephant Habitat Flyer** in the text box and then press the ENTER key.

To Move a File

Why? *At some time, you may want to move a file from one folder, called the source folder, to another, called the destination folder.* When you move a file, it no longer appears in the original folder. If the destination and the source folders are on the same media, you can move a file by dragging it. If the folders are on different media, then you will need to press and hold and then drag, or right-drag the file, and then click Move here on the shortcut menu. The following step moves the Elephant Habitat Volunteers file from the Word folder to the CIS 101 folder. If you are using Windows 7, skip these steps and instead perform the steps in the yellow box that immediately follows these Windows 8 steps.

- In File Explorer, if necessary, navigate to the location of the file to be moved (in this case, the Word folder in the CIS 101 folder [or your class folder] in the Documents library).
- If necessary, tap or click the Word folder in the navigation pane to display the files it contains in the right pane.
- Drag the Elephant Habitat Volunteers file in the right pane to the CIS 101 folder in the navigation pane and notice the ScreenTip as you drag the mouse (Figure 85).

Experiment

- Click the CIS 101 folder in the navigation pane to verify that the file was moved.

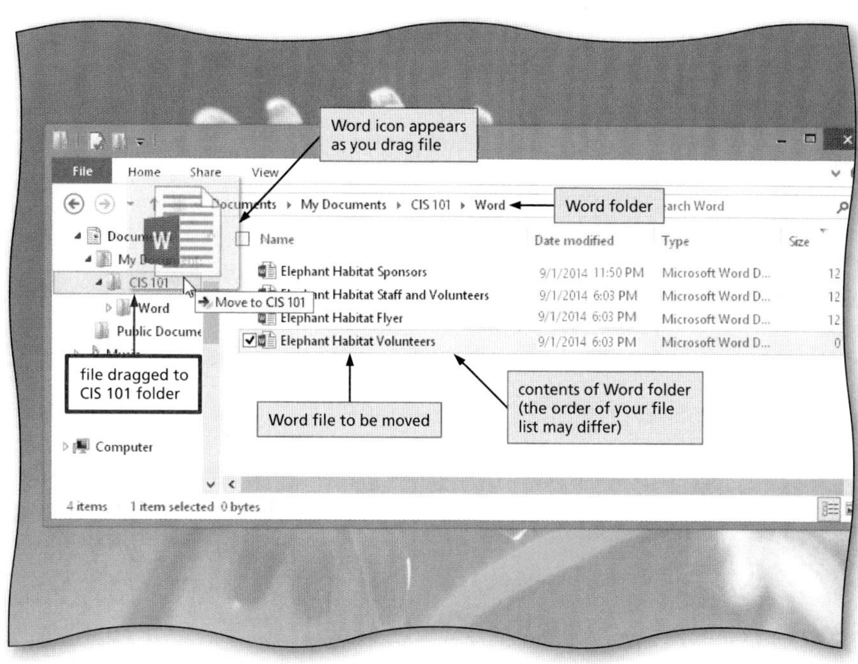

Figure 85

Other Ways

1. Press and hold or right-click file to move, tap or click Cut on shortcut menu, press and hold or right-click destination folder, tap or click Paste on shortcut menu
2. Select file to move, press CTRL+X, select destination folder, press CTRL+V

To Move a File Using Windows 7

If you are using Windows 7, perform these steps to move a file instead of the previous steps that use Windows 8.

1. In Windows Explorer, navigate to the location of the file to be moved (in this case, the Word folder in the CIS 101 folder [or your class folder] in the Documents library).
2. Click the Word folder in the navigation pane to display the files it contains in the right pane.
3. Drag the Elephant Habitat Volunteers file in the right pane to the CIS 101 folder in the navigation pane.

To Delete a File

1 SIGN IN | 2 USE WINDOWS | 3 USE APPS | 4 FILE MANAGEMENT | 5 SWITCH APPS | 6 SAVE FILES
7 CHANGE SCREEN RESOLUTION | 8 EXIT APPS | 9 USE ADDITIONAL APP FEATURES | 10 USE HELP

A final task you may want to perform is to delete a file. Exercise extreme caution when deleting a file or files. When you delete a file from a hard disk, the deleted file is stored in the Recycle Bin where you can recover it until you empty the Recycle Bin. If you delete a file from removable media, such as a USB flash drive, the file is deleted permanently. The next steps delete the Elephant Habitat Volunteers file from the CIS 101 folder. ***Why?*** *When a file no longer is needed, you can delete it to conserve space in your storage location.* If you are using Windows 7, skip these steps and instead perform the steps in the yellow box that immediately follows these Windows 8 steps.

- In File Explorer, navigate to the location of the file to be deleted (in this case, the CIS 101 folder [or your class folder] in the Documents library).
- Press and hold or right-click the Elephant Habitat Volunteers icon or file name in the right pane to select the file and display a shortcut menu (Figure 86).

- Tap or click Delete on the shortcut menu to delete the file.
- If a dialog box appears, tap or click the Yes button to delete the file.

Q&A Can I use this same technique to delete a folder?
Yes. Right-click the folder and then click Delete on the shortcut menu. When you delete a folder, all of the files and folders contained in the folder you are deleting, together with any files and folders on lower hierarchical levels, are deleted as well.

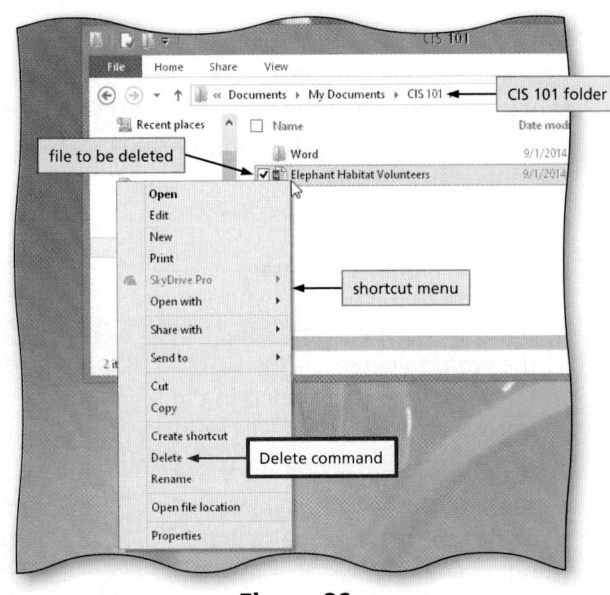

Figure 86

Other Ways

1. Select icon, press DELETE

To Delete a File Using Windows 7

If you are using Windows 7, perform these steps to delete a file instead of the previous steps that use Windows 8.

1. In Windows Explorer, navigate to the location of the file to be deleted (in this case, the CIS 101 folder [or your class folder] in the Documents library).
2. Right-click the Elephant Habitat Volunteers icon or file name in the right pane to select the file and display a shortcut menu.
3. Click Delete on the shortcut menu to delete the file.
4. If a dialog box appears, click the Yes button to delete the file.

Microsoft Office and Windows Help

At any time while you are using one of the Office apps, such as Word, you can use Office Help to display information about all topics associated with the app. This section illustrates the use of Word Help. Help in other Office apps operates in a similar fashion.

In Office, Help is presented in a window that has browser-style navigation buttons. Each Office app has its own Help home page, which is the starting Help page that is displayed in the Help window. If your computer is connected to the Internet, the contents of the Help page reflect both the local help files installed on the computer and material from Microsoft's website.

To Open the Help Window in an Office App

1 SIGN IN | 2 USE WINDOWS | 3 USE APPS | 4 FILE MANAGEMENT | 5 SWITCH APPS | 6 SAVE FILES | 7 CHANGE SCREEN RESOLUTION | 8 EXIT APPS | 9 USE ADDITIONAL APP FEATURES | **10 USE HELP**

The following step opens the Word Help window. ***Why?*** *You might not understand how certain commands or operations work in Word, so you can obtain the necessary information using help.* The step to open a Help window in other Office programs is similar.

- Run Word.
- Tap or click the Microsoft Word Help button near the upper-right corner of the app window to open the Word Help window (Figure 87).

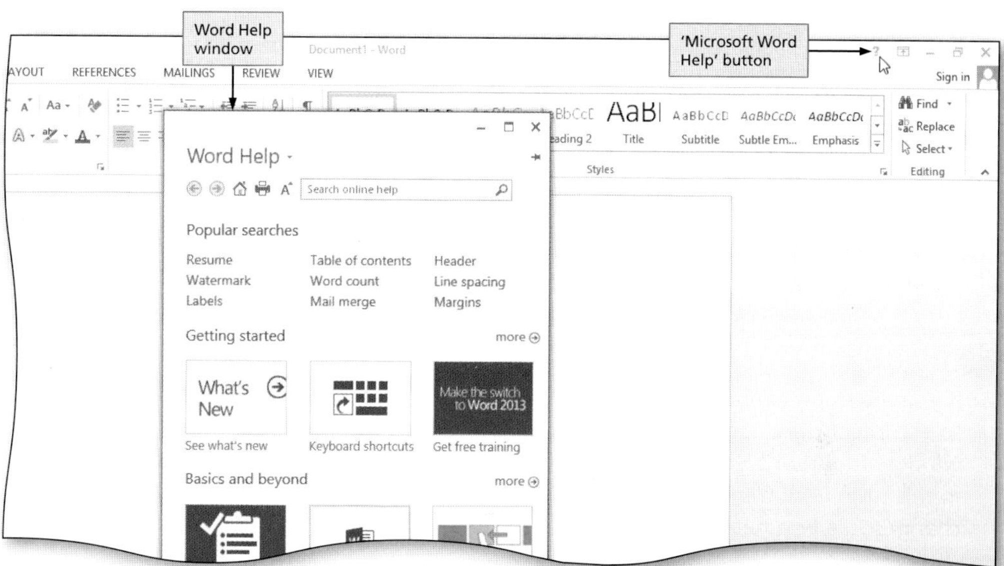

Figure 87

Other Ways

1. Press F1

Moving and Resizing Windows

At times, it is useful, or even necessary, to have more than one window open and visible on the screen at the same time. You can resize and move these open windows so that you can view different areas of and elements in the window. In the case of the Help window, for example, it could be covering document text in the Word window that you need to see.

To Move a Window by Dragging

1 SIGN IN | 2 USE WINDOWS | 3 USE APPS | 4 FILE MANAGEMENT | 5 SWITCH APPS | 6 SAVE FILES | 7 CHANGE SCREEN RESOLUTION | 8 EXIT APPS | 9 USE ADDITIONAL APP FEATURES | **10 USE HELP**

You can move any open window that is not maximized to another location on the desktop by dragging the title bar of the window. ***Why?*** *You might want to have a better view of what is behind the window or just want to move the window so that you can see it better.* The step on the next page drags the Word Help window to the upper-left corner of the desktop.

- Drag the window title bar (the Word Help window title bar, in this case) so that the window moves to the upper-left corner of the desktop, as shown in Figure 88.

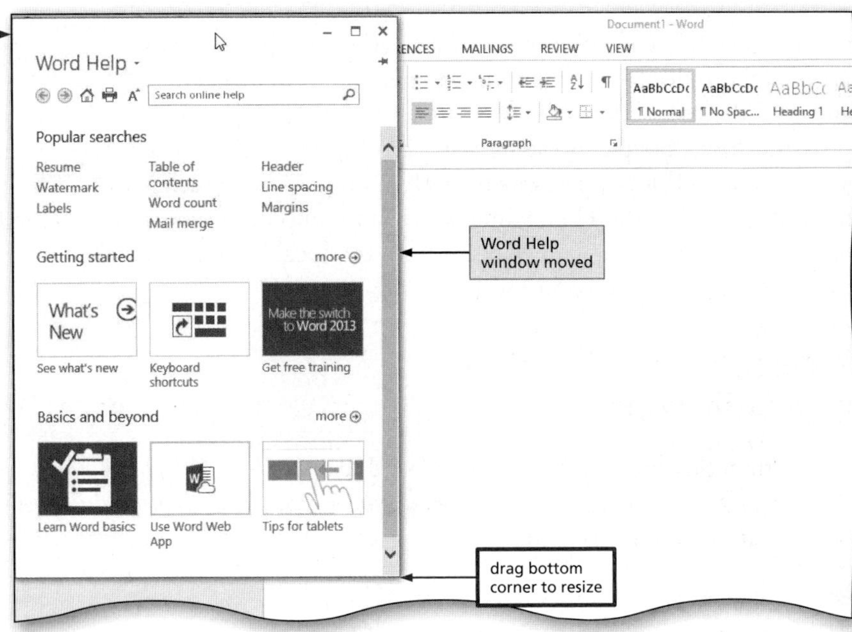

Figure 88

To Resize a Window by Dragging

1 SIGN IN | 2 USE WINDOWS | 3 USE APPS | 4 FILE MANAGEMENT | 5 SWITCH APPS | 6 SAVE FILES
7 CHANGE SCREEN RESOLUTION | 8 EXIT APPS | 9 USE ADDITIONAL APP FEATURES | 10 USE HELP

A method used to change the size of the window is to drag the window borders. The following step changes the size of the Word Help window by dragging its borders. ***Why?*** *Sometimes, information is not visible completely in a window, and you want to increase the size of the window.*

- If you are using a mouse, point to the lower-right corner of the window (the Word Help window, in this case) until the pointer changes to a two-headed arrow.
- Drag the bottom border downward to display more of the active window (Figure 89).

Q&A

Can I drag other borders on the window to enlarge or shrink the window?
Yes, you can drag the left, right, and top borders and any window corner to resize a window.

Will Windows remember the new size of the window after I close it?
Yes. When you reopen the window, Windows will display it at the same size it was when you closed it.

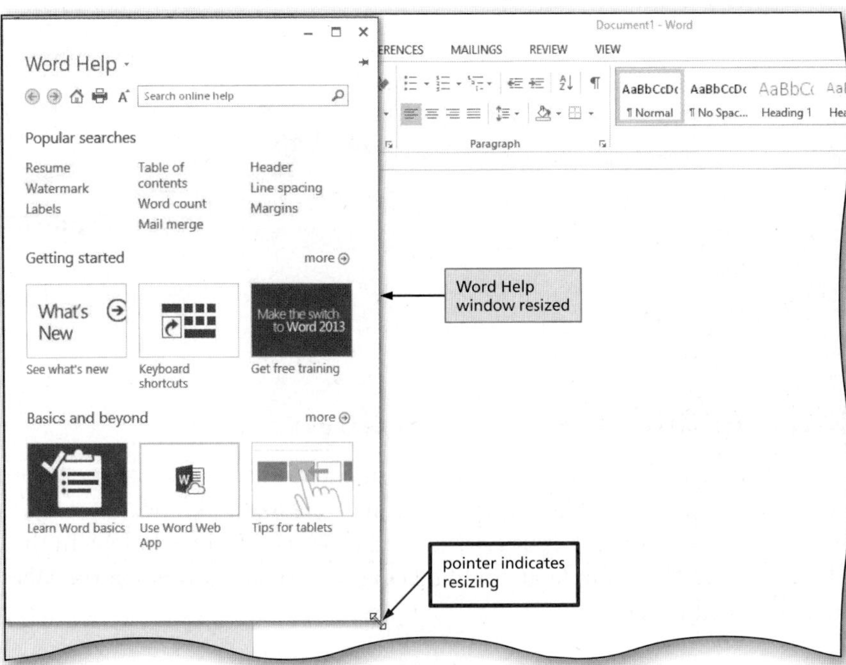

Figure 89

Using Office Help

Once an Office app's Help window is open, several methods exist for navigating Help. You can search for help by using any of the three following methods from the Help window:

1. Enter search text in the 'Search online help' text box.
2. Click the links in the Help window.
3. Use the Table of Contents.

To Obtain Help Using the 'Search online help' Text Box

1 SIGN IN | 2 USE WINDOWS | 3 USE APPS | 4 FILE MANAGEMENT | 5 SWITCH APPS | 6 SAVE FILES
7 CHANGE SCREEN RESOLUTION | 8 EXIT APPS | 9 USE ADDITIONAL APP FEATURES | **10 USE HELP**

Assume for the following example that you want to know more about fonts. The following steps use the 'Search online help' text box to obtain useful information about fonts by entering the word, fonts, as search text. ***Why?*** *You may not know the exact help topic you are looking to find, so using keywords can help narrow your search.*

1

- Type **fonts** in the 'Search online help' text box at the top of the Word Help window to enter the search text.
- Tap or click the 'Search online help' button to display the search results (Figure 90).

Q&A

Why do my search results differ?
If you do not have an Internet connection, your results will reflect only the content of the Help files on your computer. When searching for help online, results also can change as material is added, deleted, and updated on the online Help webpages maintained by Microsoft.

Why were my search results not very helpful?
When initiating a search, be sure to check the spelling of the search text; also, keep your search specific to return the most accurate results.

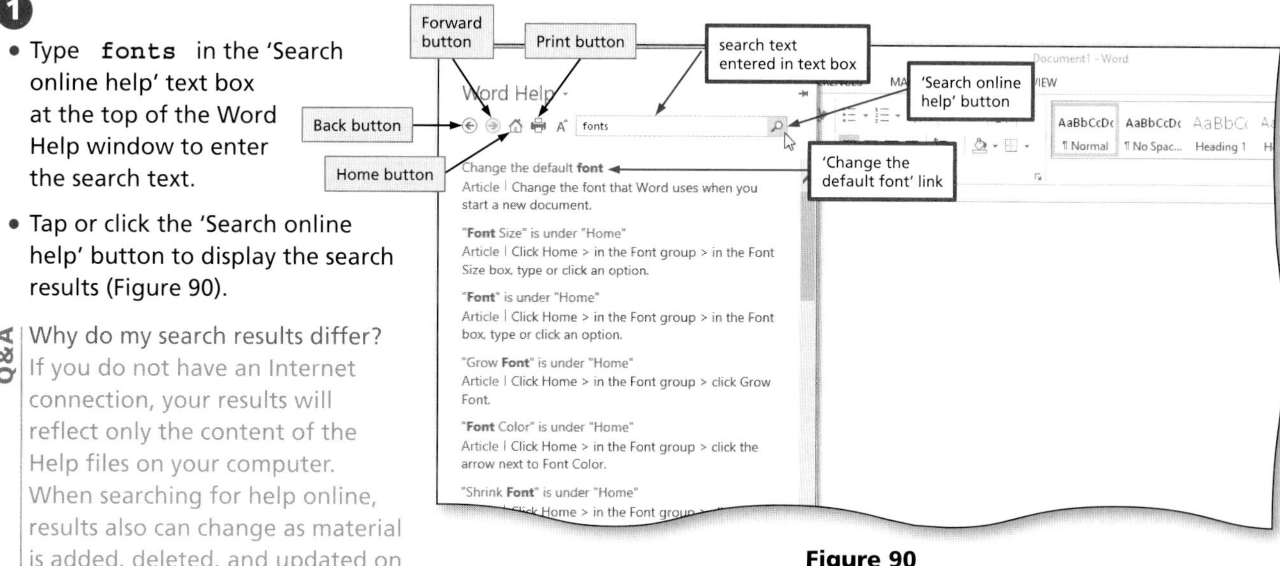

Figure 90

2

- Tap or click the 'Change the default font' link to display the Help information associated with the selected topic (Figure 91).

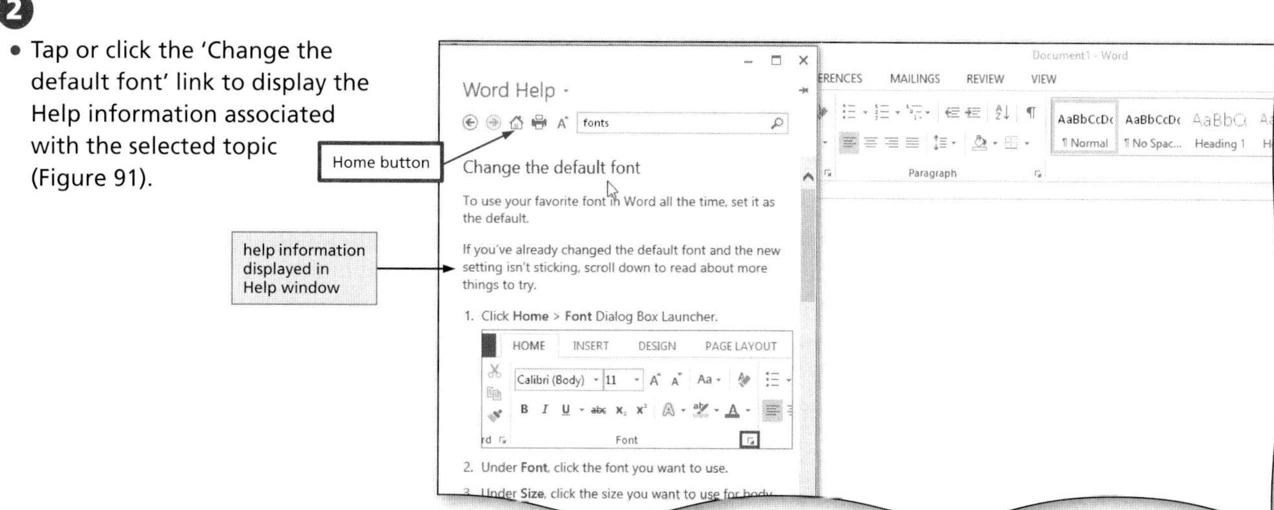

Figure 91

3

- Tap or click the Home button in the Help window to clear the search results and redisplay the Help home page (Figure 92).

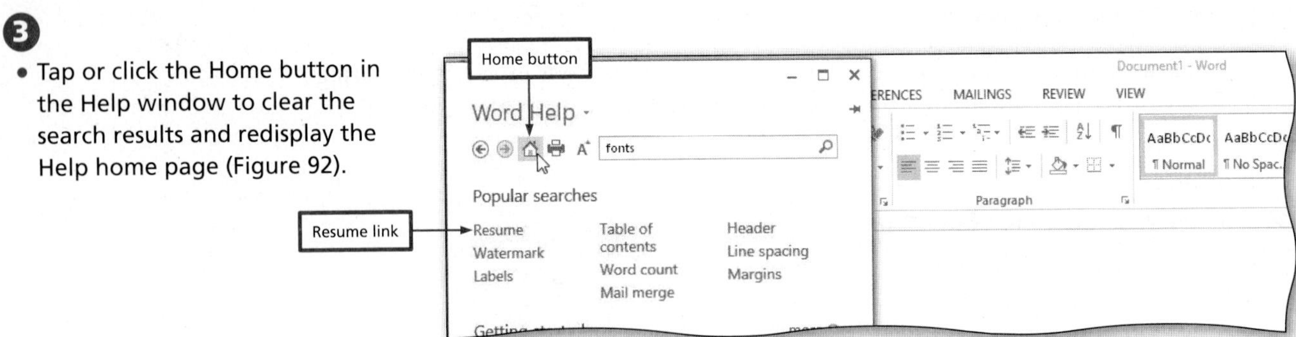

Figure 92

To Obtain Help Using Help Links

1 SIGN IN | 2 USE WINDOWS | 3 USE APPS | 4 FILE MANAGEMENT | 5 SWITCH APPS | 6 SAVE FILES
7 CHANGE SCREEN RESOLUTION | 8 EXIT APPS | 9 USE ADDITIONAL APP FEATURES | 10 USE HELP

If your topic of interest is listed in the Help window, you can click the link to begin browsing the Help categories instead of entering search text. ***Why?** You browse Help just as you would browse a website. If you know which category contains your Help information, you may wish to use these links.* The following step finds the Resume information using the Resume link from the Word Help home page.

- Tap or click the Resume link on the Help home page (shown in Figure 92) to display the Resume help links (Figure 93).

- After reviewing the page, tap or click the Close button to close the Help window.
- Tap or click Word's Close button to exit Word.

Q&A Why does my Help window display different links?
The content of your Help window may differ because Microsoft continually updates its Help information.

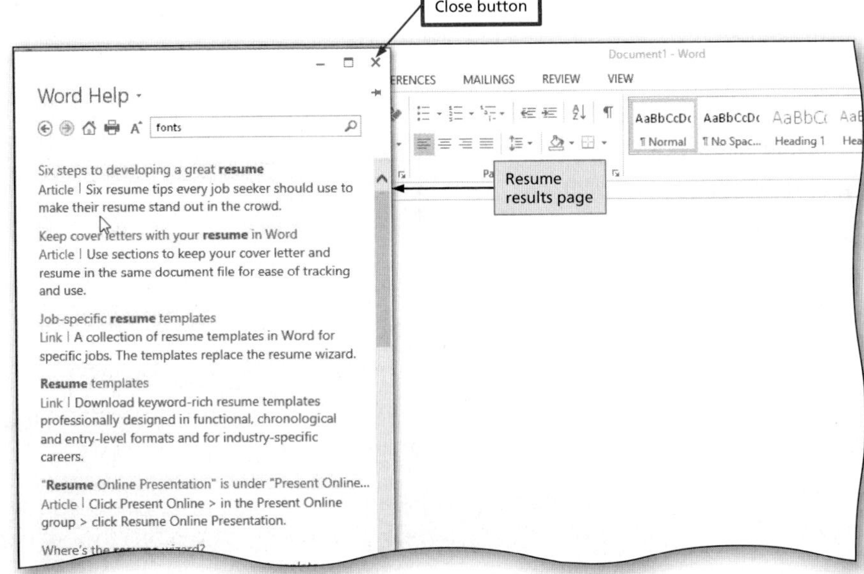

Figure 93

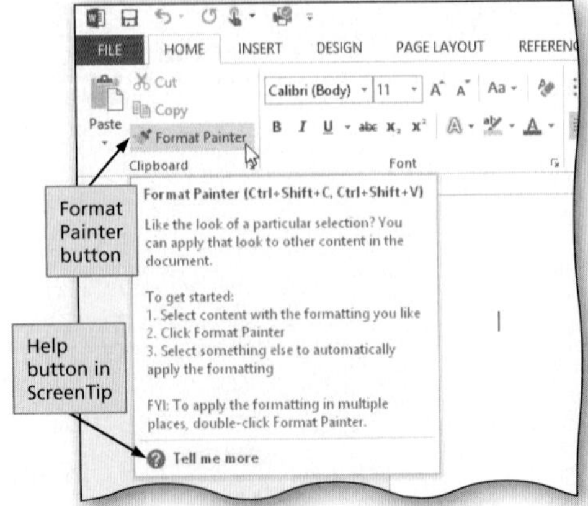

Figure 94

Obtaining Help while Working in an Office App

Help in the Office apps, such as Word, provides you with the ability to obtain help directly, without opening the Help window and initiating a search. For example, you may be unsure about how a particular command works, or you may be presented with a dialog box that you are not sure how to use.

Figure 94 shows one option for obtaining help while working in an Office app. If you want to learn more about a command, point to its button and wait for the ScreenTip to appear. If the Help icon appears in the ScreenTip, press the F1 key while pointing to the button to open the Help window associated with that command.

Figure 95 shows a dialog box that contains a Help button. Pressing the F1 key while the dialog box is displayed opens a Help window. The Help window contains help about that dialog box, if available. If no help file is available for that particular dialog box, then the main Help window opens.

Figure 95

Using Windows Help and Support

One of the more powerful Windows features is Windows Help and Support. **Windows Help and Support** is available when using Windows or when using any Microsoft app running in Windows. The same methods used for searching Microsoft Office Help can be used in Windows Help and Support. The difference is that Windows Help and Support displays help for Windows, instead of for Microsoft Office.

To Use Windows Help and Support

1 SIGN IN | 2 USE WINDOWS | 3 USE APPS | 4 FILE MANAGEMENT | 5 SWITCH APPS | 6 SAVE FILES
7 CHANGE SCREEN RESOLUTION | 8 EXIT APPS | 9 USE ADDITIONAL APP FEATURES | **10 USE HELP**

The following steps use Windows Help and Support and open the Windows Help and Support window, which contains links to more information about Windows. ***Why?*** *This feature is designed to assist you in using Windows or the various apps.* If you are using Windows 7, skip these steps and instead perform the steps in the yellow box that immediately follows these Windows 8 steps.

- Swipe in from the right edge of the screen or point to the upper-right corner of the screen to display the Charms bar (Figure 96).

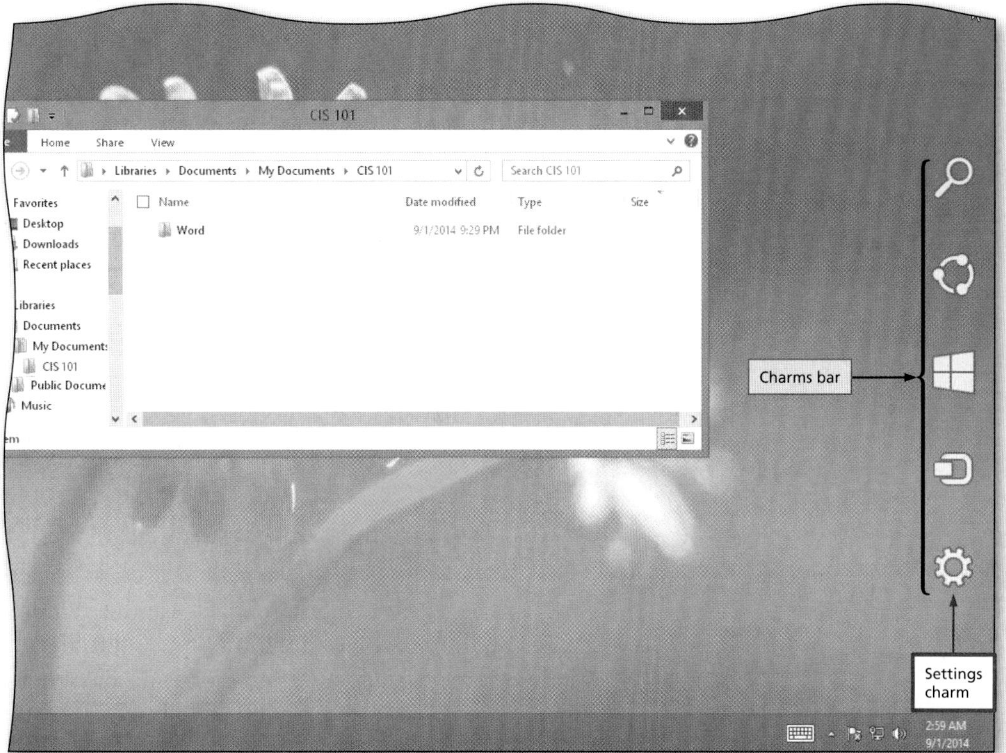

Figure 96

- Tap or click the Settings charm on the Charms bar to display the Settings menu (Figure 97).

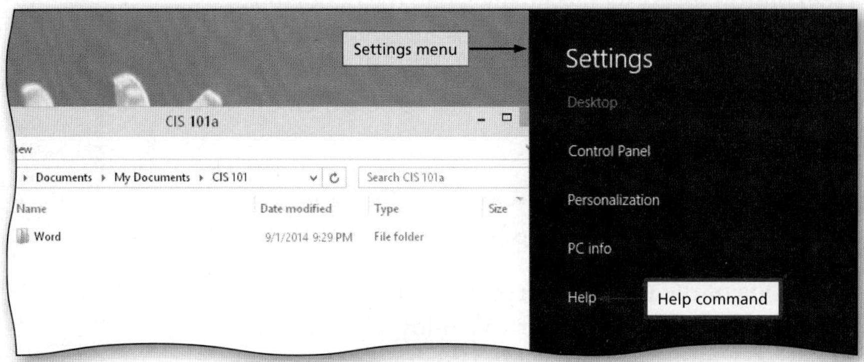

Figure 97

- Tap or click Help to open the Windows Help and Support window (Figure 98).

- After reviewing the Windows Help and Support window, tap or click the Close button to close the Windows Help and Support window.

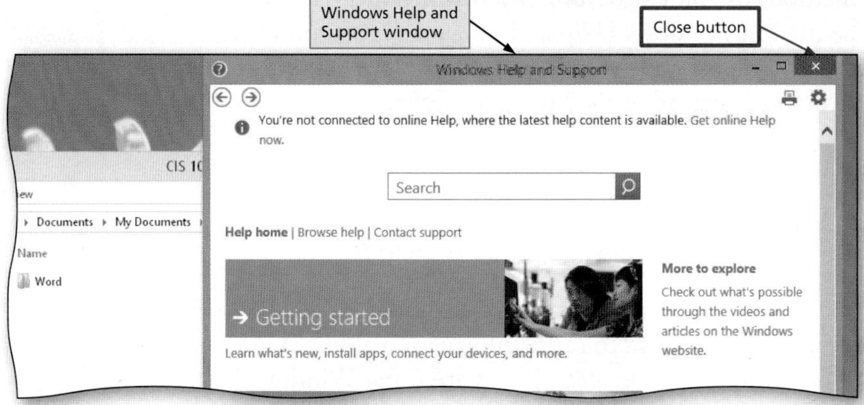

Figure 98

Other Ways

1. Press WINDOWS+F1

BTW

Certification

The Microsoft Office Specialist (MOS) program provides an opportunity for you to obtain a valuable industry credential — proof that you have the Microsoft Office 2013 skills required by employers. For more information, visit the Certification resource on the Student Companion Site located on www.cengagebrain.com. For detailed instructions about accessing available resources, visit www.cengage.com/ct/studentdownload or contact your instructor for information about accessing the required files.

BTW

Quick Reference

For a table that lists how to complete the tasks covered in this book using touch gestures, the mouse, ribbon, shortcut menu, and keyboard, see the Quick Reference Summary at the back of this book, or visit the Quick Reference resource on the Student Companion Site located on www.cengagebrain.com. For detailed instructions about accessing available resources, visit www.cengage.com/ct/studentdownload or contact your instructor for information about accessing the required files.

To Use Windows Help and Support with Windows 7

If you are using Windows 7, perform these steps to start Windows Help and Support instead of the previous steps that use Windows 8.

1. Click the Start button on the taskbar to display the Start menu.
2. Click Help and Support on the Start menu to open the Windows Help and Support window.
3. After reviewing the Windows Help and Support window, click the Close button to exit Windows Help and Support.

Chapter Summary

In this chapter, you learned how to use the Windows interface, several touch screen and mouse operations, and file and folder management. You also learned some basic features of Word and discovered the common elements that exist among Microsoft Office apps. The following items include all of the new Windows and Word skills you have learned in this chapter, with the tasks grouped by activity.

File Management

- Create a Folder (OFF 24)
- Create a Folder within a Folder (OFF 26)
- Expand a Folder, Scroll through Folder Contents, and Collapse a Folder (OFF 27)
- Copy a Folder to a USB Flash Drive (OFF 39)
- Rename a File (OFF 50)
- Move a File (OFF 51)
- Delete a File (OFF 52)

Use Help

- Open the Help Window in an Office App (OFF 53)
- Obtain Help Using the 'Search online help' Text Box (OFF 55)
- Obtain Help Using Help Links (OFF 56)
- Use Windows Help and Support (OFF 57)

Use Windows

- Sign In to an Account (OFF 7)
- Run an App from the Start Screen (OFF 11)
- Switch between an App and the Start Screen (OFF 13)
- Maximize a Window (OFF 14)
- Switch from One App to Another (OFF 29)
- Minimize and Restore a Window (OFF 32)
- Change the Screen Resolution (OFF 37)
- Run an App Using the Search Box (OFF 40)
- Run an App from File Explorer and Open a File (OFF 47)
- Move a Window by Dragging (OFF 53)
- Resize a Window by Dragging (OFF 54)

Use Word

- Display a Different Tab on the Ribbon (OFF 18)
- Collapse and Expand the Ribbon and Use Full Screen Mode (OFF 19)
- Use a Shortcut Menu to Relocate the Quick Access Toolbar (OFF 20)
- Customize the Quick Access Toolbar (OFF 21)
- Enter Text in a Document (OFF 22)
- Save a File in a Folder (OFF 29)
- Save a File on SkyDrive (OFF 33)
- Sign Out of a Microsoft Account (OFF 35)
- Exit an App with One Document Open (OFF 38)
- Open an Existing File (OFF 42)
- Create a New Document from the Backstage View (OFF 43)
- Close a File Using the Backstage View (OFF 45)
- Open a Recent File Using the Backstage View (OFF 45)
- Create a New Blank Document from File Explorer (OFF 46)
- Save an Existing File with the Same File Name (OFF 48)

CONSIDER THIS: PLAN AHEAD

What guidelines should you follow to plan your projects?

The process of communicating specific information is a learned, rational skill. Computers and software, especially Microsoft Office 2013, can help you develop ideas and present detailed information to a particular audience and minimize much of the laborious work of drafting and revising projects. No matter what method you use to plan a project, it is beneficial to follow some specific guidelines from the onset to arrive at a final product that is informative, relevant, and effective. Use some aspects of these guidelines every time you undertake a project, and others as needed in specific instances.

1. Determine the project's purpose.
   a) Clearly define why you are undertaking this assignment.
   b) Begin to draft ideas of how best to communicate information by handwriting ideas on paper; composing directly on a laptop, tablet, or mobile device; or developing a strategy that fits your particular thinking and writing style.
2. Analyze your audience.
   a) Learn about the people who will read, analyze, or view your work.
   b) Determine their interests and needs so that you can present the information they need to know and omit the information they already possess.
   c) Form a mental picture of these people or find photos of people who fit this profile so that you can develop a project with the audience in mind.
3. Gather possible content.
   a) Locate existing information that may reside in spreadsheets, databases, or other files.
   b) Conduct a web search to find relevant websites.
   c) Read pamphlets, magazine and newspaper articles, and books to gain insights of how others have approached your topic.
   d) Conduct personal interviews to obtain perspectives not available by any other means.
   e) Consider video and audio clips as potential sources for material that might complement or support the factual data you uncover.

Continued >

CONSIDER THIS: PLAN AHEAD *continued*

4. Determine what content to present to your audience.
   a) Write three or four major ideas you want an audience member to remember after reading or viewing your project.
   b) Envision your project's endpoint, the key fact you wish to emphasize, so that all project elements lead to this final element.
   c) Determine relevant time factors, such as the length of time to develop the project, how long readers will spend reviewing your project, or the amount of time allocated for your speaking engagement.
   d) Decide whether a graph, photo, or artistic element can express or enhance a particular concept.
   e) Be mindful of the order in which you plan to present the content, and place the most important material at the top or bottom of the page, because readers and audience members generally remember the first and last pieces of information they see and hear.

CONSIDER THIS

How should you submit solutions to questions in the assignments identified with a symbol?
Every assignment in this book contains one or more questions identified with a symbol. These questions require you to think beyond the assigned file. Present your solutions to the questions in the format required by your instructor. Possible formats may include one or more of these options: write the answer; create a document that contains the answer; present your answer to the class; discuss your answer in a group; record the answer as audio or video using a webcam, smartphone, or portable media player; or post answers on a blog, wiki, or website.

Apply Your Knowledge

Reinforce the skills and apply the concepts you learned in this chapter.

Creating a Folder and a Document

Instructions: You will create a Word folder and then create a Word document and save it in the folder.

Perform the following tasks:

1. Open the File Explorer window and then double-tap or double-click to open the Documents library.
2. Tap or click the New folder button on the Quick Access Toolbar to display a new folder icon and text box for the folder name.
3. Type **Word** in the text box to name the folder. Press the ENTER key to create the folder in the Documents library.
4. Run Word.
5. Enter the text shown in Figure 99 in a new blank document.
6. If requested by your instructor, enter your name in the Word document.
7. Tap or click the Save button on the Quick Access Toolbar. Navigate to the Word folder in the Documents library and then save the document using the file name, Apply 1 Class List.
8. If your Quick Access Toolbar does not show the Quick Print button, add the Quick Print button to the Quick Access Toolbar. Print the document using the Quick Print button on the Quick Access Toolbar. When you are finished printing, remove the Quick Print button from the Quick Access Toolbar.
9. Submit the printout to your instructor.
10. Exit Word.
11. What other commands might you find useful to include on the Quick Access Toolbar?

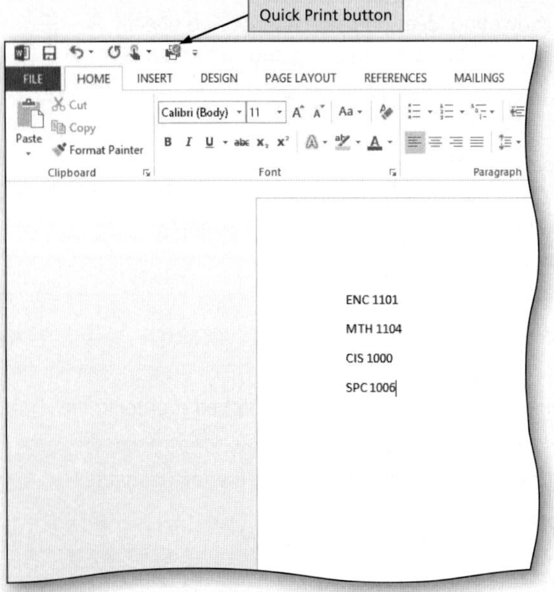

Figure 99

Extend Your Knowledge

Extend the skills you learned in this chapter and experiment with new skills. You will use Help to complete the assignment.

Using Help

Instructions: Use Word Help to perform the following tasks.

Perform the following tasks:

1. Run Word.
2. Tap or click the Microsoft Word Help button to open the Word Help window (Figure 100).
3. Search Word Help to answer the following questions.
   a) What are three features new to Word 2013?
   b) What type of training courses are available through Help?
   c) What are the steps to add a new group to the ribbon?
   d) What are Quick Parts?
   e) How do you insert clip art?
   f) What is a template?
   g) How do you use Read mode?
   h) What is a SmartArt graphic?
   i) What is cropping?
   j) What is the purpose of the Navigation Pane?

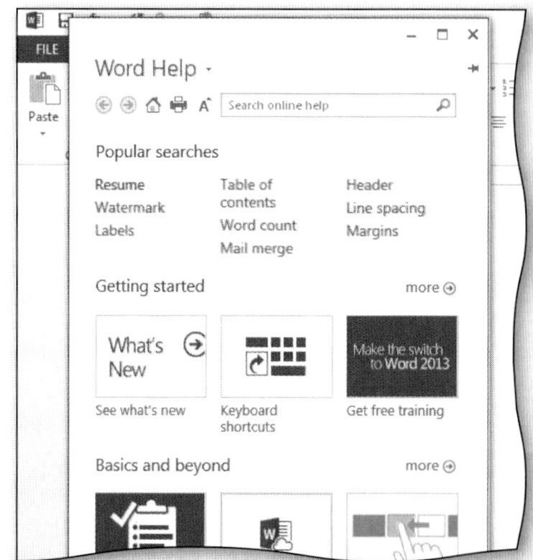

Figure 100

4. Type the answers from your searches in a new blank Word document. Save the document with a new file name and then submit it in the format specified by your instructor.
5. If requested by your instructor, enter your name in the Word document.
6. Exit Word.
7. What search text did you use to perform the searches above? Did it take multiple attempts to search and locate the exact information for which you were searching?

Analyze, Correct, Improve

Analyze a file structure, correct all errors, and improve the design.

Organizing Vacation Photos

Note: To complete this assignment, you will be required to use the Data Files for Students. Visit www.cengage.com/ct/studentdownload for detailed instructions or contact your instructor for information about accessing the required files.

Instructions: Traditionally, you have stored photos from past vacations together in one folder. The photos are becoming difficult to manage, and you now want to store them in appropriate folders. You will create the folder structure shown in Figure 101. You then will move the photos to the folders so that they will be organized properly.

1. Correct Create the folder structure in Figure 101 so that you are able to store the photos in an organized manner. If requested by your instructor, add another folder using your last name as the folder name.

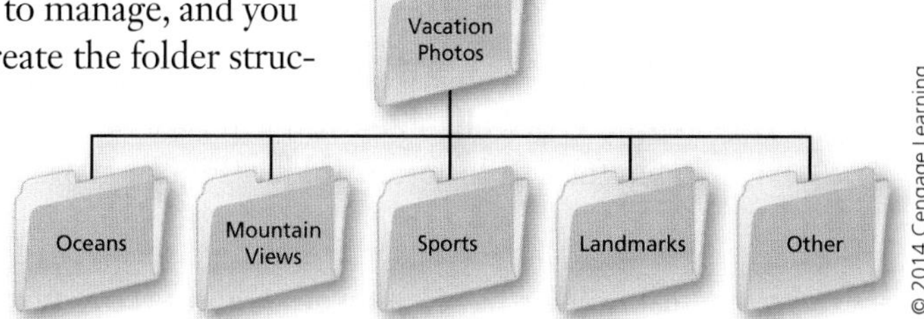

Figure 101

2. Improve View each photo and drag it to the appropriate folder to improve the organization. Submit the assignment in the format specified by your instructor.

3. In which folder did you place each photo? Think about the files you have stored on your computer. What folder hierarchy would be best to manage your files?

In the Labs

Use the guidelines, concepts, and skills presented in this chapter to increase your knowledge of Windows 8 and Word 2013. Labs 1 and 2, which increase in difficulty, require you to create solutions based on what you learned in the chapter; Lab 3 requires you to create a solution, which uses cloud and web technologies, by learning and investigating on your own from general guidance.

Lab 1: Creating Folders for a Video Store

Problem: Your friend works for Ebaird Video. He would like to organize his files in relation to the types of videos available in the store. He has six main categories: drama, action, romance, foreign, biographical, and comedy. You are to create a folder structure similar to Figure 102.

Instructions: Perform the following tasks:

1. Insert a USB flash drive in an available USB port and then open the USB flash drive window.
2. Create the main folder for Ebaird Video.
3. Navigate to the Ebaird Video folder.
4. Within the Ebaird Video folder, create a folder for each of the following: Drama, Action, Romance, Foreign, Biographical, and Comedy.

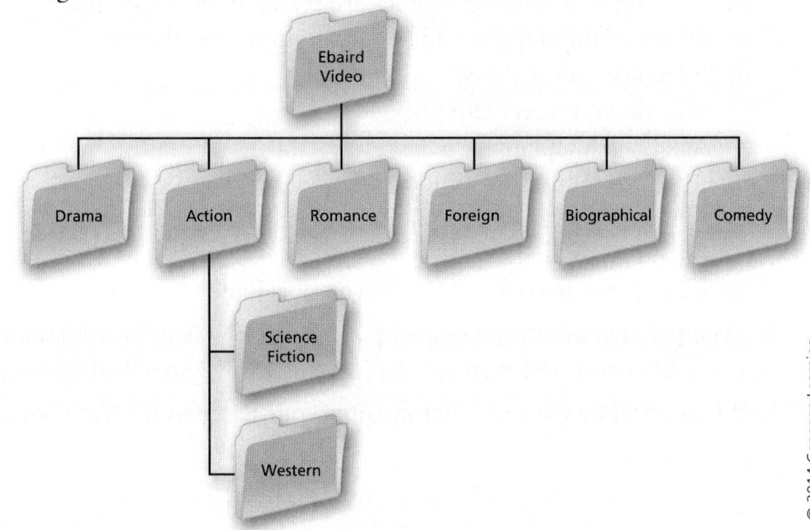

Figure 102

5. Within the Action folder, create two additional folders, one for Science Fiction and the second for Western.
6. If requested by your instructor, add another folder using your last name as the folder name.
7. Submit the assignment in the format specified by your instructor.
8. Think about how you use your computer for various tasks (consider personal, professional, and academic reasons). What folders do you think will be required on your computer to store the files you save?

Lab 2: Saving Files in Folders

Problem: You are taking a class that requires you to complete three Word chapters. You will save the work completed in each chapter in a different folder (Figure 103).

Instructions: Create the folders shown in Figure 103. Then, using Word, create three small files to save in each folder.

1. Create a Word document containing the text, First Word Chapter.
2. In the Backstage view, tap or click Save As and then tap or click Computer.

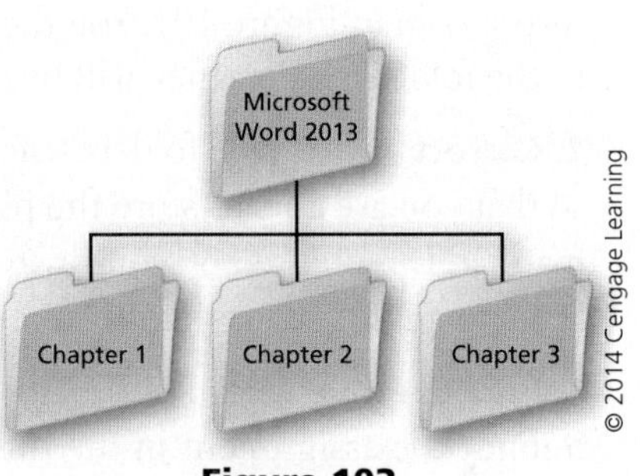

Figure 103

3. Tap or click the Browse button to display the Save As dialog box.
4. Tap or click Documents to open the Documents library. Next, create the folder structure shown in Figure 103 using the New folder button.
5. Navigate to the Chapter 1 folder and then save the file in the Chapter 1 folder using the file name, Word Chapter 1 Document.
6. Create another Word document containing the text, Second Word Chapter, and then save it in the Chapter 2 folder using the file name, Word Chapter 2 Document.
7. Create a third Word document containing the text, Third Word Chapter, and then save it in the Chapter 3 folder using the file name, Word Chapter 3 Document.
8. If requested by your instructor, add your name to each of the three Word files.
9. Submit the assignment in the format specified by your instructor.
10. Based on your current knowledge of Windows and Word, how will you organize folders for assignments in this class? Why?

Lab 3: Expand Your World: Cloud and Web Technologies

Creating Folders on SkyDrive and Using the Word Web App

Problem: You are taking a class that requires you to create folders on SkyDrive, use the Word Web App to create a document, and then save the document in a folder on SkyDrive (Figure 104).

Instructions: Perform the following tasks:

1. Sign in to SkyDrive in your browser.
2. Use the Create button to create the folder structure shown in Figure 104.
3. In the Notes folder, use the Create button to create a Word document with the file name, Notes, and containing the text, Important Test on Tuesday.
4. If requested by your instructor, add your name to the Word document.
5. Save the document in the Notes folder and then exit the app.
6. Submit the assignment in the format specified by your instructor.
7. Based on your current knowledge of SkyDrive, do you think you will use it? What about the Word Web App?

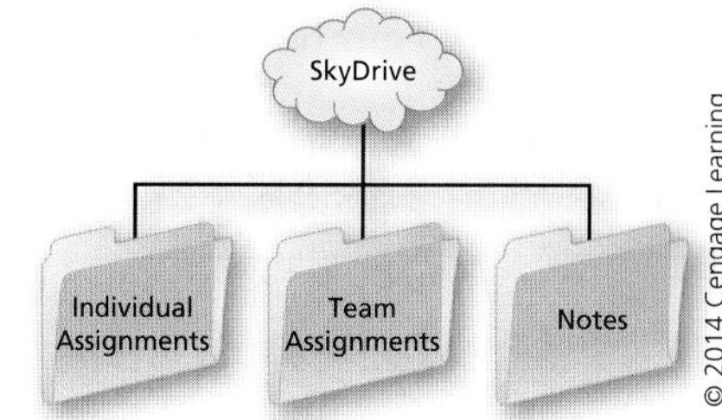

Figure 104

Consider This: Your Turn

Apply your creative thinking and problem solving skills to design and implement a solution.

1: Creating Beginning Files for Classes

Personal

Part 1: You are taking the following classes: Introduction to Sociology, Chemistry, Calculus, and Marketing. Create folders for each of the classes. Create a folder structure that will store the documents for each of these classes. Use Word to create a separate Word document for each class. Each document should contain the name of each class and the class meeting locations and times: Introduction to Sociology meets on Mondays and Wednesdays from 8:00 a.m. to 10:00 a.m.; Chemistry meets on Tuesdays and Thursdays from 11:00 a.m. to 1:00 p.m.; Calculus meets on Mondays, Wednesdays, and Fridays from 1:30 p.m. to 3:00 p.m.; and Marketing meets on Tuesdays from 5:00 p.m. to 8:00 p.m. If requested by your instructor, add your name to each of the Word

Continued >

Consider This: Your Turn *continued*

documents. Use the concepts and techniques presented in this chapter to create the folders and files, and store the files in their respective locations. Submit your assignment in the format specified by your instructor.

Part 2: You made several decisions while determining the folder structure in this assignment. What was the rationale behind these decisions? Are there any other decisions that also might have worked?

2: Creating Folders

Professional

Part 1: Your boss at the media store where you work part-time has asked for help with organizing his files. After looking through the files, you decided upon a file structure for her to use, including the following folders: CDs, DVDs, and general merchandise. Use Word to create separate Word documents that list examples in each category. For example, CDs include music [blues, rock, country, new age, pop, and soundtracks], blank discs, books, and games; DVDs include movies [action, documentary, music videos, mystery, and drama], television series, and blank discs; and general merchandise includes clothing, portable media players, cases, earbuds, chargers, and cables. If requested by your instructor, add your name to each of the Word documents. Use the concepts and techniques presented in this chapter to create the folders. Submit your assignment in the format specified by your instructor.

Part 2: You made several decisions while determining the folder structure in this assignment. What was the rationale behind these decisions? Justify why you feel this folder structure will help your boss organize her files.

3: Using Help

Research and Collaboration

Part 1: You have just installed a new computer with the Windows operating system and want to be sure that it is protected from the threat of viruses. You ask two of your friends to help research computer viruses, virus prevention, and virus removal. In a team of three people, each person should choose a topic (computer viruses, virus prevention, and virus removal) to research. Use the concepts and techniques presented in this chapter to use Help to find information regarding these topics. Create a Word document that contains steps to properly safeguard a computer from viruses, ways to prevent viruses, as well as the different ways to remove a virus should your computer become infected. Submit your assignment in the format specified by your instructor.

Part 2: You made several decisions while searching Windows Help and Support for this assignment. What decisions did you make? What was the rationale behind these decisions? How did you locate the required information about viruses in help?

Learn Online

Reinforce what you learned in this chapter with games, exercises, training, and many other online activities and resources.

Student Companion Site Reinforcement activities and resources are available at no additional cost on www.cengagebrain.com. Visit www.cengage.com/ct/studentdownload for detailed instructions about accessing the resources available at the Student Companion Site.

SAM Put your skills into practice with SAM Projects! If you have a SAM account, go to www.cengage.com/sam2013 to access SAM assignments for this chapter.

Office 365 Essentials

Objectives

You will have mastered the material in this chapter when you can:

- Describe the components of Office 365
- Compare Office 2013 to Office 365 subscription plans
- Understand the productivity tools of Office 365
- Sync multiple devices using Office 365
- Describe how business teams collaborate using SharePoint
- Describe how to use a SharePoint template to design a public website
- Describe how to conduct an online meeting with Lync

Explore Office 365

Introduction to Office 365

Microsoft Office 365 uses the cloud to deliver a subscription-based service offering the newest Office suite and much more. The Microsoft cloud provides Office software and information stored on remote servers all over the world. Your documents are located online or on the cloud, which provides you access to your information anywhere using a PC, Mac, tablet, mobile phone, or other device with an Internet connection. For businesses and students alike, Office 365 offers significant cost savings compared to the traditional cost of purchasing Microsoft Office 2013. In addition to the core desktop Office suite, Office 365 provides access to email, calendars, conferencing, file sharing, and website design, which sync across multiple devices.

Cloud Computing

Cloud computing refers to a collection of computer servers that house resources users access through the Internet (Figure 1). These resources include email messages, schedules, music, photos, videos, games, websites, programs, apps, servers, storage, and more. Instead of accessing these resources on your computer or mobile device, you access them on the cloud.

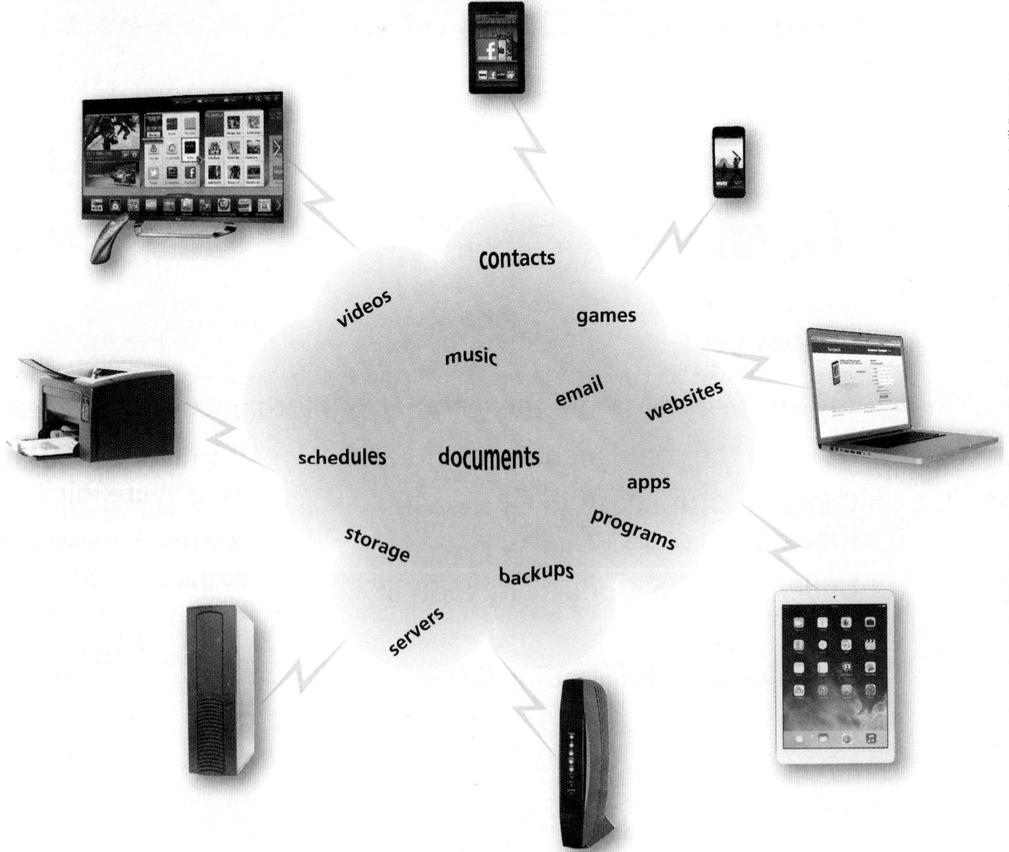

Figure 1

Cloud computing can help businesses be more efficient and save them money by shifting usage and the consumption of resources, such as servers and programs, from a local environment to the Internet. For example, an employee working during the day in California could use computing resources located in an office in London that is closed for the evening. When the company in California uses the computing resources, it pays a fee that is based on the amount of computing time and other resources it consumes, much in the same way that consumers pay utility companies for the amount of electricity they use.

Cloud computing is changing how users access and pay for software applications. Fading fast are the days when software packages were sold in boxes at a physical store location with a one-time purchase software license fee. Instead, the new pricing structure is a subscription-based model, where users pay a monthly or annual fee for the software that you can use on multiple devices. The cloud-based Office 365 offers the Office suite with added features that allow you to communicate and collaborate with others in real time.

When you create a free Microsoft account, do you get free cloud storage space?
Yes, when you create a free Microsoft account at Outlook.com, you have access to 15 GB of cloud storage for any types of files.

What Is Office 365?

Office 365 is a collection of programs and services, which includes the Microsoft Office suite, file storage, online collaboration, and file synchronization, as shown in Figure 2 on the next page. You can access these services using your computer, tablet (Windows, iPad, or Android), any browser, or supported mobile device. For example, a business has two options for providing Office to their employees. A business could purchase Office 2013 and install the software on company computers and servers; however, this traditional Office 2013 package with perpetual licensing does not include the communication and collaboration tools. Employees could not access the Office software if they were not using their work computers. In contrast, if the business purchases a monthly subscription to Office 365, each employee has access to the Office suite on up to five different computers, whether at home or work; company-wide email; web conferencing; website creation capabilities; unlimited cloud storage; and shared files. An employee can begin a departmental budget on Excel on their office PC, finish the budget on their iPad at home, and review the final budget on their smartphone using Office 365. For a lower price, Office 365 provides many more features. In addition, a business may prefer a subscription plan with predictable monthly costs and no up-front infrastructure costs.

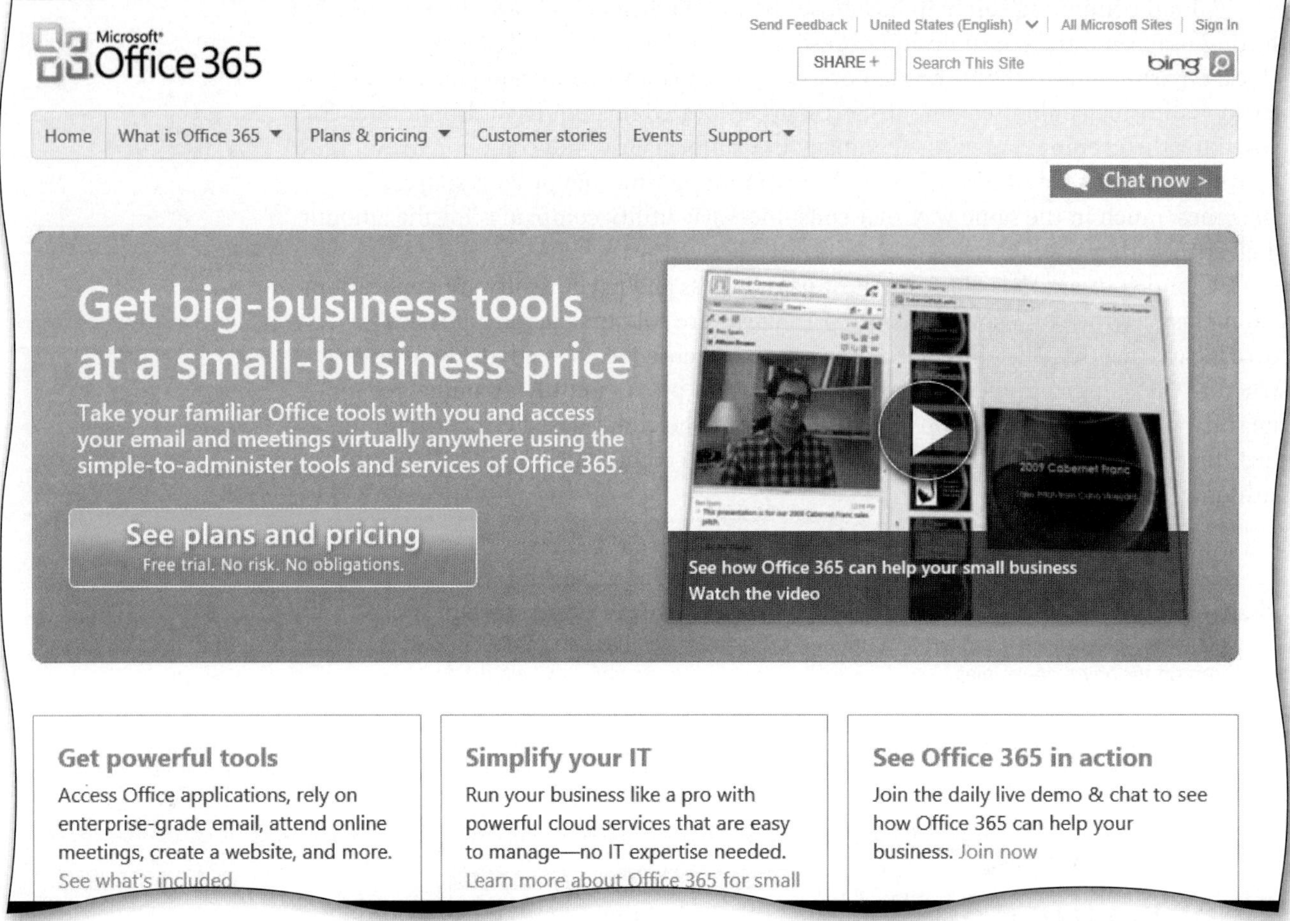

Figure 2

Office 2013 and Office 365 Features Comparison

Office 2013 is the name of the perpetual software package that includes individual applications that can be installed on a single computer. An Office 365 subscription comes with a license to install the software on multiple PCs, Macs, iPad tablets, or smartphones at the same time, giving you more flexibility to use your Office products in your home, school, or workplace, whether on a computer, tablet, or a mobile device. Office 365 provides updated Office 2013 programs as part of a subscription service that includes online storage, sharing, and syncing via Microsoft cloud services as shown in Table 1. A limited version of Office 365 including Word, Excel, PowerPoint, and OneNote can be downloaded from the appropriate app store on mobile devices, such as an iPad or smartphone. Office documents can be created, viewed, and edited using an iPhone, Android, or Windows smartphone. Office applications differ across different platforms and are tailored to work best on each device. The Office applications are available for Mac users and the version numbers may be different from those available for PC users.

Office 365 is available in business, consumer, education, and government editions. Office 365 combines the full version of the Microsoft Office desktop suite with cloud-based versions of Microsoft's communications and collaboration services. The subscription package includes:

- Microsoft Exchange online for shared email and calendars
- Microsoft SharePoint Online for shared file access and public website creation
- Microsoft Office Online for browser viewing
- Microsoft Lync Online for communication services

Table 1 Office 2013 and Office 365 Feature Comparison for PCs and Macs

Office 2013 Professional (Installed on a single device)	Office 365 Subscription (Installed on 2 to 5 devices)
Microsoft Word	Microsoft Word
Microsoft Excel	Microsoft Excel
Microsoft PowerPoint	Microsoft PowerPoint
Microsoft Access (Mac version not available)	Microsoft Access (Mac version not available)
Microsoft Outlook	Microsoft Outlook
Microsoft Publisher	Microsoft Publisher
Microsoft OneNote	Microsoft OneNote
	email and calendars (Exchange Online)
	file sharing (SharePoint Online and Yammer)
	public website design and publishing (SharePoint Online)
	browser-based Office Online
	instant messaging (Lync Online and Yammer)
	audio and video web conferencing (Lync Online)
	screen sharing with shared control (Lync Online)
	technical support

Subscription-Based Office 365 Plans

Microsoft provides various subscription plans for Office 365 with different benefits for each individual or organization. Subscription plans include Office 365 Home Premium for home users, Office 365 ProPlus programs for students and teachers, Office 365 Small Business, Office 365 Small Business Premium, Office 365 Midsize Business, and Office 365 Enterprise and Government. During the Office 365 sign-up process, you create a Microsoft email address and password to use on your multiple devices. A single subscription to an Office 365 Home Premium account can cover an entire household. The Office 365 Home Premium subscription allows up to five concurrent installations by using the same email address and password combination. This means that your mother could be on the main family computer while you use your tablet and smartphone at the same time. You each can sign in with your individual Microsoft accounts using your settings and accessing your own documents using a single Office 365 subscription.

The educational Office 365 ProPlus subscription plan is designed for K12 and higher-education full-time and part-time students, faculty, and staff. By submitting the proper credentials, such as a school email address, students, faculty, and school staff can download Office 365, including full online copies of Word, PowerPoint, Excel, Access, Outlook, Publisher, and OneNote for free if their school has an Office 2013 or 365 site wide license agreement (office.com/getoffice365). In addition, Office 365 ProPlus provides users with unlimited OneDrive cloud storage rather than the free 15 GB provided by a Microsoft account, and 60 Skype world minutes per month for videoconferencing. The Office 365 ProPlus program is limited to five home computers, tablets, or smartphones.

The Microsoft Office 365 Business Plans can provide full support for employees to work from any location, whether they are in their traditional business office, commuting to and from work across the country, or working from a home office. Office 365 Business accommodates up to 300 users. Office 365 Enterprise Plan fits organizations ranging in size from a single employee to 50,000-plus users. Each employee can install Microsoft Office 365 on five different computers.

First Look at Office 365

Microsoft Office 365 subscription plans offer all the same applications that are available in the Microsoft Office Professional 2013 suite in addition to multiple communication and collaboration tools. With Office 365 you can retrieve, edit, and save Office documents on the Office 365 cloud, coauthor documents in real time with others, and quickly initiate computer-based calls, instant messages, and web conferences with others. Microsoft continues to update Office 365 to include new features, so over time expect greater differences between Office 2013 and Office 365.

Productivity Tools

Whether you are inserting audio and video into a Word document to create a high-impact business plan proposal or utilizing the visualization tools in Excel to chart the return on investment of a new mobile marketing program, Office 365 uses a quick-start installation technology, called **Click-to-Run**, that downloads and installs the basics within minutes, so that users are able to start working almost immediately. In effect, the Office 365 subscription provides access to the full Office applications wherever you are working. When you access your Office 365 account management panel, three choices are listed: 32- and 64-bit versions of Office 2013, and Office for Mac. Selecting the third option will initiate a download of an installer that must be run in the standard OS X fashion. When you install Office 365 on a Mac, the most current Mac version of Office is installed.

CONSIDER THIS

Unlike Google, which offers online documents, spreadsheets, and presentations called Google Docs, Microsoft Office 365 installs locally on your computer in addition to being available online.

Email and Calendars

In business, sharing information is essential to meeting the needs of your customers and staff. Office 365 offers shared access to business email, calendars, and contacts using **Exchange Online** from a computer, tablet, phone, and browser. The cloud-based Exchange Online enables business people to access Outlook information from anywhere at any time, while eliminating the cost of purchasing and maintaining servers to store data. If you need to meet with a colleague about a new project, you can compare calendars to view availability, confirm conference room availability, share project contacts, search email messages related to the project, and send email invitations to the project meeting. Exchange Online also allows you to search and access your company's address list.

Online Meetings

When you are working with a team on a project that requires interaction, email and text communications can slow the communications process. Microsoft Lync connects you with others by facilitating real-time, interactive presentations and meetings over the Internet using both video and audio calling. As shown in Figure 3, you can conduct an online meeting with a team member or customer that includes an instant messaging conversation, audio, high-definition video, virtual whiteboards, and screen sharing. If the customer does not have an Office 365 subscription, they still can join the meeting through the invitation link, which runs the Lync Web App.

Skype is another tool in the Office 365 subscription, which enables users to place video calls to computers and smartphones and voice calls to landlines. Skype also supports instant message and file sharing to computers and mobile devices. While Skype may be adequate for simple communication, Lync provides for more robust, comprehensive communications. These robust features include high-definition (HD) videoconferencing capabilities, a whiteboard, and a larger audience. Using Lync, meeting attendees simultaneously can view up to five participants' videos, identify the active speaker, and associate names with faces. Lync supports up to 250 attendees per meeting. Unlike Skype, Lync meetings can be recorded for replaying at a later time. This enables businesses and schools to schedule meetings or organize online classes using Lync capabilities.

In addition to Lync, Microsoft Office 365 Business includes a business social networking tool named Yammer. With Yammer, employees create an online team workspace to discuss projects, deadlines, and share files. By sharing your profile and expertise, coworkers can easily find each other and post messages to keep all team members in the loop.

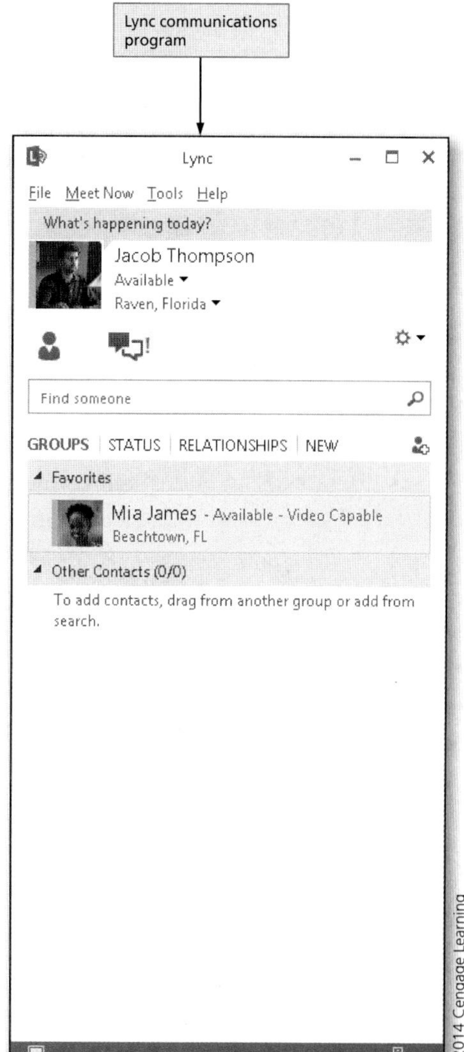

Figure 3

File Sharing

Office 365 includes a team site, which is a password-protected portal that supports sharing of large, difficult-to-email files and provides a single location for the latest versions of documents. In business, for example, colleagues working on common projects can save valuable time by being able to access instantly the latest master copy of each document. Security can be managed through different levels of user access so that users see only what they are supposed to see. Office 365 provides access to shared files using the cloud, making writing, editing, and sharing documents easier. If a construction company creates a commercial bid for a building project, the customers can be invited to view an Excel spreadsheet bid, construction timetable with a shared calendar, and an Access database of all the materials needed using the file sharing feature online.

Website Creation

Office 365 business plan subscriptions include a built-in hosted public website, where customers and clients can find an online storefront of a company. This public website, called the Website, can be customized to market a company by using various templates within the Office 365 cloud. The website creation tools include those for adding a theme, graphics, fonts, maps, directions, blogs, stock tickers, slide shows, PayPal, weather, and videos to interact with the website's visitors.

Synchronization

Office 365 subscription plans provide a central place to store and access your documents and business information. A feature of Office 365 ensures the original and backup computer files in two or more locations are identical through a process called **Active Directory Synchronization**. For example, if you open a PowerPoint presentation on your smartphone while you are riding a city bus and then add a new slide as you head to school, the PowerPoint presentation automatically is synced with Office 365. When you arrive on campus and open the PowerPoint presentation on a school computer, your new slide already is part of the finished slide show. By storing your files in Office 365, you can access your files on another computer if your home computer fails, with no loss of time or important information. When using your mobile phone's data plan, you do not need to search for a Wi-Fi hot spot to connect to the Office 365 cloud. Computer labs in schools can be configured to synchronize automatically all student files to Office 365 online.

Multiple Device Access to Office 365

With a single sign-in process, Office 365 provides access to multiple computers and mobile devices, including Android smartphones and tablets, Apple iPhones and iPads, and Windows phones. After you configure your devices' email settings, you can view your Microsoft account calendar, contacts, and email. Your personalized settings, preferences, and documents can be synchronized among all the different devices included in your Office 365 premium subscription. With the mobility of Office 365, students and employees can work anywhere, accessing information and responding to email requests immediately. If you lose your phone, Office 365 includes a feature that allows you to remotely wipe your phone clean of any data. By wiping your phone's data, you can prevent any unauthorized access to sensitive information, such as your banking information, passwords, and contacts, as well as discourage identity theft. Because your phone contacts and other information are stored on the Microsoft cloud, damaged or lost equipment is never a problem.

A thief can be quite resourceful if he or she steals your phone. Before you can alert your parents or spouse to the theft, they might receive a text from "you" asking for your ATM or credit card PIN number. Your parents or spouse might then reply with the PIN number. Your bank account could be emptied in minutes.

Teams Using Office 365 in Business

In the business world, rarely does an employee work in isolation. Companies need their employees to collaborate, whether they work in the same office or in locations around the world. Telecommuters working from home can communicate as if they were on-site by using a common team website and conferencing software. SharePoint Online and Lync Online provide seamless communication.

Small business subscription plans as low as $8.25 per user per month allow employees to create and store Word documents, Excel spreadsheets, and PowerPoint presentations online and communicate with one another via email, instant messaging, or video chat as they work on projects together. As shown in Figure 4, a team portal page is shown when you subscribe at https://portal.microsoftonline.com. Larger companies and those requiring more features can take advantage of the Office 365 business premium package, which, in addition to the features listed above, provides access to the Office 365 portal website and eliminates the effort and cost of the users maintaining their own costly computer servers.

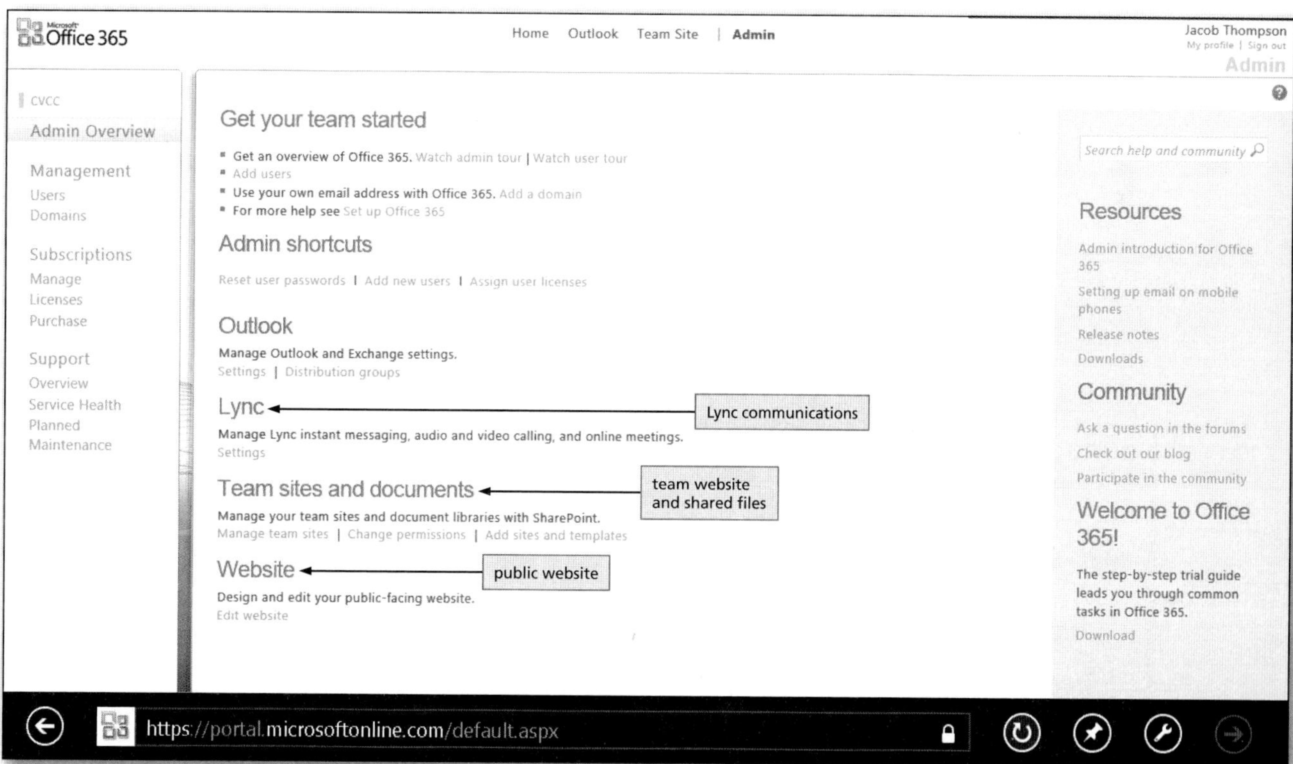

Figure 4

Email Communication Using Exchange

Office 365 includes Exchange Online, an email-based collaborative communications server for business. Exchange enables employees to be more productive by effectively managing email across multiple devices and facilitating teamwork.

Collaboration Using SharePoint

SharePoint Online, a part of Office 365 subscription plans, allows employees to collaborate with one another, share documents, post announcements, and track tasks, as shown in Table 2.

Table 2 Office 365 SharePoint Features

Team Site Feature	Description
Calendar	Track important dates
Shared Document Library	Store related documents according to topic; picture, report, and slide libraries often are included
Task List	Track team tasks according to who is responsible for completion
Team Discussion Board	Discuss the topics at hand in an open forum
Contacts List	Share contact lists of employees, customers, contractors, and suppliers

Office 365 provides the tools to plan meetings. Users can share calendars side by side, view availability, and suggest meeting times from shared calendars. Typically, a SharePoint team administrator or website owner establishes a folder structure to share and manage documents. The team website is fully searchable online, making locating and sharing data more efficient than using a local server. With a team website, everyone on the team has a central location to store and find all the information for a project, client, or department, as shown in Figure 5.

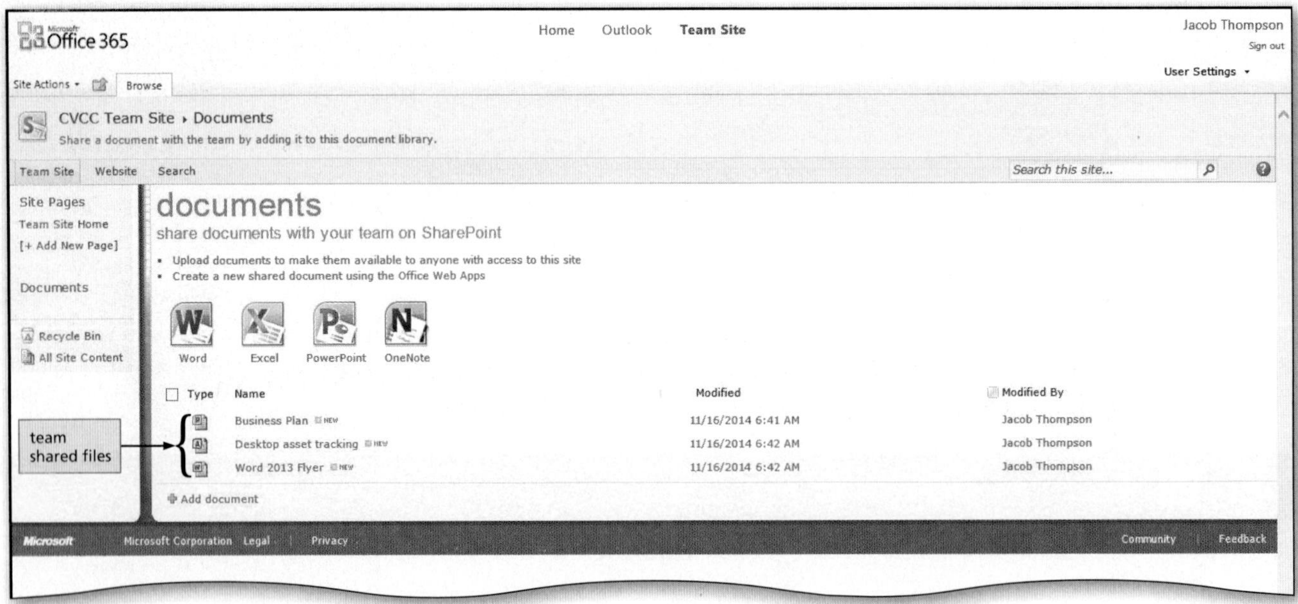

Figure 5

Website Design Using SharePoint

SharePoint provides templates to create a professional looking, public website for an online presence to market your business. As shown in Figure 6, a local pet sitting business is setting up a business website by customizing a SharePoint template. SharePoint Public Website includes features within the Design Manager that you use to customize and design your website by adding your own images, forms, style sheets, maps, themes, and social networking tools. When you finish customizing your business site, you can apply your own domain name to the site. A **domain** is a unique web address that identifies where your website can be found. Office 365 SharePoint hosts your website as part of your subscription. Your customers easily can find your business online and learn about your services.

BTW

Creating SharePoint Intranet Sites

A SharePoint website also can be customized to serve as an internal company website for private communications within the company.

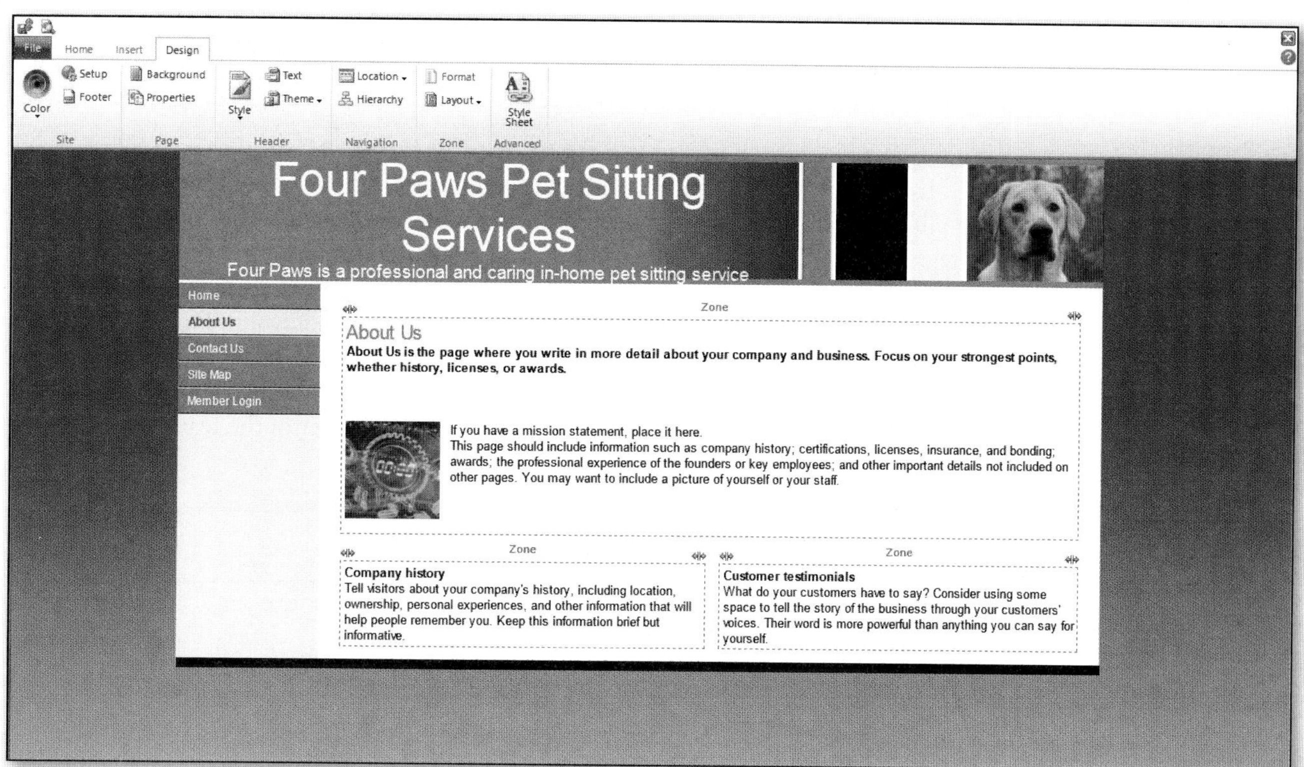

Figure 6

Real-Time Communications Using Lync

Lync Online is Microsoft's server platform for online team communications and comes bundled with Office 365 business subscriptions. As shown in Figure 7, Lync connects in real time to allow instant messaging, videoconferencing, and voice communications; it also integrates with email and Microsoft Office applications.

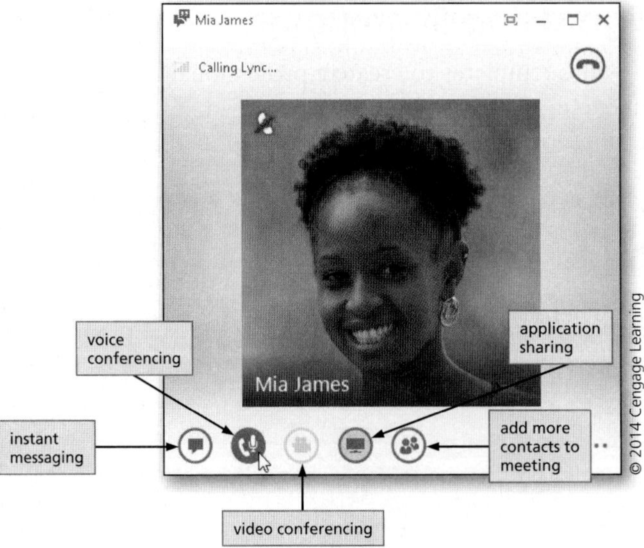

Figure 7

Lync allows you to connect with staff at remote locations using instant messaging capabilities, desktop sharing, videoconferencing, and shared agendas or documents. Lync is integrated into Office 365, which allows staff to start communicating from within the applications in which they currently are working. For example, while an employee is creating a PowerPoint presentation for a new product line, as shown in Figure 8, Lync enables him or her to collaborate with the entire team about the details of the product presentation. The team can view the presenter's screen displaying the PowerPoint presentation. The presenter can share control with any member of the team and can share his or her screen at any time during the Lync meeting.

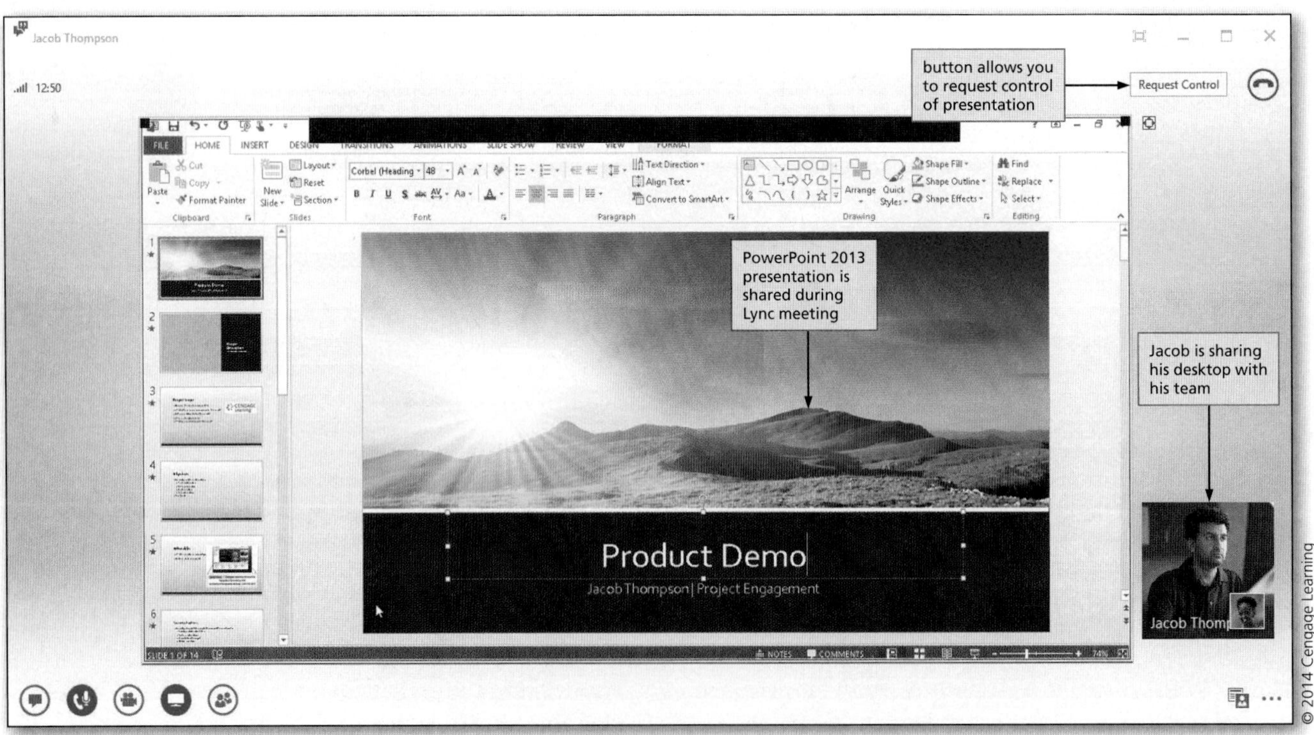

Figure 8

Users can send a Lync meeting request to schedule a team meeting, or an impromptu conversation can be started immediately using the Meet Now feature. Participants receive a Lync meeting request link via an email message, and when they click the meeting request link, Lync automatically connects them to the online conference. If the participant does not have Lync installed, the Lync Web App automatically connects to the Lync meeting through the user's PC or Mac OS X browser. If a participant is away from his or her computer, he or she still can participate using the Lync Mobile apps for Windows Phone, iOS, and Android. As shown in Figure 9, Lync utilizes **instant messaging** (IM), allowing two or more people to share text messages. They can communicate in real time, similar to a voice conversation. In addition to a simple instant message, Lync provides a feature called **persistent chat**, which allows end-users to participate in a working session of instant messages that is persistent or sustained over a specified amount of time in a moderated chat room. Consider having an instant messaging session with a group of colleagues in different parts of your organization, regardless of geographic region, where you all are working on the same project. Over the course of the project, different people post questions and concerns, and others are able to respond to all those who have subscribed to your topic or been admitted to the chat room. Instead of a long trail of email messages, a team can keep information in a controlled environment with a full history of the discussion in one location.

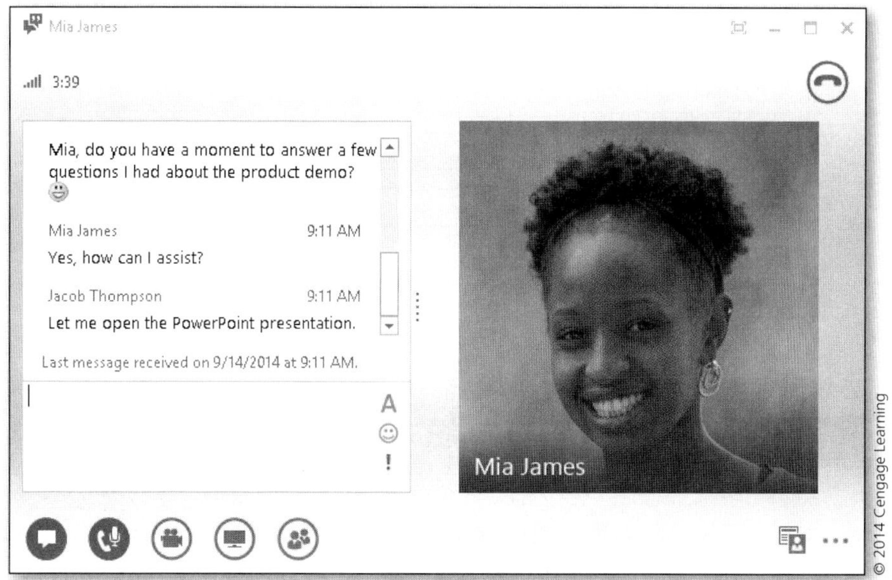

Figure 9

Lync also delivers support for full high-definition (HD) videoconferencing, so that a team can have a clear view of the participants, products, and demos. Before you join the video feed, you can preview your video feed to make sure your video camera is at the correct angle, your image is centered within the video frame, and that your room lighting provides for a clear image. The Lync preview option is important in creating a positive first impression over video. Your audio devices can be tested for clarity to make sure your headset, microphone, and speakers are functioning properly.

Lync provides a polling feature that presenters can use to ask the participants' opinions during a meeting (Figure 10). The poll question can consist of up to seven possible choices. The presenter has the option to view the results privately or share the results with the entire group.

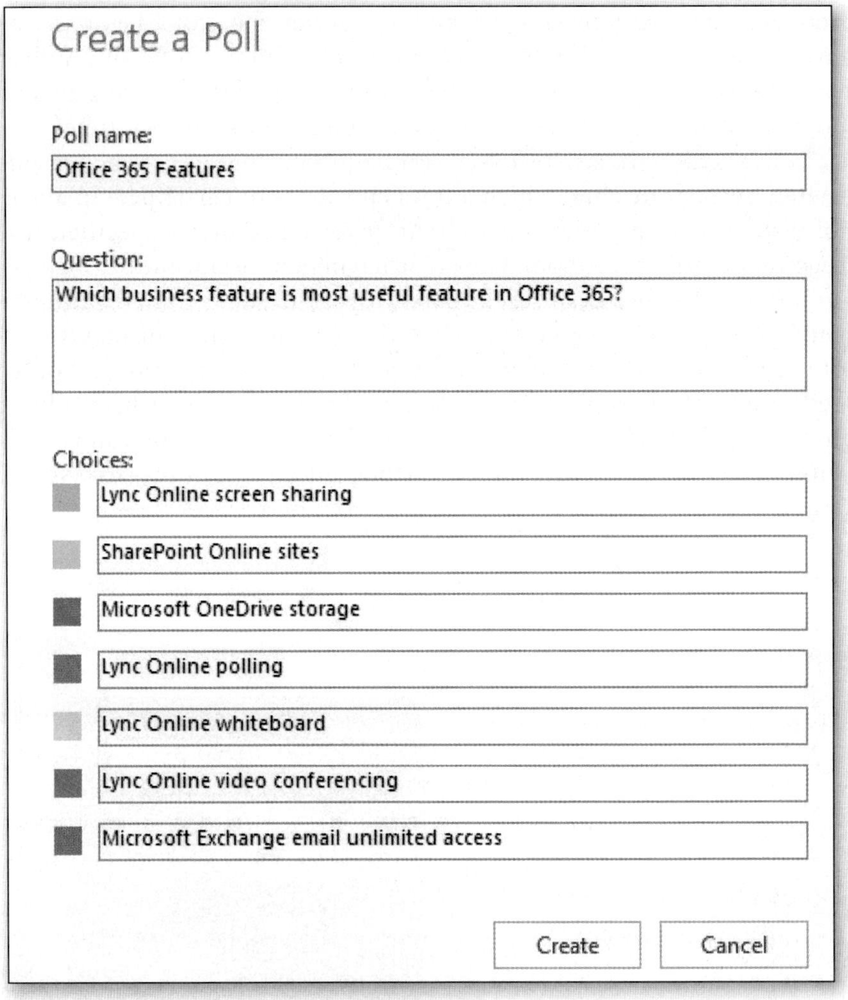

Create a Poll

Poll name:
Office 365 Features

Question:
Which business feature is most useful feature in Office 365?

Choices:
Lync Online screen sharing
SharePoint Online sites
Microsoft OneDrive storage
Lync Online polling
Lync Online whiteboard
Lync Online video conferencing
Microsoft Exchange email unlimited access

Create
Cancel

Figure 10

Finally, by enabling the recording feature, Lync meetings and conversations can be captured for viewing at a later time. For instance, you can capture the audio, video, instant messaging (IM), screen sharing, Microsoft PowerPoint presentations, whiteboard, and polling portions of the Lync session and then play them back just as they transpired during the live Lync event. The meeting recordings can be made available to others so that they can view all or part of the Lync event. Instructors can record Lync online class sessions for students who were unable to attend the original presentation. The recording starts in Microsoft Lync; recordings then can be viewed within the Recording Manager feature.

Chapter Summary

In this chapter, you have learned how to subscribe to Office 365, which provides local and online access to Office applications, email, document sharing, web conferencing, and business websites. You also learned how a business can utilize Office 365 features on the cloud to facilitate teamwork. Finally, you learned about the features of SharePoint, Yammer, and Lync, which provide collaboration and communications for business teams using Office 365.

Consider This: Your Turn

Apply your creative thinking and problem solving skills to design and implement a solution.

1: Comparing Office 365 Personal Plans

Personal

Part 1: After graduation, you are considering if it would be a better value to subscribe to Office 365 Personal or Office 365 Home Premium. Write a one-page document comparing the pros and cons of the two subscription plans. Research the different subscriptions in detail at Office365.com. Submit your assignment in the format specified by your instructor.

Part 2: Which type of computer and/or devices would you use with your Office 365 subscription? If you are at a friend's home that does not have Office 365, how could you access your Office files if you do not have your computer or mobile device with you?

2: Upgrading a Local Business to Office 365

Professional

Part 1: You are an employee at Impact Digital Marketing, a small marketing firm with 12 employees. The firm is setting up an Office 365 Business subscription next week, and you need to compose an email message with multiple paragraphs to explain the features of this new subscription plan to the members of your firm. Research the Office 365 Business subscription plan in detail at Office365.com, and compile your findings in an email message. Submit your assignment in the format specified by your instructor.

Part 2: Give three examples of how a marketing firm could use Lync. How could a marketing firm use the SharePoint Websites feature?

3: Conducting a Lync Meeting

Research and Collaboration

* Students need an Office 365 subscription to complete the following assignment.

Part 1: Using your Office 365 subscription, conduct a meeting using Lync. Working with a partner, use your Office 365 subscription to research how to use Lync. Then, conduct a 15-minute Lync meeting, including instant messaging, to discuss the features of Lync. Use the concepts and techniques presented in this chapter to create the Lync meeting. Submit your assignment in the format specified by your instructor.

Part 2: When using Lync in an online class, when would the screen recording feature best be utilized?

Chapter Summary

1 Creating, Formatting, and Editing a Word Document with a Picture

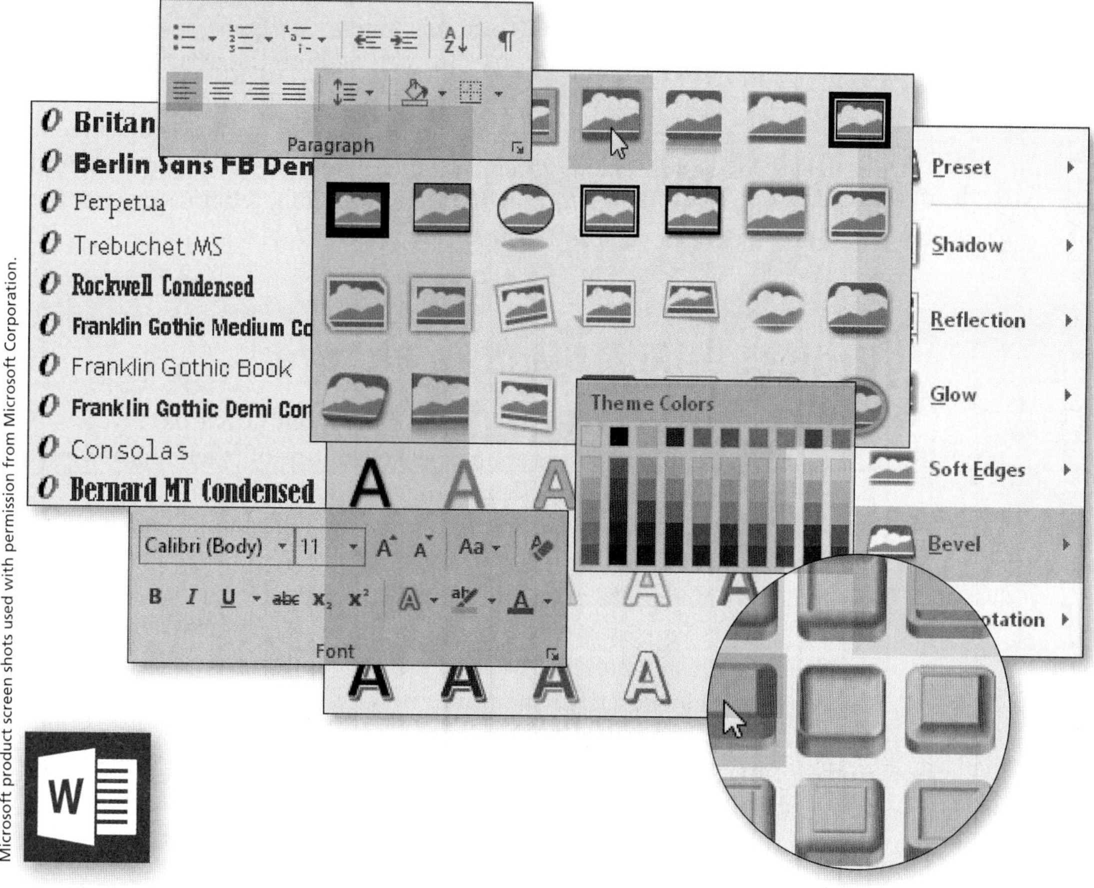

Objectives

You will have mastered the material in this chapter when you can:

- Enter text in a Word document
- Check spelling as you type
- Format paragraphs
- Format text
- Undo and redo commands or actions
- Change theme colors
- Insert digital pictures in a Word document
- Format pictures
- Add a page border
- Adjust spacing
- Change document properties
- Correct errors and revise a document
- Print and read a document

1 Creating, Formatting, and Editing a Word Document with a Picture

Introduction

To advertise a sale, promote a business, publicize an event, or convey a message to the community, you may want to create a flyer and hand it out in person or post it in a public location. Libraries, schools, religious organizations, grocery stores, coffee shops, and other places often provide bulletin boards or windows for flyers. You also see flyers posted on webpages or as email messages.

Flyers announce personal items for sale or rent (car, boat, apartment); garage or block sales; services being offered (animal care, housecleaning, lessons, tours); membership, sponsorship, or donation requests (club, religious organization, charity); and other messages, such as a lost or found pet.

Project — Flyer with a Picture

Individuals and businesses create flyers to gain public attention. Flyers, which usually are a single page in length, are an inexpensive means of reaching the community. Many flyers, however, go unnoticed because they are designed poorly.

The project in this chapter follows general guidelines and uses Word to create the flyer shown in Figure 1–1. This colorful, eye-catching flyer announces tour adventures. The picture of the tour group on the mountain trail, taken with a digital camera, entices passersby or viewers to stop and look at the flyer. The headline on the flyer is large and colorful to draw attention into the text. The body copy below the picture briefly describes the tours, along with a bulleted list that concisely highlights important tour information. The signature line of the flyer calls attention to the contact phone number. The word, breathtaking, and the signature line are in a different color so that they stand apart from the rest of the text on the flyer. Finally, the graphical page border nicely frames and complements the contents of the flyer.

For an introduction to Office and instruction about how to perform basic tasks in Office apps, read the Office and Windows chapter at the beginning of this book, where you can learn how to run an application, use the ribbon, save a file, open a file, exit an application, use Help, and much more.

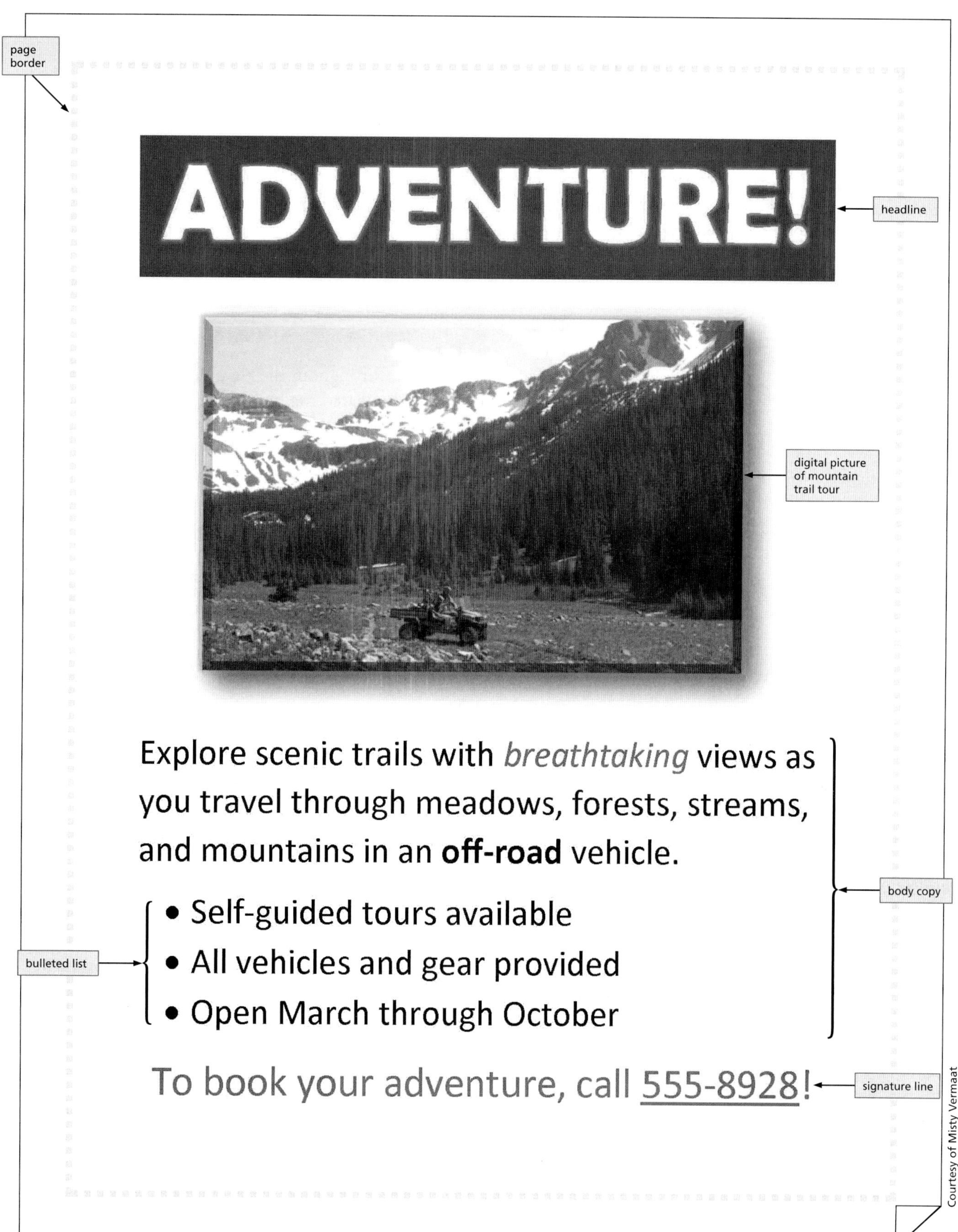
page border
ADVENTURE!
headline
digital picture of mountain trail tour
Explore scenic trails with *breathtaking* views as you travel through meadows, forests, streams, and mountains in an **off-road** vehicle.
• Self-guided tours available
• All vehicles and gear provided
• Open March through October
body copy
bulleted list
To book your adventure, call 555-8928!
signature line
Courtesy of Misty Vermaat

Figure 1–1

For an introduction to Windows and instruction about how to perform basic Windows tasks, read the Office and Windows chapter at the beginning of this book, where you can learn how to resize windows, change screen resolution, create folders, move and rename files, use Windows Help, and much more.

Roadmap

In this chapter, you will learn how to create the flyer shown in Figure 1–1. The following roadmap identifies general activities you will perform as you progress through this chapter:

1. **ENTER TEXT** in a new document.
2. **FORMAT** the **TEXT** in the flyer.
3. **INSERT** a **PICTURE**, called Mountain Trail, in the flyer.
4. **FORMAT** the **PICTURE** in the flyer.
5. **ENHANCE** the **PAGE** with a border and spacing.
6. **CORRECT** errors **AND REVISE** text in the flyer.
7. **PRINT OR READ** the flyer.

At the beginning of step instructions throughout the chapter, you will see an abbreviated form of this roadmap. The abbreviated roadmap uses colors to indicate chapter progress: gray means the chapter is beyond that activity, blue means the task being shown is covered in that activity, and black means that activity is yet to be covered. For example, the following abbreviated roadmap indicates the chapter would be showing a task in the 2 FORMAT TEXT activity.

1 ENTER TEXT | 2 FORMAT TEXT | 3 INSERT PICTURE | 4 FORMAT PICTURE
5 ENHANCE PAGE | 6 CORRECT & REVISE | 7 PRINT OR READ

Use the abbreviated roadmap as a progress guide while you read or step through the instructions in this chapter.

To Run Word and Create a Blank Document

If you are using a computer to step through the project in this chapter and you want your screens to match the figures in this book, you should change your screen's resolution to 1366 × 768. For information about how to change a computer's resolution, refer to the Office and Windows chapter at the beginning of this book.

The following steps, which assume Windows 8 is running, use the Start screen or the Search box to run Word based on a typical installation. You may need to ask your instructor how to run Word on your computer. For a detailed example of the procedure summarized below, refer to the Office and Windows chapter.

One of the few differences between Windows 7 and Windows 8 occurs in the steps to run Word. If you are using Windows 7, click the Start button, type **Word** in the 'Search programs and files' box, click Word 2013, and then, if necessary, maximize the Word window. For detailed steps to run Word in Windows 7, refer to the Office and Windows chapter at the beginning of this book. For a summary of the steps, refer to the Quick Reference located at the back of this book.

1. Scroll the Start screen for a Word 2013 tile. If your Start screen contains a Word 2013 tile, tap or click it to run Word and then proceed to Step 5; if the Start screen does not contain the Word 2013 tile, proceed to the next step to search for the Word app.
2. Swipe in from the right edge of the screen or point to the upper-right corner of the screen to display the Charms bar and then tap or click the Search charm on the Charms bar to display the Search menu.
3. Type **Word** as the search text in the Search box and watch the search results appear in the Apps list.
4. Tap or click Word 2013 in the search results to run Word.
5. Tap or click the Blank document thumbnail on the Word start screen to create a blank document and display it in the Word window.
6. If the Word window is not maximized, tap or click the Maximize button on its title bar to maximize the window.

7 If the Print Layout button on the status bar is not selected (shown in Figure 1–2), tap or click it so that your screen is in Print Layout view.

Q&A What is Print Layout view?
The default (preset) view in Word is **Print Layout view**, which shows the document on a mock sheet of paper in the document window.

8 If Normal (HOME tab | Styles group) is not selected in the Styles gallery (shown in Figure 1–2), tap or click it so that your document uses the Normal style.

Q&A What is the Normal style?
When you create a document, Word formats the text using a particular style. The default style in Word is called the **Normal style**, which is discussed later in this book.

What if rulers appear on my screen?
Tap or click VIEW on the ribbon to display the VIEW tab and then remove the check mark from the View Ruler check box (VIEW tab | Show group).

BTW
The Word Window
The chapters in this book begin with the Word window appearing as it did at the initial installation of the software. Your Word window may look different depending on your screen resolution and other Word settings.

Entering Text

The first step in creating a document is to enter its text. With the projects in this book, you enter text by typing on the keyboard. By default, Word positions text you type at the left margin. In a later section of this chapter, you will learn how to format, or change the appearance of, the entered text.

To Type Text

1 ENTER TEXT | 2 FORMAT TEXT | 3 INSERT PICTURE | 4 FORMAT PICTURE
5 ENHANCE PAGE | 6 CORRECT & REVISE | 7 PRINT OR READ

To begin creating the flyer in this chapter, type the headline in the document window. ***Why?** The headline is the first line of text in the Adventure Flyer.* The following steps type the first line of text in the document.

1

- Type **Adventure!** as the headline (Figure 1–2).

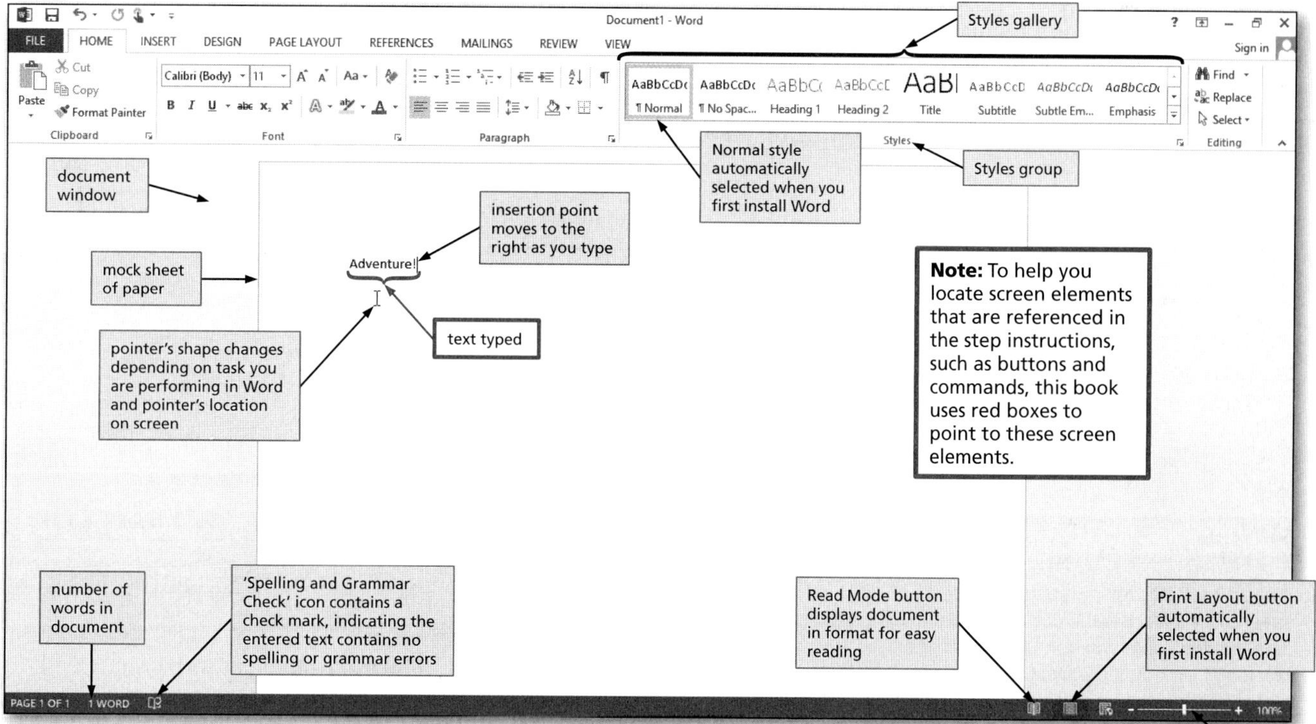

Figure 1–2

What if I make an error while typing?
You can press the BACKSPACE key until you have deleted the text in error and then retype the text correctly.

What is the purpose of the Spelling and Grammar Check icon on the status bar?
The **Spelling and Grammar Check icon** displays either a check mark to indicate the entered text contains no spelling or grammar errors, or an X to indicate that it found potential errors. Word flags potential errors in the document with a red, green, or blue wavy underline. Later in this chapter, you will learn how to fix flagged errors.

2

- Press the ENTER key to move the insertion point to the beginning of the next line (Figure 1–3).

Why did blank space appear between the headline and the insertion point?
Each time you press the ENTER key, Word creates a new paragraph and inserts blank space between the two paragraphs. Later in this chapter, you will learn how to increase and decrease the spacing between paragraphs.

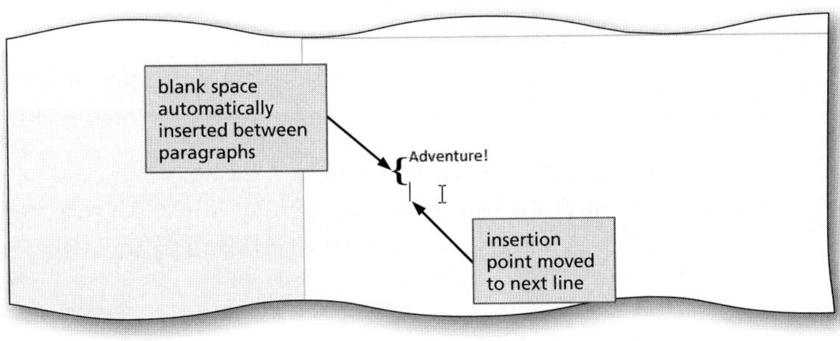

Figure 1–3

CONSIDER THIS

How do you use the touch keyboard with a touch screen?
To display the on-screen touch keyboard, tap the Touch Keyboard button on the Windows taskbar. When finished using the touch keyboard, tap the X button on the touch keyboard to close the keyboard.

To Display Formatting Marks

1 ENTER TEXT | 2 FORMAT TEXT | 3 INSERT PICTURE | 4 FORMAT PICTURE
5 ENHANCE PAGE | 6 CORRECT & REVISE | 7 PRINT OR READ

You may find it helpful to display formatting marks while working in a document. ***Why?*** *Formatting marks indicate where in a document you press the* ENTER *key,* SPACEBAR, *and other nonprinting characters.* A **formatting mark** is a character that Word displays on the screen but is not visible on a printed document. For example, the paragraph mark (¶) is a formatting mark that indicates where you pressed the ENTER key. A raised dot (·) shows where you pressed the SPACEBAR. Formatting marks are discussed as they appear on the screen.

Depending on settings made during previous Word sessions, your Word screen already may display formatting marks (Figure 1–4). The following step displays formatting marks, if they do not show already on the screen.

1

- If the HOME tab is not the active tab, tap or click HOME on the ribbon to display the HOME tab.
- If it is not selected already, tap or click the 'Show/Hide ¶' button (HOME tab | Paragraph group) to display formatting marks on the screen (Figure 1–4).

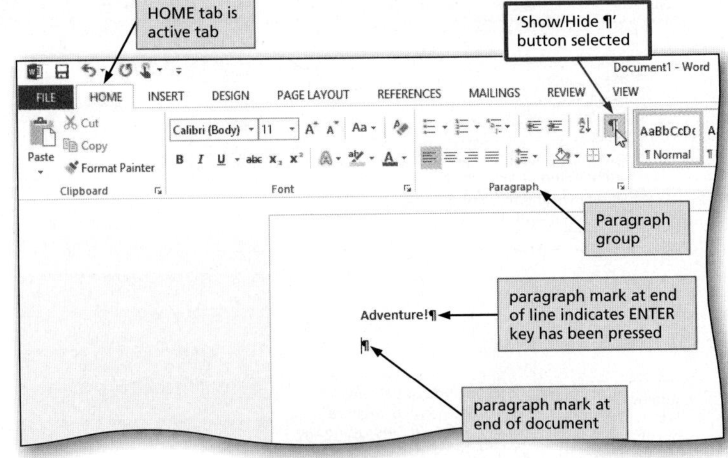

Figure 1–4

BTW
Zooming
If text is too small for you to read on the screen, you can zoom the document by dragging the Zoom slider on the status bar or tapping or clicking the Zoom Out or Zoom In buttons on the status bar. Changing the zoom has no effect on the printed document.

Q&A What if I do not want formatting marks to show on the screen?
You can hide them by tapping or clicking the 'Show/Hide ¶' button (HOME tab | Paragraph group) again. It is recommended that you display formatting marks so that you visually can identify when you press the ENTER key, SPACEBAR, and other keys associated with nonprinting characters. Most of the document windows presented in this book, therefore, show formatting marks.

Other Ways

1. Press CTRL+SHIFT+*

To Insert a Blank Line

In the flyer, the digital picture of the mountain trail appears between the headline and body copy. You will not insert this picture, however, until after you enter and format all text. ***Why?*** *Although you can format text and insert pictures in any order, for illustration purposes, this chapter formats all text first before inserting the picture. Thus, you leave a blank line in the document as a placeholder for the picture.*

To enter a blank line in a document, press the ENTER key without typing any text on the line. The following step inserts one blank line below the headline.

- Press the ENTER key to insert a blank line in the document (Figure 1–5).

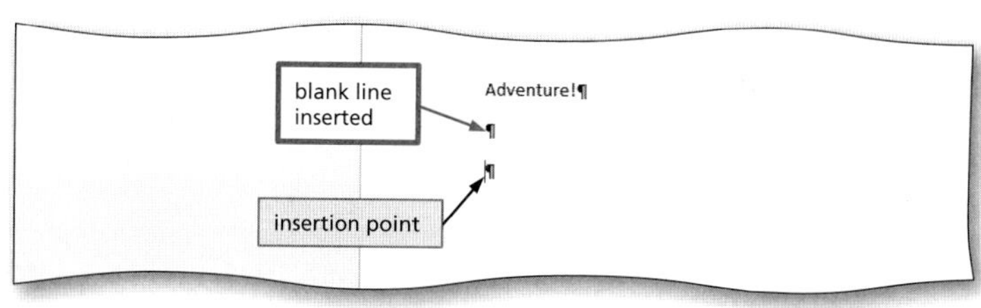

Figure 1–5

To Zoom Page Width

The next step in creating this flyer is to enlarge the contents that appear on the screen. ***Why?*** *You would like the text on the screen to be larger so that it is easier to read.* The document currently displays at 100% (shown in Figure 1–6). With Word, you can zoom page width, which zooms (enlarges or shrinks) the mock sheet of paper on the screen so that it is the width of the Word window. The following steps zoom page width.

- Tap or click VIEW on the ribbon to display the VIEW tab.

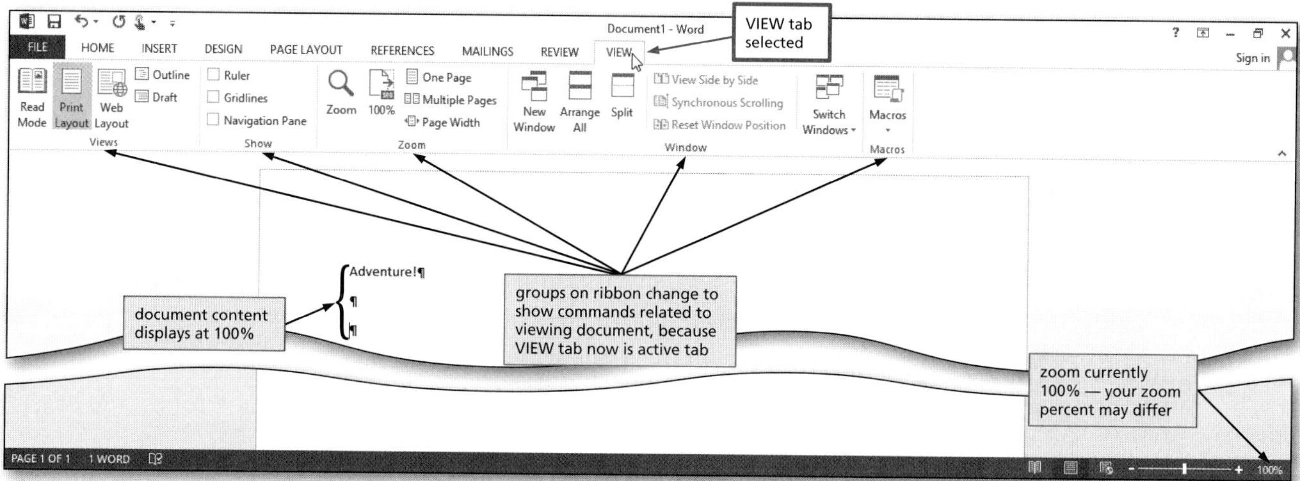

Figure 1–6

2

- Tap or click the Page Width button (VIEW tab | Zoom group) to display the page the same width as the document window (Figure 1–7).

Q&A

If I change the zoom, will the document print differently?
Changing the zoom has no effect on the printed document.

What are the other predefined zoom options?
Through the VIEW tab | Zoom group or the Zoom dialog box (Zoom button in Zoom group), you can zoom to one page (an entire single page appears in the document window), many pages (multiple pages appear at once in the document window), page width, text width, and a variety of set percentages. Whereas page width zoom places the edges of the page at the edges of the document window, text width zoom places the document contents at the edges of the document window.

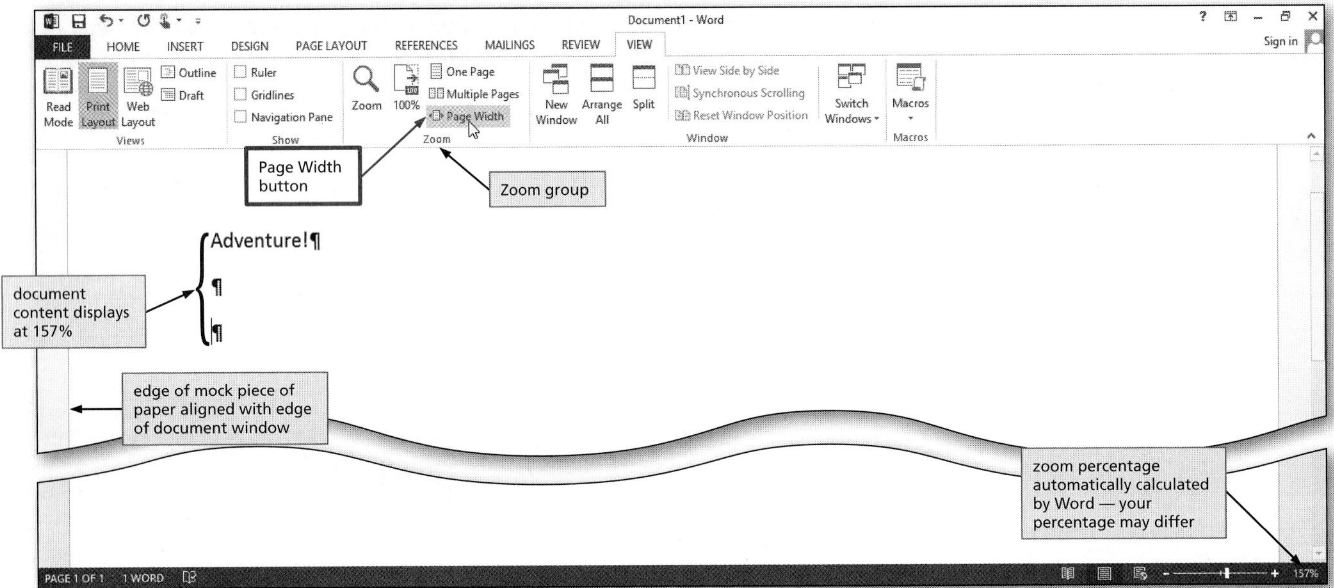

Figure 1–7

Other Ways

1. Tap or click Zoom button (VIEW tab | Zoom group), tap or click Page width (Zoom dialog box), tap or click OK button

BTW
The Ribbon and Screen Resolution
Word may change how the groups and buttons within the groups appear on the ribbon, depending on the computer's screen resolution. Thus, your ribbon may look different from the ones in this book if you are using a screen resolution other than 1366 × 768.

Wordwrap

Wordwrap allows you to type words in a paragraph continually without pressing the ENTER key at the end of each line. As you type, if a word extends beyond the right margin, Word also automatically positions that word on the next line along with the insertion point.

Word creates a new paragraph each time you press the ENTER key. Thus, as you type text in the document window, do not press the ENTER key when the insertion point reaches the right margin. Instead, press the ENTER key only in these circumstances:

1. To insert a blank line(s) in a document (as shown in the previous steps)
2. To begin a new paragraph
3. To terminate a short line of text and advance to the next line
4. To respond to questions or prompts in Word dialog boxes, task panes, and other on-screen objects

To Wordwrap Text as You Type

1 ENTER TEXT | 2 FORMAT TEXT | 3 INSERT PICTURE | 4 FORMAT PICTURE
5 ENHANCE PAGE | 6 CORRECT & REVISE | 7 PRINT OR READ

The next step in creating the flyer is to type the body copy. ***Why?*** *In many flyers, the body copy text appears below the headline.* The following steps illustrate how the body copy text wordwraps as you enter it in the document.

- Type the first sentence of the body copy: **`Explore scenic trails with breathtaking views as you travel through meadows, forests, streams, and mountains in an off-road vehicle.`**

Q&A Why does my document wrap on different words?
The printer connected to a computer is one factor that can control where wordwrap occurs for each line in a document. Thus, it is possible that the same document could wordwrap differently if printed on different printers.

2

- Press the ENTER key to position the insertion point on the next line in the document (Figure 1–8).

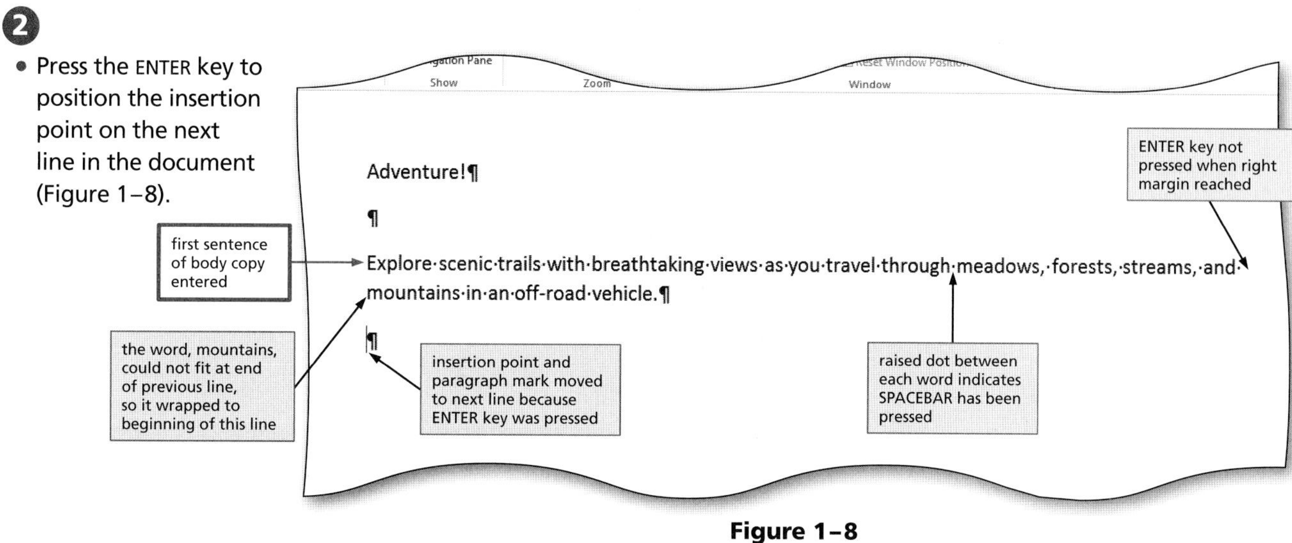

Figure 1–8

Spelling and Grammar Check

As you type text in a document, Word checks your typing for possible spelling and grammar errors. If all of the words you have typed are in Word's dictionary and your grammar is correct, as mentioned earlier, the Spelling and Grammar Check icon on the status bar displays a check mark. Otherwise, the icon shows an X. In this case, Word flags the potential error in the document window with a red, green, or blue wavy underline. A red wavy underline means the flagged text is not in Word's dictionary (because it is a proper name or misspelled). A green wavy underline indicates the text may be incorrect grammatically. A blue wavy underline indicates the text may contain a contextual spelling error, such as the misuse of homophones (words that are pronounced the same but that have different spellings or meanings, such as one and won). Although you can check the entire document for spelling and grammar errors at once, you also can check flagged errors as they appear on the screen.

A flagged word is not necessarily misspelled. For example, many names, abbreviations, and specialized terms are not in Word's main dictionary. In these cases, you can instruct Word to ignore the flagged word. As you type, Word also detects duplicate words while checking for spelling errors. For example, if your document contains the phrase, to the the store, Word places a red wavy underline below the second occurrence of the word, the.

BTW
Automatic Spelling Correction
As you type, Word automatically corrects some misspelled words. For example, if you type recieve, Word automatically corrects the misspelling and displays the word, receive, when you press the SPACEBAR or type a punctuation mark. To see a complete list of automatically corrected words, click FILE on the ribbon to open the Backstage view, click Options in the Backstage view, click Proofing in the left pane (Word Options dialog box), click the AutoCorrect Options button, and then scroll through the list near the bottom of the dialog box.

To Check Spelling and Grammar as You Type

In the following steps, the word, tours, has been misspelled intentionally as tuors. ***Why?*** *These steps illustrate Word's check spelling as you type feature. If you are completing this project on a computer, your flyer may contain different or no misspelled words, depending on the accuracy of your typing.*

1

- Type **`Self-guided tuors`** and then press the SPACEBAR, so that a red wavy line appears below the misspelled word (Figure 1–9).

Q&A What if Word does not flag my spelling and grammar errors with wavy underlines?
To verify that the check spelling and grammar as you type features are enabled, tap or click FILE on the ribbon to open the Backstage view and then tap or click Options in the Backstage view. When the Word Options dialog box is displayed, tap or click Proofing in the left pane, and then ensure the 'Check spelling as you type' and 'Mark grammar errors as you type' check boxes contain check marks. Also ensure the 'Hide spelling errors in this document only' and 'Hide grammar errors in this document only' check boxes do not contain check marks. Tap or click the OK button.

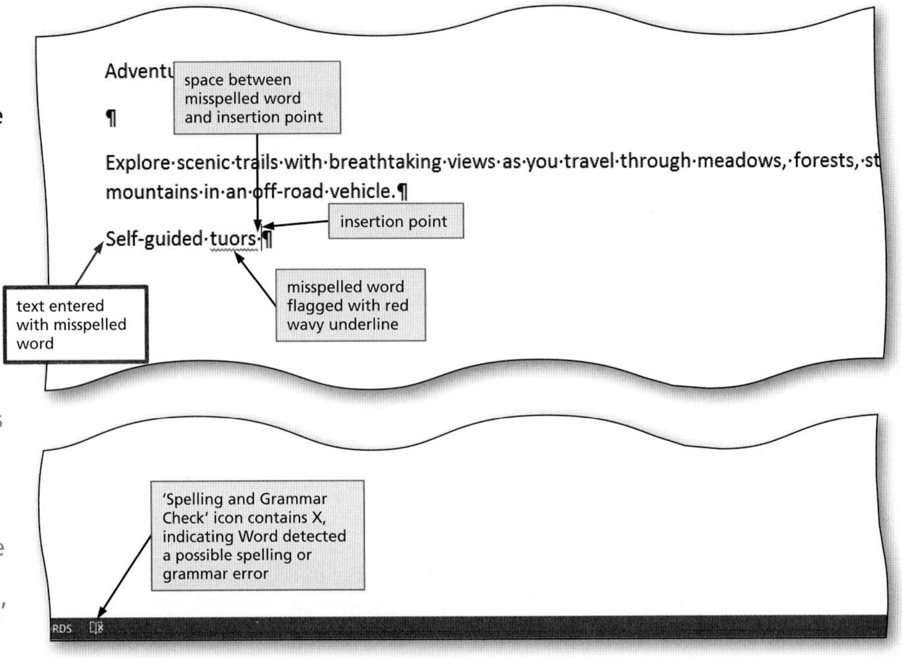

space between misspelled word and insertion point

insertion point

text entered with misspelled word

misspelled word flagged with red wavy underline

'Spelling and Grammar Check' icon contains X, indicating Word detected a possible spelling or grammar error

Figure 1–9

2

- Press and hold or right-click the flagged word (tuors, in this case) to display a shortcut menu that presents a list of suggested spelling corrections for the flagged word (Figure 1–10).

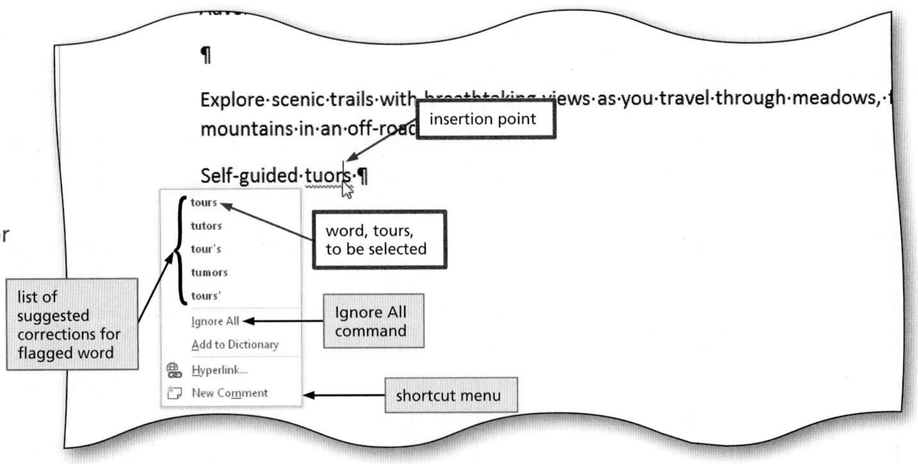

Q&A What if, when I press and hold or right-click the misspelled word, my desired correction is not in the list on the shortcut menu?
You can tap or click outside the shortcut menu to close the shortcut menu and then retype the correct word.

What if a flagged word actually is, for example, a proper name and spelled correctly?
Press and hold or right-click it and then tap or click Ignore All on the shortcut menu to instruct Word not to flag future occurrences of the same word in this document.

insertion point

word, tours, to be selected

list of suggested corrections for flagged word

Ignore All command

shortcut menu

Figure 1–10

3

- Tap or click tours on the shortcut menu to replace the misspelled word in the document with a correctly spelled word (Figure 1–11).

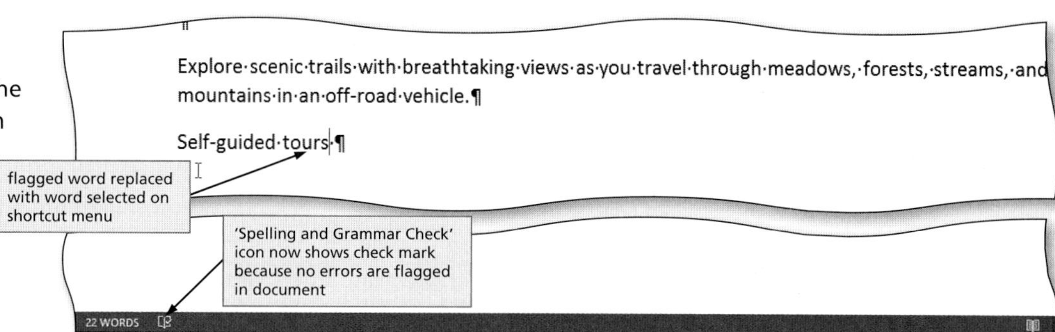

Explore·scenic·trails·with·breathtaking·views·as·you·travel·through·meadows,·forests,·streams,·and mountains·in·an·off-road·vehicle.¶
Self-guided·tours·¶
flagged word replaced with word selected on shortcut menu
'Spelling and Grammar Check' icon now shows check mark because no errors are flagged in document
22 WORDS

Figure 1–11

Other Ways

1. Tap or click 'Spelling and Grammar Check' icon on status bar, tap or click desired word in Spelling pane, tap or click Change button, tap or click OK button

To Enter More Text

In the flyer, the text yet to be entered includes the remainder of the body copy, which will be formatted as a bulleted list, and the signature line. The next steps enter the remainder of text in the flyer.

BTW

Character Widths

Many word processing documents use variable character fonts, where some characters are wider than others; for example, the letter w is wider than the letter i.

1. Press the END key to move the insertion point to the end of the current line.
2. Type **`available`** and then press the ENTER key.
3. Type **`Open March through October`** and then press the ENTER key.
4. Type **`All vehicles and gear provided`** and then press the ENTER key.
5. Type the signature line in the flyer (Figure 1–12): **`To book your adventure, call 555-8928!`**

   If requested by your instructor, enter your phone number instead of 555-8928 in the signature line.

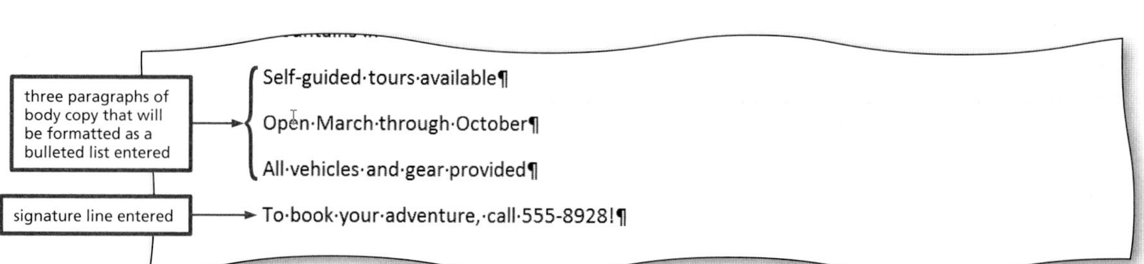

three paragraphs of body copy that will be formatted as a bulleted list entered
Self-guided·tours·available¶
Open·March·through·October¶
All·vehicles·and·gear·provided¶
signature line entered
To·book·your·adventure,·call·555-8928!¶

Figure 1–12

CONSIDER THIS

How should you organize text in a flyer?

The text in a flyer typically is organized into three areas: headline, body copy, and signature line.

- The **headline** is the first line of text on the flyer. It conveys the product or service being offered, such as a car for sale, personal lessons, or sightseeing tours, or the benefit that will be gained, such as a convenience, better performance, greater security, higher earnings, or more comfort, or it can contain a message, such as a lost or found pet.
- The **body copy** consists of text between the headline and the signature line. This text highlights the key points of the message in as few words as possible. It should be easy to read and follow. While emphasizing the positive, the body copy must be realistic, truthful, and believable.
- The **signature line**, which is the last line of text on the flyer, contains contact information or identifies a call to action.

Navigating a Document

BTW
Minimize Wrist Injury
Computer users frequently switch among touch gestures, the keyboard, and the mouse during a word processing session; such switching strains the wrist. To help prevent wrist injury, minimize switching. For instance, if your fingertips already are on the screen, use your finger to slide the document to a new location. If your fingers are already on the keyboard, use keyboard keys to scroll. If your hand already is on the mouse, use the mouse to scroll.

You view only a portion of a document on the screen through the document window. At some point when you type text or insert graphics, Word probably will **scroll** the top or bottom portion of the document off the screen. Although you cannot see the text and graphics once they scroll off the screen, they remain in the document.

You can use touch gestures, the keyboard, or a mouse to scroll to a different location in a document and/or move the insertion point around a document. If you are using a touch screen, simply use your finger to slide the document up or down to display a different location in the document and then tap to move the insertion point to a new location. When you use the keyboard, the insertion point automatically moves when you press the desired keys. For example, the previous steps used the END key to move the insertion point to the end of the current line. Table 1–1 outlines various techniques to navigate a document using the keyboard.

With the mouse, you can use the scroll arrows or the scroll box on the scroll bar to display a different portion of the document in the document window and then click the mouse to move the insertion point to that location. Table 1–2 explains various techniques for using the scroll bar to scroll vertically with the mouse.

Table 1–1 Moving the Insertion Point with the Keyboard

Insertion Point Direction	Key(s) to Press	Insertion Point Direction	Key(s) to Press
Left one character	LEFT ARROW	Up one paragraph	CTRL+UP ARROW
Right one character	RIGHT ARROW	Down one paragraph	CTRL+DOWN ARROW
Left one word	CTRL+LEFT ARROW	Up one screen	PAGE UP
Right one word	CTRL+RIGHT ARROW	Down one screen	PAGE DOWN
Up one line	UP ARROW	To top of document window	ALT+CTRL+PAGE UP
Down one line	DOWN ARROW	To bottom of document window	ALT+CTRL+PAGE DOWN
To end of line	END	To beginning of document	CTRL+HOME
To beginning of line	HOME	To end of document	CTRL+END

Table 1–2 Using the Scroll Bar to Scroll Vertically with the Mouse

Scroll Direction	Mouse Action	Scroll Direction	Mouse Action
Up	Drag the scroll box upward.	Down one screen	Click anywhere below the scroll box on the vertical scroll bar.
Down	Drag the scroll box downward.	Up one line	Click the scroll arrow at the top of the vertical scroll bar.
Up one screen	Click anywhere above the scroll box on the vertical scroll bar.	Down one line	Click the scroll arrow at the bottom of the vertical scroll bar.

To Save a Document

You have performed many tasks while creating this document and do not want to risk losing work completed thus far. Accordingly, you should save the document on your hard disk, SkyDrive, or a location that is most appropriate to your situation.

The following steps assume you already have created folders for storing your files, for example, a CIS 101 folder (for your class) that contains a Word folder (for your assignments). Thus, these steps save the document in the Word folder in the

CIS 101 folder on your desired save location. For a detailed example of the procedure for saving a file in a folder or saving a file on SkyDrive, refer to the Office and Windows chapter at the beginning of this book.

1. Tap or click the Save button on the Quick Access Toolbar, which depending on settings, will display either the Save As gallery in the Backstage view or the Save As dialog box.

2. To save on a hard disk or other storage media on your computer, proceed to Step 2a. To save on SkyDrive, proceed to Step 2b.

2a. If your screen opens the Backstage view and you want to save on storage media on your computer, tap or click Computer in the left pane, if necessary, to display options in the right pane related to saving on your computer. If your screen already displays the Save As dialog box, proceed to Step 4.

2b. If your screen opens the Backstage view and you want to save on SkyDrive, tap or click SkyDrive in the left pane to display SkyDrive saving options or a Sign In button. If your screen displays a Sign In button, tap or click it and then sign in to SkyDrive.

3. Tap or click the Browse button in the right pane to display the Save As dialog box associated with the selected save location (i.e., Computer or SkyDrive).

4. Type **Adventure Flyer** in the File name box to change the file name. Do not press the ENTER key after typing the file name because you do not want to close the dialog box at this time.

5. Navigate to the desired save location (in this case, the Word folder in the CIS 101 folder [or your class folder] on your computer or SkyDrive).

6. Tap or click the Save button (Save As dialog box) to save the document in the selected folder on the selected save location with the entered file name.

BTW

Organizing Files and Folders

You should organize and store files in folders so that you easily can find the files later. For example, if you are taking an introductory computer class called CIS 101, a good practice would be to save all Word files in a Word folder in a CIS 101 folder. For a discussion of folders and detailed examples of creating folders, refer to the Office and Windows chapter at the beginning of this book.

Formatting Paragraphs and Characters

With the text for the flyer entered, the next step is to **format**, or change the appearance of, its text. A paragraph encompasses the text from the first character in the paragraph up to and including its paragraph mark (¶). **Paragraph formatting** is the process of changing the appearance of a paragraph. For example, you can center or add bullets to a paragraph. Characters include letters, numbers, punctuation marks, and symbols. **Character formatting** is the process of changing the way characters appear on the screen and in print. You use character formatting to emphasize certain words and improve readability of a document. For example, you can color, italicize, or underline characters. Often, you apply both paragraph and character formatting to the same text. For example, you may center a paragraph (paragraph formatting) and underline some of the characters in the same paragraph (character formatting).

Although you can format paragraphs and characters before you type, many Word users enter text first and then format the existing text. Figure 1–13a on the next page shows the flyer in this chapter before formatting its paragraphs and characters. Figure 1–13b on the next page shows the flyer after formatting. As you can see from the two figures, a document that is formatted is easier to read and looks more professional. The following pages discuss how to format the flyer so that it looks like Figure 1–13b.

If you are using your finger on a touch screen and are having difficulty completing the steps in this chapter, consider using a stylus. Many people find it easier to be precise with a stylus than with a finger. In addition, with a stylus you see the pointer. If you still are having trouble completing the steps with a stylus, try using a mouse.

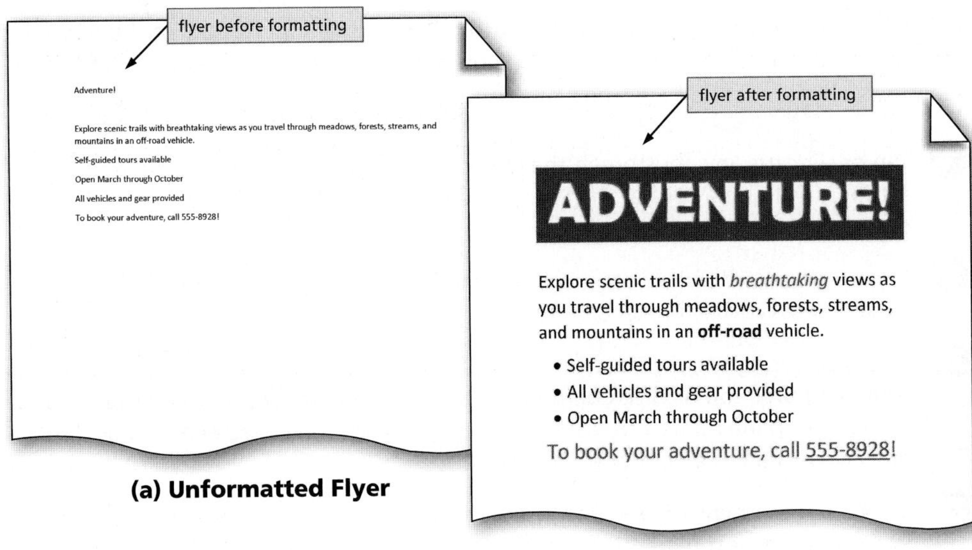
flyer before formatting
Adventure!
Explore scenic trails with breathtaking views as you travel through meadows, forests, streams, and mountains in an off-road vehicle.
Self-guided tours available
Open March through October
All vehicles and gear provided
To book your adventure, call 555-8928!
flyer after formatting
ADVENTURE!
Explore scenic trails with breathtaking views as you travel through meadows, forests, streams, and mountains in an off-road vehicle.
• Self-guided tours available
• All vehicles and gear provided
• Open March through October
To book your adventure, call 555-8928!

(a) Unformatted Flyer

(b) Formatted Flyer

Figure 1–13

Font, Font Sizes, and Themes

Characters that appear on the screen are a specific shape and size. The **font**, or typeface, defines the appearance and shape of the letters, numbers, and special characters. In Word, the default font usually is Calibri (shown in Figure 1–14). You can leave characters in the default font or change them to a different font. **Font size** specifies the size of the characters and is determined by a measurement system called points. A single **point** is about 1/72 of one inch in height. The default font size in Word typically is 11 (Figure 1–14). Thus, a character with a font size of 11 is about 11/72 or a little less than 1/6 of one inch in height. You can increase or decrease the font size of characters in a document.

A document **theme** is a set of unified formats for fonts, colors, and graphics. Word includes a variety of document themes to assist you with coordinating these visual elements in a document. The default theme fonts are Calibri Light for headings and Calibri for body text. By changing the document theme, you quickly can give your document a new look. You also can define your own document themes.

BTW

Formatting Marks

With some fonts, the formatting marks will not be displayed properly on the screen. For example, the raised dot that signifies a blank space between words may be displayed behind a character instead of in the blank space, causing the characters to look incorrect.

CONSIDER THIS

How do I know which formats to use in a flyer?

In a flyer, consider the following formatting suggestions.

- **Increase the font size of characters.** Flyers usually are posted on a bulletin board or in a window. Thus, the font size should be as large as possible so that passersby easily can read the flyer. To give the headline more impact, its font size should be larger than the font size of the text in the body copy. If possible, make the font size of the signature line larger than the body copy but smaller than the headline.
- **Change the font of characters.** Use fonts that are easy to read. Try to use only two different fonts in a flyer; for example, use one for the headline and the other for all other text. Too many fonts can make the flyer visually confusing.
- **Change the paragraph alignment.** The default alignment for paragraphs in a document is **left-aligned**, that is, flush at the left margin of the document with uneven right edges. Consider changing the alignment of some of the paragraphs to add interest and variety to the flyer.
- **Highlight key paragraphs with bullets.** A bulleted paragraph is a paragraph that begins with a dot or other symbol. Use bulleted paragraphs to highlight important points in a flyer.
- **Emphasize important words.** To call attention to certain words or lines, you can underline them, italicize them, or bold them. Use these formats sparingly, however, because overuse will minimize their effect and make the flyer look too busy.
- **Use color.** Use colors that complement each other and convey the meaning of the flyer. Vary colors in terms of hue and brightness. Headline colors, for example, can be bold and bright. Signature lines should stand out more than body copy but less than headlines. Keep in mind that too many colors can detract from the flyer and make it difficult to read.

To Center a Paragraph

1 ENTER TEXT | 2 FORMAT TEXT | 3 INSERT PICTURE | 4 FORMAT PICTURE
5 ENHANCE PAGE | 6 CORRECT & REVISE | 7 PRINT OR READ

The headline in the flyer currently is left-aligned (Figure 1–14). ***Why?*** *Word, by default left-aligns text, unless you specifically change the alignment.* You want the headline to be **centered**, that is, positioned horizontally between the left and right margins on the page. Recall that Word considers a single short line of text, such as the one-word headline, a paragraph. Thus, you will center the paragraph containing the headline. The following steps center a paragraph.

1

- Tap or click HOME on the ribbon to display the HOME tab.
- Tap or click somewhere in the paragraph to be centered (in this case, the headline) to position the insertion point in the paragraph to be formatted (Figure 1–14).

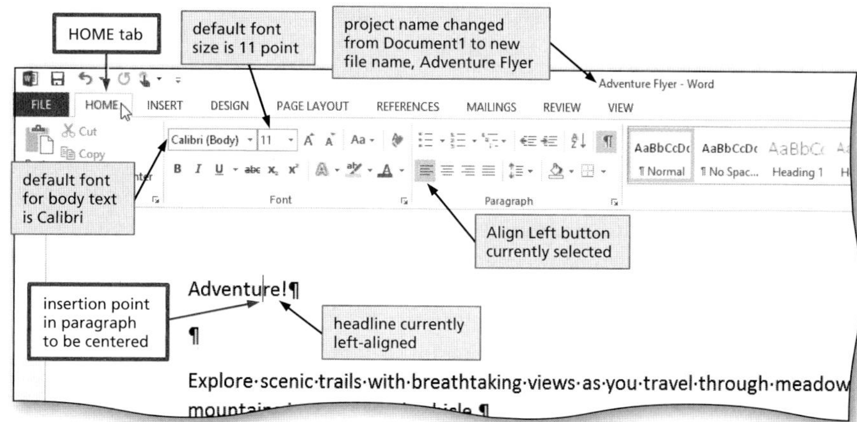

Figure 1–14

2

- Tap or click the Center button (HOME tab | Paragraph group) to center the paragraph containing the insertion point (Figure 1–15).

Q&A What if I want to return the paragraph to left-aligned?
You would tap or click the Center button again or tap or click the Align Left button (HOME tab | Paragraph group).

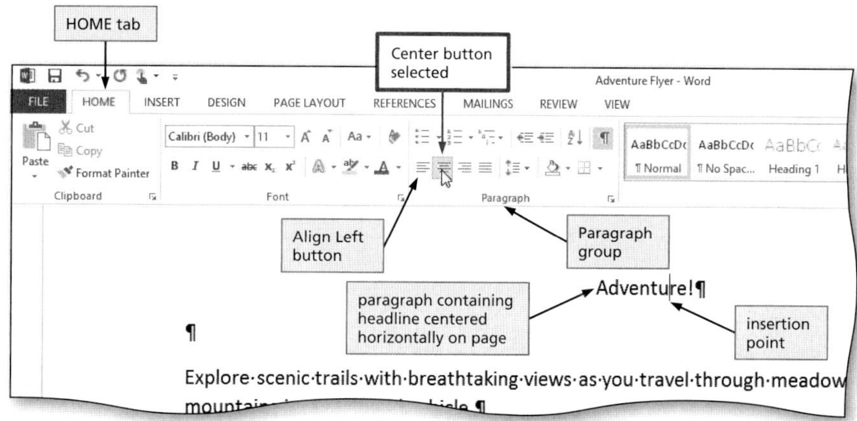

Figure 1–15

Other Ways

1. Tap 'Show Context Menu' button on mini toolbar or right-click paragraph, tap or click Paragraph on shortcut menu, tap or click Indents and Spacing tab (Paragraph dialog box), tap or click Alignment arrow, tap or click Centered, tap or click OK button
2. Tap or click Paragraph Settings Dialog Box Launcher (HOME tab or PAGE LAYOUT tab | Paragraph group), tap or click Indents and Spacing tab (Paragraph dialog box), tap or click Alignment arrow, tap or click Centered, tap or click OK button
3. Press CTRL+E

To Center Another Paragraph

In the flyer, the signature line is to be centered to match the paragraph alignment of the headline. The following steps center the signature line.

1. Tap or click somewhere in the paragraph to be centered (in this case, the signature line) to position the insertion point in the paragraph to be formatted.
2. Tap or click the Center button (HOME tab | Paragraph group) to center the paragraph containing the insertion point (shown in Figure 1–16 on the next page).

BTW
File Type
Depending on your Windows settings, the file type .docx may be displayed on the title bar immediately to the right of the file name after you save the file. The file type .docx identifies a Word 2013 document.

BTW
Touch Screen Differences
The Office and Windows interfaces may vary if you are using a touch screen. For this reason, you might notice that the function or appearance of your touch screen differs slightly from this chapter's presentation.

Formatting Single versus Multiple Paragraphs and Characters

As shown on the previous pages, to format a single paragraph, simply move the insertion point in the paragraph to make it the current paragraph, and then format the paragraph. Similarly, to format a single word, position the insertion point in the word to make it the current word, and then format the word.

To format multiple paragraphs or words, however, you first must select the paragraphs or words you want to format and then format the selection.

1 ENTER TEXT | 2 FORMAT TEXT | 3 INSERT PICTURE | 4 FORMAT PICTURE
5 ENHANCE PAGE | 6 CORRECT & REVISE | 7 PRINT OR READ

To Select a Line

The default font size of 11 point is too small for a headline in a flyer. To increase the font size of the characters in the headline, you first must select the line of text containing the headline. ***Why?*** *If you increase font size of text without selecting any text, Word will increase the font size only of the word containing the insertion point.* The following steps select a line.

- If you are using a mouse, move the pointer to the left of the line to be selected (in this case, the headline) until the pointer changes to a right-pointing block arrow (Figure 1–16).

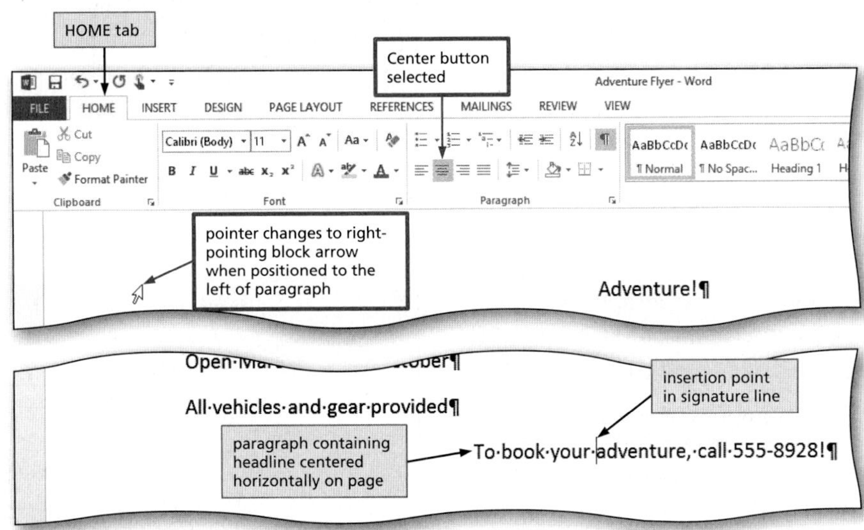

Figure 1–16

- If you are using a touch screen, double-tap to the left of the line to be selected to select the line; if you are using a mouse, while the pointer is a right-pointing block arrow, click the mouse to select the entire line to the right of the pointer (Figure 1–17).

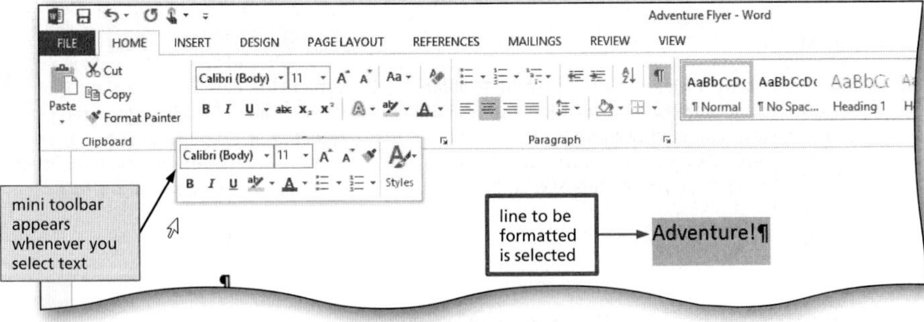

Figure 1–17

Q&A Why is the selected text shaded gray?
If your screen normally displays dark letters on a light background, which is the default setting in Word, then selected text displays with a light shading color, such as gray, on the dark letters. Note that the selection that appears on the text does not print.

Other Ways

1. Drag pointer through line
2. With insertion point at beginning of desired line, press SHIFT+DOWN ARROW

To Change the Font Size of Selected Text

The next step is to increase the font size of the characters in the selected headline. ***Why?*** *You would like the headline to be as large as possible and still fit on a single line, which in this case is 72 point.* The following steps increase the font size of the headline from 11 to 72 point.

- With the text selected, tap or click the Font Size arrow (HOME tab | Font group) to display the Font Size gallery (Figure 1–18).

Q&A Why are the font sizes in my Font Size gallery different from those in Figure 1–18?
Font sizes may vary depending on the current font and your printer driver.

What happened to the mini toolbar?
The mini toolbar disappears if you do not use it. These steps use the Font Size arrow on the HOME tab instead of the Font Size arrow on the mini toolbar.

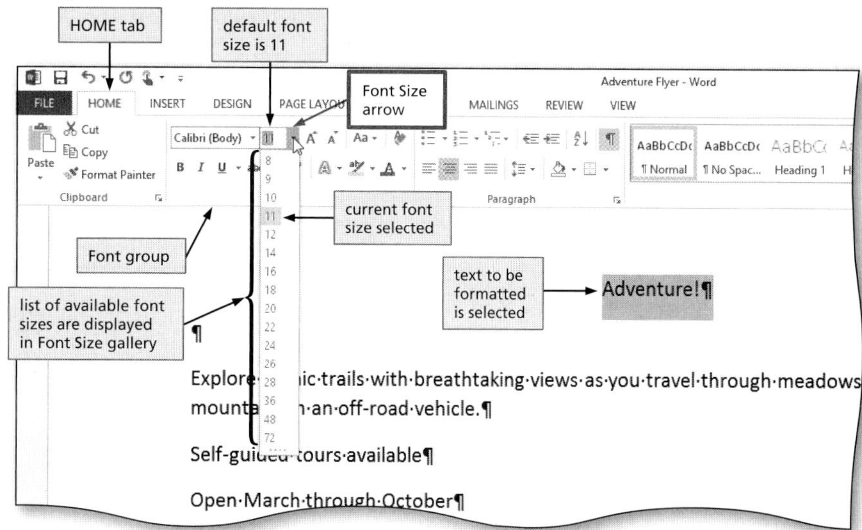

Figure 1–18

- If you are using a mouse, point to 72 in the Font Size gallery to display a live preview of the selected text at the selected point size (Figure 1–19).

Q&A Can I use live preview on a touch screen?
Live preview is not available on a touch screen.

Experiment

- If you are using a mouse, point to various font sizes in the Font Size gallery and watch the font size of the selected text change in the document window.

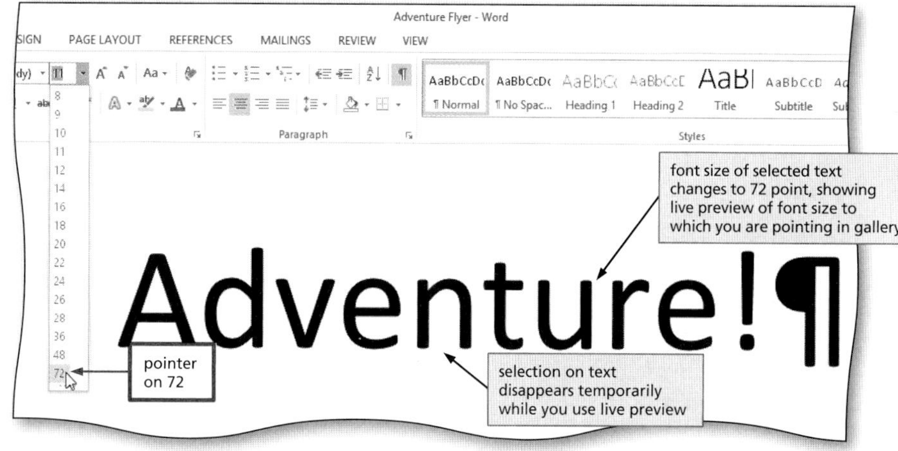

Figure 1–19

- Tap or click 72 in the Font Size gallery to increase the font size of the selected text.

Other Ways

1. Tap or click Font Size arrow on mini toolbar, tap or click desired font size in Font Size gallery
2. Tap 'Show Context Menu' button on mini toolbar or right-click selected text, tap or click Font on shortcut menu, tap or click Font tab (Font dialog box), select desired font size in Size list, tap or click OK button
3. Tap or click Font Dialog Box Launcher, tap or click Font tab (Font dialog box), select desired font size in Size list, tap or click OK button
4. Press CTRL+D, tap or click Font tab (Font dialog box), select desired font size in Size list, tap or click OK button

To Change the Font of Selected Text

The default theme font for headings is Calibri Light and for all other text, called body text in Word, is Calibri. Many other fonts are available, however, so that you can add variety to documents.

The following steps change the font of the headline from Calibri to Berlin Sans FB Demi. ***Why?*** *To draw more attention to the headline, you change its font so that it differs from the font of other text in the flyer.*

1

- With the text selected, tap or click the Font arrow (HOME tab | Font group) to display the Font gallery (Figure 1–20).

Q&A

Will the fonts in my Font gallery be the same as those in Figure 1–20?
Your list of available fonts may differ, depending on the type of printer you are using and other settings.

What if the text no longer is selected?
Follow the steps on page WD 16 to select a line.

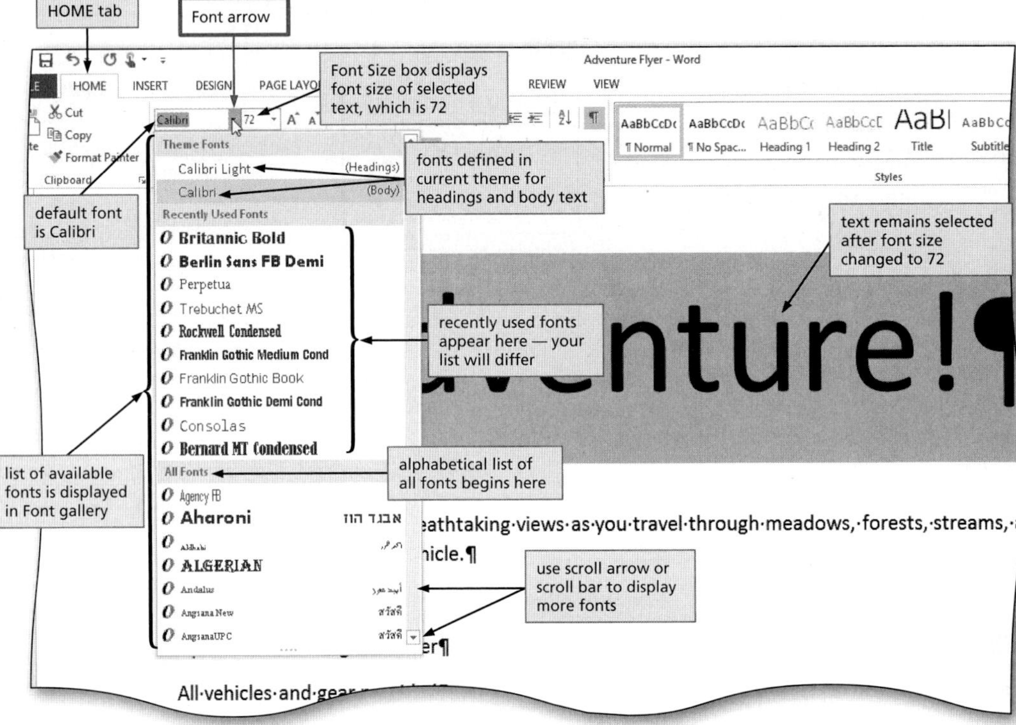

Figure 1–20

2

- If necessary, scroll through the Font gallery to display Berlin Sans FB Demi (or a similar font).
- If you are using a mouse, point to Berlin Sans FB Demi (or a similar font) to display a live preview of the selected text in the selected font (Figure 1–21).

Experiment

- If you are using a mouse, point to various fonts in the Font gallery and watch the font of the selected text change in the document window.

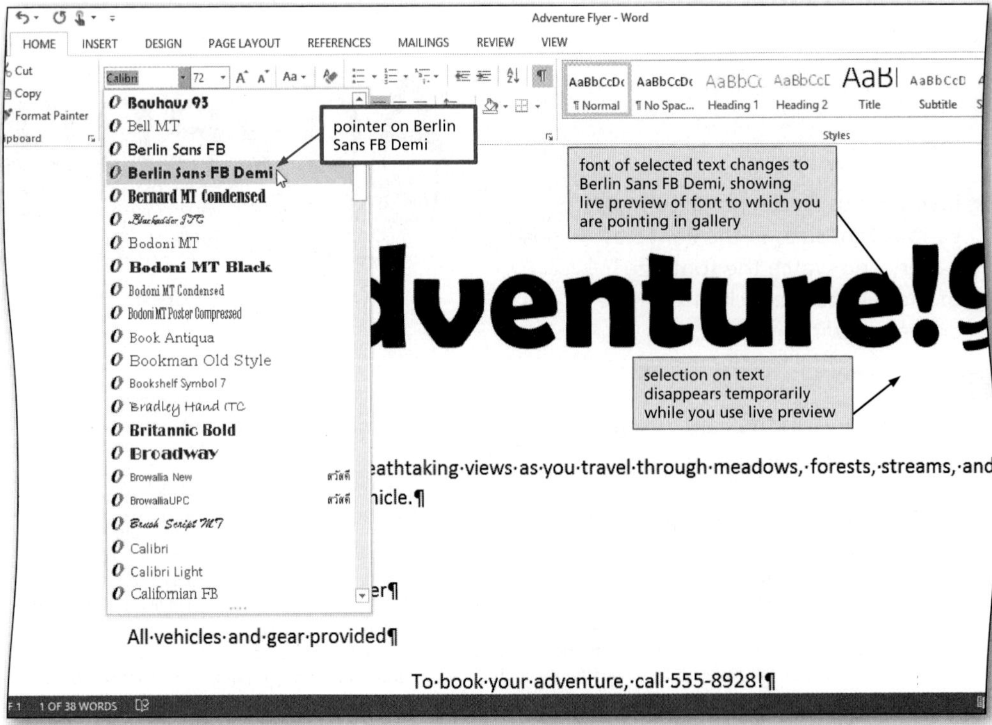

Figure 1–21

- Tap or click Berlin Sans FB Demi (or a similar font) to change the font of the selected text.

Q&A If the font I want to use appears in the Recently Used Fonts list in the Font gallery, could I tap or click it there instead?

Yes.

Other Ways

1. Tap or click Font arrow on mini toolbar, tap or click desired font in Font gallery
2. Tap 'Show Context Menu' button on mini toolbar or right-click selected text, tap or click Font on shortcut menu, tap or click Font tab (Font dialog box), select desired font in Font list, tap or click OK button
3. Tap or click Font Dialog Box Launcher (HOME tab | Font group), tap or click Font tab (Font dialog box), select desired font in Font list, tap or click OK button
4. Press CTRL+D, tap or click Font tab (Font dialog box), select desired font in Font list, tap or click OK button

To Change the Case of Selected Text

1 ENTER TEXT | 2 FORMAT TEXT | 3 INSERT PICTURE | 4 FORMAT PICTURE
5 ENHANCE PAGE | 6 CORRECT & REVISE | 7 PRINT OR READ

The headline currently shows the first letter in each word capitalized, which sometimes is referred to as initial cap. The following steps change the headline to uppercase. ***Why?*** *To draw more attention to the headline, you would like the entire line of text to be capitalized, or in uppercase letters.*

- With the text selected, tap or click the Change Case button (HOME tab | Font group) to display the Change Case gallery (Figure 1–22).

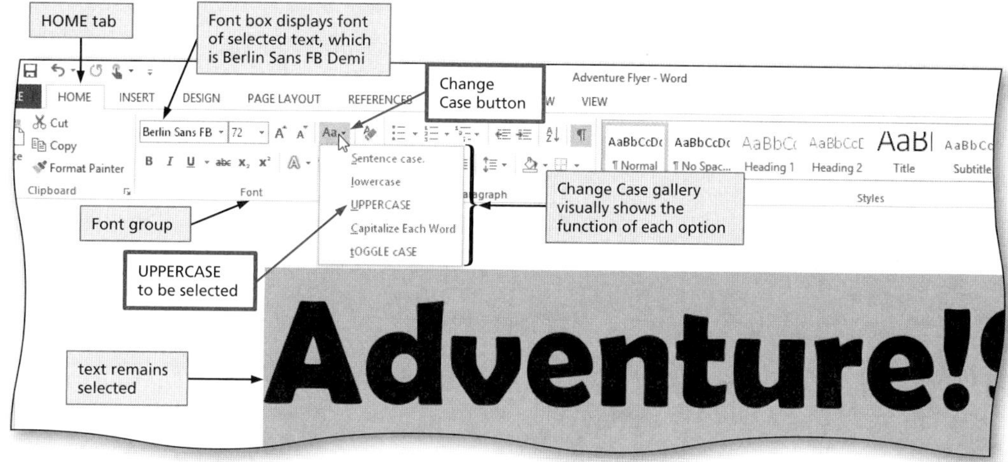

Figure 1–22

- Tap or click UPPERCASE in the Change Case gallery to change the case of the selected text (Figure 1–23).

Figure 1–23

Q&A What if a ruler appears on the screen or the pointer shape changes?

If you are using a mouse, depending on the position of your pointer and locations you click on the screen, a ruler may automatically appear or the pointer's shape may change. Simply move the mouse and the ruler should disappear and/or the pointer shape will change.

Other Ways

1. Tap 'Show Context Menu' button on mini toolbar or right-click selected text, tap or click Font on shortcut menu, tap or click Font tab (Font dialog box), select All caps in Effects area, tap or click OK button
2. Tap or click Font Dialog Box Launcher (HOME tab | Font group), tap or click Font tab (Font dialog box), select All caps in Effects area, tap or click OK button
3. Press SHIFT+F3 repeatedly until text is desired case

To Apply a Text Effect to Selected Text

Word provides many text effects to add interest and variety to text. The following steps apply a text effect to the headline. ***Why?*** *You would like the text in the headline to be even more noticeable.*

1

- With the text selected, tap or click the 'Text Effects and Typography' button (HOME tab | Font group) to display the Text Effects and Typography gallery (Figure 1–24).

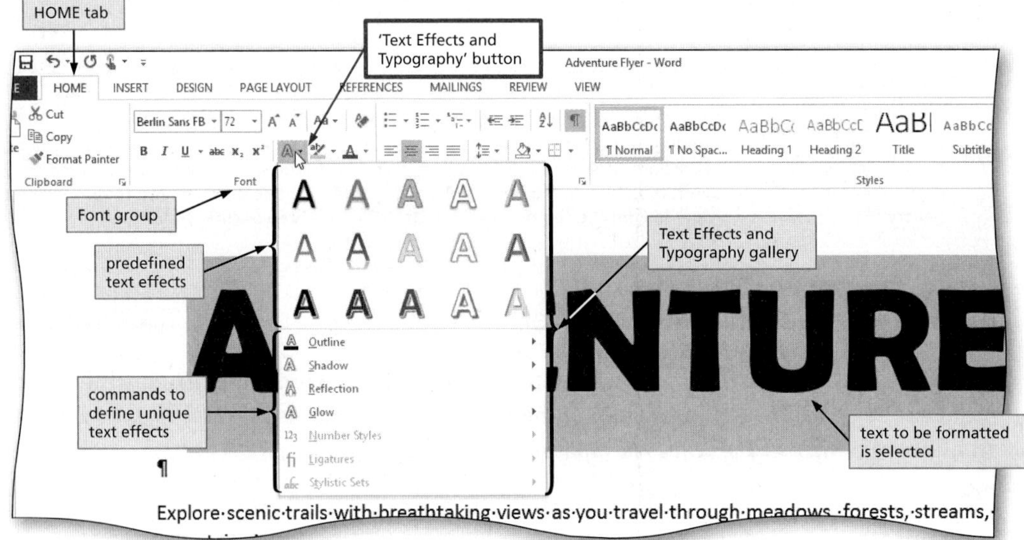

Figure 1–24

2

- If you are using a mouse, point to 'Fill - White, Outline - Accent 1, Glow - Accent 1' (fourth text effect in second row) to display a live preview of the selected text in the selected text effect (Figure 1–25).

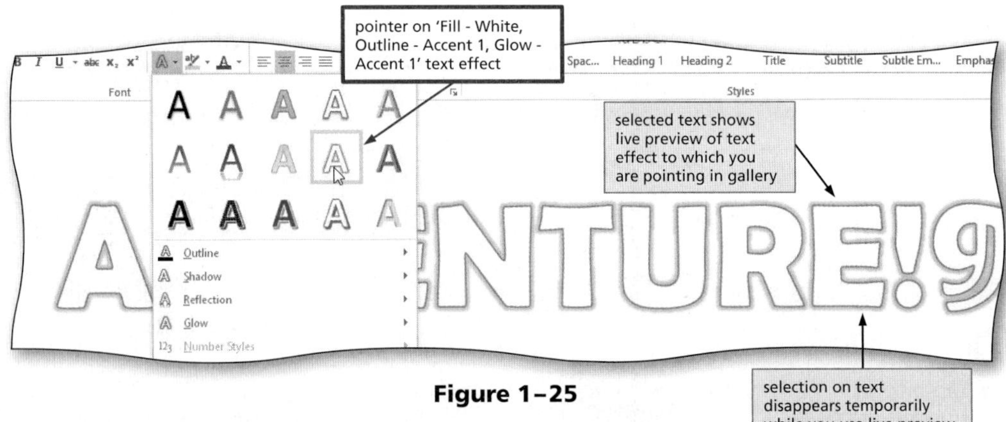

Figure 1–25

Experiment

- If you are using a mouse, point to various text effects in the Text Effects and Typography gallery and watch the text effects of the selected text change in the document window.

3

- Tap or click 'Fill - White, Outline - Accent 1, Glow - Accent 1' to change the text effect of the selected text.

4

- Tap or click anywhere in the document window to remove the selection from the selected text.

Other Ways

1. Tap 'Show Context Menu' button on mini toolbar or right-click selected text, tap or click Font on shortcut menu, tap or click Font tab (Font dialog box), tap or click Text Effects button, expand TEXT FILL or TEXT OUTLINE section and then select the desired text effect(s) (Format Text Effects dialog box), tap or click OK button, tap or click OK button
2. Tap or click Font Dialog Box Launcher (HOME tab | Font group), tap or click Font tab (Font dialog box), tap or click Text Effects button, expand TEXT FILL or TEXT OUTLINE section and then select desired text effect (Format Text Effects dialog box), tap or click OK button, tap or click OK button

To Shade a Paragraph

When you **shade** text, Word colors the rectangular area behind any text or graphics. If the text to shade is a paragraph, Word shades the area from the left margin to the right margin of the current paragraph. To shade a paragraph, place the insertion point in the paragraph. To shade any other text, you must first select the text to be shaded.

This flyer uses green as the shading color for the headline. ***Why?*** *To make the headline of the flyer more eye-catching, you shade it.* The following steps shade a paragraph.

1

- Tap or click somewhere in the paragraph to be shaded (in this case, the headline) to position the insertion point in the paragraph to be formatted.
- Tap or click the Shading arrow (HOME tab | Paragraph group) to display the Shading gallery (Figure 1–26).

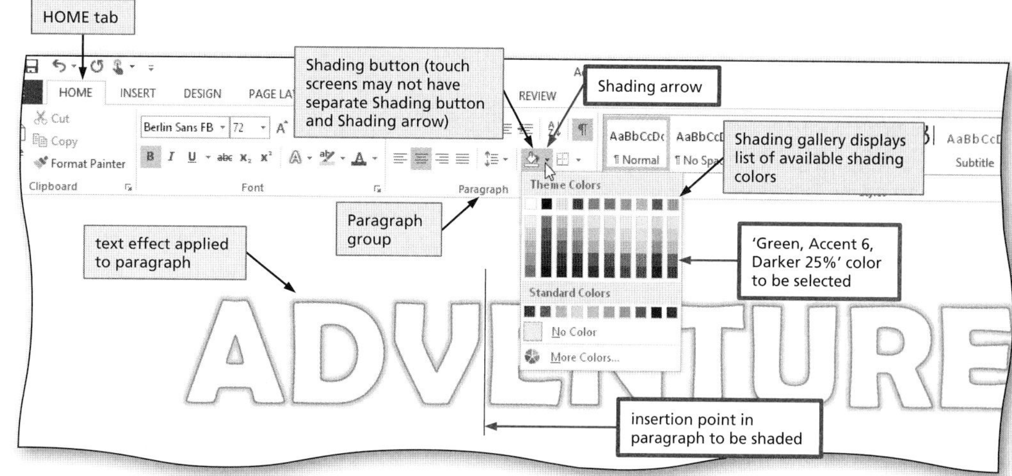

Figure 1–26

Q&A If I am using a mouse, what if I click the Shading button by mistake?
Click the Shading arrow and proceed with Step 2. If you are using a touch screen, you may not have a separate Shading button.

Experiment

- If you are using a mouse, point to various colors in the Shading gallery and watch the shading color of the current paragraph change.

2

- Tap or click 'Green, Accent 6, Darker 25%' (rightmost color in fifth row) to shade the current paragraph (Figure 1–27).

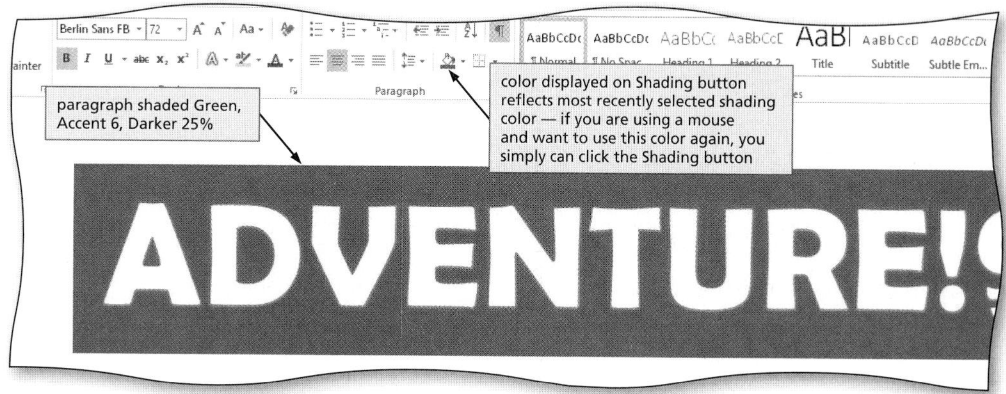

Figure 1–27

Q&A What if I apply a dark shading color to dark text?
When the font color of text is Automatic, it usually is black. If you select a dark shading color, Word automatically may change the text color to white so that the shaded text is easier to read.

Other Ways

1. Tap or click Borders arrow (HOME tab | Paragraph group), tap or click Borders and Shading, tap or click Shading tab (Borders and Shading dialog box), tap or click Fill arrow, select desired color, tap or click OK button

To Select Multiple Lines

The next formatting step for the flyer is to increase the font size of the characters between the headline and the signature line. ***Why?*** *You want this text to be easier to read from a distance.*

To change the font size of the characters in multiple lines, you first must select all the lines to be formatted. The following steps select multiple lines.

1

- Scroll, if necessary, so that all text below the headline is displayed on the screen.
- If you are using a touch screen, tap to position the insertion point in the text to select; if you are using a mouse, move the pointer to the left of the first paragraph to be selected until the pointer changes to a right-pointing block arrow (Figure 1–28).

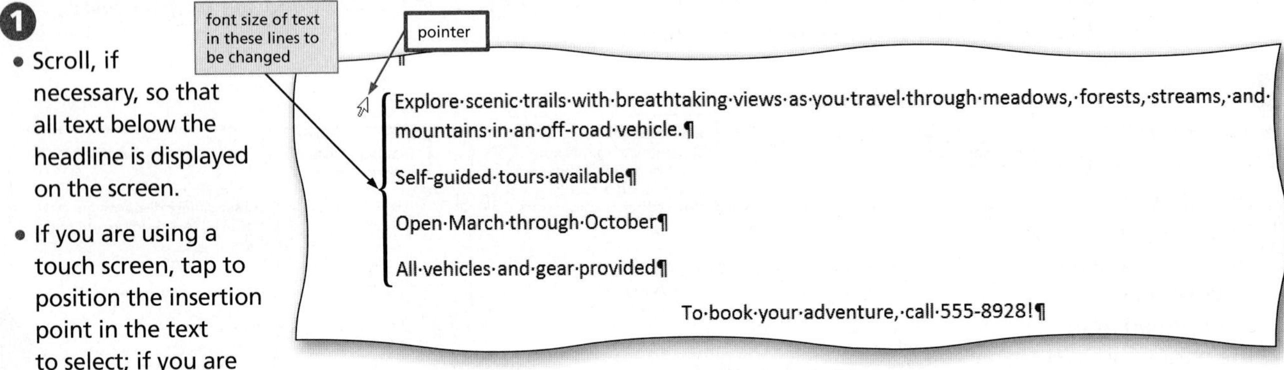
font size of text in these lines to be changed
pointer
Explore·scenic·trails·with·breathtaking·views·as·you·travel·through·meadows,·forests,·streams,·and·mountains·in·an·off-road·vehicle.¶
Self-guided·tours·available¶
Open·March·through·October¶
All·vehicles·and·gear·provided¶
To·book·your·adventure,·call·555-8928!¶

Figure 1–28

2

- If you are using a touch screen, drag the selection handle(s) as necessary to select the text that will be formatted; if you are using a mouse, while the pointer is a right-pointing block arrow, drag downward to select all lines that will be formatted (Figure 1–29).

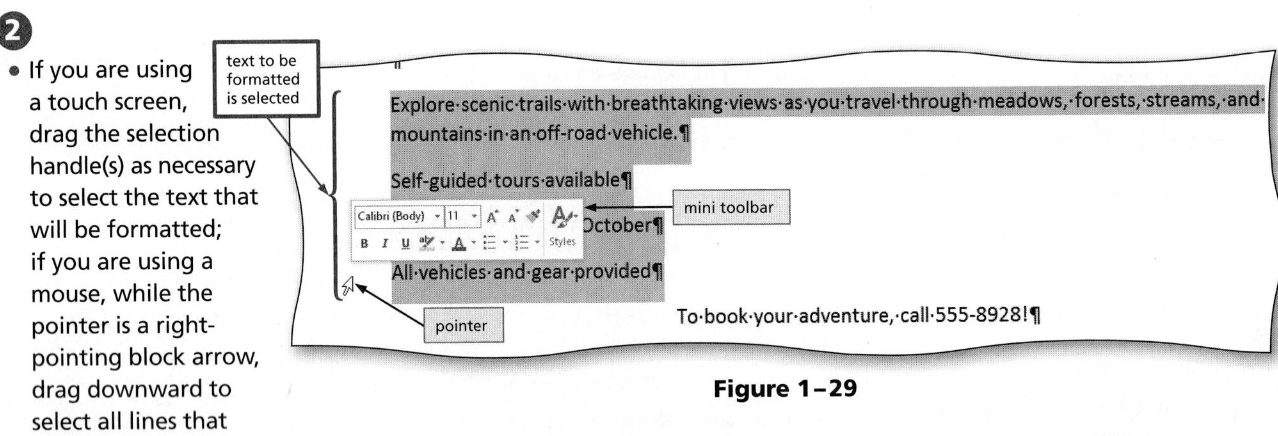
text to be formatted is selected
Explore·scenic·trails·with·breathtaking·views·as·you·travel·through·meadows,·forests,·streams,·and·mountains·in·an·off-road·vehicle.¶
Self-guided·tours·available¶
Calibri (Body)
11
Styles
October¶
mini toolbar
All·vehicles·and·gear·provided¶
pointer
To·book·your·adventure,·call·555-8928!¶

Figure 1–29

Q&A What is a selection handle?
When working on a touch screen, a **selection handle** (small circle) appears below the insertion point. Using a fingertip, you drag a selection handle to select text.

Other Ways

1. With insertion point at beginning of desired line, press SHIFT+DOWN ARROW repeatedly until all lines are selected

To Change the Font Size of Selected Text

The characters between the headline and the signature line in the flyer currently are 11 point. To make them easier to read from a distance, this flyer uses a 24-point font size for these characters. The following steps change the font size of the selected text.

1 With the text selected, tap or click the Font Size arrow (HOME tab | Font group) to display the Font Size gallery.

2 Tap or click 24 in the Font Size gallery to increase the font size of the selected text.

3 Tap or click anywhere in the document window to remove the selection from the text.

4 If necessary, scroll so that you can see all the resized text on the screen (Figure 1–30).

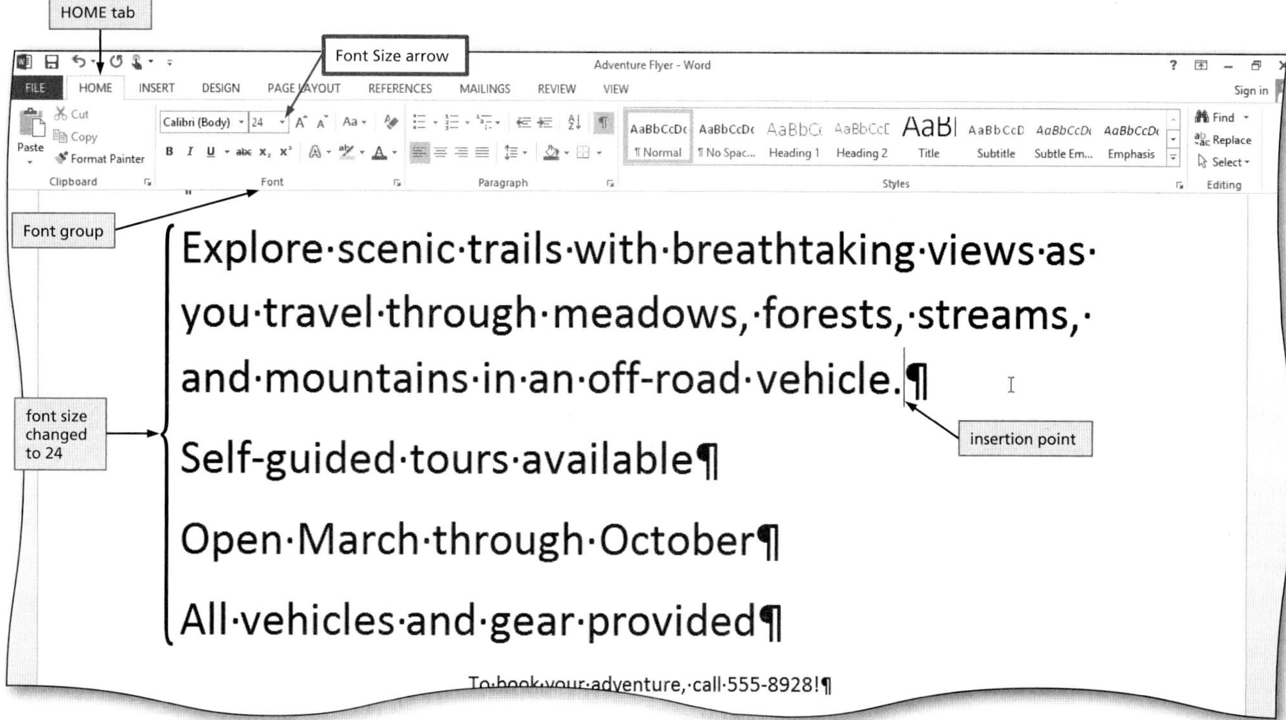
HOME tab
Font Size arrow
Font group
font size changed to 24
insertion point
Explore·scenic·trails·with·breathtaking·views·as·you·travel·through·meadows,·forests,·streams,·and·mountains·in·an·off-road·vehicle.¶
Self-guided·tours·available¶
Open·March·through·October¶
All·vehicles·and·gear·provided¶
To·book·your·adventure,·call·555-8928!¶

Figure 1–30

To Bullet a List of Paragraphs

1 ENTER TEXT | 2 FORMAT TEXT | 3 INSERT PICTURE | 4 FORMAT PICTURE
5 ENHANCE PAGE | 6 CORRECT & REVISE | 7 PRINT OR READ

A **bulleted list** is a series of paragraphs, each beginning with a bullet character. The next step is to format the three paragraphs about the tours that are above the signature line in the flyer as a bulleted list.

To format a list of paragraphs with bullets, you first must select all the lines in the paragraphs. ***Why?*** *If you do not select all paragraphs, Word will place a bullet only in the paragraph containing the insertion point.* The following steps bullet a list of paragraphs.

1

- If you are using a touch screen, tap to position the insertion point in the text to select; if you are using a mouse, move the pointer to the left of the first paragraph to be selected until the pointer changes to a right-pointing block arrow.

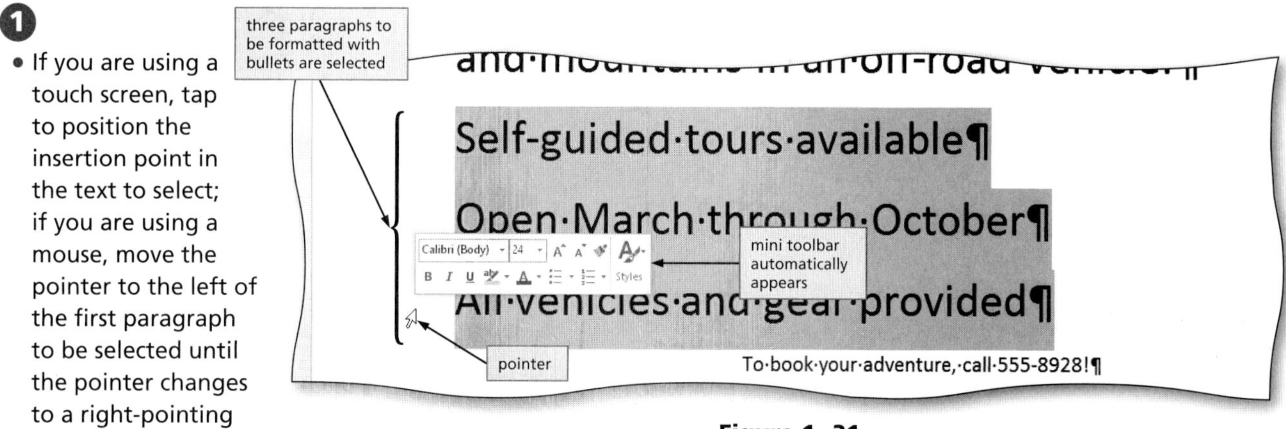
three paragraphs to be formatted with bullets are selected
Self-guided·tours·available¶
Open·March·through·October¶
All·vehicles·and·gear·provided¶
mini toolbar automatically appears
pointer
To·book·your·adventure,·call·555-8928!¶

Figure 1–31

- If you are using a touch screen, drag the selection handle(s) as necessary to select the text that will be formatted; if you are using a mouse, drag downward until all paragraphs that will be formatted with a bullet character are selected (Figure 1–31).

- Tap or click the Bullets button (HOME tab | Paragraph group) to place a bullet character at the beginning of each selected paragraph (Figure 1–32).

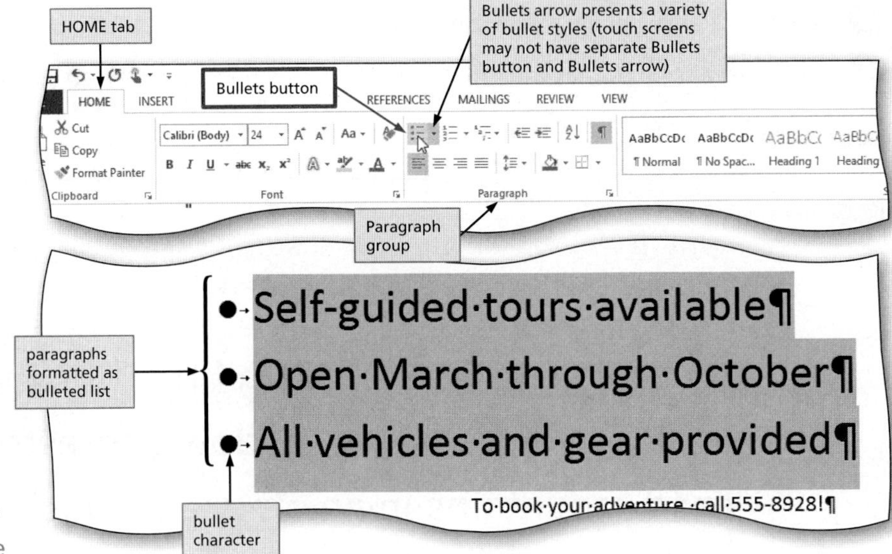

Figure 1–32

Q&A

What if my screen displays a Bullets gallery?
If you are using a touch screen, you may not have a separate Bullets button and Bullets arrow. In this case, select the desired bullet style in the Bullets gallery.

If I am using a mouse, what if I accidentally click the Bullets arrow?
Press the ESCAPE key to remove the Bullets gallery from the screen and then repeat Step 2. If you are using a touch screen, you may not have a separate Bullets button and Bullets arrow.

How do I remove bullets from a list or paragraph?
Select the list or paragraph and then tap or click the Bullets button again.

Other Ways

1. Press and hold or right-click selected paragraphs, tap or click Bullets button on mini toolbar, if necessary select bullet style in Bullets gallery

1 ENTER TEXT | 2 FORMAT TEXT | 3 INSERT PICTURE | 4 FORMAT PICTURE
5 ENHANCE PAGE | 6 CORRECT & REVISE | 7 PRINT OR READ

To Undo and Redo an Action

Word provides a means of canceling your recent command(s) or action(s). For example, if you format text incorrectly, you can undo the format and try it again. When you point to the Undo button, Word displays the action you can undo as part of a ScreenTip.

If, after you undo an action, you decide you did not want to perform the undo, you can redo the undone action. Word does not allow you to undo or redo some actions, such as saving or printing a document. The following steps undo the bullet format just applied and then redo the bullet format. ***Why?*** *These steps illustrate the undo and redo actions.*

1

- Tap or click the Undo button on the Quick Access Toolbar to reverse your most recent action (in this case, remove the bullets from the paragraphs) (Figure 1–33).

Figure 1–33

- Tap or click the Redo button on the Quick Access Toolbar to reverse your most recent undo (in this case, place a bullet character on the paragraphs again) (shown in Figure 1–32).

Other Ways

1. Press CTRL+Z to undo; press CTRL+Y to redo

To Italicize Text

Italic text has a slanted appearance. The next step is to italicize the word, breathtaking, in the flyer to further emphasize it. As with a single paragraph, if you want to format a single word, you do not need to select it. ***Why?*** *To format a single word, you simply position the insertion point somewhere in the word and apply the desired format.* The following step italicizes a word.

- Tap or click somewhere in the word to be italicized (breathtaking, in this case) to position the insertion point in the word to be formatted.
- Tap or click the Italic button (HOME tab | Font group) to italicize the word containing the insertion point (Figure 1–34).

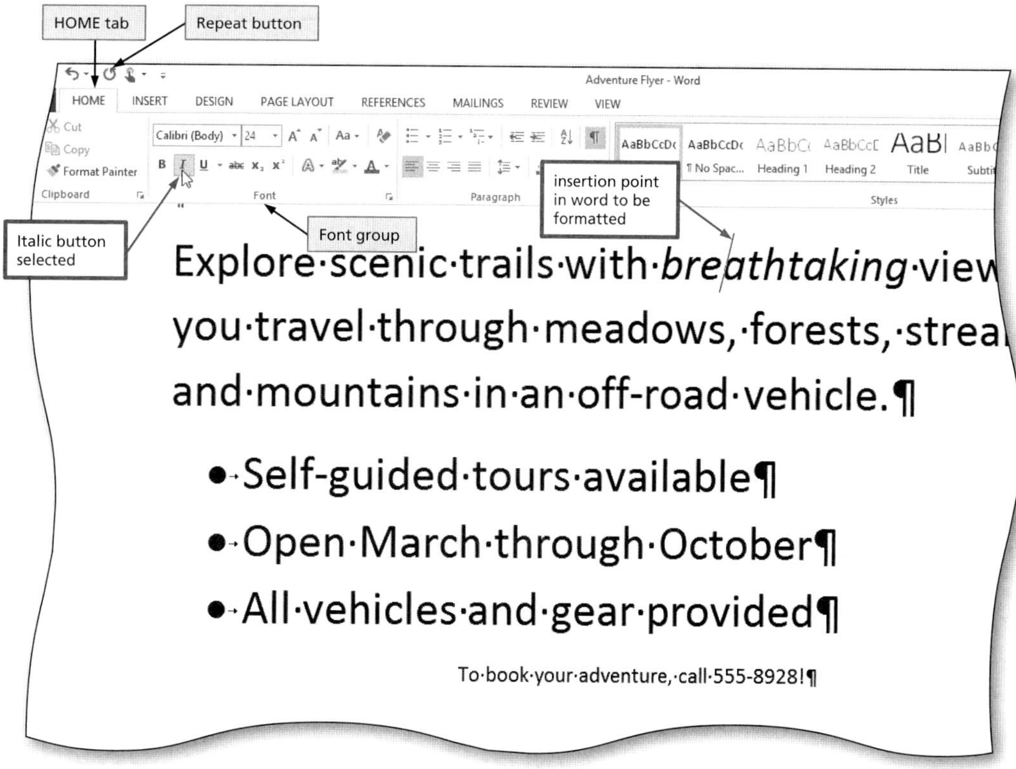

Figure 1–34

Q&A

How would I remove an italic format?
You would tap or click the Italic button a second time, or you immediately could tap or click the Undo button on the Quick Access Toolbar or press CTRL+Z.

How can I tell what formatting has been applied to text?
The selected buttons and boxes on the HOME tab show formatting characteristics of the location of the insertion point. With the insertion point in the word, breathtaking, the HOME tab shows these formats: 24-point Calibri italic font.

Why did the appearance of the Redo button change?
It changed to a Repeat button. When it is a Repeat button, you can tap or click it to repeat your last action. For example, you can select different text and then click the Repeat button to apply (repeat) the italic format to the selected text.

Other Ways

1. Tap or click Italic button on mini toolbar
2. Tap 'Show Context Menu' button on mini toolbar or right-click selected text, tap or click Font on shortcut menu, tap or click Font tab (Font dialog box), tap or click Italic in Font style list, tap or click OK button
3. Tap or click Font Dialog Box Launcher (HOME tab | Font group), tap or click Font tab (Font dialog box), tap or click Italic in Font style list, tap or click OK button
4. Press CTRL+I

To Color Text

The following steps change the color of the word, breathtaking. ***Why?*** *To emphasize the word even more, you change its color to a shade of orange.*

1

- With the insertion point in the word to format, tap or click the Font Color arrow (HOME tab | Font group) to display the Font Color gallery (Figure 1–35).

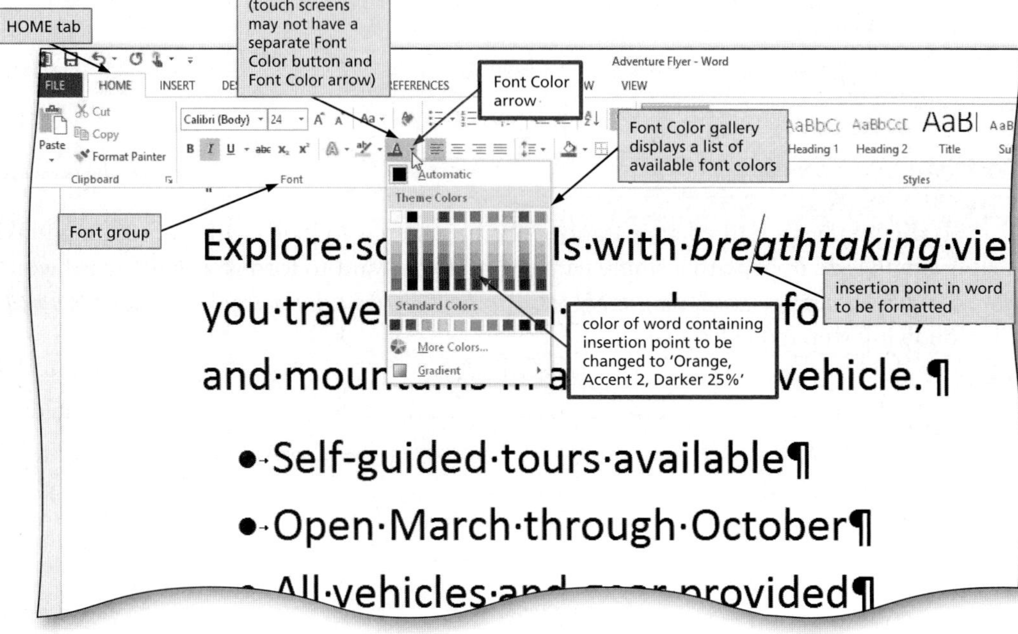

Figure 1–35

Q&A If I am using a mouse, what if I click the Font Color button by mistake?
Click the Font Color arrow and then proceed with Step 2. If you are using a touch screen, you may not have a separate Font Color button.

Experiment

- If you are using a mouse, point to various colors in the Font Color gallery and watch the color of the current word change.

2

- Tap or click 'Orange, Accent 2, Darker 25%' (sixth color in fifth row) to change the color of the text (Figure 1–36).

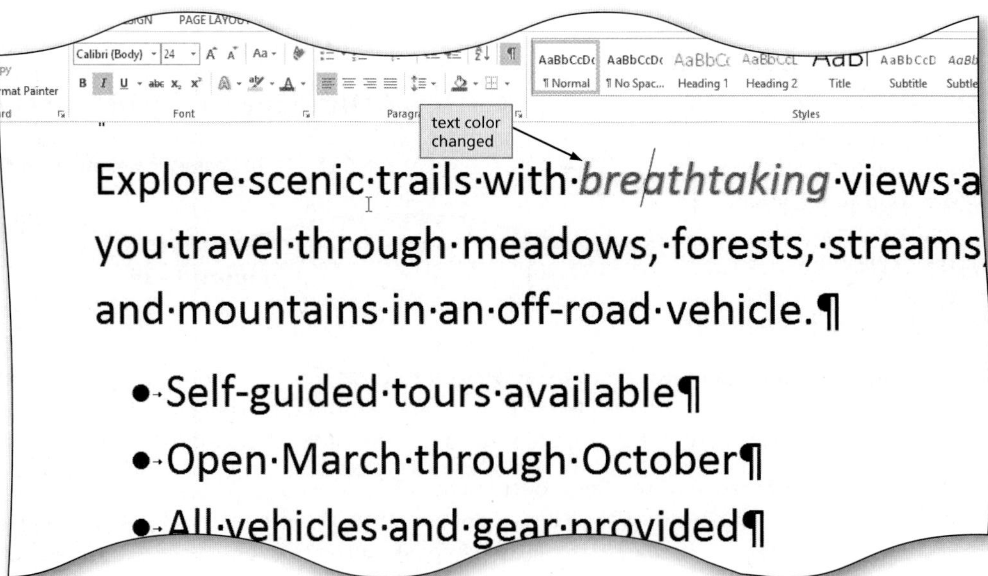

Figure 1–36

Q&A How would I change the text color back to black?
You would position the insertion point in the word or select the text, tap or click the Font Color arrow (HOME tab | Font group) again, and then tap or click Automatic in the Font Color gallery.

Other Ways

1. Tap or click Font Color arrow on mini toolbar, tap or click desired color
2. Tap 'Show Context Menu' button on mini toolbar or right-click selected text, tap or click Font on shortcut menu, tap or click Font tab (Font dialog box), tap or click Font color arrow, tap or click desired color, tap or click OK button
3. Tap or click Font Dialog Box Launcher (HOME tab | Font group), tap or click Font tab (Font dialog box), tap or click Font color arrow, tap or click desired color, tap or click OK button

To Use the Mini Toolbar to Format Text

Recall from the Office and Windows chapter at the beginning of this book that the mini toolbar automatically appears based on certain tasks you perform. ***Why?*** *Word places commonly used buttons and boxes on the mini toolbar for your convenience. If you do not use the mini toolbar, it disappears from the screen.* All commands on the mini toolbar also exist on the ribbon.

The following steps use the mini toolbar to change the color and font size of text in the signature line of the flyer.

- If you are using a touch screen, double-tap to the left of the line to be selected to select the line, and then tap the selection to display the mini toolbar; if you are using a mouse, move the pointer to the left of the line to be selected until the pointer changes to a right-pointing block arrow and then click to select the line and display the mini toolbar (Figure 1–37).

mini toolbar
line selected
pointer is right-pointing block arrow

Figure 1–37

Q&A Why does my mini toolbar look different than the one in Figure 1–37?
If you are using a touch screen, the buttons and boxes on the mini toolbar differ. For example, it contains a 'Show Context Menu' button at the far-right edge, which you tap to display a shortcut menu.

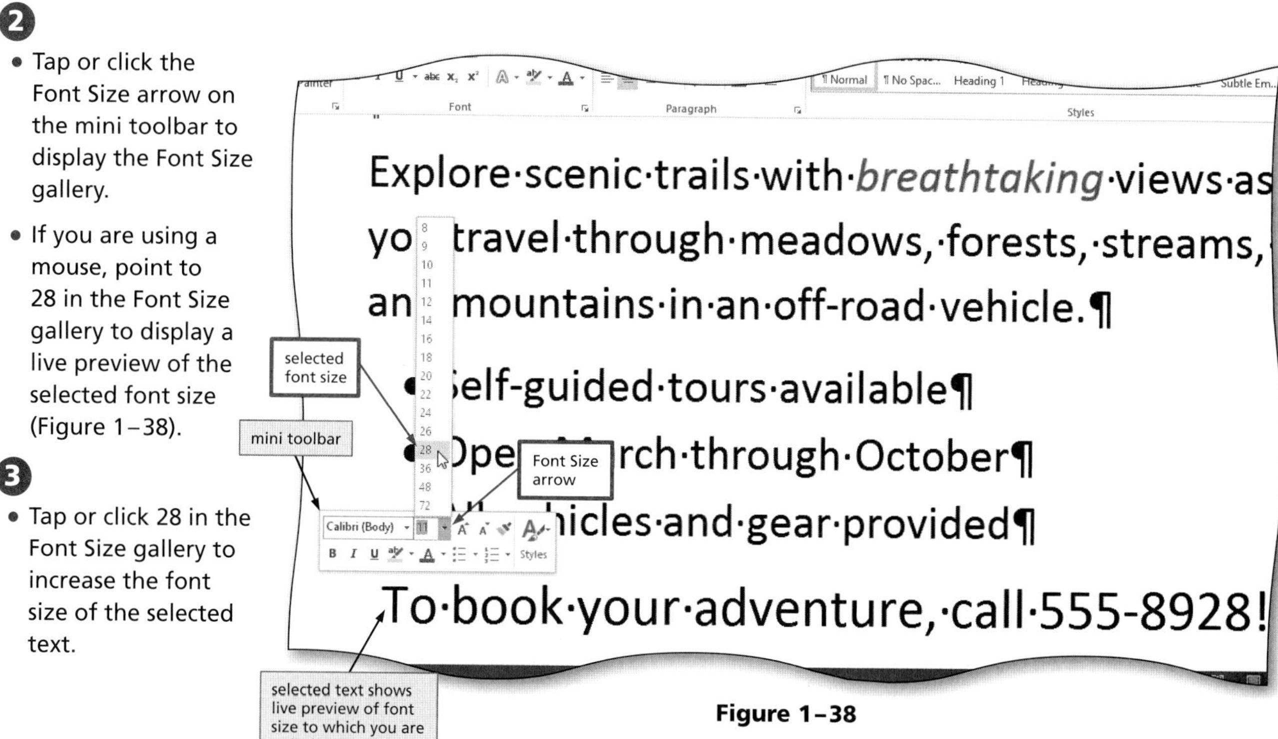

2

- Tap or click the Font Size arrow on the mini toolbar to display the Font Size gallery.
- If you are using a mouse, point to 28 in the Font Size gallery to display a live preview of the selected font size (Figure 1–38).

3

- Tap or click 28 in the Font Size gallery to increase the font size of the selected text.

Figure 1–38

- With the text still selected and the mini toolbar still displayed, tap or click the Font Color arrow on the mini toolbar to display the Font Color gallery.
- If you are using a mouse, point to 'Orange, Accent 2, Darker 25%' (sixth color in the fifth row) to display a live preview of the selected font color (Figure 1–39).

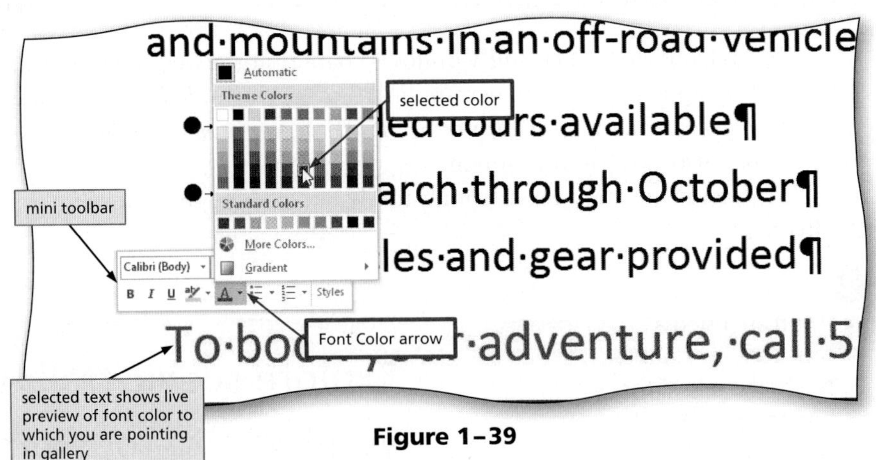

Figure 1–39

- Tap or click 'Orange, Accent 2, Darker 25%' to change the color of the selected text.
- Tap or click anywhere in the document window to remove the selection from the text.

To Select a Group of Words

1 ENTER TEXT | 2 FORMAT TEXT | 3 INSERT PICTURE | 4 FORMAT PICTURE
5 ENHANCE PAGE | 6 CORRECT & REVISE | 7 PRINT OR READ

To emphasize the contact phone number (555-8928), this text is underlined in the flyer. Because the phone number is separated with a hyphen, Word considers it a group of words. To format a group of words, you first must select them. ***Why?*** *If you underline text without selecting any text first, Word will underline only the word containing the insertion point.* The following steps select a group of words.

- If you are using a touch screen, tap to position the insertion point in the text you want to select; if you are using a mouse, position the pointer immediately to the left of the first character of the text to be selected, in this case, the 5 in 555 (Figure 1–40).

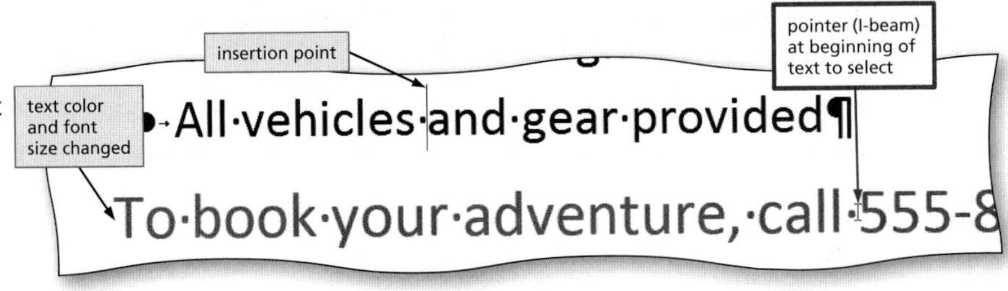

Figure 1–40

Q&A Why did the shape of the pointer change?
The pointer's shape is an I-beam when positioned in unselected text in the document window.

- If you are using a touch screen, drag the selection handle(s) to select the text to be formatted; if you are using a mouse, drag the pointer through the last character of the text to be selected, in this case, the 8 in the phone number (Figure 1–41).

Figure 1–41

Q&A Why did the pointer shape change again?
When the pointer is positioned in selected text, its shape is a left-pointing block arrow.

Other Ways

1. With insertion point at beginning of first word in group, press CTRL+SHIFT+RIGHT ARROW repeatedly until all words are selected

To Underline Text

1 ENTER TEXT | 2 FORMAT TEXT | 3 INSERT PICTURE | 4 FORMAT PICTURE
5 ENHANCE PAGE | 6 CORRECT & REVISE | 7 PRINT OR READ

Underlined text prints with an underscore (_) below each character. In the flyer, the contact phone number, 555-8928, in the signature line is underlined. ***Why?*** *Underlines are used to emphasize or draw attention to specific text.* The following step formats selected text with an underline.

1

- With the text selected, tap or click the Underline button (HOME tab | Font group) to underline the selected text (Figure 1–42).

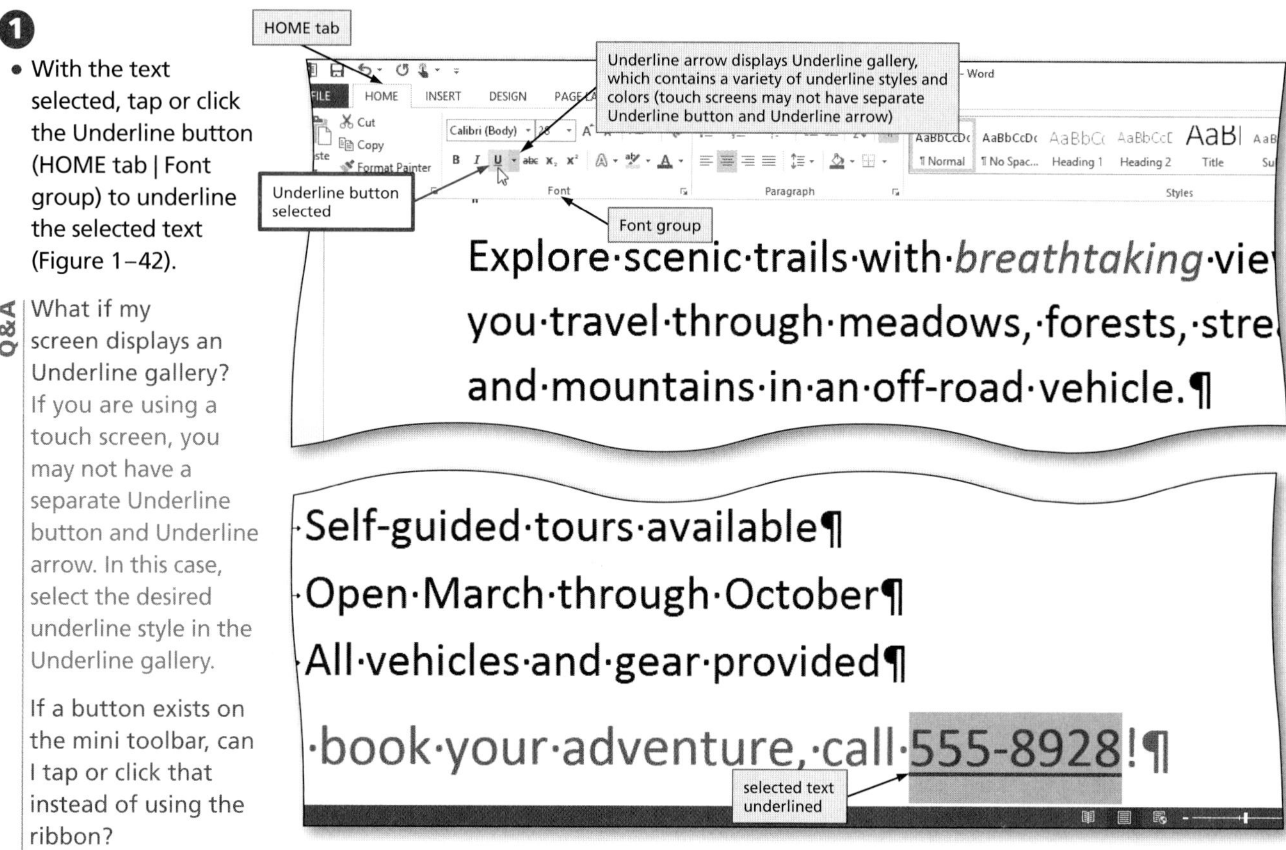

Figure 1–42

Q&A

What if my screen displays an Underline gallery?
If you are using a touch screen, you may not have a separate Underline button and Underline arrow. In this case, select the desired underline style in the Underline gallery.

If a button exists on the mini toolbar, can I tap or click that instead of using the ribbon?
Yes.

How would I remove an underline?
You would tap or click the Underline button a second time, or you immediately could tap or click the Undo button on the Quick Access Toolbar.

Other Ways

1. Tap or click Underline button on mini toolbar
2. Tap 'Show Context Menu' button on mini toolbar or right-click text, tap or click Font on shortcut menu, tap or click Font tab (Font dialog box), tap or click Underline style box arrow, tap or click desired underline style, tap or click OK button
3. Tap or click Font Dialog Box Launcher (HOME tab | Font group), tap or click Font tab (Font dialog box), tap or click Underline style arrow, tap or click desired underline style, tap or click OK button
4. Press CTRL+U

To Bold Text

1 ENTER TEXT | 2 FORMAT TEXT | 3 INSERT PICTURE | 4 FORMAT PICTURE
5 ENHANCE PAGE | 6 CORRECT & REVISE | 7 PRINT OR READ

Bold characters appear somewhat thicker and darker than those that are not bold. The steps on the next page format the text, off-road, in bold characters. ***Why?*** *To further emphasize this text, it is bold in the flyer.* Recall that if you want to format a single word, you simply position the insertion point in the word and then format the word. To format text that consists of more than one word, as you have learned previously, you select the text first.

- Select the text to be formatted (the text, off-road, in this case); that is, if you are using a touch screen, tap to position the insertion point in the text you want to select and then drag the selection handle(s) to select the text to be formatted; if you are using a mouse, position the pointer immediately to the left of the first character of the text to be selected and then drag the pointer through the last character of the text to be selected.

- With the text selected, tap or click the Bold button (HOME tab | Font group) to bold the selected text (Figure 1–43).

Q&A How would I remove a bold format?
You would tap or click the Bold button a second time, or you immediately could tap or click the Undo button on the Quick Access Toolbar.

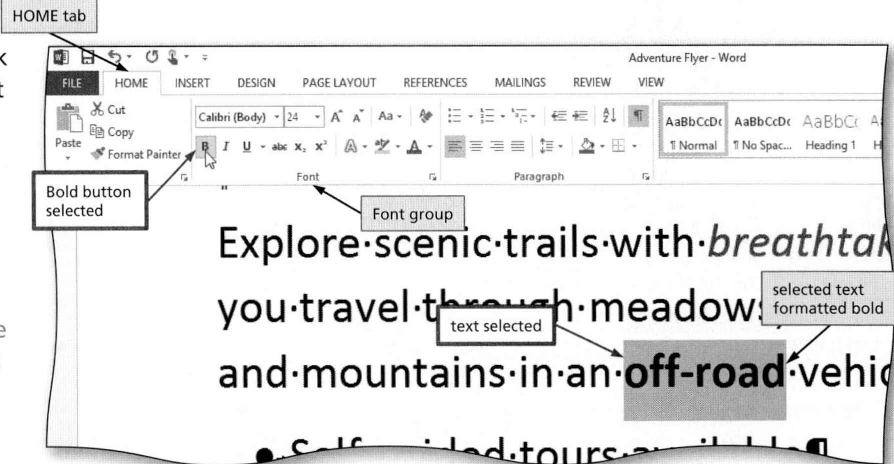
HOME tab
Bold button selected
Font group
text selected
selected text formatted bold
Explore·scenic·trails·with·breathta
you·travel·through·meadows
and·mountains·in·an·off-road·vehi

Figure 1–43

- Tap or click anywhere in the document window to remove the selection from the screen.

Other Ways

1. Tap or click Bold button on mini toolbar
2. Tap 'Show Context Menu' button on mini toolbar or right-click selected text, tap or click Font on shortcut menu, tap or click Font tab (Font dialog box), tap or click Bold in Font style list, tap or click OK button
3. Tap or click Font Dialog Box Launcher (HOME tab | Font group), tap or click Font tab (Font dialog box), tap or click Bold in Font style list, tap or click OK button
4. Press CTRL+B

1 ENTER TEXT | 2 FORMAT TEXT | 3 INSERT PICTURE | 4 FORMAT PICTURE
5 ENHANCE PAGE | 6 CORRECT & REVISE | 7 PRINT OR READ

To Zoom One Page

Earlier in this chapter, you changed the zoom to page width so that the text on the screen was larger and easier to read. In the next set of steps, you want to see the entire page (mock sheet of paper) on the screen at once. ***Why?*** *You want be able to see the effect of adjusting colors in the document as a whole.* The next step displays a single page in its entirety in the document window as large as possible.

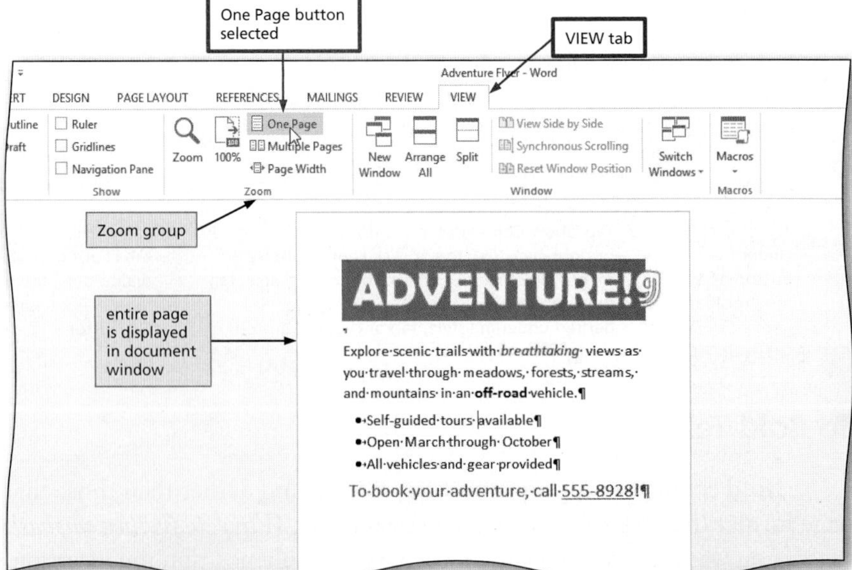
One Page button selected
VIEW tab
Zoom group
entire page is displayed in document window
ADVENTURE!
Explore·scenic·trails·with·breathtaking·views·as·
you·travel·through·meadows,·forests,·streams,·
and·mountains·in·an·off-road·vehicle.¶
•·Self-guided·tours·available¶
•·Open·March·through·October¶
•·All·vehicles·and·gear·provided¶
To·book·your·adventure,·call·555-8928!¶

- Tap or click VIEW on the ribbon to display the VIEW tab.
- Tap or click the One Page button (VIEW tab | Zoom group) to display the entire page in the document window as large as possible (Figure 1–44).

Figure 1–44

Other Ways

1. Tap or click Zoom button (VIEW tab | Zoom group), tap or click Whole page (Zoom dialog box), tap or click OK button

CONSIDER THIS

What colors should I choose when creating documents?

When choosing color, associate the meaning of the color with your message:

- Red expresses danger, power, or energy and often is associated with sports or physical exertion.
- Brown represents simplicity, honesty, and dependability.
- Orange denotes success, victory, creativity, and enthusiasm.
- Yellow suggests sunshine, happiness, hope, liveliness, and intelligence.
- Green symbolizes growth, healthiness, harmony, blooming, and healing and often is associated with safety or money.
- Blue indicates integrity, trust, importance, confidence, and stability.
- Purple represents wealth, power, comfort, extravagance, magic, mystery, and spirituality.
- White stands for purity, goodness, cleanliness, precision, and perfection.
- Black suggests authority, strength, elegance, power, and prestige.
- Gray conveys neutrality and, thus, often is found in backgrounds and other effects.

To Change Theme Colors

1 ENTER TEXT | 2 FORMAT TEXT | 3 INSERT PICTURE | 4 FORMAT PICTURE
5 ENHANCE PAGE | 6 CORRECT & REVISE | 7 PRINT OR READ

A **color scheme** in Word is a document theme that identifies 12 complementary colors for text, background, accents, and links in a document. With more than 20 predefined color schemes, Word provides a simple way to coordinate colors in a document.

The default color scheme is called Office. In the flyer, you will change the color scheme from Office to Green. ***Why?*** *You want the colors in the flyer to suggest growth, harmony, blooming, trust, and stability, which are conveyed by shades of greens and blues. In Word, the Green color scheme uses these colors.* The following steps change theme colors.

- Tap or click DESIGN on the ribbon to display the DESIGN tab.
- Tap or click the Theme Colors button (DESIGN tab | Document Formatting group) to display the Theme Colors gallery.
- If you are using a mouse, point to Green in the Theme Colors gallery to display a live preview of the selected theme color (Figure 1–45).

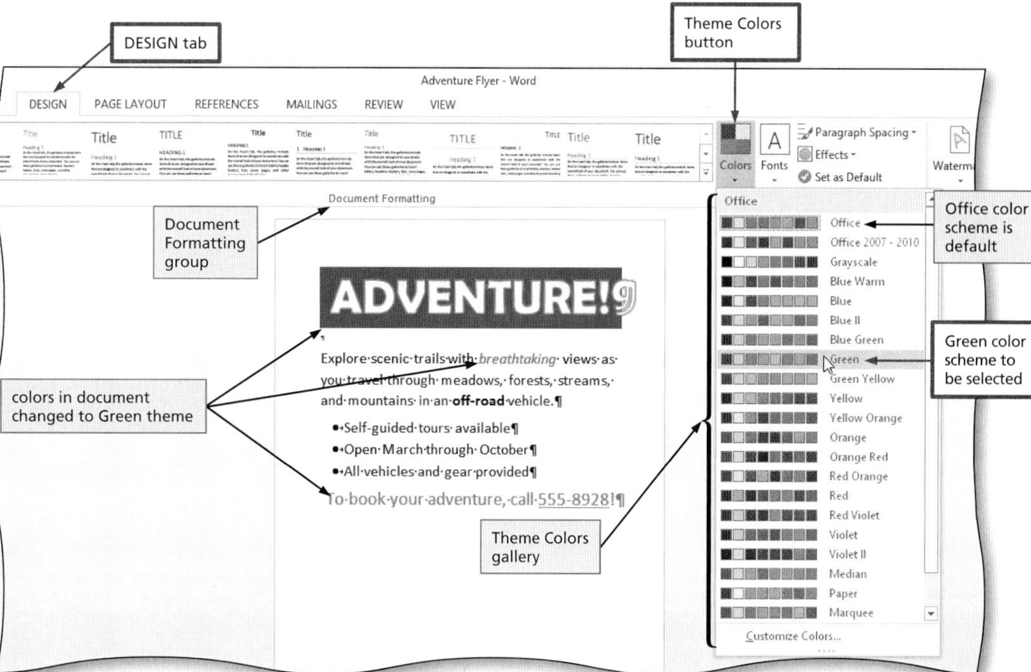

Figure 1–45

Experiment

- If you are using a mouse, point to various color schemes in the Theme Colors gallery and watch the colors change in the document.

• Tap or click Green in the Colors gallery to change the document theme colors.

Q&A What if I want to return to the original color scheme?
You would tap or click the Theme Colors button again and then tap or click Office in the Theme Colors gallery.

BTW
Selecting Nonadjacent Items
In Word, you can use keyboard keys to select nonadjacent items, that is, items not next to each other. This is helpful when you are applying the same formatting to multiple items. To select nonadjacent items (text or graphics), select the first item, such as a word or paragraph, as usual; then, press and hold down the CTRL key. While holding down the CTRL key, select additional items.

To Zoom Page Width

Because the document contents are small when displayed at one page, the next steps zoom page width again.

1. Tap or click VIEW on the ribbon to display the VIEW tab.
2. Tap or click the Page Width button (VIEW tab | Zoom group) to display the page the same width as the document window (shown in Figure 1–46 on page WD 34).

Selecting Text

In many of the previous steps, you have selected text. Table 1–3 summarizes the techniques used to select various items.

Table 1–3 Techniques for Selecting Text

Item to Select	Touch	Mouse	Keyboard (where applicable)
Block of text	Tap to position insertion point in text to select and then drag selection handle(s) to select text.	Click at beginning of selection, scroll to end of selection, position pointer at end of selection, hold down SHIFT key, and then click; or drag through text.	
Character(s)	Tap to position insertion point in text to select and then drag selection handle(s) to select text.	Drag through character(s).	SHIFT+RIGHT ARROW or SHIFT+LEFT ARROW
Document		Move pointer to left of text until pointer changes to right-pointing block arrow and then triple-click.	CTRL+A
Graphic	Tap the graphic.	Click the graphic.	
Line	Double-tap to left of line to be selected.	Move pointer to left of line until pointer changes to right-pointing block arrow and then click.	HOME, then SHIFT+END or END, then SHIFT+HOME
Lines	Tap to position insertion point in text to select and then drag selection handle(s) to select text.	Move pointer to left of first line until pointer changes to right-pointing block arrow and then drag up or down.	HOME, then SHIFT+DOWN ARROW or END, then SHIFT+UP ARROW
Paragraph	Tap to position insertion point in text to select and then drag selection handle(s) to select text.	Triple-click paragraph; or move pointer to left of paragraph until pointer changes to right-pointing block arrow and then double-click.	CTRL+SHIFT+DOWN ARROW or CTRL+SHIFT+UP ARROW
Paragraphs	Tap to position insertion point in text to select and then drag selection handle(s) to select text.	Move pointer to left of paragraph until pointer changes to right-pointing block arrow, double-click, and then drag up or down.	CTRL+SHIFT+DOWN ARROW or CTRL+SHIFT+UP ARROW repeatedly
Sentence	Tap to position insertion point in text to select and then drag selection handle(s) to select text.	Press and hold down CTRL key and then click sentence.	
Word	Double-tap word.	Double-click word.	CTRL+SHIFT+RIGHT ARROW or CTRL+SHIFT+LEFT ARROW
Words	Tap to position insertion point in text to select and then drag selection handle(s) to select text.	Drag through words.	CTRL+SHIFT+RIGHT ARROW or CTRL+SHIFT+LEFT ARROW repeatedly

To Save an Existing Document with the Same File Name

You have made several modifications to the document since you last saved it. Thus, you should save it again. The following step saves the document again. For an example of the step listed below, refer to the Office and Windows chapter at the beginning of this book.

1. Tap or click the Save button on the Quick Access Toolbar to overwrite the previously saved file.

Break Point: If you wish to take a break, this is a good place to do so. You can exit Word now (refer to page WD 46 for instructions). To resume at a later time, run Word (refer to pages WD 46 to WD 47 for instructions), open the file called Adventure Flyer (refer to page WD 47 for instructions), and continue following the steps from this location forward.

Inserting and Formatting a Picture in a Word Document

With the text formatted in the flyer, the next step is to insert a digital picture in the flyer and format the picture. Flyers usually contain a graphical image(s), such as a picture, to attract the attention of passersby. In the following pages, you will perform these tasks:

1. Insert a digital picture into the flyer and then reduce its size.
2. Enlarge the size of the picture.
3. Change the look of the picture.

CONSIDER THIS

How do I locate a graphic file to use in a document?

To use a graphic in a Word document, the image must be stored digitally in a file. Files containing graphics are available from a variety of sources:

- Microsoft has free digital images on the web for use in a document. Other websites also have images available, some of which are free, while others require a fee.
- You can take a picture with a digital camera or camera phone and **download** it, which is the process of copying the digital picture from the camera or phone to your computer.
- With a scanner, you can convert a printed picture, drawing, or diagram to a digital file.

If you receive a picture from a source other than yourself, do not use the file until you are certain it does not contain a virus. A **virus** is a computer program that can damage files and programs on your computer. Use an antivirus program to verify that any files you use are virus free.

To Center Another Paragraph

In the flyer, the digital picture of a mountain trail tour group should be centered on the blank line below the headline. The blank paragraph below the headline currently is left-aligned. The following steps center this paragraph.

1. Tap or click HOME on the ribbon to display the HOME tab.
2. Tap or click somewhere in the paragraph to be centered (in this case, the blank line below the headline) to position the insertion point in the paragraph to be formatted.
3. Tap or click the Center button (HOME tab | Paragraph group) to center the paragraph containing the insertion point (shown in Figure 1–46 on the next page).

BTW

BTWs

For a complete list of the BTWs found in the margins of this book, visit the BTW resource on the Student Companion Site located on www.cengagebrain.com. For detailed instructions about accessing available resources, visit www.cengage.com/ct/studentdownload or contact your instructor for information about accessing the required files.

To Insert a Picture

1 ENTER TEXT | 2 FORMAT TEXT | 3 INSERT PICTURE | 4 FORMAT PICTURE
5 ENHANCE PAGE | 6 CORRECT & REVISE | 7 PRINT OR READ

The next step in creating the flyer is to insert a digital picture of a mountain trail tour group in the flyer on the blank line below the headline. The picture, which was taken with a digital camera, is available on the Data Files for Students. Visit www.cengage.com/ct/studentdownload for detailed instructions or contact your instructor for information about accessing the required files.

The following steps insert a picture, which, in this example, is located in the Chapter 01 folder in the Word folder in the Data Files for Students folder. ***Why?*** *It is good practice to organize and store files in folders so that you easily can find the files at a later date.*

1

- If necessary, position the insertion point at the location where you want to insert the picture (in this case, on the centered blank paragraph below the headline).
- Tap or click INSERT on the ribbon to display the INSERT tab (Figure 1–46).

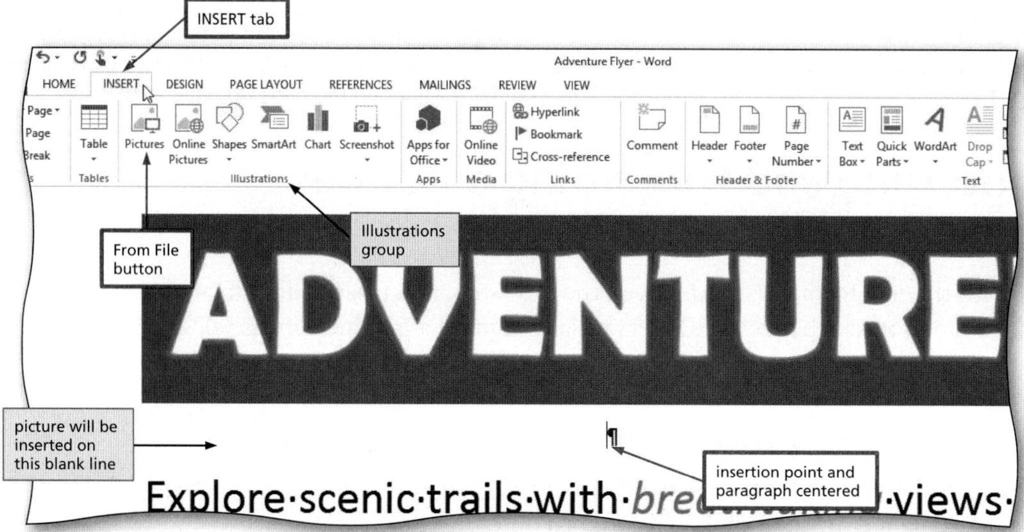

Figure 1–46

2

- Tap or click the From File button (INSERT tab | Illustrations group) (shown in Figure 1–46) to display the Insert Picture dialog box (shown in Figure 1–47).

3

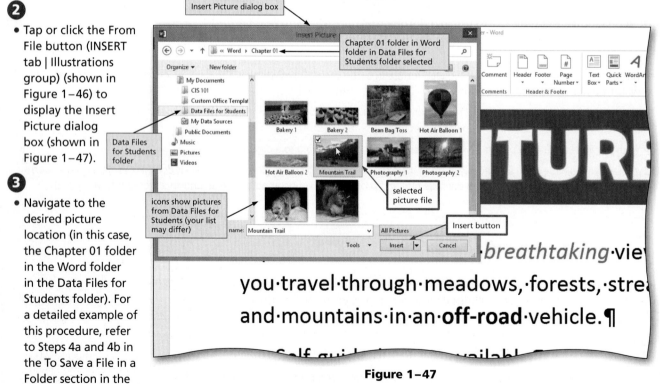

- Navigate to the desired picture location (in this case, the Chapter 01 folder in the Word folder in the Data Files for Students folder). For a detailed example of this procedure, refer to Steps 4a and 4b in the To Save a File in a Folder section in the Office and Windows chapter at the beginning of this book.
- Tap or click Mountain Trail to select the file (Figure 1–47).

Insert Picture dialog box
Chapter 01 folder in Word folder in Data Files for Students folder selected
Data Files for Students folder
icons show pictures from Data Files for Students (your list may differ)
selected picture file
Insert button

Figure 1–47

• Tap or click the Insert button (Insert Picture dialog box) to insert the picture at the location of the insertion point in the document (Figure 1–48).

Q&A

What are the symbols around the picture?
A selected graphic appears surrounded by a **selection rectangle**, which has small squares and circles, called **sizing handles**, at each corner and middle location.

What is the purpose of the Layout Options button?
When you tap or click the Layout Options button, Word provides options for changing how the graphic is positioned with text in the document.

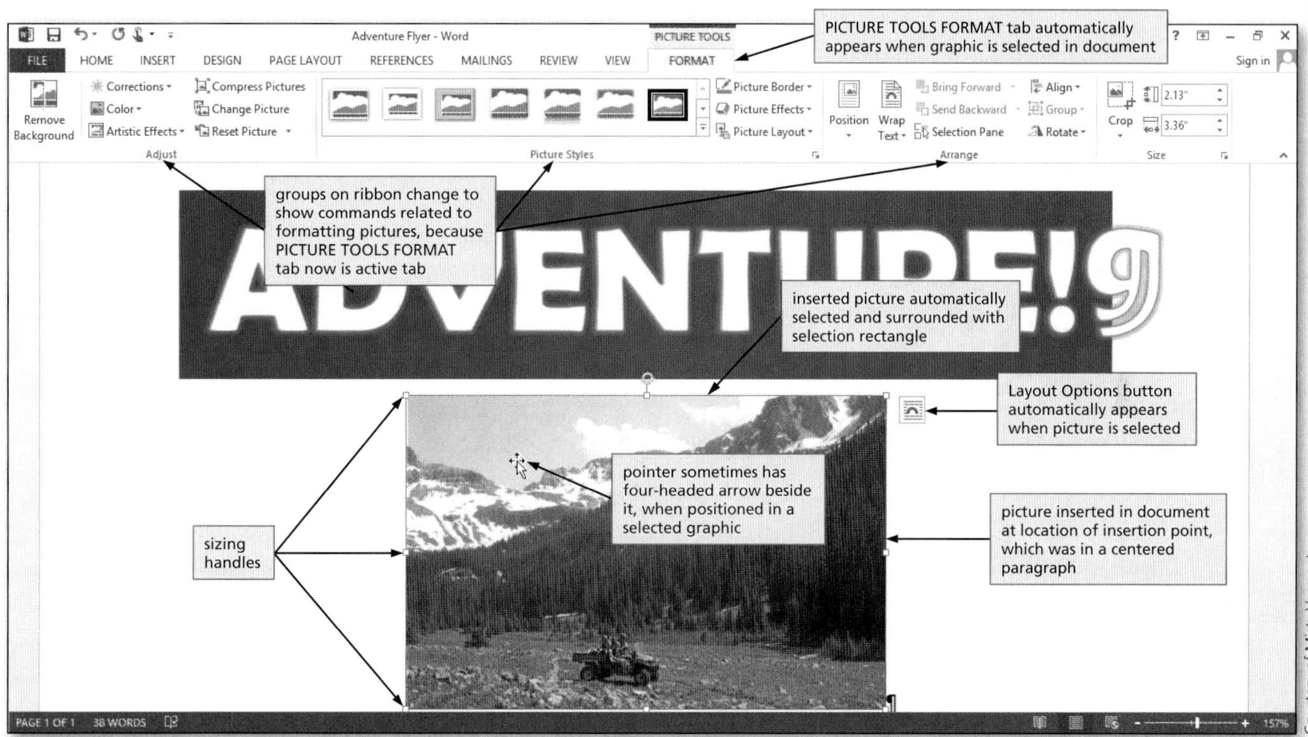

Courtesy of Misty Vermaat

Figure 1–48

CONSIDER THIS

How do you know where to position a graphic on a flyer?
The content, size, shape, position, and format of a graphic should capture the interest of passersby, enticing them to stop and read the flyer. Often, the graphic is the center of attention and visually the largest element on a flyer. If you use colors in the graphical image, be sure they are part of the document's color scheme.

To Zoom the Document

1 ENTER TEXT | 2 FORMAT TEXT | 3 INSERT PICTURE | 4 FORMAT PICTURE
5 ENHANCE PAGE | 6 CORRECT & REVISE | 7 PRINT OR READ

In the steps on the following pages, you will work with the picture just inserted. The next task is to adjust the zoom percentage. ***Why?*** *Currently, you can see only a small amount of text with the picture. Seeing more of the document at once helps you determine the appropriate size for the picture.* The following step zooms the document.

Experiment

• If you are using a mouse, repeatedly click the Zoom Out and Zoom In buttons on the status bar and watch the size of the document change in the document window.

• If you are using a touch screen, repeatedly pinch (move two fingers together) and stretch (move two fingers apart) and watch the size of the document change in the document window.

- Pinch and stretch or click the Zoom Out or Zoom In button as many times as necessary until the Zoom button on the status bar displays 80% on its face (Figure 1–49).

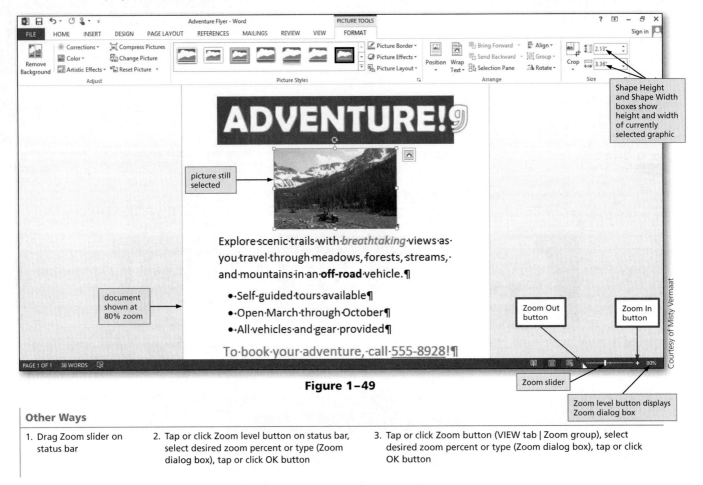

Shape Height and Shape Width boxes show height and width of currently selected graphic

picture still selected

document shown at 80% zoom

Zoom Out button

Zoom In button

Zoom slider

Zoom level button displays Zoom dialog box

Courtesy of Misty Vermaat

Figure 1–49

Other Ways

1. Drag Zoom slider on status bar
2. Tap or click Zoom level button on status bar, select desired zoom percent or type (Zoom dialog box), tap or click OK button
3. Tap or click Zoom button (VIEW tab | Zoom group), select desired zoom percent or type (Zoom dialog box), tap or click OK button

To Resize a Graphic

1 ENTER TEXT | 2 FORMAT TEXT | 3 INSERT PICTURE | **4 FORMAT PICTURE**
5 ENHANCE PAGE | **6 CORRECT & REVISE** | **7 PRINT OR READ**

Resizing includes both increasing and reducing the size of a graphic. The next step is to resize the picture so that it is larger in the flyer. ***Why?*** *You want the graphic as large as possible on a single page flyer to draw the attention of passersby.* The following steps resize a selected graphic.

- Be sure the graphic still is selected.

Q&A What if my graphic (picture) is not selected?

To select a graphic, tap or click it.

- If you are using a mouse, point to the lower-left corner sizing handle on the picture so that the pointer shape changes to a two-headed arrow (Figure 1–50).

Figure 1–50

• Drag the sizing handle diagonally outward until the lower-left corner of the picture is positioned approximately as shown in Figure 1–51. Do not lift your finger or release the mouse button at this point.

3

• Release your finger or the mouse button to resize the graphic, which in this case, should have a height of about 3.26" and a width of about 5.04".

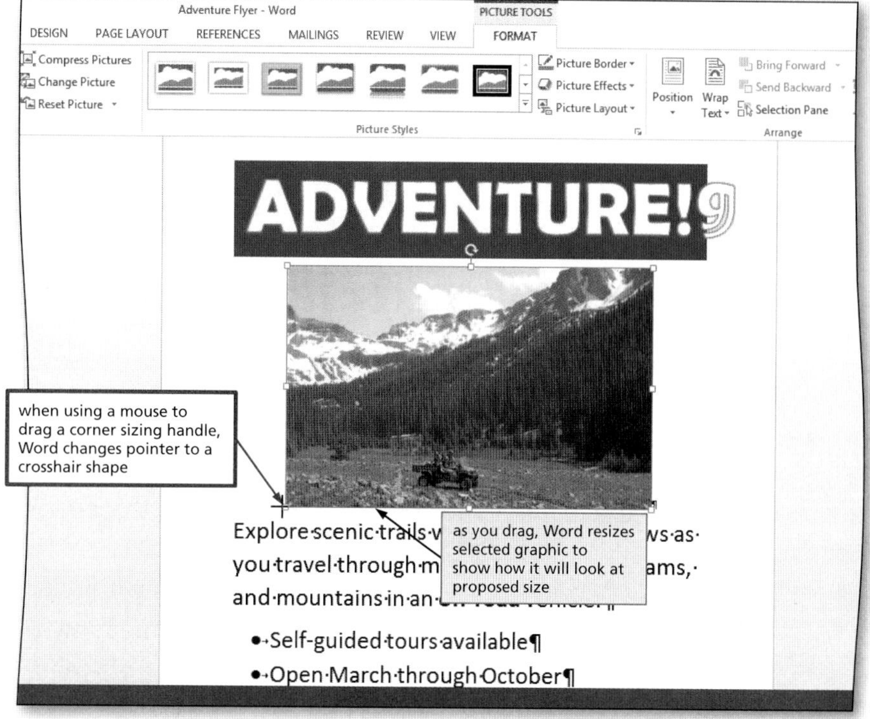

Courtesy of Misty Vermaat

Figure 1–51

Q&A

How can I see the height and width measurements?

Look in the Size group on the PICTURE TOOLS FORMAT tab to see the height and width measurements of the currently selected graphic (shown in Figure 1–49).

What if the graphic is the wrong size?

Repeat Steps 1, 2, and 3, or enter the desired height and width values in the Shape Height and Shape Width boxes (PICTURE TOOLS FORMAT tab | Size group).

What if I want to return a graphic to its original size and start again?

With the graphic selected, tap or click the Size Dialog Box Launcher (PICTURE TOOLS FORMAT tab | Size group), tap or click the Size tab (Layout dialog box), tap or click the Reset button, and then tap or click the OK button.

Other Ways

1. Enter height and width of graphic in Shape Height and Shape Width boxes (PICTURE TOOLS FORMAT tab | Size group)
2. Tap or click Advanced Layout: Size Dialog Box Launcher (PICTURE TOOLS FORMAT tab | Size group), tap or click Size tab (Layout dialog box), enter desired height and width values in boxes, tap or click OK button

To Zoom 100%

1 ENTER TEXT | 2 FORMAT TEXT | 3 INSERT PICTURE | **4 FORMAT PICTURE**
5 ENHANCE PAGE | **6 CORRECT & REVISE** | **7 PRINT OR READ**

In the next series of steps, you will format the picture. Earlier in this chapter, you changed the zoom to 80% so that you could see more of the page while resizing the graphic. The step on the next page zooms the screen to 100%. ***Why?*** *You want the contents of the image to be enlarged a bit, while still seeing some of the text in the document.*

1

- Tap or click VIEW on the ribbon to display the VIEW tab.
- Tap or click the 100% button (VIEW tab | Zoom group) to display the page at 100% in the document window (Figure 1–52).

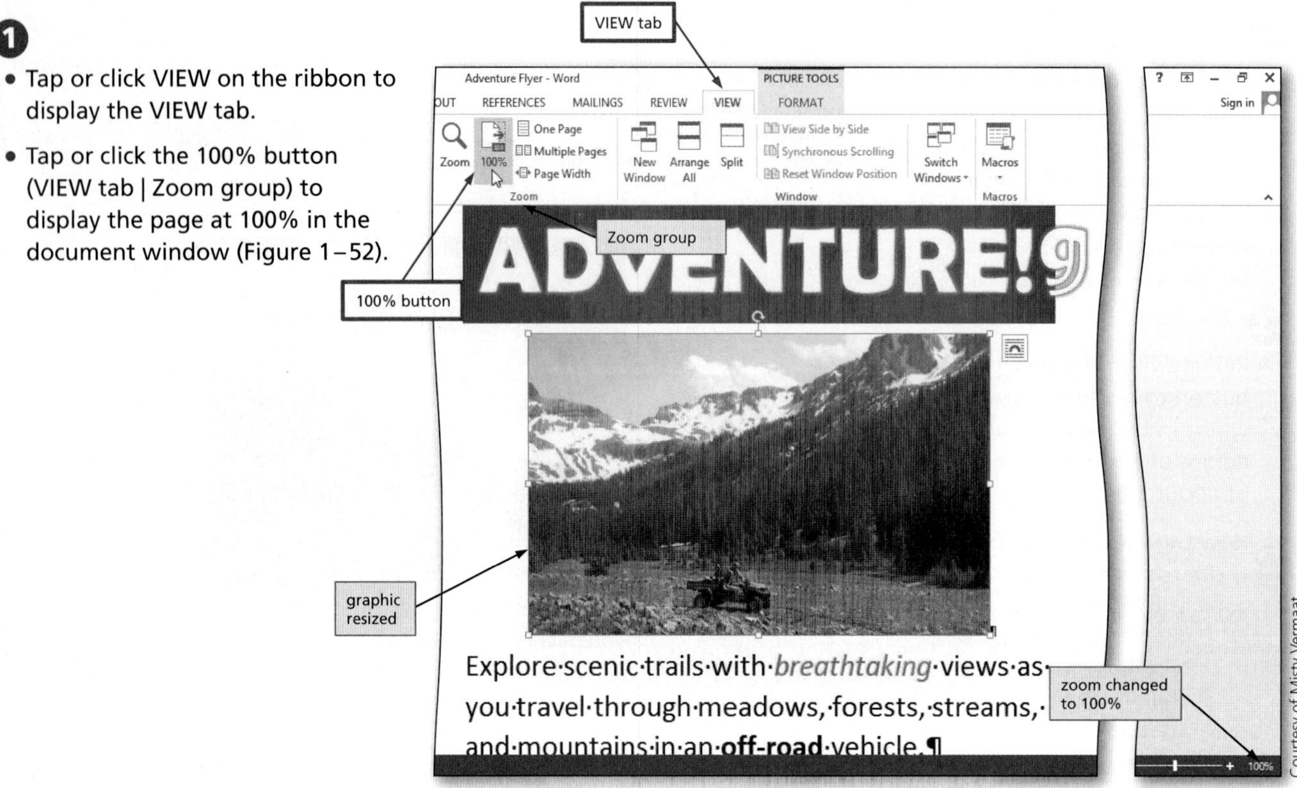

Figure 1–52

Other Ways

1. Tap or click Zoom button (VIEW tab | Zoom group), tap or click 100% (Zoom dialog box), tap or click OK button

To Apply a Picture Style

1 ENTER TEXT | 2 FORMAT TEXT | 3 INSERT PICTURE | 4 FORMAT PICTURE
5 ENHANCE PAGE | 6 CORRECT & REVISE | 7 PRINT OR READ

A **style** is a named group of formatting characteristics. Word provides more than 25 picture styles. ***Why?*** *Picture styles enable you easily to change a picture's look to a more visually appealing style, including a variety of shapes, angles, borders, and reflections.* The flyer in this chapter uses a style that applies a drop shadow to the picture. The following steps apply a picture style to a picture.

1

- Tap or click PICTURE TOOLS FORMAT on the ribbon to display the PICTURE TOOLS FORMAT tab.
- Be sure the graphic still is selected (Figure 1–53).

Q&A What if my graphic (picture) is not selected?

To select a graphic, tap or click it.

What is the white circle attached to top of the selected graphic?

It is called a rotate handle. When you drag a graphic's **rotate handle**, the graphic moves in either a clockwise or counterclockwise direction.

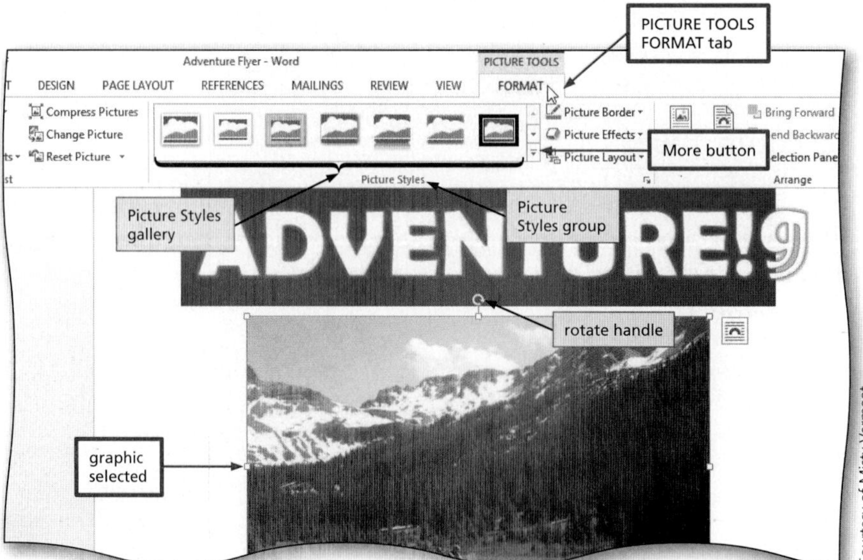

Figure 1–53

2

- Tap or click the More button in the Picture Styles gallery (PICTURE TOOLS FORMAT tab | Picture Styles group) (shown in Figure 1–53) to expand the gallery.
- If you are using a mouse, point to 'Drop Shadow Rectangle' in the Picture Styles gallery to display a live preview of that style applied to the picture in the document (Figure 1–54).

Experiment

- If you are using a mouse, point to various picture styles in the Picture Styles gallery and watch the style of the picture change in the document window.

3

- Tap or click 'Drop Shadow Rectangle' in the Picture Styles gallery (fourth style in first row) to apply the style to the selected picture.

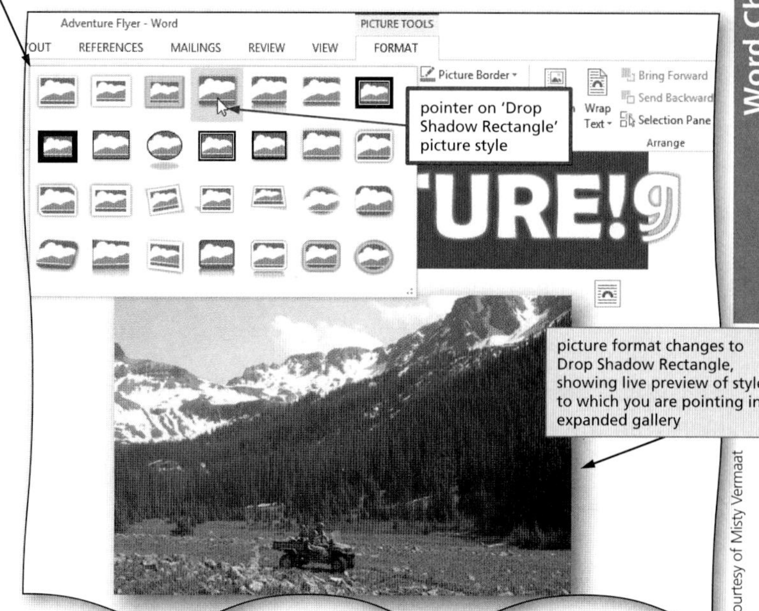

Figure 1–54

Other Ways

1. Press and hold or right-click picture, tap or click 'Picture Quick Styles' on mini toolbar, select desired style

To Apply Picture Effects

1 ENTER TEXT | 2 FORMAT TEXT | 3 INSERT PICTURE | 4 FORMAT PICTURE
5 ENHANCE PAGE | 6 CORRECT & REVISE | 7 PRINT OR READ

Word provides a variety of picture effects, such as shadows, reflections, glow, soft edges, bevel, and 3-D rotation. The difference between the effects and the styles is that each effect has several options, providing you with more control over the exact look of the image.

In this flyer, the picture has a slight green glow effect and beveled edges. The following steps apply picture effects to the selected picture. ***Why?*** *Picture effects enable you to further customize the a picture.*

1

- With the picture still selected, tap or click the Picture Effects button (PICTURE TOOLS FORMAT tab | Picture Styles group) to display the Picture Effects menu.
- Tap or point to Glow on the Picture Effects menu to display the Glow gallery.
- If you are using a mouse, point to 'Turquoise, 5 pt glow, Accent color 6' in the Glow Variations area (rightmost glow in first row) to display a live preview of the selected glow effect applied to the picture in the document window (Figure 1–55).

Experiment

- If you are using a mouse, point to various glow effects in the Glow gallery and watch the picture change in the document window

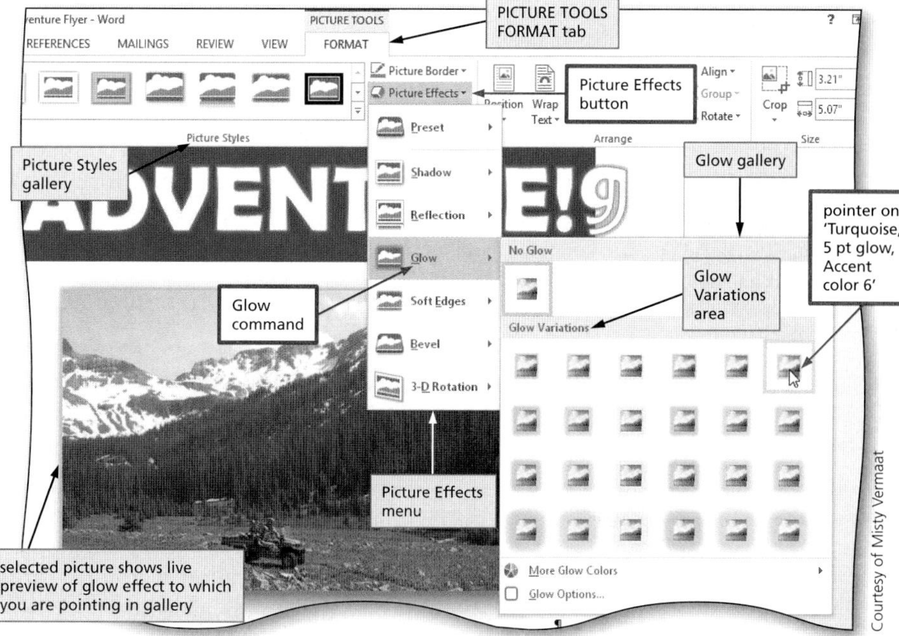

Figure 1–55

2

- Tap or click 'Turquoise, 5 pt glow, Accent color 6' in the Glow gallery to apply the selected picture effect.

Q&A What if I wanted to discard formatting applied to a picture?
You would tap or click the Reset Picture button (PICTURE TOOLS FORMAT tab | Adjust group). To reset formatting and size, you would tap or click the Reset Picture arrow (PICTURE TOOLS FORMAT tab | Adjust group) and then tap or click 'Reset Picture & Size' on the Reset Picture menu.

3

- Tap or click the Picture Effects button (PICTURE TOOLS FORMAT tab | Picture Styles group) to display the Picture Effects menu again.
- Tap or point to Bevel on the Picture Effects menu to display the Bevel gallery.
- If you are using a mouse, point to Angle in the Bevel area (first effect in second row) to display a live preview of the selected bevel effect applied to the picture in the document window (Figure 1–56).

Experiment

- If you are using a mouse, point to various bevel effects in the Bevel gallery and watch the picture change in the document window.

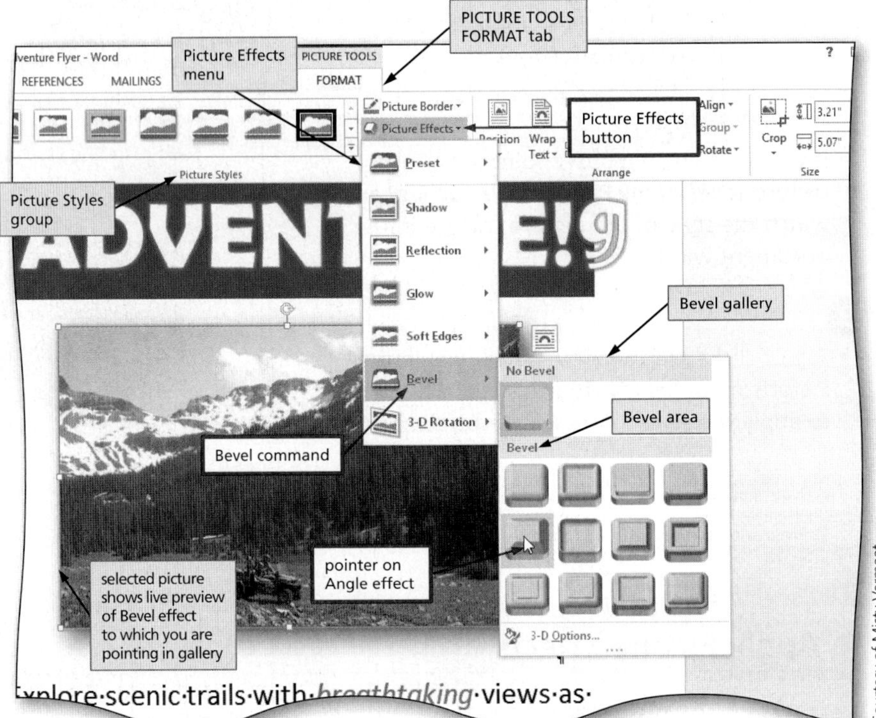

Figure 1–56

4

- Tap or click Angle in the Bevel gallery to apply the selected picture effect.

Other Ways

1. Tap 'Show Context Menu' button on mini toolbar or right-click picture, tap or click Format Object or Format Picture on shortcut menu, tap or click Effects button (Format Picture task pane), select desired options, tap or click Close button
2. Tap or click Format Shape Dialog Box Launcher (PICTURE TOOLS FORMAT tab | Picture Styles group), tap or click Effects button (Format Picture task pane), select desired options, tap or click Close button

Enhancing the Page

With the text and graphics entered and formatted, the next step is to look at the page as a whole and determine if it looks finished in its current state. As you review the page, answer these questions:

- Does it need a page border to frame its contents, or would a page border make it look too busy?
- Is the spacing between paragraphs and graphics on the page adequate? Do any sections of text or graphics look as if they are positioned too closely to the items above or below them?
- Does the flyer have too much space at the top or bottom? Should the contents be centered vertically?

You determine that a graphical, color-coordinated border would enhance the flyer. You also notice that the flyer would look better proportioned if it had a little more space above and below the picture. You also want to ensure that the contents are centered vertically. The following pages make these enhancements to the flyer.

BTW
Word Help
At any time while using Word, you can find answers to questions and display information about various topics through Word Help. Used properly, this form of assistance can increase your productivity and reduce your frustrations by minimizing the time you spend learning how to use Word. For instruction about Word Help and exercises that will help you gain confidence in using it, read the Office and Windows chapter at the beginning of this book.

To Add a Page Border

In Word, you can add a border around the perimeter of an entire page. The flyer in this chapter has a light green border. ***Why?*** *This border color complements the color of the flyer contents.* The following steps add a page border.

1

- Tap or click DESIGN on the ribbon to display the DESIGN tab.
- Tap or click the 'Borders and Shading' button (DESIGN tab | Page Background group) to display the Borders and Shading dialog box (Figure 1–57).

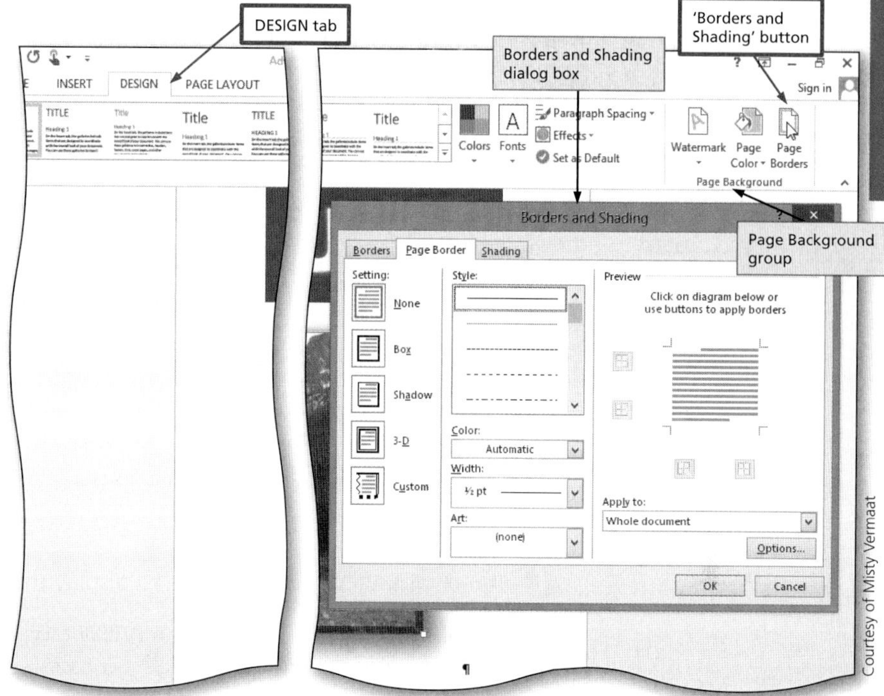

Figure 1–57

2

- Tap or click the second border style in the Style list (Borders and Shading dialog box) to select the style.
- Tap or click the Color arrow to display a Color palette (Figure 1–58).

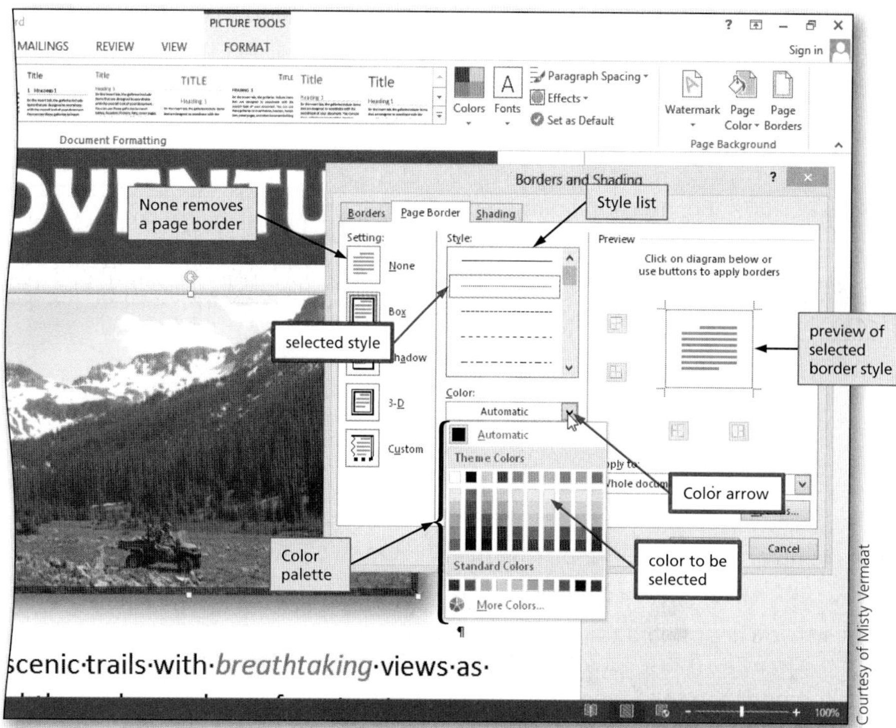

Figure 1–58

3

- Tap or click 'Lime, Accent 2, Lighter 80%' (sixth color in second row) in the Color palette to select the color for the page border.
- Tap or click the Width arrow to display the Width list and then tap or click 4 ½ pt to select the thickness of the page border (Figure 1–59).

4

- Tap or click the OK button to add the border to the page (shown in Figure 1–60).

Q&A What if I wanted to remove the border?
You would tap or click None in the Setting list in the Borders and Shading dialog box.

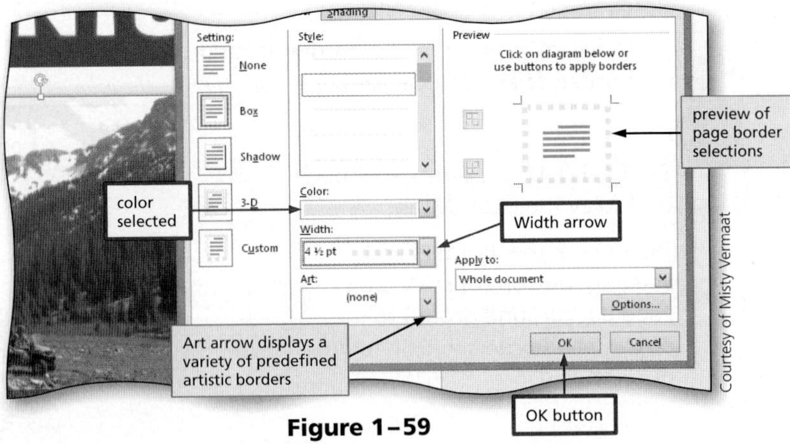

Figure 1–59

To Zoom One Page

1 ENTER TEXT | 2 FORMAT TEXT | 3 INSERT PICTURE | 4 FORMAT PICTURE
5 ENHANCE PAGE | 6 CORRECT & REVISE | 7 PRINT OR READ

The next steps zoom one page so that you can see the entire page on the screen at once.

1. Tap or click VIEW on the ribbon to display the VIEW tab.
2. Tap or click the One Page button (VIEW tab | Zoom group) to display the entire page in the document window as large as possible.

To Change Spacing before and after Paragraphs

1 ENTER TEXT | 2 FORMAT TEXT | 3 INSERT PICTURE | 4 FORMAT PICTURE
5 ENHANCE PAGE | 6 CORRECT & REVISE | 7 PRINT OR READ

The default spacing above (before) a paragraph in Word is 0 points and below (after) is 8 points. In the flyer, you want to increase the spacing below the paragraph containing the headline and above the signature line. ***Why?*** *The flyer spacing will look more balanced with spacing increased above and below these paragraphs.* The following steps change the spacing above and below a paragraph.

1

- Position the insertion point in the paragraph to be adjusted, in this case, the paragraph containing the headline.

Q&A What happened to the PICTURE TOOLS FORMAT tab?
When you tap or click outside of a graphic or press a key to scroll through a document, Word deselects the graphic and removes the PICTURE TOOLS FORMAT tab from the screen. That is, this tab appears only when a graphic is selected.

- Tap or click PAGE LAYOUT on the ribbon to display the PAGE LAYOUT tab.
- If you are using a touch screen, tap the Spacing After box (PAGE LAYOUT tab | Paragraph group) and then type 12 to change the spacing below the paragraph; if you are using a mouse, click the Spacing After up arrow (PAGE LAYOUT tab | Paragraph group) so that 12 pt is displayed in the Spacing After box to increase the space below the current paragraph (Figure 1–60).

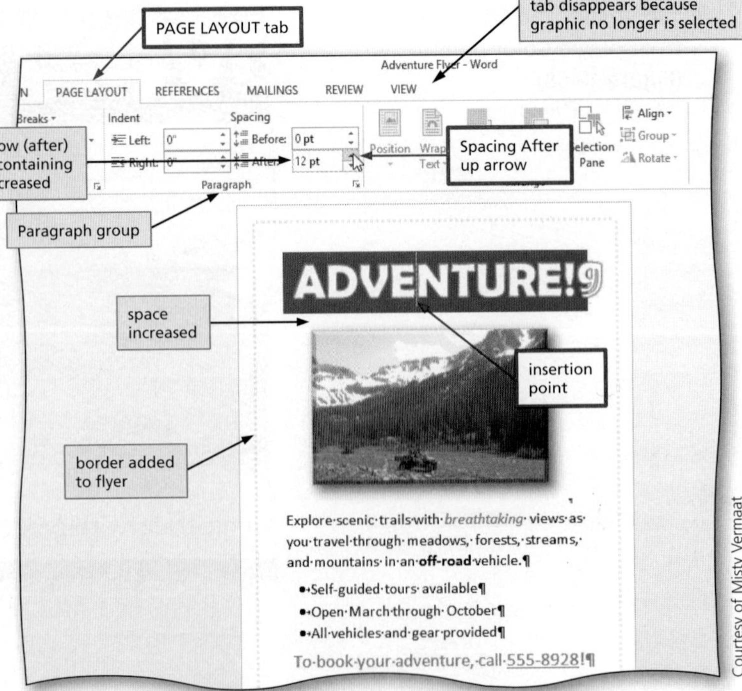

Figure 1–60

2

- Position the insertion point in the paragraph to be adjusted, in this case, the paragraph containing the signature line.
- If you are using a touch screen, tap the Spacing Before box (PAGE LAYOUT tab | Paragraph group) and then type 12 to change the spacing above the paragraph; if you are using a mouse, click the Spacing Before up arrow (PAGE LAYOUT tab | Paragraph group) as many times as necessary so that 12 pt is displayed in the Spacing Before box to increase the space above the current paragraph (Figure 1–61).
- If the text flows to two pages, reduce the spacing above and below paragraphs as necessary.

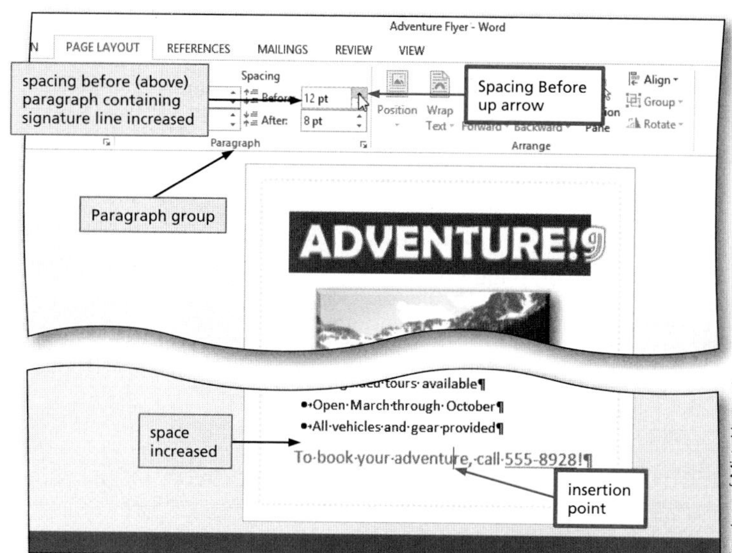

Figure 1–61

Other Ways

1. Tap 'Show Context Menu' button on mini toolbar or right-click paragraph, tap or click Paragraph on shortcut menu, tap or click Indents and Spacing tab (Paragraph dialog box), enter spacing before and after values, tap or click OK button
2. Tap or click Paragraph Settings Dialog Box Launcher (HOME tab or PAGE LAYOUT tab | Paragraph group), tap or click Indents and Spacing tab (Paragraph dialog box), enter spacing before and after values, tap or click OK button

To Center Page Contents Vertically

1 ENTER TEXT | 2 FORMAT TEXT | 3 INSERT PICTURE | 4 FORMAT PICTURE
5 ENHANCE PAGE | **6 CORRECT & REVISE** | **7 PRINT OR READ**

In Word, you can center the page contents vertically. ***Why?*** *This places the same amount of space at the top and bottom of the page.* The following steps center page contents vertically.

- If necessary, tap or click PAGE LAYOUT on the ribbon to display the PAGE LAYOUT tab.
- Tap or click the Page Setup Dialog Box Launcher (PAGE LAYOUT tab | Page Setup group) to display the Page Setup dialog box.
- Tap or click the Layout tab (Page Setup dialog box) to display the Layout sheet (Figure 1–62).

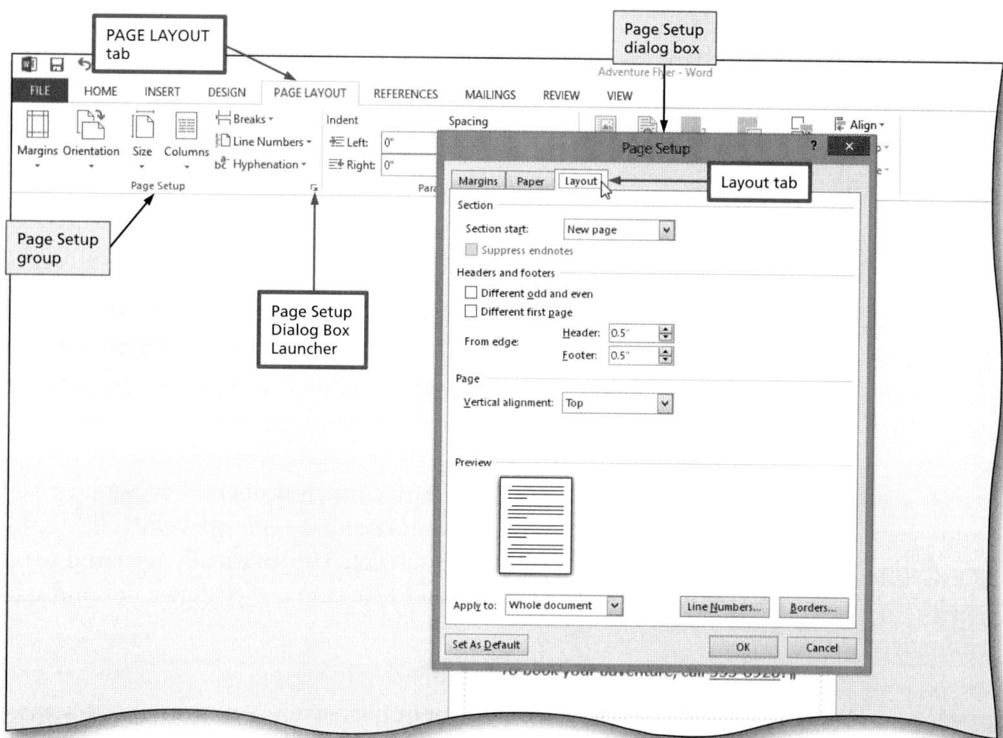

Figure 1–62

2
- Tap or click the Vertical alignment arrow (Page Setup dialog box) to display the list of alignment options and then tap or click Center in the list (Figure 1–63).

3
- Tap or click the OK button to center the page contents vertically on the screen (shown in Figure 1–1 on page WD 3).

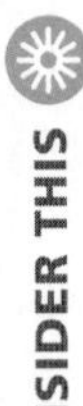

Q&A What if I wanted to change the alignment back?

You would select the Top vertical alignment from the Vertical alignment list in the Layout sheet (Page Setup dialog box).

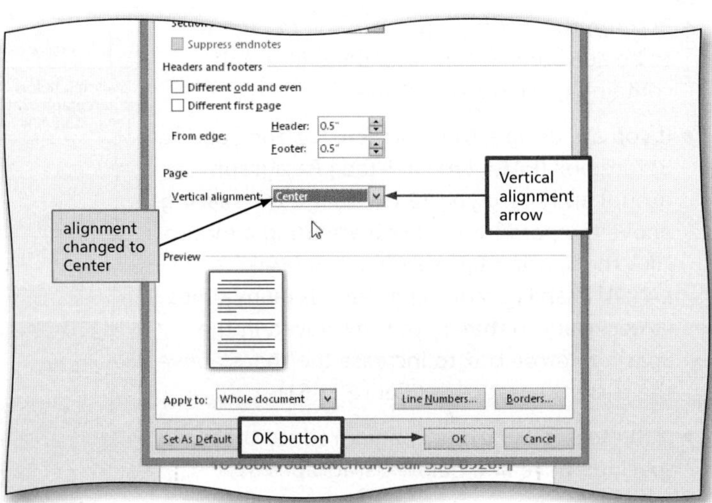

Figure 1–63

To Save an Existing Document with the Same File Name

You have made several modifications to the document since you last saved it. Thus, you should save it again. The following step saves the document again. For an example of the step listed below, refer to the Office and Windows chapter at the beginning of this book.

1 Tap or click the Save button on the Quick Access Toolbar to overwrite the previously saved file.

Document Properties

Word helps you organize and identify your files by using **document properties**, which are the details about a file such as the project author, title, and subject. For example, a class name or document topic can describe the file's purpose or content.

CONSIDER THIS

Why would you want to assign document properties to a document?

Document properties are valuable for a variety of reasons:

- Users can save time locating a particular file because they can view a file's document properties without opening the document.
- By creating consistent properties for files having similar content, users can better organize their documents.
- Some organizations require Word users to add document properties so that other employees can view details about these files.

The more common document properties are standard and automatically updated properties. **Standard properties** are associated with all Microsoft Office files and include author, title, and subject. **Automatically updated properties** include file system properties, such as the date you create or change a file, and statistics, such as the file size.

To Change Document Properties

To change document properties, you would follow these steps.

1. Tap or click FILE on the ribbon to open the Backstage view and then, if necessary, tap or click the Info tab in the Backstage view to display the Info gallery.

2. If the property you wish to change is displayed in the Properties list in the right pane of the Info gallery, try to tap or click to the right of the property. If a text box appears to the right of the property, type the text for the property in the text box, and then tap or click the Back button in the upper-left corner of the Backstage view to return to the Word window. Skip the remaining steps.
3. If the property you wish to change is not displayed in the Properties list in the right pane of the Info gallery or you cannot change it in the Info gallery, tap or click the Properties button in the right pane to display the Properties menu, and then tap or click 'Show Document Panel' on the Properties menu to close the Backstage view and display the Document Information Panel in the Word document window.

Q&A Why are some of the document properties in my Document Information Panel already filled in?
The person who installed Office 2013 on your computer or network may have set or customized the properties.

4. Type the desired text in the appropriate property text boxes.

Q&A What if the property I want to change is not displayed in the Document Information Panel?
Tap or click the Document Properties button in the Document Information Panel and then tap or click Advanced Properties on the menu to display the Properties dialog box. If necessary, tap or click the Summary tab (Properties dialog box) to display the Summary sheet, fill in the appropriate text boxes, and then tap or click the OK button.

5. Tap or click the 'Close the Document Information Panel' button at the right edge of the Document Information Panel so that the panel no longer appears in the Word document window.

To Sign Out of a Microsoft Account

If you are signed in to a Microsoft account and are using a public computer or otherwise wish to sign out of your Microsoft account, you should sign out of the account from the Account gallery in the Backstage view before exiting Word. Signing out of the account is the safest way to make sure that nobody else can access SkyDrive files or settings stored in your Microsoft account. The following steps sign out of a Microsoft account from Word. For a detailed example of the procedure summarized below, refer to the Office and Windows chapter at the beginning of this book.

1. If you wish to sign out of your Microsoft account, tap or click FILE on the ribbon to open the Backstage view and then tap or click the Account tab to display the Account gallery.

2. Tap or click the Sign out link, which displays the Remove Account dialog box. If a Can't remove Windows accounts dialog box appears instead of the Remove Account dialog box, tap or click the OK button and skip the remaining steps.

Q&A Why does a Can't remove Windows accounts dialog box appear?
If you signed in to Windows using your Microsoft account, then you also must sign out from Windows, rather than signing out from within the Word. When you are finished using Windows, be sure to sign out at that time.

3. Tap or click the Yes button (Remove Account dialog box) to sign out of your Microsoft account on this computer.

Q&A Should I sign out of Windows after signing out of my Microsoft account?
When you are finished using the computer, you should sign out of your account for maximum security.

4. Tap or click the Back button in the upper-left corner of the Backstage view to return to the document.

BTW
Q&As
For a complete list of the Q&As found in many of the step-by-step sequences in this book, visit the Q&A resource on the Student Companion Site located on www.cengagebrain.com. For detailed instructions about accessing available resources, visit www.cengage.com/ct/studentdownload or contact your instructor for information about accessing the required files.

To Exit Word

Although you still need to make some edits to this document, you want to exit Word and resume working on the project at a later time. Thus, the following steps exit Word. For a detailed example of the procedure summarized below, refer to the Office and Windows chapter at the beginning of this book.

1a If you have one Word document open, tap or click the Close button on the right side of the title bar to close the open document and exit Word.

1b If you have multiple Word documents open, press and hold or right-click the Word app button on the taskbar and then tap or click 'Close all windows' on the shortcut menu to close all open documents and exit Word.

Q&A Could I press and hold or repeatedly click the Close button to close all open documents and exit Word?
Yes.

2 If a Microsoft Word dialog box appears, tap or click the Save button to save any changes made to the document since the last save.

Break Point: If you wish to take a break, this is a good place to do so. To resume at a later time, continue following the steps from this location forward.

Correcting Errors and Revising a Document

After creating a document, you may need to change it. For example, the document may contain an error, or new circumstances may require you to add text to the document.

Types of Changes Made to Documents

The types of changes made to documents normally fall into one of the three following categories: additions, deletions, or modifications.

Additions Additional words, sentences, or paragraphs may be required in a document. Additions occur when you omit text from a document and want to insert it later. For example, you may want to add your email address to the flyer.

Deletions Sometimes, text in a document is incorrect or no longer is needed. For example, you may discover that the tours no longer provide gear. In this case, you would delete the words, and gear, from the flyer.

Modifications If an error is made in a document or changes take place that affect the document, you might have to revise a word(s) in the text. For example, the tours may start in April instead of March.

BTW
Certification
The Microsoft Office Specialist (MOS) program provides an opportunity for you to obtain a valuable industry credential — proof that you have the Word 2013 skills required by employers. For more information, visit the Certification resource on the Student Companion Site located on www.cengagebrain.com. For detailed instructions about accessing available resources, visit www.cengage.com/ct/studentdownload or contact your instructor for information about accessing the required files.

To Run Word

Once you have created and saved a document, you may need to retrieve it from your storage medium. For example, you might want to revise the document or print it. The following steps, which assume Windows 8 is running, use the Start screen or the Search box to run Word based on a typical installation. You may need to ask your instructor how to run Word on your computer. For a detailed example of the procedure summarized below, refer to the Office and Windows chapter.

1. Scroll the Start screen for a Word 2013 tile. If your Start screen contains a Word 2013 tile, tap or click it to run Word and then proceed to Step 5; if the Start screen does not contain the Word 2013 tile, proceed to the next step to search for the Word app.
2. Swipe in from the right edge of the screen or point to the upper-right corner of the screen to display the Charms bar and then tap or click the Search charm on the Charms bar to display the Search menu.
3. Type `Word` as the search text in the Search box and watch the search results appear in the Apps list.
4. Tap or click Word 2013 in the search results to run Word.
5. Tap or click the Blank document thumbnail on the Word start screen to create a blank document and display it in the Word window.
6. If the Word window is not maximized, tap or click the Maximize button on its title bar to maximize the window.

To Open a Document from Word

Earlier in this chapter you saved your flyer using the file name, Adventure Flyer. The following steps open the Adventure Flyer file from the Word folder in the CIS 101 folder. For a detailed example of the procedure summarized below, refer to the Office and Windows chapter at the beginning of this book.

1. Tap or click FILE on the ribbon to open the Backstage view and then tap or click the Open tab in the Backstage view to display the Open gallery.
2. If the file you wish to open is displayed in the Recent Documents list, tap or click the file name to open the file and display the opened document in the Word window; then, skip the remaining steps. If the file you wish to open is not displayed in the Recent Documents list, proceed to the next step to locate the file.
3. Tap or click Computer, SkyDrive, or another location in the left pane, tap or click the Browse button, and then navigate to the location of the file to be opened (in this case the Word folder in the CIS 101 folder).
4. Tap or click Adventure Flyer to select the file to be opened.
5. Tap or click the Open button (Open dialog box) to open the selected file and display the opened document in the Word window.

To Zoom the Document

While modifying the document, you prefer the document at 100% so that it is easier to read. Thus, the following step changes the zoom back to 100%.

1. Tap or click VIEW on the ribbon to display the VIEW tab.
2. Tap or click the 100% button (VIEW tab | Zoom group) to display the page at 100% in the document window.

BTW

Quick Reference
For a table that lists how to complete the tasks covered in this book using touch gestures, the mouse, ribbon, shortcut menu, and keyboard, see the Quick Reference Summary at the back of this book, or visit the Quick Reference resource on the Student Companion Site located on www.cengagebrain.com. For detailed instructions about accessing available resources, visit www.cengage.com/ct/studentdownload or contact your instructor for information about accessing the required files.

To Insert Text in an Existing Document

1 ENTER TEXT | 2 FORMAT TEXT | 3 INSERT PICTURE | 4 FORMAT PICTURE
5 ENHANCE PAGE | 6 CORRECT & REVISE | 7 PRINT OR READ

Word inserts text to the left of the insertion point. The text to the right of the insertion point moves to the right and downward to fit the new text. The following steps insert the word, today, to the left of the word, with, in the flyer. ***Why?*** *These steps illustrate the process of inserting text.*

- Scroll through the document and then tap or click to the left of the location of text to be inserted (in this case, the w in with) to position the insertion point where text should be inserted (Figure 1–64).

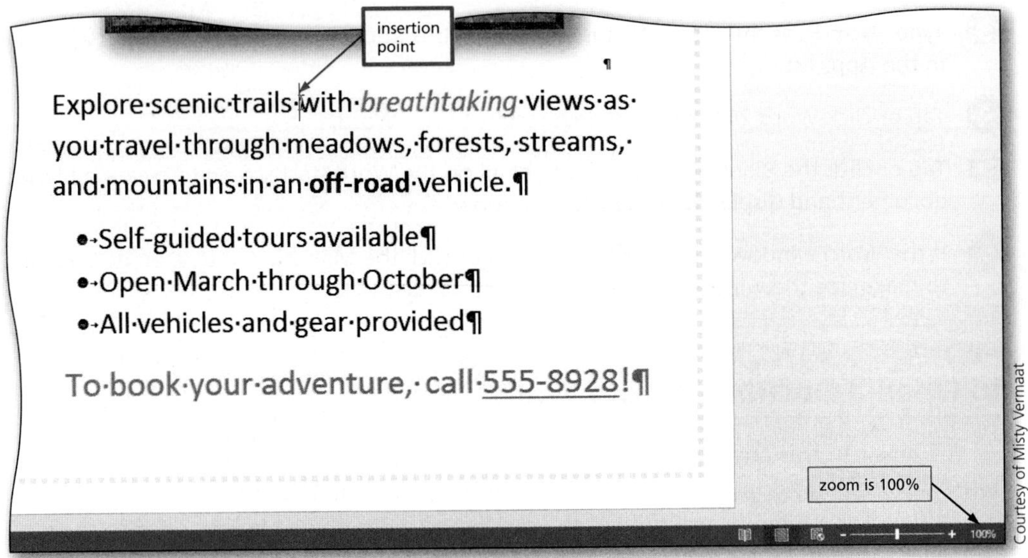
insertion point
Explore·scenic·trails·with·breathtaking·views·as·you·travel·through·meadows,·forests,·streams,·and·mountains·in·an·off-road·vehicle.¶
•·Self-guided·tours·available¶
•·Open·March·through·October¶
•·All·vehicles·and·gear·provided¶
To·book·your·adventure,·call·555-8928!¶
zoom is 100%
Courtesy of Misty Vermaat

Figure 1–64

- Type **today** and then press the SPACEBAR to insert the word to the left of the insertion point (Figure 1–65).

Q&A Why did the text move to the right as I typed?
In Word, the default typing mode is **insert mode**, which means as you type a character, Word moves all the characters to the right of the typed character one position to the right.

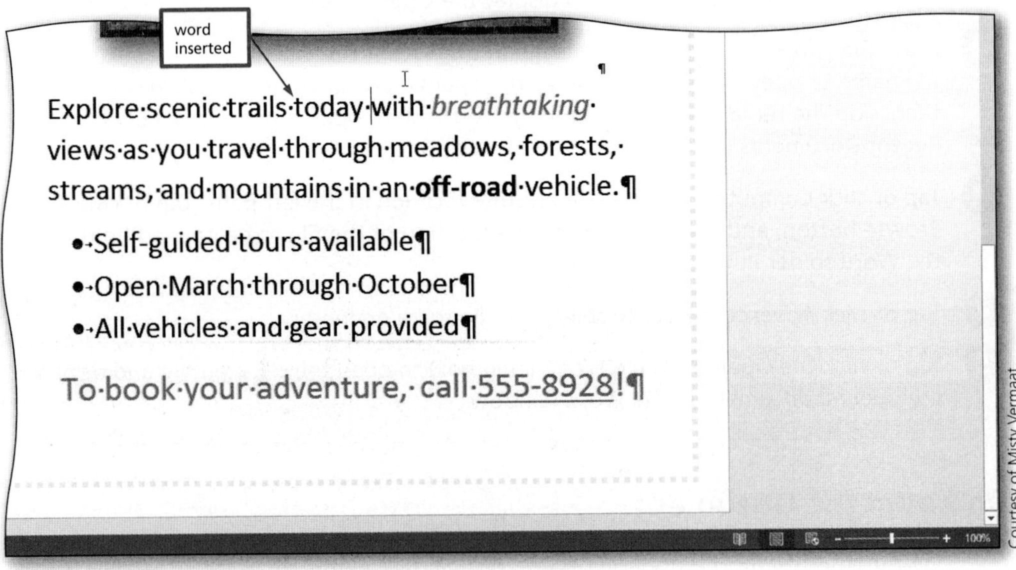
word inserted
Explore·scenic·trails·today·with·breathtaking·views·as·you·travel·through·meadows,·forests,·streams,·and·mountains·in·an·off-road·vehicle.¶
•·Self-guided·tours·available¶
•·Open·March·through·October¶
•·All·vehicles·and·gear·provided¶
To·book·your·adventure,·call·555-8928!¶
Courtesy of Misty Vermaat

Figure 1–65

To Delete Text

1 ENTER TEXT | 2 FORMAT TEXT | 3 INSERT PICTURE | 4 FORMAT PICTURE
5 ENHANCE PAGE | 6 CORRECT & REVISE | 7 PRINT OR READ

It is not unusual to type incorrect characters or words in a document. As discussed earlier in this chapter, you can tap or click the Undo button on the Quick Access Toolbar to undo a command or action immediately — this includes typing. Word also provides other methods of correcting typing errors.

To delete an incorrect character in a document, simply tap or click next to the incorrect character and then press the BACKSPACE key to erase to the left of the insertion point, or press the DELETE key to erase to the right of the insertion point.

To delete a word or phrase, you first must select the word or phrase. The following steps select the word, today, which was just added in the previous steps and then delete the selection. ***Why?*** *These steps illustrate the process of selecting a word and then deleting selected text.*

- Double-tap or double-click the word to be selected (in this case, today) to select the word (Figure 1–66).

- If you are using a touch screen, tap the selected text to display the mini toolbar and then tap the Cut button on the mini toolbar to delete the selected text; if you are using a keyboard, with the text selected, press the DELETE key to delete the selected text.

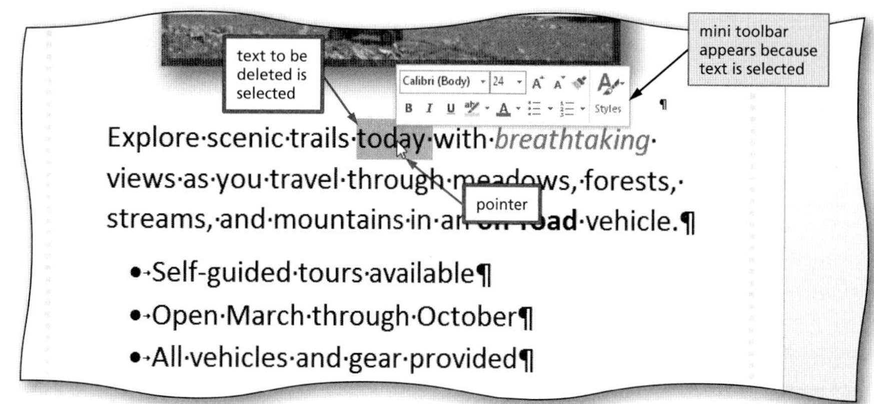
text to be deleted is selected
mini toolbar appears because text is selected
Explore·scenic·trails·today·with·breathtaking·
views·as·you·travel·through·meadows,·forests,·
streams,·and·mountains·in·an·off-road·vehicle.¶
pointer
•·Self-guided·tours·available¶
•·Open·March·through·October¶
•·All·vehicles·and·gear·provided¶
Courtesy of Misty Vermaat

Figure 1–66

Other Ways

1. Press and hold or right-click selected item, tap Cut on mini toolbar or click Cut on shortcut menu
2. Select item, press BACKSPACE to delete to left of insertion point or press DELETE to delete to right of insertion point
3. Select item, press CTRL+X

To Move Text

1 ENTER TEXT | 2 FORMAT TEXT | 3 INSERT PICTURE | 4 FORMAT PICTURE
5 ENHANCE PAGE | 6 CORRECT & REVISE | 7 PRINT OR READ

An efficient way to move text a short distance is drag-and-drop editing. With **drag-and-drop editing**, you select the item to be moved, drag the selected item to the new location, and then drop, or insert, it in the new location. Another technique for moving text is the cut-and-paste technique, which is discussed in the next chapter.

The following steps use drag-and-drop editing to move text. ***Why?*** *While proofreading the flyer, you realize that the body copy would read better if the last two bulleted paragraphs were reversed.*

- If you are using a mouse, position the pointer in the paragraph to be moved (in this case, the last bulleted item) and then triple-click to select the paragraph.
- If you are using a mouse, with the pointer in the selected text, press and hold down the mouse button, which displays a small dotted box with the pointer (Figure 1–67).

text deleted

text to be moved is selected

pointer has small box below it when you begin to drag selected text

Figure 1–67

2

- If you are using a mouse, drag the insertion point to the location where the selected text is to be moved, as shown in Figure 1–68.

selected text to be dropped at location of dotted insertion point

Figure 1–68

- If you are using a mouse, release the mouse button to move the selected text to the location of the dotted insertion point (Figure 1–69).

Q&A

What if I accidentally drag text to the wrong location?
Tap or click the Undo button on the Quick Access Toolbar and try again.

Can I use drag-and-drop editing to move any selected item?
Yes, you can select words, sentences, phrases, and graphics and then use drag-and-drop editing to move them.

What is the purpose of the Paste Options button?
If you are using a mouse and click the Paste Options button, a menu appears that allows you to change the format of the item that was moved. The next chapter discusses the Paste Options menu.

- Tap or click anywhere in the document window to remove the selection from the bulleted item.

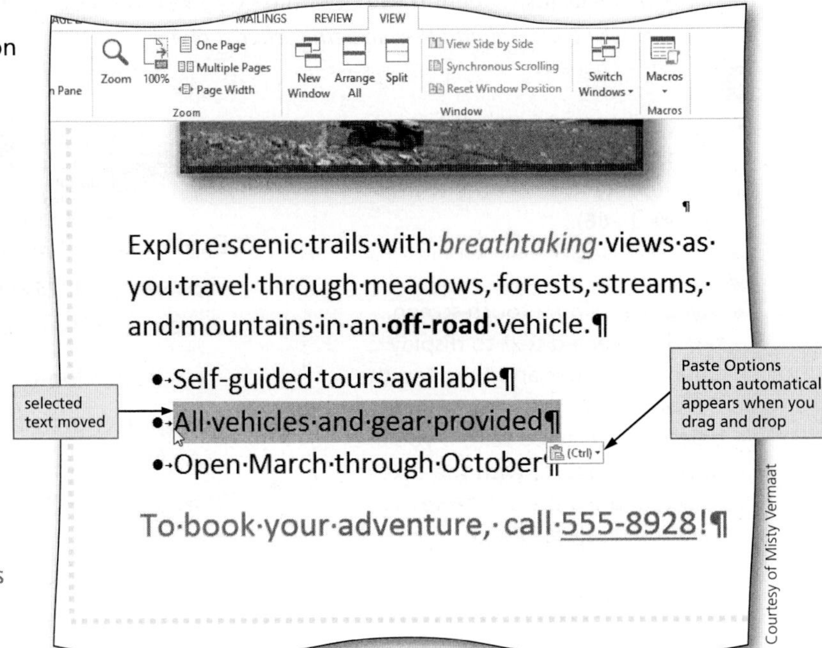

Figure 1–69

Q&A

What if I am using a touch screen?
If you have a stylus, you can follow Steps 1 through 3 using the stylus. If you are using your finger, you will need to use the cut-and-paste technique: tap to position the insertion point in the text to be moved and then drag the selection handles as necessary to select the text that you want to move; tap the selection to display the mini toolbar and then tap the Cut button on the mini toolbar to remove the text; tap to position the insertion point at the location where you want to move the text; display the HOME tab and then tap the Paste button on the HOME tab to place the text at the location of the insertion point. The next chapter discusses this procedure in more depth.

Other Ways

1. Tap or click Cut button (HOME tab | Clipboard group), tap or click where text or object is to be pasted, tap or click Paste button (HOME tab | Clipboard group)
2. Press and hold or right-click selected text, tap or click Cut on mini toolbar or shortcut menu, press and hold or right-click where text or object is to be pasted, tap Paste on mini toolbar or click Keep Source Formatting on shortcut menu
3. Press CTRL+X, position insertion point where text or object is to be pasted, press CTRL+V

BTW
Conserving Ink and Toner
If you want to conserve ink or toner, you can instruct Word to print draft quality documents by tapping or clicking FILE on the ribbon to open the Backstage view, tapping or clicking Options in the Backstage view, tapping or clicking Advanced in the left pane (Word Options dialog box), sliding or scrolling to the Print area in the right pane, placing a check mark in the 'Use draft quality' check box, and then tapping or clicking the OK button. Then, use the Backstage view to print the document as usual.

To Save an Existing Document with the Same File Name

You have made several modifications to the document since you last saved it. Thus, you should save it again. The following step saves the document again. For an example of the step listed below, refer to the Office and Windows chapter at the beginning of this book.

1. Tap or click the Save button on the Quick Access Toolbar to overwrite the previously saved file.

Printing or Reading a Document

After creating a document, you may want to print it or read it on-screen. Printing a document enables you to distribute it to others in a form that can be read or viewed but typically not edited. It is a good practice to save a document before printing it, in the event you experience difficulties printing. Some users prefer reading a document on-screen instead of on paper.

CONSIDER THIS

What is the best method for distributing a document?

The traditional method of distributing a document uses a printer to produce a hard copy. A **hard copy** or **printout** is information that exists on a physical medium such as paper. Hard copies can be useful for the following reasons:

- Some people prefer proofreading a hard copy of a document rather than viewing it on the screen to check for errors and readability.
- Hard copies can serve as a backup reference if your storage medium is lost or becomes corrupted and you need to recreate the document.

Instead of distributing a hard copy of a document, users can distribute the document as an electronic image that mirrors the original document's appearance. The electronic image of the document can be sent as an email attachment, posted on a website, or copied to a portable storage medium such as a USB flash drive. Two popular electronic image formats, sometimes called fixed formats, are PDF by Adobe Systems and XPS by Microsoft. In Word, you can create electronic image files through the Save As dialog box and the Export, Share, and Print tabs in the Backstage view. Electronic images of documents, such as PDF and XPS, can be useful for the following reasons:

- Users can view electronic images of documents without the software that created the original document (e.g., Word). Specifically, to view a PDF file, you use a program called Adobe Reader, which can be downloaded free from Adobe's website. Similarly, to view an XPS file, you use a program called XPS Viewer, which is included in the latest versions of Windows and Internet Explorer.
- Sending electronic documents saves paper and printer supplies. Society encourages users to contribute to **green computing**, which involves reducing the electricity consumed and environmental waste generated when using computers, mobile devices, and related technologies.

To Print a Document

1 ENTER TEXT | 2 FORMAT TEXT | 3 INSERT PICTURE | 4 FORMAT PICTURE
5 ENHANCE PAGE | 6 CORRECT & REVISE | **7 PRINT OR READ**

With the completed document saved, you may want to print it. ***Why?*** *Because this flyer is being posted, you will print a hard copy on a printer.* The following steps print a hard copy of the contents of the saved Adventure Flyer document.

- Tap or click FILE on the ribbon to open the Backstage view.
- Tap or click the Print tab in the Backstage view to display the Print gallery (Figure 1–70).

Q&A How can I print multiple copies of my document?
Increase the number in the Copies box in the Print gallery.

What if I decide not to print the document at this time?
Tap or click the Back button in the upper-left corner of the Backstage view to return to the document window.

- Verify that the printer listed on the Printer Status button will print a hard copy of the document. If necessary, click the Printer Status button to display a list of available printer options and then click the desired printer to change the currently selected printer.

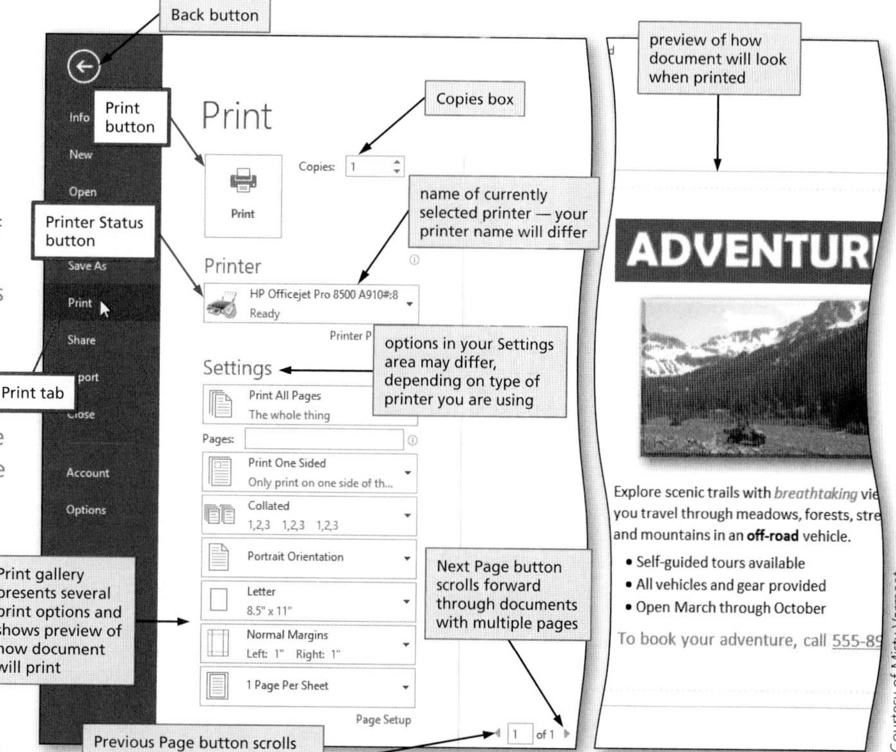

Figure 1–70

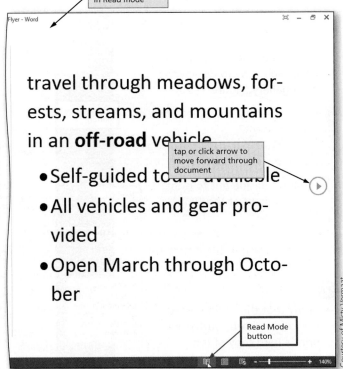

- Tap or click the Print button in the Print gallery to print the document on the currently selected printer.
- When the printer stops, retrieve the hard copy (Figure 1–71).

Q&A

Do I have to wait until my document is complete to print it?
No, you can follow these steps to print a document at any time while you are creating it.

What if I want to print an electronic image of a document instead of a hard copy?
You would click the Printer Status button in the Print gallery and then select the desired electronic image option, such as Microsoft XPS Document Writer, which would create an XPS file.

What if one or more of my borders do not print?
Tap or click the Page Borders button (DESIGN tab | Page Background group), tap or click the Options button (Borders and Shading dialog box), tap or click the Measure from arrow and click Text, change the four text boxes to 15 pt, and then tap or click the OK button in each dialog box. Try printing the document again. If the borders still do not print, adjust the boxes in the dialog box to a number smaller than 15 point.

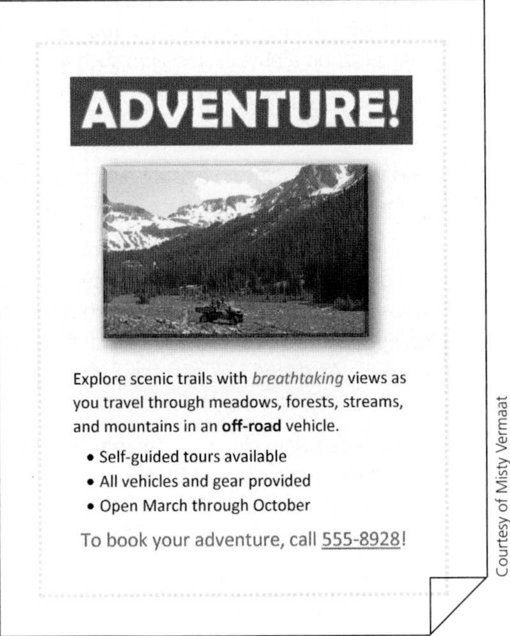

Figure 1–71

To Switch to Read Mode

1 ENTER TEXT | 2 FORMAT TEXT | 3 INSERT PICTURE | 4 FORMAT PICTURE
5 ENHANCE PAGE | 6 CORRECT & REVISE | **7 PRINT OR READ**

The next steps switch from Print Layout view to Read mode. ***Why?*** *If you are not composing a document, you can switch to* ***Read mode,*** *which hides the ribbon and other writing tools so that more content fits on the screen. Read mode is intended to make it easier to read a document.* The following step switches to Read mode.

1

- Tap or click the Read Mode button on the status bar to switch to Read mode (Figure 1–72).

Experiment

- Tap or click the arrows to advance forward and then move backward through the document.

Q&A

Besides reading, what can I do in Read mode?
You can zoom, copy text, highlight text, search, add comments, and more.

Figure 1–72

Other Ways

1. Tap or click Read Mode button (VIEW tab | Views group)
2. Tap or click VIEW on the ribbon, tap or click Edit Document

To Switch to Print Layout View

The next steps switch back to Print Layout view. ***Why?*** *If you want to show the document on a mock sheet of paper in the document window, along with the ribbon and other writing tools, you should switch to Print Layout view.* The following step switches to Print Layout view.

1

- Tap or click the Print Layout button on the status bar to switch to Print Layout view (Figure 1–73).

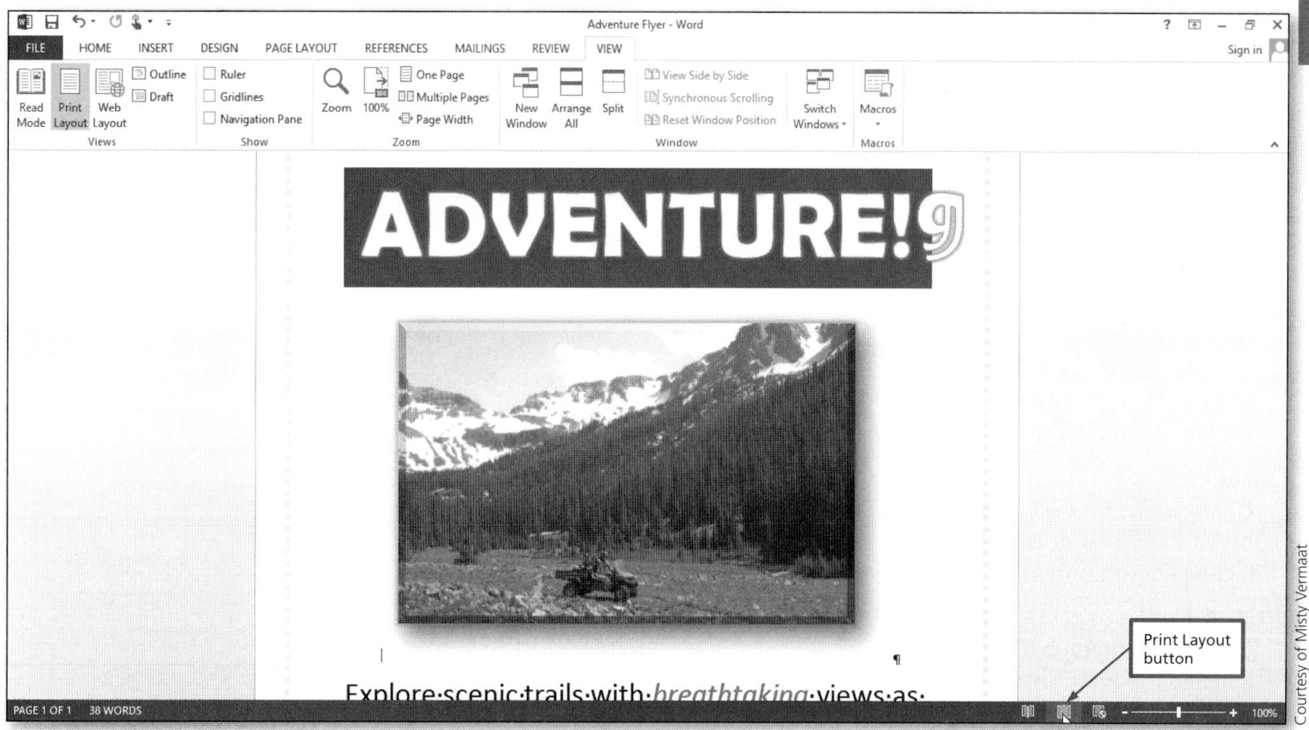

Figure 1–73

Other Ways

1. Tap or click Print Layout button (VIEW tab | Views group)

To Exit Word

This project now is complete. The following steps exit Word. For a detailed example of the procedure summarized below, refer to the Office and Windows chapter at the beginning of this book.

1a If you have one Word document open, tap or click the Close button on the right side of the title bar to close the open document and exit Word.

1b If you have multiple Word documents open, press and hold or right-click the Word app button on the taskbar and then tap or click 'Close all windows' on the shortcut menu to close all open documents and exit Word.

2 If a Microsoft Word dialog box appears, tap or click the Save button to save any changes made to the document since the last save.

BTW
Printing Document Properties
To print document properties, tap or click FILE on the ribbon to open the Backstage view, tap or click the Print tab in the Backstage view to display the Print gallery, tap or click the first button in the Settings area to display a list of options specifying what you can print, tap or click Document Info in the list to specify you want to print the document properties instead of the actual document, and then tap or click the Print button in the Print gallery to print the document properties on the currently selected printer.

Chapter Summary

In this chapter, you have learned how to enter text in a document, format text, insert and format a picture, add a page border, adjust paragraph and page spacing, and print and read a document. The items listed below include all the new Word skills you have learned in this chapter, with the tasks grouped by activity.

Enter and Edit Text
- Type Text (WD 5)
- Insert a Blank Line (WD 7)
- Wordwrap Text as You Type (WD 9)
- Check Spelling and Grammar as You Type (WD 10)
- Insert Text in an Existing Document (WD 48)
- Delete Text (WD 48)
- Move Text (WD 49)

File Management
- Run Word (WD 4)
- Save a Document (WD 12)
- Save an Existing Document with the Same File Name (WD 33)
- Change Document Properties (WD 44)
- Exit Word (WD 46)
- Open a Document from Word (WD 47)
- Print a Document (WD 51)

Format a Page
- Change Theme Colors (WD 31)
- Add a Page Border (WD 41)
- Center Page Contents Vertically (WD 43)

Format Text
- Center a Paragraph (WD 15)
- Change the Font Size of Selected Text (WD 17)
- Change the Font of Selected Text (WD 18)
- Change the Case of Selected Text (WD 19)
- Apply a Text Effect to Selected Text (WD 20)
- Shade a Paragraph (WD 21)
- Bullet a List of Paragraphs (WD 23)
- Undo and Redo an Action (WD 24)
- Italicize Text (WD 25)
- Color Text (WD 26)
- Use the Mini Toolbar to Format Text (WD 27)
- Underline Text (WD 29)
- Bold Text (WD 29)
- Change Spacing before and after Paragraphs (WD 42)

Select Text
- Select a Line (WD 16)
- Select Multiple Lines (WD 22)
- Select a Group of Words (WD 28)

Word Settings
- Display Formatting Marks (WD 6)
- Zoom Page Width (WD 7)
- Zoom One Page (WD 30)
- Zoom the Document (WD 35)
- Zoom 100% (WD 37)
- Switch to Read Mode (WD 52)
- Switch to Print Layout View (WD 53)

Work with Graphics (Pictures)
- Insert a Picture (WD 34)
- Resize a Graphic (WD 36)
- Apply a Picture Style (WD 38)
- Apply Picture Effects (WD 39)

CONSIDER THIS: PLAN AHEAD

What decisions will you need to make when creating your next flyer?

Use these guidelines as you complete the assignments in this chapter and create your own flyers outside of this class.

1. Choose the text for the headline, body copy, and signature line — using as few words as possible to make a point.
2. Format various elements of the text.
   a) Select appropriate font sizes for text in the headline, body copy, and signature line.
   b) Select appropriate fonts for text in the headline, body copy, and signature line.
   c) Adjust paragraph alignment, as appropriate.
   d) Highlight key paragraphs with bullets.
   e) Emphasize important words.
   f) Use color to convey meaning and add appeal.
3. Find an eye-catching graphic(s) that conveys the overall message and meaning of the flyer.
4. Establish where to position and how to format the graphical image(s) so that the image grabs the attention of passersby and draws them into reading the flyer.
5. Determine whether the flyer needs enhancements such as a graphical, color-coordinated border or spacing adjustments to improve readability or overall appearance.
6. Correct errors and revise the document as necessary.
   a) Post the flyer on a wall and make sure all text and images are legible from a distance.
   b) Ask someone else to read the flyer and give you suggestions for improvements.
7. Determine the best method for distributing the document such as printing, sending via email, or posting on the web.

How should you submit solutions to questions in the assignments identified with a ✲ symbol?
Every assignment in this book contains one or more questions identified with a ✲ symbol. These questions require you to think beyond the assigned document. Present your solutions to the questions in the format required by your instructor. Possible formats may include one or more of these options: write the answer; create a document that contains the answer; present your answer to the class; discuss your answer in a group; record the answer as audio or video using a webcam, smartphone, or portable media player; or post answers on a blog, wiki, or website.

Apply Your Knowledge

Reinforce the skills and apply the concepts you learned in this chapter.

Modifying Text and Formatting a Document

Note: To complete this assignment, you will be required to use the Data Files for Students. Visit www.cengage.com/ct/studentdownload for detailed instructions or contact your instructor for information about accessing the required files.

Instructions: Run Word. Open the document, Apply 1-1 County Park Flyer Unformatted, from the Data Files for Students. The document you open is an unformatted flyer. You are to modify text, format paragraphs and characters, and insert a picture in the flyer to create the flyer shown in Figure 1–74.

Perform the following tasks:

1. Delete the word, below, in the sentence below the headline.
2. Insert the word, Valley, between the words, Green County, in the second to last line of the flyer.
3. Change the period to an exclamation point in the last line so that the text reads: Thank You!
4. If requested by your instructor, change the phone number in the flyer to your phone number.
5. Center the headline and the last two paragraphs of the flyer.
6. Select the third, fourth, and fifth paragraphs in the flyer and add bullets to the selected paragraphs.
7. Change the theme colors to the Red Orange color scheme.
8. Change the font and font size of the headline to 48-point Franklin Gothic Heavy, or a similar font. Change the case of the headline text to uppercase letters. Apply the text effect called Fill - Black, Text 1, Outline - Background 1, Hard Shadow - Background 1 to the headline. Change the font color of the headline text to Dark Red, Accent 6.

Figure 1–74

Continued >

Apply Your Knowledge *continued*

9. Change the font size of the sentence below the headline, the bulleted list, and the last line of flyer to 26 point.
10. Use the mini toolbar to change the font size of the sentence below the bulleted list to 18 point.
11. Select the words, Follow these guidelines, in the paragraph below the headline and underline them.
12. Bold the word, not, in the first bulleted paragraph. Change the font color of this same word to Dark Red, Accent 6.
13. Italicize the word, all, in the second bulleted item. Undo this change and then redo the change.
14. Switch the last two bulleted paragraphs. That is, select the 'Never leave food unattended' bullet and move it so that it is the second bulleted paragraph.
15. Bold the text, Thank You!, in the last line of the flyer. Shade this same paragraph Dark Red, Accent 6, Darker 25%. If the font color does not automatically change to a lighter color, change its color to White, Background 1.
16. Change the zoom so that the entire page is visible in the document window.
17. Insert the picture of the squirrel eating the sucker centered on the blank line below the headline. The picture is called Squirrel and is available on the Data Files for Students. Apply the Soft Edge Oval picture style to the inserted picture.
18. Change the spacing before the first bulleted paragraph to 12 point and the spacing after the last bulleted paragraph to 24 point.
19. The entire flyer should fit on a single page. If it flows to two pages, resize the picture or decrease spacing before and after paragraphs until the entire flyer text fits on a single page.
20. Change the zoom to text width, then page width, then 100% and notice the differences.
21. If requested by your instructor, enter the text, Green Valley, as the keywords in the document properties. Change the other document properties, as specified by your instructor.
22. Click FILE on the ribbon and then click Save As. Save the document using the file name, Apply 1-1 County Park Flyer Formatted.
23. Print the document. Switch to Read Mode and browse pages through the document. Switch to Print Layout view.
24. Submit the revised document, shown in Figure 1–74, in the format specified by your instructor.
25. Exit Word.
26. If this flyer were announcing the park reopening instead of including a warning, which color scheme would you apply and why?

Extend Your Knowledge

Extend the skills you learned in this chapter and experiment with new skills. You may need to use Help to complete the assignment.

Modifying Text and Picture Formats and Adding Page Borders

Note: To complete this assignment, you will be required to use the Data Files for Students. Visit www.cengage.com/ct/studentdownload for detailed instructions or contact your instructor for information about accessing the required files.

Instructions: Run Word. Open the document, Extend 1-1 Baseball Tryouts Flyer Draft, from the Data Files for Students. You will enhance the look of the flyer shown in Figure 1–75. *Hint:* Remember, if you make a mistake while formatting the picture, you can reset it by using the Reset Picture button or Reset Picture arrow (PICTURE TOOLS FORMAT tab | Adjust group).

Perform the following tasks:

1. Use Help to learn about the following: remove bullets, grow font, shrink font, art page borders, decorative underline(s), picture bullets, picture border shading, picture border color, shadow picture effects, and color saturation and tone.
2. Remove the bullet from the last line of the flyer.
3. Select the text, August 30, and use the 'Increase Font Size' button (HOME tab | Font group) to increase its font size.
4. Add an art page border to the flyer. If the border is not in color, add color to it.
5. Change the solid underline below the word, Travel, to a decorative underline. Change the color of the underline.
6. Change the style of the bullets to picture bullet(s). Adjust the hanging indent, if necessary, to align the text in bulleted list.
7. Change the color of the picture border. Add the Perspective Right 3-D Rotation picture effect to the picture.
8. Change the color saturation and color tone of the picture.
9. If requested by your instructor, change the name of the field (High Crop) to your last name.
10. Save the revised document with the file name, Extend 1-1 Baseball Tryouts Flyer Final, and then submit it in the format specified by your instructor.
11. In this assignment you added an art page border to the flyer. Which border did you select and why?

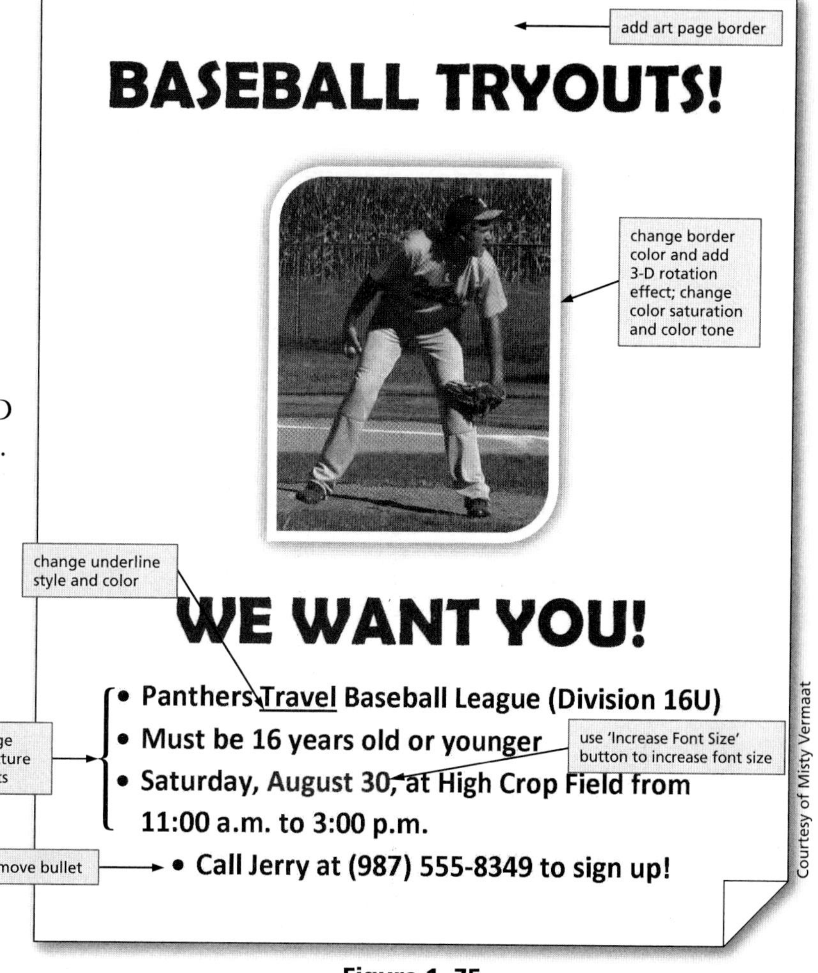

Figure 1–75

Analyze, Correct, Improve

Analyze a document, correct all errors, and improve it.

Correcting Spelling and Grammar Errors and Adding Color

Note: To complete this assignment, you will be required to use the Data Files for Students. Visit www.cengage.com/ct/studentdownload for detailed instructions or contact your instructor for information about accessing the required files.

Instructions: Run Word. Open the document, Analyze 1-1 Beauty Salon Flyer Draft, from the Data Files for Students. The document is a flyer that contains spelling and grammar errors, as shown in Figure 1–76 on the next page. It also could include color to make it more visually appealing.

Continued >

Analyze, Correct, Improve *continued*

1. Correct You are to correct each spelling (red wavy underline) and grammar (green and blue wavy underlines) error by pressing and holding or right-clicking the flagged text and then clicking the appropriate correction on the shortcut menu.

If your screen does not display the wavy underlines, tap or click FILE on the ribbon and then tap or click Options in the Backstage view. When the Word Options dialog box is displayed, tap or click Proofing in the left pane, be sure the 'Hide spelling errors in this document only' and 'Hide grammar errors in this document only' check boxes do not contain check marks, and then tap or click the OK button. If your screen still does not display the wavy underlines, redisplay the Word Options dialog box, tap or click Proofing, and then tap or click the Recheck Document button.

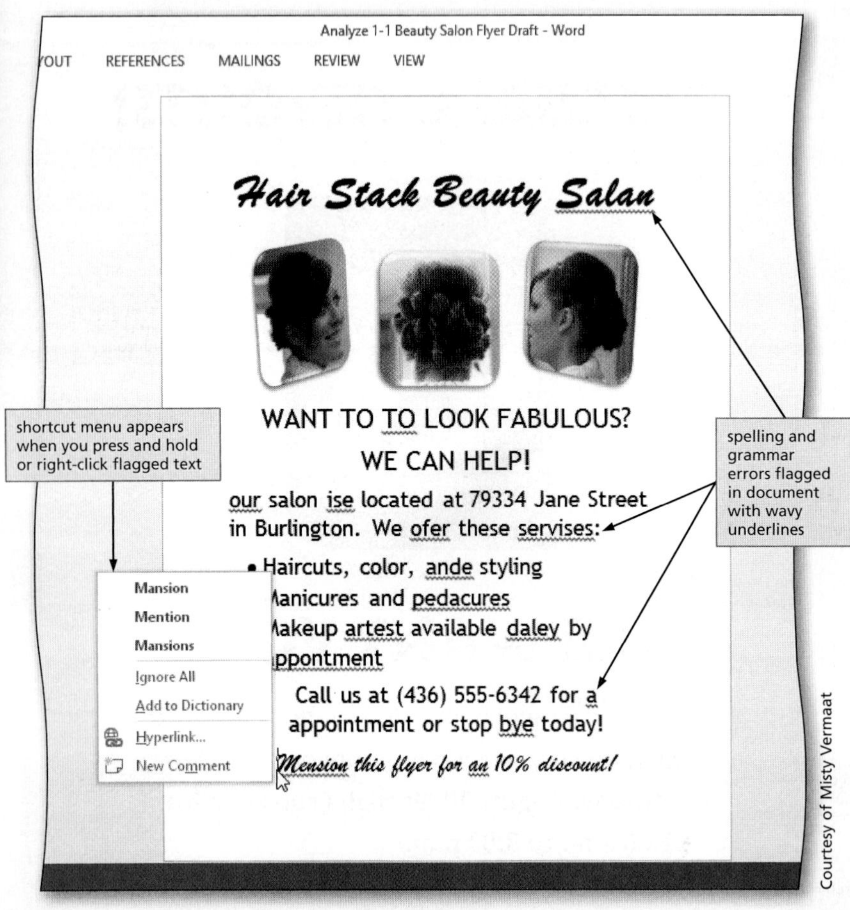

Figure 1–76

2. Improve Enhance the flyer by (a) adding a shading color to the first and last lines (paragraphs) on the flyer, (b) changing the color of the text in the first line and last line of the flyer, and (c) adding a color glow effect to the three pictures in the flyer.

If requested by your instructor, change the street name in the flyer to your first name. Save the revised document with the file name, Extend 1-1 Beauty Salon Flyer Final, and then submit it in the format specified by your instructor.

3. In this assignment, you selected color to add to the flyer. Which color(s) did you select and why?

In the Labs

Design and/or create a document using the guidelines, concepts, and skills presented in this chapter. Labs 1 and 2, which increase in difficulty, require you to create solutions based on what you learned in the chapter; Lab 3 requires you to create a solution, which uses cloud and web technologies, by learning and investigating on your own from general guidance.

Lab 1: Creating a Flyer with a Picture

Problem: Your friend asked you to prepare a flyer that advertises the puppy she has for sale. First, you prepare the unformatted flyer shown in Figure 1–77a, and then you format it so that it looks like Figure 1–77b on page WD 60. *Hint:* Remember, if you make a mistake while formatting the flyer, you can use the Undo button on the Quick Access Toolbar to undo your last action.

Note: To complete this assignment, you will be required to use the Data Files for Students. Visit www.cengage.com/ct/studentdownload for detailed instructions or contact your instructor for information about accessing the required files.

Instructions: Perform the following tasks:

1. Run Word. Display formatting marks on the screen.
2. Type the flyer text, unformatted, as shown in Figure 1–77a, inserting a blank line between the headline and the body copy. If Word flags any misspelled words as you type, check their spelling and correct them.
3. Save the document using the file name, Lab 1-1 Puppy for Sale Flyer.
4. Center the headline and the signature line.
5. Change the theme colors to Aspect.
6. Change the font size of the headline to 72 point and the font to Gil Sans Ultra Bold Condensed, or a similar font. Apply the text effect called Fill - Dark Purple, Accent 1, Outline - Background, Hard Shadow - Accent 1.
7. Change the font size of body copy between the headline and the signature line to 22 point.
8. Change the font size of the signature line to 20 point.
9. Change the font of the body copy and signature line to Comic Sans MS.
10. Bullet the three lines (paragraphs) of text above the signature line.
11. Change the color of the words, purebred American Cocker Spaniel, to Dark Green, Accent 4, Darker 50%.
12. Italicize the word, and, in the third bulleted paragraph.
13. Bold the text in the signature line. Shade this paragraph containing the signature line in Dark Purple, Accent 5, Lighter 80%.
14. Underline the phone number in the signature line.
15. Change the zoom so that the entire page is visible in the document window.
16. Insert the picture centered on a blank line below the headline. The picture is called Puppy and is available on the Data Files for Students.
17. Apply the Rotated, White picture style to the inserted picture. Apply the glow effect called Dark Purple, 5 pt glow, Accent color 5 to the picture.

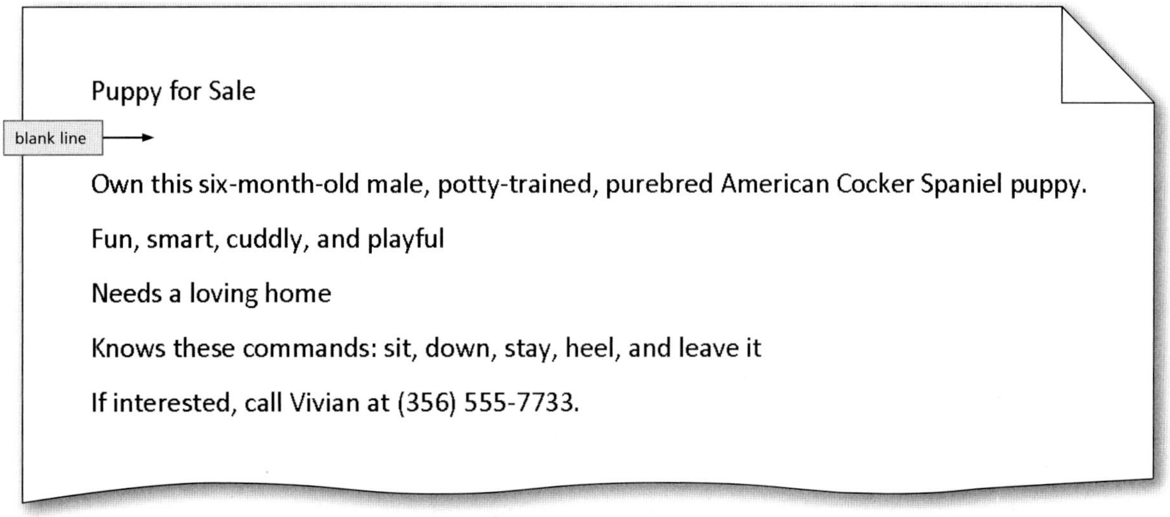

Puppy for Sale

blank line

Own this six-month-old male, potty-trained, purebred American Cocker Spaniel puppy.

Fun, smart, cuddly, and playful

Needs a loving home

Knows these commands: sit, down, stay, heel, and leave it

If interested, call Vivian at (356) 555-7733.

(a) Unformatted Text
Figure 1–77 (Continued)

Continued >

In the Labs *continued*

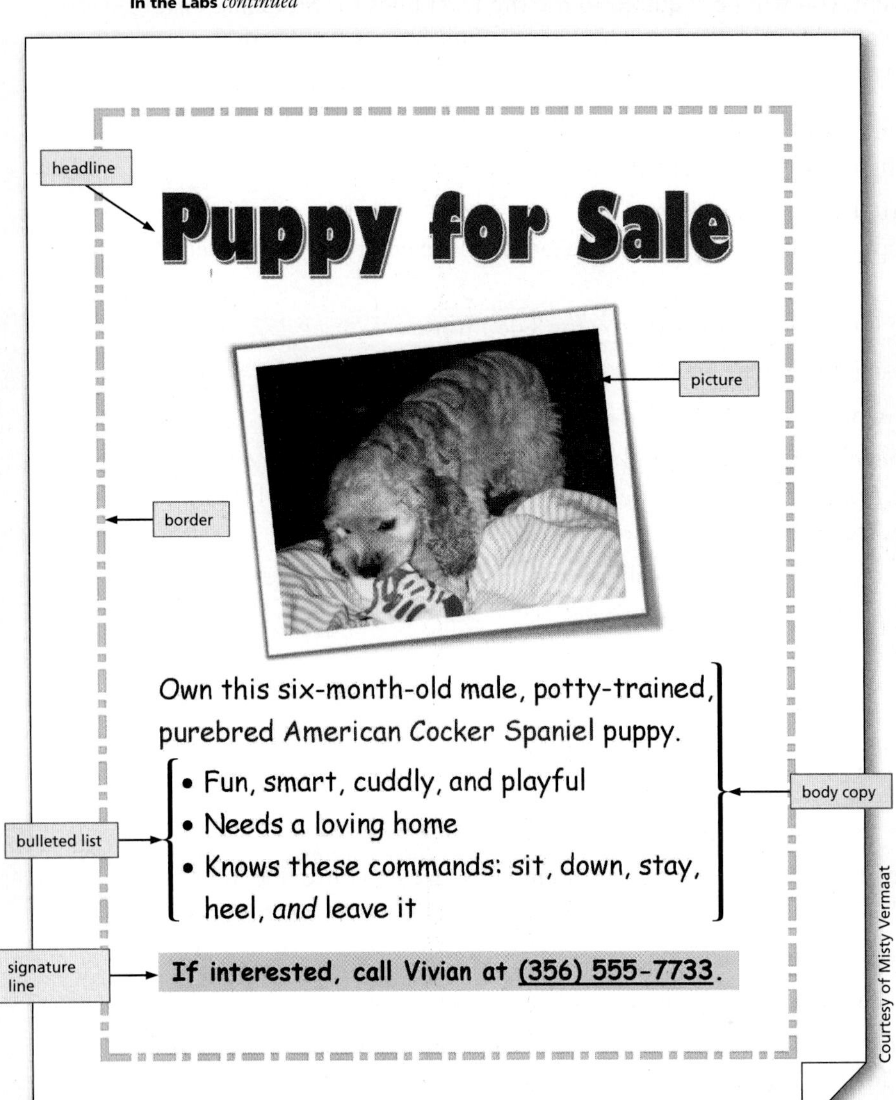

(b) Formatted Document
Figure 1–77 (Continued)

18. Change the spacing after the paragraph containing the headline to 0 pt. Change the spacing above (before) the signature line to 18 pt. The entire flyer should fit on a single page. If it flows to two pages, resize the picture or decrease spacing before and after paragraphs until the entire flyer text fits on a single page.
19. Add a 6-pt Dark Green, Accent 4, Lighter 60% page border, as shown in Figure 1–77b.
20. If requested by your instructor, change the contact name in the flyer to your first name.
21. Save the flyer again with the same file name. Submit the document, shown in Figure 1–77b, in the format specified by your instructor.
22. Why do you think this flyer used shades of purple and green?

Lab 2: Creating a Flyer with a Resized Pictures

Problem: Your boss at Junior's Wedding Bakery has asked you to prepare a flyer that promotes its business. You prepare the flyer shown in Figure 1–78. *Hint:* Remember, if you make a mistake while formatting the flyer, you can use the Undo button on the Quick Access Toolbar to undo your last action.

Note: To complete this assignment, you will be required to use the Data Files for Students. Visit www.cengage.com/ct/studentdownload for detailed instructions or contact your instructor for information about accessing the required files.

Instructions: Perform the following tasks:

1. Run Word. Type the flyer text, unformatted. If Word flags any misspelled words as you type, check their spelling and correct them.
2. Save the document using the file name, Lab 1-2 Wedding Bakery Flyer.
3. Change the theme colors to the Marquee color scheme.

4. Add bullets to the three paragraphs shown in the figure. Center all paragraphs, except the paragraphs containing the bulleted list.
5. Change the font size of the headline to 36 point and the font to Franklin Gothic Heavy, or a similar font. Apply the text effect called Fill - Orange, Accent 3, Sharp Bevel.
6. Change the font size of body copy between the headline and signature line to 20 point, except for line above the bulleted list, which is 24 point.
7. Change the font size of the signature line to 22 point. Bold the text in the signature line. Change the font color of the text in the signature line to Orange, Accent 3.
8. Italicize the word, personalize.
9. Bold the text above the bulleted list.
10. Underline the text, Junior's Wedding Bakery.
11. Shade the line above the bulleted list to the Orange, Accent 3 color. If the font color does not automatically change to a lighter color, change it to White, Background 1.
12. Change the zoom so that the entire page is visible in the document window.
13. Insert the first picture on a blank line below the headline and the second picture on a blank line below the bulleted list. The pictures are called Bakery 1 and Bakery 2, respectively, and are available on the Data Files for Students.
14. Resize the top picture so that it is approximately 2.8" × 5.39". Apply the Soft Edge Oval picture style to the top inserted picture. Apply the Offset Right Shadow picture effect to the top picture. Resize the bottom picture so that it is approximately 1.5" × 4.05". Apply the Simple Frame, Black picture style to the bottom inserted picture.
15. Change the spacing after the paragraph containing the bakery name to 0 pt and the spacing after the last bulleted paragraph to 12 pt. The entire flyer should fit on a single page. If it flows to two pages, resize the picture or decrease spacing before and after paragraphs until the entire flyer text fits on a single page.
16. Add the page border shown in Figure 1–78, using the color Gold, Accent 5.
17. Center the page contents vertically.
18. If requested by your instructor, change the bakery name to your last name.
19. Save the flyer again with the same file name. Submit the document, shown in Figure 1–78, in the format specified by your instructor.
20. Why do you think this flyer used shades of orange and yellow?

Figure 1–78

Lab 3: Expand Your World: Cloud and Web Technologies

Using the Word Web App to Create a Flyer with a Picture

Problem: You have a side business where you build bean bag toss boards. You would like to create a flyer that promotes this business. You will use the Word Web App to prepare a flyer. The text for the unformatted flyer is shown in Figure 1–79.

Note: To complete this assignment, you will be required to use the Data Files for Students. Visit www.cengage.com/ct/studentdownload for detailed instructions or contact your instructor for information about accessing the required files.

Instructions: Perform the following tasks:

1. Run a browser. Search for the text, Word Web App, using a search engine. Visit several websites to learn about the Word Web App. Navigate to the Office Web Apps website. You will need to sign in to your SkyDrive account.
2. Use the Create button to begin creating a Word document using the Word Web App. Name the document Lab 1-3 Bean Bag Toss Flyer.
3. Notice the differences between the Word Web App and the Word desktop app you used to create the project in this chapter.
4. Enter the text in the flyer, shown in Figure 1–79, checking spelling as you type.

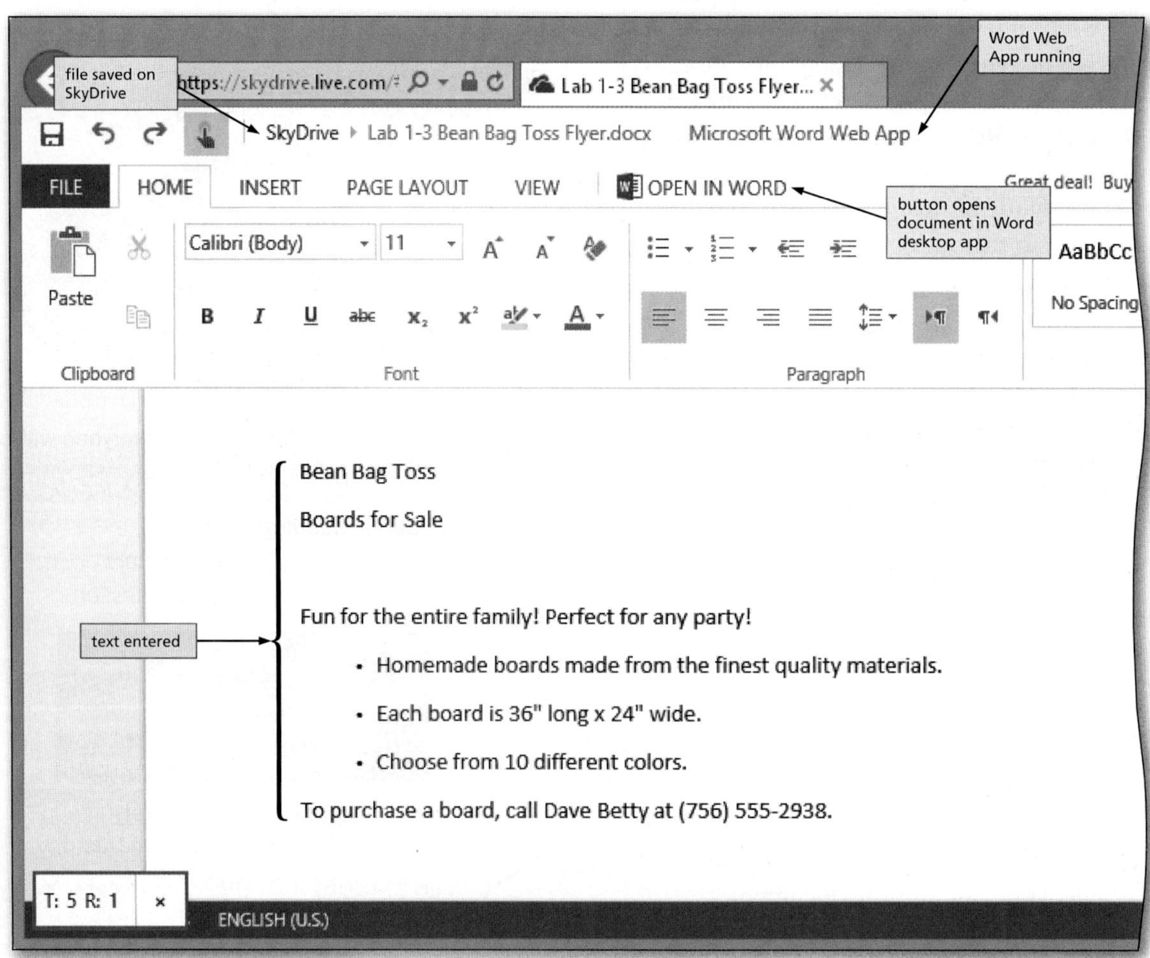

Figure 1–79

5. Insert the picture called Bean Bag Toss, which is located on the Data Files for Students.
6. Use the features available in the Word Web App, along with the concepts and techniques presented in this chapter, to format this flyer. Be sure to change the font and font size of text, center a paragraph(s), italicize text, color text, underline text, and apply a picture style. Adjust spacing above and below paragraphs as necessary. Resize the picture, if necessary.
7. If requested by your instructor, replace the contact name in the flyer with your name.
8. Save the document again. Tap or click the button to open the document in the Word desktop app. If necessary, sign in to your Microsoft account when prompted. Notice how the document appears in the Word desktop app.
9. Using either the Word Web App or Word desktop app, submit the document in the format requested by your instructor. Exit the Word Web App (FILE tab | Exit). Sign out of your SkyDrive account. Sign out of the Microsoft account in Word.
10. What is the Word Web App? Which features that are covered in this chapter are not available in the Word Web App? Do you prefer using the Word Web App or the Word desktop app? Why?

Consider This: Your Turn

Apply your creative thinking and problem solving skills to design and implement a solution.

Note: To complete these assignments, you may be required to use the Data Files for Students. Visit www.cengage.com/ct/studentdownload for detailed instructions or contact your instructor for information about accessing the required files.

1: Design and Create a Photography Club Flyer

Personal

Part 1: As secretary of your school's Photography Club, you are responsible for creating and distributing flyers announcing the club. The flyer should contain two digital pictures appropriately resized; the Data Files for Students contains two pictures called Photography 1 and Photography 2, or you can use your own digital pictures if they are appropriate for the topic of the flyer. The flyer should contain the headline, Photography Club, and this signature line: Questions? Call Emily at (883) 555-0901. The body copy consists of the following text, in any order: Do you love photography? This is the club for you! All skill levels are welcome. Meetings every Tuesday at 5:00 p.m. in the Student Center (room 232). Bring your camera. We look forward to seeing you at our next meeting!

Use the concepts and techniques presented in this chapter to create and format this flyer. Be sure to check spelling and grammar. Submit your assignment and answers to the critical thinking questions in the format specified by your instructor.

Part 2: You made several decisions while creating the flyer in this assignment: where to place text, how to format the text (i.e., font, font size, paragraph alignment, bulleted paragraphs, underlines, italics, bold, color, etc.), which graphics to use, where to position the graphics, how to format the graphics, and which page enhancements to add (i.e., borders and spacing). What was the rationale behind each of these decisions? When you proofread the document, what further revisions did you make and why? How would you recommend distributing this flyer?

2: Design and Create a Hot Air Balloon Rides Flyer

Professional

Part 1: As a part-time employee at Galaxy Recreations, your boss has asked you to create and distribute flyers announcing hot air balloon rides. The flyer should contain two digital pictures appropriately resized; the Data Files for Students contains two pictures called Hot Air Balloon 1

Continued >

Consider This: Your Turn *continued*

and Hot Air Balloon 2, or you can use your own digital pictures if they are appropriate for the topic of the flyer. The flyer should contain the headline, Hot Air Balloon Rides, and this signature line: For reservations, call (485) 555-2295. The body copy consists of the following text, in any order: Amazing sights from incredible heights! The experience of a lifetime. Fun for the whole family. No pets. Bring your camera. Open seven days a week from 10:00 a.m. to 4:00 p.m. Book your private tour with Galaxy Recreations today!

Use the concepts and techniques presented in this chapter to create and format this flyer. Be sure to check spelling and grammar. Submit your assignment in the format specified by your instructor.

Part 2: You made several decisions while creating the flyer in this assignment: where to place text, how to format the text (i.e., font, font size, paragraph alignment, bulleted paragraphs, underlines, italics, bold, color, etc.), which graphics to use, where to position the graphics, how to format the graphics, and which page enhancements to add (i.e., borders and spacing). What was the rationale behind each of these decisions? When you proofread the document, what further revisions did you make and why? How would you recommend distributing this flyer?

3: Design and Create a Water Park Flyer

Research and Collaboration

Part 1: As a part-time employee at a local water park, your boss has asked you and two other employees to create and distribute flyers for the upcoming water park season. Form a three-member team to compose and create this flyer. Research a local water park: its location, hours, prices, rules, specials, etc. As a group, determine the text for the flyer's headline, body copy, and signature line. Your team also will need to obtain at least two digital pictures appropriate for the content of this flyer. You could take the pictures with a digital camera or search for public-domain images on the web.

Use the concepts and techniques presented in this chapter to create and format this flyer. Be sure to check spelling and grammar. Submit your team assignment in the format specified by your instructor.

Part 2: You made several decisions while creating the flyer in this assignment: text to use, where to place text, how to format the text (i.e., font, font size, paragraph alignment, bulleted paragraphs, underlines, italics, bold, color, etc.), which graphics to use, where to position the graphics, how to format the graphics, and which page enhancements to add (i.e., borders and spacing). What was the rationale behind each of these decisions? When you proofread the document, what further revisions did you make and why? What research methods did you use to create the flyer? Where did you obtain your pictures? How would you recommend distributing this flyer?

Learn Online

Reinforce what you learned in this chapter with games, exercises, training, and many other online activities and resources.

Student Companion Site Reinforcement activities and resources are available at no additional cost on www.cengagebrain.com. Visit www.cengage.com/ct/studentdownload for detailed instructions about accessing the resources available at the Student Companion Site.

SAM

SAM Put your skills into practice with SAM Projects! If you have a SAM account, go to www.cengage.com/sam2013 to access SAM assignments for this chapter.

2 Creating a Research Paper with References and Sources

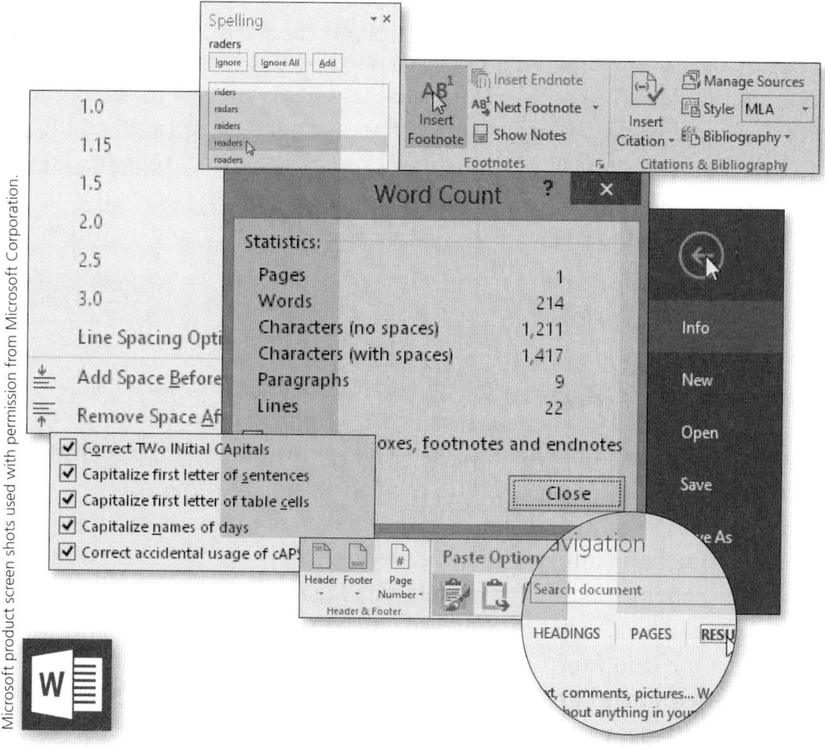

Objectives

You will have mastered the material in this chapter when you can:

- Describe the MLA documentation style for research papers
- Modify a style
- Change line and paragraph spacing in a document
- Use a header to number pages of a document
- Apply formatting using keyboard shortcuts
- Modify paragraph indentation
- Insert and edit citations and their sources
- Add a footnote to a document
- Insert a manual page break
- Create a bibliographical list of sources
- Cut, copy, and paste text
- Find text and replace text
- Find a synonym
- Check spelling and grammar at once
- Look up information

2 Creating a Research Paper with References and Sources

Introduction

In both academic and business environments, you will be asked to write reports. Business reports range from proposals to cost justifications to five-year plans to research findings. Academic reports focus mostly on research findings.

A **research paper** is a document you can use to communicate the results of research findings. To write a research paper, you learn about a particular topic from a variety of sources (research), organize your ideas from the research results, and then present relevant facts and/or opinions that support the topic. Your final research paper combines properly credited outside information along with personal insights. Thus, no two research papers — even if they are about the same topic — will or should be the same.

Project — Research Paper

When preparing a research paper, you should follow a standard documentation style that defines the rules for creating the paper and crediting sources. A variety of documentation styles exists, depending on the nature of the research paper. Each style requires the same basic information; the differences in styles relate to requirements for presenting the information. For example, one documentation style uses the term bibliography for the list of sources, whereas another uses references, and yet a third prefers the title works cited. Two popular documentation styles for research papers are the **Modern Language Association of America** (**MLA**) and **American Psychological Association** (**APA**) styles. This chapter uses the MLA documentation style because it is used in a wide range of disciplines.

BTW
APA Appendix
If your version of this book includes the Word APA Appendix and you are required to create a research paper using the APA documentation style instead of the MLA documentation style, the appendix shows the steps required to create the research paper in this chapter using following APA guidelines. If your version of this book does not include the Word APA Appendix, see online or print publications for the APA guidelines or see your instructor.

The project in this chapter follows research paper guidelines and uses Word to create the short research paper shown in Figure 2–1. This paper, which discusses biometric devices, follows the MLA documentation style. Each page contains a page number. The first two pages present the name and course information (student name, instructor name, course name, and paper due date), paper title, an introduction with a thesis statement, details that support the thesis, and a conclusion. This section of the paper also includes references to research sources and a footnote. The third page contains a detailed, alphabetical list of the sources referenced in the research paper. All pages include a header at the upper-right edge of the page.

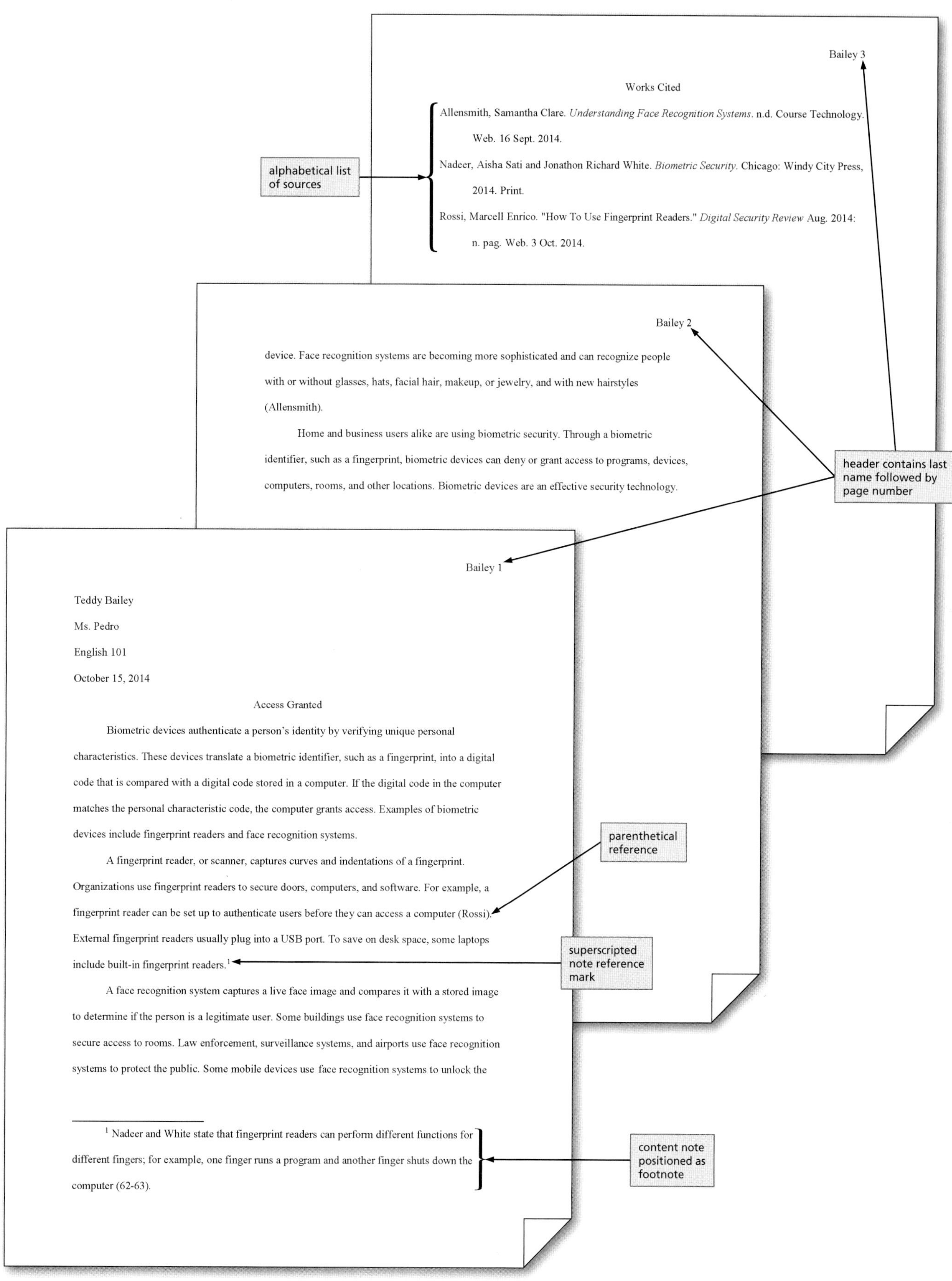
Bailey 3
Works Cited
Allensmith, Samantha Clare. *Understanding Face Recognition Systems*. n.d. Course Technology. Web. 16 Sept. 2014.
Nadeer, Aisha Sati and Jonathon Richard White. *Biometric Security*. Chicago: Windy City Press, 2014. Print.
Rossi, Marcell Enrico. "How To Use Fingerprint Readers." *Digital Security Review* Aug. 2014: n. pag. Web. 3 Oct. 2014.
alphabetical list of sources
Bailey 2
device. Face recognition systems are becoming more sophisticated and can recognize people with or without glasses, hats, facial hair, makeup, or jewelry, and with new hairstyles (Allensmith).
Home and business users alike are using biometric security. Through a biometric identifier, such as a fingerprint, biometric devices can deny or grant access to programs, devices, computers, rooms, and other locations. Biometric devices are an effective security technology.
header contains last name followed by page number
Bailey 1
Teddy Bailey
Ms. Pedro
English 101
October 15, 2014
Access Granted
Biometric devices authenticate a person's identity by verifying unique personal characteristics. These devices translate a biometric identifier, such as a fingerprint, into a digital code that is compared with a digital code stored in a computer. If the digital code in the computer matches the personal characteristic code, the computer grants access. Examples of biometric devices include fingerprint readers and face recognition systems.
A fingerprint reader, or scanner, captures curves and indentations of a fingerprint. Organizations use fingerprint readers to secure doors, computers, and software. For example, a fingerprint reader can be set up to authenticate users before they can access a computer (Rossi). External fingerprint readers usually plug into a USB port. To save on desk space, some laptops include built-in fingerprint readers.[1]
A face recognition system captures a live face image and compares it with a stored image to determine if the person is a legitimate user. Some buildings use face recognition systems to secure access to rooms. Law enforcement, surveillance systems, and airports use face recognition systems to protect the public. Some mobile devices use face recognition systems to unlock the
[1] Nadeer and White state that fingerprint readers can perform different functions for different fingers; for example, one finger runs a program and another finger shuts down the computer (62-63).
parenthetical reference
superscripted note reference mark
content note positioned as footnote

Figure 2–1

For an introduction to Windows and instruction about how to perform basic Windows tasks, read the Office and Windows chapter at the beginning of this book, where you can learn how to resize windows, change screen resolution, create folders, move and rename files, use Windows Help, and much more.

Roadmap

In this chapter, you will learn how to create the research paper shown in Figure 2–1 on the previous page. The following roadmap identifies general activities you will perform as you progress through this chapter:

1. CHANGE the DOCUMENT SETTINGS.
2. CREATE the HEADER for each page of the research paper.
3. TYPE the RESEARCH PAPER text WITH CITATIONS.
4. CREATE an ALPHABETICAL WORKS CITED page.
5. PROOFREAD AND REVISE the RESEARCH PAPER.

At the beginning of step instructions throughout the chapter, you will see an abbreviated form of this roadmap. The abbreviated roadmap uses colors to indicate chapter progress: gray means the chapter is beyond that activity, blue means the task being shown is covered in that activity, and black means that activity is yet to be covered. For example, the following abbreviated roadmap indicates the chapter would be showing a task in the 2 CREATE HEADER activity.

1 CHANGE DOCUMENT SETTINGS | 2 CREATE HEADER | 3 TYPE RESEARCH PAPER WITH CITATIONS
4 CREATE ALPHABETICAL WORKS CITED | 5 PROOFREAD & REVISE RESEARCH PAPER

Use the abbreviated roadmap as a progress guide while you read or step through the instructions in this chapter.

MLA Documentation Style

The research paper in this project follows the guidelines presented by the MLA. To follow the MLA documentation style, use a 12-point Times New Roman or similar font. Double-space text on all pages of the paper using one-inch top, bottom, left, and right margins. Indent the first word of each paragraph one-half inch from the left margin. At the right margin of each page, place a page number one-half inch from the top margin. On each page, precede the page number with your last name.

The MLA documentation style does not require a title page. Instead, place your name and course information in a block at the left margin beginning one inch from the top of the page. Center the title one double-spaced line below your name and course information.

BTW
APA Documentation Style
In the APA style, a separate title page is required instead of placing name and course information on the paper's first page. Double-space all pages of the paper with one-inch top, bottom, left, and right margins. Indent the first word of each paragraph one-half inch from the left margin. In the upper-right margin of each page, including the title page, place a running head that consists of the page number preceded by a brief summary of the paper title.

In the text of the paper, place author references in parentheses with the page number(s) of the referenced information. The MLA documentation style uses in-text **parenthetical references** instead of noting each source at the bottom of the page or at the end of the paper. In the MLA documentation style, notes are used only for optional content or bibliographic notes.

If used, content notes elaborate on points discussed in the paper, and bibliographic notes direct the reader to evaluations of statements in a source or provide a means for identifying multiple sources. Use a superscript (raised number) both to signal that a note exists and to sequence the notes (shown in Figure 2–1). Position notes at the bottom of the page as footnotes or at the end of the paper as endnotes. Indent the first line of each note one-half inch from the left margin. Place one space following the superscripted number before beginning the note text. Double-space the note text (shown in Figure 2–1).

The MLA documentation style uses the term, **works cited,** to refer to the bibliographic list of sources at the end of the paper. The works cited page alphabetically lists sources that are referenced directly in the paper. Place the list of sources on a separate numbered page. Center the title, Works Cited, one inch from the top margin. Double-space all lines. Begin the first line of each source at the left margin, indenting subsequent lines of the same source one-half inch from the left margin. List each source by the author's last name, or, if the author's name is not available, by the title of the source.

Changing Document Settings

The MLA documentation style defines some global formats that apply to the entire research paper. Some of these formats are the default in Word. For example, the default left, right, top, and bottom margin settings in Word are one inch, which meets the MLA documentation style. You will modify, however, the font, font size, and line and paragraph spacing.

For an introduction to Office and instruction about how to perform basic tasks in Office apps, read the Office and Windows chapter at the beginning of this book, where you can learn how to run an application, use the ribbon, save a file, open a file, exit an application, use Help, and much more.

To Run Word and Create a Blank Document

If you are using a computer to step through the project in this chapter and you want your screens to match the figures in this book, you should change your screen's resolution to 1366 × 768. For information about how to change a computer's resolution, refer to the Office and Windows chapter at the beginning of this book.

The following steps, which assume Windows 8 is running, use the Start screen or the Search box to run Word based on a typical installation. You may need to ask your instructor how to run Word on your computer. For a detailed example of the procedure summarized below, refer to the Office and Windows chapter.

1. Scroll the Start screen for a Word 2013 tile. If your Start screen contains a Word 2013 tile, tap or click it to run Word and then proceed to Step 5; if the Start screen does not contain the Word 2013 tile, proceed to the next step to search for the Word app.
2. Swipe in from the right edge of the screen or point to the upper-right corner of the screen to display the Charms bar and then tap or click the Search charm on the Charms bar to display the Search menu.
3. Type `Word` as the search text in the Search box and watch the search results appear in the Apps list.
4. Tap or click Word 2013 in the search results to run Word.
5. Tap or click the Blank document thumbnail on the Word start screen to create a blank document and display it in the Word window.
6. If the Word window is not maximized, tap or click the Maximize button on its title bar to maximize the window.
7. If the Print Layout button on the status bar is not selected (shown in Figure 2–2 on the next page), tap or click it so that your screen is in Print Layout view.
8. If Normal (HOME tab | Styles group) is not selected in the Styles gallery (shown in Figure 2–2), tap or click it so that your document uses the Normal style.
9. To display the page the same width as the document window, if necessary, tap or click the Page Width button (VIEW tab | Zoom group).

One of the few differences between Windows 7 and Windows 8 occurs in the steps to run Word. If you are using Windows 7, click the Start button, type `Word` in the 'Search programs and files' box, click Word 2013, and then, if necessary, maximize the Word window. For detailed steps to run Word in Windows 7, refer to the Office and Windows chapter at the beginning of this book. For a summary of the steps, refer to the Quick Reference located at the back of this book.

To Display Formatting Marks

As discussed in Chapter 1, it is helpful to display formatting marks that indicate where in the document you press the ENTER key, SPACEBAR, and other keys. The following steps display formatting marks.

1. If the HOME tab is not the active tab, tap or click HOME on the ribbon to display the HOME tab.
2. If the 'Show/Hide ¶' button (HOME tab | Paragraph group) is not selected already, tap or click it to display formatting marks on the screen.

BTW
Style Formats
To see the formats assigned to a particular style in a document, tap or click the Styles Dialog Box Launcher (HOME tab | Styles group) and then tap or click the Style Inspector button in the Styles task pane. Position the insertion point in the style in the document and then point to the Paragraph formatting or Text level formatting areas in the Style Inspector task pane to display a ScreenTip describing formats assigned to the location of the insertion point. You also can tap or click the Reveal Formatting button in the Style Inspector task pane or press SHIFT+F1 to display the Reveal Formatting task pane.

Styles

When you create a document, Word formats the text using a particular style. A **style** is a named group of formatting characteristics, including font and font size. The default style in Word is called the **Normal style**, which most likely uses an 11-point Calibri font. If you do not specify a style for text you type, Word applies the Normal style to the text. In addition to the Normal style, Word has many other built-in, or predefined, styles that you can use to format text. Styles make it easy to apply many formats at once to text. You can modify existing styles and create your own styles. Styles are discussed as they are used in this book.

1 CHANGE DOCUMENT SETTINGS | 2 CREATE HEADER | 3 TYPE RESEARCH PAPER WITH CITATIONS
4 CREATE ALPHABETICAL WORKS CITED | 5 PROOFREAD & REVISE RESEARCH PAPER

To Modify a Style

The MLA documentation style requires that all text in the research paper use a 12-point Times New Roman or similar font. If you change the font and font size using buttons on the ribbon, you will need to make the change many times during the course of creating the paper. ***Why?*** *Word formats various areas of a document based on the Normal style, which uses an 11-point Calibri font. For example, body text, headers, and bibliographies all display text based on the Normal style.*

Thus, instead of changing the font and font size for various document elements, a more efficient technique is to change the Normal style for this document to use a 12-point Times New Roman font. ***Why?*** *By changing the Normal style, you ensure that all text in the document will use the format required by the MLA.* The following steps change the Normal style.

1

- Press and hold or right-click Normal in the Styles gallery (HOME tab | Styles group) to display a shortcut menu related to styles (Figure 2–2).

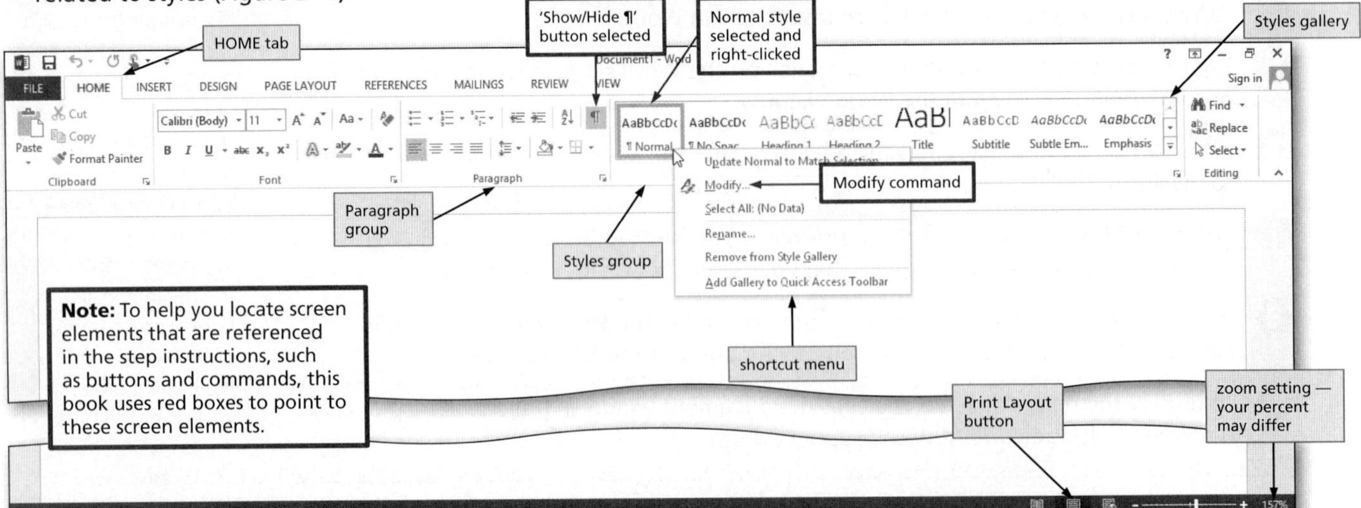

Figure 2–2

2

- Tap or click Modify on the shortcut menu to display the Modify Style dialog box (Figure 2–3).

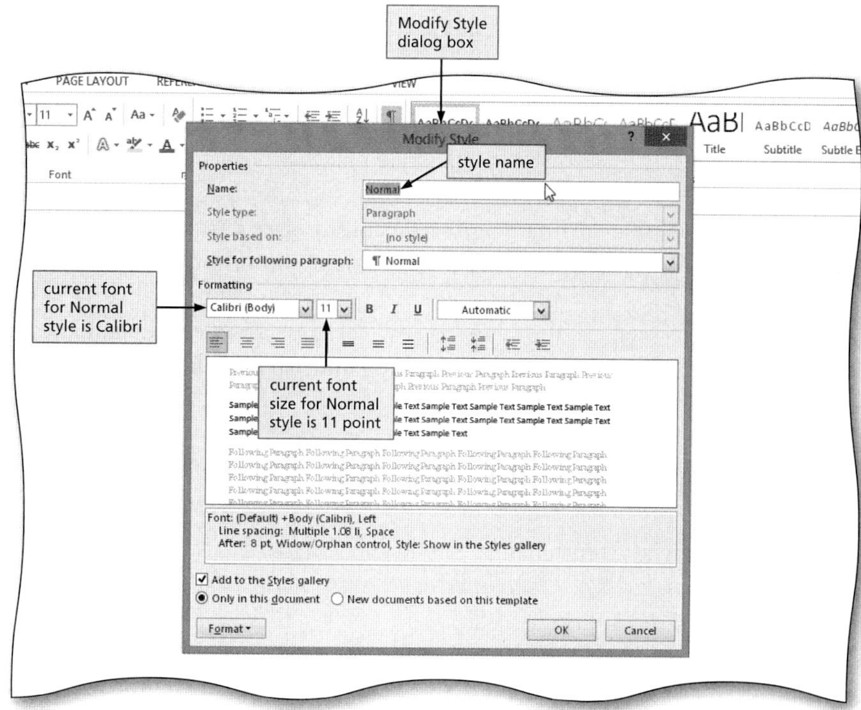

Figure 2–3

3

- Tap or click the Font arrow (Modify Style dialog box) to display the Font list. Scroll to and then click Times New Roman in the list to change the font for the style being modified.
- Tap or click the Font Size arrow (Modify Style dialog box) and then tap or click 12 in the Font Size list to change the font size for the style being modified.
- Ensure that the 'Only in this document' option button is selected (Figure 2–4).

Q&A Will all future documents use the new font and font size?
No, because the 'Only in this document' option button is selected. If you wanted all future documents to use a new setting, you would select the 'New documents based on this template' option button.

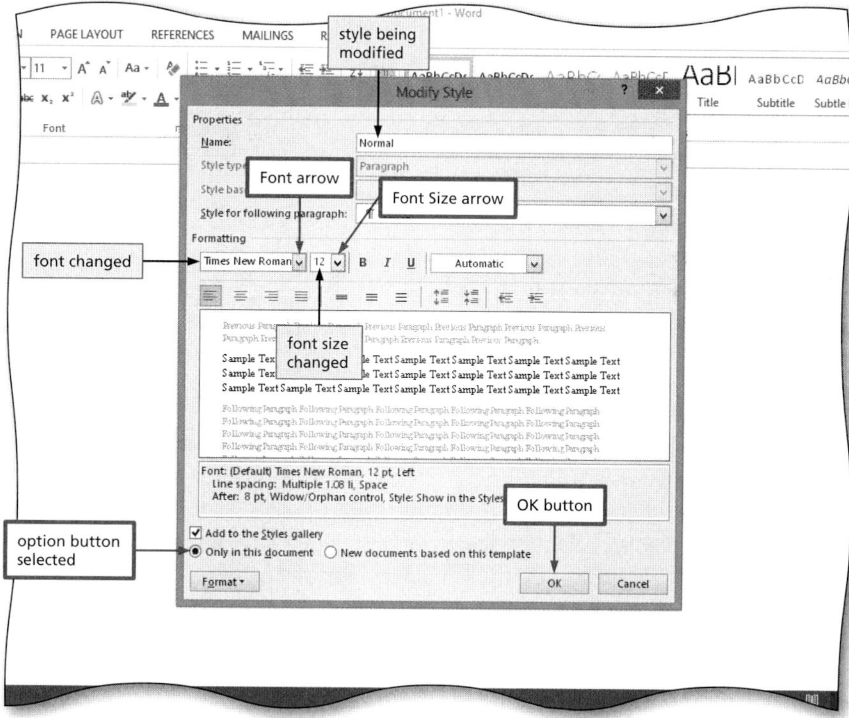

Figure 2–4

4

- Tap or click the OK button (Modify Style dialog box) to update the Normal style to the specified settings.

Other Ways

1. Tap or click Styles Dialog Box Launcher, tap or click arrow next to style name, tap or click Modify on menu, change settings (Modify Style dialog box), tap or click OK button
2. Press ALT+CTRL+SHIFT+S, tap or click arrow next to style name, tap or click Modify on menu, change settings (Modify Style dialog box), tap or click OK button

BTW
Line Spacing
If the top of a set of characters or a graphical image is chopped off, then line spacing may be set to Exactly. To remedy the problem, change line spacing to 1.0, 1.15, 1.5, 2.0, 2.5, 3.0, or At least (in the Paragraph dialog box), all of which accommodate the largest font or image.

Adjusting Line and Paragraph Spacing

Line spacing is the amount of vertical space between lines of text in a paragraph. **Paragraph spacing** is the amount of space above and below a paragraph. By default, the Normal style places 8 points of blank space after each paragraph and inserts a vertical space equal to 1.08 lines between each line of text. It also automatically adjusts line height to accommodate various font sizes and graphics.

The MLA documentation style requires that you **double-space** the entire research paper. That is, the amount of vertical space between each line of text and above and below paragraphs should be equal to one blank line. The next sets of steps adjust line spacing and paragraph spacing according to the MLA documentation style.

To Change Line Spacing

1 CHANGE DOCUMENT SETTINGS | 2 CREATE HEADER | 3 TYPE RESEARCH PAPER WITH CITATIONS
4 CREATE ALPHABETICAL WORKS CITED | 5 PROOFREAD & REVISE RESEARCH PAPER

The following steps change the line spacing to 2.0 to double-space lines in a paragraph. ***Why?*** *The lines of the research paper should be double-spaced, according to the MLA documentation style.*

- Tap or click the 'Line and Paragraph Spacing' button (HOME tab | Paragraph group) to display the Line and Paragraph Spacing gallery (Figure 2–5).

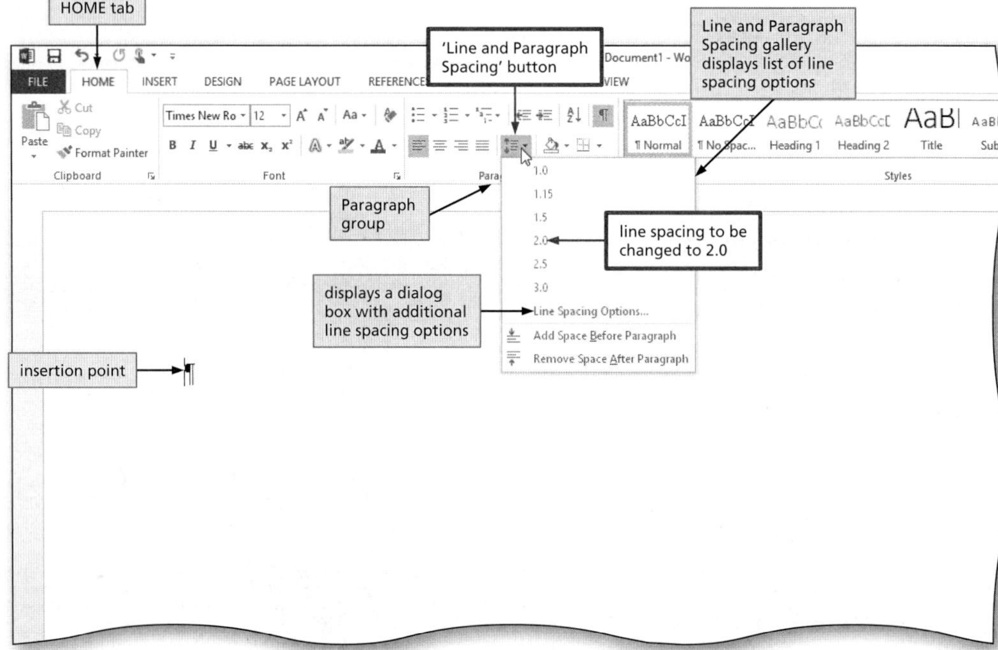

Figure 2–5

Q&A What do the numbers in the Line and Paragraph Spacing gallery represent?
The options 1.0, 2.0, and 3.0 set line spacing to single, double, and triple, respectively. Similarly, the 1.15, 1.5, and 2.5 options set line spacing to 1.15, 1.5, and 2.5 lines. All of these options adjust line spacing automatically to accommodate the largest font or graphic on a line.

- Tap or click 2.0 in the Line and Paragraph Spacing gallery to change the line spacing at the location of the insertion point.

Q&A Can I change the line spacing of existing text?
Yes. Select the text first and then change the line spacing as described in these steps.

Other Ways

1. Tap 'Show Context Menu' on mini toolbar or right-click paragraph, tap or click Paragraph on shortcut menu, tap or click Indents and Spacing tab (Paragraph dialog box), tap or click Line spacing arrow, select desired spacing, tap or click OK button
2. Tap or click Paragraph Settings Dialog Box Launcher (HOME tab or PAGE LAYOUT tab | Paragraph group), tap or click Indents and Spacing tab (Paragraph dialog box), tap or click Line spacing arrow, select desired spacing, tap or click OK button
3. Press CTRL+2 for double-spacing

To Remove Space after a Paragraph

1 CHANGE DOCUMENT SETTINGS | 2 CREATE HEADER | 3 TYPE RESEARCH PAPER WITH CITATIONS
4 CREATE ALPHABETICAL WORKS CITED | 5 PROOFREAD & REVISE RESEARCH PAPER

The following steps remove space after a paragraph. ***Why?*** *The research paper should not have additional blank space after each paragraph, according to the MLA documentation style.*

- Tap or click the 'Line and Paragraph Spacing' button (HOME tab | Paragraph group) to display the Line and Paragraph Spacing gallery (Figure 2–6).

Q&A Why is there a check mark to the left of 2.0 in the gallery?
The check mark indicates the currently selected line spacing.

- Tap or click 'Remove Space After Paragraph' in the Line and Paragraph Spacing gallery so that no blank space appears after paragraphs.

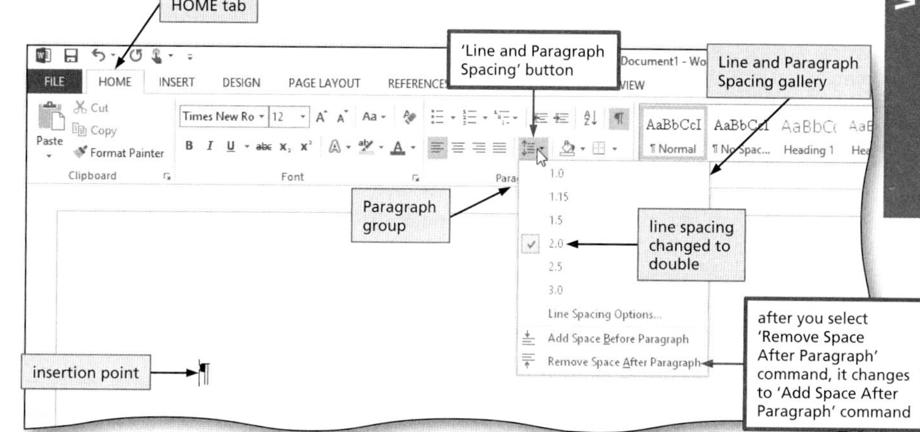

Figure 2–6

Q&A Can I remove space after existing paragraphs?
Yes. Select the paragraphs first and then remove the space as described in these steps.

Other Ways

1. Adjust Spacing After arrows (PAGE LAYOUT tab | Paragraph group) until 0 pt is displayed
2. Tap 'Show Context Menu' on mini toolbar or right-click paragraph, tap or click Paragraph on shortcut menu, tap or click Indents and Spacing tab (Paragraph dialog box), adjust After arrows until 0 pt is displayed, tap or click OK button
3. Tap or click Paragraph Settings Dialog Box Launcher (HOME tab or PAGE LAYOUT tab | Paragraph group), tap or click Indents and Spacing tab (Paragraph dialog box), adjust After arrows until 0 pt is displayed, tap or click OK button

To Update a Style to Match a Selection

1 CHANGE DOCUMENT SETTINGS | 2 CREATE HEADER | 3 TYPE RESEARCH PAPER WITH CITATIONS
4 CREATE ALPHABETICAL WORKS CITED | 5 PROOFREAD & REVISE RESEARCH PAPER

To ensure that all paragraphs in the paper will be double-spaced and do not have space after the paragraphs, you want the Normal style to include the line and paragraph spacing changes made in the previous two sets of steps. The following steps update the Normal style. ***Why?*** *You can update a style to reflect the settings of the location of the insertion point or selected text. Because no text has yet been typed in the research paper, you do not need to select text prior to updating the Normal style.*

- Press and hold or right-click Normal in the Styles gallery (HOME tab | Styles group) to display a shortcut menu (Figure 2–7).

- Tap or click 'Update Normal to Match Selection' on the shortcut menu to update the selected (or current) style to reflect the settings at the location of the insertion point.

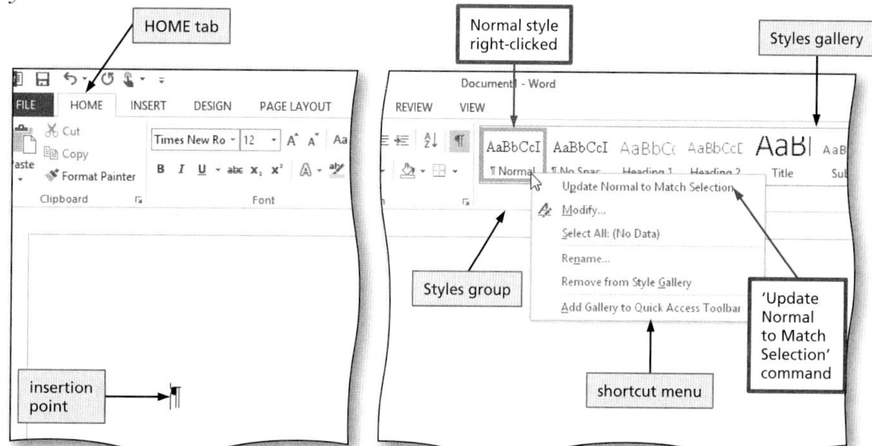

Figure 2–7

Other Ways

1. Tap or click Styles Dialog Box Launcher, tap or click arrow next to style name, tap or click 'Update Normal to Match Selection'
2. Press ALT+CTRL+SHIFT+S, tap or click arrow next to style name, tap or click 'Update Normal to Match Selection'

Creating a Header

BTW
The Ribbon and Screen Resolution
Word may change how the groups and buttons within the groups appear on the ribbon, depending on the computer's screen resolution. Thus, your ribbon may look different from the ones in this book if you are using a screen resolution other than 1366 × 768.

A **header** is text and/or graphics that print at the top of each page in a document. Similarly, a **footer** is text and/or graphics that print at the bottom of every page. In Word, headers print in the top margin one-half inch from the top of every page, and footers print in the bottom margin one-half inch from the bottom of each page, which meets the MLA documentation style. In addition to text and graphics, headers and footers can include document information such as the page number, current date, current time, and author's name.

In this research paper, you are to precede the page number with your last name placed one-half inch from the upper-right edge of each page. The procedures on the following pages enter your name and the page number in the header, as specified by the MLA documentation style.

To Switch to the Header

1 CHANGE DOCUMENT SETTINGS | 2 CREATE HEADER | 3 TYPE RESEARCH PAPER WITH CITATIONS
4 CREATE ALPHABETICAL WORKS CITED | 5 PROOFREAD & REVISE RESEARCH PAPER

The following steps switch from editing the document text to editing the header. ***Why?*** *To enter text in the header, you instruct Word to edit the header.*

1

- Tap or click INSERT on the ribbon to display the INSERT tab.
- Tap or click the 'Add a Header' button (INSERT tab | Header & Footer group) to display the Add a Header gallery (Figure 2–8).

Experiment

- Tap or click the down scroll arrow in the Add a Header gallery to see the available built-in headers.

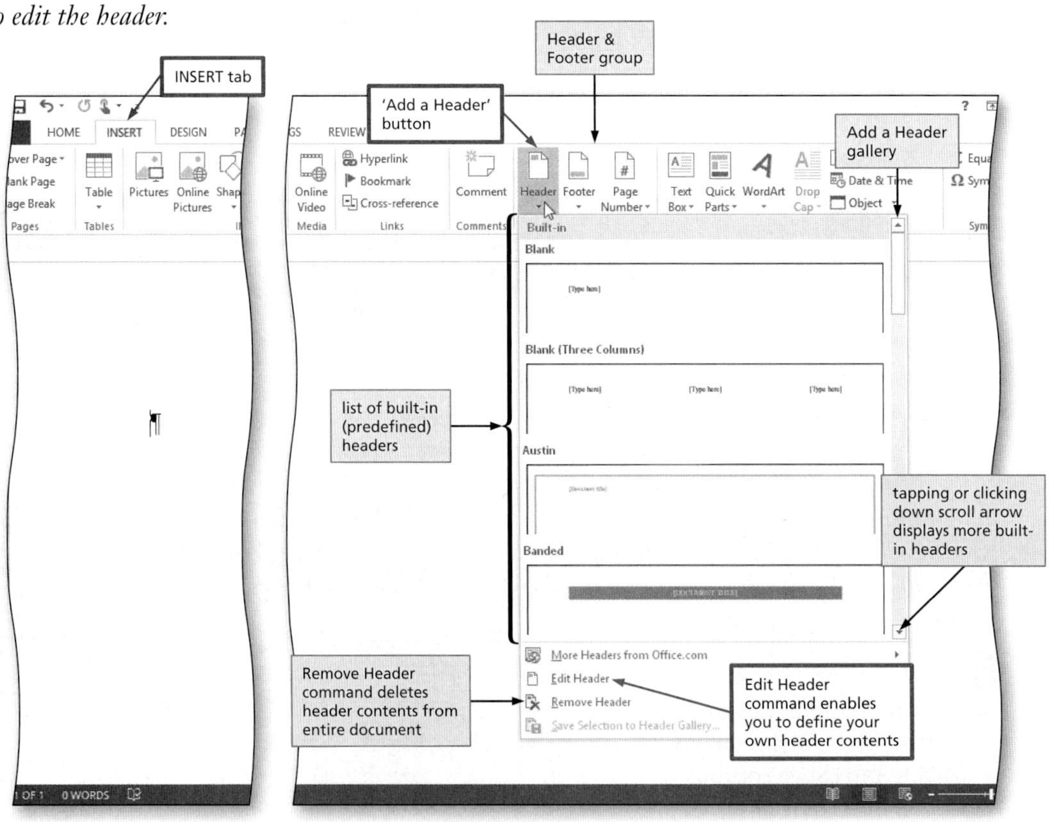

Figure 2–8

Q&A
Can I use a built-in header for this research paper?
None of the built-in headers adheres to the MLA documentation style. Thus, you enter your own header content instead of using a built-in header for this research paper.

How would I remove a header from a document?
You would tap or click Remove Header in the Add a Header gallery. Similarly, to remove a footer, you would tap or click Remove Footer in the Add a Footer gallery.

- Tap or click Edit Header in the Add a Header gallery to switch from the document text to the header, which allows you to edit the contents of the header (Figure 2–9).

Figure 2–9

Q&A How do I remove the HEADER & FOOTER TOOLS DESIGN tab from the ribbon?
When you are finished editing the header, you will close it, which removes the HEADER & FOOTER TOOLS DESIGN tab.

Other Ways

1. Double-tap or double-click dimmed header
2. Press and hold or right-click header in document, tap or click Edit Header button that appears

To Right-Align a Paragraph

1 CHANGE DOCUMENT SETTINGS | 2 CREATE HEADER | 3 TYPE RESEARCH PAPER WITH CITATIONS
4 CREATE ALPHABETICAL WORKS CITED | 5 PROOFREAD & REVISE RESEARCH PAPER

The paragraph in the header currently is left-aligned (Figure 2–9). The following steps right-align this paragraph. ***Why?*** *Your last name and the page number should print* ***right-aligned;*** *that is, they should print at the right margin, according to the MLA documentation style.*

- Tap or click HOME on the ribbon to display the HOME tab.

- Tap or click the Align Right button (HOME tab | Paragraph group) to right-align the current paragraph (Figure 2–10).

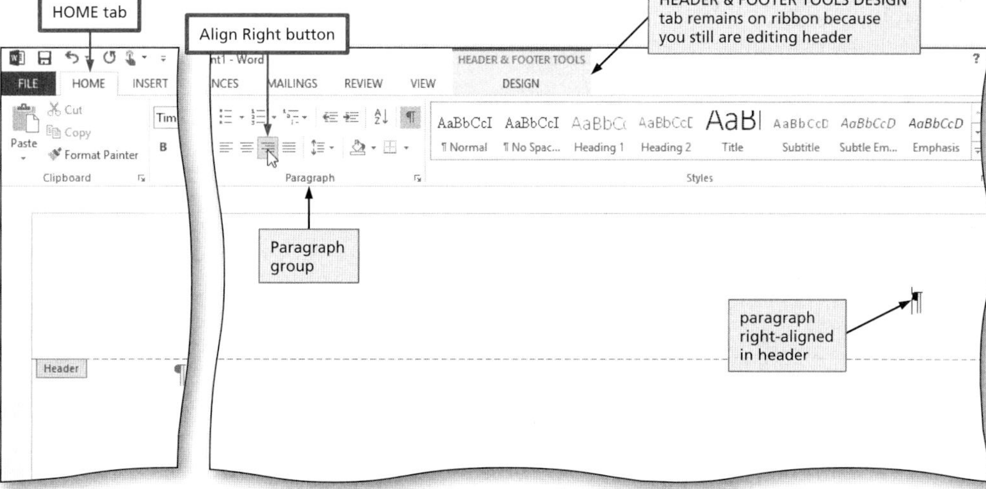

Figure 2–10

Q&A What if I wanted to return the paragraph to left-aligned?
Tap or click the Align Right button again, or tap or click the Align Left button (HOME tab | Paragraph group).

Other Ways

1. Tap 'Show Context Menu' button on mini toolbar or right-click paragraph, tap or click Paragraph on shortcut menu, tap or click Indents and Spacing tab (Paragraph dialog box), tap or click Alignment arrow, tap or click Right, tap or click OK button
2. Tap or click Paragraph Settings Dialog Box Launcher (HOME tab or PAGE LAYOUT tab | Paragraph group), tap or click Indents and Spacing tab (Paragraph dialog box), tap or click Alignment arrow, tap or click Right, tap or click OK button
3. Press CTRL+R

BTW
Footers
If you wanted to create a footer, you would click the Footer button (INSERT tab | Header & Footer group) and then select the desired built-in footer or click Edit Footer to create a customized footer; or, you could double-tap or double-click the dimmed footer.

To Enter Text

The following step enters the last name right-aligned in the header area.

Type `Bailey` and then press the SPACEBAR to enter the last name in the header.

If requested by your instructor, enter your last name instead of Bailey in the header.

To Insert a Page Number

1 CHANGE DOCUMENT SETTINGS | 2 CREATE HEADER | 3 TYPE RESEARCH PAPER WITH CITATIONS
4 CREATE ALPHABETICAL WORKS CITED | 5 PROOFREAD & REVISE RESEARCH PAPER

The following steps insert a page number at the location of the insertion point. ***Why?*** *The MLA documentation style requires a page number following the last name in the header.*

- Tap or click HEADER & FOOTER TOOLS DESIGN on the ribbon to display the HEADER & FOOTER TOOLS DESIGN tab.
- Tap or click the 'Add Page Numbers' button (HEADER & FOOTER TOOLS DESIGN tab | Header & Footer group) to display the Add Page Numbers menu.

Q&A Why does the button name in the step differ from the name on the face of the button in the figure?
The text that appears on the face of the button may vary, depending on screen resolution. The name that appears in the ScreenTip (when you point to the button), however, never changes. For this reason, this book uses the name that appears in the ScreenTip to identify buttons, boxes, and other on-screen elements.

- Tap or point to Current Position on the Add Page Numbers menu to display the Current Position gallery (Figure 2–11).

Experiment

- Tap or click the down scroll arrow in the Current Position gallery to see the available page number formats.

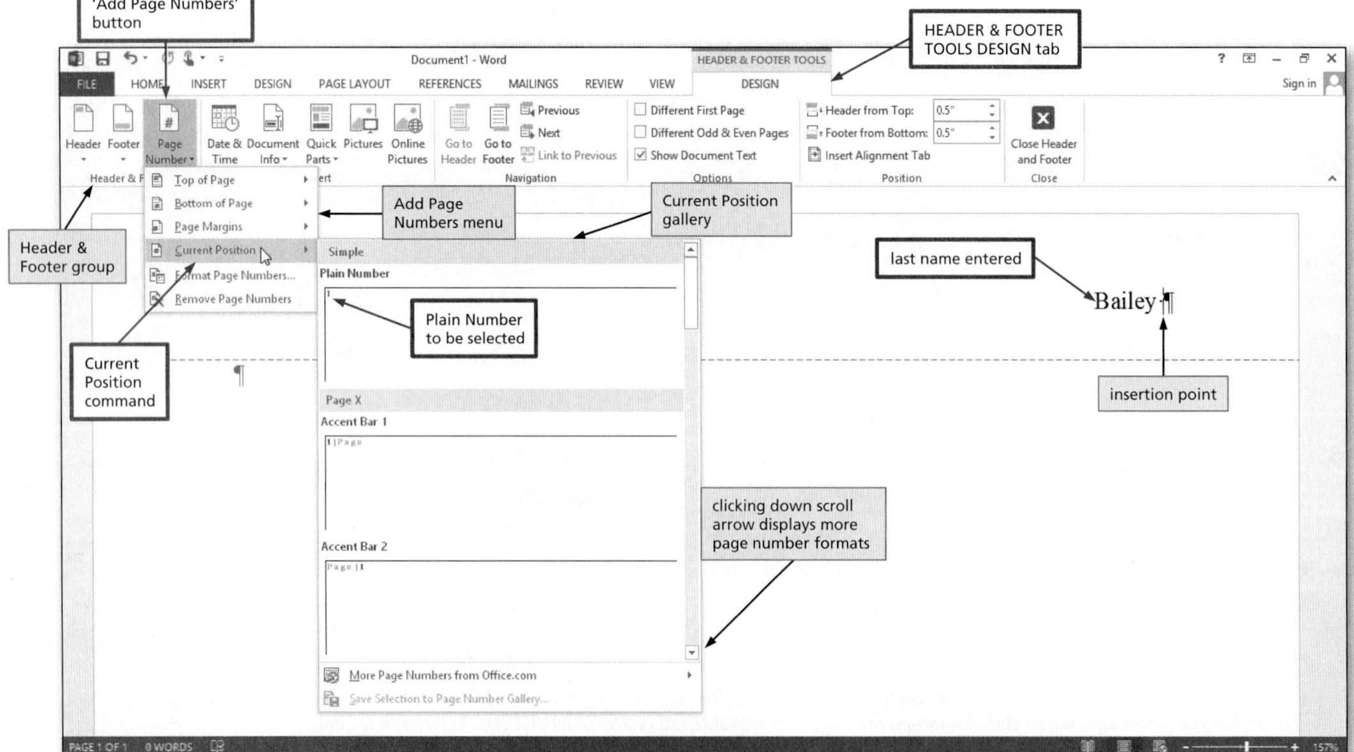

Figure 2–11

- If necessary, scroll to the top of the Current Position gallery.
- Tap or click Plain Number in the Current Position gallery to insert an unformatted page number at the location of the insertion point (Figure 2–12).

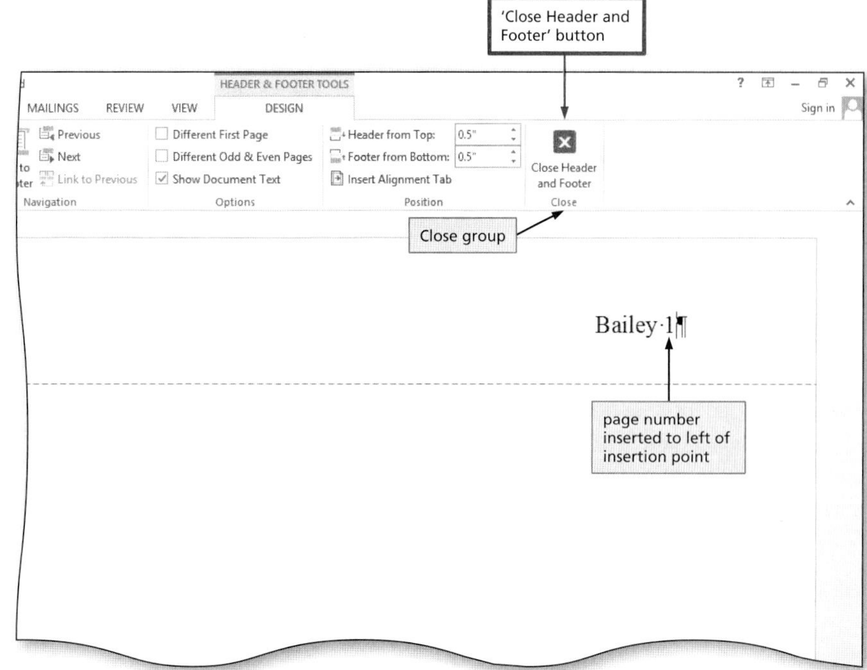

Figure 2–12

Other Ways

1. Tap or click 'Add Page Numbers' button (INSERT tab | Header & Footer group)
2. Tap or click 'Explore Quick Parts' button (INSERT tab | Text group or HEADER & FOOTER TOOLS DESIGN tab | Insert group), tap or click Field on Explore Quick Parts menu, select Page in Field names list (Field dialog box), select desired format in Format list, tap or click OK button

To Close the Header

1 CHANGE DOCUMENT SETTINGS | **2 CREATE HEADER** | **3 TYPE RESEARCH PAPER WITH CITATIONS**
4 CREATE ALPHABETICAL WORKS CITED | **5 PROOFREAD & REVISE RESEARCH PAPER**

The next task is to switch back to the document text. ***Why?*** *You are finished entering text in the header.* The following step closes the header.

- Tap or click the 'Close Header and Footer' button (HEADER & FOOTER TOOLS DESIGN tab | Close group) (shown in Figure 2–12) to close the header and switch back to the document text (Figure 2–13).

Q&A How do I make changes to existing header text?
Switch to the header using the steps described on page WD 74, edit the header as you would edit text in the document window, and then switch back to the document text.

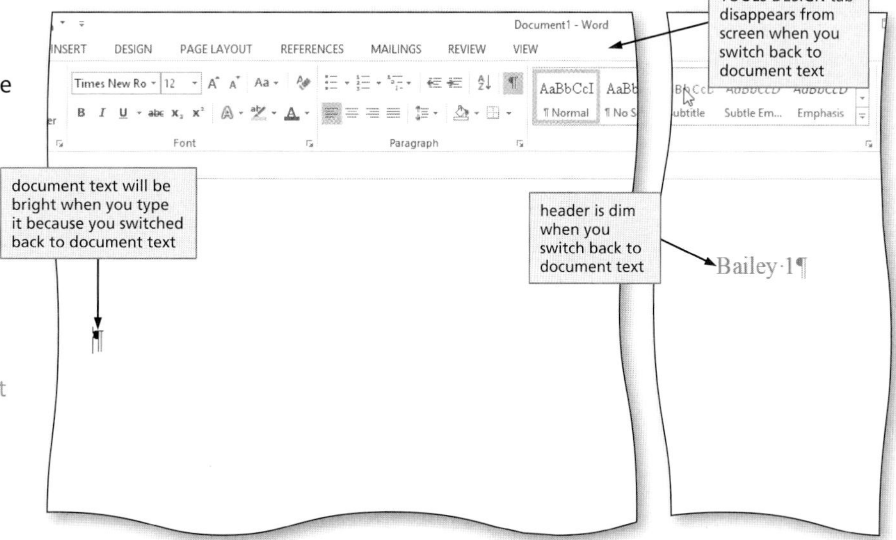

Figure 2–13

Other Ways

1. Double-tap or double-click dimmed document text

Typing the Research Paper Text

The text of the research paper in this chapter encompasses the first two pages of the paper. You will type the text of the research paper and then modify it later in the chapter, so that it matches Figure 2–1 on page WD 67.

CONSIDER THIS

What should you consider when writing the first draft of a research paper?

As you write the first draft of a research paper, be sure it includes the proper components, uses credible sources, and does not contain any plagiarized material.

- **Include an introduction, body, and conclusion.** The first paragraph of the paper introduces the topic and captures the reader's attention. The body, which follows the introduction, consists of several paragraphs that support the topic. The conclusion summarizes the main points in the body and restates the topic.
- **Evaluate sources for authority, currency, and accuracy.** Be especially wary of information obtained on the web. Any person, company, or organization can publish a webpage on the Internet. Ask yourself these questions about the source:
    - Authority: Does a reputable institution or group support the source? Is the information presented without bias? Are the author's credentials listed and verifiable?
    - Currency: Is the information up to date? Are dates of sources listed? What is the last date revised or updated?
    - Accuracy: Is the information free of errors? Is it verifiable? Are the sources clearly identified?
- **Acknowledge all sources of information; do not plagiarize.** Sources of research include books, magazines, newspapers, and the Internet. As you record facts and ideas, list details about the source: title, author, place of publication, publisher, date of publication, etc. When taking notes, be careful not to **plagiarize**. That is, do not use someone else's work and claim it to be your own. If you copy information directly, place it in quotation marks and identify its source. Not only is plagiarism unethical, but it is considered an academic crime that can have severe punishments such as failing a course or being expelled from school.

When you summarize, paraphrase (rewrite information in your own words), present facts, give statistics, quote exact words, or show a map, chart, or other graphic, you must acknowledge the source. Information that commonly is known or accessible to the audience constitutes common knowledge and does not need to be acknowledged. If, however, you question whether certain information is common knowledge, you should document it — just to be safe.

To Enter Name and Course Information

As discussed earlier in this chapter, the MLA documentation style does not require a separate title page for research papers. Instead, place your name and course information in a block at the top of the page, below the header, at the left margin. The following steps enter the name and course information in the research paper.

BTW
Date Formats
The MLA style prefers the day-month-year (15 October 2014) or month-day-year (October 15, 2014) format.

1. Type `Teddy Bailey` as the student name and then press the ENTER key.
2. Type `Ms. Pedro` as the instructor name and then press the ENTER key.
3. Type `English 101` as the course name and then press the ENTER key.
4. Type `October 15, 2014` as the paper's due date and then press the ENTER key (Figure 2–14).

   If requested by your instructor, enter your name and course information instead of the information shown above.

Q&A

Why did the word, October, appear on the screen as I began typing the month name?
Word has an AutoComplete feature, where it predicts some words or phrases as you are typing and displays its prediction in a ScreenTip. If the AutoComplete prediction is correct, you can tap the ScreenTip or press the ENTER key to instruct Word to finish your typing with the word or phrase that appears in the ScreenTip.

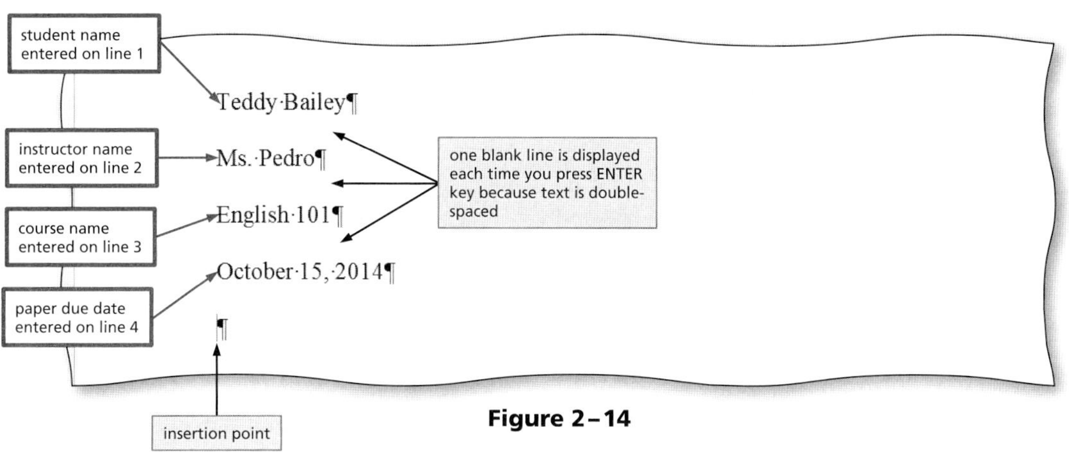

Figure 2–14

To Click and Type

1 CHANGE DOCUMENT SETTINGS | 2 CREATE HEADER | **3 TYPE RESEARCH PAPER WITH CITATIONS**
4 CREATE ALPHABETICAL WORKS CITED | 5 PROOFREAD & REVISE RESEARCH PAPER

The next task is to enter the title of the research paper centered between the page margins. In Chapter 1, you used the Center button (HOME tab | Paragraph group) to center text and graphics. As an alternative, if you are using a mouse, you can use Word's Click and Type feature to format and enter text, graphics, and other items. ***Why?** With **Click and Type**, you can double-click a blank area of the document window and Word automatically formats the item you type or insert according to the location where you double-clicked.* If you are using a mouse, the following steps use Click and Type to center and then type the title of the research paper. If you are using a touch screen, you will use a different method.

- If you are using a touch screen, tap the Center button (HOME tab | Paragraph group) and then proceed to Step 3 because the Click and Type feature does not work with a touch screen.

Experiment

- If you are using a mouse, move the pointer around the document below the entered name and course information and observe the various icons that appear with the I-beam.
- If you are using a mouse, position the pointer in the center of the document at the approximate location for the research paper title until a center icon appears below the I-beam (Figure 2–15).

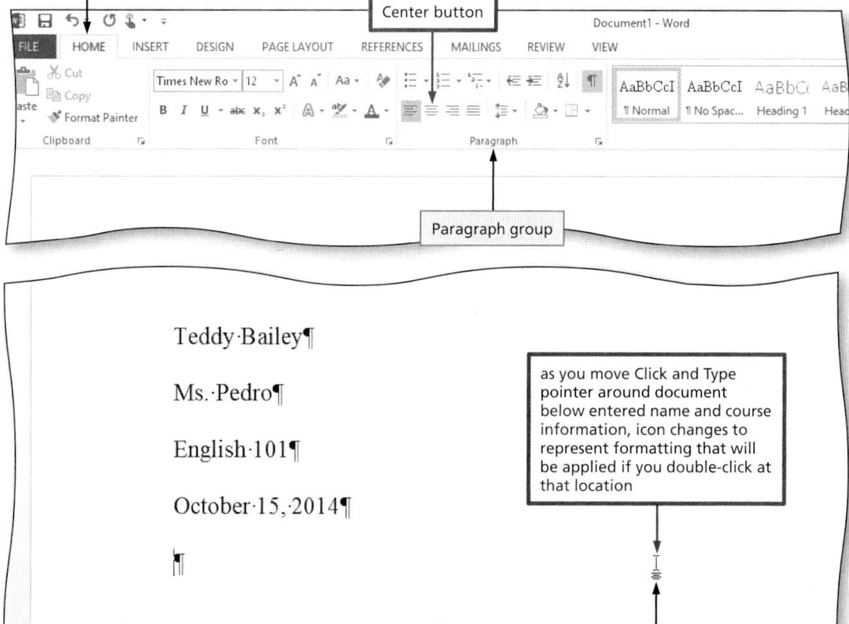

Figure 2–15

Q&A What are the other icons that appear in the Click and Type pointer?

A left-align icon appears to the right of the I-beam when the Click and Type pointer is in certain locations on the left side of the document window. A right-align icon appears to the left of the I-beam when the Click and Type pointer is in certain locations on the right side of the document window.

- If you are using a mouse, double-click to center the paragraph mark and insertion point between the left and right margins.

3

- Type **Access Granted** as the paper title and then press the ENTER key to position the insertion point on the next line (Figure 2–16).

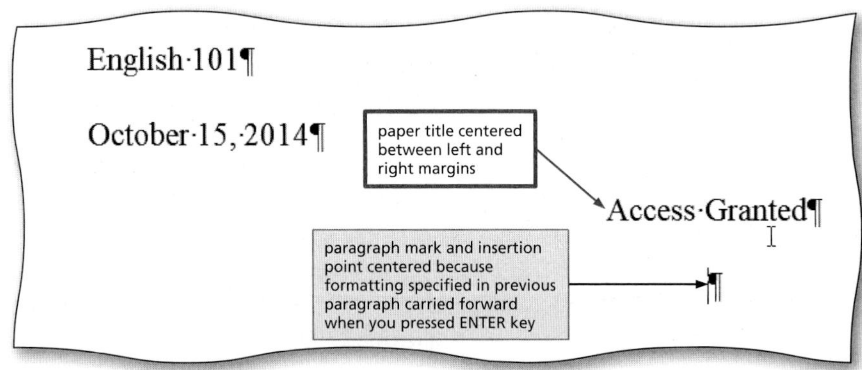

English·101¶
October·15,·2014¶
paper title centered between left and right margins
Access·Granted¶
paragraph mark and insertion point centered because formatting specified in previous paragraph carried forward when you pressed ENTER key

Figure 2–16

Keyboard Shortcuts

Word has many **keyboard shortcuts**, sometimes called shortcut keys or keyboard key combinations, for your convenience while typing. Table 2–1 lists the common keyboard shortcuts for formatting characters. Table 2–2 lists common keyboard shortcuts for formatting paragraphs.

Table 2–1 Keyboard Shortcuts for Formatting Characters

Character Formatting Task	Keyboard Shortcut	Character Formatting Task	Keyboard Shortcut
All capital letters	CTRL+SHIFT+A	Italic	CTRL+I
Bold	CTRL+B	Remove character formatting (plain text)	CTRL+SPACEBAR
Case of letters	SHIFT+F3	Small uppercase letters	CTRL+SHIFT+K
Decrease font size	CTRL+SHIFT+<	Subscript	CTRL+EQUAL SIGN
Decrease font size 1 point	CTRL+[	Superscript	CTRL+SHIFT+PLUS SIGN
Double-underline	CTRL+SHIFT+D	Underline	CTRL+U
Increase font size	CTRL+SHIFT+>	Underline words, not spaces	CTRL+SHIFT+W
Increase font size 1 point	CTRL+]		

Table 2–2 Keyboard Shortcuts for Formatting Paragraphs

Paragraph Formatting	Keyboard Shortcut	Paragraph Formatting	Keyboard Shortcut
1.5 line spacing	CTRL+5	Justify paragraph	CTRL+J
Add/remove one line above paragraph	CTRL+0 (ZERO)	Left-align paragraph	CTRL+L
Center paragraph	CTRL+E	Remove hanging indent	CTRL+SHIFT+T
Decrease paragraph indent	CTRL+SHIFT+M	Remove paragraph formatting	CTRL+Q
Double-space lines	CTRL+2	Right-align paragraph	CTRL+R
Hanging indent	CTRL+T	Single-space lines	CTRL+1
Increase paragraph indent	CTRL+M		

To Format Text Using a Keyboard Shortcut

The paragraphs below the paper title should be left-aligned, instead of centered. Thus, the next step is to left-align the paragraph below the paper title. When your fingers are already on the keyboard, you may prefer using keyboard shortcuts to format text as you type it.

The following step left-aligns a paragraph using the keyboard shortcut CTRL+L. (Recall from Chapter 1 that a notation such as CTRL+L means to press the letter L on the keyboard while holding down the CTRL key.)

1. Press CTRL+L to left-align the current paragraph, that is, the paragraph containing the insertion point (shown in Figure 2–17 on the next page).

Q&A Why would I use a keyboard shortcut instead of the ribbon to format text?
Switching between the mouse and the keyboard takes time. If your hands are already on the keyboard, use a keyboard shortcut. If your hand is on the mouse, use the ribbon.

BTW
Keyboard Shortcuts
To print a complete list of keyboard shortcuts in Word, tap or click the Microsoft Word Help button near the upper-right corner of the Word window, type **keyboard shortcuts** in the 'Search online help' text box at the top of the Word Help window, press the ENTER key, tap or click the Keyboard shortcuts for Microsoft Word link, tap or click the Show All link in the upper-right corner of the Help window, tap or click the Print button in the Help window, and then tap or click the Print button in the Print dialog box.

To Save a Document

You have performed many tasks while creating this research paper and do not want to risk losing work completed thus far. Accordingly, you should save the document. The following steps assume you already have created folders for storing your files, for example, a CIS 101 folder (for your class) that contains a Word folder (for your assignments). Thus, these steps save the document in the Word folder in the CIS 101 folder using the file name, Biometric Devices Paper.

1. Tap or click the Save button on the Quick Access Toolbar, which depending on settings, will display either the Save As gallery in the Backstage view or the Save As dialog box.

2. To save on a hard disk or other storage media on your computer, proceed to Step 2a. To save on SkyDrive, proceed to Step 2b.

2a. If your screen opens the Backstage view and you want to save on storage media on your computer, tap or click Computer in the left pane, if necessary, to display options in the right pane related to saving on your computer. If your screen already displays the Save As dialog box, proceed to Step 4.

2b. If your screen opens the Backstage view and you want to save on SkyDrive, tap or click SkyDrive in the left pane to display SkyDrive saving options or a Sign In button. If your screen displays a Sign In button, tap or click it and then sign in to SkyDrive.

3. Tap or click the Browse button in the right pane to display the Save As dialog box associated with the selected save location (i.e., Computer or SkyDrive).

4. Type **Biometric Devices Paper** in the File name box to change the file name. Do not press the ENTER key after typing the file name because you do not want to close the dialog box at this time.

5. Navigate to the desired save location (in this case, the Word folder in the CIS 101 folder [or your class folder] on your computer or SkyDrive).

6. Tap or click the Save button (Save As dialog box) to save the research paper in the selected folder on the selected save location with the entered file name.

BTW
Organizing Files and Folders
You should organize and store files in folders so that you easily can find the files later. For example, if you are taking an introductory computer class called CIS 101, a good practice would be to save all Word files in a Word folder in a CIS 101 folder. For a discussion of folders and detailed examples of creating folders, refer to the Office and Windows chapter at the beginning of this book.

To Display the Rulers

According to the MLA documentation style, the first line of each paragraph in the research paper is to be indented one-half inch from the left margin. Although you can use a dialog box to indent paragraphs, Word provides a quicker way through the **horizontal ruler**. This ruler is displayed at the top edge of the document window just below the ribbon. Word also provides a **vertical ruler** that is displayed along the left edge of the Word window. The following step displays the rulers. ***Why?*** *You want to use the horizontal ruler to indent paragraphs.*

- If necessary, scroll the document so that the research paper title is at the top of the document window.
- Tap or click VIEW on the ribbon to display the VIEW tab.
- If the rulers are not displayed, tap or click the View Ruler check box (VIEW tab | Show group) to place a check mark in the check box and display the horizontal and vertical rulers on the screen (Figure 2–17).

Q&A What tasks can I accomplish using the rulers?
You can use the rulers to indent paragraphs, set tab stops, change page margins, and adjust column widths.

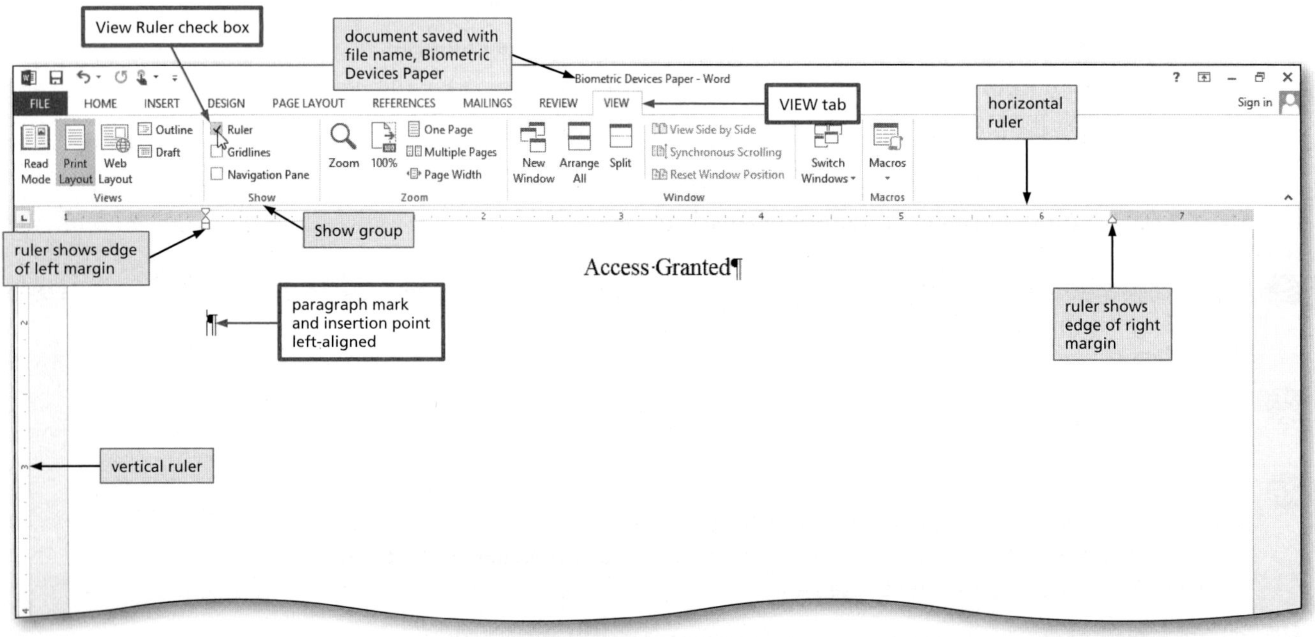

Figure 2–17

To First-Line Indent Paragraphs

If you are using a mouse, you can use the horizontal ruler, usually simply called the **ruler**, to indent just the first line of a paragraph, which is called a **first-line indent**. The left margin on the ruler contains two triangles above a square. The **'First Line Indent' marker** is the top triangle at the 0" mark on the ruler (Figure 2–18). The bottom triangle is discussed later in this chapter. The small square at the 0" mark is the Left Indent marker. The **Left Indent marker** allows you to change the entire left margin, whereas the 'First Line Indent' marker indents only the first line of the paragraph.

The next steps first-line indent paragraphs in the research paper. ***Why?*** *The first line of each paragraph in the research paper is to be indented one-half inch from the left margin, according to the MLA documentation style.*

1

- If you are using a mouse, with the insertion point on the paragraph mark below the research paper title, point to the 'First Line Indent' marker on the ruler (Figure 2–18).

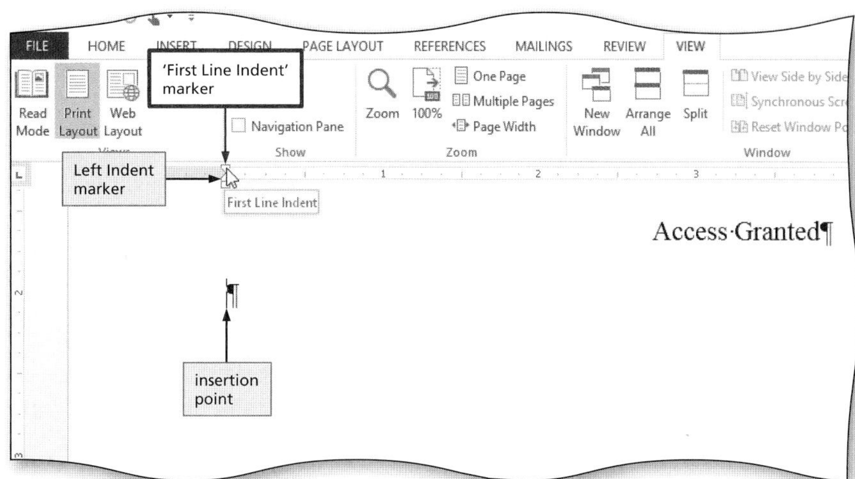

Figure 2–18

- If you are using a mouse, drag the 'First Line Indent' marker to the .5" mark on the ruler to display a vertical dotted line in the document window, which indicates the proposed indent location of the first line of the paragraph (Figure 2–19).

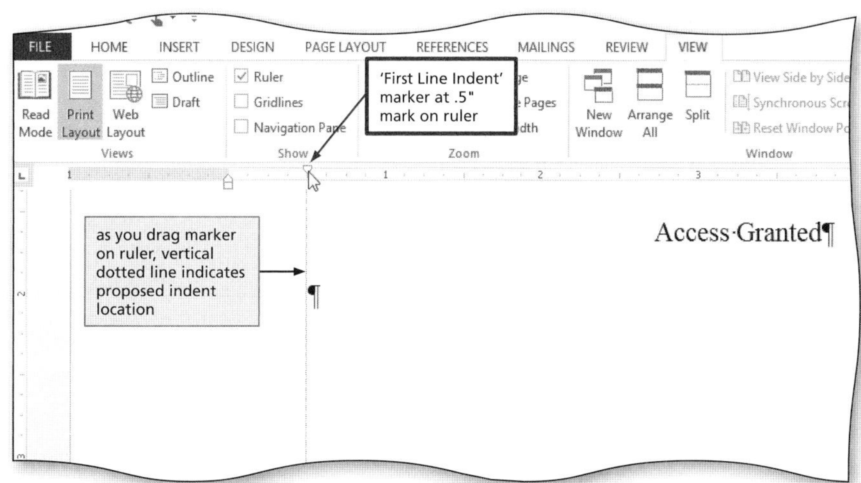

Figure 2–19

- If you are using a mouse, release the mouse button to place the 'First Line Indent' marker at the .5" mark on the ruler, or one-half inch from the left margin (Figure 2–20).
- If you are using a touch screen, you cannot drag the 'First Line Indent' marker and must follow these steps instead: tap the Paragraph Settings Dialog Box Launcher (HOME tab or PAGE LAYOUT tab | Paragraph group) to display the Paragraph dialog box, tap the Indents and Spacing tab (Paragraph dialog box), tap the Special arrow, tap First line, and then tap the OK button.

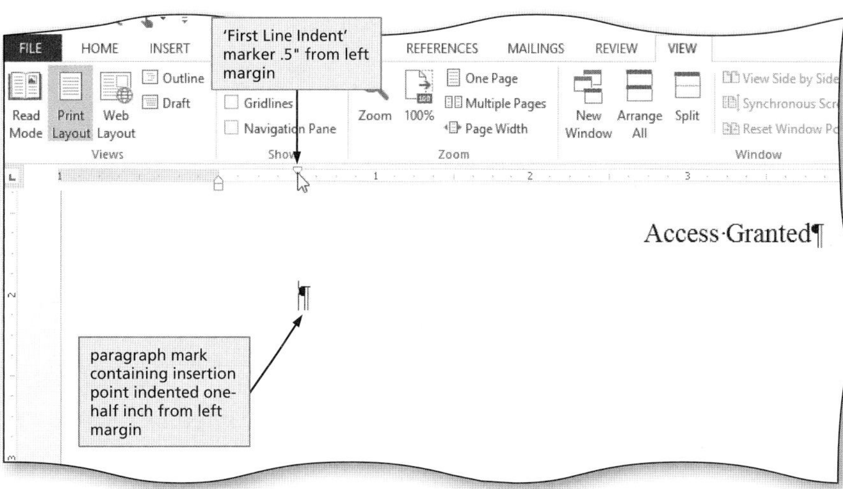

Figure 2–20

- Type **Biometric devices authenticate a person's identity by verifying unique personal characteristics.** and notice that Word automatically indented the first line of the paragraph by one-half inch (Figure 2–21).

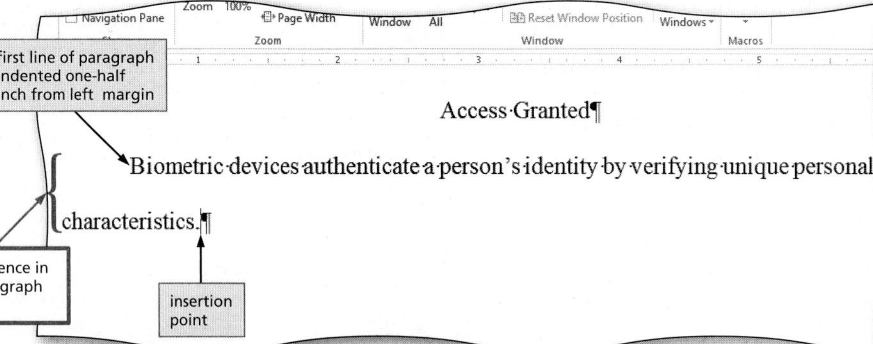
Navigation Pane
Zoom
100%
Page Width
Window
All
Reset Window Position
Windows
Zoom
Window
Macros
first line of paragraph indented one-half inch from left margin
Access·Granted¶
Biometric·devices·authenticate·a·person's·identity·by·verifying·unique·personal·
characteristics.¶
first sentence in first paragraph entered
insertion point

Figure 2–21

Q&A Will I have to set a first-line indent for each paragraph in the paper?
No. Each time you press the ENTER key, paragraph formatting in the previous paragraph carries forward to the next paragraph. Thus, once you set the first-line indent, its format carries forward automatically to each subsequent paragraph you type.

Other Ways

1. Tap 'Show Context Menu' button on mini toolbar or right-click paragraph, tap or click Paragraph on shortcut menu, tap or click Indents and Spacing tab (Paragraph dialog box), tap or click Special arrow, tap or click First line, tap or click OK button
2. Tap or click Paragraph Settings Dialog Box Launcher (HOME tab or PAGE LAYOUT tab | Paragraph group), tap or click Indents and Spacing tab (Paragraph dialog box), tap or click Special arrow, tap or click First line, tap or click OK button

To AutoCorrect as You Type

1 CHANGE DOCUMENT SETTINGS | 2 CREATE HEADER | 3 TYPE RESEARCH PAPER WITH CITATIONS
4 CREATE ALPHABETICAL WORKS CITED | 5 PROOFREAD & REVISE RESEARCH PAPER

Word has predefined many commonly misspelled words, which it automatically corrects for you. ***Why?*** *As you type, you may make typing, spelling, capitalization, or grammar errors. Word's* ***AutoCorrect*** *feature automatically corrects these kinds of errors as you type them in the document. For example, if you type ahve, Word automatically changes it to the correct spelling, have, when you press the SPACEBAR or a punctuation mark key such as a period or comma.*

The following steps intentionally misspell the word, that, as taht to illustrate the AutoCorrect feature.

1

- Press the SPACEBAR.
- Type the beginning of the next sentence, misspelling the word, that, as follows: **These devices translate a biometric element, such as a fingerprint, into a digital code taht** (Figure 2–22).

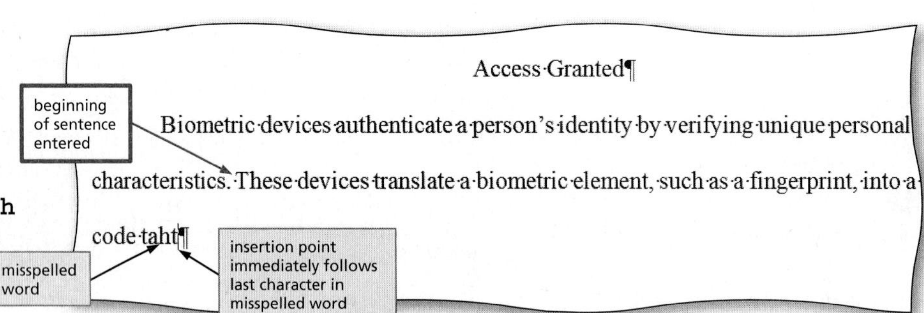
Access·Granted¶
beginning of sentence entered
Biometric·devices·authenticate·a·person's·identity·by·verifying·unique·personal
characteristics.·These·devices·translate·a·biometric·element,·such·as·a·fingerprint,·into·a·
code·taht¶
misspelled word
insertion point immediately follows last character in misspelled word

Figure 2–22

2

- Press the SPACEBAR and watch Word automatically correct the misspelled word.
- Type the rest of the sentence (Figure 2–23): **is compared with a digital code stored in a computer.**

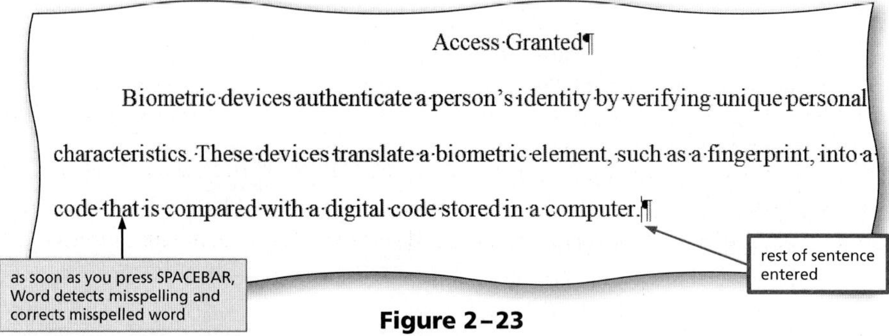
Access·Granted¶
Biometric·devices·authenticate·a·person's·identity·by·verifying·unique·personal
characteristics.·These·devices·translate·a·biometric·element,·such·as·a·fingerprint,·into·a·
code·that·is·compared·with·a·digital·code·stored·in·a·computer.¶
as soon as you press SPACEBAR, Word detects misspelling and corrects misspelled word
rest of sentence entered

Figure 2–23

To Use the AutoCorrect Options Button

The following steps illustrate the AutoCorrect Options button and menu. ***Why?*** *If you are using a mouse, when you position the pointer on text that Word automatically corrected, a small blue box appears below the text. If you point to the small blue box, Word displays the AutoCorrect Options button. When you tap or click the* ***AutoCorrect Options button****, Word displays a menu that allows you to undo a correction or change how Word handles future automatic corrections of this type.* If you are using a touch screen, read these steps without performing them.

- If you are using a mouse, position the pointer in the text automatically corrected by Word (the word, that, in this case) to display a small blue box below the automatically corrected word (Figure 2–24).

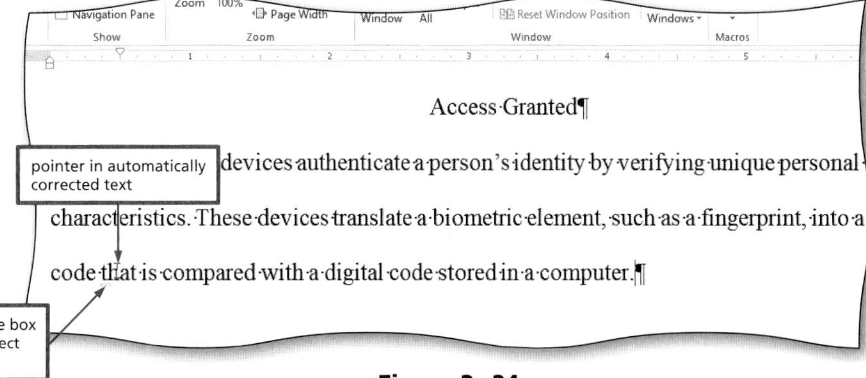

Figure 2–24

- Point to the small blue box to display the AutoCorrect Options button.
- Click the AutoCorrect Options button to display the AutoCorrect Options menu (Figure 2–25).
- Press the ESCAPE key to remove the AutoCorrect Options menu from the screen.

Q&A Do I need to remove the AutoCorrect Options button from the screen?
No. When you move the pointer, the AutoCorrect Options button will disappear from the screen. If, for some reason, you wanted to remove the AutoCorrect Options button from the screen, you could press the ESCAPE key a second time.

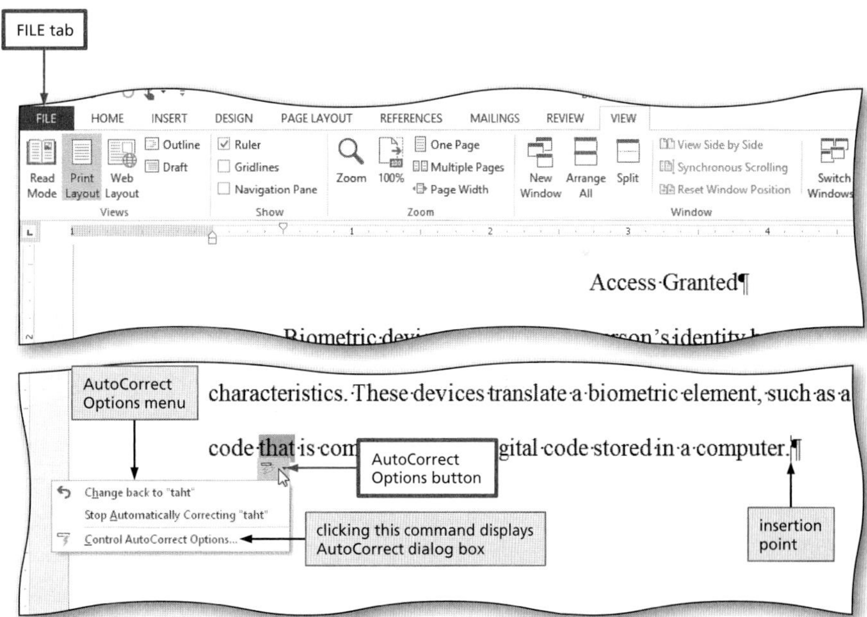

Figure 2–25

To Create an AutoCorrect Entry

The next steps create an AutoCorrect entry. ***Why?*** *In addition to the predefined list of AutoCorrect spelling, capitalization, and grammar errors, you can create your own AutoCorrect entries to add to the list. For example, if you tend to mistype the word computer as comptuer, you should create an AutoCorrect entry for it.*

- Tap or click FILE on the ribbon (shown in Figure 2–25 on the previous page) to open the Backstage view (Figure 2–26).

Backstage view

Options command

Figure 2–26

2

- Tap or click Options in the Backstage view to display the Word Options dialog box.
- Tap or click Proofing in the left pane (Word Options dialog box) to display proofing options in the right pane.
- Tap or click the AutoCorrect Options button in the right pane to display the AutoCorrect dialog box.
- When Word displays the AutoCorrect dialog box, type `comptuer` in the Replace text box.
- Press the TAB key and then type `computer` in the With text box (Figure 2–27).

Q&A How would I delete an existing AutoCorrect entry?

You would select the entry to be deleted in the list of defined entries in the AutoCorrect dialog box and then tap or click the Delete button (AutoCorrect dialog box).

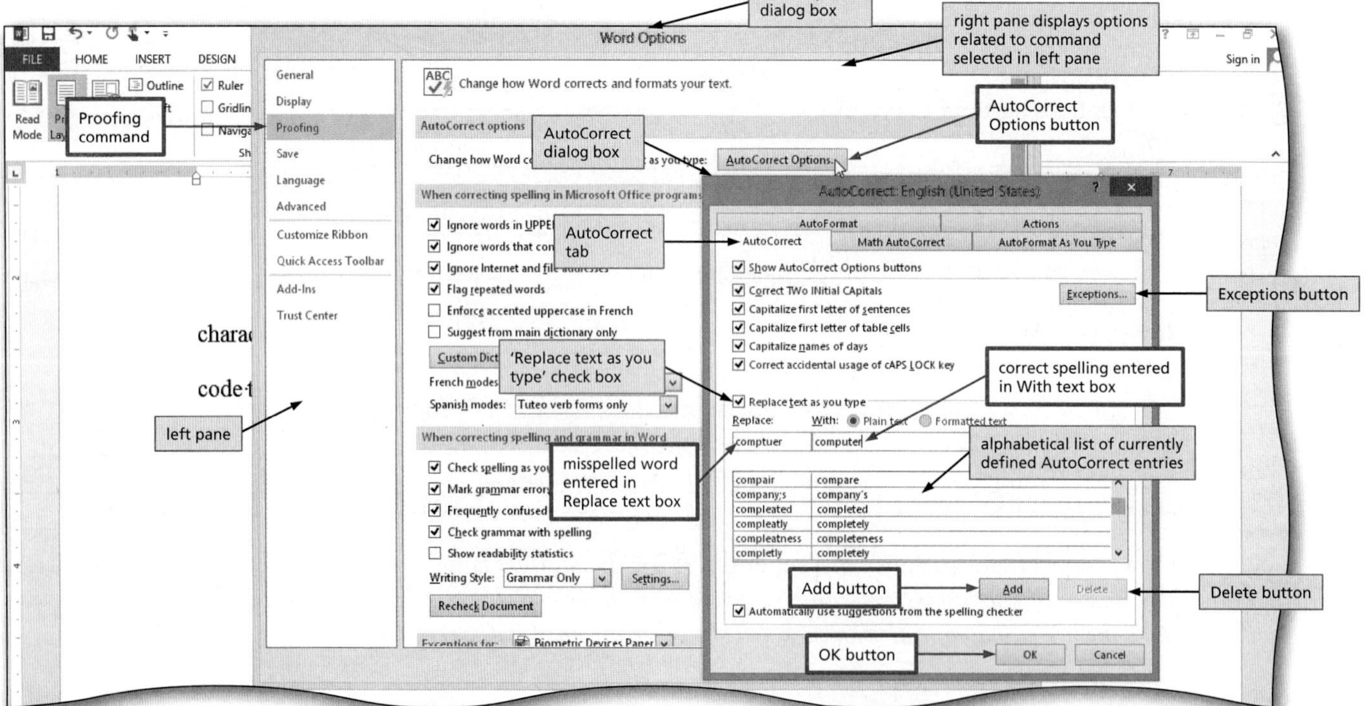

Figure 2–27

3

- Tap or click the Add button (AutoCorrect dialog box) to add the entry alphabetically to the list of words to correct automatically as you type. (If your dialog box displays a Replace button instead, tap or click it and then tap or click the Yes button in the Microsoft Word dialog box to replace the previously defined entry.)
- Tap or click the OK button (AutoCorrect dialog box) to close the dialog box.
- Tap or click the OK button (Word Options dialog box) to close the dialog box.

The AutoCorrect Dialog Box

In addition to creating AutoCorrect entries for words you commonly misspell or mistype, you can create entries for abbreviations, codes, and so on. For example, you could create an AutoCorrect entry for asap, indicating that Word should replace this text with the phrase, as soon as possible.

If, for some reason, you do not want Word to correct automatically as you type, you can turn off the Replace text as you type feature by tapping or clicking Options in the Backstage view, tapping or clicking Proofing in the left pane (Word Options dialog box), tapping or clicking the AutoCorrect Options button in the right pane (Figure 2–27), removing the check mark from the 'Replace text as you type' check box, and then tapping or clicking the OK button in each open dialog box.

The AutoCorrect sheet in the AutoCorrect dialog box (Figure 2–27) contains other check boxes that correct capitalization errors if the check boxes are selected:

- If you type two capital letters in a row, such as TH, Word makes the second letter lowercase, Th.
- If you begin a sentence with a lowercase letter, Word capitalizes the first letter of the sentence.
- If you type the name of a day in lowercase letters, such as tuesday, Word capitalizes the first letter in the name of the day, Tuesday.
- If you leave the CAPS LOCK key on and begin a new sentence, such as aFTER, Word corrects the typing, After, and turns off the CAPS LOCK key.

If you do not want Word to automatically perform any of these corrections, simply remove the check mark from the appropriate check box in the AutoCorrect dialog box.

Sometimes you do not want Word to AutoCorrect a particular word or phrase. For example, you may use the code WD. in your documents. Because Word automatically capitalizes the first letter of a sentence, the character you enter following the period will be capitalized (in the previous sentence, it would capitalize the letter i in the word, in). To allow the code WD. to be entered into a document and still leave the AutoCorrect feature turned on, you would set an exception. To set an exception to an AutoCorrect rule, tap or click Options in the Backstage view, tap or click Proofing in the left pane (Word Options dialog box), tap or click the AutoCorrect Options button in the right pane, tap or click the Exceptions button (Figure 2–27), tap or click the appropriate tab in the AutoCorrect Exceptions dialog box, type the exception entry in the text box, tap or click the Add button, tap or click the Close button (AutoCorrect Exceptions dialog box), and then tap or click the OK button in each of the remaining dialog boxes.

BTW

Automatic Corrections

If you do not want to keep a change automatically made by Word and you immediately notice the automatic correction, you can undo the change by clicking the Undo button on the Quick Access Toolbar or pressing CTRL+Z. You also can undo a correction through the AutoCorrect Options button, which was shown on page WD 85.

BTW

Touch Screen Differences

The Office and Windows interfaces may vary if you are using a touch screen. For this reason, you might notice that the function or appearance of your touch screen differs slightly from this chapter's presentation.

To Enter More Text

The next task is to continue typing text in the research paper up to the location of the in-text parenthetical reference. The following steps enter this text.

BTW
Spacing after Punctuation
Because word processing documents use variable character fonts, it often is difficult to determine in a printed document how many times someone has pressed the SPACEBAR between sentences. Thus, the rule is to press the SPACEBAR only once after periods, colons, and other punctuation marks.

1. With the insertion point positioned at the end of the first paragraph in the paper, as shown in Figure 2–25 on page WD 85, press the SPACEBAR and then type these two sentences, intentionally misspelling the word readers as raders: **If the digital code in the computer matches the personal characteristic code, the computer grants access. Examples of biometric devices include fingerprint raders and face recognition systems.**

Q&A
Why is the word, readers, misspelled?
Later in this chapter, you will use Word's check spelling and grammar at once feature to check the entire document for errors.

2. Press the ENTER key to start a new paragraph.

3. Type **A fingerprint reader, or scanner, captures curves and indentations of a fingerprint. Organizations use fingerprint readers to secure doors, computers, and software. For example, a fingerprint reader can be set up to authenticate users before they can access a computer** and then press the SPACEBAR (Figure 2–28).

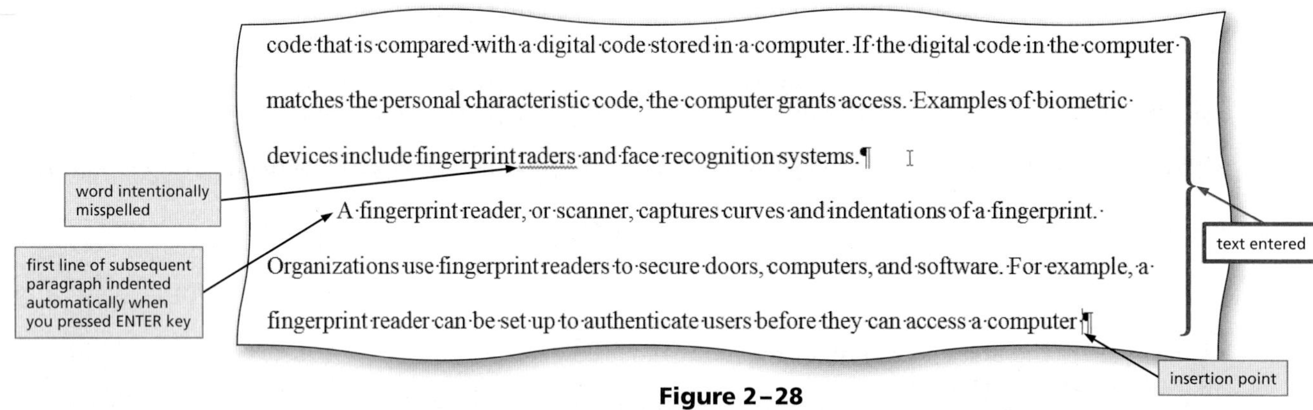

Figure 2–28

Citations

Both the MLA and APA guidelines suggest the use of in-text parenthetical references (placed at the end of a sentence), instead of footnoting each source of material in a paper. These parenthetical references, called citations in Word, guide the reader to the end of the paper for complete information about the source.

Word provides tools to assist you with inserting citations in a paper and later generating a list of sources from the citations. With a documentation style selected, Word automatically formats the citations and list of sources according to that style. The process for adding citations in Word is as follows:

1. Modify the documentation style, if necessary.
2. Insert a citation placeholder.
3. Enter the source information for the citation.

You can combine Steps 2 and 3, where you insert the citation placeholder and enter the source information at once. Or, you can insert the citation placeholder as you write and then enter the source information for the citation at a later time. While creating the research paper in this chapter, you will use both methods.

BTW
BTWs
For a complete list of the BTWs found in the margins of this book, visit the BTW resource on the Student Companion Site located on www.cengagebrain.com. For detailed instructions about accessing available resources, visit www.cengage.com/ct/studentdownload or contact your instructor for information about accessing the required files.

To Change the Bibliography Style

1 CHANGE DOCUMENT SETTINGS | 2 CREATE HEADER | 3 TYPE RESEARCH PAPER WITH CITATIONS
4 CREATE ALPHABETICAL WORKS CITED | 5 PROOFREAD & REVISE RESEARCH PAPER

The first step in inserting a citation is to be sure the citations and sources will be formatted using the correct documentation style, called the bibliography style in Word. ***Why?*** *You want to ensure that Word is using the MLA documentation style for this paper.* The following steps change the specified documentation style.

1

- Tap or click REFERENCES on the ribbon to display the REFERENCES tab.
- Tap or click the Bibliography Style arrow (REFERENCES tab | Citations & Bibliography group) to display the Bibliography Style gallery, which lists predefined documentation styles (Figure 2–29).

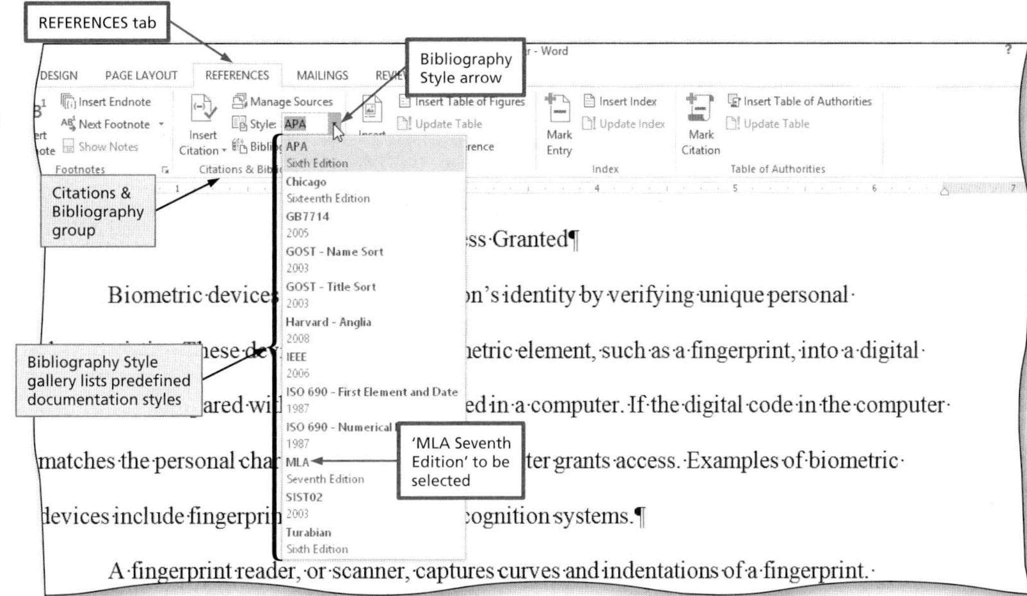

Figure 2–29

2

- Tap or click 'MLA Seventh Edition' in the Bibliography Style gallery to change the documentation style to MLA.

Q&A What if I am using a different edition of a documentation style shown in the Bibliography Style gallery?
Select the closest one and then, if necessary, perform necessary edits before submitting the paper.

CONSIDER THIS

What details are required for sources?

During your research, be sure to record essential publication information about each of your sources. Following is a sample list of types of required information for the MLA documentation style.

- Book: full name of author(s), complete title of book, edition (if available), volume (if available), publication city, publisher name, publication year, and publication medium
- Magazine: full name of author(s), complete title of article, magazine title, issue number (if available), date of magazine, page numbers of article, publication medium, and date viewed (if medium is a website)
- Website: full name of author(s), title of website, website publisher or sponsor (if none, write N.p.), publication date (if none, write n.d.), publication medium, and date viewed

To Insert a Citation and Create Its Source

1 CHANGE DOCUMENT SETTINGS | 2 CREATE HEADER | 3 TYPE RESEARCH PAPER WITH CITATIONS
4 CREATE ALPHABETICAL WORKS CITED | 5 PROOFREAD & REVISE RESEARCH PAPER

With the documentation style selected, the next task is to insert a citation at the location of the insertion point and enter the source information for the citation. You can accomplish these steps at once by instructing Word to add a new source. The steps on the next page add a new source for a magazine (periodical) article on the web. ***Why?*** *The material preceding the insertion point was summarized from an online magazine article.*

- Tap or click the Insert Citation button (REFERENCES tab | Citations & Bibliography group) to display the Insert Citation menu (Figure 2–30).

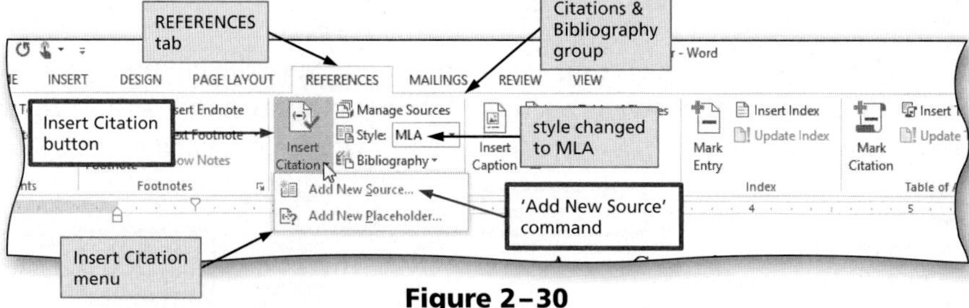

Figure 2–30

2

- Tap or click 'Add New Source' on the Insert Citation menu to display the Create Source dialog box (Figure 2–31).

Q&A What are the Bibliography Fields in the Create Source dialog box?
A **field** is a placeholder for data whose contents can change. You enter data in some fields; Word supplies data for others. In this case, you enter the contents of the fields for a particular source, for example, the author name in the Author field.

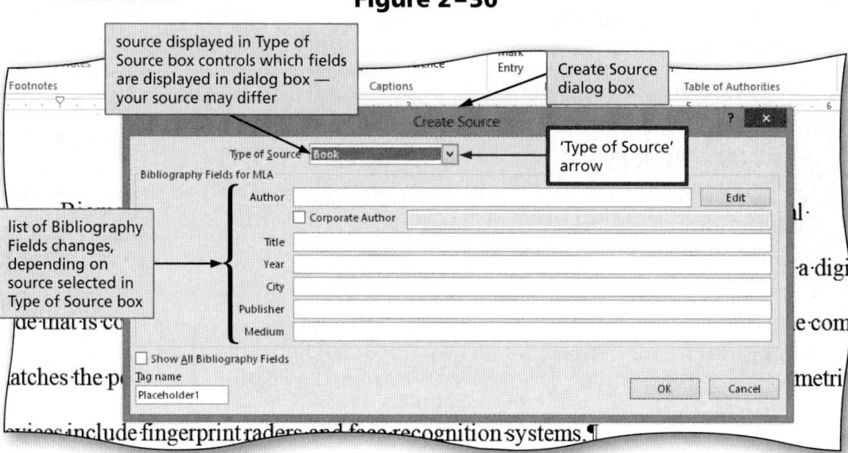

Figure 2–31

Experiment

- Tap or click the 'Type of Source' arrow and then tap or click one of the source types in the list, so that you can see how the list of fields changes to reflect the type of source you selected.

- If necessary, tap or click the 'Type of Source' arrow (Create Source dialog box) and then tap or click 'Article in a Periodical', so that the list shows fields required for a magazine (periodical).
- Tap or click the Author text box. Type **`Rossi, Marcell Enrico`** as the author.
- Tap or click the Title text box. Type **`Understanding How to Use Fingerprint Readers`** as the article title.

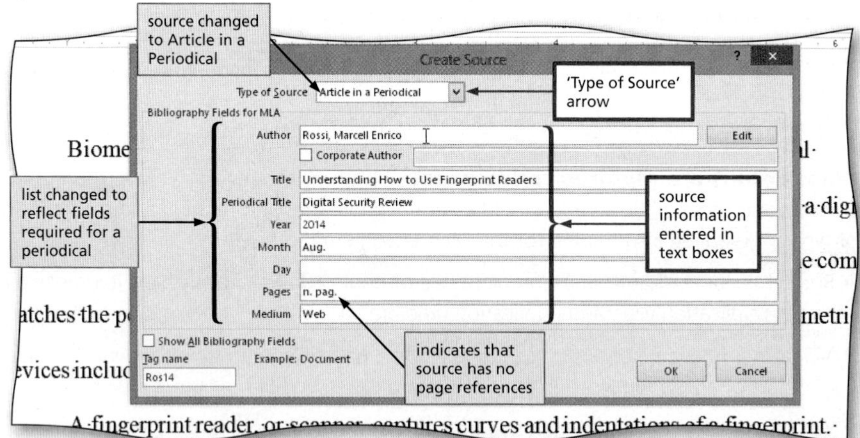

Figure 2–32

- Press the TAB key and then type **`Digital Security Review`** as the periodical title.
- Press the TAB key and then type **`2014`** as the year.
- Press the TAB key and then type **`Aug.`** as the month.
- Press the TAB key twice and then type **`n. pag.`** as the number of pages.
- Press the TAB key and then type **`Web`** as the medium (Figure 2–32).

Q&A Why is the month abbreviated?
The MLA documentation style abbreviates all months, except May, June, and July, when they appear in a source.

What does the n. pag. entry mean in the Pages text box?
The MLA documentation style uses the abbreviation n. pag. for no pagination, which indicates the source has no page references. This is common for web sources.

- Place a check mark in the 'Show All Bibliography Fields' check box so that Word displays all fields available for the selected source, including the date viewed (accessed) fields.
- If necessary, scroll to the bottom of the Bibliography Fields list to display the date viewed (accessed) fields.
- Tap or click the Year Accessed text box. Type `2014` as the year.
- Press the TAB key and then type `Oct.` as the month accessed.
- Press the TAB key and then type `3` as the day accessed (Figure 2–33).

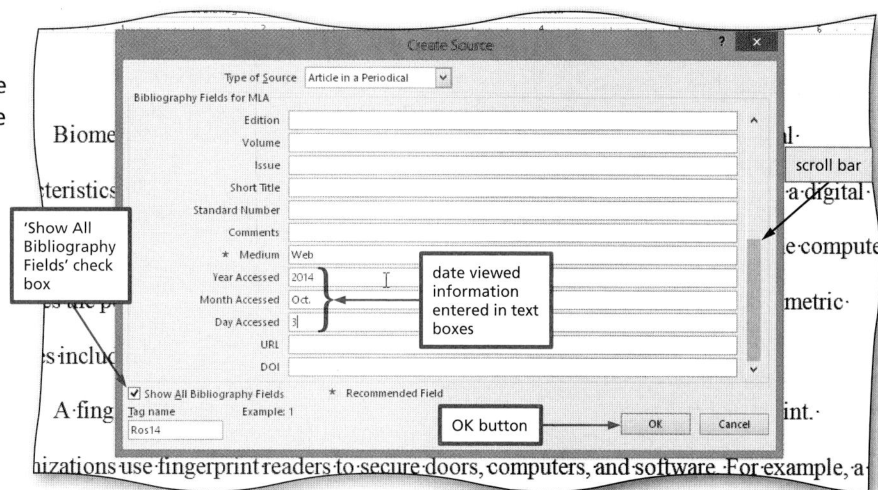

Figure 2–33

Q&A | What if some of the text boxes disappear as I enter the fields?
With the 'Show All Bibliography Fields' check box selected, the dialog box may not be able to display all fields at the same time. In this case, some may scroll up off the screen.

- Tap or click the OK button to close the dialog box, create the source, and insert the citation in the document at the location of the insertion point.
- Press the END key to move the insertion point to the end of the line, which also deselects the citation.
- Press the PERIOD key to end the sentence (Figure 2–34).

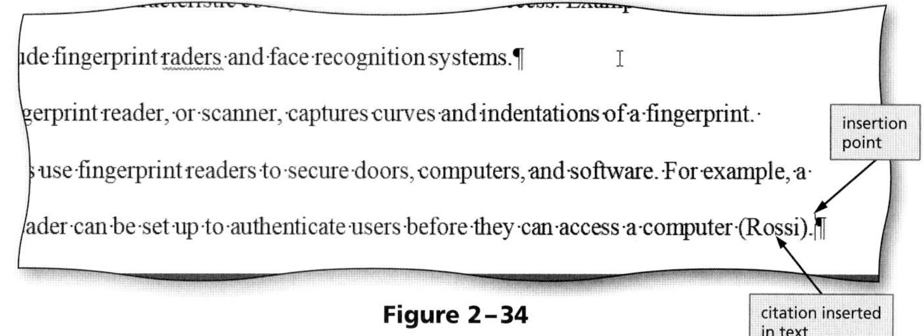

Figure 2–34

To Enter More Text

The next task is to continue typing text in the research paper up to the location of the footnote. The following steps enter this text.

1. Press the SPACEBAR.
2. Type the next sentences (Figure 2–35): **`External fingerprint readers usually plug into a USB port. To save on desk space, some laptops include built-in fingerprint readers.`**

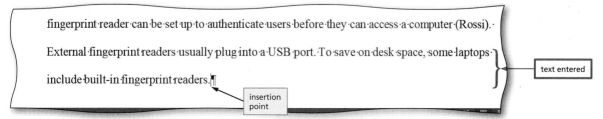

Figure 2–35

BTW

Word Help

At any time while using Word, you can find answers to questions and display information about various topics through Word Help. Used properly, this form of assistance can increase your productivity and reduce your frustrations by minimizing the time you spend learning how to use Word. For instruction about Word Help and exercises that will help you gain confidence in using it, read the Office and Windows chapter at the beginning of this book.

To Save an Existing Document with the Same File Name

You have made several modifications to the document since you last saved it. Thus, you should save it again. The following step saves the document again. For an example of the step listed below, refer to the Office and Windows chapter at the beginning of this book.

Tap or click the Save button on the Quick Access Toolbar to overwrite the previously saved file.

Footnotes

As discussed earlier in this chapter, notes are optional in the MLA documentation style. If used, content notes elaborate on points discussed in the paper, and bibliographic notes direct the reader to evaluations of statements in a source or provide a means for identifying multiple sources. The MLA documentation style specifies that a superscript (raised number) be used for a **note reference mark** to signal that a note exists either at the bottom of the page as a **footnote** or at the end of the document as an **endnote**.

In Word, **note text** can be any length and format. Word automatically numbers notes sequentially by placing a note reference mark both in the body of the document and to the left of the note text. If you insert, rearrange, or remove notes, Word renumbers any subsequent note reference marks according to their new sequence in the document.

To Insert a Footnote Reference Mark

1 CHANGE DOCUMENT SETTINGS | 2 CREATE HEADER | **3 TYPE RESEARCH PAPER WITH CITATIONS**
4 CREATE ALPHABETICAL WORKS CITED | 5 PROOFREAD & REVISE RESEARCH PAPER

The following step inserts a footnote reference mark in the document at the location of the insertion point and at the location where the footnote text will be typed. ***Why?*** *You will insert a content note elaborating on fingerprint reader functions, which you want to position as a footnote.*

1

- With the insertion point positioned as shown in Figure 2–35 on the previous page, tap or click the Insert Footnote button (REFERENCES tab | Footnotes group) to display a note reference mark (a superscripted 1) in two places: (1) in the document window at the location of the insertion point and (2) at the bottom of the page where the footnote will be positioned, just below a separator line (Figure 2–36).

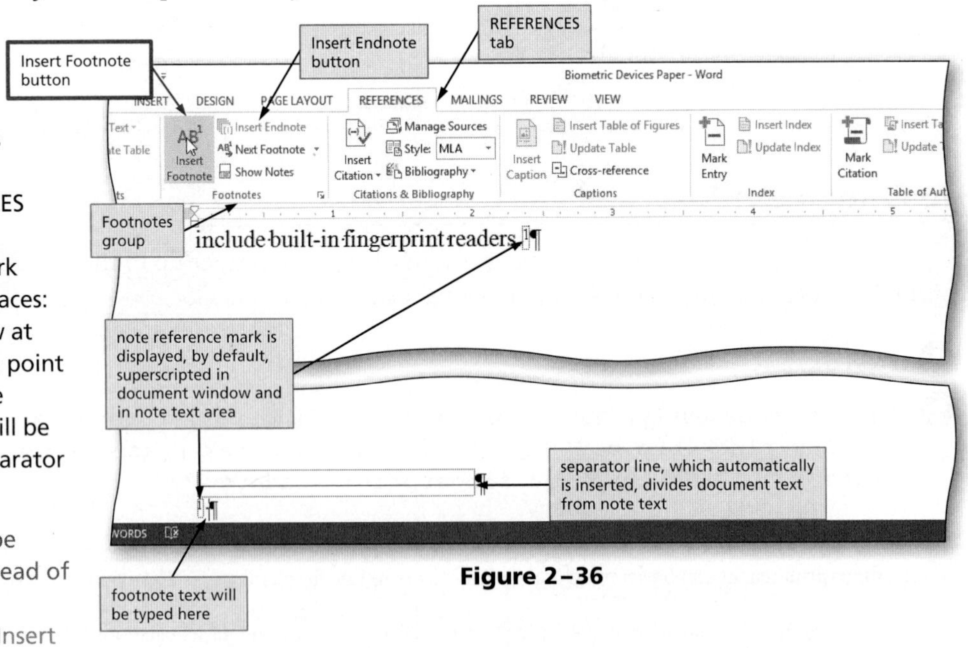

Insert Footnote button
Insert Endnote button
REFERENCES tab
Footnotes group
include built-in fingerprint readers.[1]
note reference mark is displayed, by default, superscripted in document window and in note text area
separator line, which automatically is inserted, divides document text from note text
footnote text will be typed here

Figure 2–36

Q&A What if I wanted notes to be positioned as endnotes instead of as footnotes?

You would tap or click the Insert Endnote button (REFERENCES tab | Footnotes group), which places the separator line and the endnote text at the end of the document, instead of the bottom of the page containing the reference.

Other Ways

1. Press ALT+CTRL+F

To Enter Footnote Text

The following step types the footnote text to the right of the note reference mark below the separator line.

1

Type the footnote text up to the citation (shown in Figure 2–37): **`Nadeer and White state that fingerprint readers can perform different functions for different fingers; for example, one finger runs a program and another finger shuts down the computer`** and then press the SPACEBAR.

To Insert a Citation Placeholder

1 CHANGE DOCUMENT SETTINGS | 2 CREATE HEADER | 3 TYPE RESEARCH PAPER WITH CITATIONS
4 CREATE ALPHABETICAL WORKS CITED | 5 PROOFREAD & REVISE RESEARCH PAPER

Earlier in this chapter, you inserted a citation and its source at once. In Word, you also can insert a citation without entering the source information. ***Why?*** *Sometimes, you may not have the source information readily available and would prefer to enter it at a later time.*

The following steps insert a citation placeholder in the footnote, so that you can enter the source information later.

- With the insertion point positioned as shown in Figure 2–37, tap or click the Insert Citation button (REFERENCES tab | Citations & Bibliography group) to display the Insert Citation menu (Figure 2–37).

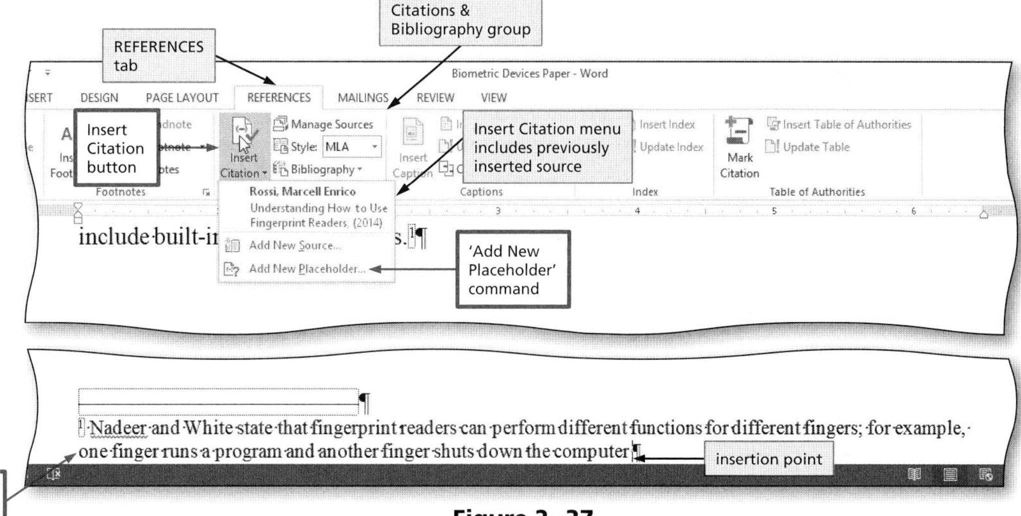

Figure 2–37

- Tap or click 'Add New Placeholder' on the Insert Citation menu to display the Placeholder Name dialog box.
- Type **`Nadeer`** as the tag name for the source (Figure 2–38).

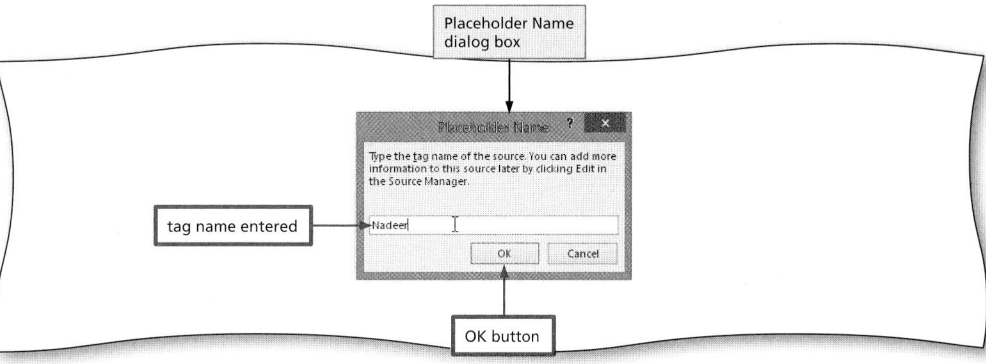

Figure 2–38

Q&A What is a tag name?
A tag name is an identifier that links a citation to a source. Word automatically creates a tag name when you enter a source. When you create a citation placeholder, enter a meaningful tag name, which will appear in the citation placeholder until you edit the source.

- Tap or click the OK button (Placeholder Name dialog box) to close the dialog box and insert the entered tag name in the citation placeholder in the document (shown in Figure 2–39).
- Press the PERIOD key to end the sentence.

Q&A What if the citation is in the wrong location?
Tap or click the citation to select it and then drag the citation tab (on the upper-left corner of the selected citation) to any location in the document.

If you are using your finger on a touch screen and are having difficulty completing the steps in this chapter, consider using a stylus. Many people find it easier to be precise with a stylus than with a finger. In addition, with a stylus you see the pointer. If you still are having trouble completing the steps with a stylus, try using a mouse.

Footnote Text Style

When you insert a footnote, Word formats it using the Footnote Text style, which does not adhere to the MLA documentation style. For example, notice in Figure 2–37 on the previous page that the footnote text is single-spaced, left-aligned, and a smaller font size than the text in the research paper. According to the MLA documentation style, notes should be formatted like all other paragraphs in the paper.

You could change the paragraph formatting of the footnote text to first-line indent and double-spacing and then change the font size from 10 to 12 point. If you use this technique, however, you will need to change the format of the footnote text for each footnote you enter into the document.

A more efficient technique is to modify the format of the Footnote Text style so that every footnote you enter in the document will use the formats defined in this style.

To Modify a Style Using a Shortcut Menu

1 CHANGE DOCUMENT SETTINGS | 2 CREATE HEADER | 3 TYPE RESEARCH PAPER WITH CITATIONS
4 CREATE ALPHABETICAL WORKS CITED | 5 PROOFREAD & REVISE RESEARCH PAPER

The Footnote Text style specifies left-aligned single-spaced paragraphs with a 10-point font size for text. The following steps modify the Footnote Text style. ***Why?*** *To meet MLA documentation style, the footnotes should be double-spaced with a first line indent and a 12-point font size for text.*

- If you are using a touch screen, press and hold the note text in the footnote and then tap the 'Show Context Menu' button on the mini toolbar; if you are using a mouse, right-click the note text in the footnote to display a shortcut menu related to footnotes (Figure 2–39).

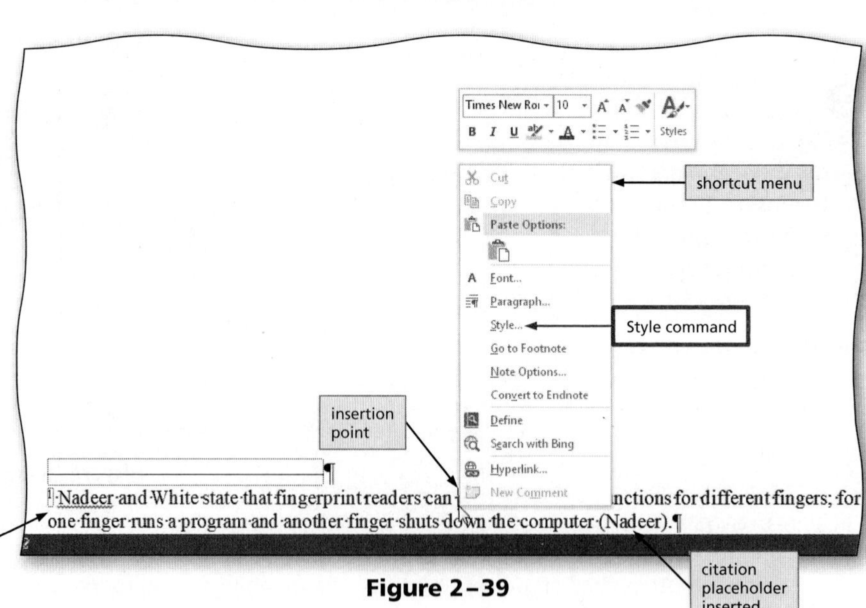

Figure 2–39

2

- Tap or click Style on the shortcut menu to display the Style dialog box. If necessary, tap or click the Category arrow, tap or click All styles in the Category list, and then tap or click Footnote Text in the Styles list to select the style to modify.
- Tap or click the Modify button (Style dialog box) to display the Modify Style dialog box.
- Tap or click the Font Size arrow (Modify Style dialog box) to display the Font Size list and then tap or click 12 in the Font Size list to change the font size.
- Tap or click the Double Space button to change the line spacing.
- Tap or click the Format button to display the Format menu (Figure 2–40).

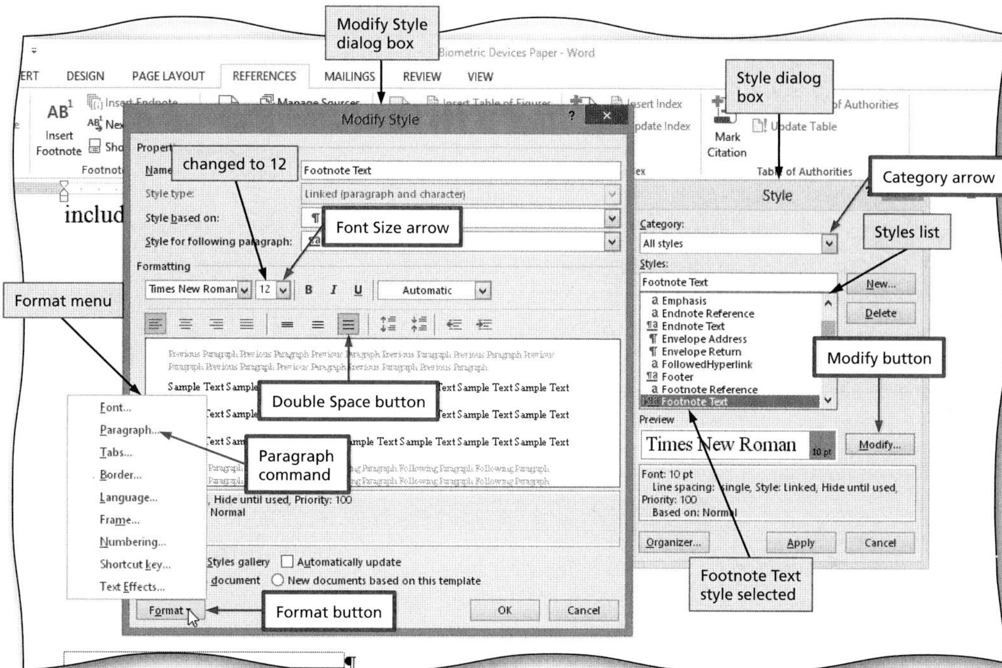

Figure 2–40

- Tap or click Paragraph on the Format menu (Modify Style dialog box) to display the Paragraph dialog box.
- Tap or click the Special arrow (Paragraph dialog box) and then tap or click First line (Figure 2–41).

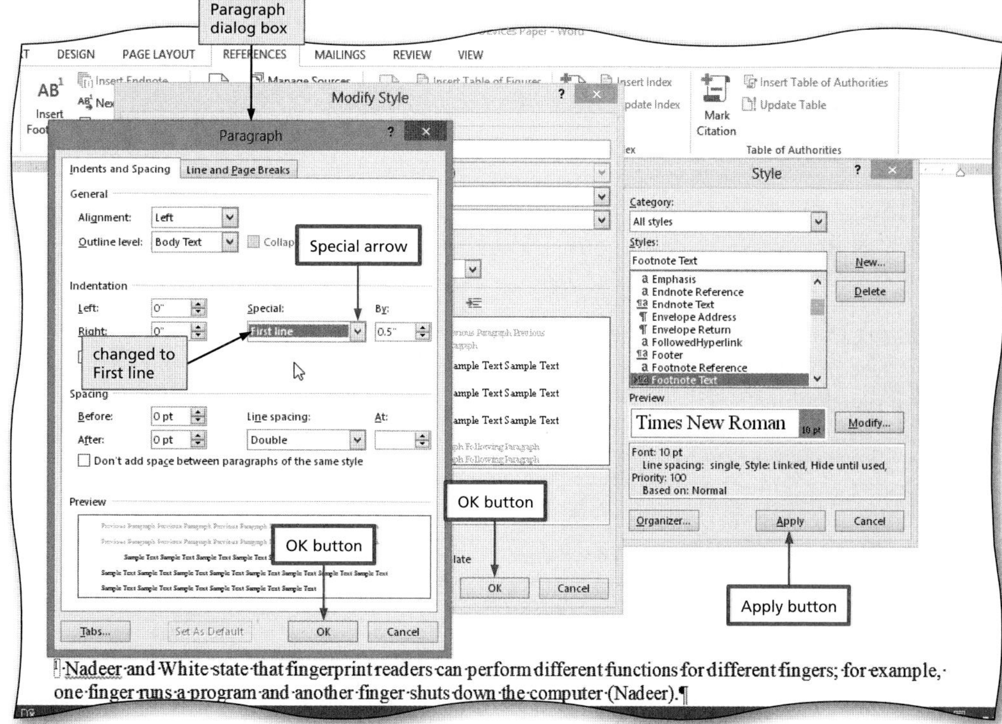

Figure 2–41

- Tap or click the OK button (Paragraph dialog box) to close the dialog box.
- Tap or click the OK button (Modify Style dialog box) to close the dialog box.
- Tap or click the Apply button (Style dialog box) to apply the style changes to the footnote text (Figure 2–42).

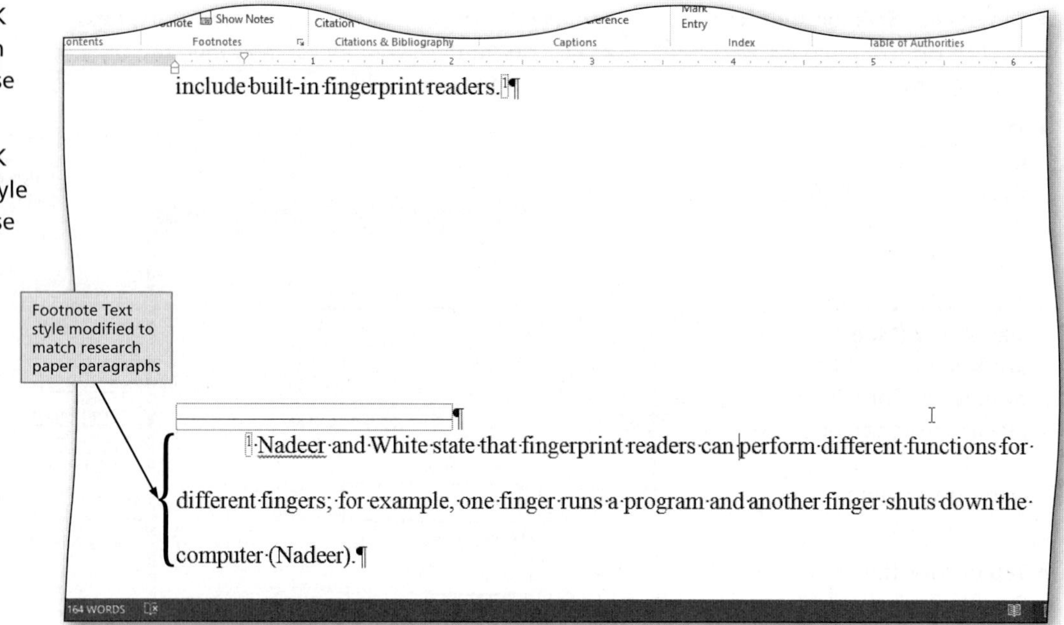

Figure 2–42

Q&A Will all footnotes use this modified style?
Yes. Any future footnotes entered in the document will use a 12-point font with the paragraphs first-line indented and double-spaced.

Other Ways

1. Tap or click Styles Dialog Box Launcher (HOME tab | Styles group), tap or point to style name in list, tap or click style name arrow, tap or click Modify, change settings (Modify Style dialog box), tap or click OK button
2. Tap or click Styles Dialog Box Launcher (HOME tab | Styles group), tap or click Manage Styles button in task pane, select style name in list, tap or click Modify button (Manage Styles dialog box), change settings (Modify Style dialog box), tap or click OK button in each dialog box

To Edit a Source

1 CHANGE DOCUMENT SETTINGS | 2 CREATE HEADER | **3 TYPE RESEARCH PAPER WITH CITATIONS**
4 CREATE ALPHABETICAL WORKS CITED | 5 PROOFREAD & REVISE RESEARCH PAPER

When you typed the footnote text for this research paper, you inserted a citation placeholder for the source. The following steps edit a source. ***Why?*** *Assume you now have the source information and are ready to enter it.*

- Tap or click somewhere in the citation placeholder to be edited, in this case (Nadeer), to select the citation placeholder.
- Tap or click the Citation Options arrow to display the Citation Options menu (Figure 2–43).

Citation Options menu
Edit Citation
Edit Source
Convert citation to static text
Update Citations and Bibliography
Edit Source command
state that fingerprint readers can perform different functions for
e, one finger runs a program and another finger shuts down the
compute (Nadeer).
citation tab is used to move citation to different location in document
citation placeholder selected
Citation Options arrow

Figure 2–43

Q&A What is the purpose of the tab to the left of the selected citation?
If, for some reason, you wanted to move a citation to a different location in the document, you would select the citation and then drag the citation tab to the desired location.

2

- Tap or click Edit Source on the Citation Options menu to display the Edit Source dialog box.
- If necessary, tap or click the 'Type of Source' arrow (Edit Source dialog box) and then tap or click Book, so that the list shows fields required for a book.
- Because this source has two authors, tap or click the Edit button to display the Edit Name dialog box, which assists you with entering multiple author names.
- Type **Nadeer** as the first author's last name; press the TAB key and then type **Aisha** as the first name; press the TAB key and then type **Sati** as the middle name (Figure 2–44).

Q&A What if I already know how to punctuate the author entry properly?

You can enter the name directly in the Author box.

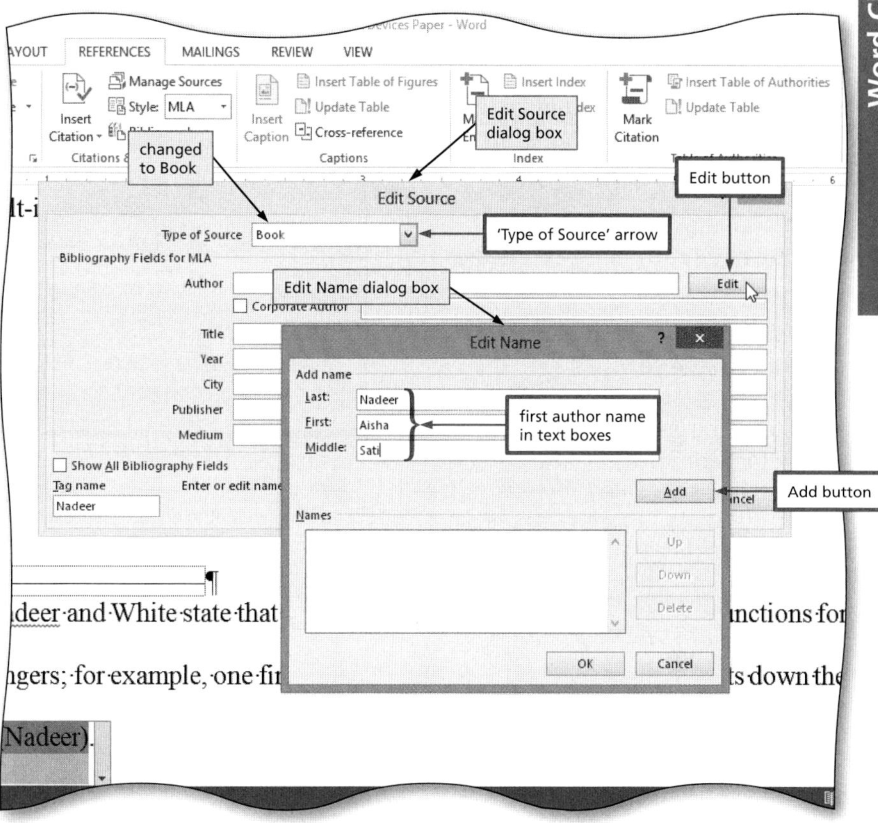

Figure 2–44

3

- Tap or click the Add button (Edit Name dialog box) to add the first author name to the Names list.
- Type **White** as the second author's last name; press the TAB key and then type **Jonathon** as the first name; press the TAB key and then type **Richard** as the middle name.
- Tap or click the Add button to add the second author name to the Names list (Figure 2–45).

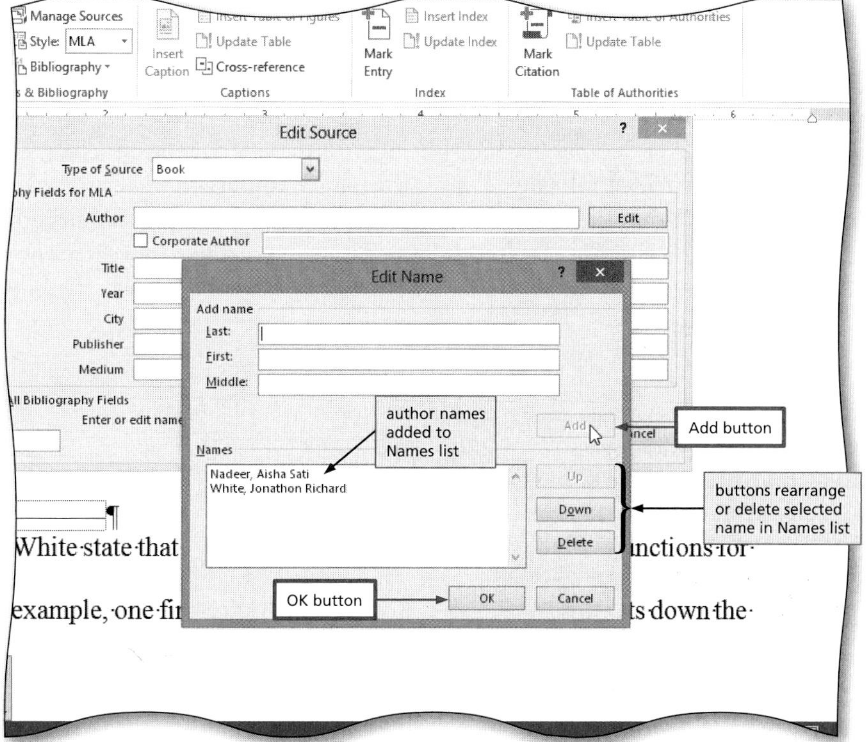

Figure 2–45

- Tap or click the OK button (Edit Name dialog box) to add the author names that appear in the Names list to the Author box in the Edit Source dialog box.
- Tap or click the Title text box (Edit Source dialog box). Type **Biometric Security** as the book title.
- Press the TAB key and then type **2014** as the year.
- Press the TAB key and then type **Chicago** as the city.
- Press the TAB key and then type **Windy City Press** as the publisher.
- Press the TAB key and then type **Print** as the medium (Figure 2–46).

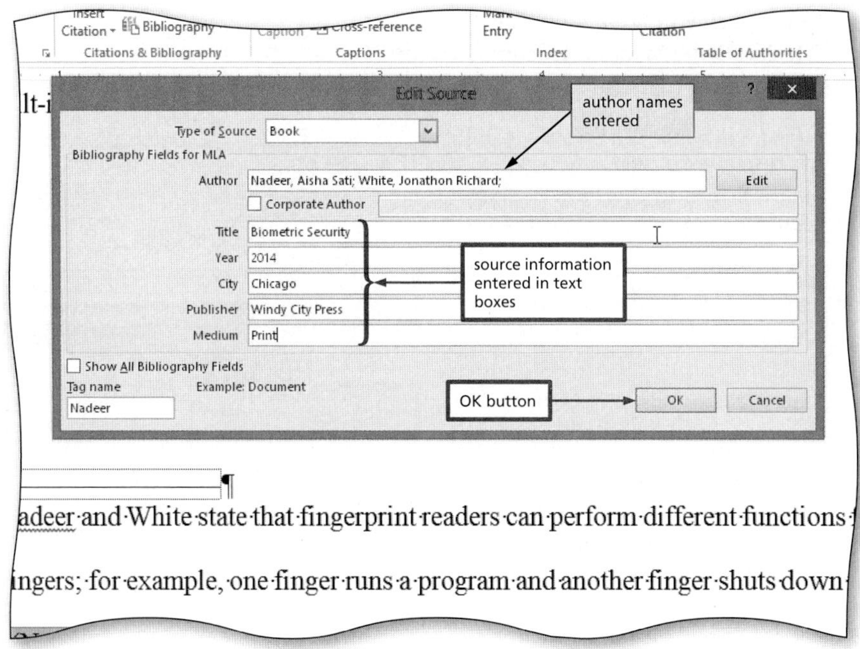

Figure 2–46

- Tap or click the OK button to close the dialog box, create the source, and update the citation to display both author last names (shown in Figure 2–47).

Other Ways

1. Tap or click Manage Sources button (REFERENCES tab | Citations & Bibliography group), tap or click placeholder source in Current List, tap or click Edit button (Source Manager dialog box)

To Edit a Citation

1 CHANGE DOCUMENT SETTINGS | 2 CREATE HEADER | **3 TYPE RESEARCH PAPER WITH CITATIONS**
4 CREATE ALPHABETICAL WORKS CITED | 5 PROOFREAD & REVISE RESEARCH PAPER

In the MLA documentation style, if a source has page numbers, you should include them in the citation. Thus, Word provides a means to enter the page numbers to be displayed in the citation. Also, if you reference the author's name in the text, you should not list it again in the parenthetical citation. Instead, just list the page number(s) in the citation. To do this, you instruct Word to suppress author and title. ***Why?*** *If you suppress the author, Word automatically displays the title, so you need to suppress both the author and title if you want just the page number(s) to be displayed.* The following steps edit the citation, suppressing the author and title but displaying the page numbers.

- If necessary, tap or click somewhere in the citation to be edited, in this case somewhere in (Nadeer and White), which selects the citation and displays the Citation Options arrow.
- Tap or click the Citation Options arrow to display the Citation Options menu (Figure 2–47).

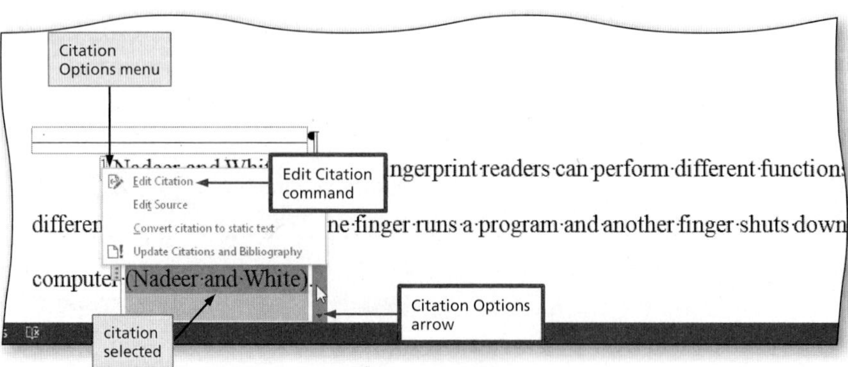

Figure 2–47

- Tap or click Edit Citation on the Citation Options menu to display the Edit Citation dialog box.
- Type 62–63 in the Pages text box (Edit Citation dialog box).
- Tap or click the Author check box to place a check mark in it.
- Tap or click the Title check box to place a check mark in it (Figure 2–48).

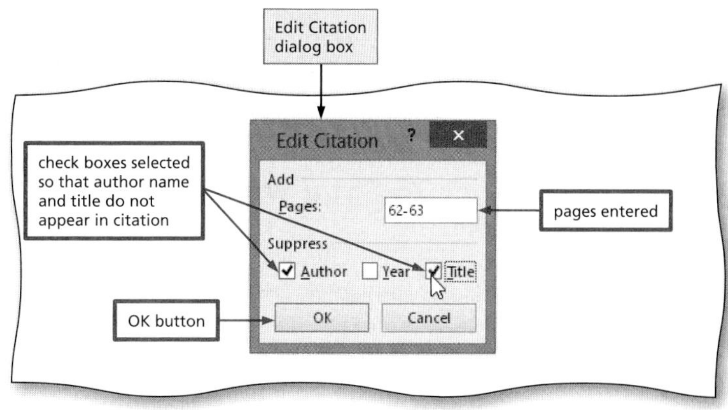

Figure 2–48

- Tap or click the OK button to close the dialog box, remove the author names from the citation in the footnote, suppress the title from showing, and add page numbers to the citation.
- Press the END key to move the insertion point to the end of the line, which also deselects the citation (Figure 2–49).

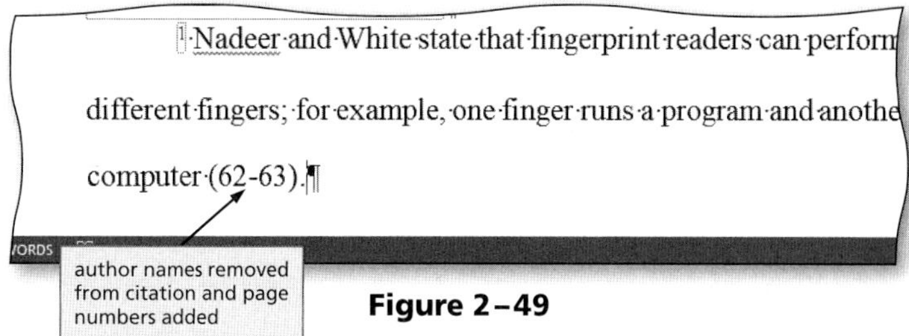

Figure 2–49

Working with Footnotes and Endnotes

You edit footnote text just as you edit any other text in the document. To delete or move a note reference mark, however, the insertion point must be in the document text (not in the footnote text).

To delete a note, select the note reference mark in the document text (not in the footnote text) by dragging through the note reference mark and then tap or click the Cut button (HOME tab | Clipboard group). Or, tap or click immediately to the right of the note reference mark in the document text and then press the BACKSPACE key twice, or tap or click immediately to the left of the note reference mark in the document text and then press the DELETE key twice.

To move a note to a different location in a document, select the note reference mark in the document text (not in the footnote text), tap or click the Cut button (HOME tab | Clipboard group), tap or click the location where you want to move the note, and then tap or click the Paste button (HOME tab | Clipboard group). When you move or delete notes, Word automatically renumbers any remaining notes in the correct sequence.

If you are using a mouse and position the pointer on the note reference mark in the document text, the note text is displayed above the note reference mark as a ScreenTip. To remove the ScreenTip, move the pointer.

If, for some reason, you wanted to change the format of note reference marks in footnotes or endnotes (i.e., from 1, 2, 3, to A, B, C), you would tap or click the Footnote & Endnote Dialog Box Launcher (REFERENCES tab | Footnotes group) to display the Footnote and Endnote dialog box, tap or click the Number format arrow (Footnote and Endnote dialog box), tap or click the desired number format in the list, and then tap or click the Apply button.

If, for some reason, you wanted to change a footnote number, you would tap or click the Footnote & Endnote Dialog Box Launcher (REFERENCES tab | Footnotes group) to display the Footnote and Endnote dialog box, enter the desired number in the Start at box, and then tap or click the Apply button (Footnote and Endnote dialog box).

If, for some reason, you wanted to convert footnotes to endnotes, you would tap or click the Footnote & Endnote Dialog Box Launcher (REFERENCES tab | Footnotes group) to display the Footnote and Endnote dialog box, tap or click the

BTW

Footnote and Endnote Location

You can change the location of footnotes from the bottom of the page to the end of the text by tapping or clicking the Footnote & Endnote Dialog Box Launcher (REFERENCES tab | Footnotes group), tapping or clicking the Footnotes arrow (Footnote and Endnote dialog box), and then tapping or clicking Below text. Similarly, tapping or clicking the Endnotes arrow (Footnote and Endnote dialog box) enables you to change the location of endnotes from the end of the document to the end of a section.

Convert button (Footnote and Endnote dialog box), select the 'Convert all footnotes to endnotes' option button, tap or click the OK button, and then tap or click the Close button (Footnote and Endnote dialog box).

To Enter More Text

The next task is to continue typing text in the body of the research paper. The following steps enter this text.

1. Position the insertion point after the note reference mark in the document and then press the ENTER key.

2. Type the first three sentences in the third paragraph of the research paper (shown in Figure 2–50): **`A face recognition system captures a live face image and compares it with a stored image to determine if the person is a legitimate user. Some buildings use face recognition systems to secure access to rooms. Law enforcement, surveillance systems, and airports use face recognition systems to protect the public.`**

1 CHANGE DOCUMENT SETTINGS | 2 CREATE HEADER | **3 TYPE RESEARCH PAPER WITH CITATIONS**
4 CREATE ALPHABETICAL WORKS CITED | **5 PROOFREAD & REVISE RESEARCH PAPER**

To Count Words

Often when you write papers, you are required to compose the papers with a minimum number of words. The minimum requirement for the research paper in this chapter is 275 words. You can look on the status bar and see the total number of words thus far in a document. For example, Figure 2–50 shows the research paper has 214 words, but you are not sure if that count includes the words in your footnote. The following steps display the Word Count dialog box. ***Why?*** *You want to verify that the footnote text is included in the count.*

- Tap or click the Word Count indicator on the status bar to display the Word Count dialog box.
- If necessary, place a check mark in the 'Include textboxes, footnotes and endnotes' check box (Word Count dialog box) (Figure 2–50).

Q&A Why do the statistics in my Word Count dialog box differ from those in Figure 2–50?
Depending on the accuracy of your typing, your statistics may differ.

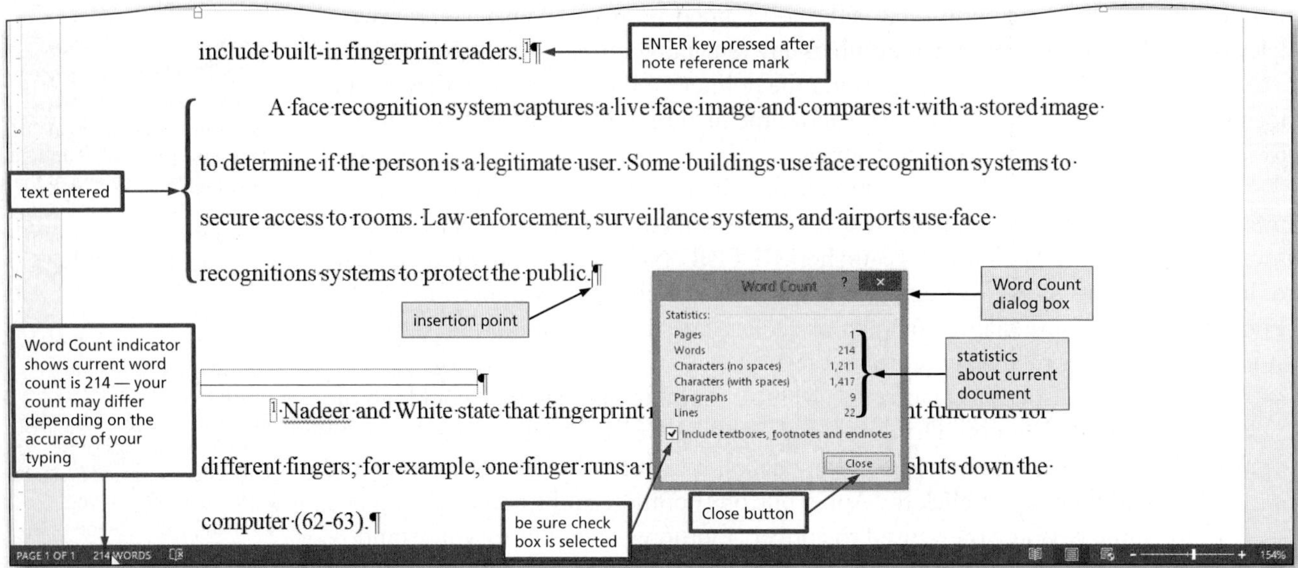

Figure 2–50

2

- Tap or click the Close button to close the dialog box.

Q&A Can I display statistics for just a section of the document?
Yes. Select the section and then click the Word Count indicator on the status bar to display statistics about the selected text.

Other Ways

1. Tap or click Word Count button (REVIEW tab | Proofing group)
2. Press CTRL+SHIFT+G

Automatic Page Breaks

As you type documents that exceed one page, Word automatically inserts page breaks, called **automatic page breaks** or **soft page breaks**, when it determines the text has filled one page according to paper size, margin settings, line spacing, and other settings. If you add text, delete text, or modify text on a page, Word recalculates the location of automatic page breaks and adjusts them accordingly.

Word performs page recalculation between the keystrokes, that is, in between the pauses in your typing. Thus, Word refers to the automatic page break task as **background repagination**. An automatic page break will occur in the next set of steps.

To Enter More Text and Insert a Citation Placeholder

The next task is to type the remainder of the third paragraph in the body of the research paper. The following steps enter this text and a citation placeholder at the end of the paragraph.

1 With the insertion point positioned at the end of the third sentence in the third paragraph, as shown in Figure 2–50, press the SPACEBAR.

2 Type the rest of the third paragraph: **`Some mobile devices use face recognition systems to unlock the device. Face recognition systems are becoming more sophisticated and can recognize people with or without glasses, hats, facial hair, makeup, or jewelry, and with new hairstyles`** and then press the SPACEBAR.

Q&A Why does the text move from the second page to the first page as I am typing?
Word, by default, will not allow the first line of a paragraph to be by itself at the bottom of a page (an **orphan**) or the last line of a paragraph to be by itself at the top of a page (a **widow**). As you type, Word adjusts the placement of the paragraph to avoid orphans and widows.

3 Tap or click the Insert Citation button (REFERENCES tab | Citations & Bibliography group) to display the Insert Citation menu. Tap or click 'Add New Placeholder' on the Insert Citation menu to display the Placeholder Name dialog box.

4 Type **`Allensmith`** as the tag name for the source.

5 Tap or click the OK button to close the dialog box and insert the tag name in the citation placeholder.

6 Press the PERIOD key to end the sentence.

BTW

Page Break Locations
As you type, your page break may occur at different locations depending on Word settings and the type of printer connected to the computer.

To Hide and Show White Space

With the page break and header, it is difficult to see the entire third paragraph at once on the screen. With the screen in Print Layout view, you can hide white space, which is the space that is displayed at the top and bottom of pages (including headers and footers) and also the space between pages. The following steps hide white space, if your screen displays it, and then shows white space. ***Why?*** *You want to see the as much of the third paragraph as possible at once, which spans the bottom of the first page and the top of the second page.*

- If you are using a mouse, position the pointer in the document window in the space between pages so that the pointer changes to a 'Hide White Space' button (Figure 2–51).

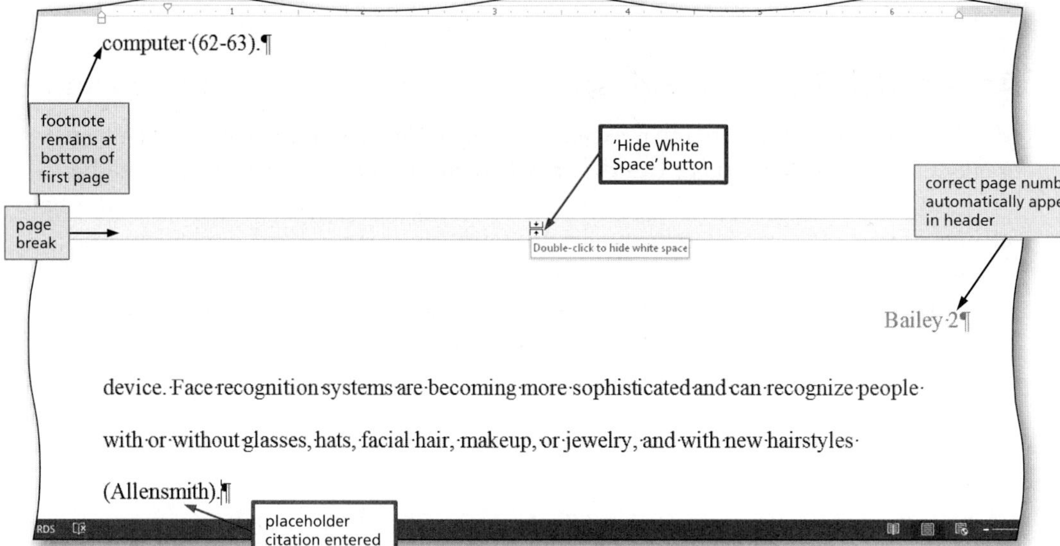

Figure 2–51

2

- If you are using a touch screen, double-tap in the space between pages; if you are using a mouse, double-click while the pointer is a 'Hide White Space' button to hide white space.

Q&A Does hiding white space have any effect on the printed document?
No.

3

- If you are using a mouse, position the pointer in the document window on the page break between pages so that the pointer changes to a 'Show White Space' button (Figure 2–52).

4

- If you are using a touch screen, double-tap the page break; if you are using a mouse, double-click while the pointer is a 'Show White Space' button to show white space.

Figure 2–52

Other Ways

1. Tap or click FILE on ribbon, tap or click Options in Backstage view, tap or click Display in left pane (Word Options dialog box), remove or select check mark from 'Show white space between pages in Print Layout view' check box, tap or click OK button

To Edit a Source

When you typed the third paragraph of the research paper, you inserted a citation placeholder, Allensmith, for the source. You now have the source information, which is for a website, and are ready to enter it. The following steps edit the source for the Allensmith citation placeholder.

1. Tap or click somewhere in the citation placeholder to be edited, in this case (Allensmith), to select the citation placeholder.
2. Tap or click the Citation Options arrow to display the Citation Options menu.
3. Tap or click Edit Source on the Citation Options menu to display the Edit Source dialog box.
4. If necessary, tap or click the Type of Source arrow (Edit Source dialog box); scroll to and then click Web site, so that the list shows fields required for a Web site.
5. Place a check mark in the 'Show All Bibliography Fields' check box to display more fields related to Web sites.
6. Tap or click the Author text box. Type `Allensmith, Samantha Clare` as the author.
7. Tap or click the Name of Web Page text box. Type `Understanding Face Recognition Systems` as the webpage name.
8. Tap or click the Production Company text box. Type `Course Technology` as the the production company.
9. Tap or click the Year Accessed text box. Type `2014` as the year accessed (Figure 2–53).
10. Press the TAB key and then type `Sept.` as the month accessed.
11. Press the TAB key and then type `16` as the day accessed.
12. Press the TAB key and then type `Web` as the Medium.

Q&A Do I need to enter a web address (URL)?
The latest MLA documentation style update does not require the web address in the source.

13. Tap or click the OK button to close the dialog box and create the source.

BTW
Q&As
For a complete list of the Q&As found in many of the step-by-step sequences in this book, visit the Q&A resource on the Student Companion Site located on www.cengagebrain.com. For detailed instructions about accessing available resources, visit www.cengage.com/ct/studentdownload or contact your instructor for information about accessing the required files.

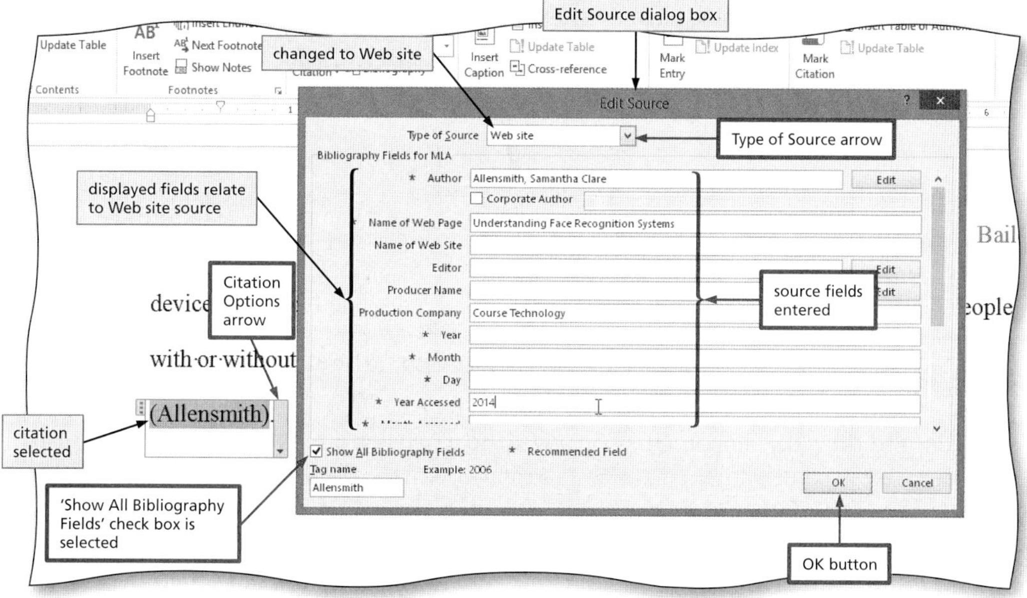

Figure 2–53

BTW
Printing Document Properties
To print document properties, tap or click FILE on the ribbon to open the Backstage view, tap or click the Print tab in the Backstage view to display the Print gallery, tap or click the first button in the Settings area to display a list of options specifying what you can print, tap or click Document Info in the list to specify you want to print the document properties instead of the actual document, and then tap or click the Print button in the Print gallery to print the document properties on the currently selected printer.

To Enter More Text

The next task is to type the last paragraph of text in the research paper. The following steps enter this text.

1. Press the END key to position the insertion point at the end of the third paragraph and then press the ENTER key.
2. Type the last paragraph of the research paper (Figure 2–54): **Home and occupational users alike are using biometric security. Through a biometric element, such as a fingerprint, devices can deny or grant access to programs, devices, computers, rooms, and other locations. Biometric devices are an effective security technology.**

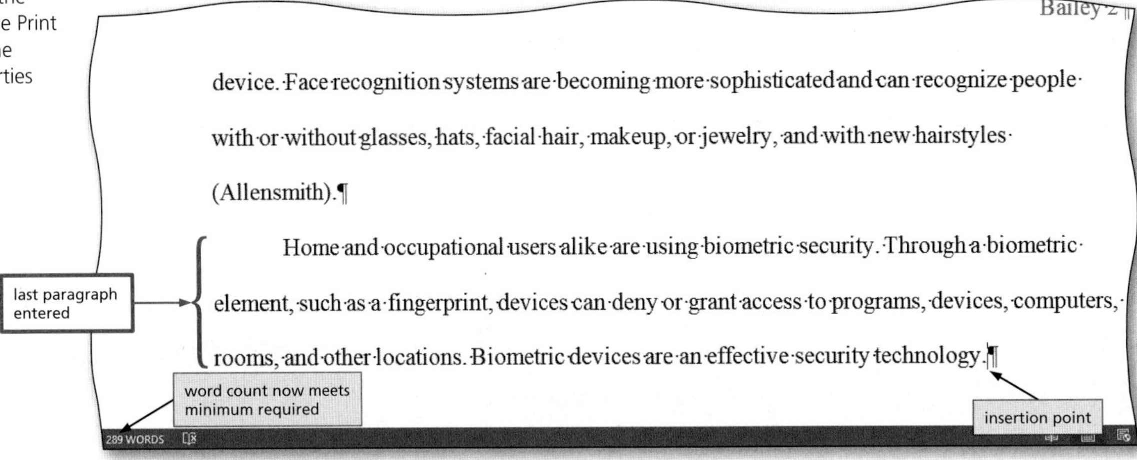

Figure 2–54

To Save an Existing Document with the Same File Name

You have made several modifications to the document since you last saved it. Thus, you should save it again. The following step saves the document again.

1. Tap or click the Save button on the Quick Access Toolbar to overwrite the previously saved file.

Break Point: If you wish to take a break, this is a good place to do so. You can exit Word now (refer to page WD 46 for instructions). To resume at a later time, run Word (refer to page WD 46 for instructions), open the file called Biometric Devices Paper (refer to page WD 47 for instructions), and continue following the steps from this location forward.

Creating an Alphabetical Works Cited Page

According to the MLA documentation style, the **works cited page** is a list of sources that are referenced directly in a research paper. You place the list on a separate numbered page with the title, Works Cited, centered one inch from the top margin. The works are to be alphabetized by the author's last name or, if the work has no author, by the work's title. The first line of each entry begins at the left margin. Indent subsequent lines of the same entry one-half inch from the left margin.

CONSIDER THIS

What is a bibliography?

A **bibliography** is an alphabetical list of sources referenced in a paper. Whereas the text of the research paper contains brief references to the source (the citations), the bibliography lists all publication information about the source. Documentation styles differ significantly in their guidelines for preparing a bibliography. Each style identifies formats for various sources, including books, magazines, pamphlets, newspapers, websites, television programs, paintings, maps, advertisements, letters, memos, and much more. You can find information about various styles and their guidelines in printed style guides and on the web.

To Page Break Manually

1 CHANGE DOCUMENT SETTINGS | 2 CREATE HEADER | 3 TYPE RESEARCH PAPER WITH CITATIONS
4 CREATE ALPHABETICAL WORKS CITED | 5 PROOFREAD & REVISE RESEARCH PAPER

The next step is to insert a manual page break following the body of the research paper. ***Why?*** *According to the MLA documentation style, the works cited are to be displayed on a separate numbered page.*

A **manual page break**, or **hard page break**, is one that you force into the document at a specific location. Word never moves or adjusts manual page breaks. Word, however, does adjust any automatic page breaks that follow a manual page break. Word inserts manual page breaks immediately above or to the left of the location of the insertion point. The following step inserts a manual page break after the text of the research paper.

1

- Verify that the insertion point is positioned at the end of the text of the research paper, as shown in Figure 2–54.
- Tap or click INSERT on the ribbon to display the INSERT tab.
- Tap or click the 'Insert a Page Break' button (INSERT tab | Pages group) to insert a manual page break immediately to the left of the insertion point and position the insertion point immediately below the manual page break (Figure 2–55).

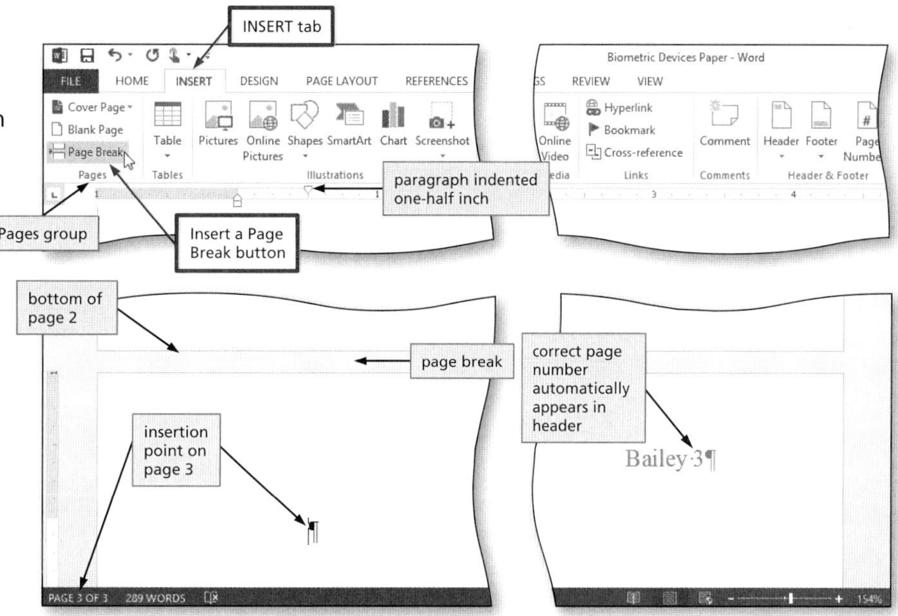

Figure 2–55

Other Ways

1. Press CTRL+ENTER

To Apply a Style

1 CHANGE DOCUMENT SETTINGS | 2 CREATE HEADER | 3 TYPE RESEARCH PAPER WITH CITATIONS
4 CREATE ALPHABETICAL WORKS CITED | 5 PROOFREAD & REVISE RESEARCH PAPER

The works cited title is to be centered between the margins of the paper. If you simply issue the Center command, the title will not be centered properly. ***Why?*** *It will be to the right of the center point because earlier you set the first-line indent for paragraphs to one-half inch.*

To properly center the title of the works cited page, you could drag the 'First Line Indent' marker back to the left margin before centering the paragraph, or you could apply the Normal style to the location of the insertion point. Recall that you modified the Normal style for this document to 12-point Times New Roman with double-spaced, left-aligned paragraphs that have no space after the paragraphs.

To apply a style to a paragraph, first position the insertion point in the paragraph and then apply the style. The step on the next page applies the modified Normal style to the location of the insertion point.

- Tap or click HOME on the ribbon to display the HOME tab.
- With the insertion point on the paragraph mark at the top of page 3 (as shown in Figure 2–55 on the previous page) even if Normal is selected, tap or click Normal in the Styles gallery (HOME tab | Styles group) to apply the Normal style to the paragraph containing the insertion point (Figure 2–56).

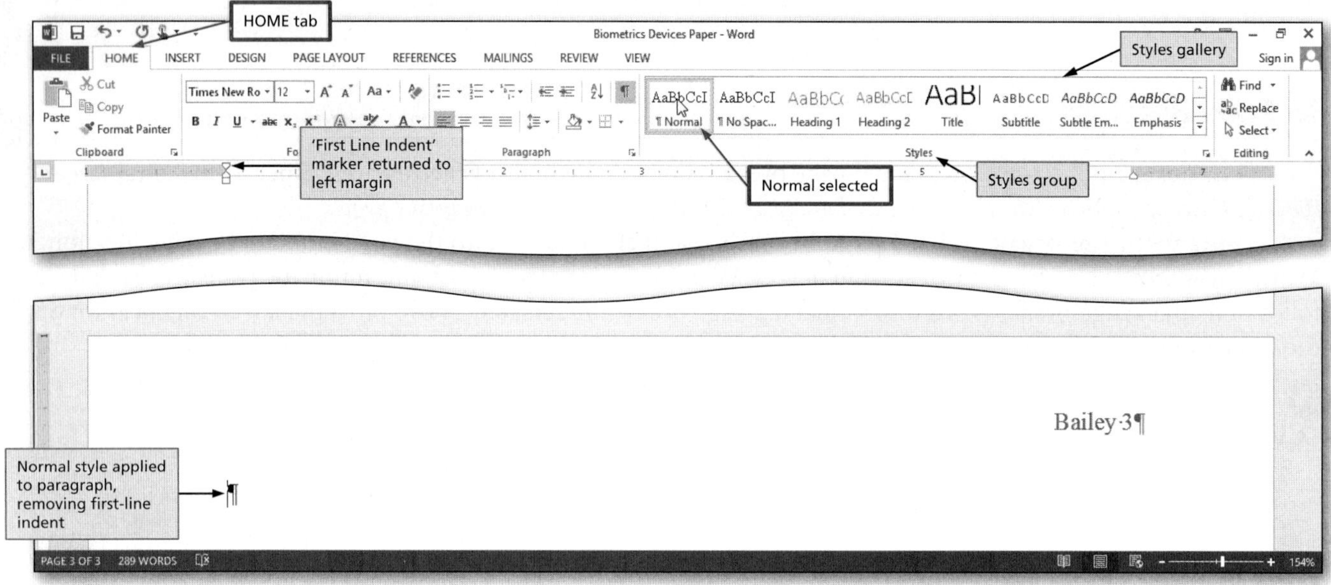

Figure 2–56

Other Ways

1. Tap or click Styles Dialog Box Launcher (HOME tab | Styles group), select desired style in Styles task pane
2. Press CTRL+SHIFT+S, tap or click Style Name arrow in Apply Styles task pane, select desired style in list

To Center Text

The next task is to enter the title, Works Cited, centered between the margins of the paper. The following steps use a keyboard shortcut to format the title.

1. Press CTRL+E to center the paragraph mark.
2. Type **`Works Cited`** as the title.
3. Press the ENTER key.
4. Press CTRL+L to left-align the paragraph mark (shown in Figure 2–57).

To Create a Bibliographical List

1 CHANGE DOCUMENT SETTINGS | 2 CREATE HEADER | 3 TYPE RESEARCH PAPER WITH CITATIONS
4 CREATE ALPHABETICAL WORKS CITED | **5 PROOFREAD & REVISE RESEARCH PAPER**

While typing the research paper, you created several citations and their sources. The next task is to use Word to format the list of sources and alphabetize them in a **bibliographical list**. ***Why?*** *Word can create a bibliographical list with each element of the source placed in its correct position with proper punctuation, according to the specified style, saving you time looking up style guidelines. For example, in this research paper, the book source will list, in this order, the author name(s), book title, publisher city, publishing company name, and publication year with the correct punctuation between each element according to the MLA documentation style.* The next steps create an MLA-styled bibliographical list from the sources previously entered.

1

- Tap or click REFERENCES on the ribbon to display the References tab.
- With the insertion point positioned as shown in Figure 2–56, tap or click the Bibliography button (REFERENCES tab | Citations & Bibliography group) to display the Bibliography gallery (Figure 2–57).

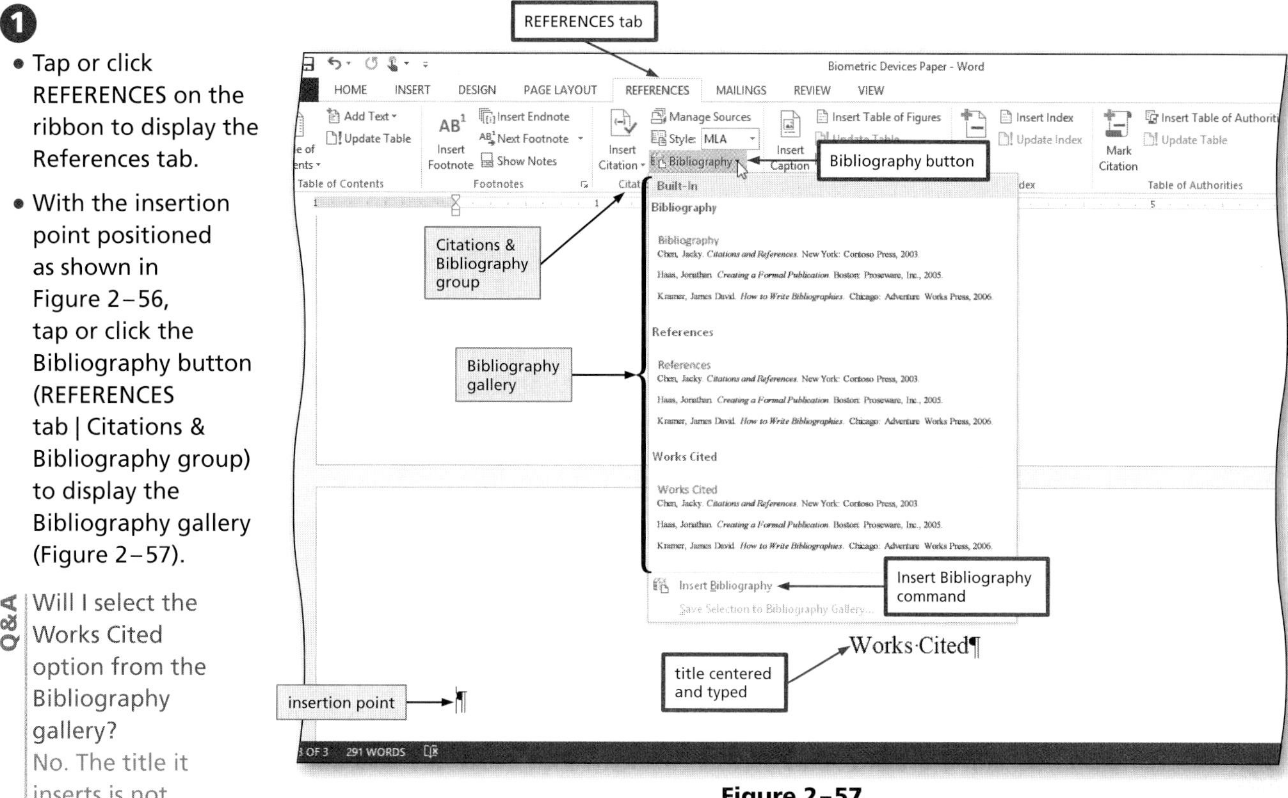

Figure 2–57

Q&A Will I select the Works Cited option from the Bibliography gallery?
No. The title it inserts is not formatted according to the MLA documentation style. Thus, you will use the Insert Bibliography command instead.

2

- Tap or click Insert Bibliography in the Bibliography gallery to insert a list of sources at the location of the insertion point.
- If necessary, scroll to display the entire list of sources in the document window (Figure 2–58).

Q&A What is the n.d. in the first work?
The MLA documentation style uses the abbreviation n.d. for no date (for example, no date appears on the webpage).

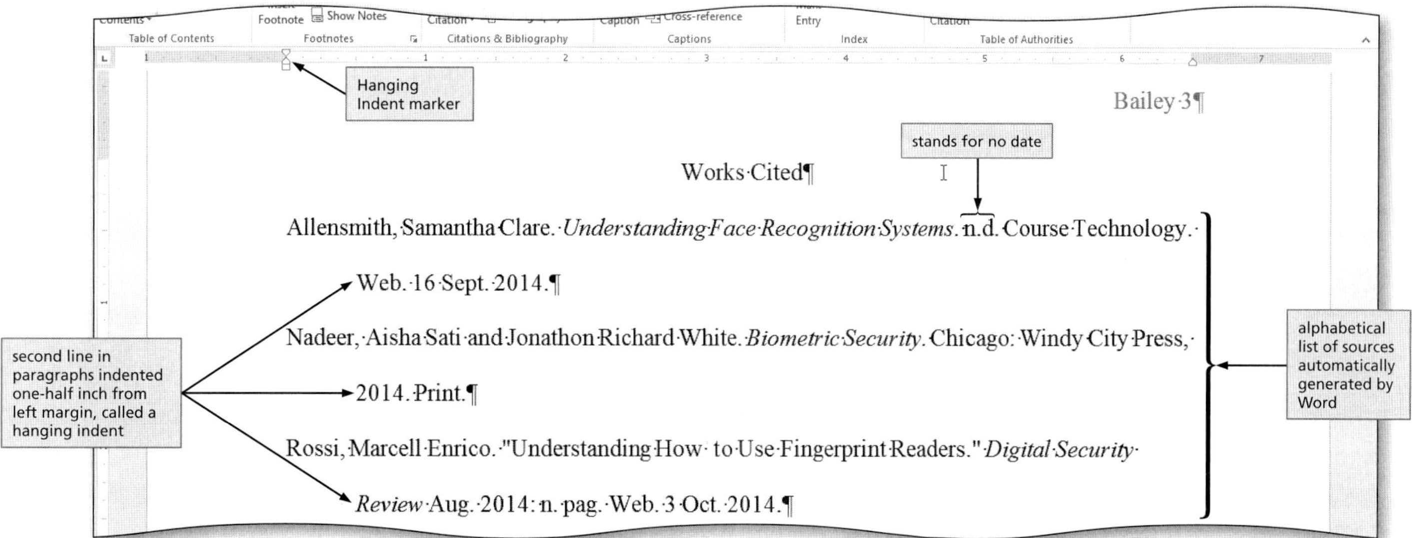

Figure 2–58

To Format Paragraphs with a Hanging Indent

Notice in Figure 2–58 on the previous page that the first line of each source entry begins at the left margin, and subsequent lines in the same paragraph are indented one-half inch from the left margin. In essence, the first line hangs to the left of the rest of the paragraph; thus, this type of paragraph formatting is called a **hanging indent**. The Bibliography style in Word automatically formats the works cited paragraphs with a hanging indent.

If you wanted to format paragraphs with a hanging indent, you would use one of the following techniques.

- With the insertion point in the paragraph to format, drag the **Hanging Indent marker** (the bottom triangle) on the ruler to the desired mark on the ruler (i.e., .5") to set the hanging indent at that location from the left margin.

or

- Tap the 'Show Context Menu' button on the mini toolbar or right-click the paragraph to format, tap or click Paragraph on shortcut menu, tap or click the Indents and Spacing tab (Paragraph dialog box), tap or click the Special arrow, tap or click Hanging, and then tap or click the OK button.

or

- Tap or click the Paragraph Dialog Box Launcher (HOME tab or PAGE LAYOUT tab | Paragraph group), tap or click the Indents and Spacing tab (Paragraph dialog box), tap or click the Special arrow, tap or click Hanging, and then tap or click the OK button.

or

- With the insertion point in the paragraph to format, press CTRL+T.

To Save an Existing Document with the Same File Name

You have made several modifications to the document since you last saved it. Thus, you should save it again. The following step saves the document again. For an example of the step listed below, refer to the Office and Windows chapter at the beginning of this book.

1 Tap or click the Save button on the Quick Access Toolbar to overwrite the previously saved file.

BTW
Certification
The Microsoft Office Specialist (MOS) program provides an opportunity for you to obtain a valuable industry credential — proof that you have the Word 2013 skills required by employers. For more information, visit the Certification resource on the Student Companion Site located on www.cengagebrain.com. For detailed instructions about accessing available resources, visit www.cengage.com/ct/studentdownload or contact your instructor for information about accessing the required files.

Proofreading and Revising the Research Paper

As discussed in Chapter 1, once you complete a document, you might find it necessary to make changes to it. Before submitting a paper to be graded, you should proofread it. While **proofreading**, ensure all the source information is correct and look for grammatical errors and spelling errors. Also ensure that transitions between sentences flow smoothly and the sentences themselves make sense.

To assist you with the proofreading effort, Word provides several tools. You can go to a page, copy text, find text, replace text, insert a synonym, check spelling and grammar, and look up information. The following pages discuss these tools.

CONSIDER THIS

What should you consider when proofreading and revising a paper?

As you proofread the paper, look for ways to improve it. Check all grammar, spelling, and punctuation. Be sure the text is logical and transitions are smooth. Where necessary, add text, delete text, reword text, and move text to different locations. Ask yourself these questions:

- Does the title suggest the topic?
- Is the thesis clear?
- Is the purpose of the paper clear?
- Does the paper have an introduction, body, and conclusion?
- Does each paragraph in the body relate to the thesis?
- Is the conclusion effective?
- Are sources acknowledged correctly?
- Are all sources acknowledged?

To Modify a Source

1 CHANGE DOCUMENT SETTINGS | 2 CREATE HEADER | 3 TYPE RESEARCH PAPER WITH CITATIONS
4 CREATE ALPHABETICAL WORKS CITED | **5 PROOFREAD & REVISE RESEARCH PAPER**

While proofreading the paper, you notice an error in the magazine title; specifically, the first word (Understanding) should be removed. If you modify the contents of any source, the list of sources automatically updates. ***Why?*** *Word automatically updates the contents of fields, and the bibliography is a field.* The following steps delete a word from the title of the magazine article.

- Tap or click the Manage Sources button (REFERENCES tab | Citations & Bibliography group) to display the Source Manager dialog box.
- Tap or click the source you wish to edit in the Current List, in this case the article by Rossi, to select the source.
- Tap or click the Edit button (Source Manager dialog box) to display the Edit Source dialog box.
- In the Title text box, delete the word, Understanding, from the beginning of the title (Figure 2–59).

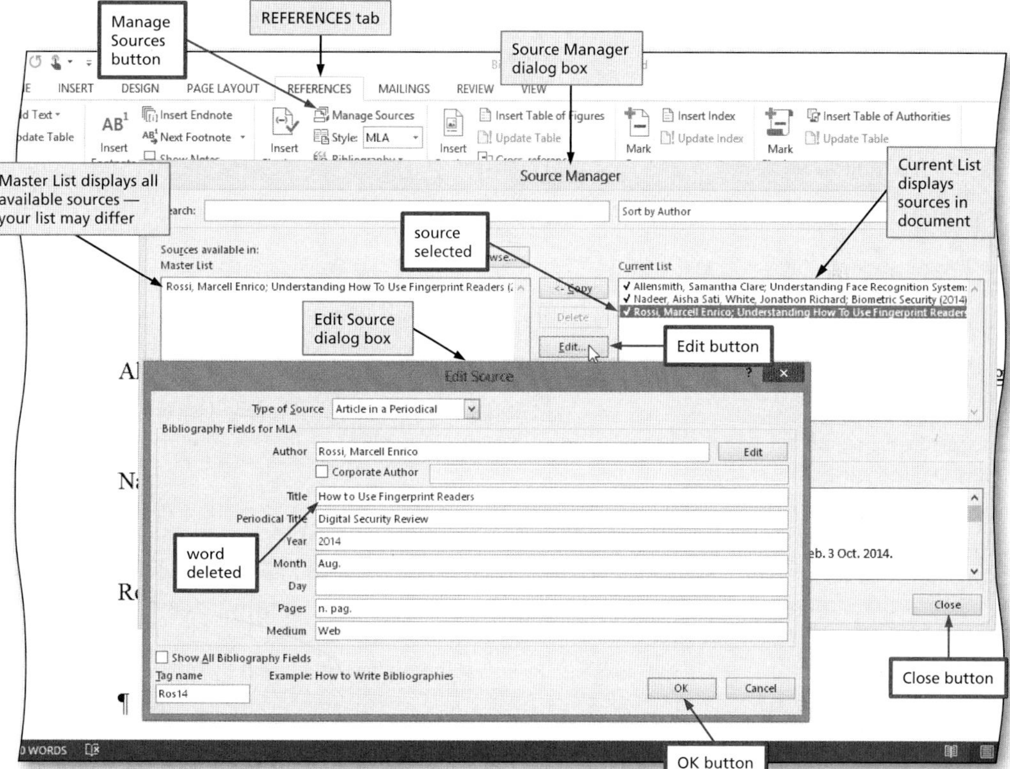

Figure 2–59

- Tap or click the OK button (Edit Source dialog box) to close the dialog box.
- If a Microsoft Word dialog box appears, tap or click its Yes button to update all occurrences of the source.
- Tap or click the Close button (Source Manager dialog box) to update the list of sources and close the dialog box.

To Update a Field

Depending on settings, the bibliography field may not automatically reflect the edited magazine title. Thus, the following steps update the bibliography field. ***Why?*** *Because the bibliography is a field, you may need to instruct Word to update its contents.*

- If you are using a touch screen, press and hold anywhere in the bibliography text and then tap the 'Show Context Menu' button on the mini toolbar; if you are using a mouse, right-click anywhere in the bibliography text to display a shortcut menu related to fields (Figure 2–60).

Q&A Why are all the words in the bibliography shaded gray?
By default, Word shades selected fields gray.

What if the bibliography field is not shaded gray?
Tap or click FILE on the ribbon to open the Backstage view, tap or click Options in the Backstage view, tap or click Advanced in the left pane (Word Options dialog box), scroll to the 'Show document content' area, tap or click the Field shading arrow, tap or click When selected, and then tap or click the OK button.

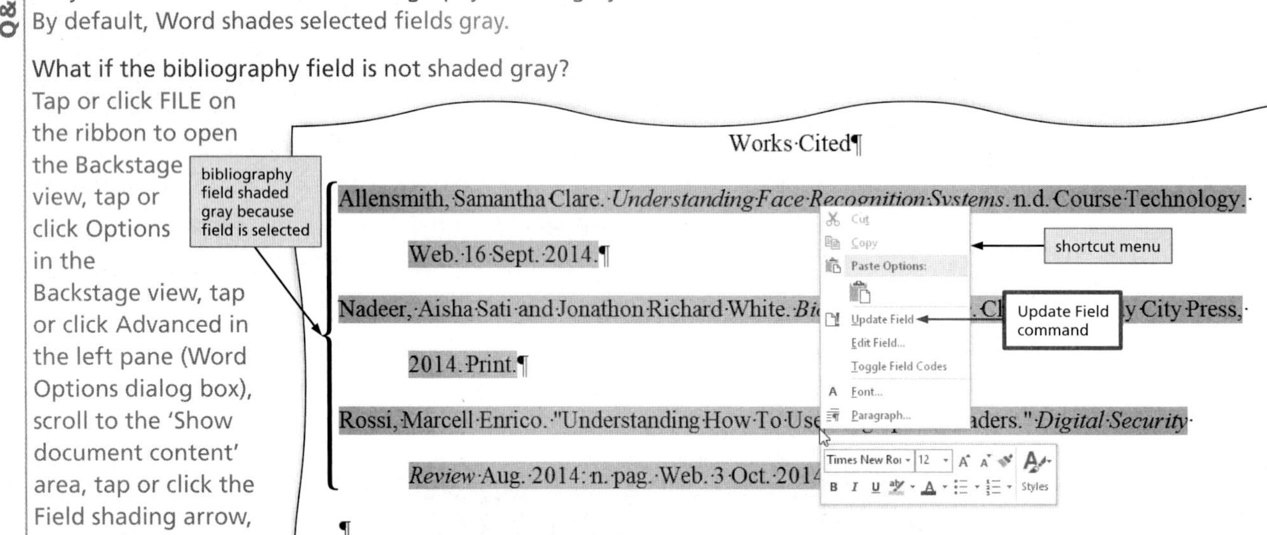

Figure 2–60

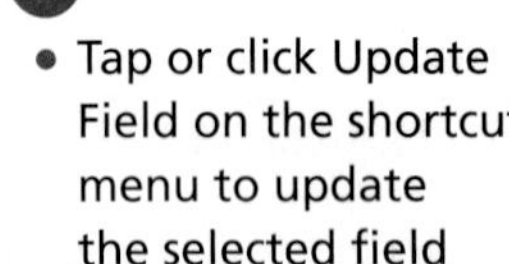

- Tap or click Update Field on the shortcut menu to update the selected field (Figure 2–61).

Q&A Can I update all fields in a document at once?
Yes. Select the entire document and then follow these steps.

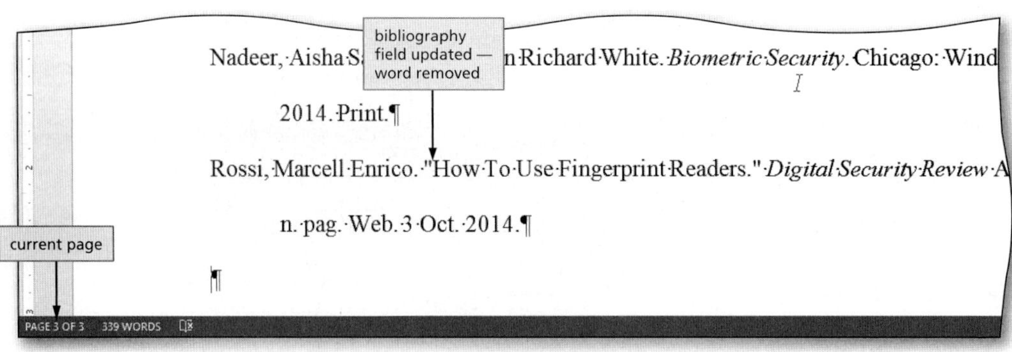

Figure 2–61

Other Ways

1. Select the field, press F9

To Convert a Field to Regular Text

If, for some reason, you wanted to convert a field, such as the bibliography field, to regular text, you would perform the following steps. Keep in mind, though, once you convert the field to regular text, it no longer is a field that can be updated.

1. Tap or click somewhere in the field to select it, in this case, somewhere in the bibliography.
2. Press CTRL+SHIFT+F9 to convert the selected field to regular text.

To Go to a Page

The next task in revising the paper is to modify text on the second page of the document. ***Why?*** *You want to copy text from one location to another on the second page.* You could scroll to the desired location in the document, or you can use the Navigation Pane to browse through pages in a document. The following steps display the top of the second page in the document window and position the insertion point at the beginning of that page.

1

- Tap or click VIEW on the ribbon to display the VIEW tab.
- Place a check mark in the 'Open the Navigation Pane' check box (VIEW tab | Show group) to open the Navigation Pane on the left side of the Word window.
- If necessary, tap or click the PAGES tab in the Navigation Pane to display thumbnails of the pages in the document.
- Scroll to and then tap or click the thumbnail of the second page to display the top of the selected page in the top of the document window (Figure 2–62).

What is the Navigation Pane?
The **Navigation Pane** is a window that enables you to browse through headings in a document, browse through pages in a document, or search for text in a document.

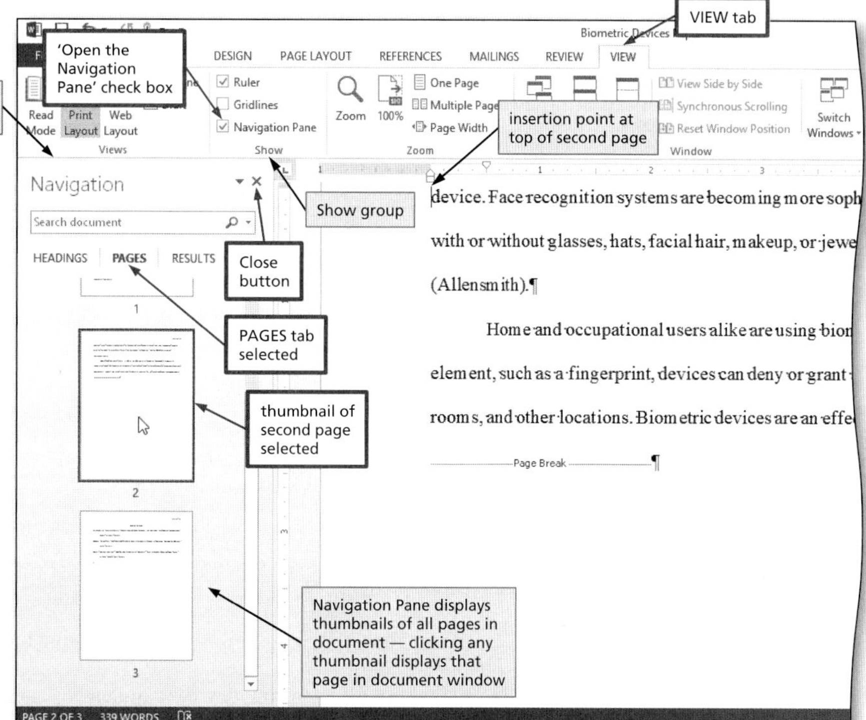

Figure 2–62

2

- Tap or click the Close button in the Navigation Pane to close the pane.

Other Ways

1. Tap or click Find arrow (HOME tab | Editing group), tap or click Go To on Find menu, tap or click Go To tab (Find and Replace dialog box), enter page number, tap or click Go To button
2. Tap or click Page Number indicator on status bar, tap or click PAGES tab in Navigation Pane, tap or click thumbnail of desired page (Navigation Pane)
3. Press CTRL+G, enter page number, tap or click Go To button

Copying, Cutting, and Pasting

While proofreading the research paper, you decide it would read better if the word, biometric, in the second sentence of the last paragraph also appeared in front of the word, devices, in the same sentence. You could type the word at the desired location, but because this is a difficult word to spell and type, you decide to use the Office Clipboard. The **Office Clipboard** is a temporary storage area that holds up to 24 items (text or graphics) copied from any Office program. The Office Clipboard works with the copy, cut, and paste commands:

- **Copying** is the process of placing items on the Office Clipboard, leaving the item in the document.
- **Cutting** removes the item from the document before placing it on the Office Clipboard.
- **Pasting** is the process of copying an item from the Office Clipboard into the document at the location of the insertion point.

BTW
Quick Reference
For a table that lists how to complete the tasks covered in this book using touch gestures, the mouse, ribbon, shortcut menu, and keyboard, see the Quick Reference Summary at the back of this book, or visit the Quick Reference resource on the Student Companion Site located on www.cengagebrain.com. For detailed instructions about accessing available resources, visit www.cengage.com/ct/studentdownload or contact your instructor for information about accessing the required files.

To Copy and Paste

In the research paper, you copy a word from one location to another. ***Why?** The sentence reads better with the word, biometric, inserted before the word, devices.* The following steps copy and paste a word.

1

- Select the item to be copied (the word, biometric, in this case).
- Tap or click HOME on the ribbon to display the HOME tab.
- Tap or click the Copy button (HOME tab | Clipboard group) to copy the selected item in the document to the Office Clipboard (Figure 2–63).

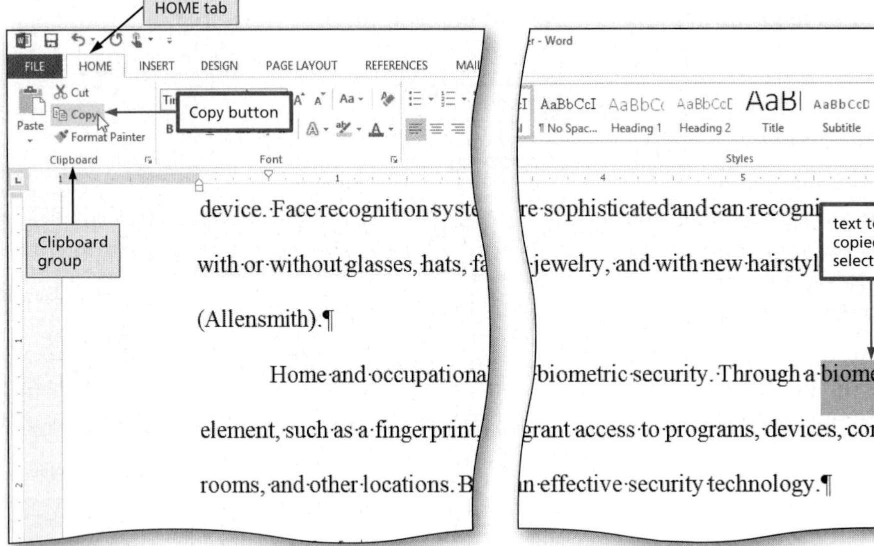

Figure 2–63

- Position the insertion point at the location where the item should be pasted (immediately to the left of the word, devices, in this case) (Figure 2–64).

insertion point located where item is to be pasted

Home and ... s alike are using biometric security. Through a biometric element, such as a fingerprint, devices can deny or grant access to programs, devices, computers, rooms, and other locations. Biometric devices are an effective security technology.¶

Figure 2–64

3

- Tap or click the Paste button (HOME tab | Clipboard group) to paste the copied item in the document at the location of the insertion point (Figure 2–65).

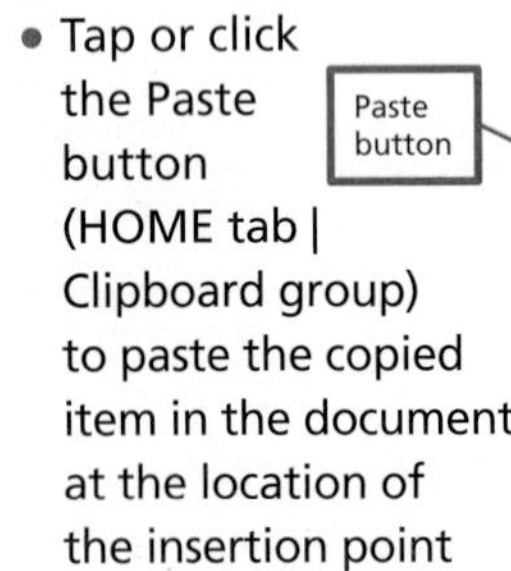

Q&A What if I click the Paste arrow by mistake?
Click the Paste arrow again to remove the Paste menu and repeat Step 3.

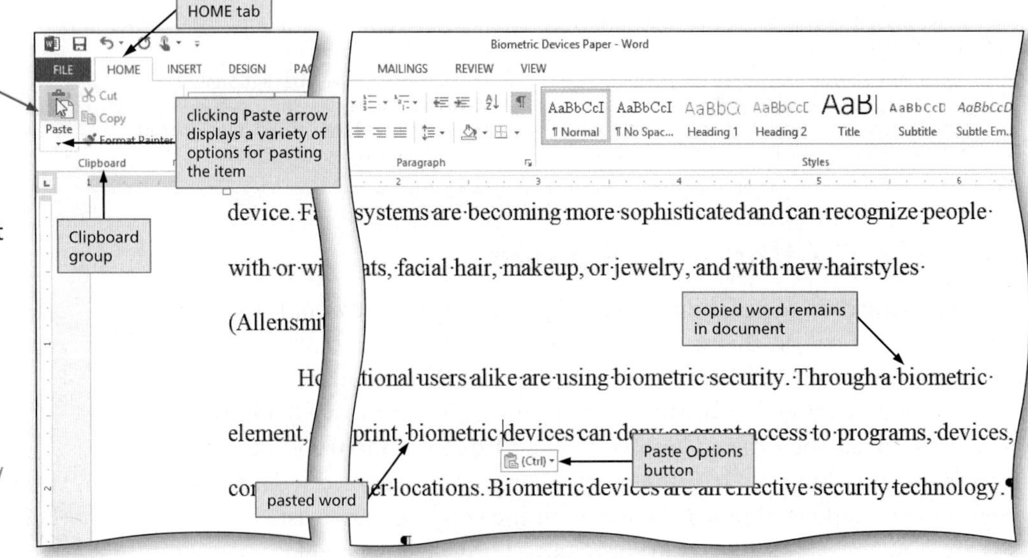

Figure 2–65

Other Ways

1. Press and hold or right-click selected item, tap Copy on mini toolbar or click Copy on shortcut menu, press and hold or right-click where item is to be pasted, tap Paste on mini toolbar or click Keep Source Formatting in Paste Options area on shortcut menu
2. Select item, press CTRL+C, position insertion point at paste location, press CTRL+V

To Display the Paste Options Menu

When you paste an item or move an item using drag-and-drop editing, which was discussed in the previous chapter, Word automatically displays a Paste Options button near the pasted or moved text (Figure 2–65). ***Why?*** *The Paste Options button allows you to change the format of a pasted item. For example, you can instruct Word to format the pasted item the same way as where it was copied (the source), or format it the same way as where it is being pasted (the destination).* The following steps display the Paste Options menu.

- Tap or click the Paste Options button to display the Paste Options menu (Figure 2–66).

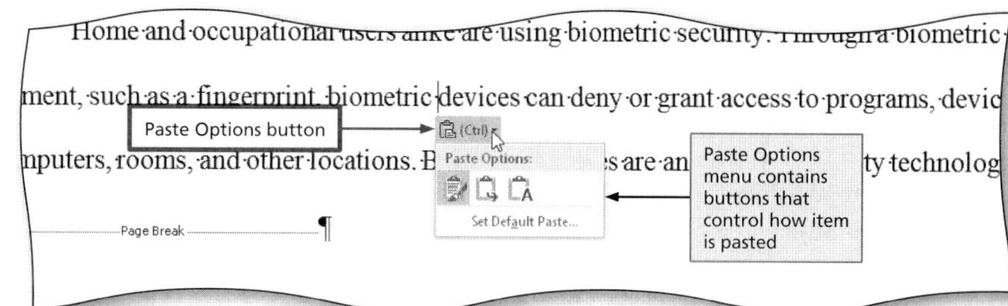

Figure 2–66

Q&A What are the functions of the buttons on the Paste Options menu?
In general, the left button indicates the pasted item should look the same as it did in its original location (the source). The second button formats the pasted text to match the rest of the item where it was pasted (the destination). The third button removes all formatting from the pasted item. The Set Default Paste command displays the Word Options dialog box. Keep in mind that the buttons shown on a Paste Options menu will vary, depending on the item being pasted.

- Tap or click anywhere to remove the Paste Options menu from the window.

Other Ways

1. CTRL (to remove the Paste Options menu)

To Find Text

While proofreading the paper, you would like to locate all occurrences of the word, element. ***Why?*** *You are contemplating changing occurrences of this word to the word, identifier.* The following steps find all occurrences of specific text in a document.

- If you are using a touch screen, tap the Find button (HOME tab | Editing group) and then tap Find on the menu; if you are using a mouse, click the Find button (HOME tab | Editing group) to display the Navigation Pane.
- If necessary, tap or click the RESULTS tab in the Navigation Pane, which displays a Search box where you can type text for which you want to search (Figure 2–67).

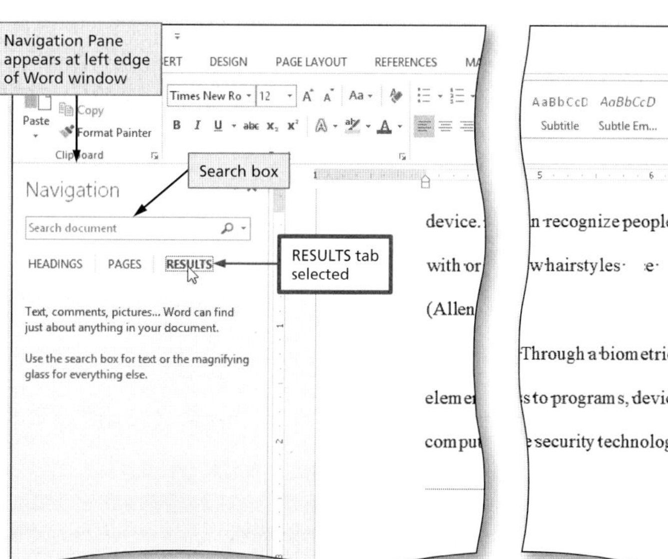

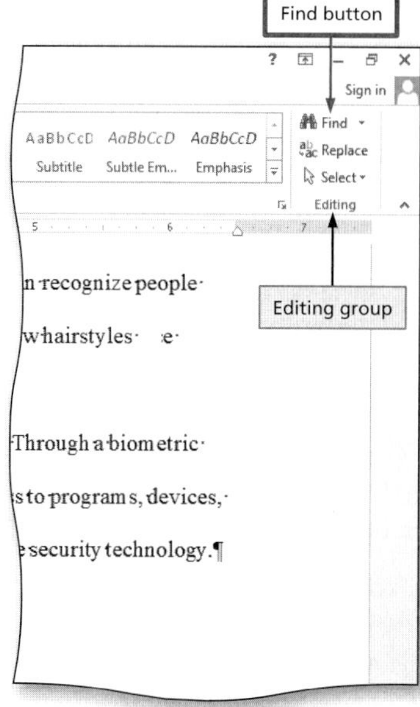

Figure 2–67

2

- Type **element** in the Navigation Pane Search box to display all occurrences of the typed text, called the search text, in the Navigation Pane and to highlight the occurrences of the search text in the document window (Figure 2–68).

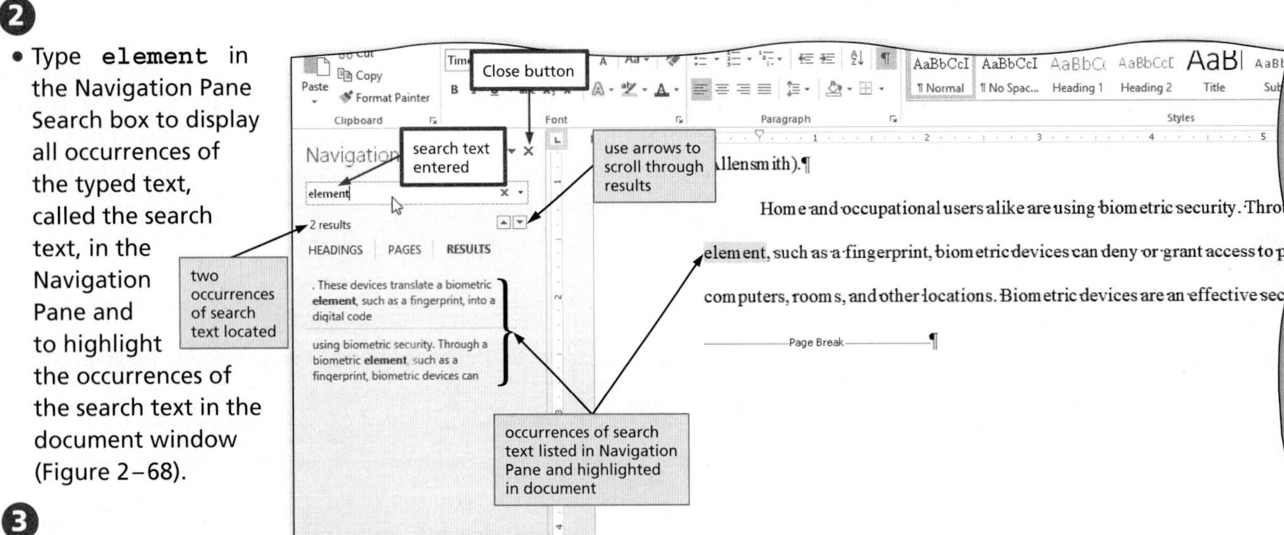

Figure 2–68

3

Experiment

- Tap or click both occurrences in the Navigation Pane and watch Word display the associated text in the document window.
- Type various search text in the Navigation Pane Search box, and watch Word both list matches in the Navigation Pane and highlight matches in the document window.
- Tap or click the Close button in the Navigation Pane to close the pane.

Other Ways

1. Tap or click Find arrow (HOME tab | Editing group), tap or click Find on Find menu, enter search text in Navigation Pane
2. Tap or click Page Number indicator on status bar, enter search text in Navigation Pane
3. Press CTRL+F, enter search text in Navigation Pane

To Replace Text

1 CHANGE DOCUMENT SETTINGS | 2 CREATE HEADER | 3 TYPE RESEARCH PAPER WITH CITATIONS
4 CREATE ALPHABETICAL WORKS CITED | 5 PROOFREAD & REVISE RESEARCH PAPER

You decide to change all occurrences of element to identifier. ***Why?** The text, biometric identifier, is a better description than biometric element.* Word's find and replace feature locates each occurrence of a word or phrase and then replaces it with text you specify. The following steps find and replace text.

- Tap or click the Replace button (HOME tab | Editing group) to display the Replace sheet in the Find and Replace dialog box.
- If necessary, type **element** in the Find what box (Find and Replace dialog box).
- Type **identifier** in the Replace with box (Figure 2–69).

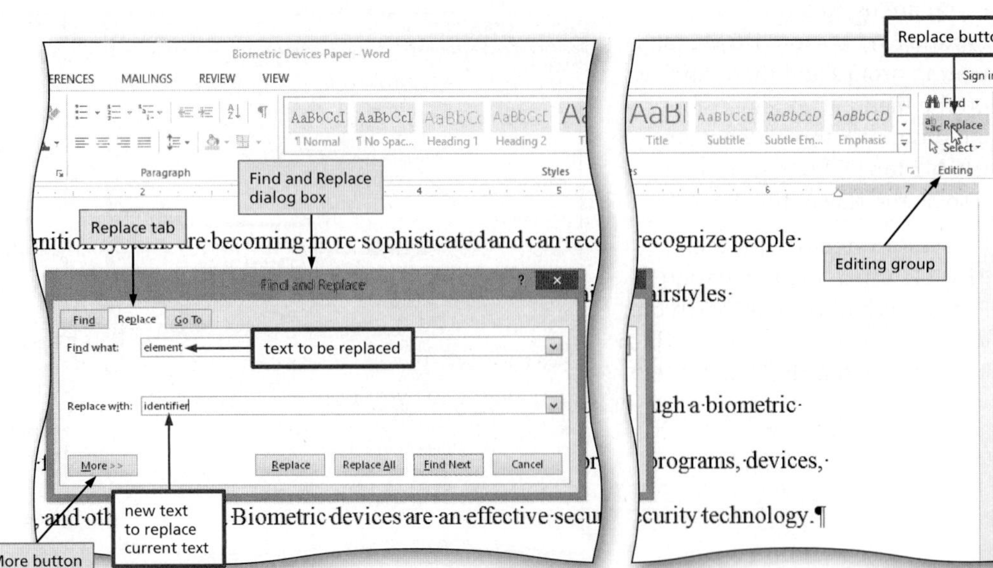

Figure 2–69

2

- Tap or click the Replace All button to instruct Word to replace all occurrences of the Find what text with the Replace with text (Figure 2–70). If Word displays a dialog box asking if you want to continue searching from the beginning of the document, tap or click the Yes button.

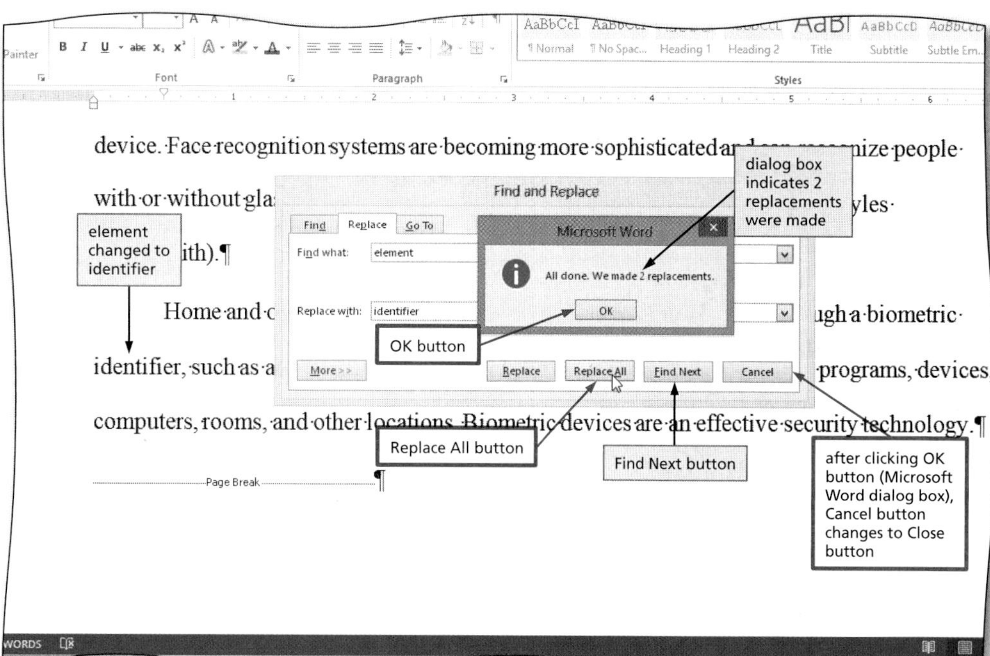

Figure 2–70

Q&A

Does Word search the entire document?

If the insertion point is at the beginning of the document, Word searches the entire document; otherwise, Word searches from the location of the insertion point to the end of the document and then displays a dialog box asking if you want to continue searching from the beginning. You also can search a section of text by selecting the text before tapping or clicking the Replace button.

3

- Tap or click the OK button (Microsoft Word dialog box) to close the dialog box.
- Tap or click the Close button (Find and Replace dialog box) to close the dialog box.

Other Ways

1. Press CTRL+H

Find and Replace Dialog Box

The Replace All button (Find and Replace dialog box) replaces all occurrences of the Find what text with the Replace with text. In some cases, you may want to replace only certain occurrences of a word or phrase, not all of them. To instruct Word to confirm each change, tap or click the Find Next button (Find and Replace dialog box) (Figure 2–70), instead of the Replace All button. When Word locates an occurrence of the text, it pauses and waits for you to tap or click either the Replace button or the Find Next button. Tapping or clicking the Replace button changes the text; tapping or clicking the Find Next button instructs Word to disregard the replacement and look for the next occurrence of the Find what text.

If you accidentally replace the wrong text, you can undo a replacement by tapping or clicking the Undo button on the Quick Access Toolbar. If you used the Replace All button, Word undoes all replacements. If you used the Replace button, Word undoes only the most recent replacement.

BTW

Finding Formatting

To search for formatting or a special character, tap or click the More button in the Find and Replace dialog box (shown in Figure 2–69). To find formatting, use the Format button in the Find dialog box. To find a special character, use the Special button.

To Find and Insert a Synonym

1 CHANGE DOCUMENT SETTINGS | 2 CREATE HEADER | 3 TYPE RESEARCH PAPER WITH CITATIONS
4 CREATE ALPHABETICAL WORKS CITED | **5 PROOFREAD & REVISE RESEARCH PAPER**

In this project, you would like a synonym for the word, occupational, in the fourth paragraph of the research paper. ***Why?*** *When writing, you may discover that you used the same word in multiple locations or that a word you used was not quite appropriate, which is the case here.* In these instances, you will want to look up a **synonym**, or a word similar in meaning, to the duplicate or inappropriate word. A **thesaurus** is a book of synonyms. Word provides synonyms and a thesaurus for your convenience. The following steps find a suitable synonym.

- If you are using a touch screen, press and hold the word for which you want a synonym and then tap the 'Show Context Menu' button on the mini toolbar; if you are using a mouse, right-click the word for which you want to find a synonym (in this case, occupational) to display a shortcut menu.
- Tap or point to Synonyms on the shortcut menu to display a list of synonyms for the word you right-clicked (Figure 2–71).

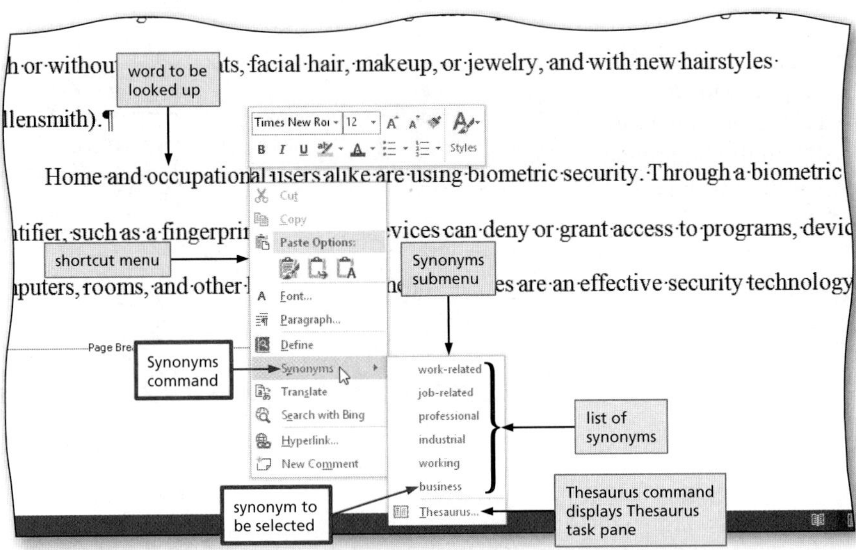

Figure 2–71

- Tap or click the synonym you want (in this case, business) on the Synonyms submenu to replace the selected word in the document with the selected synonym (Figure 2–72).

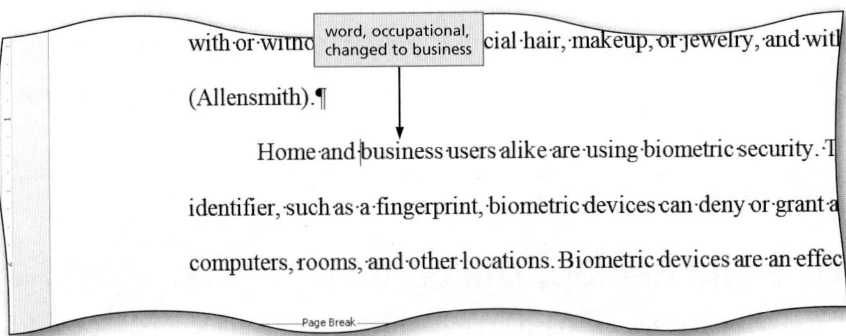

Figure 2–72

Q&A What if the synonyms list on the shortcut menu does not display a suitable word?

You can display the thesaurus in the Thesaurus task pane by tapping or clicking Thesaurus on the Synonyms submenu. The Thesaurus task pane displays a complete thesaurus, in which you can look up synonyms for various meanings of a word. You also can look up an **antonym,** or word with an opposite meaning.

Other Ways

1. Click Thesaurus button (REVIEW tab | Proofing group)
2. Press SHIFT+F7

To Check Spelling and Grammar at Once

1 CHANGE DOCUMENT SETTINGS | 2 CREATE HEADER | 3 TYPE RESEARCH PAPER WITH CITATIONS
4 CREATE ALPHABETICAL WORKS CITED | **5 PROOFREAD & REVISE RESEARCH PAPER**

As discussed in Chapter 1, Word checks spelling and grammar as you type and places a wavy underline below possible spelling or grammar errors. Chapter 1 illustrated how to check these flagged words immediately. The next steps check spelling and grammar at once. ***Why?*** *Some users prefer to wait and check their entire document for spelling and grammar errors at once.*

Note: In the following steps, the word, readers, has been misspelled intentionally as raders to illustrate the use of Word's check spelling and grammar at once feature. If you are completing this project on a personal computer, your research paper may contain different misspelled words, depending on the accuracy of your typing.

- Press CTRL+HOME because you want the spelling and grammar check to begin from the top of the document.
- Tap or click REVIEW on the ribbon to display the REVIEW tab.
- Tap or click the Spelling & Grammar button (REVIEW tab | Proofing group) to begin the spelling and grammar check at the location of the insertion point, which, in this case, is at the beginning of the document.
- Tap or click the desired word in the list of suggestions in the Spelling pane (readers, in this case) (Figure 2–73).

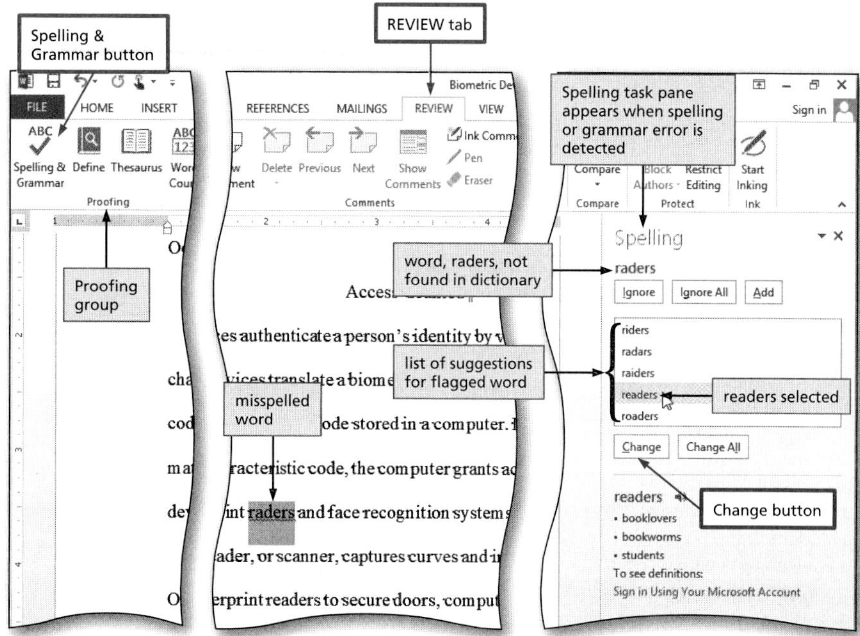

Figure 2–73

- With the word, reader, selected in the list of suggestions, tap or click the Change button (Spelling task pane) to change the flagged word to the selected suggestion and then continue the spelling and grammar check until the next error is identified or the end of the document is reached (Figure 2–74).

Figure 2–74

- Because the flagged word is a proper noun and spelled correctly, tap or click the Ignore All button (Spelling task pane) to ignore this and future occurrences of the flagged proper noun and then continue the spelling and grammar check until the next error is identified or the end of the document is reached.

- When the spelling and grammar check is finished and Word displays a dialog box, tap or click its OK button.

Q&A Can I check spelling of just a section of a document?

Yes, select the text before starting the spelling and grammar check.

Other Ways

1. Tap or click 'Spelling and Grammar Check' icon on status bar 2. Press F7

BTW
Readability Statistics
You can instruct Word to display readability statistics when it has finished a spelling and grammar check on a document. Three readability statistics presented are the percent of passive sentences, the Flesch Reading Ease score, and the Flesch-Kincaid Grade Level score. The Flesch Reading Ease score uses a 100-point scale to rate the ease with which a reader can understand the text in a document. A higher score means the document is easier to understand. The Flesch-Kincaid Grade Level score rates the text in a document on a U.S. school grade level. For example, a score of 10.0 indicates a student in the tenth grade can understand the material. To show readability statistics when the spelling check is complete, open the Backstage view, tap or click Options in the Backstage view, tap or click Proofing in the left pane (Word Options dialog box), place a check mark in the 'Show readability statistics' check box, and then click the OK button. Readability statistics will be displayed the next time you check spelling and grammar at once in the document.

The Main and Custom Dictionaries

As shown in the previous steps, Word may flag a proper noun as an error because the proper noun is not in its main dictionary. To prevent Word from flagging proper nouns as errors, you can add the proper nouns to the custom dictionary. To add a correctly spelled word to the custom dictionary, tap or click the Add button (Spelling task pane) or press and hold and then tap 'Show Context Menu' button on mini toolbar or right-click the flagged word and then tap or click Add to Dictionary on the shortcut menu. Once you have added a word to the custom dictionary, Word no longer will flag it as an error.

To View or Modify Entries in a Custom Dictionary

To view or modify the list of words in a custom dictionary, you would follow these steps.

1. Tap or click FILE on the ribbon and then tap or click Options in the Backstage view.
2. Tap or click Proofing in the left pane (Word Options dialog box).
3. Tap or click the Custom Dictionaries button.
4. When Word displays the Custom Dictionaries dialog box, place a check mark next to the dictionary name to view or modify. Tap or click the 'Edit Word List' button (Custom Dictionaries dialog box). (In this dialog box, you can add or delete entries to and from the selected custom dictionary.)
5. When finished viewing and/or modifying the list, tap or click the OK button in the dialog box.
6. Tap or click the OK button (Custom Dictionaries dialog box).
7. If the 'Suggest from main dictionary only' check box is selected in the Word Options dialog box, remove the check mark. Tap or click the OK button (Word Options dialog box).

To Set the Default Custom Dictionary

If you have multiple custom dictionaries, you can specify which one Word should use when checking spelling. To set the default custom dictionary, you would follow these steps.

1. Tap or click FILE on the ribbon and then tap or click Options in the Backstage view.
2. Tap or click Proofing in the left pane (Word Options dialog box).
3. Tap or click the Custom Dictionaries button.
4. When the Custom Dictionaries dialog box is displayed, place a check mark next to the desired dictionary name. Tap or click the Change Default button (Custom Dictionaries dialog box).
5. Tap or click the OK button (Custom Dictionaries dialog box).
6. If the 'Suggest from main dictionary only' check box is selected in the Word Options dialog box, remove the check mark. Tap or click the OK button (Word Options dialog box).

To Look Up Information

If you are signed in to your Microsoft account, you can look up a definition by tapping or clicking the Define button (REVIEW tab | Proofing group). If you are not signed in to your Microsoft account but are connected to the Internet, you can use the Research task pane to search through various forms of reference information on the web. The following steps use the Research task pane to look up a definition of a word. ***Why?*** *Assume you want to know more about the word, legitimate, but are not signed in to your Microsoft account.*

1

- While holding down the ALT key, tap or click the word you want to look up (in this case, legitimate) to open the Research task pane and display a dictionary entry for the ALT+clicked word (Figure 2–75). Release the ALT key.

Q&A Why does my Research task pane look different?
Depending on your settings and Microsoft's website search settings, your Research task pane may appear different from the figures shown here.

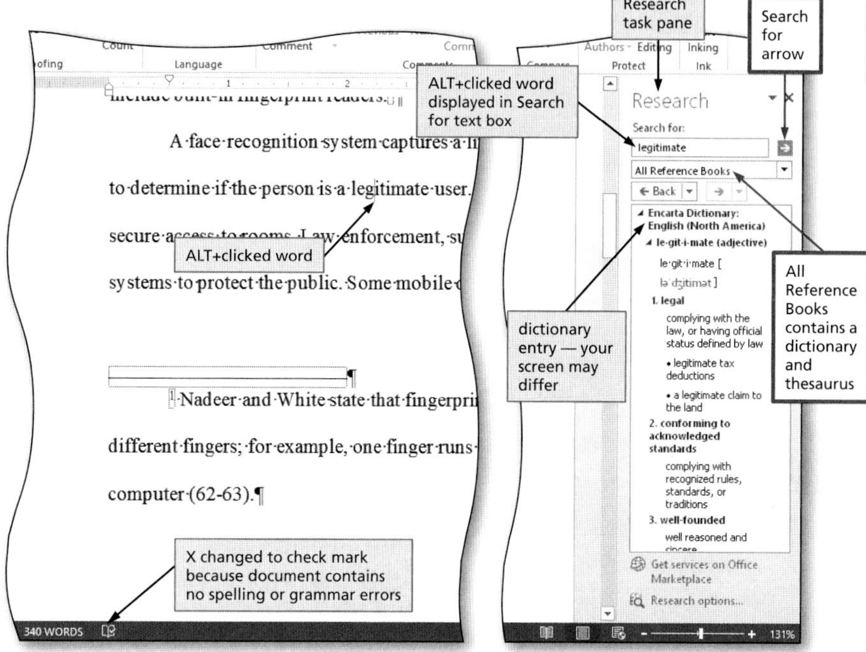

Figure 2–75

2

- Tap or click the Source arrow in the Research task pane to display a list of search locations and then tap or click 'All Research Sites' in the list (Figure 2–76).

Q&A Can I copy information from the Research task pane into my document?
Yes, you can use the Copy and Paste commands. When using Word to insert material from the Research task pane or any other online reference, however, be careful not to plagiarize.

3

- Tap or click the Close button in the Research task pane.

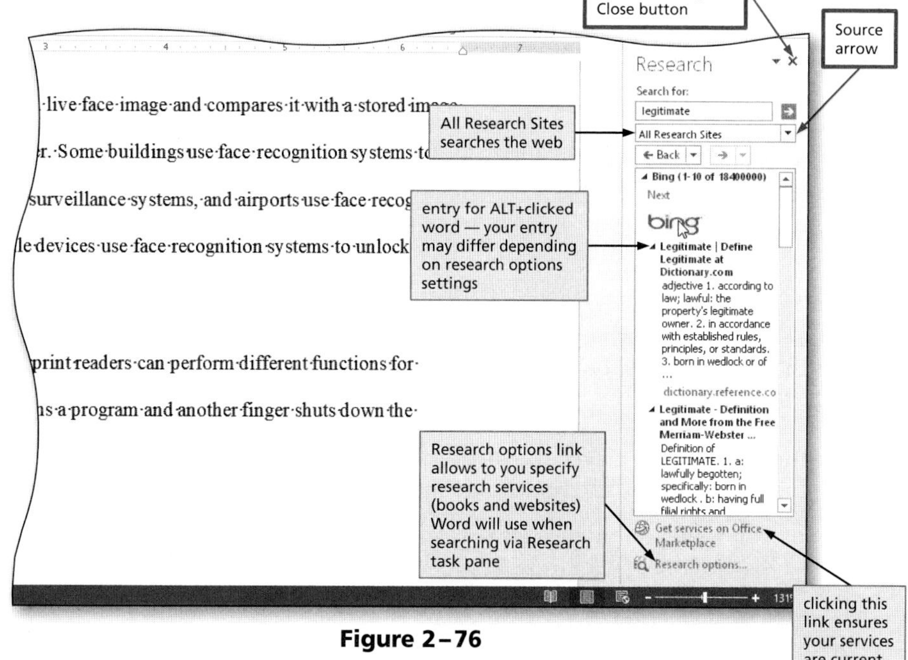

Figure 2–76

Other Ways

1. Press ALT+SHIFT+F7

Research Task Pane Options

When you install Word, it selects a series of services (reference books and websites) that it searches through when you use the Research task pane. You can view, modify, and update the list of services at any time.

Tapping or clicking the Research options link at the bottom of the Research task pane (shown in Figure 2–76 on the previous page) displays the Research Options dialog box, where you can view or modify the list of installed services. You can view information about any installed service by tapping or clicking the service in the list and then tapping or clicking the Properties button. To activate an installed service, tap or click the check box to its left; likewise, to deactivate a service, remove the check mark. To add a particular website to the list, tap or click the Add Services button, enter the web address in the Address text box, and then tap or click the Add button (Add Services dialog box). To update or remove services, tap or click the Update/Remove button, select the service in the list, tap or click the Update (or Remove) button (Update or Remove Services dialog box), and then tap or click the Close button. You also can install parental controls through the Parental Control button (Research Options dialog box), for example, if you want to prevent minor children who use Word from accessing the web.

BTW
Distributing a Document
Instead of printing and distributing a hard copy of a document, you can distribute the document electronically. Options include sending the document via email; saving it on cloud storage (such as SkyDrive) and sharing the file with others; posting it on a social networking site, blog, or other website; and sharing a link associated with an online location of the document. You also can create and share a PDF or XPS image of the document, so that users can view the file in Acrobat Reader or XPS Viewer instead of in Word.

To Save an Existing Document with the Same File Name

You have made several modifications to the document since you last saved it. Thus, you should save it again. The following step saves the document again. For an example of the step listed below, refer to the Office and Windows chapter at the beginning of this book.

Tap or click the Save button on the Quick Access Toolbar to overwrite the previously saved file.

To Zoom Multiple Pages

1 CHANGE DOCUMENT SETTINGS | 2 CREATE HEADER | 3 TYPE RESEARCH PAPER WITH CITATIONS
4 CREATE ALPHABETICAL WORKS CITED | **5 PROOFREAD & REVISE RESEARCH PAPER**

The next steps display multiple pages in the document window at once. ***Why?*** *You want be able to see all pages in the research paper on the screen at the same time. You also hide formatting marks and the rulers so that the display is easier to view.*

- Tap or click HOME on the ribbon to display the HOME tab.
- If the 'Show/Hide ¶' button (HOME tab | Paragraph group) is selected, tap or click it to hide formatting marks.
- Tap or click VIEW on the ribbon to display the VIEW tab.
- If the rulers are displayed, tap or click the View Ruler check box (VIEW tab | Show group) to remove the check mark from the check box and remove the horizontal and vertical rulers from the screen.
- Tap or click the Multiple Pages button (VIEW tab | Zoom group) to display the all three pages at once in the document window (Figure 2–77).

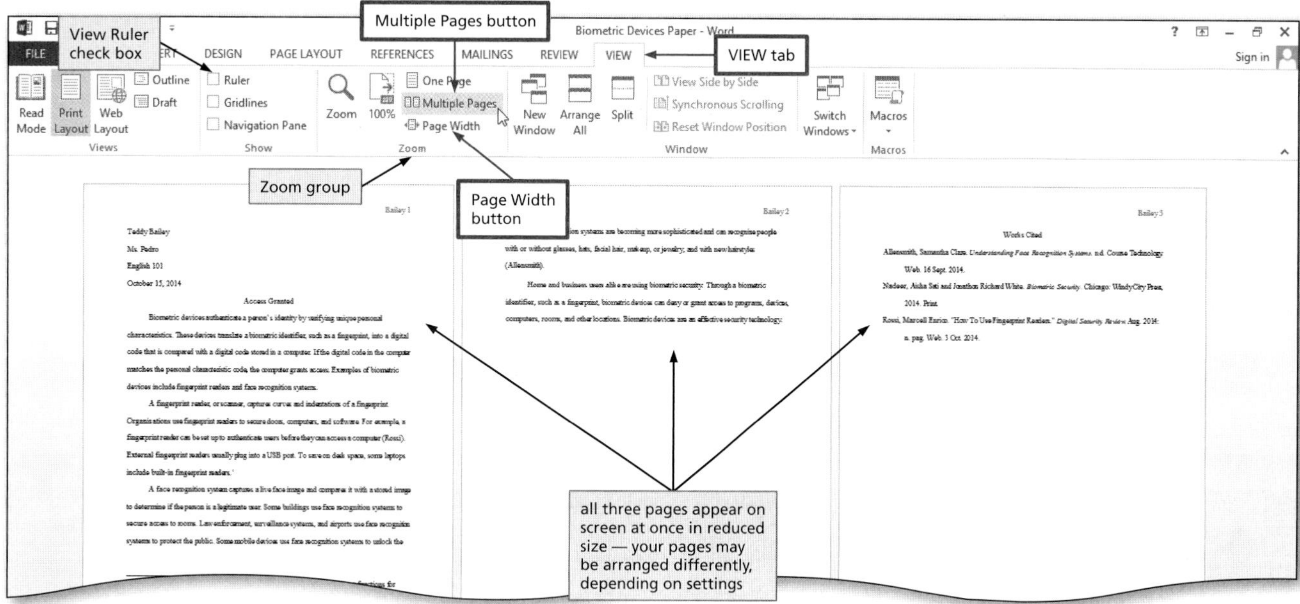

Figure 2–77

- When finished, tap or click the Page Width button (VIEW tab | Zoom group) to return to the page width zoom.

To Change Read Mode Color

You would like to read the entire research paper using Read mode but would like to change the background color of the Read mode screen. ***Why?*** *You prefer a background that is easier on your eyes when reading on the screen.* The following steps change the color of the screen in Read mode.

1

- Tap or click the Read Mode button on the status bar to switch to Read mode.
- Tap or click the VIEW tab to display the VIEW menu.
- Tap or point to Page Color on the VIEW menu to display the Page Color menu (Figure 2–78).

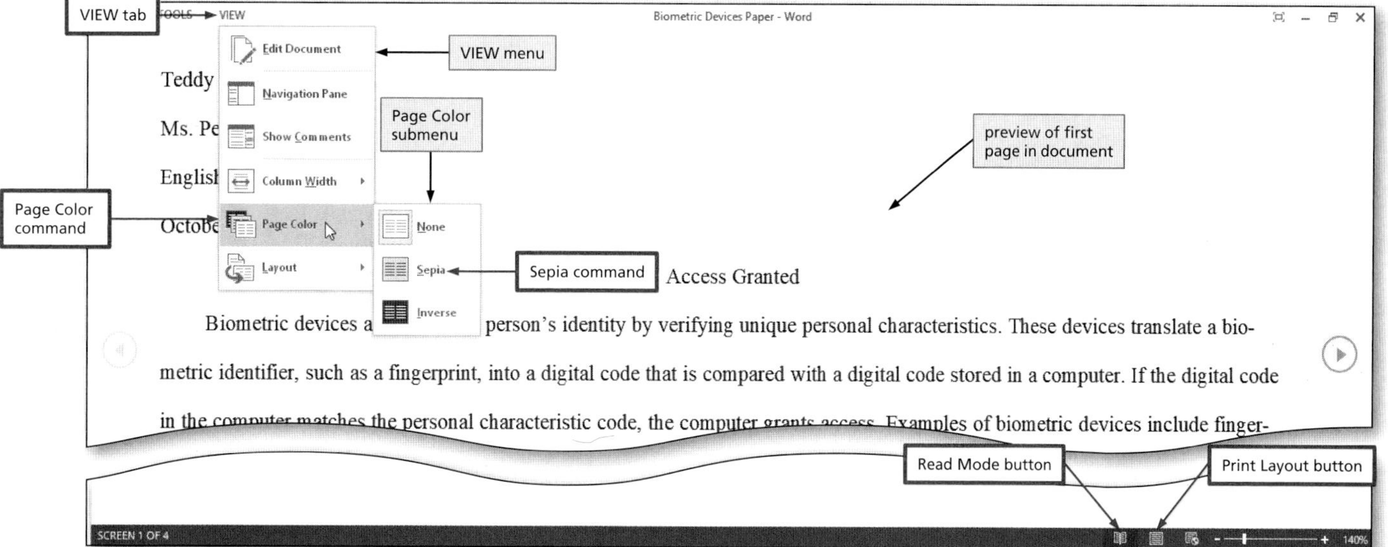

Figure 2–78

2

- Tap or click Sepia on the Page Color submenu to change the color of the Read mode screen to sepia (Figure 2–79).

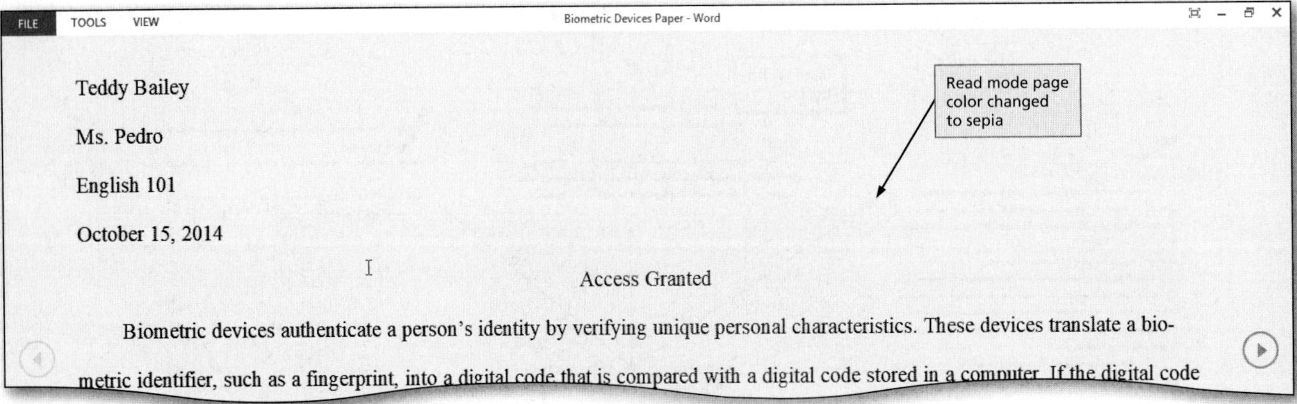

Figure 2–79

- When finished, tap or click the Print Layout button (shown in Figure 2–78 on the previous page) on the status bar to return to Print Layout view.

BTW
Conserving Ink and Toner
If you want to conserve ink or toner, you can instruct Word to print draft quality documents by tapping or clicking FILE on the ribbon to open the Backstage view, tapping or clicking Options in the Backstage view, tapping or clicking Advanced in the left pane (Word Options dialog box), sliding or scrolling to the Print area in the right pane, placing a check mark in the 'Use draft quality' check box, and then tapping or clicking the OK button. Then, use the Backstage view to print the document as usual.

To Print a Document

If you want a hard copy of the research paper, perform the following steps.

1. Tap or click FILE on the ribbon to open the Backstage view.
2. Tap or click the Print tab in the Backstage view to display the Print gallery.
3. Verify that the printer listed on the Printer Status button will print a hard copy of the document. If necessary, tap or click the Printer Status button to display a list of available printer options and then tap or click the desired printer to change the currently selected printer.
4. Tap or click the Print button in the Print gallery to print the document on the currently selected printer.
5. When the printer stops, retrieve the hard copy (shown in Figure 2–1 on page WD 67).

To Exit Word

This project now is complete. The following steps exit Word. For a detailed example of the procedure summarized below, refer to the Office and Windows chapter at the beginning of this book.

1a If you have one Word document open, tap or click the Close button on the right side of the title bar to close the open document and exit Word.

1b If you have multiple Word documents open, press and hold or right-click the Word app button on the taskbar and then tap or click 'Close all windows' on the shortcut menu to close all open documents and exit Word.

2 If a Microsoft Word dialog box appears, tap or click the Save button to save any changes made to the document since the last save.

Chapter Summary

In this chapter, you have learned how to change document settings, use headers to number pages, modify a style, insert and edit citations and their sources, add footnotes, create a bibliographical list of sources, and use proofreading tools. The items listed below include all the new Word skills you have learned in this chapter, with the tasks grouped by activity.

Enter and Edit Text

AutoCorrect as You Type (WD 84)
Use the AutoCorrect Options Button (WD 85)
Create an AutoCorrect Entry (WD 85)
Count Words (WD 100)
Update a Field (WD 110)
Copy and Paste (WD 112)
Find Text (WD 113)
Replace Text (WD 114)
Find and Insert a Synonym (WD 115)
Check Spelling and Grammar at Once (WD 116)
View or Modify Entries in a Custom Dictionary (WD 118)
Set the Default Custom Dictionary (WD 118)

Format a Page

Switch to the Header (WD 74)
Insert a Page Number (WD 76)
Close the Header (WD 77)
Page Break Manually (WD 105)

Format Text

Modify a Style (WD 70)
Change Line Spacing (WD 72)
Remove Space after a Paragraph (WD 73)
Update a Style to Match a Selection (WD 73)
Right-Align a Paragraph (WD 75)
Click and Type (WD 79)
First-Line Indent Paragraphs (WD 82)
Modify a Style Using a Shortcut Menu (WD 94)
Apply a Style (WD 105)
Format Paragraphs with a Hanging Indent (WD 108)
Convert a Field to Regular Text (WD 110)
Display the Paste Options Menu (WD 113)

Word Settings

Display the Rulers (WD 82)
Hide and Show White Space (WD 102)
Go to a Page (WD 111)
Look Up Information (WD 119)
Zoom Multiple Pages (WD 120)
Change Read Mode Color (WD 121)

Work with Citations, Sources, and Footnotes

Change the Bibliography Style (WD 89)
Insert a Citation and Create Its Source (WD 89)
Insert a Footnote Reference Mark (WD 92)
Insert a Citation Placeholder (WD 93)
Edit a Source (WD 96)
Edit a Citation (WD 98)
Create a Bibliographical List (WD 106)
Modify a Source (WD 109)

CONSIDER THIS: PLAN AHEAD

What decisions will you need to make when creating your next research paper?

Use these guidelines as you complete the assignments in this chapter and create your own research papers outside of this class.

1. Select a topic.
   a) Spend time brainstorming ideas for a topic.
   b) Choose a topic you find interesting.
   c) For shorter papers, narrow the scope of the topic; for longer papers, broaden the scope.
   d) Identify a tentative thesis statement, which is a sentence describing the paper's subject matter.
2. Research the topic and take notes, being careful not to plagiarize.
3. Organize your notes into related concepts, identifying all main ideas and supporting details in an outline.
4. Write the first draft from the outline, referencing all sources of information and following the guidelines identified in the required documentation style.
5. Create the list of sources, using the formats specified in the required documentation style.
6. Proofread and revise the paper.

STUDENT ASSIGNMENTS

CONSIDER THIS

How should you submit solutions to questions in the assignments identified with a symbol?
Every assignment in this book contains one or more questions identified with a symbol. These questions require you to think beyond the assigned document. Present your solutions to the questions in the format required by your instructor. Possible formats may include one or more of these options: write the answer; create a document that contains the answer; present your answer to the class; discuss your answer in a group; record the answer as audio or video using a webcam, smartphone, or portable media player; or post answers on a blog, wiki, or website.

Apply Your Knowledge

Reinforce the skills and apply the concepts you learned in this chapter.

Revising Text and Paragraphs in a Document

Note: To complete this assignment, you will be required to use the Data Files for Students. Visit www.cengage.com/ct/studentdownload for detailed instructions or contact your instructor for information about accessing the required files.

Instructions: Run Word. Open the document, Apply 2 - 1 Virtual Reality Paragraph Draft, from the Data Files for Students. The document you open contains a paragraph of text. You are to revise the document as follows: move a word, move another word and change the format of the moved word, change paragraph indentation, change line spacing, find all occurrences of a word, replace all occurrences of a word with another word, locate a synonym, and edit the header.

Perform the following tasks:

1. Copy the text, VR, from the first sentence and paste it in the last sentence after the underlined word, potential.
2. Select the underlined word, potential, in the paragraph. If you are using a mouse, use drag-and-drop editing to move the selected word, potential, so that it is before the word, buyers, in the same sentence. If you are using a touch screen, use the cut and paste commands to move the word. Tap or click the Paste Options button that displays to the right of the moved word, potential. Remove the underline format from the moved sentence by tapping or clicking 'Keep Text Only' on the Paste Options menu.
3. Display the ruler, if necessary. If you are using a mouse, use the ruler to indent the first line of the paragraph one-half inch; otherwise, use the Paragraph dialog box.
4. Change the line spacing of the paragraph to double.
5. Use the Navigation Pane to find all occurrences of the word, VR. How many are there?
6. Use the Find and Replace dialog box to replace all occurrences of the word, 3D, with the word, 3-D. How many replacements were made?
7. Use the Navigation Pane to find the word, endless. Use Word's thesaurus to change the word, endless, to the word, infinite. What other words are in the list of synonyms?
8. Switch to the header so that you can edit it. In the first line of the header, change the word, Draft, to the word, Modified, so that it reads: VR Paragraph Modified.
9. In the second line of the header, insert the page number (with no formatting) one space after the word, Page.
10. Change the alignment of both lines of text in the header from left-aligned to right-aligned. Switch back to the document text.
11. If requested by your instructor, enter your first and last name on a separate line below the page number in the header.
12. Tap or click FILE on the ribbon and then tap or click Save As. Save the document using the file name, Apply 2 - 1 Virtual Reality Paragraph Modified.

13. Submit the modified document, shown in Figure 2–80, in the format specified by your instructor.
14. Use the Research task pane to look up the definition of the word, simulate, in the paragraph. Which dictionary was used? If you have a Microsoft account and are signed into it, use the Define button (REVIEW tab | Proofing group) to look up a definition of the word.
15. Change the search location to All Research Sites. Submit an article from one of the sites.
16. Display the Research Options dialog box. How many currently active Reference Books and Research Sites are in the list? If your instructor approves, activate one of the services.
17. Answer the questions posed in #5, #6, #7, #14, and #16. How would you find and replace a special character, such as a paragraph mark?

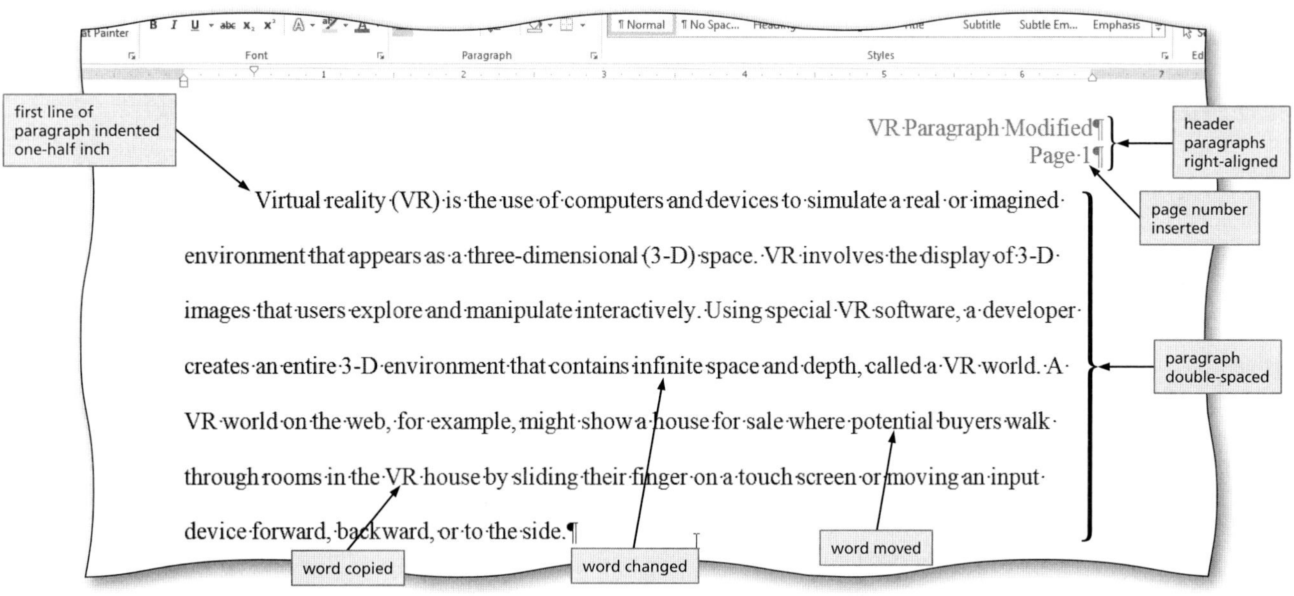

Figure 2–80

Extend Your Knowledge

Extend the skills you learned in this chapter and experiment with new skills. You may need to use Help to complete the assignment.

Working with References and Proofing Tools

Note: To complete this assignment, you will be required to use the Data Files for Students. Visit www.cengage.com/ct/studentdownload for detailed instructions or contact your instructor for information about accessing the required files.

Instructions: Run Word. Open the document, Extend 2-1 Cybercrime Paper Draft, from the Data Files for Students. You will add another footnote to the paper, convert the footnotes to endnotes, modify the Endnote Text style, change the format of the note reference marks, use Word's readability statistics, translate the document to another language (Figure 2–81 on the next page), and convert the document from MLA to APA documentation style.

Perform the following tasks:

1. Use Help to learn more about footers, footnotes and endnotes, readability statistics, bibliography styles, AutoCorrect, and the Mini Translator.
2. Delete the footer from the document.

Continued >

Extend Your Knowledge *continued*

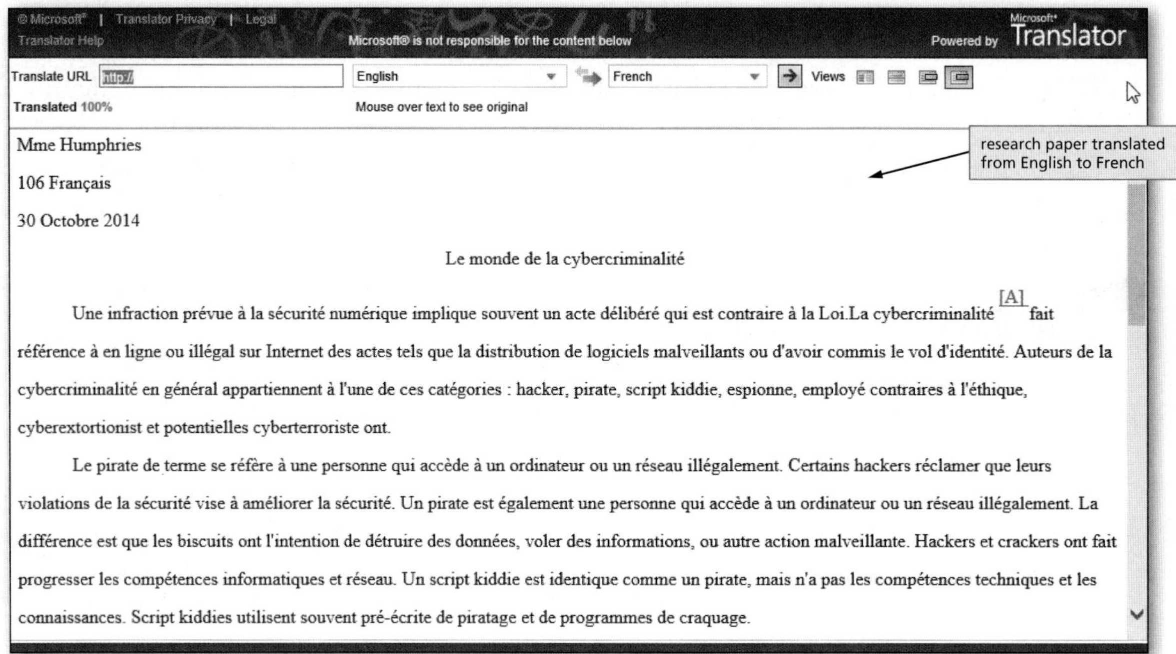

Figure 2–81

3. Insert a second footnote at an appropriate place in the research paper. Use the following footnote text: Unscrupulous companies hire corporate spies, a practice known as corporate espionage, to gain a competitive advantage.
4. Change the location of the footnotes from bottom of page to below text. How did the placement of the footnotes change?
5. Convert the footnotes to endnotes. Where are the endnotes positioned?
6. Modify the Endnote Text style to 12-point Times New Roman font, double-spaced text with a hanging-line indent.
7. Change the format of the note reference marks to capital letters (A, B, etc.).
8. Add an AutoCorrect entry that replaces the word, perpetraters, with the word, perpetrators. Add this sentence as the last sentence in the paper, misspelling the word perpetrators to test the AutoCorrect entry: These perpetraters present a growing threat to society. Delete the AutoCorrect entry that replaces perpetraters with the word, perpetrators.
9. Display the Word Count dialog box. How many words, characters without spaces, characters with spaces, paragraphs, and lines are in the document? Be sure to include footnote and endnote text in the statistics.
10. Check spelling of the document, displaying readability statistics. What are the Flesch-Kincaid Grade Level, the Flesch Reading Ease score, and the percent of passive sentences? Modify the paper to lower the grade level, increase the reading ease score, and lower the percent of passive sentences. How did you modify the paper? What are the new statistics?
11. If requested by your instructor, change the student name at the top of the paper to your name, including the last name in the header.
12. Save the revised document with the file name, Extend 2-1 Cybercrime Paper Modified, and then submit it in the format specified by your instructor.

13. If you have an Internet connection, translate the research paper into a language of your choice using the Translate button (REVIEW tab | Language group). Submit the translated document in the format specified by your instructor. Use the Mini Translator to hear how to pronounce three words in your paper.
14. Select the entire document and then change the documentation style from MLA to APA. Save the APA version of the document with a new file name. Compare the APA version to the MLA version. If you have a hard copy of each and your instructor requests it, circle the differences between the two documents.
15. Answer the questions posed in #4, #5, #9, and #10. Where did you insert the second footnote and why?

Analyze, Correct, Improve

Analyze a document, correct all errors, and improve it.

Inserting Missing Elements in an MLA-Styled Research Paper

Note: To complete this assignment, you will be required to use the Data Files for Students. Visit www.cengage.com/ct/studentdownload for detailed instructions or contact your instructor for information about accessing the required files.

Instructions: Run Word. Open the document, Analyze 2 - 1 Internet Filters Paper Draft, from the Data Files for Students. The document is a research paper that is missing several elements. You are to insert these missing elements, all formatted according to the MLA documentation style: header with a page number, name and course information, paper title, footnote, and source information for a citation.

1. Correct In the research paper, correct the following items:

(a) Insert a header with a your own last name and page number and then type the course information (your name, your instructor's name, your course name, and today's date), and an appropriate paper title, all formatted according to the MLA documentation style.

(b) The Clark citation placeholder is missing its source information (shown in Figure 2 – 82 on the next page). Use the following information to edit the source: book titled *Internet Protection*, written by Addison Lee Clark, publication year is 2014, publication city is New York, publisher is Journey Press, medium is Print. Edit the citation so that it displays the author name and the page numbers of 35–37 for this reference.

(c) Modify the website author name to include his middle name: Robert Timothy Lane. Also, change the medium in this same source from Print to Web.

(d) Use the Navigation Pane to display page 2. Insert a page break before the Works Cited heading. Use Word to insert the bibliographical list (bibliography) below the Works Cited heading.

2. Improve Enhance the paper by inserting a footnote with the note reference at an appropriate place in the paper, formatted according to the MLA documentation style, that gives a statistic about spam. (You will need to do research to obtain this statistic.) Change the Footnote Text style to 12-point Times New Roman, double-spaced paragraphs with a first-line indent. Add a citation and source for your new footnote. Be sure to update the works cited page after you add the citation and source. Save the modified document with the file name, Analyze 2 - 1 Internet Filters Paper Modified, and then submit it in the format specified by your instructor.

3. In this assignment you inserted a statistic from a web source. Why did you select that website?

Continued >

Analyze, Correct, Improve *continued*

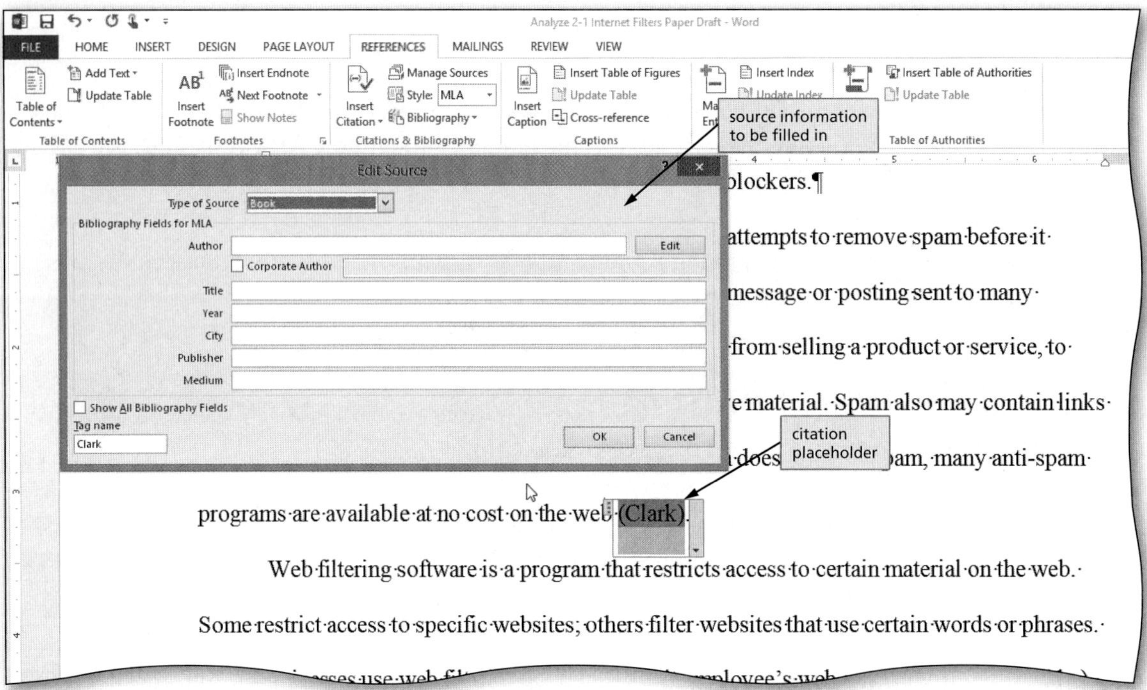

Figure 2–82

In the Labs

Design and/or create a document using the guidelines, concepts, and skills presented in this chapter. Labs 1 and 2, which increase in difficulty, require you to create solutions based on what you learned in the chapter; Lab 3 requires you to create a solution, which uses cloud and web technologies, by learning and investigating on your own from general guidance.

Lab 1: Preparing a Short Research Paper

Problem: You are a college student currently enrolled in an introductory English class. Your assignment is to prepare a short research paper (350–450 words) in any area of interest to you. The requirements are that the paper be presented according to the MLA documentation style and have three references. At least one of the three references must be from the web. You prepare the paper shown in Figure 2–83, which discusses health risks associated with technology.

Instructions: Perform the following tasks:

1. Run Word. If necessary, display formatting marks on the screen.
2. Modify the Normal style to the 12-point Times New Roman font.
3. Adjust line spacing to double.
4. Remove space below (after) paragraphs.
5. Update the Normal style to reflect the adjusted line and paragraph spacing.
6. Create a header to number pages.
7. Type the name and course information at the left margin. If requested by your instructor, use your name and course information instead of the information shown in Figure 2–83a. Center and type the title.
8. Set a first-line indent to one-half inch for paragraphs in the body of the research paper.

Delhi 1

Rajesh Delhi

Ms. June

English 102

November 9, 2014

Health Risks Associated with Technology

The widespread use of technology has led to some important user health concerns. Some of the more common physical health risks are repetitive strain injuries, computer vision syndrome, and muscular pain. These injuries are on the rise for users of technology.

A repetitive strain injury (RSI) is an injury or disorder of the muscles, nerves, tendons, ligaments, and joints. Technology-related RSIs include tendonitis and carpal tunnel syndrome (CTS). Tendonitis is inflammation of a tendon due to repeated motion or stress on that tendon. CTS is inflammation of the nerve that connects the forearm to the palm. Repeated or forceful bending of the wrist can cause tendonitis or CTS of the wrist. Factors that cause these disorders include prolonged typing or mouse usage and continual shifting between a mouse and keyboard (Jones 45-48). If untreated, these disorders can lead to permanent physical damage.

Computer vision syndrome (CVS) affects eyesight. Symptoms of CVS are sore, tired, burning, itching, or dry eyes; blurred or double vision; distance blurred vision after prolonged staring at a display device; headache or sore neck; difficulty shifting focus between a display device and documents; difficulty focusing on a screen image; color fringes or afterimages when looking away from a display device; and increased sensitivity to light. Eyestrain associated with CVS is not thought to have serious or long-term consequences (Anderson and Dean).

People who spend their workday using the computer sometimes complain of lower back pain, muscle fatigue, and emotional fatigue. Lower back pain sometimes is caused from poor

(a) Page 1

Figure 2–83

Continued >

In the Labs *continued*

Delhi 2

posture. It is advisable to sit properly in a chair while working and take periodic breaks. Users also should be sure their workplace is designed ergonomically. Ergonomic studies have shown that using the correct type and configuration of chair, keyboard, display device, and work surface helps users work comfortably and efficiently and helps protect their health (Sanchez).

Many physical health risks are associated with using technology. These risks include repetitive strain injuries, computer vision syndrome, and muscular pain. Users should take as many preventive measures as possible to avoid these risks.

(b) Page 2

Figure 2–83 (Continued)

9. Type the research paper as shown in Figures 2–83a and 2–83b. Change the bibliography style to MLA. As you insert citations, enter their source information (shown in Figure 2–83c). Edit the citations so that they are displayed according to Figures 2–83a and 2–83b.
10. At the end of the research paper text, press the ENTER key and then insert a manual page break so that the Works Cited page begins on a new page. Enter and format the works cited title (Figure 2–83c). Use Word to insert the bibliographical list (bibliography).
11. Check the spelling and grammar of the paper at once.
12. Save the document using Lab 2-1 Technology Health Risks Paper as the file name. Submit the document, shown in Figure 2–83, in the format specified by your instructor.
13. Read the paper in Print Layout view. Switch to Read mode and scroll through the pages. Do you prefer reading in Print Layout view or Read mode. Why? In Read mode, which of the page colors do you like best and why?

Delhi 3

Works Cited

Anderson, Cricket Finley and Stacey Anne Dean. "Computer Pains." *The Medical Update* Aug. 2014: n. pag. Web. 2 October 2014.

Jones, Jacob Lee. *Medical Concerns of the 21st Century*. Chicago: Smiley Incorporated, 2014. Print.

Sanchez, Jorge Mario. *Aches and Pains*. 30 Sept. 2014. Course Technology. Web. 5 Aug. 2014.

(c) Page 3

Figure 2–83 (Continued)

Lab 2: Preparing a Research Report with a Footnote

Problem: You are a college student enrolled in an introductory technology class. Your assignment is to prepare a short research paper (350–450 words) in any area of interest to you. The requirements are that the paper be presented according to the MLA documentation style, contain at least one note positioned as a footnote, and have three references. At least one ne of the three references must be from the Internet. You prepare a paper about protecting mobile devices (Figure 2–84).

Instructions: Perform the following tasks:

1. Run Word. Modify the Normal style to the 12-point Times New Roman font. Adjust line spacing to double and remove space below (after) paragraphs. Update the Normal style to include the adjusted line and paragraph spacing. Create a header to number pages. Type the name and course information at the left margin. If requested by your instructor, use your name and course information instead of the information shown in Figure 2–84a on the next page. Center and type the title. Set a first-line indent for paragraphs in the body of the research paper.

Continued >

In the Labs *continued*

Tanner 1

Camryn Tanner

Dr. Bai

Technology 101

October 16, 2014

Mobile Device Protection

The consequences of losing a smartphone or other mobile device are significant because these devices store personal and business data. The goal, therefore, for mobile device users is to make their data as secure as possible. Techniques include avoiding unsafe links, using caution when downloading apps, turning off GPS tracking, and installing mobile security software.

A high percentage of users follow unknown links, which can lead to a malicious website. Malicious links can inject malware on a mobile device. The malware may steal personal information or create toll fraud, which secretly contacts wireless messaging services that impose steep fees on a monthly bill (Bao). Users should avoid tapping or clicking unknown links.

Any device that connects to the Internet is susceptible to mobile malware.[1] Popular games are likely candidates to house malware, and it often is difficult to distinguish the legitimate apps from the fake apps. Users should check the reliability of the seller, the descriptions and reviews of the app, and the requested permissions before downloading.

GPS technology can track the mobile device's location as long as it is transmitting and receiving signals to and from satellites. Although this feature may be helpful, serious privacy concerns can arise when the technology is used in malicious ways, such as to stalk individuals or trace their whereabouts (Fields). It is best to keep this feature disabled until needed.

---

[1] According to Jameson and Bennett, cyberthieves target apps on popular devices (72).

(a) Page 1

Figure 2–84

2. Type the research paper as shown in Figures 2–84a and 2–84b. Insert the footnote as shown in Figure 2–84a. Change the Footnote Text style to the format specified in the MLA documentation style. Change the bibliography style to MLA. As you insert citations, use the following source information, entering it according to the MLA style:

   a. Type of Source: Article in a Periodical
   Author: He Gao Bao
   Article Title: Securing Mobile Devices
   Periodical Title: Technology Today
   Year: 2014
   Month: Sept.
   Pages: no pages used
   Medium: Web
   Year Accessed: 2014
   Month Accessed: Oct.
   Day Accessed: 1

   b. Type of Source: Web site
   Author: Charlotte Fields
   Name of webpage: Secure Your Mobile Device
   Year/Month/Date: none given
   Medium: Web
   Year Accessed: 2014
   Month Accessed: Sept.
   Day Accessed: 22

   c. Type of Source: Book
   Author: Lewis Taylor Jameson and Kathryn Leona Bennett
   Title: Mobile Technologies
   Year: 2014
   City: New York
   Publisher: Maxwell Press
   Medium: Print

3. At the end of the research paper text, press the ENTER key once and insert a manual page break so that the Works Cited page begins on a new page. Enter and format the works cited title. Use Word to insert the bibliographical list.
4. Check the spelling and grammar of the paper.
5. Save the document using Lab 2-2 Mobile Devices Protection Paper as the file name. Submit the document, shown in Figure 2–84, in the format specified by your instructor.
6. This paper uses web sources. What factors should you consider when selecting web sources?

Tanner 2

Users can enable the password feature on their mobile device as the first step in stopping prying eyes from viewing contents. More protection is necessary, however, to stop viruses and spyware and to safeguard personal and business data. Mobile security apps can lock a mobile device remotely, erase its memory, and activate its GPS function (Bao).

Some techniques users can take to protect their mobile devices include avoiding unsafe links, using caution when downloading, turning off GPS tracking, and using mobile security software. Users should take these measures to protect their mobile devices.

(b) Page 2

Figure 2–84 (Continued)

Continued >

In the Labs *continued*

Lab 3: Expand Your World: Cloud and Web Technologies

Using an Online Bibliography Tool to Create a List of Sources

Problem: Assume you are using a mobile device or computer that does not have Word but has Internet access. To make use of time between classes, you will use an online bibliography tool to create a list of sources that you can copy and paste into the Works Cited pages of a research paper due tomorrow.

Instructions: Perform the following tasks:

1. Run a browser. Search for the text, online bibliography tool, using a search engine. Visit several of the online bibliography tools and determine which you would like to use to create a list of sources. Navigate to the desired online bibliography tool.
2. Use the online bibliography tool to enter list of sources shown below (Figure 2–85):

   Dayton, Lacey Marie and Sally Louise Walsh. *The Wireless Revolution*. New York: New Artists Press, 2014. Print.

   Dover, Guy Sean. *Communications of Today*. Los Angeles: Sunshine Works, 2014. Print.

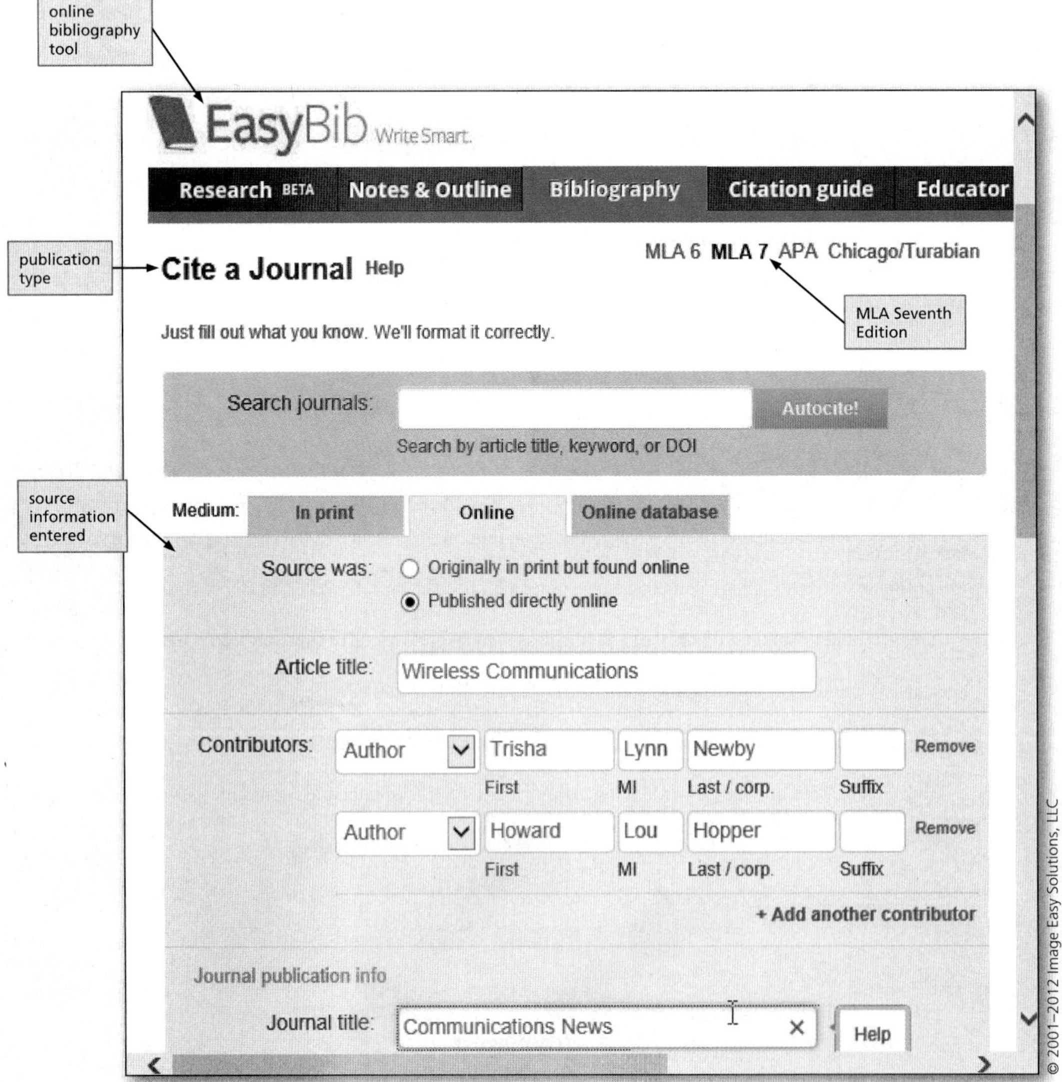

Figure 2–85

Howard, Timothy James. "The Wireless Era." *Computers and Networks* Aug. 2014. Web. 29 Aug. 2014.

Matthews, Carl James. *Wireless Trends*. Aug. 2014. Course Technology. Web. 8 Sept. 2014.

Newby, Trisha Lynn and Howard Lou Hopper. "Wireless Communications." *Communications News* Aug. 2014. Web. 4 Oct. 2014.

Newman, William Jared. *The Amazing Wireless World*. Sept. 2014. Course Technology. Web. 28 Sept. 2014.

3. If requested by your instructor, replace the name in one of the sources above with your name.
4. Search for another source that discusses wireless communications. Add that source.
5. Copy and paste the list of sources into a Word document.
6. Save the document with the name Lab 1-3 Wireless Communications Sources. Submit the document in the format specified by your instructor.
7. Which online bibliography tools did you evaluate? Which one did you select to use and why? Do you prefer using the online bibliography tool or Word to create sources? Why? What differences, if any, did you notice between the list of sources created with the online bibliography tool and the lists created when you use Word?

Consider This: Your Turn

Apply your creative thinking and problem solving skills to design and implement a solution.

Note: To complete these assignments, you may be required to use the Data Files for Students. Visit www.cengage.com/ct/studentdownload for detailed instructions or contact your instructor for information about accessing the required files.

1: Create a Research Paper about Laptops, Tablets, and Desktops

Personal

Part 1: As a student in an introductory computer class, your instructor has assigned a brief research paper that discusses types of computers. The source for the text in your research paper is in a file called Your Turn 2 - 1 Computer Notes, which is located on the Data Files for Students. If your instructor requests, use the Research task pane to obtain information from another source and include that information as a note positioned as a footnote in the paper, along with entering its corresponding source information as appropriate. Add an AutoCorrect entry to correct a word you commonly mistype. If necessary, set the default dictionary. Add one of the source last names to the dictionary.

Using the concepts and techniques presented in this chapter, organize the notes in the text in the file on the Data Files for Students, rewording as necessary, and then create and format this research paper according to the MLA documentation style. Be sure to check spelling and grammar of the finished paper. Submit your assignment and answers to the critical thinking questions in the format specified by your instructor.

Part 2: You made several decisions while creating the research paper in this assignment: how to organize the notes, where to place citations, how to format sources, and which source on the web to use for the footnote text (if requested by your instructor). What was the rationale behind each of these decisions? When you proofread the document, what further revisions did you make and why?

Continued >

Consider This: Your Turn *continued*

2: Create a Research Paper about POS Terminals, ATMs, and Self-Service Kiosks

Professional

Part 1: As a part-time employee at an advertising firm that specializes in marketing for technology, your boss has asked you to write a brief research paper that discusses types of terminals. The source for the text in your research paper is in a file called Your Turn 2 - 2 Terminals Notes, which is located on the Data Files for Students. If your instructor requests, use the Research task pane to obtain information from another source and include that information as a note positioned as a footnote in the paper, and enter its corresponding source information as appropriate. Add an AutoCorrect entry to correct a word you commonly mistype. If necessary, set the default dictionary. Add one of the source last names to the dictionary.

Using the concepts and techniques presented in this chapter, organize the notes in the file on the Data Files for Students, rewording as necessary, and then create and format this research paper according to the MLA documentation style. Be sure to check spelling and grammar of the finished paper. Submit your assignment and answers to the critical thinking questions in the format specified by your instructor.

Part 2: You made several decisions while creating the research paper in this assignment: how to organize the notes, where to place citations, how to format sources, and which source on the web to use for the footnote text (if requested by your instructor). What was the rationale behind each of these decisions? When you proofread the document, what further revisions did you make and why?

3: Create a Research Paper about Social Media Sites

Research and Collaboration

Part 1: Because all local youth groups will be creating a page on a social media site, you and two other leaders of local youth groups have been asked to prepare a research paper comparing and contrasting three different social media sites. Form a three-member team to research, compose, and create this paper. Research three separate social media sites: features, capabilities, typical uses, privacy settings, etc. Each team member should write the supporting paragraphs for the social media site he or she researched, including all citations and sources. As a group, write the introduction and conclusion. Be sure to include your team's recommendation in the conclusion.

Use the concepts and techniques presented in this chapter to create and format this paper according to the MLA documentation style. Be sure to check spelling and grammar of the finished paper. Submit your team notes and research paper in the format specified by your instructor.

Part 2: You made several decisions while creating the research paper in this assignment: the sources to use, which notes to take from the sources, how to organize the notes, how to organize each team member's submissions, what text to write for the introduction and conclusion, where to place citations, and how to format sources. What was the rationale behind each of these decisions? When you proofread the document, what further revisions did you make and why?

Learn Online

Reinforce what you learned in this chapter with games, exercises, training, and many other online activities and resources.

Student Companion Site Reinforcement activities and resources are available at no additional cost on www.cengagebrain.com. Visit www.cengage.com/ct/studentdownload for detailed instructions about accessing the resources available at the Student Companion Site.

SAM Put your skills into practice with SAM! If you have a SAM account, go to www.cengage.com/sam2013 to access SAM assignments for this chapter.

3 Creating a Business Letter with a Letterhead and Table

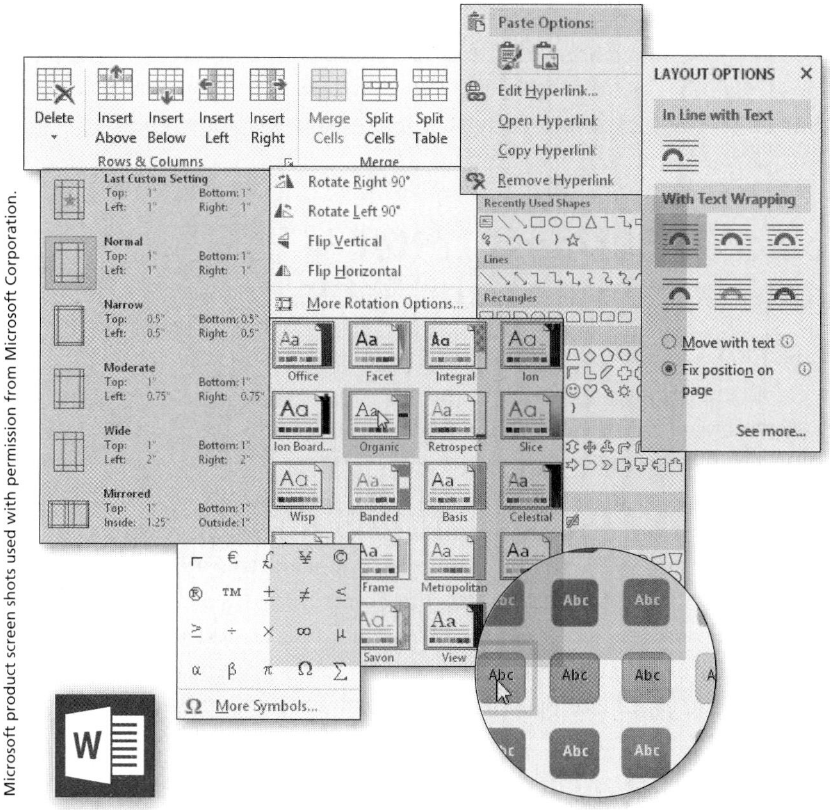

Objectives

You will have mastered the material in this chapter when you can:

- Change margins
- Insert and format a shape
- Change text wrapping
- Insert and format a clip art image
- Insert a symbol
- Add a border to a paragraph
- Clear formatting
- Convert a hyperlink to regular text
- Apply a style
- Set and use tab stops
- Insert the current date
- Create, modify, and insert a building block
- Insert a Word table, enter data in the table, and format the table
- Address and print an envelope

3 Creating a Business Letter with a Letterhead and Table

Introduction

In a business environment, people use documents to communicate with others. Business documents can include letters, memos, newsletters, proposals, and resumes. An effective business document clearly and concisely conveys its message and has a professional, organized appearance. You can use your own creative skills to design and compose business documents. Using Word, for example, you can develop the content and decide on the location of each item in a business document.

Project — Business Letter with a Letterhead and Table

At some time, you more than likely will prepare a business letter. Contents of business letters include requests, inquiries, confirmations, acknowledgements, recommendations, notifications, responses, thank you letters, invitations, offers, referrals, complaints, and more.

The project in this chapter follows generally accepted guidelines for writing letters and uses Word to create the business letter shown in Figure 3–1. This business letter is a thank you letter from a volunteer applicant to a volunteer organization (Washington Volunteer Foundation). The letter includes a custom letterhead, as well as all essential business letter components: date line, inside address, salutation, body, complimentary close, and signature block. To easily present his volunteer service background, the candidate presents this information in a table. His availability appears in a bulleted list.

For an introduction to Office and instruction about how to perform basic tasks in Office apps, read the Office and Windows chapter at the beginning of this book, where you can learn how to run an application, use the ribbon, save a file, open a file, exit an application, use Help, and much more.

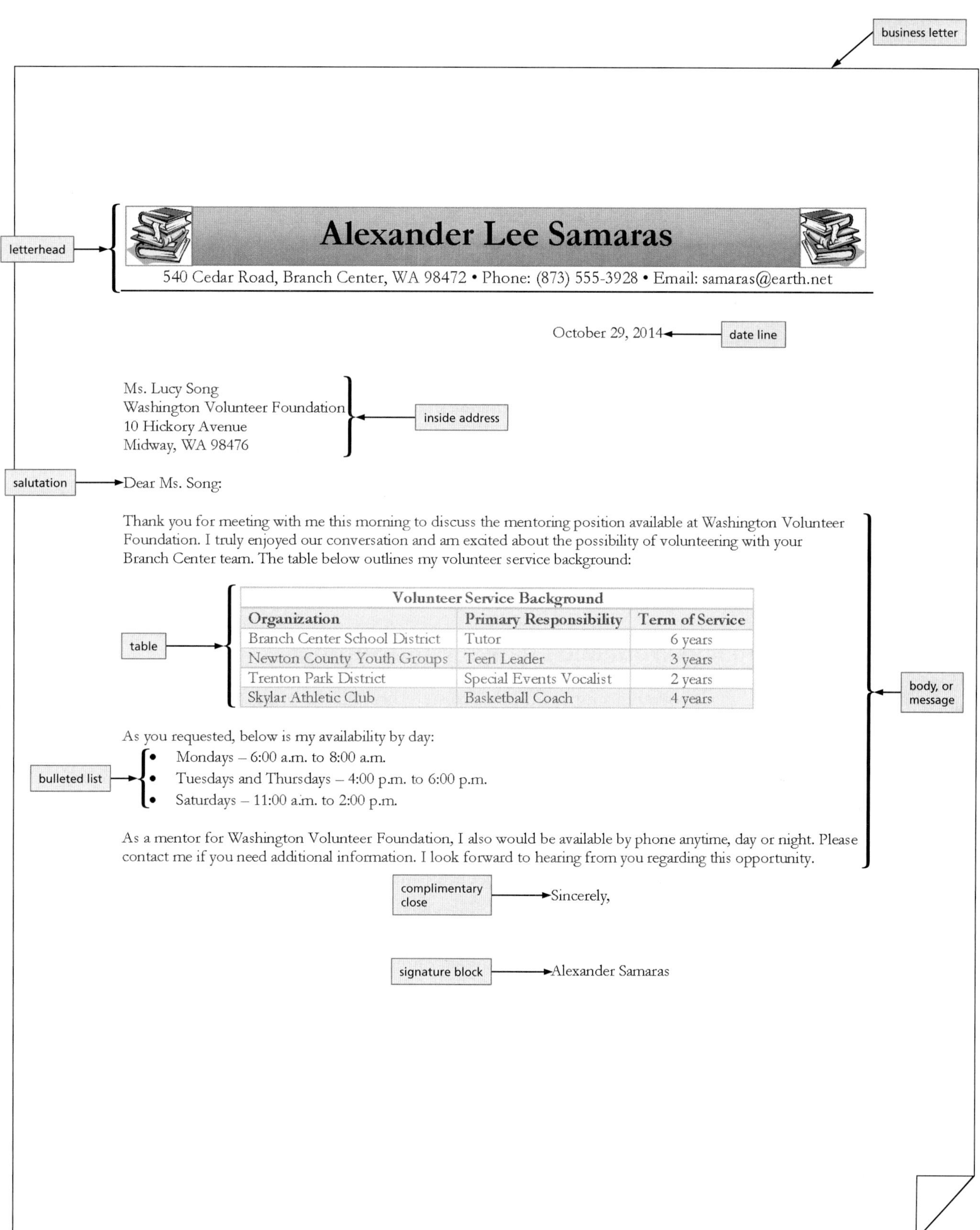
business letter
letterhead
Alexander Lee Samaras
540 Cedar Road, Branch Center, WA 98472 • Phone: (873) 555-3928 • Email: samaras@earth.net
October 29, 2014
date line
Ms. Lucy Song
Washington Volunteer Foundation
10 Hickory Avenue
Midway, WA 98476
inside address
salutation
Dear Ms. Song:
Thank you for meeting with me this morning to discuss the mentoring position available at Washington Volunteer Foundation. I truly enjoyed our conversation and am excited about the possibility of volunteering with your Branch Center team. The table below outlines my volunteer service background:
table
Volunteer Service Background
Organization | Primary Responsibility | Term of Service
Branch Center School District | Tutor | 6 years
Newton County Youth Groups | Teen Leader | 3 years
Trenton Park District | Special Events Vocalist | 2 years
Skylar Athletic Club | Basketball Coach | 4 years
body, or message
As you requested, below is my availability by day:
bulleted list
• Mondays – 6:00 a.m. to 8:00 a.m.
• Tuesdays and Thursdays – 4:00 p.m. to 6:00 p.m.
• Saturdays – 11:00 a.m. to 2:00 p.m.
As a mentor for Washington Volunteer Foundation, I also would be available by phone anytime, day or night. Please contact me if you need additional information. I look forward to hearing from you regarding this opportunity.
complimentary close
Sincerely,
signature block
Alexander Samaras

Figure 3–1

For an introduction to Windows and instruction about how to perform basic Windows tasks, read the Office and Windows chapter at the beginning of this book, where you can learn how to resize windows, change screen resolution, create folders, move and rename files, use Windows Help, and much more.

Roadmap

In this chapter, you will learn how to create the letter shown in Figure 3–1 on the previous page. The following roadmap identifies general activities you will perform as you progress through this chapter:

1. CREATE AND FORMAT a LETTERHEAD WITH GRAPHICS.
2. SPECIFY the LETTER FORMATS according to business letter guidelines.
3. INSERT a TABLE in the letter.
4. FORMAT the TABLE in the letter.
5. INSERT a BULLETED LIST in the letter.
6. ADDRESS an ENVELOPE for the letter.

At the beginning of step instructions throughout the chapter, you will see an abbreviated form of this roadmap. The abbreviated roadmap uses colors to indicate chapter progress: gray means the chapter is beyond that activity, blue means the task being shown is covered in that activity, and black means that activity is yet to be covered. For example, the following abbreviated roadmap indicates the chapter would be showing a task in the 2 SPECIFY LETTER FORMATS activity.

1 CREATE & FORMAT LETTERHEAD WITH GRAPHICS | 2 SPECIFY LETTER FORMATS
3 INSERT TABLE | 4 FORMAT TABLE | 5 INSERT BULLETED LIST | 6 ADDRESS ENVELOPE

Use the abbreviated roadmap as a progress guide while you read or step through the instructions in this chapter.

One of the few differences between Windows 7 and Windows 8 occurs in the steps to run Word. If you are using Windows 7, click the Start button, type `Word` in the 'Search programs and files' box, click Word 2013, and then, if necessary, maximize the Word window. For detailed steps to run Word in Windows 7, refer to the Office and Windows chapter at the beginning of this book. For a summary of the steps, refer to the Quick Reference located at the back of this book.

To Run Word and Change Word Settings

If you are using a computer to step through the project in this chapter and you want your screens to match the figures in this book, you should change your screen's resolution to 1366 × 768. For information about how to change a computer's resolution, refer to the Office and Windows chapter at the beginning of this book.

The following steps run Word, display formatting marks, and change the zoom to page width.

1. Run Word and create a blank document in the Word window. If necessary, maximize the Word window.
2. If the Print Layout button on the status bar is not selected (shown in Figure 3–2), tap or click it so that your screen is in Print Layout view.
3. If the 'Show/Hide ¶' button (HOME tab | Paragraph group) is not selected already, tap or click it to display formatting marks on the screen.
4. To display the page the same width as the document window, if necessary, tap or click the Page Width button (VIEW tab | Zoom group).

To Change Margin Settings

1 CREATE & FORMAT LETTERHEAD WITH GRAPHICS | 2 SPECIFY LETTER FORMATS
3 INSERT TABLE | 4 FORMAT TABLE | 5 INSERT BULLETED LIST | 6 ADDRESS ENVELOPE

Word is preset to use standard 8.5-by-11-inch paper, with 1-inch top, bottom, left, and right margins. The business letter in this chapter uses .75-inch left and right margins and 1-inch top and bottom margins. ***Why?*** *You would like more text to fit from left to right on the page.*

When you change the default (preset) margin settings, the new margin settings affect every page in the document. If you wanted the margins to affect just a portion of the document, you would divide the document into sections (discussed in a later chapter), which enables you to specify different margin settings for each section. The next steps change margin settings.

1

- Display the PAGE LAYOUT tab.
- Tap or click the Adjust Margins button (PAGE LAYOUT tab | Page Setup group) to display the Adjust Margins gallery (Figure 3–2).

2

- Tap or click Moderate in the Adjust Margins gallery to change the margins to the specified settings.

Q&A What if the margin settings I want are not in the Adjust Margins gallery?
You can tap or click Custom Margins in the Adjust Margins gallery and then enter your desired margin values in the top, bottom, left, and right boxes in the Page Setup dialog box.

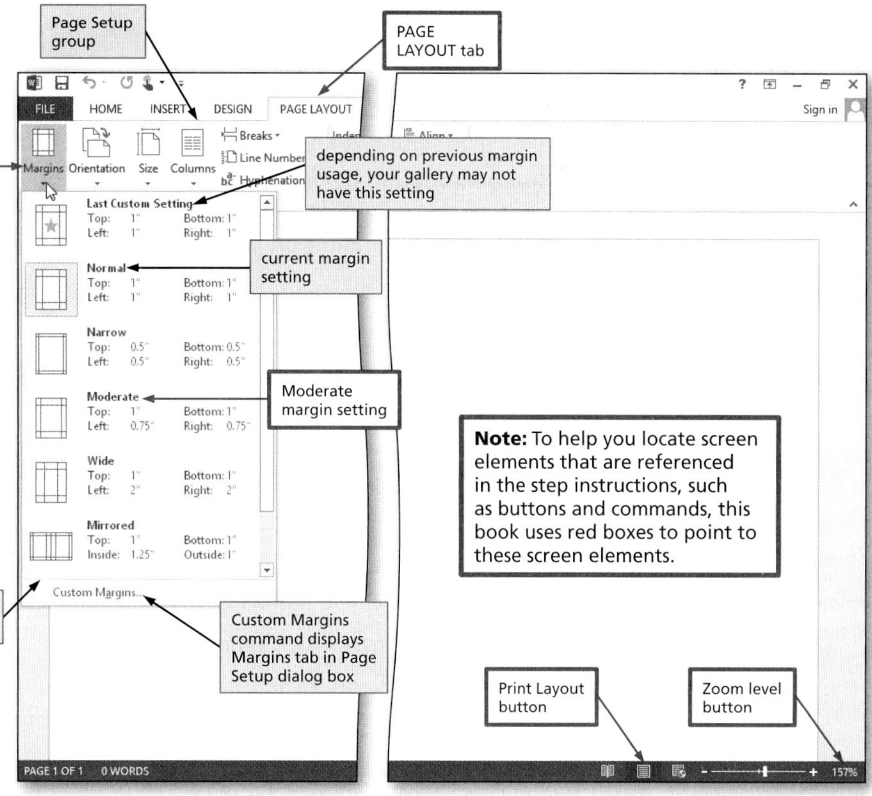

Page Setup group
PAGE LAYOUT tab
Adjust Margins button
depending on previous margin usage, your gallery may not have this setting
current margin setting
Moderate margin setting
Note: To help you locate screen elements that are referenced in the step instructions, such as buttons and commands, this book uses red boxes to point to these screen elements.
Adjust Margins gallery
Custom Margins command displays Margins tab in Page Setup dialog box
Print Layout button
Zoom level button

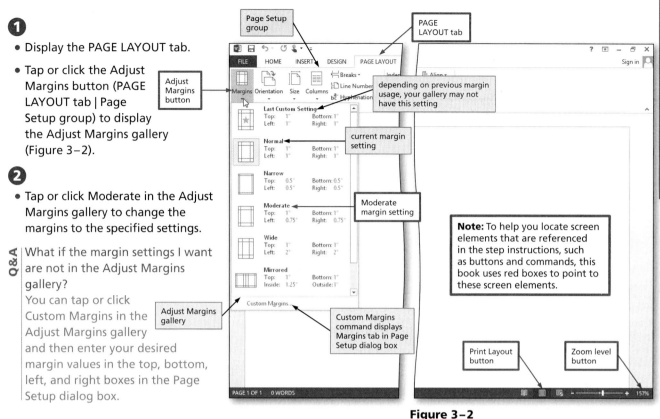

Figure 3–2

Other Ways

1. If you are using a mouse, position pointer on margin boundary on ruler; when pointer changes to two-headed arrow, drag margin boundary on ruler

Creating a Letterhead

The cost of preprinted letterhead can be high. An alternative is to create your own letterhead and save it in a file. When you want to create a letter at a later time, you can start by using the letterhead file. The following pages create a letterhead and then save it in a file for future use.

CONSIDER THIS

What is a letterhead?

A **letterhead** is the section of a letter that identifies an organization or individual. Often, the letterhead appears at the top of a letter. Although you can design and print a letterhead yourself, many businesses pay an outside firm to design and print their letterhead, usually on higher-quality paper. They then use the professionally preprinted paper for external business communications.

If you do not have preprinted letterhead paper, you can design a creative letterhead. It is important the letterhead appropriately reflect the essence of the organization or individual (i.e., formal, technical, creative, etc.). That is, it should use text, graphics, formats, and colors that reflect the organization or individual. The letterhead should leave ample room for the contents of the letter.

When designing a letterhead, consider its contents, placement, and appearance.

- **Contents of letterhead.** A letterhead should contain these elements:
  - Complete legal name of the individual, group, or company
  - Complete mailing address: street address including building, room, suite number, or post office box, along with city, state, and postal code
  - Phone number(s) and fax number, if applicable
  - Email address
  - Web address, if applicable
  - Many letterheads also include a logo or other image; if an image is used, it should express the organization or individual's personality or goals

Continued

Continued

- **Placement of elements in the letterhead.** Many letterheads center their elements across the top of the page. Others align some or all of the elements with the left or right margins. Sometimes, the elements are split between the top and bottom of the page. For example, a name and logo may be at the top of the page with the address at the bottom of the page.
- **Appearance of letterhead elements.** Use fonts that are easy to read. Give the organization or individual name impact by making its font size larger than the rest of the text in the letterhead. For additional emphasis, consider formatting the name in bold, italic, or a different color. Choose colors that complement each other and convey the goals of the organization or individual.

When finished designing the letterhead, determine if a divider line would help to visually separate the letterhead from the remainder of the letter.

BTW
The Ribbon and Screen Resolution
Word may change how the groups and buttons within the groups appear on the ribbon, depending on the computer's screen resolution. Thus, your ribbon may look different from the ones in this book if you are using a screen resolution other than 1366 × 768.

The letterhead for the letter in this chapter consists of the individual's name, appropriate graphics, postal address, phone number, and email address. The name and graphics are enclosed in a rectangular shape (Figure 3–1 on page WD 139), and the contact information is below the shape. You will follow these general steps to create the letterhead in this chapter:

1. Insert and format a shape.
2. Enter and format the individual's name in the shape.
3. Insert, format, and position the images in the shape.
4. Enter the contact information below the shape.
5. Add a border below the contact information.

To Insert a Shape

1 CREATE & FORMAT LETTERHEAD WITH GRAPHICS | 2 SPECIFY LETTER FORMATS
3 INSERT TABLE | 4 FORMAT TABLE | 5 INSERT BULLETED LIST | 6 ADDRESS ENVELOPE

Word has a variety of predefined shapes, which are a type of drawing object, that you can insert in documents. A **drawing object** is a graphic that you create using Word. Examples of shape drawing objects include rectangles, circles, triangles, arrows, flowcharting symbols, stars, banners, and callouts. The following steps insert a rectangle shape in the letterhead. ***Why?*** *The individual's name is placed in a rectangle for emphasis and visual appeal.*

- Display the INSERT tab.
- Tap or click the 'Draw a Shape' button (INSERT tab | Illustrations group) to display the Draw a Shape gallery (Figure 3–3).

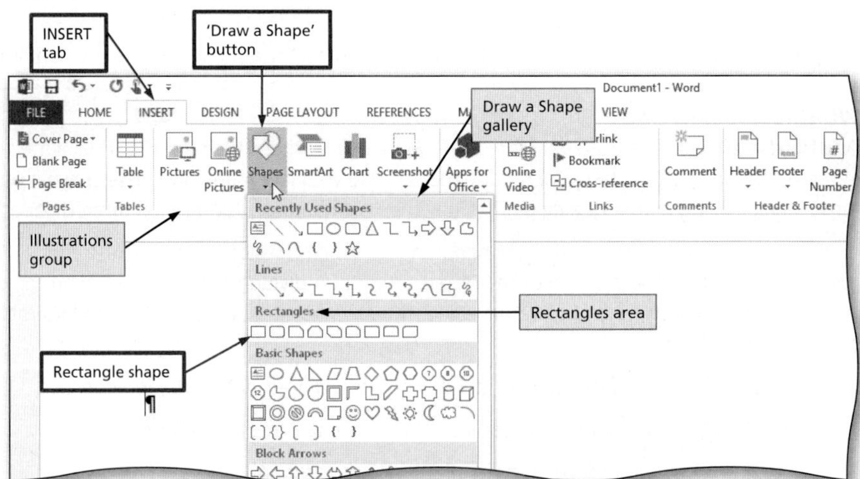

Figure 3–3

- Tap or click the Rectangle shape in the Rectangles area of the Draw a Shape gallery, which removes the gallery. If you are using a touch screen, the shape is inserted in the document window; if you are using a mouse, the pointer changes to the shape of a crosshair in the document window.
- If you are using a mouse, position the pointer (a crosshair) in the approximate location for the upper-left corner of the desired shape (Figure 3–4).

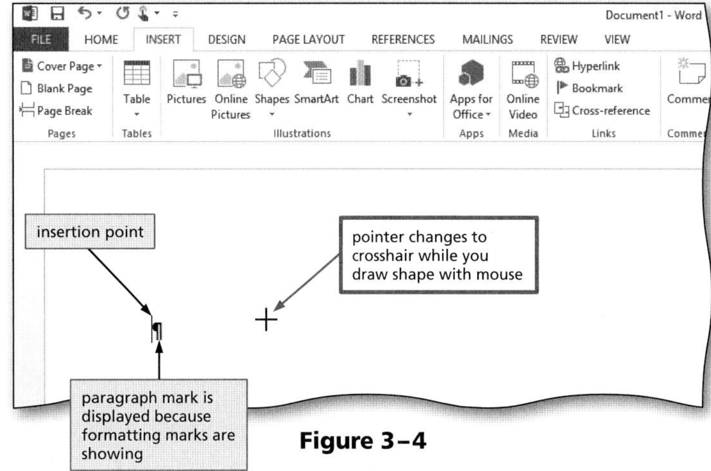

Figure 3–4

Q&A What is the purpose of the crosshair pointer?
With a mouse, you drag the crosshair pointer from the upper-left corner to the lower-right corner to form the desired location and size of the shape.

3

- Drag the mouse to the right and downward to form the boundaries of the shape, as shown in Figure 3–5. Do not release the mouse button.

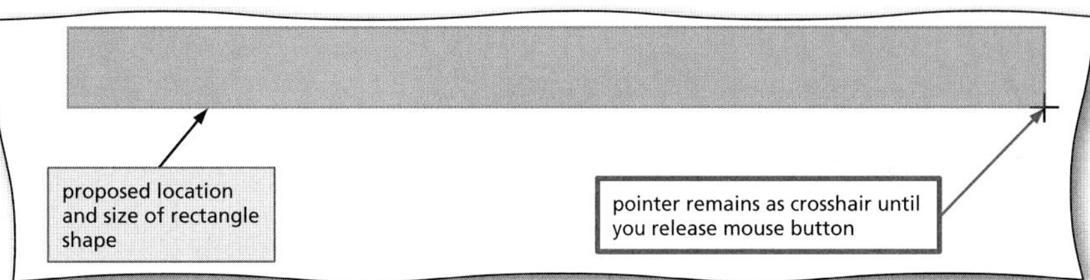

Figure 3–5

- Release the mouse button so that Word draws the shape according to your drawing in the document window.

- If you are using a touch screen, change the values in the Shape Height and Shape Width boxes (DRAWING TOOLS FORMAT tab | Size group) to 0.53" and 5.7" by typing each value in the respective box and then pressing the ENTER key; if you are using a mouse, verify your shape is the same approximate height and width as the one in this project by reviewing, and if necessary changing, the values in the Shape Height box and Shape Width boxes to 0.53" and 5.7" by typing each value in the respective box and then pressing the ENTER key (Figure 3–6).

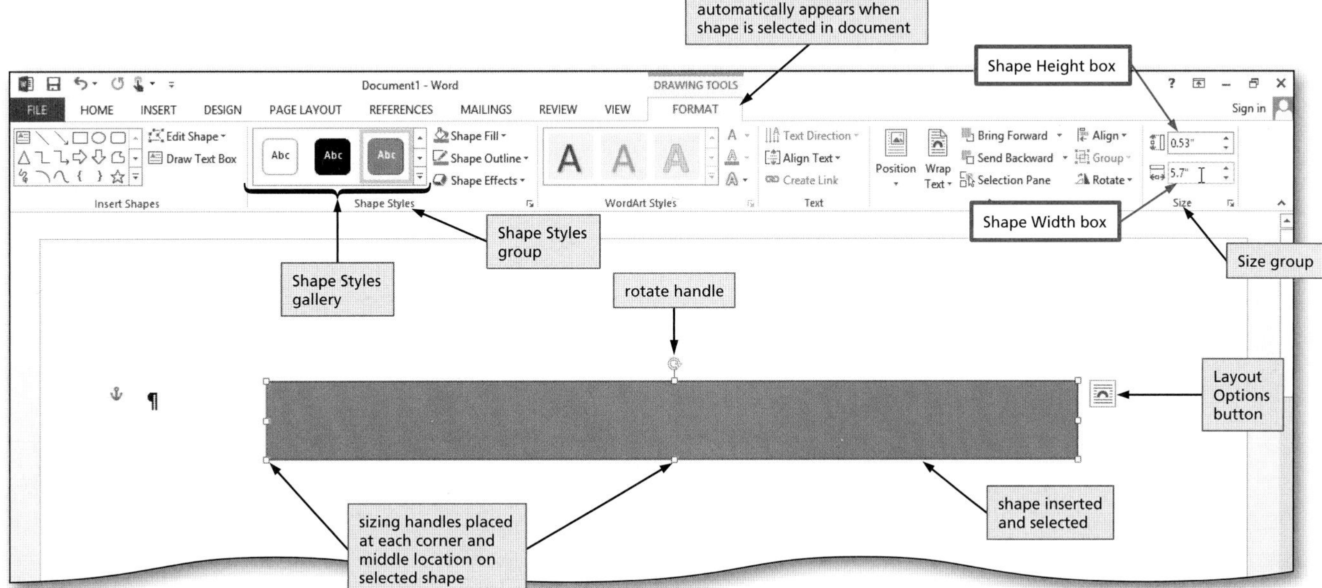

Figure 3–6

Q&A

What is the purpose of the rotate handle?
When you drag an object's **rotate handle**, which is the white circle on the top of the object, Word rotates the object in the direction you drag the mouse.

What if I wanted to delete a shape and start over?
With the shape selected, you would press the DELETE key.

Floating versus Inline Objects

When you insert an object in a document, Word inserts it as either an inline object or a floating object. An **inline object** is an object that is part of a paragraph. With inline objects, you change the location of the object by setting paragraph options, such as centered, right-aligned, and so on. For example, when you inserted the picture in Chapter 1, Word inserted it as an inline object. A **floating object**, by contrast, is an object that can be positioned at a specific location in a document or in a layer over or behind text in a document. The shape you just inserted is a floating object. You have more flexibility with floating objects because you can position a floating object anywhere on the page.

In addition to changing an object from inline to floating and vice versa, Word provides several floating options, which along with inline, are called text wrapping options because they affect how text wraps with or around the object. Table 3–1 presents the various text wrapping options.

Table 3–1 Text Wrapping Options

Text Wrapping Option	Object Type	How It Works
In Line with Text	Inline	Object positioned according to paragraph formatting; for example, if paragraph is centered, object will be centered with any text in the paragraph.
Square	Floating	Text wraps around object, with text forming a box around the object.
Tight	Floating	Text wraps around object, with text forming to shape of the object.
Through	Floating	Object appears at beginning, middle, or end of text. Moving object changes location of text.
Top and Bottom	Floating	Object appears above or below text. Moving object changes location of text.
Behind Text	Floating	Object appears behind text.
In Front of Text	Floating	Object appears in front of text and may cover the text.

To Change an Object's Position

1 CREATE & FORMAT LETTERHEAD WITH GRAPHICS | 2 SPECIFY LETTER FORMATS
3 INSERT TABLE | 4 FORMAT TABLE | 5 INSERT BULLETED LIST | 6 ADDRESS ENVELOPE

You can specify that an object's vertical position on a page (top, middle, bottom) and its horizontal position (left, center, right). The following steps change the position of an object, specifically, the rectangle shape. ***Why?*** *You want the shape to be centered at the top of the page in the letterhead.*

1

- With the shape still selected, tap or click the Position Object button (DRAWING TOOLS FORMAT tab | Arrange group) to display the Position Object gallery (Figure 3–7).

Q&A What if the shape is not still selected?
Tap or click the shape to select it.

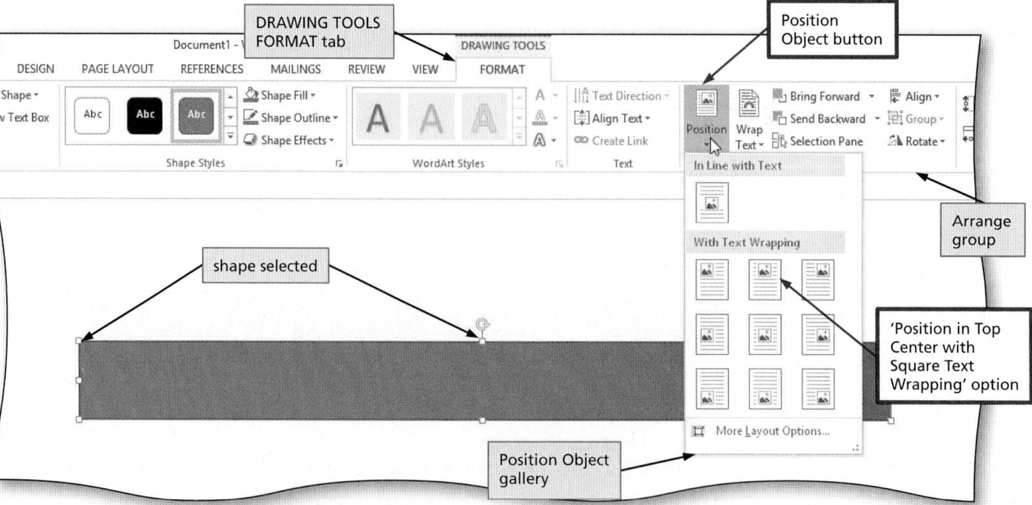

Figure 3–7

Experiment

- If you are using a mouse, point to various text options in the Position Object gallery and watch the shape move to the selected position option.

2

- Tap or click 'Position in Top Center with Square Text Wrapping' in the Position Object gallery so that the object does not cover the document and is centered at the top of the document.

Other Ways

1. Tap or click Layout Options button attached to graphic, tap or click See more link in Layout Options gallery, tap or click Horizontal Alignment arrow and select alignment (Layout dialog box), tap or click Vertical Alignment arrow and select alignment, tap or click OK button
2. Tap or click Advanced Layout: Size Dialog Box Launcher (DRAWING TOOLS FORMAT tab | Size group), tap or click Position tab (Layout dialog box), tap or click Horizontal Alignment arrow and select alignment, tap or click Vertical Alignment arrow and select alignment, tap or click OK button

To Change an Object's Text Wrapping

When you insert a shape in a Word document, the default text wrapping is In Front of Text, which means the object will cover any text behind it. The previous steps, which changed the shape's position, changed the text wrapping to Square. In the letterhead, you want the shape's text wrapping to be Top and Bottom. ***Why?*** *You want the letterhead above the contents of the letter when you type it, instead of covering the contents of the letter.* The following steps change an object's text wrapping.

- With the shape still selected, tap or click the Layout Options button attached to the graphic to display the Layout Options gallery (Figure 3–8).

- Tap or click 'Top and Bottom' in the Layout Options gallery so that the object does not cover the document text (shown in Figure 3–9 on the next page).

Q&A How can I tell that the text wrapping has changed?
Because the letter has no text, you need to look at the paragraph mark, which now is positioned below the shape instead of to its left.

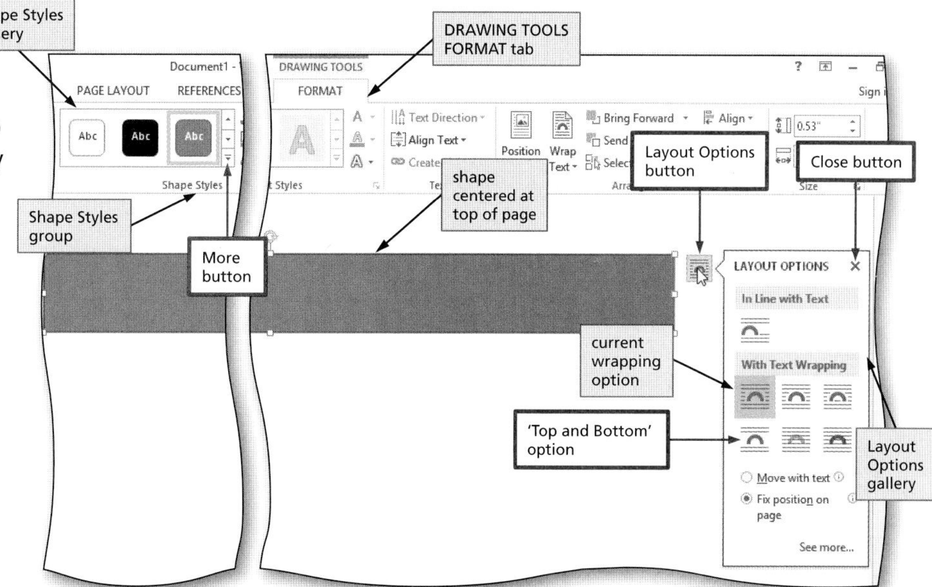

Figure 3–8

- Tap or click the Close button in the Layout Options gallery to close the gallery.

Other Ways

1. Tap 'Show Context Menu' button on mini toolbar or right-click object, tap or point to Wrap Text on shortcut menu, tap or click desired wrapping option
2. Tap or click Wrap Text button (DRAWING TOOLS FORMAT tab | Arrange group), select desired wrapping option

To Apply a Shape Style

Why apply a shape style? *Word provides a Shape Styles gallery so that you easily can change the appearance of the shape.* The steps on the next page apply a shape style to the rectangle shape.

1

- With the shape still selected, tap or click the More button (shown in Figure 3–8 on the previous page) in the Shape Styles gallery (DRAWING TOOLS FORMAT tab | Shape Styles group) to expand the gallery.

Q&A What if the shape is no longer selected?
Tap or click the shape to select it.

- If you are using a mouse, point to 'Subtle Effect - Blue, Accent 1' (second effect in fourth row) in the Shape Styles gallery to display a live preview of that style applied to the shape in the document (Figure 3–9).

Experiment

- If you are using a mouse, point to various styles in the Shape Styles gallery and watch the style of the shape change in the document.

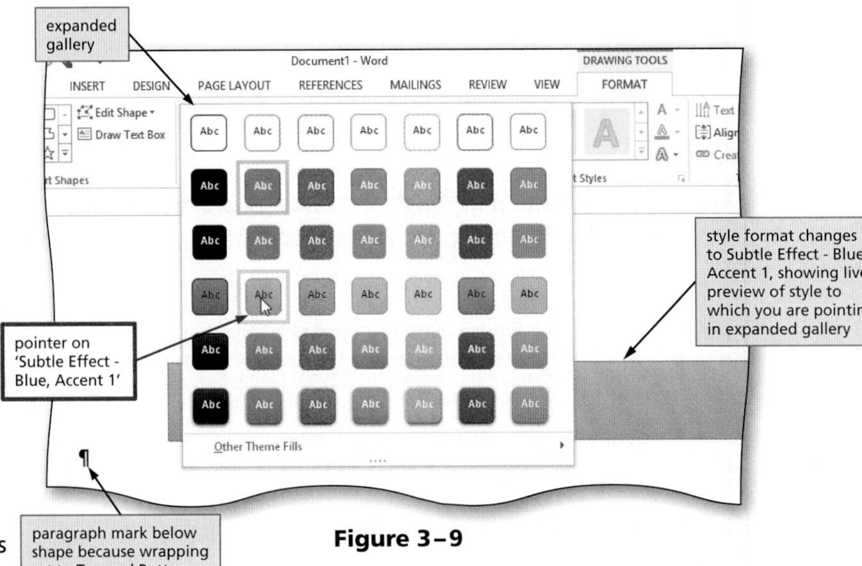

Figure 3–9

2

- Tap or click 'Subtle Effect - Blue, Accent 1' in the Shape Styles gallery to apply the selected style to the shape.

Other Ways

1. Press and hold or right-click shape, tap or click 'Shape Quick Styles' button on mini toolbar, select desired style
2. Tap or click Format Shape Dialog Box Launcher (DRAWING TOOLS FORMAT tab | Shape Styles group), tap or click 'Fill & Line' button (Format Shape task pane), expand FILL section, select desired colors, tap or click Close button

To Add Text to a Shape

1 CREATE & FORMAT LETTERHEAD WITH GRAPHICS | 2 SPECIFY LETTER FORMATS
3 INSERT TABLE | 4 FORMAT TABLE | 5 INSERT BULLETED LIST | 6 ADDRESS ENVELOPE

The following steps add text (the individual's name) to a shape. ***Why?*** *In the letterhead for this chapter, the name is in the shape. Similarly, an organization could put its name in a shape on a letterhead.*

- Press and hold or right-click the shape to display a mini toolbar and/or shortcut menu (Figure 3–10).

- If you are using a touch screen, tap the Edit Text button on the mini toolbar; if you are using a mouse, click Add Text on the shortcut menu to place an insertion point in the shape.

Q&A I do not see an Edit Text button on the mini toolbar. Why not?
If you are using a mouse in Mouse mode, the buttons on your mini toolbar will differ from those that appear when you use a touch screen in Touch mode.

- If the insertion point and paragraph mark are not centered in the shape, tap or click the Center button (HOME tab | Paragraph group) to center them.
- Type `Alexander Lee Samaras` as the name in the shape (Figure 3–11).

If requested by your instructor, enter your name instead of the name shown in Figure 3–11.

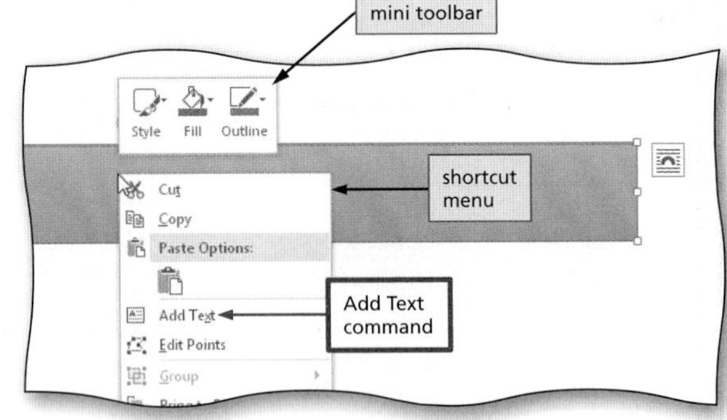

Figure 3–10

Figure 3–11

To Use the 'Increase Font Size' Button

In previous chapters, you used the Font Size arrow (HOME tab | Font group) to change the font size of text. Word also provides an 'Increase Font Size' button (HOME tab | Font group), which increases the font size of selected text each time you tap or click the button. The following steps use the 'Increase Font Size' button to increase the font size of the name in the shape to 24 point. ***Why?*** *You want the name to be as large as possible in the shape.*

1

- Drag through the text to be formatted (in this case, the name in the shape).

2

- If necessary, display the HOME tab.
- Repeatedly tap or click the 'Increase Font Size' button (HOME tab | Font group) until the Font Size box displays 24 to increase the font size of the selected text (Figure 3–12).

Q&A What if I tap or click the 'Increase Font Size' button (HOME tab | Font group) too many times, causing the font size to be too big?

Tap or click the 'Decrease Font Size' button (HOME tab | Font group) until the desired font size is displayed.

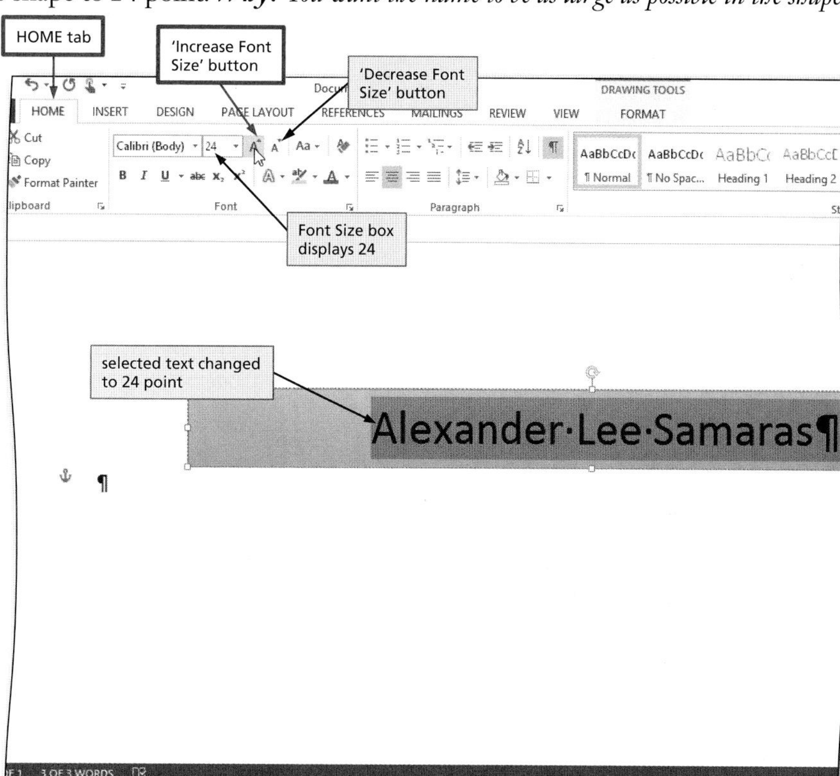

Figure 3–12

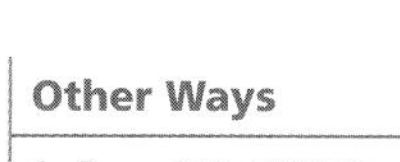

Experiment

- Repeatedly tap or click the 'Increase Font Size' and 'Decrease Font Size' buttons (HOME tab | Font group) and watch the font size of the selected name change in the document window. When you are finished experimenting with these two buttons, set the font size to 24.

Other Ways

1. Press CTRL+SHIFT+>

To Bold Selected Text

To make the name stand out even more, bold it. The following steps bold the selected text.

1. With the text selected, tap or click the Bold button (HOME tab | Font group) to bold the selected text.
2. Tap or click anywhere in the text in the shape to remove the selection and place the insertion point in the shape.

BTW
Touch Screen Differences
The Office and Windows interfaces may vary if you are using a touch screen. For this reason, you might notice that the function or appearance of your touch screen differs slightly from this chapter's presentation.

To Change the Document Theme

1 CREATE & FORMAT LETTERHEAD WITH GRAPHICS | 2 SPECIFY LETTER FORMATS
3 INSERT TABLE | 4 FORMAT TABLE | 5 INSERT BULLETED LIST | 6 ADDRESS ENVELOPE

A **document theme** is a coordinated combination of colors, fonts, and effects. The current default document theme is Office, which uses Calibri and Calibri Light as its font and shades of grays and blues primarily. The following steps change the document theme to Organic for the letter in this chapter. ***Why?*** *You want to use shades of greens, browns, and blues in the letterhead because those colors are associated with growth, honesty, dependability, and integrity. You also want to use a serif font, which is a font that has short decorative lines on some characters. The Organic theme meets both of these requirements.*

1

- Display the DESIGN tab.
- Tap or click the Themes button (DESIGN tab | Document Formatting group) to display the Themes gallery.
- If you are using a mouse, point to Organic in the Themes gallery to display a live preview of that theme applied to the document (Figure 3–13).

Experiment

- If you are using a mouse, point to various themes in the Themes gallery and watch the color scheme and font set change in the document window.

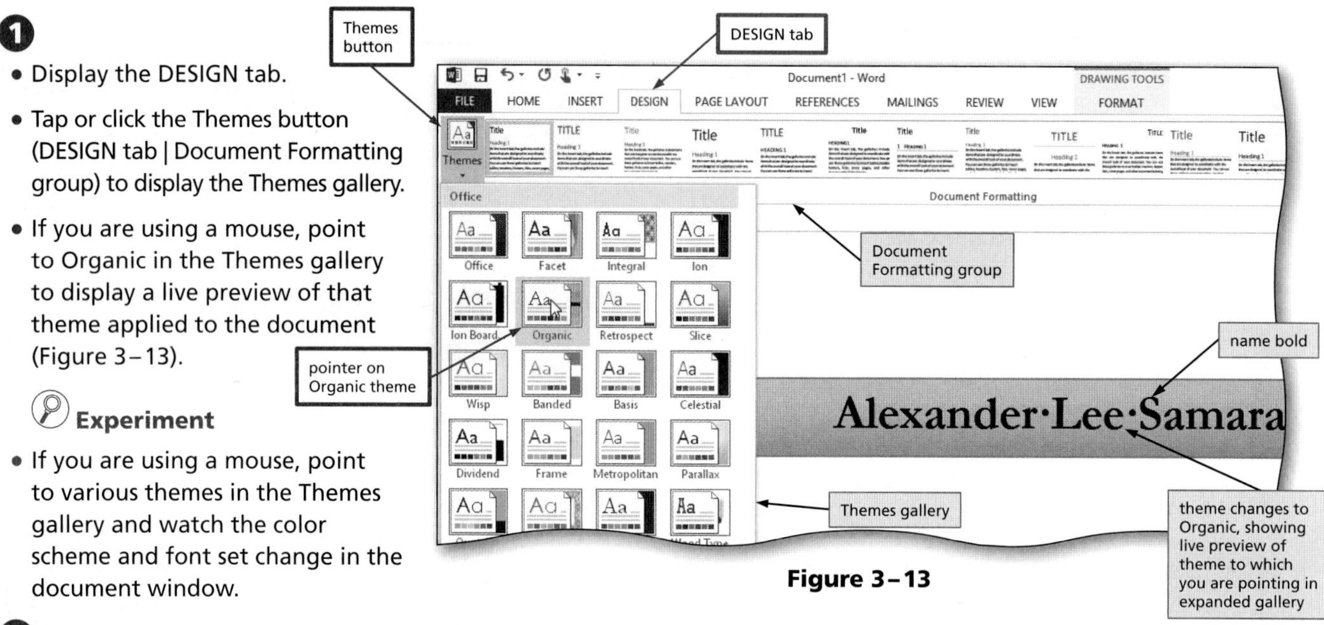

Figure 3–13

2

- Tap or click Organic in the Themes gallery to change the document theme.

To Insert Clip Art

1 CREATE & FORMAT LETTERHEAD WITH GRAPHICS | 2 SPECIFY LETTER FORMATS
3 INSERT TABLE | 4 FORMAT TABLE | 5 INSERT BULLETED LIST | 6 ADDRESS ENVELOPE

Files containing graphics are available from a variety of sources. In the Chapter 1 flyer, you inserted a digital picture taken with a camera phone. In this project, you insert **clip art**, which is a predefined graphic. Microsoft Office applications can access a collection of royalty-free clip art, photos, and animations.

The letterhead in this project contains clip art of books (Figure 3–1 on page WD 139). ***Why?*** *Because the writer of the letter enjoys reading and teaching, he selects an image of books for his letterhead.* The following steps insert clip art in the document.

1

- If necessary, tap or click the paragraph mark below the shape to position the insertion point where you want to insert the clip art.
- Display the INSERT tab.
- Tap or click the Online Pictures button (INSERT tab | Illustrations group) to display the Insert Pictures dialog box.
- Type `books` in the Search box (Insert Pictures dialog box) to specify the search text, which indicates the type of image you want to locate (Figure 3–14).

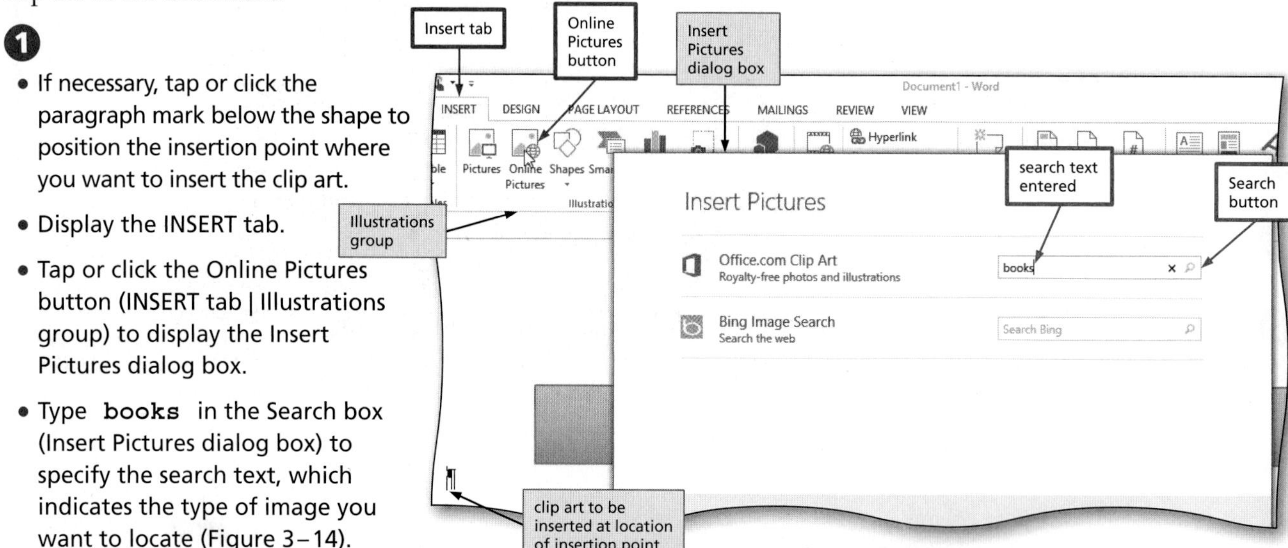

Figure 3–14

2

- Tap or click the Search button to display a list of clip art that matches the entered search text.
- Scroll through the list of clip art to locate the one shown in Figure 3–15 (or a similar image) and then tap or click the clip art to select it.

Why is my list of clip art different from Figure 3–15?
Microsoft continually updates the online images.

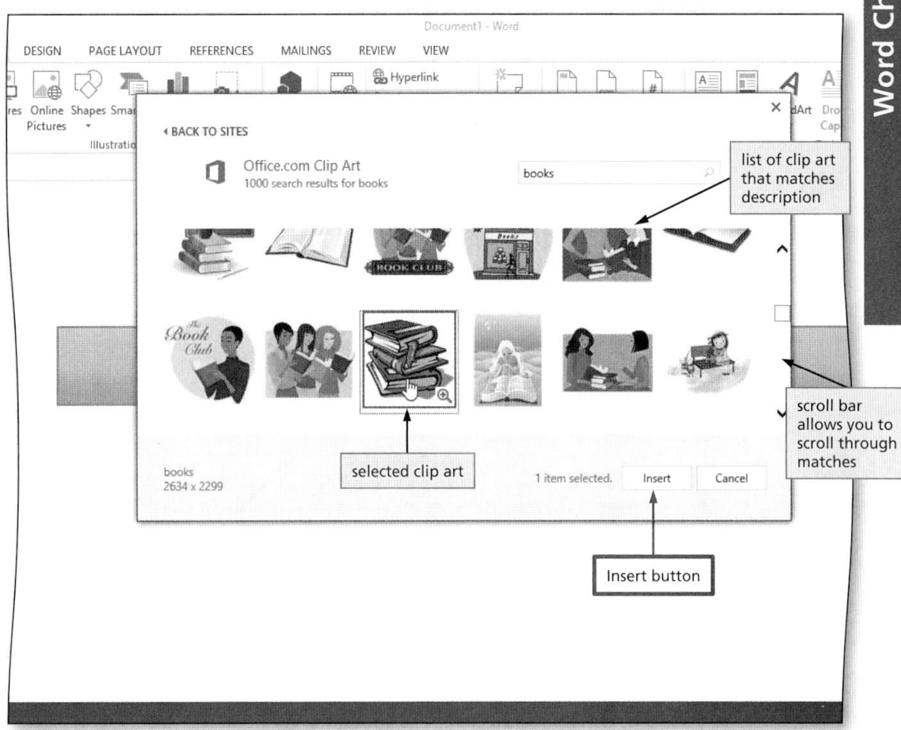

Figure 3–15

3

- Tap or click the Insert button to insert the selected clip art in the document at the location of the insertion point (Figure 3–16).

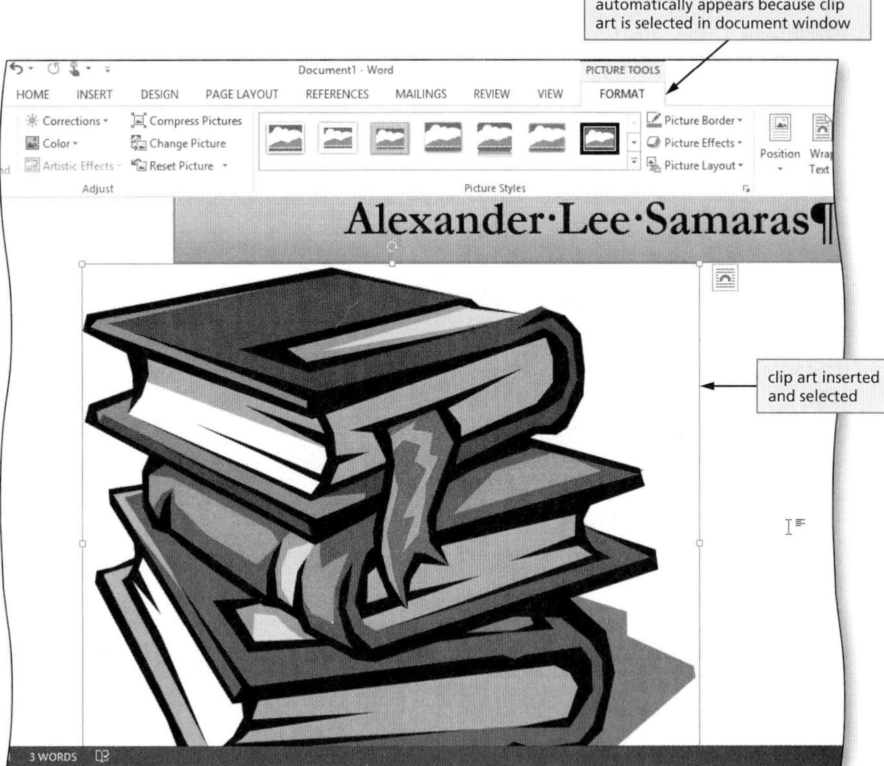

Figure 3–16

To Resize a Graphic to a Percent of the Original

1 CREATE & FORMAT LETTERHEAD WITH GRAPHICS | 2 SPECIFY LETTER FORMATS
3 INSERT TABLE | 4 FORMAT TABLE | 5 INSERT BULLETED LIST | 6 ADDRESS ENVELOPE

Instead of dragging a sizing handle to change the graphic's size, as you learned in Chapter 1, you can specify that the graphic be resized to a percent of its original size. In this project, the graphic is resized to 14 percent of its original size. ***Why?*** *The original size of the clip art is too large for the letterhead.* The following steps resize a graphic to a percent of the original.

1

- With the graphic still selected, tap or click the Advanced Layout: Size Dialog Box Launcher (PICTURE TOOLS FORMAT tab | Size group) to display the Size sheet in the Layout dialog box.

Q&A What if the graphic is not selected or the PICTURE TOOLS FORMAT tab is not on the ribbon?
Tap or click the graphic to select it or double-tap or double-click the graphic to make the PICTURE TOOLS FORMAT tab the active tab.

2

- In the Scale area (Layout dialog box), double-tap or double-click the current value in the Height box to select it.
- Type `14` in the Height box and then press the TAB key to display the same percent value in the Width box (Figure 3–17).

Q&A Why did Word automatically fill in the value in the Width box?
When the 'Lock aspect ratio' check box (Layout dialog box) is selected, Word automatically maintains the size proportions of the graphic.

How do I know to use 14 percent for the resized graphic?
The larger graphic consumed too much room on the page. Try various percentages to determine the size that works best in the letterhead design.

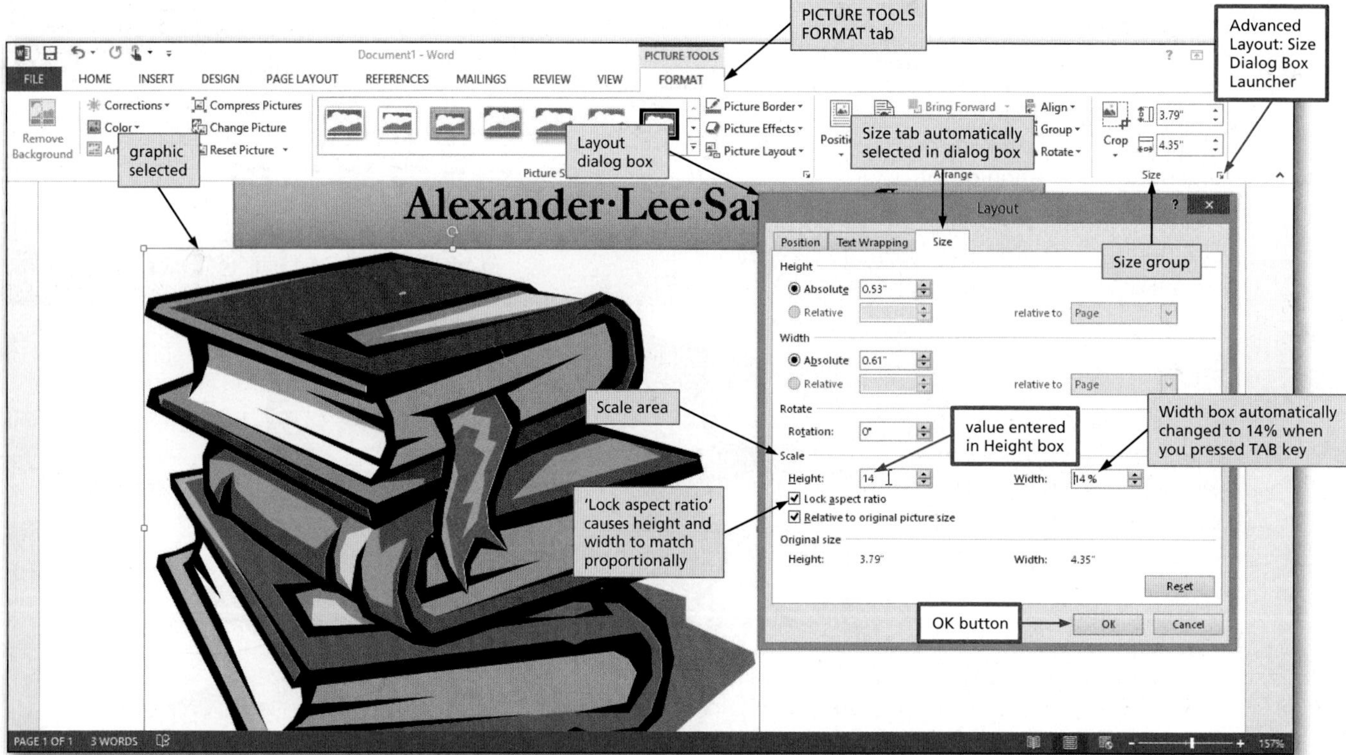

Figure 3–17

- Tap or click the OK button to close the dialog box and resize the selected graphic.
- If necessary, scroll to display the top of the document (Figure 3–18).

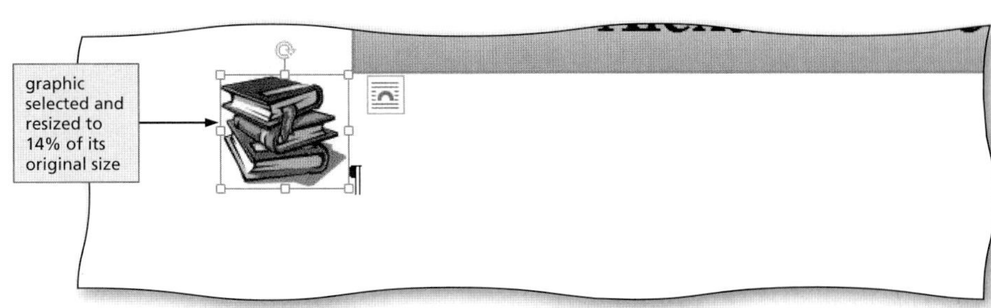

Figure 3–18

Other Ways

1. Tap or click Layout Options button attached to graphic, tap or click See more link in the Layout Options gallery, tap or click Size tab (Layout dialog box), enter height and width values, tap or click OK button
2. If you are using a mouse, right-click graphic, click 'Size and Position' on shortcut menu, enter height and width values (Layout dialog box), click OK button

To Change the Color of a Graphic

1 CREATE & FORMAT LETTERHEAD WITH GRAPHICS | 2 SPECIFY LETTER FORMATS
3 INSERT TABLE | 4 FORMAT TABLE | 5 INSERT BULLETED LIST | 6 ADDRESS ENVELOPE

In Word, you can change the color of a graphic. The clip art currently uses a variety of colors including red, orange, and blue. The following steps change the color of the clip art (graphic). ***Why?*** *Because the clip art in this project will be placed beside the rectangle shape, you prefer to use colors that blend better with the current color scheme.*

- With the graphic still selected (shown in Figure 3–18), tap or click the Color button (PICTURE TOOLS FORMAT tab | Adjust group) to display the Color gallery.
- If you are using a mouse, point to 'Green, Accent color 1 Dark' in the Color gallery (second color in second row) to display a live preview of that color applied to the selected graphic in the document (Figure 3–19).

Experiment

- If you are using a mouse, point to various colors in the Color gallery and watch the color of the graphic change in the document.

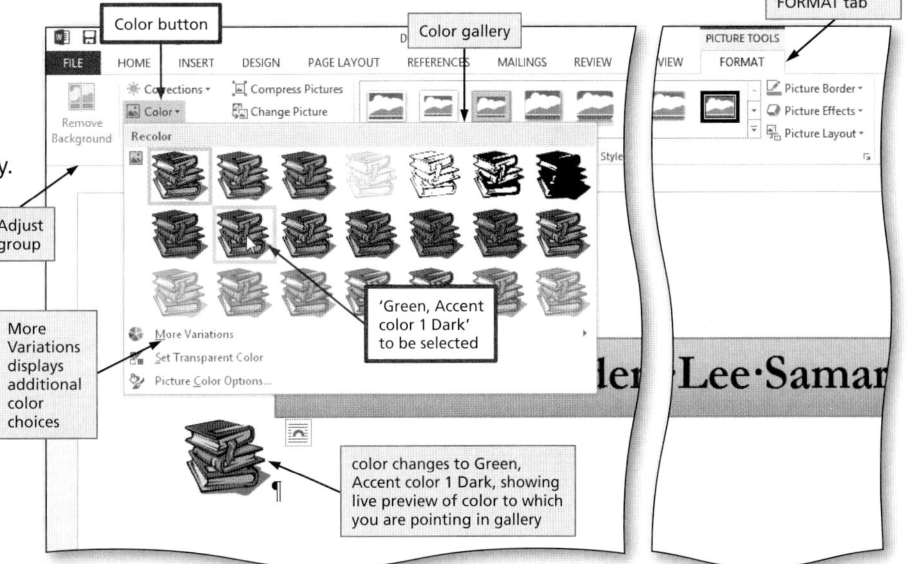

Figure 3–19

- Tap or click 'Green, Accent color 1 Dark' in the Color gallery to change the color of the selected graphic.

Q&A How would I change a graphic back to its original colors?
With the graphic selected, you would tap or click No Recolor, which is the upper-left color in the Color gallery.

Other Ways

1. Tap or click Format Shape Dialog Box Launcher (PICTURE TOOLS FORMAT tab | Picture Styles group), tap or click Picture button (Format Picture task pane), expand PICTURE COLOR section, select desired options
2. Tap 'Show Context Menu' button on mini toolbar or right-click graphic, tap Format Object or click Format Picture on shortcut menu, tap or click Picture button (Format Picture task pane), expand PICTURE COLOR section, select desired options

To Set a Transparent Color in a Graphic

In Word, you can make one color in a graphic transparent, that is, remove the color. You would make a color transparent if you wanted to remove part of a graphic or see text or colors behind a graphic. The following steps set part of the bookmark in the books graphic in a transparent color. ***Why?*** *Instead of its current dark green color, the bookmark will be easier to see if it is transparent.*

1

- Increase the zoom percent enough so that you easily can see the bookmark in the graphic.
- With the graphic still selected, tap or click the Color button (PICTURE TOOLS FORMAT tab | Adjust group) to display the Color gallery (Figure 3–20).

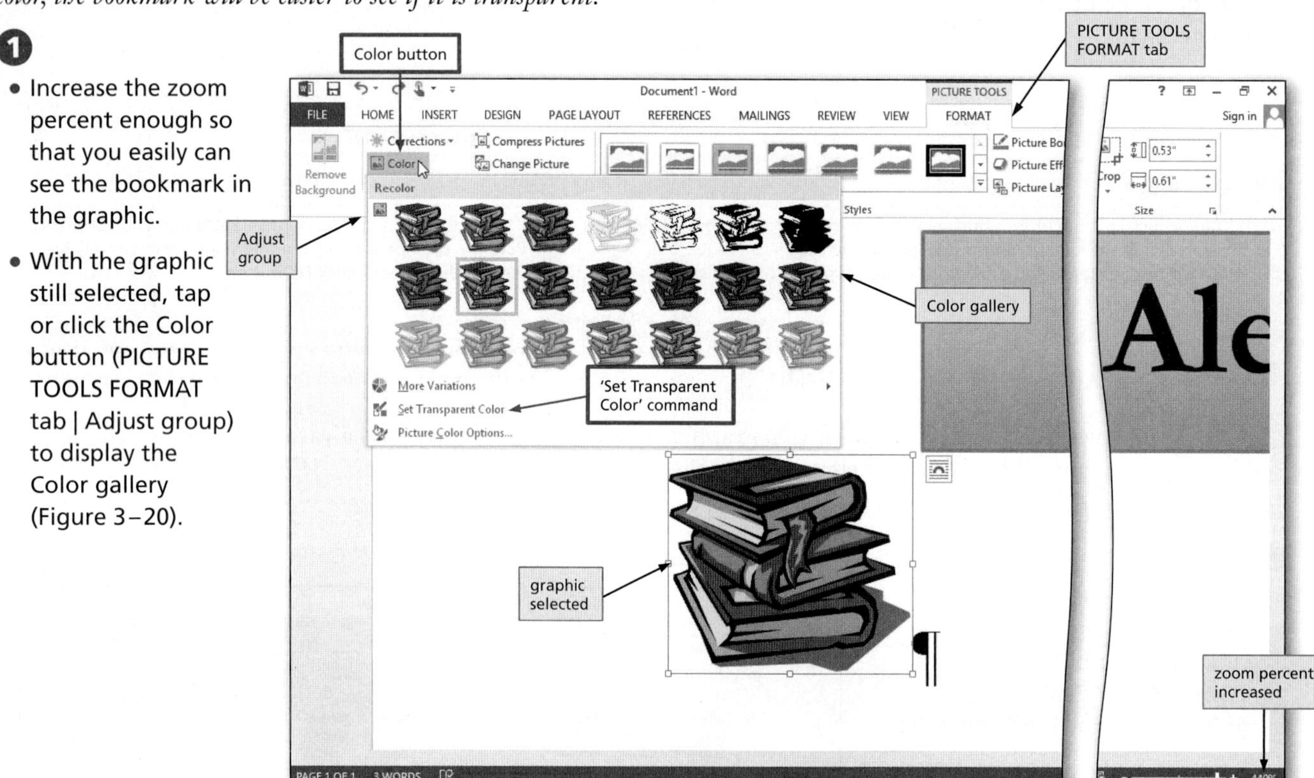

Figure 3–20

2

- Tap or click 'Set Transparent Color' in the Color gallery to display a pen pointer in the document window.
- If you are using a mouse, position the pen pointer in the graphic where you want to make the color transparent (Figure 3–21).

Figure 3–21

Q&A Can I make multiple colors in a graphic transparent?
No, you can make only one color transparent.

3

- Tap or click the location in the graphic where you want the color to be transparent (Figure 3–22).

Q&A What if this step does not work on a touch screen?
You may need to use a stylus or mouse to perform these steps.

What if I make the wrong color transparent?
Tap or click the Undo button on the Quick Access Toolbar, or press CTRL+Z, and then repeat these steps.

- Change the zoom back to page width.

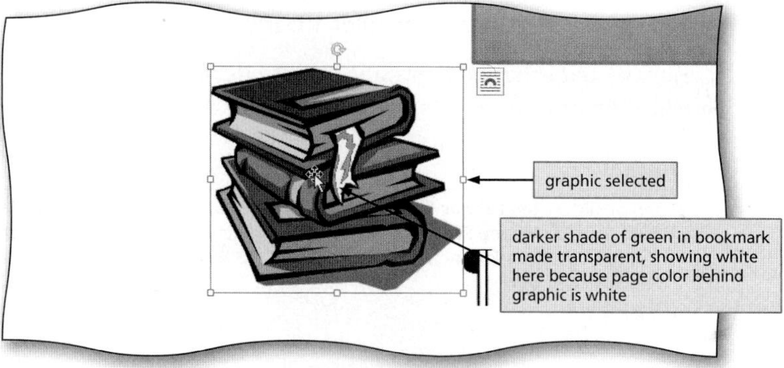

Figure 3–22

To Adjust the Brightness and Contrast of a Graphic

In Word, you can adjust the brightness, or lightness, of a graphic and also the contrast, or the difference between the lightest and darkest areas of the graphic. The following steps increase the brightness and contrast of the books graphic, each by 20%. ***Why?*** *You want to lighten the graphic slightly to decrease its emphasis on the page and, at the same time, increase the difference between the light and dark areas of the graphic.*

1

- Display the PICTURE TOOLS FORMAT tab.
- With the graphic still selected (shown in Figure 3–22), tap or click the Corrections button (PICTURE TOOLS FORMAT tab | Adjust group) to display the Corrections gallery.
- If you are using a mouse, point to 'Brightness: +20% Contrast: +20%' (fourth image in fourth row) in the Corrections gallery to display a live preview of that correction applied to the graphic in the document (Figure 3–23).

Experiment

- If you are using a mouse, point to various corrections in the Corrections gallery and watch the brightness and contrast of the graphic change in the document.

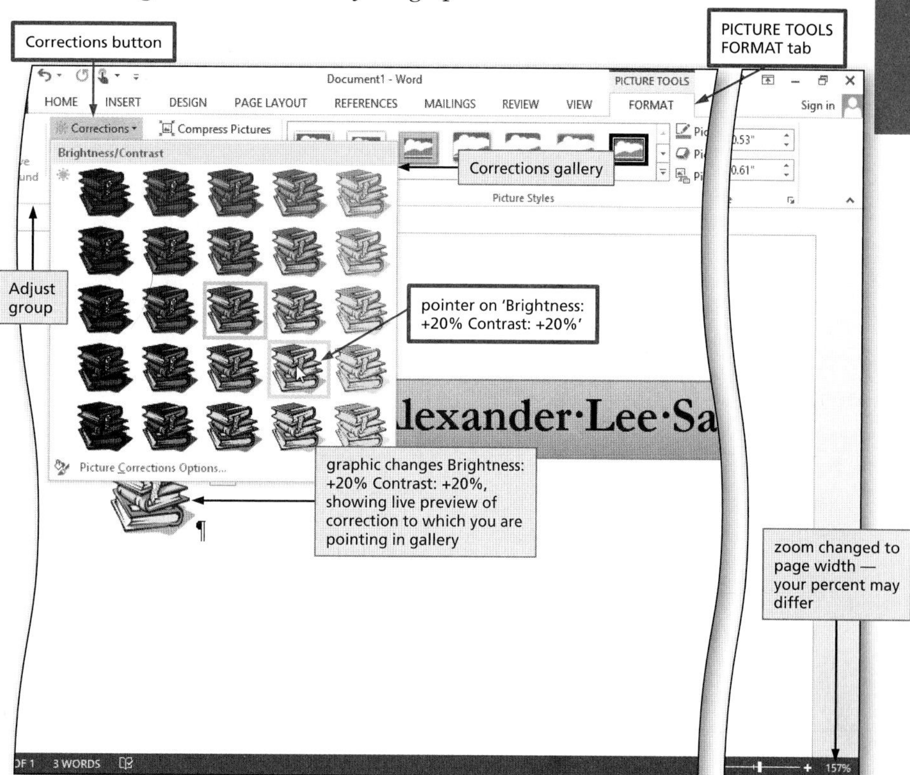

Figure 3–23

2

- Tap or click 'Brightness: +20% Contrast: +20%' in the Corrections gallery (fourth image in fourth row) to change the brightness and contrast of the selected graphic.

Other Ways

1. Tap or click Format Shape Dialog Box Launcher (PICTURE TOOLS FORMAT tab | Picture Styles group), tap or click Picture button (Format Picture task pane), expand PICTURE CORRECTIONS section, select desired options
2. Tap 'Show Context Menu' button on mini toolbar or right-click graphic, tap Format Object or click Format Picture on shortcut menu, tap or click Picture button (Format Picture task pane), expand PICTURE CORRECTIONS section, select desired options

If you are using your finger on a touch screen and are having difficulty completing the steps in this chapter, consider using a stylus. Many people find it easier to be precise with a stylus than with a finger. In addition, with a stylus you see the pointer. If you still are having trouble completing the steps with a stylus, try using a mouse.

To Change the Border Color on a Graphic

The books graphic currently has no border (outline). The following steps change the border color on the graphic. ***Why?*** *You would like the graphic to have a green border so that it matches the border on the shape.*

1

- Tap or click the Picture Border arrow (PICTURE TOOLS FORMAT tab | Picture Styles group) to display the Picture Border gallery.
- If you are using a mouse, point to 'Green, Accent 1' (fifth theme color from left in the first row) in the Picture Border gallery to display a live preview of that border color around the picture (Figure 3–24).

Q&A If I am using a mouse, what if I click the Picture Border button by mistake?
Click the Picture Border arrow and proceed with Step 2. If you are using a touch screen, you may not have a separate Picture Border button.

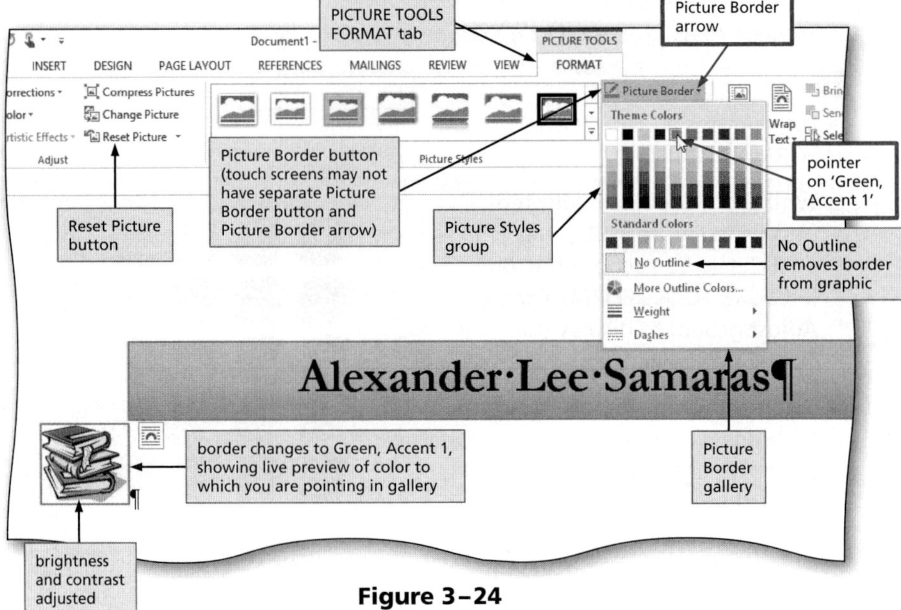

Figure 3–24

Experiment

- If you are using a mouse, point to various colors in the Picture Border gallery and watch the border color on the graphic change in the document window.

2

- Tap or click 'Green, Accent 1' in the Picture Border gallery to change the picture border color.

Q&A How would I remove a border from a graphic?
With the graphic selected, you would tap or click the No Outline in the Picture Border gallery.

Can I remove all formatting applied to a graphic and start over?
Yes. With the graphic selected, you would tap or click the Reset Picture button (PICTURE TOOLS FORMAT tab | Adjust group).

To Change an Object's Text Wrapping

The books graphic is to be positioned to the right of the shape. Clip art, by default, is formatted as an inline graphic, which cannot be moved to a precise location on a page. Recall that inline graphics are part of a paragraph and, thus, can be positioned according to paragraph formatting, such as centered or left-aligned. To move the graphic to the right of a shape, you format it as a floating object with 'In Front of Text' wrapping. The following steps change a graphic's text wrapping.

1. If necessary, tap or click the graphic to select it.
2. Tap or click the Layout Options button attached to the graphic to display the Layout Options gallery.
3. Tap or click 'In Front of Text' in the Layout Options gallery so that you can position the object on top of any item in the document, in this case, on top of the rectangular shape.
4. Tap or click the Close button to close the gallery.

BTW
Q&As
For a complete list of the Q&As found in many of the step-by-step sequences in this book, visit the Q&A resource on the Student Companion Site located on www.cengagebrain.com. For detailed instructions about accessing available resources, visit www.cengage.com/ct/studentdownload or contact your instructor for information about accessing the required files.

To Move a Graphic

The following steps move a graphic. ***Why?*** *In this letterhead, the books graphic is positioned to the right of the shape.*

- If you are using a mouse, position the pointer in the graphic so that the pointer has a four-headed arrow attached to it (Figure 3–25).

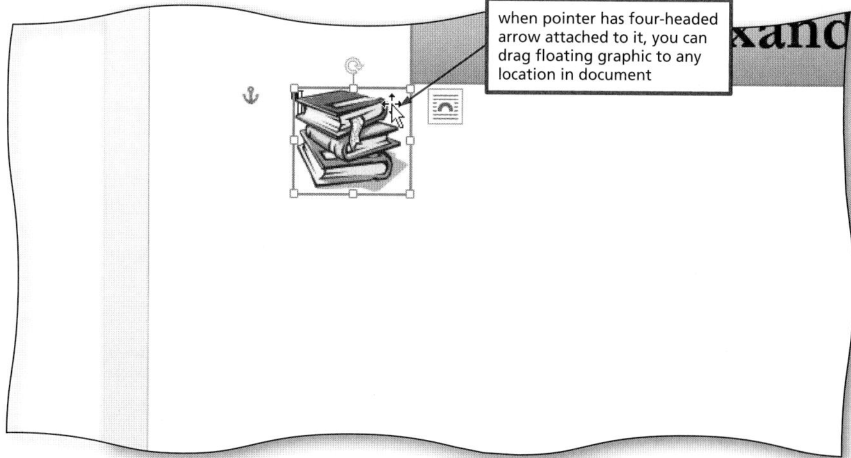
when pointer has four-headed arrow attached to it, you can drag floating graphic to any location in document
xand

Figure 3–25

- Drag the graphic to the right of the shape, as shown in Figure 3–26.

Q&A

What if I moved the graphic to the wrong location?
Repeat these steps. You can drag a floating graphic to any location in a document.

Why do green lines appear on my screen as I drag a graphic?
You have alignment guides set, which help you line up graphics. To set alignment guides, tap or click the Align Objects button (PICTURE TOOLS FORMAT tab | Arrange group) and then tap or click 'Use Alignment Guides'.

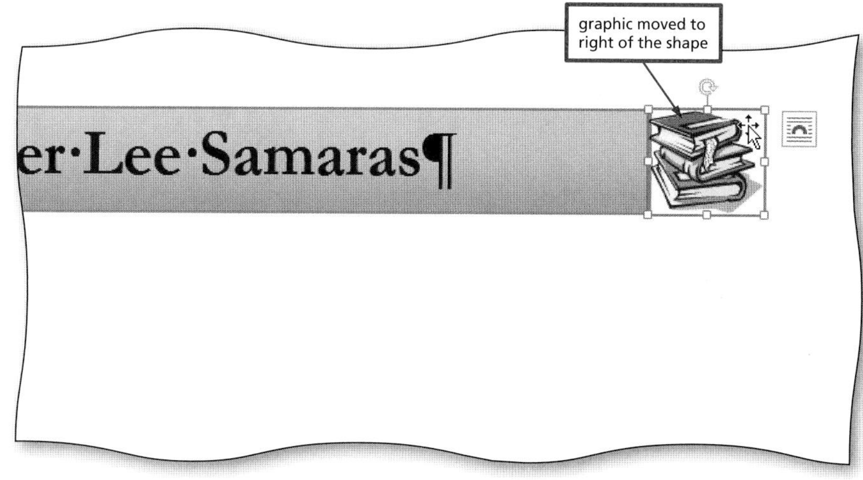
graphic moved to right of the shape
er·Lee·Samaras¶

Figure 3–26

To Copy a Graphic

In this project, the same books graphic is to be placed to the left of the shape. Instead of performing the same steps to insert and format another books graphic, you can copy the graphic to the Office Clipboard, paste the graphic from the Office Clipboard, and then move the graphic to the desired location.

You use the same steps to copy a graphic as you used in Chapter 2 to copy text. The following steps copy a graphic.

1. If necessary, tap or click the graphic to select it.
2. Display the HOME tab.
3. Tap or click the Copy button, shown in Figure 3–27 on the next page (HOME tab | Clipboard group), to copy the selected item to the Office Clipboard.

BTW

BTWs
For a complete list of the BTWs found in the margins of this book, visit the BTW resource on the Student Companion Site located on www.cengagebrain.com. For detailed instructions about accessing available resources, visit www.cengage.com/ct/studentdownload or contact your instructor for information about accessing the required files.

To Use Paste Options

1 CREATE & FORMAT LETTERHEAD WITH GRAPHICS | 2 SPECIFY LETTER FORMATS
3 INSERT TABLE | 4 FORMAT TABLE | 5 INSERT BULLETED LIST | 6 ADDRESS ENVELOPE

The following steps paste a graphic using the Paste Options gallery. ***Why?*** *Recall from Chapter 2 that you can specify the format of a pasted item using Paste Options.*

1

- Tap or click the Paste arrow (HOME tab | Clipboard group) to display the Paste gallery.

Q&A If I am using a mouse, what if I accidentally click the Paste button?
Click the Paste Options button below the graphic pasted in the document to display a Paste Options gallery. If you are using a touch screen, you may not have a separate Paste button.

- If you are using a mouse, point to the 'Keep Source Formatting' button in the Paste gallery to display a live preview of that paste option (Figure 3–27).

Experiment

- Point to the two buttons in the Paste gallery and watch the appearance of the pasted graphic change.

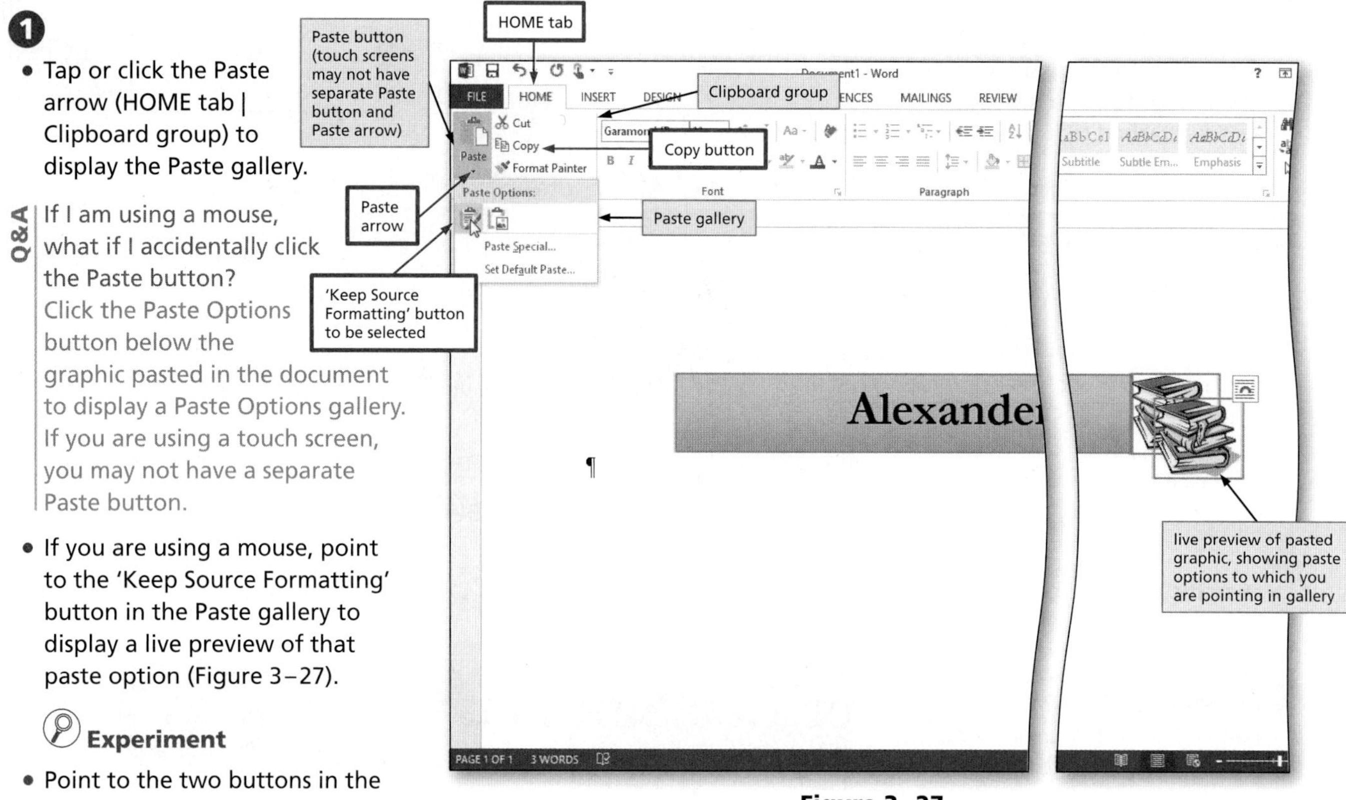

Figure 3–27

Q&A What do the buttons in the Paste gallery mean?
The 'Keep Source Formatting' button indicates the pasted graphic should have the same formats as it did in its original location. The Picture button removes some formatting from the graphic.

Why are these paste buttons different from the ones in Chapter 2?
The buttons that appear in the Paste gallery differ depending on the item you are pasting. Use live preview to see how the pasted object will look in the document.

2

- Tap or click the 'Keep Source Formatting' button in the Paste gallery to paste the object using the same formatting as the original.

To Move a Graphic

The next step is to move the second books graphic so that it is positioned to the left of the rectangle shape. The following steps move a graphic.

1. If you are using a mouse, position the pointer in the graphic so that the pointer has a four-headed arrow attached to it.
2. Drag the graphic to the location shown in Figure 3–28.

To Flip a Graphic

The following steps flip a graphic horizontally. ***Why?*** *In this letterhead, you want the books graphics to face each other.*

1

- If necessary, display the PICTURE TOOLS FORMAT tab.

2

- With the graphic still selected, tap or click the Rotate Objects button (PICTURE TOOLS FORMAT tab | Arrange group) to display the Rotate Objects gallery (Figure 3–28).

Experiment

- If you are using a mouse, point to the various rotate options in the Rotate Options gallery and watch the picture rotate in the document window.

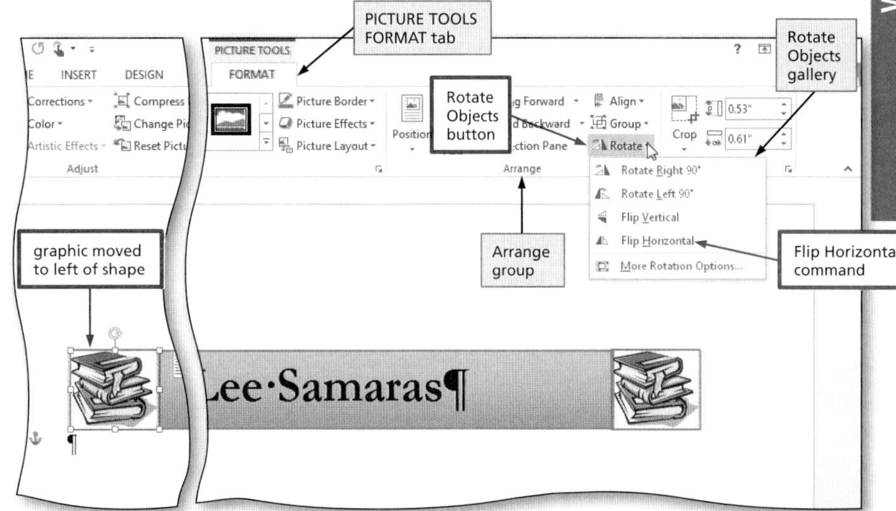

Figure 3–28

3

- Tap or click Flip Horizontal in the Rotate Options gallery, so that Word flips the graphic to display its mirror image.

Q&A Can I flip a graphic vertically?
Yes, you would tap or click Flip Vertical in the Rotate Options gallery. You also can rotate a graphic clockwise or counterclockwise by tapping or clicking the 'Rotate Right 90°' and 'Rotate Left 90°' commands, respectively, in the Rotate Options gallery.

To Save a Document

You have performed many tasks while creating this letterhead and do not want to risk losing work completed thus far. Accordingly, you should save the document. The following steps assume you already have created folders for storing your files, for example, a CIS 101 folder (for your class) that contains a Word folder (for your assignments). Thus, these steps save the document in the Word folder in the CIS 101 folder using the file name, Samaras Letterhead.

1 Tap or click the Save button on the Quick Access Toolbar, which depending on settings, will display either the Save As gallery in the Backstage view or the Save As dialog box.

2 To save on a hard disk or other storage media on your computer, proceed to Step 2a. To save on SkyDrive, proceed to Step 2b.

2a If your screen opens the Backstage view and you want to save on storage media on your computer, tap or click Computer in the left pane, if necessary, to display options in the right pane related to saving on your computer. If your screen already displays the Save As dialog box, proceed to Step 4.

2b If your screen opens the Backstage view and you want to save on SkyDrive, tap or click SkyDrive in the left pane to display SkyDrive saving options or a Sign In button. If your screen displays a Sign In button, tap or click it and then sign in to SkyDrive.

3 Tap or click the Browse button in the right pane to display the Save As dialog box associated with the selected save location (i.e., Computer or SkyDrive).

4 Type `Samaras Letterhead` in the File name box to change the file name. Do not press the ENTER key after typing the file name because you do not want to close the dialog box at this time.

BTW
Organizing Files and Folders
You should organize and store files in folders so that you easily can find the files later. For example, if you are taking an introductory computer class called CIS 101, a good practice would be to save all Word files in a Word folder in a CIS 101 folder. For a discussion of folders and detailed examples of creating folders, refer to the Office and Windows chapter at the beginning of this book.

BTW
Word Help
At any time while using Word, you can find answers to questions and display information about various topics through Word Help. Used properly, this form of assistance can increase your productivity and reduce your frustrations by minimizing the time you spend learning how to use Word. For instruction about Word Help and exercises that will help you gain confidence in using it, read the Office and Windows chapter at the beginning of this book.

5. Navigate to the desired save location (in this case, the Word folder in the CIS 101 folder [or your class folder] on your computer or SkyDrive).

6. Tap or click the Save button (Save As dialog box) to save the letterhead in the selected folder on the selected save location with the entered file name.

To Format and Enter Text

The contact information for the letterhead in this project is located on the line below the shape containing the name. The following steps format and then enter the postal address in the letterhead.

1. Position the insertion point on the line below the shape containing the name.

2. If necessary, display the HOME tab. Tap or click the Center button (HOME tab | Paragraph group) to center the paragraph.

3. Tap or click the 'Increase Font Size' button (HOME tab | Font group) to increase the font size to 12 point.

4. Type **`540 Cedar Road, Branch Center, WA 98472`** and then press the SPACEBAR (shown in Figure 3–29).

To Insert a Symbol from the Symbol Dialog Box

1 CREATE & FORMAT LETTERHEAD WITH GRAPHICS | 2 SPECIFY LETTER FORMATS
3 INSERT TABLE | 4 FORMAT TABLE | 5 INSERT BULLETED LIST | 6 ADDRESS ENVELOPE

Word provides a method of inserting dots and other symbols, such as letters in the Greek alphabet and mathematical characters, that are not on the keyboard. The following steps insert a dot symbol, sometimes called a bullet symbol, in the letterhead. ***Why?*** *You want a visual separator between the postal address and phone number in the letterhead, and also between the phone number and email address.*

1

- If necessary, position the insertion point as shown in Figure 3–29.
- Display the INSERT tab.
- Tap or click the 'Insert a Symbol' button (INSERT tab | Symbols group) to display the Insert a Symbol gallery (Figure 3–29).

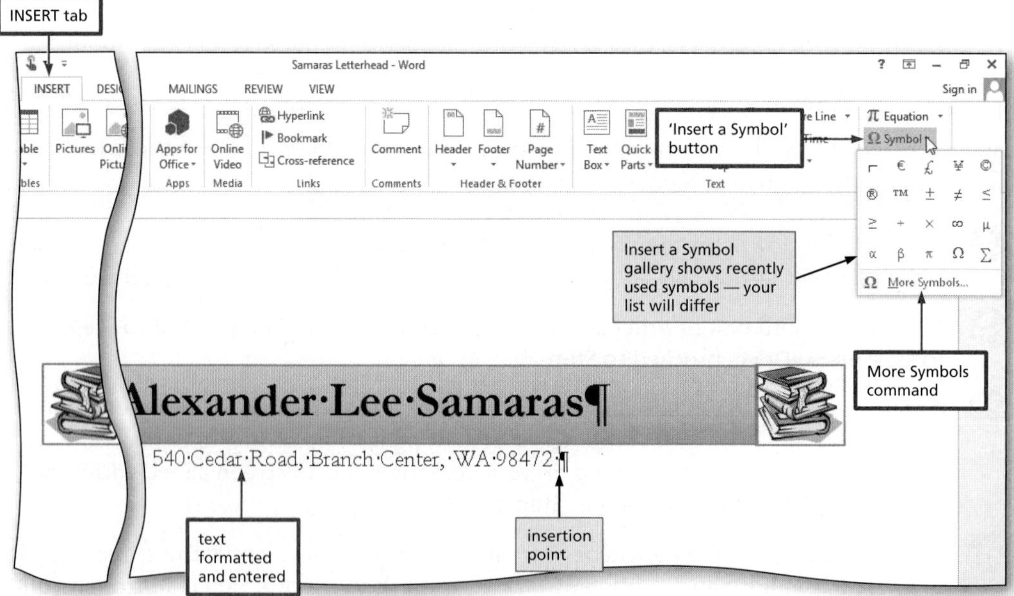

Figure 3–29

Q&A What if the symbol I want to insert already appears in the Insert a Symbol gallery?
You can tap or click any symbol shown in the Insert a Symbol gallery to insert it in the document.

2

- Tap or click More Symbols in the Insert a Symbol gallery to display the Symbol dialog box.
- If the font in the Font box is not (normal text), tap or click the Font arrow (Symbol dialog box) and then scroll to and tap or click (normal text) to select this font.
- If the subset in the Subset box is not General Punctuation, tap or click the Subset arrow and then scroll and tap or click General Punctuation to select this subset.
- In the list of symbols, if necessary, scroll to the dot symbol shown in Figure 3–30 and then tap or click the symbol to select it.
- Tap or click the Insert button (Symbol dialog box) to place the selected symbol in the document to the left of the insertion point (Figure 3–30).

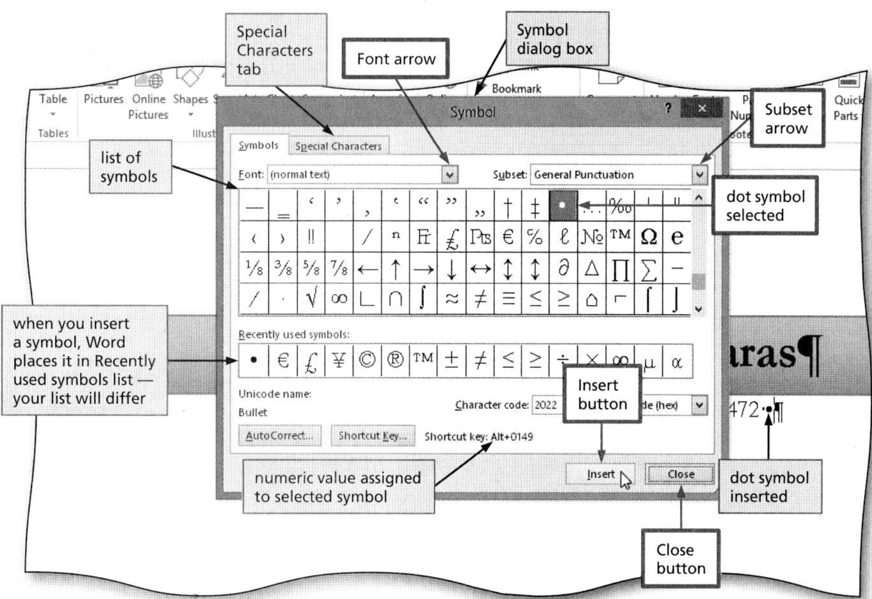

Figure 3–30

Q&A Why is the Symbol dialog box still open?
The Symbol dialog box remains open, allowing you to insert additional symbols.

- Tap or click the Close button (Symbol dialog box) to close the dialog box.

To Insert a Symbol from the Insert a Symbol Gallery

1 CREATE & FORMAT LETTERHEAD WITH GRAPHICS | 2 SPECIFY LETTER FORMATS
3 INSERT TABLE | 4 FORMAT TABLE | 5 INSERT BULLETED LIST | 6 ADDRESS ENVELOPE

In the letterhead, another dot symbol separates the phone number from the email address. The following steps use the Insert a Symbol gallery to insert a dot symbol between the phone number and email address. ***Why?*** *Once you insert a symbol using the Symbol dialog box, Word adds that symbol to the Insert a Symbol gallery so that it is more readily available.*

- Press the SPACEBAR, type `Phone: (873) 555-3928` and then press the SPACEBAR.

- Tap or click the 'Insert a Symbol' button (INSERT tab | Symbols group) to display the Insert a Symbol gallery (Figure 3–31).

Q&A Why is the dot symbol now in the Insert a Symbol gallery?
When you insert a symbol from the Symbol dialog box, Word automatically adds the symbol to the Insert a Symbol gallery.

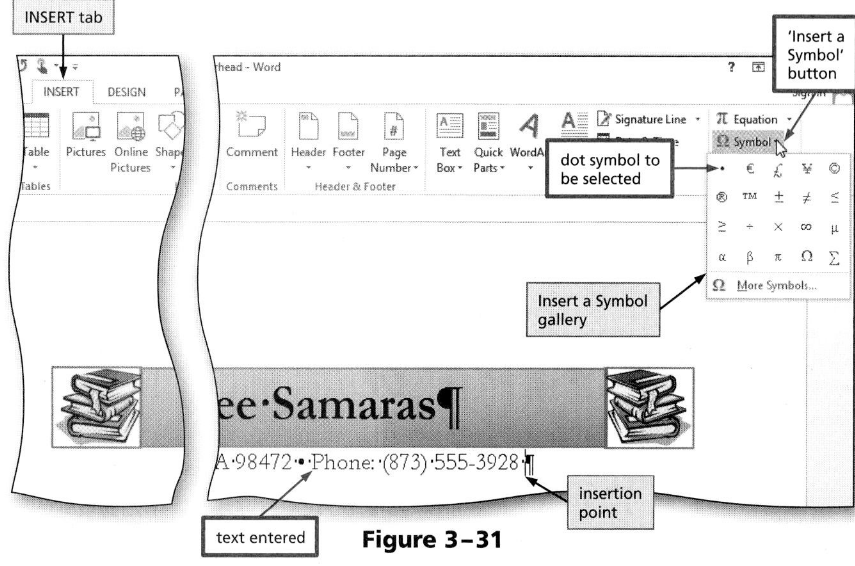

Figure 3–31

3

- Tap or click the dot symbol in the Insert a Symbol gallery to insert the symbol at the location of the insertion point (shown in Figure 3–32 on the next page).

BTW
Inserting Special Characters
In addition to symbols, you can insert a variety of special characters, including dashes, hyphens, spaces, apostrophes, and quotation marks. Tap or click the Special Characters tab in the Symbols dialog box (Figure 3–30 on the previous page), tap or click the desired character in the Character list, tap or click the Insert button, and then tap or click the Close button.

To Enter Text

The following steps enter the email address in the letterhead.

1. Press the SPACEBAR.
2. Type **`Email: samaras@earth.net`** to finish the text in the letterhead (Figure 3–32).

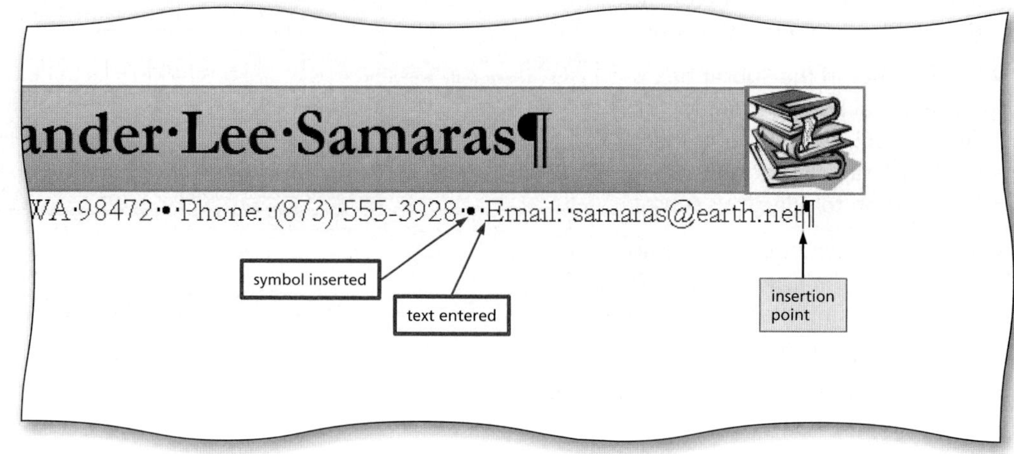

Figure 3–32

To Bottom Border a Paragraph

1 CREATE & FORMAT LETTERHEAD WITH GRAPHICS | 2 SPECIFY LETTER FORMATS
3 INSERT TABLE | 4 FORMAT TABLE | 5 INSERT BULLETED LIST | 6 ADDRESS ENVELOPE

In Word, you can draw a solid line, called a **border**, at any edge of a paragraph. That is, borders may be added above or below a paragraph, to the left or right of a paragraph, or in any combination of these sides.

The letterhead in this project has a border that extends from the left margin to the right margin immediately below the address, phone, and email address information. ***Why?*** *The horizontal line separates the letterhead from the rest of the letter.* The following steps add a bottom border to a paragraph.

1
- Display the HOME tab.
- With the insertion point in the paragraph to border, tap or click the Borders arrow (HOME tab | Paragraph group) to display the Borders gallery (Figure 3–33).

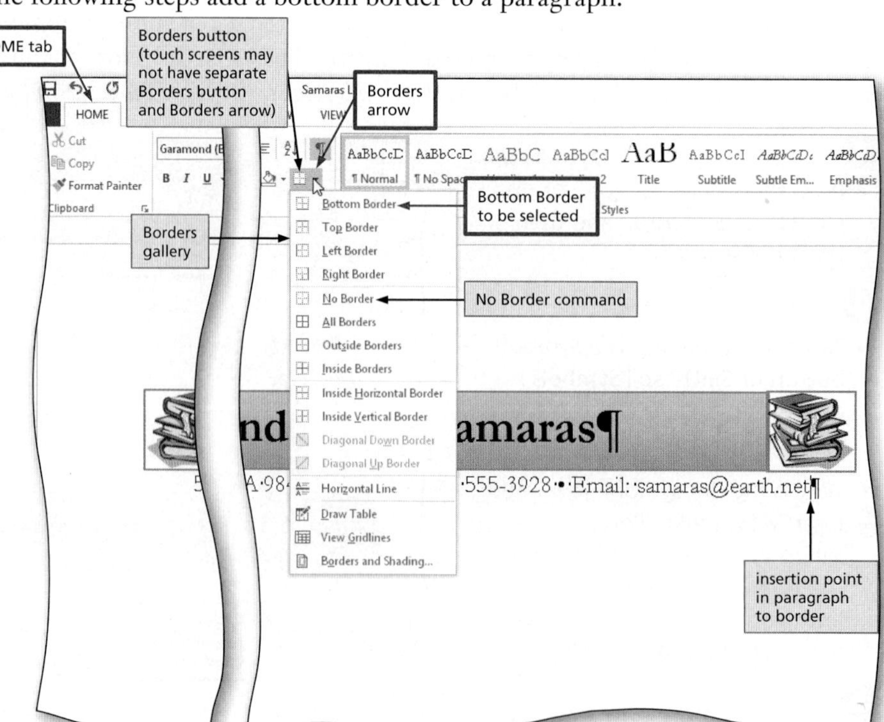

Figure 3–33

- Tap or click Bottom Border in the Borders gallery to place a border below the paragraph containing the insertion point (Figure 3–34).

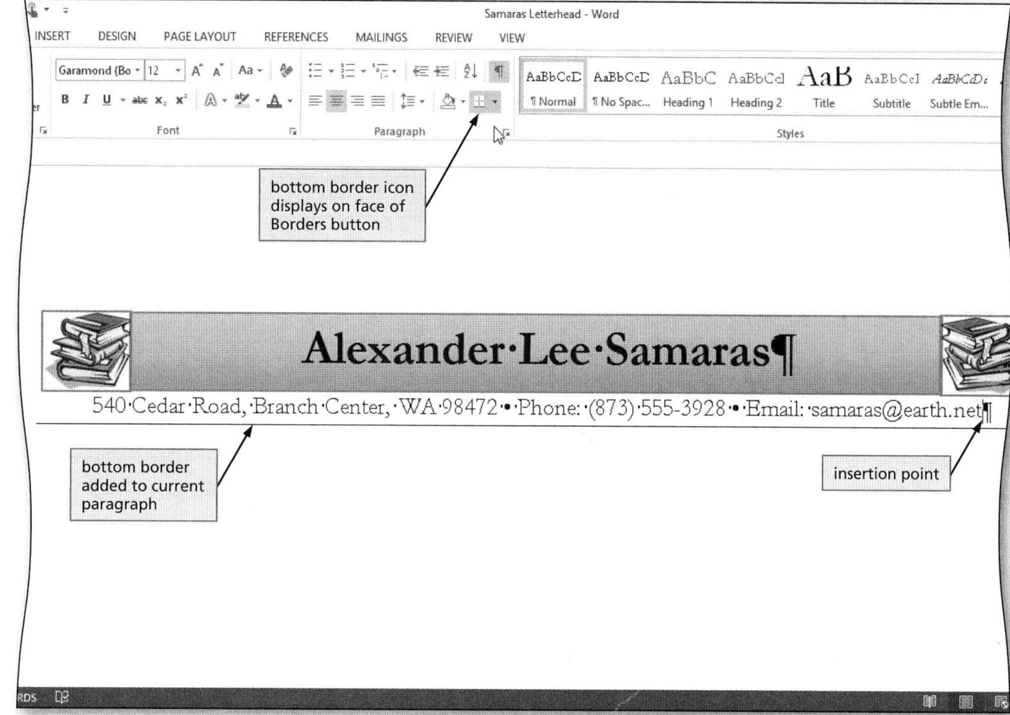

Figure 3–34

Q&A

If the face of the Borders button displays the border icon I want to use and if I am using a mouse, can I click the Borders button instead of using the Borders arrow?

Yes.

How would I remove an existing border from a paragraph?

If, for some reason, you wanted to remove a border from a paragraph, you would position the insertion point in the paragraph, tap or click the Borders arrow (HOME tab | Paragraph group), and then tap or click No Border in the Borders gallery.

Other Ways

1. Tap or click 'Borders and Shading' button (DESIGN tab | Page Background group), tap or click Borders tab (Borders and Shading dialog box), select desired border options, tap or click OK button

To Clear Formatting

1 CREATE & FORMAT LETTERHEAD WITH GRAPHICS | **2 SPECIFY LETTER FORMATS**
3 INSERT TABLE | **4 FORMAT TABLE** | **5 INSERT BULLETED LIST** | **6 ADDRESS ENVELOPE**

The next step is to position the insertion point below the letterhead, so that you can type the contents of the letter. When you press the ENTER key at the end of a paragraph containing a border, Word moves the border forward to the next paragraph. The paragraph also retains all current settings, such as the center format. Instead, you want the paragraph and characters on the new line to use the Normal style: black font with no border.

Word uses the term, **clear formatting**, to refer to returning the formats to the Normal style. The following steps clear formatting at the location of the insertion point. ***Why?*** *You do not want to retain the current formatting in the new paragraph.*

- With the insertion point between the email address and paragraph mark at the end of the contact information line (as shown in Figure 3–34 on the previous page), press the ENTER key to move the insertion point and paragraph to the next line (Figure 3–35).

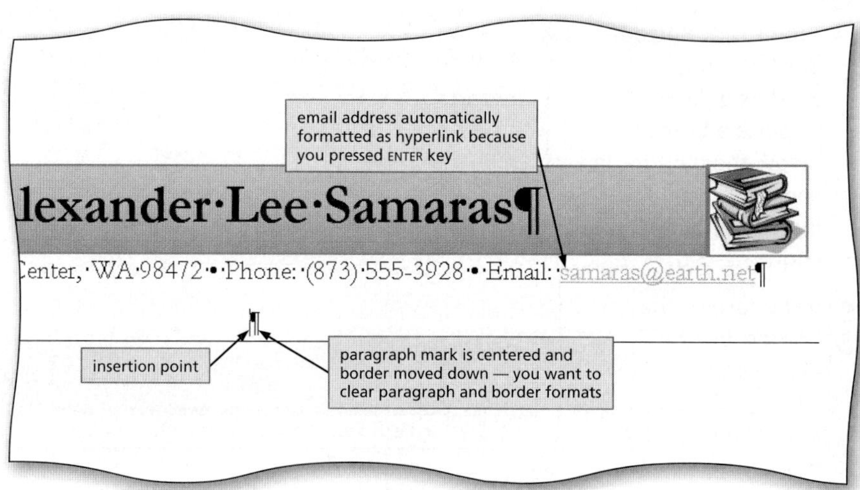

Figure 3–35

2

- Tap or click the 'Clear All Formatting' button (HOME tab | Font group) to apply the Normal style to the location of the insertion point (Figure 3–36).

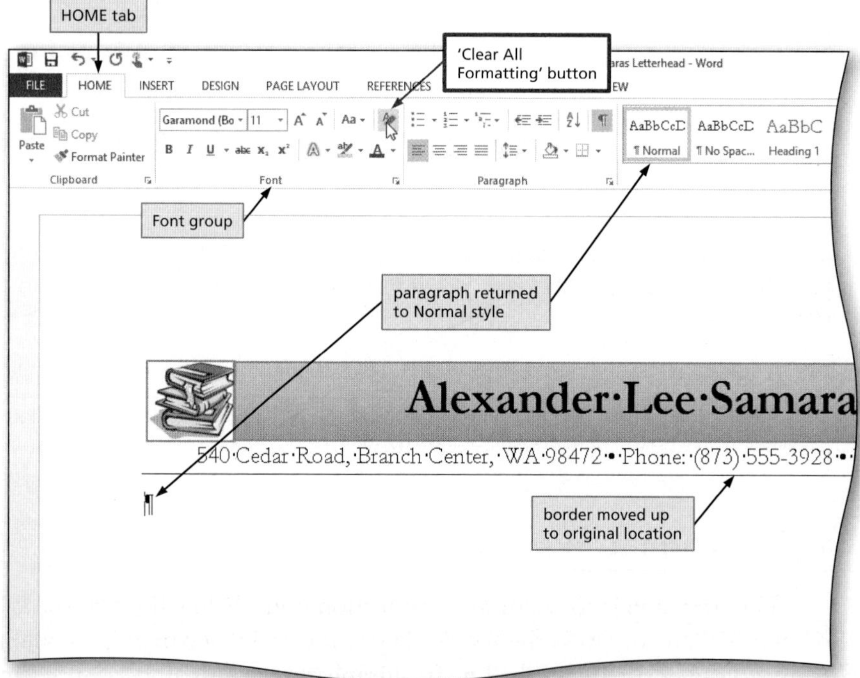

Figure 3–36

Other Ways

1. Tap or click More button in Styles gallery (HOME tab | Styles group), tap or click Clear Formatting
2. Tap or click Styles Dialog Box Launcher (HOME tab | Styles group), tap or click Clear All in Styles task pane
3. Select text, press CTRL+SPACEBAR, press CTRL+Q

AutoFormat as You Type

As you type text in a document, Word automatically formats some of it for you. For example, when you press the ENTER key or SPACEBAR after typing an email address or web address, Word automatically formats the address as a hyperlink, that is, in a different color and underlined. In Figure 3–35, for example, Word formatted the email address as a hyperlink because you pressed the ENTER key at the end of the line. Table 3–2 outlines commonly used AutoFormat As You Type options and their results.

Table 3–2 Commonly Used AutoFormat As You Type Options

Typed Text	AutoFormat Feature	Example
Quotation marks or apostrophes	Changes straight quotation marks or apostrophes to curly ones	"the" becomes “the”
Text, a space, one hyphen, one or no spaces, text, space	Changes the hyphen to an en dash	ages 20-45 becomes ages 20–45
Text, two hyphens, text, space	Changes the two hyphens to an em dash	Two types--yellow and red becomes Two types—yellow and red
Web or email address followed by SPACEBAR or ENTER key	Formats web or email address as a hyperlink	www.cengagebrain.com becomes www.cengagebrain.com
Number followed by a period, hyphen, right parenthesis, or greater than sign and then a space or tab followed by text	Creates a numbered list	1. Word 2. PowerPoint becomes 1. Word 2. PowerPoint
Asterisk, hyphen, or greater than sign and then a space or tab followed by text	Creates a bulleted list	* HOME tab * INSERT tab becomes • HOME tab • INSERT tab
Fraction and then a space or hyphen	Condenses the fraction entry so that it consumes one space instead of three	1/2 becomes ½
Ordinal and then a space or hyphen	Makes part of the ordinal a superscript	3rd becomes 3rd

To Convert a Hyperlink to Regular Text

1 CREATE & FORMAT LETTERHEAD WITH GRAPHICS | 2 SPECIFY LETTER FORMATS
3 INSERT TABLE | 4 FORMAT TABLE | 5 INSERT BULLETED LIST | 6 ADDRESS ENVELOPE

The email address in the letterhead should be formatted as regular text; that is, it should not be a different color or underlined. ***Why?*** *Hyperlinks are useful only in online documents, and this letter will be printed instead of distributed electronically.* The following steps remove a hyperlink format.

- If you are using a touch screen, press and hold the hyperlink and then tap the 'Show Context Menu' button on the mini toolbar; if you are using a mouse, right-click the hyperlink (in this case, the email address) to display a shortcut menu (Figure 3–37).

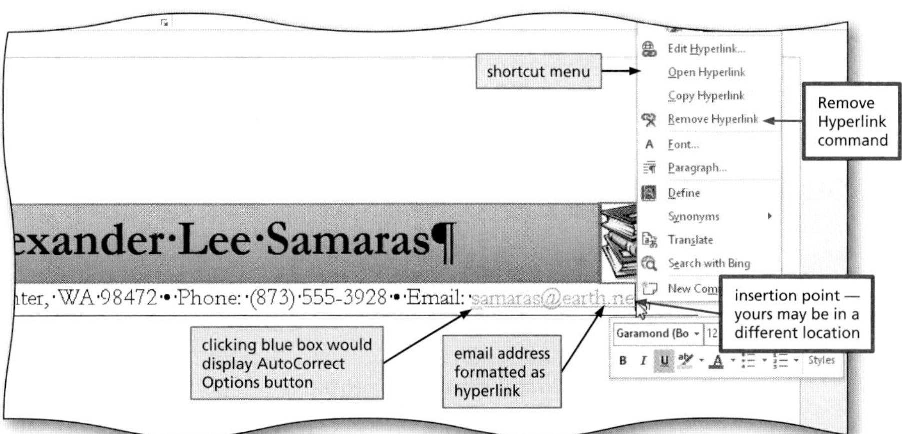

Figure 3–37

2

- Tap or click Remove Hyperlink on the shortcut menu to remove the hyperlink format from the text.
- Position the insertion point on the paragraph mark below the border because you are finished with the letterhead (Figure 3–38).

Q&A Could I have used the AutoCorrect Options button instead of the Remove Hyperlink command?
Yes. Alternatively, if you are using a mouse, you could have pointed to the small blue box at the beginning of the hyperlink, clicked the AutoCorrect Options button, and then clicked Undo Hyperlink on the AutoCorrect Options menu.

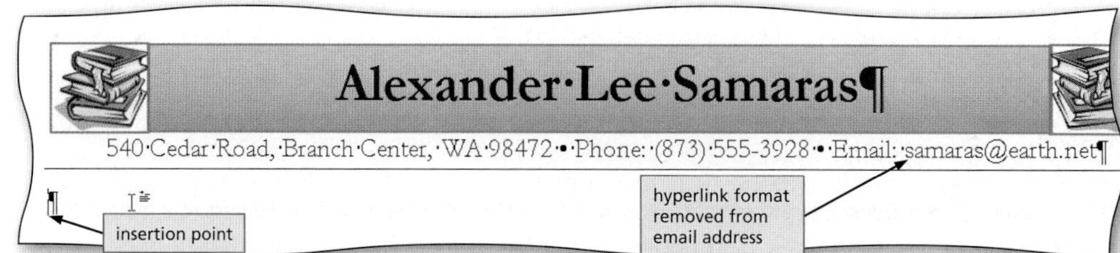

Figure 3–38

Other Ways

1. With insertion point in hyperlink, tap or click 'Add a Hyperlink' button (INSERT tab | Links group), tap or click Remove Link button

To Save an Existing Document with the Same File Name

You have made several modifications to the letterhead since you last saved it. Thus, you should save it again. The following step saves the document again. For an example of the step listed below, refer to the Office and Windows chapter at the beginning of this book.

 Tap or click the Save button on the Quick Access Toolbar to overwrite the previously saved file.

Break Point: If you wish to take a break, this is a good place to do so. You can exit Word now. To resume at a later time, run Word, open the file called Samaras Letterhead, and continue following the steps from this location forward.

Creating a Business Letter

With the letterhead for the business letter complete, the next task is to create the remainder of the content in the letter. The following pages use Word to create a business letter that contains a table and a bulleted list.

CONSIDER THIS

What should you consider when writing a business letter?

A finished business letter should look like a symmetrically framed picture with evenly spaced margins, all balanced below an attractive letterhead. The letter should be well written, properly formatted, logically organized, and use visuals where appropriate. The content of a letter should contain proper grammar, correct spelling, logically constructed sentences, flowing paragraphs, and sound ideas.

Be sure to include all essential elements, use proper spacing and formats, and determine which letter style to use.

- **Include all essential letter elements.** All business letters contain the same basic elements, including the date line, inside address, message, and signature block (shown in Figure 3–1 on page WD 139). If a business letter does not use a letterhead, then the top of the letter should include return address information in a heading.
- **Use proper spacing and formats for the contents of the letter below the letterhead.** Use a font that is easy to read, in a size between 8 and 12 point. Add emphasis with bold, italic, and bullets where appropriate, and use tables to present numeric information. Paragraphs should be single-spaced, with double-spacing between paragraphs.
- **Determine which letter style to use.** You can follow many different styles when creating business letters. A letter style specifies guidelines for the alignment and spacing of elements in the business letter.

If possible, keep the length of a business letter to one page. Be sure to proofread the finished letter carefully.

To Save a Document with a New File Name

The current open file has the name Samaras Letterhead, which is the name of the personal letterhead. Because you want the letterhead file to remain intact so that you can reuse it, you save the document with a new name. The following steps save a document with a new name.

1. Tap or click FILE on the ribbon to open the Backstage view and then tap or click the Save As tab in the Backstage view, which depending on settings, will display either the Save As gallery in the Backstage view or the Save As dialog box.
2. To save on a hard disk or other storage media on your computer, proceed to Step 2a. To save on SkyDrive, proceed to Step 2b.

2a. If your screen opens the Backstage view and you want to save on storage media on your computer, tap or click Computer in the left pane, if necessary, to display options in the right pane related to saving on your computer. If your screen already displays the Save As dialog box, proceed to Step 4.

2b. If your screen opens the Backstage view and you want to save on SkyDrive, tap or click SkyDrive in the left pane to display SkyDrive saving options or a Sign In button. If your screen displays a Sign In button, tap or click it and then sign in to SkyDrive.

3. Tap or click the Browse button in the right pane to display the Save As dialog box associated with the selected save location (i.e., Computer or SkyDrive).
4. Type `Samaras Thank You Letter` in the File name box to change the file name. Do not press the ENTER key after typing the file name because you do not want to close the dialog box at this time.
5. Navigate to the desired save location (in this case, the Word folder in the CIS 101 folder [or your class folder] on your computer or SkyDrive).
6. Tap or click the Save button (Save As dialog box) to save the letter in the selected folder on the selected save location with the entered file name.

BTW

Saving a Template

As an alternative to saving the letterhead as a Word document, you could save it as a template. To do so, tap or click FILE on the ribbon to open the Backstage view, tap or click the Export tab to display the Export gallery, tap or click 'Change File Type', tap or click Template in the right pane, tap or click the Save As button, enter the template name (Save As dialog box), if necessary select the Templates folder, and then tap or click the Save button in the dialog box. To use the template, tap or click FILE on the ribbon to open the Backstage view, tap or click the New tab to display the New gallery, tap or click the Personal tab in the New gallery, and then tap or click the template icon or name.

To Apply a Style

Recall that the Normal style in Word places 8 points of blank space after each paragraph and inserts a vertical space equal to 1.08 lines between each line of text. You will need to modify the spacing used for the paragraphs in the business letter. ***Why?*** *Business letters should use single spacing for paragraphs and double spacing between paragraphs.*

Word has many built-in, or predefined, styles that you can use to format text. The No Spacing style, for example, defines line spacing as single and does not insert any additional blank space between lines when you press the ENTER key. To apply a style to a paragraph, you first position the insertion point in the paragraph. The following step applies the No Spacing style to a paragraph.

1

- With the insertion point positioned in the paragraph to be formatted, tap or click No Spacing in the Styles gallery (HOME tab | Styles group) to apply the selected style to the current paragraph (Figure 3–39).

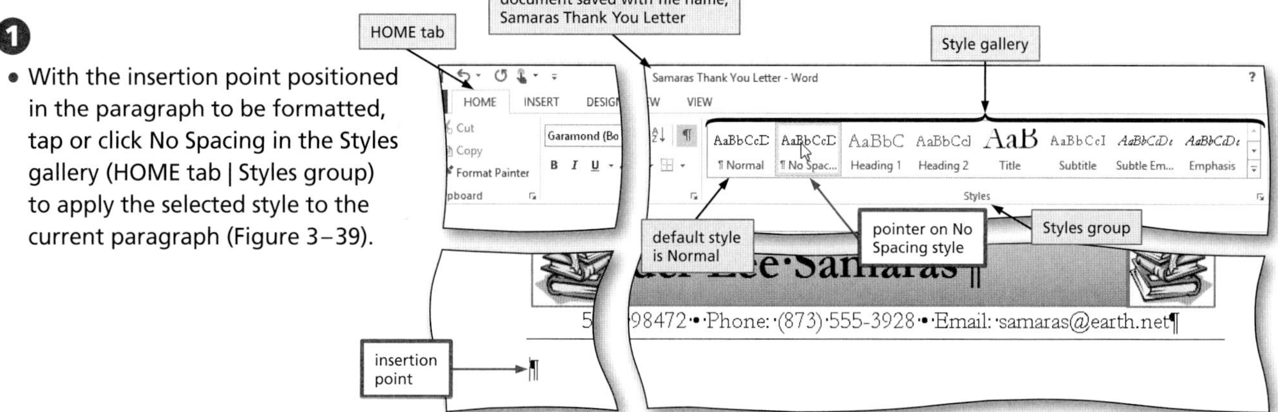

Figure 3–39

Q&A

Will this style be used in the rest of the document?

Yes. The paragraph formatting, which includes the style, will carry forward to subsequent paragraphs each time you press the ENTER key.

Other Ways

1. Tap or click Styles Dialog Box Launcher (HOME tab | Styles group), tap or click desired style in Styles task pane
2. Press CTRL+SHIFT+S, tap or click Style Name arrow in Apply Styles task pane, tap or click desired style in list

CONSIDER THIS

What elements should a business letter contain?

Be sure to include all essential business letter elements, properly spaced, in your letter:

- The **date line**, which consists of the month, day, and year, is positioned two to six lines below the letterhead.
- The **inside address**, placed three to eight lines below the date line, usually contains the addressee's courtesy title plus full name, job title, business affiliation, and full geographical address.
- The **salutation**, if present, begins two lines below the last line of the inside address. If you do not know the recipient's name, avoid using the salutation "To whom it may concern" — it is impersonal. Instead, use the recipient's title in the salutation, e.g., Dear Personnel Director. In a business letter, use a colon (:) at the end of the salutation; in a personal letter, use a comma.
- The body of the letter, the **message**, begins two lines below the salutation. Within the message, paragraphs are single-spaced with one blank line between paragraphs.
- Two lines below the last line of the message, the **complimentary close** is displayed. Capitalize only the first word in a complimentary close.
- Type the **signature block** at least four blank lines below the complimentary close, allowing room for the author to sign his or her name.

CONSIDER THIS

What are the common styles of business letters?

Three common business letter styles are the block, the modified block, and the modified semi-block. Each style specifies different alignments and indentations.

- In the block letter style, all components of the letter begin flush with the left margin.
- In the modified block letter style, the date, complimentary close, and signature block are positioned approximately one-half inch to the right of center or at the right margin. All other components of the letter begin flush with the left margin.
- In the modified semi-block letter style, the date, complimentary close, and signature block are centered, positioned approximately one-half inch to the right of center or at the right margin. The first line of each paragraph in the body of the letter is indented one-half to one inch from the left margin. All other components of the letter begin flush with the left margin.

The business letter in this project follows the modified block style.

Using Tab Stops to Align Text

A **tab stop** is a location on the horizontal ruler that tells Word where to position the insertion point when you press the TAB key on the keyboard. Word, by default, places a tab stop at every one-half inch mark on the ruler. You also can set your own custom tab stops. Tab settings are a paragraph format. Thus, each time you press the ENTER key, any custom tab stops are carried forward to the next paragraph.

To move the insertion point from one tab stop to another, press the TAB key on the keyboard. When you press the TAB key, a **tab character** formatting mark appears in the empty space between the tab stops.

When you set a custom tab stop, you specify how the text will align at a tab stop. The tab marker on the ruler reflects the alignment of the characters at the location of the tab stop. Table 3–3 shows types of tab stop alignments in Word and their corresponding tab markers.

Table 3–3 Types of Tab Stop Alignments

Tab Stop Alignment	Tab Marker	Result of Pressing TAB Key	Example
Left Tab	∟	Left-aligns text at the location of the tab stop	toolbar ruler
Center Tab	⊥	Centers text at the location of the tab stop	toolbar ruler
Right Tab	┘	Right-aligns text at the location of the tab stop	toolbar ruler
Decimal Tab	⊥:	Aligns text on decimal point at the location of the tab stop	45.72 223.75
Bar Tab	I	Aligns text at a bar character at the location of the tab stop	| toolbar | ruler

To Display the Ruler

If you are using a mouse, one way to set custom tab stops is by using the horizontal ruler. Thus, the following steps display the ruler in the document window.

1. If the rulers are not showing, display the VIEW tab.
2. Tap or click the View Ruler check box (VIEW tab | Show group) to place a check mark in the check box and display the horizontal and vertical rulers on the screen (shown in Figure 3–40).

To Set Custom Tab Stops

The first required element of the business letter is the date line, which in this letter is positioned two lines below the letterhead. The date line contains the month, day, and year, and begins four inches from the left margin. ***Why?*** *Business letter guidelines specify to begin the date line approximately one-half inch to the right of center. Thus, you should set a custom tab stop at the 4" mark on the ruler.* The following steps set a left-aligned tab stop.

1

- With the insertion point on the paragraph mark below the border (shown in Figure 3–39 on page WD 165), press the ENTER key so that a blank line appears above the insertion point.
- If you are using a touch screen, proceed to Step 3 on the next page because you have to use a different method to set custom tabs.
- If you are using a mouse, if necessary, click the tab selector at the left edge of the horizontal ruler until it displays the type of tab you wish to use, which is the Left Tab icon in this case.
- If you are using a mouse, position the pointer on the 4" mark on the ruler, which is the location of the desired custom tab stop (Figure 3–40).

Q&A What is the purpose of the tab selector?
Before using the ruler to set a tab stop, ensure the correct tab stop icon appears in the tab selector. Each time you click the tab selector, its icon changes. The Left Tab icon is the default. For a list of the types of tab stops, see Table 3–3.

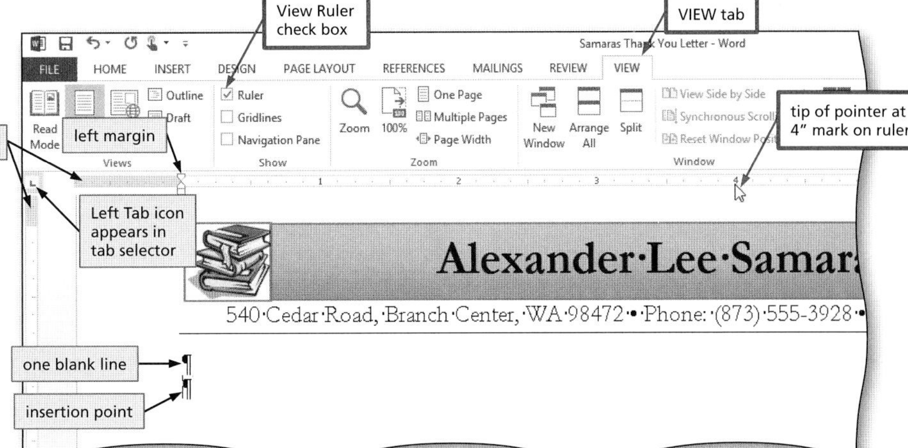

Figure 3–40

- If you are using a mouse, click the 4" mark on the ruler to place a tab marker at that location (Figure 3–41).

Q&A What if I click the wrong location on the ruler?

You can move a custom tab stop by dragging the tab marker to the desired location on the ruler. Or, you can remove an existing custom tab stop by pointing to the tab marker on the ruler and then dragging the tab marker down and out of the ruler.

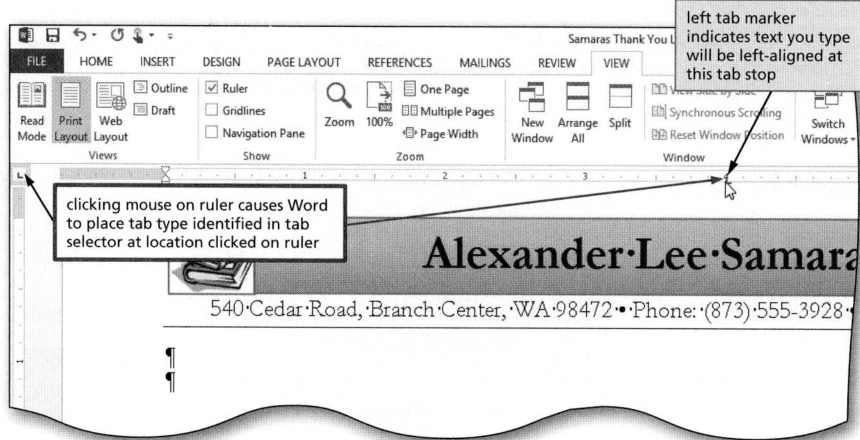

Figure 3–41

- If you are using a touch screen, display the HOME tab, tap the Paragraph Settings Dialog Box Launcher (HOME tab | Paragraph group), tap the Tabs button (Paragraph dialog box), type `4` in the Tab stop position box (Tabs dialog box), tap the Set button, and then tap the OK button to set a custom tab stop and place a corresponding tab marker on the ruler.

Other Ways

1. Tap or click Paragraph Dialog Box Launcher (HOME tab or PAGE LAYOUT tab | Paragraph group), tap or click Tabs button (Paragraph dialog box), type tab stop position (Tabs dialog box), tap or click Set button, tap or click OK button

To Insert the Current Date in a Document

1 CREATE & FORMAT LETTERHEAD WITH GRAPHICS | 2 SPECIFY LETTER FORMATS
3 INSERT TABLE | 4 FORMAT TABLE | 5 INSERT BULLETED LIST | 6 ADDRESS ENVELOPE

The next step is to enter the current date at the 4" tab stop in the document. ***Why?*** *The date in this letter will be positioned according to the guidelines for a modified block style letter.* In Word, you can insert a computer's system date in a document. The following steps insert the current date in the letter.

- Press the TAB key to position the insertion point at the location of the tab stop in the current paragraph.
- Display the INSERT tab.
- Tap or click the 'Insert Date and Time' button (INSERT tab | Text group) to display the Date and Time dialog box.
- Select the desired format (Date and Time dialog box), in this case October 29, 2014.
- If the Update automatically check box is selected, tap or click the check box to remove the check mark (Figure 3–42).

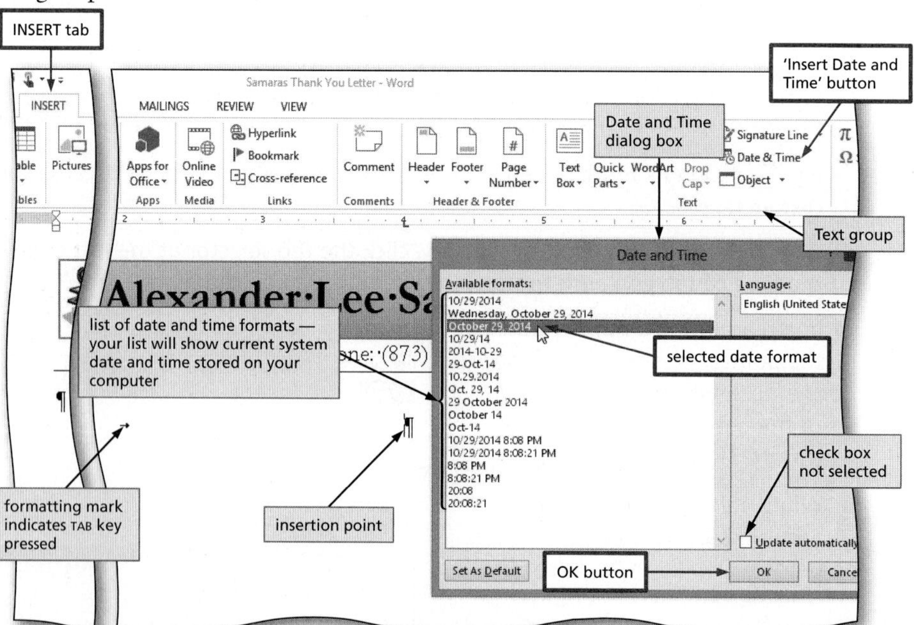

Figure 3–42

Q&A Why should the Update automatically check box not be selected?

In this project, the date at the top of the letter always should show today's date (for example, October 29, 2014). If, however, you wanted the date always to change to reflect the current computer date (for example, showing the date you open or print the letter), then you would place a check mark in this check box.

2

- Tap or click the OK button to insert the current date at the location of the insertion point (Figure 3–43).

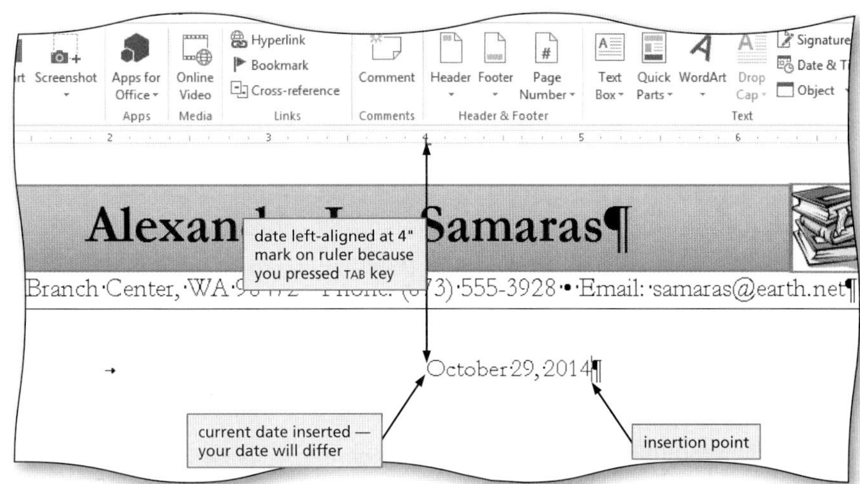

Figure 3–43

To Enter the Inside Address and Salutation

The next step in composing the business letter is to type the inside address and salutation. The following steps enter this text.

1. With the insertion point at the end of the date (shown in Figure 3–43), press the ENTER key three times.
2. Type **`Ms. Lucy Song`** and then press the ENTER key.
3. Type **`Washington Volunteer Foundation`** and then press the ENTER key.
4. Type **`10 Hickory Avenue`** and then press the ENTER key.
5. Type **`Midway, WA 98476`** and then press the ENTER key twice.
6. Type **`Dear Ms. Song:`** to complete the inside address and salutation entries (Figure 3–44).

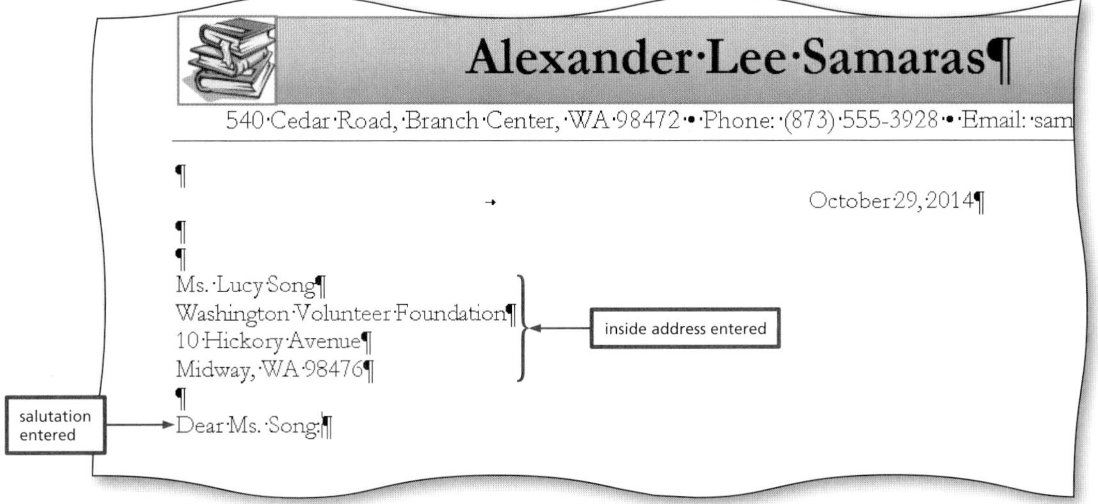

Figure 3–44

BTW

Tabs Dialog Box

You can use the Tabs dialog box to set, change the alignment of, and remove custom tab stops. To display the Tabs dialog box, tap or click the Paragraph Settings Dialog Box Launcher (HOME tab or PAGE LAYOUT tab | Paragraph group) and then tap or click the Tabs button (Paragraph dialog box). To set a custom tab stop, enter the desired tab position (Tabs dialog box) and then tap or click the Set button. To change the alignment of a custom tab stop, tap or click the tab stop position to be changed, tap or click the new alignment, and then tap or click the Set button. To remove an existing tab stop, tap or click the tab stop position to be removed and then tap or click the Clear button. To remove all tab stops, tap or click the Clear All button in the Tabs dialog box.

To Create a Building Block

1 CREATE & FORMAT LETTERHEAD WITH GRAPHICS | 2 SPECIFY LETTER FORMATS
3 INSERT TABLE | 4 FORMAT TABLE | 5 INSERT BULLETED LIST | 6 ADDRESS ENVELOPE

If you use the same text or graphic frequently, you can store the text or graphic as a **building block** and then insert the stored building block entry in the open document, as well as in future documents. That is, you can create the entry once as a building block and then insert the building block when you need it. In this way, you avoid entering text or graphics inconsistently or incorrectly in different locations throughout the same or multiple documents.

The following steps create a building block for the volunteer organization name, Washington Volunteer Foundation. ***Why?*** *Later, you will insert the building block in the document instead of typing the volunteer organization name.*

1

- Select the text to be a building block, in this case Washington Volunteer Foundation. Do not select the paragraph mark at the end of the text because you do not want the paragraph to be part of the building block.

Q&A Why is the paragraph mark not part of the building block?
Select the paragraph mark only if you want to store paragraph formatting, such as indentation and line spacing, as part of the building block.

- Tap or click the 'Explore Quick Parts' button (INSERT tab | Text group) to display the Explore Quick Parts gallery (Figure 3–45).

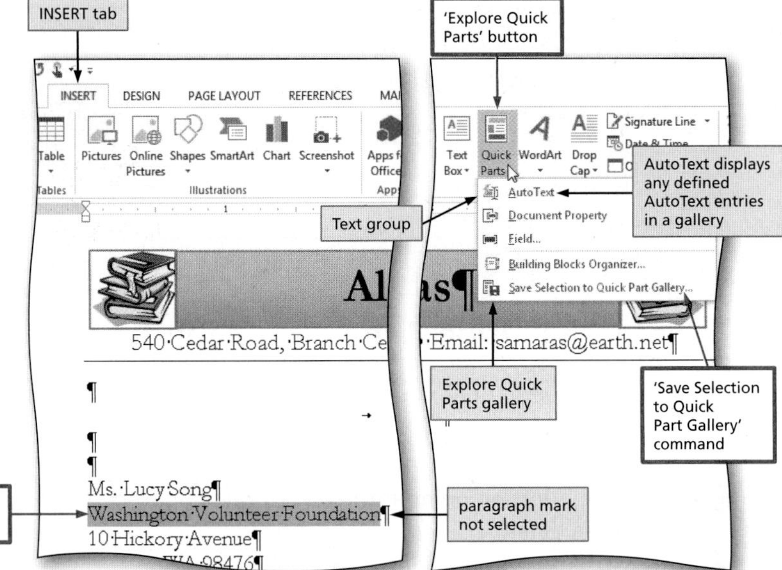

Figure 3–45

2

- Tap or click 'Save Selection to Quick Part Gallery' in the Explore Quick Parts gallery to display the Create New Building Block dialog box.
- Type **wvf** in the Name text box (Create New Building Block dialog box) to replace the proposed building block name (Washington, in this case) with a shorter building block name (Figure 3–46).

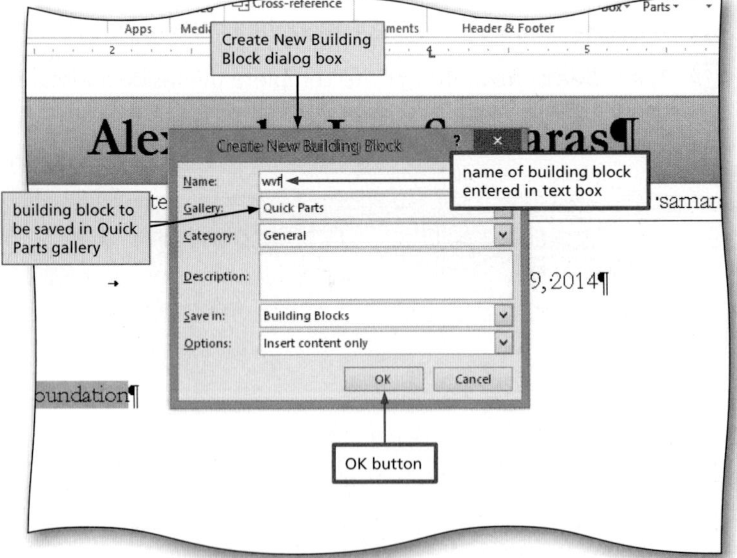

Figure 3–46

3

- Tap or click the OK button to store the building block entry and close the dialog box.
- If Word displays another dialog box, tap or click the Yes button to save changes to the building blocks.

Q&A Will this building block be available in future documents?
When you exit Word, a dialog box may appear asking if you want to save changes to the building blocks. Tap or click the Save button if you want to use the new building block in future documents.

Other Ways

1. Select text, press ALT+F3

To Modify a Building Block

When you save a building block in the Explore Quick Parts gallery, the building block is displayed at the top of the Explore Quick Parts gallery. When you point to the building block in the Explore Quick Parts gallery, a ScreenTip displays the building block name. If you want to display more information when the user points to the building block, you can include a description in the ScreenTip.

The following steps modify a building block to include a description and change its category to AutoText. ***Why?*** *Because you want to reuse this text, you place it in the AutoText gallery, which also is accessible through the Explore Quick Parts gallery.*

1

- Tap or click the 'Explore Quick Parts' button (INSERT tab | Text group) to display the Explore Quick Parts gallery.
- Press and hold or right-click the Washington Volunteer Foundation building block to display a shortcut menu (Figure 3–47).

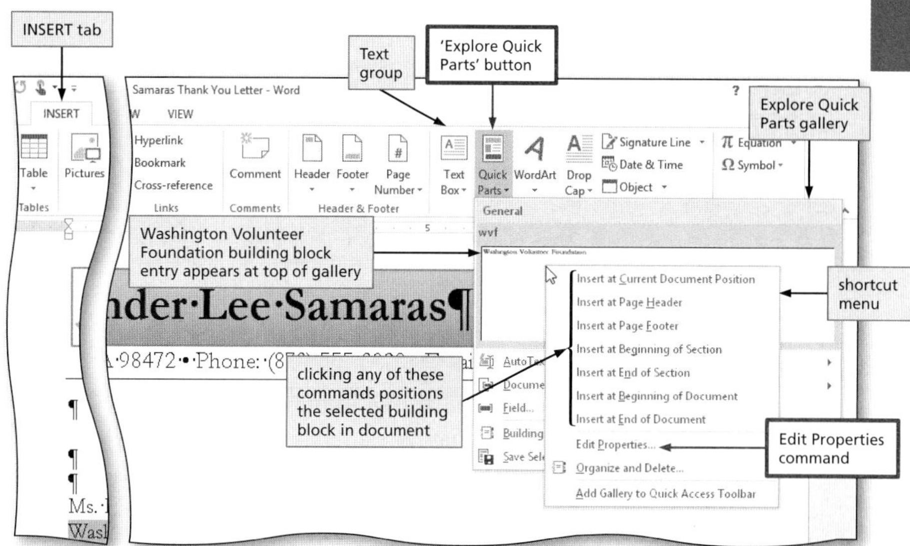

Figure 3–47

2

- Tap or click Edit Properties on the shortcut menu to display the Modify Building Block dialog box, filled in with information related to the selected building block.
- Tap or click the Gallery arrow (Modify Building Block dialog box) and then tap or click AutoText to change the gallery in which the building block will be placed.
- Type `Potential Volunteer Opportunity` in the Description text box (Figure 3–48).

3

- Tap or click the OK button to store the building block entry and close the dialog box.
- Tap or click the Yes button when asked if you want to redefine the building block entry.

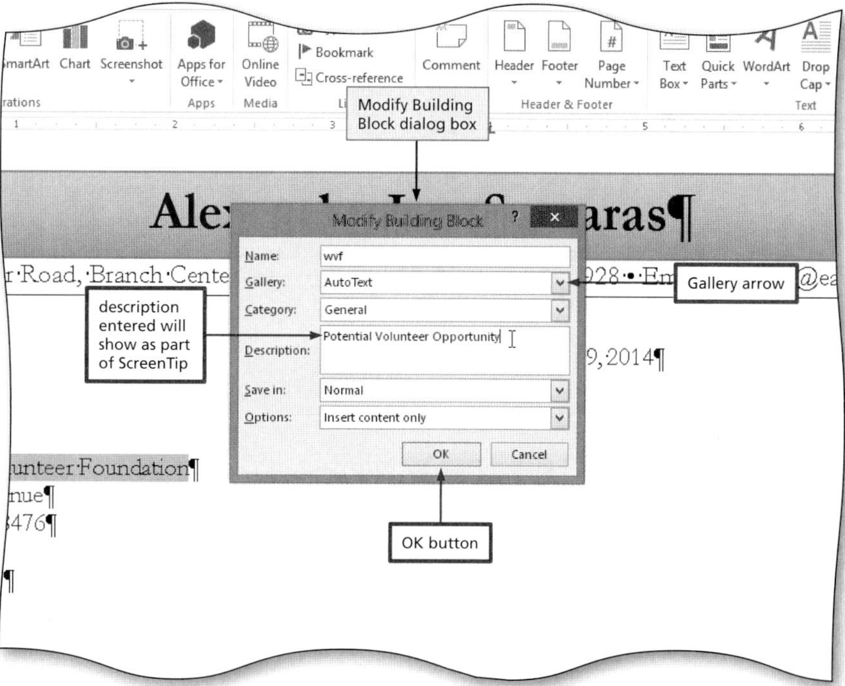

Figure 3–48

To Insert a Building Block

The prospective volunteer organization, Washington Volunteer Foundation, appears in the first sentence in the body of the letter. You will type the building block name, wvf, and then instruct Word to replace this building block name with the stored building block entry, Washington Volunteer Foundation. The following steps insert a building block. ***Why?*** *Instead of typing the name, you will insert the stored building block.*

- Tap or click to the right of the colon in the salutation and then press the ENTER key twice to position the insertion point one blank line below the salutation.
- Type the beginning of the first sentence as follows, entering the building block name as shown: **Thank you for meeting with me this morning to discuss the mentoring position available at wvf** (Figure 3–49).

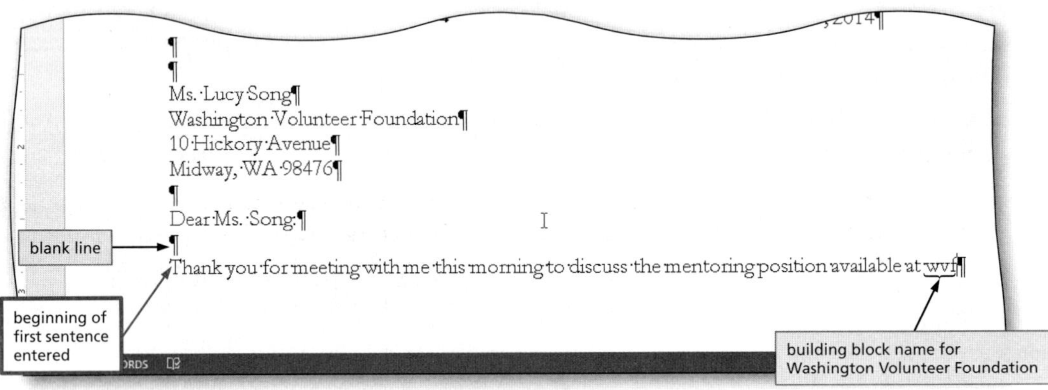

Figure 3–49

- Press the F3 key to instruct Word to replace the building block name (wvf) with the stored building block entry (Washington Volunteer Foundation).
- Press the PERIOD key (Figure 3–50).

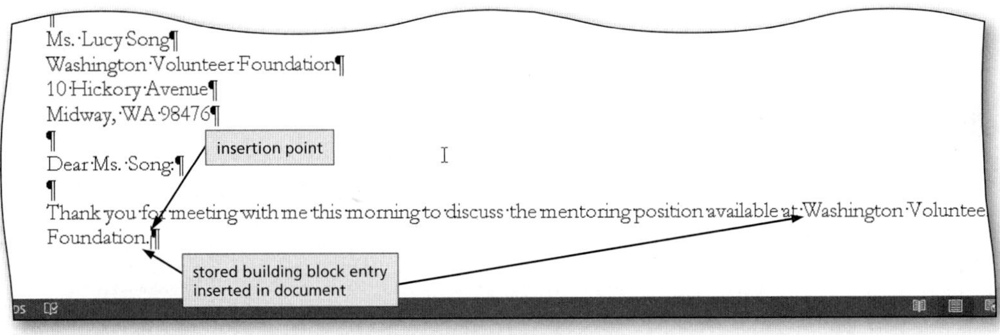

Figure 3–50

Other Ways

1. Tap or click 'Explore Quick Parts' button (INSERT tab | Text group), if necessary point to AutoText, select desired building block
2. Tap or click 'Explore Quick Parts' button (INSERT tab | Text group), tap or click Building Blocks Organizer, select desired building block, tap or click Insert button

BTW

Certification

The Microsoft Office Specialist (MOS) program provides an opportunity for you to obtain a valuable industry credential — proof that you have the Word 2013 skills required by employers. For more information, visit the Certification resource on the Student Companion Site located on www.cengagebrain.com. For detailed instructions about accessing available resources, visit www.cengage.com/ct/studentdownload or contact your instructor for information about accessing the required files.

Building Blocks versus AutoCorrect

In Chapter 2, you learned how to use the AutoCorrect feature, which enables you to insert and create AutoCorrect entries, similarly to how you created and inserted building blocks in this chapter. The difference between an AutoCorrect entry and a building block entry is that the AutoCorrect feature makes corrections for you automatically as soon as you press the SPACEBAR or type a punctuation mark, whereas you must instruct Word to insert a building block. That is, you enter the building block name and then press the F3 key, or tap or click the Explore Quick Parts button and select the building block from one of the galleries or the Building Blocks Organizer.

To Insert a Nonbreaking Space

Some compound words, such as proper nouns, dates, units of time and measure, abbreviations, and geographic destinations, should not be divided at the end of a line. These words either should fit as a unit at the end of a line or be wrapped together to the next line.

Word provides two special characters to assist with this task: the nonbreaking space and the nonbreaking hyphen. A **nonbreaking space** is a special space character that prevents two words from splitting if the first word falls at the end of a line. Similarly, a **nonbreaking hyphen** is a special type of hyphen that prevents two words separated by a hyphen from splitting at the end of a line.

The following steps insert a nonbreaking space between the two words in the city name, Branch Center. ***Why?*** *You want these two words in the city name to appear on the same physical line.*

- With the insertion point at the end of the first sentence in the body of the letter (as shown in Figure 3–50), press the SPACEBAR.
- Type **`I truly enjoyed our conversation and am excited about the possibility of volunteering with your Branch`** and then press CTRL+SHIFT+SPACEBAR to insert a nonbreaking space after the entered word (Figure 3–51).

nonbreaking space character inserted

Ms.·Song:¶

nk·you·for·meeting·with·me·this·morning·to·discuss·the·mentoring·position·available·at·Washington·Volunteer·
dation.·I·truly·enjoyed·our·conversation·and·am·excited·about·the·possibility·of·volunteering·with·your·Branch°¶

Figure 3–51

2

- Type **`Center team`** and then press PERIOD key (Figure 3–52).

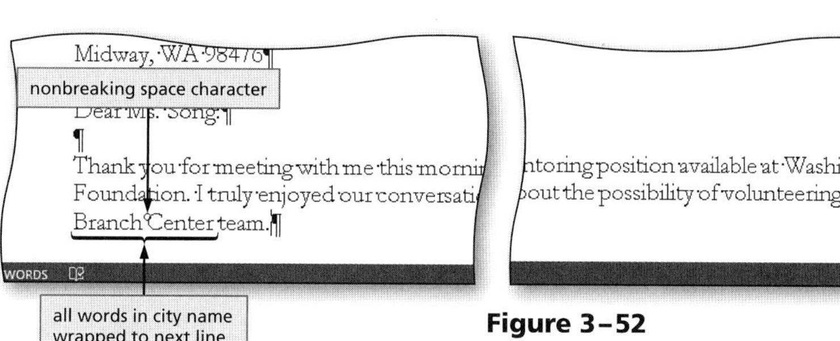

Figure 3–52

Other Ways

1. Tap or click 'Insert a Symbol' button (INSERT tab | Symbols group), tap or click More Symbols, tap or click Special Characters tab (Symbol dialog box), tap or click Nonbreaking Space in Character list, tap or click Insert button, tap or click Close button

To Enter Text

The next step in creating the letter is to enter the rest of the text in the first paragraph. The following steps enter this text.

1. Press the SPACEBAR.
2. Type this sentence: **`The table below outlines my volunteer service background:`**
3. Press the ENTER key twice to place a blank line between paragraphs (shown in Figure 3–53 on the next page).

Q&A Why does my document wrap on different words?

Differences in wordwrap may relate to the printer connected to your computer. Thus, it is possible that the same document could wordwrap differently if associated with a different printer.

BTW

Nonbreaking Hyphen

If you wanted to insert a nonbreaking hyphen, you would press CTRL+SHIFT+HYPHEN.

To Save an Existing Document with the Same File Name

You have made several modifications to the document since you last saved it. Thus, you should save it again. The following step saves the document again.

Tap or click the Save button on the Quick Access Toolbar to overwrite the previously saved file.

Break Point: If you wish to take a break, this is a good place to do so. You can exit Word now. To resume at a later time, run Word, open the file called Samaras Thank You Letter, and continue following the steps from this location forward.

Tables

The next step in composing the business letter is to place a table listing the volunteer service background (shown in Figure 3–1 on page WD 139). A Word **table** is a collection of rows and columns. The intersection of a row and a column is called a **cell**, and cells are filled with data.

The first step in creating a table is to insert an empty table in the document. When inserting a table, you must specify the total number of rows and columns required, which is called the **dimension** of the table. The table in this project has three columns. You often do not know the total number of rows in a table. Thus, many Word users create one row initially and then add more rows as needed. In Word, the first number in a dimension is the number of columns, and the second is the number of rows. For example, in Word, a 3 × 1 (pronounced "three by one") table consists of three columns and one row.

To Insert an Empty Table

1 CREATE & FORMAT LETTERHEAD WITH GRAPHICS | 2 SPECIFY LETTER FORMATS
3 INSERT TABLE | 4 FORMAT TABLE | 5 INSERT BULLETED LIST | 6 ADDRESS ENVELOPE

The next step is to insert an empty table in the letter. The following steps insert a table with three columns and one row at the location of the insertion point. ***Why?*** *The first column will identify the organization, the second will identify the primary responsibility, and the third will identify the term of service in years. You will start with one row and add them as needed.*

- Scroll the document so that you will be able to see the table in the document window.
- Display the INSERT tab.
- With the insertion point positioned as shown in Figure 3–53, tap or click the 'Add a Table' button (INSERT tab | Tables group) to display the Add a Table gallery (Figure 3–53).

Experiment

- If you are using a mouse, point to various cells on the grid to see a preview of various table dimensions in the document window.

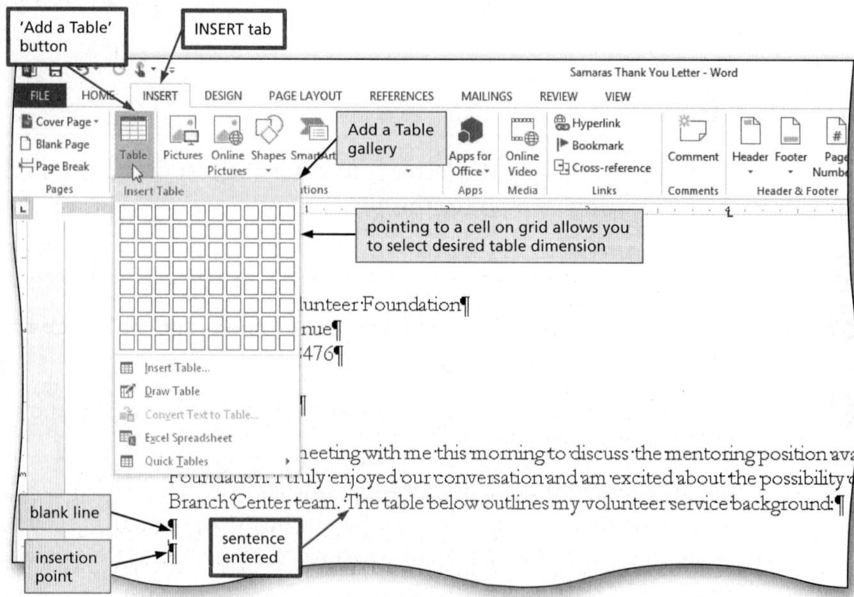

Figure 3–53

2

- If you are using a mouse, position the pointer on the cell in the first row and third column of the grid to preview the desired table dimension in the document (Figure 3–54).

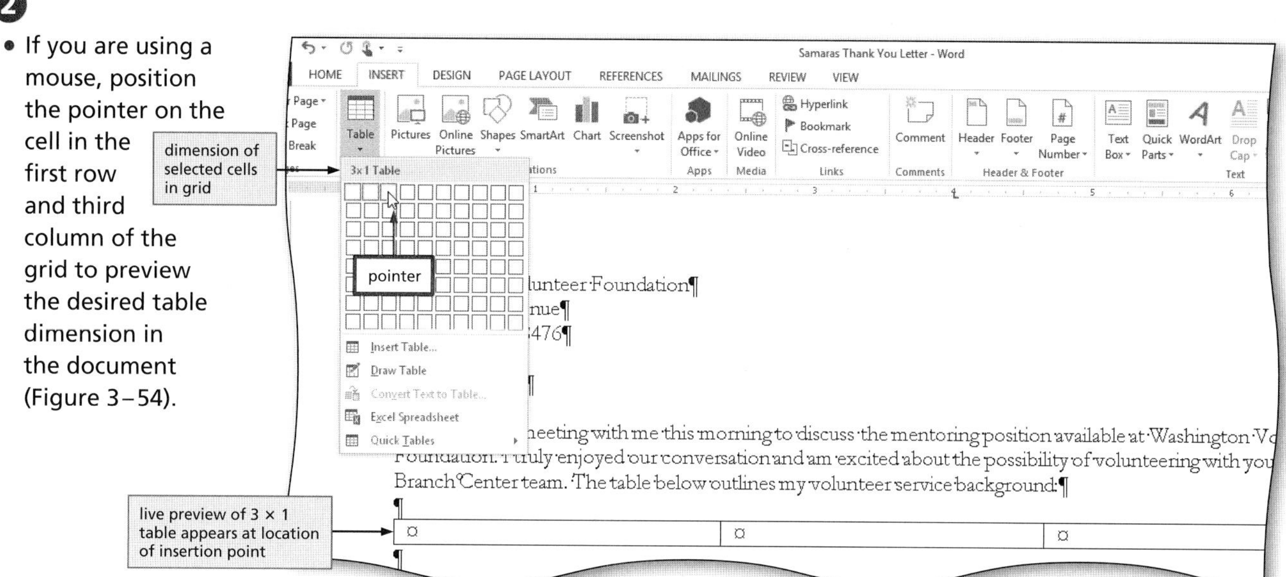

Figure 3–54

3

- Tap or click the cell in the first row and third column of the grid to insert an empty table with one row and three columns in the document.
- If necessary, scroll the document so that the table is visible (Figure 3–55).

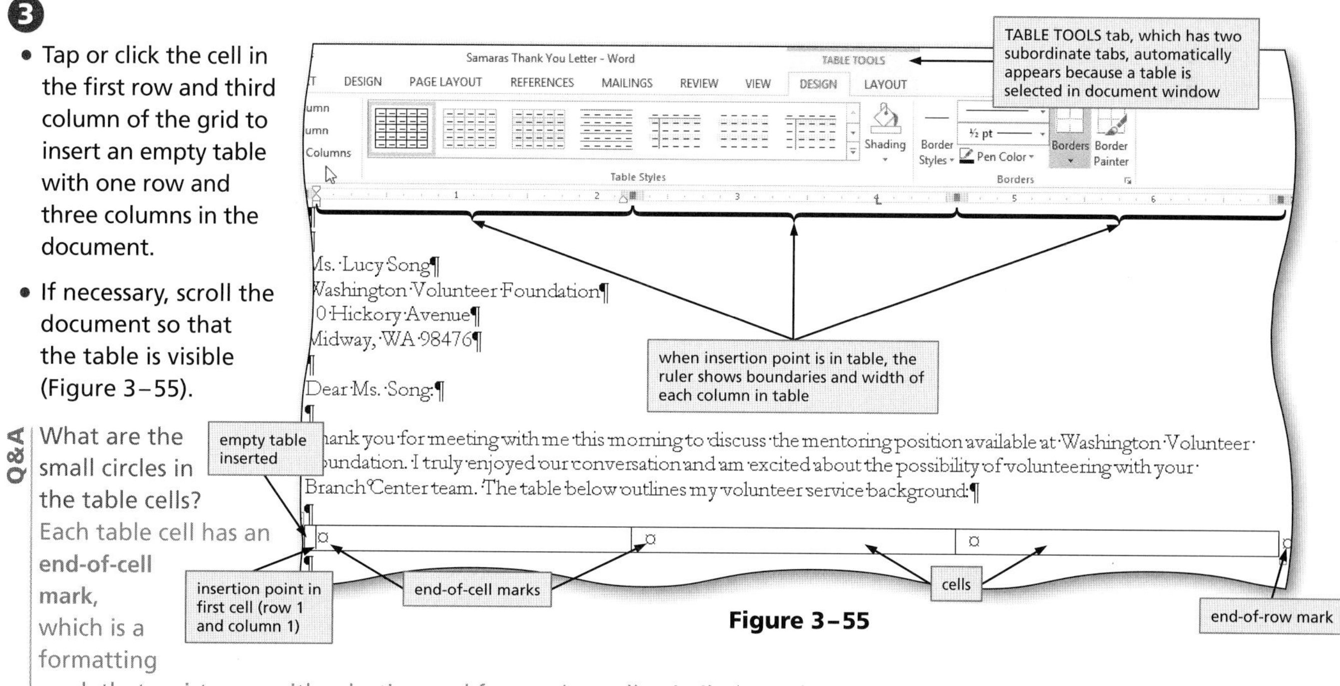

Figure 3–55

Q&A What are the small circles in the table cells?

Each table cell has an **end-of-cell mark,** which is a formatting mark that assists you with selecting and formatting cells. Similarly, each row has an **end-of-row mark,** which you can use to add columns to the right of a table. Recall that formatting marks do not print on a hard copy. The end-of-cell marks currently are left-aligned, that is, positioned at the left edge of each cell.

Other Ways

1. Tap or click 'Add a Table' button (INSERT tab | Tables group), tap or click Insert Table in Add a Table gallery, enter number of columns and rows (Insert Table dialog box), tap or click OK button

To Enter Data in a Table

1 CREATE & FORMAT LETTERHEAD WITH GRAPHICS | 2 SPECIFY LETTER FORMATS
3 INSERT TABLE | 4 FORMAT TABLE | 5 INSERT BULLETED LIST | 6 ADDRESS ENVELOPE

The next step is to enter data in the cells of the empty table. The data you enter in a cell wordwraps just as text wordwraps between the margins of a document. To place data in a cell, you tap or click the cell and then type.

To advance rightward from one cell to the next, press the TAB key. When you are at the rightmost cell in a row, press the TAB key to move to the first cell in the next row; do not press the ENTER key. ***Why?*** *The* ENTER *key is used to begin a new paragraph within a cell.* One way to add new rows to a table is to press the TAB key when the insertion point is positioned in the bottom-right corner cell of the table. The step on the next page enters data in the first row of the table and then inserts a blank second row.

- With the insertion point in the left cell of the table, type **`Organization`** and then press the TAB key to advance the insertion point to the next cell.
- Type **`Primary Responsibility`** and then press the TAB key to advance the insertion point to the next cell.
- Type **`Term of Service`** and then press the TAB key to add a second row at the end of the table and position the insertion point in the first column of the new row (Figure 3–56).

Figure 3–56

Q&A How do I edit cell contents if I make a mistake?
Tap or click in the cell and then correct the entry.

BTW
Tables
For simple tables, such as the one just created, Word users often select the table dimension in the Add a Table gallery to create the table. For a more complex table, such as one with a varying number of columns per row, Word has a Draw Table feature that allows users to draw a table in the document using a pencil pointer. To use this feature, click the 'Add a Table' button (INSERT tab | Tables group) and then click Draw Table on the Add a Table menu.

To Enter More Data in a Table

The following steps enter the remaining data in the table.

1. Type **`Branch Center School District`** and then press the TAB key to advance the insertion point to the next cell. Type **`Tutor`** and then press the TAB key to advance the insertion point to the next cell. Type **`6 years`** and then press the TAB key to add a row at the end of the table and position the insertion point in the first column of the new row.

2. In the third row, type **`Newton County Youth Groups`** in the first column, **`Teen Leader`** in the second column, and **`3 years`** in the third column. Press the TAB key to position the insertion point in the first column of a new row.

3. In the fourth row, type **`Trenton Park District`** in the first column, **`Special Events Vocalist`** in the second column, and **`2 years`** in the third column. Press the TAB key.

4. In the fifth row, type **`Skylar Athletic Club`** in the first column, **`Basketball Coach`** in the second column, and **`4 years`** in the third column (Figure 3–57).

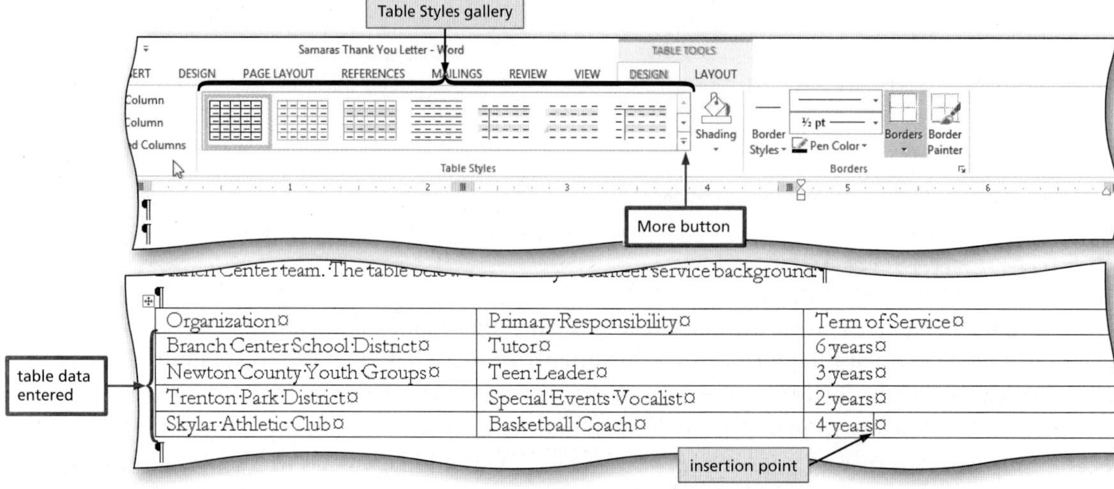

Figure 3–57

To Apply a Table Style

Word provides a gallery of more than 90 table styles, which include a variety of colors and shading. ***Why?*** *Table styles allow you to change the basic table format to a more visually appealing style.* The following steps apply a table style to the table in the letter.

1

- If the First Column check box in the Table Style Options group (TABLE TOOLS DESIGN tab) contains a check mark, tap or click the check box to remove the check mark. Be sure the remaining check marks match those in the Table Style Options group (TABLE TOOLS DESIGN tab) as shown in Figure 3–58.

Q&A

What if the TABLE TOOLS DESIGN tab no longer is the active tab?
Tap or click in the table and then display the TABLE TOOLS DESIGN tab.

What do the options in the Table Style Options group mean?
When you apply table styles, if you want the top row of the table (header row), a row containing totals (total row), first column, or last column to be formatted differently, select those check boxes. If you want the rows or columns to alternate with colors, select Banded Rows or Banded Columns, respectively.

2

- With the insertion point in the table, tap or click the More button in the Table Styles gallery (TABLE TOOLS DESIGN tab | Table Styles group), shown in Figure 3–57, to expand the gallery.
- If you are using a mouse, scroll and then point to 'Grid Table 6 Colorful - Accent 1' in the Table Styles gallery to display a live preview of that style applied to the table in the document (Figure 3–58).

Experiment

- If you are using a mouse, point to various styles in the Table Styles gallery and watch the format of the table change in the document window.

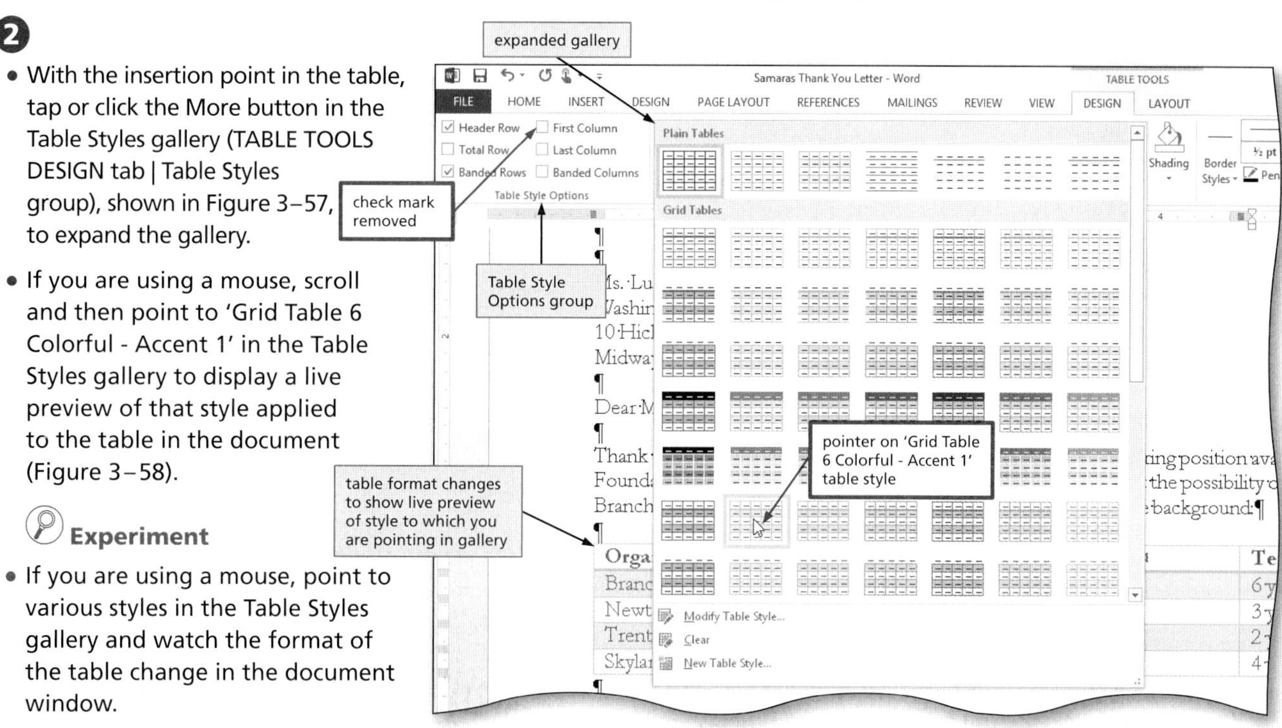

Figure 3–58

3

- Tap or click 'Grid Table 6 Colorful - Accent 1' in the Table Styles gallery to apply the selected style to the table (Figure 3–59).

Experiment

- Select and remove check marks from various check boxes in the Table Style Options group and watch the format of the table change in the document window. When finished experimenting, be sure the check marks match those shown in Figure 3–58.

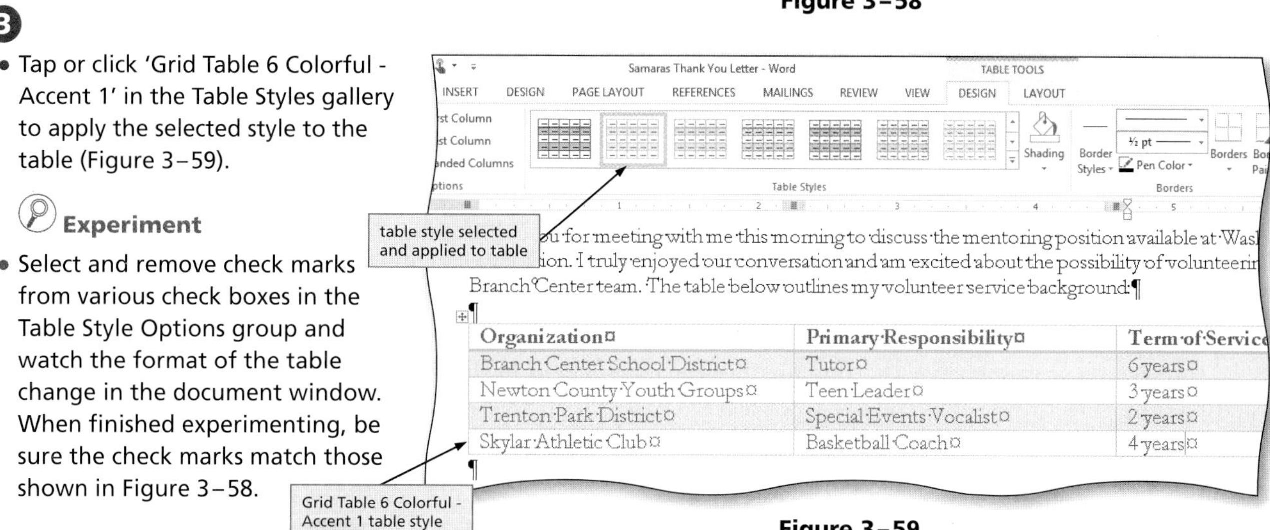

Figure 3–59

1 CREATE & FORMAT LETTERHEAD WITH GRAPHICS | 2 SPECIFY LETTER FORMATS
3 INSERT TABLE | 4 FORMAT TABLE | 5 INSERT BULLETED LIST | 6 ADDRESS ENVELOPE

To Resize Table Columns to Fit Table Contents

The table in this project currently extends from the left margin to the right margin of the document. The following steps instruct Word to fit the width of the columns to the contents of the table automatically. ***Why?*** *You want each column to be only as wide as the longest entry in the table. That is, the first column must be wide enough to accommodate the words, Newton County Youth Groups, and the second column should be only as wide as the title, Special Events Vocalist, and so on.*

- With the insertion point in the table, display the TABLE TOOLS LAYOUT tab.
- Tap or click the AutoFit button (TABLE TOOLS LAYOUT tab | Cell Size group) to display the AutoFit menu (Figure 3–60).

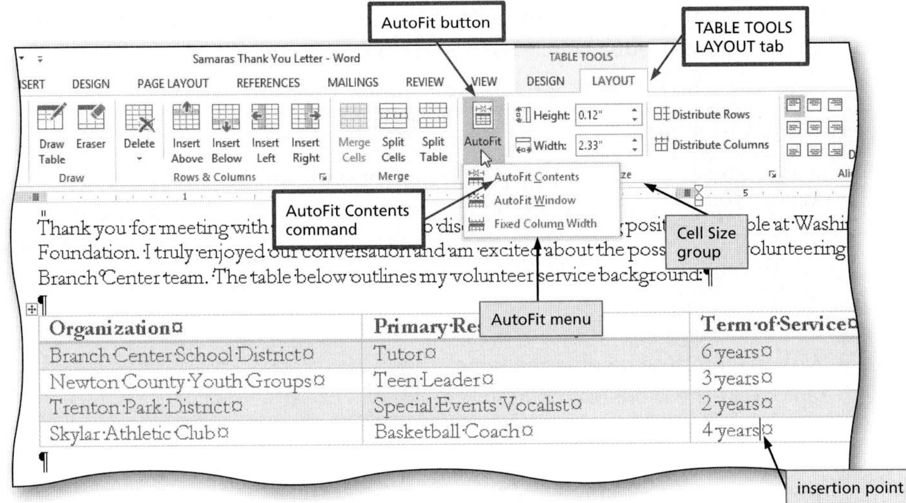

Figure 3–60

- Tap or click AutoFit Contents on the AutoFit menu, so that Word automatically adjusts the widths of the columns based on the text in the table (Figure 3–61).

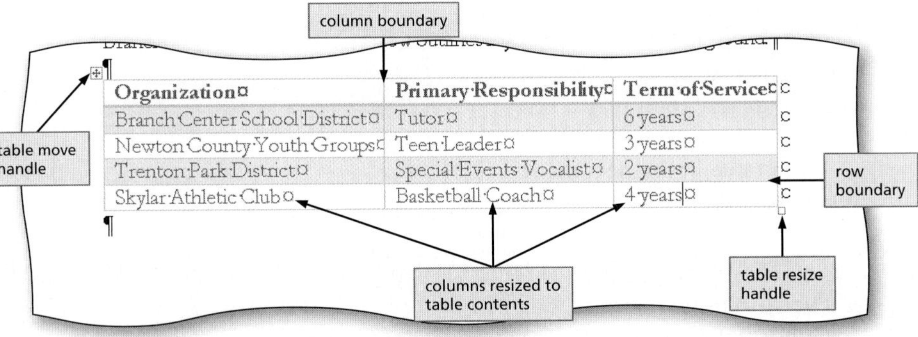

Figure 3–61

Q&A

Can I resize columns manually?

Yes, you can drag a **column boundary**, the border to the right of a column, until the column is the desired width. Similarly, you can resize a row by dragging the **row boundary**, the border at the bottom of a row, until the row is the desired height. You also can resize the entire table by dragging the **table resize handle**, which is a small square that appears when you point to a corner of the table.

What causes the table move handle and table resize handle to appear and disappear from the table?

They appear whenever you position the pointer in the table.

Other Ways

1. If you are using a mouse, double-click column boundary

1 CREATE & FORMAT LETTERHEAD WITH GRAPHICS | 2 SPECIFY LETTER FORMATS
3 INSERT TABLE | 4 FORMAT TABLE | 5 INSERT BULLETED LIST | 6 ADDRESS ENVELOPE

To Select a Column

The next task is to change the alignment of the data in cells in the third column of the table. To do this, you first must select the column. ***Why?*** *If you want to format the contents of a single cell, simply position the insertion point in the cell. To format a series of cells, you first must select them.* The next step selects a column.

- If you are using a mouse, position the pointer at the boundary above the column to be selected, the third column in this case, so that the pointer changes to a downward pointing arrow and then click to select the column (Figure 3–62).
- If you are using a touch screen, position the insertion point in the third column, tap the Select Table button (TABLE TOOLS LAYOUT tab | Table group), and then tap Select Column on the Select Table menu.

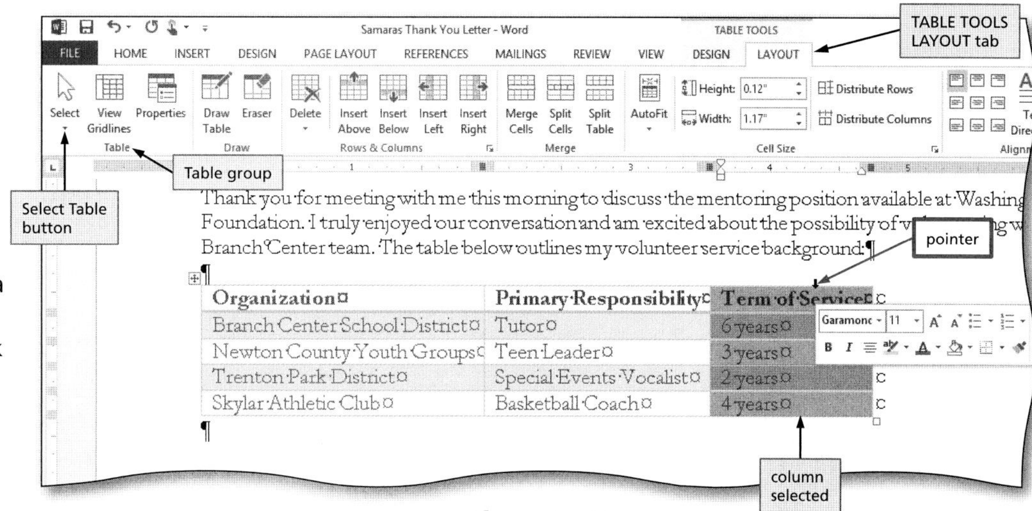

Figure 3–62

Other Ways

1. Tap or click Select Table button (TABLE TOOLS LAYOUT tab | Table group), tap or click Select Column in Select Table gallery

Selecting Table Contents

When working with tables, you may need to select the contents of cells, rows, columns, or the entire table. Table 3–4 identifies ways to select various items in a table.

Table 3–4 Selecting Items in a Table

Item to Select	Action
Cell	If you are using a mouse, point to left edge of cell and then click when the pointer changes to a small solid upward angled pointing arrow. Or, position insertion point in cell, click Select Table button (TABLE TOOLS LAYOUT tab | Table group), and then click Select Cell on the Select Table menu.
Column	If you are using a mouse, point to border at top of column and then click when the pointer changes to a small solid downward-pointing arrow. Or, position insertion point in column, click Select Table button (TABLE TOOLS LAYOUT tab | Table group), and then click Select Column on the Select Table menu.
Row	If you are using a mouse, point to the left of the row and then click when pointer changes to a right-pointing block arrow. Or, position insertion point in row, click Select Table button (TABLE TOOLS LAYOUT tab | Table group), and then click Select Row on the Select Table menu.
Multiple cells, rows, or columns adjacent to one another	Drag through cells, rows, or columns.
Multiple cells, rows, or columns not adjacent to one another	Select first cell, row, or column (as described above) and then hold down CTRL key while selecting next cell, row, or column.
Next cell	Press TAB key.
Previous cell	Press SHIFT+TAB.
Table	If you are using a mouse, point somewhere in table and then click table move handle that appears in upper-left corner of table. Or, position insertion point in table, click Select Table button (TABLE TOOLS LAYOUT tab | Table group), and then click Select Table on the Select Table menu.

To Align Data in Cells

The next step is to change the alignment of the data in cells in the third column of the table. In addition to aligning text horizontally in a cell (left, center, or right), you can align it vertically within a cell (top, center, bottom). When the height of the cell is close to the same height as the text, however, differences in vertical alignment are not readily apparent, which is the case for this table. The following step centers data in cells. ***Why?*** *The column containing the term of service would look better if its contents are centered.*

1

- With the cells selected, as shown in Figure 3–62 on the previous page, tap or click the desired alignment, in this case the 'Align Top Center' button (TABLE TOOLS LAYOUT tab | Alignment group) to center the contents of the selected cells (Figure 3–63).

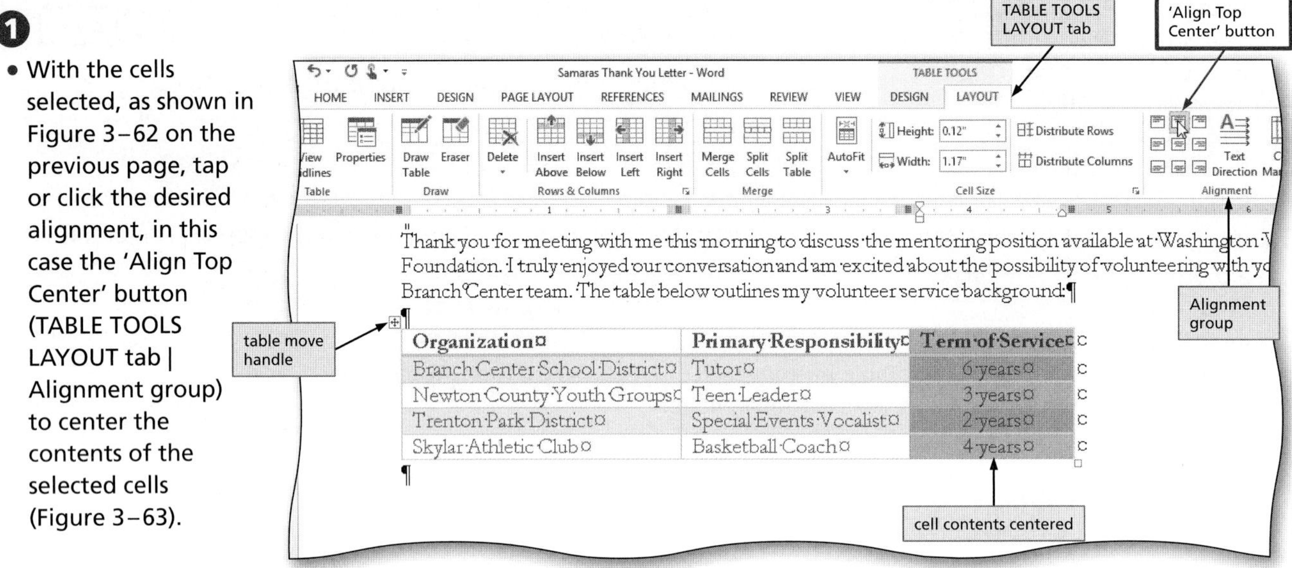

Figure 3–63

To Center a Table

When you first create a table, it is left-aligned; that is, it is flush with the left margin. In this letter, the table should be centered between the margins. To center a table, you first select the entire table. The following steps select and center a table using the mini toolbar. ***Why?*** *Recall that you can use buttons and boxes on the mini toolbar instead of those on the ribbon.*

1

- If you are using a mouse, position the pointer in the table so that the table move handle appears (shown in Figure 3–63).

Q&A What if the table move handle does not appear?

You also can select a table by clicking the Select Table button (TABLE TOOLS LAYOUT tab | Table group) and then clicking Select Table on the menu.

2

- If you are using a mouse, click the table move handle to select the entire table (Figure 3–64).
- If you are using a touch screen, tap the Select Table button (TABLE TOOLS LAYOUT tab | Table group) and then tap Select Table on the Select Table menu to select the table.

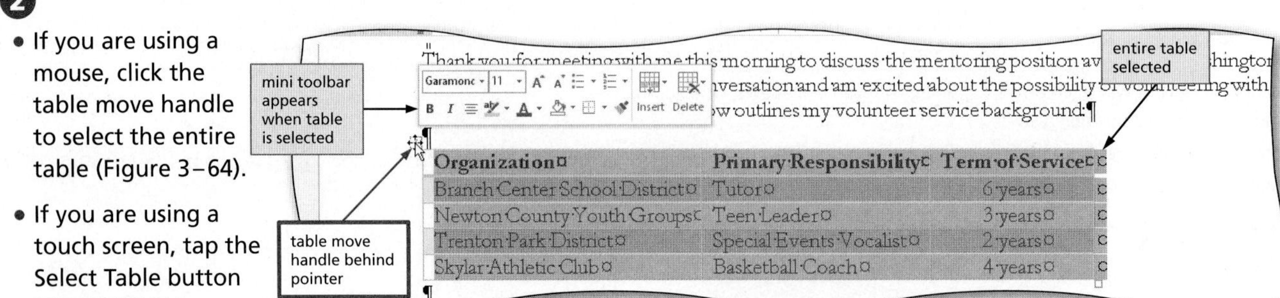

Figure 3–64

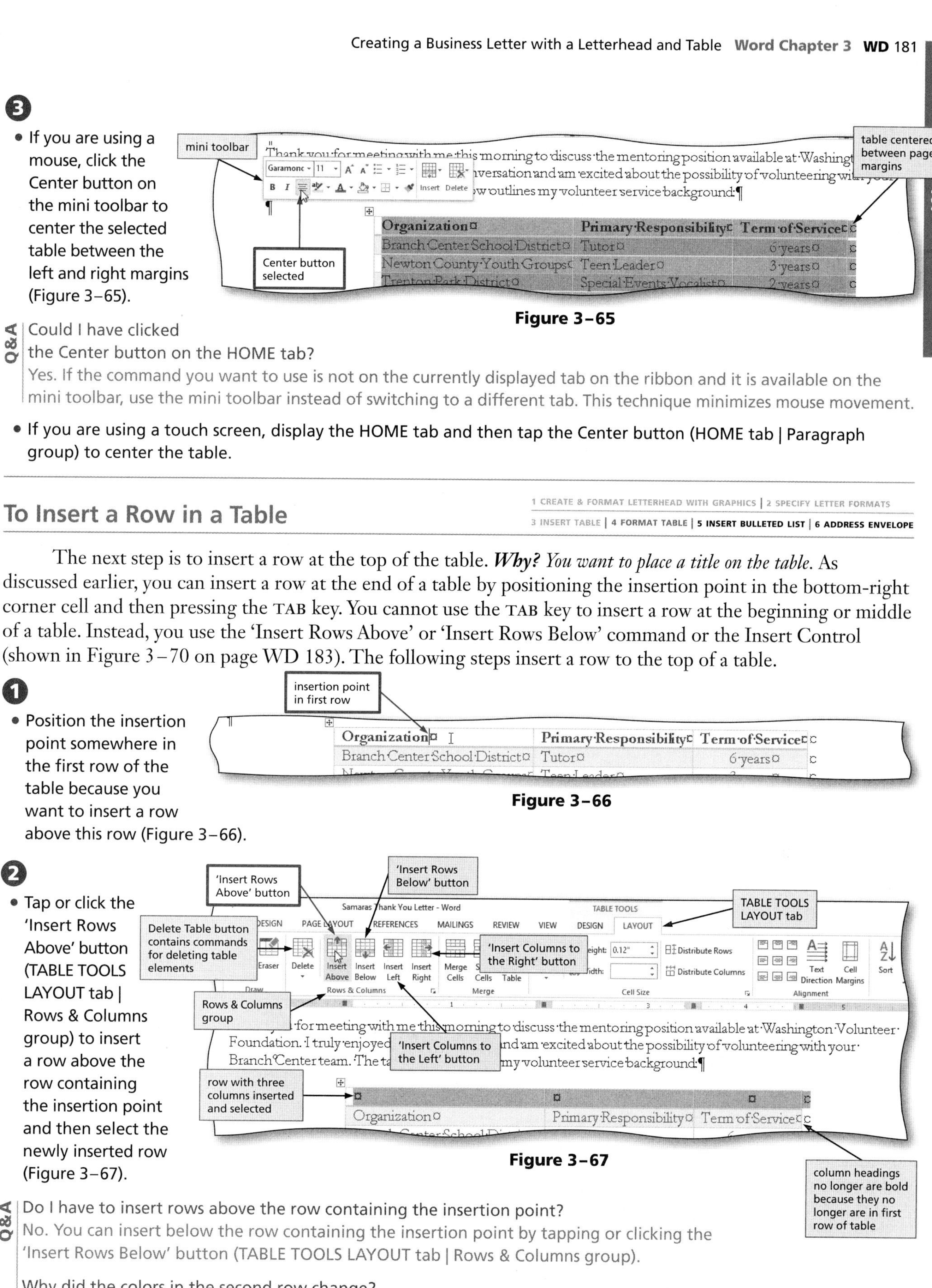

3

- If you are using a mouse, click the Center button on the mini toolbar to center the selected table between the left and right margins (Figure 3–65).

Figure 3–65

Q&A Could I have clicked the Center button on the HOME tab?

Yes. If the command you want to use is not on the currently displayed tab on the ribbon and it is available on the mini toolbar, use the mini toolbar instead of switching to a different tab. This technique minimizes mouse movement.

- If you are using a touch screen, display the HOME tab and then tap the Center button (HOME tab | Paragraph group) to center the table.

To Insert a Row in a Table

1 CREATE & FORMAT LETTERHEAD WITH GRAPHICS | 2 SPECIFY LETTER FORMATS
3 INSERT TABLE | **4 FORMAT TABLE** | **5 INSERT BULLETED LIST** | **6 ADDRESS ENVELOPE**

The next step is to insert a row at the top of the table. ***Why?*** *You want to place a title on the table.* As discussed earlier, you can insert a row at the end of a table by positioning the insertion point in the bottom-right corner cell and then pressing the TAB key. You cannot use the TAB key to insert a row at the beginning or middle of a table. Instead, you use the 'Insert Rows Above' or 'Insert Rows Below' command or the Insert Control (shown in Figure 3–70 on page WD 183). The following steps insert a row to the top of a table.

1

- Position the insertion point somewhere in the first row of the table because you want to insert a row above this row (Figure 3–66).

Figure 3–66

2

- Tap or click the 'Insert Rows Above' button (TABLE TOOLS LAYOUT tab | Rows & Columns group) to insert a row above the row containing the insertion point and then select the newly inserted row (Figure 3–67).

Figure 3–67

Q&A Do I have to insert rows above the row containing the insertion point?

No. You can insert below the row containing the insertion point by tapping or clicking the 'Insert Rows Below' button (TABLE TOOLS LAYOUT tab | Rows & Columns group).

Why did the colors in the second row change?

The table style specifies to format the Header row differently, which is the first row.

Other Ways

1. If you are using a mouse, point to the left of the table and click the desired Insert Control
2. Press and hold or right-click row, tap Insert Table button on mini toolbar or point to Insert on shortcut menu, tap or click desired command on Insert submenu

BTW
Resizing Table Columns and Rows
To change the width of a column or height of a row to an exact measurement, hold down the ALT key while dragging markers on the ruler. Or, enter values in the 'Table Column Width' or 'Table Row Height' boxes (TABLE TOOLS LAYOUT tab | Cell Size group).

To Insert a Column in a Table

If you wanted to insert a column in a table, instead of inserting rows, you would perform the following steps.

1. If you are using a mouse, point above the table and then click the desired Insert Control.

or

1. Position the insertion point in the column to the left or right of where you want to insert the column.
2. Tap or click the 'Insert Columns to the Left' button (TABLE TOOLS LAYOUT tab | Rows & Columns group) to insert a column to the left of the current column, or tap or click the 'Insert Columns to the Right' button (TABLE TOOLS LAYOUT tab | Rows & Columns group) to insert a column to the right of the current column.

or

1. Press and hold or right-click the table, tap Insert Table button on mini toolbar or point to Insert on the shortcut menu, and then tap Insert Left or Insert Right or click 'Insert Columns to the Left' or 'Insert Columns to the Right' on the Insert submenu.

To Merge Cells

1 CREATE & FORMAT LETTERHEAD WITH GRAPHICS | 2 SPECIFY LETTER FORMATS
3 INSERT TABLE | 4 FORMAT TABLE | 5 INSERT BULLETED LIST | 6 ADDRESS ENVELOPE

The row just inserted has one cell for each column, in this case, three cells (shown in Figure 3–67). The top row of the table, however, is to be a single cell that spans all rows. ***Why?*** *The top row contains the table title, which should be centered above the columns of the table.* Thus, the following steps merge the three cells into a single cell.

- With the cells to merge selected (as shown in Figure 3–67 on the previous page), tap or click the Merge Cells button (TABLE TOOLS LAYOUT tab | Merge group) to merge the selected cells into a single cell (Figure 3–68).

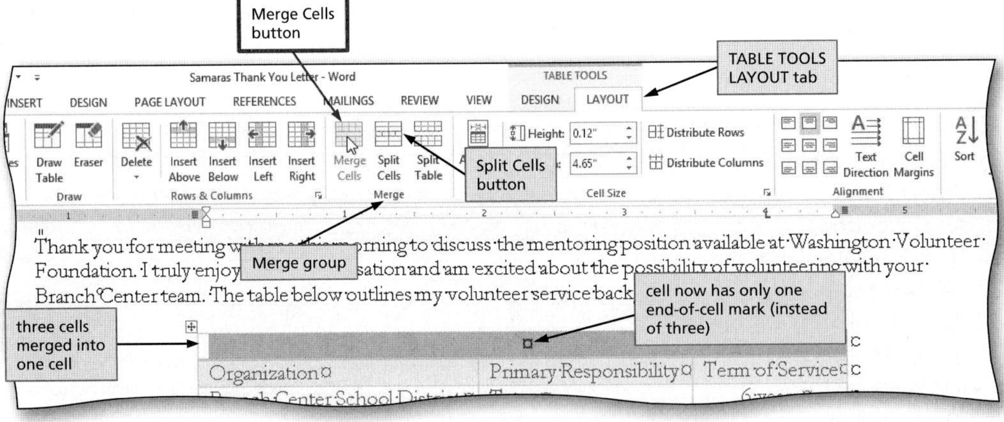

Figure 3–68

- Position the insertion point in the first row and then type `Volunteer Service Background` as the table title (Figure 3–69).

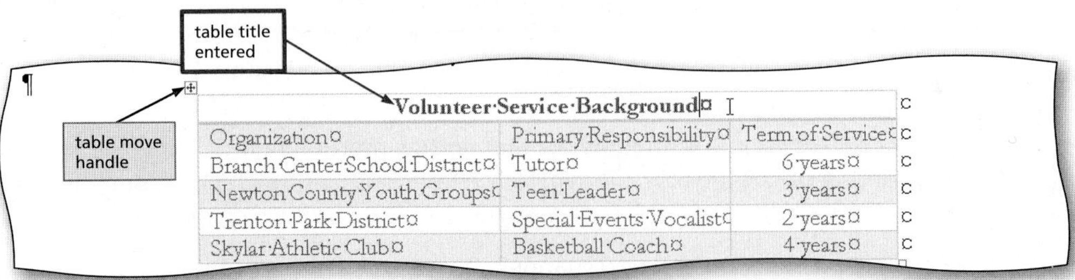

Figure 3–69

Other Ways

1. Tap 'Show Context Menu' button on mini toolbar or right-click selected cells, tap or click Merge Cells on shortcut menu

To Split Table Cells

Instead of merging multiple cells into a single cell, sometimes you want to split a single cell into multiple cells. If you wanted to split cells, you would perform the following steps.

1. Position the insertion point in the cell to split.
2. Tap or click the Split Cells button (TABLE TOOLS LAYOUT tab | Merge group); or tap 'Show Context Menu' button on mini toolbar or right-click the cell and then tap or click Split Cells on the shortcut menu to display the Split Cells dialog box.
3. Enter the number of columns and rows into which you want the cell split (Split Cells dialog box).
4. Tap or click the OK button.

BTW
Moving Tables
If you wanted to move a table to a new location, you would point to the upper-left corner of the table until the table move handle appears (shown in Figure 3–69), point to the table move handle, and then drag it to move the entire table to a new location.

To Split a Table

Instead of splitting table cells into multiple cells, sometimes you want to split a single table into multiple cells. If you wanted to split a table, you would perform the following steps.

1. Position the insertion point in the cell where you want the table to be split.
2. Tap or click the Split Table button (TABLE TOOLS LAYOUT tab | Merge group) to split the table into two tables at the location of the insertion point.

To Change the Font of Text in a Table Row

When you added a row to the top of the table for the title, Word moved the bold format from the column headings (which originally were in the first row of the table) to the title row (which now is the first row). Because you would like the columns headings bold also, the following steps select a table row and bold its contents.

1. Select the row containing the column headings (Figure 3–70).
2. With the text selected, tap or click the Bold button (HOME tab | Font group) to bold the selected text.

Q&A What is the symbol that appeared to the left of the table?
When you use a mouse to select a row or column in a table, Word displays an Insert Control. You can click the **Insert Control** to add a row or column to the table at that location.

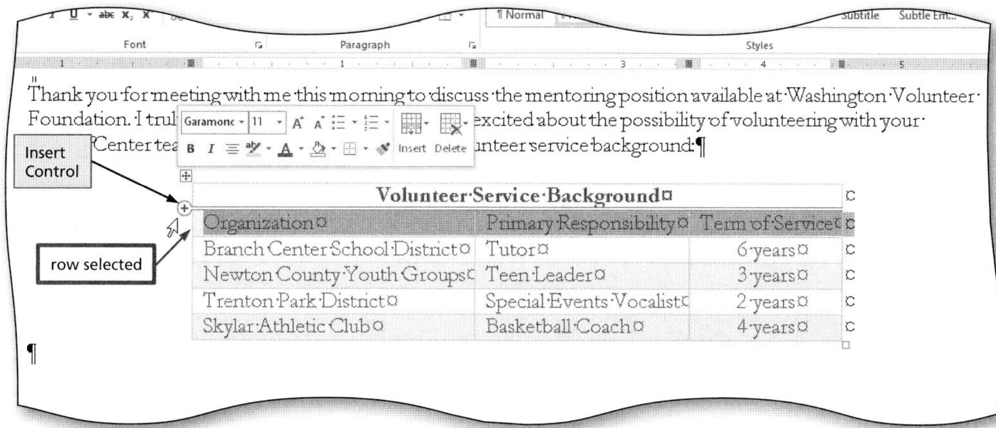

Figure 3–70

BTW
Tab Character in Tables
In a table, the TAB key advances the insertion point from one cell to the next. To insert a tab character in a cell, you must press CTRL+TAB.

Deleting Table Data

If you want to delete row(s) or delete column(s) from a table, position the insertion point in the row(s) or column(s) to delete, tap or click the Delete Table button (TABLE TOOLS LAYOUT tab | Rows & Columns group), and then tap or click Delete Rows or Delete Columns on the Delete Table menu. Or, select the row or column to delete, press and hold or right-click the selection, and then tap or click Delete Rows or Delete Columns on the mini toolbar or shortcut menu.

To delete the contents of a cell, select the cell contents and then press the DELETE or BACKSPACE key. You also can drag and drop or cut and paste the contents of cells. To delete an entire table, select the table, tap or click the Delete Table button (TABLE TOOLS LAYOUT tab | Rows & Columns group), and then tap or click Delete Table on the Delete menu. To delete the contents of a table and leave an empty table, you would select the table and then press the DELETE key.

BTW

AutoFormat Settings

Before you can use them, AutoFormat options must be enabled. To check if an AutoFormat option is enabled, tap or click FILE on the ribbon to open the Backstage view, tap or click Options in the Backstage view, tap or click Proofing in the left pane (Word Options dialog box), tap or click the AutoCorrect Options button, tap or click the AutoFormat As You Type tab, select the appropriate check boxes, and then tap or click the OK button in each open dialog box.

To Add More Text

The table now is complete. The next step is to enter text below the table. The following steps enter text.

1. Position the insertion point on the paragraph mark below the table and then press the ENTER key.
2. Type **`As you requested, below is my availability by day:`** and then press the ENTER key (shown in Figure 3–71).

To Bullet a List As You Type

1 CREATE & FORMAT LETTERHEAD WITH GRAPHICS | 2 SPECIFY LETTER FORMATS
3 INSERT TABLE | 4 FORMAT TABLE | 5 INSERT BULLETED LIST | 6 ADDRESS ENVELOPE

In Chapter 1, you learned how to apply bullets to existing paragraphs. If you know before you type that a list should be bulleted, you can use Word's AutoFormat As You Type feature to bullet the paragraphs as you type them (see Table 3–2 on page WD 163). ***Why?*** *The AutoFormat As You Type feature saves you time because it applies formats automatically.* The following steps add bullets to a list as you type.

- Press the ASTERISK key (*) as the first character on the line (Figure 3–71).

- Press the SPACEBAR to convert the asterisk to a bullet character.

Volunteer Service Background		
Organization	**Primary Responsibility**	**Term of Service**
Branch Center School District	Tutor	6 years
Newton County Youth Groups	Teen Leader	3 years
Trenton Park District	Special Events Vocalist	2 years
Skylar Athletic Club	Basketball Coach	4 years

As you requested, below is my availability by day:

*

bold text
blank line
text entered
asterisk entered at beginning of line

Figure 3–71

Q&A What if I did not want the asterisk converted to a bullet character?

You could undo the AutoFormat by tapping or clicking the Undo button; pressing CTRL+Z; tapping or clicking the AutoCorrect Options button that appears to the left of the bullet character as soon as you press the SPACEBAR and then tapping or clicking Undo Automatic Bullets on the AutoCorrect Options menu; or tapping or clicking the Bullets button (HOME tab | Paragraph group).

- Type **`Mondays - 6:00 a.m. to 8:00 a.m.`** as the first bulleted item.
- Press the ENTER key to place another bullet character at the beginning of the next line (Figure 3–72).

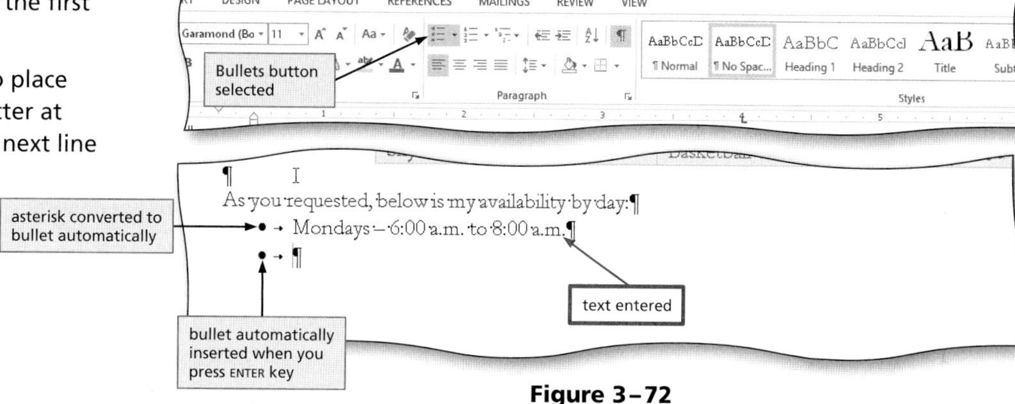

Figure 3–72

4

- Type **`Tuesdays and Thursdays - 4:00 p.m. to 6:00 p.m.`** and then press the ENTER key.
- Type **`Saturdays - 11:00 a.m. to 2:00 p.m.`** and then press the ENTER key.
- Press the ENTER key to turn off automatic bullets as you type (Figure 3–73).

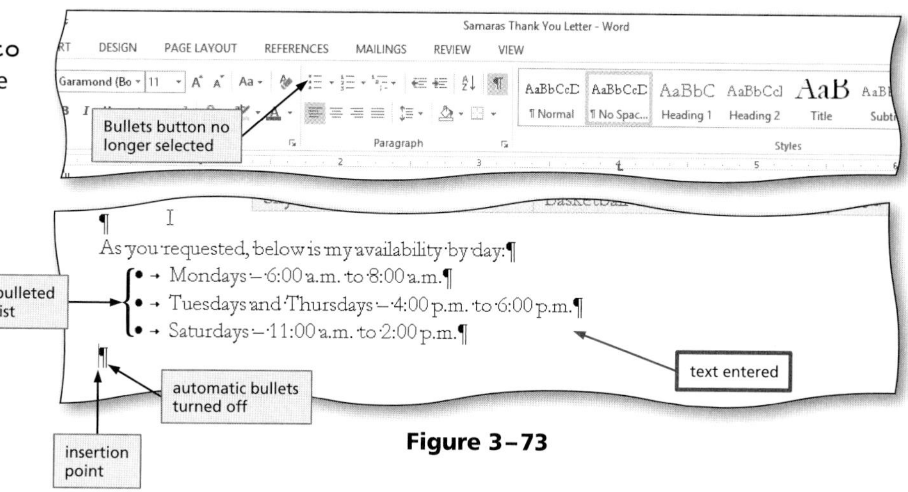

Figure 3–73

Q&A Why did automatic bullets stop?
When you press the ENTER key without entering any text after the automatic bullet character, Word turns off the automatic bullets feature.

Other Ways

1. Tap or click Bullets button (HOME tab | Paragraph group)
2. Press and hold or right-click paragraph to be bulleted, tap or click Bullets button on mini toolbar, tap or click desired bullet style, if necessary

To Enter More Text

The following steps enter the remainder of text in the letter.

1. With the insertion point positioned on the paragraph below the bulleted list, press the ENTER key and then type the paragraph shown in Figure 3–74 on the next page, making certain you use the building block name, wvf, to insert the organization name.
2. Press the ENTER key twice. Press the TAB key to position the insertion point at the tab stop set at the 4" mark on the ruler. Type **`Sincerely,`** and then press the ENTER key four times.
3. Press the TAB key to position the insertion point at the tab stop set at the 4" mark on the ruler. Type **`Alexander Samaras`** and then press the ENTER key (Figure 3–74).

   If requested by your instructor, enter your name instead of the name shown above.

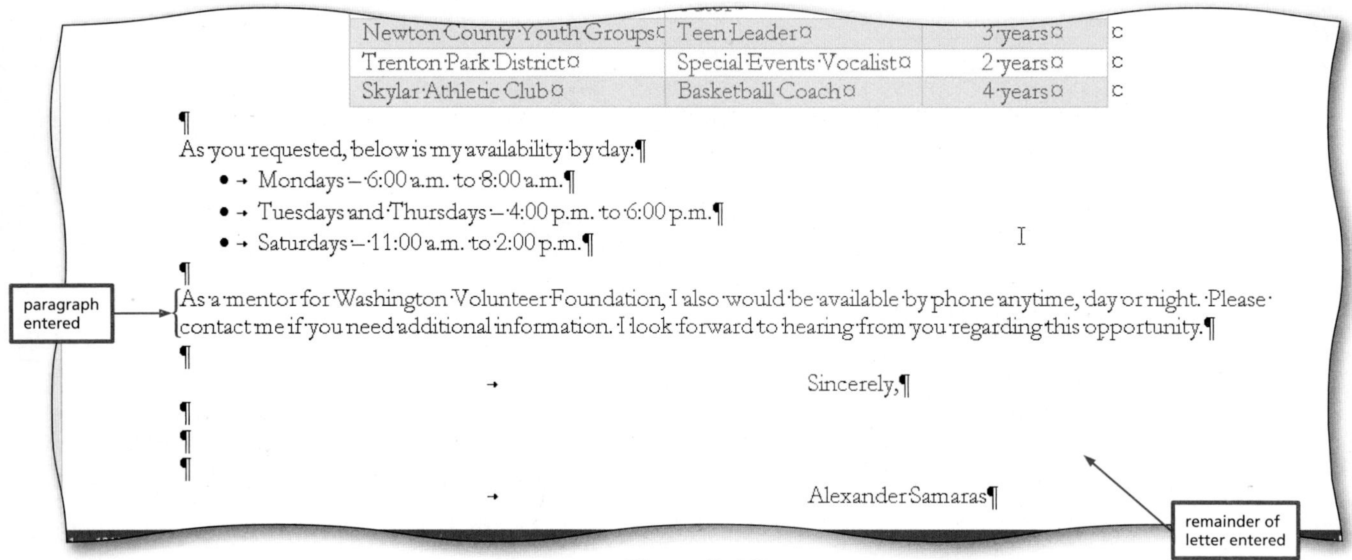

Newton County Youth Groups | Teen Leader | 3 years
Trenton Park District | Special Events Vocalist | 2 years
Skylar Athletic Club | Basketball Coach | 4 years
As you requested, below is my availability by day:
Mondays – 6:00 a.m. to 8:00 a.m.
Tuesdays and Thursdays – 4:00 p.m. to 6:00 p.m.
Saturdays – 11:00 a.m. to 2:00 p.m.
paragraph entered
As a mentor for Washington Volunteer Foundation, I also would be available by phone anytime, day or night. Please contact me if you need additional information. I look forward to hearing from you regarding this opportunity.
Sincerely,
Alexander Samaras
remainder of letter entered

Figure 3–74

To Save an Existing Document with the Same File Name

You have made several modifications to the document since you last saved it. Thus, you should save it again. The following step saves the document again. For an example of the step listed below, refer to the Office and Windows chapter at the beginning of this book.

1. Tap or click the Save button on the Quick Access Toolbar to overwrite the previously saved file.

BTW
Conserving Ink and Toner
If you want to conserve ink or toner, you can instruct Word to print draft quality documents by tapping or clicking FILE on the ribbon to open the Backstage view, tapping or clicking Options in the Backstage view to display the Word Options dialog box, tapping or clicking Advanced in the left pane (Word Options dialog box), sliding or scrolling to the Print area in the right pane, placing a check mark in the 'Use draft quality' check box, and then tapping or clicking the OK button. Then, use the Backstage view to print the document as usual.

To Print a Document

If you want a hard copy of the letter, perform the following steps.

1. Tap or click FILE on the ribbon to open the Backstage view.
2. Tap or click the Print tab in the Backstage view to display the Print gallery.
3. Verify that the printer listed on the Printer Status button will print a hard copy of the document. If necessary, tap or click the Printer Status button to display a list of available printer options and then tap or click the desired printer to change the currently selected printer.
4. Tap or click the Print button in the Print gallery to print the document on the currently selected printer.
5. When the printer stops, retrieve the hard copy (shown in Figure 3–1 on page WD 139).

Addressing and Printing Envelopes and Mailing Labels

With Word, you can print address information on an envelope or on a mailing label. Computer-printed addresses look more professional than handwritten ones.

To Address and Print an Envelope

The following steps address and print an envelope. If you are in a lab environment, check with your instructor before performing these steps. ***Why?*** *Some printers may not accommodate printing envelopes; others may stop printing until an envelope is inserted.*

- Scroll through the letter to display the inside address in the document window.
- Drag through the inside address to select it (Figure 3–75).

Figure 3–75

- Display the MAILINGS tab.
- Tap or click the Create Envelopes button (MAILINGS tab | Create group) to display the Envelopes and Labels dialog box.
- If necessary, tap or click the Envelopes tab (Envelopes and Labels dialog box), which automatically displays the selected delivery address in the dialog box.
- Type the return address as shown in Figure 3–76.

- Insert an envelope in your printer, as shown in the Feed area of the dialog box (your Feed area may be different depending on your printer).
- If your printer can print envelopes, tap or click the Print button (Envelopes and Labels dialog box) to print the envelope.

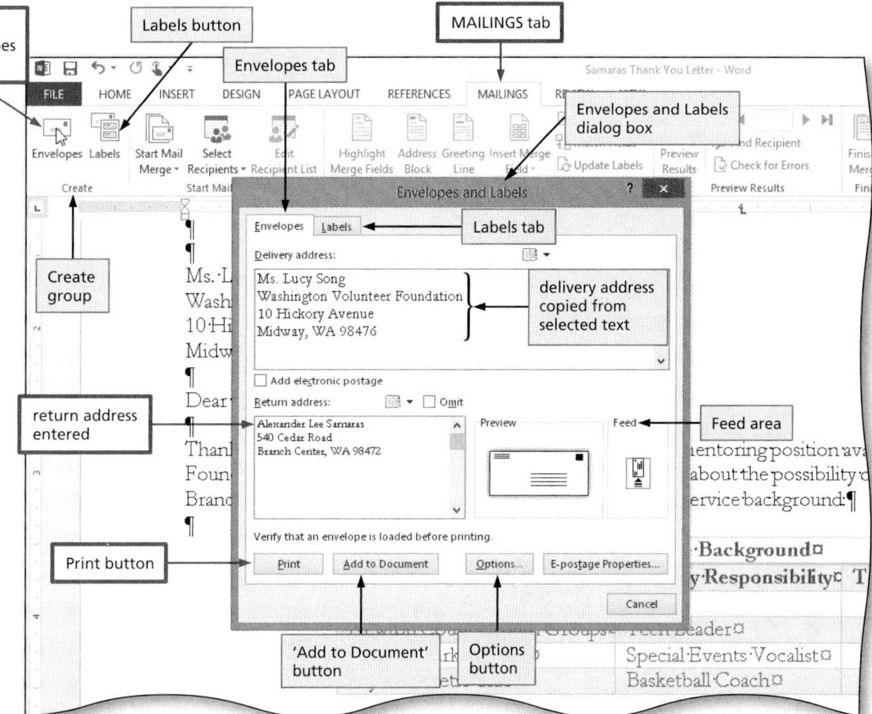

Figure 3–76

Envelopes and Labels

Instead of printing the envelope immediately, you can add it to the document by tapping or clicking the 'Add to Document' button (Envelopes and Labels dialog box). To specify a different envelope or label type (identified by a number on the box of envelopes or labels), tap or click the Options button (Envelopes and Labels dialog box).

Instead of printing an envelope, you can print a mailing label. To do this, tap or click the Labels button (MAILINGS tab | Create group) (shown in Figure 3–76) and then type the delivery address in the Delivery address box. To print the same address on all labels on the page, tap or click 'Full page of the same label' in the Print area. Tap or click the Print button (Envelopes and Labels dialog box) to print the label(s).

To Sign Out of a Microsoft Account

If you are signed in to a Microsoft account and are using a public computer or otherwise wish to sign out of your Microsoft account, you should sign out of the account from the Account gallery in the Backstage view before exiting Word. Signing out of the account is the safest way to make sure that nobody else can access SkyDrive files or settings stored in your Microsoft account. The following steps sign out of a Microsoft account from Word. For a detailed example of the procedure summarized below, refer to the Office and Windows chapter at the beginning of this book.

1. If you wish to sign out of your Microsoft account, tap or click FILE on the ribbon to open the Backstage view and then tap or click the Account tab to display the Account gallery.

2. Tap or click the Sign out link, which displays the Remove Account dialog box. If a Can't remove Windows accounts dialog box appears instead of the Remove Account dialog box, tap or click the OK button and skip the remaining steps.

   Q&A Why does a Can't remove Windows accounts dialog box appear?
   If you signed in to Windows using your Microsoft account, then you also must sign out from Windows, rather than signing out from within Word. When you are finished using Windows, be sure to sign out at that time.

3. Tap or click the Yes button (Remove Account dialog box) to sign out of your Microsoft account on this computer.

   Q&A Should I sign out of Windows after signing out of my Microsoft account?
   When you are finished using the computer, you should sign out of your account for maximum security.

4. Tap or click the Back button in the upper-left corner of the Backstage view to return to the document.

BTW
Distributing a Document
Instead of printing and distributing a hard copy of a document, you can distribute the document electronically. Options include sending the document via email; posting it on cloud storage (such as SkyDrive) and sharing the file with others; posting it on a social networking site, blog, or other website; and sharing a link associated with an online location of the document. You also can create and share a PDF or XPS image of the document, so that users can view the file in Acrobat Reader or XPS Viewer instead of in Word.

To Exit Word

This project now is complete. The following steps exit Word. For a detailed example of the procedure summarized below, refer to the Office and Windows chapter at the beginning of this book.

1a. If you have one Word document open, tap or click the Close button on the right side of the title bar to close the open document and exit Word.

1b. If you have multiple Word documents open, press and hold or right-click the Word app button on the taskbar and then tap or click 'Close all windows' on the shortcut menu to close all open documents and exit Word.

2. If a Microsoft Word dialog box appears, tap or click the Save button to save any changes made to the document since the last save.

BTW
Quick Reference
For a table that lists how to complete the tasks covered in this book using touch gestures, the mouse, ribbon, shortcut menu, and keyboard, see the Quick Reference Summary at the back of this book, or visit the Quick Reference resource on the Student Companion Site located on www.cengagebrain.com. For detailed instructions about accessing available resources, visit www.cengage.com/ct/studentdownload or contact your instructor for information about accessing the required files.

Chapter Summary

In this chapter, you have learned how to use Word to change margins, insert and format a shape, change text wrapping, insert and format clip art, move and copy graphics, insert symbols, add a border, clear formatting, convert a hyperlink to regular text, set and use tab stops, insert the current date, create and insert building blocks, insert and format tables, and address and print envelopes and mailing labels. The items listed below include all the new Word skills you have learned in this chapter, with the tasks grouped by activity.

Enter and Edit Text

Insert a Symbol from the Symbol Dialog Box (WD 158)
Insert a Symbol from the Insert a Symbol Gallery (WD 159)
Set Custom Tab Stops (WD 167)
Insert the Current Date in a Document (WD 168)
Create a Building Block (WD 170)
Modify a Building Block (WD 171)
Insert a Building Block (WD 172)
Insert a Nonbreaking Space (WD 173)
Bullet a List as You Type (WD 184)
Address and Print an Envelope (WD 187)

Format a Page

Change Margin Settings (WD 140)
Change the Document Theme (WD 148)

Format Text

Use the 'Increase Font Size' Button (WD 147)
Bottom Border a Paragraph (WD 160)
Clear Formatting (WD 161)
Convert a Hyperlink to Regular Text (WD 163)
Apply a Style (WD 165)

Work with Graphics

Insert a Shape (WD 142)
Change an Object's Position (WD 144)
Change an Object's Text Wrapping (WD 145)
Apply a Shape Style (WD 145)
Add Text to a Shape (WD 146)
Insert Clip Art (WD 148)
Resize a Graphic to a Percent of the Original (WD 150)
Change the Color of a Graphic (WD 151)
Set a Transparent Color in a Graphic (WD 152)
Adjust the Brightness and Contrast of a Graphic (WD 153)
Change the Border Color on a Graphic (WD 154)
Move a Graphic (WD 155)
Copy a Graphic (WD 155)
Use Paste Options (WD 156)
Flip a Graphic (WD 157)

Work with Tables

Insert an Empty Table (WD 174)
Enter Data in a Table (WD 175)
Apply a Table Style (WD 177)
Resize Table Columns to Fit Table Contents (WD 178)
Select a Column (WD 178)
Align Data in Cells (WD 180)
Center a Table (WD 180)
Insert a Row in a Table (WD 181)
Insert a Column in a Table (WD 182)
Merge Cells (WD 182)
Split Table Cells (WD 183)
Split a Table (WD 183)

CONSIDER THIS: PLAN AHEAD

What decisions will you need to make when creating your next business letter?

Use these guidelines as you complete the assignments in this chapter and create your own business letters outside of this class.

1. Create a letterhead.
   a) Ensure that the letterhead contains a complete legal name, mailing address, phone number, and if applicable, fax number, email address, web address, logo, or other image.
   b) Place elements in the letterhead in a visually appealing location.
   c) Format the letterhead with appropriate fonts, font sizes, font styles, and color.
2. Compose an effective business letter.
   a) Include date line, inside address, message, and signature block.
   b) Use proper spacing and formats for letter contents.
   c) Follow the alignment and spacing guidelines based on the letter style used (i.e., block, modified block, or modified semi-block).
   d) Ensure the message is well written, properly formatted, and logically organized.

CONSIDER THIS

How should you submit solutions to questions in the assignments identified with a symbol?

Every assignment in this book contains one or more questions identified with a symbol. These questions require you to think beyond the assigned document. Present your solutions to the questions in the format required by your instructor. Possible formats may include one or more of these options: write the answer; create a document that contains the answer; present your answer to the class; discuss your answer in a group; record the answer as audio or video using a webcam, smartphone, or portable media player; or post answers on a blog, wiki, or website.

Apply Your Knowledge

Reinforce the skills and apply the concepts you learned in this chapter.

Working with Tabs and a Table

Note: To complete this assignment, you will be required to use the Data Files for Students. Visit www.cengage.com/ct/studentdownload for detailed instructions or contact your instructor for information about accessing the required files.

Instructions: Run Word. Open the document called Apply 3-1 October Work Schedule Draft located on the Data Files for Students. The document is a Word table that you are to edit and format. The revised table is shown in Figure 3–77.

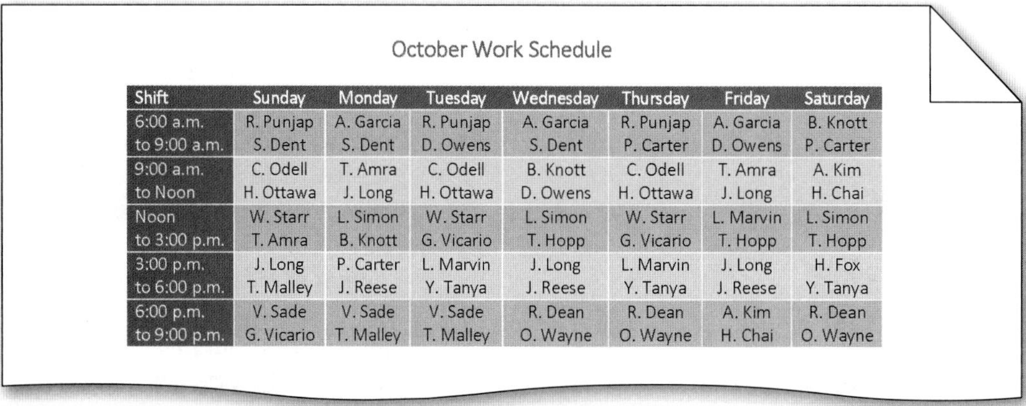

October Work Schedule

Shift	Sunday	Monday	Tuesday	Wednesday	Thursday	Friday	Saturday
6:00 a.m. to 9:00 a.m.	R. Punjap S. Dent	A. Garcia S. Dent	R. Punjap D. Owens	A. Garcia S. Dent	R. Punjap P. Carter	A. Garcia D. Owens	B. Knott P. Carter
9:00 a.m. to Noon	C. Odell H. Ottawa	T. Amra J. Long	C. Odell H. Ottawa	B. Knott D. Owens	C. Odell H. Ottawa	T. Amra J. Long	A. Kim H. Chai
Noon to 3:00 p.m.	W. Starr T. Amra	L. Simon B. Knott	W. Starr G. Vicario	L. Simon T. Hopp	W. Starr G. Vicario	L. Marvin T. Hopp	L. Simon T. Hopp
3:00 p.m. to 6:00 p.m.	J. Long T. Malley	P. Carter J. Reese	L. Marvin Y. Tanya	J. Long J. Reese	L. Marvin Y. Tanya	J. Long J. Reese	H. Fox Y. Tanya
6:00 p.m. to 9:00 p.m.	V. Sade G. Vicario	V. Sade T. Malley	V. Sade T. Malley	R. Dean O. Wayne	R. Dean O. Wayne	A. Kim H. Chai	R. Dean O. Wayne

Figure 3–77

Perform the following tasks:

1. Change the document theme to Metropolitan.
2. In the line containing the table title, October Work Schedule, remove the tab stop at the 1" mark on the ruler.
3. Set a centered tab at the 3" mark on the ruler. Move the centered tab stop to the 3.5" mark on the ruler.
4. Bold the characters in the title. Use the 'Increase Font Size' button to increase their font size to 14. Change their color to Blue-Gray, Accent 4.
5. In the table, delete the row containing the 1:00 p.m. to 4:00 p.m. shift.
6. Insert a column between the Monday and Wednesday columns. Fill in the column as follows, pressing the ENTER key between each name so that each name appears on a separate line:

   Column Title – Tuesday

   6:00 a.m. to 9:00 a.m. – R. Punjap D. Owens

   9:00 a.m. to Noon – C. Odell H. Ottawa

   Noon to 3:00 p.m. – W. Starr G. Vicario

   3:00 p.m. to 6:00 p.m. – L. Marvin Y. Tanya

   If the column heading, Tuesday, is not bold, apply the bold format to the text in this cell.

7. Insert a new row at the bottom of the table. In the first cell of the new row, enter 6:00 p.m. to 9:00 p.m. in the cell, pressing the ENTER key before the word, to, so that the text appears on two separate lines. (*Hint: You can use the AutoCorrect Options button to turn off the automatic capitalization of the first letter of the sentence, which will stop capitalizing the T in to each time you type it.*) If this cell's contents are bold, remove the bold format. Fill in the cells in the remainder of the row as follows, pressing the ENTER key between each name so that each name appears on a separate line:

   Sunday – V. Sade G. Vicario

   Monday – V. Sade T. Malley

   Tuesday – V. Sade T. Malley

   Wednesday – R. Dean O. Wayne

   Thursday – R. Dean O. Wayne

   Friday – A. Kim H. Chai

   Saturday – R. Dean O. Wayne
8. In the Table Style Options group (TABLE TOOLS DESIGN tab), ensure that these check boxes have check marks: Header Row, Banded Rows, and First Column. The Total Row, Last Column, and Banded Columns check boxes should not be selected.
9. Apply the Grid Table 5 Dark - Accent 4 style to the table.
10. Make all columns as wide as their contents (AutoFit Contents).
11. Align center left all cells in the first column.
12. Align center the column headings containing the weekday names and also all cells containing employee names in the table.
13. Center the table between the left and right margins of the page.
14. If requested by your instructor, change O. Wayne in the bottom-right cell of the table to your first initial and last name.
15. Save the document using the file name, Apply 3-1 October Work Schedule Modified, and submit it (shown in Figure 3–77) in the format specified by your instructor.
16. If you wanted the employee names to appear on the same line in each cell with a comma between each name, how would you modify the data in the table?

Extend Your Knowledge

Extend the skills you learned in this chapter and experiment with new skills. You may need to use Help to complete the assignment.

Working with Formulas, Graphics, Sorting, Picture Bullets, and Mailing Labels

Note: To complete this assignment, you will be required to use the Data Files for Students. Visit www.cengage.com/ct/studentdownload for detailed instructions or contact your instructor for information about accessing the required files.

Instructions: Run Word. Open the document called Extend 3-1 Sponsor Letter Draft located on the Data Files for Students. You will enter formulas in the table, use the Format Picture task pane, group objects, change the table style, sort paragraphs, use picture bullets, move tabs, and print mailing labels.

Perform the following tasks:

1. Use Help to learn about entering formulas, grouping objects, sorting, picture bullets, and printing mailing labels.

Continued >

Extend Your Knowledge *continued*

2. Add a row to the bottom of the table. Insert the word, Total, in the first column of the new row. In the last cell of the new row, use the Formula dialog box to insert a formula that adds the cells in the column so that the total approximate cost is displayed; in the dialog box, select a number format and then modify it in the dialog box so that the total displays with dollar signs and no cents. Which formula did you use? What number format?
3. Select the graphic of the tiger head and then click the Format Shape Dialog Box Launcher (PICTURE TOOLS FORMAT tab | Picture Styles group) to display the Format Picture task pane (Figure 3–78). Experiment with all the buttons in the task pane and modify the look of the graphic to your preferences.

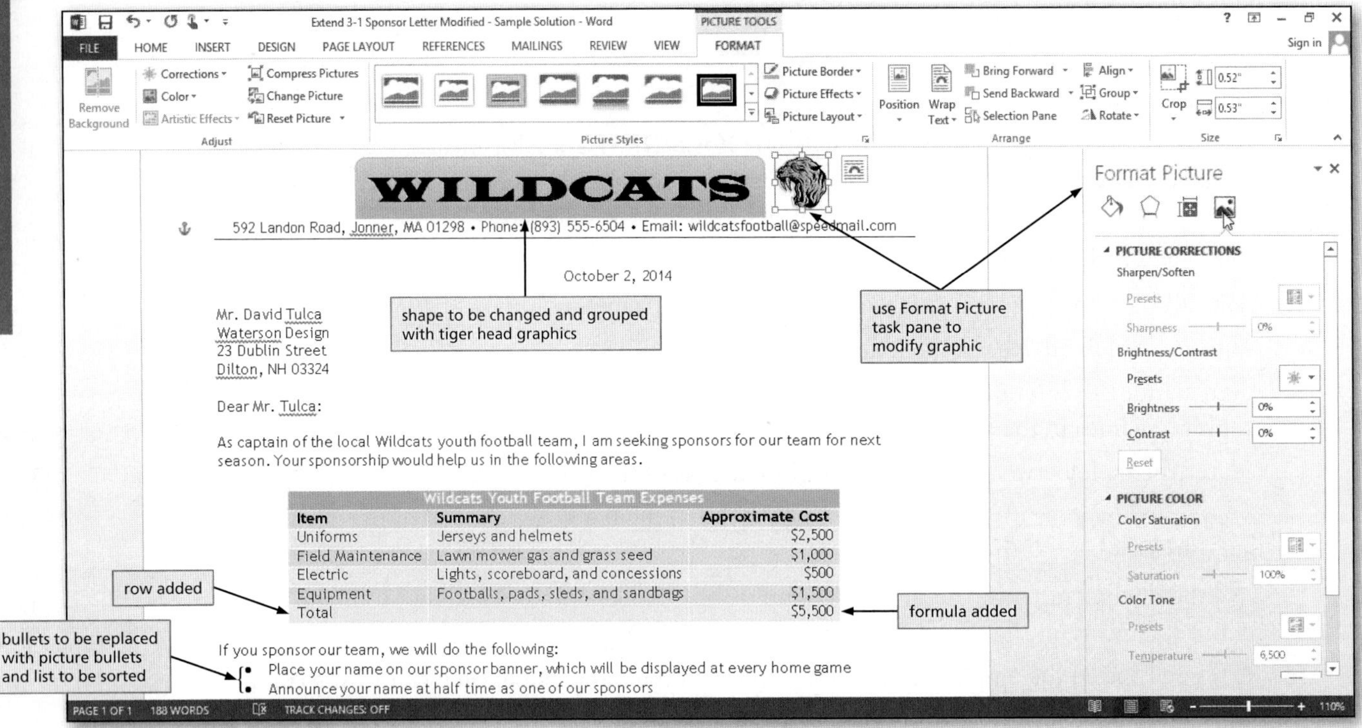

Figure 3–78

4. Select the shape around the WILDCATS title and then use the Edit Shape button (DRAWING TOOLS FORMAT tab | Insert Shapes group) to change the shape to your preference. Position the tiger head graphic in the desired location to the right of the shape.
5. Copy and paste the modified tiger head graphic, flip it horizontally, and then position it on the opposite site of the shape. Group the two tiger head graphics with the shape at the top of the letterhead. Change the text wrapping of the grouped shape to Top and Bottom.
6. Position the insertion point in the table and one at a time, select and deselect each check box in the Table Style Options group. What are the functions of each check box: Header Row, Total Row, Banded Rows, First Column, Last Column, and Banded Columns? Select the check boxes you prefer for the table.
7. Sort the paragraphs in the bulleted list.
8. Change the bullets in the bulleted list to picture bullets.
9. Move the tab stops in the date line, complimentary close, and signature block from the 3.5" mark to the 4" mark on the ruler.
10. If requested by your instructor, change the name in the signature block to your name.
11. Save the revised document using the file name, Extend 3-1 Sponsor Letter Modified, and then submit it in the format specified by your instructor.

12. If requested by your instructor, print a single mailing label for the letter and then a full page of mailing labels, each containing the address shown in Figure 3–78.
13. Answer the questions posed in #2 and #6. Why would you group objects? Which picture bullet did you use and why?

Analyze, Correct, Improve

Analyze a document, correct all errors, and improve it.

Formatting a Business Letter

Note: To complete this assignment, you will be required to use the Data Files for Students. Visit www.cengage.com/ct/studentdownload for detailed instructions or contact your instructor for information about accessing the required files.

Instructions: Run Word. Open the document, Analyze 3-1 Recommendation Letter Draft, located on the Data Files for Students. The document is a business letter that is missing elements and is formatted poorly or incorrectly (Figure 3–79). You are to change the color of the text, insert symbols, remove a hyperlink, change the letter style from block to modified block, insert and format clip art, and format the table.

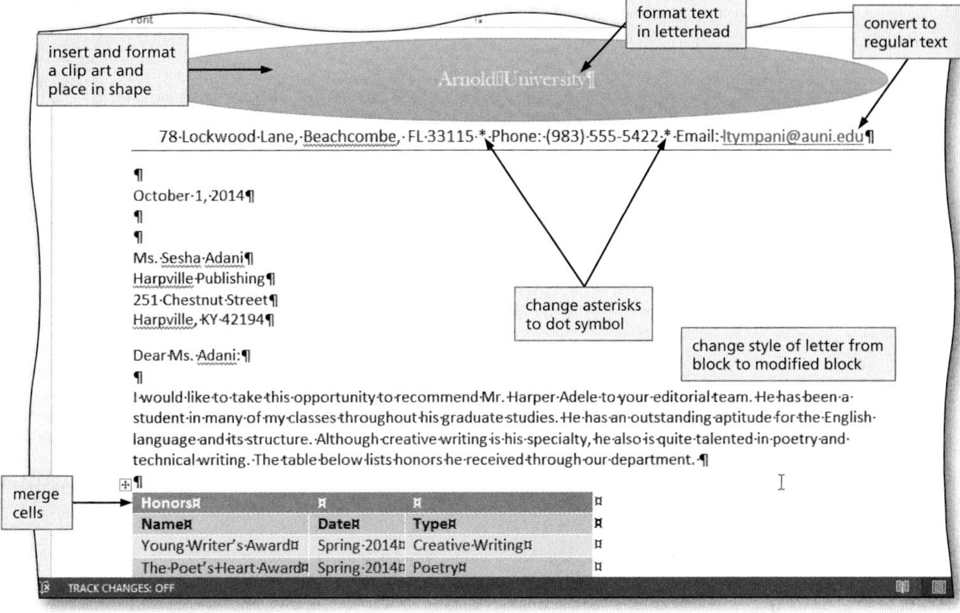

Figure 3–79

1. Correct In the letter, correct the following items:

a. Increase the font size of the text in the letterhead. Change the color of the text in the letterhead so that the text is readable.

b. Change the asterisks in the contact information to the dot symbol.

c. Convert the email address hyperlink to regular text.

d. The letter currently is the block letter style. It should be the modified block letter style. Format the appropriate paragraphs by setting custom tab stops and then positioning those paragraphs at the tab stops. Be sure to position the insertion point in the paragraph before setting the tab stop.

e. Merge the three cells in the first row of the table into one cell and then center the title in the cell. Center the entire table between the page margins.

2. Improve Enhance the letterhead by changing the theme to one you prefer. Then, locate and insert at least one appropriate clip art image in the letterhead. If necessary, resize the graphic(s). Change the text wrapping of the clip art to In Front of Text and move the graphic(s) into the shape. Change the color of the graphic to match the color of the text or shape. Adjust the brightness and contrast of the graphic. Format one color in the graphic as transparent. Change the picture border color. If requested by your instructor, change the name in the signature block to your name. Save the modified document with the file name, Analyze 3-1 Recommendation Letter Modified, and then submit it in the format specified by your instructor.

3. In this assignment, you located and inserted clip art. What image did you select and why?

In the Labs

Design and/or create a document using the guidelines, concepts, and skills presented in this chapter. Labs 1 and 2, which increase in difficulty, require you to create solutions based on what you learned in the chapter; Lab 3 requires you to create a solution, which uses cloud and web technologies, by learning and investigating on your own from general guidance.

Lab 1: Creating a Letter with a Letterhead

Problem: As office manager for a fitness club, you send membership renewal letters to members. One letter you prepare is shown in Figure 3–80.

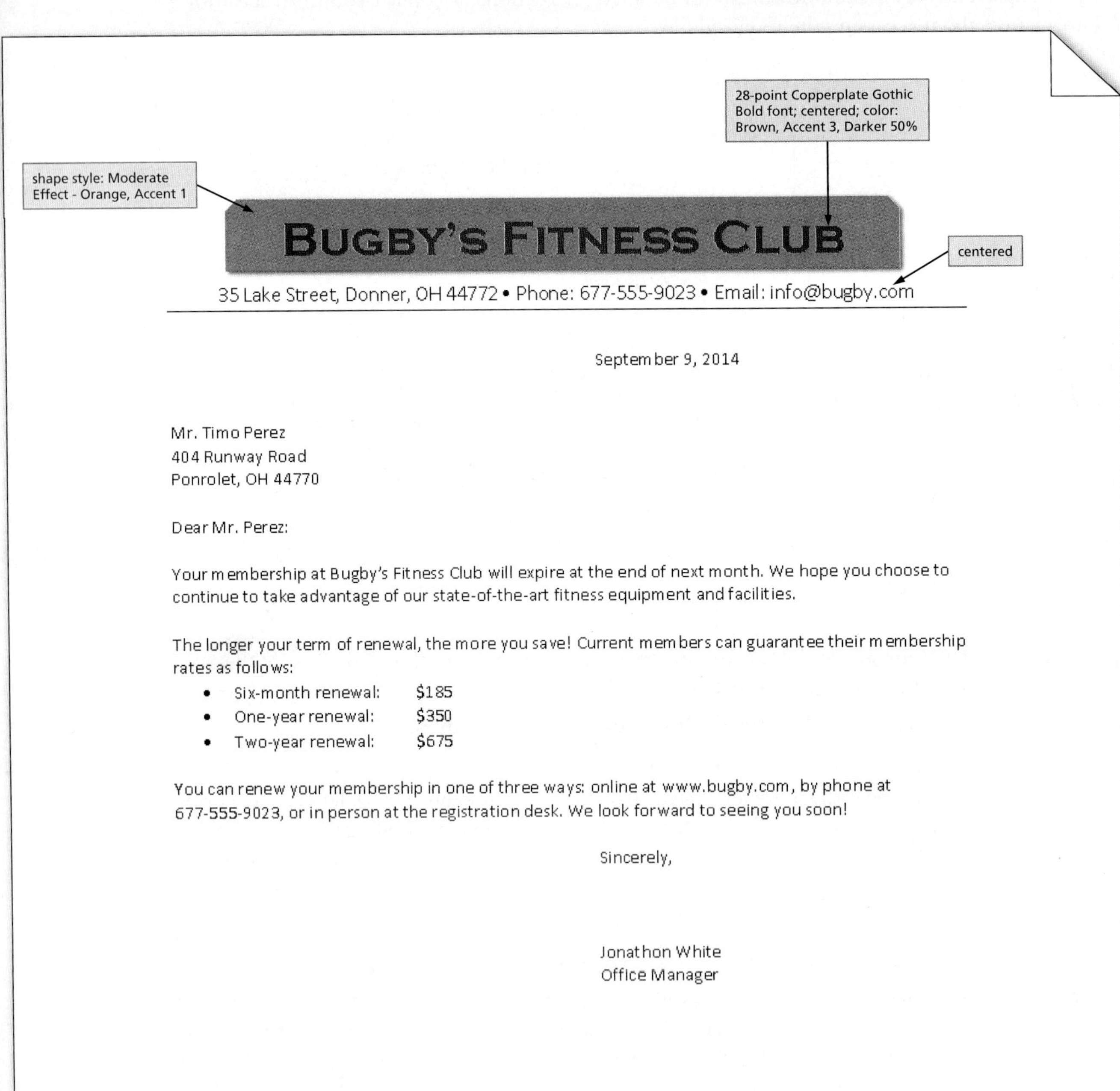

BUGBY'S FITNESS CLUB

35 Lake Street, Donner, OH 44772 • Phone: 677-555-9023 • Email: info@bugby.com

September 9, 2014

Mr. Timo Perez
404 Runway Road
Ponrolet, OH 44770

Dear Mr. Perez:

Your membership at Bugby's Fitness Club will expire at the end of next month. We hope you choose to continue to take advantage of our state-of-the-art fitness equipment and facilities.

The longer your term of renewal, the more you save! Current members can guarantee their membership rates as follows:

- Six-month renewal: $185
- One-year renewal: $350
- Two-year renewal: $675

You can renew your membership in one of three ways: online at www.bugby.com, by phone at 677-555-9023, or in person at the registration desk. We look forward to seeing you soon!

Sincerely,

Jonathon White
Office Manager

Figure 3–80

Perform the following tasks:

1. Change the theme to Retrospect.
2. Create the letterhead shown at the top of Figure 3–80, following these guidelines:
   a. Insert the Snip Same Side Corner Rectangle shape at an approximate height of 0.56" and width of 5.5". Change position of the shape to 'Position in Top Center with Square Text Wrapping'. Change the text wrapping for the shape to Top and Bottom. Add the company name, Bugby's Fitness Club, to the shape. Format the shape and its text as indicated in the figure.
   b. Insert the dot symbols as shown in the contact information. Remove the hyperlink format from the email address. If necessary, clear formatting after entering the bottom border.
   c. Save the letterhead with the file name, Lab 3-1 Fitness Club Letterhead.
3. Create the letter shown in Figure 3–80 using the modified block letter style, following these guidelines:
   a. Apply the No Spacing Quick Style to the document text (below the letterhead).
   b. Set a left-aligned tab stop at the 3.5" mark on the ruler for the date line, complimentary close, and signature block. Insert the current date.
   c. Bullet the list as you type it.
   d. Set a left-aligned tab stop at the 2" mark for the dollar amounts in the bulleted list.
   e. Convert the web address to regular text.
   f. Enter nonbreaking hyphens in the phone number.
   g. If requested by your instructor, change the name in the signature block to your name.
   h. Check the spelling of the letter. Save the letter with Lab 3-1 Fitness Club Letter as the file name and then submit it in the format specified by your instructor.
4. If your instructor permits, address and print an envelope or a mailing label for the letter.
5. What is the purpose of the nonbreaking hyphens in this letter? The letter in this assignment uses the modified block letter style. If you wanted to use the modified semi-block letter style, what changes would you make to this letter?

Lab 2: Creating a Letter with a Letterhead and Table

Problem: As a junior at your school, you are seeking an internship for the upcoming summer break. You prepare the letter shown in Figure 3–81 on the next page.

Perform the following tasks:

1. Change the theme to Celestial. Change the margins to 1" top and bottom and .75" left and right (Moderate).
2. Create the letterhead shown at the top of Figure 3–81, following these guidelines:
   a. Insert the Up Ribbon shape at an approximate height of 0.7" and width of 6". Change the position of the shape to 'Position in Top Center with Square Text Wrapping'. Change the text wrapping for the shape to Top and Bottom. Add the name to the shape. If requested by your instructor, place your name in the shape instead of the name shown in the figure. Format the shape and its text as indicated in the figure.

Continued >

In the Labs *continued*

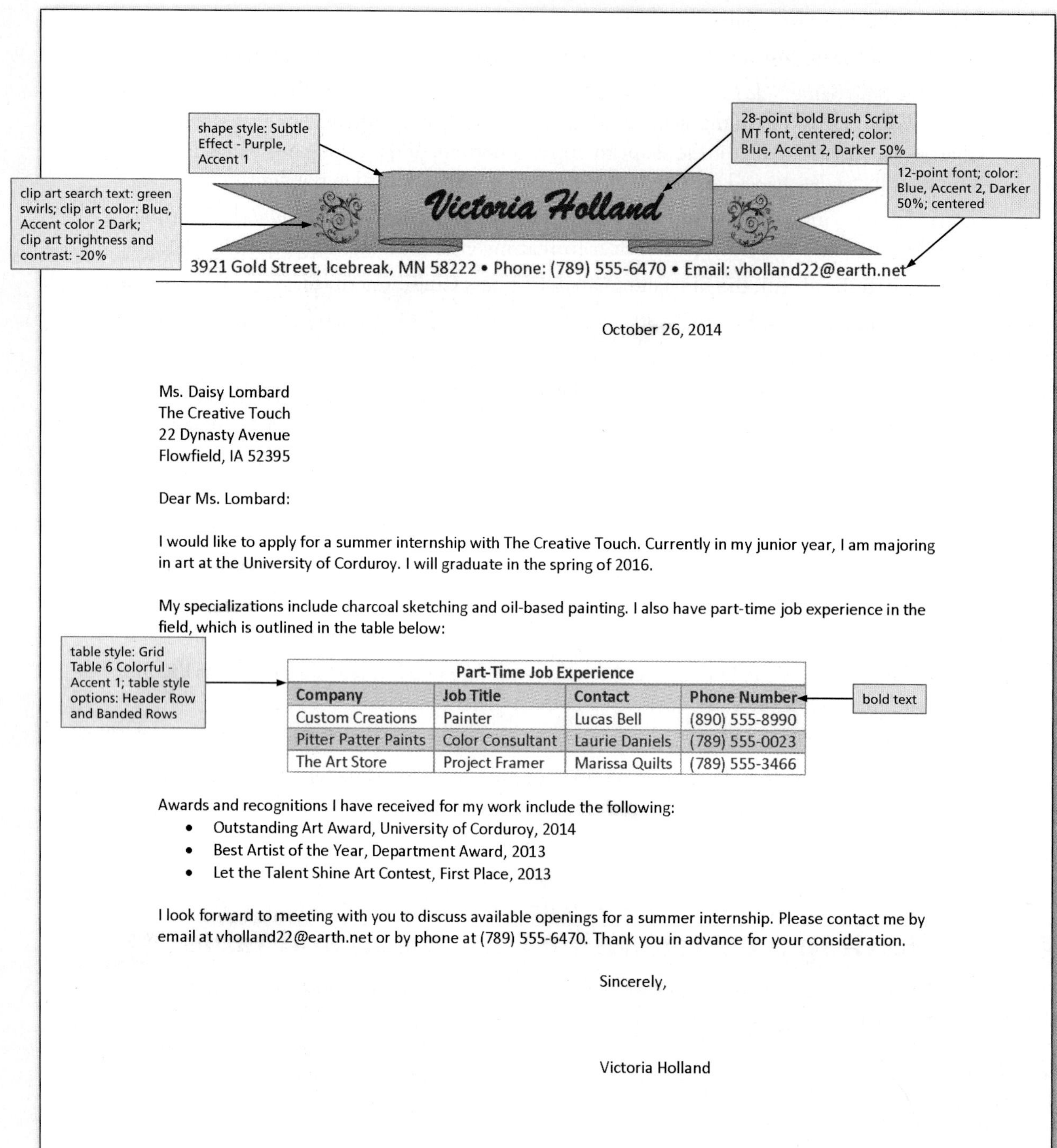

Victoria Holland

3921 Gold Street, Icebreak, MN 58222 • Phone: (789) 555-6470 • Email: vholland22@earth.net

October 26, 2014

Ms. Daisy Lombard
The Creative Touch
22 Dynasty Avenue
Flowfield, IA 52395

Dear Ms. Lombard:

I would like to apply for a summer internship with The Creative Touch. Currently in my junior year, I am majoring in art at the University of Corduroy. I will graduate in the spring of 2016.

My specializations include charcoal sketching and oil-based painting. I also have part-time job experience in the field, which is outlined in the table below:

Part-Time Job Experience			
Company	**Job Title**	**Contact**	**Phone Number**
Custom Creations	Painter	Lucas Bell	(890) 555-8990
Pitter Patter Paints	Color Consultant	Laurie Daniels	(789) 555-0023
The Art Store	Project Framer	Marissa Quilts	(789) 555-3466

Awards and recognitions I have received for my work include the following:

- Outstanding Art Award, University of Corduroy, 2014
- Best Artist of the Year, Department Award, 2013
- Let the Talent Shine Art Contest, First Place, 2013

I look forward to meeting with you to discuss available openings for a summer internship. Please contact me by email at vholland22@earth.net or by phone at (789) 555-6470. Thank you in advance for your consideration.

Sincerely,

Victoria Holland

Figure 3–81

b. Insert the clip art, resize it, change text wrapping to In Front of Text, move it to the left on the shape, and format it as indicated in the figure. Copy the clip art and move the copy of the image to the right on the shape, as shown in the figure. Flip the copied image horizontally.

c. Insert the small dot symbols as shown in the contact information. Remove the hyperlink format from the email address. If necessary, clear formatting after entering the bottom border.

d. Save the letterhead with the file name, Lab 3-2 Internship Letterhead.

3. Create the letter shown in Figure 3–81, following these guidelines:
   a. Apply the No Spacing Quick Style to the document text (below the letterhead).
   b. Set a left-aligned tab stop at the 4" mark on the ruler for the date line, complimentary close, and signature block. Insert the current date.
   c. Insert and center the table. Format the table as specified in the figure. Make all columns as wide as their contents (AutoFit Contents).
   d. Bullet the list as you type it.
   e. Convert the email address to regular text.
   f. Check the spelling of the letter. Save the letter with Lab 3-2 Internship Letter as the file name, and then submit it in the format specified by your instructor.
4. If your instructor permits, address and print an envelope or a mailing label for the letter.
5. Why do you think the clip art in this letter used a text wrapping of In Front of Text? If the table used banded columns instead of banded rows, how would its appearance change?

Lab 3: Expand Your World: Cloud and Web Technologies

Using Google Docs to Upload and Edit Files

Problem: You have created a letter in Word at work and want to proofread and edit it at home. The problem is that you do not have Word at home. You do, however, have an Internet connection at home. Because you have a Google account, you upload your Word document to Google Drive so that you can view and edit it later from a computer that does not have Word installed.

Notes:

- You will use a Google account, which you can create at no cost, to complete this assignment. If you do not have a Google account and do not want to create one, read this assignment without performing the instructions.
- To complete this assignment, you will be required to use the Data Files for Students. Visit www.cengage.com/ct/studentdownload for detailed instructions or contact your instructor for information about accessing the required files.

Instructions: Perform the following tasks:

1. In Word, open the document, Lab 3-3 Compliment Letter in Word, from the Data Files for Students. Look through the letter so that you are familiar with its contents and formats. If desired, print the letter so that you easily can compare it to the Google Docs converted file. Close the document.
2. Run a browser. Search for the text, google docs, using a search engine. Visit several websites to learn about Google Docs and Google Drive. Navigate to the Google website. If you do not have a Google account and you want to create one, click the SIGN UP button and follow the instructions. If you do not have a Google account and you do not want to create one, read the remaining instructions without performing them. If you have a Google account, sign in to your account.
3. If necessary, click Drive to display Google Drive. Click the UPLOAD, or similar, button and then follow the instructions to navigate to the location of the file, Lab 3-3 Compliment Letter in Word, and then upload the file.
4. Rename the file on Google Drive to Lab 3-3 Compliment Letter in Google. Open the file in Google Docs (Figure 3–82 on the next page). What differences do you see between the Word document and the Google Docs converted document? Fix the document in Google Docs so

Continued >

In the Labs *continued*

that it looks appealing. Download the revised document to your local storage media, changing its format to Microsoft Word. Submit the document in the format requested by your instructor.

5. What is Google Drive? What is Google Docs? Answer the question posed in #4. Do you prefer using Google Docs or Word? Why?

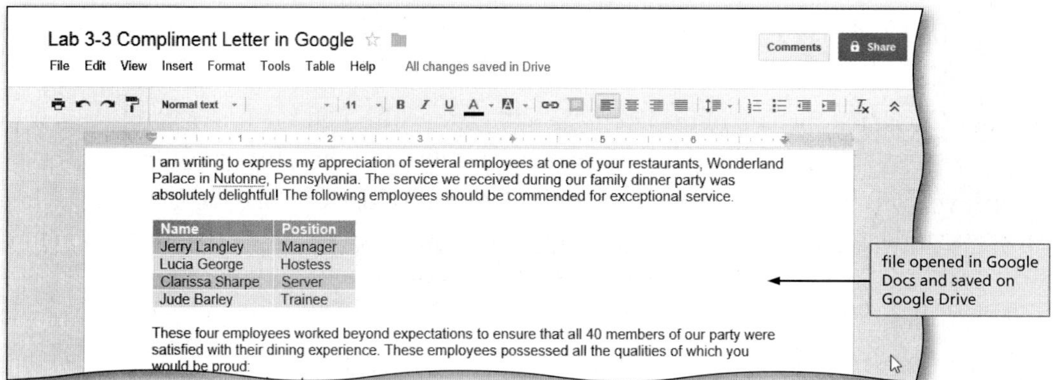

Figure 3–82

Consider This: Your Turn

Apply your creative thinking and problem solving skills to design and implement a solution.

Note: To complete these assignments, you may be required to use the Data Files for Students. Visit www.cengage.com/ct/studentdownload for detailed instructions or contact your instructor for information about accessing the required files.

1: Design and Create an Admissions Acceptance Letter

Personal

Part 1: As a part-time student in your school's office of admissions, you send acceptance letters to new students. You have been asked to design a new letterhead using this information: Frottingham College, Home of the Huskies, 77 Husky Lane, Graber, OK 74877; Phone: (439) 555-6899; website: www.frottinghamcollege.edu. Once the letterhead is designed, you then write an acceptance letter to this new student: Mr. Donald Dillenger at 13 Allison Avenue, Graber, OK 74877.

The draft wording for the letter is as follows. First paragraph: Congratulations on your admission to the School of Biological Sciences at Frottingham College for the Fall 2014 semester. We are excited to welcome you to Frottingham College. Our decision to admit you to our college is an acknowledgment of your potential and our confidence in you as a valuable addition to our student body. Second paragraph: We would like to inform you of important upcoming dates. Although not mandatory, we would advise you to attend each of these activities. The schedule is as follows:

New Student Guide Schedule		
Activity	**Date & Time**	**Location**
Get to Know Your School Campus Tour	August 14, 2014 8:00 a.m. to 5:00 p.m.	Conner Student Center, Room 134
Meet the Teachers and Advisors	August 15, 2014 9:00 a.m. to 3:00 p.m.	Milton Student Center, Room 222
Fun Night! Get to Know Your Fellow Classmates	August 19, 2014 6:00 p.m. to Midnight	Bowling & Billiards Center
What Is My Major? Learn about What Is Offered	August 20, 2014 9:00 a.m. to 7:00 p.m.	Leonardo Auditorium

Third paragraph: Before the first day of classes, you must do the following: Bulleted list: Make sure your campus email account works properly. If it does not, call (439) 555-2898 for technical support.; Verify that you can sign in online to all of your semester classes. If you cannot, call (439) 555-2898 for technical support.; Purchase all course materials from the campus bookstore. Last paragraph: Again, congratulations on your admission to Frottingham College. We look forward to your success on campus.

The letter should contain a letterhead that uses a shape and clip art, a table with an appropriate table style applied (unformatted table shown above), and a bulleted list (to present the items to complete before classes start). Insert nonbreaking spaces in the college name. Create a building block for the college name, edit the building block so that it has a ScreenTip, and insert the building block whenever you have to enter the college name.

Use the concepts and techniques presented in this chapter to create and format a letter according to a letter style, creating appropriate paragraph breaks and rewording the draft as necessary. The unformatted paragraphs in the letter are in a file called Your Turn 2-1 Letter Paragraphs, which is located on the Data Files for Students. If you prefer, you can copy and paste this text into your letter instead of typing the paragraphs yourself. If requested by your instructor, use your name in the signature line in the letter. Be sure to check the spelling and grammar of the finished letter. Submit your assignment in the format specified by your instructor.

Part 2: You made several decisions while creating the letter in this assignment: where to position elements in the letterhead, how to format elements in the letterhead, which graphic to use in the letterhead, which theme to use in the letter, which font size to use for the letter text, which table style to use, and which letter style to use. What was the rationale behind each of these decisions?

2: Design and Create a Confirmation Letter

Professional

Part 1: As a CEO of Addy Lane & Company, a retailer, you communicate the conditions of a revised business agreement with Turner Industries in a letter. You design a letterhead using this information: Addy Lane & Company, 121 Rapture Road, Harrust, NH 03891; Phone: (657) 555-7744; Email: carlosdiaz@addyemail.com. Then, you write a confirmation letter to this contact: Ms. Joyce Adams at Turner Industries, 356 Thorn Avenue, Vigil, CT 06802.

The draft wording for the letter is as follows. First paragraph: Per our phone conversation, yesterday I approved the new conditions of the business agreement with Turner Industries. The table below outlines the revised terms. Please review this list and confirm receipt either by return letter to me or email message at carlosdiaz@addyemail.com. If you have any revisions to these terms, please also include them in your reply.

Revised Business Agreement Terms		
Section	**Title**	**Summary of Revision**
2b	Materials	Addy Lane & Company will split the cost with Turner Industries for any materials used to manufacture products for Addy Lane & Company.
11a–c	Resources	Resources from each company shall be shared for mutual benefit.
33a	Communications	Addy Lane & Company and Turner Industries shall meet every other week for an assessment.
109b–d	Profits	The profits between the companies on shared merchandise now will be split 50/50.

Second paragraph: Please also confirm these new employee names and positions at Turner Industries: Bulleted list: Doreen Liner, Administrative Assistant; Frank Cart, Manager; Anthony Boyd, Web Administrator. Last paragraph: Thank you in advance for your assistance with these details. I look forward to a long-term business relationship.

The letter should contain a letterhead that uses a shape and clip art, a table with an appropriate table style applied (unformatted table shown above), and a bulleted list (to present the new employees). Insert nonbreaking spaces in the company name, Turner Industries. Create a building

Continued >

Consider This: Your Turn *continued*

block for the company name, Turner Industries, edit the building block so that it has a ScreenTip, and insert the building block whenever you have to enter the company name.

Use the concepts and techniques presented in this chapter to create and format a letter according to a letter style, creating appropriate paragraph breaks and rewording the draft as necessary. The unformatted paragraphs in the letter are in a file called Your Turn 2-2 Letter Paragraphs, which is located on the Data Files for Students. If you prefer, you can copy and paste this text into your letter instead of typing the paragraphs yourself. If requested by your instructor, use your name in the signature line in the letter. Be sure to check the spelling and grammar of the finished letter. Submit your assignment in the format specified by your instructor.

Part 2: You made several decisions while creating the letter in this assignment: where to position elements in the letterhead, how to format elements in the letterhead, which graphic to use in the letterhead, which theme to use in the letter, which font size to use for the letter text, which table style to use, and which letter style to use. What was the rationale behind each of these decisions?

3: Design and Create a Letter to a Potential Employer

Research and Collaboration

Part 1: As assistants in the Office of Career Development at your school, you and two others have been asked to prepare a sample letter to a potential employer; students seeking employment will use this letter as a reference document when creating their own letters. Form a three-member team to research, compose, and create this letter. As a group, locate a job advertisement for which your team could write a sample letter. One team member should design a letterhead. Another team member should create a table of educational background that relates to the advertisement, and the third team member should compose a list of activities that would be important to the potential employer. As a group, compose the letter using the individual elements where appropriate.

Use the concepts and techniques presented in this chapter to create and format a letter according to a letter style. If requested by your instructor, use team members' names in the letter. Be sure to check the spelling and grammar of the finished letter. Submit your team assignment in the format specified by your instructor.

Part 2: You made several decisions while creating the letter in this assignment: text to use, where to position elements in the letterhead, how to format elements in the letterhead, which graphic to use in the letterhead, which theme to use in the letter, which font size to use for the letter text, which table style to use, and which letter style to use. What was the rationale behind each of these decisions?

Learn Online

Reinforce what you learned in this chapter with games, exercises, training, and many other online activities and resources.

Student Companion Site Reinforcement activities and resources are available at no additional cost on www.cengagebrain.com. Visit www.cengage.com/ct/studentdownload for detailed instructions about accessing the resources available at the Student Companion Site.

SAM Put your skills into practice with SAM! If you have a SAM account, go to www.cengage.com/sam2013 to access SAM assignments for this chapter.

4 Creating a Document with a Title Page, Lists, Tables, and a Watermark

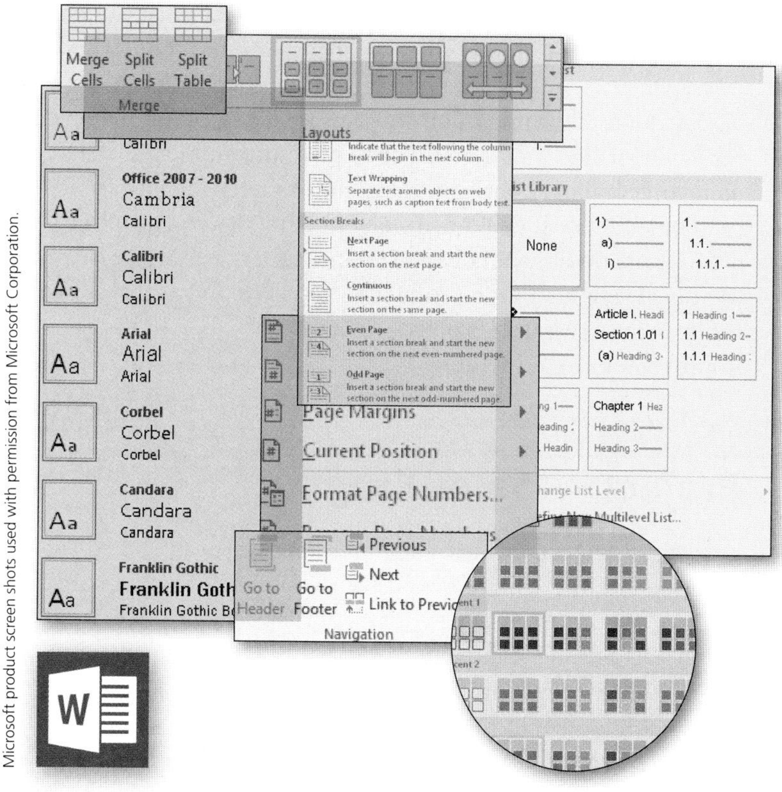

Objectives

You will have mastered the material in this project when you can:

- Border a paragraph
- Change paragraph indentation
- Insert and format a SmartArt graphic
- Apply character effects
- Insert a section break
- Insert a Word document in an open document
- Insert formatted headers and footers
- Sort paragraphs and tables
- Use the format painter
- Add picture bullets to a list
- Create a multilevel list
- Modify and format Word tables
- Sum columns in a table
- Create a watermark
- Change theme fonts

4 Creating a Document with a Title Page, Lists, Tables, and a Watermark

Introduction

During the course of your business and personal endeavors, you may want or need to provide a recommendation to a person or group of people for their consideration. You might suggest they purchase a product, such as a vehicle or books, or contract a service, such as designing their webpage or remodeling their house. Or, you might try to convince an audience to take an action, such as signing a petition, joining a club, visiting an establishment, or donating to a cause. You may be asked to request funds for a new program or activity or to promote an idea, such as a benefits package to company employees or a budget plan to upper management. To present these types of recommendations, you may find yourself writing a proposal.

A proposal generally is one of three types: sales, research, or planning. A **sales proposal** sells an idea, a product, or a service. A **research proposal** usually requests funding for a research project. A **planning proposal** offers solutions to a problem or improvement to a situation.

Project — Sales Proposal

Sales proposals describe the features and value of products and services being offered, with the intent of eliciting a positive response from the reader. Desired outcomes include the reader accepting ideas, purchasing products, contracting services, volunteering time, contributing to a cause, or taking an action. A well-written proposal can be the key to obtaining the desired results.

The project in this chapter follows generally accepted guidelines for writing short sales proposals and uses Word to create the sales proposal shown in Figure 4–1. The sales proposal in this chapter is designed to persuade readers to visit a state park. The proposal has a colorful title page to attract readers' attention. To add impact, the sales proposal has a watermark consisting of animal paw prints and tracks, positioned behind the content on each page. It also uses lists and tables to summarize and highlight important data.

Paw Ridge
State Park
paragraph border
paragraph border
watermark
SmartArt graphic
Lodging
Cabins
Camp
Inn
Rent
Recreation
Canoe
Fish
Hike
Swim
Plan your next outing with us!

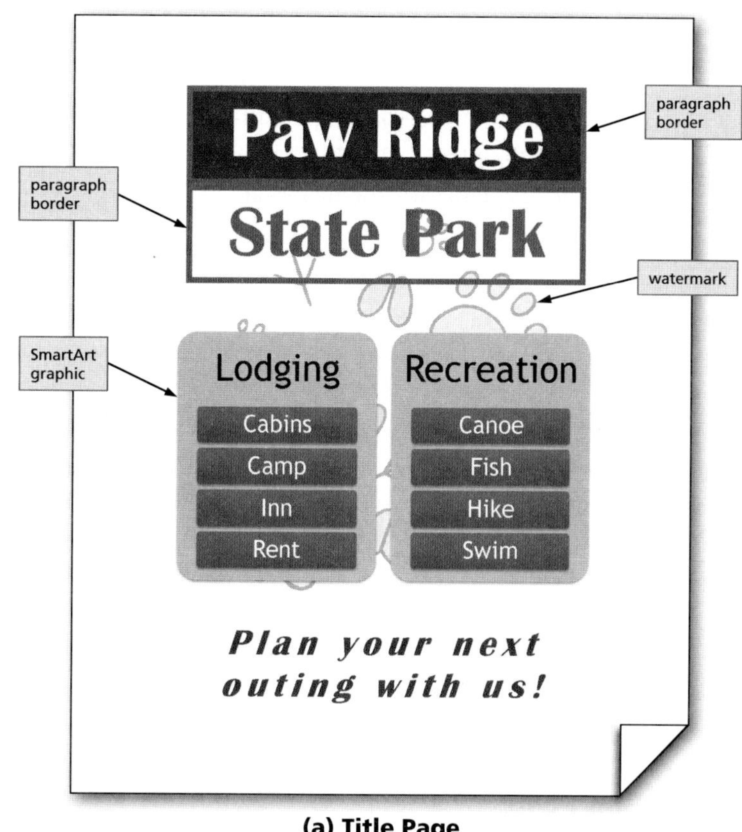

(a) Title Page

header
PAW RIDGE STATE PARK
OUR PARK
Paw Ridge State Park is located just minutes from Deer Creek Dam in Green Valley County. After entering our state park off of Highway 50 just north of the dam, you will marvel at the breathtaking views as you explore our 2,500-acre public park. Hike the trails, reserve a pavilion for an event, relax at the beach, swim in the public pool, canoe or fish in the creek, tour the nature center, or visit our historic sites.
The park is open year-round from 7:00 a.m. until 10:00 p.m. Dine in our restaurant for breakfast, lunch, or dinner. Spend the evening in a room at our rustic inn or in one of our private cabins. Overnight guests are invited to join park rangers at evening outdoor activities, including storytelling and stargazing programs.
Lodging Descriptions
Cabins (premium): sleeps six people, towels and linens included
Cabins (standard): sleeps four people, towels and linens not included
Campsites (electric): 30 amp hookup, picnic table, fire ring, modern showers
Campsites (primitive): tents only, picnic table, fire ring, modern showers
Inn Room (premium): sleeps six people, includes balcony
Inn Room (standard): sleeps four people
Rentals: pop-up campers, travel trailers, motorhomes
Lodging Rates per Night
Peak Weekend
Peak Weekday
Nonpeak Weekend
Nonpeak Weekday
Primitive Campsite $ 15 $ 10 $ 10 $ 5
Electric Campsite $ 30 $ 20 $ 25 $ 15
Cabin (Standard) $ 60 $ 45 $ 50 $ 40
Cabin (Premium) $ 90 $ 75 $ 80 $ 70
Inn Room (Standard) $ 75 $ 60 $ 65 $ 55
Inn Room (Premium) $ 115 $ 100 $ 105 $ 95
Pop-Up Rental $ 40 $ 35 $ 30 $ 25
Travel Trailer Rental $ 60 $ 45 $ 50 $ 40
Motorhome Rental $ 90 $ 75 $ 80 $ 70
watermark
picture bullets
formatted table
footer
1

(b) First Page of Body of Proposal

header
PAW RIDGE STATE PARK
Recreation
1. Canoe
a. 3-mile, 5-mile, or 10-mile trips
b. Rent a canoe, kayak, or tube
c. Open daily from May 1 through September 30
2. Fish
a. Private boats welcome or rentals available
b. Fishing license required
3. Hike
a. 15 trails, ranging from 1 to 5 miles in length
i. 2 easy
ii. 10 moderate
iii. 3 rugged
b. Bicycles not allowed on hiking trails
4. Swim
a. Public beach
b. Olympic-sized outdoor pool
c. Indoor pool for overnight guests
d. No lifeguards on duty
e. Open May 15 through September 15
PARK FEES
You can purchase access to certain recreational activities or to the entire park. Day, week, and annual passes are available.
Although the park is open all year, some areas are accessible seasonally.
Access
Day
Week
Annual
Park Fees
Docks Boat and canoe docks $ 3 $ 15 $ 45
Hiking All trails $ 3 $ 15 $ 45
Self-guided tours Nature center, pavilions, and historic sites $ 1 $ 5 $ 25
Swimming Public beach and outdoor pool $ 2 $ 10 $ 50
Access to all park recreation $ 9 $ 45 $ 165
multilevel list
watermark
formatted table
footer
2

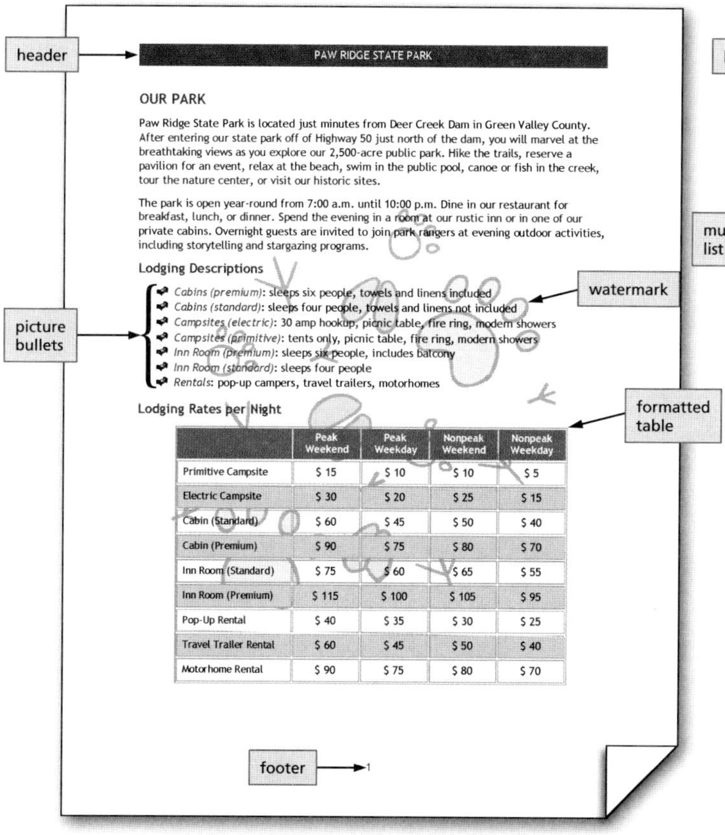

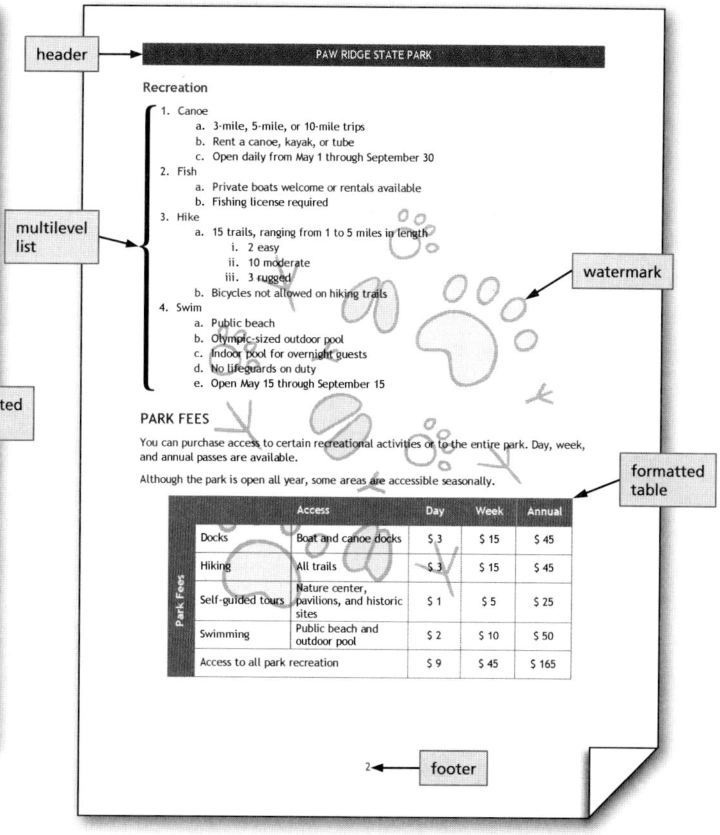

(c) Second Page of Body of Proposal

Figure 4–1

Roadmap

In this chapter, you will learn how to create the sales proposal shown in Figure 4–1. The following roadmap identifies general activities you will perform as you progress through this chapter:

1. CREATE a TITLE PAGE for the proposal.
2. INSERT an EXISTING Word DOCUMENT in the proposal.
3. CREATE a HEADER AND FOOTER in the proposal.
4. EDIT AND FORMAT LISTS in the proposal.
5. EDIT AND FORMAT TABLES in the proposal.
6. CREATE a WATERMARK in the proposal.

At the beginning of step instructions throughout the chapter, you will see an abbreviated form of this roadmap. The abbreviated roadmap uses colors to indicate chapter progress: gray means the chapter is beyond that activity, blue means the task being shown is covered in that activity, and black means that activity is yet to be covered. For example, the following abbreviated roadmap indicates the chapter would be showing a task in the 2 INSERT EXISTING DOCUMENT activity.

1 CREATE TITLE PAGE | 2 INSERT EXISTING DOCUMENT | 3 CREATE HEADER & FOOTER
3 EDIT & FORMAT LISTS | 4 EDIT & FORMAT TABLES | 5 CREATE WATERMARK

Use the abbreviated roadmap as a progress guide while you read or step through the instructions in this chapter.

One of the few differences between Windows 7 and Windows 8 occurs in the steps to run Word. If you are using Windows 7, click the Start button, type `Word` in the 'Search programs and files' box, click Word 2013, and then, if necessary, maximize the Word window. For a summary of the steps to run Word in Windows 7, refer to the Quick Reference located at the back of this book.

To Run Word and Change Word Settings

If you are using a computer to step through the project in this chapter and you want your screens to match the figures in this book, you should change your screen's resolution to 1366 × 768. For information about how to change a computer's resolution, refer to the Office and Windows chapter at the beginning of this book.

The following steps run Word, display formatting marks, and change the zoom to page width.

1. Scroll the Start screen for a Word 2013 tile. If your Start screen contains a Word 2013 tile, tap or click it to run Word and then proceed to Step 5; if the Start screen does not contain the Word 2013 tile, proceed to the next step to search for the Word app.
2. Swipe in from the right edge of the screen or point to the upper-right corner of the screen to display the Charms bar and then tap or click the Search charm on the Charms bar to display the Search menu.
3. Type `Word` as the search text in the Search box and watch the search results appear in the Apps list.
4. Tap or click Word 2013 in the search results to run Word.
5. Tap or click the Blank document thumbnail on the Word start screen to create a blank document and display it in the Word window.
6. If the Word window is not maximized, tap or click the Maximize button on its title bar to maximize the window.
7. If the Print Layout button on the status bar is not selected (shown in Figure 4–2 on page WD 206), tap or click it so that your screen is in Print Layout view.
8. If the 'Show/Hide ¶' button (HOME tab | Paragraph group) is not selected already, tap or click it to display formatting marks on the screen.
9. To display the page the same width as the document window, if necessary, tap or click the Page Width button (VIEW tab | Zoom group).
10. If the rulers are not displayed already, tap or click the View Ruler check box (VIEW tab | Show group), because you will use the rulers for several tasks in the creation of this project.

To Change Theme Colors

Recall that Word provides document themes, which contain a variety of color schemes and other effects. You should select a theme that includes colors that reflect the goals of a sales proposal. This proposal uses the Wisp document theme. The following steps the document theme.

1. Tap or click DESIGN on the ribbon to display the DESIGN tab.
2. Tap or click the Themes button (DESIGN tab | Document Formatting group) to display the Themes gallery.
3. Tap or click Wisp in the Themes gallery to change the document theme to the selected theme.

Creating a Title Page

A **title page** is a separate cover page that contains, at a minimum, the title of a document. For a sales proposal, the title page usually is the first page of the document. Solicited proposals often have a specific format for the title page. Guidelines for the title page of a solicited proposal may stipulate the margins, spacing, layout, and required contents, such as title, sponsor name, author name, date, etc. With an unsolicited proposal, by contrast, you can design the title page in a way that best presents its message.

CONSIDER THIS

How do you design an eye-catching title page?

The title page is the first section a reader sees on a sales proposal. Thus, it is important that the title page appropriately reflects the goal of the sales proposal. When designing the title page, consider its text and graphics.

- **Use concise, descriptive text.** The title page should contain a short, descriptive title that accurately reflects the message of the sales proposal. The title page also may include a theme or slogan. Do not place a page number on the title page.
- **Identify appropriate fonts, font sizes, and colors for the text.** Use fonts that are easy to read. Avoid using more than three different fonts because too many fonts can make the title page visually confusing. Use larger font sizes to add impact to the title page. To give the title more emphasis, its font size should be larger than any other text on the title page. Use colors that complement one another and convey the meaning of the proposal.
- **Use graphics to reinforce the goal.** Select simple graphics that clearly communicate the fundamental nature of the proposal. Possible graphics include shapes, pictures, and logos.
- **Use colors that complement text colors.** Be aware that too many graphics and colors can be distracting. Arrange graphics with the text so that the title page is attractive and uncluttered.

The title page of the sales proposal in this chapter (Figure 4–1a on page WD 203) contains a colorful title that is surrounded by a border with some shading, an artistic graphic with text, a colorful slogan, and the faded paw prints image in the background. The steps on the next several pages create this title page. The faded image of the paw prints is added to all pages at the end of the chapter.

To Format Characters

The title in the sales proposal should use a large font size and an easy-to-read font, and should be the focal point on the page. ***Why?*** *To give the title more emphasis, its font size should be larger than any other text on the title page.* The steps on the next page enter the title, Paw Ridge State Park, with the first two words centered on the first line and the second two words centered on the second line.

If you are using your finger on a touch screen and are having difficulty completing the steps in this chapter, consider using a stylus. Many people find it easier to be precise with a stylus than with a finger. In addition, with a stylus you see the pointer. If you still are having trouble completing the steps with a stylus, try using a mouse.

1. Tap or click HOME on the ribbon to display the HOME tab.
2. Tap or click the Center button (HOME tab | Paragraph group) to center the paragraph that will contain the title.
3. Tap or click the Font arrow (HOME tab | Font group). Scroll to and then tap or click Britannic Bold (or a similar font) in the Font gallery, so that the text you type will use the selected font.
4. Tap or click the Font Size arrow (HOME tab | Font group) and then tap or click 72 in the Font Size gallery, so that the text you type will use the selected font size.
5. Type `Paw Ridge` and then press the ENTER key to enter the first line of the title.
6. Tap or click the Font Color arrow (HOME tab | Font group) and then tap or click Brown, Accent 3 (seventh color, first row) in the Font Color gallery, so that the text you type will use the selected font color.
7. Type `State Park` as the second line of the title (shown in Figure 4–2).

To Border a Paragraph

1 CREATE TITLE PAGE | 2 INSERT EXISTING DOCUMENT | 3 CREATE HEADER & FOOTER
4 EDIT & FORMAT LISTS | 5 EDIT & FORMAT TABLES | 6 CREATE WATERMARK

If you are using a mouse and you click the Borders button (HOME tab | Paragraph group), Word applies the most recently defined border, or, if one has not been defined, it applies the default border to the current paragraph. To specify a border different from the most recently defined border, you click the Borders arrow (HOME tab | Paragraph group). If you are using a touch screen, recall that touch screens may not have a separate Borders button and Borders arrow.

In this project, the first line of the title in the sales proposal (Paw Ridge) has a 6-point brown border around it. ***Why?*** *You want the title to stand out more than the rest of the text on the title page.* The following steps add a border to all edges of a paragraph.

1

- Position the insertion point in the paragraph to border, in this case, the first line of the document.
- Tap or click the Borders arrow (HOME tab | Paragraph group) to display the Borders gallery (Figure 4–2).

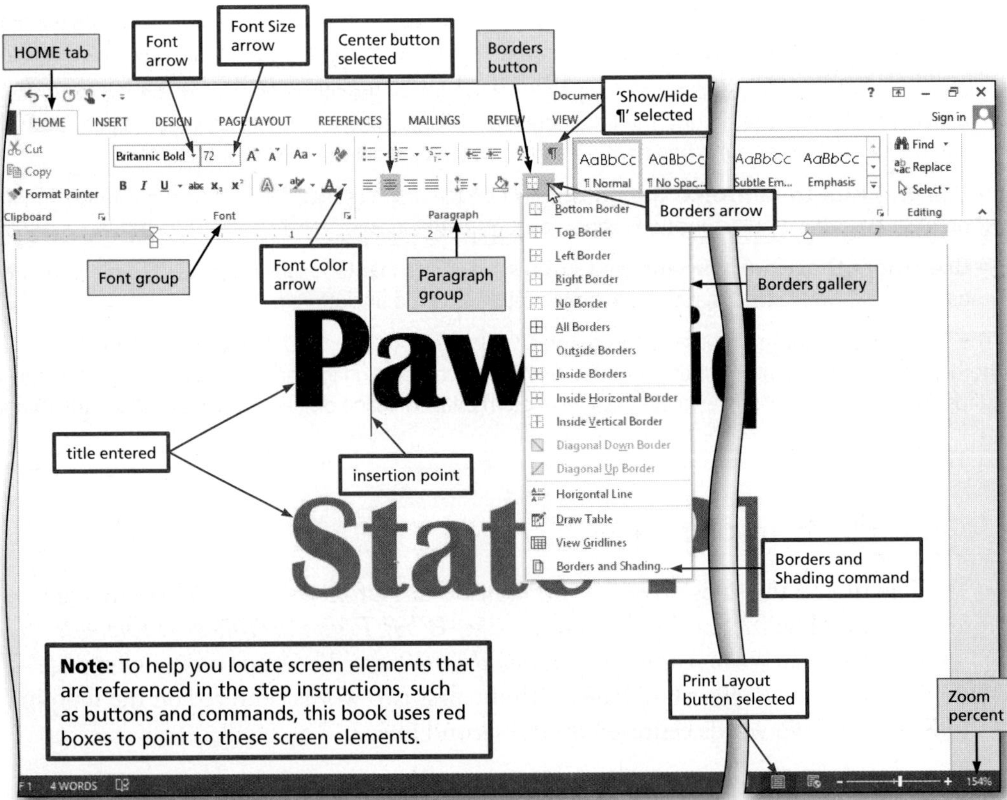

Figure 4–2

2

- Tap or click Borders and Shading in the Borders gallery to display the Borders and Shading dialog box.
- Tap or click Box in the Setting area (Borders and Shading dialog box), which will place a border on each edge of the current paragraph.
- Tap or click the Color arrow and then tap or click Brown, Accent 3 (seventh color, first row) in the Color palette to specify the border color.
- Tap or click the Width arrow and then tap or click 6 pt to specify the thickness of the border (Figure 4–3).

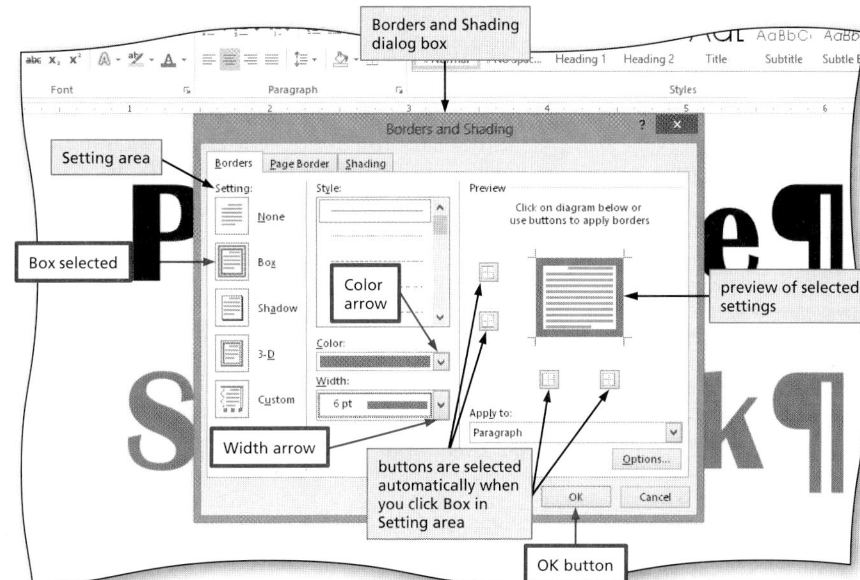

Figure 4–3

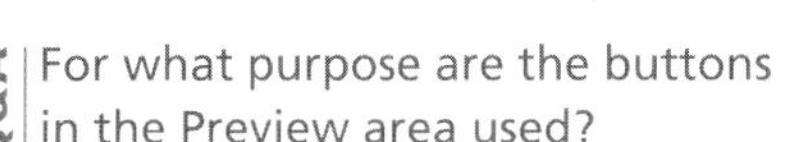

Q&A For what purpose are the buttons in the Preview area used?

They are toggles that display and remove the top, bottom, left, and right borders from the diagram in the Preview area.

3

- Tap or click the OK button (Borders and Shading dialog box) to place the border shown in the preview area of the dialog box around the current paragraph in the document (Figure 4–4).

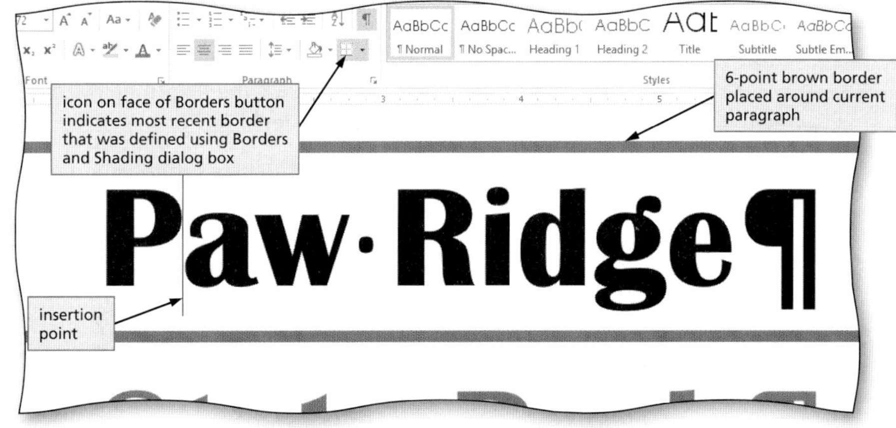

Figure 4–4

Q&A How would I remove an existing border from a paragraph?

Tap or click the Borders arrow (HOME tab | Paragraph group) and then tap or click the border in the Borders gallery that identifies the border you wish to remove, or tap or click No Border to remove all borders.

Other Ways

1. Tap or click 'Borders and Shading' button (DESIGN tab | Page Background group), tap or click Borders tab (Borders and Shading dialog box), select desired border, tap or click OK button

To Shade a Paragraph and Change Font Color

To make the first line of the title of the sales proposal more eye-catching, it is shaded in dark red. When you shade a paragraph, Word shades the rectangular area behind any text or graphics in the paragraph from the left margin of the paragraph to the right margin. If the paragraph is surrounded by a border, Word shades inside the border. The following steps shade a paragraph and change font color.

1 With the insertion point in the paragraph to shade, the first line in this case (shown in Figure 4–4), tap or click the Shading arrow (HOME tab | Paragraph group) to display the Shading gallery.

BTW
Normal Style
If your screen settings differ from Figure 4-2, it is possible the default settings in your Normal style have been changed. Normal style settings are saved in a file called normal.dotm file. To restore the original Normal style settings, exit Word and use File Explorer to locate the normal.dotm file (be sure that hidden files and folders are displayed, and include system and hidden files in your search — you may need to use Help to assist you with these tasks). Rename the normal.dotm file as oldnormal.dotm. After renaming the normal.dotm file, it no longer will exist as normal.dotm. The next time you start Word, it will recreate a normal.dotm file using the original default settings.

2. Tap or click 'Dark Red, Accent 1' (fifth color, first row) in the Shading gallery to shade the current paragraph (shown in Figure 4–5).
3. Drag through the words, Paw Ridge, in the first line of the title to select the text.
4. Tap or click the Font Color arrow (HOME tab | Font group) to display the Font Color gallery and then tap or click 'White, Background 1' (first color, first row) to change the color of the selected text (shown in Figure 4–5).

To Border Another Paragraph

To make the second line of the title of the sales proposal (State Park) more eye-catching, it has a 6-point olive green border around it. The following steps add a border to all edges of a paragraph.

1. Position the insertion point in the paragraph to border (in this case, the second paragraph containing the text, State Park).
2. Tap or click the Borders arrow (HOME tab | Paragraph group) to display the Borders gallery and then tap or click Borders and Shading in the Border gallery to display the Borders and Shading dialog box.
3. Tap or click Box in the Setting area (Borders and Shading dialog box), which will place a border on each edge of the current paragraph.
4. Tap or click the Color arrow and then tap or click 'Olive Green, Accent 4' (eighth color, first row) in the Color palette to specify the border color.
5. If necessary, tap or click the Width arrow and then tap or click 6 pt to specify the thickness of the border.
6. Tap or click the OK button to place the defined border shown around the current paragraph in the document (Figure 4–5).

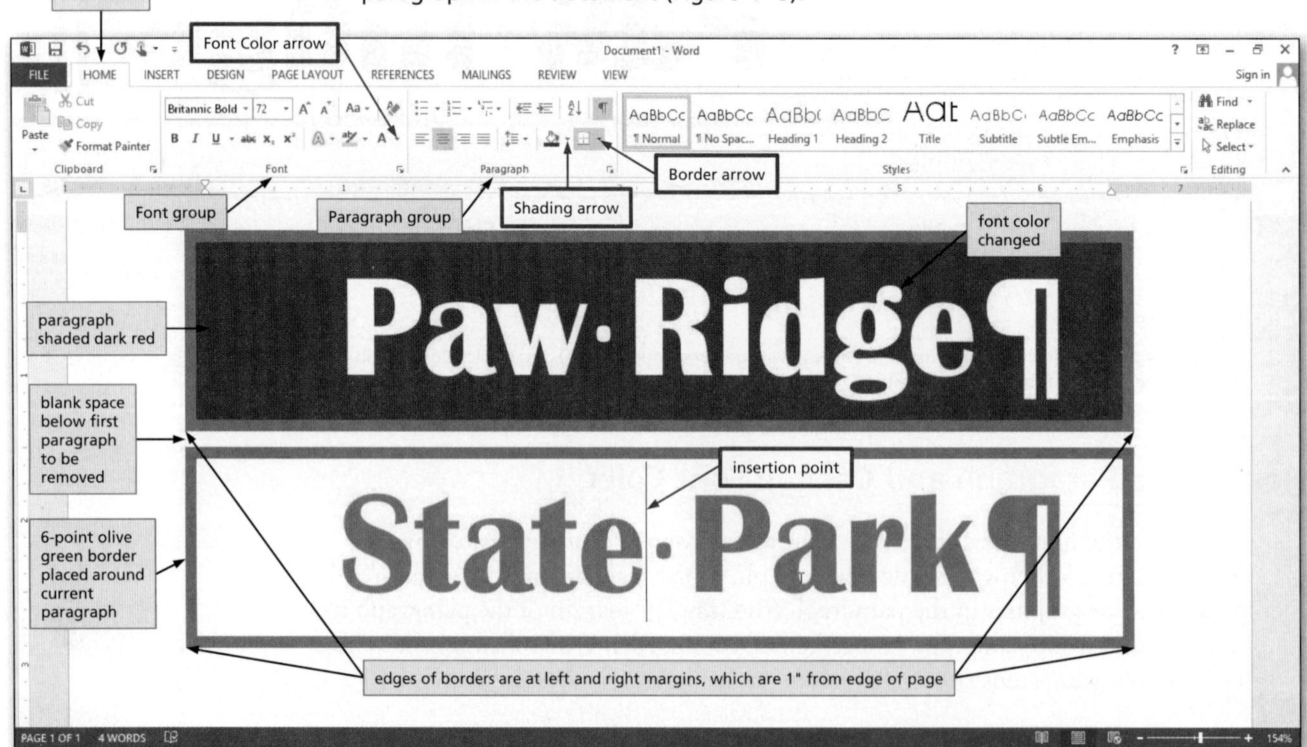

Figure 4–5

To Change Spacing after a Paragraph

Currently, a small amount of blank space exists between the two paragraph borders because Word automatically places 8 points of blank space below paragraphs (shown in Figure 4–5). The following steps remove the blank space below the first paragraph.

1. Position the insertion point in the paragraph to be adjusted (in this case, the paragraph containing the text, Paw Ridge).

2. Display the PAGE LAYOUT tab. If you are using a touch screen, tap the Spacing After box (PAGE LAYOUT tab | Paragraph group) and then type `0` to change the spacing below the paragraph; if you are using a mouse, click the Spacing After down arrow (PAGE LAYOUT tab | Paragraph group) as many times as necessary until 0 pt is displayed in the Spacing After box to remove the space below the current paragraph (shown in Figure 4–6).

To Change Left and Right Paragraph Indent

1 CREATE TITLE PAGE | 2 INSERT EXISTING DOCUMENT | 3 CREATE HEADER & FOOTER
4 EDIT & FORMAT LISTS | 5 EDIT & FORMAT TABLES | 6 CREATE WATERMARK

The borders around the first and second paragraphs and the shading in the first paragraph currently extend from the left margin to the right margin (shown in Figure 4–5). In this project, the edges of the border and shading are closer to the text in the title. ***Why?*** *You do not want such a large gap between the edge of the text and the border.* If you want the border and shading to start and end at a location different from the margin, you change the left and right paragraph indent.

The Increase Indent and Decrease Indent buttons (HOME tab | Paragraph group) change the left indent by ½-inch, respectively. In this case, however, you cannot use these buttons because you want to change both the left and right indent. The following steps change the left and right paragraph indent.

- Be sure the insertion point is positioned in the paragraph to indent (the first paragraph in this case). If you are using a touch screen, tap the Indent Left box (PAGE LAYOUT tab | Paragraph group) and then type `0.5` to change the left indent; if you are using a mouse, click the Indent Left up arrow (PAGE LAYOUT tab | Paragraph group) five times so that 0.5" is displayed in the Indent Left box because you want to adjust the paragraph left indent by this amount.
- If you are using a touch screen, tap the Indent Right box (PAGE LAYOUT tab | Paragraph group) and then type `0.5` to change the right indent; if you are using a mouse, click the Indent Right up arrow (PAGE LAYOUT tab | Paragraph group) five times so that 0.5" is displayed in the Indent Right box because you want to adjust the paragraph right indent by this amount (Figure 4–6).

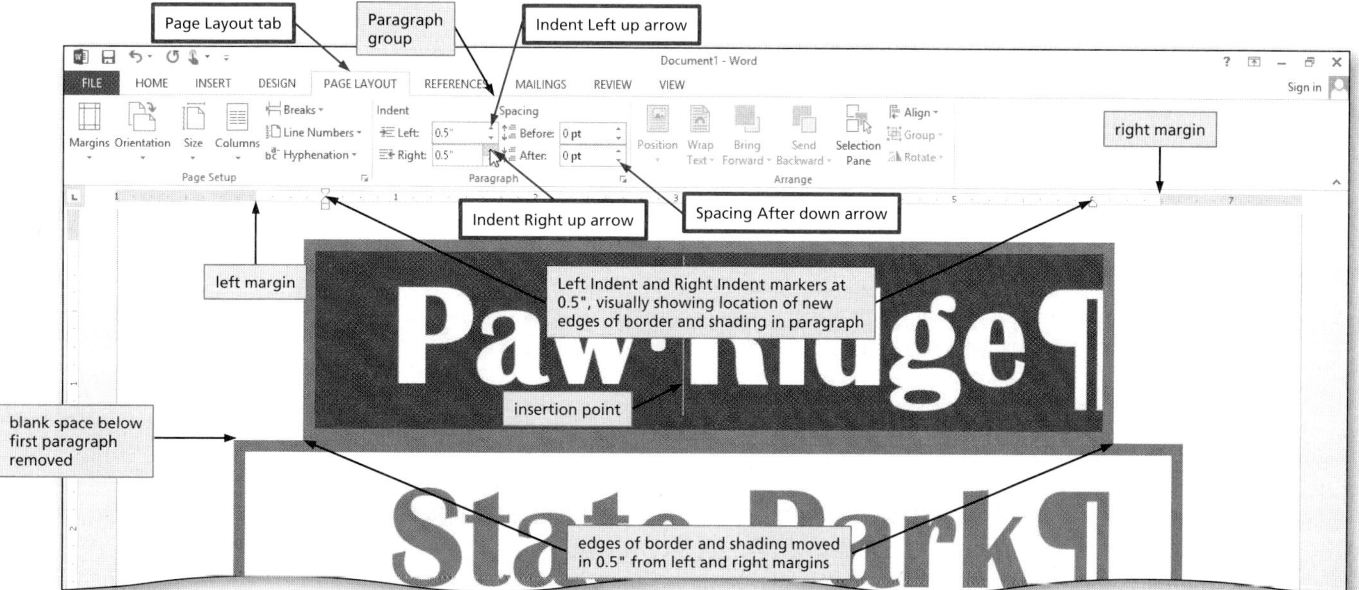

Figure 4–6

Experiment

- If you are using a mouse, repeatedly click the Indent Right and Indent Left up and down scroll arrows (PAGE LAYOUT tab | Paragraph group) and watch the left and right edges of the current paragraph change in the document window. When you have finished experimenting, set the left and right indent each to 0.5".

2

- Repeat Step 1 for the second paragraph, so that the paragraph containing the words, State Park, also has a left and right indent of 0.5" (shown in Figure 4–7).

Other Ways

1. Drag Left Indent and Right Indent markers on ruler
2. Tap or click Paragraph Settings Dialog Box Launcher (HOME tab | Paragraph group), tap or click Indents and Spacing tab (Paragraph dialog box), set indentation values, tap or click OK button
3. Tap 'Show Context Menu' button on mini toolbar or right-click paragraph, tap or click Paragraph on shortcut menu, tap or click Indents and Spacing tab (Paragraph dialog box), set indentation values, tap or click OK button

To Clear Formatting

The title is finished. When you press the ENTER key to advance the insertion point from the end of the second line to the beginning of the third line on the title page, the border will be carried forward to line 3, and any text you type will be a 72-point Britannic Bold Brown, Accent 3 font. The paragraphs and characters on line 3 should not have the same paragraph and character formatting as line 2. Instead, they should be formatted using the Normal style. The following steps clear formatting, which applies the Normal style formats to the location of the insertion point.

BTW
The Ribbon and Screen Resolution
Word may change how the groups and buttons within the groups appear on the ribbon, depending on the computer's screen resolution. Thus, your ribbon may look different from the ones in this book if you are using a screen resolution other than 1366 × 768.

1. If necessary, press the END key to position the insertion point at the end of line 2, that is, after the k in Park.
2. Press the ENTER key.
3. Display the HOME tab. Tap or click the 'Clear All Formatting' button (HOME tab | Font group) to apply the Normal style to the location of the insertion point (Figure 4–7).

Q&A Could I have tapped or clicked Normal in the Styles gallery instead of the Clear All Formatting button?
Yes.

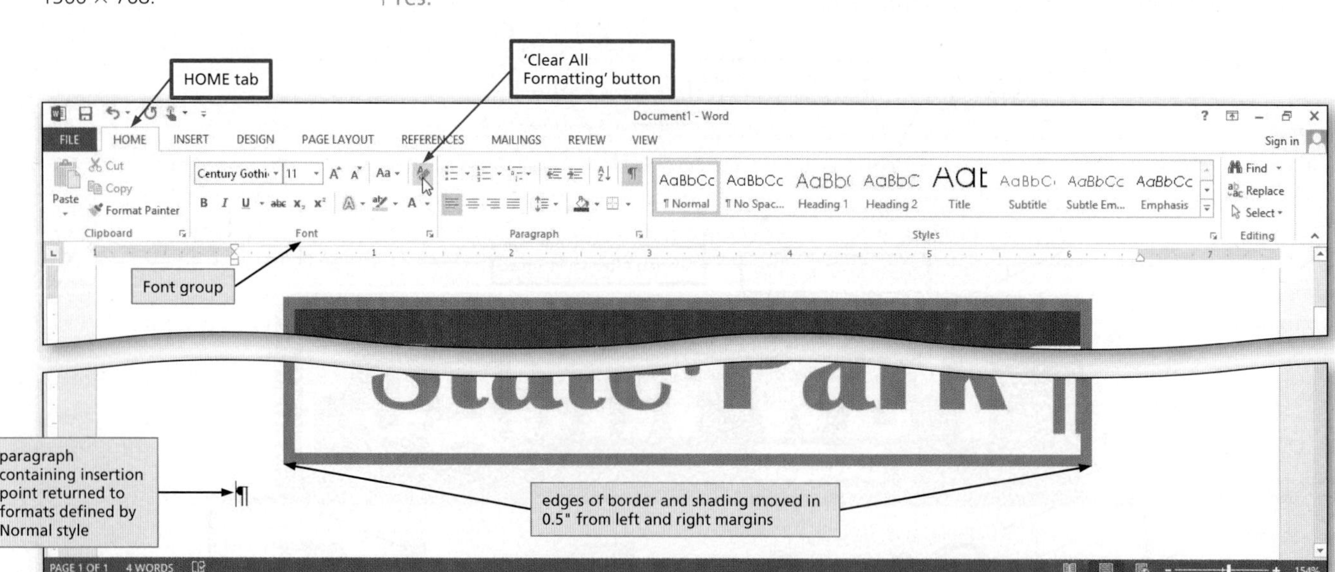

Figure 4–7

To Save a Document

You have performed many tasks while creating this title page and do not want to risk losing work completed thus far. Accordingly, you should save the document. The following steps assume you already have created folders for storing your files, for example, a CIS 101 folder (for your class) that contains a Word folder (for your assignments). Thus, these steps save the document in the Word folder in the CIS 101 folder using the file name, Paw Ridge Title Page.

BTW

Touch Screen Differences

The Office and Windows interfaces may vary if you are using a touch screen. For this reason, you might notice that the function or appearance of your touch screen differs slightly from this chapter's presentation.

1 Tap or click the Save button on the Quick Access Toolbar, which depending on settings, will display either the Save As gallery in the Backstage view or the Save As dialog box.

2 To save on a hard disk or other storage media on your computer, proceed to Step 2a. To save on SkyDrive, proceed to Step 2b.

2a If your screen opens the Backstage view and you want to save on storage media on your computer, tap or click Computer in the left pane, if necessary, to display options in the right pane related to saving on your computer. If your screen already displays the Save As dialog box, proceed to Step 4.

2b If your screen opens the Backstage view and you want to save on SkyDrive, tap or click SkyDrive in the left pane to display SkyDrive saving options or a Sign In button. If your screen displays a Sign In button, tap or click it and then sign in to SkyDrive.

3 Tap or click the Browse button in the right pane to display the Save As dialog box associated with the selected save location (i.e., Computer or SkyDrive).

4 Type `Paw Ridge Title Page` in the File name box to change the file name. Do not press the ENTER key after typing the file name because you do not want to close the dialog box at this time.

5 Navigate to the desired save location (in this case, the Word folder in the CIS 101 folder [or your class folder] on your computer or SkyDrive).

6 Tap or click the Save button (Save As dialog box) to save the title page in the selected folder on the selected save location with the entered file name.

SmartArt Graphics

Microsoft Office 2013 includes **SmartArt graphics**, which are visual representations of information. Many different types of SmartArt graphics are available, allowing you to choose one that illustrates your message best. Table 4–1 identifies the purpose of some of the more popular types of SmartArt graphics. Within each type, Office provides numerous layouts. For example, you can select from 40 different layouts of the list type.

Table 4–1 SmartArt Graphic Types

Type	Purpose
List	Shows nonsequential or grouped blocks of information.
Process	Shows progression, timeline, or sequential steps in a process or workflow.
Cycle	Shows continuous sequence of steps or events.
Hierarchy	Illustrates organization charts, decision trees, and hierarchical relationships.
Relationship	Compares or contrasts connections between concepts.
Matrix	Shows relationships of parts to a whole.
Picture	Uses images to present a message.
Pyramid	Shows proportional or interconnected relationships with the largest component at the top or bottom.

SmartArt graphics contain shapes. You can add text or pictures to shapes, add more shapes, or delete shapes. You also can modify the appearance of a SmartArt graphic by applying styles and changing its colors. The next several pages demonstrate the following general tasks to create the SmartArt graphic on the title page in this project:

1. Insert a SmartArt graphic.
2. Delete unneeded shapes from the SmartArt graphic.
3. Add shapes to the SmartArt graphic.
4. Add text to the shapes in the SmartArt graphic.
5. Change colors of the SmartArt graphic.
6. Apply a style to the SmartArt graphic.

To Insert a SmartArt Graphic

1 CREATE TITLE PAGE | 2 INSERT EXISTING DOCUMENT | 3 CREATE HEADER & FOOTER
4 EDIT & FORMAT LISTS | 5 EDIT & FORMAT TABLES | 6 CREATE WATERMARK

Below the title on the title page is a grouped list SmartArt graphic. ***Why?*** *The Grouped List SmartArt graphic allows you to place multiple lists side by side on the document, which works well for the content on this title page.* The following steps insert a SmartArt graphic centered below the title on the title page.

- With the insertion point on the blank paragraph below the title (shown in Figure 4–7), tap or click the Center button (HOME tab | Paragraph group) so that the inserted SmartArt graphic will be centered below the title.
- Display the INSERT tab.
- Tap or click the 'Insert a SmartArt Graphic' button (INSERT tab | Illustrations group) to display the Choose a SmartArt Graphic dialog box (Figure 4–8).

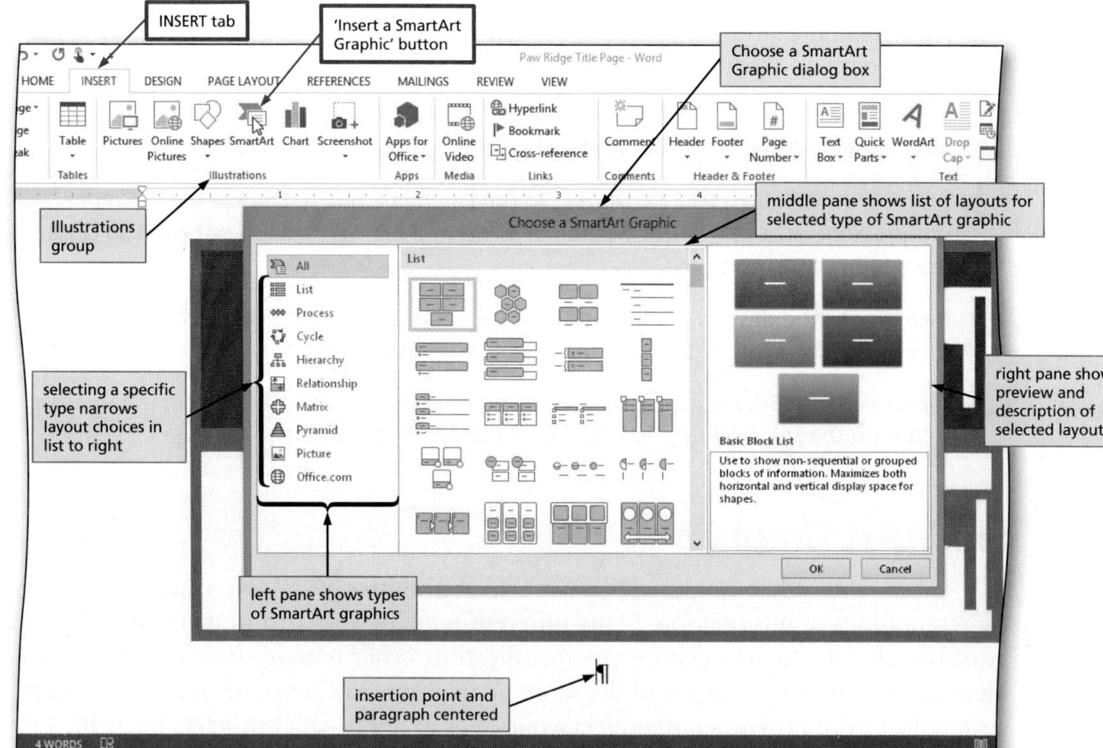

Figure 4–8

Experiment

- Tap or click various SmartArt graphic types in the left pane of the dialog box and watch the related layout choices appear in the middle pane.
- Tap or click various layouts in the list of layouts in the middle pane to see the preview and description of the layout appear in the right pane of the dialog box.

- Tap or click List in the left pane (Choose a SmartArt Graphic dialog box) to display the layout choices related to the selected SmartArt graphic type.
- Tap or click Grouped List in the middle pane, which displays a preview and description of the selected layout in the right pane (Figure 4–9).

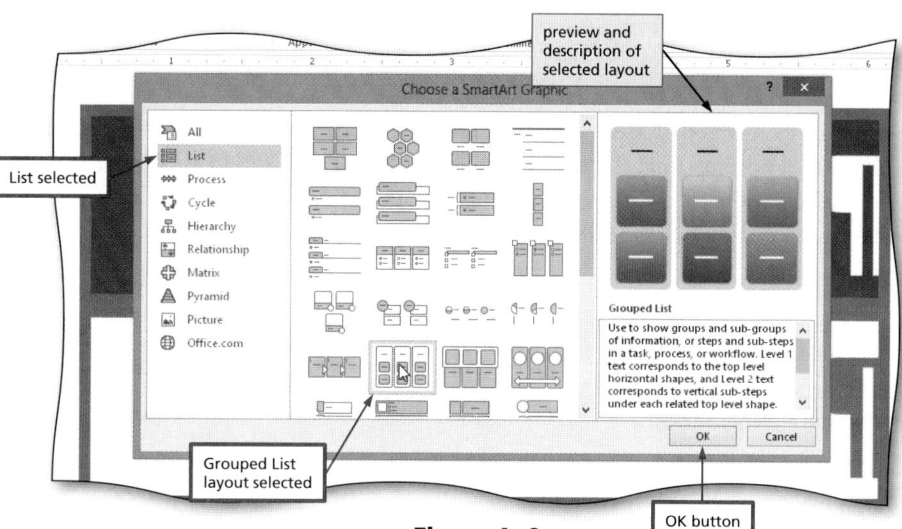

Figure 4–9

3

- Tap or click the OK button to insert the selected SmartArt graphic in the document at the location of the insertion point (Figure 4–10).

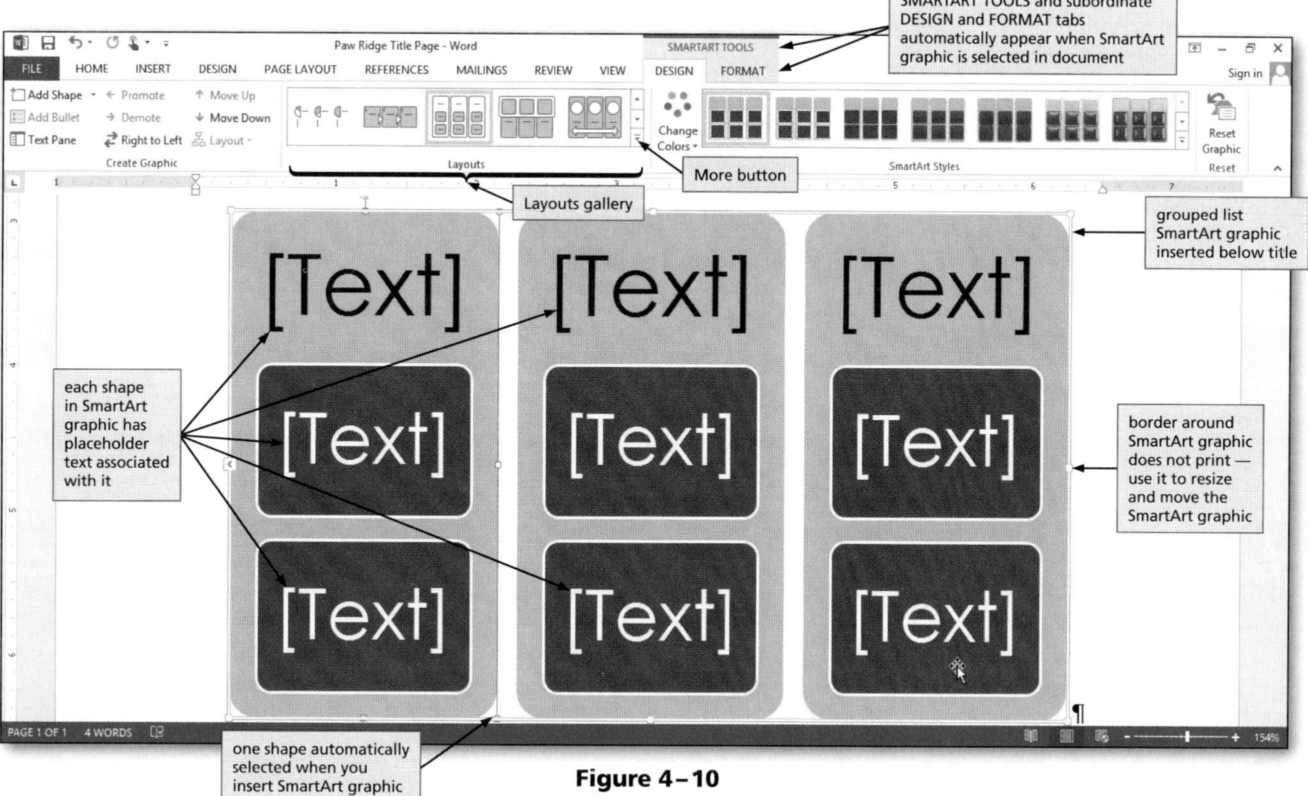

Figure 4–10

Q&A

What if the Text Pane appears next to the SmartArt graphic?

Close the Text Pane by tapping or clicking its Close button or tapping or clicking the Text Pane button (SMARTART TOOLS DESIGN tab | Create Graphic group).

Can I change the layout of the inserted SmartArt graphic?

Yes. Tap or click the More button in the Layouts gallery (SMARTART TOOLS DESIGN tab | Layouts group) to display the list of layouts and then select the desired layout.

To Delete Shapes from a SmartArt Graphic

1 CREATE TITLE PAGE | 2 INSERT EXISTING DOCUMENT | 3 CREATE HEADER & FOOTER
4 EDIT & FORMAT LISTS | 5 EDIT & FORMAT TABLES | 6 CREATE WATERMARK

The Grouped List SmartArt graphic initially has three outer groups that consist of nine different shapes (shown in Figure 4–10). Notice that each shape in the SmartArt graphic initially shows **placeholder text**, which indicates where text can be typed in a shape. The next step in this project is to delete one entire group. ***Why?*** *The SmartArt graphic in this project consists of only two major groups (Lodging and Recreation).* The following step deletes one entire group, or three shapes, in the SmartArt graphic.

- Be sure a shape is selected in the SmartArt graphic. If you are using a touch screen, tap the Cut button (HOME tab | Clipboard group) three times; if you are using a mouse, press the DELETE key three times to delete the three vertical shapes from the graphic (which is an entire group) and notice the other shapes resize and relocate in the graphic (Figure 4–11).

Q&A What if a shape is no longer selected?
Tap or click the edge of any shape to select the shape.

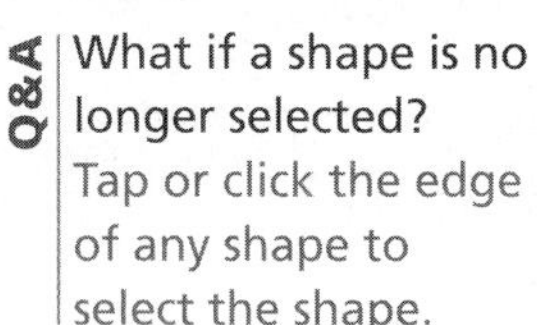

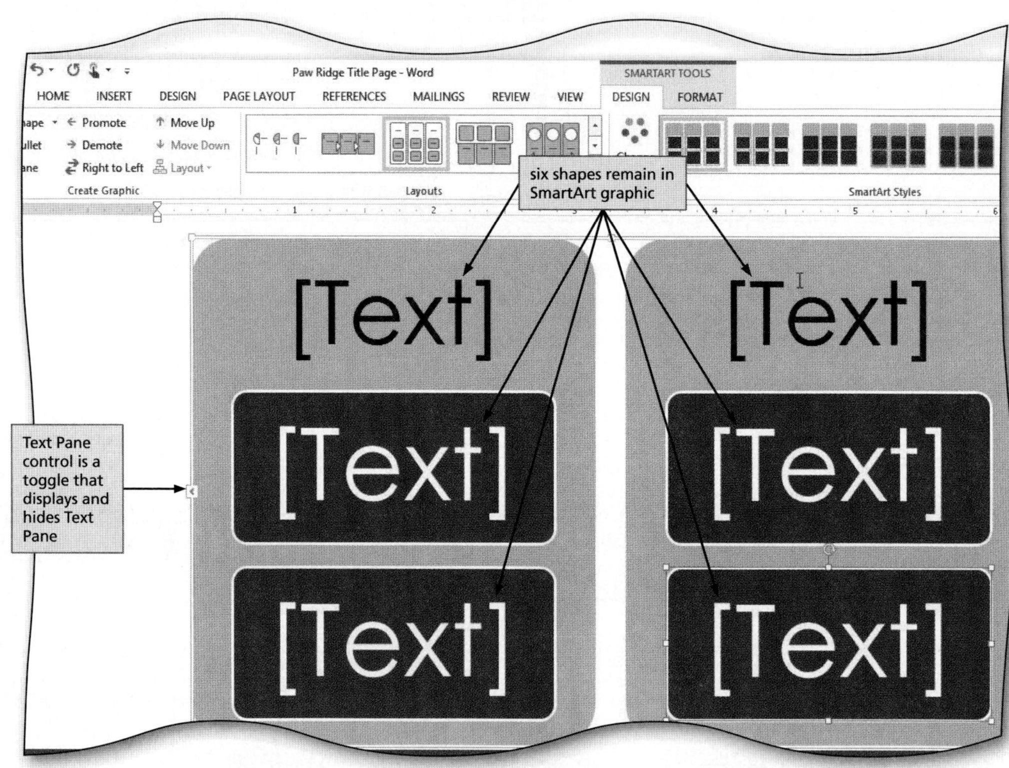

Figure 4–11

Other Ways

1. Tap or click Cut button (HOME tab | Clipboard group)

To Add Text to Shapes in a SmartArt Graphic

1 CREATE TITLE PAGE | 2 INSERT EXISTING DOCUMENT | 3 CREATE HEADER & FOOTER
4 EDIT & FORMAT LISTS | 5 EDIT & FORMAT TABLES | 6 CREATE WATERMARK

The placeholder text in a shape indicates where text can be typed in the shape. The following steps add text to the three shapes in the first group via their placeholder text. ***Why?*** *After entering the text in these three shapes, you will need to add two more shapes to finish the content in the group.*

- Tap or click the top-left shape to select it and then type `Lodging` to replace the placeholder text, [Text], with the entered text.

Q&A How do I edit placeholder text if I make a mistake?
Tap or click the placeholder text to select it and then correct the entry.

What if my typed text is longer than the shape?
The font size of the text may be adjusted or the text may wordwrap within the shape.

- Tap or click the middle-left shape to select it and then type `Cabins` as the new text.
- Tap or click the lower-left shape to select it and then type `Camp` as the new text (Figure 4–12).

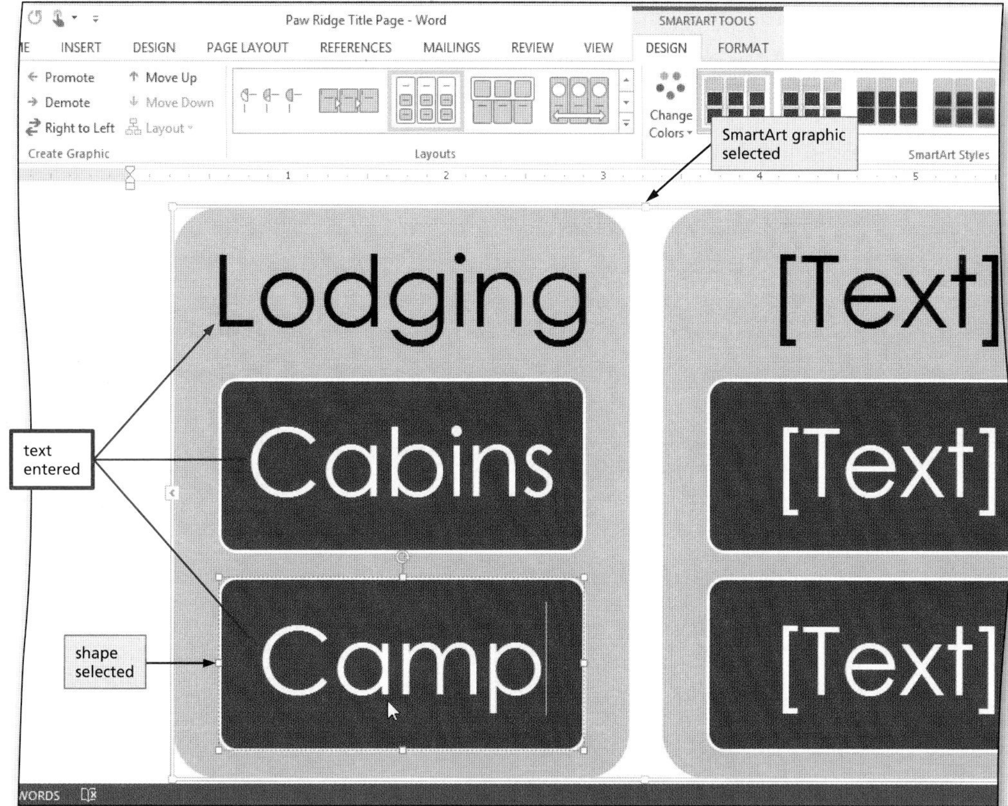

Figure 4–12

Other Ways

1. Tap or click Text Pane control, enter text in Text Pane, close Text Pane
2. Tap or click Text Pane button (SMARTART TOOLS DESIGN tab | Create Graphic group), enter text in Text Pane, tap or click Text Pane button again
3. Tap Edit Text button on mini toolbar or right-click shape and then click Edit Text on shortcut menu, enter text

To Add Shapes to a SmartArt Graphic

1 CREATE TITLE PAGE | 2 INSERT EXISTING DOCUMENT | 3 CREATE HEADER & FOOTER
4 EDIT & FORMAT LISTS | 5 EDIT & FORMAT TABLES | 6 CREATE WATERMARK

The following steps add shapes to the SmartArt graphic. ***Why?*** *Each group has four subordinate items, which means two shapes need to be added to each group.*

- If you are using a touch screen, tap the Add Shape button (SMARTART TOOLS DESIGN tab | Create Graphic group) and then tap 'Add Shape After'; if you are using a mouse, click the Add Shape button (SMARTART TOOLS DESIGN tab | Create Graphic group) to add a shape to the SmartArt graphic.

- Repeat Step 1 to add the final shape to the group.

3

- Tap or click a subordinate shape on the right (one of the brown shapes) to select it.
- Repeat Steps 1 and 2 so that the same number of shapes appear on the right and left sides of the SmartArt graphic.

4

- Enter the text in the shapes shown in Figure 4–13.

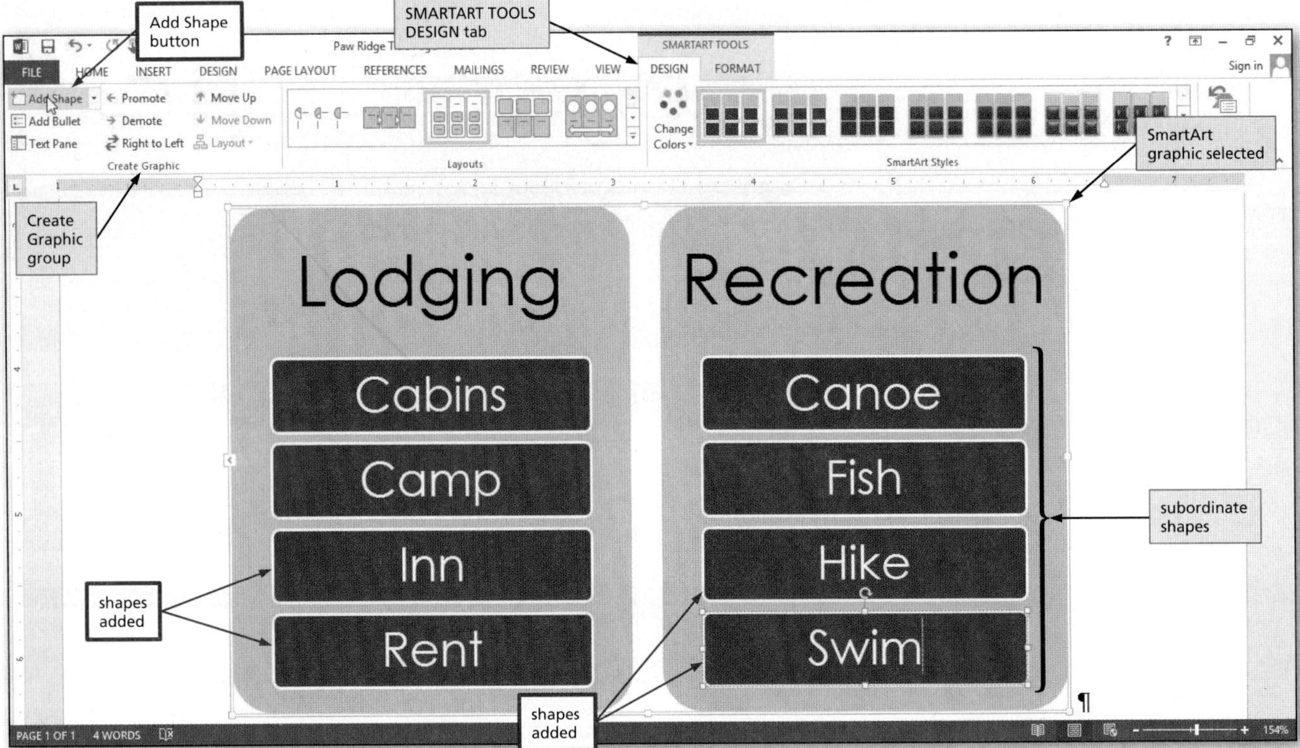

Figure 4–13

Other Ways

1. If you are using a mouse, click Add Shape arrow (SMARTART TOOLS DESIGN tab), click desired shape position
2. Tap 'Show Context Menu' button on mini toolbar or right-click paragraph, tap or point to Add Shape on shortcut menu, tap or click desired shape position

To Change Colors of a SmartArt Graphic

1 CREATE TITLE PAGE | 2 INSERT EXISTING DOCUMENT | 3 CREATE HEADER & FOOTER
4 EDIT & FORMAT LISTS | 5 EDIT & FORMAT TABLES | 6 CREATE WATERMARK

Word provides a variety of colors for a SmartArt graphic and the shapes in the graphic. In this project, the inside shapes are tan, instead of red. ***Why?*** *The dark red color competes with the title, so you want a softer color for the shapes.* The following steps change the colors of a SmartArt graphic.

1

- With the SmartArt graphic selected (shown in Figure 4–13), tap or click the Change Colors button (SMARTART TOOLS DESIGN tab | SmartArt Styles group) to display the Change Colors gallery.

Q&A What if the SmartArt graphic is not selected?
Tap or click the SmartArt graphic to select it.

BTW

Resetting Graphics

If you want to remove all formats from a SmartArt graphic and start over, you would tap or click the Reset Graphic button (SMARTART TOOLS DESIGN tab | Reset group), which is shown in Figure 4-15 on page WD 217.

- If you are using a mouse, point to 'Colored Fill - Accent 3' in the Change Colors gallery to display a live preview of the selected color applied to the SmartArt graphic in the document (Figure 4–14).

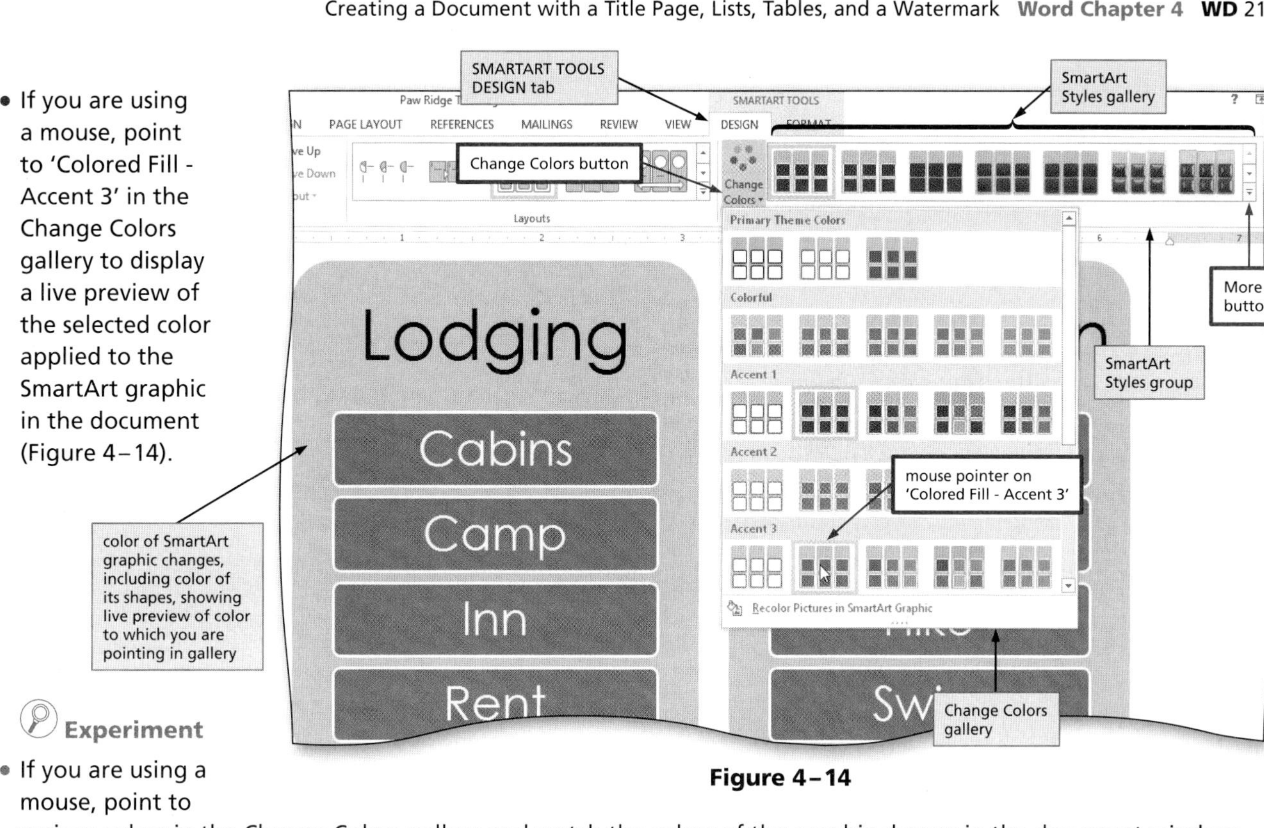

Figure 4–14

Experiment

- If you are using a mouse, point to various colors in the Change Colors gallery and watch the colors of the graphic change in the document window.

2

- Tap or click 'Colored Fill - Accent 3' in the Change Colors gallery to apply the selected color to the SmartArt graphic.

To Apply a SmartArt Style

1 CREATE TITLE PAGE | 2 INSERT EXISTING DOCUMENT | 3 CREATE HEADER & FOOTER
4 EDIT & FORMAT LISTS | 5 EDIT & FORMAT TABLES | 6 CREATE WATERMARK

The next step is to apply a SmartArt style to the SmartArt graphic. ***Why?*** *Word provides a SmartArt Styles gallery, allowing you to change the SmartArt graphic's format to a more visually appealing style.* The following steps apply a SmartArt style to a SmartArt graphic.

1

- With the SmartArt graphic still selected, tap or click the More button in the SmartArt Styles gallery (shown in Figure 4–14) to expand the SmartArt Styles gallery.
- If you are using a mouse, point to Moderate Effect in the SmartArt Styles gallery to display a live preview of that style applied to the graphic in the document (Figure 4–15).

Experiment

- If you are using a mouse, point to various SmartArt styles in the SmartArt Styles gallery and watch the style of the graphic change in the document window.

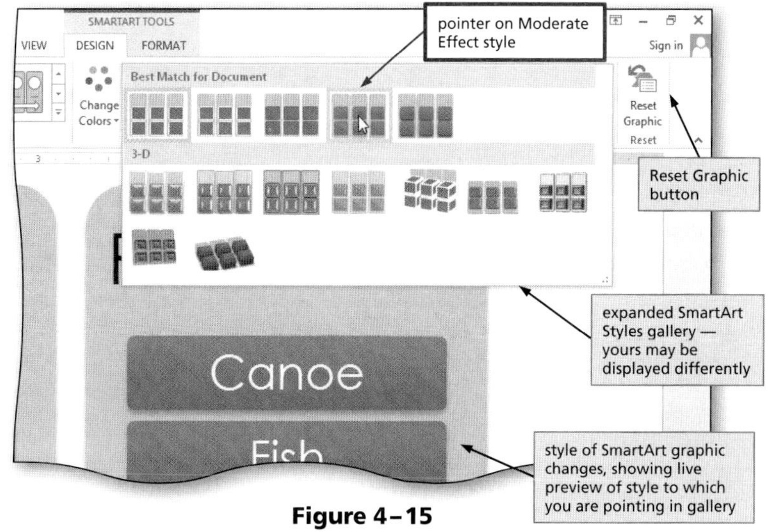

Figure 4–15

2

- Tap or click Moderate Effect in the SmartArt Styles gallery to apply the selected style to the SmartArt graphic.

To Modify Character Spacing and Format Characters Using the Font Dialog Box

1 CREATE TITLE PAGE | 2 INSERT EXISTING DOCUMENT | 3 CREATE HEADER & FOOTER
4 EDIT & FORMAT LISTS | 5 EDIT & FORMAT TABLES | 6 CREATE WATERMARK

In this project, the next step is to enter and format the text at the bottom of the title page. This text is the theme of the proposal and is formatted so that it is noticeable. Its characters are 36-point, italic, dark red Britannic Bold. Each letter in this text is formatted in **small caps**, which are letters that look like capital letters but are not as tall as a typical capital letter. Also, you want extra space between each character so that the text spans the width of the page.

Thus, the next steps apply all of the formats mentioned above using the Font dialog box. ***Why?*** *Although you could use buttons on the HOME tab to apply some of these formats, the small caps effect and expanded spacing are applied using the Font dialog box. Thus, you apply all the formats using the Font dialog box.*

1

- Position the insertion point on the paragraph mark to the right of the SmartArt graphic and then press the ENTER key to position the insertion point centered below the SmartArt graphic.
- Type `Plan your next outing with us!`
- Select the sentence you just typed and then tap or click the Font Dialog Box Launcher (HOME tab | Font group) to display the Font dialog box. If necessary, tap or click the Font tab in the dialog box to display the Font sheet.
- Scroll to and then tap or click Britannic Bold in the Font list (Font dialog box) to change the font of the selected text.
- Tap or click Italic in the Font style list to italicize the selected text.
- Scroll through the Size list and then tap or click 36 to change the font size of the selected text.
- Tap or click the Font color arrow and then tap or click 'Dark Red, Accent 1' (fifth color, first row) in the Font color palette to change the color of the selected text.
- Tap or click the Small caps check box in the Effects area so that each character is displayed as a small capital letter (Figure 4–16).

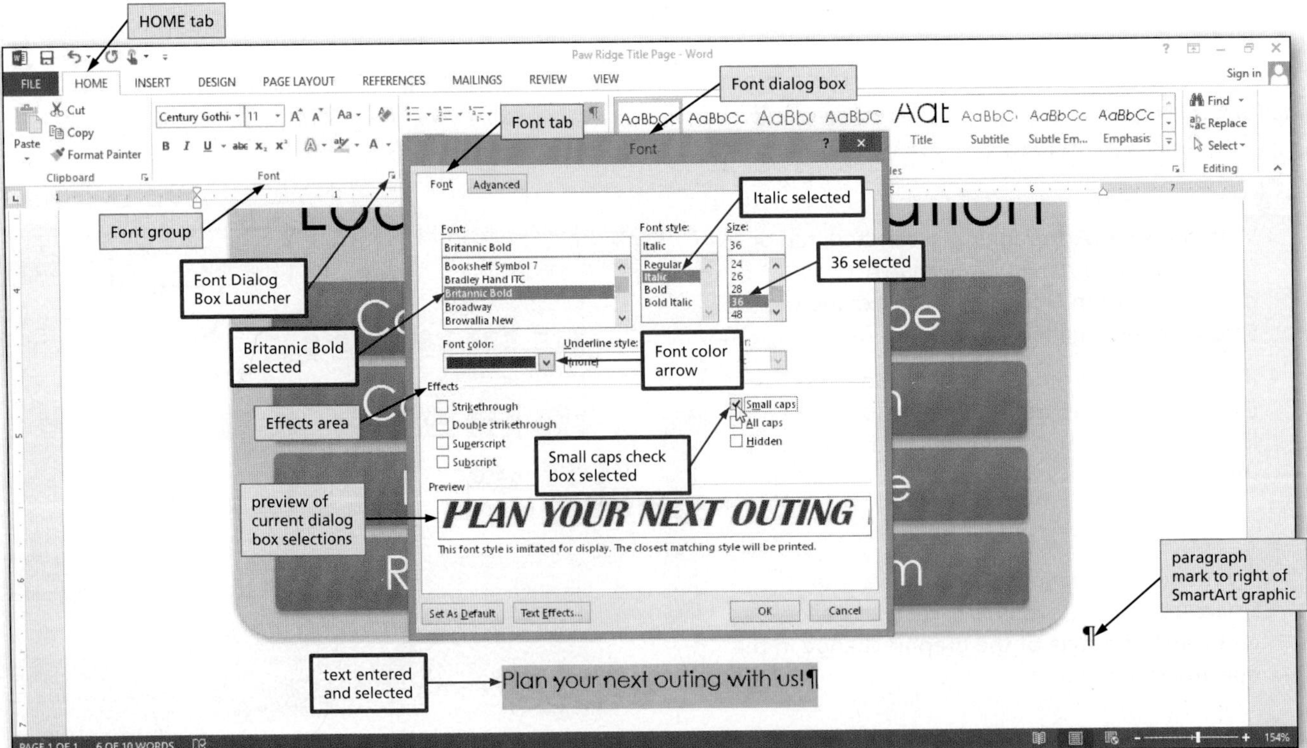

Figure 4–16

2

- Tap or click the Advanced tab (Font dialog box) to display the Advanced sheet in the Font dialog box.
- Tap or click the Spacing arrow and then tap or click Expanded to increase the amount of space between characters by 1 pt, which is the default.
- Double-tap or double-click the value in the Spacing By box to select it and then type **7** because you want this amount of blank space to be displayed between each character.
- Click in any box in the dialog box for the change to take effect and display a preview of the entered value in the Preview area (Figure 4–17).

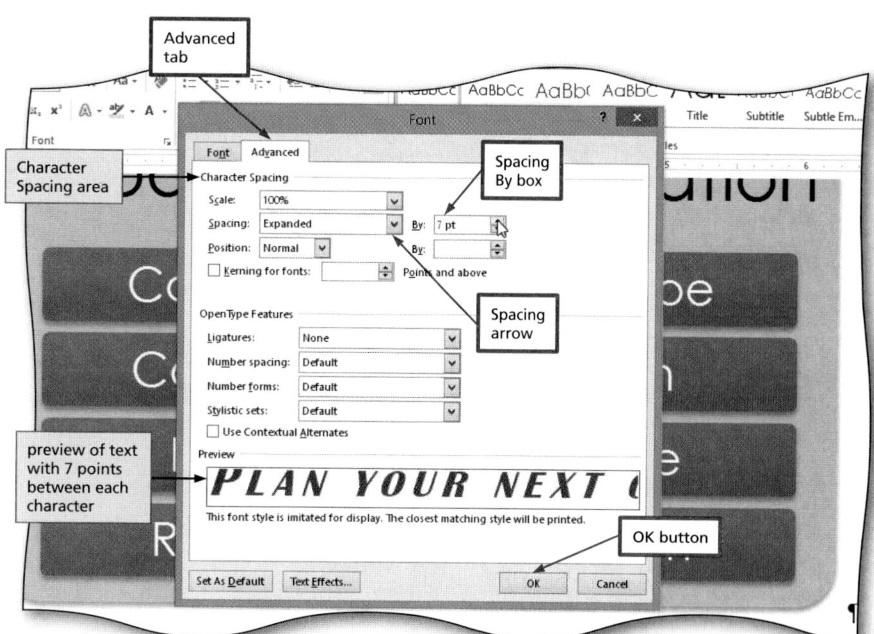

Figure 4–17

Q&A Can I tap or click the Spacing By arrows instead of typing a value in the box?
Yes.

3

- Tap or click the OK button to apply font changes to the selected text. If necessary, scroll so that the selected text is displayed completely in the document window.
- Tap or click to remove the selection from the text (Figure 4–18).

Figure 4–18

Other Ways

1. Tap 'Show Context Menu' button on mini toolbar or right-click selected text, tap or click Font on shortcut menu, select formats (Font dialog box), tap or click OK button
2. Press CTRL+D, select formats (Font dialog box), tap or click OK button

To Zoom One Page, Change Spacing before and after a Paragraph, and Set Zoom Level

The final step in creating the title page is to adjust spacing above and below the SmartArt graphic. You want to see the entire page while adjusting the spacing. Thus, the following steps zoom one page, increase spacing before and after the paragraph containing the SmartArt graphic, and then set the zoom level back to page width because you will be finished with the title page.

1 Display the VIEW tab. Tap or click the One Page button (VIEW tab | Zoom group) to display the entire page as large as possible centered in the document window.

2 Position the insertion point in the paragraph to adjust, in this case, on the paragraph mark to the right of the SmartArt graphic.

3. Display the PAGE LAYOUT tab. If you are using a touch screen, tap the Spacing After box (PAGE LAYOUT tab | Paragraph group) and then type **48** to change the spacing below the paragraph; if you are using a mouse, click the Spacing Before up arrow (PAGE LAYOUT tab | Paragraph group) as many times as necessary until 48 pt is displayed in the Spacing Before box because you want to increase the space above the graphic.

4. If you are using a touch screen, tap the Spacing After box (PAGE LAYOUT tab | Paragraph group) and then type **36** to change the spacing below the paragraph; if you are using a mouse, click the Spacing After up arrow (PAGE LAYOUT tab | Paragraph group) as many times as necessary until 36 pt is displayed in the Spacing After box because you want to increase the space below the graphic (Figure 4–19).

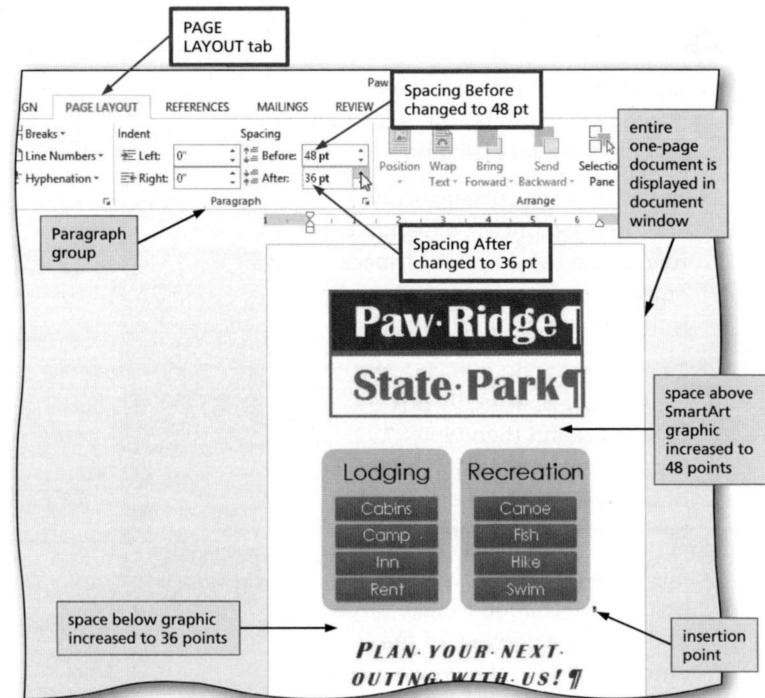

Figure 4–19

Q&A
What if the document spills to two pages?
Decrease the spacing above or below the SmartArt graphic until the title page contents fit on a single page.

5. Display the VIEW tab. Tap or click the Page Width button (VIEW tab | Zoom group) to change the zoom to page width.

To Save an Existing Document with the Same File Name

You have made several modifications to the document since you last saved it. Thus, you should save it again. The following step saves the document again.

1. Tap or click the Save button on the Quick Access Toolbar to overwrite the previously saved file.

Break Point: If you wish to take a break, this is a good place to do so. You can exit Word now. To resume at a later time, run Word, open the file called Paw Ridge Title Page, and continue following the steps from this location forward.

Inserting an Existing Document in an Open Document

Assume you already have prepared a draft of the body of the proposal and saved it with the file name, Paw Ridge Draft. You would like the draft to be displayed on a separate page following the title page.

In the following pages, you will insert the draft of the proposal below the title page and then edit the draft by deleting a page break, changing theme fonts, and applying styles.

To Save an Active Document with a New File Name

The current file name on the title bar is Paw Ridge Title Page, yet the document you will work on from this point forward in the chapter will contain both the title page and the body of the sales proposal. To keep the title page as a separate document called Paw Ridge Title Page, you should save the active document with a new file name. If you save the active document by using the Save button on the Quick Access Toolbar, Word will assign it the current file name. You want the active document to have a new file name. The following steps save the active document with a new file name.

1. Tap or click FILE on the ribbon to open the Backstage view and then tap or click the Save As tab to display the Save As gallery.
2. To save on a hard disk or other storage media on your computer, proceed to Step 2a. To save on SkyDrive, proceed to Step 2b.

2a. Tap or click Computer in the left pane, if necessary, to display options in the right pane related to saving on your computer.

2b. Tap or click SkyDrive in the left pane to display SkyDrive saving options or a Sign In button. If your screen displays a Sign In button, tap or click it and then sign in to SkyDrive.

3. Tap or click the Browse button in the right pane to display the Save As dialog box associated with the selected save location (i.e., Computer or SkyDrive).
4. Type `Paw Ridge Sales Proposal` in the File name box to change the file name. Do not press the ENTER key after typing the file name because you do not want to close the dialog box at this time.
5. Navigate to the desired save location (in this case, the Word folder in the CIS 101 folder [or your class folder] on your computer or SkyDrive).
6. Tap or click the Save button (Save As dialog box) to save the title page in the selected folder on the selected save location with the entered file name.

BTW

Inserting Documents

When you insert a Word document in another Word document, the entire inserted document is placed at the location of the insertion point. If the insertion point, therefore, is positioned in the middle of the open document when you insert another Word document, the open document continues after the last character of the inserted document.

Sections

All Word documents have at least one section. A Word document can be divided into any number of sections. During the course of creating a document, you will create a new **section** if you need to change the top margin, bottom margin, page alignment, paper size, page orientation, page number position, or contents or position of headers, footers, or footnotes in just a portion of the document.

The pages in the body of the sales proposal require page formatting different from that of the title page. The title page will not have a header or footer; the next two pages will have a header and footer.

When you want to change page formatting for a portion of a document, you create a new section in the document. Each section then may be formatted differently from the others. Thus, the title page formatted with no header or footer will be in one section, and the next two pages of the proposal, which will have a header and footer, will be in another section.

BTW

Section Numbers

If you want to display the current section number on the status bar, press and hold or right-click the status bar to display the Customize Status Bar menu and then tap or click Section on the Customize Status Bar menu. The section number appears at the left edge of the status bar. To remove the section number from the status bar, perform the same steps.

To Insert a Next Page Section Break

When you insert a section break, you specify whether the new section should begin on a new page. ***Why?*** *Sometimes you want a page break to occur with a section break, as in this project. Other times, you do not want a page break to occur with a section break (which will be illustrated in a later chapter).* In this project, the title page is separate from the next two pages. Thus, the section break should contain a page break. The following steps insert a next page section break, which instructs Word to begin the new section on a new page in the document.

1

- Position the insertion point at the end of the title page (following the exclamation point), which is the location where you want to insert the next page section break.
- Display the PAGE LAYOUT tab. Tap or click the 'Insert Page and Section Breaks' button (PAGE LAYOUT tab | Page Setup group) to display the Insert Page and Section Breaks gallery (Figure 4–20).

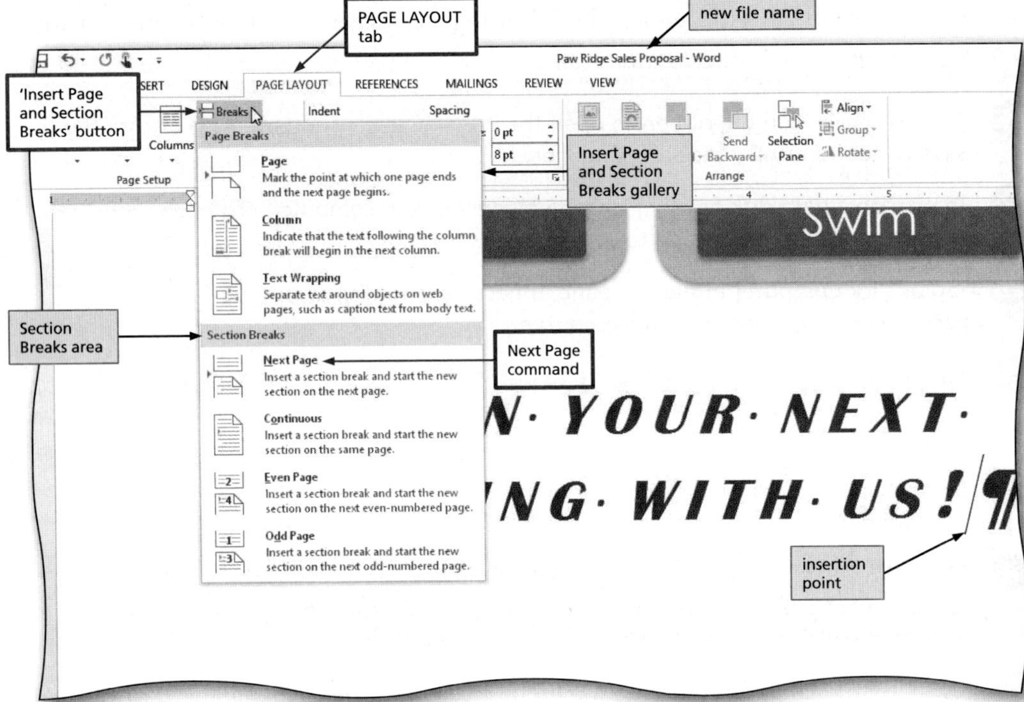

Figure 4–20

2

- Tap or click Next Page in the Section Breaks area of the Insert Page and Section Breaks gallery to insert a next page section break in the document at the location of the insertion point. If necessary, scroll so that your screen matches Figure 4–21.

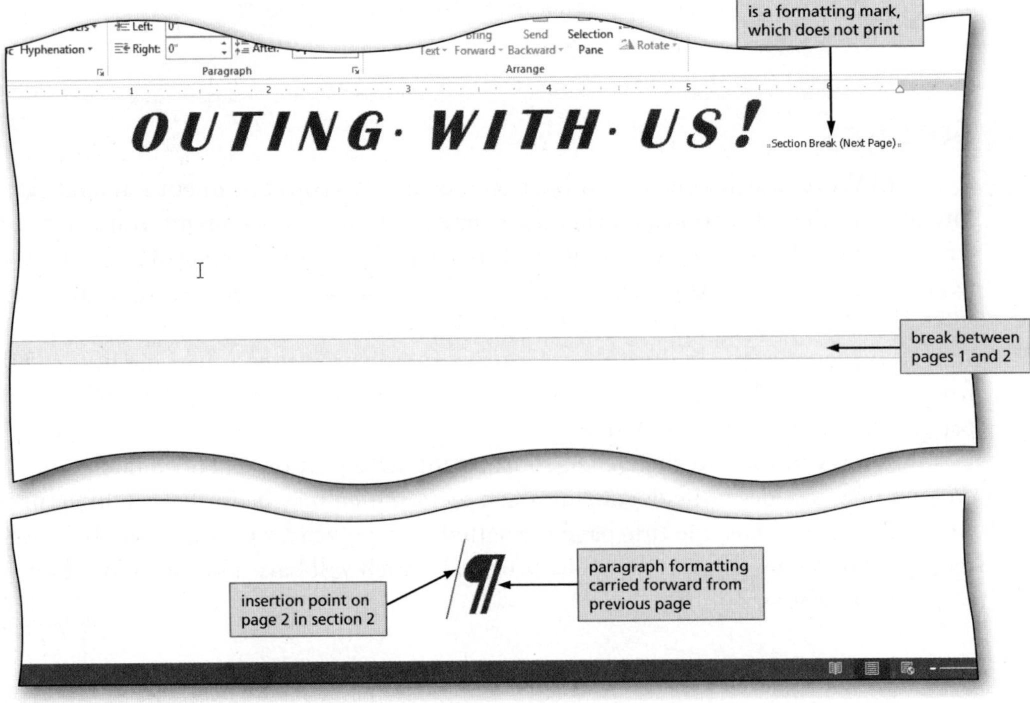

Figure 4–21

To Delete a Section Break

Word stores all section formatting in the section break. If you wanted to delete a section break and all associated section formatting, you would perform the following tasks.

1. Select the section break notation by dragging through it.
2. Press and hold or right-click the selection to display a mini toolbar or shortcut menu and then tap or click Cut on the mini toolbar or shortcut menu to delete the selection.

or

1. Position the insertion point immediately to the left or right of the section break notation.
2. Press the DELETE key to delete a section break to the right of the insertion point or press the BACKSPACE key to delete a section break to the left of the insertion point.

BTW

Sections

To see the formatting associated with a section, double-tap or double-click the section break notation or tap or click the Page Setup Dialog Box Launcher (PAGE LAYOUT tab | Page Setup group) to display the Page Setup dialog box. You can change margin settings and page orientation for a section in the Margins sheet. To change paper sizes for a section, tap or click the Paper tab. The Layout tab allows you to change header and footer specifications and vertical alignment for the section. To add a border to a section, tap or click the Borders button in the Layout sheet.

To Clear Formatting

When you create a section break, Word carries forward any formatting at the location of the insertion point to the next section. Thus, the current paragraph is formatted the same as the last line of the title page. In this project, the paragraphs and characters on the second page should be returned to the Normal style. Thus, the following step clears formatting.

Display the HOME tab. With the insertion point positioned on the paragraph mark on the second page (shown in Figure 4–21), tap or click the 'Clear All Formatting' button (HOME tab | Font group) to apply the Normal style to the location of the insertion point (shown in Figure 4–22).

To Insert a Word Document in an Open Document

1 CREATE TITLE PAGE | 2 INSERT EXISTING DOCUMENT | 3 CREATE HEADER & FOOTER
4 EDIT & FORMAT LISTS | 5 EDIT & FORMAT TABLES | 6 CREATE WATERMARK

The next step is to insert the draft of the sales proposal at the top of the second page of the document. ***Why?*** *You will modify a draft of the body of the proposal, which is located on the Data Files for Students. Visit www.cengage.com/ct/studentdownload for detailed instructions or contact your instructor for information about accessing the required files.* The following steps insert an existing Word document in an open document.

1

- Be sure the insertion point is positioned on the paragraph mark at the top of page 2, which is the location where you want to insert the contents of the Word document.
- Display the INSERT tab.
- Tap or click the Object arrow (INSERT tab | Text group) to display the Object menu (Figure 4–22).

Q&A If I am using a mouse, what if I click the Object button by mistake?

Click the Cancel button (Object dialog box) and then repeat this step.

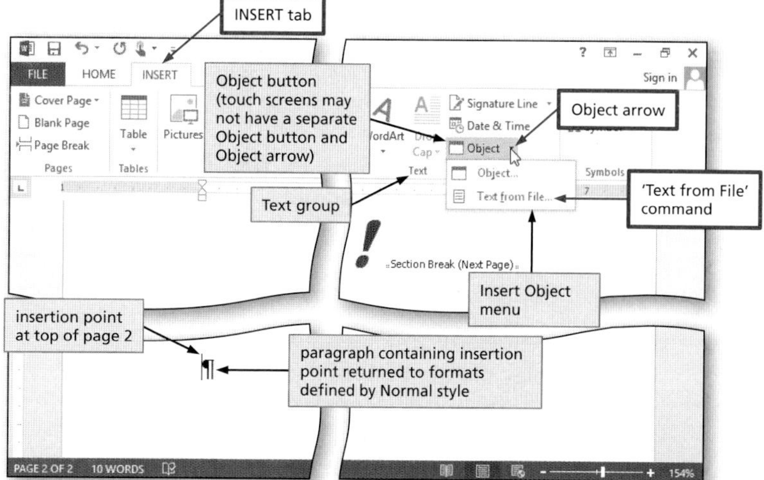

Figure 4–22

- Tap or click 'Text from File' on the Object menu to display the Insert File dialog box.
- Navigate to the location of the file to be inserted (in this case, the Chapter 04 folder in the Word folder in the Data Files for Students folder).
- Tap or click Paw Ridge Draft to select the file name (Figure 4–23).

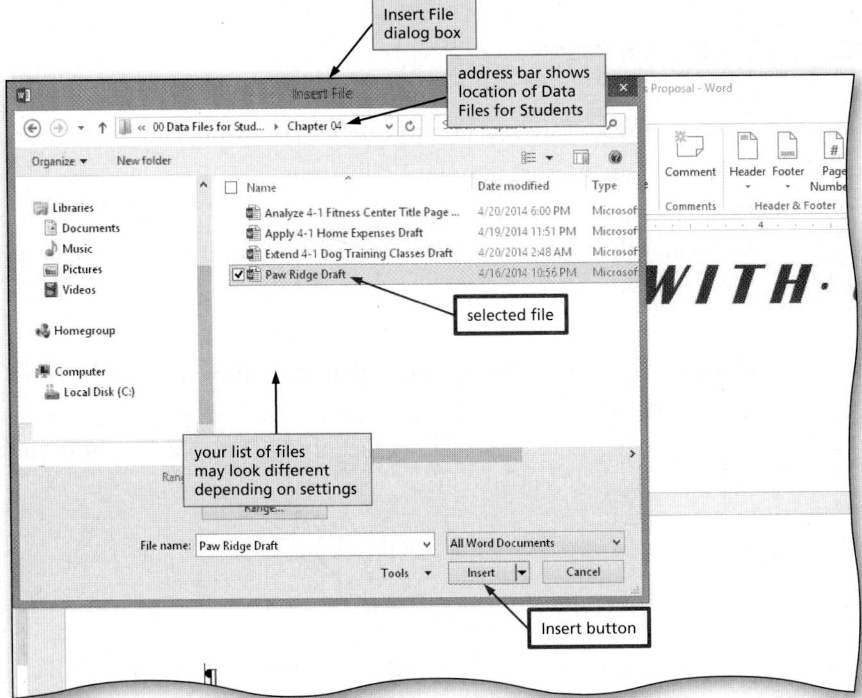

Figure 4–23

- Tap or click the Insert button (Insert File dialog box) to insert the file, Paw Ridge Draft, in the open document at the location of the insertion point.

Q&A Where is the insertion point now?
When you insert a file in an open document, Word positions the insertion point at the end of the inserted document.

- Press SHIFT+F5 to position the insertion point on line 1 of page 2, which was its location prior to inserting the new Word document (Figure 4–24).

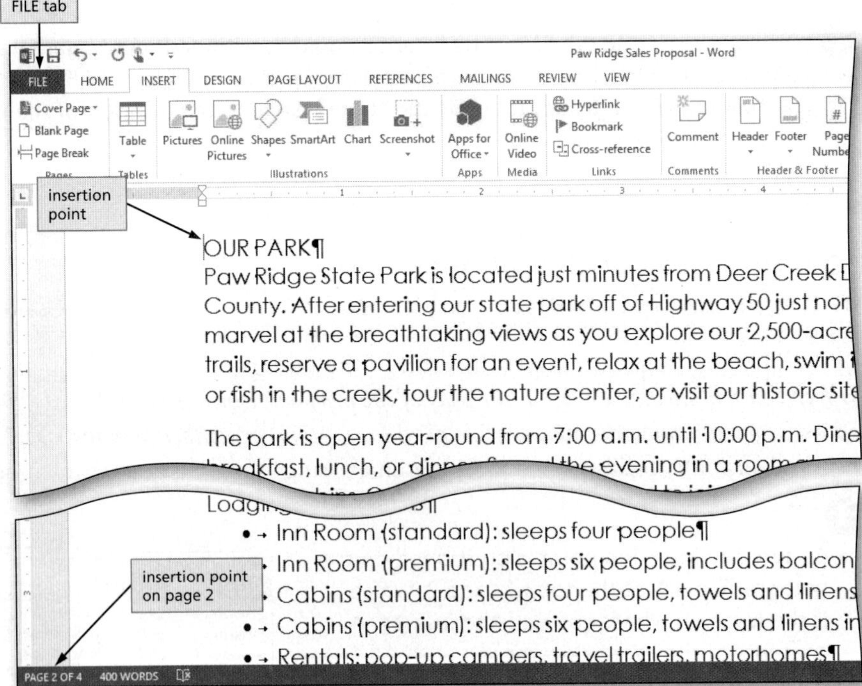

Figure 4–24

Q&A What is the purpose of SHIFT+F5?
The keyboard shortcut, SHIFT+F5, positions the insertion point at your last editing location. Word remembers your last three editing locations, which means you can press this keyboard shortcut repeatedly to return to one of your three most recent editing locations.

What if my keyboard does not have function keys?
Scroll to display the top of page 2 in the document window.

Other Ways

1. Tap or click Object button (INSERT tab | Text group), tap or click 'Create from File' tab (Object dialog box), tap or click Browse button, locate file, tap or click Insert button (Browse dialog box), tap or click OK button (Object dialog box)

To Print Specific Pages in a Document

The title page is the first page of the proposal. The body of the proposal spans the second and third pages. The following steps print a hard copy of only the body of the proposal, that is, pages 2 and 3. ***Why?** You would like to see the contents of the body of the proposal before you begin modifying it.*

1

- Tap or click FILE on the ribbon to open the Backstage view and then tap or click the Print tab in the Backstage view to display the Print gallery.
- Verify that the printer listed on the Printer Status button will print a hard copy of the document. If necessary, tap or click the Printer Status button to display a list of available printer options and then tap or click the desired printer to change the selected printer.
- Type **2–3** in the Pages text box in the Settings area of the Print gallery (Figure 4–25).

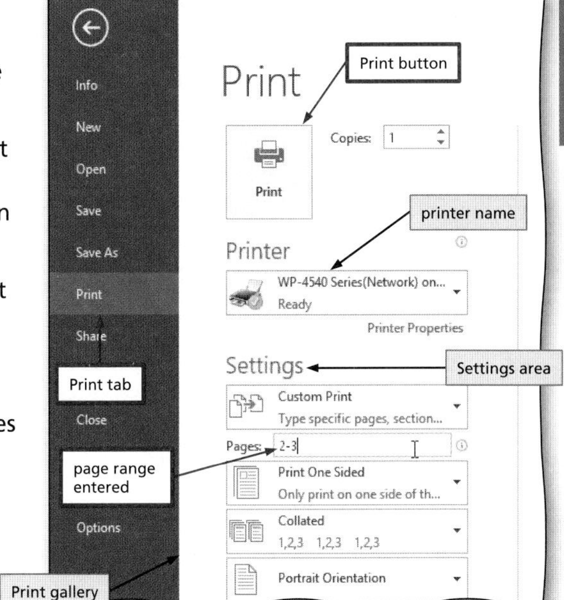

Figure 4–25

2

- Tap or click the Print button to print the inserted draft of the sales proposal (Figure 4–26).

Q&A

How would I print pages from a certain point to the end of a document?

You would enter the page number followed by a dash in the Pages text box. For example, 5- will print from page 5 to the end of the document. To print up to a certain page, put the dash first (e.g., -5 will print pages 1 through 5).

Why does my document wrap on different words than Figure 4–26?

Differences in wordwrap may be related to the printer used by your computer.

Why does my screen show the document has four pages?

You may have an extra blank page at the end of the document. This blank page will be deleted later in the chapter.

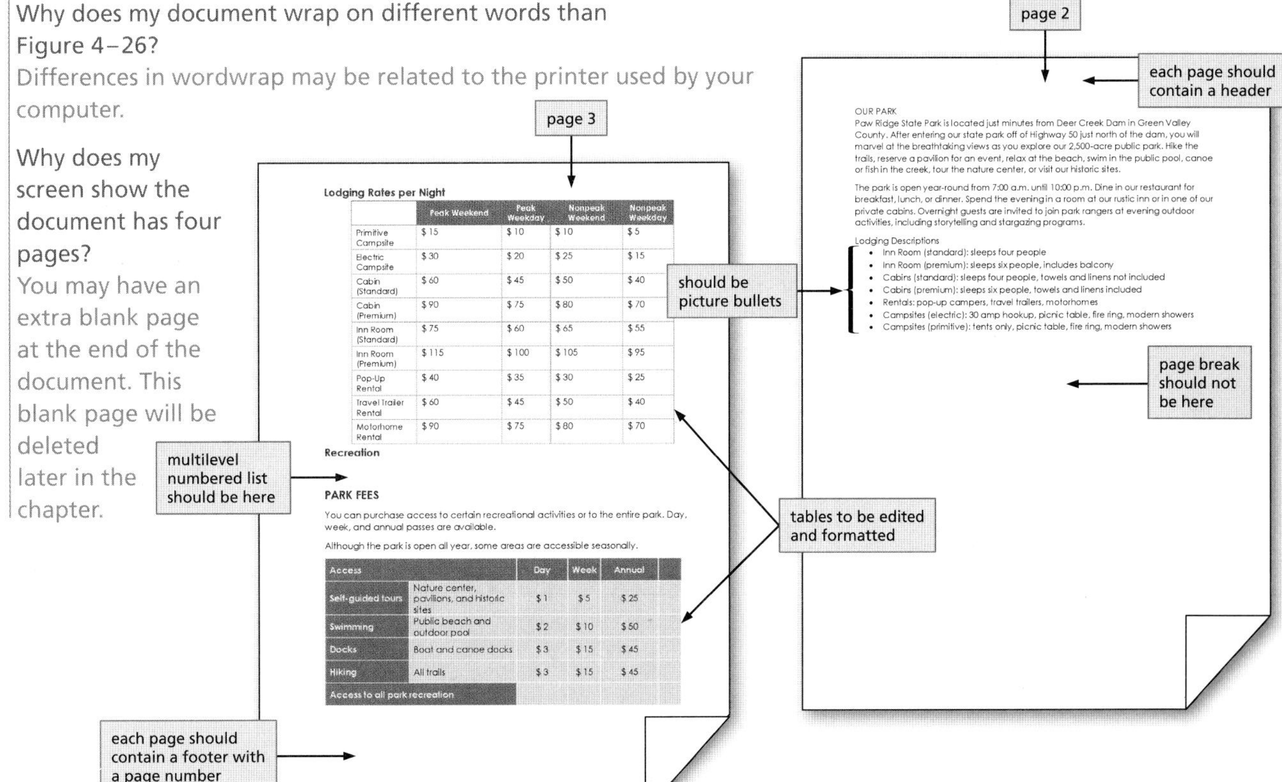

	Peak Weekend	Peak Weekday	Nonpeak Weekend	Nonpeak Weekday
Primitive Campsite	$ 15	$ 10	$ 10	$ 5
Electric Campsite	$ 30	$ 20	$ 25	$ 15
Cabin (Standard)	$ 60	$ 45	$ 50	$ 40
Cabin (Premium)	$ 90	$ 75	$ 80	$ 70
Inn Room (Standard)	$ 75	$ 60	$ 65	$ 55
Inn Room (Premium)	$ 115	$ 100	$ 105	$ 95
Pop-Up Rental	$ 40	$ 35	$ 30	$ 25
Travel Trailer Rental	$ 60	$ 45	$ 50	$ 40
Motorhome Rental	$ 90	$ 75	$ 80	$ 70

Access		Day	Week	Annual
Self-guided tours	Nature center, pavilions, and historic sites	$ 1	$ 5	$ 25
Swimming	Public beach and outdoor pool	$ 2	$ 10	$ 50
Docks	Boat and canoe docks	$ 3	$ 15	$ 45
Hiking	All trails	$ 3	$ 15	$ 45
Access to all park recreation				

Other Ways

1. Press CTRL+P, press ENTER

CONSIDER THIS

What elements should the body of a sales proposal contain?

Be sure to include basic elements in your sales proposals:

- **Include an introduction, body, and conclusion.** The introduction could contain the subject, purpose, statement of problem, need, background, or scope. The body may include costs, benefits, supporting documentation, available or required facilities, feasibility, methods, timetable, materials, or equipment. The conclusion summarizes key points or requests an action.
- **Use headers and footers.** Headers and footers help to identify every page. A page number should be in either the header or footer. If the sales proposal should become disassembled, the reader can use the headers and footers to determine the order and pieces of your proposal.

To Delete a Page Break

1 CREATE TITLE PAGE | 2 INSERT EXISTING DOCUMENT | 3 CREATE HEADER & FOOTER
4 EDIT & FORMAT LISTS | 5 EDIT & FORMAT TABLES | 6 CREATE WATERMARK

After reviewing the draft in Figure 4–26, you notice it contains a page break below the bulleted list. The following steps delete a page break. *Why? This page break below the bulleted list should not be in the proposal.*

- Scroll to display the page break notation.
- To select the page break notation, double-tap or double-click it (Figure 4–27).

- Press and hold and then tap the Cut button on the mini toolbar or press the DELETE key to remove the page break from the document.

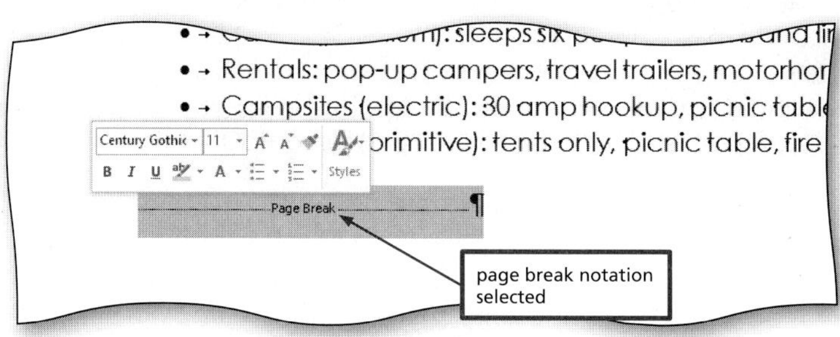

Figure 4–27

Other Ways

1. With page break notation selected, tap or click Cut button (HOME tab | Clipboard group)
2. With page break notation selected, press and hold or right-click selection and then tap or click Cut on mini toolbar or shortcut menu
3. With the insertion point to the left or right of the page break notation, press DELETE or BACKSPACE, respectively

To Apply Heading Styles

Word has many built-in, or predefined, styles that you can use to format text. Three of the Styles shown in the Styles gallery in Figure 4–28 are for headings: Heading 1 for the major headings and Heading 2 and Heading 3 for minor headings. In the Paw Ridge Draft, all headings except for the first two were formatted using heading styles.

The following steps apply the Heading 1 style to the paragraph containing the text, OUR PARK, and the Heading 2 style to the paragraph containing the text, Lodging Descriptions.

BTW

Q&As

For a complete list of the Q&As found in many of the step-by-step sequences in this book, visit the Q&A resource on the Student Companion Site located on www.cengagebrain.com. For detailed instructions about accessing available resources, visit www.cengage.com/ct/studentdownload or contact your instructor for information about accessing the required files.

1. Position the insertion point in the paragraph to be formatted to the Heading 1 style, in this case, the first line on the second page with the text, OUR PARK.
2. Tap or click Heading 1 in the Style gallery (HOME tab | Styles group) to apply the selected style to the paragraph containing the insertion point.

Q&A Why did a square appear on the screen near the left edge of the paragraph formatted with the Heading 1 style?

The square is a nonprinting character, like the paragraph mark, that indicates text to its right has a special paragraph format applied to it.

3. Position the insertion point in the paragraph to be formatted to the Heading 2 style, in this case, the line above the bulleted list with the text, Lodging Descriptions.

4. Tap or click Heading 2 in the Style gallery (HOME tab | Styles group) to apply the selected style to the paragraph containing the insertion point (Figure 4–28).

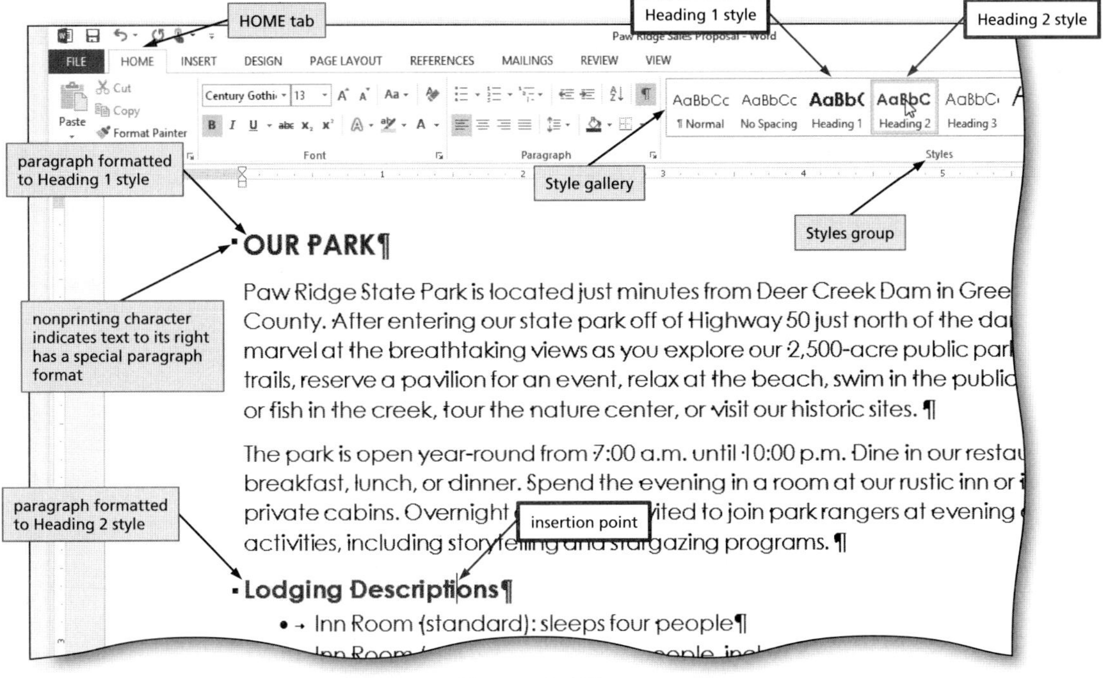

Figure 4–28

To Change Spacing before and after a Paragraph

The next step is to adjust spacing above and below the current paragraph, that is, the heading above the bulleted list. This paragraph is formatted using the Heading 2 style, which places no space above the paragraph and 8 points below the paragraph. You would like this paragraph, and all other paragraphs formatted using the Heading 2 style, to have 12 points of space above them and 6 points of space below them. Thus, the following steps adjust the spacing before and after a paragraph.

1. Display the PAGE LAYOUT tab. Position the insertion point as shown in Figure 4–29 on the next page. If you are using a touch screen, tap the Spacing Before box (PAGE LAYOUT tab | Paragraph group) and then type `12` to change the spacing above the paragraph; if you are using a mouse, tap or click the Spacing Before up arrow (PAGE LAYOUT tab | Paragraph group) as many times as necessary so that 12 pt is displayed in the Spacing Before box.

2. If you are using a touch screen, tap the Spacing After box (PAGE LAYOUT tab | Paragraph group) and then type `6` to change the spacing below the paragraph; if you are using a mouse, tap or click the Spacing After up arrow (PAGE LAYOUT tab | Paragraph group) so that 6 pt is displayed in the Spacing After box.

To Update a Style to Match a Selection

You want all paragraphs formatted in the Heading 2 style in the proposal to use this adjusted spacing. Thus, the steps on the next page update the Heading 2 style so that this adjusted spacing is applied to all Heading 2 paragraphs in the document.

1. If necessary, position the insertion point in the paragraph containing the style to be updated.

2. Display the HOME tab. Press and hold or right-click Heading 2 in the Styles gallery (HOME tab | Styles group) to display a shortcut menu (Figure 4–29).

3. Tap or click 'Update Heading 2 to Match Selection' on the shortcut menu to update the Heading 2 style to reflect the settings at the location of the insertion point.

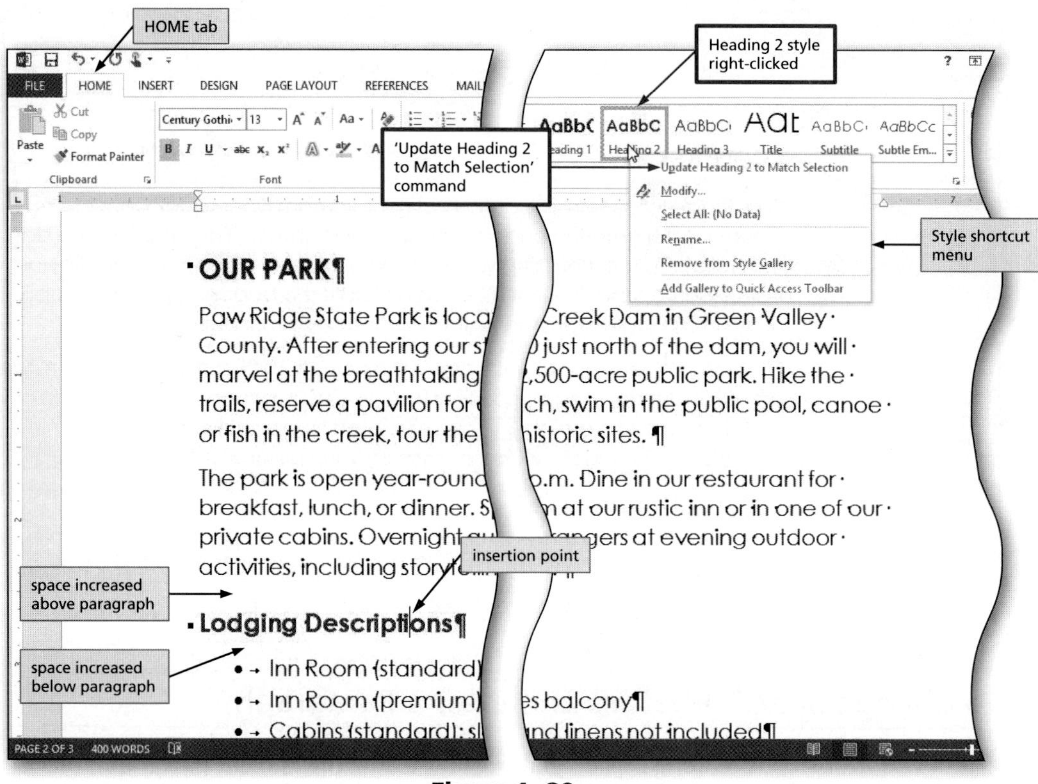

Figure 4–29

BTW

Headers and Footers

If a portion of a header or footer does not print, it may be in a nonprintable area. Check the printer user instructions to see how close the printer can print to the edge of the paper. Then, tap or click the Page Setup Dialog Box Launcher (PAGE LAYOUT tab | Page Setup group), tap or click the Layout tab (Page Setup dialog box), adjust the From edge text box to a value that is larger than the printer's minimum margin setting, tap or click the OK button, and then print the document again.

Creating Headers and Footers

A header is text that prints at the top of each page in the document. A footer is text that prints at the bottom of each page. In this proposal, you want the header and footer to appear on each page after the title page; that is, you do not want the header and footer on the title page. Recall that the title page is in a separate section from the rest of the sales proposal. Thus, the header and footer should not be in section 1, but they should be in section 2. The steps on the following pages explain how to create a header and footer in section 2 only.

To Insert a Formatted Header Different from the Previous Header

1 CREATE TITLE PAGE | 2 INSERT EXISTING DOCUMENT | **3 CREATE HEADER & FOOTER**
4 EDIT & FORMAT LISTS | **5 EDIT & FORMAT TABLES** | **6 CREATE WATERMARK**

Word provides several built-in preformatted header designs for you to insert in documents. The following steps insert a formatted header in section 2 of the sales proposal that is different from the previous header. ***Why?*** *You do not want the header to appear on the title page, so you will instruct Word to not place the header in the previous section. Recall that the title page is in section 1 and the body of the proposal is in section 2.*

- Display the INSERT tab. Tap or click the 'Add a Header' button (INSERT tab | Header & Footer group) and then tap or click Edit Header in the Header gallery to switch to the header for section 2.
- If the 'Link to Previous' button (HEADER & FOOTER TOOLS DESIGN tab | Navigation group) is selected, tap or click it to deselect the button because you do not want the header in this section to be copied to the previous section (that is, the header should not be on the title page).

- Tap or click the 'Add a Header' button (HEADER & FOOTER TOOLS DESIGN tab | Header & Footer group) to display the Add a Header gallery (Figure 4–30).

Experiment

- Scroll through the list of built-in headers to see the variety of available formatted header designs.

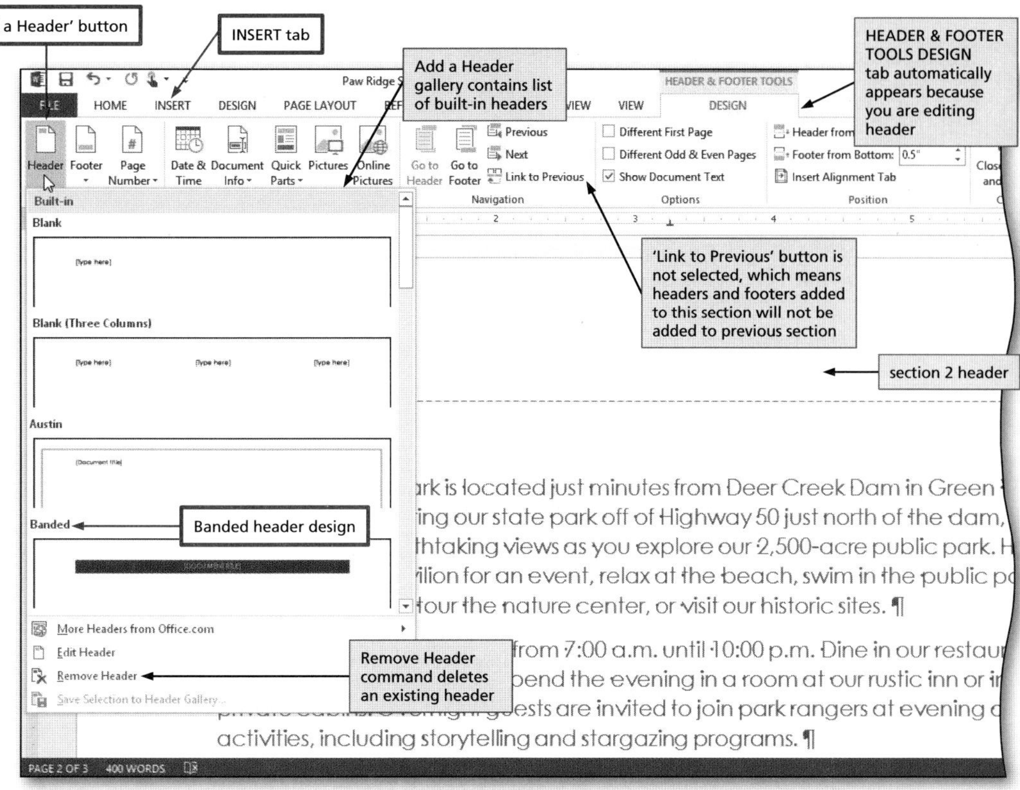

Figure 4–30

2

- If necessary, scroll to and then tap or click the Banded header design in the Add a Header gallery to insert the formatted header in the header of section 2, which contains a content control (Figure 4–31).

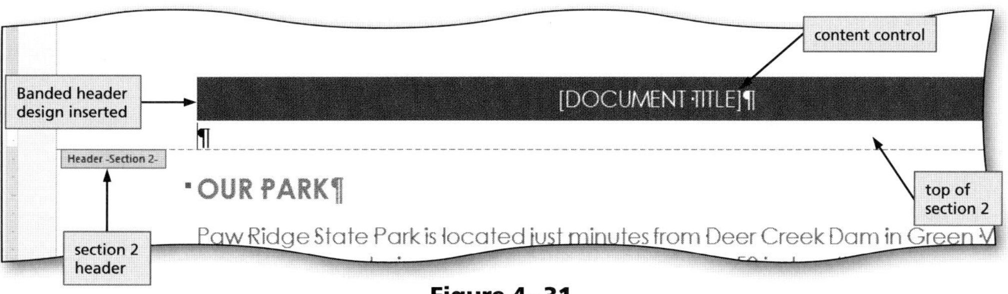

Figure 4–31

Q&A What is a content control?

A **content control** is an object that contains sample text or instructions for filling in text and graphics.

3

- Tap or click the content control, DOCUMENT TITLE, to select it and then type **Paw Ridge State Park** in the content control (Figure 4–32).

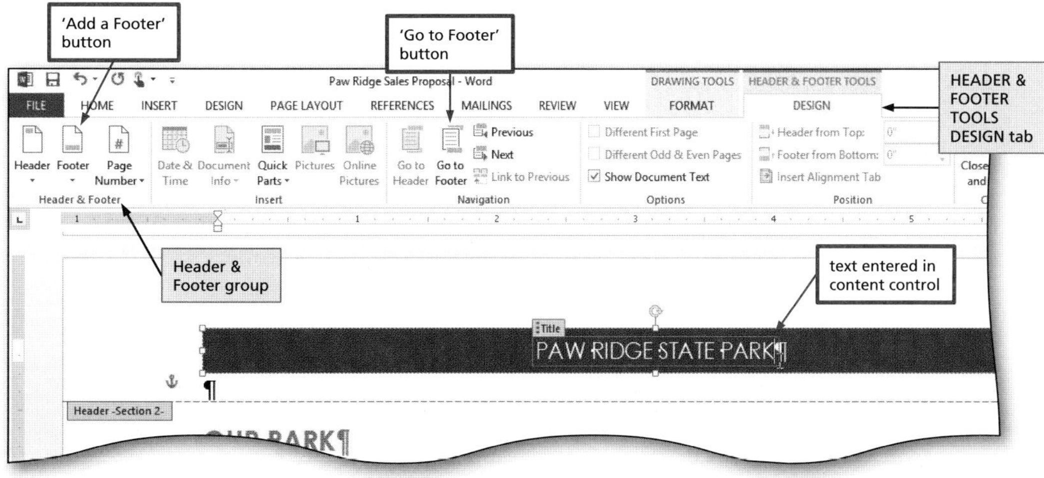

Figure 4–32

If requested by your instructor, enter your name instead of the state park name shown in Figure 4–31.

Q&A How would I delete a header?
You would tap or click Remove Header in the Header gallery.

Other Ways

1. Tap or click 'Add a Header' button (INSERT tab | Header & Footer group), select desired header in list
2. Tap or click 'Explore Quick Parts' button (INSERT tab | Text group), tap or click 'Building Blocks Organizer' on Quick Parts menu, select desired header (Building Blocks Organizer dialog box), tap or click Insert button

To Insert a Formatted Footer

The next step is to insert the footer. Word provides the same built-in preformatted footer designs as header designs. The footer design that corresponds to the header just inserted contains a centered page number. The following steps insert a formatted footer in section 2 of the sales proposal that corresponds to the header just inserted.

1. Tap or click the 'Go to Footer' button (shown in Figure 4–32) (HEADER & FOOTER TOOLS DESIGN tab | Header & Footer group) to display the Add a Footer gallery.
2. If the 'Link to Previous' button (HEADER & FOOTER TOOLS DESIGN tab | Navigation group) is selected, tap or click it to deselect the button because you do not want the footer in this section to be copied to the previous section (that is, the footer should not be on the title page).
3. Tap or click the 'Add a Footer' button (shown in Figure 4–32) (HEADER & FOOTER TOOLS DESIGN tab | Header & Footer group) to display the Add a Footer gallery.
4. Tap or click the Banded footer design to insert the formatted footer in the footer of section 2 (shown in Figure 4–33).

Q&A Why is the page number a 2?
The page number is 2 because, by default, Word begins numbering pages from the beginning of the document.

BTW

Page Numbers
If Word displays {PAGE} instead of the actual page number, press ALT+F9 to turn off field codes. If Word prints {PAGE} instead of the page number, open the Backstage view, tap or click Options to display the Word Options dialog box, tap or click Advanced in the left pane (Word Options dialog box), scroll to the Print area, remove the check mark from the 'Print field codes instead of their values' check box, and then tap or click the OK button.

To Format Page Numbers to Start at a Different Number

1 CREATE TITLE PAGE | 2 INSERT EXISTING DOCUMENT | 3 CREATE HEADER & FOOTER
4 EDIT & FORMAT LISTS | 5 EDIT & FORMAT TABLES | 6 CREATE WATERMARK

On the page after the title page in the proposal, you want to begin numbering with a number 1, instead of a 2 as shown in Figure 4–33. ***Why?*** *Word begins numbering pages from the beginning of the document and you want it to begin numbering on the body of the proposal.* Thus, you need to instruct Word to begin numbering the pages in section 2 with the number 1. The next steps format the page numbers so that they start at a different number.

- Tap or click the 'Add Page Numbers' button (HEADER & FOOTER TOOLS DESIGN tab | Header & Footer group) to display the Add Page Numbers menu (Figure 4–33).

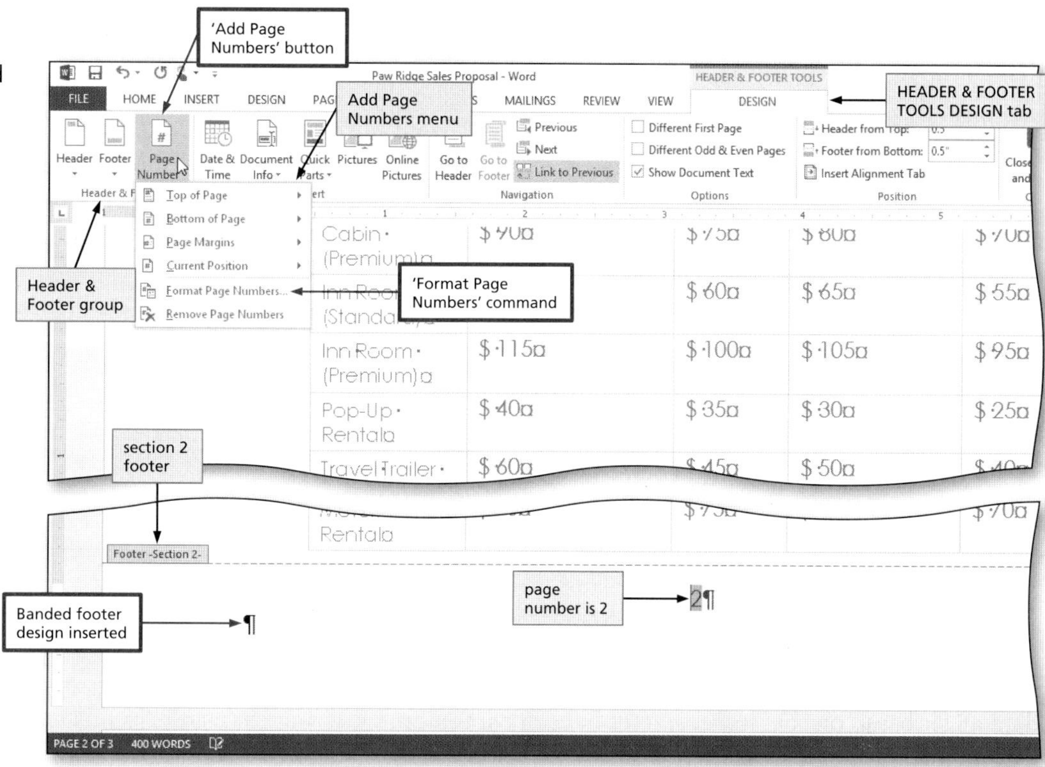

Figure 4–33

- Tap or click 'Format Page Numbers' on the Add Page Numbers menu to display the Page Number Format dialog box.
- Tap or click Start at in the Page numbering area (Page Number Format dialog box), which displays a 1 by default as the starting page number (Figure 4–34).

Q&A Can I also change the look of the page number?

Yes. Tap or click the Number format arrow (Page Number Format dialog box) for a list of page number variations.

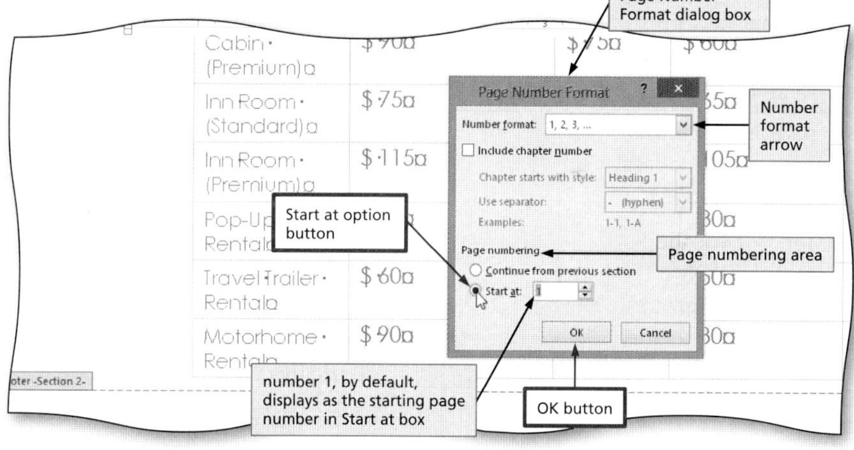

Figure 4–34

- Tap or click the OK button to change the starting page number for section 2 to the number 1 (Figure 4–35).
- Tap or click the 'Close Header and Footer' button (HEADER & FOOTER TOOLS DESIGN tab | Close group) to close the header and footer.

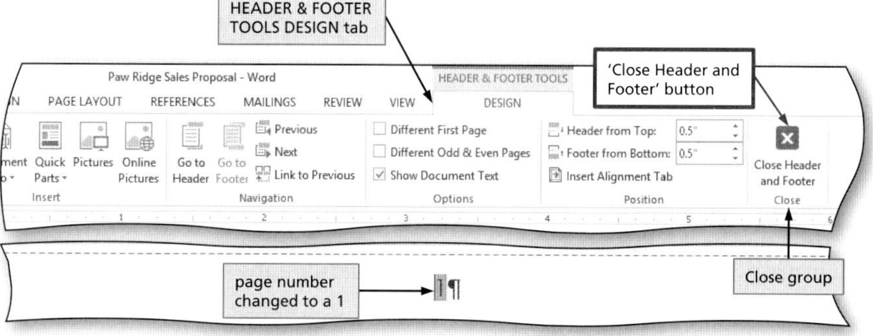

Figure 4–35

Other Ways

1. Tap or click 'Add Page Numbers' button (INSERT tab | Header & Footer group), tap or click 'Format Page Numbers' on Add Page Numbers menu, set page formats (Page Number Format dialog box), tap or click OK button

Editing and Formatting Lists

The finished sales proposal in this chapter has two lists: a bulleted list and a numbered list (shown in Figures 4–1b and 4–1c on page WD 203). The bulleted list is in alphabetical (sorted) order, the first word of each list item is emphasized, and the bullets are graphical instead of simple round dots. The numbered listed has multiple levels for each numbered item. The following pages illustrate steps used to edit and format the lists in the proposal:

1. Sort a list of paragraphs.
2. Format text in the first list item and then copy the format to text in each of the remaining list items.
3. Customize bullets in a list of paragraphs.
4. Create a multilevel numbered list.

To Sort Paragraphs

The next step is to alphabetize the paragraphs in the bulleted list. ***Why?*** *It is easier for readers to locate information in lists that are in alphabetical order.* In Word, you can arrange paragraphs in alphabetic, numeric, or date order based on the first character in each paragraph. Ordering characters in this manner is called **sorting**. The following steps sort paragraphs.

1

- Scroll up to display the paragraphs to be sorted.
- Drag through the paragraphs to be sorted, in this case, the bulleted list.
- Tap or click the Sort button (HOME tab | Paragraph group) to display the Sort Text dialog box (Figure 4–36).

What does ascending mean?
Ascending means to sort in alphabetic, numeric, or earliest-to-latest date order.

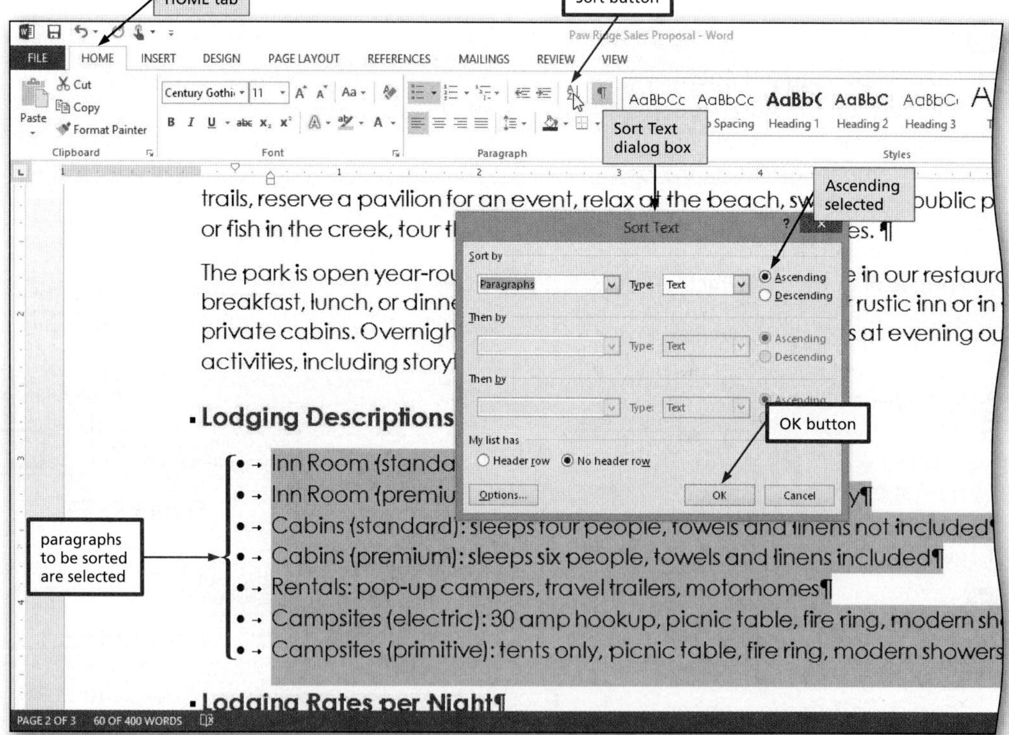

Figure 4–36

2

- Tap or click the OK button (Sort Text dialog box) to instruct Word to alphabetize the selected paragraphs (shown in Figure 4–37).
- Tap or click anywhere to remove the selection from the text.

To Apply a Style Using the Mini Toolbar

The text up to the colon in each list item is to be formatted in bold, dark red, and italic. Although you could apply formatting using buttons in the Font group on the ribbon, it is more efficient to use the Intense Emphasis style. If you use a style and decide at a later time that you want to modify the formatting, you simply modify the style and Word will apply the changes to all text formatted with that style. Thus, the following steps format text using a style.

1. Drag through the text to be formatted (in this case, the text, Cabins (premium), in the first list item).
2. Tap or click the Styles button on the mini toolbar to display the Styles gallery (Figure 4–37).
3. Tap or click Intense Emphasis in the Styles gallery to apply the selected style to the selected text.

Q&A Could I use the Styles gallery on the HOME tab instead of the mini toolbar?
Yes.

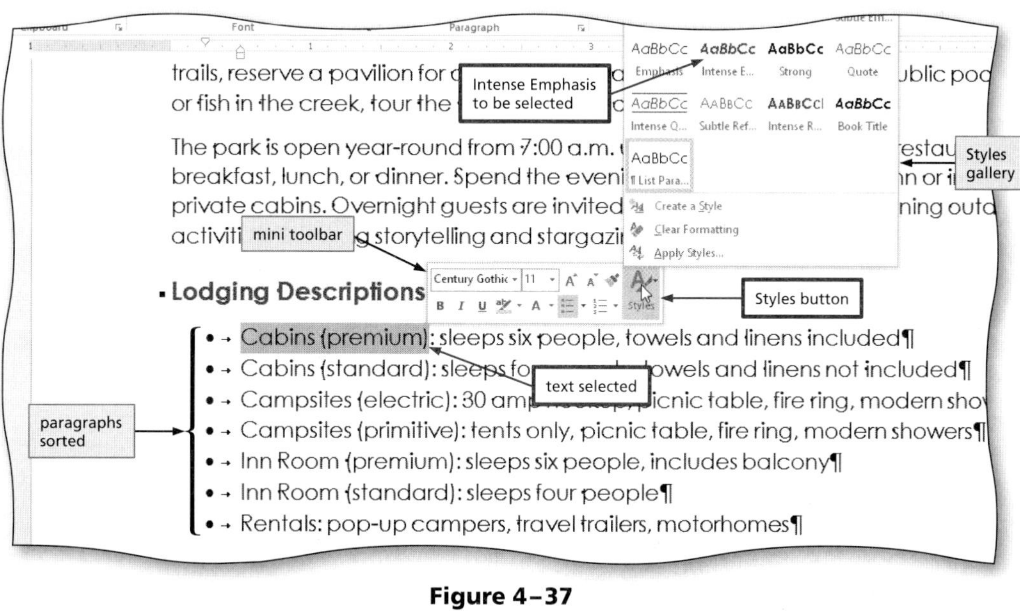

Figure 4–37

BTW
Format Painter
If you also want to copy paragraph formatting, such as alignment and line spacing, select the paragraph mark at the end of the paragraph prior to tapping or clicking the Format Painter button. If you want to copy only character formatting, such as fonts and font sizes, do not include the paragraph mark in your selected text.

To Use the Format Painter Button

1 CREATE TITLE PAGE | 2 INSERT EXISTING DOCUMENT | 3 CREATE HEADER & FOOTER
4 EDIT & FORMAT LISTS | **5 EDIT & FORMAT TABLES** | **6 CREATE WATERMARK**

The first words in each of the remaining list items is to be formatted the same as the first words in the first list item. ***Why?*** *You would like the lists to be formatted consistently.* Instead of selecting the text in each list item one at a time and then formatting it, you will copy the format from the first word to the remaining words. The following steps copy formatting.

- Position the insertion point in the text that contains the formatting you wish to copy (in this case, the text, Cabins (premium)).
- Double-tap or double-click the Format Painter button (HOME tab | Clipboard group) to turn on the format painter.

Q&A Why double-tap or double-click the Format Painter button?
To copy formats to only one other location, tap or click the Format Painter button (HOME tab | Clipboard group) once. If you want to copy formatting to multiple locations, however, double-tap or double-click the Format Painter button so that the format painter remains active until you turn it off.

- If you are using a mouse, move the pointer to where you want to copy the formatting (the text, Cabins (standard), in this case) and notice that the format painter is active (Figure 4–38).

Q&A How can I tell if the format painter is active?
The pointer has a paintbrush attached to it when the format painter is active.

- Drag through the text in the next list item (the text, Cabins (standard), in this case) to paste the copied format to the selected text.

Q&A What if the Format Painter button no longer is selected?
Repeat Step 1.

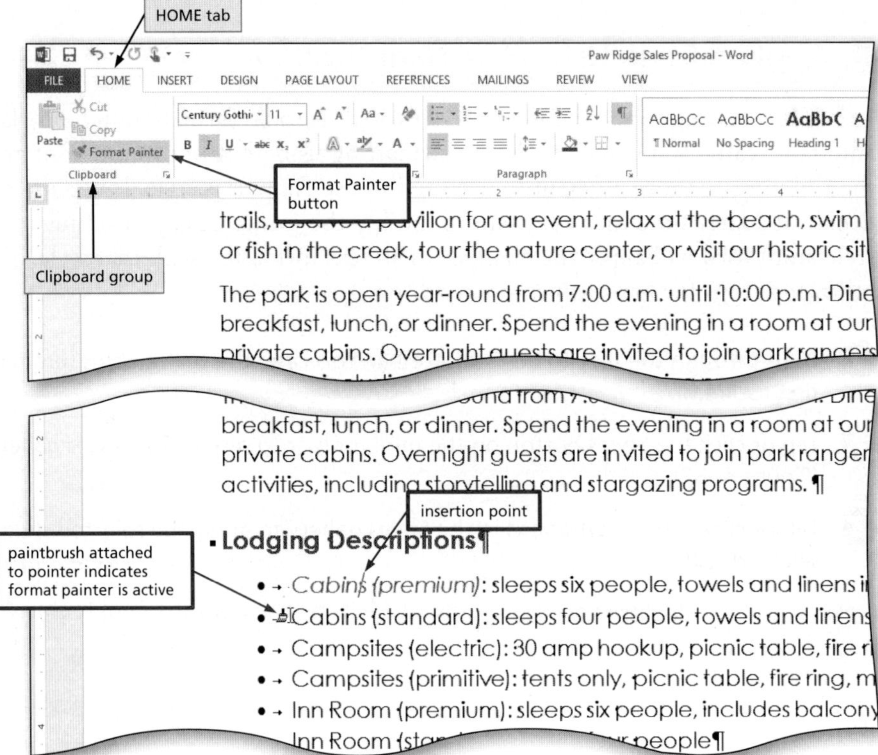

Figure 4–38

3

- Repeat Step 2 for the remaining the list items, selecting text up to the colon in Campsites (electric), Campsites (primitive), Inn Room (premium), Inn Room (standard), and Rentals.
- Tap or click the Format Painter button (HOME tab | Clipboard group) to turn off the format painter (Figure 4–39).

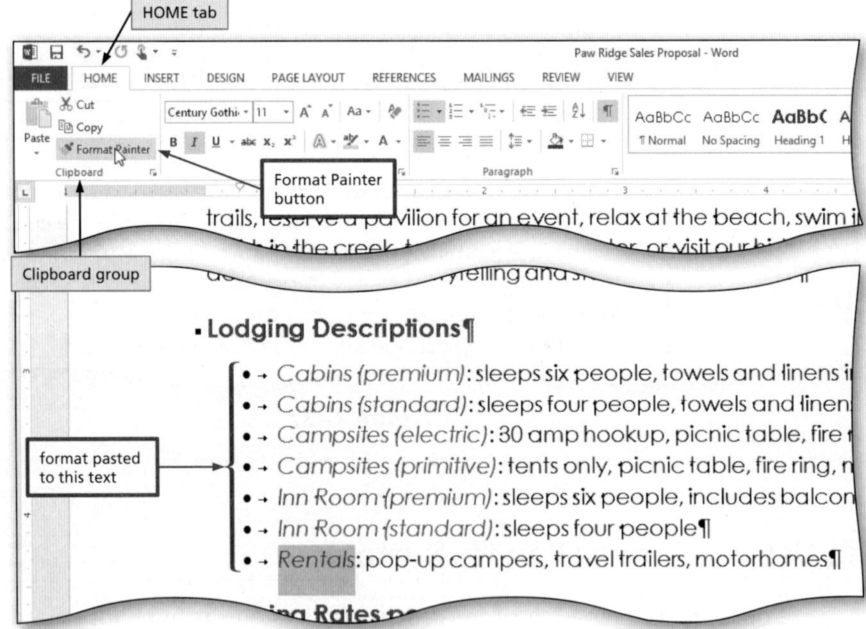

Figure 4–39

To Customize Bullets in a List

1 CREATE TITLE PAGE | 2 INSERT EXISTING DOCUMENT | 3 CREATE HEADER & FOOTER
4 EDIT & FORMAT LISTS | **5 EDIT & FORMAT TABLES** | **6 CREATE WATERMARK**

The bulleted list in the sales proposal draft uses default bullet characters, that is, the dot symbol. The following steps change the bullets in a list from the default to picture bullets. ***Why?*** *You want to use a more visually appealing bullet that looks like bed and pillow. Word refers to these graphical bullets as picture bullets.*

1

- Select all the paragraphs in the bulleted list.
- Tap or click the Bullets arrow (HOME tab | Paragraph group) to display the Bullets gallery (Figure 4–40).

Q&A Can I select any of the bullet characters in the Bullet Library area of the Bullets gallery?
Yes, but if you prefer a different bullet character, follow the rest of these steps.

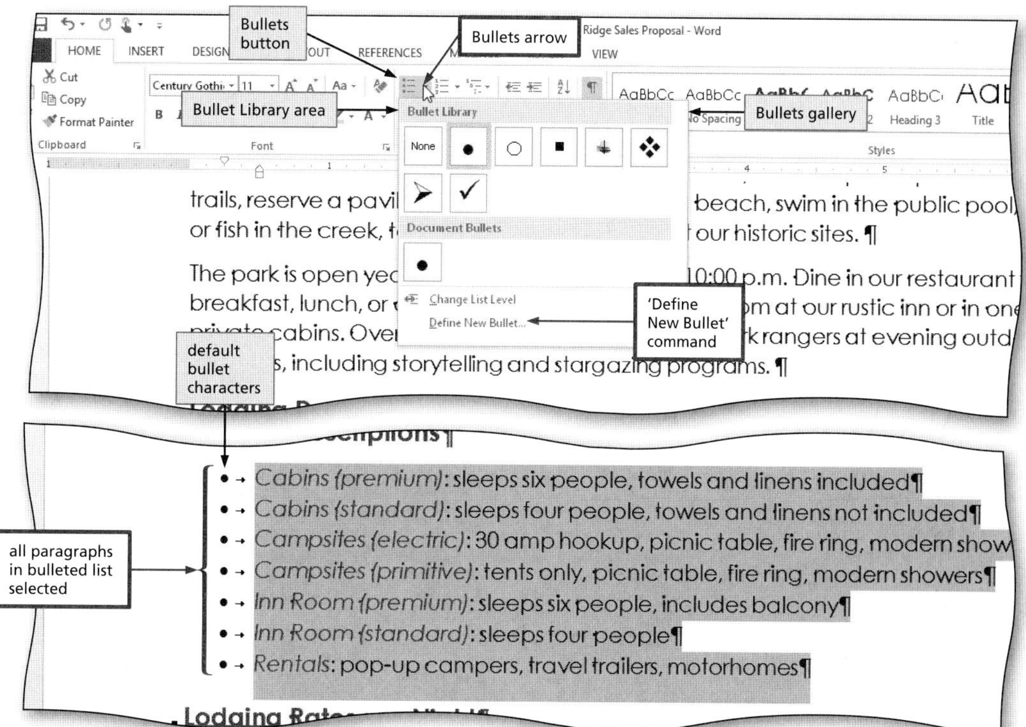

Figure 4–40

2

- Tap or click 'Define New Bullet' in the Bullets gallery to display the Define New Bullet dialog box.
- Tap or click the Picture button (Define New Bullet dialog box) to display the Insert Pictures dialog box.

Q&A Is this the same dialog box I use to locate clip art?
Yes.

- Type **pillow** in the Office.com Clip Art Search box (Insert Pictures dialog box) and then tap or click the Search button to display a list of clip art that matches the entered search text.
- Scroll through the list of clip art to locate the one shown in Figure 4–41 (or a similar image), if necessary, and then tap or click the clip art to select it.

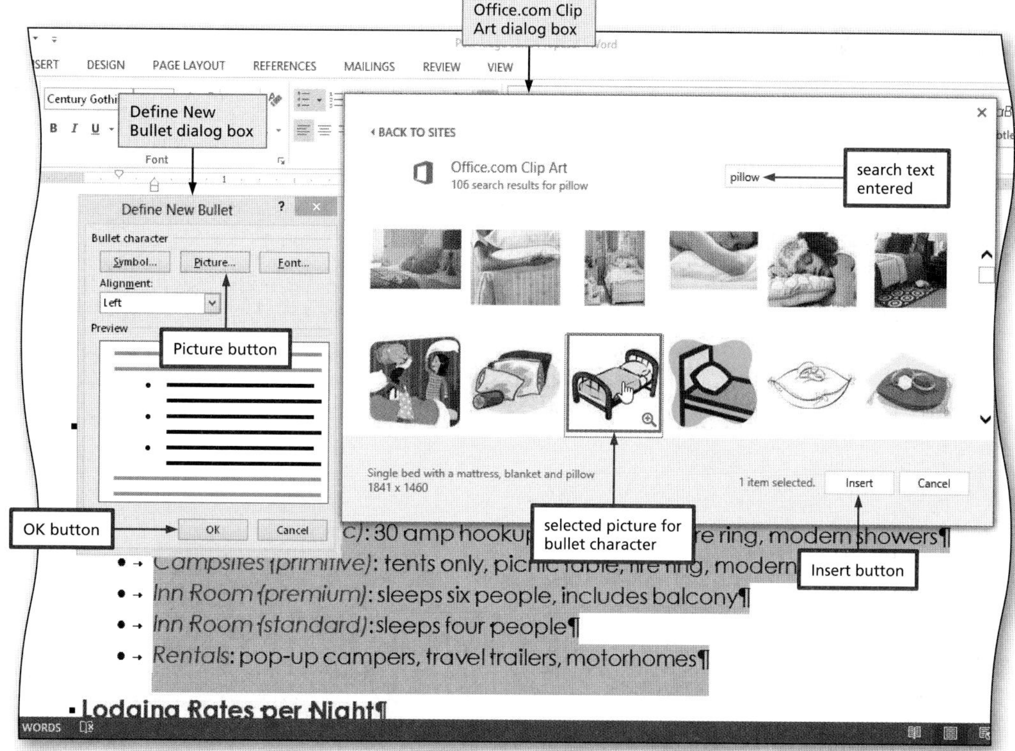

Figure 4–41

- Tap or click the Insert button (Office.com Clip Art dialog box) to download the image, close the dialog box, and show a preview of the selected picture bullet in the Define New Bullet dialog box.
- Tap or click the OK button (Define New Bullet dialog box) to change the bullets in the selected list to picture bullets.
- When the Word window is visible again, tap or click in the selected list to remove the selection (Figure 4–42).

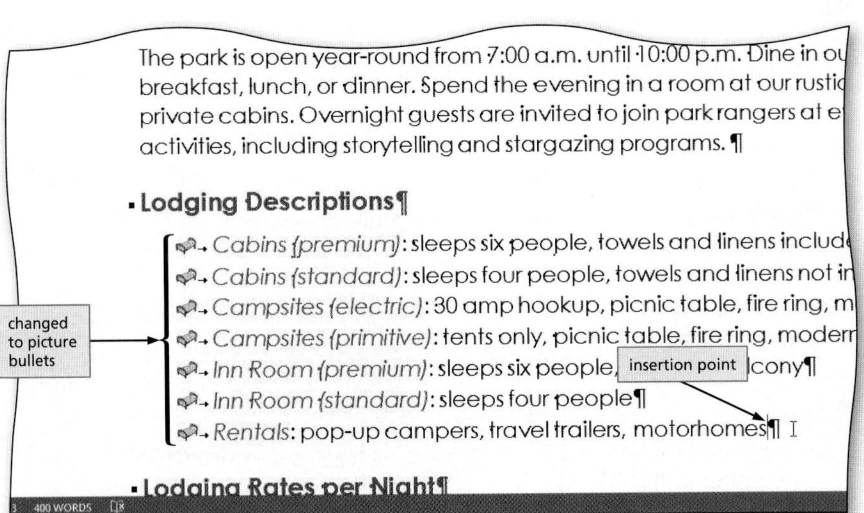

Figure 4–42

To Create a Multilevel Numbered List

1 CREATE TITLE PAGE | 2 INSERT EXISTING DOCUMENT | 3 CREATE HEADER & FOOTER
4 EDIT & FORMAT LISTS | 5 EDIT & FORMAT TABLES | 6 CREATE WATERMARK

The next step is to create a multilevel numbered list below the Recreation heading on the last page of the sales proposal in this chapter (shown in Figure 4–1c on page WD 203). ***Why?*** *You would like to list the various types of recreation available at the state park.*

A **multilevel list** is a list that contains several levels of list items, with each lower level displaying a different numeric, alphabetic, or bullet character. In a multilevel list, the first level is displayed at the left edge of the list and subsequent levels are indented; that is, the second level is indented below the first, the third level is indented below the second level, and so on. The list is referred to as a numbered list if the first level contains numbers or letters and is referred to as a bulleted list if the first level contains a character other than a number or letter.

For the list in this project, the first level uses numbers (i.e., 1., 2., 3.), the second level uses lowercase letters (a., b., c.), and the third level uses lowercase Roman numerals (for example, i., ii., iii.). The following steps create a multilevel numbered list.

- Position the insertion point at the location for the multilevel numbered list, which in this case is the blank line below the Recreation heading on the last page of the sales proposal.
- Tap or click the Multilevel List button (HOME tab | Paragraph group) to display the Multilevel List gallery (Figure 4–43).

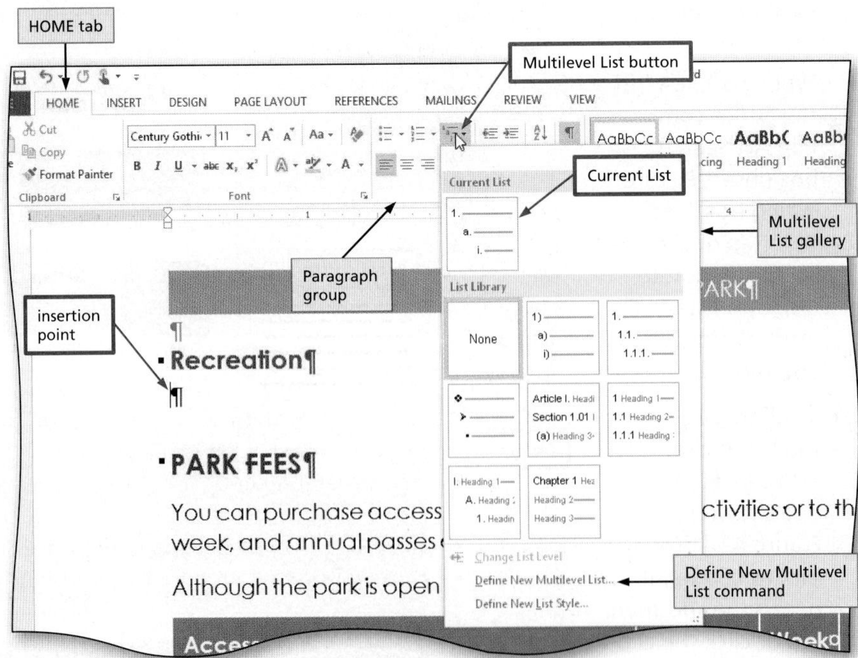

Figure 4–43

2

- Tap or click the Current List format in the Multilevel List gallery to display the current paragraph as a multilevel list item using the current number format, which in this case is an indented 1 followed by a period.

Q&A What if I wanted a different number format?
You would tap or click the Multilevel List button (HOME tab | Paragraph group) and then select the desired format in the Multilevel List gallery, or tap or click the Define New Multilevel List command in the Multilevel List gallery to define your own format.

- Type **Canoe** as a first-level list item and then press the ENTER key, which automatically places the next sequential number for the current level at the beginning of the next line (in this case, 2.) (Figure 4–44).

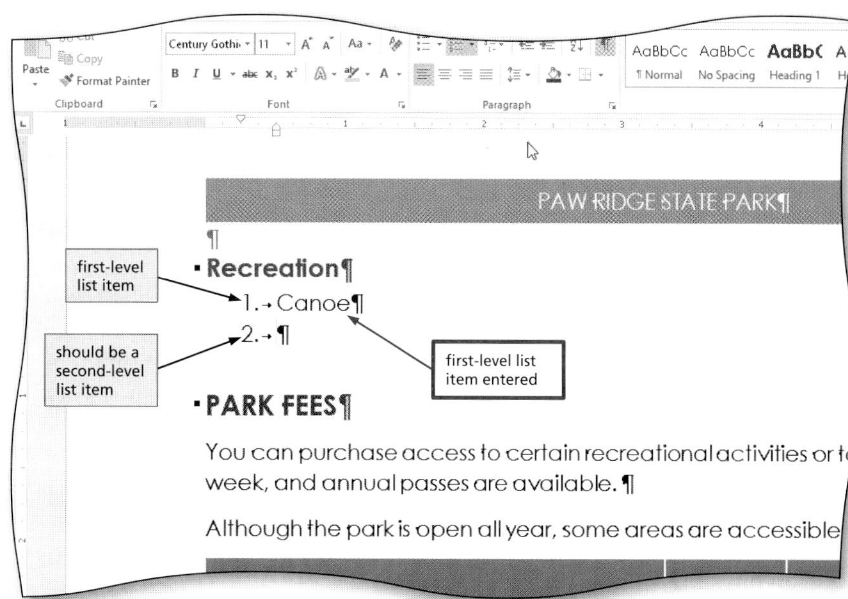

Figure 4–44

- Press the TAB key to demote the current list item (the 2.) to the next lower level, which is indented below the higher-level list item (in this case, converting 2. to a.).

- Type the text for list item 1-a as shown in Figure 4–45 and then press the ENTER key, which automatically places the next sequential list item for the current level on the next line (in this case, b.).
- Type the text for list item 1-b as shown in Figure 4–45 and then press the ENTER key, which automatically places the next sequential list item on the next line (in this case, c.).

PAW RIDGE STATE PARK¶
Recreation¶
1. Canoe¶
a. 3-mile, 5-mile, and 10-mile trips¶
b. Rent a canoe, kayak, or tube¶
c. Open daily from May 1 through September 30¶
d. ¶
PARK FEES¶
You can purchase access to certain recreational activities or to the ent
week, and annual passes are available. ¶
converted to second-level list item
should be promoted to first-level list item, aligned below number 1
text entered

Figure 4–45

- Type the text for list item 1-c as shown in Figure 4–45 and then press the ENTER key, which automatically places the next sequential list item on the next line (Figure 4–45).

- Press SHIFT+TAB to promote the current-level list item to a higher-level list item (in this case, converting d. to 2.).

Q&A Can I use buttons on the ribbon instead of pressing TAB or SHIFT+TAB to promote and demote list items?
Yes. With the insertion point in the item to adjust, you can tap or click the Increase Indent or Decrease Indent button (HOME tab | Paragraph group) or press and hold or right-click the list item and then tap or click the desired command on the shortcut menu.

6

- Type **Fish** as a first-level list item and then press the ENTER key.
- Press the TAB key to demote the current level list item to a lower-level list item (in this case, converting 3. to a.).
- Type the text for list item 2-a as shown in Figure 4–46 and then press the ENTER key.
- Type the text for list item 2-b as shown in Figure 4–46 and then press the ENTER key.
- Press SHIFT+TAB to promote the current-level list item to a higher-level list item (in this case, converting c. to 3.).
- Type **Hike** as a first-level list item, press the ENTER key, and then press the TAB key to demote the current-level list item to a lower-level list item (in this case, converting 4. to a.).
- Type the text for list item 3-a as shown in Figure 4–46 and then press the ENTER key.

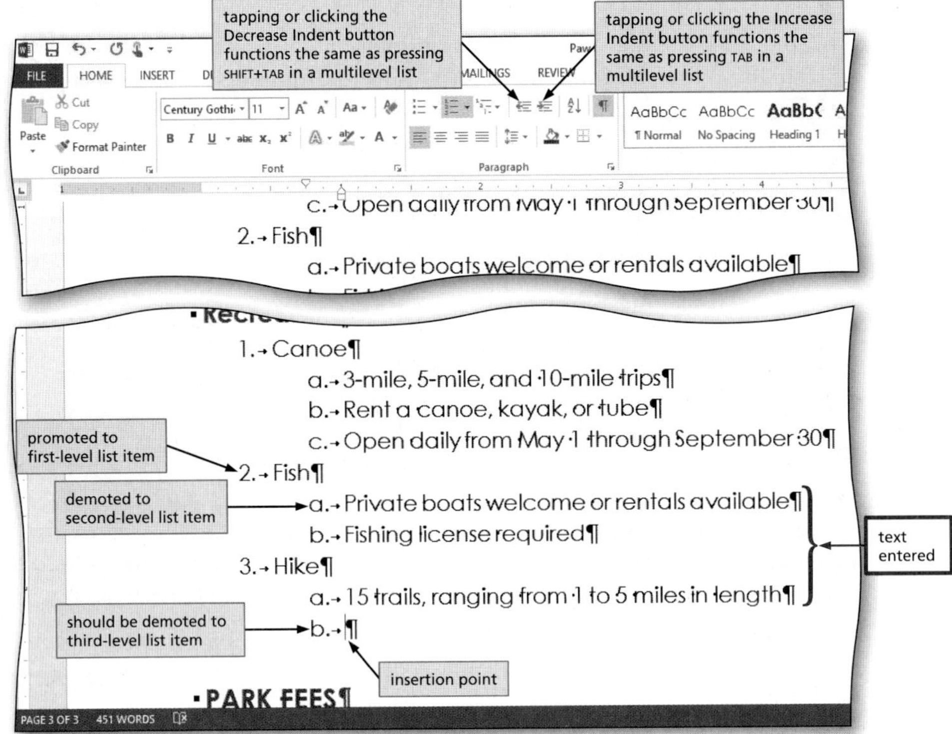

Figure 4–46

7

- Press the TAB key to demote the current-level list item to a lower-level list item (in this case, converting b. to i.).
- Type the text for list item 3-a-i as shown in Figure 4–47 and then press the ENTER key.
- Type the text for list item 3-a-ii as shown in Figure 4–47 and then press the ENTER key.
- Type the text for list item 3-a-iii as shown in Figure 4–47 and then press the ENTER key.
- Press SHIFT+TAB to promote the current-level list item to a higher-level list item (in this case, converting iii. to b.).
- Type the text for list item 3-b as shown in Figure 4–47 and then press the ENTER key.
- Press SHIFT+TAB to promote the current-level list item to a higher-level list item (in this case, converting c. to 4.).
- Finish entering the list as shown in Figure 4–47.

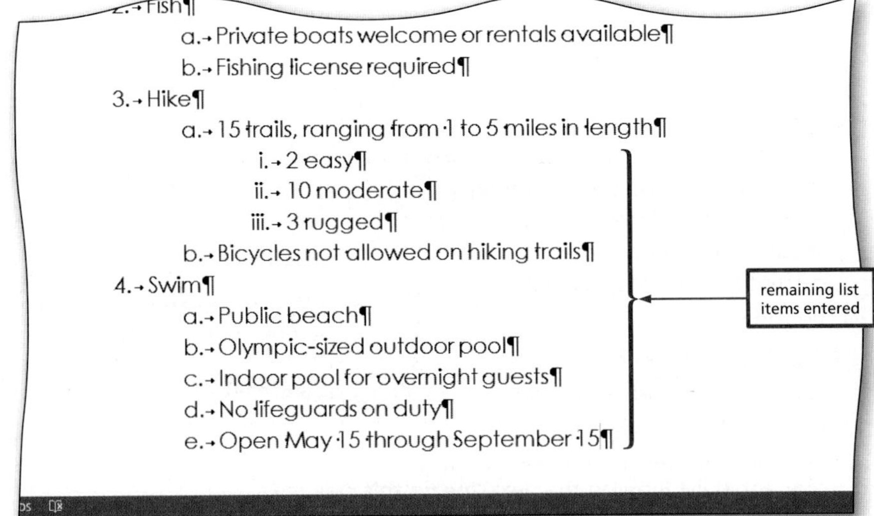

Figure 4–47

Other Ways

1. Type **1.,** press the SPACEBAR, and then type the numbered list

To Save an Existing Document with the Same File Name

You have made several modifications to the document since you last saved it. Thus, you should save it again. The following step saves the document again.

 Tap or click the Save button on the Quick Access Toolbar to overwrite the previously saved file.

Break Point: If you wish to take a break, this is a good place to do so. You can exit Word now. To resume at a later time, run Word, open the file called Paw Ridge Title Page, and continue following the steps from this location forward.

Editing and Formatting Tables

The sales proposal draft contains two Word tables: the lodging rates table and the park fees table (shown in Figure 4–26 on page WD 227). The lodging rates table shows the rates for several types of overnight accommodations, and the park fees table shows the costs of accessing various areas in the park. In this section, you will make several modifications to these two tables so that they appear as shown in Figure 4–1 on page WD 203.

The following pages explain how to modify the tables in the sales proposal draft:

1. Lodging rates table
   a. Change the column width for the column containing the type of lodging.
   b. Change row heights so that they are not so tall.
   c. Shade table cells.
   d. Change cell spacing.
   e. Change the column width of columns containing costs.
2. Park fees table
   a. Delete the extra column on the right edge of the table.
   b. Sort the table contents by type of access.
   c. Split table cells so that the heading, Access, is above the second column.
   d. Display text in a cell vertically to the left of the table.
   e. Remove cell shading from the table.
   f. Add borders to the table.
   g. Sum columns in the table.

BTW
Table Wrapping
If you want text to wrap around a table, instead of displaying above and below the table, do the following: either press and hold or right-click the table and then tap or click Table Properties on the shortcut menu or tap or click the Table Properties button (TABLE TOOLS LAYOUT tab | Table group), tap or click the Table tab (Table Properties dialog box), tap or click Around in the Text wrapping area, and then tap or click the OK button.

CONSIDER THIS

Why should you include visuals in a sales proposal?
Studies have shown that most people are visually oriented, preferring images to text. Use tables to clarify ideas and illustrate points. Be aware, however, that too many visuals can clutter a document.

To Show Gridlines

1 CREATE TITLE PAGE | 2 INSERT EXISTING DOCUMENT | 3 CREATE HEADER & FOOTER
4 EDIT & FORMAT LISTS | 5 EDIT & FORMAT TABLES | 6 CREATE WATERMARK

When a table contains no borders or light borders, it may be difficult to see the individual cells in the table. Thus, the step on the next page shows gridlines. ***Why?*** *To help identify the location of cells, you can display gridlines, which show cell outlines on the screen.* **Gridlines** are formatting marks, which means the gridlines do not print.

- Display the table to be edited in the document window (in this case, the lodging rates table).
- Position the insertion point in any cell in the table.
- Display the TABLE TOOLS LAYOUT tab.
- If gridlines are not displayed on the screen, tap or click the 'View Table Gridlines' button (TABLE TOOLS LAYOUT tab | Table group) to show gridlines in the table (Figure 4–48).

Q&A How do I turn off table gridlines?

Tap or click the 'View Table Gridlines' button again.

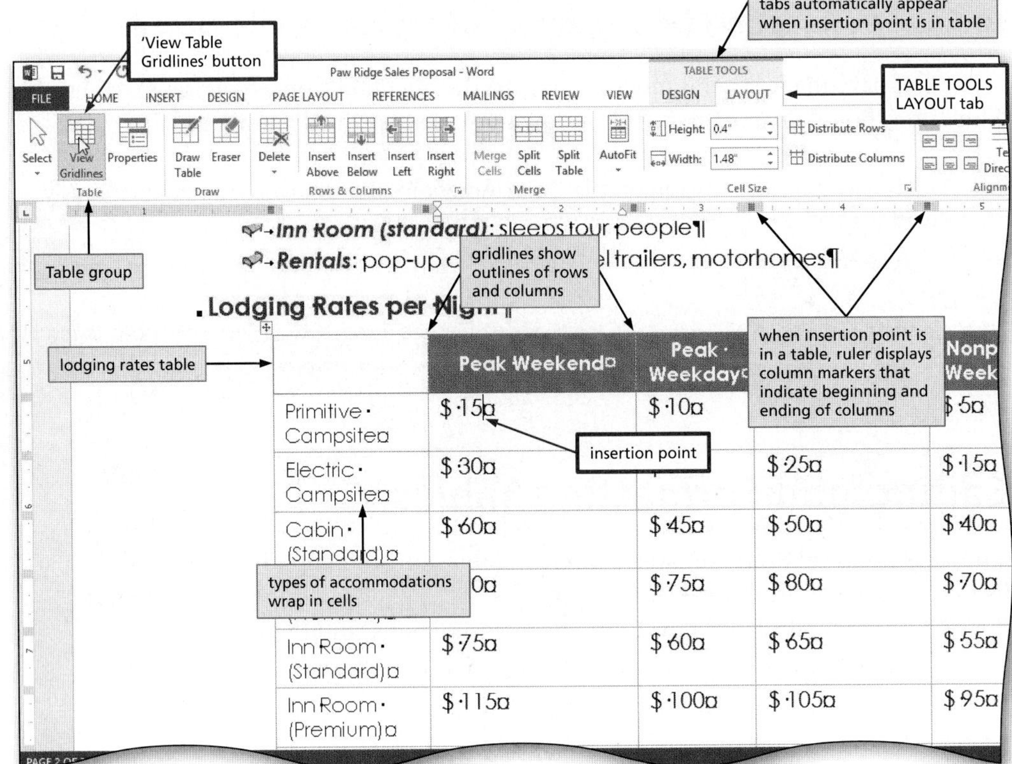

Figure 4–48

To Change Column Width

1 CREATE TITLE PAGE | 2 INSERT EXISTING DOCUMENT | 3 CREATE HEADER & FOOTER
4 EDIT & FORMAT LISTS | 5 EDIT & FORMAT TABLES | 6 CREATE WATERMARK

Notice in Figure 4–48 that the leftmost column containing the types of accommodations is not wide enough to fit the contents; that is, the accommodations wrap in the cells. Thus, you will change the column width of just this single column. ***Why?*** *In this proposal, the accommodations should appear on a single line that is just wide enough to accommodate the types of accommodations.*

You can change a column width by entering a specific value on the ribbon or in a dialog box, or by using a marker on the ruler or the column boundary. The following steps change column width by dragging a column's boundary.

- If you are using a mouse, position the pointer on the column boundary to the right of the column to adjust (in this case, to the right of the first column) so that the pointer changes to a double-headed arrow split by two vertical bars (Figure 4–49).

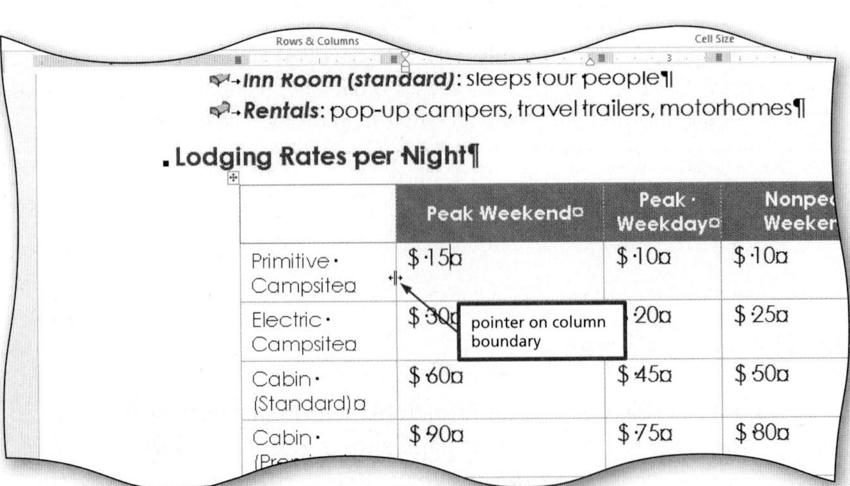

Figure 4–49

- If you are using a mouse, double-click the column boundary so that Word adjusts the column width according to the column contents. If all of the contents in the column still are not displayed on a single line, double-click the column boundary again so that all contents are displayed on a single line (Figure 4–50).

Figure 4–50

Q&A What if I am using a touch screen?
Position the insertion point in the column to adjust, tap the AutoFit button (TABLE TOOLS LAYOUT tab | Cell Size group), and then tap AutoFit Contents on the AutoFit menu.

Experiment

- Practice changing this column's width using other techniques: drag the 'Move Table Column' marker on the horizontal ruler to the right and then to the left. Tap or click the 'Table Column Width' box up and down arrows (TABLE TOOLS LAYOUT tab | Cell Size group). When you have finished experimenting, type `1.48` in the 'Table Column Width' box (TABLE TOOLS LAYOUT tab | Cell Size group).

Other Ways

1. Drag 'Move Table Column' marker on horizontal ruler to desired width
2. Enter desired value in 'Table Column Width' box (TABLE TOOLS LAYOUT tab | Cell Size group)
3. Tap or click Table Properties button (TABLE TOOLS LAYOUT tab | Table group), tap or click Column tab, enter width, tap or click OK button

To Change Row Height

1 CREATE TITLE PAGE | 2 INSERT EXISTING DOCUMENT | 3 CREATE HEADER & FOOTER
4 EDIT & FORMAT LISTS | **5 EDIT & FORMAT TABLES** | **6 CREATE WATERMARK**

The next step in this project is to narrow the height of the rows containing the accommodations and rates. ***Why?*** *This table extends close to the bottom of the page, and you want to ensure that it does not spill onto the next page. Note that it already may spill onto a second page.*

You change row height in the same ways you change column width. That is, you can change row height by entering a specific value on the ribbon or in a dialog box, or by using a marker on the ruler or the row boundary. The latter two methods, however, work only for a single row at a time. The following steps change row height by entering a value on the ribbon.

- Select the rows to change (in this case, all the rows below the first row).

Q&A How do I select rows?
If you are using a touch screen, drag through the rows; if you are using a mouse, point to the left of the first row and then drag downward when the pointer changes to a right-pointing arrow.

2

- If you are using a touch screen, enter `0.3` in the 'Table Row Height' box (TABLE TOOLS LAYOUT tab | Cell Size group); if you are using a mouse, click the 'Table Row Height' box up or down arrows (TABLE TOOLS LAYOUT tab | Cell Size group) as many times as necessary until the box displays 0.3" to change the row height to this value (Figure 4–51).
- Tap or click anywhere to remove the selection from the table.

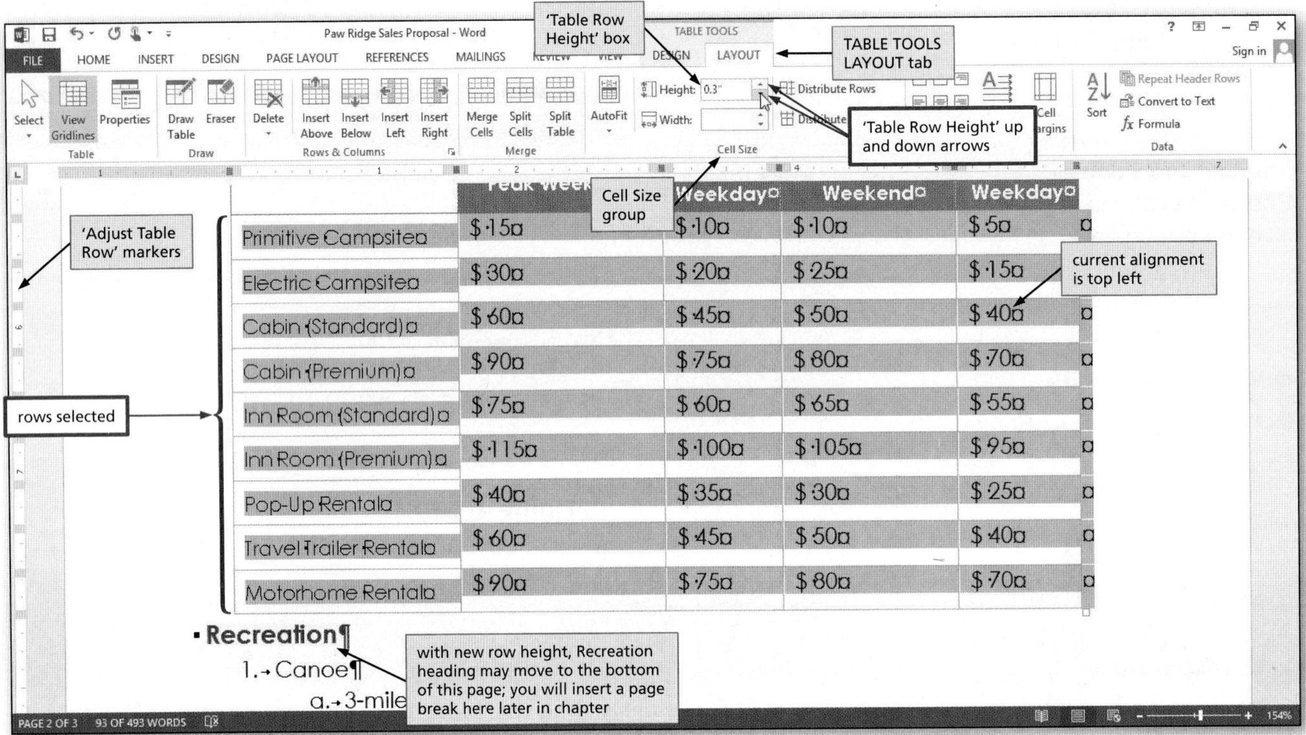

Figure 4–51

Other Ways

1. Tap or click Table Properties button (TABLE TOOLS LAYOUT tab | Table group), tap or click Row tab (Table Properties dialog box), enter row height, tap or click OK button
2. Tap 'Show Context Menu' button on mini toolbar or right-click selected row, tap or click Table Properties on shortcut menu, tap or click Row tab, enter row height (Table Properties dialog box), tap or click OK button
3. For a single row, drag row boundary (horizontal gridline at bottom of row in table) to desired height
4. Drag 'Adjust Table Row' marker on vertical ruler to desired height

BTW

Page Breaks and Tables

If you do not want a page break to occur in the middle of a table, position the insertion point in the table, tap or click the Table Properties button (TABLE TOOLS LAYOUT tab | Table group), tap or click the Row tab (Table Properties dialog box), remove the check mark from the 'Allow row to break across pages' check box, and then tap or click the OK button. To force a table to break across pages at a particular row, tap or click in the row that you want to appear on the next page and then press CTRL+ENTER.

To Align Data in Cells

The next step is to change the alignment of the data in cells that contain the dollar amounts. Recall that, in addition to aligning text horizontally in a cell (left, center, or right), you can align it vertically within a cell (top, center, or bottom). Currently, the dollar amounts have a top left alignment (shown in Figure 4–51). In this project, they should be aligned center so that they are more centered within the row height and width. The following steps change the alignment of data in cells.

1 Select the cells containing dollar amounts, as shown in Figure 4–52.

Q&A How do I select a series of cells?

Drag through the cells.

2. Tap or click the Align Center button (TABLE TOOLS LAYOUT tab | Alignment group) to center the contents of the selected cells (Figure 4–52).

3. Tap or click anywhere to remove the selection from the table.

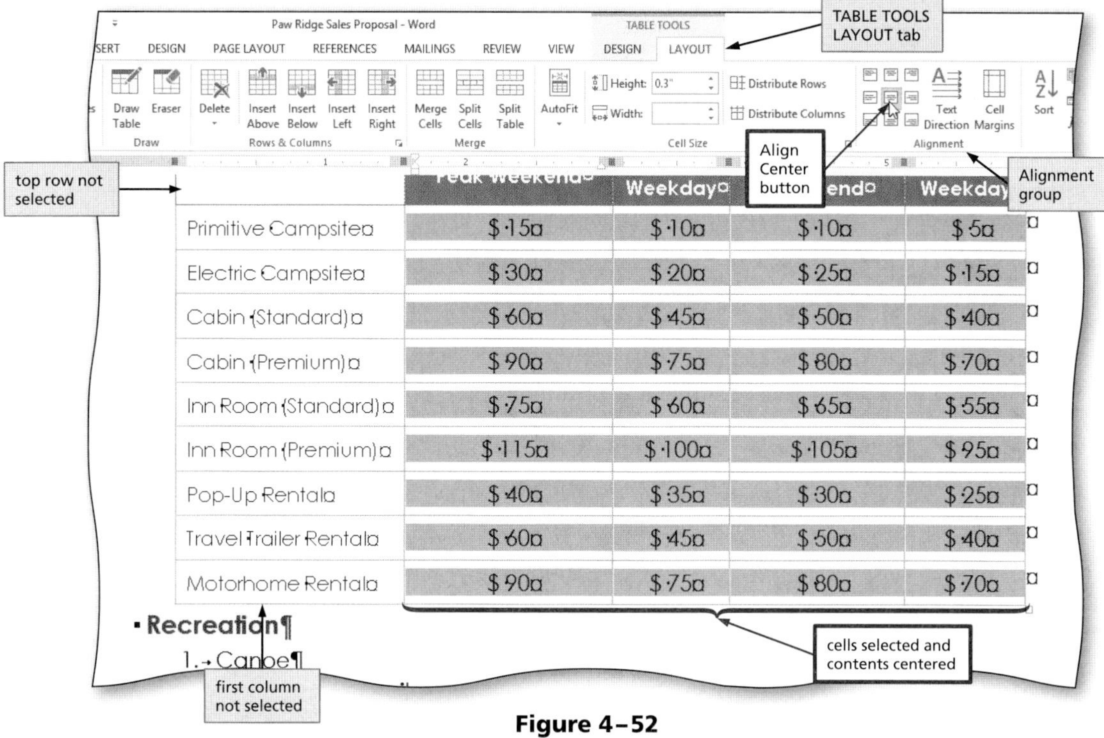

Figure 4–52

To Shade a Table Cell

1 CREATE TITLE PAGE | 2 INSERT EXISTING DOCUMENT | 3 CREATE HEADER & FOOTER
4 EDIT & FORMAT LISTS | 5 EDIT & FORMAT TABLES | **6 CREATE WATERMARK**

In this table, the cell in the upper-left corner of the table is to be shaded brown. ***Why?*** *You want all cells in the top row shaded the same color.* The following steps shade a cell.

1.
- Position the insertion point in the cell to shade (in this case, the cell in the upper-left corner of the table).
- Display the TABLE TOOLS DESIGN tab.
- Tap or click the Shading arrow (TABLE TOOLS DESIGN tab | Table Styles group) to display the Shading gallery (Figure 4–53).

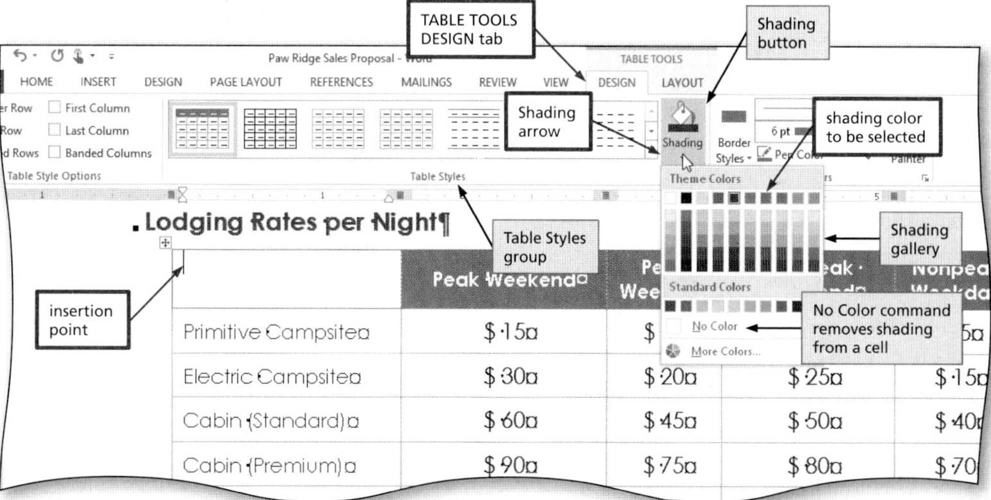

Figure 4–53

Experiment

- If you are using a mouse, point to various colors in the Shading gallery and watch the shading color of the current cell change.

- Tap or click 'Brown, Accent 3' (seventh color, first row) in the Shading gallery to apply the selected shading color to the current cell.

Q&A How do I remove shading from a cell?
Tap or click the Shading arrow (TABLE TOOLS DESIGN tab | Table Styles group) and then tap or click No Color in the Shading gallery.

To Select Nonadjacent Items

1 CREATE TITLE PAGE | 2 INSERT EXISTING DOCUMENT | 3 CREATE HEADER & FOOTER
4 EDIT & FORMAT LISTS | **5 EDIT & FORMAT TABLES** | **6 CREATE WATERMARK**

The next step is to select every other row in the table and shade it light brown. ***Why?*** *You feel that using shading on alternating rows will make it easier to read across individual rows.* If you are using a mouse, Word provides a method of selecting nonadjacent items, which are items such as text, cells, or graphics that are not next to each other, that is, not to the immediate right, left, top, or bottom. When you select nonadjacent items, you can format all occurrences of the items at once. The following steps select nonadjacent cells.

- Select the first row to format (in this case, the row containing the Electric Campsite accommodation).

2

- While holding down the CTRL key, select the next row to format (in this case, the row containing Cabin (Premium) accommodation) to select the nonadjacent row.
- While holding down the CTRL key, select the remaining nonadjacent rows (that is, the rows containing the Inn Room (Premium) and Travel Trailer Rental accommodations), as shown in Figure 4–54.

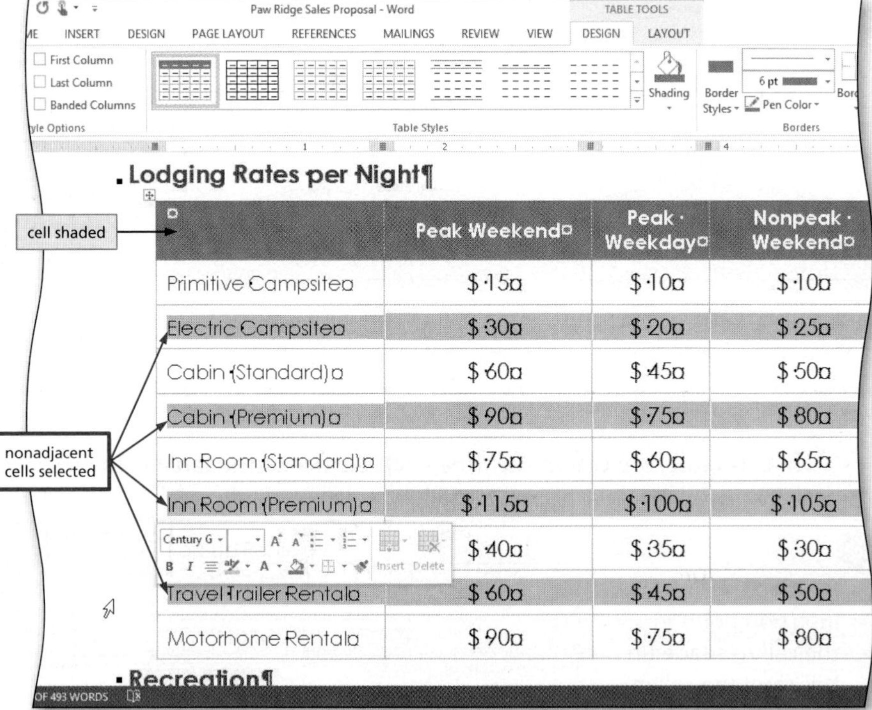

Figure 4–54

Q&A Do I follow the same procedure to select any nonadjacent item?
Yes. Select the first item and then hold down the CTRL key while selecting the remaining items.

What if my keyboard does not have a CTRL key?
You will need to format each row individually, one at a time.

To Shade Selected Cells

With the alternating rows selected, the next step is to shade them light brown. The following steps shade selected cells.

1. With the rows selected, tap or click the Shading arrow (TABLE TOOLS DESIGN tab | Table Styles group) to display the Shading gallery and then tap or click 'Brown, Accent 3, Lighter 80%' (seventh color, second row) in the Shading gallery to shade the selected rows with the selected color (Figure 4–55).

2. Tap or click anywhere to remove the selection from the table.

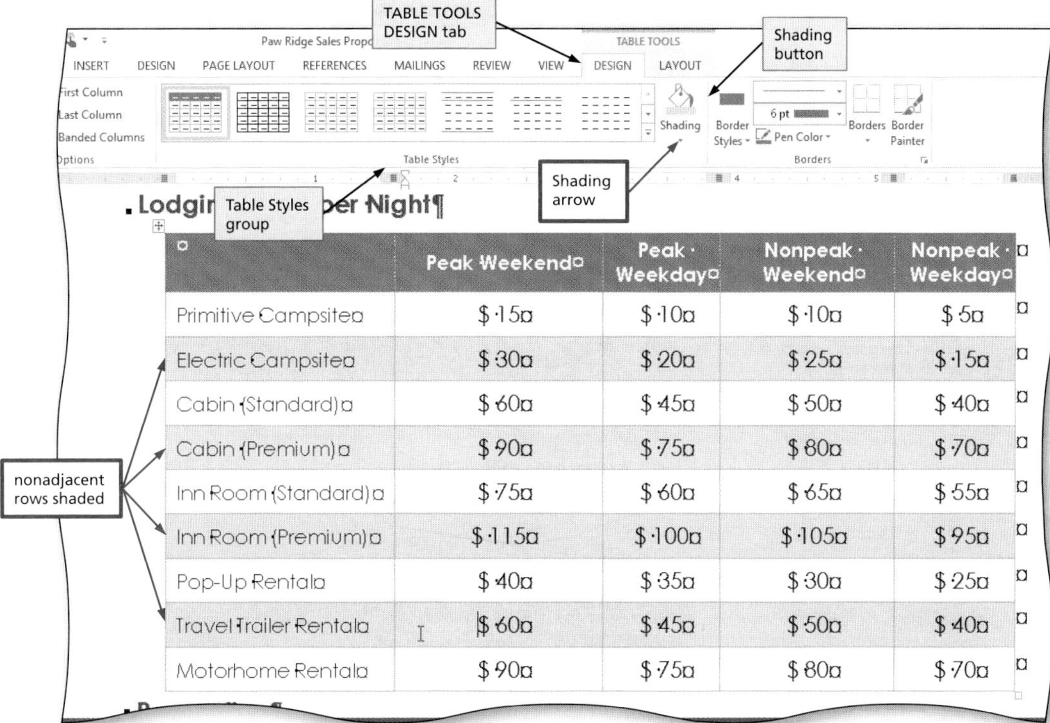

Figure 4–55

BTW

Table Headings

If a table continues on the next page, you can instruct Word to repeat the table headings at the top of the subsequent page(s) containing the table. To do this, select the first row in the table and then tap or click the 'Repeat Header Rows' button (TABLE TOOLS LAYOUT tab | Data group).

To Hide Gridlines

You no longer need to see the gridlines in the table. Thus, you can hide the gridlines. The following steps hide gridlines.

1. If necessary, position the insertion point in a table cell.
2. Display the TABLE TOOLS LAYOUT tab.
3. Tap or click the 'View Table Gridlines' button (TABLE TOOLS LAYOUT tab | Table group) to hide gridlines in the table on the screen.

To Change Cell Spacing

1 CREATE TITLE PAGE | 2 INSERT EXISTING DOCUMENT | 3 CREATE HEADER & FOOTER
4 EDIT & FORMAT LISTS | 5 EDIT & FORMAT TABLES | 6 CREATE WATERMARK

The next step in formatting the lodging rates table is to place a small amount of white space between every cell in the table. ***Why?*** *You feel the table would be easier to read with shite space surrounding each cell.* The following steps change spacing between cells.

- With the insertion point somewhere in the table, tap or click the Cell Margins button (TABLE TOOLS LAYOUT tab | Alignment group) to display the Table Options dialog box.

- Place a check mark in the 'Allow spacing between cells' check box and then tap or click the up arrow once so that 0.02" is displayed in this box, because you want to increase space between cells by this value (Figure 4–56).

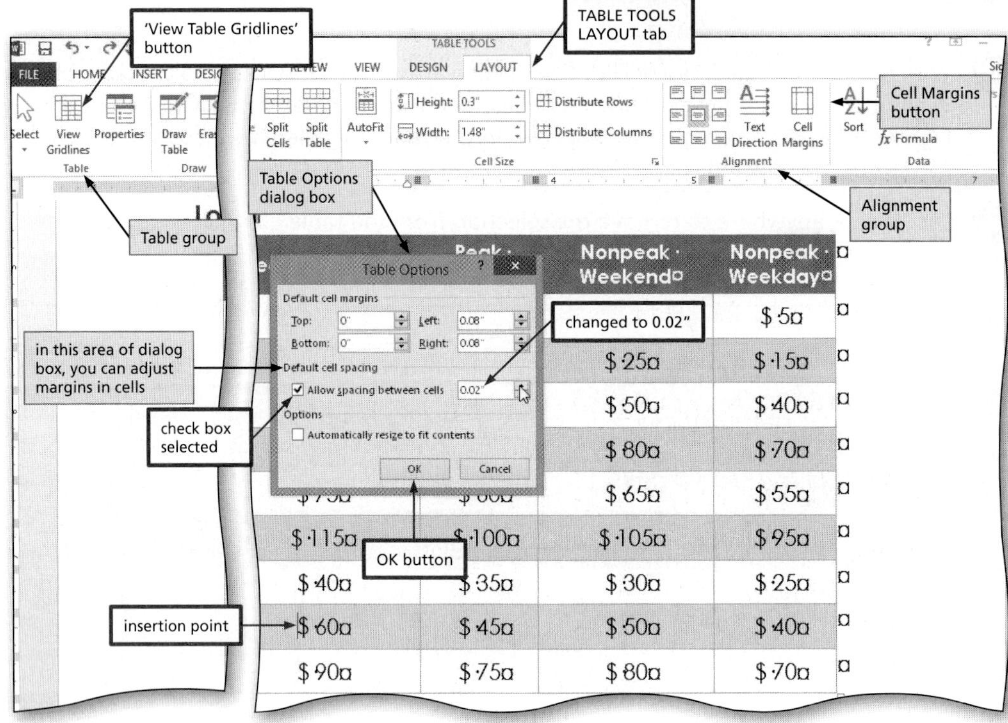

Figure 4–56

2

- Tap or click the OK button (Table Options dialog box) to apply the cell spacing changes to the current table (Figure 4–57).

Lodging Rates per Night¶

space added between cells

	Peak Weekend	Peak Weekday	Nonpeak Weekend	Nonpeak Weekday
Primitive Campsite	$15	$10	$10	$5
Electric Campsite	$30	$20	$25	$15
Cabin (Standard)	$60	$45	$50	$40
Cabin (Premium)	$90	$75	$80	$70
Inn Room (Standard)	$75	$60	$65	$55
Inn Room (Premium)	$115	$100	$105	$95

Figure 4–57

Other Ways

1. Tap or click Table Properties button (TABLE TOOLS LAYOUT tab | Table group), tap or click Table tab (Table Properties dialog box), tap or click Options button, select desired options (Table Options dialog box), tap or click OK button in each dialog box
2. Tap 'Show Context Menu' button on mini toolbar or right-click table, tap or click Table Properties on shortcut menu, tap or click Table tab (Table Properties dialog box), tap or click Options button, select desired options (Table Options dialog box), tap or click OK button in each dialog box

BTW

Table Columns

If you hold down the ALT key while dragging a column marker on the ruler or a column boundary in the table, the width measurements of all columns appear on the ruler as you drag the column marker or boundary.

To Change Column Width

In reviewing the lodging rates table, you notice that the columns containing the rates are different widths. Thus, the final step in formatting the lodging rates table is to change the column widths because you want the columns containing the rates to all be the same width, specifically .95". The following steps change column widths by specifying a value on the ribbon.

1. Select the columns to be resized, in this case, all columns except the first.
2. Tap or click the 'Table Column Width' box (TABLE TOOLS LAYOUT tab | Cell Size group) to select it.

3. Type **.95** in the 'Table Column Width' box and then press the ENTER key to change the width of the selected table columns (Figure 4–58).

4. Tap or click anywhere to remove the selection from the table.

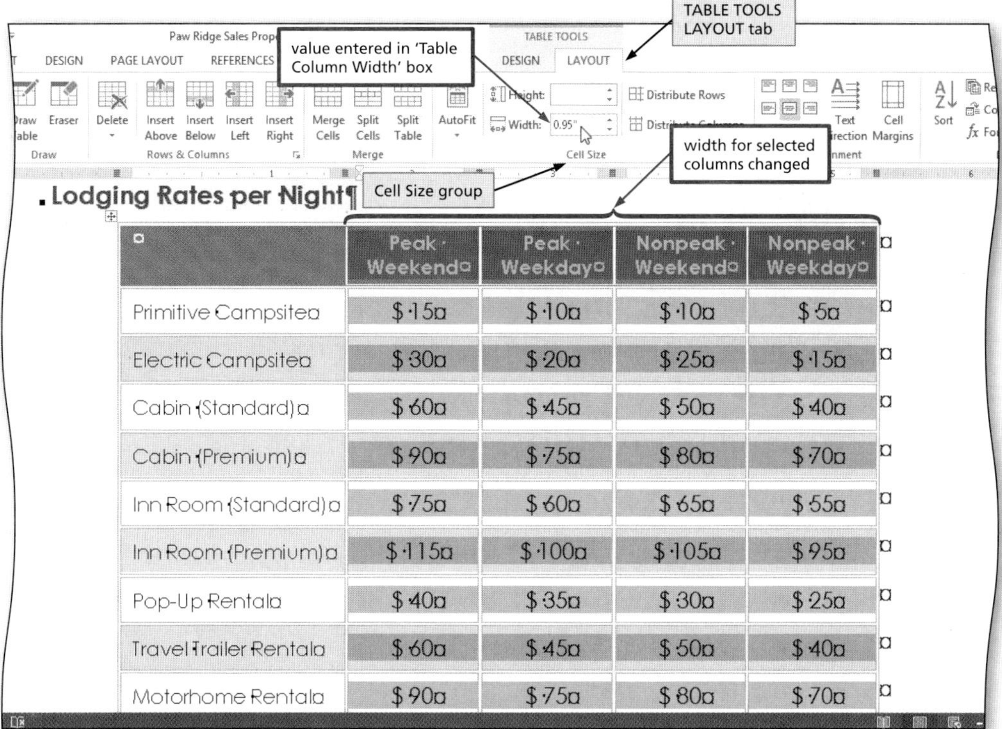

Figure 4–58

To Page Break Manually

If the Recreation heading appears below the lodging rates table, insert a page break immediately to its left so that this heading appears at the top of the last page of the proposal (as shown in Figure 4–1 on page WD 203). The following steps insert a manual page break, if necessary.

1. If the Recreation heading is not on the last page of the proposal, position the insertion point immediately to the left of the R in Recreation.

2. Display the INSERT tab.

3. Tap or click the 'Insert a Page Break' button (INSERT tab | Pages group) to insert a manual page break at the location of the insertion point, which will move the Recreation heading to the last page of the proposal.

BTW

BTWs

For a complete list of the BTWs found in the margins of this book, visit the BTW resource on the Student Companion Site located on www.cengagebrain.com. For detailed instructions about accessing available resources, visit www.cengage.com/ct/studentdownload or contact your instructor for information about accessing the required files.

To Delete a Column

1 CREATE TITLE PAGE | 2 INSERT EXISTING DOCUMENT | 3 CREATE HEADER & FOOTER
4 EDIT & FORMAT LISTS | 5 EDIT & FORMAT TABLES | **6 CREATE WATERMARK**

With the lodging rates table finished, the next task is to format the park fees table. The following steps delete a column from a table. ***Why?*** *The table in the draft of the proposal contains a blank column that should be deleted.*

- Scroll to display the park fees table in the document window.
- Position the insertion point in the column to be deleted (in this case, the rightmost column).

- Tap or click the Delete Table button (TABLE TOOLS LAYOUT tab | Rows & Columns group) to display the Delete Table menu (Figure 4–59).

2

- Tap or click Delete Columns on the Delete Table menu to delete the column containing the insertion point (shown in Figure 4–60).

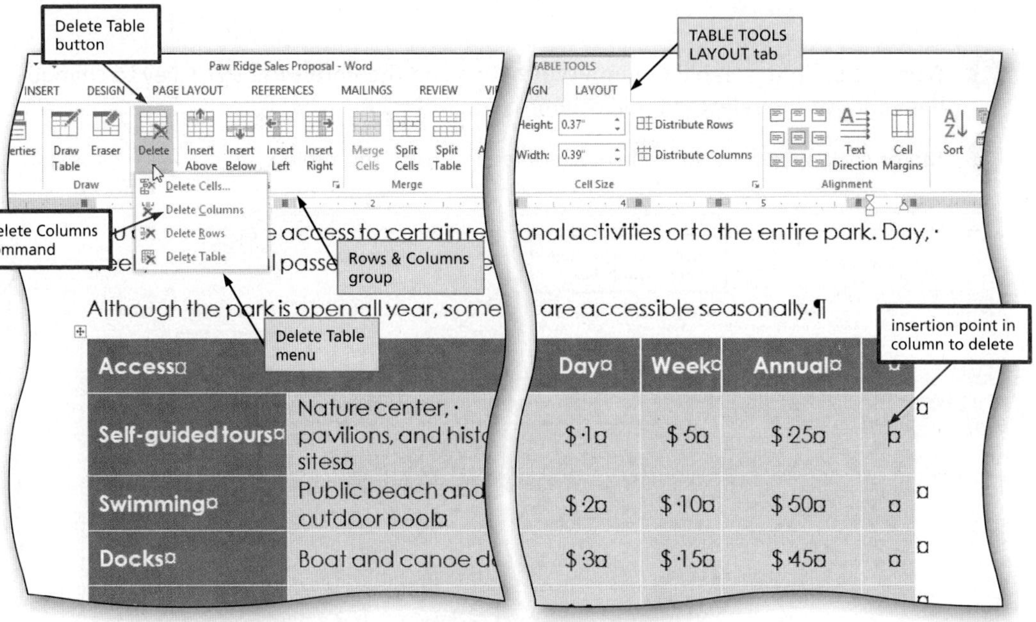

Figure 4–59

Other Ways

1. Press and hold column to delete, tap Delete Table button on mini toolbar, tap Delete Columns
2. Right-click column to delete, click Delete Cells on shortcut menu, click 'Delete entire column' (Delete Cells dialog box), click OK button
3. Select column, right-click selection, click Delete Columns on shortcut menu

BTW

Quick Reference

For a table that lists how to complete the tasks covered in this book using touch gestures, the mouse, ribbon, shortcut menu, and keyboard, see the Quick Reference Summary at the back of this book, or visit the Quick Reference resource on the Student Companion Site located on www.cengagebrain.com. For detailed instructions about accessing available resources, visit www.cengage.com/ct/studentdownload or contact your instructor for information about accessing the required files.

To Delete a Row

If you wanted to delete a row, you would perform the following tasks.

- Position the insertion point in the row to be deleted; tap or click the Delete Table button (TABLE TOOLS LAYOUT tab | Rows & Columns group) and then tap or click Delete Rows on the Delete Table menu.

or

- Press and hold row to delete, tap Delete Table button on mini toolbar, tap Delete Rows.

or

- Right-click the row to delete, click Delete Cells on the shortcut menu, click 'Delete entire row' (Delete Cells dialog box), and then click the OK button.

or

- Select the row to be deleted, right-click the selected row, and then click Delete Rows on the shortcut menu.

To Sort a Table

1 CREATE TITLE PAGE | 2 INSERT EXISTING DOCUMENT | 3 CREATE HEADER & FOOTER
4 EDIT & FORMAT LISTS | 5 EDIT & FORMAT TABLES | **6 CREATE WATERMARK**

In the draft of this sales proposal, the access fees are grouped by category: self-guided tours, swimming, docks, and hiking. The next task is to sort rows in the table. ***Why?*** *The categories should be listed in alphabetical order: docks, hiking, self-guided tours, and then swimming.* The following steps sort rows in a table.

1

- Select the rows to be sorted (in this case, the four middle rows).

Q&A What if I want to sort all rows in the table?

Place the insertion point anywhere in the table instead of selecting the rows.

- Tap or click the Sort button (TABLE TOOLS LAYOUT tab | Data group) to display the Sort dialog box (Figure 4–60).

Q&A What is the purpose of the Then by area (Sort dialog box)?
If you have multiple values for a particular column, you can sort by columns within columns. For example, if the table had a city column and a last name column, you could sort by last names within cities.

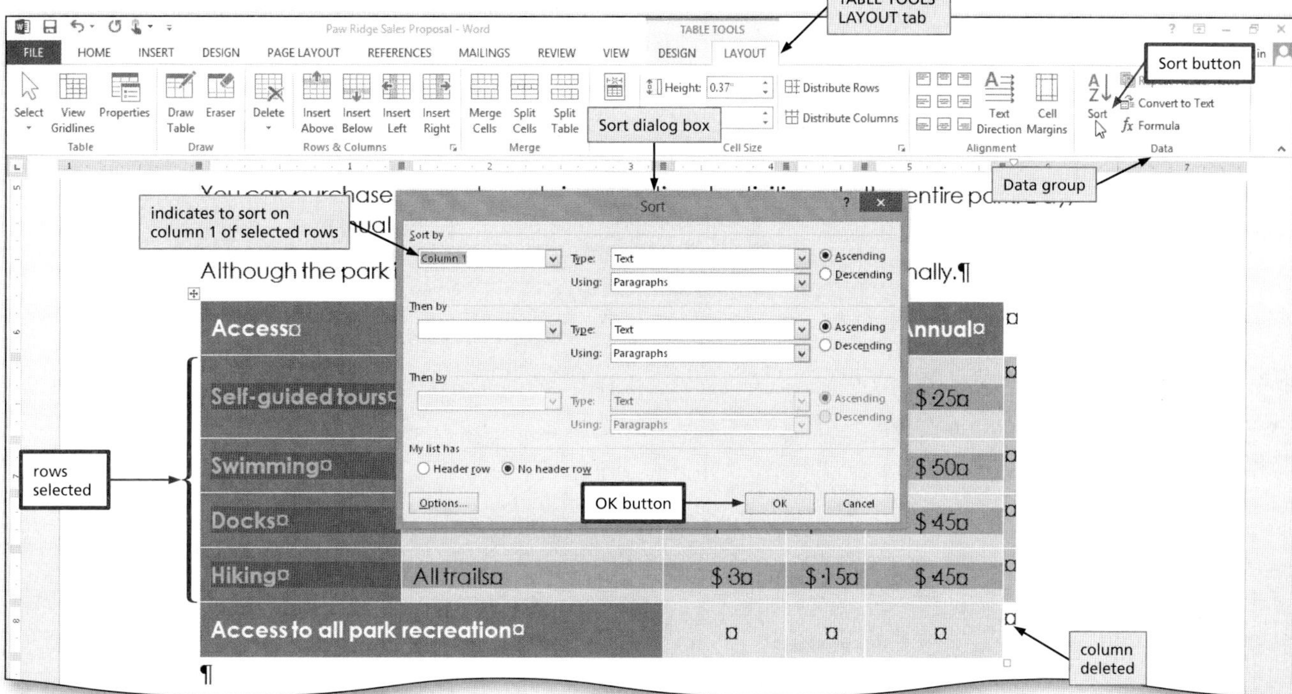

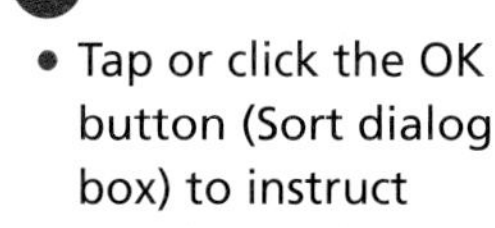

Figure 4–60

2

- Tap or click the OK button (Sort dialog box) to instruct Word to alphabetize the selected rows.
- Tap or click anywhere to remove the selection from the text (Figure 4–61).

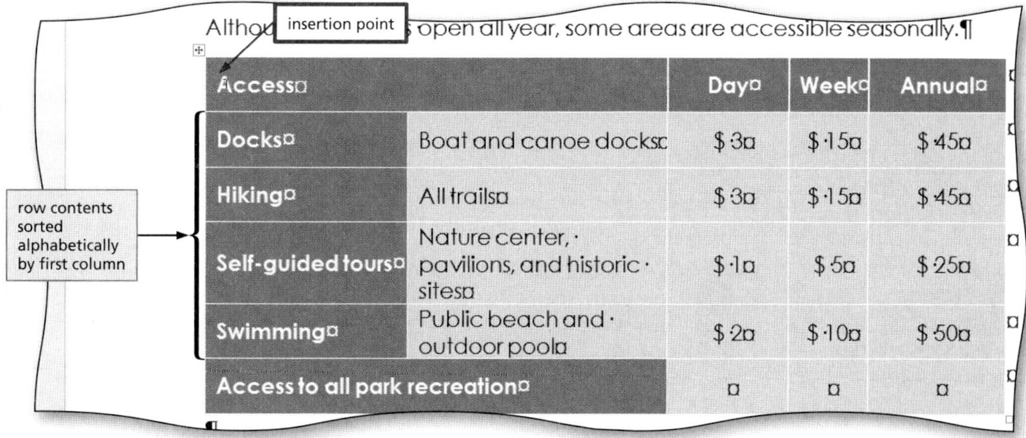

Figure 4–61

To Split Cells

1 CREATE TITLE PAGE | 2 INSERT EXISTING DOCUMENT | 3 CREATE HEADER & FOOTER
4 EDIT & FORMAT LISTS | 5 EDIT & FORMAT TABLES | 6 CREATE WATERMARK

The top, left cell of the table contains the text, Access. In the draft of the sales proposal, this row is above the first two columns in the table (the categories and their descriptions). This heading, Access, should be above the descriptions of the facilities, that is, above the second column. Thus, you will split the cell into two cells. ***Why?*** *With the cell split, you can reposition the heading, Access, above the second column.* The steps on the next page split a single cell into two separate cells.

- Position the insertion point in the cell to split, in this case the top left cell as shown in Figure 4–61.
- Tap or click the Split Cells button (TABLE TOOLS LAYOUT tab | Merge group) to display the Split Cells dialog box (Figure 4–62).

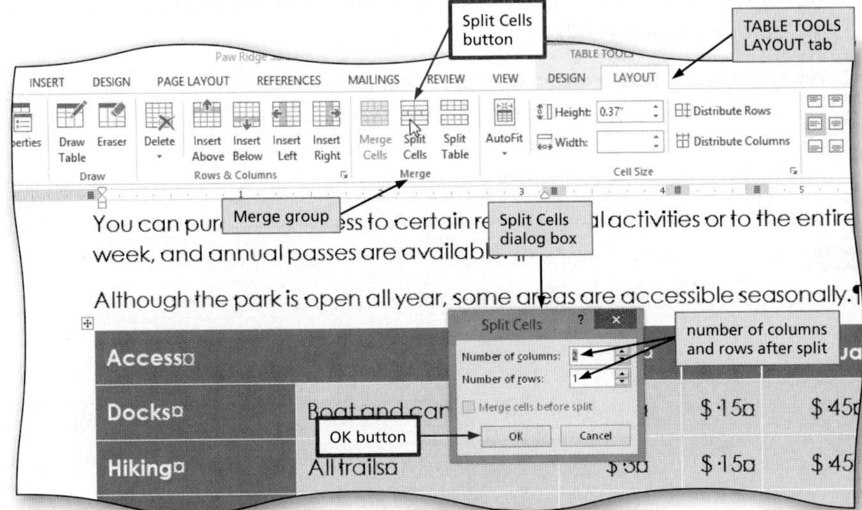

Figure 4–62

- Verify the number of columns and rows into which you want the cell split, in this case, 2 columns and 1 row.
- Tap or click the OK button (Split Cells dialog box) to split the one cell into two columns (Figure 4–63).

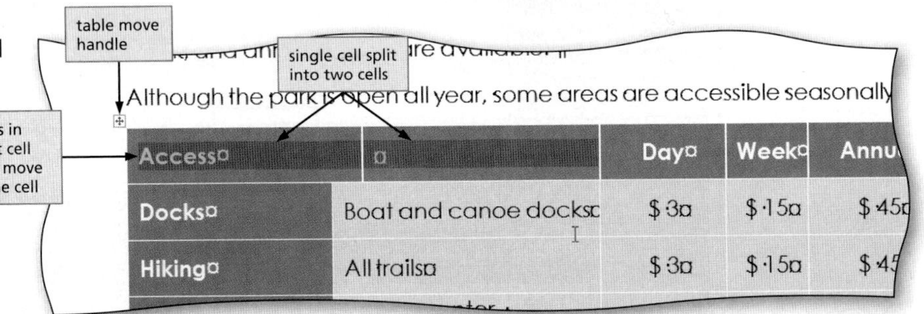

Figure 4–63

Other Ways

1. Tap 'Show Context Menu' button on mini toolbar or right-click cell, tap or click Split Cells on shortcut menu

BTW
Moving Tables
If you wanted to move a table to a new location, you would tap or click in the table to display the table move handle in the upper-left corner of the table (shown in Figure 4-63) and then drag the table move handle to move the entire table to a new location.

To Move Cell Contents

When you split a cell into two cells, Word places the contents of the original cell in the leftmost cell after the split. In this case, the contents (Access) should be in the right cell. Thus, the following steps move cell contents.

1. Select the cell contents to be moved (in this case, Access).
2. Drag the cell contents to the desired location (in this case, the second cell in the first row) (shown in Figure 4–64).

Q&A What if I cannot drag the cell contents properly?
Use the Cut and Paste commands.

To Move a Cell Boundary

1 CREATE TITLE PAGE | 2 INSERT EXISTING DOCUMENT | 3 CREATE HEADER & FOOTER
4 EDIT & FORMAT LISTS | 5 EDIT & FORMAT TABLES | 6 CREATE WATERMARK

Notice in Figure 4–64 that the cell boundary to the left of the Access label does not line up with the boundary to the right of the category types. ***Why not?*** *This is because when you split a cell, Word divides the cell into evenly sized cells.* If you want the boundary to line up with other column boundaries, drag it to the desired location. The next steps move a cell boundary.

- If you are using a mouse, position the pointer on the cell boundary you wish to move so that the pointer changes to a double-headed arrow split by two vertical bars (Figure 4–64).

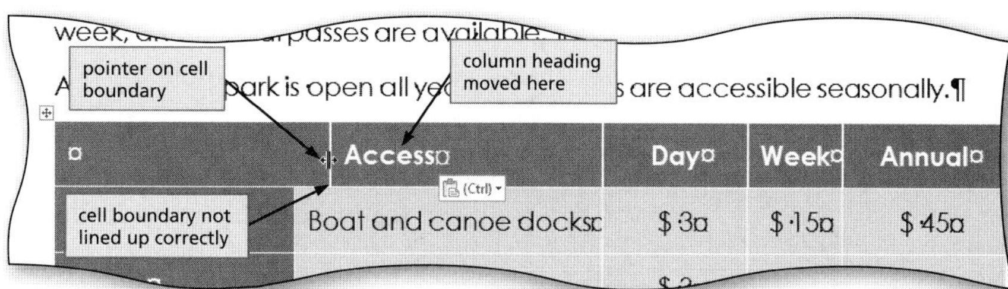

Figure 4–64

2

- Drag the cell boundary to the desired new location, in this case, to line up with the column boundary to its left, as shown in Figure 4–65.

Q&A What if I am using a touch screen?
Position the insertion point in the upper-left cell, tap the Table Properties button (TABLE TOOLS LAYOUT tab | Table group), tap the Cell tab (Table Properties dialog box), type `1.44` in the Preferred width box, and then tap the OK button.

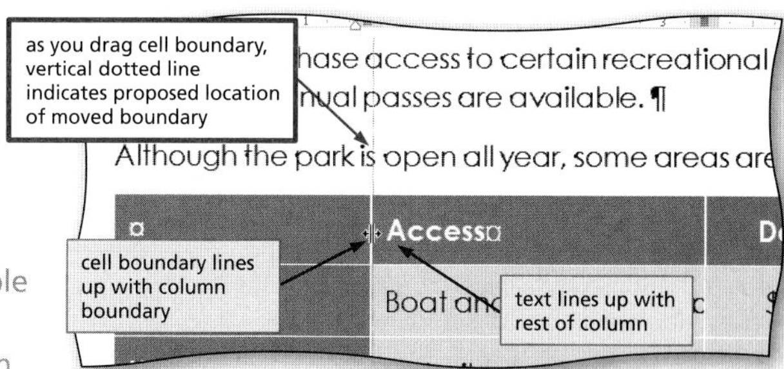

Figure 4–65

Other Ways

1. Drag 'Move Table Column' marker on horizontal ruler to desired width

To Distribute Columns

1 CREATE TITLE PAGE | 2 INSERT EXISTING DOCUMENT | 3 CREATE HEADER & FOOTER
4 EDIT & FORMAT LISTS | 5 EDIT & FORMAT TABLES | 6 CREATE WATERMARK

The next step in formatting the park fees table is to make the width of the day, week, and annual columns uniform, that is, the same width. The next step distributes selected columns. ***Why?*** *Instead of checking and adjusting the width of each column individually, you can make all columns uniform at the same time.*

- Select the columns to format, in this case, the three rightmost columns.
- Tap or click the Distribute Columns button (TABLE TOOLS LAYOUT tab | Cell Size group) to make the width of the selected columns uniform (Figure 4–66).

Q&A How would I make all columns in the table uniform?
Simply place the insertion point somewhere in the table before tapping or clicking the Distribute Columns button.

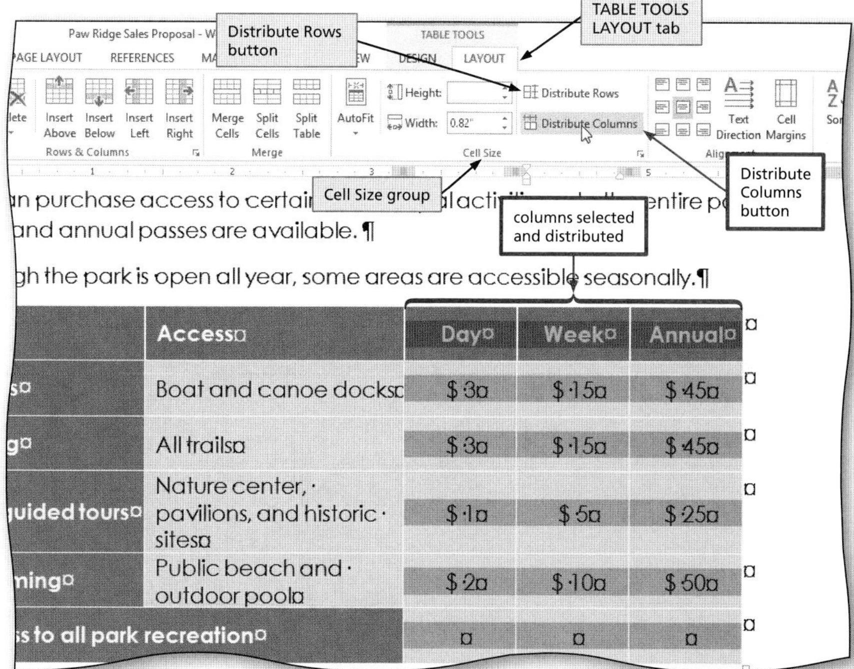

Figure 4–66

Other Ways

1. Tap 'Show Context Menu' button on mini toolbar or right-click selected columns, tap or click 'Distribute Columns Evenly' on shortcut menu

To Distribute Rows

If you wanted to make rows the same height, you would perform the following tasks.

1. Select the rows to format.
2. Tap or click the Distribute Rows button (TABLE TOOLS LAYOUT tab | Cell Size group) to make the width of the selected rows uniform.

or

1. Tap the 'Show Context Menu' button on the mini toolbar or right-click selected columns and then tap or click 'Distribute Rows Evenly' on the shortcut menu.

BTW

Draw Table

If you want to draw the boundary, rows, and columns of a table, tap or click the 'Add a Table' button (INSERT tab | Tables group) and then tap or click Draw Table in the Add a Table gallery. Use the pencil-shaped pointer to draw the perimeter of the table and the inside rows and columns. Use the Table Eraser button (TABLE TOOLS DESIGN tab | Draw group) to erase lines in the table. To continue drawing, tap or click the Draw Table button (TABLE TOOLS DESIGN tab | Draw group).

To Insert a Column

In this project, the left edge of the park fees table has a column that displays the label, Park Fees. Thus, the following steps insert a column at the left edge of the table.

1. Position the insertion point somewhere in the first column of the table.
2. Tap or click the 'Insert Columns to the Left' button (TABLE TOOLS LAYOUT tab | Rows & Columns group) to insert a column to the left of the column containing the insertion point (Figure 4–67).
3. Tap or click anywhere in the table to remove the selection.

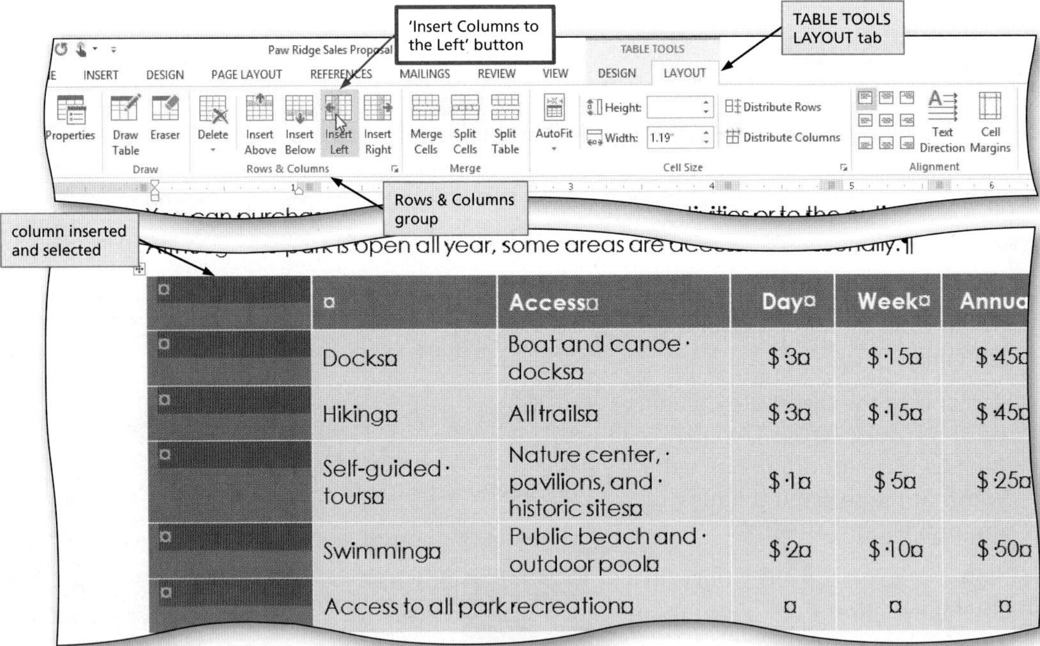

Figure 4–67

To Merge Cells and Enter Text

The label, Park Fees, is to be displayed vertically to the left of the bottom five rows in the table. To display this text, the five cells should be merged into a single cell. The following steps merge cells and then enter text in the merged cell.

1. Select the cells to merge, in this case, the bottom five cells in the first column of the table.
2. Tap or click the Merge Cells button (TABLE TOOLS LAYOUT tab | Merge group) to merge the five selected cells into one cell.

3 Type **Park Fees** in the merged cell.

4 If necessary, center the entered text (Figure 4–68).

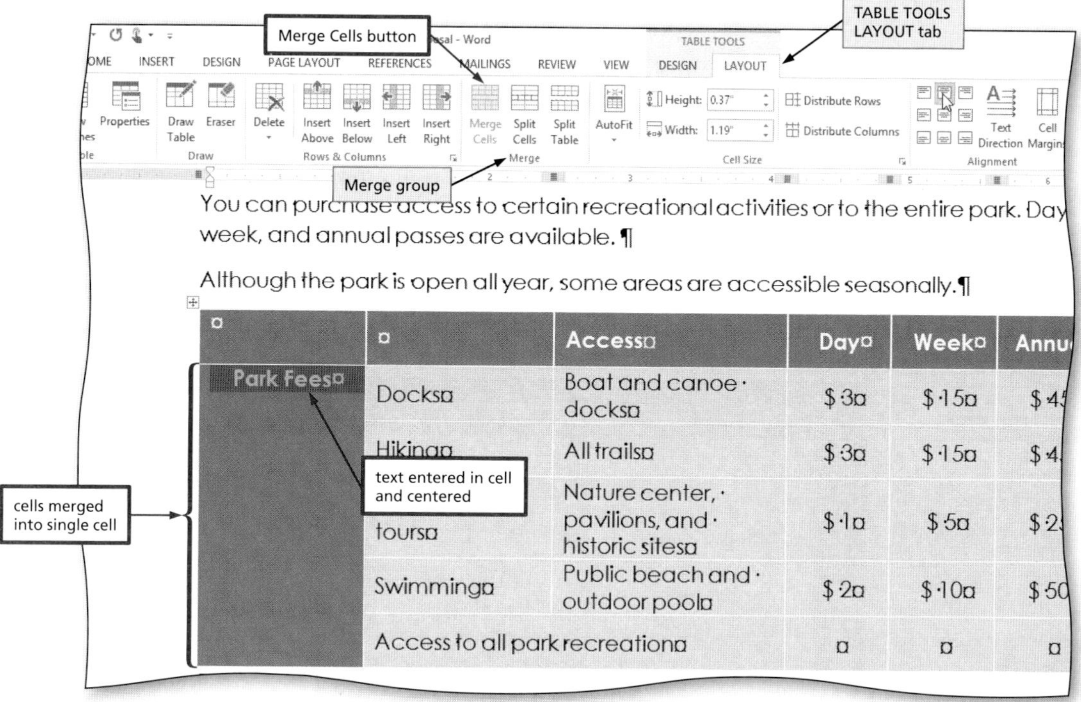

Figure 4–68

To Display Text in a Cell Vertically

1 CREATE TITLE PAGE | 2 INSERT EXISTING DOCUMENT | 3 CREATE HEADER & FOOTER
4 EDIT & FORMAT LISTS | 5 EDIT & FORMAT TABLES | 6 CREATE WATERMARK

The data you enter in cells is displayed horizontally by default. You can rotate the text so that it is displayed vertically. Changing the direction of text adds variety to your tables. The following step displays text vertically in a cell. ***Why?*** *The label, Park Fees, is displayed vertically at the left edge of the table.*

1

- Position the insertion point in the cell that contains the text to rotate (in this case, Park Fees).
- Tap or click the Text Direction button twice (TABLE TOOLS LAYOUT tab | Alignment group) so that the text reads from bottom to top in the cell (Figure 4–69).

Q&A Why tap or click the Text Direction button twice?
The first time you tap or click the Text Direction button (TABLE TOOLS LAYOUT tab | Alignment group), the text in the cell reads from top to bottom. The second time you tap or click it, the text is displayed so that it reads from bottom to top (Figure 4–69). If you were to tap or click the button a third time, the text would be displayed horizontally again.

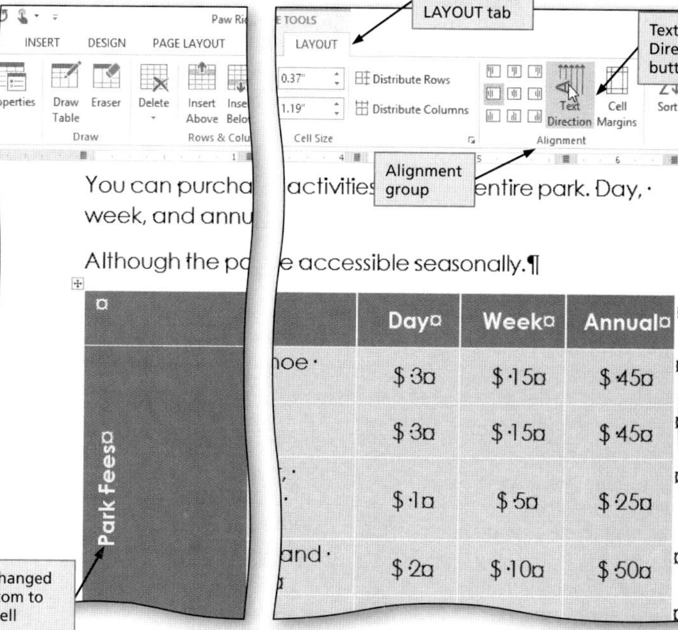

Figure 4–69

To Change Column Width

The cell containing the vertical text is too wide. Thus, the next step is to change the width of that column. The following step changes column width using the ruler.

1 If you are using a mouse, drag the column's boundary inward, as shown in Figure 4–70, to resize the column.

Q&A What if I am using a touch screen?
Position the insertion point in the column to adjust. Tap the 'Table Column Width' box (TABLE TOOLS LAYOUT tab | Cell Size group), type `.34` as the column width, and then press the ENTER key.

column resized

pointer on column boundary

Although the park is open all year, some areas are accessible seasonally.¶

¤	¤	Access¤	Day¤	Week¤
Park Fees¤	Docks¤	Boat and canoe docks¤	$3¤	$15¤
	Hiking¤	All trails¤	$3¤	$15¤
	Self-guided tours¤	Nature center, pavilions, and historic sites¤	$1¤	$5¤
	Swimming¤	Public beach and outdoor pool¤	$2¤	$10¤

Figure 4–70

To Center a Table

The next step in formatting this table is to center it horizontally between the page margins. The following steps center a table.

1 Select the table.

2 Display the HOME tab. Tap or click the Center button (HOME tab | Paragraph group) to center the selected table between the left and right margins.

3 Tap or click anywhere to remove the selection from the table.

BTW
Certification
The Microsoft Office Specialist (MOS) program provides an opportunity for you to obtain a valuable industry credential — proof that you have the Word 2013 skills required by employers. For more information, visit the Certification resource on the Student Companion Site located on www.cengagebrain.com. For detailed instructions about accessing available resources, visit www.cengage.com/ct/studentdownload or contact your instructor for information about accessing the required files.

To Remove Cell Shading

In this table, only the first row and first column should have shading. Thus, the following steps remove shading from table cells.

1 Select the cells that should not contain shading (in this case, all of the cells below the first row and to the right of the first column).

2 Display the TABLE TOOLS DESIGN tab. Tap or click the Shading arrow (TABLE TOOLS DESIGN tab | Table Styles group) to display the Shading gallery (Figure 4–71).

3 Tap or click No Color in the Shading gallery to remove the shading from the selected cells (shown in Figure 4–72).

4 Tap or click anywhere in the table to remove the selection.

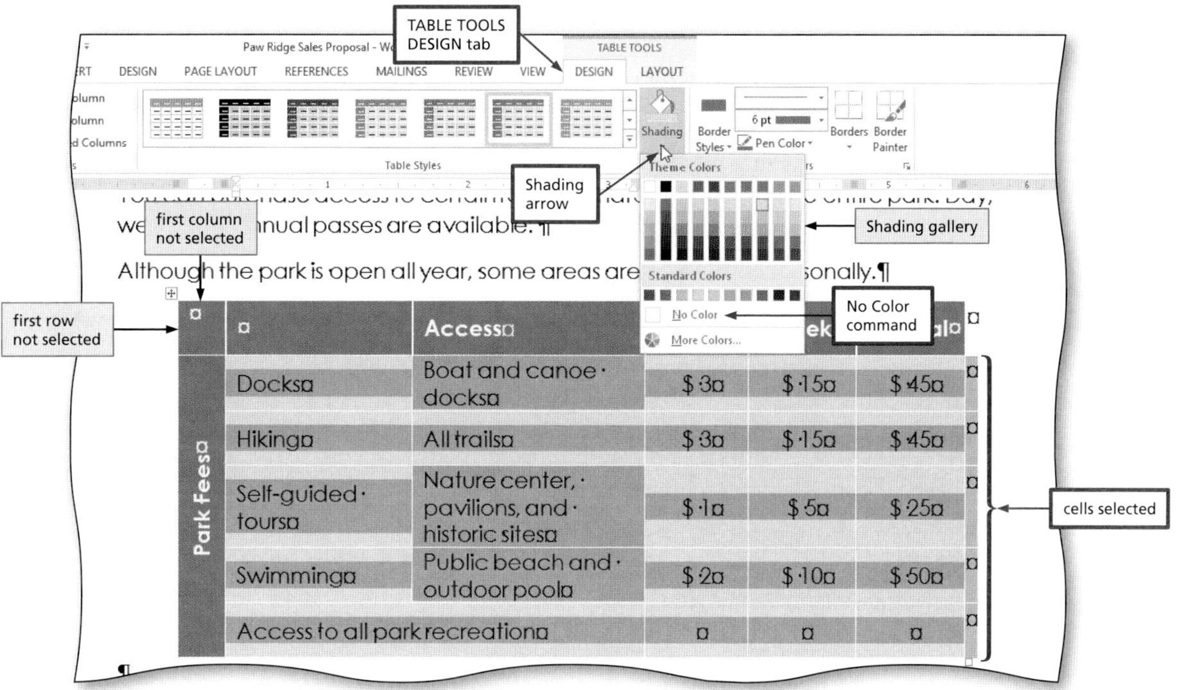

Figure 4–71

To Border a Table

The table in this project has a 1-point, olive green border around all cells. The following steps add a border to a table using the Borders and Shading dialog box. ***Why?*** *Earlier in this chapter when you created the title page, the border line weight was changed to 6 point. Because the table border should be ½ point, you will use the Borders and Shading dialog box to change the line weight before adding the border to the table.*

1

- Position the insertion point somewhere in the table.
- Tap or click the Borders arrow (TABLE TOOLS DESIGN tab | Table Styles group) to display the Borders gallery.
- Tap or click Borders and Shading in the Borders gallery to display the Borders and Shading dialog box.
- Tap or click All in the Setting area (Borders and Shading dialog box), which will place a border on every cell in the table.
- Tap or click the Color arrow and then tap or click 'Olive Green, Accent 4' (eighth color, first row) in the Color palette to specify the border color (Figure 4–72).

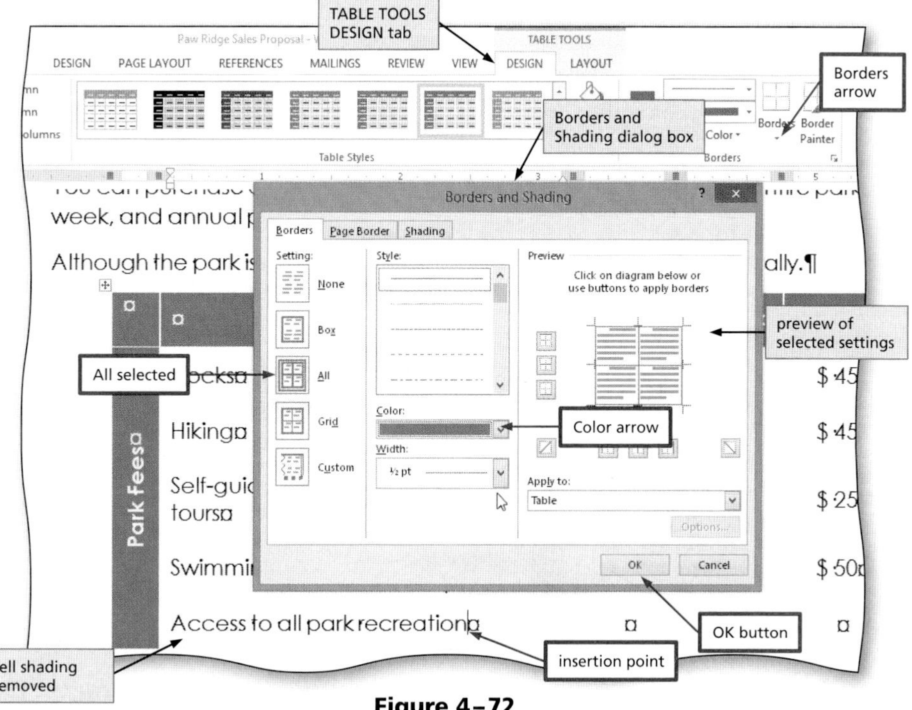

Figure 4–72

2

- Tap or click the OK button to place the border shown in the preview area of the dialog box around the table cells in the document (shown in Figure 4–73 on the next page).

To Sum Columns in a Table

1 CREATE TITLE PAGE | 2 INSERT EXISTING DOCUMENT | 3 CREATE HEADER & FOOTER
4 EDIT & FORMAT LISTS | 5 EDIT & FORMAT TABLES | 6 CREATE WATERMARK

Word can calculate the totals of rows and columns. You also can specify the format for how the totals will be displayed. The following steps sum the columns in a table. ***Why?*** *In this project, the last row should display the sum (total) of the values in the last two columns: Day, Week, and Annual.*

1

- Position the insertion point in the cell to contain the sum (last row, Day column).

2

- Type $ (a dollar sign) and then press the SPACEBAR.
- Display the TABLE TOOLS LAYOUT tab.
- Tap or click the Formula button (TABLE TOOLS LAYOUT tab | Data group) to display the Formula dialog box (Figure 4–73).

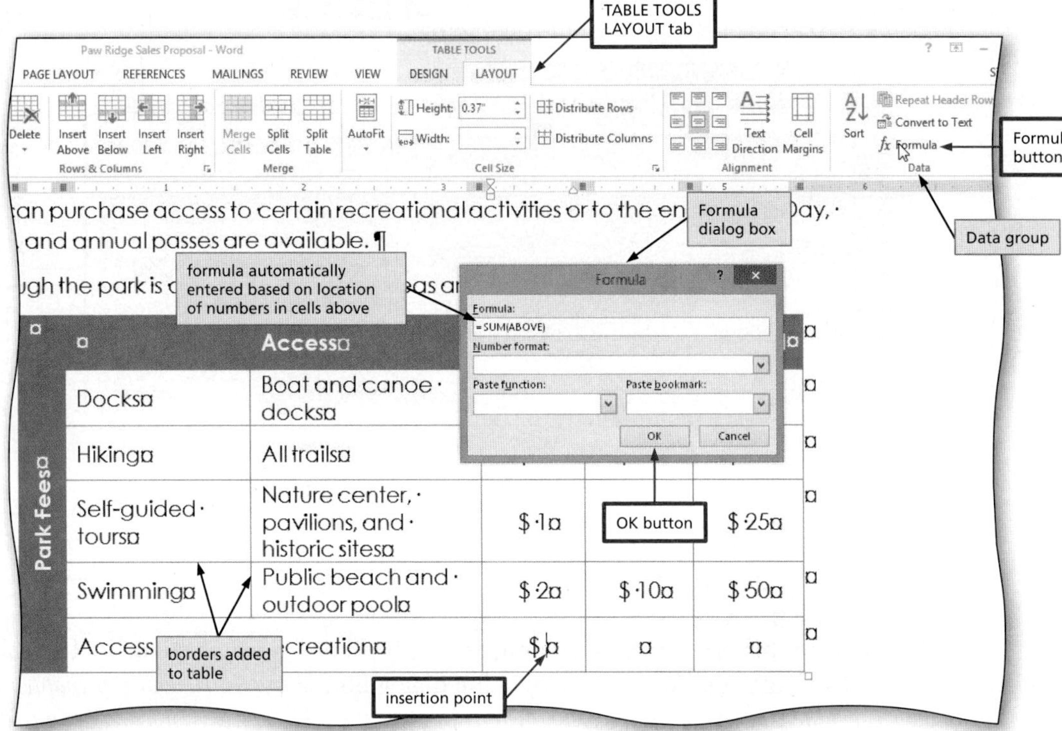

Figure 4–73

Q&A What is the formula that shows in the Formula box, and can I change it?
Word places a default formula in the Formula box, depending on the location of the numbers in surrounding cells. In this case, because numbers are above the current cell, Word displays a formula that will add the numbers above the current cell. You can change the formula that Word proposes, or type a different formula. For example, instead of summing numbers you can multiply them.

3

- Tap or click the Number format arrow (Formula dialog box) and then tap or click the desired format for the result of the computation, in this case, the format with the numeral 0 (Figure 4–74).

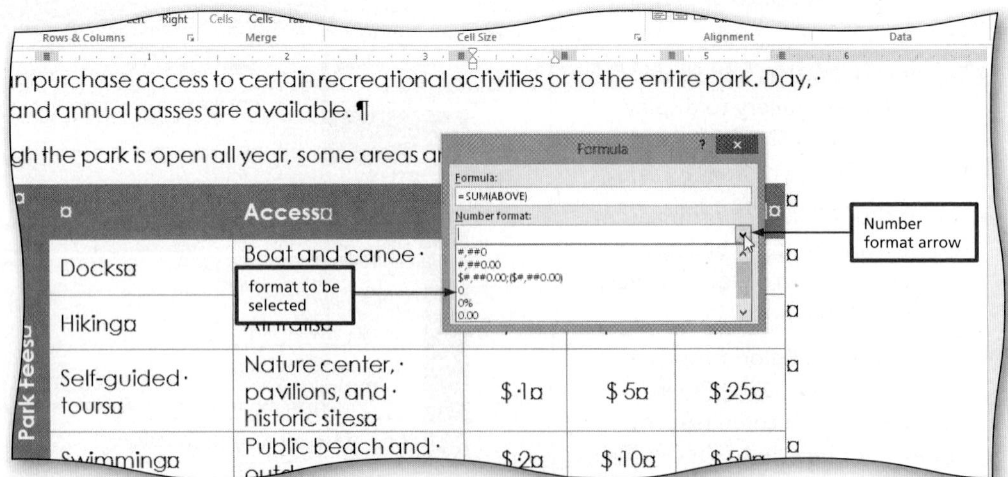

Figure 4–74

Q&A Why select the format with the numeral 0?
You want the result to be displayed as a whole number so you select the numeral 0. If you wanted the result to display with cents, you would select the format #,##0.00 (the # symbol means to display a blank if the number has a value of zero).

4

- Tap or click the OK button (Formula dialog box) to place the sum of the numbers using the specified format in the current cell.

5

- Press the TAB key to move the insertion point to the next cell to sum.
- Repeat Steps 2, 3, and 4 for the next two cells (Figure 4–75).

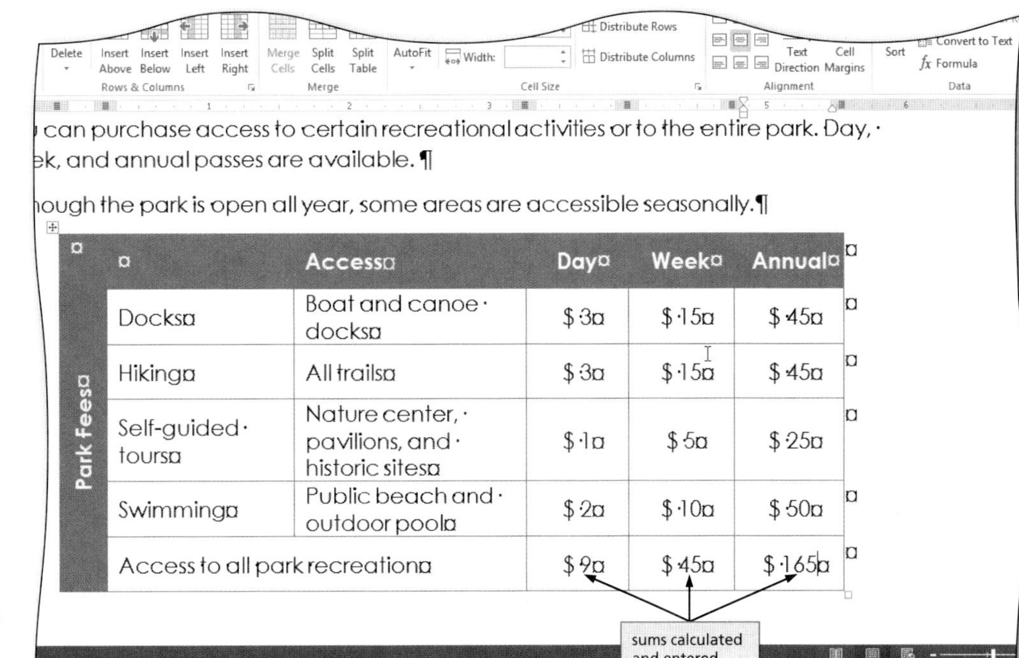

Figure 4–75

Q&A Can I sum a row instead of a column?

Yes. You would position the insertion point in an empty cell at the right edge of the row before tapping or clicking the Formula button.

If I make a change to a number in a table, does Word automatically recalculate the sum?

No. You will need to update the field by pressing and holding or right-clicking it and then tapping or clicking Update Field on the shortcut menu, or selecting the field and then pressing the F9 key.

To Delete a Blank Paragraph

If you notice an extra paragraph mark below the park fees table that it is causing an extra blank page in the document, you should delete the blank paragraph. If necessary, the following steps delete a blank paragraph.

1. Press CTRL+END to position the insertion point at the end of the document.
2. If necessary, press the BACKSPACE key to remove the extra blank paragraph and delete the blank page.
3. If text spills onto a fourth page, remove space above paragraphs in the sales proposal until the entire proposal fits on three pages, as shown in Figure 4–1 on page WD 203.

BTW

Distributing a Document

Instead of printing and distributing a hard copy of a document, you can distribute the document electronically. Options include sending the document via email; posting it on cloud storage (such as SkyDrive) and sharing the file with others; posting it on a social networking site, blog, or other website; and sharing a link associated with an online location of the document. You also can create and share a PDF or XPS image of the document, so that users can view the file in Acrobat Reader or XPS Viewer instead of in Word.

Creating a Watermark

The final task in this chapter is to create a watermark for the pages of the sales proposal. A **watermark** is text or a graphic that is displayed on top of or behind the text in a document. For example, a catalog may print the words, Sold Out, on top of sold-out items. The first draft of a five-year-plan may have the word, Draft, printed behind the text of the document. Some companies use their logos or other graphics as watermarks to add visual appeal to their documents.

To Zoom Multiple Pages

The following steps display multiple pages in their entirety in the document window as large as possible, so that you can see the position of the watermark as you create it.

1. Press CTRL+HOME to position the insertion point at the beginning of the document.
2. Display the VIEW tab. Tap or click the Multiple Pages button (VIEW tab | Zoom group) to display all three pages in the document window as large as possible.

To Create a Watermark

1 CREATE TITLE PAGE | 2 INSERT EXISTING DOCUMENT | 3 CREATE HEADER & FOOTER
4 EDIT & FORMAT LISTS | 5 EDIT & FORMAT TABLES | **6 CREATE WATERMARK**

In this project, the image of paw tracks is displayed behind all content in the proposal as a watermark. ***Why?*** *The graphic adds visual appeal to the document, enticing readers to look at its contents.* The following steps create a watermark.

1

- Display the DESIGN tab.
- Tap or click the Watermark button (DESIGN tab | Page Background group) to display the Watermark gallery (Figure 4–76).

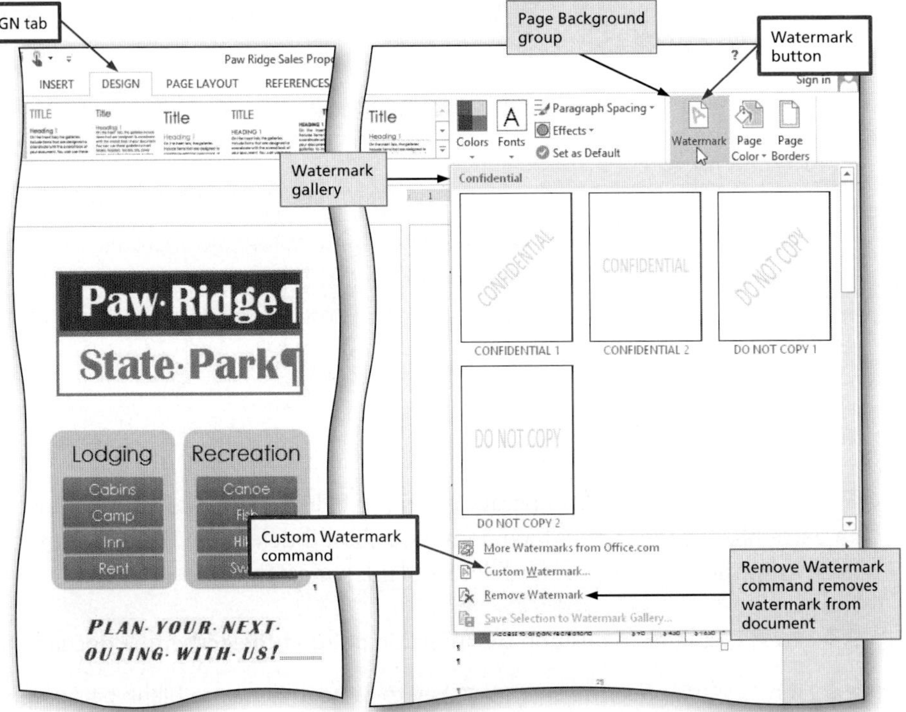

Figure 4–76

- Tap or click Custom Watermark in the Watermark gallery to display the Printed Watermark dialog box.
- Tap or click Picture watermark (Printed Watermark dialog box) so that you can select a clip art image for the watermark.
- Tap or click the Select Picture button to display the Insert Pictures dialog box.
- Type `paw prints` in the Search box and then tap or click the Search button. Tap or click the paw prints image shown in Figure 4–1 on page WD 203 (or a similar image) and then tap or click the Insert button to download the image and close the dialog box.

- Tap or click the Apply button to show a preview of the watermark on the pages in the document window (Figure 4–77).

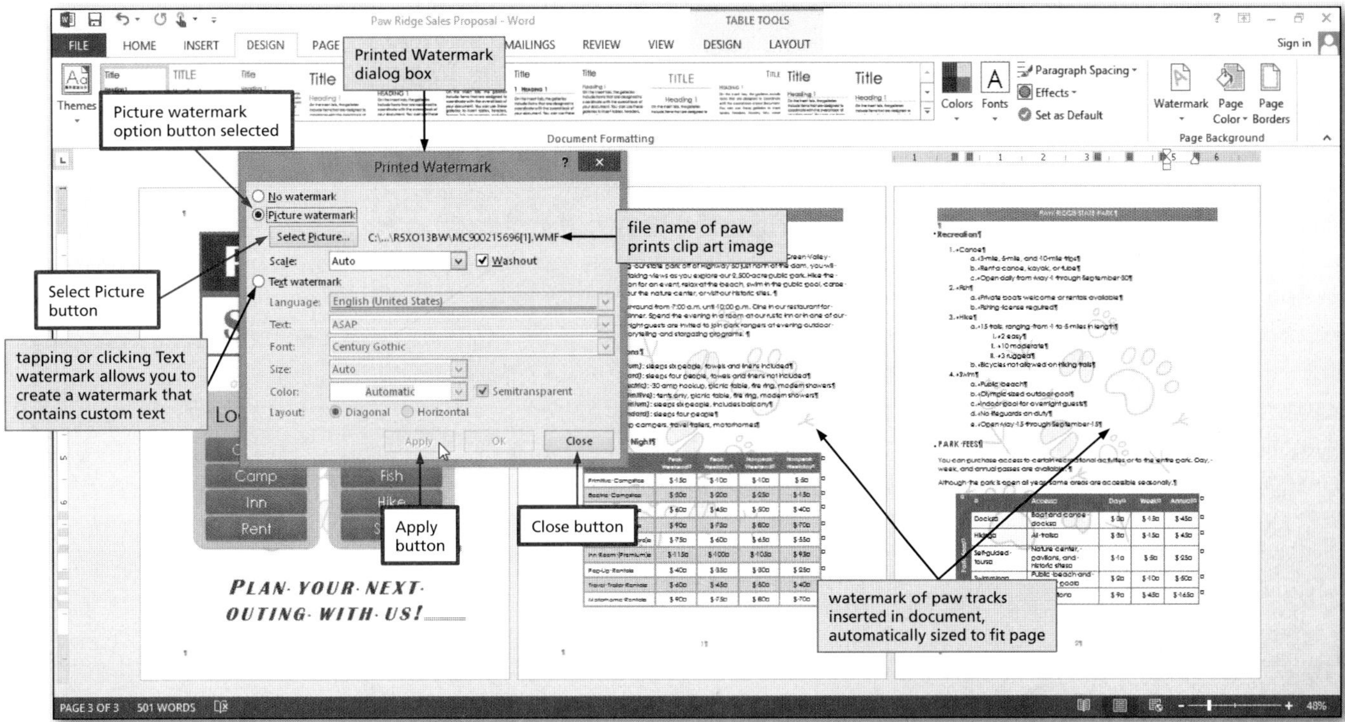

Figure 4–77

- Tap or click the Close button (Printed Watermark dialog box) to close the dialog box.

Q&A

How do I remove a watermark from a document?

Tap or click the Watermark button (DESIGN tab | Page Background group) and then tap or click Remove Watermark in the Watermark gallery.

How do I create a text watermark?

Tap or click Text watermark in the Printed Watermark dialog box, select or type the text for the watermark, select format options, and then tap or click the OK button.

Other Ways

1. Tap or click 'Explore Quick Parts' button (INSERT tab | Text group), tap or click 'Building Blocks Organizer' on Explore Quick Parts menu, select desired watermark (Building Blocks Organizer dialog box), tap or click Insert button

To Change Theme Fonts

1 CREATE TITLE PAGE | 2 INSERT EXISTING DOCUMENT | 3 CREATE HEADER & FOOTER
4 EDIT & FORMAT LISTS | 5 EDIT & FORMAT TABLES | **6 CREATE WATERMARK**

The final step in formatting this project is to change the fonts used for text in the document. ***Why?*** *With the watermark, some of the text is difficult to read. You would prefer a bolder font.* If text is entered using the headings and body text fonts, you easily can change the font in the entire document by changing the theme fonts, or font set. A **font set** defines one font for headings and another for body text. The default font set is Office, which uses the Cambria font for headings and the Calibri font for body text. In Word, you can select from more than 20 predefined, coordinated font sets to give the document's text a new look.

If you previously changed a font using buttons on the ribbon or mini toolbar, Word will not alter those when you change the font set because changes to the font set are not applied to individually changed fonts. This means the font of the title on the title page will remain as Britannic Bold if you change the font set. The following steps change the theme fonts to TrebuchetMs for headings and for body text.

1

- Display the DESIGN tab.
- Tap or click the Theme Fonts button (DESIGN tab | Document Formatting group) to display the Theme Fonts gallery (Figure 4–78).

Experiment

- If you are using a mouse, point to various font sets in the Theme Fonts gallery and watch the fonts of text in the document change.

2

- Scroll through the Theme Fonts gallery and then tap or click TrebuchetMs in the Fonts gallery to set the document theme fonts to the selected font.

Q&A What if I want to return to the default font set?
You would tap or click the Theme Fonts button and then tap or click Office in the Fonts gallery.

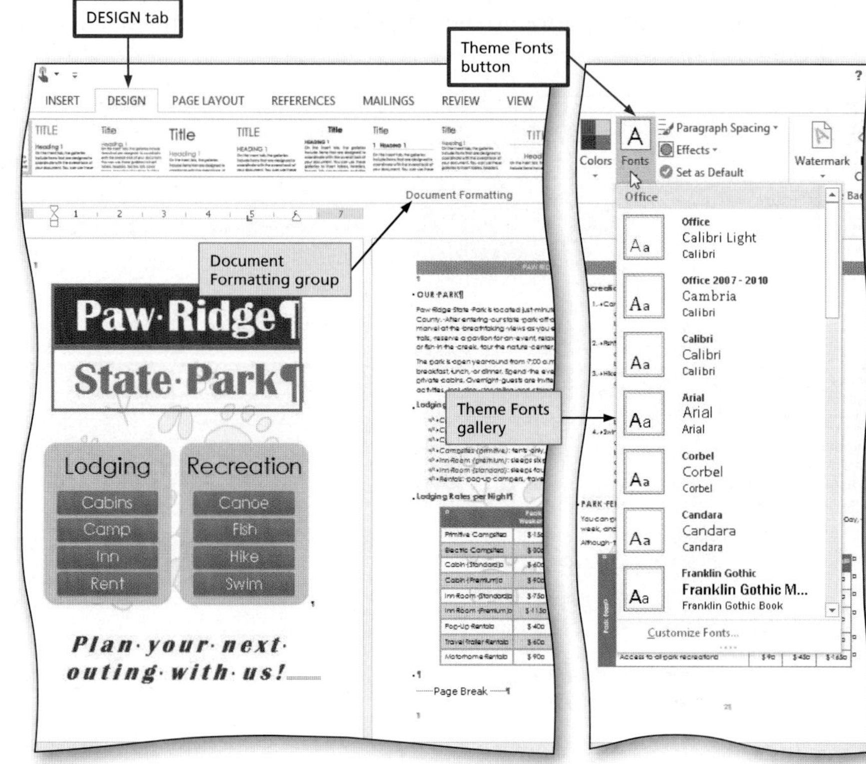

Figure 4–78

- If necessary, insert a page break before the Recreation heading (see instructions on page WD 247).

BTW
Conserving Ink and Toner
If you want to conserve ink or toner, you can instruct Word to print draft quality documents by tapping or clicking FILE on the ribbon to open the Backstage view, tapping or clicking Options in the Backstage view to display the Word Options dialog box, tapping or clicking Advanced in the left pane (Word Options dialog box), sliding or scrolling to the Print area in the right pane, placing a check mark in the 'Use draft quality' check box, and then tapping or clicking the OK button. Then, use the Backstage view to print the document as usual.

To Check Spelling, Save, Print, and Exit Word

The following steps check the spelling of the document, save and print the document, and then exit Word.

1. Display the REVIEW tab. Tap or click the 'Spelling & Grammar' button (REVIEW tab | Proofing group) to begin the spelling and grammar check. Correct any misspelled words.
2. Save the sales proposal again with the same file name.
3. Print the sales proposal (shown in Figure 4–1 on page WD 203).
4. Exit Word.

Chapter Summary

In this chapter, you learned how to add a border to a paragraph, change paragraph indentation, insert and format a SmartArt graphic, apply character effects, insert a section break, insert a Word document in an open document, change theme fonts, insert formatted headers and footers, sort lists and tables, modify and format existing Word tables, sum columns in a table, and insert a watermark. The items listed below include all the new Word skills you have learned in this chapter, with the tasks grouped by activity.

Enter and Edit Text

Insert a Word Document in an Open Document (WD 223)

Format a Page

Insert a Next Page Section Break (WD 222)
Delete a Section Break (WD 223)
Delete a Page Break (WD 226)
Insert a Formatted Header Different from the Previous Header (WD 230)
Insert a Formatted Footer (WD 230)
Format Page Numbers to Start at a Different Number (WD 230)
Create a Watermark (WD 258)
Change Theme Fonts (WD 259)

Format Text

Border a Paragraph (WD 206)
Change Left and Right Paragraph Indent (WD 209)
Modify Character Spacing and Format Characters Using the Font Dialog Box (WD 218)
Sort Paragraphs (WD 232)
Use the Format Painter Button (WD 233)
Customize Bullets in a List (WD 234)
Create a Multilevel Numbered List (WD 236)

Word Settings

Print Specific Pages in a Document (WD 225)

Work with Graphics

Insert a SmartArt Graphic (WD 212)
Delete Shapes from a SmartArt Graphic (WD 214)
Add Text to Shapes in a SmartArt Graphic (WD 214)
Add Shapes to a SmartArt Graphic (WD 215)
Change Colors of a SmartArt Graphic (WD 216)
Apply a SmartArt Style (WD 217)

Work with Tables

Show Gridlines (WD 239)
Change Column Width (WD 240)
Change Row Height (WD 241)
Shade a Table Cell (WD 243)
Select Nonadjacent Items (WD 244)
Change Cell Spacing (WD 245)
Delete a Column (WD 247)
Delete a Row (WD 248)
Sort a Table (WD 248)
Split Cells (WD 249)
Move a Cell Boundary (WD 250)
Distribute Columns (WD 251)
Distribute Rows (WD 252)
Display Text in a Cell Vertically (WD 253)
Border a Table (WD 255)
Sum Columns in a Table (WD 256)

CONSIDER THIS: PLAN AHEAD

What decisions will you need to make when creating your next proposal?

Use these guidelines as you complete the assignments in this chapter and create your own proposals outside of this class.

1. Identify the nature of the proposal.
   a) If someone else requests that you develop the proposal, it is solicited. Be sure to include all requested information in a **solicited proposal**.
   b) When you write a proposal because you recognize a need, the proposal is unsolicited. With an **unsolicited proposal**, you must gather information you believe will be relevant and of interest to the intended audience.
2. Design an eye-catching title page.
   a) The title page should convey the overall message of the sales proposal.
   b) Use text, graphics, formats, and colors that reflect the goals of the sales proposal.
   c) Be sure to include a title.
3. Compose the text of the sales proposal.
   a) Sales proposals vary in length, style, and formality, but all should be designed to elicit acceptance from the reader.
   b) The sales proposal should have a neat, organized appearance.
   c) A successful sales proposal uses succinct wording and includes lists for textual messages.
   d) Write text using active voice, instead of passive voice.
   e) Assume that readers of unsolicited sales proposals have no previous knowledge about the topic.
   f) Be sure the goal of the proposal is clear.
   g) Establish a theme and carry it throughout the proposal.

(Continued)

CONSIDER THIS: PLAN AHEAD *continued*

4. Enhance the sales proposal with appropriate visuals.
   a) Use visuals to add interest, clarify ideas, and illustrate points.
   b) Visuals include tables, charts, and graphical images (i.e., photos, clip art, etc.).
5. Proofread and edit the proposal.
   a) Carefully review the sales proposal to be sure it contains no spelling, grammar, mathematical, or other errors.
   b) Check that transitions between sentences and paragraphs are smooth. Ensure that the purpose of the proposal is stated clearly.
   c) Ask others to review the proposal and give you suggestions for improvements.

CONSIDER THIS

How should you submit solutions to questions in the assignments identified with a symbol?
Every assignment in this book contains one or more questions identified with a symbol. These questions require you to think beyond the assigned document. Present your solutions to the questions in the format required by your instructor. Possible formats may include one or more of these options: write the answer; create a document that contains the answer; present your answer to the class; discuss your answer in a group; record the answer as audio or video using a webcam, smartphone, or portable media player; or post answers on a blog, wiki, or website.

Apply Your Knowledge

Reinforce the skills and apply the concepts you learned in this chapter.

Working with a Table

Note: To complete this assignment, you will be required to use the Data Files for Students. Visit www.cengage.com/ct/studentdownload for detailed instructions or contact your instructor for information about accessing the required files.

Instructions: Run Word. Open the document called Apply 4-1 Home Expenses Draft located the Data Files for Students. The document contains a Word table that you are to modify. The modified table is shown in Figure 4–79.

Home Expenses					
Year-to-Date					
	January	February	March	April	Total
Electric	55.38	52.22	40.28	33.18	$ 181.06
Gas	15.20	13.89	19.56	14.74	$ 63.39
Insurance	55.00	55.00	55.00	55.00	$ 220.00
Rent	525.00	525.00	525.00	525.00	$2,100.00
Water	48.74	48.74	43.25	43.25	$ 183.98
Total	$ 699.32	$ 694.85	$ 683.09	$ 671.17	$2,748.43

Figure 4–79

Perform the following tasks:

1. Show gridlines.
2. Delete the blank column between the March and April columns.
3. Use the Distribute Rows command to evenly space all the rows in the table.
4. Use the Distribute Columns command to make the January, February, March, April, and Total columns evenly spaced.

5. Change the width of the January, February, March, April, and Total columns to 1".
6. Use the Formula button (TABLE TOOLS LAYOUT tab | Data group) to place totals in the bottom row for the January, February, March, and April columns. The totals should be formatted to display dollar signs and cents.
7. Use the Formula button (TABLE TOOLS LAYOUT tab | Data group) to place totals in the right column using a dollars and cents format. Start in the bottom-right cell and work your way up the column.
8. Add a row to the top of the table. Merge all cells in the first row into a single cell. Enter the title, Home Expenses, as the table title. Align top center the title.
9. Split the cell in the first row into two rows (one column). In the new cell below the title, enter the text, Year-to-Date, as the subtitle.
10. Shade the first row Blue, Accent 1, Darker 50%. Change the font color of text in the first row to White, Background 1. Shade the second row Blue, Accent 1, Lighter 80%.
11. Add a 1 pt, White, Background 1, Darker 50% border to all cells in the table.
12. Hide gridlines.
13. Change the height of the row containing the month headings (row 3) to 0.1". Change the alignment of these headings to Align Top Center.
14. Change the height of all expense rows and the total row (rows 4 through 9) to 0.3".
15. Change the alignment of the cells in the first column to Align Center Left.
16. Change the alignment of the cells containing dollar amounts to Align Center Right.
17. Center the entire table across the width of the page.
18. Sort the rows containing the expenses.
19. If requested by your instructor, add your last name to the first row of the table before the words, Home Expenses.
20. Save the modified file with the file name, Apply 4-1 Home Expenses Modified, and submit it (shown in Figure 4–79) in the format specified by your instructor.
21. Which number format did you use in the Formula dialog box in #6 above? Why do some totals have a space after the dollar sign and others do not? Which Formula appeared in #7?

Extend Your Knowledge

Extend the skills you learned in this chapter and experiment with new skills. You may need to use Help to complete the assignment.

Modifying Multilevel List Formats, Drawing Tables, and Creating Text Watermarks

Note: To complete this assignment, you will be required to use the Data Files for Students. Visit www.cengage.com/ct/studentdownload for detailed instructions or contact your instructor for information about accessing the required files.

Instructions: Run Word. Open the document, Extend 4-1 Dog Training Classes Draft, from the Data Files for Students. You will define a new number format for the multilevel list, insert a text watermark, and use Word's Draw Table feature to draw a table.

Perform the following tasks:

1. Use Help to learn about defining multilevel list number formats, text watermarks, and Draw Table.
2. For each level in the multilevel list, define a new number format that is different from the format in the draft file. Be sure to change (at a minimum) the number style, font, font size, and font color of the number format.

Continued >

Extend Your Knowledge *continued*

3. Insert a text watermark using the text, TRAINING!, in a font, size, color, and layout that you feel works best on the page.
4. Below the multilevel list, draw the table shown in Figure 4–80. That is, use the Draw Table button to create the blank table.

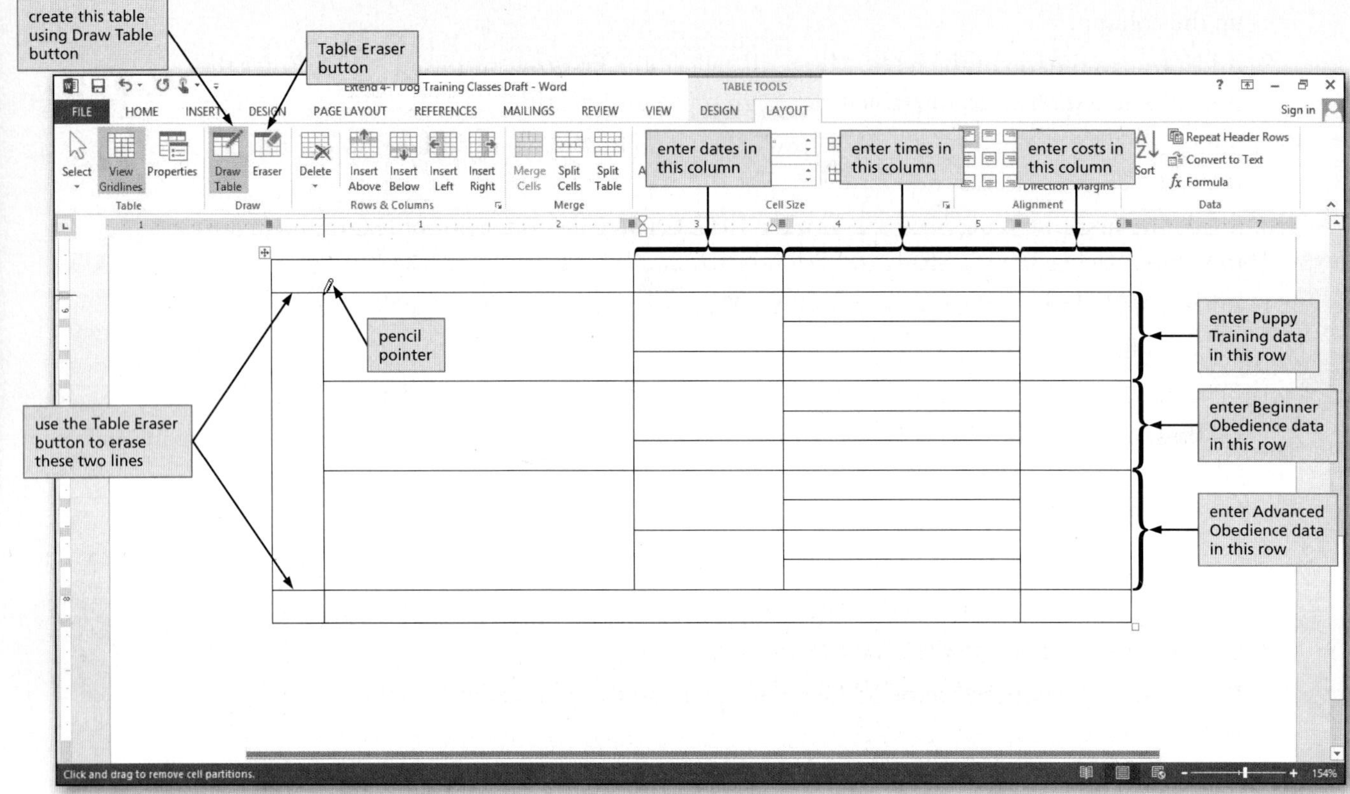

Figure 4–80

5. In the leftmost column of the table, enter the text, Dog Training, so that it displays vertically in the cell.
6. In the second column of the table, enter these labels in the second, third, and fourth rows: Puppy Training, Beginner Obedience, and Advanced Obedience.
7. In the top row, enter these headings in the last three columns: Start Date, Times, and Cost.
8. For Puppy Training, use this data for the table: January 17 class times are 9:00 – 10:00 a.m. and 7:00 – 8:00 p.m.; January 31 class times are 1:00 – 2:00 p.m.; cost is $120.
9. For Beginner Obedience, use this data for the table: January 10 class times are 9:00 – 10:00 a.m. and 7:30 – 8:30 p.m.; January 24 class times are 1:30 – 2:30 p.m.; cost is $140.
10. For Advanced Obedience, use this data for the table: January 3 class times are 9:00 – 10:00 a.m. and 7:00 – 8:00 p.m.; January 10 class times are 2:00 – 3:00 p.m. and 5:00 – 6:00 p.m.; cost is $125.
11. Enter the text, Special Offer: Sign up in advance for all three classes, in the bottom row. The cost for the bottom, right cell is $350.
12. Enhance the table as you deem appropriate.
13. If requested by your instructor, change the phone number in the footer to your phone number.
14. Save the revised document using the file name, Extend 4-1 Dog Training Classes Modified, and then submit it in the format specified by your instructor.
15. For the text watermark, which font, font size, color, and layout did you choose and why?

Analyze, Correct, Improve

Analyze a document, correct all errors, and improve it.

Formatting a Title Page

Note: To complete this assignment, you will be required to use the Data Files for Students. Visit www.cengage.com/ct/studentdownload for detailed instructions or contact your instructor for information about accessing the required files.

Instructions: Run Word. Open the document, Analyze 4-1 Fitness Center Title Page Draft, from the Data Files for Students. The document is a title page that is missing elements and that is not formatted ideally (Figure 4–81). You are to remove the header and footer, edit the border, change paragraph indents, modify the SmartArt graphic, change the character spacing, and adjust the font sizes.

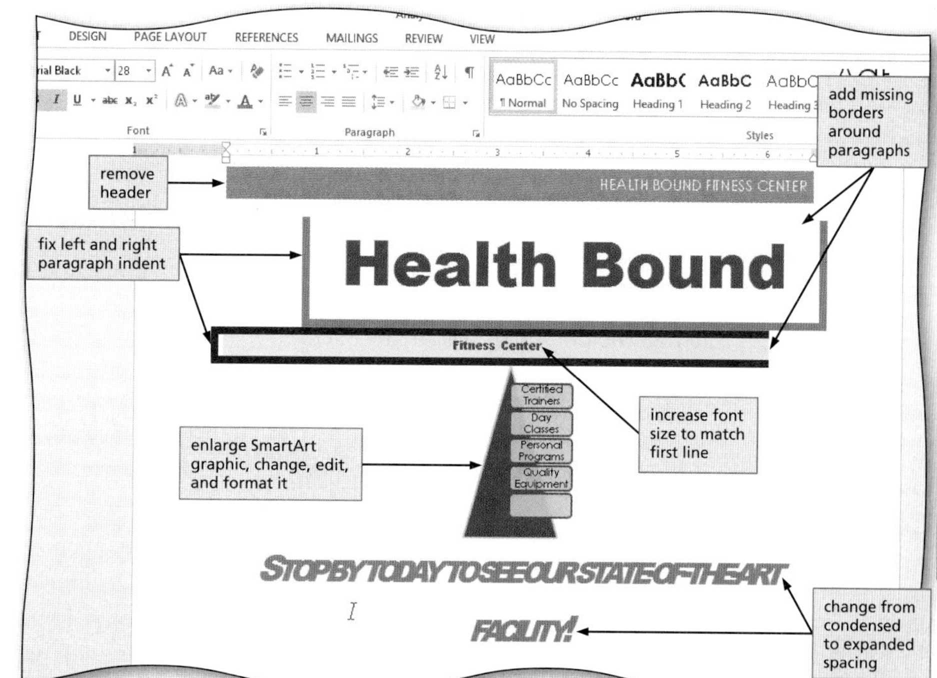

Figure 4–81

1. Correct On the title page, correct the following items:

a. Remove the header and footer from the title page.

b. Modify the borders on the first and second lines so that they surround all edges of each paragraph.

c. Change the left and right paragraph indent of the first two lines (paragraphs) so that they have a 0.5" left and right indent.

d. Increase the font size of the text in the second line to match the font size of the text in the first line.

e. Increase the size of the SmartArt graphic on the title page. Delete the shape that has no text in it. Change the word, Day, to Daily in the second shape.

f. Change the character spacing of the last two lines on the title page from condensed to expanded.

2. Improve Enhance the title page by changing the layout of the SmartArt graphic to one you feel is appropriate for the content. Then, change the colors and style of the SmartArt graphic to those that complement the rest of the content on the title page. Resize it appropriately. Increase the font size of the text in the shapes so that the text is easy to read. Add or remove space above or below paragraphs so that all contents of the title page fit on a single page and the contents are evenly spaced. If requested by your instructor, add a shape to the SmartArt graphic that contains your name. Save the modified document with the file name, Analyze 4-1 Fitness Center Title Page Modified, and then submit it in the format specified by your instructor.

3. In this assignment, you changed the layout of the SmartArt graphic. What layout did you select and why?

STUDENT ASSIGNMENTS

In the Labs

Design and/or create a document using the guidelines, concepts, and skills presented in this chapter. Labs 1 and 2, which increase in difficulty, require you to create solutions based on what you learned in the chapter; Lab 3 requires you to create a solution, which uses cloud and web technologies, by learning and investigating on your own from general guidance.

Lab 1: Creating a Proposal with a SmartArt Graphic, a Bulleted List, and a Table

Problem: The owner of Donna's Deli has hired you to prepare a sales proposal her menu and prices (Figure 4–82).

Perform the following tasks:

1. Change the document theme to Facet.
2. Change the theme fonts to the Century Gothic font set.
3. Create the title page as shown in Figure 4–82a. Be sure to do the following:

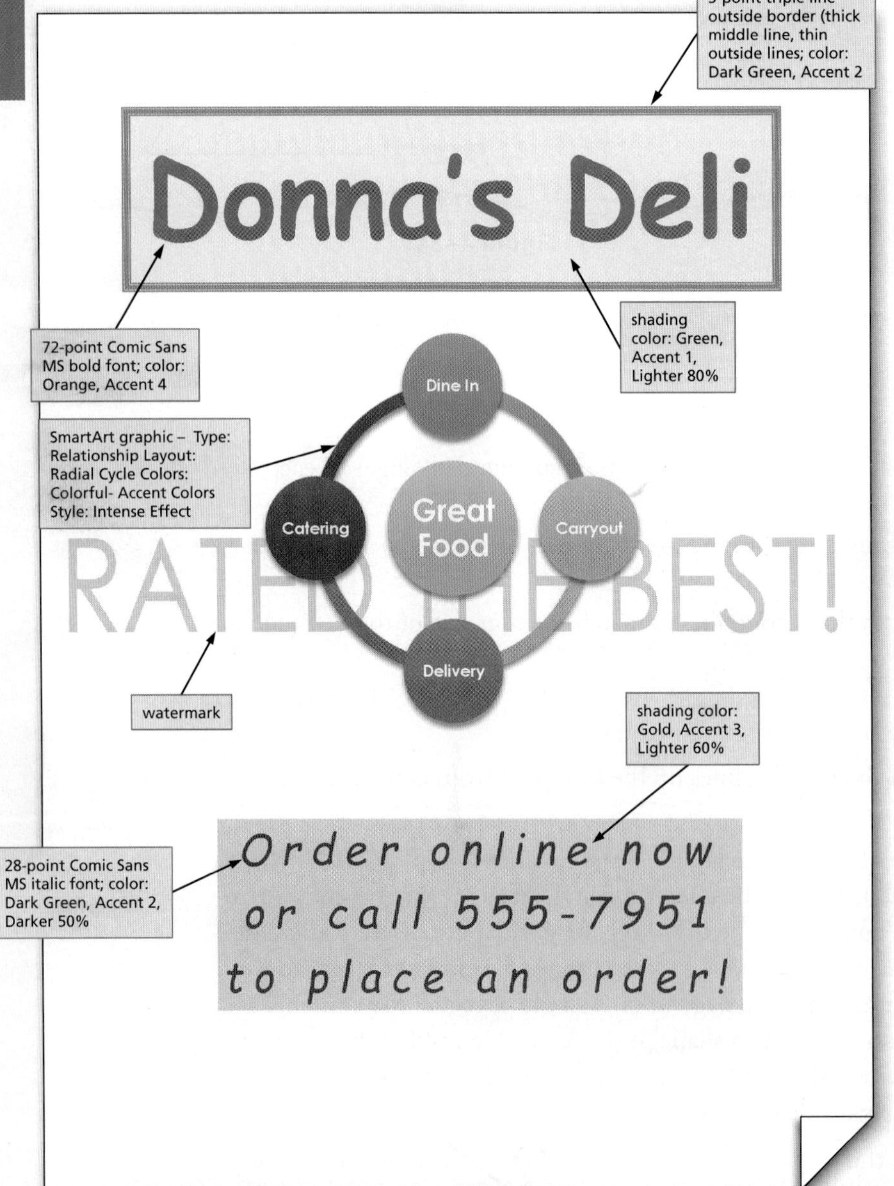

Figure 4–82 (a)

   a. Insert the SmartArt graphic, add text to it, bold the text, and make all the shapes one size larger. (*Hint*: Use the Larger button (SMARTART TOOLS FORMAT tab | Shapes group).) Change the colors and style of the SmartArt graphic as shown. Change the spacing above the SmartArt graphic to 24 points and the spacing after the graphic to 54 points.
   b. Change the fonts, font sizes, and font colors as specified in the figure. Add the paragraph border. Indent the left and right edges of the title paragraph by 0.25 inches and the left and right edges of the paragraph below the SmartArt graphic by 1 inch. Expand the characters in the sentence at the bottom of the page by 7 points.

4. At the bottom of the title page, insert a next page section break. Clear formatting.

5. Create the second page of the proposal as shown in Figure 4–82b.
   a. Insert the formatted header using the Retrospect design. The header should appear only on the second page (section) of the proposal. Enter the header text as shown.
   b. Enter the multilevel list as shown.
   c. Format the Heading 1 style as shown and update the Heading 1 style accordingly.
   d. Create the table as shown. Border the table as specified. Distribute rows so that they are all the same height. Change the row height to 0.21 inches. Center the table between the margins. Align top left the text in the first column, and align top center all other text in the table. Shade the table cells as specified. Change cell spacing to 0.04 inches between cells.
   e. Insert the formatted footer using the Retrospect design. The footer should appear only on the second page (section) of the proposal. Enter the footer text as shown. If requested by your instructor, change the phone number in the footer to your phone number.
6. Add a text watermark, RATED THE BEST!, using a 72-point Century Gothic font.
7. Adjust the spacing above and below paragraphs as necessary to fit all content as shown in the figure.
8. Check the spelling. Save the document with Lab 4-1 Deli Proposal as the file name.
9. This proposal contains a text watermark, which is semitransparent by default. For what type of text would you want to remove the check mark from the semitransparent check box?

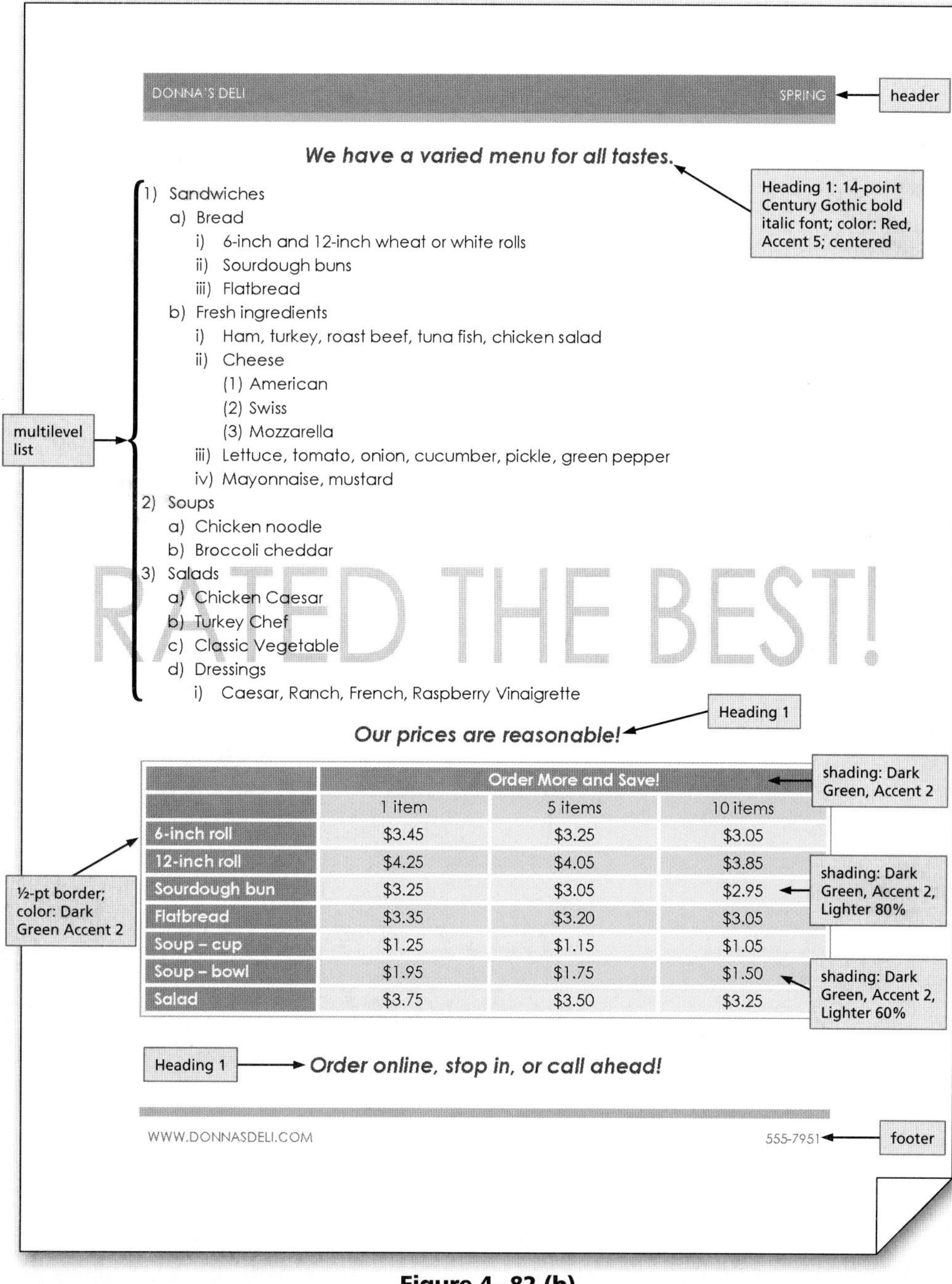

	Order More and Save!		
	1 item	5 items	10 items
6-inch roll	$3.45	$3.25	$3.05
12-inch roll	$4.25	$4.05	$3.85
Sourdough bun	$3.25	$3.05	$2.95
Flatbread	$3.35	$3.20	$3.05
Soup – cup	$1.25	$1.15	$1.05
Soup – bowl	$1.95	$1.75	$1.50
Salad	$3.75	$3.50	$3.25

Figure 4–82 (b)

Continued >

Lab 2: Creating a Proposal with a SmartArt Graphic, a Complex Table, Picture Bullets, and a Numbered List

Problem: The owner of the Cedar Trail Music Academy has hired you to prepare a sales proposal that describes the academy's focus, class times, and costs (Figure 4–83).

Instructions: Perform the following tasks:

1. Change the document theme to the Slice theme.
2. Change the theme fonts to the Consolas-Verdana font set.
3. Create the title page as shown in Figure 4–83a. Be sure to do the following:
   a. Insert the Picture Caption List SmartArt graphic and add shapes as necessary; insert the pictures using this search text: piano notes, guitar notes, drum notes, trumpet notes, and song notes; and add text below each picture. (*Hint*: If you have difficulty adding text below the pictures, display the Text Pane and type the text in the Text Pane.) Resize the SmartArt graphic as necessary.

Figure 4–83 (a)

b. Change the fonts, font sizes, font colors, and shading as indicated in the figure. Indent the left and right edges of the title paragraph by 0.5 inches. Expand the characters in the sentence at the bottom of the page by 7 points.

4. At the bottom of the title page, insert a next page section break. Clear formatting.

5. Create the second page of the proposal as shown in Figure 4–83b.

a. Insert the formatted header using the Viewmaster design. The header should appear only on the second page of the proposal. Enter the header text as shown.

b. Format the headings using the heading styles specified. Adjust spacing before the Heading 1 style to 18 point and after to 6 point, and before the Heading 2 style to 12 point and after to 6 point. Update both heading styles.

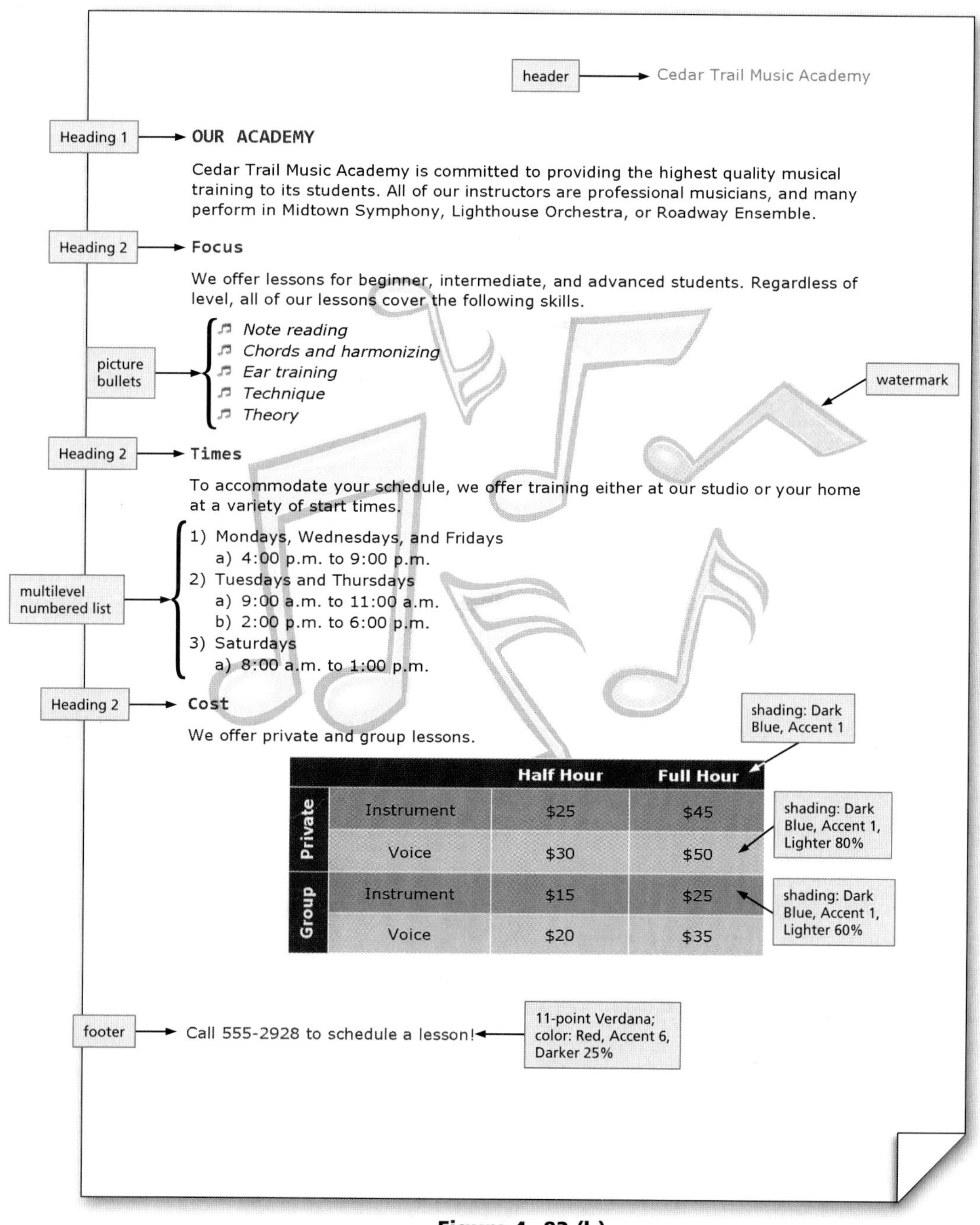

		Half Hour	Full Hour
Private	Instrument	$25	$45
	Voice	$30	$50
Group	Instrument	$15	$25
	Voice	$20	$35

Figure 4–83 (b)

Continued >

In the Labs *continued*

c. Create the bulleted list using the picture bullets shown (search for the text, music note). Apply the Emphasis style to the text in the first bulleted item. Use the format painter to copy the formatting to the text in the remaining bulleted items.
d. Create the multilevel numbered list as shown.
e. Create the table as shown. Distribute rows so that they are all the same height (about 0.42"). Distribute the last two columns so that they are the same width (about 1.30"). Align center all text. Center the table. Change the direction of the Group and Private headings. Shade the table cells as indicated in the figure.
f. Insert the formatted footer using the Blank design. The footer should appear only on the second page of the proposal. Enter the footer text as shown in the figure. If requested by your instructor, change the phone number in the footer to your phone number.

6. Create a picture watermark of music notes. If necessary, adjust spacing above and below paragraphs to fit all content as shown in the figure.
7. Check the spelling of the proposal. Save the document with Lab 4-2 Music Academy Proposal as the file name and then submit it in the format specified by your instructor.
8. This proposal contains a multilevel numbered list. How would you change the font size of the numbers and letters at the beginning of each list item?

Lab 3: Expand Your World: Cloud and Web Technologies

Using the Word Web App to Create a Table

Problem: You are using a mobile device or computer at school that does not have Word but has Internet access. To make use of time between classes, you use Word to create a table showing your college expenses (Figure 4–84).

Instructions: Perform the following tasks:

1. Run a browser. Navigate to the Office Web Apps website. You will need to sign in to your SkyDrive account.
2. Use the Create button to begin creating a Word document using the Word Web App. Name the document Lab 4-3 College Budget.
3. Enter and format the table, as shown in Figure 4–84.
4. Save the document again. Tap or click the button to open the document in the Word desktop app. If necessary, sign in to your Microsoft account when prompted.
5. In the Word desktop app, apply a table style to the table (any style). Save the table on your SkyDrive account with the file name, Lab 4-3 College Budget Modified.
6. Redisplay your SkyDrive account and open the file Lab 4-3 College Budget Modified in the Word Web App. Select the option to edit the modified document in the Word Web App. Did the file retain the table style you applied?
7. Using either the Word Web App or the Word desktop app, submit the Lab 4-3 College Budget document in the format requested by your instructor. Sign out of your SkyDrive account. Sign out of the Microsoft account in Word.
8. Which table features that are covered in the chapter are not available in the Word Web App? Answer the question posed in #6.

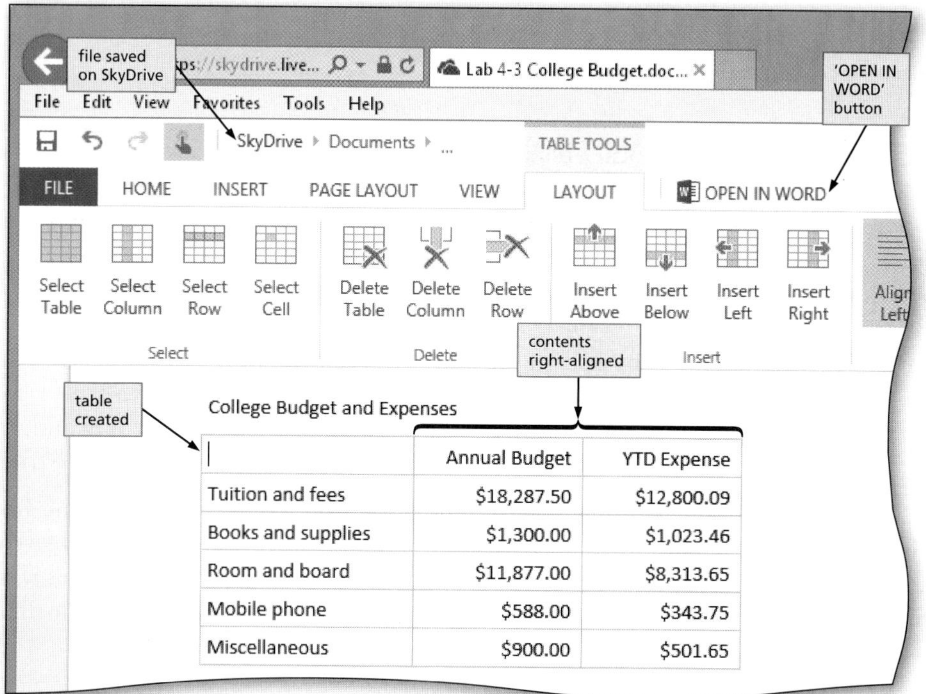

	Annual Budget	YTD Expense
Tuition and fees	$18,287.50	$12,800.09
Books and supplies	$1,300.00	$1,023.46
Room and board	$11,877.00	$8,313.65
Mobile phone	$588.00	$343.75
Miscellaneous	$900.00	$501.65

Figure 4–84

Consider This: Your Turn

Apply your creative thinking and problem solving skills to design and implement a solution.

Note: To complete these assignments, you may be required to use the Data Files for Students. Visit www.cengage.com/ct/studentdownload for detailed instructions or contact your instructor for information about accessing the required files.

1: Create a Proposal for Tutoring

Personal

Part 1: As a member of the investment club at your school, you have been asked to design a multipage sales proposal that can be distributed on campus to recruit new members. The proposal should contain a title page, followed by two pages of information about the club. The title page is to contain the club name, Moraine College Investment Club (MCIC), formatted with a border and shading. Include an appropriate SmartArt graphic that contains these words, at a minimum: finance, business, investing. Include this text on the title page: Make a difference by assisting with the management of our school's endowment fund!

The source for the text, tables, and lists in the body of the proposal is in a file called Your Turn 4-1 MCIC Draft. Use the concepts and techniques presented in this chapter to create and format the sales proposal. Include an appropriate watermark. Be sure to check the spelling and grammar of the finished document. Submit your assignment in the format specified by your instructor.

Part 2: You made several decisions while creating the sales proposal in this assignment: how to organize and format the title page (fonts, font sizes, colors, shading, styles, etc.), which SmartArt graphic to use on the title page, and how to organize and format the tables and lists. What was the rationale behind each of these decisions? When you proofread the document, what further revisions did you make and why?

Continued >

Consider This: Your Turn *continued*

2: Create a Proposal for a Family Business

Professional

Part 1: As a part-time employee at a local office supply store, you have been asked to design a multipage sales proposal that can be distributed to the local community. The proposal should contain a title page, followed by two pages of information about the store. The title page is to contain the store name, Malcom's Office Warehouse, formatted with a border and shading. Include an appropriate SmartArt graphic that contains these words, at a minimum: office supplies, technology, furniture. Include this text on the title page: Shop with us for all of your office needs!

The source for the text, tables, and lists in the body of the proposal is in a file called Your Turn 4-2 Office Draft. Use the concepts and techniques presented in this chapter to create and format the sales proposal. Include an appropriate watermark. Be sure to check the spelling and grammar of the finished document. Submit your assignment in the format specified by your instructor.

Part 2: You made several decisions while creating the sales proposal in this assignment: how to organize and format the title page (fonts, font sizes, colors, shading, styles, etc.), which SmartArt graphic to use on the title page, and how to organize and format the tables and lists. What was the rationale behind each of these decisions? When you proofread the document, what further revisions did you make and why?

3: Create a Research Proposal

Research and Collaboration

Part 1: You and two of your coworkers have been asked to prepare a multipage research proposal that recommends the type of vehicle your organization should purchase for its outside sales representatives this year. The proposal should provide comparisons and quotations on leasing, renting, and purchasing three different makes of vehicles, along with the suggested recommendation. The quotations must list the source from where the figures were obtained. Form a three-member team to research, compose, and create this proposal. Along with researching the makes of vehicles, also research how to write research proposals.

Use the concepts and techniques presented in this chapter to create and format the research proposal. The proposal should contain a title page, along with at least one table, at least one list, and an appropriate watermark. Be sure to check the spelling and grammar of the finished document. Submit your assignment in the format specified by your instructor.

Part 2: You made several decisions while creating the research proposal in this assignment: text to use, sources to use, how to organize and format the title page (fonts, font sizes, colors, shading, styles, etc.), which SmartArt graphic to use on the title page, and how to organize and format the tables and lists. What was the rationale behind each of these decisions? When you proofread the document, what further revisions did you make and why?

Learn Online

Reinforce what you learned in this chapter with games, exercises, training, and many other online activities and resources.

Student Companion Site Reinforcement activities and resources are available at no additional cost on www.cengagebrain.com. Visit www.cengage.com/ct/studentdownload for detailed instructions about accessing the resources available at the Student Companion Site.

SAM

SAM Put your skills into practice with SAM! If you have a SAM account, go to www.cengage.com/sam2013 to access SAM assignments for this chapter.

5 Using a Template to Create a Resume and Sharing a Finished Document

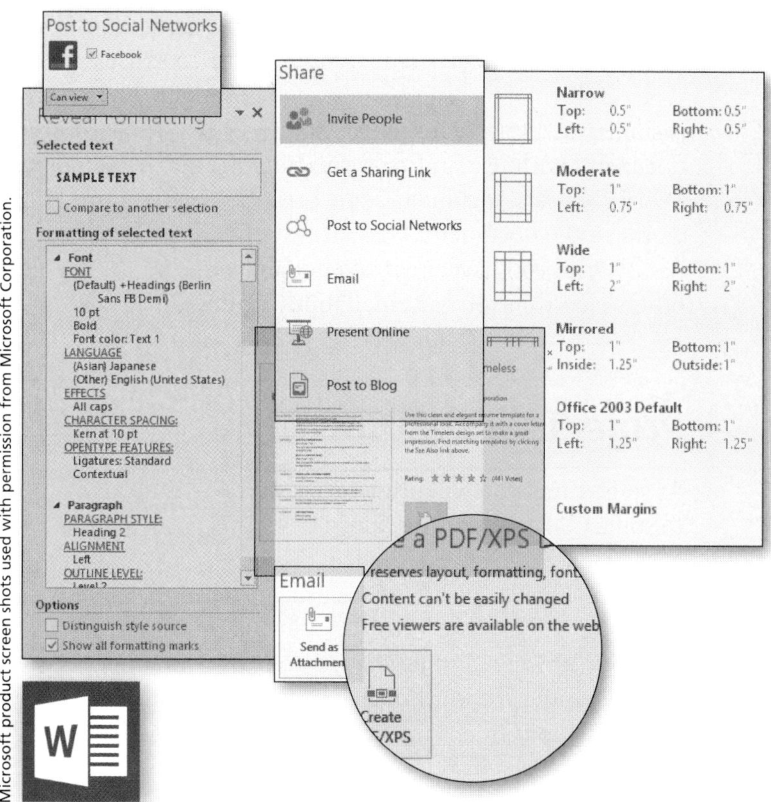

Objectives

You will have mastered the material in this chapter when you can:

- Use a template to create a document
- Change document margins
- Personalize a document template
- Indent a paragraph
- Customize theme fonts
- Create and modify a style
- Insert a building block
- Save a Word document as a PDF document and edit a PDF document
- Run the compatibility checker
- Enable others to access a document on SkyDrive or an online social network
- Send a Word document using email
- Save a Word document as a webpage
- Format text as a hyperlink
- Change a style set

5 Using a Template to Create a Resume and Sharing a Finished Document

Introduction

Some people prefer to use their own creative skills to design and compose Word documents. Using Word, for example, you can develop the content and decide the location of each item in a document. On occasion, however, you may have difficulty composing a particular type of document. To assist with the task of creating certain types of documents, such as resumes and letters, Word provides templates. A **template** is similar to a form with prewritten text; that is, Word prepares the requested document with text and/or formatting common to all documents of this nature. After Word creates a document from a template, you fill in the blanks or replace prewritten words in the document.

Once you have created a document, such as a resume, you often share it with others electronically via email, links, online social networks, or webpages.

Project — Resume

At some time, you will prepare a resume to send to prospective employers. In addition to some personal information, a **resume** usually contains the applicant's educational background and job experience. Employers review many resumes for each vacant position. Thus, you should design your resume carefully so that it presents you as the best candidate for the job.

The project in this chapter follows generally accepted guidelines for creating resumes and uses Word to create the resume shown in Figure 5–1. The resume for Jordan Taylor Green, an upcoming graduate of a criminal justice program, uses a Word template to present relevant information to a potential employer.

Roadmap

In this chapter, you will learn how to create the resume shown in Figure 5–1. The following roadmap identifies general activities you will perform as you progress through this chapter:

1. CREATE a new resume DOCUMENT FROM a Word TEMPLATE.
2. MODIFY AND FORMAT the resume TEMPLATE.
3. SAVE the resume DOCUMENT IN OTHER FORMATS so that you can share it with others.
4. MAKE the resume DOCUMENT AVAILABLE ONLINE so that others can access it.
5. CREATE a WEBPAGE FROM the resume WORD DOCUMENT.
6. FORMAT the resume WEBPAGE.

1931 Elm Street
Beachcombe, FL 33115
583-555-2772 (cell)
jgreen@earth.com

JORDAN TAYLOR GREEN

OBJECTIVE To obtain a full-time investigator position with a local or state law enforcement agency.

EDUCATION

B.A. CRIMINAL JUSTICE – GROVE COLLEGE
December 2014

- Dean's List, every semester
- Outstanding Student Award, May 2014
- *Justice Journal,* 1st Place, cross-cultural perspectives article
- Areas of concentration:
  Criminal law
  International justice systems
  Research methods
  Victims' rights

A.A. LEGAL STUDIES – PARKER COMMUNITY COLLEGE
December 2012, GPA 3.95/4.00

EXPERIENCE

TEACHERS' ASSISTANT – GROVE COLLEGE
August 2013 - Present
Research trends in course projects, grade student assignments, guide students with projects, manage student communications, present lectures when instructors are off campus.

MEMBERSHIPS

- Criminal Justice Club, Grove College
- Phi Kappa Sigma National Honor Society
- Student Government Association, Grove College

COMMUNITY SERVICE

VICTIM ADVOCATE – GROVE COMMUNITY SERVICES
October 2013 - Present
Volunteer eight hours a week at the call center. Offer emotional support and provide information on victims' legal rights and the criminal justice process.

Figure 5–1

At the beginning of step instructions throughout the chapter, you will see an abbreviated form of this roadmap. The abbreviated roadmap uses colors to indicate chapter progress: gray means the chapter is beyond that activity, blue means the task being shown is covered in that activity, and black means that activity is yet to be covered. For example, the following abbreviated roadmap indicates the chapter would be showing a task in the 2 MODIFY & FORMAT TEMPLATE activity.

1 CREATE DOCUMENT FROM TEMPLATE | 2 MODIFY & FORMAT TEMPLATE | 3 SAVE DOCUMENT IN OTHER FORMATS
4 MAKE DOCUMENT AVAILABLE ONLINE | 5 CREATE WEBPAGE FROM WORD DOCUMENT | 6 FORMAT WEBPAGE

Use the abbreviated roadmap as a progress guide while you read or step through the instructions in this chapter.

To Run Word and Change Word Settings

One of the few differences between Windows 7 and Windows 8 occurs in the steps to run Word. If you are using Windows 7, click the Start button, type `Word` in the 'Search programs and files' box, click Word 2013, and then, if necessary, maximize the Word window. For a summary of the steps to run Word in Windows 7, refer to the Quick Reference located at the back of this book.

If you are using a computer to step through the project in this chapter and you want your screens to match the figures in this book, you should change your screen's resolution to 1366 × 768. The following steps run Word, display formatting marks, and change the zoom to page width.

1. Run Word and create a blank document in the Word window. If necessary, maximize the Word window.
2. If the Print Layout button on the status bar is not selected (shown in Figure 5–4 on page WD 278), tap or click it so that your screen is in Print Layout view.
3. If the 'Show/Hide ¶' button (HOME tab | Paragraph group) is not selected already, tap or click it to display formatting marks on the screen.
4. To display the page the same width as the document window, if necessary, tap or click the Page Width button (VIEW tab | Zoom group).

Using a Template to Create a Resume

Although you could compose a resume in a blank document window, this chapter shows how to use a template instead, where Word formats the resume with appropriate headings and spacing. You then customize the resume that the template generated by filling in blanks and by selecting and replacing text.

To Create a New Document from an Online Template

1 CREATE DOCUMENT FROM TEMPLATE | 2 MODIFY & FORMAT TEMPLATE | 3 SAVE DOCUMENT IN OTHER FORMATS
4 MAKE DOCUMENT AVAILABLE ONLINE | 5 CREATE WEBPAGE FROM WORD DOCUMENT | 6 FORMAT WEBPAGE

Word has a variety of templates available online to assist you with creating documents. Available online templates include agendas, award certificates, calendars, expense reports, greeting cards, invitations, invoices, letters, meeting minutes, memos, resumes, and statements. When you select an online template, Word downloads (or copies) it from the Office.com website to your computer or mobile device. Many of the templates use the same design or style. ***Why?*** *If you create related documents, such as a resume and a letter, you can use the same template design or style so that the documents complement one another.* The next steps create a resume using the Basic resume (Timeless design) template.

1

- Tap or click FILE on the ribbon to open the Backstage view and then tap or click the New tab in the Backstage view to display the New gallery, which initially lists several featured templates.
- Type `resume` in the 'Search for online templates' box and then tap or click the Start searching button to display a list of online resume templates (Figure 5–2).

Q&A Can I select a template from the Word start screen that appears when I initially run Word?
Yes, instead of selecting Blank document from the Word start screen, you can select any of the available templates.

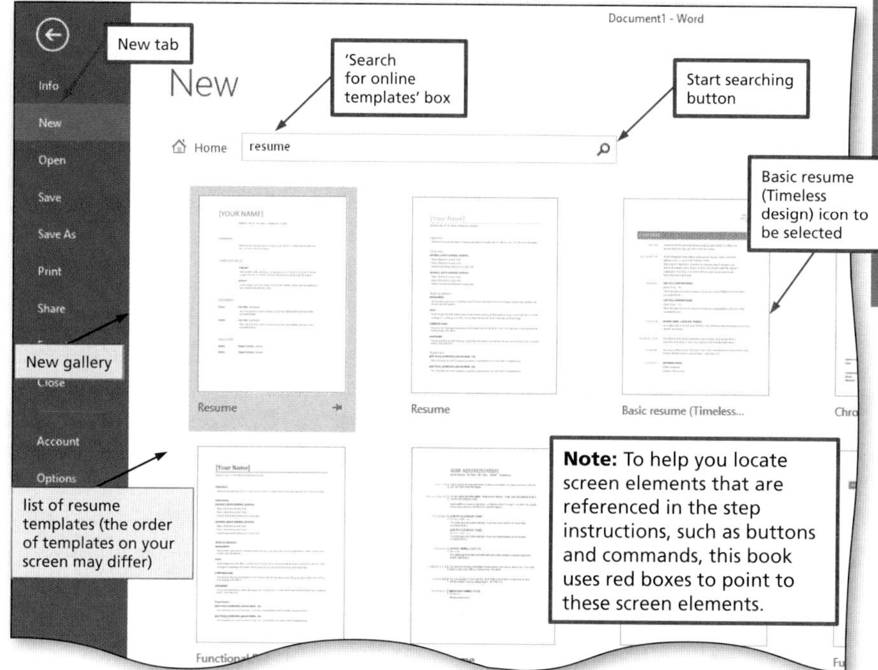

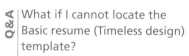

Figure 5–2

2

- If necessary, scroll through the list of templates to display the Basic resume (Timeless design) thumbnail.
- Tap or click the Basic resume (Timeless design) thumbnail to select the template and display it in a preview window (Figure 5–3).

Experiment

- Tap or click the Back and Forward buttons on the sides of the preview window to view previews of other templates. When finished, display the Basic resume (Timeless design) thumbnail in the preview window.

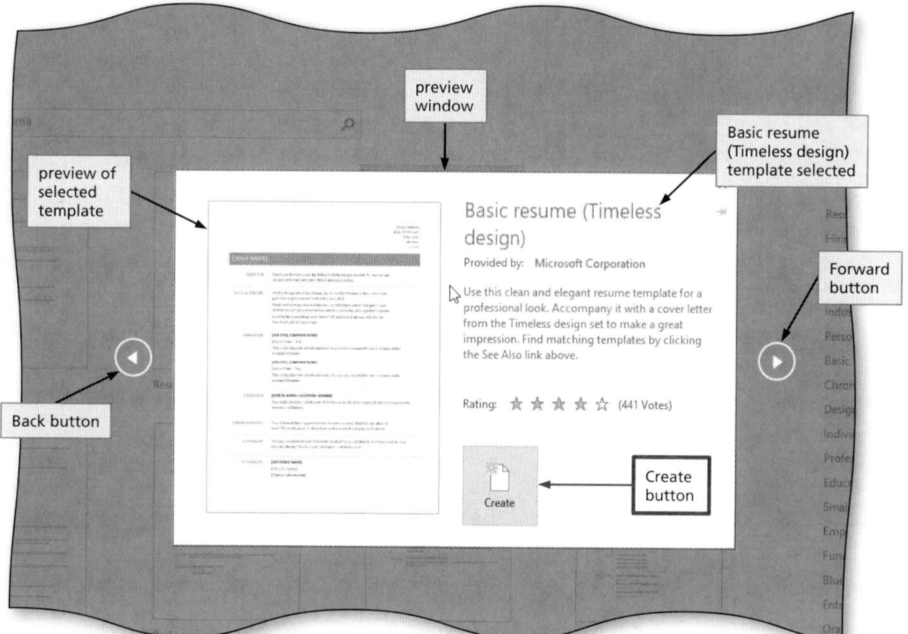

Figure 5–3

Q&A What if I cannot locate the Basic resume (Timeless design) template?
Exit the Backstage view and then proceed to the steps called To Open a Document Created from a Template that are shaded yellow and immediately follow these steps.

• Tap or click the Create button to create a new document based on the selected template (Figure 5–4).

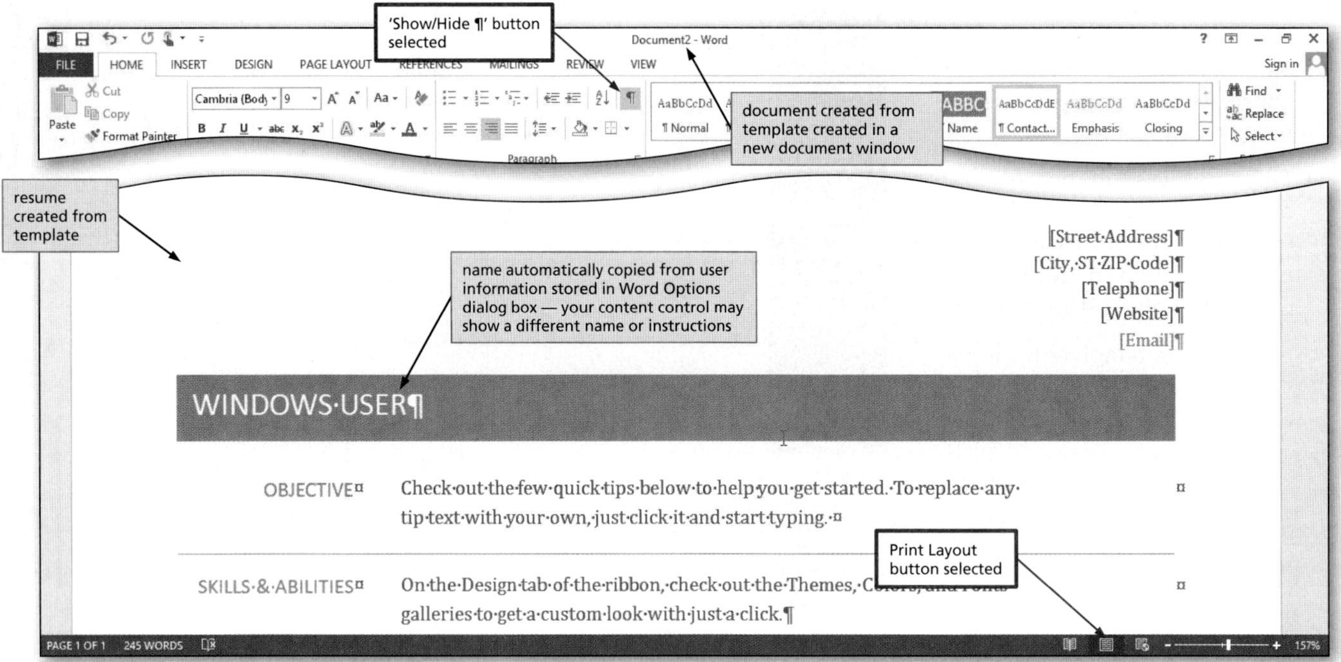

Figure 5–4

BTW
Touch Screen Differences
The Office and Windows interfaces may vary if you are using a touch screen. For this reason, you might notice that the function or appearance of your touch screen differs slightly from this chapter's presentation.

To Open a Document Created from a Template

If you are unable to locate the Basic resume (Timeless design) template in the previous steps, you can open it from the Data Files for Students. Visit www.cengage .com/ct/studentdownload for detailed instructions or contact your instructor for information about accessing the required files. The following steps open a document. NOTE: PERFORM THE STEPS IN THIS YELLOW BOX ONLY IF YOU WERE UNABLE TO LOCATE THE BASIC RESUME (TIMELESS DESIGN) TEMPLATE IN THE PREVIOUS STEPS.

1. Open the Backstage view and then, if necessary, tap or click the Open tab in the Backstage view to display the Open gallery.
2. Tap or click Computer, SkyDrive, or another location in the left pane that references the location of the Data Files for Students, tap or click the Browse button, and then navigate to the location of the Basic resume (Timeless design) file to be opened (in this case, the Chapter 5 folder in the Word folder in the CIS 101 folder).
3. Tap or click the Open button (Open dialog box) to open the file.

To Print the Resume

To see the entire resume created by the resume template using the Basic resume (Timeless design), print the document shown in the Word window. The following steps print a document.

1. Tap or click FILE on the ribbon to open the Backstage view and then tap or click the Print tab in the Backstage view to display the Print gallery.

2 Verify that the printer listed on the Printer Status button will print a hard copy of the document. If necessary, change the selected printer.

3 Tap or click the Print button in the Print gallery to print the current document (Figure 5–5).

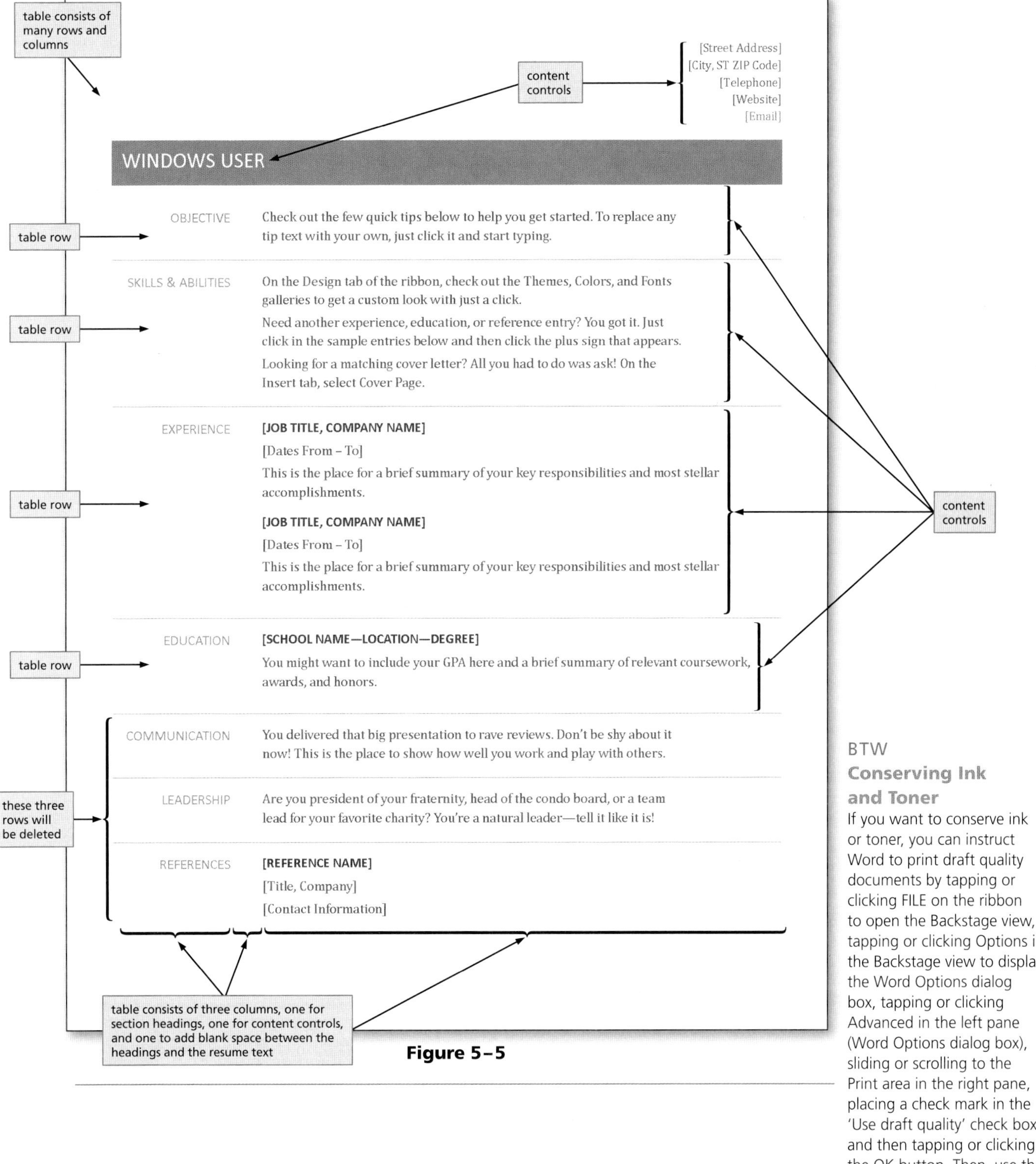

Figure 5–5

BTW

Conserving Ink and Toner

If you want to conserve ink or toner, you can instruct Word to print draft quality documents by tapping or clicking FILE on the ribbon to open the Backstage view, tapping or clicking Options in the Backstage view to display the Word Options dialog box, tapping or clicking Advanced in the left pane (Word Options dialog box), sliding or scrolling to the Print area in the right pane, placing a check mark in the 'Use draft quality' check box, and then tapping or clicking the OK button. Then, use the Backstage view to print the document as usual.

CONSIDER THIS

How do you craft a successful resume?

Two types of resumes are the chronological resume and the functional resume. A chronological resume sequences information by time, with the most recent listed first. This type of resume highlights a job seeker's job continuity and growth. A functional resume groups information by skills and accomplishments. This resume emphasizes a job seeker's experience and qualifications in specialized areas. Some resumes use a combination of the two formats. For an entry-level job search, experts recommend a chronological resume or a combination of the two types of resumes.

When creating a resume, be sure to include necessary information and present it appropriately. Keep descriptions concise, using action words and bulleted lists.

- **Include necessary information.** Your resume should include contact information, a clearly written objective, educational background, and experience. Use your legal name and mailing address, along with your phone number and email address, if you have one. Other sections you might consider including are memberships, skills, recognitions and awards, and/or community service. Do not include your Social Security number, marital status, age, height, weight, gender, physical appearance, health, citizenship, previous pay rates, reasons for leaving a prior job, current date, high-school information (if you are a college graduate), and references. Employers assume you will provide references, if asked, and this information simply clutters a resume.
- **Present your resume appropriately.** For printed resumes, use a high-quality ink-jet or laser printer to print your resume on standard letter-sized white or ivory paper. Consider using paper that contains cotton fibers for a professional look.

Resume Template

If you are using your finger on a touch screen and are having difficulty completing the steps in this chapter, consider using a stylus. Many people find it easier to be precise with a stylus than with a finger. In addition, with a stylus you see the pointer. If you still are having trouble completing the steps with a stylus, try using a mouse.

The resume created from the template, shown in Figure 5–5 on the previous page, contains several content controls and a table. A **content control** is an object that contains instructions for filling in text and graphics. To select a content control, you tap or click it. As soon as you begin typing in the selected content control, your typing replaces the instructions in the control. Thus, you do not need to delete the selected instructions before you begin typing.

The table below the name in the document consists of seven rows and three columns. Each resume section is contained in one row (i.e., objective, skills & abilities, experience, etc.) The section headings are in the first column, followed by a blank column, followed by the third column that contains the content controls.

The following pages personalize the resume created by the resume template using these general steps:

1. Change the name at the top of the resume.
2. Fill in the contact information at the top of the resume.
3. Fill in the Objective section.
4. Move the Education and Experience sections above the Skills & Abilities section.
5. Fill in the Education and Experience sections.
6. Change the Skills & Abilities heading to Memberships and fill in this section.
7. Add a row for the Community Service section and fill in this section.
8. Delete the last three unused rows.

To Set Custom Margins

1 CREATE DOCUMENT FROM TEMPLATE | 2 MODIFY & FORMAT TEMPLATE | 3 SAVE DOCUMENT IN OTHER FORMATS
4 MAKE DOCUMENT AVAILABLE ONLINE | 5 CREATE WEBPAGE FROM WORD DOCUMENT | 6 FORMAT WEBPAGE

The resume template selected in this project uses .75-inch top, bottom, left, and right margins. You prefer slightly wider margins for the top, left, and right edges of the resume and a smaller bottom margin. ***Why?*** *You do not want the text to run so close to the top edge and sides of the page and do not want the resume to spill to a second page.* In earlier chapters, you changed the margins by selecting predefined settings in the Margins gallery. The margins you will use for the resume in this chapter, however, are not predefined. Thus, the next steps set custom margins.

- Display the PAGE LAYOUT tab.
- Tap or click the Adjust Margins button (PAGE LAYOUT tab | Page Setup group) to display the Margins gallery (Figure 5–6).

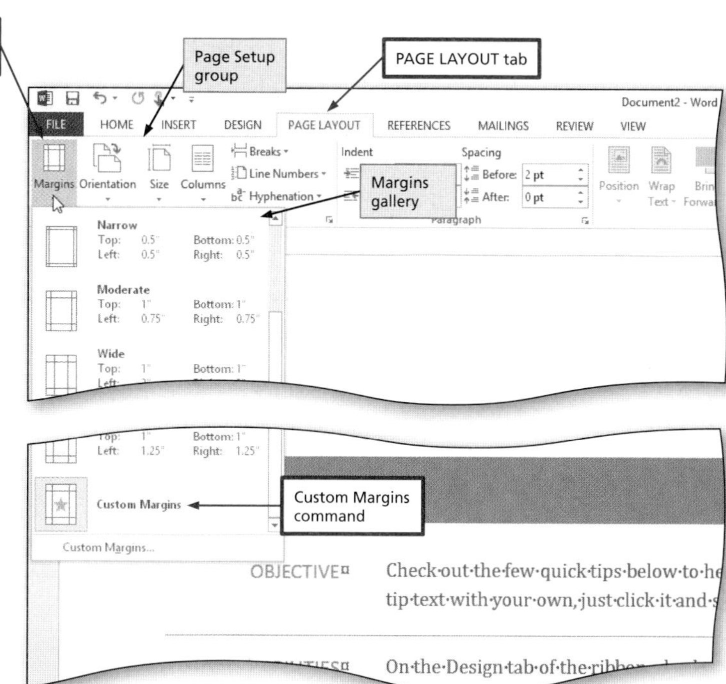

Figure 5–6

- Tap or click Custom Margins in the Margins gallery to display the Page Setup dialog box. If necessary, tap or click the Margins tab (Page Setup dialog box) to display the Margins sheet.
- Type `1` in the Top box to change the top margin setting and then press the TAB key to position the insertion point in the Bottom box.
- Type `.5` in the Bottom box to change the bottom margin setting and then press the TAB key to position the insertion point in the Left box.
- Type `1` in the Left box to change the left margin setting and then press the TAB key to position the insertion point in the Right box.
- Type `1` in the Right box to change the right margin setting (Figure 5–7).

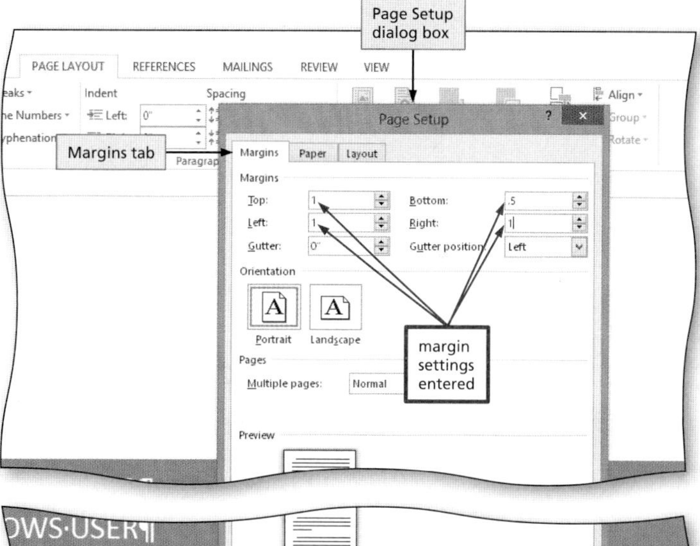

- Tap or click the OK button to set the custom margins for this document.

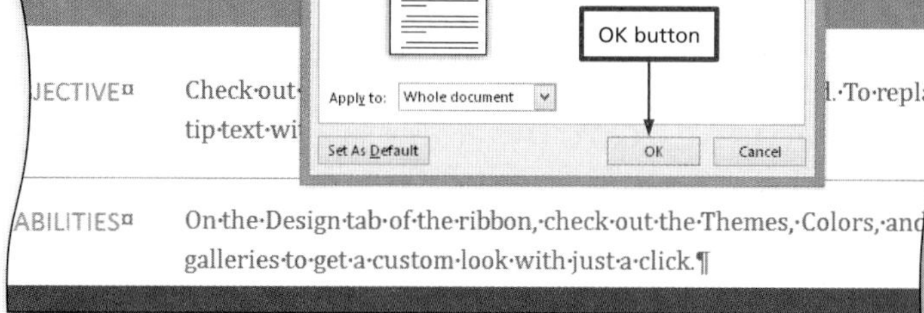

Figure 5–7

Other Ways

1. Drag margin boundaries on ruler

BTW
The Ribbon and Screen Resolution
Word may change how the groups and buttons within the groups appear on the ribbon, depending on the computer's screen resolution. Thus, your ribbon may look different from the ones in this book if you are using a screen resolution other than 1366 x 768.

To View Gridlines

When tables contain no borders, such as those in this resume, it can be difficult to see the individual cells in the table. To help identify the location of cells, you can display gridlines, which show cell outlines on the screen. The following steps show gridlines.

1. Position the insertion point in any table cell (in this case, the cell containing the OBJECTIVE heading).
2. Display the TABLE TOOLS LAYOUT tab.
3. If it is not selected already, tap or click the 'View Table Gridlines' button (TABLE TOOLS LAYOUT tab | Table group) to show gridlines in the table (Figure 5–8).

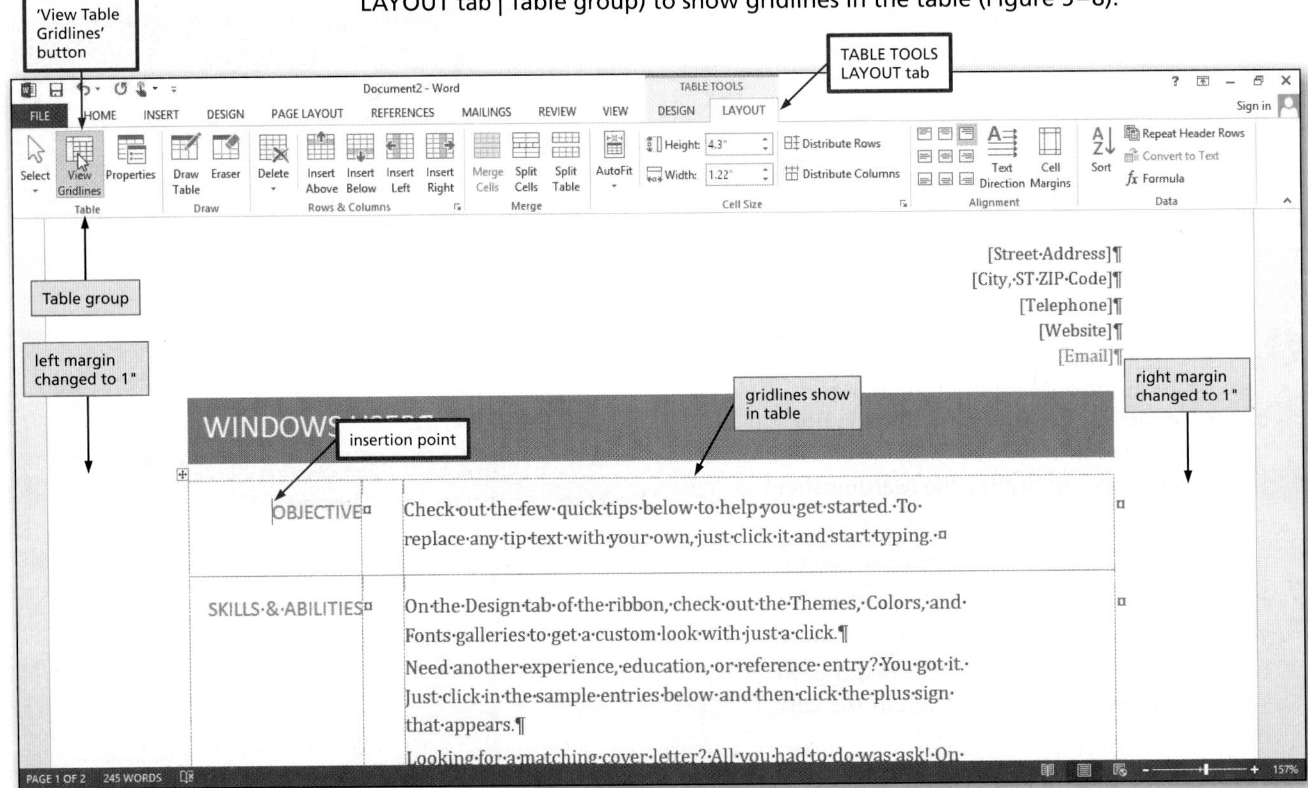

Figure 5–8

To Modify Text in a Content Control

1 CREATE DOCUMENT FROM TEMPLATE | 2 MODIFY & FORMAT TEMPLATE | 3 SAVE DOCUMENT IN OTHER FORMATS
4 MAKE DOCUMENT AVAILABLE ONLINE | 5 CREATE WEBPAGE FROM WORD DOCUMENT | 6 FORMAT WEBPAGE

The next step is to select the text that the template inserted in the resume and replace it with personal information. The name area on your resume may already contain your name. ***Why?*** *Word copies the user name from the Word Options dialog box and places it in the Your Name content control.* The next steps modify the text in a content control.

- Tap or click the content control to be modified (in this case, the Your Name content control) to select it.

Q&A How can I tell if a content control is selected?
The appearance of selected content controls varies. When you select some content controls, they are surrounded by a rectangle. Selected content controls also may have a name that is attached to the top, and/or a tag that appears to the left. With others, the text inside the content control appears selected.

- If necessary, tap or click the content control name (in this case, the words Your Name) to select the contents of the content control (Figure 5–9).

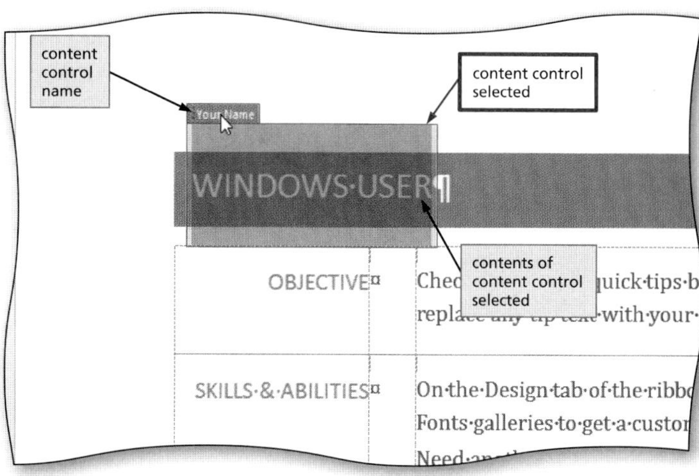

Figure 5–9

- Type **Jordan Taylor Green** as the name (Figure 5–10).

  If requested by your instructor, enter your name instead of the job seeker's name shown in Figure 5–10.

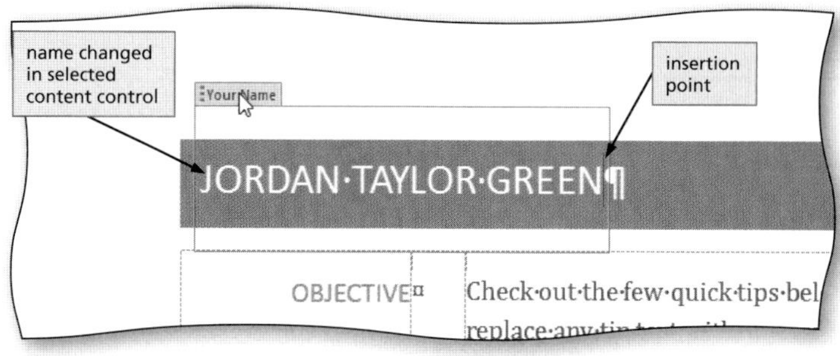

Figure 5–10

To Format a Content Control

1 CREATE DOCUMENT FROM TEMPLATE | 2 MODIFY & FORMAT TEMPLATE | 3 SAVE DOCUMENT IN OTHER FORMATS
4 MAKE DOCUMENT AVAILABLE ONLINE | 5 CREATE WEBPAGE FROM WORD DOCUMENT | 6 FORMAT WEBPAGE

The next step is to format the text in the name content control. ***Why?*** *You want the name slightly larger so that is stands out more.* To modify text in a content control, select the content control and then modify the formats. That is, you do not need to select the text in the content control. The following step formats the name content control.

- If the Your Name content control is not selected, tap or click it.
- Tap or click the 'Increase Font Size' button (HOME tab | Font group) to increase the font size of the text in the selected content control to the next font size (Figure 5–11).

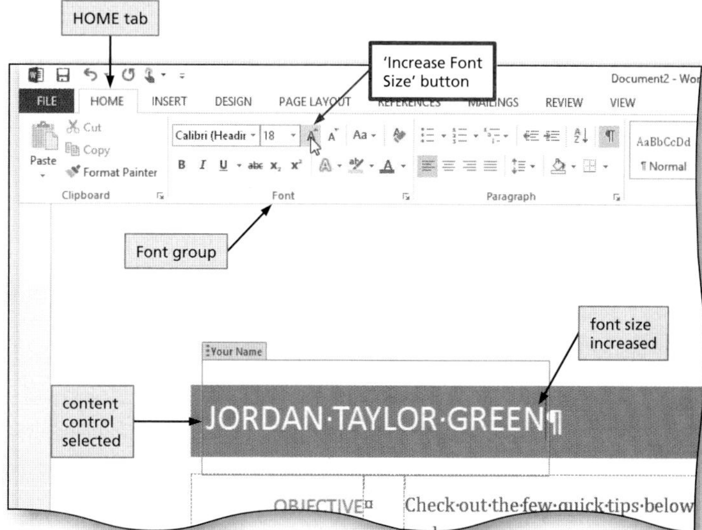

Figure 5–11

To Replace Placeholder Text

The next step is to select the Street Address content control and replace its placeholder text with a street address. Word uses **placeholder text** to indicate where text can be typed. To replace placeholder text in a content control, you select the content control and then type. ***Why?*** *The typed text automatically replaces the selected placeholder text.* The following steps replace the placeholder text in the Street Address content control.

1

- Tap or click the Street Address content control to select it (Figure 5–12).

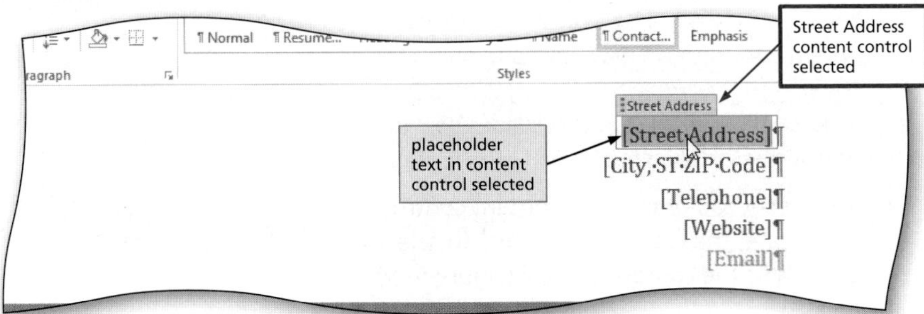

Figure 5–12

2

- Type **`1931 Elm Street`** as the street address (Figure 5–13).

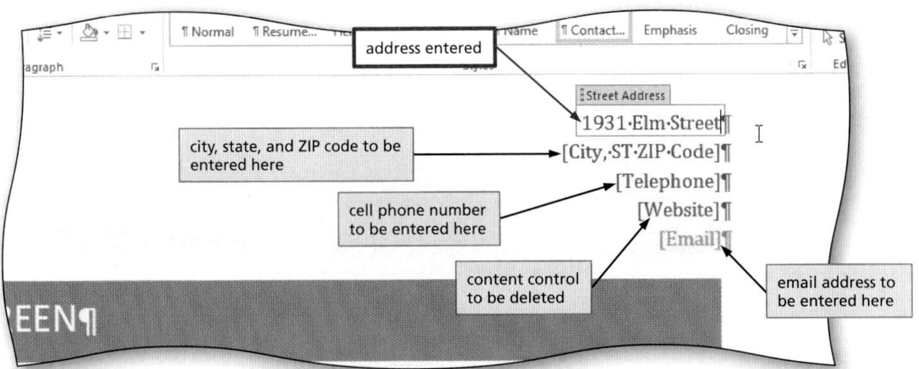

Figure 5–13

To Replace Placeholder Text in Content Controls

The next step is to select the placeholder text in the remaining content controls for your contact information and replace their instructions with personal information. You will enter city, state, and ZIP code; cell phone number; and email address in the respective content controls. Because you do not have a website, you will leave the website contact control as is and delete it in later steps. The following steps replace placeholder text in content controls.

BTW
Remove Content Control
If you discover that Word ignores entries in placeholder text due to certain settings, you can use the 'Remove Content Control' command illustrated in the steps beside Figure 5–14 to convert values entered in placeholder text to regular text.

1. Tap or click the Category content control (with the placeholder text: City, ST ZIP Code) to select it.
2. Type **`Beachcombe, FL 33115`** as the city, state, and ZIP code.
3. Tap or click the Telephone content control to select it.
4. Type **`583-555-2772 (cell)`** as the cell phone number.
5. Tap or click the Email content control to select it.
6. Type **`jgreen@earth.com`** as the email address.

To Delete a Content Control

The following steps delete the Website content control. ***Why?*** *You do not have a website.*

- Tap or click the Website content control to select it.
- Press and hold and then tap the 'Show Context Menu' button on the mini toolbar or right-click the selected content control to display a shortcut menu (Figure 5–14).

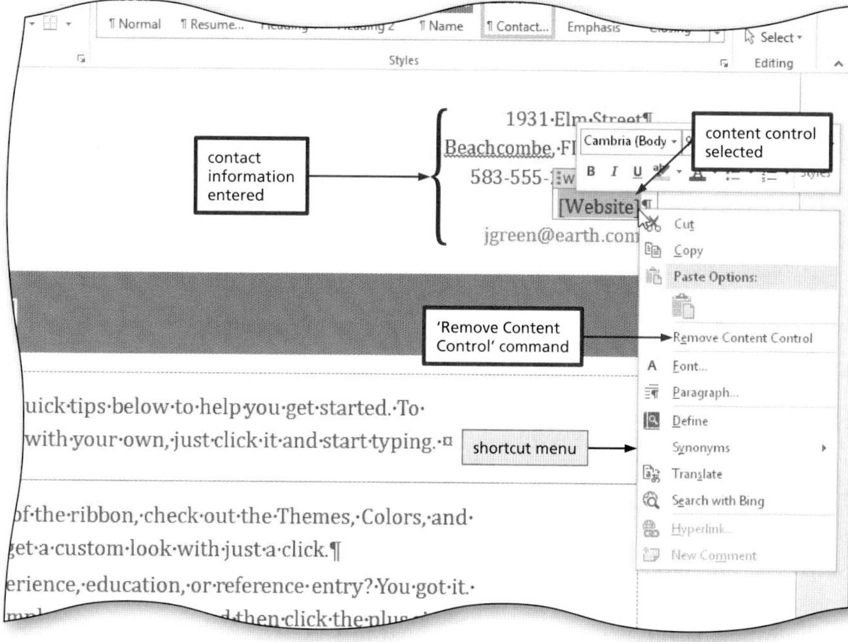

Figure 5–14

2

- Tap or click 'Remove Content Control' on the shortcut menu to delete the selected content control, which also deletes the placeholder text contained in the content control.
- Press the DELETE key to remove the blank line between the phone number and the email address (Figure 5–15).

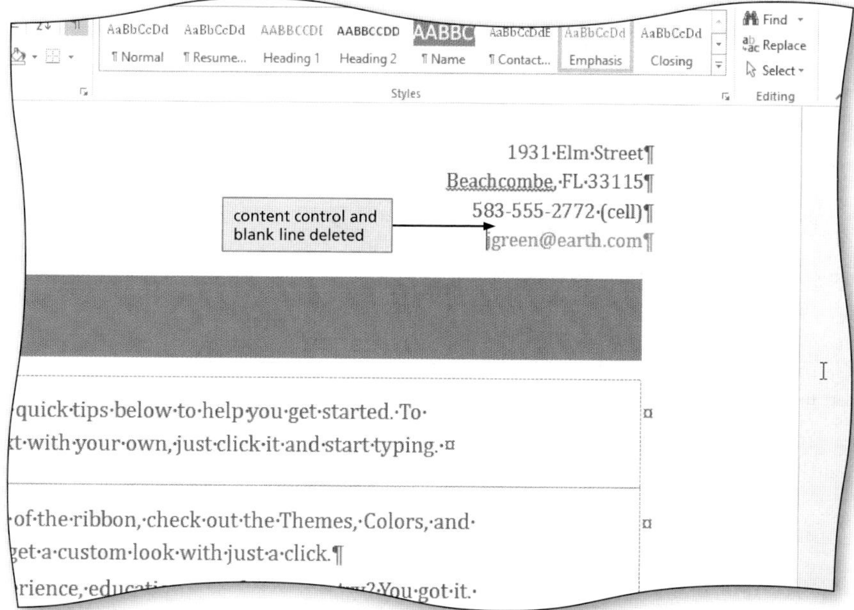

Figure 5–15

Other Ways

1. With content control selected, tap or click Cut button (HOME tab | Clipboard group)
2. With content control selected, press CTRL+X or DELETE or BACKSPACE

To Save a Document

You have performed several tasks while creating this resume and do not want to risk losing work completed thus far. Accordingly, you should save the document. The following steps assume you already have created folders for storing your files, for example, a CIS 101 folder (for your class) that contains a Word folder (for your assignments). Thus, these steps save the document in the Word folder in the CIS 101 folder using the file name, Green Resume.

BTW
Selecting Rows
To move table rows, you must select them first. Recall that if you are using a touch screen, drag the selection handles to select the rows; if you are using a mouse, point to the left of the first row to select and then drag downward or upward when the pointer changes to a right-pointing block arrow.

1. Tap or click the Save button on the Quick Access Toolbar, which depending on settings, will display either the Save As gallery in the Backstage view or the Save As dialog box.
2. Save the file in the desired location (in this case, Word folder in the CIS 101 folder [or your class folder]) using the file name, Green Resume.

To Move Table Rows

1 CREATE DOCUMENT FROM TEMPLATE | 2 MODIFY & FORMAT TEMPLATE | 3 SAVE DOCUMENT IN OTHER FORMATS
4 MAKE DOCUMENT AVAILABLE ONLINE | 5 CREATE WEBPAGE FROM WORD DOCUMENT | 6 FORMAT WEBPAGE

In the resume, you would like the Education and Experience sections immediately below the Objective section, in that order. ***Why?*** *You want to emphasize your educational background and experience.* Thus, the next step is to move rows in the resume. Each row contains a separate section in the resume. You will move the row containing the Education section below the row containing the Objective section. Then, you will move the row containing the Experience section so that it is below the moved row containing the Education section.

You use the same procedure to move table rows as to move text. That is, select the rows to move and then drag them to the desired location. The following steps use drag-and-drop editing to move table rows.

1

- Display the VIEW tab. Tap or click the 100% button (VIEW tab | Zoom group) to display the resume at 100 percent zoom in the document window.
- Scroll so that the Objective, Experience, and Education sections appear in the document window at the same time.

2

- Select the row to be moved, in this case, the row containing the Education section.
- If you are using a mouse, position the pointer in the selected row, press and hold down the mouse button and then drag the insertion point to the location where the selected row is to be moved (Figure 5–16).

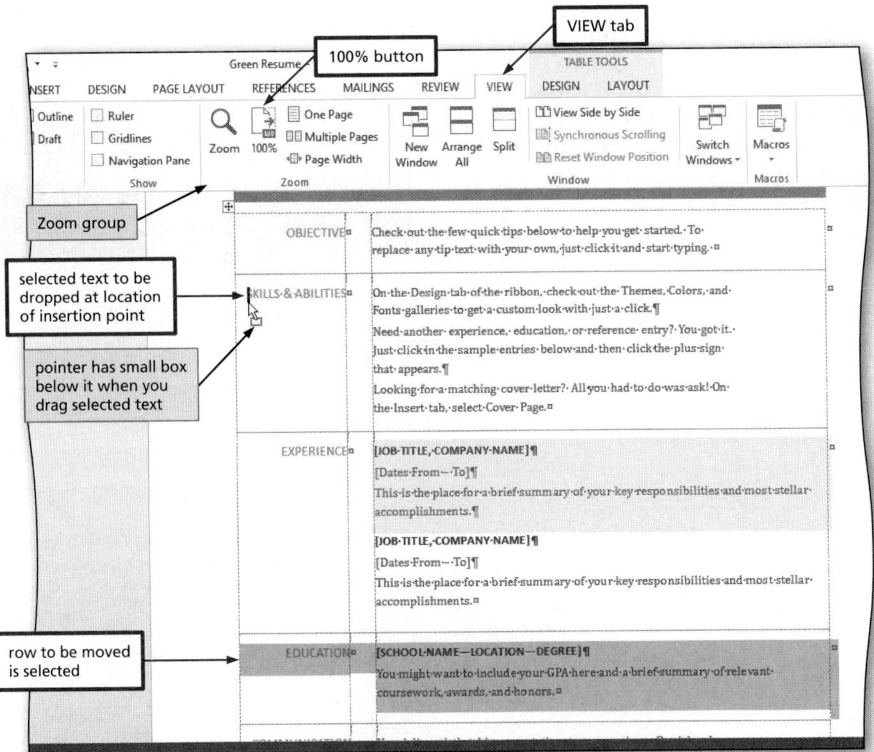

Figure 5–16

3

- If you are using a mouse, release the mouse button to move the selected row to the location of the insertion point (Figure 5–17).

Q&A What if I accidentally drag text to the wrong location?
Tap or click the Undo button on the Quick Access Toolbar and try again.

What if I am using a touch screen?
If you have a stylus, you can follow Steps 1 through 3 using the stylus. If you are using your finger, you will need to use the cut-and-paste technique: tap to position the insertion point in the row to be moved, tap the Select Table button (TABLE TOOLS LAYOUT tab | Table group), and then tap Select Row; press the selection to display the mini toolbar and then tap the Cut button on the mini toolbar to remove the row; tap to position the insertion point at the location where you want to move the row; display the HOME tab and then tap the Paste button (HOME tab | Clipboard group) to place the row at the location of the insertion point.

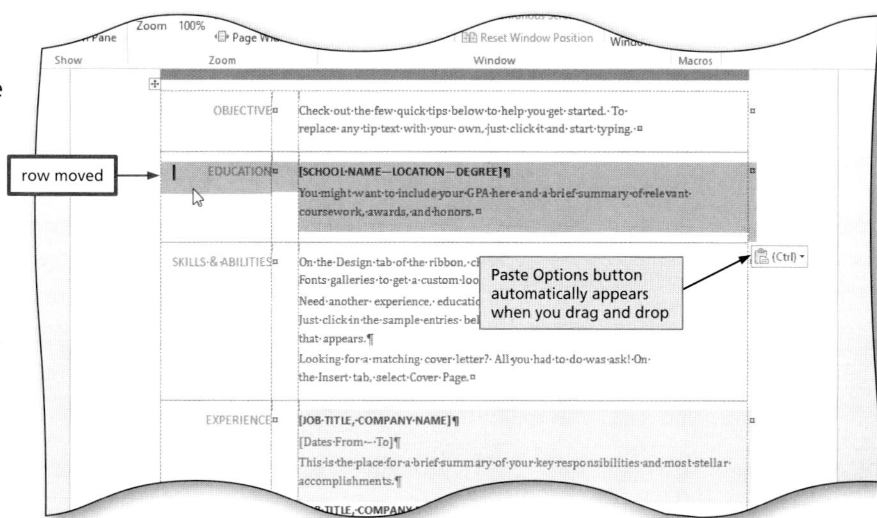

Figure 5–17

4

- Repeat Steps 2 and 3 to move the row containing the Experience section so that it is positioned below the row containing the Education section (Figure 5–18).

5

- Tap or click anywhere to remove the selection.
- Change the zoom to page width.

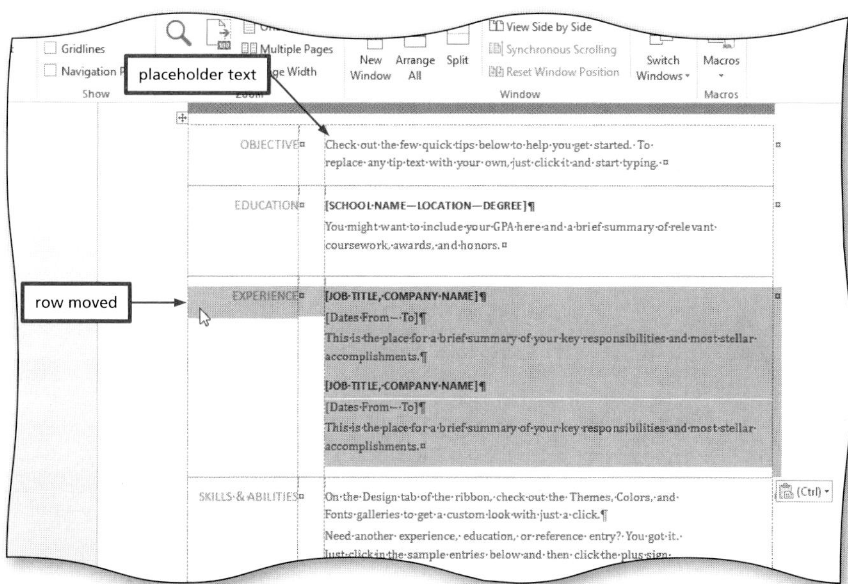

Figure 5–18

Other Ways

1. Tap or click Cut button (HOME tab | Clipboard group), tap or click where text or object is to be pasted, tap or click Paste button (HOME tab | Clipboard group)
2. Press and hold or right-click selected text, tap Cut button on mini toolbar or click Cut shortcut menu, press and hold or right-click where text or object is to be pasted, tap Paste on mini toolbar or click 'Keep Source Formatting' on shortcut menu
3. Press CTRL+X, position insertion point where text or object is to be pasted, press CTRL+V

To Modify Text in a Content Control

The following steps select the placeholder text in the Objective content control in the resume and then replaces with personal information.

1. If necessary, scroll to display the Objective section of the resume in the document window.

2. In the Objective section of the resume, tap or click the placeholder text that begins, 'Check out the few...', in the Objective content control (shown in Figure 5–18 on the previous page) to select it.

3. Type the objective: `To obtain a full-time investigator position with a local or state law enforcement agency.`

To Add an Item to a Content Control

1 CREATE DOCUMENT FROM TEMPLATE | 2 MODIFY & FORMAT TEMPLATE | 3 SAVE DOCUMENT IN OTHER FORMATS
4 MAKE DOCUMENT AVAILABLE ONLINE | 5 CREATE WEBPAGE FROM WORD DOCUMENT | 6 FORMAT WEBPAGE

Some content controls contain repeating items. For example, the Experience section currently contains two identical items, for two separate job entries. You can add items or delete items from repeating item content controls. The following steps add an item to the Education content control. ***Why?*** *You would like to add two degrees to the resume.*

1

- Tap or click the Education content control to select it (Figure 5–19).

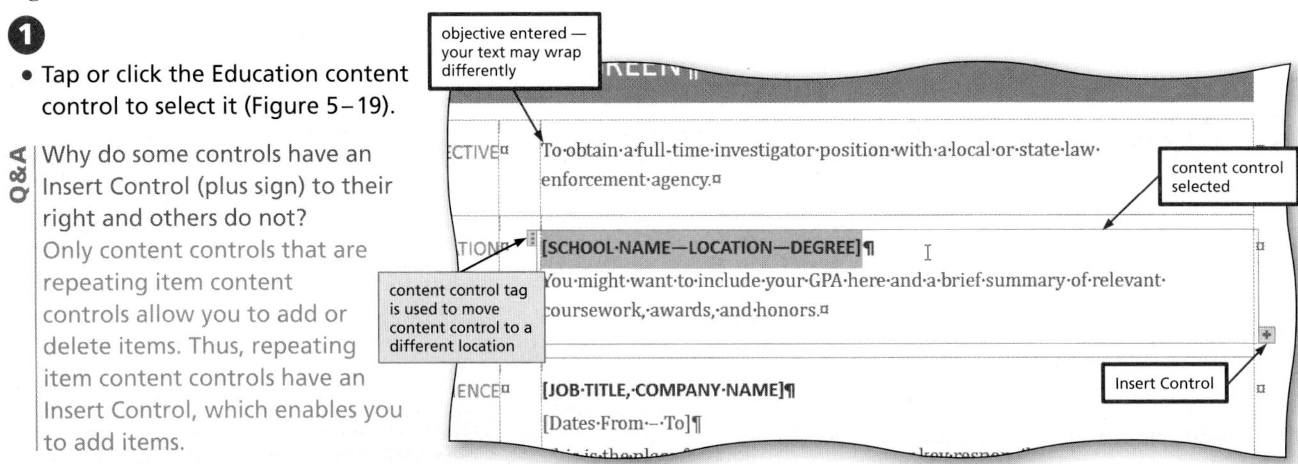

Q&A Why do some controls have an Insert Control (plus sign) to their right and others do not?
Only content controls that are repeating item content controls allow you to add or delete items. Thus, repeating item content controls have an Insert Control, which enables you to add items.

Figure 5–19

2

- Tap or click the Insert Control on the right edge of the Education content control to add another item to the content control (Figure 5–20).

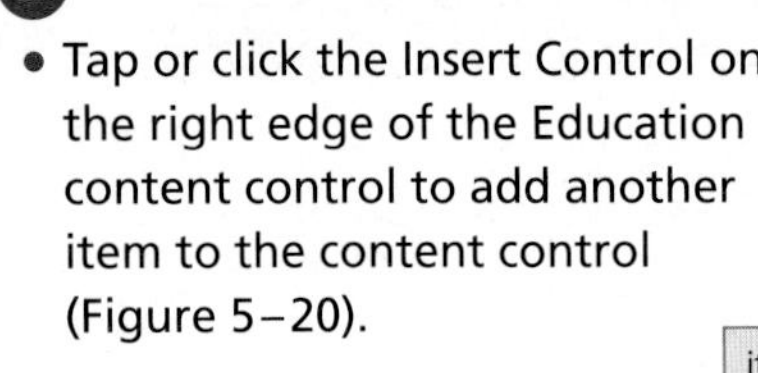

Q&A Could I add more items to the content control?
Yes.

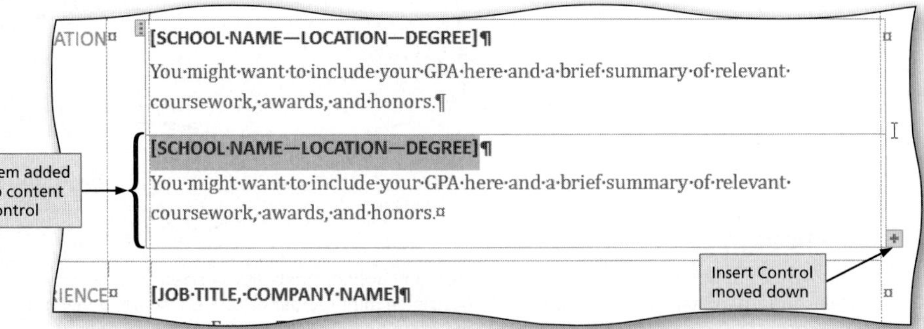

Figure 5–20

Other Ways

1. Tap 'Show Context Menu' button on mini toolbar or right-click content control, tap or click 'Insert Item Before' or 'Insert Item After' on shortcut menu

To Replace Placeholder Text in a Content Control

The next step is to begin to enter text in the Education section of the resume. The following step replaces placeholder text.

1 In the Education section of the resume, select the placeholder text, [SCHOOL NAME–LOCATION–DEGREE], in the first content control and then type `B.A. CRIMINAL JUSTICE - GROVE COLLEGE` as the degree and school name.

To Use AutoComplete

As you begin typing, Word may display a ScreenTip that presents a suggestion for the rest of the word or phrase you are typing. ***Why?*** *With its* ***AutoComplete*** *feature, Word predicts the word or phrase you are typing and displays its prediction in a ScreenTip.* If the AutoComplete prediction is correct, you can instruct Word to finish your typing with its prediction, or you can ignore Word's prediction. Word draws its AutoComplete suggestions from its dictionary and from AutoText entries you create and save in the Normal template.

The following steps use the AutoComplete feature as you type the graduation date in the Education section of the resume.

1

- In the Education section of the resume, tap or click the placeholder text that begins, 'You might want to…', in the first content control and then type `Dece` and notice the AutoComplete ScreenTip that appears on the screen (Figure 5–21).

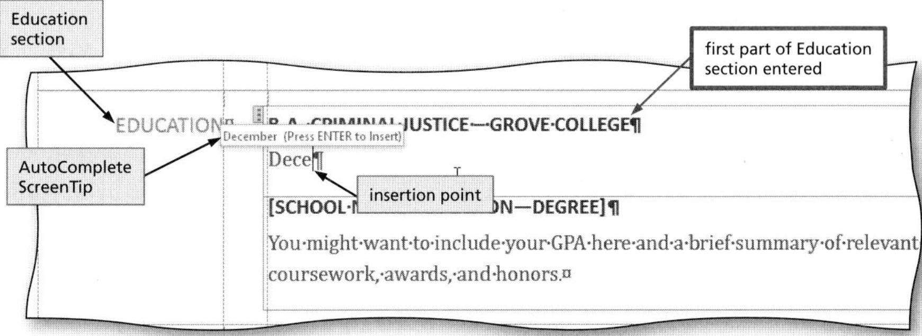

Figure 5–21

Q&A Why would my screen not display the AutoComplete ScreenTip?
Depending on previous Word entries, you may need to type more characters in order for Word to predict a particular word or phrase accurately. Or, you may need to turn on AutoComplete by tapping or clicking FILE on the ribbon to open the Backstage view, tapping or clicking Options in the Backstage view to display the Word Options dialog box, tapping or clicking Advanced in the left pane (Word Options dialog box), placing a check mark in the 'Show AutoComplete suggestions' check box, and then tapping or clicking the OK button.

2

- Tap the ScreenTip or press the ENTER key to instruct Word to finish your typing with the word or phrase that appeared in the AutoComplete ScreenTip.

Q&A What if I do not want to use the text proposed in the AutoComplete ScreenTip?
Simply continue typing and the AutoComplete ScreenTip will disappear from the screen.

3

- Press the SPACEBAR. Type `2014` and then press the ENTER key (Figure 5–22).

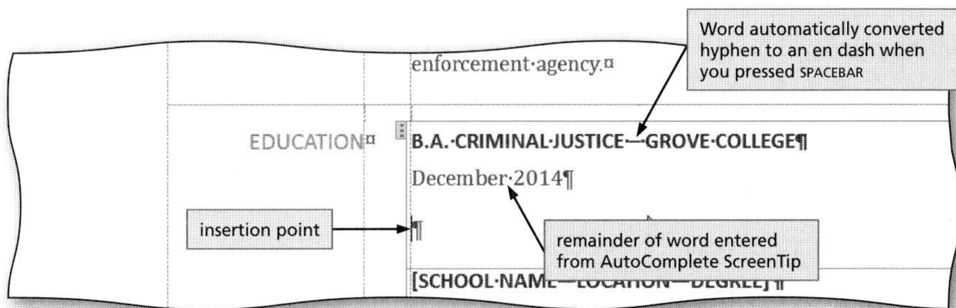

Figure 5–22

BTW

AutoFormat

Word automatically formats quotation marks, dashes, lists, fractions, ordinals, and other items depending on your typing and settings. To check if an AutoFormat option is enabled, tap or click FILE on the ribbon to open the Backstage view, tap or click Options in the Backstage view, tap or click Proofing in the left pane (Word Options dialog box), tap or click the AutoCorrect Options button, tap or click the 'AutoFormat As You Type' tab (AutoCorrect dialog box), select the appropriate check boxes, and then tap or click the OK button in each open dialog box.

To Enter More Text

The following steps continue entering text in the Education section of the resume.

1. Type **Dean's List, every semester** and then press the ENTER key.
2. Type **Outstanding Student Award, May 2014** and then press the ENTER key.
3. Type **Justice Journal, 1st Place, cross-cultural perspectives article** and then italicize the journal title.
4. Bullet the three paragraphs just entered (Figure 5–23).

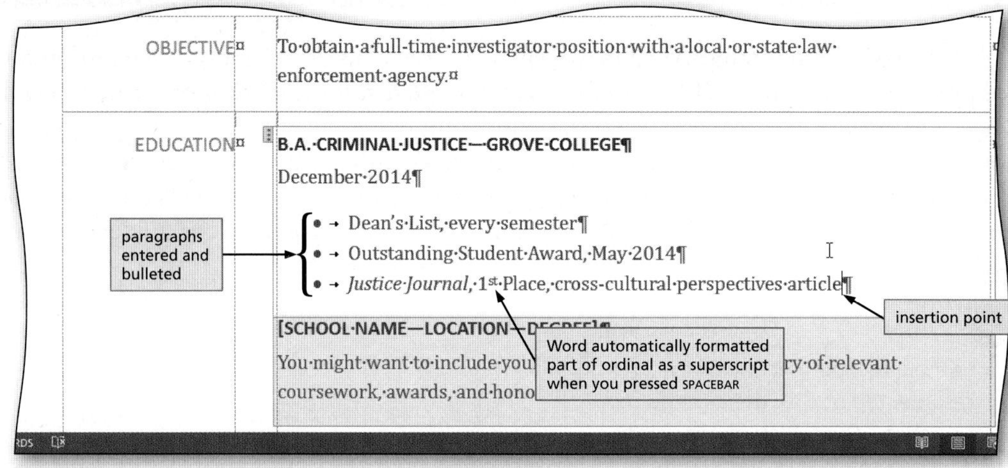

Figure 5–23

To Enter a Line Break

The next step in personalizing the resume is to enter the areas of concentration in the Education section. You want only the first line, which says, Areas of concentration:, to begin with a bullet. If you press the ENTER key on subsequent lines, Word automatically will carry forward the paragraph formatting, which includes the bullet. Thus, you will not press the ENTER key between each line. Instead, you will create a line break. ***Why?*** *A **line break** advances the insertion point to the beginning of the next physical line, ignoring any paragraph formatting.* The following steps enter the areas of concentration using a line break, instead of a paragraph break, between each line.

- With the insertion point positioned as shown in Figure 5–23, press the ENTER key.
- If necessary, turn off italics. Type **Areas of concentration:** and then press SHIFT+ENTER to insert a line break character and move the insertion point to the beginning of the next physical line (Figure 5–24).

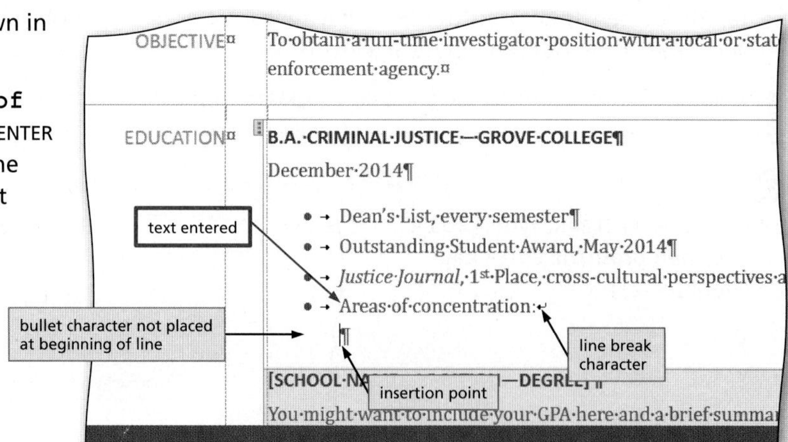

Figure 5–24

2

- Type **`Criminal law`** and then press SHIFT+ENTER.
- Type **`International justice systems`** and then press SHIFT+ENTER.
- Type **`Research methods`** and then press SHIFT+ENTER.
- Type **`Victims' rights`** as the last entry. Do not press SHIFT+ENTER at the end of this line (Figure 5–25).

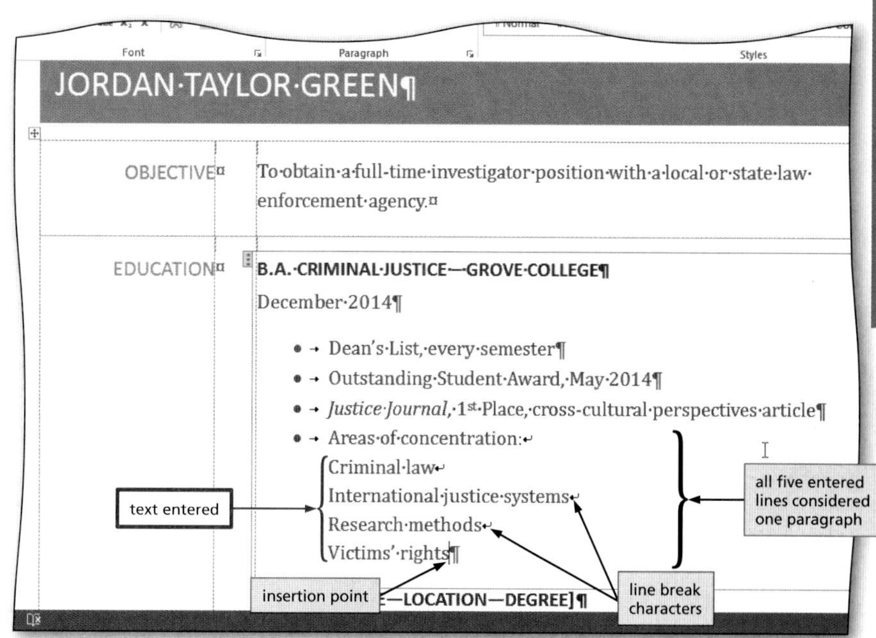

Figure 5–25

To Replace Placeholder Text in Content Controls

The next step is to enter the information for the second degree in the Education section of the resume. The following steps replace placeholder text.

1 In the Education section of the resume, select the placeholder text, [SCHOOL NAME–LOCATION–DEGREE], in the second content control and then type **`A.A. LEGAL STUDIES - PARKER COMMUNITY COLLEGE`** as the degree and school name.

2 Select the placeholder text that begins, 'You might want to...', in the second content control and then type **`December 2012, GPA 3.95/4.00`** (Figure 5–26).

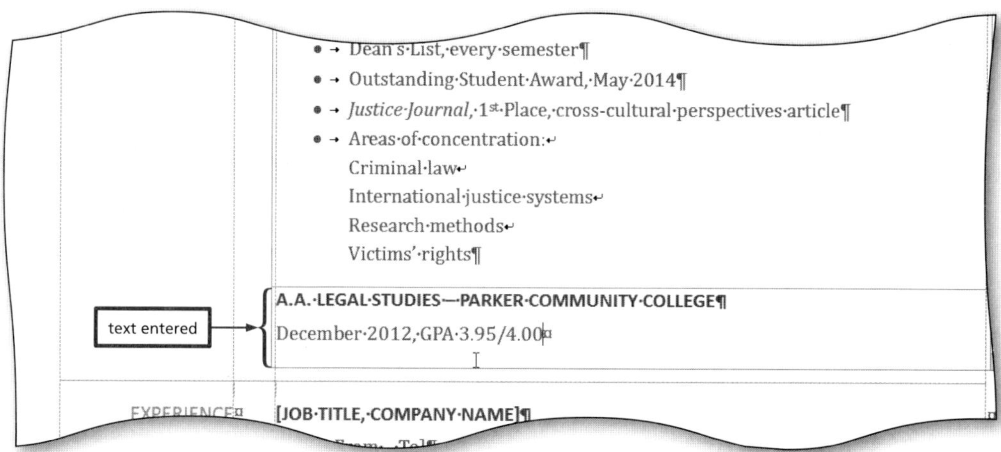

Figure 5–26

BTW

Line Break Character

Line break characters do not print. A line break character is a formatting mark that indicates a line break at the end of the line.

To Delete an Item from a Content Control

1 CREATE DOCUMENT FROM TEMPLATE | 2 MODIFY & FORMAT TEMPLATE | 3 SAVE DOCUMENT IN OTHER FORMATS
4 MAKE DOCUMENT AVAILABLE ONLINE | 5 CREATE WEBPAGE FROM WORD DOCUMENT | 6 FORMAT WEBPAGE

You can delete items from repeating item content controls. The following steps delete an item from the Experience content control. ***Why?*** *You only have one job experience entry for the resume.*

- Tap or click the second item in the Experience content control to select it.
- Press and hold and then tap the 'Show Context Menu' button or right-click the selected item to display a shortcut menu (Figure 5–27).

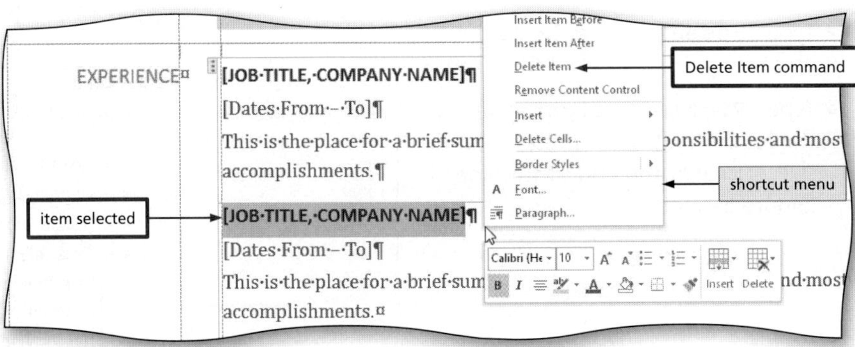

Figure 5–27

Q&A What is the difference between the Delete Item command and the Remove Content Control command?

The Delete Item command deletes one item from a repeating item content control, whereas the Remove Content Control deletes the entire content control (all items). If you personalized text in the content control, the Remove Content Control removes the content control but leaves your personalized text.

2

- Tap or click Delete Item on the shortcut menu to delete the second item from the content control.
- Press the BACKSPACE key to remove the blank line below the remaining item in the content control (Figure 5–28).

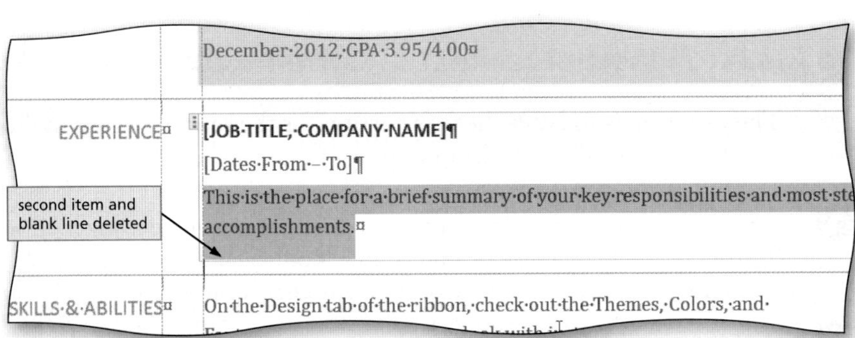

Figure 5–28

To Replace Placeholder Text in Content Controls

The next step is to enter the job information for the Experience section of the resume. The following steps replace placeholder text.

1. In the Experience section of the resume, select the placeholder text, [JOB TITLE, COMPANY NAME], in the content control and then type **`TEACHERS' ASSISTANT - GROVE COLLEGE`** as the job title and company name.
2. Select the placeholder text that begins, 'Dates From...', in the content control and then type **`August 2013 - Present`** as the dates.
3. Select the placeholder text that begins, 'This is the place...', in the content control and then type this text (Figure 5–29): **`Research trends in course topics, grade student assignments, guide students with projects, manage student communications, present lectures when instructors are off campus.`**

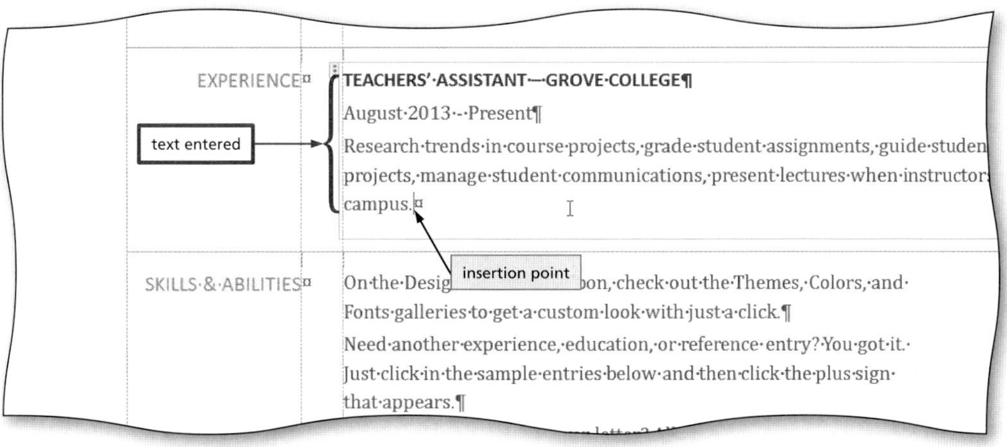

EXPERIENCE
TEACHERS'·ASSISTANT—GROVE·COLLEGE¶
August·2013·-·Present¶
text entered
Research·trends·in·course·projects,·grade·student·assignments,·guide·studen
projects,·manage·student·communications,·present·lectures·when·instructor
campus.
insertion point
SKILLS·&·ABILITIES
On·the·Desig
on,·check·out·the·Themes,·Colors,·and·
Fonts·galleries·to·get·a·custom·look·with·just·a·click.¶
Need·another·experience,·education,·or·reference·entry?·You·got·it.·
Just·click·in·the·sample·entries·below·and·then·click·the·plus·sign·
that·appears.¶

Figure 5–29

To Indent a Paragraph

1 CREATE DOCUMENT FROM TEMPLATE | 2 MODIFY & FORMAT TEMPLATE | 3 SAVE DOCUMENT IN OTHER FORMATS
4 MAKE DOCUMENT AVAILABLE ONLINE | 5 CREATE WEBPAGE FROM WORD DOCUMENT | 6 FORMAT WEBPAGE

In the resume, the lines below the job start date and end date that contain the job responsibilities are to be indented. ***Why?*** *You feel the responsibilities would be easier to read if they are indented.* The following step indents the left edge of a paragraph.

- With the insertion point in the paragraph to indent, tap or click the Increase Indent button (HOME tab | Paragraph group) to indent the current paragraph one-half inch (Figure 5–30).

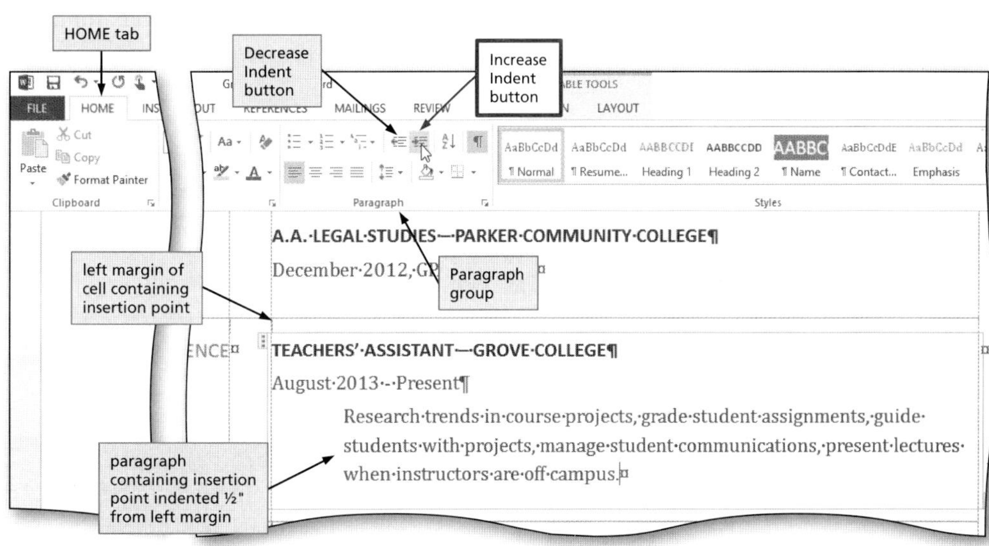

Figure 5–30

Experiment

- Repeatedly tap or click the Increase Indent and Decrease Indent buttons (HOME tab | Paragraph group) and watch the left indent of the current paragraph change. When you have finished experimenting, use the Increase Indent and Decrease Indent buttons until the paragraph is indented one-half inch.

Q&A Why is the paragraph indented one-half inch?

Each time you tap or click the Increase Indent button (HOME tab | Paragraph group), the current paragraph is indented one-half inch. Similarly, tapping or clicking the Decrease Indent button (HOME tab | Paragraph group) decreases the paragraph indent by one-half inch.

Other Ways

1. Drag Left Indent marker on horizontal ruler
2. Enter value in Indent Left box (PAGE LAYOUT tab | Paragraph group)
3. Tap or click Paragraph Dialog Box Launcher (HOME tab | Paragraph group), tap or click Indents and Spacing tab (Paragraph dialog box), set indentation in Left box, tap or click OK button
4. Tap 'Show Context Menu' button on mini toolbar or right-click text, tap or click Paragraph on shortcut menu, tap or click Indents and Spacing tab (Paragraph dialog box), set indentation in Left box, tap or click OK button
5. Press CTRL+M

To Replace Placeholder Text in Content Controls

The next step is to enter the membership information. You will replace the text in the Skills & Abilities section with membership information. The following steps replace placeholder text.

1. Select the text, SKILLS & ABILITIES, and then type **`MEMBERSHIPS`** as the new section heading.
2. In the Memberships section, select the placeholder text that begins, 'On the Design tab...', in the content control and then type **`Criminal Justice Club, Grove College`** and then press the ENTER key.
3. Type **`Phi Kappa Sigma National Honor Society`** and then press the ENTER key.
4. Type **`Student Government Association, Grove College`** and then bullet the three paragraphs just entered (shown in Figure 5–31).

To Copy and Paste a Table Item

1 CREATE DOCUMENT FROM TEMPLATE | 2 MODIFY & FORMAT TEMPLATE | **3 SAVE DOCUMENT IN OTHER FORMATS**
4 MAKE DOCUMENT AVAILABLE ONLINE | 5 CREATE WEBPAGE FROM WORD DOCUMENT | 6 FORMAT WEBPAGE

The next section of the resume in this chapter is the Community Service section, which is organized exactly like the Experience section. Thus, you copy of the Experience section and paste it below the Memberships section. ***Why?*** *It will be easier to edit the Experience section rather than format the Community Service section from scratch.*

You use the same procedure to copy table rows that you use to copy text. That is, select the rows to copy and then paste them at the desired location. The following steps copy table rows.

1

- Display the VIEW tab. Tap or click the 100% button (VIEW tab | Zoom group) to display the resume at 100 percent zoom in the document window.
- If necessary, scroll so that the Experience and Memberships sections appear in the document window at the same time.
- Select the row to be copied, in this case, the row containing the Experience section in the resume.
- Display the HOME tab.
- Tap or click the Copy button (HOME tab | Clipboard group) to copy the selected rows in the document to the Office Clipboard (Figure 5–31).

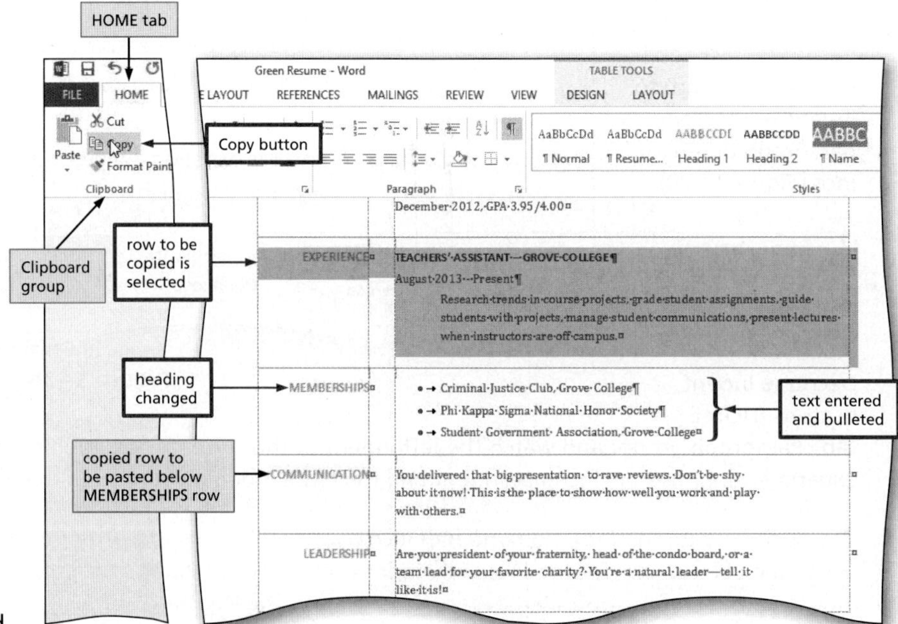

Figure 5–31

- Position the insertion point at the location where the copied row should be pasted, in this case, to the left of the M in the MEMBERSHIPS heading.
- Tap or click the Paste arrow (HOME tab | Clipboard group) to display the Paste gallery.

Q&A What if I tap or click the Paste button by mistake?
Tap or click the Undo button on the Quick Access Toolbar and then try again.

- If you are using a mouse, point to the Merge Table button in the Paste gallery to display a live preview of that paste option applied to the row in the table (Figure 5–32).

Experiment

- Point to the four options in the Paste gallery and watch the format of the pasted row change in the document window.

3

- Tap or click the Merge Table button in the Paste gallery to apply the selected option to the pasted table row because you want the pasted row to use the same formatting as the copied row.
- Tap or click anywhere to remove the selection.
- Change the zoom to page width.

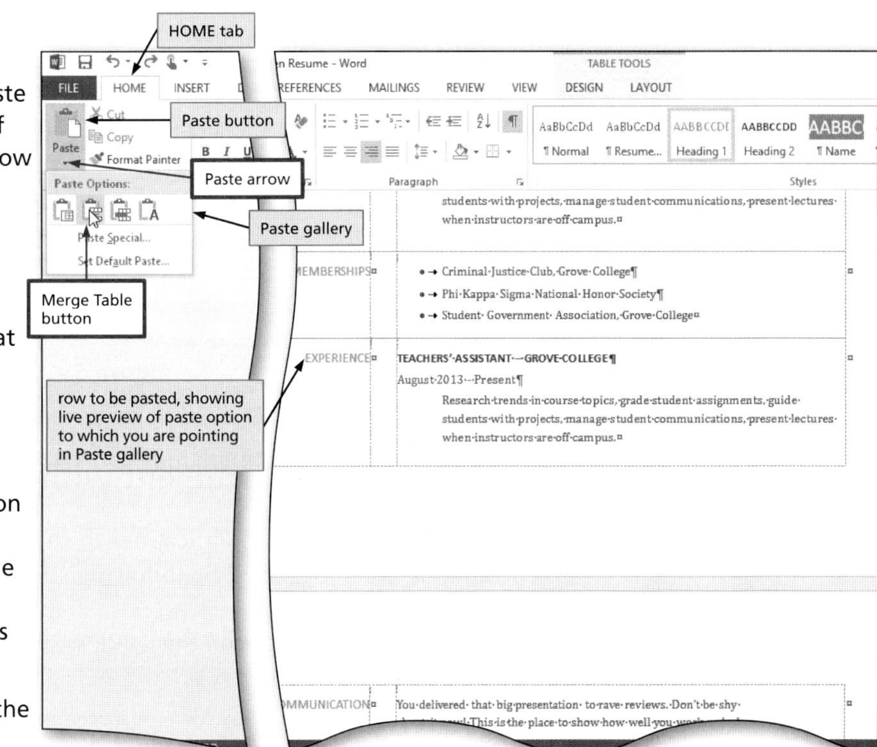

Figure 5–32

Other Ways

1. Press and hold or right-click selected item, tap or click Copy on mini toolbar or shortcut menu, press and hold or right-click where item is to be pasted, tap or click desired option in Paste Options area on shortcut menu
2. Select item, press CTRL+C, position insertion point at paste location, press CTRL+V

To Delete Rows and Edit Text

Because you will not be using the last three rows of the resume template, the next step is to delete them and then enter the remainder of the text in the resume, that is, the Community Service section. The following steps delete rows and edit text.

1. If necessary, display the TABLE TOOLS LAYOUT tab.
2. Select the last three rows of the table (COMMUNICATION, LEADERSHIP, and REFERENCES), which might appear on a second page, tap or click the Delete Table button (TABLE TOOLS LAYOUT tab | Rows & Columns group), and then tap or click Delete Rows on the Delete Table menu.
3. Below the MEMBERSHIPS heading, select the text, EXPERIENCE, and then type `COMMUNITY SERVICE` as the new section heading.
4. In the Community Service section of the resume, replace the text that begins, TEACHERS' ASSISTANT…, with the text `VICTIM ADVOCATE - GROVE COMMUNITY SERVICES` as the title and organization name.
5. Replace the month of August with the text `October` as the month.
6. Select the indented paragraph of text and then type this text (Figure 5–33 on the next page): `Volunteer eight hours a week at the call center. Offer emotional support and provide information on victims' legal rights and the criminal justice process.`

Figure 5–33

To Save an Existing Document with the Same File Name

You have made several modifications to the document since you last saved it. Thus, you should save it again. The following step saves the document again.

 Tap or click the Save button on the Quick Access Toolbar to overwrite the previously saved file.

To Customize Theme Fonts

1 CREATE DOCUMENT FROM TEMPLATE | 2 MODIFY & FORMAT TEMPLATE | 3 SAVE DOCUMENT IN OTHER FORMATS
4 MAKE DOCUMENT AVAILABLE ONLINE | 5 CREATE WEBPAGE FROM WORD DOCUMENT | 6 FORMAT WEBPAGE

Recall that a font set defines one font for headings in a document and another font for body text. This resume currently uses the Calibri-Cambria font set, which specifies the Calibri font for the headings and the Cambria font for body text. The resume in this chapter creates a customized font set (theme font). ***Why?*** *You want the headings to use the Berlin Sans FB Demi font and the body text to use the Bookman Old Style font.* The following steps create a customized theme font set with the name Resume Text.

- Display the DESIGN tab.
- Tap or click the Theme Fonts button (DESIGN tab | Document Formatting group) to display the Theme Fonts gallery (Figure 5–34).

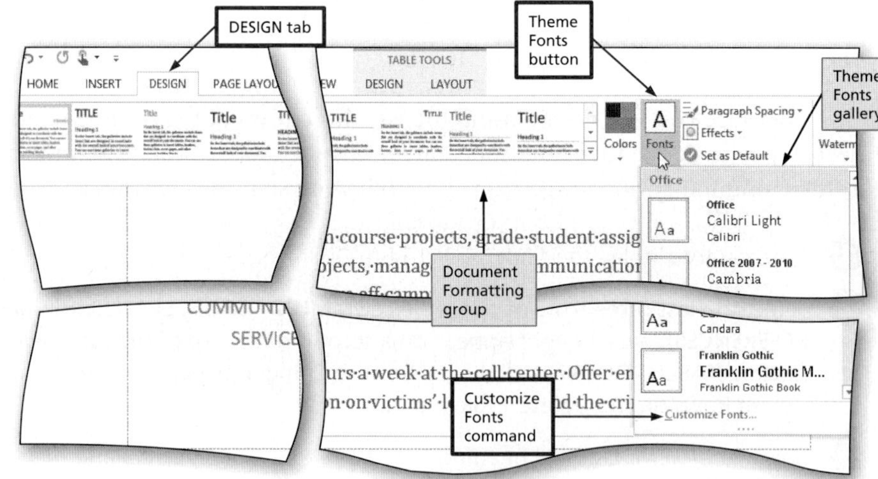

Figure 5–34

- Tap or click Customize Fonts in the Theme Fonts gallery to display the Create New Theme Fonts dialog box.
- Tap or click the Heading font arrow (Create New Theme Fonts dialog box); scroll to and then tap or click 'Berlin Sans FB Demi' (or a similar font).
- Tap or click the Body font arrow; scroll to and then tap or click Bookman Old Style (or a similar font).
- Type **`Resume Text`** in the Name text box as the name for the new theme font (Figure 5–35).

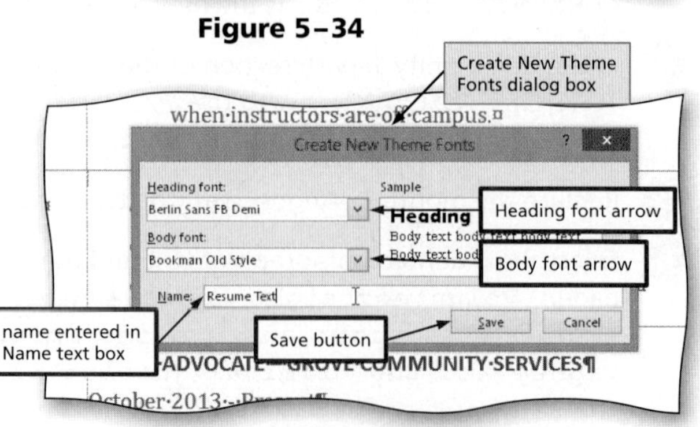

Figure 5–35

- Tap or click the Save button (Create New Theme Fonts dialog box) to create the customized theme font with the entered name (Resume Text, in this case) and apply the new heading fonts to the current document (Figure 5–36).

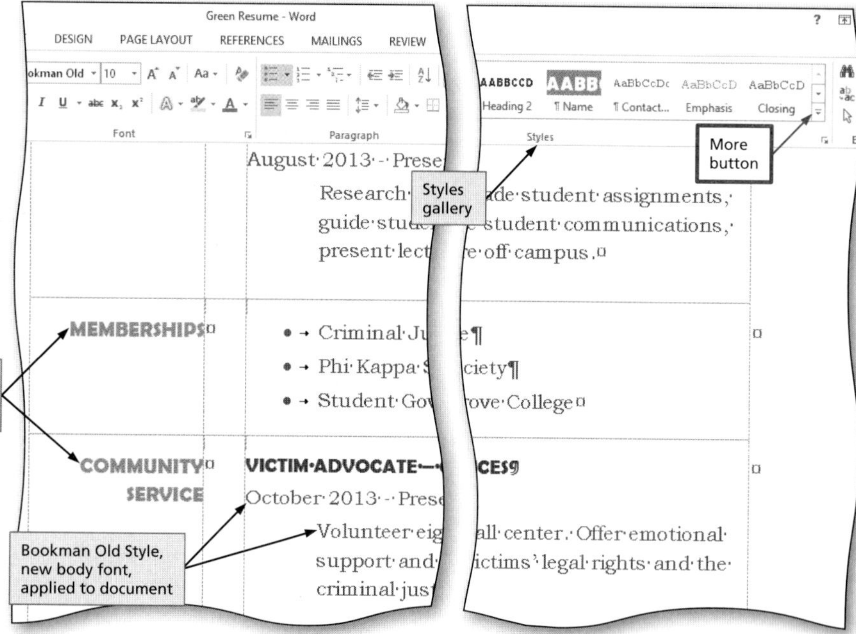

Figure 5–36

To Create a Style

1 CREATE DOCUMENT FROM TEMPLATE | 2 MODIFY & FORMAT TEMPLATE | 3 SAVE DOCUMENT IN OTHER FORMATS
4 MAKE DOCUMENT AVAILABLE ONLINE | 5 CREATE WEBPAGE FROM WORD DOCUMENT | 6 FORMAT WEBPAGE

Recall that a style is a predefined style that appears in the Styles gallery. You have used styles in the Styles gallery to apply defined formats to text and have updated existing styles. You also can create your own styles.

The next task in this project is to create a style for the section headings in the resume. ***Why?*** *To illustrate creating a style, you will increase the font size of a section heading and save the new format as a style. Then, you will apply the newly defined style to the remaining section headings.* The following steps format text and then create a style based on the formats in the selected paragraph.

1

- Position the insertion point in the MEMBERSHIPS heading, display the HOME tab, and then tap or click the 'Increase Font Size' button (HOME tab | Font group).
- Tap or click the More button (shown in Figure 5–36) in the Styles gallery (HOME tab | Styles group) to expand the gallery (Figure 5–37).

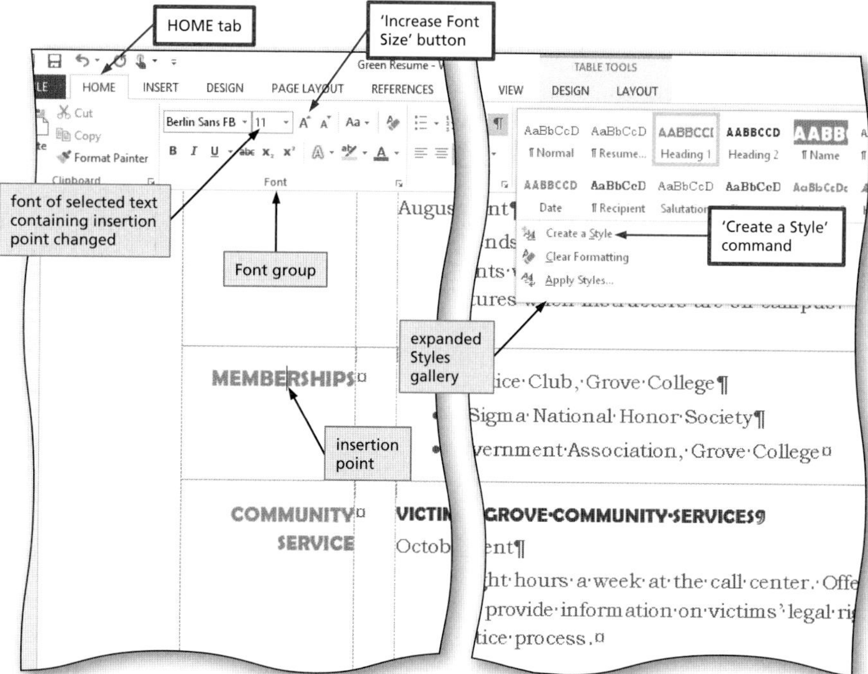

Figure 5–37

2

- Tap or click 'Create a Style' in the Styles gallery to display the Create New Style from Formatting dialog box.
- Type `Resume Headings` in the Name text box (Create New Style from Formatting dialog box) (Figure 5–38).

3

- Tap or click the OK button to create the new style and add it to the Styles gallery.

Q&A How can I see the style just created?
If the style name does not appear in the in-ribbon Styles gallery, tap or click the More button in the Styles gallery (HOME tab | Styles group) to display the expanded Styles gallery.

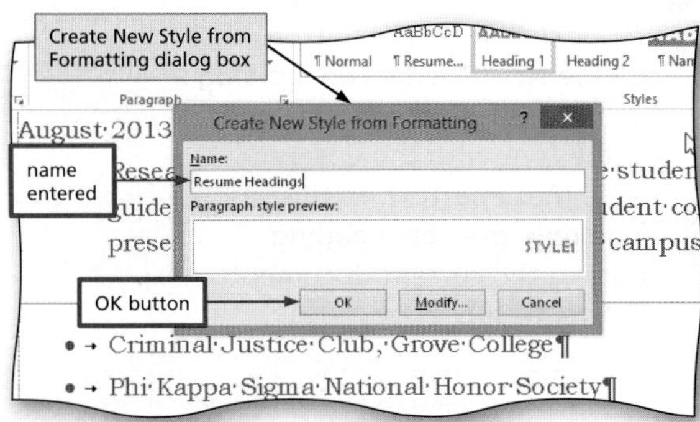

Figure 5–38

To Apply a Style

The next step is to apply the style just created to the lines other section headings in the resume. The following step applies a style.

1 One at a time, position the insertion point in the remaining section headings (OBJECTIVE, EDUCATION, EXPERIENCE, and COMMUNITY SERVICE) and then tap or click Resume Headings in the Styles gallery.

To Reveal Formatting

Sometimes, you want to know what formats were applied to certain text items in a document. ***Why?*** *For example, you may wonder what font, font size, font color, and other effects were applied to the degree and job titles in the resume.* To display formatting applied to text, use the Reveal Formatting task pane. The following steps open and then close the Reveal Formatting task pane.

1

- Position the insertion point in the text for which you want to reveal formatting (in this case, the degree name in the Education section).
- Press SHIFT+F1 to open the Reveal Formatting task pane, which shows formatting applied to the location of the insertion point in (Figure 5–39).

 **Experiment**

- Tap or click the Font collapse button to hide the Font formats. Tap or click the Font expand button to redisplay the Font formats.

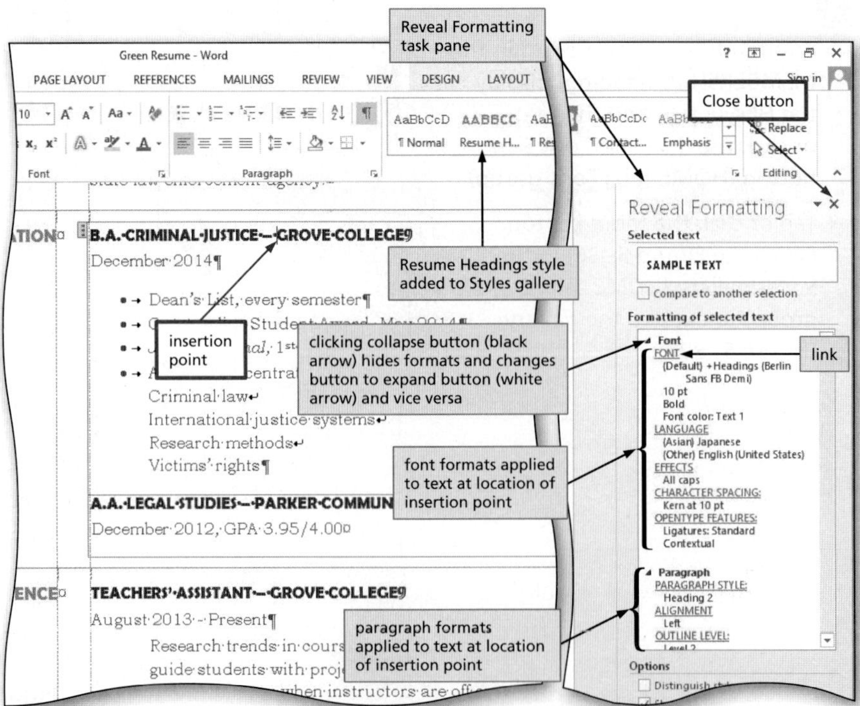

Figure 5–39

Q&A Why do some of the formats in the Reveal Formatting task pane appear as links?
Tapping or clicking a link in the Reveal Formatting task pane displays an associated dialog box, allowing you to change the format of the current text. For example, tapping or clicking the Font link in the Reveal Formatting task pane would display the Font dialog box. If you made changes in the Font dialog box and then tapped or clicked the OK button, Word would change the format of the current text.

- Close the Reveal Formatting task pane by tapping or clicking its Close button.

To Modify a Style Using the Styles Dialog Box

1 CREATE DOCUMENT FROM TEMPLATE | 2 MODIFY & FORMAT TEMPLATE | 3 SAVE DOCUMENT IN OTHER FORMATS
4 MAKE DOCUMENT AVAILABLE ONLINE | 5 CREATE WEBPAGE FROM WORD DOCUMENT | 6 FORMAT WEBPAGE

The next step is to modify the Heading 2 style. ***Why?*** *The degree and job names in the resume currently have a different font than the other text in the resume. You prefer that all text in the resume use the same font.* Thus, the following steps modify a style.

1

- Press and hold or right-click the style name to modify in the Styles gallery (Heading 2, in this case) to display a shortcut menu (Figure 5–40).

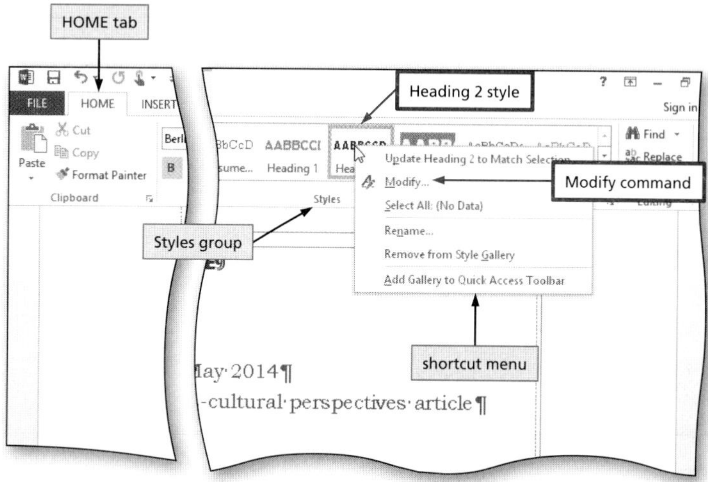

Figure 5–40

- Tap or click Modify on the shortcut menu to display the Modify Style dialog box.
- Tap or click the Font arrow (Modify Style dialog box) and then tap or click Bookman Old Style in the Font gallery to change the font of the current style.
- Place a check mark in the Automatically update check box so that any future changes you make to the style in the document will update the current style automatically (Figure 5–41).

Q&A What is the purpose of the Format button in the Modify Style dialog box?
If the formatting you wish to change for the style is not available in the Modify Style dialog box, you can tap or click the Format button and then select the desired command after you tap or click the Format button to display a dialog box that contains additional formatting options.

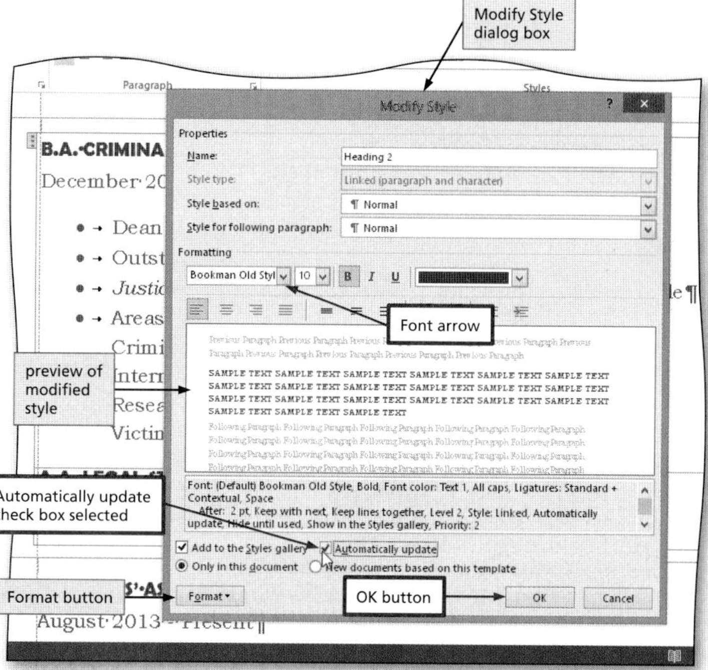

Figure 5–41

• Tap or click the OK button to close the dialog box and apply the style changes to the paragraphs in the document (Figure 5–42).

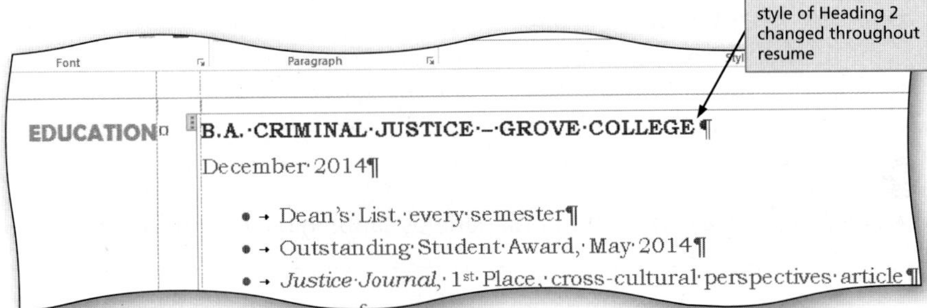

Figure 5–42

Other Ways

1. Tap or click Styles Dialog Box Launcher (HOME tab | Styles group), tap or click arrow to right of style to modify, tap or click Modify on menu, change settings (Modify Style dialog box), tap or click OK button
2. Tap or click Styles Dialog Box Launcher, tap or click Manage Styles button, scroll to style and then select it (Manage Styles dialog box), tap or click Modify button, change settings (Modify Style dialog box), tap or click OK button in each dialog box

To Save and Print the Document

The resume is complete. Thus, you should save it again. The following steps save the document again and print it.

1. Tap or click the Save button on the Quick Access Toolbar to overwrite the previously saved file.
2. Print the resume (shown in Figure 5–1 on page WD 275).

Break Point: If you wish to take a break, this is a good place to do so. You can exit Word now. To resume at a later time, run Word, open the file called Green Resume, and continue following the steps from this location forward.

Sharing a Document with Others

You may want to share Word documents with others electronically, such as via email, USB flash drive, or cloud storage. To ensure that others can read and/or open the files successfully, Word provides a variety of formats and tools to assist with sharing documents. This section uses the Green Resume created in this chapter to present a variety of these formats and tools.

To Insert a Building Block Using the Building Blocks Organizer

1 CREATE DOCUMENT FROM TEMPLATE | 2 MODIFY & FORMAT TEMPLATE | **3 SAVE DOCUMENT IN OTHER FORMATS**
4 MAKE DOCUMENT AVAILABLE ONLINE | 5 CREATE WEBPAGE FROM WORD DOCUMENT | 6 FORMAT WEBPAGE

You would like to place the text, DRAFT, as a watermark on the resume before you share it, so that others are aware you might be making additional changes to the document. In an earlier chapter, you inserted a watermark using the ribbon. Because watermarks are a type of building block, you also can use the Building Blocks Organizer to insert them.

A **building block** is a reusable formatted object that is stored in a gallery. Examples of building blocks include cover pages, headers, footers, page numbers, watermarks, and text boxes. You can see a list of every available building block in the **Building Blocks Organizer**. From the Building Blocks Organizer, you can sort building blocks, change their properties, or insert them in a document.

The next steps sort the Building Blocks Organizer by gallery and then insert the Draft 1 building block in the document. ***Why?*** *Sorting the building blocks by gallery makes it easier to locate them.*

- Display the VIEW tab. Tap or click the One Page button (VIEW tab | Zoom group) to display the resume in its entirety in the document window.
- Display the INSERT tab.
- Tap or click the 'Explore Quick Parts' button (INSERT tab | Text group) to display the Explore Quick Parts menu (Figure 5–43).

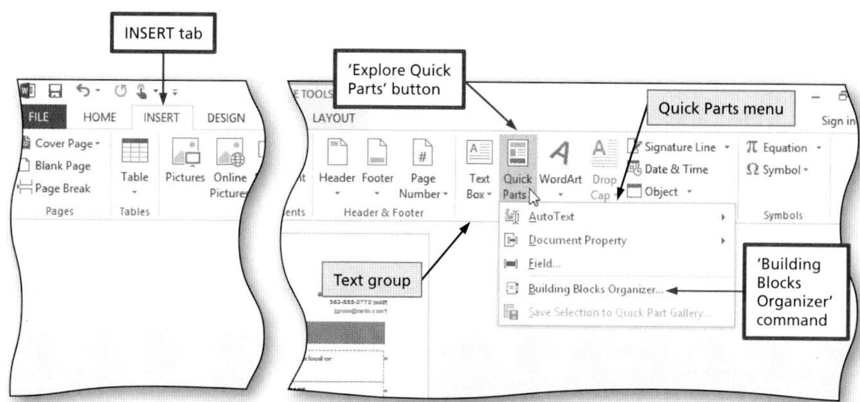

Figure 5–43

- Tap or click 'Building Blocks Organizer' on the Explore Quick Parts menu to display the Building Blocks Organizer dialog box.

- Drag the scroll bars in the Building Blocks Organizer so that you can look at all the columns and rows in the dialog box.
- Tap or click the Gallery heading (Building Blocks Organizer dialog box) in the building blocks list to sort the building blocks by gallery (Figure 5–44).

- Tap or click various names in the building blocks list and notice that a preview of the selected building block appears in the dialog box.

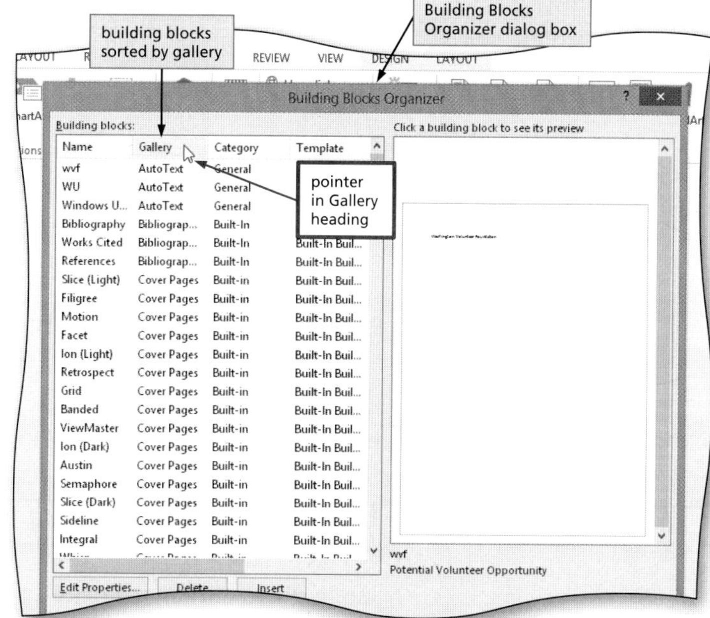

Figure 5–44

- Scroll through the building blocks list to the Watermarks group in the Gallery column and then tap or click DRAFT 1 to select this building block (Figure 5–45).

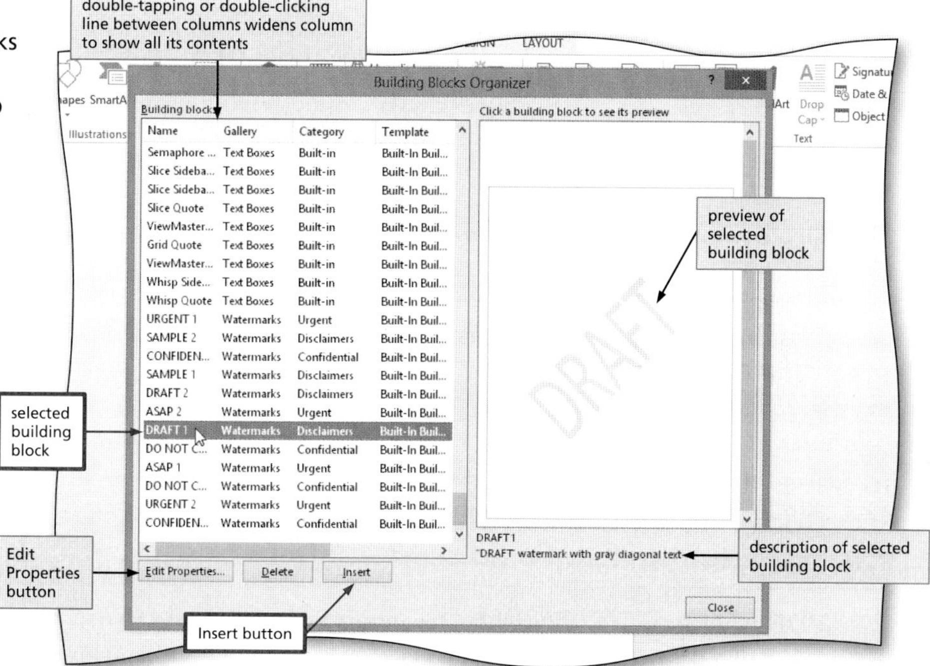

Figure 5–45

- Tap or click the Insert button to insert the selected building block in the document (Figure 5–46).

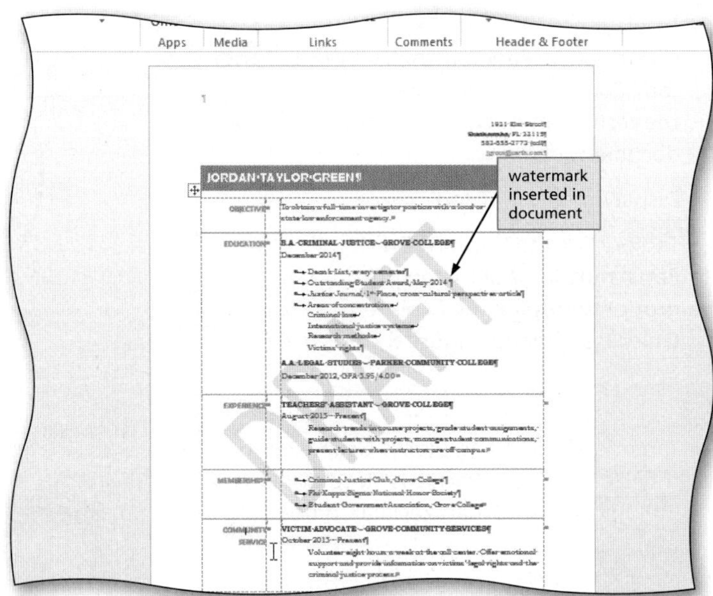

Figure 5–46

To Edit Properties of Building Block Elements

Properties of a building block include its name, gallery, category, description, location where it is saved, and how it is inserted in the document. If you wanted to change any of these building block properties for a particular building block, you would perform these steps.

1. Tap or click the 'Explore Quick Parts' button (INSERT tab | Text group) to display the Explore Quick Parts menu.
2. Tap or click 'Building Blocks Organizer' on the Explore Quick Parts menu to display the Building Blocks Organizer dialog box.
3. Select the building block you wish to edit (Building Blocks Organizer dialog box).
4. Tap or click the Edit Properties button (shown in Figure 5–45) to display the Modify Building Block dialog box.
5. Edit any property (Modify Building Block dialog box) and then tap or click the OK button. Close the Building Blocks Organizer dialog box.

CONSIDER THIS

Will a document look the same on another computer when you share it electronically?

When sharing a Word document with others, you cannot be certain that it will look or print the same on their computers or mobile devices as on your computer or mobile device. For example, the document may wordwrap text differently on others' computers and mobile devices. If others do not need to edit the document, that is, they need only to view and/or print the document, you could save the file in a format that allows others to view the document as you see it. Two popular such formats are PDF and XPS.

To Save a Word Document as a PDF Document and View the PDF Document in Adobe Reader

1 CREATE DOCUMENT FROM TEMPLATE | 2 MODIFY & FORMAT TEMPLATE | **3 SAVE DOCUMENT IN OTHER FORMATS**
4 MAKE DOCUMENT AVAILABLE ONLINE | 5 CREATE WEBPAGE FROM WORD DOCUMENT | 6 FORMAT WEBPAGE

PDF, which stands for Portable Document Format, is a file format created by Adobe Systems that shows all elements of a printed document as an electronic image. Users can view a PDF document without the software that created the original document. Thus, the PDF format enables users to share documents with others easily.

To view, navigate, and print a PDF file, you use an application called **Adobe Reader**, which can be downloaded free from Adobe's website.

When you save a Word document as a PDF document, the original Word document remains intact; that is, Word creates a copy of the file in the PDF format. The following steps save the Green Resume Word document as a PDF document and then open the Green Resume PDF document in Adobe Reader. ***Why?*** *You want to share the resume with others but want to ensure it looks the same on their computer or mobile device as it does on yours.*

- Open the Backstage view and then tap or click the Export tab in the Backstage view to display the Export gallery.
- If necessary, tap or click 'Create PDF/XPS Document' in the Export gallery to display information about creating PDF/XPS documents in the right pane (Figure 5–47).

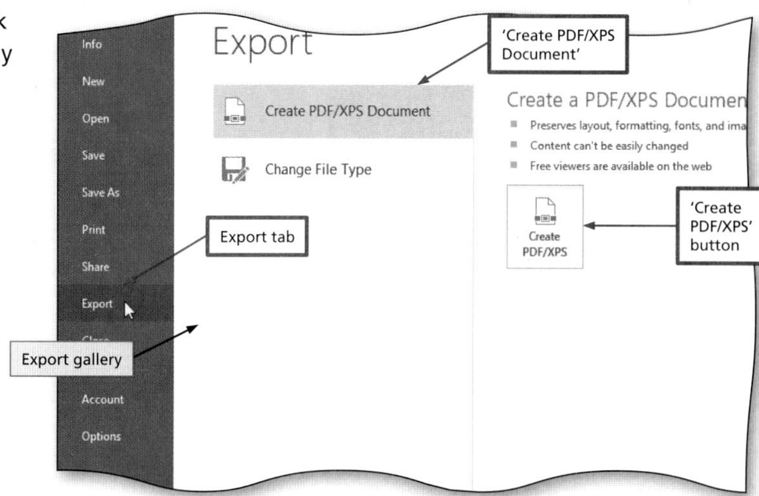

Figure 5–47

2

- Tap or click the 'Create PDF/XPS' button in the right pane to display the Publish as PDF or XPS dialog box.
- Navigate to the desired save location (in this case, the Word folder in the CIS 101 folder [or your class folder] on the USB flash drive) (Publish as PDF or XPS dialog box).

Q&A Can the file name be the same for the Word document and the PDF document?
Yes. The file names can be the same because the file types are different: one is a Word document and the other is a PDF document.

- If necessary, tap or click the 'Save as type' arrow and then tap or click PDF.
- If necessary, place a check mark in the 'Open file after publishing' check box so that Word will display the resulting PDF document in Adobe Reader (Figure 5–48).

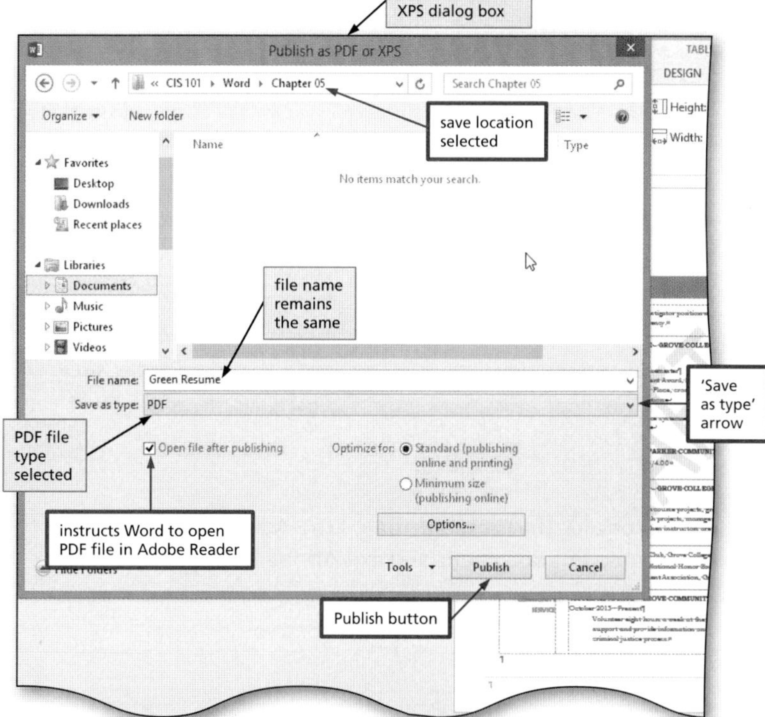

Figure 5–48

Q&A Why is my 'Open file after publishing' check box dimmed?
You do not have Adobe Reader installed on your computer. Use a search engine, such as Google, to search for the text, get adobe reader. Then, tap or click the link in the search results to download Adobe Reader and follow the on-screen instructions to install the program. After installing Adobe Reader, repeat these steps.

- Tap or click the Publish button to create the PDF document from the Word document and then, because the check box was selected, open the resulting PDF document in Adobe Reader.
- If necessary, tap or click the Maximize button in the Adobe Reader window to maximize the window (Figure 5–49).

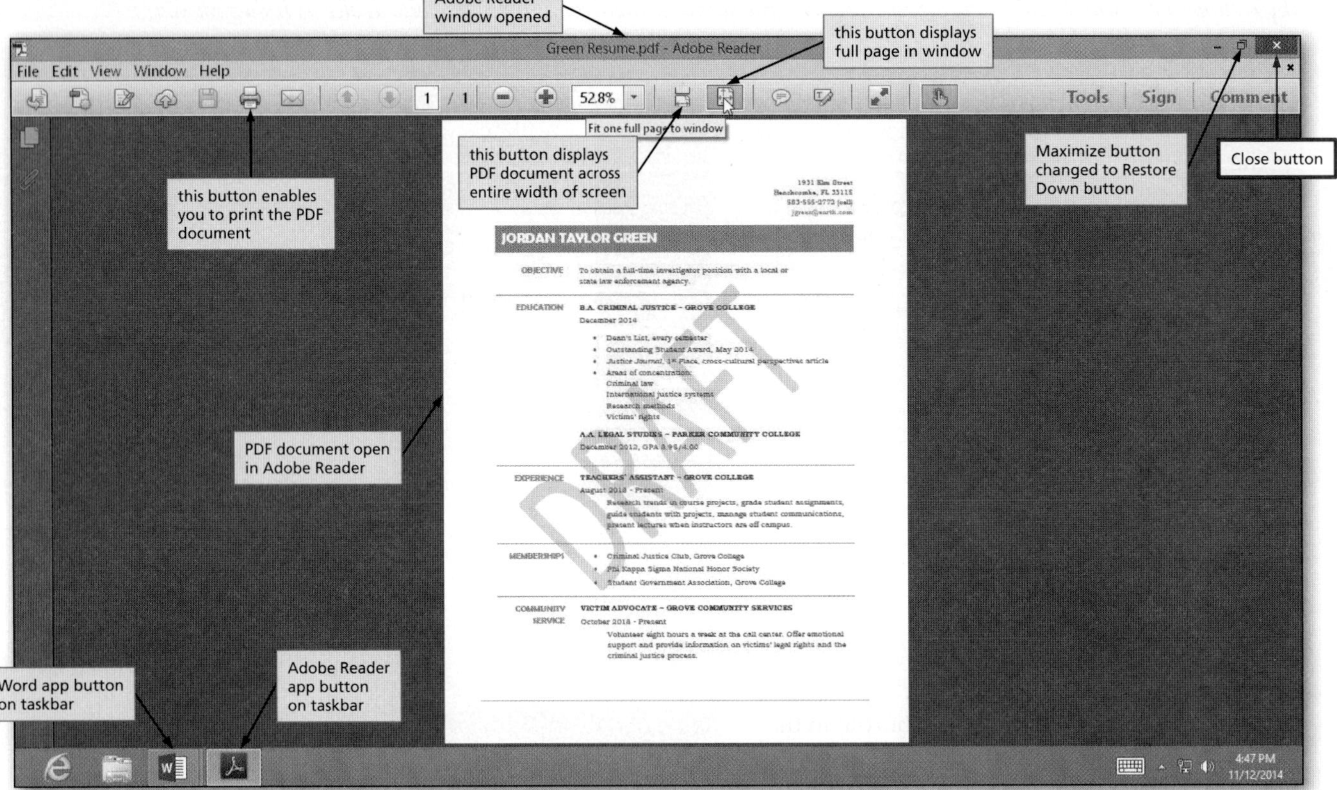

Figure 5–49

Q&A Do I have to display the resulting PDF document in Adobe Reader?
No. If you do not want to display the document in Adobe Reader, you would not place a check mark in the 'Open file after publishing' check box in the Publish as PDF or XPS dialog box (shown in Figure 5-48 on the previous page).

Is the Green Resume Word document still open?
Yes. Word still is running with the Green Resume document opened.

What if a blank screen appears instead of Adobe Reader?
You may not have Adobe reader installed. Press the Start key on the keyboard to redisplay the Start screen and then navigate back to Word.

- Tap or click the Close button on the Adobe Reader title bar to close the Green Resume.pdf document and exit Adobe Reader.

Q&A Can I edit documents in Adobe Reader?
No, you need Adobe Acrobat or some other program that enables editing of PDF files.

Other Ways

1. Press F12, tap or click 'Save as type' box arrow (Save As dialog box), select PDF in list, tap or click Save button

To Open a PDF Document from Word

1 CREATE DOCUMENT FROM TEMPLATE | 2 MODIFY & FORMAT TEMPLATE | **3 SAVE DOCUMENT IN OTHER FORMATS**
4 MAKE DOCUMENT AVAILABLE ONLINE | 5 CREATE WEBPAGE FROM WORD DOCUMENT | 6 FORMAT WEBPAGE

When you use Word to open a PDF file, Word converts it to an editable document. ***Why?*** *You may want to change the contents of a PDF file.* The editable PDF document that Word creates from the PDF document may appear slightly different from the PDF due to the conversion process. To illustrate this feature, the next steps open the PDF document just saved.

1

- Open the Backstage view and then tap or click the Open tab in the Backstage view to display the Open gallery.
- Tap or click Computer, SkyDrive, or another location in the left pane that references the location of the saved PDF file, tap or click the Browse button, and then navigate to the location of the PDF file to be opened (in this case, the Word folder in the CIS 101 folder).
- If necessary, tap or click the File Types arrow to display a list of file types that can be opened by Word (Figure 5–50).

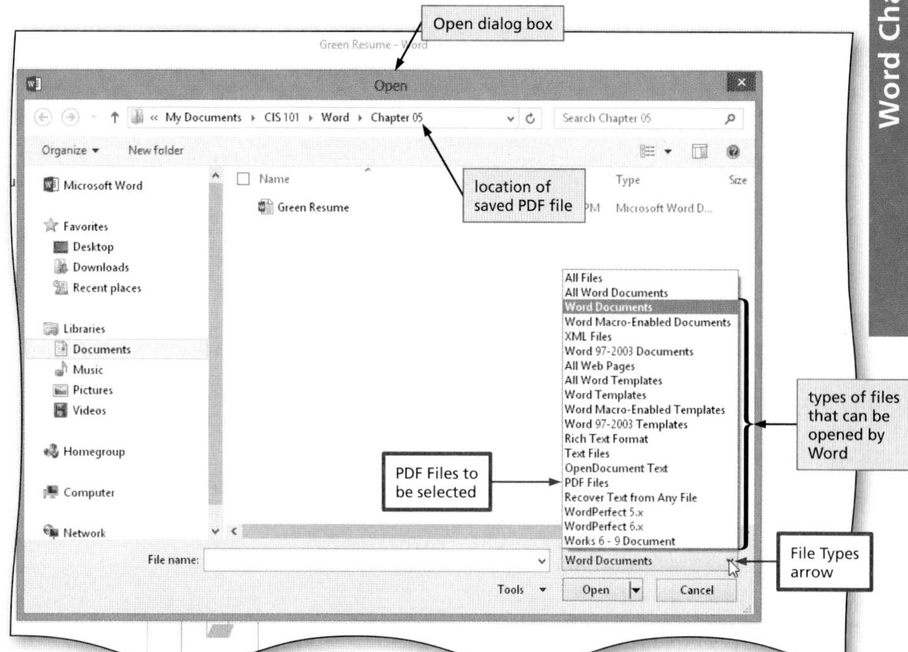

Figure 5–50

Q&A Why does the PDF file already appear in my list?
If the file type is All Word Documents, Word displays all file types that it can open in the file list.

- Tap or click PDF Files in the File Types list, so that Word displays PDF file names in the dialog box.
- Tap or click Green Resume to select the PDF file to be opened (Figure 5–51).

- Tap or click the Open button (Open dialog box) to open the selected file and display the opened document in the Word window.
- If Word displays a dialog box indicating it will begin converting the document, tap or click its OK button.

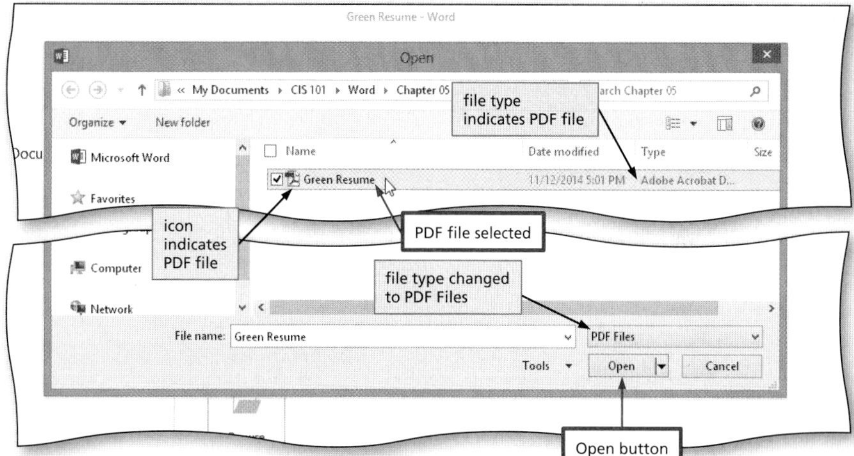

Figure 5–51

- If necessary, click the Print Layout button on the status bar to switch to print layout view.

Experiment

- Scroll through the PDF that Word converted, noticing any differences between it and the original resume created in this chapter.
- Close the Word window and do not save this converted PDF document.

To Save a Word Document as an XPS Document

XPS, which stands for XML Paper Specification, is a file format created by Microsoft that shows all elements of a printed document as an electronic image. As with the PDF format, users can view an XPS document without the software that created the original document. Thus, the XPS format also enables users to share documents with others easily. Windows includes an XPS Viewer, which enables you to view, navigate, and print XPS files.

When you save a Word document as an XPS document, the original Word document remains intact; that is, Word creates a copy of the file in the XPS format. If you wanted to save a Word document as an XPS document, you would perform the following steps.

1. Open the Backstage view and then tap or click the Export tab in the Backstage view to display the Export gallery.
2. Tap or click 'Create PDF/XPS Document' in the Export gallery to display information about PDF/XPS documents in the right pane and then tap or click the 'Create PDF/XPS' button to display the Publish as PDF or XPS dialog box.

or

1. Press F12 to display the Save As dialog box.
2. If necessary, navigate to the desired save location.
3. If necessary, tap or click the 'Save as type' arrow and then tap or click XPS Document.
4. Tap or click the Publish or Save button to create the XPS document from the Word document and then, if the 'Open file after publishing' check box was selected, open the resulting XPS document in the XPS Viewer.

Q&A What if I do not have an XPS Viewer?
The document will open in a browser window.

5. If necessary, exit the XPS Viewer.

BTW
Q&As
For a complete list of the Q&As found in many of the step-by-step sequences in this book, visit the Q&A resource on the Student Companion Site located on www.cengagebrain.com. For detailed instructions about accessing available resources, visit www.cengage.com/ct/studentdownload or contact your instructor for information about accessing the required files.

To Run the Compatibility Checker

1 CREATE DOCUMENT FROM TEMPLATE | 2 MODIFY & FORMAT TEMPLATE | **3 SAVE DOCUMENT IN OTHER FORMATS**
4 MAKE DOCUMENT AVAILABLE ONLINE | 5 CREATE WEBPAGE FROM WORD DOCUMENT | 6 FORMAT WEBPAGE

Word 2013 enables you to determine if a document is compatible (will work with) with earlier versions of Microsoft Word. ***Why?*** *If you would like to save a document, such as your resume, in the Word 97-2003 format so that it can be opened by users with earlier versions of Microsoft Word, you want to ensure that all of its elements (such as building blocks, content controls, and graphics) are compatible with earlier versions of Word.* The following steps run the compatibility checker.

- Open the Backstage view and then, if necessary, tap or click the Info tab in the Backstage view to display the Info gallery.
- Tap or click the 'Check for Issues' button in the Info gallery to display the Check for Issues menu (Figure 5–52).

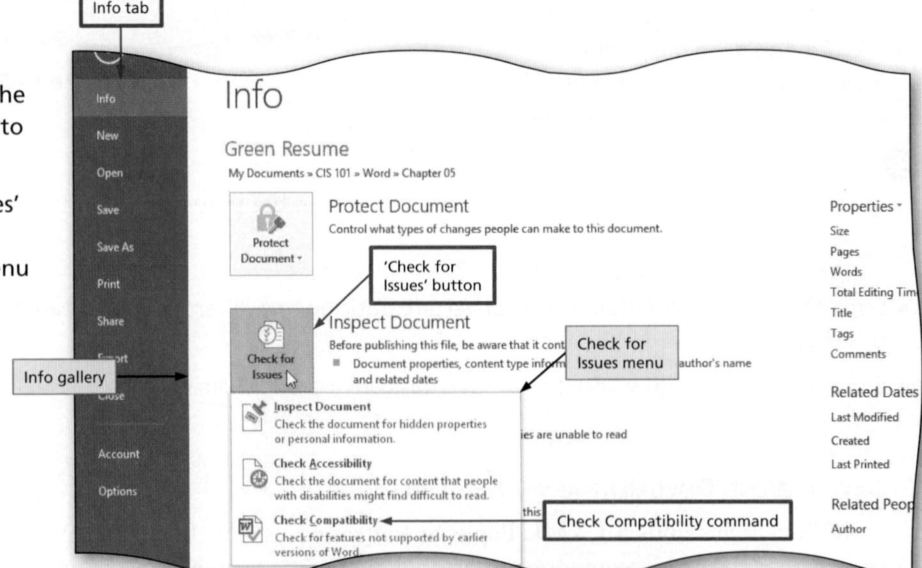

Figure 5–52

- Tap or click Check Compatibility on the Check for Issues menu to display the Microsoft Word Compatibility Checker dialog box, which shows any content that may not be supported by earlier versions of Word (Figure 5–53).

- Tap or click the OK button (Microsoft Word Compatibility Checker dialog box) to close the dialog box.

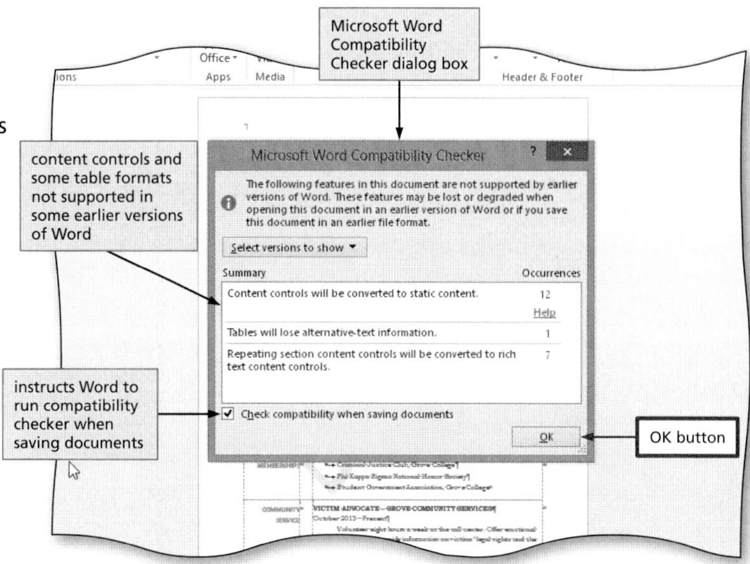

Figure 5–53

To Save a Word 2013 Document in an Earlier Word Format

1 CREATE DOCUMENT FROM TEMPLATE | 2 MODIFY & FORMAT TEMPLATE | **3 SAVE DOCUMENT IN OTHER FORMATS**
4 MAKE DOCUMENT AVAILABLE ONLINE | 5 CREATE WEBPAGE FROM WORD DOCUMENT | 6 FORMAT WEBPAGE

If you send a document created in Word 2013 to users who have a version of Word earlier than Word 2007, they will not be able to open the Word 2013 document. ***Why?*** *Word 2013 saves documents in a format that is not backward compatible with versions earlier than Word 2007. Word 2013 documents have a file type of .docx, and versions prior to Word 2007 have a .doc file type.* To ensure that all Word users can open your Word 2013 document, you should save the document in a Word 97-2003 format. The following steps save the Word 2013 format of the Green Resume document in the Word 97-2003 format.

1

- Open the Backstage view and then tap or click the Export tab in the Backstage view to display the Export gallery.
- Tap or click 'Change File Type' in the Export gallery to display information in the right pane about various Word file types.
- Tap or click 'Word 97-2003' in the right pane to specify the new file type (Figure 5–54).

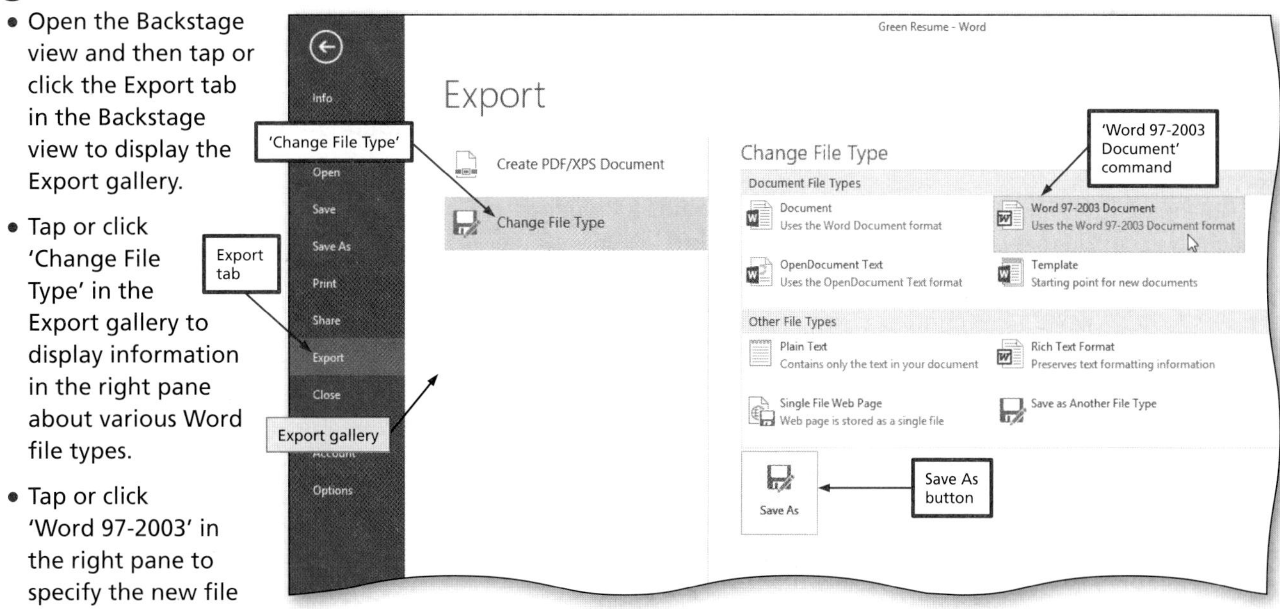

Figure 5–54

2

- Tap or click the Save As button in the right pane to display the Save As dialog box.
- If necessary, navigate to the desired save location (in this case, the Word folder in the CIS 101 folder [or your class folder]) (Save As dialog box) (Figure 5–55).

Q&A Can the file name be the same for the Word 2013 document and the Word 97-2003 document?

Yes. The file names can be the same because the file types are different: one is a Word document with a .docx extension, and the other is a Word document with a .doc extension. The next section discusses file types and extensions.

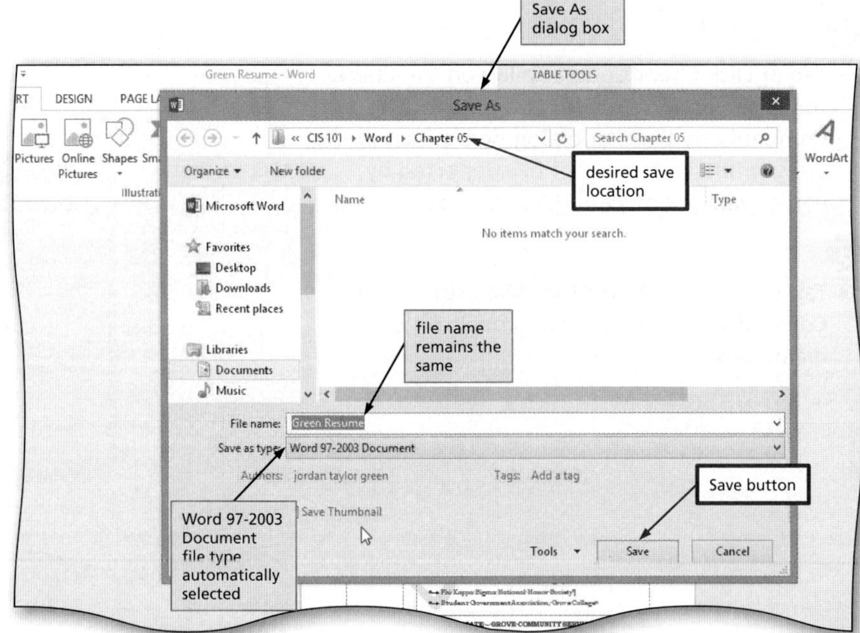

Figure 5–55

3

- Tap or click the Save button, which may display the Microsoft Word Compatibility Checker dialog box before saving the document (Figure 5–56).

Q&A My screen did not display the Microsoft Word Compatibility Checker dialog box. Why not?

If the 'Check compatibility when saving documents' check box is not selected (as shown in Figure 5–53 on the previous page), Word will not check compatibility when saving a document.

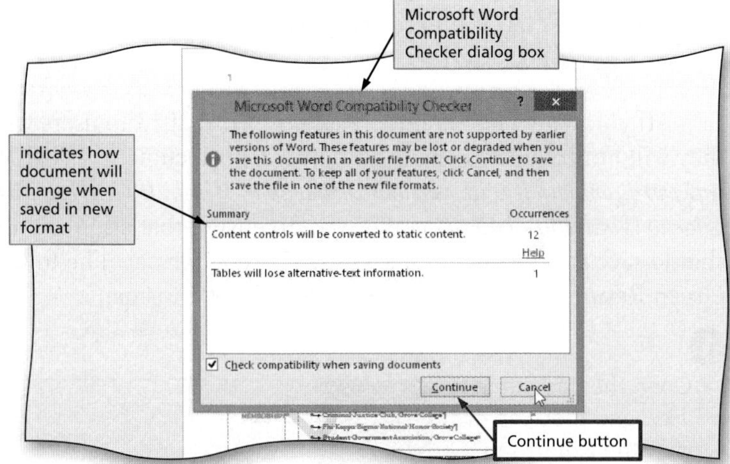

Figure 5–56

4

- If the Microsoft Word Compatibility Checker dialog box is displayed, tap or click its Continue button to save the document on the selected drive with the current file name in the specified format (Figure 5–57).

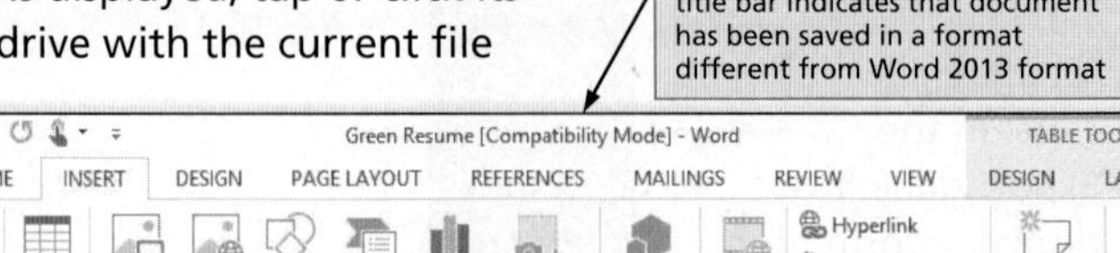

Q&A Is the Word 2013 format of the Green Resume document still open?

No. Word closed the original document (the Word 2013 format of the Green Resume).

Can I use Word 2013 to open a document created in an earlier version of Word?

Yes, but you may notice that the appearance of the document differs when opened in Word 2013.

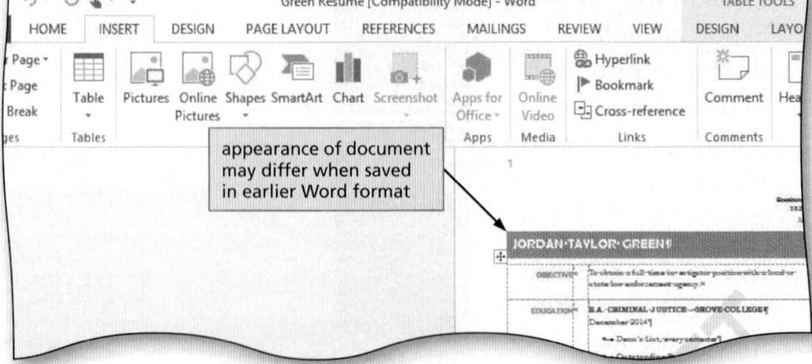

Figure 5–57

Other Ways

1. Press F12, tap or click 'Save as type' arrow (Save As dialog box), select 'Word 97-2003 Document' in list, tap or click Save button

File Types

When saving documents in Word, you can select from a variety of file types that can be opened in Word using the Export gallery in the Backstage view (shown in Figure 5–54 on page WD 307) or by tapping or clicking the 'Save as type' arrow in the Save As dialog box. To save in these varied formats (Table 5–1), you follow the same basic steps as just illustrated.

Table 5–1 File Types

File Type	File Extension	File Explorer Image	Description
OpenDocument Text	.odt		Format used by other word processing programs, such as Google Docs and OpenOffice.org
PDF	.pdf		Portable Document Format, which can be opened in Adobe Reader
Plain Text	.txt		Format where all or most formatting is removed from the document
Rich Text Format	.rtf		Format designed to ensure file can be opened and read in many programs; some formatting may be lost to ensure compatibility
Single File Web Page	.mht		HTML (Hypertext Markup Language) format that can be opened in a browser; all elements of the webpage are saved in a single file
Web Page	.htm		HTML format that can be opened in a browser; various elements of the webpage, such as graphics, saved in separate files and folders
Word 97-2003 Document	.doc		Format used for documents created in versions of Word from Word 97 to Word 2003
Word 97-2003 Template	.dot		Format used for templates created in versions of Word from Word 97 and Word 2003
Word Document	.docx		Format used for Word 2013, Word 2010, or Word 2007 documents
Word Template	.dotx		Format used for Word 2010 or Word 2007 templates
XPS	.xps		XML (Extensible Markup Language) Paper Specification, which can be opened in the XPS Viewer

To Save a Word 2013 Document as a Different File Type

To save a Word 2013 document as a different file type, you would follow these steps.

1. Open the Backstage view and then tap or click the Export tab in the Backstage view to display the Export gallery.
2. Tap or click 'Change File Type' in the Export gallery to display information in the right pane about various file types that can be opened in Word.
3. Tap or click the desired file type in the right pane to display the Save As dialog box.
4. Navigate to the desired save location (in this case, the Word folder in the CIS 101 folder [or your class folder]) (Save As dialog box) and then tap or click the Save button in the dialog box.
5. If the Microsoft Word Compatibility Checker dialog box appears and you agree with the changes that will be made to the document, tap or click the Continue button (Microsoft Word Compatibility Checker dialog box) to save the document on the selected drive with the current file name in the specified format.

To Close a Document

You are finished with the Word 97-2003 format of the Green Resume. Thus, the next step is to close this document. The following steps close a document.

1. Open the Backstage view.
2. Tap or click Close in the Backstage view to close the current open document.

To Open a Recent Document

You would like to reopen the Word 2013 format of the Green Resume. Thus, the next step is to open this document. Because it recently was open, the following steps open a document from Recent Documents.

1. Open the Backstage view and then, if necessary, tap or click the Open tab in the Backstage view to display the Open gallery.
2. If necessary, tap or click Recent Documents in the Open gallery to display the list of recent documents.
3. To be sure you open the Word 2013 format of the Green Resume, if you are using a mouse, point to the file name and verify the file name is Green Resume.docx in the ScreenTip.
4. Tap or click the desired file name (in this case, Green Resume [the Word 2013 format]) in the list of recent documents in the Recent gallery to open the document in the Word document window.

BTW
Distributing a Document
Instead of printing and distributing a hard copy of a document, you can distribute the document electronically. Options include sending the document via email; posting it on cloud storage (such as SkyDrive) and sharing the file with others; posting it on a social networking site, blog, or other website; and sharing a link associated with an online location of the document. You also can create and share a PDF or XPS image of the document, so that users can view the file in Acrobat Reader or XPS Viewer instead of in Word.

To Save a File on SkyDrive

The steps on the next several pages require that you have a Microsoft account and an Internet connection. If you do not have a Microsoft account or an Internet connection, read these steps without performing them. The following steps save a file on SkyDrive so that you can share it online with others.

1. Open the Backstage view and then, if necessary, tap or click the Save As tab in the Backstage view to display the Save As gallery.
2. Tap or click SkyDrive to display SkyDrive saving options or a Sign In button, if you are not signed in already to your Microsoft account. If your screen displays a Sign In button, tap or click it and then follow the instructions to sign in to your account.
3. Tap or click your SkyDrive, if necessary, and then tap or click the Browse button to contact the SkyDrive server and then display the Save As dialog box.
4. Navigate to the desired save location on your SkyDrive and then tap or click the Save button (Save As dialog box) to save the file on SkyDrive.

To Invite Others to View or Edit a Document

1 CREATE DOCUMENT FROM TEMPLATE | 2 MODIFY & FORMAT TEMPLATE | 3 SAVE DOCUMENT IN OTHER FORMATS
4 MAKE DOCUMENT AVAILABLE ONLINE | **5 CREATE WEBPAGE FROM WORD DOCUMENT** | **6 FORMAT WEBPAGE**

If you have a SkyDrive account, you can share a Word document saved on your SkyDrive with others through email message invitations. ***Why?*** *Invited users can tap or click a link in an email message that displays a webpage enabling them to view or edit the document on SkyDrive.* The next steps invite a user to view the resume document. If you do not have a Microsoft account or an Internet connection, read these steps without performing them.

1

- Open the Backstage view and then tap or click the Share tab in the Backstage view to display the Share gallery.
- If necessary, tap or click Invite People in the Share gallery to display text boxes for entering email addresses and a message in the right pane.
- Type the email address(es) of the person(s) with whom you want to share the document, tap or click the box arrow so that you can specify Can view, and then type a message to the recipient(s) (Figure 5–58).

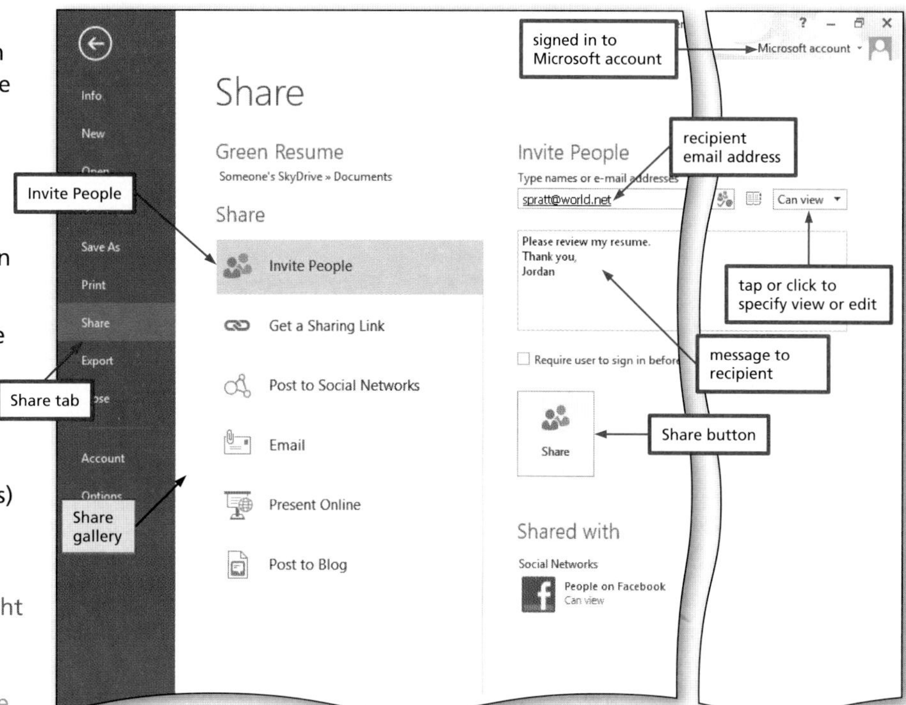

Figure 5–58

Q&A

Why does my screen display a 'Save To Cloud' button in the right pane?

The document has not been saved on SkyDrive and/or you are not signed in to your Microsoft account.

2

- Tap or click the Share button in the right pane to send the message along with a link to the document on SkyDrive to the listed recipients.

CONSIDER THIS

How does a recipient access the shared document?

The recipient receives an email message that indicates it contains a link to a shared document (Figure 5–59). When the recipient taps or clicks the link in the email message, the document opens in the Word Web App on SkyDrive (Figure 5–60 on the next page).

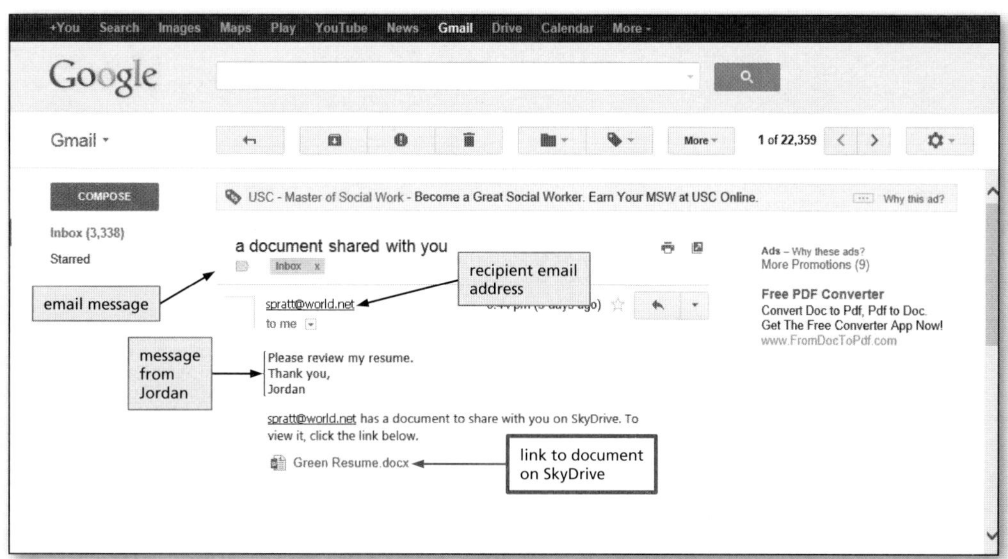

Figure 5–59

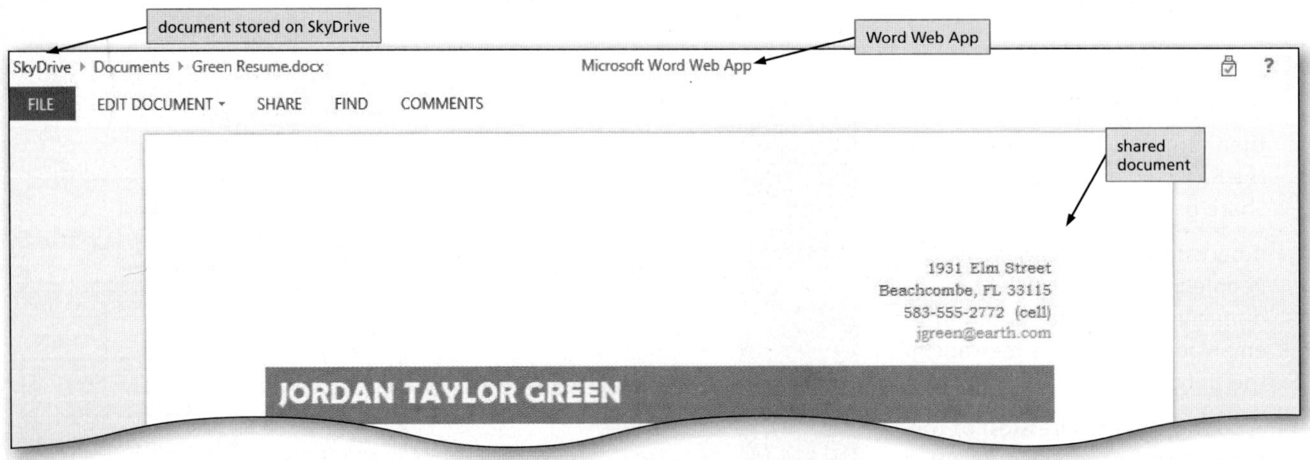

Figure 5–60

To Get a Sharing Link

1 CREATE DOCUMENT FROM TEMPLATE | 2 MODIFY & FORMAT TEMPLATE | 3 SAVE DOCUMENT IN OTHER FORMATS
4 MAKE DOCUMENT AVAILABLE ONLINE | **5 CREATE WEBPAGE FROM WORD DOCUMENT** | 6 FORMAT WEBPAGE

Why share a link? *Instead of inviting people to view or edit a document, you can create a link to the document's location on SkyDrive and then send others the link via an email message or text message, post it on a website, or communicate it via some other means.* The following steps get a sharing link. If you do not have a Microsoft account or an Internet connection, read these steps without performing them.

1

- If necessary, open the Backstage view and then tap or click the Share tab in the Backstage view to display the Share gallery.
- Tap or click 'Get a Sharing Link' in the Share gallery to display options for obtaining a link to a document on SkyDrive in the right pane (Figure 5–61).

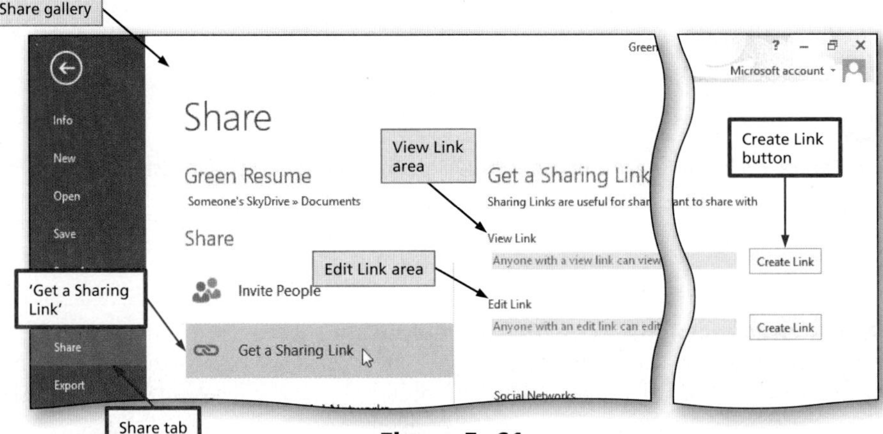

Figure 5–61

Q&A Why does my screen display a 'Save To Cloud' button in the right pane?
The document has not been saved on SkyDrive and/or you are not signed in to your Microsoft account.

- Tap or click the Create Link button in the View Link area in the right pane to create the link associated with the file on SkyDrive (Figure 5–62).

Green Resume - Word
Microsoft account
link created that enables others to view document on SkyDrive
Get a Sharing Link
Sharing Links are useful for sharing with large groups of people, or when you don't know the e-mail addresses of everyone you want to share with
View Link
https://skydrive.live.com/redir?page=view&resid=8218CE0C95F22EB5!113&authkey=!AGpgUVH7KHhXvK4
Disable Link
Edit Link
Anyone with an edit link can edit this document
Create Link button changes to Disable Link button, which you tap or click if you want to remove the link
Create Link

Figure 5–62

Q&A What do I do with the link?
You can copy and paste the link in an email or text message, on a webpage, or some other location.

What is the difference between a view link and an edit link?
A view link enables others to read the document but not modify it, while an edit link enables others to both view and edit the document.

To Post a Document to a Social Network

If you belong to an online social network such as Facebook, Twitter, or LinkedIn, and you have connected that social network service to your Microsoft account, you can post a document directly to your online social network. The following steps post the resume document to Facebook, which is connected to the Microsoft account. ***Why?*** *You want your Facebook friends to review your resume.* If you do not have a Microsoft account connected to an online social network or do not have an Internet connection, read these steps without performing them.

1

- If necessary, open the Backstage view and then tap or click the Share tab in the Backstage view to display the Share gallery.
- If necessary, tap or click 'Post to Social Networks' in the Share gallery to display online social networks connected to your Microsoft account, along with text boxes for a post, in the right pane.
- Type the post content (Figure 5–63).

Q&A Why does my screen display a 'Save To Cloud' button in the right pane? The document has not been saved on SkyDrive and/or you are not signed in to your Microsoft account.

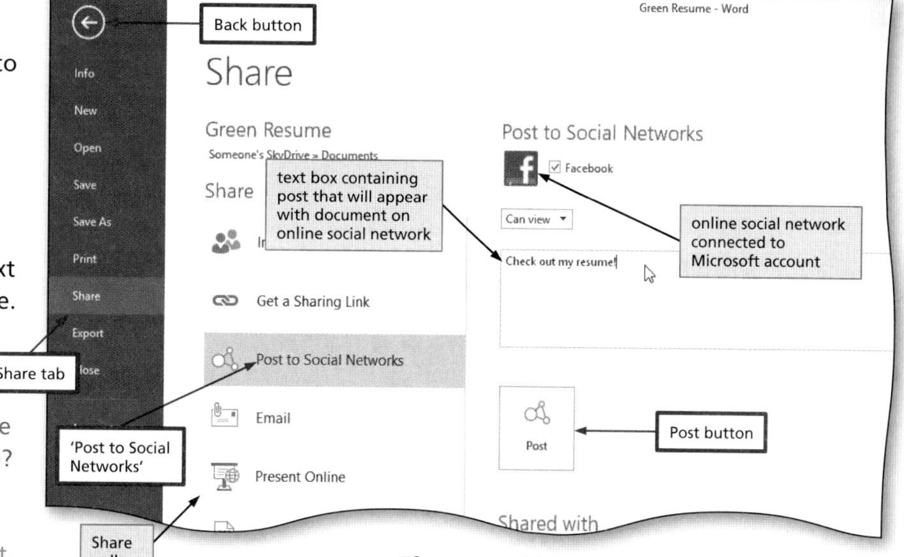

Figure 5–63

2

- Tap or click the Post button in the right pane to post the document on the social network(s) connected to your Microsoft account.

3

- If necessary, tap or click the Back button to return to the document window.

CONSIDER THIS

How do you see the resume post on Facebook?

Display your Facebook newsfeed to see the message and post (Figure 5–64).

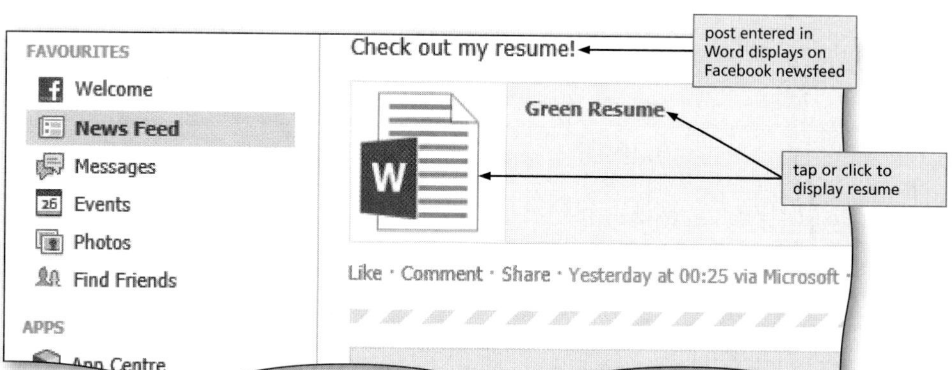

Figure 5–64

To Remove a Watermark

The following steps remove the DRAFT watermark from the resume in the document window, if it was saved with the document, because you now consider the document final and would like to distribute it to potential employers.

1. If necessary, open the Green Resume (Word 2013 format).
2. Display the DESIGN tab.
3. Tap or click the Watermark button (DESIGN tab | Page Background group) to display the Watermark gallery.
4. Tap or click Remove Watermark in the Watermark gallery to remove the watermark.
5. Save the document again with the same file name.

CONSIDER THIS

What file type should you use when emailing documents?

If you email a document, such as your resume, consider that the recipient, such as a potential employer, may not have the same software you used to create the resume and, thus, may not be able to open the file. As an alternative, you could save the file in a format, such as a PDF or XPS, that can be viewed with a reader program. Many job seekers also post their resumes on the web.

To Send a Document Using Email

1 CREATE DOCUMENT FROM TEMPLATE | 2 MODIFY & FORMAT TEMPLATE | 3 SAVE DOCUMENT IN OTHER FORMATS
4 MAKE DOCUMENT AVAILABLE ONLINE | **5 CREATE WEBPAGE FROM WORD DOCUMENT** | **6 FORMAT WEBPAGE**

In Word, you can include the current document as an attachment to an email message. An attachment is a file included with an email message. The following steps send the Green Resume as an email attachment, assuming you use Outlook as your default email program. ***Why?*** *When you attach an email document from within Word, it automatically uses the default email program, which is Outlook in this case.*

1

- Open the Backstage view and then tap or click the Share tab in the Backstage view to display the Share gallery.
- If necessary, tap or click Email in the Share gallery to display information in the right pane about various ways to send a document via email from within Word (Figure 5–65).

Q&A

Why is my list of share options in the Share gallery shorter?
You have not saved the document previously on SkyDrive.

What are the purpose of the 'Send as PDF' and 'Send as XPS' buttons?
Depending on which button you tap or click, Word converts the current document either to the PDF or XPS format and then attaches the PDF or XPS document to the email message.

Why is my 'Send a Link' button dimmed?
You have not saved the document previously on SkyDrive.

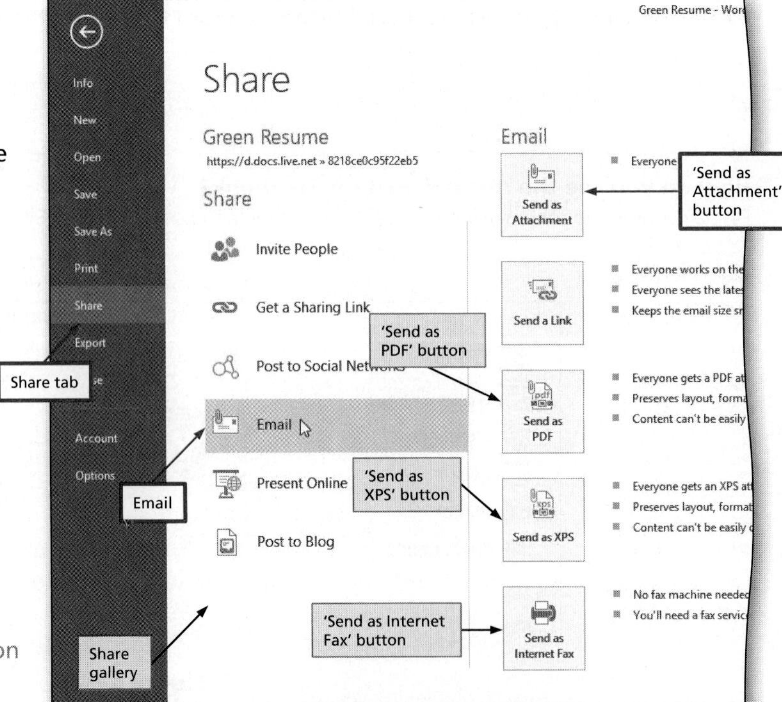

Figure 5–65

- Tap or click the 'Send as Attachment' button to start your default email program (Outlook, in this case), which automatically attaches the active Word document to the email message.
- Fill in the To text box with the recipient's email address.
- Fill in the message text (Figure 5–66).

3

- Tap or click the Send button to send the email message along with its attachment to the recipient named in the To text box and then close the email window.

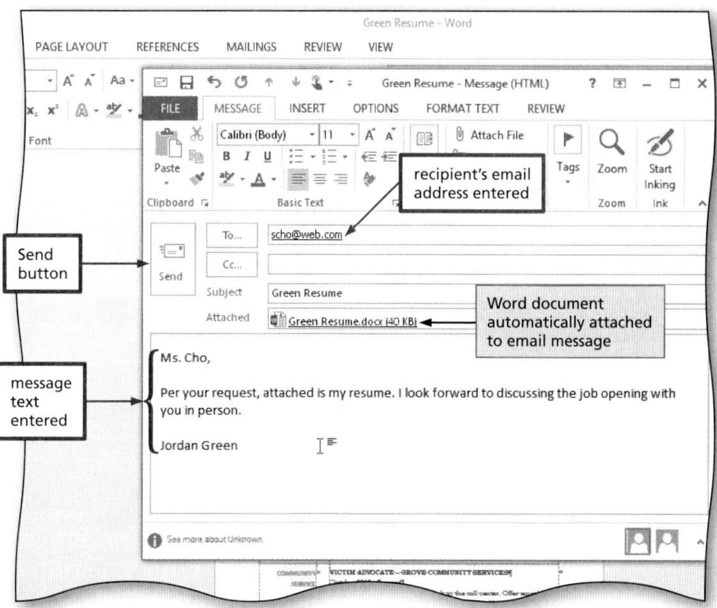

Figure 5–66

To Use the Document Inspector

Word includes a Document Inspector that checks a document for content you might not want to share with others, such as personal information. Before sharing a document with others, you may want to check for this type of content. If you wanted to use the Document Inspector, you would do the following:

1. Open the Backstage view and then tap or click the Info tab in the Backstage view to display the Info gallery.
2. Tap or click the 'Check for Issues' button in the Info gallery to display the Check for Issues menu.
3. Tap or click Inspect Document on the Check for Issues menu to display the Document Inspector dialog box.
4. Tap or click the Inspect button (Document Inspector dialog box) to instruct Word to inspect the document.
5. Review the results (Document Inspector dialog box) and then tap or click the Remove All button(s) for any item that you do not want to be saved with the document.
6. When finished removing information, tap or click the Close button to close the dialog box.

To Customize How Word Opens Email Attachments

When a user sends you an email message that contains a Word document as an attachment, Word may display the document in Read mode. This view is designed to increase the readability and legibility of an on-screen document. Read mode, however, does not represent how the document will look when it is printed. For this reason, many users prefer working in Print Layout view to read documents. To exit Read mode, press the ESC key.

BTW

Internet Fax

If you do not have a stand-alone fax machine, you can send and receive faxes in Word by tapping or clicking the 'Send as Internet Fax' button in the Backstage view (shown in Figure 5-65). To send or receive faxes using Word, you first must sign up with a fax service provider by tapping or clicking the OK button in the Microsoft Office dialog box that appears the first time you tap or click the 'Send as Internet Fax' button, which displays an Available Fax Services webpage. You also may need to install either the Windows Fax printer driver or Windows Fax Services component on your computer. When sending a fax, Word converts the document to an image file and attaches it to an email message where you enter the recipient's fax number, name, subject, and message for the cover sheet, and then tap or click a Send button to deliver the fax.

BTW
BTWs
For a complete list of the BTWs found in the margins of this book, visit the BTW resource on the Student Companion Site located on www.cengagebrain.com. For detailed instructions about accessing available resources, visit www.cengage.com/ct/studentdownload or contact your instructor for information about accessing the required files.

If you wanted to customize how Word opens email attachments, you would do the following.

1. Open the Backstage view and then tap or click Options in the Backstage view to display the Word Options dialog box.
2. If necessary, tap or click General in the left pane (Word Options dialog box).
3. If you want email attachments to open in Read mode, place a check mark in the 'Open e-mail attachments and other uneditable files in reading view' check box; otherwise, remove the check mark to open email attachments in Print Layout view.
4. Tap or click the OK button to close the dialog box.

To Sign Out of a Microsoft Account

You are finished working with the Green Resume on SkyDrive. If you are signed in to a Microsoft account and are using a public computer or otherwise wish to sign out of your Microsoft account, you should sign out of the account from the Account gallery in the Backstage view before exiting Word. Signing out of the account is the safest way to make sure that nobody else can access SkyDrive files or settings stored in your Microsoft account. The following steps sign out of a Microsoft account from Word.

1. If you wish to sign out of your Microsoft account, open the Backstage view and then tap or click the Account tab to display the Account gallery.

2. Tap or click the Sign out link, which displays the Remove Account dialog box. If a Can't remove Windows accounts dialog box appears instead of the Remove Account dialog box, tap or click the OK button and skip the remaining steps.

   Q&A Why does a Can't remove Windows accounts dialog box appear?
   If you signed in to Windows using your Microsoft account, then you also must sign out from Windows, rather than signing out from within the Word. When you are finished using Windows, be sure to sign out at that time.

3. Tap or click the Yes button (Remove Account dialog box) to sign out of your Microsoft account on this computer.

   Q&A Should I sign out of Windows after signing out of my Microsoft account?
   When you are finished using the computer, you should sign out of your account for maximum security.

4. Tap or click the Back button in the upper-left corner of the Backstage view to return to the document.

5. To be certain that the connection with SkyDrive no longer is active, exit Word, run Word, and then open the Green Resume document again.

Creating a Webpage from a Word Document

If you have created a document, such as a resume, using Word, you can save it in a format that can be opened by a browser, such as Internet Explorer. When you save a file as a webpage, Word converts the contents of the document into **HTML** (Hypertext Markup Language), which is a set of codes that browsers can interpret. Some of Word's formatting features are not supported by webpages. Thus, your webpage may look slightly different from the original Word document.

When saving a document as a webpage, Word provides you with three choices:

- The **single file Web page format** saves all of the components of the webpage in a single file that has a **.mht** extension. This format is particularly useful for sending documents via email in HTML format.
- The **Web Page format** saves some of the components of the webpage in a folder, separate from the webpage. This format is useful if you need access to the individual components, such as images, that make up the webpage.
- The **filtered Web Page format** saves the file in webpage format and then reduces the size of the file by removing specific Microsoft Office formats. This format is useful if you want to speed up the time it takes to download a webpage that contains graphics, video, audio, or animations.

The webpage created in this section uses the single file Web page format.

BTW

Saving as a Webpage
Because you might not have access to SkyDrive or a web server, the webpage you create in this feature is saved in your class folder rather than on SkyDrive or a web server.

To Save a Word Document as a Webpage

1 CREATE DOCUMENT FROM TEMPLATE | 2 MODIFY & FORMAT TEMPLATE | 3 SAVE DOCUMENT IN OTHER FORMATS
4 MAKE DOCUMENT AVAILABLE ONLINE | 5 CREATE WEBPAGE FROM WORD DOCUMENT | 6 FORMAT WEBPAGE

The following steps save the Green Resume created earlier in this chapter as a webpage. ***Why?** You intend to post your resume online.*

1

- With the Word 2013 format of the resume file open in the document window, open the Backstage view and then tap or click the Export tab in the Backstage view to display the Export gallery.
- Tap or click 'Change File Type' in the Export gallery to display information in the right pane about various file types that are supported by Word.
- Tap or click 'Single File Web Page' in the right pane to specify a new file type (Figure 5–67).

Q&A What if I wanted to save the document as a Web Page instead of a Single File Web Page?
You would tap or click 'Save as Another File Type' in the Change File Type area, tap or click the Save As button, tap or click the 'Save as type' arrow in the Save As dialog box, and then tap or click Web Page in the Save as type list.

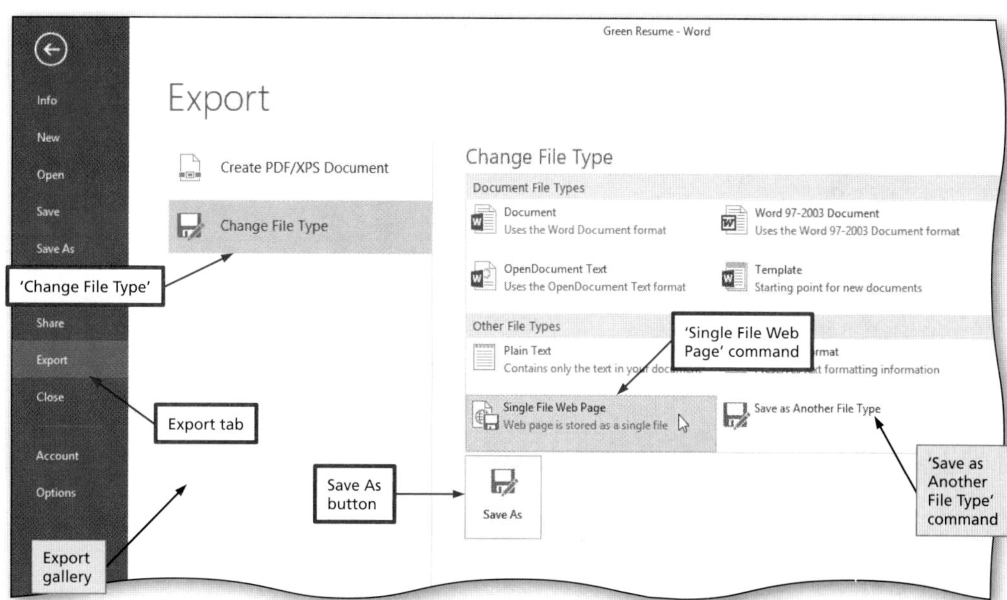

Figure 5–67

2

- Tap or click the Save As button in the right pane to display the Save As dialog box.
- If necessary, navigate to the desired save location (in this case, the Word folder in the CIS 101 folder [or your class folder]) (Save As dialog box).
- If necessary, type `Green Resume` in the File name box to change the file name.

- Tap or click the Change Title button to display the Enter Text dialog box.
- Type **`Green Resume`** in the Page title text box (Enter Text dialog box) (Figure 5–68).

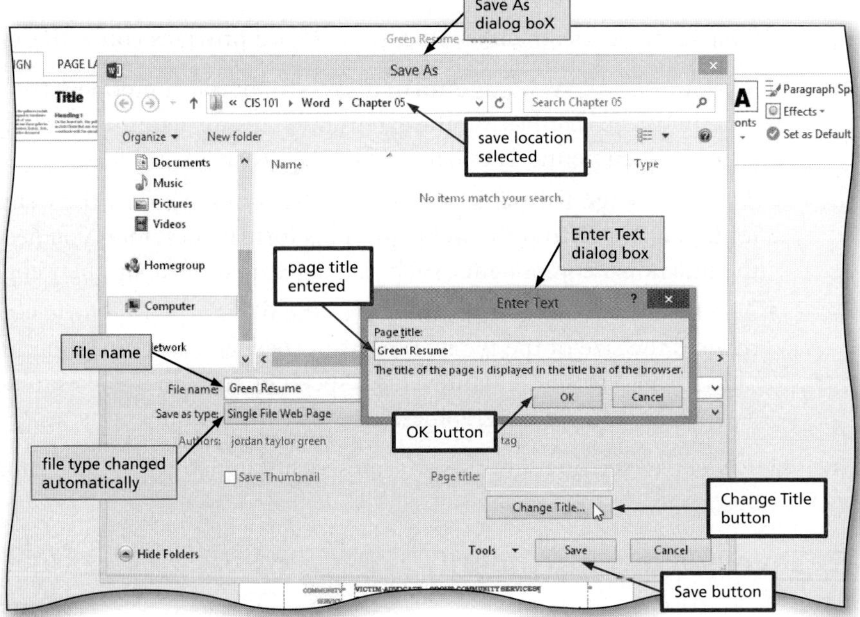

Figure 5–68

- Tap or click the OK button (Enter Text dialog box) to close the dialog box.
- Tap or click the Save button (Save As dialog box) to save the resume as a webpage and then display it in the document window in Web Layout view.
- If necessary, change the zoom to 100% (Figure 5–69).
- If the Microsoft Word Compatibility Checker dialog box appears, tap or click its Continue button.

Q&A

Can I switch to Web Layout view at any time by tapping or clicking the Web Layout button?
Yes.

Can I save the webpage to a web server?
If you have access to a web server, you can save the webpage from Word directly to the web server.

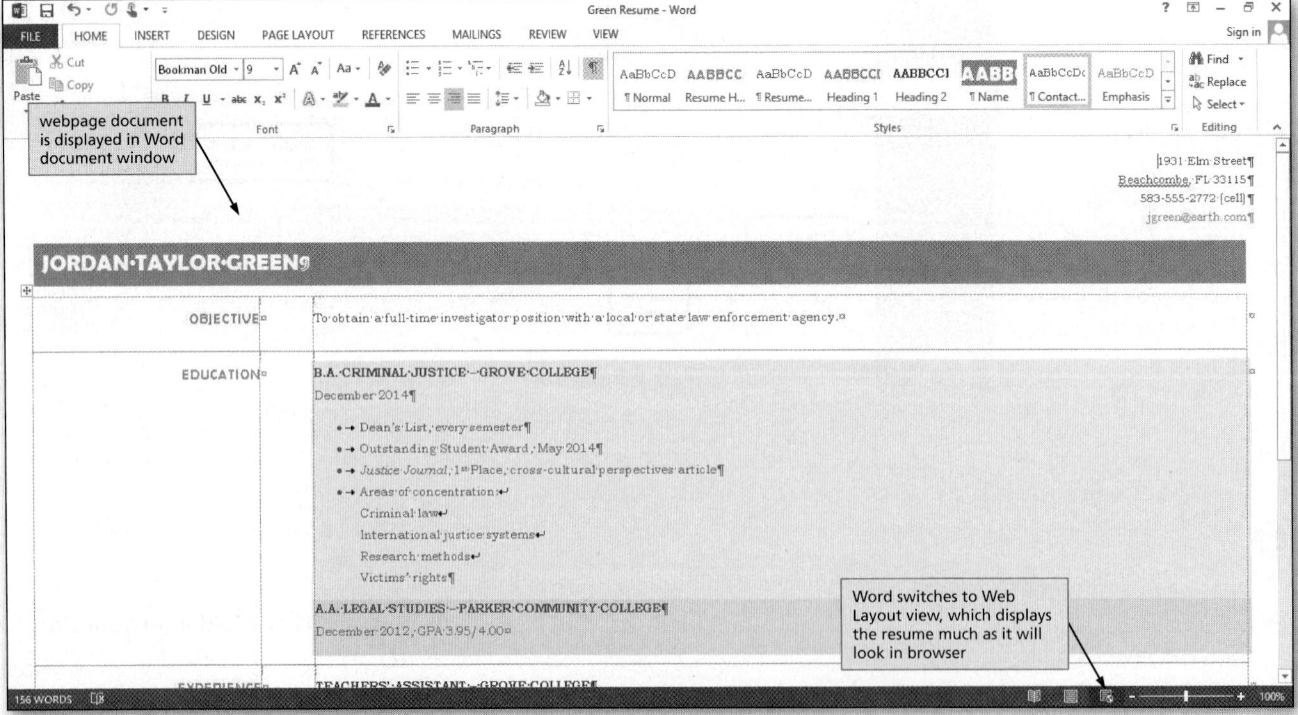

Figure 5–69

To Set a Default Save Location

If you wanted to change the default location that Word uses when it saves a document, you would do the following.

1. Open the Backstage view and then tap or click the Options in the Backstage view to display the Word Options dialog box.
2. Tap or click Save in the left pane (Word Options dialog box) to display options for saving documents in the right pane.
3. In the 'Default file location' text box, type the new desired save location.
4. Tap or click the OK button to close the dialog box.

BTW

Certification

The Microsoft Office Specialist (MOS) program provides an opportunity for you to obtain a valuable industry credential — proof that you have the Word 2013 skills required by employers. For more information, visit the Certification resource on the Student Companion Site located on www.cengagebrain.com. For detailed instructions about accessing available resources, visit www.cengage.com/ct/studentdownload or contact your instructor for information about accessing the required files.

To Delete a Content Control

Recall that the email address is a content control. In the next step, you will format the email address as a hyperlink. To do this, you first must delete the content control. The following steps delete a content control.

1. Tap or click the Email content control to select it.

2. Press and hold and then tap the 'Show Context Menu' button on the mini toolbar or right-click the selected content control to display a shortcut menu and then tap or click 'Remove Content Control' on the shortcut menu to delete the selected content control.

To Format Text as a Hyperlink

1 CREATE DOCUMENT FROM TEMPLATE | 2 MODIFY & FORMAT TEMPLATE | 3 SAVE DOCUMENT IN OTHER FORMATS
4 MAKE DOCUMENT AVAILABLE ONLINE | 5 CREATE WEBPAGE FROM WORD DOCUMENT | **6 FORMAT WEBPAGE**

The email address in the resume webpage should be formatted as a hyperlink. ***Why?*** *When webpage visitors tap or click the hyperlink-formatted email address, you want their email program to run automatically and open an email window with the email address already filled in.* The following steps format the email address as a hyperlink.

1

- Select the email address in the resume webpage (jgreen@earth.com, in this case).
- Display the INSERT tab.
- Tap or click the 'Add a Hyperlink' button (INSERT tab | Links group) to display the Insert Hyperlink dialog box (Figure 5–70).

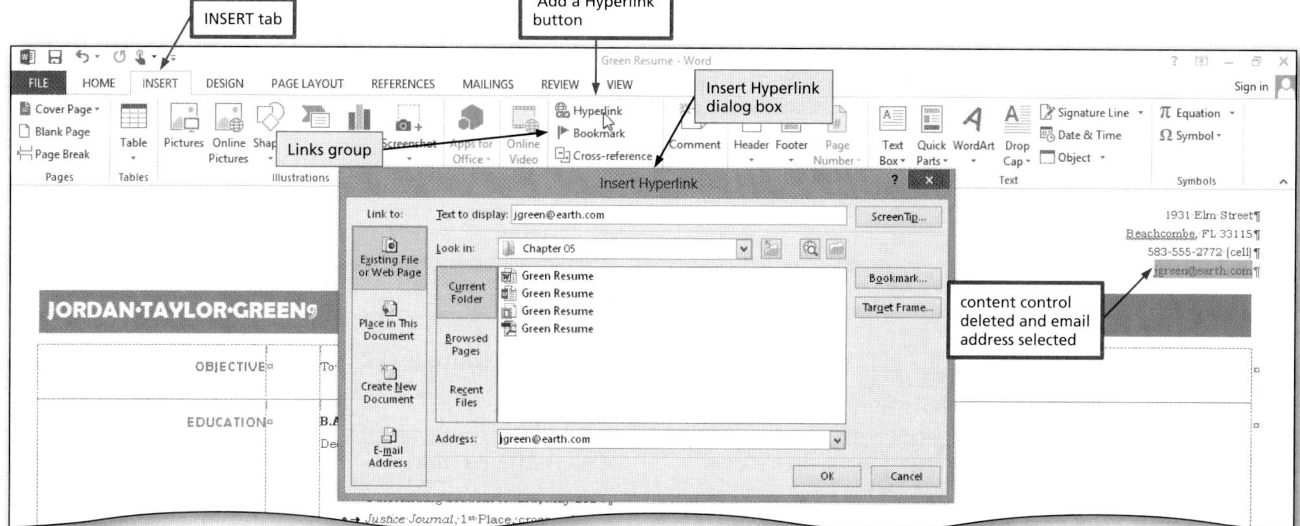

Figure 5–70

2

- Tap or click E-mail Address in the Link to bar (Insert Hyperlink dialog box) so that the dialog box displays email address settings instead of webpage settings.
- In the E-mail address text box, type **`jgreen@earth.com`** to specify the email address that the browser uses when a user taps or clicks the hyperlink.

Q&A Can I change the text that automatically appeared in the 'Text to display' text box?
Yes. Word assumes that the hyperlink text should be the same as the email address, so as soon as you enter the email address, the same text is entered in the 'Text to display' text box.

- If the email address in the 'Text to display' text box is preceded by the text, mailto:, delete this leading text because you want only the email address to appear in the document.
- Tap or click the ScreenTip button to display the Set Hyperlink ScreenTip dialog box.
- Type **`Send email message to Jordan Green.`** in the 'ScreenTip text' text box (Set Hyperlink ScreenTip dialog box) to specify the text that will be displayed when a user points to the hyperlink (Figure 5–71).

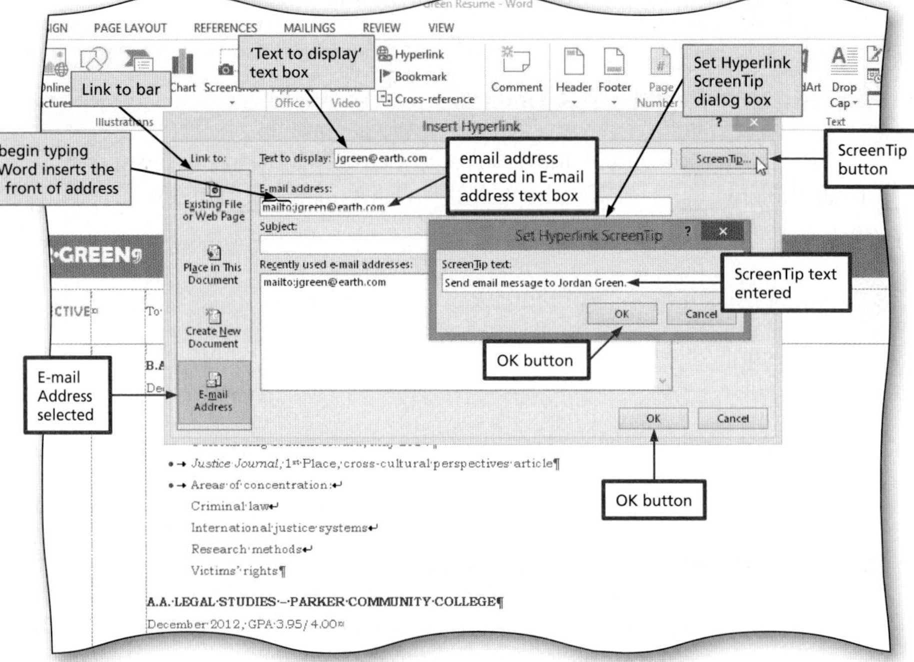

Figure 5–71

3

- Tap or click the OK button in each dialog box to format the email address as a hyperlink (Figure 5–72).

Q&A How do I know if the hyperlink works?
In Word, if you are using a mouse, you can test the hyperlink by holding down the CTRL key while clicking the hyperlink. In this case, CTRL+clicking the email address should open an email window.

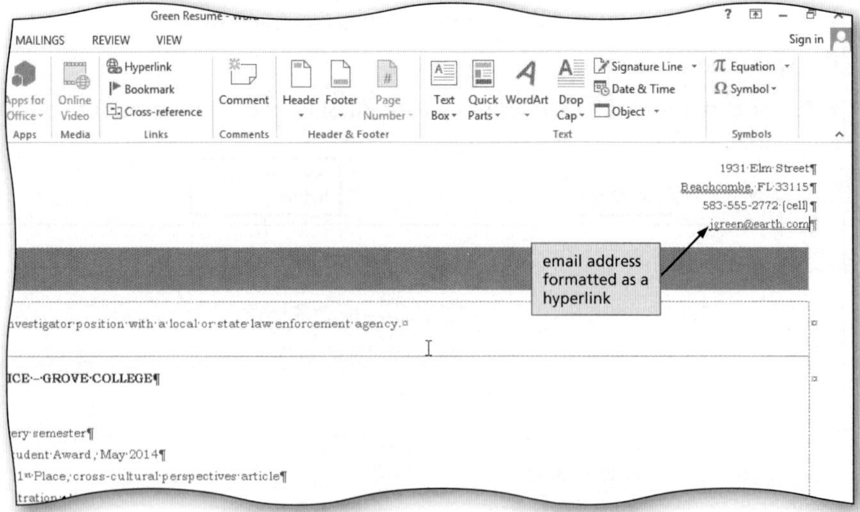

Figure 5–72

Other Ways

1. Tap 'Show Context Menu' on mini toolbar or right-click selected text, tap or click Hyperlink on shortcut menu
2. Select text, press CTRL+K

To Edit a Hyperlink

If you needed to edit a hyperlink, for example, to change its ScreenTip or its link, you would follow these steps.

1. Position the insertion point in the hyperlink.
2. Tap or click the 'Add a Hyperlink' button (INSERT tab | Links group) or press CTRL+K to display the Edit Hyperlink dialog box.

or

1. Tap 'Show Context Menu' on mini toolbar or right-click the hyperlink to display a shortcut menu.
2. Tap or click Edit Hyperlink on the shortcut menu to display the Edit Hyperlink dialog box.

BTW

Quick Reference

For a table that lists how to complete the tasks covered in this book using touch gestures, the mouse, ribbon, shortcut menu, and keyboard, see the Quick Reference Summary at the back of this book, or visit the Quick Reference resource on the Student Companion Site located on www.cengagebrain.com. For detailed instructions about accessing available resources, visit www.cengage.com/ct/studentdownload or contact your instructor for information about accessing the required files.

To Change the Style Set

1 CREATE DOCUMENT FROM TEMPLATE | 2 MODIFY & FORMAT TEMPLATE | 3 SAVE DOCUMENT IN OTHER FORMATS
4 MAKE DOCUMENT AVAILABLE ONLINE | 5 CREATE WEBPAGE FROM WORD DOCUMENT | **6 FORMAT WEBPAGE**

Word provides several built-in style sets to help you quickly change the look of an entire document. ***Why?*** *A style set contains formats for fonts and paragraphs.* The following steps change the style set to the Shaded style set.

1

- Display the DESIGN tab.
- Tap or click the More button (DESIGN tab | Document Formatting group) (shown in Figure 5–74 on the next page) to display the expanded Style Set gallery (Figure 5–73).

Experiment

- If you are using a mouse, point to various style sets in the Style Set gallery and watch the font and paragraph formatting change in the document window.

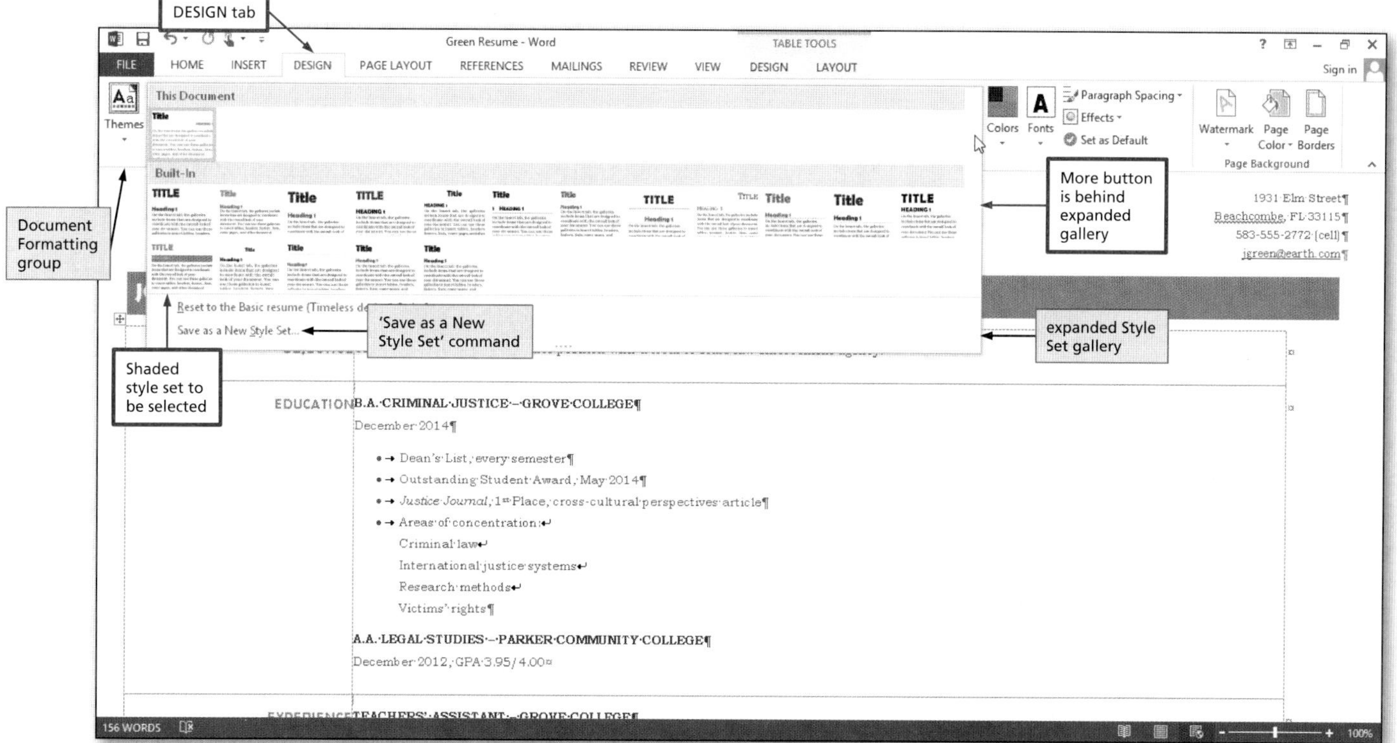

Figure 5–73

2

- Tap or click Shaded to change the style set to the selected style set (Figure 5–74).

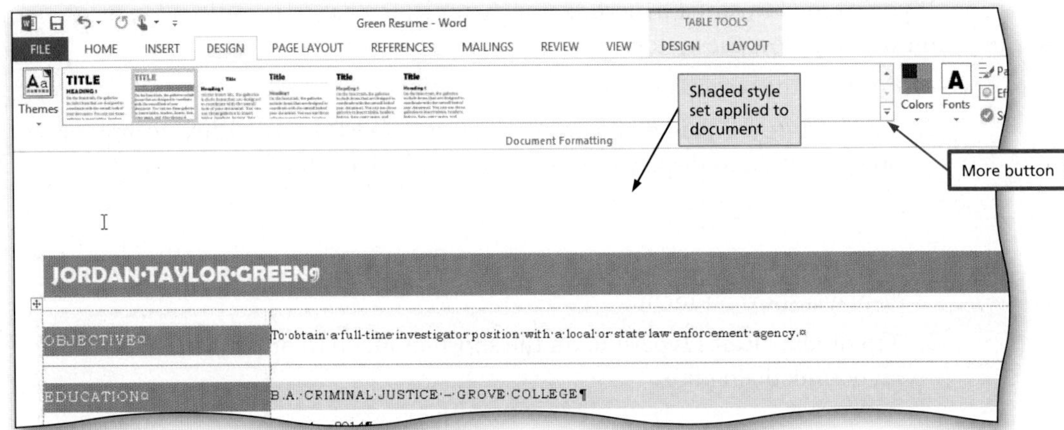

Figure 5–74

Q&A Can I create my own style sets?
Yes. Modify the fonts and other formats as desired, tap or click 'Save as a New Style Set' on the expanded Style Set gallery (shown in Figure 5–73 on the previous page), enter the name for the style set (Save as a New Style Set dialog box), and then click the Save button to create the custom style set. You then can access the custom style set through the Style Set gallery.

To Save an Existing Document and Exit Word

The webpage document now is complete. The following steps save the document again and exit Word.

1. Tap or click the Save button on the Quick Access Toolbar to overwrite the previously saved file.
2. Exit Word.

To Test a Webpage in a Browser

1 CREATE DOCUMENT FROM TEMPLATE | 2 MODIFY & FORMAT TEMPLATE | 3 SAVE DOCUMENT IN OTHER FORMATS
4 MAKE DOCUMENT AVAILABLE ONLINE | 5 CREATE WEBPAGE FROM WORD DOCUMENT | **6 FORMAT WEBPAGE**

After creating and saving a webpage, you will want to test it in at least one browser. ***Why?*** *You want to be sure it looks and works the way you intended.* The following steps use File Explorer to display the resume webpage in the Internet Explorer browser.

1

- Tap or click the File Explorer app button on the Windows taskbar to open the File Explorer window.
- Navigate to the desired save location (in this case, the Word folder in the CIS 101 folder [or your class folder]) (Figure 5–75).

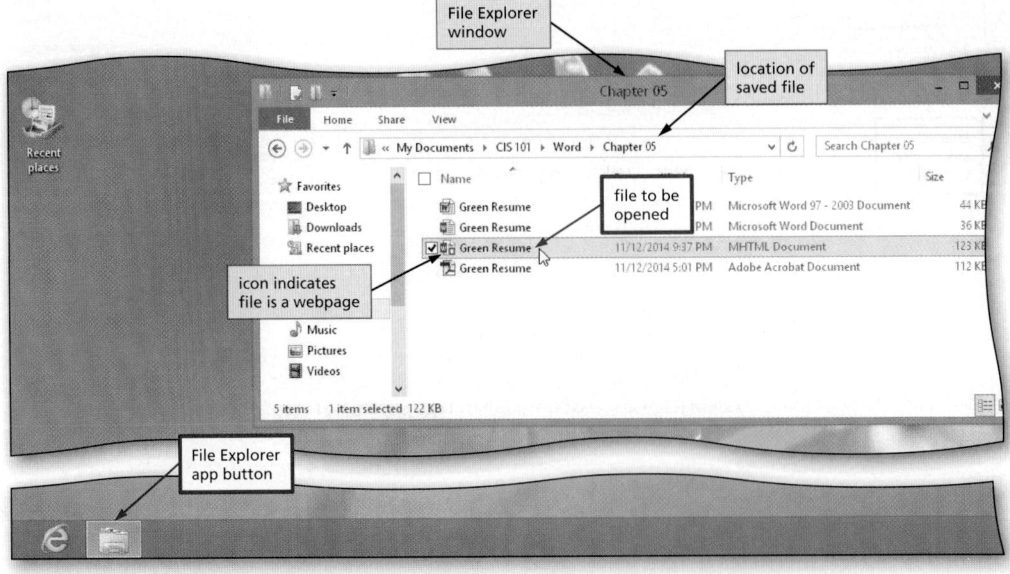

Figure 5–75

2

- Double-tap or double-click the webpage file name, Green Resume, to run Internet Explorer and display the webpage file in the browser window (Figure 5–76).

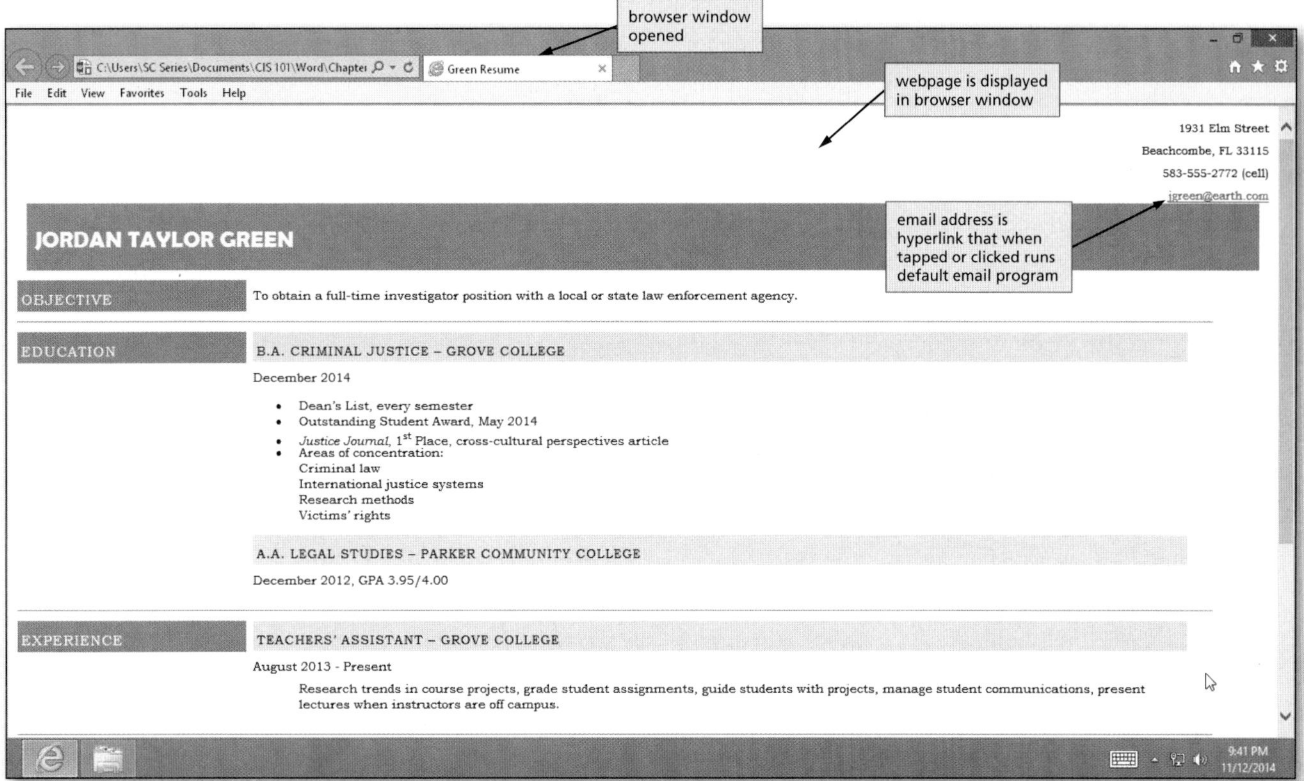

Figure 5–76

- With the webpage document displayed in the browser, tap or click the email address link to run the email program with the email address displayed in the email window (Figure 5–77).
- If Internet Explorer displays a security dialog box, tap or click its Allow button.

- Close all open windows.

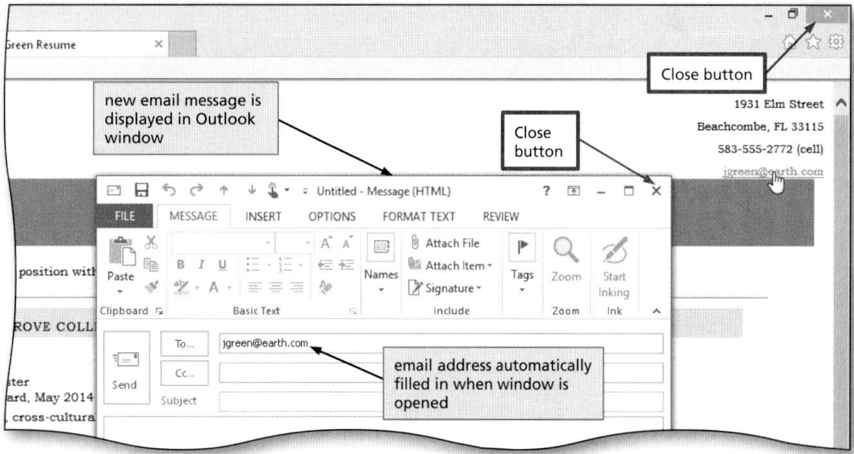

Figure 5–77

How do you publish a webpage?

Once you have created a webpage, you can publish it. **Publishing** is the process of making a webpage available to others on a network, such as the Internet or a company's intranet. Many Internet service providers (ISPs) offer storage space on their web servers at no cost to their subscribers.

Chapter Summary

In this chapter, you learned how to use Word to use a template to create a document, set custom margins, personalize a document template, indent a paragraph, customize theme fonts, create a style, modify a style, insert building blocks, save a Word document in a variety of formats, share a document online via SkyDrive and an online social network, insert a hyperlink, and change the style set. The items listed below include all the new Word skills you have learned in this chapter, with the tasks grouped by activity.

Enter and Edit Text

Create a New Document from an Online Template (WD 276)
Modify Text in a Content Control (WD 282)
Replace Placeholder Text (WD 284)
Delete a Content Control (WD 285)
Add an Item to a Content Control (WD 288)
Use AutoComplete (WD 289)
Enter a Line Break (WD 290)
Delete an Item from a Content Control (WD 292)

File Management

Save a Word Document as a PDF Document in Adobe Reader (WD 302)
Open a PDF Document from Word (WD 304)
Save a Word Document as an XPS Document (WD 305)
Save a Word 2013 Document in an Earlier Word Format (WD 307)
Save a Word 2013 Document as a Different File Type (WD 309)
Invite Others to View or Edit a Document (WD 310)
Get a Sharing Link (WD 312)
Post a Document to a Social Network (WD 313)
Send a Document Using Email (WD 314)
Save a Word Document as a Webpage (WD 317)

Format a Page

Set Custom Margins (WD 280)
Insert a Building Block Using the Building Block Organizer (WD 300)
Edit Properties of Building Block Elements (WD 302)
Change the Style Set (WD 321)

Format Text

Format a Content Control (WD 283)
Indent a Paragraph (WD 293)
Customize Theme Fonts (WD 296)
Create a Style (WD 297)
Modify a Style Using the Styles Dialog Box (WD 299)
Format Text as a Hyperlink (WD 319)
Edit a Hyperlink (WD 321)

Word Settings

Reveal Formatting (WD 298)
Run the Compatibility Checker (WD 306)
Use the Document Inspector (WD 315)
Customize How Word Opens Email Attachments (WD 315)
Set a Default Save Location (WD 319)

Work with Tables

Move Table Rows (WD 286)
Copy and Paste a Table Item (WD 294)

CONSIDER THIS: PLAN AHEAD

What decisions will you need to make when creating your next resume?

Use these guidelines as you complete the assignments in this chapter and create your own resumes outside of this class.

1. Craft a successful resume.
   a) Include necessary information (at a minimum, your contact information, objective, educational background, and work experience).
   b) Honestly present all your positive points.
   c) Organize information appropriately.
   d) Ensure the resume is error free.
2. For electronic distribution, such as email or online social media, ensure the document is in the proper format.
   a) Save the resume in a format that can be shared with others.
   b) Ensure that others will be able to open the resume using software on their computers and that the look of the resume will remain intact when recipients open the resume.
3. If desired, create a resume webpage from your resume Word document.
   a) Improve the usability of the resume webpage by making your email address a link to an email program.
   b) Enhance the look of the webpage by adding, for example, a background color.
   c) Test your finished webpage document in at least one browser to be sure it looks and works as intended.
   d) Publish your resume webpage.

CONSIDER THIS

How should you submit solutions to questions in the assignments identified with a symbol?

Every assignment in this book contains one or more questions identified with a symbol. These questions require you to think beyond the assigned document. Present your solutions to the questions in the format required by your instructor. Possible formats may include one or more of these options: write the answer; create a document that contains the answer; present your answer to the class; discuss your answer in a group; record the answer as audio or video using a webcam, smartphone, or portable media player; or post answers on a blog, wiki, or website.

Apply Your Knowledge

Reinforce the skills and apply the concepts you learned in this chapter.

Saving a Word Document in a Variety of Formats

Note: To complete this assignment, you will be required to use the Data Files for Students. Visit www.cengage.com/ct/studentdownload for detailed instructions or contact your instructor for information about accessing the required files.

Instructions: Run Word. Open the document, Apply 5-1 Online Job Searching, from the Data Files for Students. You are to save the document as a Single File Web Page (Figure 5–78), a PDF document, an XPS document, and in the Word 97-2003 format.

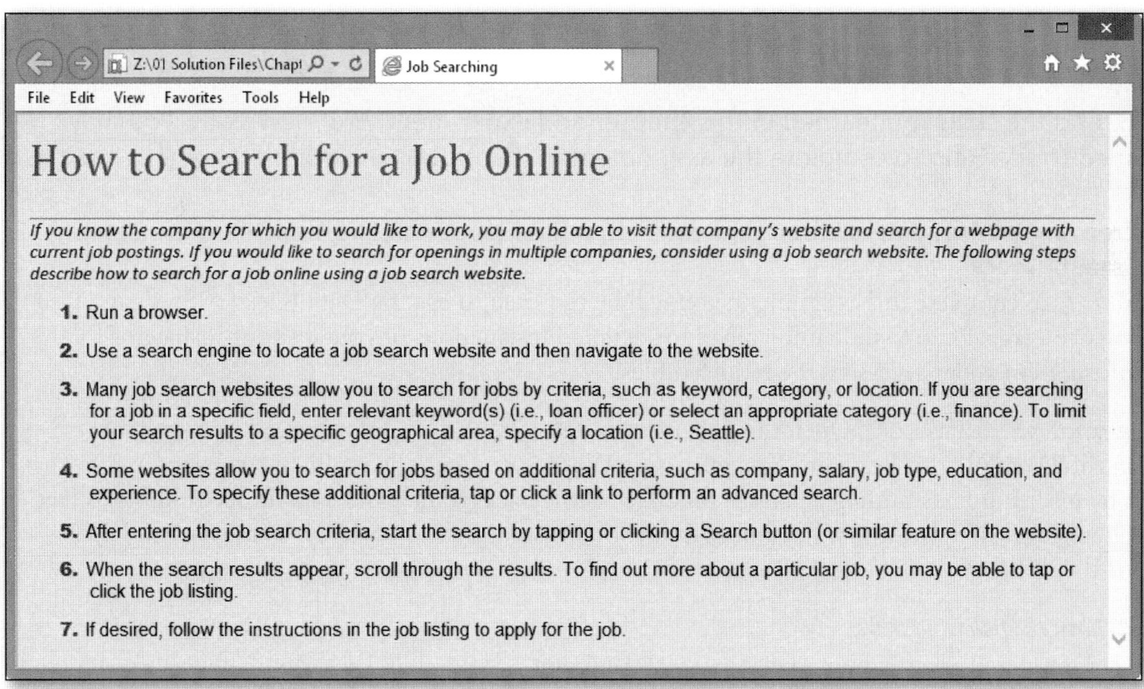

Figure 5–78

Perform the following tasks:

1. Save the document as a Single File Web Page using the file name, Apply 5-1 Online Job Searching Webpage. In the Save As dialog box, tap or click the Change Title button change the webpage title to Job Searching. If requested by your instructor, change the text, finance, in the third list item in the resume to your major.
2. Add the background color Tan, Background 2 to the webpage document. Save the file again.

Continued >

Apply Your Knowledge *continued*

3. Use Internet Explorer, or another browser, to view the webpage (shown in Figure 5–78). What differences do you notice between the Word document format and the Single File Web Page format? Exit Internet Explorer and then close the webpage document in Word.
4. Open the original Apply 5-1 Online Job Searching document. If requested by your instructor, change the text, finance, in the third list item in the resume to your major. Save the document as a PDF document and then view the PDF document in Adobe Reader. Submit the document as specified by your instructor. Exit Adobe Reader. In Word, open the PDF document just created. What differences do you notice between the Word document format and the PDF format? Close the converted PDF document without saving it.
5. If necessary, open the original Apply 5-1 Online Job Searching document. If requested by your instructor, change the text, finance, in the third list item in the resume to your major. Save the document as an XPS Document and then view the XPS document in the XPS Viewer. What differences do you notice between the Word document format and the XPS format? Exit the XPS Viewer.
6. If necessary, open the original Apply 5-1 Online Job Searching document. Run the compatibility checker. What issue(s) were identified by the compatibility checker? Save the document in the Word 97-2003 format.
7. If your instructor allows, email the document saved in #6 to his or her email account.
8. Answer the questions posed in #3, #4, #5, and #6. If you wanted to email this document to others, which format would you choose and why?

Extend Your Knowledge

Extend the skills you learned in this chapter and experiment with new skills. You may need to use Help to complete the assignment.

Creating a Multi-File Webpage, Applying a Fill Effect and Highlights, and Inserting Screen Shots

Note: To complete this assignment, you will be required to use the Data Files for Students. Visit www.cengage.com/ct/studentdownload for detailed instructions or contact your instructor for information about accessing the required files.

Instructions: Run Word. Open the document called Extend 5-1 Online Social Network located on the Data Files for Students. You will save a Word document as a multi-file webpage and format it by inserting links, adding a pattern fill effect as the background, and applying highlights to text. Then, you will create a new document that contains screen shots of the webpage and files created for the webpage.

Perform the following tasks:

1. Use Help to learn about saving as a webpage (not a Single File Web Page), hyperlinks, pattern fill effects, text highlight color, and screen shots.
2. If requested by your instructor, add your name on a separate line at the end of the document. Save the Extend 5-1 Online Social Networks file in the Web Page format (not as a Single File Web Page) using the file name, Extend 5-1 Online Social Networks Webpage.
3. Determine the web address of your favorite social network. At the end of the document, type a line of text that directs the reader to that web address for more information. Format the web address in the document as a hyperlink so that when a user clicks the web address, the associated webpage is displayed in the browser window.

4. Add a page color of your choice to the document. Add a pattern fill effect of your choice to the page color.
5. Apply a text highlight color of your choice to at least five words in the document.
6. Save the document again. Test the webpage by tapping or clicking its name in File Explorer. Test the web address link on the webpage. Leave this window open so that you can include its screenshot in the next step.
7. Redisplay the Word window. Create a new Word document. Insert a screen shot of the webpage displaying in the File Explorer window. Below the screen shot of the webpage, insert a screen shot(s) of File Explorer that shows all the files and folders created by saving the document as a webpage. Insert callout shapes with text that points to and identifies the files and folders created by saving the document as a webpage (Figure 5–79). Save the document with the file name, Extend 5-1 Online Social Networks Screen Shots.
8. Close all open windows. Submit the files in the format specified by your instructor.
9. Why would you add a pattern fill effect to a background?

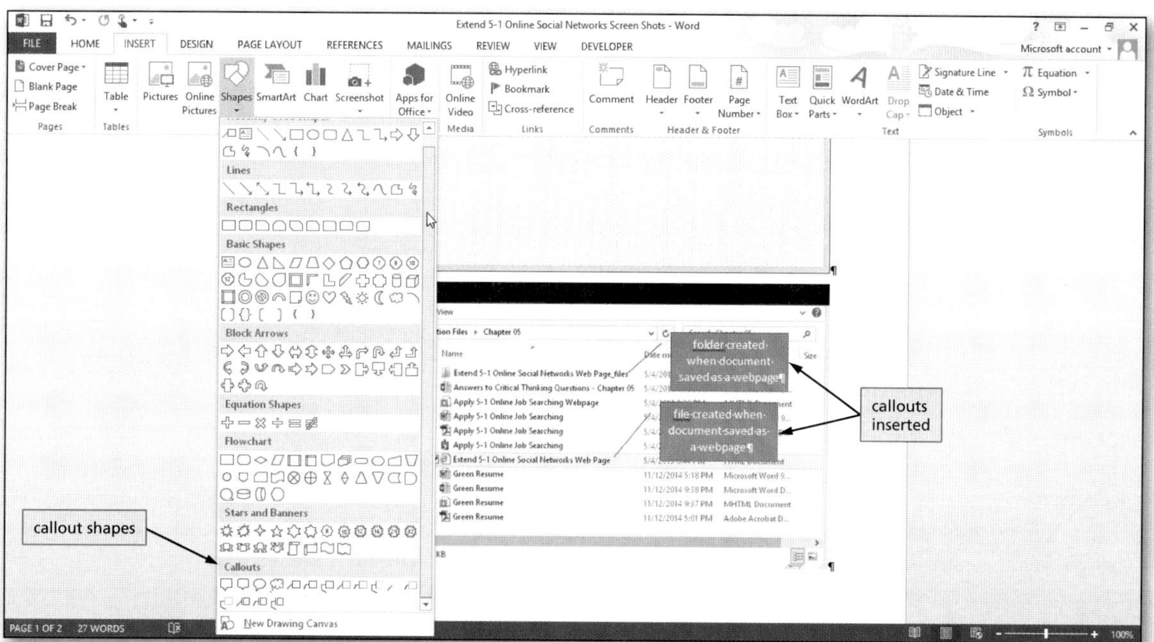

Figure 5–79

Analyze, Correct, Improve

Analyze a document, correct all errors, and improve it.

Formatting a Resume Created from a Template

Note: To complete this assignment, you will be required to use the Data Files for Students. Visit www.cengage.com/ct/studentdownload for detailed instructions or contact your instructor for information about accessing the required files.

Instructions: Run Word. Open the document, Analyze 5-1 Ames Resume Draft, located on the Data Files for Students. The document is a resume created from a template that is formatted incorrectly (Figure 5–80 on the next page). You are to change the margins, delete table rows, move table rows, modify styles, adjust the paragraph indent, modify a content control, remove a hyperlink format, and change the document theme.

Continued >

Analyze, Correct, Improve *continued*

Perform the following tasks:

1. Correct In the resume, correct the following items:

a. Change the margins so that the resume text does not run off the page and its contents are centered (Figure 5–80).

b. Modify the Normal style so that the text is a color other than red.

c. Delete the SKILLS & ABILITIES, LEADERSHIP, and REFERENCES rows.

d. Move the EDUCATION row above the EXPERIENCE row.

e. Decrease the indent of the objective text so it is aligned at the left edge of the cell.

f. Increase the indent of items in the activities section so that they all line up with each other.

g. Increase the font size of the name content control so that it is predominant on the page.

h. Use the Reveal Formatting task pane to determine the font size of the section headings (i.e., OBJECTIVE) and section text (i.e., To secure a nursing…). Modify the Heading 1 style so that it uses a font size that is greater than the font size of the section text.

i. Remove the hyperlink format from the email address.

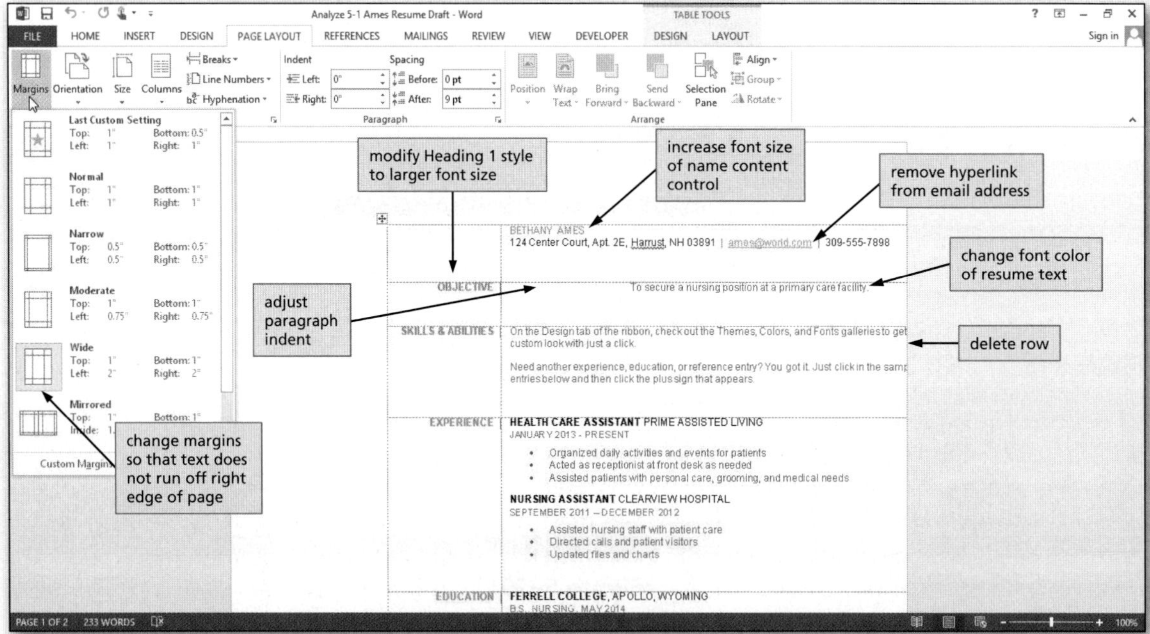

Figure 5–80

2. Improve Enhance the resume by customizing theme fonts, name the theme fonts. If necessary, edit the theme fonts until you are satisfied with the look of the resume. Adjust the font size of the contact line, if necessary, so that it all fits on a single line. If requested by your instructor, change the name at the top of the resume to your name. Save the modified document with the file name, Analyze 5-1 Ames Resume Modified, and then submit it in the format specified by your instructor.

3. In this assignment, you customized theme fonts. Which fonts did you select for the headings and body text and why?

In the Labs

Design and/or create a document using the guidelines, concepts, and skills presented in this chapter. Labs 1 and 2, which increase in difficulty, require you to create solutions based on what you learned in the chapter; Lab 3 requires you to create a solution, which uses cloud and web technologies, by learning and investigating on your own from general guidance.

Lab 1: Creating a Resume from a Template

Problem: You are hospitality management student at California College. As graduation quickly is approaching, you prepare the resume shown in Figure 5–81 on the next page using one of Word's resume templates.

Perform the following tasks:

1. Use the Basic resume (Timeless design) template to create a resume. If you cannot locate this template, open the file called Basic resume (Timeless design) from the Data Files for Students.
2. Change the document theme to Wisp.
3. Personalize the resume as shown in Figure 5–81. Following are some guidelines for some sections of the resume:
    a. Change the margins to 1" on the top, left, and right, and .5" on the bottom.
    b. If requested by your instructor, use your own name and contact information in the content controls. Delete the line containing the Website content control.
    c. Move the Education and Experience rows so that they appear as shown in Figure 5–81. Insert line breaks in the areas of concentration section of the education information.
    d. Add an item to the Education content control so that you can enter both degrees.
    e. Delete the second item from the Experience content control because the resume lists only one job.
    f. In the Experience section, indent the job responsibilities paragraphs one-half inch.
    g. Change the heading, SKILLS & ABILITIES, to MEMBERSHIPS.
    h. Copy the Experience section to below the Memberships section. Change the added row to show the community service information.
    i. Customize the theme fonts so that the headings are Arial Black and the body text is Verdana. Name the customized font Lab 1 Resume.
    j. Modify the Heading 2 style to the Verdana font.
    k. Change the Style Set to Shaded.
    l. Delete any unused rows in the resume.
4. The entire resume should fit on a single page. If it flows to two pages, decrease spacing before and after paragraphs until the entire resume text fits on a single page.
5. Check the spelling of the resume. Save the resume with Lab 5-1 Garlapati Resume as the file name and submit it in the format specified by your instructor.
6. Look through the other resume templates available. Which would work best for your resume? Why?

Continued >

In the Labs *continued*

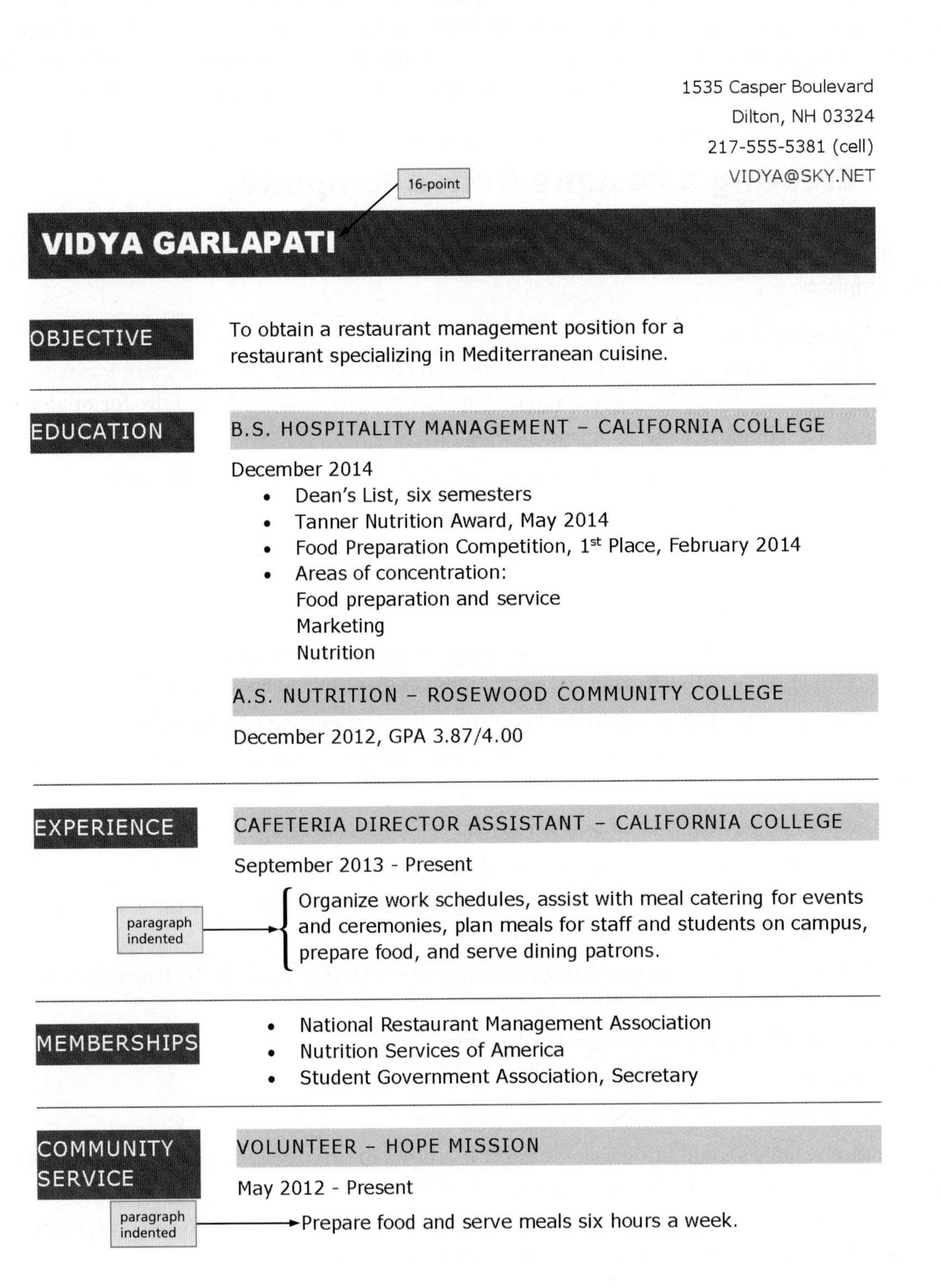

Figure 5–81

Lab 2: Creating a Resume from a Template

Problem: You are an industrial engineering technology student at Alamo College. As graduation is approaching quickly, you prepare the resume shown in Figure 5–82 on the next page using one of Word's resume templates.

Perform the following tasks:

1. Use the Resume template to create a resume. If you cannot locate this template, open the file called Resume from the Data Files for Students.
2. Personalize and format the resume as shown in Figure 5–82. Remove and insert content controls and items as necessary so that the resume appears as in the figure. If requested by your instructor, use your own name and contact information in the content controls. Following are some guidelines for some sections of the resume:
   a. Create a customized theme font set that uses Rockwell for headings and Arial for body text. Save the theme font with the name Lab 2 Resume.
   b. Modify the Section style to contain paragraph shading of White, Background 1, Darker 5%. Reduce spacing to 24 point before paragraphs. Update the style so that it applies to the entire resume.
   c. Increase the font size of the name to 28 point and the Address content control to 10 point. Create a style called Contact Info using the format in the Address content control. Apply the Contact Info style to the phone and email content controls.
3. The entire resume should fit on a single page. If it flows to two pages, decrease spacing before and after paragraphs until the entire resume text fits on a single page.
4. Check the spelling of the resume. Save the resume with Lab 5-2 Chung Resume as the file name and submit it in the format specified by your instructor.
5. Look through the templates available besides resumes. Which ones might you find useful? Why?

Continued >

In the Labs *continued*

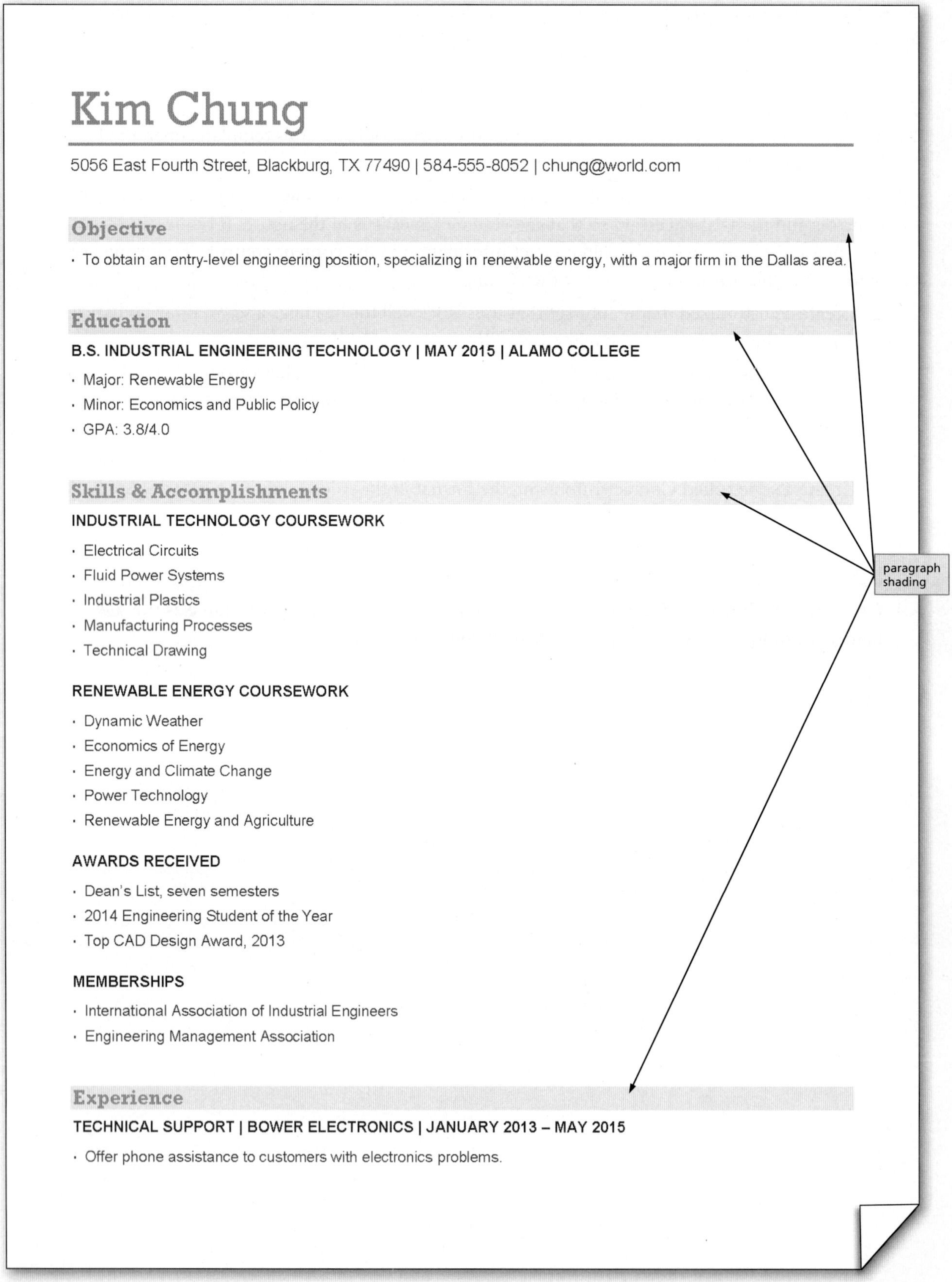

Kim Chung

5056 East Fourth Street, Blackburg, TX 77490 | 584-555-8052 | chung@world.com

Objective

- To obtain an entry-level engineering position, specializing in renewable energy, with a major firm in the Dallas area.

Education

B.S. INDUSTRIAL ENGINEERING TECHNOLOGY | MAY 2015 | ALAMO COLLEGE

- Major: Renewable Energy
- Minor: Economics and Public Policy
- GPA: 3.8/4.0

Skills & Accomplishments

INDUSTRIAL TECHNOLOGY COURSEWORK

- Electrical Circuits
- Fluid Power Systems
- Industrial Plastics
- Manufacturing Processes
- Technical Drawing

RENEWABLE ENERGY COURSEWORK

- Dynamic Weather
- Economics of Energy
- Energy and Climate Change
- Power Technology
- Renewable Energy and Agriculture

AWARDS RECEIVED

- Dean's List, seven semesters
- 2014 Engineering Student of the Year
- Top CAD Design Award, 2013

MEMBERSHIPS

- International Association of Industrial Engineers
- Engineering Management Association

Experience

TECHNICAL SUPPORT | BOWER ELECTRONICS | JANUARY 2013 – MAY 2015

- Offer phone assistance to customers with electronics problems.

paragraph shading

Figure 5–82

Lab 3: Expand Your World: Cloud and Web Technologies

Sharing a Resume Online

Problem: You are a technical writing graduate from Midway College. You have prepared a resume and are ready to share it with potential employers. You will save it on your SkyDrive account, invite others to view it, get a sharing link, post it on your online social network, send it via email, and post it on a job sharing website (Figure 5-83 on the next page).

Notes:

- You will use a SkyDrive, online social network, and job sharing website accounts, all of which you can create at no cost, to complete this assignment. If you do not have these accounts and do not want to create them, read this assignment without performing the instructions.
- To complete this assignment, you will be required to use the Data Files for Students. Visit www.cengage.com/ct/studentdownload for detailed instructions or contact your instructor for information about accessing the required files.

Instructions: Perform the following tasks:

1. In Word, open the document, Lab 5-3 Mendez Resume, from the Data Files for Students. Look through the resume so that you are familiar with its contents and formats.
2. Save the resume to your SkyDrive account.
3. In Word, invite at least one of your classmates to view your resume document. If requested, include your instructor in the invitation.
4. In Word, get a sharing link for the resume. Email the sharing link to at least one of your classmates. If requested, email the sharing link to your instructor.
5. If your Microsoft account is not connected to an online social network, connect it to one and then, in Word, post your resume document to the connected social network. Submit the posting in the format requested by your instructor.
6. Save the resume as a PDF file. Search for the text, post resume online, using a search engine. Visit several of the job search websites and determine on which one you would like to post a resume. If requested, create an account or profile, fill in the requested information, and then upload the PDF format of the resume (Figure 5–83). Submit the posting in the format requested by your instructor. Delete the posted resume from the job search website.
7. Which job search websites did you evaluate? Which one did you select to use and why? What would cause the file size of your resume to be too large to upload (post)? How can you reduce the file size?

Continued >

In the Labs *continued*

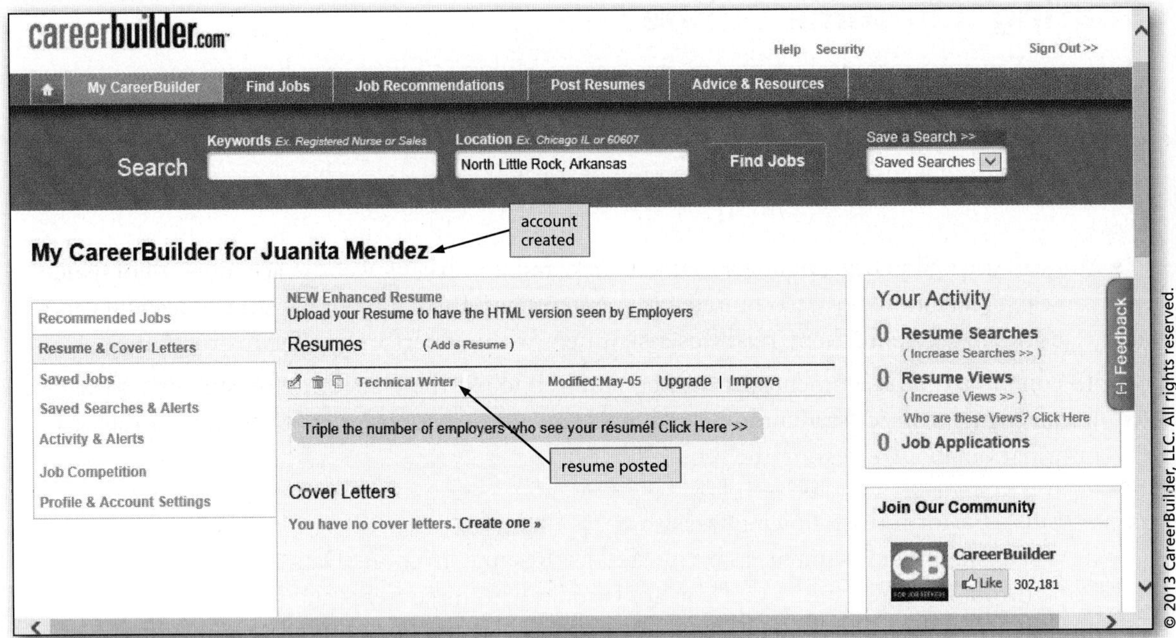

Figure 5–83

Consider This: Your Turn

Apply your creative thinking and problem solving skills to design and implement a solution.

1: Create a Graduation Invitation and a Calendar

Personal

Part 1: To help organize your appointments and important dates, you use a calendar template. While filling in the calendar, you decide to schedule your graduation party for which you will need to send out invitations. Browse through Word's online templates and download appropriate invitation and calendar templates and then use the text in the next two paragraphs for content. Use the concepts and techniques presented in this chapter to create and format the invitation and calendar. Be sure to check the spelling and grammar of the finished documents. Submit your assignment in the format specified by your instructor.

Calendar information: May 1 – send out graduation party invitations; May 2 – Golf tournament at 3:00 p.m., May 5 – capstone project due, May 7 – internship presentation at 2:00 p.m., May 10 – call mom (Mother's Day); May 11 – Kristina's birthday and Psychology final at 10:00 a.m., May 12 – Literature final term paper due by 11:59 p.m., May 15 – Grandpa's birthday, May 16 – volunteer at Community Center from 6:00 to 9:00 p.m., May 19 – Dentist appointment at 9:00 a.m., May 23 – My Graduation Party! from noon to ?? p.m., May 26 – First day of work!, and May 31 – Mom and Dad's anniversary (28th). If the template requires, insert appropriate clip art or an image of your own. If requested by your instructor, insert a personal event in the calendar.

Invitation information: Congratulations Marianne!; Graduation Party!; Saturday, May 30, Noon - ??; 143 Baker Avenue, Donner Grove, NH; Come hungry!; Bring your swimsuit and towel!; Hope you can join us! If the template requires, insert appropriate clip art or an image of your own. If requested by your instructor, use your name and contact information instead of the information listed here.

Part 2: You made several decisions while creating the calendar and invitation in this assignment: which template to use, where to position elements, how to format elements, and which graphic(s) to use. What was the rationale behind each of these decisions?

2: Create Business Cards and a Sales Receipt

Professional

Part 1: As a part-time employee at Annika's Flowers, your boss has asked you to create business cards and a sales receipt form. Browse through Word's online templates and download appropriate business cards and sales receipts templates and then use the information in the next two paragraphs for content. Use the concepts and techniques presented in this chapter to create and format the business cards and sales receipt form. Be sure to check the spelling and grammar of the finished documents. Submit your assignment in the format specified by your instructor.

Business card information: business name: Annika's Flowers; owner: Annika Lundsteen; address: 76 Main Street, Mitcheltown, DE 19722; phone: 555-907-9400; fax: 555-908-9400; web address: www.annikasflowers.com; email: annika@earth.net; slogan: Celebrating all special occasions! Insert an appropriate clip art or photo on the business card. If requested by your instructor, use your name and contact information instead of the information listed here.

Sales receipt information: business name: Annika's Flowers; address: 76 Main Street, Mitcheltown, DE 19722; phone: 555-907-9400; fax: 555-908-9400; web address: www.annikasflowers.com; email: annika@earth.net; slogan: Celebrating all special occasions! Insert an appropriate clip art or photo as the logo on the sales receipt. Sales tax rate is 5.5 percent. Delete all placeholder text that will be handwritten by sales clerks. If requested by your instructor, use your name and contact information instead of the information listed here. Print out the sales receipt form and fill in a sample with this information: customer name: Scarlett Winters; customer address: 882 Elm Street, Micheltown, DE 19722; phone: 555-272-2653; payment method: cash; purchased one vase for $9.99 and a dozen tulips for $4.99.

Part 2: You made several decisions while creating the business cards and sales receipt in this assignment: which template to use, where to position elements, how to format elements, and which graphic(s) to use. What was the rationale behind each of these decisions?

3: Create a Meeting Agenda, Invoice, and Travel Expense Report

Research and Collaboration

Part 1: As partners in a new business venture, you and two others have been developing documents needed in the business. Documents yet to be created include meeting agenda forms, travel expense report forms, and invoice forms. Form a three-member team to research, create, and fill in sample data for these forms. Decide on a business name, slogan, logo, mailing address, web address, and email address as a group. One team member should design the meeting agenda forms, another should design the travel expense forms, and a third should design the invoice forms using Word's online templates. In addition to the form, each also should create a sample filled-in form.

Use the concepts and techniques presented in this chapter to create and format the forms. If requested by your instructor, use team members' names in the forms. Be sure to check the spelling and grammar of the finished forms. Submit your team assignment in the format specified by your instructor.

Part 2: You made several decisions while creating the forms in this assignment: text to use, graphic(s) to use, which template to use, where to position elements, and how to format elements. What was the rationale behind each of these decisions?

Learn Online

Reinforce what you learned in this chapter with games, exercises, training, and many other online activities and resources.

Student Companion Site Reinforcement activities and resources are available at no additional cost on www.cengagebrain.com. Visit www.cengage.com/ct/studentdownload for detailed instructions about accessing the resources available at the Student Companion Site.

SAM Put your skills into practice with SAM! If you have a SAM account, go to www.cengage .com/sam2013 to access SAM assignments for this chapter.

6 Generating Form Letters, Mailing Labels, and a Directory

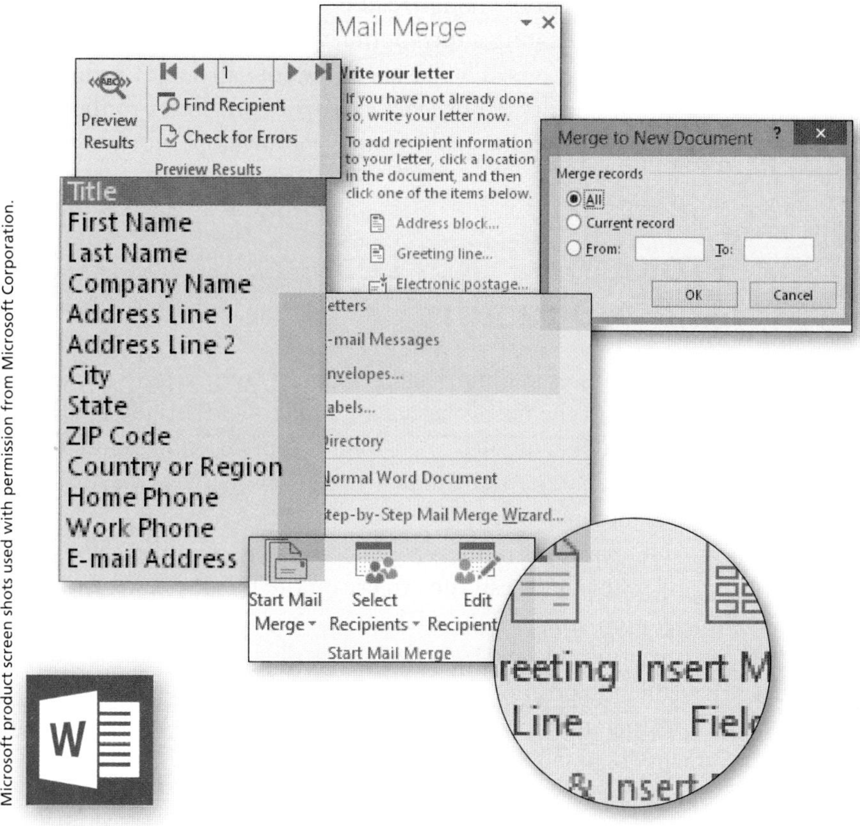

Objectives

You will have mastered the material in this chapter when you can:

- Explain the merge process
- Use the Mail Merge task pane and the MAILINGS tab on the ribbon
- Use a letter template as the main document for a mail merge
- Create and edit a data source
- Insert merge fields in a main document
- Use an IF field in a main document
- Merge form letters
- Select records to merge
- Sort data records
- Address and print mailing labels and envelopes
- Change page orientation
- Merge all data records to a directory
- Convert text to a table

6 Generating Form Letters, Mailing Labels, and a Directory

Introduction

People are more likely to open and read a personalized letter than a letter addressed as Dear Sir, Dear Madam, or To Whom It May Concern. Creating individual personalized letters, though, can be a time-consuming task. Thus, Word provides the capability of creating a form letter, which is an easy way to generate mass mailings of personalized letters. The basic content of a group of form letters is similar. Items such as name and address, however, vary from one letter to the next. With Word, you easily can address and print mailing labels or envelopes for the form letters.

Project — Form Letters, Mailing Labels, and a Directory

Both businesses and individuals regularly use form letters to communicate with groups of people via the postal service or email. Types of form letter correspondence include announcements of sales to customers, notices of benefits to employees, invitations to the public to participate in a sweepstakes giveaway, and job application letters to potential employers.

The project in this chapter follows generally accepted guidelines for writing form letters and uses Word to create the form letters shown in Figure 6–1. The form letters inform potential employers of your interest in a job opening at their organization. Each form letter states the potential employer's name and address, available job position, and location of the job fair they attended.

To generate form letters, such as the ones shown in Figure 6–1, you create a main document for the form letter (Figure 6–1a), create or specify a data source (Figure 6–1b), and then merge, or **blend**, the main document with the data source to generate a series of individual letters (Figure 6–1c). In Figure 6–1a, the main document represents the portion of the form letter that is repeated from one merged letter to the next. In Figure 6–1b, the data source contains the name, address, available position, and job fair attended for various potential employers. To personalize each letter, you merge the potential employer data in the data source with the main document for the form letter, which generates or prints an individual letter for each potential employer listed in the data source.

Word provides two methods of merging documents: the Mail Merge task pane and the MAILINGS tab on the ribbon. The Mail Merge task pane displays a wizard, which is a step-by-step progression that guides you through the merging process. The MAILINGS tab provides buttons and boxes you use to merge documents. This chapter illustrates both techniques.

If you are using your finger on a touch screen and are having difficulty completing the steps in this chapter, consider using a stylus. Many people find it easier to be precise with a stylus than with a finger. In addition, with a stylus you see the pointer. If you still are having trouble completing the steps with a stylus, try using a mouse.

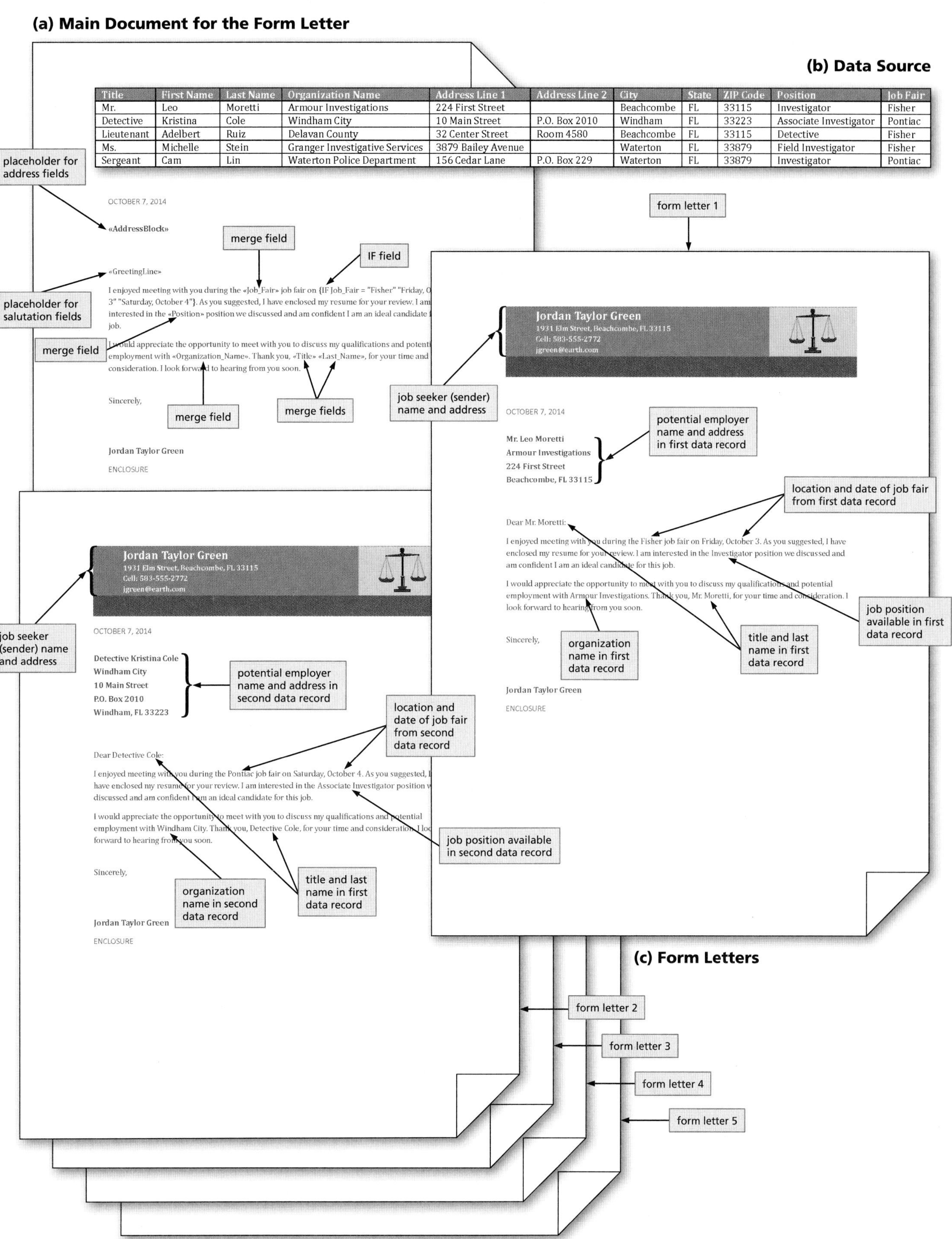

Title	First Name	Last Name	Organization Name	Address Line 1	Address Line 2	City	State	ZIP Code	Position	Job Fair
Mr.	Leo	Moretti	Armour Investigations	224 First Street		Beachcombe	FL	33115	Investigator	Fisher
Detective	Kristina	Cole	Windham City	10 Main Street	P.O. Box 2010	Windham	FL	33223	Associate Investigator	Pontiac
Lieutenant	Adelbert	Ruiz	Delavan County	32 Center Street	Room 4580	Beachcombe	FL	33115	Detective	Fisher
Ms.	Michelle	Stein	Granger Investigative Services	3879 Bailey Avenue		Waterton	FL	33879	Field Investigator	Fisher
Sergeant	Cam	Lin	Waterton Police Department	156 Cedar Lane	P.O. Box 229	Waterton	FL	33879	Investigator	Pontiac

Figure 6–1

Roadmap

In this chapter, you will learn how to create the form letters shown in Figure 6–1 on the previous page. The following roadmap identifies general activities you will perform as you progress through this chapter:

1. IDENTIFY the MAIN DOCUMENT for the form letters.
2. CREATE a DATA SOURCE.
3. COMPOSE the MAIN DOCUMENT for the form letters.
4. MERGE the DATA SOURCE with the main document.
5. ADDRESS the MAILING LABELS.
6. MERGE all data records TO a DIRECTORY.

At the beginning of step instructions throughout the chapter, you will see an abbreviated form of this roadmap. The abbreviated roadmap uses colors to indicate chapter progress: gray means the chapter is beyond that activity, blue means the task being shown is covered in that activity, and black means that activity is yet to be covered. For example, the following abbreviated roadmap indicates the chapter would be showing a task in the 2 CREATE DATA SOURCE activity.

1 IDENTIFY MAIN DOCUMENT | 2 CREATE DATA SOURCE | 3 COMPOSE MAIN DOCUMENT
4 MERGE DATA SOURCE | 5 ADDRESS MAILING LABELS | 6 MERGE TO DIRECTORY

Use the abbreviated roadmap as a progress guide while you read or step through the instructions in this chapter.

To Run Word and Change Word Settings

One of the few differences between Windows 7 and Windows 8 occurs in the steps to run Word. If you are using Windows 7, click the Start button, type `Word` in the 'Search programs and files' box, click Word 2013, and then, if necessary, maximize the Word window. For a summary of the steps to run Word in Windows 7, refer to the Quick Reference located at the back of this book.

If you are using a computer to step through the project in this chapter and you want your screens to match the figures in this book, you should change your screen's resolution to 1366 × 768. The following steps run Word, display formatting marks, and change the zoom to page width.

1. Run Word and create a blank document in the Word window. If necessary, maximize the Word window.
2. If the Print Layout button on the status bar is not selected, tap or click it so that your screen is in Print Layout view.
3. If the 'Show/Hide ¶' button (HOME tab | Paragraph group) is not selected already, tap or click it to display formatting marks on the screen.
4. To display the page the same width as the document window, if necessary, tap or click the Page Width button (VIEW tab | Zoom group).

Identifying the Main Document for Form Letters

The first step in the mail merge process is to identify the type of document you are creating for the main document. Typical installations of Word support five types of main documents: letters, email messages, envelopes, labels, and a directory. In this section of the chapter, you create letters as the main document. Later in this chapter, you will specify labels and a directory as the main document.

CONSIDER THIS

How should you create the letter for the main document?

When creating form letters, you either can type the letter for the main document from scratch in a blank document window or use a letter template. If you enter the contents of the main document from scratch, you can compose it according to the block, modified block, or semi-block letter style, formatted appropriately with business letter spacing. Alternatively, you can use a letter template to save time because Word prepares a letter with text and/or formatting common to all letters. Then, you customize the resulting letter by selecting and replacing prewritten text.

To Identify the Main Document for the Form Letter Using the Mail Merge Task Pane

1 IDENTIFY MAIN DOCUMENT | 2 CREATE DATA SOURCE | 3 COMPOSE MAIN DOCUMENT
4 MERGE DATA SOURCE | 5 ADDRESS MAILING LABELS | 6 MERGE TO DIRECTORY

This chapter uses a template for the main document for the form letter, where you select predefined content controls and replace them with personalized content, adjusting formats as necessary. ***Why?*** *You use the same style that you used with the resume in the previous chapter so that the two documents complement one another.* The following steps use the Mail Merge task pane to identify the Timeless letter template as the main document for a form letter.

- Tap or click MAILINGS on the ribbon to display the MAILINGS tab.
- Tap or click the 'Start Mail Merge' button (MAILINGS tab | Start Mail Merge group) to display the Start Mail Merge menu (Figure 6–2).

Q&A What is the function of the E-mail Messages command?
Instead of sending individual letters, you can send individual email messages using email addresses in the data source or using a Microsoft Outlook Contacts list.

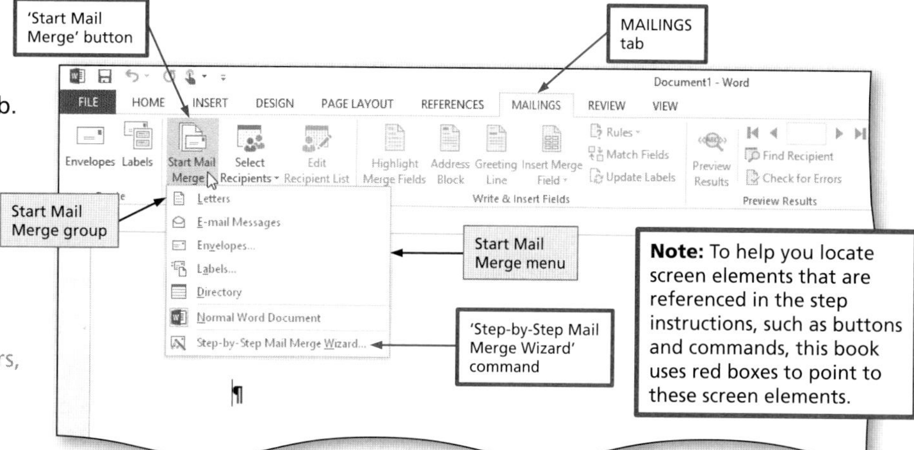

Figure 6–2

- Tap or click 'Step-by-Step Mail Merge Wizard' on the Start Mail Merge menu to display Step 1 of the Mail Merge wizard in the Mail Merge task pane (Figure 6–3).

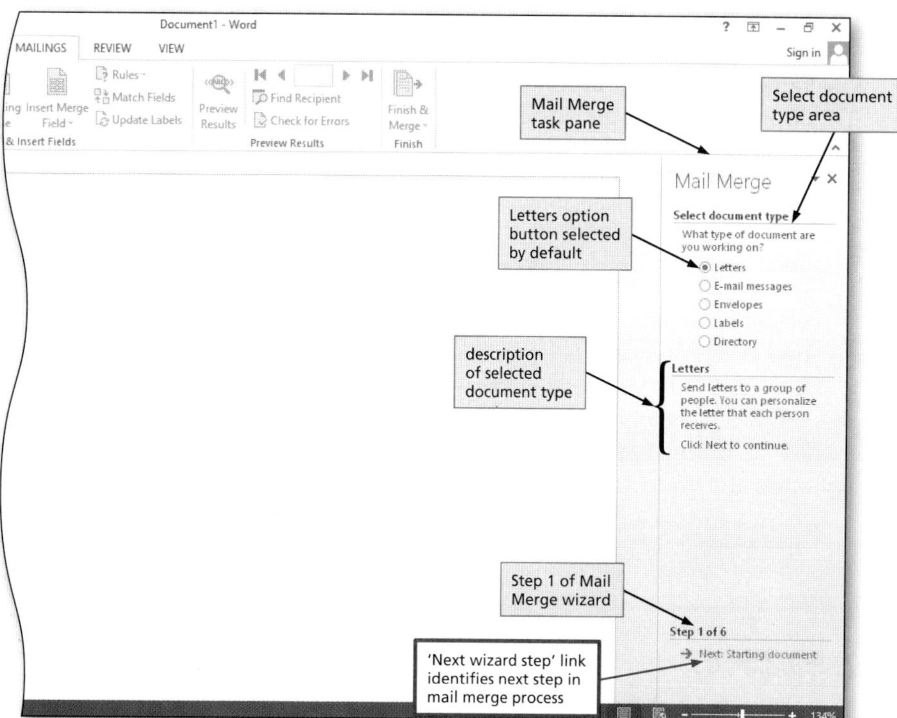

Figure 6–3

3

- Tap or click the 'Next wizard step' link at the bottom of the Mail Merge task pane to display Step 2 of the Mail Merge wizard, which requests you select a starting document.
- Tap or click 'Start from a template' in the Select starting document area and then tap or click the 'Select mail merge template' link to display the Select Template dialog box.

Q&A Why does the link name in the step differ from the name displayed in the Mail Merge task pane?
As with buttons and boxes, the text that appears on the screen may vary, depending on your screen resolution. The name that appears in the ScreenTip (when you point to the link), however, never changes. For this reason, this book uses the name that appears in the ScreenTip to identify links, buttons, boxes, and other on-screen elements.

- Tap or click the Letters tab (Select Template dialog box) to display the Letters sheet and then tap or click Timeless letter, which shows a preview of the selected template in the Preview area (Figure 6–4).

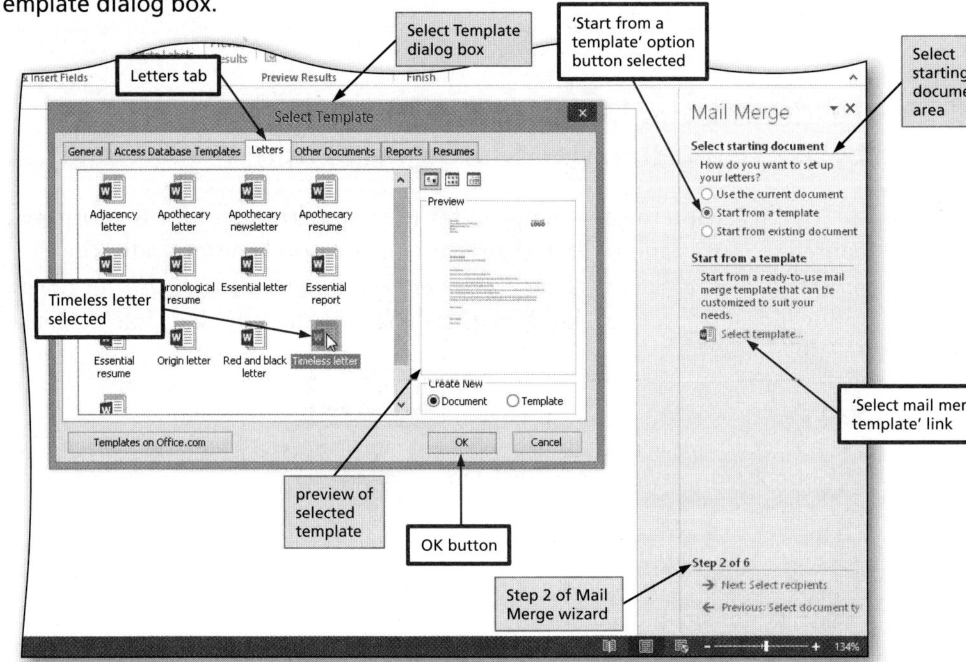

Figure 6–4

 **Experiment**

- Tap or click various Letter templates in the Letters sheet and watch the preview change in the right pane of the dialog box. When you are finished experimenting, tap or click the Timeless letter template to select it.

Q&A What if I cannot locate the Timeless letter template?
Skip the remainder of these steps and proceed to the steps called To Start a Mail Merge from an Existing Document that are shaded yellow at the top of the next page.

4

- Tap or click the OK button to display a letter in the document window that is based on the Timeless letter template (Figure 6–5).

Q&A Can I close the Mail Merge task pane?
Yes, you can close the Mail Merge task pane at any time by tapping or clicking its Close button. When you want to continue with the merge process, you repeat these steps and Word will resume the merge process at the correct step in the Mail Merge wizard.

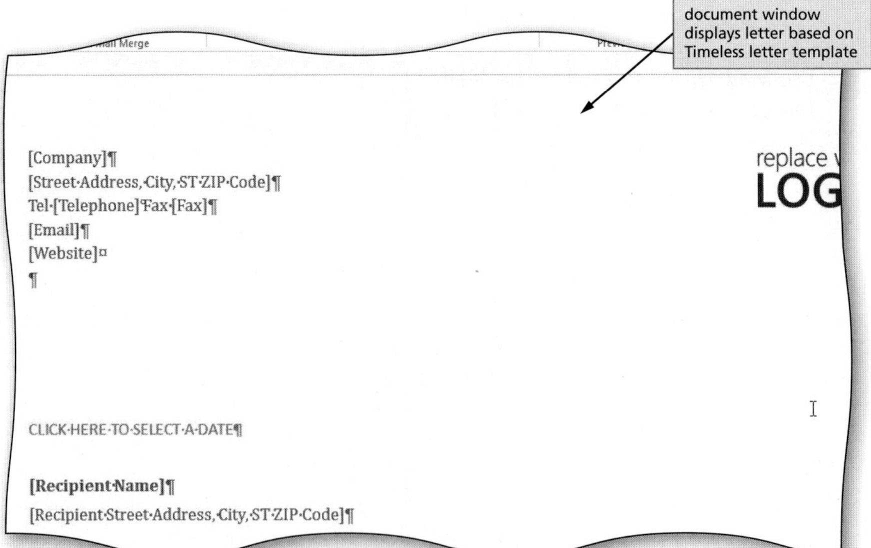

Figure 6–5

Other Ways

1. Open Backstage view, tap or click New, type `letters` in the 'Search for online templates' box, tap or click Start searching button, tap or click desired letter template, tap or click Create button

To Start a Mail Merge from an Existing Document

If you are unable to locate the Timeless letter template in the previous steps, you can open it from the Data Files for Students. Visit www.cengage.com/ct/studentdownload for detailed instructions or contact your instructor for information about accessing the required files. The following steps open a document. NOTE: PERFORM THE STEPS IN THIS YELLOW BOX ONLY IF YOU WERE UNABLE TO LOCATE THE TIMELESS LETTER TEMPLATE IN THE PREVIOUS STEPS.

1. Tap or click the 'Start from existing document' link in the Mail Merge task pane to display options for opening a document in the task pane.
2. Tap or click the Open button that appears in the Mail Merge task pane to display the Open dialog box.
3. Navigate to the location of the Timeless letter file to be opened (in this case, the Chapter 6 folder in the Word folder in the Data Files for Students folder).
4. Tap or click the Open button (Open dialog box) to open the file.

BTW

Conserving Ink and Toner

If you want to conserve ink or toner, you can instruct Word to print draft quality documents by tapping or clicking FILE on the ribbon to open the Backstage view, tapping or clicking Options in the Backstage view to display the Word Options dialog box, tapping or clicking Advanced in the left pane (Word Options dialog box), sliding or scrolling to the Print area in the right pane, placing a check mark in the 'Use draft quality' check box, and then tapping or clicking the OK button. Then, use the Backstage view to print the document as usual.

To Print the Document

The next step is to print the letter that Word generated, which is based on the Timeless letter template, so that you easily can see the entire letter contents.

1. Ready the printer. Open the Backstage view and then tap or click the Print tab. If necessary, select the desired printer, and then tap or click the Print button to print the document (Figure 6–6).

Q&A

What are the content controls in the document?
Recall that a content control contains instructions for filling in areas of the document. To select a content control, tap or click it. Later in this chapter, you will personalize the content controls.

Why is Windows User displayed in the signature block?
Word places the user name associated with your copy of Microsoft Word as the sender name. Windows User is the user name associated with this copy of Word.

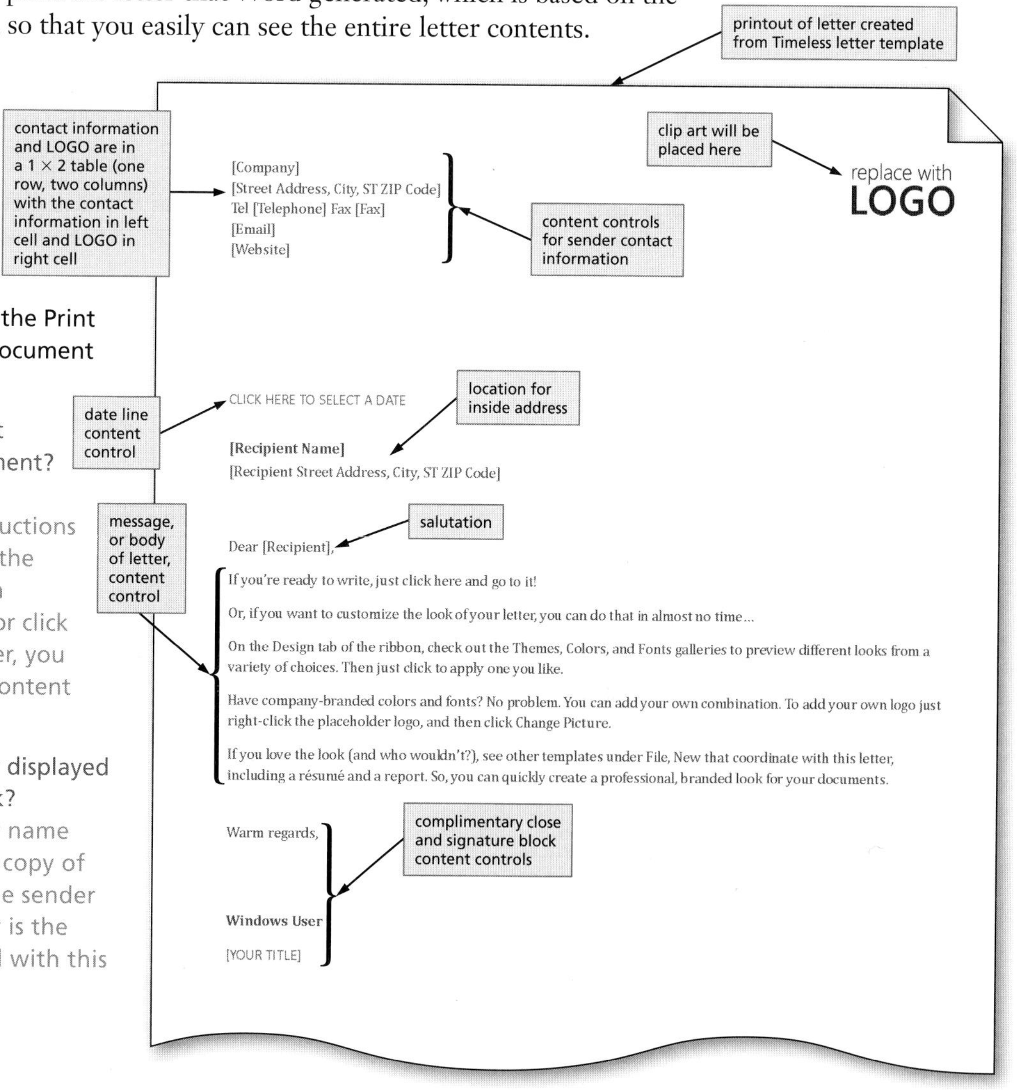

Figure 6–6

To Change the User Name and Initials

If you wanted to change the user name and initials associated with your copy of Microsoft Word, you would perform the following steps.

1. Open the Backstage view and then tap or click Options to display the Word Options dialog box.
2. If necessary, tap or click General in the left pane (Word Options dialog box).
3. Enter your name in the User name text box.
4. Enter your initials in the Initials text box.
5. Tap or click the OK button.

To Enter and Format the Sender Information

The next step is to enter the sender's contact information at the top of the letter. You will use the Company content control for the sender's name. You will delete the Fax and Website content controls because this sender does not have a fax or website. Then, you will change the font size of the text and indent the paragraphs one-half inch. The following steps enter and format the sender information.

1. Select the placeholder text, [Company], and then type **Jordan Taylor Green** as the sender name.
   If requested by your instructor, enter your name instead of the job seeker's name.
2. Select the placeholder text, [Street Address, City, ST ZIP Code], and then type **1931 Elm Street, Beachcombe, FL 33115** as the sender's address.
3. Select the text, Tel, and then type **Cell:** as the label. Select the placeholder text, [Telephone], and then type **583-555-2772** as the sender's cell phone.
4. Delete the Fax label and [Fax] content control.
5. Select the placeholder text, [Email], and then type **jgreen@earth.com** as the sender's email address.
6. Delete the [Website] content control and then press the BACKSPACE key to delete the blank line.
7. Increase the font size of the name to 14 point, and decrease the font size of the street address, cell phone, and email address to 9 point.
8. Select the name and all contact information. Bold the text and indent it one-half inch (Increase Indent button | HOME tab), shown in Figure 6–7.

BTW
Touch Screen Differences
The Office and Windows interfaces may vary if you are using a touch screen. For this reason, you might notice that the function or appearance of your touch screen differs slightly from this chapter's presentation.

To Change a Picture and Format It

The current picture in the letter contains the text, replace the LOGO, which is a placeholder for a picture. The following steps change a picture.

1. Press and hold and then tap the 'Show Context Menu' button on the mini toolbar or right-click the picture to be changed (in this case, the picture placeholder with the text, replace the LOGO) to display a shortcut menu (Figure 6–7).

2. Tap or click Change Picture on the shortcut menu to display the Insert Pictures dialog box.

   Q&A Can I use the Change Picture button (PICTURE TOOLS FORMAT tab | Adjust group) instead of the shortcut menu to display the Insert Pictures dialog box?
   Yes.

3. Type **scales of justice** in the Office.com Clip Art Search box (Insert Pictures dialog box) and then tap or click the Search button to display a list of clip art that matches the entered search text.

4. Scroll through the list of clip art to locate the one shown in Figure 6–8 (or a similar image), tap or click the clip art to select it, and then tap or click the Insert button (Office.com Clip Art dialog box) to download the image, close the dialog box, and replace the selected placeholder with the new picture file (shown in Figure 6–8 on the next page).

   Q&A What if I cannot locate the same clip art?
   Tap or click the Cancel button and then tap or click the Browse button (Insert Pictures dialog box), navigate to the scales of justice file on the Data Files for Students, and then tap or click the Insert button (Insert Picture dialog box) to insert the picture.

5. Use the Shape Height and Shape Width boxes (PICTURE TOOLS FORMAT tab | Size group) to change the picture height to .75" and width to .8", respectively.

   Tap or click the Center button (HOME tab | Paragraph group) to center the picture in the cell.

   Q&A Why center the picture?
   Currently, the picture is right-aligned in the cell. To balance the indent of the contact information, you center the picture.

BTW
The Ribbon and Screen Resolution
Word may change how the groups and buttons within the groups appear on the ribbon, depending on the computer's screen resolution. Thus, your ribbon may look different from the ones in this book if you are using a screen resolution other than 1366 × 768.

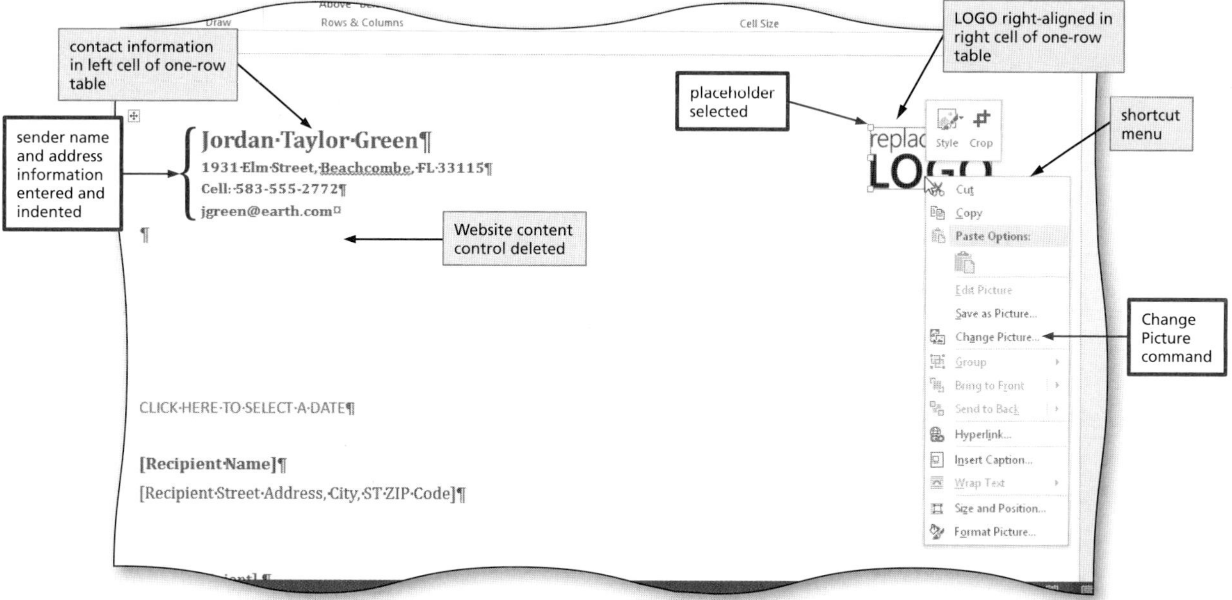

Figure 6–7

To Shade Cells and a Shape

In the letter in this chapter, the left and right cells of the table containing the contact information and picture are shaded different colors. The one-row table is contained in a rectangular shape that extends below the table. By shading the shape a different color, you create a letterhead with three different colors. The following steps shade table cells and a shape.

1. Position the insertion point in the contact information (left cell of the one-row table). Display the TABLE TOOLS LAYOUT tab and then, if necessary, tap or click the 'View Table Gridlines' button (TABLE TOOLS LAYOUT tab | Table group) to show table gridlines.

   Q&A Why show table gridlines?
   With table gridlines showing, the cells are easier to see.

2. Display the TABLE TOOLS DESIGN tab. With the insertion point in the left cell, tap or click the Shading arrow (TABLE TOOLS DESIGN tab | Table Styles group) and then tap or click 'Blue-Gray, Accent 1' (fifth color, first row) to shade the current cell with the selected color.

3. Select the contact information in the left cell and change its font color to 'White, Background 1' (first color, first row).

4. Position the insertion point in the cell with the picture, tap or click the Shading arrow (TABLE TOOLS DESIGN tab | Table Styles group) and then tap or click 'Brown, Accent 3, Lighter 80%' (seventh color, second row) to shade the current cell with the selected color.

5. Position the insertion point on the paragraph mark below the table to select the rectangle drawing object. Display the DRAWING TOOLS FORMAT tab. Tap or click the Shape Fill arrow (DRAWING TOOLS FORMAT tab | Shape Styles group) to display the Shape Fill gallery (Figure 6–8) and then tap or click 'Tan, Accent 2, Darker 25%' (sixth color, fifth row) to shade the selected shape with the selected color.

6. Hide table gridlines.

BTW
Q&As
For a complete list of the Q&As found in many of the step-by-step sequences in this book, visit the Q&A resource on the Student Companion Site located on www.cengagebrain.com. For detailed instructions about accessing available resources, visit www.cengage.com/ct/studentdownload or contact your instructor for information about accessing the required files.

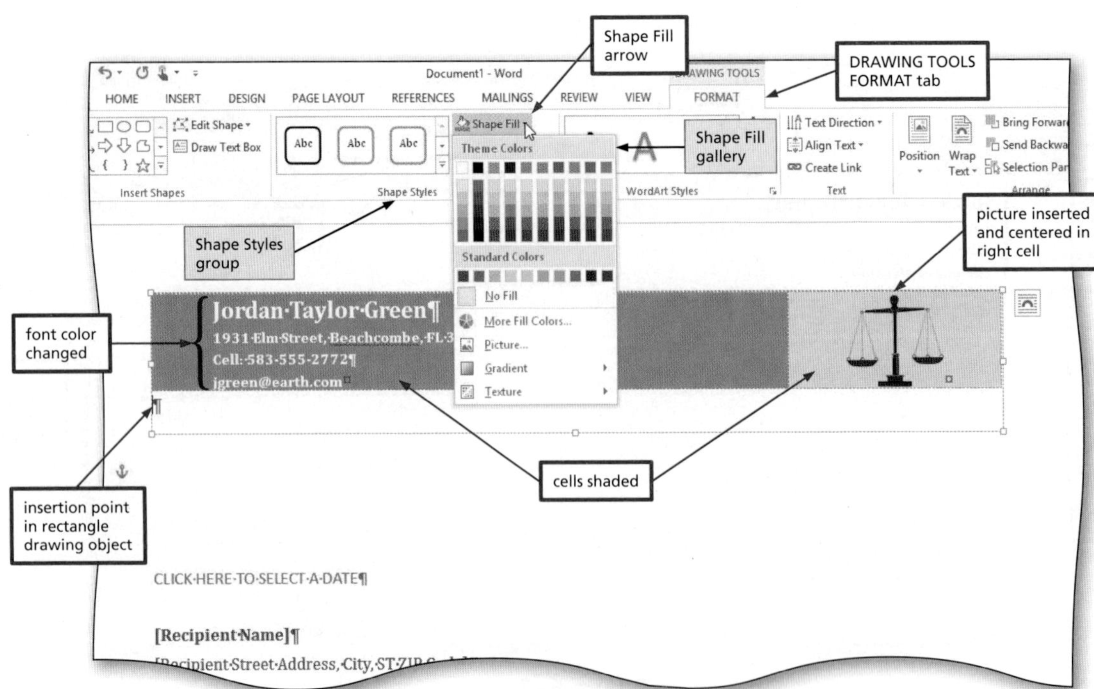

Figure 6–8

To Change Spacing above and below Paragraphs and Margin Settings

You would like to increase the space below the email address slightly, and decrease the space above the date line. Also, the Timeless letter template uses 0.9-inch top and .75-inch bottom, left, and right margins. You want the form letter to use 1-inch top and bottom margins and 1.25-inch left and right margins. The following steps change paragraph and margin settings.

1. Position the insertion point in the email address. Display the PAGE LAYOUT tab. Adjust the Spacing After box to 2 pt (PAGE LAYOUT tab | Paragraph group).
2. Tap or click the Date content control to select it. Adjust the Spacing Before box to 36 pt (PAGE LAYOUT tab | Paragraph group)
3. Tap or click the Adjust Margins button (PAGE LAYOUT tab | Page Setup group) to display the Margins gallery and then tap or click Custom Margins to display the Page Setup dialog box.
4. Change the values in the Top, Bottom, Left, and Right boxes (Page Setup dialog box) to 1", 1", 1.25", and 1.25", respectively (Figure 6–9).
5. Tap or click the OK button to change the margin values.

Q&A Why is the top margin unchanged?
The template specifies that the rectangle shape be positioned a certain distance from the top of the page, regardless of margin settings. The next steps change the position of the shape.

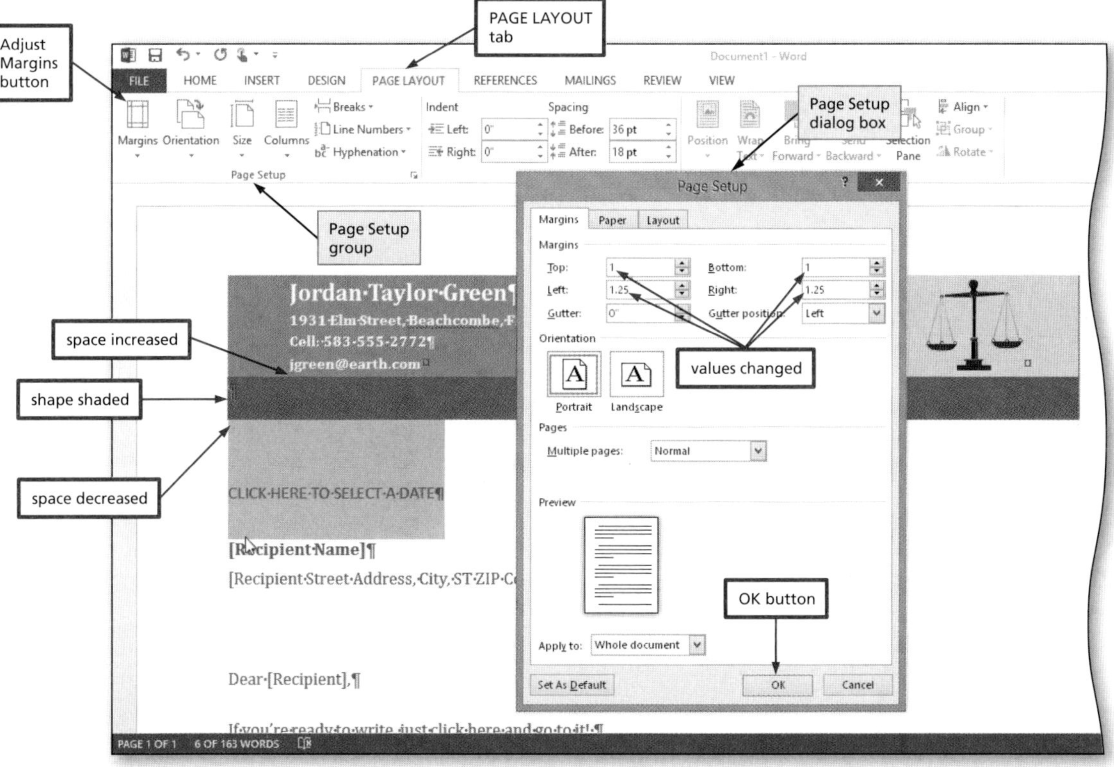

Figure 6–9

To Specify the Position of a Graphic

The next step is to change the distance between the shape and the top of the page. ***Why?*** *You want a one-inch space above the shape.* The following steps specify the position of a graphic.

1

- Tap or click the rectangle shape to select it.
- Tap or click the Layout Options button attached to the shape to display the Layout Options gallery (Figure 6–10).

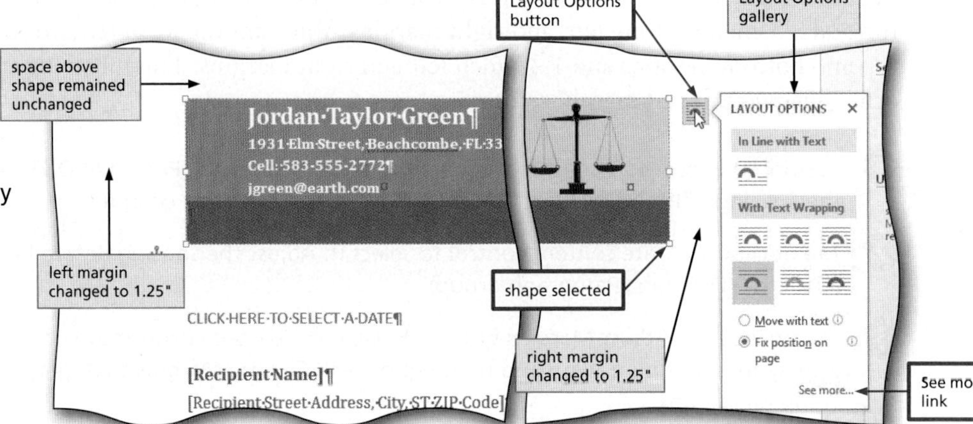

Figure 6–10

2

- Tap or click the See more link (Layout Options gallery) to display the Position tab in the Layout dialog box.
- Tap or click Absolute position in the Vertical area (Layout dialog box), select the value in the Absolute position box, and then type 1 to specify the distance in inches from the top of the page.
- If necessary, tap or click the below arrow and select Page (Figure 6–11).

Q&A What is the difference between the specifications in the Horizontal and Vertical areas?
Horizontal settings specify the graphic's position left to right on the page, whereas vertical settings specify the graphic's position top to bottom on the page.

- Tap or click the OK button to change the position of the selected graphic (Figure 6–12).

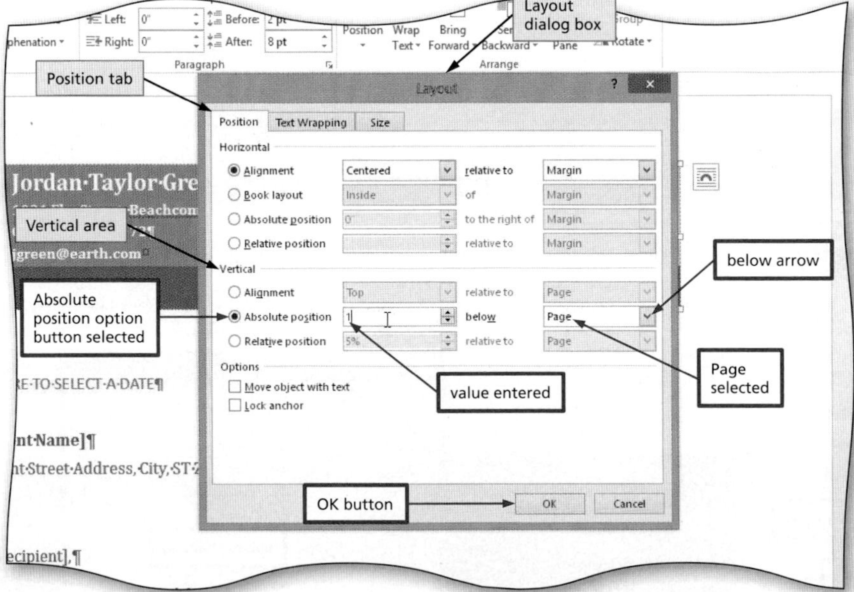

Figure 6–11

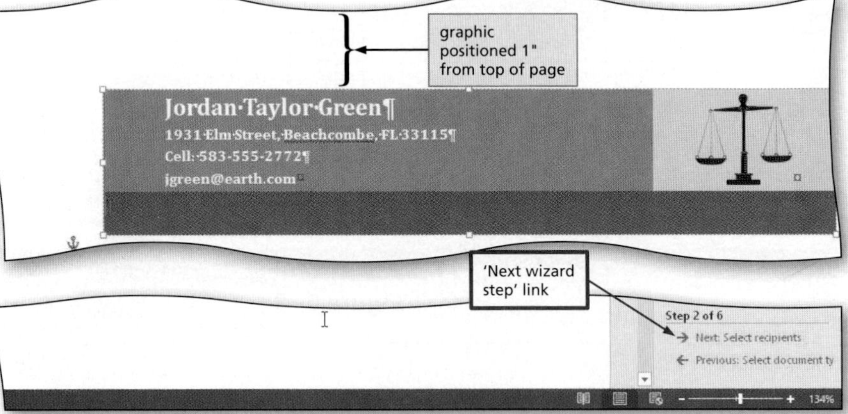

Figure 6–12

To Create a Folder while Saving

You have performed several tasks while creating this project and, thus, should save it. The following steps assume you already have created folders for storing files, for example, a CIS 101 folder (for your class) that contains a Word folder and chapter folders. You want to save this and all other documents created in this chapter in a folder called Job Hunting in the Word folder. The following steps create a folder during the process of saving a document. ***Why?*** *This folder does not exist, so you must create it. Rather than creating the folder in Windows, you can create folders in Word.*

1

- Tap or click the Save button on the Quick Access Toolbar, which depending on settings, will display either the Save As gallery in the Backstage view or the Save As dialog box. If necessary, select the save location (i.e., Computer or SkyDrive) and then tap or click the Browse button to display the Save As dialog box associated with the selected save location.
- Type **Green Cover Letter** in the File name box (Save As dialog box) to change the file name. Do not press the ENTER key after typing the file name because you do not want to close the dialog box at this time.
- Navigate to the desired save location for the new folder (in this case, the Word folder in the CIS 101 folder [or your class folder]).
- Tap or click the 'Create a new folder' button to display a new folder icon with the name, New folder, selected in the dialog box (Figure 6–13).

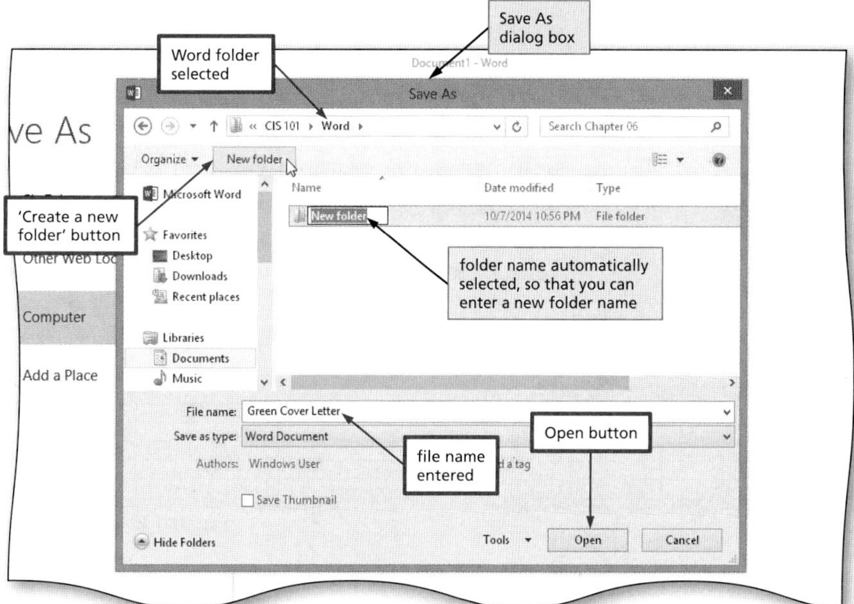

Figure 6–13

- Type **Job Hunting** as the new folder name and then press the ENTER key to create the new folder.
- Tap or click the Open button to open the selected folder, in this case, the Job Hunting folder (Figure 6–14).

- Tap or click the Save button (Save As dialog box) to save the current document in the selected folder on the selected drive.

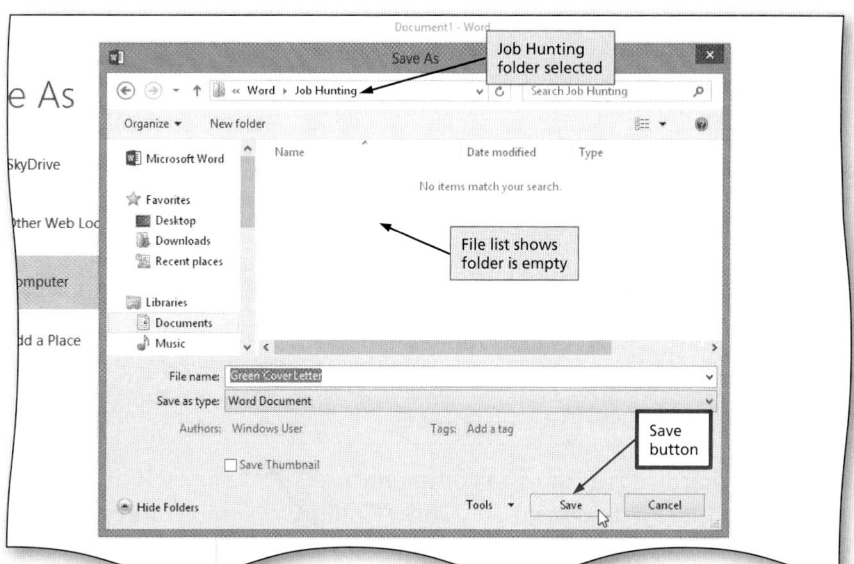

Figure 6–14

Q&A Can I create a folder in any other dialog box?

Yes. Any dialog box that displays a File list, such as the Open and Insert File dialog boxes, also has the 'Create a new folder' button, allowing you to create a new folder in Word instead of using Windows for this task.

Creating a Data Source

BTW
Fields and Records
Field and record are terms that originate from the computer programming field. Do not be intimidated by these terms. A field is simply a column in a table, and a record is a row. Instead of as a field, some programmers identify a column of data as a variable or an attribute. All three terms (field, variable, and attribute) have the same meaning.

The **data source** is a file that contains the variable, or changing, values from one merged document to the next. A data source can be an Access database table, an Outlook contacts list, or an Excel worksheet. If the necessary and properly organized data already exists in one of these Office programs, you can instruct Word to use the existing file as the data source for the mail merge. Otherwise, you can create a new data source using one of these programs.

As shown in Figure 6–15, a data source often is shown as a table that consists of a series of rows and columns. Each row is called a **record**. The first row of a data source is called the **header record** because it identifies the name of each column. Each row below the header row is called a **data record**. Data records contain the text that varies in each occurrence of the merged document. The data source for the project in this chapter contains five data records. In this project, each data record identifies a different potential employer. Thus, five form letters will be generated from this data source.

Each column in the data source is called a **data field**. A data field represents a group of similar data. Each data field must be identified uniquely with a name, called a **field name**. For example, Position is the name of the data field (column) that contains the available job position. In this chapter, the data source contains 11 data fields with the following field names: Title, First Name, Last Name, Organization Name, Address Line 1, Address Line 2, City, State, ZIP Code, Position, and Job Fair.

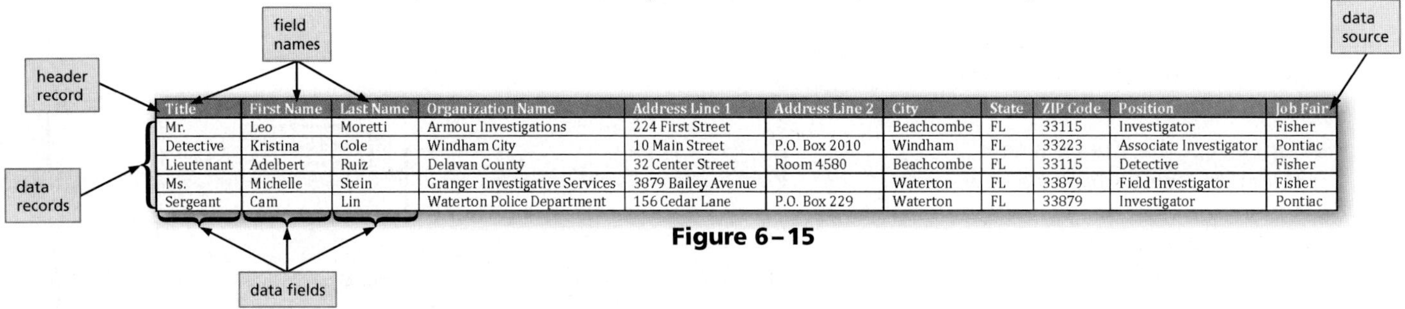

Title	First Name	Last Name	Organization Name	Address Line 1	Address Line 2	City	State	ZIP Code	Position	Job Fair
Mr.	Leo	Moretti	Armour Investigations	224 First Street		Beachcombe	FL	33115	Investigator	Fisher
Detective	Kristina	Cole	Windham City	10 Main Street	P.O. Box 2010	Windham	FL	33223	Associate Investigator	Pontiac
Lieutenant	Adelbert	Ruiz	Delavan County	32 Center Street	Room 4580	Beachcombe	FL	33115	Detective	Fisher
Ms.	Michelle	Stein	Granger Investigative Services	3879 Bailey Avenue		Waterton	FL	33879	Field Investigator	Fisher
Sergeant	Cam	Lin	Waterton Police Department	156 Cedar Lane	P.O. Box 229	Waterton	FL	33879	Investigator	Pontiac

Figure 6–15

CONSIDER THIS

What guidelines should you follow when creating a data source?

When you create a data source, you will need to determine the fields it should contain. That is, you will need to identify the data that will vary from one merged document to the next. Following are a few important points about fields:

- For each field, you may be required to create a field name. Because data sources often contain the same fields, some programs create a list of commonly used field names that you may use.
- Field names must be unique; that is, no two field names may be the same.
- Fields may be listed in any order in the data source. That is, the order of fields has no effect on the order in which they will print in the main document.
- Organize fields so that they are flexible. For example, separate the name into individual fields: title, first name, and last name. This arrangement allows you to print a person's title, first name, and last name (e.g., Mr. Leo Moretti) in the inside address but only the title and last name in the salutation (Dear Mr. Moretti).

To Create a New Data Source

1 IDENTIFY MAIN DOCUMENT | 2 CREATE DATA SOURCE | 3 COMPOSE MAIN DOCUMENT
4 MERGE DATA SOURCE | 5 ADDRESS MAILING LABELS | 6 MERGE TO DIRECTORY

Word provides a list of 13 commonly used field names. This project uses 9 of the 13 field names supplied by Word: Title, First Name, Last Name, Company Name, Address Line 1, Address Line 2, City, State, and ZIP Code. This project does not use the other four field names supplied by Word: Country or Region, Home Phone, Work Phone, and E-mail Address. Thus, you will delete these four field names. Then, you will change the Company Name field name to Organization Name. ***Why?*** *The term, organization, better describes the potential employers in this project.* You also will add two new field names (Position and Job Fair) to the data source. ***Why?*** *You want to reference the available position, as well as the job fair at which you met with the potential employer.* The next steps create a new data source for a mail merge.

1

- Tap or click the 'Next wizard step' link at the bottom of the Mail Merge task pane (shown in Figure 6–12 on page WD 348) to display Step 3 of the Mail Merge wizard, which requests you select recipients.
- Tap or click 'Type a new list' in the Select recipients area, which displays the Type a new list area.
- Tap or click the 'Create new recipient list' link to display the New Address List dialog box (Figure 6–16).

Q&A When would I use the other two option buttons in the Select recipients area?

If a data source already was created, you would use the first option: Use an existing list. If you wanted to use your Outlook contacts list as the data source, you would choose the second option.

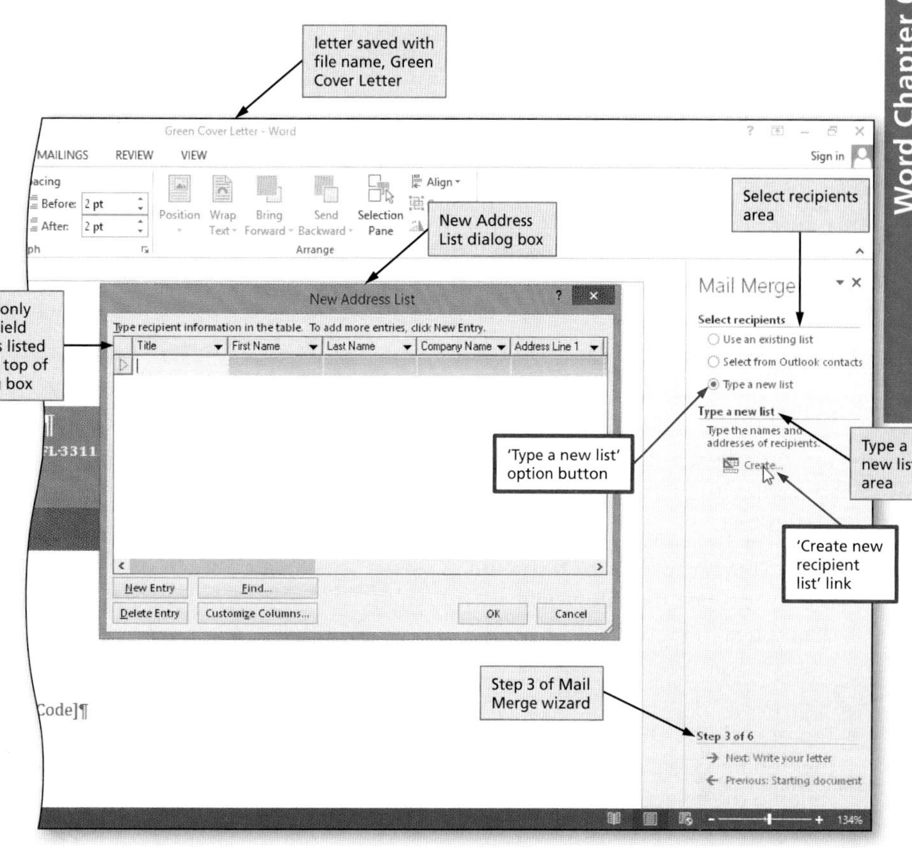

Figure 6–16

2

- Tap or click the Customize Columns button (New Address List dialog box) to display the Customize Address List dialog box (Figure 6–17).

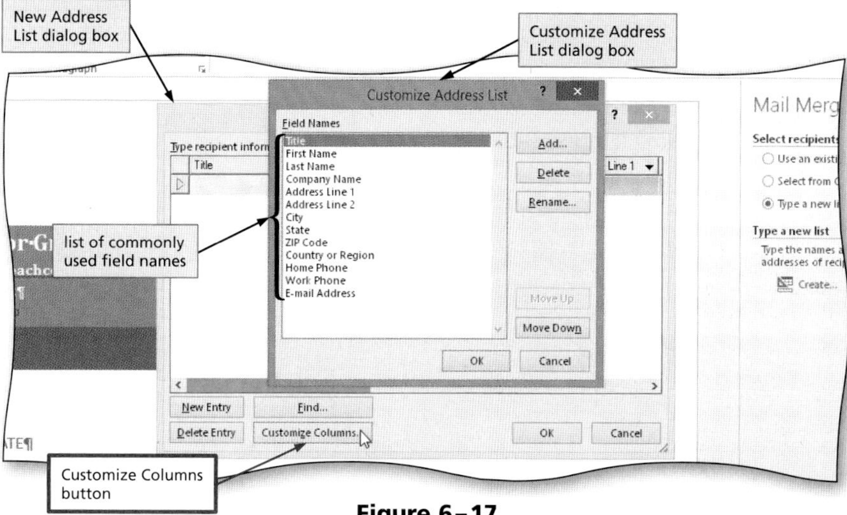

Figure 6–17

- Tap or click 'Country or Region' in the Field Names list (Customize Address List dialog box) to select the field to be deleted and then tap or click the Delete button to display a dialog box asking if you are sure you want to delete the selected field (Figure 6–18).

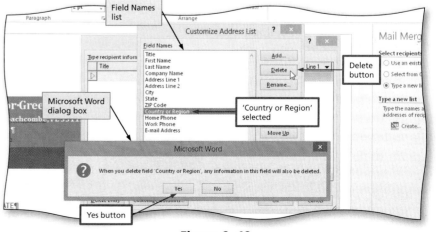

Field Names list

Delete button

Microsoft Word dialog box

'Country or Region' selected

Yes button

When you delete field 'Country or Region', any information in this field will also be deleted.

Figure 6–18

- Tap or click the Yes button (Microsoft Word dialog box) to delete the field.
- Tap or click Home Phone in the Field Names list to select the field. Tap or click the Delete button (Customize Address List dialog box) and then tap or click the Yes button (Microsoft Word dialog box) to delete the field.
- Use this same procedure to delete the Work Phone and E-mail Address fields.

- Tap or click Company Name in the Field Names list to select the field to be renamed.
- Tap or click the Rename button to display the Rename Field dialog box.
- Type `Organization Name` in the To text box (Rename Field dialog box) (Figure 6–19).

- Tap or click the OK button to close the Rename Field dialog box and rename the selected field.

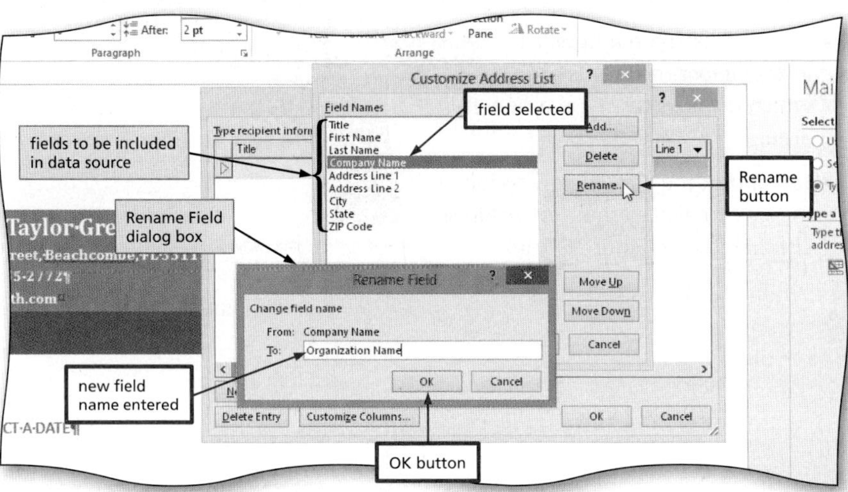

Figure 6–19

7

- Tap or click the Add button to display the Add Field dialog box.
- Type `Position` in the 'Type a name for your field' text box (Add Field dialog box) (Figure 6–20).

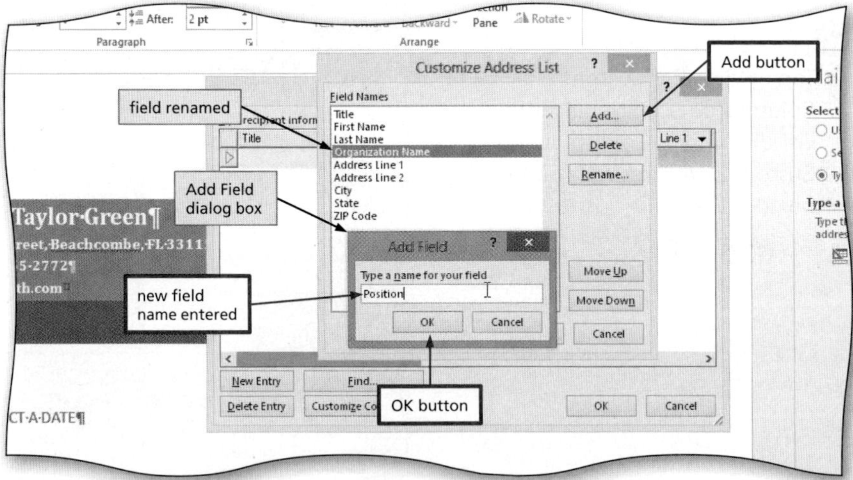

Figure 6–20

- Tap or click the OK button to close the Add Field dialog box and add the Position field name to the Field Names list immediately below the selected field (Figure 6–21).

Q&A Can I change the order of the field names in the Field Names list?
Yes. Select the field name and then tap or click the Move Up or Move Down button to move the selected field in the direction of the button name.

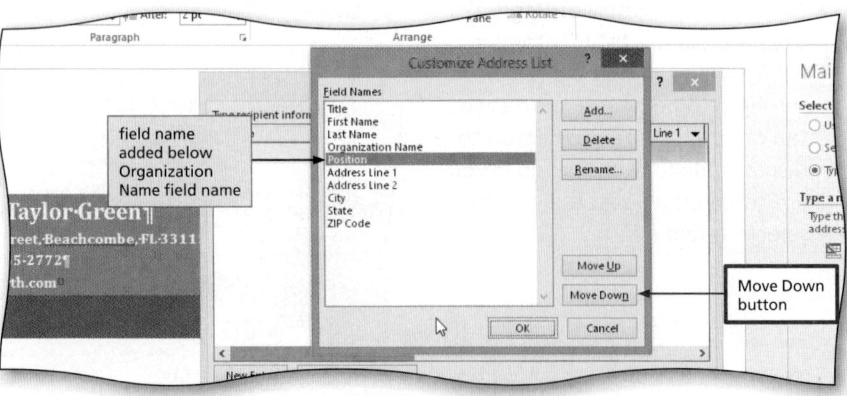

Figure 6–21

9

- With the Position field selected, tap or click the Move Down button five times to position the selected field at the end of the Field Names list.
- Tap or click the Add button to display the Add Field dialog box.
- Type **Job Fair** (Add Field dialog box) in the 'Type a name for your field' text box and then tap or click the OK button to close the Add Field dialog box and add the Job Fair field name to the bottom of the Field Names list (Figure 6–22).

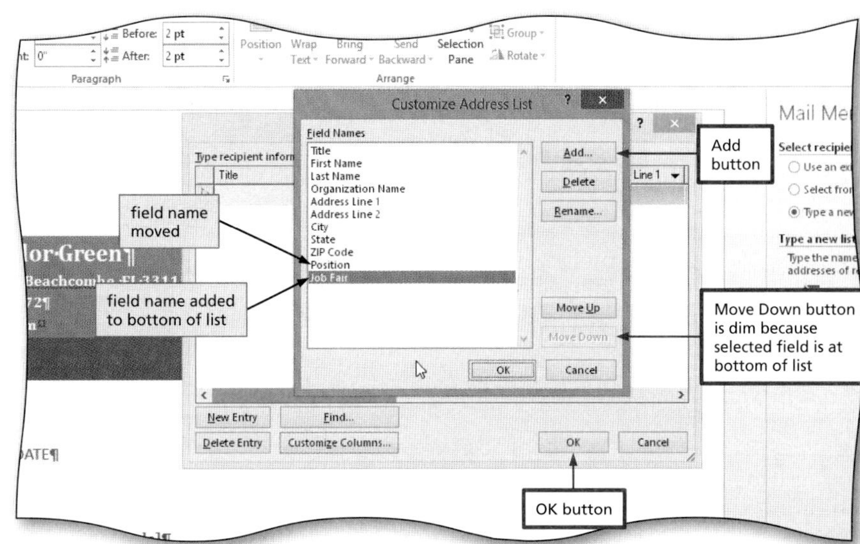

Figure 6–22

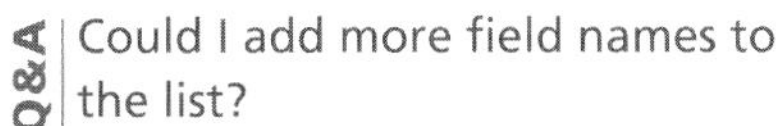

Q&A Could I add more field names to the list?
Yes. You would tap or click the Add button for each field name you want to add.

10

- Tap or click the OK button to close the Customize Address List dialog box, which positions the insertion point in the Title text box for the first record (row) in the New Address List dialog box (Figure 6–23).

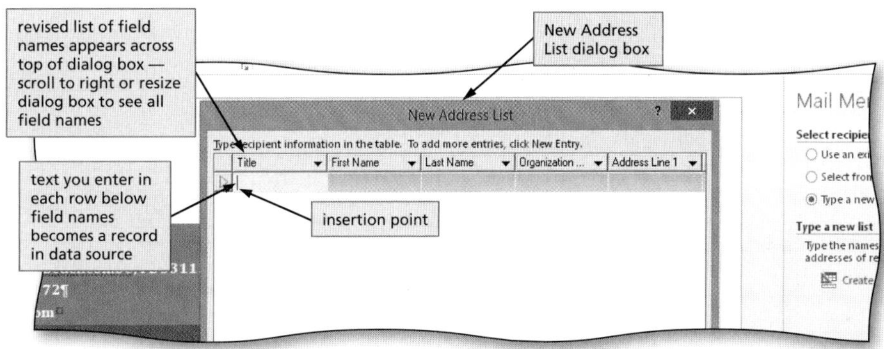

Figure 6–23

11

- Type **Mr.** and then press the TAB key to enter the title for the first data record.
- Type **Leo** and then press the TAB key to enter the first name.
- Type **Moretti** and then press the TAB key to enter the last name.
- Type **Armour Investigations** and then press the TAB key to enter the organization name.
- Type **224 First Street** to enter the first address line (Figure 6–24).

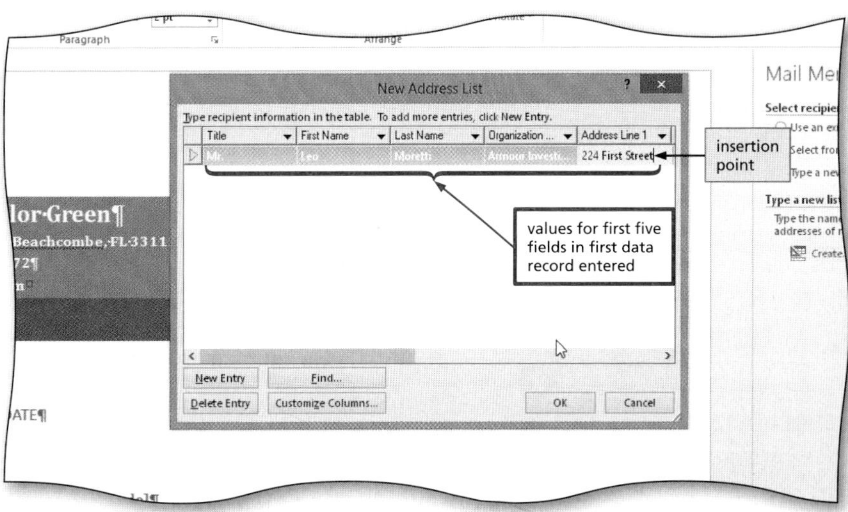

Figure 6–24

Q&A What if I notice an error in an entry?
Tap or click the entry and then correct the error as you would in the document window.

What happened to the rest of the Organization Name entry?
It is stored in the field, but you cannot see the entire entry because it is longer than the display area.

- Press the TAB key twice to leave the second address line empty.
- Type **Beachcombe** and then press the TAB key to enter the city.
- Type **FL** and then press the TAB key to enter the state code.
- Type **33115** and then press the TAB key to enter the ZIP code.
- Type **Investigator** and then press the TAB key to enter the Position.
- Type **Fisher** to enter the job fair (Figure 6–25).

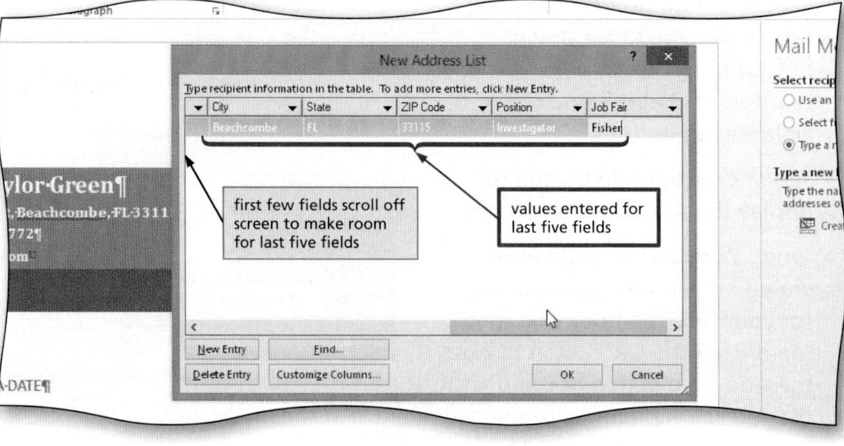

Figure 6–25

- Press the TAB key to add a new blank record and position the insertion point in the Title field of the new record (Figure 6–26).

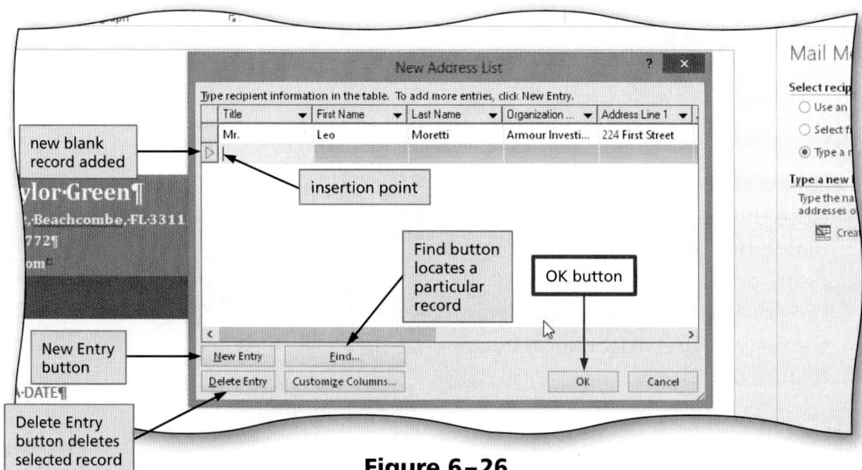

Figure 6–26

Other Ways

1. Tap or click Select Recipients button (MAILINGS tab | Start Mail Merge group)

To Enter More Records

The following steps enter the remaining four records in the New Address List dialog box.

1. Type **Detective** and then press the TAB key. Type **Kristina** and then press the TAB key. Type **Cole** and then press the TAB key. Type **Windham City** and then press the TAB key.
2. Type **10 Main Street** and then press the TAB key. Type **P.O. Box 2010** and then press the TAB key.
3. Type **Windham** and then press the TAB key. Type **FL** and then press the TAB key. Type **33223** and then press the TAB key.
4. Type **Associate Investigator** and then press the TAB key. Type **Pontiac** and then press the TAB key.

Q&A Instead of pressing the TAB key, can I tap or click the New Entry button at the end of one row to add a new blank record?

Yes. Tapping or clicking the New Entry button at the end of a row has the same effect as pressing the TAB key.

5 Type **Lieutenant** and then press the TAB key. Type **Adelbert** and then press the TAB key. Type **Ruiz** and then press the TAB key. Type **Delavan County** and then press the TAB key.

6 Type **32 Center Street** and then press the TAB key. Type **Room 4580** and then press the TAB key.

7 Type **Beachcombe** and then press the TAB key. Type **FL** and then press the TAB key. Type **33115** and then press the TAB key.

8 Type **Detective** and then press the TAB key. Type **Fisher** and then press the TAB key.

9 Type **Ms.** and then press the TAB key. Type **Michelle** and then press the TAB key. Type **Stein** and then press the TAB key. Type **Granger Investigative Services** and then press the TAB key.

10 Type **3879 Bailey Avenue** and then press the TAB key twice. Type **Waterton** and then press the TAB key. Type **FL** and then press the TAB key. Type **33879** and then press the TAB key.

11 Type **Field Investigator** and then press the TAB key. Type **Fisher** and then press the TAB key.

12 Type **Sergeant** and then press the TAB key. Type **Cam** and then press the TAB key. Type **Lin** and then press the TAB key. Type **Waterton Police Department** and then press the TAB key.

13 Type **156 Cedar Lane** and then press the TAB key. Type **P.O. Box 229** and then press the TAB key.

14 Type **Waterton** and then press the TAB key. Type **FL** and then press the TAB key. Type **33879** and then press the TAB key.

15 Type **Investigator** and then press the TAB key. Type **Pontiac** and then tap or click the OK button (shown in Figure 6–26), which displays the Save Address List dialog box (shown in Figure 6–27).

To Save a Data Source when Prompted by Word

1 IDENTIFY MAIN DOCUMENT | 2 CREATE DATA SOURCE | 3 COMPOSE MAIN DOCUMENT
4 MERGE DATA SOURCE | 5 ADDRESS MAILING LABELS | 6 MERGE TO DIRECTORY

When you tap or click the OK button in the New Address List dialog box, Word displays the Save Address List dialog box. ***Why?*** *You immediately save the data source so that you do not lose any entered information.* By default, the save location is the My Data Sources folder on your computer's hard drive. In this chapter, you save the data source to the Job Hunting folder created earlier in this chapter. The following steps save the data source.

1

- Type **Green Prospective Employers** in the File name box (Save Address List dialog box) as the name for the data source. Do not press the ENTER key after typing the file name because you do not want to close the dialog box at this time.
- Navigate to the desired save location for the data source (for example, the Job Hunting folder in the Word folder in the CIS 101 folder [or your class folder]) (Figure 6–27).

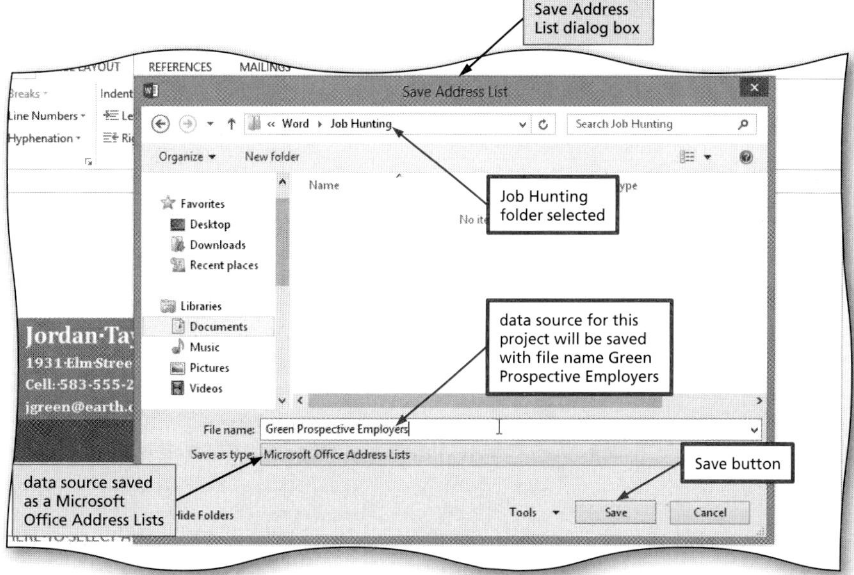

Figure 6–27

Q&A What is a Microsoft Office Address Lists file type?
It is a Microsoft Access database file. If you are familiar with Microsoft Access, you can open the Green Prospective Employers file in Access. You do not have to be familiar with Access or have Access installed on your computer, however, to continue with this mail merge process. Word simply stores a data source as an Access table because it is an efficient method of storing a data source.

2

- Tap or click the Save button (Save Address List dialog box) to save the data source in the selected folder using the entered file name and then display the Mail Merge Recipients dialog box (Figure 6–28).

Q&A What if the fields in my Mail Merge Recipients list are in a different order?
The order of fields in the Mail Merge Recipients list has no effect on the mail merge process. If Word rearranges the order, you can leave them in the revised order.

- Tap or click the OK button to close the Mail Merge Recipients dialog box.

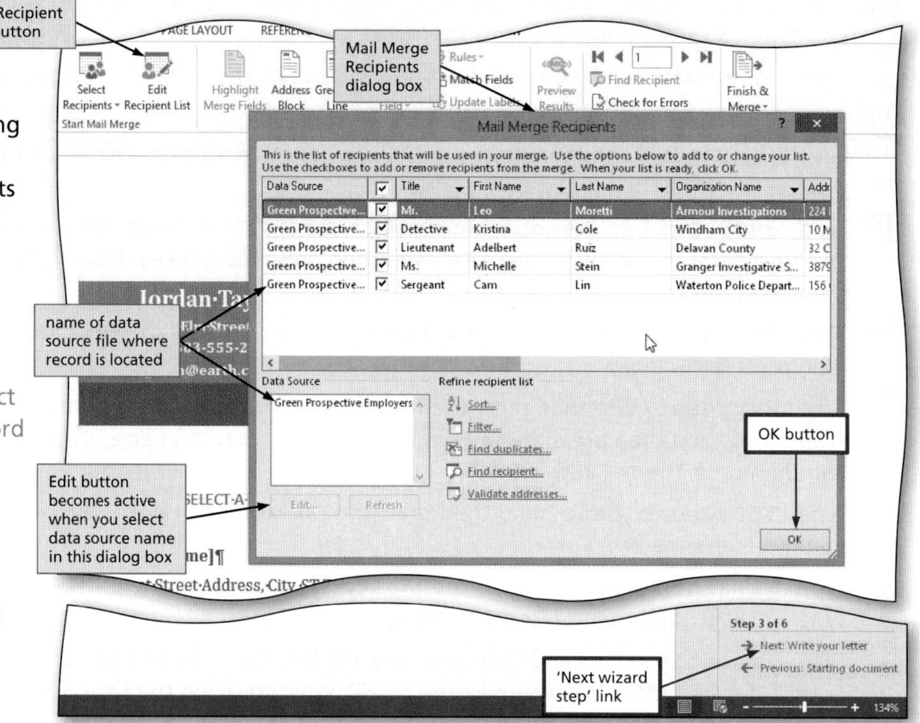

Figure 6–28

BTW
Saving Data Sources
Word, by default, saves a data source in the My Data Sources folder on your computer or mobile device's hard drive. Likewise, when you open a data source, Word initially looks in the My Data Sources folder for the file. Because the data source files you create in Word are saved as Microsoft Access database file types, if you are familiar with Microsoft Access, you can open and view these files in Access.

Editing Records in the Data Source

All of the data records have been entered in the data source and saved with the file name, Green Prospective Employers. To add or edit data records in the data source, you would tap or click the 'Edit Recipient List' button (MAILINGS tab | Start Mail Merge group) to display the Mail Merge Recipients dialog box (shown in Figure 6–28). Tap or click the data source name in the Data Source list and then tap or click the Edit button (Mail Merge Recipients dialog box) to display the data records in a dialog box similar to the one shown in Figure 6–26 on page WD 354. Then, add or edit records as described in the previous steps. If you want to edit a particular record and the list of data records is long, you can tap or click the Find button to locate an item, such as a last name, quickly in the list.

To delete a record, select it using the same procedure described in the previous paragraph. Then, tap or click the Delete Entry button in the dialog box (Figure 6–26).

Using an Existing Data Source

Instead of creating a new data source, you can use an existing Microsoft Outlook Contacts list, an Access database table, an Excel table, or a Word table as a data source in a mail merge. To use an existing data source, select the appropriate option in the Select recipients area in the Mail Merge task pane or tap or click the Select Recipients button (MAILINGS tab | Start Mail Merge group) and then tap or click the desired option on the Select Recipients menu.

For a Microsoft Outlook Contacts list, tap or click 'Select from Outlook contacts' in the Mail Merge task pane or 'Choose from Outlook Contacts' on the Select Recipients menu to display the Select Contacts dialog box. Next, select the contact folder you wish to import (Select Contacts dialog box) and then tap or click the OK button.

For other existing data source types such as an Access database table, an Excel worksheet, or a Word table, tap or click 'Use an existing list' in the Mail Merge task pane or on the Select Recipients menu to display the Select Data Source dialog box. Next, select the file name of the data source you wish to use and then tap or click the Open button.

With Access, you can use any field in the database in the main document. (Later in this chapter you use an existing Access database table as the data source.) For the merge to work correctly with an Excel table or a Word table, you must ensure data is arranged properly and that the table is the only element in the file. The first row of the table should contain unique field names, and the table cannot contain any blank rows.

BTW

BTWs
For a complete list of the BTWs found in the margins of this book, visit the BTW resource on the Student Companion Site located on www.cengagebrain.com. For detailed instructions about accessing available resources, visit www.cengage.com/ct/studentdownload or contact your instructor for information about accessing the required files.

Composing the Main Document for the Form Letters

The next step in this project is to enter and format the text and fields in the main document for the form letters (shown in Figure 6–1a on page WD 339). A **main document** contains the constant, or unchanging, text, punctuation, spaces, and graphics, as well as references to the data in the data source. You will follow these steps to compose the main document for the form letter.

1. Enter the date.
2. Enter the address block.
3. Enter the greeting line (salutation).
4. Enter text and insert a merge field.
5. Insert an IF field.
6. Enter the remainder of the text and merge fields.
7. Merge the letters.

CONSIDER THIS

What guidelines should you follow when composing the main document for a form letter?

The finished main document letter should look like a symmetrically framed picture with evenly spaced margins, all balanced below an attractive letterhead or return address. The content of the main document for the form letter should contain proper grammar, correct spelling, logically constructed sentences, flowing paragraphs, and sound ideas; it also should reference the data in the data source properly.

Be sure the main document for the form letter includes all essential business letter elements. All business letters should contain a date line, inside address, message, and signature block. Many business letters contain additional items such as a special mailing notation(s), an attention line, a salutation, a subject line, a complimentary close, reference initials, and an enclosure notation. When finished, proofread your letter carefully.

To Display the Next Step in the Mail Merge Wizard

The following step displays the next step in the Mail Merge wizard, which is to write the letter.

1. Tap or click the 'Next wizard step' link at the bottom of the Mail Merge task pane (shown in Figure 6–28) to display Step 4 of the Mail Merge wizard in the Mail Merge task pane (shown in Figure 6–29 on the next page).

To Enter the Date

The next step is to enter the date in the letter. ***Why?*** *All business letters should contain a date, which usually is positioned below the letterhead or return address.* You can tap or click the date content control and type the correct date, or you can tap or click the arrow and select the date from a calendar. The following steps use the calendar to select the date.

- Tap or click the Date content control to select it and then tap or click its arrow to display a calendar.
- Scroll through the calendar months until the desired month appears, October, 2014, in this case (Figure 6–29).

- Tap or click 7 in the calendar to display the selected month, day, and year in the date line of the form letter (shown in Figure 6–30).
- Tap or click outside the content control to deselect it.

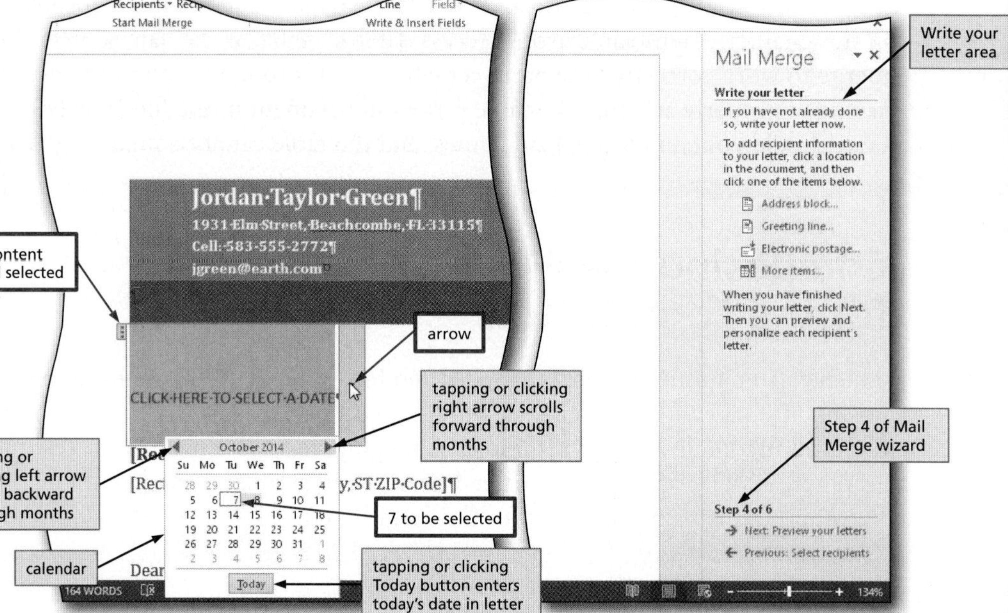

Figure 6–29

Other Ways

1. Type date in Date content control
2. Tap or click 'Insert Date & Time' button (INSERT tab | Text group)

Merge Fields

In this form letter, the inside address appears below the date line, and the salutation is placed below the inside address. The contents of the inside address and salutation are located in the data source. To link the data source to the main document, you insert the field names from the data source in the main document.

In the main document, field names linked to the data source are called **merge fields** because they merge, or combine, the main document with the contents of the data source. When a merge field is inserted in the main document, Word surrounds the field name with **merge field characters**, which are chevrons (« ») that mark the beginning and ending of a merge field. Merge field characters are not on the keyboard; therefore, you cannot type them directly in the document. Word automatically displays them when a merge field is inserted in the main document.

Most letters contain an address and salutation. For this reason, Word provides an AddressBlock merge field and a GreetingLine merge field. The **AddressBlock merge field** contains several fields related to an address: Title, First Name, Middle Name, Last Name, Suffix, Company, Street Address 1, Street Address 2, City, State, and ZIP Code. When Word uses the AddressBlock merge field, it automatically looks for any fields in the associated data source that are related to an address and then formats the address block properly when you merge the data source with the main document. For example, if your inside address does not use a middle name, suffix, or company, Word omits these items from the inside address and adjusts the spacing so that the address prints correctly.

To Insert the AddressBlock Merge Field

The default format for the AddressBlock merge field is the first name and last name on one line, followed by the street address on the next line, and then the city, state, and postal code on the next line. In this letter, you want the potential employer's title (i.e., Ms.) to appear to the left of the first name. ***Why?*** *You want to address the potential employers formally.* You also want the organization name to appear above the street address, if it does not already. The following steps insert the AddressBlock merge field in this format.

- Delete the content control that contains placeholder text for the recipient's address and then press the DELETE key to delete the blank paragraph.
- Delete the [Recipient Name] placeholder text but leave the paragraph mark; position the insertion point to the left of the paragraph mark because you will insert the AddressBlock merge field in that location.
- Tap or click the 'Insert formatted address' link in the Mail Merge task pane to display the Insert Address Block dialog box.
- Scroll through the list of recipient name formats (Insert Address Block dialog box) and then tap or click the format, Mr. Joshua Randall Jr., in this list, because that format places the title to the left of the first name and last name (Figure 6–30).

Experiment

- Tap or click various recipient name formats and watch the preview change in the dialog box. When finished experimenting, tap or click the format: Mr. Joshua Randall Jr.
- If necessary, tap or click the 'Insert company name' check box to select it, and notice the preview area shows the organization name in the sample formatted address (Figure 6–30).

Q&A Why is my 'Insert company name' check box dimmed?

If your data source does not have a match to the Company Name in the AddressBlock merge field, this check box will be dimmed. Recall that earlier in this project the Company Name field was renamed as Organization Name, which may cause the fields to be unmatched. The next step shows how to match the fields.

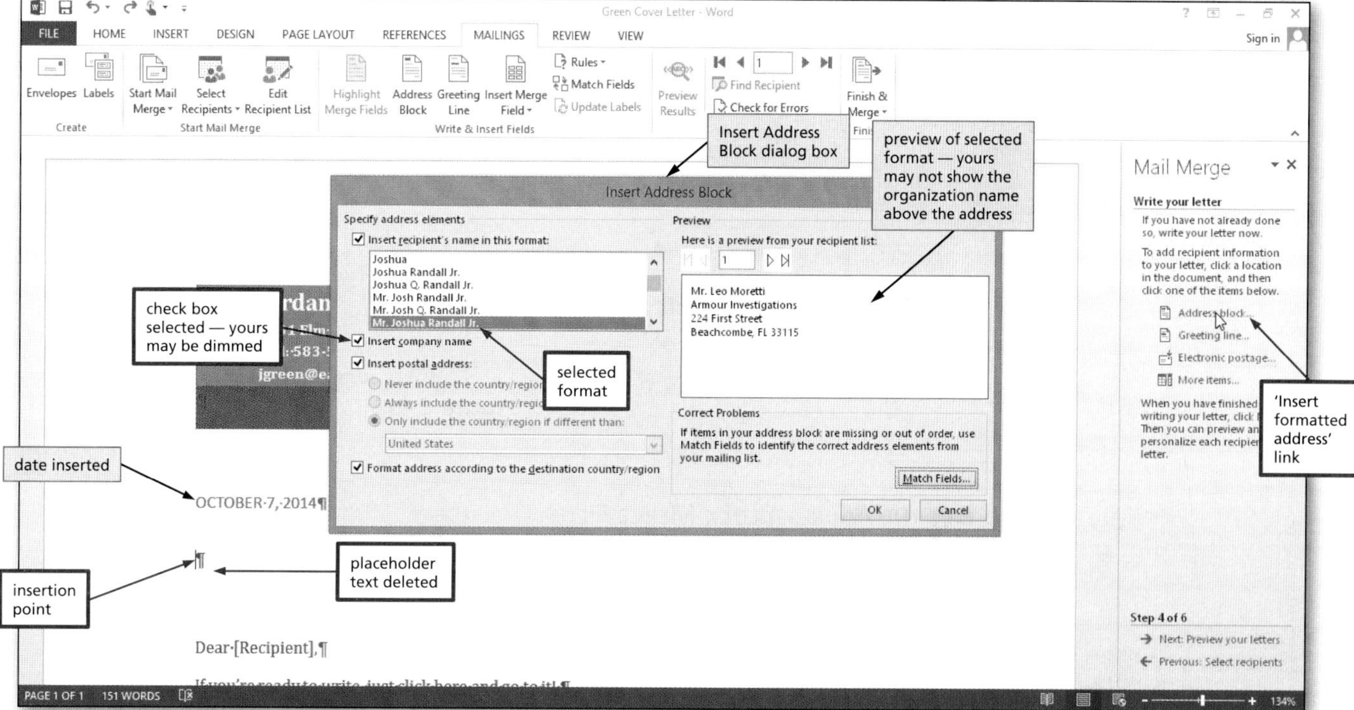

Figure 6–30

- If your AddressBlock merge field does not show the Organization Name above the address or if your 'Insert company name' check box is dimmed, tap or click the Match Fields button (Insert Address Block dialog box) to display the Match Fields dialog box; if the Organization Name already appears in your AddressBlock merge field, proceed to Step 4.
- If necessary, scroll through the Match Fields dialog box until Company appears.
- Tap or click the Company arrow (Match Fields dialog box) to display a list of fields in the data source and then tap or click Organization Name to place that selected field as the match field (Figure 6–31).

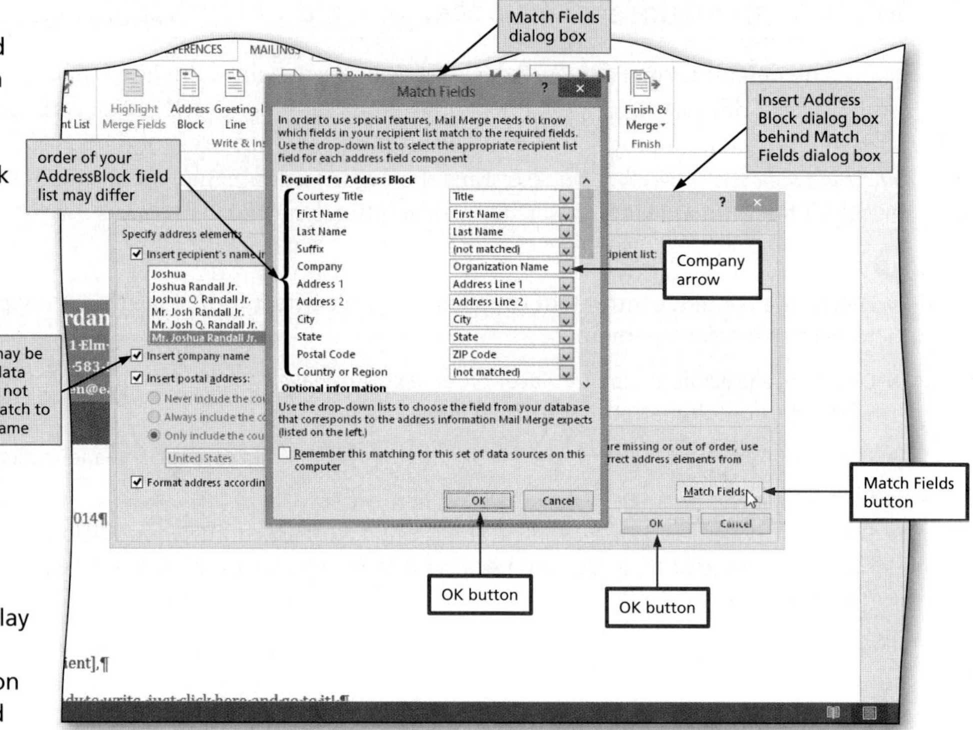

Figure 6–31

- Tap or click the OK button (Match Fields dialog box) to close the dialog box, and notice the 'Insert company name' check box no longer is dimmed because the Company field now has a matched field in the data source.
- If necessary, tap or click the 'Insert company name' check box to select it, and notice the preview area shows the organization name in the sample formatted address.

- Tap or click the OK button (Insert Address Block dialog box) to insert the AddressBlock merge field at the location of the insertion point (Figure 6–32).

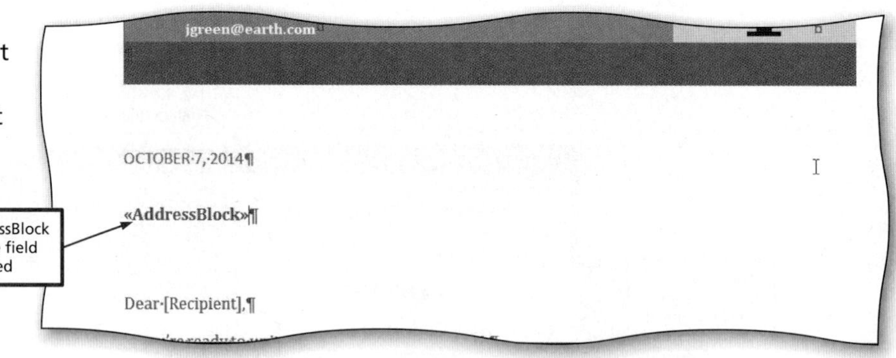

Figure 6–32

To Edit the AddressBlock Merge Field

If you wanted to change the format of or match fields in the AddressBlock merge field, you would perform the following steps.

1. Press and hold or right-click the AddressBlock merge field to display a shortcut menu.
2. Tap or click 'Edit Address Block' on the shortcut menu to display the Modify Address Block dialog box.
3. Make necessary changes and then tap or click the OK button (Modify Address Block dialog box).

To View Merged Data in the Main Document

1 IDENTIFY MAIN DOCUMENT | 2 CREATE DATA SOURCE | 3 COMPOSE MAIN DOCUMENT
4 MERGE DATA SOURCE | 5 ADDRESS MAILING LABELS | 6 MERGE TO DIRECTORY

Instead of displaying merge fields, you can display merged data. ***Why?*** *One way to see how fields, such as the AddressBlock fields, will look in the merged letter, is to view merged data.* The following step views merged data.

- Tap or click the 'View Merged Data' button (MAILINGS tab | Preview Results group) to display the values in the current data record, instead of the merge fields (Figure 6–33).

Q&A How can I tell which record is showing?
The current record number is displayed in the Preview Results group.

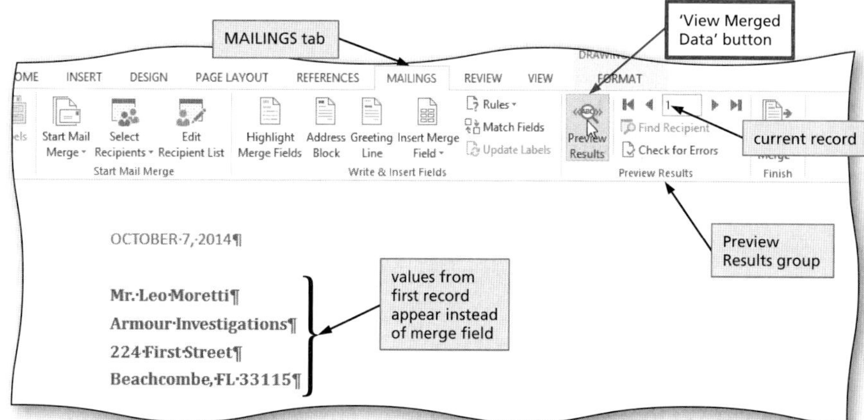

Figure 6–33

To Insert the GreetingLine Merge Field

1 IDENTIFY MAIN DOCUMENT | 2 CREATE DATA SOURCE | 3 COMPOSE MAIN DOCUMENT
4 MERGE DATA SOURCE | 5 ADDRESS MAILING LABELS | 6 MERGE TO DIRECTORY

The **GreetingLine merge field** contains text and fields related to a salutation. The default greeting for the salutation is in the format, Dear Leo, followed by a comma. In this letter, you want the salutation to be followed by a colon. ***Why?*** *Business letters use a more formal salutation (Dear Mr. Moretti:) in the cover letter.* The following steps insert the GreetingLine merge field.

- Delete the word, Dear, the [Recipient] placeholder text, and the comma in the salutation but leave the paragraph mark; position the insertion point to the left of the paragraph mark because you will insert the GreetingLine merge field in that location.
- Tap or click the 'Insert formatted salutation' link in the Mail Merge task pane to display the Insert Greeting Line dialog box.
- If necessary, tap or click the middle arrow in the Greeting line format area (Insert Greeting Line dialog box); scroll to and then tap or click the format, Mr. Randall, in this list because you want the title followed by the last name format.
- If necessary, tap or click the rightmost arrow in the Greeting line format area and then tap or click the colon (:) in the list (Figure 6–34).

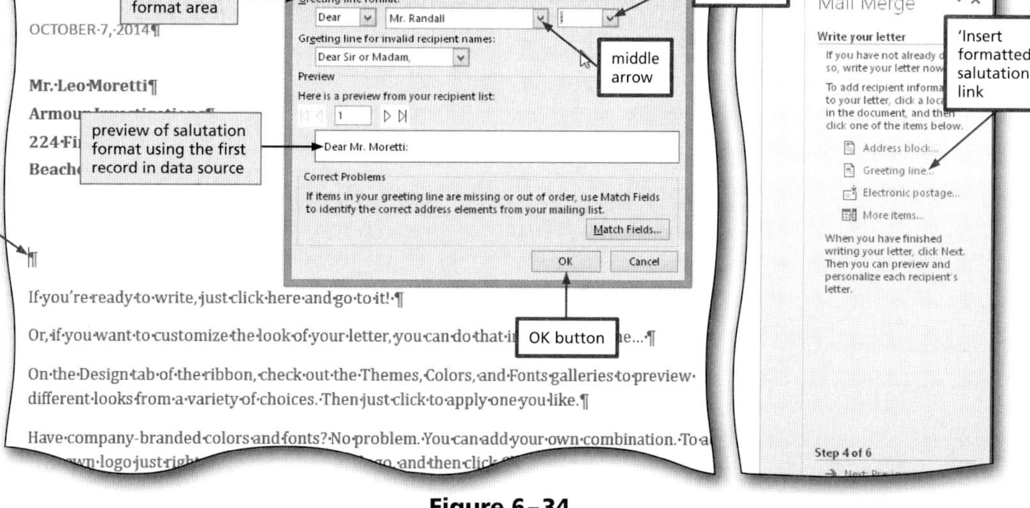

Figure 6–34

- Tap or click the OK button to insert the GreetingLine merge field at the location of the insertion point (Figure 6–35).

Q&A Why are the values for the title and last name displayed instead of the merge field names?
With the 'View Merged Data' button (MAILINGS tab | Preview Results group) still selected, the field values are displayed instead of the field names.

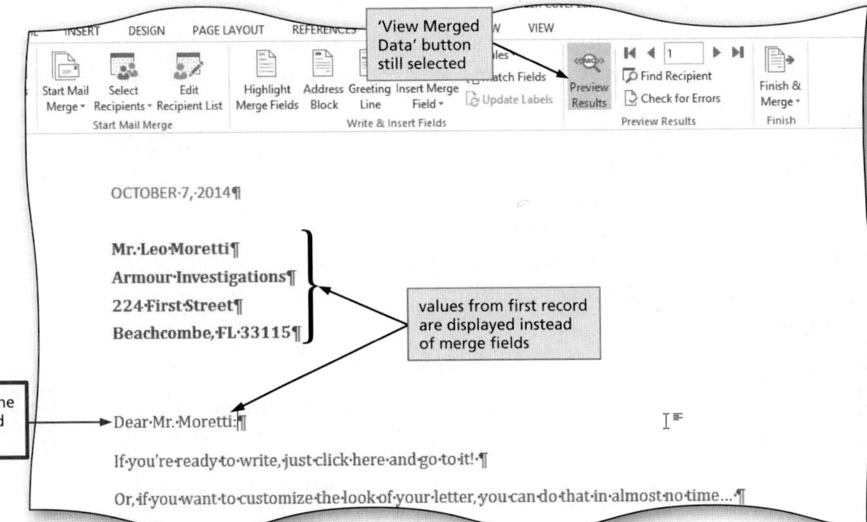

Figure 6–35

To Edit the GreetingLine Merge Field

If you wanted to change the format of or match fields in the GreetingLine merge field, you would perform the following steps.

1. Press and hold or right-click the GreetingLine merge field to display a shortcut menu.
2. Tap or click 'Edit Greeting Line' on the shortcut menu to display the Modify Greeting Line dialog box.
3. Make the necessary changes and then tap or click the OK button (Modify Greeting Line dialog box).

To View Merge Fields in the Main Document

Because you will be entering merge fields in the document next, you wish to display the merge fields instead of the merged data. The following step views merge fields instead of merged data.

1 Tap or click the 'View Merged Data' button (MAILINGS tab | Preview Results group) to display the merge fields instead of the values in the current data record (shown in Figure 6–36).

To Begin Typing the Body of the Form Letter

The next step is to begin typing the message, or body of the letter, which is located at the content control that begins with the placeholder text, If you're ready to write..., below the GreetingLine merge field. The following steps begin typing the letter in the location of the content control.

1. Tap or click the body of the letter to select the content control (Figure 6–36).
2. With the content control selected, type `I enjoyed meeting with you during the` and then press the SPACEBAR (shown in Figure 6–37).

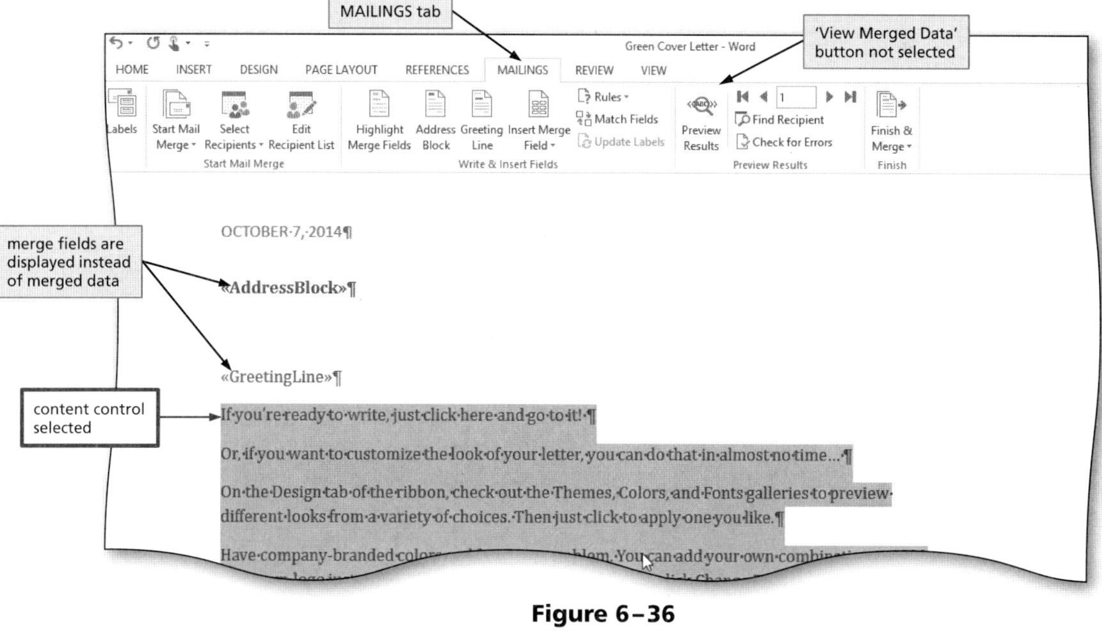

Figure 6–36

BTW

'Insert Merge Field' Button

If you tap or click the 'Insert Merge Field' button instead of the 'Insert Merge Field' arrow (Figure 6–37), Word displays the Insert Merge Field dialog box instead of the Insert Merge Field menu. To insert fields from the dialog box, tap or click the field name and then tap or click the Insert button. The dialog box remains open so that you can insert multiple fields, if necessary. When you have finished inserting fields, tap or click the Close button in the dialog box.

To Insert a Merge Field in the Main Document

1 IDENTIFY MAIN DOCUMENT | 2 CREATE DATA SOURCE | **3 COMPOSE MAIN DOCUMENT**
4 MERGE DATA SOURCE | 5 ADDRESS MAILING LABELS | 6 MERGE TO DIRECTORY

The next step is to insert the Job Fair merge field into the main document. ***Why?*** *The first sentence in the first paragraph of the letter identifies the job fair, which is a merge field, at which the student met the prospective employer.* To instruct Word to use data fields from the data source, you insert merge fields in the main document for the form letter. The following steps insert a merge field at the location of the insertion point.

1

- Tap or click the 'Insert Merge Field' arrow (MAILINGS tab | Write & Insert Fields group) to display the Insert Merge Field menu (Figure 6–37).

Q&A What if I accidentally tap or click the 'Insert Merge Field' button instead of the arrow?
Tap or click the Cancel button in the Insert Merge Field dialog box and repeat Step 1.

Why is the underscore character in some of the field names?
Word places an underscore character in place of the space in merge fields.

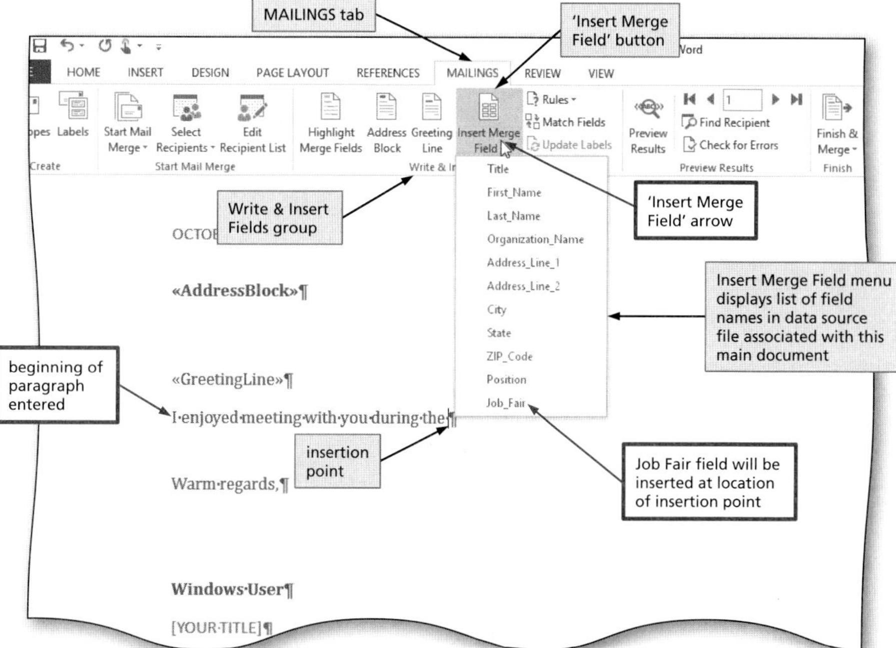

Figure 6–37

2

- Tap or click Job_Fair on the Insert Merge Field menu to insert the selected merge field in the document at the location of the insertion point (Figure 6–38).

Q&A Will the word, Job_Fair, and the chevron characters print when I merge the form letters?

No. When you merge the data source with the main document, the value in the Job Fair field (e.g., Fisher) will print at the location of the merge field, Job_Fair.

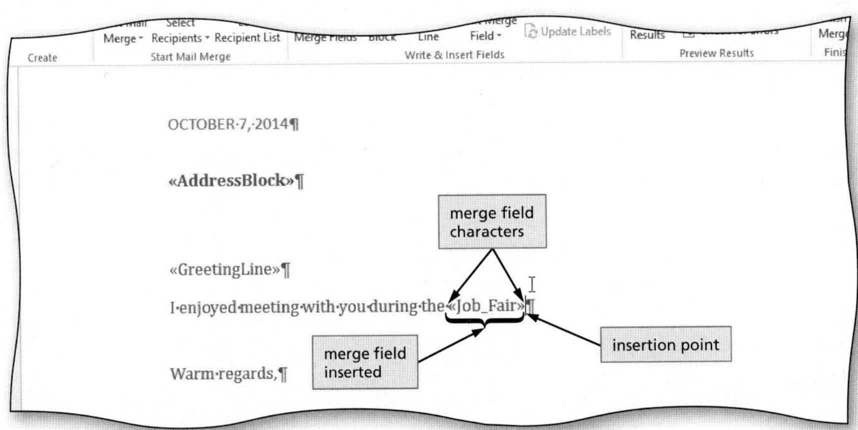

Figure 6–38

3

- Press the SPACEBAR. Type `job fair on` and then press the SPACEBAR again.

Other Ways

1. Tap or click 'Insert Merge Field' button (MAILINGS tab | Write & Insert fields group), tap or click desired field (Insert Merge Field dialog box), tap or click Insert button, tap or click Close button

BTW

Merge Fields

When you insert fields in a document, the displayed fields may be surrounded by braces instead of chevrons, and extra instructions may appear between the braces. If this occurs, then field codes have been turned on. To turn off field codes so that they are not displayed, press ALT+F9.

IF Fields

In addition to merge fields, you can insert Word fields that are designed specifically for a mail merge. An **IF field** is an example of a Word field. One form of the IF field is called an **If...Then:** If a condition is true, then perform an action. For example, If Mary owns a house, then send her information about homeowner's insurance. Another form of the IF field is called an **If...Then...Else:** If a condition is true, then perform an action; else perform a different action. For example, If John has an email address, then send him an email message; else send him the message via the postal service.

In this project, the form letter checks the job fair location and displays the corresponding date the job fair was held. If the job fair was held in Fisher, then the form letter should print the text, Friday, October 3; else if the job fair was held in Pontiac, then the form letter should print the text, Saturday, October 4. Thus, you will use an If...Then...Else: If the Job_Fair is equal to Fisher, then insert Friday, October 3; else insert Saturday, October 4.

The phrase that appears after the word If is called a rule, or condition. A **condition** consists of an expression, followed by a comparison operator, followed by a final expression.

Expression The expression in a condition can be a merge field, a number, a series of characters, or a mathematical formula. Word surrounds a series of characters with quotation marks ("). To indicate an empty, or null, expression, Word places two quotation marks together ("").

Comparison operator The comparison operator in a condition must be one of six characters: = (equal to or matches the text), <> (not equal to or does not match text), < (less than), <= (less than or equal to), > (greater than), or >= (greater than or equal to).

If the result of a condition is true, then Word evaluates the **true text**. If the result of the condition is false, Word evaluates the **false text** if it exists. In this project, the first expression in the condition is a merge field (Job_Fair); the comparison operator is equal to (=); and the second expression is the text "Fisher". The true text is "Friday, October 3". The false text is "Saturday, October 4". The complete IF field is as follows:

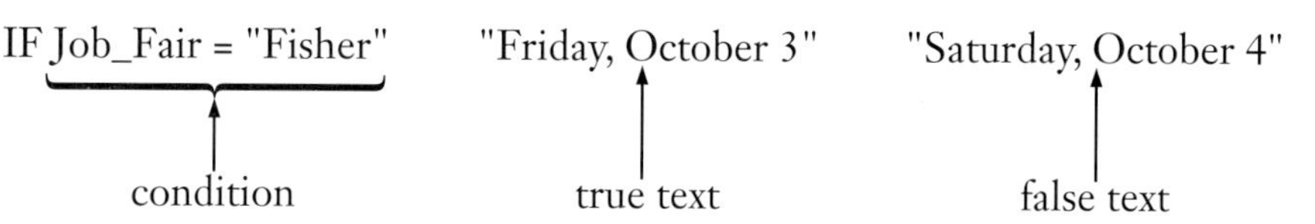

> BTW
> **IF Fields**
> The phrase, IF field, originates from computer programming. Do not be intimidated by the terminology. An IF field simply specifies a decision. Some programmers refer to it as an IF statement. Complex IF statements include one or more nested IF fields, which is a second IF field inside the true or false text of the first IF field.

To Insert an IF Field in the Main Document

1 IDENTIFY MAIN DOCUMENT | 2 CREATE DATA SOURCE | 3 COMPOSE MAIN DOCUMENT
4 MERGE DATA SOURCE | 5 ADDRESS MAILING LABELS | 6 MERGE TO DIRECTORY

The next step is to insert an IF field in the main document. ***Why?*** *You want to print the date of the job fair where you met the potential employer.* The following steps insert this IF field in the form letter: If the Job_Fair is equal to Fisher, then insert Friday, October 3, else insert Saturday, October 4.

- With the insertion point positioned as shown in Figure 6–39, tap or click the Rules button (MAILINGS tab | Write & Insert Fields group) to display the Rules menu (Figure 6–39).

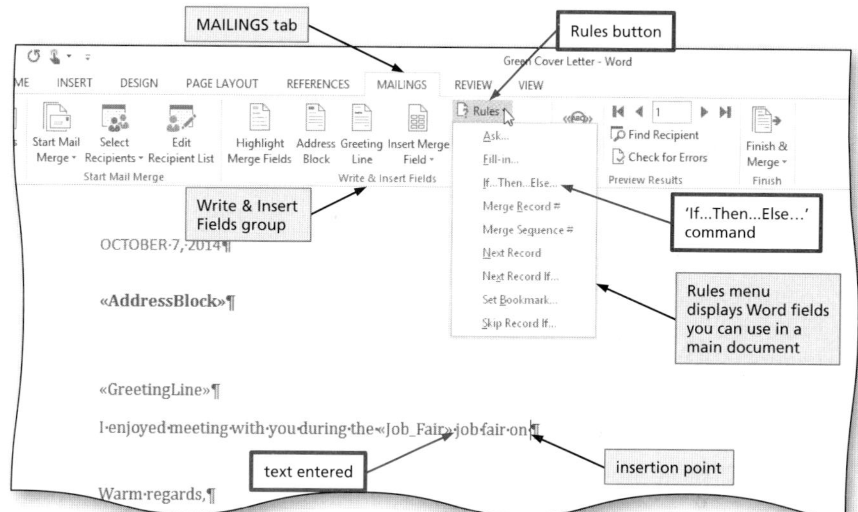

Figure 6–39

- Tap or click 'If...Then...Else...' on the Rules menu to display the Insert Word Field: IF dialog box, which is where you enter the components of the IF field (Figure 6–40).

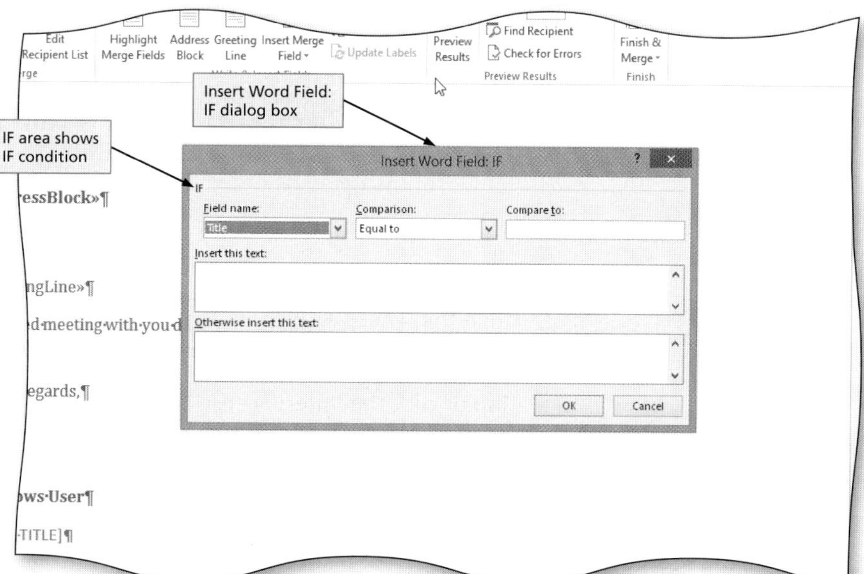

Figure 6–40

3

- Tap or click the Field name arrow (Insert Word Field: IF dialog box) to display the list of fields in the data source.
- Scroll through the list of fields in the Field name list and then tap or click Job_Fair to select the field.
- Position the insertion point in the Compare to text box and then type **`Fisher`** as the comparison text.
- Press the TAB key and then type **`Friday, October 3`** as the true text.
- Press the TAB key and then type **`Saturday, October 4`** as the false text (Figure 6–41).

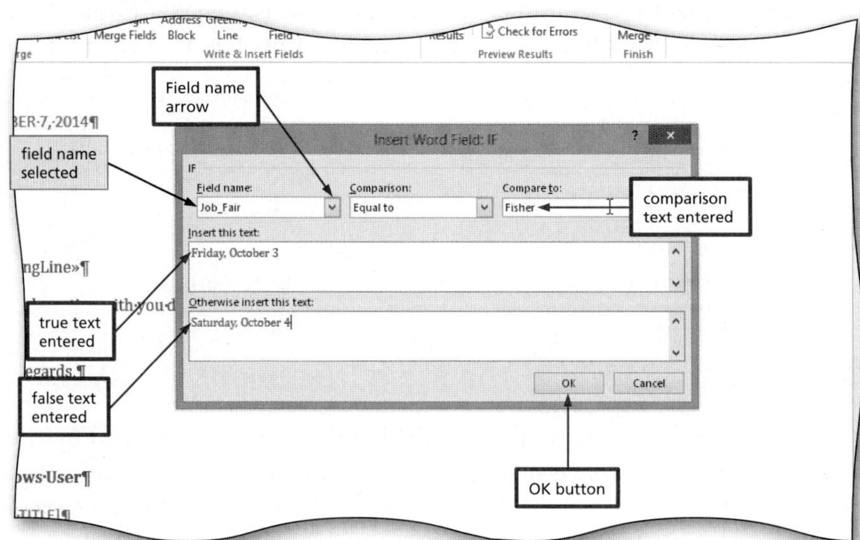

Figure 6–41

Does the capitalization matter in the comparison text?
Yes. The text, Fisher, is different from the text, fisher, in a comparison. Be sure to enter the text exactly as you entered it in the data source.

4

- Tap or click the OK button to insert the IF field at the location of the insertion point (Figure 6–42).

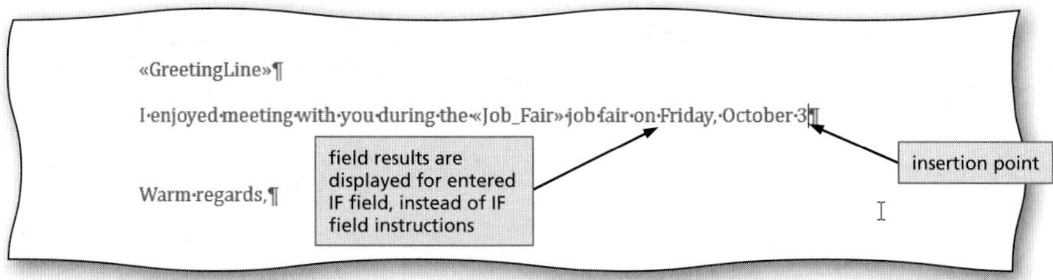

Figure 6–42

Q&A Why does the main document display the text, Friday, October 3, instead of the IF field instructions?
The text, Friday, October 3, is displayed because the first record in the data source has a job fair equal to Fisher. Word, by default, evaluates the IF field using the current record and displays the results, called the **field results**, in the main document instead of displaying the IF field instructions. Later in the chapter, you will view the IF field instructions.

To Enter More Text and Merge Fields in the Main Document

The following steps enter the remainder of the text and merge fields into the form letter.

1. With the insertion point at the location shown in Figure 6–42, press the PERIOD and then the SPACEBAR. Type **`As you suggested, I have enclosed my resume for your review. I am interested in the`** and then press the SPACEBAR.
2. Tap or click the 'Insert Merge Field' arrow (MAILINGS tab | Write & Insert Fields group) and then tap or click Position on the Insert Merge Field menu to insert the selected merge field in the document.
3. Press the SPACEBAR. Type **`position we discussed and am confident I am an ideal candidate for this job.`** Press the ENTER key. Type **`I would appreciate the opportunity to meet with you to discuss my qualifications and potential employment with`** and then press the SPACEBAR.

4. Tap or click the 'Insert Merge Field' arrow (MAILINGS tab | Write & Insert Fields group) and then tap or click Organization_Name on the Insert Merge Field menu to insert the selected merge field in the document.

5. Press the PERIOD key. Type **`Thank you,`** and then press the SPACEBAR. Insert the Title merge field, press the SPACEBAR, and then insert the Last Name merge field. Type **`, for your time and consideration. I look forward to hearing from you soon.`**

6. Change the closing to the word, Sincerely. Change the Your Name content control to Jordan Taylor Green, and change the Your Title content control to the word, ENCLOSURE, to complete the letter (Figure 6–43).

   If requested by your instructor, enter your name instead of the job seeker's name.

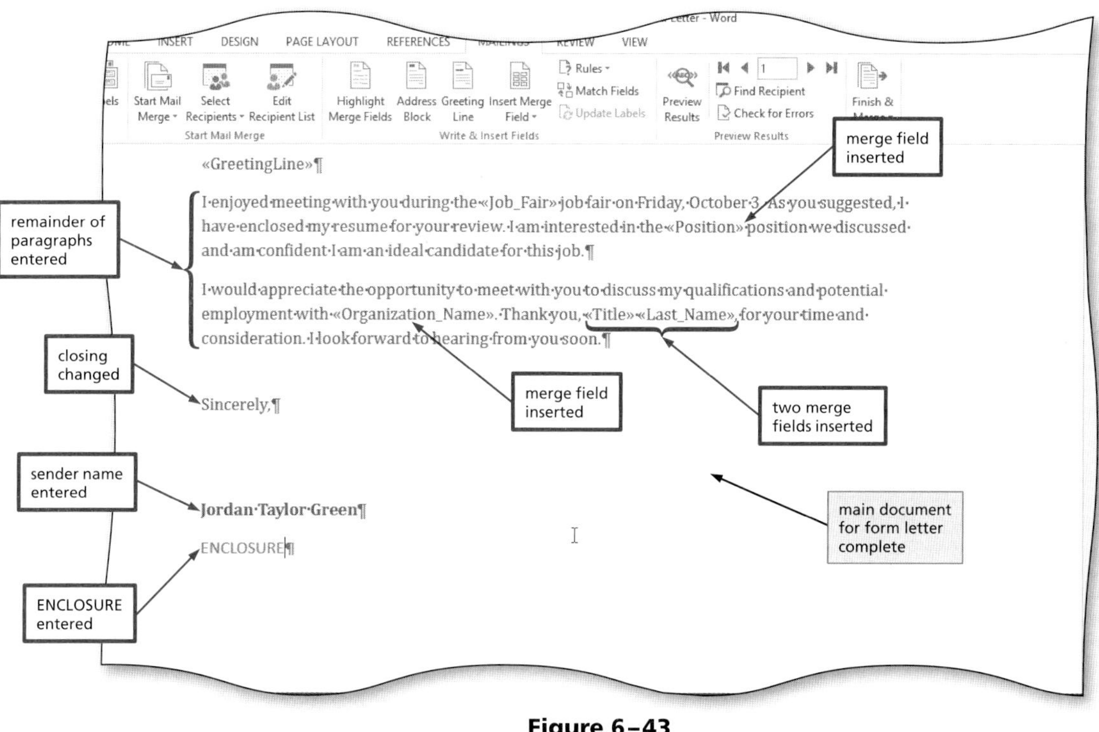

Figure 6–43

To Highlight Merge Fields

If you wanted to highlight all the merge fields in a document so that you could identify them quickly, you would perform the following steps.

1. Tap or click the 'Highlight Merge Fields' button (MAILINGS tab | Write & Insert Fields group) to highlight the merge fields in the document.
2. When finished viewing merge fields, tap or click the 'Highlight Merge Fields' button (MAILINGS tab | Write & Insert Fields group) again to remove the highlight from the merge fields in the document.

BTW

Word Fields

In addition to the IF field, Word provides other fields that may be used in form letters. For example, the ASK and FILLIN fields prompt the user to enter data for each record in the data source. The SKIP RECORD IF field instructs the mail merge not to generate a form letter for a data record if a specific condition is met.

To Display a Field Code

1 IDENTIFY MAIN DOCUMENT | 2 CREATE DATA SOURCE | **3 COMPOSE MAIN DOCUMENT**
4 MERGE DATA SOURCE | 5 ADDRESS MAILING LABELS | 6 MERGE TO DIRECTORY

The instructions in the IF field are not displayed in the document; instead, the field results are displayed for the current record (Figure 6–42). The instructions of an IF field are called **field codes**, and the default for Word is for field codes not to be displayed. Thus, field codes do not print or show on the screen unless you turn them on. You use one procedure to show field codes on the screen and a different procedure to print them on a hard copy.

The following steps show a field code on the screen. ***Why?*** *You might want to turn on a field code to verify its accuracy or to modify it. Field codes tend to clutter the screen. Thus, most Word users turn them off after viewing them.*

1

- If necessary, scroll to display the body of the letter in the document window.
- Press and hold the field results and then tap the 'Show Context Menu' button on the mini toolbar or right-click the field results showing the text, Friday, October 3, to display a shortcut menu (Figure 6–44).

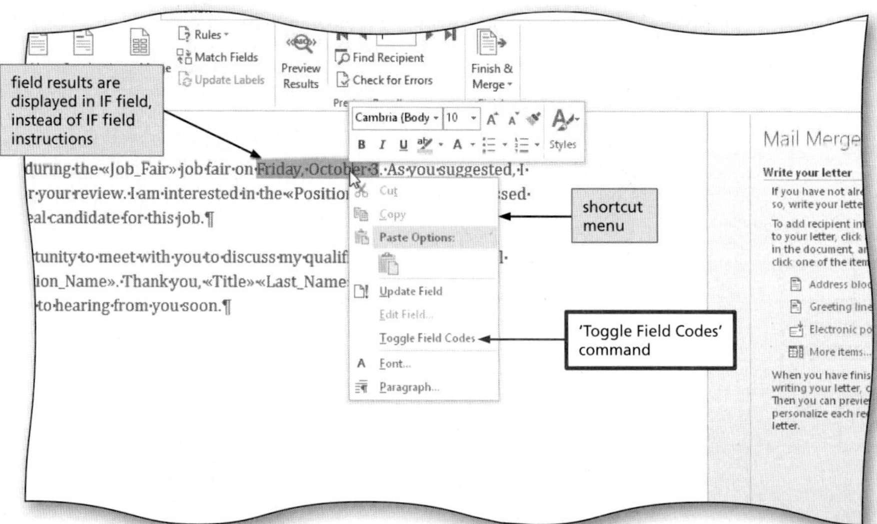

Figure 6–44

2

- Tap or click 'Toggle Field Codes' on the shortcut menu to display the field codes instead of the field results for the IF field (Figure 6–45).

Q&A

Will displaying field codes affect the merged documents?
No. Displaying field codes has no effect on the merge process.

What if I wanted to display all field codes in a document?
You would press ALT+F9. Then, to hide all the field codes, press ALT+F9 again.

Why does the IF field turn gray?
Word, by default, shades a field in gray when the field is selected. The shading displays on the screen to help you identify fields; the shading does not print on a hard copy.

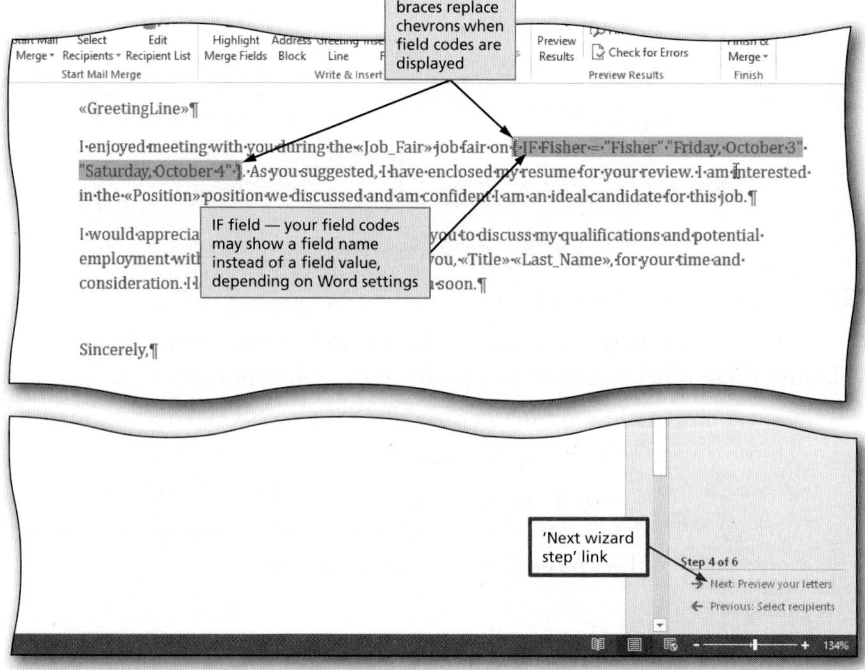

Figure 6–45

Other Ways

1. With insertion point in field, press SHIFT+F9

To Print Field Codes in the Main Document

When you merge or print a document, Word automatically converts field codes that show on the screen to field results. You may want to print the field codes version of the form letter, however, so that you have a hard copy of the field codes for future reference. When you print field codes, you must remember to turn off the field codes option so that merged documents print field results instead of field codes. If you wanted to print the field codes in the main document, you would perform the following steps.

1. Open the Backstage view and then tap or click Options to display the Word Options dialog box.
2. Tap or click Advanced in the left pane (Word Options dialog box) to display advanced options in the right pane and then scroll to the Print area in the right pane of the dialog box.
3. Place a check mark in the 'Print field codes instead of their values' check box.
4. Tap or click the OK button to instruct Word to show field codes when the document prints.
5. Open the Backstage view, tap or click the Print tab, and then tap or click the Print button to print the document with all field codes showing.
6. Open the Backstage view and then tap or click Options to display the Word Options dialog box.
7. Tap or click Advanced in the left pane (Word Options dialog box) to display advanced options in the right pane and then scroll to the Print area in the right pane of the dialog box.
8. Remove the check mark from the 'Print field codes instead of their values' check box.
9. Tap or click the OK button to instruct Word to show field results the next time you print the document.

BTW

Data Source and Main Document Files

When you open a main document, if Word cannot locate the associated data source file or it does not display a dialog box with the 'Find Data Source' button, then the data source may not be associated with the main document. To associate the data source with the main document, tap or click the Select Recipients button (MAILINGS tab | Start Mail Merge group), tap or click 'Use an Existing List' on the Select Recipients menu, and then locate the data source file. When you save the main document, Word will associate the data source with the main document.

To Save a Document Again

The main document for the form letter now is complete. Thus, you should save it again. The following step saves the document again.

1. Save the main document for the form letter again with the same file name, Green Cover Letter.

Opening a Main Document

You open a main document as you open any other Word document (i.e., tapping or clicking Open in the Backstage view). If Word displays a dialog box indicating it will run an SQL command, tap or click the Yes button (Figure 6–46).

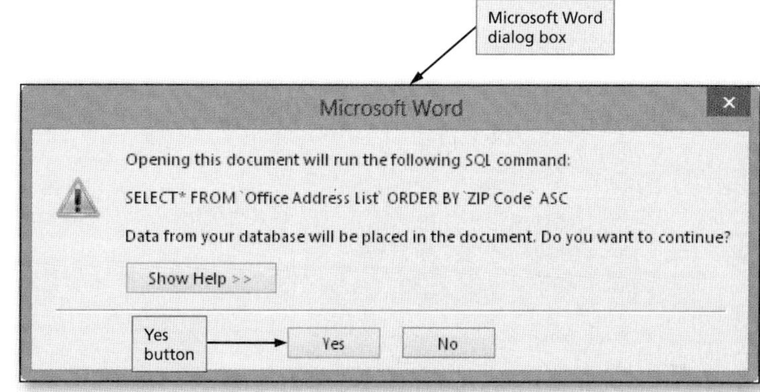

Figure 6–46

When you open a main document, Word attempts to open the associated data source file, too. If the data source is not in exactly the same location (i.e., drive and folder)

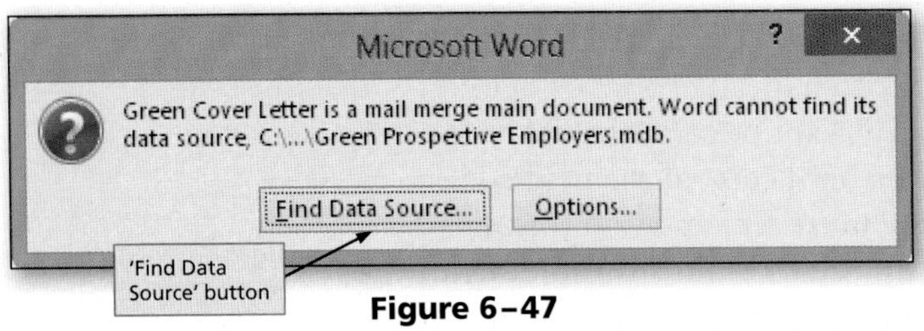

Figure 6–47

as when it originally was saved, Word displays a dialog box indicating that it could not find the data source (Figure 6–47). When this occurs, tap or click the 'Find Data Source' button to display the Open Data Source dialog box, which allows you to locate the data source file. (Word may display several dialog boxes requiring you to tap or click an OK (or similar) button until the one shown in Figure 6–47 appears.)

Break Point: If you wish to take a break, this is a good place to do so. You can exit Word now. To resume at a later time, run Word, open the file called Green Cover Letter, and continue following the steps from this location forward.

BTW

Locking Fields

If you wanted to lock a field so that its field results cannot be changed, tap or click the field and then press CTRL+F11. To subsequently unlock a field so that it may be updated, tap or click the field and then press CTRL+SHIFT+F11.

Merging the Data Source with the Main Document to Generate Form Letters

The next step in this project is to merge the data source with the main document to generate the form letters (shown in Figure 6–1c on page WD 339). **Merging** is the process of combining the contents of a data source with a main document.

You can merge the form letters to a new document, which you can edit, or merge them directly to a printer. You also have the option of merging all data in a data source or merging just a portion of it. The following pages discuss various ways to merge.

1 IDENTIFY MAIN DOCUMENT | 2 CREATE DATA SOURCE | 3 COMPOSE MAIN DOCUMENT
4 MERGE DATA SOURCE | 5 ADDRESS MAILING LABELS | 6 MERGE TO DIRECTORY

To Preview the Merged Letters

Earlier in this chapter, you previewed the data in the letters using a button on the ribbon. The following step uses the Mail Merge wizard to preview the letters. ***Why?*** *The next wizard step previews the letters so that you can verify the content is accurate before performing the merge.*

1

- Tap or click the 'Next wizard step' link at the bottom of the Mail Merge task pane (shown in Figure 6–45) to display Step 5 of the Mail Merge wizard in the Mail Merge task pane (Figure 6–48).

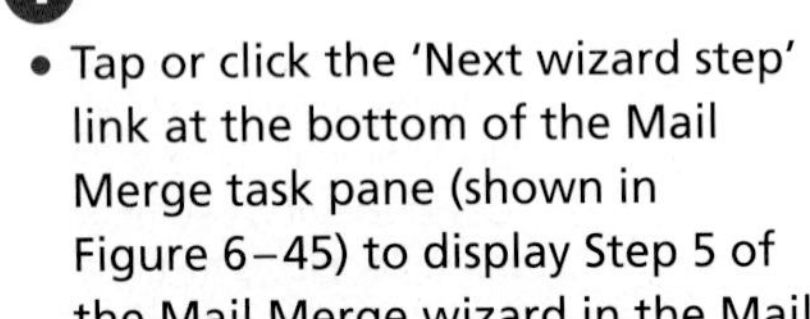

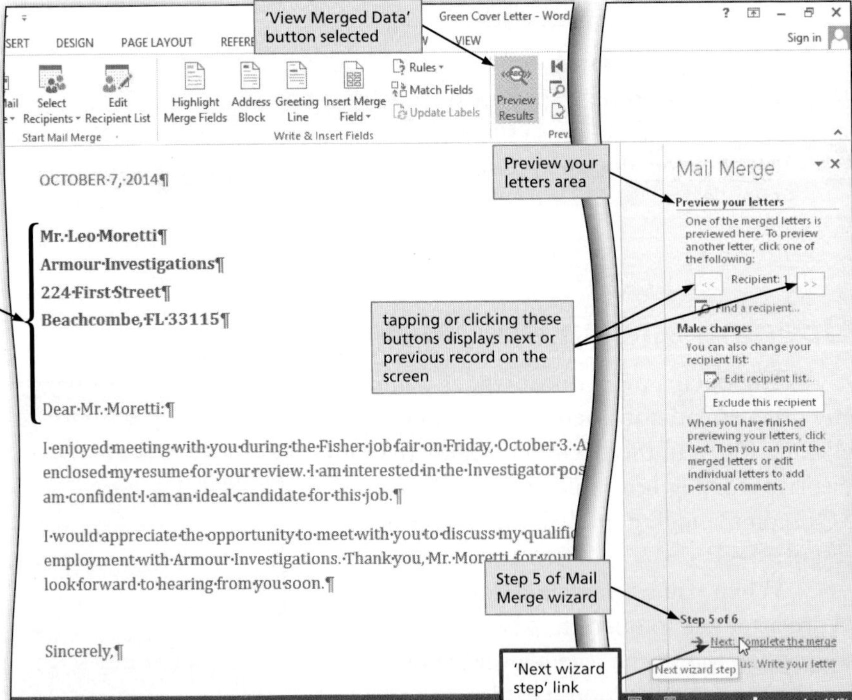

Figure 6–48

To Check for Errors

Before merging documents, you can instruct Word to check for errors that might occur during the merge process. If you wanted to check for errors, you would perform the following steps.

1. Tap or click the 'Auto Check for Errors' button (MAILINGS tab | Preview Results group) or press ALT+SHIFT+K to display the Checking and Reporting Errors dialog box.
2. Select the desired option and then tap or click the OK button.

BTW
Converting Main Document Files
If you wanted to convert a mail merge main document to a regular Word document, you would open the main document, tap or click the 'Start Mail Merge' button (MAILINGS tab | Start Mail Merge group), and then tap or click 'Normal Word Document' on the Start Mail Merge menu.

To Merge the Form Letters to a New Document

1 IDENTIFY MAIN DOCUMENT | 2 CREATE DATA SOURCE | 3 COMPOSE MAIN DOCUMENT
4 MERGE DATA SOURCE | **5 ADDRESS MAILING LABELS** | **6 MERGE TO DIRECTORY**

With the data source and main document for the form letter complete, the next step is to merge them to generate the individual form letters. You can merge the letters to the printer or to a new document. ***Why?*** *If you merge the documents to a new document, you can save the merged documents in a file and then print them later, review the merged documents for accuracy and edit them as needed, or you can add personal messages to individual merged letters.* The following steps merge the form letters to a new document.

- Tap or click the 'Next wizard step' link at the bottom of the Mail Merge task pane (shown in Figure 6–48) to display Step 6 of the Mail Merge wizard in the Mail Merge task pane.
- Tap or click the 'Merge to new document' link in the Mail Merge task pane to display the Merge to New Document dialog box (Figure 6–49).

Q&A What if I wanted to print the merged letters immediately instead of reviewing them first in a new document window?
You would tap or click the 'Merge to printer' link instead of the 'Merge to new document' link.

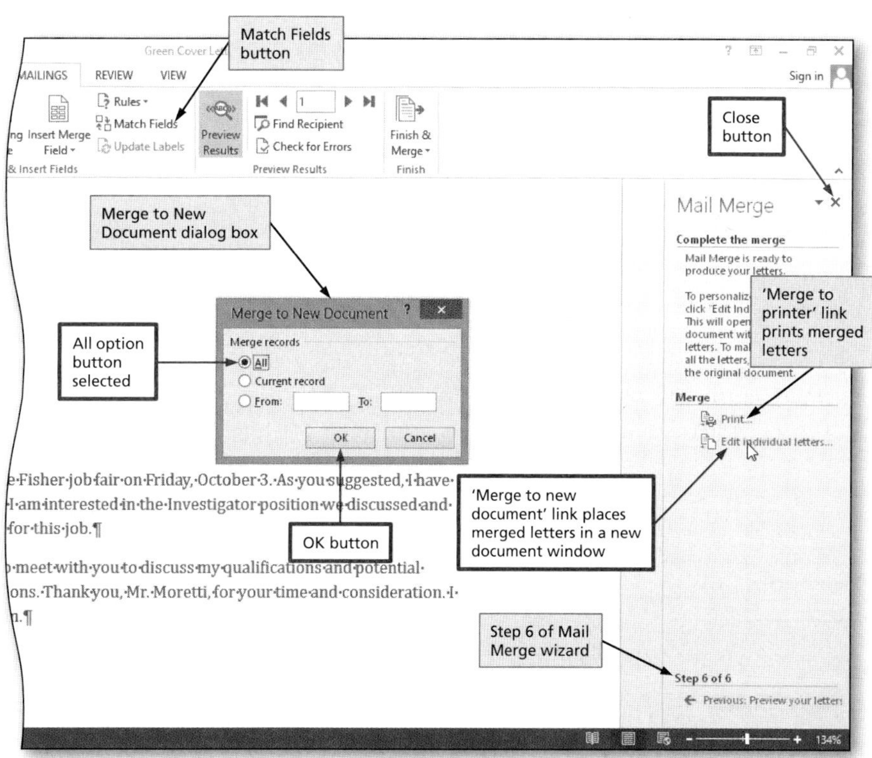

Figure 6–49

2

- If necessary, tap or click All (Merge to New Document dialog box) so that all records in the data source are merged.

Q&A Do I have to merge all records?
No. Through this dialog box, you can merge the current record or a range of record numbers.

- Tap or click the OK button to merge the letters to a new document, in this case, five individual letters — one for each potential employer in the data source (Figure 6–50). (If Word displays a dialog box containing a message about locked fields, tap or click its OK button.)

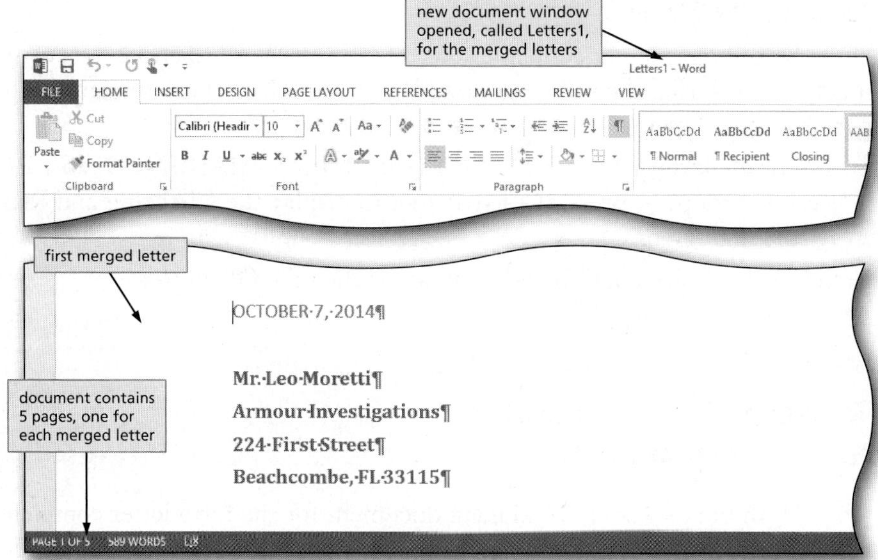

Figure 6–50

 **Experiment**

- Scroll through the merged documents so that you can see all five letters.

Q&A Why does my screen show an extra blank page at the end?
You might have a blank record in the data source, or the spacing may cause an overflow to a blank page.

Other Ways

1. Tap or click 'Finish & Merge' button (MAILINGS tab | Finish group), tap or click 'Edit Individual Documents'

To Edit a Merged Letter, Save the Merged Documents in a File, and Close the Document Window

You should proofread the merged letters to be sure that the grammar and punctuation surrounding the merged fields is correct. After reviewing the merged letters, you notice a grammatical error in the last form letter. The word, the, should be inserted before the organization name. The following steps edit text in a form letter, save the merged letters in a file, and then close the document window containing the merged letters.

1 Scroll to the last form letter in the document and then insert the word, the, in front of the organization name, Waterton Police Department (Figure 6–51).

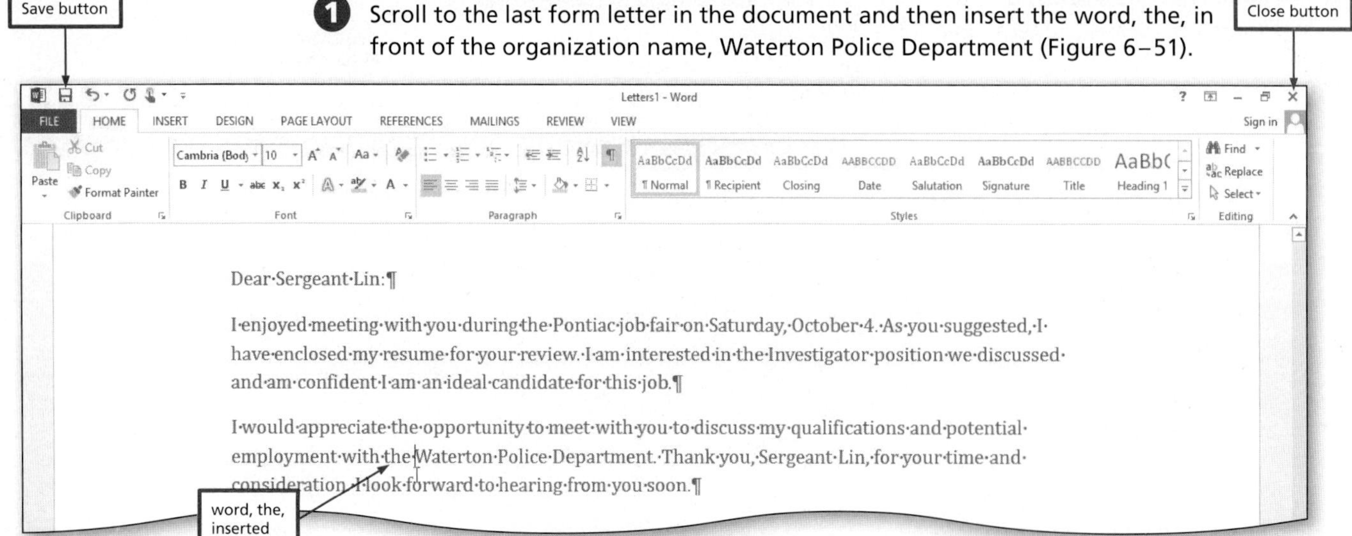

Figure 6–51

Q&A

Is it common to edit the text in the merged letters?

Sentence structure may be awkward or incorrect for some field values following a merge. Always proofread the merged letters for accuracy before distributing them.

2. Tap or click the Save button on the Quick Access Toolbar, which depending on settings, will display either the Save As gallery in the Backstage view or the Save As dialog box.

3. Save the file in the desired location (in this case, the Job Hunting folder in the Word folder in the CIS 101 folder [or your class folder]) using the file name, Green Merged Letters.

Q&A

Do I have to save the document containing the merged letters?

No. You can close the document without saving it.

4. Tap or click the Close button on the right side of the document window to close the document.

5. Tap or click the Close button on the Mail Merge task pane title bar (shown in Figure 6–49 on page WD 371) because you are finished with the Mail Merge wizard.

Correcting Merge Field Errors in Merged Documents

If the wrong field results appear, Word may be mapping the fields incorrectly. To view fields, tap or click the Match Fields button (MAILINGS tab | Write & Insert Fields group) (shown in Figure 6–49). Then, review the list of fields in the list. For example, Last Name should map to the Last Name field in the data source. If it does not, tap or click the arrow to change the name of the data source field.

If the fields are mapped correctly, the data in the data source may be incorrect. For a discussion about editing records in the data source, refer to page WD 356.

To Merge the Form Letters to a Printer

If you are certain contents of the merged letters will be correct and do not need individual editing, you can perform the following steps to merge the form letters directly to the printer.

1. If necessary, display the MAILINGS tab.
2. Tap or click the 'Finish & Merge' button (MAILINGS tab | Finish group) and then tap or click Print Documents on the Finish & Merge menu, or tap or click the 'Merge to printer' link (Mail Merge task pane), to display the Merge to Printer dialog box.
3. If necessary, tap or click All (Merge to Printer dialog box) and then tap or click the OK button to display the Print dialog box.
4. Select desired printer settings. Tap or click the OK button (Print dialog box) to print five separate letters, one for each potential employer in the data source, as shown in Figure 6–1c on page WD 339. (If Word displays a message about locked fields, tap or click its OK button.)

To Select Records to Merge

1 IDENTIFY MAIN DOCUMENT | 2 CREATE DATA SOURCE | 3 COMPOSE MAIN DOCUMENT
4 MERGE DATA SOURCE | 5 ADDRESS MAILING LABELS | 6 MERGE TO DIRECTORY

Instead of merging all of the records in the data source, you can choose which records to merge, based on a condition you specify. The dialog box in Figure 6–49 allows you to specify by record number which records to merge. Often, though, you want to merge based on the contents of a specific field. The following steps select records for a merge. ***Why?*** *You want to merge just those potential employers who were at the Pontiac job fair.*

1

- Tap or click the 'Edit Recipient List' button (MAILINGS tab | Start Mail Merge group) to display the Mail Merge Recipients dialog box (Figure 6–52).

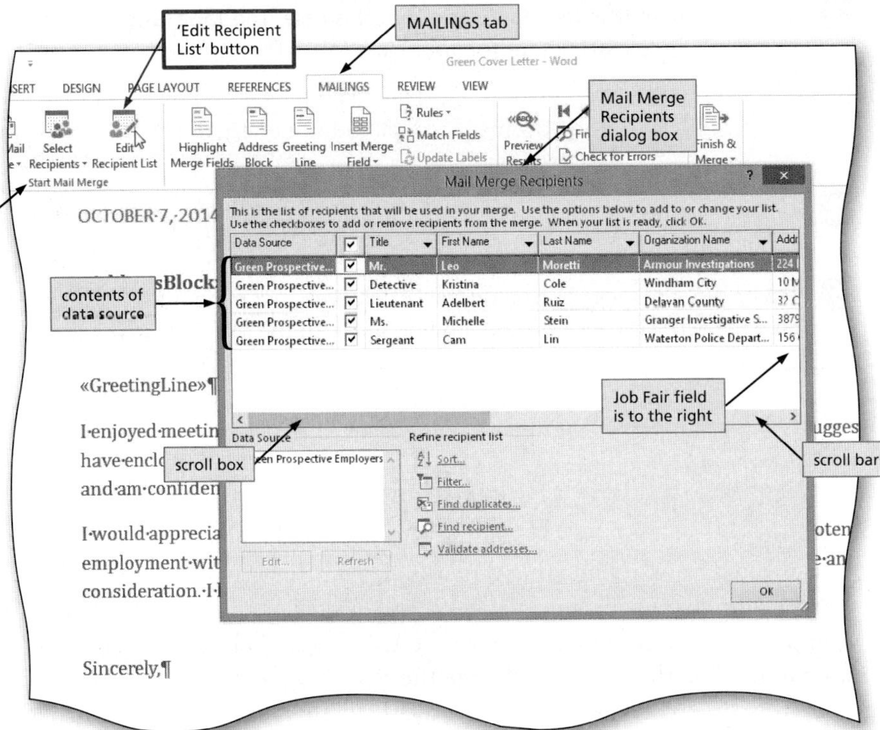

Figure 6–52

2

- Drag the scroll box to the right edge of the scroll bar (Mail Merge Recipients dialog box) so that the Job Fair field appears in the dialog box.
- Tap or click the arrow to the right of the field name, Job Fair, to display sort and filter criteria for the selected field (Figure 6–53).

Q&A What are the filter criteria in the parentheses?

The (All) option clears any previously set filter criteria. The (Blanks) option selects records that contain blanks in that field, and the (Nonblanks) option selects records that do not contain blanks in that field. The (Advanced) option displays the Filter and Sort dialog box, which allows you to perform more advanced record selection operations.

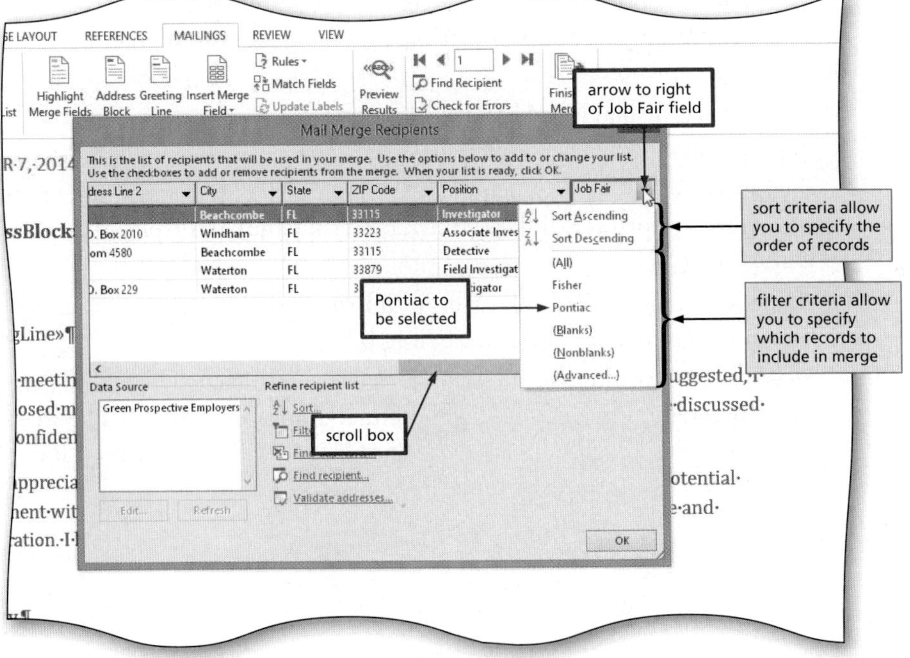

Figure 6–53

3

- Tap or click Pontiac to reduce the number of data records displayed (Mail Merge Recipients dialog box) to two, because two potential employers attended the Pontiac job fair (Figure 6–54).

What happened to the other three records that did not meet the criteria?
They still are part of the data source; they just are not appearing in the Mail Merge Recipients dialog box. When you clear the filter, all records will reappear.

4

- Tap or click the OK button to close the Mail Merge Recipients dialog box.

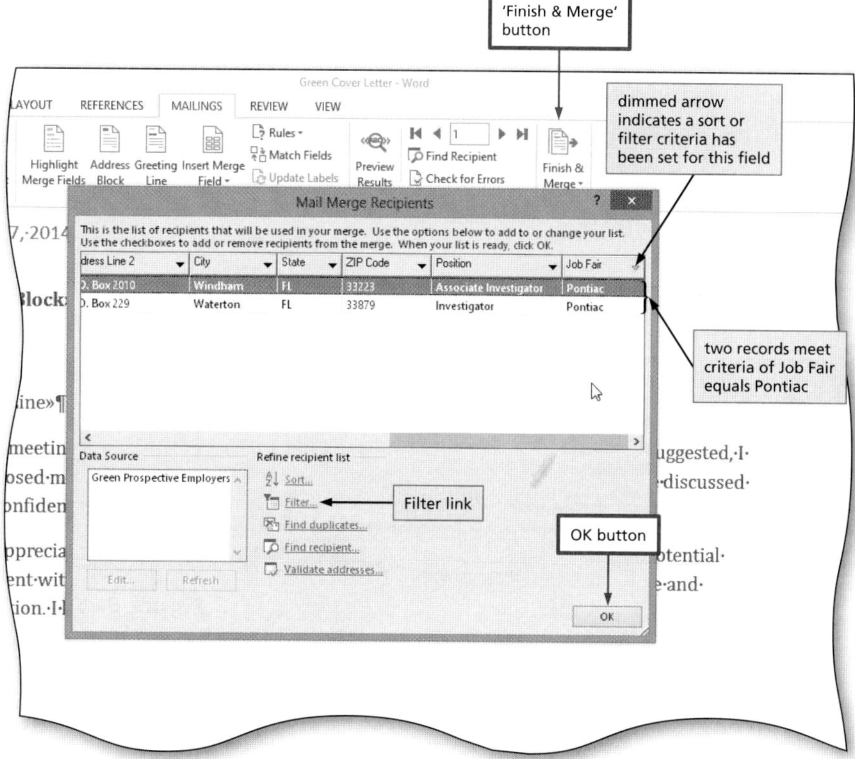

Figure 6–54

Other Ways

1. Tap or click Filter link (Mail Merge Recipients dialog box), tap or click Filter Records tab (Sort and Filter dialog box), enter filter criteria, tap or click OK button

To Merge the Form Letters to the New Document

The next step is to merge the selected records. To do this, you follow the same steps described earlier. The difference is that Word will merge only those records that meet the criteria specified, that is, just those with a job fair equal to Pontiac. The following steps merge the filtered records to a new document using the ribbon.

1. Tap or click the 'Finish & Merge' button (MAILINGS tab | Finish group) to display the Finish & Merge menu.

2. Tap or click 'Edit Individual Documents' to display the Merge to New Document dialog box. If necessary, tap or click All in the dialog box.

3. Tap or click the OK button (Merge to New Document dialog box) to display the merged documents in a new document window.

4. Change the zoom so that both documents, one for each potential employer whose job fair field equals Pontiac, appear in the document window at the same time (Figure 6–55 on the next page). (If Word displays a message about locked fields, tap or click its OK button.)

Q&A Should I add the word, the, in these letters in front of the organization name of Waterton Police Department?
Because you are not saving this document, it is not necessary to edit its grammar.

5. Close the window. Do not save the merged documents.

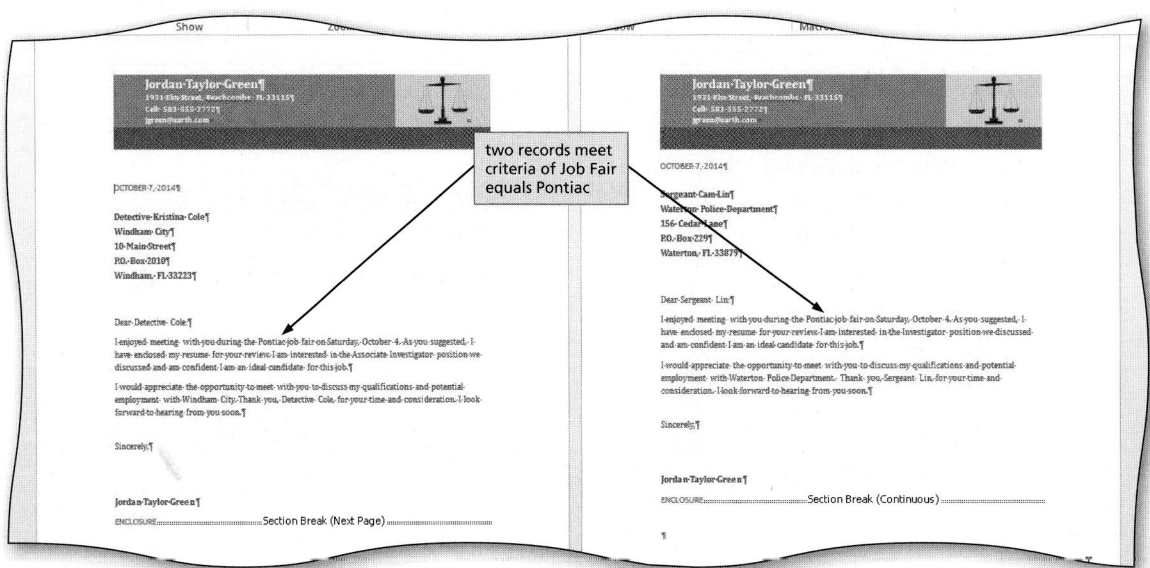

Figure 6–55

To Remove a Merge Condition

1 IDENTIFY MAIN DOCUMENT | 2 CREATE DATA SOURCE | 3 COMPOSE MAIN DOCUMENT
4 MERGE DATA SOURCE | 5 ADDRESS MAILING LABELS | 6 MERGE TO DIRECTORY

You should remove the merge condition. ***Why?*** *You do not want future merges be restricted to potential employers with a job fair equal to Pontiac.* The following steps remove a merge condition.

1

- Tap or click the 'Edit Recipient List' button (MAILINGS tab | Start Mail Merge group) to display the Mail Merge Recipients dialog box.

2

- Tap or click the Filter link (Mail Merge Recipients dialog box) to display the Filter and Sort dialog box.
- If necessary, tap or click the Filter Records tab to display the Filter Records sheet (Figure 6–56).

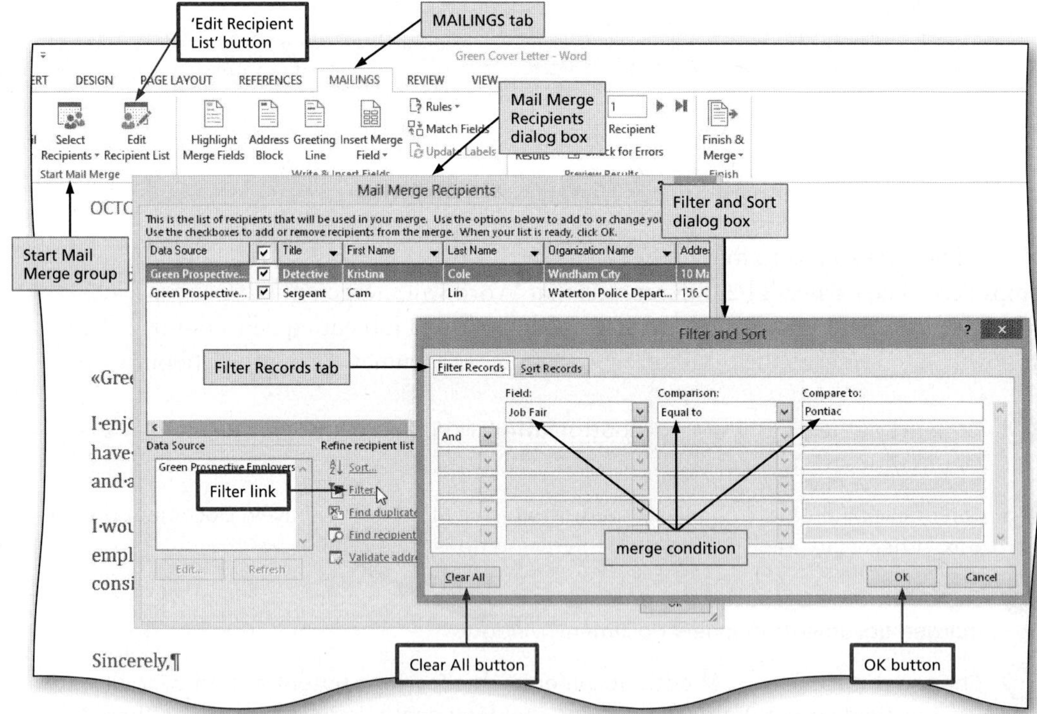

Figure 6–56

Q&A Can I specify a merge condition in this dialog box instead of using the box arrow in the Mail Merge Recipients dialog box?

Yes.

3

- Tap or click the Clear All button (Filter and Sort dialog box).
- Tap or click the OK button in each of the two open dialog boxes to remove the merge condition.

To Sort the Data Records in a Data Source

The following steps sort the data records by ZIP code. ***Why?*** *You may want the form letters printed in a certain order. For example, if you mail the form letters using the U.S. Postal Service's bulk rate mailing service, the post office requires that you sort and group the form letters by ZIP code.*

1

- Tap or click the 'Edit Recipient List' button (MAILINGS tab | Start Mail Merge group) to display the Mail Merge Recipients dialog box.
- Scroll to the right until the ZIP Code field shows in the dialog box.
- Tap or click the arrow to the right of the field name, ZIP Code, to display a menu of sort and filter criteria (Figure 6–57).

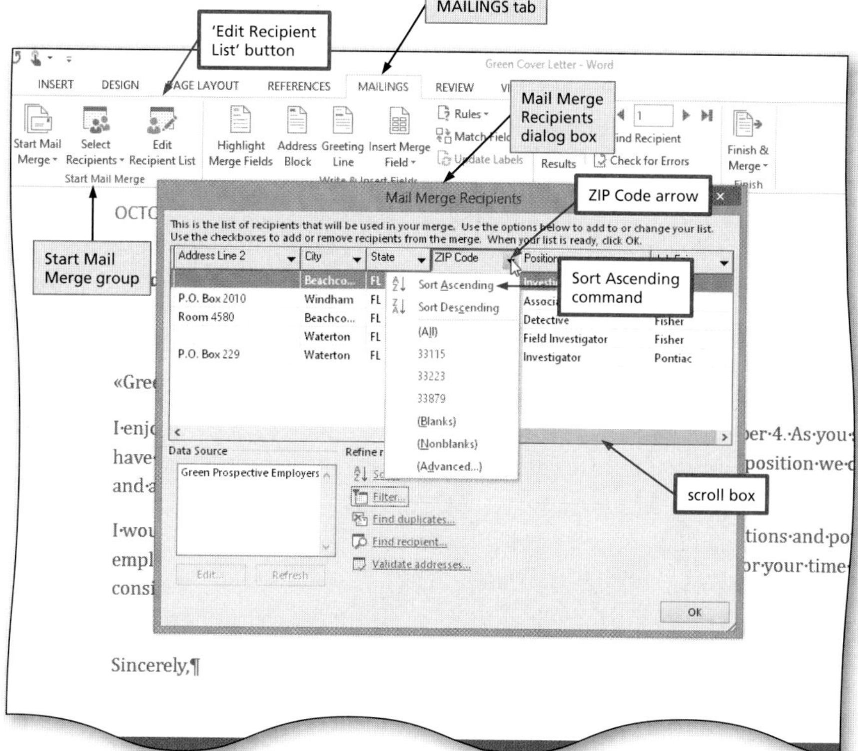

Figure 6–57

- Tap or click Sort Ascending on the menu to sort the data source records in ascending (smallest to largest) order by ZIP Code (Figure 6–58).

- Tap or click the OK button to close the Mail Merge Recipients dialog box.

Q&A In what order would the form letters print if I merged them again now?
Word would merge them in ZIP code order; that is, the records with ZIP code 33115 would appear first, and the records with ZIP code 33879 would appear last.

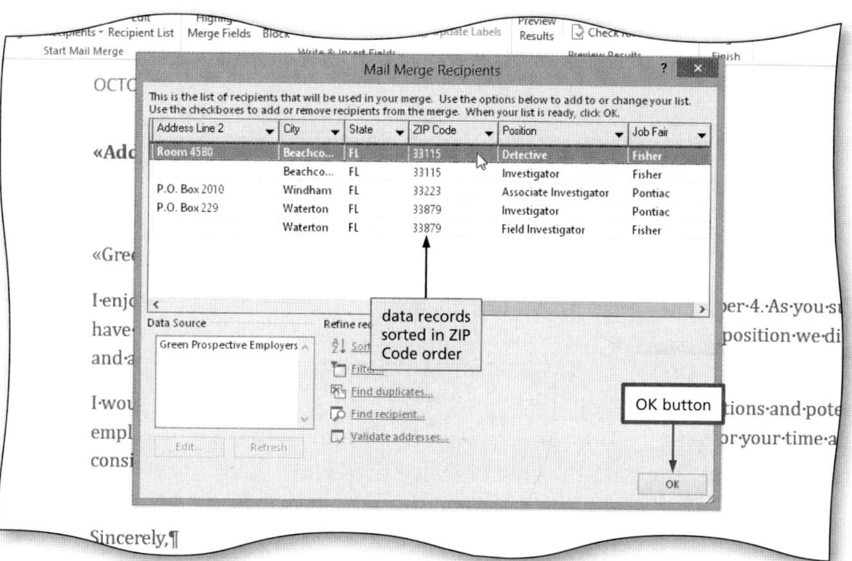

Figure 6–58

Other Ways

1. Tap or click Sort link (Mail Merge Recipients dialog box), enter sort criteria (Sort and Filter dialog box), tap or click OK button

To Find and Display Data

1 IDENTIFY MAIN DOCUMENT | 2 CREATE DATA SOURCE | 3 COMPOSE MAIN DOCUMENT
4 MERGE DATA SOURCE | 5 ADDRESS MAILING LABELS | 6 MERGE TO DIRECTORY

***Why?** If you wanted to find a particular record in the data source and display that record's data in the main document on the screen, you can search for a field value.* The following steps find Stein, which is a last name in the data source, and display that record's values in the form letter currently displaying on the screen.

- If necessary, tap or click the 'View Merged Data' button (MAILINGS tab | Preview Results group) to show field results instead of merged fields on the screen.
- Tap or click the Find Recipient button (MAILINGS tab | Preview Results group) to display the Find Entry dialog box.
- Type `Stein` in the Find text box (Find Entry dialog box) as the search text.
- Tap or click the Find Next button to display the record containing the entered text (Figure 6–59).

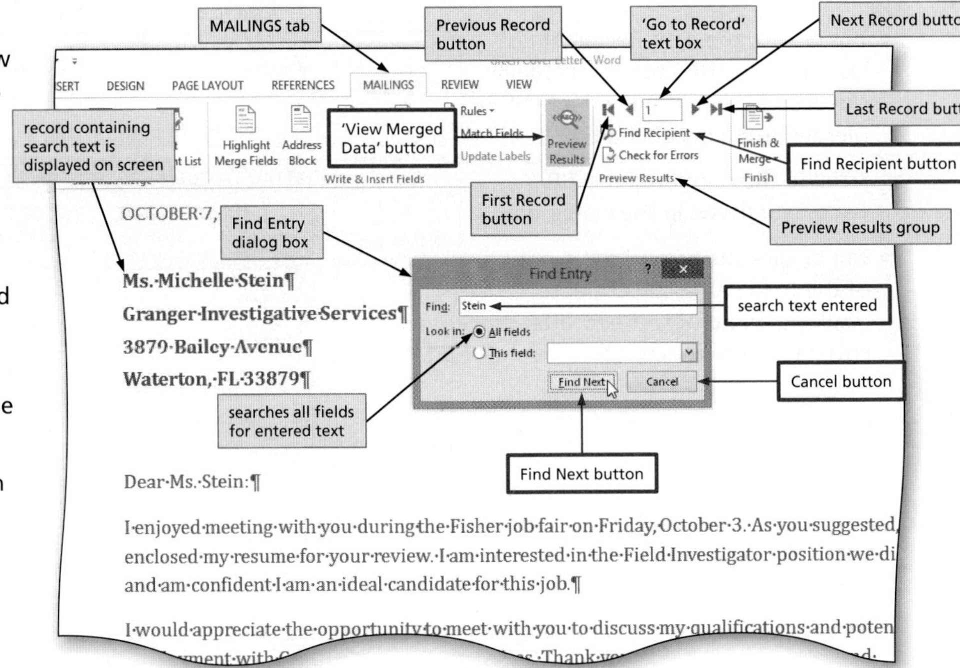

Figure 6–59

2

- Tap or click the Cancel button (Find Entry dialog box) to close the dialog box.

Displaying Data Source Records in the Main Document

When you are viewing merged data in the main document (Figure 6–59) — that is, the 'View Merged Data' button (MAILINGS tab | Preview Results group) is selected — you can tap or click buttons and boxes in the Preview Results group on the MAILINGS tab to display different results and values. For example, tap or click the Last Record button to display the values from the last record in the data source, the First Record button to display the values in record one, the Next Record button to display the values in the next consecutive record number, or the Previous Record button to display the values from the previous record number. You also can display a specific record by tapping or clicking the 'Go to Record' text box, typing the record number you would like to be displayed in the main document, and then pressing the ENTER key.

BTW
Closing Main Document Files
Word always asks if you want to save changes when you close a main document, even if you just saved the document. If you are sure that no additional changes were made to the document, tap or click the Don't Save button; otherwise, tap or click the Save button — just to be safe.

To Close a Document

The cover letter is complete. Thus, the following steps close the document.

1. Open the Backstage view and then tap or click Close.
2. If a Microsoft Word dialog box is displayed, tap or click the Save button to save the changes.

Addressing Mailing Labels and Envelopes

Now that you have merged and printed the form letters, the next step is to print addresses on mailing labels to be affixed to envelopes for the form letters. The mailing labels will use the same data source as the form letter, Green Prospective Employers. The format and content of the mailing labels will be exactly the same as the inside address in the main document for the form letter. That is, the first line will contain the title and first name followed by the last name. The second line will contain the organization name, and so on. Thus, you will use the AddressBlock merge field in the mailing labels.

You follow the same basic steps to create the main document for the mailing labels as you did to create the main document for the form letters. That is, determine the appropriate data source, create the label main document, and then merge the main document with the data source to generate the mailing labels and envelopes. The major difference here is that the data source already exists because you created it earlier in this project.

To Address and Print Mailing Labels Using an Existing Data Source

1 IDENTIFY MAIN DOCUMENT | 2 CREATE DATA SOURCE | 3 COMPOSE MAIN DOCUMENT
4 MERGE DATA SOURCE | **5 ADDRESS MAILING LABELS** | **6 MERGE TO DIRECTORY**

To address mailing labels, you specify the type of labels you intend to use. Word will request the label information, including the label vendor and product number. You can obtain this information from the box of labels. For illustration purposes in addressing these labels, the label vendor is Avery and the product number is J8158. The following steps address and print mailing labels using an existing data source. ***Why?*** *You already created the data source earlier in this chapter, so you will use that data source.*

Note: If your printer does not have the capability of printing mailing labels, read these steps without performing them. If you are in a laboratory environment, ask your instructor if you should perform these steps or read them without performing them.

1

- Open the Backstage view. Tap or click the New tab in the Backstage view to display the New gallery. Tap or click the Blank document thumbnail to open a new blank document window.
- If necessary, change the zoom to page width.
- Display the MAILINGS tab. Tap or click the 'Start Mail Merge' button (MAILINGS tab | Start Mail Merge group) and then tap or click 'Step-by-Step Mail Merge Wizard' on the Start Mail Merge menu to display Step 1 of the Mail Merge wizard in the Mail Merge task pane.
- Tap or click Labels in the Select document type area to specify labels as the main document type (Figure 6–60).

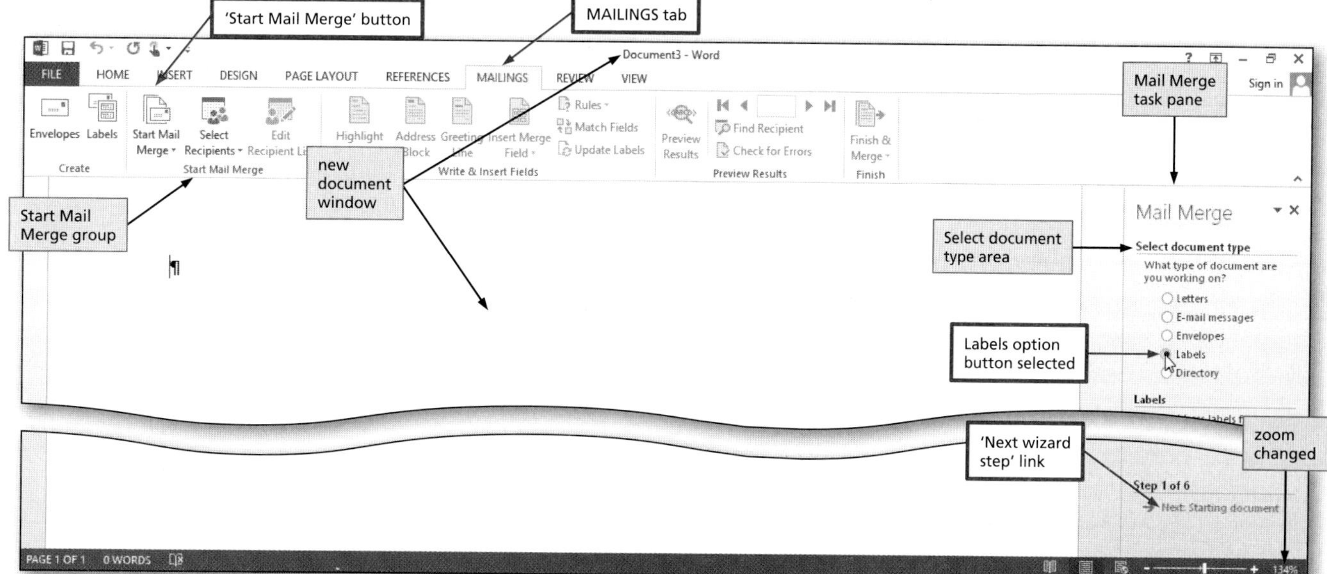

Figure 6–60

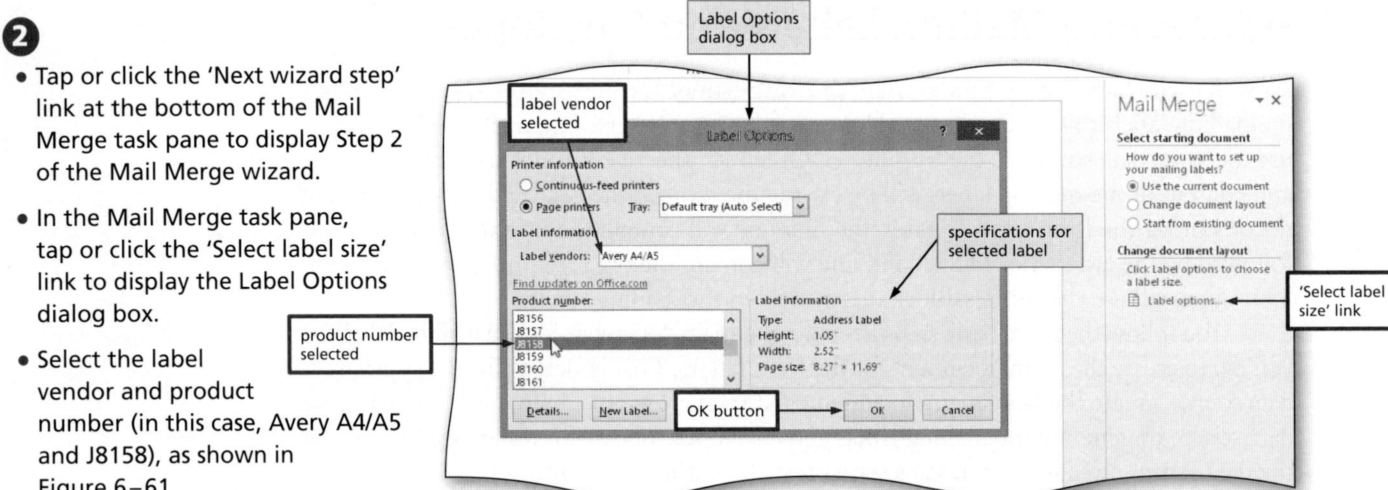

2

- Tap or click the 'Next wizard step' link at the bottom of the Mail Merge task pane to display Step 2 of the Mail Merge wizard.
- In the Mail Merge task pane, tap or click the 'Select label size' link to display the Label Options dialog box.
- Select the label vendor and product number (in this case, Avery A4/A5 and J8158), as shown in Figure 6–61.

Figure 6–61

3

- Tap or click the OK button (Label Options dialog box) to display the selected label layout as the main document (Figure 6–62).
- If necessary, scroll to display the left edge of the main document in the window.
- If gridlines are not displayed, tap or click the 'View Table Gridlines' button (TABLE TOOLS LAYOUT tab | Table group) to show gridlines.

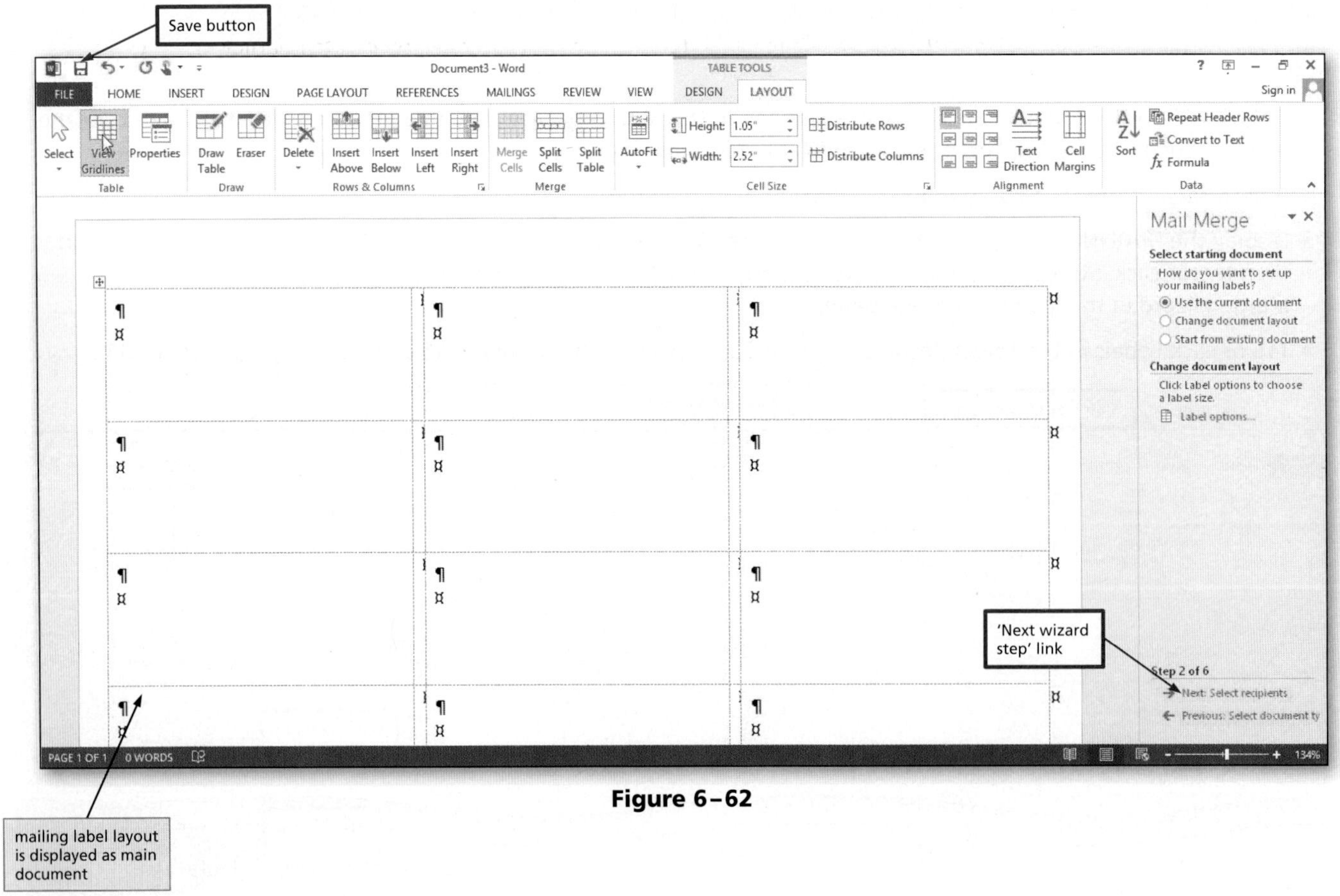

Save button

'Next wizard step' link

mailing label layout is displayed as main document

Figure 6–62

- Tap or click the 'Next wizard step' link at the bottom of the Mail Merge task pane to display Step 3 of the Mail Merge wizard, which allows you to select the data source.
- If necessary, tap or click 'Use an existing list' in the Select recipients area. Tap or click the 'Select recipient list file' link to display the Select Data Source dialog box.
- If necessary, navigate to the location of the data source (in this case, the Job Hunting folder in the Word folder in the CIS 101 folder [or your class folder]).
- Tap or click the file name, Green Prospective Employers, to select the data source you created earlier in the chapter (Figure 6–63).

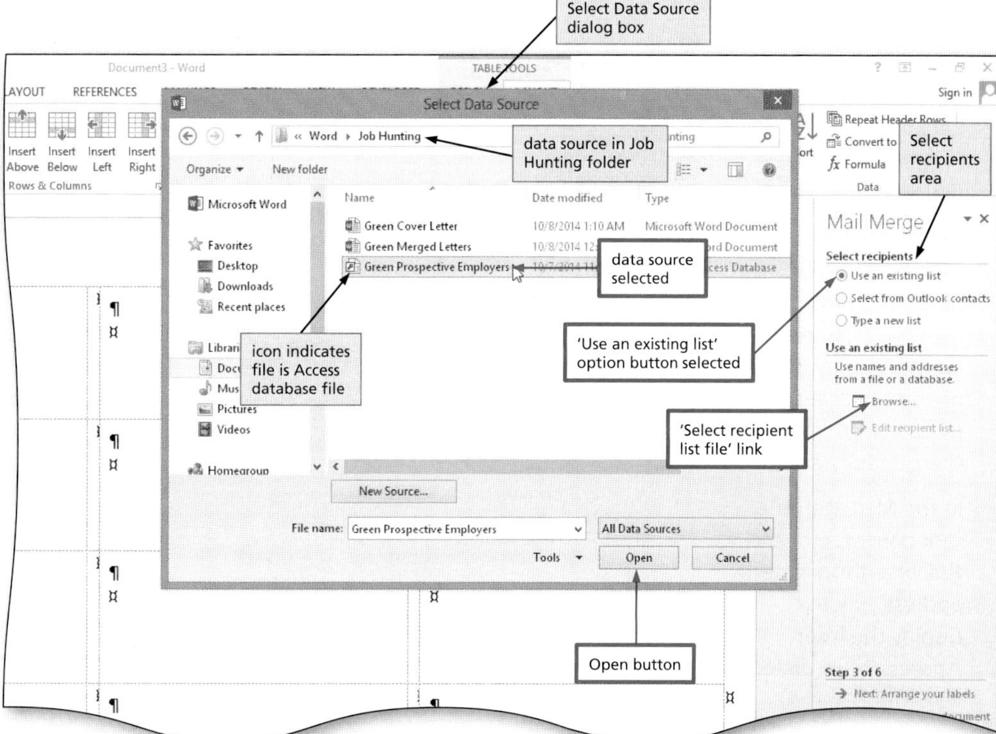

Figure 6–63

Q&A What is the folder initially displayed in the Select Data Source dialog box?

It is the default folder for storing data source files. Word looks in that folder first for an existing data source.

- Tap or click the Open button (Select Data Source dialog box) to display the Mail Merge Recipients dialog box (Figure 6–64).

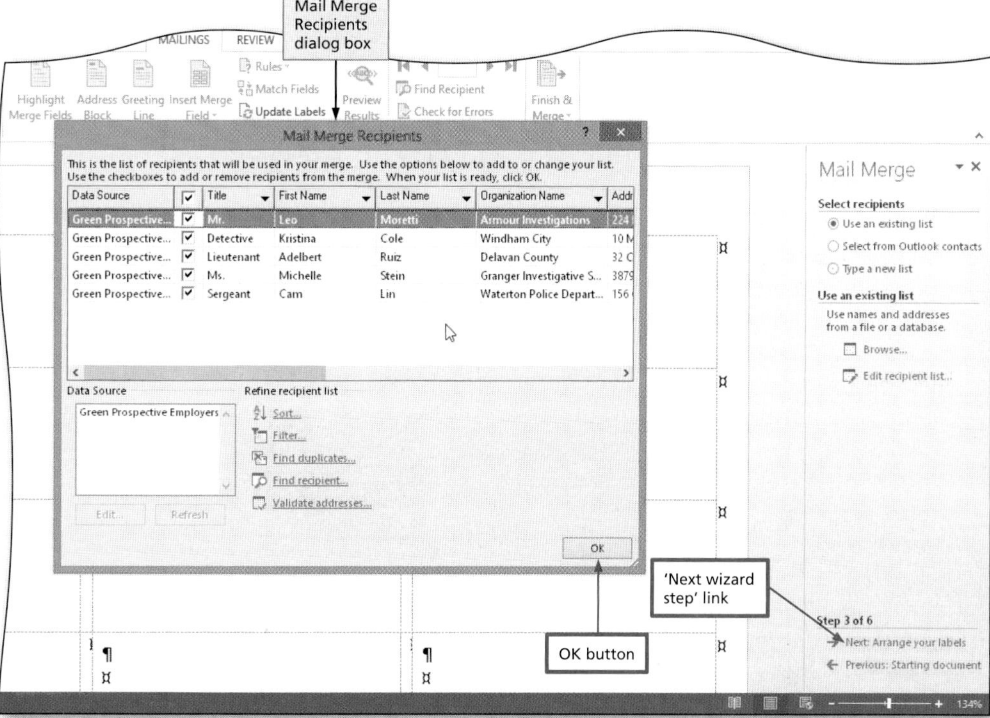

Figure 6–64

6

- Tap or click the OK button (Mail Merge Recipients dialog box) to close the dialog box.
- At the bottom of the Mail Merge task pane, tap or click the 'Next wizard step' link to display Step 4 of the Mail Merge wizard in the Mail Merge task pane.
- In the Mail Merge task pane, tap or click the 'Insert formatted address' link to display the Insert Address Block dialog box (Figure 6–65).
- If necessary, match the company name to the organization name (as shown on page WD 360).

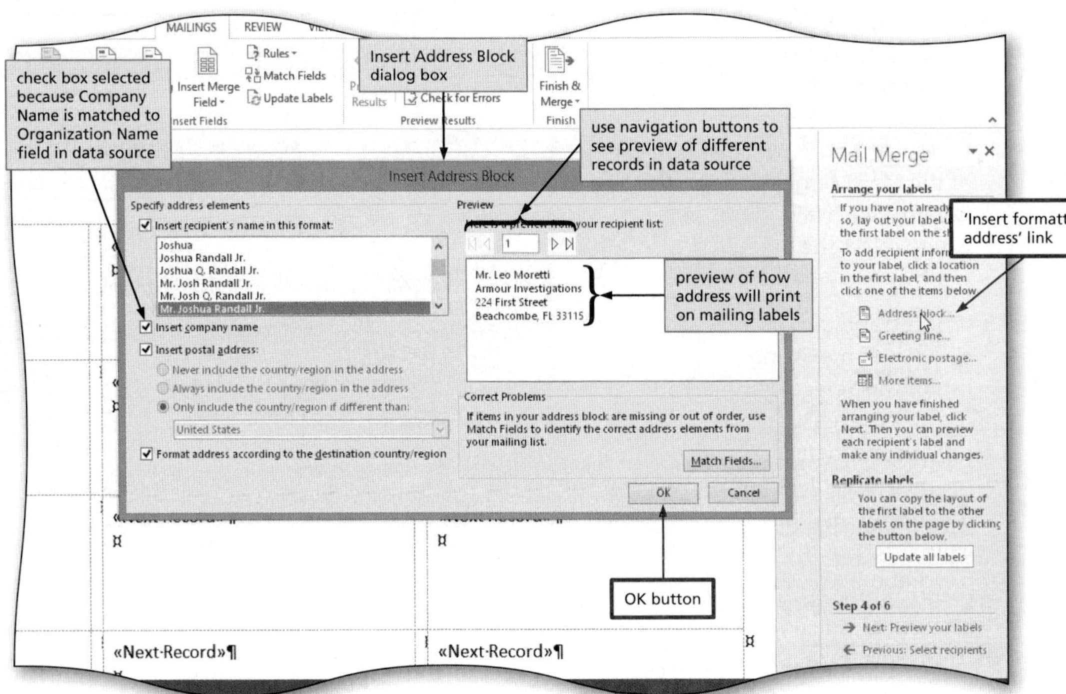

Figure 6–65

Remember – Ctrl+A no spacing before update all labels

7

- Tap or click the OK button to close the dialog box and insert the AddressBlock merge field in the first label of the main document (Figure 6–66).

Q&A Do I have to use the AddressBlock merge field?

No. You can tap or click the Insert Merge Field button (MAILINGS tab | Write & Insert Fields group) and then select the preferred fields for the mailing labels, organizing labels, organizing the fields as desired.

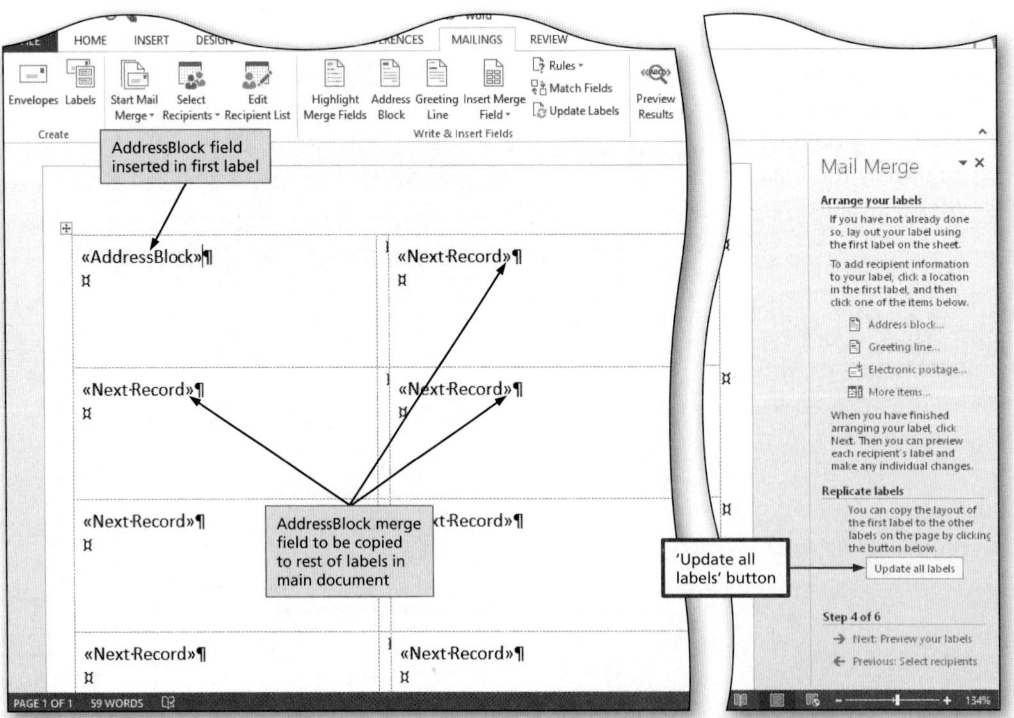

Figure 6–66

8

- Tap or click the 'Update all labels' button in the Mail Merge task pane to copy the layout of the first label to the remaining label layouts in the main document (Figure 6–67).

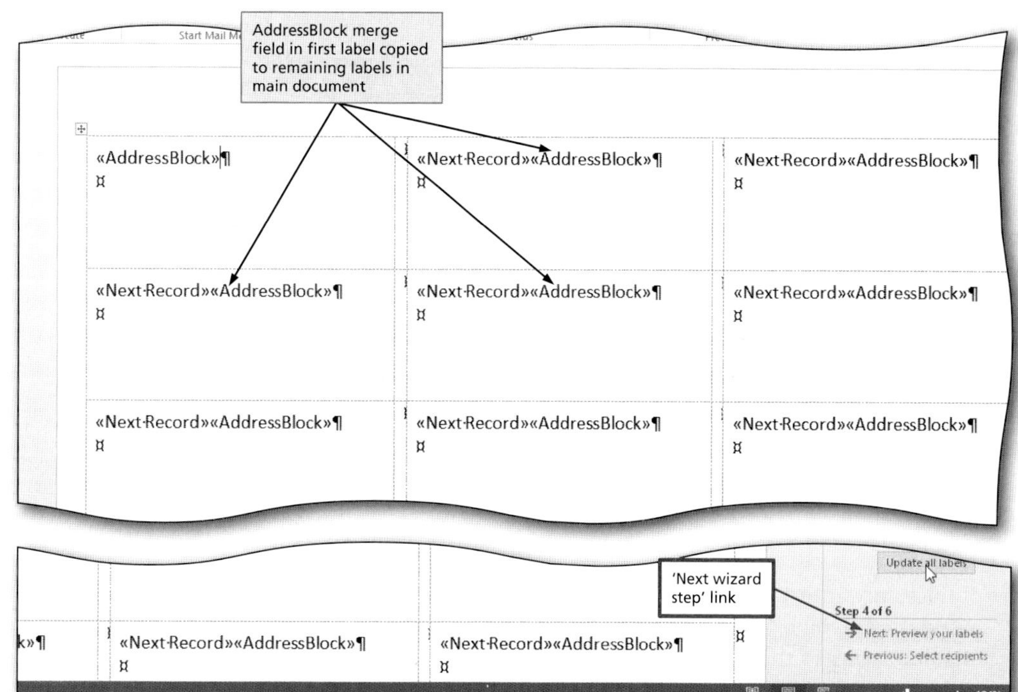

Figure 6–67

9

- Tap or click the 'Next wizard step' link at the bottom of the Mail Merge task pane to display Step 5 of the Mail Merge wizard, which shows a preview of the mailing labels in the document window.
- Because you do not want a blank space between each line in the printed mailing address, select the table containing the label layout (that is, tap or click the table move handle in the upper-left corner of the table), display the PAGE LAYOUT tab, change the Spacing Before and After boxes to 0 pt, and then tap or click anywhere to remove the selection (Figure 6–68).

Q&A What if the spacing does not change? Drag through the labels and try changing the Spacing Before and After boxes to 0 again.

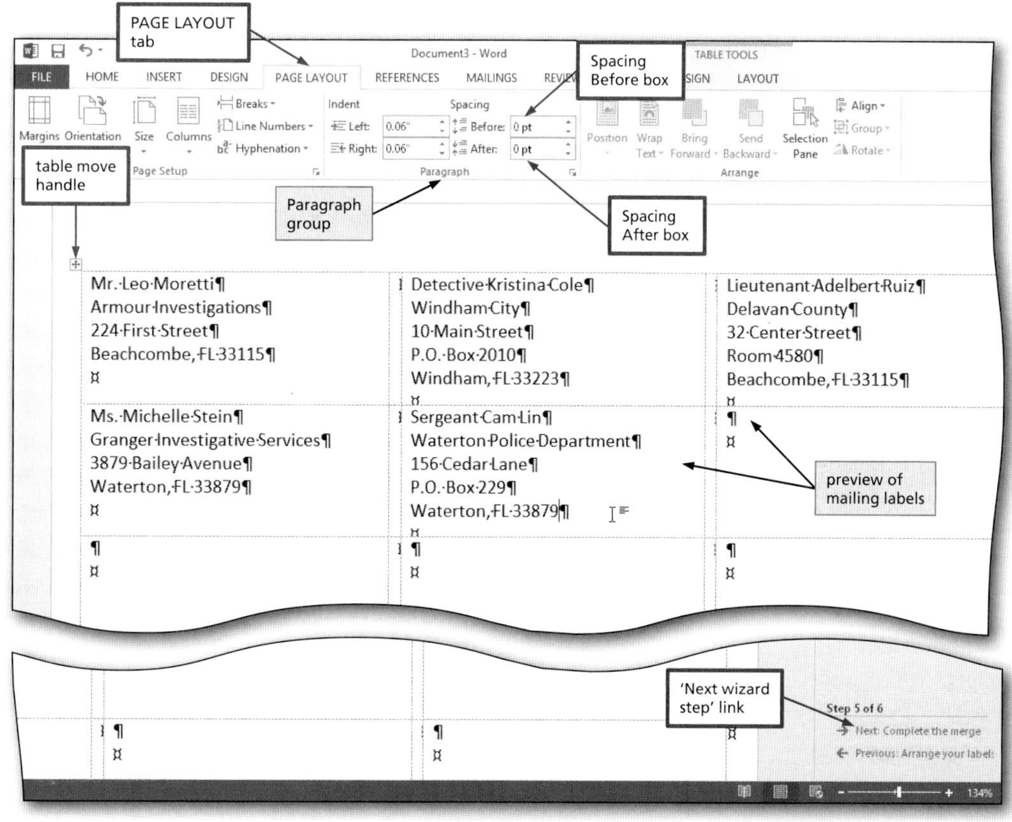

Figure 6–68

- Tap or click the 'Next wizard step' link at the bottom of the Mail Merge task pane to display Step 6 of the Mail Merge wizard.
- In the Mail Merge task pane, if you want to print the mailing labels, tap or click the 'Merge to printer' link to display the Merge to Printer dialog box.
- If necessary, tap or click All (Merge to Printer dialog box) so that all records in the data source will be included in the merge (Figure 6–69).

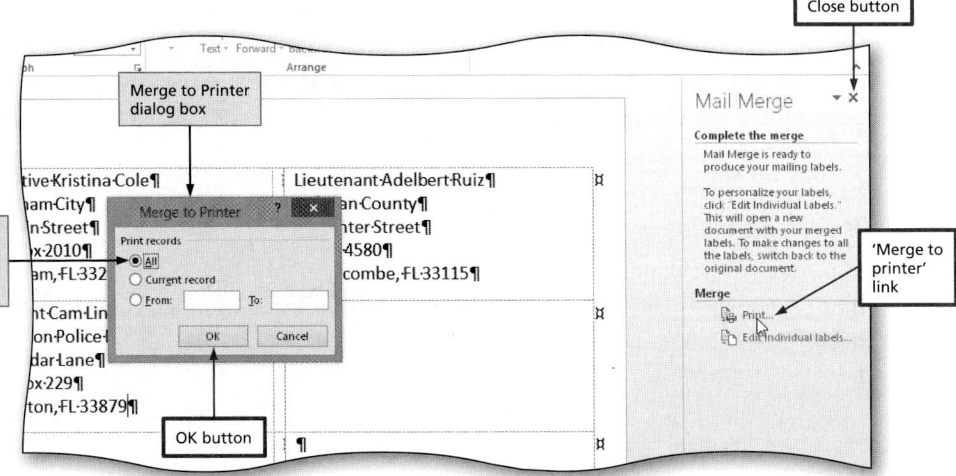

Figure 6–69

- If necessary, insert a sheet of blank mailing labels in the printer.
- Tap or click the OK button (Merge to Printer dialog box) to display the Print dialog box.
- Tap or click the OK button (Print dialog box) to print the mailing labels (Figure 6–70).

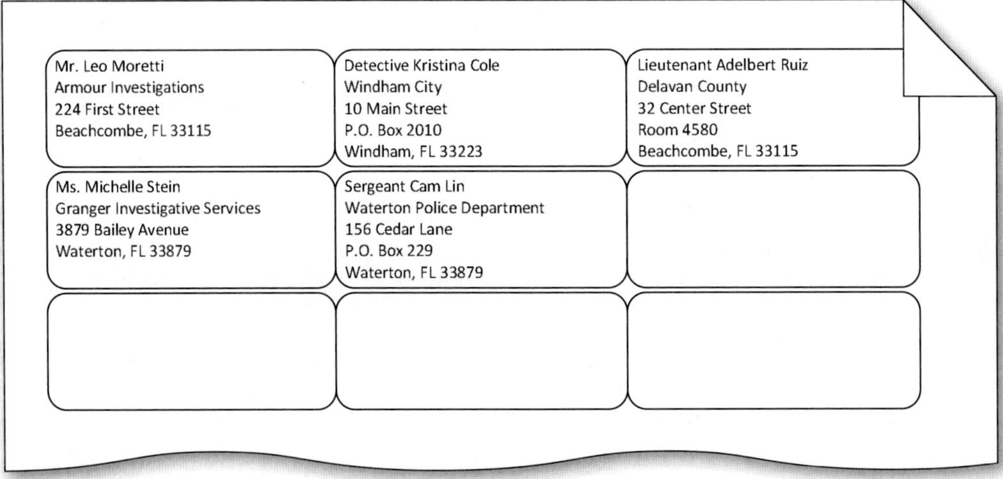

Figure 6–70

12

- Tap or click the Close button at the right edge of the Mail Merge task pane.

To Save the Mailing Labels

The following steps save the mailing labels.

1. Tap or click the Save button on the Quick Access Toolbar, which depending on settings, will display either the Save As gallery in the Backstage view or the Save As dialog box.
2. Save the file in the desired location (in this case, the Job Hunting folder in the Word folder in the CIS 101 folder [or your class folder]) using the file name, Green Mailing Labels.
3. Close the label file.

BTW

Validating Addresses

If you have installed address validation software, you can tap or click the Validate addresses link in the Mail Merge Recipients dialog box to validate your recipients' addresses. If you have not yet installed address validation software and would like information about doing so, tap or click the Validate addresses link in the Mail Merge Recipients dialog box and then tap or click the Yes button in the Microsoft Word dialog box to display a related Microsoft Office webpage.

CONSIDER THIS

How should you position addresses on an envelope?

An envelope should contain the sender's full name and address in the upper-left corner of the envelope. It also should contain the addressee's full name and address, positioned approximately in the vertical and horizontal center of the envelope. The address can be printed directly on the envelope or on a mailing label that is affixed to the envelope.

To Address and Print Envelopes

Instead of addressing mailing labels to affix to envelopes, your printer may have the capability of printing directly on envelopes. If you wanted to print address information directly on envelopes, you would perform the following steps to merge the form letters directly to the printer.

Note: Before printing address information directly on a printer, ensure your printer has the capability of printing on envelopes. If you are in a laboratory environment, ask your instructor if you should perform these steps.

1. Open the Backstage view. Tap or click the New tab in the Backstage view to display the New gallery. Tap or click the Blank document thumbnail to open a new blank document window.
2. Display the MAILINGS tab. Tap or click the 'Start Mail Merge' button (MAILINGS tab | Start Mail Merge group) and then tap or click 'Step-by-Step Mail Merge Wizard' on the Start Mail Merge menu to display Step 1 of the Mail Merge wizard in the Mail Merge task pane. Specify envelopes as the main document type by tapping or clicking Envelopes in the Select document type area.
3. Tap or click the 'Next wizard step' link at the bottom of the Mail Merge task pane to display Step 2 of the Mail Merge wizard. In the Mail Merge task pane, tap or click the 'Set Envelope Options' link to display the Envelope Options dialog box.
4. Select the envelope size and then tap or click the OK button (Envelope Options dialog box), which displays the selected envelope layout as the main document.
5. If your envelope does not have a preprinted return address, position the insertion point in the upper-left corner of the envelope layout and then type a return address.
6. Tap or click the 'Next wizard step' link at the bottom of the Mail Merge task pane to display Step 3 of the Mail Merge wizard, which allows you to select the data source. Select an existing data source or create a new one. At the bottom of the Mail Merge task pane, tap or click the 'Next wizard step' link to display Step 4 of the Mail Merge wizard in the Mail Merge task pane.
7. Position the insertion point in the middle of the envelope. In the Mail Merge task pane, tap or click the 'Insert formatted address' link to display the Insert Address Block dialog box. Select desired settings and then tap or click the OK button to close the dialog box and insert the AddressBlock merge field in the envelope layout of the main document.
8. Tap or click the 'Next wizard step' link at the bottom of the Mail Merge task pane to display Step 5 of the Mail Merge wizard, which shows a preview of an envelope in the document window.
9. Tap or click the 'Next wizard step' link at the bottom of the Mail Merge task pane to display Step 6 of the Mail Merge wizard. In the Mail Merge task pane, tap or click the 'Merge to printer' link to display the Merge to Printer dialog box. If necessary, tap or click All (Merge to Printer dialog box) so that all records in the data source will be included in the merge.
10. If necessary, insert blank envelopes in the printer. Tap or click the OK button to display the Print dialog box. Tap or click the OK button (Print dialog box) to print the addresses on the envelopes. Close the Mail Merge task pane.

BTW

AddressBlock Merge Field

Another way to insert the AddressBlock merge field in a document is to tap or click the Address Block button (MAILINGS tab | Write & Insert Fields group).

Merging All Data Records to a Directory

You may want to print the data records in the data source. Recall that the data source is saved as a Microsoft Access database table. Thus, you cannot open the data source in Word. To view the data source, you tap or click the 'Edit Recipient List' button (MAILINGS tab | Start Mail Merge group), which displays the Mail Merge Recipients dialog box. This dialog box, however, does not have a Print button.

One way to print the contents of the data source is to merge all data records in the data source into a single document, called a directory. A **directory** is a listing from the contents of the data source. A directory does not merge each data record to a separate document; instead, a directory lists all records together in a single document. When you merge to a directory, the default organization of a directory places each record one after the next, similar to the look of entries in a telephone book.

To create a directory, follow the same process as for the form letters. That is, determine the appropriate data source, create the directory main document, and then merge the main document with the data source to create the directory.

The directory in this chapter is more organized with the rows and columns divided and field names placed above each column (shown in Figure 6–83 on page WD 393). To accomplish this look, the following steps are required:

1. Change the page orientation from portrait to landscape, so that each record fits on a single row.
2. Create a directory layout, placing a separating character between each merge field.
3. Merge the directory to a new document, which creates a list of all records in the data source.
4. Convert the directory to a table, using the separator character as the identifier for each new column.
5. Format the table containing the directory.
6. Sort the table by organization name within city, so that it is easy to locate a particular record.

To Create a New Blank Document

The following steps create a new blank document.

1. Open the Backstage view.
2. Tap or click the New tab in the Backstage view to display the New gallery.
3. Tap or click the Blank document thumbnail to open a new blank document window (shown in Figure 6–71).
4. If necessary, change the zoom to page width.

BTW
Certification
The Microsoft Office Specialist (MOS) program provides an opportunity for you to obtain a valuable industry credential — proof that you have the Word 2013 skills required by employers. For more information, visit the Certification resource on the Student Companion Site located on www.cengagebrain.com. For detailed instructions about accessing available resources, visit www.cengage.com/ct/studentdownload or contact your instructor for information about accessing the required files.

To Change Page Orientation

1 IDENTIFY MAIN DOCUMENT | 2 CREATE DATA SOURCE | 3 COMPOSE MAIN DOCUMENT
4 MERGE DATA SOURCE | 5 ADDRESS MAILING LABELS | **6 MERGE TO DIRECTORY**

When a document is in **portrait orientation**, the short edge of the paper is the top of the document. You can instruct Word to lay out a document in **landscape orientation**, so that the long edge of the paper is the top of the document. The following steps change the orientation of the document from portrait to landscape. ***Why?*** *You want an entire record to fit on a single line in the directory.*

1

- Display the PAGE LAYOUT tab.
- Tap or click the 'Change Page Orientation' button (PAGE LAYOUT tab | Page Setup group) to display the Change Page Orientation gallery (Figure 6–71).

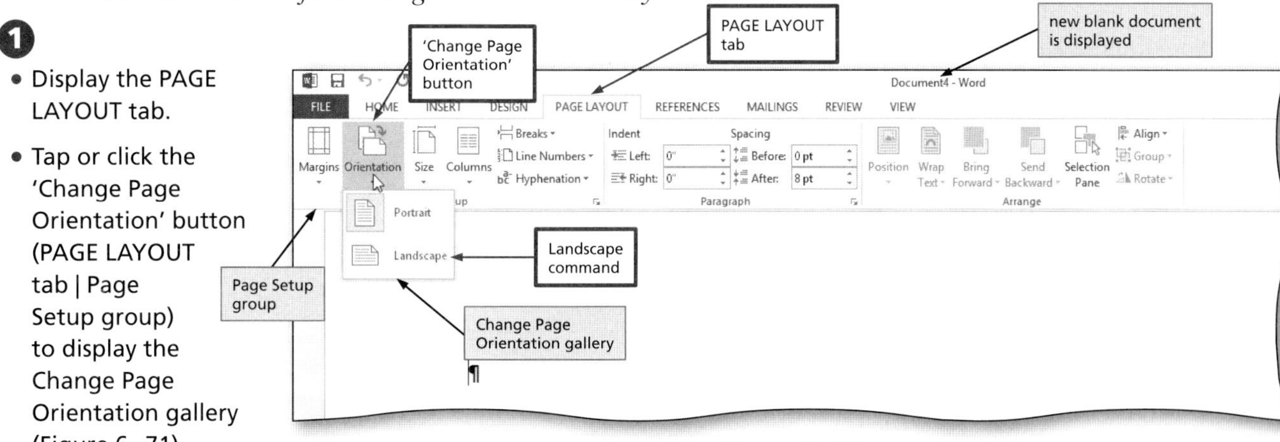

Figure 6–71

2

- Tap or click Landscape in the Change Page Orientation gallery to change the page orientation to landscape.

To Merge to a Directory

1 IDENTIFY MAIN DOCUMENT | 2 CREATE DATA SOURCE | 3 COMPOSE MAIN DOCUMENT
4 MERGE DATA SOURCE | 5 ADDRESS MAILING LABELS | **6 MERGE TO DIRECTORY**

The next steps merge the data records in the data source to a directory. ***Why?*** *You would like a listing of all records in the data source.* For illustration purposes, the following steps use the buttons on the MAILINGS tab rather than using the Mail Merge task pane to merge to a directory.

1

- Display the MAILINGS tab.
- Tap or click the 'Start Mail Merge' button (MAILINGS tab | Start Mail Merge group) to display the Start Mail Merge menu (Figure 6–72).

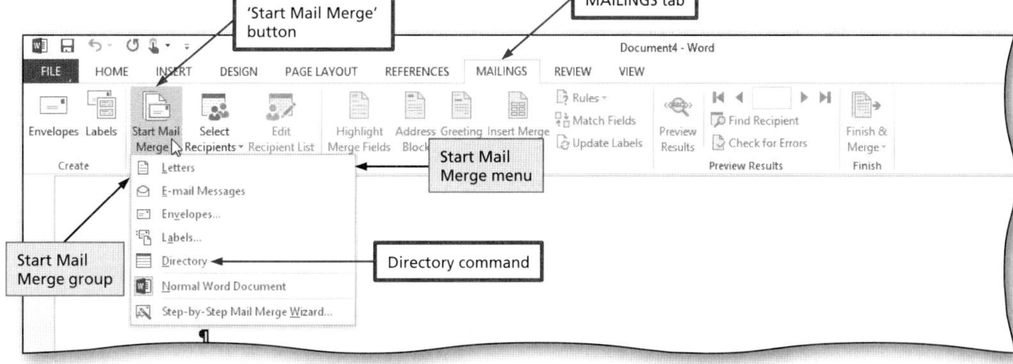

Figure 6–72

2

- Tap or click Directory on the Start Mail Merge menu to select the main document type.

3

- Tap or click the Select Recipients button (MAILINGS tab | Start Mail Merge group) to display the Select Recipients menu (Figure 6–73).

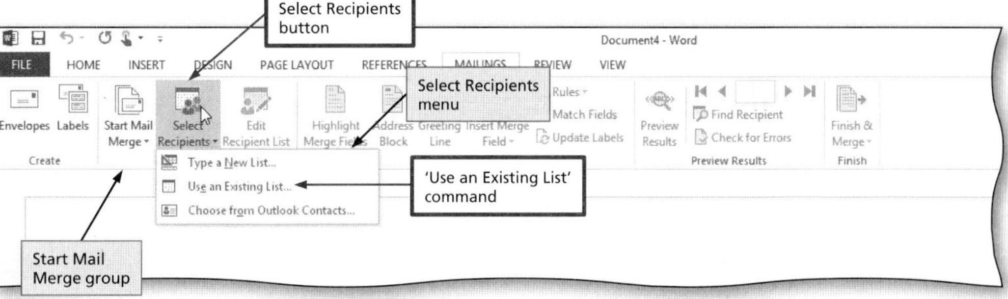

Figure 6–73

4

- Tap or click 'Use an Existing List' on the Select Recipients menu to display the Select Data Source dialog box.
- If necessary, navigate to the location of the data source (in this case, the Job Hunting folder in the Word folder in the CIS 101 folder [or your class folder]).
- Tap or click the file name, Green Prospective Employers, to select the data source you created earlier in the chapter (Figure 6–74).

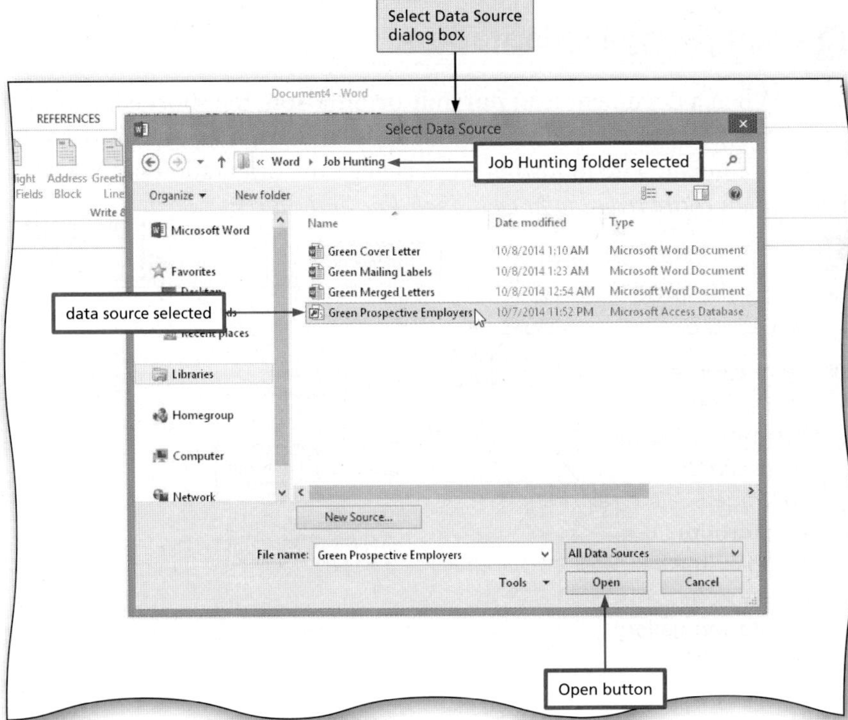

Figure 6–74

5

- Tap or click the Open button (Select Data Source dialog box) to associate the selected data source with the current main document.

6

- Tap or click the 'Insert Merge Field' arrow (MAILINGS tab | Write & Insert Fields group) to display the Insert Merge Field menu (Figure 6–75).

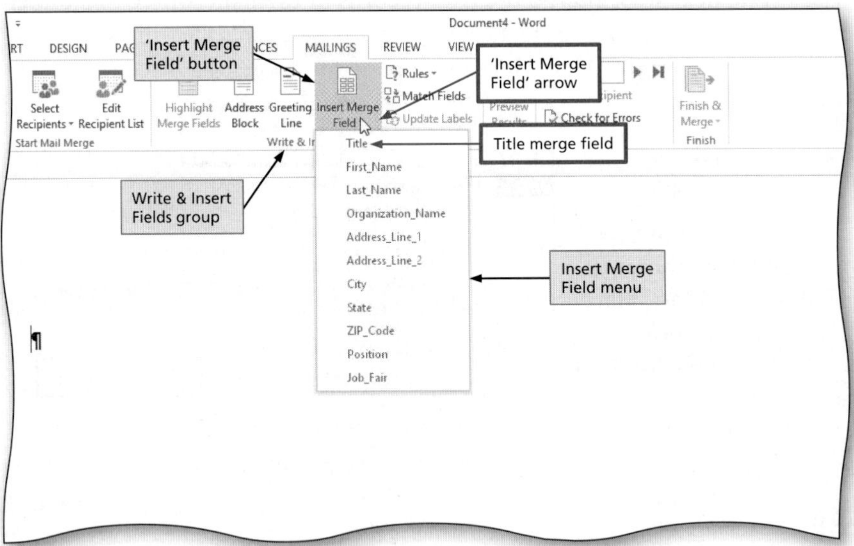

Figure 6–75

7

- Tap or click Title on the Insert Merge Field menu to insert the selected merge field in the document.
- Press the COMMA (,) key to place a comma after the inserted merge field.

Q&A Why insert a comma after the merge field?

In the next steps, you will convert the entered merge fields to a table format with the records in rows and the fields in columns. To do this, Word divides the columns based on a character separating each field. In this case, you use the comma to separate the merge fields.

8

- Repeat Steps 6 and 7 for the First_Name, Last_Name, Organization_Name, Address_Line_1, Address_Line_2, City, State, and ZIP_Code fields on the Insert Merge Field menu, so that these fields in the data source appear in the main document separated by a comma, except do not type a comma after the last field: ZIP_Code.
- Press the ENTER key (Figure 6–76).

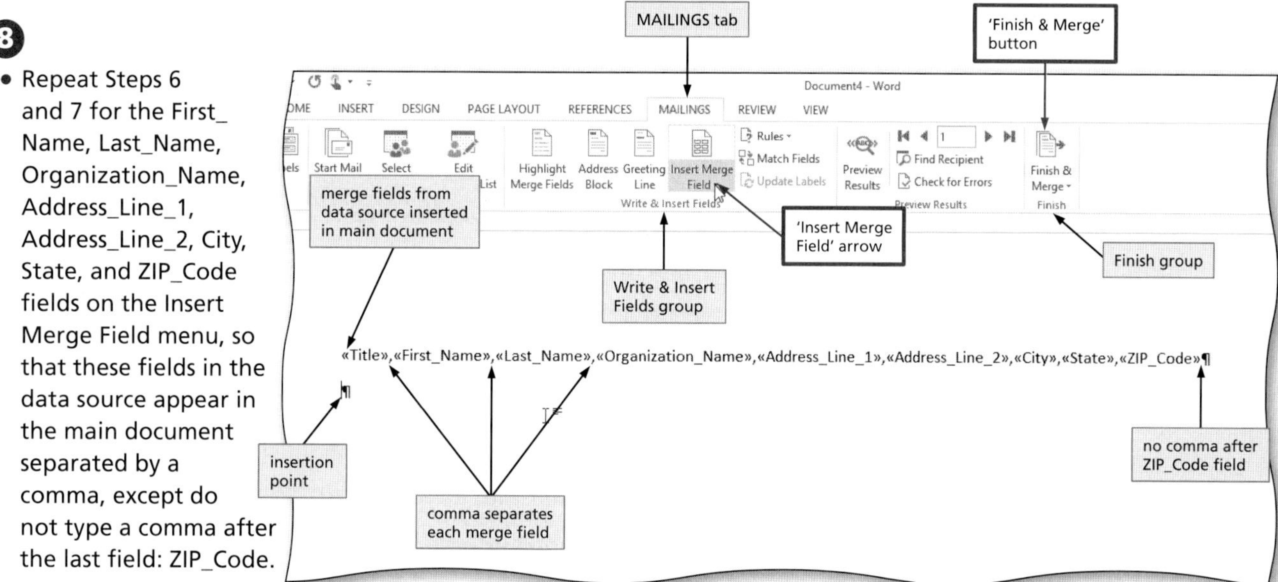

Figure 6–76

Q&A Why press the ENTER key after entering the merge fields names?
This will place the first field in each record at the beginning of a new line.

To Save the Directory

The following steps save the directory main document.

1. Tap or click the Save button on the Quick Access Toolbar, which depending on settings, will display either the Save As gallery in the Backstage view or the Save As dialog box.
2. Save the file in the desired location (in this case, the Job Hunting folder in the Word folder in the CIS 101 folder [or your class folder]) using the file name, Green Potential Employer Directory.

To Merge to a New Document

The next step is to merge the data source and the directory main document to a new document, so that you can edit the resulting document. The following steps merge to a new document.

1. Tap or click the 'Finish & Merge' button (MAILINGS tab | Finish group) to display the Finish & Merge menu.
2. Tap or click 'Edit Individual Documents' on the Finish & Merge menu to display the Merge to New Document dialog box.
3. If necessary, tap or click All (Merge to New Document dialog box).
4. Tap or click the OK button to merge the data records to a directory in a new document window (Figure 6–77 on the next page).

BTW

Quick Reference

For a table that lists how to complete the tasks covered in this book using touch gestures, the mouse, ribbon, shortcut menu, and keyboard, see the Quick Reference Summary at the back of this book, or visit the Quick Reference resource on the Student Companion Site located on www.cengagebrain.com. For detailed instructions about accessing available resources, visit www.cengage.com/ct/studentdownload or contact your instructor for information about accessing the required files.

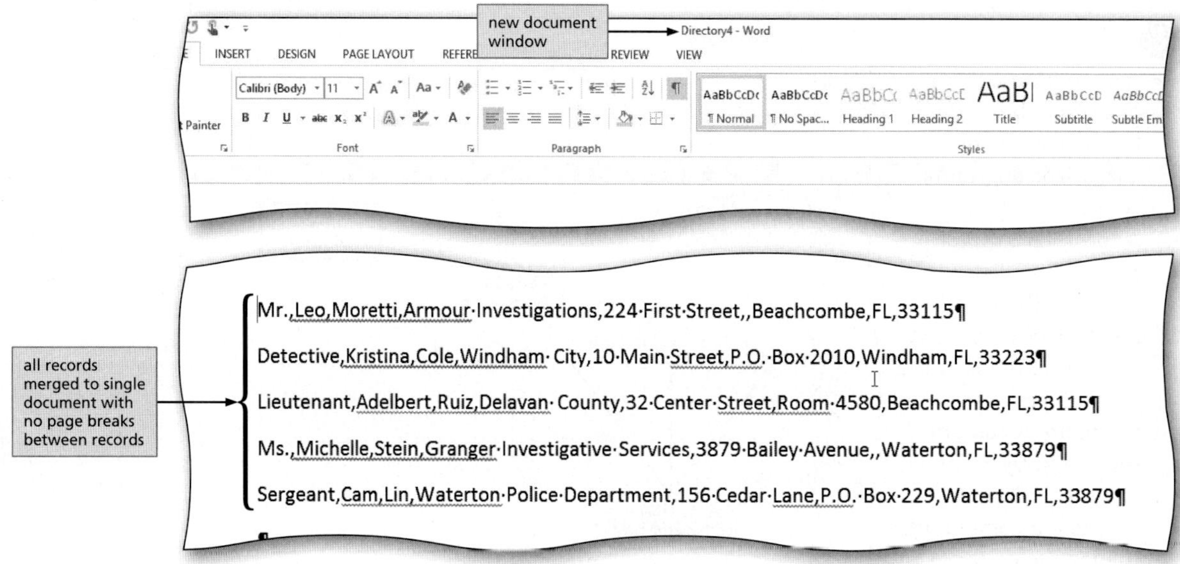

Figure 6–77

To Convert Text to a Table

1 IDENTIFY MAIN DOCUMENT | 2 CREATE DATA SOURCE | 3 COMPOSE MAIN DOCUMENT
4 MERGE DATA SOURCE | 5 ADDRESS MAILING LABELS | **6 MERGE TO DIRECTORY**

You want each data record to be in a single row and each merge field to be in a column. ***Why?*** *The directory will be easier to read if it is in table form.* The following steps convert the text containing the merge fields to a table.

1

- Press CTRL+A to select the entire document, because you want all document contents to be converted to a table.
- Display the INSERT tab.
- Tap or click the 'Add a Table' button (INSERT tab | Tables group) to display the Add a Table gallery (Figure 6–78).

Q&A Can I convert a section of a document to a table?
Yes, simply select the characters, lines, or paragraphs to be converted before displaying the Convert Text to Table dialog box.

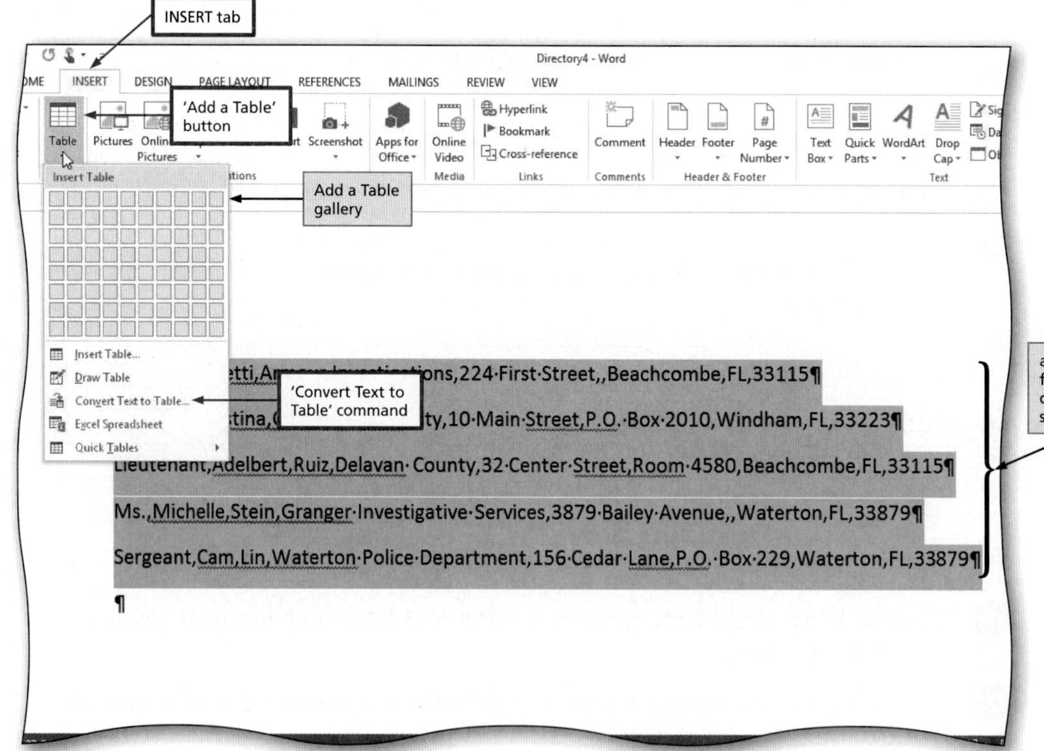

Figure 6–78

2

- Tap or click 'Convert Text to Table' in the Add a Table gallery to display the Convert Text to Table dialog box.
- If necessary, type 9 in the 'Number of columns' box (Convert Text to Table dialog box) to specify the number of columns for the resulting table.
- Tap or click 'AutoFit to window', which instructs Word to fit the table and its contents to the width of the window.
- If necessary, tap or click Commas to specify the character that separates the merge fields in the document (Figure 6–79).

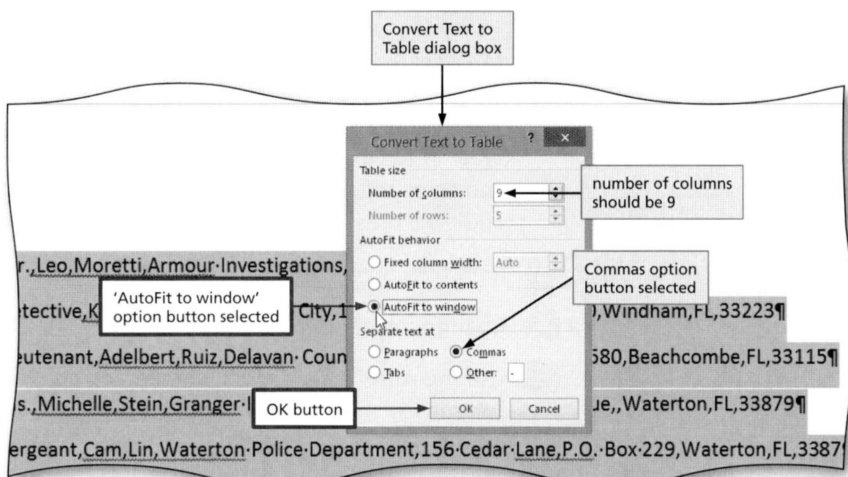

Figure 6–79

3

- Tap or click the OK button to convert the selected text to a table and then, if necessary, tap or click to remove the selection from the table (Figure 6–80).

Q&A Can I format the table?

Yes. You can use any of the commands on the TABLE TOOLS DESIGN and TABLE TOOLS LAYOUT tabs to change the look of the table.

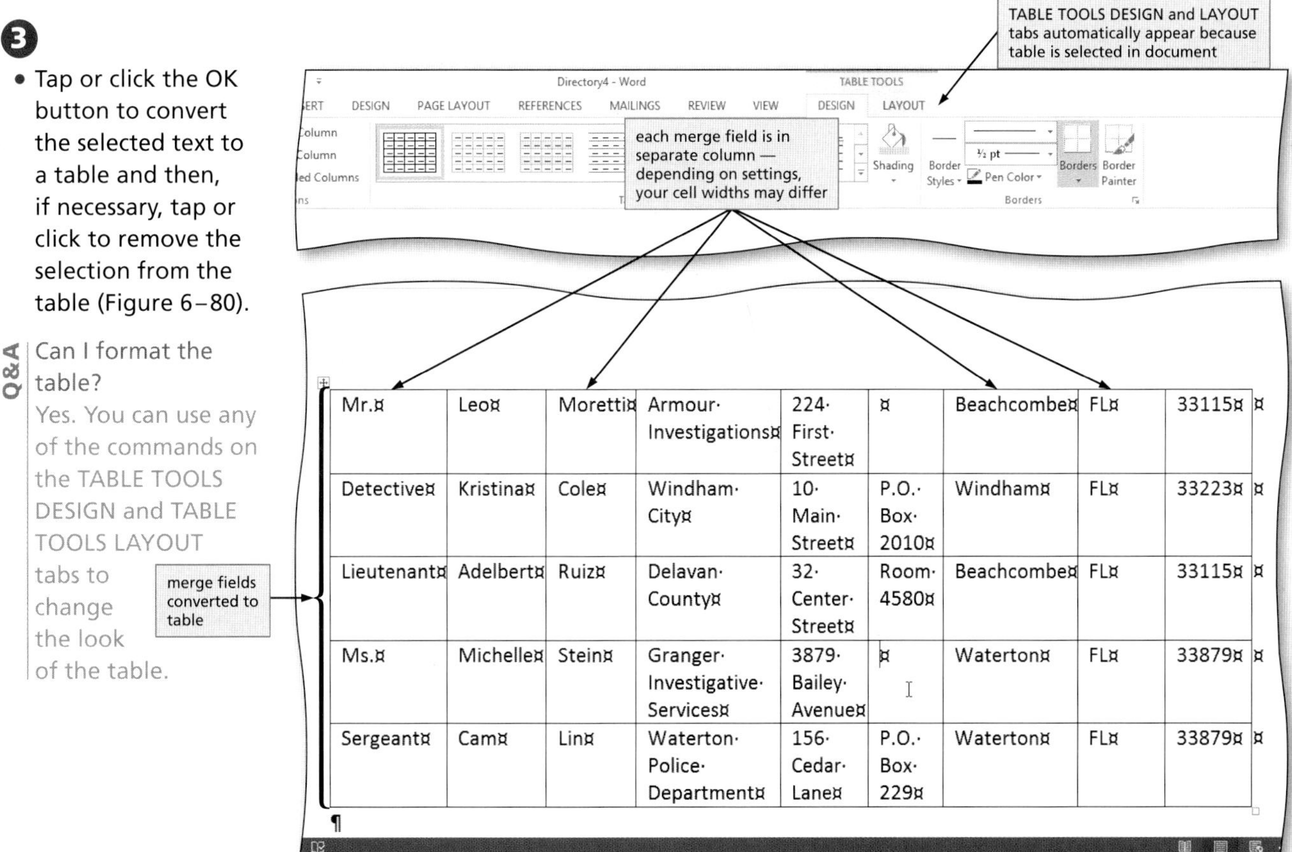

Mr.	Leo	Moretti	Armour Investigations	224 First Street		Beachcombe	FL	33115
Detective	Kristina	Cole	Windham City	10 Main Street	P.O. Box 2010	Windham	FL	33223
Lieutenant	Adelbert	Ruiz	Delavan County	32 Center Street	Room 4580	Beachcombe	FL	33115
Ms.	Michelle	Stein	Granger Investigative Services	3879 Bailey Avenue		Waterton	FL	33879
Sergeant	Cam	Lin	Waterton Police Department	156 Cedar Lane	P.O. Box 229	Waterton	FL	33879

Figure 6–80

To Modify and Format a Table

The table would be more descriptive if the field names were displayed in a row above the actual data. The following steps add a row to the top of a table and format the data in the new row.

1 Add a row to the top of the table by positioning the insertion point in the first row of the table and then tapping or clicking the 'Insert Rows Above' button (TABLE TOOLS LAYOUT tab | Rows & Columns group).

2. Tap or click in the first (leftmost) cell of the new row. Type **`Title`** and then press the TAB key. Type **`First Name`** and then press the TAB key. Type **`Last Name`** and then press the tab key. Type **`Organization Name`** and then press the tab key. Type **`Address Line 1`** and then press the TAB key. Type **`Address Line 2`** and then press the TAB key. Type **`City`** and then press the TAB key. Type **`State`** and then press the TAB key. Type **`ZIP Code`** as the last entry in the row.

3. Bold the contents of the first row.

4. Change the page margins to Narrow.

5. Use the AutoFit Contents command on the ribbon or the shortcut menu to make all columns as wide as their contents (Figure 6–81).

header row added and bold

Title	**First Name**	**Last Name**	**Organization Name**	**Address Line 1**	**Address Line 2**	**City**	**State**	**ZIP Code**
Mr.	Leo	Moretti	Armour Investigations	224 First Street		Beachcomber	FL	33115
Detective	Kristina	Cole	Windham City	10 Main Street	P.O. Box 2010	Windham	FL	33223
Lieutenant	Adelbert	Ruiz	Delavan County	32 Center Street	Room 4580	Beachcomber	FL	33115
Ms.	Michelle	Stein	Granger Investigative Services	3879 Bailey Avenue		Waterton	FL	33879
Sergeant	Cam	Lin	Waterton Police Department	156 Cedar Lane	P.O. Box 229	Waterton	FL	33879

Figure 6–81

To Repeat Header Rows

If you had a table that exceeded a page in length and you wanted the header row (the first row) to appear at the top of the table on each continued page, you would perform the following steps.

1. Position the insertion point in the header row.
2. Tap or click the 'Repeat Header Rows' button (TABLE TOOLS LAYOUT tab | Data group) to repeat the row containing the insertion point at the top of every page on which the table continues.

To Sort a Table by Multiple Columns

1 IDENTIFY MAIN DOCUMENT | 2 CREATE DATA SOURCE | 3 COMPOSE MAIN DOCUMENT
4 MERGE DATA SOURCE | 5 ADDRESS MAILING LABELS | **6 MERGE TO DIRECTORY**

The next step is to sort the table. ***Why?*** *In this project, the table records are displayed by organization name within city.* The following steps sort a table by multiple columns.

- With the table selected or the insertion point in the table, tap or click the Sort button (TABLE TOOLS LAYOUT tab | Data group) to display the Sort dialog box.
- Tap or click the Sort by arrow (Sort dialog box); scroll to and then tap or click City in the list.
- Tap or click the first Then by arrow and then tap or click Organization Name in the list.
- If necessary, tap or click Header row so that the first row remains in its current location when the table is sorted (Figure 6–82).

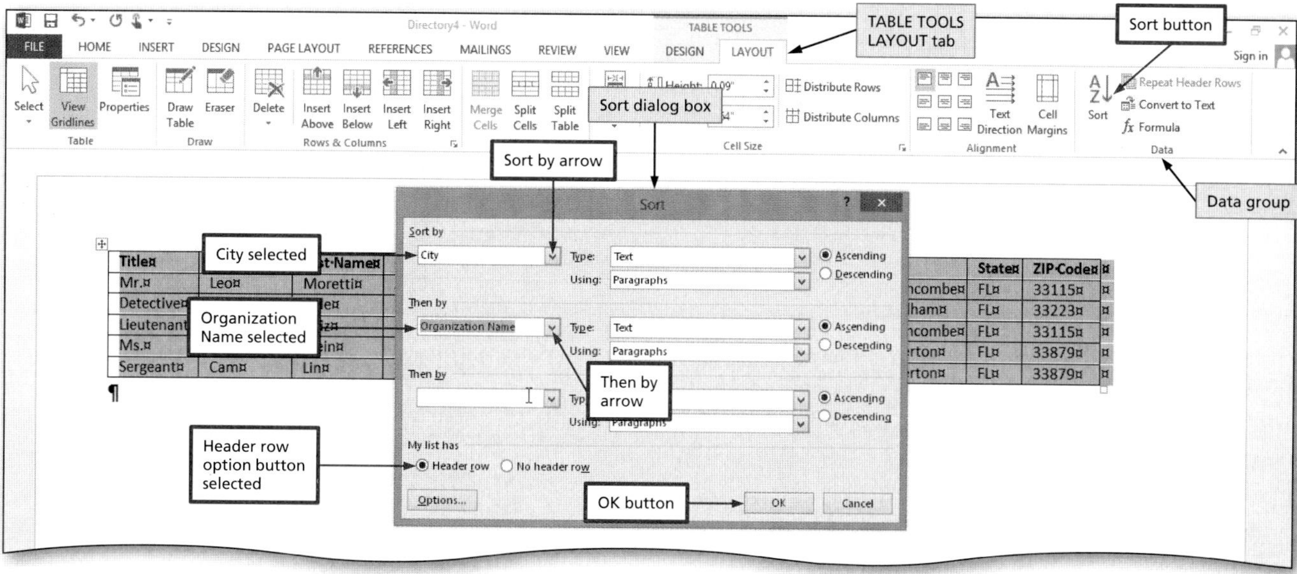

Figure 6–82

2

- Tap or click the OK button to sort the records in the table in ascending Organization Name order within ascending City order (Figure 6–83).
- If necessary, tap or click to deselect the table.

header row left in row 1

records sorted by Organization Name within City

Title	First Name	Last Name	Organization Name	Address Line 1	Address Line 2	City	State	ZIP Code
Mr.	Leo	Moretti	Armour Investigations	224 First Street		Beachcomber	FL	33115
Lieutenant	Adelbert	Ruiz	Delavan County	32 Center Street	Room 4580	Beachcomber	FL	33115
Ms.	Michelle	Stein	Granger Investigative Services	3879 Bailey Avenue		Waterton	FL	33879
Sergeant	Cam	Lin	Waterton Police Department	156 Cedar Lane	P.O. Box 229	Waterton	FL	33879
Detective	Kristina	Cole	Windham City	10 Main Street	P.O. Box 2010	Windham	FL	33223

Figure 6–83

To Save the Directory Listing and Exit Word

The following steps save and print the directory listing.

1 Tap or click the Save button on the Quick Access Toolbar, which depending on settings, will display either the Save As gallery in the Backstage view or the Save As dialog box.

2 Save the file in the desired location (in this case, the Job Hunting folder in the Word folder in the CIS 101 folder [or your class folder]) using the file name, Green Potential Employer Directory Listing.

3 If desired, print the directory file and then close all open files.

Q&A If Microsoft Access is installed on my computer, can I use that to print the data source?
As an alternative to merging to a directory and printing the results, if you are familiar with Microsoft Access and it is installed on your computer, you can open and print the data source in Access.

4 Exit Word.

BTW

Distributing a Document

Instead of printing and distributing a hard copy of a document, you can distribute the document electronically. Options include sending the document via email; posting it on cloud storage (such as SkyDrive) and sharing the file with others; posting it on a social networking site, blog, or other website; and sharing a link associated with an online location of the document. You also can create and share a PDF or XPS image of the document, so that users can view the file in Acrobat Reader or XPS Viewer instead of in Word.

Chapter Summary

In this chapter, you have learned how to create and print form letters, create and edit a data source, address mailing labels and envelopes from a data source, and merge to a directory. The items listed below include all the new Word skills you have learned in this chapter, with the tasks grouped by activity.

Enter and Edit Text
Enter the Date (WD 358)

File Management
Create a Folder while Saving (WD 349)

Format a Page
Change Page Orientation (WD 387)

Word Settings
Change the User Name and Initials (WD 344)

Work with Graphics
Specify the Position of a Graphic (WD 348)

Work with Mail Merge
Identify the Main Document for the Form Letter Using the Mail Merge Task Pane (WD 341)
Create a New Data Source (WD 350)
Save a Data Source when Prompted by Word (WD 355)
Insert the AddressBlock Merge Field (WD 359)
Edit the AddressBlock Merge Field (WD 360)
View Merged Data in the Main Document (WD 361)
Insert the GreetingLine Merge Field (WD 361)
Edit the GreetingLine Merge Field (WD 362)
Insert a Merge Field in the Main Document (WD 363)
Insert an IF Field in the Main Document (WD 365)
Highlight Merge Fields (WD 367)
Display a Field Code (WD 368)
Print Field Codes in the Main Document (WD 369)
Preview the Merged Letters (WD 370)
Check for Errors (WD 371)
Merge the Form Letters to a New Document (WD 371)
Merge the Form Letters to a Printer (WD 373)
Select Records to Merge (WD 374)
Remove a Merge Condition (WD 376)
Sort the Data Records in a Data Source (WD 377)
Find and Display Data (WD 378)
Address and Print Mailing Labels Using an Existing Data Source (WD 379)
Address and Print Envelopes (WD 385)
Merge to a Directory (WD 387)

Work with Tables
Convert Text to a Table (WD 390)
Repeat Header Rows (WD 392)
Sort a Table by Multiple Columns (WD 392)

CONSIDER THIS: PLAN AHEAD

What decisions will you need to make when creating your next form letter?

Use these guidelines as you complete the assignments in this chapter and create your own form letters outside of this class.

1. Identify the main document for the form letter.
   a) Determine whether to type the letter from scratch in a blank document window or use a letter template.
2. Create or specify the data source.
   a) Determine if the data exists already in an Access database table, an Outlook contacts list, or an Excel worksheet.
   b) If you cannot use an existing data source, create a new one using appropriate field names.
3. Compose the main document for the form letter.
   a) Ensure the letter contains all essential business letter elements and is visually appealing.
   b) Be sure the letter contains proper grammar, correct spelling, logically constructed sentences, flowing paragraphs, and sound ideas.
   c) Properly reference the data in the data source.
4. Merge the main document with the data source to create the form letters.
   a) Determine the destination for the merge (i.e., a new document, the printer, etc.).
   b) Determine which records to merge (all of them or a portion of them).

5. Determine whether to generate mailing labels or envelopes.
    a) Create or specify the data source.
    b) Ensure the mailing label or envelope contains all necessary information.
6. Create a directory of the data source.
    a) Create or specify the data source.
    b) If necessary, format the directory appropriately.

CONSIDER THIS

How should you submit solutions to questions in the assignments identified with a symbol?

Every assignment in this book contains one or more questions identified with a symbol. These questions require you to think beyond the assigned document. Present your solutions to the questions in the format required by your instructor. Possible formats may include one or more of these options: write the answer; create a document that contains the answer; present your answer to the class; discuss your answer in a group; record the answer as audio or video using a webcam, smartphone, or portable media player; or post answers on a blog, wiki, or website.

Apply Your Knowledge

Reinforce the skills and apply the concepts you learned in this chapter.

Editing, Printing, and Merging a Form Letter and Its Data Source

Note: To complete this assignment, you will be required to use the Data Files for Students. Visit www.cengage.com/ct/studentdownload for detailed instructions or contact your instructor for information about accessing the required files.

Instructions: Run Word. Open the document, Apply 6-1 Fund-Raising Letter Draft, from the Data Files for Students. When you open the main document, if Word displays a dialog box about an SQL command, tap or click the Yes button. If Word prompts for the name of the data source, select Apply 6-1 Member List on the Data Files for Students.

The document is a main document for the Valley View Golf Club form letter (Figure 6–84 on the next page). You are to edit the date content control and GreetingLine merge field, print the form letter, add a record to the data source, and merge the form letters to a file.

Perform the following tasks:

1. Edit the date content control so that it contains the date 8/26/2014.
2. Edit the GreetingLine merge field so that the salutation ends with a comma (,).
3. Save the modified main document for the form letter with the name Apply 6-1 Fund-Raising Letter Modified.
4. Highlight the merge fields in the document. How many are there? Remove the highlight from the merge fields.
5. View merged data in the document. Use the navigation buttons in the Preview Results group to display merged data from various records in the data source. What is the last name shown in the first record? The third record? The fifth record? View merge fields (that is, turn off the view merged data).
6. Print the main document for the form letter by opening the Backstage view, clicking the Print tab, and then clicking the Print button (Figure 6–84).

Continued >

Apply Your Knowledge *continued*

7. If requested by your instructor, add a record to the data source that contains your personal information. Type `student` in the Membership Type field.
8. In the data source, change Kim Chung's last name to Weavers.
9. Sort the data source by the Last Name field.
10. Save the main document for the form letter again.
11. Merge the form letters to a new document. Save the new document with the file name, Apply 6-1 Fund-Raising Merged Letters. Edit the merged letters by changing the word, a, to the word, an, before those members who are associate members.
12. If requested by your instructor, merge the form letters directly to the printer.
13. Submit the saved documents in the format specified by your instructor.
14. Answer the questions posed in #4 and #5. The form letter used in this assignment was based on one of Word's online mail merge letter templates called 'Mail merge letter (Apothecary design)'. What other online mail merge letter templates are available through Word? (*Hint*: In the New gallery, search for the text, mail merge template.) What merge fields are included in the mail merge letter templates? Which template do you like best and why?

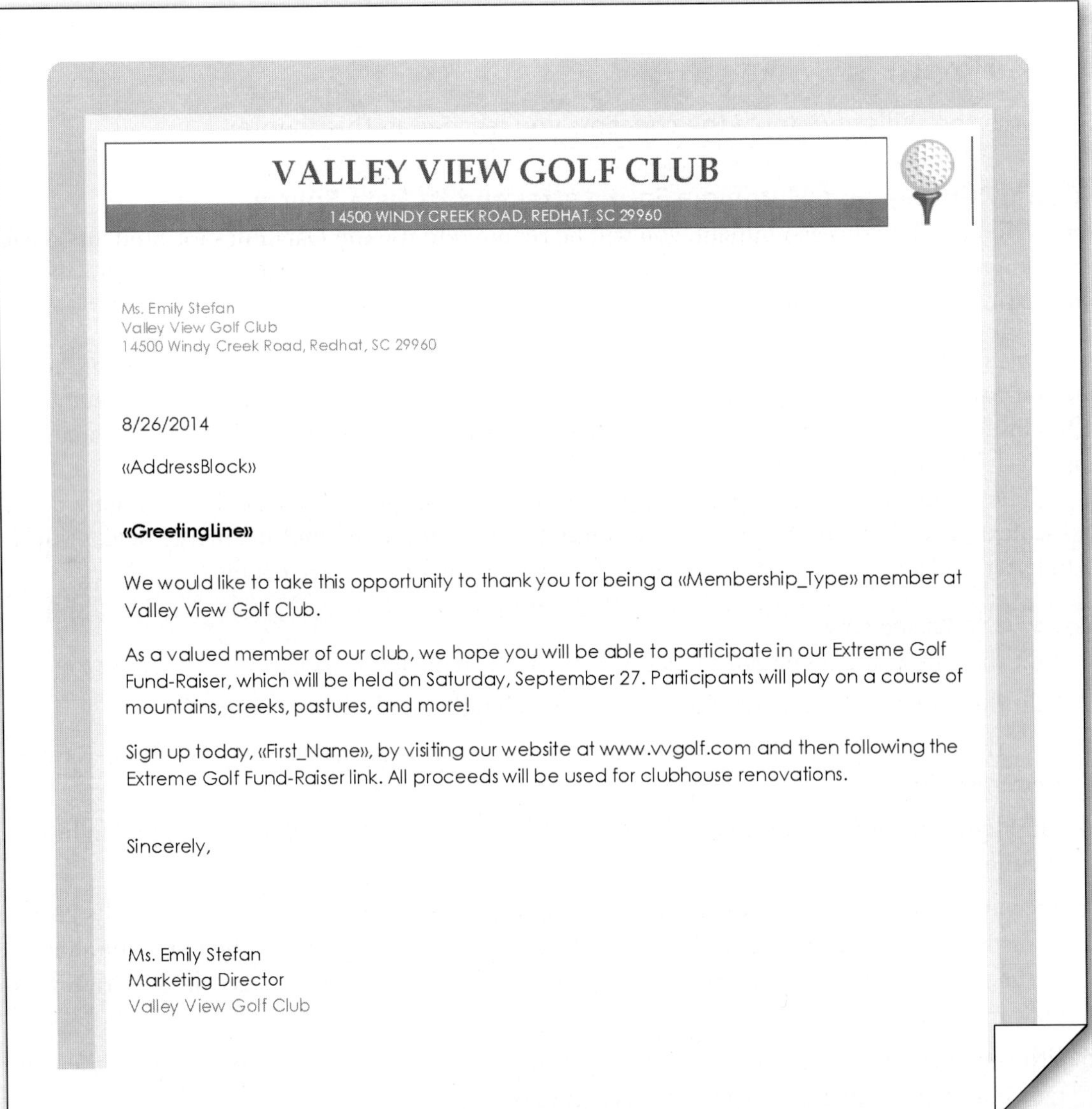

VALLEY VIEW GOLF CLUB

14500 WINDY CREEK ROAD, REDHAT, SC 29960

Ms. Emily Stefan
Valley View Golf Club
14500 Windy Creek Road, Redhat, SC 29960

8/26/2014

«AddressBlock»

«GreetingLine»

We would like to take this opportunity to thank you for being a «Membership_Type» member at Valley View Golf Club.

As a valued member of our club, we hope you will be able to participate in our Extreme Golf Fund-Raiser, which will be held on Saturday, September 27. Participants will play on a course of mountains, creeks, pastures, and more!

Sign up today, «First_Name», by visiting our website at www.vvgolf.com and then following the Extreme Golf Fund-Raiser link. All proceeds will be used for clubhouse renovations.

Sincerely,

Ms. Emily Stefan
Marketing Director
Valley View Golf Club

Figure 6–84

Extend Your Knowledge

Extend the skills you learned in this chapter and experiment with new skills. You may need to use Help to complete the assignment.

Editing an IF Field, Inserting a Fill-In Field, Formatting a Letter, and Merging Using Outlook and Access

Note: To complete this assignment, you will be required to use the Data Files for Students. Visit www.cengage.com/ct/studentdownload for detailed instructions or contact your instructor for information about accessing the required files.

Instructions: Run Word. Open the document called Extend 6-1 Vitamin Sale Letter Draft located on the Data Files for Students. When you open the main document, if Word displays a dialog box about an SQL command, tap or click the Yes button. If Word prompts for the name of the data source, select Extend 6-1 Customer List on the Data Files for Students.

The document is a main document for a form letter announcing a store moving (Figure 6–85). You will modify an IF field, and add a Fill-in field, print field codes, reformat the letter according to the block style for business letters, create envelopes for records in the data source, using an Access database file as a data source, and merge to email addresses.

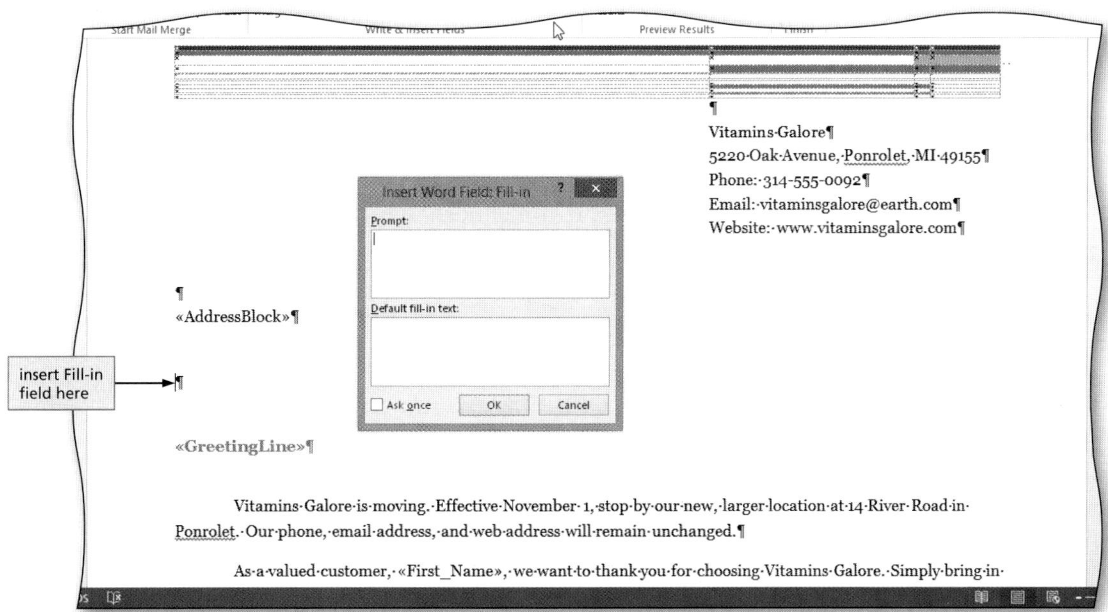

Figure 6–85

Perform the following tasks:

1. Use Help to learn about mail merge, IF fields, Fill-in fields, and merging to email addresses.
2. Edit the IF field so that the preferred customers receive a 20 percent discount and all others receive a 10 percent discount. (*Hint*: Use the 'Toggle Field Codes' command on the shortcut menu [press and hold or right-click the IF field code in the document window] and edit the IF field directly in the document.)
3. Below the AddressBlock merge field, insert a Fill-in field (Figure 6–85) that asks this question: What date will you be mailing these letters? Select the Ask once check box so that the question is asked only once, instead of for each letter. When merging the letters, use a date in September of 2014. What is the purpose of the Fill-in field?

Continued >

Extend Your Knowledge *continued*

4. If requested by your instructor, add a record to the data source that contains your personal information. Save the modified letter with the file name, Extend 6-1 Vitamin Sale Letter Modified.
5. Merge the letters to a new document. Save the merged letters using the file name, Extend 6-1 Vitamin Sale Merged Letters.
6. Print the main document for the form letter by opening the Backstage view, tapping or clicking the Print tab, and then tapping or clicking the Print button.
7. Print the form letter with field codes showing, that is, with the 'Print field codes instead of their values' check box selected in the Word Options dialog box. Be sure to deselect this check box after printing the field codes version of the letter. How does this printout differ from the one printed in #5?
8. Submit the merged letters in the format specified by your instructor.
9. If your instructor requests, create envelopes for each letter in the data source. Submit the merged envelopes in the format specified by your instructor.
10. Reformat the form letter so that it is properly spaced and sized according to the block style for business letters. Save the letter with the file name, Extend 6-1 Vitamin Sale Block Letter.
11. If you know Access and your instructor requests, create the data source in Access and then open the main document with the Access database file as the data source.
12. If your instructor requests, display your record on the screen and merge the form letter to an email message, specifying only the current record to receive the message. Submit the merged email message in the format specified by your instructor.
13. Answer the questions posed in #3 and #7. If you choose to merge to email addresses, what is the purpose of the various email formats?

Analyze, Correct, Improve

Analyze a document, correct all errors, and improve it.

Editing Merge Fields, Editing a Data Source, and Specifying Filter Conditions

Note: To complete this assignment, you will be required to use the Data Files for Students. Visit www.cengage.com/ct/studentdownload for detailed instructions or contact your instructor for information about accessing the required files.

Instructions: Run Word. Open the document, Analyze 6-1 Admissions Letter Draft, located on the Data Files for Students. When you open the main document, if Word displays a dialog box about an SQL command, tap or click the Yes button. If Word prompts for the name of the data source, select Analyze 6-1 Student List on the Data Files for Students.

The document is a form letter that is missing fields and requires editing (Figure 6–86). You are to insert an AddressBlock merge field and a GreetingLine merge field, insert and delete merge fields in the form letter, edit data source records, and filter and sort records.

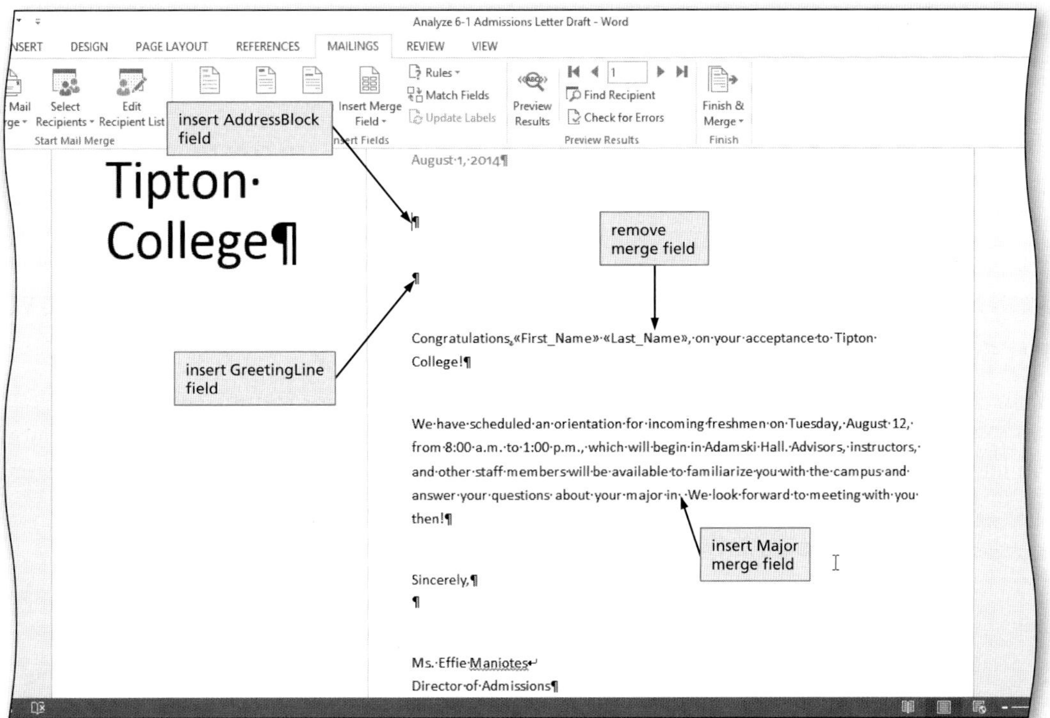

Figure 6–86

Perform the following tasks:

1. Correct In the form letter, correct the following items:

a. Add a field to the data source called Major. Enter these majors in the five records: general engineering, biology, business, animal and poultry sciences, and psychology.

b. In the data source, find the record whose last name is Johnson. Fix the State entry so that it reads, NC, and ZIP Code entry so that it reads 38761.

c. In the data source, find the misspelled address, Bakr, and correct its spelling to Baker.

d. If requested by your instructor, add a record to the data source that contains your personal information.

e. In the main document, insert the AddressBlock merge field below the date.

f. In the main document, insert the GreetingLine merge field below the AddressBlock. Use an appropriate salutation and punctuation.

g. In the first sentence, delete the merge field, Last_Name, and the space that precedes it, so that just the First_Name merge field appears.

h. At the end of the second sentence in the second paragraph, insert the Major merge field.

i. Save the modified document with the file name, Analyze 6-1 Admissions Letter Modified, and then submit it in the format specified by your instructor.

2. Improve Enhance the letter specifying merge filters. Merge to a new document only those students who live in Georgia. Clear the filter. Identify another type of filter and merge those form letters to a new document. Clear the filter. Merge all records in last name order and merge to a new document. Clear the sort order. Identify another type of sort order and merge those form letters to a new document. Clear the sort order. If requested by your instructor, submit the filtered and sorted documents in the format specified.

3. This assignment contains only a few records in the data source. If it contained records for the entire school, what filters might be useful? Why?

In the Labs

Design and/or create a document using the guidelines, concepts, and skills presented in this chapter. Labs 1 and 2, which increase in difficulty, require you to create solutions based on what you learned in the chapter; Lab 3 requires you to create a solution, which uses cloud and web technologies, by learning and investigating on your own from general guidance.

Lab 1: Creating a Form Letter Using a Template, a Data Source, Mailing Labels, and a Directory

Problem: You are graduating this December and have prepared your resume (shown in Figure 5–81 on page WD 329 in Chapter 5). You decide to create a cover letter for your resume as a form letter that you will send to potential employers. The main document for the form letter is shown in Figure 6–87a.

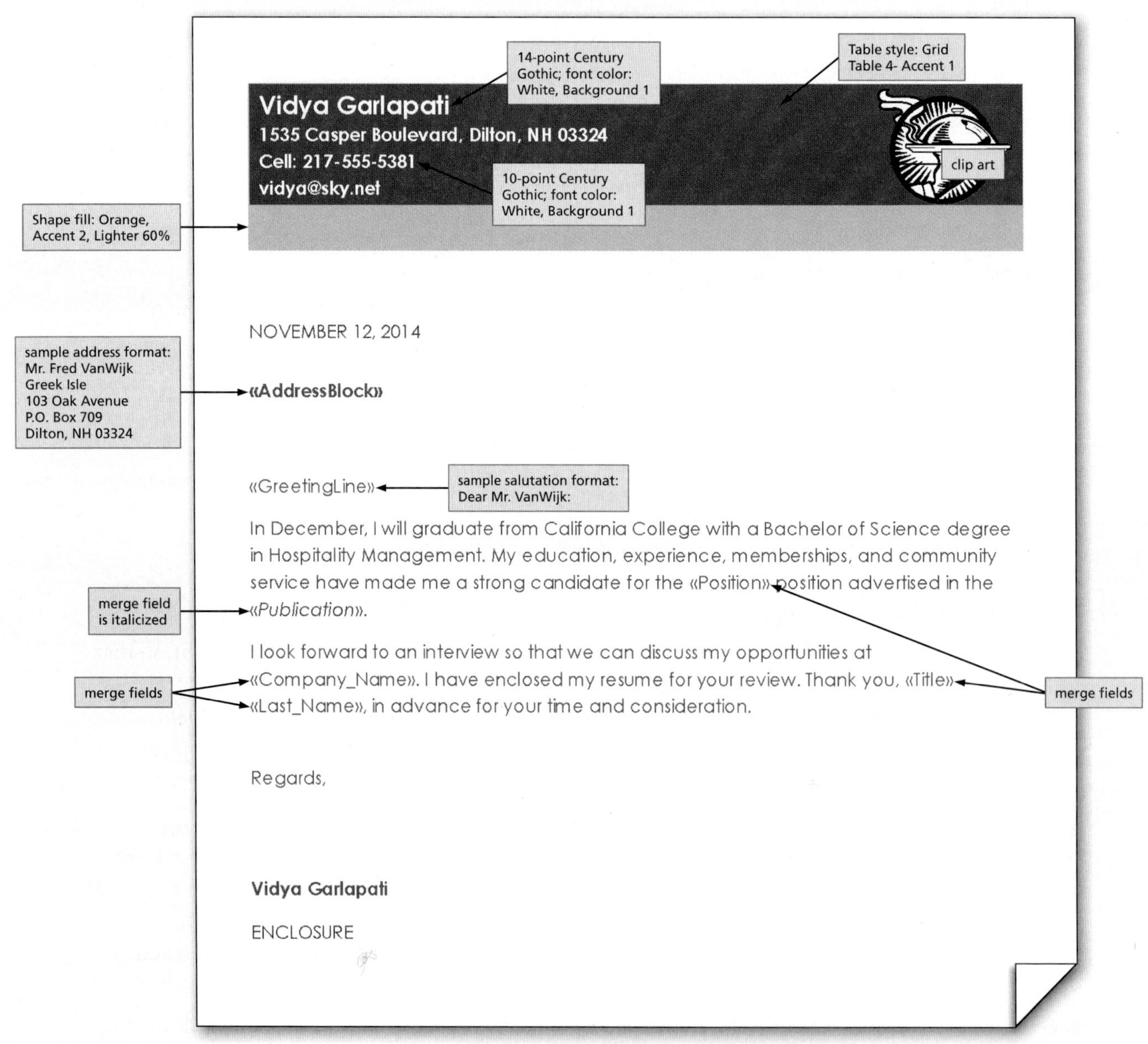

(a) Main Document for Form Letter

Figure 6–87

Perform the following tasks:

1. Use the Timeless letter template to begin creating the main document for the form letter. If you cannot locate this template, open the file called Basic resume (Timeless design) from the Data Files for Students. If necessary, change the document theme to Wisp (or a similar theme). Save the main document for the form letter with the file name, Lab 6-1 Garlapati Cover Letter.
2. Type a new data source using the data shown in Figure 6–87b. Delete the field names not used and add two field names: Position and Publication. If requested by your instructor, add a record to the data source that contains your personal information. Save the data source with the file name, Lab 6-1 Garlapati Potential Employers.

Title	First Name	Last Name	Company Name	Address Line 1	Address Line 2	City	State	ZIP Code	Position	Publication
Ms.	Dawn	Nitz	Garden Grill	145 Sunset Road		Dilton	NH	03324	Assistant Manager	Dilton Press
Mr.	Fred	VanWijk	Greek Isle	103 Oak Avenue	P.O. Box 709	Dilton	NH	03324	Restaurant Supervisor	Moraine Weekly
Ms.	Lynette	Galens	Lynette's Mediterranean Eatery	312 Center Street		Harrust	NH	03891	Manager	Weekly Gazette
Ms.	Latisha	Adams	Starlight Hotels	85 Cottage Grove Lane	P.O. Box 8722	Harrust	NH	03891	Associate Food Service Director	Tipton News
Mr.	Milton	Brewer	Paradise Cuisine	198 Shilling Boulevard	P.O. Box 239	Dilton	NH	03324	Management Trainee	Dilton Press

(b) Data Source

Figure 6–87 (continued)

3. Save the main document for the form letter again. Enter the text, clip art, merge fields, and formats as shown in the figure. Insert the AddressBlock and GreetingLine merge fields according to the sample formats shown in the figure. Italicize the Publication merge field. Change the top and bottom margins to 1 inch and the left and right margins to 1.25 inches. Specify the position of the rectangle graphic to 1 inch from the top of the page. Reduce the space above the paragraph containing the date to 36 point.
4. Merge the form letters to a new document. Save the merged letters in a file called Lab 6-1 Garlapati Merged Letters.
5. In a new document window, address mailing labels using the same data source you used for the form letters. Save the mailing label layout with the name, Lab 6-1 Garlapati Mailing Labels. If required by your instructor, merge the mailing labels to the printer.
6. In a new document window, specify the main document type as a directory. Change the page layout to landscape orientation. Change the margins to narrow. Insert all merge fields in the document, separating each with a comma. Merge the directory layout to a new document window. Convert the list of fields to a Word table (the table will have 11 columns). Add a row to the top of the table and insert field names in the empty cells. Change the font size of all text in the table to 8 point. Apply the List Table 3 - Accent 2 table style (remove formatting from the first column). Resize the table columns so that the table looks like Figure 6–87b. Center the table. Sort the table in the directory by the Last Name field. Save the merged directory with the file name, Lab 6-1 Garlapati Directory.
7. Submit all documents in the format specified by your instructor.
8. Why is the Publication merge field italicized in this letter?

Continued >

In the Labs *continued*

Lab 2: Designing a Data Source, Form Letter, and Directory from Sample Letters

Problem: You are graduating this May and have prepared your resume (shown in Figure 5–82 on page WD 331 in Chapter 5). You decide to create a cover letter for your resume as a form letter that you will send to potential employers. Sample drafted letters for the cover letter are shown in Figure 6–88a and Figure 6–88b.

KIM CHUNG

5056 East Fourth Street, Blackburg, TX 77490 • Phone: 584-555-8052 • Email: chung@world.com

April 22, 2015

Ms. Teresa McGill
Twin Power
1250 East Washington Street
Blackburg, TX 77490

Dear Ms. McGill:

I have enclosed my resume in response to your advertisement for an Industrial Engineer. I will graduate in May with a Bachelor of Science degree in Industrial Engineering Technology from Alamo College.

My coursework and experience make me an ideal candidate to work as an employee at Twin Power. I look forward to the opportunity to meet with you, Ms. McGill, to discuss my qualifications.

Sincerely,

Kim Chung
Enclosure

(a) Sample First Letter

KIM CHUNG

5056 East Fourth Street, Blackburg, TX 77490 • Phone: 584-555-8052 • Email: chung@world.com

April 22, 2015

Mr. Ronald Hidalgo
Fluid Energy Corporation
7685 Independence Parkway
P.O. Box 2283
Gartner, TX 77399

Dear Mr. Hidalgo:

I have enclosed my resume in response to your advertisement for an Energy System Control Engineer. I will graduate in May with a Bachelor of Science degree in Industrial Engineering Technology from Alamo College.

My coursework and experience make me an ideal candidate to work as a contractor at Fluid Energy Corporation. I look forward to the opportunity to meet with you, Mr. Hidalgo, to discuss my qualifications.

Sincerely,

Kim Chung
Enclosure

(b) Sample Second Letter

Figure 6–88

Perform the following tasks:

1. Review the letters in Figure 6–88 and determine the fields that should be in the data source. Write the field names on a piece of paper.
2. Do not use a template to create this form letter. In Word, create a main document for the letters using the block letter style. Apply the No Spacing style to all paragraphs. Save the main document for the form letter with the file name, Lab 6-2 Chung Cover Letter.
3. Create a data source containing five records, consisting of data from the two letters shown in Figure 6–88 and then add three more records with your own data. If requested by your instructor, add a record to the data source that contains your personal information. Save the data source with the file name, Lab 6-2 Chung Potential Employers.

Continued >

In the Labs *continued*

4. Enter the text and merge fields into the letter. The letter requires one IF field that displays the words, an employee, if the available job position is for an employee; otherwise, it displays the words, a contractor, if the available job position is for a contractor. Merge the form letters to a new document. Save the merged letters with the file name, Lab 6-2 Chung Merged Letters. Submit the merged letters in the format specified by your instructor.
5. Merge the data source to a directory. Convert it to a Word table. Add an attractive border to the table and apply any other formatting you feel necessary. Submit the directory in the format specified by your instructor.
6. Which fields did you use in your data source?

Lab 3: Expand Your World: Cloud and Web Technologies

Exploring Apps for Office

Problem: You use apps on your phone and tablet regularly to look up a variety of information. You see that you can use apps not only in Word, but in other Office apps. You would like to investigate some of the apps available for Word to determine which ones would be helpful for you to use.

Note: You will be required to use your Microsoft Account to complete this assignment. If you do not have a Microsoft account and do not want to create one, read this assignment without performing the instructions.

Instructions: Perform the following tasks:

1. Use Help to learn about Apps for Office. If necessary, sign in to your Windows account.
2. If you are not signed in already, sign in to your Microsoft Account in Word.
3. Display the INSERT tab and then tap or click the 'Insert an App' button (INSERT tab | Apps group) to display the Apps for Office dialog box. (If a menu is displayed, tap or click the See All link to display the Apps for Office dialog box.) Tap or click the Office Store button to visit the online Office Store. Tap or click the 'What are apps?' link and read the information. Tap or click the Back button to return to the Office Store.
4. Scroll through the 'New Apps for Word', the 'Featured Apps for Word' (Figure 6–89), and the 'Top Downloaded Apps for Word'. Tap or click the More button in one of these categories to display more information about your selection. Locate a free app that you feel would be helpful to you while you use Word, tap or click the Add button, and then follow the instructions to add the app to Word.
5. In Word, tap or click the 'Insert an App' button (INSERT tab | Apps group) to display the Apps for Office dialog box. Tap or click the app you added and then tap or click the Insert button to add the app. Tap or click the 'Insert an App' arrow (INSERT tab | Apps group) to see the added app in the list.
6. Practice using the app. Does the app work as you intended? Would you recommend the app to others?
7. Which app did you download and why? Answer the questions in #6. If you download a dictionary app, how else in Word can you access that app?

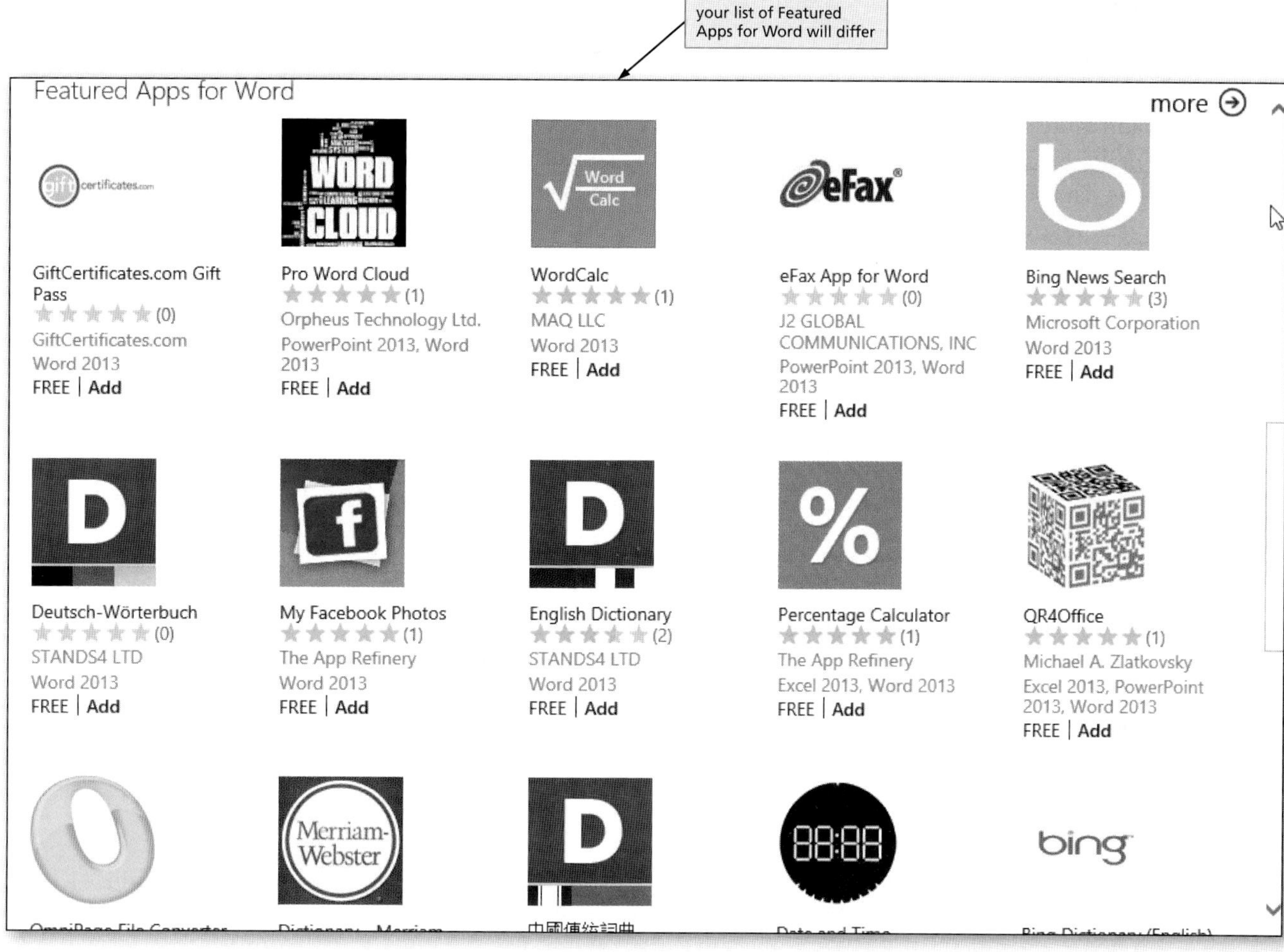

Figure 6–89

Consider This: Your Turn

Apply your creative thinking and problem solving skills to design and implement a solution.

1: Create a Form Letter for a Family Reunion

Personal

Part 1: You are coordinating the 10th annual family reunion for all of your relatives. The reunion will be held in Wilmington Park in Graber on Saturday, September 6. The pavilion at the park has been reserved from 11:00 a.m. until 10:00 p.m. If anyone has a volleyball set, horseshoes, or other outdoor equipment, ask them to contact you. Anyone who wants to play baseball should bring bats and mitts. Everyone is being assigned a food and beverage item to bring, along with a table service such as plates, napkins, and condiments. Each person should bring enough of their assigned items to serve 20 people.

No spacing set 1st before anything else

Continued >

Consider This: Your Turn *continued*

Use the concepts and techniques presented in this chapter to create and format a form letter announcing the family reunion to your relatives and assigning respective food, beverage, and table service items. Use your name and contact information as the sender information in the main document. The merge fields for the data source are shown in Table 6–1. All merge fields in the data source should be used at least once in the form letter. Be sure to check the spelling and grammar of the finished documents. Create a directory of the data source records. If required by your instructor, address and print accompanying labels for the form letters. Submit your assignment in the format specified by your instructor.

Table 6–1

Relative Name	Address Line 1	Address Line 2	City	State	ZIP Code	Assigned food	Assigned Beverage	Assigned Table Service
Tom and Betty Warner	32 Tipton Avenue		Graber	OK	74877	hamburgers	iced tea	plastic cups
George Peterson	127 First Placess	Apt. 52	Elwood	OK	74891	hamburger and hot dog buns	lemonade	paper plates and napkins
Henrietta Gilbert	58 Ohio Court	Unit 2B	Melville	OK	74770	brats and hot dogs	water	ketchup and mustard
The Carter Family	359 Hillside Lane	P.O. Box 17	Elwood	OK	74891	chips	regular soda	pickles and onions
The Wakefield Family	887 East Street		Graber	OK	74877	cookies	diet soda	salt and pepper

Part 2: You made several decisions while creating the form letter, data source, and directory in this assignment: whether to use a template or create the letter from scratch, wording to use, where to position text and merge fields in the letter, how to format elements, how to set up the data source, and how to format the directory. What was the rationale behind each of these decisions?

2: Create a Form Letter for a Vehicle Service Center

Professional

Part 1: As office manager at Total Vehicle Care, you send reminder letters to customers for service to their vehicles. Your business is located at 983 Independence Parkway, Rocktown, AR 71672; phone number is (847) 555-3838; website is www.tvc.com. In the form letters, you inform customers of the month of their last vehicle service and the type of service performed on their vehicle. You ask them to call to schedule an appointment for a service appointment at their earliest convenience. If they bring their letter, they will receive a 10 percent discount on any service performed.

Use the concepts and techniques presented in this chapter to create and format a form letter reminding customers of service due on their vehicle. Use your name and contact information as the sender information in the main document. The merge fields for the data source are shown in Table 6–2. All merge fields in the data source should be used at least once in the form letter. Be sure to check the spelling and grammar of the finished documents. Create a directory of the data source records. If required by your instructor, address and print accompanying labels for the form letters. Submit your assignment in the format specified by your instructor.

Table 6–2

Title	First Name	Last Name	Address Line 1	Address Line 2	City	State	ZIP Code	Vehicle Type	Month of Last Service	Last Service Performed
Ms.	Lana	Canaan	202 Park Boulevard		Rocktown	AR	71672	pickup truck	January	oil change
Mr.	Raul	Ramos	22 Fifth Street	Apt. 2B	Hill City	AR	71630	SUV	May	oil change
Ms.	Laura	Ennis	74 MacEnroe Court	P.O. Box 77	Fairview	AR	71622	compact car	March	tune-up
Mr.	Max	Henreich	322 County Line Road		Rocktown	AR	71672	van	February	tire rotation and alignment
Ms.	Constance	Marsh	5421 Crestview Circle	Unit 10C	Horizon	AR	74642	sports car	March	inspection

Part 2: You made several decisions while creating the form letter, data source, and directory in this assignment: whether to use a template or create the letter from scratch, wording to use, where to position text and merge fields in the letter, how to format elements, how to set up the data source, and how to format the directory. What was the rationale behind each of these decisions?

3: Create Form Letters Using Different Types of Data Sources

Research and Collaboration

Part 1: This chapter illustrated using one type of data source for merging form letters. As mentioned in the chapter, however, other types of data sources can be used for a merge operation. As a starting point for this assignment, select the form letter created in this chapter, the Apply Your Knowledge letter, or any of the other assignments completed, along with the corresponding data source. Form a three-member team to research, create, and merge form letters as follows:

a. If necessary, add an email field to the data source and then merge the contents of the data source to email addresses.

b. Use Access 2013 to view and format the contents of a data source created in Word. It may be necessary to use Help in Access.

c. Use Access 2013 to create a table and then use that table as the data source in the merge document. It may be necessary to use Help in both Word and Access for instructions about creating and saving an Access table in the proper format for a mail merge.

d. Use Excel 2013 to create a table and then use that table as the data source in the merge document. It may be necessary to use Help in both Word and Excel for instructions about creating and saving an Excel table in the proper format for a mail merge.

e. Use Outlook 2013 recipients as a data source in the merge document. It may be necessary to use Help in both Word and Outlook.

Summarize the steps you followed for each of the above tasks. Submit your team assignment in the format specified by your instructor.

Part 2: Of the various data source types used in this assignment, which do you prefer and why? Do you prefer to create data sources in Word or to use one of the techniques in this assignment? Why?

Learn Online

Reinforce what you learned in this chapter with games, exercises, training, and many other online activities and resources.

Student Companion Site Reinforcement activities and resources are available at no additional cost on www.cengagebrain.com. Visit www.cengage.com/ct/studentdownload for detailed instructions about accessing the resources available at the Student Companion Site.

SAM Put your skills into practice with SAM! If you have a SAM account, go to www.cengage.com/sam2013 to access SAM assignments for this chapter.

7 Creating a Newsletter with a Pull-Quote and Graphics

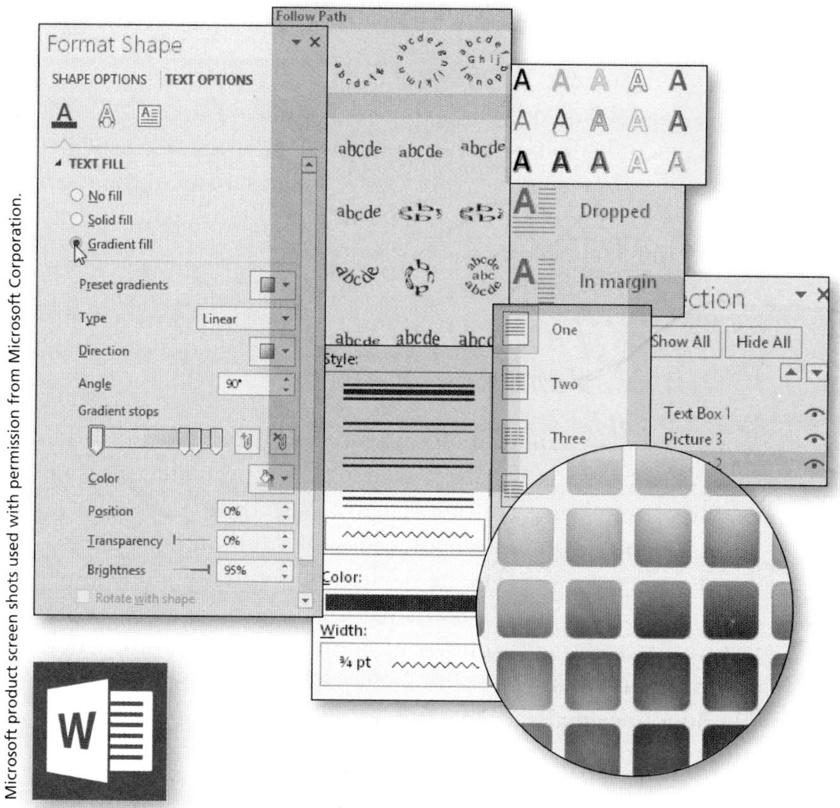

Objectives

You will have mastered the material in this chapter when you can:

- Insert and format WordArt
- Set custom tab stops
- Crop a graphic
- Rotate a graphic
- Format a document in multiple columns
- Justify a paragraph
- Hyphenate a document
- Format a character as a drop cap
- Insert a column break
- Insert and format a text box
- Copy and paste using a split window
- Balance columns
- Modify and format a SmartArt graphic
- Copy and paste using the Office Clipboard
- Add an art page border

7 Creating a Newsletter with a Pull-Quote and Graphics

Introduction

Professional-looking documents, such as newsletters and brochures, often are created using desktop publishing software. With desktop publishing software, you can divide a document in multiple columns, wrap text around diagrams and other graphical images, change fonts and font sizes, add color and lines, and so on, to create an attention-grabbing document. Desktop publishing software, such as Microsoft Publisher, Adobe PageMaker, or QuarkXpress, enables you to open an existing word processing document and enhance it through formatting tools not provided in your word processing software. Word, however, provides many of the formatting features that you would find in a desktop publishing program. Thus, you can use Word to create eye-catching newsletters and brochures.

Project — Newsletter

A newsletter is a publication geared for a specific audience that is created on a recurring basis, such as weekly, monthly, or quarterly. The audience may be subscribers, club members, employees, customers, patrons, students, etc.

The project in this chapter uses Word to produce the two-page newsletter shown in Figure 7–1. The newsletter is a monthly publication, called *Campus Post*. Each issue of *Campus Post* contains a feature article and announcements. This month's feature article discusses information literacy. The feature article spans the first two columns of the first page of the newsletter and then continues on the second page. The announcements, which are located in the third column of the first page, inform students about discounts and spirit wear and announce the topic of the next issue's feature article.

The *Campus Post* newsletter in this chapter incorporates the desktop publishing features of Word. The body of each page of the newsletter is divided in three columns. A variety of fonts, font sizes, and colors add visual appeal to the document. The first page has text wrapped around a pull-quote, and the second page has text wrapped around a graphic. Horizontal and vertical lines separate distinct areas of the newsletter, including a page border around the perimeter of each page.

The project in this chapter involves several steps requiring you to drag and drop. If you drag to the wrong location, you may want to cancel an action. Remember that you always can tap or click the Undo button on the Quick Access Toolbar to cancel your most recent action.

If you are using your finger on a touch screen and are having difficulty completing the steps in this chapter, consider using a stylus. Many people find it easier to be precise with a stylus than with a finger. In addition, with a stylus you see the pointer. If you still are having trouble completing the steps with a stylus, try using a mouse.

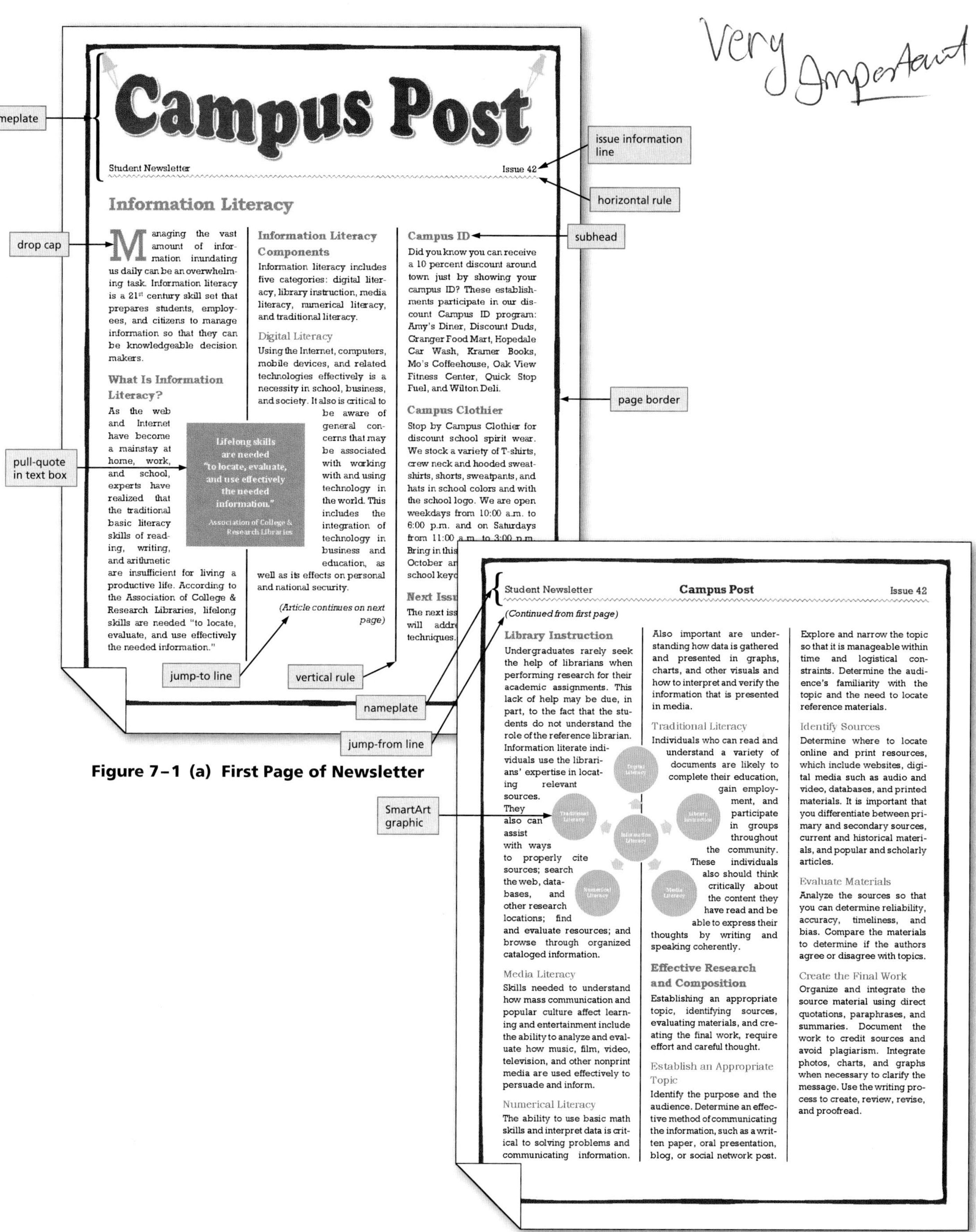

Campus Post

Student Newsletter — Issue 42

Information Literacy

Managing the vast amount of information inundating us daily can be an overwhelming task. Information literacy is a 21st century skill set that prepares students, employees, and citizens to manage information so that they can be knowledgeable decision makers.

What Is Information Literacy?

As the web and Internet have become a mainstay at home, work, and school, experts have realized that the traditional basic literacy skills of reading, writing, and arithmetic are insufficient for living a productive life. According to the Association of College & Research Libraries, lifelong skills are needed "to locate, evaluate, and use effectively the needed information."

> Lifelong skills are needed "to locate, evaluate, and use effectively the needed information."
> Association of College & Research Libraries

Information Literacy Components

Information literacy includes five categories: digital literacy, library instruction, media literacy, numerical literacy, and traditional literacy.

Digital Literacy

Using the Internet, computers, mobile devices, and related technologies effectively is a necessity in school, business, and society. It also is critical to be aware of general concerns that may be associated with working with and using technology in the world. This includes the integration of technology in business and education, as well as its effects on personal and national security.

(Article continues on next page)

Campus ID

Did you know you can receive a 10 percent discount around town just by showing your campus ID? These establishments participate in our discount Campus ID program: Amy's Diner, Discount Duds, Granger Food Mart, Hopedale Car Wash, Kramer Books, Mo's Coffeehouse, Oak View Fitness Center, Quick Stop Fuel, and Wilton Deli.

Campus Clothier

Stop by Campus Clothier for discount school spirit wear. We stock a variety of T-shirts, crew neck and hooded sweatshirts, shorts, sweatpants, and hats in school colors and with the school logo. We are open weekdays from 10:00 a.m. to 6:00 p.m. and on Saturdays from 11:00 a.m. to 3:00 p.m. Bring in this ... October ar... school keyc...

Next Issu...

The next iss... will addre... techniques.

Student Newsletter — **Campus Post** — Issue 42

(Continued from first page)

Library Instruction

Undergraduates rarely seek the help of librarians when performing research for their academic assignments. This lack of help may be due, in part, to the fact that the students do not understand the role of the reference librarian. Information literate individuals use the librarians' expertise in locating relevant sources. They also can assist with ways to properly cite sources; search the web, databases, and other research locations; find and evaluate resources; and browse through organized cataloged information.

Media Literacy

Skills needed to understand how mass communication and popular culture affect learning and entertainment include the ability to analyze and evaluate how music, film, video, television, and other nonprint media are used effectively to persuade and inform.

Numerical Literacy

The ability to use basic math skills and interpret data is critical to solving problems and communicating information. Also important are understanding how data is gathered and presented in graphs, charts, and other visuals and how to interpret and verify the information that is presented in media.

Traditional Literacy

Individuals who can read and understand a variety of documents are likely to complete their education, gain employment, and participate in groups throughout the community. These individuals also should think critically about the content they have read and be able to express their thoughts by writing and speaking coherently.

Effective Research and Composition

Establishing an appropriate topic, identifying sources, evaluating materials, and creating the final work, require effort and careful thought.

Establish an Appropriate Topic

Identify the purpose and the audience. Determine an effective method of communicating the information, such as a written paper, oral presentation, blog, or social network post. Explore and narrow the topic so that it is manageable within time and logistical constraints. Determine the audience's familiarity with the topic and the need to locate reference materials.

Identify Sources

Determine where to locate online and print resources, which include websites, digital media such as audio and video, databases, and printed materials. It is important that you differentiate between primary and secondary sources, current and historical materials, and popular and scholarly articles.

Evaluate Materials

Analyze the sources so that you can determine reliability, accuracy, timeliness, and bias. Compare the materials to determine if the authors agree or disagree with topics.

Create the Final Work

Organize and integrate the source material using direct quotations, paraphrases, and summaries. Document the work to credit sources and avoid plagiarism. Integrate photos, charts, and graphs when necessary to clarify the message. Use the writing process to create, review, revise, and proofread.

Figure 7–1 (a) First Page of Newsletter

Figure 7–1 (b) Second Page of Newsletter

Roadmap

In this chapter, you will learn how to create the newsletter shown in Figure 7–1 on the previous page. The following roadmap identifies general activities you will perform as you progress through this chapter:

1. CREATE the NAMEPLATE FOR the FIRST PAGE of the newsletter.
2. FORMAT the FIRST PAGE of the body of the newsletter.
3. CREATE a PULL-QUOTE on the first page of the newsletter.
4. CREATE the NAMEPLATE FOR the SECOND PAGE of the newsletter.
5. FORMAT the SECOND PAGE of the body of the newsletter.
6. ADD a PAGE BORDER to the newsletter.

At the beginning of step instructions throughout the chapter, you will see an abbreviated form of this roadmap. The abbreviated roadmap uses colors to indicate chapter progress: gray means the chapter is beyond that activity, blue means the task being shown is covered in that activity, and black means that activity is yet to be covered. For example, the following abbreviated roadmap indicates the chapter would be showing a task in the 2 FORMAT FIRST PAGE activity.

1 CREATE NAMEPLATE FOR FIRST PAGE | 2 FORMAT FIRST PAGE | 3 CREATE PULL-QUOTE
4 CREATE NAMEPLATE FOR SECOND PAGE | 5 FORMAT SECOND PAGE | 6 ADD PAGE BORDER

Use the abbreviated roadmap as a progress guide while you read or step through the instructions in this chapter.

Desktop Publishing Terminology

As you create professional-looking newsletters and brochures, you should be familiar with several desktop publishing terms. Figure 7–1 identifies these terms:

- A **nameplate**, or **banner**, is the portion of a newsletter that contains the title of the newsletter and usually an issue information line.
- The **issue information line** identifies the specific publication.
- A **ruling line**, usually identified by its direction as a **horizontal rule** or **vertical rule**, is a line that separates areas of the newsletter.
- A **subhead** is a heading within the body of the newsletter.
- A **pull-quote** is text that is *pulled*, or copied, from the text of the document and given graphical emphasis.

One of the few differences between Windows 7 and Windows 8 occurs in the steps to run Word. If you are using Windows 7, click the Start button, type `Word` in the 'Search programs and files' box, click Word 2013, and then, if necessary, maximize the Word window. For a summary of the steps to run Word in Windows 7, refer to the Quick Reference located at the back of this book.

To Run Word and Change Word Settings

If you are using a computer to step through the project in this chapter and you want your screens to match the figures in this book, you should change your screen's resolution to 1366 × 768. The following steps run Word, display formatting marks, and change the zoom to page width.

1. Run Word and create a blank document in the Word window. If necessary, maximize the Word window.
2. If the Print Layout button on the status bar is not selected, tap or click it so that your screen is in Print Layout view.
3. If the 'Show/Hide ¶' button (HOME tab | Paragraph group) is not selected already, tap or click it to display formatting marks on the screen.
4. To display the page the same width as the document window, if necessary, tap or click the Page Width button (VIEW tab | Zoom group).

To Change Spacing above and below Paragraphs and Margin Settings

Recall that Word is preset to use standard 8.5-by-11-inch paper, with 1-inch top, bottom, left, and right margins. In earlier chapters, you changed the margins by selecting predefined settings in the Margins gallery. For the newsletter in this chapter, all margins (left, right, top, and bottom) are .75 inches, which is not a predefined setting in the Margins gallery. Thus, the following steps set custom margins.

1. Display the PAGE LAYOUT tab.
2. Tap or click the Adjust Margins button (PAGE LAYOUT tab | Page Setup group) to display the Margins gallery and then tap or click Custom Margins to display the Page Setup dialog box.
3. Change each value in the Top, Bottom, Left, and Right boxes (Page Setup dialog box) to .75" (Figure 7–2).
4. Tap or click the OK button to change the margin values.

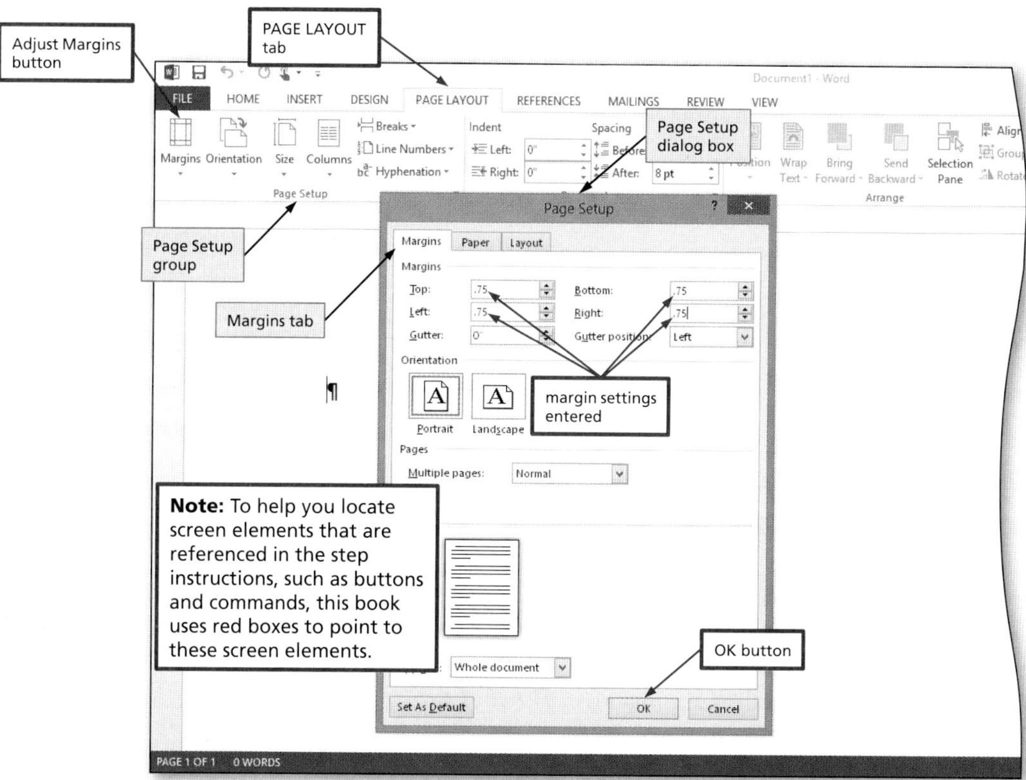

Figure 7–2

BTW

The Ribbon and Screen Resolution

Word may change how the groups and buttons within the groups appear on the ribbon, depending on the computer's screen resolution. Thus, your ribbon may look different from the ones in this book if you are using a screen resolution other than 1366 × 768.

To Change Theme Colors

The newsletter in this chapter uses the Damask theme. The following steps change the theme to Damask.

1. Display the DESIGN tab.
2. Tap or click the Themes button (DESIGN tab | Document Formatting group) and then tap or click Damask in the Themes gallery to change the document theme.

Creating the Nameplate

The nameplate on the first page of this newsletter consists of the information above the multiple columns (Figure 7–1a on page WD 411). In this project, the nameplate includes the newsletter title, Campus Post, images of thumbtacks, and the issue information line. The steps on the following pages create the nameplate for the first page of the newsletter in this chapter.

The following pages use the steps outlined below to create the nameplate for the newsletter in this chapter.

1. Enter and format the newsletter title using WordArt.
2. Set custom tab stops for the issue information line.
3. Enter text in the issue information line.
4. Add a horizontal rule below the issue information line.
5. Insert and format the clip art images.

CONSIDER THIS

How should you design a nameplate?

A nameplate visually identifies a newsletter. It should catch the attention of readers, enticing them to read a newsletter. Usually, the nameplate is positioned horizontally across the top of the newsletter, although some nameplates are vertical. The nameplate typically consists of the title of the newsletter and the issue information line. Some also include a subtitle, a slogan, and a graphical image or logo.

Guidelines for the newsletter title and other elements in the nameplate are as follows:

- Compose a title that is short, yet conveys the contents of the newsletter. In the newsletter title, eliminate unnecessary words such as these: the, newsletter. Use a decorative font in as large a font size as possible so that the title stands out on the page.
- Other elements on the nameplate should not compete in size with the title. Use colors that complement the title. Select easy-to-read fonts.
- Arrange the elements of the nameplate so that it does not have a cluttered appearance. If necessary, use ruling lines to visually separate areas of the nameplate.

To Insert WordArt

1 CREATE NAMEPLATE FOR FIRST PAGE | **2 FORMAT FIRST PAGE** | **3 CREATE PULL-QUOTE**
4 CREATE NAMEPLATE FOR SECOND PAGE | **5 FORMAT SECOND PAGE** | **6 ADD PAGE BORDER**

In Chapter 3, you inserted a shape drawing object in a document. Recall that a drawing object is a graphic you create using Word. Another type of drawing object, called **WordArt**, enables you to create text with special effects such as shadowed, rotated, stretched, skewed, and wavy effects.

This project uses WordArt for the newsletter title, Campus Post. ***Why?*** *A title created with WordArt is likely to draw the reader's attention.* The following steps insert WordArt.

1

- Display the INSERT tab.
- Tap or click the Insert WordArt button (INSERT tab | Text group) to display the Insert WordArt gallery (Figure 7–3).

Q&A Once I select a WordArt style, can I customize its appearance?
Yes. The next steps customize the WordArt style selected here.

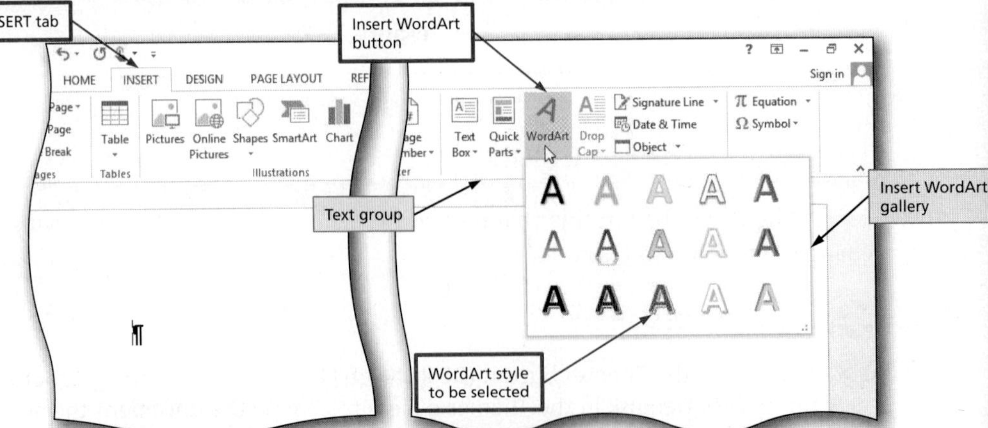

Figure 7–3

2

- Tap or click 'Fill - Pink, Accent 1, Outline - Background 1, Hard Shadow - Accent 1' in the WordArt gallery (third WordArt style in last row) to insert a drawing object in the document that is formatted according to the selected WordArt style, which contains the placeholder text, Your text here (Figure 7–4).

3

- Type **Campus Post** to replace the selected placeholder text in the WordArt drawing object (shown in Figure 7–5).

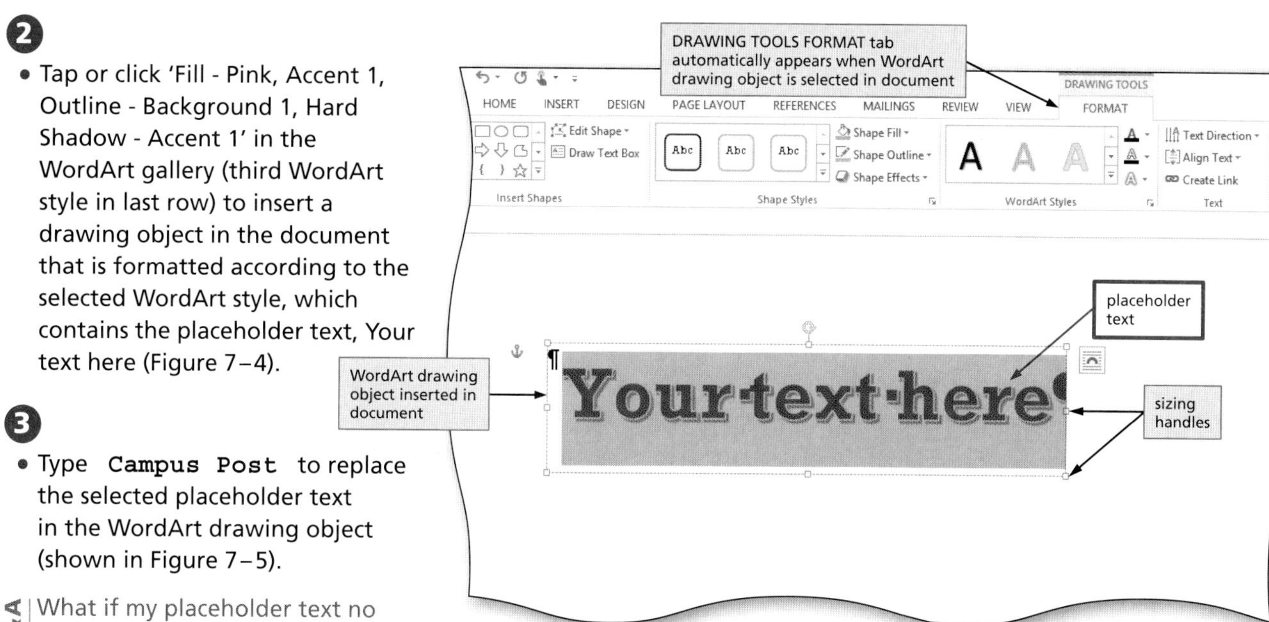

Figure 7–4

Q&A

What if my placeholder text no longer is selected?
Drag through it to select it.

How do I correct a mistake in the WordArt text?
You correct WordArt text using the same techniques you use to correct document text.

To Resize WordArt

You resize WordArt the same way you resize any other graphic. That is, you can drag its sizing handles or enter values in the Shape Height and Shape Width boxes. The next steps resize the WordArt drawing object.

1. With the WordArt drawing object selected, if necessary, display the DRAWING TOOLS FORMAT tab.
2. Change the value in the Shape Height box to 1.44 and the value in the Shape Width box to 7 (Figure 7–5).

BTW

Deleting WordArt

If you want to delete a WordArt drawing object, press and hold or right-click it and then tap Cut on the mini toolbar or click Cut on the shortcut menu, or select the WordArt drawing object and then tap or click the Cut button (HOME tab | Clipboard group).

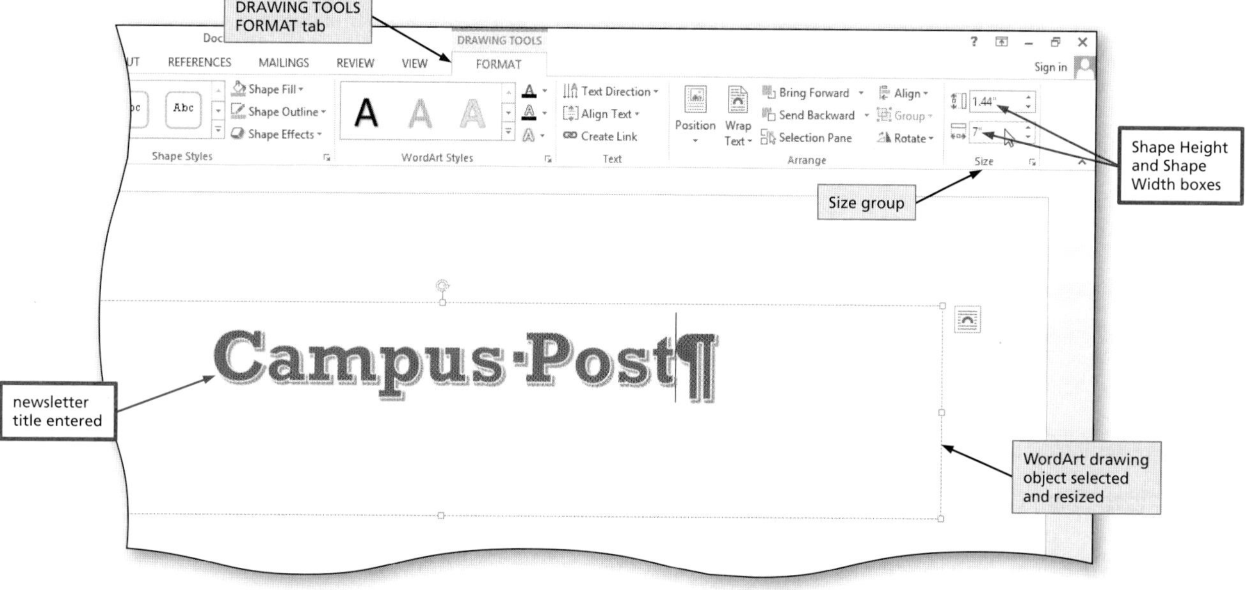

Figure 7–5

To Change the Font and Font Size of WordArt Text

You change the font and font size of WordArt text the same way you change the font and font size of any other text. That is, you select the text and then change its font and font size. The next steps change the font and font size of WordArt text.

1. Select the WordArt text, in this case, Campus Post.
2. Change the font of the selected text to Cooper Black.
3. Change the font size of the selected text to 72 point (shown in Figure 7–6).

To Change an Object's Text Wrapping

BTW
Touch Screen Differences
The Office and Windows interfaces may vary if you are using a touch screen. For this reason, you might notice that the function or appearance of your touch screen differs slightly from this chapter's presentation.

When you insert a drawing object in a Word document, the default text wrapping is Square, which means text will wrap around the object in the shape of a square. Because you want the nameplate above the rest of the newsletter, you change the text wrapping for the drawing object to Top and Bottom. The following steps change a drawing object's text wrapping.

1. With the WordArt drawing object selected, tap or click the Layout Options button that is attached to the WordArt drawing object to display the Layout Options gallery.
2. Tap or click 'Top and Bottom' in the Layout Options gallery so that the WordArt drawing object will not cover the document text; in this case, the paragraph mark moves below the WordArt drawing object (Figure 7–6).
3. Close the Layout Options gallery.

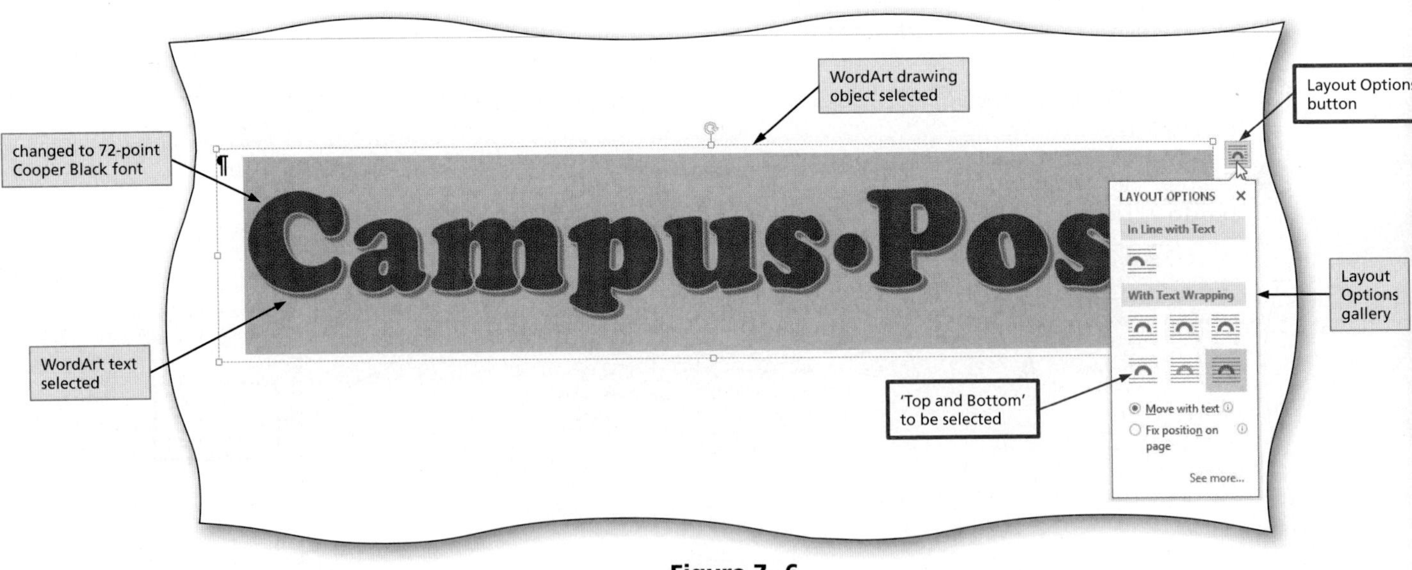

Figure 7–6

1 CREATE NAMEPLATE FOR FIRST PAGE | 2 FORMAT FIRST PAGE | 3 CREATE PULL-QUOTE
4 CREATE NAMEPLATE FOR SECOND PAGE | 5 FORMAT SECOND PAGE | 6 ADD PAGE BORDER

To Change the WordArt Fill Color

The next step is to change the color of the WordArt text so that it displays a purple and pink gradient fill color. **Gradient** means the colors blend into one another. Word includes several built-in gradient fill colors, or you can customize one for use in drawing objects. The next steps change the fill color of the WordArt drawing object to a built-in gradient fill color and then customize the selected fill color. ***Why?*** *Using a gradient fill color will add interest to the title.*

1

- With the WordArt drawing object selected, tap or click the Text Fill arrow (DRAWING TOOLS FORMAT tab | WordArt Styles group) to display the Text Fill gallery.

Q&A The Text Fill gallery did not appear. Why not?
If you are using a mouse, be sure you click the Text Fill arrow, which is to the right of the Text Fill button. If you mistakenly click the Text Fill button, Word places a default fill in the selected WordArt instead of displaying the Text Fill gallery.

- Tap or point to Gradient in the Text Fill gallery to display the Gradient gallery (Figure 7–7).

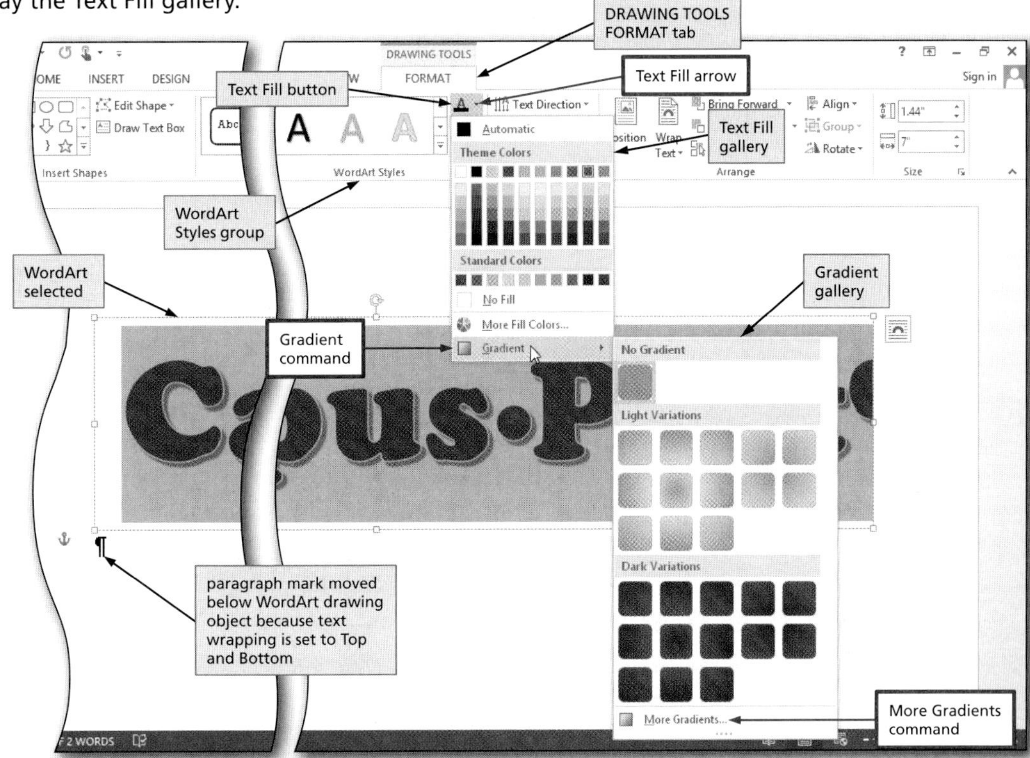

Figure 7–7

- Tap or click More Gradients in the Gradient gallery to display the Format Shape task pane. If necessary, tap or click the TEXT OPTIONS tab (Format Shape task pane) and then, if necessary, tap or click the 'Text Fill & Outline' button. If necessary, expand the TEXT FILL section.

- Tap or click Gradient fill in the TEXT FILL section to display options related to gradient colors in the task pane (Figure 7–8).

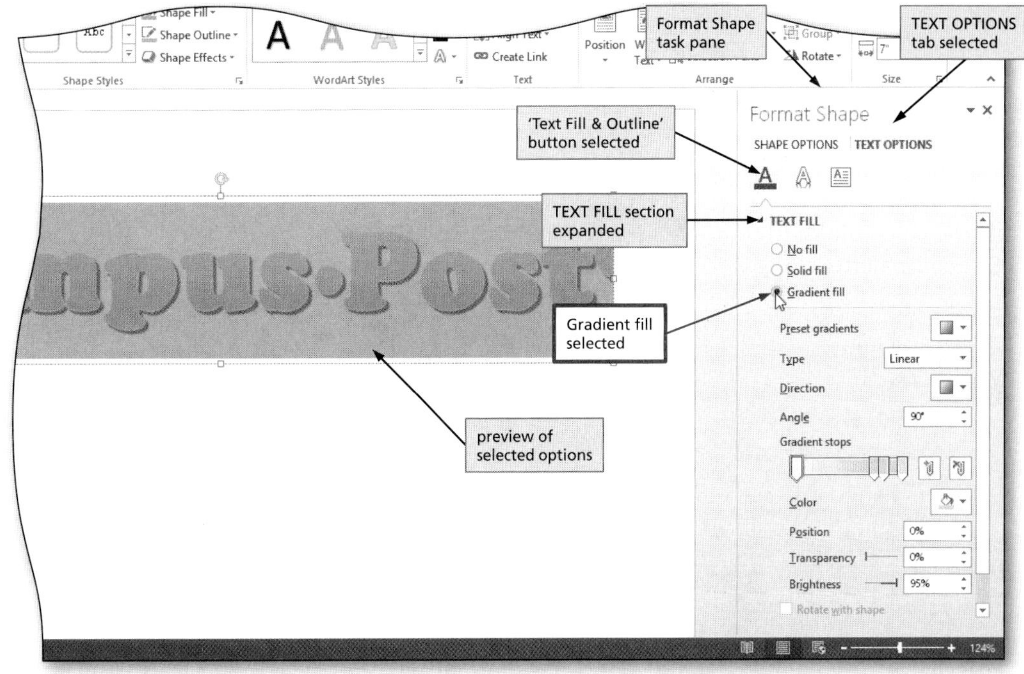

Figure 7–8

4

- Tap or click the Preset gradients button to display a palette of built-in gradient fill colors (Figure 7–9).

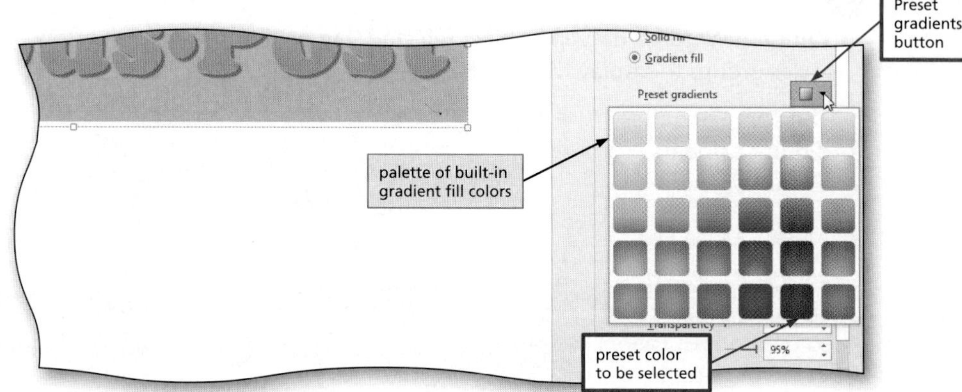

Figure 7–9

5

- Tap or click 'Radial Gradient - Accent 5' (bottom row, fifth column) in the Preset gradients palette to select the built-in gradient color, which shows a preview in the Gradient stops area (Figure 7–10).

Q&A What is a gradient stop?
A gradient stop is the location where two colors blend. You can change the color of a stop so that Word changes the color of the blend. You also can add or delete stops, with a minimum of two stops and a maximum of ten stops per gradient fill color.

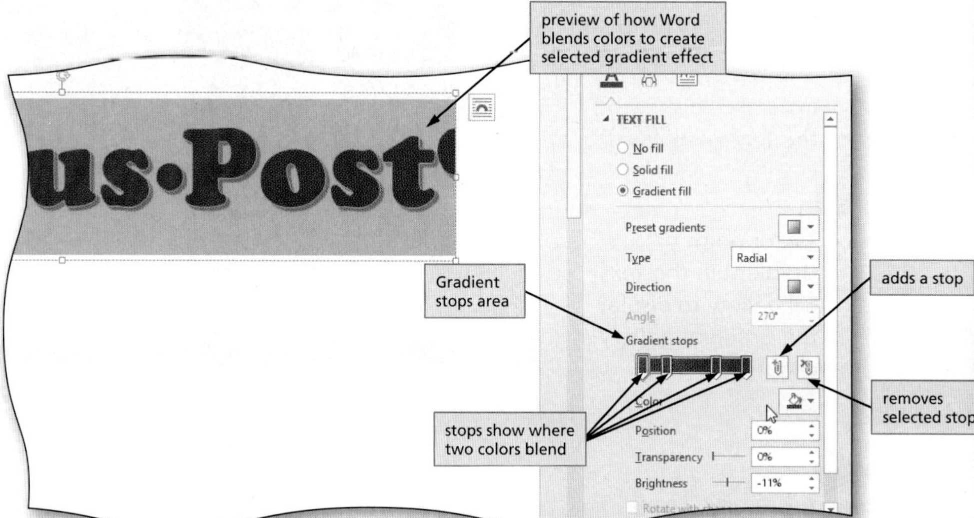

Figure 7–10

6

- Tap or click the second gradient stop to select it and then tap or click the Color button to display a Color palette, from which you can select a color for the selected stop (Figure 7–11).

7

- Tap or click 'Lavender, Accent 4, Darker 25%' (fifth row, eighth column) in the Color palette to change the color of the selected stop and the gradient between the selected stop and the next stop.

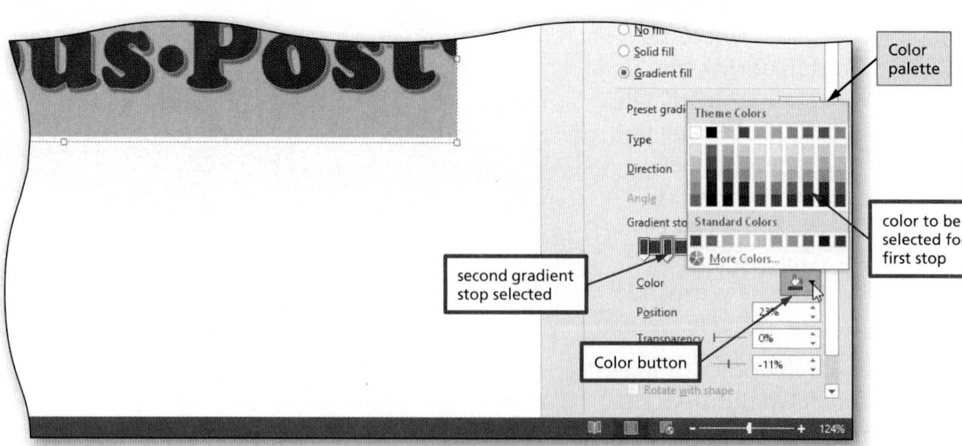

Figure 7–11

- Tap or click the rightmost gradient stop to select it and then tap or click the Color button to display a Color palette. Tap or click 'Lavender, Accent 4, Darker 25%' (fifth row, eighth column) in the Color palette to change the color of the selected stop and the gradient between the selected stop and the previous stop.

Q&A Can I move a gradient stop?
Yes. You can drag a stop to any location along the color bar. You also can adjust the position, brightness, and transparency of any selected stop.

8

- Tap or click the Direction button to display a gallery that shows a variety of directions for the gradient colors (Figure 7–12).

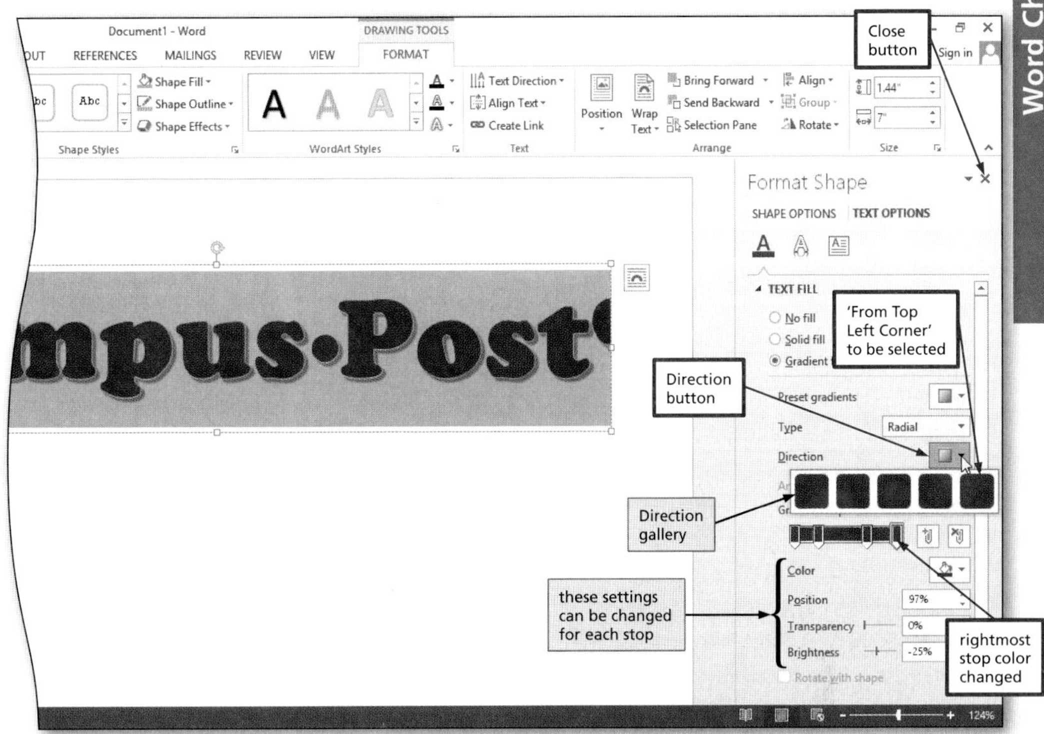

Figure 7–12

9

- Tap or click 'From Top Left Corner' (rightmost direction) in the Direction gallery to specify the direction to blend the colors.
- Tap or click the Close button in the task pane.
- Tap or click the paragraph mark below the WordArt drawing object to deselect the text so that you can see its gradient fill colors (Figure 7–13).

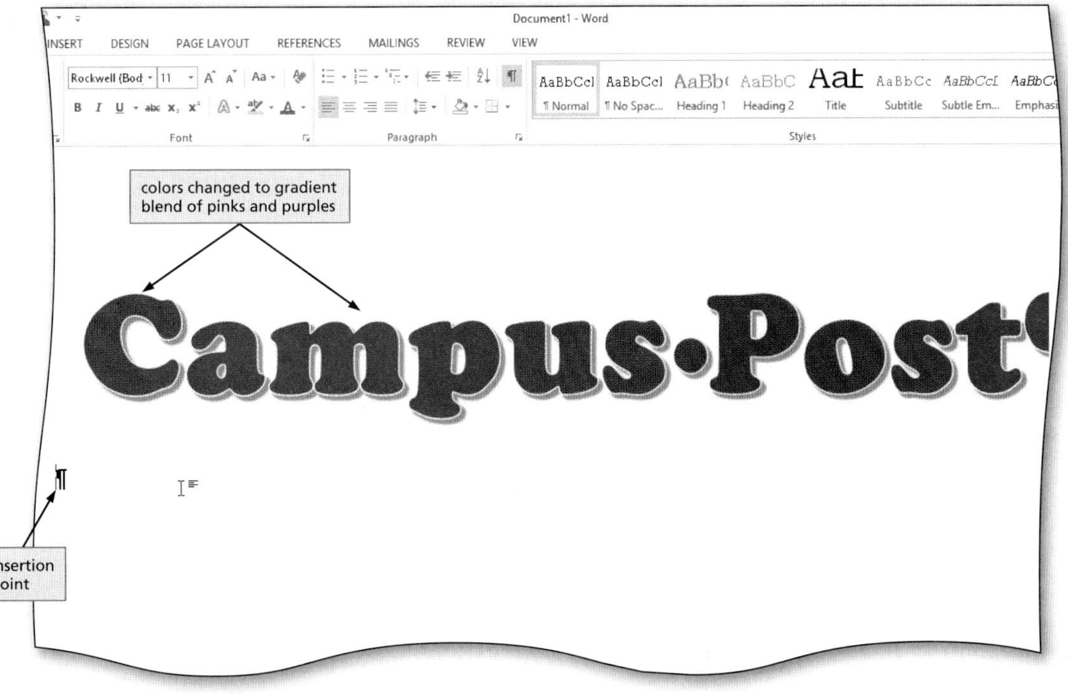

Figure 7–13

To Change the WordArt Shape

1 CREATE NAMEPLATE FOR FIRST PAGE | 2 FORMAT FIRST PAGE | 3 CREATE PULL-QUOTE
4 CREATE NAMEPLATE FOR SECOND PAGE | 5 FORMAT SECOND PAGE | 6 ADD PAGE BORDER

Word provides a variety of shapes to make your WordArt more interesting. The following steps change the WordArt shape. ***Why?*** *The WordArt in this newsletter has a wavy appearance.*

1

- Tap or click the WordArt drawing object to select it.
- If necessary, display the DRAWING TOOLS FORMAT tab.
- Tap or click the Text Effects button (DRAWING TOOLS FORMAT tab | WordArt Styles group) to display the Text Effects gallery.
- Tap or point to Transform in the Text Effects gallery to display the Transform gallery.
- If you are using a mouse, point to Double Wave 1 (third effect, fifth row in Warp area) in the Transform gallery to display a live preview of the selected transform effect applied to the selected drawing object (Figure 7–14).

Experiment

- If you are using a mouse, point to various text effects in the Transform gallery and watch the selected drawing object conform to that transform effect.

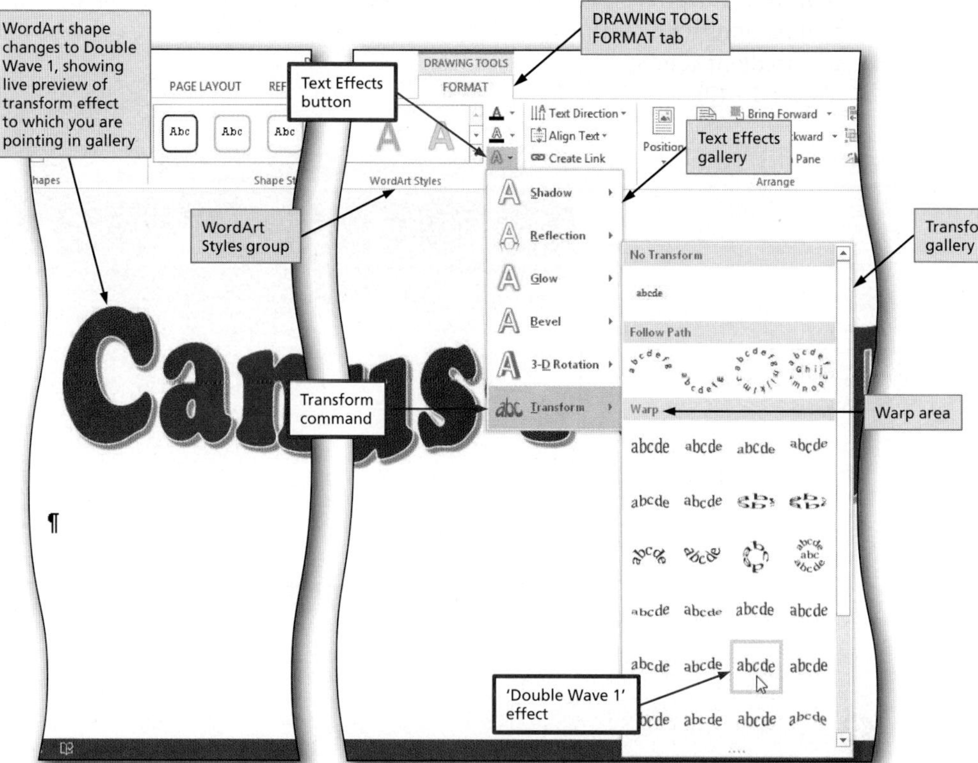

Figure 7–14

2

- Tap or click 'Double Wave 1' in the Transform gallery to change the shape of the WordArt drawing object.

To Set Custom Tab Stops Using the Tabs Dialog Box

1 CREATE NAMEPLATE FOR FIRST PAGE | 2 FORMAT FIRST PAGE | 3 CREATE PULL-QUOTE
4 CREATE NAMEPLATE FOR SECOND PAGE | 5 FORMAT SECOND PAGE | 6 ADD PAGE BORDER

The issue information line in this newsletter contains the text, Student Newsletter, at the left margin and the issue number at the right margin (shown in Figure 7–1a on page WD 411). In Word, a paragraph cannot be both left-aligned and right-aligned. ***Why?*** *If you tap or click the 'Align Text Right' button (HOME tab | Paragraph group), for example, all text will be right-aligned.* To place text at the right margin of a left-aligned paragraph, you set a tab stop at the right margin.

One method of setting custom tab stops is to tap or click the ruler at the desired location of the tab stop, which you learned in an earlier chapter. You cannot tap or click, however, at the right margin location. Thus, the next steps use the Tabs dialog box to set a custom tab stop.

1

- If necessary, display the HOME tab.
- Position the insertion point on the paragraph mark below the WordArt drawing object, which is the paragraph to be formatted with the custom tab stops.
- Tap or click the Paragraph Settings Dialog Box Launcher to display the Paragraph dialog box (Figure 7–15).

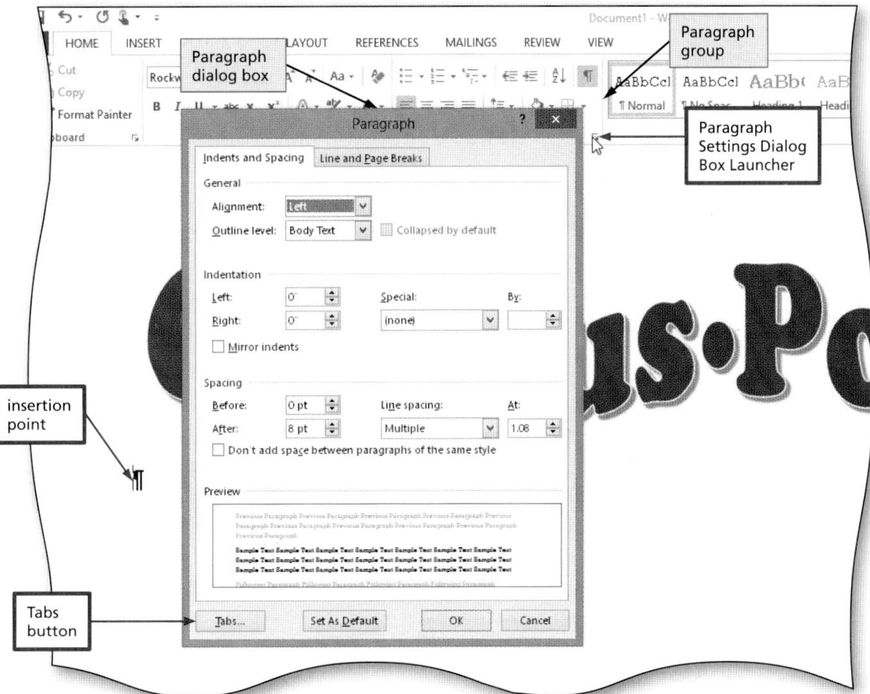

Figure 7–15

2

- Tap or click the Tabs button (Paragraph dialog box) to display the Tabs dialog box.
- Type 7 in the 'Tab stop position' text box (Tabs dialog box).
- Tap or click Right in the Alignment area to specify alignment for text at the tab stop (Figure 7–16).

3

- Tap or click the Set button (Tabs dialog box) to set a right-aligned custom tab stop at the specified position.
- Tap or click the OK button to set the defined tab stops.

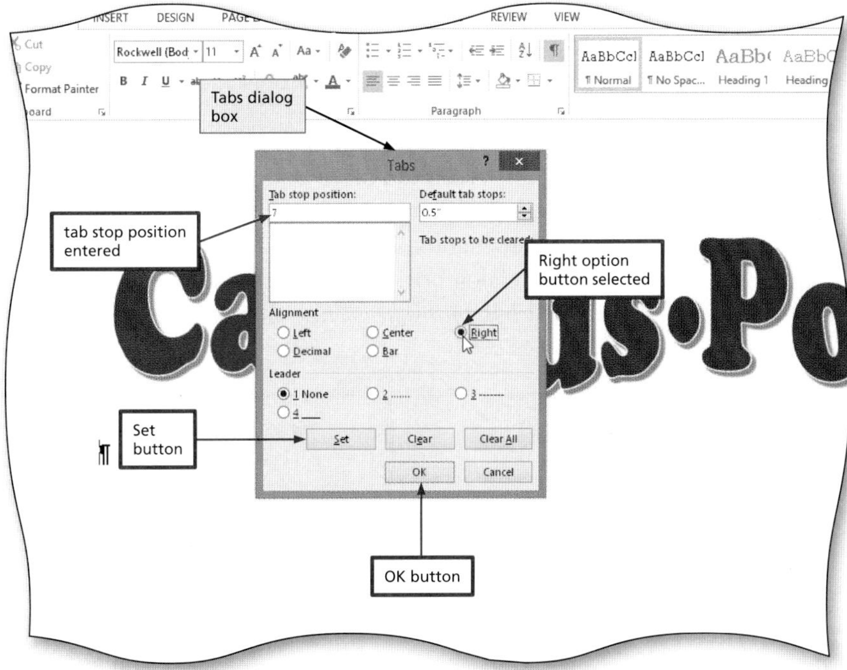

Figure 7–16

Other Ways

1. Tap 'Show Context Menu' button on mini toolbar or right-click paragraph, tap or click Paragraph on shortcut menu, tap or click Tabs button (Paragraph dialog box), enter desired settings, tap or click OK button

To Enter Text

The following steps enter the issue information line text.

1. With the insertion point on the paragraph below the WordArt, type **Student Newsletter** on line 2 of the newsletter.

   If requested by your instructor, enter your name instead of the word, Student.

2. Press the TAB key and then type **Issue 42** to complete the issue information line (Figure 7–17).

Figure 7–17

To Border One Edge of a Paragraph

1 CREATE NAMEPLATE FOR FIRST PAGE | 2 FORMAT FIRST PAGE | 3 CREATE PULL-QUOTE
4 CREATE NAMEPLATE FOR SECOND PAGE | 5 FORMAT SECOND PAGE | 6 ADD PAGE BORDER

In Word, you use borders to create ruling lines. As discussed in previous projects, Word can place borders on any edge of a paragraph; that is, Word can place a border on the top, bottom, left, and right edges of a paragraph.

One method of bordering paragraphs is by tapping or clicking the desired border in the Borders gallery, which you learned in an earlier chapter. If you want to specify a particular border, for example, one with color, you use the Borders and Shading dialog box. The following steps use the Borders and Shading dialog box to place a border below a paragraph. ***Why?*** *In this newsletter, the issue information line has a ¾-point wavy pink border below it.*

- Tap or click the Borders arrow (HOME tab | Paragraph group) to display the Borders gallery (Figure 7–18).

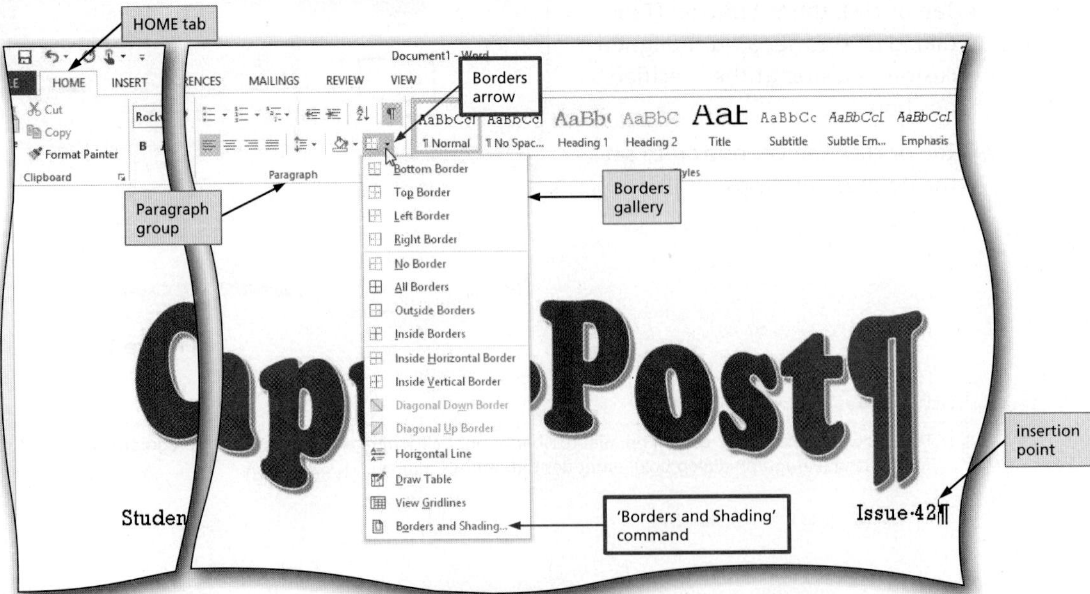

Figure 7–18

2

- Tap or click 'Borders and Shading' in the Borders gallery to display the Borders and Shading dialog box.
- Tap or click Custom in the Setting area (Borders and Shading dialog box) because you are setting just a bottom border.
- Scroll through the style list and tap or click the style shown in Figure 7–19, which has a wavy line as the border.
- Tap or click the Color button and then tap or click 'Pink, Accent 5, Darker 50%' (ninth column, sixth row) in the Color gallery.
- Tap or click the Bottom Border button in the Preview area of the dialog box to show a preview of the selected border style (Figure 7–19).

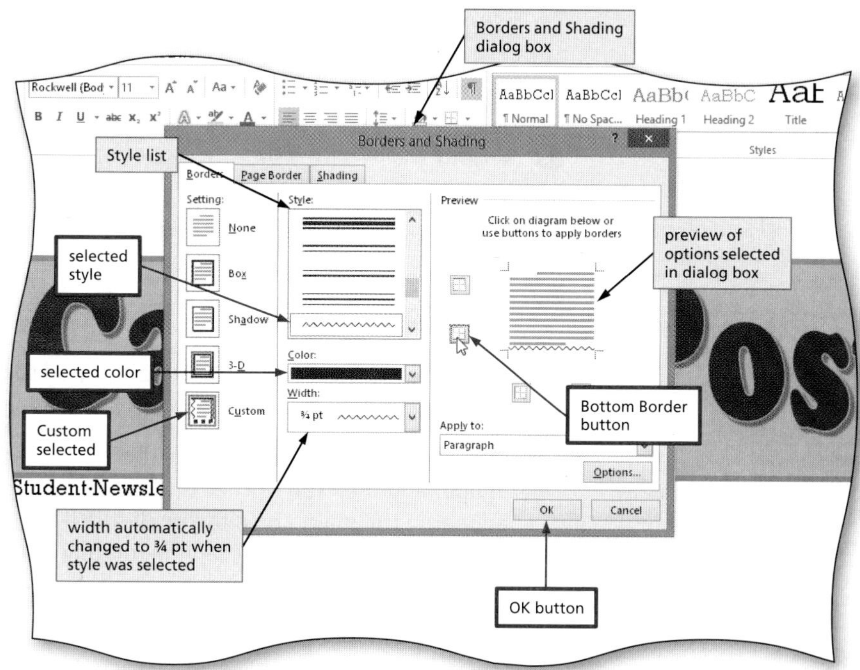

Figure 7–19

Q&A What is the purpose of the buttons in the Preview area?
They are toggles that display and remove the top, bottom, left, and right borders from the diagram in the Preview area.

3

- Tap or click the OK button to place the defined border on the paragraph containing the insertion point (Figure 7–20).

Q&A How would I change an existing border?
You first remove the existing border by tapping or clicking the Borders arrow (HOME tab | Paragraph group) and then tapping or clicking the border in the Borders gallery that identifies the border you wish to remove. Then, add a new border as described in these steps.

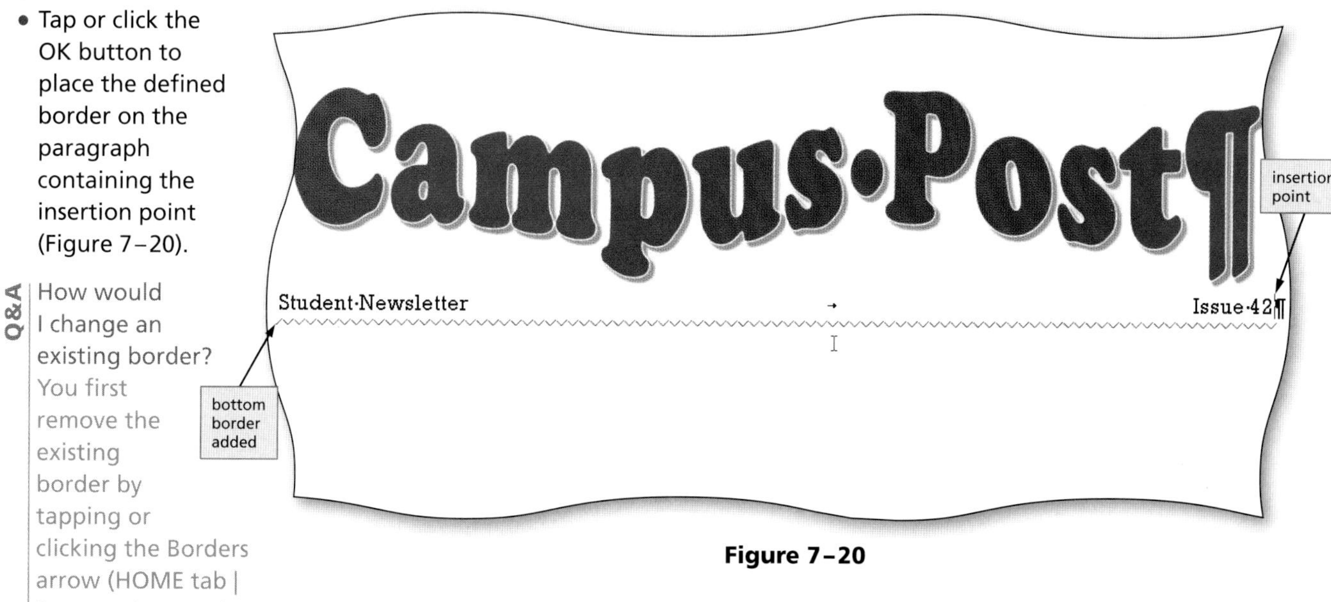

Figure 7–20

Other Ways

1. Tap or click 'Borders and Shading' button (DESIGN tab | Page Background group), tap or click Borders tab (Borders and Shading dialog box), select desired border, tap or click OK button

To Insert Clip Art

The next steps insert a clip art image of a thumbtack in the nameplate.

1. Display the INSERT tab.
2. Tap or click the Online Pictures button (INSERT tab | Illustrations group) to display the Insert Pictures dialog box.
3. Type `tack` in the Search box to specify the search text, which indicates the type of image you want to locate.
4. Tap or click the Search button to display a list of clip art that matches the entered search text.
5. Scroll through the list of clip art to locate the one shown in Figure 7–21 (or a similar image) and then tap or click the clip art to select it. (If the clip art image does not appear in the dialog box, tap or click the Cancel button in each dialog box and then proceed to the shaded steps immediately following these steps.)
6. Tap or click the Insert button to insert the selected clip art in the document at the location of the insertion point.

Q&A What if my clip art image is not in the same location as in Figure 7–21?
The clip art image may be in a different location, depending on the position of the insertion point when you inserted the image. In a later section, you will move the image to a different location.

BTW
Q&As
For a complete list of the Q&As found in many of the step-by-step sequences in this book, visit the Q&A resource on the Student Companion Site located on www.cengagebrain.com. For detailed instructions about accessing available resources, visit www.cengage.com/ct/studentdownload or contact your instructor for information about accessing the required files.

To Insert a Graphic File from the Data Files for Students

If you do not have access to the Internet, you can insert the clip art file in the Word document from the Data Files for Students. Visit www.cengage.com/ct/studentdownload for detailed instructions or contact your instructor for information about accessing the required files. NOTE: PERFORM THE STEPS IN THIS YELLOW BOX ONLY IF YOU WERE NOT ABLE TO INSERT THE TACK CLIP ART FROM THE WEB IN THE PREVIOUS STEPS.

1. Display the INSERT tab. Tap or click the From File button (INSERT tab | Illustrations group) to display the Insert Picture dialog box.
2. Navigate to the location of the picture to be inserted.
3. Tap or click the Tack file (Insert Picture dialog box) to select the file.
4. Tap or click the Insert button in the dialog box to insert the picture in the document at the location of the insertion point (shown in Figure 7–21).

To Change the Color of a Graphic

The next steps change the color of the graphic (the tack) to a lime green.

1. With the graphic still selected, tap or click the Color button (PICTURE TOOLS FORMAT tab | Adjust group) to display the Color gallery (Figure 7–21).
2. Tap or click 'Lime, Accent color 1 Light' (second color, third row) in the Recolor area in the Color gallery to change the color of the selected graphic.

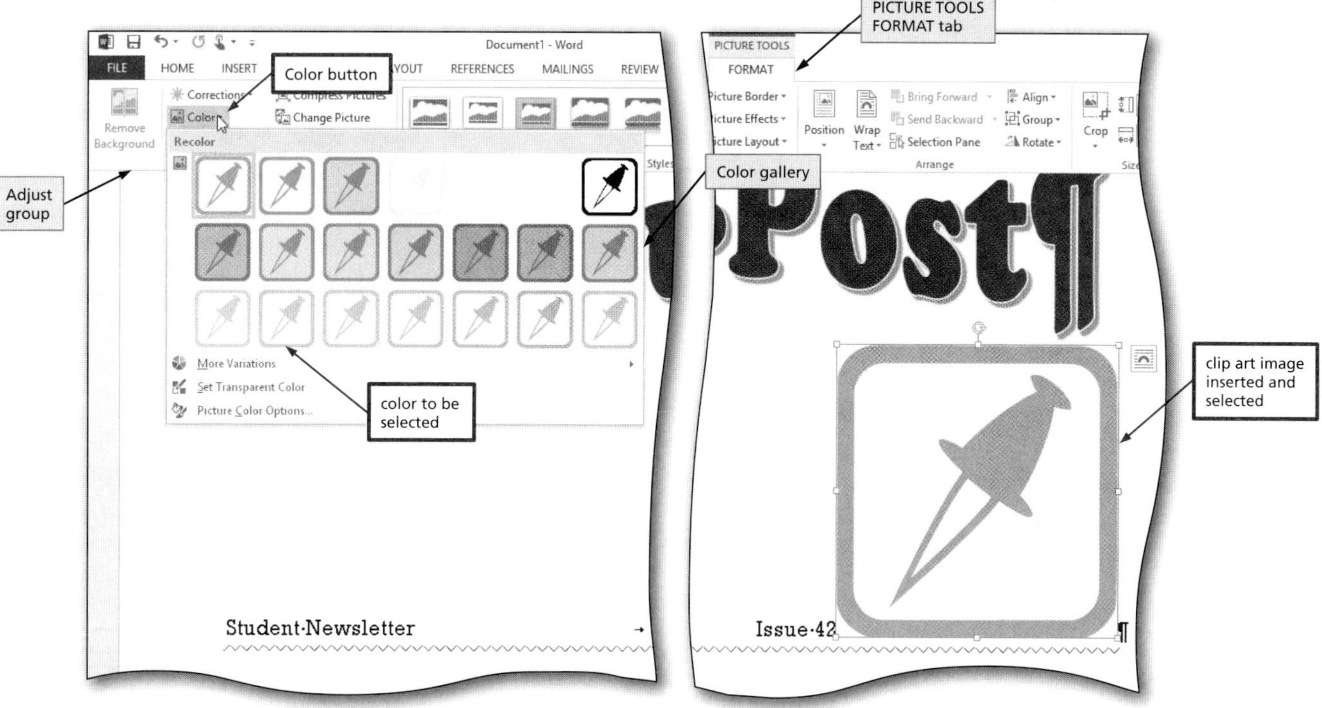

Figure 7–21

To Crop a Graphic

1 CREATE NAMEPLATE FOR FIRST PAGE | 2 FORMAT FIRST PAGE | 3 CREATE PULL-QUOTE
4 CREATE NAMEPLATE FOR SECOND PAGE | 5 FORMAT SECOND PAGE | 6 ADD PAGE BORDER

The next step is to format the clip art image just inserted. You would like to remove the rounded frame from the perimeter of the image. ***Why?*** *You want just the tack to appear in the newsletter.* Word allows you to **crop**, or remove edges from, a graphic. The following steps crop a graphic.

1

- With the graphic selected, tap or click the Crop button (PICTURE TOOLS FORMAT tab | Size group), which places cropping handles on the image in the document.

Q&A What if I mistakenly tap or click the Crop arrow?
Tap or click the Crop button.

- If you are using a mouse, position the pointer on the top-middle cropping handle so that it looks like an upside-down letter T (Figure 7–22).

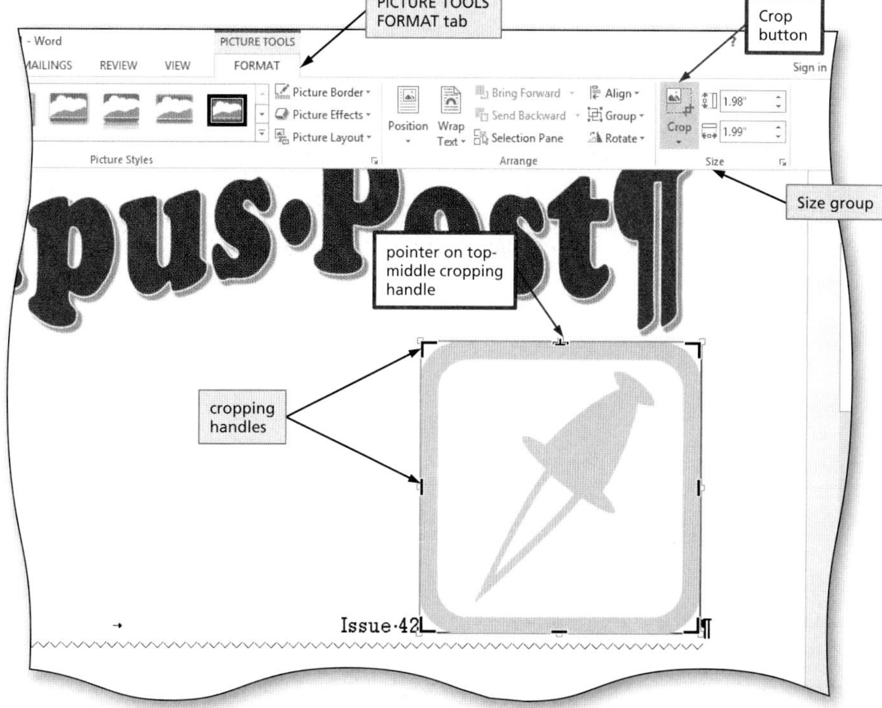

Figure 7–22

- Drag the top-middle cropping handle downward to the location of the shown in Figure 7–23 to remove the frame at the top of the image.

- If you are using a mouse, release the mouse button to crop the graphic to the location shown in Figure 7–23.

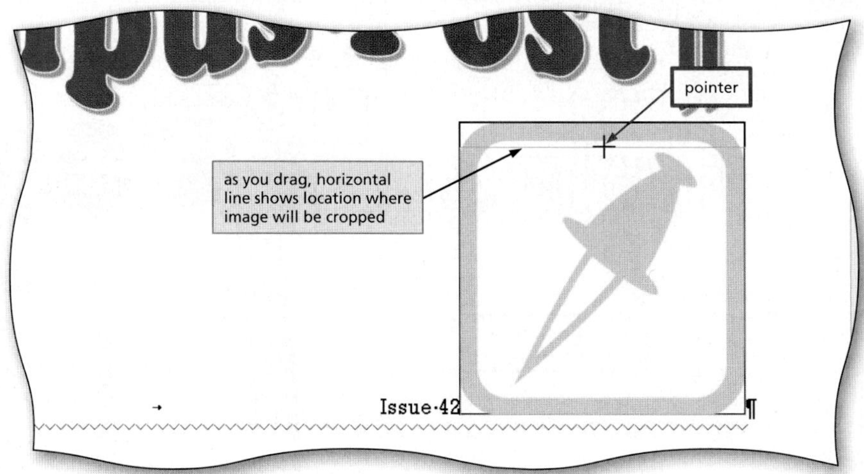

Figure 7–23

- Drag the left-middle cropping handle inward until the frame at the left edge of the image disappears, as shown in Figure 7–24.
- Drag the right-middle cropping handle inward until the frame at the right edge of the image disappears, as shown in Figure 7–24.
- Drag the bottom-middle cropping handle upward until the frame at the bottom edge of the image disappears, as shown in Figure 7–24.

- Tap or click the Crop button (PICTURE TOOLS FORMAT tab | Size group) to deactivate the cropping tool, which removes the cropping handles from the selected image.

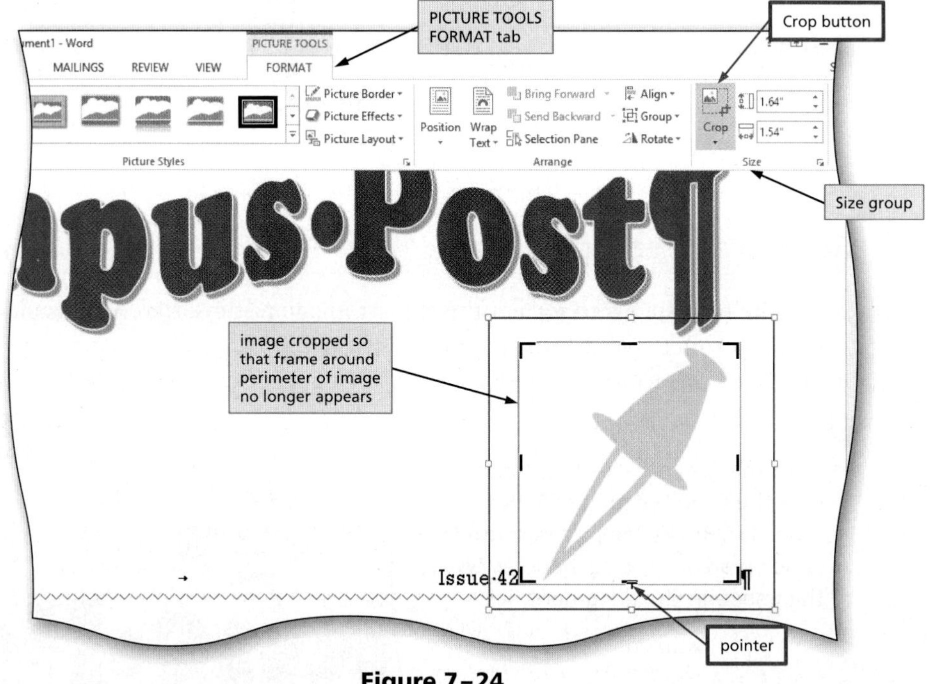

Figure 7–24

Other Ways

1. Press and hold or right-click graphic, tap or click Crop button on mini toolbar, drag cropping handles, tap or click Crop button

To Change an Object's Text Wrapping and Size

When you insert clip art in a Word document, the default text wrapping is In Line with Text, which means the object is part of the current paragraph. Because you want the clip art images behind the newsletter title, you change the text wrapping for the clip art image to Behind Text. The next steps change a drawing object's text wrapping and also change its size.

1. With the clip art image selected, tap or click the Layout Options button attached to the graphic to display the Layout Options gallery.
2. Tap or click Behind Text in the Layout Options gallery so that the clip art image is positioned behind text in the document.
3. Close the Layout Options gallery.
4. Change the values in the Shape Height and Shape Width boxes (PICTURE TOOLS FORMAT tab | Size group) to .5" and .45", respectively.

To Move a Graphic

The clip art image needs to be moved up so that the tip of the tack is on the t in the word, Post, in the newsletter title. The following steps move a graphic.

1. Hide formatting marks so that you can see exactly where the letter t ends.
2. Drag the graphic to the location shown in Figure 7–25.

To Copy a Graphic, Flip It, and Move It

The next step is to copy the cropped thumbtack image, flip it so that it faces the opposite direction, and then move it so that it is positioned above the C in the word, Campus, in the nameplate. The following steps copy, flip, and move a graphic.

1. If necessary, tap or click the graphic (the tack) to select it.
2. If necessary, display the HOME tab.
3. Tap or click the Copy button (HOME tab | Clipboard group) to copy the selected item to the Office Clipboard.
4. Tap or click the Paste arrow (HOME tab | Clipboard group) to display the Paste gallery and then tap or click 'Keep Source Formatting' to paste the object using the same formatting as the original.
5. Display the PICTURE TOOLS FORMAT tab. With the graphic still selected, tap or click the Rotate Objects button (PICTURE TOOLS FORMAT tab | Arrange group) to display the Rotate Objects gallery and then tap or click Flip Horizontal in the Rotate Options gallery, so that Word flips the graphic to display its mirror image.
6. Drag the graphic to the location shown in Figure 7–25.

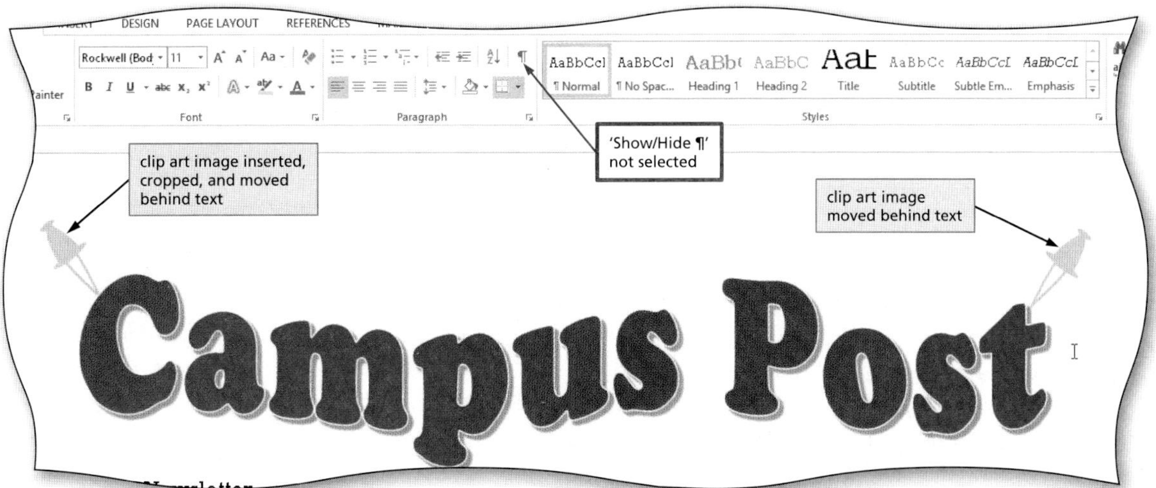

Figure 7–25

To Use the Selection Task Pane

1 CREATE NAMEPLATE FOR FIRST PAGE | 2 FORMAT FIRST PAGE | 3 CREATE PULL-QUOTE
4 CREATE NAMEPLATE FOR SECOND PAGE | 5 FORMAT SECOND PAGE | 6 ADD PAGE BORDER

The next step is to rotate the clip art images, but because they are positioned behind the text, it may be difficult to select them. The following step displays the Selection task pane. ***Why?*** *The Selection task pane enables you easily to select items on the screen that are layered behind other objects.*

1

- If necessary, tap or click in a graphic to display the PICTURE TOOLS FORMAT tab.
- Tap or click the 'Display the Selection Pane' button (PICTURE TOOLS FORMAT tab | Arrange group) to display the Selection task pane (Figure 7–26).

Experiment

- Tap or click Text Box 1 in the Selection task pane to select the WordArt drawing object. Tap or click Picture 3 in the Selection task pane to select the first tack image. Tap or click Picture 2 in the Selection task pane to select the second tack image.

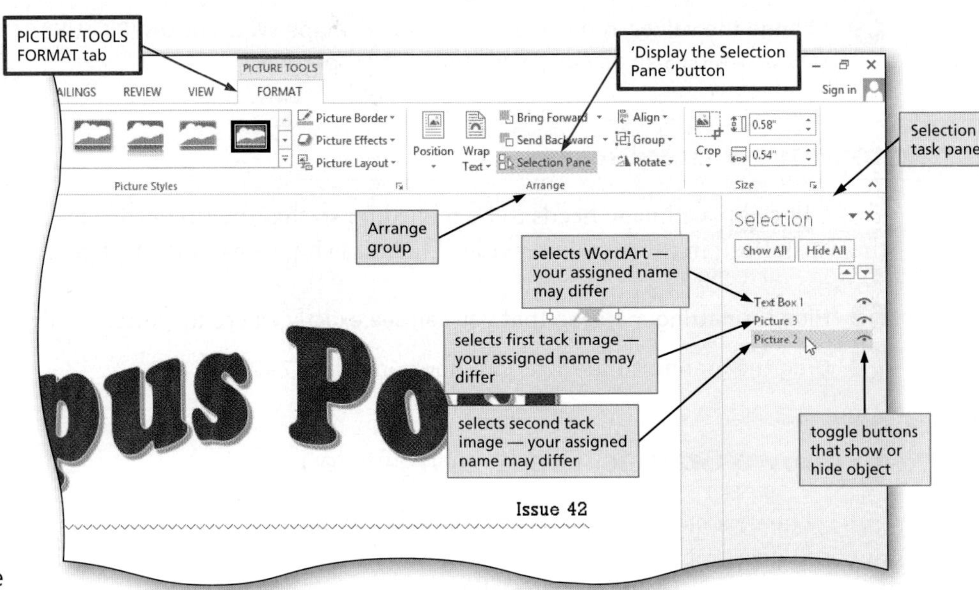

Figure 7–26

Q&A What are the displayed names in the Selection task pane?
Word assigns names to each object in the document. The names displayed on your screen may differ.

To Rotate a Graphic

1 CREATE NAMEPLATE FOR FIRST PAGE | 2 FORMAT FIRST PAGE | 3 CREATE PULL-QUOTE
4 CREATE NAMEPLATE FOR SECOND PAGE | 5 FORMAT SECOND PAGE | 6 ADD PAGE BORDER

The following steps rotate a graphic. ***Why?*** *You would like the tack images angled inward a bit more.*

1

- If necessary, tap or click Picture 2 in the Selection task pane to select the image of the tack on the right side of the screen.
- If you are using a mouse, position the pointer on the graphic's rotate handle (Figure 7–27).

Figure 7–27

2

- If you are using a mouse, drag the rotate handle leftward and downward to rotate the graphic slightly as shown in Figure 7–28.

Q&A Can I drag the rotate handle in any direction?
You can drag the rotate handle clockwise or counterclockwise.

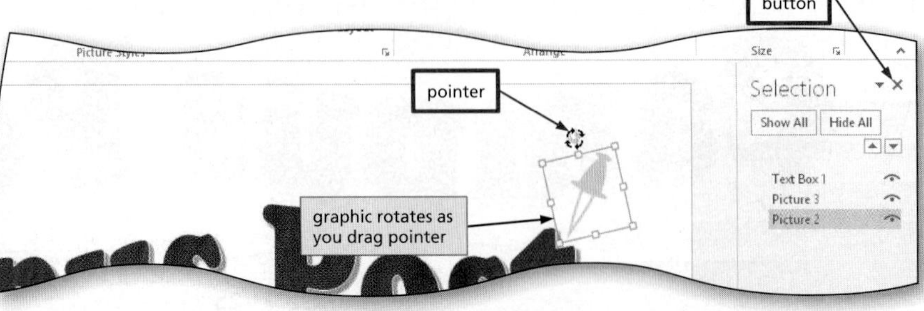

Figure 7–28

- If you are using a mouse, release the mouse button to position the graphic at the location where you dragged the rotate handle (shown in Figure 7–28). (You may need to rotate the graphic a few times to position it in the desired location.)

Q&A What if I am using a touch screen?
Because the rotate handle is not available on a touch screen, you enter the degree of rotation in the Size dialog box. Tap the Rotate Objects button (PICTURE TOOLS FORMAT tab | Arrange group) to display the Rotate Objects menu, tap the More Rotation Options command on the Rotate Objects menu to display the Size tab in the Layout dialog box, change the Rotation value to 347, and then tap the OK button.

4

- Tap or click Picture 3 in the Selection task pane to select the tack image on the left side of the screen.
- If you are using a mouse, drag the rotate handle rightward and downward to rotate the graphic slightly as shown in Figure 7–29.

Q&A What if I am using a touch screen?
Follow the same steps outlined above, except change the rotation value to 14.

- If necessary, move the images or rotate them again or resize them so that they look the same as those shown in Figure 7–29 and then close the Selection task pane.
- Tap or click somewhere in the issue information to deselect the graphic (Figure 7–29).

Figure 7–29

To Save a Document

You have performed several tasks while creating this resume and do not want to risk losing work completed thus far. Accordingly, you should save the document. The following steps assume you already have created folders for storing your files, for example, a CIS 101 folder (for your class) that contains a Word folder (for your assignments). Thus, these steps save the document in the Word folder in the CIS 101 folder using the file name, Campus Post Newsletter.

1. Tap or click the Save button on the Quick Access Toolbar, which depending on settings, will display either the Save As gallery in the Backstage view or the Save As dialog box.

2. Save the file in the desired location (in this case, Word folder in the CIS 101 folder [or your class folder]) using the file name, Campus Post Newsletter.

Break Point: If you wish to take a break, this is a good place to do so. You can exit Word now. To resume at a later time, run Word, open the file called Campus Post Newsletter, and continue following the steps from this location forward.

Formatting the First Page of the Body of the Newsletter

The next step is to format the first page of the body of the newsletter. The body of the newsletter in this chapter is divided in three columns (Figure 7–1a on page WD 411). The first two columns contain the feature article, and the third column contains announcements. The characters in the paragraphs are aligned on both the right and left edges — similar to newspaper columns. The first letter in the first paragraph is much larger than the rest of the characters in the paragraph. A vertical rule separates the columns. The steps on the following pages format the first page of the body of the newsletter using these desktop publishing features.

CONSIDER THIS

What guidelines should you follow when creating the body of a newsletter?

While content and subject matter of newsletters may vary, the procedures used to create newsletters are similar:

- **Write the body copy.** Newsletters should contain articles of interest and relevance to readers. Some share information, while others promote a product or service. Use active voice in body copy, which is more engaging than passive voice. Proofread the body copy to be sure it is error free. Check all facts for accuracy.
- **Organize body copy in columns.** Most newsletters arrange body copy in columns. The body copy in columns, often called **snaking columns** or newspaper-style columns, flows from the bottom of one column to the top of the next column.
- **Format the body copy.** Begin the feature article on the first page of the newsletter. If the article spans multiple pages, use a continuation line, called a jump or jump line, to guide the reader to the remainder of the article. The message at the end of the article on the first page of the newsletter is called a **jump-to line**, and a **jump-from line** marks the beginning of the continuation, which is usually on a subsequent page.
- **Maintain consistency.** Be consistent with placement of body copy elements in newsletter editions. If the newsletter contains announcements, for example, position them in the same location in each edition so that readers easily can find them.
- **Maximize white space.** Allow plenty of space between lines, paragraphs, and columns. Tightly packed text is difficult to read. Separate the text adequately from graphics, borders, and headings.
- **Incorporate color.** Use colors that complement those in the nameplate. Be careful not to overuse color. Restrict color below the nameplate to drop caps, subheads, graphics, and ruling lines. If you do not have a color printer, still change the colors because the colors will print in shades of black and gray, which add variety to the newsletter.
- **Select and format subheads.** Develop subheads with as few words as possible. Readers should be able to identify content of the next topic by glancing at a subhead. Subheads should be emphasized in the newsletter but should not compete with text in the nameplate. Use a larger, bold, or otherwise contrasting font for subheads so that they stand apart from the body copy. Use this same format for all subheads for consistency. Leave a space above subheads to visually separate their content from the previous topic. Be consistent with spacing above and below subheads throughout the newsletter.
- **Divide sections with vertical rules.** Use vertical rules to guide the reader through the newsletter.
- **Enhance the document with visuals.** Add energy to the newsletter and emphasis to important points with graphics, pull-quotes, and other visuals, such as drop caps, to mark beginning of an article. Use these elements sparingly, however, so that the newsletter does not have a crowded appearance. Fewer, large visuals are more effective than several smaller ones. If you use a graphic that you did not create, be sure to obtain permission to use it in the newsletter and give necessary credit to the creator of the graphic.

To Clear Formatting

The next step is to enter the title of the feature article below the horizontal rule. To do this, you position the insertion point at the end of the issue information line (after the 2 in Issue 42) and then press the ENTER key. Recall that the issue information line has a bottom border. When you press the ENTER key in a bordered paragraph, Word carries forward any borders to the next paragraph. Thus, after you press the ENTER key, you should clear formatting to format the new paragraph as the Normal style. The following steps clear formatting.

1. Tap or click at the end of line 2 (the issue information line) so that the insertion point is immediately after the 2 in Issue 42. Press the ENTER key to advance the insertion point to the next line, which also moves the border down one line.
2. If necessary, display the HOME tab. Tap or click the 'Clear All Formatting' button (HOME tab | Font group) to apply the Normal style to the location of the insertion point, which in this case moves the new paragraph below the border on the issue information line.

To Format Text as a Heading Style, Modify a Heading Style, and Adjust Spacing before and after the Paragraph

Below the bottom border in the nameplate is the title of the feature article, Information Literacy. The following steps apply the Heading 1 style to this paragraph, modify the style, and adjust the paragraph spacing.

1. If necessary, display formatting marks.
2. With the insertion point on the paragraph mark below the border, tap or click Heading 1 (HOME tab | Styles group) to apply the Heading 1 style to the paragraph containing the insertion point.
3. Increase the font size 20 point. Bold the paragraph. Update the Heading 1 style to reflect these changes.
4. Type `Information Literacy` as the title of the feature article.
5. Display the PAGE LAYOUT tab. Change the Spacing Before box to 18 pt and the Spacing After box to 12 pt (Figure 7–30).

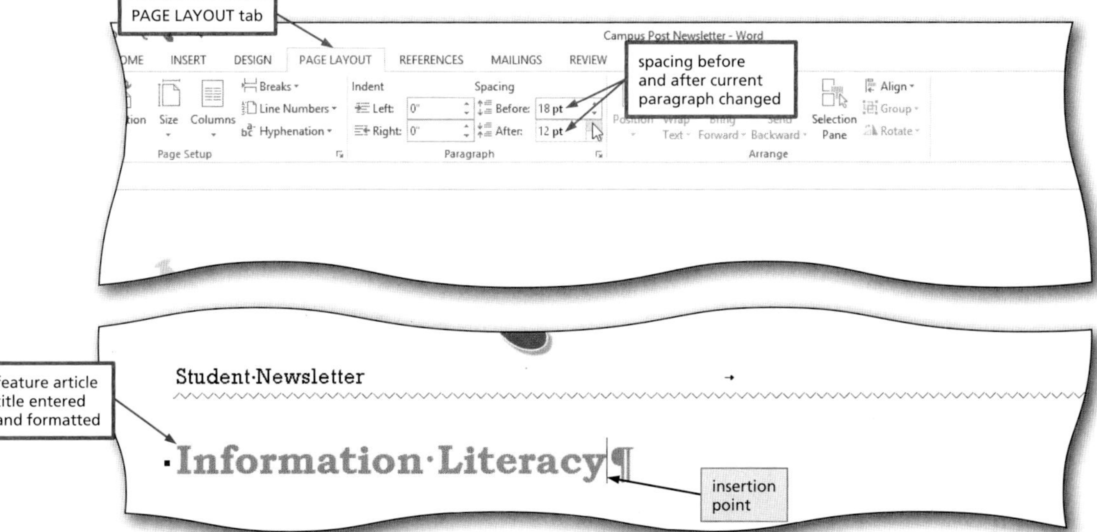

Figure 7–30

Columns

When you begin a document in Word, it has one column. You can divide a portion of a document or the entire document in multiple columns. Within each column, you can type, modify, or format text.

To divide a portion of a document in multiple columns, you use section breaks. Word requires that a new section be created each time you alter the number of columns in a document. Thus, if a document has a nameplate (one column) followed by an article of three columns followed by an article of two columns, the document would be divided in three separate sections.

CONSIDER THIS

How should you organize the body copy in columns?

Be consistent from page to page with the number of columns. Narrow columns generally are easier to read than wide ones. Columns, however, can be too narrow. A two- or three-column layout generally is appealing and offers a flexible design. Try to have between five and fifteen words per line. To do this, you may need to adjust the column width, the font size, or the leading (line spacing). Font size of text in columns should be no larger than 12 point but not so small that readers must strain to read the text.

To Insert a Continuous Section Break

1 CREATE NAMEPLATE FOR FIRST PAGE | 2 FORMAT FIRST PAGE | 3 CREATE PULL-QUOTE
4 CREATE NAMEPLATE FOR SECOND PAGE | 5 FORMAT SECOND PAGE | 6 ADD PAGE BORDER

The next step is to insert a continuous section break below the nameplate. ***Why?*** *In this chapter, the nameplate is one column and the body of the newsletter is three columns.* The term, continuous, means the new section should be on the same page as the previous section, which, in this case, means that the three columns of body copy will be positioned directly below the nameplate on the first page of the newsletter. The following steps insert a continuous section break.

1

- With the insertion point at the end of the feature article title (shown in Figure 7–30), press the ENTER key to position the insertion point below the article title.
- Tap or click the 'Insert Page and Section Breaks' button (PAGE LAYOUT tab | Page Setup group) to display the Insert Page and Section Breaks gallery (Figure 7–31).

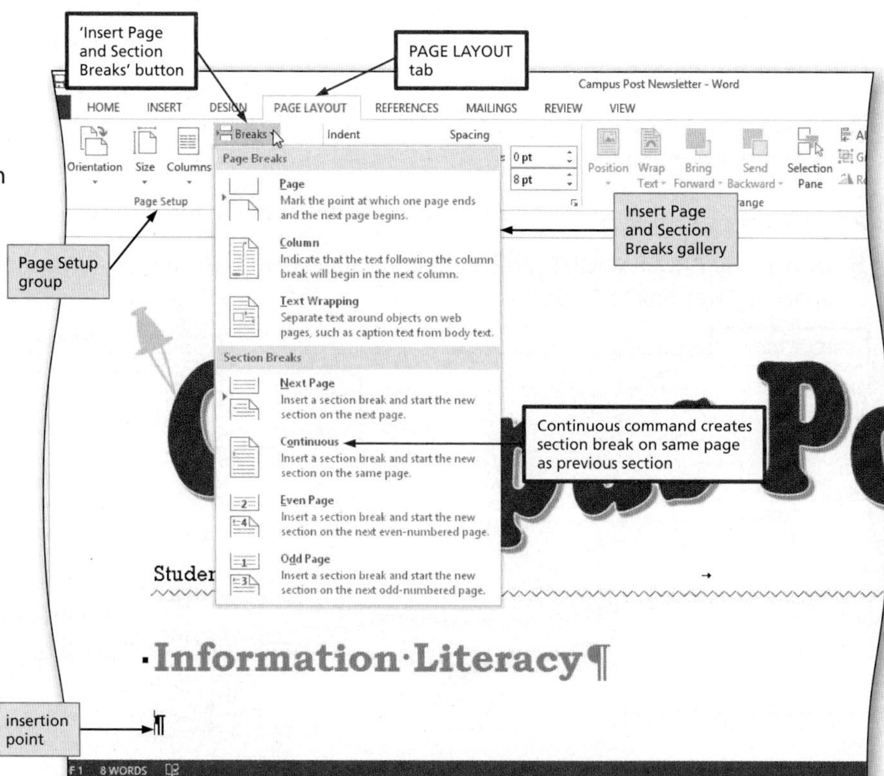

Figure 7–31

2

- Tap or click Continuous in the Insert Page and Section Breaks gallery to insert a continuous section break above the insertion point (Figure 7–32).

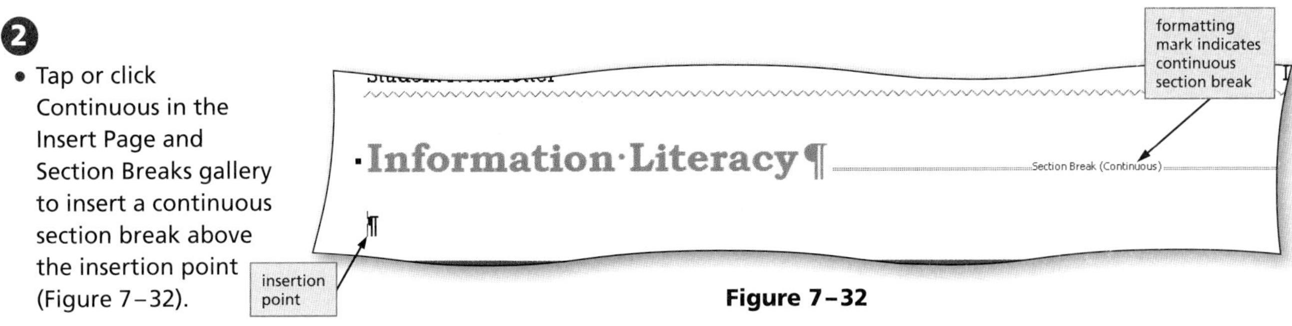

Figure 7–32

To Change the Number of Columns

1 CREATE NAMEPLATE FOR FIRST PAGE | 2 FORMAT FIRST PAGE | 3 CREATE PULL-QUOTE
4 CREATE NAMEPLATE FOR SECOND PAGE | 5 FORMAT SECOND PAGE | 6 ADD PAGE BORDER

The document now has two sections. The nameplate is in the first section, and the insertion point is in the second section. The second section should be formatted to three columns. ***Why?*** *The feature article and announcements appear in three columns that snake across the page.* Thus, the following steps format the second section in the document as three columns.

1

- Tap or click the 'Add or Remove Columns' button (PAGE LAYOUT tab | Page Setup group) to display the Add or Remove Columns gallery (Figure 7–33).

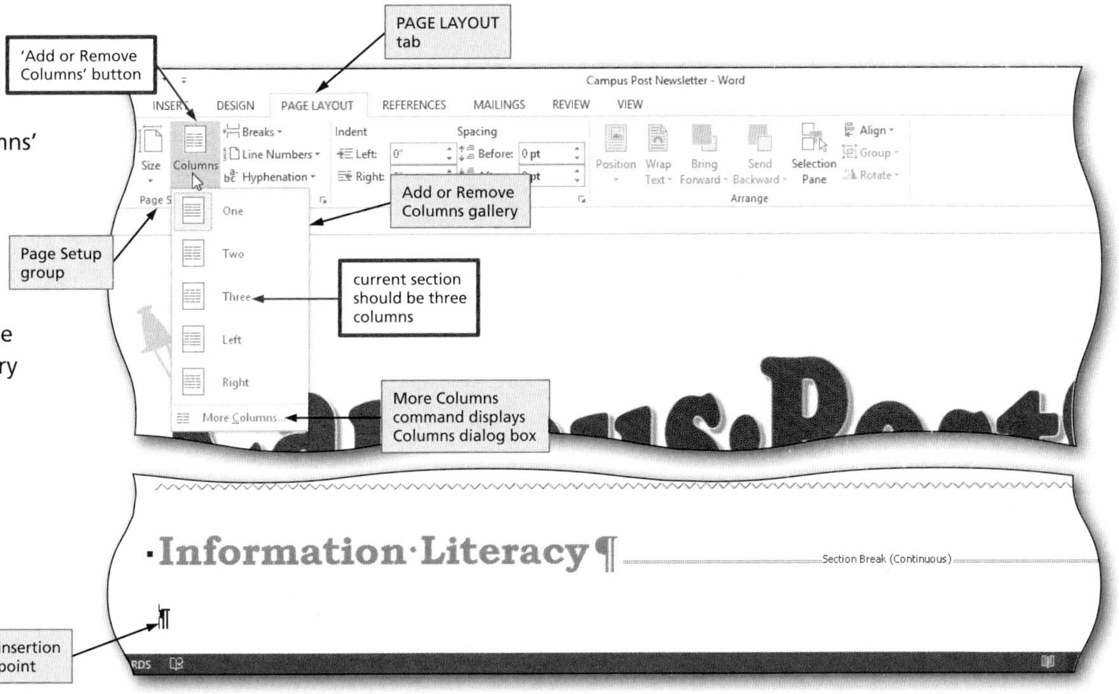

'Add or Remove Columns' button

PAGE LAYOUT tab

Add or Remove Columns gallery

Page Setup group

current section should be three columns

More Columns command displays Columns dialog box

insertion point

Figure 7–33

2

- Tap or click Three in the Add or Remove Columns gallery to divide the section containing the insertion point in three evenly sized and spaced columns
- Display the VIEW tab and then, if necessary, tap or click the View Ruler check box so that the rulers appear on the screen (Figure 7–34).

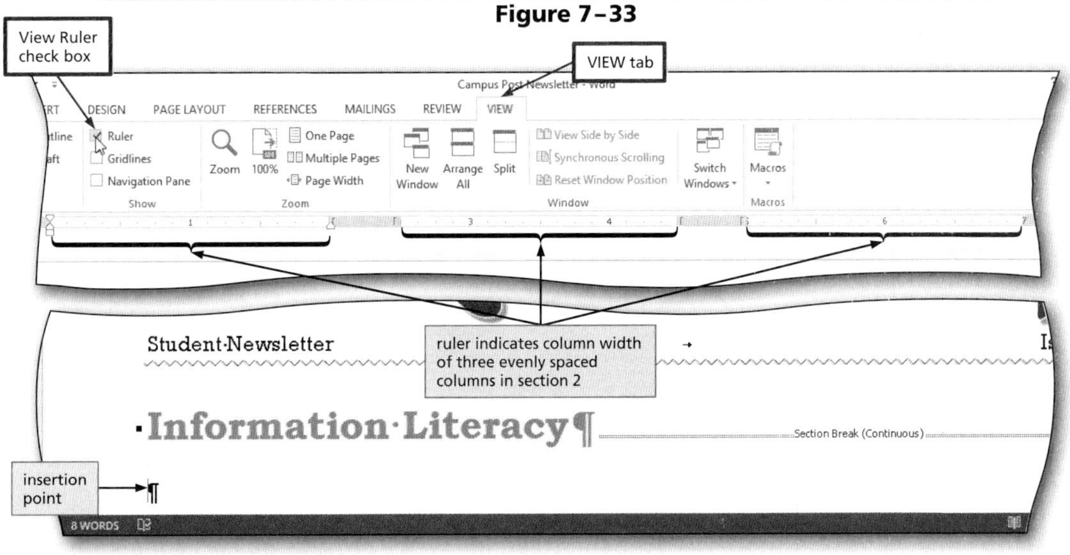

View Ruler check box

VIEW tab

ruler indicates column width of three evenly spaced columns in section 2

insertion point

Figure 7–34

Q&A Why display the rulers?
You want to see the column widths on the ruler.

What if I want columns of different widths?
You would tap or click the More Columns command in the Add or Remove Columns gallery, which displays the Columns dialog box. In this dialog box, you can specify varying column widths and spacing.

To Justify a Paragraph

1 CREATE NAMEPLATE FOR FIRST PAGE | 2 FORMAT FIRST PAGE | 3 CREATE PULL-QUOTE
4 CREATE NAMEPLATE FOR SECOND PAGE | 5 FORMAT SECOND PAGE | 6 ADD PAGE BORDER

The following step enters the first paragraph of the feature article using justified alignment. ***Why?*** *The text in the paragraphs of the body of the newsletter is* ***justified****, which means that the left and right margins are aligned, like the edges of newspaper columns.*

1

- Display the HOME tab.
- Tap or click the Justify button (HOME tab | Paragraph group) so that Word aligns both the left and right margins of typed text.
- Type the first paragraph of the feature article (Figure 7–35): **Managing the vast amount of information inundating us daily can be an overwhelming task. Information literacy is a 21st century skill set that prepares students, employees, and citizens to manage information so that they can be knowledgeable decision makers.** and then press the ENTER key.

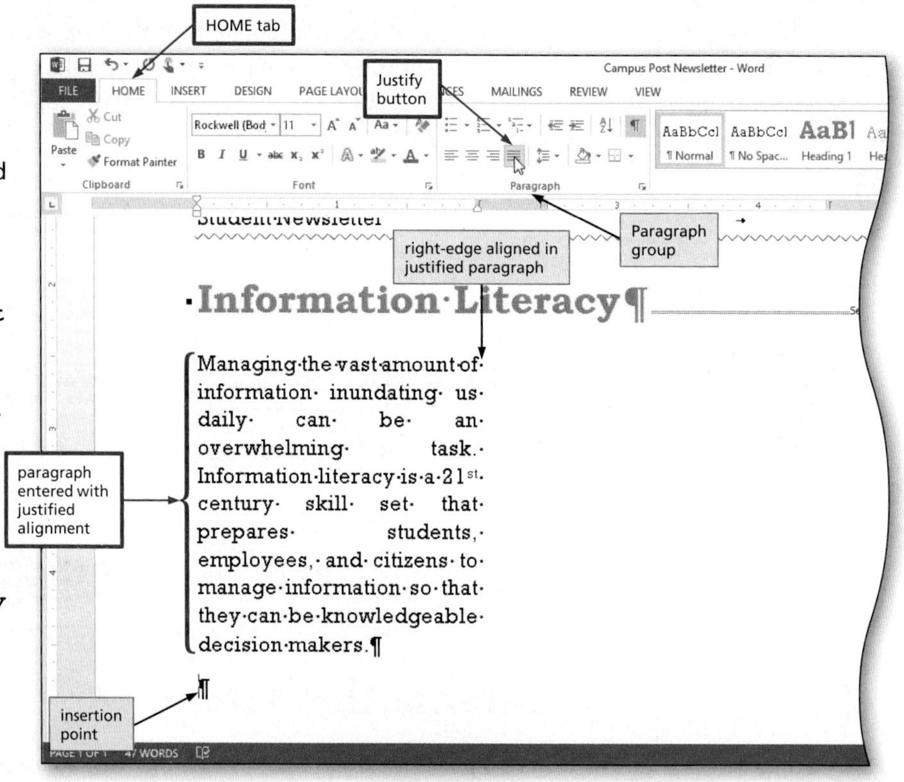

Figure 7–35

Q&A Why do some words have extra space between them?
When a paragraph is formatted to justified alignment, Word places extra space between words so that the left and right edges of the paragraph are aligned. To remedy big gaps, sometimes called rivers, you can add or rearrange words, change the column width, change the font size, and so on.

Other Ways

1. Tap 'Show Context Menu' button on mini toolbar or right-click paragraph, tap or click Paragraph on shortcut menu, tap or click 'Indents and Spacing' tab (Paragraph dialog box), tap or click Alignment arrow, tap or click Justified, tap or click OK button
2. Tap or click Paragraph Settings Dialog Box Launcher (HOME tab or PAGE LAYOUT tab | Paragraph group), tap or click Indents and Spacing tab (Paragraph dialog box), tap or click Alignment arrow, tap or click Justified, tap or click OK button
3. Press CTRL+J

To Insert a File in a Column of the Newsletter

1 CREATE NAMEPLATE FOR FIRST PAGE | 2 FORMAT FIRST PAGE | 3 CREATE PULL-QUOTE
4 CREATE NAMEPLATE FOR SECOND PAGE | 5 FORMAT SECOND PAGE | 6 ADD PAGE BORDER

The next step is to insert a file named Information Literacy Article in the newsletter. ***Why?*** *To save you time typing, the rest of the feature article is located on the Data Files for Students.* Visit www.cengage.com/ct/studentdownload for detailed instructions or contact your instructor for information about accessing the required files. The next steps insert the Information Literacy Article file in a column of the newsletter.

1

- Display the INSERT tab.
- With the insertion point positioned in the left column as shown in Figure 7–35, tap or click the Object arrow (INSERT tab | Text group) to display the Object menu.
- Tap or click 'Text from File' on the Object menu to display the Insert File dialog box.
- Navigate to the location of the file to be inserted (in this case, the Data Files for Students folder).
- Tap or click the file named, Information Literacy Article, to select the file (Figure 7–36).

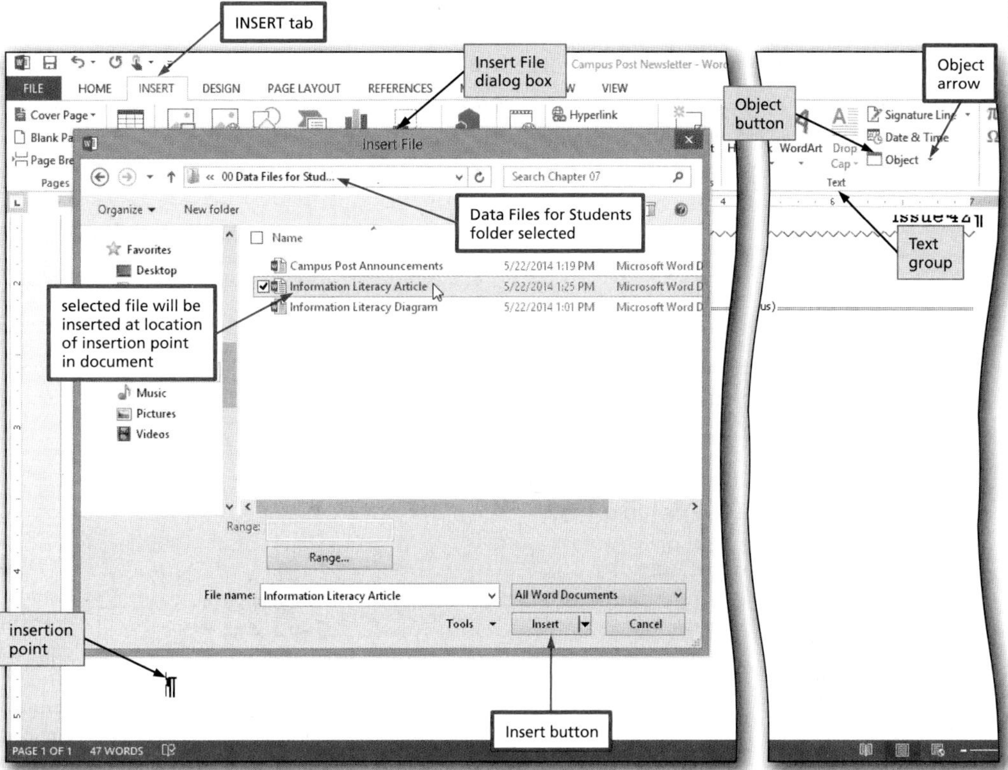

Figure 7–36

2

- Tap or click the Insert button (Insert File dialog box) to insert the file, Information Literacy Article, in the current document at the location of the insertion point.
- So that you can see the entire inserted article, display multiple pages on the screen by tapping or clicking the Multiple Pages button (VIEW tab | Zoom group) (Figure 7–37).

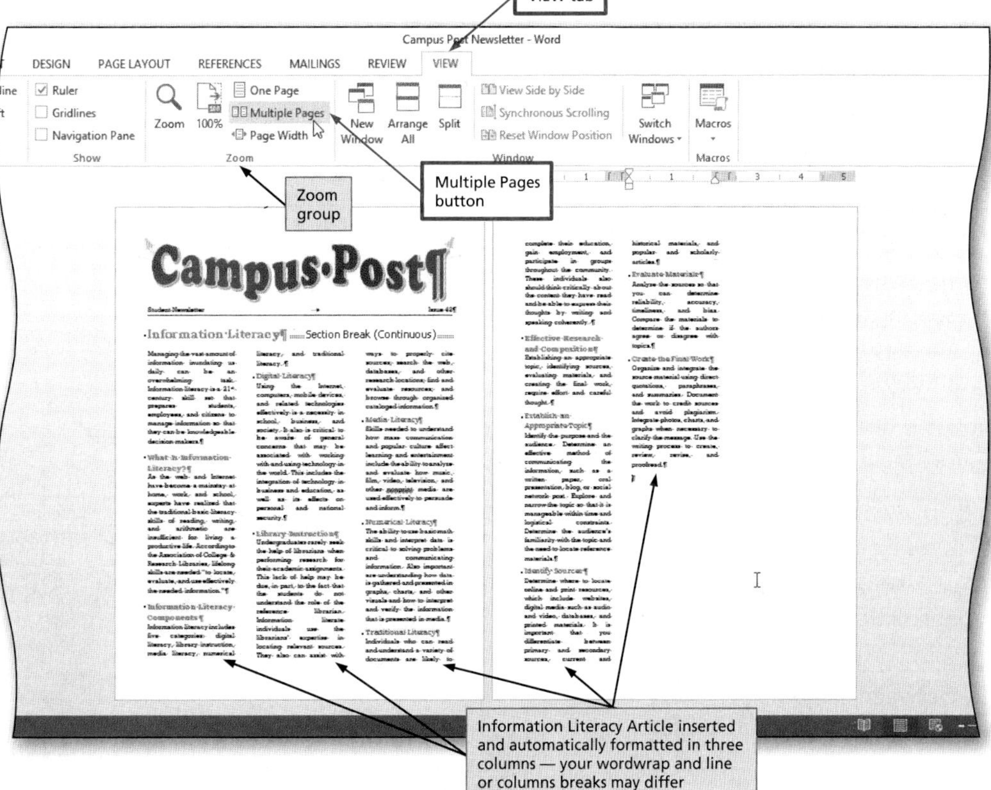

Figure 7–37

3

- When you are finished viewing the document, change the zoom to page width so that the newsletter content is larger on the screen.

To Increase Column Width and Place a Vertical Rule between Columns

The columns in the newsletter currently contain many rivers. ***Why?*** *The justified alignment in the narrow column width often causes large gaps between words.* To eliminate some of the rivers, you increase the size of the columns slightly in this newsletter. In newsletters, you often see a vertical rule separating columns. Through the Columns dialog box, you can change column width and add vertical rules. The following steps increase column widths and add vertical rules between columns.

- Position the insertion point somewhere in the feature article text.
- Display the PAGE LAYOUT tab.
- Tap or click the 'Add or Remove Columns' button (PAGE LAYOUT tab | Page Setup group) to display the Add or Remove Columns gallery (Figure 7–38).

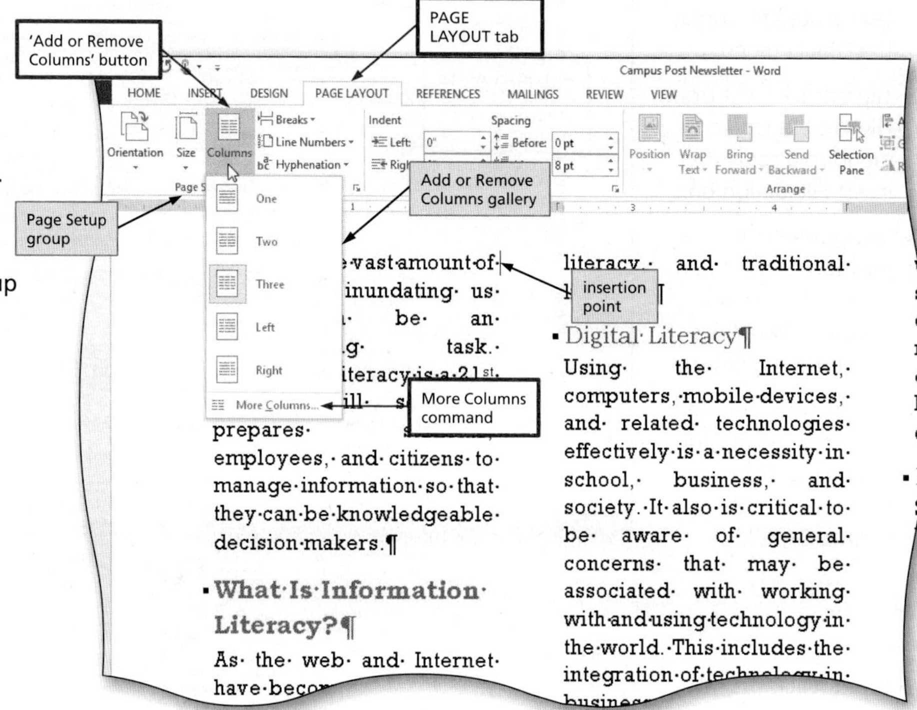

Figure 7–38

- Tap or click More Columns in the Add or Remove Columns gallery to display the Columns dialog box.
- If necessary, in the Width and spacing area (Columns dialog box), tap or click the Width up arrow until the Width box reads 2.1".

Q&A How would I make the columns different widths?

You would remove the check mark from the 'Equal column width' check box and then set the individual column widths in the dialog box.

- Place a check mark in the Line between check box to select the check box (Figure 7–39).

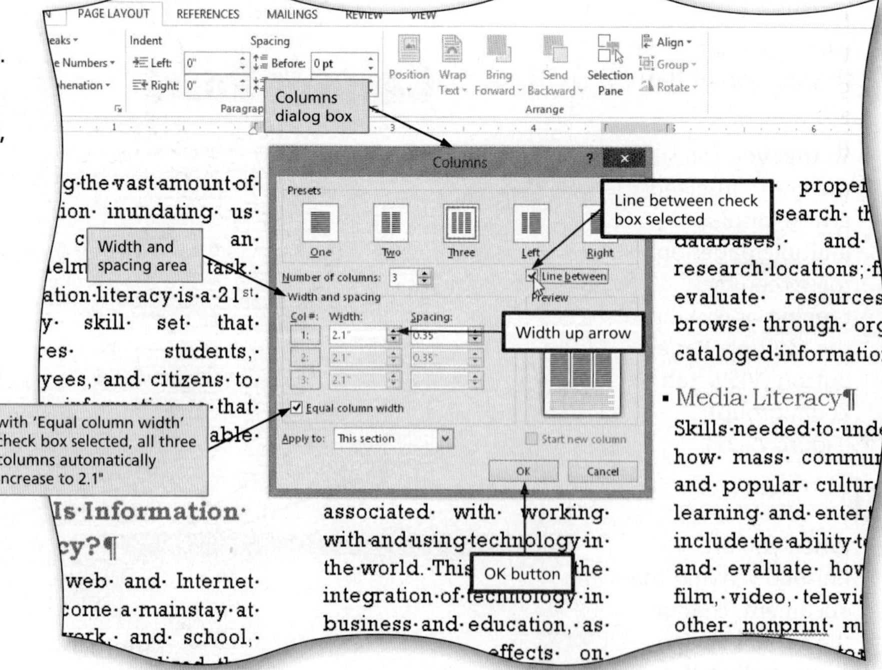

Figure 7–39

- Tap or click the OK button to make the columns slightly wider and place a line (vertical rule) between each column in the document (Figure 7–40).

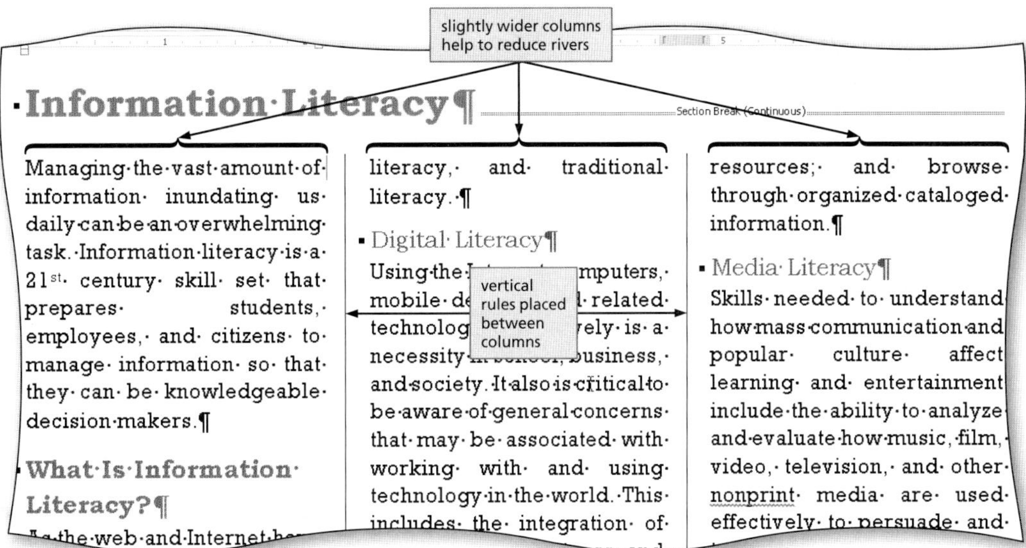

Figure 7–40

Other Ways

1. Double-tap or double-click shaded space between columns on ruler, enter settings (Columns dialog box), tap or click OK button
2. To adjust column widths, drag column boundaries on ruler
3. To insert single rule, tap or click Borders arrow (HOME tab | Paragraph group)

To Hyphenate a Document

1 CREATE NAMEPLATE FOR FIRST PAGE | **2 FORMAT FIRST PAGE** | **3 CREATE PULL-QUOTE**
4 CREATE NAMEPLATE FOR SECOND PAGE | **5 FORMAT SECOND PAGE** | **6 ADD PAGE BORDER**

The following steps turn on the hyphenation feature. ***Why?*** *To further eliminate some of the rivers in the columns of the newsletter, you turn on Word's hyphenation feature so that words with multiple syllables are hyphenated at the end of lines instead of wrapped in their entirety to the next line.*

1

- Tap or click the Change Hyphenation button (PAGE LAYOUT tab | Page Setup group) to display the Change Hyphenation gallery (Figure 7–41).

Q&A What is the difference between Automatic and Manual hyphenation?
Automatic hyphenation places hyphens wherever words can break at a syllable in the document. With manual hyphenation, Word displays a dialog box for each word it could hyphenate, enabling you to accept or reject the proposed hyphenation.

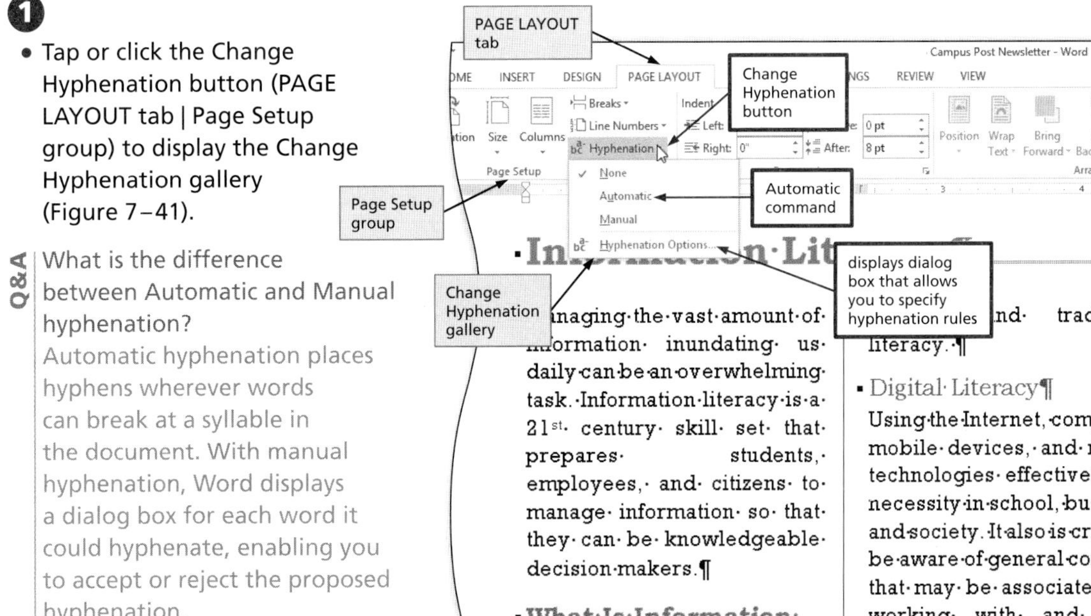

Figure 7–41

2

- Tap or click Automatic in the Change Hyphenation gallery to hyphenate the document (Figure 7–42).

Q&A What if I do not want a particular word hyphenated?
You can reword text, and Word will redo the hyphenation automatically.

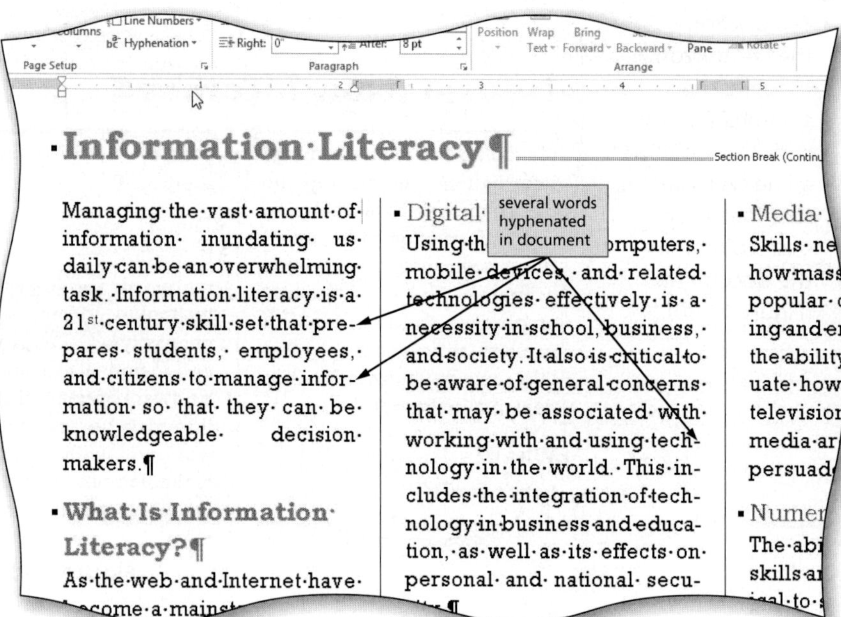

Figure 7–42

To Format a Character as a Drop Cap

1 CREATE NAMEPLATE FOR FIRST PAGE | 2 FORMAT FIRST PAGE | 3 CREATE PULL-QUOTE
4 CREATE NAMEPLATE FOR SECOND PAGE | 5 FORMAT SECOND PAGE | 6 ADD PAGE BORDER

The first character in the feature article in this newsletter, that is, the capital letter M, is formatted as a drop cap. ***Why?*** *To add interest to an article, you often see a* ***drop cap****, which is a capital letter whose font size is larger than the rest of the characters in the paragraph.* In Word, the drop cap can sink into the first few lines of text, or it can extend into the left margin, which often is called a stick-up cap. In this newsletter, the paragraph text wraps around the drop cap.

The following steps create a drop cap in the first paragraph of the feature article in the newsletter.

1

- Position the insertion point somewhere in the first paragraph of the feature article.
- Display the INSERT tab.
- Tap or click the 'Add a Drop Cap' button (INSERT tab | Text group) to display the Add a Drop Cap gallery (Figure 7–43).

Experiment

- If you are using a mouse, point to various commands in the Add a Drop Cap gallery to see a live preview of the drop cap formats in the document.

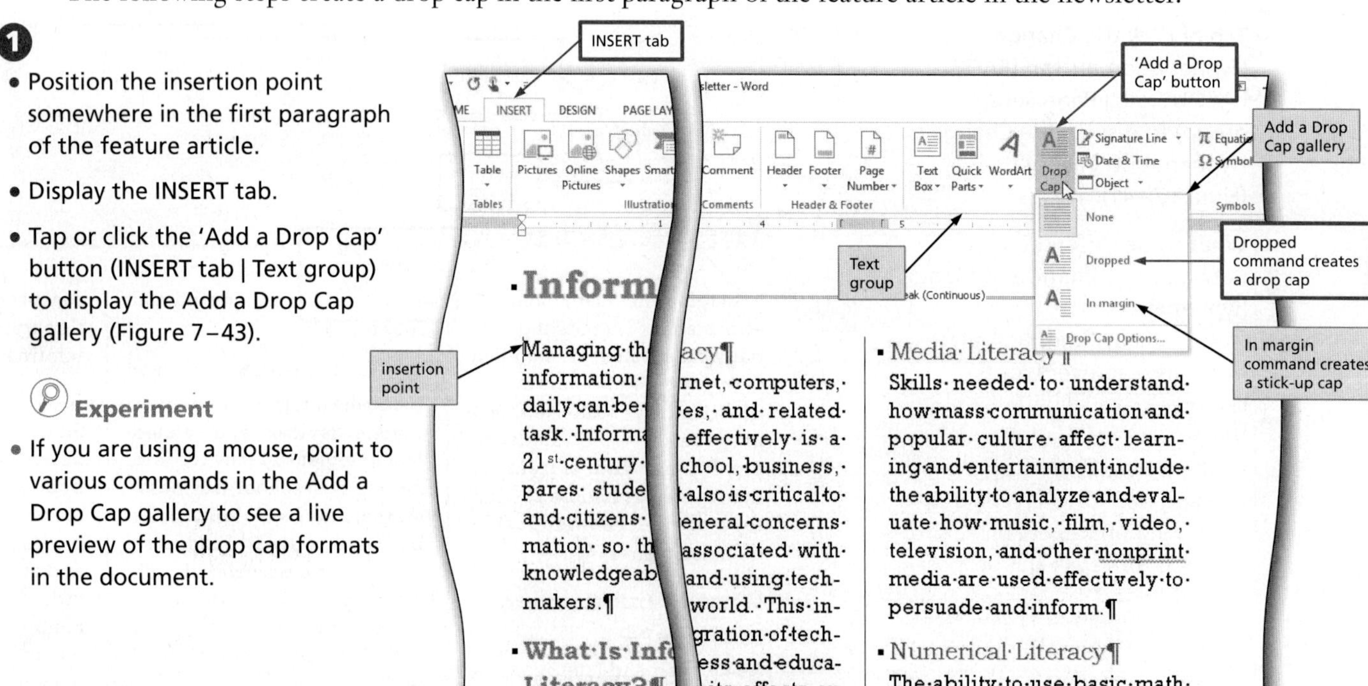

Figure 7–43

- Tap or click Dropped in the Add a Drop Cap gallery to format the first letter in the paragraph containing the insertion point (the M in Managing, in this case) as a drop cap and wrap subsequent text in the paragraph around the drop cap (Figure 7–44).

Q&A What is the outline around the drop cap in the document?
When you format a letter as a drop cap, Word places a frame around it. A **frame** is a container for text that allows you to position the text anywhere on the page. Word formats a frame for the drop cap so that text wraps around it. The frame also contains a paragraph mark nonprinting character to the right of the drop cap, which may or may not be visible on your screen.

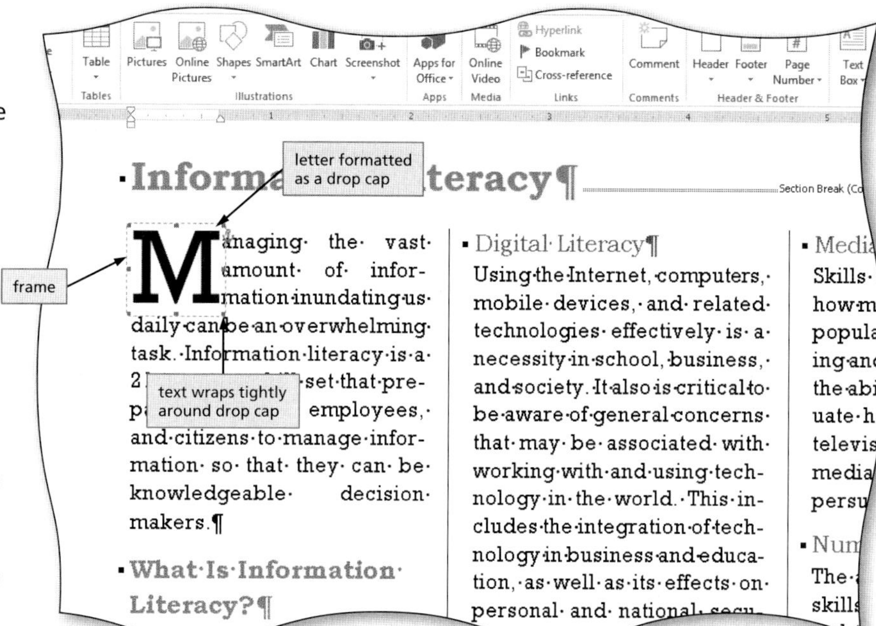

Figure 7–44

To Format the Drop Cap

The following steps change the font color of the drop cap and make it slightly wider to eliminate the river near the end of the paragraph.

1. With the drop cap selected, display the HOME tab and then change the font color of the drop cap to 'Lime, Accent 1, Darker 25%' (fifth color, fifth row) in Font Color gallery.

Q&A What if my frame no longer is displayed?
Tap or click the drop cap to select it. Then, tap or click the blue selection rectangle to display the frame.

2. If necessary, drag the right-middle sizing handles on the frame until the drop cap and the text in the paragraph look like Figure 7–45. If necessary, reposition the drop cap again.

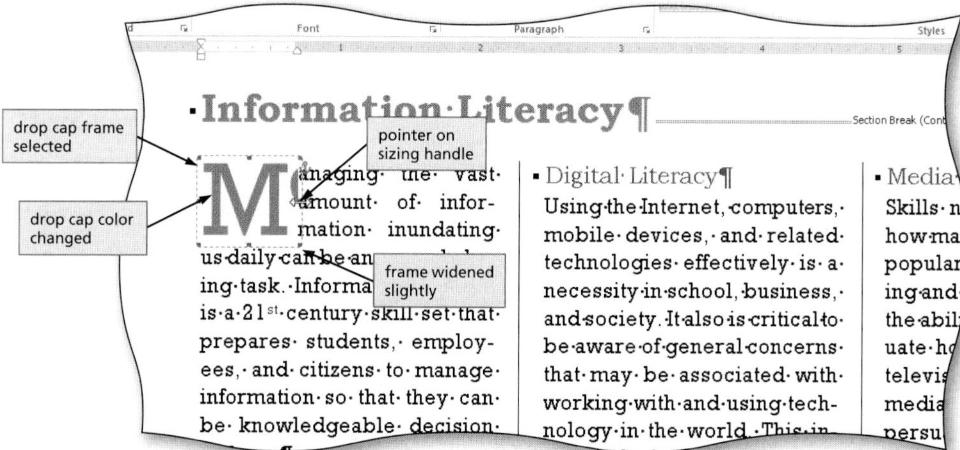

Figure 7–45

To Insert a Next Page Section Break

The third column on the first page of the newsletter is not a continuation of the feature article. ***Why not?*** *The third column, instead, contains several member announcements. The feature article continues on the second page of the newsletter (shown in Figure 7–1b on page WD 411).* Thus, you must insert a next page section break, which is a section break that also contains a page break, at the bottom of the second column so that the remainder of the feature article moves to the second page. The following steps insert a next page section break in the second column.

1

- Position the insertion point at the location for the section break, in this case, to the left of the L in the Library Instruction heading.
- Display the PAGE LAYOUT tab.
- Tap or click the 'Insert Page and Section Breaks' button (PAGE LAYOUT tab | Page Setup group) to display the Insert Page and Section Breaks gallery (Figure 7–46).

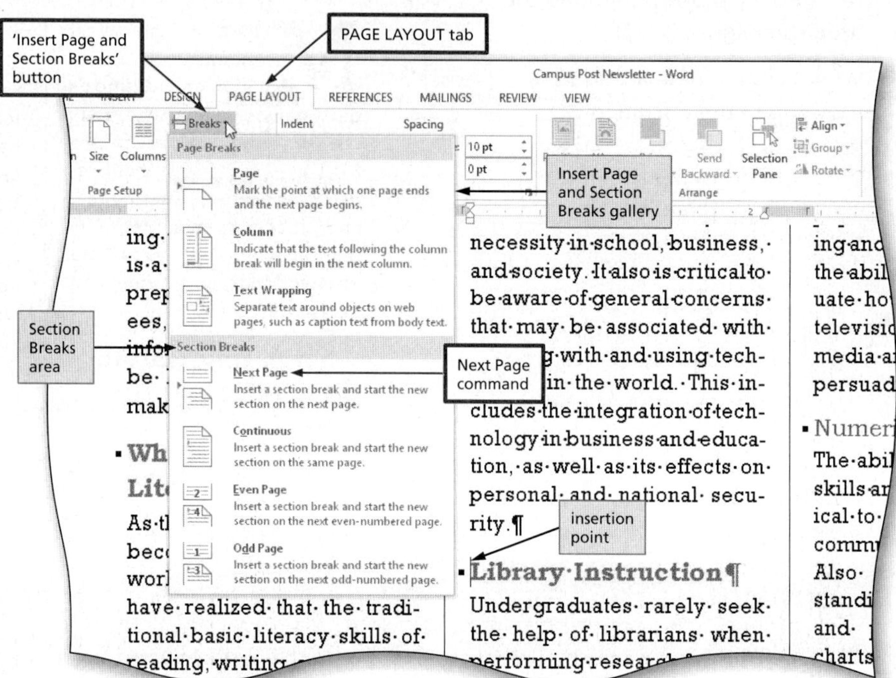

Figure 7–46

- In the Section Breaks area in the gallery, tap or click Next Page to insert a next page section break, which positions the insertion point on the next page.
- Scroll to the bottom of the first page so that you can see the moved text (Figure 7–47).

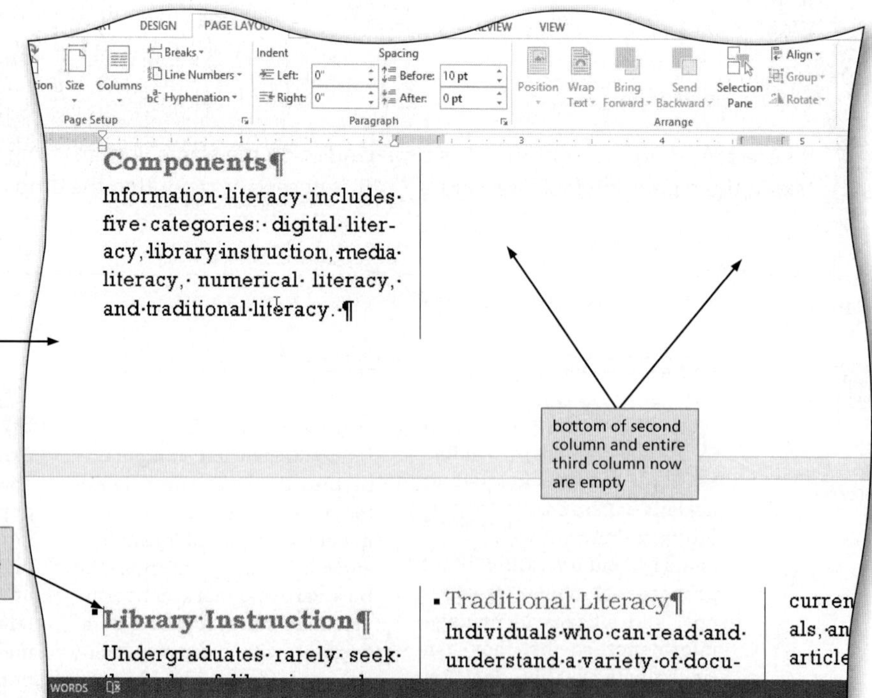

Figure 7–47

To Enter Text

The next step is to insert a jump-to line at the end of the second column, informing the reader where to look for the rest of the feature article. The following steps insert a jump-to line at the end of the text in the second column on the first page of the newsletter.

1. Scroll to display the end of the text in the second column of the first page of the newsletter and then position the insertion point between the paragraph mark and the section break notation.
2. Press the ENTER key twice to insert a blank line for the jump-to text above the section break notation.
3. Press the UP ARROW key to position the insertion point on the blank line. If the blank line is formatted in the Heading 1 style, tap or click the 'Clear All Formatting' button (HOME tab | Font group) so that the entered text follows the Normal style.
4. Press CTRL+R to right align the paragraph mark. Press CTRL+I to turn on the italic format. Type **`(Article continues on next page)`** as the jump-to text and then press CTRL+I again to turn off the italic format.

To Insert a Column Break

In the Campus Post newsletters, for consistency, the student announcements always begin at the top of the third column. If you insert the Campus Post Announcements at the current location of the insertion point, however, they will begin at the bottom of the second column. ***Why?*** *The insertion point currently is at the bottom of the second column.*

For the student announcements to be displayed in the third column, you insert a **column break** at the bottom of the second column, which places the insertion point at the top of the next column. Thus, the following steps insert a column break at the bottom of the second column.

1.
- Position the insertion point to the left of the paragraph mark on the line containing the next page section break, which is the location where the column break should be inserted.
- Tap or click the 'Insert Page and Section Breaks' button (PAGE LAYOUT tab | Page Setup group) to display the Insert Page and Section Breaks gallery (Figure 7–48).

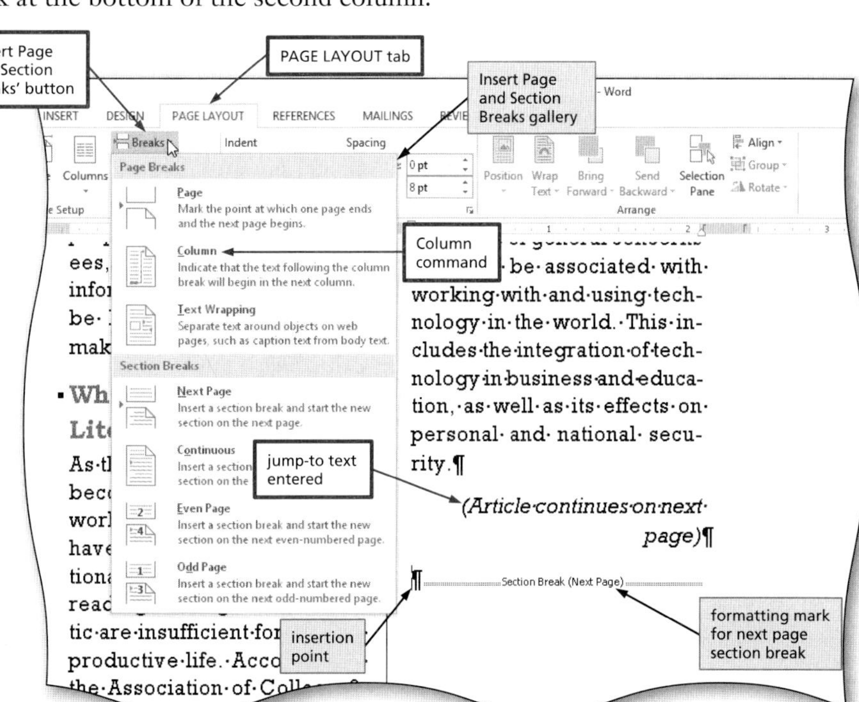

Figure 7–48

- Tap or click Column in the Insert Page and Section Breaks gallery to insert a column break at the location of the insertion point and move the insertion point to the top of the next column (Figure 7–49).

Q&A What if I wanted to remove a column break?

You would double-tap or double-click it to select it and then tap or click the Cut button (HOME tab | Clipboard group) or press the DELETE key.

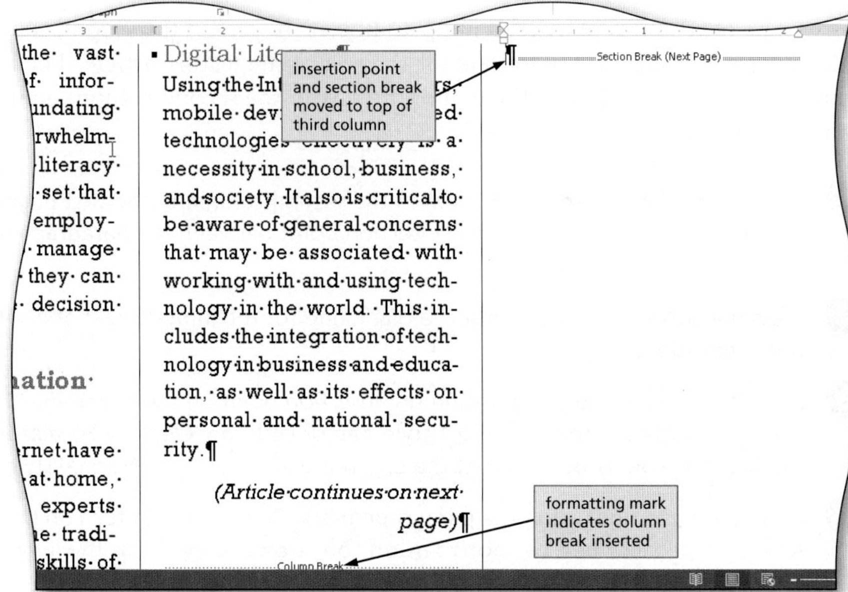

Figure 7–49

Other Ways

1. Press CTRL+SHIFT+ENTER

To Insert a File in a Column of the Newsletter

So that you do not have to enter the entire third column of announcements in the newsletter, the next step in the project is to insert the file named Campus Post Announcements in the third column of the newsletter. This file contains the three announcements: the first about student discounts, the second about spirit wear, and the third about the topic of the next newsletter issue.

The Campus Post Announcements file is located on the Data Files for Students. Visit www.cengage.com/ct/studentdownload for detailed instructions or contact your instructor for information about accessing the required files. The following steps insert a file in a column of the newsletter.

1. With the insertion point at the top of the third column, display the INSERT tab.
2. Tap or click the Object arrow (INSERT tab | Text group) to display the Object menu and then tap or click 'Text from File' on the Object menu to display the Insert File dialog box.
3. Navigate to the location of the file to be inserted (in this case, the Data Files for Students folder).
4. Tap or click Campus Post Announcements to select the file.
5. Tap or click the Insert button (Insert File dialog box) to insert the file, Campus Post Announcements, in the document at the location of the insertion point.

   Q&A What if text from the announcements column spills onto the second page of the newsletter?

   You will format text in the announcements column so that all of its text fits in the third column of the first page.
6. Press SHIFT+F5 to return the insertion point to the last editing location, in this case, the top of the third column on the first page of the newsletter (Figure 7–50).

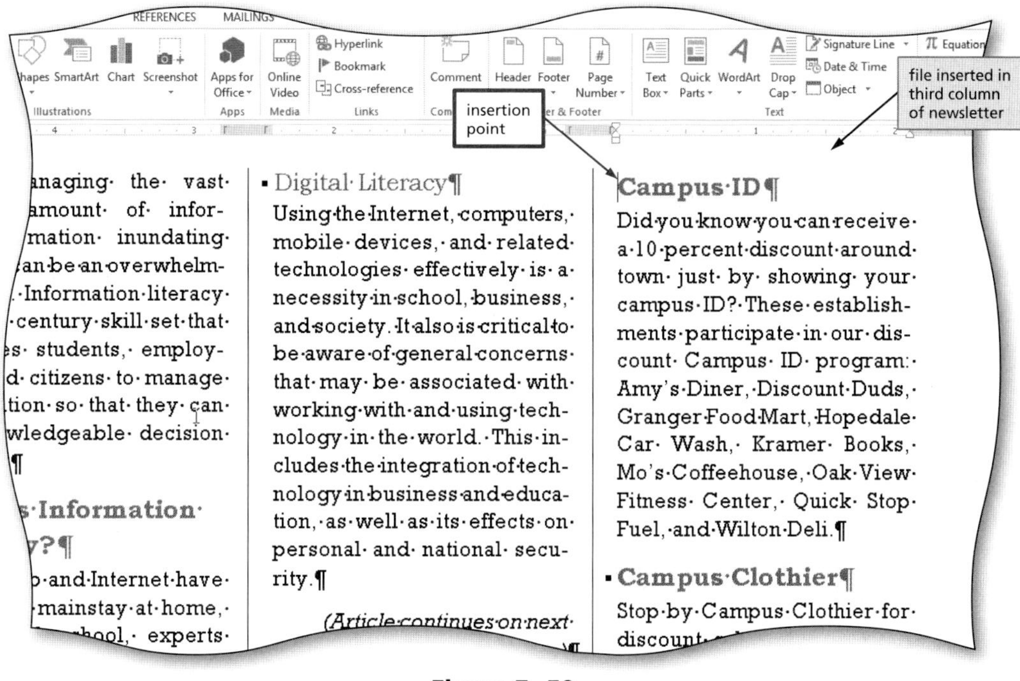

Figure 7–50

To Save a Document Again

You have performed several steps since the last save. Thus, you should save the newsletter again.

 Save the newsletter again with the same file name, Campus Post Newsletter.

Creating a Pull-Quote

A pull-quote is text pulled, or copied, from the text of the document and given graphical emphasis so that it stands apart and commands the reader's attention. The newsletter in this project copies text from the second page of the newsletter and places it in a pull-quote on the first page between the first and second columns (Figure 7–1a on page WD 411).

CONSIDER THIS

What guidelines should you follow when using pull-quote?

Because of their bold emphasis, pull-quotes should be used sparingly in a newsletter. Pull-quotes are useful for breaking the monotony of long columns of text. Typically, quotation marks are used only if you are quoting someone directly. If you use quotation marks, use curly (or smart) quotation marks instead of straight quotation marks.

To create the pull-quote in this newsletter, follow this general procedure:

1. Create a **text box**, which is a container for text that allows you to position the text anywhere on the page.
2. Copy the text from the existing document to the Office Clipboard and then paste the text from the Office Clipboard to the text box.
3. Resize and format the text box.
4. Move the text box to the desired location.

To Insert a Text Box

1 CREATE NAMEPLATE FOR FIRST PAGE | 2 FORMAT FIRST PAGE | 3 CREATE PULL-QUOTE
4 CREATE NAMEPLATE FOR SECOND PAGE | 5 FORMAT SECOND PAGE | 6 ADD PAGE BORDER

The first step in creating the pull-quote is to insert a text box. A text box is like a frame; the difference is that a text box has more graphical formatting options than does a frame. The following steps insert a built-in text box. ***Why?*** *Word provides a variety of built-in text boxes, saving you the time of formatting the text box.*

- Tap or click the 'Choose a Text Box' button (INSERT tab | Text group) to display the Choose a Text Box gallery.

Experiment

- Scroll through the Choose a Text Box gallery to see the variety of available text box styles.
- Scroll to display Whisp Quote in the Choose a Text Box gallery (Figure 7–51).

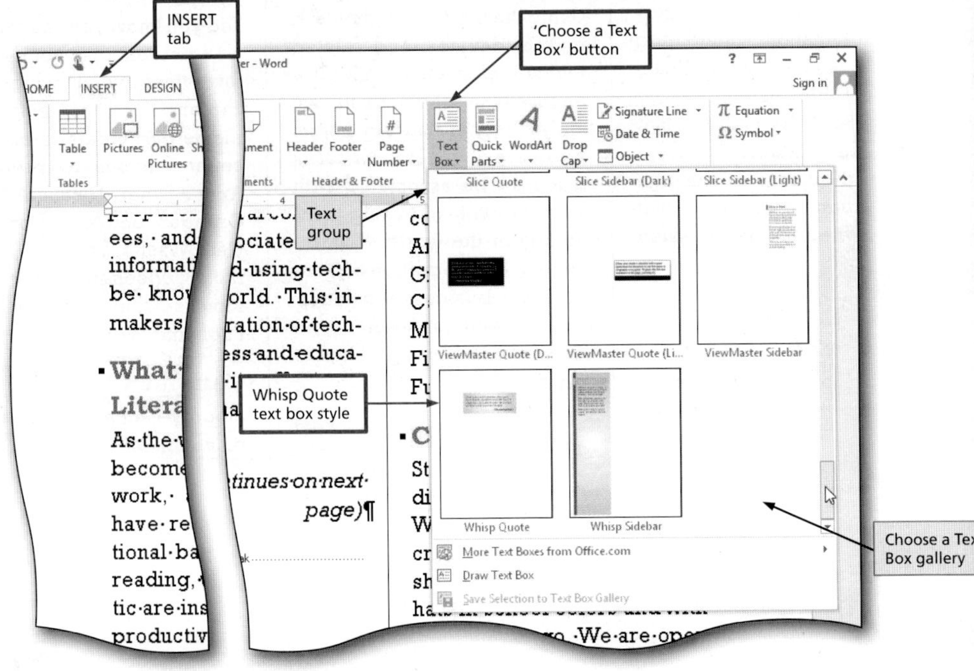

Figure 7–51

- Tap or click Whisp Quote in the Text Box gallery to insert that style of text box in the document. If necessary, scroll to display the entire text box in the document window (Figure 7–52).

Q&A Does my text box need to be in the same location as in Figure 7–52?
No. You will move the text box later.

The layout of the first page is not correct because of the text box. What do I do?
You will enter text in the text box and then position it in the correct location. At that time, the layout of the first page will be fixed.

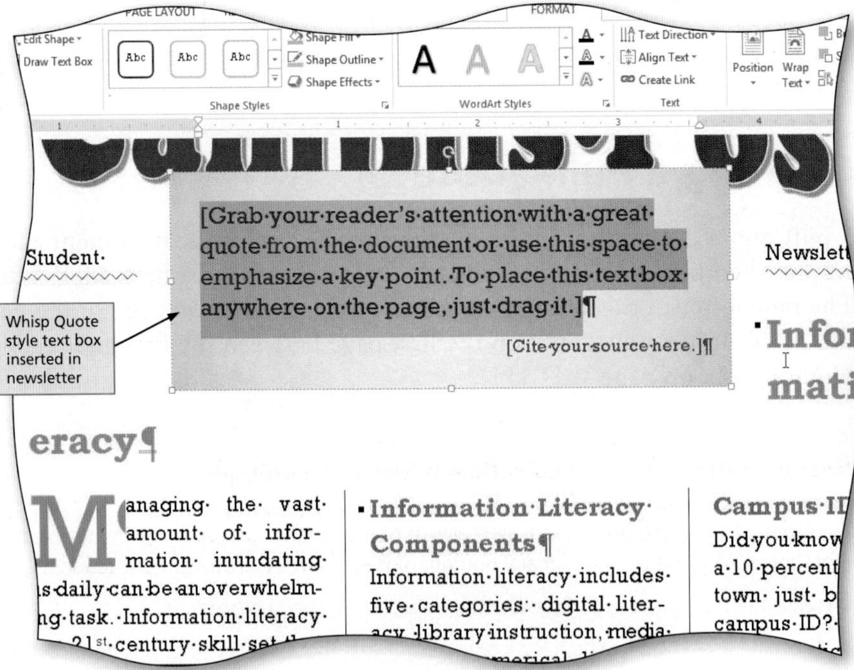

Figure 7–52

Other Ways

1. Tap or click 'Explore Quick Parts' button (INSERT tab | Text group), tap or click 'Building Blocks Organizer' on Explore Quick Parts menu, select desired text box name in Building blocks list, tap or click Insert button, tap or click OK button

To Split the Window

The text that you will copy for the pull-quote is at the bottom of the first page on the newsletter and the pull-quote (text box) is at the top of the first page of the newsletter. Thus, the next step is to copy the pull-quote text from the bottom of the first page and then paste it in the pull-quote at the top of the first page. You would like to view the pull-quote and the text to be copied on the screen at the same time. ***Why?*** *Viewing both simultaneously will simplify the copying and pasting process.*

Word allows you to split the window in two separate panes, each containing the current document and having its own scroll bar. This enables you to scroll to and view two different portions of the same document at the same time. The following step splits the Word window.

1

- Display the VIEW tab.
- Tap or click the Split Window button (VIEW tab | Windows group) to divide the document window in two separate panes — both the upper and lower panes display the current document (Figure 7–53).

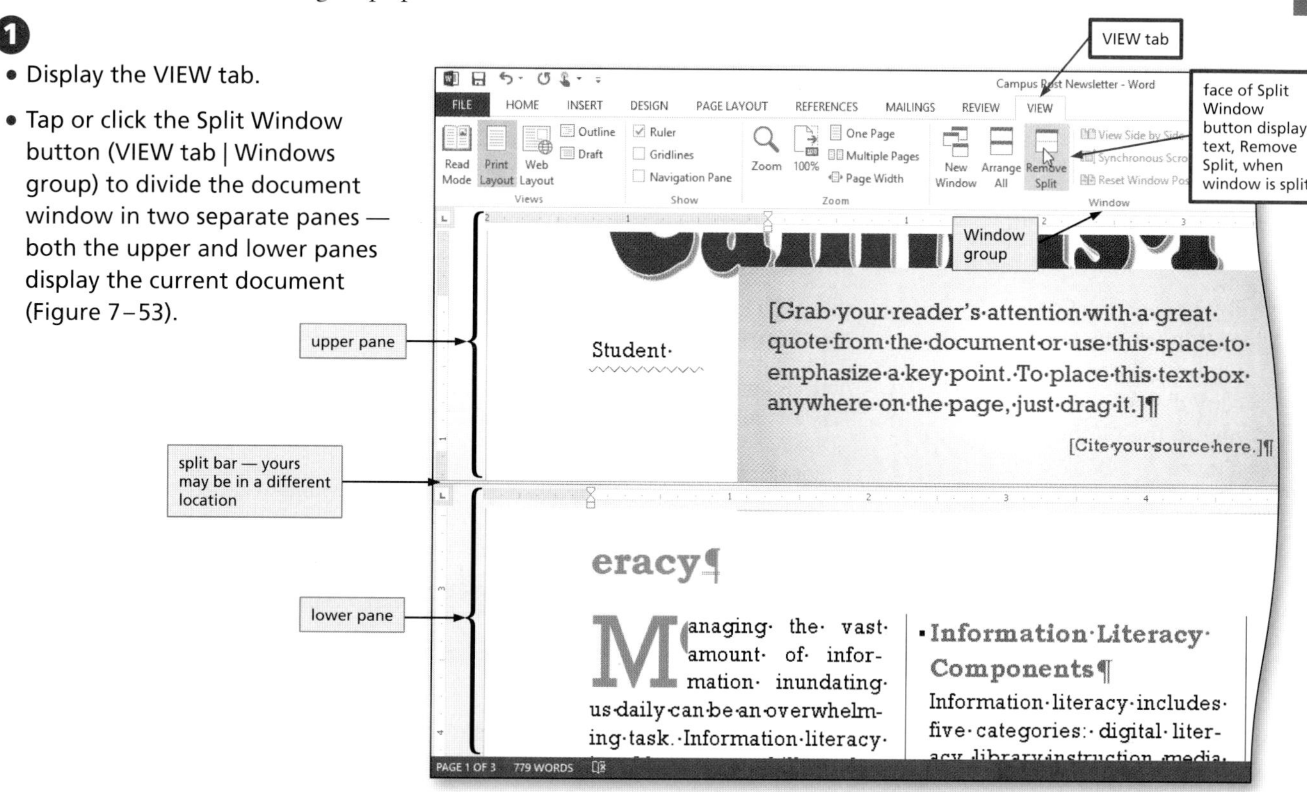

Figure 7–53

Other Ways

1. Press ALT+CTRL+S, then ENTER

BTW

Quick Reference

For a table that lists how to complete the tasks covered in this book using touch gestures, the mouse, ribbon, shortcut menu, and keyboard, see the Quick Reference Summary at the back of this book, or visit the Quick Reference resource on the Student Companion Site located on www.cengagebrain.com. For detailed instructions about accessing available resources, visit www.cengage.com/ct/studentdownload or contact your instructor for information about accessing the required files.

To Arrange All Open Word Documents on the Screen

If you have multiple Word documents open and want to view all of them at the same time on the screen, you can instruct Word to arrange all the open documents on the screen from top to bottom. If you wanted to arrange all open Word documents on the same screen, you would perform the following steps.

1. Tap or click the Arrange All button (VIEW tab | Window group) to display each open Word document on the screen.
2. To make one of the arranged documents fill the entire screen again, maximize the window by tapping or clicking its Maximize button or double-tapping or double-clicking its title bar.

To Copy and Paste Using Split Windows

1 CREATE NAMEPLATE FOR FIRST PAGE | 2 FORMAT FIRST PAGE | 3 CREATE PULL-QUOTE
4 CREATE NAMEPLATE FOR SECOND PAGE | 5 FORMAT SECOND PAGE | 6 ADD PAGE BORDER

The following steps copy text from bottom of the first page of the newsletter to the Clipboard (the source) and then paste the text into the text box (the destination). ***Why?*** *The item being copied is called the* ***source****. The location to which you are pasting is called the* ***destination****.*

1

- In the lower pane, scroll to display text to be copied, as shown in Figure 7–54, and then select the text to be copied: lifelong skills are needed "to locate, evaluate, and use effectively the needed information."
- Tap or click the Copy button (HOME tab | Clipboard group) to copy the selected text to the Clipboard (Figure 7–54).

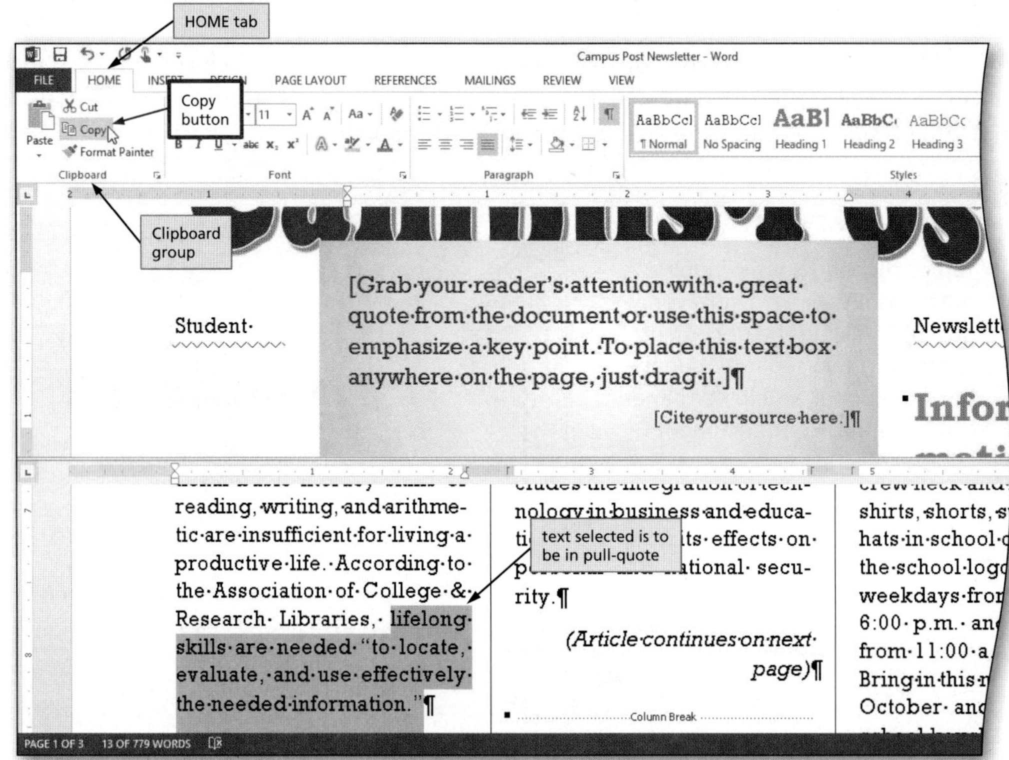

Figure 7–54

2

- In the upper pane, if necessary, scroll to display a portion of the text box. Tap or click the text in the text box to select it.
- Tap or click the Paste arrow (HOME tab | Clipboard group) to display the Paste menu.

Q&A What if I tap or click the Paste button by mistake?
Tap or click the Paste Options button to the right of the pasted text in the text box to display the Paste Options menu.

- If you are using a mouse, point to the Merge Formatting button on the Paste menu and notice the text box shows a live preview of the selected paste option (Figure 7–55).

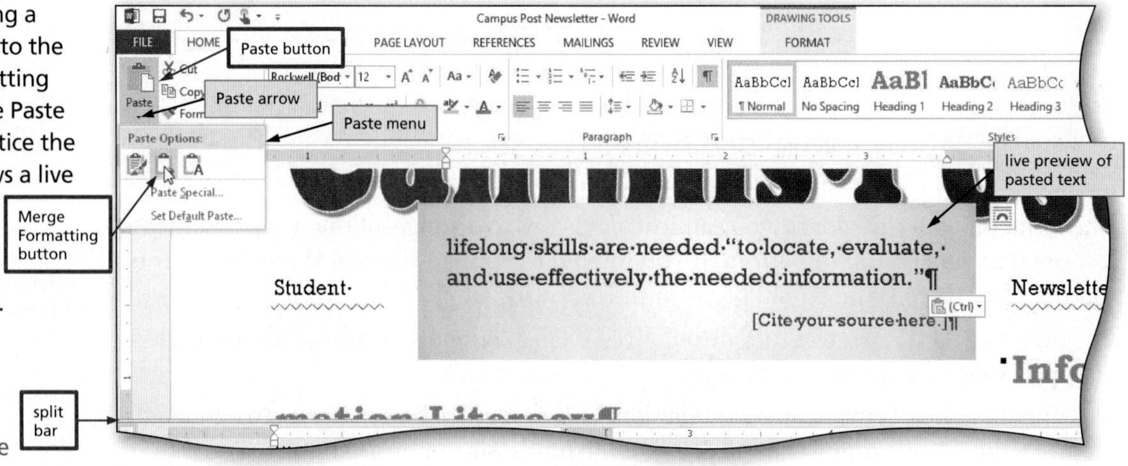

Figure 7–55

Q&A Why select the Merge Formatting button on the Paste menu?
You want the pasted text to use the formats that were in the text box (the destination) instead of the formats of the copied text (the source).

3

- Tap or click the Merge Formatting button on the Paste menu to paste the copied text into the text box.

4

- Repeat Steps 1, 2, and 3 for the source text, Association of College & Research Libraries, pasting it into the placeholder, [Cite your source here.].

Q&A Why does a hyphen appear in the source?
Word may have hyphenated the word automatically. You will format the pull-quote text next.

Other Ways

1. Select text to copy, press CTRL+C; select destination for pasted text, press CTRL+V

To Remove a Split Window

The next step is to remove the split window so that you can position the pull-quote. The following step removes a split window.

1. Double-click the split bar (shown in Figure 7–55), or tap or click the Split Window button again (VIEW tab | Window group), or press ALT+SHIFT+C, to remove the split window and return to a single Word window on the screen.

To Format Text in the Text Box

The next steps format text in the pull-quote.

1. If necessary, scroll to display the text box in the document window.
2. Capitalize the L in the word, Lifelong.
3. Select all the text in the text box, change its font to Cambria, and bold the text.
4. Select the first paragraph of text in the text box and change its font size to 11 point. Center this paragraph.
5. Tap or click in the text box to deselect the text, but leave the text box selected.

BTW
Rotating Text Box Text
To rotate text in a text box, select the text box, tap or click the Text Direction button (DRAWING TOOLS FORMAT tab | Text group), and then tap or click the desired direction on the Text Direction menu.

To Resize a Text Box and Insert Line Break Characters

The next step in formatting the pull-quote is to resize the text box. You resize a text box the same way as any other object. That is, you drag its sizing handles or enter values in the height and width boxes through the Size button (DRAWING TOOLS FORMAT tab | Size group). You do not want any hyphenated words in the text box. Once the text box is resized, you insert line break characters to eliminate any hyphenated words. The following steps resize the text box and insert line break characters.

1. Drag the sizing handles so that the pull-quote looks about the same size as Figure 7–56 on the next page.
2. Verify the pull-quote dimensions in the Shape Height and Shape Width boxes (DRAWING TOOLS FORMAT tab | Size group) and, if necessary, change the value in the Shape Height box to 2 and the Shape Width box to 1.94.
3. Position the insertion point to the left of the a in the word, are, and then press SHIFT+ENTER to insert a line break character, which places the word on the next line and removes the hyphen.
4. Insert line break characters to the left of the first quotation mark and also to the left of the words, Information and Research. If necessary, delete the hyphen in the word, Research (Figure 7–56).

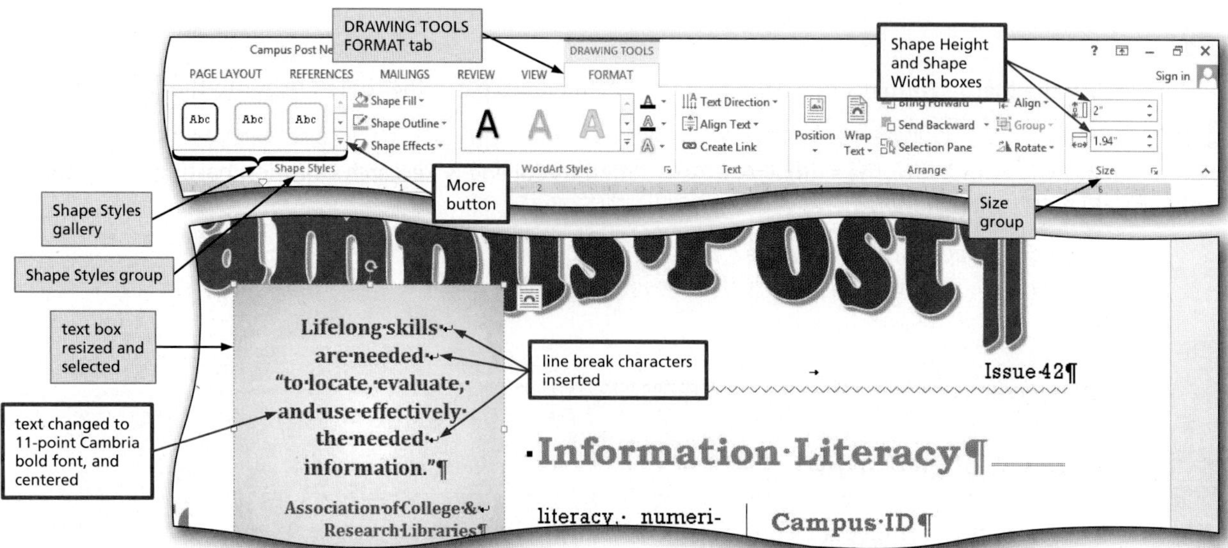

Figure 7–56

BTW

Text Box Styles

Like other drawing objects or pictures, text boxes can be formatted or have styles applied. You can change the fill in a text box by tapping or clicking the Shape Fill button (DRAWING TOOLS FORMAT tab | Shape Styles group), add an outline to a text box by clicking the Shape Outline button (DRAWING TOOLS FORMAT tab | Shape Styles group), and apply an effect such as shadow or 3-D effects by tapping or clicking the Shape Effects button (DRAWING TOOLS FORMAT tab | Shape Styles group).

To Apply a Shape Style to a Text Box

The next step in formatting the pull-quote is to apply a shape style to the text box to coordinate its colors with the rest of the newsletter. The following steps apply a shape style to a text box.

1. With the text box still selected, tap or click the More button (shown in Figure 7–56) in the Shape Styles gallery (DRAWING TOOLS FORMAT tab | Shape Styles group) to expand the gallery (Figure 7–57).
2. If you are using a mouse, point to 'Light 1 Outline, Colored Fill - Orange, Accent 6' (rightmost style, third row) in the Shape Styles gallery to display a live preview of that style applied to the text box.
3. Tap or click 'Light 1 Outline, Colored Fill - Orange, Accent 6' in the Shape Styles gallery to apply the selected style to the shape.
4. If the text in the text box did not change to white, select the text, tap or click the Font Color arrow (HOME tab | Font group), and then tap or click 'White, Background 1' to change the text color.

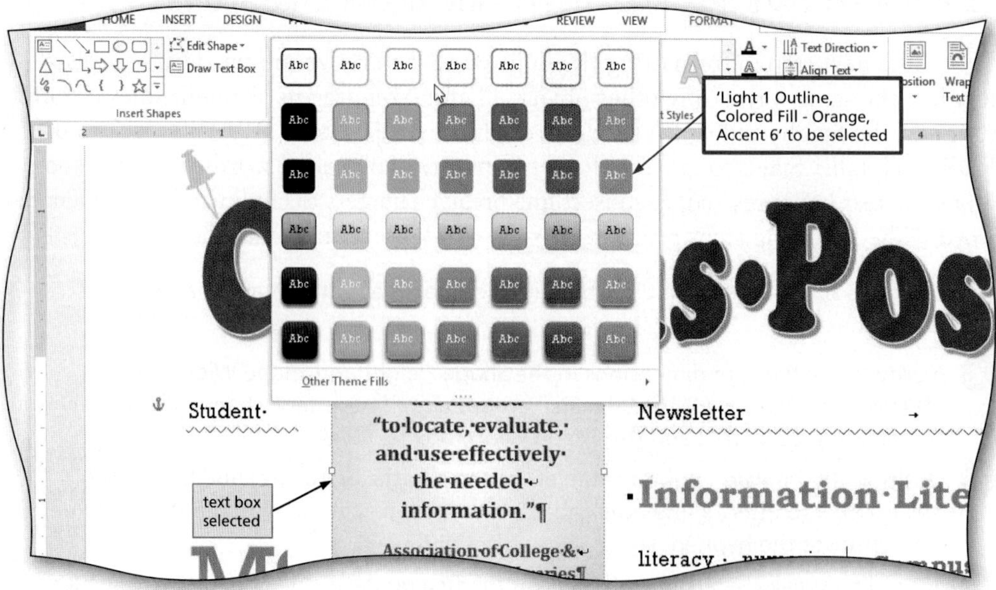

Figure 7–57

To Position a Text Box

The following step moves the text box to the desired location. ***Why?*** *The pull-quote text box should be positioned between the first and second columns of the newsletter.*

- With the text box still selected, drag the text box to its new location (Figure 7–58). You may need to drag and/or resize the text box a couple of times so that it looks similar to this figure.
- Tap or click outside the text box to remove the selection.

Q&A Why does my text wrap differently around the text box?
Differences in wordwrap often relate to the printer used by your computer. Thus, your document may wordwrap around the text box differently.

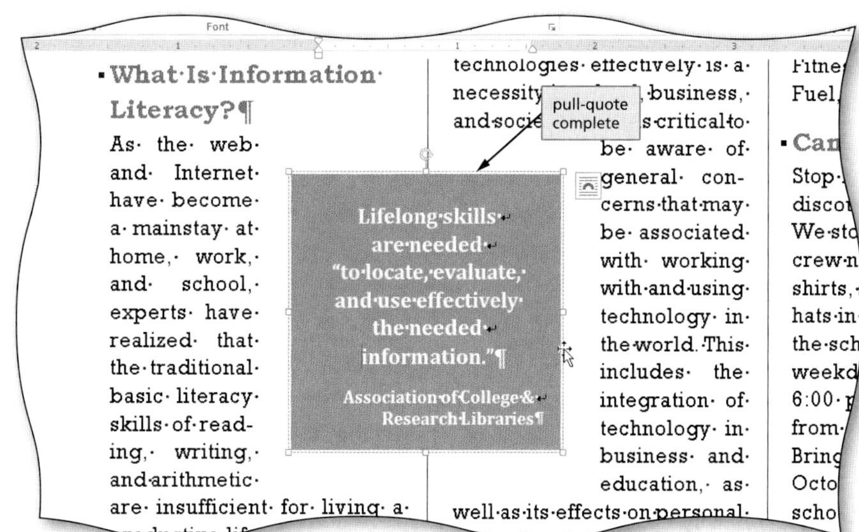

Figure 7–58

To Save a Document Again

You have performed several steps since the last save. You should save the newsletter again.

 Save the newsletter again with the same file name, Campus Post Newsletter.

BTW
Moving Text Boxes
To move a text box using the keyboard, select the text box and then press the arrow keys on the keyboard. For example, each time you press the DOWN ARROW key, the selected text box moves down one line.

Break Point: If you wish to take a break, this is a good place to do so. You can exit Word now. To resume at a later time, run Word, open the file called Campus Post Newsletter, and continue following the steps from this location forward.

Formatting the Second Page of the Newsletter

The second page of the newsletter (Figure 7–1b on page WD 411) continues the feature article that began in the first two columns on the first page. The nameplate on the second page is less elaborate than the one on the first page of the newsletter. In addition to the text in the feature article, page two contains a graphic. The following pages format the second page of the newsletter in this project.

CONSIDER THIS

How do you create a nameplate for inner pages of a newsletter?
The top of the inner pages of a newsletter may or may not have a nameplate. If you choose to create one for your inner pages, it should not be the same as, or compete with, the one on the first page. Inner page nameplates usually contain only a portion of the nameplate from the first page of a newsletter.

To Change Column Formatting

The document currently is formatted in three columns. The nameplate at the top of the second page, however, should be in a single column. ***Why?*** *The nameplate should span across the top of the three columns below it.* The next step, then, is to change the number of columns at the top of the second page from three to one.

As discussed earlier in this project, Word requires a new section each time you change the number of columns in a document. Thus, you first must insert a continuous section break and then format the section to one column so that the nameplate can be entered on the second page of the newsletter. The following steps insert a continuous section break and then change the column format.

1

- If you have a blank page between the first and second pages of the newsletter, position the insertion point to the left of the paragraph mark at the end of the third column on the first page of the newsletter and then press the DELETE key as many times as necessary to delete the blank line causing the overflow.
- Position the insertion point at the upper-left corner of the second page of the newsletter (to the left of L in Library).
- Display the PAGE LAYOUT tab.
- Tap or click the 'Insert Page and Section Breaks' button (PAGE LAYOUT tab | Page Setup group) to display the Insert Page and Section Breaks gallery (Figure 7–59).

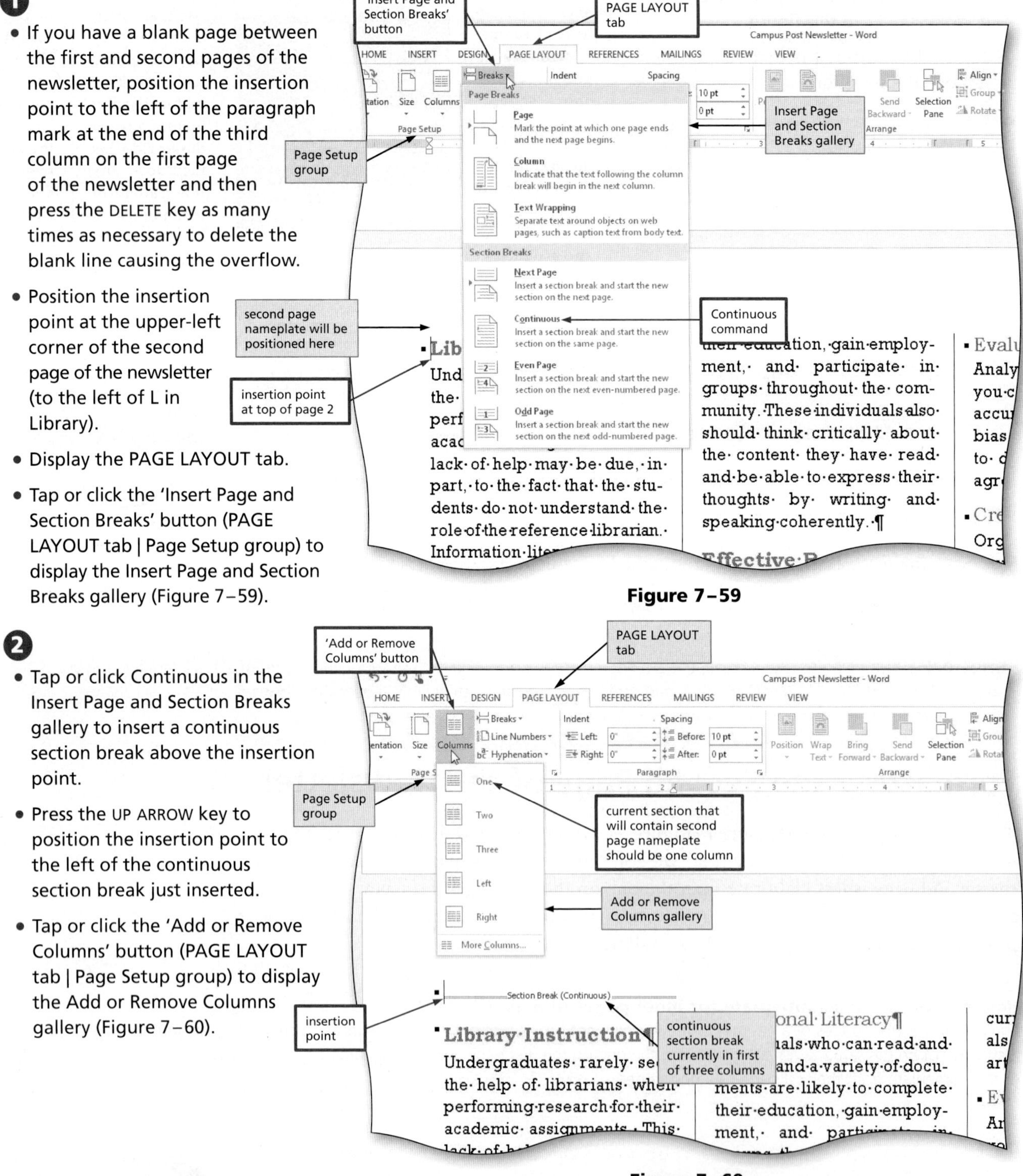

Figure 7–59

2

- Tap or click Continuous in the Insert Page and Section Breaks gallery to insert a continuous section break above the insertion point.
- Press the UP ARROW key to position the insertion point to the left of the continuous section break just inserted.
- Tap or click the 'Add or Remove Columns' button (PAGE LAYOUT tab | Page Setup group) to display the Add or Remove Columns gallery (Figure 7–60).

Figure 7–60

3

- Tap or click One in the Add or Remove Columns gallery to format the current section to one column, which now is ready for the second page nameplate.
- If necessary, scroll to display the bottom of the first page and the top of the second page, so that you can see the varying columns in the newsletter (Figure 7–61).

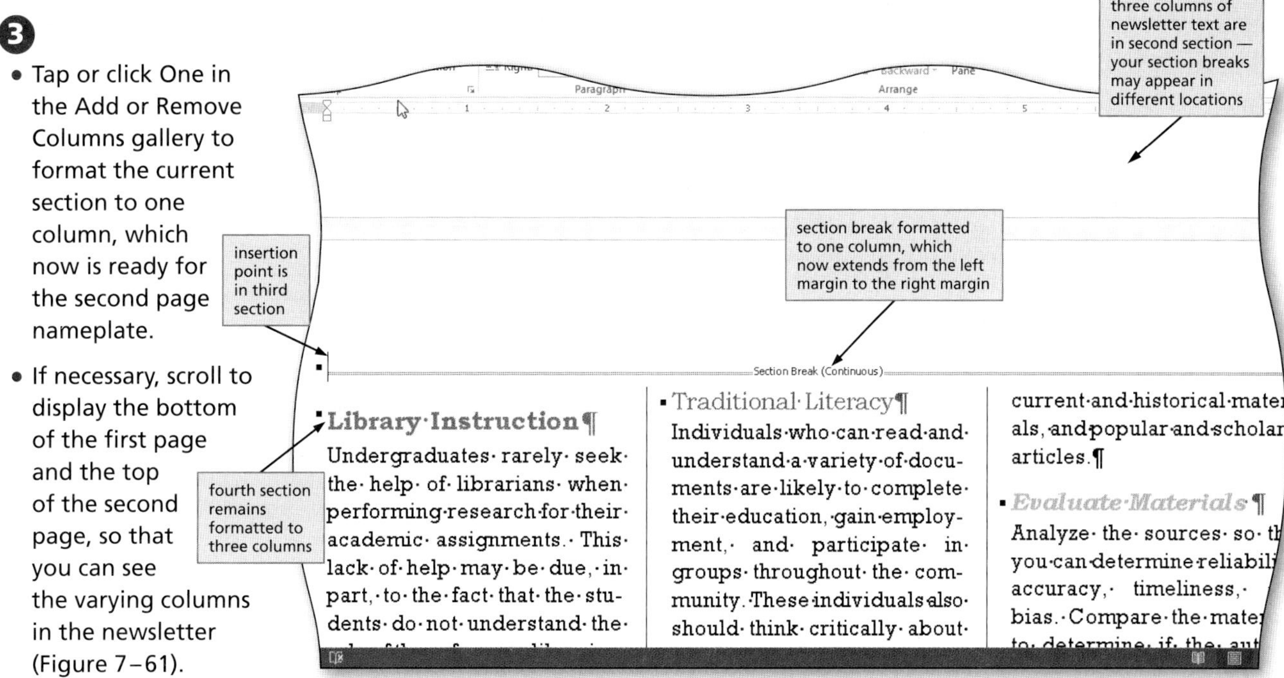

Figure 7–61

Q&A Can I change the column format of existing text?

Yes. If you already have typed text and would like it to be formatted in a different number of columns, select the text, tap or click the 'Add or Remove Columns' button (PAGE LAYOUT tab | Page Setup group), and then tap or click the number of columns desired in the Add or Remove Columns gallery. Word automatically creates a new section for the newly formatted columns.

To Set Custom Tab Stops Using the Tabs Dialog Box

The nameplate on the second page of the newsletter contains the text, Student Newsletter, at the left margin, the newsletter title in the center, and the issue number at the right margin (shown in Figure 7–1a on page WD 411). To properly align the text in the center and at the right margin, you will set custom tab stops at these locations. The following steps set custom tab stops.

1. Press the ENTER key twice and then position the insertion point on the first line of the second page of the newsletter, which is the paragraph to be formatted with the custom tab stops.
2. Tap or click the 'Clear All Formatting' button (HOME tab | Font group) to apply the Normal style to the first line on the second page of the newsletter.
3. Tap or click the Paragraph Settings Dialog Box Launcher (PAGE LAYOUT tab | Paragraph group) to display the Paragraph dialog box and then tap or click the Tabs button (Paragraph dialog box) to display the Tabs dialog box.
4. Type `3.5` in the Tab stop position text box (Tabs dialog box), tap or click Center in the Alignment area to specify the tab stop alignment, and then tap or click the Set button to set the custom tab stop.
5. Type `7` in the Tab stop position text box (Tabs dialog box), tap or click Right in the Alignment area to specify the tab stop alignment, and then tap or click the Set button to set the custom tab stop (Figure 7–62 on the next page).
6. Tap or click the OK button to set custom tab stops using the specified alignments.

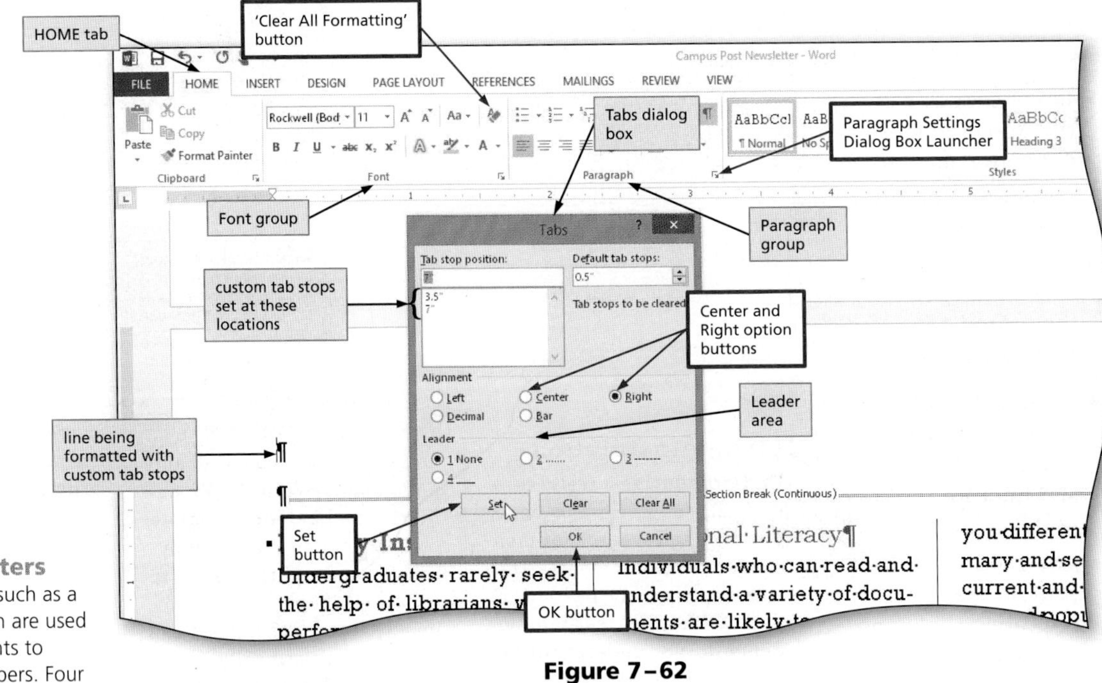

Figure 7–62

BTW

Leader Characters

Leader characters, such as a series of dots, often are used in a table of contents to precede page numbers. Four types of leader characters, which Word places in the space occupied by a tab character, are available in the Leader area of the Tabs dialog box (shown in Figure 7-62).

To Format and Enter Text and Add a Border

The following steps enter the newsletter title at the top of the second page in the third section.

1. With the insertion point on the first line of the second page of the newsletter, tap or click the Font Color arrow and then change the font of the current text to 'Pink, Accent 5, Darker 50%' (ninth column, sixth row). Increase the font size to 12 point. Type **`Student Newsletter`** at the left margin.

   If requested by your instructor, enter your name instead of the word, Student.

2. Press the TAB key to advance the insertion point to the centered tab stop. Increase the font size to 14 point and then tap or click the Bold button (HOME tab | Font group) to bold the text. Type **`Campus Post`** at the centered tab stop.

3. Press the TAB key to advance the insertion point to the right-aligned tab stop. Reduce the font size to 12 point and then tap or click the Bold button (HOME tab | Font group) to turn off the bold format. Type **`Issue 42`** at the right-aligned tab stop.

4. Tap or click the Borders button (HOME tab | Paragraph group) to add a bottom border (shown in Figure 7–63).

   Q&A Why is the border formatted already?

   When you define a custom border, Word uses that custom border the next time you tap or click the Borders button in the Borders gallery.

To Enter Text

The second page of the feature article on the second page of this newsletter begins with a jump-from line (the continued message) immediately below the nameplate. The next steps enter the jump-from line.

1. Position the insertion point on the blank line above the heading, Library Instruction, to the left of the paragraph mark.
2. Tap or click the 'Clear All Formatting' button (HOME tab | Font group) to apply the Normal style to the location of the insertion point.
3. Press CTRL+I to turn on the italic format.
4. Type `(Continued from first page)` and then press CTRL+I to turn off the italic format (Figure 7–63).

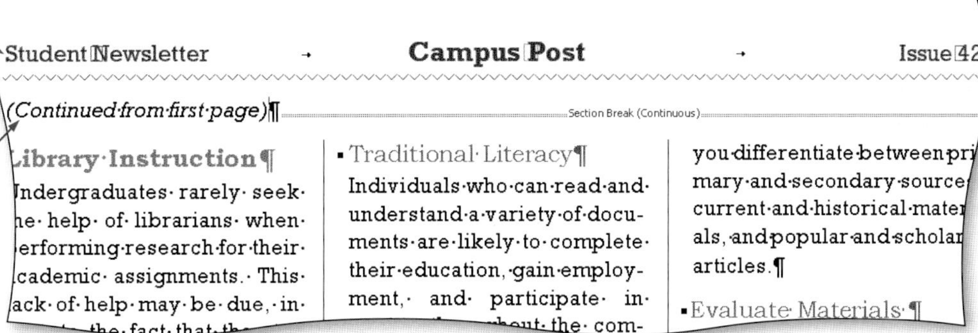

Figure 7–63

To Balance Columns

1 CREATE NAMEPLATE FOR FIRST PAGE | 2 FORMAT FIRST PAGE | 3 CREATE PULL-QUOTE
4 CREATE NAMEPLATE FOR SECOND PAGE | 5 FORMAT SECOND PAGE | **6 ADD PAGE BORDER**

Currently, the text on the second page of the newsletter completely fills up the first and second columns and almost fills the third column. The text in the three columns should consume the same amount of vertical space. ***Why?*** *Typically, the text in columns of a newsletter is balanced.* To balance columns, you insert a continuous section break at the end of the text. The following steps balance columns.

1.
- Scroll to the bottom of the text in the third column on the second page of the newsletter and then position the insertion point at the end of the text.
- If an extra paragraph mark is below the last line of text, press the DELETE key to remove the extra paragraph mark.
- Display the PAGE LAYOUT tab.
- Tap or click the 'Insert Page and Section Breaks' button (PAGE LAYOUT tab | Page Setup group) to display the Insert Page and Section Breaks gallery (Figure 7–64).

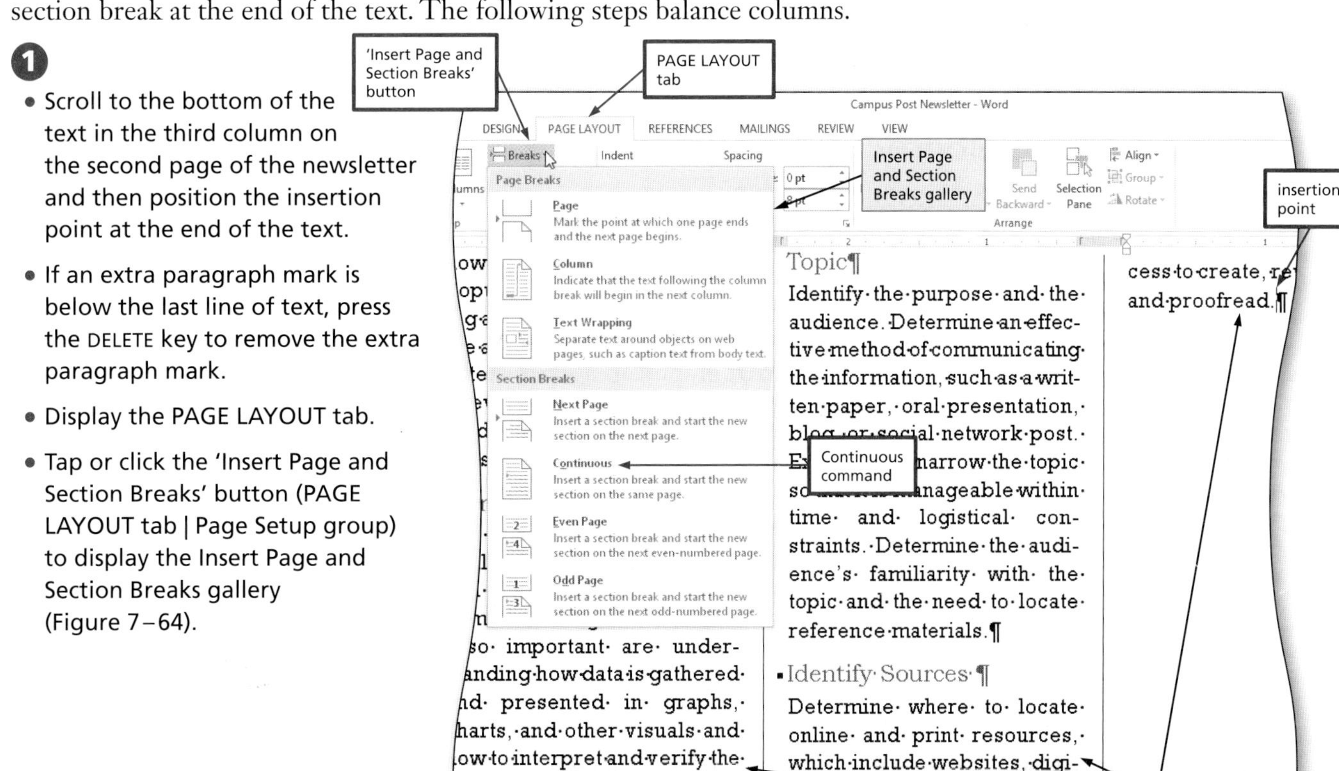

Figure 7–64

- Tap or click Continuous in the Insert Page and Section Breaks gallery to insert a continuous section break, which balances the columns on the second page of the newsletter (Figure 7–65).

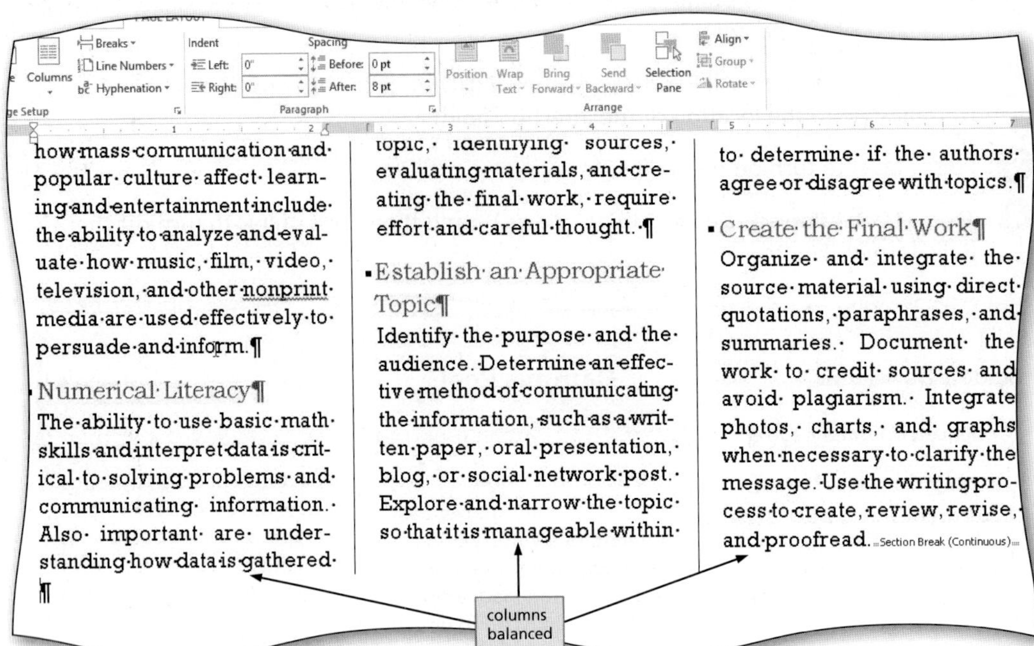

Figure 7–65

To Save a Document Again

You have performed several steps since the last save. Thus, you should save the newsletter again. The following step saves the newsletter again.

Save the newsletter again with the same file name, Campus Post Newsletter.

Modifying and Formatting a SmartArt Graphic

Recall from Chapter 4 that Microsoft Office includes **SmartArt graphics**, which are visual representations of ideas. Many different types of SmartArt graphics are available, allowing you to choose one that illustrates your message best.

In this newsletter, a SmartArt graphic is positioned on the second page, in the first and second columns. Because the columns are small in the newsletter, it is best to work with a SmartArt graphic in a separate document window so that you easily can see all of its components. When finished editing the graphic, you can copy and paste it in the newsletter. You will follow these steps for the SmartArt graphic in this newsletter:

1. Open the document that contains the SmartArt graphic for the newsletter.
2. Modify the layout of the graphic.
3. Add a shape and text to the graphic.
4. Format a shape and the graphic.
5. Copy and paste the graphic in the newsletter.
6. Resize the graphic and position it in the desired location.

BTW

BTWs

For a complete list of the BTWs found in the margins of this book, visit the BTW resource on the Student Companion Site located on www.cengagebrain.com. For detailed instructions about accessing available resources, visit www.cengage.com/ct/studentdownload or contact your instructor for information about accessing the required files.

To Open a Document from Word

The first draft of the SmartArt graphic is in a file called Information Literacy Diagram on the Data Files for Students. Visit www.cengage.com/ct/studentdownload for detailed instructions or contact your instructor for information about accessing the required files. The following steps open the Information Literacy Diagram file.

1. Open the Backstage view and then tap or click the Open tab to display the Open gallery.
2. Navigate to the location of the file to be opened (in this case, the Data Files for Students folder).
3. Tap or click Information Literacy Diagram to select the file name.
4. Tap or click the Open button (Open dialog box) to open the selected file.
5. Tap or click the graphic to select it and display the SMARTART TOOLS DESIGN and FORMAT tabs (Figure 7–66).

Q&A Is the Campus Post Newsletter file still open?
Yes. Leave it open because you will copy the modified diagram to the second page of the newsletter.

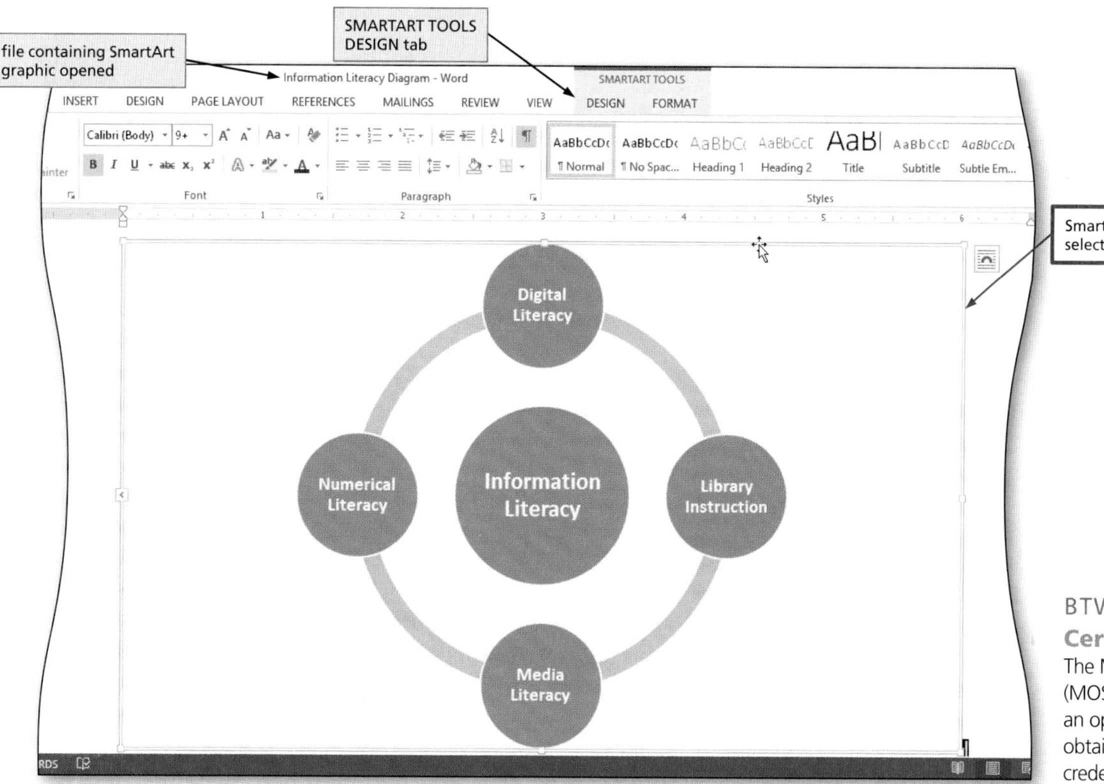

Figure 7–66

BTW

Certification

The Microsoft Office Specialist (MOS) program provides an opportunity for you to obtain a valuable industry credential — proof that you have the Word 2013 skills required by employers. For more information, visit the Certification resource on the Student Companion Site located on www.cengagebrain.com. For detailed instructions about accessing available resources, visit www.cengage.com/ct/studentdownload or contact your instructor for information about accessing the required files.

To Change the Layout of a SmartArt Graphic

The following step changes the layout of an existing SmartArt graphic. ***Why?*** *The SmartArt graphic currently uses the Radial Cycle layout, and this newsletter uses the Diverging Radial layout.*

1

- If necessary, display the SMARTART TOOLS DESIGN tab.
- Scroll through the layouts in the Layouts gallery until Diverging Radial appears (that is, tap or click the up or down scroll arrows to scroll through the in-ribbon gallery) and then tap or click Diverging Radial to change the layout of the SmartArt graphic (Figure 7–67).

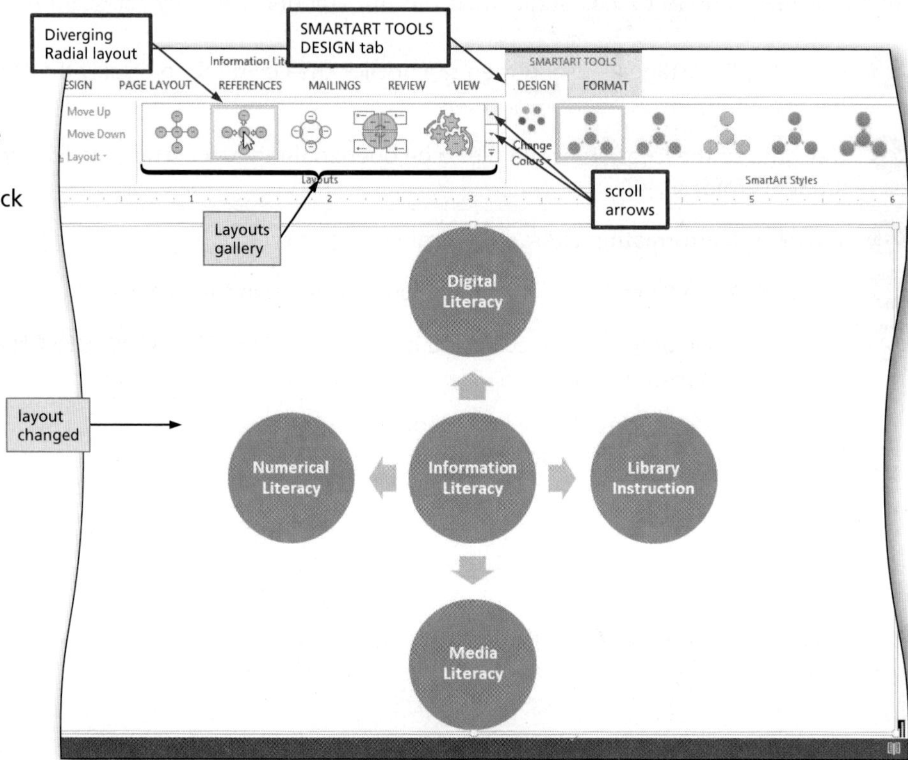

Figure 7–67

Other Ways

1. Press and hold or right-click the selected graphic, tap or click Layout button or 'More Layout Options' on mini toolbar or shortcut menu, select desired layout, if necessary, tap or click OK button

To Add a Shape to a SmartArt Graphic

The current SmartArt graphic has four perimeter shapes. This newsletter has a fifth shape. The following step adds a shape to a SmartArt graphic.

1 With the diagram selected, tap or click the Add Shape button (SMARTART TOOLS DESIGN tab | Create Graphic group) to add a shape to the SmartArt graphic (Figure 7–68).

Q&A

Why did my screen display a menu instead of adding a shape?

You tapped or clicked the Add Shape arrow instead of the Add Shape button. Tapping or clicking the Add Shape button adds the shape automatically; tapping or clicking the Add Shape arrow displays a menu allowing you to specify the location of the shape.

How do I delete a shape?

Select the shape by tapping or clicking it and then press the DELETE key, or press and hold or right-click the shape and then tap or click Cut on the mini toolbar or shortcut menu.

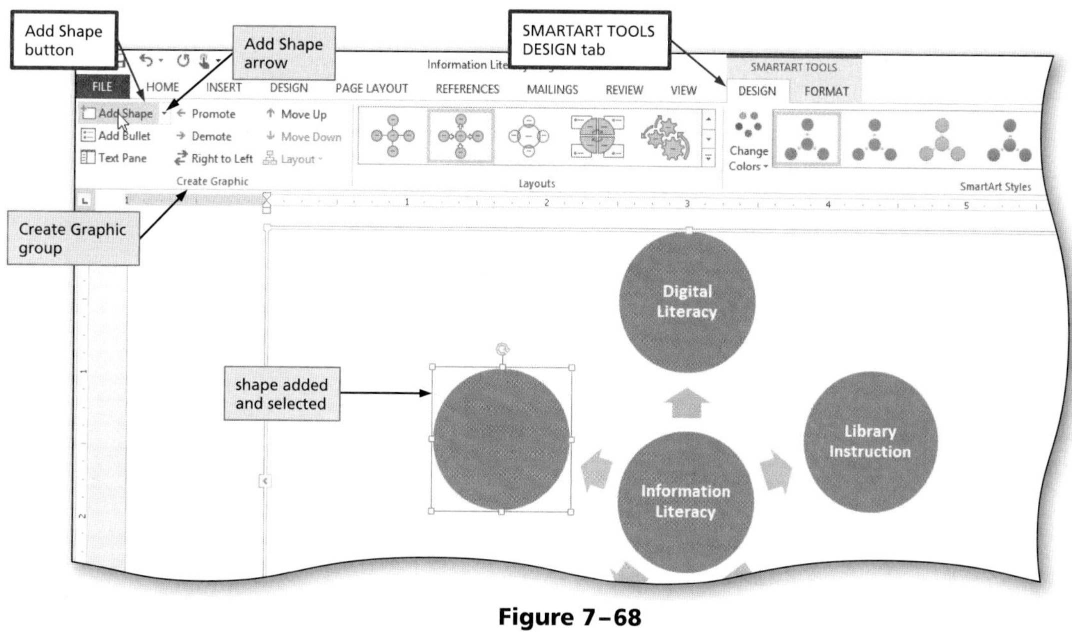

Figure 7–68

BTW

Demoting Text Pane Text

Instead of pressing the TAB key in the Text Pane, you could tap or click the Demote Selection button (SMARTART TOOLS DESIGN tab | Create Graphic group) to increase (or move to the right) the indent for a bulleted item. You also can tap or click the Promote Selection button (SMARTART TOOLS DESIGN tab | Create Graphic group) to decrease (or move to the left) the indent for a bulleted item.

To Add Text to a SmartArt Graphic through the Text Pane

1 CREATE NAMEPLATE FOR FIRST PAGE | 2 FORMAT FIRST PAGE | 3 CREATE PULL-QUOTE
4 CREATE NAMEPLATE FOR SECOND PAGE | 5 FORMAT SECOND PAGE | **6 ADD PAGE BORDER**

In Chapter 4, you added text directly to the shapes in a SmartArt graphic. In this project, you enter the text through the Text Pane. ***Why?*** *Some users prefer to enter text in the Text Pane instead of in the shape.* The following steps use the Text Pane to add text to a shape.

1

- Tap or click the Text Pane control, which is on the left side of the SmartArt graphic, to display the Text Pane to the left of the SmartArt graphic.

2

- In the Text Pane, if necessary, position the insertion point to the right of the bullet that has no text to its right.
- Type **Traditional Literacy** as the text for the shape (Figure 7–69).

3

- Tap or click the Close button in the Text Pane to close the Text Pane.

Q&A Can I instead close the Text Pane by tapping or clicking the Text Pane button (SMARTART TOOLS DESIGN tab | Create Graphic group)?
Yes.

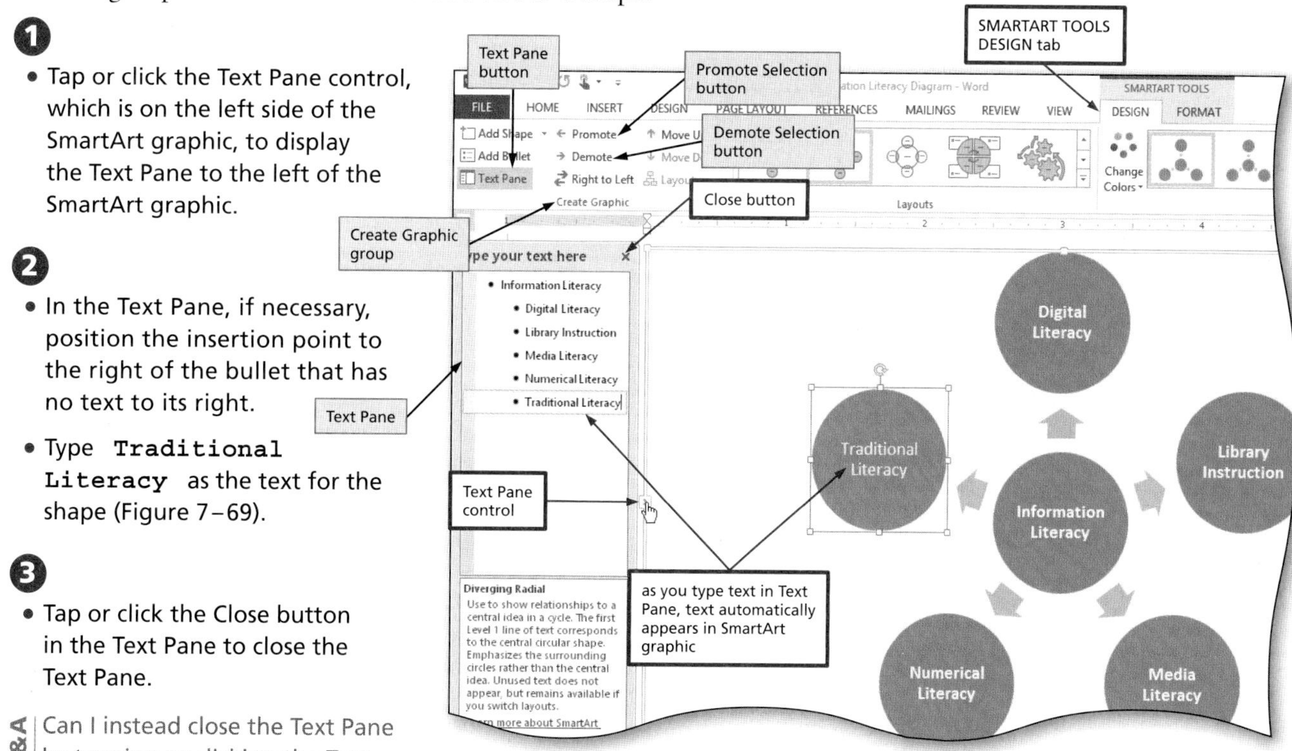

Figure 7–69

To Format SmartArt Graphic Text

To format text in an entire SmartArt graphic, select the graphic and then apply the format. The following steps bold the text in the SmartArt graphic.

1. If necessary, double-tap or double-click the shape just added to select it.
2. Display the HOME tab. Tap or click the Bold button (HOME tab | Font group) to bold the text in the SmartArt graphic (shown in Figure 7–70).

To Modify Theme Effects

If you wanted to change the look of graphics such as SmartArt graphics, you could perform the following steps to change the theme effects.

1. Tap or click the Theme Effects button (DESIGN tab | Document Formatting group).
2. Tap or click the desired effect in the Theme Effects gallery.

To Save Customized Themes

When you modify the theme effects, theme colors, or theme fonts, you can save the modified theme for future use. If you wanted to save a customized theme, you would perform the following steps.

1. Tap or click the Themes button (DESIGN tab | Document Formatting group) to display the Themes gallery.
2. Tap or click 'Save Current Theme' in the Themes gallery.
3. Enter a theme name in the File name box (Save Current Theme dialog box).
4. Tap or click the Save button to add the saved theme to the Themes gallery.

To Save an Active Document with a New File Name

To preserve the contents of the original Information Literacy Diagram file, you should save the active document with a new file name. The following steps save the active document with a new file name.

1. Open the Backstage view and then tap or click the Save As tab to display the Save As gallery.
2. Navigate to the location of the file to be saved.
3. Save the document with the file name, Information Literacy Diagram Modified.

BTW
Clipboard Task Pane and Office Clipboard Icon
You can control when the Clipboard task pane appears on the Word screen and the Office Clipboard icon appears in the notification area on the taskbar. To do this, first display the Clipboard task pane by tapping or clicking the Clipboard Dialog Box Launcher on the HOME tab. Next, tap or click the Options button at the bottom of the Clipboard task pane and then tap or click the desired option on the menu. For example, if you want to be able to display the Clipboard task pane by tapping or clicking the Office Clipboard icon on the Windows taskbar, tap or click 'Show Office Clipboard Icon on Taskbar' on the Options menu.

Copying and Pasting

The next step is to copy the SmartArt graphic from this document window and then paste it in the newsletter. To copy from one document and paste into another, you can use the Office Clipboard. Through the Office Clipboard, you can copy multiple items from any Office document and then paste them into the same or another Office document by following these general guidelines:

1. Items are copied *from* a **source document**. If the source document is not the active document, display it in the document window.
2. Display the Office Clipboard task pane and then copy items from the source document to the Office Clipboard.
3. Items are copied *to* a **destination document**. If the destination document is not the active document, display the destination document in the document window.
4. Paste items from the Office Clipboard to the destination document.

To Copy a SmartArt Graphic Using the Office Clipboard

1 CREATE NAMEPLATE FOR FIRST PAGE | 2 FORMAT FIRST PAGE | 3 CREATE PULL-QUOTE
4 CREATE NAMEPLATE FOR SECOND PAGE | 5 FORMAT SECOND PAGE | **6 ADD PAGE BORDER**

The following step copies the SmartArt graphic to the Office Clipboard. ***Why?*** *Sometimes you want to copy multiple items to the Office Clipboard through the Clipboard task pane and then paste them later.*

- Tap or click the Clipboard Dialog Box Launcher (HOME tab | Clipboard group) to display the Clipboard task pane.
- If the Office Clipboard in the Clipboard task pane is not empty, tap or click the Clear All button in the Clipboard task pane.
- With the SmartArt graphic selected in the document window, tap or click the Copy button (HOME tab | Clipboard group) to copy the selected text to the Clipboard (Figure 7–70).

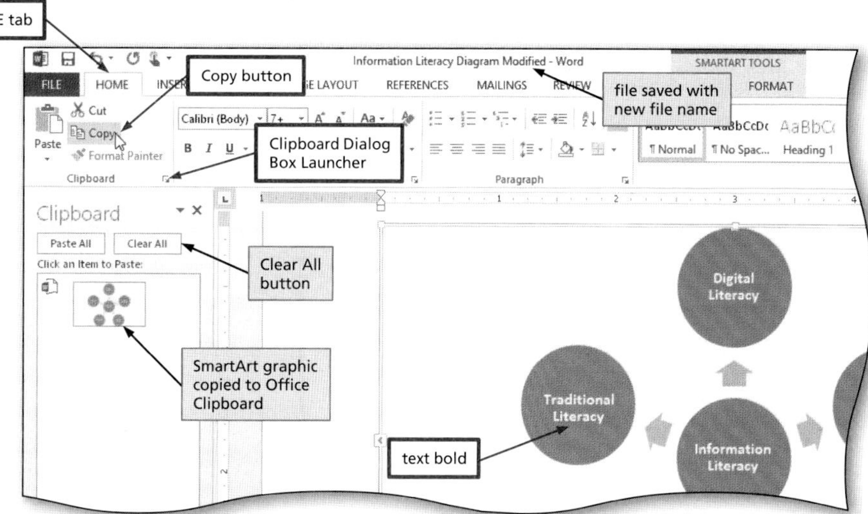

Figure 7–70

Other Ways

1. With Clipboard task pane displayed, press and hold or right-click selected item, tap or click Copy on mini toolbar or shortcut menu
2. With Clipboard task pane displayed and item to copy selected, press CTRL+C

To Switch from One Open Document to Another

1 CREATE NAMEPLATE FOR FIRST PAGE | 2 FORMAT FIRST PAGE | 3 CREATE PULL-QUOTE
4 CREATE NAMEPLATE FOR SECOND PAGE | 5 FORMAT SECOND PAGE | **6 ADD PAGE BORDER**

The steps below switch from the open Information Literacy Diagram Modified document (the source document) to the open Campus Post Newsletter document (the destination document). ***Why?*** *You want to paste the copied diagram into the newsletter document.*

- If you are using a touch screen, tap the Word app button on the taskbar; if you are using a mouse, point to the Word app button on the taskbar to display a live preview of the open documents or window titles of the open documents, depending on your computer's configuration (Figure 7–71).

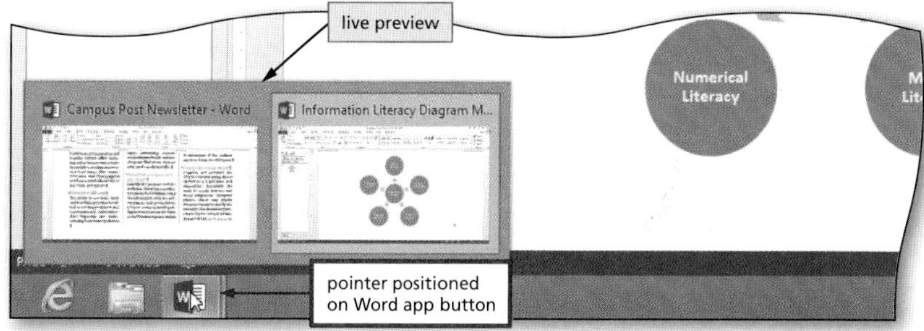

Figure 7–71

2

- Tap or click the live preview of the Campus Post Newsletter on the Windows taskbar to display the selected document in the document window (shown in Figure 7–72 on the next page).

Other Ways

1. Tap or click Switch Windows button (VIEW tab | Window group), tap or click document name
2. Press ALT+TAB

To Paste from the Office Clipboard

1 CREATE NAMEPLATE FOR FIRST PAGE | 2 FORMAT FIRST PAGE | 3 CREATE PULL-QUOTE
4 CREATE NAMEPLATE FOR SECOND PAGE | 5 FORMAT SECOND PAGE | 6 ADD PAGE BORDER

The following steps paste from the Office Clipboard. ***Why?*** *You want to paste the copied SmartArt graphic into the destination document, in this case, the newsletter document.*

1

- If the Clipboard task pane is not displayed on the screen, display the HOME tab and then tap or click the Clipboard Dialog Box Launcher (HOME tab | Clipboard group) to display the Clipboard task pane.
- Tap or click the SmartArt graphic entry in the Office Clipboard to paste it in the document at the location of the insertion point (Figure 7–72).

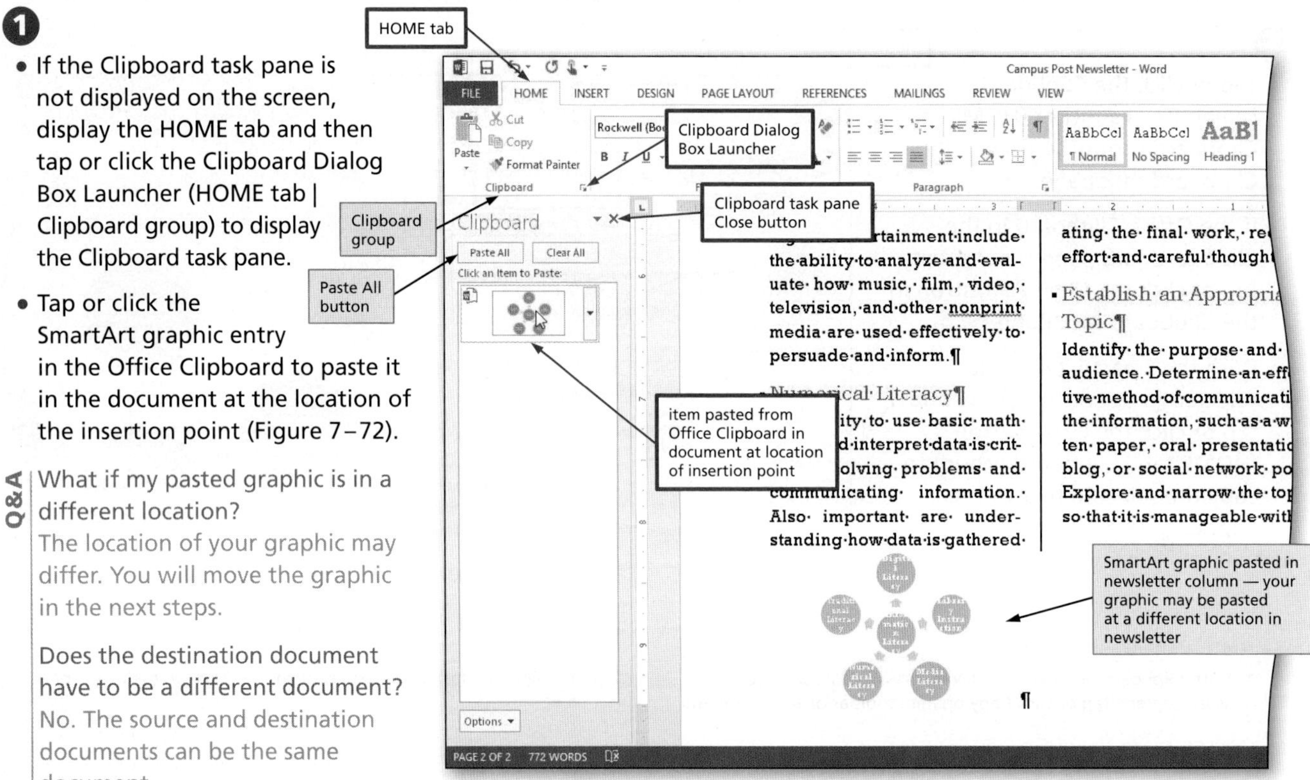

Figure 7–72

Q&A

What if my pasted graphic is in a different location?
The location of your graphic may differ. You will move the graphic in the next steps.

Does the destination document have to be a different document?
No. The source and destination documents can be the same document.

What is the function of the Paste All button?
If you have multiple items in the Office Clipboard, it pastes all items in a row, without any characters between them, at the location of the insertion point or selection.

2

- Tap or click the Close button in the Clipboard task pane.

Other Ways

1. With Clipboard task pane displayed, press and hold or right-click selected item, tap or click Paste on shortcut menu
2. With Clipboard task pane displayed, press CTRL+V

To Format a Graphic as Floating

The text in the newsletter should wrap tightly around the graphic; that is, the text should conform to the graphic's shape. Thus, the next step is to change the graphic from inline to floating with a wrapping style of tight. The following steps format the graphic as floating with tight wrapping.

1. Tap or click the SmartArt graphic to select it.
2. With the SmartArt graphic selected, tap or click the Layout Options button that is attached to the graphic to display the Layout Options gallery.
3. Tap or click Tight in the Layout Options gallery to change the graphic from inline to floating with tight wrapping.
4. Close the Layout Options gallery.

To Resize and Position the SmartArt Graphic

The next task is to increase the size of the SmartArt graphic and then position it in the first and second columns on the second page. The following steps resize and then position the graphic.

1. Drag the sizing handles outward until the graphic is approximately the same size as shown in Figure 7–73, which has a height of 2.74" and a width of 4.26".
2. Drag the edge of the graphic to the location shown in Figure 7–73. You may have to drag the graphic a couple of times to position it similarly to the figure.
3. If the newsletter spills onto a third page, reduce the size of the SmartArt graphic. You may need to delete an extra paragraph mark at the end of the document, as well.

BTW

Space around Graphics
The space between a graphic and the text, which sometimes is called the run-around, should be at least 1/8" and should be the same for all graphics in a document. Adjust the run-around of a selected floating graphic by doing the following: tap or click the Wrap Text button (SMARTART TOOLS FORMAT tab | Arrange group), tap or click 'More Layout Options' on the Wrap Text menu, tap or click the Position tab (Layout dialog box), adjust the values in the Horizontal and Vertical boxes, and then tap or click the OK button.

To Layer the SmartArt Graphic in Front of Text

1 CREATE NAMEPLATE FOR FIRST PAGE | 2 FORMAT FIRST PAGE | 3 CREATE PULL-QUOTE
4 CREATE NAMEPLATE FOR SECOND PAGE | **5 FORMAT SECOND PAGE** | **6 ADD PAGE BORDER**

In Word, you can layer objects on top of or behind other objects. The following steps layer the SmartArt graphic on top of all text. ***Why?*** *You want to ensure that the ruling line is positioned behind the SmartArt graphic.*

1

- If necessary, tap or click the SmartArt graphic to select it. Tap or click the Bring Forward arrow (SMARTART TOOLS FORMAT tab | Arrange group) to display the Bring Forward menu (Figure 7–73).

2

- Tap or click 'Bring in Front of Text' on the Bring Forward menu to position the selected object on top of all text.
- Tap or click outside the graphic so that it no longer is selected.

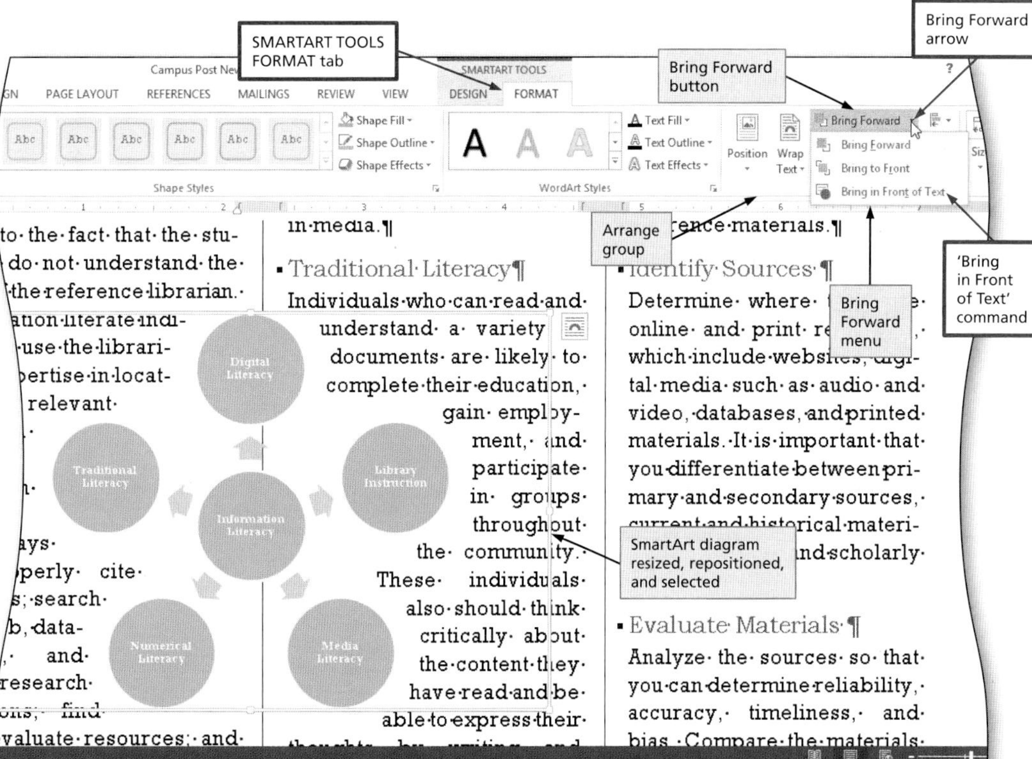

Figure 7–73

Finishing the Newsletter

With the text and graphics in the newsletter entered and formatted, the next step is to view the newsletter as a whole and determine if it looks finished in its current state. To give the newsletter a finished appearance, you will add a border to its edges.

To Turn Off Formatting Marks and Zoom Multiple Pages

The last step in formatting the newsletter is to place a border around its edges. First, you turn off formatting marks to remove the clutter from the screen. Then, you place both pages in the document window at once so that you can see all the page borders applied. The following steps turn off formatting marks and zoom multiple pages.

1. If necessary, display the HOME tab and then turn off formatting marks.
2. Display the VIEW tab and then display multiple pages on the screen.

To Add an Art Page Border

1 CREATE NAMEPLATE FOR FIRST PAGE | 2 FORMAT FIRST PAGE | 3 CREATE PULL-QUOTE
4 CREATE NAMEPLATE FOR SECOND PAGE | 5 FORMAT SECOND PAGE | **6 ADD PAGE BORDER**

The following steps add a page border around the pages of the newsletter. ***Why?*** *This newsletter has a purple art border around the perimeter of each page.*

- Display the DESIGN tab.
- Tap or click the 'Borders and Shading' button (DESIGN tab | Page Background group) to display the Borders and Shading dialog box. If necessary, tap or click the Page Border tab.

Q&A What if I cannot select the Page Borders button because it is dimmed?
Tap or click somewhere in the newsletter to make the newsletter the active document and then repeat Step 1.

2

- Tap or click Box in the Setting area (Borders and Shading dialog box) to specify a border on all four sides of the page.
- Tap or click the Art arrow, scroll to and then tap or click the art border shown in Figure 7–74.
- Tap or click the Color arrow and then tap or click 'Lavender, Accent 4, Darker 50%' (sixth row, eighth column) on the palette (Figure 7–74).

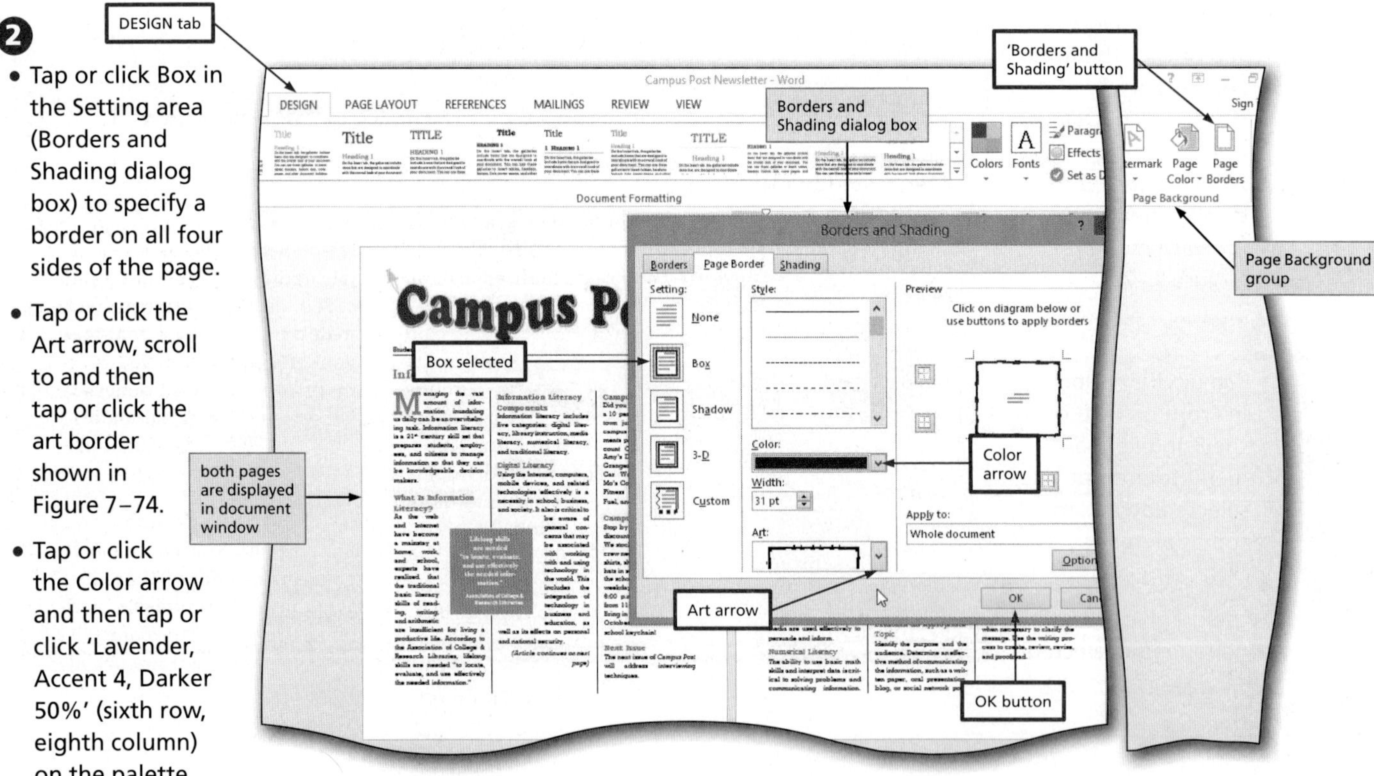

Figure 7–74

3

- Tap or click the OK button to place the defined border on each page of the newsletter (Figure 7–75).

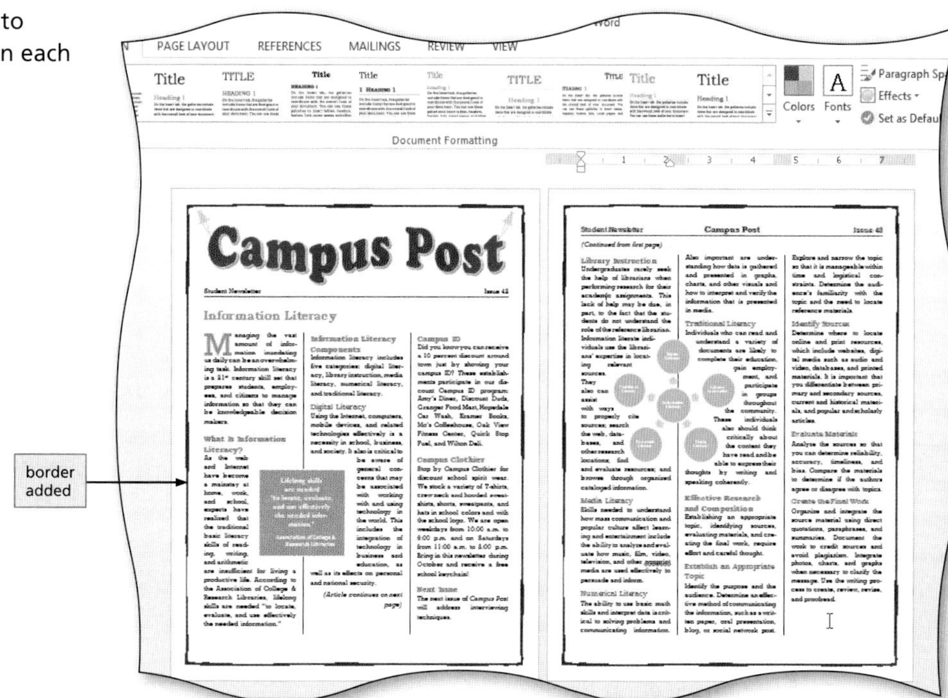

Figure 7–75

To Save and Print the Document, Then Exit Word

The newsletter now is complete. You should save the document, print it, and then exit Word.

1. Save the newsletter again with the same file name.
2. If desired, print the newsletter (shown in Figure 7–1 on page WD 411).

Q&A
What if an error message appears about margins?
Depending on the printer you are using, you may need to set the margins differently for this project.

What if one or more of the borders do not print?
Tap or click the 'Borders and Shading' button (DESIGN tab | Page Background group), tap or click the Options button (Borders and Shading dialog box), tap or click the Measure from arrow and tap or click Text, change the four text boxes to 15 pt, and then tap or click the OK button in each dialog box. Try printing the document again. If the borders still do not print, adjust the text boxes in the dialog box to a number smaller than 15 pt.

3. Exit Word, closing all open documents.

BTW
Conserving Ink and Toner
If you want to conserve ink or toner, you can instruct Word to print draft quality documents by tapping or clicking FILE on the ribbon to open the Backstage view, tapping or clicking Options in the Backstage view to display the Word Options dialog box, tapping or clicking Advanced in the left pane (Word Options dialog box), sliding or scrolling to the Print area in the right pane, placing a check mark in the 'Use draft quality' check box, and then tapping or clicking the OK button. Then, use the Backstage view to print the document as usual.

BTW
Distributing a Document
Instead of printing and distributing a hard copy of a document, you can distribute the document electronically. Options include sending the document via email; posting it on cloud storage (such as SkyDrive) and sharing the file with others; posting it on a social networking site, blog, or other website; and sharing a link associated with an online location of the document. You also can create and share a PDF or XPS image of the document, so that users can view the file in Acrobat Reader or XPS Viewer instead of in Word.

Chapter Summary

In this chapter, you have learned how to create a professional-looking newsletter using Word's desktop publishing features such as WordArt, columns, horizontal and vertical rules, and pull-quotes. The items listed below include all the new Word skills you have learned in this chapter, with the tasks grouped by activity.

Enter and Edit Text

Copy and Paste Using Split Windows (WD 446)

File Management

Insert a File in a Column of the Newsletter (WD 434)
Switch from One Open Document to Another (WD 459)

Format a Page

Modify Theme Effects (WD 458)
Save Customized Themes (WD 458)
Add an Art Page Border (WD 462)

Format Text

Set Custom Tab Stops Using the Tabs Dialog Box (WD 420)
Border One Edge of a Paragraph (WD 422)
Insert a Continuous Section Break (WD 432)
Change the Number of Columns (WD 433)
Justify a Paragraph (WD 434)
Increase Column Width and Place a Vertical Rule between Columns (WD 436)
Hyphenate a Document (WD 437)
Format a Character as a Drop Cap (WD 438)
Insert a Next Page Section Break (WD 440)
Insert a Column Break (WD 441)
Change Column Formatting (WD 450)
Balance Columns (WD 453)

Word Settings

Split the Window (WD 445)
Arrange All Open Word Documents on the Screen (WD 445)
Remove a Split Window (WD 447)

Work with Graphics

Insert WordArt (WD 414)
Change the WordArt Fill Color (WD 416)
Change the WordArt Shape (WD 420)
Crop a Graphic (WD 425)
Use the Selection Task Pane (WD 428)
Rotate a Graphic (WD 428)
Insert a Text Box (WD 444)
Position a Text Box (WD 449)
Change the Layout of a SmartArt Graphic (WD 456)
Add Text to a SmartArt Graphic through the Text Pane (WD 457)
Copy a SmartArt Graphic Using the Office Clipboard (WD 459)
Paste from the Office Clipboard (WD 460)
Layer the SmartArt Graphic in Front of Text (WD 461)

CONSIDER THIS: PLAN AHEAD

What decisions will you need to make when creating your next newsletter?

Use these guidelines as you complete the assignments in this chapter and create your own newsletters outside of this class.

1. Create the nameplate.
   a) Determine the location of the nameplate.
   b) Determine content, formats, and arrangement of text and graphics.
   c) If appropriate, use ruling lines.
2. Determine content for the body of the newsletter.
   a) Write the body copy.
   b) Organize the body copy in columns.
   c) Format the body copy and subheads.
   d) Incorporate color.
   e) Divide sections with vertical rules.
   f) Enhance with visuals.
3. Bind and distribute the newsletter.
   a) Determine if newsletters should be printed, posted on bulletin boards, sent as an email message, or posted on websites.
   b) For multipage newsletters that will be printed, determine the appropriate method of binding the pages.
   c) For online newsletters, select a format that most users will be able to open.

CONSIDER THIS

How should you submit solutions to questions in the assignments identified with a ✲ symbol?
Every assignment in this book contains one or more questions identified with a ✲ symbol. These questions require you to think beyond the assigned document. Present your solutions to the questions in the format required by your instructor. Possible formats may include one or more of these options: write the answer; create a document that contains the answer; present your answer to the class; discuss your answer in a group; record the answer as audio or video using a webcam, smartphone, or portable media player; or post answers on a blog, wiki, or website.

Apply Your Knowledge

Reinforce the skills and apply the concepts you learned in this chapter.

Working with Desktop Publishing Elements of a Newsletter

Note: To complete this assignment, you will be required to use the Data Files for Students. Visit www.cengage.com/ct/studentdownload for detailed instructions or contact your instructor for information about accessing the required files.

Instructions: Run Word. Open the document, Apply 7-1 Meteor Shower Newsletter Draft, from the Data Files for Students. The document contains a newsletter that you are to modify (Figure 7–76).

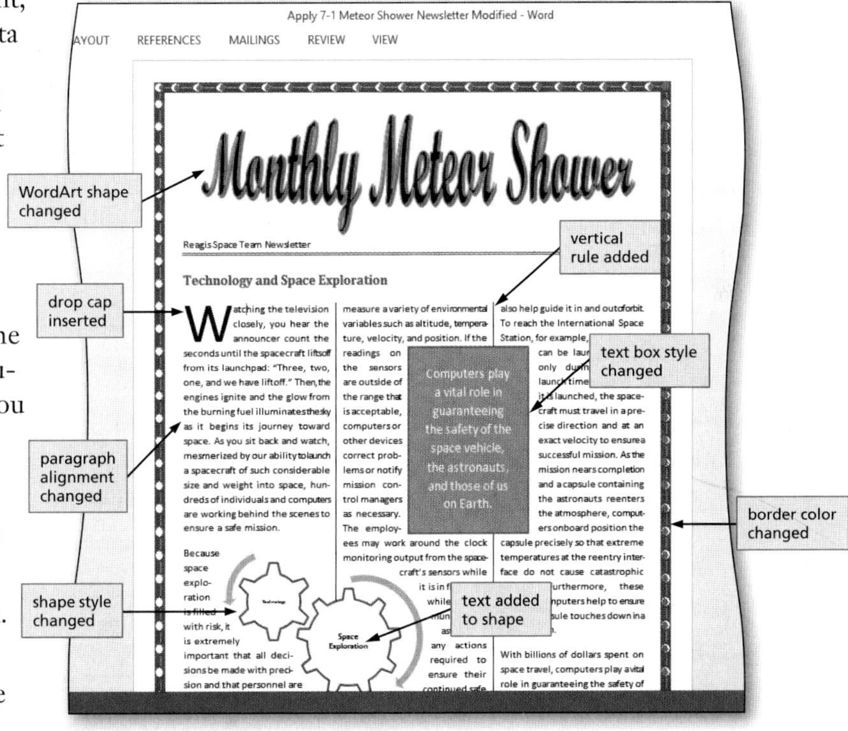

Figure 7–76

Perform the following tasks:

1. Change the WordArt shape to Inflate.
2. Turn on automatic hyphenation.
3. Change the column width of the columns in the body of the newsletter to 2.2".
4. Add a vertical rule (line) between each column.
5. Change the style of the pull-quote (text box) to 'Colored Fill - Tan, Accent 6' (DRAWING TOOLS FORMAT tab | Shape Styles group).
6. Format the first paragraph with a drop cap.
7. Change the alignment of the paragraph containing the drop cap from left-aligned to justified.
8. Change the layout of the SmartArt graphic to Gear.
9. Use the Text Pane to add the text, Space Exploration, to the right shape in the SmartArt graphic.
10. If necessary, move the SmartArt graphic and the pull-quote so that they are positioned similarly to the ones in Figure 7–76.
11. Change the color of the page border to Dark Blue, Accent 3.
12. If requested by your instructor, change the name Reagis in the issue information line to your name.
13. If the newsletter flows to two pages, reduce the size of elements such as WordArt or pull-quote, or adjust spacing above or below paragraphs so that the newsletter fits on a single page. Make any other necessary adjustments to the newsletter.
14. Save the modified file with the file name, Apply 7-1 Meteor Shower Newsletter Modified.

Continued >

Apply Your Knowledge *continued*

15. Submit the revised newsletter in the format specified by your instructor.
16. When you use hyphenation to divide words at the end of a line, what are the accepted guidelines for dividing the words? (*Hint:* Use a search engine to search the text, end of line hyphenation.)

Extend Your Knowledge

Extend the skills you learned in this chapter and experiment with new skills. You may need to use Help to complete the assignment.

Adding a Equations to a Newsletter and Enhancing a Nameplate

Note: To complete this assignment, you will be required to use the Data Files for Students. Visit www.cengage.com/ct/studentdownload for detailed instructions or contact your instructor for information about accessing the required files.

Instructions: Run Word. Open the document, Extend 7-1 Mathletes Newsletter Draft, from the Data Files for Students. You will add equations to the newsletter, change the format of the WordArt, format the drop cap, adjust the hyphenation rules, move the page border closer to the text, clear tabs, and insert leader characters.

Perform the following tasks:

1. Use Help to learn about equations, WordArt options, borders, hyphenation, and tabs.
2. Insert the equations shown in Figure 7–77 in the newsletter in their appropriate locations. *Hint:* Use the 'Insert an Equation' button (INSERT tab | Symbols group).
3. Change the WordArt by adding at least two WordArt style text effects. Change the color of the WordArt text outline. Change the color of the WordArt text fill color.
4. Add a shape fill color to the text box surrounding the WordArt.
5. Add a drop cap to the first paragraph in the body of the newsletter. Change the number of lines to drop from three to two lines.

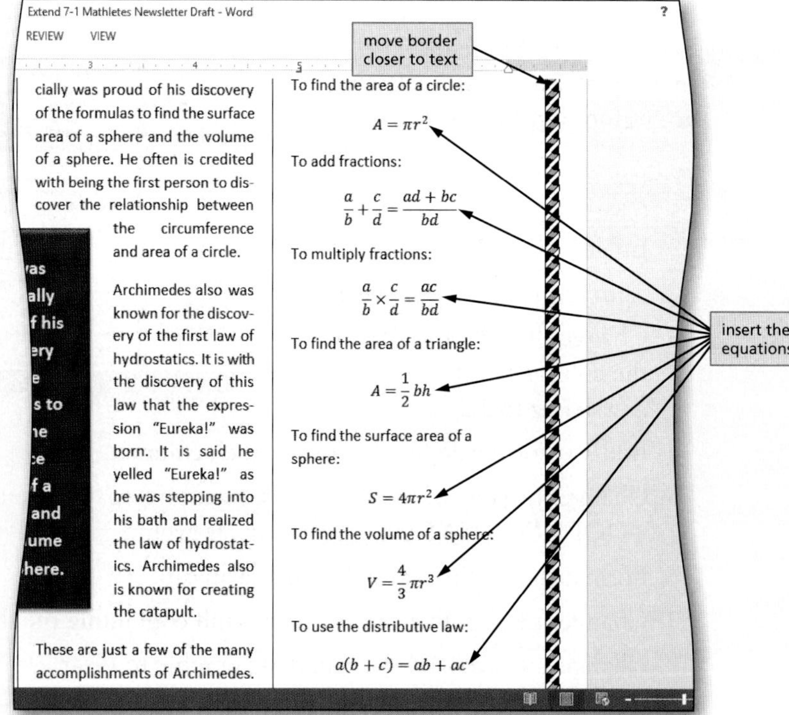

Figure 7–77

6. Change the hyphenation rules to limit consecutive hyphens to two.
7. Change the page border so that the border is closer to the text.
8. If the newsletter flows to two pages, reduce the size of elements such as WordArt or the pull-quote or the table, or adjust spacing above or below paragraphs so that the newsletter fits on a single page. Make any other necessary adjustments to the newsletter.
9. Clear the tabs in the issue information line in the nameplate. Use the Tabs dialog box to insert a right-aligned tab stop at the 6.5" mark. Fill the tab space with a leader character of your choice.

10. If requested by your instructor, change the name, Juniper, in the issue information line to your last name.
11. Submit the revised newsletter in the format specified by your instructor.
12. Which equations are predefined in Word? Which structures are available on the EQUATION TOOLS DESIGN tab? How do you change the alignment of an equation?

Analyze, Correct, Improve

Analyze a document, correct all errors, and improve it.

Formatting a Newsletter

Note: To complete this assignment, you will be required to use the Data Files for Students. Visit www.cengage.com/ct/studentdownload for detailed instructions or contact your instructor for information about accessing the required files.

Instructions: Run Word. Open the document, Analyze 7-1 Saddle Bits Newsletter Draft, from the Data Files for Students. The document is a newsletter whose elements are not formatted properly (Figure 7–78). You are to edit and format the WordArt, format the clip art image and columns, change tab stop alignment, change paragraph alignment, add a drop cap, format the pull-quote (text box), and add a border.

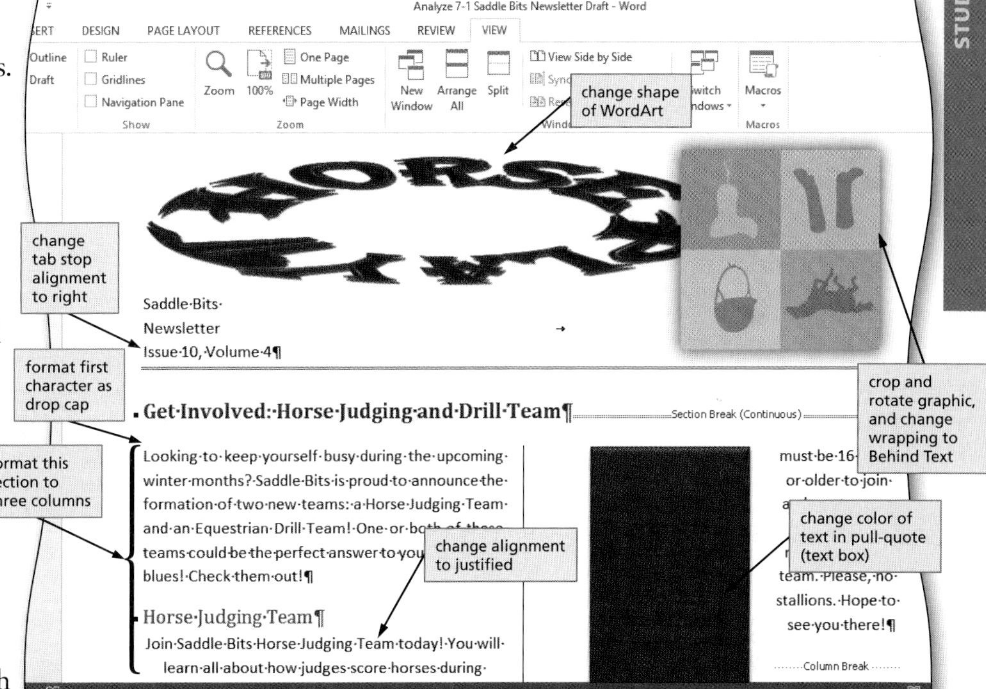

Figure 7–78

Perform the following tasks:

1. Correct In the newsletter, correct the following items:

a. Change the shape of the WordArt so that the text is more readable.
b. Format the clip art image in the nameplate to Behind Text.
c. Rotate the clip art image so it is upright and angled so that it fits the space. Adjust the location and size of the clip art image so that it has a pleasing appearance in the nameplate.
d. Crop the clip art image so that just the horse and boots show.
e. Change the alignment of the custom tab stop at the 7" mark in the issue information line from left-aligned to right-aligned.
f. Change the number of columns in the body of the newsletter from two to three.
g. Change the paragraphs in the Horse Judging Team and Equestrian Drill Team sections from centered to justified paragraph alignment.
h. Format the first letter in the first paragraph of text as a drop cap.
i. Change the color of the text in the pull-quote (text box) so that it is easier to read. Position the pull-quote between the first and second columns.

Continued >

Analyze, Correct, Improve *continued*

2. Improve Enhance the newsletter by adding color to the drop cap. Add an attractive art border around the edge of the newsletter. Do not use the default single line, black border. If the newsletter flows to two pages, reduce the size of elements such as WordArt or clip art or the pull-quote, or adjust spacing above or below paragraphs so that the newsletter fits on a single page. Make any other adjustments you deem appropriate to the newsletter. If requested by your instructor, change the stable name in the newsletter to your name. Save the modified document with the file name, Analyze 7-1 Saddle Bits Newsletter Modified, and then submit it in the format specified by your instructor.

3. In this assignment, you added an art border. Which border did you select and why?

In the Labs

Design and/or create a document using the guidelines, concepts, and skills presented in this chapter. Labs 1 and 2, which increase in difficulty, require you to create solutions based on what you learned in the chapter; Lab 3 requires you to create a solution, which uses cloud and web technologies, by learning and investigating on your own from general guidance.

Lab 1: Creating a Newsletter with a Pull-Quote (Text Box) and an Article on File

Note: To complete this assignment, you will be required to use the Data Files for Students. Visit www.cengage.com/ct/studentdownload for detailed instructions or contact your instructor for information about accessing the required files.

Problem: You are an editor of the newsletter, *Weekly Woofer*. The next edition is due out in one week (Figure 7–79). The text for the articles in the newsletter is in a file on the Data Files for Students. You need to create the nameplate and the text box for the pull-quote.

Perform the following tasks:

1. Change all margins to .75 inches. Depending on your printer, you may need different margin settings. Change the theme to Parallax.
2. Create the nameplate using the formats identified in Figure 7–79. Create the title using WordArt. Set the WordArt wrapping to Top and Bottom. If necessary, drag the bottom of the Word Art up to shorten the image. Set a right-aligned custom tab stop at the right margin. Search for and insert the clip art image (or a similar image). Resize the image to the size shown in the figure and apply the Beveled Oval, Black picture style to the image. Copy the image and flip the copied image horizontally. Format the images as Behind Text, rotate them, and then position them as shown.
3. Below the nameplate, enter the heading, Upcoming Events: Training, Shows, and More, as shown in the figure. Format the heading using the Heading 1 style. Change the spacing above this paragraph to 24 pt and the spacing after to 12 pt.
4. Create a continuous section break below the heading, Upcoming Events: Training, Shows, and More.
5. Format section 2 to three columns.
6. Insert the Lab 7-1 PAWS Article file, which is located on the Data Files for Students, in section 2 below the nameplate.
7. Format the newsletter according to Figure 7–79. Insert a column break before these headings: Shows and Dog of the Week. Columns should have a width of 2.1" with spacing of 0.35". Place a vertical rule between the columns.
8. If necessary, insert a continuous section break at the end of the document to balance the columns.

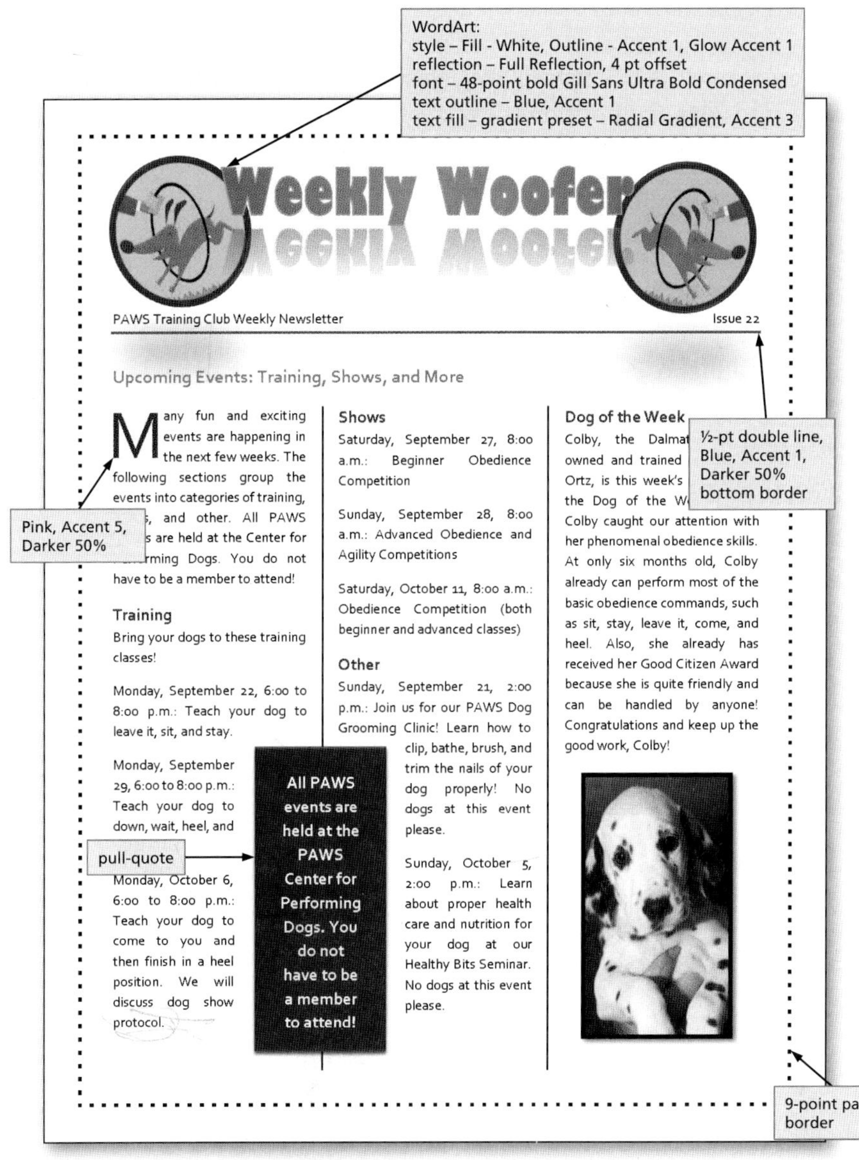

Figure 7–79

9. Format the subheads using the Heading 2 style.
10. Insert a text box using the Simple Text Box built-in text box. The text for the pull-quote is in the first paragraph of the article. Split the window. Use the split window to copy the text and then paste it in the text box. Remove the split window. Change the fill color (shape fill) of the text box to Black, Text 1, Lighter 15%. Resize the text box so that it is similar in size to Figure 7–79. Position the text box as shown in Figure 7–79.
11. Add the page border as shown in the figure.
12. If the document does not fit on a single page, adjust spacing above and below paragraphs.
13. If requested by your instructor, change the trainer name from Leonard Ortz to your name.
14. Save the document with Lab 7-1 PAWS Newsletter as the file name and then submit it in the format specified by your instructor.
15. This newsletter used a pull-quote. What other text in the newsletter could appear in the pull-quote?

Lab 2: Creating a Newsletter with a SmartArt Graphic and an Article on File

Note: To complete this assignment, you will be required to use the Data Files for Students. Visit www.cengage.com/ct/studentdownload for detailed instructions or contact your instructor for information about accessing the required files.

Problem: You are responsible for the weekly preparation of *Help Desk!*, a newsletter for college students. The next edition discusses how to search for a job online (Figure 7–80 on the next page). This article already has been prepared and is on the Data Files for Students. You need to create the nameplate, the SmartArt graphic, and the section at the bottom of the newsletter.

Perform the following tasks:

1. Change all margins to .75 inches. Depending on your printer, you may need different margin settings. Change the document theme to Slice.
2. Create the nameplate using the formats identified in Figure 7–80. Create the title using WordArt. Set a right-aligned custom tab stop at the right margin. Set the WordArt wrapping to Top and Bottom. If necessary, drag the bottom of the Word Art up to shorten the image.

Continued >

In the Labs *continued*

Search for and insert the clip art image (or a similar image). Resize the image as shown in the figure. Format the image as Behind Text and position the images as shown.

3. Below the nameplate, enter the heading, Search for a Job Online, as shown in the figure.
4. Create a continuous section break below the heading.
5. Format section 2 to two columns.
6. Insert the Lab 7-2 Help Desk Article file, which is located on the Data Files for Students, in section 2 below the nameplate.
7. Format the newsletter according to Figure 7–80. Columns should have a width of 3.33" with spacing of 0.35". Place a vertical rule between the columns.
8. Use Word's automatic hyphenation feature to hyphenate the document.
9. Insert a continuous section break at the end of the document to balance the columns.
10. In the next section, change the number of columns from two to one. Enter the text shown at the bottom of the newsletter.
11. Add the page border as shown in the figure.
12. Open a new document window and create the SmartArt graphic shown in Figure 7–80. Use the Radial Venn layout. Add the text shown in the figure (you will need to add shapes). Use the Office Clipboard to copy and paste the SmartArt graphic from the current window to the newsletter. Resize the pasted graphic as shown in the figure. Change the colors to Colorful Range - Accent Colors 2 to 3. Note that your graphic may look slightly different from the figure due to variations in the shape size.
13. If the document does not fit on a single page, adjust spacing above and below paragraphs.
14. If requested by your instructor, change the hall name from Bantam to your last name.
15. Save the newsletter using Lab 7-2 Help Desk Newsletter as the file name and submit it in the format specified by your instructor.
16. How many sections are in this newsletter? How many columns are in each section? If you wanted to add a second page to this newsletter, what type of section break would appear at the end of the first page?

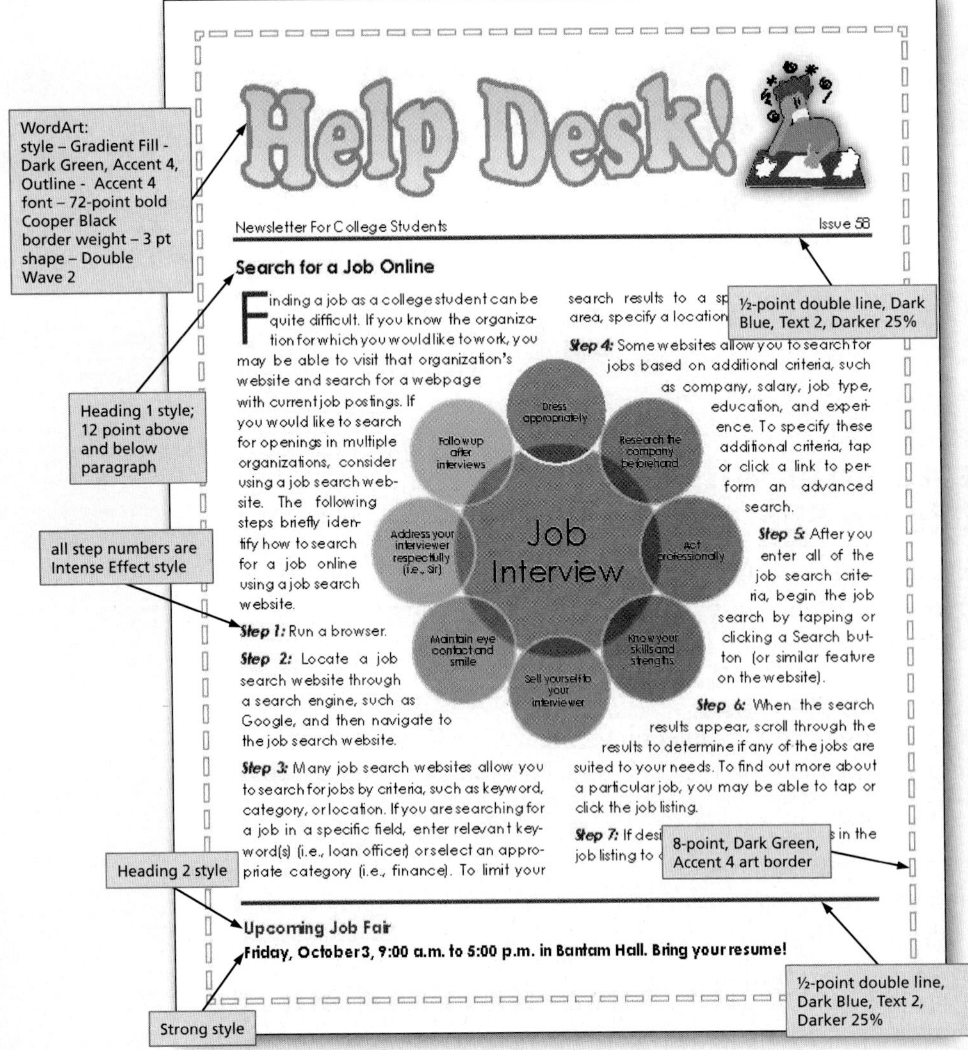

Figure 7–80

Lab 3: Expand Your World: Cloud and Web Technologies

Using Windows Essentials

Problem: You have heard that Windows Essentials includes some useful programs, so you decide to learn about it, download it, and use its programs.

Note: You may be required to use your Microsoft account to complete this assignment. If you do not have a Microsoft account and do not want to create one, read the assignment without performing the instructions.

Instructions: Perform the following tasks:

1. Run a browser. Search for the text, Windows Essentials, using a search engine. Tap or click a link to learn about Windows Essentials.
2. Navigate to the website to download Windows Essentials (Figure 7–81) and then follow the instructions to download Windows Essentials.
3. One at a time, run each program included with Windows Essentials. Browse through the features and functions of each program.
4. What programs are included with Windows Essentials? What is the purpose of each program? Which programs will you use and why? Which programs required you to sign in to your Microsoft account?

Figure 7–81

Consider This: Your Turn

Apply your creative thinking and problem solving skills to design and implement a solution.

Note: To complete these assignments, you may be required to use the Data Files for Students. Visit www.cengage.com/ct/studentdownload for detailed instructions or contact your instructor for information about accessing the required files.

1: Create a Newsletter about E-Books

Personal

Part 1: As a part-time assistant in the library at your school, you have been assigned the task of creating a newsletter called Bookmark It, which will be distributed to all enrolled students. The article in Issue 54 of the Library Newsletter covers e-books. The text for the article is in a file called Your Turn 7-1 E-Books Draft on the Data Files for Students.

The newsletter should contain at least two of these graphical elements: a clip art image, a SmartArt graphic, a pull-quote, or a table. Enhance the newsletter with a drop cap, WordArt, color, ruling lines, and a page border. Be sure to use appropriate desktop publishing elements, including a nameplate, columns of text, balanced columns, and a variety of font sizes, font colors, and shading. Use the concepts and techniques presented in this chapter to create and format the newsletter. Be sure to check spelling and grammar of the finished newsletter. Submit your assignment in the format specified by your instructor.

Part 2: You made several decisions while creating the newsletter in this assignment: how to organize and format the nameplate (location, content, formats, arrangement of text and graphics, ruling lines, etc.), which two graphics to use (clip art, SmartArt graphic, text box, or table), and how to organize and format the body copy (columns, formats, headings and subheads, color, vertical rules, etc.). What was the rationale behind each of these decisions? When you proofread the document, what further revisions did you make and why?

Continued >

Consider This: Your Turn *continued*

2: Create a Newsletter about Safe Web Browsing

Professional

Part 1: As a part-time employee at JD Systems Technology, you have been asked to create a newsletter called Megabits, which is placed in the office lobby and on the company's website. The article in Issue 11 of the Technology Center Newsletter covers web browsing safety tips. The text for the article is in a file called Your Turn 7-2 Web Browsing Draft on the Data Files for Students.

The newsletter should contain at least two of these graphical elements: a clip art image, a SmartArt graphic, a pull-quote, or a table. Enhance the newsletter with a drop cap, WordArt, color, ruling lines, and a page border. Be sure to use appropriate desktop publishing elements, including a nameplate, columns of text, balanced columns, and a variety of font sizes, font colors, and shading. Use the concepts and techniques presented in this chapter to create and format the newsletter. Be sure to check spelling and grammar of the finished newsletter. Submit your assignment in the format specified by your instructor.

Part 2: You made several decisions while creating the newsletter in this assignment: how to organize and format the nameplate (location, content, formats, arrangement of text and graphics, ruling lines, etc.), which two graphics to use (clip art, SmartArt graphic, text box, or table), and how to organize and format the body copy (columns, formats, headings and subheads, color, vertical rules, etc.). What was the rationale behind each of these decisions? When you proofread the document, what further revisions did you make and why?

3: Create a Review Newsletter

Research and Collaboration

Part 1: The local newspaper has a two-page newsletter in its Wednesday edition each week that reviews current movies, live performances, books, restaurants, and local events. You and two other team members have been assigned the task of designing and writing the next newsletter. The newsletter should have a feature article that contains at least three separate reviews. One column of the newsletter should contain community calendar announcements.

Each team member should independently see or rent a current movie, watch a live performance, read a book, dine at a local restaurant, or attend a local event and then write at least a three paragraph review. Then, the team should meet as a group to combine all the reviews into a single article. As a team, compose the newsletter. The newsletter should contain at least one of each of these graphical elements: a clip art image, a SmartArt graphic, and a pull-quote. Enhance the newsletter with a drop cap, WordArt, color, ruling lines, and a page border. Be sure to use appropriate desktop publishing elements, including a nameplate, columns of text, balanced columns, and a variety of font sizes, font colors, and shading. Use the concepts and techniques presented in this chapter to create and format the newsletter. Be sure to check spelling and grammar of the finished newsletter. Submit your assignment in the format specified by your instructor.

Part 2: You made several decisions while creating the newsletter in this assignment: text to use, how to organize and format the nameplate (location, content, formats, arrangement of text and graphics, ruling lines, etc.), which graphics to use, and how to organize and format the body copy (columns, formats, headings and subheads, color, vertical rules, etc.). What was the rationale behind each of these decisions? When you proofread the document, what further revisions did you make and why?

Learn Online

Reinforce what you learned in this chapter with games, exercises, training, and many other online activities and resources.

Student Companion Site Reinforcement activities and resources are available at no additional cost on www.cengagebrain.com. Visit www.cengage.com/ct/studentdownload for detailed instructions about accessing the resources available at the Student Companion Site.

SAM Put your skills into practice with SAM! If you have a SAM account, go to www.cengage.com/sam2013 to access SAM assignments for this chapter.

8 Using Document Collaboration, Integration, and Charting Tools

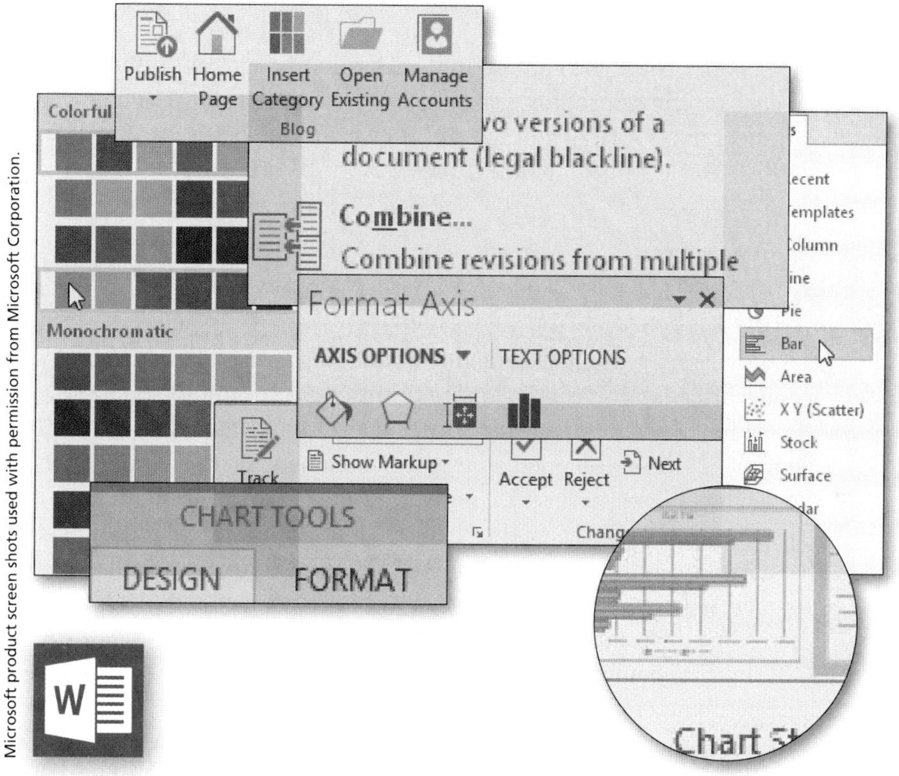

Objectives

You will have mastered the material in this chapter when you can:

- Insert, edit, view, and delete comments
- Track changes
- Review tracked changes
- Compare documents
- Combine documents
- Link an Excel worksheet to a Word document
- Break a link
- Create a chart in Word
- Format a Word chart
- View and scroll through side-by-side documents
- Create a new document for a blog post
- Insert a quick table
- Publish a blog post

8 Using Document Collaboration, Integration, and Charting Tools

Introduction

Word provides the capability for users to work with other users, or **collaborate**, on a document. For example, you can show edits made to a document so that others can review the edits. You also can merge edits from multiple users or compare two documents to determine the differences between them.

From Word, you can interact with other programs and incorporate the data and objects from those programs in a Word document. For example, you can link an Excel worksheet in a Word document or publish a blog post from Word. You also use the charting features of Microsoft Office 2013 in Word.

Project — Memo with Chart

A memo is an informal document that businesses use to correspond with others. Memos often are internal to an organization, for example, to employees or coworkers.

The project in this chapter uses Word to produce the memo shown in Figure 8–1. First, you open an existing document that contains the memo and the Word table. Next, you insert comments and edit the document, showing the changes so that other users can review the changes. The changes appear on the screen with options that allow the author of the document to accept or reject the changes and delete the comments. Then, you chart the Word table using charting features available in several Microsoft Office applications.

In this chapter, you also learn how to link an Excel worksheet to a Word document and create a document for a blog post.

If you are using your finger on a touch screen and are having difficulty completing the steps in this chapter, consider using a stylus. Many people find it easier to be precise with a stylus than with a finger. In addition, with a stylus you see the pointer. If you still are having trouble completing the steps with a stylus, try using a mouse.

INTEROFFICE MEMORANDUM

TO: MOLLY PADRO
FROM: ZACH ANDERSON
SUBJECT: FUND-RAISING RESULTS
DATE: SEPTEMBER 19, 2014

Our August fund-raiser was a huge success. I would like to thank you and your staff for all of the help before and during the event. Below are a table and chart that summarize the results for our fund-raising efforts this year. In the next few days, you will see a post on our blog, indicating key dates associated with our next fund-raising event.

YTD Fund-Raising Results

Fund-Raising Category	May Event	August Event
Bake Sale	$ 498.50	$ 665.00
Donations	$ 2,200.25	$ 3,241.75
Food Booth	$ 956.25	$ 1,064.50
Gate	$ 4,125.50	$ 5,503.00
Raffle	$ 515.00	$ 795.00
Silent Auction	$ 1,058.95	$ 1,125.51
Vendors	$ 5,025.00	$ 6,470.50

Word table

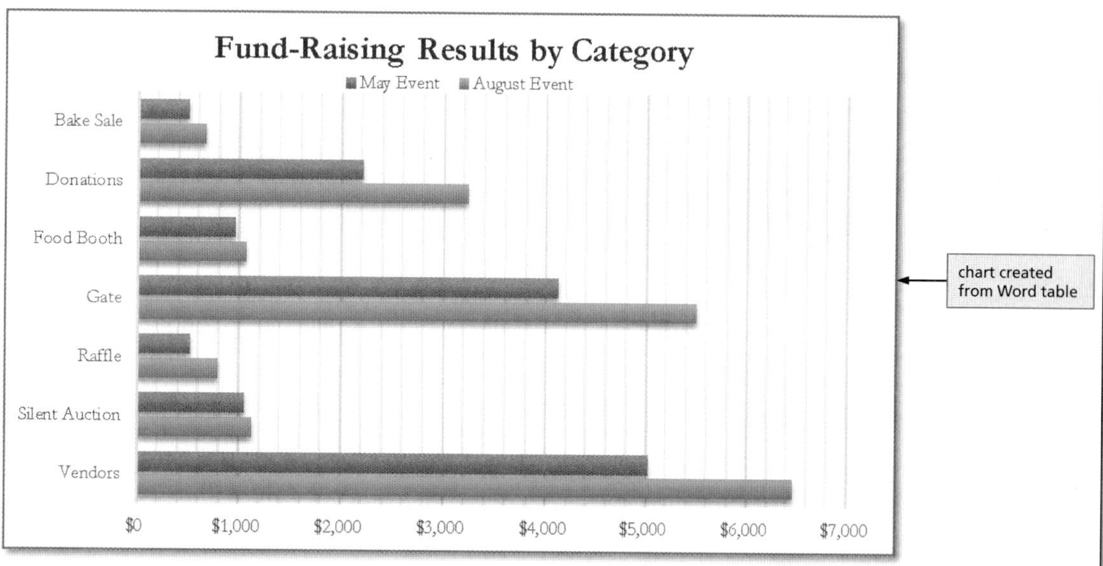

Figure 8–1

Roadmap

In this chapter, you will learn how to create the document shown in Figure 8–1 on the previous page. The following roadmap identifies general activities you will perform as you progress through this chapter:

1. INSERT COMMENTS AND TRACK CHANGES in the memo with the table.
2. REVIEW the COMMENTS AND TRACKED CHANGES.
3. LINK an EXCEL WORKSHEET TO a WORD DOCUMENT.
4. CHART a WORD TABLE using Word's CHART TOOLS tab.
5. CREATE AND PUBLISH a BLOG POST.

At the beginning of step instructions throughout the chapter, you will see an abbreviated form of this roadmap. The abbreviated roadmap uses colors to indicate chapter progress: gray means the chapter is beyond that activity, blue means the task being shown is covered in that activity, and black means that activity is yet to be covered. For example, the following abbreviated roadmap indicates the chapter would be showing a task in the 2 REVIEW COMMENTS & TRACKED CHANGES activity.

1 INSERT COMMENTS & TRACK CHANGES | 2 REVIEW COMMENTS & TRACKED CHANGES

3 LINK EXCEL WORKSHEET TO WORD DOCUMENT | 4 CHART WORD TABLE | 5 CREATE & PUBLISH BLOG POST

Use the abbreviated roadmap as a progress guide while you read or step through the instructions in this chapter.

One of the few differences between Windows 7 and Windows 8 occurs in the steps to run Word. If you are using Windows 7, click the Start button, type **Word** in the 'Search programs and files' box, click Word 2013, and then, if necessary, maximize the Word window. For a summary of the steps to run Word in Windows 7, refer to the Quick Reference located at the back of this book.

To Run Word and Change Word Settings

If you are using a computer to step through the project in this chapter and you want your screens to match the figures in this book, you should change your screen's resolution to 1366 × 768. For information about how to change a computer's resolution, refer to the Office and Windows chapter at the beginning of this book.

The following steps run Word, display formatting marks, and change the zoom to page width.

1. Scroll the Start screen for a Word 2013 tile. If your Start screen contains a Word 2013 tile, tap or click it to run Word and then proceed to Step 5; if the Start screen does not contain the Word 2013 tile, proceed to the next step to search for the Word app.
2. Swipe in from the right edge of the screen or point to the upper-right corner of the screen to display the Charms bar and then tap or click the Search charm on the Charms bar to display the Search menu.
3. Type **Word** as the search text in the Search box and watch the search results appear in the Apps list.
4. Tap or click Word 2013 in the search results to run Word.
5. Tap or click the Blank document thumbnail on the Word start screen to create a blank document and display it in the Word window.
6. If the Word window is not maximized, tap or click the Maximize button on its title bar to maximize the window.
7. If the Print Layout button on the status bar is not selected, tap or click it so that your screen is in Print Layout view.

8 If the 'Show/Hide ¶' button (HOME tab | Paragraph group) is not selected already, tap or click it to display formatting marks on the screen.

9 To display the page the same width as the document window, if necessary, tap or click the Page Width button (VIEW tab | Zoom group).

Reviewing a Document

Word provides many tools that allow users to **collaborate** on a document. One set of collaboration tools within Word allows you to track changes in a document and review the changes. That is, one computer user can create a document and another user(s) can make changes and insert comments in the same document. Those changes then appear on the screen with options that allow the originator (author) to accept or reject the changes and delete the comments. With another collaboration tool, you can compare and/or merge two or more documents to determine the differences between them.

To illustrate Word collaboration tools, this section follows these general steps:

1. Open a document to be reviewed.
2. Insert comments in the document for the originator (author).
3. Track changes in the document.
4. View and delete the comments.
5. Accept and reject the tracked changes. For illustration purposes, you assume the role of originator (author) of the document in this step.
6. Compare the reviewed document to the original to view the differences.
7. Combine the original document with the reviewed document and with another reviewer's suggestions.

To Open a Document and Save It with a New File Name

Assume your coworker has created a draft of a memo and is sending it to you for review. The file, called Fund-Raising Results Memo Draft, is located on the Data Files for Students. Visit www.cengage.com/ct/studentdownload for detailed instructions or contact your instructor for information about accessing the required files. To preserve the original memo, you save the open document with a new file name. The following steps save an open document with a new file name.

1 Tap or click FILE on the ribbon to open the Backstage view and then, if necessary, tap or click the Open tab to display the Open gallery.

2 Navigate to the Data Files for Students and then open the file called Fund-Raising Results Memo Draft.

3 Tap or click FILE on the ribbon to open the Backstage view and then tap or click the Save As tab to display the Save As gallery.

4 To save on a hard disk or other storage media on your computer, proceed to Step 4a. To save on SkyDrive, proceed to Step 4b.

4a Tap or click Computer in the left pane, if necessary, to display options in the right pane related to saving on your computer.

BTW
The Ribbon and Screen Resolution
Word may change how the groups and buttons within the groups appear on the ribbon, depending on the computer's screen resolution. Thus, your ribbon may look different from the ones in this book if you are using a screen resolution other than 1366 × 768.

4b Tap or click SkyDrive in the left pane to display SkyDrive saving options or a Sign In button. If your screen displays a Sign In button, tap or click it and then sign in to SkyDrive.

5 Tap or click the Browse button in the right pane to display the Save As dialog box associated with the selected save location (i.e., Computer or SkyDrive).

6 Type **`Fund-Raising Results Memo with Comments and Tracked Changes`** in the File name box to change the file name. Do not press the ENTER key after typing the file name because you do not want to close the dialog box at this time.

7 Navigate to the desired save location (in this case, the Word folder in the CIS 101 folder [or your class folder] on your computer or SkyDrive).

8 Tap or click the Save button (Save As dialog box) to save the file in the selected folder on the selected save location with the entered file name.

If requested by your instructor, change the name, Molly Padro, in the memo to your name.

To Insert a Comment

1 INSERT COMMENTS & TRACK CHANGES | **2 REVIEW COMMENTS & TRACKED CHANGES**
3 LINK EXCEL WORKSHEET TO WORD DOCUMENT | **4 CHART WORD TABLE** | **5 CREATE & PUBLISH BLOG POST**

Reviewers often use comments to communicate suggestions, tips, and other messages to the author of a document. A **comment** is a note inserted in a document. Comments do not affect the text of the document.

After reading through the memo, you have two comments for the originator (author) of the document. The following steps insert a comment in the document. ***Why?*** *You insert a comment that requests that the author insert a graph in the document.*

1

- Position the insertion point at the location where the comment should be located (in this case, in the third sentence of the memo immediately to the left of the t in the word, table).
- Display the REVIEW tab (Figure 8–2).
- If the 'Display for Review' box (REVIEW tab | Tracking group) does not show All Markup, tap or click the 'Display for Review' arrow (REVIEW tab | Tracking group) and then tap or click All Markup on the Display for Review menu to instruct Word to display the document with all proposed edits shown as markup.

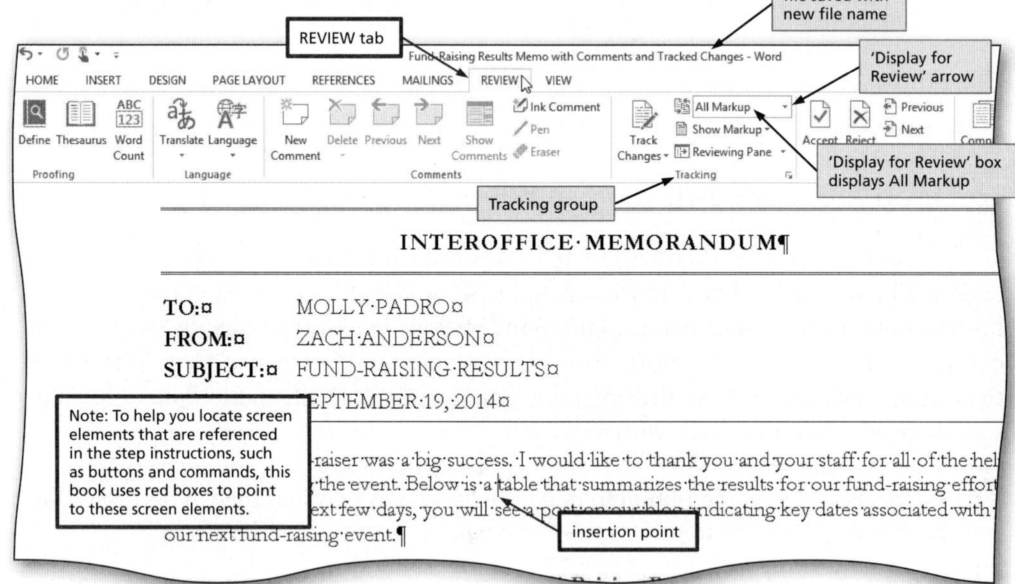

Figure 8–2

Q&A What are the other Display for Review options?
If you tap or click the 'Display for Review' arrow, several options appear. Simple Markup means Word incorporates proposed changes in the document and places a vertical line near the margin of the line containing the proposed change or a comment balloon at the location of a user comment. All Markup means that all proposed changes are highlighted and all comments appear in full. No Markup shows the proposed edits as part of the final document, instead of as markup. Original shows the document before changes.

2

- Tap or click the 'Insert a Comment' button (REVIEW tab | Comments group) to display a comment balloon in the markup area in the document window and place comment marks around the commented text in the document window.
- Change the zoom so that the entire document and markup area are visible in the document window (Figure 8–3).

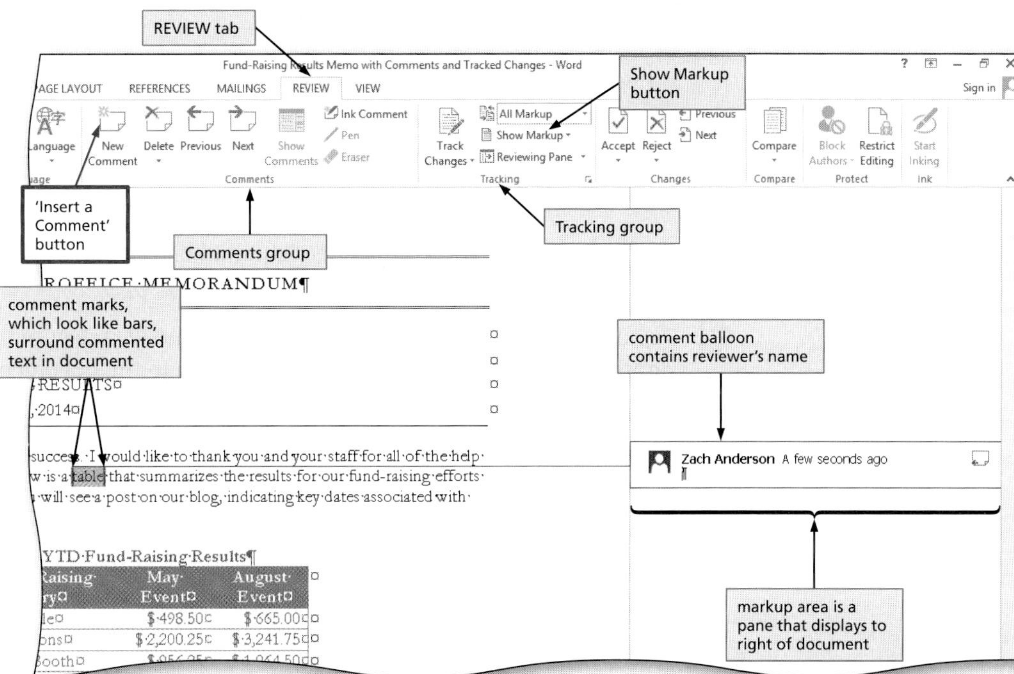

Figure 8–3

Q&A

What if the markup area does not appear with the comment balloon?

The balloons setting has been turned off. Tap or click the Show Markup button (REVIEW tab | Tracking group) and then if a check mark does not appear to the left of Comments on the Show Markup menu, tap or click Comments. If comments still do not appear, tap or click the Show Markup button again, tap or point to Balloons on the Show Markup menu, and then tap or click 'Show Only Comments and Formatting in Balloons' on the Balloons submenu, which is the default setting.

Why do comment marks surround selected text?

A comment is associated with text. If you do not select text on which you wish to comment, Word automatically selects the text to the right or left of the insertion point for the comment.

3

- In the comment balloon, type the following comment text: **Add a graph of the data below the table.**
- If necessary, scroll to the right so that the entire comment is visible on the screen (Figure 8–4).

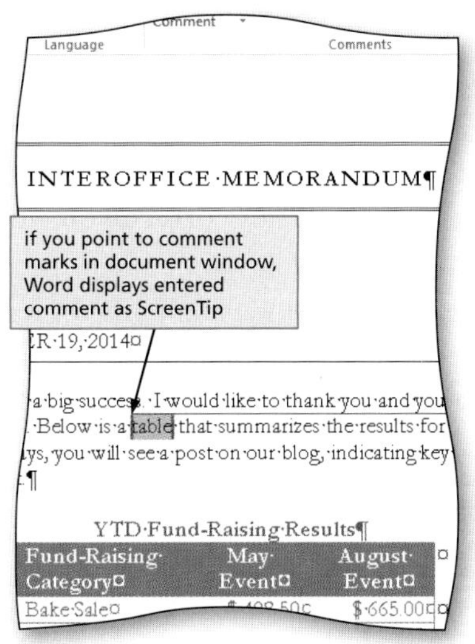

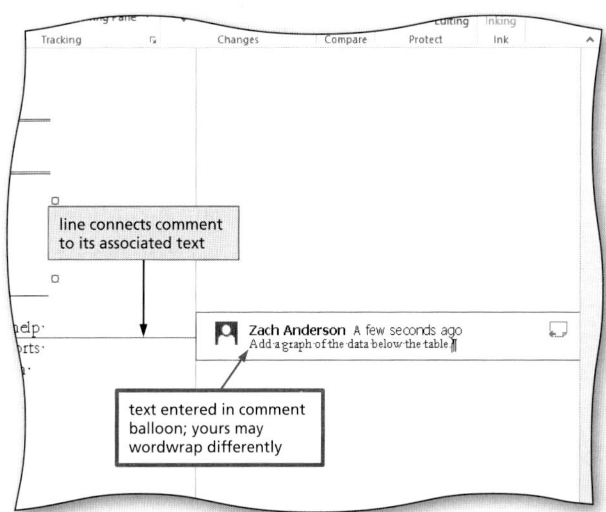

Figure 8–4

Other Ways

1. Press CTRL+ALT+M

BTW
Touch Screen Differences
The Office and Windows interfaces may vary if you are using a touch screen. For this reason, you might notice that the function or appearance of your touch screen differs slightly from this chapter's presentation.

To Insert Another Comment

The second comment you want to insert in the document is to request that the blog post also contain a calendar. Because you want the comment associated with several words, you select the text before inserting the comment. The following steps insert another comment in the document.

1. Select the text where the comment should be located (in this case, the text, post on our blog, in the last sentence of the memo).
2. Tap or click the 'Insert a Comment' button (REVIEW tab | Comments group) to display another comment balloon in the markup area in the document window.
3. In the new comment balloon, type the following comment text: **`Suggest posting a calendar on the blog.`** (Figure 8–5).

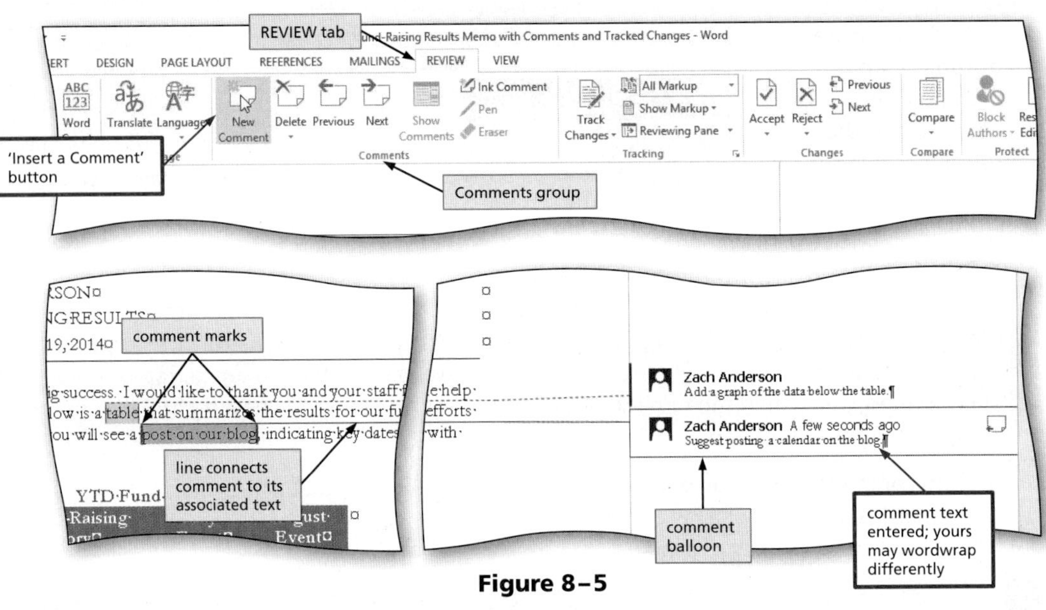

Figure 8–5

To Change Reviewer Information

Word uses predefined settings for the reviewer's initials and/or name that appears in the document window, the comment balloon, and the Reviewing task pane. If the reviewer's name or initials are not correct, you would change them by performing the following steps.

1a. Tap or click the Change Tracking Options Dialog Box Launcher (REVIEW tab | Tracking group) to display the Track Changes Options dialog box. Tap or click the 'Change User Name' button (Track Changes Options dialog box) to display the Word Options dialog box.

or

1b. Open the Backstage view and then tap or click Options to display the Word Options dialog box. If necessary, tap or click General in the left pane.

2. Enter the correct name in the User name text box (Word Options dialog box), and enter the correct initials in the Initials text box.

3. Tap or click the OK button to change the reviewer information. If necessary, tap or click the OK button in the Track Changes Options dialog box.

To Edit a Comment in a Comment Balloon

You modify comments in a comment balloon by tapping or clicking inside the comment balloon and editing the same way you edit text in the document window. In this project, you change the word, graph, to the word, chart, in the first comment. The following steps edit a comment in a balloon.

BTW
Q&As
For a complete list of the Q&As found in many of the step-by-step sequences in this book, visit the Q&A resource on the Student Companion Site located on www.cengagebrain.com. For detailed instructions about accessing available resources, visit www.cengage.com/ct/studentdownload or contact your instructor for information about accessing the required files.

1 Tap or click the first comment balloon to select it.

Q&A How can I tell if a comment is selected?
A selected comment appears surrounded by a rectangle and contains a Reply button to the right of the comment.

2 Position the insertion point at the location of the text to edit (in this case, to the left of the g in graph in the first comment) (Figure 8–6).

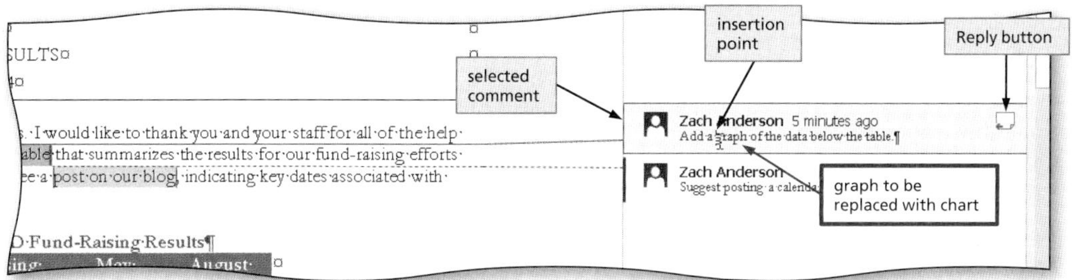

Figure 8–6

3 Replace the word, graph, with the word, chart, to edit the comment (shown in Figure 8–7).

To Reply to a Comment

1 INSERT COMMENTS & TRACK CHANGES | 2 REVIEW COMMENTS & TRACKED CHANGES
3 LINK EXCEL WORKSHEET TO WORD DOCUMENT | 4 CHART WORD TABLE | 5 CREATE & PUBLISH BLOG POST

Sometimes, you want to reply to an existing comment. ***Why?*** *You may want to respond to a question by another reviewer or provide additional information to a previous comment you inserted.* The following steps reply to the first comment you inserted in the document.

1

- If necessary, tap or click the comment to which you wish to reply so that the comment is selected (in this case, the first comment).

2

- Tap or click the Reply button in the selected comment to display a reply comment for the selected comment.

3

- In the new indented comment, type the following comment text: `Suggest using horizontal bars to plot the categories.` (Figure 8–7).

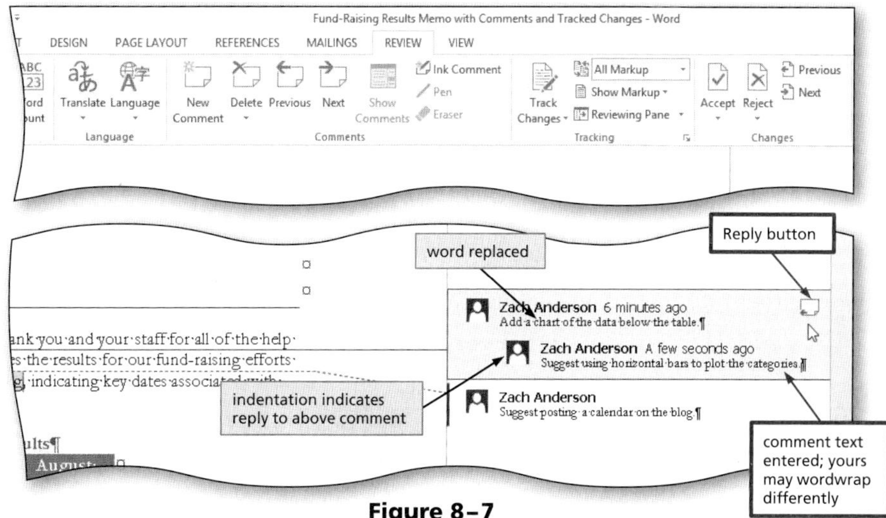

Figure 8–7

Other Ways

1. Tap or click 'Insert a Comment' button (REVIEW tab | Comments group)
2. Press CTRL+ALT+M

To Customize the Status Bar

1 INSERT COMMENTS & TRACK CHANGES | 2 REVIEW COMMENTS & TRACKED CHANGES
3 LINK EXCEL WORKSHEET TO WORD DOCUMENT | 4 CHART WORD TABLE | 5 CREATE & PUBLISH BLOG POST

You can customize the items that appear on the status bar. Recall that the status bar presents information about a document, the progress of current tasks, the status of certain commands and keys, and controls for viewing. Some indicators and buttons appear and disappear as you type text or perform certain commands. Others remain on the status bar at all times.

The following steps customize the status bar to show the Track Changes indicator. ***Why?*** *The TRACK CHANGES indicator does not appear by default on the status bar.*

- If the status bar does not show a desired item (in this case, the TRACK CHANGES indicator), press and hold or right-click anywhere on the status bar to display the Customize Status Bar menu.

2

- Tap or click the item on the Customize Status Bar menu that you want to show (in this case, Track Changes) to place a check mark beside the item, which also immediately may show as an indicator on the status bar (Figure 8–8).

Q&A Can I show or hide any of the items listed on the Customize Status Bar menu?
Yes, tap or click the item to display or remove its check mark.

- Tap or click anywhere outside of the Customize Status Bar menu or press the ESC key to remove the menu from the screen.

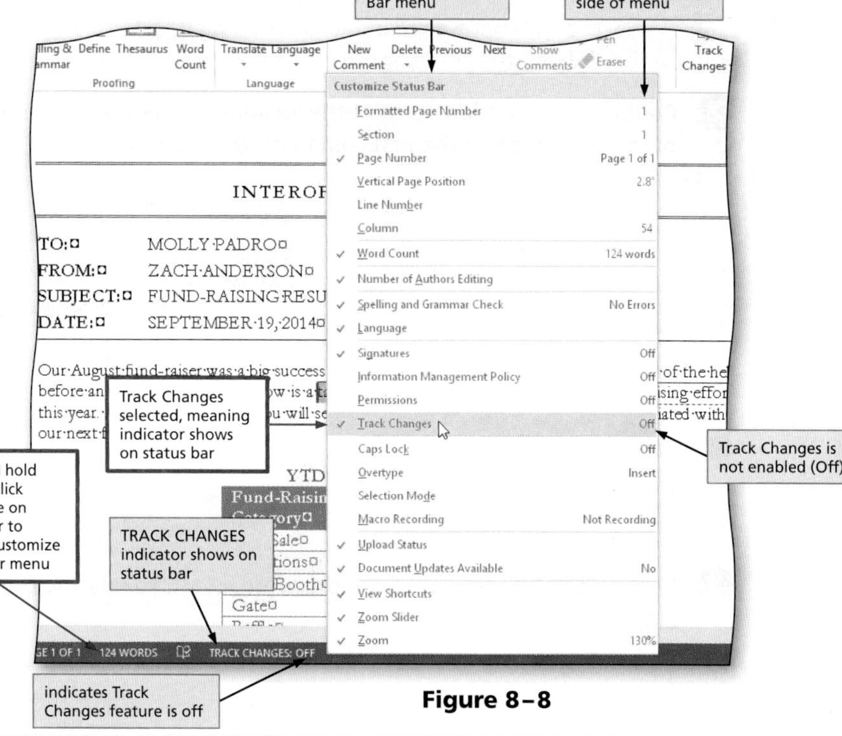

Figure 8–8

To Enable Tracked Changes

1 INSERT COMMENTS & TRACK CHANGES | 2 REVIEW COMMENTS & TRACKED CHANGES
3 LINK EXCEL WORKSHEET TO WORD DOCUMENT | 4 CHART WORD TABLE | 5 CREATE & PUBLISH BLOG POST

When you edit a document that has the track changes feature enabled, Word marks all text or graphics that you insert, delete, or modify and refers to the revisions as **markups** or **revision marks**. An author can identify the changes a reviewer has made by looking at the markups in a document. The author also has the ability to accept or reject any change that a reviewer has made to a document.

The following step enables tracked changes. ***Why?*** *To track changes in a document, you must enable (turn on) the track changes feature.*

- If the TRACK CHANGES indicator on the status bar shows that the track changes feature is off, tap or click the TRACK CHANGES indicator on the status bar to enable the track changes feature (Figure 8–9).

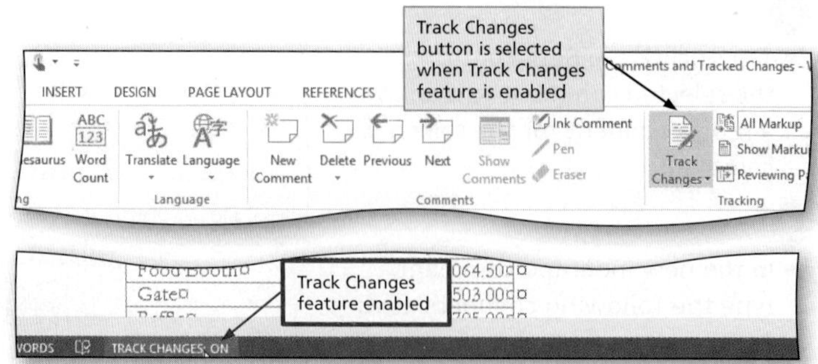

Figure 8–9

Other Ways

1. Tap or click Track Changes button (REVIEW tab | Tracking group)
2. Tap or click Track Changes arrow (REVIEW tab | Tracking group), tap or click Track Changes
3. Press CTRL+SHIFT+E

To Track Changes

You have four suggested changes for the current document:

1. Insert the words, and chart, after the word, table, in the third sentence so that it reads: ... a table and chart that ...
2. Delete the letter, s, at the end of the word, summarizes.
3. Insert the word, upcoming, before the word, next, in the last sentence so that it reads: ... our upcoming next fund-raising event.
4. Change the word, big, to the word, huge, in the first sentence so that it reads: ... a huge success.

The following steps track these changes as you enter them in the document. ***Why?*** *You want edits you make to the document to show so that others can review the edits.*

- Position the insertion point immediately to the left of the word, that, in the third sentence of the memo to position the insertion point at the location for the tracked change.
- Type **and chart** and then press the SPACEBAR to insert the typed text as a tracked change (Figure 8–10).

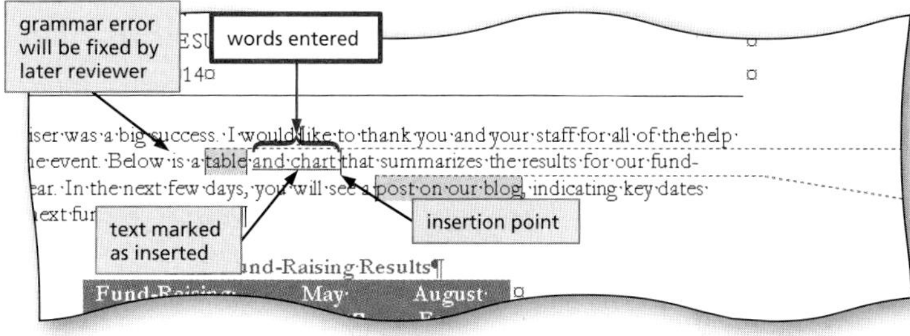

Figure 8–10

Q&A Why is the inserted text in color and underlined?
When the track changes feature is enabled, Word marks (signals) all text inserts by underlining them and changing their color, and marks all deletions by striking through them and changing their color.

When I scroll left, I see a vertical bar in the margin. What is the bar?
The bar is called a changed line (shown in Figure 8–16 on page WD 486), which indicates a tracked change is on the line to the right of the bar.

- In the same sentence, delete the s at the end of the word, summarizes (so that it reads, summarize), to mark the letter for deletion (Figure 8–11).

Figure 8–11

- In the next sentence, position the insertion point immediately to the left of the word, next. Type **upcoming** and then press the SPACEBAR to insert the typed text as a tracked change.
- In the first sentence, double-tap or double-click the word, big, to select it.
- Type **huge** as the replacement text, which tracks a deletion and an insertion change (Figure 8–12).

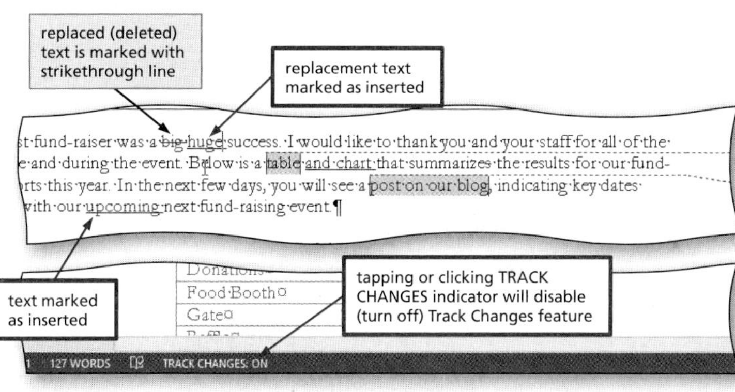

Figure 8–12

Q&A Can I see the name of the person who tracked a change?
If you are using a mouse, you can point to a tracked change in the document window; Word then will display a ScreenTip that identifies the reviewer's name and the type of change made by that reviewer.

To Change How Markups and Comments Are Displayed

The tracked changes entered in the previous steps appeared inline instead of in markup balloons. Inline means that the inserts are underlined and the deletions are shown as strikethroughs. The default Word setting displays comments and formatting changes in balloons and all other changes inline. If you wanted all changes and comments to appear in balloons or all changes and comments to appear inline, you would perform the following steps.

1. Tap or click the Show Markup button (REVIEW tab | Tracking group) to display the Show Markup menu and then tap or point to Balloons on the Show Markup menu.
2. If you want all revisions and comments to appear in balloons, tap or click 'Show Revisions in Balloons' on the Balloons submenu. If you want all revisions and comments to appear inline, tap or click 'Show All Revisions Inline' on the Balloons submenu. If you want to use the default Word setting, tap or click 'Show Only Comments and Formatting in Balloons' on the Balloons submenu.

To Disable Tracked Changes

When you have finished tracking changes, you should disable (turn off) the track changes feature so that Word stops marking your revisions. You follow the same steps to disable tracked changes as you did to enable them; that is, the indicator or button or keyboard shortcut functions as a toggle, turning the track changes feature on or off each time the command is issued. The following step disables tracked changes.

1 To turn the track changes feature off, tap or click the TRACK CHANGES indicator on the status bar (shown in Figure 8–12 on the previous page), or tap or click the Track Changes button (REVIEW tab | Tracking group), or press CTRL+SHIFT+E.

To Use the Reviewing Task Pane

1 INSERT COMMENTS & TRACK CHANGES | 2 REVIEW COMMENTS & TRACKED CHANGES
3 LINK EXCEL WORKSHEET TO WORD DOCUMENT | 4 CHART WORD TABLE | 5 CREATE & PUBLISH BLOG POST

Word provides a Reviewing task pane that can be displayed either at the left edge (vertically) or the bottom (horizontally) of the screen. ***Why?*** *As an alternative to reading through tracked changes in the document window and comment balloons in the markup area, some users prefer to view tracked changes and comments in the Reviewing task pane.* The following steps display the Reviewing task pane on the screen.

- Tap or click the Reviewing Pane arrow (REVIEW tab | Tracking group) to display the Reviewing Pane menu (Figure 8–13).

- Tap or click 'Reviewing Pane Vertical' on the Reviewing Pane menu to display the Reviewing task pane on the left side of the Word window.

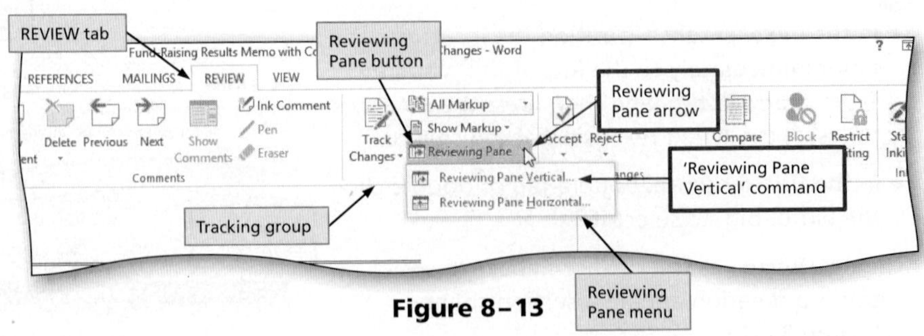

Figure 8–13

Q&A What if I tap or click the Reviewing Pane button instead of the button arrow?
Word displays the Reviewing task pane in its most recent location, that is, either vertically on the left side of the screen or horizontally on the bottom of the screen.

3

- Tap or click the Show Markup button (REVIEW tab | Tracking group) to display the Show Markup menu.
- Tap or point to Balloons on the Show Markup menu to display the Balloons submenu (Figure 8–14).

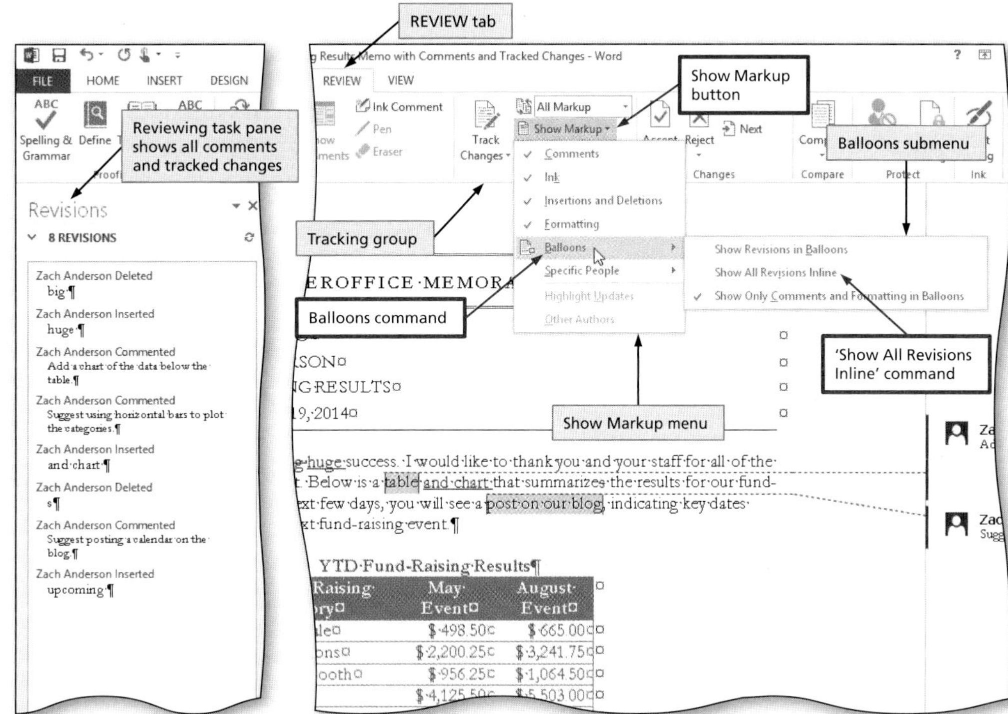

Figure 8–14

Q&A Why display the Balloons submenu?
Because the Reviewing task pane shows all comments, you do not need the markup area to display comment balloons. Thus, you will display all revisions inline.

4

- Tap or click 'Show All Revisions Inline' on the Balloons submenu to remove the markup area from the Word window and place all markups inline (Figure 8–15).

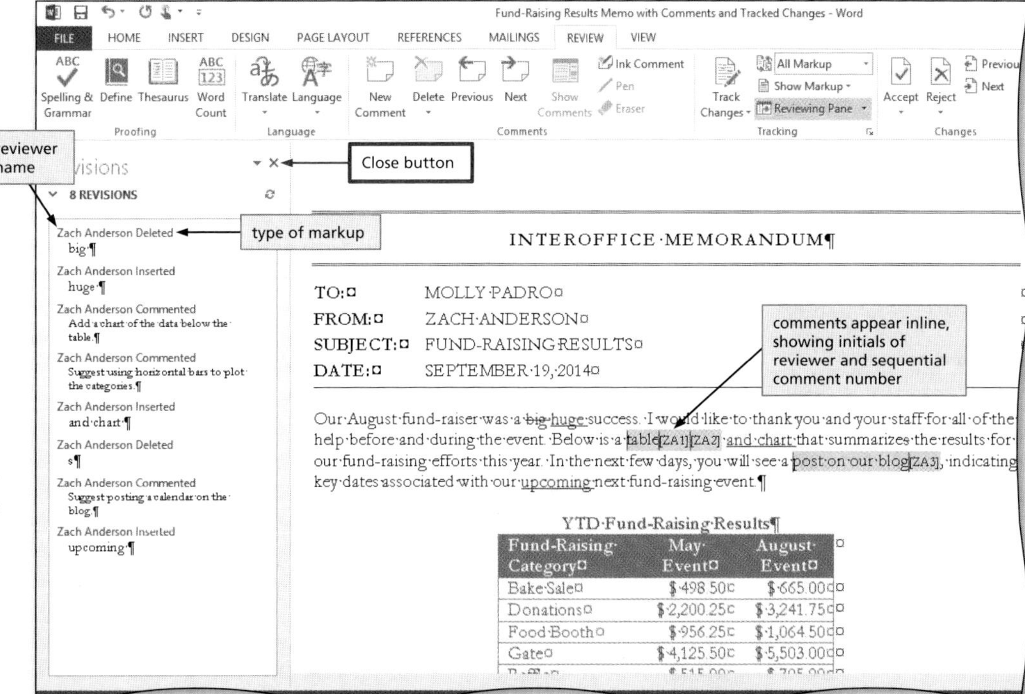

Figure 8–15

Q&A Can I edit revisions in the Reviewing task pane?
Yes. Simply tap or click in the Reviewing task pane and edit the text the same way you edit in the document window.

5

- Tap or click the Close button in the Reviewing task pane to close the task pane.

Q&A Can I also tap or click the Reviewing Pane button on the ribbon to close the task pane?
Yes.

To Display Tracked Changes and Comments as Simple Markup

1 INSERT COMMENTS & TRACK CHANGES | 2 REVIEW COMMENTS & TRACKED CHANGES
3 LINK EXCEL WORKSHEET TO WORD DOCUMENT | 4 CHART WORD TABLE | 5 CREATE & PUBLISH BLOG POST

Word provides a Simple Markup option instead of the All Markup option for viewing tracked changes and comments. ***Why?*** *Some users feel the All Markup option clutters the screen and prefer the cleaner look of the Simple Markup option.* The following step displays tracked changes using the Simple Markup option.

1

- Tap or click the 'Display for Review' arrow (REVIEW tab | Tracking group) to display the Display for Review menu.
- Tap or click Simple Markup on the Display for Review menu to show a simple markup instead of all markups in the document window (Figure 8–16).

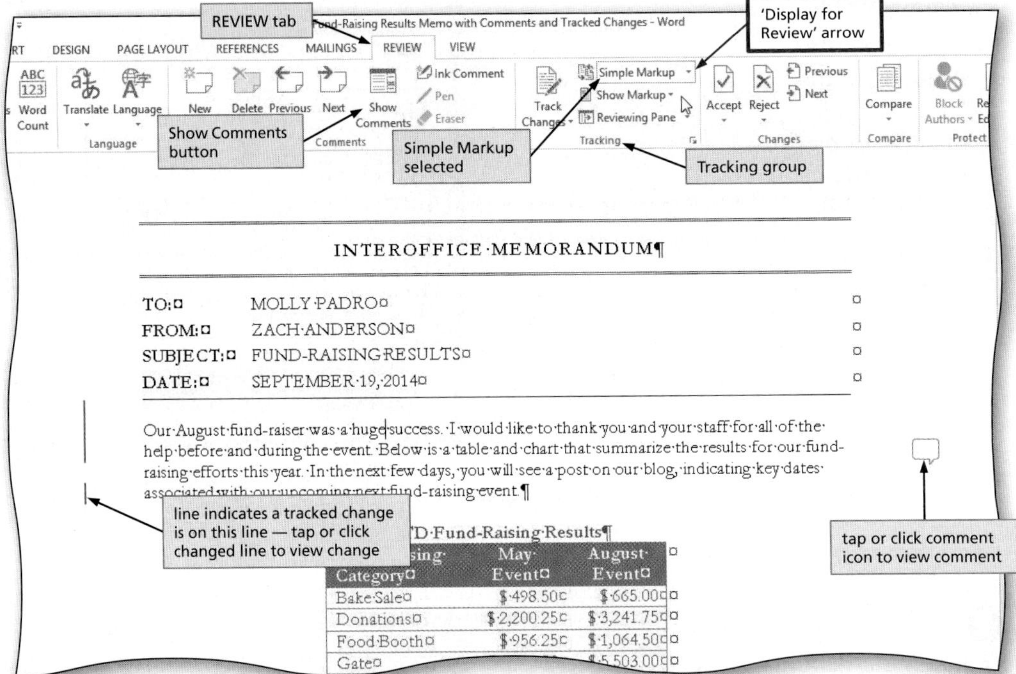

Figure 8–16

Q&A What if the comments appear in the markup area instead of as icons in the document?

Be sure the Show Comments button (REVIEW tab | Comments group) is not selected. When the Show Comments button is selected, the comments appear in the markup area to the right of the document.

Experiment

- Tap or click the comment icon to display the comments. Tap or click the comment icon again to hide the comments. Tap or click one of the changed lines to display the tracked changes. Tap or click one of the changed lines to hide the tracked changes.

To Show All Markup

You prefer to show all markup where comments appear in the markup area and have tracked changes visible in the document window. The following steps show all markup and comments in balloons.

1. Tap or click the 'Display for Review' arrow (REVIEW tab | Tracking group) and then tap or click All Markup on the Display for Review menu to instruct Word to display the document with all proposed edits shown as markup.

2. Tap or click the Show Markup button (REVIEW tab | Tracking group) to display the Show Markup menu, tap or point to Balloons on the Show Markup menu, and then tap or click 'Show Only Comments and Formatting in Balloons', so that the markup area reappears with the comment balloons.

To Print Markups

When you print a document with comments and tracked changes, Word chooses the zoom percentage and page orientation that will best show the comments on the printed document. You can print the document with its markups, which looks similar to how the Word window shows the markups on the screen, or you can print just the list of the markups. If you wanted to print markups, you would perform the following steps.

1. Open the Backstage view and then tap or click the Print tab in the Backstage view to display the Print gallery.
2. Tap or click the first button in the Settings area to display a list of options specifying what you can print. To print the document with the markups, if necessary, place a check mark to the left of Print Markup. To print just the markups (without printing the document), tap or click 'List of Markup' in the Document Info area.
3. Tap or click the Print button.

BTW

Limiting Authors

If you wanted to restrict formatting or editing, you would tap or click the Restrict Editing button (REVIEW tab | Protect group) to display the Restrict Editing task pane. To restrict formatting, select the 'Limit formatting to a selection of styles' check box, tap or click the Settings link, select the styles to allow and disallow (Formatting Restrictions dialog box), and then tap or click the OK button. To restrict editing, select the 'Allow only this type of editing in the document' check box, tap or click the box arrow, and then select the desired editing restriction. To restrict formatting or editing to certain authors, select part of the document and select the users who are allowed to edit the selected areas, and then tap or click the 'Yes, Start Enforcing Protection' button. To block authors from making changes to selected text, tap or click the Block Authors button (REVIEW tab | Protect group) and then select the authors to block in the list.

To Save an Existing Document with the Same File Name

You are finished reviewing the document and have performed several steps since the last save. Thus, you should save the document again, as described in the following step.

Tap or click the Save button on the Quick Access Toolbar to save the document again with the same file name, Fund-Raising Results Memo with Comments and Tracked Changes.

Reviewing Tracked Changes and Comments

After tracking changes and entering comments in a document, you send the document to the originator for his or her review. For demonstration purposes in this chapter, you assume the role of originator and review the tracked changes and comments in the document.

To do this, be sure the markups are displayed on the screen. Tap or click the Show Markup button (REVIEW tab | Tracking group) and verify that Comments, 'Insertions and Deletions', and Formatting each have a check mark beside them. Ensure the 'Display for Review' box (REVIEW tab | Tracking group) shows All Markup; if it does not, tap or click the 'Display for Review' arrow (REVIEW tab | Tracking group) and then tap or click All Markup on the Display for Review menu. This option shows the final document with tracked changes.

If you wanted to see how a document would look if you accepted all the changes, without actually accepting them, tap or click the 'Display for Review' arrow (REVIEW tab | Tracking group) and then tap or click No Markup on the Display for Review menu. If you print this view of the document, it will print how the document will look if you accept all the changes. If you wanted to see how the document looked before any changes were made, tap or click the 'Display for Review' arrow (REVIEW tab | Tracking group) and then tap or click Original on the Display for Review menu. When you have finished reviewing the various options, if necessary, tap or click the 'Display for Review' arrow (REVIEW tab | Tracking group) and then tap or click All Markup on the Display for Review menu.

To View Comments

1 INSERT COMMENTS & TRACK CHANGES | 2 REVIEW COMMENTS & TRACKED CHANGES
3 LINK EXCEL WORKSHEET TO WORD DOCUMENT | 4 CHART WORD TABLE | 5 CREATE & PUBLISH BLOG POST

The next step is to read the comments in the marked-up document using the REVIEW tab. ***Why?*** *You could scroll through the document and read each comment that appears in the markup area, but you might overlook one or more comments using this technique. Thus, it is more efficient to use the REVIEW tab.* The following step views comments in the document.

- Position the insertion point at the beginning of the document, so that Word begins searching for comments from the top of the document.
- Tap or click the Next Comment button (REVIEW tab | Comments group), which causes Word to locate and select the first comment in the document (Figure 8–17).

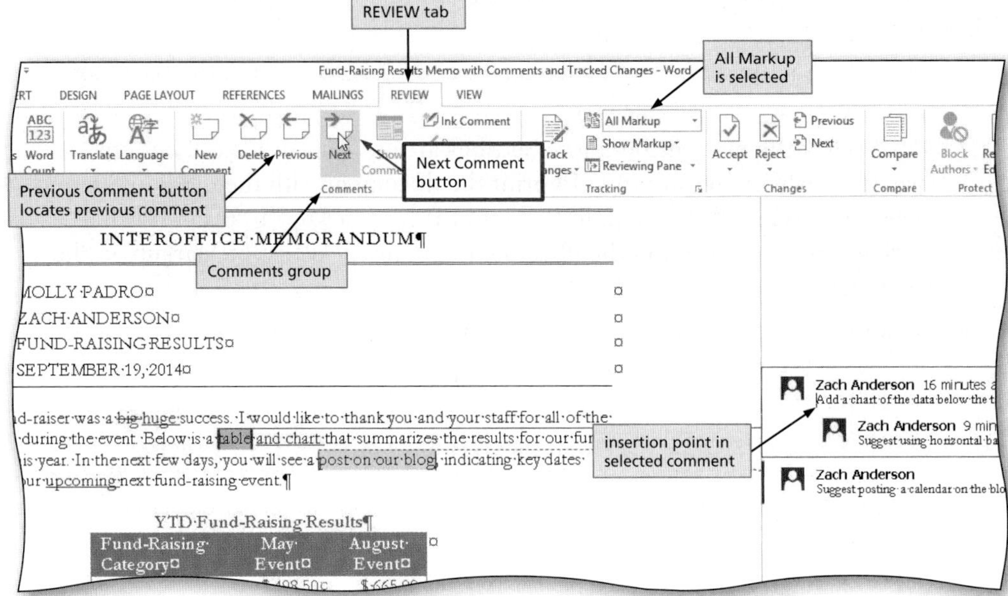

Figure 8–17

To Delete a Comment

1 INSERT COMMENTS & TRACK CHANGES | 2 REVIEW COMMENTS & TRACKED CHANGES
3 LINK EXCEL WORKSHEET TO WORD DOCUMENT | 4 CHART WORD TABLE | 5 CREATE & PUBLISH BLOG POST

The following step deletes a comment. ***Why?*** *You have read the comment and want to remove it from the document.*

- Tap or click the Delete Comment button (REVIEW tab | Comments group) to remove the comment balloon from the markup area (Figure 8–18).

Q&A What if I accidentally tap or click the Delete Comment arrow?
Tap or click Delete on the Delete Comment menu.

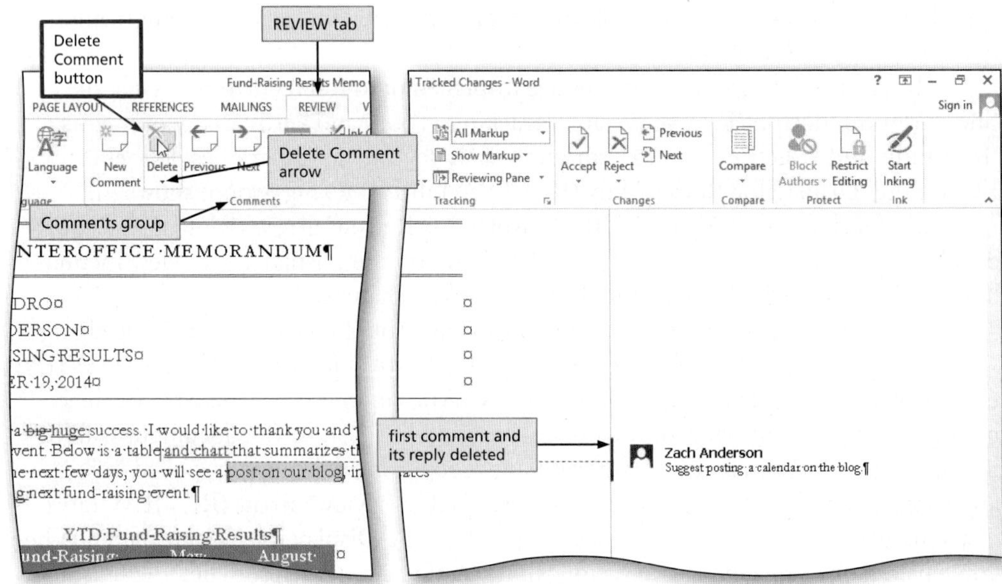

Figure 8–18

Other Ways

1. Tap 'Show Context Menu' button on mini toolbar or right-click comment, tap or click Delete Comment on shortcut menu

To Mark Comments as Done

Instead of deleting comments, some users prefer to leave them in the document but mark them as done. When you mark a comment as done, it changes color. If you wanted to mark a comment as done, you would perform the following steps.

1. Press and hold the comment and then tap the 'Show Context Menu' button on the mini toolbar or right-click the comment to display a shortcut menu.
2. Tap or click 'Mark Comment Done' on the shortcut menu.

To Delete All Comments

1 INSERT COMMENTS & TRACK CHANGES | 2 REVIEW COMMENTS & TRACKED CHANGES
3 LINK EXCEL WORKSHEET TO WORD DOCUMENT | 4 CHART WORD TABLE | 5 CREATE & PUBLISH BLOG POST

The following steps delete all comments at once. ***Why?*** *Assume you now want to delete all the comments in the document at once because you have read them all.*

- Tap or click the Delete Comment arrow (REVIEW tab | Comments group) to display the Delete Comment menu (Figure 8–19).

- Tap or click 'Delete All Comments in Document' on the Delete Comment menu to remove all comments from the document, which also closes the markup area (shown in Figure 8–20).

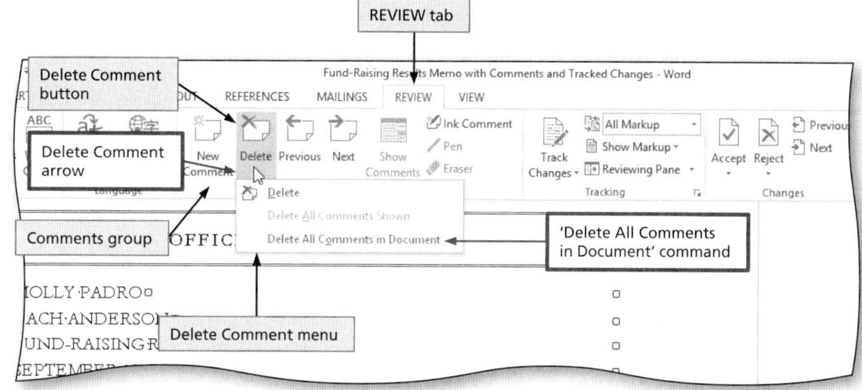

Figure 8–19

To Review Tracked Changes

1 INSERT COMMENTS & TRACK CHANGES | 2 REVIEW COMMENTS & TRACKED CHANGES
3 LINK EXCEL WORKSHEET TO WORD DOCUMENT | 4 CHART WORD TABLE | 5 CREATE & PUBLISH BLOG POST

The next step is to review the tracked changes in the marked-up document using the REVIEW tab. ***Why?*** *As with the comments, you could scroll through the document and point to each markup to read it, but you might overlook one or more changes using this technique. A more efficient method is to use the REVIEW tab to review the changes one at a time, deciding whether to accept, modify, or delete each change.* The following steps review the changes in the document.

- Position the insertion point at the beginning of the document, so that Word begins the review of tracked changes from the top of the document.
- Tap or click the Next Change button (REVIEW tab | Changes group), which causes Word to locate and select the first markup in the document (in this case, the deleted word, big) (Figure 8–20).

Q&A What if my document also had contained comments?

When you tap or click the Next Change button (REVIEW tab | Changes group), Word locates the next tracked change or comment, whichever appears first.

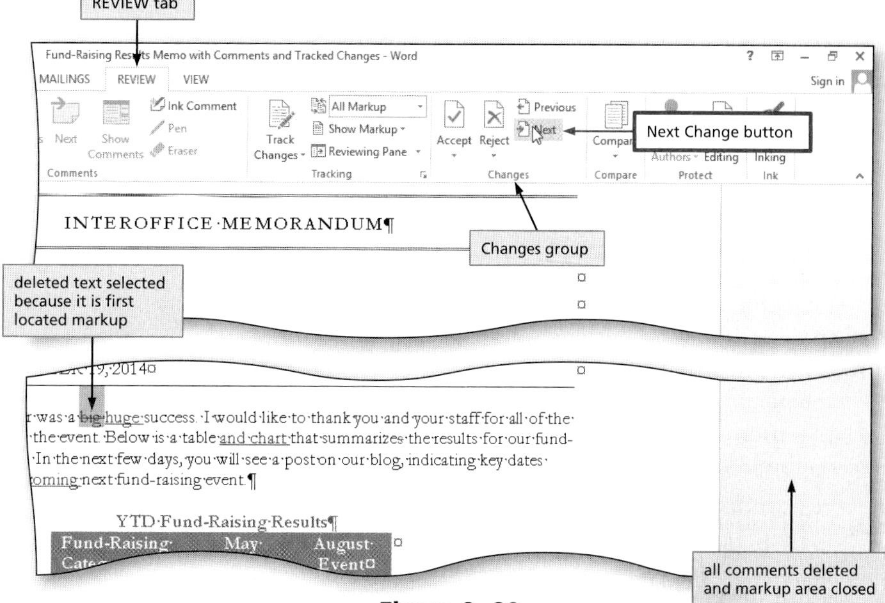

Figure 8–20

2

- Because you agree with this change, tap or click the 'Accept and Move to Next' button (REVIEW tab | Changes group) to accept the deletion of the word, big, and instruct Word to locate and select the next markup (in this case, the inserted word, huge) (Figure 8–21).

Q&A What if I accidentally tap or click the 'Accept and Move to Next' arrow (REVIEW tab | Changes group)?

Tap or click 'Accept and Move to Next' on the Accept and Move to Next menu.

What if I wanted to accept the change but not search for the next tracked change?

You would tap or click the 'Accept and Move to Next' arrow and then tap or click 'Accept This Change' on the Accept and Move to Next menu.

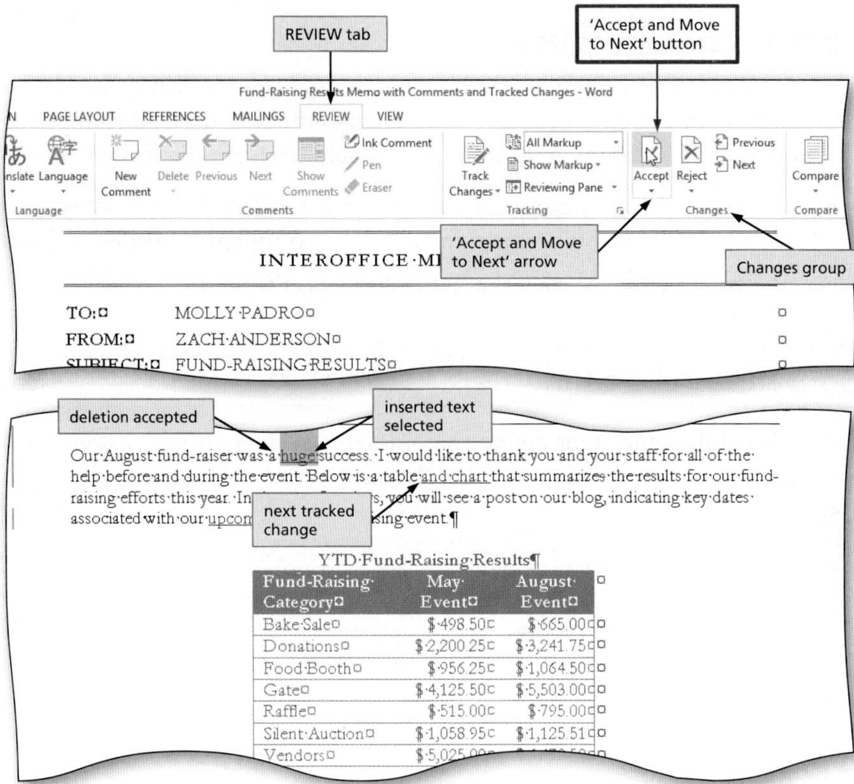

Figure 8–21

3

- Tap or click the 'Accept and Move to Next' button (REVIEW tab | Changes group) to accept the insertion of the word, huge, and instruct Word to locate and select the next markup (in this case, the inserted words, and chart).
- Tap or click the 'Accept and Move to Next' button (REVIEW tab | Changes group) to accept the insertion of the words, and chart, and instruct Word to locate and select the next markup (in this case, the deleted letter s).
- Tap or click the 'Accept and Move to Next' button (REVIEW tab | Changes group) to accept the deletion of the letter s, and instruct Word to locate and select the next markup (in this case, the inserted word, upcoming) (Figure 8–22).

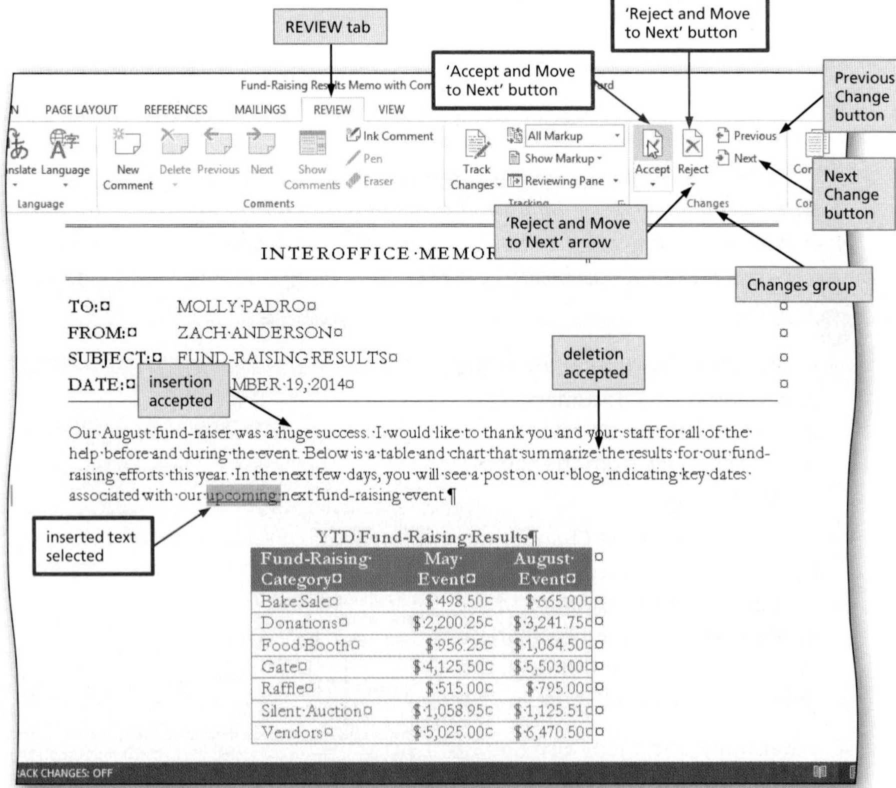

Figure 8–22

- Because you do not agree with this change, tap or click the 'Reject and Move to Next' button (REVIEW tab | Changes group) to reject the marked deletion, and instruct Word to locate and select the next markup. If you are using a touch screen, also tap 'Reject and Move to Next' on the Reject and Move to Next menu.

Q&A

If I am using a mouse, what if I accidentally click the 'Reject and Move to Next' arrow (REVIEW tab | Changes group)?
Click 'Reject and Move to Next' on the Reject and Move to Next menu.

What if I wanted to reject the change but not search for the next tracked change?
You would tap or click the 'Reject and Move to Next' arrow (REVIEW tab | Changes group) and then tap or click Reject Change on the Reject and Move to Next menu.

What if I did not want to accept or reject a change but wanted to locate the next tracked change?
You would tap or click the Next Change button (REVIEW tab | Changes group) to locate the next tracked change or comment. Likewise, to locate the previous tracked change or comment, you would tap or click the Previous Change button (REVIEW tab | Changes group).

- Tap or click the OK button in the dialog box that appears, which indicates the document contains no more comments or tracked changes.

Other Ways

1. Tap 'Show Context Menu' button on mini toolbar or right-click comment or tracked change, tap or click desired command on shortcut menu

To Accept or Reject All Tracked Changes

If you wanted to accept or reject all tracked changes in a document at once, you would perform the following step.

1. To accept all tracked changes, tap or click the 'Accept and Move to Next' arrow (REVIEW tab | Changes group) to display the Accept and Move to Next menu and then tap or click 'Accept All Changes' on the menu to accept all changes in the document and continue tracking changes or tap or click 'Accept All Changes and Stop Tracking' to accept all changes in the document and stop tracking changes.

or

1. To reject all tracked changes, tap or click the 'Reject and Move to Next' arrow (REVIEW tab | Changes group) to display the Reject and Move to Next menu and then tap or click 'Reject All Changes' on the menu to reject all changes in the document and continue tracking changes or tap or click 'Reject All Changes and Stop Tracking' to reject all changes in the document and stop tracking changes.

BTW

Document Inspector

If you wanted to ensure that all comments were removed from a document, you could use the document inspector. Open the Backstage view, display the Info gallery, tap or click the 'Check for Issues' button, and then tap or click Inspect Document. Place a check mark in the 'Comments, Revisions, Versions, and Annotations' check box and then tap or click the Inspect button (Document Inspector dialog box). If any comments are located, tap or click the Remove All button.

Changing Tracking Options

If you wanted to change the color and markings reviewers use for tracked changes and comments or change how balloons are displayed, use the Advanced Track Changes Options dialog box (Figure 8–23 on the next page). To display the Advanced Track Changes Options dialog box, tap or click the Change Tracking Options Dialog Box Launcher (REVIEW tab | Tracking group) and then tap or click the Advanced Options button (Track Changes Options dialog box).

BTW
Mark as Final
If you wanted to mark a document as final so that users could not make further edits to it, you would perform these steps. Open the Backstage view, display the Info gallery, tap or click the Protect Document button, tap or click 'Mark as Final', and then tap or click the OK button in the Word dialog box that appears. This makes the document a read-only file, which prevents any further edits.

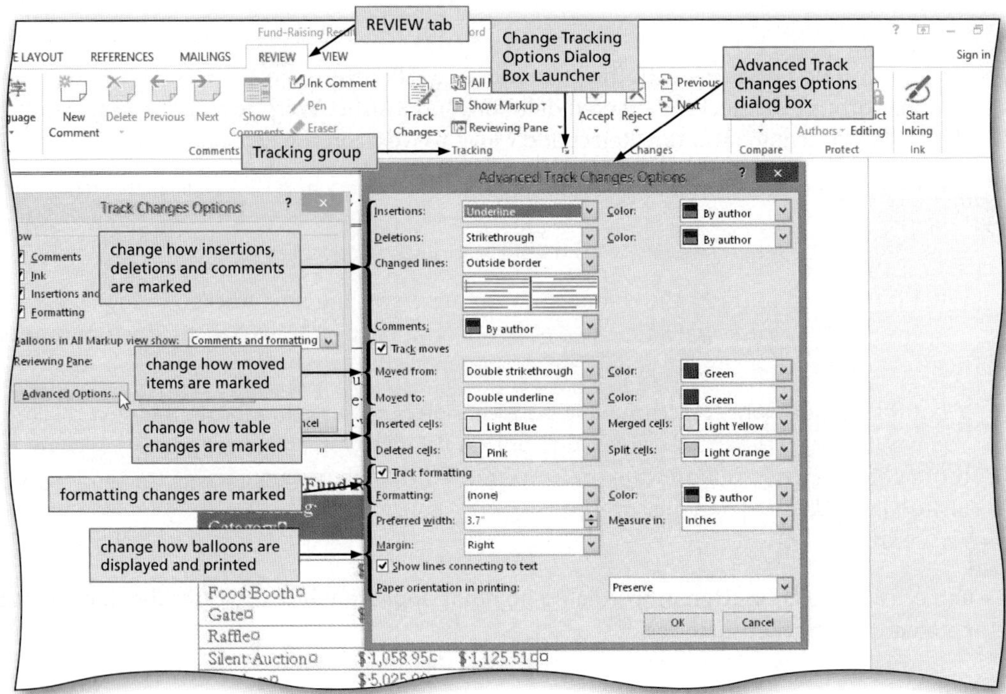

Figure 8–23

To Save an Active Document with a New File Name and Close the File

The current file name is Fund-Raising Results Memo with Comments and Tracked Changes. Because you would like to keep the document with comments and tracked changes, as well as the current one, you will save the current document with a new file name. The following steps save the active document with a new file name.

1. Tap or click FILE on the ribbon to open the Backstage view and then tap or click the Save As tab to display the Save As gallery.

2. To save on a hard disk or other storage media on your computer, proceed to Step 2a. To save on SkyDrive, proceed to Step 2b.

2a. Tap or click Computer in the left pane, if necessary, to display options in the right pane related to saving on your computer.

2b. Tap or click SkyDrive in the left pane to display SkyDrive saving options or a Sign In button. If your screen displays a Sign In button, tap or click it and then sign in to SkyDrive.

3. Tap or click the Browse button in the right pane to display the Save As dialog box associated with the selected save location (i.e., Computer or SkyDrive).

4. Type `Fund-Raising Results Memo Reviewed` in the File name box to change the file name. Do not press the ENTER key after typing the file name because you do not want to close the dialog box at this time.

5. Navigate to the desired save location (in this case, the Word folder in the CIS 101 folder [or your class folder] on your computer or SkyDrive).

6. Tap or click the Save button (Save As dialog box) to save the memo in the selected folder on the selected save location with the entered file name.

BTW
Compare and Merge
If you wanted to compare two documents and merge the changes into an existing document instead of into a new document, you would tap or click Original document (Compare Documents dialog box) to merge into the original document or tap or click Revised document (Compare Documents dialog box) to merge into the revised document (Figure 8–25), and then tap or click the OK button.

To Compare Documents

With Word, you can compare two documents to each other. ***Why?*** *Comparing documents allows you easily to identify any differences between two files because Word displays the differences between the documents as tracked changes for your review. By comparing files, you can verify that two separate files have the same or different content. If no tracked changes are found, then the two documents are identical.*

Assume you want to compare the original Fund-Raising Results Memo Draft document with the Fund-Raising Results Memo Reviewed document so that you can identify the changes made to the document. The following steps compare two documents.

1

- If necessary, display the REVIEW tab.
- Tap or click the Compare button (REVIEW tab | Compare group) to display the Compare menu (Figure 8–24).

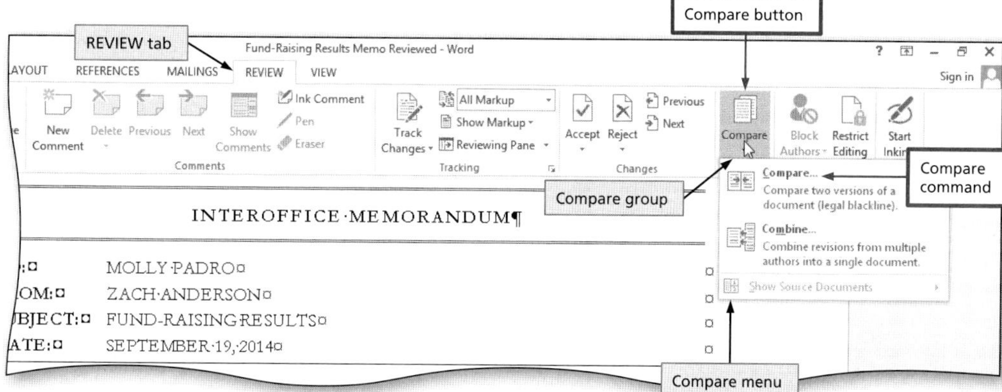

Figure 8–24

2

- Tap or click Compare on the Compare menu to display the Compare Documents dialog box.
- Tap or click the Original document arrow (Compare Documents dialog box) and then tap or click the file, Fund-Raising Results Memo Draft, in the Original document list to select the first file to compare and place the file name in the Original document box.

Q&A What if the file is not in the Original document list?
Tap or click the Open button to the right of the Original document arrow, locate the file, and then tap or click the Open button (Open dialog box).

- Tap or click the Revised document arrow (Compare Documents dialog box) and then tap or click the file, Fund-Raising Results Memo Reviewed, in the Revised document list to select the second file to compare and place the file name in the Revised document box.

Q&A What if the file is not in the Revised document list?
Tap or click the Open button to the right of the Revised document arrow, locate the file, and then tap or click the Open button (Open dialog box).

- If a More button appears in the dialog box, tap or click it to expand the dialog box, which changes the More button to a Less button.
- If necessary, in the Show changes in area, tap or click New document so that tracked changes are marked in a new document. Ensure that all your settings in the expanded dialog box (below the Less button) match those in Figure 8–25.

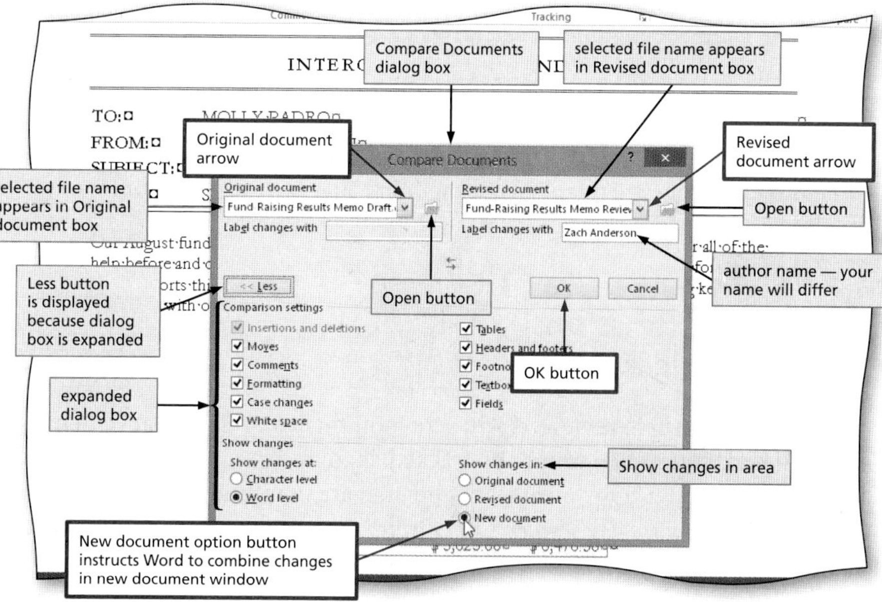

Figure 8–25

3

- Tap or click the OK button to open a new document window and display the differences between the two documents as tracked changes in a new document window; if the Reviewing task pane appears on the screen, tap or click its Close button (Figure 8–26).

Q&A What if the original and source documents do not appear on the screen with the compared document?
Tap or click the Compare button (REVIEW tab | Compare group) to display the Compare menu, tap or point to 'Show Source Documents' on the Compare menu, and then tap or click Show Both on the Show Source Documents submenu.

Experiment

- Tap or click the Next Change button (REVIEW tab | Changes group) to display the first tracked change in the compared document. Continue tapping or clicking the Next Change or Previous Change buttons. You can accept or reject changes in the compared document using the same steps described earlier in the chapter.

- Scroll through the windows and watch them scroll synchronously.

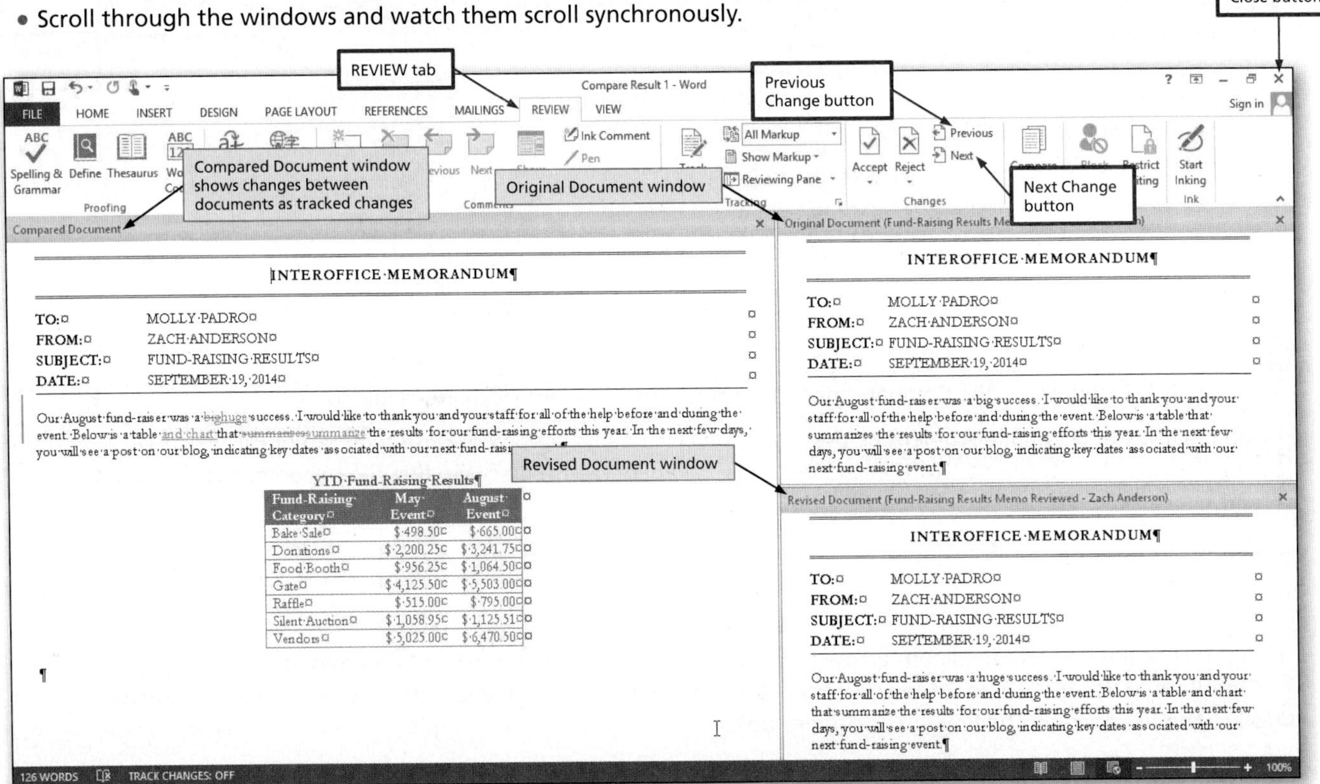

Figure 8–26

4

- When you have finished comparing the documents, tap or click the Close button in the document window (shown in Figure 8–26), and then tap or click the Don't Save button when Word asks if you want to save the compare results.

To Combine Revisions from Multiple Authors

1 INSERT COMMENTS & TRACK CHANGES | 2 REVIEW COMMENTS & TRACKED CHANGES
3 LINK EXCEL WORKSHEET TO WORD DOCUMENT | 4 CHART WORD TABLE | 5 CREATE & PUBLISH BLOG POST

Often, multiple reviewers will send you their markups (tracked changes) for the same original document. Using Word, you can combine the tracked changes from multiple reviewers' documents into a single document, two documents at a time, until all documents are combined. ***Why?*** *Combining documents allows you to review all markups from a single document, from which you can accept and reject changes and read comments. Each reviewer's markups are shaded in a different color to help you visually differentiate among multiple reviewers' markups.*

Assume you want to combine the original Fund-Raising Results Memo Draft document with the Fund-Raising Results Memo with Comments and Tracked Changes document and also with a document called Fund-Raising Results Memo - Review by L Jones, which is on the Data Files for Students. Visit www.cengage.com/ct/studentdownload for detailed instructions or contact your instructor for information about accessing the required files. The file by L Jones identifies another grammar error in the memo. The following steps combine these three documents, two at a time.

- Tap or click the Compare button (REVIEW tab | Compare group) to display the Compare menu (Figure 8–27).

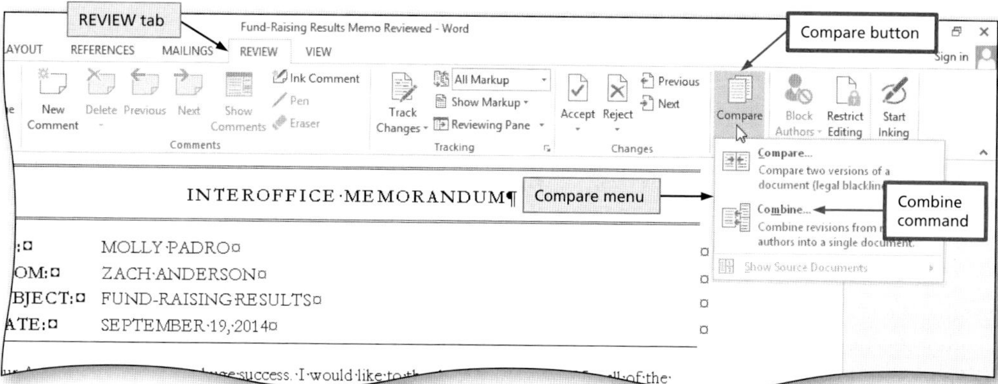

Figure 8–27

- Tap or click Combine on the Compare menu to display the Combine Documents dialog box.
- Tap or click the Original document arrow (Combine Documents dialog box) and then tap or click the file, Fund-Raising Results Memo Draft, in the Original document list to select the first file to combine and place the file name in the Original document box.

Q&A What if the file is not in the Original document list?
Tap or click the Open button to the right of the Original document arrow, locate the file, and then tap or click the Open button (Open dialog box).

- Tap or click the Revised document arrow (Combine Documents dialog box) and then tap or click the file, Fund-Raising Results Memo with Comments and Tracked Changes, in the Revised document list to select the second file to combine and place the file name in the Revised document box.

Q&A What if the file is not in the Revised document list?
Tap or click the Open button to the right of the Revised document arrow, locate the file, and then tap or click the Open button (Open dialog box).

- If a More button appears in the dialog box, tap or click it to expand the dialog box, which changes the More button to a Less button.
- In the Show changes in area, if necessary, tap or click Original document so that tracked changes are marked in the original document (Fund-Raising Results Memo Draft). Ensure that all your settings in the expanded dialog box (below the Less button) match those in Figure 8–28.

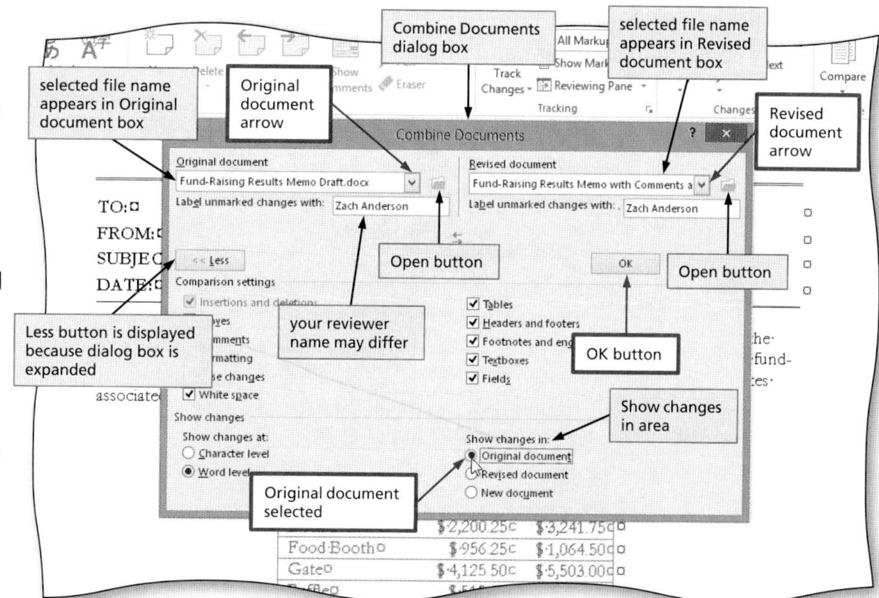

Figure 8–28

3

- Tap or click the OK button to combine the Fund-Raising Results Memo Draft document with the Fund-Raising Results Memo with Comments and Tracked Changes document and display the differences between the two documents as tracked changes in the original document.
- Tap or click the Compare button again (REVIEW tab | Compare group) and then tap or click Combine on the Compare menu to display the Combine Documents dialog box.
- Locate and display the file name, Fund-Raising Results Memo Draft, in the Original document text box (Combine Documents dialog box) to select the first file and place the file name in the Original document box.
- Tap or click the Open button to the right of the Revised document box arrow (Combine Documents dialog box) to display the Open dialog box.
- Locate the file name, Fund-Raising Results Memo - Review by L Jones, in the Data Files for Students and then tap or click the Open button (Open dialog box) to display the selected file name in the Revised document box (Combine Documents dialog box).
- If a More button appears in the Combine Documents dialog box, tap or click it to expand the dialog box.
- If necessary, in the 'Show changes in' area, tap or click Original document so that tracked changes are marked in the original document (Fund-Raising Results Memo Draft). Ensure that all your settings in the expanded dialog box (below the Less button) match those in Figure 8–29.

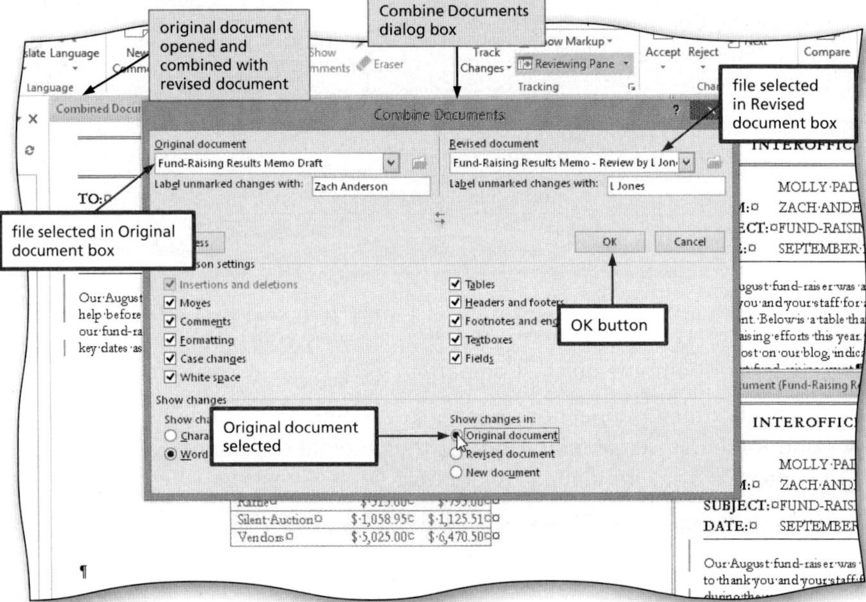

Figure 8–29

4

- Tap or click the OK button to combine the Fund-Raising Results Memo - Review by L Jones document with the currently combined document and display the differences among the three documents as tracked changes in the original document (Figure 8–30).

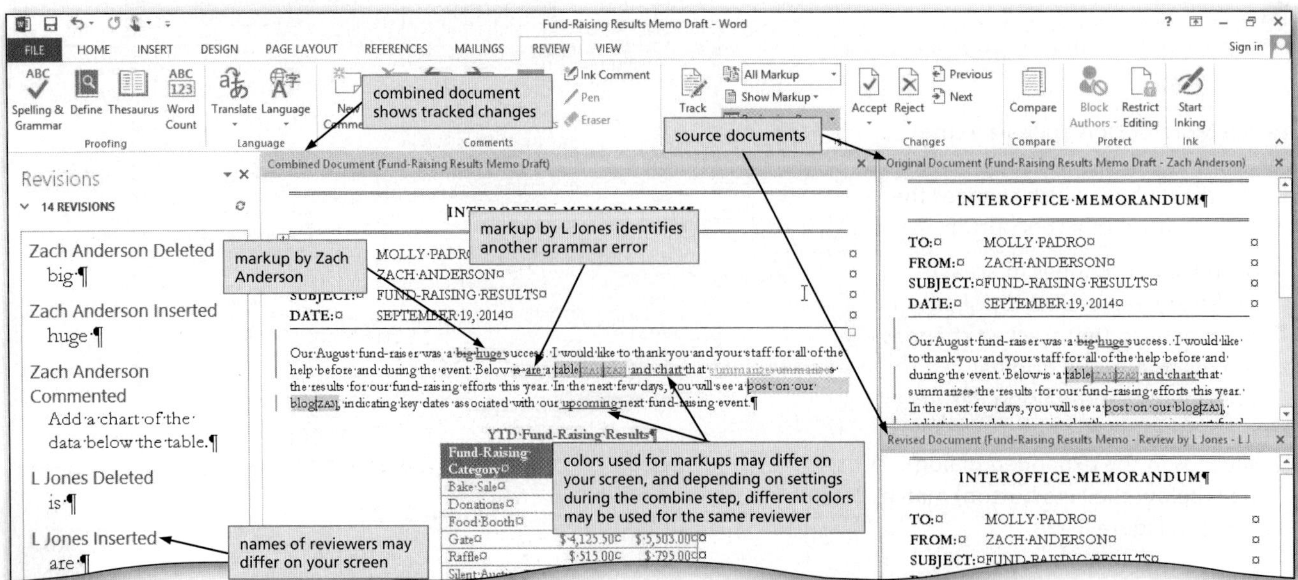

Figure 8–30

Q&A What if my screen does not display the original and source documents?
Tap or click the Compare button (REVIEW tab | Compare group) to display the Compare menu, tap or point to 'Show Source Documents' on the Compare menu, and then tap or click Show Both on the Show Source Documents submenu.

- Tap or click the Next Change button (REVIEW tab | Changes group) to display the first tracked change in the combined document. Continue tapping or clicking the Next Change or Previous Change buttons. You can accept or reject changes in the combined document using the same steps described earlier in the chapter.

To Show Tracked Changes and Comments by a Single Reviewer

1 INSERT COMMENTS & TRACK CHANGES | 2 REVIEW COMMENTS & TRACKED CHANGES
3 LINK EXCEL WORKSHEET TO WORD DOCUMENT | 4 CHART WORD TABLE | 5 CREATE & PUBLISH BLOG POST

***Why?** Instead of looking through a document for a particular reviewer's markups, you can show markups by reviewer.* The following steps show the markups by the reviewer named L Jones.

- Tap or click the Show Markup button (REVIEW tab | Tracking group) to display the Show Markup menu and then tap or point to Specific People on the Show Markup menu to display the Specific People submenu (Figure 8–31).

Q&A What if my Specific People submenu differs?
Your submenu may have additional, different, or duplicate reviewer names or colors, depending on your Word settings.

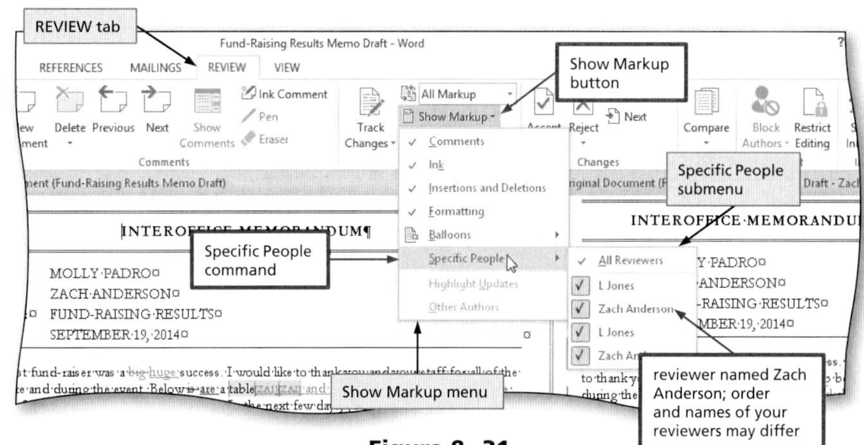

Figure 8–31

- Tap or click Zach Anderson on the Reviewers submenu to hide the selected reviewer's markups and leave other markups on the screen.

Q&A Are the Zach Anderson reviewer markups deleted?
No. They are hidden from view.

- If necessary, repeat Steps 1 and 2 to hide the second occurrence of reviewer markups for Zach Anderson (Figure 8–32).

- Practice hiding and showing reviewer markups in this document.

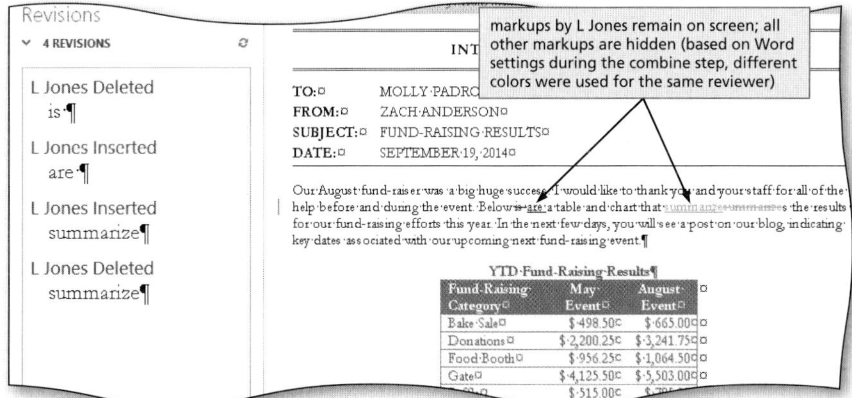

Figure 8–32

- Redisplay all reviewer comments by tapping or clicking the Show Markup button (REVIEW tab | Tracking group), tapping or pointing to Specific People, and then tapping or clicking All Reviewers on the Specific People submenu.

BTW
Locating Comments by Reviewer
You can find a comment from a specific reviewer through the Go To dialog box. Tap or click the Find arrow (HOME tab | Editing group) and then tap or click Go To or press CTRL+G to display the Go To sheet in the Find and Replace dialog box. Tap or click Comment in the Go to what list (Find and Replace dialog box). Select the reviewer whose comments you wish to find and then tap or click the Next button.

To Customize the Status Bar

You are finished working with tracked changes in this chapter. The following steps remove the TRACK CHANGES indicator from the status bar.

1. Press and hold or right-click anywhere on the status bar to display the Customize Status Bar menu.
2. Remove the check mark to the left of Track Changes on the Customize Status Bar menu, which removes the TRACK CHANGES indicator from the status bar.
3. Tap or click anywhere outside of the Customize Status Bar menu, or press the ESCAPE key, to remove the Customize Status Bar menu from the screen.

To Close the Document without Saving It

The next step is to close the combined document without saving it.

1. Open the Backstage view and then tap or click Close.
2. When Word displays the dialog box, tap or click the Don't Save button.
3. Close any other open Word documents.

Break Point: If you wish to take a break, this is a good place to do so. You can exit Word now. To resume at a later time, run Word and continue following the steps from this location forward.

Linking an Excel Worksheet to a Word Document

With Microsoft Office, you can copy part or all of a document created in one Office program to a document created in another Office program. The item being copied is called the **object**. For example, you could copy an Excel worksheet (the object) that is located in an Excel workbook (the source file) to a Word document (the destination file). That is, an object is copied from a source to a destination.

You can use one of three techniques to copy objects from one program to another: copy and paste, embed, or link.

- **Copy and paste:** When you copy an object and then paste it, the object becomes part of the destination document. You edit a pasted object using editing features of the destination program. For example, when you select an Excel worksheet in an Excel workbook, tap or click the Copy button (HOME tab | Clipboard group) in Excel, and then tap or click the Paste button (HOME tab | Clipboard group) in Word, the Excel worksheet becomes a Word table.
- **Embed:** When you embed an object, like a pasted object, it becomes part of the destination document. The difference between an embedded object and a pasted object is that you edit the contents of an embedded object using the editing features of the source program. The embedded object, however, contains static data; that is, any changes made to the object in the source program are not reflected in the destination document. If you embed an Excel worksheet in a Word document, the Excel worksheet remains as an Excel worksheet in the Word document. When you edit the Excel worksheet from within the Word document, you will use Excel editing features.

- **Link:** A linked object, by contrast, does not become a part of the destination document even though it appears to be a part of it. Rather, a connection is established between the source and destination documents so that when you open the destination document, the linked object appears as part of it. When you edit a linked object, the source program runs and opens the source document that contains the linked object. For example, when you edit a linked worksheet, Excel runs and displays the Excel workbook that contains the worksheet; you then edit the worksheet in Excel. Unlike an embedded object, if you open the Excel workbook that contains the Excel worksheet and then edit the Excel worksheet, the linked object will be updated in the Word document, too.

CONSIDER THIS

How do I determine which method to use: copy/paste, embed, or link?

- If you simply want to use the object's data and have no desire to use the object in the source program, then copy and paste the object.
- If you want to use the object in the source program but you want the object's data to remain static if it changes in the source file, then embed the object.
- If you want to ensure that the most current version of the object appears in the destination file, then link the object. If the source file is large, such as a video clip or a sound clip, link the object to keep the size of the destination file smaller.

The steps in this section show how to link an Excel worksheet (the object), which is located in an Excel workbook (the source file), to a Word document (the destination file). The Word document is similar to the same memo used in the previous section, except that all grammar errors are fixed and it does not contain the table. To link the worksheet to the memo, you will follow these general steps:

1. Run Excel and open the Excel workbook that contains the object (worksheet) you want to link to the Word document.
2. Select the object (worksheet) in Excel and then copy the selected object to the Clipboard.
3. Switch to Word and then link the copied object to the Word document.

Note: The steps in this section assume you have Microsoft Excel installed on your computer. If you do not have Excel, read the steps in this section without performing them.

To Open a Document

The first step in this section is to open the memo that is to contain the link to the Excel worksheet object. The memo file, named Fund-Raising Memo without Table, is located on the Data Files for Students. Visit www.cengage.com/ct/studentdownload for detailed instructions or contact your instructor for information about accessing the required files. The following steps open a document.

1. Tap or click FILE on the ribbon to open the Backstage view and then, if necessary, tap or click the Open tab to display the Open gallery.
2. Navigate to the Data Files for Students and then open the file called Fund-Raising Results Memo without Table.

BTW

Linked Objects

When you open a document that contains linked objects, Word displays a dialog box asking if you want to update the Word document with data from the linked file. Tap or click the Yes button only if you are certain the linked file is from a trusted source; that is, you should be confident that the source file does not contain a virus or other potentially harmful program before you instruct Word to link the source file to the destination document.

Excel Basics

The Excel window contains a rectangular grid that consists of columns and rows. A column letter above the grid identifies each column. A row number on the left side of the grid identifies each row. The intersection of each column and row is a cell. A cell is referred to by its unique address, which is the coordinates of the intersection of a column and a row. To identify a cell, specify the column letter first, followed by the row number. For example, cell reference A1 refers to the cell located at the intersection of column A and row 1 (Figure 8–33).

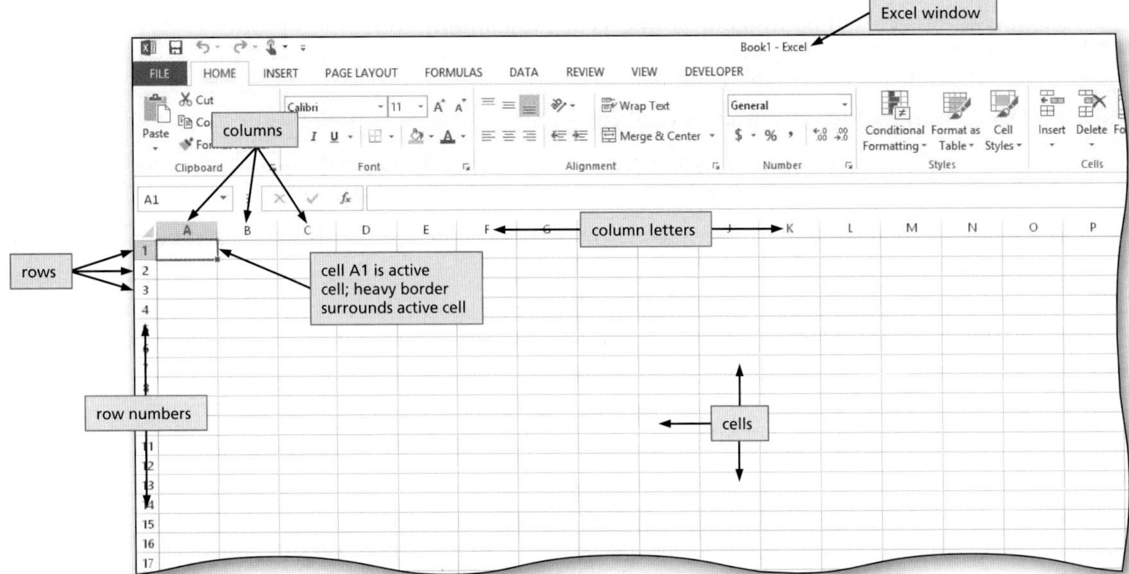

Figure 8–33

To Run Excel and Open an Excel Workbook

The Excel worksheet to be linked to the memo is in an Excel workbook called Fund-Raising Results in Excel, which is located on the Data Files for Students. Visit www.cengage.com/ct/studentdownload for detailed instructions or contact your instructor for information about accessing the required files.

The following steps run Excel and open a workbook. (Do not exit Word or close the open Word document before starting these steps.)

1. Display the Windows Start screen and then scroll the Start screen for an Excel 2013 tile. If your Start screen contains an Excel 2013 tile, tap or click it to run Excel and then proceed to Step 5; if the Start screen does not contain the Excel 2013 tile, proceed to the next step to search for the Excel app.
2. Swipe in from the right edge of the screen or point to the upper-right corner of the screen to display the Charms bar and then tap or click the Search charm on the Charms bar to display the Search menu.
3. Type `Excel` as the search text in the Search box and watch the search results appear in the Apps list.
4. Tap or click Excel 2013 in the search results to run Excel.
5. Tap or click 'Open Other Workbooks' in the left pane of the Excel start screen, navigate to the Data Files for Students, and then tap or click the file called Fund-Raising Results in Excel (Open dialog box).
6. Tap or click the Open button to open the selected file and display the opened workbook in the Excel window.

To Link an Excel Worksheet to a Word Document

1 INSERT COMMENTS & TRACK CHANGES | 2 REVIEW COMMENTS & TRACKED CHANGES
3 LINK EXCEL WORKSHEET TO WORD DOCUMENT | 4 CHART WORD TABLE | 5 CREATE & PUBLISH BLOG POST

The following steps link an Excel worksheet to a Word document. ***Why?*** *You want to copy the Excel worksheet to the Clipboard and then link the Excel worksheet to the Word document.*

1

- In the Excel window, drag through the cells in the range A1 through C8 to select them.
- In the Excel window, if you are using a touch screen, tap the Copy button (HOME tab | Clipboard group) and then tap Copy on the Copy menu; if you are using a mouse, click the Copy button (HOME tab | Clipboard group) to copy the selected cells to the Clipboard (Figure 8–34).

Q&A If I am using a mouse, what if I click the Copy arrow by mistake?
Click Copy on the Copy menu.

What is the dotted line around the selected cells?
Excel surrounds copied cells with a moving marquee to help you visually identify the copied cells.

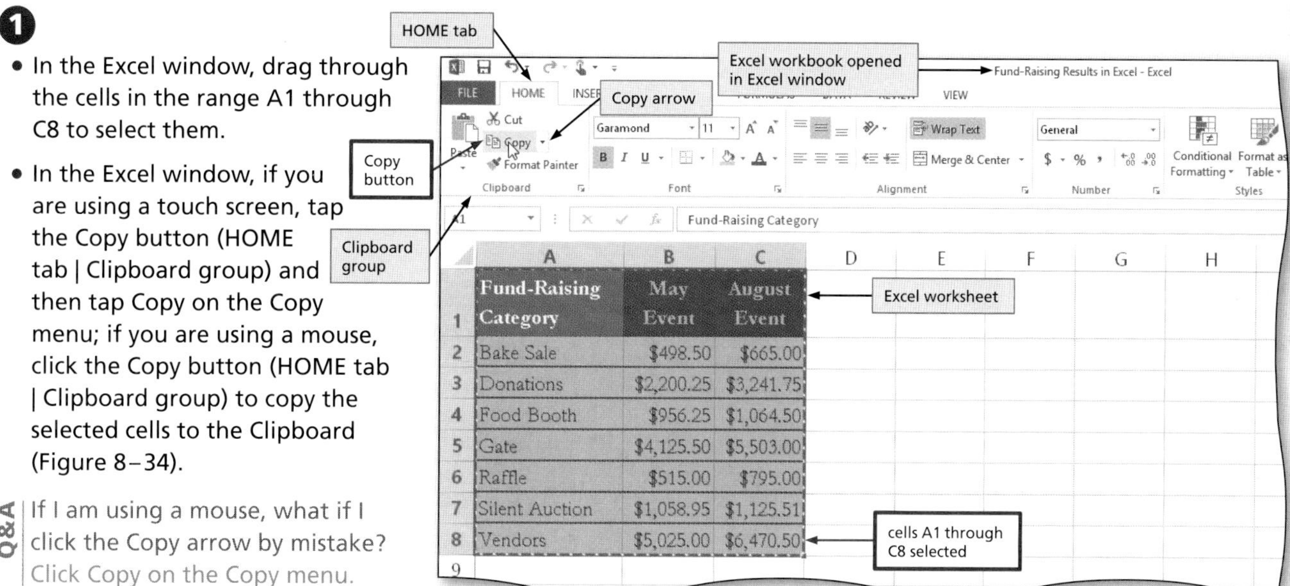

Figure 8–34

2

- Tap or click the Word app button on the taskbar switch to Word and display the open document in the Word window.
- Position the insertion point on the paragraph mark below the table title.
- In Word, tap or click the Paste arrow (HOME tab | Clipboard group) to display the Paste gallery.

Q&A What if I accidentally tap or click the Paste button instead of the Paste arrow?
Tap or click the Undo button on the Quick Access Toolbar and then tap or click the Paste arrow.

- If you are using a mouse, point to the 'Link & Keep Source Formatting' button in the Paste gallery to display a live preview of that paste option (Figure 8–35).

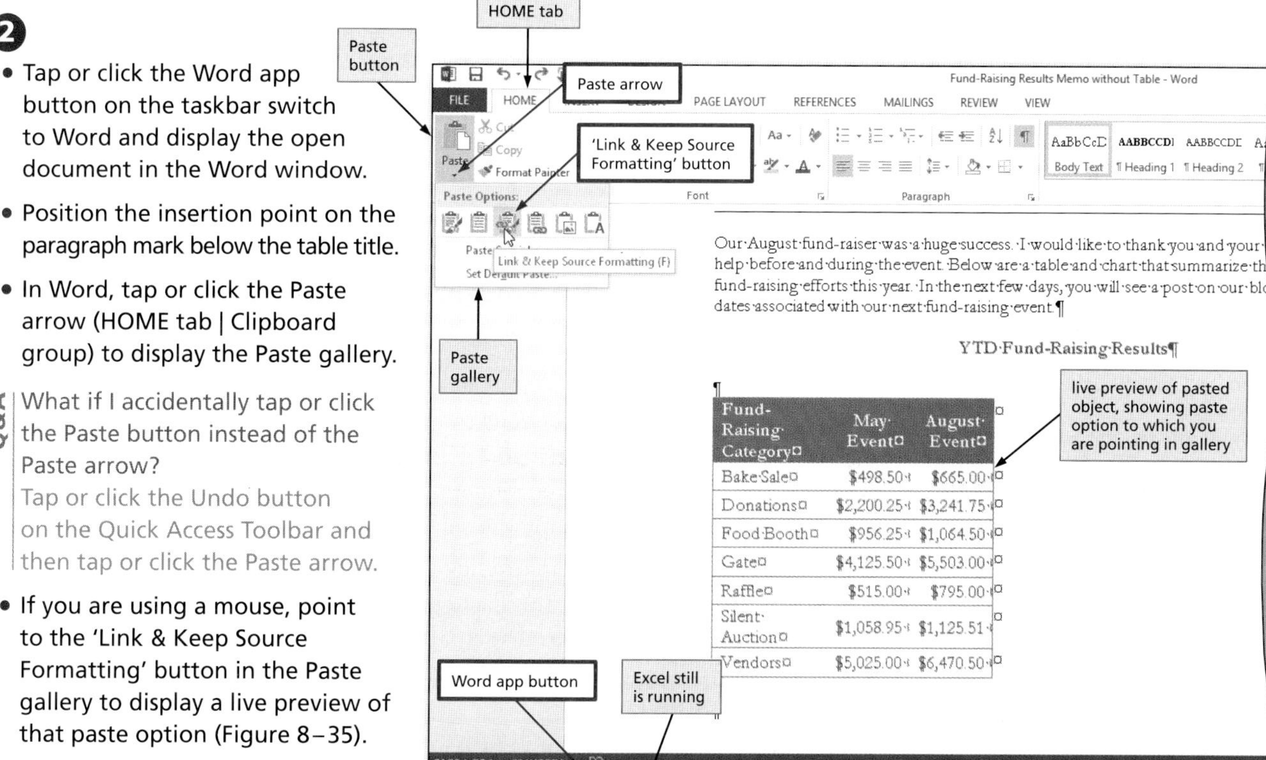

Figure 8–35

Experiment

- If you are using a mouse, point to the various buttons in the Paste gallery to display a live preview of each paste option.

- Tap or click the 'Link & Keep Source Formatting' button in the Paste gallery to paste and link the object at the location of the insertion point in the document.

Q&A What if I wanted to copy an object instead of link it?
To copy an object, you would tap or click the 'Keep Source Formatting' button in the Paste gallery. To convert the object to a picture so that you can use tools on Word's PICTURE TOOLS tab to format it, you would tap or click the Picture button in the Paste gallery.

- Select and then center the linked Excel table using the same technique you use to select and center a Word table.
- Resize the linked Excel table until the table is approximately the same size as Figure 8–36.

Q&A What if I wanted to delete the linked worksheet?
You would select the linked worksheet and then press the DELETE key.

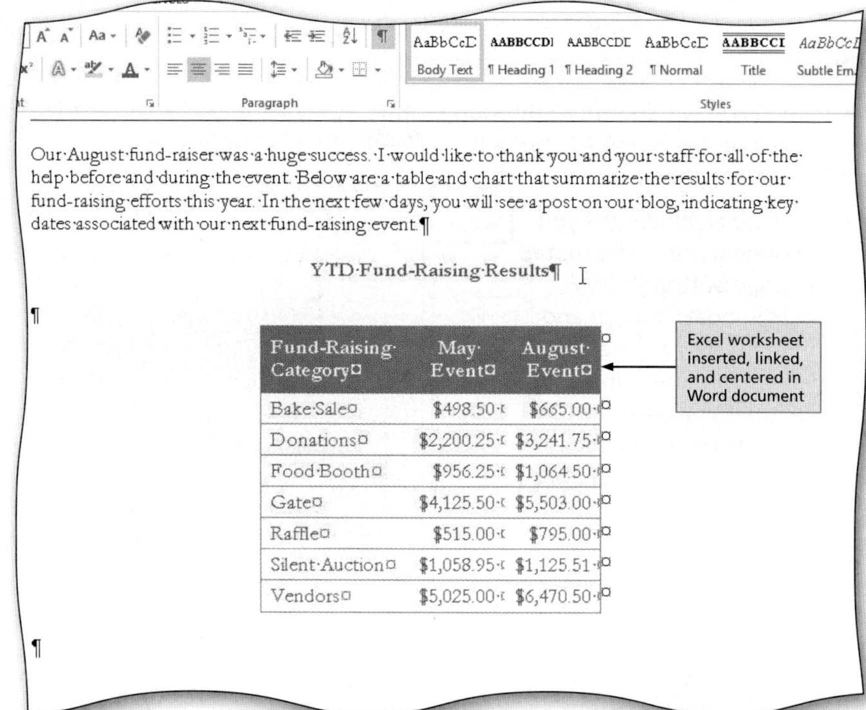

Figure 8–36

Other Ways

1. Tap or click Paste arrow (HOME tab | Clipboard group), tap or click Paste Special, tap or click Paste link (Paste Special dialog box), tap or click 'Microsoft Excel Worksheet Object' in As list, tap or click OK button
2. To link an entire source file, tap or click Object button (INSERT tab | Text group), tap Object on Object menu if using a touch screen, tap or click Create from File tab (Object dialog box), locate file, tap or click 'Link to file' check box, tap or click OK button

To Embed an Excel Worksheet in a Word Document

If you wanted to embed an Excel worksheet in a Word document, instead of link it, you would perform the following steps.

1. Run Excel.
2. In Excel, select the worksheet cells to embed. If you are using a touch screen, tap the Copy button (HOME tab | Clipboard group) and then tap Copy on the Copy menu; if you are using a mouse, click the Copy button (HOME tab | Clipboard group) to copy the selected cells to the Clipboard.
3. Switch to Word. In Word, tap or click the Paste arrow (HOME tab | Clipboard group) to display the Paste gallery and then tap or click Paste Special in the Paste gallery to display the Paste Special dialog box.
4. Select the Paste option button (Paste Special dialog box), which indicates the object will be embedded.
5. Select 'Microsoft Excel Worksheet Object' as the type of object to embed.
6. Tap or click the OK button to embed the contents of the Clipboard in the Word document at the location of the insertion point.

BTW
Editing Embedded Objects
If you wanted to edit an embedded object in the Word document, you would double-tap or double-click the object to display the source program's interface in the destination program. For example, double-tapping or double-clicking an embedded Excel worksheet in a Word document displays the Excel ribbon in the Word window. To redisplay the Word ribbon in the Word window, double-tap or double-click outside of the embedded object.

To Edit a Linked Object

At a later time, you may find it necessary to change the data in the Excel worksheet. Any changes you make to the Excel worksheet while in Excel will be reflected in the Excel worksheet in the Word document because the objects are linked to the Word document. If you wanted to edit a linked object, such as an Excel worksheet, you would perform these steps.

1. In the Word document, press and hold the linked Excel worksheet and then tap the 'Show Context Menu' button on mini toolbar or right-click the linked Excel worksheet, tap or point to 'Linked Worksheet Object' on the shortcut menu, and then tap or click Edit Link on the Linked Worksheet Object submenu to run Excel and open the source file that contains the linked worksheet.
2. In Excel, make changes to the Excel worksheet.
3. Tap or click the Save button on the Quick Access Toolbar to save the changes.
4. Exit Excel.
5. If necessary, redisplay the Word window.
6. If necessary, to update the worksheet with the edited Excel data, tap or click the Excel worksheet in the Word document and then press the F9 key, or press and hold the linked object and then tap the 'Show Context Menu' button on the mini toolbar, or right-click the linked object and then tap or click Update Link on the shortcut menu to update the linked object with the revisions made to the source file.

BTW

Opening Word Documents with Links

When you open a document that contains a linked object, Word attempts to locate the source file associated with the link. If Word cannot find the source file, open the Backstage view, display the Info tab, then tap or click 'Edit Links to Files' at the bottom of the right pane to display the Links dialog box. Next, select the appropriate source file in the list (Links dialog box), tap or click the Change Source button, locate the source file, and then tap or click the OK button.

To Break a Link

1 INSERT COMMENTS & TRACK CHANGES | 2 REVIEW COMMENTS & TRACKED CHANGES
3 LINK EXCEL WORKSHEET TO WORD DOCUMENT | **4 CHART WORD TABLE** | 5 CREATE & PUBLISH BLOG POST

Why? *You can convert a linked or embedded object to a Word object by breaking the link. That is, you break the connection between the source file and the destination file.* When you break a linked object, such as an Excel worksheet, the linked object becomes a Word object, a Word table in this case. The following steps break the link to the Excel worksheet.

- If you are using a touch screen, press and hold the linked object and then tap the 'Show Context Menu' button on the mini toolbar; if you are using a mouse, right-click the linked object (the linked Excel worksheet, in this case) to display a shortcut menu.
- Tap or point to 'Linked Worksheet Object' on the shortcut menu to display the Linked Worksheet Object submenu (Figure 8–37).

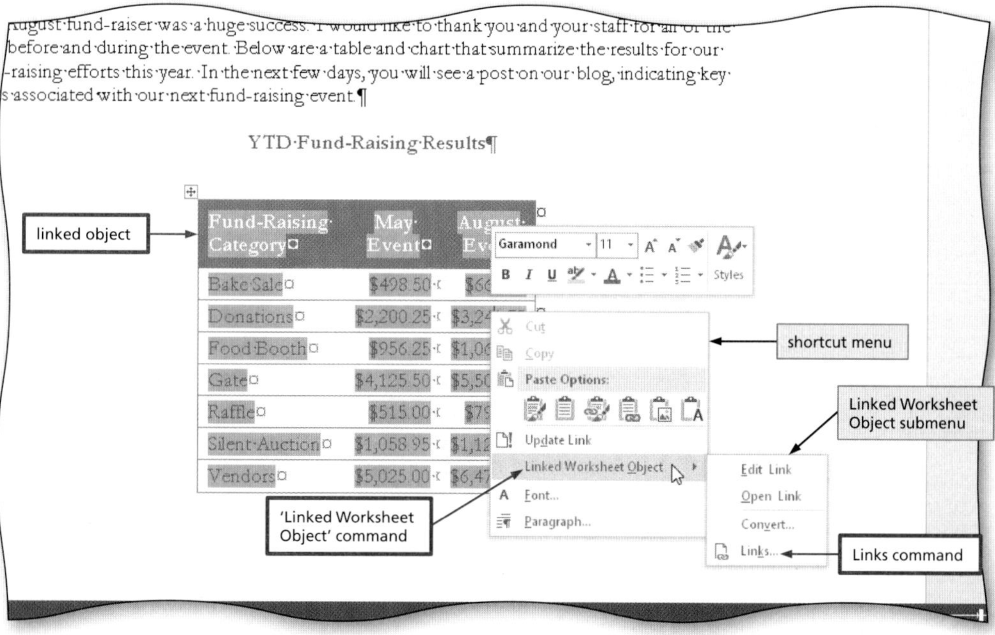

Figure 8–37

- Tap or click Links on the Linked Worksheet Object submenu to display the Links dialog box.
- If necessary, tap or click the source file listed in the dialog box to select it (Links dialog box).
- Tap or click the Break Link button, which displays a dialog box asking if you are sure you want to break the selected links (Figure 8–38).

- Tap or click the Yes button in the dialog box to remove the source file from the list (break the link).

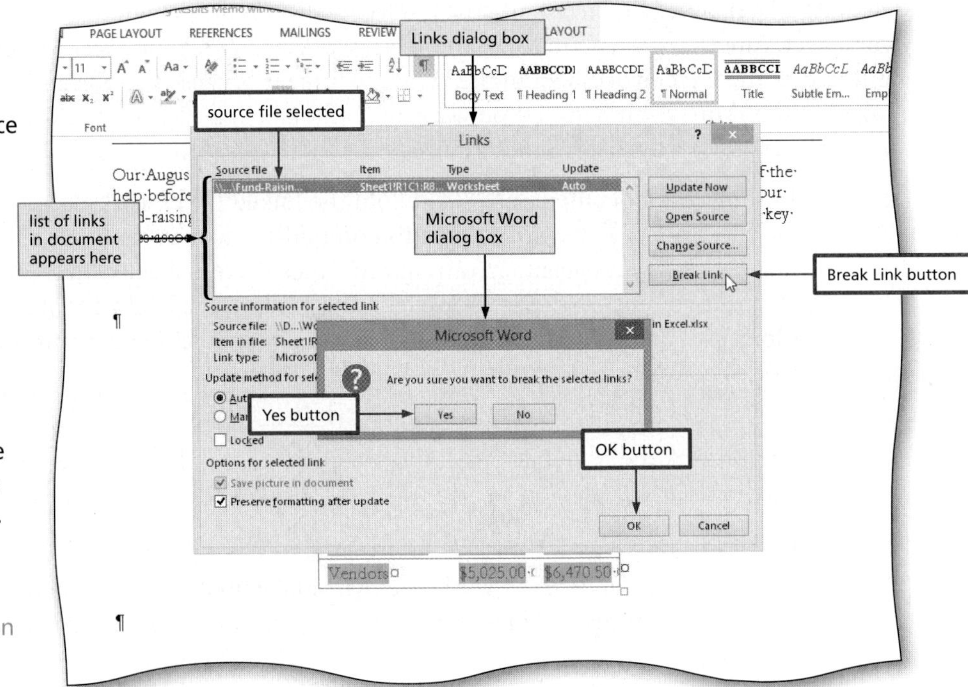

Figure 8–38

Q&A How can I verify the link is broken?

Press and hold the table and then tap the 'Show Context Menu button' or right-click the table in the Word document to display a shortcut menu. If the shortcut menu does not contain a 'Linked Worksheet Object' command, a link does not exist for the object. Or, when you double-tap or double-click the table, Excel should not open an associated workbook.

Other Ways

1. Select link, press CTRL+SHIFT+F9

CONSIDER THIS

Why would you break a link?

If you share a Word document that contains a linked object, such as an Excel worksheet, users will be asked by Word if they want to update the links when they open the Word document. If users are unfamiliar with links, they will not know how to answer the question. Further, if they do not have the source program, such as Excel, they may not be able to open the Word document. When sharing documents, it is recommended you convert links to a regular Word object; that is, break the link.

BTW

BTWs

For a complete list of the BTWs found in the margins of this book, visit the BTW resource on the Student Companion Site located on www.cengagebrain.com. For detailed instructions about accessing available resources, visit www.cengage.com/ct/studentdownload or contact your instructor for information about accessing the required files.

To Close a Document without Saving It and Exit Excel

The next step is to close the document without saving it. The following steps close the Word document and the Excel window.

1. Open the Backstage view and then tap or click Close.
2. When Word displays the dialog box, tap or click the Don't Save button.
3. Press and hold or right-click the Excel app button on the taskbar and then tap or click Close window on the shortcut menu.
4. If an Excel dialog box is displayed, tap or click the Don't Save button.

Charting a Word Table

Several Office applications, including Word, enable you to create charts from data. In the following pages, you will insert and format a chart of the Fund-Raising Results Word table using the CHART TOOLS tab in Word. You will follow these general steps to insert and then format the chart:

1. Create a chart of the table.
2. Remove a data series from the chart.
3. Apply a chart style to the chart.
4. Change the colors of the chart.
5. Add a chart element.
6. Edit a chart element.
7. Format chart elements.
8. Add an outline to the chart.

To Open a Document

The next step is to open the Fund-Raising Results Memo file that contains the final wording so that you can create a chart of its Word table. This file, called Fund-Raising Results Memo with Table, is located on the Data Files for Students. Visit www.cengage.com/ct/studentdownload for detailed instructions or contact your instructor for information about accessing the required files. The following steps open a document.

1. Tap or click FILE on the ribbon to open the Backstage view and then, if necessary, tap or click the Open tab to display the Open gallery.
2. Navigate to the Data Files for Students and then open the file called Fund-Raising Results Memo with Table.

To Chart a Table

1 INSERT COMMENTS & TRACK CHANGES | 2 REVIEW COMMENTS & TRACKED CHANGES
3 LINK EXCEL WORKSHEET TO WORD DOCUMENT | 4 CHART WORD TABLE | **5 CREATE & PUBLISH BLOG POST**

The following steps insert a default chart and then copy the data to be charted from the Word table in the Word document to a chart spreadsheet. ***Why?*** *To chart a table, you fill in or copy the data into a chart spreadsheet that automatically opens after you insert the chart.*

1

- Center the paragraph mark below the table so that the inserted chart will be centered. Leave the insertion point on this paragraph mark because the chart will be inserted at the location of the insertion point.
- Display the INSERT tab.
- Tap or click the 'Add a Chart' button (INSERT tab | Illustrations group) to display the Insert Chart dialog box.
- Tap or click Bar in the left pane (Insert Chart dialog box) to display the available types of bar charts in the right pane.

Experiment

- Tap or click the various types of charts in the left pane and watch the subtypes appear in the right pane. When finished experimenting, tap or click Bar in the left pane.

- If necessary, tap or click Clustered Bar in the right pane to select the chart type (Figure 8–39).

Experiment

- Tap or click the various types of bar charts in the right pane and watch the graphic change in the right pane. When finished experimenting, tap or click Clustered Bar in the right pane.

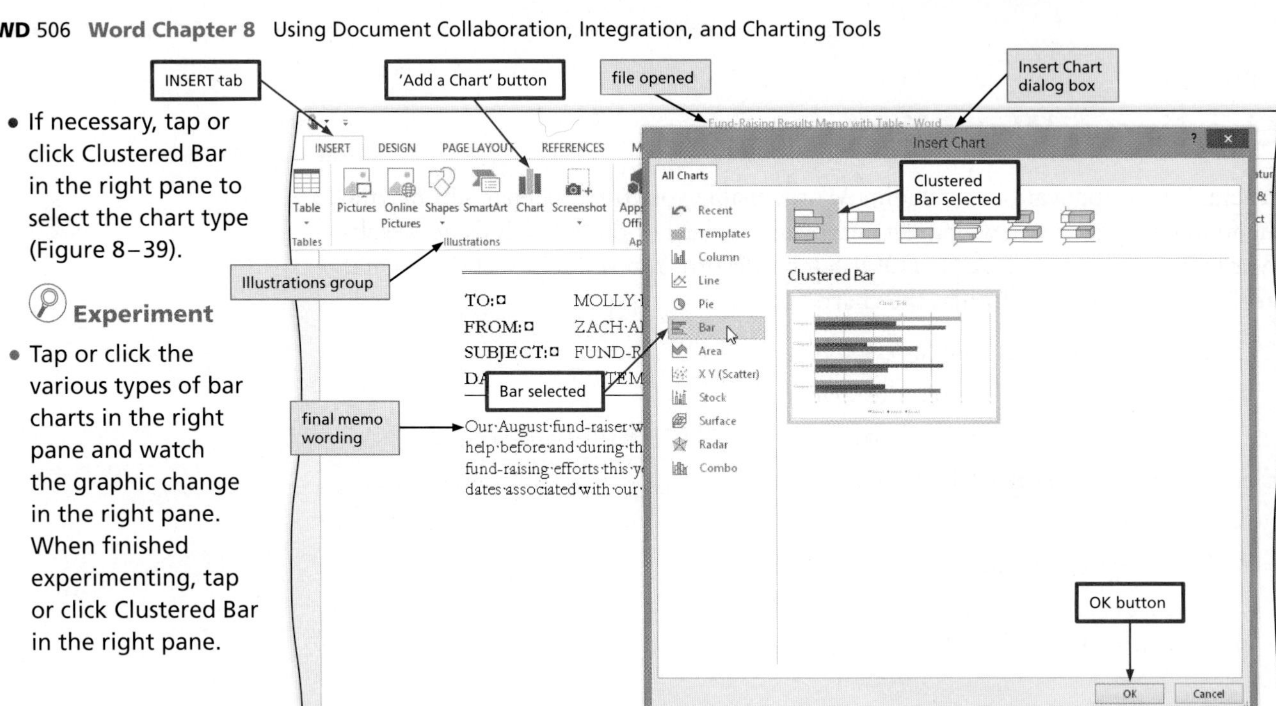

Figure 8–39

2

- Tap or click the OK button so that Word creates a default clustered bar chart in the Word document at the location of the insertion point (Figure 8–40).

Q&A What are the requirements for the format of a table that can be charted?

The chart spreadsheet window shows the layout for the selected chart type. In this case, the categories are in the rows and the series are in the columns. Notice the categories appear in the chart in reverse order.

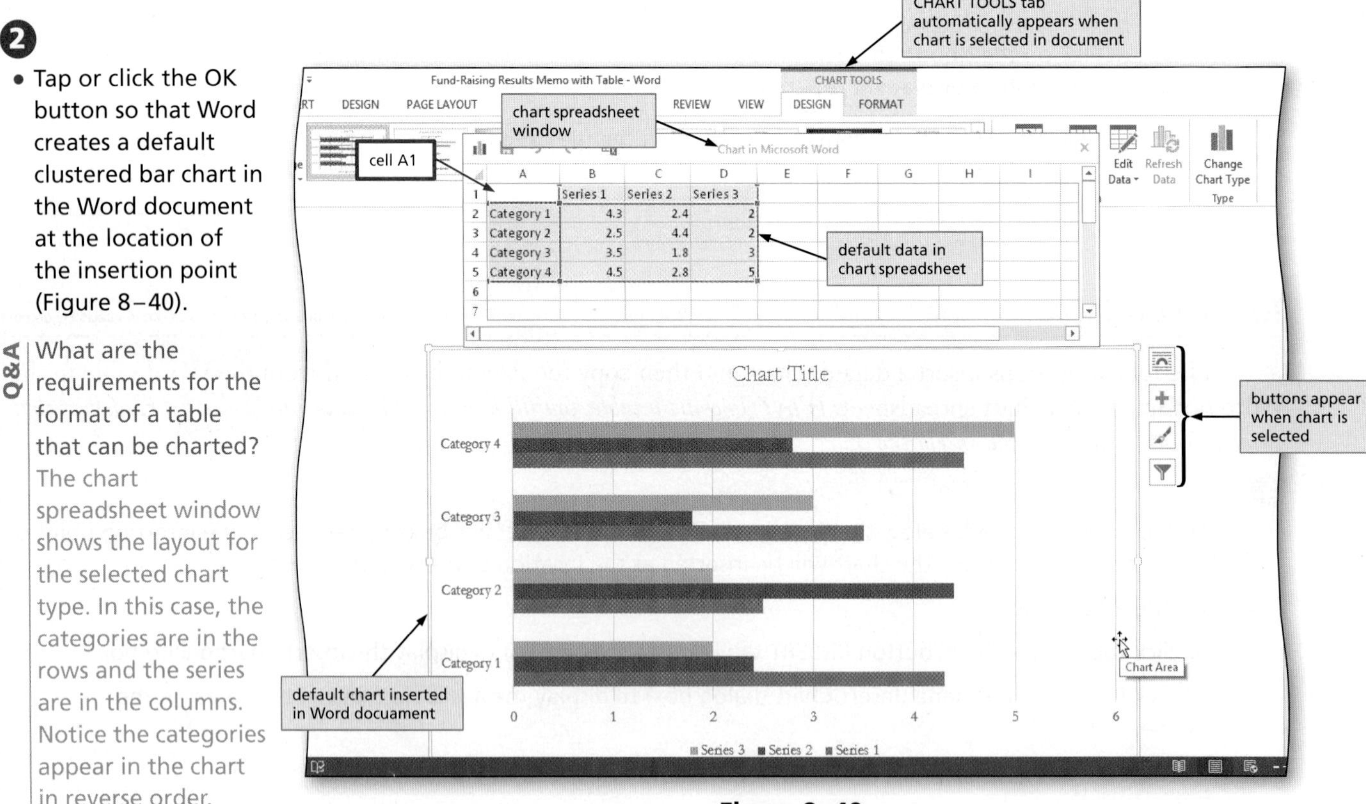

Figure 8–40

3

- In the Word document, select the table to be charted.
- Tap or click the Copy button (HOME tab | Clipboard group) to copy the selected table to the Clipboard (Figure 8–41).

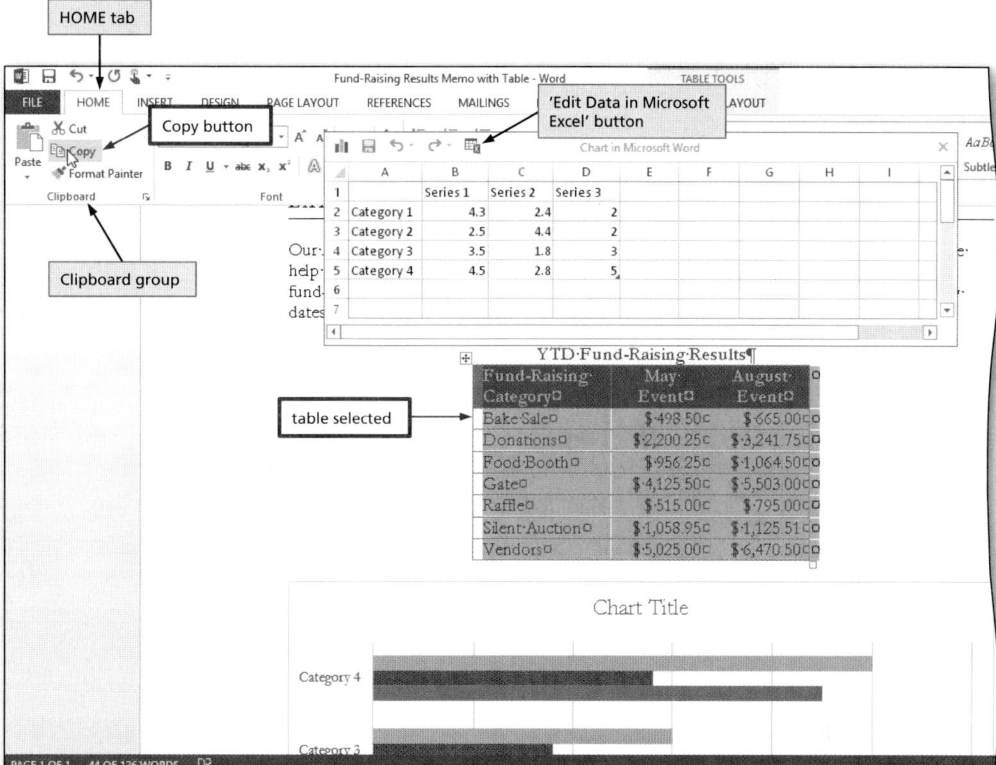

Figure 8–41

Q&A Instead of copying table data to the chart spreadsheet, could I type the data directly into the spreadsheet? Yes. If the chart spreadsheet window does not appear, tap or click the Edit Data arrow (CHART TOOLS DESIGN tab | Data group) and then tap or click Edit Data on the menu. You also can tap or click the 'Edit Data in Microsoft Excel' button to use Excel to enter the data (if Excel is installed on your computer), or tap or click the Edit Data arrow (CHART TOOLS DESIGN tab | Data group) and then tap or click 'Edit Data in Excel 2013' on the Edit Data menu.

4

- In the chart spreadsheet window, tap or click the Select All button (upper-left corner of worksheet) to select the entire worksheet.
- Press and hold or right-click the selected worksheet to display a mini toolbar or shortcut menu (Figure 8–42).

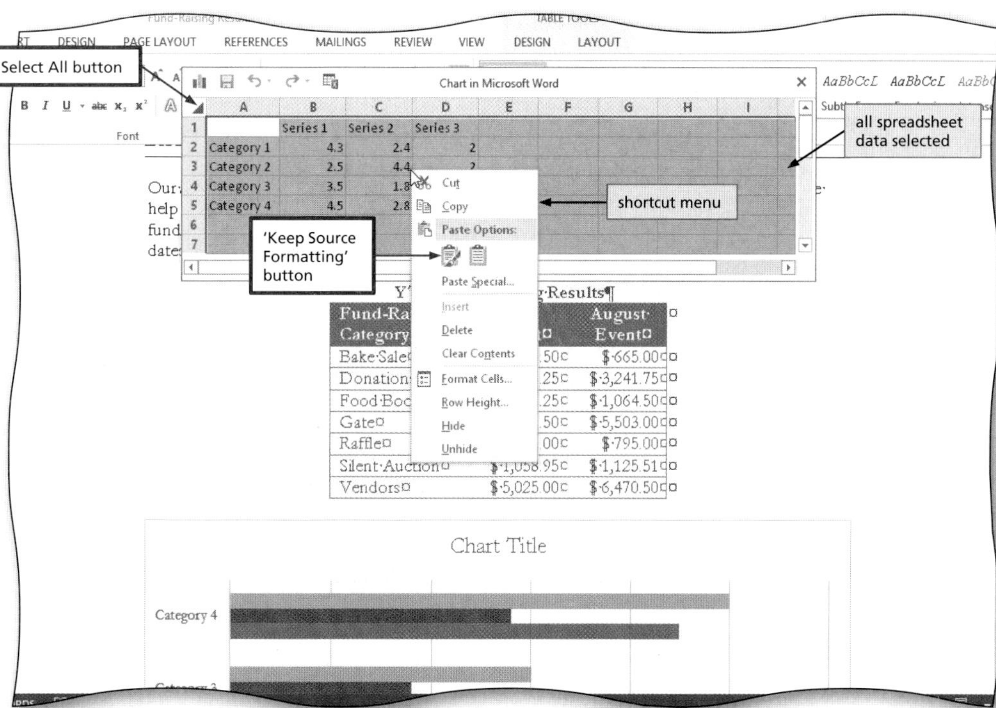

Figure 8–42

- In the chart spreadsheet window, tap the Paste button or click the 'Keep Source Formatting' button to paste the contents of the Clipboard starting in the upper-left corner of the worksheet.
- When Word displays a dialog box indicating that the pasted contents are a different size from the selection, tap or click the OK button.

Q&A Why did Word display this dialog box?

The source table contains three columns, and the target worksheet has four columns. In the next section, you will delete the fourth column from the chart spreadsheet.

- Resize the chart worksheet window by dragging its window edges and move it by dragging its title bar so it appears as shown in Figure 8–43. Notice that the chart in the Word window automatically changes to reflect the new data in the chart worksheet (Figure 8–43).

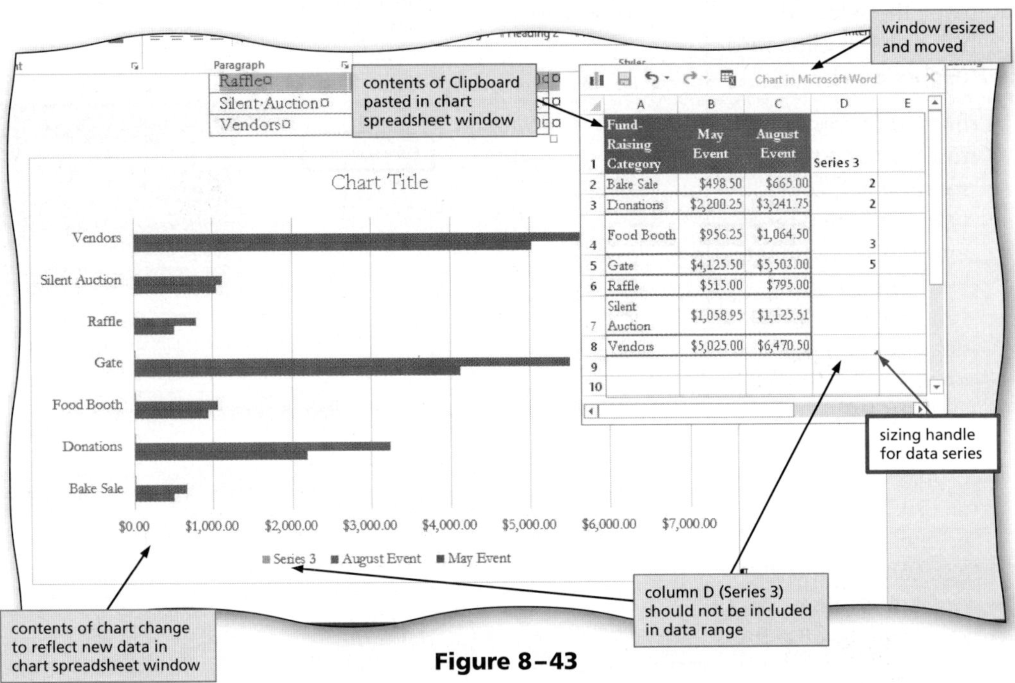

Figure 8–43

To Remove a Data Series from the Chart

1 INSERT COMMENTS & TRACK CHANGES | 2 REVIEW COMMENTS & TRACKED CHANGES
3 LINK EXCEL WORKSHEET TO WORD DOCUMENT | 4 CHART WORD TABLE | 5 CREATE & PUBLISH BLOG POST

The following steps remove the data in column D from the chart, which is plotted as Series 3 (shown in Figure 8–43). ***Why?*** *By default, Word selects the first four columns in the chart spreadsheet window. The chart in this project covers only the first three columns: the fund-raising categories and two data series — May Event and August Event.*

- Drag the sizing handle in cell D8 of the chart spreadsheet leftward so that the selection ends at cell C8; that is the selection should encompass cells A1 through C8 (Figure 8–44).

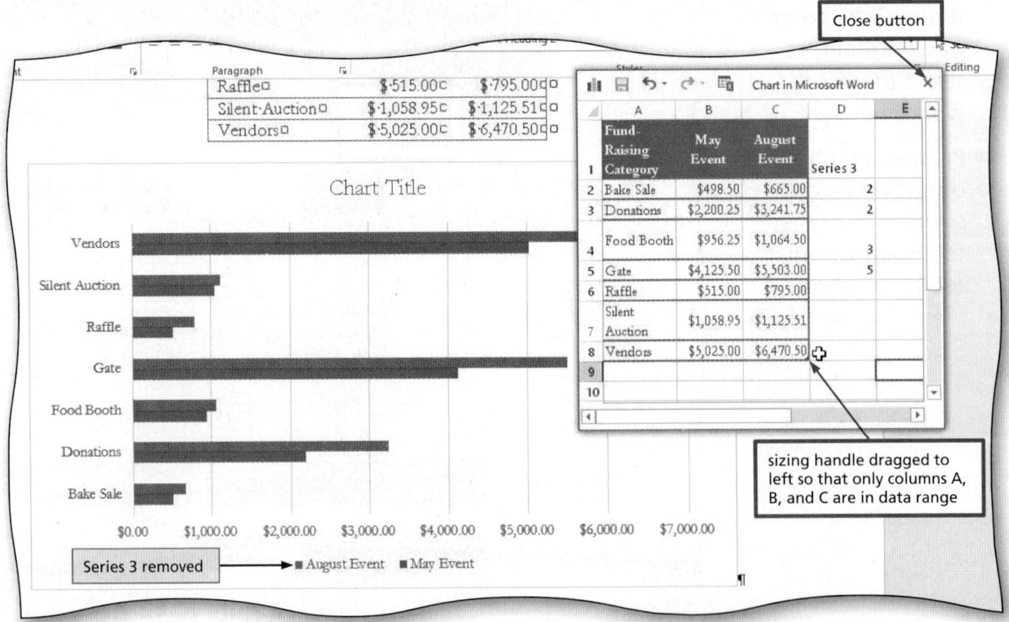

Figure 8–44

Q&A How would I add a data series?

Add a column of data to the chart spreadsheet. Drag the sizing handle outward to include the series, or you could tap or click the Select Data button (CHART TOOLS DESIGN tab | Data group), tap or click the Add button (Select Data Source dialog box), tap or click the Select Range button (Edit Series dialog box), drag through the data range in the worksheet, and then tap or click the OK button.

How would I add or remove data categories?

Follow the same steps to add or remove data series, except work with spreadsheet rows instead of columns.

2

- Close the chart spreadsheet window by tapping or clicking its Close button.

Other Ways

1. Tap or click Select Data button (CHART TOOLS DESIGN tab | Data group), tap or click series to remove (Select Data Source dialog box), tap or click Remove button, tap or click OK button

To Apply a Chart Style

1 INSERT COMMENTS & TRACK CHANGES | 2 REVIEW COMMENTS & TRACKED CHANGES
3 LINK EXCEL WORKSHEET TO WORD DOCUMENT | 4 CHART WORD TABLE | 5 CREATE & PUBLISH BLOG POST

The next step is to apply a chart style to the chart. ***Why?*** *Word provides a Chart Styles gallery, allowing you to change the chart's format to a more visually appealing style.* The following steps apply a chart style to a chart.

1

- Display the CHART TOOLS DESIGN tab.
- Tap or click the chart to select it.
- If you are using a mouse, point to Style 5 in the Chart Styles gallery (CHART TOOLS DESIGN tab | Chart Styles group) to display a live preview of that style applied to the graphic in the document (Figure 8–45).

Experiment

- If you are using a mouse, point to various styles in the Chart Styles gallery and watch the style of the chart change in the document window.

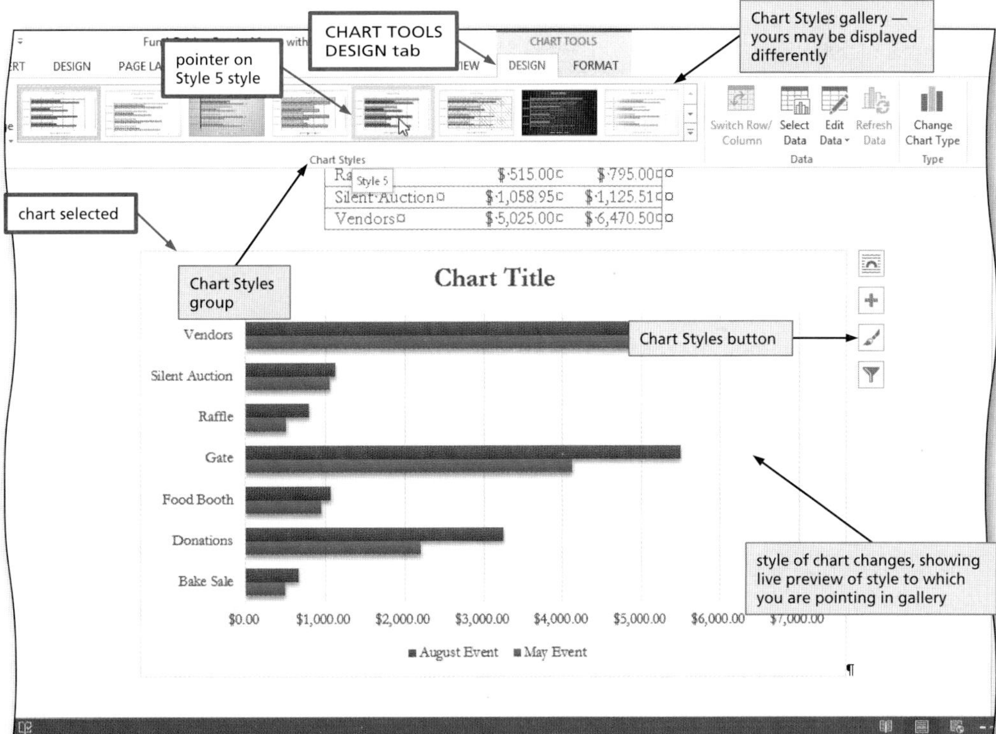

Figure 8-45

2

- Tap or click Style 5 in the Chart Styles gallery (CHART TOOLS DESIGN tab | Chart Styles group) to apply the selected style to the chart.

Other Ways

1. Tap or click Chart Styles button attached to chart, tap or click STYLE tab, tap or click desired style

To Change Colors of a Chart

1 INSERT COMMENTS & TRACK CHANGES | 2 REVIEW COMMENTS & TRACKED CHANGES
3 LINK EXCEL WORKSHEET TO WORD DOCUMENT | 4 CHART WORD TABLE | **5 CREATE & PUBLISH BLOG POST**

The following steps change the colors of the chart. ***Why?*** *Word provides a predefined variety of colors for charts. You select one that best matches the colors already used in the letter.*

1

- With the chart selected, tap or click the 'Chart Quick Colors' button (CHART TOOLS DESIGN tab | Chart Styles group) to display the Chart Quick Colors gallery.

Q&A What if the chart is not selected?
Tap or click the chart to select it.

- If you are using a mouse, point to Color 4 in the Chart Quick Colors gallery to display a live preview of the selected color applied to the chart in the document (Figure 8–46).

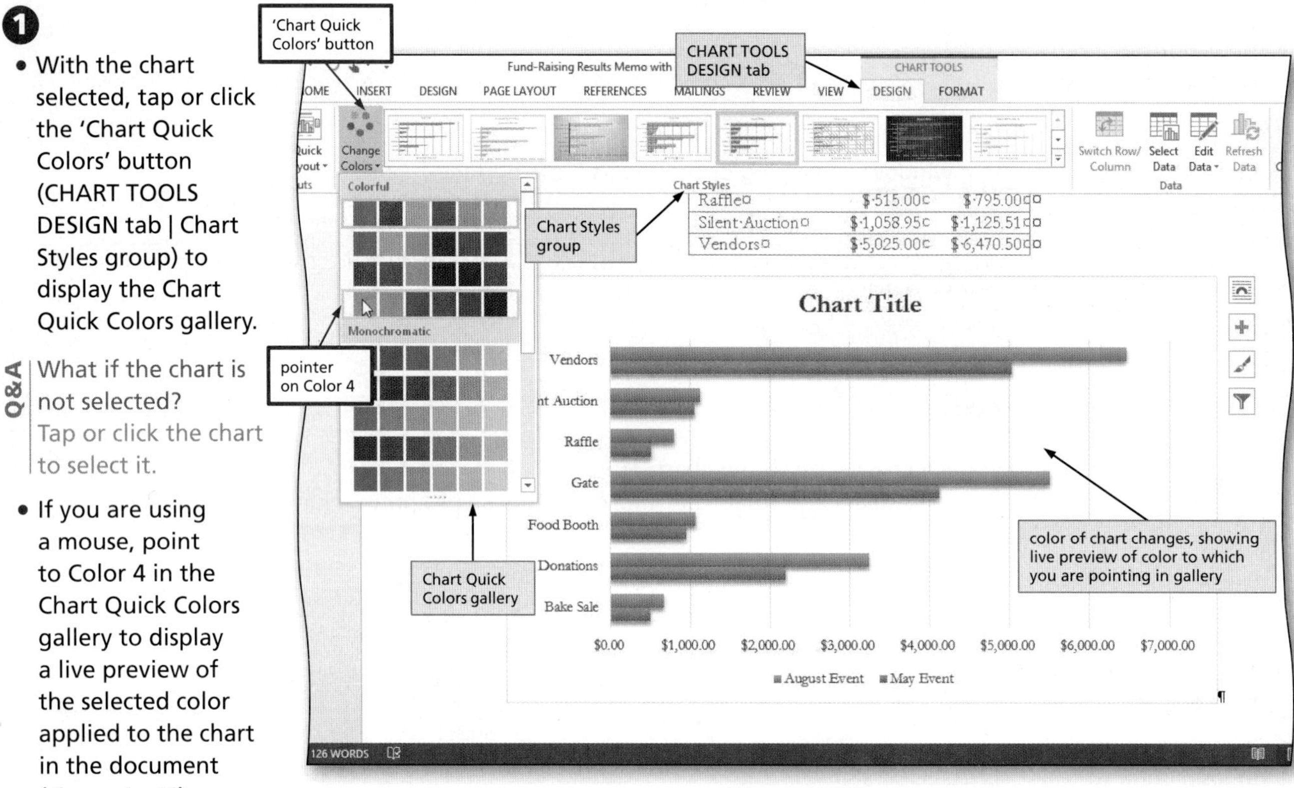

Figure 8-46

Experiment

- If you are using a mouse, point to various colors in the Chart Quick Colors gallery and watch the colors of the graphic change in the document window.

- Tap or click Color 4 in the Chart Quick Colors gallery to apply the selected color to the chart.

Other Ways

1. Tap or click Chart Styles button attached to chart, tap or click COLOR tab, tap or click desired style

To Add a Chart Element

1 INSERT COMMENTS & TRACK CHANGES | 2 REVIEW COMMENTS & TRACKED CHANGES
3 LINK EXCEL WORKSHEET TO WORD DOCUMENT | 4 CHART WORD TABLE | **5 CREATE & PUBLISH BLOG POST**

The following steps add minor vertical gridlines to the chart. ***Why?*** *You want to add more vertical lines to the chart so that it is easier to see the dollar values associated with each bar length.*

1

- With the chart selected, tap or click the 'Add Chart Element' button (CHART TOOLS DESIGN tab | Chart Layouts group) to display the Add Chart Element gallery and then tap or point to Gridlines to display the Gridlines submenu (Figure 8–47).

Experiment

- If you are using a mouse, point to various elements in the Add Chart Element gallery so that you can see the other types of elements you can add to a chart. When finished, point to Gridlines.

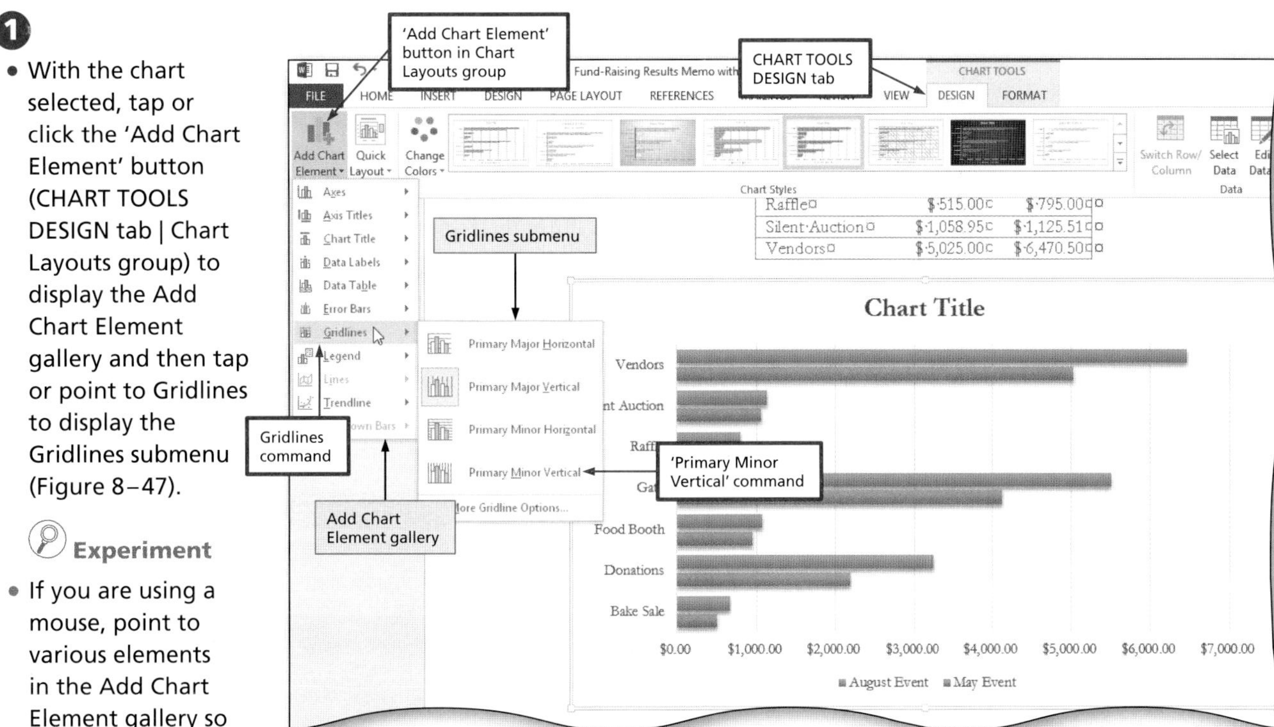

Figure 8–47

2

- Tap or click 'Primary Minor Vertical' on the Gridline submenu to add vertical minor gridlines to the chart (Figure 8–48).

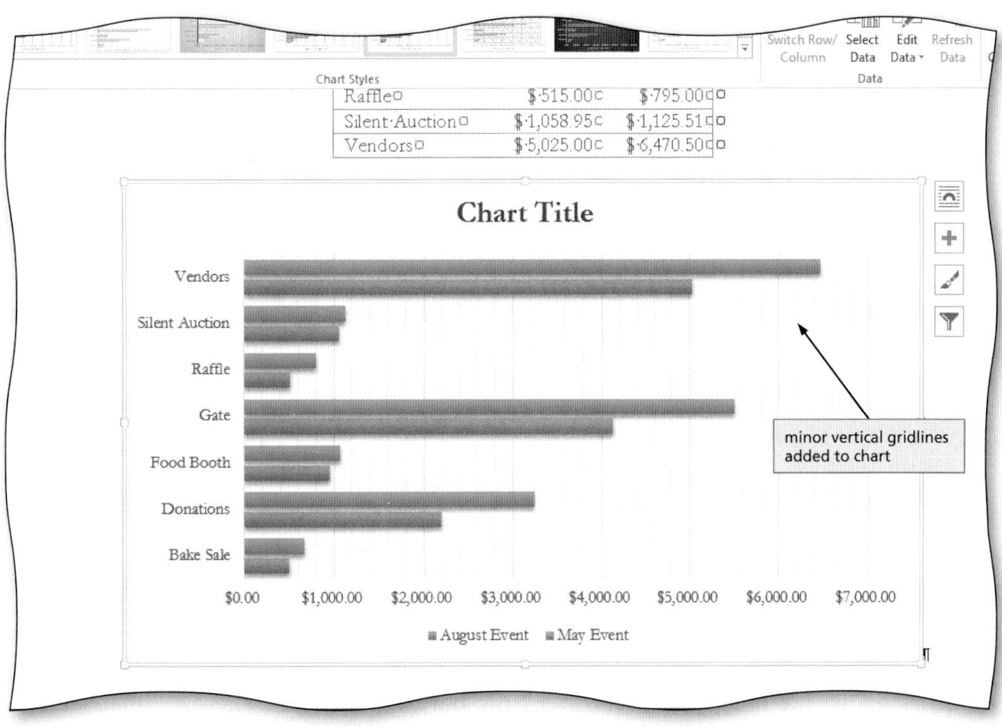

Figure 8–48

To Select a Chart Element and Edit It

1 INSERT COMMENTS & TRACK CHANGES | 2 REVIEW COMMENTS & TRACKED CHANGES
3 LINK EXCEL WORKSHEET TO WORD DOCUMENT | 4 CHART WORD TABLE | 5 CREATE & PUBLISH BLOG POST

The following steps change the chart title. ***Why?*** *You want to change the title from the default to a more meaningful name.*

- Display the CHART TOOLS FORMAT tab.
- With the chart selected, tap or click the Chart Elements arrow (CHART TOOLS FORMAT tab | Current Selection group) to display the Chart Elements list (Figure 8–49).

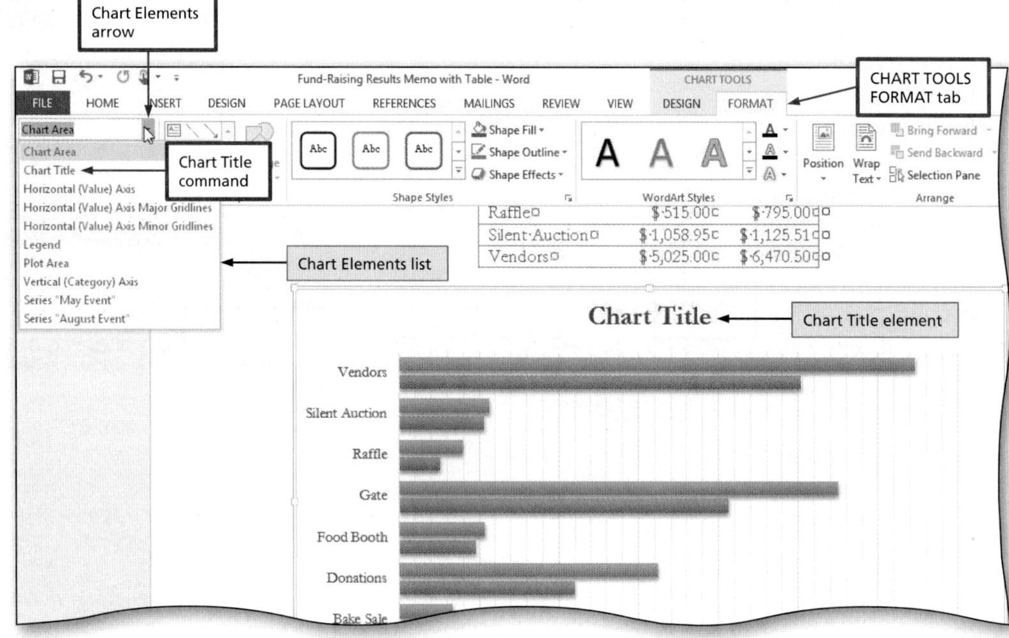

Figure 8–49

2

- Tap or click Chart Title in the Chart Elements list to select the chart's title.
- Type **`Fund-Raising Results by Category`** as the new title (Figure 8–50).

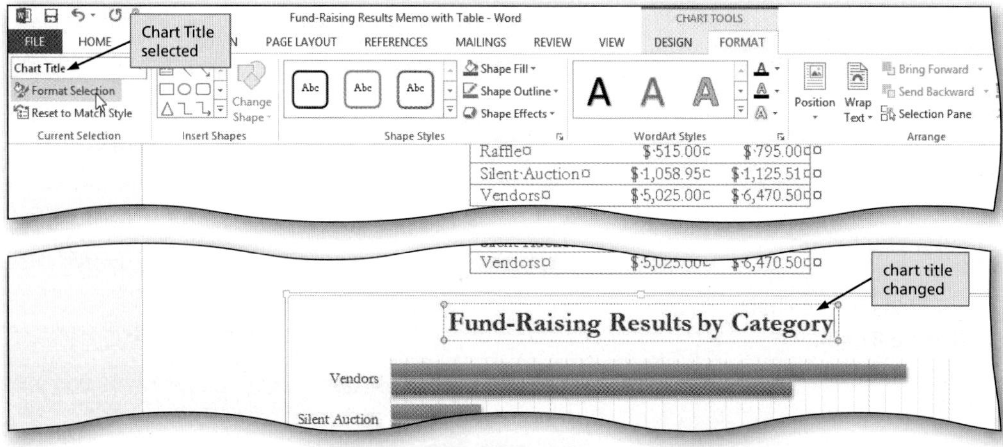

Figure 8–50

Other Ways

1. Tap or click the chart element in the chart to select the element

To Format Chart Elements

1 INSERT COMMENTS & TRACK CHANGES | 2 REVIEW COMMENTS & TRACKED CHANGES
3 LINK EXCEL WORKSHEET TO WORD DOCUMENT | 4 CHART WORD TABLE | 5 CREATE & PUBLISH BLOG POST

Currently, the category names on the vertical axis are in reverse order of the row labels in the table; that is, category names are in alphabetical order from bottom to top and the row labels in the table are in alphabetical order from top to bottom. Also, the numbers across the bottom display with no cents following the dollar values. The following steps format axis elements. ***Why?*** *You want the categories to display in the same order as the table, the numbers to display as whole numbers, and the legend to appear at the top of the chart.*

1

- If necessary, select the chart by tapping or clicking it.
- With the chart selected, tap or click the Chart Elements arrow (CHART TOOLS FORMAT tab | Current Selection group) to display the Chart Elements list and then tap or click 'Vertical (Category) Axis'.
- Tap or click the Chart Elements button attached to the right of the chart to display the CHART ELEMENTS gallery.
- Tap or point to and then click the Axes arrow in the CHART ELEMENTS gallery to display the Axes fly-out menu (Figure 8–51).

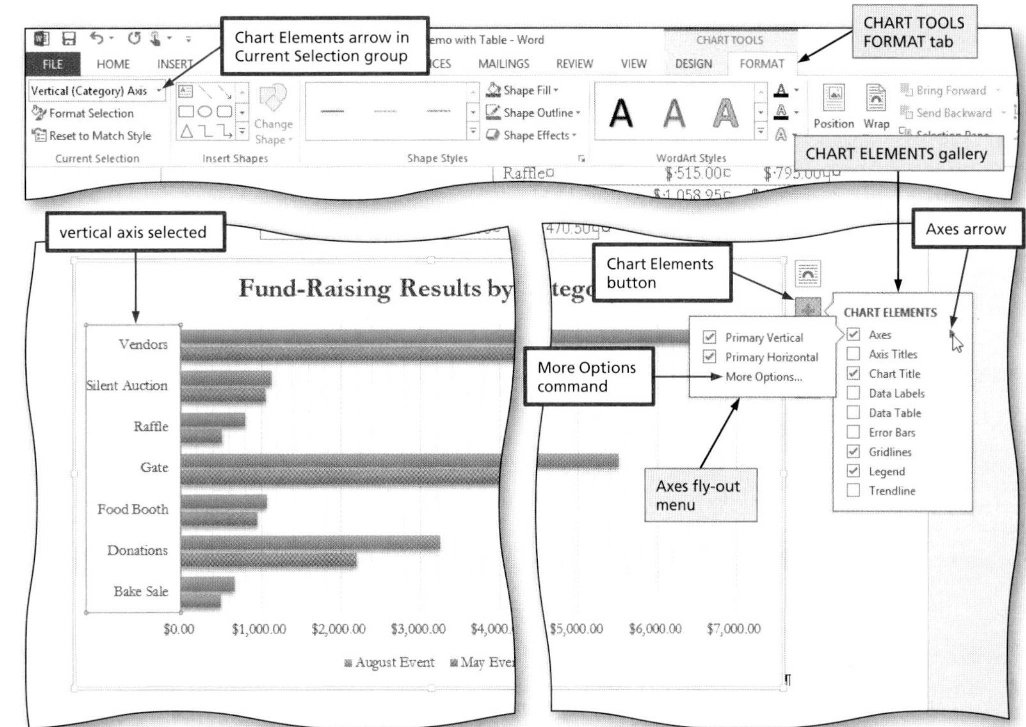

Figure 8–51

2

- Tap or click More Options on the Axes fly-out menu to display the Format Axis task pane.
- If necessary, tap or click AXIS OPTIONS to expand the section.
- If necessary, tap or click the Chart Elements arrow (CHART TOOLS FORMAT tab | Current Selection group) to display the Chart Elements list and then tap or click 'Vertical (Category) Axis'.
- Place a check mark in the 'Categories in reverse order' check box so that the order of the categories in the chart matches the order of the categories in the table (Figure 8–52).

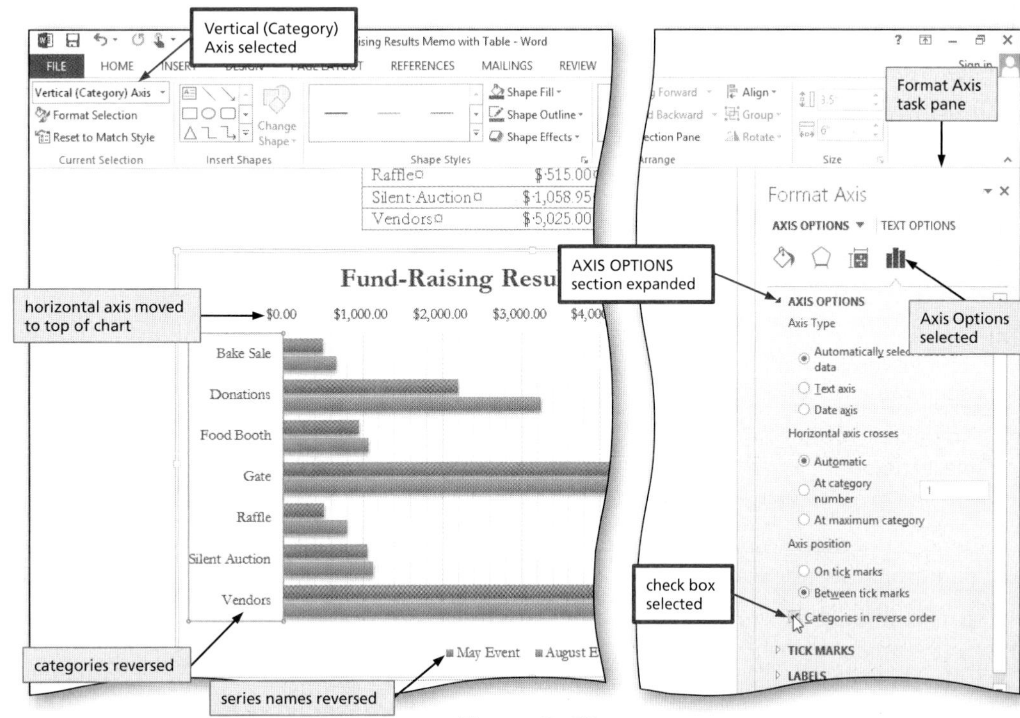

Figure 8–52

Q&A Why did the horizontal axis move from the bottom of the chart to the top?

When you reverse the categories, the horizontal axis automatically moves from the bottom of the chart to the top of the chart. Notice that the series names below the chart also are reversed.

3

- With the chart selected, tap or click the Chart Elements arrow (CHART TOOLS FORMAT tab | Current Selection group) to display the Chart Elements list and then tap or click 'Horizontal (Value) Axis'.
- If necessary, tap or click LABELS and NUMBER at the bottom of the Format Axis task pane to expand the sections in the task pane.
- If necessary, scroll the task pane to display the entire LABELS and NUMBER sections.
- In the LABELS section, tap or click the Label Position arrow and then tap or click High to move the axis to the bottom of the chart.
- In the NUMBER section, change the value in the Decimal places text box to 0 (the number zero) and then press the ENTER key (Figure 8–53).

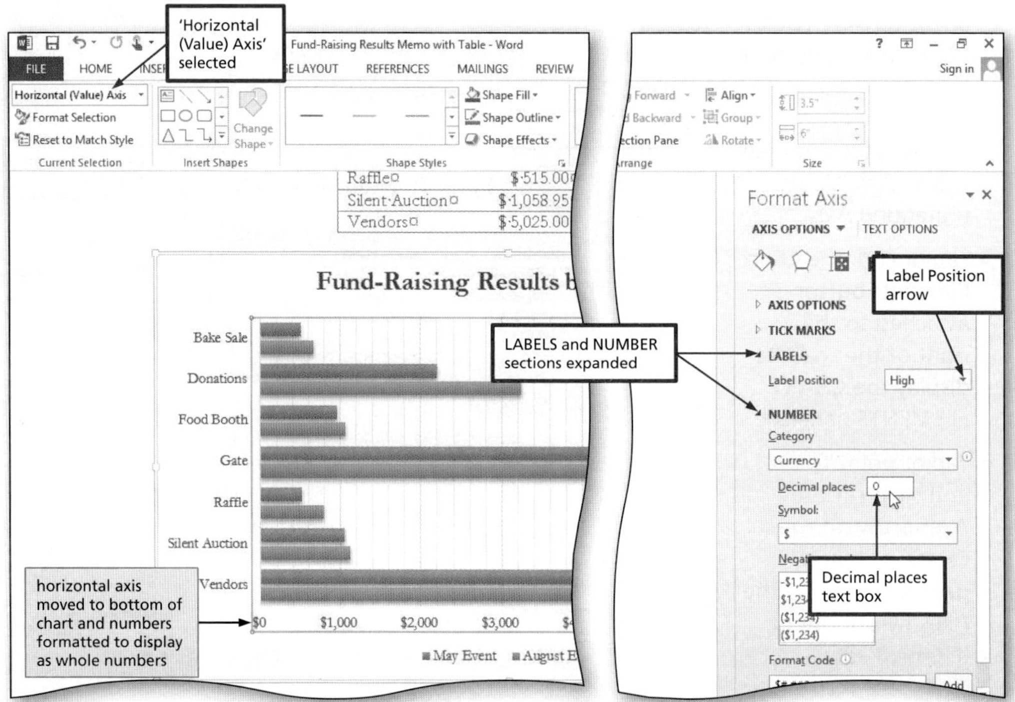

Figure 8–53

4

- With the chart selected, tap or click the Chart Elements arrow (CHART TOOLS FORMAT tab | Current Selection group) to display the Chart Elements list and then tap or click Legend.

Q&A What happened to the Format Axis task pane?
It now is the Format Legend task pane. The task pane title and options change, depending on the element you are using or formatting.

- If necessary, tap or click LEGEND OPTIONS to expand the section in the Legend task pane.
- Tap or click Top to select the option button.
- Remove the check mark from the 'Show the legend without overlapping the chart' check box so that the legend drops down into the chart a bit (Figure 8–54).

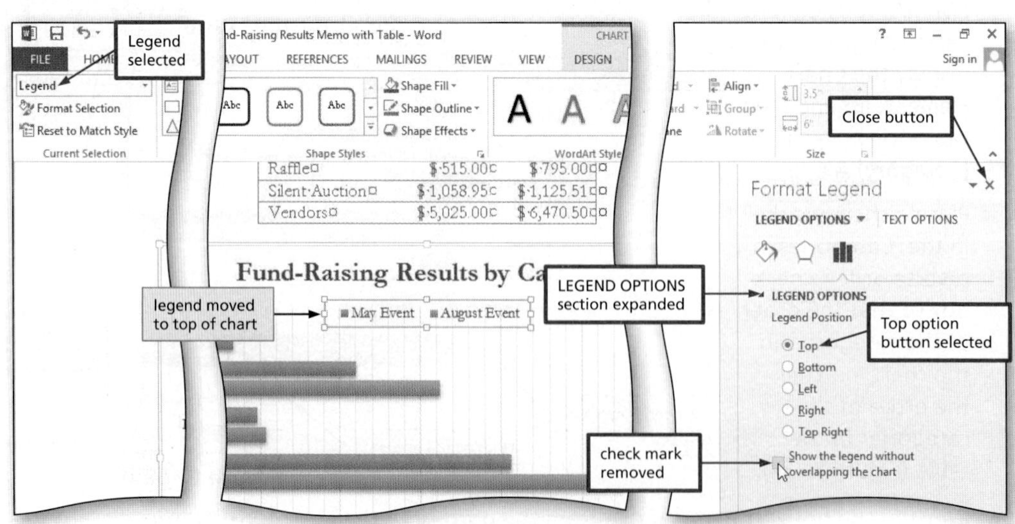

Figure 8–54

- Drag the legend up slightly so that it rests on top of the vertical lines in the chart.
- Close the task pane by tapping or clicking its close button.

To Add an Outline to a Chart

1 INSERT COMMENTS & TRACK CHANGES | 2 REVIEW COMMENTS & TRACKED CHANGES
3 LINK EXCEL WORKSHEET TO WORD DOCUMENT | 4 CHART WORD TABLE | 5 CREATE & PUBLISH BLOG POST

The following steps add an outline to the chart with a shadow. ***Why?*** *You want a border surrounding the chart.*

- With the chart selected, tap or click the Chart Elements arrow (CHART TOOLS FORMAT tab | Current Selection group) to display the Chart Elements list and then tap or click Chart Area.
- Tap or click the Shape Outline arrow (CHART TOOLS FORMAT tab | Shape Styles group) to display the Shape Outline gallery.

2

- Tap or click 'Blue, Accent 1' (fifth color, first row) in the Shape Outline gallery to change the outline color.
- Tap or click the Shape Outline arrow (CHART TOOLS FORMAT tab | Shape Styles group) again and then tap or point to Weight in the Shape Outline gallery to display the Weight gallery (Figure 8–55).

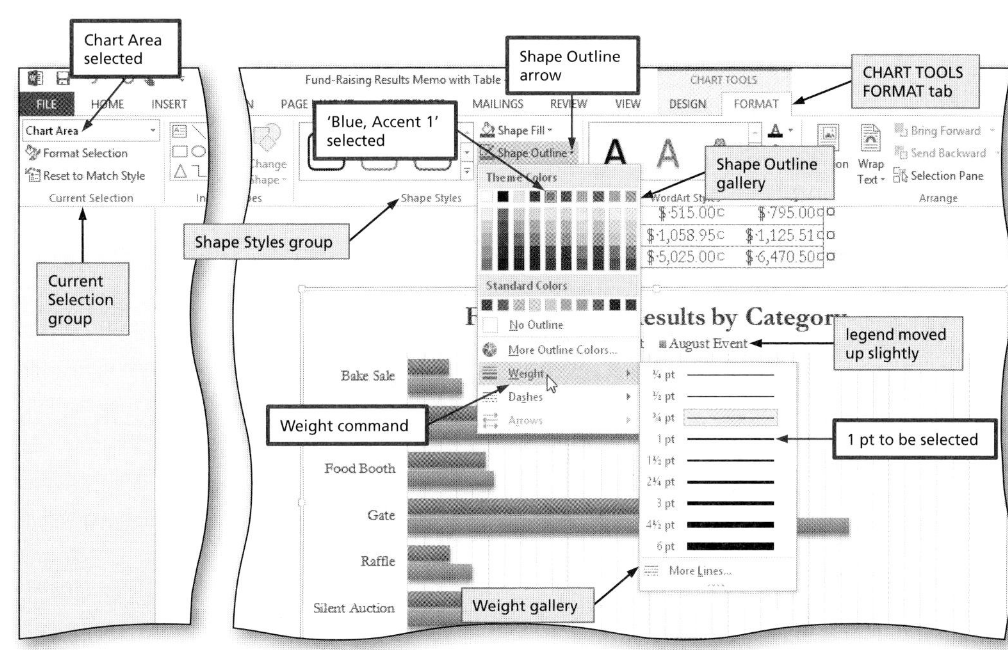

Figure 8–55

- Tap or click 1 pt in the Weight gallery to apply the selected weight to the outline.
- Tap or click the Shape Effects button (CHART TOOLS FORMAT tab | Shape Styles group) and then tap or point to Shadow in the Shape Effects gallery to display the Shadow gallery (Figure 8–56).

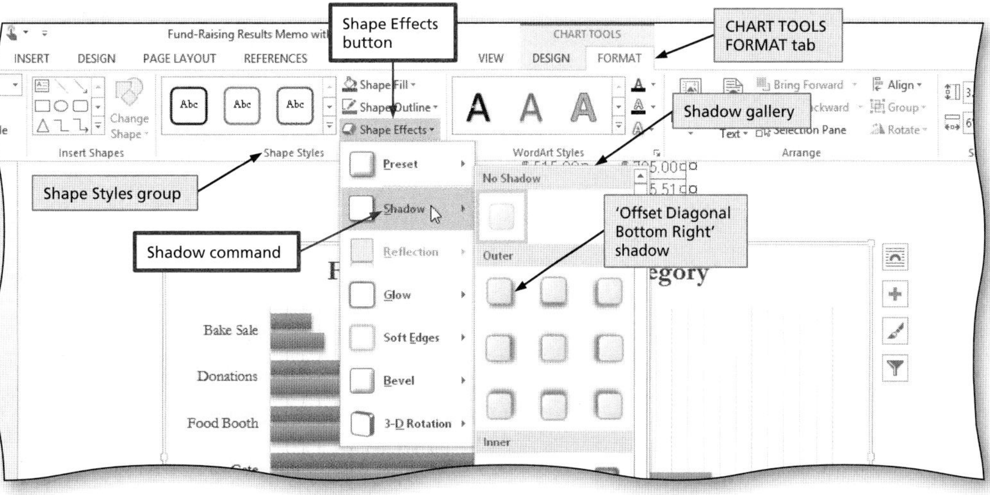

Figure 8–56

- Tap or click 'Offset Diagonal Bottom Right' in the Shadow gallery to apply the selected shadow to the outline.

To Save an Active Document with a New File Name and Close the File

You are finished charting the Word table with a clustered chart. Thus, the following steps save the document.

1. Open the Backstage view and then tap or click the Save As tab to display the Save As gallery.
2. Navigate to the desired save location and save the document with the file name, Fund-Raising Results Memo with Table and Clustered Chart.

To Change a Chart Type

1 INSERT COMMENTS & TRACK CHANGES | 2 REVIEW COMMENTS & TRACKED CHANGES
3 LINK EXCEL WORKSHEET TO WORD DOCUMENT | 4 CHART WORD TABLE | **5 CREATE & PUBLISH BLOG POST**

The following steps change the chart type. ***Why?*** *After reviewing the document, you would like to see how the chart looks as a 3-D clustered bar chart.*

- Display the CHART TOOLS DESIGN tab.
- Tap or click the 'Change Chart Type' button (CHART TOOLS DESIGN tab | Type group) to display the Change Chart Type dialog box.
- Tap or click '3-D Clustered Bar' (Change Chart Type dialog box) in the right pane to change the chart type (Figure 8–57).

Experiment

- If you are using a mouse, point to the chart preview in the dialog box to see in more detail how the chart will look in the document.

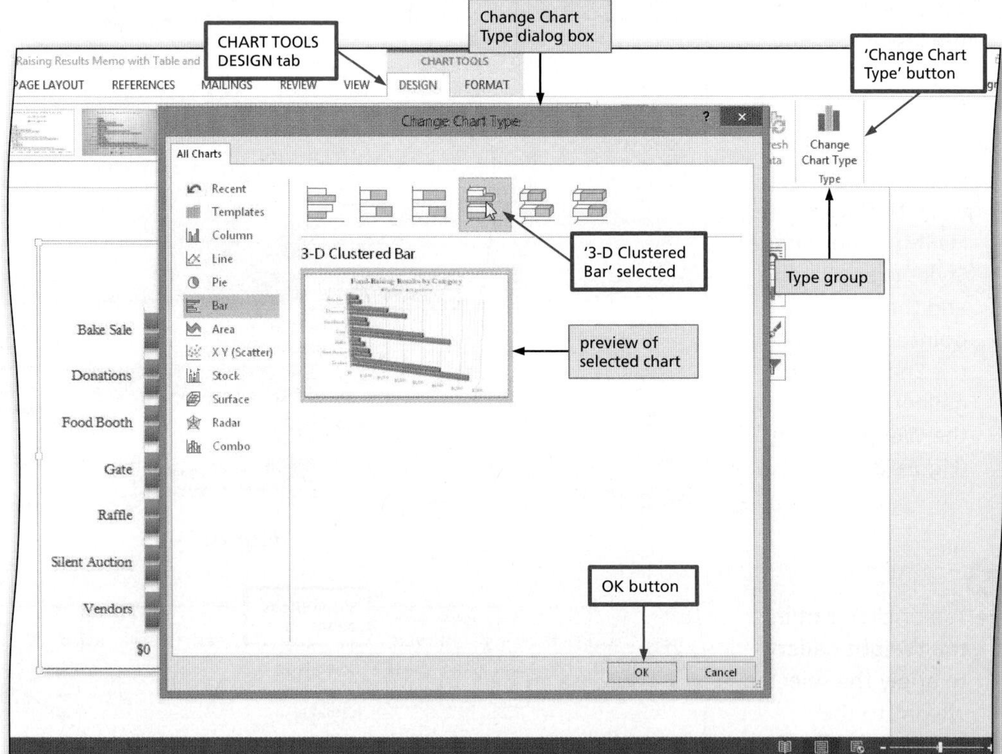

Figure 8–57

- Tap or click the OK button to change the chart type (Figure 8–58).

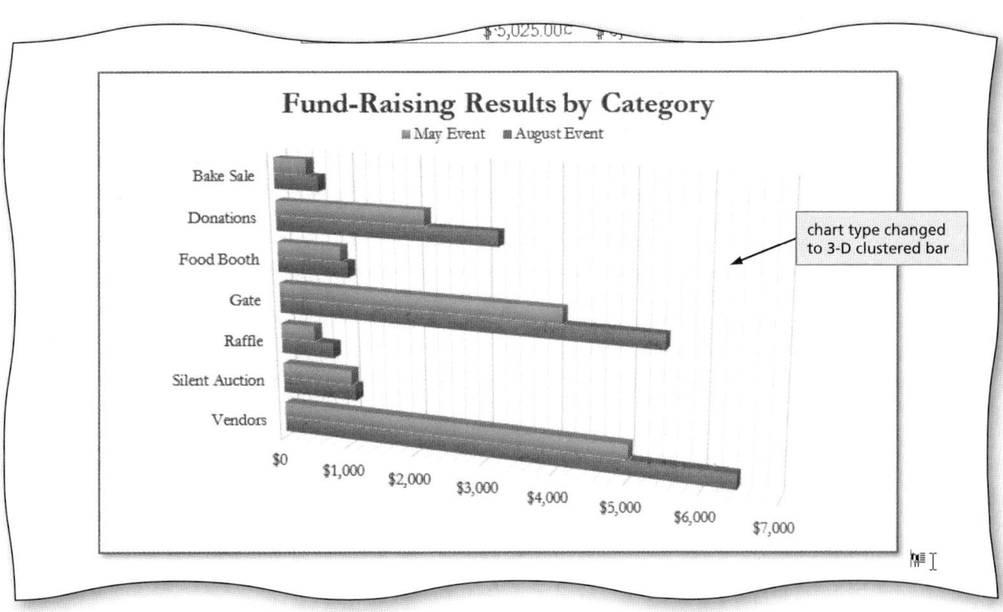

Figure 8–58

To Save an Active Document with a New File Name and Close the File

You would like to save the document with the 3-D clustered chart with a different file name. Thus, the following steps save the document.

1. Open the Backstage view and then tap or click the Save As tab to display the Save As gallery.
2. Navigate to the desired save location and save the document with the file name, Fund-Raising Results Memo with Table and 3-D Clustered Chart.

To Chart a Word Table Using Microsoft Graph

In previous versions of Word, you charted Word tables using an embedded program called Microsoft Graph, or simply Graph. When working with the chart, Graph has its own menus and commands because it is a program embedded in Word. Using Graph commands, you can modify the appearance of the chart after you create it. If you wanted to create a chart using the legacy Graph program, you would perform these steps.

1. Select the rows and columns or table to be charted.
2. Display the INSERT tab.
3. Tap or click the Object button (INSERT tab | Text group) to display the Object dialog box.
4. If necessary, tap or click the Create New tab (Object dialog box).
5. Scroll to and then select 'Microsoft Graph Chart' in the Object type list to specify the object being inserted.
6. Tap or click the OK button to start the Microsoft Graph program, which creates a chart of the selected table or selected rows and columns.

To View and Scroll through Documents Side by Side

Word provides a way to display two documents side by side, each in a separate window. By default, the two documents scroll synchronously, that is, together. If necessary, you can turn off synchronous scrolling so that you can scroll through each document individually. The following steps display documents side by side. ***Why?*** *You would like to see the how the document with the clustered chart looks alongside the document with the 3-D clustered chart.*

- Position the insertion point at the top of the document because you want to begin viewing side by side from the top of the documents.
- Open the file called Fund-Raising Results Memo with Table and Clustered Chart so that both documents are open in Word.
- Display the VIEW tab (Figure 8–59).

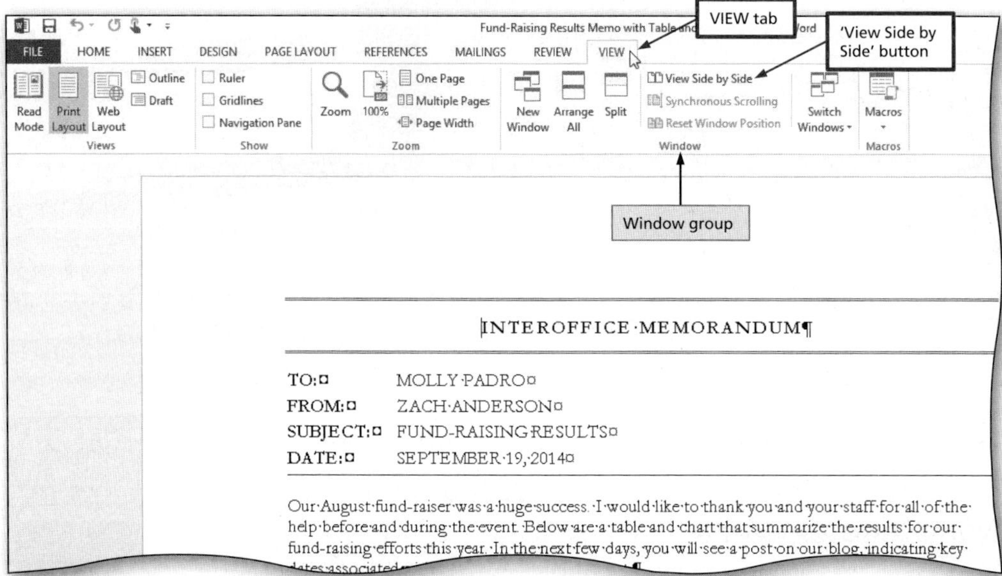

Figure 8–59

2

- Tap or click the 'View Side by Side' button (VIEW tab | Window group) to display each open window side by side (Figure 8–60).

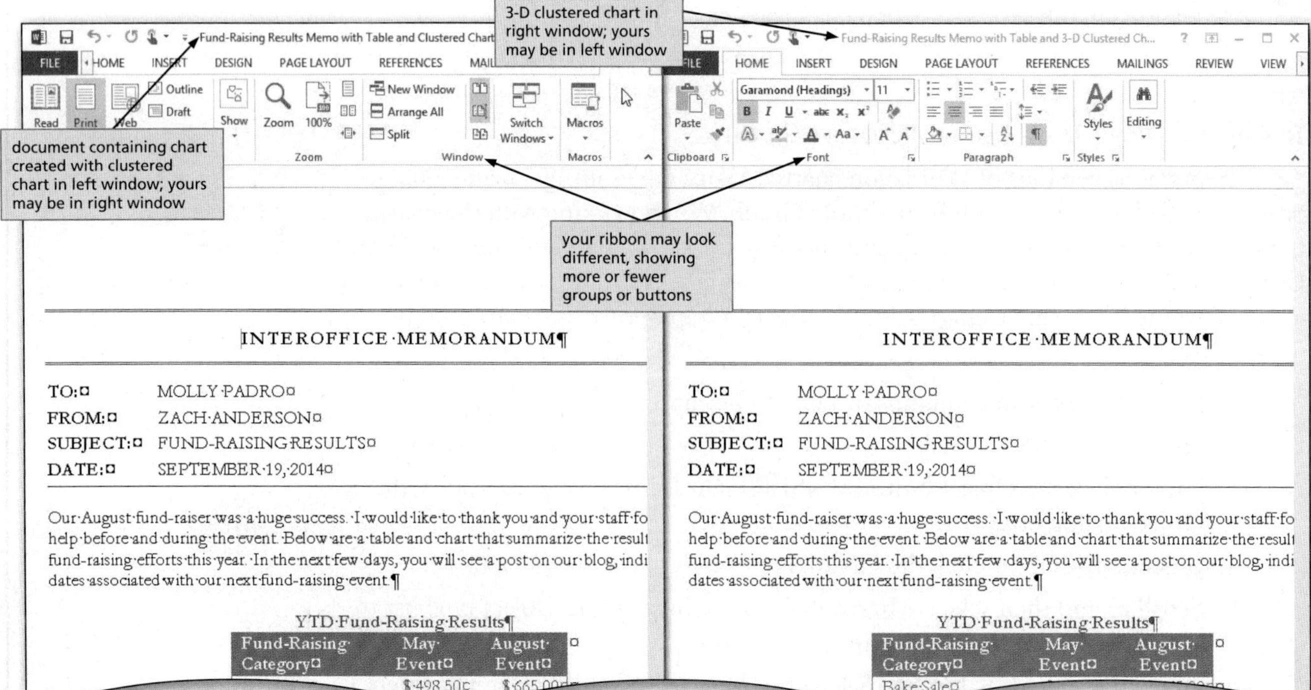

Figure 8–60

- If necessary, adjust the zoom to fit the memo contents in each window.
- Scroll to the bottom of one of the windows and notice how both windows (documents) scroll together (Figure 8–61).

Q&A Can I scroll through one window separately from the other?
By default, synchronous scrolling is active when you display windows side by side. If you want to scroll separately through the windows, simply turn off synchronous scrolling.

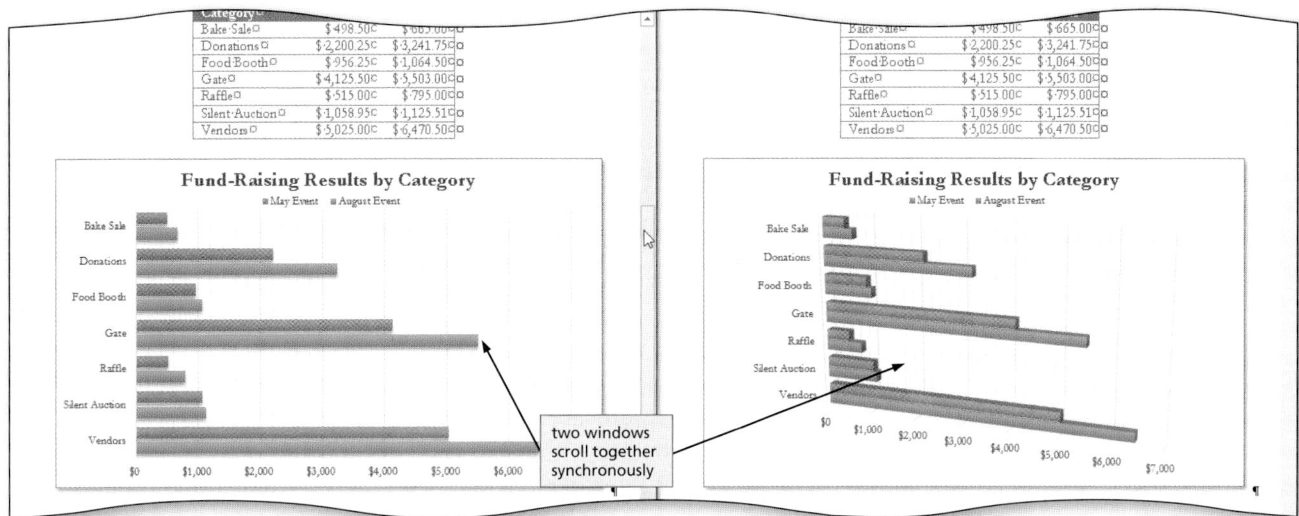

Figure 8–61

4

- If necessary, display the VIEW tab (in either window).
- Tap or click the Synchronous Scrolling button (VIEW tab | Window group) to turn off synchronous scrolling.

5

- Scroll to the top of the window on the right and notice that the window on the left does not scroll because you turned off synchronous scrolling (Figure 8–62).

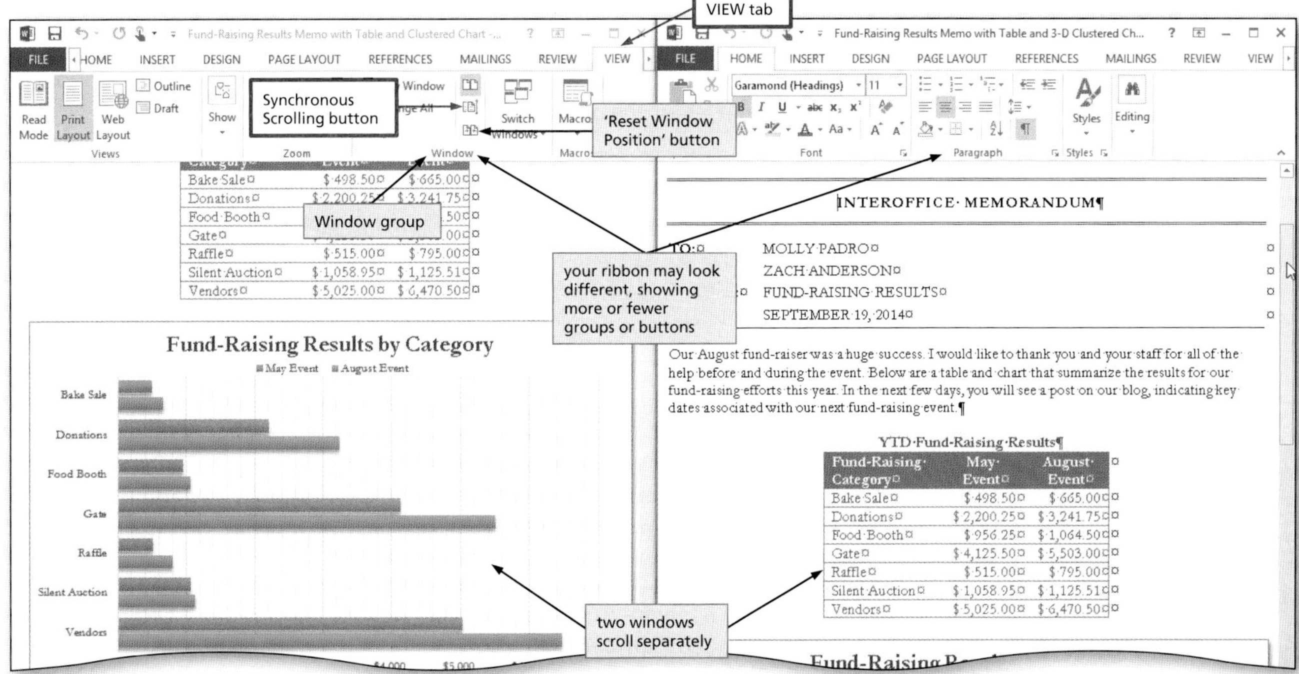

Figure 8–62

Q&A | What is the purpose of the 'Reset Window Position' button?
It repositions the side-by-side windows so that each consumes the same amount of screen space.

6

- In either window, tap or click the 'View Side by Side' button (VIEW tab | Window group) to turn off side-by-side viewing and display each window in the full screen.
- Close each open Word document, saving them if prompted.

Break Point: If you wish to take a break, this is a good place to do so. You can exit Word now. To resume at a later time, run Word and continue following the steps from this location forward.

Creating a Blog Post

A **blog**, short for **weblog**, is an informal website consisting of date- or time-stamped articles, or **posts**, in a diary or journal format, usually listed in reverse chronological order. Blogs reflect the interests, opinions, and personalities of the author, called the **blogger**, and sometimes of the website visitors as well.

Blogs have become an important means of worldwide communications. Businesses create blogs to communicate with employees, customers, and vendors. Teachers create blogs to collaborate with other teachers and students, and home users create blogs to share aspects of their personal life with family, friends, and others.

This section of the chapter creates a blog post and then publishes it to a registered blog account at WordPress, which is a blogging service on the web. The blog relays current events for the Yellville Community Center. This specific blog post is a communication about the fund-raisers.

CONSIDER THIS

What should you consider when creating and posting on a blog?

When creating a blog post, you should follow these general guidelines:

1. **Create a blog account on the web.** Many websites exist that allow users to set up a blog free or for a fee. Blogging services that work with Word 2013 include Blogger, SharePoint blog, Telligent Community, TypePad, and WordPress. For illustration purposes in this chapter, a free blog account was created at WordPress.com.
2. **Register your blog account in Word.** Before you can use Word to publish a blog post, you must register your blog account in Word. This step establishes a connection between Word and your blog account. The first time you create a new blog post, Word will ask if you want to register a blog account. You can tap or click the Register Later button if you want to learn how to create a blog post without registering a blog account.
3. **Create a blog post.** Use Word to enter the text and any graphics in your blog post. Some blogging services accept graphics directly from a Word blog post. Others require that you use a picture hosting service to store pictures you use in a blog post.
4. **Publish a blog post.** When you publish a blog post, the blog post in the Word document is copied to your account at the blogging service. Once the post is published, it appears at the top of the blog webpage. You may need to tap or click the Refresh button in the browser window to display the new post.

To Register a Blog Account

Once you set up a blog account with a blog provider, you must register it in Word so that you can publish your Word post on the blog account. Examples of blog providers are Blogger, SharePoint blog, Telligent Community, TypePad, and WordPress. To register a blog account, with WordPress for example, you would perform the following steps.

1. Tap or click the Manage Accounts button (BLOG POST tab | Blog group) to display the Blog Accounts dialog box.
2. Tap or click the New button (Blog Accounts dialog box) to display the New Blog Account dialog box.

3. Tap or click the Blog arrow (New Blog Account dialog box) to display a list of blog providers and then select your provider in the list.
4. Tap or click the Next button to display the New [Provider] Account dialog box (i.e., a New WordPress Account dialog box would appear if you selected WordPress as the provider).
5. In the Blog Post URL text box, replace the <Enter your blog URL here> text with the web address for your blog account. (Note that your dialog box may differ, depending on the provider you select.)

Q&A What is a URL?

A URL (Uniform Resource Locator), often called a web address, is the unique address for a webpage. For example, the web address for a WordPress blog account might be smith.wordpress.com; in that case, the complete blog post URL would read as http://smith.wordpress.com/xhlrpc.php in the text box.

6. In the Enter account information area, enter the user name and password you use to access your blog account.

Q&A Should I tap or click the Remember Password check box?

If you do not select this check box, Word will prompt you for a password each time you publish to the blog account.

7. If your blog provider does not allow pictures to be stored, tap or click the Picture Options button, select the correct option for storing your posted pictures, and then tap or click the OK button (Picture Options dialog box).
8. Tap or click the OK button to register the blog account.
9. When Word displays a dialog box indicating the account registration was successful, tap or click the OK button.

To Create a Blank Document for a Blog Post

1 INSERT COMMENTS & TRACK CHANGES | 2 REVIEW COMMENTS & TRACKED CHANGES
3 LINK EXCEL WORKSHEET TO WORD DOCUMENT | 4 CHART WORD TABLE | 5 CREATE & PUBLISH BLOG POST

The following steps create a new blank Word document for a blog post. ***Why?*** *Word provides a blog post template you can use to create a blank blog post document.*

- Open the Backstage view.
- Tap or click the New tab in the Backstage view to display the New gallery.
- Tap or click the Blog post thumbnail to select the template and display it in a preview window (Figure 8–63).

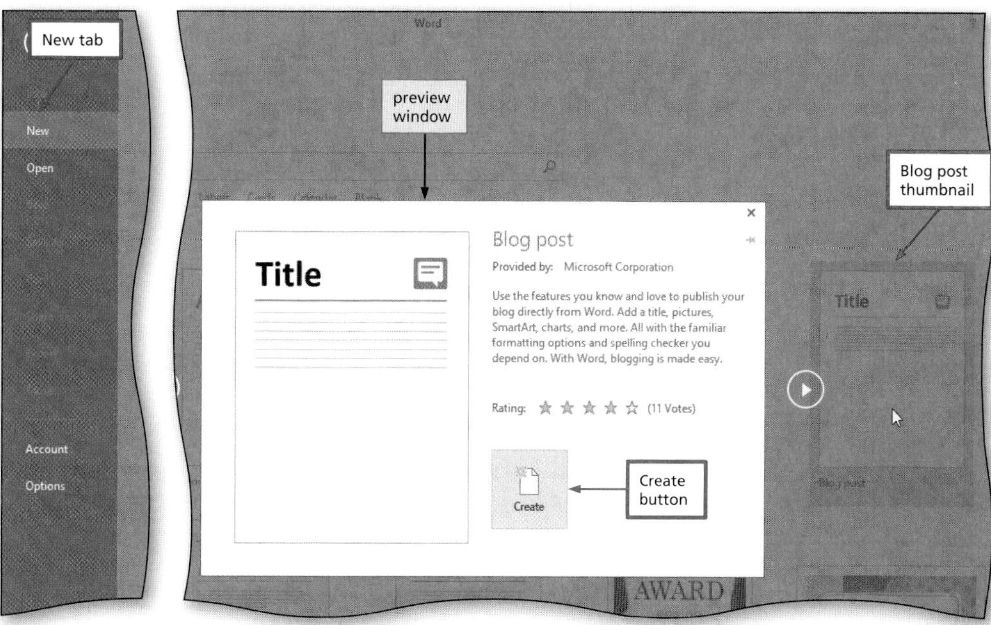

Figure 8–63

2

- Tap or click the Create button in the preview window to create a new document based on the selected template (Figure 8–64).

Q&A What if a Register a Blog Account dialog box appears?
Tap or click the Register Later button to skip the registration process at this time. Or, if you have a blog account, you can tap or click the Register Now button and follow the instructions to register your account.

Why did the ribbon change?
When creating a blog post, the ribbon in Word changes to display only the tabs required to create and publish a blog post.

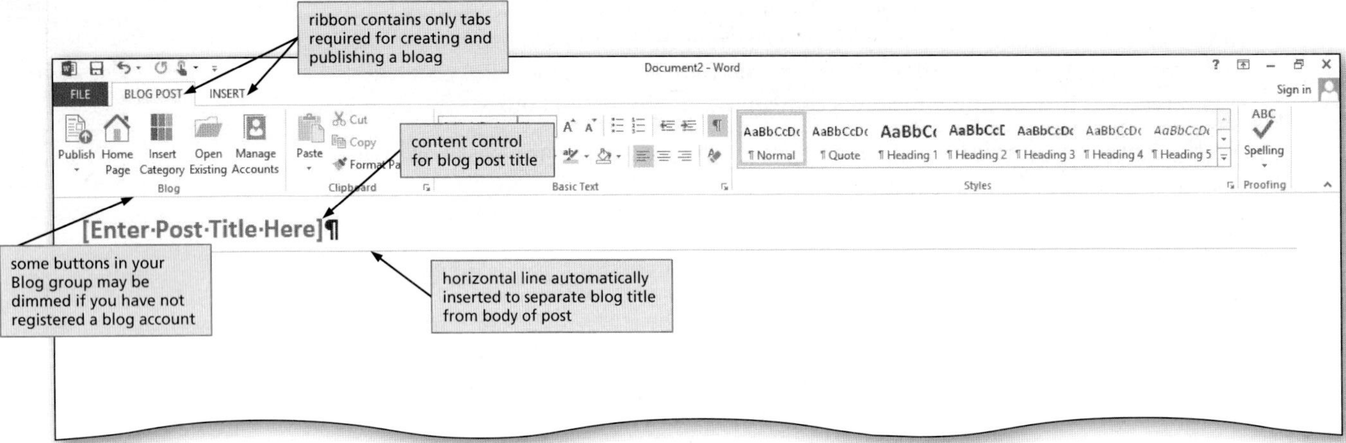

Figure 8–64

To Enter Text

The next step is to enter the blog post title and text in the blog post. The following steps enter text in the blog post.

1 Tap or click the 'Enter Post Title Here' content control and then type `Fund-Raiser Update` as the blog title.

2 Position the insertion point below the horizontal line and then type these three lines of text, pressing the ENTER key at end of each line (Figure 8–65):

`Our latest fund-raiser was a huge success!`

`Thank you to everyone who helped before and during the event!`

`See the following calendar for key dates for our next event. We hope we can count on you again.`

Q&A Can I format text in the blog post?
Yes, you can use the Basic Text and other groups on the ribbon to format the post. You also can check spelling using the Proofing group.

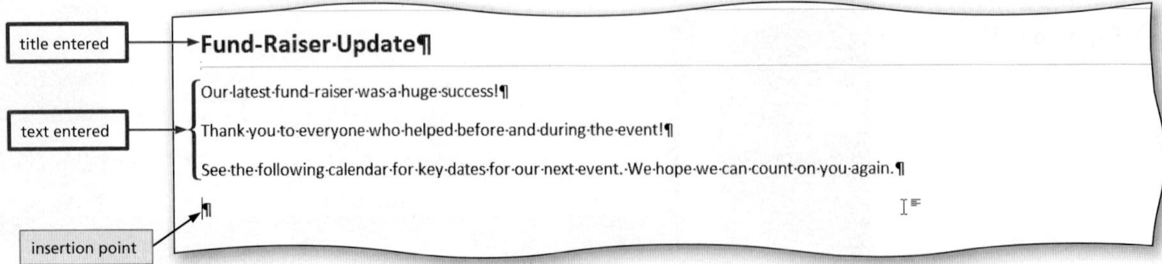

Figure 8–65

To Insert a Quick Table

Word provides several quick tables, which are preformatted table styles that you can customize. Calendar formats are one type of quick table. The following steps insert a calendar in the blog. ***Why?*** *You will post the upcoming key fund-raiser dates in the calendar.*

1

- Display the INSERT tab.
- With the insertion point positioned as shown in Figure 8–65, tap or click the 'Add a Table' button (INSERT tab | Tables group) to display the Add a Table gallery.
- Tap or point to Quick Tables in the Add a Table gallery to display the Quick Tables gallery (Figure 8–66).

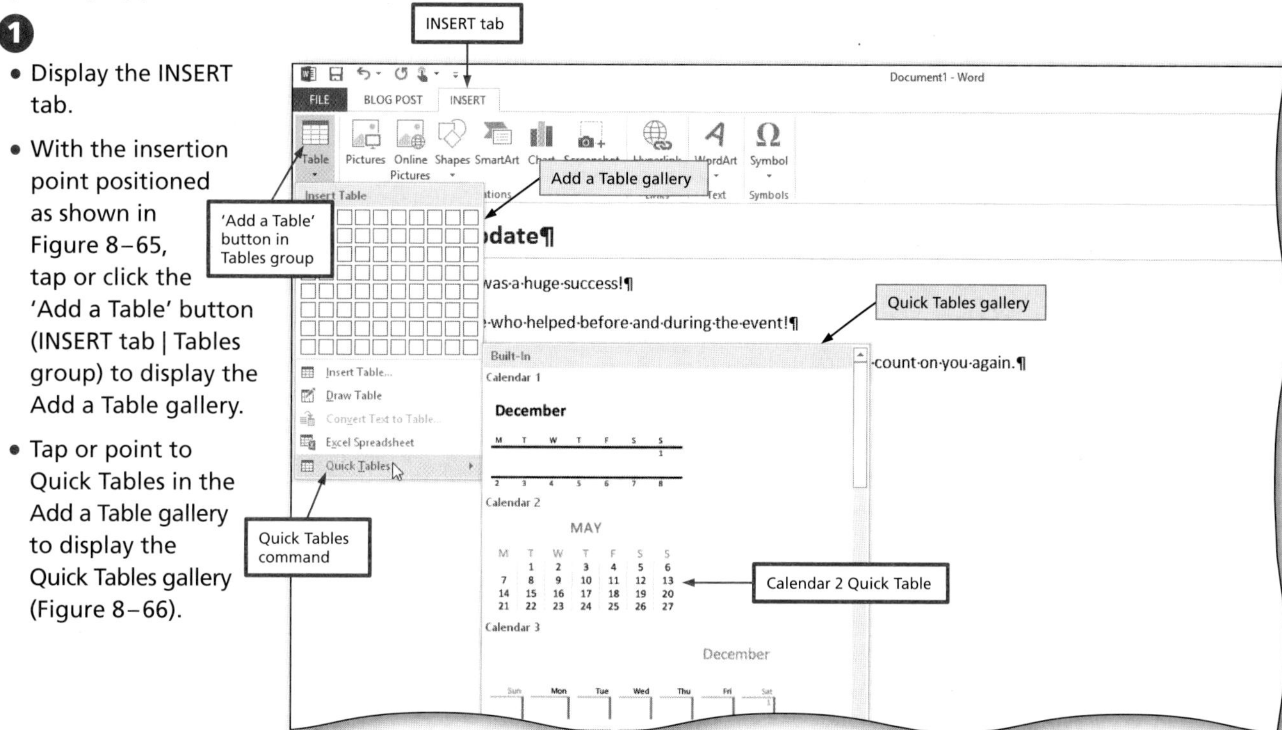

Figure 8–66

- Tap or click Calendar 2 in the Quick Tables gallery to insert the selected Quick Table in the document at the location of the insertion point (Figure 8–67).

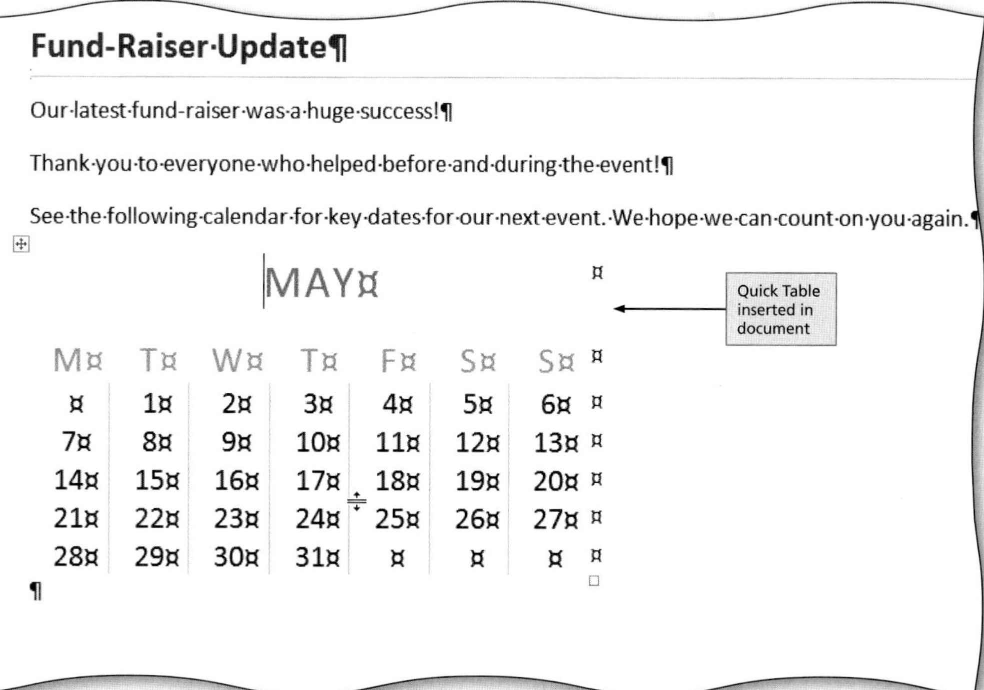

Figure 8–67

To Edit and Format a Table

The calendar in the blog post should show the month of October with a first day of the month starting on Wednesday. The following steps edit the table and apply a quick style.

1. Change the month in the first cell of the table from May to October.
2. Edit the contents of the cells in the table so that the first day of the month starts on a Wednesday and the 31 (the last day of the month) is on a Friday.
3. Enter the text in the appropriate cells for October 1, 7, 16, 22, and 25, as shown in Figure 8–68.
4. If necessary, display the TABLE TOOLS DESIGN tab.
5. Remove the check mark from the First Column check box (TABLE TOOLS DESIGN tab | Table Style Options group) because you do not want the first column in the table formatted differently.
6. Apply the 'Grid Table 1 Light - Accent 5' table style to the table.
7. If necessary, left-align the heading and resize the table column widths to 0.8".
8. Make any other necessary adjustments so that the table appears as shown in Figure 8–68.

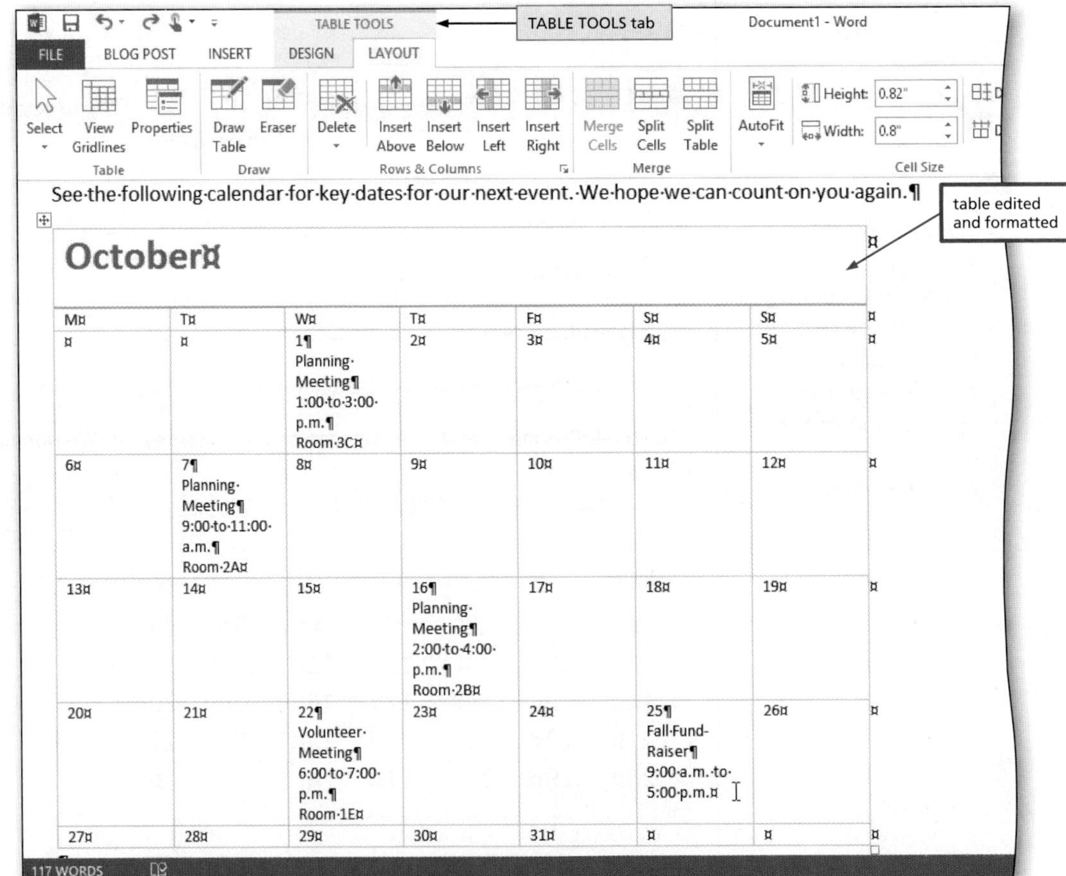

Figure 8–68

BTW

Certification

The Microsoft Office Specialist (MOS) program provides an opportunity for you to obtain a valuable industry credential — proof that you have the Word 2013 skills required by employers. For more information, visit the Certification resource on the Student Companion Site located on www.cengagebrain.com. For detailed instructions about accessing available resources, visit www.cengage.com/ct/studentdownload or contact your instructor for information about accessing the required files.

To Save an Active Document with a New File Name and Close the File

You are finished entering and formatting the content of the blog post. Thus, the following steps save the blog post.

1. Tap or click FILE on the ribbon to open the Backstage view and then tap or click the Save As tab to display the Save As gallery.

2. Navigate to the desired save location and save the document with the file name, Fund-Raising Blog.

BTW

Deleting Blog Posts
If you want to delete a blog post from your blog account, sign in to your blog account and then follow the instructions from your blog provider to delete a post from your blog.

Note: If you have not registered a blog account, read the next series of steps without performing them.

To Publish a Blog Post

1 INSERT COMMENTS & TRACK CHANGES | 2 REVIEW COMMENTS & TRACKED CHANGES
3 LINK EXCEL WORKSHEET TO WORD DOCUMENT | 4 CHART WORD TABLE | **5 CREATE & PUBLISH BLOG POST**

The following step publishes the blog post. ***Why?*** *Publishing the blog post places the post at the top of the webpage associated with this blog account.*

1

- Display the BLOG POST tab.
- Tap or click the Publish button (BLOG POST tab | Blog group), which causes Word to display a brief message that it is contacting the blog provider and then display a message on the screen that the post was published (Figure 8–69).

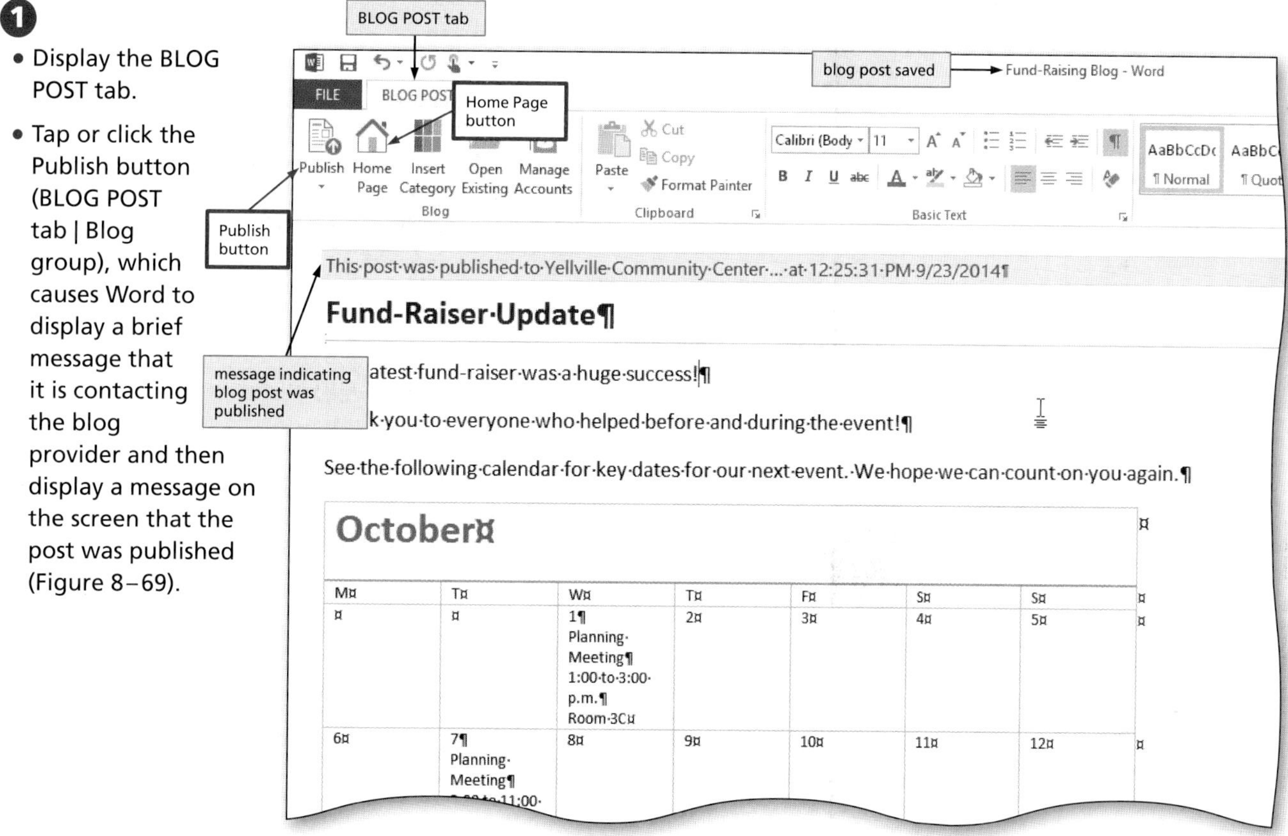

Figure 8–69

To Display a Blog Webpage in a Browser Window

1 INSERT COMMENTS & TRACK CHANGES | 2 REVIEW COMMENTS & TRACKED CHANGES
3 LINK EXCEL WORKSHEET TO WORD DOCUMENT | 4 CHART WORD TABLE | **5 CREATE & PUBLISH BLOG POST**

The step on the next page displays the current blog account's webpage in a browser window. ***Why?*** *You can view a blog account associated with Word if you want to verify a post was successful.*

1

- Tap or click the Home Page button (BLOG POST tab | Blog group) (shown in Figure 8–69 on the previous page), which runs the default browser (Internet Explorer, in this case) and displays the webpage associated with the registered blog account in the browser window. You may need to tap or click the Refresh button in your browser window to display the most current webpage contents (Figure 8–70).

Figure 8–70

Q&A What if the wrong webpage is displayed?
You may have multiple blog accounts registered with Word. To select a different blog account registered with Word, switch back to Word, tap or click the Manage Accounts button (BLOG POST tab | Blog group), tap or click the desired account (Blog Accounts dialog box), and then tap or click the Close button. Then, repeat Step 1.

To Open an Existing Blog Post

If you wanted to open an existing blog post to modify or view it in Word, you would perform the following steps.

1. Tap or click the Open Existing button (BLOG POST tab | Blog group) to display the Open Existing Post dialog box.
2. Select the title of the post you wish to open and then tap or click the OK button (Open Existing Post dialog box).

BTW
Quick Reference
For a table that lists how to complete the tasks covered in this book using touch gestures, the mouse, ribbon, shortcut menu, and keyboard, see the Quick Reference Summary at the back of this book, or visit the Quick Reference resource on the Student Companion Site located on www.cengagebrain.com. For detailed instructions about accessing available resources, visit www.cengage.com/ct/studentdownload or contact your instructor for information about accessing the required files.

To Exit Word

You are finished with the project in this chapter. Thus, the following steps close the open browser window and exit Word.

1 Close your browser window.

2 Exit Word.

Chapter Summary

In this chapter, you have learned how to insert comments, track changes, review tracked changes, compare documents and combine documents, link or embed an Excel worksheet to a Word document, chart a table and format the chart, and create and publish a blog post. The items listed below include all the new Word skills you have learned in this chapter, with the tasks grouped by activity.

Enter and Edit Text

Insert a Comment (WD 478)
Reply to a Comment (WD 481)
Enable Tracked Changes (WD 482)
Track Changes (WD 483)
Disable Tracked Changes (WD 484)
Use the Reviewing Task Pane (WD 484)
Display Tracked Changes and Comments as Simple Markup (WD 486)
Show All Markup (WD 486)
View Comments (WD 488)
Delete a Comment (WD 488)
Mark Comments as Done (WD 489)
Delete All Comments (WD 489)
Review Tracked Changes (WD 489)
Accept or Reject All Tracked Changes (WD 491)
Compare Documents (WD 493)
Combine Revisions from Multiple Authors (WD 494)
Show Tracked Changes and Comments by a Single Reviewer (WD 497)
Link an Excel Worksheet to a Word Document (WD 501)
Embed an Excel Worksheet in a Word Document (WD 502)
Edit a Linked Object (WD 503)
Break a Link (WD 503)

File Management

Print Markups (WD 487)

Word Settings

Change Reviewer Information (WD 480)
Customize the Status Bar (WD 482)
Change How Markups and Comments Are Displayed (WD 484)
View and Scroll through Documents Side by Side (WD 518)

Work with Blogs

Register a Blog Account (WD 520)
Create a Blank Document for a Blog Post (WD 521)
Publish a Blog Post (WD 525)
Display a Blog Webpage in a Browser Window (WD 525)
Open an Existing Blog Post (WD 526)

Work with Charts

Chart a Table (WD 505)
Remove a Data Series from a Chart (WD 508)
Apply a Chart Style (WD 509)
Change Colors of a Chart (WD 510)
Add a Chart Element (WD 510)
Select a Chart Element and Edit It (WD 512)
Format Chart Elements (WD 512)
Add an Outline to a Chart (WD 515)
Change a Chart Type (WD 516)
Chart a Word Table Using Microsoft Graph (WD 517)

Work with Tables

Insert a Quick Table (WD 523)

CONSIDER THIS: PLAN AHEAD

What decisions will you need to make when creating documents to share or publish?

Use these guidelines as you complete the assignments in this chapter and create your own shared documents outside of this class.

1. If sharing documents, be certain received files and copied objects are virus free.
   a) Do not open files created by others until you are certain they do not contain a virus or other malicious program (malware).
   b) Use an antivirus program to verify that any files you use are free of viruses and other potentially harmful programs.
2. If necessary, determine how to copy an object.
   a) Your intended use of the Word document will help determine the best method for copying the object: copy and paste, embed, or link.
3. Enhance a document with appropriate visuals.
   a) Use visuals to add interest, clarify ideas, and illustrate points. Visuals include tables, charts, and graphical images (i.e., pictures or clip art).
4. If desired, post communications on a blog.

CONSIDER THIS

How should you submit solutions to questions in the assignments identified with a symbol?
Every assignment in this book contains one or more questions identified with a symbol. These questions require you to think beyond the assigned document. Present your solutions to the questions in the format required by your instructor. Possible formats may include one or more of these options: write the answer; create a document that contains the answer; present your answer to the class; discuss your answer in a group; record the answer as audio or video using a webcam, smartphone, or portable media player; or post answers on a blog, wiki, or website.

Apply Your Knowledge

Reinforce the skills and apply the concepts you learned in this chapter.

Working with Comments and Tracked Changes

Note: To complete this assignment, you will be required to use the Data Files for Students. Visit www.cengage.com/ct/studentdownload for detailed instructions or contact your instructor for information about accessing the required files.

Instructions: Run Word. Open the document Apply 8-1 Near Field Communications Draft from the Data Files for Students. The document includes two paragraphs of text that contain tracked changes and comments. You are to insert additional tracked changes and comments, accept and reject tracked changes, and delete comments.

Perform the following tasks:

1. If necessary, customize the status bar so that it displays the TRACK CHANGES indicator.
2. Enable (turn on) tracked changes.
3. If requested by your instructor, change the user name and initials so that your name and initials are displayed in the tracked changes and comments.
4. Use the REVIEW tab to navigate to the first comment. Follow the instruction in the comment. Be sure tracked changes are on when you add the required text to the document.
5. When you have finished making the change, reply to the comment with a new comment that includes a message stating you completed the requested task. Mark the comment as done. How does a comment marked as done differ from the other comments? What color are the WU markups? What color are your markups?
6. Navigate to the remaining comments and read through each one.
7. Insert the following comment for the word, wristbands, in the last sentence of the first paragraph: Should this be two words?
8. With tracked changes on, change the word, items, in the third sentence to the word, objects.
9. Edit the comment entered in Step 7 to add this sentence: Be sure to look it up in the dictionary or a dictionary app.
10. Print the document with tracked changes.
11. Print only the tracked changes.
12. Save the document with the file name, Apply 8-1 Near Field Communications Reviewed (Figure 8–71).
13. Show only your tracked changes in the document. Show all users' tracked changes in the document.
14. Reject the insertion of the words, that are, in the first sentence.
15. Delete the comment that begins with the words, Reject the tracked change…
16. Insert the word, successful, as a tracked change at the beginning of the second paragraph as instructed in the comment.

17. Accept all the remaining edits in the document.
18. Delete all the remaining comments.
19. Disable (turn off) tracked changes. Remove the TRACK CHANGES indicator from the status bar.
20. If requested by your instructor, add your name on a line below the second paragraph. Save the modified file with a new file name, Apply 8-1 Near Field Communications Final. Submit the documents in the format specified by your instructor.
21. Answer the questions posed in #5. How would you change the color of your tracked changes?

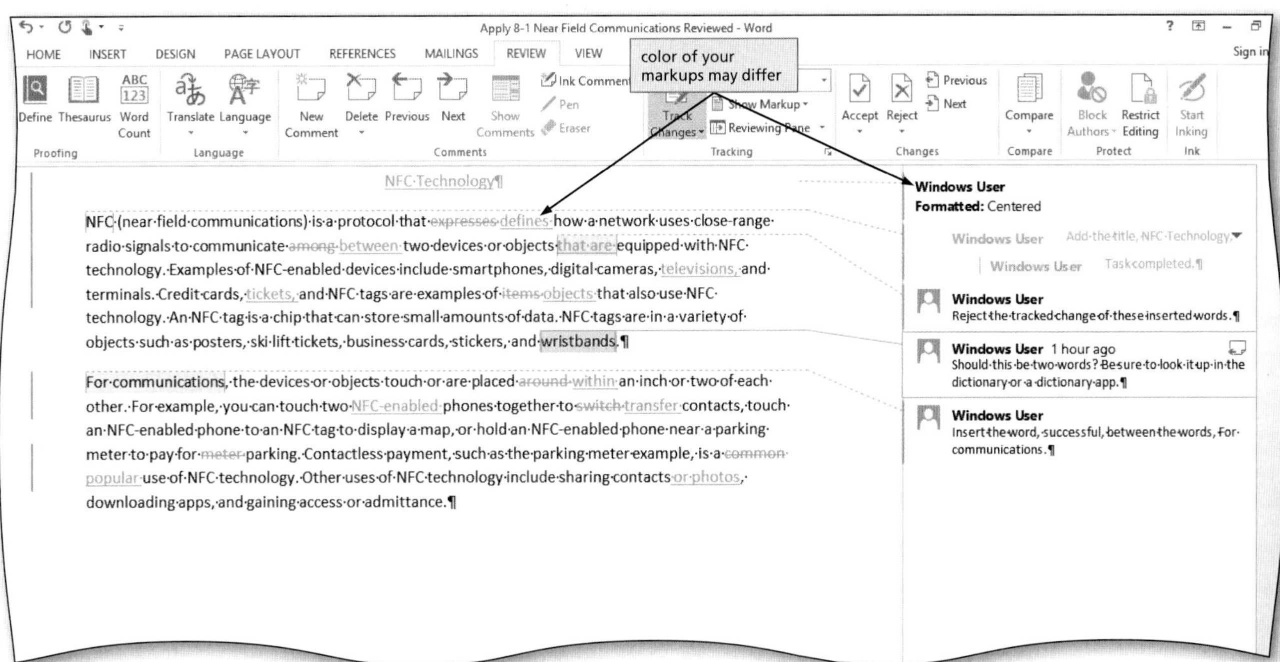

Figure 8–71

Extend Your Knowledge

Extend the skills you learned in this chapter and experiment with new skills. You may need to use Help to complete the assignment.

Using Microsoft Graph to Create a Chart

Note: To complete this assignment, you will be required to use the Data Files for Students. Visit www.cengage.com/ct/studentdownload for detailed instructions or contact your instructor for information about accessing the required files.

Instructions: Run Word. Open the document Extend 8-1 Library Seminar Attendees Memo Draft from the Data Files for Students. You will use Microsoft Graph to chart the table in the memo (Figure 8–72 on the next page).

Continued >

Extend Your Knowledge *continued*

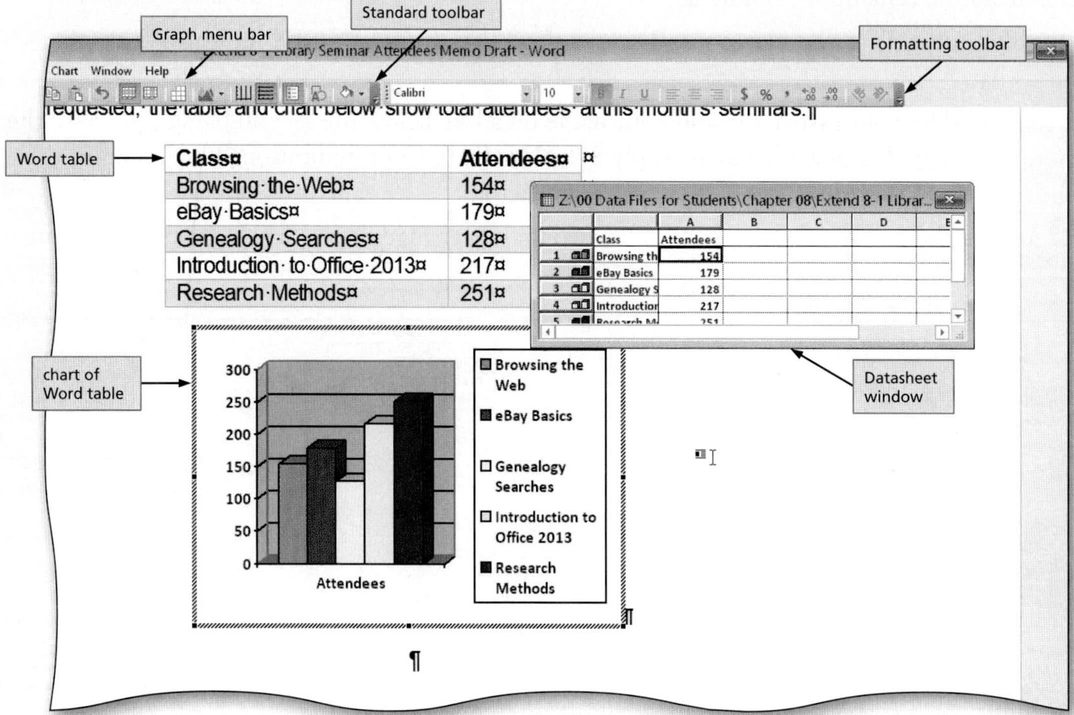

Figure 8–72

Perform the following tasks:

1. Search the web to learn about Microsoft Graph. What is Microsoft Graph?
2. Select the table in the memo to be charted and then follow the steps on page WD 517 to insert a Microsoft Graph chart. Close the Datasheet window.
3. Tap or click the Help on the menu bar in the Graph window and then tap or click 'Microsoft Graph Help' to open the Graph Help window. Browse through the help information to learn how to use Graph.
4. Tap or click the By Column button on the Standard toolbar to plot the data by column instead of by row. What text appears along the horizontal axis now?
5. Move the legend to the bottom of the chart.
6. Change the chart type to a bar chart.
7. Display the categories on the category axis in reverse order, leaving the value axis at the bottom. (*Hint*: Select the Scale tab in Format Axis dialog box and then place check marks in all three check boxes.) If necessary, also change the number of tick marks between items to show all classes.
8. Change the color of the chart area.
9. Change the color of the series "Attendees," which changes the color of the bars.
10. If they are not displayed already, display value axis gridlines.
11. If necessary, drag the chart to center it below the table.
12. If requested by your instructor, change the name at the top of the memo to your name. Save the modified file with a new file name, Apply 8-1 Library Seminar Attendees Memo Final. Submit the documents in the format specified by your instructor.
13. Answer the question posed in #4. Do you prefer using Microsoft Graph or the CHART TOOLS tab to create a chart in Word? Why?

Analyze, Correct, Improve

Analyze a document, correct all errors, and improve it.

Editing and Formatting a Quick Table and a Chart

Note: To complete this assignment, you will be required to use the Data Files for Students. Visit www.cengage.com/ct/studentdownload for detailed instructions or contact your instructor for information about accessing the required files.

Instructions: Run Word. Open the document Analyze 8-1 Home Plans Memo Draft from the Data Files for Students. The document is a memo that is missing a table and whose chart is not formatted properly. You are to insert, format, and edit a Quick Table and edit a chart.

Perform the following tasks:

1. Correct In the letter, correct the following items:

a. Above the chart and below the Home Plan Breakdown title, insert the Tabular List Quick Table (Figure 8–73). Change the values in the header row and first six table rows as follows: Header row, first column: Style; Header row, second column: Plans; first data row, first column: Colonial; first data row, second column: 1,728; second data row, first column: Contemporary; second data row, second column: 2,582; third data row, first column: European; third data row, second column: 4,820; fourth data row, first column: Ranch; fourth data row, second column: 3,928; fifth data row, first column: Tudor; fifth data row, second column: 1,882; sixth data row, first column: Victorian; sixth data row, second column: 2,058. Delete the last two rows in the table.

b. Select the chart and then display the chart spreadsheet window. Edit the contents of the chart spreadsheet window to match the table in the document.

c. Resize the chart so that all data is readable.

d. Delete the legend.

e. Change the chart type to a type other than line.

f. Format the numbers on the vertical axis to show a comma separator.

g. Change the color of the data series.

h. Add a chart title, category (x) axis title, and horizontal (value) axis title. Add color to each of these titles.

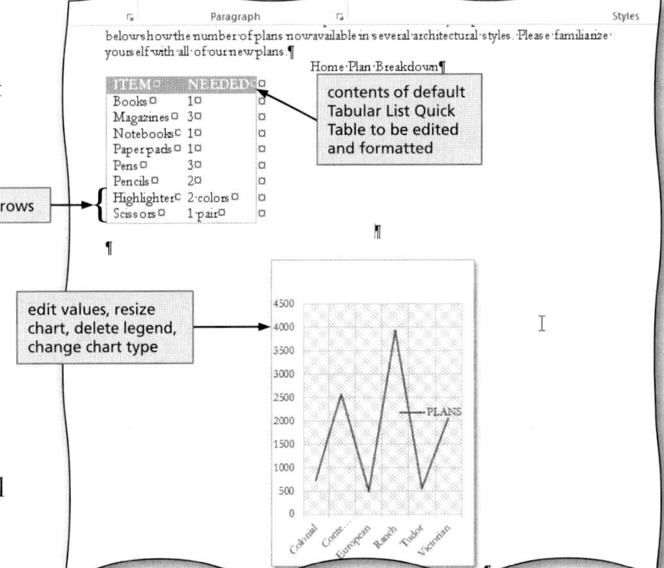

Figure 8–73

2. Improve Enhance the letter by applying a table style of your choice to the table, centering the table, right-aligning the number values in the table, and resizing columns as appropriate. Apply a chart style of your choice to the chart. Make any other adjustments you deem appropriate to the letter. If requested by your instructor, change the name of the sales manager to your name. Save the modified document with the file name, Analyze 8-1 Home Plans Memo Final, and then submit it in the format specified by your instructor.

3. Would you prefer to edit the chart values in Excel instead of the chart spreadsheet window? Why or why not?

In the Labs

Design and/or create a document using the guidelines, concepts, and skills presented in this chapter. Labs 1 and 2, which increase in difficulty, require you to create solutions based on what you learned in the chapter; Lab 3 requires you to create a solution, which uses cloud and web technologies, by learning and investigating on your own from general guidance.

Lab 1: Creating a Memo with an Excel Table and Chart

Note: To complete this assignment, you will be required to use the Data Files for Students. Visit www.cengage.com/ct/studentdownload for detailed instructions or contact your instructor for information about accessing the required files.

Problem: Your supervisor has asked you to prepare a memo that contains an Excel table and a chart comparing current and projected school enrollments. (*Note:* If you do not have Excel on your computer, create the table using Word instead of importing it from Excel.) You prepare the document shown in Figure 8–74.

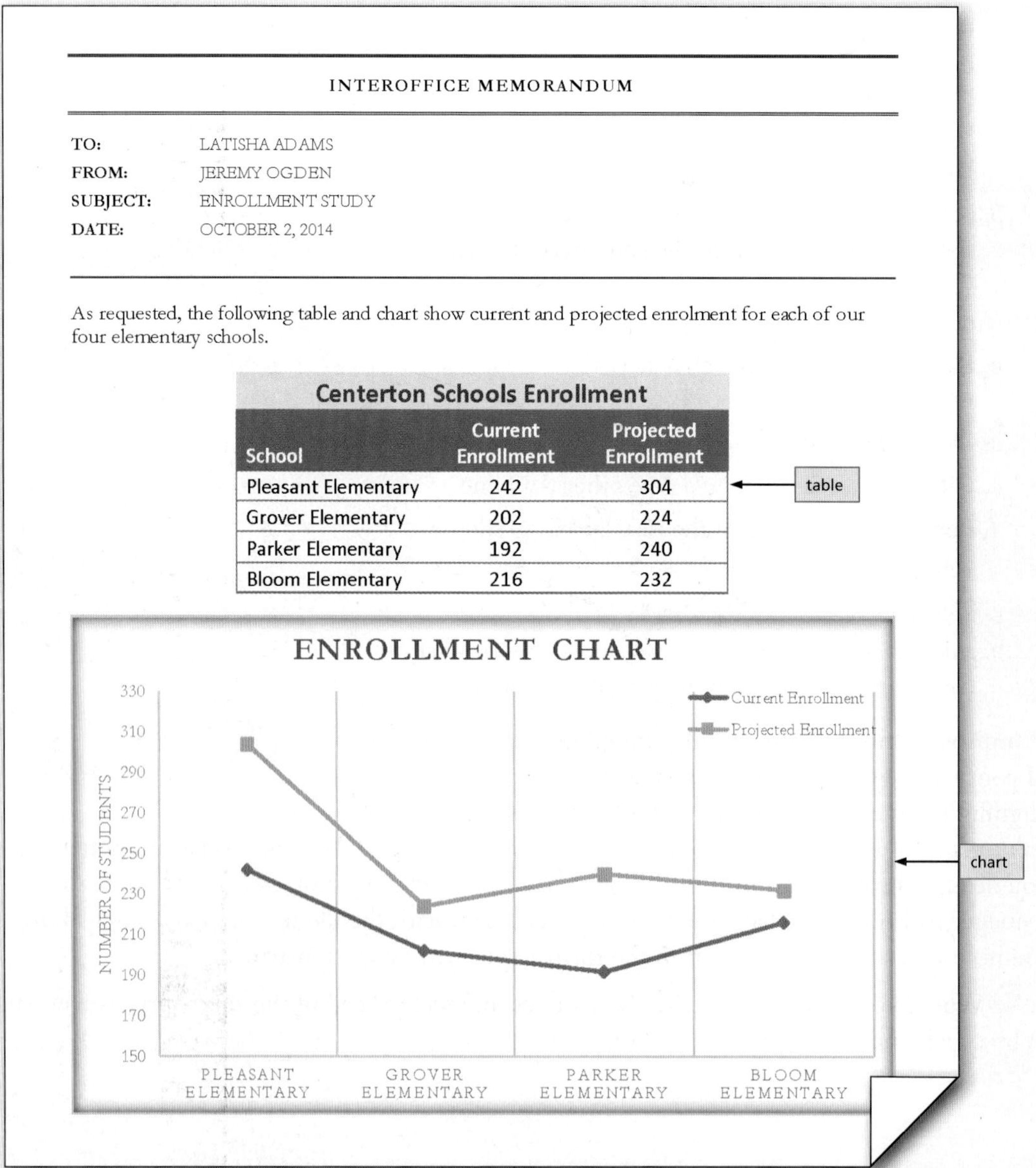

INTEROFFICE MEMORANDUM

TO: LATISHA ADAMS
FROM: JEREMY OGDEN
SUBJECT: ENROLLMENT STUDY
DATE: OCTOBER 2, 2014

As requested, the following table and chart show current and projected enrolment for each of our four elementary schools.

Centerton Schools Enrollment		
School	Current Enrollment	Projected Enrollment
Pleasant Elementary	242	304
Grover Elementary	202	224
Parker Elementary	192	240
Bloom Elementary	216	232

Figure 8–74

Perform the following tasks:

1. Use the Memo (elegant) template to create a new memo and then enter all text in the memo, as shown in the figure. Delete the row containing the cc in the header. Remove the first line indent from the paragraphs below the header. (*Hint*: Use the Paragraph Settings Dialog Box Launcher.)
2. Link the worksheet in the Lab 8-1 School Enrollment in Excel workbook, which is on the Data Files for Students, to the Word memo below the paragraph. If you do not have Excel on your computer, create the table in Word. Change the column width to AutoFit Contents. Center the table.
3. Break the link between the Excel table in the Word document and the Excel worksheet in the Excel workbook. If necessary, resize the table so that it looks like the one in Figure 8–74.
4. Insert a Line with Markers chart, centered below the table.
   a. Copy the rows from the table to the chart spreadsheet window. Remove the Series 3 data series from the chart spreadsheet.
   b. Apply the Style 11 chart style to the chart.
   c. Change the colors to Color 2.
   d. Add a vertical axis title, NUMBER OF STUDENTS.
   e. Change the chart title to ENROLLMENT CHART.
   f. Move the legend so that it appears at the top, right of the chart. Remove the check mark from the 'Show the legend without overlapping the chart' check box. If necessary, position the legend as shown in the figure.
   g. Format the vertical axis so that its minimum value (starting point) is 150.
   h. Adjust spacing above and below paragraphs as necessary so that all of the memo contents fit on a single page.
5. If requested by your instructor, change the name at the top of the memo from Latisha Adams to your name.
6. Save the document with Lab 8-1 School Enrollment Projections as the file name and then submit it in the format specified by your instructor.
7. This lab instructed you to remove the first line indent from the paragraphs in the memo. Why do you think this was requested?

Lab 2: Working with Comments and Tracked Changes

Note: To complete this assignment, you will be required to use the Data Files for Students. Visit www.cengage.com/ct/studentdownload for detailed instructions or contact your instructor for information about accessing the required files.

Problem: Your supervisor has asked you to prepare a draft of a memo, showing all tracked changes and comments. You mark up the document shown in Figure 8–75.

Perform the following tasks:

1. Open the document Lab 8-2 ATM Safety Draft from the Data Files for Students.
2. Insert the comments and track all changes shown in Figure 8–75 on the next page.
3. Save the document with the file name, Lab 8-2 ATM Safety Draft with Markups.
4. Make the changes indicated in the comments and then delete the comments in the document.
5. Accept all tracked changes in the document.
6. Save the document with the file name, Lab 8-2 ATM Safety Final.

Continued >

In the Labs *continued*

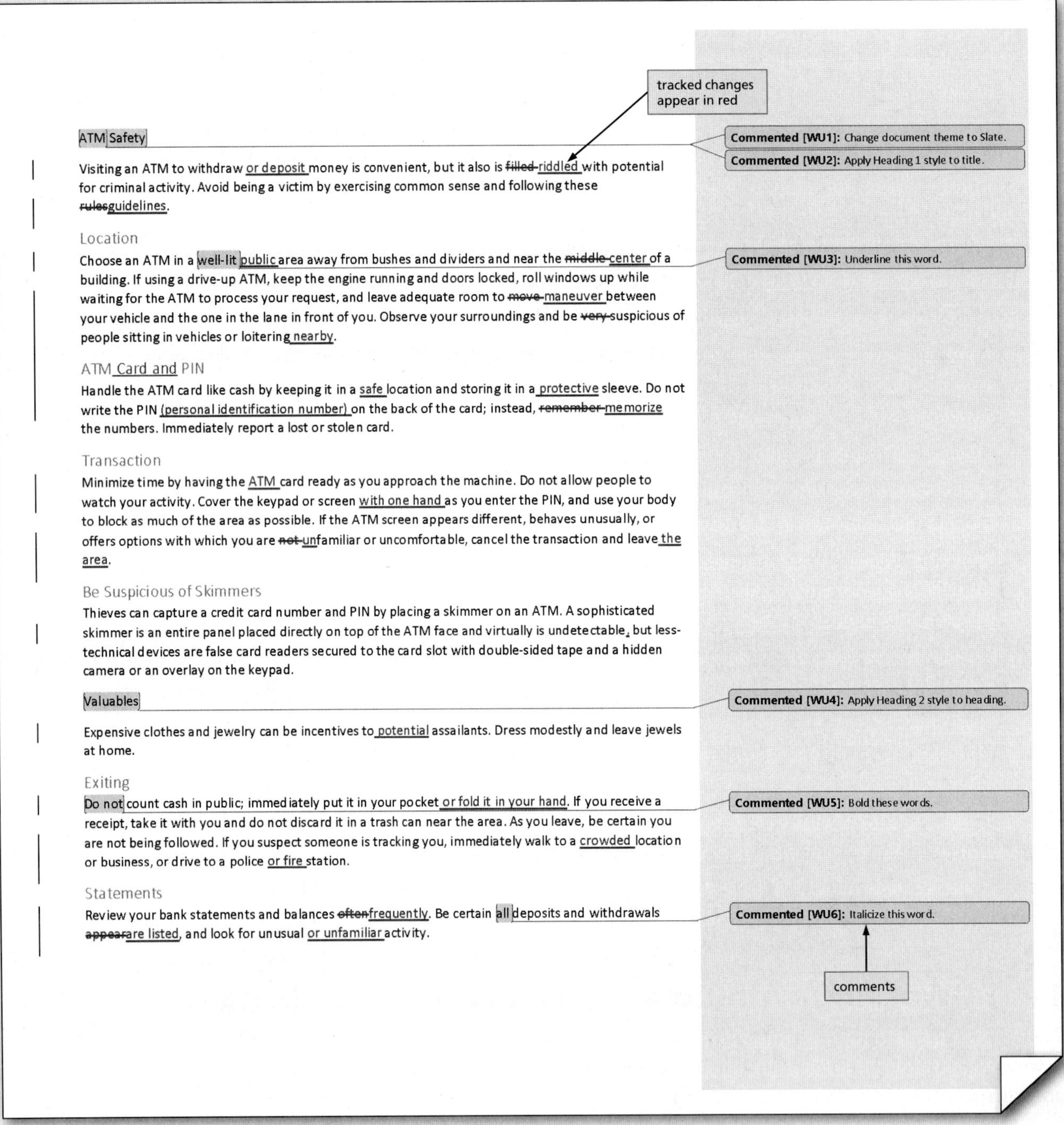

ATM Safety

Commented [WU1]: Change document theme to Slate.

Commented [WU2]: Apply Heading 1 style to title.

Visiting an ATM to withdraw or deposit money is convenient, but it also is ~~filled~~ riddled with potential for criminal activity. Avoid being a victim by exercising common sense and following these ~~rules~~guidelines.

Location

Choose an ATM in a well-lit public area away from bushes and dividers and near the ~~middle~~ center of a building. If using a drive-up ATM, keep the engine running and doors locked, roll windows up while waiting for the ATM to process your request, and leave adequate room to ~~move~~ maneuver between your vehicle and the one in the lane in front of you. Observe your surroundings and be ~~very~~ suspicious of people sitting in vehicles or loitering nearby.

Commented [WU3]: Underline this word.

ATM Card and PIN

Handle the ATM card like cash by keeping it in a safe location and storing it in a protective sleeve. Do not write the PIN (personal identification number) on the back of the card; instead, ~~remember~~ memorize the numbers. Immediately report a lost or stolen card.

Transaction

Minimize time by having the ATM card ready as you approach the machine. Do not allow people to watch your activity. Cover the keypad or screen with one hand as you enter the PIN, and use your body to block as much of the area as possible. If the ATM screen appears different, behaves unusually, or offers options with which you are ~~not~~ unfamiliar or uncomfortable, cancel the transaction and leave the area.

Be Suspicious of Skimmers

Thieves can capture a credit card number and PIN by placing a skimmer on an ATM. A sophisticated skimmer is an entire panel placed directly on top of the ATM face and virtually is undetectable, but less-technical devices are false card readers secured to the card slot with double-sided tape and a hidden camera or an overlay on the keypad.

Valuables

Commented [WU4]: Apply Heading 2 style to heading.

Expensive clothes and jewelry can be incentives to potential assailants. Dress modestly and leave jewels at home.

Exiting

Do not count cash in public; immediately put it in your pocket or fold it in your hand. If you receive a receipt, take it with you and do not discard it in a trash can near the area. As you leave, be certain you are not being followed. If you suspect someone is tracking you, immediately walk to a crowded location or business, or drive to a police or fire station.

Commented [WU5]: Bold these words.

Statements

Review your bank statements and balances ~~often~~frequently. Be certain all deposits and withdrawals ~~appear~~are listed, and look for unusual or unfamiliar activity.

Commented [WU6]: Italicize this word.

Figure 8–75

7. Compare the Lab 8-2 ATM Safety Draft file (original document) with the Lab 8-2 ATM Safety Final file (revised document). Save the compare result with the file name, Lab 8-2 Safety Compared.
8. Close all windows and then open the Lab 8-2 ATM Safety Compared file. Print the document with markups. Use the REVIEW tab to review each change. Close the document without saving.
9. How could you determine if two documents contained the same content?

Lab 3: Expand Your World: Cloud and Web Technologies
Creating a Blog Account Using a Blogger Service

Problem: You would like to create a blog account so that you can use Word for blog posts. You research a variety of blogging services and select one for use (Figure 8–76).

Note: You will use a blog account, many of which you can create at no cost, to complete this assignment. If you do not want to create a blog account, read this assignment without performing the instructions.

Instructions: Perform the following tasks:

1. Run a browser. Research these blogging services: Blogger, SharePoint blog, Telligent Community, TypePad, and WordPress.
2. Navigate to the blogger service with which you want to set up an account and then follow the instructions to set up an account.
3. Set up your blog in the blogger service.
4. In Word, register your blog account (see instructions on page WD 520 and WD 521).
5. Create a blog post in Word and then publish your blog post to your account.
6. Which blogger service did you select and why? Would you recommend this blogger service? Why or why not?

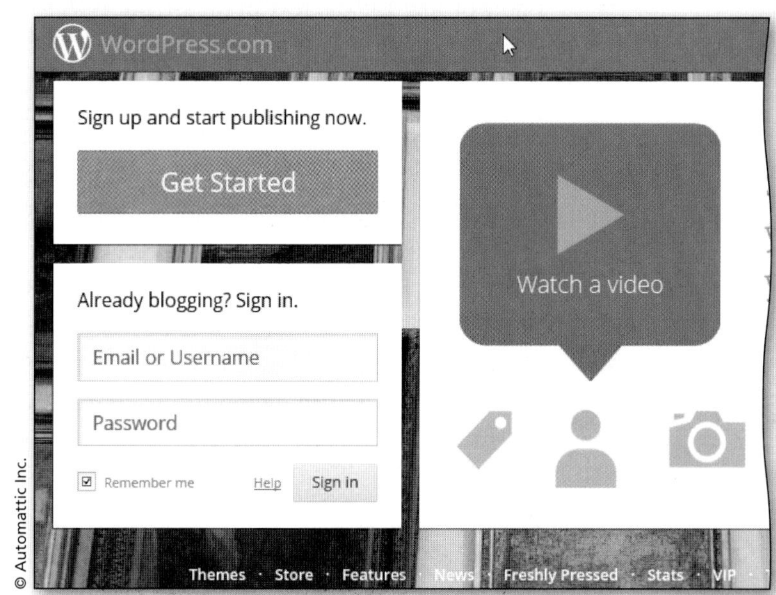

Figure 8–76

Consider This: Your Turn

Apply your creative thinking and problem solving skills to design and implement a solution.

1: Create a Memo for a Side Job

Personal

Part 1: You and a friend have decided to wash, wax, and detail cars to earn extra cash while attending school. To advertise your services on campus, you need to write a memo to the office of career development that outlines prices of your services. Write the memo to Julio Martinez. Use today's date. The memo should contain a table and chart as specified below.

The wording for the text in the memo is as follows: Jon and Jim at Two Friends Cleaning Services wash, wax, and detail all sizes of cars, pick-up trucks, vans, and SUVs. The table and chart below show prices of our services.

The data for the table is as follows: compact car – wash $8.50, wax $40.00, detailing $55.00; mid-sized car – wash $10.50, wax $50.00, detailing $62.50; full-sized car – wash $12.50, wax $60.00, detailing $70.00; pick-up truck/van/SUV – wash $15.50, wax $70.00, detailing $82.50. Create a chart of all table data.

Use the concepts and techniques presented in this chapter to create and format the memo and its text, table, and chart. Be sure to check the spelling and grammar of the finished memo. Submit your assignment in the format specified by your instructor.

Part 2: You made several decisions while creating the memo in this assignment: whether to use a memo template or create a memo from scratch, and how to organize and format the memo, table, and chart (fonts, font sizes, colors, shading, styles, etc.). What was the rationale behind each of these decisions? When you proofread the document, what further revisions did you make and why?

Continued >

Consider This: Your Turn *continued*

2: Create a Memo Showing First Quarter Sales

Professional

Part 1: As assistant to the manager of a party supply store, you have been asked to create a memo showing the first quarter sales figures for the top four items. You are to write the memo to all sales staff with a subject of First Quarter Sales. Use today's date. The memo should contain a table and chart as specified below.

The wording for the text in the memo is as follows: Sales figures for the first quarter have been compiled. The table and chart below show sales for the first quarter for the top four items sold.

The data for the table is as follows: decorations – January $10,210.32, February $12,291.28, March $11,382.99; gift wrap/bags – January $7,218.31, February $10,887.19, March $6,485.21; greeting cards – January $1,986.23, February $3,798.25, March $2,669.47; and paper products – January $5,002.36, February $7,652.54, March $6,795.33. Create a chart of all table data.

Use the concepts and techniques presented in this chapter to create and format the memo and its text, table, and chart. Be sure to check the spelling and grammar of the finished memo. Submit your assignment in the format specified by your instructor.

Part 2: You made several decisions while creating the memo in this assignment: whether to use a memo template or create a memo from scratch, and how to organize and format the memo, table, and chart (fonts, font sizes, colors, shading, styles, etc.). What was the rationale behind each of these decisions? When you proofread the document, what further revisions did you make and why?

3: Create a Memo about Travel Expenses

Research and Collaboration

Your employer has asked you and two of your coworkers to research the flight, hotel, and rental car expenses for a six-day business trip from the home office in Chicago, Illinois, to a conference in Orlando, Florida. Form a three-member team to research the expenses for at least four options in each area (flight, hotel, and rental car). Each team member should research one area. As a group, create a memo that contains a table and chart presenting your findings.

Use the concepts and techniques presented in this chapter to create and format the memo and its text, table, and chart. If requested by your instructor, use team members' names in the memo. Be sure to check the spelling and grammar of the finished memo. Submit your team assignment in the format specified by your instructor.

Part 2: You made several decisions while creating the memo in this assignment: text to use, whether to use a memo template or create a memo from scratch, and how to organize and format the memo, table, and chart (fonts, font sizes, colors, shading, styles, etc.). What was the rationale behind each of these decisions? When you proofread the document, what further revisions did you make and why?

Learn Online

Reinforce what you learned in this chapter with games, exercises, training, and many other online activities and resources.

Student Companion Site Reinforcement activities and resources are available at no additional cost on www.cengagebrain.com. Visit www.cengage.com/ct/studentdownload for detailed instructions about accessing the resources available at the Student Companion Site.

SAM

SAM Put your skills into practice with SAM! If you have a SAM account, go to www.cengage.com/sam2013 to access SAM assignments for this chapter.

9 Creating a Reference Document with a Table of Contents and an Index

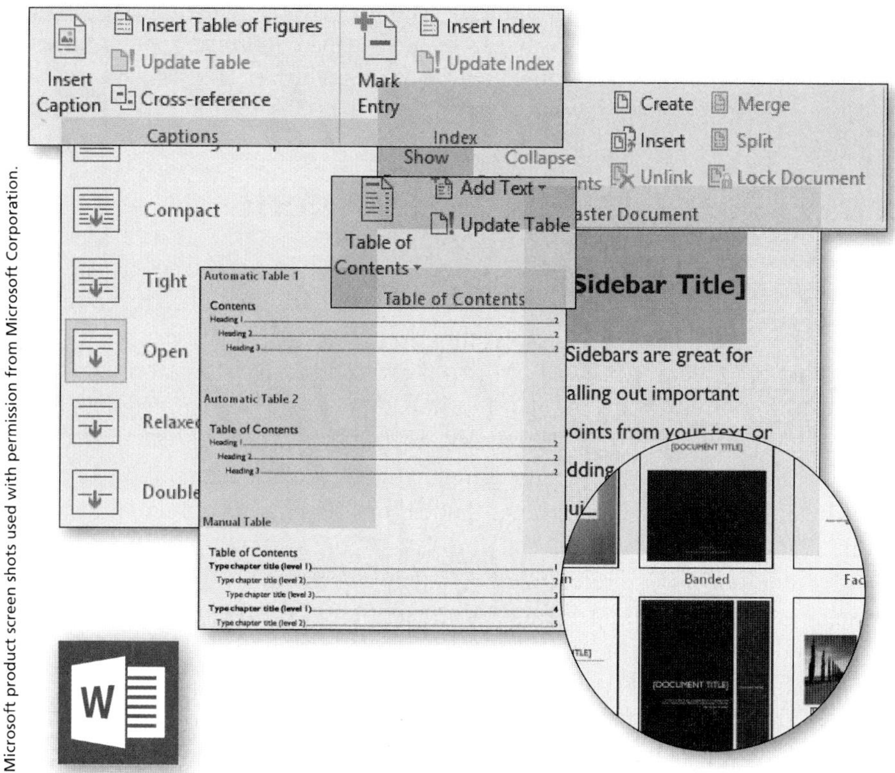

Objectives

You will have mastered the material in this chapter when you can:

- Insert a screenshot
- Add and modify a caption
- Create a cross-reference
- Insert and link text boxes
- Compress pictures
- Work in Outline view
- Work with a master document and subdocuments
- Insert a cover page
- Create and modify a table of contents
- Use the Navigation Pane
- Create and update a table of figures
- Build, modify, and update an index
- Create alternating footers
- Add bookmarks

9 Creating a Reference Document with a Table of Contents and an Index

Introduction

During the course of your academic studies and professional activities, you may find it necessary to compose a document that is many pages or even hundreds of pages in length. When composing a long document, you must ensure that the document is organized so that a reader easily can locate material in that document. Sometimes a document of this nature is called a **reference document**.

Project — Reference Document

A reference document is any multipage document organized so that users easily can locate material and navigate through the document. Examples of reference documents include user guides, term papers, pamphlets, manuals, proposals, and plans.

The project in this chapter uses Word to produce the reference document shown in Figure 9–1. This reference document, titled the *Learn Word*, is a multipage information guide that is distributed by Gardner College to students and staff. Notice that the inner margin between facing pages has extra space to allow duplicated copies of the document to be bound (i.e., stapled or fastened in some manner) — without the binding covering the words.

The *Learn Word* reference document begins with a title page designed to entice the target audience to open the document and read it. Next is the copyright page, followed by the table of contents. The document then describes how to insert four types of graphics in a Word document: clip art, picture, shape, and screenshot. The end of this reference document has a table of figures and an index to assist readers in locating information contained within the document. A miniature version of the *Learn Word* reference document is shown in Figure 9–1.

The section of the *Learn Word* reference document that is titled, Inserting Various Types of Graphics in a Word Document, is a draft document that you will modify. The draft document is located on the Data Files for Students. Visit www.cengage.com/ct/studentdownload for detailed instructions or contact your instructor for information about accessing the required files. After editing the content, you will incorporate a final version in the reference document.

If you are using your finger on a touch screen and are having difficulty completing the steps in this chapter, consider using a stylus. Many people find it easier to be precise with a stylus than with a finger. In addition, with a stylus you see the pointer. If you still are having trouble completing the steps with a stylus, try using a mouse.

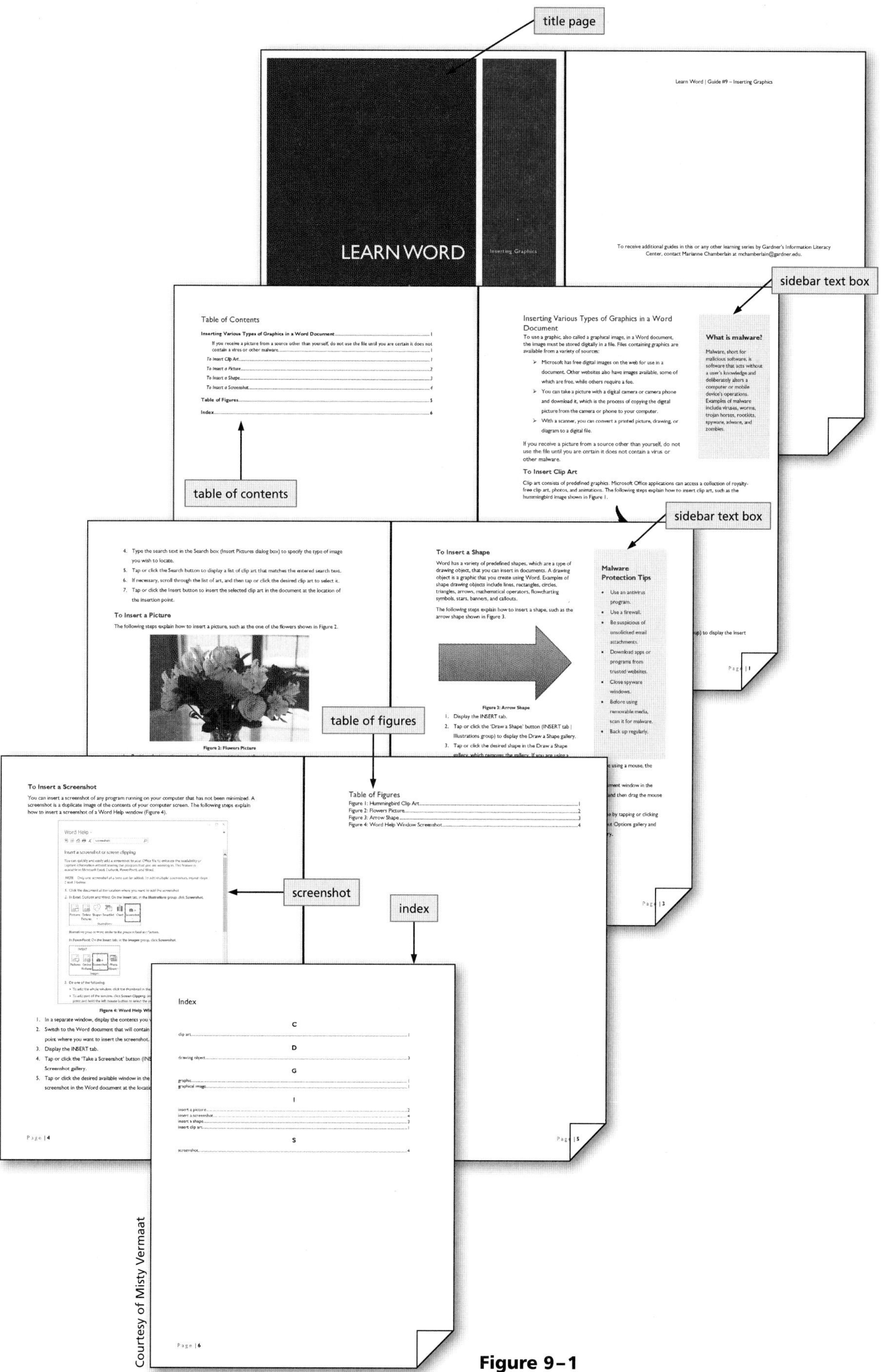
title page
LEARN WORD
sidebar text box
table of contents
sidebar text box
table of figures
screenshot
index
Courtesy of Misty Vermaat

Figure 9–1

Roadmap

In this chapter, you will learn how to create the document shown in Figure 9–1. The following roadmap identifies general activities you will perform as you progress through this chapter:

1. MODIFY a draft of a REFERENCE DOCUMENT.
2. CREATE a MASTER DOCUMENT for the reference document.
3. ORGANIZE the REFERENCE DOCUMENT.

At the beginning of step instructions throughout the chapter, you will see an abbreviated form of this roadmap. The abbreviated roadmap uses colors to indicate chapter progress: gray means the chapter is beyond that activity, blue means the task being shown is covered in that activity, and black means that activity is yet to be covered. For example, the following abbreviated roadmap indicates the chapter would be showing a task in the 2 CREATE MASTER DOCUMENT activity.

1 MODIFY REFERENCE DOCUMENT | 2 CREATE MASTER DOCUMENT | 3 ORGANIZE REFERENCE DOCUMENT

Use the abbreviated roadmap as a progress guide while you read or step through the instructions in this chapter.

One of the few differences between Windows 7 and Windows 8 occurs in the steps to run Word. If you are using Windows 7, click the Start button, type `Word` in the 'Search programs and files' box, click Word 2013, and then, if necessary, maximize the Word window. For a summary of the steps to run Word in Windows 7, refer to the Quick Reference located at the back of this book.

To Run Word and Change Word Settings

If you are using a computer to step through the project in this chapter and you want your screens to match the figures in this book, you should change your screen's resolution to 1366 × 768. The following steps run Word, display formatting marks, and change the zoom to page width.

1. Run Word and create a blank document in the Word window. If necessary, maximize the Word window.
2. If the Print Layout button on the status bar is not selected, tap or click it so that your screen is in Print Layout view.
3. To display the page the same width as the document window, if necessary, tap or click the Page Width button (VIEW tab | Zoom group).

Preparing a Document to Be Included in a Reference Document

Before including the Inserting Various Types of Graphics Draft document in a longer document, you will make several modifications to the document:

1. Insert a screenshot.
2. Add captions to the images in the document.
3. Insert references to the figures in the text.
4. Mark an index entry.
5. Insert text boxes that contain information about malware.
6. Compress the pictures.
7. Change the bullet symbol.

The following pages outline these changes.

CONSIDER THIS

How should you prepare a document to be included in a longer document?
Ensure that reference elements in a document, such as captions and index entries, are formatted properly and entered consistently.

- **Captions:** A **caption** is text that appears outside of an illustration, usually below it. If the illustration is identified with a number, the caption may include the word, Figure, along with the illustration number (i.e., Figure 1). In the caption, separate the figure number from the text of the figure by a space or punctuation mark such as a period or colon (Figure 1: Hummingbird Clip Art Image).
- **Index Entries:** If your document will include an index, read through the document and mark any terms or headings that you want to appear in the index. Include any term that the reader may want to locate quickly. Omit figures from index entries if the document will have a table of figures; otherwise, include figures in the index if appropriate.

To Open a Document from Word and Then Save It with a New File Name

The draft document that you will insert in the reference document is called Inserting Various Types of Graphics Draft. To preserve the original draft document, you create a file from the original document. The draft document is located on the Data Files for Students. Visit www.cengage.com/ct/studentdownload for detailed instructions or contact your instructor for information about accessing the required files. To preserve the contents of the original draft, you save it with a new file name. The following steps open the draft file and save it with a new file name.

1. Open the Backstage view and then tap or click the Open tab to display the Open gallery.
2. Navigate to the location of the file to be opened (in this case, the Data Files for Students folder).
3. Tap or click the file name, Inserting Various Types of Graphics Draft, to select it.
4. Tap or click the Open button (Open dialog box) to open the selected file.
5. Open the Backstage view and then tap or click the Save As tab to display the Save As gallery.
6. Display the Save As dialog box and then type `Inserting Various Types of Graphics Final` in the File name box to change the file name. Do not press the ENTER key after typing the file name because you do not want to close the dialog box at this time.
7. Navigate to the desired save location (in this case, the Word folder in the CIS 101 folder [or your class folder] on your computer or SkyDrive).
8. Tap or click the Save button (Save As dialog box) to save the document in the selected folder on the selected save location with the entered file name.
9. If the 'Show/Hide ¶' button (HOME tab | Paragraph group) is selected, tap or click it to hide formatting marks.

Q&A What if some formatting marks still appear after tapping or clicking the 'Show/Hide ¶' button?
Open the Backstage view, tap or click Options in the left pane in the Backstage view to display the Word Options dialog box, tap or click Display in the left pane (Word Options dialog box), remove the check mark from the Hidden text check box, and then tap or click the OK button.

BTW
Protected View
To keep your computer safe from potentially dangerous files, Word may automatically open certain files in a restricted mode, called Protected view. To see the Protected view settings, tap or click FILE on the ribbon to open the Backstage view, tap or click Options to display the Word Options dialog box, tap or click Trust Center in the left pane (Word Options dialog box), tap or click the 'Trust Center Settings' button in the right pane to display the Trust Center dialog box, and then tap or click Protected View in the left pane to show the current Protected view settings.

BTW
The Ribbon and Screen Resolution
Word may change how the groups and buttons within the groups appear on the ribbon, depending on the computer's screen resolution. Thus, your ribbon may look different from the ones in this book if you are using a screen resolution other than 1366 × 768.

10 Display the VIEW tab and then tap or click the Multiple Pages button (VIEW tab | Zoom group) to see all three pages of the document at once (Figure 9–2).

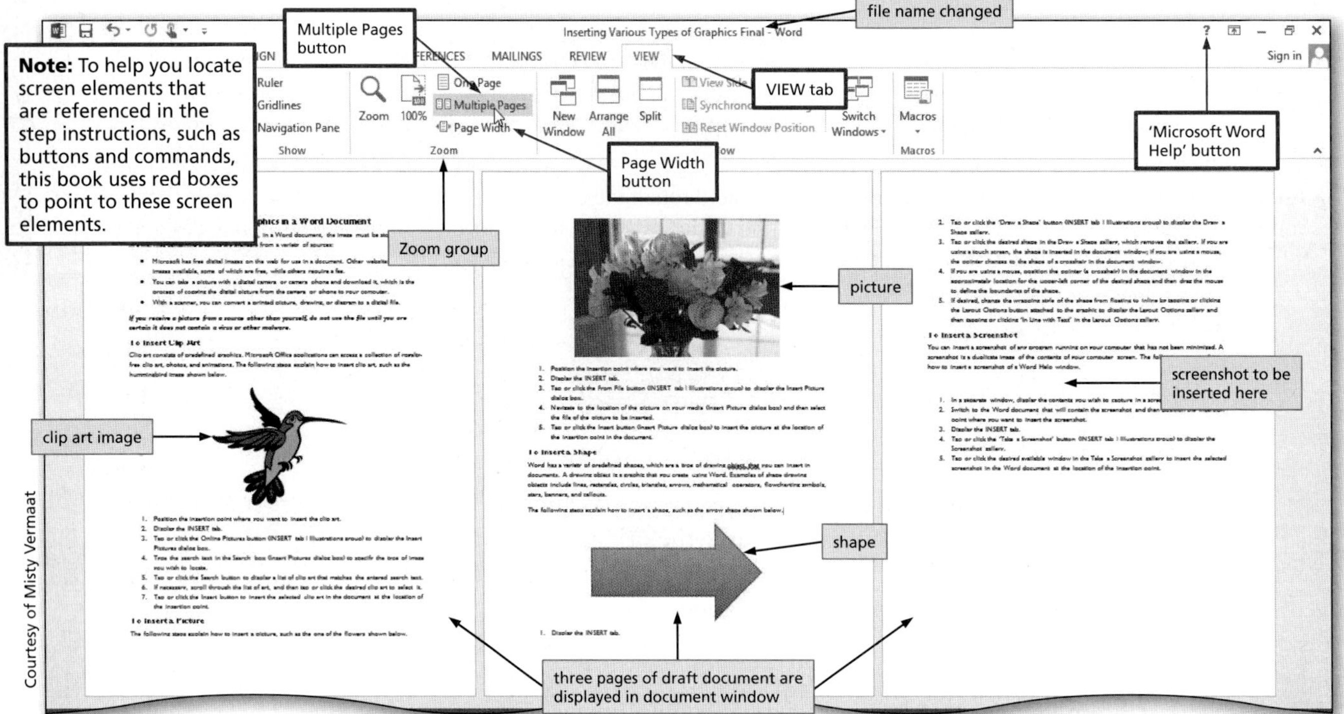

Figure 9–2

11 When you have finished viewing the document, tap or click the Page Width button (VIEW tab | Zoom group) to display the document as wide as possible in the document window.

To Insert a Screenshot

1 MODIFY REFERENCE DOCUMENT | **2 CREATE MASTER DOCUMENT** | **3 ORGANIZE REFERENCE DOCUMENT**

A **screenshot** is a duplicate image of the contents of your computer or mobile device's screen. The current document is missing a screenshot of a Word Help window. To insert a screenshot, you first must display the screen of which you want a screenshot in a window on your computer or mobile device. ***Why?*** *From within Word, you can insert a screenshot of any program running on your computer, provided the program has not been minimized.* The following steps insert a screenshot in a document.

1

- Display the contents you want to capture in a screenshot (in this case, tap or click the 'Microsoft Word Help' button on the title bar to open the Help window, type `screenshots` in the 'Search online help' text box, tap or click the 'Search online help' button, tap or click the 'Insert a screenshot or clipping' link to display the associated help information. If necessary, resize the Word Help window. (Figure 9–3).

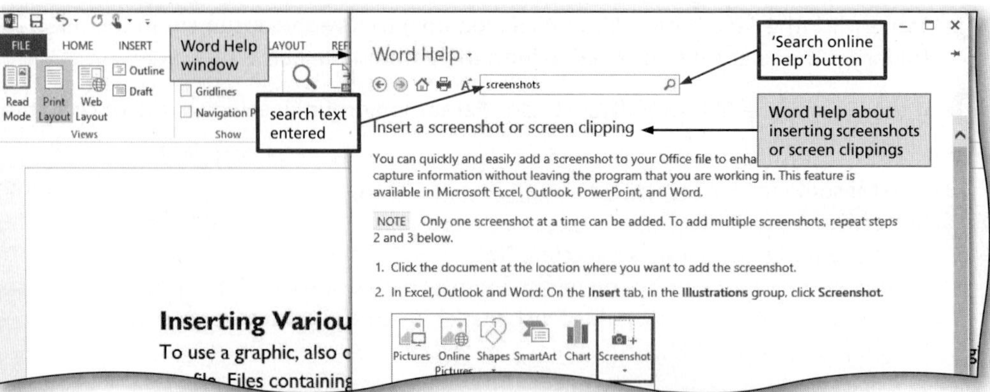

Figure 9–3

- In the Word window, position the insertion point in the document where the screenshot should be inserted (in this case, on the centered blank line above the numbered list in the To Insert a Screenshot section at the bottom of the document).
- Display the INSERT tab.
- Tap or click the 'Take a Screenshot' button (INSERT tab | Illustrations group) to display the Take a Screenshot gallery (Figure 9–4).

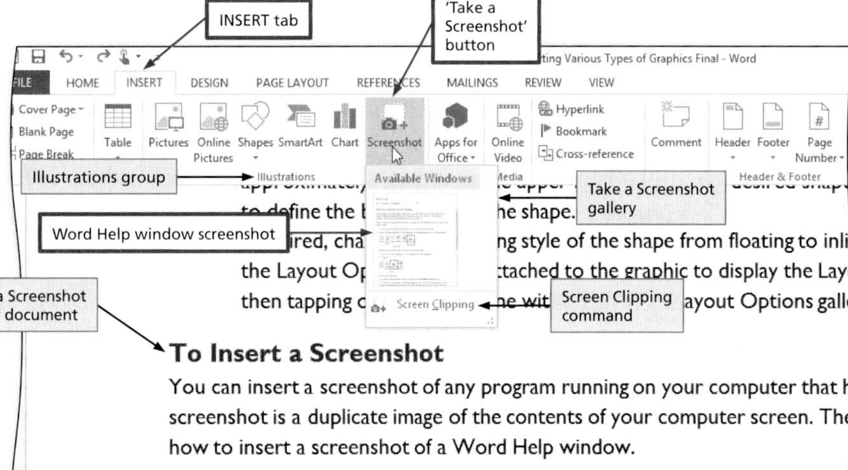

Figure 9–4

Q&A What is a screen clipping?
A screen clipping is a section of a window. When you select Screen Clipping in the Take a Screenshot gallery, the window turns opaque so that you can drag through the part of the window to be included in the document.

Why does my Take a Screenshot gallery show more windows?
You have additional programs running in windows on your desktop.

- Tap or click the Word Help window screenshot in the Take a Screenshot gallery to insert the selected screenshot in the Word document at the location of the insertion point.
- Tap or click the Shape Height and Shape Width box down arrows (PICTURE TOOLS FORMAT tab | Size group) as many times as necessary to resize the screenshot to approximately 5" tall by 4.76" wide (Figure 9–5).

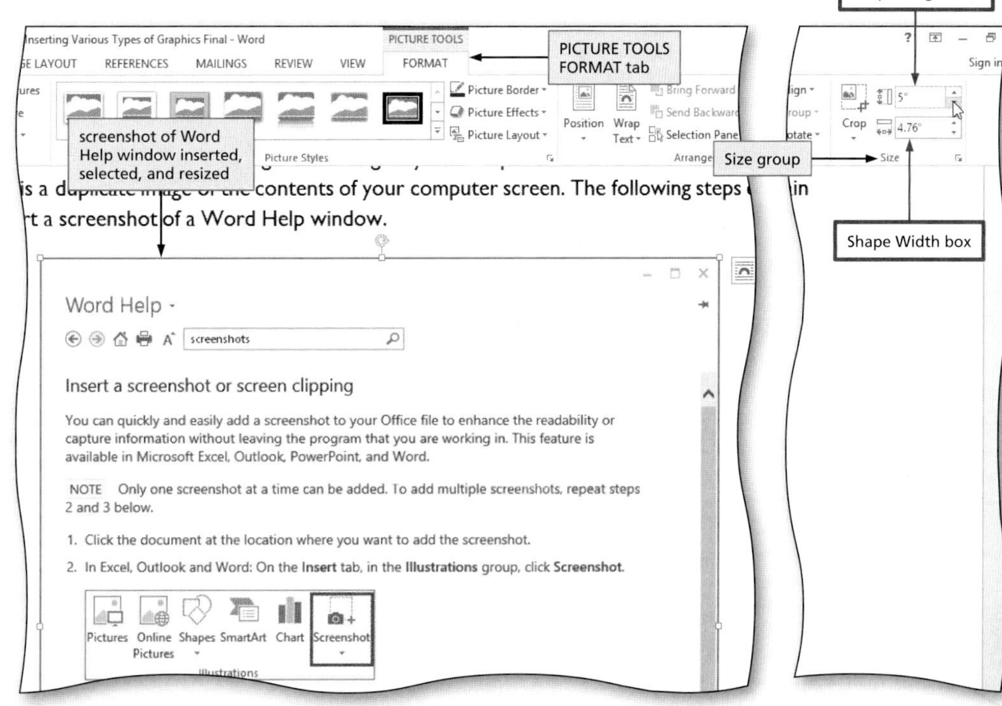

Figure 9–5

Q&A What if my text appears on a separate page from the screenshot?
Depending on settings, the text may move to the next page.

To Add a Caption

1 MODIFY REFERENCE DOCUMENT | **2 CREATE MASTER DOCUMENT** | **3 ORGANIZE REFERENCE DOCUMENT**

In Word, you can add a caption to an equation, a figure, and a table. If you move, delete, or add captions in a document, Word renumbers remaining captions in the document automatically. In this reference document, the captions contain the word, Figure, followed by the figure number, a colon, and a figure description. The following steps add a caption to a graphic, specifically, the screenshot. ***Why?*** *The current document contains four images: a clip art image, a picture, a shape, and a screenshot. All of these images should have captions.*

1

- If the screenshot is not selected already, tap or click it to select the graphic for which you want a caption.
- Display the REFERENCES tab.
- Tap or click the Insert Caption button (REFERENCES tab | Captions group) to display the Caption dialog box with a figure number automatically assigned to the selected graphic (Figure 9–6).

Q&A Why is the figure number a 1?
No other captions have been assigned in this document yet. When you insert a new caption, or move or delete items containing captions, Word automatically updates caption numbers throughout the document.

What if the Caption text box has the label Table or Equation instead of Figure?
Tap or click the Label arrow (Caption dialog box) and then tap or click Figure in the Label list.

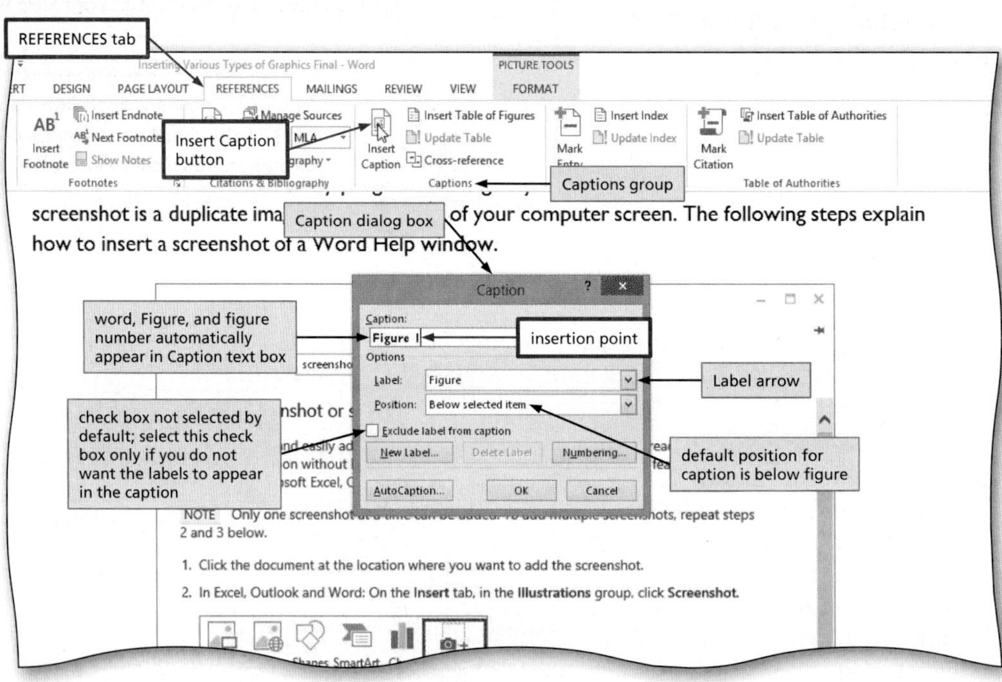

Figure 9–6

2

- Press the COLON (:) key and then press the SPACEBAR in the Caption text box (Caption dialog box) to place separating characters between the figure number and description.
- Type **Help Window Screenshot** as the figure description (Figure 9–7).

Q&A Can I change the format of the caption number?
Yes, tap or click the Numbering button (Caption dialog box), adjust the format as desired, and then tap or click the OK button.

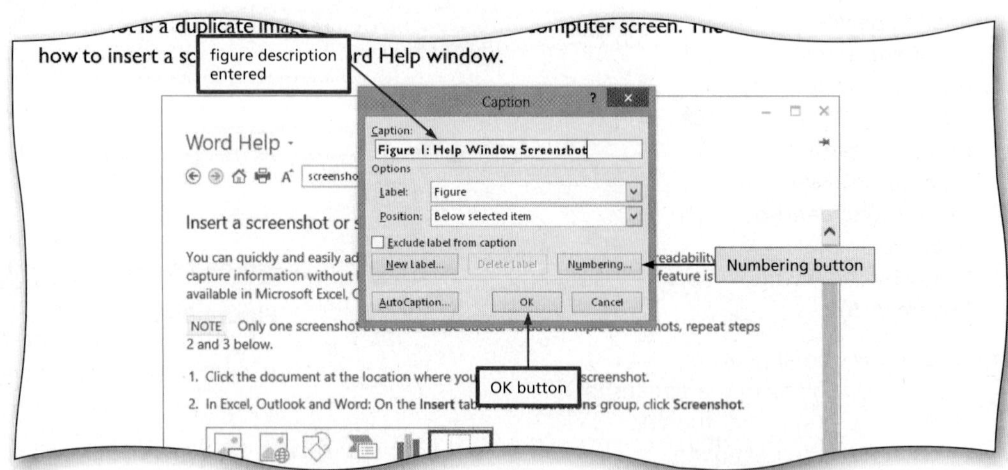

Figure 9–7

- Tap or click the OK button to insert the caption below the selected graphic.
- If necessary, scroll to display the caption in the document window (Figure 9–8).

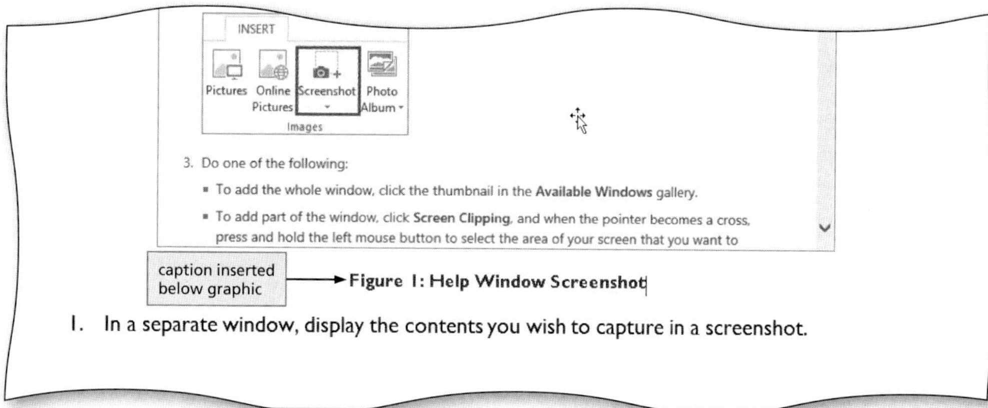

Figure 9–8

Q&A How do I change the position of a caption?
Tap or click the Position arrow (Caption dialog box) and then select the desired position of the caption.

Caption Numbers

Each caption number contains a field. In Word, recall that a **field** is a placeholder for data that can change in a document. Examples of fields you have used in previous projects are page numbers, merge fields, IF fields, and the current date. You update caption numbers using the same technique used to update any other field. That is, to update all caption numbers, select the entire document and then press the F9 key, or press and hold or right-click the field and then tap or click Update Field on the shortcut menu. When you print a document, Word updates the caption numbers automatically, regardless of whether the document window displays the updated caption numbers.

BTW
Captions
If a caption appears with extra characters inside curly braces ({ }), Word is displaying field codes instead of field results. Press ALT+F9 to display captions correctly as field results. If Word prints fields codes for captions, tap or click FILE on the ribbon to open the Backstage view, tap or click Options in the Backstage view to display the Word Options dialog box, tap or click Advanced in the left pane (Word Options dialog box), scroll to the Print section in the right pane, remove the check mark from the 'Print field codes instead of their values' check box, tap or click the OK button, and then print the document again.

To Hide White Space

White space is the space displayed in the margins at the top and bottom of pages (including any headers and footers) and also space between pages. To make it easier to see the text in this document as you scroll through it, the following step hides white space.

If you are using a touch screen, double-tap in the space between pages; if you are using a mouse, position the pointer in the document window in the space between the pages and then double-click when the pointer changes to a 'Hide White Space' button to hide white space.

To Create a Cross-Reference

1 MODIFY REFERENCE DOCUMENT | **2 CREATE MASTER DOCUMENT** | **3 ORGANIZE REFERENCE DOCUMENT**

The next step in this project is to add a reference to the new figure. ***Why?*** *In reference documents, the text should reference each figure specifically and, if appropriate, explain the contents of the figure.*

Because figures may be inserted, deleted, or moved, you may not know the actual figure number in the final document. For this reason, Word provides a method of creating a **cross-reference**, which is a link to an item, such as a heading, caption, or footnote in a document. By creating a cross-reference to the caption, the text that mentions the figure will be updated whenever the caption to the figure is updated. The steps on the next page create a cross-reference.

- At the end of the last sentence below the To Insert a Screenshot heading, position the insertion point to the left of the period, press the SPACEBAR, and then press the LEFT PARENTHESIS key.
- Display the INSERT tab.
- Tap or click the 'Insert Cross-reference' button (INSERT tab | Links group) to display the Cross-reference dialog box (Figure 9–9).

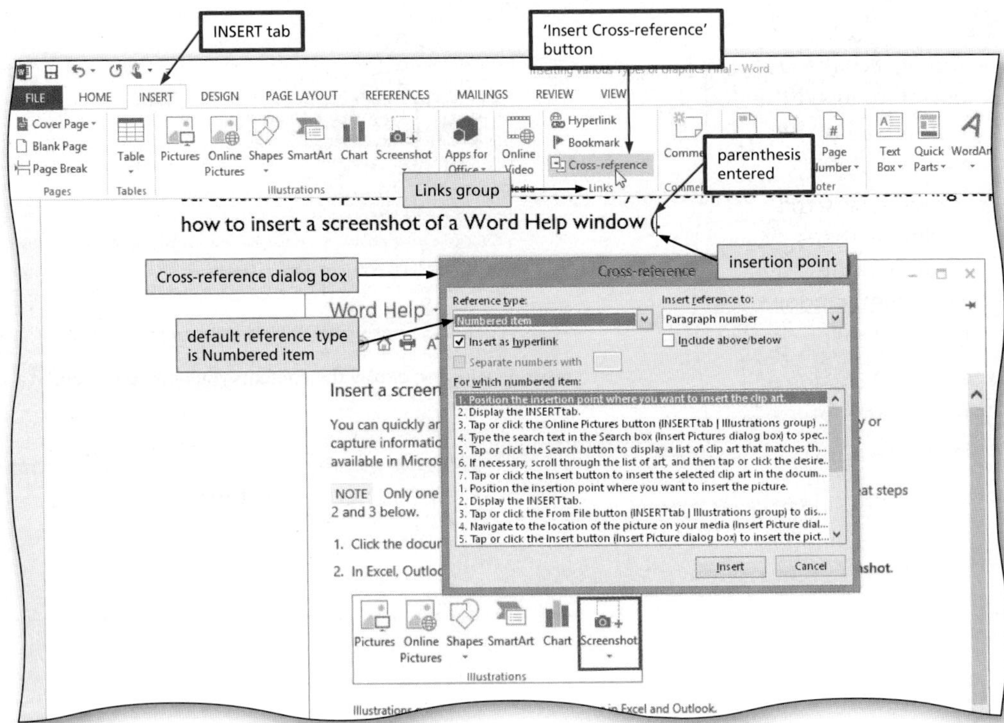

Figure 9–9

- Tap or click the Reference type arrow (Cross-reference dialog box) to display the Reference type list; scroll to and then tap or click Figure, which displays a list of figures from the document in the For which caption list (which, at this point, is only one figure).
- If necessary, tap or click 'Figure 1: Help Window Screenshot' in the For which caption list to select the caption to reference.
- Tap or click the 'Insert reference to' arrow and then tap or click 'Only label and number' to instruct Word that the cross-reference in the document should list just the label, Figure, followed by the figure number (Figure 9–10).

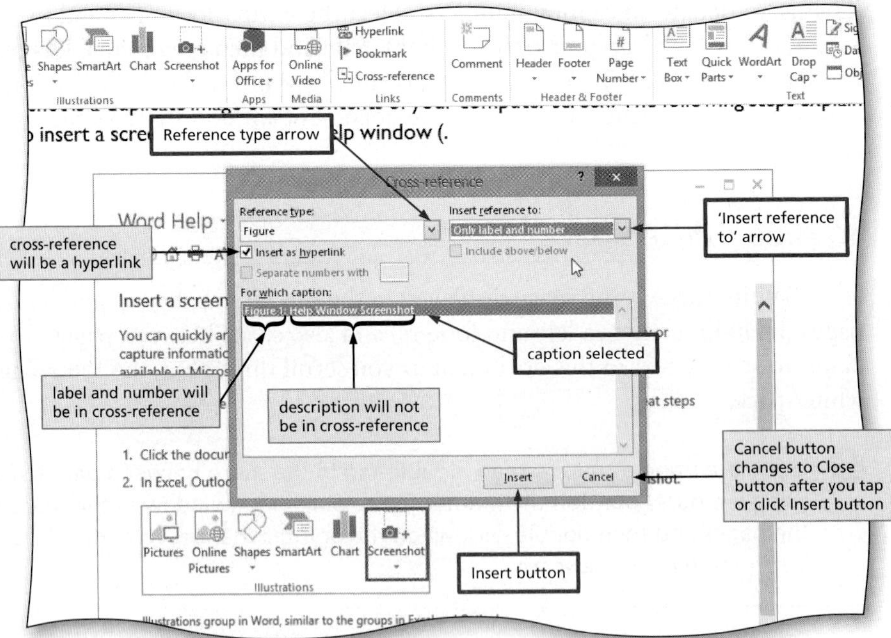

Figure 9–10

- Tap or click the Insert button to insert the cross-reference in the document at the location of the insertion point.

Q&A

What if my cross-reference is shaded in gray?

The cross-reference is a field. Depending on your Word settings, fields may appear shaded in gray to help you identify them on the screen.

4

- Tap or click the Close button (Cross-reference dialog box).
- Press the RIGHT PARENTHESIS key to close off the cross-reference (Figure 9–11).

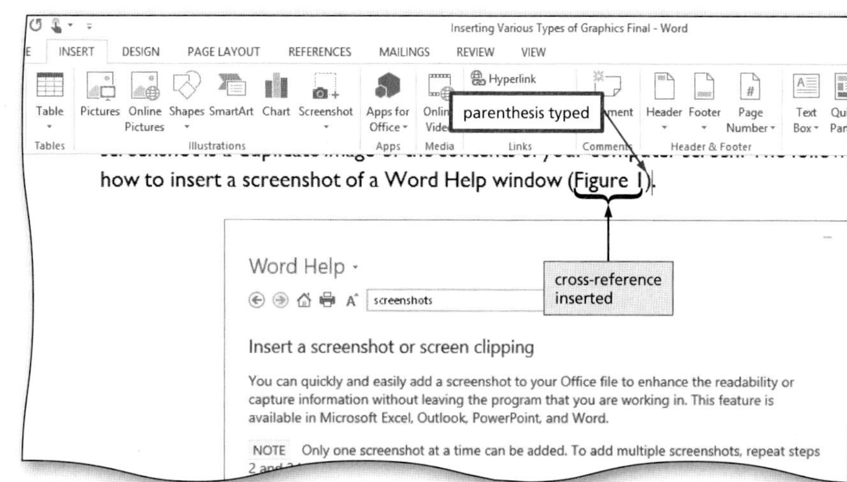

Figure 9–11

Q&A How do I update a cross-reference if a caption is added, deleted, or moved?

In many cases, Word automatically updates a cross-reference in a document if the item to which it refers changes. To update a cross-reference manually, select the cross-reference and then press the F9 key, or press and hold or right-click the cross-reference and then tap or click Update Field on the shortcut menu.

Other Ways

1. Tap or click 'Insert Cross-reference' button (REFERENCES tab | Captions group)

To Go to an Object

1 MODIFY REFERENCE DOCUMENT | **2 CREATE MASTER DOCUMENT** | **3 ORGANIZE REFERENCE DOCUMENT**

Often, you would like to bring a certain page, graphic, or other part of a document into view in the document window. Although you could scroll through the document to find a desired page, graphic, or part of the document, Word enables you to go to a specific location via the Go To sheet in the Find and Replace dialog box.

The following steps go to a graphic. ***Why?*** *The next step in this chapter is to add a caption to another graphic in the document, so you want to display the graphic in the document window.*

1

- Display the HOME tab.
- Tap or click the Find arrow (HOME tab | Editing group) to display the Find menu (Figure 9–12).

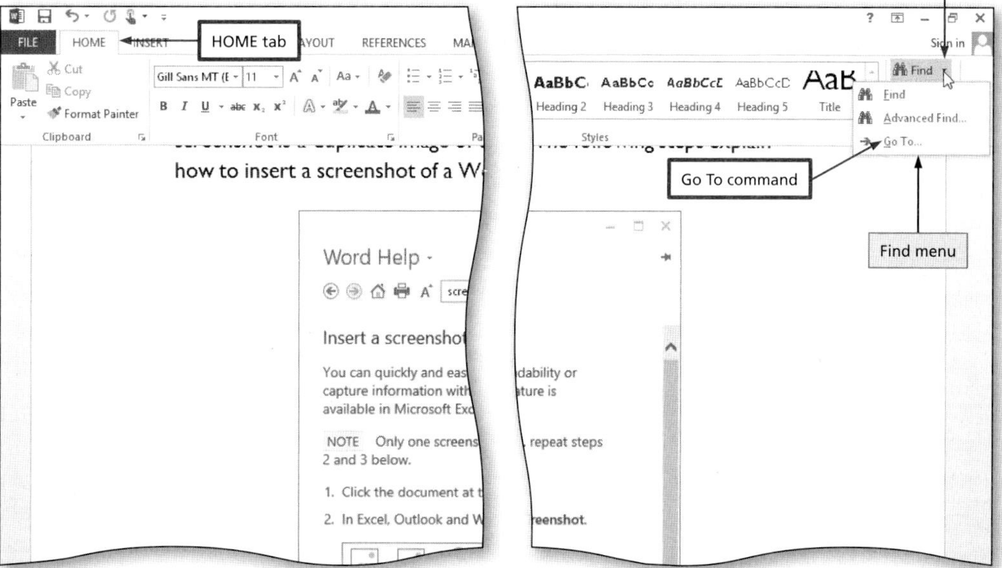

Figure 9–12

- Tap or click Go To on the Find menu to display the Find and Replace dialog box.
- Scroll through the Go to what list and then tap or click Graphic to select it.
- Tap or click the Previous button to display the previous graphic in the document window (which is the arrow shape, in this case) (Figure 9–13).

- Tap or click Close button to close the dialog box.

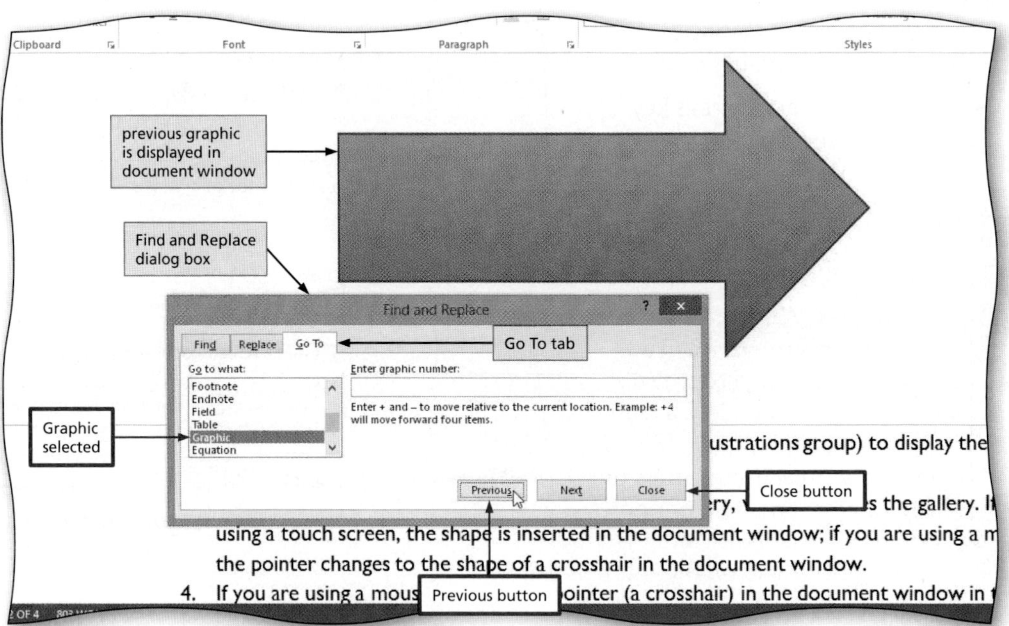

Figure 9–13

Other Ways

1. Press CTRL+G

To Add Captions and Create Cross-References

The previous steps added a caption to the screenshot graphic and then created a cross-reference to that caption. The following steps add captions to the remaining three graphics in the document (that is, the shape, the picture, and the clip art).

1. Tap or click the arrow shape to select the graphic for which you want to add a caption.
2. Tap or click the Insert Caption button (REFERENCES tab | Captions group) to display the Caption dialog box with a figure number automatically assigned to the selected graphic.
3. Press the COLON (:) key and then press the SPACEBAR in the Caption text box (Caption dialog box) to place separating characters between the figure number and description.
4. Type `Arrow Shape` as the figure description and then tap or click the OK button to insert the caption below the selected graphic.
5. At the end of the last sentence above the graphic, change the word, below, to the word, in, and then press the SPACEBAR.
6. Tap or click the 'Insert Cross-reference' button (INSERT or REFERENCES tab | Links or Captions group) to display the Cross-reference dialog box, if necessary, tap or click 'Figure 1: Arrow Shape' in the For which caption list to select the caption to reference, tap or click the Insert button to insert the cross-reference at the location of the insertion point, and then tap or click the Close button in the Cross-reference dialog box.

Q&A Why did I not need to change the settings for the reference type and reference to in the dialog box?
Word retains the previous settings in the dialog box.

BTW
Q&As
For a complete list of the Q&As found in many of the step-by-step sequences in this book, visit the Q&A resource on the Student Companion Site located on www.cengagebrain.com. For detailed instructions about accessing available resources, visit www.cengage.com/ct/studentdownload or contact your instructor for information about accessing the required files.

7 Tap or click the Find arrow (HOME tab | Editing group) to display the Find menu and then tap or click Go To on the Find menu to display the Go To dialog box. With Graphic selected in the Go to what list, tap or click the Previous button to display the previous graphic in the document window (which is the flowers picture in this case). Tap or click the Close button to close the dialog box.

8 Repeat Steps 1 though 7 to add the caption, Flowers Picture, to the picture of the flowers and the caption, Hummingbird Clip Art, to the clip art of the hummingbird. Also add a cross-reference at the end of the sentences above each image (Figure 9–14).

9 Close the Cross-reference dialog box.

BTW
Touch Screen Differences
The Office and Windows interfaces may vary if you are using a touch screen. For this reason, you might notice that the function or appearance of your touch screen differs slightly from this chapter's presentation.

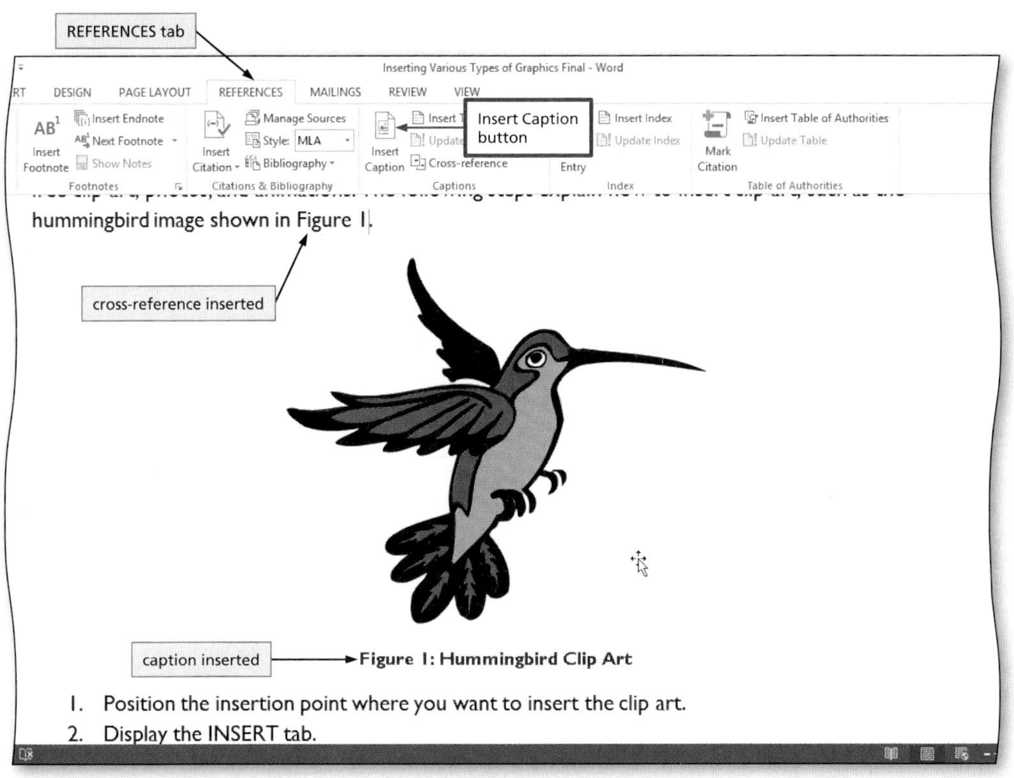

Figure 9–14

To Mark an Index Entry

1 MODIFY REFERENCE DOCUMENT | 2 CREATE MASTER DOCUMENT | 3 ORGANIZE REFERENCE DOCUMENT

The last page of the reference document in this project is an index, which lists important terms discussed in the document along with each term's corresponding page number. For Word to generate the index, you first must mark any text you wish to appear in the index. ***Why?*** *When you mark an index entry, Word creates a field that it uses to build the index.* Index entry fields are hidden and are displayed on the screen only when you show formatting marks, that is, when the 'Show/Hide ¶' button (HOME tab | Paragraph group) is selected.

In this document, you want the words, graphical image, in the first sentence below the Inserting Various Types of Graphics in a Word Document heading to be marked as an index entry. The steps on the next page mark an index entry.

- Select the text you wish to appear in the index (the words, graphical image, in the first sentence of the document in this case).
- Tap or click the Mark Entry button (REFERENCES tab | Index group) to display the Mark Index Entry dialog box (Figure 9–15).

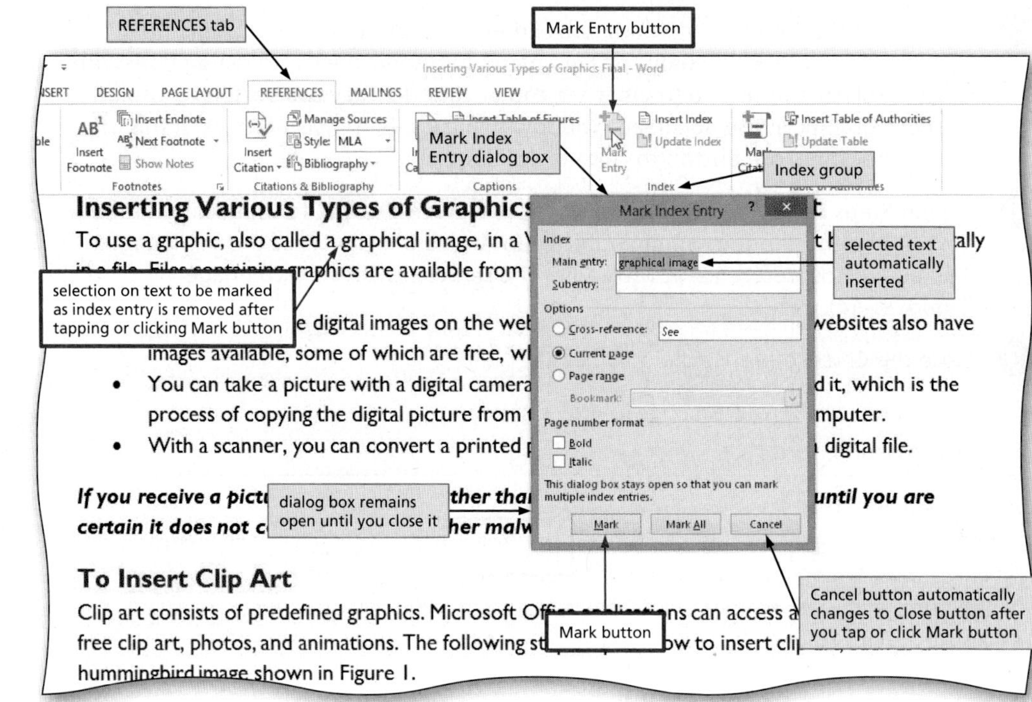

Figure 9–15

- Tap or click the Mark button (Mark Index Entry dialog box) to mark the selected text in the document as an index entry.

Q&A Why do formatting marks now appear on the screen?
When you mark an index entry, Word automatically shows formatting marks (if they are not showing already) so that you can see the index entry field. Notice that the marked index entry begins with the letters, XE.

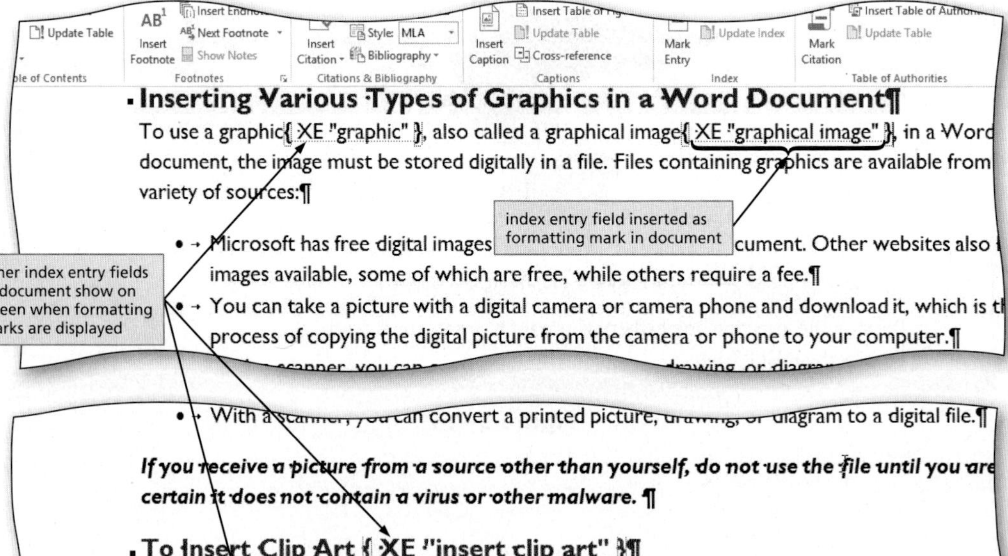

Figure 9–16

- Tap or click the Close button in the Mark Index Entry dialog box to close the dialog box (Figure 9–16).

Q&A How could I see all index entries marked in a document?
With formatting marks displaying, you could scroll through the document, scanning for all occurrences of XE, or you could use the Navigation Pane (that is, place a check mark in the 'Open the Navigation Pane' check box (VIEW tab | Show group)) to find all occurrences of XE.

Other Ways

1. Select text, press ALT+SHIFT+X

To Mark Multiple Index Entries

Word leaves the Mark Index Entry dialog box open until you close it, which allows you to mark multiple index entries without having to reopen the dialog box repeatedly. To mark multiple index entries, you would perform the following steps.

1. With the Mark Index Entry dialog box displayed, tap or click in the document window; scroll to and then select the next index entry.
2. If necessary, tap or click the Main entry text box (Mark Index Entry dialog box) to display the selected text in the Main entry text box.
3. Tap or click the Mark button.
4. Repeat Steps 1 through 3 for all entries. When finished, tap or click the Close button in the Mark Index Entry dialog box.

BTW

Index Entries

Index entries may include a switch, which is a slash followed by a letter inserted after the field text. Switches include \b to apply bold formatting to the entry's page number, \f to define an entry type, \i to make the entry's page number italic, \r to insert a range of page numbers, \t to insert specified text in place of a page number, and \y to specify that the subsequent text defines the pronunciation for the index entry. A colon in an index entry precedes a subentry keyword in the index.

To Hide Formatting Marks

To remove the clutter of index entry fields from the document, you should hide formatting marks. The following step hides formatting marks.

1 If the 'Show/Hide ¶' button (HOME tab | Paragraph group) is selected, tap or click it to hide formatting marks.

Q&A What if the index entries still appear after tapping or clicking the 'Show/Hide ¶' button? Open the Backstage view, tap or click Options in the left pane in the Backstage view to display the Word Options dialog box, tap or click Display in the left pane (Word Options dialog box), remove the check mark from the Hidden text check box, and then tap or click the OK button.

To Change Paragraph Spacing in a Document

1 MODIFY REFERENCE DOCUMENT | **2 CREATE MASTER DOCUMENT** | **3 ORGANIZE REFERENCE DOCUMENT**

In Word, you easily can expand or condense the amount of space between lines in all paragraphs in a document. The following steps expand paragraph spacing. ***Why?*** *You feel the document text would be easier to read if the paragraphs were more open.*

1

- Display the DESIGN tab.
- Tap or click the Paragraph Spacing button (DESIGN tab | Document Formatting group) to display the Paragraph Spacing gallery (Figure 9–17).

Experiment

- If you are using a mouse, point to various spacing commands in the Paragraph Spacing gallery and watch the paragraphs conform to that spacing.

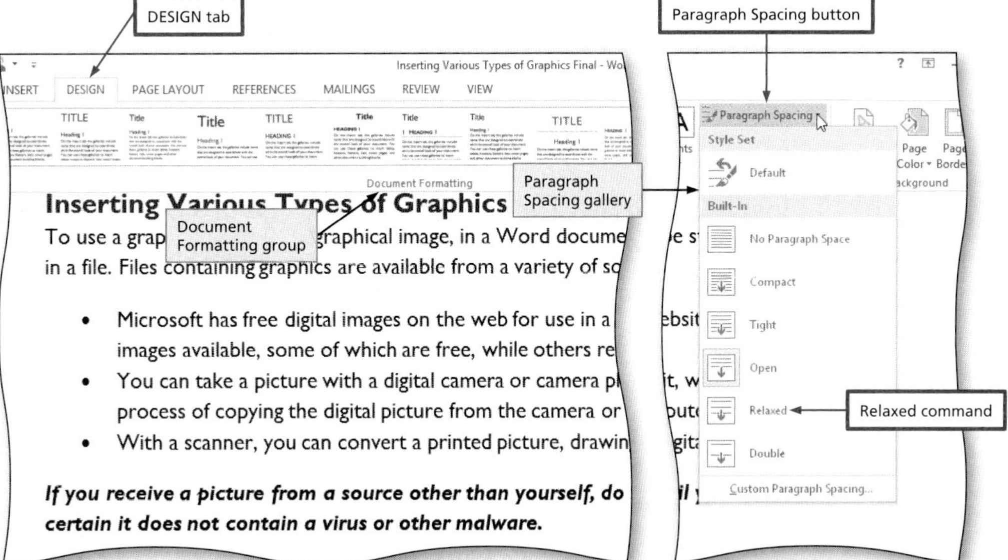

Figure 9–17

- Tap or click Relaxed in the Paragraph Spacing gallery to expand the spacing of paragraphs in the document.

To Show White Space

For the remainder of creating this project, you would like to see headers, footers, and margins. Thus, you should show white space. The following step shows white space.

If you are using a touch screen, double-tap the page break notation; if you are using a mouse, position the pointer in the document window on the page break and then double-click when the pointer changes to a 'Show White Space' button to show white space.

To Insert a Sidebar Text Box

1 MODIFY REFERENCE DOCUMENT | 2 CREATE MASTER DOCUMENT | 3 ORGANIZE REFERENCE DOCUMENT

A **sidebar text box** is a text box that runs across the top or bottom of a page or along the edge of the right or left of a page. The following steps insert a built-in sidebar text box. ***Why?*** *Sidebar text boxes take up less space on the page than text boxes positioned in the middle of the page.*

- Be sure the insertion point is near the top of page 1 of the document, as shown in Figure 9–18.

Q&A | Does the insertion point need to be at the top of the page?
The insertion point should be close to where you want to insert the text box.

- Display the INSERT tab.
- Tap or click the 'Choose a Text Box' button (INSERT tab | Text group) to display the Choose a Text Box gallery.

Experiment

- Scroll through the Choose a Text Box gallery to see the variety of available text box styles.
- Scroll to display Grid Sidebar in the Choose a Text Box gallery (Figure 9–18).

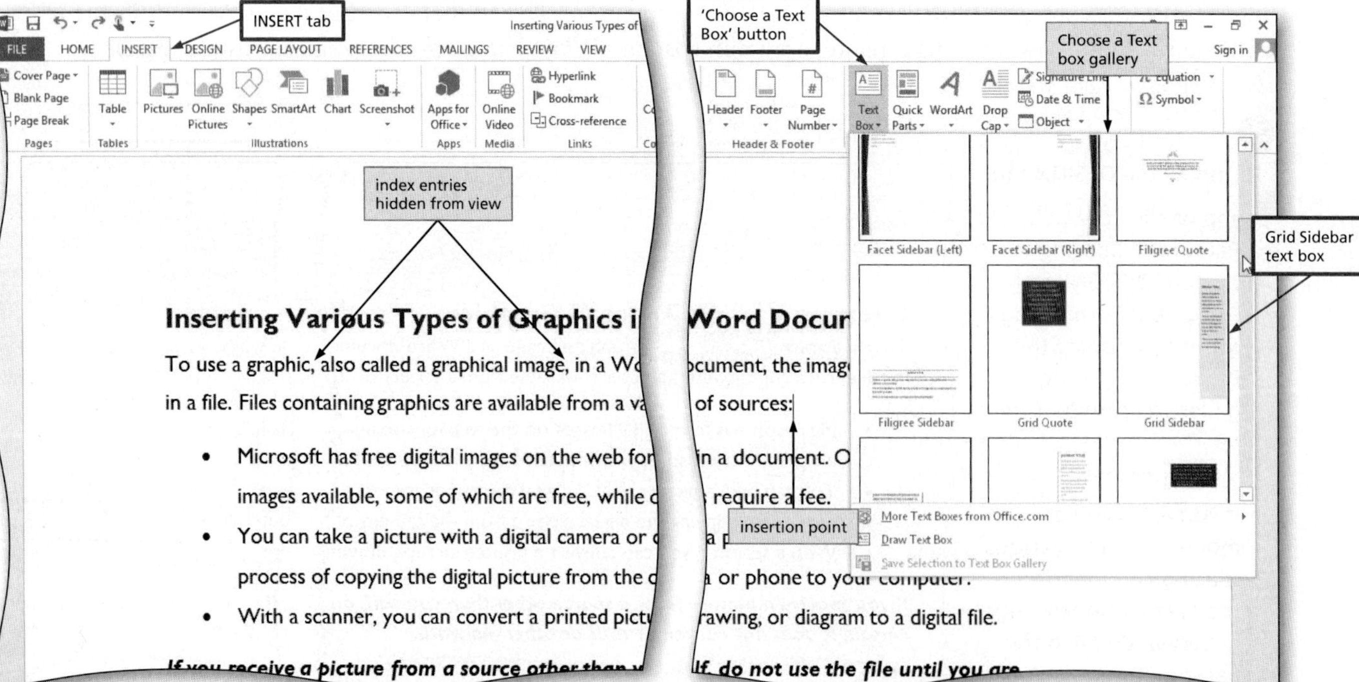

Figure 9–18

2

- Tap or click Grid Sidebar in the Choose a Text Box gallery to insert that text box style in the document (Figure 9–19).

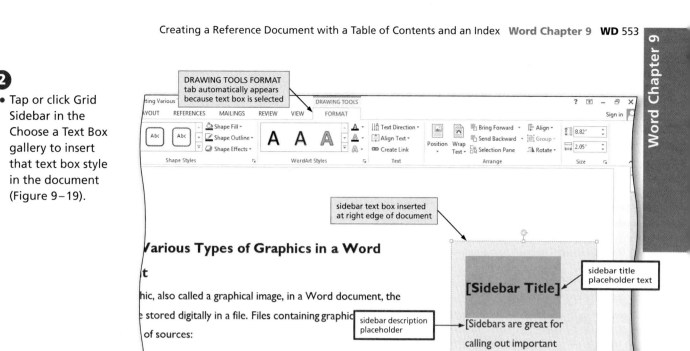

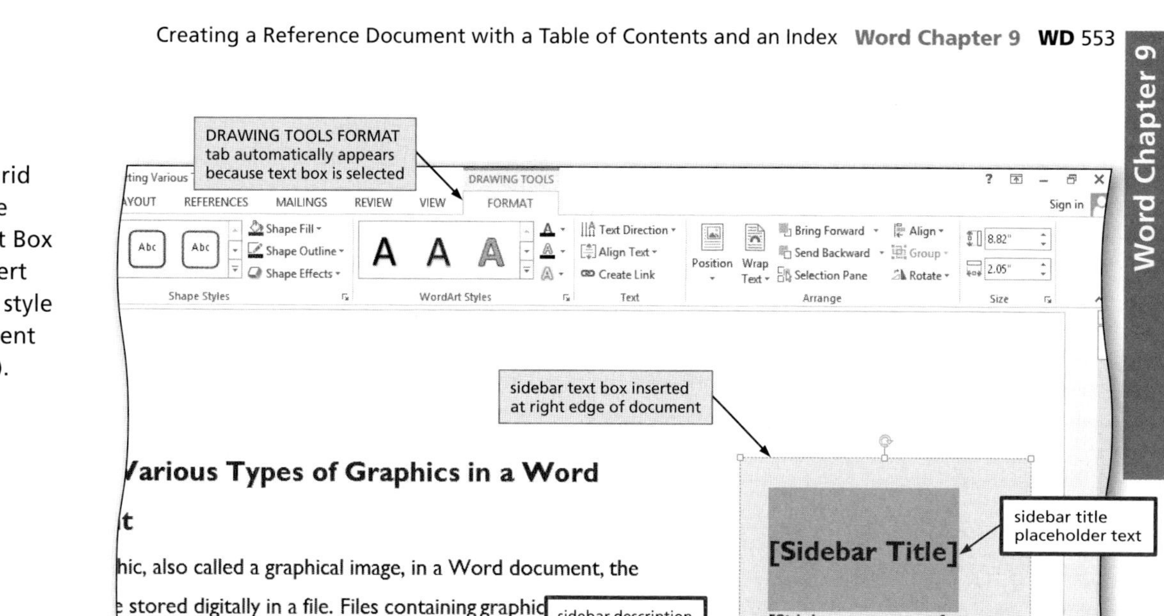

Figure 9–19

Other Ways

1. Tap or click 'Explore Quick Parts' button (INSERT tab | Text group), tap or click 'Building Blocks Organizer' on Explore Quick Parts menu, select desired text box name in Building blocks list, tap or click Insert button

To Enter and Format Text in the Sidebar Text Box

The next step is to enter the text in the sidebar text box. The following steps enter text in the text box.

1. If necessary, tap or click the sidebar title placeholder in the text box to select it.
2. Type `What is malware?`
3. Tap or click the sidebar description placeholder and then type the following paragraph: `Malware, short for malicious software, is software that acts without a user's knowledge and deliberately alters a computer or mobile device's operations. Examples of malware include viruses, worms, trojan horses, rootkits, spyware, adware, and zombies.`
4. Press the ENTER key. Change the font size to 14 point and bold the text. Type `Malware Protection Tips` and then press the ENTER key.
5. Change the font size to 11 point and remove the bold format from the text. Tap or click the Bullets button (HOME tab | Paragraph group) to bullet the list. Tap or click the Decrease Indent button (HOME tab | Paragraph group) to move the bullet symbol left one-half inch. Type `Use an antivirus program.`
6. Press the ENTER key. Type `Use a firewall.`
7. Press the ENTER key. Type `Be suspicious of unsolicited email attachments.`
8. Press the ENTER key. Type `Download apps or programs from trusted websites.`
9. Press the ENTER key. Type `Close spyware windows.`

BTW
Building Blocks
Many of the objects that you can insert through the Building Blocks gallery are available as built-in objects in galleries on the ribbon. Some examples are cover pages in the Add a Cover Page gallery (INSERT tab | Pages group), equations in the Insert an Equation gallery (INSERT tab | Symbols group), footers in the Add a Footer gallery (INSERT tab | Header & Footer group), headers in the Add a Header gallery (INSERT tab | Header & Footer group), page numbers in the Add Page Numbers gallery (INSERT tab | Header & Footer group), text boxes in the Choose a Text Box gallery (INSERT tab | Text group), and watermarks in the Watermark gallery (DESIGN tab | Page Background group).

BTW
Deleting Building Blocks
To delete an existing building block, tap or click the 'Explore Quick Parts' button (INSERT tab | Text group) to display the Explore Quick Parts menu, tap or click 'Building Blocks Organizer' on the Explore Quick Parts menu to display the Building Blocks Organizer dialog box, select the building block to delete (Building Blocks Organizer dialog box), tap or click the Delete button, tap or click the Yes button in the dialog box that appears, and then close the Building Blocks Organizer dialog box.

10. Press the ENTER key. Type **`Before using removable media, scan it for malware.`** If necessary, drag the bottom of the text box down to make it longer so that all of the entered text is visible.

11. Press the ENTER key. Type **`Back up regularly.`**

12. Tap or click the One Page button (VIEW tab | Zoom group) so that you can see all of the entered text at once (Figure 9–20).

13. Change the zoom to page width.

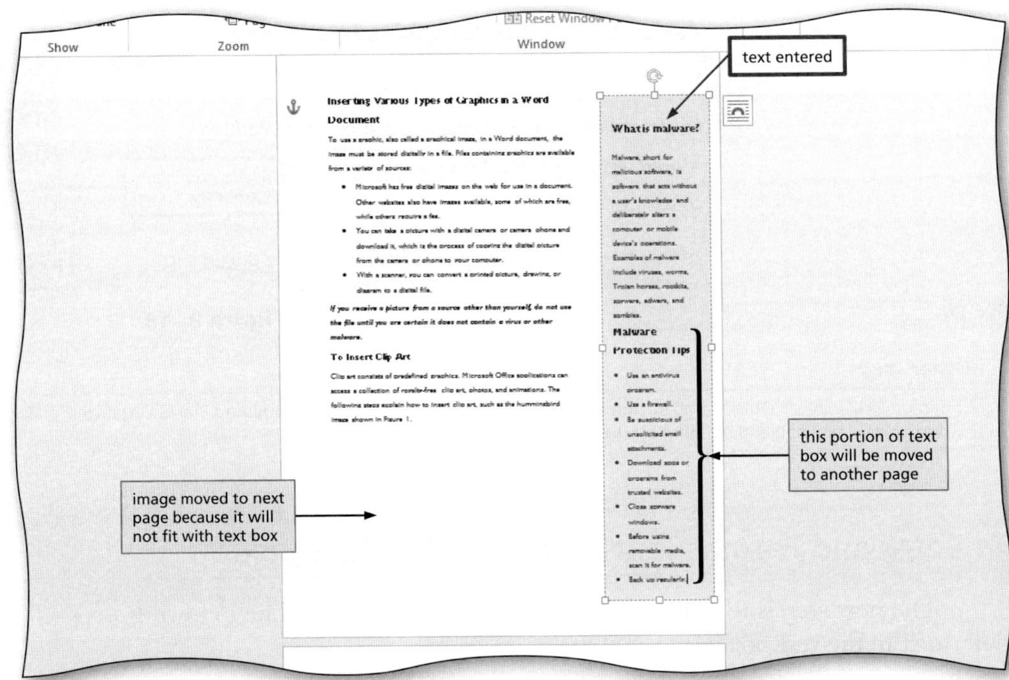

Figure 9–20

To Use the Navigation Pane to Go to a Page

Instead of one long text box, this project splits the text box across the top of two pages, specifically, the first and third pages of this document. The following steps use the Navigation Pane to display page 3 in the document window so that you can insert another text box on that page.

1. Display the VIEW tab. Place a check mark in the 'Open the Navigation Pane' check box (VIEW tab | Show group) to display the Navigation Pane at the left edge of the Word window.

2. Tap or click the PAGES tab in the Navigation Pane to display thumbnail images of the pages in the document.

3. Scroll to and then tap or click the thumbnail of the third page in the Navigation Pane to display the top of the selected page in the top of the document window.

4. Position the insertion point near the bottom of the third page at the approximate location for the sidebar text box (Figure 9–21).

5. Leave the Navigation Pane open for use in the next several steps.

BTW
Field Codes
If your index, table of contents, or table of figures displays odd characters inside curly braces ({ }), then Word is displaying field codes instead of field results. Press ALT+F9 to display the index or table correctly.

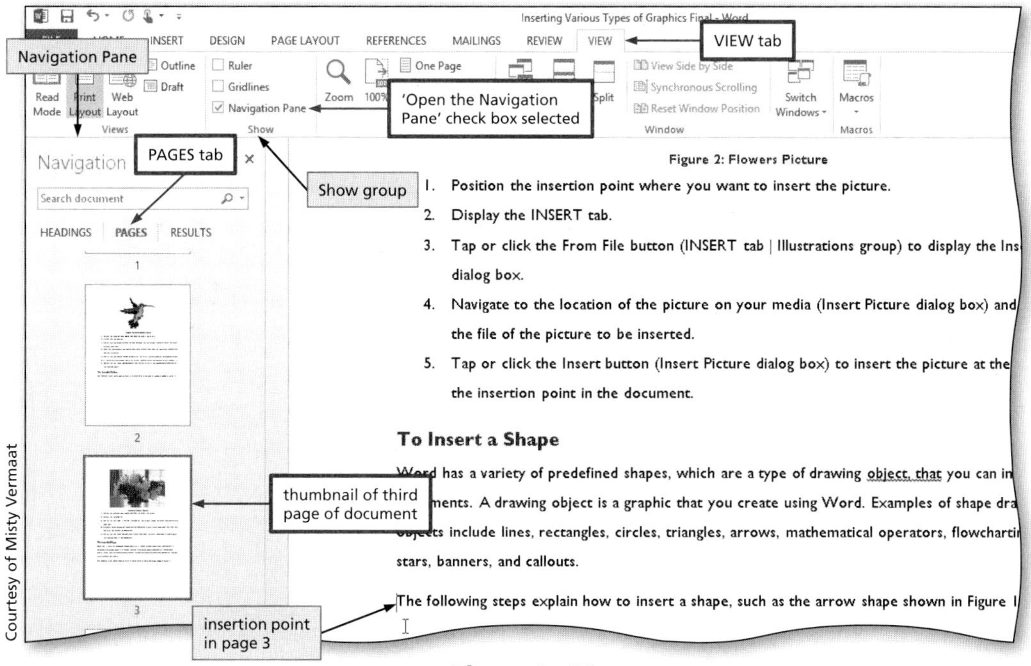

Figure 9–21

To Insert Another Sidebar Text Box

The following steps insert a Grid Sidebar text box building block on the third page in the document.

1. Ensure that the insertion point is near the bottom of the third page in the document.

   Q&A Why position the insertion point near the bottom of the page?
   The content of the first and second text boxes will be shared, which means the content currently at the top of page three may move to page two after you link the text boxes. You want to ensure the text box will be positioned on the third page after linking the two text boxes together. If the text box moves to the second page, you can drag it back to the third page.

2. Display the INSERT tab.

3. Tap or click the 'Choose a Text Box' button (INSERT tab | Text group) to display the Choose a Text Box gallery and then locate and select Grid Sidebar in the Choose a Text Box gallery to insert that text box style in the document.

4. Press the DELETE key four times to delete the current contents from the text box (Figure 9–22).

Figure 9–22

BTW

BTWs

For a complete list of the BTWs found in the margins of this book, visit the BTW resource on the Student Companion Site located on www.cengagebrain.com. For detailed instructions about accessing available resources, visit www.cengage.com/ct/studentdownload or contact your instructor for information about accessing the required files.

To Link Text Boxes

Word allows you to link two separate text boxes. ***Why?*** *You can flow text from one text box into the other.* To link text boxes, the second text box must be empty, which is why you deleted the contents of the text box in the previous steps. The following steps link text boxes.

1

- Tap or click the thumbnail of the first page in the Navigation Pane to display the top of the selected page in the document window.
- Tap or click the text box on the first page to select it.
- If necessary, display the DRAWING TOOLS FORMAT tab.
- Tap or click the Create Link button (DRAWING TOOLS FORMAT tab | Text group), which changes the pointer to the shape of a cup if you are using a mouse.
- If you are using a mouse, move the pointer in the document window to see its new shape (Figure 9–23).

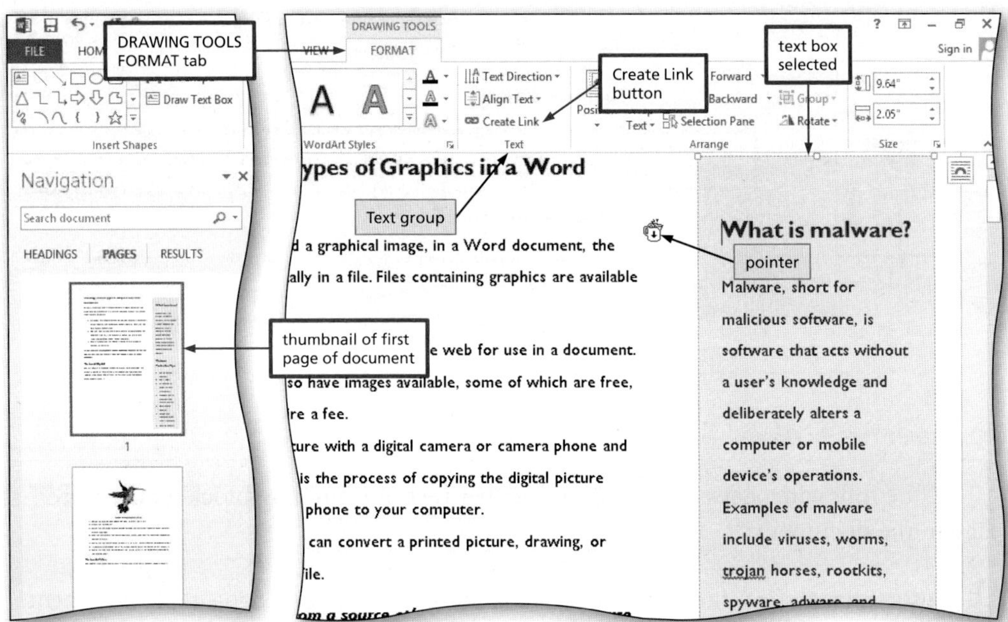

Figure 9–23

2

- Scroll through the document to display the second text box on the third page in the document window.

Q&A Can I use the Navigation Pane to go to the second text box?
No. If you tap or click in the Navigation Pane, the link process will stop and the pointer will return to its default shape.

- If you are using a mouse, position the pointer in the empty text box, so that the pointer shape changes to a pouring cup (Figure 9–24).

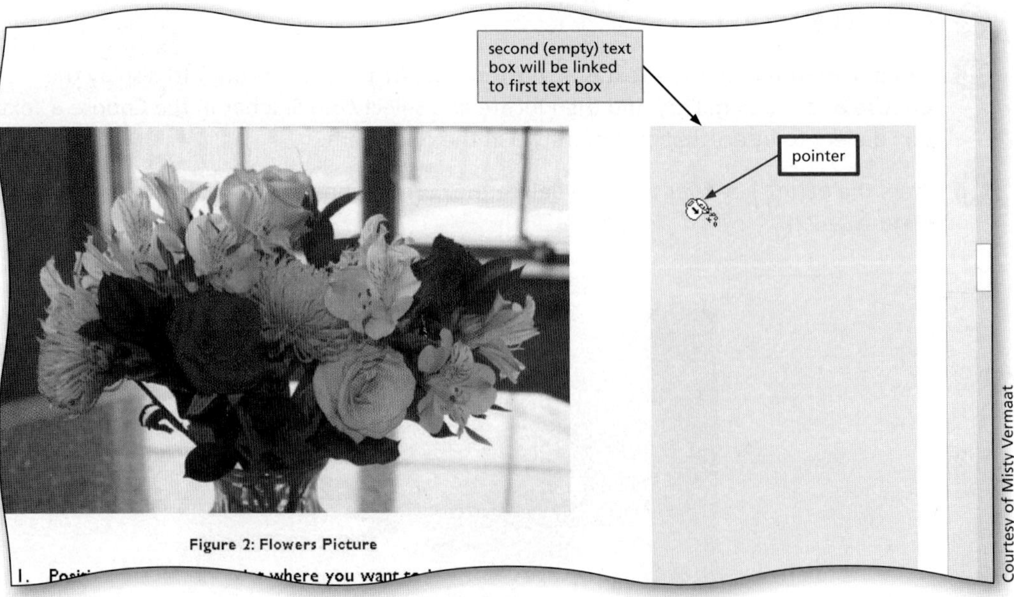

Figure 9–24

3

- If you are using a mouse, click the empty text box to link it to the first text box. If you are using a touch screen, you will need to use a stylus to tap the empty text box.
- Use the Navigation Pane to display the first page in the document window.
- If necessary, scroll to display the first text box in the document window and then select the text box.
- Resize the text box by dragging its bottom-middle sizing handle until the amount of text that is displayed in the text box is similar to Figure 9–25.

Q&A How would I remove a link?
Select the text box in which you created the link and then tap or click the Break Link button (DRAWING TOOLS FORMAT tab | Text group).

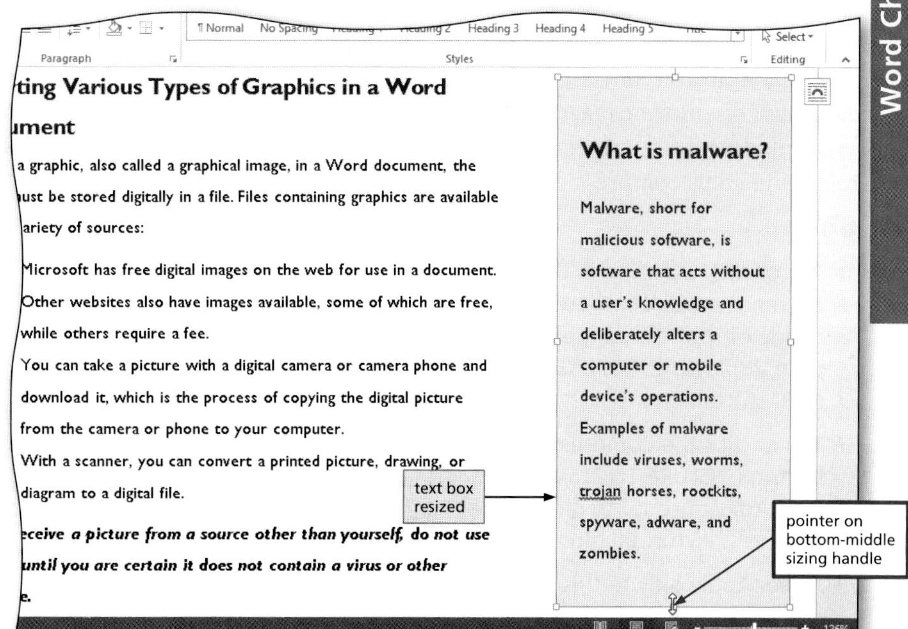

Figure 9–25

4

- Use the Navigation Pane to display the third page in the document window.
- If necessary, scroll to display the second text box in the document window and then select the text box.
- Resize the text box by dragging its bottom-middle sizing handle until the amount of text that is displayed in the text box is similar to Figure 9–26.
- If necessary drag the entire text box to position it as shown in Figure 9–26.
- If necessary, insert a page break to the left of the To Insert a Shape heading so that the heading begins at the top of third page.

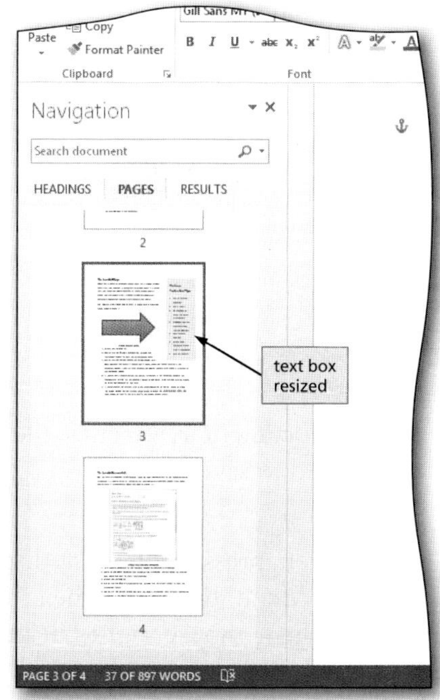

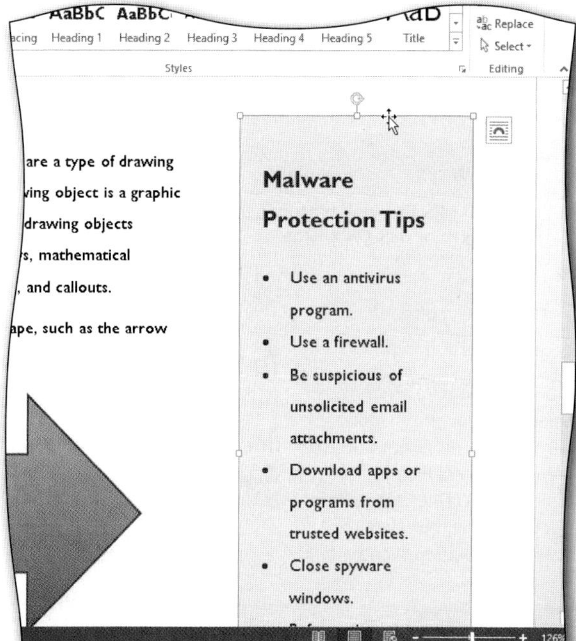

Figure 9–26

To Compress Pictures

1 MODIFY REFERENCE DOCUMENT | 2 CREATE MASTER DOCUMENT | 3 ORGANIZE REFERENCE DOCUMENT

If you plan to email a Word document that contains pictures or graphics or post it for downloading, you may want to reduce its file size to speed up file transmission time. ***Why?*** *Pictures and other graphics in Word documents can increase the size of these files.* In Word, you can compress pictures, which reduces the size of the Word document. Compressing the pictures in Word does not cause any loss in their original quality. The following steps compress pictures in a document.

- Tap or click a picture in the document to select it, such as the image of the hummingbird, and then display the PICTURE TOOLS FORMAT tab.
- Tap or click the Compress Pictures button (PICTURE TOOLS FORMAT tab | Adjust group) to display the Compress Pictures dialog box.
- If the 'Apply only to this picture' check box (Compress Pictures dialog box) contains a check mark, remove the check mark so that all pictures in the document are compressed.
- If necessary, tap or click 'Print (220 ppi): excellent quality on most printers and screens' in the Target output area to specify how images should be compressed (Figure 9–27).

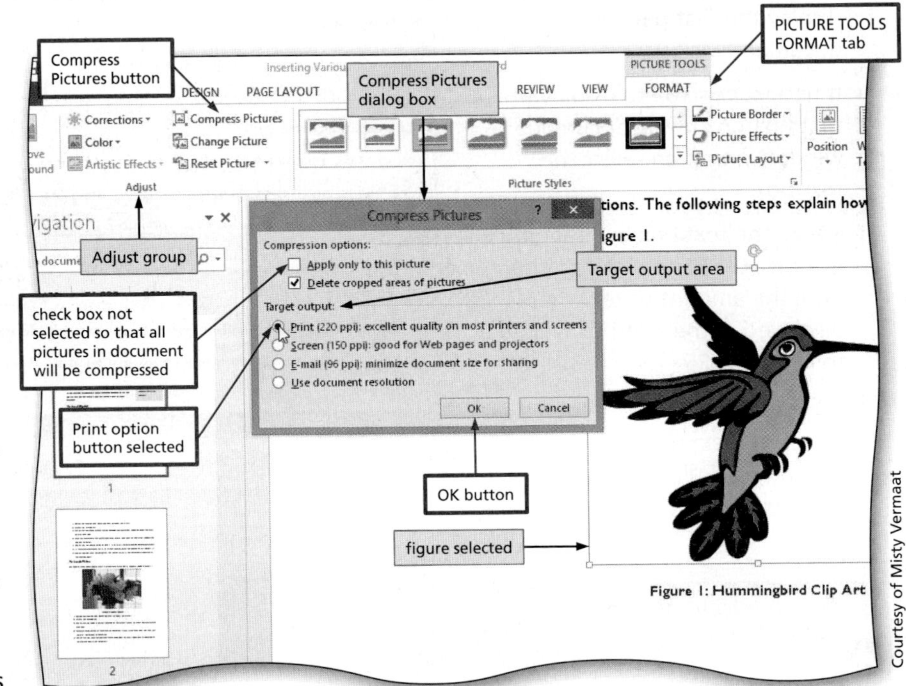

Figure 9–27

- Tap or click the OK button to compress all pictures in the document.

Q&A Can I compress a single picture?

Yes. Select the picture and then place a check mark in the 'Apply only to this picture' check box (Compress Pictures dialog box).

Other Ways

1. Tap or click the Tools button in the Save As dialog box, tap or click Compress Pictures on Tools menu, select options (Compress Pictures dialog box), tap or click OK button

BTW

Compressing Pictures

Selecting a lower ppi (pixels per inch) in the Target output area (Compress Picture dialog box) creates a smaller document file, but also lowers the quality of the images.

To Save Pictures in Other Formats

You can save any graphic in a document as a picture file for use in other documents or programs. If you wanted to save a graphic in a Word document, you would perform these steps.

1. If you are using a touch screen, press and hold to display a mini toolbar and then tap the 'Show Context Menu' button on the mini toolbar to display a shortcut menu; if you are using a mouse, right-click the graphic to display a shortcut menu.
2. Tap or click 'Save as Picture' on the shortcut menu to display the File Save dialog box.
3. Navigate to the location you want to save the graphic.

4. Tap or click the 'Save as type' arrow (File Save dialog box) and then select the graphic type for the saved graphic.
5. Tap or click the Save button (File Save dialog box) to save the graphic in the specified location using the specified graphic type.

To Change the Symbol Format in a Bulleted List

1 MODIFY REFERENCE DOCUMENT | **2 CREATE MASTER DOCUMENT** | **3 ORGANIZE REFERENCE DOCUMENT**

The following steps change the symbol in a bulleted list. ***Why?*** *The project in this chapter uses an arrow-type bullet symbol for the bulleted list instead of the default round bullet symbol.* Word provides several predefined bullet symbols for use in bulleted lists.

1

- Navigate to the first page and then select the bulleted list for which you want to change the bullet symbol (in this case, the three bulleted paragraphs on the first page).
- Tap or click the Bullets arrow (HOME tab | Paragraph group) to display the Bullets gallery (Figure 9–28).

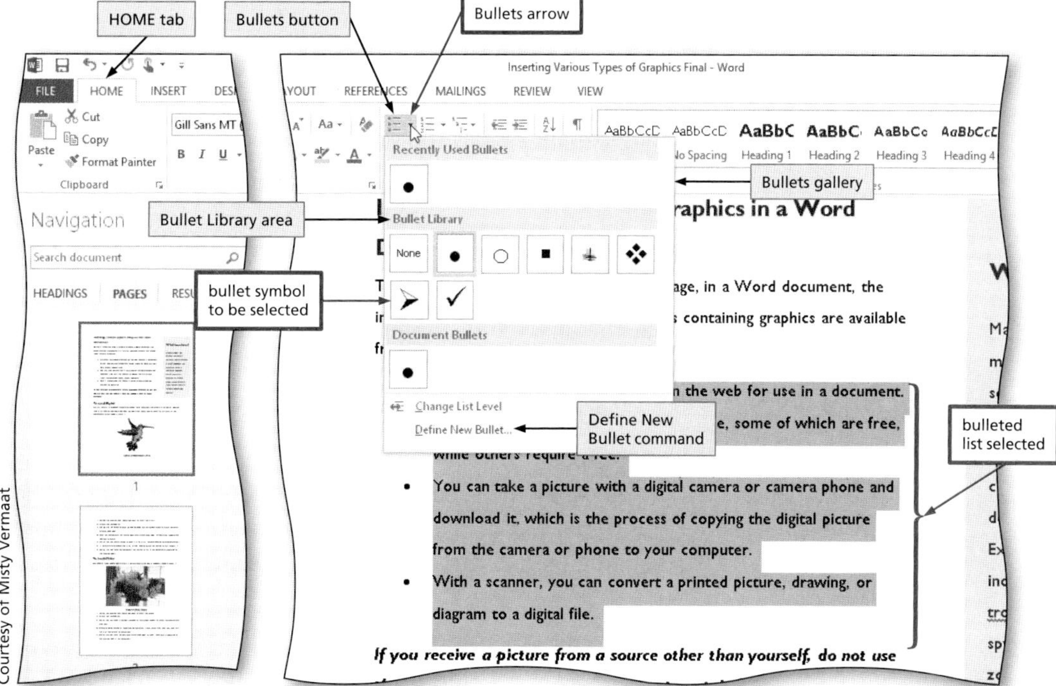

Figure 9–28

2

- Tap or click the desired bullet symbol in the Bullet Library area to change the bullet symbol on the selected bulleted list (Figure 9–29).

Q&A Can I select any bullet symbol in the Bullet Library area?
Yes. You also can tap or click 'Define New Bullet' in the Bullets gallery if the bullet symbol you desire is not shown in the Bullet Library area.

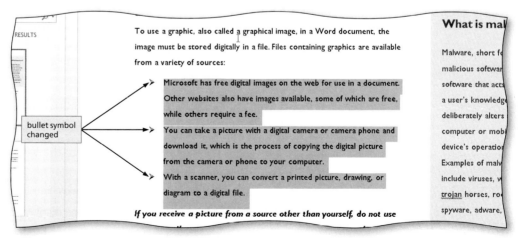

Figure 9–29

- Tap or click anywhere to remove the selection from the text.

BTW
Bullets
You can select from a variety of other bullet symbols or change the font attributes of a bullet by tapping or clicking 'Define New Bullet' in the Bullets gallery and then tapping or clicking the Symbol button or Font button in the Define New Bullet dialog box. You also can change the level of a bullet by tapping or clicking the 'Change List Level' command in the Bullets gallery.

To Save an Existing Document with the Same File Name

You are finished modifying the document and have performed several steps since the last save. Thus, you should save the document again, as described in the following step.

Tap or click the Save button on the Quick Access Toolbar to save the document again with the same file name, Inserting Various Types of Graphics Final.

To Close a Document

The following steps close the open Word document and the Word Help window.

1. Close the Navigation Pane.
2. Open the Backstage view and then tap or click Close to close the open document.
3. If necessary, display the Word Help window and close it.

To Recover Unsaved Documents (Draft Versions)

If you accidently exit Word without saving a document, you may be able to recover the unsaved document, called a **draft version**, in Word. If you wanted to recover an unsaved document, you would perform these steps.

1. Run Word and create a blank document in the Word window.
2. Open the Backstage view and then, if necessary, tap or click the Open tab to display the Open gallery. Scroll to the bottom of the Recent Documents list. Tap or click the 'Recover Unsaved Documents' button to display an Open dialog box that lists unsaved files retained by Word.

   or

2. Open the Backstage view and then, if necessary, tap or click the Info tab to display the Info gallery. Tap or click the Manage Versions button to display the Manage Versions menu. Tap or click 'Recover Unsaved Documents' on the Manage Versions menu to display an Open dialog box that lists unsaved files retained by Word.
3. Select the file to recover and then tap or click the Open button to display the unsaved file in the Word window.
4. To save the document, tap or click the Save As button on the Message Bar.

To Delete All Unsaved Documents (Draft Versions)

If you wanted to delete all unsaved documents, you would perform these steps.

1. Run Word and create a blank document in the Word window.
2. If necessary, open a document. Open the Backstage view and then, if necessary, tap or click the Info tab to display the Info gallery.
3. Tap or click the Manage Versions button to display the Manage Versions menu.
4. If available, tap or click 'Delete All Unsaved Documents' on the Manage Versions menu.
5. When Word displays a dialog box asking if you are sure you want to delete all copies of unsaved files, tap or click the Yes button to delete all unsaved documents.

Break Point: If you wish to take a break, this is a good place to do so. You can exit Word now. To resume at a later time, run Word and continue following the steps from this location forward.

Working with a Master Document

When you are creating a document that includes other files, you may want to create a master document to organize the documents. A **master document** is simply a document that contains links to one or more other documents, each of which is called a **subdocument**. In addition to subdocuments, a master document can contain its own text and graphics.

In this project, the master document file is named Learn Word – Guide #9. This master document file contains a link to one subdocument: Inserting Graphical Images Final. The master document also contains other items: a title page, a copyright page, a table of contents, a table of figures, and an index. The following pages create this master document and insert the necessary elements in the document to create the finished Learn Word - Guide #9 document.

BTW
Master Documents
Master documents can be used when multiple people prepare different sections of a document or when a document contains separate elements such as the chapters in a book. If multiple people in a network need to work on the same document simultaneously, each person can work on a section (subdocument); all subdocuments can be stored together collectively in a master document on the network server.

To Change the Document Theme

The first step in creating this master document is to change its document theme to Dividend. The following steps change the document theme.

1. If necessary, run Word and create a new blank document.
2. Tap or click DESIGN on the ribbon to display the DESIGN tab.
3. Tap or click the Themes button (DESIGN tab | Document Formatting group) to display the Themes gallery.
4. Tap or click Dividend in the Themes gallery to change the document theme to the selected theme.

Outlines

To create a master document, Word must be in Outline view. You then enter the headings of the document as an outline using Word's built-in heading styles. In an outline, the major heading is displayed at the left margin with each subordinate, or lower-level, heading indented. In Word, the built-in Heading 1 style is displayed at the left margin in outline view. Heading 2 style is indented below Heading 1 style, Heading 3 style is indented further, and so on. (Outline view works similarly to multilevel lists.)

You do not want to use a built-in heading style for the paragraphs of text within the document because when you create a table of contents, Word places all lines formatted using the built-in heading styles in the table of contents. Thus, the text below each heading is formatted using the Body Text style.

Each heading should print at the top of a new page. Because you might want to format the pages within a heading differently from those pages in other headings, you insert next page section breaks between each heading.

To Switch to Outline View

1 MODIFY REFERENCE DOCUMENT | 2 CREATE MASTER DOCUMENT | **3 ORGANIZE REFERENCE DOCUMENT**

The following steps switch to Outline view. ***Why?*** *To create a master document, Word must be in Outline view.*

- Display the VIEW tab (Figure 9–30).

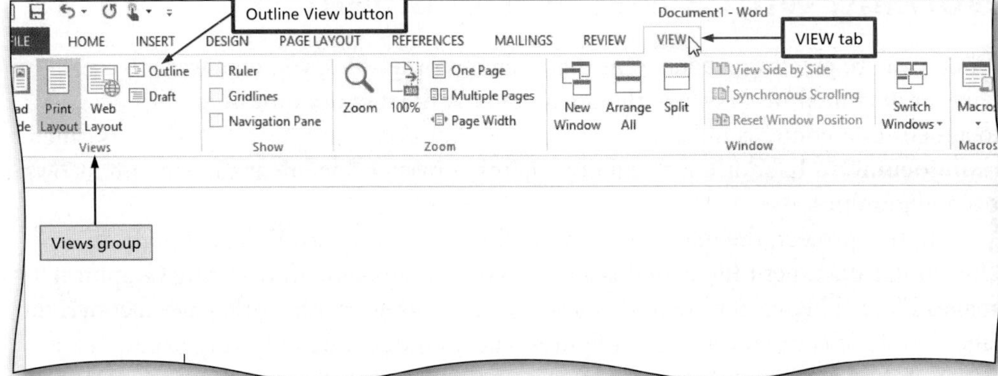

Figure 9–30

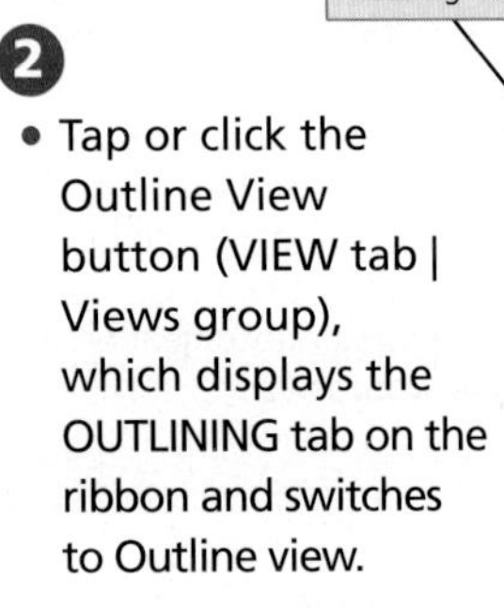

- Tap or click the Outline View button (VIEW tab | Views group), which displays the OUTLINING tab on the ribbon and switches to Outline view.
- Be sure the 'Show Text Formatting' check box is selected (OUTLINING tab | Outline Tools group) (Figure 9–31).

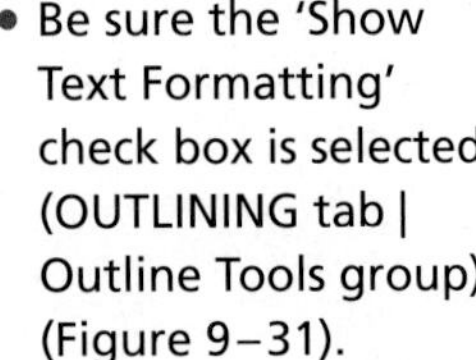

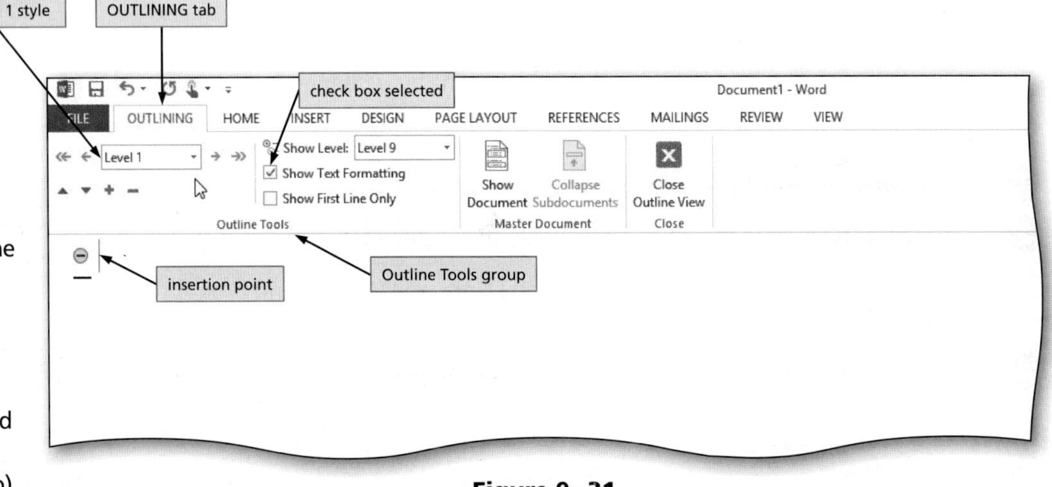

Figure 9–31

To Add Entries in Outline View

1 MODIFY REFERENCE DOCUMENT | 2 CREATE MASTER DOCUMENT | **3 ORGANIZE REFERENCE DOCUMENT**

The Learn Word – Guide #9 document contains these three major headings: Inserting Various Types of Graphics in a Word Document, Table of Figures, and Index. The heading, Inserting Various Types of Graphics in a Word Document, is not entered in the outline. ***Why not?*** *It is part of the subdocument inserted in the master document.*

The first page of the outline (the copyright page) does not contain a heading; instead it contains three paragraphs of body text, which you enter directly in the outline. The Inserting Various Types of Graphics in a Word Document content is inserted from the subdocument. You will instruct Word to create the content for the Table of Figures and Index later in this chapter. The following steps create an outline that contains headings and body text to be used in the master document.

1

- Tap or click the 'Demote to Body Text' button (OUTLINING tab | Outline Tools group), so that you can enter the paragraphs of text for the copyright page.
- Type `Learn Word | Guide #9 - Inserting Graphics` as the first paragraph in the outline and then press the ENTER key.
- Type `To receive additional guides in this or any other learning series by Gardner's Information Literacy Center, contact Marianne Chamberlain at mchamberlain@gardner.edu.` as the second paragraph in the outline and then press the ENTER key.

  If requested by your instructor, change the name, Marianne Chamberlain, on the copyright page to your name.

Q&A Why is only my first line of text in the paragraph displayed?
Remove the check mark from the 'Show First Line Only' check box (OUTLINING tab | Outline Tools group).

- If you are using a touch screen, press and hold the hyperlink and then tap the 'Show Context Menu' button on the mini toolbar; if you are using a mouse, right-click the hyperlink (in this case, the email address) to display a shortcut menu.
- Tap or click Remove Hyperlink on the shortcut menu.
- Tap or click the third Body Text style bullet and then type `Copyright 2014` as the third paragraph and then press the ENTER key.
- Tap or click the 'Promote to Heading 1' button (OUTLINING tab | Outline Tools group) because you are finished entering body text and will enter the remaining headings in the outline next (Figure 9–32).

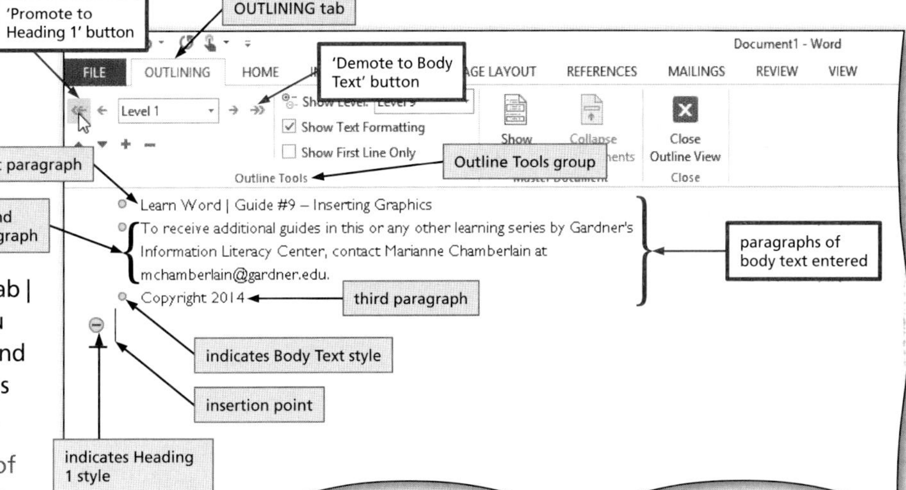

Figure 9–32

Q&A Could I press SHIFT+TAB instead of tapping or clicking the 'Promote to Heading 1' button?
Yes.

2

- Display the PAGE LAYOUT tab.
- Tap or click the 'Insert Page and Section Breaks' button (PAGE LAYOUT tab | Page Setup group) and then tap or click Next Page in the Section Breaks area in the Insert Page and Section Breaks gallery because you want to enter a next page section break before the next heading.

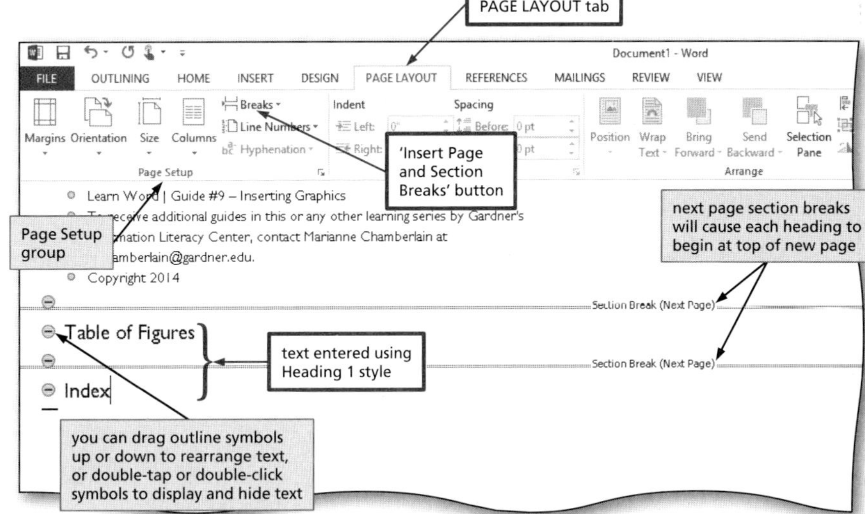

Figure 9–33

3

- Type `Table of Figures` and then press the ENTER key.
- Repeat Step 2.

4

- Type `Index` as the last entry (Figure 9–33).

Q&A Why do the outline symbols contain a minus sign?
The minus sign means the outline level does not have any subordinate levels. If an outline symbol contains a plus sign, it means the outline level has subordinate levels.

To Show First Line Only

1 MODIFY REFERENCE DOCUMENT | 2 CREATE MASTER DOCUMENT | 3 ORGANIZE REFERENCE DOCUMENT

Users often instruct Word to display just the first line of each paragraph of body text. ***Why?*** *When only the first line of each paragraph is displayed, the outline often is more readable.* The following step displays only the first line of body text paragraphs.

- Display the OUTLINING tab.
- Place a check mark in the 'Show First Line Only' check box (OUTLINING tab | Outline Tools group), so that Word displays only the first line of each paragraph (Figure 9–34).

Q&A How would I redisplay all lines of the paragraphs of body text?
Remove the check mark from the 'Show First Line Only' check box (OUTLINING tab | Outline Tools group).

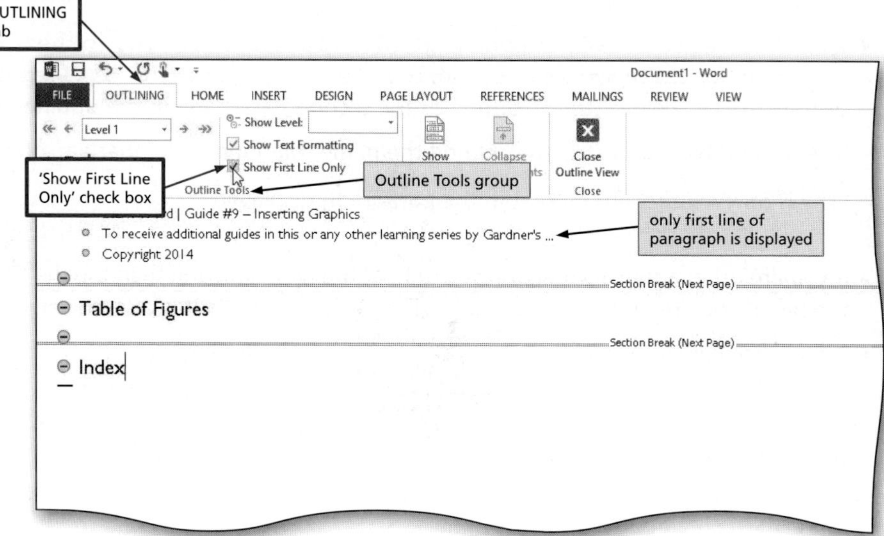

Figure 9–34

BTW
Distributing a Document
Instead of printing and distributing a hard copy of a document, you can distribute the document electronically. Options include sending the document via email; posting it on cloud storage (such as SkyDrive) and sharing the file with others; posting it on a social networking site, blog, or other website; and sharing a link associated with an online location of the document. You also can create and share a PDF or XPS image of the document, so that users can view the file in Acrobat Reader or XPS Viewer instead of in Word.

To Save a Document

The next step is to save the master document because you have performed many steps thus far. The following steps save a document.

1. Open the Backstage view and then tap or click the Save As tab to display the Save As gallery.
2. Display the Save As dialog box and then type `Learn Word - Guide #9` in the File name box to change the file name. Do not press the ENTER key after typing the file name because you do not want to close the dialog box at this time.
3. Navigate to the desired save location (in this case, the Word folder in the CIS 101 folder [or your class folder] on your computer or SkyDrive).
4. Tap or click the Save button (Save As dialog box) to save the document in the selected folder on the selected save location with the entered file name.

To Insert a Subdocument

1 MODIFY REFERENCE DOCUMENT | 2 CREATE MASTER DOCUMENT | 3 ORGANIZE REFERENCE DOCUMENT

The next step is to insert a subdocument in the master document. The subdocument to be inserted is the Inserting Various Types of Graphics Final file, which you created earlier in the chapter. Word places the first line of text in the subdocument at the first heading level in the master document. ***Why?*** *The first line in the subdocument was defined using the Heading 1 style.* The following steps insert a subdocument in a master document.

1

- Display the HOME tab. If formatting marks do not appear, tap or click the 'Show/Hide ¶' button (HOME tab | Paragraph group).
- Position the insertion point where you want to insert the subdocument (on the section break above the Table of Figures heading).
- Display the OUTLINING tab. Tap or click the Show Document button (OUTLINING tab | Master Document group) so that all commands in the Master Document group appear.
- Tap or click the Insert Subdocument button (OUTLINING tab | Master Document group) to display the Insert Subdocument dialog box.
- Locate and select the Inserting Various Types of Graphics Final file (Insert Subdocument dialog box) (Figure 9–35).

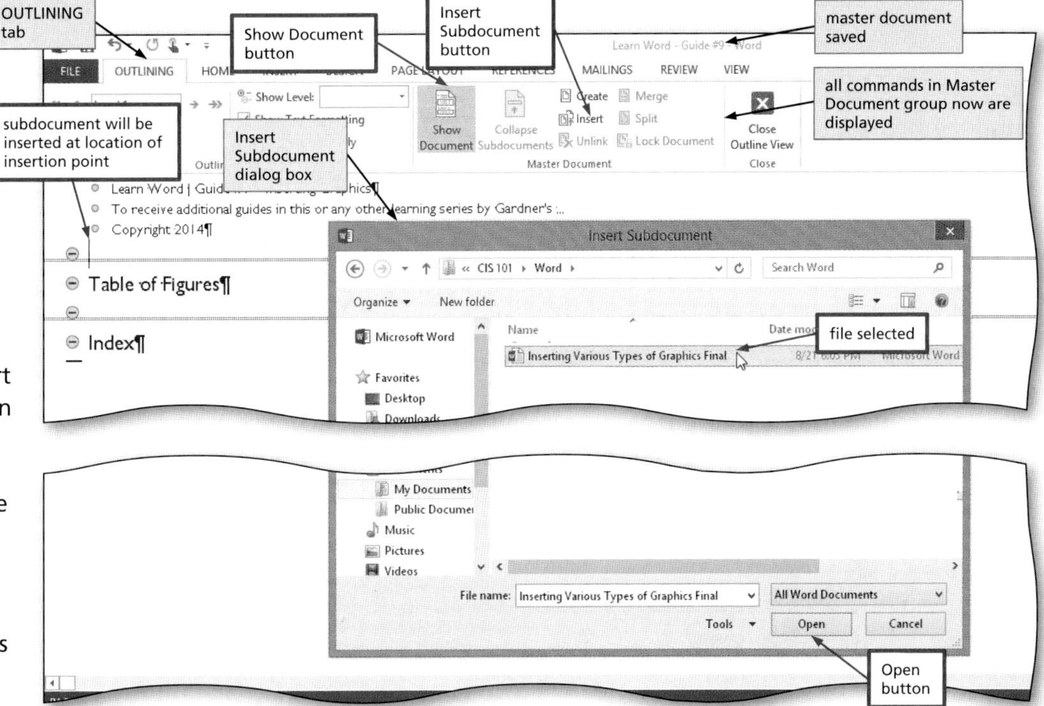

Figure 9–35

2

- Tap or click the Open button (Insert Subdocument dialog box) to insert the selected file as a subdocument.
- If Word displays a dialog box about styles, tap or click the 'No to All' button.
- Press CTRL+HOME to position the insertion point at the top of the document (Figure 9–36).

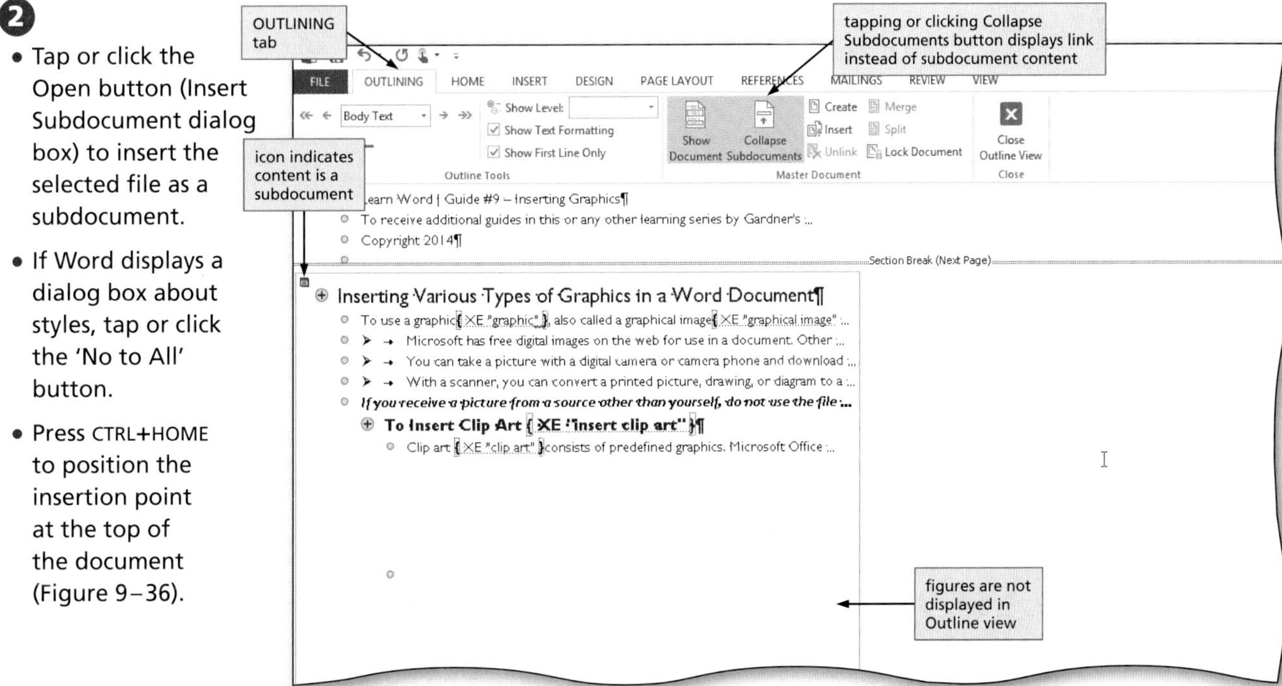

Figure 9–36

Master Documents and Subdocuments

When you open the master document, the subdocuments initially are collapsed; that is, they are displayed as hyperlinks (Figure 9–37). To work with the contents of a master document after you open it, switch to Outline view and then expand the subdocuments by tapping or clicking the Expand Subdocuments button (OUTLINING tab | Master Document group).

You can open a subdocument in a separate document window and modify it. To open a collapsed subdocument, tap or click the hyperlink. To open an expanded subdocument, double-tap or double-click the subdocument icon to the left of the document heading (shown in Figure 9–37).

If, for some reason, you wanted to remove a subdocument from a master document, you would expand the subdocuments, tap or click the subdocument icon to the left of the subdocument's first heading, and then press the DELETE key. Although Word removes the subdocument from the master document, the subdocument file remains on the storage media.

Occasionally, you may want to convert a subdocument to part of the master document — breaking the connection between the text in the master document and the subdocument. To do this, expand the subdocuments, tap or click the subdocument icon, and then tap or click the Remove Subdocument button (OUTLINING tab | Master Document group).

BTW
Locked Subdocuments
If a lock icon is displayed next to a subdocument's name, either the master document is collapsed or the subdocument is locked. If the master document is collapsed, simply tap or click the Expand Subdocuments button (OUTLINING tab | Master Document group). If the subdocument is locked, you will be able to display the contents of the subdocument but will not be able to modify it.

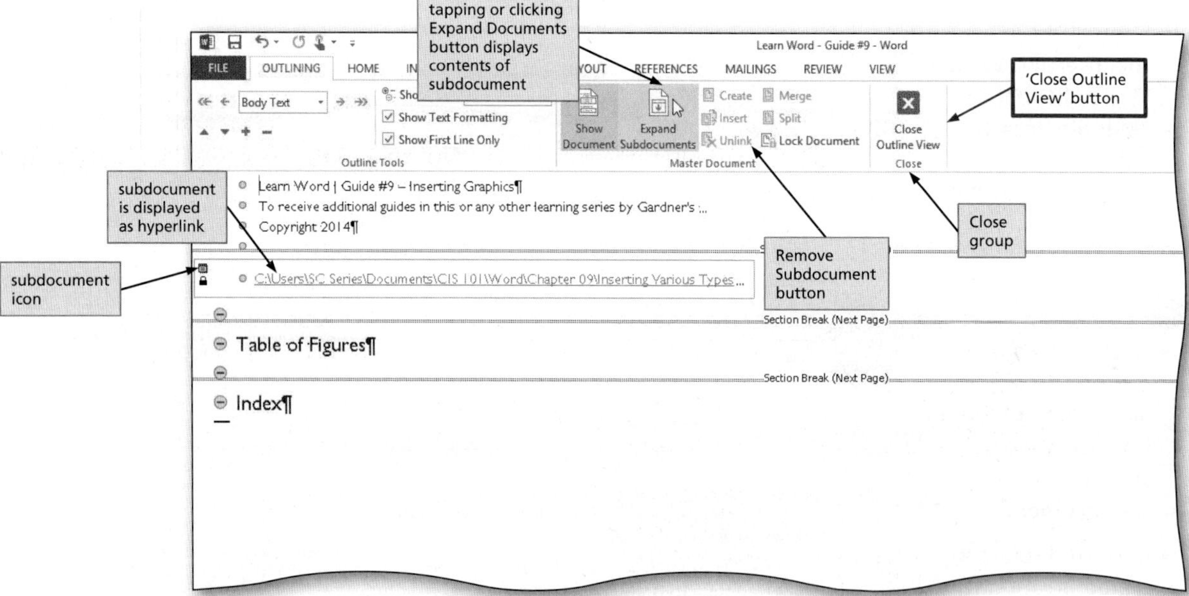

Figure 9–37

To Hide Formatting Marks

To remove the clutter of index entry fields from the document, you should hide formatting marks. The following step hides formatting marks.

1. Display the HOME tab. If the 'Show/Hide ¶' button (HOME tab | Paragraph group) is selected, tap or click it to hide formatting marks.

To Exit Outline View

1 MODIFY REFERENCE DOCUMENT | 2 CREATE MASTER DOCUMENT | **3 ORGANIZE REFERENCE DOCUMENT**

The following step exits Outline view. ***Why?*** *You are finished organizing the master document.*

1

- Display the OUTLINING tab.
- Tap or click the 'Close Outline View' button (shown in Figure 9–37) (OUTLINING tab | Close group) to redisplay the document in Print Layout view, which selects the Print Layout button on the status bar.
- If necessary, press CTRL+HOME to display the top of the document (Figure 9–38).

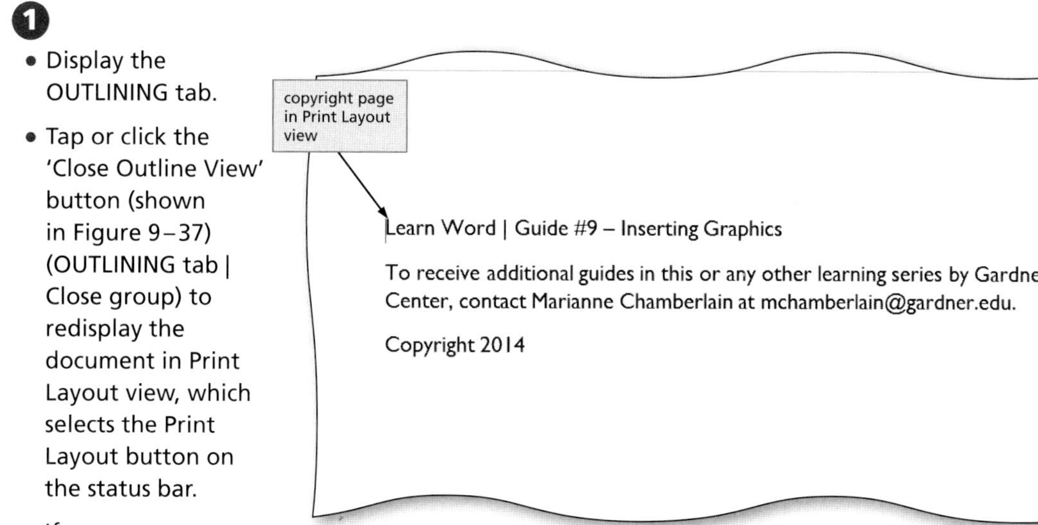
copyright page in Print Layout view
Learn Word | Guide #9 – Inserting Graphics
To receive additional guides in this or any other learning series by Gardner's Information Literacy Center, contact Marianne Chamberlain at mchamberlain@gardner.edu.
Copyright 2014

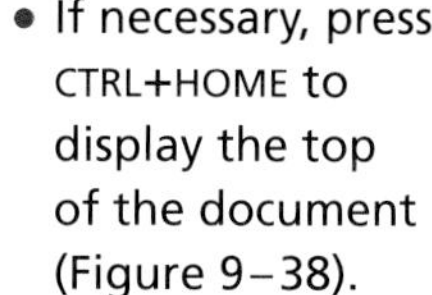

Experiment

- Scroll through the document to familiarize yourself with the sections. When finished, display the top of the subdocument in the document window.

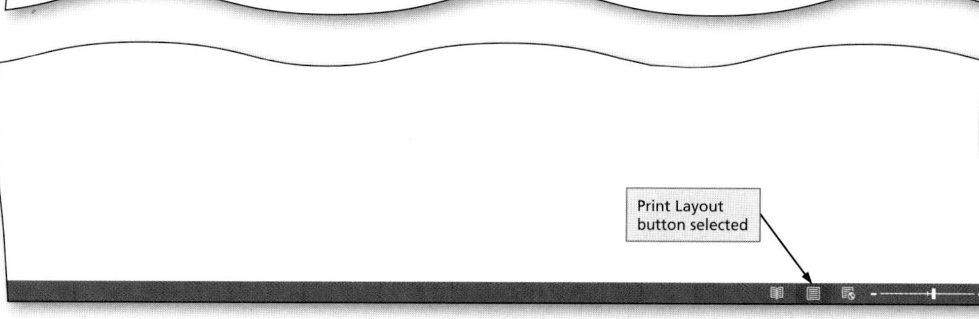
Print Layout button selected

Figure 9–38

To Save an Existing Document with the Same File Name

The following step saves the master document again with the same file name.

1 Tap or click the Save button on the Quick Access Toolbar to save the document again with the same file name, Learn Word - Guide #9.

BTW
Certification
The Microsoft Office Specialist (MOS) program provides an opportunity for you to obtain a valuable industry credential — proof that you have the Word 2013 skills required by employers. For more information, visit the Certification resource on the Student Companion Site located on www.cengagebrain.com. For detailed instructions about accessing available resources, visit www.cengage.com/ct/studentdownload or contact your instructor for information about accessing the required files.

Organizing a Reference Document

Reference documents are organized and formatted so that users easily can navigate through and read the document. The reference document in this chapter includes the following elements: a copyright page, a title page, a table of contents, a table of figures, an index, alternating footers, and a gutter margin. This section illustrates the tasks required to include these elements.

CONSIDER THIS

What elements are common to reference documents?

Reference documents often include a title page, a table of contents, a table of figures or list of tables (if one exists), and an index.

- **Title Page.** A title page should contain, at a minimum, the title of the document. Some also contain the author, a subtitle, an edition or volume number, and the date written.
- **Table of Contents.** The table of contents should list the title (heading) of each chapter or section and the starting page number of the chapter or section. You may use a leader character, such as a dot or hyphen, to fill the space between the heading and the page number. Sections preceding the table of contents are not listed in it — only list material that follows the table of contents.
- **Table of Figures or List of Tables.** If you have multiple figures or tables in a document, consider identifying all of them in a table of figures or a list of tables. The format of the table of figures or list of tables should match the table of contents.
- **Index.** The index usually is set in two columns or one column. The index can contain any item a reader might want to look up, such as a heading or a key term. If the document does not have a table of figures or list of tables, also include figures and tables in the index.

To Insert a Cover Page

1 MODIFY REFERENCE DOCUMENT | 2 CREATE MASTER DOCUMENT | 3 **ORGANIZE REFERENCE DOCUMENT**

Word has many predefined cover page formats that you can use for the title page in a document. The following steps insert a cover page. ***Why?*** *The reference document in this chapter includes a title page.*

1

- Display the INSERT tab.
- Tap or click the 'Add a Cover Page' button (INSERT tab | Pages group) to display the Add a Cover Page gallery (Figure 9–39).

Experiment

- Scroll through the Add a Cover Page gallery to see the variety of available predefined cover pages.

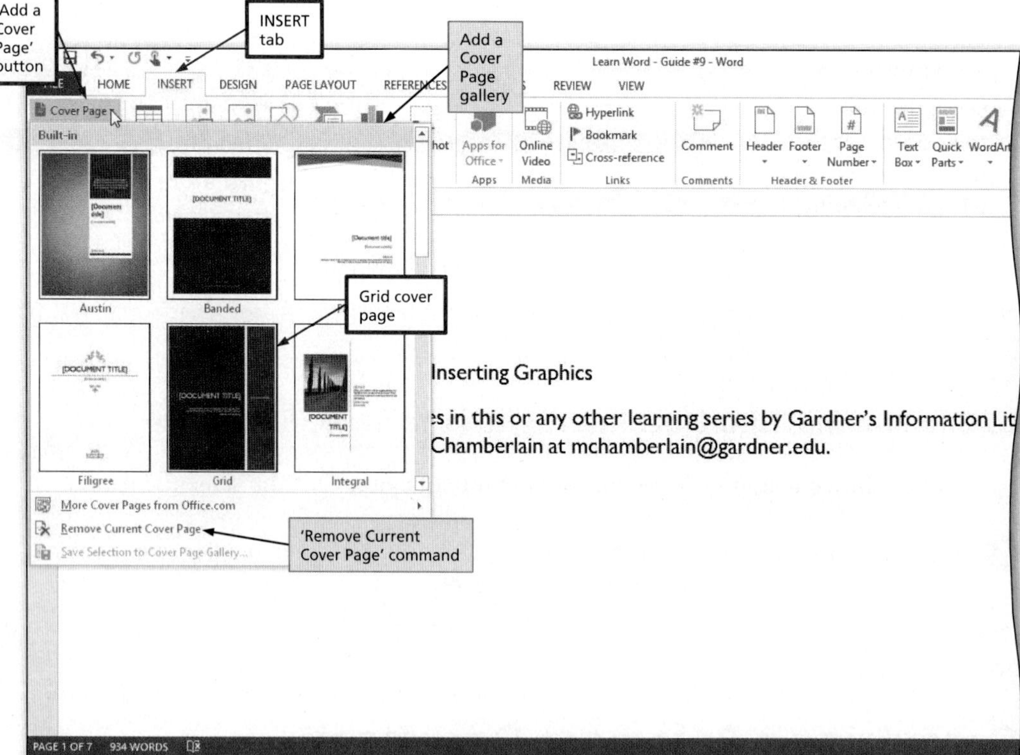

Figure 9–39

Q&A

Does it matter where I position the insertion point before inserting a cover page?

No. By default, Word inserts the cover page as the first page in a document.

2

- Tap or click Grid in the Add a Cover Page gallery to insert the selected cover page as the first page in the current document.
- Display the VIEW tab. Tap or click the One Page button (VIEW tab | Zoom group) to display the entire cover page in the document window (Figure 9–40).

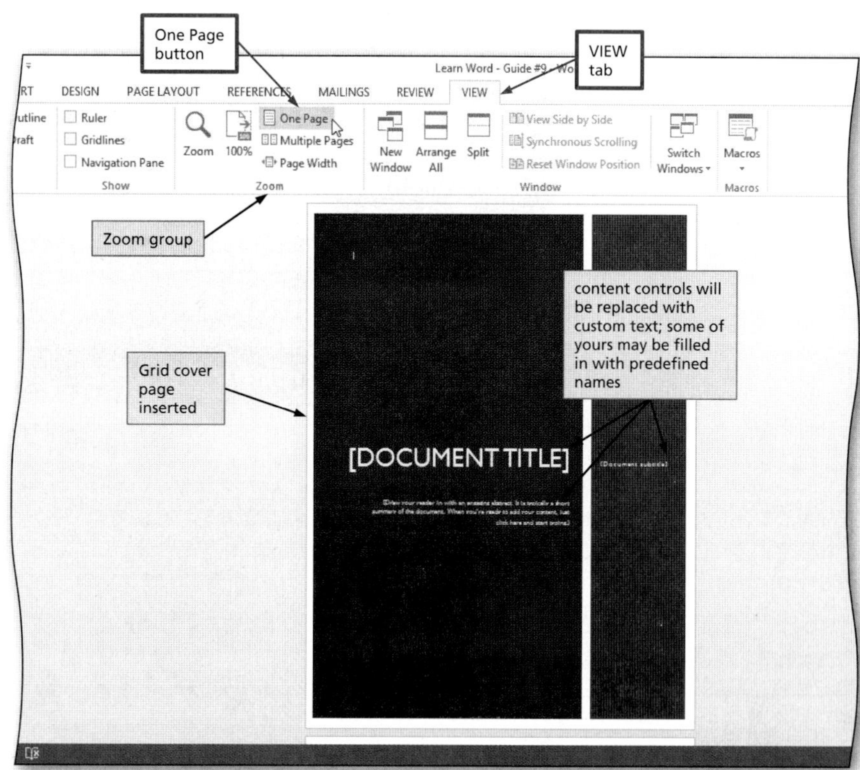

Figure 9–40

Q&A

Does the cover page have to be the first page?

No. You can press and hold or right-click the desired cover page and then tap or click the desired location on the submenu.

How would I delete a cover page?

You would tap or click the 'Add a Cover Page' button (INSERT tab | Pages group) and then tap or click 'Remove Current Cover Page' in the Add a Cover Page gallery.

3

- Change the zoom back to page width.

Other Ways

1. Tap or click 'Explore Quick Parts' button (INSERT tab | Text group), tap or click 'Building Blocks Organizer', select desired cover page building block (Building Blocks Organizer dialog box), tap or click Insert button, tap or click Close button

To Enter Text in Content Controls

The next step is to select content controls on the cover page and replace their instructions or text with the title page information. Keep in mind that the content controls present suggested text. Depending on settings on your computer or mobile device, some content controls already may contain customized text, which you will change. You can enter any appropriate text in any content control. The following steps enter title page text on the cover page.

1. Tap or click the DOCUMENT TITLE content control and then type **LEARN WORD** as the title.
2. Tap or click the Document subtitle content control and then type **Inserting Graphics** as the subtitle.
3. Tap or click the content control that begins with the instruction, Draw your reader in with an engaging abstract. Type **A series of guides designed to strengthen your information literacy skills.** in the content control. (Figure 9–41 on the next page).

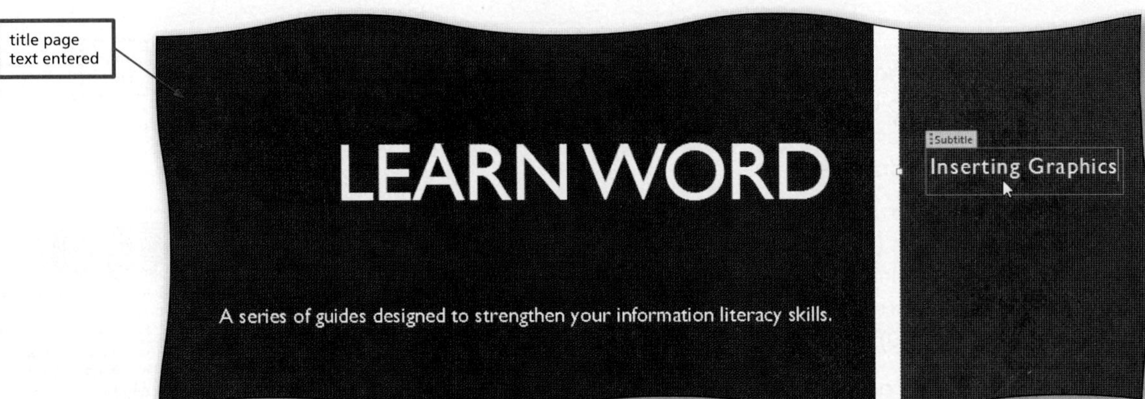

Figure 9–41

To Center Text

The next step is to center the text on the copyright page. The following steps center text.

1. Scroll to display the copyright page text in the document window.
2. Select the text on the copyright page and then center it.
3. Deselect the text.

To Insert a Continuous Section Break and Change the Margins in the Section

The margins on the copyright page are wider than the rest of the document. To change margins for a page, the page must be in a separate section. The next steps insert a continuous section break and then change the margins.

1. Position the insertion point at the location for the section break, in this case, to the left of L in Learn on the copyright page.
2. Display the PAGE LAYOUT tab. Tap or click the 'Insert Page and Section Breaks' button (PAGE LAYOUT tab | Page Setup group) to display the Insert Page and Section Breaks gallery.
3. Tap or click Continuous in the Insert Page and Section Breaks gallery to insert a continuous section break to the left of the insertion point.
4. Tap or click the Adjust Margins button (PAGE LAYOUT tab | Page Setup group) to display the Adjust Margins gallery and then tap or click Wide in the Adjust Margins gallery to change the margins on the copyright page to the selected settings (Figure 9–42).

BTW

Quick Reference

For a table that lists how to complete the tasks covered in this book using touch gestures, the mouse, ribbon, shortcut menu, and keyboard, see the Quick Reference Summary at the back of this book, or visit the Quick Reference resource on the Student Companion Site located on www.cengagebrain.com. For detailed instructions about accessing available resources, visit www.cengage.com/ct/studentdownload or contact your instructor for information about accessing the required files.

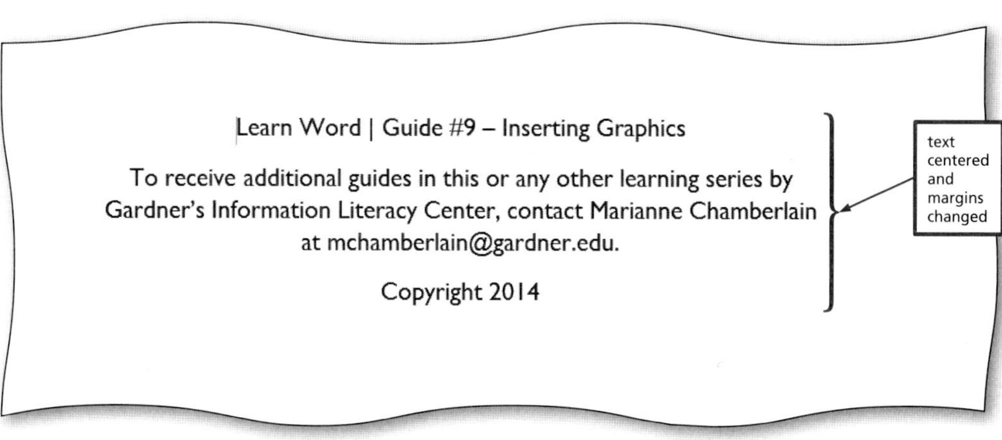

Figure 9–42

To Adjust Vertical Alignment on a Page

1 MODIFY REFERENCE DOCUMENT | 2 CREATE MASTER DOCUMENT | **3 ORGANIZE REFERENCE DOCUMENT**

You can instruct Word to center the contents of a page vertically using one of two options: place an equal amount of space above and below the text on the page, or evenly space each paragraph between the top and bottom margins. The following steps vertically center text on a page. ***Why?*** *The copyright page in this project evenly spaces each paragraph on a page between the top and bottom margins, which is called justified vertical alignment.*

1

- Tap or click the Page Setup Dialog Box Launcher (PAGE LAYOUT tab | Page Setup group) to display the Page Setup dialog box.
- Tap or click the Layout tab (Page Setup dialog box) to display the Layout sheet.
- Tap or click the Vertical alignment arrow and then tap or click Justified (Figure 9–43).

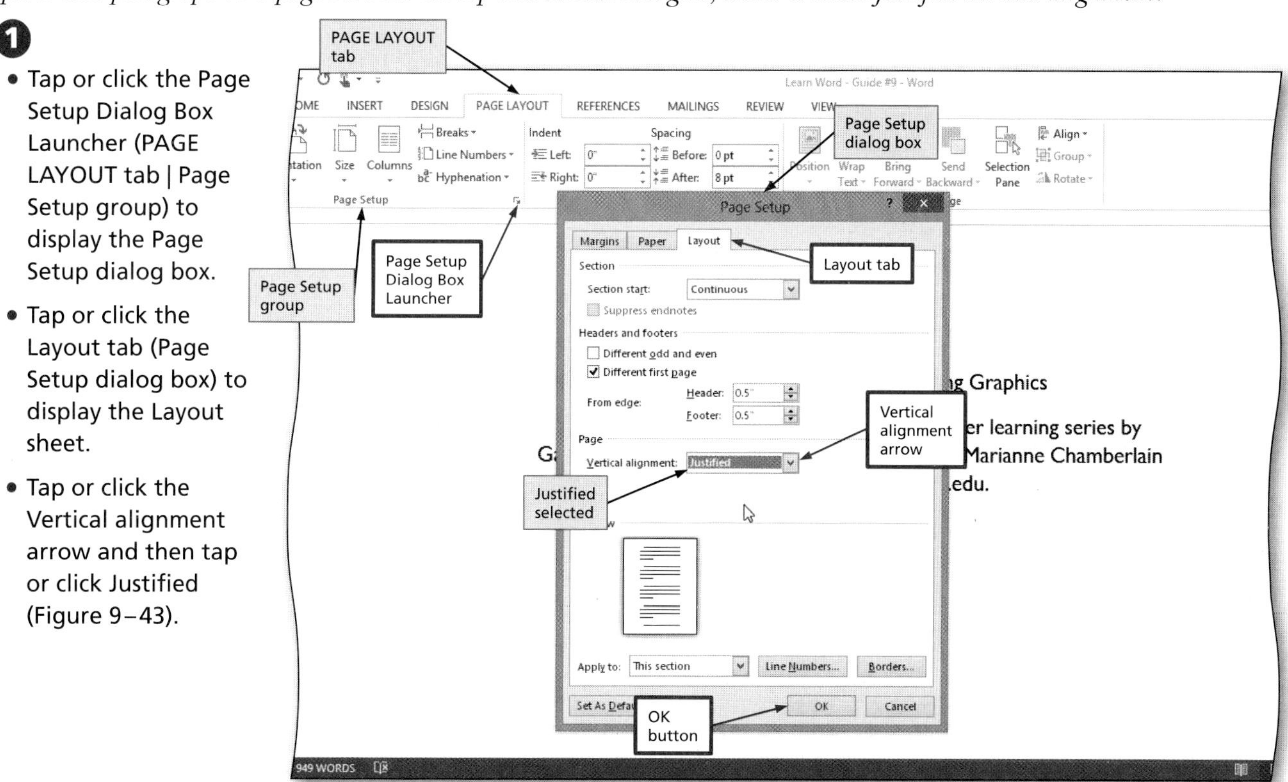

Figure 9–43

- Tap or click the OK button to justify the text in the current section.
- To see the entire justified page, display the VIEW tab and then tap or click the One Page button (VIEW tab | Zoom group) (Figure 9–44).

- Change the zoom back to page width.

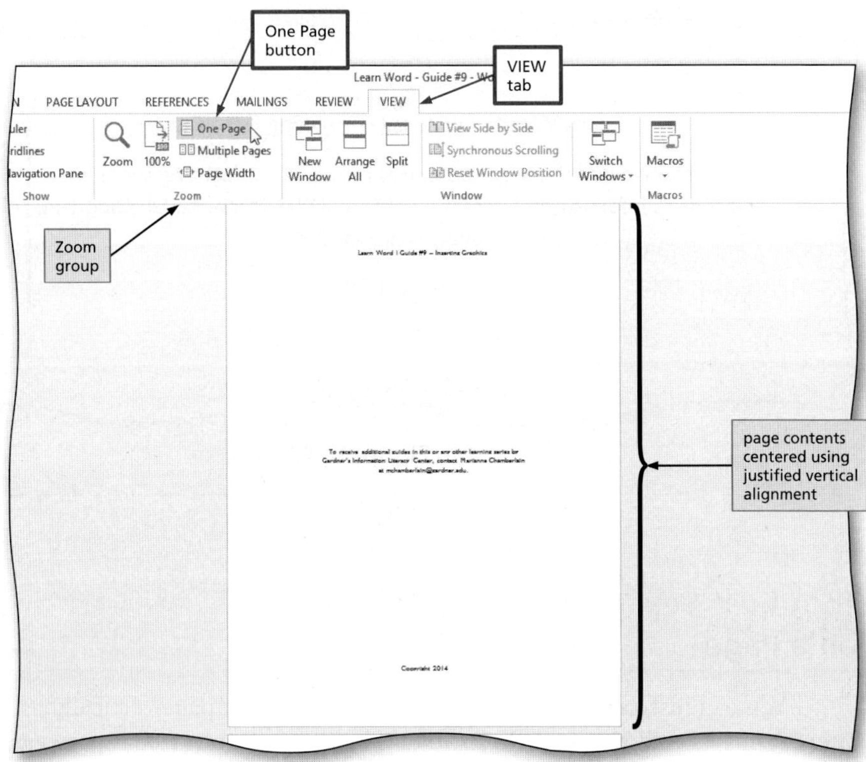

Figure 9–44

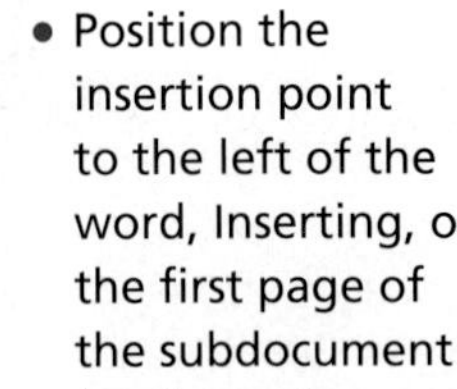

Q&A What are the other vertical alignments?
Top, the default, aligns contents starting at the top margin on the page. Center places all contents centered vertically on the page, and Bottom places contents at the bottom of the page.

To Insert a Blank Page

The following step inserts a blank page. ***Why?*** *In the reference document in this chapter, the table of contents is on a page between the copyright page and the first page of the subdocument.*

1

- Position the insertion point to the left of the word, Inserting, on the first page of the subdocument (as shown in Figure 9–45).
- Display the INSERT tab.
- Tap or click the 'Add a Blank Page' button (INSERT tab | Pages group) to insert a blank page at the location of the insertion point.
- If necessary, scroll to display the blank page in the document window (Figure 9–45).

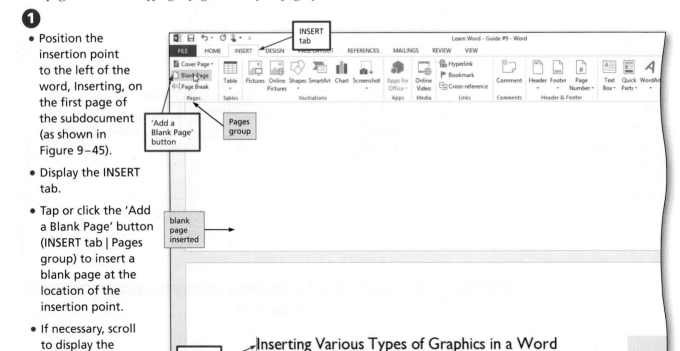

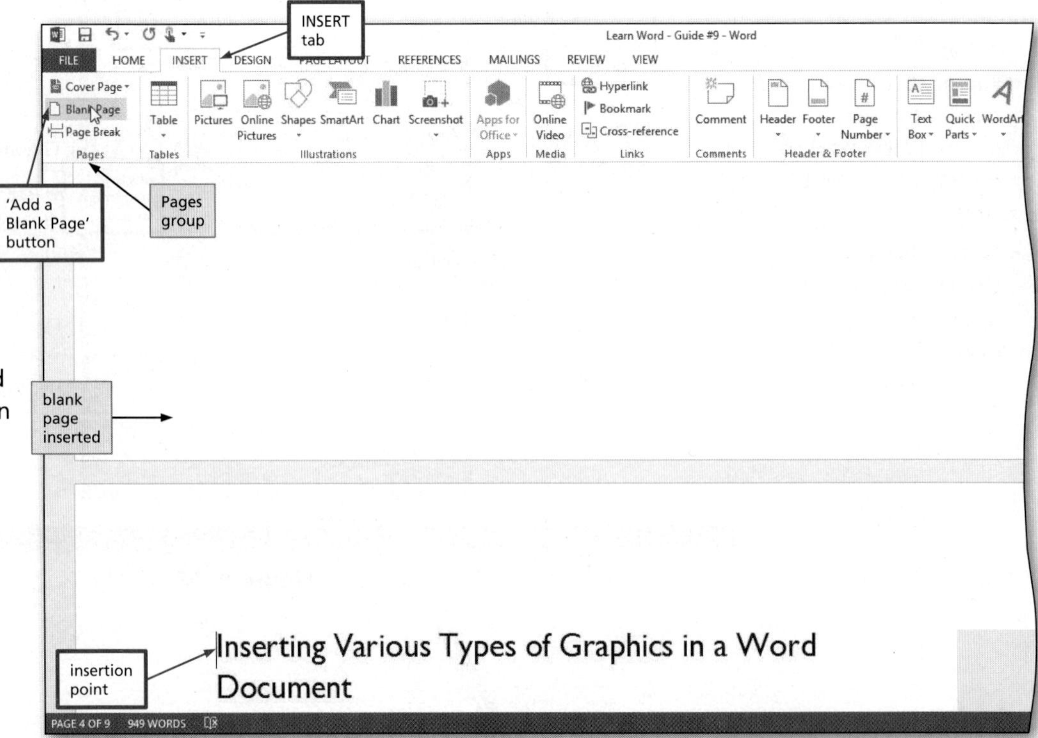

Figure 9–45

To Create a Table of Contents

A table of contents lists all headings in a document and their associated page numbers. When you use Word's built-in heading styles (for example, Heading 1, Heading 2, and so on), you can instruct Word to create a table of contents from these headings. In the reference document in this chapter, the heading of each section uses the Heading 1 style, and subheadings use the Heading 2 style.

The following steps use a predefined building block to create a table of contents. ***Why?*** *Using Word's predefined table of contents formats can be more efficient than creating a table of contents from scratch.*

1

- Position the insertion point at the top of the blank page 3, which is the location for the table of contents. (If necessary, show formatting marks so that you easily can see the paragraph mark at the top of the page.)
- Ensure that formatting marks do not show.

Q&A Why should I hide formatting marks?
Formatting marks, especially those for index entries, sometimes can cause wrapping to occur on the screen that will be different from how the printed document will wrap. These differences could cause a heading to move to the next page. To ensure that the page references in the table of contents reflect the printed pages, be sure that formatting marks are hidden when you create a table of contents.

- Display the REFERENCES tab.
- Tap or click the 'Table of Contents' button (REFERENCES tab | Table of Contents group) to display the Table of Contents gallery (Figure 9–46).

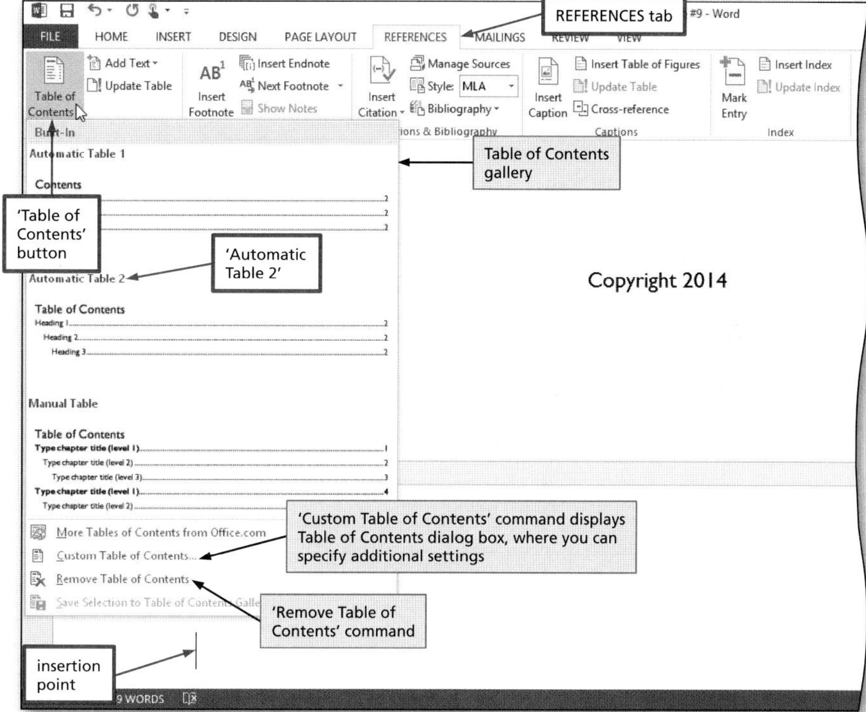

Figure 9–46

2

- Tap or click 'Automatic Table 2' in the Table of Contents gallery to insert the table of contents at the location of the insertion point (Figure 9–47). If necessary, scroll to see the table of contents.

Q&A How would I delete a table of contents?
You would tap or click the 'Table of Contents' button (REFERENCES tab | Table of Contents group) and then tap or click 'Remove Table of Contents' in the Table of Contents gallery.

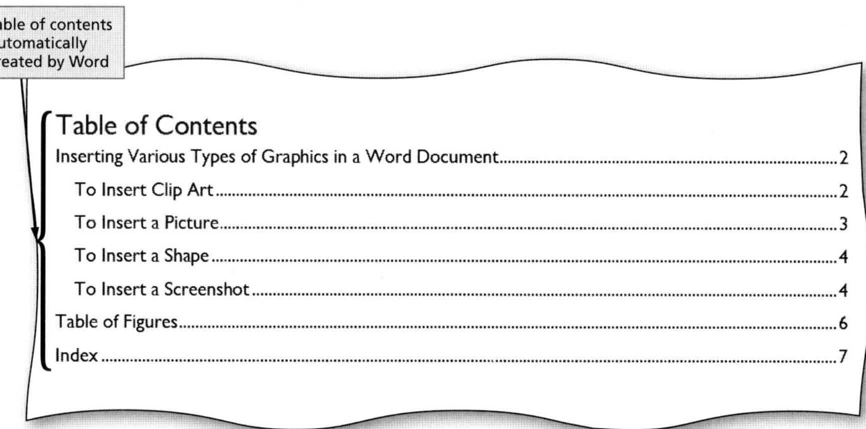

Figure 9–47

Other Ways

1. Tap or click 'Table of Contents' button (REFERENCES tab | Table of Contents group), tap or click 'Custom Table of Contents', select table of contents options (Table of Contents dialog box), tap or click OK button
2. Tap or click 'Explore Quick Parts' button (INSERT tab | Text group), tap or click 'Building Blocks Organizer', select desired table of contents building block (Building Blocks Organizer dialog box), tap or click Insert button, tap or click Close button

To Insert a Continuous Section Break and Change the Starting Page Number in the Section

The table of contents should not be the starting page number; instead, the subdocument should be the starting page number in the document. To change the starting page number, the page must be in a separate section. The following steps insert a continuous section break and then change the starting page number for the table of contents.

1. Position the insertion point at the location for the section break, in this case, to the left of I in Inserting Various Types of Graphics in a Word Document.
2. Display the PAGE LAYOUT tab. Tap or click the 'Insert Page and Section Breaks' button (PAGE LAYOUT tab | Page Setup group) to display the Insert Page and Section Breaks gallery.
3. Tap or click Continuous in the Insert Page and Section Breaks gallery to insert a continuous section break to the left of the insertion point.
4. Position the insertion point in the table of contents.
5. Display the INSERT tab. Tap or click the 'Add Page Numbers' button (INSERT tab | Header & Footer group) to display the Add Page Numbers menu and then tap or click 'Format Page Numbers' on the Add Page Numbers menu to display the Page Number Format dialog box.
6. Tap or click the Start at down arrow (Page Number Format dialog box) until 0 is displayed in the Start at box (Figure 9–48).
7. Tap or click the OK button to change the starting page for the current section.

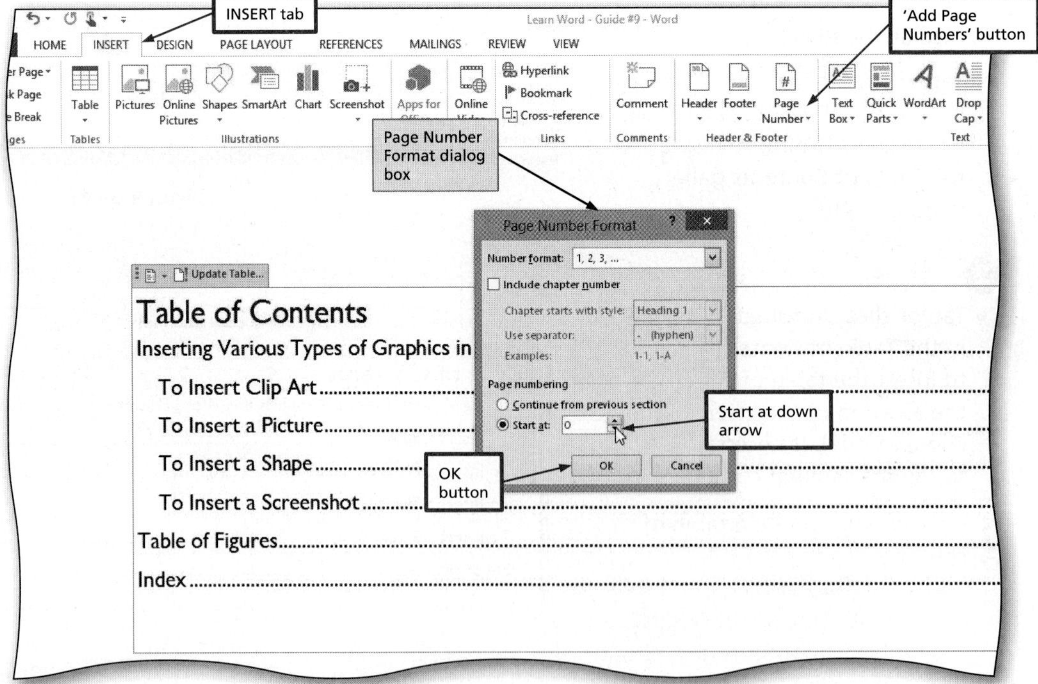

Figure 9–48

BTW
Advanced Layout Options
You can adjust Word's advanced layout options by tapping or clicking FILE on the ribbon to open the Backstage view, tapping or clicking Options in the Backstage view to display the Word Options dialog box, tapping or clicking Advanced in the left pane (Word Options dialog box), sliding or scrolling to the Layout options for area in the right pane, placing a check mark in the desired settings, and then tapping or clicking the OK button.

To Update Page Numbers in a Table of Contents

When you change a document, you should update the associated table of contents. The following steps update the page numbers in the table of contents. ***Why?*** *The starting page number change will affect the page numbers in the table of contents.*

- If necessary, tap or click the table of contents to select it.

Q&A If I am using a mouse, why does the ScreenTip say 'CTRL+Click to follow link'?
Each entry in the table of contents is a link. If you hold down the CTRL key while clicking an entry in the table of contents, Word will display the associated heading in the document window.

- Tap or click the Update Table button that is attached to the table of contents to display the Update Table of Contents dialog box.
- Ensure the 'Update page numbers only' option button is selected because you want to update only the page numbers in the table of contents (Figure 9–49).

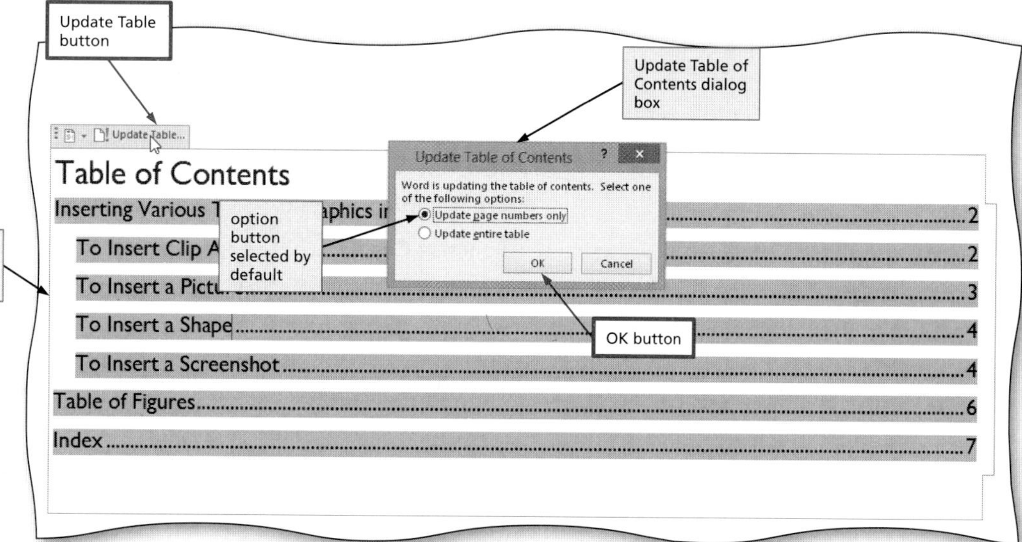

Figure 9–49

- Tap or click the OK button (Update Table of Contents dialog box) to update the page numbers in the table of contents.

- Tap or click outside the table of contents to remove the selection from the table (Figure 9–50).

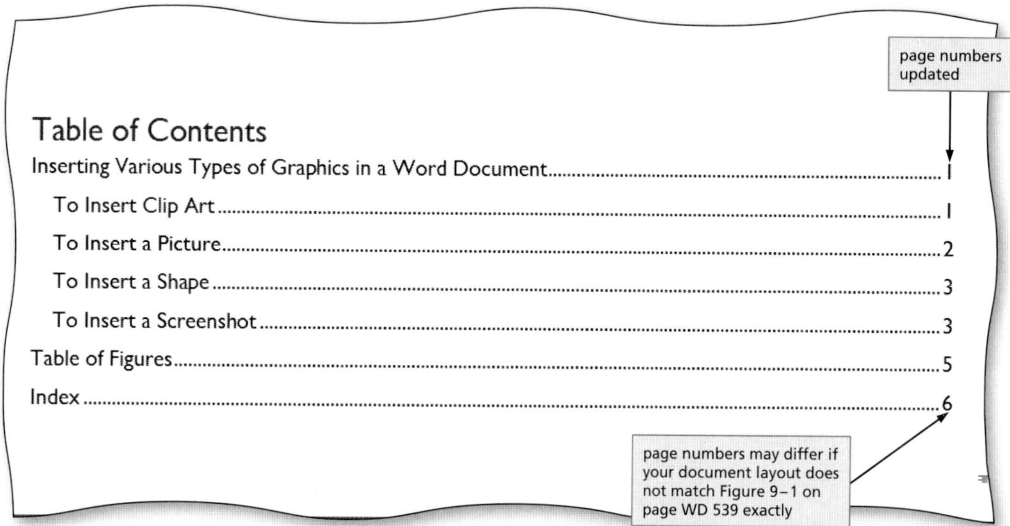

Figure 9–50

Other Ways

1. Select table, tap or click Update Table button (REFERENCES tab | Table of Contents group)
2. Select table, press F9 key

To Find a Format

The subdocument contains a sentence of text formatted as bold italic. To find this text in the document, you could scroll through the document until it is displayed on the screen. A more efficient way is to find the bold, italic format using the Find and Replace dialog box. The following steps find a format. ***Why?*** *You want to add the text to the table of contents.*

- If necessary, display the HOME tab.
- Tap or click the Find arrow (HOME tab | Editing group) to display the Find menu (Figure 9–51).

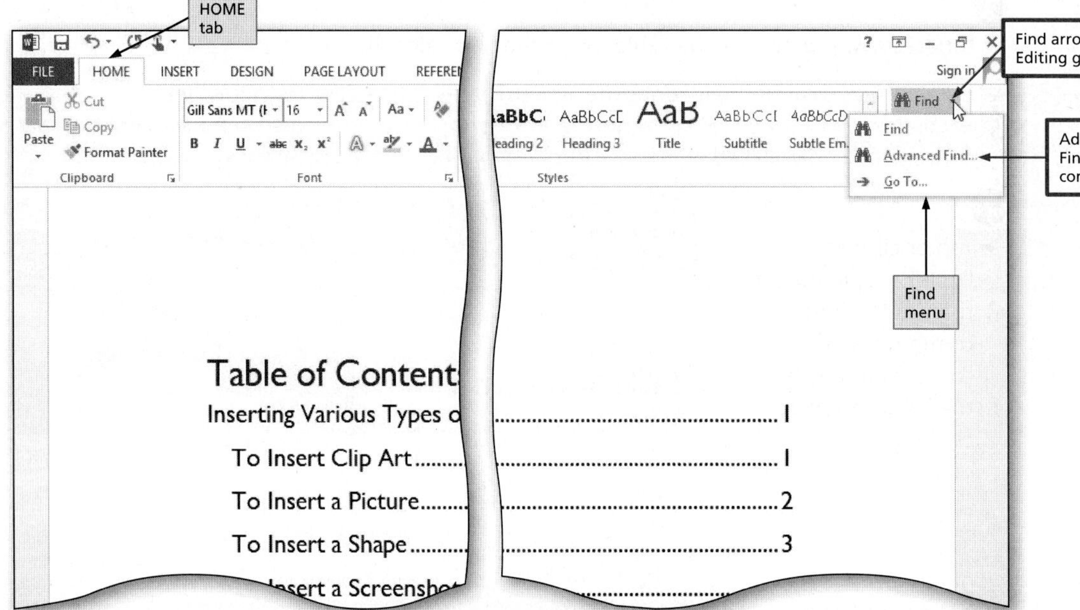

Figure 9–51

- Tap or click Advanced Find on the Find menu to display the Find and Replace dialog box.
- If Word displays a More button in the Find and Replace dialog box, tap or click it so that it changes to a Less button and expands the dialog box.
- Tap or click the Format button (Find and Replace dialog box) to display the Format menu (Figure 9–52).

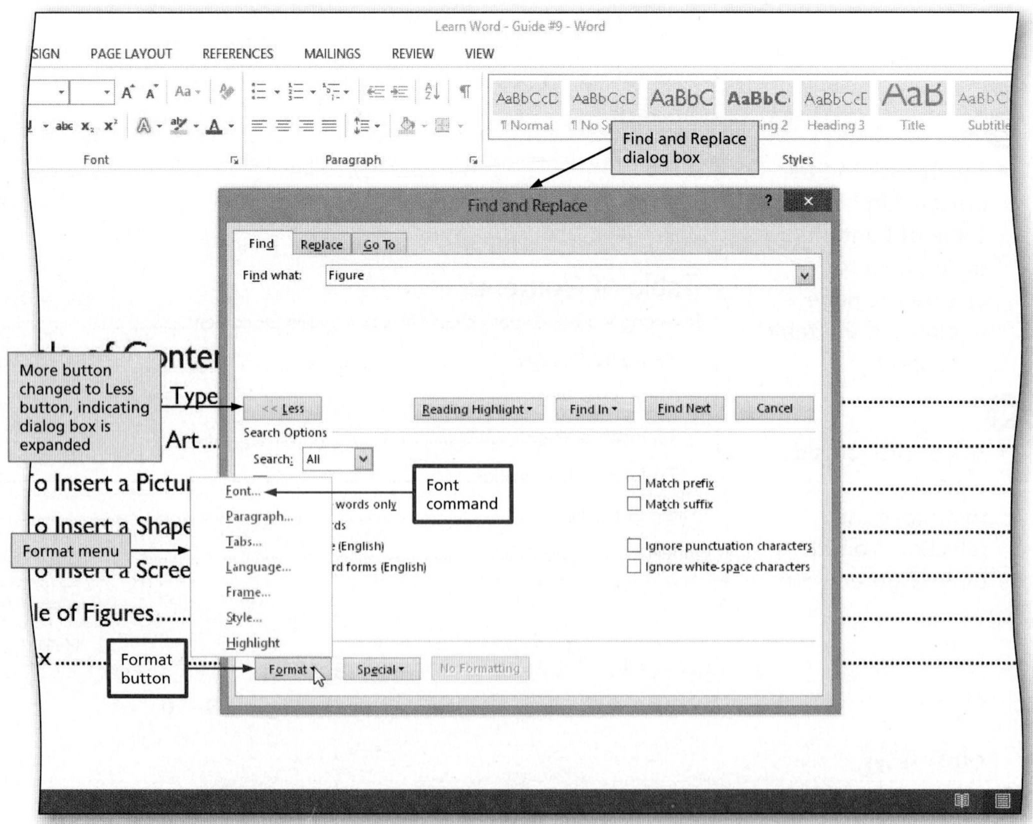

Figure 9–52

- Tap or click Font on the Format menu to display the Find Font dialog box. If necessary, tap or click the Font tab (Find Font dialog box) to display the Font sheet.
- Tap or click Bold Italic in the Font style list because that is the format you want to find (Figure 9–53).

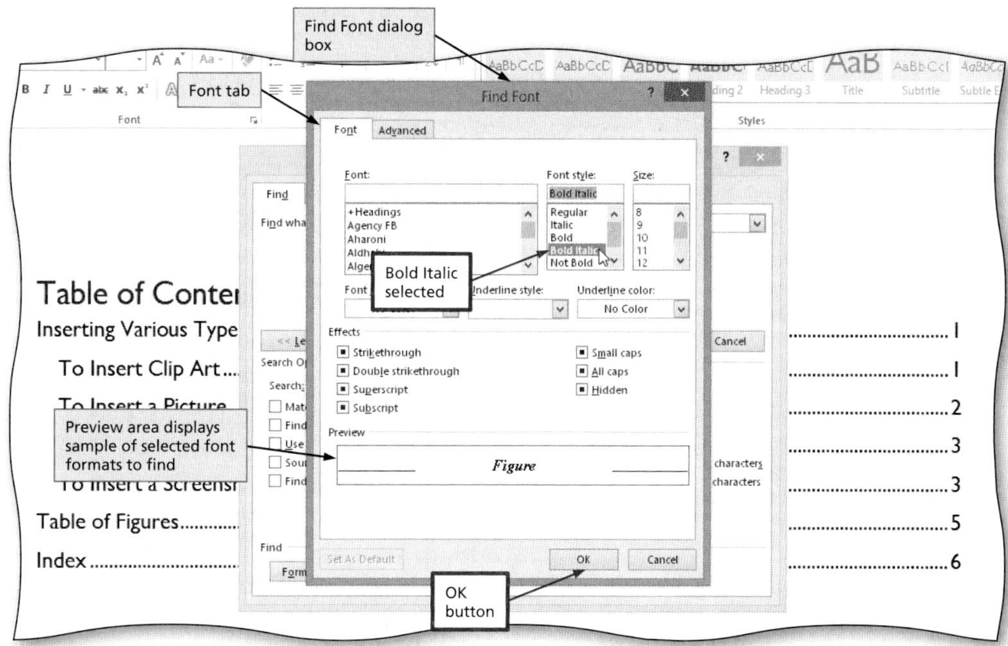

Figure 9–53

- Tap or click the OK button to close the Find Font dialog box.
- Be sure no text is in the Find what text box (or tap or click the Find what arrow and then click [Formatting Only]).
- Be sure all check boxes in the Search Options area are cleared.
- When the Find and Replace dialog box is active again, tap or click its Find Next button to locate and highlight in the document the first occurrence of the specified format (Figure 9–54).

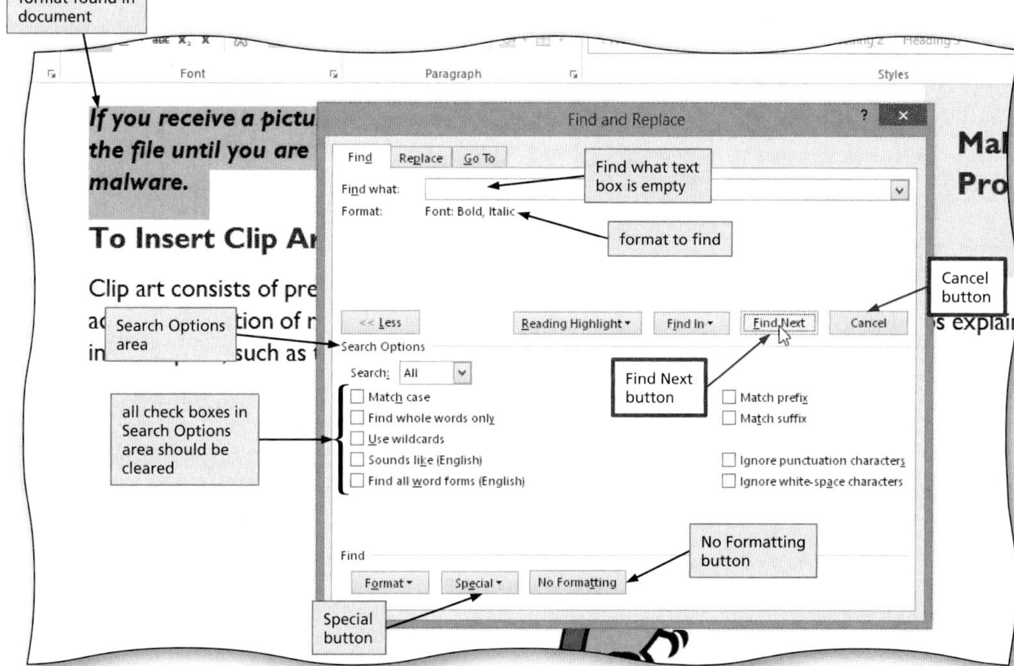

Figure 9–54

Q&A How do I remove a find format?
You would tap or click the No Formatting button in the Find and Replace dialog box.

- Tap or click the Cancel button (Find and Replace dialog box) because the located occurrence is the one you wanted to find.

Q&A Can I search for (find) special characters such as page breaks?
Yes. To find special characters, you would tap or click the Special button in the Find and Replace dialog box.

Other Ways

1. Press CTRL+F

BTW
Find and Replace
The expanded Find and Replace dialog box allows you to specify how Word locates search text. For example, selecting the Match case check box instructs Word to find the text exactly as you typed it, and selecting the 'Find whole words only' check box instructs Word to ignore text that contains the search text (i.e., the word, then, contains the word, the). If you select the Use wildcard check box, you can use wildcard characters in a search. For example, with this check box selected, the search text of *ing would search for all words that end with the characters, ing.

To Format Text as a Heading

The following steps format a paragraph of text as a Heading 3 style. Occasionally, you may want to add a paragraph of text, which normally is not formatted using a heading style, to a table of contents. One way to add the text is to format it as a heading style.

1. With the paragraph still selected (shown in Figure 9–54), if necessary, display the HOME tab.
2. Tap or click Heading 3 in the Styles gallery to apply the selected style to the current paragraph in the document. Tap or click outside the paragraph to deselect it (Figure 9–55).

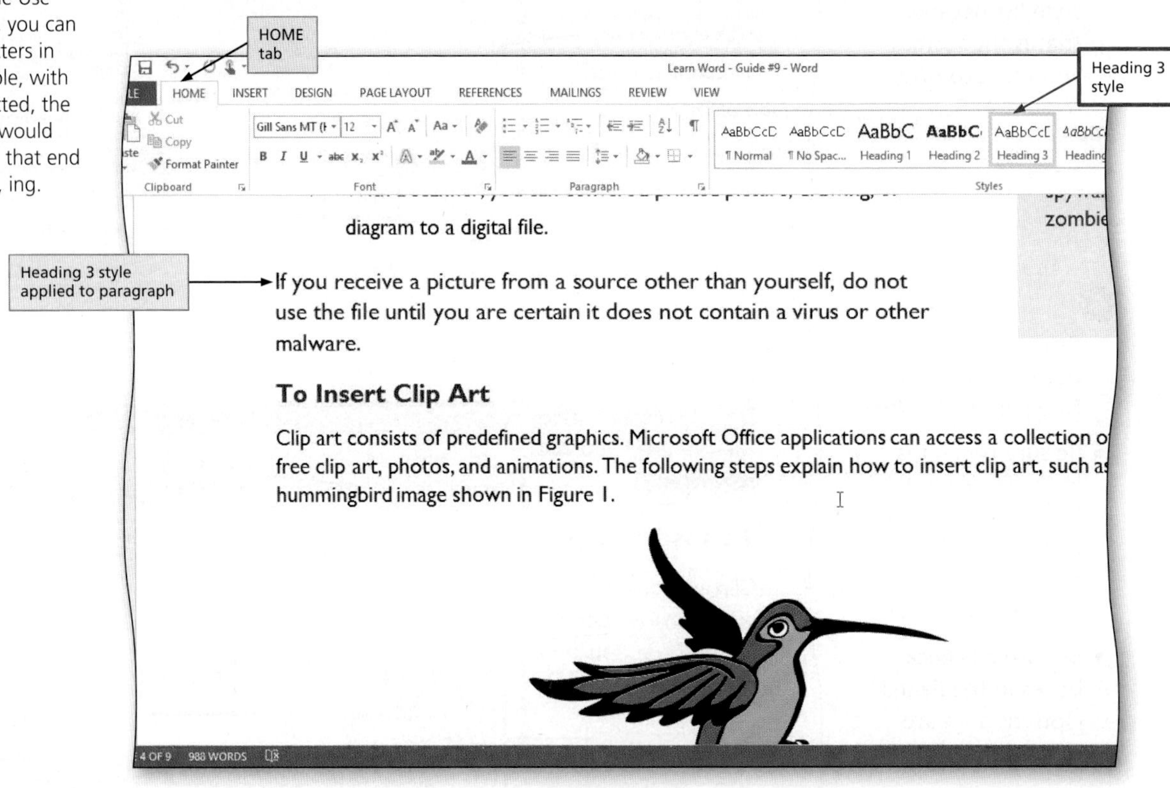

Figure 9–55

BTW
Replace Formats
You can tap or click the Replace tab (Find and Replace dialog box) to find and replace formats. Follow the steps on the previous two pages to enter the format to find in the Find what text box and then follow the same steps to enter the format to replace in the Replace with text box. Next, tap or click the Replace or Replace All button to replace the next occurrence of the format or all occurrences of the format in the document.

To Retain Formatting when Adding Text to the Table of Contents

If you wanted to retain formatting of text when adding it to the table of contents, you would perform the following steps.

1. Position the insertion point in the paragraph of text that you want to add to the table of contents.
2. Tap or click the Add Text button (REFERENCES tab | Table of Contents group) to display the Add Text menu.
3. Tap or click the desired level on the Add Text menu, which adds the format of the selected style to the selected paragraph and adds the paragraph of text to the table of contents.

To Update the Entire Table of Contents

The following steps update the entire table of contents. ***Why?*** *The text changed to the Heading 3 style should appear in the table of contents.*

- Display the table of contents in the document window.
- Tap or click the table of contents to select it.
- Tap or click the Update Table button that is attached to the table of contents to display the Update Table of Contents dialog box.
- Tap or click the 'Update entire table' option button (Update Table of Contents dialog box) because you want to update the entire table of contents (Figure 9–56).

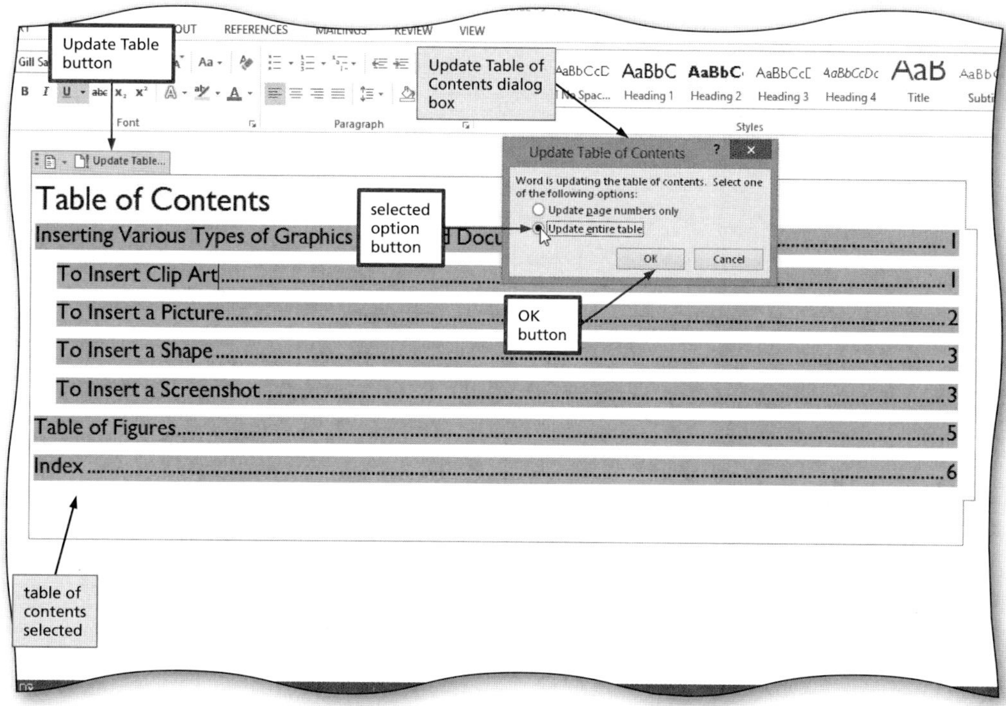

Figure 9–56

- Tap or click the OK button (Update Table of Contents dialog box) to update the entire table of contents (Figure 9–57).

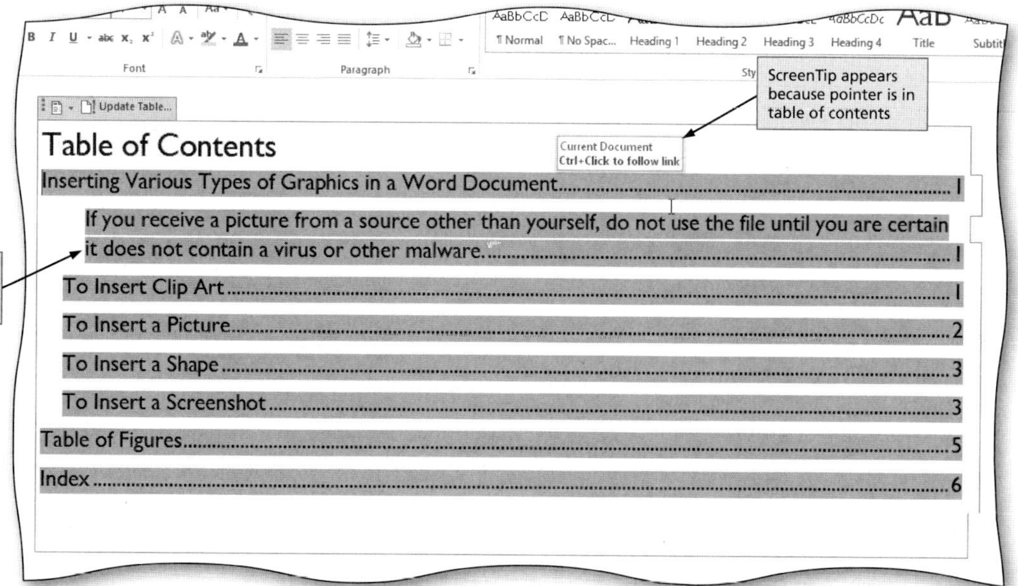

Figure 9–57

Other Ways

1. Select table, tap or click Update Table button (REFERENCES tab | Table of Contents group)
2. Select table, press F9 key

To Change the Format of a Table of Contents

1 MODIFY REFERENCE DOCUMENT | 2 CREATE MASTER DOCUMENT | **3 ORGANIZE REFERENCE DOCUMENT**

You can change the format of the table of contents to any of the predefined table of contents styles or to custom settings. The following steps change the table of contents format. ***Why?*** *In this table of contents, you specify the format, page number alignment, and tab leader character.*

- Display the REFERENCES tab.
- Tap or click the 'Table of Contents' button (REFERENCES tab | Table of Contents group) to display the Table of Contents gallery (Figure 9–58).

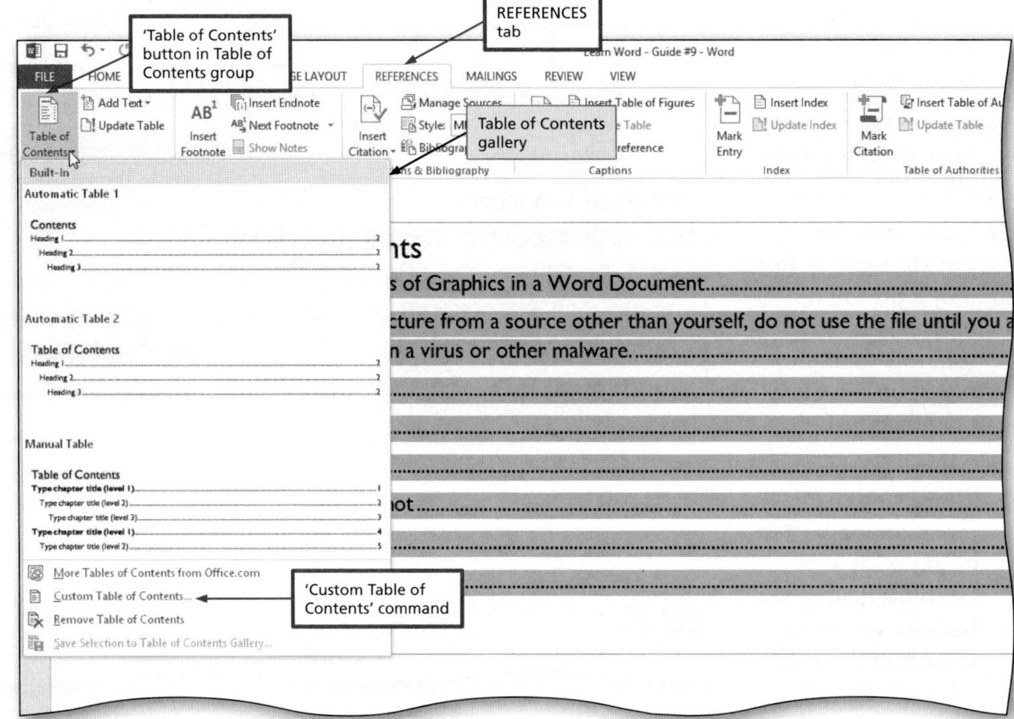

Figure 9–58

- Tap or click 'Custom Table of Contents' in the Table of Contents gallery to display the Table of Contents dialog box.
- Tap or click the Formats arrow (Table of Contents dialog box) and then tap or click Simple to change the format style for the table of contents.
- Place a check mark in the 'Right align page numbers' check box so that the page numbers appear at the right margin in the table of contents.
- Tap or click the Tab leader arrow and then tap or click the first leader type in the list so that the selected leader characters appear between the heading name and the page numbers in the table of contents (Figure 9–59).

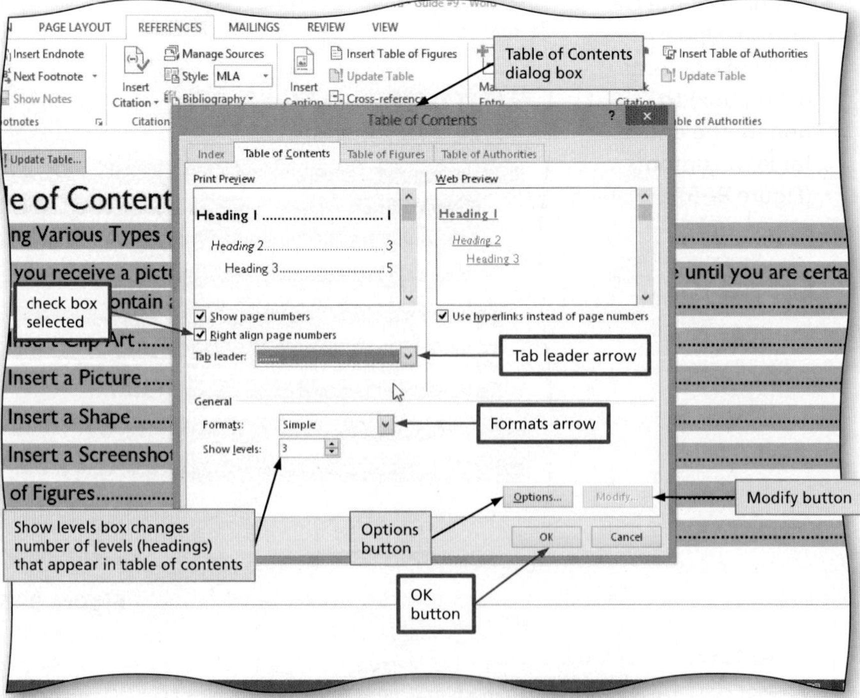

Figure 9–59

- Tap or click the OK button to modify the table of contents according to the specified settings. When Word displays a dialog box asking if you want to replace the selected table of contents, tap or click the Yes button (Figure 9–60).

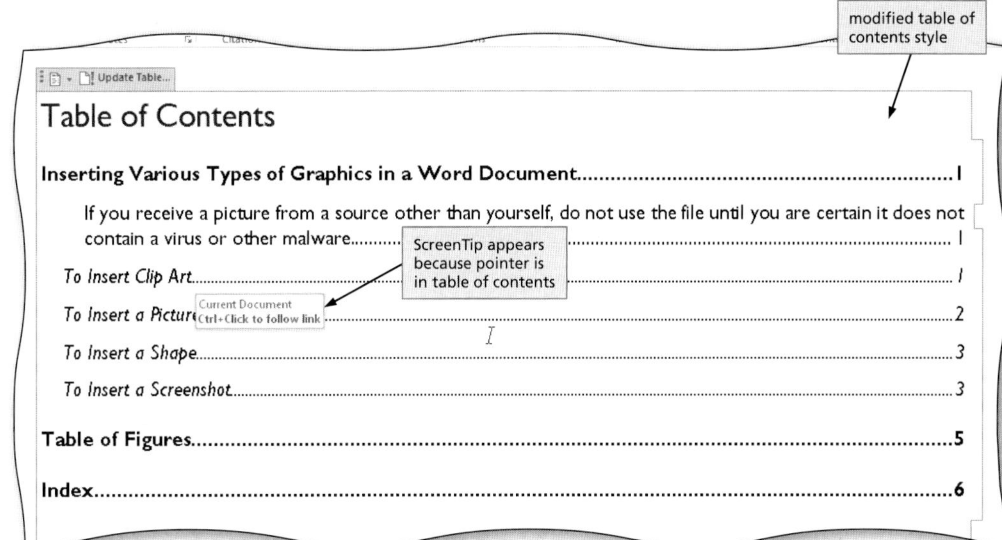

Figure 9–60

To Use the Navigation Pane to Go to a Heading in a Document

1 MODIFY REFERENCE DOCUMENT | 2 CREATE MASTER DOCUMENT | **3 ORGANIZE REFERENCE DOCUMENT**

When you use Word's built-in heading styles in a document, you can use the Navigation Pane to go to headings in a document quickly. ***Why?*** *When you tap or click a heading in the Navigation Pane, Word displays the page associated with that heading in the document window.* The following step uses the Navigation Pane to display an associated heading in the document window.

- Display the VIEW tab. Place a check mark in the 'Open the Navigation Pane' check box (VIEW tab | Show group) to display the Navigation Pane at the left edge of the Word window.
- If necessary, tap or click the HEADINGS tab in the Navigation Pane to display the text that is formatted using Heading styles.
- Tap or click the Table of Figures heading in the Navigation Pane to display the top of the selected page in the top of the document window (Figure 9–61).

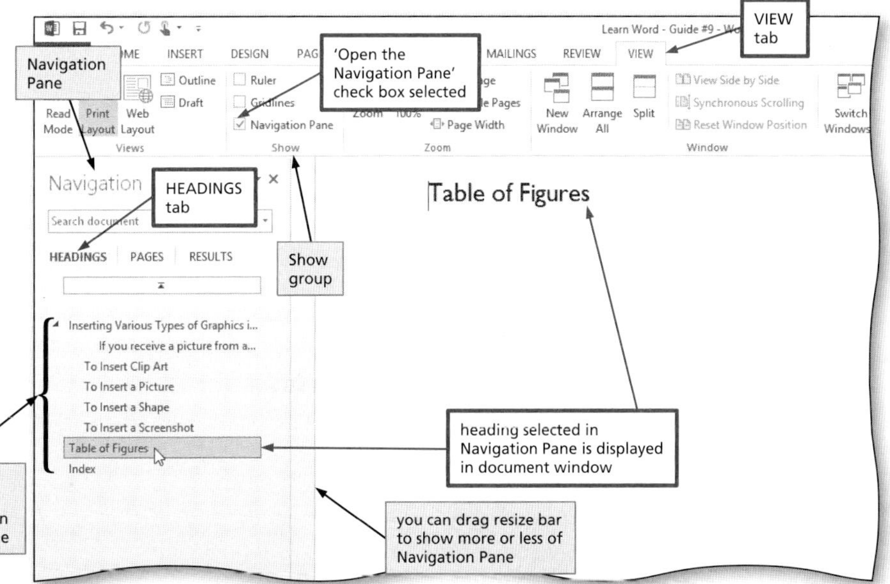

Figure 9–61

Q&A What if all of the headings are not displayed?

Press and hold or right-click a heading in the Navigation Pane and then tap or click Expand All on the shortcut menu to ensure that all headings are displayed. If a heading still is not displayed, verify that the heading is formatted with a heading style. To display or hide subheadings below a heading in the Navigation Pane, tap or click the triangle to the left of the heading. If a heading is too wide for the Navigation Pane, you can point to the heading to display a ScreenTip that shows the complete title.

To Create a Table of Figures

The following steps create a table of figures. ***Why?*** *At the end of the reference document is a table of figures, which lists all figures and their corresponding page numbers. Word generates this table of figures from the captions in the document.*

- Ensure that formatting marks are not displayed.
- Position the insertion point at the end of the Table of Figures heading and then press the ENTER key, so that the insertion point is on the line below the heading.
- Display the REFERENCES tab.
- Tap or click the 'Table of Figures Dialog' button (REFERENCES tab | Captions group) to display the Table of Figures dialog box.
- Be sure that all settings in your dialog box match those in Figure 9–62.

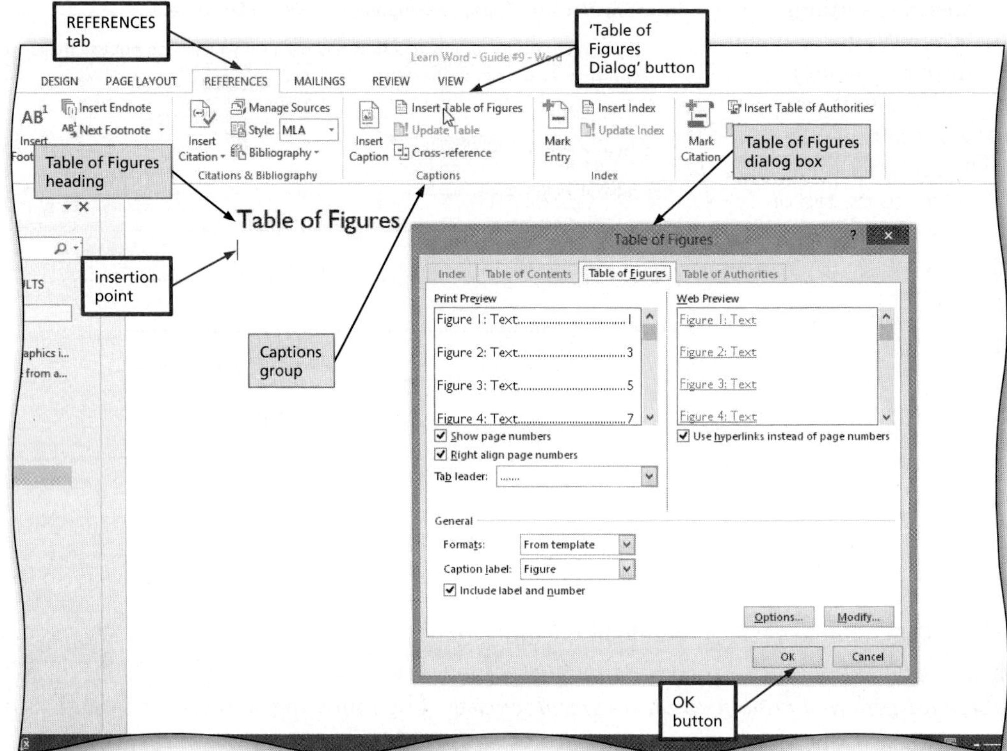

Figure 9–62

- Tap or click the OK button (Table of Figures dialog box) to create a table of figures at the location of the insertion point (Figure 9–63).

table of figures created by Word

Table of Figures

Figure 1: Hummingbird Clip Art.. 1
Figure 2: Flowers Picture.. 2
Figure 3: Arrow Shape.. 3
Figure 4: Help Window Screenshot.. 4

Figure 9–63

TO CHANGE THE FORMAT OF THE TABLE OF FIGURES

If you wanted to change the format of the table of figures, you would perform the following steps.

1. Tap or click the table of figures to select it.
2. Tap or click the 'Table of Figures Dialog' button (REFERENCES tab | Captions group) to display the Table of Figures dialog box.
3. Change settings in the dialog box as desired.
4. Tap or click the OK button (Table of Figures dialog box) to apply the changed settings.
5. Tap or click the OK button when Word asks if you want to replace the selected table of figures.

BTW
Table of Contents Styles
If you wanted to change the level associated with each style used in a table of contents, tap or click the Options button in the Table of Contents dialog box (shown in Figure 9–59 on page WD 580), enter the desired level number in the text box beside the appropriate heading or other styled item, and then tap or click the OK button. To change the formatting associated with a style, tap or click the Modify button in the Table of Contents dialog box.

To Edit a Caption and Update the Table of Figures

1 MODIFY REFERENCE DOCUMENT | 2 CREATE MASTER DOCUMENT | **3 ORGANIZE REFERENCE DOCUMENT**

The following steps change the Figure 4 caption and then update the table of figures. ***Why?*** *When you modify captions in a document or move illustrations to a different location in the document, you will have to update the table of figures.*

- Tap or click the heading, To Insert a Screenshot, in the Navigation Pane to display the selected heading in the document window. (If this heading is not at the top of page 7, insert a page break to position the heading at the top of a new page.)
- Insert the text, Word, in the Figure 4 caption so that it reads: Word Help Window Screenshot (Figure 9–64).

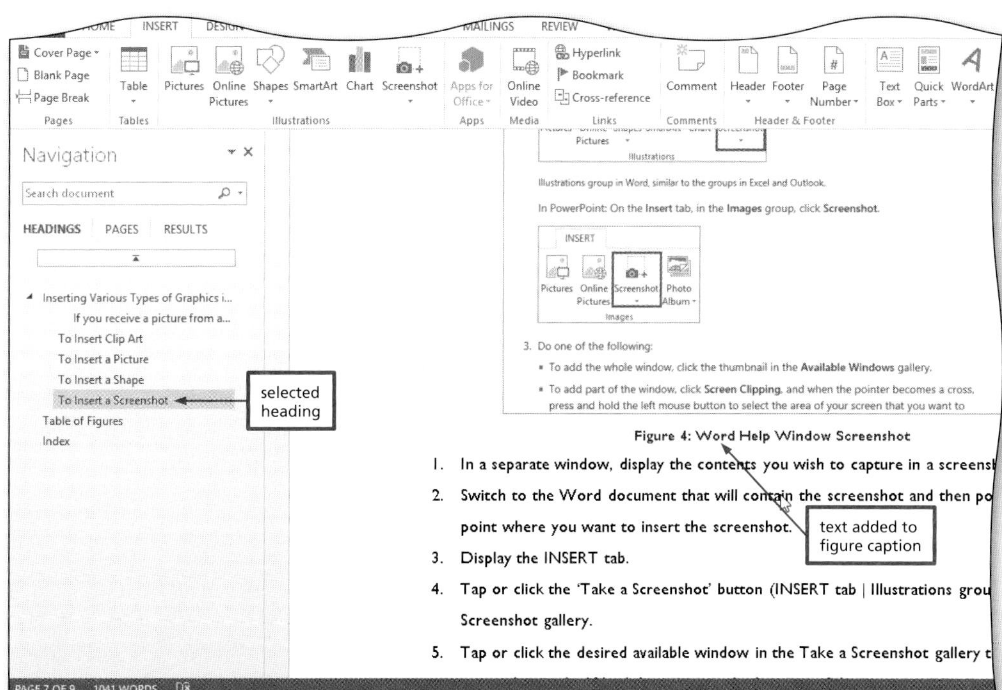

Figure 9–64

2

- Tap or click the heading, Table of Figures, in the Navigation Pane to display the Table of Figures heading in the document window.
- Tap or click the table of figures to select it.
- Tap or click the 'Update Table of Figures' button (REFERENCES tab | Captions group) to display the Update Table of Figures dialog box.
- Tap or click 'Update entire table' (Update Table of Figures dialog box), so that Word updates the contents of the entire table of figures instead of updating only the page numbers (Figure 9–65).

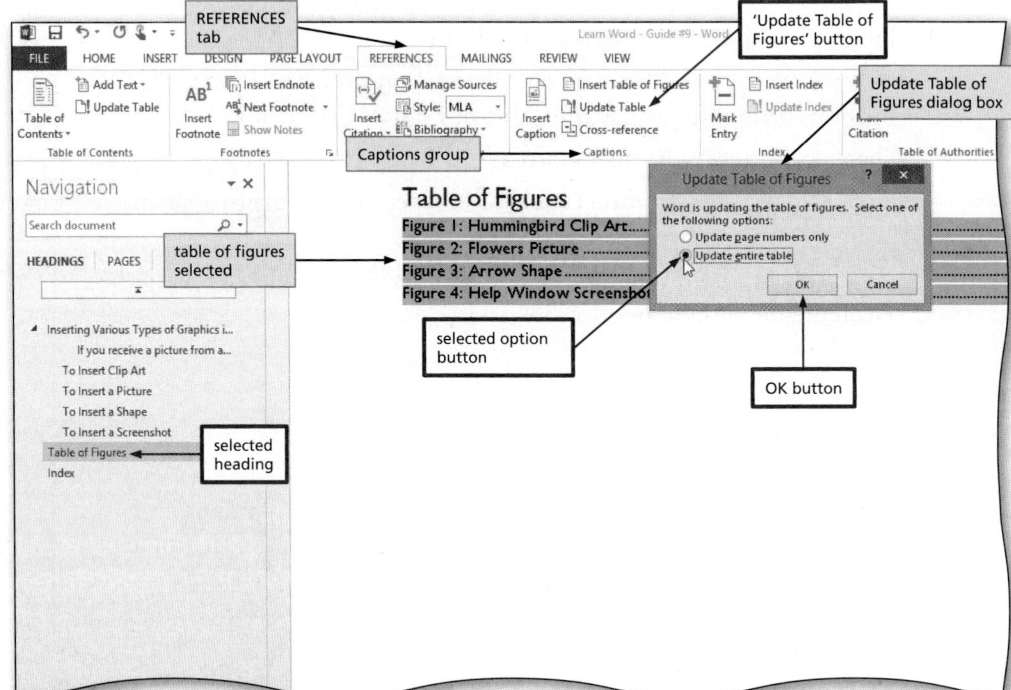

Figure 9–65

3

- Tap or click the OK button to update the table of figures and then tap or click outside the table to deselect it (Figure 9–66).

Q&A Are the entries in the table of figures links?
Yes. As with the table of contents, if you are using a mouse, you can CTRL+click any entry in the table of figures and Word will display the associated figure in the document window.

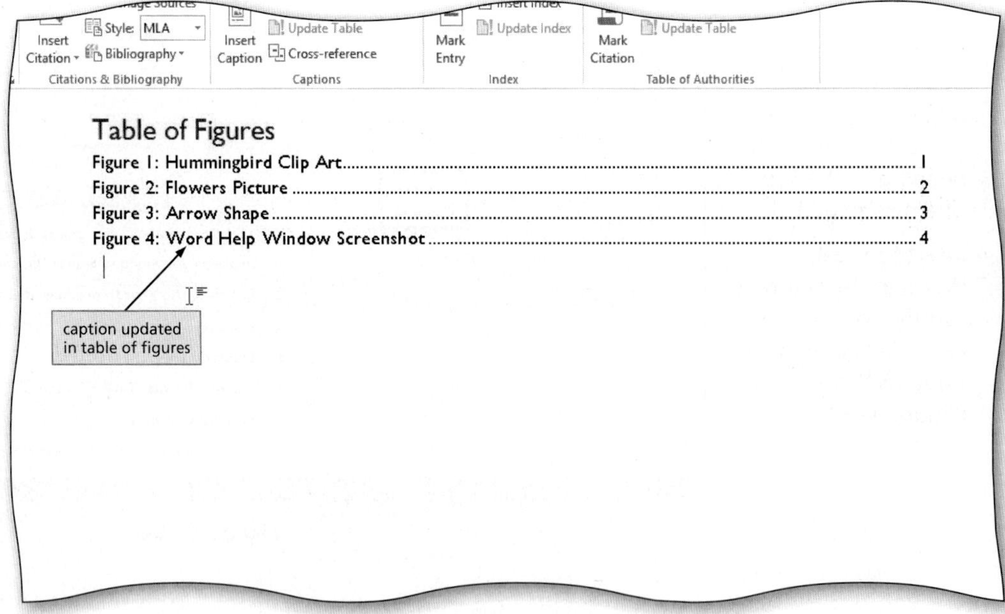

Figure 9–66

Other Ways

1. Select table of figures, press F9 key

To Build an Index

The reference document in this chapter ends with an index. Earlier, this chapter showed how to mark index entries. ***Why?*** *For Word to generate the index, you first must mark any text you wish to appear in the index.*

Once all index entries are marked, Word can build the index from the index entry fields in the document. Recall that index entry fields begin with XE, which appears on the screen when formatting marks are displayed. When index entry fields show on the screen, the document's pagination probably will be altered because of the extra text in the index entries. Thus, be sure to hide formatting marks before building an index. The following steps build an index.

1

- Tap or click the heading, Index, in the Navigation Pane to display the Index heading in the document window.
- Tap or click to the right of the Index heading and then press the ENTER key, so that the insertion point is on the line below the heading.
- Ensure that formatting marks are not displayed.
- Tap or click the Insert Index button (REFERENCES tab | Index group) to display the Index dialog box.
- If necessary, tap or click the Formats arrow in the dialog box and then tap or click Classic in the Formats list to change the index format.
- Place a check mark in the 'Right align page numbers' check box.
- Tap or click the Tab leader arrow and then tap or click the first leader character in the list to specify the leader character to be displayed between the index entry and the page number.
- Tap or click the Columns down arrow until the number of columns is 1 to change the number of columns in the index (Figure 9–67).

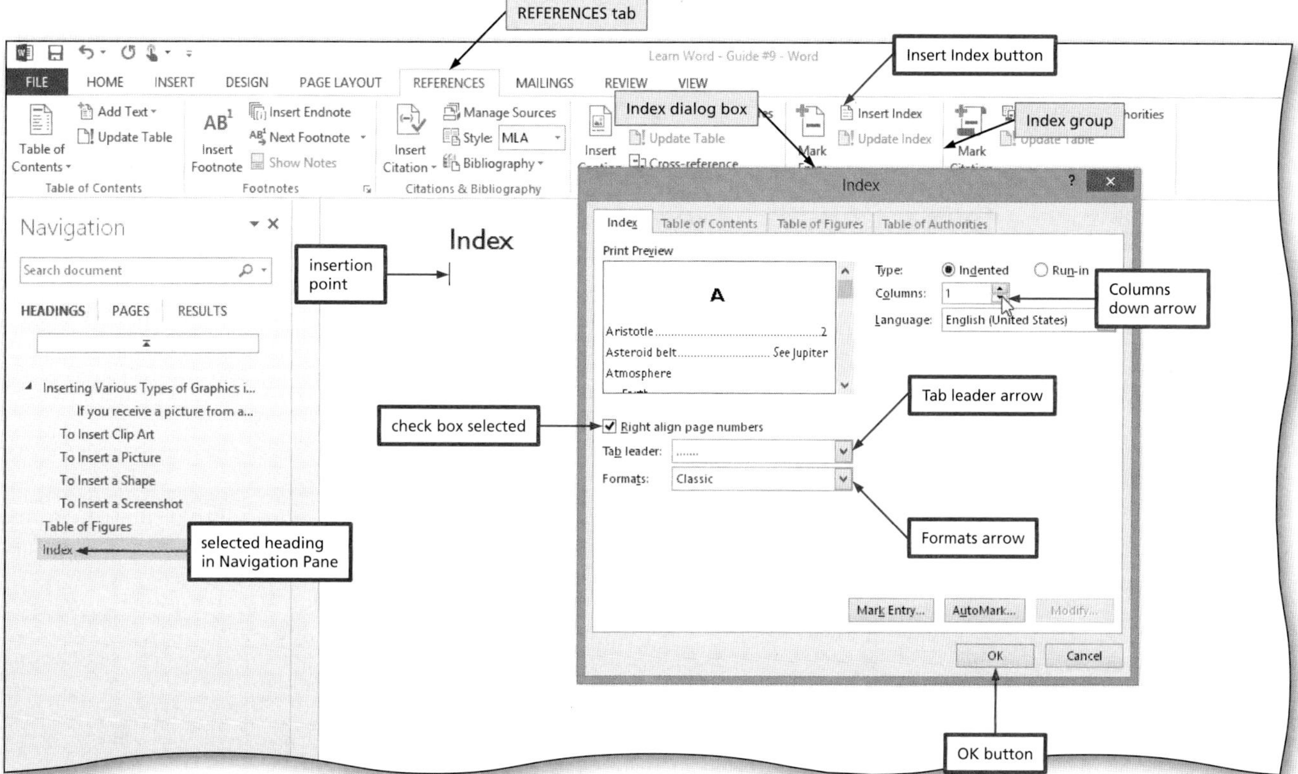

Figure 9–67

- Tap or click the OK button (Index dialog box) to create an index at the location of the insertion point (Figure 9–68).

Q&A How would I change the language used in the index?

Tap or click the Language arrow (Index dialog box) and then tap or click the desired language.

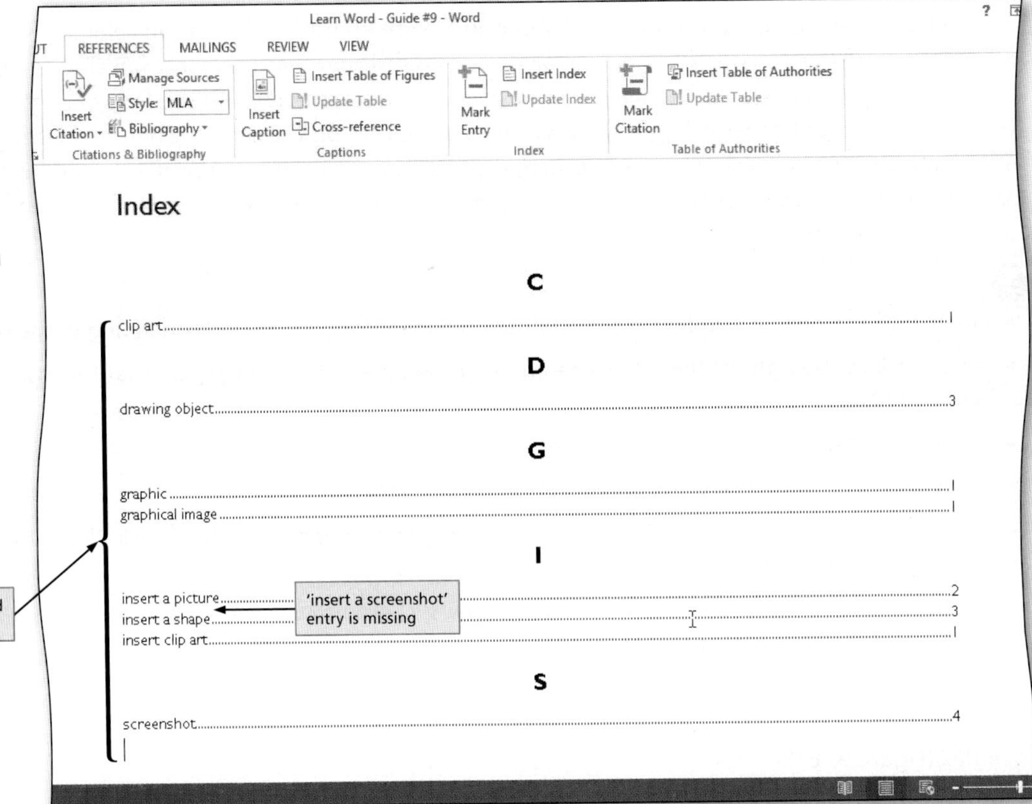

Figure 9–68

To Mark Another Index Entry

Notice in Figure 9–68 that the 'insert a screenshot' index entry is missing. The following steps mark an index entry in the Insert a Screenshot section.

1. Tap or click the heading, To Insert a Screenshot, in the Navigation Pane to display the selected heading in the document window.
2. Select the words, Insert a Screenshot, in the heading.
3. Tap or click the Mark Entry button (REFERENCES tab | Index group) to display the Mark Index Entry dialog box.
4. Type `insert a screenshot` in the Main entry text box (Mark Index Entry dialog box) so that the entry is all lowercase (Figure 9–69).
5. Tap or click the Mark button to mark the entry.
6. Close the dialog box.
7. Hide formatting marks.

BTW
Index Files
Instead of marking index entries in a document, you can create a concordance file that contains all index entries you wish to mark. A **concordance file** contains two columns: the first column identifies the text in the document you want Word to mark as an index entry, and the second column lists the index entries to be generated from the text in the first column. To mark entries in the concordance file, tap or click the AutoMark button in the Index and Tables dialog box.

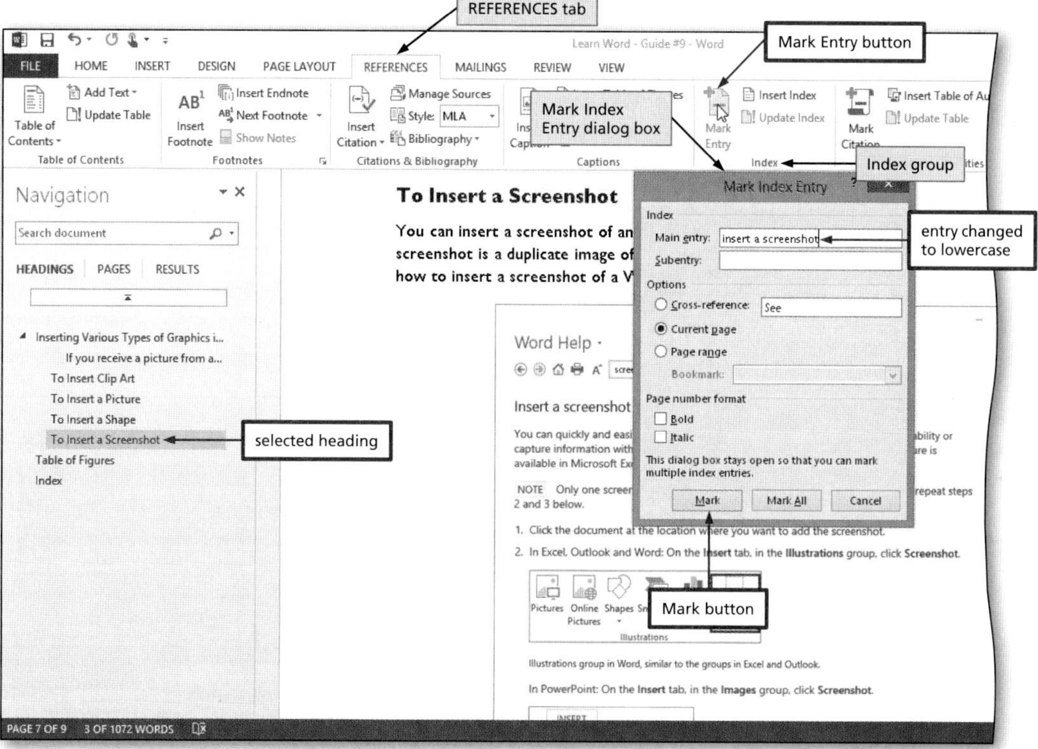

Figure 9–69

To Edit an Index Entry

At some time, you may want to change an index entry after you have marked it. For example, you may forget to lowercase the entry for the headings. If you wanted to change an index entry, you would perform the following steps.

1. Display formatting marks.
2. Locate the XE field for the index entry you wish to change (i.e., { XE "Insert a Screenshot" }).
3. Change the text inside the quotation marks (i.e., { XE "insert a screenshot" }).
4. Update the index as described in the steps on the next page.

To Delete an Index Entry

If you wanted to delete an index entry, you would perform the following steps.

1. Display formatting marks.
2. Select the XE field for the index entry you wish to delete (i.e., { XE "insert a screenshot" }).
3. Press the DELETE key.
4. Update the index as described in the steps on the next page.

BTW
Navigation Pane
You can drag any heading in the Navigation Pane to reorganize document content. For example, you could drag the 'To Insert a Screenshot' heading upward in the Navigation Pane so that its content appears earlier in the document.

To Update an Index

The following step updates an index. ***Why?*** *After marking a new index entry, you must update the index.*

1

- Tap or click the heading, Index, in the Navigation Pane to display the selected heading in the document window.
- In the document window, tap or click the index to select it.
- If necessary, display the REFERENCES tab.
- Tap or click the Update Index button (REFERENCES tab | Index group) to update the index (Figure 9–70).

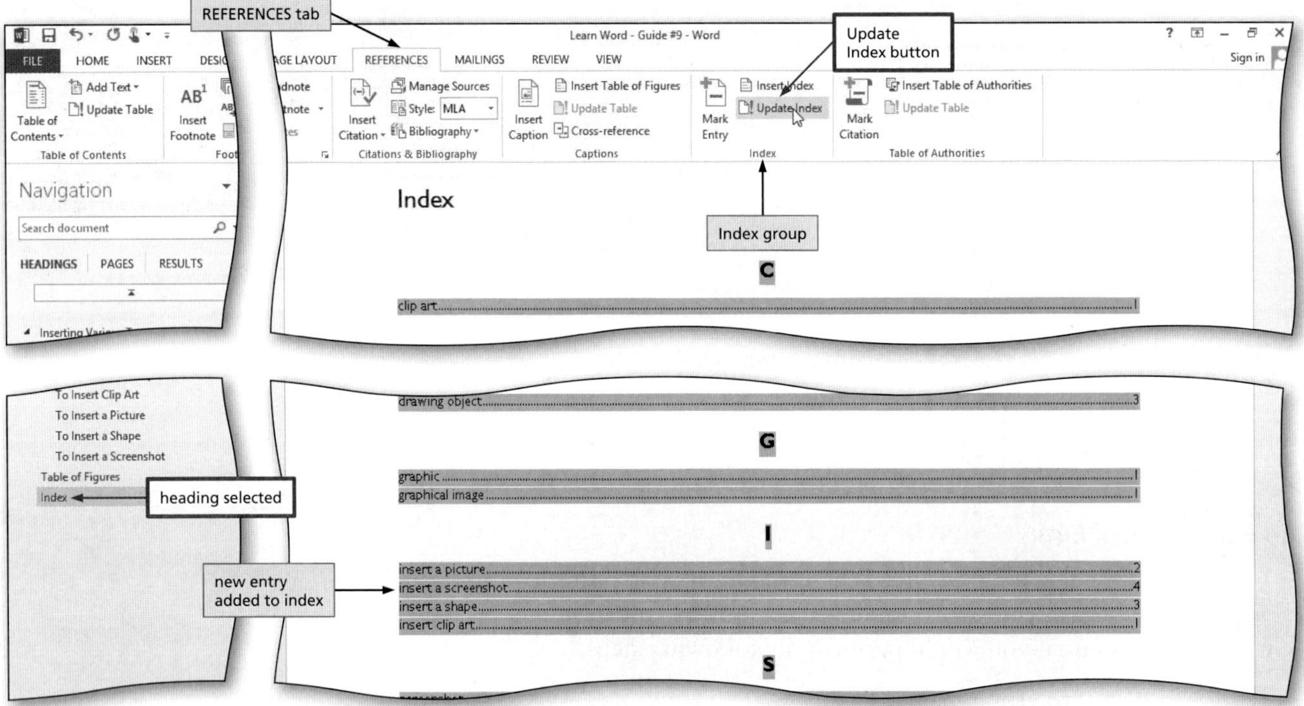

Figure 9–70

Other Ways

1. Select index, press F9 key

To Change the Format of the Index

If you wanted to change the format of the index, you would perform the following steps.

1. Tap or click the index to select it.
2. Tap or click the Insert Index button (REFERENCES tab | Index group) to display the Index dialog box.
3. Change settings in the dialog box as desired. If you want to modify the style used for the index, tap or click the Modify button.
4. Tap or click the OK button (Index dialog box) to apply the changed settings.
5. Tap or click the OK button when Word asks if you want to replace the selected index.

To Delete an Index

If you wanted to delete an index, you would perform the following steps.

1. Tap or click the index to select it.
2. Press SHIFT+F9 to display field codes.
3. Drag through the entire field code, including the braces, and then press the DELETE key.

Table of Authorities

In addition to creating an index, table of figures, and table of contents, you can use Word to create a table of authorities. Legal documents often include a **table of authorities** to list references to cases, rules, statutes, etc. To create a table of authorities, mark the citations first and then build the table of authorities.

The procedures for marking citations, editing citations, creating the table of authorities, changing the format of the table of authorities, and updating the table of authorities are the same as those for indexes. The only difference is you use the buttons in the Table of Authorities group on the REFERENCES tab instead of the buttons in the Index group.

BTW
Table of Authorities
See pages WD 723 through WD 726 in the Supplementary Word Tasks section of Chapter 11 for additional instructions related to creating a table of authorities.

To Create Alternating Footers Using a Footer Building Block

1 MODIFY REFERENCE DOCUMENT | 2 CREATE MASTER DOCUMENT | **3 ORGANIZE REFERENCE DOCUMENT**

The *Learn Word* documents are designed so that they can be duplicated back-to-back. That is, the document prints on nine separate pages. When they are duplicated, however, pages one and two are printed on opposite sides of the same sheet of paper. ***Why?*** *Back-to-back duplicating saves resources because it enables the nine-page document to use only five sheets of paper.*

In many books and documents that have facing pages, the page number is always on the same side of the page — often on the outside edge. In Word, you accomplish this task by specifying one type of header or footer for even-numbered pages and another type of header or footer for odd-numbered pages. The following steps create alternating footers beginning on the fourth page of the document (the beginning of the subdocument).

- If necessary, hide formatting marks.
- Use the Navigation Pane to display the page with the heading, Inserting Various Types of Graphics in a Word Document.
- Display the INSERT tab.
- Tap or click the 'Add a Footer' button (INSERT tab | Header & Footer group) and then tap or click Edit Footer to display the footer area.
- Be sure the 'Link to Previous' button (HEADER & FOOTER TOOLS DESIGN tab | Navigation group) is not selected.
- Place a check mark in the 'Different Odd & Even Pages' check box (HEADER & FOOTER TOOLS DESIGN tab | Options group), so that you can enter a different footer for odd and even pages.
- If necessary, tap or click the Show Next button (HEADER & FOOTER TOOLS DESIGN tab | Navigation group) to display the desired footer page (in this case, the Odd Page Footer – Section 4).

- Tap or click the 'Insert Alignment Tab' button (HEADER & FOOTER TOOLS DESIGN tab | Position group) to display the Alignment Tab dialog box.
- Tap or click Right (Alignment Tab dialog box) because you want to place a right-aligned tab stop in the footer (Figure 9–71).

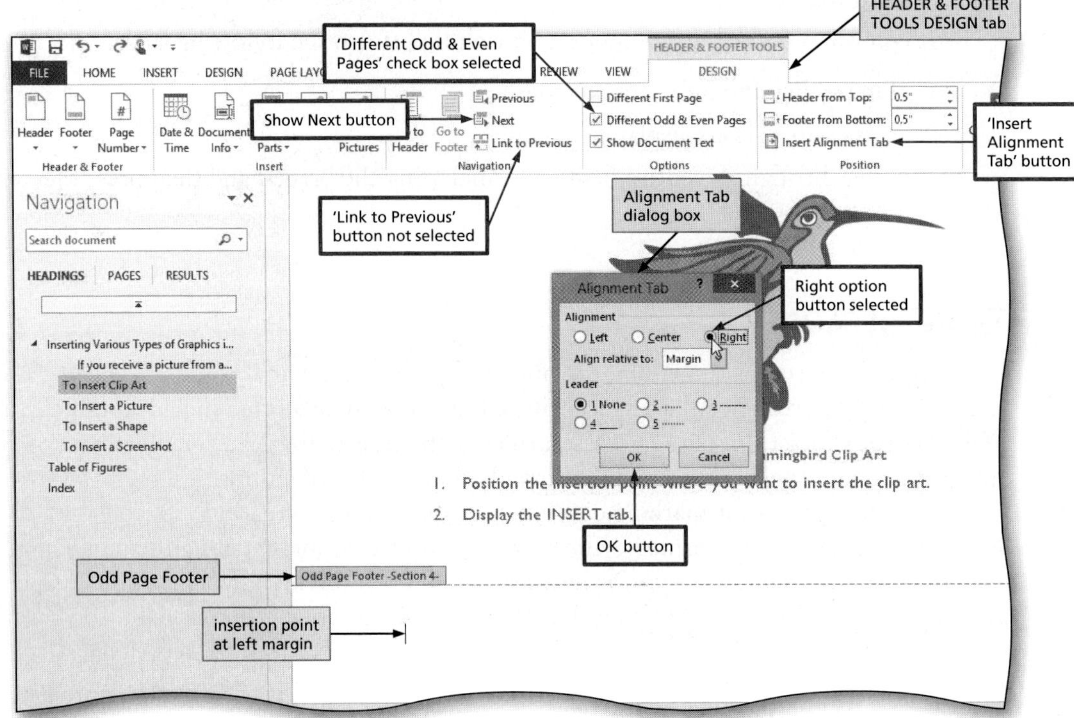

Figure 9–71

- Tap or click the OK button to align the paragraph and insertion point in the footer at the right margin.
- Tap or click the 'Add Page Numbers' button (HEADER & FOOTER TOOLS DESIGN tab | Header & Footer group) to display the Add Page Numbers gallery.
- Tap or point to Current Position in the Add Page Numbers gallery to display the Current Position gallery (Figure 9–72).

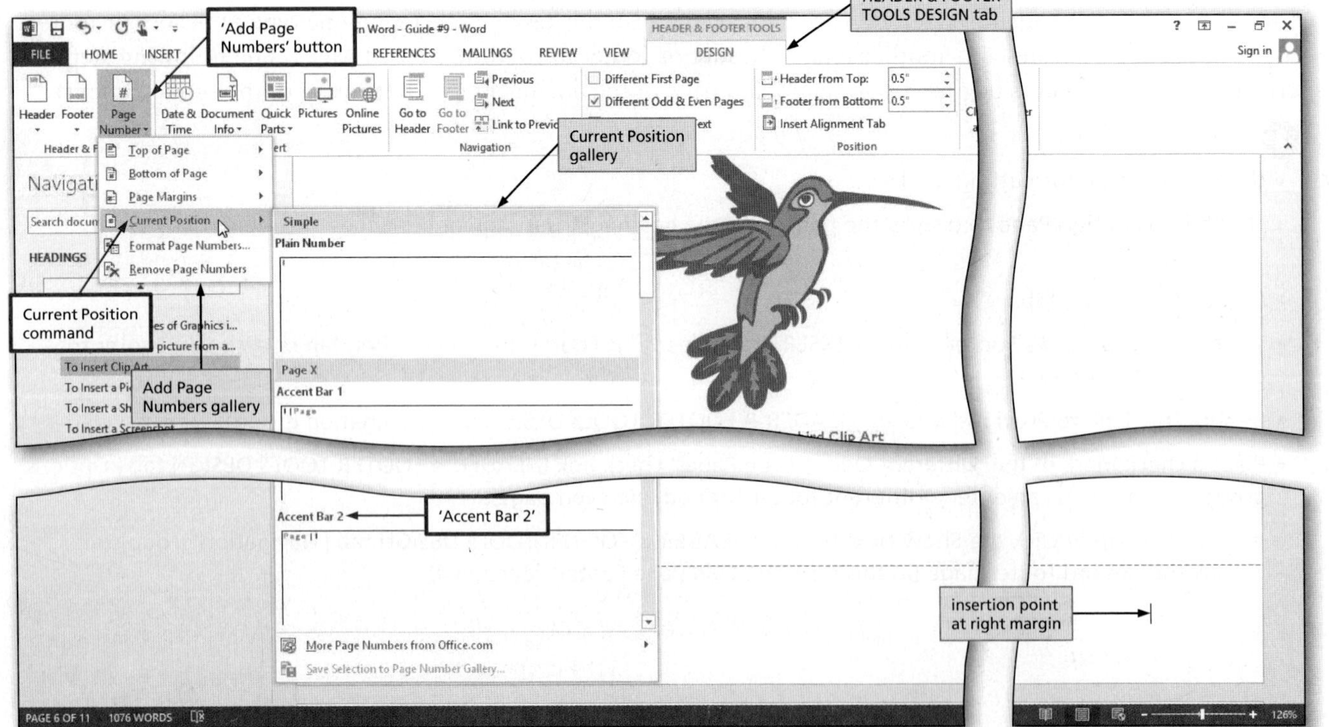

Figure 9–72

4

- Tap or click 'Accent Bar 2' in the Current Position gallery to insert the selected page number in the footer (Figure 9–73).

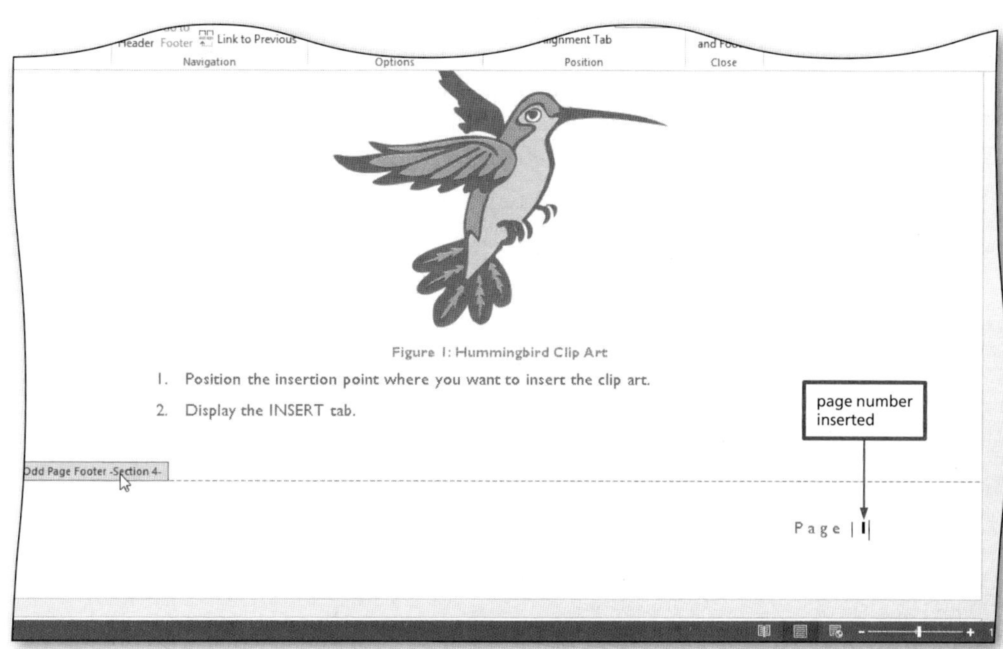

Figure 9–73

5

- Tap or click the Show Next button to display the next footer, in this case, Even Page Footer -Section 4-.
- Be sure the 'Link to Previous' button (HEADER & FOOTER TOOLS DESIGN tab | Navigation group) is not selected.
- Tap or click the 'Add Page Numbers' button (HEADER & FOOTER TOOLS DESIGN tab | Header & Footer group) to display the Add Page Numbers gallery.
- Tap or point to Current Position in the Add Page Numbers gallery to display the Current Position gallery.
- Tap or click 'Accent Bar 2' in the Current Position gallery to insert the selected page number in the footer (Figure 9–74).

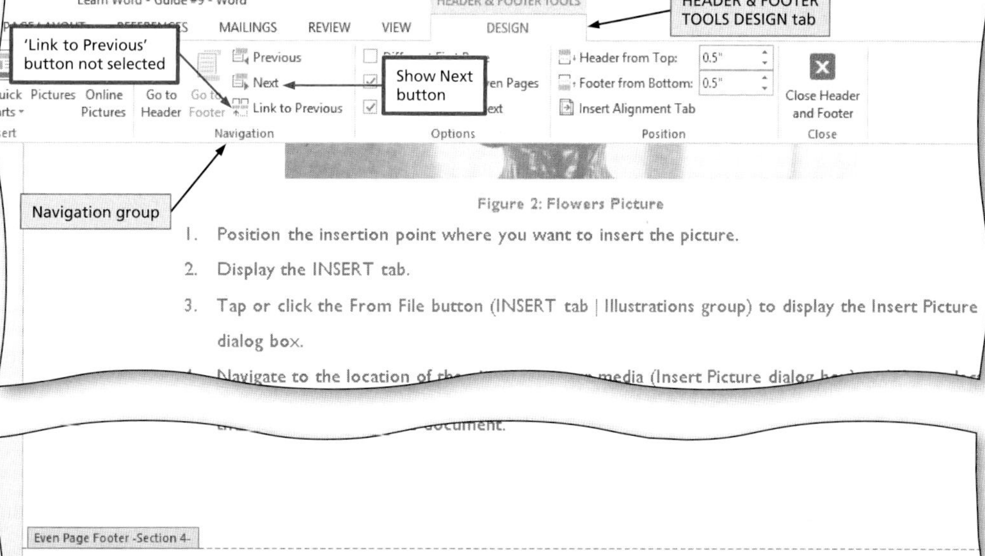

Figure 9–74

Q&A Can I create alternating headers?
Yes. Follow the same basic procedure, except insert a header building block or header text.

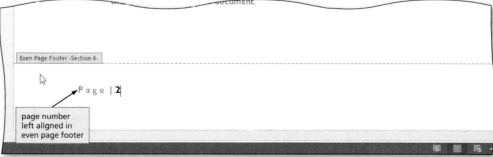

To Set a Gutter Margin

The reference document in this chapter is designed so that the inner margin between facing pages has extra space. ***Why?*** *Extra space on facing pages allows printed versions of the documents to be bound (such as stapled) — without the binding covering the words.* This extra space in the inner margin is called the **gutter margin**. The following steps set a three-quarter-inch left and right margin and a one-half-inch gutter margin.

- Display the PAGE LAYOUT tab.
- Tap or click the Adjust Margins button (PAGE LAYOUT tab | Page Setup group) and then tap or click Custom Margins in the Adjust Margins gallery to display the Page Setup dialog box.
- Type `.75` in the Left box, `.75` in the Right box, and `.5` in the Gutter box (Page Setup dialog box).
- Tap or click the Apply to arrow and then tap or click Whole document (Figure 9–75).

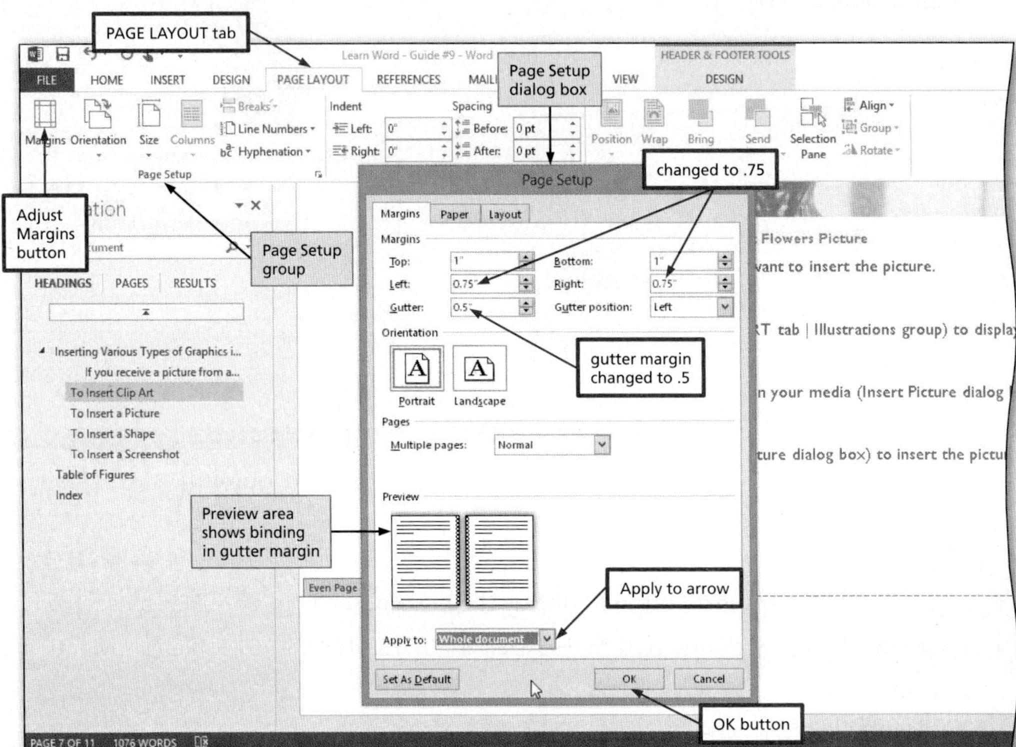

Figure 9–75

- Tap or click the OK button (Page Setup dialog box) to set the new margins for the entire document.

BTW
Header and Footer Margins
If you want the margin of the header or footer to be different from the default of one-half inch, you would adjust the margin in the 'Header Position from Top' or 'Footer Position from Bottom' boxes (HEADER & FOOTER TOOLS DESIGN tab | Position group) or in the Layout sheet of the Page Setup dialog box through the Page Setup Dialog Box Launcher (PAGE LAYOUT tab | Page Setup group). You also can specify alignment of items in the header or footer by tapping or clicking the 'Insert Alignment Tab' button (HEADER & FOOTER TOOLS DESIGN tab | Position group) and then tapping or clicking the desired alignment in the Alignment Tab dialog box.

To Check the Layout of the Printed Pages

To view the layout of all the pages in the document, the following steps display all the pages as they will print.

1. Open the Backstage view.
2. Tap or click the Print tab to display all pages of the document in the right pane, as shown in Figure 9–76. (If all pages are not displayed, change the Zoom level to 10%.)

Q&A Why do blank pages appear in the middle of the document?
When you insert even and odd headers or footers, Word may add pages to fill the gaps.

3. Close the Backstage view.

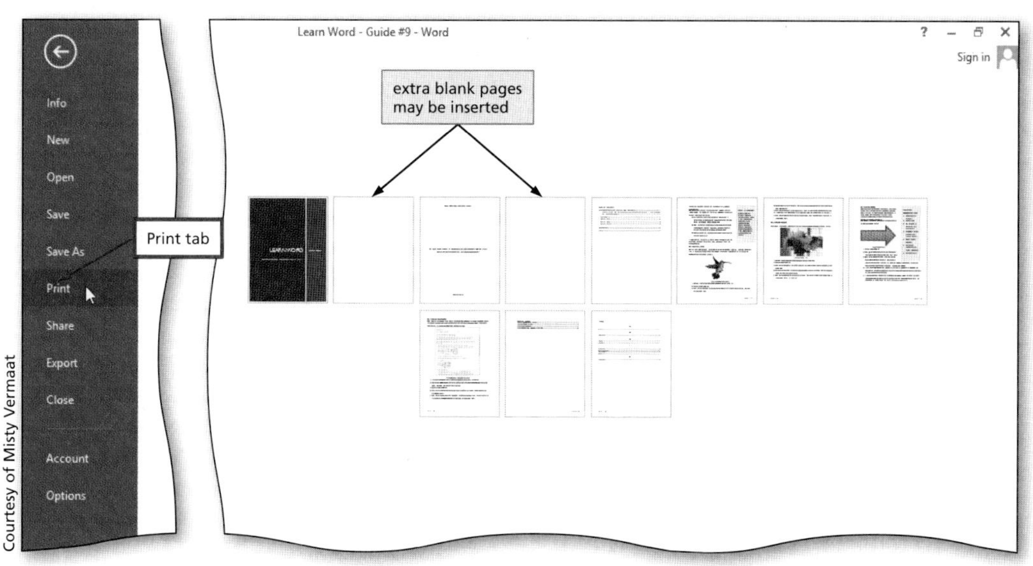

Figure 9–76

BTW

Set Print Scaling

If you wanted to ensure a document prints on a certain paper size, you can scale the document by opening the Backstage view, tapping or clicking the Print tab to display the Print gallery, tapping or clicking the bottom option in the Settings area (Print gallery), tapping or pointing to 'Scale to Paper Size', and then tapping or clicking the desired paper size before printing the document.

To Switch to Draft View

1 MODIFY REFERENCE DOCUMENT | 2 CREATE MASTER DOCUMENT | **3 ORGANIZE REFERENCE DOCUMENT**

To adjust the blank pages automatically inserted in the printed document by Word, you change the continuous section break at the top of the document to an odd page section break. The following step switches to Draft view. ***Why?*** *Section breaks are easy to see in Draft view.*

- Display the VIEW tab. Tap or click the Draft View button (VIEW tab | Views group) to switch to Draft view.
- Scroll to the top of the document and notice how different the document looks in Draft view (Figure 9–77).

Q&A What happened to the graphics, footers, and other items?

They do not appear in Draft view because Draft view is designed to make editing text in a document easier.

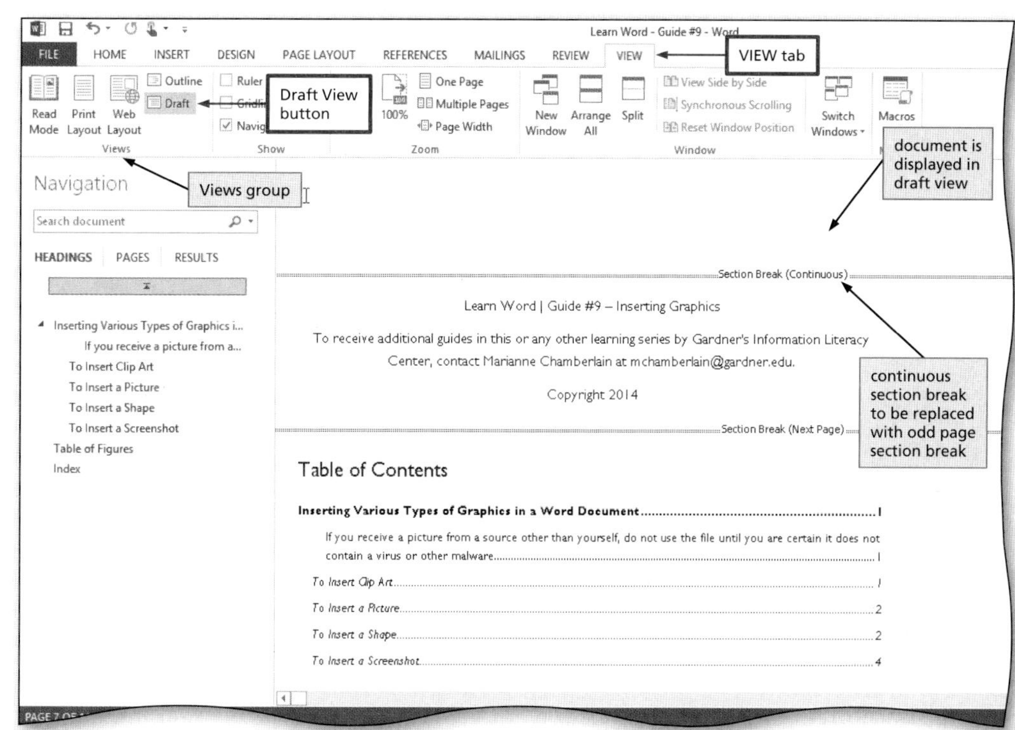

Figure 9–77

BTW
Different First Page
If you wanted only the first page of a document to have a different header or footer, you could place a check mark in the 'Different First Page' check box (HEADER & FOOTER TOOLS DESIGN tab | Options group). Doing so instructs Word to create a First Page Header or First Page Footer that can contain content that differs from the rest of the headers or footers.

To Insert an Odd Page Section Break

To fix the extra pages in the printed document, replace the continuous section break at the end of the title page with an odd page section break. With an odd page section break, Word starts the next section on an odd page instead of an even page.

1. Select the continuous section break at the bottom of the title page and then press the DELETE key to delete the selected section break.
2. If necessary, display the PAGE LAYOUT tab.
3. To insert an odd page section break, tap or click the 'Insert Page and Section Breaks' button (PAGE LAYOUT tab | Page Setup group) and then tap or click Odd Page in the Section Breaks area in the Insert Page and Section Breaks gallery (Figure 9–78).

Q&A
Can I insert even page section breaks?
Yes. To instruct Word to start the next section on an even page, tap or click Even Page in the Insert Page and Section Breaks gallery.

4. Tap or click the Print Layout button on the status bar to switch to Print Layout view.

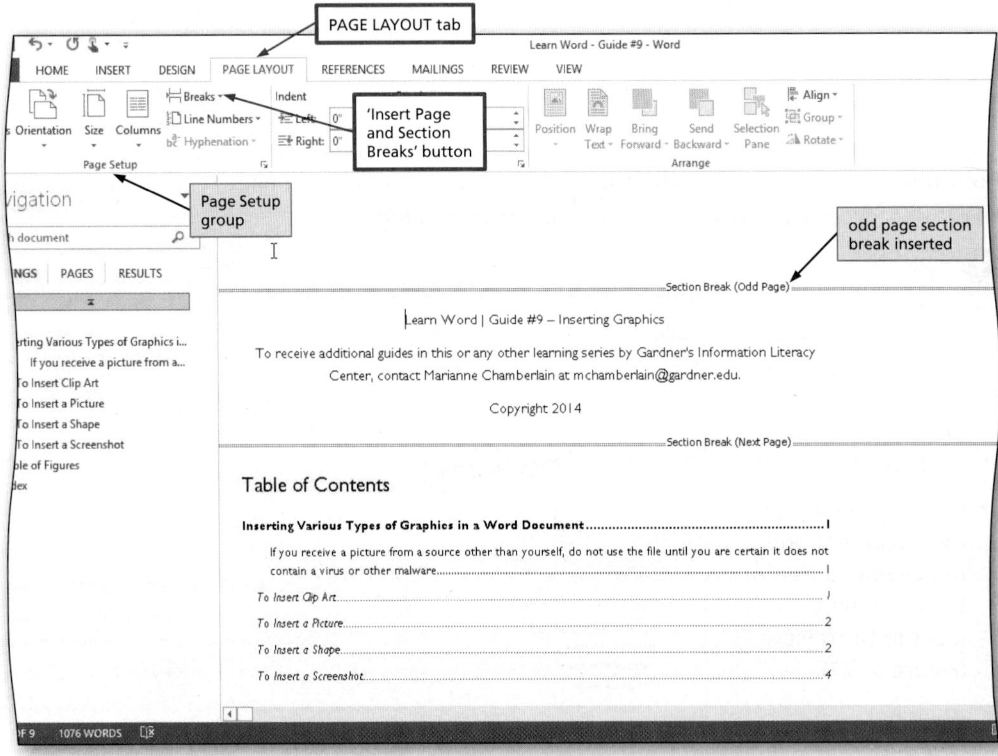

Figure 9–78

To Add a Bookmark

1 MODIFY REFERENCE DOCUMENT | 2 CREATE MASTER DOCUMENT | 3 ORGANIZE REFERENCE DOCUMENT

A **bookmark** is an item in a document that you name for future reference. The next steps add bookmarks. ***Why?*** *Bookmarks assist users in navigating through a document online. For example, you could bookmark the headings in the document, so that users easily could jump to these areas of the document.*

- Use the Navigation Pane to display the To Insert Clip Art heading in the document window and then select the heading.
- Display the INSERT tab.
- Tap or click the 'Insert a Bookmark' button (INSERT tab | Links group) to display the Bookmark dialog box.
- Type **ClipArt** in the Bookmark name text box (Figure 9–79).

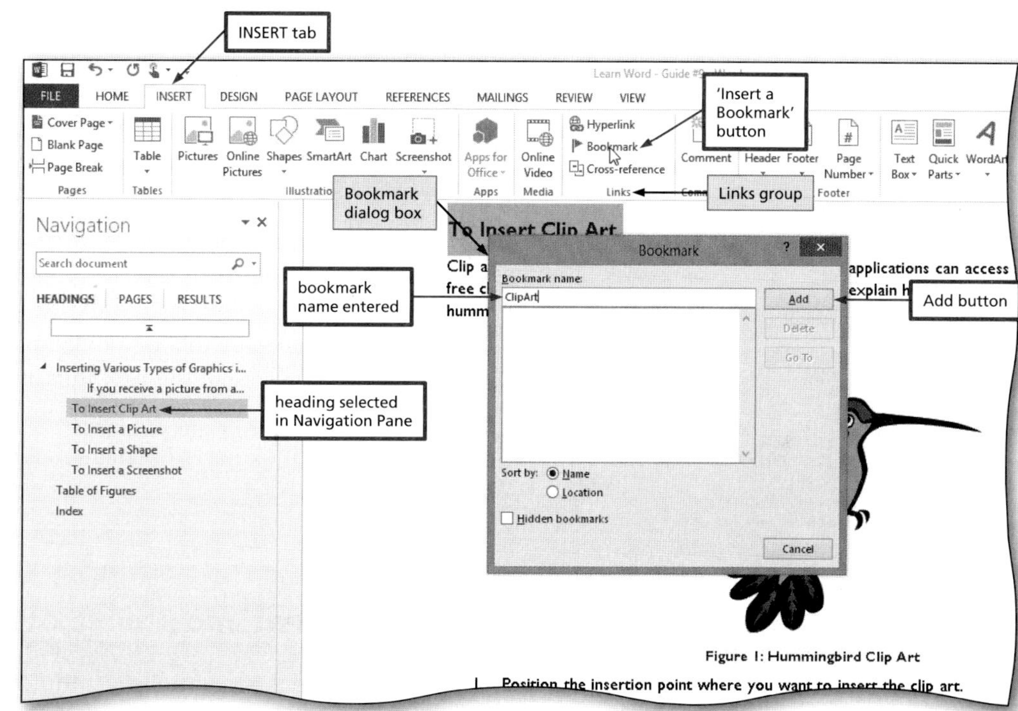

Figure 9–79

Q&A What are the rules for bookmark names?

Bookmark names can contain only letters, numbers, and the underscore character (_). They also must begin with a letter and cannot contain spaces.

- Tap or click the Add button (Bookmark dialog box) to add the bookmark name to the list of existing bookmarks in the document.

- Repeat Steps 1 and 2 for these headings in the document: To Insert a Picture, To Insert a Shape, and To Insert a Screenshot (use bookmark names Picture, Shape, and Screenshot).

To Go to a Bookmark

Once you have added bookmarks, you can jump to them by performing these steps.

1. Tap or click the 'Insert a Bookmark' button (INSERT tab | Links group) to display the Bookmark dialog box (Figure 9–79).
2. Tap or click the bookmark name in the Bookmark name list (Bookmark dialog box) and then tap or click the Go To button.

or

1. Press the F5 key to display the Go To sheet in the Find and Replace dialog box.
2. Tap or click Bookmark in the list (Find and Replace dialog box), select the bookmark name, and then tap or click the Go To button.

BTW
Link to Graphic
If you wanted to link a graphic in a document to a webpage, you would tap or click the 'Add a Hyperlink' button (INSERT tab | Links group), enter the web address in the Address text box (Insert Hyperlink dialog box), and then tap or click the OK button. To display the webpage associated with the graphic, tap or CTRL+click the graphic.

To Insert a Hyperlink

Instead of or in addition to bookmarks in online documents, you can insert hyperlinks that link one part of a document to another. If you wanted to insert a hyperlink that links to a heading or bookmark in the document, you would follow these steps.

1. Select the text to be a hyperlink.
2. Tap or click the 'Add a Hyperlink' button (INSERT tab | Links group) to display the Insert Hyperlink dialog box.
3. In the Link to bar (Insert Hyperlink dialog box), tap or click 'Place in This Document', so that Word displays all the headings and bookmarks in the document.
4. Tap or click the heading or bookmark to which you want to link.
5. Tap or click the OK button.

BTW
Conserving Ink and Toner
If you want to conserve ink or toner, you can instruct Word to print draft quality documents by tapping or clicking FILE on the ribbon to open the Backstage view, tapping or clicking Options in the Backstage view to display the Word Options dialog box, tapping or clicking Advanced in the left pane (Word Options dialog box), sliding or scrolling to the Print area in the right pane, placing a check mark in the 'Use draft quality' check box, and then tapping or clicking the OK button. Then, use the Backstage view to print the document as usual.

To Save and Print a Document and Then Exit Word

The reference document for this project now is complete. Save the document, print it, and then exit Word.

1. Save the document with the same file name.
2. If requested by your instructor, print the finished document (shown in Figure 9–1 on page WD 539). Another option is to save the document as a PDF file and submit the PDF in the format requested by your instructor.
3. Exit Word.

Chapter Summary

In this chapter, you have learned how to insert a screenshot, add captions, create cross-references, use the Building Blocks Organizer, work with master documents and subdocuments, and create a table of contents, a table of figures, and an index. The items listed below include all the new Word skills you have learned in this chapter, with the tasks grouped by activity.

Enter and Edit Text
Switch to Outline View (WD 562)
Add Entries in Outline View (WD 562)
Show First Line Only (WD 564)
Insert a Subdocument (WD 564)
Exit Outline View (WD 567)
Insert a Cover Page (WD 568)
Insert a Blank Page (WD 572)
Find a Format (WD 576)
Use the Navigation Pane to Go to a Heading in a Document (WD 581)
Switch to Draft View (WD 593)
Add a Bookmark (WD 594)
Go to a Bookmark (WD 595)
Insert a Hyperlink (WD 596)

Format a Page
Change Paragraph Spacing in a Document (WD 551)
Adjust Vertical Alignment on a Page (WD 571)
Create Alternating Footers Using a Footer Building Block (WD 589)
Set a Gutter Margin (WD 592)

Reference Settings
Add a Caption (WD 544)
Create a Cross-Reference (WD 545)
Mark an Index Entry (WD 549)
Mark Multiple Index Entries (WD 551)
Create a Table of Contents (WD 573)
Update Page Numbers in a Table of Contents (WD 575)

Retain Formatting when Adding Text to the Table of Contents (WD 578)
Update the Entire Table of Contents (WD 579)
Change the Format of a Table of Contents (WD 580)
Create a Table of Figures (WD 582)
Change the Format of the Table of Figures (WD 583)
Edit a Caption and Update the Table of Figures (WD 583)
Build an Index (WD 585)
Edit an Index Entry (WD 587)
Delete an Index Entry (WD 587)
Update an Index (WD 588)
Change the Format of the Index (WD 588)
Delete an Index (WD 589)

Word Settings
Recover Unsaved Documents (Draft Versions) (WD 560)
Delete All Unsaved Documents (Draft Versions) (WD 560)

Work with Graphics
Insert a Screenshot (WD 542)
Go to an Object (WD 547)
Insert a Sidebar Text Box (WD 552)
Link Text Boxes (WD 556)
Compress Pictures (WD 558)
Save Pictures in Other Formats (WD 558)
Change the Symbol Format in a Bulleted List (WD 559)

CONSIDER THIS: PLAN AHEAD

What decisions will you need to make when creating reference documents?
Use these guidelines as you complete the assignments in this chapter and create your own reference documents outside of this class.

1. Prepare a document to be included in a longer document.
   a) If a document contains multiple illustrations (figures), each figure should have a caption and be referenced from within the text.
   b) All terms in the document that should be included in the index should be marked as an index entry.
2. Include elements common to a reference document such as a title page, a table of contents, and an index.
   a) The title page entices passersby to take a copy of the document.
   b) A table of contents at the beginning of the document and an index at the end helps a reader locate topics within the document.
   c) If a document contains several illustrations, you also should include a table of figures.
3. Prepare the document for distribution, including gutter margins for binding, bookmarks, and hyperlinks as appropriate.

CONSIDER THIS

How should you submit solutions to questions in the assignments identified with a symbol?
Every assignment in this book contains one or more questions identified with a symbol. These questions require you to think beyond the assigned document. Present your solutions to the questions in the format required by your instructor. Possible formats may include one or more of these options: write the answer; create a document that contains the answer; present your answer to the class; discuss your answer in a group; record the answer as audio or video using a webcam, smartphone, or portable media player; or post answers on a blog, wiki, or website.

Apply Your Knowledge

Reinforce the skills and apply the concepts you learned in this chapter.

Working with Outline View

Note: To complete this assignment, you will be required to use the Data Files for Students. Visit www.cengage.com/ct/studentdownload for detailed instructions or contact your instructor for information about accessing the required files.

Instructions: Run Word. Open the document, Apply 9-1 Information Literacy Outline Draft, from the Data Files for Students. The document is an outline for a paper. You are to modify the outline in Outline view. The final outline is shown in Figure 9–80.

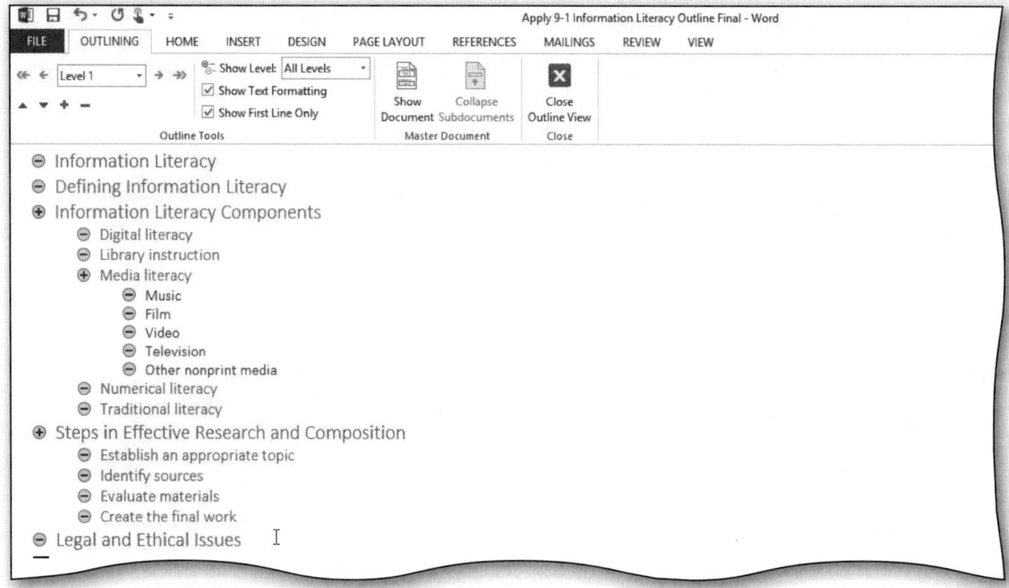

Figure 9–80

Perform the following tasks:

1. If necessary, switch to Outline view.
2. Move the item on the third line, Information Literacy, up two lines so that it is at the top of the outline.
3. In the Information Literacy Components section, move the item, Library instruction, down one line.
4. Practice collapsing and expanding by collapsing the Information Literacy Components item and then expanding the Information Literacy Components item.
5. Demote the five items in the outline below the item, Media literacy (Music, Film, Video, Television, and Other nonprint media) so that they are Level 3 instead of Level 2.
6. Promote the item, Identify sources, so that it is Level 2 instead of Level 3.
7. Change the word, Reading, in the Steps in Effective Reading and Composition item to the word, Research, so that it reads: Steps in Effective Research and Composition.
8. Insert an item, called Traditional literacy, as a Level 2 item below the Numerical literacy item.
9. Delete the item called Review media.
10. Promote the item, Legal and Ethical Issues, to Heading 1 (Level 1).
11. Remove the check mark in the 'Show Text Formatting' check box (OUTLINING tab | Outline Tools group). Place the check mark in the check box again. What is the purpose of this check box?

12. Close Outline view. How does the document differ when displayed in Print Layout view?
13. If requested by your instructor, add your name at the end of the first line of the outline. Save the modified file with a new file name, Apply 9-1 Information Literacy Outline Final. Submit the document in the format specified by your instructor.
14. Answer the questions posed in #11 and #12. What are two different ways to expand and collapse items in an outline, to move items up and down an outline, and to demote and promote items in an outline?

Extend Your Knowledge

Extend the skills you learned in this chapter and experiment with new skills. You may need to use Help to complete the assignment.

Working with Screenshots

Note: To complete this assignment, you will be required to use the Data Files for Students. Visit www.cengage.com/ct/studentdownload for detailed instructions or contact your instructor for information about accessing the required files.

Instructions: Run Word. Open the document, Extend 9-1 Word Screenshots Draft, from the Data Files for Students. You will insert a screenshot and a screen clipping in the document.

Perform the following tasks:

1. Use Help to expand your knowledge about screenshots, screen clippings, saving images, and print scaling.
2. Change the page from portrait to landscape orientation.
3. Run Word again and create a blank document so that you have two separate Word windows open. Switch to the Word window with the Extend 9-1 Word Screenshots Draft file open. Insert a screenshot, centered on the blank line below the first paragraph.
4. Insert a screen clipping of the ribbon, centered on the blank line below the second paragraph.
5. Save the Word screenshot as a JPEG file with the name, Extend 9-1 Word Screenshot.
6. Save the screen clipping of the ribbon as a JPEG file with the file name, Extend 9-1 Word Ribbon Screen Clipping.
7. Add a border or shadow to the screenshot and the screen clipping.
8. Add these callouts to the screenshot: Quick Access Toolbar, ribbon, status bar.
9. Add these callouts to the screen clipping: tab, group, button (Figure 9–81).

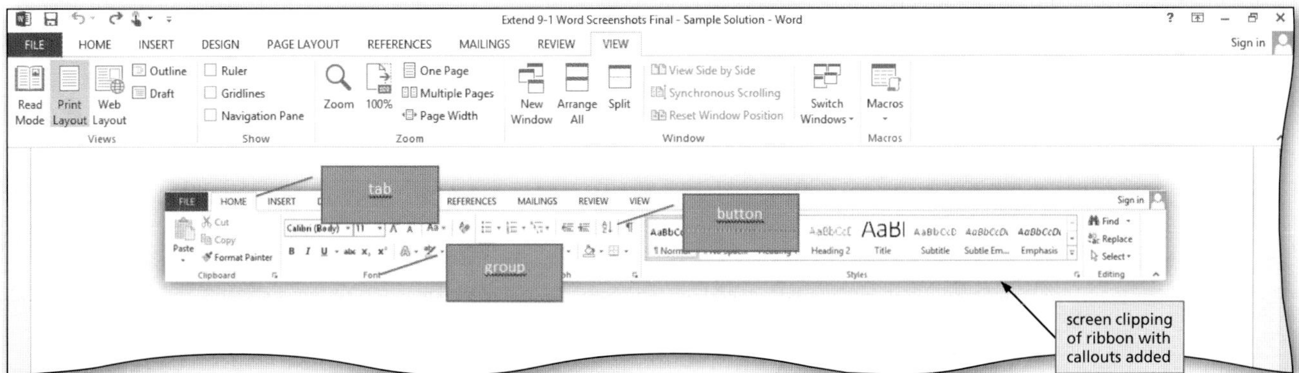

Figure 9–81

Continued >

STUDENT ASSIGNMENTS

Extend Your Knowledge *continued*

10. Print the document so that it fits on a single page; that is, make sure it is scaled to the paper size.
11. Locate the saved JPEG files and then double-tap or double-click them. In what program did they open?
12. If requested by your instructor, add a text box to the Word screen with your name in it. Save the modified file with a new file name, Extend 9-1 Word Screenshots Final. Submit the documents in the format specified by your instructor.
13. Answer the question posed in #11. How did you print the document so that it fits on a single page? What changes could you make to the document so that it all fits on a single page when you view it on the screen?

Analyze, Correct, Improve

Analyze a document, correct all errors, and improve it.

Formatting a Reference Document

Note: To complete this assignment, you will be required to use the Data Files for Students. Visit www.cengage.com/ct/studentdownload for detailed instructions or contact your instructor for information about accessing the required files.

Instructions: Run Word. Open the document, Analyze 9-1 Operating Systems Draft, from the Data Files for Students. The document is a reference document whose elements are not formatted properly (Figure 9–82). You are to edit, modify, and update the table of contents and index; insert and delete section breaks; change bullet symbols; and add and delete bookmarks. Open the Navigation Pane so that you can use it to go to specific headings and pages as referenced in this exercise.

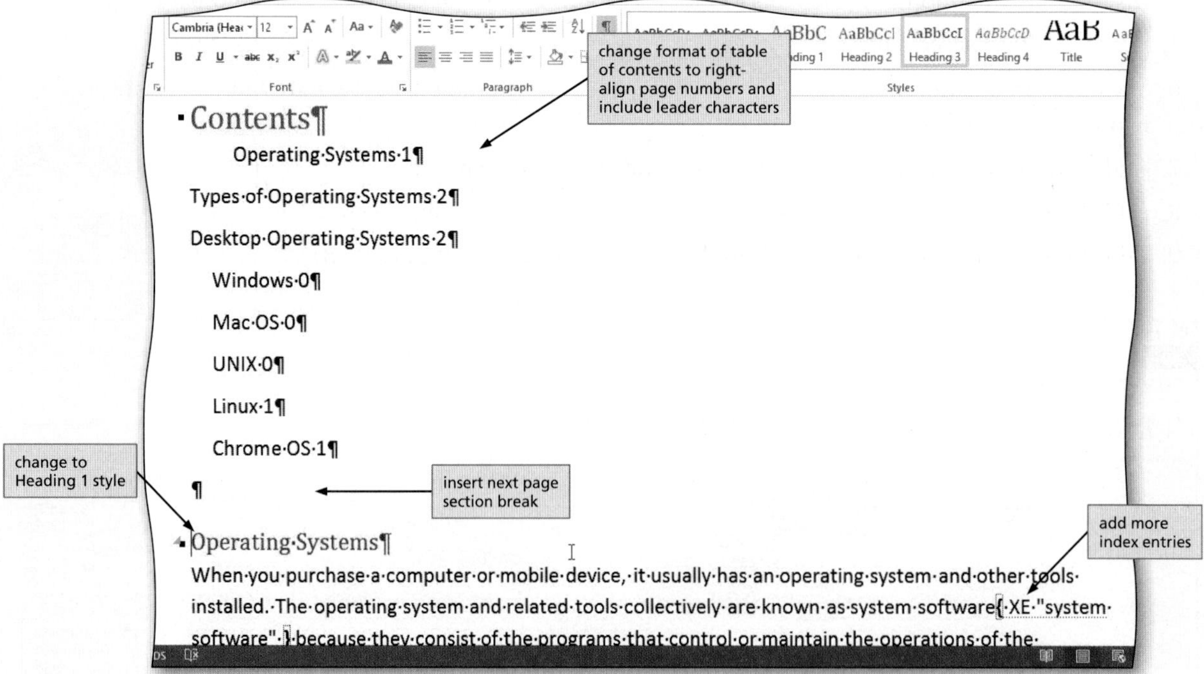

Figure 9–82

Perform the following tasks:

1. Correct In the reference document, correct the following items:

a. Change the title, ALL ABOUT COMPUTER OPERATING SYSTEMS, on the cover page to a color that is easier to see.

b. Insert a next page section break between the table of contents and the Operating Systems heading. Change the Operating Systems heading from a Heading 3 style to a Heading 1 style.

c. Insert a page number in the section starting with the Operating Systems heading. Change the starting page number of the page with the Operating Systems heading to 1. Update the table of contents. Change the format of the table of contents to Automatic Table 2.

d. Notice the page numbers are not correct at the end of the table of contents because an extra section break is in the document. Switch to Draft view and then delete the next page section break above the Windows heading. Switch back to Print Layout view. Update the table of contents again. If necessary, adjust starting page numbers again and then update the table of contents again.

e. Change the format of the Index heading to Heading 1. Update the table of contents again. Change the format of the index to a format other than From template. Right-align the page numbers and place a tab leader character between the index entries and the page numbers.

f. The document currently contains eight index entries. Read through the document and mark at least 15 more entries. Lowercase the C in the Client operating systems index entry so that it reads: client operating systems. Update the index.

2. Improve Enhance the document by changing the bullet symbol in both bulleted lists to one other than the dot symbol. Insert a bookmark for each heading in the document. Use the Go To command to practice locating bookmarks in the document. Delete the bookmark for the Index heading. Make any other adjustments you deem appropriate to the reference document. If requested by your instructor, change the name on the title page to your name. Save the modified document with the file name, Analyze 9-1 Operating Systems Final, and then submit it in the format specified by your instructor.

3. Do you prefer working in Draft view or Print Layout view? Why?

In the Labs

Design and/or create a document using the guidelines, concepts, and skills presented in this chapter. Labs 1 and 2, which increase in difficulty, require you to create solutions based on what you learned in the chapter; Lab 3 requires you to create a solution, which uses cloud and web technologies, by learning and investigating on your own from general guidance.

Lab 1: Creating a Reference Document with a Cover Page, a Table of Contents, and an Index

Note: To complete this assignment, you will be required to use the Data Files for Students. Visit www.cengage.com/ct/studentdownload for detailed instructions or contact your instructor for information about accessing the required files.

Problem: As a part-time assistant at Learning Computers Institute you have been asked to prepare a guide briefly describing input, output, and storage. A miniature version of this document is shown in Figure 9–83 on the next page. A draft of the body of the document is on the Data Files for Students.

Continued >

In the Labs *continued*

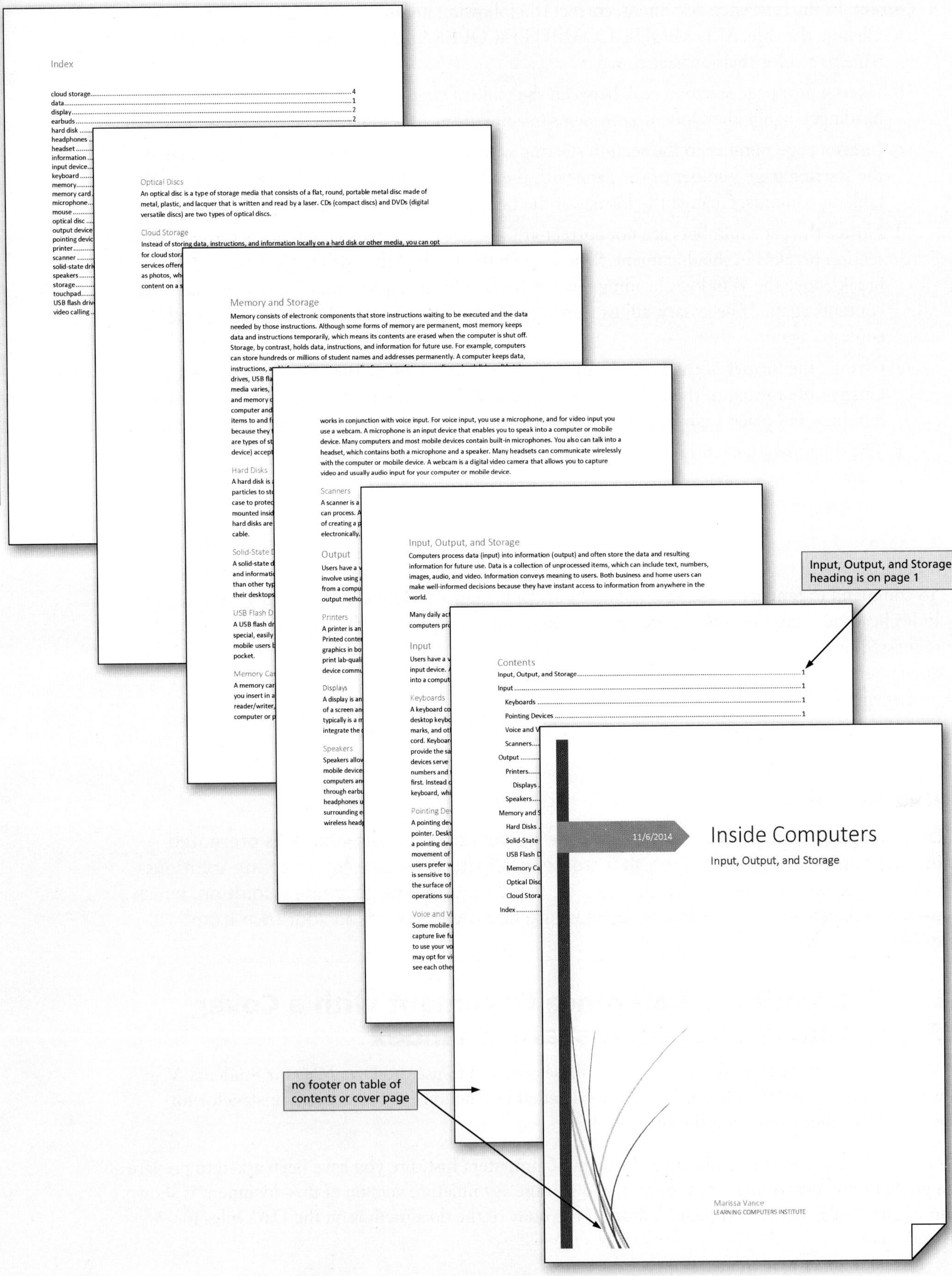

Index

Optical Discs

An optical disc is a type of storage media that consists of a flat, round, portable metal disc made of metal, plastic, and lacquer that is written and read by a laser. CDs (compact discs) and DVDs (digital versatile discs) are two types of optical discs.

Cloud Storage

Instead of storing data, instructions, and information locally on a hard disk or other media, you can opt

Memory and Storage

Memory consists of electronic components that store instructions waiting to be executed and the data needed by those instructions. Although some forms of memory are permanent, most memory keeps data and instructions temporarily, which means its contents are erased when the computer is shut off. Storage, by contrast, holds data, instructions, and information for future use. For example, computers can store hundreds or millions of student names and addresses permanently. A computer keeps data,

works in conjunction with voice input. For voice input, you use a microphone, and for video input you use a webcam. A microphone is an input device that enables you to speak into a computer or mobile device. Many computers and most mobile devices contain built-in microphones. You also can talk into a headset, which contains both a microphone and a speaker. Many headsets can communicate wirelessly with the computer or mobile device. A webcam is a digital video camera that allows you to capture video and usually audio input for your computer or mobile device.

Input, Output, and Storage

Computers process data (input) into information (output) and often store the data and resulting information for future use. Data is a collection of unprocessed items, which can include text, numbers, images, audio, and video. Information conveys meaning to users. Both business and home users can make well-informed decisions because they have instant access to information from anywhere in the world.

Contents

11/6/2014

Inside Computers

Input, Output, and Storage

Marissa Vance

LEARNING COMPUTERS INSTITUTE

Input, Output, and Storage heading is on page 1

no footer on table of contents or cover page

Figure 9–83

Perform the following tasks:

1. Open the document, Lab 9-1 Input Output Storage Draft, from the Data Files for Students. Save the document with a new file name, Lab 9-1 Input Output Storage Final.
2. Create a title page by inserting the Whisp style cover page. Use the following information on the title page: title – Inside Computers; subtitle – Input, Output, and Storage; date – *use today's date*; author – *use your name*; company name – Learning Computers Institute.
3. Insert a blank page between the title page and the Input, Output, and Storage heading.
4. Create a table of contents on the blank page using the Automatic Table 1 style. Insert a continuous section break at the end of the table of contents. Insert the Banded built-in footer starting on the page with the section titled Input, Output, and Storage. Update the table of contents.
5. Mark the following terms in the document as index entries: Data, Information, input device, keyboard, pointing device, mouse, touchpad, video calling, microphone, headset, scanner, output device, printer, display, Speakers, earbuds, headphones, Memory, Storage, hard disk, solid-state drive, USB flash drive, memory card, optical disc, and Cloud storage. Lowercase the first letter in the index entries for the words, Data, Information, Speakers, Memory, Storage, and Cloud storage so that the entire entry appears in lowercase letters in the index.
6. On a separate page at the end of the document, insert the word Index formatted in the Heading 1 style and then build an index for the document. Remember to hide formatting marks prior to building the index. Use the From template format using one column, with right-aligned page numbers and leader characters. Update the table of contents so that it includes the index.
7. Save the document again and then submit it in the format specified by your instructor.
8. If you wanted the index entries to appear in bold in the index but remain not bold in the document, what steps would you take to accomplish this?

Lab 2: Using a Master Document and Subdocument for a Reference Document

Note: To complete this assignment, you will be required to use the Data Files for Students. Visit www.cengage.com/ct/studentdownload for detailed instructions or contact your instructor for information about accessing the required files.

Problem: Your supervisor at your part-time job has asked you to prepare a guide about the history of the Internet and how the Internet works. A miniature version of this document is shown in Figure 9–84 on the next page. The document is a master document with one subdocument. The subdocument is on the Data Files for Students.

Perform the following tasks:

1. Open the file Lab 9-2 Internet Subdocument Draft, from the Data Files for Students. Save the document with the file name, Lab 9-2 Internet Subdocument Final.
2. Add the following captions to the figures: first figure – Figure 1: Popular Broadband Internet Service Technologies; second figure – Figure 2: Data Usage Examples; third figure – Figure 3: IPv4 and IPv6 Addresses and Domain Name for Google's Website.
3. Replace the occurrences of XX in the document with cross-references to the figure captions.
4. Insert a Retrospect Sidebar text box on the first page. Enter this text in the text box: **`Who owns the Internet?`** Select the description placeholder and then type: **`No single person, company, or government agency owns the Internet. Each organization on the Internet is responsible only for maintaining its own network.`** Press the ENTER key. Type: **`What is the W3C?`** Press the ENTER key.

Continued >

In the Labs *continued*

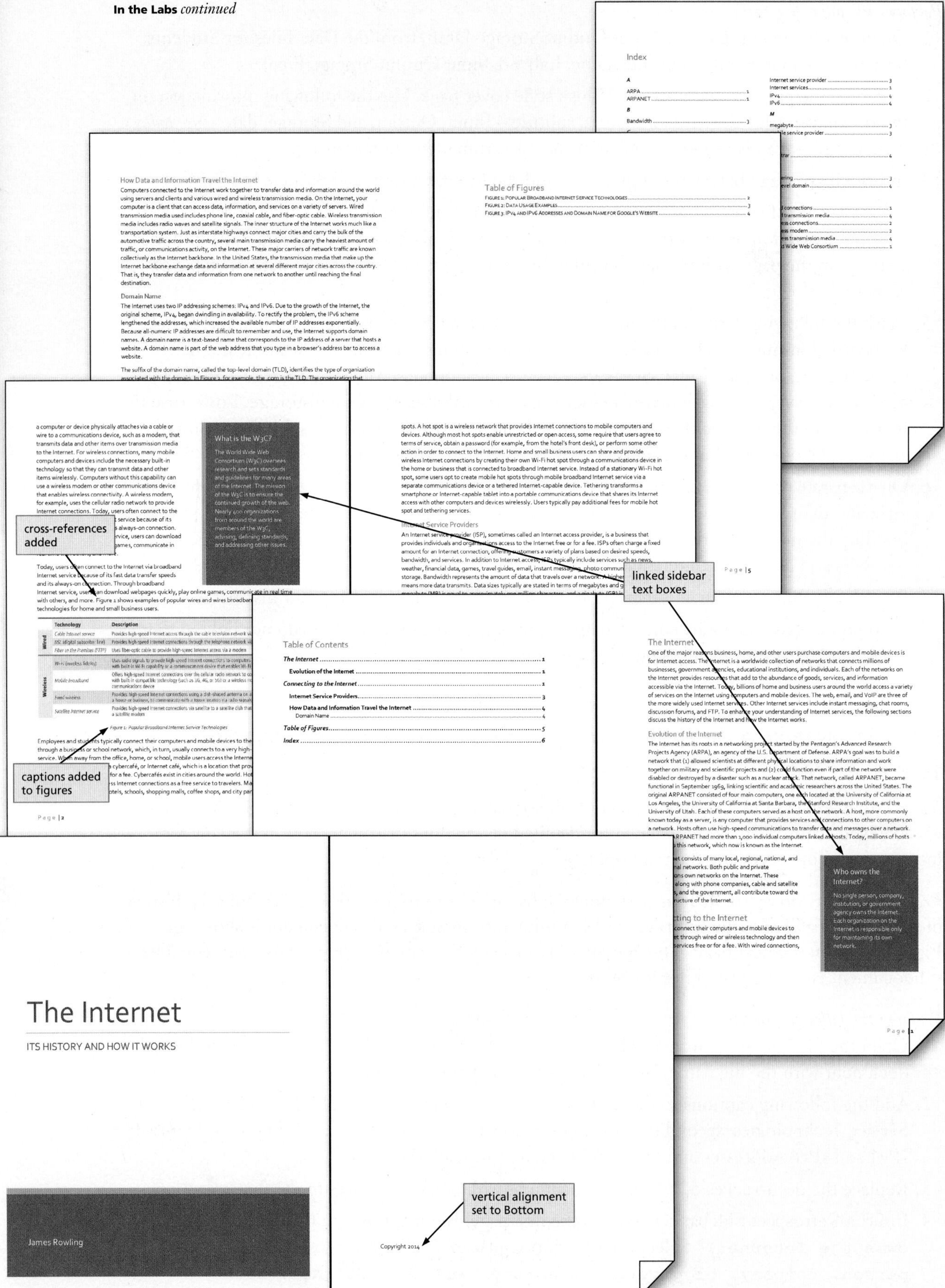

Figure 9–84

Type: **`The World Wide Web Consortium (W3C) oversees research and sets standards and guidelines for many areas of the Internet. The mission of the W3C is to ensure the continued growth of the web. Nearly 400 organizations from around the world are members of the W3C, advising, defining standards, and addressing other issues.`** Format the second question the same as the first.

5. On the next page, insert another Retrospect Sidebar text box and then delete the contents of the second text box. Link the two text boxes together. Resize each text box so that each one contains just one question and answer. Move the first text box to the bottom of the first page and the second text box to the top of the second page. Save and close the document.
6. Create a new document. In Outline view, type **`Copyright 2014`** as the first line formatted as Body Text, and the remaining lines containing the headings Table of Figures and Index. Insert a next page section break between each line.
7. Save the master document with the file name, Lab 9-2 Internet Master Document.
8. Between the Copyright line and Table of Figures headings, insert the subdocument named Lab 9-2 Internet Subdocument Final.
9. Switch to Print Layout view.
10. Create a cover page by inserting the Retrospect style cover page. Use the following information on the title page: title – The Internet; subtitle – ITS HISTORY AND HOW IT WORKS; author – *use your name*. Delete the company name and company address placeholders.
11. Format the copyright page with a vertical alignment of Bottom.
12. Insert a blank page between the copyright page and the heading, The Internet.
13. Create a table of contents on the blank page using the Distinctive style, right-aligned page numbers, and dots for leader characters.
14. At the end of the document, format the Table of Figures heading using the Heading 1 style. Then, add a table of figures below the heading using the Formal format with right-aligned page numbers and a tab leader character.
15. Build an index for the document. Remember to hide formatting marks prior to building the index. Use the Formal format in two columns with right-aligned page numbers.
16. Beginning on the fourth page (with the heading, The Internet), create alternating footers. Insert a right tab for the odd page footer. Align left the even page footer. Insert the Accent Bar 2 page number style. The cover page, copyright page, or table of contents should not contain the footer.
17. Resize Figure 2 so that it fits at the bottom of page 3, and resize Figure 3 so that the body text ends on page 4.
18. For the entire document, set the left and right margins to .75" (Moderate) and set a gutter margin of .5".
19. Insert a bookmark for each Heading 2 in the document.
20. Compress the pictures in the document.
21. Update the table of contents, table of figures, and index.
22. Make any additional adjustments so that the document looks like Figure 9–84.
23. Save the document again and then submit it in the format specified by your instructor. If requested by your instructor, print the document back to back.
24. If you added a figure in the Evolution of the Internet section, how would you renumber the remaining figures in the document?

Continued >

STUDENT ASSIGNMENTS

In the Labs *continued*

Lab 3: Expand Your World: Cloud and Web Technologies
Using an Online Photo Editor

Note: To complete this assignment, you will be required to use the Data Files for Students. Visit www.cengage.com/ct/studentdownload for detailed instructions or contact your instructor for information about accessing the required files.

Problem: Assume you have a digital photo that you want to edit before including it in a Word document.

Instructions: Perform the following tasks:

1. Run a browser. Search for the text, online photo editor, using a search engine. Visit several of the online photo editors and determine which you would like to use to edit a photo. Navigate to the desired online photo editor.
2. In the photo editor, open the image called Balloon from the Data Files for Students (Figure 9–85). Use the photo editor to enhance the image. Apply at least five enhancements. Which enhancements did you apply?

Figure 9–85

3. If requested by your instructor, add your name as a text element to the photo.
4. Save the photo with the file name, Lab 9-3 Revised Balloon. In what format did the online photo editor save the file? Submit the photo in the format specified by your instructor.
5. Answer the questions posed in #2 and #4. Which online photo editors did you evaluate? Which one did you select to use, and why? Do you prefer using the online photo editor or Word to enhance images?

Consider This: Your Turn

Apply your creative thinking and problem solving skills to design and implement a solution.

Note: To complete these assignments, you may be required to use the Data Files for Students. See the inside back cover of this book for instructions on downloading the Data Files for Students, or contact your instructor for information about accessing the required files.

1: Create a Reference Document about File and Disk Manager Tools

Personal

Part 1: In your Introduction to Computers class, you have been asked to create a reference document that discusses various file and disk manager tools. You decide to use master documents and subdocuments. The subdocument you created is a file named, Your Turn 9-1 - File and Disk Manager Draft, located on the Data Files for Students. In this subdocument, mark at least 20 terms as index entries. Insert at least three screenshots of various file and disk manager tools on your computer or mobile device and then add captions to the screenshot images. Compress the images and then save the subdocument file using a different file name. Create a master document that contains the subdocument file. The master document also should have a title page (cover page), a table of contents, a table of figures, and an index. Format the document with a footer that contains a page number. Use the concepts and techniques presented in this chapter to organize and format the document. Submit your assignment in the format specified by your instructor.

Part 2: You made several decisions while creating the reference document in this assignment: which terms to mark as index entries, which screenshot images to include, what text to use for captions, and how to organize and format the subdocument and master document (table of contents, table of figures, index, etc.). What was the rationale behind each of these decisions? When you proofread the document, what further revisions did you make and why?

2: Create a Reference Document about Productivity Office Applications

Professional

Part 1: As an assistant at a local computer store, your supervisor has asked you to create a reference document that discusses types of productivity office applications. You decide to use master documents and subdocuments. The subdocument you created is a file named, Your Turn 9-2 - Productivity Office Applications Draft, located on the Data Files for Students. In this subdocument, mark at least 20 terms as index entries. Insert at least three screenshots of various productivity applications on your computer or mobile device and then add captions to the screenshot images. Compress the images and then save the subdocument file using a different file name. Create a master document that contains the subdocument file. The master document also should have a title page (cover page), a table of contents, a table of figures, and an index. Format the document with a footer that contains a page number. Use the concepts and techniques presented in this chapter to organize and format the document. Submit your assignment in the format specified by your instructor.

Part 2: You made several decisions while creating the reference document in this assignment: which terms to mark as index entries, which screenshot images to include, what text to use for captions, and how to organize and format the subdocument and master document (table of contents, table of figures, index, etc.). What was the rationale behind each of these decisions? When you proofread the document, what further revisions did you make and why?

Continued >

Consider This: Your Turn *continued*

3: Create a Reference Document about Local Entertainment

Research and Collaboration

Part 1: As coworkers at the village hall, your team has been asked to create a reference document that discusses local community events and activities. You decide to use master documents and subdocuments. Each team member should research three events or activities and create a subdocument that presents these events and activities under separate headings. Each subdocument should contain at least one figure. For the figures, you can use screenshots, digital photos, or scanned images. As a group, create the master document that includes the three subdocuments. The master document also should have a title page (cover page), a table of contents, a table of figures, and an index.

Use the concepts and techniques presented in this chapter to organize and format the document. Be sure to check the spelling and grammar of the finished document. Submit your team assignment in the format specified by your instructor.

Part 2: You made several decisions while creating the reference document in this assignment: text to use, which terms to mark as index entries, which images to include, and how to organize and format the subdocuments and master document (table of contents, table of figures, index, etc.). What was the rationale behind each of these decisions? When you proofread the document, what further revisions did you make and why?

Learn Online

Reinforce what you learned in this chapter with games, exercises, training, and many other online activities and resources.

Student Companion Site Reinforcement activities and resources are available at no additional cost on www.cengagebrain.com. Visit www.cengage.com/ct/studentdownload for detailed instructions about accessing the resources available at the Student Companion Site.

SAM Put your skills into practice with SAM! If you have a SAM account, go to www.cengage.com/sam2013 to access SAM assignments for this chapter.

10 Creating a Template for an Online Form

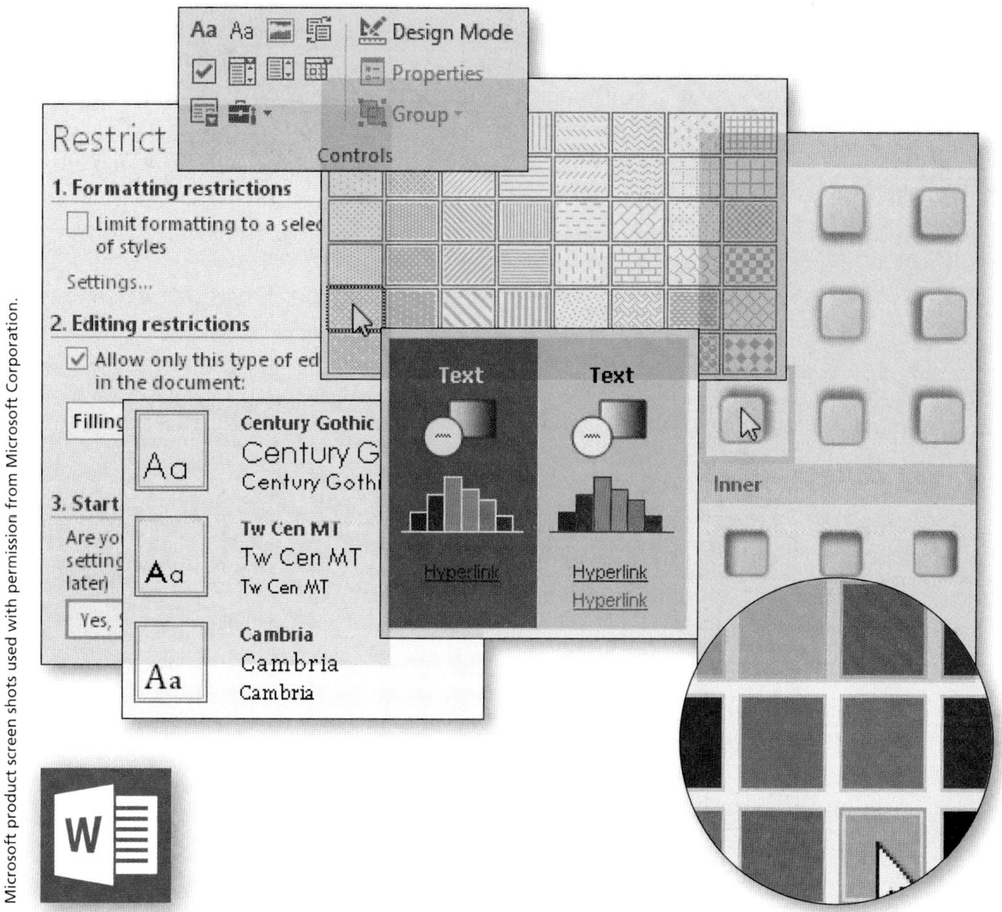

Objectives

You will have mastered the material in this chapter when you can:

- Save a document as a template
- Change paper size
- Change page color
- Insert a borderless table in a form
- Show the DEVELOPER tab
- Insert plain text, drop-down list, check box, rich text, combo box, and date picker content controls
- Edit placeholder text
- Change properties of content controls
- Insert and format a rectangle shape
- Customize a theme
- Protect a form
- Open a new document based on a template
- Fill in a form

10 Creating a Template for an Online Form

Introduction

During your personal and professional life, you undoubtedly have filled in countless forms. Whether a federal tax form, a time card, a job application, an order, a deposit slip, a request, or a survey, a form is designed to collect information. In the past, forms were printed; that is, you received the form on a piece of paper, filled it in with a pen or pencil, and then returned it manually. With an **online form**, you use a computer to access, fill in, and then return the form. In Word, you easily can create an online form for electronic distribution; you also can fill in that same form using Word.

Project — Online Form

Today, people are concerned with using resources efficiently. To minimize paper waste, protect the environment, enhance office efficiency, and improve access to data, many businesses have moved toward a paperless office. Thus, online forms have replaced many paper forms. You access online forms on a website, on your company's intranet, or from your inbox if you receive the form via email.

The project in this chapter uses Word to produce the online form shown in Figure 10–1. Happy Homes is a cleaning service interested in customer feedback. Instead of sending a survey via the postal service, Happy Homes will send the survey via email to customers for whom it has email addresses. Upon receipt of the online form (a survey), the customer fills in the form, saves it, and then sends it back via email to Happy Homes.

If you are using your finger on a touch screen and are having difficulty completing the steps in this chapter, consider using a stylus. Many people find it easier to be precise with a stylus than with a finger. In addition, with a stylus you see the pointer. If you still are having trouble completing the steps with a stylus, try using a mouse.

Figure 10–1a shows how the form is displayed on a user's screen initially, Figure 10–1b shows the form partially filled in by one user, and Figure 10–1c shows how this user filled in the entire form.

The data entry area of the form contains three text boxes (named First Name, Last Name, and Other Services Used), one drop-down list box (named Frequency of Service Use), five check boxes (named Standard Cleaning, Green Cleaning, Window Washing, Carpet Cleaning, and Other Services Used), a combination text box/drop-down list box (named Cleaning Staff Rating), and a date picker (named Today's Date).

The form is designed so that it fits completely within a Word window that is set at a page width zoom and has the ribbon collapsed, which prevents a user from having to scroll while filling in the form. The data entry area of the form is enclosed by a rectangle that has a shadow on its top and right edges. The line of text above the data entry area is covered with the color gray, giving it the look of text that has been marked with a gray highlighter pen.

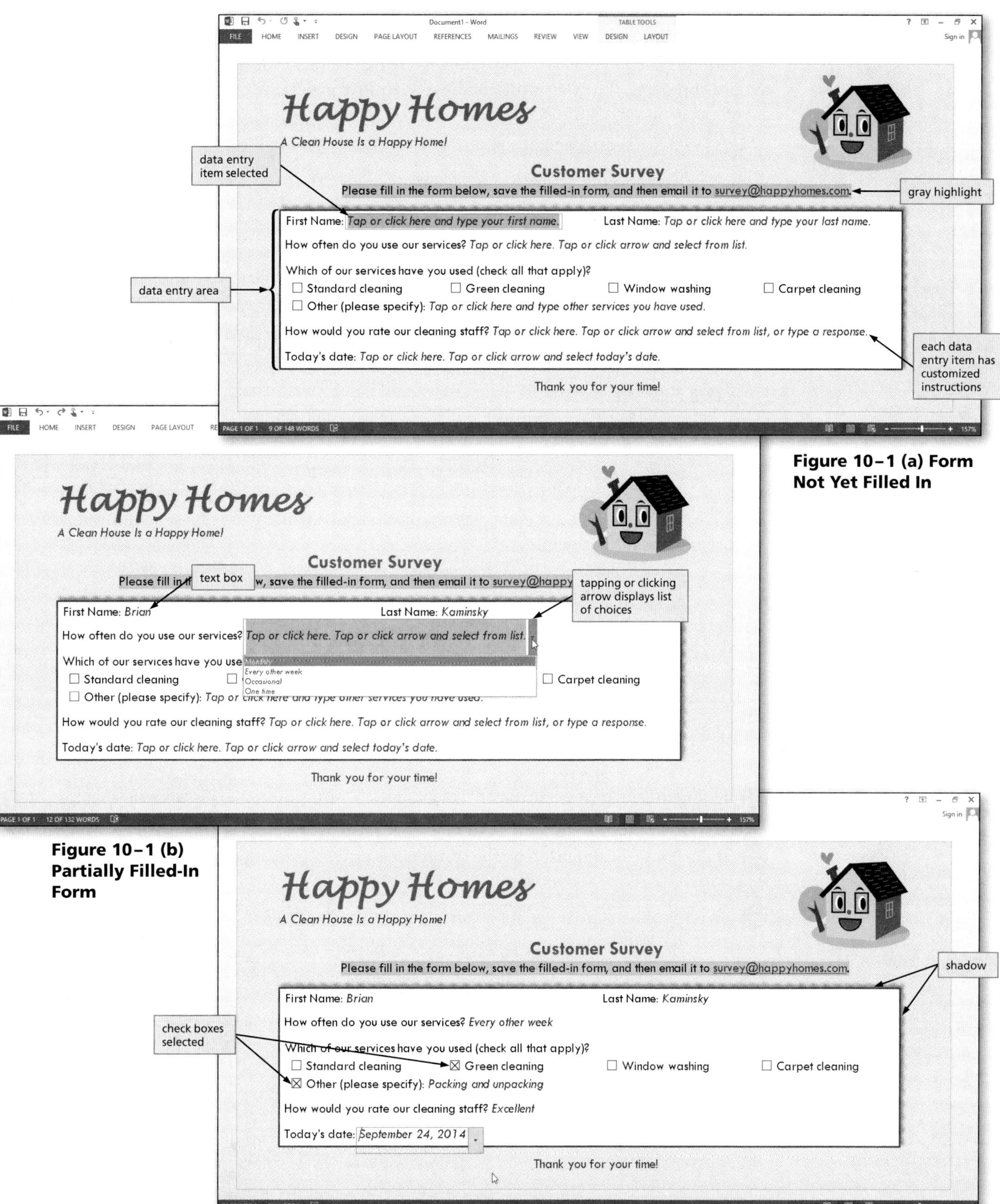

Figure 10–1 (a) Form Not Yet Filled In

Figure 10–1 (b) Partially Filled-In Form

Figure 10–1 (c) Filled-In Form

Roadmap

In this chapter, you will learn how to create the form shown in Figure 10–1 on the previous page. The following roadmap identifies general activities you will perform as you progress through this chapter:

1. SAVE a DOCUMENT as a TEMPLATE.
2. SET FORM FORMATS FOR the TEMPLATE.
3. ENTER TEXT, GRAPHICS, AND CONTENT CONTROLS in the form.
4. PROTECT the FORM.
5. USE the FORM.

At the beginning of step instructions throughout the chapter, you will see an abbreviated form of this roadmap. The abbreviated roadmap uses colors to indicate chapter progress: gray means the chapter is beyond that activity, blue means the task being shown is covered in that activity, and black means that activity is yet to be covered. For example, the following abbreviated roadmap indicates the chapter would be showing a task in the 2 SET FORM FORMATS FOR TEMPLATE activity.

1 SAVE DOCUMENT TEMPLATE | 2 SET FORM FORMATS FOR TEMPLATE
3 ENTER TEXT, GRAPHICS, & CONTENT CONTROLS | 4 PROTECT FORM | 5 USE FORM

Use the abbreviated roadmap as a progress guide while you read or step through the instructions in this chapter.

One of the few differences between Windows 7 and Windows 8 occurs in the steps to run Word. If you are using Windows 7, click the Start button, type **Word** in the 'Search programs and files' box, click Word 2013, and then, if necessary, maximize the Word window. For a summary of the steps to run Word in Windows 7, refer to the Quick Reference located at the back of this book.

To Run Word and Change Word Settings

If you are using a computer to step through the project in this chapter and you want your screens to match the figures in this book, you should change your screen's resolution to 1366 × 768. The following steps run Word, display formatting marks, and change the zoom to page width.

1. Run Word and create a blank document in the Word window. If necessary, maximize the Word window.
2. If the Print Layout button on the status bar is not selected, tap or click it so that your screen is in Print Layout view.
3. To display the page the same width as the document window, if necessary, tap or click the Page Width button (VIEW tab | Zoom group).
4. If the 'Show/Hide ¶' button (HOME tab | Paragraph group) is not selected already, tap or click it to display formatting marks on the screen.

Saving a Document as a Template

A **template** is a file that contains the definition of the appearance of a Word document, including items such as default font, font size, margin settings, and line spacing; available styles; and even placement of text. Every Word document you create is based on a template. When you select the Blank document thumbnail on the Word start screen or in the New gallery of the Backstage view, Word creates a document based on the Normal template. Word also provides other templates for more specific types of documents, such as memos, letters, and resumes, some of which you have used in previous chapters. Creating a document based on these templates can improve your productivity because Word has defined much of the document's appearance for you.

In this chapter, you create an online form. If you create and save an online form as a Word document, users will be required to open that Word document to display the form on the screen. Next, they will fill in the form. Then, to preserve the content of the original form, they will have to save the form with a new file name. If they accidentally tap or click the Save button on the Quick Access Toolbar during the process of filling in the form, Word will replace the original blank form with a filled-in form.

If you create and save the online form as a template instead, users will open a new document window that is based on that template. This displays the form on the screen as a brand new Word document; that is, the document does not have a file name. Thus, the user fills in the form and then taps or clicks the Save button on the Quick Access Toolbar to save his or her filled-in form. By creating a Word template for the form, instead of a Word document, the original template for the form remains intact when the user taps or clicks the Save button.

BTW
The Ribbon and Screen Resolution
Word may change how the groups and buttons within the groups appear on the ribbon, depending on the computer's screen resolution. Thus, your ribbon may look different from the ones in this book if you are using a screen resolution other than 1366 × 768.

To Save a Document as a Template

1 SAVE DOCUMENT TEMPLATE | **2 SET FORM FORMATS FOR TEMPLATE**
3 ENTER TEXT, GRAPHICS, & CONTENT CONTROLS | **4 PROTECT FORM** | **5 USE FORM**

The following steps save a new blank document as a template. ***Why?*** *The template will be used to create the online form shown in Figure 10–1 on page WD 611.*

- With a new blank document in the Word window, open the Backstage view and then tap or click the Export tab in the left pane of the Backstage view to display the Export gallery.
- Tap or click 'Change File Type' in the Export gallery to display information in the right pane about various file types that can be opened in Word.
- Tap or click Template in the right pane to specify the file type for the current document (Figure 10–2).

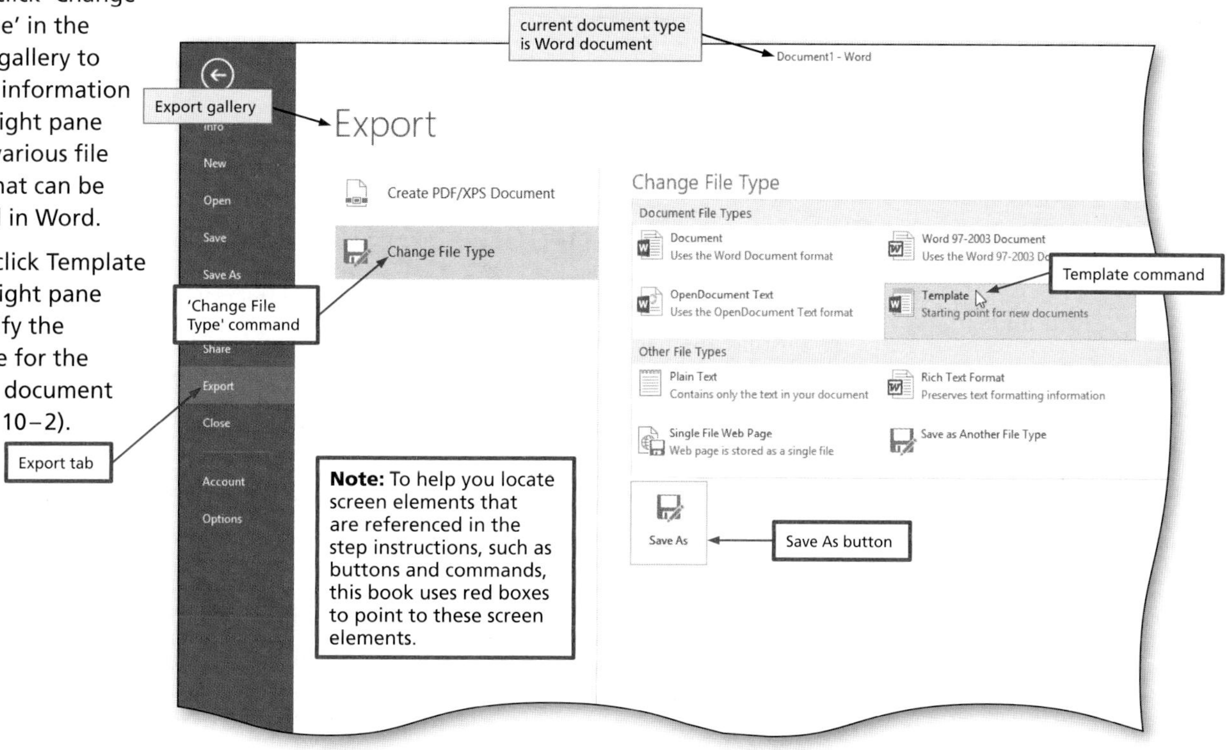

current document type is Word document
Export gallery
'Change File Type' command
Template command
Export tab
Save As button

Note: To help you locate screen elements that are referenced in the step instructions, such as buttons and commands, this book uses red boxes to point to these screen elements.

Figure 10–2

- Tap or click the Save As button to display the Save As dialog box with the file type automatically changed to Word Template.

Q&A How does Word differentiate between a saved Word template and a saved Word document?
Files typically have a file name and a file extension. The file extension identifies the file type. The source program often assigns a file type to a file. A Word document has an extension of .docx, whereas a Word template has an extension of .dotx. Thus, a file named July Report.docx is a Word document, and a file named Fitness Form.dotx is a Word template.

- Type **Customer Survey** in the File name box to change the file name.
- Navigate to the desired save location (in this case, the Word folder in the CIS 101 folder [or your class folder]) (Figure 10–3).

- Tap or click the Save button (Save As dialog box) to save the document as a Word template with the entered file name in the specified location.

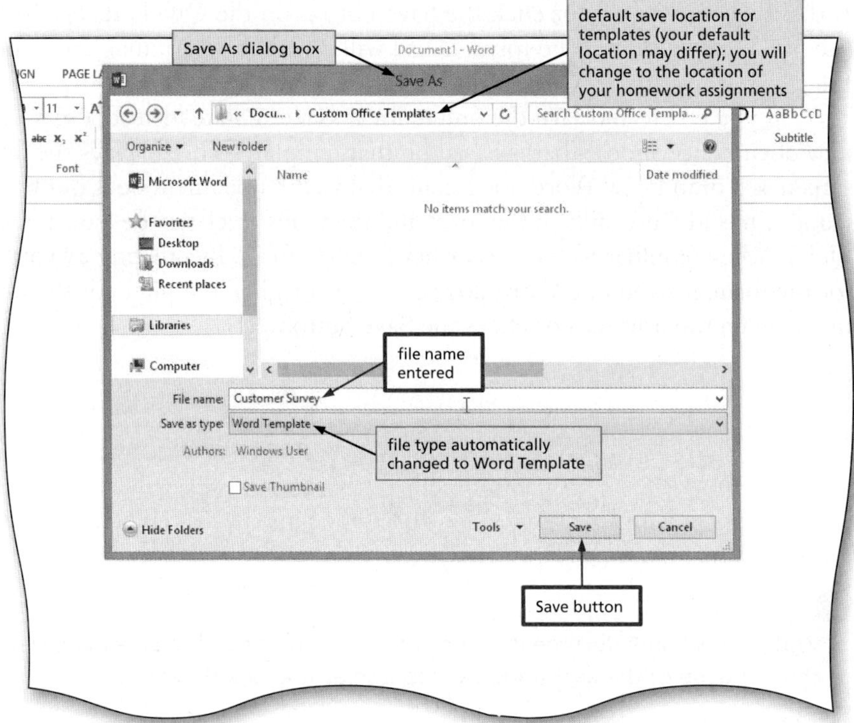

Figure 10–3

Other Ways

1. Press F12, change document type to Word Template
2. Open Backstage view, tap or click Save As, change document type to Word Template

Changing Document Settings

To enhance the look of the form, you change several default settings in Word:

1. Display the page as wide as possible in the document window to maximize the amount of space for text and graphics on the form, called page width zoom.
2. Change the size of the paper so that it fits completely within the document window.
3. Adjust the margins so that as much text as possible will fit in the document.
4. Change the document theme to Slice and the theme fonts to the Tw Cen MT font set.
5. Change the page color to a shade of green with a pattern.

The first item was completed earlier in the chapter. The following pages make the remaining changes to the document.

BTW
Touch Screen Differences
The Office and Windows interfaces may vary if you are using a touch screen. For this reason, you might notice that the function or appearance of your touch screen differs slightly from this chapter's presentation.

To Change Paper Size

For the online form in this chapter, all edges of the paper appear in the document window. Currently, only the top, left, and right edges are displayed in the document window. The following steps change paper size. ***Why?*** *To display all edges of the document in the document window in the current resolution, change the height of the paper from 11 inches to 4 inches.*

1

- Display the PAGE LAYOUT tab.
- Tap or click the 'Choose Page Size' button (PAGE LAYOUT tab | Page Setup group) to display the Choose Page Size gallery (Figure 10–4).

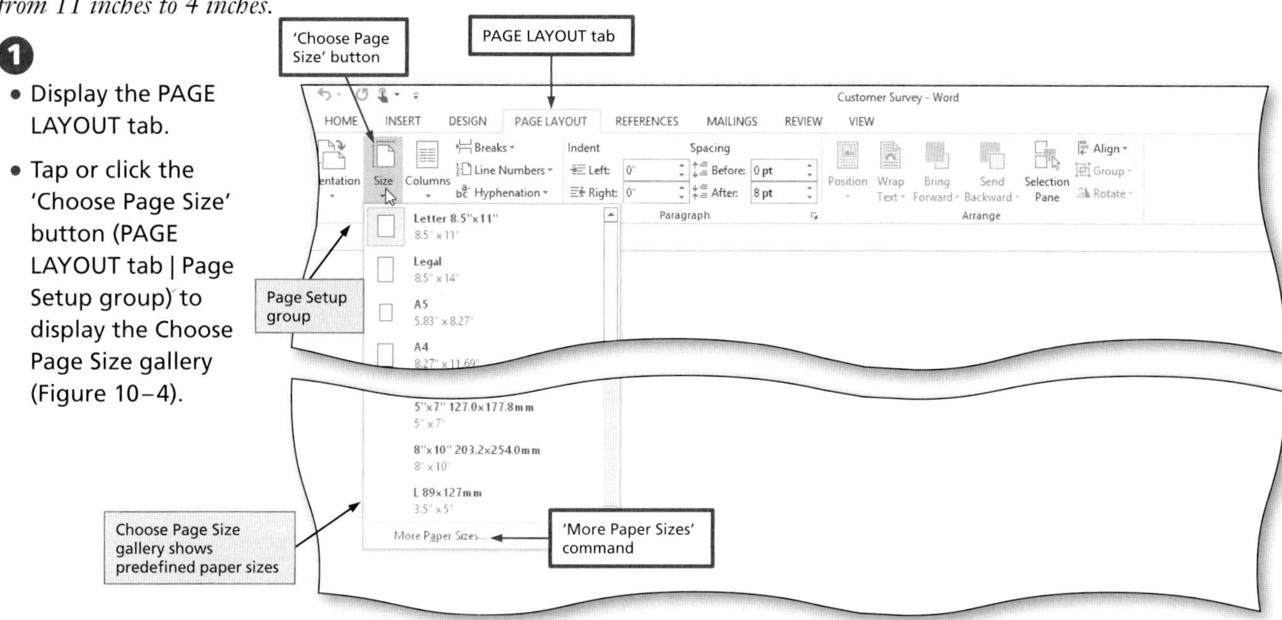

Figure 10–4

- Tap or click 'More Paper Sizes' in the Choose Page Size gallery to display the Paper sheet in the Page Setup dialog box.
- In the Height box (Page Setup dialog box), type **4** as the new height (Figure 10–5).

- Tap or click the OK button to change the paper size to the entered measurements, which, in this case, are 8.5 inches wide by 4 inches tall.

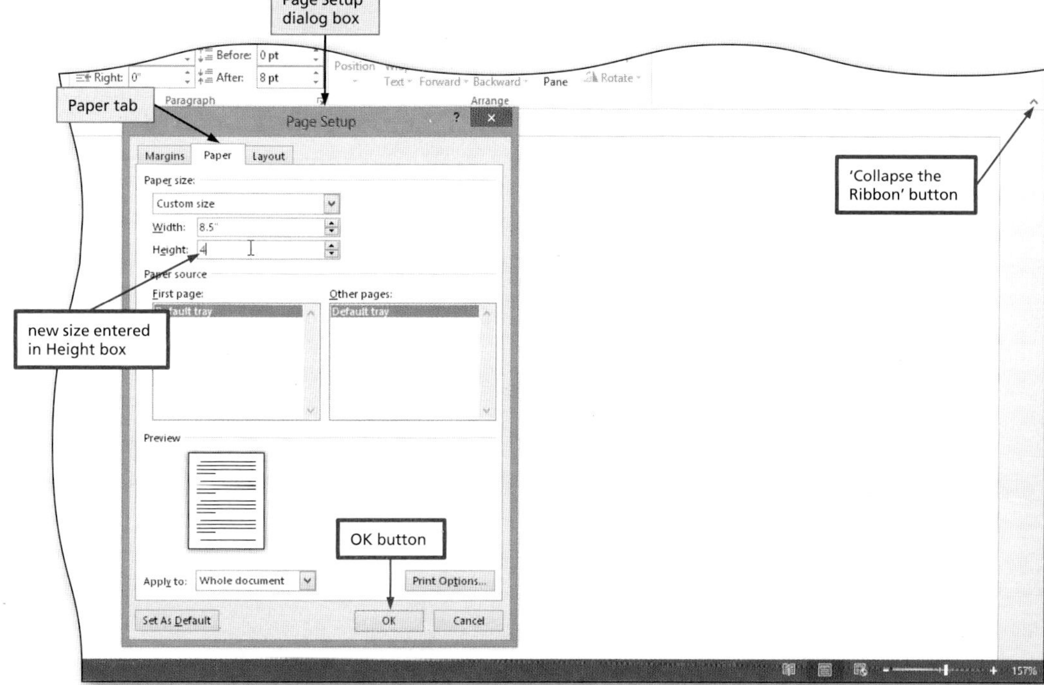

Figure 10–5

To Collapse the Ribbon

To display more of a document or other item in the Word window, you can collapse the ribbon, which hides the groups on the ribbon and displays only the main tabs. For the online form to fit entirely in the Word window, you collapse the ribbon. The following step collapses the ribbon so that you can see how the form fits in the document window.

1. Tap or click the 'Collapse the Ribbon' button on the ribbon (shown in Figure 10–5 on the previous page) to collapse the ribbon (Figure 10–6).

Q&A

What happened to the 'Collapse the Ribbon' button?
The 'Pin the ribbon' button replaces the 'Collapse the Ribbon' button when the ribbon is collapsed. You will see the 'Pin the ribbon' button only when you expand a ribbon by tapping or clicking a tab.

What if the height of my document does not match the figure?
You may need to show white space. To do this, if you are using a mouse, position the pointer above the top of the page below the ribbon and then double-click when the pointer changes to a 'Show White Space' button; if you are using a touch screen, double-tap below the page. Or, your screen resolution may be different; if so, you may need to adjust the page height or width values.

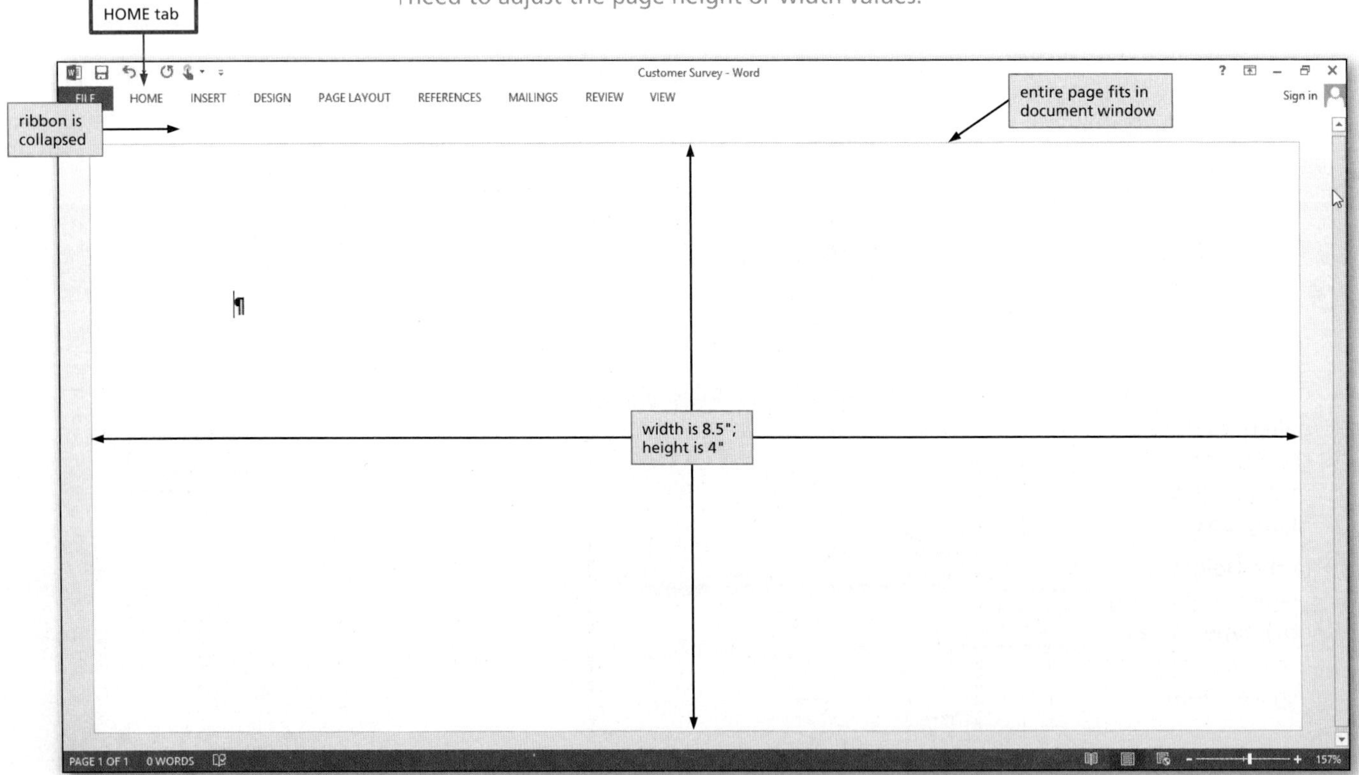

Figure 10–6

To Expand the Ribbon

After you verify that the entire form will fit in the document window, you should expand the ribbon so that you can see the groups while creating the online form. The following steps expand the ribbon.

1. Tap or click HOME on the collapsed ribbon to expand the HOME tab.
2. Tap or click the 'Pin the ribbon' button on the expanded HOME tab to restore the ribbon.

To Set Custom Margins

Recall that Word is preset to use 1-inch top, bottom, left, and right margins. To maximize the space for the contents of the form, this chapter sets the left and right margins to .5 inches, the top margin to .25 inches, and the bottom margin to 0 inches. The following steps set custom margins.

BTW

Quick Reference

For a table that lists how to complete the tasks covered in this book using touch gestures, the mouse, ribbon, shortcut menu, and keyboard, see the Quick Reference Summary at the back of this book, or visit the Quick Reference resource on the Student Companion Site located on www.cengagebrain.com. For detailed instructions about accessing available resources, visit www.cengage.com/ct/studentdownload or contact your instructor for information about accessing the required files.

1. Display the PAGE LAYOUT tab. Tap or click the Adjust Margins button (PAGE LAYOUT tab | Page Setup group) to display the Adjust Margins gallery.
2. Tap or click Custom Margins in the Adjust Margins gallery to display the Margins sheet in the Page Setup dialog box.
3. Type `.25` in the Top box (Page Setup dialog box) to change the top margin setting.
4. Type `0` (zero) in the Bottom box to change the bottom margin setting.

Q&A Why set the bottom margin to zero?
This allows you to place form contents at the bottom of the page, if necessary.

5. Type `.5` in the Left box to change the left margin setting.
6. Type `.5` in the Right box to change the right margin setting (Figure 10–7).
7. Tap or click the OK button to set the custom margins for this document.

Q&A What if Word displays a dialog box indicating margins are outside the printable area?
Tap or click the Ignore button because this is an online form that is not intended for printing.

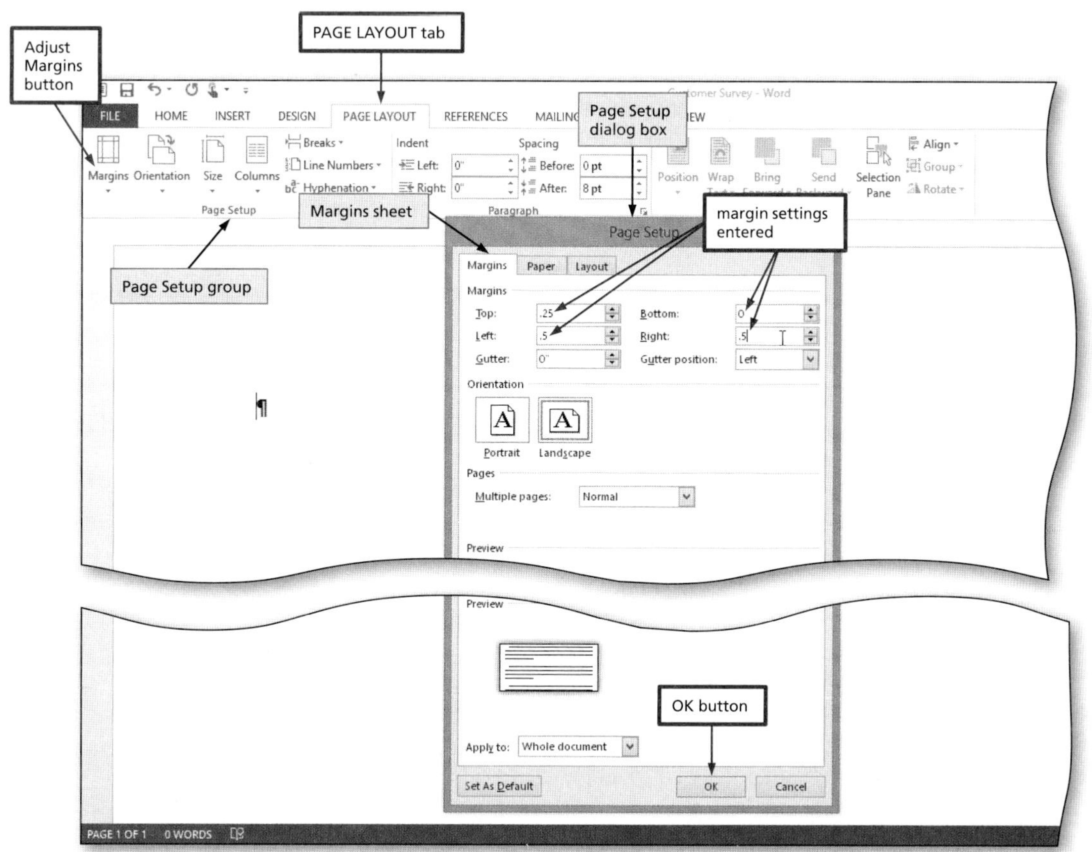

Figure 10–7

To Change the Document Theme and Theme Fonts

BTW
Set a Theme as the Default
If you wanted to change the default theme, you would select the theme you want to be the default theme, or select the color scheme, font set, and theme effects you would like to use as the default. Then, tap or click the 'Set as Default' button (DESIGN tab | Document Formatting group), which uses the current settings as the new default.

The following steps change the document theme colors to Slice and the theme fonts to Tw Cen MT.

1. Display the DESIGN tab. Tap or click the Themes button (DESIGN tab | Document Formatting group) and then tap or click Slice in the Themes gallery to change the document theme.

2. Tap or click the Theme Fonts button (DESIGN tab | Document Formatting group) and then scroll through the Theme Fonts gallery to display the Tw Cen MT font set (Figure 10–8).

3. Tap or click Tw Cen MT in the Theme Fonts gallery to change the font set.

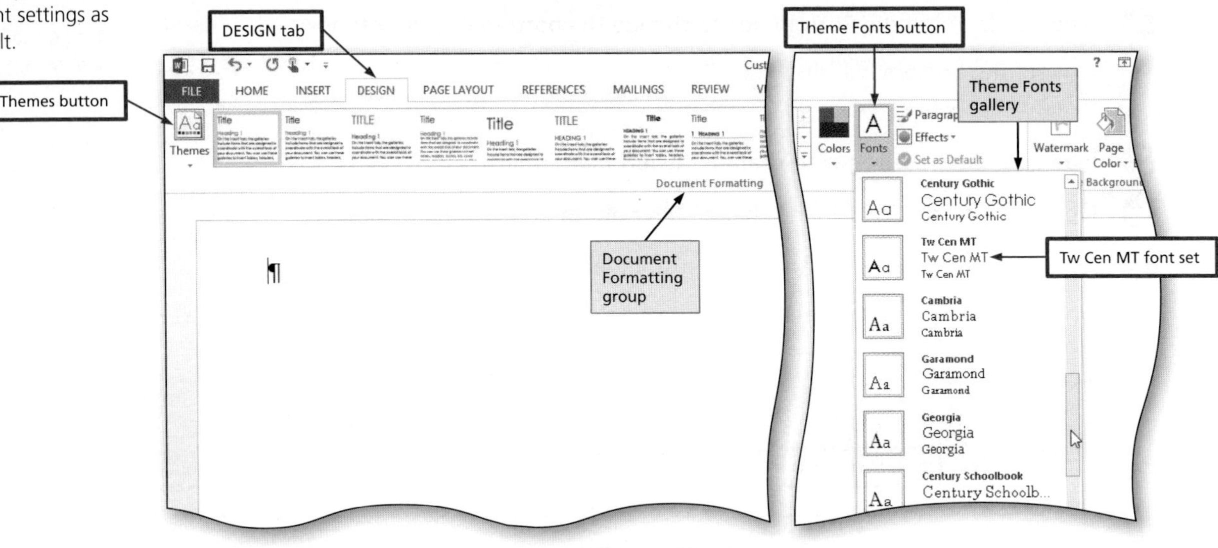

Figure 10–8

To Add a Page Color

1 SAVE DOCUMENT TEMPLATE | 2 SET FORM FORMATS FOR TEMPLATE
3 ENTER TEXT, GRAPHICS, & CONTENT CONTROLS | 4 PROTECT FORM | 5 USE FORM

The following steps change the page color. ***Why?*** *This online form uses a shade of green for the page color (background color) so that the form is more visually appealing.*

1.
- Tap or click the Page Color button (DESIGN tab | Page Background group) to display the Page Color gallery.
- If you are using a mouse, point to 'Dark Green, Accent 3, Lighter 40%' (seventh color in the fourth row) in the Page Color gallery to display a live preview of the selected background color (Figure 10–9).

 **Experiment**

- If you are using a mouse, point to various colors in the Page Color gallery and watch the page color change in the document window.

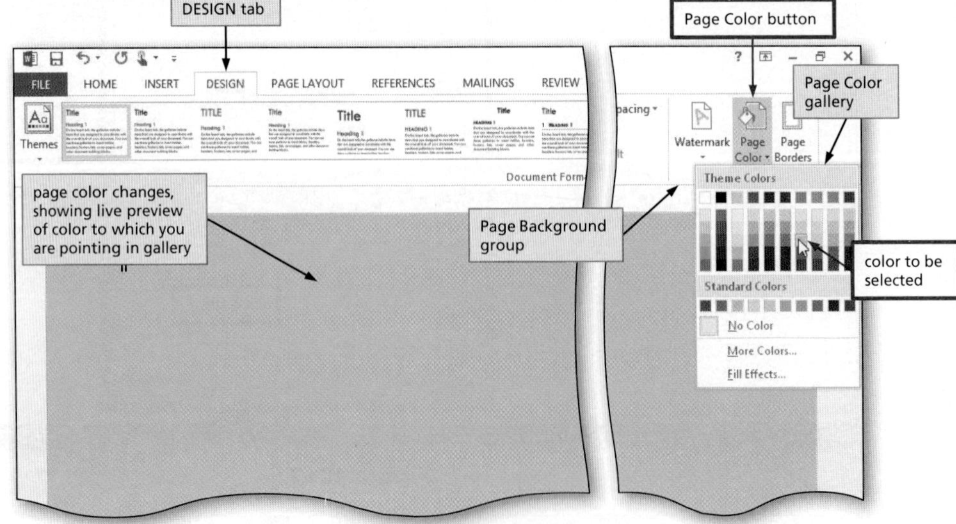

Figure 10–9

2

- Tap or click 'Dark Green, Accent 3, Lighter 40%' to change the page color to the selected color.

Q&A Do page colors print?
When you change the page color, it appears only on the screen. Changing the page color does not affect a printed document.

To Add a Pattern Fill Effect to a Page Color

1 SAVE DOCUMENT TEMPLATE | 2 SET FORM FORMATS FOR TEMPLATE
3 ENTER TEXT, GRAPHICS, & CONTENT CONTROLS | 4 PROTECT FORM | 5 USE FORM

When you changed the page color in the previous steps, Word placed a solid color on the screen. The following steps add a pattern to the page color. ***Why?*** *For this online form, the solid background color is a little too bright. To soften the color, you can add a pattern to it.*

1

- Tap or click the Page Color button (DESIGN tab | Page Background group) to display the Page Color gallery (Figure 10–10).

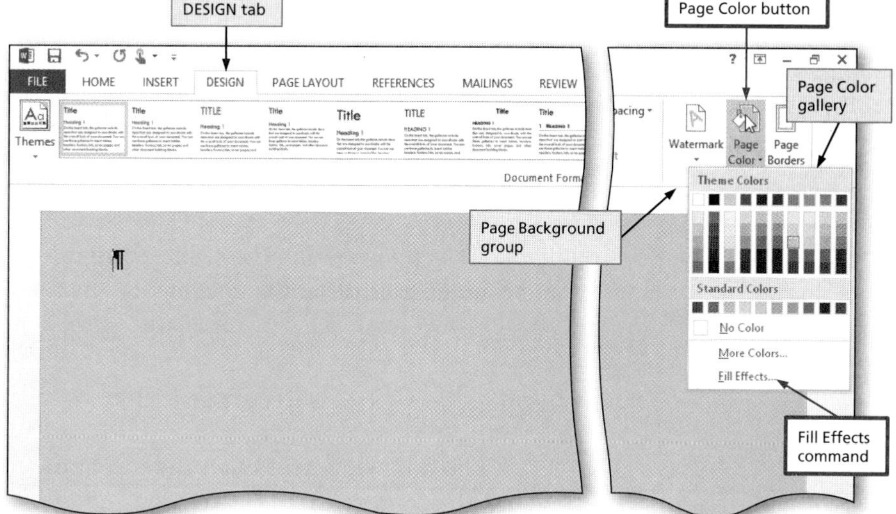

Figure 10–10

2

- Tap or click Fill Effects in the Page Color gallery to display the Fill Effects dialog box.
- Tap or click the Pattern tab (Fill Effects dialog box) to display the Pattern sheet in the dialog box.
- Tap or click the 30% pattern (first pattern in the fifth row) to select it (Figure 10–11).

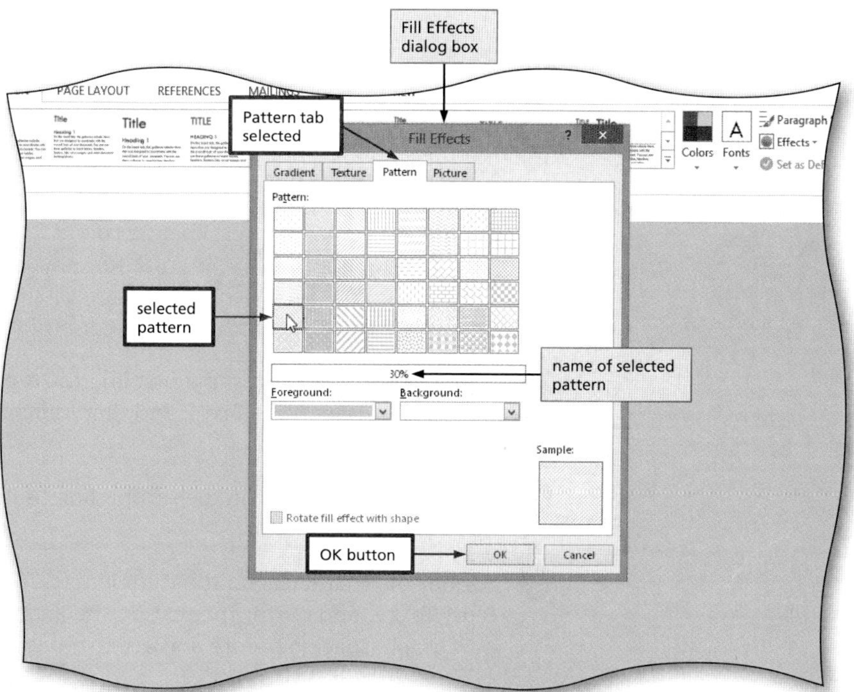

Figure 10–11

- Tap or click the OK button to add the selected pattern to the current page color (Figure 10–12).

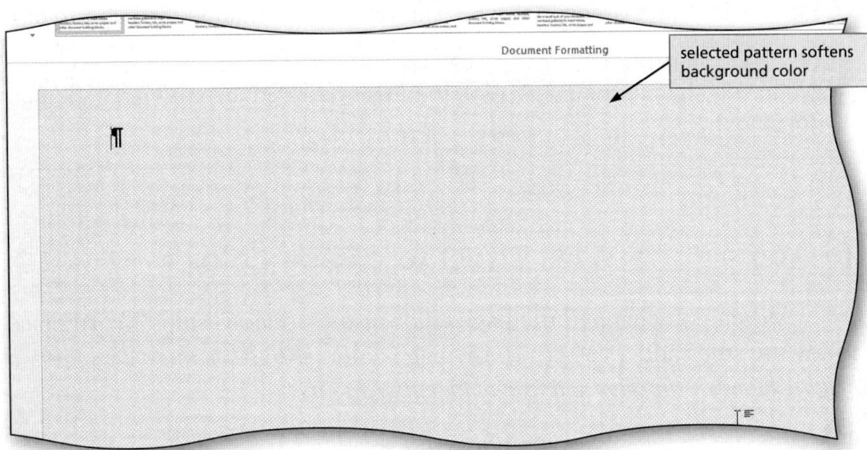

Figure 10–12

Enter Content in the Online Form

The next step in creating the online form in this chapter is to enter the text, graphics, and content controls in the document. The following pages describe this process.

To Enter and Format Text

The following steps enter the text at the top of the online form.

1. Type `Happy Homes` and then press the ENTER key.
2. Type `A Clean House Is a Happy Home!` and then press the ENTER key.
3. Type `Customer Survey` and then press the ENTER key.
4. Type `Please fill in the form below, save the filled-in form, and email it to survey@happyhomes.com.` and then press the ENTER key.

   If requested by your instructor, change the name, happyhomes, in the email address to your name.

   Q&A Why did the email address change color?
   In this document theme, the color for a hyperlink is a shade of blue. When you pressed the ENTER key, Word automatically formatted the hyperlink in this color. Later in this chapter, you will change the color of the hyperlink.

5. Format the characters on the first line to 28-point Lucida Handwriting font, bold, with the color of Dark Blue, Text 2 and then remove space after the paragraph (spacing after should be 0 pt).
6. Format the characters on the second line to italic with the color of Red, Accent 6, Darker 25%.
7. Format the characters on the third line to 16-point bold font with the color of Dark Blue, Text 2, and center the text on the line. Remove space before and after this paragraph (spacing before and after should be 0 pt).

8. Center the text on the fourth line and increase the spacing after this line to 12 point.

9. Position the insertion point on the blank line below the text (Figure 10–13).

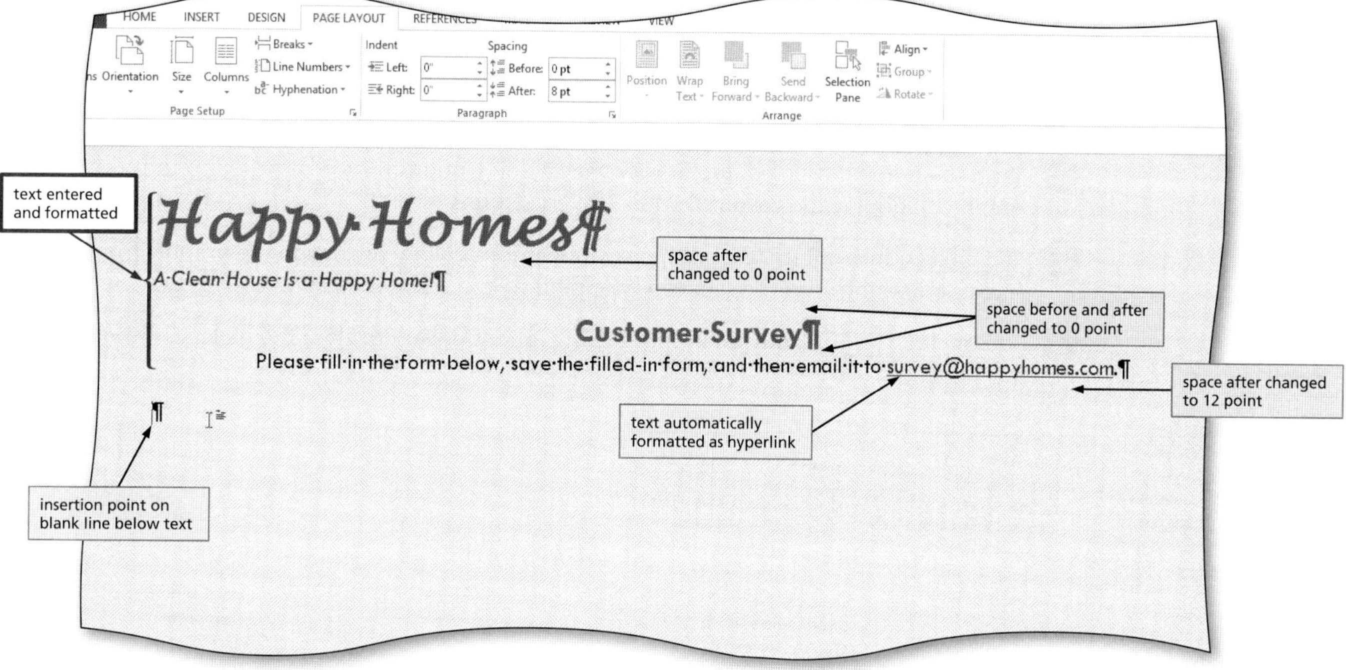

Figure 10–13

To Insert Clip Art and Scale It

The next step is to insert a graphic of a house in the form. Because the graphic's original size is too large, you will reduce its size. The following steps insert and scale a graphic.

1. Display the INSERT tab. Tap or click the Online Pictures button (INSERT tab | Illustrations group) to display the Insert Pictures dialog box.

2. Type **`happy house`** in the Search box (Insert Pictures dialog box) and then tap or click the Search button to display a list of clip art that matches the entered search text.

3. Tap or click the house clip art that matches the one in Figure 10–14 on the next page (or a similar image) and then tap or click the Insert button to download the image, close the dialog box, and insert the graphic in the document at the location of the insertion point.

Q&A What if I cannot locate the same clip art?
Tap or click the Cancel button and then close the Insert Pictures dialog box. Tap or click the From File button (INSERT tab | Illustrations group) to display the Insert Picture dialog box, navigate to the Happy House file on the Data Files for Students (Insert Picture dialog box), and tap or click the Insert button to insert the picture.

4. With the graphic still selected, use the Shape Height and Shape Width boxes (PICTURE TOOLS FORMAT tab | Size group) to change the graphic height to approximately 1.1" and width to 1.34", respectively (shown in Figure 10–14).

Q&A What if the PICTURE TOOLS FORMAT tab is not the active tab on my ribbon?
Double-tap or double-click the graphic, or tap or click the PICTURE TOOLS FORMAT tab on the ribbon.

To Format a Graphic's Text Wrapping

Word inserted the clip art as an inline graphic, that is, as part of the current paragraph. In this online form, the graphic should be positioned to the right of the company name (shown in Figure 10–1 on page WD 611). Thus, the graphic should be a floating graphic instead of an inline graphic. The text in the online form should not wrap around the graphic. Thus, the graphic should float in front of the text. The following steps change the graphic's text wrapping to In Front of Text.

1. With the graphic selected, tap or click the Layout Options button attached to the graphic to display the Layout Options gallery (Figure 10–14).
2. Tap or click 'In Front of Text' in the Layout Options gallery to change the graphic from inline to floating with the selected wrapping style.
3. Tap or click the Close button in the Layout Options gallery to close the gallery.

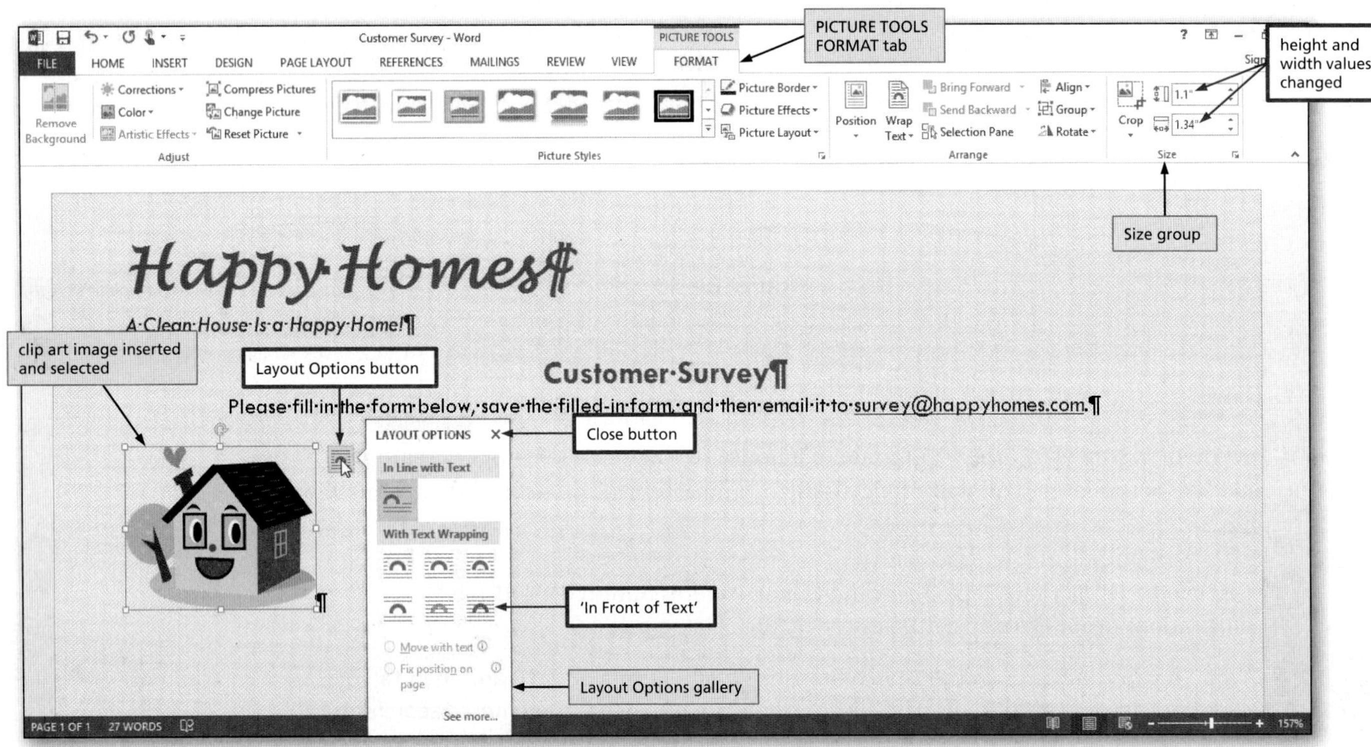

Figure 10–14

BTW

Ordering Graphics

If you have multiple graphics displaying on the screen and would like them to overlap, you can change their stacking order by using the Bring Forward and Send Backward arrows (PICTURE TOOLS FORMAT tab | Arrange group). The 'Bring to Front' command on the Bring Forward menu displays the selected object at the top of the stack, and the 'Send to Back' command on the Send Backward menu displays the selected object at the bottom of the stack. The Bring Forward and Send Backward commands each move the graphic forward or backward one layer in the stack. These commands also are available through the shortcut menu that is displayed when you press and hold or right-click a graphic.

To Move a Graphic

The final step associated with the graphic is to move it so that it is positioned on the right side of the online form. The following steps move a graphic.

1. If necessary, scroll to display the top of the form in the document window.
2. Drag the graphic to the location shown in Figure 10–15.

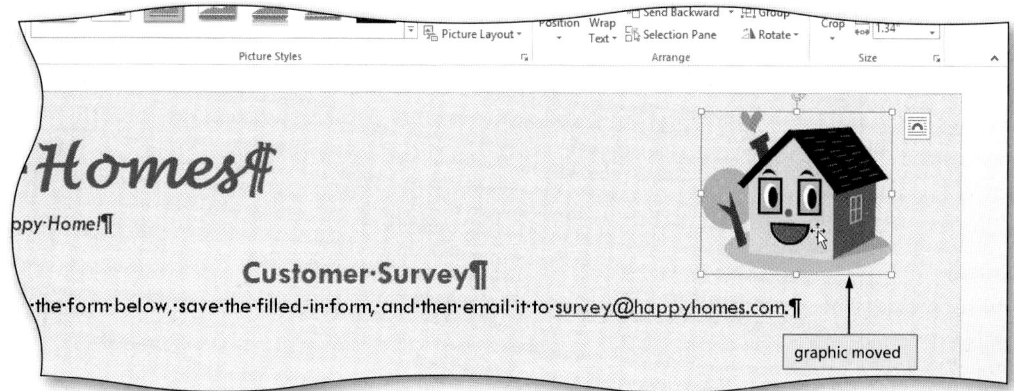

Figure 10–15

To Use a Table to Control Layout

The first line of data entry in the form consists of the First Name content control, which begins at the left margin, and the Last Name content control, which begins at the center point of the same line. At first glance, you might decide to set a tab stop at each content control location. This, however, can be a complex task. For example, to place two content controls evenly across a row, you must calculate the location of each tab stop. If you insert a 2 × 1 table instead, Word automatically calculates the size of two evenly spaced columns. Thus, to enter multiple content controls on a single line, insert a table to control layout.

In this online form, the line containing the First Name and Last Name content controls will be a 2 × 1 table, that is, a table with two columns and one row. By inserting a 2 × 1 table, Word automatically positions the second column at the center point. The following steps insert a 2 × 1 table in the form and remove its border. ***Why?*** *When you insert a table, Word automatically surrounds it with a border. Because you are using the tables solely to control layout, you do not want the table borders visible.*

1.
- Position the insertion point where the table should be inserted, in this case, on the blank paragraph mark below the text on the form.
- Display the INSERT tab. Tap or click the 'Add a Table' button (INSERT tab | Tables group) to display the Add a Table gallery (Figure 10–16).

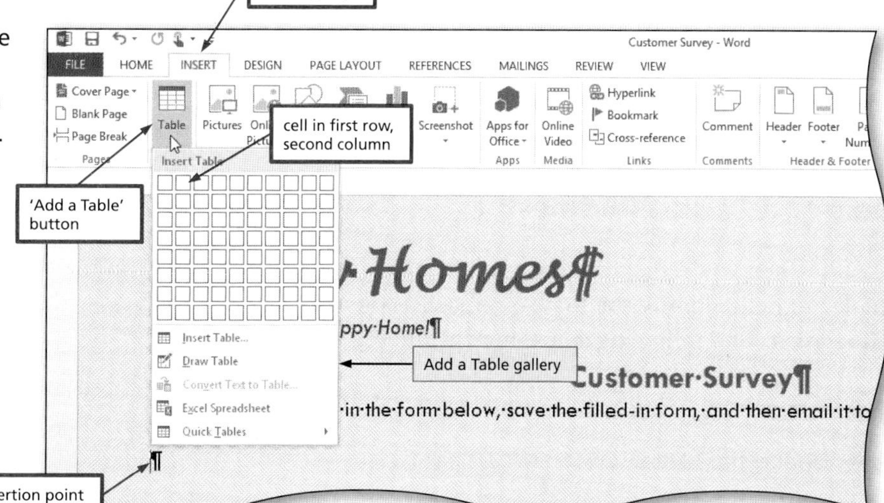

Figure 10–16

2

- Tap or click the cell in the first row and second column of the grid to insert an empty 2 × 1 table at the location of the insertion point.
- Select the table.

Q&A How do I select a table?

If you are using a mouse, point somewhere in the table and then click the table move handle that appears in the upper-left corner of the table; if you are using a touch screen, tap the Select Table button (TABLE TOOLS LAYOUT tab | Table group) and then tap Select Table on the Select Table menu.

- Tap or click the Borders arrow (TABLE TOOLS DESIGN tab | Borders group) to display the Borders gallery (Figure 10–17).

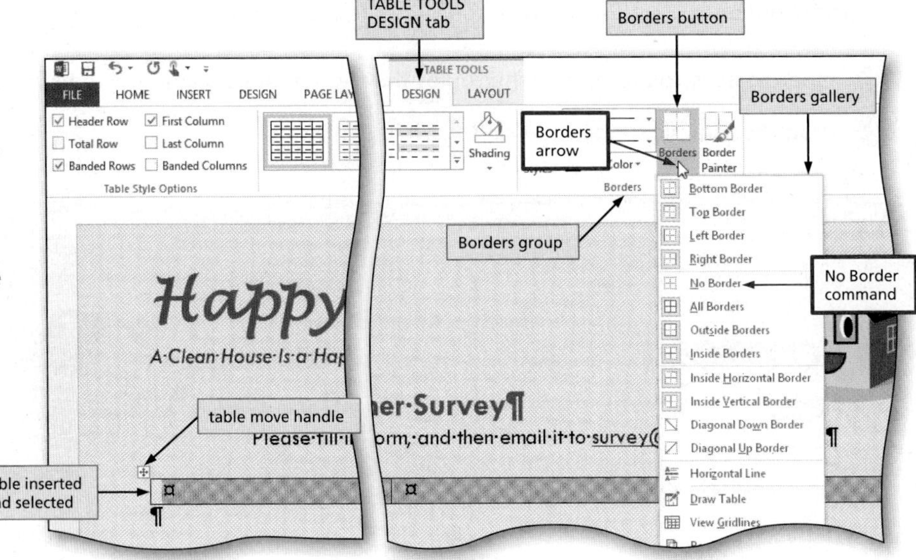

Figure 10–17

3

- Tap or click No Border in the Borders gallery to remove the borders from the table.

4

- Tap or click the first cell of the table to remove the selection (Figure 10–18).

Q&A My screen does not display the end-of-cell marks. Why not?

Display formatting marks by tapping or clicking the 'Show/Hide ¶' button (HOME tab | Paragraph group).

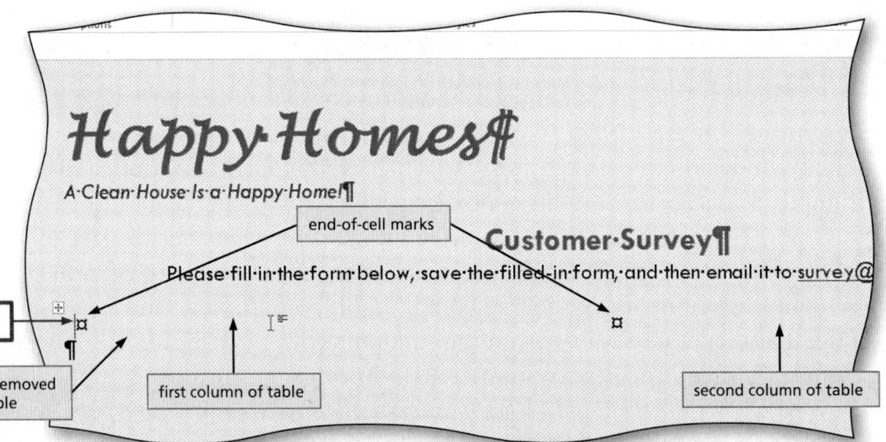

Figure 10–18

Other Ways

1. Tap or click 'Add a Table' button (INSERT tab | Tables group), tap or click Insert Table in Add a Table gallery, enter number of columns and rows, tap or click OK button (Insert Table dialog box)

To Show Table Gridlines

When you remove the borders from a table, you no longer can see the individual cells in the table. To help identify the location of cells, you can display **gridlines**, which show cell outlines on the screen. The following steps show gridlines.

1. If necessary, position the insertion point in a table cell.
2. Display the TABLE TOOLS LAYOUT tab.

3 If gridlines do not show already, tap or click the 'View Table Gridlines' button (TABLE TOOLS LAYOUT tab | Table group) to show table gridlines on the screen (Figure 10–19).

Q&A Do table gridlines print?
No. Gridlines are formatting marks that show only on the screen. Gridlines help users easily identify cells, rows, and columns in borderless tables.

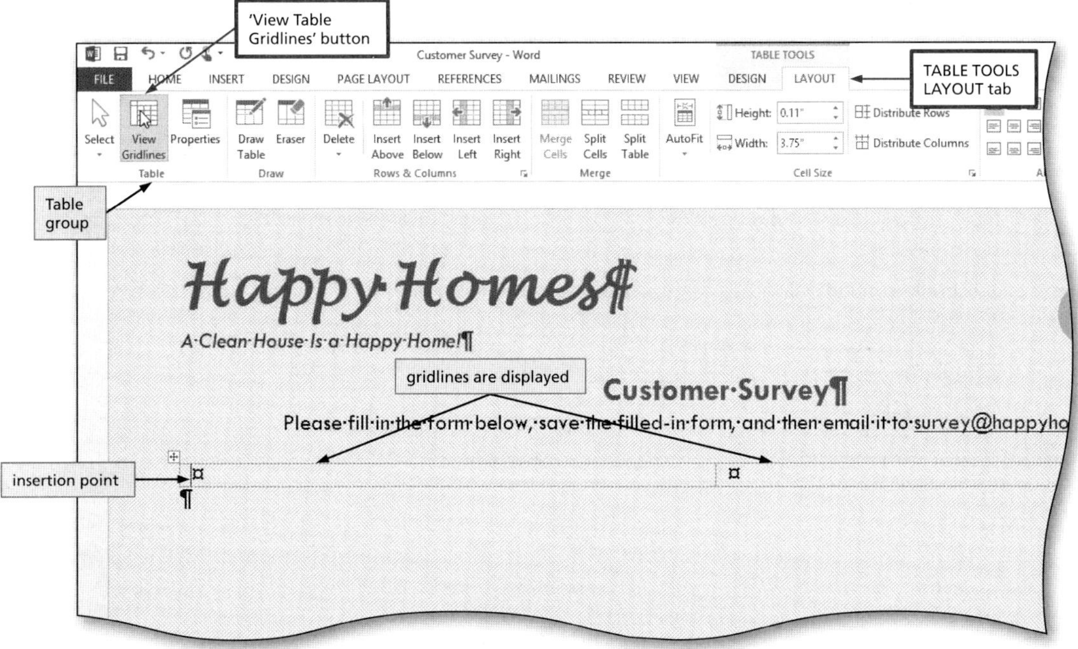

Figure 10–19

Content Controls

To add data entry fields in a Word form, you insert content controls. Word includes nine different content controls you can insert in your online forms. Table 10–1 outlines the use of each of these controls.

Table 10–1 Content Controls

Type	Icon	Use
Building Block Gallery		User selects a built-in building block from the gallery.
Check Box		User selects or deselects a check box.
Combo Box		User types text entry or selects one item from a list of choices.
Date Picker		User interacts with a calendar to select a date or types a date in the placeholder.
Drop-Down List		User selects one item from a list of choices.
Picture		User inserts a drawing, a shape, a picture, clip art, or a SmartArt graphic.
Plain Text	Aa	User enters text, which may not be formatted.
Repeating Section		Users can instruct Word to create a duplicate of the content control.
Rich Text	**Aa**	User enters text and, if desired, may format the entered text.

CONSIDER THIS

How do you determine the correct content control to use for each data entry field?

For each data entry field, decide which content control best maps to the type of data the field will contain. The field specifications for the fields in this chapter's online form are listed below:

- The First Name, Last Name, and Other Services Used data entry fields will contain text. The first two will be plain text content controls and the last will be a rich text content control.
- The Frequency of Service Use data entry field must contain one of these four values: Monthly, Every other week, Occasional, One time. This field will be a drop-down list content control.
- The Standard Cleaning, Green Cleaning, Window Washing, Carpet Cleaning, and Other Services Used data entry fields will be check boxes that the user can select or deselect.
- The Cleaning Staff Rating data entry field can contain one of these four values: Excellent, Good, Fair, and Poor. In addition, users should be able to enter their own value in this data entry field if none of these four values is applicable. A combo box content control will be used for this field.
- The Today's Date data entry field should contain only a valid date value. Thus, this field will be a date picker content control.

The following pages insert content controls in the online form.

To Show the DEVELOPER Tab

1 SAVE DOCUMENT TEMPLATE | 2 SET FORM FORMATS FOR TEMPLATE
3 ENTER TEXT, GRAPHICS, & CONTENT CONTROLS | 4 PROTECT FORM | 5 USE FORM

To create a form in Word, you use buttons on the DEVELOPER tab. The following steps display the DEVELOPER tab on the ribbon. ***Why?** Because it allows you to perform more advanced tasks not required by everyday Word users, the DEVELOPER tab does not appear on the ribbon by default.*

- Open the Backstage view (Figure 10–20).

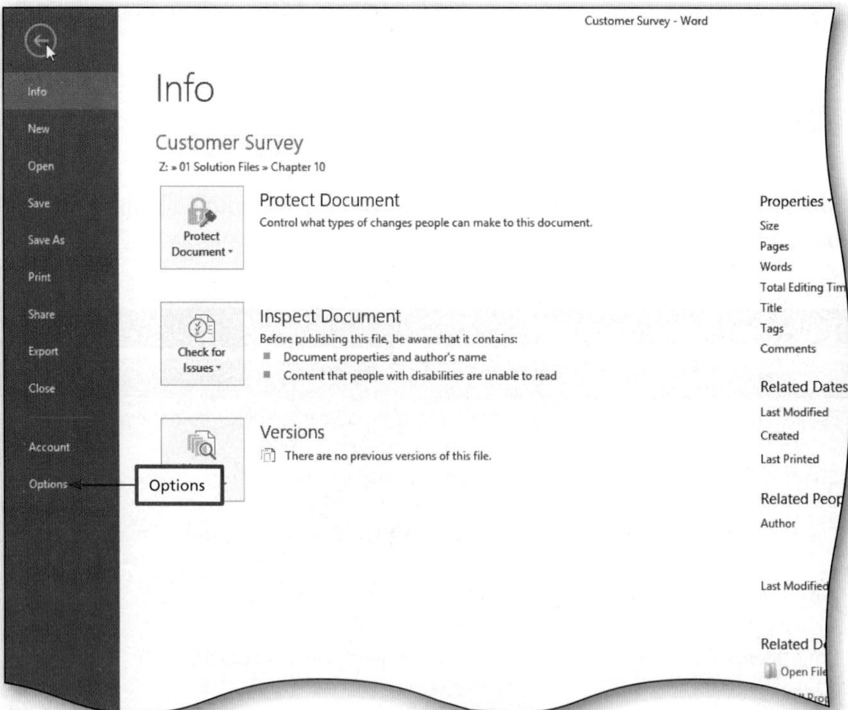

Figure 10–20

- Tap or click Options in the left pane of the Backstage view to display the Word Options dialog box.
- Tap or click Customize Ribbon in the left pane (Word Options dialog box) to display associated options in the right pane.
- Place a check mark in the Developer check box in the Main Tabs list (Figure 10–21).

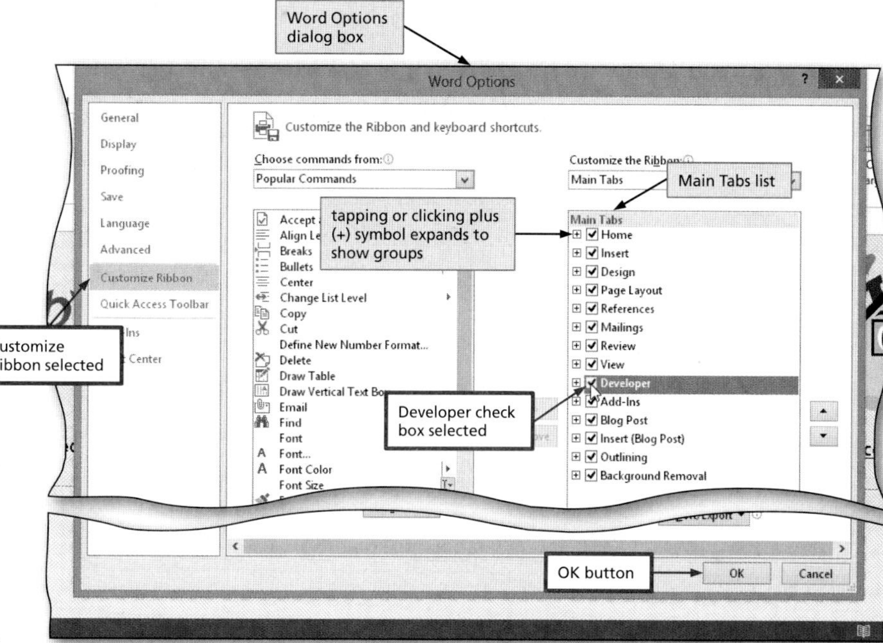

Figure 10–21

Q&A

What are the plus symbols to the left of each tab name?

Tapping or clicking the plus symbol expands to show the groups.

Can I show or hide any tab in this list?

Yes. Place a check mark in the check box to show the tab, or remove the check mark to hide the tab.

- Tap or click the OK button to show the DEVELOPER tab on the ribbon (Figure 10–22).

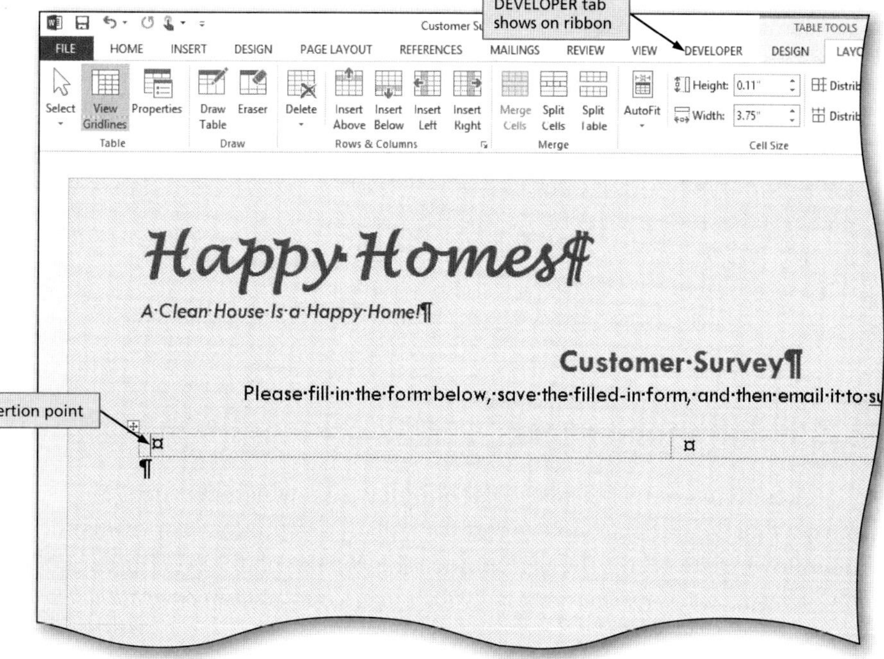

Figure 10–22

Q&A

How do I remove the DEVELOPER tab from the ribbon?

Follow these same steps, except remove the check mark from the Developer check box (Word Options dialog box).

To Insert a Plain Text Content Control

1 SAVE DOCUMENT TEMPLATE | 2 SET FORM FORMATS FOR TEMPLATE
3 ENTER TEXT, GRAPHICS, & CONTENT CONTROLS | 4 PROTECT FORM | 5 USE FORM

The first item that a user enters in the Customer Survey is his or her first name. Because the first name entry contains text that the user should not format, this online form uses a plain text content control for the First Name data entry field. The steps on the next page enter the label, First Name:, followed by a plain text content control. ***Why?*** *The label, First Name:, is displayed to the left of the plain text content control. To improve readability, a colon or some other character often separates a label from the content control.*

- With the insertion point in the first cell of the table as shown in Figure 10–22 on the previous page, type **`First Name:`** as the label for the content control.
- Press the SPACEBAR (Figure 10–23).

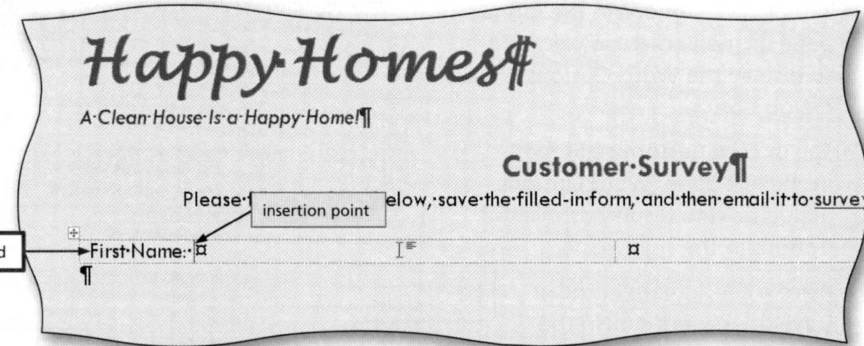

Figure 10–23

2

- Display the DEVELOPER tab.
- Tap or click the 'Plain Text Content Control' button (DEVELOPER tab | Controls group) to insert a plain text content control at the location of the insertion point (Figure 10–24).

Q&A Is the plain text content control similar to the content controls that I have used in templates installed with Word, such as in the letter, memo, and resume templates?

Yes. The content controls you insert through the DEVELOPER tab have the same functionality as the content controls in the templates installed with Word.

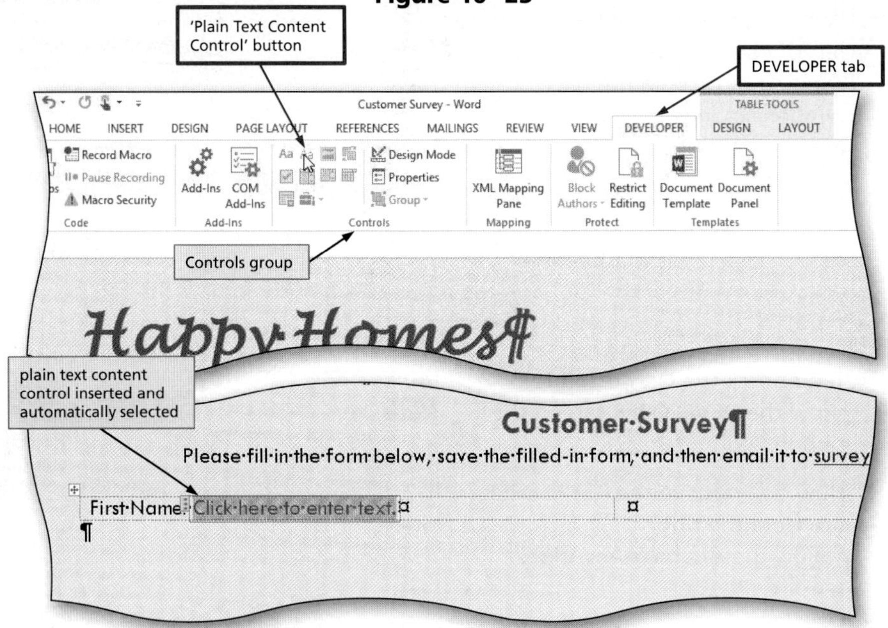

Figure 10–24

To Edit Placeholder Text

1 SAVE DOCUMENT TEMPLATE | 2 SET FORM FORMATS FOR TEMPLATE
3 ENTER TEXT, GRAPHICS, & CONTENT CONTROLS | 4 PROTECT FORM | 5 USE FORM

A content control displays **placeholder text**, which instructs the user how to enter values in the content control. The default placeholder text for a plain text content control is the instruction, Click here to enter text. The following steps edit the placeholder text for the plain text content control just entered. ***Why?*** *You can change the wording in the placeholder text so that it is more instructional or applicable to the current form.*

- With the plain text content control selected (shown in Figure 10–24), tap or click the Design Mode button (DEVELOPER tab | Controls group) to turn on Design mode, which displays tags at the beginning and ending of the placeholder text (Figure 10–25).

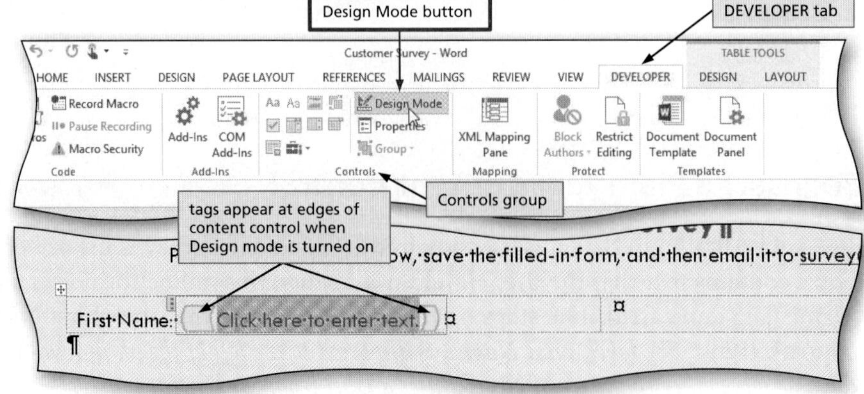

Figure 10–25

2

- Drag through the text to replace in the placeholder text (Figure 10–26).

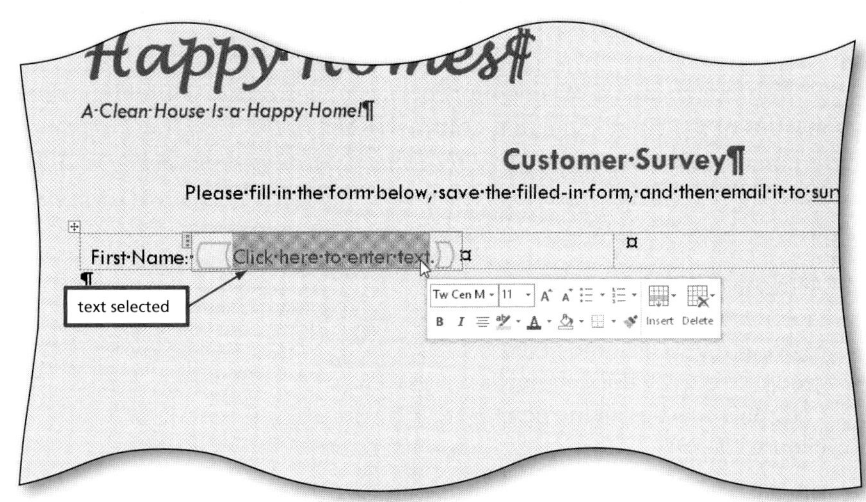

Figure 10–26

3

- Edit the placeholder text so that it contains the text, Tap or click here and type your first name., as the instruction (Figure 10–27).

Q&A Why did the placeholder text wrap to the next line?
Because of the tags at each edge of the placeholder text, the entered text may wrap in the table cell. Once you turn off Design mode, the placeholder text should fit on a single line. If it does not, you can adjust the font size of the placeholder text to fit.

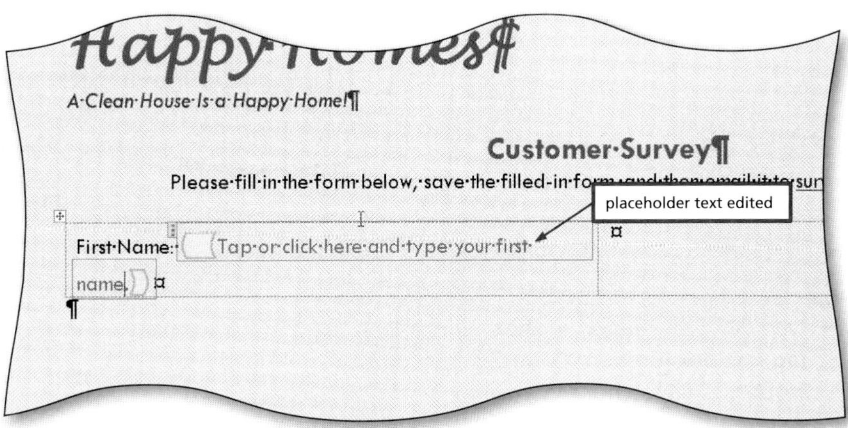

Figure 10–27

4

- Tap or click the Design Mode button (DEVELOPER tab | Controls group) to turn off Design mode (Figure 10–28).

Q&A What if I notice an error in the placeholder text?
Follow these steps to turn on Design mode, correct the error, and then turn off Design mode.

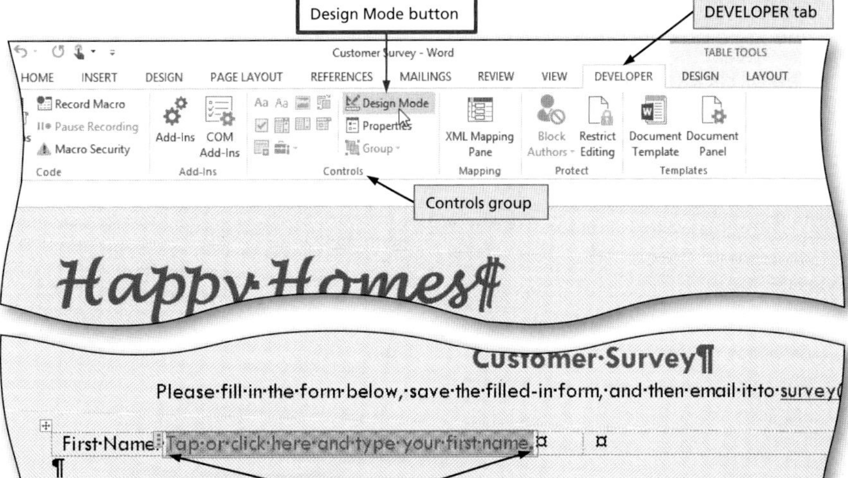

Figure 10–28

To Change the Properties of a Plain Text Content Control

You can change a variety of properties to customize content controls. The following steps change the properties of a plain text content control. ***Why?*** *In this form, you assign a tag name to a content control for later identification. You also apply a style to the content control to define how text will look as a user types data or makes selections, and you lock the content control so that a user cannot delete the content control during the data entry process.*

1

- With the content control selected, tap or click the Control Properties button (DEVELOPER tab | Controls group) to display the Content Control Properties dialog box (Figure 10–29).

Q&A How do I know the content control is selected?

A selected content control is surrounded by an outline. It also may be shaded.

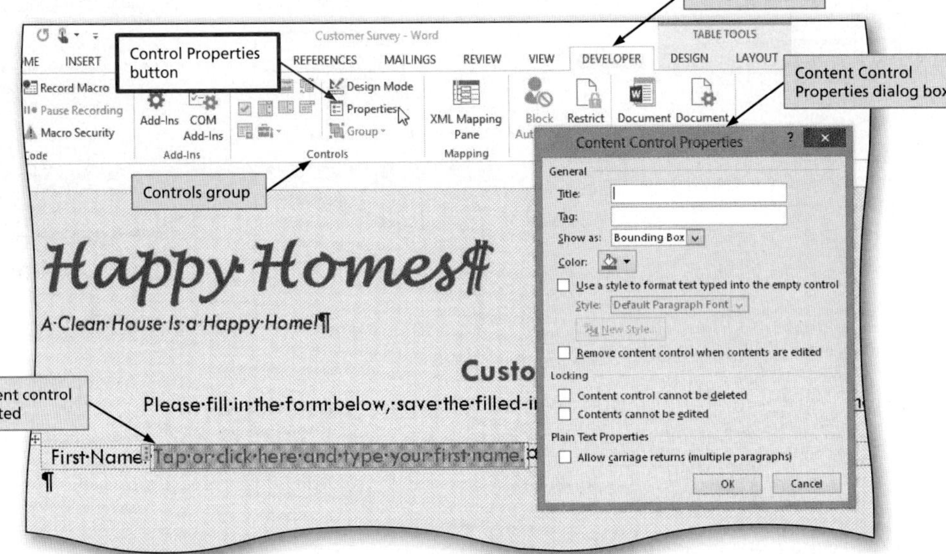

Figure 10–29

2

- Type **First Name** in the Tag text box (Content Control Properties dialog box).
- Place a check mark in the 'Use a style to format text typed into the empty control' check box so that the Style box becomes active.
- Tap or click the Style arrow to display the Style list (Figure 10–30).

Q&A Why leave the Title text box empty?

When you tap or click a content control in a preexisting Word template, the content control may display an identifier in its top-left corner. For templates that you create, you can instruct Word to display this identifier, called the Title, by changing the properties of the content control. In this form, you do not want the identifier to appear.

What is a bounding box?

A bounding box is a rectangle that surrounds the content control on the form. You can show content controls with a bounding box, with tags, or with no visible markings.

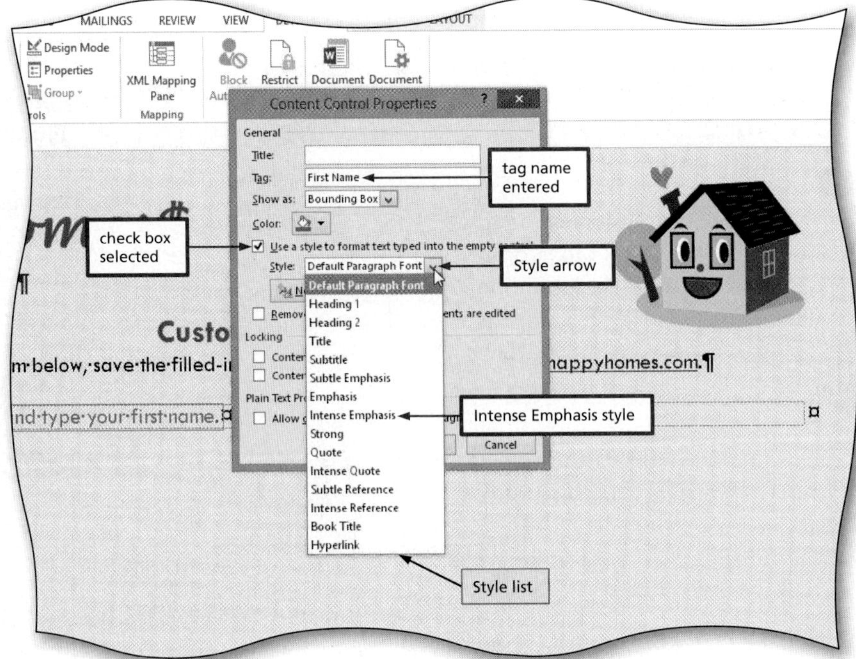

Figure 10–30

3

- Tap or click Intense Emphasis to select the style for the content control.
- Place a check mark in the 'Content control cannot be deleted' check box so that the user cannot delete the content control (Figure 10–31).

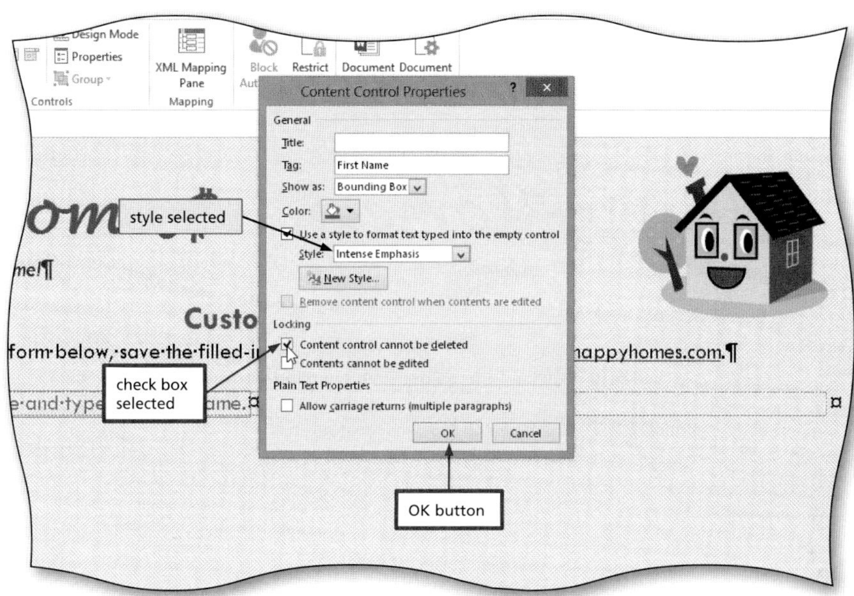

Figure 10–31

4

- Tap or click the OK button to assign the modified properties to the content control (Figure 10–32).

Q&A Why is the placeholder text not formatted to the selected style, Intense Emphasis, in this case?

When you apply a style to a content control, as described in these steps, the style is applied to the text the user types during the data entry process. To change the appearance of the placeholder text, apply a style using the HOME tab as described in the next steps.

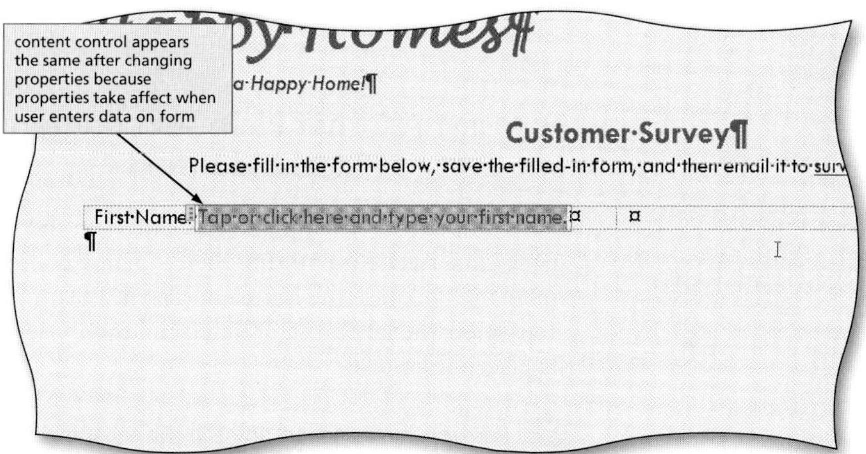

Figure 10–32

To Format Placeholder Text

In this online form, the placeholder text has the same style applied to it as the content control. The following steps format placeholder text.

1. With the placeholder text selected, display the HOME tab.
2. If you are using a mouse, click the Styles gallery down arrow (HOME tab | Styles group) to scroll through the Styles gallery to display the Intense Emphasis style or click the More button (HOME tab | Styles group); if you are using a touch screen, tap the More button (HOME tab | Styles group) to expand the Styles gallery.
3. Tap or click Intense Emphasis in the Styles gallery (even if it is selected already) to apply the selected style to the selected placeholder text (Figure 10–33 on the next page).

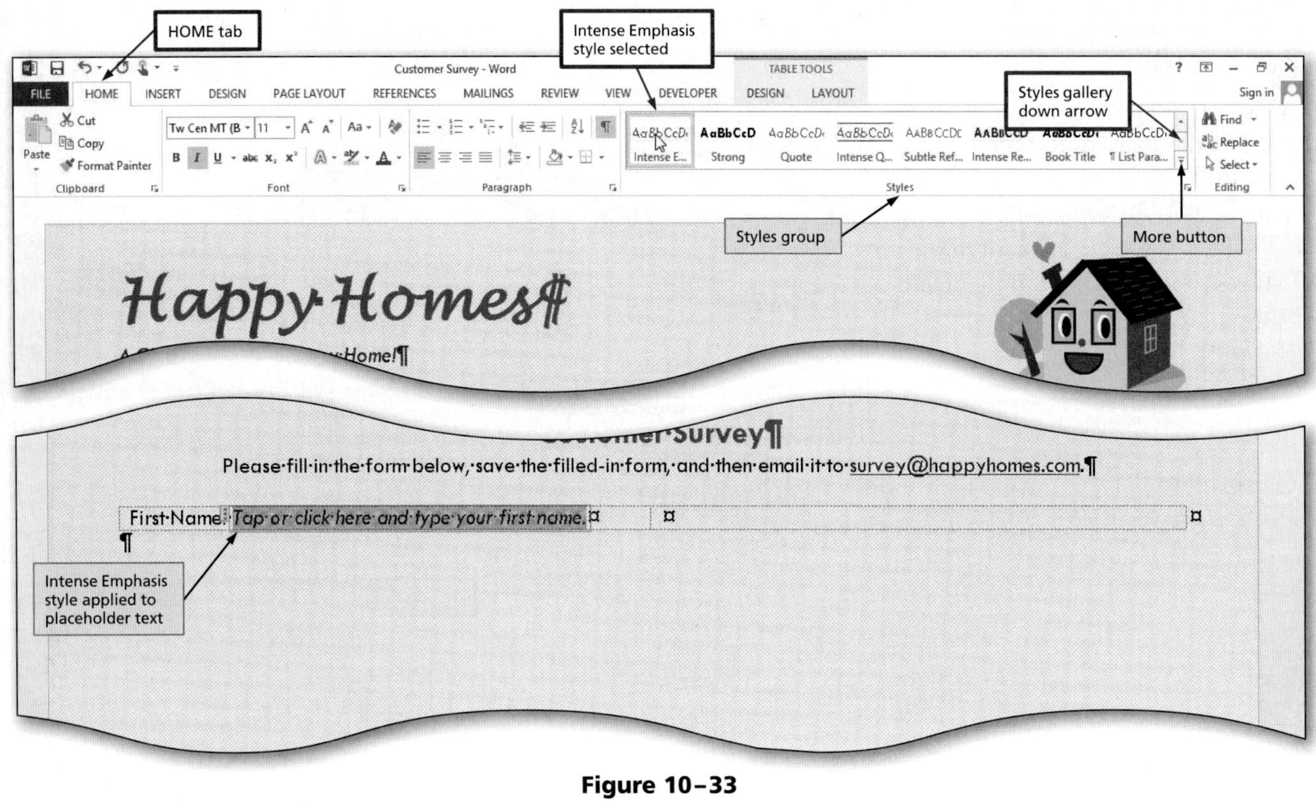

Figure 10–33

To Insert Another Plain Text Content Control and Edit Its Placeholder Text

The second item that a user enters in the Customer Survey is his or her last name. The steps for entering the last name content control are similar to those for the first name, because the last name also is a plain text content control. The following steps enter the label, Last Name:, and then insert a plain text content control and edit its placeholder text.

1. Position the insertion point in the second cell (column) in the table.
2. With the insertion point in the second cell of the table, type `Last Name:` as the label for the content control and then press the SPACEBAR.
3. Display the DEVELOPER tab. Tap or click the 'Plain Text Content Control' button (DEVELOPER tab | Controls group) to insert a plain text content control at the location of the insertion point.
4. With the plain text content control selected, tap or click the Design Mode button (DEVELOPER tab | Controls group) to turn on Design mode (Figure 10–34).
5. If necessary, select the placeholder text to be changed.
6. Edit the placeholder text so that it contains the text, Tap or click here and type your last name., as the instruction.
7. Tap or click the Design Mode button (DEVELOPER tab | Controls group) to turn off Design mode.

BTW

Deleting Content Controls

To delete a content control, select it and then press the DELETE key or tap or click the Cut button (HOME tab | Clipboard group), or press and hold or right-click it and then tap or click Cut on the shortcut menu.

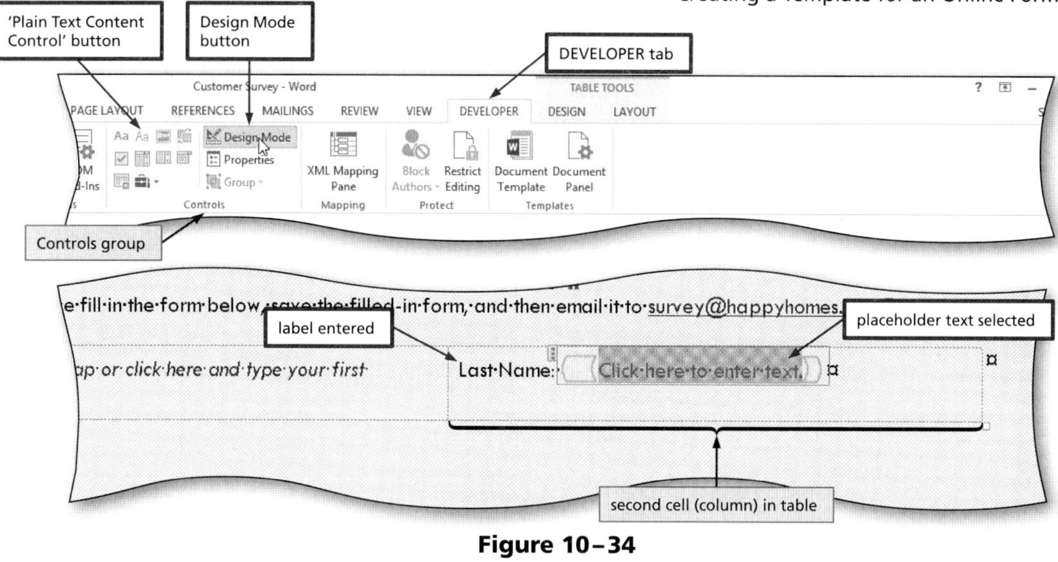

Figure 10–34

To Change the Properties of a Plain Text Content Control

The next step is to change the title, style, and locking properties of the Last Name content control, just as you did for the First Name content control. The following steps change properties of a plain text content control.

1. With the content control selected, tap or click the Control Properties button (DEVELOPER tab | Controls group) to display the Content Control Properties dialog box.
2. Type `Last Name` in the Tag text box (Content Control Properties dialog box).
3. Place a check mark in the 'Use a style to format text typed into the empty control' check box to activate the Style box.
4. Tap or click the Style arrow and then select Intense Emphasis in the list to specify the style for the content control.
5. Place a check mark in the 'Content control cannot be deleted' check box (Figure 10–35).
6. Tap or click the OK button to assign the properties to the content control.

BTW

BTWs

For a complete list of the BTWs found in the margins of this book, visit the BTW resource on the Student Companion Site located on www.cengagebrain.com. For detailed instructions about accessing available resources, visit www.cengage.com/ct/studentdownload or contact your instructor for information about accessing the required files.

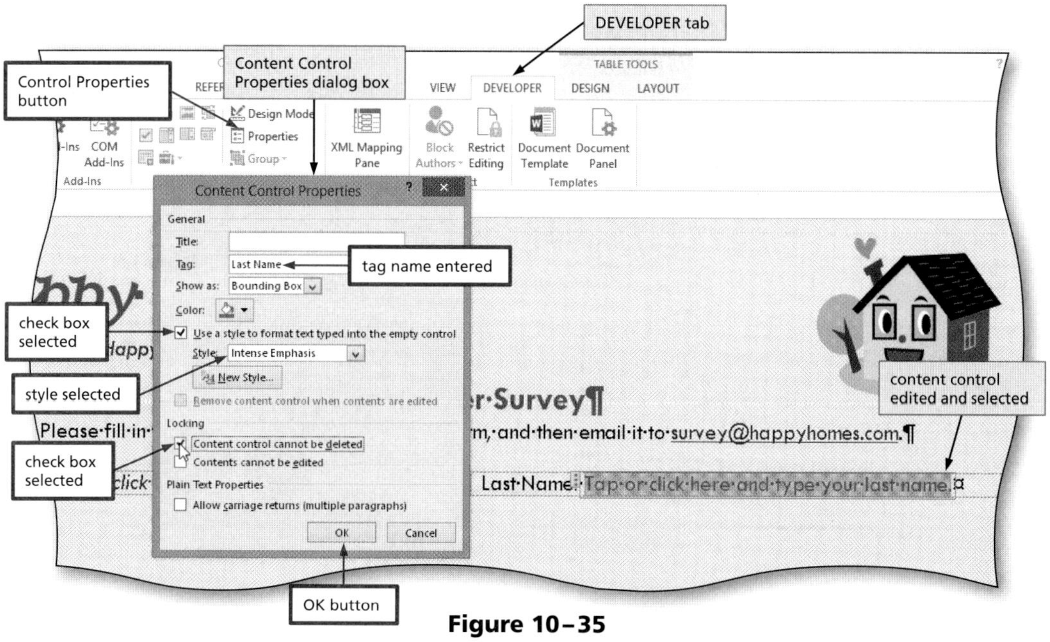

Figure 10–35

To Format Placeholder Text

As with the placeholder text for the first name, the placeholder text for the last name should use the Intense Emphasis style. The following steps format placeholder text.

1. With the last name placeholder text selected, display the HOME tab.
2. Locate and select the Intense Emphasis style in the Styles gallery (HOME tab | Styles group) to apply the selected style to the selected placeholder text.

To Increase Space before a Paragraph

The next step in creating this online form is to increase space before a paragraph so that the space below the table is consistent with the space between other elements on the form. The following steps increase space before a paragraph.

1. Position the insertion point on the blank line below the table.
2. Display the PAGE LAYOUT tab.
3. Change the value in the Spacing Before box (PAGE LAYOUT tab | Paragraph group) to 8 pt to increase the space between the table and the paragraph (shown in Figure 10–36).

To Insert a Drop-Down List Content Control

1 SAVE DOCUMENT TEMPLATE | 2 SET FORM FORMATS FOR TEMPLATE
3 ENTER TEXT, GRAPHICS, & CONTENT CONTROLS | **4 PROTECT FORM** | **5 USE FORM**

In the online form in this chapter, the user selects from one of these four choices for the Frequency of Service Use content control: Monthly, Every other week, Occasional, or One time. The following steps insert a drop-down list content control. ***Why?*** *To present a set of choices to a user in the form of a drop-down list, from which the user selects one, insert a drop-down list content control. To view the set of choices, the user taps or clicks the arrow at the right edge of the content control.*

- With the insertion point positioned on the blank paragraph mark below the First Name content control, using either the ruler or the PAGE LAYOUT tab, change the left indent to 0.06" so that the entered text aligns with the text immediately above it (that is, the F in First).
- Type **`How often do you use our services?`** and then press the SPACEBAR.

- Display the DEVELOPER tab.
- Tap or click the 'Drop-Down List Content Control' button (DEVELOPER tab | Controls group) to insert a drop-down list content control at the location of the insertion point (Figure 10–36).

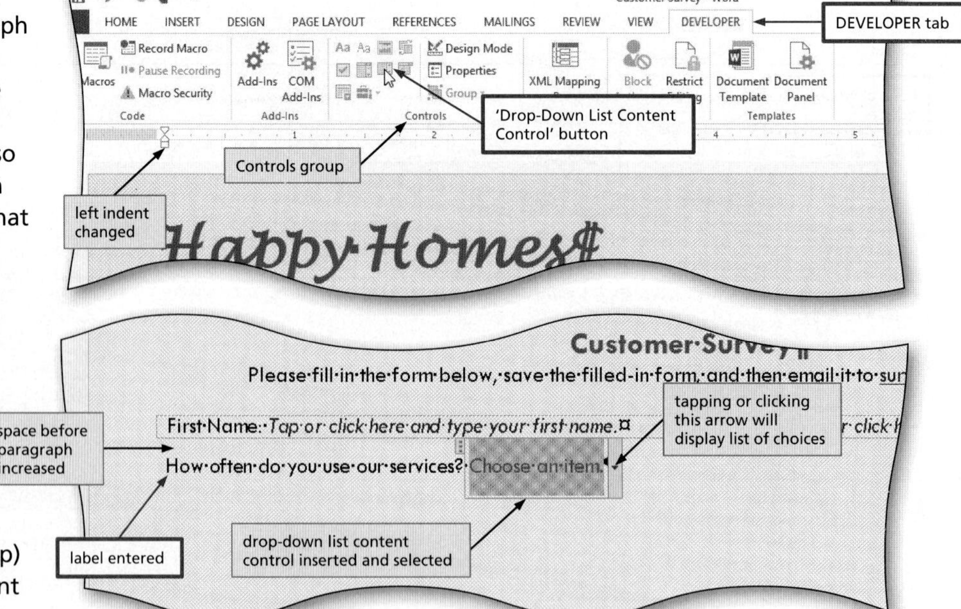

Figure 10–36

To Edit Placeholder Text

The following steps edit the placeholder text for the drop-down list content control.

1. If necessary, display the DEVELOPER tab. With the drop-down list content control selected, tap or click the Design Mode button (DEVELOPER tab | Controls group) to turn on Design mode.
2. Edit the placeholder text so that it contains this instruction, which contains two separate sentences: Tap or click here. Tap or click arrow and select from list.
3. Tap or click the Design Mode button (DEVELOPER tab | Controls group) to turn off Design mode.

To Change the Properties of a Drop-Down List Content Control

The following steps change the properties of a drop-down list content control. ***Why?*** *In addition to identifying a tag, selecting a style, and locking the drop-down list content control, you can specify the choices that will be displayed when a user taps or clicks the arrow to the right of the content control.*

- With the drop-down list content control selected, tap or click the Control Properties button (DEVELOPER tab | Controls group) to display the Content Control Properties dialog box.
- Type `Frequency of Service Use` in the Tag text box (Content Control Properties dialog box).
- Place a check mark in the 'Use a style to format text typed into the empty control' check box to activate the Style box.
- Tap or click the Style arrow and then select Intense Emphasis in the list to specify the style for the content control.
- Place a check mark in the 'Content control cannot be deleted' check box.
- In the Drop-Down List Properties area, tap or click 'Choose an item.' to select it (Figure 10–37).

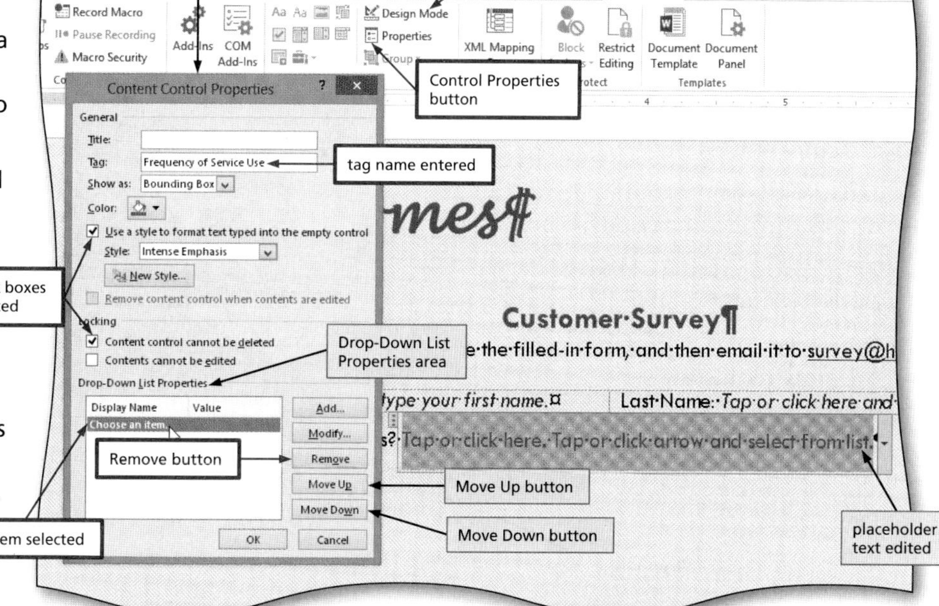

Figure 10–37

2

- Tap or click the Remove button (Content Control Properties dialog box) to delete the 'Choose an item.' entry.

Q&A Why delete the 'Choose an item.' entry?
If you leave it in the list, it will appear as the first item in the list when the user taps or clicks the content control arrow. You do not want it in the list, so you delete it.

Can I delete any entry in a drop-down list using the Remove button?
Yes, select the entry in this dialog box and then tap or click the Remove button. You also can rearrange the order of entries in a list by selecting the entry and then tapping or clicking the Move Up or Move Down buttons.

3

- Tap or click the Add button to display the Add Choice dialog box.
- Type **`Monthly`** in the Display Name text box (Add Choice dialog box), and notice that Word automatically enters the same text in the Value text box (Figure 10–38).

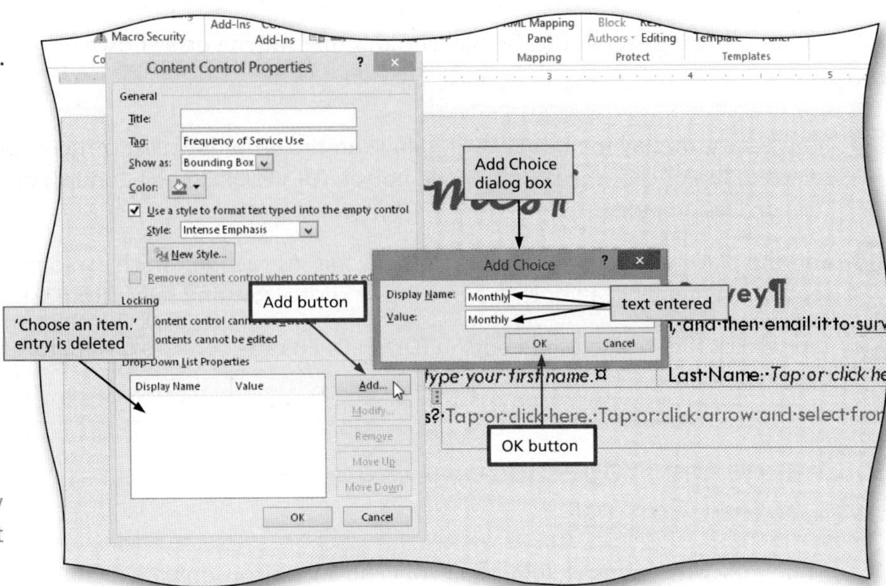

Figure 10–38

Q&A What is the difference between a display name and a value?
Often, they are the same, which is why when you type the display name, Word automatically enters the same text in the Value text box. Sometimes, however, you may want to store a shorter or different value. If the display name is long, entering shorter values makes it easier for separate programs to analyze and interpret entered data.

4

- Tap or click the OK button (Add Choice dialog box) to add the entered display name and value to the list of choices in the Drop-Down List Properties area (Content Control Properties dialog box).

5

- Tap or click the Add button to display the Add Choice dialog box.
- Type **`Every other week`** in the Display Name text box.
- Tap or click the OK button to add the entry to the list.
- Tap or click the Add button to display the Add Choice dialog box.
- Type **`Occasional`** in the Display Name text box.
- Tap or click the OK button to add the entry to the list.
- Tap or click the Add button to display the Add Choice dialog box.
- Type **`One time`** in the Display Name text box.
- Tap or click the OK button to add the entry to the list (Figure 10–39).

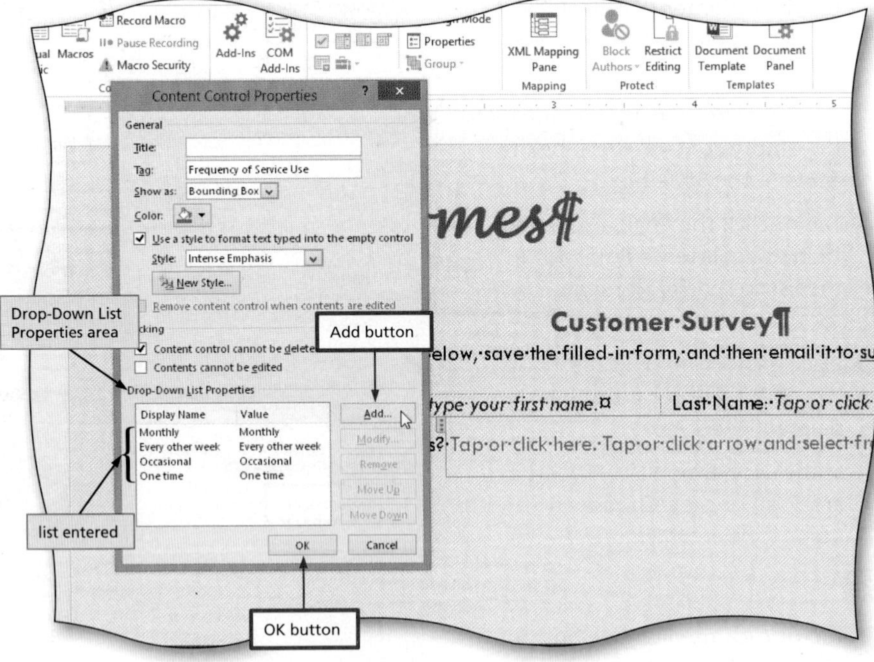

Figure 10–39

6

- Tap or click the OK button (Content Control Properties dialog box) to change the content control properties.

Q&A What if I want to change an entry in the drop-down list?
You would select the drop-down list content control, tap or click the Control Properties button (DEVELOPER tab | Controls group) to display the Content Control Properties dialog box, select the entry to change, tap or click the Modify button, adjust the entry, and then tap or click the OK button.

To Format Placeholder Text

As with the previous placeholder text, the placeholder text for the Frequency of Service Use content control should use the Intense Emphasis style. The following steps format placeholder text.

1. With the Frequency of Service Use placeholder text selected, display the HOME tab.
2. Locate and select the Intense Emphasis style in the Styles gallery (HOME tab | Styles group) to apply the selected style to the selected placeholder text.
3. Press the END key to position the insertion point at the end of the current line and then press the ENTER key to position the insertion point below the Frequency of Service Use content control.

To Enter Text and Use a Table to Control Layout

The next step is to enter the user instructions for the check box content controls and insert a 4 × 1 borderless table so that four evenly spaced check boxes can be displayed horizontally below the check box instructions. The following steps enter text and insert a borderless table.

1. With the insertion point positioned on the paragraph below the Frequency of Service Use content control, tap or click Normal in the Styles gallery (HOME tab | Styles group) to format the current paragraph to the Normal style.
2. Using either the ruler or the PAGE LAYOUT tab, change the left indent to 0.06" so that the entered text aligns with the text immediately above it (that is, the H in How).
3. Type **`Which of our services have you used (check all that apply)?`** as the instruction.
4. Tap or click the 'Line and Paragraph Spacing' button (HOME tab | Paragraph group) and then tap or click 'Remove Space After Paragraph' so that the check boxes will appear one physical line below the instructions.
5. Press the ENTER key to position the insertion point on the line below the check box instructions.
6. Display the INSERT tab. Tap or click the 'Add a Table' button (INSERT tab | Tables group) to display the Add a Table gallery and then tap or click the cell in the first row and fourth column of the grid to insert an empty 4 × 1 table at the location of the insertion point.
7. Select the table.
8. Tap or click the Borders arrow (TABLE TOOLS DESIGN tab | Borders group) to display the Borders gallery and then tap or click No Border in the Borders gallery to remove the borders from the table.
9. Tap or click the first cell of the table to remove the selection (shown in Figure 10–40 on the next page).

BTW

Certification

The Microsoft Office Specialist (MOS) program provides an opportunity for you to obtain a valuable industry credential — proof that you have the Word 2013 skills required by employers. For more information, visit the Certification resource on the Student Companion Site located on www.cengagebrain.com. For detailed instructions about accessing available resources, visit www.cengage.com/ct/studentdownload or contact your instructor for information about accessing the required files.

To Insert a Check Box Content Control

The following step inserts the first check box content control. ***Why?*** *In the online form in this chapter, the user can select up to five check boxes: Standard cleaning, Green cleaning, Window washing, Carpet cleaning, and Other.*

- Position the insertion point at the location for the check box content control, in this case, the leftmost cell in the 4 × 1 table.
- Display the DEVELOPER tab.
- Tap or click the 'Check Box Content Control' button (DEVELOPER tab | Controls group) to insert a check box content control at the location of the insertion point (Figure 10–40).

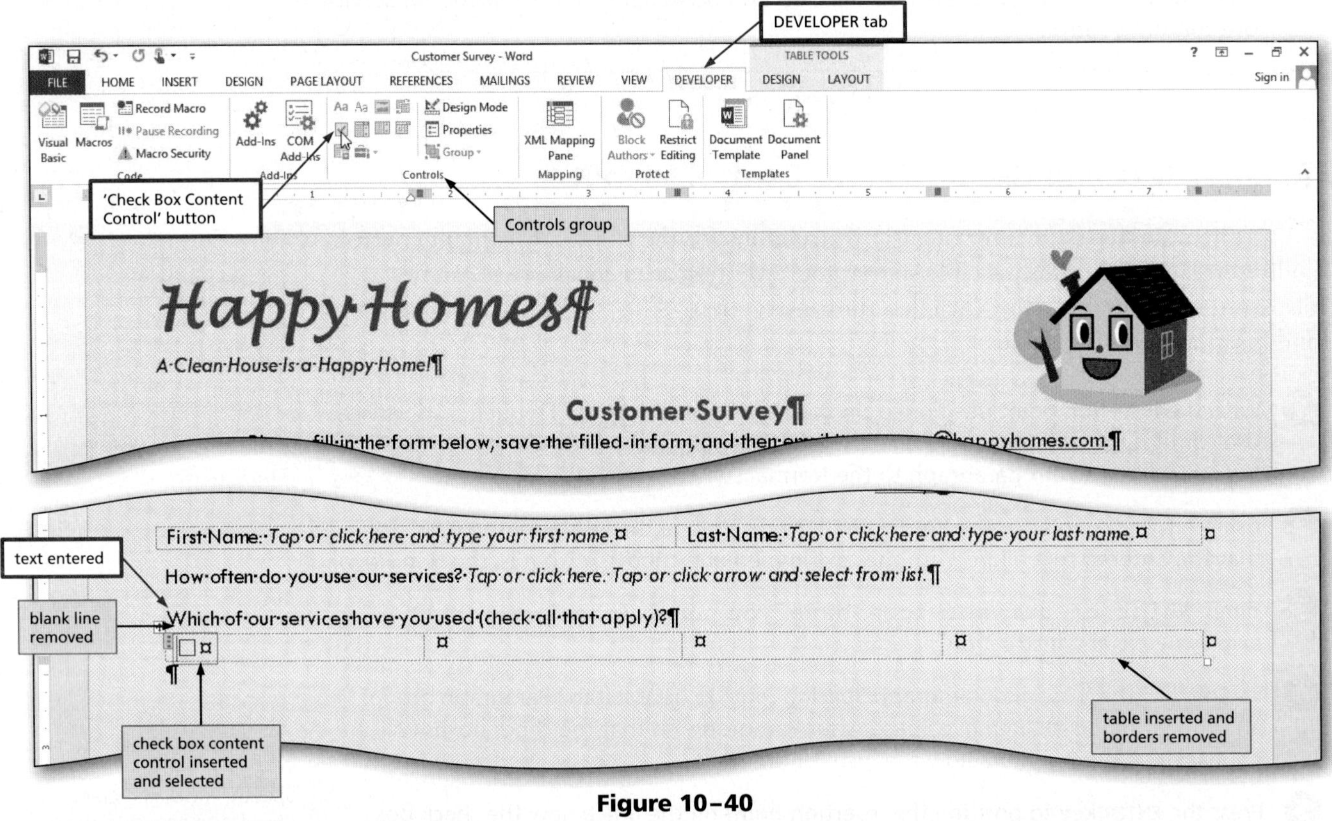

Figure 10–40

To Change the Properties of a Check Box Content Control

The next step is to change the title and locking properties of the content control. The following steps change properties of a check box content control.

1. With the content control selected, tap or click the Control Properties button (DEVELOPER tab | Controls group) to display the Content Control Properties dialog box.
2. Type `Standard Cleaning` in the Tag text box (Content Control Properties dialog box).
3. Tap or click the Show as arrow and then select None in the list, because you do not want a border surrounding the check box content control.
4. Place a check mark in the 'Content control cannot be deleted' check box (Figure 10–41).
5. Tap or click the OK button to assign the properties to the selected content control.

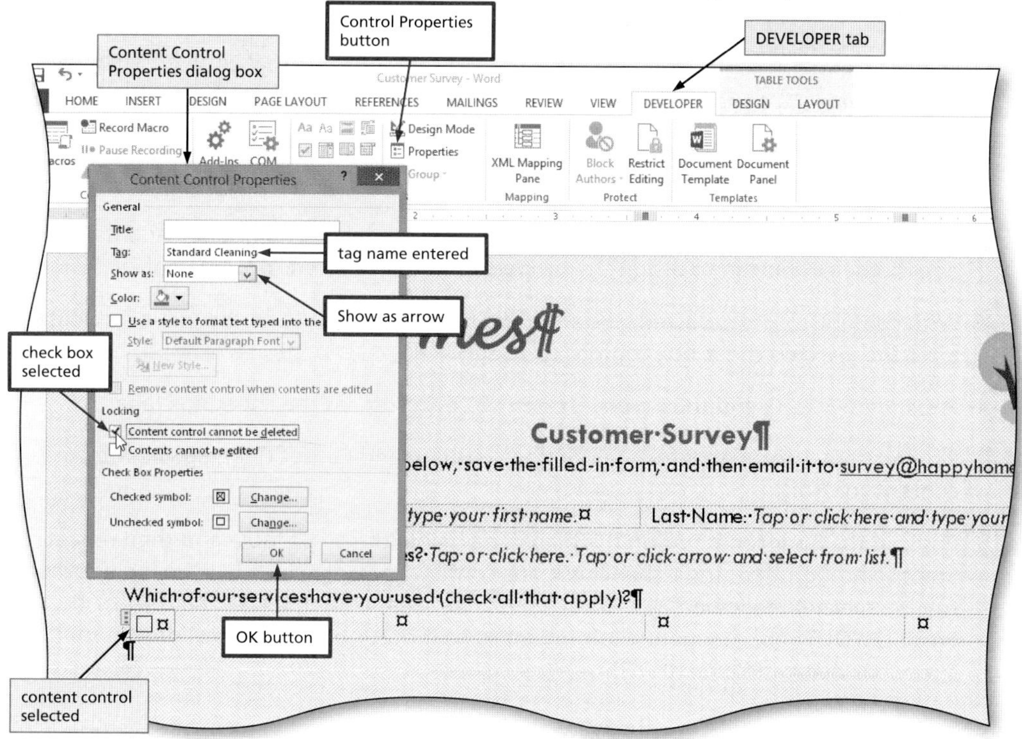

Figure 10–41

To Add a Label to a Check Box Content Control

The following steps add a label to the right of a check box content control.

1. With content control selected, press the END key twice to position the insertion point after the inserted check box content control.

2. Press the SPACEBAR and then type `Standard cleaning` as the check box label (Figure 10–42).

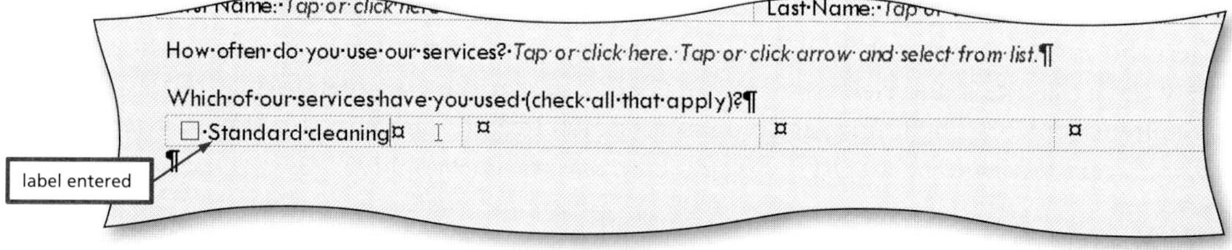

Figure 10–42

To Insert Additional Check Box Content Controls

The following steps insert the remaining check box content controls and their labels.

1. Press the TAB key to position the insertion point in the next cell, which is the location for the next check box content control.

2. Tap or click the 'Check Box Content Control' button (DEVELOPER tab | Controls group) to insert a check box content control at the location of the insertion point.

3. With the content control selected, tap or click the Control Properties button (DEVELOPER tab | Controls group) to display the Content Control Properties dialog box.

4. Type `Green Cleaning` in the Tag text box (Content Control Properties dialog box).

5. Tap or click the Show as arrow and then select None in the list because you do not want a border surrounding the check box content control.

6. Place a check mark in the 'Content control cannot be deleted' check box and then tap or click the OK button to assign the properties to the selected content control.

7. With content control selected, press the END key twice to position the insertion point after the inserted check box content control.

8. Press the SPACEBAR and then type `Green cleaning` as the check box label.

9. Repeat Steps 1 through 8 for the Window washing and Carpet cleaning check box content controls.

10. Position the insertion point on the blank line below the 4 × 1 table and then repeat Steps 1 through 8 for the Other check box content control, which has the label, Other (please specify):, followed by the SPACEBAR. If necessary, using either the ruler or the PAGE LAYOUT tab, change the left indent so that check box above is aligned with the check box below (Figure 10–43).

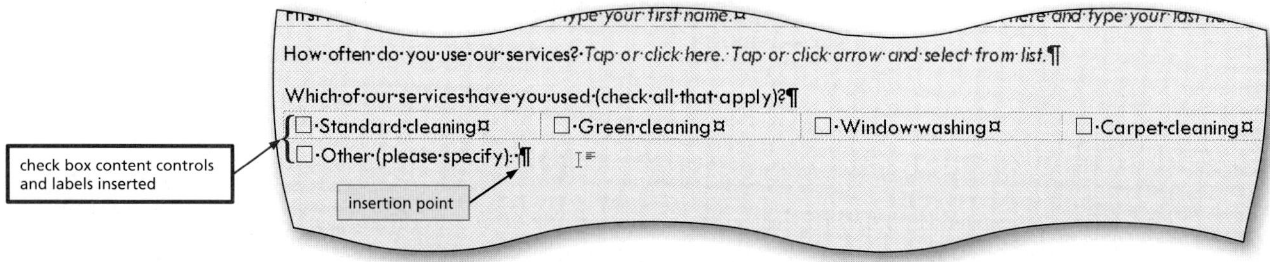

Figure 10–43

To Insert a Rich Text Content Control

1 SAVE DOCUMENT TEMPLATE | 2 SET FORM FORMATS FOR TEMPLATE
3 ENTER TEXT, GRAPHICS, & CONTENT CONTROLS | **4 PROTECT FORM** | **5 USE FORM**

The next step is to insert the content control that enables users to type in any other types of services they have used. The difference between a plain text and rich text content control is that the users can format text as they enter it in the rich text content control. The following step inserts a rich text content control. ***Why?*** *Because you want to allow users to format the text they enter in the Other Services Used content control, you use the rich text content control.*

- If necessary, position the insertion point at the location for the rich text content control (shown in Figure 10–43).
- Tap or click the 'Rich Text Content Control' button (DEVELOPER tab | Controls group) to insert a rich text content control at the location of the insertion point (Figure 10–44).

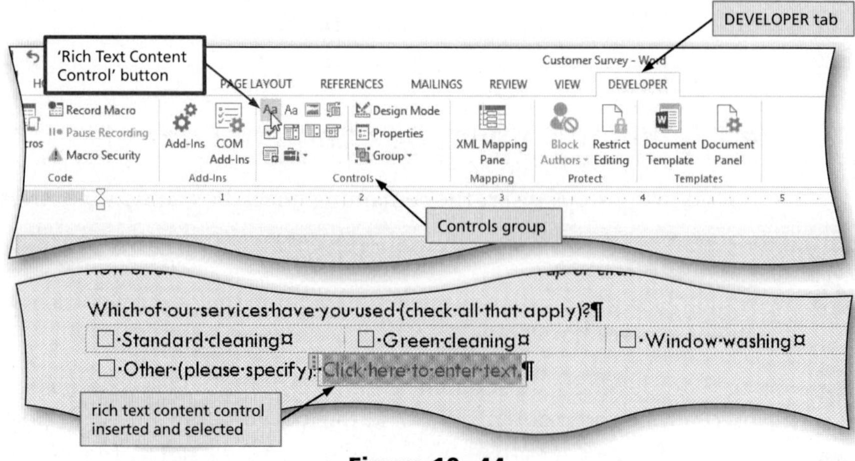

Figure 10–44

To Edit Placeholder Text

The following steps edit placeholder text for the rich text content control.

1. With the rich text content control selected, tap or click the Design Mode button (DEVELOPER tab | Controls group) to turn on Design mode.
2. If necessary, scroll to display the content control in the document window.
3. Edit the placeholder text so that it contains the text, Tap or click here and type other services you have used., as the instruction.
4. Tap or click the Design Mode button (DEVELOPER tab | Controls group) to turn off Design mode. If necessary, scroll to display the top of the form in the document window.

To Change the Properties of a Rich Text Content Control

In the online form in this chapter, you change the same three properties for the rich text content control as for the plain text content control. That is, you enter a tag name, specify the style, and lock the content control. The following steps change the properties of the rich text content control.

1. With the content control selected, tap or click the Control Properties button (DEVELOPER tab | Controls group) to display the Content Control Properties dialog box.
2. Type `Other Services Used` in the Tag text box (Content Control Properties dialog box).
3. Place a check mark in the 'Use a style to format text typed into the empty control' check box to activate the Style box.
4. Tap or click the Style arrow and then select Intense Emphasis in the list to specify the style for the content control.
5. Place a check mark in the 'Content control cannot be deleted' check box (Figure 10–45).
6. Tap or click the OK button to assign the properties to the content control.

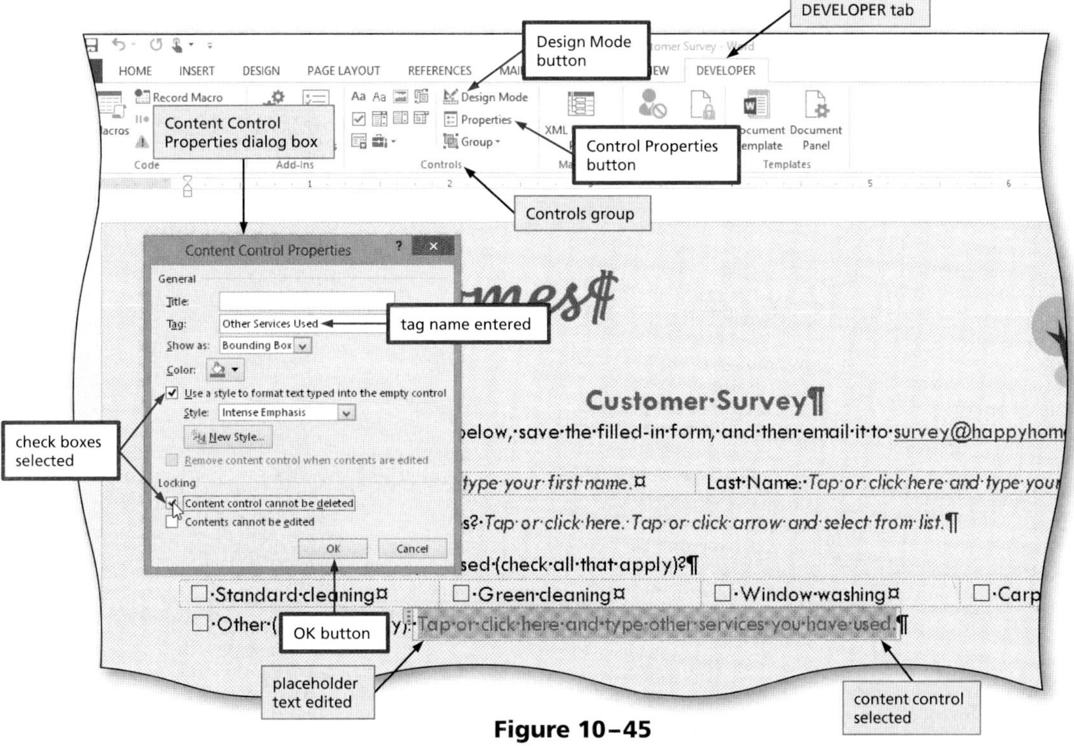

Figure 10–45

To Format Placeholder Text and Add Space before a Paragraph

The placeholder text for the Other Services Used text entry should use the Intense Emphasis style, and the space below the check boxes should be consistent with the space between other elements on the form. The next steps format placeholder text and increase space before a paragraph.

1. With the Other Services Used placeholder text selected, display the HOME tab.
2. Locate and select the Intense Emphasis style in the Styles gallery (HOME tab | Styles group) to apply the selected style to the selected placeholder text.
3. Press the END key to position the insertion point on the paragraph mark after the Other Services Used content control and then press the ENTER key to position the insertion point below the Other Services Used content control.
4. If necessary, display the HOME tab. With the insertion point positioned on the paragraph below the Other Services Used content control, tap or click Normal in the Styles gallery (HOME tab | Styles group) to format the current paragraph to the Normal style.
5. Using either the ruler or the PAGE LAYOUT tab, change the left indent to 0.06" so that the entered text aligns with the text two lines above it (that is, the W in Which).
6. Display the PAGE LAYOUT tab. Change the value in the Spacing Before box (PAGE LAYOUT tab | Paragraph group) to 8 pt to increase the space between the Other Services Used check box and the paragraph.

To Insert a Combo Box Content Control

1 SAVE DOCUMENT TEMPLATE | 2 SET FORM FORMATS FOR TEMPLATE
3 ENTER TEXT, GRAPHICS, & CONTENT CONTROLS | **4 PROTECT FORM** | **5 USE FORM**

In Word, a combo box content control allows a user to type text or select from a list. The following steps insert a combo box content control. ***Why?*** *In the online form in this chapter, users can type their own entry in the Cleaning Staff Rating content control or select from one of these four choices: Excellent, Good, Fair, or Poor.*

1

- With the insertion point positioned on the blank paragraph mark, type **How would you rate our cleaning staff?** and then press the SPACEBAR.

2

- Display the DEVELOPER tab.
- Tap or click the 'Combo Box Content Control' button (DEVELOPER tab | Controls group) to insert a combo box content control at the location of the insertion point (Figure 10–46).

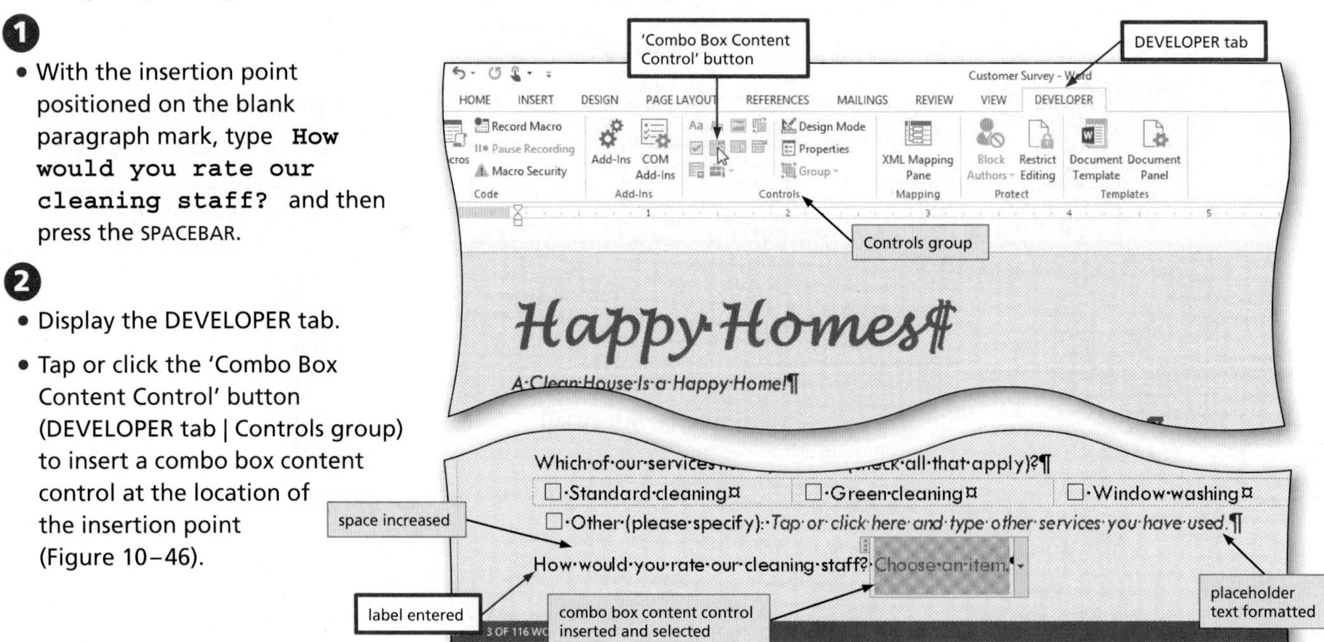

Figure 10–46

To Edit Placeholder Text

The following steps edit the placeholder text for the combo box content control.

1. With the combo box content control selected, tap or click the Design Mode button (DEVELOPER tab | Controls group) to turn on Design mode.

2. If necessary, scroll to page 2 to display the combo box content control.

Q&A Why did the content control move to another page?
Because Design mode displays tags, the content controls and placeholder text are not displayed in their proper positions on the screen. When you turn off Design mode, the content controls will return to their original locations and the extra page should disappear.

3. Edit the placeholder text so that it contains this instruction, which contains two sentences (Figure 10–47): Tap or click here. Tap or click arrow and select from list, or type a response.

4. Tap or click the Design Mode button (DEVELOPER tab | Controls group) to turn off Design mode.

5. Scroll to display the top of the form in the document window.

BTW
Q&As
For a complete list of the Q&As found in many of the step-by-step sequences in this book, visit the Q&A resource on the Student Companion Site located on www.cengagebrain.com. For detailed instructions about accessing available resources, visit www.cengage.com/ct/studentdownload or contact your instructor for information about accessing the required files.

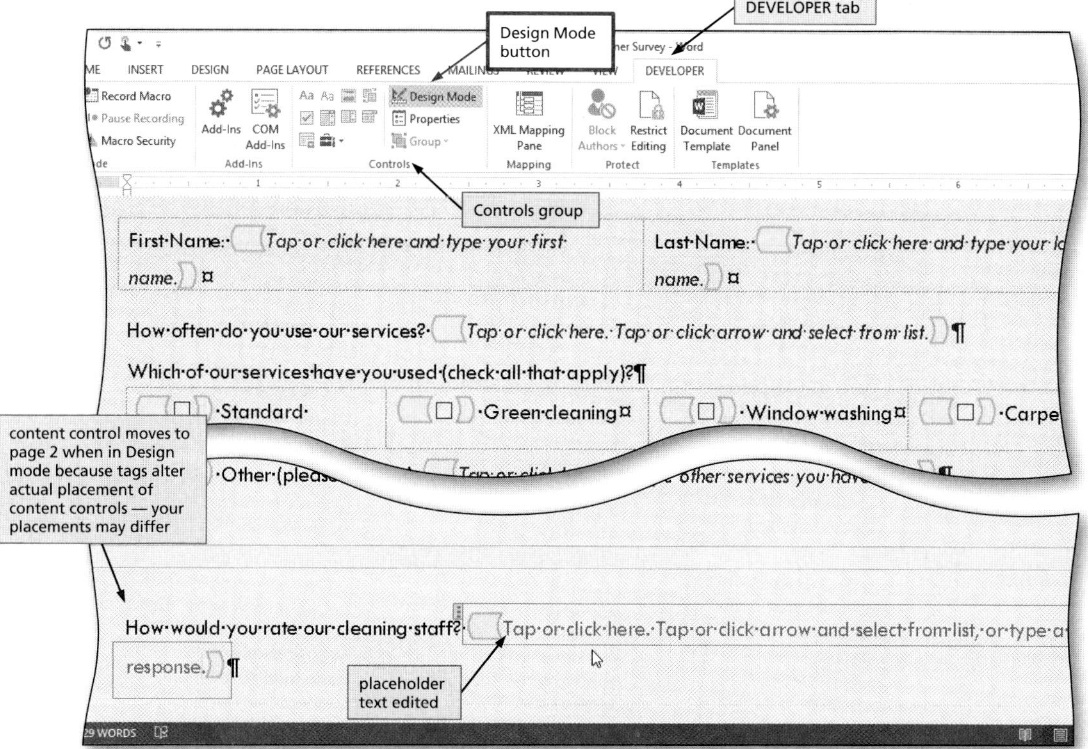

Figure 10–47

To Change the Properties of a Combo Box Content Control

1 SAVE DOCUMENT TEMPLATE | 2 SET FORM FORMATS FOR TEMPLATE
3 ENTER TEXT, GRAPHICS, & CONTENT CONTROLS | **4 PROTECT FORM** | **5 USE FORM**

You follow similar steps to enter the list for a combo box content control as you do for the drop-down list content control. The next steps change the properties of a combo box content control. ***Why?*** *You enter the tag name, specify the style for typed text, and enter the choices for the drop-down list.*

1

- With content control selected, tap or click the Control Properties button (DEVELOPER tab | Controls group) to display the Content Control Properties dialog box.
- Type **`Cleaning Staff Rating`** in the Tag text box (Content Control Properties dialog box).
- Place a check mark in the 'Use a style to format text typed into the empty control' check box to activate the Style box.
- Tap or click the Style arrow and then select Intense Emphasis in the list to specify the style for the content control.
- Place a check mark in the 'Content control cannot be deleted' check box.
- In the Drop-Down List Properties area, tap or click 'Choose an item.' to select it (Figure 10–48).

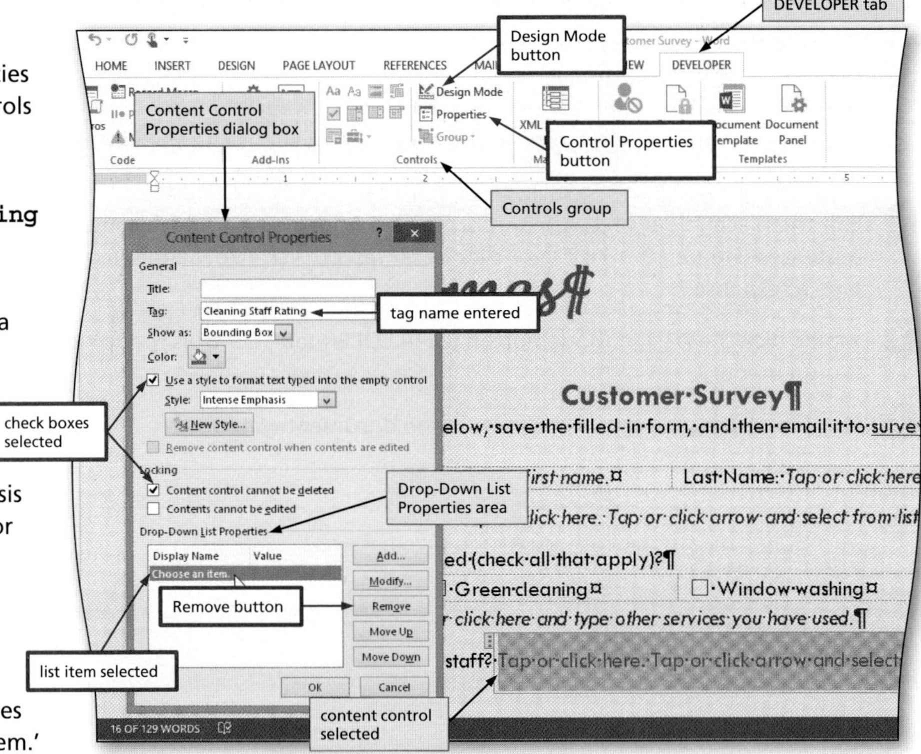

Figure 10–48

- Tap or click the Remove button (Content Control Properties dialog box) to delete the selected entry.

- Tap or click the Add button to display the Add Choice dialog box.
- Type **`Excellent`** in the Display Name text box (Add Choice dialog box).
- Tap or click the OK button to add the entered display name to the list of choices in the Drop-Down List Properties area (Content Control Properties dialog box).
- Tap or click the Add button and add **`Good`** to the list.
- Tap or click the Add button and add **`Fair`** to the list.
- Tap or click the Add button and add **`Poor`** to the list (Figure 10–49).

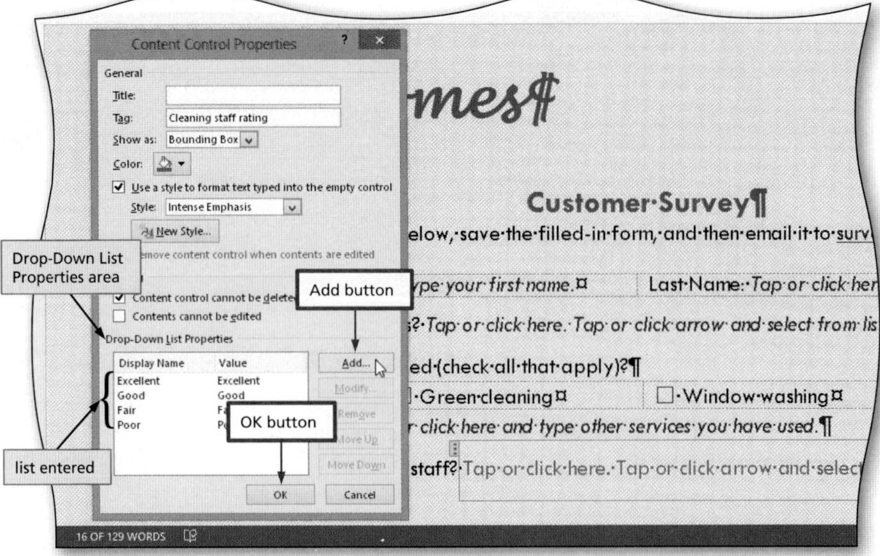

Figure 10–49

4

- Tap or click the OK button (Content Control Properties dialog box) to change the content control properties.

Q&A How do I make adjustments to entries in the list?
Follow the same procedures as you use to make adjustments to entries in a drop-down list content control (see page WD 636).

To Format Placeholder Text

As with the previous placeholder text, the placeholder text for the Cleaning Staff Rating should use the Intense Emphasis style. The following steps format placeholder text.

1. With the Cleaning Staff Rating placeholder text selected, display the HOME tab.
2. Locate and select the Intense Emphasis style in the Styles gallery (HOME tab | Styles group) to apply the selected style to the selected placeholder text.
3. Press the END key to position the insertion point at the end of the current line and then press the ENTER key to position the insertion point below the Cleaning Staff Rating content control.
4. Tap or click Normal in the Styles list (HOME tab | Styles group) to format the current paragraph to the Normal style.
5. Using either the ruler or the PAGE LAYOUT tab, change the left indent to 0.06" so that the entered text aligns with the text above it (that is, the H in How).

To Insert a Date Picker Content Control

1 SAVE DOCUMENT TEMPLATE | 2 SET FORM FORMATS FOR TEMPLATE
3 ENTER TEXT, GRAPHICS, & CONTENT CONTROLS | **4 PROTECT FORM** | **5 USE FORM**

To assist users with entering dates, Word provides a date picker content control, which displays a calendar when the user taps or clicks the arrow to the right of the content control. Users also can enter a date directly in the content control without using the calendar. The following steps enter the label, Today's Date:, and a date picker content control. ***Why?*** *The last item that users enter in the Customer Survey is today's date.*

1

- With the insertion point below the Cleaning Staff Rating content control, type **`Today's date:`** as the label for the content control and then press the SPACEBAR.

2

- Display the DEVELOPER tab.
- Tap or click the 'Date Picker Content Control' button (DEVELOPER tab | Controls group) to insert a date picker content control at the location of the insertion point (Figure 10–50).

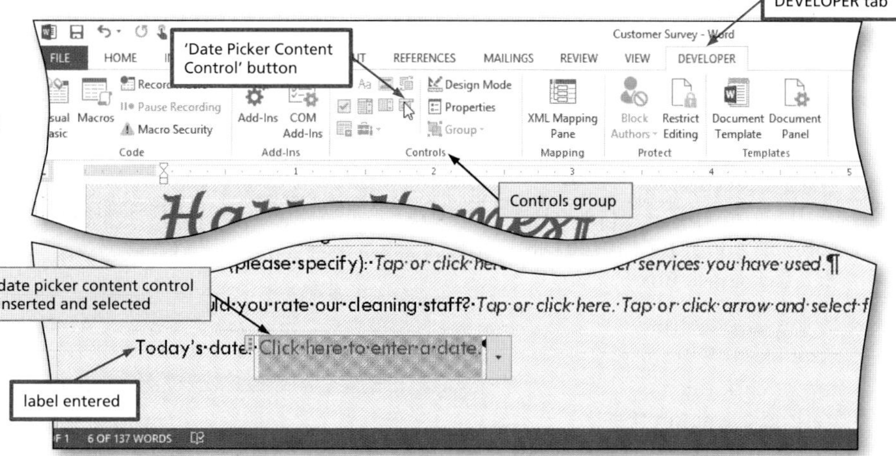

Figure 10–50

To Edit Placeholder Text

The following steps edit the placeholder text for the date picker content control.

1. With the date picker content control selected, tap or click the Design Mode button (DEVELOPER tab | Controls group) to turn on Design mode.
2. If necessary, scroll to page 2 to display the date picker content control.
3. Edit the placeholder text so that it contains this instruction, which contains two sentences: Tap or click here. Tap or click arrow and select today's date.
4. Tap or click the Design Mode button (DEVELOPER tab | Controls group) to turn off Design mode.
5. If necessary, scroll to display the top of the form in the document window.

To Change the Properties of a Date Picker Content Control

1 SAVE DOCUMENT TEMPLATE | 2 SET FORM FORMATS FOR TEMPLATE
3 ENTER TEXT, GRAPHICS, & CONTENT CONTROLS | **4 PROTECT FORM** | **5 USE FORM**

The following steps change the properties of a date picker content control. ***Why?*** *In addition to identifying a tag name for a date picker content control, specifying a style, and locking the control, you will specify how the date will be displayed when the user selects it from the calendar.*

- With the content control selected, tap or click the Control Properties button (DEVELOPER tab | Controls group) to display the Content Control Properties dialog box.
- Type `Today's Date` in the Tag text box.
- Place a check mark in the 'Use a style to format text typed into the empty control' check box to activate the Style box.
- Tap or click the Style arrow and then select Intense Emphasis in the list to specify the style for the content control.
- Place a check mark in the 'Content control cannot be deleted' check box.
- In the Display the date like this area, tap or click the desired format in the list (Figure 10–51).

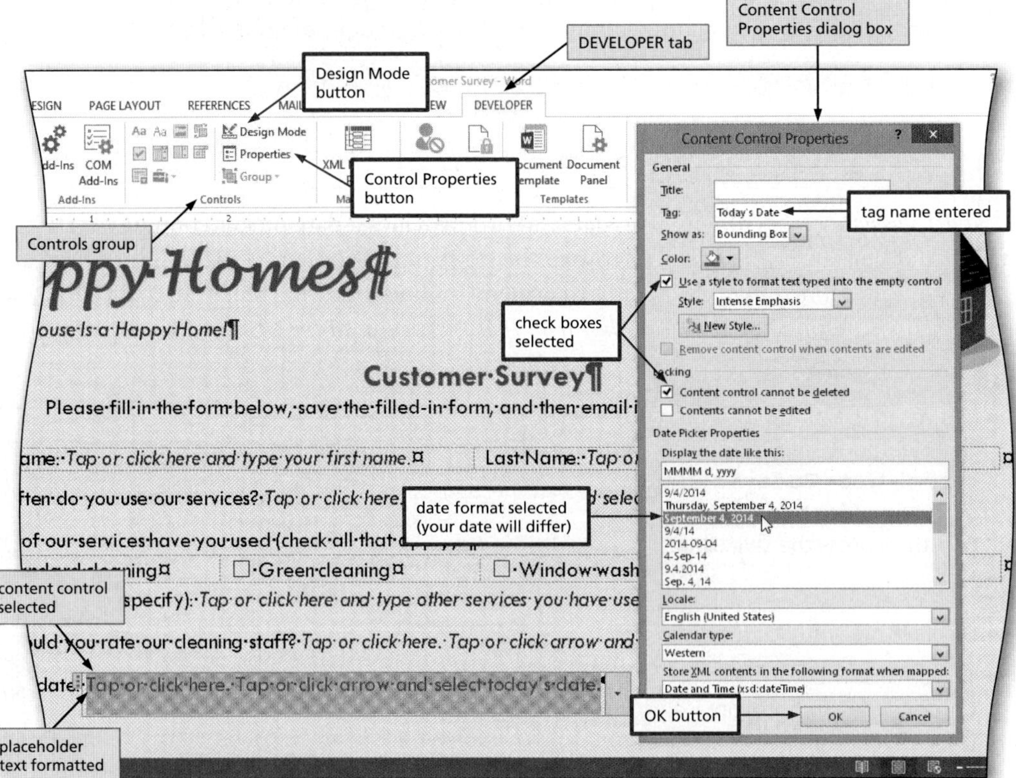

Figure 10–51

- Tap or click the OK button to change the content control properties.

To Format Placeholder Text

As with the previous placeholder text, the placeholder text for today's date should use the Intense Emphasis style. The following steps format placeholder text.

1. With the today's date placeholder text selected, display the HOME tab.
2. Locate and select the Intense Emphasis style in the Styles gallery (HOME tab | Styles group) to apply the selected style to the selected placeholder text.
3. Press the END key to position the insertion point at the end of the current line and then press the ENTER key to position the insertion point below the Today's Date content control.
4. Tap or click Normal in the Styles gallery (HOME tab | Styles group) to format the current paragraph to the Normal style.

To Enter and Format Text

The following steps enter and format the line of text at the bottom of the online form.

1. Be sure the insertion point is on the line below the Today's Date content control.
2. Center the paragraph mark.
3. Format the text to be typed with the color of Red, Accent 6, Darker 25%.
4. Type **`Thank you for your time!`**
5. Change the space before the paragraph to 12 point (Figure 10–52).
6. If the text flows to a second page, reduce spacing before paragraphs in the form so that all lines fit on a single page.

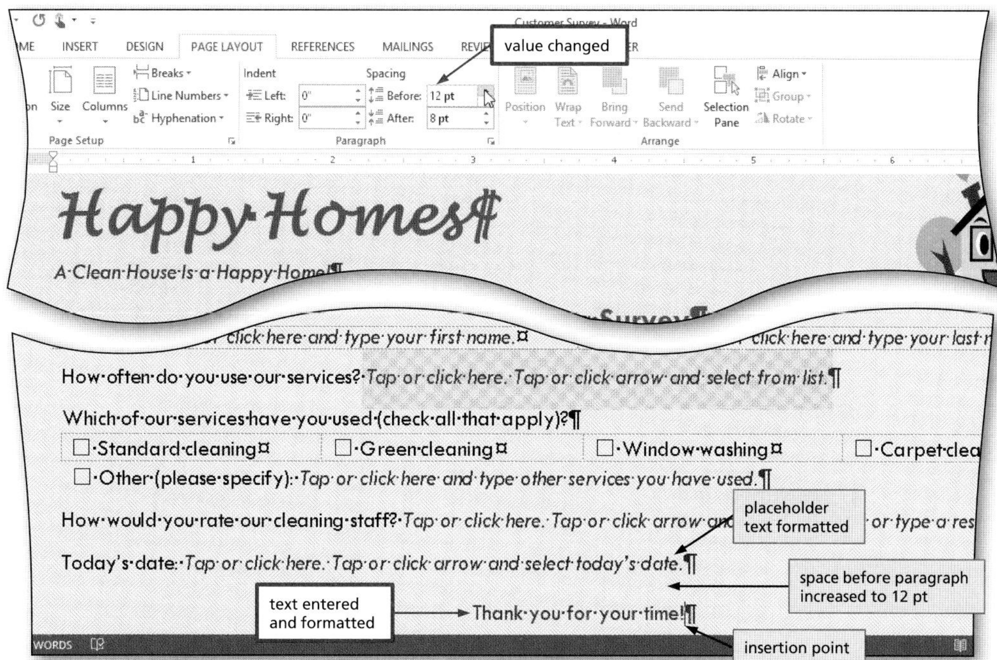

Figure 10–52

To Hide Gridlines and Formatting Marks

Because you are finished with the tables in this form and will not enter any additional tables, you will hide the gridlines. You also are finished with entering and formatting text on the screen. To make the form easier to view, you hide the formatting marks, which can clutter the screen. The following steps hide gridlines and formatting marks.

1. If necessary, position the insertion point in a table cell.
2. Display the TABLE TOOLS LAYOUT tab. If gridlines are showing, tap or click the 'View Table Gridlines' button (TABLE TOOLS LAYOUT tab | Table group) to hide table gridlines.
3. Display the HOME tab. If the 'Show/Hide ¶' button (HOME tab | Paragraph group) is selected, tap or click it to remove formatting marks from the screen.

To Save an Existing Template with the Same File Name

You have made several modifications to the template since you last saved it. Thus, you should save it again. The following step saves the template again.

1. Tap or click the Save button on the Quick Access Toolbar to overwrite the previously saved file.

Break Point: If you wish to take a break, this is a good place to do so. You can exit Word now. To resume at a later time, run Word, open the file called Customer Survey, and continue following the steps from this location forward.

To Draw a Rectangle

1 SAVE DOCUMENT TEMPLATE | 2 SET FORM FORMATS FOR TEMPLATE
3 ENTER TEXT, GRAPHICS, & CONTENT CONTROLS | **4 PROTECT FORM** | **5 USE FORM**

The next step is to emphasize the data entry area of the form. The data entry area includes all the content controls in which a user enters data. The following steps draw a rectangle around the data entry area, and subsequent steps format the rectangle. ***Why?*** *To call attention to the data entry area of the form, this chapter places a rectangle around the data entry area, changes the style of the rectangle, and then adds a shadow to the rectangle.*

1

- Position the insertion point on the last line in the document (shown in Figure 10–52 on the previous page).
- Display the INSERT tab.
- Tap or click the 'Draw a Shape' button (INSERT tab | Illustrations group) to display the Draw a Shape gallery (Figure 10–53).

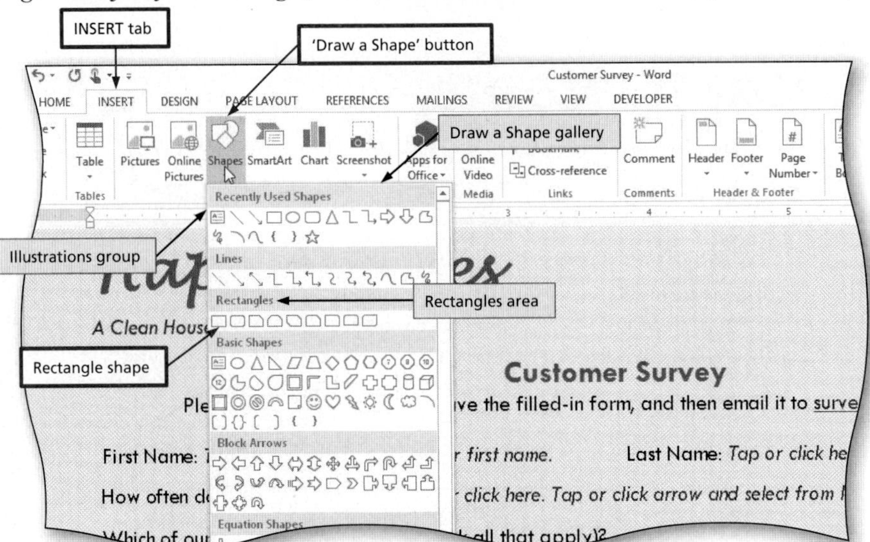

Figure 10–53

2

- Tap or click the rectangle shape in the Rectangles area of the Draw a Shape gallery, which removes the gallery. If you are using a touch screen, the shape is inserted in the document window; if you are using a mouse, the pointer changes to the shape of a crosshair in the document window.
- If you are using a mouse, position the pointer (a crosshair) in the approximate location for the upper-left corner of the desired shape (Figure 10–54).

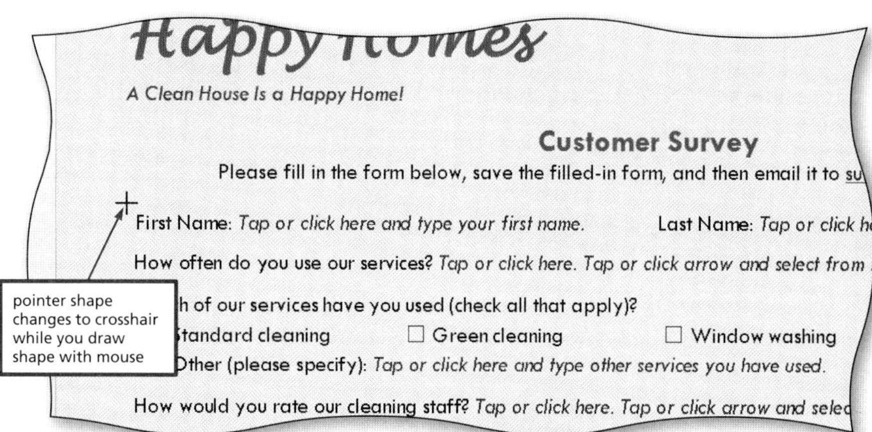

Figure 10–54

3

- If you are using a mouse, drag the pointer downward and rightward to form a rectangle around the data entry area, as shown in Figure 10–55.

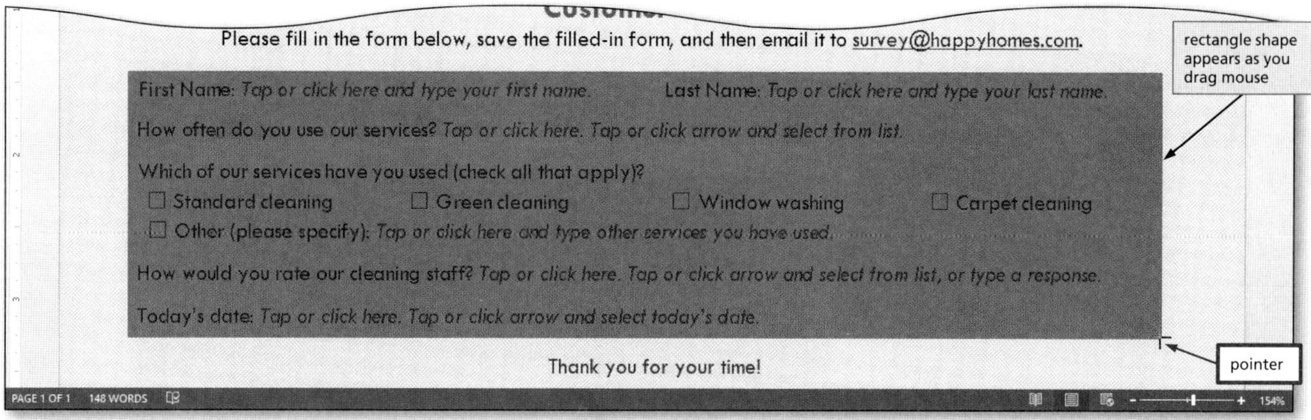

Figure 10–55

4

- If you are using a mouse, release the mouse button to draw the rectangle shape on top of the data entry area (Figure 10–56).

Q&A What happened to all the text in the data entry area?
When you draw a shape in a document, Word initially places the shape in front of, or on top of, any text in the same area. You can change the stacking order of the shape so that it is displayed behind the text. Thus, the next steps move the shape behind text.

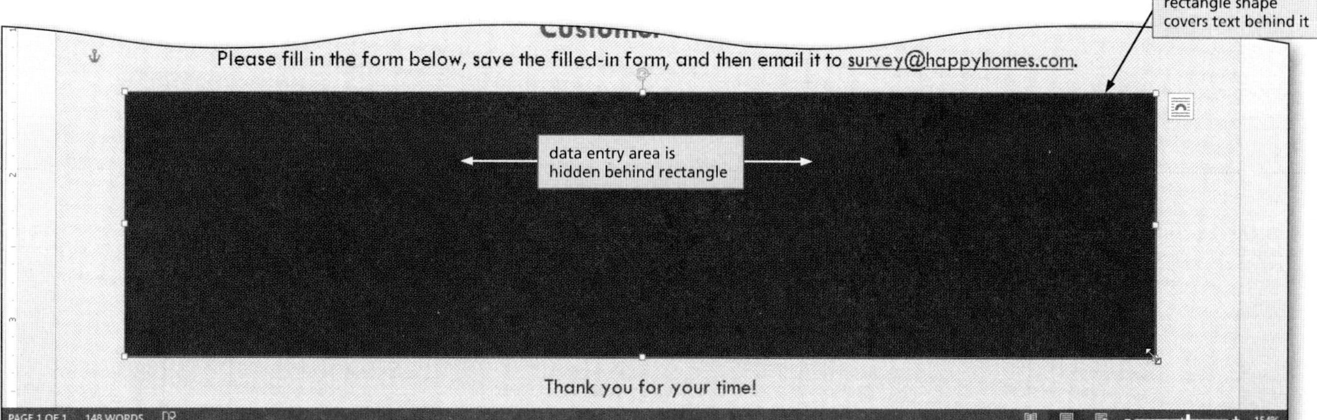

Figure 10–56

- If you are using a touch screen, change the values in the Shape Height and Shape Width boxes (DRAWING TOOLS FORMAT tab | Size group) to 1.82" and 7.39" (shown in Figure 10–58); if you are using a mouse, verify your shape is the same approximate height and width and, if necessary, change the values in the Shape Height and Shape Width boxes accordingly.

To Send a Graphic behind Text

1 SAVE DOCUMENT TEMPLATE | 2 SET FORM FORMATS FOR TEMPLATE
3 ENTER TEXT, GRAPHICS, & CONTENT CONTROLS | 4 PROTECT FORM | 5 USE FORM

The following steps send a graphic behind text. ***Why?*** *You want the rectangle shape graphic to be positioned behind the data entry area text, so that you can see the text in the data entry area along with the shape.*

- If necessary, display the DRAWING TOOLS FORMAT tab.
- With the rectangle shape selected, tap or click the Layout Options button attached to the graphic to display the Layout Options gallery (Figure 10–57).

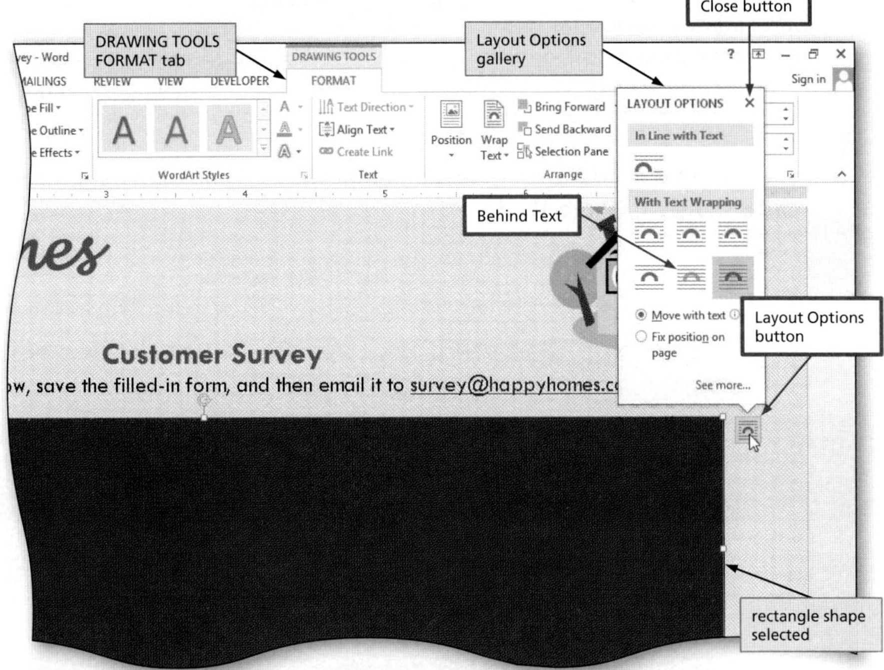

Figure 10–57

2

- Tap or click Behind Text in the Layout Options gallery to position the rectangle shape behind the text (Figure 10–58).

Q&A What if I want a shape to cover text?
You would tap or click 'In Front of Text' in the Layout Options gallery.

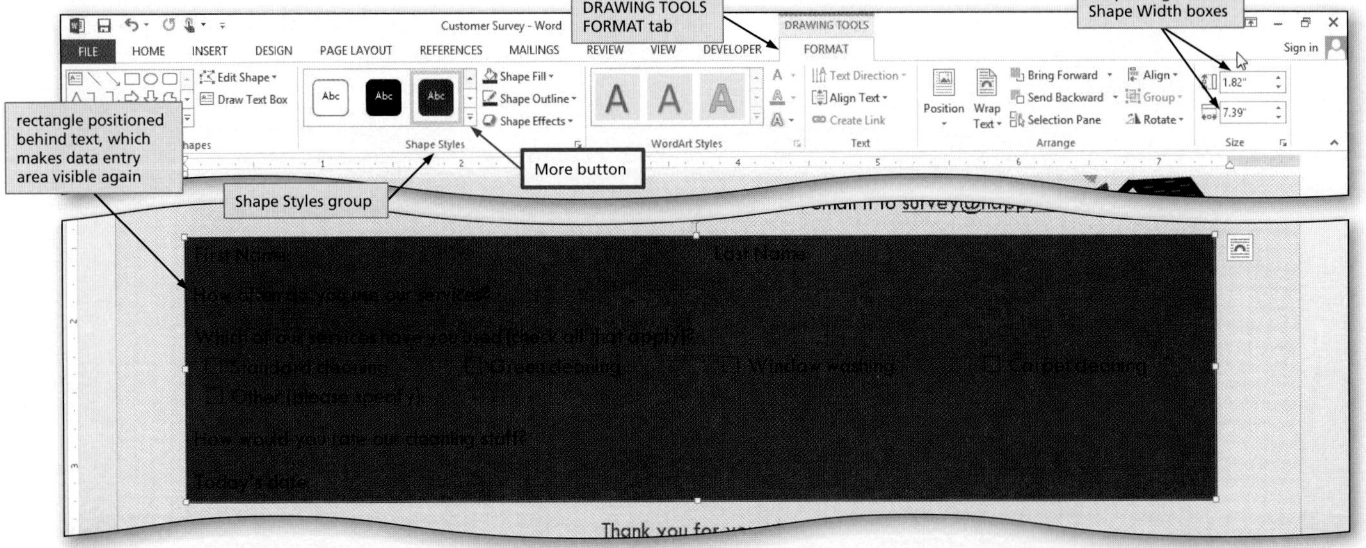

Figure 10–58

3

- Tap or click the Close button in the Layout Options gallery to close the gallery.

Other Ways

1. Tap or click Wrap Text button (DRAWING TOOLS FORMAT tab | Arrange group), select desired option
2. Tap 'Show Context Menu' button on mini toolbar or right-click object, tap or point to Wrap Text on shortcut menu, tap or click desired option

To Apply a Shape Style

The next step is to apply a shape style to the rectangle, so that the text in the data entry area is easier to read. The following steps apply a style to the rectangle shape.

1 With the shape still selected, tap or click the More button in the Shape Styles gallery (DRAWING TOOLS FORMAT tab | Shape Styles group) (shown in Figure 10–58) to expand the Shape Styles gallery.

2 If you are using a mouse, point to 'Colored Outline - Dark Blue, Accent 1' in the Shape Styles gallery (second effect in first row) to display a live preview of that style applied to the rectangle shape in the form (Figure 10–59).

3 Tap or click 'Colored Outline - Dark Blue, Accent 1' in the Shape Styles gallery to apply the selected style to the selected shape.

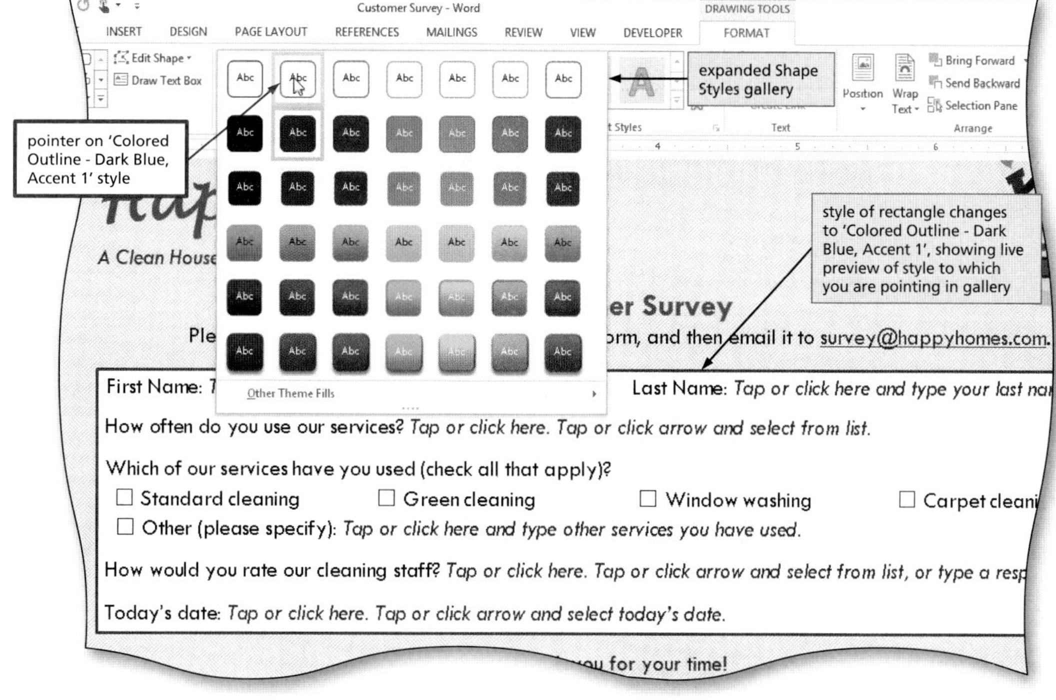

Figure 10–59

BTW

Formatting Shapes

Like other drawing objects or pictures, shapes can be formatted or have styles applied. You can change the fill in a shape by tapping or clicking the Shape Fill arrow (DRAWING TOOLS FORMAT tab | Shape Styles group), add an outline or border to a shape by tapping or clicking the Shape Outline arrow (DRAWING TOOLS FORMAT tab | Shape Styles group), and apply an effect such as shadow or 3-D effects by tapping or clicking the Shape Effects arrow (DRAWING TOOLS FORMAT tab | Shape Styles group).

To Add a Shadow to a Shape

1 SAVE DOCUMENT TEMPLATE | 2 SET FORM FORMATS FOR TEMPLATE
3 ENTER TEXT, GRAPHICS, & CONTENT CONTROLS | 4 PROTECT FORM | 5 USE FORM

The next steps add a shadow to the rectangle shape. ***Why?*** *To further offset the data entry area of the form, this online form has a shadow on the outside top and right edges of the rectangle shape.*

1

- With the shape still selected, tap or click the Shape Effects button (DRAWING TOOLS FORMAT tab | Shape Styles group) to display the Shape Effects menu.

2

- Tap or point to Shadow on the Shape Effects menu to display the Shadow gallery.
- If you are using a mouse, point to 'Offset Diagonal Top Right' in the Outer area in the Shadow gallery to display a live preview of that shadow effect applied to the selected shape in the document (Figure 10–60).

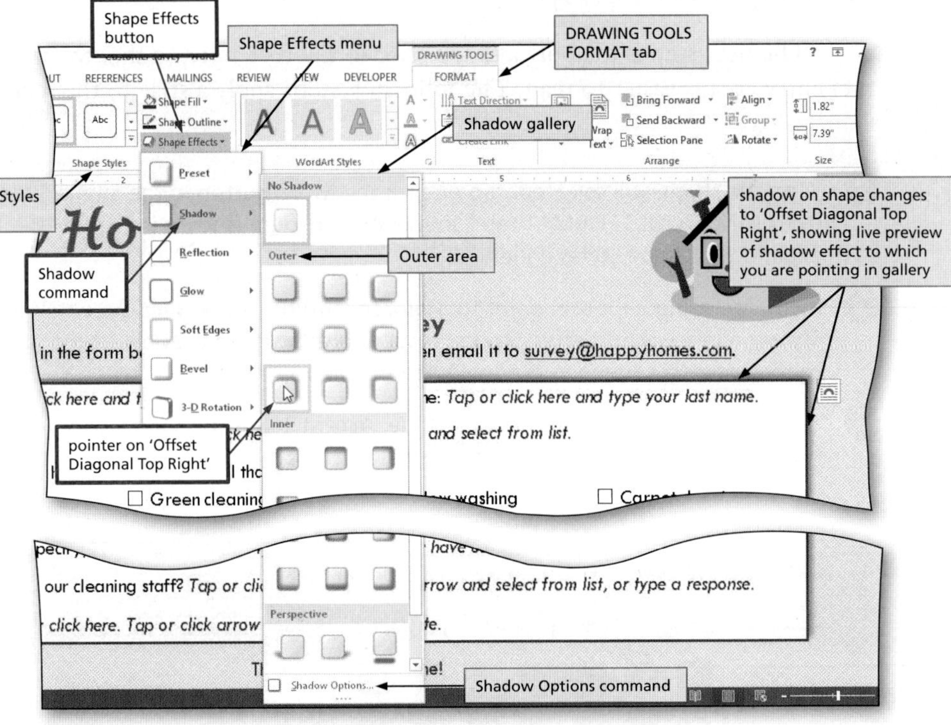

Figure 10–60

Experiment

- If you are using a mouse, point to various shadows in the Shadow gallery and watch the shadow on the selected shape change.

3

- Tap or click 'Offset Diagonal Top Right' in the Shadow gallery to apply the selected shadow to the selected shape.

Q&A Can I change the color of a shadow?
Yes. Tap or click Shadow Options in the Shadow gallery.

To Highlight Text

1 SAVE DOCUMENT TEMPLATE | 2 SET FORM FORMATS FOR TEMPLATE
3 ENTER TEXT, GRAPHICS, & CONTENT CONTROLS | 4 PROTECT FORM | 5 USE FORM

To emphasize text in an online document, you can highlight it. **Highlighting** alerts a reader to online text's importance, much like a highlighter pen does on a printed page. Word provides 15 colors you can use to highlight text, including the traditional yellow and green, as well as some nontraditional highlight colors such as gray, dark blue, and dark red. The following steps highlight the fourth line of text in the color gray. ***Why?*** *You want to emphasize the line of text on the form that contains instructions related to completing the form.*

- Select the text to be highlighted, which, in this case, is the fourth line of text.

Q&A Why is the selection taller than usual?
Earlier in this project you increased the space after this paragraph. The selection includes this vertical space.

- If necessary, display the HOME tab.
- Tap or click the 'Text Highlight Color' arrow (HOME tab | Font group) to display the Text Highlight Color gallery.

Q&A The Text Highlight Color gallery did not appear. Why not?
If you are using a mouse, you clicked the 'Text Highlight Color' button instead of the 'Text Highlight Color' arrow. Click the Undo button on the Quick Access Toolbar and then repeat Step 1.

What if the icon on the 'Text Highlight Color' button already displays the color I want to use?
If you are using a mouse, you can click the 'Text Highlight Color' button instead of the arrow.

- If you are using a mouse, point to Gray-25% in the Text Highlight Color gallery to display a live preview of this highlight color applied to the selected text (Figure 10–61).

Experiment

- If you are using a mouse, point to various colors in the Text Highlight Color gallery and watch the highlight color on the selected text change.

- Tap or click Gray-25% in the Text Highlight Color gallery to highlight the selected text in the selected highlight color.

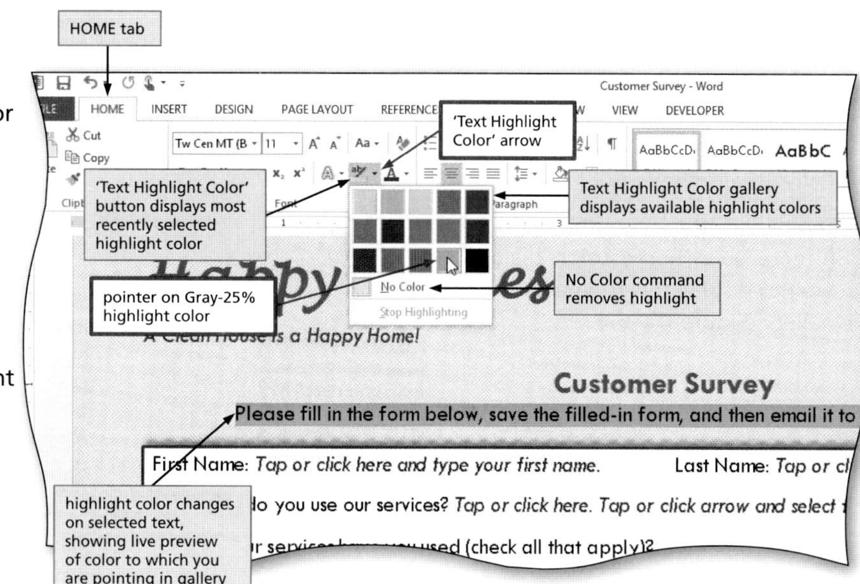

Figure 10–61

Q&A How would I remove a highlight from text?
Select the highlighted text, tap or click the 'Text Highlight Color' arrow, and then tap or click No Color in the Text Highlight Color gallery.

Other Ways

1. Tap or click 'Text Highlight Color' arrow (HOME tab | Font group), select desired color, select text to be highlighted in document, select any additional text to be highlighted, tap or click 'Text Highlight Color' button to turn off highlighting

To Customize a Theme Color and Save It with a New Theme Name

1 SAVE DOCUMENT TEMPLATE | 2 SET FORM FORMATS FOR TEMPLATE
3 ENTER TEXT, GRAPHICS, & CONTENT CONTROLS | **4 PROTECT FORM** | **5 USE FORM**

The final step in formatting the online form in this chapter is to change the color of the hyperlink. A document theme has 12 predefined colors for various on-screen objects including text, backgrounds, and hyperlinks. You can change any of the theme colors. The following steps customize the Slice theme, changing its designated theme color for hyperlinks. ***Why?*** *You would like the hyperlink to be red, to match the 'thank you' line on the form.*

1

- Display the DESIGN tab.
- Tap or click the Theme Colors button (DESIGN tab | Document Formatting group) to display the Theme Colors gallery (Figure 10–62).

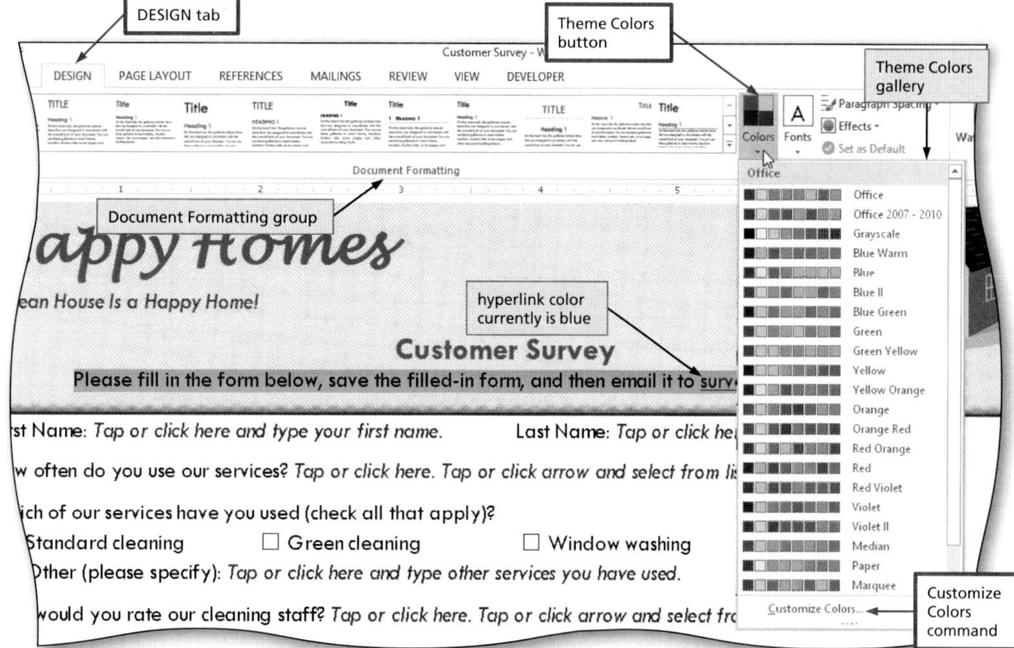

Figure 10–62

2

- Tap or click Customize Colors in the Theme Colors gallery to display the Create New Theme Colors dialog box.
- Tap or click the Hyperlink button (Create New Theme Colors dialog box) to display the Theme Colors gallery (Figure 10–63).

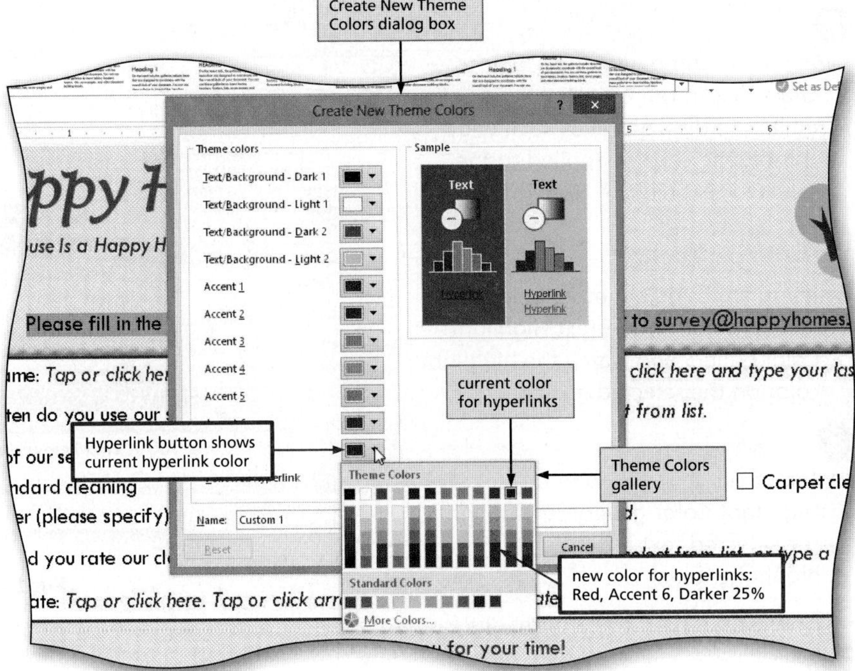

Figure 10–63

3

- Tap or click 'Red, Accent 6, Darker 25%' in the Hyperlink column (tenth color in fifth row) as the new hyperlink color.
- Type **Customer Survey** in the Name text box (Figure 10–64).

Q&A What if I wanted to reset all the original theme colors?
You would tap or click the Reset button (Create New Theme Colors dialog box) before tapping or clicking the Save button.

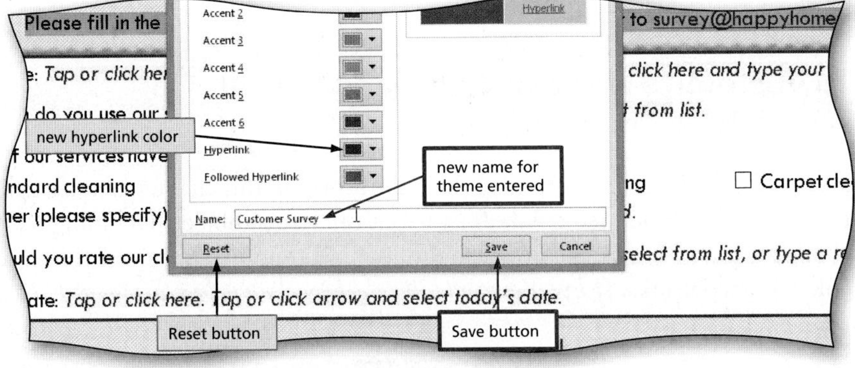

Figure 10–64

- Tap or click the Save button (Create New Theme Colors dialog box) to save the modified theme with the name, Customer Survey, which will be positioned at the top of the Theme Colors gallery for future access (Figure 10–65).

Q&A What if I do not enter a name for the modified theme?
Word assigns a name that begins with the letters, Custom, followed by a number (i.e., Custom8).

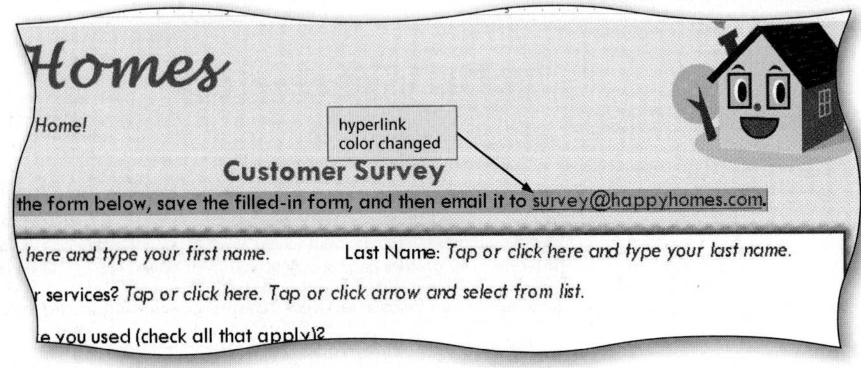

Figure 10–65

Other Ways

1. Make changes to theme colors, fonts, and/or effects; tap or click Themes button (DESIGN tab | Document Formatting group), tap or click 'Save Current Theme' in Themes gallery

To Protect a Form

When you **protect a form**, you are allowing users to enter data only in designated areas — specifically, the content controls. The following steps protect the online form. ***Why?*** *To prevent unwanted changes and edits to the form, it is crucial that you protect a form before making it available to users.*

1

- Display the DEVELOPER tab.
- Tap or click the Restrict Editing button (DEVELOPER tab | Protect group) to display the Restrict Editing task pane (Figure 10–66).

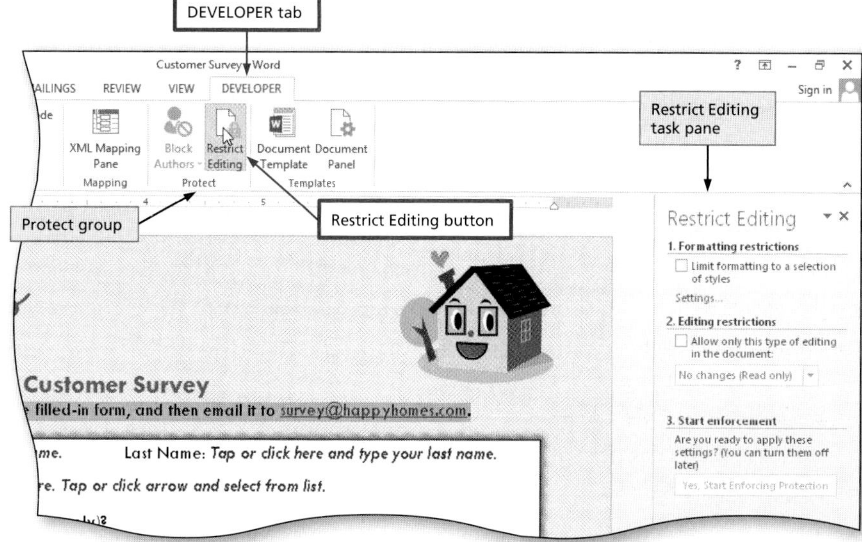

Figure 10–66

- In the Editing restrictions area, place a check mark in the 'Allow only this type of editing in the document' check box and then tap or click its arrow to display a list of the types of allowed restrictions (Figure 10–67).

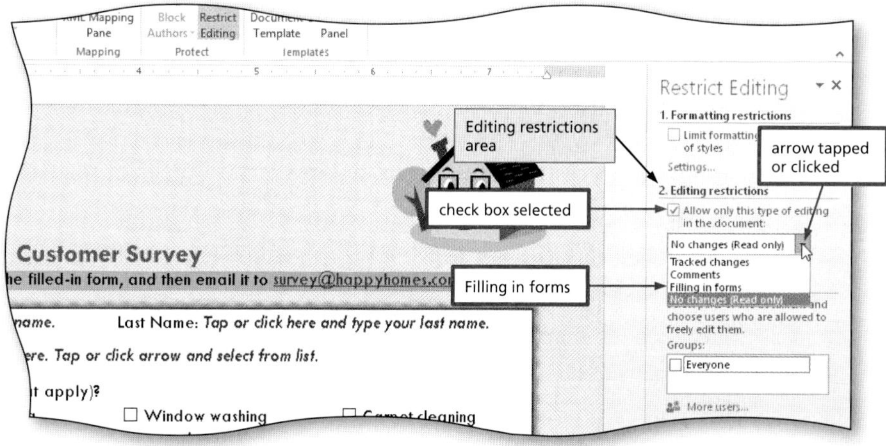

Figure 10–67

- Tap or click 'Filling in forms' in the list to instruct Word that the only editing allowed in this document is to the content controls.
- In the Start enforcement area, tap or click the 'Yes, Start Enforcing Protection' button, which displays the Start Enforcing Protection dialog box (Figure 10–68).

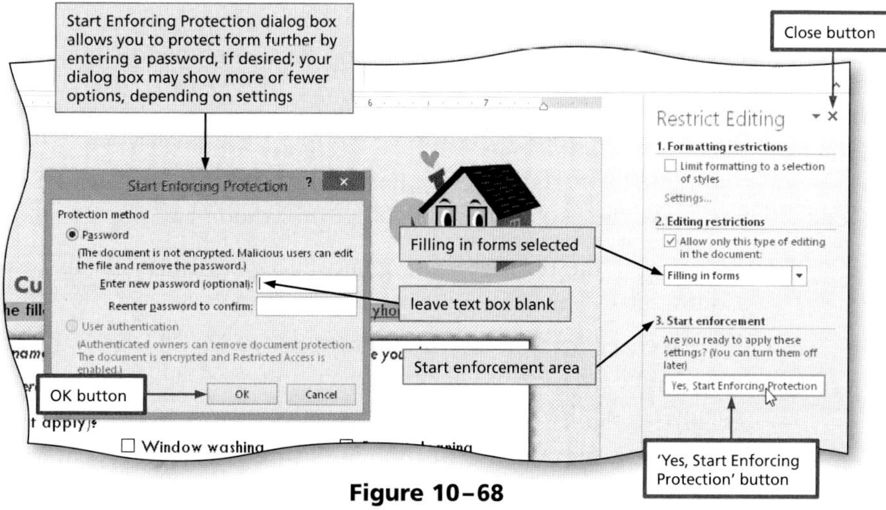

Figure 10–68

4

- Tap or click the OK button (Start Enforcing Protection dialog box) to protect the document without a password.

Q&A What if I enter a password?
If you enter a password, only a user who knows the password will be able to unprotect the document.

- Close the Restrict Editing task pane to show the protected form (Figure 10–69).

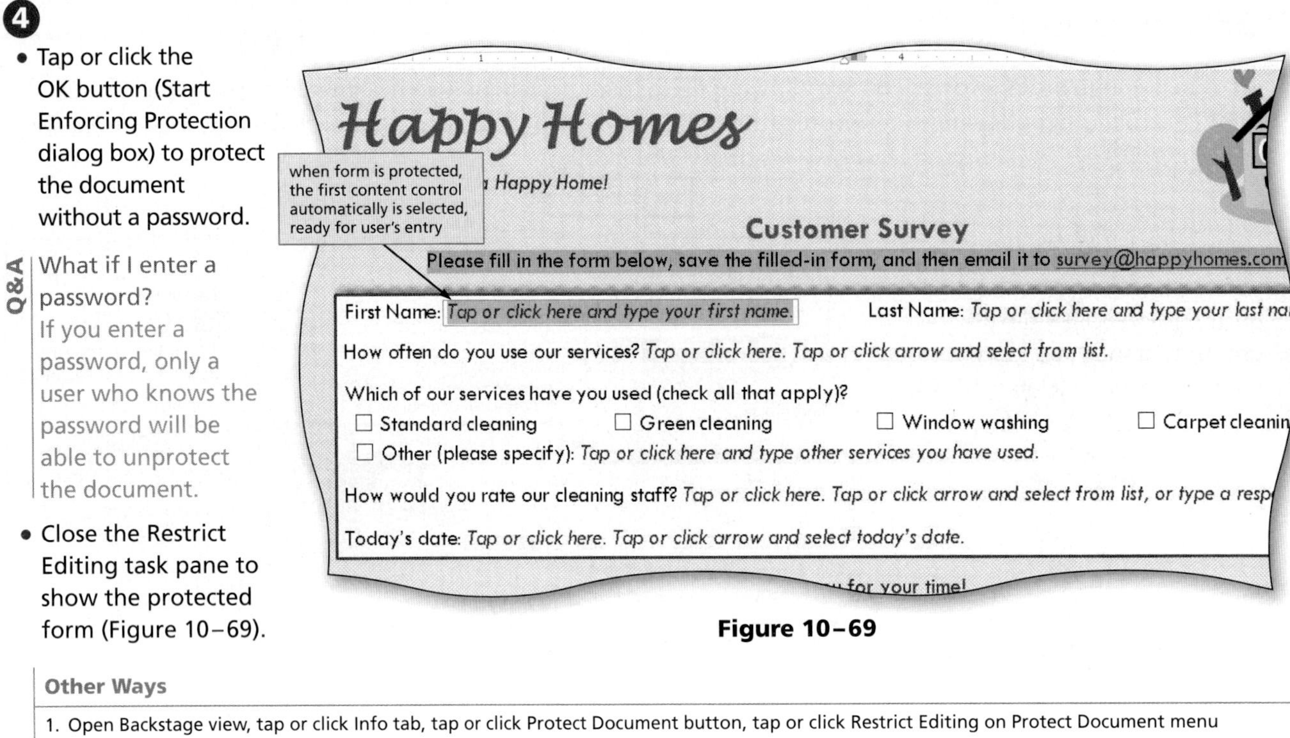

Happy Homes
a Happy Home!
when form is protected, the first content control automatically is selected, ready for user's entry
Customer Survey
Please fill in the form below, save the filled-in form, and then email it to survey@happyhomes.com
First Name: Tap or click here and type your first name.
Last Name: Tap or click here and type your last na
How often do you use our services? Tap or click here. Tap or click arrow and select from list.
Which of our services have you used (check all that apply)?
Standard cleaning
Green cleaning
Window washing
Carpet cleanin
Other (please specify): Tap or click here and type other services you have used.
How would you rate our cleaning staff? Tap or click here. Tap or click arrow and select from list, or type a resp
Today's date: Tap or click here. Tap or click arrow and select today's date.
for your time!

Figure 10–69

Other Ways

1. Open Backstage view, tap or click Info tab, tap or click Protect Document button, tap or click Restrict Editing on Protect Document menu

Protecting Documents

In addition to protecting a form so that it only can be filled in, Word provides several other options in the Restrict Editing task pane.

To Set Formatting Restrictions

If you wanted to restrict users from making certain types of formatting changes to a document, you would perform the following steps.

1. Tap or click the Restrict Editing button (DEVELOPER tab | Protect group) to display the Restrict Editing task pane.
2. Place a check mark in the 'Limit formatting to a selection of styles' check box in the Formatting restrictions area.
3. Tap or click the Settings link and then select the types of formatting you want to allow (Formatting Restrictions dialog box).
4. Tap or click the OK button.
5. Tap or click the 'Yes, Start Enforcing Protection' button, enter a password if desired, and then tap or click the OK button (Start Enforcing Protection dialog box).

To Set Editing Restrictions to Tracked Changes or Comments or No Edits

If you wanted to restrict users' edits to allow only tracked changes, allow only comments, or not allow any edits (that is, make the document read only), you would perform the following steps.

1. Tap or click the Restrict Editing button (DEVELOPER tab | Protect group) to display the Restrict Editing task pane.
2. Place a check mark in the 'Allow only this type of editing in the document' check box in the Editing restrictions area, tap or click the arrow, and then tap or click the desired option — that is, Tracked changes, Comments, or No changes (Read only) — to specify the types of edits allowed in the document.
3. Tap or click the 'Yes, Start Enforcing Protection' button, enter a password if desired, and then tap or click the OK button (Start Enforcing Protection dialog box).

To Hide the DEVELOPER Tab

You are finished using the commands on the DEVELOPER tab. Thus, the following steps hide the DEVELOPER tab from the ribbon.

1. Open the Backstage view and then tap or click Options in the left pane of the Backstage view to display the Word Options dialog box.
2. Tap or click Customize Ribbon in the left pane (Word Options dialog box).
3. Remove the check mark from the Developer check box in the Main Tabs list.
4. Tap or click the OK button to hide the DEVELOPER tab from the ribbon.

To Hide the Ruler

You are finished using the ruler. Thus, the following steps hide the ruler.

1. Display the VIEW tab.
2. If the ruler is displayed on the screen, remove the check mark from the View Ruler check box (VIEW tab | Show group).

To Collapse the Ribbon

The following step collapses the ribbon so that when you test the form in the next steps, the ribbon is collapsed.

1. Tap or click the 'Collapse the Ribbon' button on the ribbon (shown in Figure 10–5 on page WD 615) to collapse the ribbon.

To Save the Template Again and Exit Word

The online form template for this project now is complete. Thus, the following steps save the template and exit Word.

1. Tap or click the Save button on the Quick Access Toolbar to overwrite the previously saved file.
2. Exit Word.

Working with an Online Form

When you create a template, you use the Open command in the Backstage view to open the template so that you can modify it. After you have created a template, you then can make it available to users. Users do not open templates with the Open command in Word. Instead, a user creates a new Word document that is based on the template, which means the title bar displays the default file name, Document1 (or a similar name) rather than the template name. When Word creates a new document that is based on a template, the document window contains any text and formatting associated with the template. If a user accesses a letter template, for example, Word displays the contents of a basic letter in a new document window.

BTW

Highlighter

If you tap or click the 'Text Highlight Color' button (HOME tab | Font group) without first selecting any text, the highlighter remains active until you turn it off. This allows you to continue selecting text that you want to be highlighted. To deactivate the highlighter, tap or click the 'Text Highlight Color' button (HOME tab | Font group) and then tap or click Stop Highlighting on the Text Highlight Color menu, or press the ESC key.

BTW

Password-Protecting Documents

You can save documents with a password to keep unauthorized users from accessing files. To do this, type the password in the Start Enforcing Protection dialog box (shown in Figure 10–68 on page WD 655); or open the Backstage view, tap or click Save As, display the Save As dialog box, tap or click the Tools button (Save As dialog box), tap or click General Options on the Tools menu, type the password in the appropriate text box (General Options dialog box), type the password again (Confirm Password dialog box), and then tap or click the OK button and Save button (Save As dialog box). As you type a password in the text box, Word displays a series of dots instead of the actual characters so that others cannot see your password as you type it.

Be sure to keep the password confidential. Choose a password that is easy to remember and that no one can guess. Do not use any part of your first or last name, Social Security number, birthday, and so on. Use a password that is at least six characters long, and if possible, use a mixture of numbers and letters.

To Use File Explorer to Create a New Document That Is Based on a Template

1 SAVE DOCUMENT TEMPLATE | 2 SET FORM FORMATS FOR TEMPLATE
3 ENTER TEXT, GRAPHICS, & CONTENT CONTROLS | 4 PROTECT FORM | **5 USE FORM**

When you save a template on storage media, as instructed earlier in this chapter, a user can create a new document that is based on the template through File Explorer. ***Why?*** *This allows the user to work with a new document instead of risking the chance of altering the original template.* The following steps create a new Word document that is based on the Customer Survey template.

1

- Tap or click the File Explorer app button on the Windows taskbar to open the File Explorer window.
- Navigate to the location of the saved template (in this case, the Chapter 10 folder in the Word folder in the CIS 101 folder [or your class folder]) (Figure 10–70).

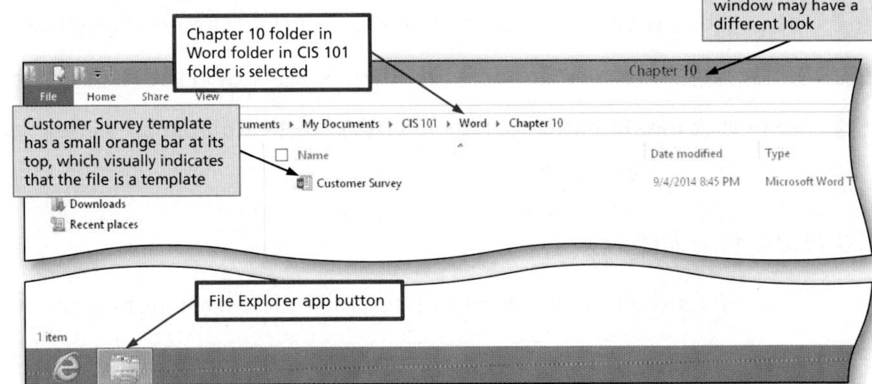

Figure 10–70

2

- Double-tap or double-click the Customer Survey file in the File Explorer window, which runs Word and creates a new document that is based on the contents of the selected template (Figure 10–71).

Q&A Why did my background page color disappear?
If the background page color does not appear, open the Backstage view, tap or click Options to display the Word Options dialog box, tap or click Advanced in the left pane (Word Options dialog box), scroll to the Show document content section, place a check mark in the 'Show background colors and images in Print Layout view' check box, and then tap or click the OK button.

Why does my ribbon only show three tabs: FILE, TOOLS, and VIEW?
Your screen is in Read mode. Tap or click the VIEW tab and then tap or click Edit Document to switch to Print Layout view.

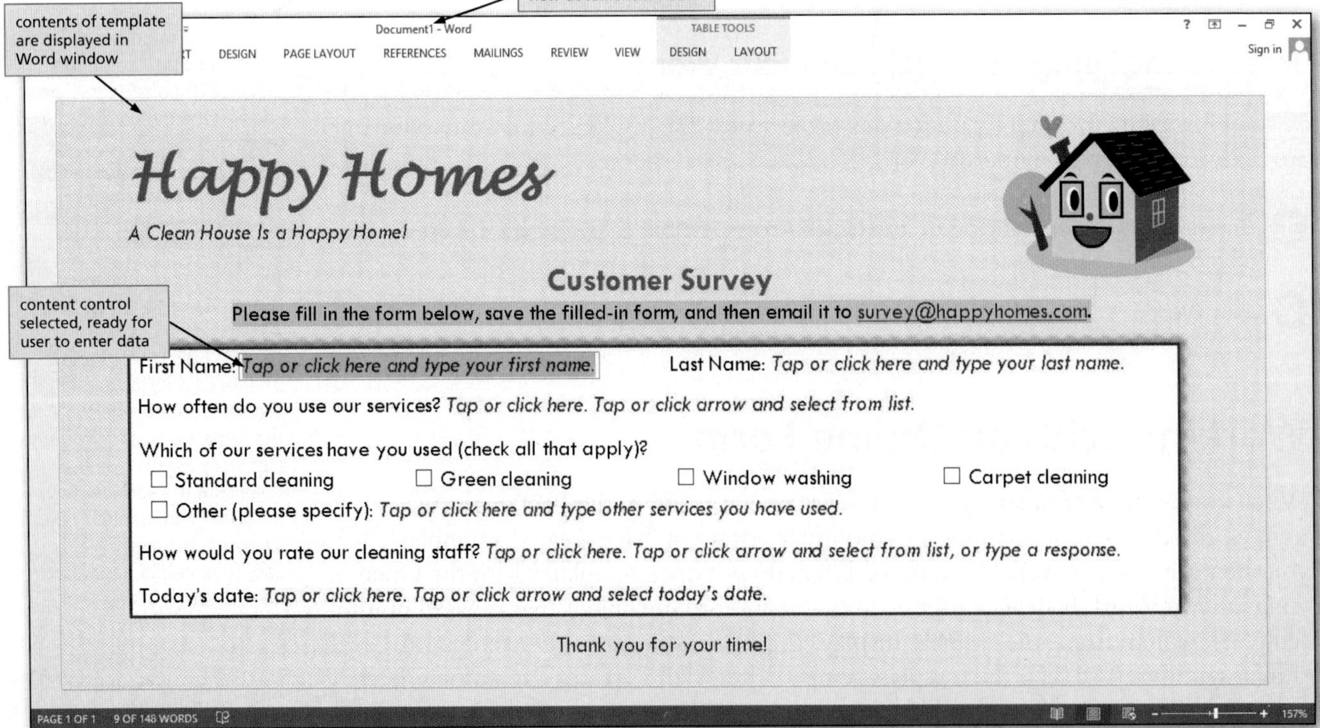

Figure 10–71

To Fill In a Form and Save It

The next step is to enter data in the form. To advance from one content control to the next, a user can tap or click the content control or press the TAB key. To move to a previous content control, a user can tap or click it or press SHIFT+TAB. The following steps fill in the Customer Survey form. ***Why?*** *You want to test the form to be sure it works as you intended.*

1

- With the First Name content control selected, type **Brian** and then press the TAB key.
- Type **Kaminsky** in the Last Name content control.

  If requested by your instructor, use your first and last name instead of the name, Brian Kaminsky.
- Press the TAB key to select the Frequency of Service Use content control and then tap or click its arrow to display the list of choices (shown in Figure 10–1b on page WD 611).
- Tap or click 'Every other week' in the list.
- Tap or click the Green cleaning and Other check boxes to select them.
- Type **Packing and unpacking** in the Other Services Used content control.
- Tap or click the Cleaning Staff Rating content control and then tap or click its arrow to display the list of choices (Figure 10–72).

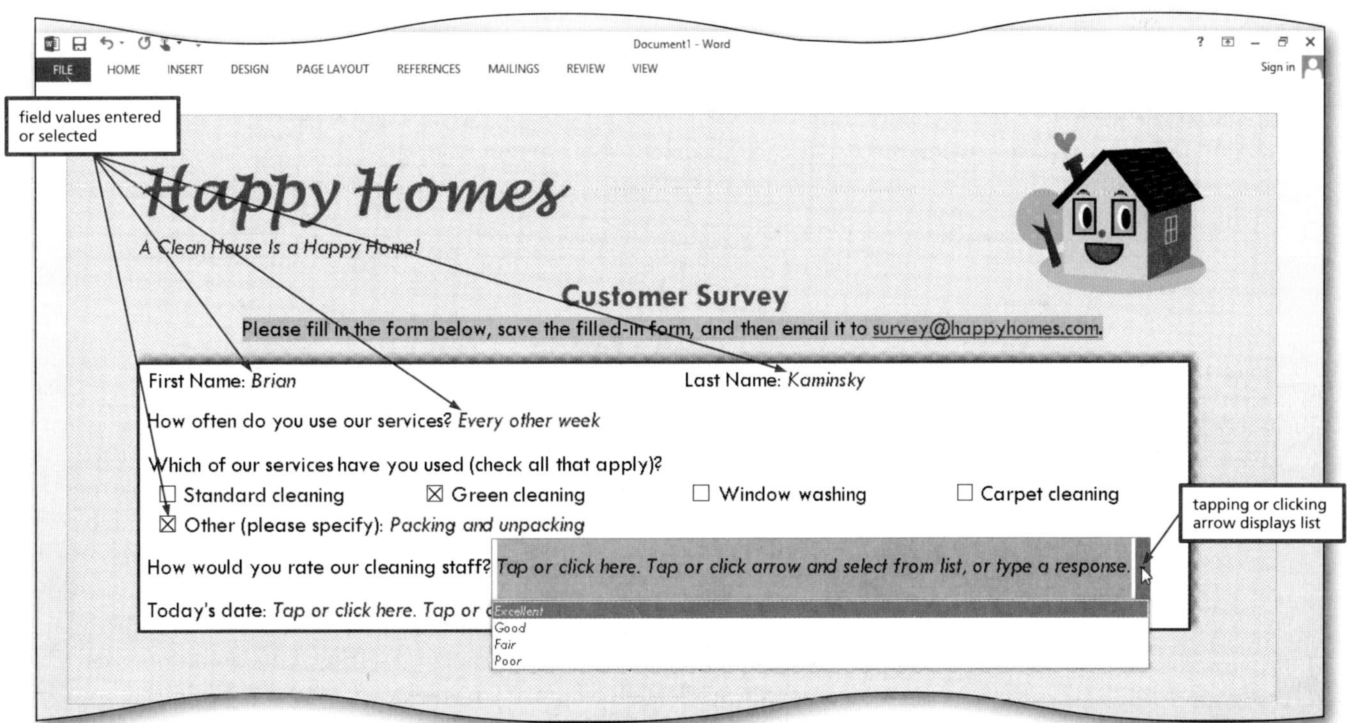

Figure 10–72

BTW
Internet Explorer vs. Windows Explorer
Internet Explorer is a browser included with the Windows operating system. File Explorer is a file manager that is included with the Windows operating system. It enables you to perform functions related to file management, such as displaying a list of files, organizing files, and copying files.

2

- Select Excellent in the list.
- Tap or click the Today's date arrow to display the calendar (Figure 10–73).

3

- Tap or click September 24, 2014 in the calendar to complete the data entry (shown in Figure 10–1c on page WD 611).

4

- Tap or click the Save button on the Quick Access Toolbar and then save the file on your storage media with the file name, Kaminsky Survey. If Word asks if you want to also save changes to the document template, tap or click the No button.

If requested by your instructor, use your last name in the file name instead of the name, Kaminsky.

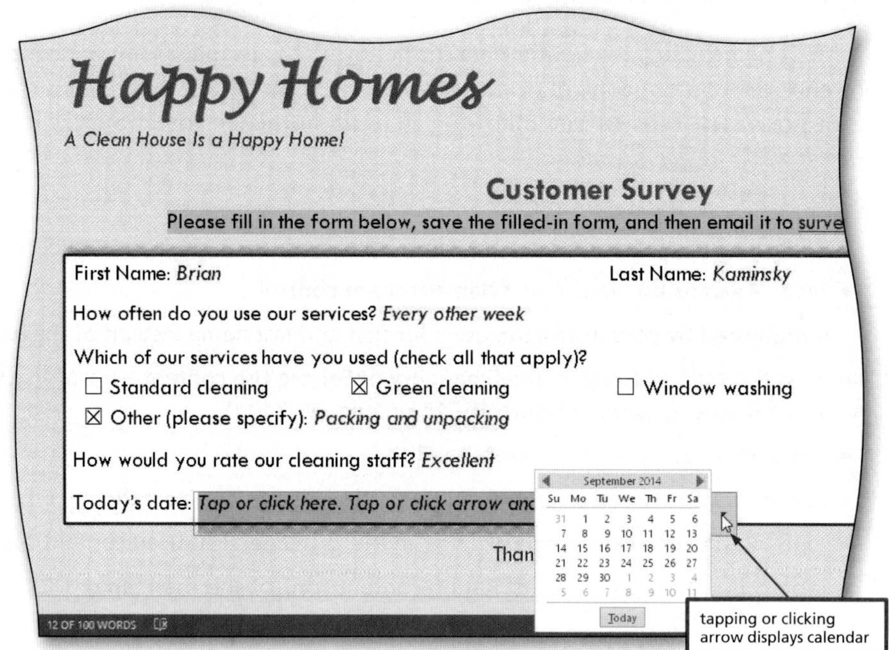

Figure 10–73

Q&A Can I print the form?

You can print the document as you print any other document. Keep in mind, however, that the colors used were designed for viewing online. Thus, different color schemes would have been selected if the form had been designed for a printout.

BTW

Protected Documents

If you open an existing form that has been protected, Word will not allow you to modify the form's appearance until you unprotect it. To unprotect a form (or any protected document), display the Restrict Formatting and Editing task pane by tapping or clicking the Restrict Editing button (DEVELOPER tab | Protect group) or opening the Backstage view, displaying the Info gallery, tapping or clicking the Protect Document button, and tapping or clicking Restrict Editing on the Protect Document menu. Then, tap or click the Stop Protection button in the Restrict Editing task pane and close the task pane. If a document has been protected with a password, you will be asked to enter the password when you attempt to unprotect the document.

Working with Templates

If you want to modify the template, open it by tapping or clicking the Open command in the Backstage view, tapping or clicking the template name, and then tapping or clicking the Open button in the dialog box. Then, you must **unprotect the form** by tapping or clicking the Restrict Editing button (DEVELOPER tab | Protect group) and then tapping or clicking the Stop Protection button in the Restrict Editing task pane.

When you created the template in this chapter, you saved it on your local storage media. In environments other than an academic setting, you would not save the template on your own storage media; instead, you would save the file in the Custom Office Templates folder (shown in Figure 10–3 on page WD 614). When you save a template in the Custom Office Templates folder, you can locate the template by opening the Backstage view, tapping or clicking the New tab to display the New gallery, and then tapping or clicking the PERSONAL tab in the New gallery, which displays the template in the New gallery (Figure 10–74).

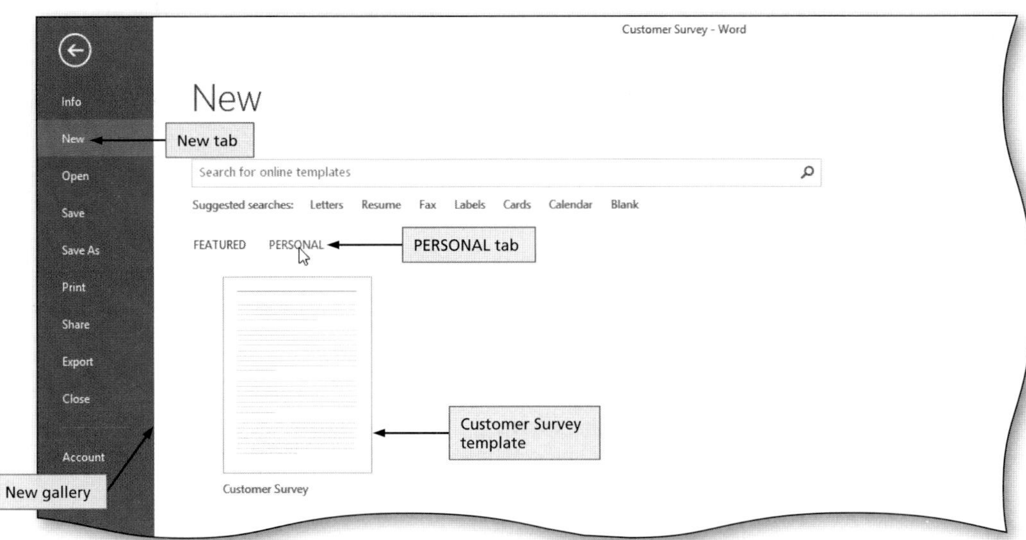

Figure 10–74

BTW

Linking a Form to a Database

If you want to use or analyze the data that a user enters into a form in an Access database or an Excel worksheet, you could save the form data in a comma-delimited text file. This file separates each data item with a comma and places quotation marks around text data items. Then, you can use Access or Excel to import the comma-delimited text file for use in the respective program. To save form data, open the Backstage view, tap or click Save As in the Backstage view, and then display the Save As dialog box. Tap or click the Tools button (Save As dialog box) and then tap or click Save Options on the Tools menu to display the Word Options dialog box. Tap or click Advanced in the left pane (Word Options dialog box), scroll to the Preserve fidelity when sharing this document area in the right pane, place a check mark in the 'Save form data as delimited text file' check box, and then tap or click the OK button. Next, be sure the file type is Plain Text (Save As dialog box) and then tap or click the Save button to save the file as a comma-delimited text file. You can import the resulting comma-delimited file in an Access database or an Excel worksheet. To convert successfully, you should use the legacy controls (i.e., text form field, check box form field, etc.), which are available through the Legacy Tools button (DEVELOPER tab | Controls group). To use Word 2013 content controls, use the 'XML Mapping Pane' button (DEVELOPER tab | Mapping group) and refer to pages WD 726 and WD 727 in the Supplementary Word Tasks section in Chapter 11 for instructions about working with XML.

To Exit Word

The following steps exit Word and close the File Explorer window.

1. Exit Word. (If Word asks if you want to save the modified styles, tap or click the Don't Save button.)
2. If the File Explorer window still is open, close it.

Chapter Summary

In this chapter, you have learned how to create an online form. Topics covered included saving a document as a template, changing paper size, using a table to control layout, showing the DEVELOPER tab, inserting content controls, editing placeholder text, changing properties of content controls, and protecting a form. The items listed below include all the new Word skills you have learned in this chapter, with the tasks grouped by activity.

Create a Template

Insert a Plain Text Content Control (WD 627)
Edit Placeholder Text (WD 628)
Change the Properties of a Plain Text Content Control (WD 630)
Insert a Drop-Down List Content Control (WD 634)
Change the Properties of a Drop-Down List Content Control (WD 634)
Insert a Check Box Content Control (WD 638)
Insert a Rich Text Content Control (WD 640)
Insert a Combo Box Content Control (WD 642)
Change the Properties of a Combo Box Content Control (WD 644)
Insert a Date Picker Content Control (WD 645)
Change the Properties of a Date Picker Content Control (WD 646)

Enter and Edit Text

Fill In a Form and Save It (WD 659)

File Management

Save a Document as a Template (WD 613)
Protect a Form (WD 655)
Use File Explorer to Create a New Document That Is Based on a Template (WD 658)

Format a Page

Change Paper Size (WD 615)
Add a Page Color (WD 618)
Add a Pattern Fill Effect to a Page Color (WD 619)
Customize a Theme Color and Save It with a New Theme Name (WD 653)

Format Text

Highlight Text (WD 652)

Word Settings

Collapse the Ribbon (WD 616)
Expand the Ribbon (WD 616)
Show the DEVELOPER Tab (WD 626)
Set Formatting Restrictions (WD 656)
Set Editing Restrictions to Tracked Changes or Comments or No Edits (WD 656)

Work with Graphics

Draw a Rectangle (WD 648)
Send a Graphic behind Text (WD 650)
Add a Shadow to a Shape (WD 652)

Work with Tables

Use a Table to Control Layout (WD 623)

CONSIDER THIS: PLAN AHEAD

What decisions will you need to make when creating online forms?

Use these guidelines as you complete the assignments in this chapter and create your own online forms outside of this class.

1. Design the form.
   a) To minimize the time spent creating a form while using a computer or mobile device, consider sketching the form on a piece of paper first.
   b) Design a well-thought-out draft of the form — being sure to include all essential form elements, including the form's title, text and graphics, data entry fields, and data entry instructions.
2. For each data entry field, determine its field type and/or list of possible values that it can contain.
3. Save the form as a template, instead of as a Word document, to simplify the data entry process for users of the form.
4. Create a functional and visually appealing form.
   a) Use colors that complement one another.
   b) Draw the user's attention to important sections.
   c) Arrange data entry fields in logical groups on the form and in an order that users would expect.
   d) Data entry instructions should be succinct and easy to understand.
   e) Ensure that users can enter and edit data only in designated areas of the form.
5. Determine how the form data will be analyzed.
   a) If the data entered in the form will be analyzed by a program outside of Word, create the data entry fields so that the entries are stored in separate fields that can be shared with other programs.
6. Test the form, ensuring it works as you intended.
   a) Fill in the form as if you are a user.
   b) Ask others to fill in the form to be sure it is organized in a logical manner and is easy to understand and complete.
   c) If any errors or weaknesses in the form are identified, correct them and test the form again.
7. Publish or distribute the form.
   a) Not only does an online form reduce the need for paper, it saves the time spent making copies of the form and distributing it.
   b) When the form is complete, post it on social media, the web, or your company's intranet, or email it to targeted recipients.

CONSIDER THIS

How should you submit solutions to questions in the assignments identified with a ☼ symbol?

Every assignment in this book contains one or more questions identified with a ☼ symbol. These questions require you to think beyond the assigned document. Present your solutions to the questions in the format required by your instructor. Possible formats may include one or more of these options: write the answer; create a document that contains the answer; present your answer to the class; discuss your answer in a group; record the answer as audio or video using a webcam, smartphone, or portable media player; or post answers on a blog, wiki, or website.

Apply Your Knowledge

Reinforce the skills and apply the concepts you learned in this chapter.

Filling In an Online Form

Note: To complete this assignment, you will be required to use the Data Files for Students. Visit www.cengage.com/ct/studentdownload for detailed instructions or contact your instructor for information about accessing the required files.

Instructions: In this assignment, you access a template through File Explorer. The template is located on the Data Files for Students. The template contains an online form (Figure 10–75). You are to fill in the form.

The Bradley Times

News You Can Use

Email Notification Request Form

Please fill in the form below, save the filled-in form, and then email it to requests@bradleytimes.com.

Email Address: Tap or click here and type your email address.

How often would you like to receive notifications? Tap or click here. Tap or click arrow and select from list.

What are your interests (check all that apply)?

☐ Local news ☐ National news ☐ Celebrity news ☐ Science advancements

☐ Other (please specify): Tap or click here and type your other interests.

How did you hear about our publications? Tap or click here. Tap or click arrow and select from list, or type a response.

Today's date: Tap or click here. Tap or click arrow and select today's date.

Thank you for your time!

Figure 10–75

Perform the following tasks:

1. Run File Explorer. Double-tap or double-click the Apply 10-1 Bradley Times Survey template in File Explorer.
2. When Word displays a new document based on the Apply 10-1 Bradley Times Survey template, if necessary, collapse the ribbon, hide formatting marks, and change the zoom to page width. Your screen should look like Figure 10–75.
3. With the Email Address content control selected, type **`avery@earth.net`** or, if requested by your instructor, enter your email address.
4. Tap or click the Notifications content control and then tap or click the arrow. Tap or click Weekly in the list.
5. Tap or click the Local news and Science advancements check boxes to select them.
6. Tap or click the Other check box. If necessary, tap or click the Other text box and then type **`Health news`** in the text box.
7. Tap or click the 'Hear About Publications' content control to select it. Tap or click the 'Hear About Publications' arrow and then review the list. Press the ESC key because none of these choices answers the question. Type **`Friend`** as the response.

Continued >

Apply Your Knowledge *continued*

8. Tap or click the Today's Date content control and then click the arrow to display a calendar. If necessary, scroll to display the calendar for October 2014. Tap or click 'October 21, 2014', (or today's date, if requested by your instructor) in the calendar.
9. Save the modified file with a new file name, Apply 10-1 Avery Survey (or, if requested by your instructor, replace the name, Avery, with your name). Submit the document in the format specified by your instructor. Close the document.
10. Open the Apply 10-1 Bradley Times Survey template from the Data Files for Students.
11. Unprotect the Apply 10-1 Bradley Times Survey template.
12. Save the template with a new name, Apply 10-1 Bradley Times Survey Modified.
13. Change the Today's Date content control to the format d-MMM-yy (i.e., 21-Oct-14).
14. Protect the modified template.
15. Save the modified template. Submit the revised template in the format specified by your instructor.
16. In this form, what are the options in the Notifications and Hear About Publications lists? What items might you add to those lists? How would you add those items?

Extend Your Knowledge

Extend the skills you learned in this chapter and experiment with new skills. You may need to use Help to complete the assignment.

Working with Picture Content Controls, Grouping Objects, Themes, and Passwords

Note: To complete this assignment, you will be required to use the Data Files for Students. Visit www.cengage.com/ct/studentdownload for detailed instructions or contact your instructor for information about accessing the required files.

Instructions: Run Word. Open the document, Extend 10-1 Baby Contest Form Draft, from the Data Files for Students. You will add a picture content control in a text box and then format the text box, group the graphical images, change the text highlight color, change the shadow color, change the shape fill, change theme colors, reset theme colors, save a modified theme, and protect a form with a password.

Perform the following tasks:

1. Use Help to review and expand your knowledge about these topics: picture content controls, text boxes, grouping objects, shadows, shape fill effects, changing theme colors, and protecting forms with passwords.
2. Add a simple text box to the empty space in the right side of the data entry area. Resize the text box so that it fits completely in the data entry area.
3. In the text box, type the label, Baby Photo:, and then below the label, insert a picture content control. Resize the picture content control so that it fits in the text box and then center both the picture and label in the text box (Figure 10–76). Remove the border from the text box.
4. Change the fill effect in the rectangle shape to a texture of your choice. If necessary, change the font color or style of text in the data entry area so that it is readable on the texture.
5. Group the three graphics at the top of the form together. Move the grouped graphics. Return them to their original location.
6. Change the text highlight color of the third line of text to a color other than yellow. If necessary, change the text color so that you can read the text in the new highlight color.
7. Add a shadow to the rectangle and then change the color of the shadow on the rectangle to a color other than the default.

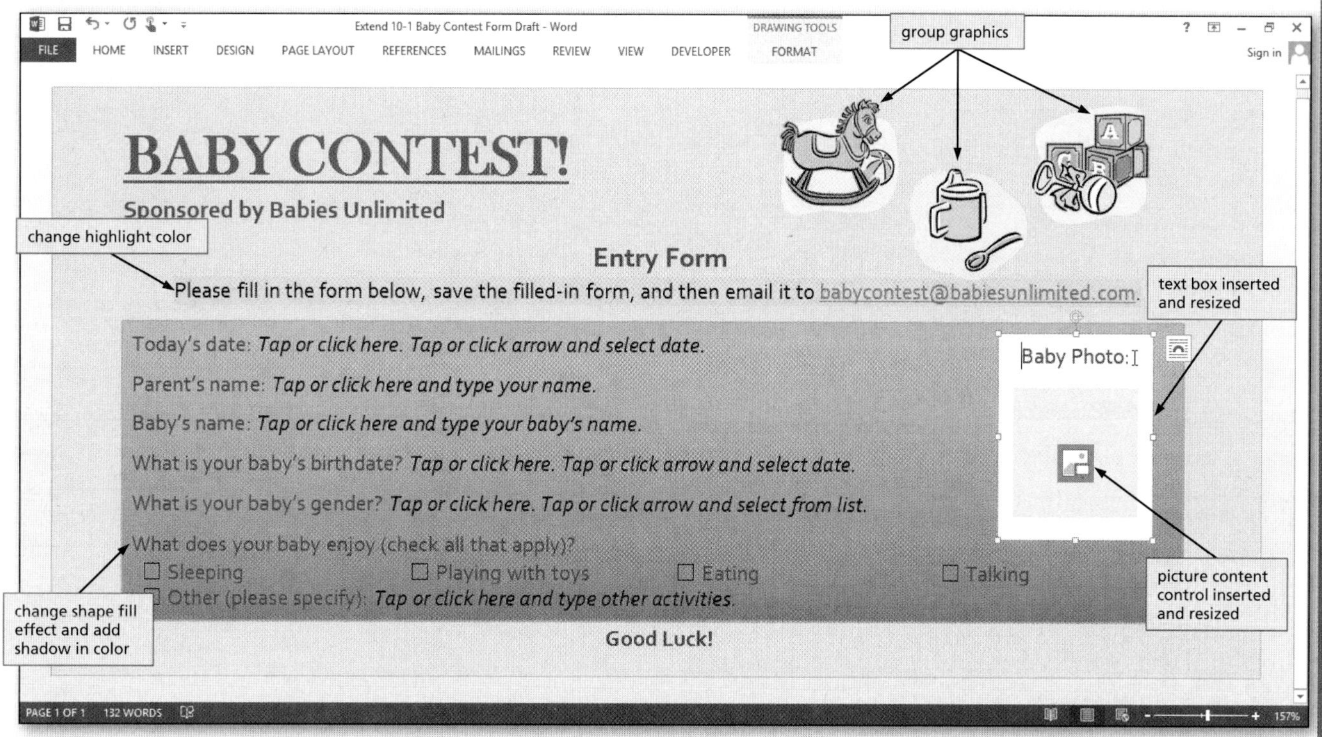

Figure 10–76

8. Change the theme colors for Accent 3. Reset the theme colors before closing the dialog box. Change the theme colors for Accent 1 and Hyperlink. Change theme colors for other items as desired. Save the modified theme colors.
9. Make any necessary formatting changes to the form.
10. Protect the form using the word, baby, as the password.
11. If requested by your instructor, change the sponsoring company name to include your last name. Save the revised document with a new file name, Extend 10-1 Baby Contest Form Modified.
12. Test the form. When filling in the form, use your own baby picture or the picture called Baby Photo on the Data Files for Students for the picture content control. Submit the online form in the format specified by your instructor.
13. Which texture did you select and why? What is the advantage of grouping graphics? Besides changing the color of the shadow, what other shadow settings can you adjust?

Analyze, Correct, Improve

Analyze a document, correct all errors, and improve it.

Formatting an Online Form

Note: To complete this assignment, you will be required to use the Data Files for Students. Visit www.cengage.com/ct/studentdownload for detailed instructions or contact your instructor for information about accessing the required files.

Instructions: Run Word. Open the document, Analyze 10-1 Harper Survey Draft, from the Data Files for Students. The document is an online form that contains unformatted elements (Figure 10–77 on the next page).

You are to change the graphic's wrapping style; change the page color; change fonts, font sizes, font colors, and text highlight color; remove the table border; edit placeholder text; change content control properties; draw a rectangle and format it; and protect the form.

Continued >

Analyze, Correct, Improve *continued*

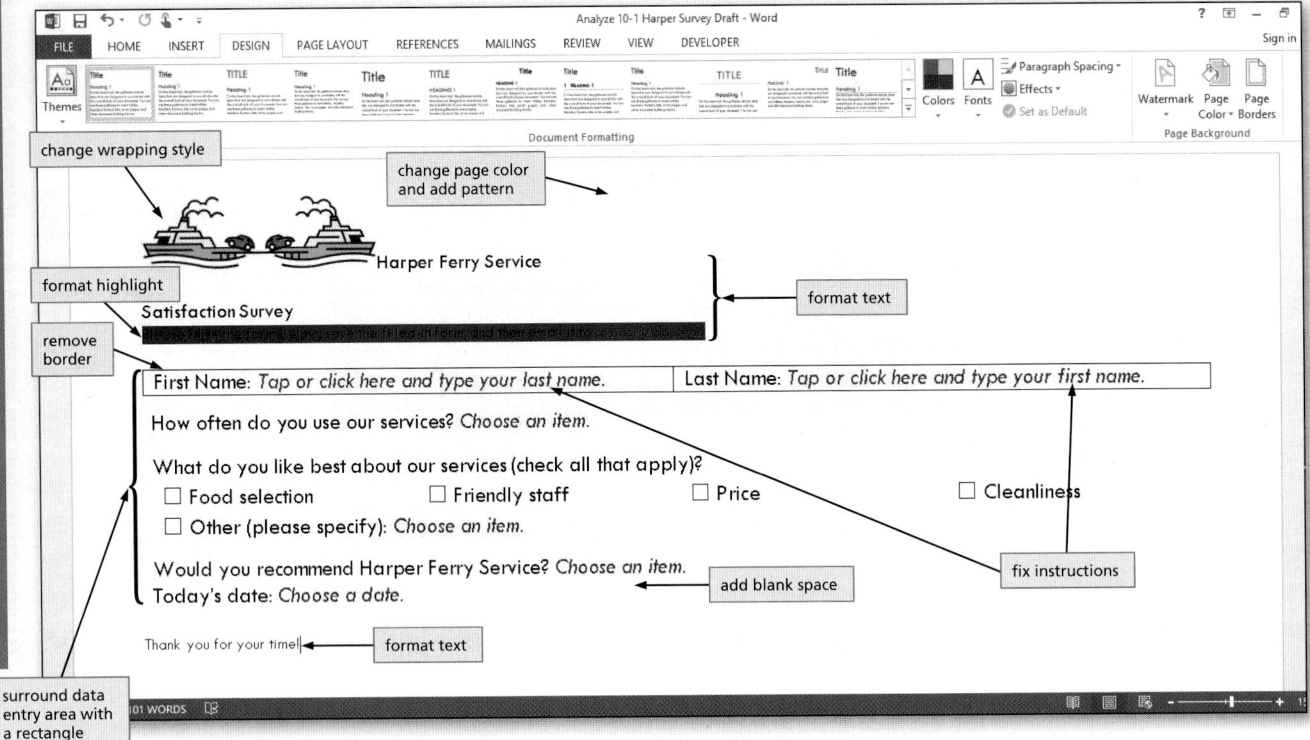

Figure 10–77

Perform the following tasks:

1. Correct In the online form, correct the following items:

a. Change the wrapping style of each graphic from inline to floating. Resize the graphics as necessary. Position one graphic at each edge of the top of the form. Format the graphics as desired.

b. On the third line of text, change the text highlight color so that the text is visible.

c. Change the font, font size, and font color for the first three lines and last line of text. Add font styles as desired. Center these four lines.

d. Remove the border from the 2 × 1 table that surrounds the First Name and Last Name content controls. Show table gridlines.

e. Add blank space between the Recommendation and Today's Date lines at the bottom of the data entry area.

f. Fix the placeholder text for the First Name content control so that it reads: Tap or click here and type your first name. Similarly, fix the placeholder text for the Last Name content control. For the remaining placeholder text, change the instructions so that they are more meaningful.

g. For the content control that lists how often services are used, change the properties as follows: add the tag name, Frequency of Use, and set the locking so that the content control cannot be deleted.

h. In the Recommendation content control, fix the spelling of the option, Maybe.

2. Improve Enhance the online form by changing the page color to a color of your choice (other than white) and then adding a pattern fill effect to the color. Draw a rectangle around the data entry area. Format the rectangle so that it is behind the text. Add a shape style and a shadow to the rectangle. Make any necessary adjustments to the form so that it fits on a single page. Hide table gridlines. Protect the form. If requested by your instructor, change the name, Harper, to your name. Save the modified document with the file name, Analyze 10-1 Harper Survey Modified, test the form, and then submit it in the format specified by your instructor.

3. Which page color did you choose, and why?

In the Labs

Design and/or create a document using the guidelines, concepts, and skills presented in this chapter. Labs 1 and 2, which increase in difficulty, require you to create solutions based on what you learned in the chapter; Lab 3 requires you to create a solution, which uses cloud and web technologies, by learning and investigating on your own from general guidance.

Lab 1: Creating an Online Form with Plain Text and Drop-Down List Content Controls

Problem: Your uncle owns Ozzie's Creamery and has asked you to prepare an online survey, shown in Figure 10–78.

Perform the following tasks:

1. Save a blank document as a template, called Lab 10-1 Creamery Survey, for the online form.
2. If necessary, change the view to page width.
3. Change the paper size to a width of 8.5 inches and a height of 4 inches.
4. Change the margins as follows: top - 0.25", bottom - 0", left - 0.5", and right - 0.5".
5. Change the document theme to Dividend.
6. Change the page color to Plum, Accent 1, Lighter 50%. Change the fill effect to the Outlined diamond pattern.
7. Enter and format the company name, message, and form title as shown in Figure 10–78 (or with similar fonts). If requested by your instructor, change the creamery name from Ozzie's to

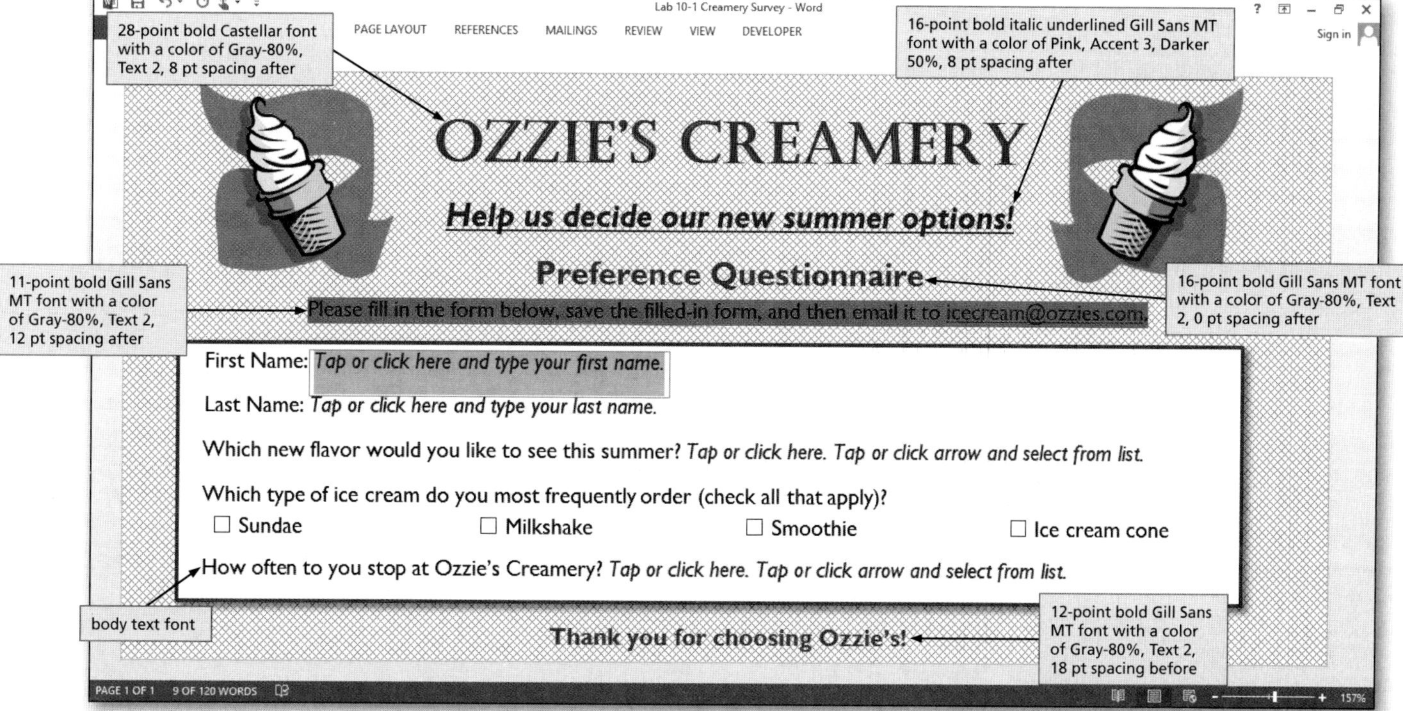

Figure 10–78

Continued >

In the Labs *continued*

your first name. Insert the clip art shown (or a similar image) using the term, ice cream cone, as the search text. Change the wrapping style of the graphics to In Front of Text. If necessary, resize the graphics and position them in the locations shown.

8. Enter the instructions above the data entry area and highlight the line Pink.
9. Customize the colors so that the hyperlink color is Blue-Gray, Accent 6, Darker 50%. Save the modified theme.
10. In the data entry area, enter the labels as shown in Figure 10–78 on the previous page and the content controls as follows: First Name and Last Name are plain text content controls. Summer Flavor is a drop-down list content control with these choices: Blueberry pomegranate, Cinnamon roll, Espresso, Key lime, and Red velvet. Sundae, Milkshake, Smoothie, and Ice cream cone are check boxes. Number of Visits is a drop-down list content control with these choices: Everyday, Several times a week, Once a week, Occasionally through the month, Once a month, A few times a year, and Never.
11. Format the placeholder text to the Intense Emphasis style. Edit the placeholder text of all content controls to match Figure 10–78. Change the properties of the content controls so that each contains a tag name, uses the Intense Emphasis style, and has locking set so that the content control cannot be deleted.
12. Enter the line below the data entry area as shown in Figure 10–78.
13. Adjust spacing above and below paragraphs as necessary so that all contents fit on a single screen.
14. Draw a rectangle around the data entry area. Change the shape style of the rectangle to Colored Outline - Plum, Accent 2. Apply the Offset Diagonal Bottom Right shadow to the rectangle.
15. Protect the form.
16. Save the form again and then submit it in the format specified by your instructor.
17. Access the template through File Explorer. Fill in the form using personal data and then submit the filled-in form in the format specified by your instructor.
18. If the creamery sold six different types of ice cream instead of four different types, how would you evenly space the six items across the line?

Lab 2: Creating an Online Form with Plain Text, Drop-Down List, Combo Box, Rich Text, Check Box, and Date Picker Content Controls

Problem: You work part-time for Bard's Gym. Your supervisor has asked you to prepare a member survey (Figure 10–79).

Perform the following tasks:

1. Save a blank document as a template, called Lab 10-2 Fitness Survey, for the online form.
2. If necessary, change the view to page width.
3. Change the paper size to a width of 8.5 inches and a height of 4 inches.
4. Change the margins as follows: top - 0.25", bottom - 0", left - 0.5", and right - 0.5".
5. Change the document theme to Droplet.
6. Change the page color to Black, Text 1. Change the fill effect to a 5% pattern.
7. Enter and format the company name, business tag line, and form title as shown in Figure 10–79 (or with similar fonts). If requested by your instructor, change the gym name from

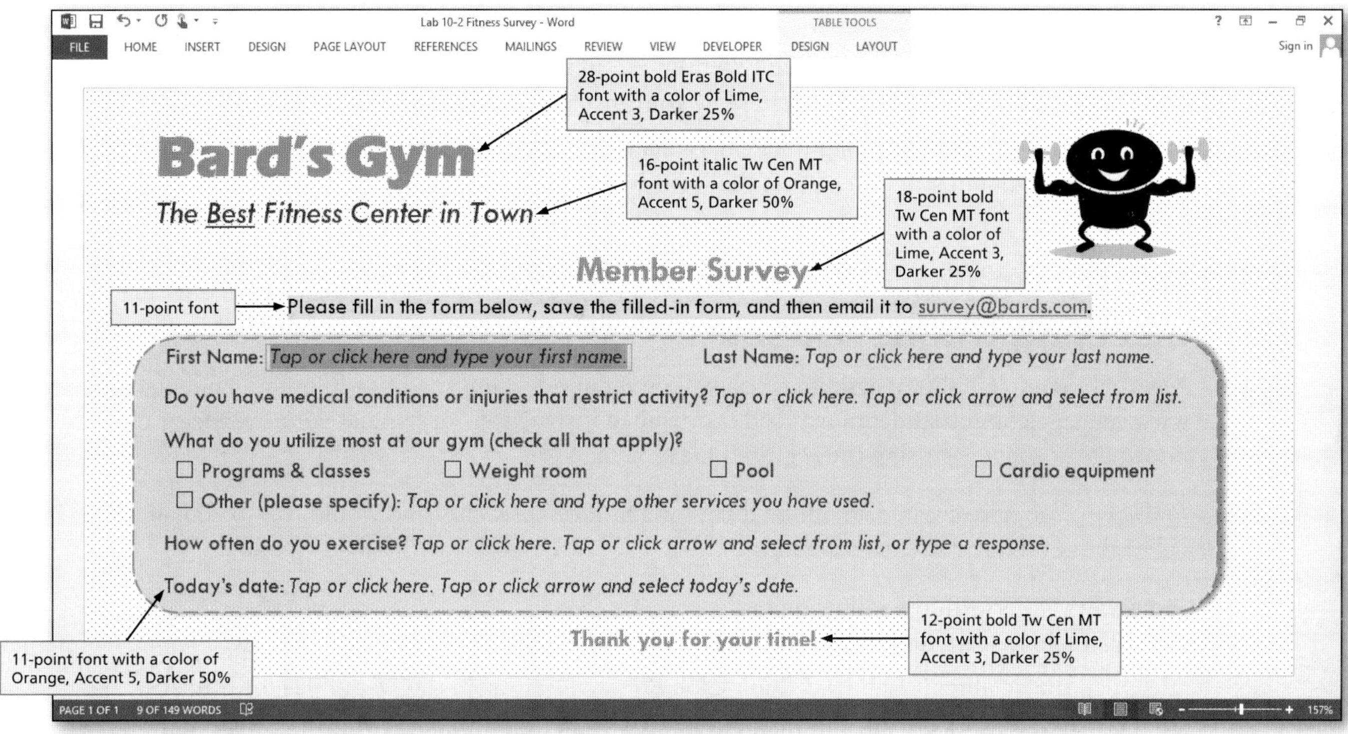

Figure 10–79

Bard's to your last name. Insert the clip art using the text, lifting weights, as the search text. Change the wrapping style of the graphic to In Front of Text. If necessary, resize the graphic and move it to the location shown.

8. Enter the instructions above the data entry area and highlight the line yellow.
9. In the data entry area, enter the labels as shown in Figure 10–79 and the content controls as follows: First Name and Last Name are plain text content controls. Activity Restrictions is a drop-down list content control with these choices: Yes, I have a long-term restriction; Yes, I have a short-term restriction; No; and I am not sure. Programs & classes, Weight room, Pool, Cardio equipment, and Other are check boxes. Other Services is a rich text content control. Exercise Frequency is a combo box content control with these choices: Daily, Three to five times a week, Once to twice a week, Not very often, and Never. Today's date is a date picker content control.
10. Format the placeholder text to Subtle Emphasis. Edit the placeholder text of all content controls to match Figure 10–79. Change the properties of the content controls so that each contains a tag name, uses the Subtle Emphasis style, and has locking specified so that the content control cannot be deleted.
11. Customize the colors so that the hyperlink color is Lime, Accent 3, Darker 50%. Save the modified theme.
12. Enter the line below the data entry area as shown in Figure 10–79.
13. Change the color of labels in the data entry area as shown in the figure.
14. Adjust spacing above and below paragraphs as necessary so that all contents fit on the screen.
15. Draw a Rounded Rectangle around the data entry area. Change the shape style of the rectangle to Subtle Effect - Lime, Accent 3. Change the shape outline to Long Dash. Add an Offset Right shadow.
16. Protect the form.
17. Save the form again and then submit it in the format specified by your instructor.

Continued >

In the Labs *continued*

18. Access the template through File Explorer. Fill in the form using personal data and submit the filled-in form in the format specified by your instructor.
19. What other question might a gym ask its members? If you were to add this question to the form, how would you fit it so that the form still displays in its entirety on a single page?

Lab 3: Expand Your World: Cloud and Web Technologies

Inserting Online Videos

Note: To complete this assignment, you will be required to use the Data Files for Students. Visit www.cengage.com/ct/studentdownload for detailed instructions or contact your instructor for information about accessing the required files.

Problem: You have created an online form for a library book club and would like to add an online video about e-book readers to the form.

Instructions: Perform the following tasks:

1. Use Help to learn about inserting online videos.
2. Open the document Lab 10-3 Book Club Survey Draft from the Data Files for Students.
3. Display the INSERT tab and then tap or click the Online Video button (INSERT tab | Media group) to display the Insert Video dialog box. Type **`e-book reader`** in the 'Enter your search term' box (Figure 10–80) and then tap or click the Search button to display a list of videos that match your search criteria.
4. Scroll through the list of videos, tapping or clicking several to see their name, length, and source. Tap or click the View Larger button in the lower-right corner of the video so that you can watch the video. Select an appropriate video and then tap or click the Insert button to insert it on the form. Change the layout to In Front of Text and position the video in the upper-right corner of the form. Resize the video if necessary.
5. Protect the form. Save the form again and then submit it in the format specified by your instructor.
6. Access the template through File Explorer. Test the video.
7. What options are available in the search results dialog box while you are watching a video? What are some of the sources for the videos in the dialog box? Which video did you insert in the form, and why? How do you play the video inserted on the form? Does the video play where you inserted it on the form? If not, where does it play?

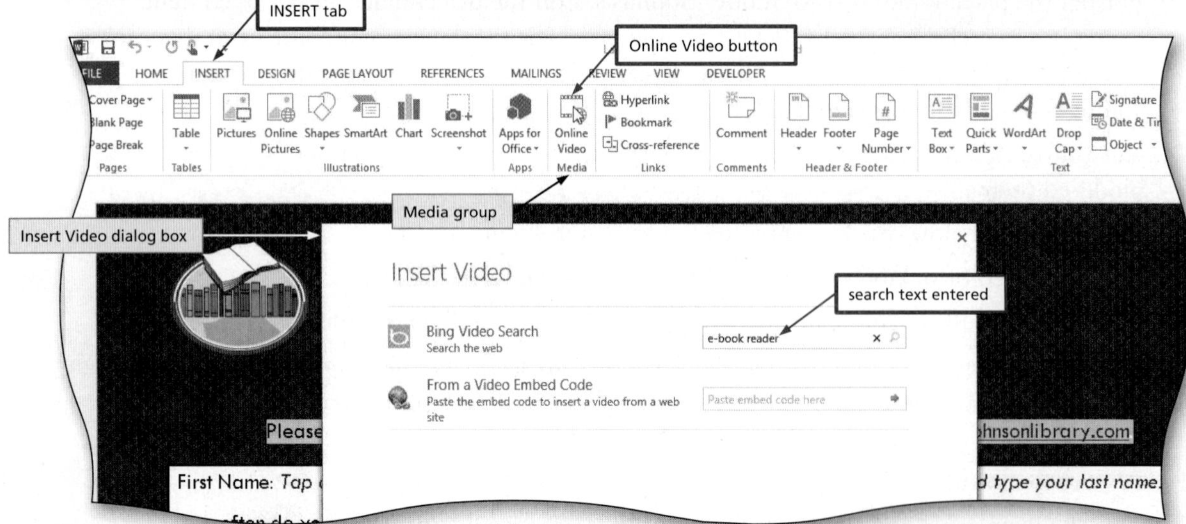

Figure 10–80

Consider This: Your Turn

Apply your creative thinking and problem solving skills to design and implement a solution.

1: Create an Online Form for a School

Personal

Part 1: As an assistant in the adult education center, you have been asked to create an online student survey. Create a template that contains the school name (Holland College), the school's tag line (A Great Place to Learn), and appropriate clip art. The third line should have the text, Seminar Survey. The fourth line should be highlighted and should read: Please fill in the form below, save the filled-in form, and then email it to seminars@hollandcollege.edu. The data entry area should contain the following. First Name and Last Name are plain text content controls within a table. A drop-down list content control with the label, What is your age range?, has these choices: 18-24, 25-40, 41-55, and over 55. The following instruction should appear above these check boxes: What skills have you learned in our seminars (check all that apply)?; the check boxes are Computer, Cooking, Dance, Language, Photography, and Other. A rich text content control has the label, Other (please specify), where students can enter other skills they have learned. A combo box content control with the label, How would you rate our seminars?, has these choices: Excellent, Good, Fair, and Poor. Today's Date is a date picker content control. On the last line, include the text: Thank you for attending our classes!

Use the concepts and techniques presented in this chapter to create and format the online form. Use meaningful placeholder text for all content controls. (For example, the placeholder text for the First Name plain text content control could be as follows: Click here and then type your first name.) Draw a rectangle around the data entry area of the form. Add a shadow to the rectangle. Apply a style to the placeholder text. Assign names, styles, and locking to each content control. Protect the form, test it, and submit it in the format specified by your instructor.

Part 2: You made several decisions while creating the online form in this assignment: placeholder text to use, graphics to use, and how to organize and format the online form (fonts, font sizes, styles, colors, etc.). What was the rationale behind each of these decisions? When you proofread and tested the online form, what further revisions did you make, and why?

2: Create an Online Form for a Law Office

Professional

Part 1: As a part-time employee at a local law office, you have been asked to create an online client survey. Create a template that contains the firm name (Clark Law), the firm's tag line (Serving You for More than 55 Years), and appropriate clip art. The third line should have the text, Client Survey. The fourth line should be highlighted and should read: Please fill in the form below, save the filled-in form, and then email it to info@clarklaw.com. The data entry area should contain the following. First Name and Last Name are plain text content controls within a table. A drop-down list content control with the label, Which lawyer has been handling your case?, has these choices: Clarissa Door, Gregory Hersher, Diane Lee, and Maria Sanchez. The following instruction should appear above these check boxes: Which category describes your case (check all that apply)?; the check boxes are Adoption, Auto incident, Estate planning, Personal injury, Workers' compensation, and Other. A rich text content control has the label, Other (please specify), where clients can enter other case areas. A combo box content control with the label, How would you rate our services to date?, has these choices: Excellent, Good, Fair, and Poor. Today's Date is a date picker content control. On the last line, include the text: Thank you for your business!

Use the concepts and techniques presented in this chapter to create and format the online form. Use meaningful placeholder text for all content controls. (For example, the placeholder text for the First Name plain text content control could be as follows: Click here and then type your first name.) Draw a rectangle around the data entry area of the form. Add a shadow to the rectangle. Apply a style to the placeholder text. Assign names, styles, and locking to each content control. Protect the form, test it, and submit it in the format specified by your instructor.

Continued >

Consider This: Your Turn *continued*

Part 2: You made several decisions while creating the online form in this assignment: placeholder text to use, graphics to use, and how to organize and format the online form (fonts, font sizes, styles, colors, etc.). What was the rationale behind each of these decisions? When you proofread and tested the online form, what further revisions did you make, and why?

3: Create an Online Form for a Campus Group

Research and Collaboration

Part 1: Your team will investigate a campus organization, club, or facility that could benefit from an online survey. For example, the fitness center might benefit from knowing time preferences for the racquetball court, or a club might benefit from knowing members' interests for scheduling upcoming events. Once you have made your choice for the online form, determine what information is required for the form to be effective and helpful and then decide which choices to include in the various content controls. Be sure to include at least one of each of the following content controls: plain text, rich text, drop-down list, combo box, picture, check box, and date picker. As a team, select a title, tag line, and appropriate clip art and/or other graphics.

Use the concepts and techniques presented in this chapter to create and format the online form. Decide on the overall design of the form, as well as the fonts, colors, and other visual elements. Each member should design an area of the form. Use meaningful placeholder text for all content controls. Be sure to check the spelling and grammar of the finished form. Protect the form, test it, and submit the team assignment in the format specified by your instructor.

Part 2: You made several decisions while creating the online form in this assignment: text and instructions to use, placeholder text to use, graphics to use, and how to organize and format the online form (fonts, font sizes, styles, colors, etc.). What was the rationale behind each of these decisions? When you proofread and tested the online form, what further revisions did you make, and why?

Learn Online

Learn Online – Reinforce what you learned in this chapter with games, exercises, training, and many other online activities and resources.

Student Companion Site Reinforcement activities and resources are available at no additional cost on www.cengagebrain.com. Visit www.cengage.com/ct/studentdownload for detailed instructions about accessing the resources available at the Student Companion Site.

SAM Put your skills into practice with SAM! If you have a SAM account, go to www.cengage.com/sam2013 to access SAM assignments for this chapter.

11 Enhancing an Online Form and Using Macros

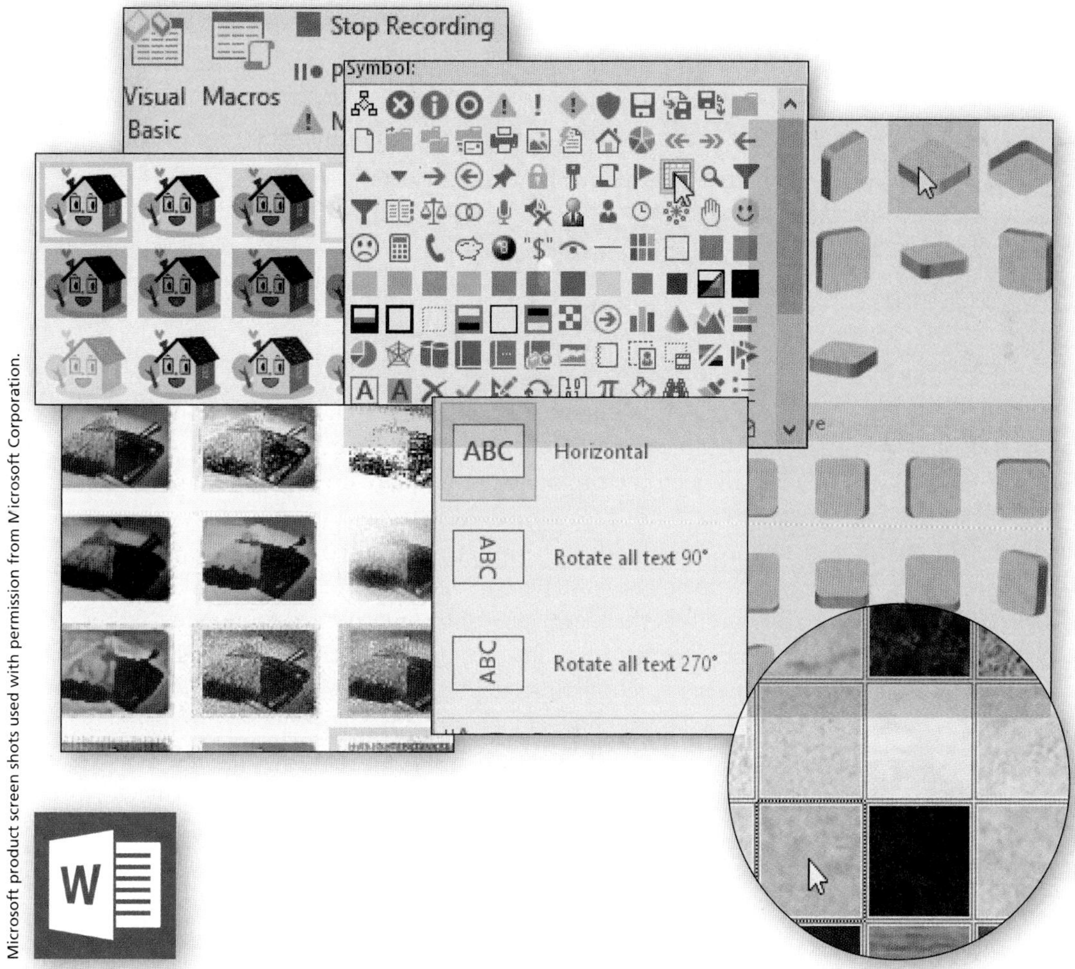

Objectives

You will have mastered the material in this chapter when you can:

- Unprotect a document
- Specify macro settings
- Convert a table to text
- Insert and edit a field
- Create a character style
- Apply and modify fill effects
- Change a shape
- Remove a background from a graphic
- Apply an artistic effect to a graphic
- Insert and format a text box
- Group objects
- Record and execute a macro
- Customize the Quick Access Toolbar
- Edit a macro's VBA code

11 Enhancing an Online Form and Using Macros

Introduction

Word provides many tools that allow you to improve the appearance, functionality, and security of your documents. This chapter discusses tools used to perform the following tasks:

- Modify text and content controls.
- Enhance with color, shapes, effects, and graphics.
- Automate a series of tasks with a macro.

Project — Online Form Revised

This chapter uses Word to improve the visual appearance of and add macros to the online form created in Chapter 10, producing the online form shown in Figure 11–1a. This project begins with the Customer Survey online form created in Chapter 10. Thus, you will need the online form template created in Chapter 10 to complete this project. (If you did not create the template, see your instructor for a copy.)

If you are using your finger on a touch screen and are having difficulty completing the steps in this chapter, consider using a stylus. Many people find it easier to be precise with a stylus than with a finger. In addition, with a stylus you see the pointer. If you still are having trouble completing the steps with a stylus, try using a mouse.

This project modifies the fonts and font colors of the text in the Customer Survey online form and enhances the contents of the form to include a texture fill effect, a picture fill effect, and a text box and picture grouped together. The date in the form automatically displays the computer or mobile device's system date, instead of requiring the user to enter the date.

This form also includes macros to automate tasks. A **macro** is a set of commands and instructions grouped together to allow a user to accomplish a task automatically. One macro allows the user to hide formatting marks and the ruler by pressing a keyboard shortcut (sometimes called a shortcut key) or tapping or clicking a button on the Quick Access Toolbar. Another macro specifies how the form is displayed initially on a user's Word screen. As shown in Figure 11–1b, when a document contains macros, Word may generate a security warning. If you are sure the macros are from a trusted source and free of viruses, then enable the content. Otherwise, do not enable the content, which protects your computer from potentially harmful viruses or other malicious software.

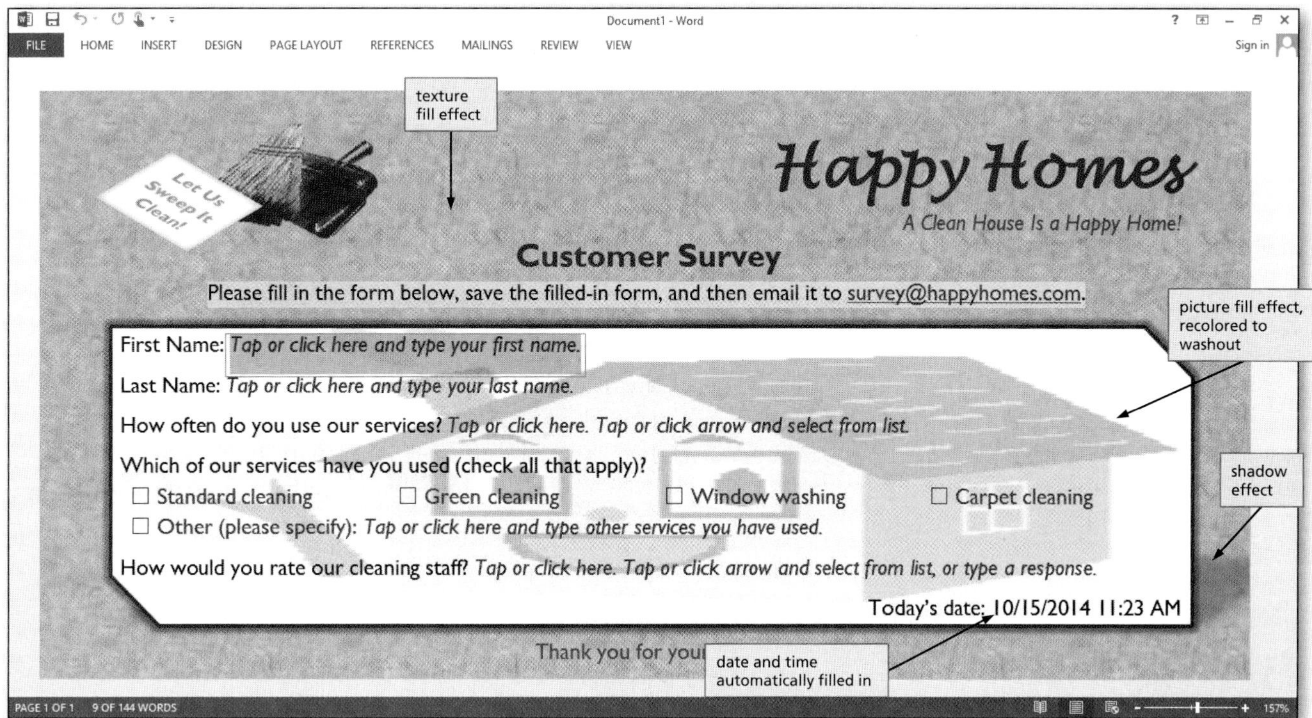

(a) Modified and Enhanced Online Form

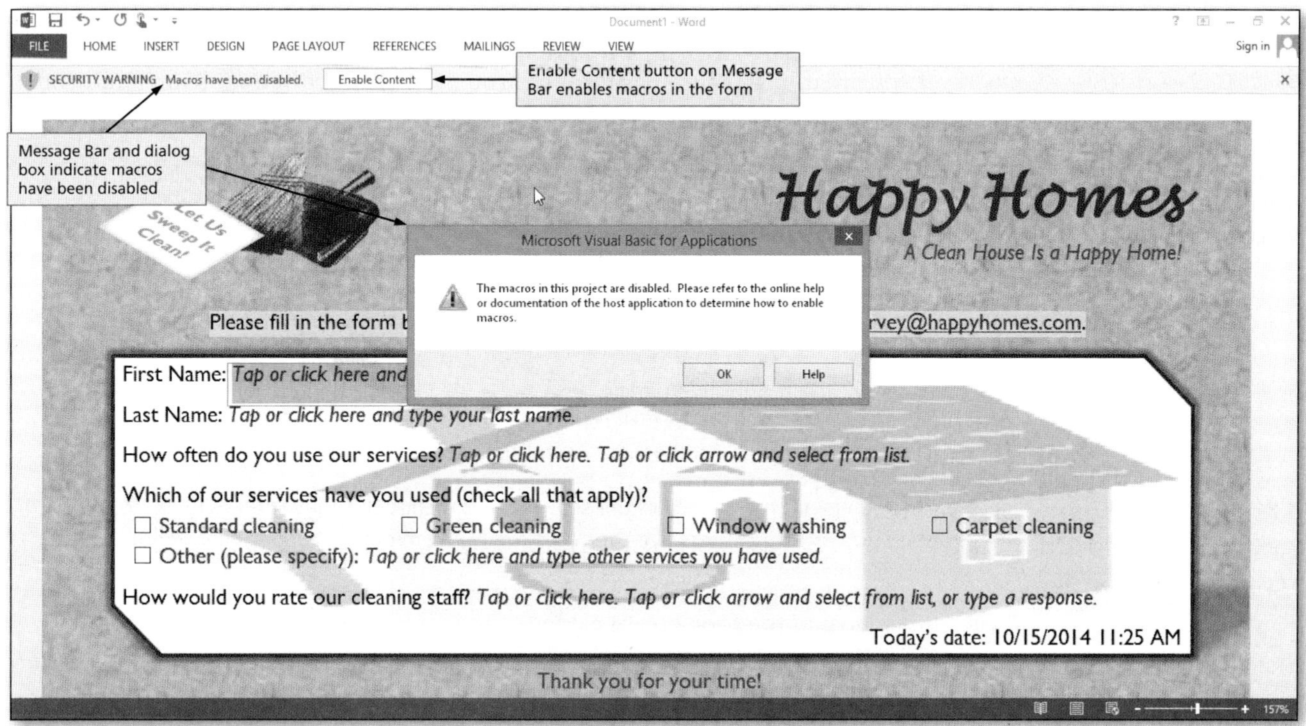

(b) Macros in Online Form Generate Security Warning

Figure 11–1

Roadmap

In this chapter, you will learn how to create the form shown in Figure 11–1 on the previous page. The following roadmap identifies general activities you will perform as you progress through this chapter:

1. SAVE a DOCUMENT AS a MACRO-ENABLED TEMPLATE.
2. MODIFY the TEXT AND FORM CONTENT CONTROLS.
3. ENHANCE the FORM'S VISUAL APPEAL.
4. CREATE MACROS TO AUTOMATE TASKS in the form.

At the beginning of step instructions throughout the chapter, you will see an abbreviated form of this roadmap. The abbreviated roadmap uses colors to indicate chapter progress: gray means the chapter is beyond that activity, blue means the task being shown is covered in that activity, and black means that activity is yet to be covered. For example, the following abbreviated roadmap indicates the chapter would be showing a task in the 2 MODIFY TEXT & FORM CONTENT CONTROLS activity.

1 SAVE DOCUMENT AS MACRO-ENABLED TEMPLATE | 2 MODIFY TEXT & FORM CONTENT CONTROLS
3 ENHANCE FORM'S VISUAL APPEAL | 4 CREATE MACROS TO AUTOMATE TASKS

Use the abbreviated roadmap as a progress guide while you read or step through the instructions in this chapter.

One of the few differences between Windows 7 and Windows 8 occurs in the steps to run Word. If you are using Windows 7, click the Start button, type **Word** in the 'Search programs and files' box, click Word 2013, and then, if necessary, maximize the Word window. For a summary of the steps to run Word in Windows 7, refer to the Quick Reference located at the back of this book.

To Run Word and Change Word Settings

If you are using a computer to step through the project in this chapter and you want your screens to match the figures in this book, you should change your screen's resolution to 1366 × 768. The following steps run Word, display formatting marks, and change the zoom to page width.

1. Run Word and create a blank document in the Word window. If necessary, maximize the Word window.
2. If the Print Layout button on the status bar is not selected, tap or click it so that your screen is in Print Layout view.
3. If the 'Show/Hide ¶' button (HOME tab | Paragraph group) is selected, tap or click it to hide formatting marks because you will not use them in this project.
4. If the rulers are displayed on the screen, tap or click the View Ruler check box (VIEW tab | Show group) to remove the rulers from the Word window because you will not use the rulers in this project.
5. If the edges of the page do not extend to the edge of the document window, display the VIEW tab and then tap or click the Page Width button (VIEW tab | Zoom group).

BTW
The Ribbon and Screen Resolution
Word may change how the groups and buttons within the groups appear on the ribbon, depending on the computer's screen resolution. Thus, your ribbon may look different from the ones in this book if you are using a screen resolution other than 1366 x 768.

To Save a Macro-Enabled Template

1 SAVE DOCUMENT AS MACRO-ENABLED TEMPLATE | 2 MODIFY TEXT & FORM CONTENT CONTROLS
3 ENHANCE FORM'S VISUAL APPEAL | 4 CREATE MACROS TO AUTOMATE TASKS

The project in this chapter contains macros. Thus, the first step in this chapter is to open the Customer Survey template created in Chapter 10 (see your instructor for a copy if you did not create the template) and then save the template as a macro-enabled template. ***Why?*** *To provide added security to templates, a basic Word template cannot store macros. Word instead provides a specific type of template, called a* ***macro-enabled template****, in which you can store macros.*

- Open the template named Customer Survey created in Chapter 10.

- Open the Backstage view, tap or click the Save As tab to display the Save As gallery, navigate to the desired save location, and display the Save As dialog box.
- Type `Customer Survey Modified` in the File name text box (Save As dialog box) to change the file name.
- Tap or click the 'Save as type' arrow to display the list of available file types and then tap or click 'Word Macro-Enabled Template' in the list to change the file type (Figure 11–2).

- Tap or click the Save button (Save As dialog box) to save the file using the entered file name as a macro-enabled template.

Q&A How does Word differentiate between a Word template and a Word macro-enabled template?
A Word template has an extension of .dotx, whereas a Word macro-enabled template has an extension of .dotm. Also, the icon for a macro-enabled template contains an exclamation point.

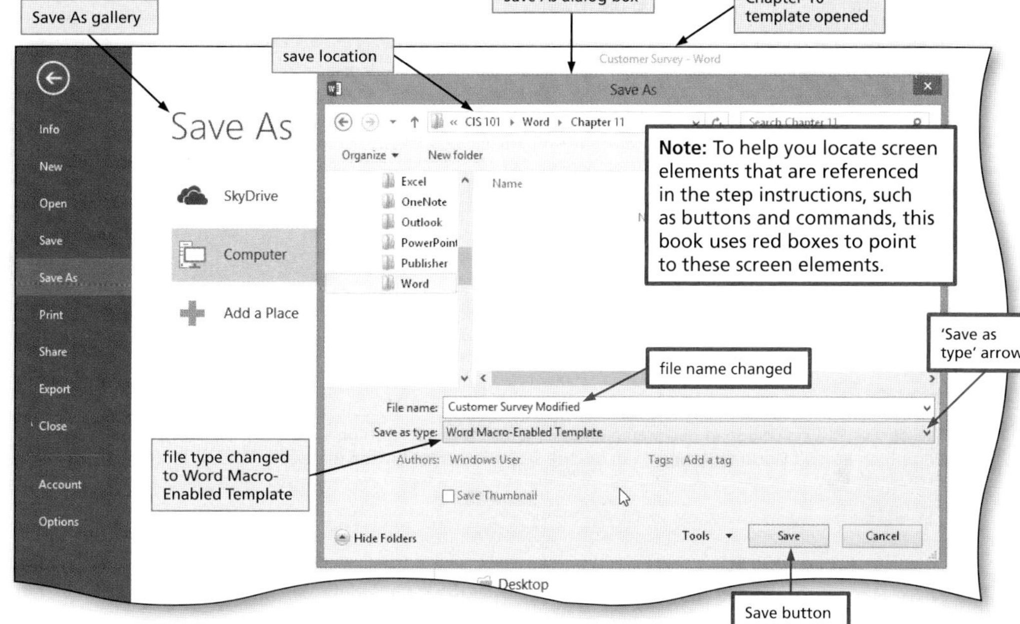

Figure 11–2

To Show the DEVELOPER Tab

Many of the tasks you will perform in this chapter use commands on the DEVELOPER tab. Thus, the following steps show the DEVELOPER tab on the ribbon.

1. Open the Backstage view and then tap or click Options in the left pane of the Backstage view to display the Word Options dialog box.
2. Tap or click Customize Ribbon in the left pane (Word Options dialog box) to display associated options in the right pane.
3. If it is not selected already, place a check mark in the Developer check box in the Main Tabs list.
4. Tap or click the OK button to show the DEVELOPER tab on the ribbon.

BTW
Macro-Enabled Documents
The above steps showed how to create a macro-enabled template. If you wanted to create a macro-enabled document, you would tap or click the 'Save as type' arrow (Save As dialog box), tap or click 'Word Macro-Enabled Document', and then tap or click the Save button.

To Unprotect a Document

The Customer Survey Modified template is protected. Recall that Chapter 10 showed how to protect a form so that users could enter data only in designated areas, specifically, the content controls. The following steps unprotect a document. ***Why?*** *Before this form can be modified, it must be unprotected. Later in this project, after you have completed the modifications, you will protect it again.*

- Display the DEVELOPER tab.
- Tap or click the Restrict Editing button (DEVELOPER tab | Protect group) to display the Restrict Editing task pane (Figure 11–3).

- Tap or click the Stop Protection button in the Restrict Editing task pane to unprotect the form.
- Tap or click the Close button in the Restrict Editing task pane to close the task pane.

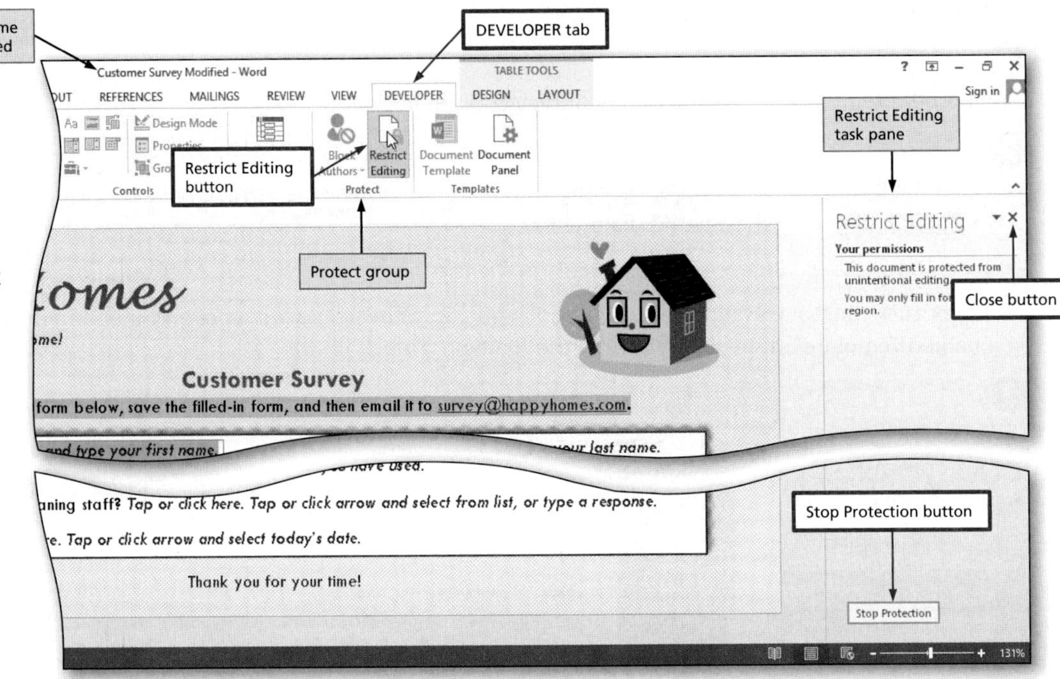

Figure 11–3

Other Ways

1. Tap or click FILE on ribbon, if necessary, tap or click Info tab in Backstage view, tap or click Protect Document button, tap or click Restrict Editing on Protect Document menu, tap or click Stop Protection button in Restrict Editing task pane

CONSIDER THIS

How do you protect a computer from macro viruses?

A **computer virus** is a type of malicious software, or malware, which is a potentially damaging computer program that affects, or infects, a computer or mobile device negatively by altering the way the computer or mobile device works without the user's knowledge or permission. Millions of known viruses and other malicious programs exist. The increased use of networks, the Internet, and email has accelerated the spread of computer viruses and other malicious programs.

- To combat these threats, most computer users run an **antivirus program** that searches for viruses and other malware and destroys the malicious programs before they infect a computer or mobile device. Macros are known carriers of viruses and other malware. For this reason, you can specify a macro setting in Word to reduce the chance your computer will be infected with a macro virus. These macro settings allow you to enable or disable macros. An **enabled macro** is a macro that Word will execute, and a **disabled macro** is a macro that is unavailable to Word.
- As shown in Figure 11–1b on page WD 675, you can instruct Word to display a security warning on a Message Bar if it opens a document that contains a macro(s). If you are confident of the source (author) of the document and macros, enable the macros. If you are uncertain about the reliability of the source of the document and macros, then do not enable the macros.

To Specify Macro Settings in Word

Why? *When you open the online form in this chapter, you want the macros enabled. At the same time, your computer should be protected from potentially harmful macros. Thus, you will specify a macro setting that allows you to enable macros each time you open this chapter's online form or any document that contains a macro from an unknown source.* The following steps specify macro settings.

- Tap or click the Macro Security button (DEVELOPER tab | Code group) to display the Trust Center dialog box.
- If it is not selected already, tap or click the 'Disable all macros with notification' option button (Trust Center dialog box), which causes Word to alert you when a document contains a macro so that you can decide whether to enable the macro(s) (Figure 11–4).

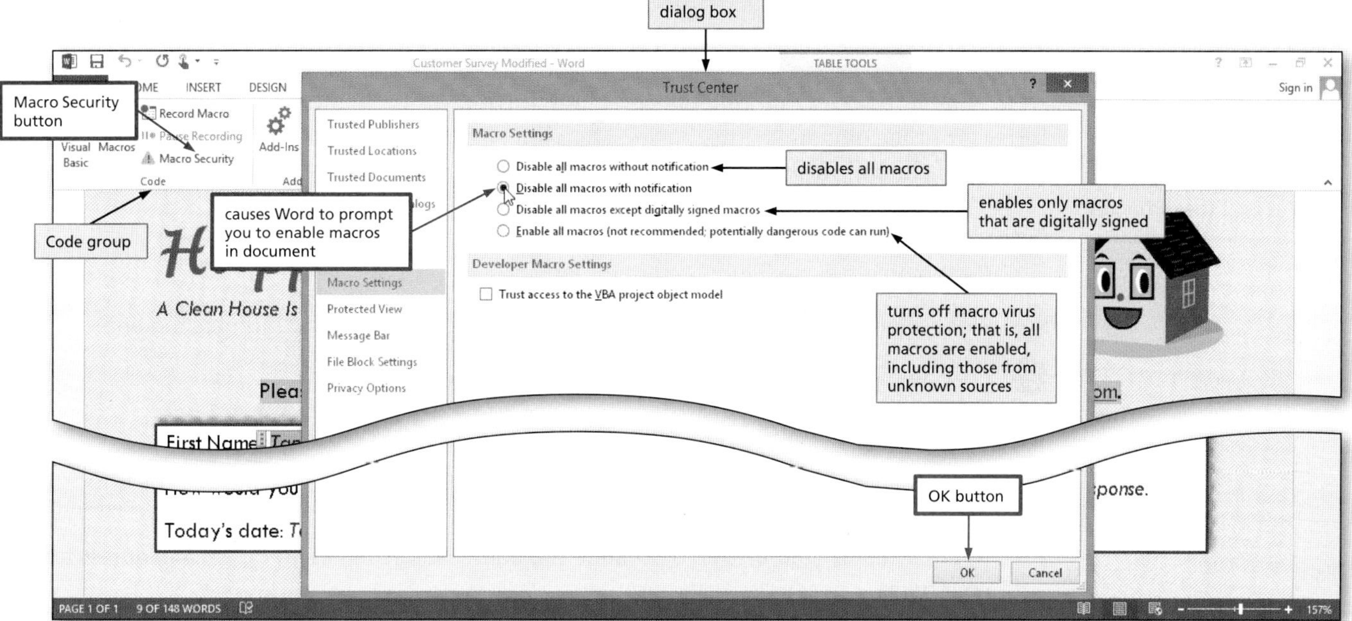

Figure 11–4

- Tap or click the OK button to close the dialog box.

Other Ways

1. Tap or click FILE on ribbon, tap or click Options in Backstage view, tap or click Trust Center in left pane (Word Options dialog box), tap or click 'Trust Center Settings' button in right pane, if necessary, tap or click Macro Settings in left pane (Trust Center dialog box), select desired setting, tap or click OK button in each dialog box

Modifying Text and Form Content Controls

The form created in Chapter 10 is enhanced in this chapter by performing these steps:

1. Delete the current clip art.
2. Change the document theme.
3. Change the fonts, colors, and alignments of the first four lines of text.
4. Convert the 2 × 1 table containing the First Name and Last Name content controls to text so that each of these content controls is on a separate line.
5. Delete the date picker content control and replace it with a date field.
6. Modify the color of the hyperlink and the check box labels.

The following pages apply these changes to the form.

To Delete a Graphic and Change the Document Theme

BTW
Saving and Resetting Themes
If you have changed the color scheme and font set and want to save this combination for future use, save it as a new theme by tapping or clicking the Themes button (DESIGN tab | Themes group), tapping or clicking 'Save Current Theme' in the Themes gallery, entering a theme name in the File name box (Save Current Theme dialog box), and then tapping or clicking the Save button. If you want to reset the theme template to the default, you would tap or click the Themes button (DESIGN tab | Themes group) and then tap or click 'Reset to Theme from Template' in the Themes gallery.

The online form in this chapter has a different clip art and uses the Dividend document theme. The following steps delete the current clip art and change the document theme.

1. Tap or click the happy house clip art to select it and then press the DELETE key to delete the selected clip art.
2. Display the DESIGN tab. Tap or click the Themes button (DESIGN tab | Document Formatting group) and then tap or click Dividend in the Themes gallery to change the document theme.

To Format Text and Change Paragraph Alignment

The next step in modifying the online form for this chapter is to change the formats of the company name, business tag line, form name, form instructions, and date line. The following steps format text and change paragraph alignment.

1. Change the color of the first line of text, Happy Homes, and third line of text, Customer Survey, to 'Plum, Accent 2, Darker 25%'.
2. Right-align the first and second lines of text (company name and business tag line).
3. Change the highlight color on the fourth line of text to Yellow.
4. Right-align the line of text containing the Today's date content control.
5. If necessary, widen the text box surrounding the data entry area to include the entire date placeholder (Figure 11–5).

   If requested by your instructor, change the name, happyhomes, in the email address to your name.

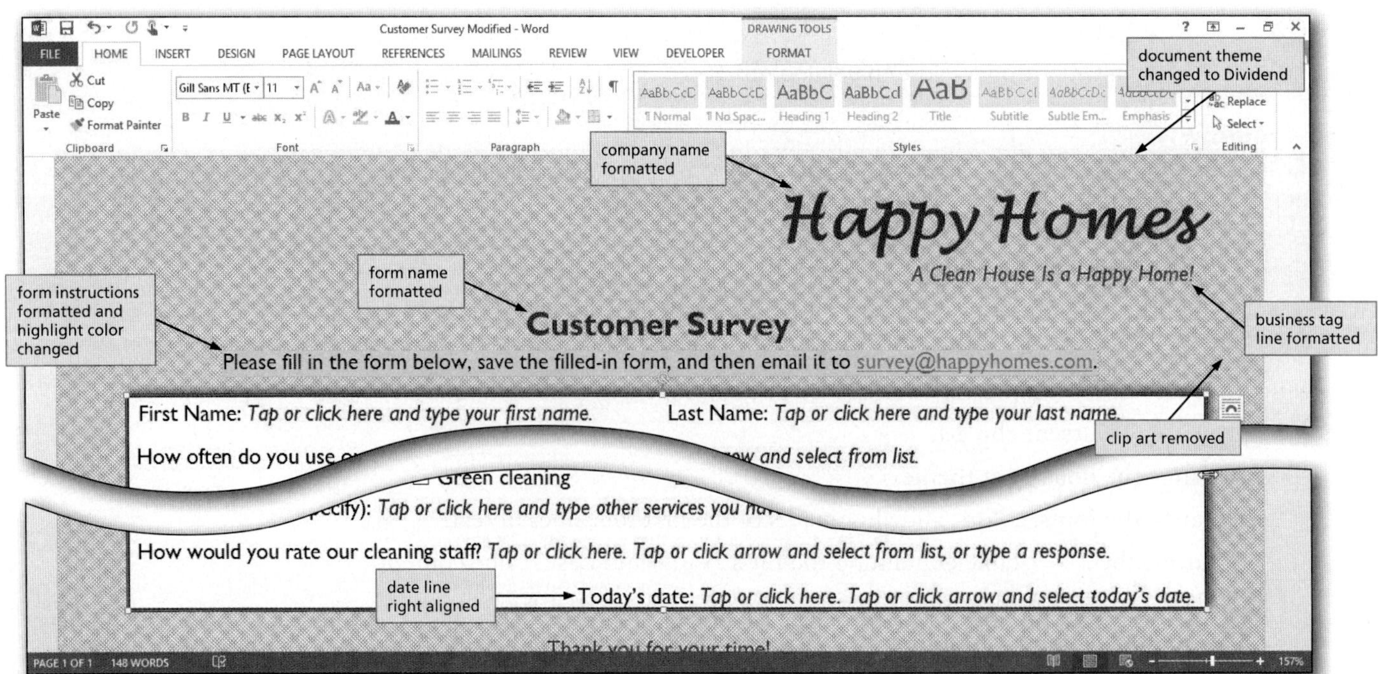

Figure 11–5

To Change the Properties of a Plain Text Content Control

In this online form, the First Name and Last Name content controls are on separate lines. In Chapter 10, you selected the 'Content control cannot be deleted' check box in the Content Control Properties dialog box so that users could not delete the content control accidentally while filling in the form. With this check box selected, however, you cannot move a content control from one location to another on the form. Thus, the following steps change the locking properties of the First Name and Last Name content controls so that you can rearrange them.

BTW

Touch Screen Differences

The Office and Windows interfaces may vary if you are using a touch screen. For this reason, you might notice that the function or appearance of your touch screen differs slightly from this chapter's presentation.

1. Display the DEVELOPER tab.
2. Tap or click the First Name content control to select it.
3. Tap or click the Control Properties button (DEVELOPER tab | Controls group) to display the Content Control Properties dialog box.
4. Remove the check mark from the 'Content control cannot be deleted' check box (Content Control Properties dialog box) (Figure 11–6).
5. Tap or click the OK button to assign the modified properties to the content control.
6. Tap or click the Last Name content control to select it and then tap or click the Control Properties button (DEVELOPER tab | Controls group) to display the Content Control Properties dialog box.
7. Remove the check mark from the 'Content control cannot be deleted' check box (Content Control Properties dialog box) and then tap or click the OK button to assign the modified properties to the content control.

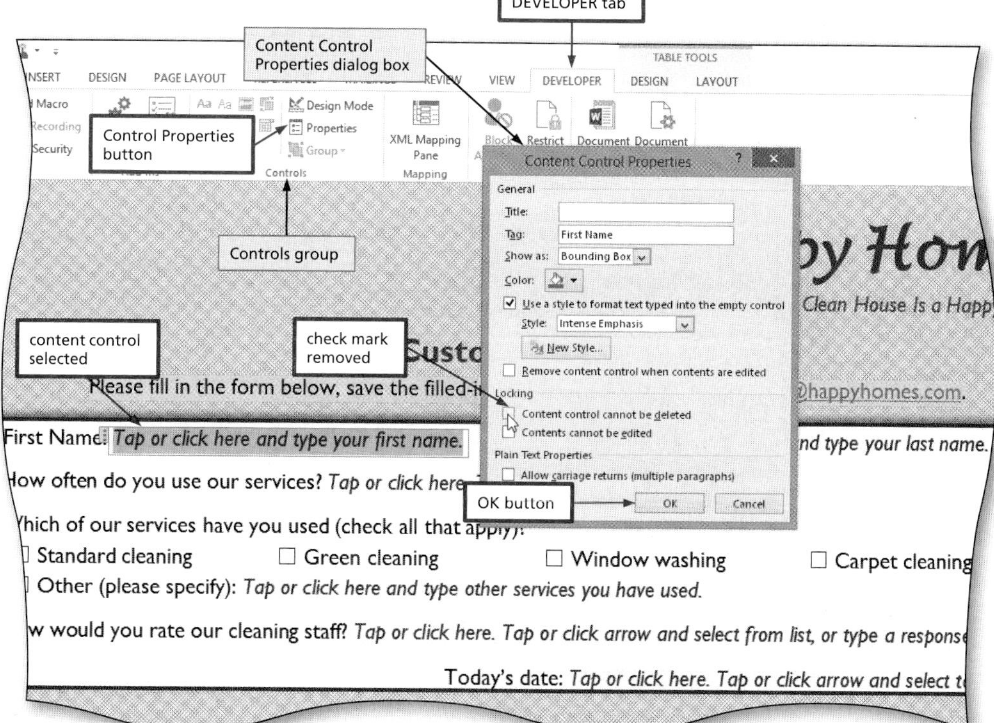

Figure 11–6

To Convert a Table to Text

The First Name and Last Name content controls currently are in a 2×1 table. The following steps convert the table to regular text, placing a paragraph break at the location of the second column. ***Why?*** *In this online form, these content controls are on separate lines, one below the other. That is, they are not in a table.*

- Position the insertion point somewhere in the table.
- Display the TABLE TOOLS LAYOUT tab.
- Tap or click the 'Convert to Text' button (TABLE TOOLS LAYOUT tab | Data group) to display the Convert Table To Text dialog box.
- Tap or click Paragraph marks (Convert Table To Text dialog box), which will place a paragraph mark at the location of each new column in the table (Figure 11–7).

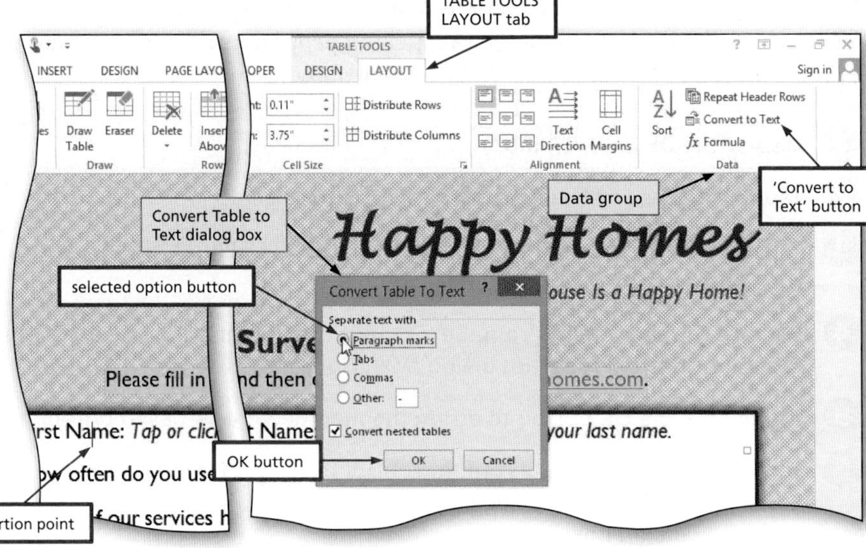

Figure 11–7

2

- Tap or click the OK button to convert the table to text, separating each column with the specified character, a paragraph mark in this case.

Q&A Why did the Last Name content control move below the First Name content control?
The Separate text with area (Convert Table To Text dialog box) controls how the table is converted to text. The Paragraph marks setting converts each column in the table to a line of text below the previous line. The Tabs setting places a tab character where each column was located, and the Commas setting places a comma where each column was located.

- With the First Name and Last Name lines selected, using either the ruler or the PAGE LAYOUT tab, change the left indent to 0.06" so that the text aligns with the text immediately below it (that is, the H in How), as shown in Figure 11–8.

- Tap or click anywhere to remove the selection from the text.

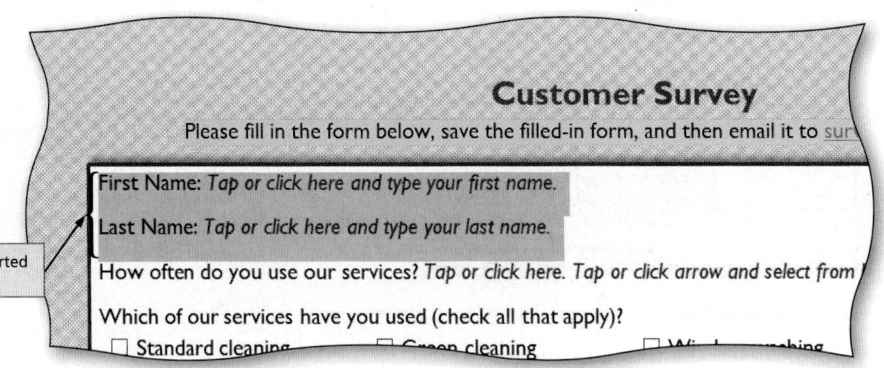

Figure 11–8

To Change the Properties of a Plain Text Content Control

You are finished moving the First Name and Last Name content controls. The following steps reset the locking properties of these content controls.

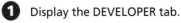

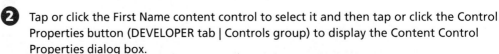

1. Display the DEVELOPER tab.
2. Tap or click the First Name content control to select it and then tap or click the Control Properties button (DEVELOPER tab | Controls group) to display the Content Control Properties dialog box.

3. Place a check mark in the 'Content control cannot be deleted' check box (Content Control Properties dialog box) and then tap or click the OK button to assign the modified properties to the content control.

4. Repeat Steps 2 and 3 for the Last Name content control.

To Adjust Paragraph Spacing and Resize the Rectangle Shape

With the First Name and Last Name content controls on separate lines, the thank you line moved to a second page, and the rectangle outline in the data entry area now is too short to accommodate the text. The following steps adjust paragraph spacing and extend the rectangle shape downward so that it surrounds the entire data entry area.

1. Position the insertion point in the second line of text on the form (the tag line) and then adjust the spacing after to 0 pt (PAGE LAYOUT tab | Paragraph group).

2. Adjust the spacing after to 6 pt for the First Name and Last Name lines.

3. Adjust the spacing before and after to 6 pt for the line that begins, How often do you use..., and the line that begins, How would you rate...

4. Adjust the spacing before to 6 pt for the thank you line.

5. Scroll to display the entire form in the document window. If necessary, reduce spacing after other paragraphs so that the entire form fits in a single document window.

6. Tap or click the rectangle shape to select it.

7. Position the pointer on the bottom-middle sizing handle of the rectangle shape.

8. Drag the bottom-middle sizing handle downward so that the shape includes the bottom content control, in this case, the Today's Date content control (Figure 11–9). If necessary, resize the other edges of the shape to fit the text.

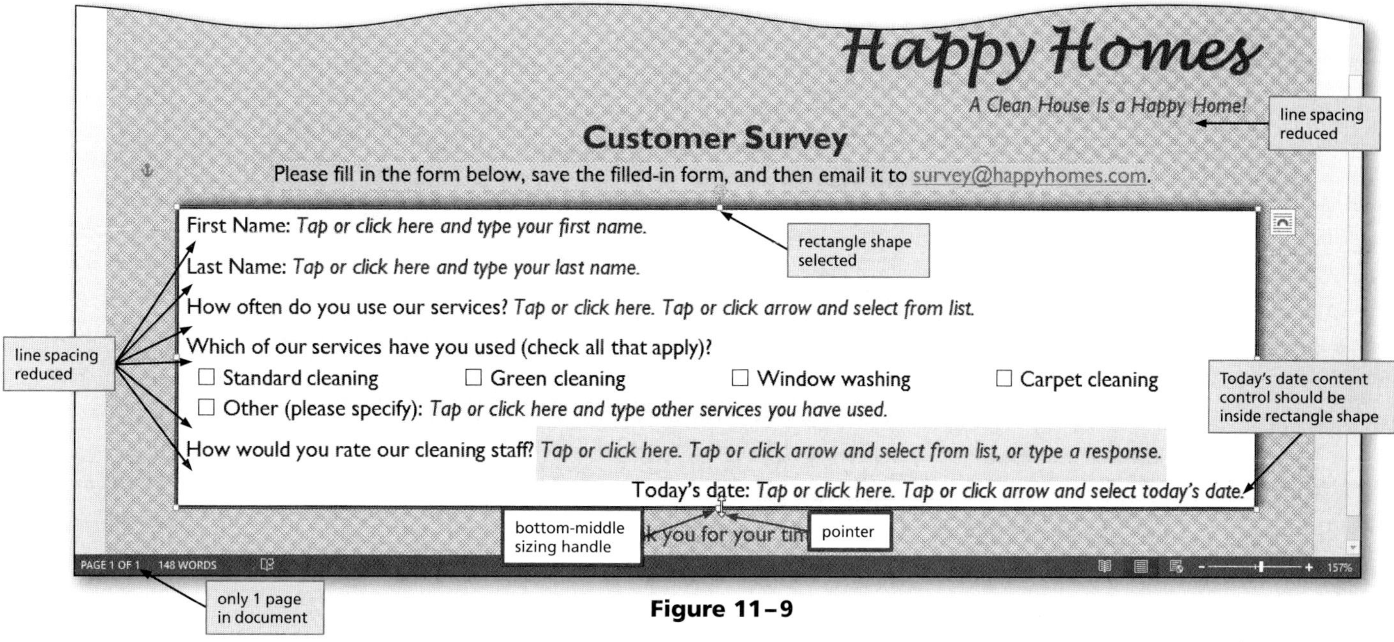

Figure 11–9

To Change the Properties of a Date Picker Content Control

In this online form, instead of the user entering the current date, the computer or mobile device's system date will be filled in automatically by Word. Thus, the Today's date content control is not needed and can be deleted. To delete the content control, you first will need to remove the check mark from the 'Content control cannot be deleted' check box in the Content Control Properties dialog box. The following steps change the locking properties of the Today's date content control and then delete the content control.

BTW
Document Properties
If you wanted to insert document properties into a document, you would tap or click the 'Explore Quick Parts' button (INSERT tab | Text group) to display the Explore Quick Parts menu, tap or point to Document Property on the Explore Quick Parts menu, and then tap or click the property you want to insert on the Document Property menu. To create custom document properties for a document, open the Backstage view, tap or click the Info tab to display the Info gallery, tap or click the Properties button in the far right pane to display the Properties menu, tap or click Advanced Properties on the Properties menu to display the Document Properties dialog box, tap or click the Custom tab (Document Properties dialog box) to display the Custom sheet, enter the name of the new property in the Name text box, select its type and value in the dialog box, tap or click the Add button to add the property to the document, and then tap or click the OK button to close the dialog box.

1. Display the DEVELOPER tab.
2. Tap or click the Today's Date content control to select it.
3. Tap or click the Control Properties button (DEVELOPER tab | Controls group) to display the Content Control Properties dialog box.
4. Remove the check mark from the 'Content control cannot be deleted' check box (Content Control Properties dialog box) (Figure 11–10).
5. Tap or click the OK button to assign the modified properties to the content control.
6. Press and hold and then tap the 'Show Context Menu' button on the mini toolbar or right-click the Today's Date content control to display a shortcut menu; tap or click 'Remove Content Control' on the shortcut menu to delete the selected content control.

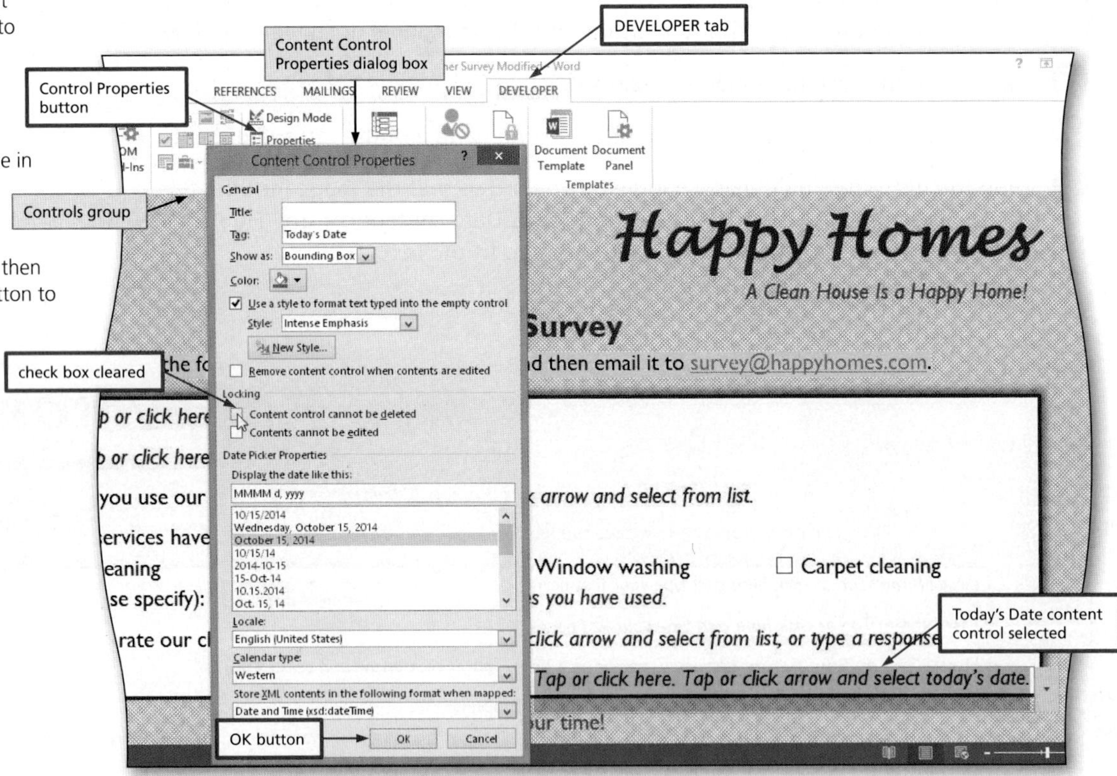

Figure 11–10

To Insert a Date Field

The following steps insert the date and time as a field in the form at the location of the insertion point. ***Why?*** *The current date and time is a field so that the form automatically displays the current date and time. Recall that a field is a set of codes that instructs Word to perform a certain action.*

1

- Display the INSERT tab.
- With the insertion point positioned as shown in Figure 11–11, which is the location for the date and time, tap or click the 'Explore Quick Parts' button (INSERT tab | Text group) to display the Explore Quick Parts menu.

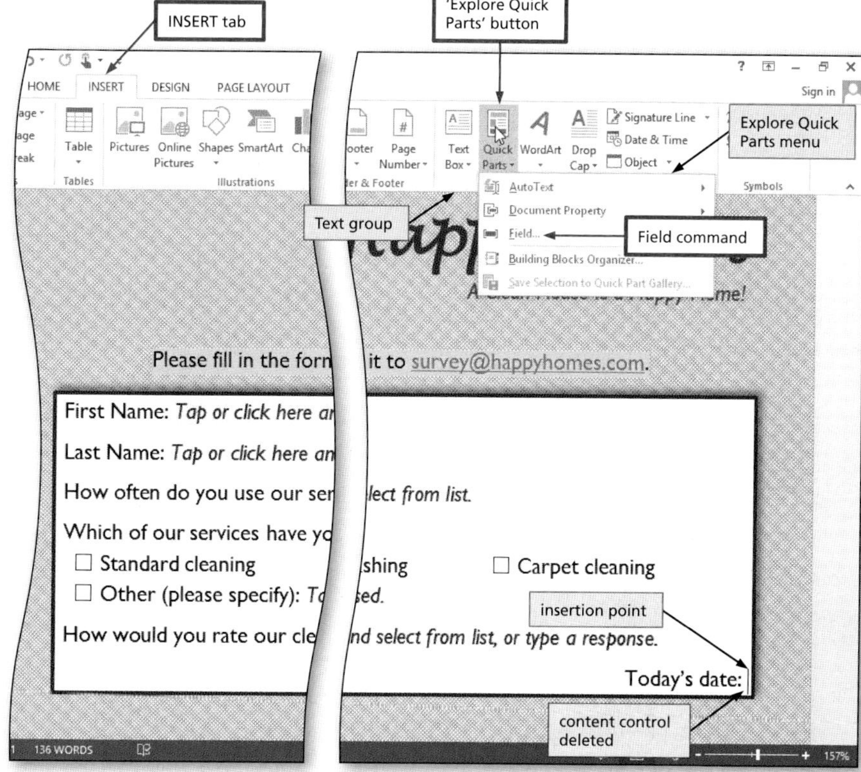

Figure 11–11

2

- Tap or click Field on the Explore Quick Parts menu to display the Field dialog box.
- Scroll through the Field names list (Field dialog box) and then tap or click Date, which displays the Date formats list in the Field properties area.
- Tap or click the date in the format of 10/15/2014 9:45:54 AM in the Date formats list to select a date format — your date and time will differ (Figure 11–12).

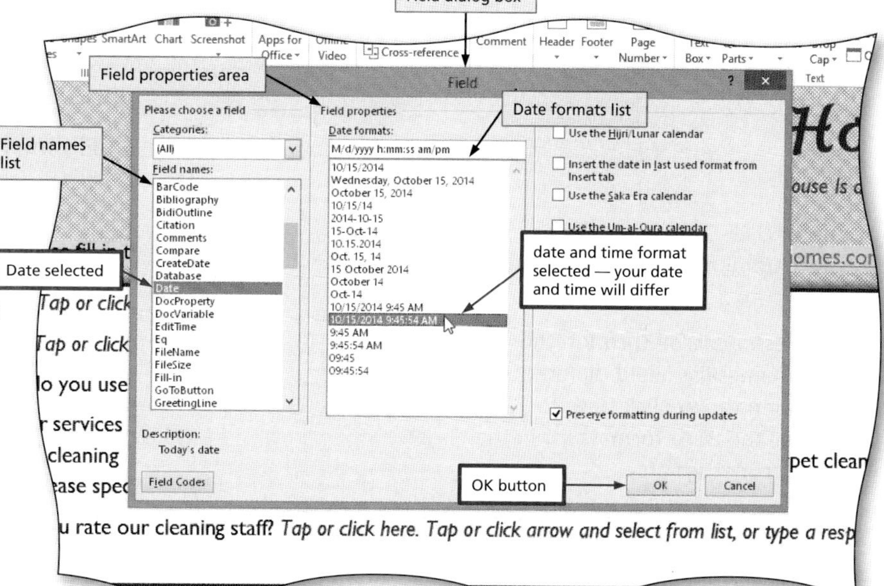

Figure 11–12

Q&A What controls the date that appears?

Your current computer or mobile device date appears in this dialog box. The format for the selected date shows in the Date formats box. In this case, the format for the selected date is M/d/yyyy h:mm:ss am/pm, which displays the date as month/day/year hours:minutes:seconds AM/PM.

3

- Tap or click the OK button to insert the current date and time at the location of the insertion point (Figure 11–13).

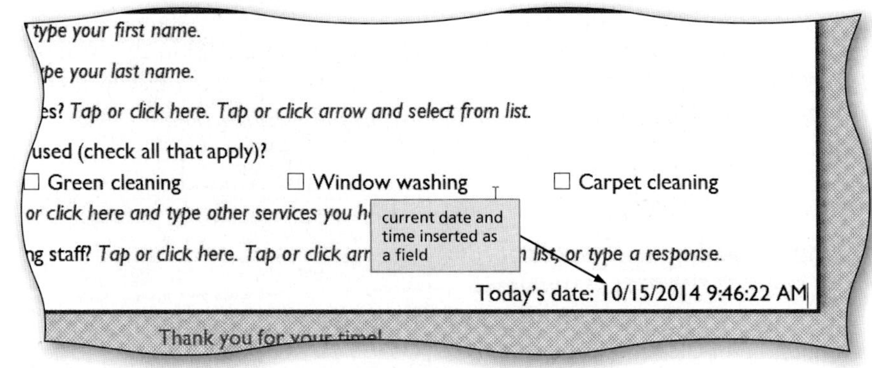

Figure 11–13

Q&A How do I delete a field?
Select it and then press the DELETE key or tap or click the Cut button (HOME tab | Clipboard group), or press and hold or right-click it and then tap the Cut button on the mini toolbar or click Cut on the shortcut menu.

Other Ways

1. Tap or click 'Insert Date and Time' button (INSERT tab | Text group), select date format (Date and Time dialog box), place check mark in Update automatically check box, tap or click OK button

To Edit a Field

1 SAVE DOCUMENT AS MACRO-ENABLED TEMPLATE | 2 MODIFY TEXT & FORM CONTENT CONTROLS
3 ENHANCE FORM'S VISUAL APPEAL | 4 CREATE MACROS TO AUTOMATE TASKS

The following steps edit the field. ***Why?*** *After you see the date and time in the form, you decide not to include the seconds in the time. That is, you want just the hours and minutes to be displayed.*

1

- Press and hold or right-click the date field to display a shortcut menu (Figure 11–14).

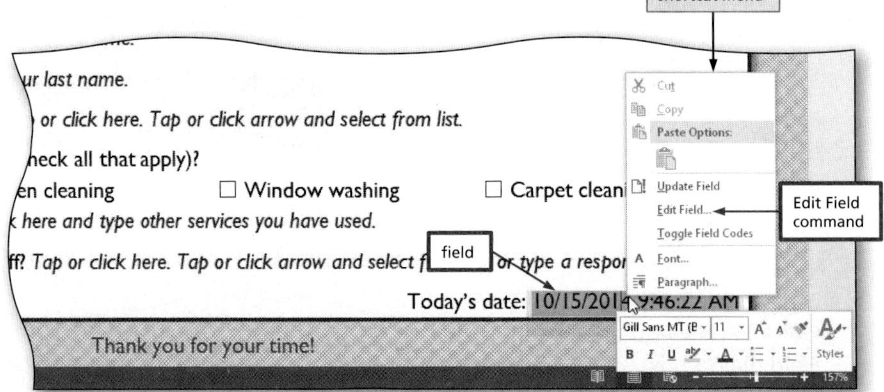

Figure 11–14

2

- Tap or click Edit Field on the shortcut menu to display the Field dialog box.
- If necessary, scroll through the Field names list (Field dialog box) and then tap or click Date to display the Date formats list in the Field properties area.
- Select the desired date format, in this case 10/15/2014 9:47 AM (Figure 11–15).

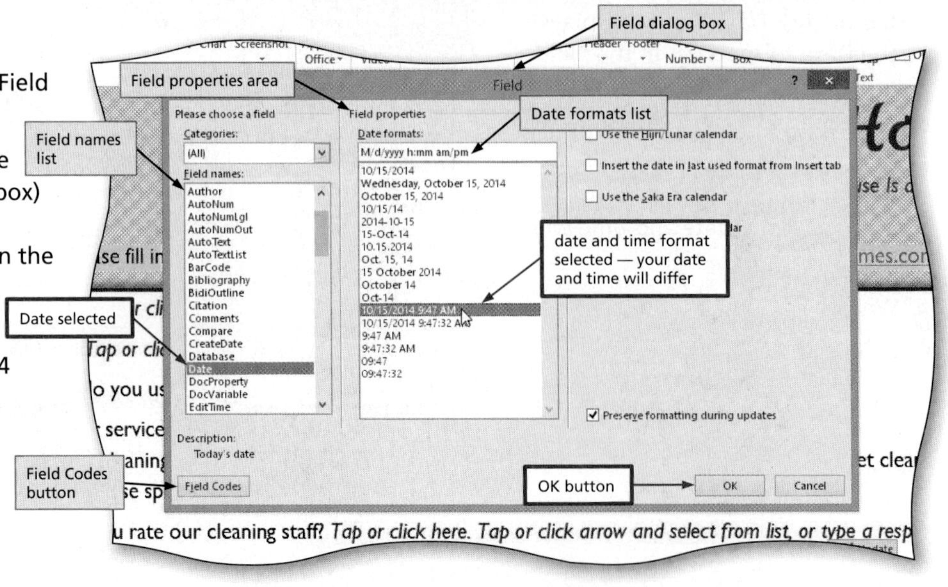

Field dialog box
Field properties area
Field names list
Date formats list
date and time format selected — your date and time will differ
Date selected
Field Codes button
OK button

Figure 11–15

- Tap or click the OK button to insert the edited field at the location of the insertion point (Figure 11–16).

BTW
Field Formats
If you wanted to create custom field formats, you would tap or click the Field Codes button (Field dialog box) (shown in Figure 11-15) to display advanced field properties in the right pane in the dialog box, tap or click the Options button to display the Field Options dialog box, select the format to apply in the Formatting list, tap or click the 'Add to Field' button, and then tap or click the OK button in each open dialog box.

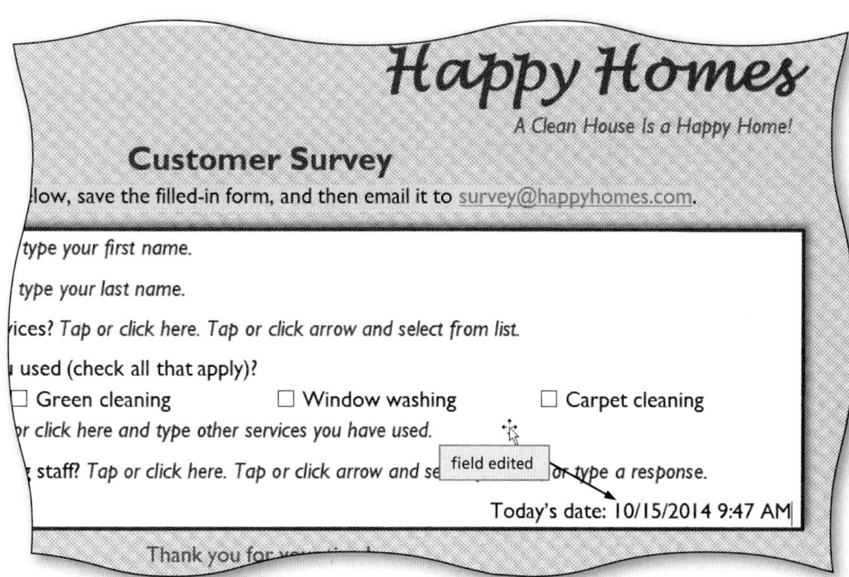

Figure 11–16

To Modify a Style Using the Styles Task Pane

1 SAVE DOCUMENT AS MACRO-ENABLED TEMPLATE | 2 MODIFY TEXT & FORM CONTENT CONTROLS
3 ENHANCE FORM'S VISUAL APPEAL | 4 CREATE MACROS TO AUTOMATE TASKS

The new text highlight color of the form instructions makes it difficult to see the hyperlink. In this online form, the hyperlink should be the same color as the company name so that the hyperlink is noticeable. The following steps modify a style using the Styles task pane. ***Why?*** *The Hyperlink style is not in the Styles gallery. To modify a style that is not in the Styles gallery, you can use the Styles task pane.*

- Position the insertion point in the hyperlink in the form.
- Display the HOME tab.
- Tap or click the Styles Dialog Box Launcher (HOME tab | Styles group) to display the Styles task pane.
- If necessary, tap or click Hyperlink in the list of styles in the task pane to select it and then tap or click the Hyperlink arrow to display the Hyperlink menu (Figure 11–17).

Q&A What if the style I want to modify is not in the list?
Tap or click the Manage Styles button at the bottom of the task pane (shown in Figure 11–18 on the next page), locate the style, and then tap or click the Modify button in the dialog box.

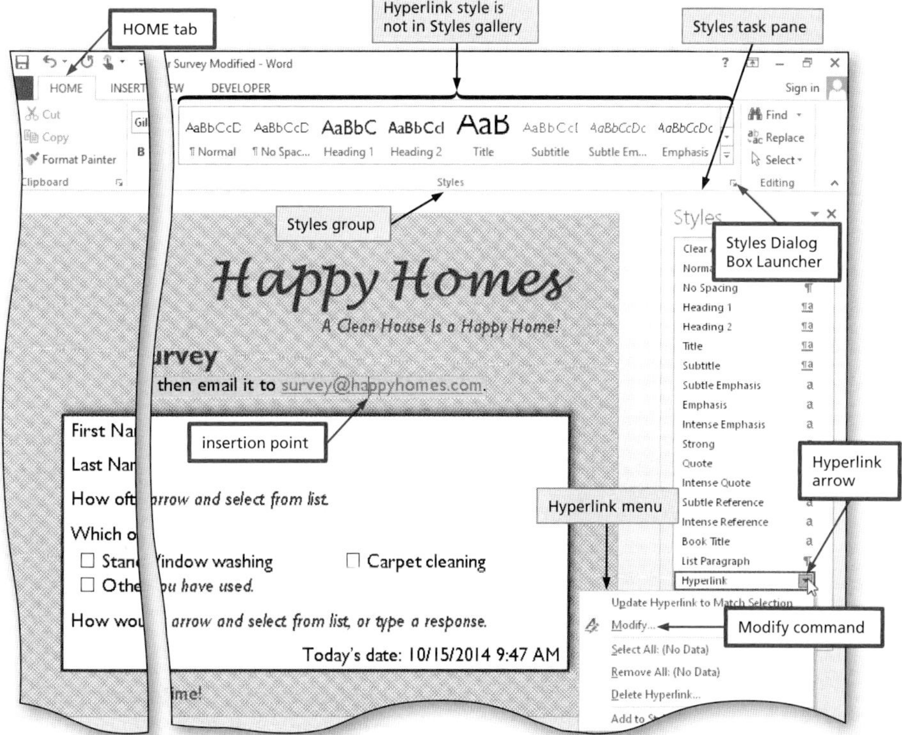

Figure 11–17

2

- Tap or click Modify on the Hyperlink menu to display the Modify Style dialog box.
- Tap or click the Font Color arrow (Modify Style dialog box) to display the Font Color gallery (Figure 11–18).

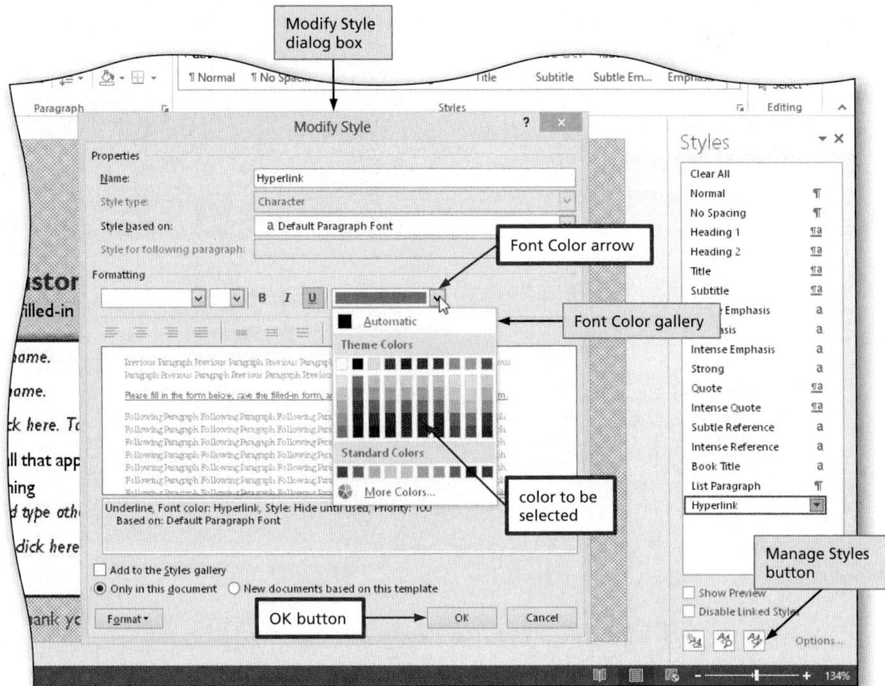

Figure 11–18

3

- Tap or click 'Plum, Accent 2, Darker 25%' (sixth color in fifth row) as the new hyperlink color.
- Tap or click the OK button to close the dialog box. Close the Styles task pane (Figure 11–19).

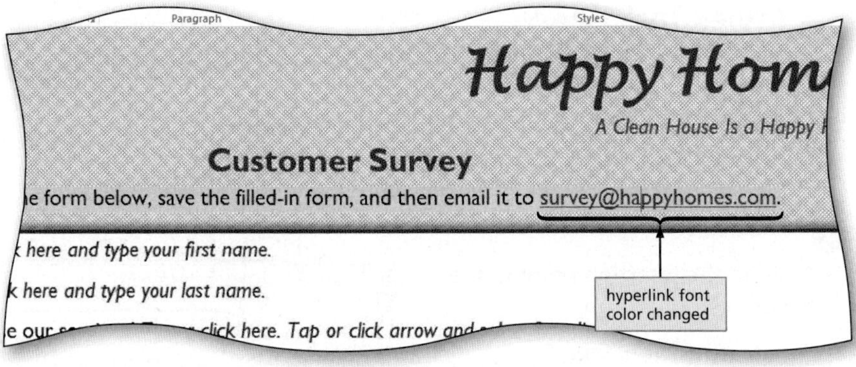

Figure 11–19

BTW
Hidden Styles
Some styles are hidden, which means they do not appear in the Styles task pane. You can display all styles, including hidden styles, by tapping or clicking the Manage Styles button in the Styles task pane (Figure 11–18), which displays the Manage Styles dialog box. Tap or click the Edit tab, if necessary, and then locate the style name in the Select a style to edit list.

To Modify a Style

In this online form, the placeholder text is to be the same color as the company name. Currently, the placeholder text is formatted using the Intense Emphasis style, which uses a light shade of plum as the font color. Thus, the following steps modify the color of the Intense Emphasis style to a darker shade of plum.

1. Scroll through the Styles gallery (HOME tab | Styles group) to locate the Intense Emphasis style.
2. Press and hold or right-click Intense Emphasis in the Styles gallery to display a shortcut menu and then tap or click Modify on the shortcut menu to display the Modify Style dialog box.

3. Tap or click the Font Color arrow (Modify Style dialog box) to display the Font Color gallery (Figure 11–20).

4. Tap or click 'Plum, Accent 2, Darker 25%' (sixth color in fifth row) as the new color.

5. Tap or click the OK button to change the color of the style, which automatically changes the color of every item formatted using this style in the document.

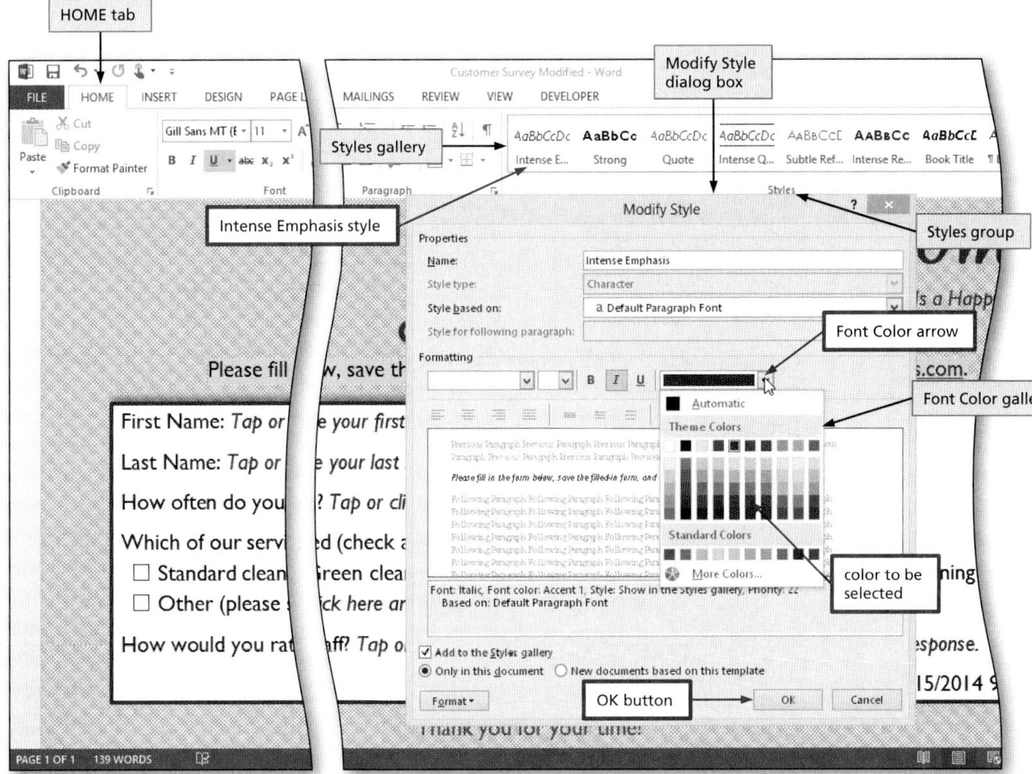

Figure 11–20

BTW

Character vs. Paragraph Styles

In the Styles task pane, character styles display a lowercase letter a to the right of the style name, and paragraph styles show a paragraph mark. With a character style, Word applies the formats to the selected text. With a paragraph style, Word applies the formats to the entire paragraph.

BTW

Assign a Shortcut Key to a Style

If you wanted to assign a shortcut key to a style, you would press and hold or right-click the style name in the Styles gallery (HOME tab | Styles group) or display the Styles task pane and then tap or click the style arrow, tap or click Modify on the menu to display the Modify Style dialog box, tap or click the Format button (Modify Style dialog box), tap or click Shortcut key on the Format menu to display the Customize Keyboard dialog box, press the desired shortcut key(s) (Customize Keyboard dialog box), tap or click the Assign button to assign the shortcut key to the style, tap or click the Close button to close the Customize Keyboard dialog box, and then tap or click the OK button to close the Modify Style dialog box.

To Modify the Default Font Settings

You can change the default font so that the current document and all future documents use the new font settings. That is, if you exit Word, restart the computer, and run Word again, documents you create will use the new default font. If you wanted to change the default font from 11-point Calibri to another font, font style, font size, font color, and/or font effects, you would perform the following steps.

1. Tap or click the Font Dialog Box Launcher (HOME tab | Font group) to display the Font dialog box.
2. Make desired changes to the font settings in the Font dialog box.
3. Tap or click the 'Set As Default' button to change the default settings to those specified in Step 2.
4. When the Microsoft Word dialog box is displayed, select the desired option button and then tap or tap or click the OK button.

To Reset the Default Font Settings

BTW
Advanced Character Attributes
If you wanted to set advanced character attributes, you would tap or click the Font Dialog Box Launcher (HOME tab | Font group) to display the Font dialog box, tap or click the Advanced tab (Font dialog box) to display the Advanced sheet, select the desired Character Spacing or OpenType Features settings, and then tap or click the OK button.

To change the font settings back to the default, you would follow the steps at the bottom of the previous page, using the default font settings when performing Step 2. If you do not remember the default settings, you would perform the following steps to restore the original Normal style settings.

1. Exit Word.
2. Use File Explorer to locate the Normal.dotm file (be sure that hidden files and folders are displayed and include system and hidden files in your search), which is the file that contains default font and other settings.
3. Rename the Normal.dotm file to oldnormal.dotm file so that the Normal.dotm file no longer exists.
4. Run Word, which will recreate a Normal.dotm file using the original default settings.

To Create a Character Style

1 SAVE DOCUMENT AS MACRO-ENABLED TEMPLATE | 2 MODIFY TEXT & FORM CONTENT CONTROLS
3 ENHANCE FORM'S VISUAL APPEAL | 4 CREATE MACROS TO AUTOMATE TASKS

In this online form, the check box labels are to be the same color as the company name. The following steps create a character style called Check Box Labels. ***Why?*** *Although you could select each of the check box labels and then format them, a more efficient technique is to create a character style.* If you decide to modify the formats of the check box labels at a later time, you simply change the formats assigned to the style to automatically change all characters in the document based on that style.

- Position the insertion point in one of the check box labels.
- Tap or click the Styles Dialog Box Launcher (HOME tab | Styles group) to display the Styles task pane.
- Tap or click the Manage Styles button in the Styles task pane to display the Manage Styles dialog box (Figure 11–21).

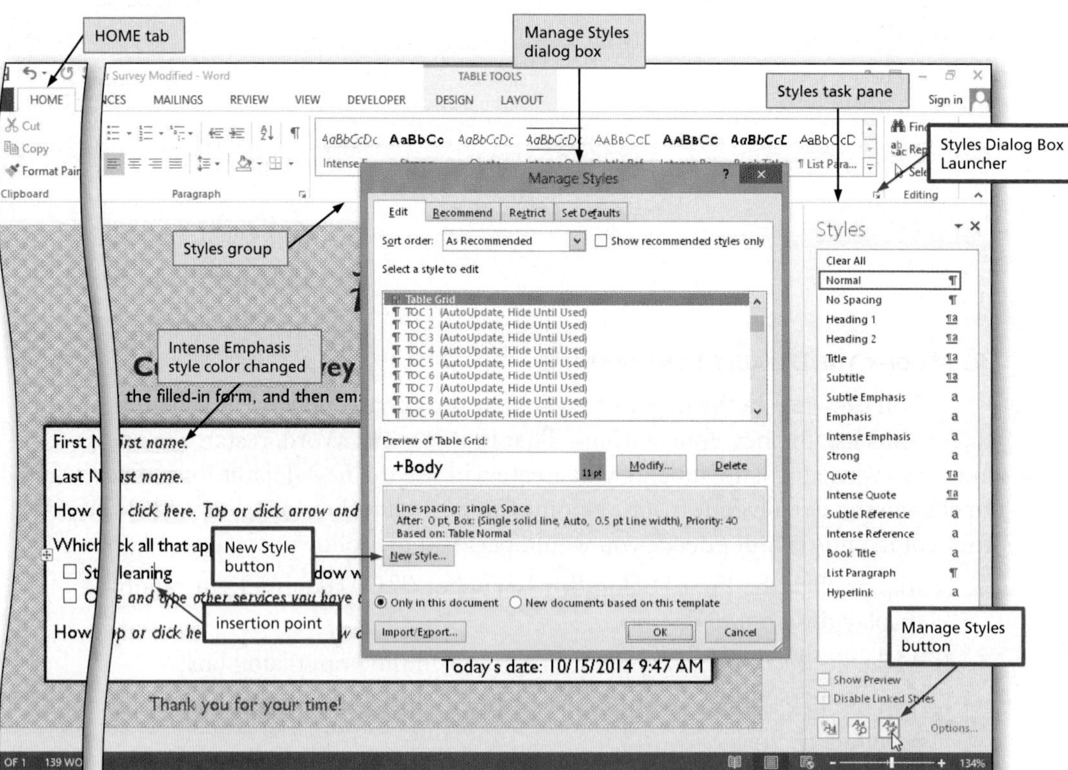

Figure 11–21

- Tap or click the New Style button (Manage Styles dialog box) to display the Create New Style from Formatting dialog box.
- Type `Check Box Labels` in the Name text box (Create New Style from Formatting dialog box) as the name of the new style.
- Tap or click the Style type arrow and then tap or click Character so that the new style does not contain any paragraph formats.
- Tap or click the Font Color arrow to display the Font Color gallery and then tap or click 'Plum, Accent 2, Darker 25%' (sixth color in fifth row) as the new color (Figure 11–22).

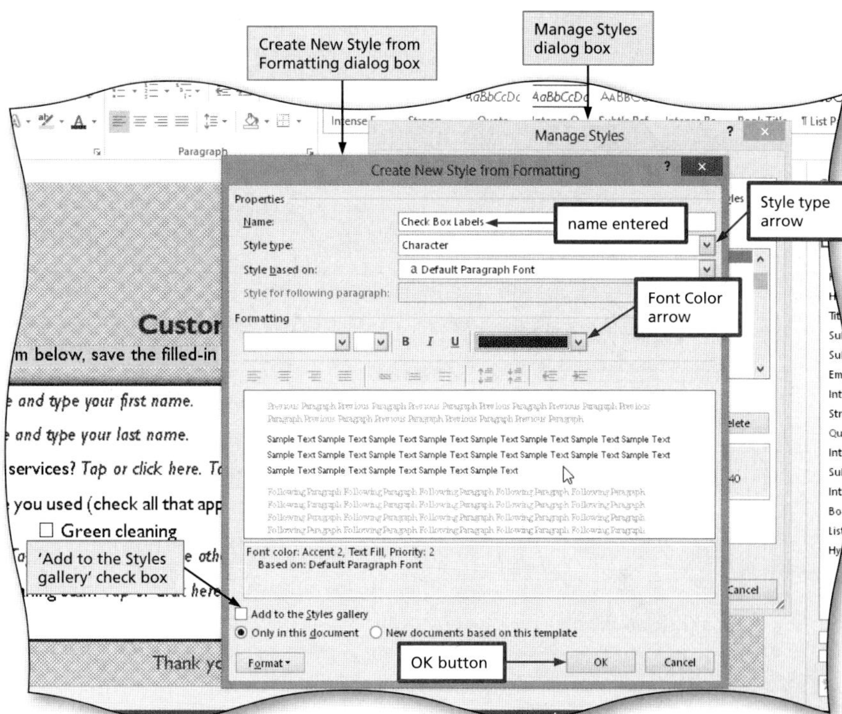

Figure 11–22

- Tap or click the OK button in each open dialog box to create the new character style, Check Box Labels in this case, and insert the new style name in the Styles task pane (Figure 11–23).

Q&A What if I wanted the style added to the Styles gallery?

You would place a check mark in the 'Add to the Styles gallery' check box (Create New Style from Formatting dialog box), shown in Figure 11–22.

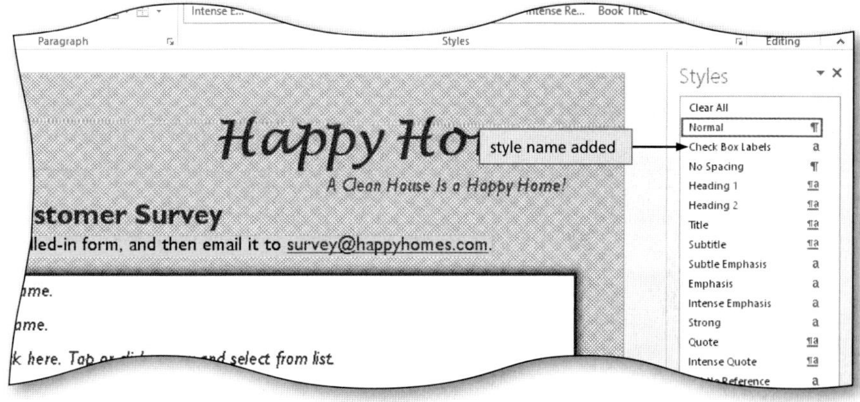

Figure 11–23

To Apply a Style

The next step is to apply the Check Box Labels style just created to the check box labels in the form. The following steps apply a style.

1. Drag through the check box label, Standard cleaning, to select it and then tap or click Check Box Labels in the Styles task pane to apply the style to the selected text.
2. Repeat Step 1 for these check box labels (Figure 11–24 on the next page): Green cleaning, Window washing, Carpet cleaning, and Other (please specify).
3. Close the Styles task pane.
4. Tap or click anywhere to remove the selection from the check box label.

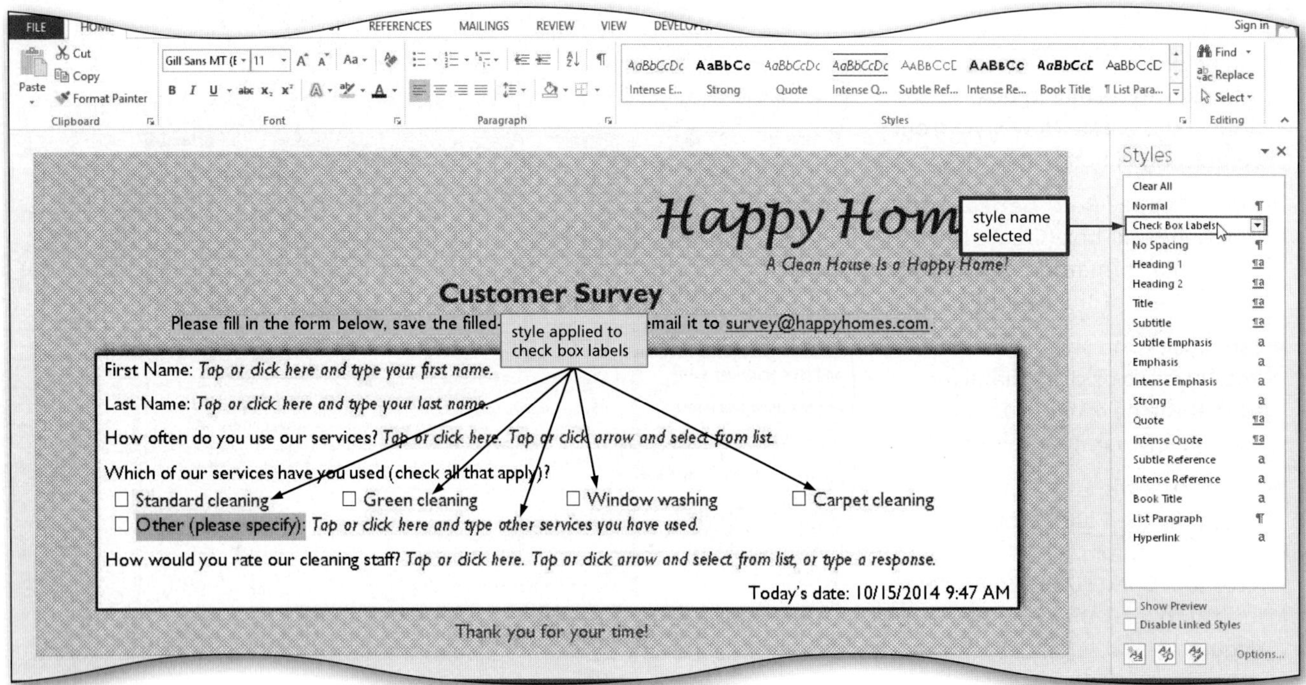

Figure 11–24

To Save an Existing Template with the Same File Name

BTW
Saving Templates
When you save a template that contains building blocks, the building blocks are available to all users who access the template.

You have made several modifications to the template since you last saved it. Thus, you should save it again. The following step saves the template again.

1 Tap or click the Save button on the Quick Access Toolbar to overwrite the previously saved file.

Break Point: If you wish to take a break, this is a good place to do so. You can exit Word now. To resume at a later time, run Word, open the file called Customer Survey Modified, and continue following the steps from this location forward.

Enhancing with Color, Shapes, Effects, and Graphics

You will enhance the form created in Chapter 10 by performing these steps:

1. Apply a texture fill effect for the page color.
2. Change the appearance of the shape.
3. Change the color of a shadow on the shape.
4. Fill a shape with a picture.
5. Insert a picture, remove its background, and apply an artistic effect.
6. Insert and format a text box.
7. Group the picture and the text box together.

The following pages apply these changes to the form.

To Use a Fill Effect for the Page Color

Word provides a gallery of 24 predefined textures you can use as a page background. These textures resemble various wallpaper patterns. The following steps change the page color to a texture fill effect. ***Why?*** *Instead of a simple color for the background page color, this online form uses a texture for the page color.*

- Display the DESIGN tab.
- Tap or click the Page Color button (DESIGN tab | Page Background group) to display the Page Color gallery (Figure 11–25).

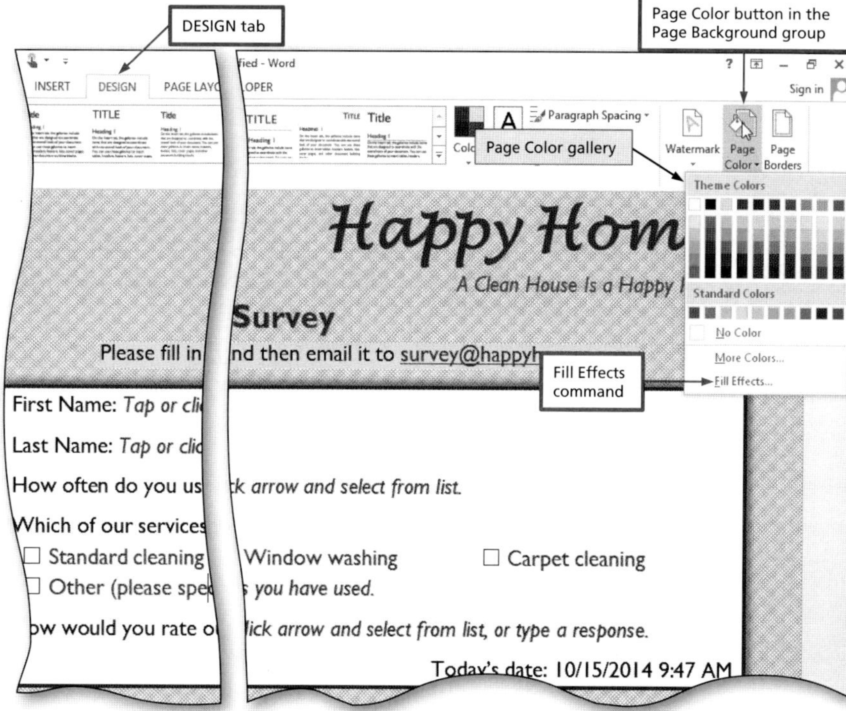

Figure 11–25

- Tap or click Fill Effects in the Page Color gallery to display the Fill Effects dialog box.
- Tap or click the Texture tab (Fill Effects dialog box) to display the Texture sheet.
- Scroll to, if necessary, and then tap or click the 'Pink tissue paper' texture in the Texture gallery to select the texture (Figure 11–26).

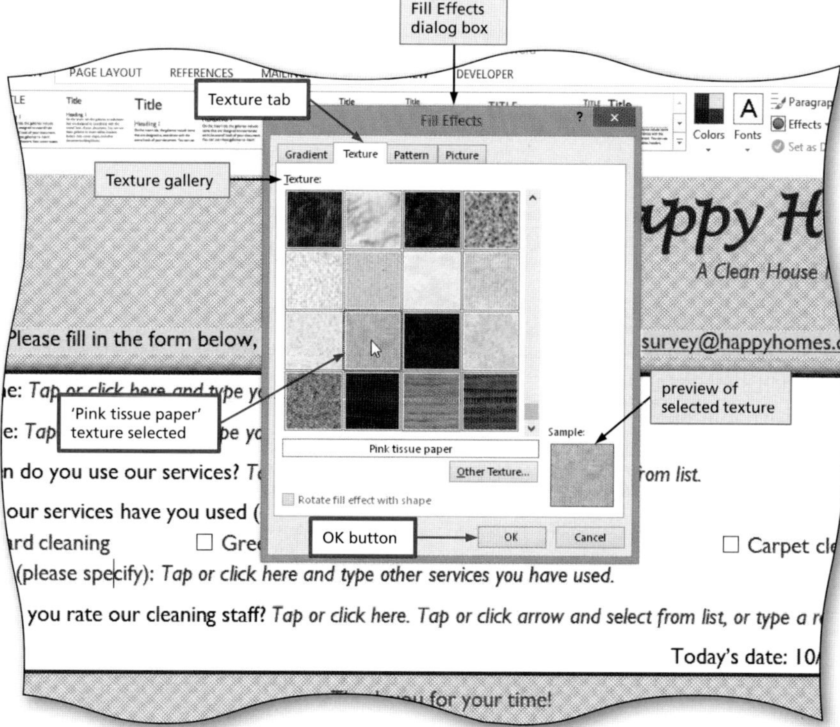

Figure 11–26

- Tap or click the OK button to apply the selected texture as the page color in the document (Figure 11–27).

Q&A How would I remove a texture page color?
You would tap or click the Page Color button (DESIGN tab | Page Background group) and then tap or click No Color in the Page Color gallery.

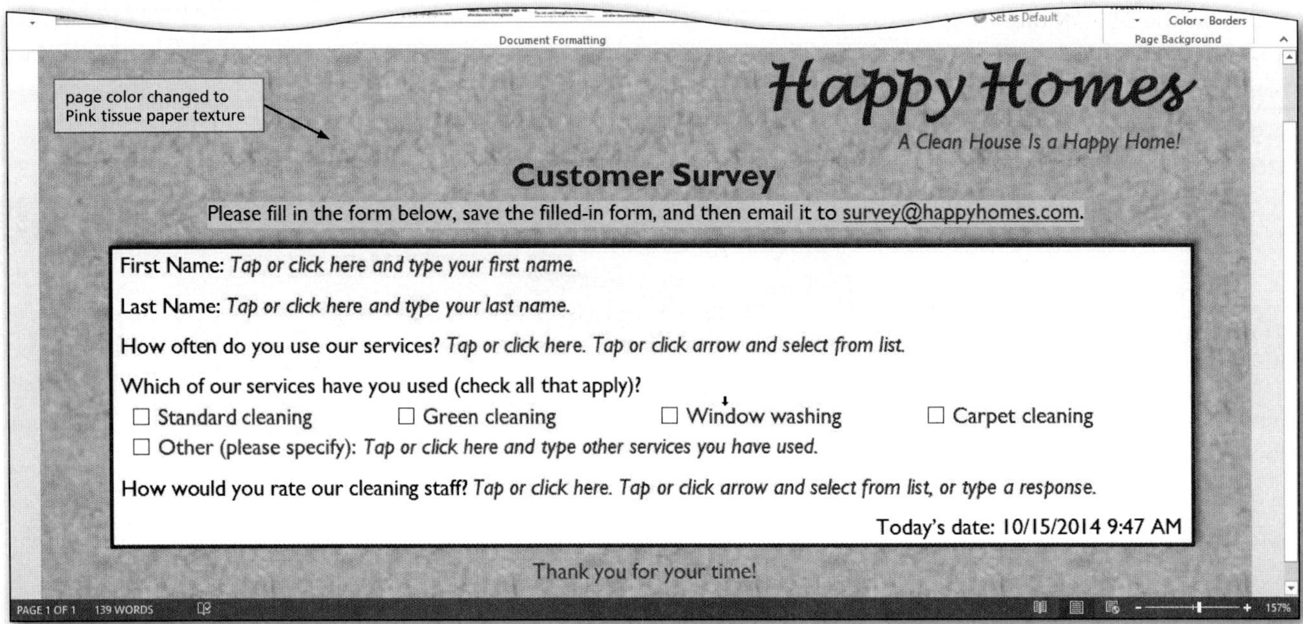

Figure 11–27

To Change a Shape

1 SAVE DOCUMENT AS MACRO-ENABLED TEMPLATE | 2 MODIFY TEXT & FORM CONTENT CONTROLS
3 ENHANCE FORM'S VISUAL APPEAL | **4 CREATE MACROS TO AUTOMATE TASKS**

The following steps change a shape. ***Why?*** *This online form uses a variation of the standard rectangle shape.*

1

- Tap or click the rectangle shape to select it.
- Display the DRAWING TOOLS FORMAT tab.
- Tap or click the Edit Shape button (DRAWING TOOLS FORMAT tab | Insert Shapes group) to display the Edit Shape menu.
- Tap or point to Change Shape on the Edit Shape menu to display the Change Shape gallery (Figure 11–28).

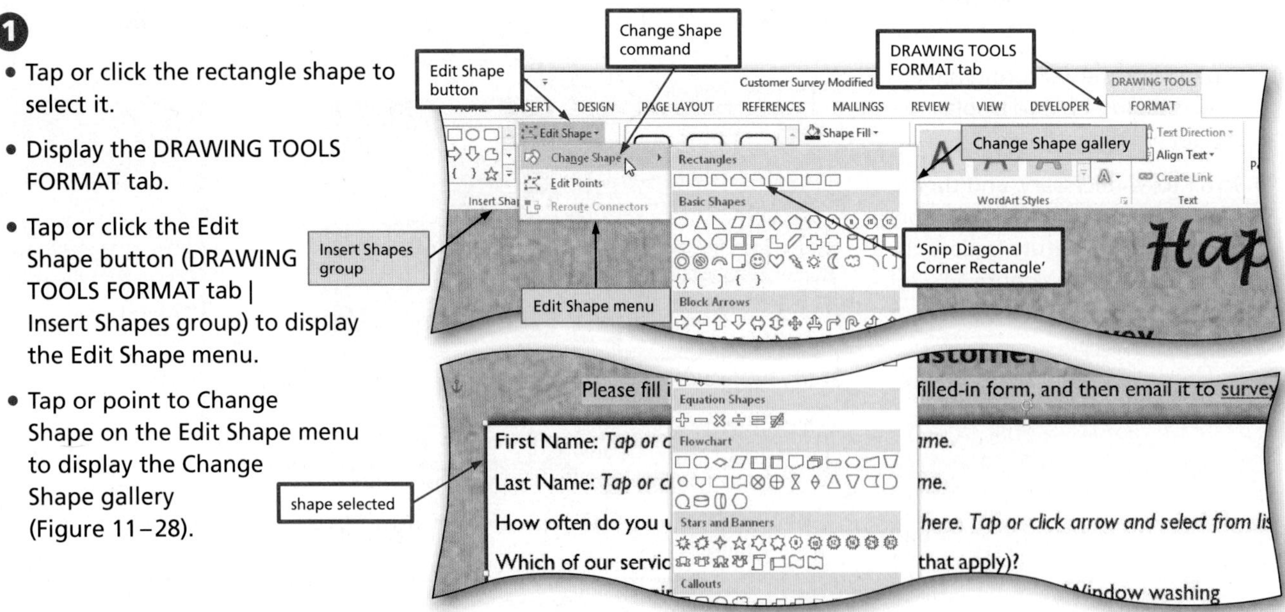

Figure 11–28

2

- Tap or click 'Snip Diagonal Corner Rectangle' in the Rectangles area in the Change Shape gallery to change the selected shape (Figure 11–29).

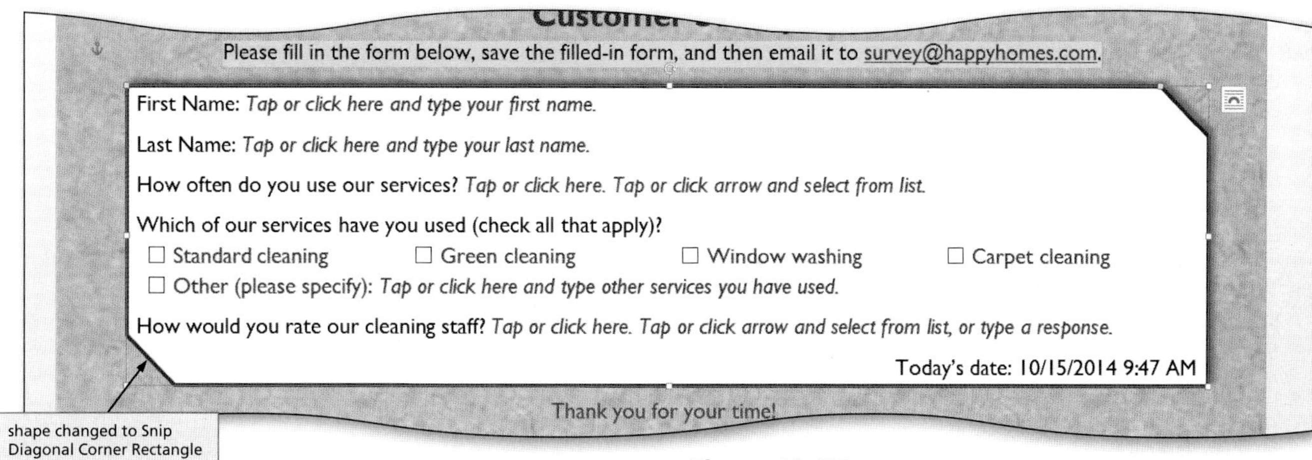

Figure 11–29

To Apply a Glow Shape Effect

The next step is to apply a glow effect to the rectangle shape. You can apply the same effects to shapes as to pictures. That is, you can apply shadows, reflections, glows, soft edges, bevels, and 3-D rotations to pictures and shapes. The following steps apply a shape effect.

1. With the rectangle shape selected, tap or click the Shape Effects button (DRAWING TOOLS FORMAT tab | Shape Styles group) to display the Shape Effects menu.
2. Tap or point to Glow on the Shape Effects menu to display the Glow gallery.
3. If you are using a mouse, point to 'Plum, 5 pt glow, Accent color 1' in the Glow Variations area (first glow in first row) to display a live preview of the selected glow effect applied to the selected shape in the document window (Figure 11–30).
4. Tap or click 'Plum, 5 pt glow, Accent color 1' in the Glow gallery (first glow in first row) to apply the shape effect to the selected shape.

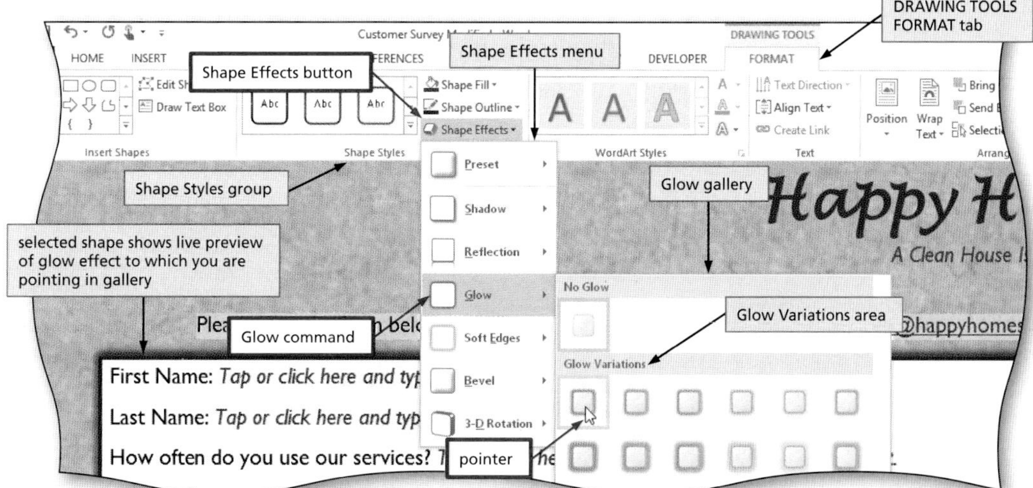

Figure 11–30

To Apply a Shadow Shape Effect

1 SAVE DOCUMENT AS MACRO-ENABLED TEMPLATE | 2 MODIFY TEXT & FORM CONTENT CONTROLS
3 ENHANCE FORM'S VISUAL APPEAL | 4 CREATE MACROS TO AUTOMATE TASKS

The following steps apply a shadow effect and change its color. ***Why?*** *The rectangle in this online form has a shadow that is a similar color to the company tag line.*

1

- With the rectangle shape still selected, tap or click the Shape Effects button (DRAWING TOOLS FORMAT tab | Shape Styles group) again to display the Shape Effects menu.
- Tap or point to Shadow in the Shape Effects menu to display the Shadow gallery.
- If you are using a mouse, point to 'Perspective Diagonal Upper Right' in the Perspective area at the bottom of the Shadow gallery to display a live preview of that shadow applied to the shape in the document (Figure 11–31).

Experiment

- If you are using a mouse, point to various shadows in the Shadow gallery and watch the shadow on the selected shape change.

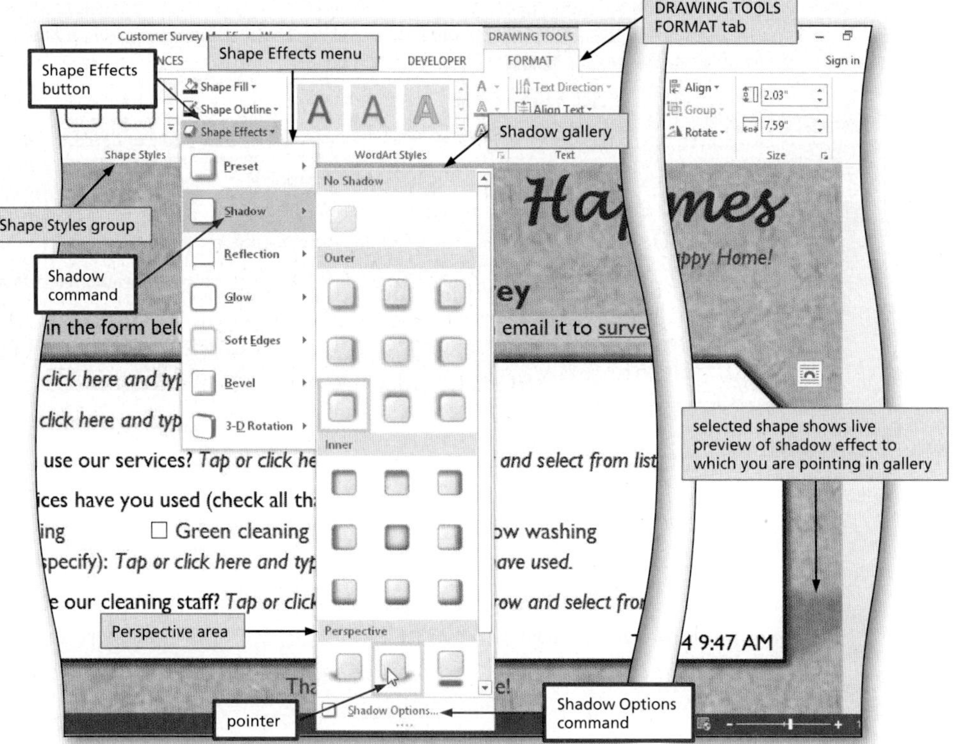

Figure 11–31

2

- Tap or click 'Perspective Diagonal Upper Right' in the Shadow gallery to apply the selected shadow to the selected shape.
- Tap or click the Shape Effects button (DRAWING TOOLS FORMAT tab | Shape Styles group) again to display the Shape Effects menu.
- Tap or point to Shadow in the Shape Effects menu to display the Shadow gallery.
- Tap or click Shadow Options in the Shadow gallery to open the Format Shape task pane.
- Tap or click the Shadow Color button (Format Shape task pane) and then tap or click 'Blue-Gray, Accent 6, Darker 25%' (last color in fifth row) in the Shadow Color gallery to change the shadow color.
- Tap or click the Transparency down arrow as many times as necessary until the Transparency box displays 60% to change the amount of transparency in the shadow (Figure 11–32).

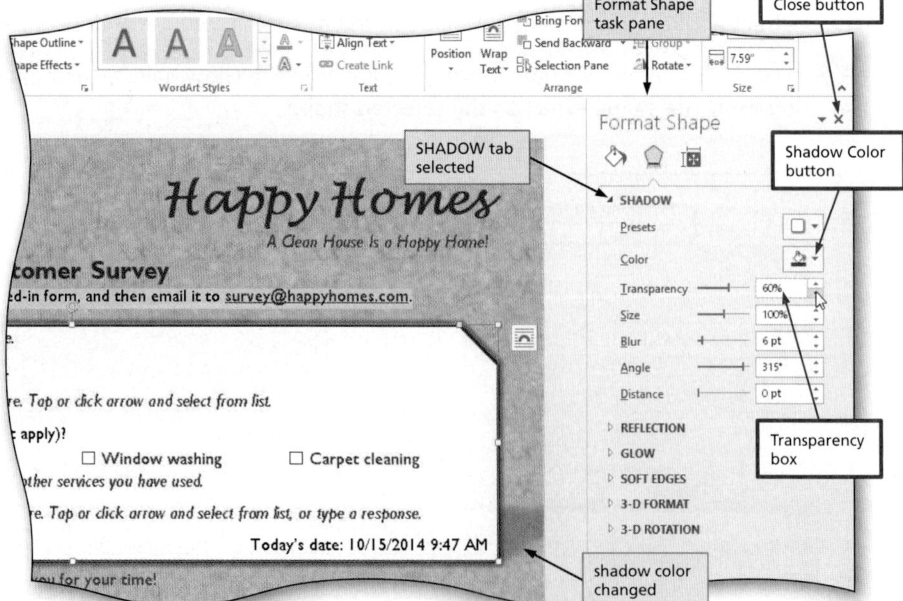

Figure 11–32

- Tap or click the Close button to close the Format Shape task pane.

To Fill a Shape with a Picture

The following steps fill a shape with a picture. ***Why?*** *The rectangle in this online form contains the happy house picture. The picture, called Happy House, is located on the Data Files for Students. Visit www.cengage.com/ct/studentdownload for detailed instructions or contact your instructor for information about accessing the required files.*

1

- With the rectangle shape still selected, tap or click the Shape Fill arrow (DRAWING TOOLS FORMAT tab | Shape Styles group) to display the Shape Fill gallery (Figure 11–33).

Q&A My Shape Fill gallery did not display. Why not?
If you are using a mouse, you clicked the Shape Fill button instead of the Shape Fill arrow. Repeat Step 1.

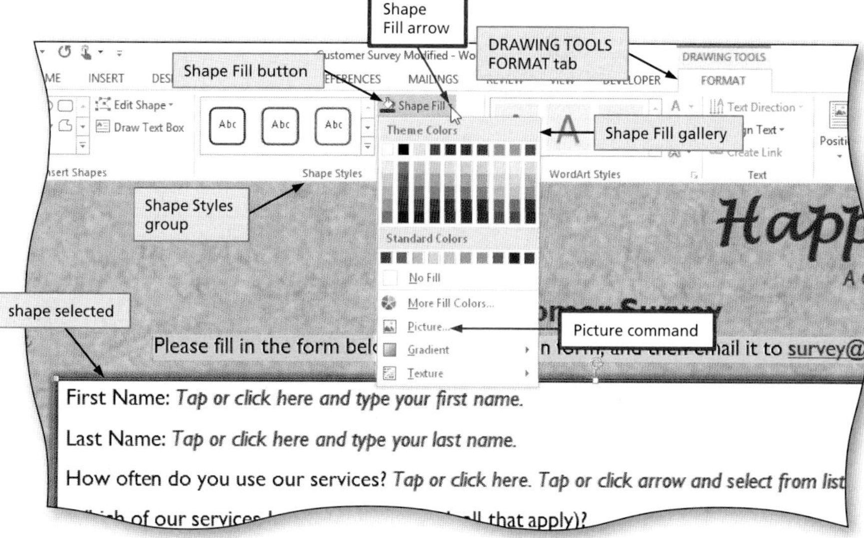

Figure 11–33

2

- Tap or click Picture in the Shape Fill gallery to display the Insert Pictures dialog box.
- Tap or click the Browse button (Insert Pictures dialog box) to display the Insert Picture dialog box. Locate and then select the file called Happy House (Insert Picture dialog box).
- Tap or click the Insert button (Insert Picture dialog box) to fill the rectangle shape with the picture (Figure 11–34).

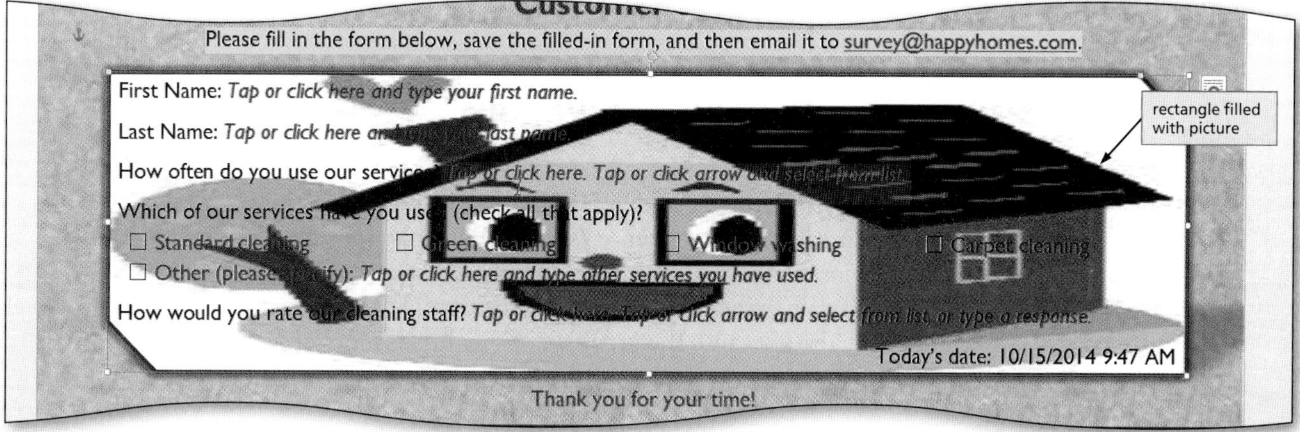

Figure 11–34

To Change the Color of a Picture

The text in the rectangle shape is difficult to read because the picture just inserted is too colorful. You can experiment with adjusting the brightness, contrast, and color of a picture so that the text is readable. In this project, the color is changed to the washout setting so that the text is easier to read. The steps on the next page change the color of the picture to washout.

1. Display the PICTURE TOOLS FORMAT tab.
2. With the rectangle shape still selected, tap or click the Color button (PICTURE TOOLS FORMAT tab | Adjust group) to display the Color gallery.
3. If you are using a mouse, point to Washout in the Recolor area in the Color gallery to display a live preview of the selected color applied to the selected picture (Figure 11–35).
4. Tap or click Washout in the Color gallery to apply the selected color to the selected picture.

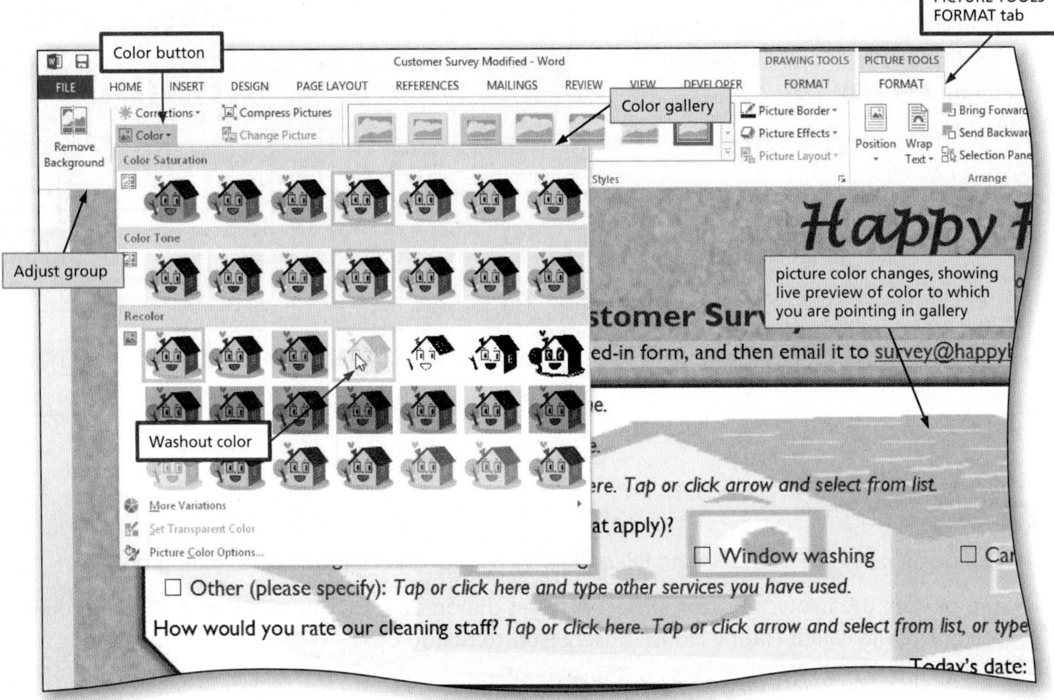

Figure 11–35

To Insert, Change Wrapping Style, and Resize a Picture

The top of the online form in this chapter contains a picture of a whisk broom and dustpan. The picture, called Whisk Broom, is located on the Data Files for Students. Visit www.cengage.com/ct/studentdownload for detailed instructions or contact your instructor for information about accessing the required files.

You will change the wrapping style of the inserted picture so that it can be positioned in front of the text. Because the graphic's original size is too large, you also will resize it. The following steps insert a picture, change its wrapping style, and resize it.

BTW
Drawing Canvas
Some users prefer inserting graphics on a drawing canvas, which is a rectangular boundary between a shape and the rest of the document; it also is a container that helps you resize and arrange shapes on the page. To insert a drawing canvas, tap or click the 'Draw a Shape' button (INSERT tab | Illustrations group) and then tap or click 'New Drawing Canvas' in the Draw a Shape gallery. You can use the DRAWING TOOLS FORMAT tab to insert objects in the drawing canvas or format the appearance of the drawing canvas.

1. Position the insertion point in a location near where the picture will be inserted, in this case, near the top of the online form.
2. Display the INSERT tab. Tap or click the From File button (INSERT tab | Illustrations group) to display the Insert Picture dialog box.
3. Locate and then tap or click the file called Whisk Broom (Insert Picture dialog box) to select the file.
4. Tap or click the Insert button to insert the picture at the location of the insertion point.

5 With the picture selected, tap or click the Wrap Text button (PICTURE TOOLS FORMAT tab | Arrange group) and then tap or click 'In Front of Text' so that the graphic can be positioned on top of text.

6 Change the value in the Shape Height box (PICTURE TOOLS FORMAT tab | Size group) to 1" and the value in the Shape Width box (PICTURE TOOLS FORMAT tab | Size group) to 1.4".

7 If necessary, scroll to display the online form in the document window (Figure 11–36).

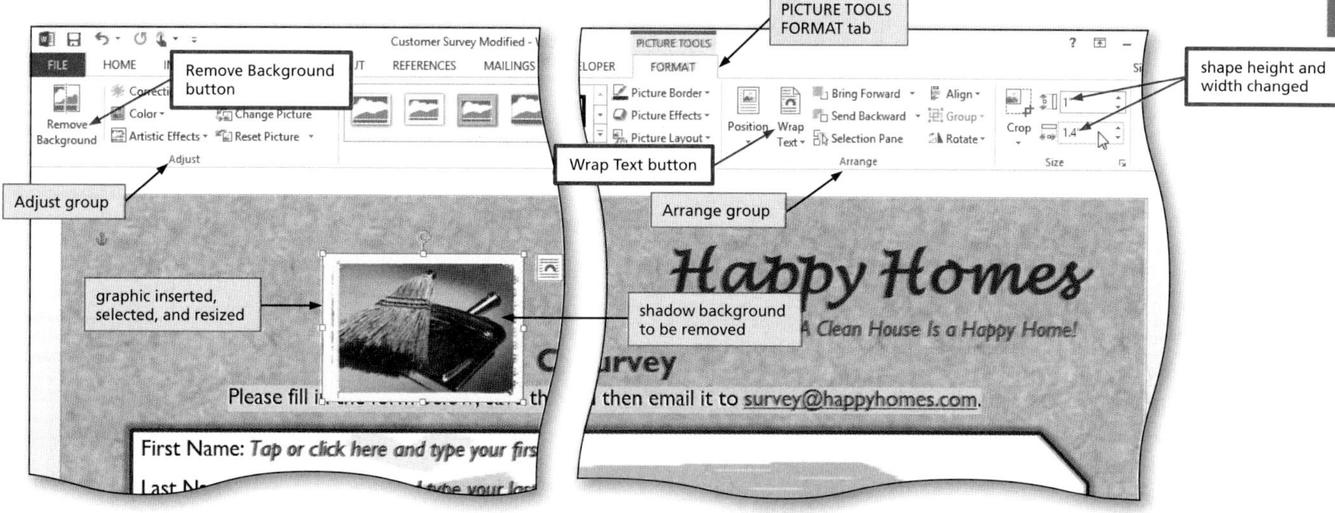

Figure 11–36

To Remove a Background

1 SAVE DOCUMENT AS MACRO-ENABLED TEMPLATE | 2 MODIFY TEXT & FORM CONTENT CONTROLS
3 ENHANCE FORM'S VISUAL APPEAL | 4 CREATE MACROS TO AUTOMATE TASKS

In Word, you can remove a background from a picture. The following steps remove a background. ***Why?*** *You remove the shadow background from the picture of the whisk broom and dustpan.*

1

- Tap or click the Remove Background button (PICTURE TOOLS FORMAT tab | Adjust group) (shown in Figure 11–36), to display the BACKGROUND REMOVAL tab and show the proposed area to be deleted in purple (Figure 11–37).

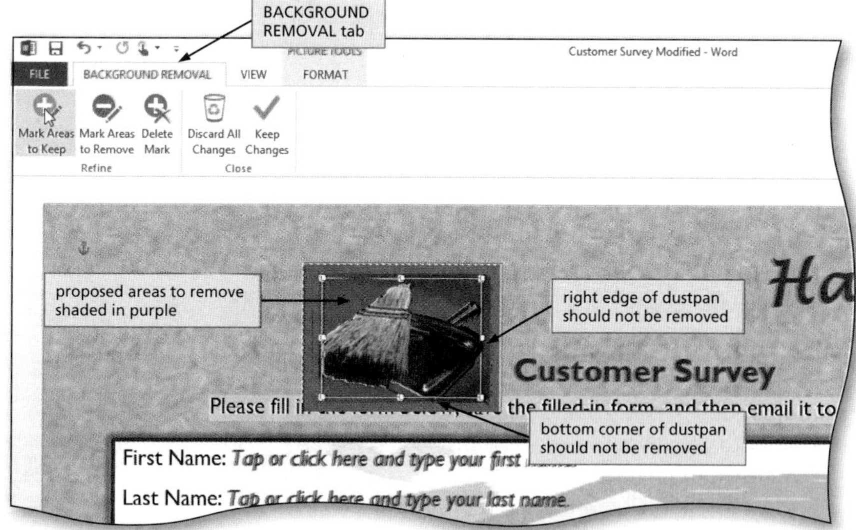

Figure 11–37

Q&A What is the BACKGROUND REMOVAL tab?
You can draw around areas to keep or areas to remove by tapping or clicking the respective buttons on the BACKGROUND REMOVAL tab. If you mistakenly mark too much, use the Delete Mark button. You also can drag the proposed rectangle to adjust the proposed removal area. When finished marking, tap or click the 'Close Background Removal and Keep Changes' button, or to start over, tap or click the 'Close Background Removal and Discard Changes' button.

2

- Drag the proposed marking lines downward and rightward slightly, as shown in Figure 11–38, so that the entire dustpan shows and the entire shadow background is shaded purple. If necessary, drag the marking lines a few times.

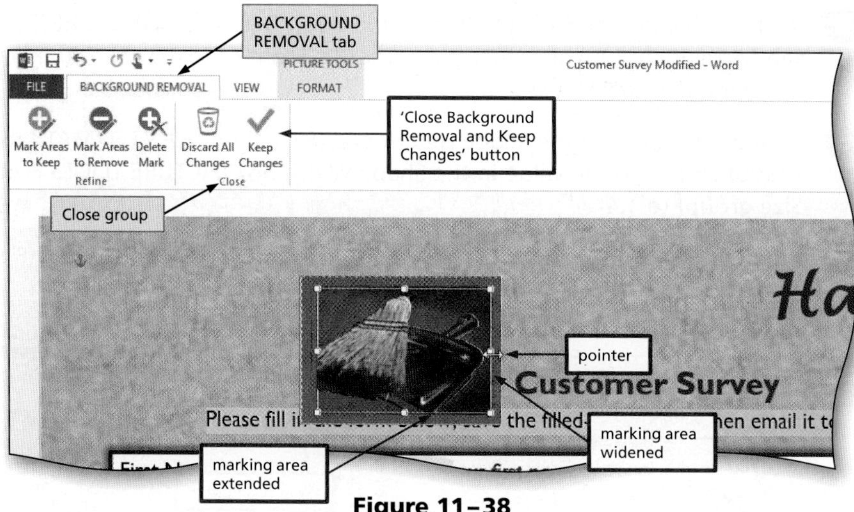

Figure 11–38

3

- Tap or click the 'Close Background Removal and Keep Changes' button (BACKGROUND REMOVAL tab | Close group) to remove the area shaded purple to close the BACKGROUND REMOVAL tab (Figure 11–39).

Figure 11–39

To Apply an Artistic Effect

Word provides several different artistic effects, such as blur, line drawing, and paint brush, that alter the appearance of a picture. The following steps apply an artistic effect to the picture. ***Why?*** *You want to soften the look of the picture a bit.*

1

- With the picture still selected, tap or click the Artistic Effects button (PICTURE TOOLS FORMAT tab | Adjust group) to display the Artistic Effects gallery.
- If you are using a mouse, point to Pastels Smooth (fourth effect in fourth row) in the Artistic Effects gallery to display a live preview of the effect applied to the selected picture in the document window (Figure 11–40).

2

- Tap or click Pastels Smooth in the Artistic Effects gallery to apply the selected effect to the selected picture.

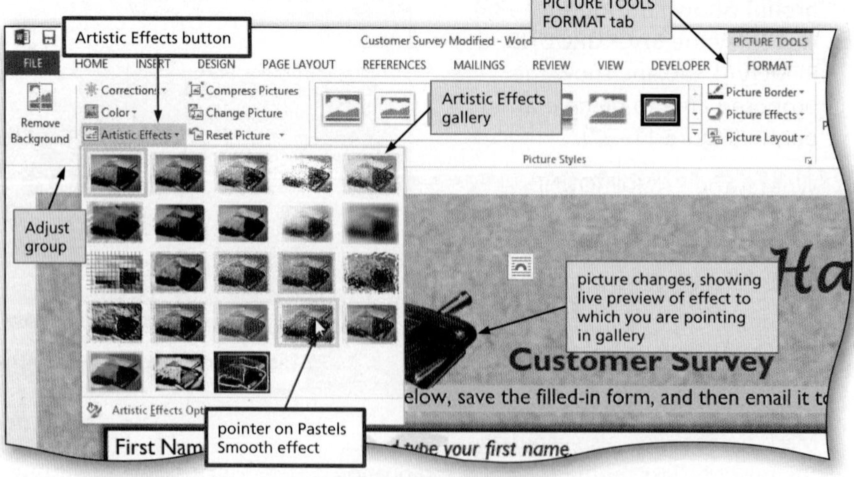

Figure 11–40

To Change the Color of a Graphic and Move the Graphic

In this project, the color of the whisk broom and dustpan is changed to match the colors in the company name. Then, the graphic is to be positioned on the left edge of the form. The following steps change the color of the picture and then move it.

1. With the picture still selected, tap or click the Color button (PICTURE TOOLS FORMAT tab | Adjust group) to display the Color gallery.
2. Tap or click 'Plum, Accent color 1 Light' in the Recolor area in the Color gallery (second color in last row) to apply the selected color to the selected picture.
3. Drag the graphic to the location shown in Figure 11–41.

To Draw a Text Box

The picture of the whisk broom and dustpan in this form has a text box with the words, Let Us Sweep It Clean!, positioned near the bottom of the broom. The following steps draw a text box. ***Why?*** *The first step in creating the text box is to draw its perimeter. You draw a text box using the same procedure as you do to draw a shape.*

1

- Position the insertion point somewhere in the top of the online form.
- Display the INSERT tab.
- Tap or click the 'Choose a Text Box' button (INSERT tab | Text group) to display the Choose a Text Box gallery (Figure 11–41).

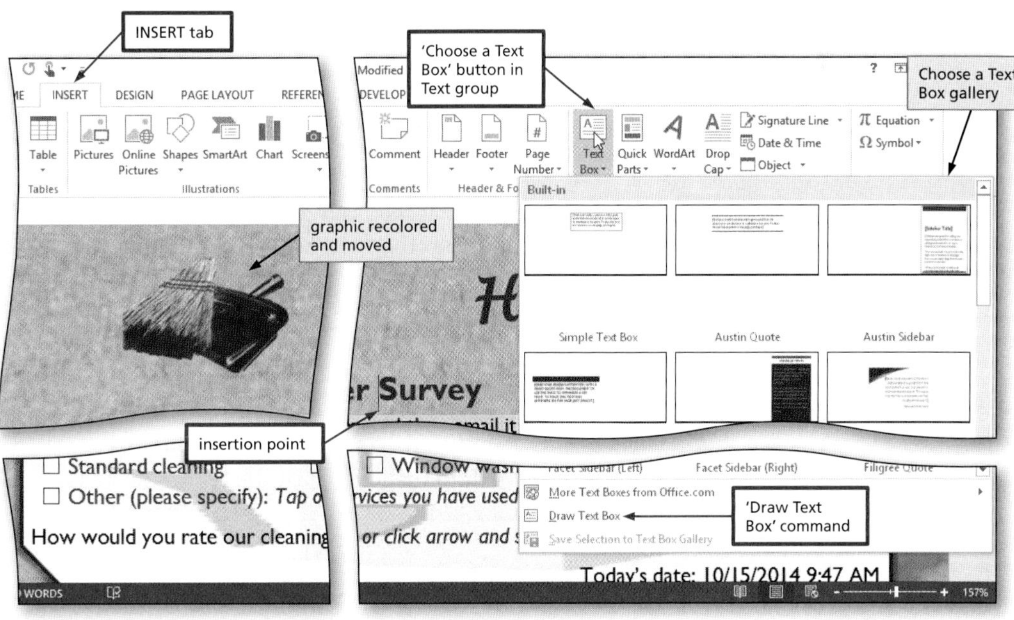

Figure 11–41

2

- Tap or click 'Draw Text Box' in the Text Box gallery, which removes the gallery. If you are using a touch screen, the text box is inserted in the document window; if you are using a mouse, the pointer changes to the shape of a crosshair.
- If you are using a mouse, drag the pointer to the right and downward to form the boundaries of the text box, as shown in Figure 11–42.

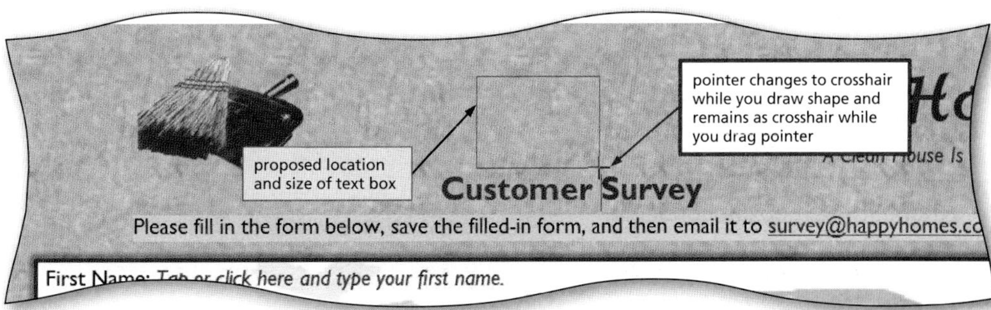

Figure 11–42

- If you are using a mouse, release the mouse button so that Word draws the text box according to your drawing in the document window.
- Verify your shape is the same approximate height and width as the one in this project by changing the values in the Shape Height and Shape Width boxes (DRAWING TOOLS FORMAT tab | Size group) to 0.9" and 0.75", respectively (Figure 11–43).

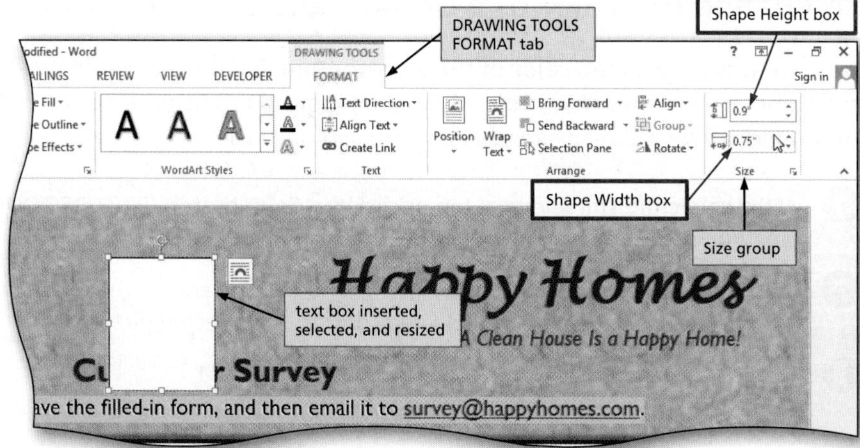

Figure 11–43

To Add Text to a Text Box and Format the Text

The next step is to add the phrase, Let Us Sweep It Clean!, centered in the text box using a text effect. You add text to a text box using the same procedure you do when adding text to a shape. The following steps add text to a text box.

1. Display the HOME tab. With the text box selected, tap or click the Center button (HOME tab | Paragraph group) so that the text you enter is centered in the text box.
2. With the text box selected, tap or click the 'Text Effects and Typography' button (HOME tab | Font group) and then tap or click 'Fill - Blue-Gray, Accent 4, Soft Bevel' (last effect in first row) in the Text Effects gallery to specify the format for the text in the text box.
3. If your insertion point is not positioned in the text box (shape), press and hold or right-click the shape to display a shortcut menu and the mini toolbar and then tap or click Edit Text on the mini toolbar or shortcut menu to place an insertion point centered in the text box.
4. Type `Let Us Sweep It Clean!` as the text for the text box (shown in Figure 11–44). (If necessary, adjust the width of the text box to fit the text.)

To Change Text Direction in a Text Box

1 SAVE DOCUMENT AS MACRO-ENABLED TEMPLATE | 2 MODIFY TEXT & FORM CONTENT CONTROLS
3 ENHANCE FORM'S VISUAL APPEAL | 4 CREATE MACROS TO AUTOMATE TASKS

The following steps change text direction in a text box. ***Why?*** *The direction of the text in the text box should be vertical instead of horizontal.*

- Display the DRAWING TOOLS FORMAT tab.
- With the shape still selected, tap or click the Text Direction button (DRAWING TOOLS FORMAT tab | Text group) to display the Text Direction gallery (Figure 11–44).

Q&A What if my text box no longer is selected?

Tap or click the text box to select it.

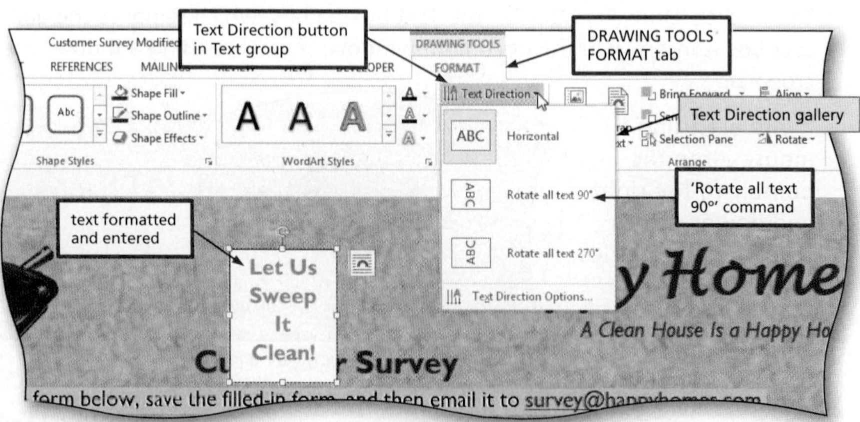

Figure 11–44

2

- Tap or click 'Rotate all text 90°' in the Text Direction gallery to display the text in the text box vertically from top to bottom (Figure 11–45).

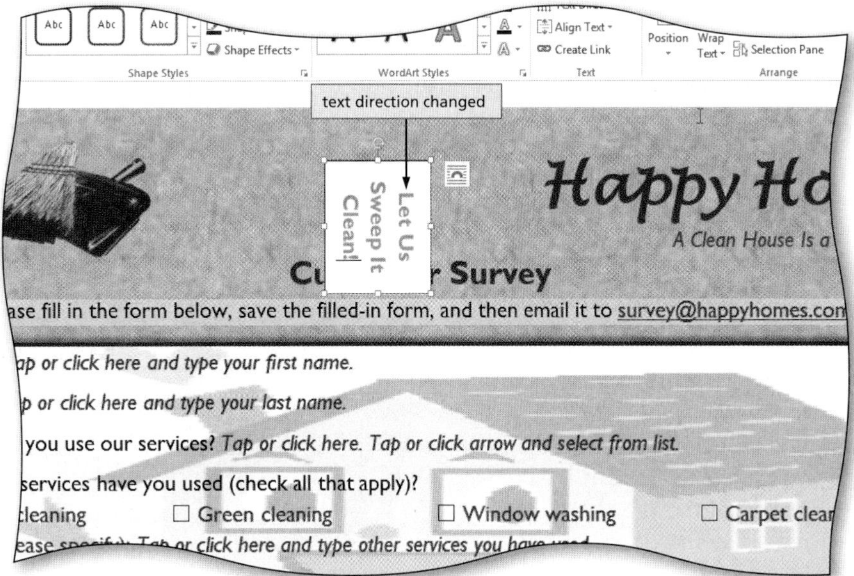

Figure 11–45

Other Ways

1. Tap 'Show Context Menu' button on mini toolbar or right-click text box, tap or click Format Shape on shortcut menu, tap or click TEXT OPTIONS tab (Format Shape task pane), expand TEXT BOX section, tap or click Text direction box, select desired direction, tap or click Close button

To Apply a Shadow Shape Effect to a Text Box

The text box in this online form has an inside shadow that is in the same color as the tag line. The following steps apply a shadow effect and change its color.

1. Move the text box to the left so that it is visible when you change the shadows and colors.
2. With the text box still selected, tap or click the Shape Effects button (DRAWING TOOLS FORMAT tab | Shape Styles group) to display the Shape Effects menu.
3. Tap or point to Shadow in the Shape Effects menu to display the Shadow gallery and then tap or click Inside Center in the Inner area of the Shadow gallery to apply the selected shadow to the selected shape.
4. Tap or click the Shape Effects button (DRAWING TOOLS FORMAT tab | Shape Styles group) again to display the Shape Effects menu.
5. Tap or point to Shadow in the Shape Effects menu to display the Shadow gallery and then tap or click Shadow Options in the Shadow gallery to display the Format Shape task pane.
6. Tap or click the Shadow Color button (Format Shape task pane) and then tap or click 'Blue-Gray, Accent 6, Darker 25%' (last color in fifth row) in the Color gallery to change the shadow color.
7. Change the value in the Transparency box to 60% to change the amount of transparency in the shadow (shown in Figure 11–46 on the next page).
8. Tap or click the Close button to close the Format Shape task pane.

To Change a Shape Outline of a Text Box

1 SAVE DOCUMENT AS MACRO-ENABLED TEMPLATE | 2 MODIFY TEXT & FORM CONTENT CONTROLS
3 ENHANCE FORM'S VISUAL APPEAL | **4 CREATE MACROS TO AUTOMATE TASKS**

You change an outline on a text box (shape) using the same procedure as you do with a picture. The following steps remove the shape outline on the text box. ***Why?*** *The text box in this form has no outline.*

- With the text box still selected, tap or click the Shape Outline arrow (DRAWING TOOLS FORMAT tab | Shape Styles group) to display the Shape Outline gallery (Figure 11–46).

Q&A The Shape Outline gallery did not display. Why not?
If you are using a mouse, you clicked the Shape Outline button instead of the Shape Outline arrow. Repeat Step 1.

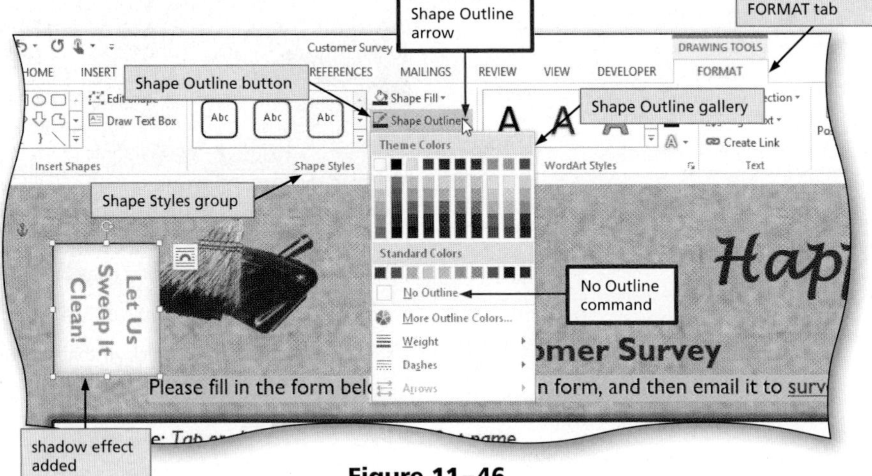

Figure 11–46

Experiment

- If you are using a mouse, point to various colors in the Shape Outline gallery and watch the color of the outline on the text box change in the document.

- Tap or click No Outline in the Shape Outline gallery to remove the outline from the selected shape.

Other Ways

1. Tap or click Format Shape Dialog Box Launcher (DRAWING TOOLS FORMAT tab | Shape Styles group); expand LINE section (Format Shape task pane); tap or click No line to remove line, or tap or click Solid line, tap or click Outline color button, and select desired color to change line color; tap or click Close button
2. Tap 'Show Context Menu' button on mini toolbar or right-click text box, tap or click Format Shape on shortcut menu, expand LINE section (Format Shape task pane), tap or click No line to remove line, or tap or click Solid line, tap or click Outline color button, and select desired color to change line color; tap or click Close button

To Apply a 3-D Effect to a Text Box

1 SAVE DOCUMENT AS MACRO-ENABLED TEMPLATE | 2 MODIFY TEXT & FORM CONTENT CONTROLS
3 ENHANCE FORM'S VISUAL APPEAL | **4 CREATE MACROS TO AUTOMATE TASKS**

Word provides 3-D effects for shapes (such as text boxes) that are similar to those it provides for pictures. The following steps apply a 3-D rotation effect to a text box. ***Why?*** *In this form, the text box is rotated using a 3-D rotation effect.*

- With the text box selected, tap or click the Shape Effects button (DRAWING TOOLS FORMAT tab | Shape Styles group) to display the Shape Effects gallery.
- Tap or point to '3-D Rotation' in the Shape Effects gallery to display the 3-D Rotation gallery.
- If you are using a mouse, point to 'Isometric Top Up' in the Parallel area (third rotation in first row) to display a live preview of the selected 3-D effect applied to the text box in the document window (Figure 11–47).

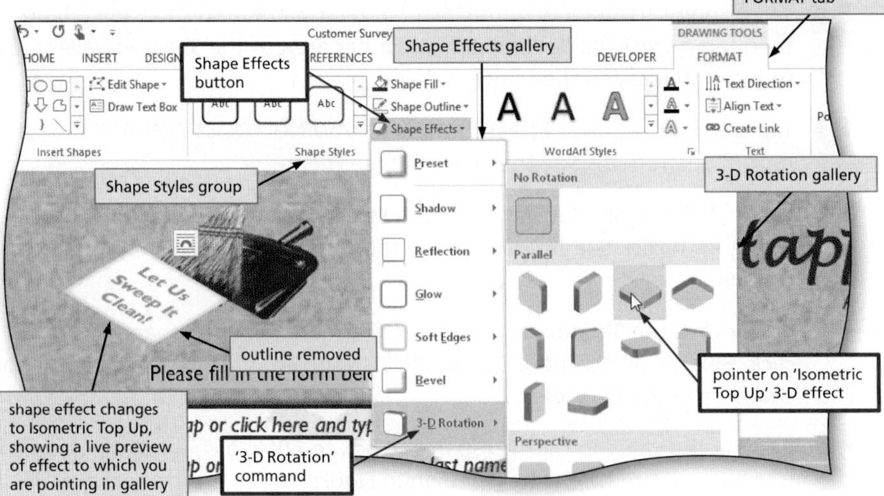

Figure 11–47

Experiment

- If you are using a mouse, point to various 3-D rotation effects in the 3-D Rotation gallery and watch the text box change in the document window.

- Tap or click 'Isometric Top Up' in the 3-D Rotation gallery to apply the selected 3-D effect.

Other Ways

1. Tap or click Format Shape Dialog Box Launcher (DRAWING TOOLS FORMAT tab | Shape Styles group), tap or click TEXT OPTIONS tab (Format Shape task pane), tap or click Text Effects button, if necessary expand 3-D ROTATION SECTION, select desired options, tap or click Close button
2. Tap 'Show Context Menu' button on mini toolbar or right-click text box, tap or click Format Shape on shortcut menu, tap or click TEXT OPTIONS tab (Format Shape task pane), tap or click Text Effects button, if necessary expand 3-D ROTATION SECTION, select desired options, tap or click Close button

To Move the Text Box

In this project, the text box is to be positioned near the bristles of the whisk broom graphic. The following step moves the text box.

1 Drag the text box to the location shown in Figure 11–48. (You may need to drag the text box a couple of times to position it as shown in the figure.)

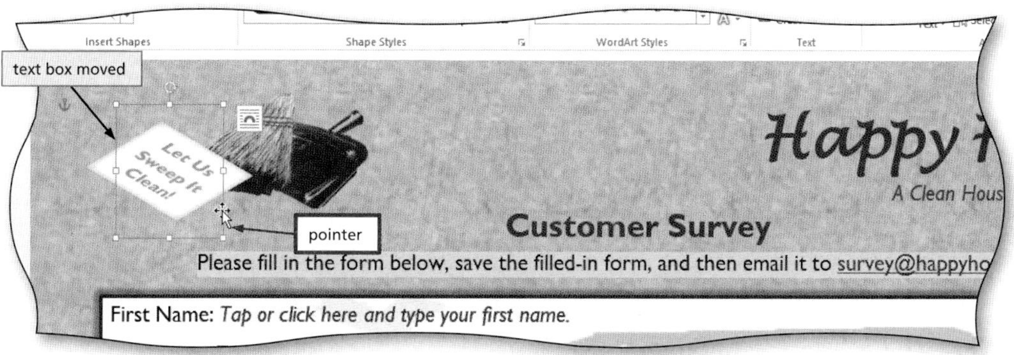

Figure 11–48

To Group Objects

1 SAVE DOCUMENT AS MACRO-ENABLED TEMPLATE | 2 MODIFY TEXT & FORM CONTENT CONTROLS
3 ENHANCE FORM'S VISUAL APPEAL | **4 CREATE MACROS TO AUTOMATE TASKS**

When you have multiple graphics, such as pictures, clip art, shapes, and text boxes, positioned on a page, you can group them so that they are a single graphic instead of separate graphics. The following steps group the whisk broom graphic and the text box together. ***Why?*** *Grouping the graphics makes it easier to move them because they all move together as a single graphic.*

- With the text box selected, hold down the CTRL key while tapping or clicking the whisk broom picture (that is, CTRL+tap or click), so that both graphics are selected at the same time.

Q&A What if I had more than two graphics that I wanted to group?
For each subsequent graphic to select, CTRL+tap or click the graphic, which enables you to select multiple objects at the same time.

- Tap or click the Group Objects button (DRAWING TOOLS FORMAT tab | Arrange group) to display the Group Objects menu (Figure 11–49).

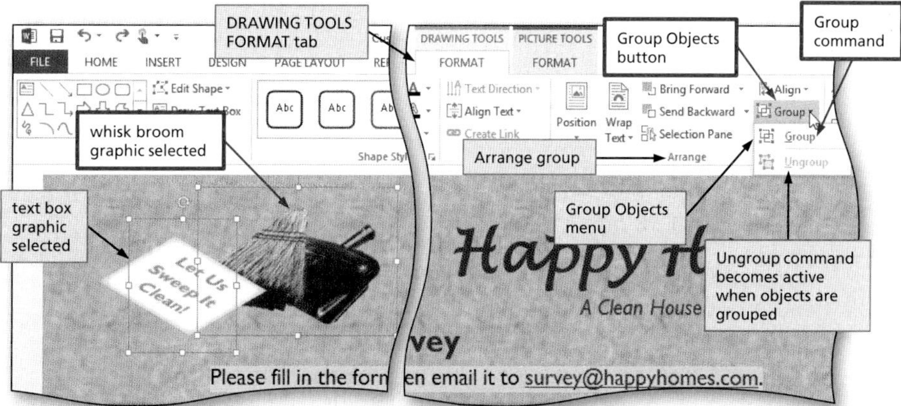

Figure 11–49

2

- Tap or click Group on the Group Objects menu to group the selected objects into a single selected object (Figure 11–50).

Q&A What if I wanted to ungroup grouped objects?
Select the object to ungroup, tap or click the Group Objects button (DRAWING TOOLS FORMAT tab | Arrange group), and then tap or click Ungroup on the Group Objects menu.

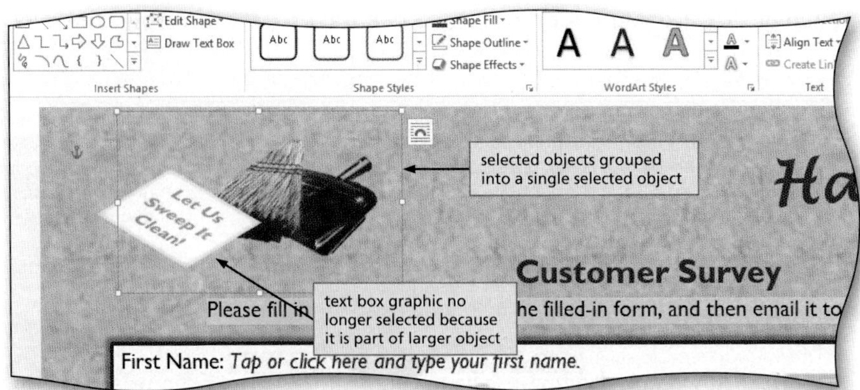

Figure 11–50

3

- Tap or click outside of the graphic to position the insertion point in the document and deselect the graphic.

To Save an Existing Template with the Same File Name

You have made several modifications to the template since you last saved it. Thus, you should save it again. The following step saves the template again.

1. Tap or click the Save button on the Quick Access Toolbar to overwrite the previously saved file.

Break Point: If you wish to take a break, this is a good place to do so. You can exit Word now. To resume at a later time, run Word, open the file called Customer Survey Modified, and continue following the steps from this location forward.

Using a Macro to Automate a Task

BTW
Naming Macros
If you give a new macro the same name as an existing built-in command in Microsoft Word, the new macro's actions will replace the existing actions. Thus, you should be careful not to name a macro a name reserved for automatic macros (see Table 11–1 on page WD 713) or after any Word commands. To view a list of built-in macros in Word, tap or click the View Macros button (VIEW tab | Macros group) to display the Macros dialog box. Tap or click the Macros in arrow and then tap or click Word commands.

A **macro** consists of a series of Word commands or instructions that are grouped together as a single command. This single command is a convenient way to automate a difficult or lengthy task. Macros often are used to simplify formatting or editing activities, to combine multiple commands into a single command, or to select an option in a dialog box using a shortcut key.

To create a macro, you can use the macro recorder or the Visual Basic Editor. With the macro recorder, Word generates the VBA instructions associated with the macro automatically as you perform actions in Word. If you wanted to write the VBA instructions yourself, you would use the Visual Basic Editor. This chapter uses the macro recorder to create a macro and the Visual Basic Editor to modify it.

The **macro recorder** creates a macro based on a series of actions you perform while the macro recorder is recording. The macro recorder is similar to a video camera: after you start the macro recorder, it records all actions you perform while working in a document and stops recording when you stop the macro recorder. To record a macro, you follow this sequence of steps:

1. Start the macro recorder and specify options about the macro.
2. Execute the actions you want recorded.
3. Stop the macro recorder.

After you record a macro, you can execute the macro, or play it, any time you want to perform the same set of actions.

To Record a Macro and Assign It a Shortcut Key

In Word, you can assign a shortcut key to a macro so that you can execute the macro by pressing the shortcut key instead of using a dialog box to execute it. The following steps record a macro that hides formatting marks and the rulers; the macro is assigned the shortcut key, ALT+H. ***Why?*** *Assume you find that you are repeatedly hiding the formatting marks and rulers while designing the online form. To simplify this task, the macro in this project hides these screen elements.*

- Display formatting marks and the rulers on the screen.
- Display the DEVELOPER tab.
- Tap or click the Record Macro button (DEVELOPER tab | Code group) to display the Record Macro dialog box.
- Type **`HideScreenElements`** in the Macro name text box (Record Macro dialog box).

Q&A Do I have to name a macro?
If you do not enter a name for the macro, Word assigns a default name. Macro names can be up to 255 characters in length and can contain only numbers, letters, and the underscore character. A macro name cannot contain spaces or other punctuation.

- Tap or click the 'Store macro in' arrow and then tap or click 'Documents Based On Customer Survey Modified'.

Q&A What is the difference between storing a macro with the document template versus the Normal template?
Macros saved in the Normal template are available to all future documents; macros saved with the document template are available only with a document based on the template.

- In the Description text box, type this sentence (Figure 11–51): **`Hide formatting marks and the rulers.`**

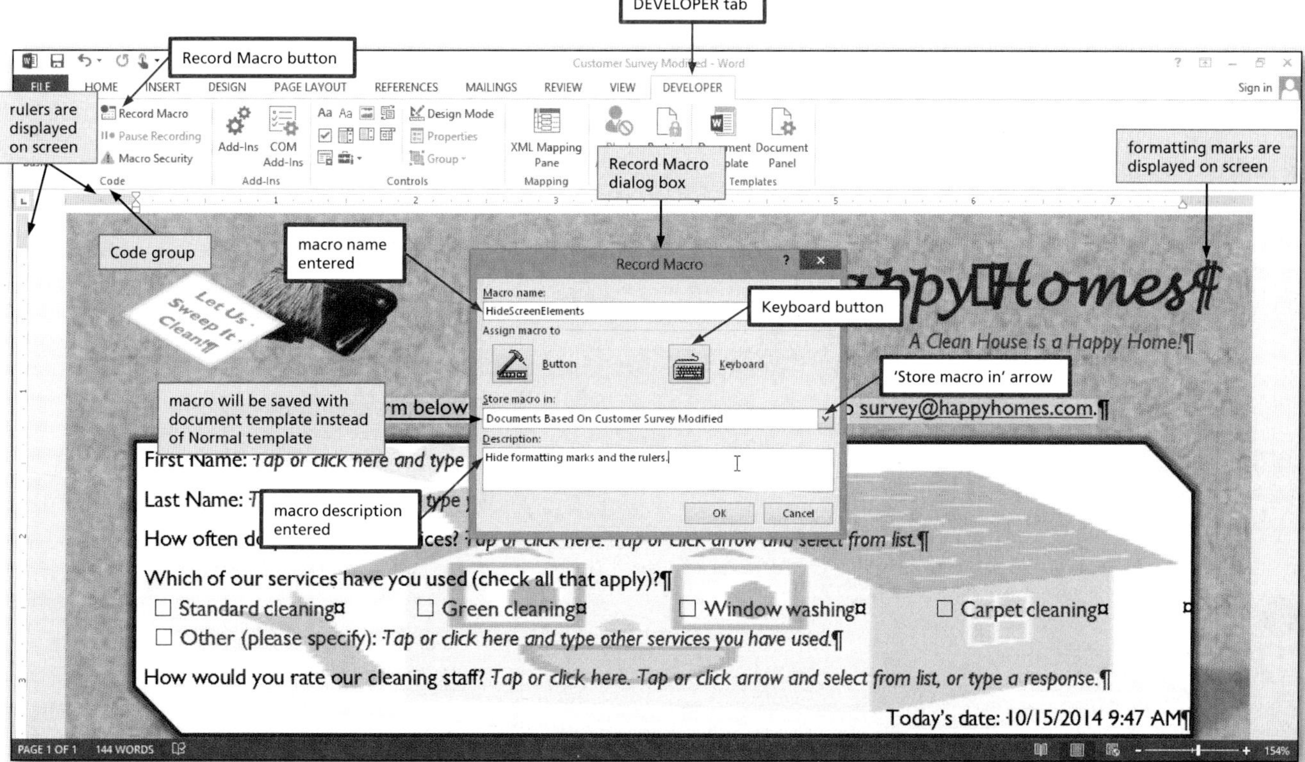

Figure 11–51

2

- Tap or click the Keyboard button to display the Customize Keyboard dialog box.
- Press ALT+H to display the characters ALT+H in the 'Press new shortcut key' text box (Customize Keyboard dialog box) (Figure 11–52).

Q&A Can I type the letters in the shortcut key (ALT+H) in the text box instead of pressing them?
No. Although typing the letters places them in the text box, the shortcut key is valid only if you press the shortcut key combination itself.

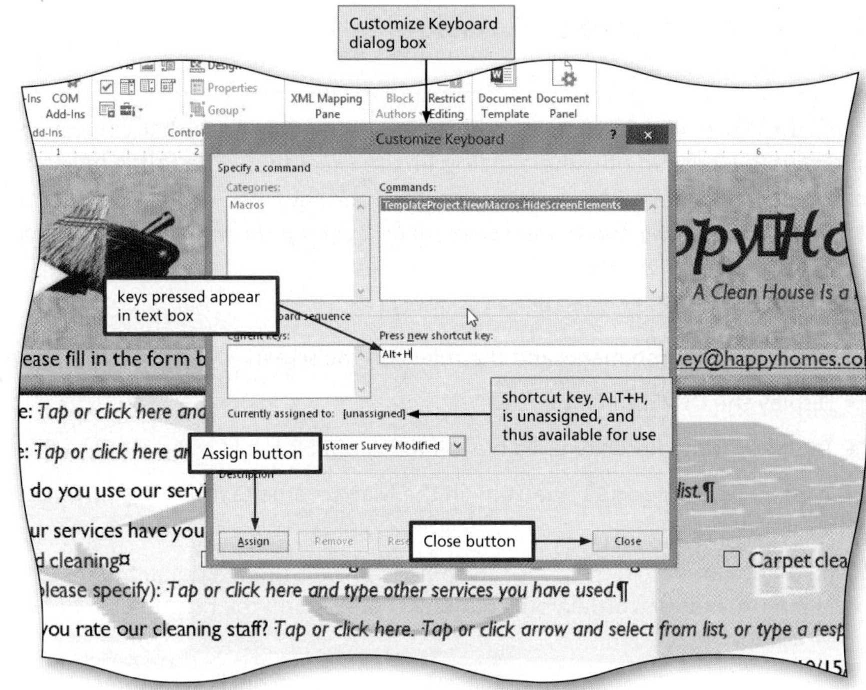

Figure 11–52

3

- Tap or click the Assign button (Customize Keyboard dialog box) to assign the shortcut key, ALT+H, to the macro named, HideScreenElements.
- Tap or click the Close button (Customize Keyboard dialog box), which closes the dialog box, displays a Macro Recording button on the status bar, and starts the macro recorder (Figure 11–53).

Q&A How do I record the macro?
While the macro recorder is running, any action you perform in Word will be part of the macro — until you stop or pause the macro.

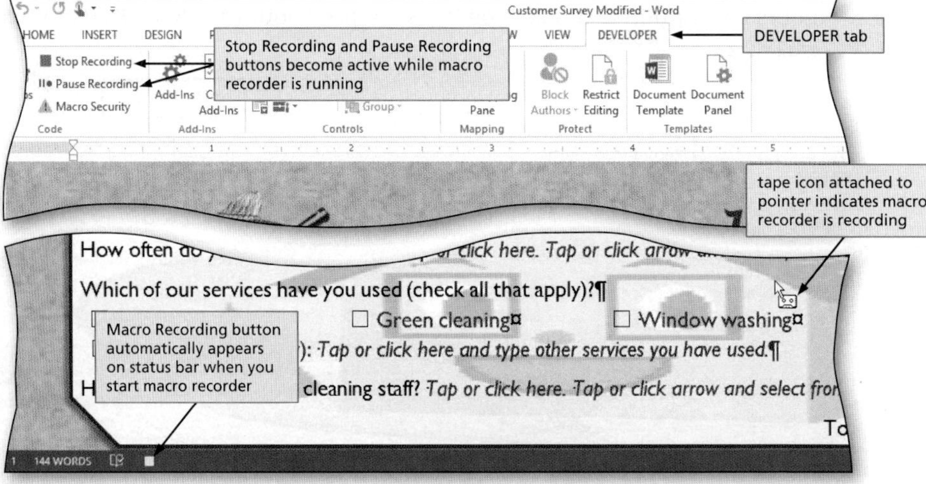

Figure 11–53

What is the purpose of the Pause Recording button (DEVELOPER tab | Code group)?
If, while recording a macro, you want to perform some actions that should not be part of the macro, tap or click the Pause Recording button to suspend the macro recorder. The Pause Recording button changes to a Resume Recorder button that you tap or click when you want to continue recording.

4

- Display the HOME tab.

Q&A What happened to the tape icon?
While recording a macro, the tape icon might disappear from the pointer when the pointer is in a menu, on the ribbon, or in a dialog box.

- Tap or click the 'Show/Hide ¶' button (HOME tab | Paragraph group) to hide formatting marks.
- Display the VIEW tab. Remove the check mark from the View Ruler check box (VIEW tab | Show group) to hide the rulers (Figure 11–54).

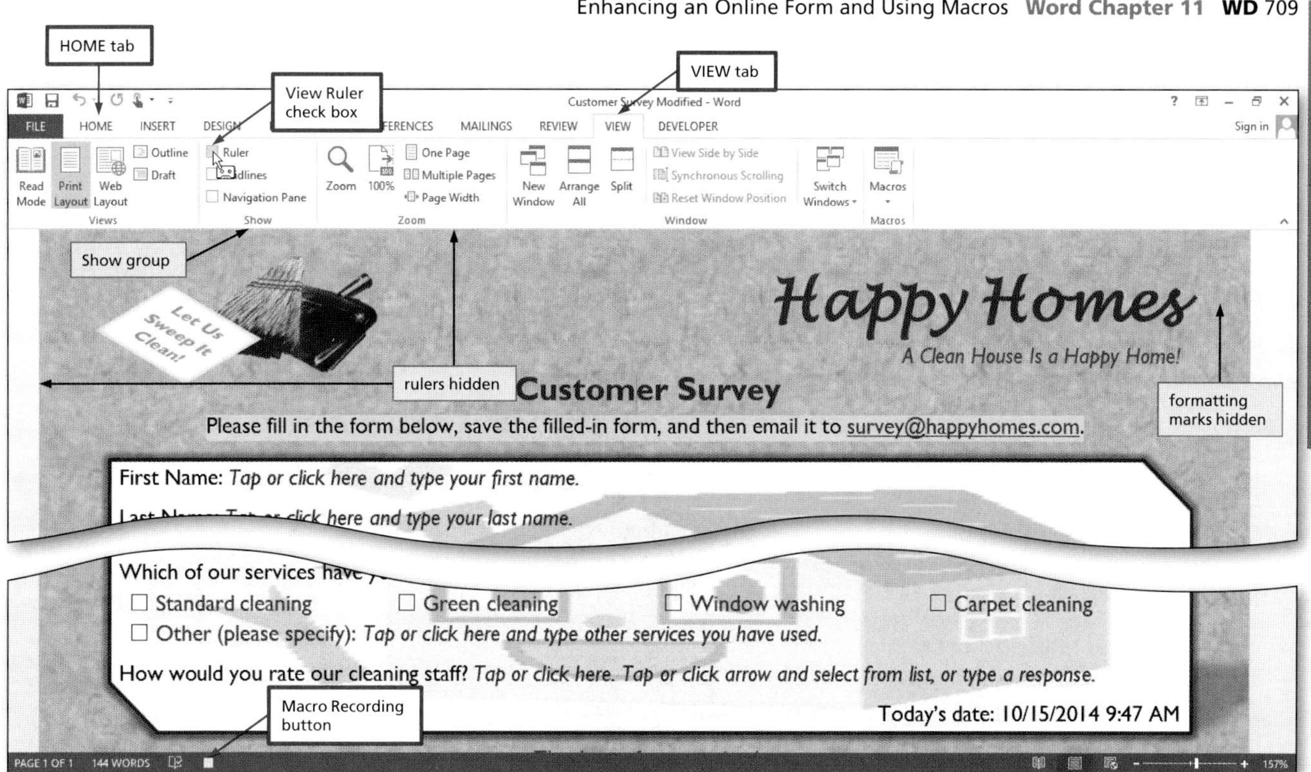

Figure 11–54

5

- Tap or click the Macro Recording button on the status bar to turn off the macro recorder, that is, to stop recording actions you perform in Word.

Q&A What if I made a mistake while recording the macro?
Delete the macro and record it again. To delete a macro, tap or click the View Macros button (DEVELOPER tab | Code group), select the macro name in the list (Macros dialog box), tap or click the Delete button, and then tap or click the Yes button.

What if I wanted to assign the macro to a button instead of a shortcut key?
You would tap or click the Button button in the Record Macro dialog box (Figure 11–51 on page WD 707) and then follow Steps 4 and 5 above.

Other Ways

1. Tap or click View Macros arrow (VIEW tab | Macros group), tap or click Record Macro on View Macros menu
2. Press ALT+F8, tap or click Create button (Macros dialog box)

To Run a Macro

The next step is to execute, or run, the macro to ensure that it works. Recall that this macro hides formatting marks and the rulers, which means you must be sure the formatting marks and rulers are displayed on the screen before running the macro. Because you created a shortcut key for the macro in this project, the following steps show formatting marks and the rulers so that you can run the HideScreenElements macro using the shortcut key, ALT+H.

1. Display formatting marks on the screen.
2. Display rulers on the screen.
3. Press ALT+H, which causes Word to perform the instructions stored in the HideScreenElements macro, that is, to hide formatting marks and rulers.

BTW
Running Macros
You can run a macro by tapping or clicking the View Macros button (DEVELOPER tab | Code group or VIEW tab | Macros group) or by pressing ALT+F8 to display the Macros dialog box, selecting the macro name in the list, and then tapping or clicking the Run button (Macros dialog box).

To Add a Command and a Macro as Buttons on the Quick Access Toolbar

1 SAVE DOCUMENT AS MACRO-ENABLED TEMPLATE | 2 MODIFY TEXT & FORM CONTENT CONTROLS
3 ENHANCE FORM'S VISUAL APPEAL | 4 CREATE MACROS TO AUTOMATE TASKS

Word allows you to add buttons to and delete buttons from the Quick Access Toolbar. You also can assign a command, such as a macro, to a button on the Quick Access Toolbar. The following steps add an existing command to the Quick Access Toolbar and assign a macro to a new button on the Quick Access Toolbar. ***Why?*** *This chapter shows how to add the New command to the Quick Access Toolbar and also shows how to create a button for the HideScreenElements macro so that instead of pressing the shortcut keys, you can tap or click the button to hide formatting marks and the rulers.*

1

- Tap or click the 'Customize Quick Access Toolbar' button on the Quick Access Toolbar to display the Customize Quick Access Toolbar menu (Figure 11–55).

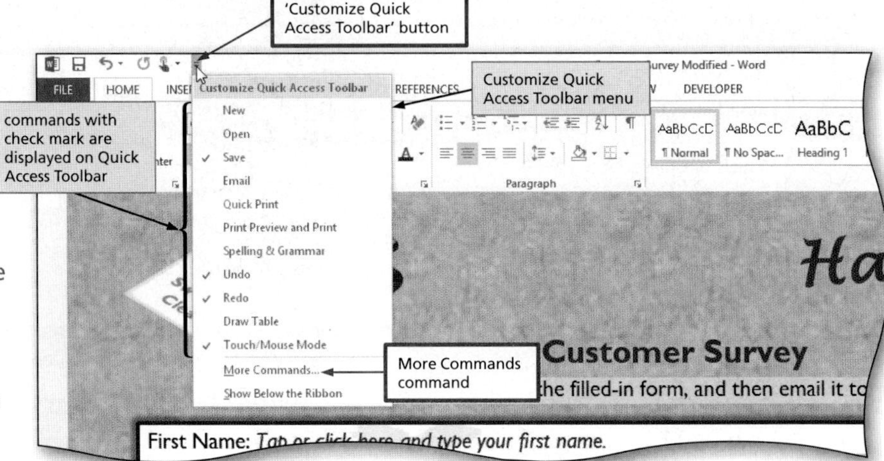

Figure 11–55

Q&A What happens if I tap or click the commands listed on the Customize Quick Access Toolbar menu?
If the command does not have a check mark beside it and you tap or click it, Word places the button associated with the command on the Quick Access Toolbar. If the command has a check mark beside it and you tap or click (deselect) it, Word removes the command from the Quick Access Toolbar.

2

- Tap or click More Commands on the Customize Quick Access Toolbar menu to display the Word Options dialog box with Quick Access Toolbar selected in the left pane.
- Scroll through the list of popular commands (Word Options dialog box) and then click New to select the command.
- Tap or click the Add button to add the selected command (New, in this case) to the Customize Quick Access Toolbar list (Figure 11–56).

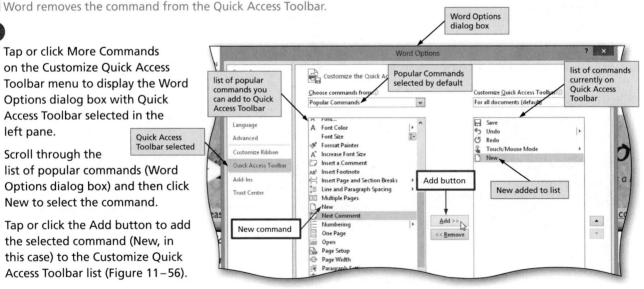

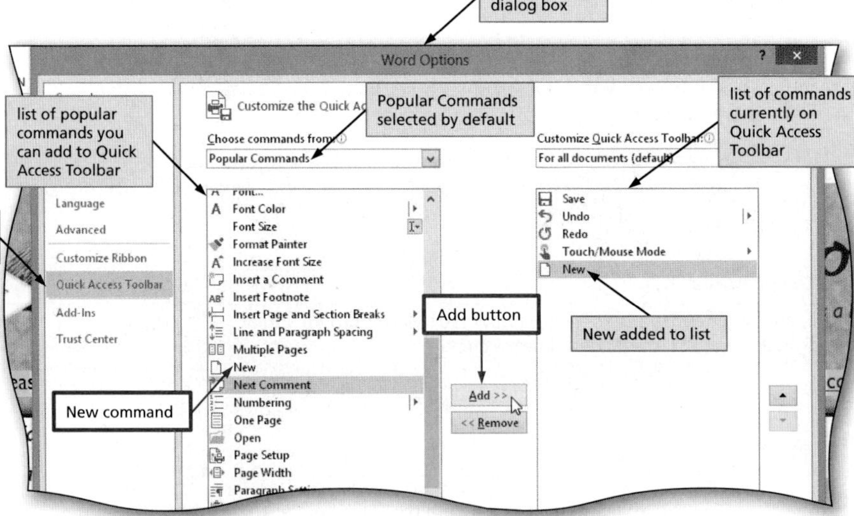

Figure 11–56

3

- Tap or click the 'Choose commands from' arrow to display a list of categories of commands (Figure 11–57).

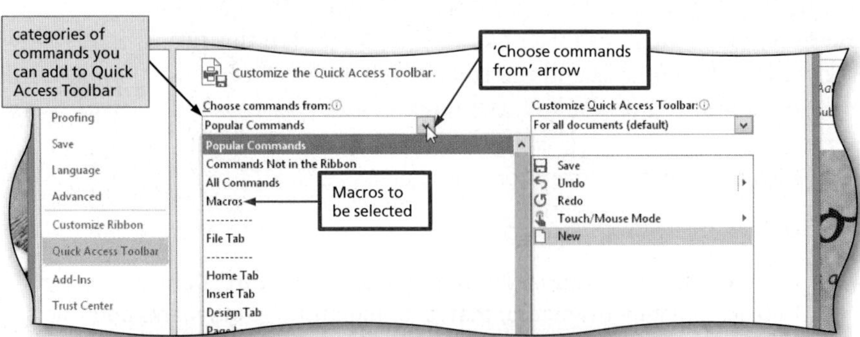

Figure 11–57

4

- Tap or click Macros in the Choose commands from list to display the macro in this document.
- If necessary, tap or click the macro to select it.
- Tap or click the Add button (Word Options dialog box) to display the selected macro in the Customize Quick Access Toolbar list.
- Tap or click the Modify button to display the Modify Button dialog box.
- Change the name in the Display name text box to **`Hide Screen Elements`** (Modify Button dialog box), which will be the text that appears in the ScreenTip for the button.
- In the list of symbols, tap or click the screen icon as the new face for the button (Figure 11–58).

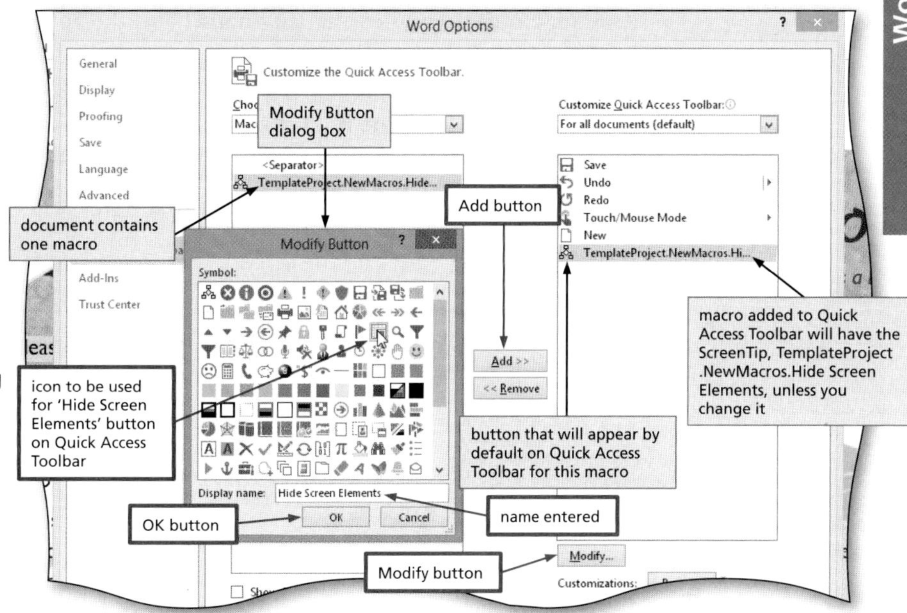

Figure 11–58

- Tap or click the OK button (Modify Button dialog box) to change the button characteristics in the Customize Quick Access Toolbar list (Figure 11–59).

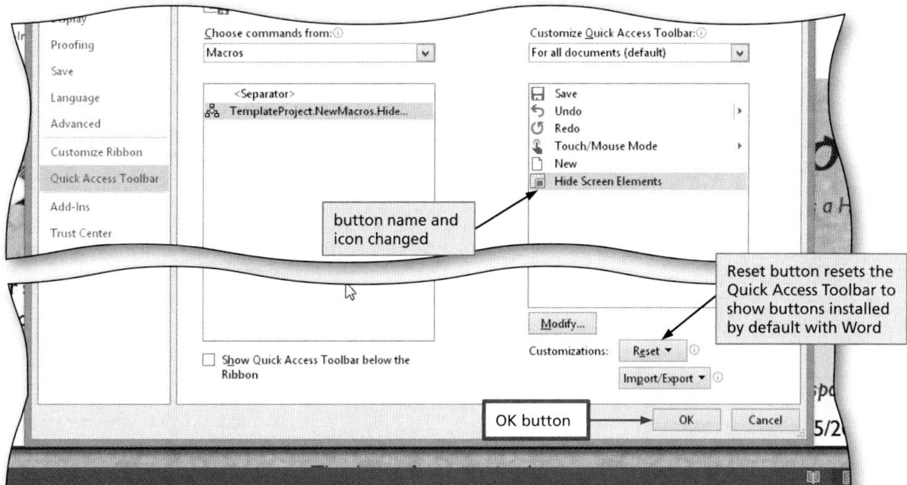

Figure 11–59

- Tap or click the OK button (Word Options dialog box) to add the buttons to the Quick Access Toolbar (Figure 11–60).

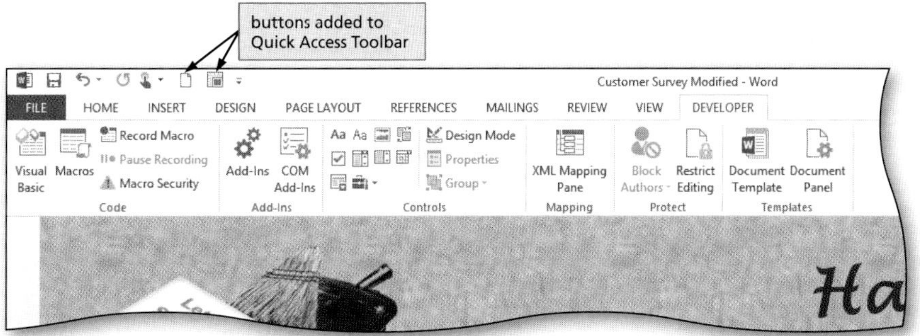

Figure 11–60

Other Ways

1. Press and hold or right-click Quick Access Toolbar, tap or click 'Customize Quick Access Toolbar' on shortcut menu

To Use the New Buttons on the Quick Access Toolbar

The next step is to test the new buttons on the Quick Access Toolbar, that is, the New button and the 'Hide Screen Elements' button, which will execute, or run, the macro that hides formatting marks and the rulers. The following steps use buttons on the Quick Access Toolbar.

1. Tap or click the New button on the Quick Access Toolbar to display a new blank document window. Close the new blank document window.
2. Display formatting marks on the screen.
3. Display rulers on the screen.
4. Tap or click the 'Hide Screen Elements' button on the Quick Access Toolbar, which causes Word to perform the instructions stored in the HideScreenElements macro, that is, to hide formatting marks and the rulers.

To Delete Buttons from the Quick Access Toolbar

1 SAVE DOCUMENT AS MACRO-ENABLED TEMPLATE | 2 MODIFY TEXT & FORM CONTENT CONTROLS
3 ENHANCE FORM'S VISUAL APPEAL | 4 CREATE MACROS TO AUTOMATE TASKS

The following steps delete the New button and the 'Hide Screen Elements' button from the Quick Access Toolbar. ***Why?*** *If you no longer plan to use a button on the Quick Access Toolbar, you can delete it.*

- Press and hold or right-click the button to be deleted from the Quick Access Toolbar, in this case the 'Hide Screen Elements' button, to display a shortcut menu (Figure 11–61).

- Tap or click 'Remove from Quick Access Toolbar' on the shortcut menu to remove the button from the Quick Access Toolbar.

3

- Repeat Steps 1 and 2 for the New button on the Quick Access Toolbar.

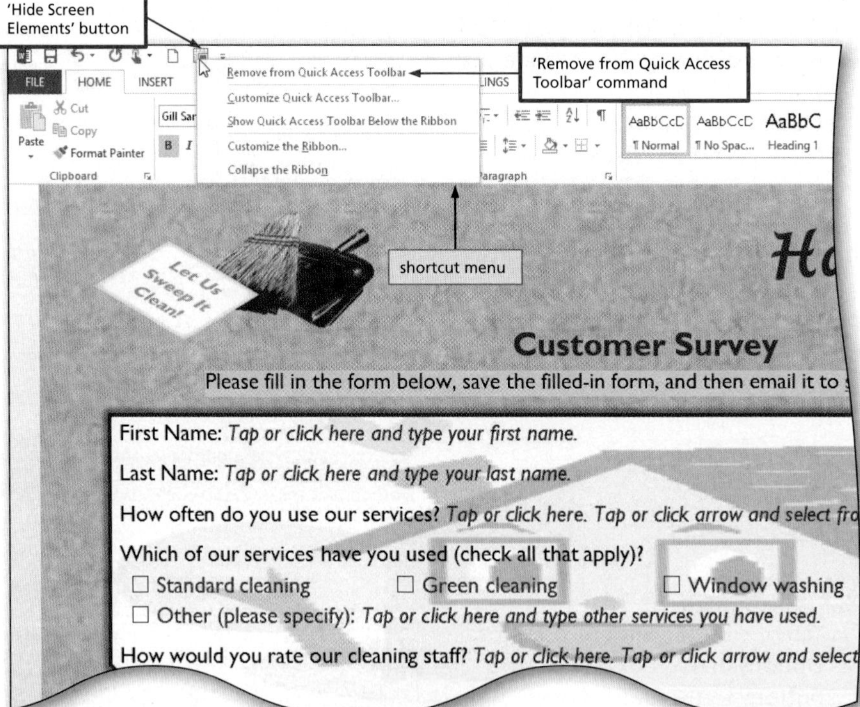

Figure 11–61

To Delete a Macro

If you wanted to delete a macro, you would perform the following steps.

1. Tap or click the View Macros button (DEVELOPER tab | Code group) to display the Macros dialog box.
2. Tap or click the macro to delete and then tap or click the Delete button (Macros dialog box) to display a dialog box asking if you are sure you want to delete the macro. Tap or click the Yes button in the dialog box.
3. Close the Macros dialog box.

Automatic Macros

The previous section showed how to create a macro, assign it a unique name (HideScreenElements) and a shortcut key, and then add a button that executes the macro on the Quick Access Toolbar. This section creates an **automatic macro**, which is a macro that executes automatically when a certain event occurs. Word has five prenamed automatic macros. Table 11–1 lists the name and function of these automatic macros.

Table 11–1 Automatic Macros

Macro Name	Event That Causes Macro to Run
AutoClose	Closing a document that contains the macro
AutoExec	Running Word
AutoExit	Exiting Word
AutoNew	Creating a new document based on a template that contains the macro
AutoOpen	Opening a document that contains the macro

BTW
Automatic Macros
A document can contain only one AutoClose macro, one AutoNew macro, and one AutoOpen macro. The AutoExec and AutoExit macros, however, are not stored with the document; instead, they must be stored in the Normal template. Thus, only one AutoExec macro and only one AutoExit macro can exist for all Word documents.

The automatic macro you choose depends on when you want certain actions to occur. In this chapter, when a user creates a new Word document that is based on the Customer Survey template, you want to be sure that the zoom is set to page width. Thus, the AutoNew automatic macro is used in this online form.

To Create an Automatic Macro

1 SAVE DOCUMENT AS MACRO-ENABLED TEMPLATE | 2 MODIFY TEXT & FORM CONTENT CONTROLS
3 ENHANCE FORM'S VISUAL APPEAL | 4 CREATE MACROS TO AUTOMATE TASKS

The following steps use the macro recorder to create an AutoNew macro. ***Why?*** *The online form in this chapter is displayed properly when the zoom is set to page width. Thus, you will record the steps to zoom to page width in the AutoNew macro.*

1

- Display the DEVELOPER tab.
- Tap or click the Record Macro button (DEVELOPER tab | Code group) to display the Record Macro dialog box.
- Type `AutoNew` in the Macro name text box (Record Macro dialog box).
- Tap or click the 'Store macro in' arrow and then click 'Documents Based On Customer Survey Modified'.
- In the Description text box, type this sentence (Figure 11–62): `Specifies how the form initially is displayed.`

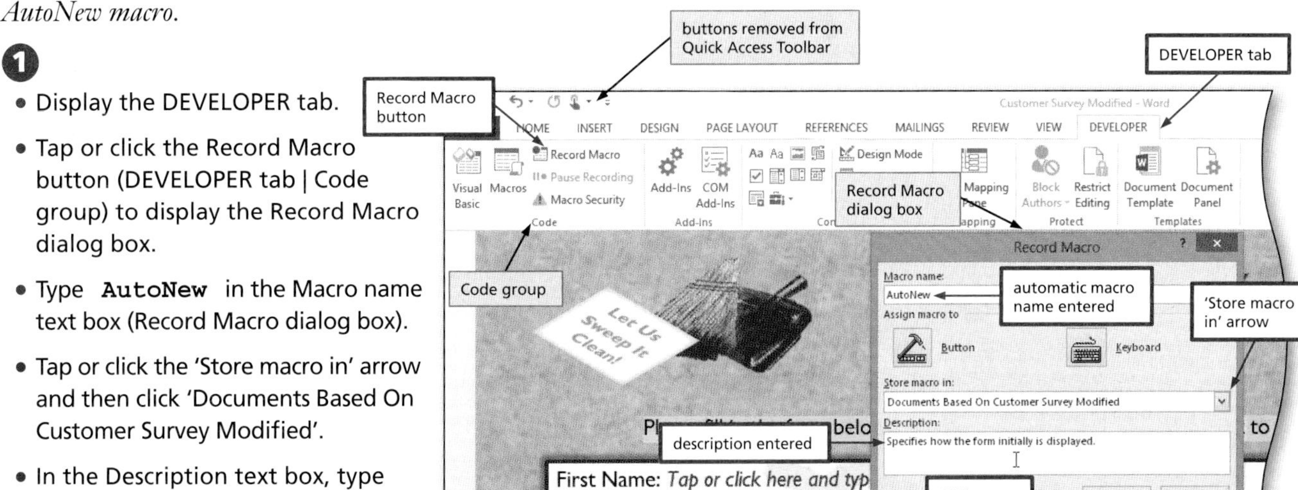

Figure 11–62

2

- Tap or click the OK button to close the Record Macro dialog box and start the macro recorder.
- Display the VIEW tab.
- Tap or click the Page Width button (VIEW tab | Zoom group) to zoom page width (Figure 11–63).

3

- Tap or click the Macro Recording button on the status bar to turn off the macro recorder, that is, stop recording actions you perform in Word.

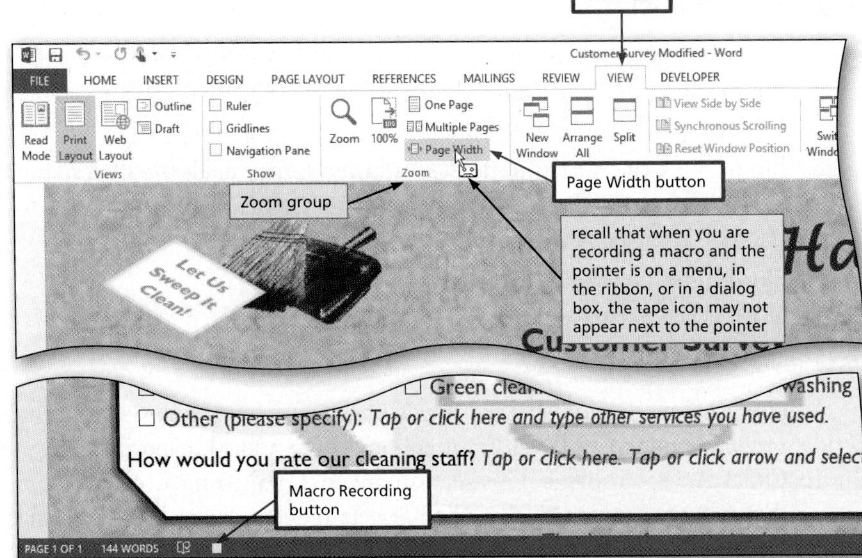

Figure 11–63

Q&A How do I test an automatic macro?
Activate the event that causes the macro to execute. For example, the AutoNew macro runs whenever you create a new Word document that is based on the template.

To Run the AutoNew Macro

The next step is to execute, or run, the AutoNew macro to ensure that it works. To run the AutoNew macro, you need to create a new Word document that is based on the Customer Survey Modified template. This macro contains instructions to zoom page width. To verify that the macro works as intended, you will change the zoom to 100% before testing the macro. The following steps run a macro.

1. Use the Zoom Out button on the status bar to change the zoom to 100%.
2. Save the template with the same file name, Customer Survey Modified.
3. Tap or click the File Explorer button on the taskbar to open the File Explorer window.
4. Locate and then double-tap or double-click the file named Customer Survey Modified to display a new document window that is based on the contents of the Customer Survey Modified template, which should be zoomed to page width as shown in Figure 11–1a on page WD 675. (If Word displays a dialog box about disabling macros, tap or click its OK button. If the Message Bar displays a security warning, tap or click the Enable Content button.)
5. Close the new document that displays the form in the Word window. Tap or click the Don't Save button when Word asks if you want to save the changes to the new document.
6. Close the File Explorer window.
7. Change the zoom back to page width.

BTW
VBA
VBA includes many more statements than those presented in this chapter. You may need a background in computer programming if you plan to write VBA code instructions in macros you develop and if the VBA code instructions are beyond the scope of those instructions presented in this chapter.

To Edit a Macro's VBA Code

As mentioned earlier, a macro consists of VBA instructions. To edit a recorded macro, you use the Visual Basic Editor. The following steps use the Visual Basic Editor to add VBA instructions to the AutoNew macro. ***Why?*** *In addition to zooming page width when the online form is displayed in a new document window, you would like to be sure that the DEVELOPER tab is hidden and the ribbon is collapsed. These steps are designed to show the basic composition of a VBA procedure and illustrate the power of VBA code statements.*

1

- Display the DEVELOPER tab.
- Tap or click the View Macros button (DEVELOPER tab | Code group) to display the Macros dialog box.
- If necessary, select the macro to be edited, in this case, AutoNew (Figure 11–64).

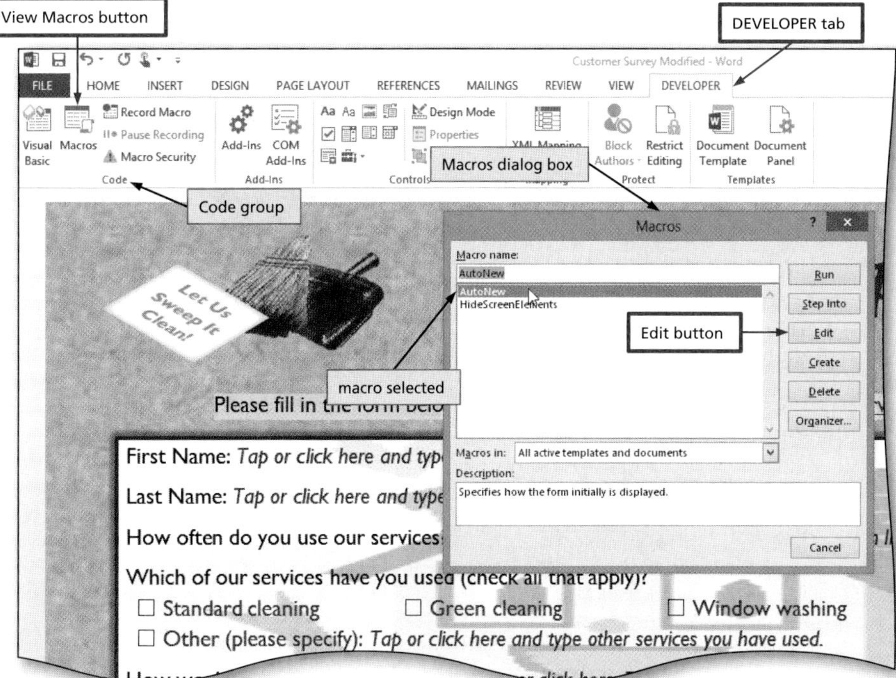

Figure 11–64

2

- Tap or click the Edit button (Macros dialog box) to start the Visual Basic Editor and display the VBA code for the AutoNew macro in the Code window — your screen may look different depending on previous Visual Basic Editor settings (Figure 11–65).

Q&A What if the Code window does not appear in the Visual Basic Editor?

In the Visual Basic Editor, tap or click View on the menu bar and then tap or click Code. If it still does not appear and you are in a network environment, this feature may be disabled for some users.

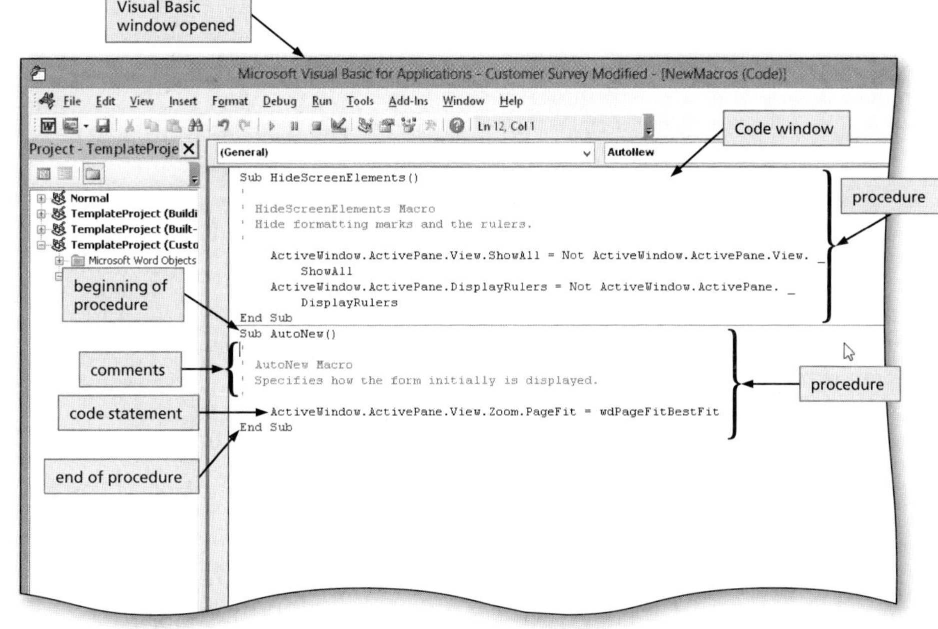

Figure 11–65

What are the lines of text (instructions) in the Code window?

The named set of instructions associated with a macro is called a **procedure**. It is this set of instructions — beginning with the word, Sub, and continuing sequentially to the line with the words, End Sub — that executes when you run the macro. The instructions within a procedure are called **code statements**.

- Position the insertion point at the end of the second-to-last line in the AutoNew macro and then press the ENTER key to insert a blank line for a new code statement.
- On a single line, type **`Options.ShowDevTools = False`** and then press the ENTER key, which enters the VBA code statement that hides the DEVELOPER tab.

Q&A What are the lists that appear in the Visual Basic Editor as I enter code statements?
The lists present valid statement elements to assist you with entering code statements. Because they are beyond the scope of this chapter, ignore them.

- On a single line, type **`If Application.CommandBars.Item("Ribbon").Height > 100 Then`** and then press the ENTER key, which enters the beginning VBA if statement that determines whether to collapse the ribbon.
- On a single line, press the TAB key, type **`ActiveWindow.ToggleRibbon`** and then press the ENTER key, which enters the beginning VBA code statement that collapses the ribbon.
- On a single line, press SHIFT+TAB, type **`End If`** and then press the ENTER key, which enters the beginning VBA code statement that collapses the ribbon (Figure 11–66).

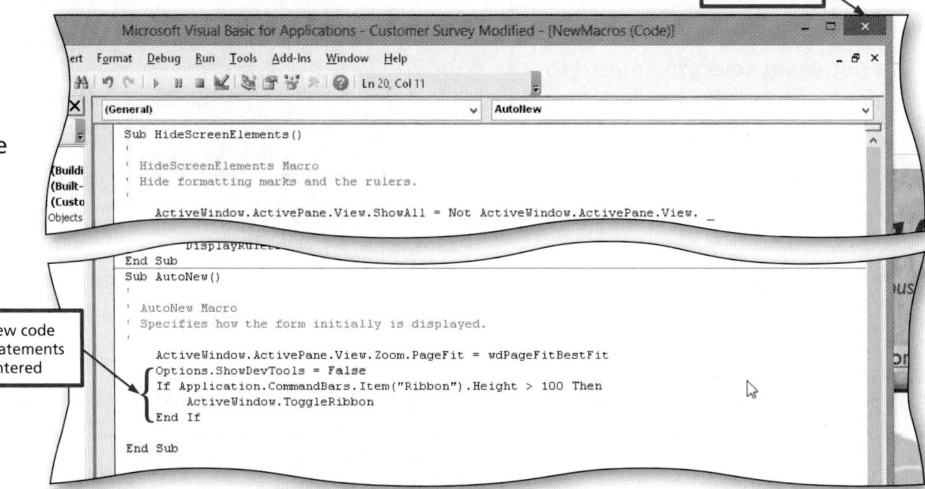

Figure 11–66

4

- Tap or click the Close button on the right edge of the Microsoft Visual Basic window title bar.

To Run the AutoNew Macro

The next step is to execute, or run, the AutoNew macro again to ensure that it works. To be sure the macro works as intended, ensure the DEVELOPER tab is displayed on the ribbon. The AutoNew macro should hide the DEVELOPER tab. The following steps run the automatic macro.

1. If necessary, display the DEVELOPER tab.
2. Save the template with the same file name, Customer Survey Modified.
3. Tap or click the File Explorer button on the taskbar to open the File Explorer window.
4. Locate and then double-tap or double-click the file named Customer Survey Modified to open a new document that is based on the contents of the Customer Survey Modified template, which should be zoomed to page width and display no DEVELOPER tab. (If Word displays a dialog box about disabling macros, tap or click its OK button. If the Message Bar displays a security warning, tap or click the Enable Content button.)
5. Close the new document that displays the form in the Word window. Tap or click the Don't Save button when Word asks if you want to save the changes to the new document.
6. Close the File Explorer window.

VBA

As shown in the steps on pages WD 715 and WD 716, a VBA procedure begins with a Sub statement and ends with an End Sub statement. The Sub statement is followed by the name of the procedure, which is the macro name (AutoNew). The parentheses following the macro name in the Sub statement are required. They indicate that arguments can be passed from one procedure to another. Passing arguments is beyond the scope of this chapter, but the parentheses still are required. The End Sub statement signifies the end of the procedure and returns control to Word.

Comments often are added to a procedure to help you remember the purpose of the macro and its code statements at a later date. Comments begin with an apostrophe (') and appear in green in the Code window. The macro recorder, for example, placed four comment lines below the Sub statement. These comments display the name of the macro and its description, as entered in the Record Macro dialog box. Comments have no effect on the execution of a procedure; they simply provide information about the procedure, such as its name and description, to the developer of the macro.

For readability, code statement lines are indented four spaces. Table 11–2 explains the function of each element of a code statement.

Table 11–2 Elements of a Code Statement

Code Statement Element	Definition	Examples
Keyword	Recognized by Visual Basic as part of its programming language; keywords appear in blue in the Code window	Sub End Sub
Variable	An item whose value can be modified during program execution	ActiveWindow.ActivePane.View.Zoom.PageFit
Constant	An item whose value remains unchanged during program execution	False
Operator	A symbol that indicates a specific action	=

To Protect a Form Using the Backstage View

You now are finished enhancing the online form and adding macros to it. Because the last macro hid the DEVELOPER tab on the ribbon, you will use the Backstage view to protect the form. The following steps use the Backstage view to protect the online form so that users are restricted to entering data only in content controls.

1. Open the Backstage view and then, if necessary, display the Info gallery.
2. Tap or click the Protect Document button to display the Protect Document menu.
3. Tap or click Restrict Editing on the Protect Document menu to display the Restrict Editing task pane.
4. In the Editing restrictions area, if necessary, place a check mark in the 'Allow only this type of editing in the document' check box, tap or click its arrow, and then select 'Filling in forms' in the list.
5. Tap or click the 'Yes, Start Enforcing Protection' button and then tap or click the OK button (Start Enforcing Protection dialog box) to protect the document without a password.
6. Close the Restrict Editing task pane.

BTW

Setting Exceptions to Editing Restrictions

You can use the Restrict Editing task pane to allow editing in just certain areas of the document, a procedure called adding users excepted from restrictions. To do this, place a check mark in the 'Allow only this type of editing in the document' check box and then change the associated text box to 'No changes (Read only)', which instructs Word to prevent any editing to the document. Next, select the placeholder text for which you want to except users from restrictions and place a check mark in the Everyone check box in the Exceptions (optional) area to instruct Word that the selected item can be edited — the rest of the form will be read only.

To Save an Existing Template with the Same File Name and Exit Word

You have made several modifications to the template since you last saved it. Thus, you should save it again. The following steps save the template again, exit Word, and close the File Explorer window.

1. Tap or click the Save button on the Quick Access Toolbar to overwrite the previously saved file.
2. Exit Word.
3. If the File Explorer window still is open, close it.

BTW

Opening Files

In addition to current and previous versions of Word documents and templates, XML and PDF files, and webpage files, all discussed previously, you can open a variety of other types of documents through the Open dialog box, including rich text format, text files, OpenDocument text, WordPerfect files, and Works files. To open these documents, open the Backstage view, tap or click the Open tab to display the Open gallery, tap or click the Browse button to display the Open dialog box, tap or click the file type arrow (Open dialog box), tap or click the desired file type to open, locate the file, and then tap or click the Open button to open the file and display its contents in a Word window. Through the Save dialog box, you can save these open files in their native format or save them as a Word document or template.

Supplementary Word Tasks

If you plan to take the certification exam, you should be familiar with the skills in the following sections.

Adding a Digital Signature to a Document

Some users attach a **digital signature** to a document to verify its authenticity. A digital signature is an electronic, encrypted, and secure stamp of authentication on a document. This signature confirms that the file originated from the signer (file creator) and that it has not been altered.

A digital signature references a digital certificate. A **digital certificate** is an attachment to a file, macro project, email message, or other digital content that vouches for its authenticity, provides secure encryption, or supplies a verifiable signature. Many users who receive online forms enable the macros based on whether they are digitally signed by a developer on the user's list of trusted sources. You can obtain a digital certificate from a commercial certification authority or from your network administrator.

Once a digital signature is added, the document becomes a read-only document, which means that modifications cannot be made to it. Thus, you should create a digital signature only when the document is final. In Word, you can add two types of digital signatures to a document: (1) an invisible digital signature or (2) a signature line.

To Add an Invisible Digital Signature to a Document

An invisible digital signature does not appear as a tangible signature in the document. If the status bar displays a Signatures button, the document has an invisible digital signature. If you wanted to add an invisible digital signature to a document, you would perform the following steps.

1. Open the Backstage view and then, if necessary, display the Info gallery.
2. Tap or click the Protect Document button to display the Protect Document menu and then tap or click 'Add a Digital Signature' on the Protect Document menu to display the Sign dialog box. (If a dialog box appears indicating you need a digital ID, tap or click the OK button and then follow the on-screen instructions. If a dialog box about signature services appears, tap or click its OK button.)
3. Type the purpose of the digital signature in the Purpose for signing this document text box.

4. Tap or click the Sign button to add the digital signature, show the Signatures button on the status bar, and display Marked as Final on a Message Bar.

Q&A How can I view or remove the digital signatures in a document?
Open the Backstage view, if necessary, display the Info tab, and then tap or click the View Signatures button to display the Signatures task pane. To remove a digital signature, tap or click the arrow beside the signature name, tap or click Remove Signature on the menu, and then tap or click the Yes button in the dialog box.

To Add a Signature Line to a Document

A **digital signature line**, which resembles a printed signature placeholder, allows a recipient of the electronic file to type a signature, include an image of his or her signature, or write a signature using the ink feature on a Tablet PC. Digital signature lines enable organizations to use paperless methods of obtaining signatures on official documents such as contracts. If you wanted to add a digital signature line to a document, you would perform the following steps.

1. Position the insertion point at the location for the digital signature.
2. Display the INSERT tab. Tap or click the 'Add a Signature Line' button (INSERT tab | Text group) to display the Signature Setup dialog box. (If a dialog box appears about signature services, tap or click its OK button.)
3. Type the name of the person who should sign the document in the appropriate text box.
4. If available, type the signer's title and email address in the appropriate text boxes.
5. Place a checkmark in the 'Allow the signer to add comments in the Sign dialog' check box so that the recipient can send a response back to you.
6. Tap or click the OK button (Signature Setup dialog box) to insert a signature line in the document at the location of the insertion point.

Q&A How does a recipient insert his or her digital signature?
When the recipient opens the document, a Message Bar appears that contains a View Signatures button. The recipient can tap or click the View Signatures button to display the Signatures task pane, tap or click the requested signature arrow, and then tap or click Sign on the menu (or double-tap or double-click the signature line in the document) to display a dialog box that the recipient then completes.

Copying and Renaming Styles and Macros

If you have created a style or macro in one document or template, you can copy the style or a macro to another so that you can use it in a second document or template.

BTW
Certification
The Microsoft Office Specialist (MOS) program provides an opportunity for you to obtain a valuable industry credential — proof that you have the Word 2013 skills required by employers. For more information, visit the Certification resource on the Student Companion Site located on www.cengagebrain.com. For detailed instructions about accessing available resources, visit www.cengage.com/ct/studentdownload or contact your instructor for information about accessing the required files.

To Copy a Style from One Template or Document to Another

If you wanted to copy a style from one template or document to another, you would perform the following steps.

1. Open the document or template into which you want to copy the style.
2. If necessary, tap or click the Styles Dialog Box Launcher (HOME tab | Styles group) to display the Styles task pane, tap or click the Manage Styles button at the bottom of the Styles task pane to display the Manage Styles dialog box, and then tap or click the Import/Export button (Manage Styles dialog box) to display Styles sheet in the Organizer dialog box. Or, tap or click the Document Template button (DEVELOPER tab | Templates group) to display the Templates and Add-ins dialog box, tap or click the Organizer button (Templates

and Add-ins dialog box) to display the Organizer dialog box, and then, if necessary, tap or click the Styles tab to display the Styles sheet in the dialog box. Notice that the left side of the dialog box displays the style names in the currently open document or template.

3. Tap or click the Close File button (Organizer dialog box) to clear the right side of the dialog box.

Q&A What happened to the Close File button?
It changed to an Open File button.

4. Tap or click the Open File button (Organizer dialog box) and then locate the file that contains the style you wish to copy. Notice that the styles in the located document or template appear on the right side of the dialog box.
5. On the ride side of the dialog box, select the style you wish to copy and then tap or click the Copy button to copy the selected style to the document or template on the left. You can continue to copy as many styles as necessary.
6. When finished copying styles, tap or click the Close button to close the dialog box.

To Rename a Style

If you wanted to rename a style, you would perform the following steps.

1. Open the document or template that contains the style to rename.
2. If necessary, tap or click the Styles Dialog Box Launcher (HOME tab | Styles group) to display the Styles task pane, tap or click the Manage Styles button at the bottom of the Styles task pane to display the Manage Styles dialog box, and then tap or click the Import/Export button (Manage Styles dialog box) to display the Styles sheet in the Organizer dialog box. Or, tap or click the Document Template button (DEVELOPER tab | Templates group) to display the Templates and Add-ins dialog box, tap or click the Organizer button (Templates and Add-ins dialog box) to display the Organizer dialog box, and then, if necessary, tap or click the Styles tab to display the Styles sheet in the dialog box. Notice that the left side of the dialog box displays the style names in the currently open document or template.
3. Select the style you wish to rename and then tap or click the Rename button (Organizer dialog box) to display the Rename dialog box.
4. Type the new name of the style in the text box and then tap or click the OK button (Rename dialog box).

Q&A Can I delete styles too?
Yes, tap or click the Delete button (Organizer dialog box) to delete any selected styles.

5. When finished renaming styles, tap or click the Close button (Organizer dialog box) to close the dialog box.

BTW
Q&As
For a complete list of the Q&As found in many of the step-by-step sequences in this book, visit the Q&A resource on the Student Companion Site located on www.cengagebrain.com. For detailed instructions about accessing available resources, visit www.cengage.com/ct/studentdownload or contact your instructor for information about accessing the required files.

To Copy a Macro from One Template or Document to Another

If you wanted to copy a macro from one template or document to another, you would perform the following steps.

1. Open the document or template into which you want to copy the macro.
2. If necessary, tap or click the View Macros button (DEVELOPER tab | Code group or VIEW tab | Macros group) to display the Macros dialog box, tap or click the Organizer button (Macros dialog box) to display Macro Project Items sheet in the Organizer dialog box. Or, tap or click the Document Template button (DEVELOPER tab | Templates group) to display the Templates and

Add-ins dialog box, tap or click the Organizer button (Templates and Add-ins dialog box) to display the Organizer dialog box, and then, if necessary, tap or click the Macro Project Items tab to display the Macro Project Items sheet in the dialog box. Notice that the left side of the dialog box displays the macro names in the currently open document or template.

3. Tap or click the Close File button (Organizer dialog box) to clear the right side of the dialog box.

Q&A What happened to the Close File button?
It changed to an Open File button.

4. Tap or click the Open File button (Organizer dialog box) and then locate the file that contains the macro you wish to copy. Notice that the macros in the located document or template appear on the right side of the dialog box.
5. On the ride side of the dialog box, select the macro you wish to copy and then tap or click the Copy button to copy the selected macro to the document or template on the left. You can continue to copy as many macros as necessary.
6. When finished copying macros, tap or click the Close button (Organizer dialog box) to close the dialog box.

To Rename a Macro

If you wanted to rename a macro, you would perform the following steps.

1. Open the document that contains the macro to rename.
2. If necessary, tap or click the View Macros button (DEVELOPER tab | Code group or VIEW tab | Macros group) to display the Macros dialog box, tap or click the Organizer button (Macros dialog box) to display Macro Project Items sheet in the Organizer dialog box. Or, tap or click the Document Template button (DEVELOPER tab | Templates group) to display the Templates and Add-ins dialog box, tap or click the Organizer button (Templates and Add-ins dialog box) to display the Organizer dialog box, and then, if necessary, tap or click the Macro Project Items tab to display the Macro Project Items sheet in the dialog box. Notice that the left side of the dialog box displays the macro names in the currently open document or template.
3. Select the macro you wish to rename and then tap or click the Rename button (Organizer dialog box) to display the Rename dialog box.
4. Type the new name of the macro in the text box and then tap or click the OK button (Rename dialog box).

Q&A Can I delete macros, too?
Yes, tap or click the Delete button (Organizer dialog box) to delete any selected macros.

5. When finished renaming macros, tap or click the Close button to close the dialog box.

Preparing a Document for Internationalization

Word provides internationalization features you can use when creating documents and templates. Use of features should be determined based on the intended audience of the document or template. By default, Word uses formatting consistent with the country or region selected when installing Windows. In addition to inserting symbols, such as those for currency, and using date and time formats that are recognized internationally or in other countries, you can set the language used for proofing tools and other language preferences.

BTW
BTWs
For a complete list of the BTWs found in the margins of this book, visit the BTW resource on the Student Companion Site located on www.cengagebrain.com. For detailed instructions about accessing available resources, visit www.cengage.com/ct/studentdownload or contact your instructor for information about accessing the required files.

To Set the Language for Proofing Tools

If you wanted to change the language that Word uses to proof documents or templates, you would perform the following steps.

1. Tap or click the Language button (REVIEW tab | Language group) to display the Language menu.
2. Tap or click 'Set Proofing Language' on the Language menu to display the Language dialog box. (If you want to set this language as the default, tap or click the 'Set As Default' button.)
3. Select the desired language to use for proofing tools and then tap or click the OK button.

To Set Language Preferences

If you wanted to change the language that Word uses for editing, display, Help, and ScreenTips, you would perform the following steps.

1. Tap or click the Language button (REVIEW tab | Language group) to display the Language menu and then tap or click Language Preferences on the Language menu to display the language settings in the Word Options dialog box. Or, open the Backstage view, tap or click Options in the left pane to display the Word Options dialog box, and then tap or click Language in the left pane (Word Options dialog box) to display the language settings.
2. Select language preferences for editing, display and Help, and ScreenTips, and then tap or click the OK button.

BTW

Removing Metadata

If you wanted to remove document metadata, such as personal information and comments, you would do the following with the document open in a document window: open the Backstage view, tap or click the Info tab in the Backstage view to display the Info gallery, tap or click the 'Check for Issues' button in the Info gallery to display the Check for Issues menu, tap or click Inspect Document on the Check for Issues menu to display the Document Inspector dialog box, tap or click the Inspect button (Document Inspector dialog box) to instruct Word to inspect the document, review the results (Document Inspector dialog box), and then tap or click the Remove All button(s) for any item that you do not want to be saved with the document. When you have finished removing information, tap or click the Close button to close the dialog box.

Enhancing a Document's Accessibility

Word provides several options for enhancing the accessibility of documents for individuals who have difficulty reading. Some previously discussed tasks you can perform to assist users include increasing zoom and font size, customizing the ribbon, ensuring tab/reading order in tables is logical, and using Read mode. You also can use the accessibility checker to locate and address problematic issues, and you can add alternative text to graphics and tables.

To Use the Accessibility Checker

The accessibility checker scans a document and identifies issues that could affect a person's ability to read the content. Once identified, you can address each individual issue in the document. If you wanted to check accessibility of a document, you would perform the following steps.

1. Open the Backstage view and then, if necessary, display the Info gallery.
2. Tap or click the 'Check for Issues' button to display the Check for Issues menu.
3. Tap or click Check Accessibility on the Check for Issues menu, which scans the document and then displays accessibility issues in the Accessibility Checker task pane.
4. Address the errors and warnings in the Accessibility Checker task pane and then close the task pane.

To Add Alternative Text to Graphics

For users who have difficulty seeing images on the screen, you can include **alternate text**, also called **alt text**, to your graphics so that these users can see or hear the alternate text when working with your document. Graphics you can add alt text to include pictures, shapes, text boxes, SmartArt graphics, and charts. If you wanted to add alternative text to graphics, you would perform the following steps.

1. Tap or click the Format Shape Dialog Box Launcher (PICTURE TOOLS FORMAT tab | Picture Styles group or DRAWING TOOLS FORMAT tab or SMARTART TOOLS FORMAT tab or CHART TOOLS FORMAT tab | Shape Styles group); or press and hold the object, tap the 'Show Context Menu' button on the mini toolbar, and then tap Format Picture, Format Shape, Format Object, or Format Chart Area on the shortcut menu; or right-click the object and then click Format Picture, Format Shape, Format Object, or Format Chart Area on the shortcut menu to display the Format Picture, Format Shape, or Format Chart Area task pane.
2. Tap or click the 'Layout & Properties' button (Format Picture, Format Shape, or Format Chart Area task pane) and then, if necessary, expand the ALT TEXT section.
3. Type a brief title and then type a narrative description of the picture in the respective text boxes.
4. Close the task pane.

To Add Alternative Text to Tables

For users who have difficulty seeing tables on the screen, you can include alternative text to your tables so that these users can see or hear the alternative text when working with your document. If you wanted to add alternative text to a table, sometimes called a table title, you would perform the following steps.

1. Tap or click the Table Properties button (TABLE TOOLS LAYOUT tab | Table group); or press and hold the table, tap the 'Show Context Menu' button on the mini toolbar, and tap Table Properties on the shortcut menu; or right-click the table and then click Table Properties on the shortcut menu to display the Table Properties dialog box.
2. Tap or click the Alt Text tab (Table Properties dialog box) to display the Alt Text sheet.
3. Type a brief title and then type a narrative description of the table in the respective text boxes.
4. Tap or click the OK button to close the dialog box.

Table of Authorities

Legal documents often include a **table of authorities** to list references to cases, rules, statutes, etc., along with the page number(s) on which the references appear. To create a table of authorities, mark the citations first and then build the table of authorities. The procedures for marking citations, editing citations, creating the table of authorities, changing the format of the table of authorities, and updating the table of authorities are the same as those for indexes. The only difference is that you use the buttons in the Table of Authorities group on the REFERENCES tab instead of the buttons in the Index group.

To Mark a Citation

If you wanted to mark a citation, creating a citation entry, you would perform the following steps.

1. Select the long, full citation that you wish to appear in the table of authorities (for example, State v. Smith 220 J.3d 167 (UT, 1997)).
2. Tap or click the Mark Citation button (REFERENCES tab | Table of Authorities group) or press ALT+SHIFT+I to display the Mark Citation dialog box.
3. If necessary, tap or click the Category arrow (Mark Citation dialog box) and then select a new category type.
4. If desired, enter a short version of the citation in the Short citation text box.
5. Tap or click the Mark button to mark the selected text in the document as citation.

Q&A

Why do formatting marks now appear on the screen?
When you mark a citation, Word automatically shows formatting marks (if they are not showing already) so that you can see the citation field. The citation entry begins with the letters, TA.

6. Tap or click the Close button in the Mark Citation dialog box.

Q&A

How could I see all marked citation entries in a document?
With formatting marks displaying, you could scroll through the document, scanning for all occurrences of TA, or you could use the Navigation Pane (that is, place a check mark in the 'Open the Navigation Pane' check box (VIEW tab | Show group)) to find all occurrences of TA.

To Mark Multiple Citations

Word leaves the Mark Citation dialog box open until you close it, which allows you to mark multiple citations without having to redisplay the dialog box repeatedly. To mark multiple citations, you would perform the following steps.

1. With the Mark Citation dialog box displayed, tap or click in the document window; scroll to and then select the next citation.
2. If necessary, tap or click the Selected text text box (Mark Citation dialog box) to display the selected text in the Selected text text box.
3. Tap or click the Mark button.
4. Repeat Steps 1 through 3 for all citations you wish to mark. When finished, tap or click the Close button in the dialog box.

To Edit a Citation Entry

At some time, you may want to change a citation entry after you have marked it. For example, you may need to change the case of a letter. If you wanted to change a citation entry, you would perform the following steps.

1. Display formatting marks.
2. Locate the TA field for the citation entry you wish to change.
3. Change the text inside the quotation marks.
4. Update the table of authorities as described in the steps at the end of this section.

To Delete a Citation Entry

If you wanted to delete a citation entry, you would perform the following steps.

1. Display formatting marks.
2. Select the TA field for the citation entry you wish to delete.
3. Press the DELETE key, or tap or click the Cut button (HOME tab | Clipboard group), or press and hold or right-click the field and then tap or click Cut on the mini toolbar or shortcut menu.
4. Update the table of authorities as described in the steps at the end of this section.

To Build a Table of Authorities

Once all citations are marked, Word can build a table of authorities from the citation entries in the document. Recall that citation entries begin with TA, and they appear on the screen when formatting marks are displayed. When citation entries show on the screen, the document's pagination probably will be altered because of the extra text in the citation entries. Thus, be sure to hide formatting marks before building a table of authorities. To build a table of authorities, you would perform the following steps.

1. Position the insertion point at the location for the table of authorities.
2. Ensure that formatting marks are not displayed.
3. Tap or click the 'Insert Table of Authorities' button (REFERENCES tab | Table of Authorities group) to display the Table of Authorities dialog box.
4. If necessary, select the category to appear in the table of authorities by tapping or clicking the desired option in the Category list, or leave the default selection of All so that all categories will be displayed in the table of authorities.
5. If necessary, tap or click the Formats arrow (Table of Authorities dialog box) and then select the desired format for the table of authorities.
6. If necessary, tap or click the Tab leader arrow and then select the desired leader character in the list to specify the leader character to be displayed between the marked citation and the page number.
7. If you wish to display the word, passim, instead of page numbers for citations with more than four page references, select the Use passim check box.

Q&A
What does the word, passim, mean?
Here and there.

8. Tap or click the OK button (Table of Authorities dialog box) to create a table of authorities using the specified settings at the location of the insertion point.

To Update a Table of Authorities

If you add, delete, or modify citation entries, you must update the table of authorities to display the new or modified citation entries. If you wanted to update a table of authorities, you would perform the following steps.

1. In the document window, tap or click the table of authorities to select it.
2. Tap or click the 'Update Table of Authorities' button (REFERENCES tab | Table of Authorities group) or press the F9 key to update the table of authorities.

To Change the Format of the Table of Authorities

If you wanted to change the format of the table of authorities, you would perform the following steps.

1. Tap or click the table of authorities to select it.
2. Tap or click the 'Insert Table of Authorities' button (REFERENCES tab | Table of Authorities group) to display the Table of Authorities dialog box.
3. Change settings in the dialog box as desired. To change the style of headings, alignment, etc., tap or click the Formats arrow and then tap or click From template; next tap or click the Modify button to display the Style dialog box, make necessary changes and then tap or click the OK button (Style dialog box).
4. Tap or click the OK button (Table of Authorities dialog box) to apply the changed settings.
5. Tap or click the OK button when Word asks if you want to replace the selected category of the table of authorities.

To Delete a Table of Authorities

If you wanted to delete a table of authorities, you would perform the following steps.

1. Tap or click the table of authorities to select it.
2. Press SHIFT+F9 to display field codes.
3. Drag through the entire field code, including the braces, and then press the DELETE key, or tap or click the Cut button (HOME tab | Clipboard group), or press and hold or right-click the field and then tap or click Cut on the mini toolbar or shortcut menu.

Working with XML

You can convert an online form to the XML format so that the data in the form can be shared with other programs, such as Microsoft Access. XML is a popular format for structuring data, which allows the data to be reused and shared. **XML**, which stands for Extensible Markup Language, is a language used to encapsulate data and a description of the data in a single text file, the **XML file**. XML uses **tags** to describe data items. Each data item is called an **element**. Businesses often create standard XML file layouts and tags to describe commonly used types of data.

In Word, you can save a file in a default XML format, in which Word parses the document into individual components that can be used by other programs. Or, you can identify specific sections of the document as XML elements; the elements then can be used in other programs, such as Access. This feature is available only in the stand-alone version of Microsoft Word and in Microsoft Office Professional.

To Save a Document in the Default XML Format

If you wanted to save a document in the XML format, you would perform the following steps.

1. Open the file to be saved in the XML format (for example, a form containing content controls).
2. Open the Backstage view and then tap or click Save As to display the Save As gallery.
3. Navigate to the desired save location and then display the Save As dialog box.
4. Tap or click the 'Save as type' arrow (Save As dialog box), tap or click 'Word XML Document' in the list, and then tap or click the Save button to save the template as an XML document.

Q&A

How can I identify an XML document?

XML documents typically have an .xml extension.

To Attach a Schema File

To identify sections of a document as XML elements, you first attach an XML schema to the document, usually one that contains content controls. An **XML schema** is a special type of XML file that describes the layout of elements in other XML files. Word users typically do not create XML schema files. Computer programmers or other technical personnel create an XML schema file and provide it to Word users. XML schema files, often simply called **schema files**, usually have an extension of .xsd. Once the schema is attached, you can use the XML Mapping Pane (DEVELOPER tab | Mapping group) to insert controls from the schema into the document. If you wanted to attach a schema file to a document, such as an online form, you would perform the following steps.

1. Open the file to which you wish to attach the schema, such as an online form that contains content controls.
2. Open the Backstage view and then use the Save As command to save the file with a new file name, to preserve the contents of the original file.
3. Tap or click the Document Template button (DEVELOPER tab | Templates group) to display the Templates and Add-ins dialog box.
4. Tap or click the XML Schema tab (Templates and Add-ins dialog box) to display the XML Schema sheet and then tap or click the Add Schema button to display the Add Schema dialog box.
5. Locate and select the schema file (Add Schema dialog box) and then tap or click the Open button to display the Schema Settings dialog box.
6. Enter the URI and alias in the appropriate text boxes (Schema Settings dialog box) and then tap or click the OK button to add the schema to the Schema Library and to add the namespace alias to the list of available schemas in the XML Schema sheet (Templates and Add-ins dialog box).

Q&A What is a URI and an alias?
Word uses the URI, also called a **namespace**, to refer to the schema. Because these names are difficult to remember, you can define a namespace alias. In a setting outside of an academic environment, a computer administrator would provide you with the appropriate namespace entry.

7. If necessary, place a check mark in the desired schema's check box.
8. Tap or click the OK button, which causes Word to attach the selected schema to the open document and display the XML Structure task pane in the Word window.

To Delete a Schema from the Schema Library

To delete a schema from a document, you would remove the check mark from the schema name's check box in the XML Schema sheet in the Templates and Add-ins dialog box. If you wanted to delete a schema altogether from the Schema Library, you would do the following.

1. Tap or click the Document Template button (DEVELOPER tab | Templates group) to display the Templates and Add-ins dialog box.
2. Tap or click the XML Schema tab (Templates and Add-ins dialog box) to display the XML Schema sheet and then tap or click the Schema Library button to display the Schema Library dialog box.
3. Tap or click the schema you want to delete in the Select a schema list (Schema Library dialog box) and then tap or click the Delete Schema button.
4. When Word displays the Schema Library dialog box asking if you are sure you wish to delete the schema, tap or click the Yes button.
5. Tap or click the OK button (Schema Library dialog box) and then tap or click the Cancel button (Templates and Add-ins dialog box).

BTW
Quick Reference
For a table that lists how to complete the tasks covered in this book using touch gestures, the mouse, ribbon, shortcut menu, and keyboard, see the Quick Reference Summary at the back of this book, or visit the Quick Reference resource on the Student Companion Site located on www.cengagebrain.com. For detailed instructions about accessing available resources, visit www.cengage.com/ct/studentdownload or contact your instructor for information about accessing the required files.

Chapter Summary

In this chapter, you learned how to enhance the look of text and graphics and automate a series of tasks with a macro. You also learned about several supplementary tasks that you should know if you plan to take the certification exam. The items listed below include all the new Word skills you have learned in this chapter, with the tasks grouped by activity.

Enter and Edit Text

Insert a Date Field (WD 685)
Edit a Field (WD 686)

File Management

Save a Macro-Enabled Template (WD 677)
Unprotect a Document (WD 718)
Add an Invisible Digital Signature to a Document (WD 718)
Add a Signature Line to a Document (WD 719)
Copy a Style from One Template or Document to Another (WD 719)
Copy a Macro from One Template or Document to Another (WD 720)
Save a Document in the Default XML Format (WD 726)
Attach a Schema File (WD 727)
Delete a Schema from the Schema Library (WD 727)

Format a Page

Use a Fill Effect for the Page Color (WD 693)

Format Text

Modify a Style Using the Styles Task Pane (WD 687)
Create a Character Style (WD 690)

Word Settings

Modify the Default Font Settings (WD 689)
Reset the Default Font Settings (WD 690)
Specify Macro Settings in Word (WD 679)
Record a Macro and Assign It a Shortcut Key (WD 707)
Run a Macro (WD 709)
Add a Command and a Macro as Buttons on the Quick Access Toolbar (WD 710)
Delete Buttons from the Quick Access Toolbar (WD 712)
Rename a Macro (WD 721)
Delete a Macro (WD 713)
Create an Automatic Macro (WD 713)
Edit a Macro's VBA Code (WD 715)
Rename a Style (WD 720)
Set the Language for Proofing Tools (WD 722)
Set Language Preferences (WD 722)
Use the Accessibility Checker (WD 722)

Work with Graphics

Change a Shape (WD 694)
Apply a Shadow Shape Effect (WD 696)
Fill a Shape with a Picture (WD 697)
Remove a Background (WD 699)
Apply an Artistic Effect (WD 699)
Draw a Text Box (WD 701)
Change Text Direction in a Text Box (WD 702)
Change a Shape Outline of a Text Box (WD 704)
Apply a 3-D Effect to a Text Box (WD 704)
Group Objects (WD 705)
Add Alternative Text to Graphics (WD 723)

Work with Tables

Convert a Table to Text (WD 682)
Add Alternative Text to Tables (WD 723)

Work with Tables of Authorities

Mark a Citation (WD 724)
Mark Multiple Citations (WD 724)
Edit a Citation Entry (WD 724)
Delete a Citation Entry (WD 725)
Build a Table of Authorities (WD 725)
Update a Table of Authorities (WD 725)
Change the Format of the Table of Authorities (WD 726)
Delete a Table of Authorities (WD 726)

CONSIDER THIS: PLAN AHEAD

What decisions will you need to make when creating macro-enabled and enhanced online forms?

Use these guidelines as you complete the assignments in this chapter and create your own online forms outside of this class.

1. Save the form to be modified as a macro-enabled template, if you plan to include macros in the template for the form.
2. Enhance the visual appeal of a form.
   a) Arrange data entry fields in logical groups on the form and in an order that users would expect.
   b) Draw the user's attention to important sections.
   c) Use colors and images that complement one another.
3. Add macros to automate tasks.
   a) Record macros, if possible.
   b) If you are familiar with computer programming, write VBA code to extend capabilities of recorded macros.
4. Determine how the form data will be analyzed.
   a) If the data entered in the form will be analyzed by a program outside of Word, create the data entry fields so that the entries are stored in a format that can be shared with other programs.

CONSIDER THIS

How should you submit solutions to questions in the assignments identified with a ❋ symbol?
Every assignment in this book contains one or more questions identified with a ❋ symbol. These questions require you to think beyond the assigned document. Present your solutions to the questions in the format required by your instructor. Possible formats may include one or more of these options: write the answer; create a document that contains the answer; present your answer to the class; discuss your answer in a group; record the answer as audio or video using a webcam, smartphone, or portable media player; or post answers on a blog, wiki, or website.

Apply Your Knowledge

Reinforce the skills and apply the concepts you learned in this chapter.

Working with Graphics, Shapes, and Fields

Note: To complete this assignment, you will be required to use the Data Files for Students. Visit www.cengage.com/ct/studentdownload for detailed instructions or contact your instructor for information about accessing the required files.

Instructions: Run Word. Open the template, Apply 11-1 Bradley Times Survey, from the Data Files for Students. In this assignment, you add an artistic effect to pictures, group images, change a shape, use a texture fill effect, and insert a date field (Figure 11–67).

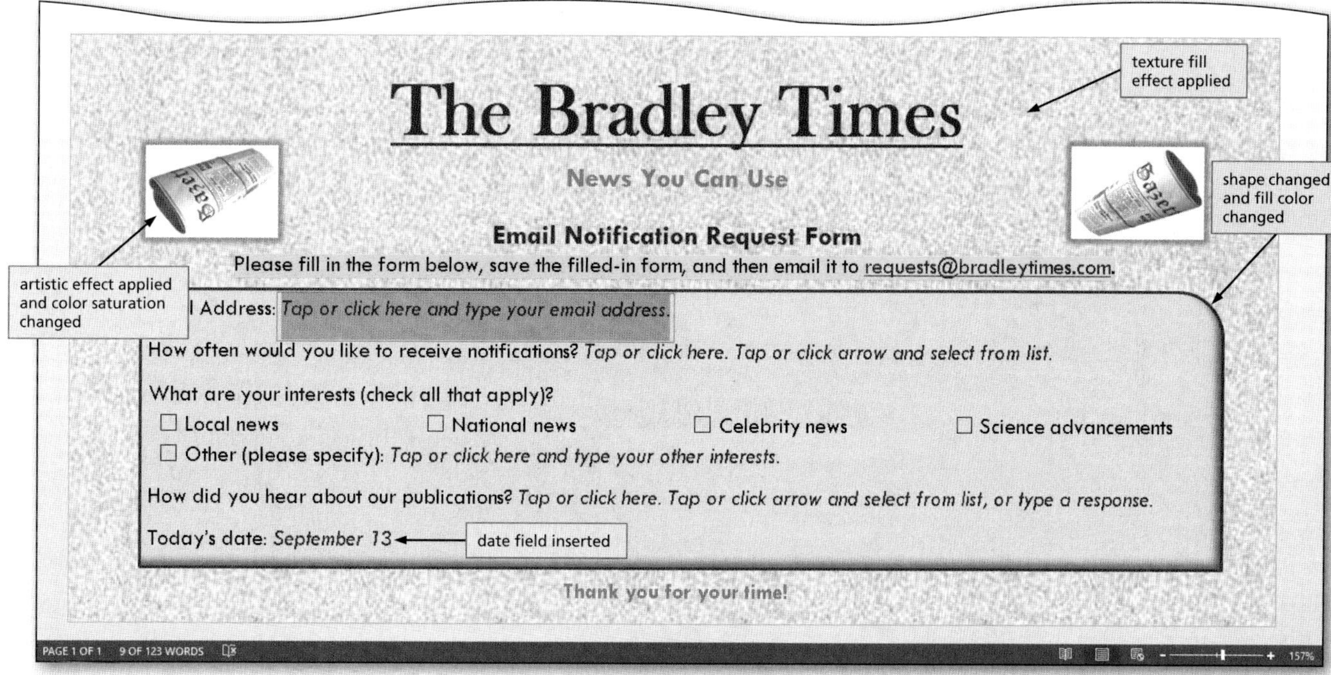

Figure 11–67

Perform the following tasks:

1. Unprotect the template.
2. Apply the Crisscross Etching artistic effect to both of the newspaper images. Change the color saturation of each image to 0%. Apply the following glow effect to each image: Dark Blue, 5 pt glow, Accent color 1.
3. Group the two newspaper images together. Move the grouped images down so that they are positioned just above the instruction line highlighted in yellow.
4. Change the page color to the Newsprint fill effect.
5. Change the shape around the data entry area from Rectangle to Round Single Corner Rectangle.
6. Change the fill color of the rectangle shape to Orange, Accent 5, Lighter 80%.

Continued >

Apply Your Knowledge *continued*

7. Apply the Inside Diagonal Bottom Right shadow to the rectangle shape.
8. Display the DEVELOPER tab. Change the properties of the date picker content control so that its contents can be deleted and then delete the content control. Insert a date field after the Today's Date: label in the format month day (i.e., September 13). Change the format of the displayed date field to Intense Emphasis. Hide the DEVELOPER tab.
9. If requested by your instructor, change the email address on the form to your email address.
10. Protect the form. Save the modified form using the file name, Apply 11-1 Bradley Times Survey Modified. Submit the revised template in the format specified by your instructor.
11. If you wanted to change the picture on the form, you could delete the current pictures and then insert new ones, or you could use the Change Picture button (PICTURE TOOLS FORMAT tab | Adjust group)? Which technique would you use and why?

Extend Your Knowledge

Extend the skills you learned in this chapter and experiment with new skills. You may need to use Help to complete the assignment.

Working with Document Security

Note: To complete this assignment, you will be required to use the Data Files for Students. Visit www.cengage.com/ct/studentdownload for detailed instructions or contact your instructor for information about accessing the required files.

Instructions: Run Word. Open the document, Extend 11-1 Credit Card Letter Draft, from the Data Files for Students. You will add a digital signature line, encrypt the document with a password, remove the password, and mark the document as final.

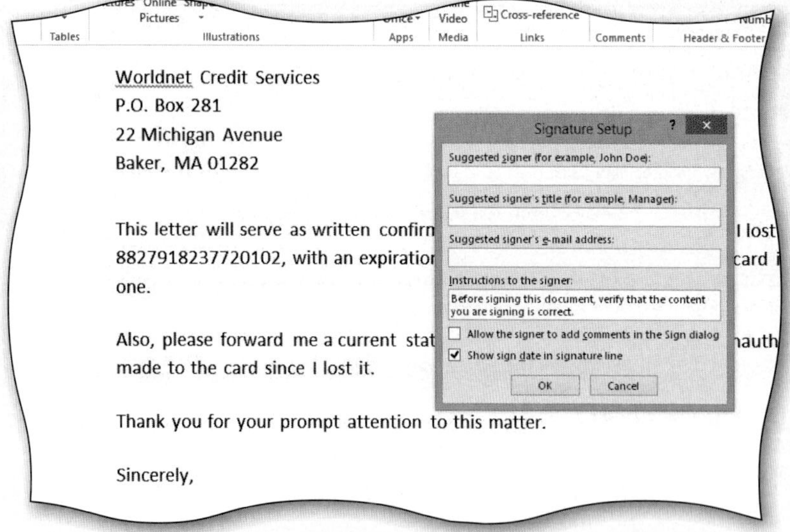

Figure 11–68

Perform the following tasks:

1. Use Help to review and expand your knowledge about these topics: signature lines, passwords, document encryption, and marking the document as final.
2. Add a digital signature line to end of the document (Figure 11–68). Use your personal information in the signature line.
3. Encrypt the document. Be sure to use a password you will remember.
4. Save the revised document with a new file name, Extend 11-1 Credit Card Letter Modified. Then, close the document and reopen it. Enter the password when prompted.
5. Remove the password from the document.
6. Mark the document as final.
7. Submit the document in the format specified by your instructor.
8. When you encrypted the document, what password did you use? Why did you choose that password? When you marked the document as final, what text appeared on the title bar? What text appeared in the Message Bar? What appeared on the status bar?

Analyze, Correct, Improve

Analyze a document, correct all errors, and improve it.

Formatting an Online Form

Note: To complete this assignment, you will be required to use the Data Files for Students. Visit www.cengage.com/ct/studentdownload for detailed instructions or contact your instructor for information about accessing the required files.

Instructions: Run Word. Open the template, Analyze 11-1 Harper Survey Draft, from the Data Files for Students. In this assignment, you change fill effects and a shape, modify a style, ungroup graphics, and format a text box (Figure 11–69).

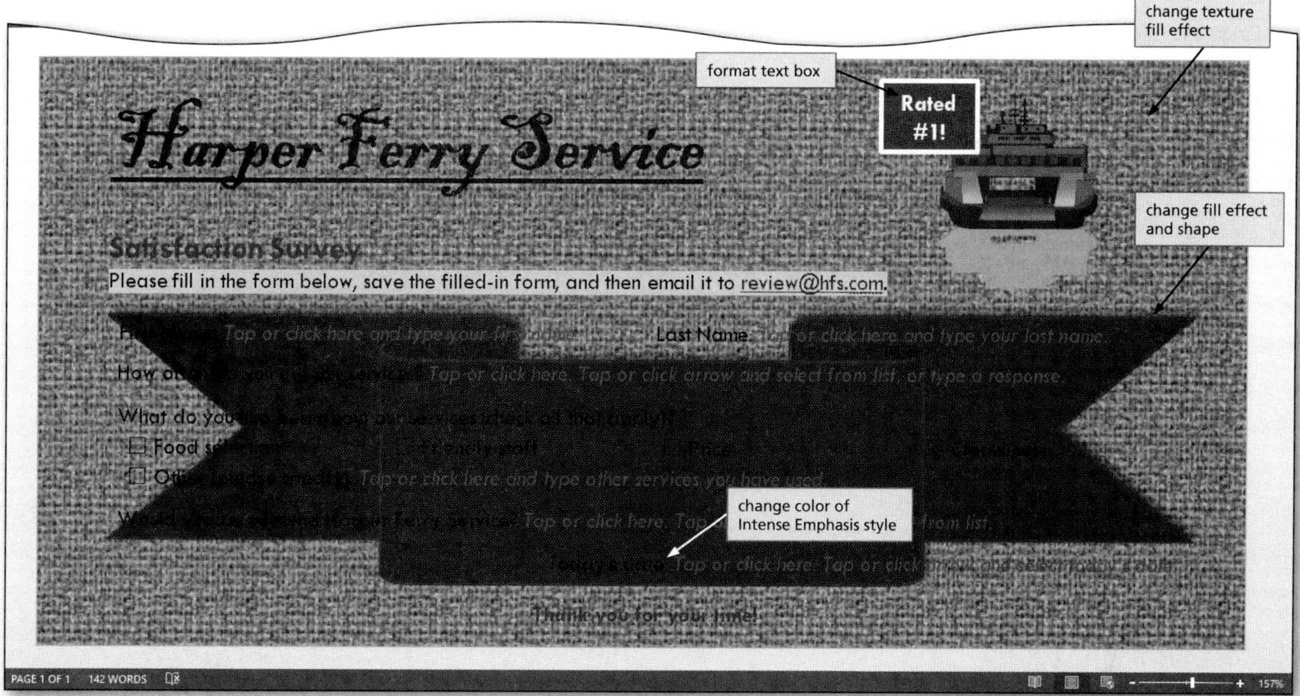

Figure 11–69

Perform the following tasks:

1. Correct In the online form, correct the following items:

a. Unprotect the template.

b. Change the page color fill effect to a texture that does not compete with the colors of the text on the form.

c. Change the shape covering the data entry area to one of the rectangle shapes.

d. Change the fill effect of the rectangle shape to a color that does not compete with the colors of the data entry instructions.

2. Improve Enhance the online form by changing the color of the Intense Emphasis style from the current color. Ungroup the graphic and text box. Add a glow effect to the graphic. Change the size of the text box so that the text fits on a single line. Change the shape style of the text box to one of your liking. Apply a 3-D rotation effect to the text box. Position the text box in a noticeable location on the form. Protect the form, changing the editing restrictions from Tracked changes to Filling in forms. If requested by your instructor, change the name, Harper, to your name. Save the modified document with the file name, Analyze 11-1 Harper Survey Modified, test the form, and then submit it in the format specified by your instructor.

3. Which texture fill effect did you choose and why?

In the Labs

Design and/or create a document using the guidelines, concepts, and skills presented in this chapter. Labs 1 and 2, which increase in difficulty, require you to create solutions based on what you learned in the chapter; Lab 3 requires you to create a solution, which uses cloud and web technologies, by learning and investigating on your own from general guidance.

Lab 1: Enhancing the Graphics, Shapes, and Text Boxes on an Online Form

Problem: You created the online form shown in Figure 10–78 on page WD 667 for Ozzie's Creamery. Your uncle has asked you to change the form's appearance and add a text box. You modify the form so that it looks like the one shown in Figure 11–70.

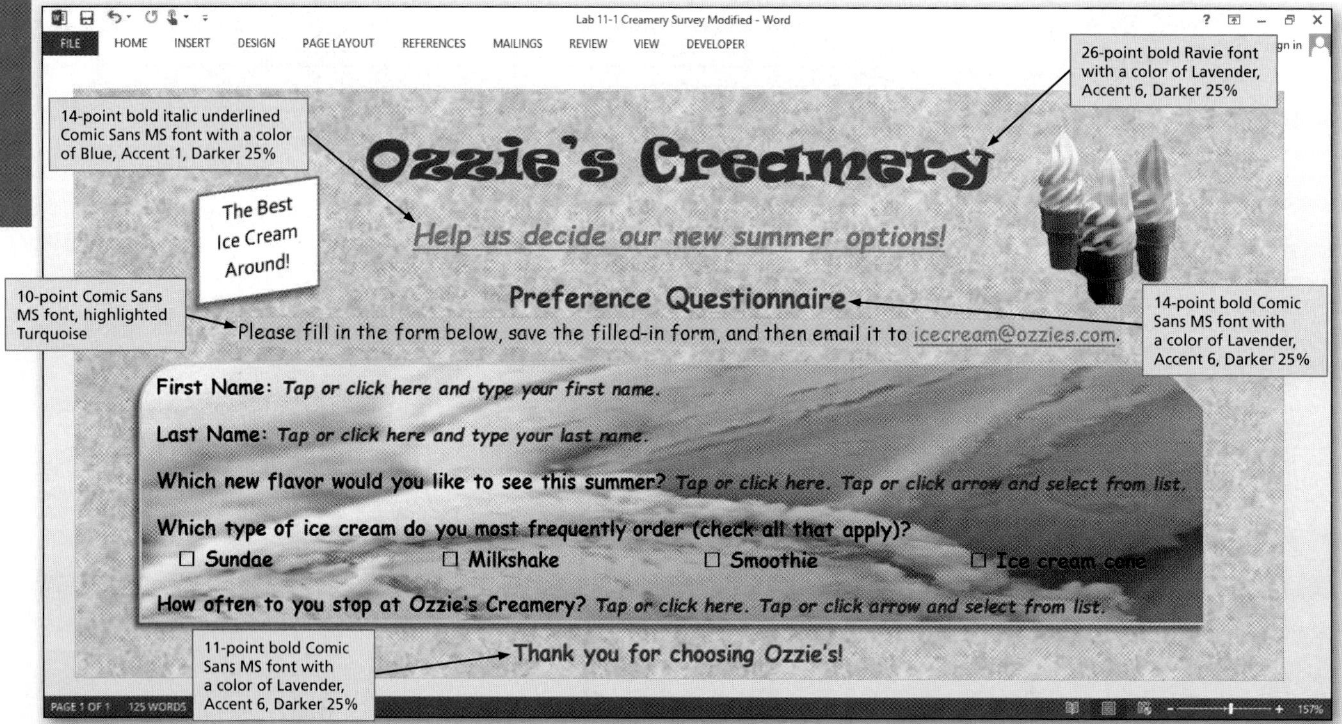

Figure 11–70

Perform the following tasks:

1. Open the template called Lab 10-1 Creamery Survey that you created in Lab 1 of Chapter 10. Save the template with a new file name of Lab 11-1 Creamery Survey Modified. If you did not complete the lab in Chapter 10, see your instructor for a copy. Unprotect the template.
2. Change the document theme to Parallax.
3. Use the Bouquet fill effect for the page color.
4. Modify the formats of the company name, business tag line, form title, user instruction, and thank you lines as shown in Figure 11–70 (or with similar fonts). If requested by your instructor, change the creamery name from Ozzie's to your first name.
5. Use the picture fill effect to place a picture in the rectangle shape. Use the picture called Ice Cream from the Data Files for Students. Change the color of the picture in the rectangle to Red, Accent color 4 Light.
6. Create a character style, with the name Data Entry Labels, for all labels in the data entry that starts with the current format and applies the bold format, uses 10-point Comic Sans MS font, and a color of Black, Text 1, Lighter 5%.

7. Change the shape of the rectangle to Snip and Round Single Corner Rectangle. Change the shape outline color (border) to Pink, Accent 5, Lighter 80%.
8. Apply the Offset Diagonal Bottom Left shadow effect to the rectangle shape. Change the shadow color to Lavender, Accent 6, Darker 25%. Change the transparency of the shadow to 20%.
9. Modify the Intense Emphasis style to the color Lavender, Accent 6, Darker 25% and apply the bold format.
10. Change the clip art on the right with the picture called Ice Cream Cones from the Data Files for Students. Remove the background, as shown in the figure. Apply the Marker artistic effect to the picture. Save the modified image with the file name, Ice Cream Cones Modified.
11. Delete the clip art on the left. Draw a text box that is approximately 0.77" × 0.93" that contains the text, The Best Ice Cream Around!, centered in the text box. Apply the Colored Outline – Lavender, Accent 6 shape style to the text box. Apply the Off Axis 1 Right 3-D rotation to the text box. Add an Offset Diagonal Bottom Left shadow to the text box. Position the text box as shown in the figure.
12. Adjust spacing above and below paragraphs as necessary so that all contents fit on a single screen. Protect the form. Save the form again and submit it in the format specified by your instructor.
13. Access the template through File Explorer. Fill in the form using personal data and submit the filled-in form in the format specified by your instructor.
14. What is the advantage of creating a style for the data entry labels?

Lab 2: Enhancing the Look of an Online Form and Adding Macros to the Form

Problem: You created the online form shown in Figure 10–79 on page WD 669 for Bard's Gym. Your supervisor has asked you to change the form's appearance, add a field, and add some macros. You modify the form so that it looks like the one shown in Figure 11–71.

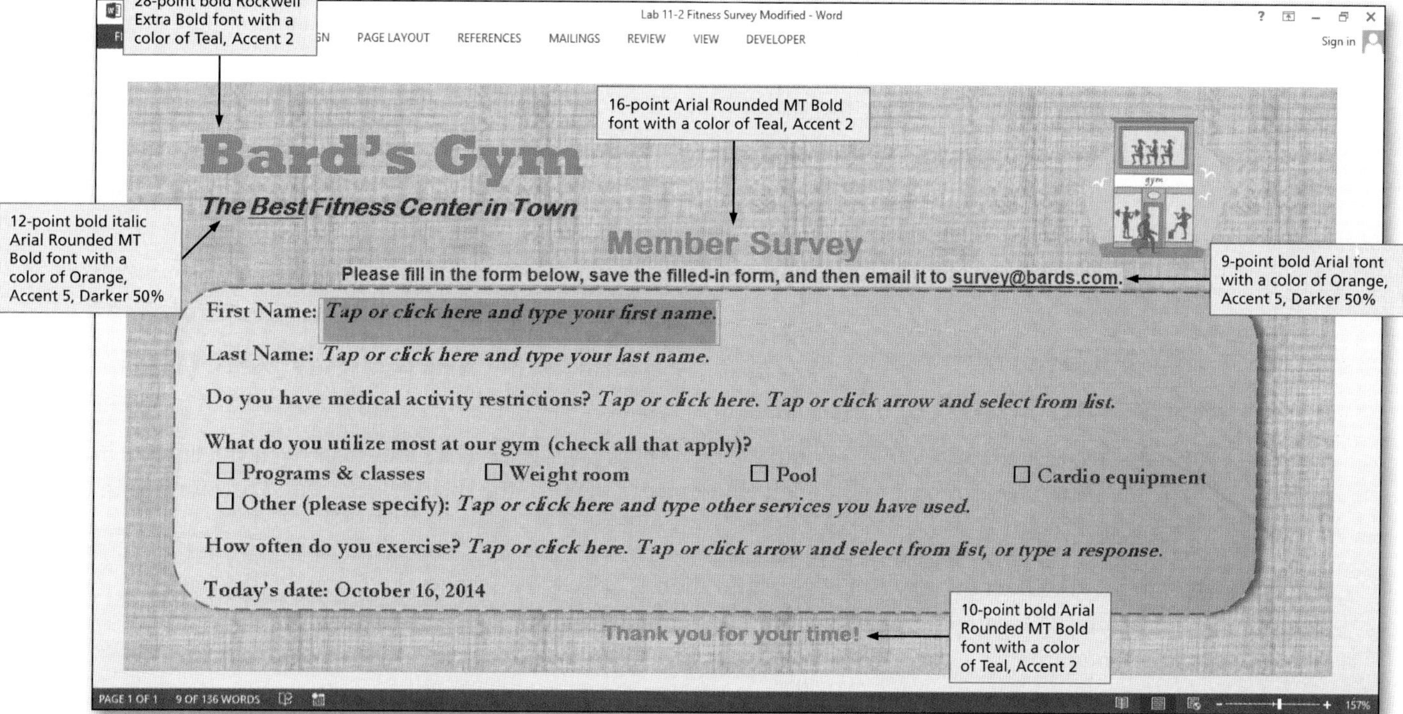

Figure 11–71

Continued >

In the Labs *continued*

Perform the following tasks:

1. Open the template called Lab 10-2 Fitness Survey that you created in Lab 2 of Chapter 10. Save the template as a macro-enabled template with a new file name of Lab 11-2 Fitness Survey Modified. If you did not complete the lab in Chapter 10, see your instructor for a copy. Unprotect the template.
2. Change the document theme to Organic.
3. Use the Papyrus fill effect for the page color.
4. Change the fill color in the rectangle shape to Green, Accent 1, Darker 25%. Apply the From Bottom Right Corner gradient fill effect to the rectangle shape, which lightens the fill color.
5. Modify the formats of the company name, business tag line, form title, user instruction, and thank you line as shown in Figure 11–71 on the previous page (or with similar fonts).
6. Convert the table to text for the 2 × 1 table containing the First Name and Last Name content controls. Change the left indent to 0.06".
7. Remove the Today's Date content control. Insert a date field from the Quick Parts gallery in the format October 16, 2014.
8. Modify the Normal style to include the bold format.
9. Change the text, Do you have medical conditions or injuries that restrict activity?, to the text, Do you have any medical activity restrictions?. Adjust spacing above and below paragraphs as necessary so that all contents fit on a single screen. Adjust the rectangle so that it covers the entire data entry area.
10. Change the current clip art to the one shown in the figure (or a similar image). Change the color of the image to Green, Accent color 1 Light. If necessary, resize the image and position it as shown.
11. Record a macro that hides the formatting marks and the rulers. Name it HideScreenElements. Assign it the shortcut key, ALT+H. Run the macro to test it.
12. Add a button to the Quick Access Toolbar for the macro created in Step 11. Test the button and then delete the button from the Quick Access Toolbar.
13. Create an automatic macro called AutoNew using the macro recorder. The macro should change the view to page width.
14. Edit the AutoNew macro so that it also hides the DEVELOPER tab and the ribbon.
15. Protect the form. Save the form again and submit it in the format specified by your instructor.
16. Access the template through File Explorer. Fill in the form and submit the filled-in form in the format specified by your instructor.
17. If a recorded macro does not work as intended when you test it, how would you fix it?

Lab 3: Expand Your World: Cloud and Web Technologies
Inserting Online Videos

Problem: You are interested in obtaining a digital ID so that you can digitally sign your documents in Word. You plan to research various digital ID services to determine the one best suited to your needs.

Instructions: Perform the following tasks:

1. Run Word. Open the Backstage view and then, if necessary, display the Info tab. Tap or click the Protect Document button and then tap or click 'Add a Digital Signature' on the Protect Document menu.
2. When Word displays the Get a Digital ID dialog box, tap or click the Yes button, which runs a browser and displays an Office Help window with a list of services that issue digital IDs (Figure 11–72).

3. Tap or click the link beside each service to learn more about each one.
4. Use a search engine to read reviews about these services.
5. Compose a Word document comparing and contrasting the digital ID services suggested by Microsoft. Be sure to cite your sources. In your report, recommend the service you feel best suits your needs.
6. Which digital ID services did you evaluate? When you read the reviews, were there other services not listed on the Office website? If so, what were their names? Which digital ID service would you recommend? Why?

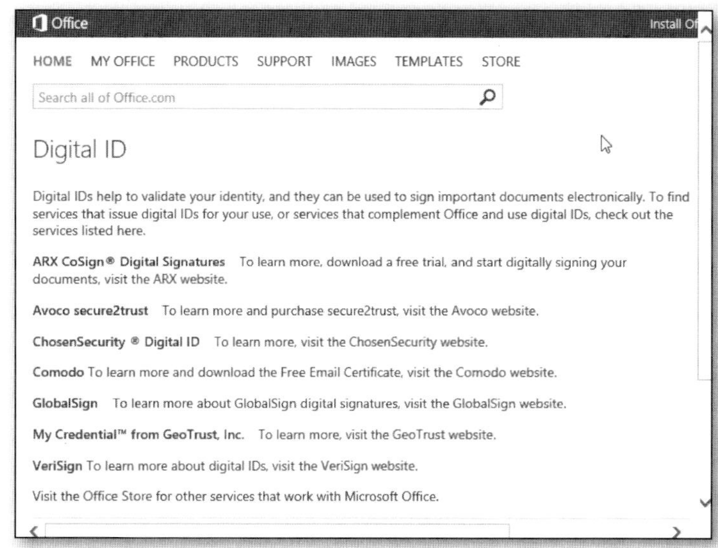

Figure 11–72

Consider This: Your Turn

Apply your creative thinking and problem solving skills to design and implement a solution.

1: Modify an Online Form for a School

Personal

Part 1: You created the student seminar survey online form for Holland College that was defined in Consider This: Your Turn Assignment 1 in Chapter 10 on page WD 671. Your supervisor was pleased with the initial design. You and your supervisor, however, believe the form can be improved by enhancing its appearance. Make the following modifications to the form: Change the school name, tag line, and form title to a different font and color; change the page color to a texture; change the highlight color; and change the font and color of the last line. Change the rectangle shape around the data entry area. In the rectangle, add a picture fill effect using the School Building file on the Data Files for Students (or a similar image) and recolor it using the Washout color. Change the color of the shadow in the rectangle. Delete the existing clip art, replace it with the picture called Tulips on the Data Files for Students (or a similar image), and apply an artistic effect to the picture. Draw a text box with the text, Your opinion counts!, and apply a 3-D effect to the text box.

Specify the appropriate macro security level. Record a macro that hides screen elements and then assign the macro to a button on the Quick Access Toolbar. Record another macro for a task you would like to automate. Add another button to the Quick Access Toolbar for any Word command not on the ribbon.

Use the concepts and techniques presented in this chapter to modify the online form. Be sure to save it as a macro-enabled template. Protect the form, test it, and submit it in the format specified by your instructor.

Part 2: You made several decisions while creating the online form in this assignment: formats to use (i.e., fonts, font sizes, colors, styles, etc.), graphics to use, which task to automate, and which button to add to the Quick Access Toolbar. What was the rationale behind each of these decisions? When you proofread and tested the online form, what further revisions did you make, and why?

2: Modify an Online Form for a Law Office

Professional

Part 1: You created the client survey online form for Clark Law that was defined in Consider This: Your Turn Assignment 2 in Chapter 10 on page WD 671. Your supervisor was pleased with the initial design. You and your supervisor, however, believe the form can be improved by enhancing its appearance. Make the following modifications to the form: Change the firm name, tag line, and

Continued >

Consider This: Your Turn *continued*

form title to a different font and color; change the page color to a texture; change the highlight color; and change the font and color of the last line. Change the rectangle shape around the data entry area. In the rectangle, add a picture fill effect using the Scales of Justice file on the Data Files for Students (or a similar image) and recolor it using the Washout color. Change the color of the shadow in the rectangle. Delete the existing clip art, replace it with the picture called Courthouse on the Data Files for Students (or a similar image), and apply an artistic effect to the picture. Draw a text box with the text, Your opinion counts!, and apply a 3-D effect to the text box.

Specify the appropriate macro security level. Record a macro that hides screen elements and then assign the macro to a button on the Quick Access Toolbar. Record another macro for a task you would like to automate. Add another button to the Quick Access Toolbar for any Word command not on the ribbon.

Use the concepts and techniques presented in this chapter to modify the online form. Be sure to save it as a macro-enabled template. Protect the form, test it, and submit it in the format specified by your instructor.

Part 2: You made several decisions while creating the online form in this assignment: formats to use (i.e., fonts, font sizes, colors, styles, etc.), graphics to use, which task to automate, and which button to add to the Quick Access Toolbar. What was the rationale behind each of these decisions? When you proofread and tested the online form, what further revisions did you make, and why?

3: Modify an Online Form for a Campus Group

Research and Collaboration

Part 1: Your team created the online form for a campus group at your school, which was defined in Consider This: Your Turn Assignment 3 in Chapter 10 on page WD 672. Your team was pleased with the initial design but believe the form can be improved by enhancing its appearance. Make the following modifications to the form: Change the school name, tag line, and form title to a different font and color; change the page color to a texture; change the highlight color; and change the font and color of the last line. Change the shape around the data entry area. In the rectangle, add a picture fill effect using an appropriate picture of your choice and recolor it accordingly. Change the color of the shadow in the rectangle. Delete the existing clip art, replace it with a picture of your choice, and apply an artistic effect to the picture. Add a text box to the form and apply a 3-D effect to the text box.

Specify the appropriate macro security level. Record a macro that hides screen elements and then assign the macro to a button on the Quick Access Toolbar. Record another macro for a task you would like to automate. Add another button to the Quick Access Toolbar for any Word command not on the ribbon.

Use the concepts and techniques presented in this chapter to modify the online form. Be sure to save it as a macro-enabled template. Protect the form, test it, and submit it in the format specified by your instructor.

Part 2: You made several decisions while creating the online form in this assignment: formats to use (i.e., fonts, font sizes, colors, styles, etc.), graphics to use, which task to automate, and which button to add to the Quick Access Toolbar. What was the rationale behind each of these decisions? When you proofread and tested the online form, what further revisions did you make, and why?

Learn Online

Learn Online – Reinforce what you learned in this chapter with games, exercises, training, and many other online activities and resources.

Student Companion Site Reinforcement activities and resources are available at no additional cost on www.cengagebrain.com. Visit www.cengage.com/ct/studentdownload for detailed instructions about accessing the resources available at the Student Companion Site.

SAM

SAM Put your skills into practice with SAM! If you have a SAM account, go to www.cengage.com/sam2013 to access SAM assignments for this chapter.

Appendix

APA Research Paper — Chapter 2 Supplement

Project — Research Paper Based on APA Documentation Style

As described in Chapter 2, two popular documentation styles for research papers are the Modern Language Association of America (MLA) and American Psychological Association (APA). This appendix creates the same research paper shown in Chapter 2, except it uses the APA documentation style instead of the MLA documentation style (Figure 1 on the next page).

This appendix is intended as a supplement for Chapter 2. It assumes you have completed the Chapter 2 project and, thus, presents only the steps required to create the research paper following the APA guidelines. That is, this appendix does not repeat background, explanations, boxes, or steps from Chapter 2 that are not required specifically to create this APA research paper. For example, this appendix does not present proofing tools, citation placeholders, footnotes, copy and paste, Research task pane, etc. It does not contain the roadmap, Q&As, or BTWs. You should know the material presented in Chapter 2 because it will help you to complete later chapters in the book successfully and can help you prepare if you intend to take the Word Certification exam.

APA Documentation Style

The research paper in this appendix follows the guidelines presented by the APA. To follow the APA documentation style, format the text with a 12-point Times New Roman or a similar font. Double-space text on all pages of the paper using one-inch top, bottom, left, and right margins. Indent the first word of each paragraph in the body of the paper, and in footnotes if they are used, one-half inch from the left margin. At the top of each page, place a left-aligned running head and a right-aligned page number. The **running head** consists of the text, Running head:, followed by an abbreviated paper title (no more than 50 characters) in all uppercase letters.

The APA documentation style requires a title page. In addition to the running head and page number at the top of the page, the title page contains the complete paper title, author name, and institutional affiliation, all centered on separate lines in the upper half of the page. The paper title should not exceed 12 words and should be written so that it easily can be shortened to an abbreviated title for the running head. The author name,

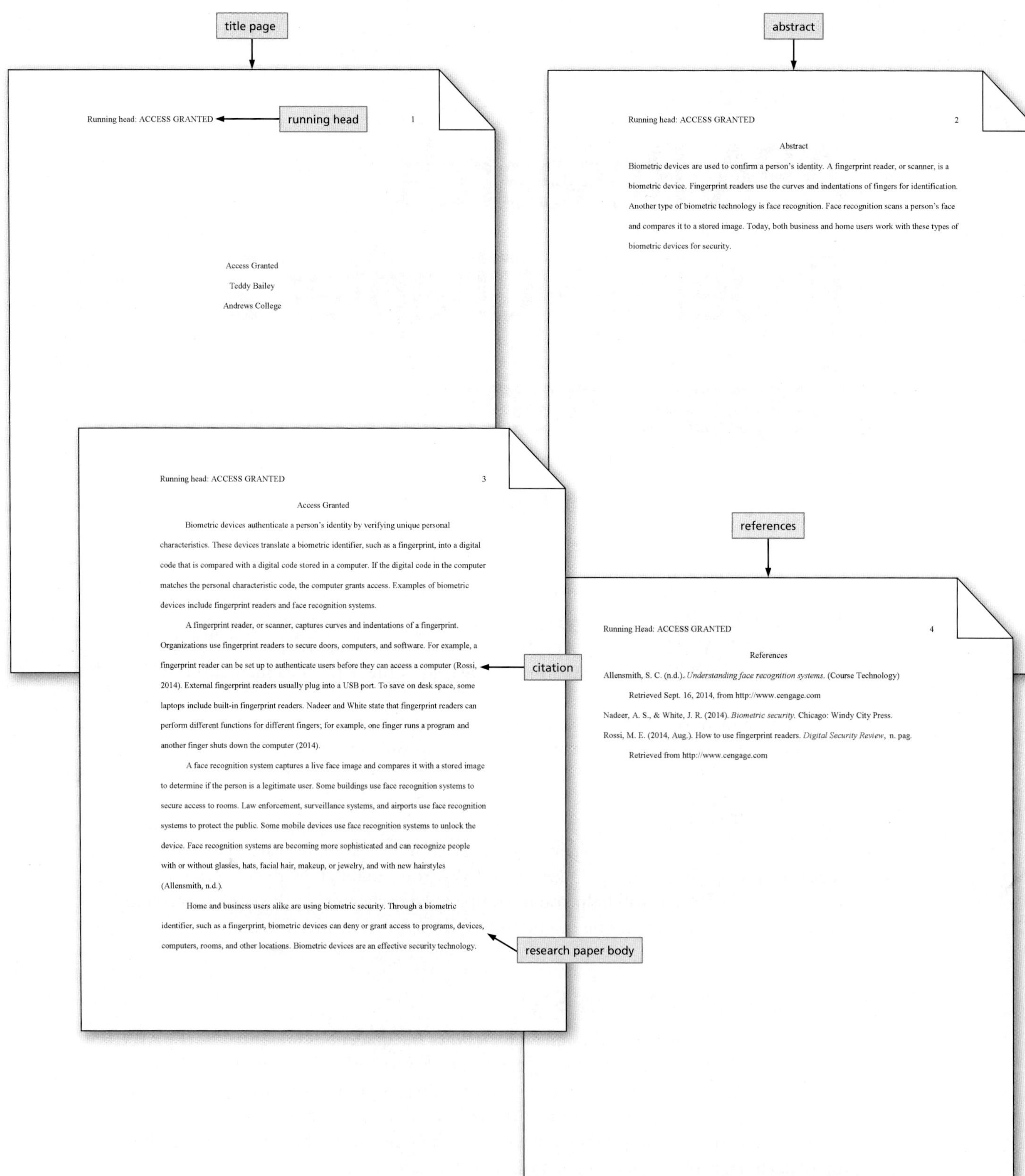
title page
abstract
running head
citation
references
research paper body
Running head: ACCESS GRANTED 1
Access Granted
Teddy Bailey
Andrews College
Running head: ACCESS GRANTED 2
Abstract
Biometric devices are used to confirm a person's identity. A fingerprint reader, or scanner, is a biometric device. Fingerprint readers use the curves and indentations of fingers for identification. Another type of biometric technology is face recognition. Face recognition scans a person's face and compares it to a stored image. Today, both business and home users work with these types of biometric devices for security.
Running head: ACCESS GRANTED 3
Access Granted
Biometric devices authenticate a person's identity by verifying unique personal characteristics. These devices translate a biometric identifier, such as a fingerprint, into a digital code that is compared with a digital code stored in a computer. If the digital code in the computer matches the personal characteristic code, the computer grants access. Examples of biometric devices include fingerprint readers and face recognition systems.
A fingerprint reader, or scanner, captures curves and indentations of a fingerprint. Organizations use fingerprint readers to secure doors, computers, and software. For example, a fingerprint reader can be set up to authenticate users before they can access a computer (Rossi, 2014). External fingerprint readers usually plug into a USB port. To save on desk space, some laptops include built-in fingerprint readers. Nadeer and White state that fingerprint readers can perform different functions for different fingers; for example, one finger runs a program and another finger shuts down the computer (2014).
A face recognition system captures a live face image and compares it with a stored image to determine if the person is a legitimate user. Some buildings use face recognition systems to secure access to rooms. Law enforcement, surveillance systems, and airports use face recognition systems to protect the public. Some mobile devices use face recognition systems to unlock the device. Face recognition systems are becoming more sophisticated and can recognize people with or without glasses, hats, facial hair, makeup, or jewelry, and with new hairstyles (Allensmith, n.d.).
Home and business users alike are using biometric security. Through a biometric identifier, such as a fingerprint, biometric devices can deny or grant access to programs, devices, computers, rooms, and other locations. Biometric devices are an effective security technology.
Running Head: ACCESS GRANTED 4
References
Allensmith, S. C. (n.d.). Understanding face recognition systems. (Course Technology) Retrieved Sept. 16, 2014, from http://www.cengage.com
Nadeer, A. S., & White, J. R. (2014). Biometric security. Chicago: Windy City Press.
Rossi, M. E. (2014, Aug.). How to use fingerprint readers. Digital Security Review, n. pag. Retrieved from http://www.cengage.com

Figure 1

also called an author byline, should not contain any title (e.g., Professor) or degrees (e.g., PhD). If the author is not affiliated with an institution, list the author's city and state of residence. The title page also can include an author note centered at the bottom of the page, which can contain separate paragraphs identifying the author's departmental affiliation, changes in affiliation during research, acknowledgments, and contact information. If the title page contains an author note, the text, Author Note, should be centered above the notes.

Research papers that follow the APA documentation style include an abstract. The **abstract** is a one-paragraph summary (usually 250 words or less) of the most important topics in the paper. The abstract appears after the title page on its own numbered page, which includes the running head. The title, Abstract, is centered above a single paragraph that is double-spaced and not indented.

The APA documentation style cites references in the text of the paper, called **citations**, instead of noting each source at the bottom of the page or at the end of the paper. This documentation style also uses the term, **references,** to refer to the bibliographic list of sources at the end of the paper. The references page alphabetically lists sources that are cited in the paper. Place the list of sources on a separate numbered page. Center the title, References, one inch from the top margin. Double-space all entries and format them with a **hanging indent**, in which the first line of a paragraph begins at the left margin and subsequent lines in the same paragraph are indented. The APA guidelines specify the hanging indent should be one-half inch from the left margin. List each source by the author's last name, or, if the author's name is not available, by the title of the source. Capitalize only the first letter of the first word in a title, along with any proper nouns.

To Start Word

If you are using a computer to step through the project in this chapter and you want your screens to match the figures in this book, you should change your screen's resolution to 1366 × 768. For information about how to change a computer's resolution, refer to the Office and Windows chapter at the beginning of this book.

The following steps, which assume Windows 8 is running, use the Start screen or the Search box to run Word based on a typical installation. You may need to ask your instructor how to run Word on your computer. For a detailed example of the procedure summarized below, refer to the Office and Windows chapter.

1. Scroll the Start screen for a Word 2013 tile. If your Start screen contains a Word 2013 tile, tap or click it to run Word and then proceed to Step 5; if the Start screen does not contain the Word 2013 tile, proceed to the next step to search for the Word app.
2. Swipe in from the right edge of the screen or point to the upper-right corner of the screen to display the Charms bar and then tap or click the Search charm on the Charms bar to display the Search menu.
3. Type `Word` as the search text in the Search box and watch the search results appear in the Apps list.
4. Tap or click Word 2013 in the search results to run Word.
5. Tap or click the Blank document thumbnail on the Word start screen to create a blank document and display it in the Word window.
6. If the Word window is not maximized, tap or click the Maximize button on its title bar to maximize the window.

7. If the Print Layout button on the status bar is not selected (shown in Figure 2), tap or click it so that your screen is in Print Layout view.

8. If Normal (HOME tab | Styles group) is not selected in the Styles gallery (shown in Figure 2), tap or click it so that your document uses the Normal style.

9. To display the page the same width as the document window, if necessary, tap or click the Page Width button (VIEW tab | Zoom group).

10. If the 'Show/Hide ¶' button (HOME tab | Paragraph group) is not selected already, tap or click it to display formatting marks on the screen.

To Modify the Normal Style for the Current Document

The APA documentation style requires that all text in the research paper use a 12-point Times New Roman or similar font. If you change the font and font size using buttons on the ribbon, you will need to make the change many times during the course of creating the paper. ***Why?*** *Word formats various areas of a document based on the Normal style, which uses an 11-point Calibri font. For example, body text, headers, and bibliographies all display text based on the Normal style.*

Thus, instead of changing the font and font size for various document elements, a more efficient technique is to change the Normal style for this document to use a 12-point Times New Roman font. ***Why?*** *By changing the Normal style, you ensure that all text in the document will use the format required by the APA.* The following steps change the Normal style.

- Press and hold or right-click Normal in the Styles gallery (HOME tab | Styles group) to display a shortcut menu related to styles (Figure 2).

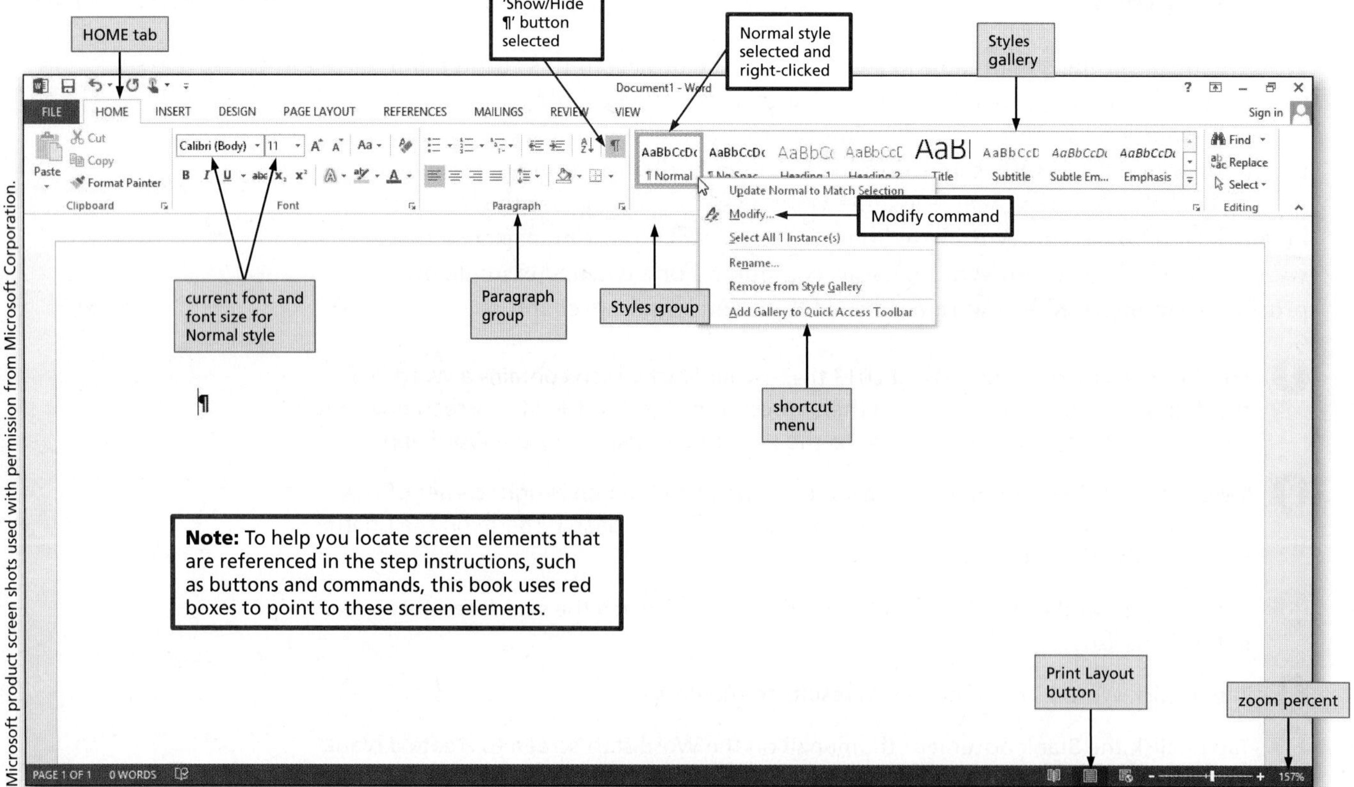

Figure 2

2

- Tap or click Modify on the shortcut menu to display the Modify Style dialog box.

3

- Tap or click the Font arrow (Modify Style dialog box) to display the Font list. Scroll to and then click Times New Roman in the list to change the font for the style being modified.
- Tap or click the Font Size arrow (Modify Style dialog box) and then tap or click 12 in the Font Size list to change the font size for the style being modified.
- Ensure that the 'Only in this document' option button is selected (Figure 3).

4

- Tap or click the OK button (Modify Style dialog box) to update the Normal style to the specified settings.

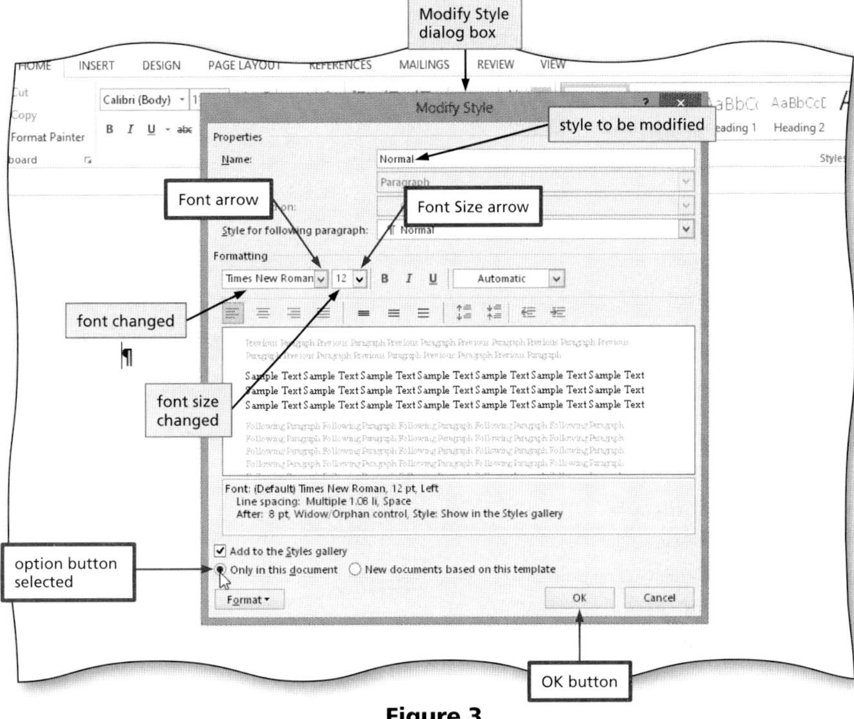

Figure 3

To Change Line Spacing to Double

The following steps change the line spacing to 2.0 to double-space lines in a paragraph. ***Why?*** *The lines of the research paper should be double-spaced, according to the APA documentation style.*

1

- Tap or click the 'Line and Paragraph Spacing' button (HOME tab | Paragraph group) to display the Line and Paragraph Spacing gallery (Figure 4).

2

- Tap or click 2.0 in the Line and Paragraph Spacing gallery to change the line spacing at the location of the insertion point.

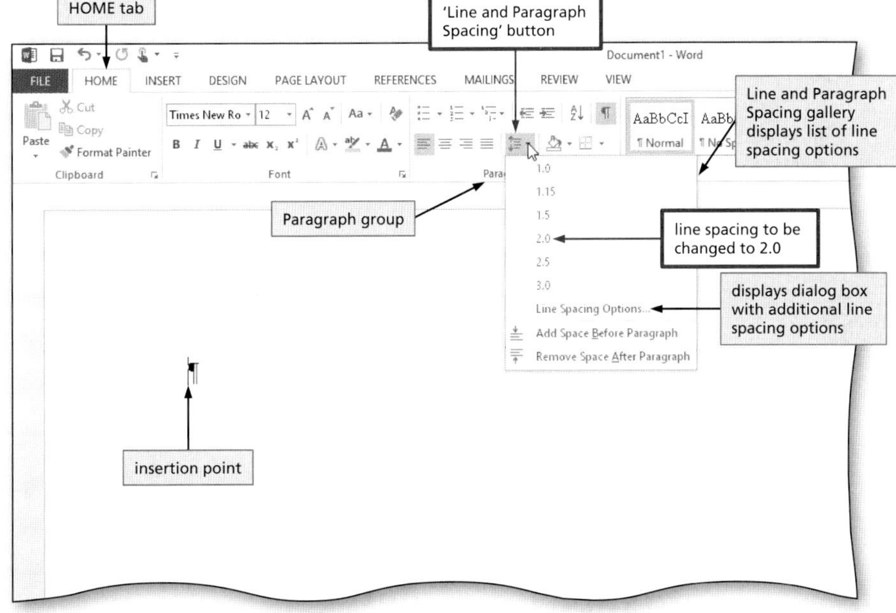

Figure 4

To Remove Space after a Paragraph

The following steps remove space after a paragraph. ***Why?*** *The research paper should not have additional blank space after each paragraph, according to the APA documentation style.*

- Tap or click the 'Line and Paragraph Spacing' button (HOME tab | Paragraph group) to display the Line and Paragraph Spacing gallery (Figure 5).

- Tap or click 'Remove Space After Paragraph' in the Line and Paragraph Spacing gallery so that no blank space appears after paragraphs.

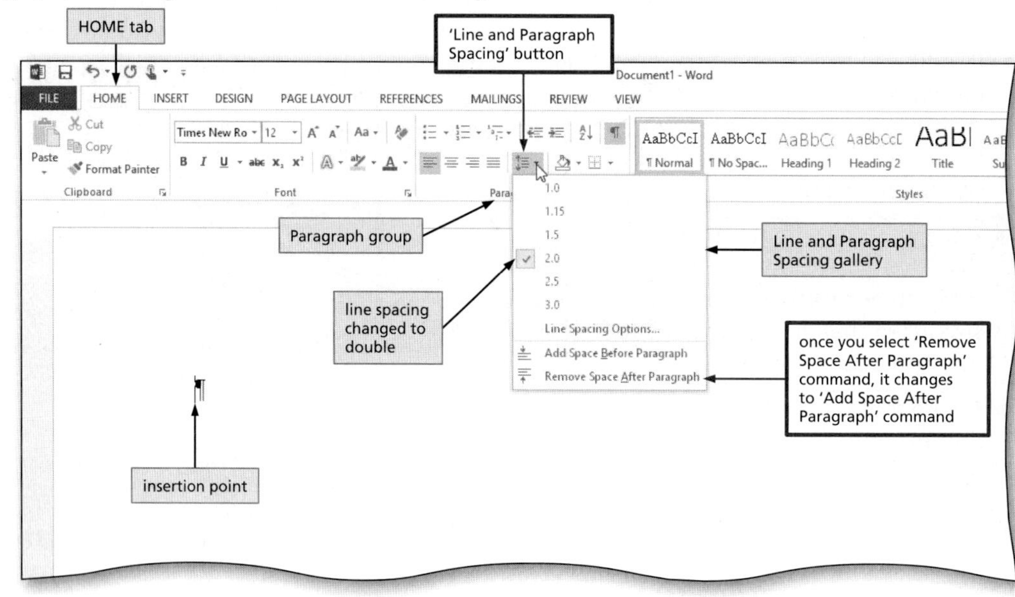

Figure 5

To Update a Style to Match a Selection

To ensure that all paragraphs in the paper will be double-spaced and do not have space after the paragraphs, you want the Normal style to include the line and paragraph spacing changes made in the previous two sets of steps. The following steps update the Normal style. ***Why?*** *You can update a style to reflect the settings of the location of the insertion point or selected text. Because no text has yet been typed in the research paper, you do not need to select text prior to updating the Normal style.*

- Press and hold or right-click Normal in the Styles gallery (HOME tab | Styles group) to display a shortcut menu (Figure 6).

2

- Tap or click 'Update Normal to Match Selection' on the shortcut menu to update the selected (or current) style to reflect the settings at the location of the insertion point.

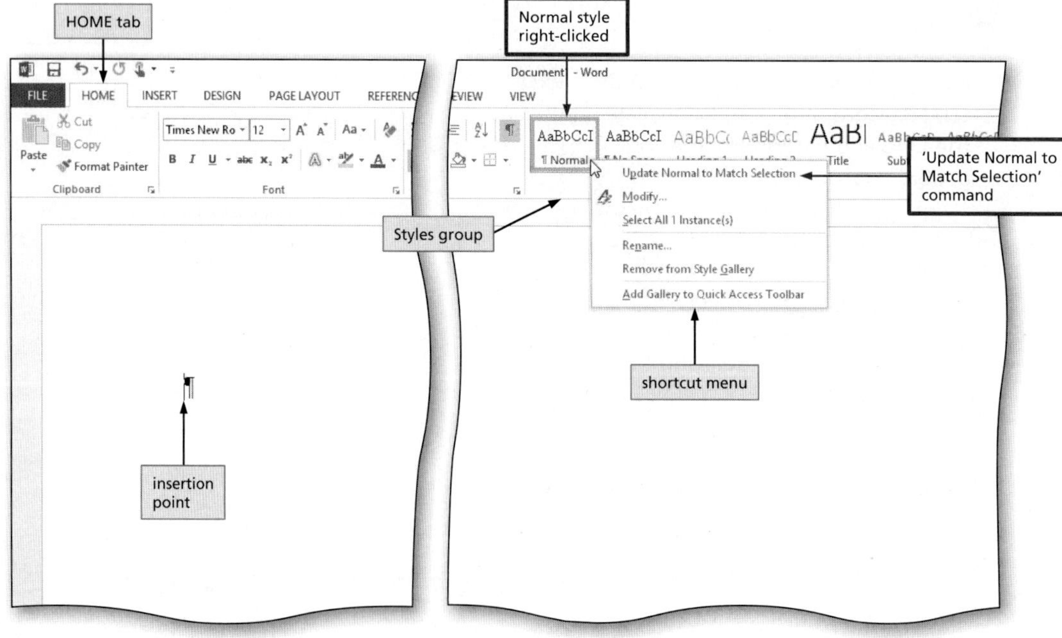

Figure 6

To Insert a Formatted Header and Switch to the Header

In this research paper, the running head is to be placed at the left margin and the page number at the right margin, both on the same line one-half inch from the top of each page. You can insert a formatted header that contains placeholders for text at the left, center, and right locations of the header. ***Why?*** *The APA documentation style requires text at both the left and right margins.* The following steps insert a formatted header and then switch from editing the document text to editing the header.

- Tap or click INSERT on the ribbon to display the INSERT tab.
- Tap or click the 'Add a Header' button (INSERT tab | Header & Footer group) to display the Add a Header gallery (Figure 7).

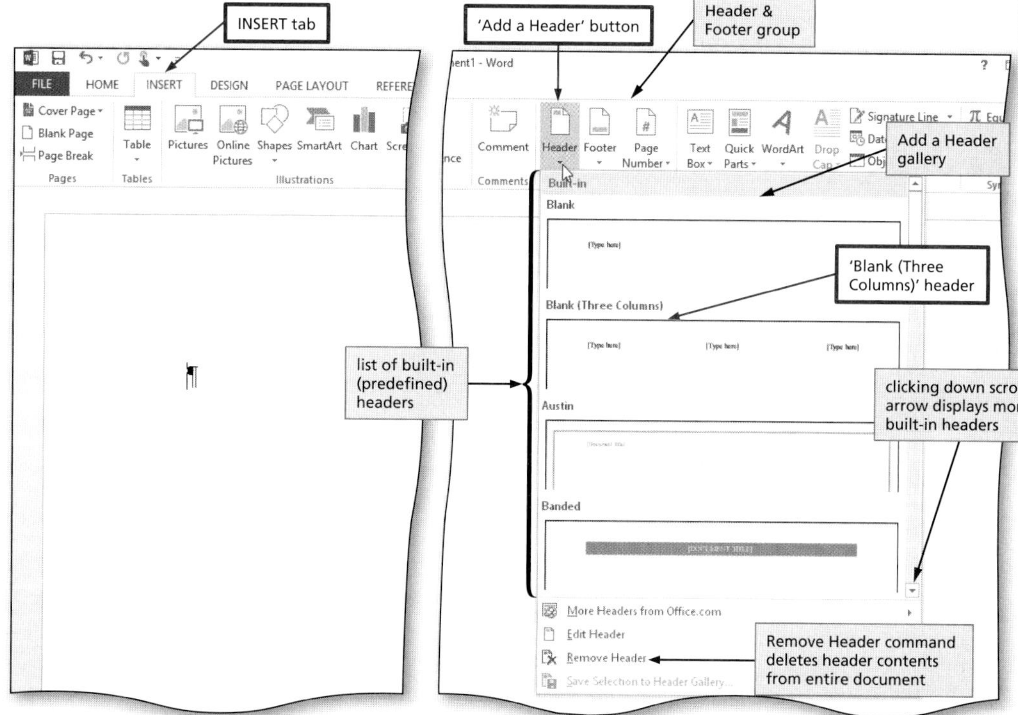

Figure 7

2

- Tap or click 'Blank (Three Columns)' in the Add a Header gallery to insert the selected header design in the document and switch from the document text to the header, which allows you to edit the contents of the header (Figure 8).

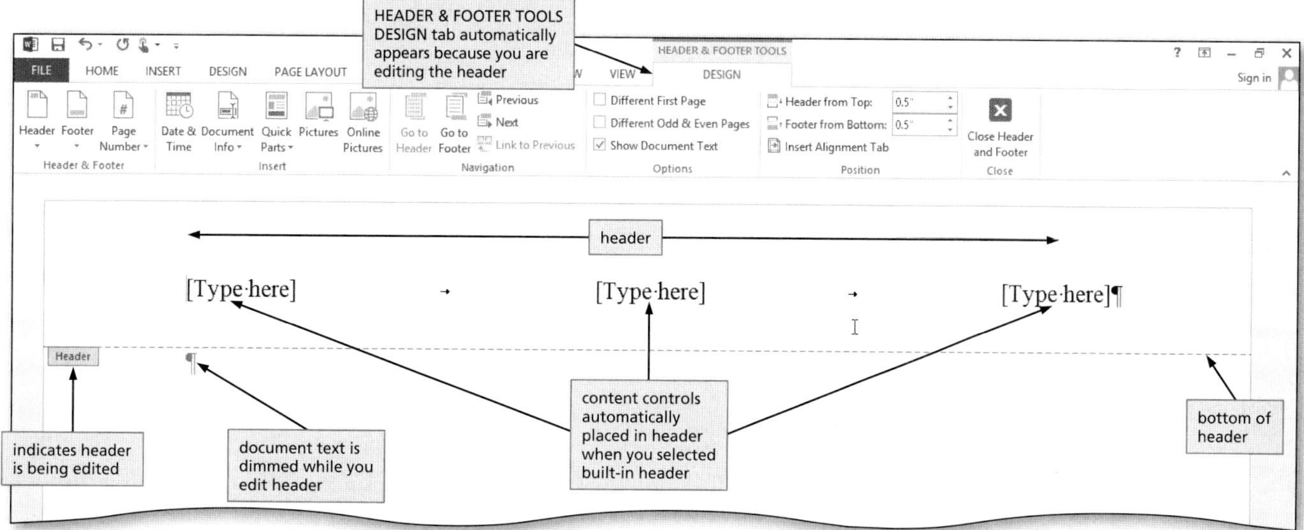

Figure 8

To Enter Text in a Header Content Control

The formatted header contains three content controls (one at the left margin, one centered, and one at the right margin) with a tab character between each content control. A **content control** contains instructions for filling areas of text or graphics. The tab characters, which are formatting marks that indicate the TAB key has been pressed, are displayed because Word uses tab stops to align these content controls. Chapter 3 discusses tab stops in more depth.

To select a content control, you tap or click it. You do not need to delete the selection unless you wish to remove the content control and not enter any replacement text. ***Why?*** *As soon as you begin typing in a selected content control, the text you type replaces the instruction in the control.* The following steps delete the centered content control and then enter the running head at the location of the leftmost content control in the header.

- Tap or click the centered content control in the header to select the content control.
- Press the DELETE key to delete the selected content control.
- Tap or click the leftmost content control in the header to select the content control (Figure 9).

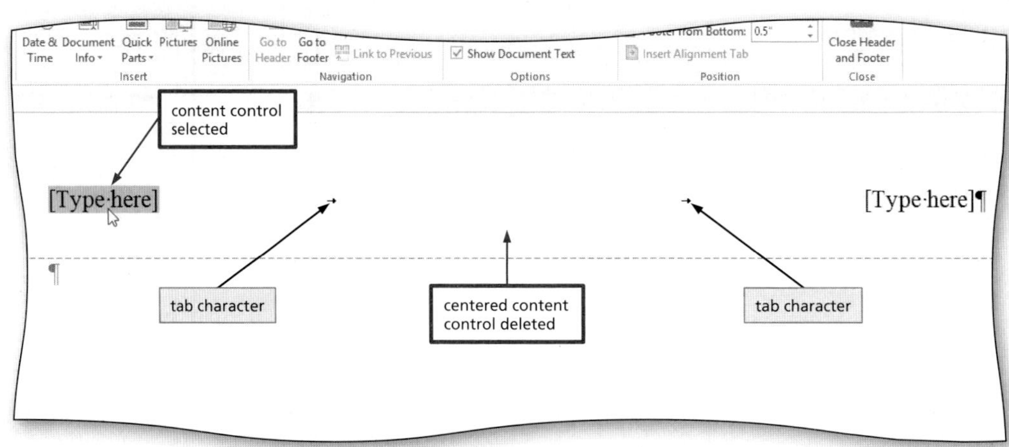

Figure 9

- Type **Running head: ACCESS GRANTED** as the text in the leftmost content control (Figure 10).

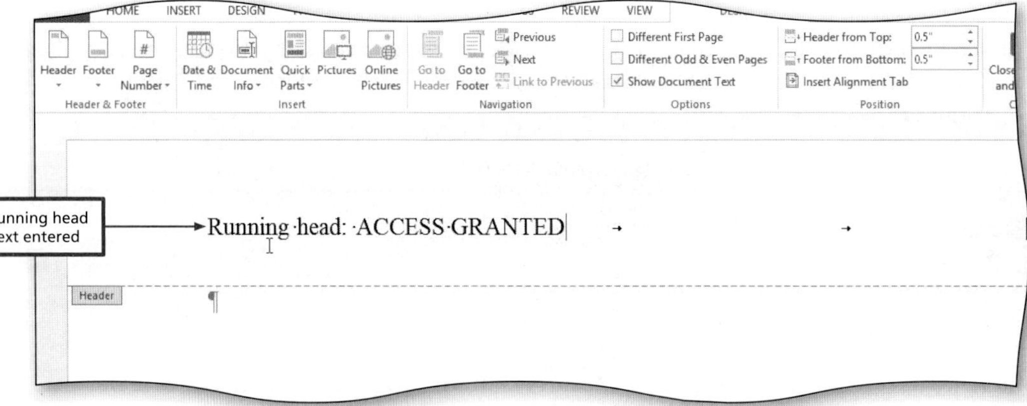

Figure 10

To Count Characters

The next steps count the characters in the running head. ***Why?*** *The running head should be no more than 50 characters, according to the APA documentation style.*

- Drag through the running head text, ACCESS GRANTED, to select the text.
- With the running head selected, tap or click the Word Count indicator on the status bar to display the Word Count dialog box (Figure 11).

- Tap or click the Close button (Word Count dialog box) to close the dialog box.

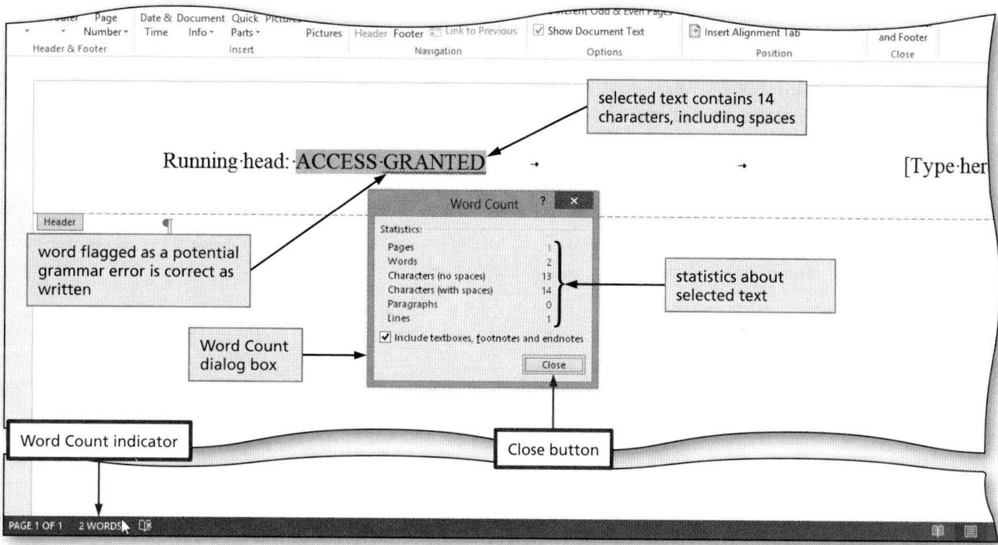

Figure 11

To Insert a Page Number in a Header Content Control

The next task is to insert the current page number in the header. ***Why?*** *The APA documentation style requires a page number in the upper-right corner of each page in the paper.* The following steps insert a page number at the location of the rightmost content control in the header.

- Tap or click the rightmost content control in the header to select the content control.
- Tap or click the 'Add Page Numbers' button (HEADER & FOOTER TOOLS DESIGN tab | Header & Footer group) to display the Add Page Numbers menu.
- Tap or point to Current Position on the Add Page Numbers menu to display the Current Position gallery (Figure 12).

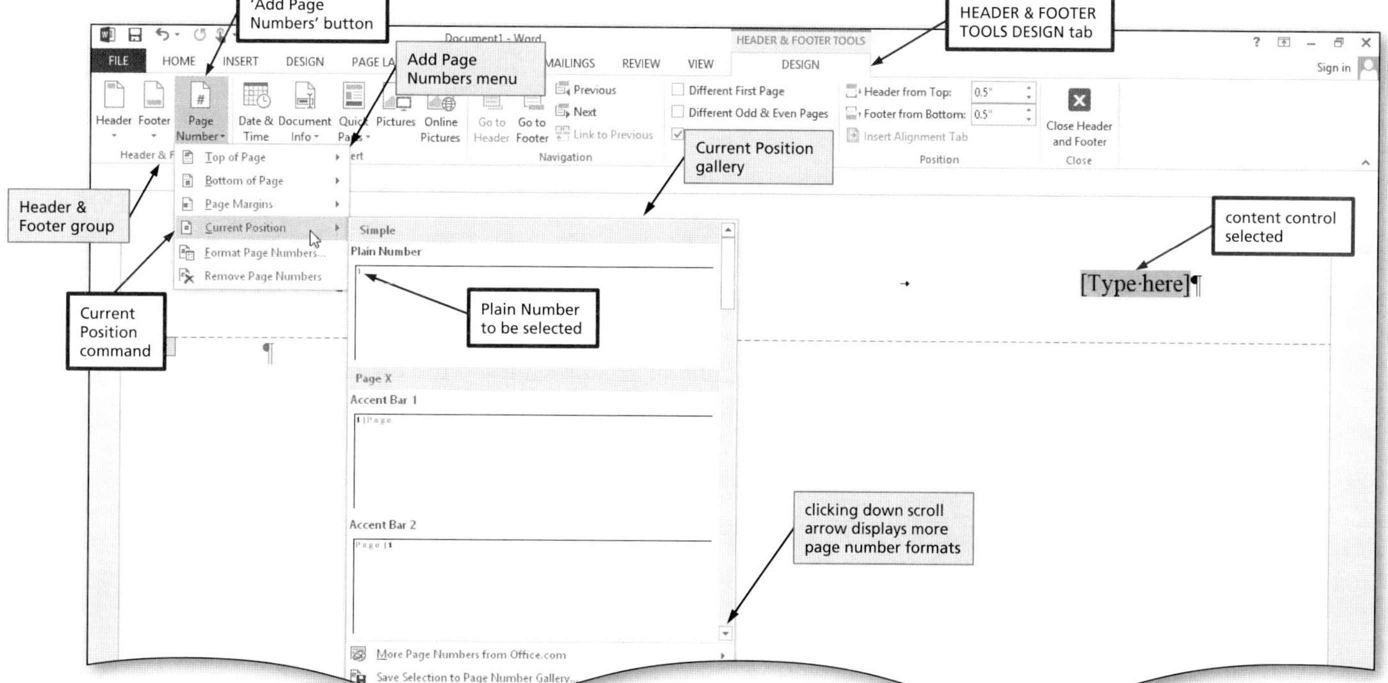

Figure 12

2

- Tap or click Plain Number in the Current Position gallery to insert an unformatted page number at the location of the selected content control in the header (Figure 13).

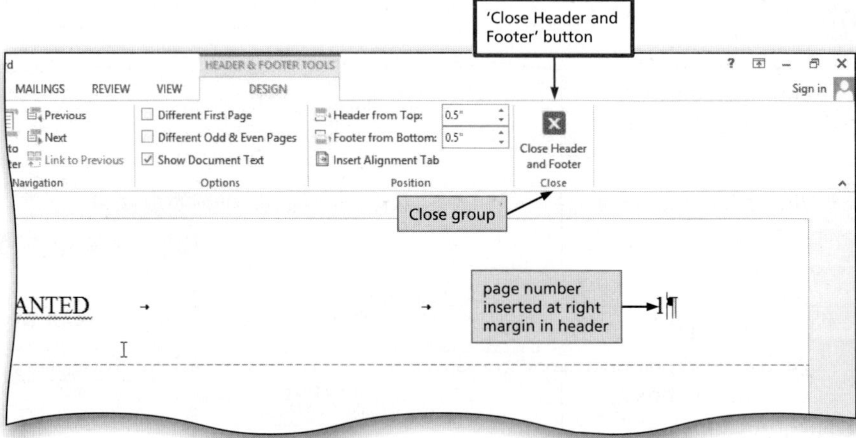

Figure 13

To Close the Header

The next task is to switch back to the document text. ***Why?*** *You are finished entering text in the header.* The following step closes the header.

- Tap or click the 'Close Header and Footer' button (HEADER & FOOTER TOOLS DESIGN tab | Close group) (shown in Figure 13) to close the header and switch back to the document text (Figure 14).

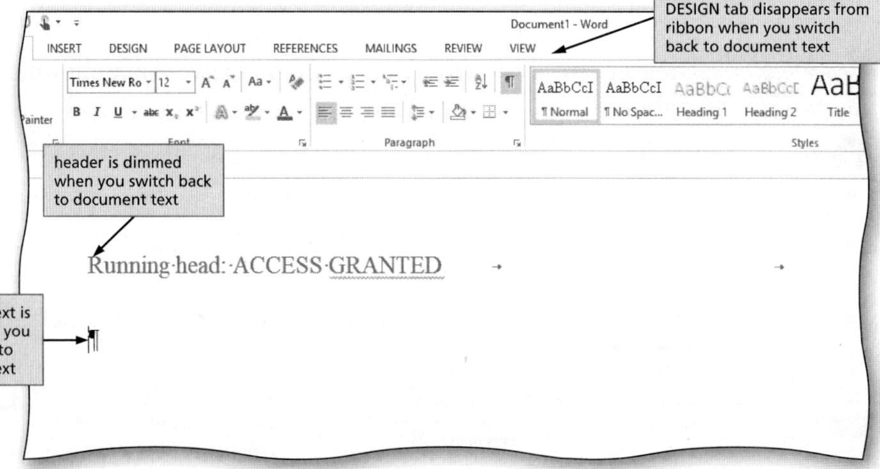

Figure 14

To Type the Title Page Text

In addition to the header, which appears on every page in the paper, the title page for this research paper should contain the complete paper title, author name, and institutional affiliation, all centered on separate lines in the upper-half of the page. The next steps type the title page text.

1. With the insertion point at the top of the document, press the ENTER key six times.
2. Tap or click the Center button (HOME tab | Paragraph group) to center the insertion point.
3. Type `Access Granted` and then press the ENTER key.
4. Type `Teddy Bailey` and then press the ENTER key.
5. Type `Andrews College` and then press the ENTER key (Figure 15).

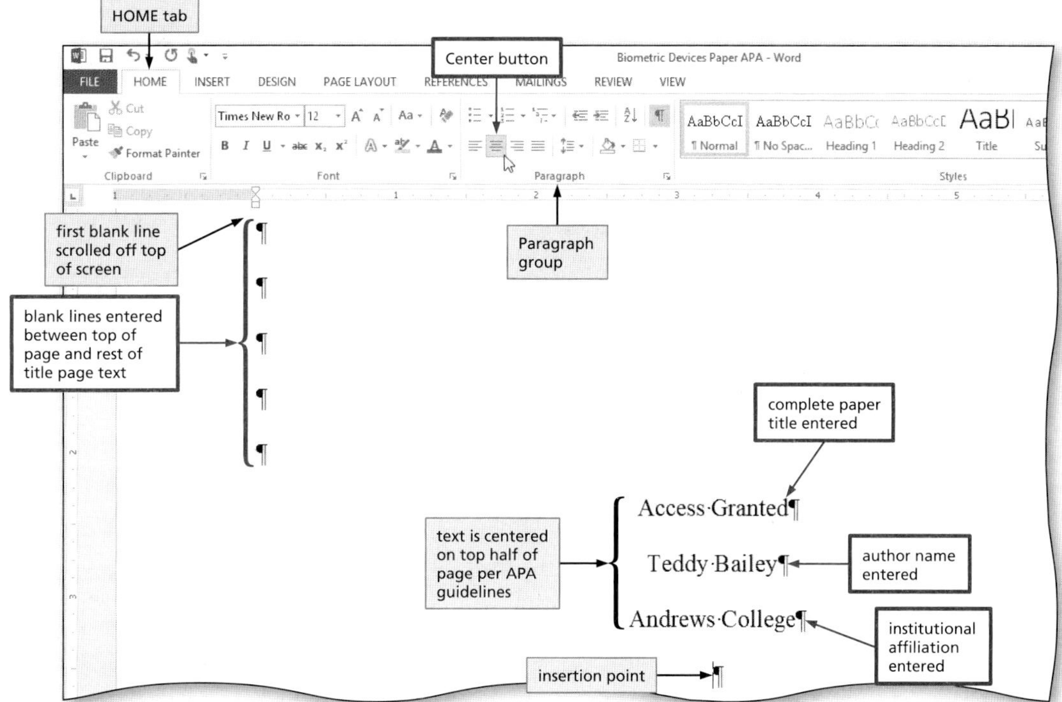

Figure 15

To Page Break Manually

To move the insertion point to the next page, you insert a manual page break. ***Why?*** *According to the APA documentation style, the abstract page is to be displayed on a separate numbered page.*

A **manual page break**, or **hard page break**, is one that you force into the document at a specific location. Word never moves or adjusts manual page breaks. Word, however, does adjust any automatic page breaks that follow a manual page break. Word inserts manual page breaks immediately above or to the left of the location of the insertion point. The following step inserts a manual page break after the title page text of the research paper.

- Verify that the insertion point is positioned below the name of the college on the title page, as shown in Figure 15.
- Tap or click INSERT on the ribbon to display the INSERT tab.
- Tap or click the 'Insert a Page Break' button (INSERT tab | Pages group) to insert a manual page break immediately to the left of the insertion point and position the insertion point immediately below the manual page break (Figure 16).

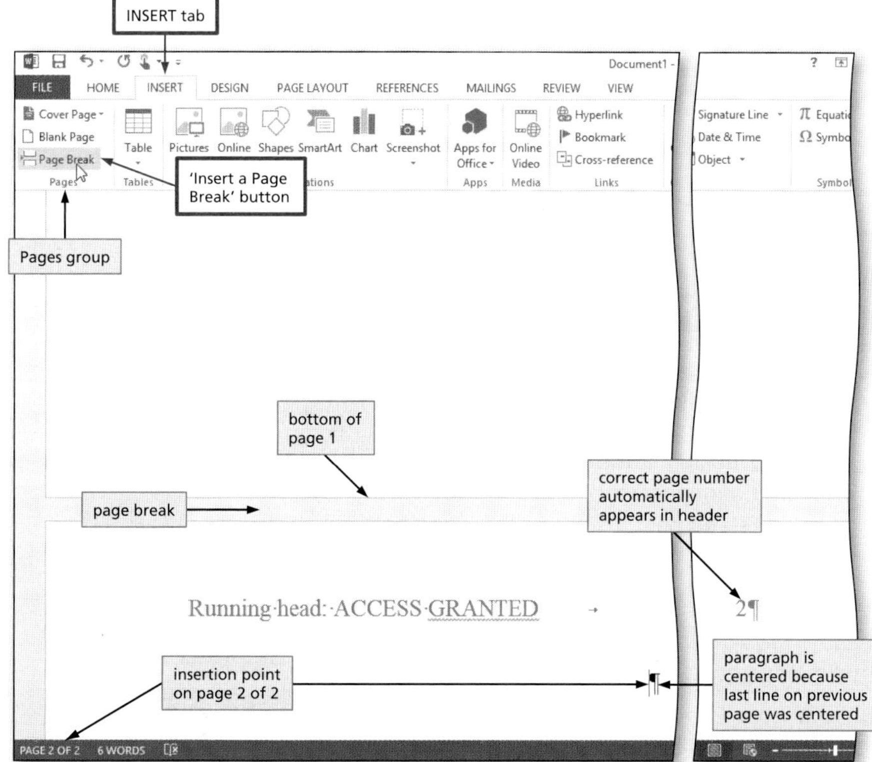

Figure 16

To Type the Abstract

The abstract is a one-page or less summary of the most important points in the research paper. The title should be centered, and the paragraph below the title should be left-aligned. The following steps type the title centered, left-align a paragraph, and then type the abstract in the research paper.

1. Type **Abstract** and then press the ENTER key to enter the title for the page containing the abstract.
2. Press CTRL+L to left-align the current paragraph, that is, the paragraph containing the insertion point. (Recall from Chapter 1 that a notation such as CTRL+L means to press the letter L on the keyboard while holding down the CTRL key.)
3. Type the abstract text as shown in Figure 17.

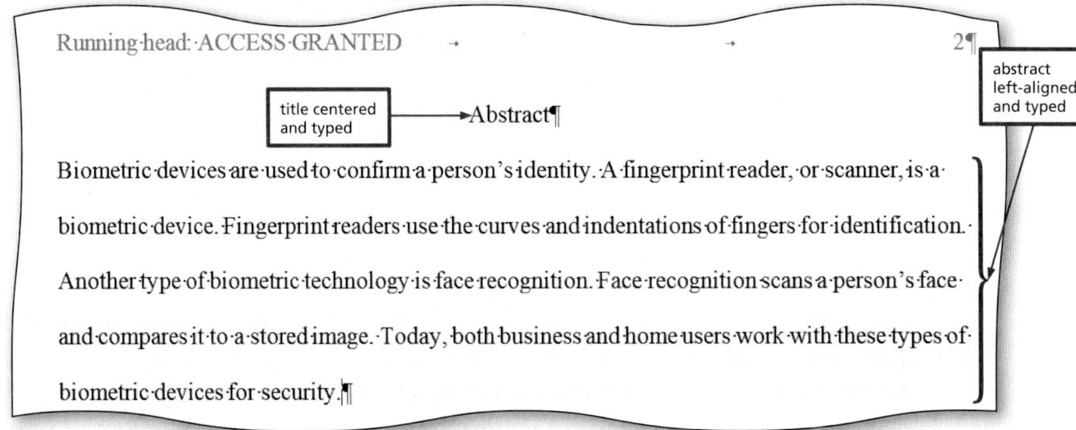

Figure 17

To Count Words

When you write papers, you often are required to compose the papers with a minimum number of words. The following steps verify the number of words in the abstract. ***Why?*** *The APA documentation style specifies that the abstract in a research paper should contain no more than 250 words, sometimes no more than 150 words.*

- Select the paragraph containing the abstract.
- Verify the number of words in the selected text by looking at the Word Count indicator on the status bar (Figure 18).

- Tap or click anywhere in the abstract to remove the selection from the text.

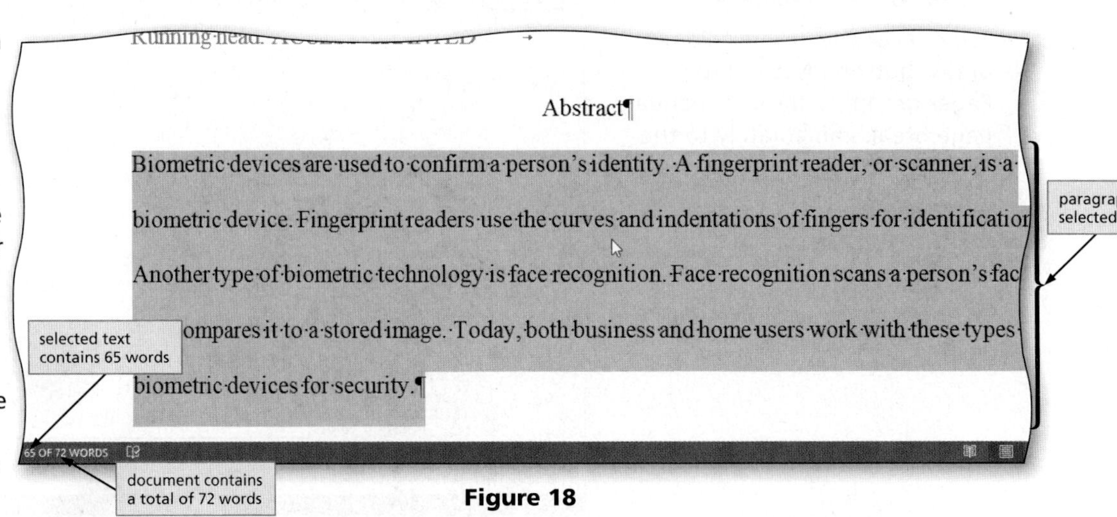

Figure 18

To Page Break Manually

The abstract is complete, and the text for the research paper should begin on a new page. The following steps insert a manual page break after the abstract.

1. Press CTRL+END to position the insertion point at the end of the document, which is the end of the abstract in this case.
2. Tap or click the 'Insert a Page Break' button (INSERT tab | Pages group) to insert a manual page break immediately to the left of the insertion point and position the insertion point immediately below the manual page break.

To Enter the Paper Title

The following steps enter the title of the research paper centered between the page margins.

1. Center the paragraph containing the insertion point.
2. Type **`Access Granted`** and then press the ENTER key to enter the title of the paper (Figure 19).

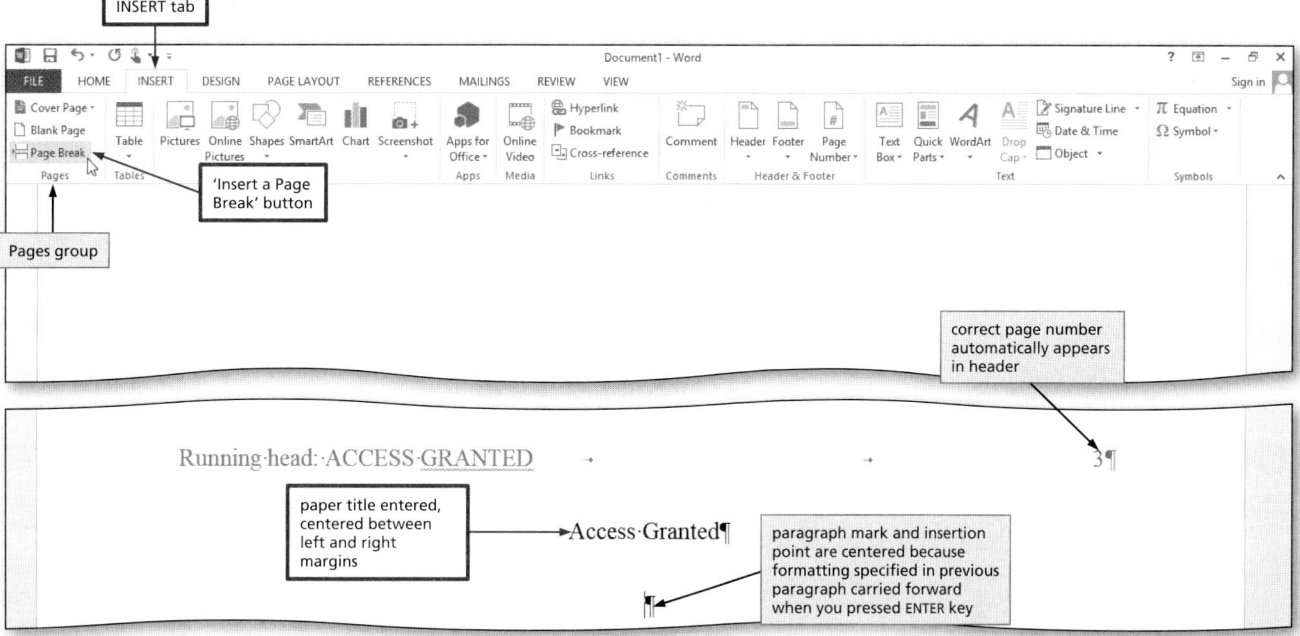

Figure 19

To Format Text

The paragraphs below the paper title should be left-aligned, instead of centered. Thus, the following step left-aligns the paragraph below the paper title.

1. Press CTRL+L to left-align the current paragraph, that is, the paragraph containing the insertion point.

To Display Rulers and First-Line Indent Paragraphs

If you are using a mouse, you can use the horizontal ruler, usually simply called the **ruler**, to indent just the first line of a paragraph, which is called a **first-line indent**. The left margin on the ruler contains two triangles above a square. The **First Line Indent marker** is the top triangle at the 0" mark on the ruler (Figure 20). The bottom triangle is discussed later in this appendix. The small square at the 0" mark is the Left Indent marker. The **Left Indent marker** allows you to change the entire left margin, whereas the First Line Indent marker indents only the first line of the paragraph.

The following steps first-line indent paragraphs in the research paper. ***Why?*** *The first line of each paragraph in the research paper is to be indented one-half inch from the left margin, according to the APA documentation style.*

- Tap or click VIEW on the ribbon to display the VIEW tab.
- If the rulers are not displayed, tap or click the View Ruler check box (VIEW tab | Show group) to place a check mark in the check box and display the horizontal and vertical rulers on the screen.

- If you are using a mouse, with the insertion point on the paragraph mark below the research paper title, point to the 'First Line Indent' marker on the ruler (Figure 20).

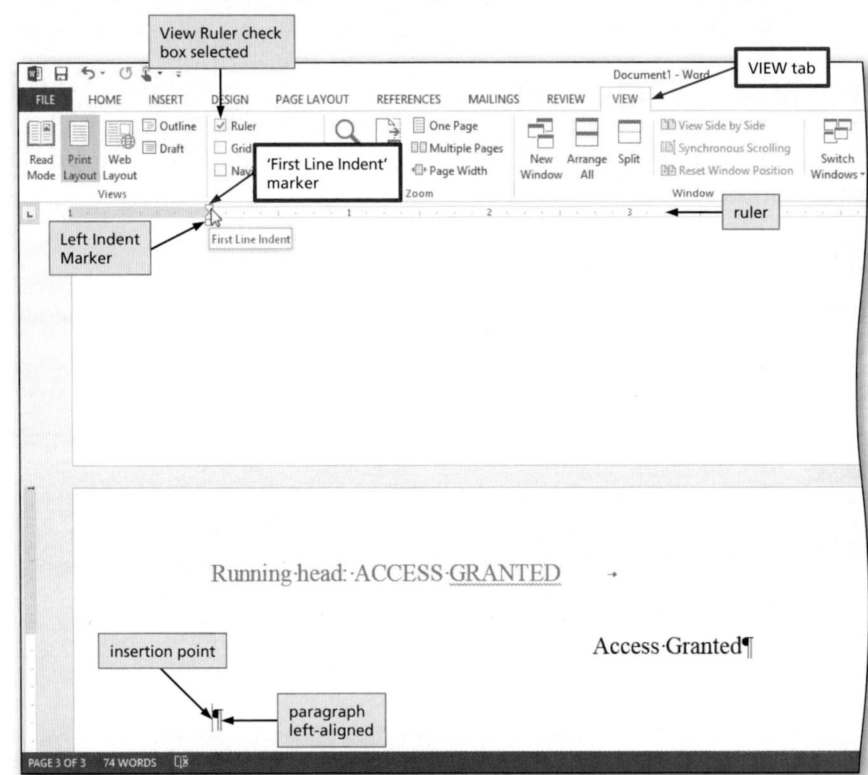

Figure 20

- If you are using a mouse, drag the 'First Line Indent' marker to the .5" mark on the ruler to display a vertical dotted line in the document window, which indicates the proposed indent location of the first line of the paragraph (Figure 21).

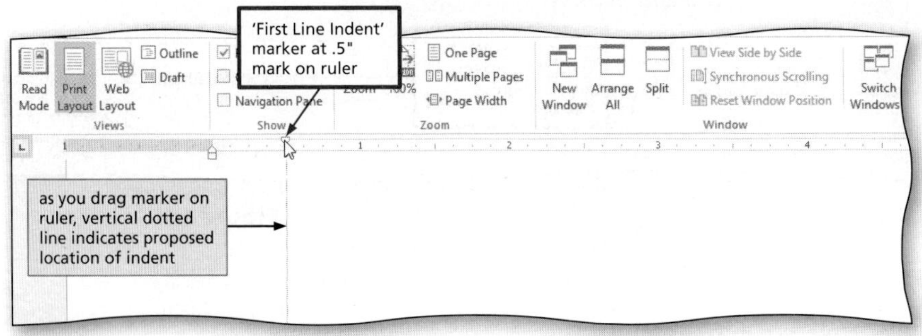

Figure 21

- If you are using a mouse, release the mouse button to place the 'First Line Indent' marker at the .5" mark on the ruler, or one-half inch from the left margin.
- If you are using a touch screen, you cannot drag the 'First Line Indent' marker and must follow these steps instead: tap the Paragraph Settings Dialog Box Launcher (HOME tab or PAGE LAYOUT tab | Paragraph group) to display the Paragraph dialog box, tap the Indents and Spacing tab (Paragraph dialog box), tap the Special arrow, tap First line, and then tap the OK button.

5
- Type **Biometric devices authenticate a person's identity by verifying unique personal characteristics.** and notice that Word automatically indented the first line of the paragraph by one-half inch (Figure 22).

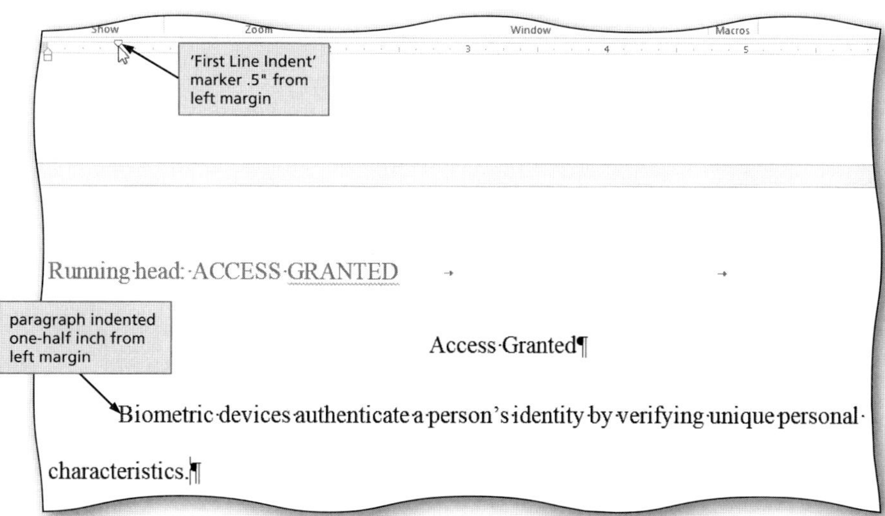

Figure 22

To Type the First and Second Paragraphs

The following steps type the remainder of the first paragraph and the second paragraph in the research paper.

1. Press the SPACEBAR. Type the remainder of the first paragraph of the research paper as shown in Figure 23 and then press the ENTER key.

2. Type the second paragraph of the research paper as shown in Figure 23.

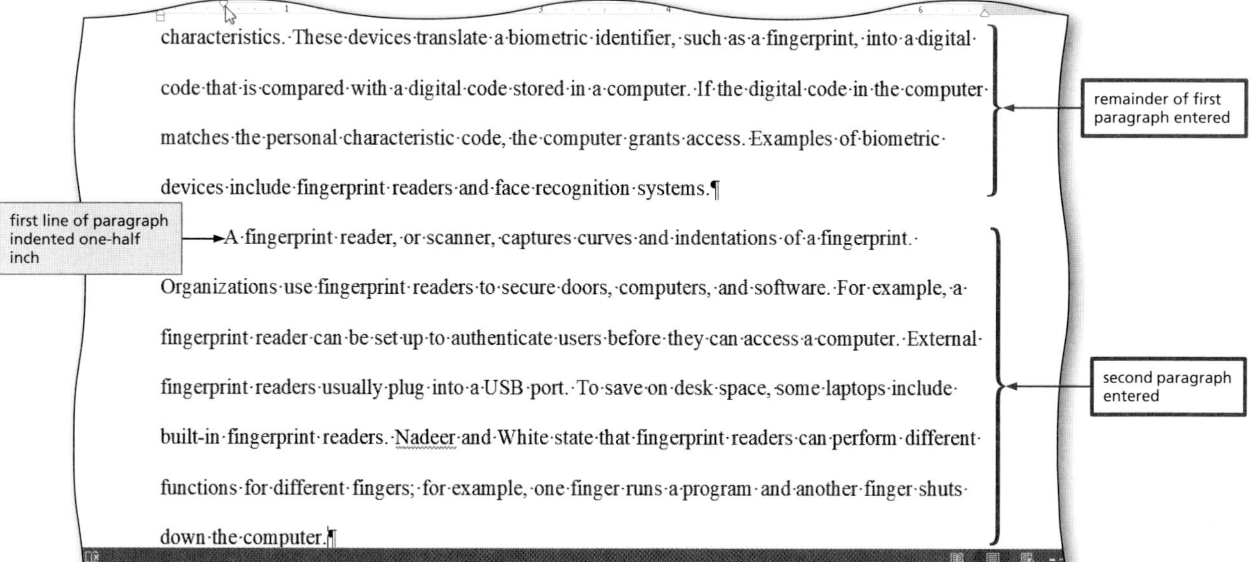

Figure 23

To Save a Document

You have performed many tasks while creating this research paper and do not want to risk losing work completed thus far. Accordingly, you should save the document. The following steps assume you already have created folders for storing your files, for example, a CIS 101 folder (for your class) that contains a Word folder (for your assignments). Thus, these steps save the document in the Word folder in the CIS 101 folder using the file name, Biometric Devices Paper APA.

1. Tap or click the Save button on the Quick Access Toolbar, which depending on settings, will display either the Save As gallery in the Backstage view or the Save As dialog box.

2. To save on a hard disk or other storage media on your computer, proceed to Step 2a. To save on SkyDrive, proceed to Step 2b.

2a. If your screen opens the Backstage view and you want to save on storage media on your computer, tap or click Computer in the left pane, if necessary, to display options in the right pane related to saving on your computer. If your screen already displays the Save As dialog box, proceed to Step 4.

2b. If your screen opens the Backstage view and you want to save on SkyDrive, tap or click SkyDrive in the left pane to display SkyDrive saving options or a Sign In button. If your screen displays a Sign In button, tap or click it and then sign in to SkyDrive.

3. Tap or click the Browse button in the right pane to display the Save As dialog box associated with the selected save location (i.e., Computer or SkyDrive).

4. Type **`Biometric Devices Paper APA`** in the File name box to change the file name. Do not press the ENTER key after typing the file name because you do not want to close the dialog box at this time.

5. Navigate to the desired save location (in this case, the Word folder in the CIS 101 folder [or your class folder] on your computer or SkyDrive).

6. Tap or click the Save button (Save As dialog box) to save the research paper in the selected folder on the selected save location with the entered file name.

To Change the Bibliography Style

The APA guidelines suggest the use of in-text citations instead of footnoting each source of material in a paper. These parenthetical acknowledgments guide the reader to the end of the paper for complete information about the source.

The first step in inserting a citation is to be sure the citations and sources will be formatted using the correct documentation style, called the bibliography style in Word. ***Why?*** *You want to ensure that Word is using the APA documentation style for this paper.* The following steps change the specified documentation style.

- Tap or click REFERENCES on the ribbon to display the REFERENCES tab.
- Tap or click the Bibliography Style arrow (REFERENCES tab | Citations & Bibliography group) to display the Bibliography Style gallery, which lists predefined documentation styles (Figure 24).

- Tap or click 'APA Sixth Edition' in the Bibliography Style gallery to change the documentation style to APA.

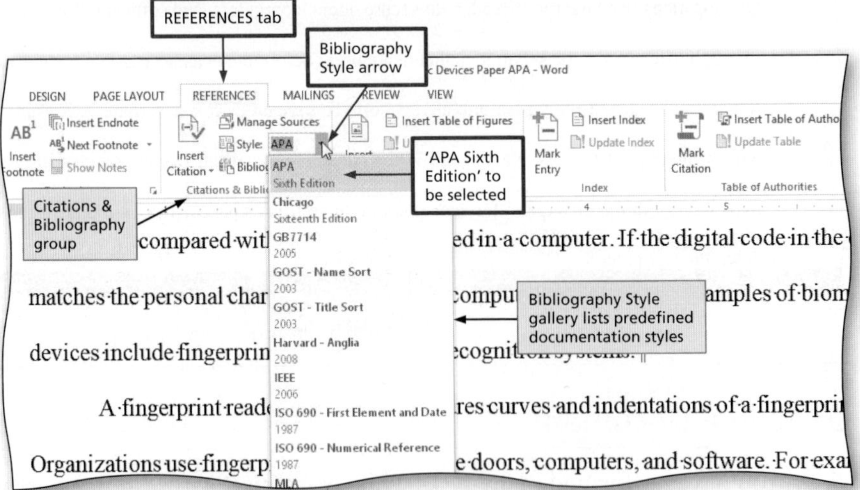

Figure 24

To Insert a Citation and Create Its Source

With the documentation style selected, the next task is to insert a citation at the location of the insertion point and enter the source information for the citation. You can accomplish these steps at once by instructing Word to add a new source. The following steps add a new source for a magazine (periodical) article on the web. ***Why?*** *The material preceding the insertion point was summarized from a magazine article on the web.*

- Position the insertion point at the location for the citation (in this case, after the word, computer, in the third sentence of the second paragraph before the period) and then press the SPACEBAR.

- Tap or click the Insert Citation button (REFERENCES tab | Citations & Bibliography group) to display the Insert Citation menu (Figure 25).

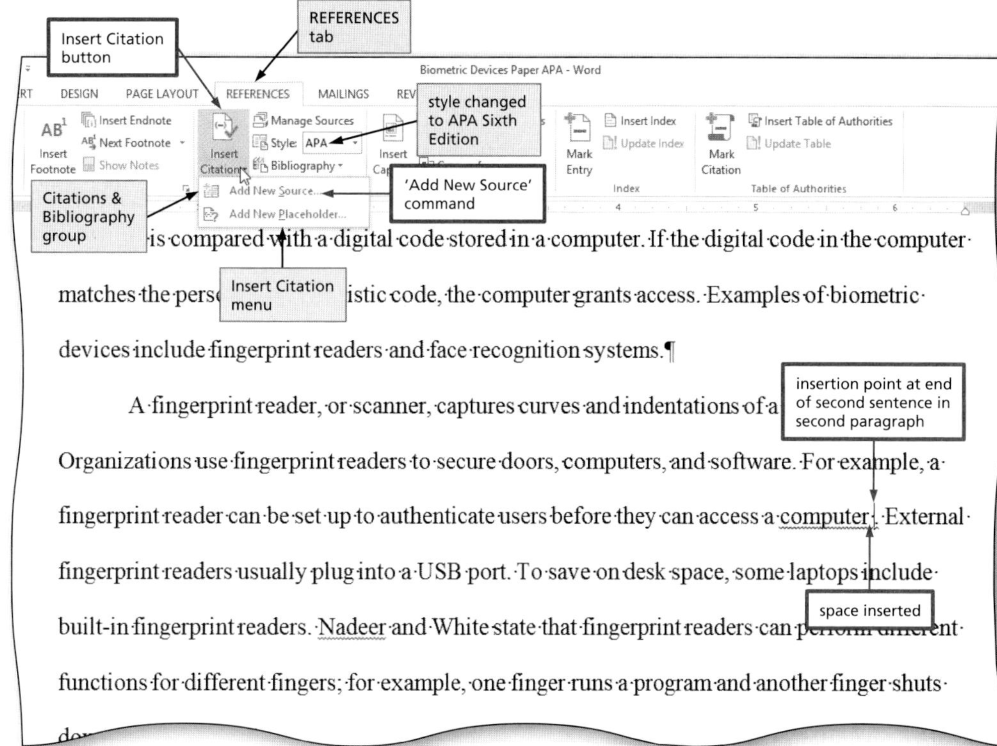

Figure 25

3

- Tap or click 'Add New Source' on the Insert Citation menu to display the Create Source dialog box (Figure 26).

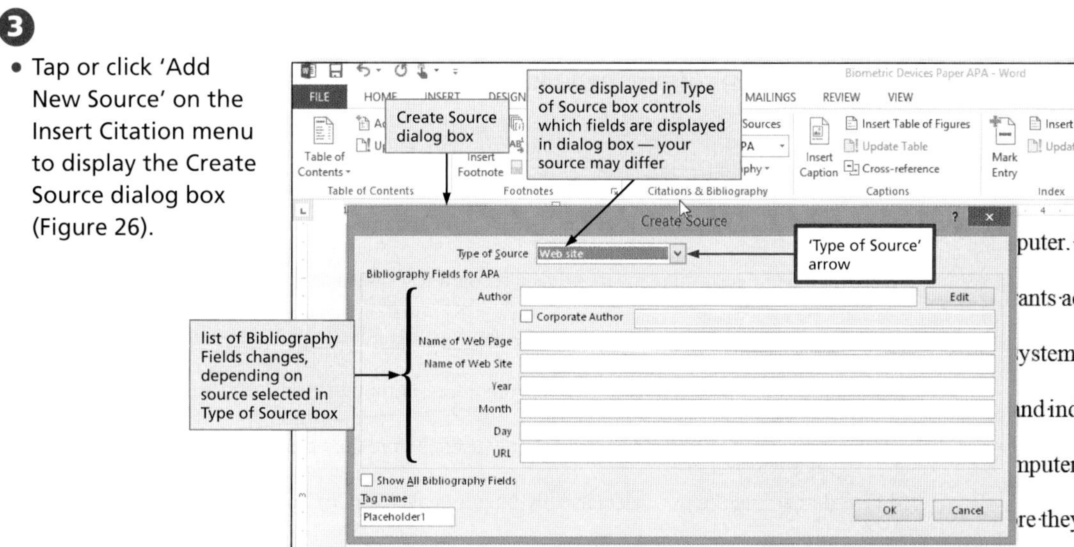

Figure 26

4

- If necessary, tap or click the 'Type of Source' arrow (Create Source dialog box) and then tap or click 'Article in a Periodical', so that the list shows fields required for a magazine (periodical).
- Tap or click the Author text box. Type **`Rossi, M. E.`** as the author.
- Tap or click the Title text box. Type **`How to use fingerprint readers`** as the article title.
- Press the TAB key and then type **`Digital Security Review`** as the periodical title.
- Press the TAB key and then type **`2014`** as the year.
- Press the TAB key and then type **`Aug.`** as the month.
- Press the TAB key twice and then type **`n. pag.`** as the number of pages (Figure 27).

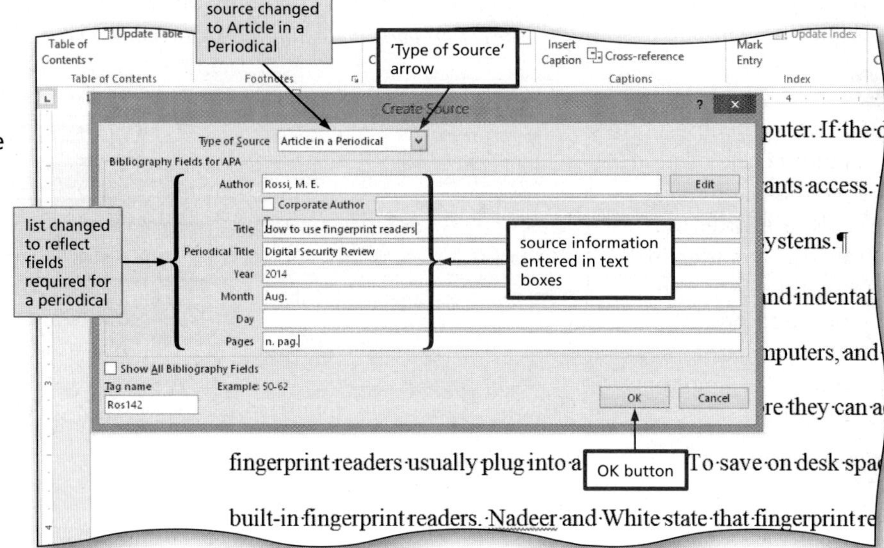

Figure 27

- Place a check mark in the 'Show All Bibliography Fields' check box so that Word displays all fields available for the selected source, including the date viewed (accessed) fields.
- If necessary, scroll to the bottom of the Bibliography Fields list to display the URL field.

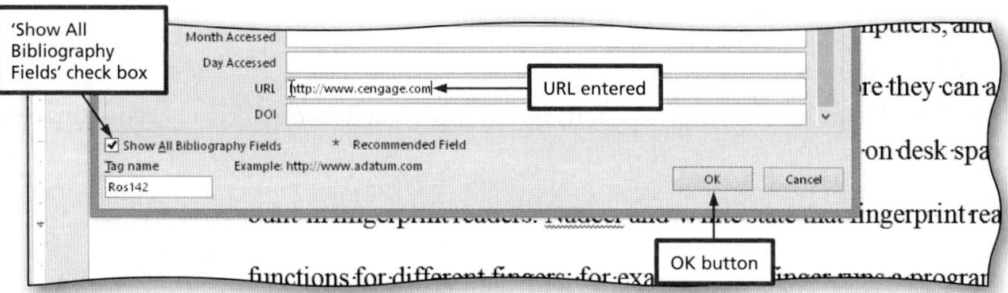

Figure 28

- Tap or click the URL text box and then type **`http://www.cengage.com`** (Figure 28).

6

- Tap or click the OK button to close the dialog box, create the source, and insert the citation in the document at the location of the insertion point (Figure 29).

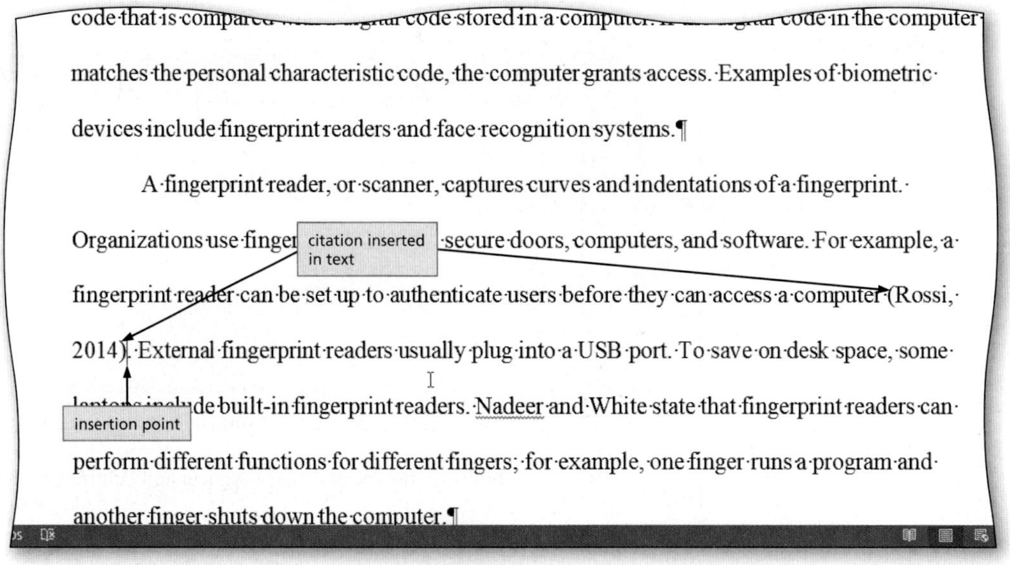

Figure 29

To Insert Another Citation and Create Its Source

The following steps add a new source for a book.

1. Position the insertion point at the location for the citation (in this case, after the word, computer, in the last sentence of the second paragraph) and then press the SPACEBAR.
2. If necessary, display the REFERENCES tab. Tap or click the Insert Citation button (REFERENCES tab | Citations & Bibliography group) to display the Insert Citation menu.
3. Tap or click 'Add New Source' on the Insert Citation menu to display the Create Source dialog box.
4. If necessary, tap or click the 'Type of Source' arrow (Create Source dialog box) and then tap or click Book, so that the list shows fields required for a Book.
5. Type `Nadeer, A. S.; White, J. R.` in the Author text box.
6. Type `Biometric security` the Title text box.
7. Type `2014` in the Year text box.
8. Type `Chicago` in the City text box.
9. Type `Windy City Press` in the Publisher text box (Figure 30).
10. Click the OK button to close the dialog box, create the source, and insert the citation in the document at the location of the insertion point.

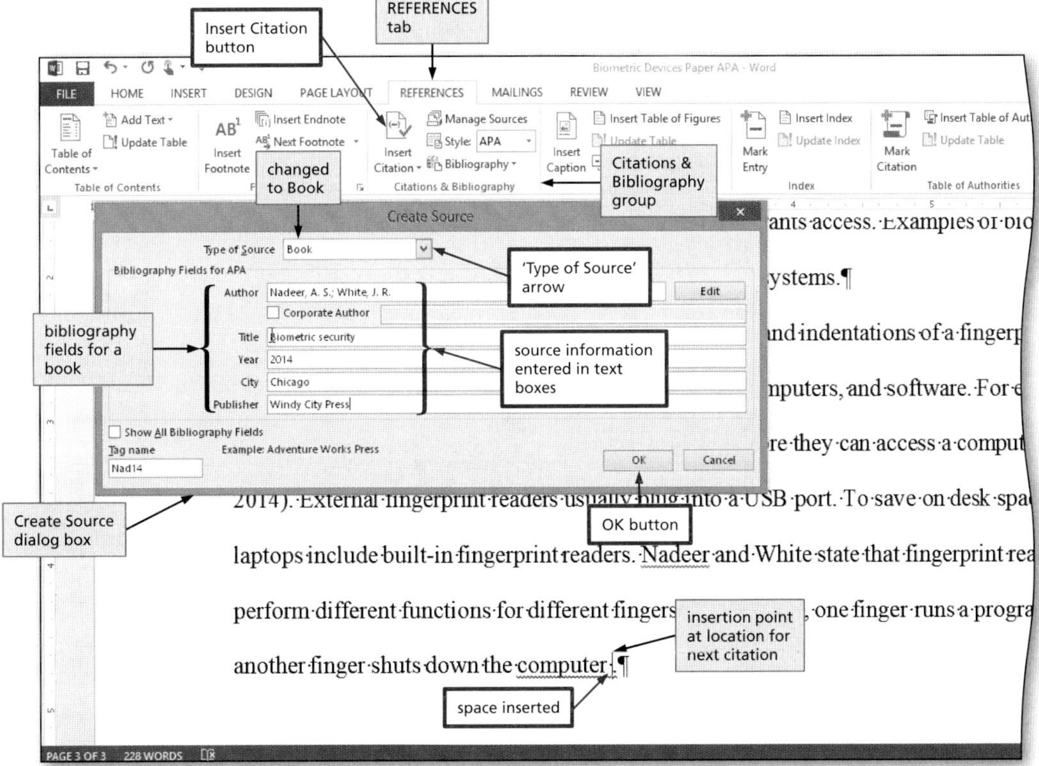

Figure 30

To Edit a Citation

In the APA documentation style, if you reference the author's name in the text, you should not list it again in the citation. Instead, just list the publication year in the citation. To do this, instruct Word to suppress the author and title. ***Why?*** *If you suppress the author, Word automatically displays the title, so you need to suppress both the author and title if you want just the page number(s) to be displayed.* The steps on the next page edit the citation, suppressing the author and title but displaying the year.

- If necessary, tap or click somewhere in the citation to be edited, in this case somewhere in (Nadeer and White), which selects the citation and displays the Citation Options arrow.
- Tap or click the Citation Options arrow to display the Citation Options menu (Figure 31).

- Tap or click Edit Citation on the Citation Options menu to display the Edit Citation dialog box.
- Tap or click the Author check box (Edit Citations dialog box) to place a check mark in it.
- Tap or click the Title check box to place a check mark in it (Figure 32).

- Tap or click the OK button to close the dialog box, remove the author name from the citation, and suppress the title from showing.
- Press CTRL+END to move the insertion point to the end of the document (paragraph, in this case), which also removes the selection from the citation (Figure 33).

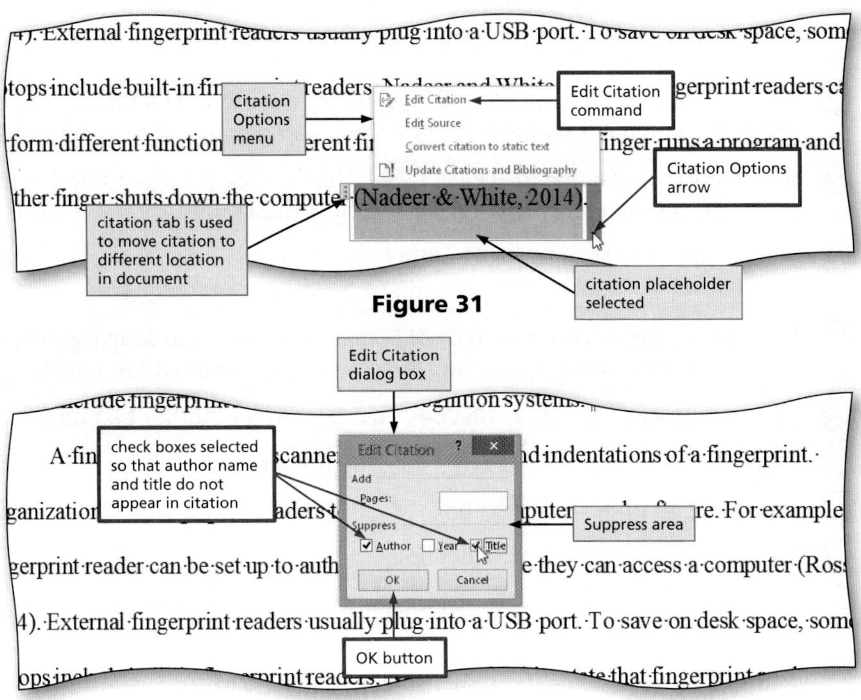

Figure 31

Figure 32

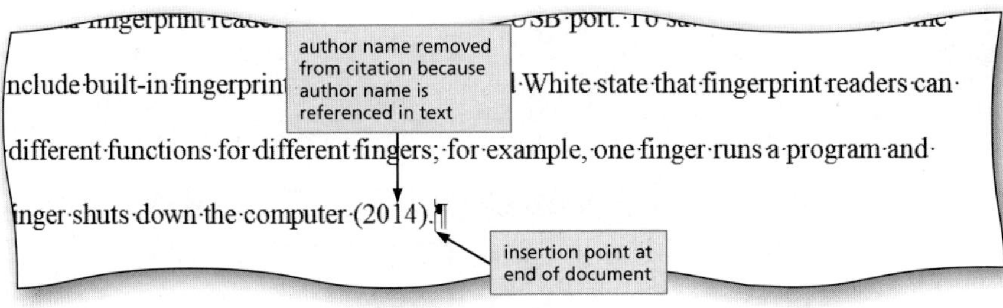

Figure 33

To Type the Third Paragraph

The following steps continue typing text in the research paper.

1. Press the ENTER key.
2. Type the third paragraph of the research paper as shown in Figure 34.

A·face·recognition·system·captures·a·live·face·image·and·compares·it·with·a·stored·image·to·determine·if·the·person·is·a·legitimate·user.·Some·buildings·use·face·recognition·systems·to·secure·access·to·rooms.·Law·enforcement,·surveillance·systems,·and·airports·use·face·recognition·systems·to·protect·the·public.·Some·mobile·devices·use·face·recognition·systems·to·unlock·the·device.·Face·recognition·systems·are·becoming·more·sophisticated·and·can·recognize·people·with·or·without·glasses,·hats,·facial·hair,·makeup,·or·jewelry,·and·with·new·hairstyles.¶

third paragraph entered

Figure 34

To Insert Another Citation and Create Its Source

The following steps add a new source for a Web site.

1. Position the insertion point at the location for the citation (in this case, after the word, hairstyles, in the last sentence of the third paragraph but before the period) and then press the SPACEBAR to insert a space.
2. Tap or click the Insert Citation button (REFERENCES tab | Citations & Bibliography group) to display the Insert Citation menu.
3. Tap or click 'Add New Source' on the Insert Citation menu to display the Create Source dialog box.
4. If necessary, tap or click the 'Type of Source' arrow (Create Source dialog box) and then tap or click Web site, so that the list shows fields required for a Web site.
5. Place a check mark in the 'Show All Bibliography Fields' check box so that Word displays all fields available for the selected source, including the date viewed (accessed) fields.
6. Type **`Allensmith, S. C.`** in the Author text box.
7. Type **`Understanding face recognition systems`** in the 'Name of Web Page' text box.
8. Type **`2014`** in the Year Accessed text box.
9. Type **`Sept.`** in the Month Accessed text box.
10. Type **`16`** in the Day Accessed text box.
11. Type **`http://www.cengage.com`** in the URL text box (Figure 35).
12. Tap or click the OK button to close the dialog box, create the source, and insert the citation in the document at the location of the insertion point.

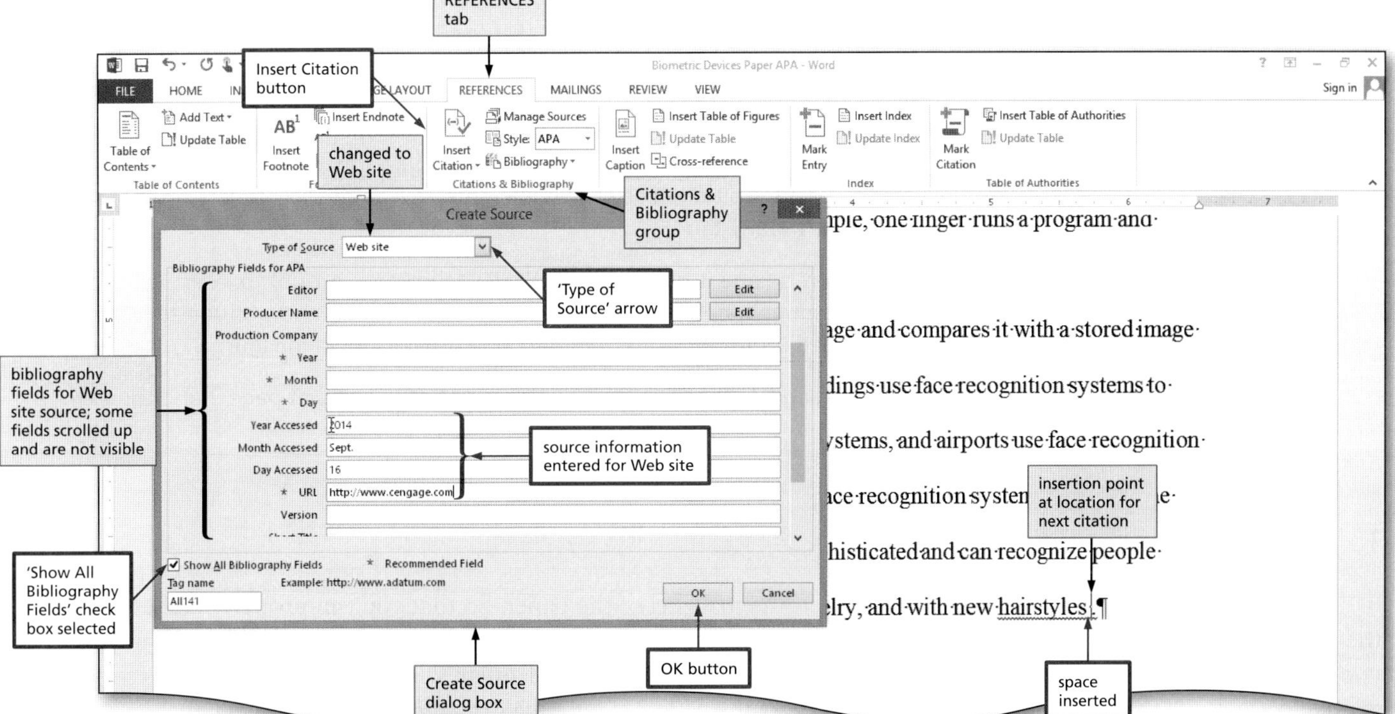

Figure 35

To Type the Fourth Paragraph

The following steps type the last paragraph in the research paper.

1. Press CTRL+END to move the insertion point to the end of the last paragraph and then press the ENTER key.
2. Type the fourth paragraph of the research paper as shown in Figure 36.

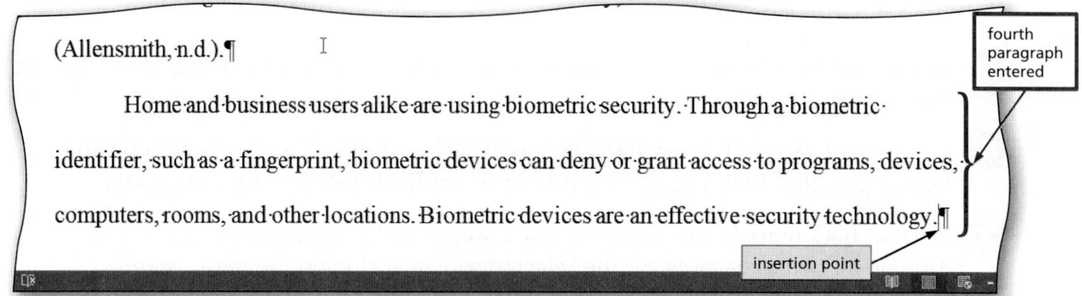

(Allensmith, n.d.).¶
Home and business users alike are using biometric security. Through a biometric identifier, such as a fingerprint, biometric devices can deny or grant access to programs, devices, computers, rooms, and other locations. Biometric devices are an effective security technology.¶
fourth paragraph entered
insertion point

Figure 36

To Save an Existing Document with the Same File Name

You have made several modifications to the document since you last saved it. Thus, you should save it again. The following step saves the document again. For an example of the step listed below, refer to the Office and Windows chapter at the beginning of this book.

1. Tap or click the Save button on the Quick Access Toolbar to overwrite the previously saved file.

To Page Break Manually

The research paper text is complete. The next step is to create the references on a separate numbered page. The following steps insert a manual page break.

1. With the insertion point positioned as shown in Figure 36, tap or click INSERT on the ribbon to display the INSERT tab.
2. Tap or click the 'Insert a Page Break' button (INSERT tab | Pages group) to insert a manual page break immediately to the left of the insertion point and position the insertion point immediately below the manual page break (shown in Figure 37).
3. If you have a blank page 4, position the insertion point at the end of page 3 and then press the DELETE key.

To Apply the Normal Style

The references title is to be centered between the margins of the paper. So that you can properly center the title of the reference page, you will apply the Normal style to the location of the insertion point. Recall that you modified the Normal style for this document to 12-point Times New Roman with double-spaced, left-aligned paragraphs that have no space after the paragraphs. ***Why?*** *If you simply issue the Center command, the title will not be centered properly. Instead, it will be to the right of the center point because earlier you set first-line indent for paragraphs to one-half inch from the left margin.*

To apply a style to a paragraph, first position the insertion point in the paragraph and then apply the style. The following step applies the modified Normal style to the location of the insertion point.

- Tap or click HOME on the ribbon to display the HOME tab.
- With the insertion point on the paragraph mark at the top of page 4, as shown in Figure 37, even if Normal is selected, tap or click Normal in the Styles gallery (HOME tab | Styles group) to apply the selected style to the paragraph containing the insertion point (Figure 37).

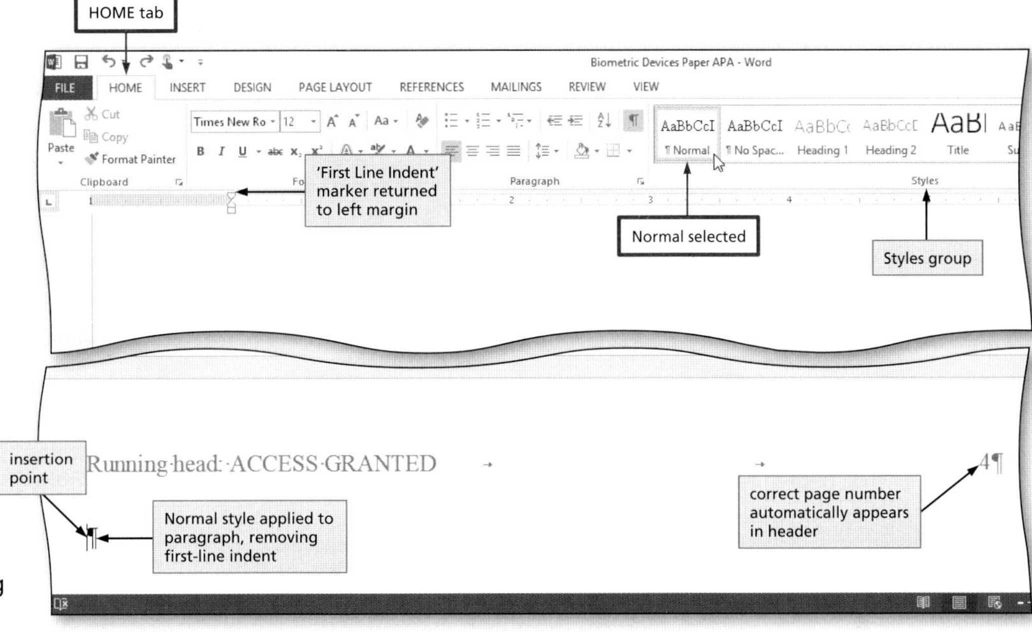

Figure 37

To Enter the References Page Title

The next step is to enter the title, References, centered between the margins of the paper. The following steps use shortcut keys to format the title.

1. Press CTRL+E to center the paragraph mark.
2. Type **References** as the title.
3. Press the ENTER key.
4. Press CTRL+L to left-align the paragraph mark (shown in Figure 38 on the next page).

To Create the Bibliographical List

While typing the research paper, you created several citations and their sources. The next task is to use Word to format the list of sources and alphabetize them in a **bibliographical list**. ***Why?*** *Word can create a bibliographical list with each element of the source placed in its correct position with proper punctuation, according to the specified style, saving you time looking up style guidelines. For example, in this research paper, the book source will list, in this order, the author name(s), publication year, book title, publisher city, and publishing company name with the correct punctuation between each element according to the APA documentation style.* The steps on the next page create an APA-styled bibliographical list from the sources previously entered.

1

- Tap or click REFERENCES on the ribbon to display the References tab.
- With the insertion point positioned as shown in Figure 38, tap or click the Bibliography button (REFERENCES tab | Citations & Bibliography group) to display the Bibliography gallery (Figure 38).

2

- Tap or click Insert Bibliography in the Bibliography gallery to insert a list of sources at the location of the insertion point.
- If necessary, scroll to display the entire list of sources in the document window (Figure 39).

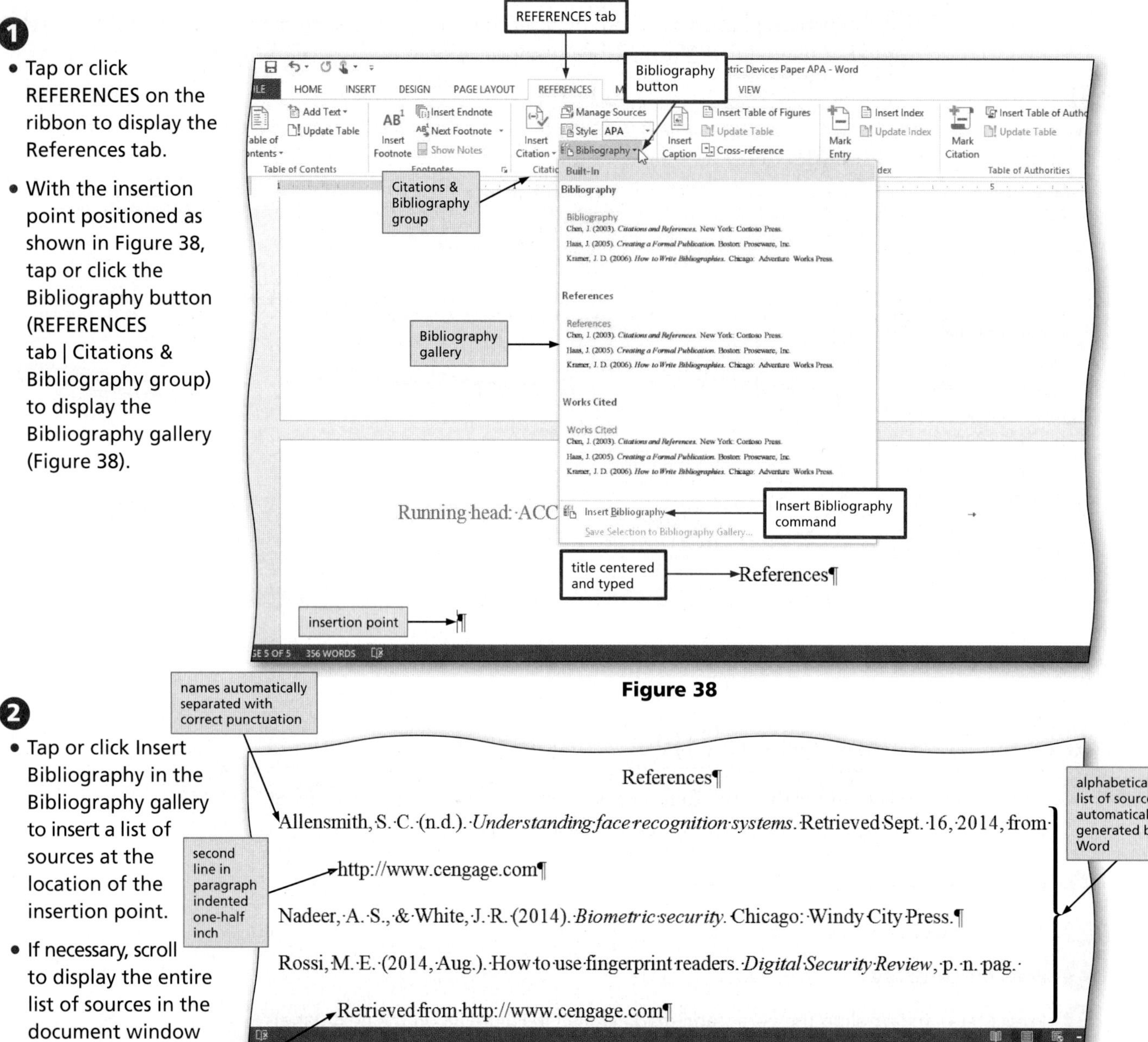

Figure 38

Figure 39

To Convert a Field to Regular Text

If, for some reason, you wanted to convert a field, such as the bibliography field, to regular text, you would perform the following steps. Keep in mind, though, once you convert the field to regular text, it no longer is a field that can be updated. For example, the latest guidelines for the APA documentation style state that the page number in magazine articles should not be preceded with the p. notation.

1. Tap or click somewhere in the field to select it, in this case, somewhere in the bibliography.
2. Press CTRL+SHIFT+F9 to convert the selected field to regular text.
3. Tap or click anywhere in the document to remove the selection from the text.
4. Drag through the p. notation in the magazine entry to select it and press the DELETE key to delete the selected text (Figure 40).

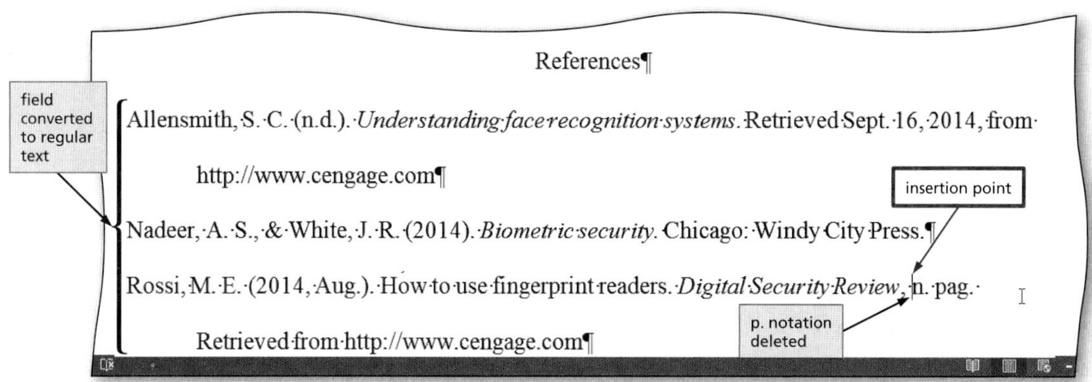

Figure 40

To Save an Existing Document, Print the Document, and Exit Word

The document now is complete. You should save the research paper again before exiting Word. The following steps save the document again, print the document, and then exit Word. For a detailed example of the procedure summarized below, refer to the Office and Windows chapter at the beginning of this book.

1. Tap or click the Save button on the Quick Access Toolbar to overwrite the previously saved file.
2. Tap or click FILE on the ribbon to open the Backstage view.
3. Tap or click the Print tab in the Backstage view to display the Print gallery.
4. Verify that the printer listed on the Printer Status button will print a hard copy of the document. If necessary, tap or click the Printer Status button to display a list of available printer options and then tap or click the desired printer to change the currently selected printer.
5. Tap or click the Print button in the Print gallery to print the document on the currently selected printer.
6. When the printer stops, retrieve the hard copy.

7a. If you have one Word document open, tap or click the Close button on the right side of the title bar to close the open document and exit Word.

7b. If you have multiple Word documents open, press and hold or right-click the Word app button on the taskbar and then tap or click 'Close all windows' on the shortcut menu to close all open documents and exit Word.

8. If a Microsoft Word dialog box appears, tap or click the Save button to save any changes made to the document since the last save.

Appendix Summary

In this appendix, you have learned how to create the same research paper as the one shown in Chapter 2, except you used the APA documentation style instead of the MLA documentation style. This appendix presented only the steps required to create this APA-styled research paper.

STUDENT ASSIGNMENTS

CONSIDER THIS

How should you submit solutions to questions in the assignments identified with a symbol?
Every assignment in this book contains one or more questions identified with a symbol. These questions require you to think beyond the assigned document. Present your solutions to the questions in the format required by your instructor. Possible formats may include one or more of these options: write the answer; create a document that contains the answer; present your answer to the class; discuss your answer in a group; record the answer as audio or video using a webcam, smartphone, or portable media player; or post answers on a blog, wiki, or website.

Apply Your Knowledge

Reinforce the skills and apply the concepts you learned in this chapter.

Revising Text and Paragraphs in a Document

Note: To complete this assignment, you will be required to use the Data Files for Students. Visit www.cengage.com/ct/studentdownload for detailed instructions or contact your instructor for information about accessing the required files.

Instructions: Run Word. Open the document, Apply A-1 Virtual Reality Paragraph Draft, from the Data Files for Students. The document you open contains a paragraph of text. You are to revise the document as follows: move a word, move another word and change the format of the moved word, change paragraph indentation, change line spacing, find all occurrences of a word, replace all occurrences of a word with another word, locate a synonym, and edit the header. The modified document is shown in Figure 41.

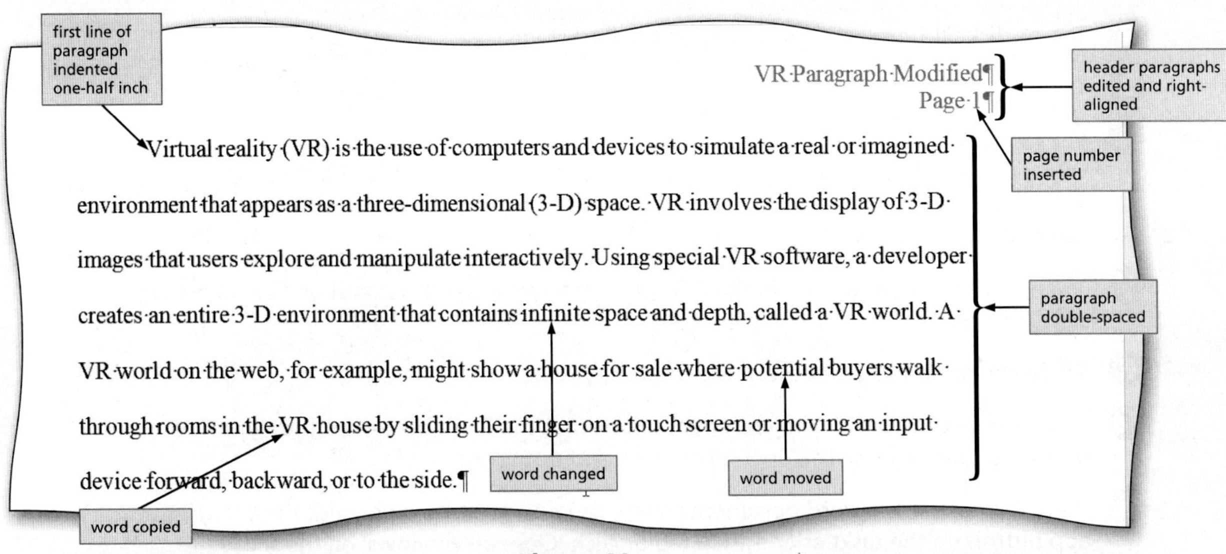

Figure 41

Perform the following tasks:

1. Copy the text, VR, from the first sentence and paste it in the last sentence after the underlined word, potential.
2. Select the underlined word, potential, in the paragraph. If you are using a mouse, use drag-and-drop editing to move the selected word, potential, so that it is before the word, buyers, in the same sentence. If you are using a touch screen, use the cut and paste commands to move the word. Tap or click the Paste Options button that displays to the right of the moved word, potential. Remove the underline format from the moved sentence by tapping or clicking 'Keep Text Only' on the Paste Options menu.

3. Display the ruler, if necessary. If you are using a mouse, use the ruler to indent the first line of the paragraph one-half inch; otherwise, use the Paragraph dialog box.
4. Change the line spacing of the paragraph to double.
5. Use the Navigation Pane to find all occurrences of the word, VR. How many were found?
6. Use the Find and Replace dialog box to replace all occurrences of the word, 3D, with the word, 3-D. How many replacements were made?
7. Use the Navigation Pane to find the word, endless. Use Word's thesaurus to change the word, endless, to the word, infinite. What other words are in the list of synonyms?
8. Switch to the header so that you can edit it. In the first line of the header, change the word, Draft, to the word, Modified, so that it reads: VR Paragraph Modified.
9. In the second line of the header, insert the page number (with no formatting) one space after the word, Page.
10. Change the alignment of both lines of text in the header from left-aligned to right-aligned. Switch back to the document text.
11. If requested by your instructor, enter your first and last name on a separate line below the page number in the header.
12. Tap or click FILE on the ribbon and then tap or click Save As. Save the document using the file name, Apply A-1 Virtual Reality Paragraph Modified.
13. Submit the modified document, shown in Figure 41, in the format specified by your instructor.
14. Use the Research task pane to look up the definition of the word, simulate, in the paragraph. Which dictionary was used? If you have a Microsoft account and are signed into it, use the Define button (REVIEW tab | Proofing group) to look up a definition of the word.
15. Change the search location to All Research Sites. Submit an article from one of the sites.
16. Display the Research Options dialog box. How many currently active Reference Books and Research Sites are in the list? If your instructor approves, activate one of the services.
17. Answer the questions posed in #5, #6, #7, #14, and #16. How would you find and replace a special character, such as a paragraph mark?

Extend Your Knowledge

Extend the skills you learned in this chapter and experiment with new skills. You may need to use Help to complete the assignment.

Working with References and Proofing Tools

Note: To complete this assignment, you will be required to use the Data Files for Students. Visit www.cengage.com/ct/studentdownload for detailed instructions or contact your instructor for information about accessing the required files.

Instructions: Run Word. Open the document, Extend A-1 Cybercrime Paper Draft APA, from the Data Files for Students. You will add another footnote to the paper, convert the footnotes to endnotes, modify the Endnote Text style, change the format of the note reference marks, use Word's readability statistics, translate the document to another language, and convert the document from APA to MLA documentation style.

Perform the following tasks:

1. Use Help to learn more about footers, footnotes and endnotes, readability statistics, bibliography styles, AutoCorrect, and the Mini Translator.
2. Delete the footer from the document.

Continued >

Extend Your Knowledge *continued*

3. Determine the APA guidelines for footnotes. Insert the following footnote at an appropriate place in the research paper: According to Ross, any illegal act involving the use of a computer or related devices generally is referred to as a computer crime (2014).
4. Insert this second footnote at an appropriate place in the research paper: Both hackers and crackers have advanced computer and network skills.
5. Convert the footnotes to endnotes, so that the footnotes are on a separate numbered page after the references. Place the title, Footnotes, at the top of the page.
6. Modify the Endnote Text style to 12-point Times New Roman font, double-spaced with a hanging indent.
7. Change the format of the note reference marks to capital letters (A, B, etc.).
8. Use the Find and Replace dialog box to find the word, excellent, in the document and then replace it with the word of your choice.
9. Add an AutoCorrect entry that replaces the word, perpetraters, with the word, perpetrators. Add this sentence as the last sentence in the paper, misspelling the word, perpetrators, to test the AutoCorrect entry: These perpetraters present a growing threat to society. Delete the AutoCorrect entry that replaces perpetraters with the word, perpetrators.
10. Display the Word Count dialog box. How many words, characters without spaces, characters with spaces, paragraphs, and lines are in the document? Be sure to include footnote and endnote text in the statistics.
11. Check spelling of the document, displaying readability statistics. What are the Flesch-Kincaid Grade Level, the Flesch Reading Ease score, and the percent of passive sentences? Modify the paper to lower the grade level, increase the reading ease score, and lower the percentage of passive sentences. How did you modify the paper? What are the new statistics?
12. If requested by your instructor, change the student name at the top of the paper to your name.
13. Save the revised document with the file name, Extend A-1 Cybercrime Paper Modified APA, and then submit it in the format specified by your instructor.
14. If you have an Internet connection, translate the research paper into a language of your choice (Figure 42) using the Translate button (REVIEW tab | Language group). Submit the

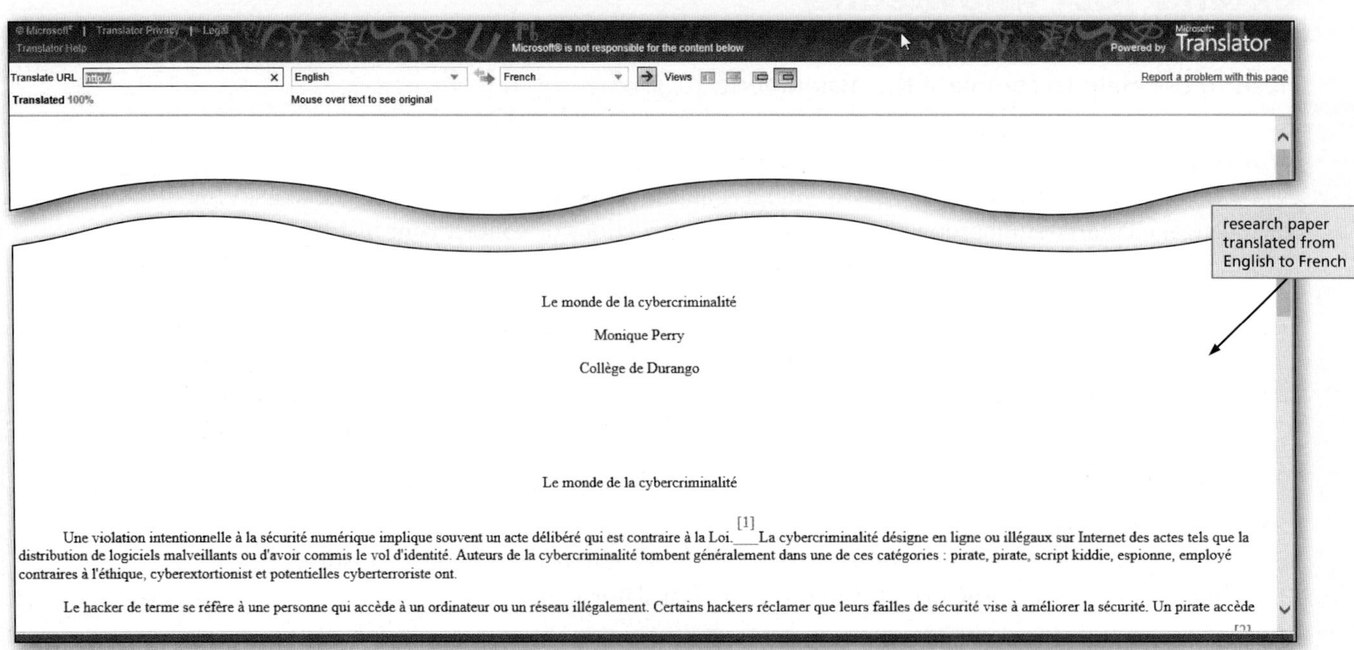

Figure 42

translated document in the format specified by your instructor. Use the Mini Translator to hear how to pronounce three words in your paper.

15. Select the entire document and then change the documentation style from APA to MLA. Save the MLA version of the document with a new file name. Compare the APA version to the MLA version. If you have a hard copy of each and your instructor requests it, circle the differences between the two documents.

16. Answer the questions posed in #10 and #11. Where did you insert the second footnote and why?

Analyze, Correct, Improve

Analyze a document, correct all errors, and improve it.

Inserting Missing Elements in an APA-Styled Research Paper

Note: To complete this assignment, you will be required to use the Data Files for Students. Visit www.cengage.com/ct/studentdownload for detailed instructions or contact your instructor for information about accessing the required files.

Instructions: Run Word. Open the document, Analyze A-1 Internet Filters Paper Draft APA, from the Data Files for Students. The document is a research paper that is missing several elements. You are to insert these missing elements, all formatted according to the APA documentation style: header with a running head and page number, title page, paper title, footnote, and source information for a citation.

1. Correct In the research paper, correct the following items:

a. Insert a header with a running head (Running head: INTERNET FILTERS) and a page number, formatted according to the APA documentation style.

b. Insert a title page that contains the header, along with the paper title (Internet Filters), author name (use your name), and school affiliation (use your school). If necessary, insert a manual page break after the end of the title page.

c. On the Abstract page, center the title and then remove the first-line indent from the paragraph below the title.

d. The Clark citation placeholder is missing its source information (shown in Figure 43). Use the following information to edit the source: book titled *Internet protection* written by Addison Lee Clark, publication year is 2014, publication city is New York, and the publisher is Journey Press.

e. Modify the website author name to include his middle name (the APA documentation style will display only the initials for the first and middle name on the references page): Robert Timothy Lane.

f. Use the Navigation Pane to display page 4. Insert a page break before the References heading.

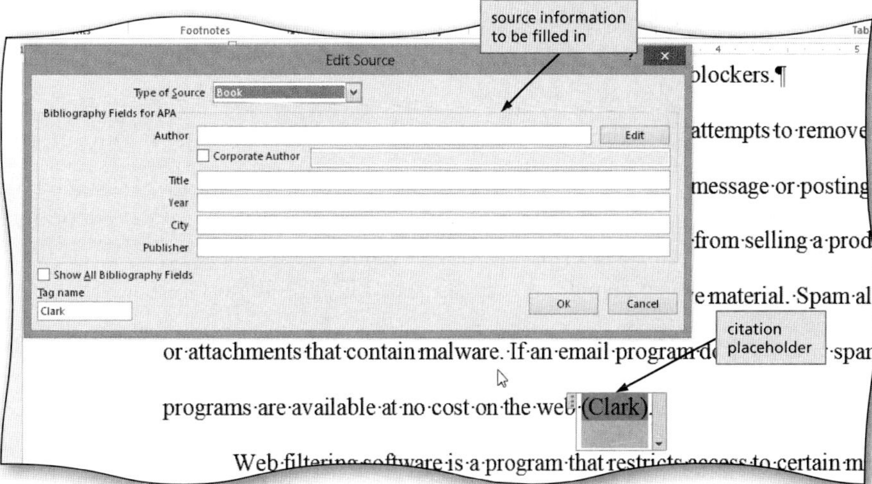

Figure 43

Continued >

Analyze, Correct, Improve *continued*

2. Improve Enhance the paper by finishing the contents of the abstract page and using Word to insert the bibliographical list (bibliography) below the References heading. Save the modified document with the file name, Analyze A-1 Internet Filters Paper Modified APA, and then submit it in the format specified by your instructor.

3. This assignment uses a web source. How can you determine if a web source is reliable?

In the Labs

Design and/or create a document using the guidelines, concepts, and skills presented in this chapter. Labs 1 and 2, which increase in difficulty, require you to create solutions based on what you learned in the chapter; Lab 3 requires you to create a solution, which uses cloud and web technologies, by learning and investigating on your own from general guidance.

Lab 1: Preparing a Short Research Paper

Problem: You are a college student currently enrolled in an introductory English class. Your assignment is to prepare a short research paper (400–500 words) in any area of interest to you. The requirements are that the paper be presented according to the APA documentation style and have three references. At least one of the three references must be from the web. You prepare the paper shown in Figure 44, which discusses health risks associated with technology.

Instructions: Perform the following tasks:

1. Run Word. If necessary, display formatting marks on the screen.
2. Modify the Normal style to the 12-point Times New Roman font.
3. Adjust line spacing to double.
4. Remove space below (after) paragraphs.
5. Update the Normal style to reflect the adjusted line and paragraph spacing.
6. Create a header that includes the running head (Running head: HEALTH RISKS) at the left margin and the page number at the right margin.
7. Insert the title page as shown in Figure 44a, ensuring that it includes a header, along with the complete paper title (Health Risks Associated with Technology), author name, and school affiliation. If requested by your instructor, use your name and course information instead of the information shown in Figure 44a. Insert a manual page break after the last line on the title page.
8. Type the Abstract as shown in Figure 44b. Insert a manual page break after the last line of the abstract.
9. Set a first-line indent to one-half inch for paragraphs in the body of the research paper.
10. Type the research paper as shown in Figure 44c (on page APP 32) and Figure 44d (on page APP 33). Change the bibliography style to APA. As you insert citations, enter their source information (shown in Figure 44e on page APP 33). If necessary, edit the citations so that they are displayed according to Figure 44c and 44d.
11. At the end of the research paper text, press the ENTER key and then insert a manual page break so that the References page begins on a new page. Enter and format the references title (Figure 44e). Use Word to insert the bibliographical list (bibliography). Convert the bibliography field to text. Remove the p. notion from the page numbers in the magazine article entry (shown in Figure 44e).
12. Check the spelling and grammar of the paper at once.

Running head: HEALTH RISKS 1

Health Risks Associated with Technology

Rajesh Delhi

Lowland College

(a) Page 1

Running head: HEALTH RISKS 2

Abstract

Technology has led to a rising number of important user health concerns. Repetitive strain injuries (RSI) are injuries or disorders of the muscles, nerves, tendons, ligaments, and joints. Computer vision syndrome (CVS) is a health concern that affects eyesight. Other complaints associated with technology use are lower back pain, muscle fatigue, and emotional fatigue.

(b) Page 2

Figure 44 (Continued)

Continued >

In the Labs *continued*

Running head: HEALTH RISKS 3

Health Risks Associated with Technology

The widespread use of technology has led to some important user health concerns. Some of the more common physical health risks are repetitive strain injuries, computer vision syndrome, and muscular pain. These injuries are on the rise for users of technology.

A repetitive strain injury (RSI) is an injury or disorder of the muscles, nerves, tendons, ligaments, and joints. Technology-related RSIs include tendonitis and carpal tunnel syndrome (CTS). Tendonitis is inflammation of a tendon due to repeated motion or stress on that tendon. CTS is inflammation of the nerve that connects the forearm to the palm. Repeated or forceful bending of the wrist can cause tendonitis or CTS of the wrist. Factors that cause these disorders include prolonged typing or mouse usage and continual shifting between a mouse and keyboard (Jones, 2014, pp. 45-48). If untreated, these disorders can lead to permanent physical damage.

Computer vision syndrome (CVS) affects eyesight. Symptoms of CVS are sore, tired, burning, itching, or dry eyes; blurred or double vision; distance blurred vision after prolonged staring at a display device; headache or sore neck; difficulty shifting focus between a display device and documents; difficulty focusing on a screen image; color fringes or afterimages when looking away from a display device; and increased sensitivity to light. Eyestrain associated with CVS is not thought to have serious or long-term consequences (Anderson & Dean, 2014).

People who spend their workday using the computer sometimes complain of lower back pain, muscle fatigue, and emotional fatigue. Lower back pain sometimes is caused from poor posture. It is advisable to sit properly in a chair while working and take periodic breaks. Users also should be sure their workplace is designed ergonomically. Ergonomic studies have shown that using the correct type and configuration of chair, keyboard, display device, and work surface helps users work comfortably and efficiently and helps protect their health (Sanchez, 2014).

(c) Page 3

Figure 44

Running head: HEALTH RISKS 4

Many physical health risks are associated with using technology. These risks include repetitive strain injuries, computer vision syndrome, and muscular pain. Users should take as many preventive measures as possible to avoid these risks.

(d) Page 4

Running head: HEALTH RISKS 5

References

Anderson, C. F., & Dean, S. A. (2014, Aug.). Computer pains. *The Medical Update*, n. pag. Retrieved October 2, 2014, from http://www.cengage.com

Jones, J. L. (2014). *Medical concerns of the 21st century.* Chicago: Smiley Incorporated.

Sanchez, J. M. (2014, Sept. 30). *Aches and pains.* Retrieved Aug. 5, 2014, from The Tech Spot: http://www.cengage.com

(e) Page 5

Figure 44 (Continued)

Continued >

In the Labs *continued*

13. Save the document using Lab A-1 Technology Health Risks Paper APA as the file name. Submit the document, shown in Figure 44, in the format specified by your instructor.
14. Read the paper in Print Layout view. Switch to Read mode and scroll through the pages. Do you prefer reading in Print Layout view or Read mode? Why? In Read mode, which of the page colors do you like best and why?

Lab 2: Preparing a Research Report

Problem: You are a college student enrolled in an introductory technology class. Your assignment is to prepare a short research paper (400–500 words) in any area of interest to you. The requirements are that the paper be presented according to the APA documentation style and have three references. At least one of the three references must be from the Internet. You prepare a paper about protecting mobile devices (Figure 45).

Instructions: Perform the following tasks:

1. Run Word. Modify the Normal style to the 12-point Times New Roman font. Adjust line spacing to double and remove space below (after) paragraphs. Update the Normal style to include the adjusted line and paragraph spacing. Create a header that includes a running head at the left margin and the page number at the right margin. Create an appropriate title page, using your name and school affiliation (page 1). Create the abstract (page 2) as shown in Figure 45a. Center and type the title (page 3). Set a first-line indent for paragraphs in the body of the research paper.

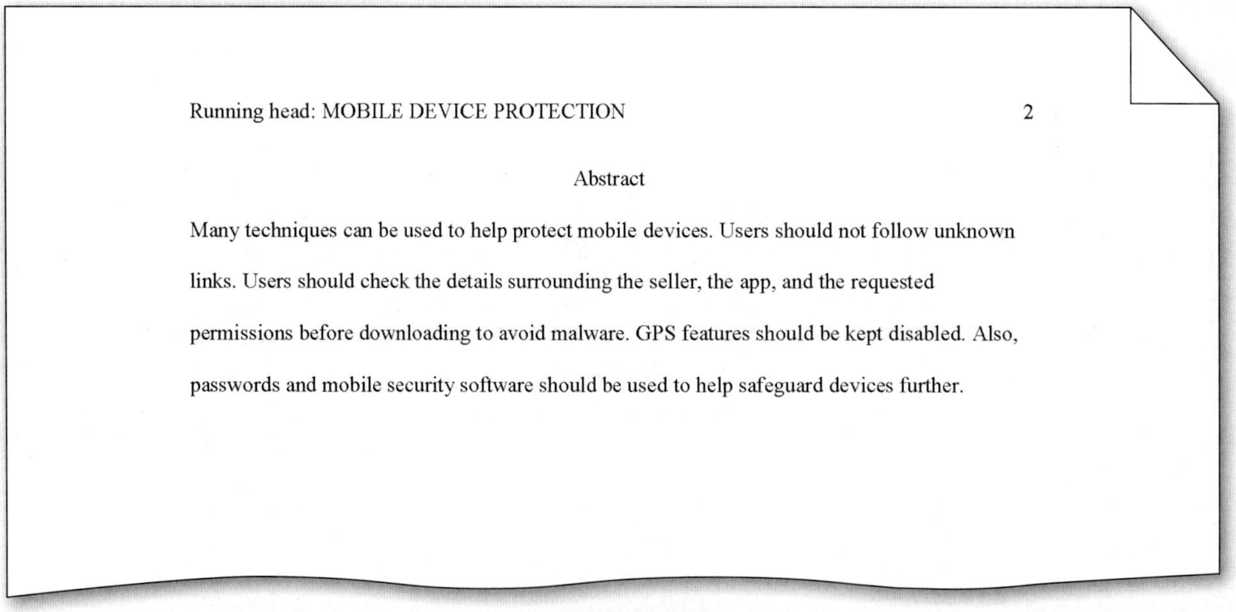

Running head: MOBILE DEVICE PROTECTION 2

Abstract

Many techniques can be used to help protect mobile devices. Users should not follow unknown links. Users should check the details surrounding the seller, the app, and the requested permissions before downloading to avoid malware. GPS features should be kept disabled. Also, passwords and mobile security software should be used to help safeguard devices further.

(a) Abstract

Figure 45

Running head: MOBILE DEVICE PROTECTION 3

Mobile Device Protection

The consequences of losing a smartphone or other mobile device are significant because these devices store personal and business data. The goal, therefore, for mobile device users is to make their data as secure as possible. Techniques include avoiding unsafe links, using caution when downloading apps, turning off GPS tracking, and installing mobile security software.

A high percentage of users follow unknown links, which can lead to a malicious website. Malicious links can inject malware on a mobile device. The malware may steal personal information or create toll fraud, which secretly contacts wireless messaging services that impose steep fees on a monthly bill (Bao, 2014). Users should avoid tapping or clicking unknown links.

Any device that connects to the Internet is susceptible to mobile malware. According to Jameson and Bennett, cyberthieves target apps on popular devices (2014, p. 72). Popular games are likely candidates to house malware, and it often is difficult to distinguish the legitimate apps from the fake apps. Users should check the reliability of the seller, the descriptions and reviews of the app, and the requested permissions before downloading.

GPS technology can track the mobile device's location as long as it is transmitting and receiving signals to and from satellites. Although this feature may be helpful, serious privacy concerns can arise when the technology is used in malicious ways, such as to stalk individuals or trace their whereabouts (Fields, n.d.). It is best to keep this feature disabled until needed.

Users can enable the password feature on their mobile device as the first step in stopping prying eyes from viewing contents. More protection is necessary, however, to stop viruses and spyware and to safeguard personal and business data. Mobile security apps can lock a mobile device remotely, erase its memory, and activate its GPS function (Bao, 2014).

(b) Body of Paper

Figure 45 (Continued)

Continued >

In the Labs *continued*

Running head: MOBILE DEVICE PROTECTION 4

Some techniques users can take to protect their mobile devices include avoiding unsafe links, using caution when downloading, turning off GPS tracking, and using mobile security software. Users should take these measures to protect their mobile devices.

(c) Body of Paper

Figure 45 (Continued)

2. Type the research paper (pages 3 and 4) as shown in Figure 45b (on page APP 35) and Figure 45c. Change the bibliography style to APA. As you insert citations, use the following source information, entering it according to the APA style:
   a. Type of Source: Article in a Periodical
      Author: H. G. Bao
      Article Title: Securing Mobile Devices
      Periodical Title: Technology Today
      Year: 2014
      Month: Sept.
      Pages: no pages used
      Year Accessed: 2014
      Month Accessed: Oct.
      Day Accessed: 1
   b. Type of Source: Web site
      Author: C. Fields
      Name of web page: Secure Your Mobile Device
      Year/Month/Date: none given
      Year Accessed: 2014
      Month Accessed: Sept.
      Day Accessed: 22

c. Type of Source: Book
   Author: L. T. Jameson and K. L. Bennett
   Title: Mobile Technologies
   Year: 2014
   City: New York
   Publisher: Maxwell Press

3. At the end of the research paper text, press the ENTER key once and insert a manual page break so that the References page begins on a new page (page 5). Enter and format the references title. Use Word to insert the bibliographical list.
4. Check the spelling and grammar of the paper.
5. Save the document using Lab A-2 Mobile Devices Protection Paper APA as the file name. Submit the document in the format specified by your instructor.
6. This paper uses web sources. What factors should you consider when selecting web sources?

Lab 3: Expand Your World: Cloud and Web Technologies

Using an Online Bibliography Tool to Create a List of Sources

Problem: Assume you are using a mobile device or computer that does not have Word but has Internet access. To make use of time between classes, you will use an online bibliography tool to create a list of sources that you can copy and paste into the References page of a research paper due tomorrow.

Instructions: Perform the following tasks:

1. Run a browser. Search for the text, online bibliography tool, using a search engine. Visit several of the online bibliography tools and determine which you would like to use to create a list of sources formatted according to the APA documentation style. Navigate to the desired online bibliography tool.
2. Use the online bibliography tool (Figure 46 on the next page) to enter the following list of sources:

   Dayton, L. M., & Walsh, S. L. (2014) The wireless revolution. New York: New Artists Press.

   Dover, G. S. (2014) Communications of today. Los Angeles: Sunshine Works.

   Howard, T. J. (2014, Aug.) The wireless era. Computers and networks, n. pag. Retrieved August 29, 2014, from http://www.cengage.com

   Matthews, C. J. (2014, Aug.) Wireless trends. Retrieved September 8, 2014, from http://www.cengage.com

   Newby, T. L., & Hopper, H. L. (2014, Aug.) Wireless communications. Communications News, n. pag. Retrieved October 4, 2014, from http://www.cengage.com

   Newman, W. J. (2014, Sept.) The amazing wireless world. Retrieved September 28, 2014, from http://www.cengage.com

3. If requested by your instructor, replace the name in one of the sources above with your name.
4. Search for another source that discusses wireless communications. Add that source.
5. Copy and paste the list of sources into a Word document.
6. Save the document with the name Lab A-3 Wireless Communications Sources APA. Submit the document in the format specified by your instructor.

Continued >

In the Labs *continued*

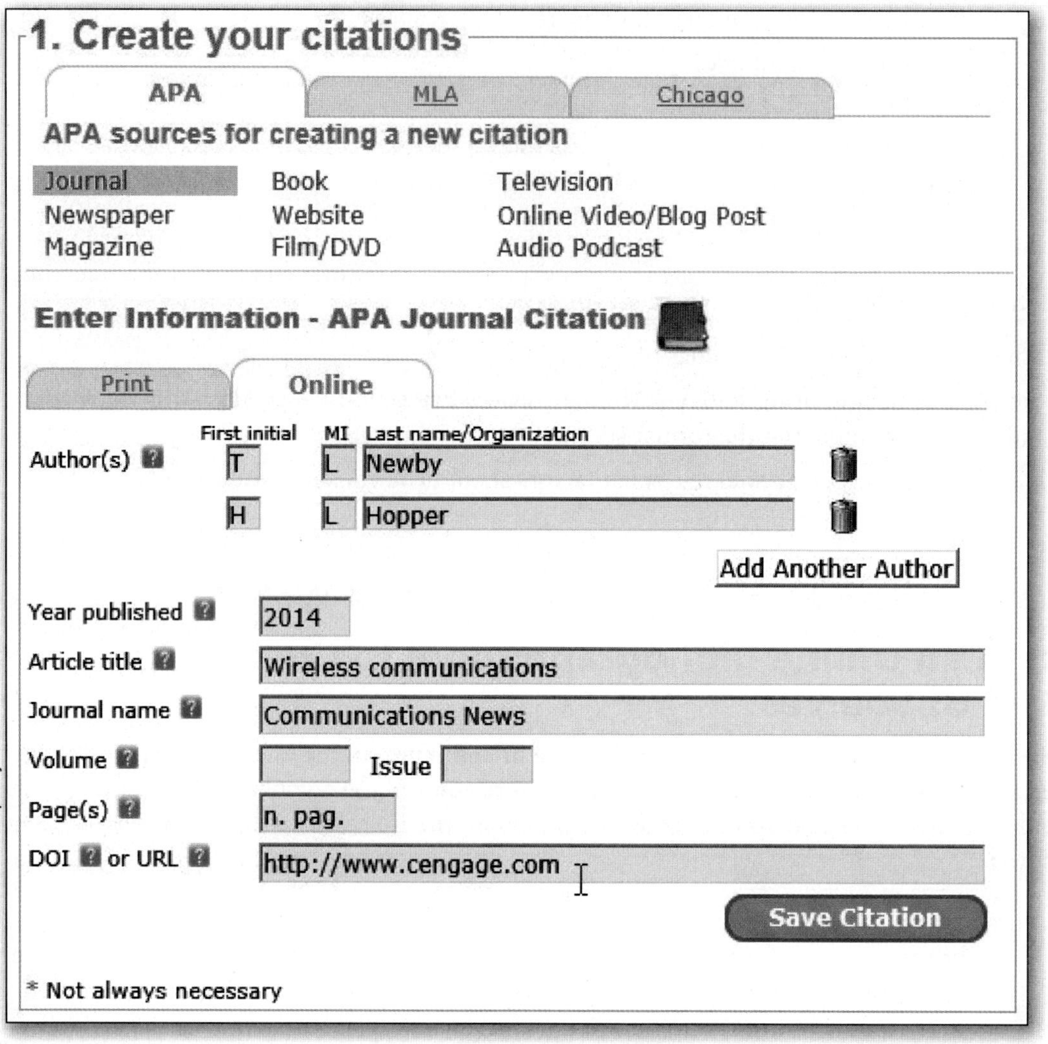

1. Create your citations

APA | MLA | Chicago

APA sources for creating a new citation

Journal Book Television
Newspaper Website Online Video/Blog Post
Magazine Film/DVD Audio Podcast

Enter Information - APA Journal Citation

Print | Online

Author(s) First initial T MI L Last name/Organization Newby
H L Hopper

Add Another Author

Year published 2014

Article title Wireless communications

Journal name Communications News

Volume Issue

Page(s) n. pag.

DOI or URL http://www.cengage.com

Save Citation

* Not always necessary

Figure 46

7. Which online bibliography tools did you evaluate? Which one did you select to use and why? Do you prefer using the online bibliography tool or Word to create sources? Why? What differences, if any, did you notice between the list of sources created with the online bibliography tool and the lists created when you use Word?

Consider This: Your Turn

Apply your creative thinking and problem solving skills to design and implement a solution.

Note: To complete these assignments, you may be required to use the Data Files for Students. Visit www.cengage.com/ct/studentdownload for detailed instructions or contact your instructor for information about accessing the required files.

1: Create a Research Paper about Laptops, Tablets, and Desktops

Personal

Part 1: As a student in an introductory computer class, your instructor has assigned a brief research paper that discusses types of computers. The source for the text in your research paper is in a file called Your Turn A-1 Computers Notes APA, which is located on the Data Files for Students. If your instructor requests, use the Research task pane to obtain information from another source and include that information as a note positioned as a footnote in the paper, along with entering its corresponding source information as appropriate. Add an AutoCorrect entry to correct a word you commonly mistype. If necessary, set the default dictionary. Add one of the source last names to the dictionary.

Using the concepts and techniques presented in this chapter, organize the notes in the text in the file on the Data Files for Students, rewording as necessary, and then create and format this research paper according to the APA documentation style. Be sure to check spelling and grammar of the finished paper. Submit your assignment and answers to the critical thinking questions in the format specified by your instructor.

Part 2: You made several decisions while creating the research paper in this assignment: how to organize the notes, where to place citations, how to format sources, and which source on the web to use for the footnote text (if requested by your instructor). What was the rationale behind each of these decisions? When you proofread the document, what further revisions did you make and why?

2: Create a Research Paper about POS Terminals, ATMs, and Self-Service Kiosks

Professional

Part 1: As a part-time employee at an advertising firm that specializes in marketing for technology, your boss has asked you to write a brief research paper that discusses types of terminals. The source for the text in your research paper is in a file called Your Turn A-2 Terminals Notes APA, which is located on the Data Files for Students. If your instructor requests, use the Research task pane to obtain information from another source and include that information as a note positioned as a footnote in the paper, and enter its corresponding source information as appropriate. Add an AutoCorrect entry to correct a word you commonly mistype. If necessary, set the default dictionary. Add one of the source last names to the dictionary.

Using the concepts and techniques presented in this chapter, organize the notes in the file on the Data Files for Students, rewording as necessary, and then create and format this research paper according to the APA documentation style. Be sure to check spelling and grammar of the finished paper. Submit your assignment and answers to the critical thinking questions in the format specified by your instructor.

Part 2: You made several decisions while creating the research paper in this assignment: how to organize the notes, where to place citations, how to format sources, and which source on the web to use for the footnote text (if requested by your instructor). What was the rationale behind each of these decisions? When you proofread the document, what further revisions did you make and why?

3: Create a Research Paper about Social Media Sites

Research and Collaboration

Part 1: Because all local youth groups will be creating a page on a social media site, you and two other leaders of local youth groups have been asked to prepare a research paper comparing and contrasting three different social media sites. Form a three-member team to research, compose, and create this paper. Research three separate social media sites: features, capabilities, typical uses, privacy settings, etc. Each team member should write the supporting paragraphs for the social media site he or she researched, including all citations and sources. As a group, write the introduction and conclusion. Be sure to include your team's recommendation in the conclusion.

Use the concepts and techniques presented in this chapter to create and format this paper according to the APA documentation style. Be sure to check spelling and grammar of the finished paper. Submit your team notes and research paper in the format specified by your instructor.

Part 2: You made several decisions while creating the research paper in this assignment: the sources to use, which notes to take from the sources, how to organize the notes, how to organize each team member's submissions, what text to write for the introduction and conclusion, where to place citations, and how to format sources. What was the rationale behind each of these decisions? When you proofread the document, what further revisions did you make and why?

Learn Online

Reinforce what you learned in this chapter with games, exercises, training, and many other online activities and resources.

Student Companion Site Reinforcement activities and resources are available at no additional cost on www.cengagebrain.com. Visit www.cengage.com/ct/studentdownload for detailed instructions about accessing the resources available at the Student Companion Site.

SAM Put your skills into practice with SAM! If you have a SAM account, go to www.cengage.com/sam2013 to access SAM assignments for this chapter.

Appendix B

SAM Projects

Introduction

With SAM Projects—SAM's hands-on, live-in-the-application projects—students master Microsoft Office skills that are essential to academic and career success. SAM Projects engage students in applying the latest Microsoft Office 2013 skills to real-world scenarios. Immediate grading and feedback allow students to fix errors and understand where they may need more practice.

This appendix provides the printed instructions for one SAM Project that corresponds to this text. This project was created by an instructor currently teaching an Introduction to Computing course:

- Word Project: created by Brad West, Associate Professor, Sinclair Community College

To complete the project in this appendix, you must log into your SAM account. Go to sam .cengage.com for more information or contact your instructor.

Word 2013: Student Engagement Project 1a

SAM Creating a Resume

Getting the Job You Want

Project Description

Created by Brad West, Associate Professor, Sinclair Community College

Now that you have mastered Office 2013, you are ready to apply for a job that will utilize your skills. You have already organized an outline that you will use to enter your information into your partially completed resume. After you complete the resume and proofread it, you will format it appropriately.

Getting Started

- Download the following file from the SAM website:
  - **SAM_Word2013_SE_P1a_*FirstLastName*_1.docx**
- Open the file you just downloaded and save it with the name:
  - **SAM_Word2013_SE_P1a_*FirstLastName*_2.docx**
  - *Hint*: If you do not see the **.docx** file extension in the Save file dialog box, do not type it. Word will add the file extension for you automatically.
- To complete this Project, you will also need to download and save the following support file from the SAM website:
  - **support_SAM_W13_SE_P1a_resume_outline.docx**
- With the file **SAM_Word2013_SE_P1a_*FirstLastName*_2.docx** still open, ensure that your first and last name is displayed in the footer. If the footer does not display your name, delete the file and download a new copy from the SAM website.

Project Steps

1. Replace "Student Name" with your name.
2. Replace "Student Contact Information" with the address from the Resume Outline in **support_SAM_W13_SE_P1a_resume_outline.docx** available for download from the SAM website. Insert a tab, then insert the phone number, another tab, and the email address.
   - *Hint*: Each time you paste text from the support file, use the **Keep Text Only** option.
3. Replace "Insert Duties from Job 1 Here" with the duties from **Job 1** in the Resume Outline.
4. Replace "Insert Duties from Job 2 Here" with the duties from **Job 2** in the Resume Outline.
5. Run the Spelling & Grammar check. Correct all spelling mistakes, but ignore the punctuation error.
6. Change the document margins to **Normal**.
7. Change the document theme to **Depth**.
8. Change the document theme colors to **Blue**.
9. In the address line of the document, set a center tab stop at **3.5"** and a right tab stop at **6.5"**.
10. On the lines that begin with "Associate of Applied…," "Binder Clips…," and "Burgers!...," set right tab stops at **6.5"**.
11. Apply the **Title** style to your name at the top of the resume.
12. Apply the **Heading 1** style to "OBJECTIVE," "EDUCATION," "QUALIFICATIONS," "RELATED EXPERIENCE," and "OTHER EXPERIENCE."
13. Apply the **Heading 2** style to "Intern" and "Team Leader."
14. Apply **bold** to "Binder Clips" and "Burgers!"
15. Change the case of "OBJECTIVE," "EDUCATION," "QUALIFICATIONS," "RELATED EXPERIENCE," and "OTHER EXPERIENCE" to **Capitalize Each Word**.
   - *Hint*: Use the **Change Case** tool.
16. Create a bulleted list that begins with "Entered and updated account information in Access database for over 300 clients" and ends with "Greeted visitors and presented appropriate company information." Create a second bulleted list that begins with "Took cash, credit card, and debit card payments at cash register" and ends with "Closed register and prepared cash and transaction reports, investigated and rectified errors as appropriate."
17. Change the style of the bullets used in both bulleted lists to the arrow style:

   ➢

Save your changes, close the document, and exit Word. Follow the directions on the SAM website to submit your completed project.

Appendix C

Capstone Projects

Capstone Project 1

Note: To complete these assignments, you will be required to use the Data Files for Students. Visit www.cengage.com/ct/studentdownload for detailed instructions or contact your instructor for information about accessing the required files.

Problem: For your local park district, you are helping to promote the fifth annual recycling drop-off event. The head of public relations has created a document with the details of the event. You will format the document as a one-page flyer that presents the main information in a bulleted list. You will add formatting, a clip art image, a table, a shape with text, and a photo to enhance the text.

Instructions: Run Word. Open the document SC_Word2013_Capstone_1-1.docx and save it with the name SC_Word2013_Capstone_1-2.docx. You will also need the following support files from the student data files:

SC_Word2013_Capstone_recycling_globe.png
SC_Word2013_Capstone_bench.jpg

Perform the following tasks:

1. Change document margins to Normal.
2. Change the document theme to Circuit and the theme colors to Green Yellow (9th row in the Office section of the Colors palette).
3. Select the text "Recycle Your E-Waste!" and format it with the attributes listed in Steps 4 to 6.
4. Center-align the text.
5. Change the font to 34 pt. Arial Black.
6. Apply the Fill – Lime, Accent 1, Shadow text effect (2nd column, 1st row in the Text Effects and Typography palette).
7. Add a bottom paragraph border to the text "Recycle Your E-Waste!" using the following attributes: Use the Aqua, Accent 5, Darker 25% border color (9th column, 5th row in the Theme Colors palette). Use a 3 pt. width. Move the insertion point to the left of the text, "Are you feeling…" and insert the picture SC_Word2013_Capstone_recycling_globe.png, available from the student data files.
8. Next, make the following formatting changes to the picture: Apply Square text wrapping.
9. Resize the image proportionally so it has a height of 0.85".
10. Change the Before paragraph spacing of the paragraph beginning "Are you feeling weighed down…" to 12 pt. and the After spacing to 18 pt.
11. Format the text "What can you drop off?" with the following attributes: Change the font size to 16 pt. Apply bold and the font case Capitalize Each Word. Apply Lime, Accent 1, Darker 25% paragraph shading (5th column, 5th row in the Shading palette). Apply the White, Background 1 font color (1st column, 1st row in the Theme Colors palette).

12. Format the text from "Batteries" through "...Plasma" as a bulleted list. (Hint: Your list should contain exactly 12 list items.)
13. Move the insertion point to the right of the first bulleted list item, after the word "car," and insert the picture SC_Word2013_Capstone_bench.jpg, available from the student data files. Next, make the following formatting changes to the picture: Resize the picture so it has a height of 2" and a width of 2.4". Apply Square text wrapping. Apply the Reflected Bevel, White picture style.
14. Using Smart Guides, move the image horizontally to the right edge of the document.
15. Insert a Rounded Rectangle (2nd column, 1st row in the Rectangles area of the Shapes gallery) that is 0.50" tall and 2.4" wide positioned immediately below the picture inserted in Step 13.
16. Apply Square text wrapping to the shape.
17. Add text to the shape that reads: Picture yourself here enjoying a clean world!
18. Format the text in bold and UPPERCASE.
19. Right-align the text that begins "Do you have..." and ends with "...take the item.," and then format it in bold with 14 pt. font size. Set the paragraph's After spacing to 0.
20. Place the insertion point after the text that ends "...if we can take the item.," press Enter two times, and select left-align. Then, insert a table with two columns and five rows at that point.
21. Merge the cells in row 1, and then enter the text exactly as shown in Table 1–1.

Table 1–1 Remember to Mark Your Calendars	
What	Recycle your e-waste
When	Saturday, April 14
Where	Arlington Park District parking lot
Why	To recycle electronic waste and keep it out of landfills

22. Format the table with the following attributes: Apply the Grid Table 2 – Accent 1 table style and AutoFit Window. Format the text in column 2 in bold with a Lime, Accent 1, Darker 50% font color (6th column, 6th row in the Theme Colors palette). Format all the text in the table to 14 pt.
23. Insert a footnote at the end of the first paragraph following the period in the text "...7th annual e-waste drop off." with the following text: In case of inclement weather, the drop off will be moved inside the Park District warehouse at the same address as noted in the table. Use the north entrance, which will be clearly marked.
24. Add a blank header to the document with the text:

    Distributed by the Arlington Park District
25. Apply bold formatting and center-align the header text.
26. Check the Spelling & Grammar in the document to identify and correct any spelling errors. (Hint: You should find and correct at least two spelling errors.) Save your changes, close the document, and exit Word. Submit the assignment as specified by your instructor.

Capstone Project 2

Problem: As a volunteer at the Easton Humane Society, you are helping to create a newsletter updating local residents on fund-raising and volunteer efforts. You will format the two-page newsletter by adding a WordArt heading, creating one table and revising another, creating and applying a new style, formatting text in columns, adding a textbox, and editing a photo.

Instructions: Run Word. Open the document SC_Word2013_Capstone_2-1.docx and save it with the name SC_Word2013_Capstone_2-2.docx. You will also need the following support file from the student data files:

SC_Word2013_Capstone_volunteers.docx

Perform the following tasks:

1. Set custom document margins by changing the top and bottom margins to 0.5".
2. Turn on automatic hyphenation for the document.
3. Change the heading font of the document theme to Bookman Old Style and save the customized theme font using the name Easton.
4. Move the insertion point to the blank paragraph after "Our Animal Friends Need Our Help." Insert WordArt using the Fill – Aqua, Accent 1, Shadow option (2nd column, 1st row of the WordArt gallery). Type Easton Humane Society as the WordArt text.
5. Apply the following formatting to the WordArt shape: Change the text wrapping to In Line with Text. Resize the WordArt to a height of 0.89" and a width of 5.32". Apply the Chevron Up text effect (1st column, 2nd row in the Warp section of the Transform gallery).
6. Format the "Our Animal Friends Need Our Help" paragraph as follows: Add a Box paragraph border. Apply the Gold, Accent 5 border color (9th column, 1st row in the Color palette in the Borders and Shading dialog box). Use a 3 pt. border width. Apply the Aqua, Accent 1 shading color (5th column, 1st row in the Shading gallery). Change the font color to White, Background 1 (1st column, 1st row in the Theme Colors palette). Apply the Small Caps font effect.
7. Create a style based on the formats in the "Our Animal Friends Need Our Help" heading. Name the new style Easton.
8. At the top of page two, apply the new Boxed Heading style to the "Easton Wish List" heading.
9. In the table on page one, in the "TOTAL" row of the "Amount" column, insert a formula that sums the numeric values above the "Total" row.
10. In the "Amount" column, change the amount of the city grant from $10,000 to $15,000. Update the formula in the "TOTAL" row for the "Amount" column to display the correct total.
11. Distribute the columns so they are of equal width.
12. Move the insertion point to the blank paragraph above the paragraph that begins "To join our volunteer crew...." Insert text from the file SC_Word2013_Capstone_volunteers.docx, available from the student data files, and then create a table as follows: Convert the inserted text to a table with four columns. In row 1 of the table, merge the cells in columns 3 and 4. In each of the remaining rows (rows 2–5), merge the cells in columns 3 and 4.
13. Insert a row at the bottom of the table and enter the text shown in the bottom row in Figure 2–1.

Volunteers	Hours Per Week	Favorite Shifts
Michael J. Porter	40	Monday–Friday All day
Gertrude Dronzek	25	Monday, Wednesday–Friday Afternoons
Susan Samuelson	23	Tuesday–Thursday Afternoons
Charles Anufrom	12	Monday, Wednesday Mornings
Petra Johansson	25	Thursday–Saturday All day

Figure 2–1 Table with New Last Row

14. Format the new table as follows: Apply the Grid Table 4 – Accent 5 style to the table. AutoFit the table to its contents. Sort the table so that the hours per week appear in ascending order.
15. In the last paragraph of page one, delete the Company Email content control and replace it with the following email address: bakersfield@easton.cengage.com.

16. Format the "bakersfield@easton.cengage.com" email address as a hyperlink using the information shown in bold in Table 2–1.

Table 2–1 Hyperlink Settings

Field	Text to Insert
Text to display	bakersfield@easton.cengage.com
Email address	mailto:bakersfield@prairie.cengage.com
ScreenTip text	Create a new email message addressed to Jessica Bakersfield

17. In the blank paragraph at the bottom of page one, insert a SmartArt graphic as follows: Use the Equation style (1st column, 10th row in the Process category).
18. Insert the text Donors into the first shape. Insert the text Volunteers into the second shape. Insert the text Happy Pets into the third shape.
19. Resize the entire SmartArt to a height of 2" and a width of 6.35".
20. On page two, move the insertion point to the beginning of the "Dog Supplies," and then insert a Continuous section break.
21. Format the new section to display text in three columns.
22. With the insertion point at the beginning of the "Dog Supplies" heading, insert the Banded Quote text box (1st column, 2nd row in the Text Box gallery).
23. Enter the following text into the text box: We're always in need of supplies for our animals. Consider donating any of the items on our wish list.
24. Change the text wrapping around the text box to Tight.
25. At the bottom of the first column, insert a Column break at the beginning of the "Cat Supplies" heading.
26. Move the text box down so that it appears between columns 1 and 2, below "Collars" in the "Dog Supplies" list, as shown in Figure 2–2.
27. Flip the photo of the dog horizontally, and then move the photo to just above the "Small-Animal Supplies" heading, as shown in Figure 2–3.

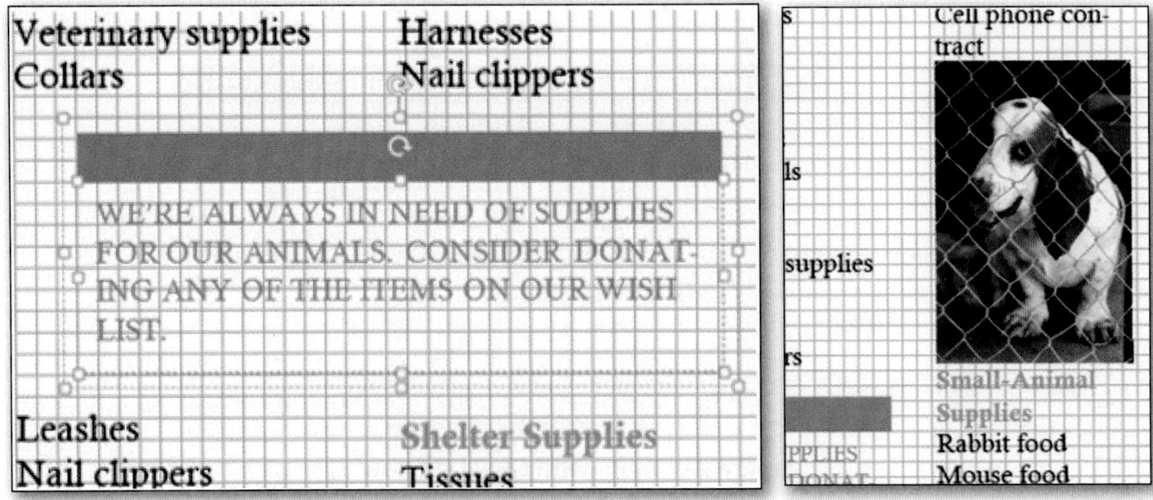

Figure 2–2 Text Box Placement

Figure 2–3 Photo Placement

28. Save your changes, close the document, and exit Word. Submit the assignment as specified by your instructor.

Capstone Project 3

Problem: Spring Time Gymnastics needs to increase its enrollment for the upcoming competitive season. Spring Time's operations manager, Kelly Randall, has asked you to prepare some marketing materials that the gym can use to attract successful gymnasts who can help the team win competitions. You will need to create a flyer, track changes on a memo, add a photo index, and design a form.

Note: To complete this assignment, you will be required to use the Data Files for Students. Visit www.cengage.com/ct/studentdownload for detailed instructions or contact your instructor for information about accessing the required files.

Instructions, Part 1: Create the brochure shown in Figure 3–1 for Kelly to send to prospective gymnasts. Start Word and create a new blank document. Save the new document with the file name, Cap 1 Brochure Text. Change the layout to a landscape page orientation and change the column layout to a three-column layout. Open the Brochure Template document from the Data Files for students, copy the text, and paste it into the Cap 1 Brochure Text document. Add a page break at the beginning of the brochure text so that the brochure text begins on page 2. Format the text as shown in Figure 3–1.

Begin by changing the page color to Lavender, Accent 6, Lighter 40%. Update the template's document styles to match the figure. Enter the text shown on page 1 of the brochure for the back and front panels, as shown in Figure 3-1a. For the back panel text, use the Heading 1 Brochure title style and change the font to Tempus Sans ITC. Change the title font size to 26 and the color to Lavender, Accent 6, Darker 25%. Add the Cap 1 beam figure from the Data Files for Students to the opening panel of the brochure and resize the image as necessary. Apply the Metal Frame picture style to the figure.

On the second page of the brochure, format the paragraph headlines with the Heading Top of Column text style and change the text to Tempus Sans ITC, size 14. Change the body text to Eras Medium ITC, size 11. Change the spacing of the body text paragraphs to 1.25. Save the file as Spring Time Brochure.

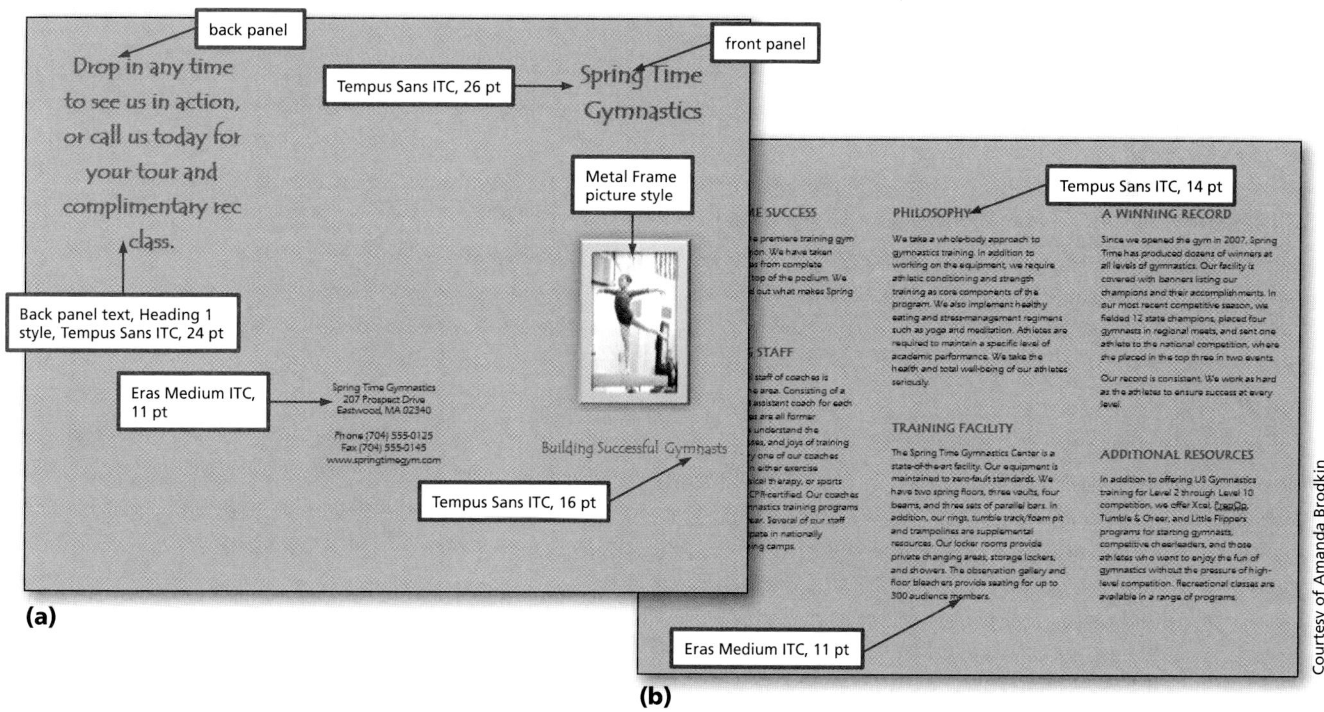

Courtesy of Amanda Brodkin

Figure 3–1

Instructions, Part 2: Kelly is working on a poster to advertise the gym's upcoming spring invitational meet. She needs to collect feedback on the meet's poster, participants, and other details from Spring Time's owner, Stephen Grimaldi. Modify a memo for review by Stephen. Open the Spring Time Memo.docx file from the Data Files for Students. Enable Track Changes, and then annotate the memo with Stephen's edits as shown in Figure 3–2. Correct the spelling, capitalization, and other language as shown in the figure. Add the three comments from Stephen.

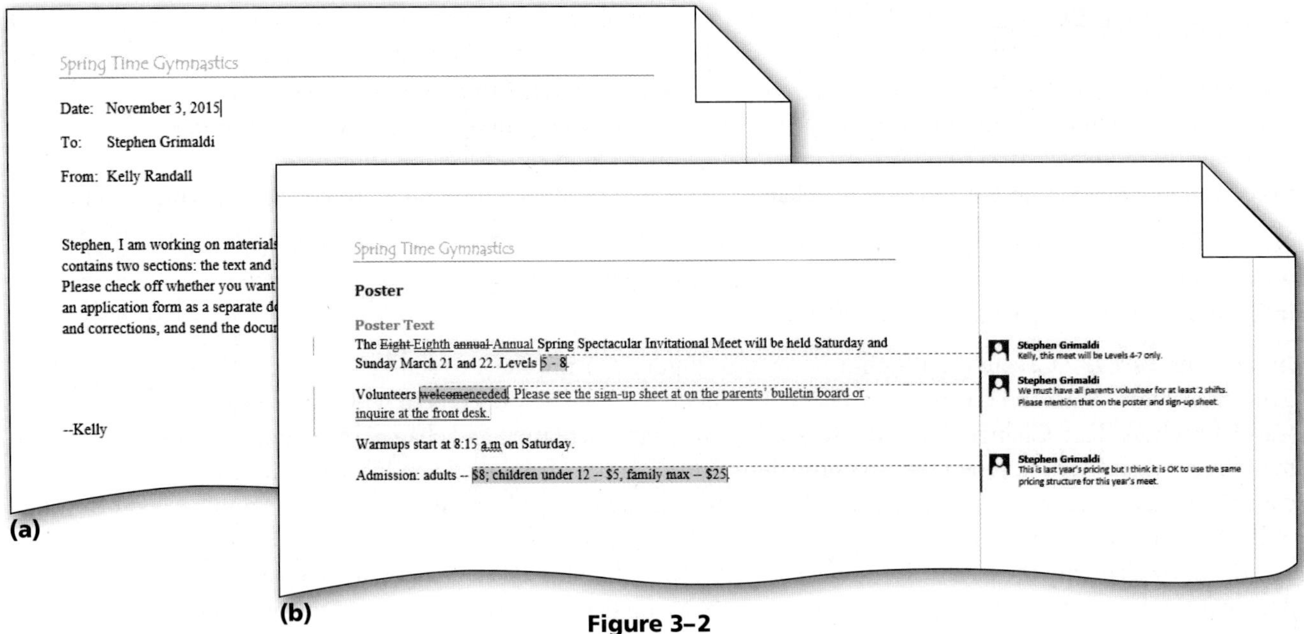

Figure 3–2

Add captions for the four photos on pages 3, 4, and 5 of the memo, as shown in Figure 3–3 and 3–4, and then create a table of figures, as shown in Figure 3–4.

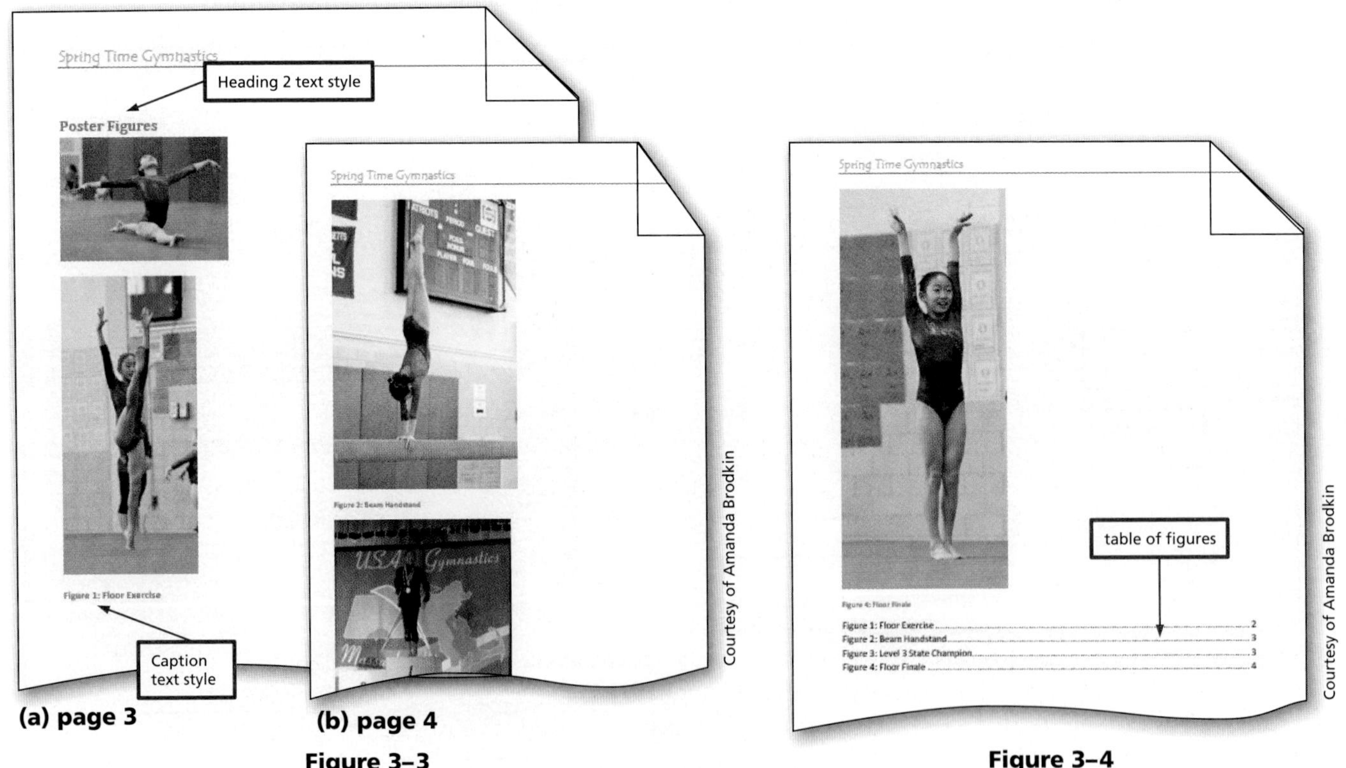

Figure 3–3

Figure 3–4

Page 6 of the memo consists of a table to track potential participating gyms, as shown in Figure 3–5. Use the Heading 1 text style for the table title and change the font color to Purple, Accent 4, Darker 50%. With the List Table 4-Accent 4 table style, create the table shown in Figure 3–5, and add a check box content control to the Invite? column. Save the memo with the name Spring Time Memo SG, where S is your first initial and G is your last initial.

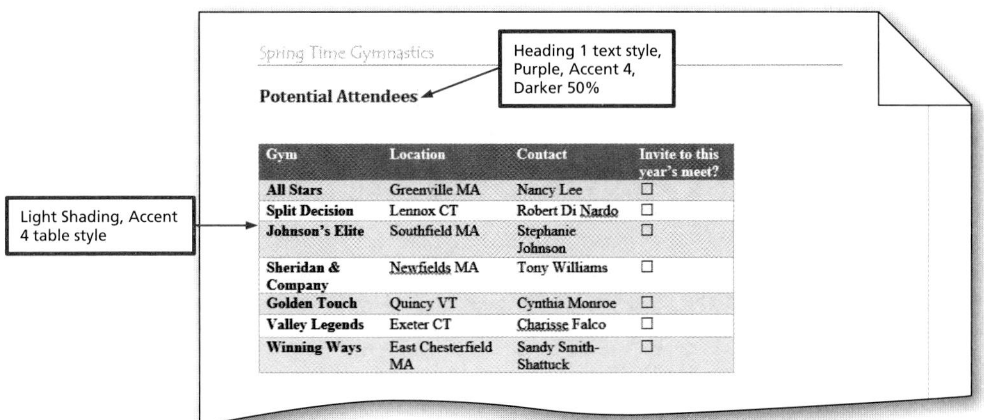

Figure 3–5

Instructions, Part 3: To collect information on the gyms that will be participating in the meet, Kelly wants to use an electronic form that she can send as an email attachment. Create the form shown in Figure 3–6. Open a new document and save it with the name, Spring Time Meet Form. The form should be 8" tall and 4" wide.

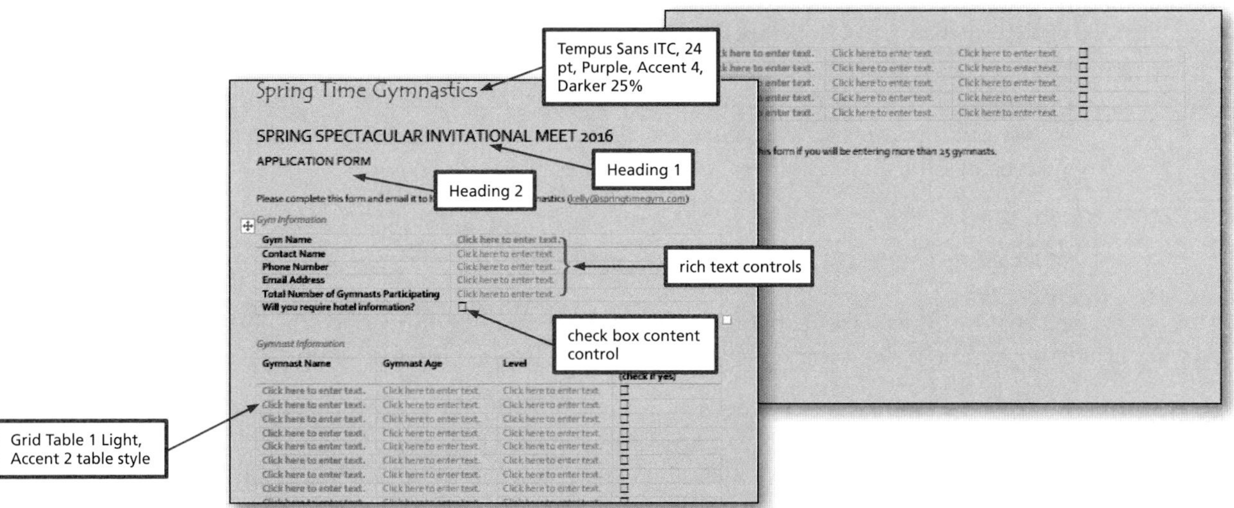

Figure 3–6

Use Narrow margins and apply the Basis theme. Change the document colors to the Violet II color scheme. Change the page color to Lavender, Background 2, Darker 10%. Create the form content as shown in Figure 3–6. Insert a two-column table in the position indicated in the figure to use for the form fields. Enter the text for the first field, Gym Name, and turn on Design Mode. Format the right column with plain text controls and modify the placeholder text for each row as shown in the figure.

Create a second form for recording the gymnast info. Use a four-column table. Format the first row with 11 point Tw Cent MT, bold text. Format the first three fields as plain text controls and modify the placeholder text as shown in the figure. The fourth field should contain a check box content control. Copy and paste the second row 24 times for a total of 25 gymnast rows.

Save the form and submit it, along with the flyer and memo, in the format requested by your instructor.

Appendix D

Microsoft Office 2013 Specialist and Expert Certifications

What Are Microsoft Office Specialist and Expert Certifications?

Microsoft Corporation has developed a set of standardized, performance-based examinations that you can take to demonstrate your overall expertise with Microsoft Office 2013 programs, including Microsoft Word 2013, Microsoft PowerPoint 2013, Microsoft Excel 2013, Microsoft Access 2013, and Microsoft Outlook 2013. When you successfully complete an examination for one of these Office programs, you will have earned the designation as a specialist or as an expert in that particular Office program. These examinations collectively are called the Microsoft Office 2013 Specialist and Microsoft Office 2013 Expert certification exams.

Why Should You Be Certified?

Microsoft Office 2013 certification provides a number of benefits for both you and your potential employer. The benefits for you include the following:

- You can differentiate yourself in the employment marketplace from those who are not Microsoft Office Specialist or Expert certified.
- You have proved your skills and expertise when using Microsoft Office 2013.
- You will be able to perform at a higher skill level in your job.
- You will be working at a higher professional level than those who are not certified.
- You will broaden your employment opportunities and advance your career more rapidly.

For employers, Microsoft Office 2013 certification offers the following advantages:

- When hiring or promoting employees, employers have immediate verification of employees' skills.
- Companies can maximize their productivity and efficiency by employing Microsoft Office 2013 certified individuals.

Skills Mapping

The following mapping information shows where each skill in the Word 2013 certification exams is covered in this text.

Table D–1 Specialist-Level Skill Sets and Locations in Book for Microsoft Word 2013

Skill Set	Page Number
1.0 Create and Manage Documents	
1.1 Create a Document	
creating new blank documents	OFF 11, OFF 43, OFF 46, WD 4
creating new documents using templates	WD 276, WD 342
importing files	WD 223, WD 304, WD 718 (BTW)
opening non-native files directly in Word	WD 718 (BTW)
opening a PDF in Word for editing	WD 304 (To-Do B open pdf from Word)
1.2 Navigate through a Document	
searching for text within document	WD 113, WD 115, WD 578 (BTW)
inserting hyperlinks	WD 163 (Table 3-2), WD 319, WD 321, WD 595 (BTW), WD 596
creating bookmarks	WD 594, WD 595
using Go To	WD 111, WD 378, WD 498 (BTW), WD 547, WD 554, WD 581, WD 595
1.3 Format a Document	
modifying page setup	WD 43, WD 140, WD 141 (Q&A), WD 280, WD 387, WD 433, WD 571, WD 592
changing document themes	WD 31, WD 148, WD 259, WD 458, WD 618 (BTW)
changing document style sets	WD 321
inserting simple headers and footers	WD 74, WD 76 (BTW), WD 77, WD 228, WD 230
inserting watermarks	WD 257, WD 258, WD 259 (Q&A)
inserting page numbers	WD 76, WD 230, WD 300, WD 553 (BTW), WD 574
1.4 Customize Options and Views for Documents	
changing document views	WD 5, WD 52, WD 53, WD 121, WD 318 (Q&A), WD 561, WD 562, WD 593
using zoom	WD 6 (BTW), WD 7, WD 8 (Q&A), WD 30, WD 35, WD 37, WD 258
customizing the Quick Access toolbar	OFF 20, OFF 21, WD 710, WD 712
customizing the Ribbon	OFF 44 (BTW), WD 616, WD 626, WD 657
splitting the window	WD 445, WD 446, WD 447
adding values to document properties	WD 44, WD 684 (BTW)
using Show/Hide	WD 6, WD 7 (Q&A)
recording simple macros	WD 707, WD 709
assigning shortcut keys	WD 689 (BTW), WD 708
managing macro security	WD 679
1.5 Configure Documents to Print or Save	
configuring documents to print	WD 50, WD 51, WD 53 (BTW), WD 122 (BTW), WD 225, WD 487
saving documents in alternate file formats	WD 165, WD 302, WD 305, WD 307, WD 309, WD 317, WD 613, WD 661 (BTW), WD 677
printing document sections	WD 225

Table D–1 Specialist-Level Skill Sets and Locations in Book for Microsoft Word 2013 *(continued)*

Skill Set	Page Number
saving files to remote locations	OFF 33, WD 310, WD 313
protecting documents with passwords	WD 655, WD 656, WD 657 (BTW)
setting print scaling	WD 593 (BTW)
maintaining backward compatibility	WD 306, WD 307, WD 309
2.0 Format Text, Paragraphs, and Sections	
2.1 Insert Text and Paragraphs	
appending text to documents	WD 5, WD 11, WD 46, WD 48, WD 49, WD 79, WD 220, WD 221 (BTW), WD 223, WD 434
finding and replacing text	WD 113, WD 114, WD 115, WD 115 (BTW), WD 116, WD 576, WD 578
copying and pasting text	WD 112, WD 113, WD 446
inserting text via AutoCorrect	WD 9 (BTW), WD 84, WD 85, WD 85, WD 87, WD 163 (Table 3-2)
removing blank paragraphs	WD 257, WD 359 (Step 1)
inserting built-in fields	WD 77 (Other Ways), WD 168, WD 230 (BTW), WD 350, WD 358, WD 359, WD 361, WD 363, WD 364, WD 365, WD 366, WD 367, WD 368, WD 449, WD 545, WD 685, WD 686
inserting special characters (©, ™, £)	WD 158, WD 159, WD 160 (BTW), WD 173 (BTW)
2.2 Format Text and Paragraphs	
changing font attributes	WD 13, WD 14, WD 17, WD 18, WD 19, WD 20, WD 25, WD 26, WD 27, WD 29, WD 80 (Table 2-1), WD 147, WD 652
using Find and Replace to format text	WD 114, WD 115 (BTW), WD 576, WD 577 (Q&A), WD 578 (BTWs)
using Format Painter	WD 233
setting paragraph spacing	WD 72, WD 73, WD 80 (Table 2–2), WD 431, WD 551
setting line spacing	WD 72, WD 80 (Table 2–2)
clearing existing formatting	WD 161, WD 210
setting indentation	WD 80 (Table 2–2), WD 82, WD 108, WD 209, WD 293
highlighting text selections	WD 367, WD 652, WD 657 (BTW)
adding styles to text	WD 5 (Q&A), WD 70, WD 105, WD 165, WD 226, WD 233, WD 297, WD 298, WD 431
changing text to WordArt	WD 414, WD 416, WD 420
modifying existing style attributes	WD 73, WD 94, WD 227, WD 299
2.3 Order and Group Text and Paragraphs	
preventing paragraph orphans	WD 101 (Q&A)
inserting breaks to create sections	WD 221, WD 222, WD 223, WD 432, WD 440
creating multiple columns within sections	WD 433, WD 441
adding titles to sections	*Functionality not found in Word 2013
forcing page breaks	WD 101, WD 105, WD 226, WD 242 (BTW), WD 247
3.0 Create Tables and Lists	
3.1 Create a Table	
converting text to tables	WD 390
converting tables to text	WD 682
defining table dimensions	WD 174, WD 176

Table D–1 Specialist-Level Skill Sets and Locations in Book for Microsoft Word 2013 *(continued)*

Skill Set	Page Number
setting AutoFit options	WD 178, WD 241 (Q&A), WD 391 (Step 2)
using Quick Tables	WD 523
establishing titles	WD 723
3.2 Modify a Table	
applying styles to tables	WD 177, WD 391 (Q&A), WD 243, WD 254, WD 255, WD 524
modifying fonts within tables	WD 183
sorting table data	WD 248, WD 392
configuring cell margins	WD 178, WD 182 (BTW), WD 245
using formulas	WD 192 (EYK), WD 256, WD 466 (EYK), WD 553 (BTW)
modifying table dimensions	WD 178 (Q&A), WD 181, WD 182
merging cells	WD 182, WD 183, WD 252
3.3 Create and Modify a List	
adding numbering or bullets	WD 23, WD 163 (Table 3–2), WD 184, WD 236
creating custom bullets	WD 191 (EYK), WD 234, WD 559
modifying list indentation	WD 236, WD 237, WD 238
modifying line spacing	WD 72
increasing and decreasing list levels	WD 236, WD 237, WD 238
modifying numbering	WD 237 (Q&A)
4.0 Apply References	
4.1 Create Endnotes, Footnotes, and Citations	
inserting endnotes	WD 92, WD 99, WD 125–126 (EYK)
managing footnote locations	WD 99
configuring endnote formats	WD 99
modifying footnote numbering	WD 99
inserting citation placeholders	WD 93
inserting citations	WD 89, WD 96, WD 109
inserting bibliography	WD 106, WD 110
changing citation styles	WD 98
4.2 Create Captions	
adding captions	WD 544, WD 548
setting caption positions	WD 544, WD 545 (Q&A)
changing caption formats	WD 544 (Q&A)
changing caption labels	WD 544 (Q&A)
excluding labels from captions	WD 544
5.0 Insert and Format Objects	
5.1 Insert and Format Building Blocks	
inserting Quick Parts	WD 77 (OW), WD 170, WD 172, WD 230 (OW), WD 259 (OW), WD 300, WD 444 (OW), WD 553 (OW), WD 569 (OW), WD 573 (OW), WD 589, WD 684 (BTW), WD 685
inserting textboxes	WD 300, WD 444, WD 447, WD 448, WD 449, WD 552
utilizing Building Blocks Organizer	WD 172, WD 230 (OW), WD 259 (OW), WD 300, WD 302, WD 444 (OW), WD 553, WD 554 (BTW), WD 569 (OW), WD 573 (OW)
customizing building blocks	WD 171, WD 302

Table D–1 Specialist-Level Skill Sets and Locations in Book for Microsoft Word 2013 *(continued)*

Skill Set	Page Number
5.2 Insert and Format Shapes and SmartArt	
inserting simple shapes	WD 142, WD 648
inserting SmartArt	WD 211, WD 212
modifying SmartArt properties (color, size, shape)	WD 213 (Q&A), WD 214, WD 215, WD 216, WD 217, WD 454, WD 456, WD 457
wrapping text around shapes	WD 144, WD 145, WD 154, WD 460, WD 461
positioning shapes	WD 144, WD 145, WD 155, WD 157, WD 461
5.3 Insert and Format Images	
inserting images	WD 33, WD 34, WD 142, WD 148, WD 414, WD 424, WD 505, WD 542
applying artistic effects	WD 700
applying picture effects	WD 39
modifying image properties (color, size, shape)	WD 36, WD 37 (Q&A), WD 38, WD 150, WD 151, WD 152, WD 153, WD 154, WD 157, WD 216, WD 217, WD 415, WD 416, WD 420, WD 424, WD 425, WD 509, WD 510, WD 651, WD 699
adding Quick Styles to images	WD 38, WD 145, WD 217, WD 448, WD 509, WD 510, WD 651
wrapping text around images	WD 144, WD 145, WD 154, WD 416, WD 426, WD 622
positioning images	WD 35, WD 38 (Q&A), WD 155, WD 157, WD 385, WD 427, WD 428

Table D-2 Expert-Level Skill Sets and Locations in Book for Microsoft Word 2013

Skill Set	Page Number
1.0 Manage and Share Documents	
1.1 Manage Multiple Documents	
modifying existing templates	WD 276–WD 300, WD 341–WD 378, WD 521–WD 525, WD 613–WD 657, WD 660, WD 677–WD 718
merging multiple documents	WD 223, WD 494, WD 561–WD 567
managing versions of documents	WD 307, WD 493, WD 560
copying styles from template to template	WD 719
using the style organizer	WD 719, WD 720, WD 721
copying macros from document to document	WD 720
linking to external data	WD 319, WD 321, WD 498, WD 499, WD 501, WD 502, WD 503, WD 504, WD 595, WD 596, WD 661 (BTW)
moving building blocks between documents	WD 692 (BTW)
1.2 Prepare Documents for Review	
setting tracking options	WD 480, WD 482, WD 484, WD 486, WD 491, WD 492
limiting authors	WD 487 (BTW)
restricting editing	WD 487, WD 655, WD 656, WD 660, WD 678, WD 717
deleting document draft version	WD 560
removing document metadata	WD 315, WD 491 (BTW), WD 722

Table D-2 Expert-Level Skill Sets and Locations in Book for Microsoft Word 2013 *(continued)*

Skill Set	Page Number
marking as final	WD 492 (BTW), WD 719, WD 730 (EYK)
protecting a document with a password	WD 655, WD 656, WD 657, WD 660, WD 664 (EYK)
1.3 Manage Document Changes	
tracking changes	WD 482, WD 483, WD 484, WD 486, WD 489, WD 491, WD 497
managing comments	WD 478, WD 480, WD 481, WD 484, WD 486, WD 488, WD 489, WD 497
using markup options	WD 482, WD 484, WD 486, WD 487, WD 491, WD 492
resolving a multi-document style conflicts	WD 492 (BTW), WD 493, WD 494
displaying all changes	WD 484, WD 486, WD 487
2.0 Design Advanced Documents	
2.1 Apply Advanced Formatting	
using wildcards in find and replace searches	WD 578 (BTW)
creating custom field formats	WD 687 (BTW)
setting advanced layout options	WD 571, WD 574 (BTW), WD 615, WD 618, WD 619, WD 623
setting character space options	WD 218
setting advanced character attributes	WD 690 (BTW)
creating and breaking section links	WD 222, WD 223, WD 228, WD 230, WD 432, WD 440, WD 589
linking textboxes	WD 556
2.2 Apply Advanced Styles	
creating custom styles	WD 297, WD 322 (Q&A), WD 690
customizing settings for existing styles	WD 70, WD 94, WD 299
creating character-specific styles	WD 690
assigning keyboard shortcuts to styles	WD 689 (BTW)
2.3 Apply Advanced Ordering and Grouping	
creating outlines	WD 236, WD 561, WD 562, WD 562, WD 564, WD 567
promoting sections in outlines	WD 563
creating master documents	WD 561, WD 564, WD 566
inserting subdocuments	WD 564, WD 566
linking document elements	WD 162, WD 228, WD 319, WD 321,WD 498, WD 501, WD 503, WD 545, WD 548, WD 556
3.0 Create Advanced References	
3.1 Create and Manage Indexes	
creating indexes	WD 585, WD 587, WD 588, WD 589
updating indexes	WD 588
marking index entries	WD 549, WD 551
using index auto-mark files	WD 586
3.2 Create and Manage Reference Tables	
creating a table of contents	WD 573, WD 575, WD 579
creating a table of figures	WD 582, WD 583, WD 583
formatting a table of contents	WD 578, WD 580, WD 583 (BTW)

Table D-2 Expert-Level Skill Sets and Locations in Book for Microsoft Word 2013 *(continued)*	
Skill Set	**Page Number**
updating a table of authorities	WD 589, WD 723–WD 726
setting advanced reference options (captions, footnotes, citations)	WD 99, WD 120, WD 545 (BTW), WD 561 (BTW), WD 722
3.3 Manage Forms, Fields, and Mail Merge Operations	
adding custom fields	WD 363, WD 365, WD 684 (BTW), WD 685, WD 686, WD 687 (BTW)
modifying field properties	WD 44, WD 630, WD 635, WD 638, WD 641, WD 644, WD 646, WD 684 (BTW), WD 686
adding controls	WD 625, WD 627, WD 634, WD 638, WD 640, WD 642, WD 645
modifying control properties	WD 630, WD 635, WD 638, WD 641, WD 644, WD 646
performing mail merges	WD 341–WD 379, WD 371, WD 373, WD 375, WD 376, WD 379–WD 384, WD 385, WD 387–WD 393
managing recipient lists	WD 350, WD 355, WD 356, WD 374, WD 377, WD 378
inserting merged fields	WD 358, WD 359, WD 360, WD 361, WD 362, WD 363, WD 364, WD 365, WD 367, WD 368
previewing results	WD 361, WD 362, WD 370, WD 371
4.0 Create Custom Word Elements	
4.1 Create and Modify Building Blocks	
creating custom building blocks	WD 170
saving selections as Quick Parts	WD 170
editing building block properties	WD 171, WD 302
deleting building blocks	WD 554 (BTW)
4.2 Create Custom Style Sets and Templates	
creating custom color themes	WD 458, WD 653
creating custom font themes	WD 296, WD 458
creating custom templates	WD 612, WD 625–WD 647, WD 655, WD 677
creating and managing style sets	WD 321
4.3 Prepare a Document for Internationalization and Accessibility	
configuring language options in documents	WD 722
adding alt-text to document elements	WD 723
creating documents for use with accessibility tools	WD 722, WD 723
managing multiple options for +Body and +Heading fonts	WD 17, WD 18, WD 80 (Table 2-1 and Table 2-2), WD 147, WD 218, WD 226, WD 259, WD 298, WD 689, WD 690
utilizing global content standards	WD 722, WD 723
modifying Tab order in document elements and objects	WD 662 (4c), WD 722, WD 728 (2a)

Index

Note: **Boldface** page numbers indicate key terms.

E

G

H

P

Q

R

U

V

W

X

Z

Quick Reference Summary

Microsoft Word 2013 Quick Reference Summary

Task	Page Number	Ribbon	Other On-Screen Element	Shortcut Menu	Keyboard Shortcut
Accessibility Checker	WD 722	FILE tab | Info tab, 'Check for Issues' button, Check Accessibility			
AddressBlock Merge Field, Edit	WD 360			'Edit Address Block'	
AddressBlock Merge Field, Insert	WD 359		'Insert formatted address' link in Mail Merge task pane		
All Caps	WD 19	Change Case button (HOME tab | Font group), UPPERCASE			CTRL+SHIFT+A
Alternative Text, Add to Graphics	WD 723	Format Shape Dialog Box Launcher (PICTURE TOOLS FORMAT tab | Picture Styles group or DRAWING TOOLS FORMAT tab or SMARTART TOOLS FORMAT tab or CHART TOOLS FORMAT tab | Shape Styles group), 'Layout & Properties' button (Format Picture, Format Shape, or Format Chart Area task pane), ALT TEXT section in task pane		Format Picture, Format Shape, Format Object, or Format Chart Area on shortcut menu Touch mode: 'Show Context Menu' button on mini toolbar, Format Picture, Format Shape, Format Object, or Format Chart Area on shortcut menu	
Alternative Text, Add to Tables	WD 723	Table Properties button (TABLE TOOLS LAYOUT tab | Table group), Alt Text tab (Table Properties dialog box)		Table Properties Touch mode: 'Show Context Menu' button on mini toolbar, Table Properties on shortcut menu, Alt Text tab (Table Properties dialog box)	
Arrange All Open Word Documents on Screen	WD 445	Arrange All button (VIEW tab | Window group)			
Art Page Border	WD 462	'Borders and Shading' button (DESIGN tab | Page Background group), Page Border tab (Borders and Shading dialog box)			

Microsoft Word 2013 Quick Reference Summary *(continued)*

Task	Page Number	Ribbon	Other On-Screen Element	Shortcut Menu	Keyboard Shortcut
Artistic Effect	WD 700	Artistic Effects button (PICTURE TOOLS FORMAT tab | Adjust group)			
AutoCorrect, Delete Entry	WD 86	Options (FILE tab), Proofing (Word Options dialog box), AutoCorrect Options button			
AutoCorrect, Set Exceptions	WD 87	Options (FILE tab), Proofing (Word Options dialog box), AutoCorrect Options button, Exceptions button (Auto Correction Exceptions dialog box)			
AutoCorrect Entry, Create	WD 85	Options (FILE tab), Proofing (Word Options dialog box)			
AutoCorrect Options Button, Use	WD 85		Point to AutoCorrect Options button in flagged word		
Background, Remove	WD 699	Remove Background button (PICTURE TOOLS FORMAT tab | Adjust group), adjust marking lines, 'Close Background Removal and Keep Changes' button (BACKGROUND REMOVAL tab | Close group)			
Bibliographical List, Create	WD 106	Bibliography button (REFERENCES tab | Citations & Bibliography group)			
Bibliography Style, Change	WD 89	Bibliography Style arrow (REFERENCES tab | Citations & Bibliography group)			
Blank Page, Insert	WD 572	'Add a Blank Page' button (INSERT tab | Pages group)			
Blog, Create Blank Document for Posting	WD 521	Blog post thumbnail (FILE tab | New tab), Create button			
Blog, Display in Browser	WD 525	Home Page button (BLOG POST tab | Blog group)			
Blog, Open Existing Post	WD 526	Open Existing button (BLOG POST tab | Blog group)			
Blog, Register Account	WD 520	Manage Accounts button (BLOG POST tab | Blog group), New (Blog Accounts dialog box)			
Blog Post, Publish	WD 525	Publish button (BLOG POST tab | Blog group)			
Bold	WD 29	Bold button (HOME tab | Font group)	Bold button on mini toolbar	Font, Font tab (Font dialog box) Touch mode: 'Show Context Menu' button on mini toolbar, Font on shortcut menu, Font tab (Font dialog box)	CTRL+B

Microsoft Word 2013 Quick Reference Summary *(continued)*

Task	Page Number	Ribbon	Other On-Screen Element	Shortcut Menu	Keyboard Shortcut
Bookmark, Add	WD 594	'Insert a Bookmark' button (INSERT tab | Links group)			
Bookmark, Go To	WD 595	'Insert a Bookmark' button (INSERT tab | Links group), tap or click bookmark name (Bookmark dialog box)			F5, Bookmark (Find and Replace dialog box)
Border Paragraph	WD 206	Borders arrow (HOME tab | Paragraph group), 'Borders and Shading' in Borders gallery			
Border Paragraph, Default Border	WD 160	Borders arrow (HOME tab | Paragraph group)			
Border Paragraph, One Edge	WD 422	Borders arrow (HOME tab | Paragraph group), 'Borders and Shading' in Borders gallery, Custom (Borders and Shading dialog box)			
Building Block, Create	WD 170	'Explore Quick Parts' button (INSERT tab | Text group)			ALT+F3
Building Block, Edit Properties	WD 302	'Explore Quick Parts' button (INSERT tab | Text group), 'Building Blocks Organizer', select building block to edit, Edit Properties button (Building Blocks Organizer dialog box)			
Building Block, Insert	WD 172	'Explore Quick Parts' button (INSERT tab | Text group), 'Building Blocks Organizer'			F3
Building Block, Modify	WD 171	'Explore Quick Parts' button (INSERT tab | Text group), press and hold or right-click building block, Edit Properties			
Bulleted List, Change Symbol Format	WD 559	Bullets arrow (HOME tab | Paragraph group)			
Bullets, Apply	WD 23	Bullets button (HOME tab | Paragraph group)	Bullets button on mini toolbar		* (ASTERISK), SPACEBAR
Bullets, Change Font Attributes	WD 560	Bullets arrow (HOME tab | Paragraph group), 'Define New Bullet'			
Bullets, Change Level	WD 560	Bullets arrow (HOME tab | Paragraph group), 'Change List Level'			
Bullets, Custom	WD 234	Bullets arrow (HOME tab | Paragraph group), 'Define New Bullet' in Bullets gallery			
Caption, Add	WD 544	Insert Caption button (REFERENCES tab | Captions group)			
Caption, Edit	WD 583		locate caption, edit as desired		

Microsoft Word 2013 Quick Reference Summary *(continued)*

Task	Page Number	Ribbon	Other On-Screen Element	Shortcut Menu	Keyboard Shortcut
Center	WD 15	Center button (HOME tab | Paragraph group)	Center button on mini toolbar	Paragraph, Indents and Spacing tab (Paragraph dialog box)	CTRL+E
Center Page Vertically	WD 43	Page Setup Dialog Box Launcher (PAGE LAYOUT tab | Page Setup group), Layout tab (Page Setup dialog box)			
Change Case	WD 19	Change Case button (HOME tab | Font group)		Font, Font tab (Font dialog box) Touch mode: 'Show Context Menu' on mini toolbar, Font on shortcut menu, Font tab (Font dialog box)	SHIFT+F3
Change Spacing before or after Paragraph	WD 42	Spacing Before or Spacing After box (PAGE LAYOUT tab | Paragraph group)		Paragraph, Indents and Spacing tab (Paragraph dialog box) Touch mode: 'Show Context Menu' button on mini toolbar, Paragraph on shortcut menu, Indents and Spacing tab (Paragraph dialog box)	
Character Attribute, Advanced	WD 690	Font Dialog Box Launcher (HOME tab | Font group), Advanced tab (Font dialog box)			
Character Spacing	WD 218	Font Dialog Box Launcher (HOME tab | Font group), Advanced tab (Font dialog box)		Font	CTRL+D
Character Style, Create	WD 690	Styles Dialog Box Launcher (HOME tab | Styles group), Manage Styles button in Styles task pane, New Style button (Manage Styles dialog box)			
Chart, Add Data Series	WD 509	Select Data button (CHART TOOLS DESIGN tab | Data group), Add button (Select Data Source dialog box)	Drag sizing handle to include desired series		
Chart, Add Element	WD 511	'Add Chart Element' button (CHART TOOLS DESIGN tab | Chart Layouts group)			
Chart, Add Outline	WD 515	Chart Elements arrow (CHART TOOLS FORMAT tab | Current Selection group), Chart Area, Shape Outline button (CHART TOOLS FORMAT tab | Shape Styles group)			
Chart, Apply Style	WD 509	Select chart, tap or click desired style (CHART TOOLS DESIGN tab | Chart Styles group)	Chart Styles button attached to chart, STYLE tab		
Chart, Change Colors	WD 510	'Chart Quick Colors' button (CHART TOOLS DESIGN tab | Chart Styles group)	Chart Styles button attached to chart, COLOR tab		

Microsoft Word 2013 Quick Reference Summary *(continued)*

Task	Page Number	Ribbon	Other On-Screen Element	Shortcut Menu	Keyboard Shortcut
Chart, Change Type	WD 516	'Change Chart Type' button (CHART TOOLS DESIGN tab | Type group)			
Chart, Edit Element	WD 512	Chart Elements arrow (CHART TOOLS FORMAT tab | Current Selection group)	Tap or click element to select		
Chart, Format Element	WD 512	Chart Elements arrow (CHART TOOLS FORMAT tab | Current Selection group), select from list, tap or click Chart Elements button			
Chart, Remove Data Series	WD 508	Select Data button (CHART TOOLS DESIGN tab | Data group), Remove button (Select Data Source dialog box)	Drag sizing handle to include desired series		
Chart Table	WD 505	'Add a Chart' button (INSERT tab | Illustrations group)			
Citation, Edit	WD 98		Tap or click citation, Citations Options arrow, Edit Citation		
Citation, Insert	WD 89	Insert Citation button (REFERENCES tab | Citations & Bibliography group), 'Add New Source'			
Citation Placeholder, Insert	WD 93	Insert Citation button (REFERENCES tab | Citations & Bibliography group), 'Add New Placeholder'			
Clear Formatting	WD 161	'Clear All Formatting' button (HOME tab | Font group)			CTRL+SPACEBAR, CTRL+Q
Click and Type	WD 79		Position pointer until desired icon appears, then double-tap or double-click		
Clip Art, Insert	WD 148	Online Pictures button (INSERT tab | Illustrations group)			
Color Text	WD 26	Font Color arrow (HOME tab | Font group)	Font Color arrow on mini toolbar	Font, Font tab (Font dialog box) Touch mode: 'Show Context Menu' on mini toolbar, Font on shortcut menu	
Column Break, Insert	WD 441	'Insert Page and Section Breaks' button (PAGE LAYOUT tab | Page Setup group), Column			CTRL+SHIFT+ENTER
Column Break, Remove	WD 442	Select column break, Cut button (HOME tab | Clipboard group)			Select column break, DELETE
Columns, Balance	WD 453	'Insert Page and Section Breaks' button (PAGE LAYOUT tab | Page Setup group), Continuous			
Columns, Change Number	WD 450	'Add or Remove Columns' button (PAGE LAYOUT tab | Page Setup group)			

Microsoft Word 2013 Quick Reference Summary *(continued)*

Task	Page Number	Ribbon	Other On-Screen Element	Shortcut Menu	Keyboard Shortcut
Columns, Change Width	WD 436	'Add or Remove Columns' button (PAGE LAYOUT tab | Page Setup group), More Columns in Add or Remove Columns gallery			
Columns, Different Widths	WD 434	'Add or Remove Columns' button (PAGE LAYOUT tab | Page Setup group), More Columns in Add or Remove Columns gallery, clear 'Equal column width' check box (Columns dialog box)	Double-tap or double-click between columns, enter settings (Column dialog box) or drag column boundaries		
Combine Revisions from Multiple Authors	WD 494	Compare button (REVIEW tab | Compare group), Combine			
Comment, Delete	WD 488	Delete Comment button (REVIEW tab | Comments group)		Delete Comment Touch mode: 'Show Context Menu' button on mini toolbar, Delete Comment on shortcut menu	
Comment, Insert	WD 478	'Insert a Comment'button (REVIEW tab | Comments group)			CTRL+ALT+M
Comment, Reply To	WD 481	'Insert a Comment' button (REVIEW tab | Comments group)	Reply button in selected comment		CTRL+ALT+M
Comments, Delete All	WD 489	Delete Comment arrow (REVIEW tab | Comments group), 'Delete All Comments in Document'			
Comments, Locate Reviewer	WD 498	Find arrow (HOME tab | Editing group), Go To, Comment			CTRL+G, Comment
Comments, Mark as Done	WD 489			'Mark Comment Done' Touch mode: 'Show Context Menu' button on mini toolbar, 'Mark Comment Done' on shortcut menu	
Comments, View	WD 488	NextComment button (REVIEW tab | Comments group)			
Compare and Merge	WD 492	Compare button (REVIEW tab | Compare group), Original document or Revised document			
Compare Documents	WD 493	Compare button (REVIEW tab | Compare group)			
Compatibility Checker	WD 306	'Check for Issues' button (FILE tab | Info tab)			
Compress Picture	WD 558	Compress Pictures button (PICTURE TOOLS FORMAT tab | Adjust group)			
Concordance File, Create	WD 586	Insert Index button (REFERENCES tab | Index group), AutoMark button (Index dialog box)			

Microsoft Word 2013 Quick Reference Summary *(continued)*

Task	Page Number	Ribbon	Other On-Screen Element	Shortcut Menu	Keyboard Shortcut
Content Control, Add Item	WD 288		Select content control, Insert Control on right edge of content control	'Insert Item Before' or 'Insert Item After'	
Content Control, Change Properties	WD 630	Control Properties button (DEVELOPER tab | Controls group)			
Content Control, Check Box, Insert	WD 638	'Check Box Content Control' button (DEVELOPER tab | Controls group)			
Content Control, Combo Box, Insert	WD 642	'Combo Box Content Control' button (DEVELOPER tab | Controls group)			
Content Control, Date Picker, Insert	WD 645	'Date Picker Content Control' button (DEVELOPER tab | Controls group)			
Content Control, Delete	WD 285	Cut button (HOME tab | Clipboard group)		'Remove Content Control'	CTRL+X or DELETE or BACKSPACE
Content Control, Delete Item	WD 292			Delete Item	
Content Control, Drop-Down List, Insert	WD 634	'Drop-Down List Content Control' button (DEVELOPER tab | Controls group)			
Content Control, Edit Placeholder Text	WD 628	Design Mode button (DEVELOPER tab | Controls group)			
Content Control, Modify Text	WD 282		Tap or click content control name, type new text		
Content Control, Plain Text, Insert	WD 627	'Plain Text Content Control' button (DEVELOPER tab | Controls group)			
Content Control, Rich Text, Insert	WD 640	'Rich Text Content Control' button (DEVELOPER tab | Controls group)			
Convert Text to Table	WD 390	'Add a Table' button (INSERT tab | Tables group), 'Convert Text to Table' in Add a Table gallery			
Copy	WD 112	Copy button (HOME tab | Clipboard group)		Copy	CTRL+C
Count Words	WD 100	Word Count button (REVIEW tab | Proofing group)	Word Count indicator on status bar		CTRL+SHIFT+G
Cover Page	WD 568	'Add a Cover Page' button (INSERT tab | Pages group)			
Create New Document Based on Template	WD 658	FILE tab | New tab	Double-click or double-tap file in File Explorer		
Cross-Reference, Create	WD 545	'Insert Cross-reference' button (INSERT tab | Links group)			

Microsoft Word 2013 Quick Reference Summary *(continued)*

Task	Page Number	Ribbon	Other On-Screen Element	Shortcut Menu	Keyboard Shortcut
Cross-Reference, Update Manually	WD 547				Select cross-reference, CTRL+F9
Custom Dictionary, Set Default, View or Modify Entries	WD 118	Options (FILE tab), Proofing (Word Options dialog box), Custom Dictionaries button			
Customize Status Bar	WD 482			Tap or click item on Customize Status Bar menu	
Customized Themes, Save	WD 458	Themes button (DESIGN tab | Document Formatting group) 'Save Current Theme' in Themes gallery			
Data, Find and Display	WD 378	Find Recipient button (MAILINGS tab | Preview Results group)			
Data Source, Create	WD 350		'Type a new list' in Mail Merge task pane, 'Create new recipient list' in Type a new list area, Customize Columns button (New Address List dialog box)		
Data Source, Save	WD 355		Enter file name in File name box (Save Address List dialog box)		
Data Source, Sort Records	WD 377	'Edit Recipient List' button (MAILINGS tab | Start Mail Merge group), arrow to right of field name on which to sort			
Data Source, Use Outlook Contacts, Access Table, Excel Table or Word Table	WD 356	Select Recipients button (MAILINGS tab | Start Mail Merge group)	'Select from Outlook contacts' or 'Use an existing list' in Mail Merge task pane		
Date, Insert Current	WD 168	'Insert Date and Time' button (INSERT tab | Text group)			
Date, Insert from Calendar	WD 358	'Insert Date & Time' button (INSERT tab | Text group)	Tap or click content control, tap or click arrow		
Date Field, Insert	WD 685	'Explore Quick Parts' button (INSERT tab | Text group), Field			
Default Font Settings, Modify	WD 689	Font Dialog Box Launcher (HOME tab | Font group), 'Set As Default' button (Font dialog box)			

Microsoft Word 2013 Quick Reference Summary *(continued)*

Task	Page Number	Ribbon	Other On-Screen Element	Shortcut Menu	Keyboard Shortcut
Default Font Settings, Reset	WD 690		In File Explorer, locate Normal. dotm file, rename as oldnormal.dotm, run Word		
Delete Unsaved (Draft Version) Documents	WD 560	Manage Versions button (FILE tab | Info tab), 'Delete All Unsaved Documents'			
DEVELOPER Tab, Show/Hide	WD 626	FILE tab | Options, Customize Ribbon, Developer check box (Word Options dialog box)			
Digital Signature	WD 718	Protect Document button (FILE tab | Info tab), 'Add a Digital Signature'			
Document Inspector	WD 315	'Check for Issues' button (FILE tab | Info tab), Inspect Document			
Document Properties, Change	WD 44	Properties button (FILE tab | Info tab)			
Document Properties, Custom	WD 684	FILE tab | Info tab, Properties button, Advanced Properties, Custom tab (Document Properties dialog box)			
Document Properties, Insert	WD 684	'Explore Quick Parts' button (INSERT tab | Text group), Document Property, tap or click property			
Document Properties, Print	WD 104	FILE tab | Print tab, first button in Settings area			
Document Theme, Change	WD 148	Themes button (DESIGN tab | Document Formatting group)			
Double-Space	WD 72	'Line and Paragraph Spacing' button (HOME tab | Paragraph group)		Paragraph, Indents and Spacing tab (Paragraph dialog box)	CTRL+2
Double-Underline	WD 80	Underline arrow (HOME tab | Font group)		Font, Font tab (Font dialog box)	CTRL+SHIFT+D
Draft View	WD 593	Draft View button (VIEW tab | Views group)			
Draw Rectangle	WD 648	'Draw a Shape' button (INSERT tab | Illustrations group)			
Drawing Canvas	WD 698	'Draw a Shape' button (INSERT tab | Illustrations group), 'New Drawing Canvas' in Draw a Shape gallery			
Drop Cap	WD 438	'Add a Drop Cap' button (INSERT tab | Text group)			
Editing Restrictions	WD 715	FILE tab | Info tab, Protect Document button, 'Allow only this type of editing in the document' check box in Restrict Editing task pane, 'No changes (Read only)'			

Microsoft Word 2013 Quick Reference Summary *(continued)*

Task	Page Number	Ribbon	Other On-Screen Element	Shortcut Menu	Keyboard Shortcut
Email, Send Document Using	WD 314	Email (FILE tab | Share tab), 'Send as Attachment' button			
Email Attachments, Customize How Word Opens	WD 315	Options (FILE tab), General (Word Options dialog box)			
Embed Excel Worksheet in Word Document	WD 502	Copy button (HOME tab | Clipboard group); Paste arrow (HOME tab | Clipboard group), Paste Special, Paste option button (Paste Special dialog box) Touch mode: Copy button (HOME tab | Clipboard group), Copy; Paste arrow (HOME tab | Clipboard group), Paste Special, Paste option button (Paste Special dialog box)			
Envelope, Address and Print	WD 187	Create Envelopes button (MAILINGS tab | Create group), Envelopes tab (Envelopes and Labels dialog box)			
Envelopes, Mail Merge	WD 385	'Start Mail Merge' button (MAILINGS tab | Start Mail Merge group), 'Step-by-Step Mail Merge Wizard' on Start Mail Merge Menu, Envelopes in Mail Merge task pane			
Exit Word	WD 46		Close button on title bar		
Field, Convert to Regular Text	WD 110				Tap or click field, CTRL+SHIFT+F9
Field, Delete	WD 686	Select field, Cut button (HOME tab | Clipboard group)	Select field, DELETE	Cut Touch mode: Cut button on mini toolbar	
Field, Edit	WD 686			Edit Field	
Field, Update	WD 110			Update Field Touch mode: 'Show Context Menu' button on mini toolbar, Update Field on shortcut menu	Tap or click field, F9
Field Code, Display	WD 368			'Toggle Field Codes'	SHIFT+F9
Field Codes, Display All	WD 368				ALT+F9
Field Codes, Print	WD 369	Options (FILE tab), Advanced (Word Options dialog box), Print area			
Field Formats, Custom	WD 687	'Explore Quick Parts' button (INSERT tab | Text group), Field, Field Code button (Field dialog box), Options button, select format, 'Add to Field' button			

Microsoft Word 2013 Quick Reference Summary *(continued)*

Task	Page Number	Ribbon	Other On-Screen Element	Shortcut Menu	Keyboard Shortcut
Find Text	WD 113	Find button (HOME tab | Editing group)	Page Number indicator on status bar		CTRL+F
Folder, Create while Saving	WD 349		Save As button (Quick Access Toolbar), 'Create a new folder' button (Save As dialog box)		
Font, Change	WD 18	Font arrow (HOME tab | Font group)	Font arrow on mini toolbar Touch mode: 'Show Context Menu' on mini toolbar, Font on shortcut menu	Font, Font tab (Font dialog box)	CTRL+D
Font Size, Change	WD 17	Font Size arrow (HOME tab | Font group)	Font Size arrow on mini toolbar	Font, Font tab (Font dialog box) Touch mode: 'Show Context Menu' button on mini toolbar, Font on shortcut menu, Font tab (Font dialog box)	CTRL+D
Font Size, Decrease	WD 147	'Decrease Font Size' button (HOME tab | Font group)	Font button on mini toolbar	Font	CTRL+SHIFT+<
Font Size, Decrease 1 point	WD 80				CTRL+[
Font Size, Increase	WD 147	'Increase Font Size' button (HOME tab | Font group)	Font button on mini toolbar	Font	CTRL+SHIFT+>
Font Size, Increase 1 point	WD 80				CTRL+]
Footers, Alternating	WD 589	'Add a Footer' button (INSERT tab | Header & Footer group), Edit Footer, deselect 'Link to Previous' button (HEADER & FOOTER DESIGN tab | Navigation group), 'Different Odd & Even Pages' check box (HEADER & FOOTER DESIGN tab | Options group)			
Footnote, Change Format	WD 99	Footnote & Endnote Dialog Box Launcher (REFERENCES tab | Footnotes group)			
Footnote, Delete	WD 99	Select note reference mark, Cut button (HOME tab | Clipboard group)			CTRL+X
Footnote, Insert	WD 92	Insert Footnote button (REFERENCES tab | Footnotes group)			ALT+CTRL+F
Footnote, Move	WD 99	Select note reference mark, Cut button (HOME tab | Clipboard group); Paste button (HOME tab | Clipboard group)			CTRL+X; CTRL+V
Format, Find	WD 576	Find arrow (HOME tab | Editing group), Advanced Find			CTRL+F

Microsoft Word 2013 Quick Reference Summary *(continued)*

Task	Page Number	Ribbon	Other On-Screen Element	Shortcut Menu	Keyboard Shortcut
Formatting Marks	WD 6	'Show/Hide ¶' button (HOME tab | Paragraph group)			CTRL+SHIFT+*
Format Painter	WD 233	Format Painter button (HOME tab | Clipboard group)			
Go to a Page	WD 111	'Open the Navigation Pane' check box (VIEW tab | Show group), PAGES tab	Page Number indicator on status bar, PAGES tab		CTRL+G
Go to Heading Using Navigation Pane	WD 581	'Open the Navigation Pane' check box (VIEW tab | Show group), HEADINGS tab in Navigation Pane			
Go To Object	WD 547	Find arrow (HOME tab | Editing group), Go To			CTRL+G
Graphic, Adjust Brightness and Contrast	WD 153	Corrections button (PICTURE TOOLS FORMAT tab | Adjust group)	Format Picture, Picture button in Format Picture task pane		
Graphic, Change Border Color	WD 154	Picture Border arrow (PICTURE TOOLS FORMAT tab | Picture Styles group)			
Graphic, Change Color	WD 151	Color button (PICTURE TOOLS FORMAT tab | Adjust group)		Format Picture or Format Object, Picture Color button (Format Picture dialog box)	
Graphic, Change Order	WD 622	Bring Forward or Send Backward arrows (PICTURE TOOLS FORMAT tab | Arrange group)			
Graphic, Crop	WD 425	Crop button (PICTURE TOOLS FORMAT tab | Size group)	Crop button on mini toolbar		
Graphic, Flip	WD 157	Rotate Objects button (PICTURE TOOLS FORMAT tab | Arrange group)			
Graphic, Link to Webpage	WD 595	'Add a Hyperlink' button (INSERT tab | Links group), enter web address in Address text box			
Graphic, Move	WD 155		Drag graphic		
Graphic, Resize	WD 36	Shape Height and Shape Width boxes (PICTURE TOOLS FORMAT tab | Size group)	Drag sizing handle	More Layout Options, Size tab (Layout dialog box)	
Graphic, Resize to % of Original	WD 150	Advanced Layout: Size Dialog Box Launcher (PICTURE TOOLS FORMAT tab | Size group), enter height and width (Layout dialog box)	Layout Options button attached to graphic, See more link in Layout Options gallery, Size tab (Layout dialog box)	'Size and Position'	
Graphic, Rotate	WD 428	Rotate Objects button (PICTURE TOOLS FORMAT tab | Arrange group), 'More Rotation Options' on Rotate Objects menu	Drag rotate handle		

Microsoft Word 2013 Quick Reference Summary *(continued)*

Task	Page Number	Ribbon	Other On-Screen Element	Shortcut Menu	Keyboard Shortcut
Graphic, Send behind Text	WD 650	Wrap Text button (DRAWING TOOLS FORMAT tab | Arrange group)	Layout Options button attached to graphic, Behind Text	Wrap Text	
Graphic, Set Transparent Color	WD 152	Color button (PICTURE TOOLS FORMAT tab | Adjust group), 'Set Transparent Color' in Color gallery			
Graphic, Specify Position	WD 348		Layout Options button attached to graphic, See more link in Layout Options gallery		
GreetingLine Merge Field, Edit	WD 362			'Edit Greeting Line'	
GreetingLine Merge Field, Insert	WD 361		'Insert formatted salutation' link in Mail Merge task pane		
Group Objects	WD 705	Select objects, Group Objects button (DRAWING TOOLS FORMAT tab | Arrange group), Group			
Gutter Margin	WD 592	Adjust Margins button (PAGE LAYOUT tab | Page Setup group), Custom Margins			
Hanging Indent, Create	WD 108	Paragraph Dialog Box Launcher (HOME tab | Paragraph group), Indents and Spacing tab (Paragraph dialog box)	Drag Hanging Indent marker on ruler	Paragraph, Indents and Spacing tab (Paragraph dialog box)	CTRL+T
Hanging Indent, Remove	WD 80	Paragraph Dialog Box Launcher (HOME tab | Paragraph group), Indents and Spacing tab (Paragraph dialog box)	Drag Hanging Indent marker on ruler	Paragraph, Indents and Spacing tab (Paragraph dialog box)	CTRL+SHIFT+T
Header, Delete	WD 230	'Add a Header' button (INSERT tab | Header & Footer group), Remove Header in Add a Header gallery			
Header, Different from Previous	WD 228	'Add a Header' button (INSERT tab | Header & Footer group), Edit Header, deselect 'Link to Previous' button (HEADER & FOOTERS TOOLS DESIGN tab | Navigation group)			
Header, Switch to	WD 74	'Add a Header' button (INSERT tab | Header & Footer group)	Double-tap or double-click dimmed header	Edit Header	
Header and Footer, Change Default Margin	WD 592	'Header Position from Top' or 'Header Position from Bottom' box (HEADER & FOOTER TOOLS DESIGN tab | Position group)			
Header and Footer, Different First Page	WD 594	'Different First Page' check box (HEADER & FOOTER TOOLS DESIGN tab | Options group)			

Microsoft Word 2013 Quick Reference Summary *(continued)*

Task	Page Number	Ribbon	Other On-Screen Element	Shortcut Menu	Keyboard Shortcut
Header and Footer, Close	WD 77	'Close Header and Footer' button (HEADER & FOOTER TOOLS DESIGN tab | Close group)	Double-tap or double-click dimmed document text		
Hide/Show White Space	WD 102	Options (FILE tab), Display (Word Options dialog box)	Double-tap or double-click white space between pages		
Highlight Text	WD 652	'Text Highlight Color' arrow (HOME tab | Font group)			
Hyperlink, Convert to Regular Text	WD 163	'Add a Hyperlink' button (INSERT tab | Links group)	Undo Hyperlink (AutoCorrect Options menu)	Remove Hyperlink	
Hyperlink, Edit	WD 321	'Add a Hyperlink' button (INSERT tab | Links group)		Edit Hyperlink	CTRL+K
Hyperlink, Format Text As	WD 319	'Add a Hyperlink' button (INSERT tab | Links group)		Hyperlink	CTRL+K
Hyperlink, Insert	WD 596	'Add a Hyperlink' button (INSERT tab | Links group)			
Hyphenate	WD 437	Change Hyphenation button (PAGE LAYOUT tab | Page Setup group)			
IF Field, Insert	WD 365	Rules button (MAILINGS tab | Write & Insert Fields group)			
Indent, Decrease	WD 80	Decrease Indent button (HOME tab | Paragraph group)	Drag 'First Line Indent' marker on ruler	Paragraph, Indents and Spacing tab (Paragraph dialog box)	CTRL+SHIFT+M
Indent, First-Line	WD 82	Paragraph Settings Dialog Box Launcher (HOME tab | Paragraph group)	Drag 'First Line Indent' marker on ruler	Paragraph, Indents and Spacing tab (Paragraph dialog box)	TAB
Indent, Increase	WD 80	Increase Indent button (HOME tab | Paragraph group)			CTRL+M
Indent Paragraph	WD 293	Increase Indent button (HOME tab | Paragraph group)	Drag Left Indent marker on horizontal ruler	Paragraph, Indents and Spacing tab (Paragraph dialog box)	CTRL+M
Index, Build	WD 585	Insert Index button (REFERENCES tab | Index group)			
Index, Change Format	WD 588	Insert Index button (REFERENCES tab | Index group), change settings (Index dialog box)			
Index, Delete	WD 589		Drag through field code, DELETE		
Index, Update	WD 588	Update Index button (REFERENCES tab | Index group)			
Index Entry, Delete	WD 587		Select field, DELETE		
Index Entry, Edit	WD 587		Locate field, change text inside quotation marks		
Index Entry, Mark	WD 549	Mark Entry button (REFERENCES tab | Index group)			ALT+SHIFT+X

Microsoft Word 2013 Quick Reference Summary ***(continued)***

Task	Page Number	Ribbon	Other On-Screen Element	Shortcut Menu	Keyboard Shortcut
Index Entry, Mark Multiple	WD 551	Mark Entry button (REFERENCES tab | Index group), Mark button (Mark Index Entry dialog box)			
Insert File in Column	WD 434	Object arrow (INSERT tab | Text group), 'Text from File'			
Insert Word Document in Existing Document	WD 223	Object arrow (INSERT tab | Text group), 'Text from File'			
Insertion Point, Move Down/Up One Line	WD 12				DOWN ARROW/ UP ARROW
Insertion Point, Move Down/Up One Paragraph	WD 12				CTRL+DOWN ARROW/ CTRL+UP ARROW
Insertion Point, Move Down/Up One Screen	WD 12				PAGE DOWN/ PAGE UP
Insertion Point, Move Left/ Right One Character	WD 12				LEFT ARROW/ RIGHT ARROW
Insertion Point, Move Left/ Right One Word	WD 12				CTRL+LEFT ARROW/ CTRL+RIGHT ARROW
Insertion Point, Move to Beginning/End of Document	WD 12				CTRL+HOME/ CTRL+END
Insertion Point, Move to Beginning/ End of Line	WD 12				HOME/ END
Insertion Point, Move to Bottom of Document Window	WD 12				ALT+CTRL+PAGE DOWN/ ALT+CTRL+PAGE UP
Invite Others to View or Edit Document	WD 310	Invite People (FILE tab | Share tab)			
Italicize	WD 25	Italic button (HOME tab | Font group)	Italic button on mini toolbar	Font, Font tab (Font dialog box) Touch mode: 'Show Context Menu' on mini toolbar, Font on shortcut menu, Font tab (Font dialog box)	CTRL+I
Justify Paragraph	WD 80	Justify button (HOME tab | Paragraph group)		Paragraph, Indents and Spacing tab (Paragraph dialog box)	CTRL+J
Language, Set for Proofing Tools	WD 722	Language button (REVIEW tab | Language group), 'Set Proofing Language'			

Microsoft Word 2013 Quick Reference Summary *(continued)*					
Task	**Page Number**	**Ribbon**	**Other On-Screen Element**	**Shortcut Menu**	**Keyboard Shortcut**
Language, Set Preferences	WD 722	Language button (REVIEW tab | Language group), Language Preferences			
Last Editing Location, Go To	WD 224				SHIFT+F5
Layout Options, Advanced	WD 574	FILE tab | Options, Advanced (Word Options dialog box)			
Left-Align Paragraph	WD 80	Align Left button (HOME tab | Paragraph group)		Paragraph, Indents and Spacing tab (Paragraph dialog box)	CTRL+L
Left and Right Paragraph Indent	WD 209	Indent Left and Indent Right box (PAGE LAYOUT tab | Paragraph group)	Drag Left Indent or Right Indent markers on ruler	Paragraph, Indents and Spacing tab (Paragraph dialog box)	
Line Break	WD 290				SHIFT+ENTER
Line Spacing, Change	WD 72	'Line and Paragraph Spacing' button (HOME tab | Paragraph group)	Touch mode: 'Show Context button' on mini toolbar, Paragraph	Paragraph, Indents and Spacing tab (Paragraph dialog box) Touch mode: 'Show Context button' on mini toolbar, Paragraph, Indents and Spacing tab (Paragraph dialog box)	CTRL+[number of desired line spacing, i.e., 2 for double-spacing]
Link, Break	WD 503			'Linked Worksheet Object', Links, Break Link button (Links dialog box)	CTRL+SHIFT+F9
Link Excel Worksheet to Word Document	WD 501	Copy button (HOME tab | Clipboard group); Paste arrow (HOME tab | Clipboard group), 'Link & Keep Source Formatting' Touch mode: Copy button (HOME tab | Clipboard group), Copy; Paste arrow (HOME tab | Clipboard group), 'Link & Keep Source Formatting'			
Link Form to Database	WD 661	FILE tab | Save As, Tools button (Save As dialog box), Save Options on Tools menu, Advanced (Word Options dialog box), 'Save form data as delimited text file' check box			
Linked Object, Edit	WD 503			'Linked Worksheet Object', Edit Link	
Macro, Automatic	WD 713	Record Macro button (DEVELOPER tab | Code group), type macro name (Record Macro dialog box)			
Macro, Copy from One Template or Document to Another	WD 720	View Macros button (DEVELOPER tab | Code group or VIEW tab | Macros group), Organizer button (Macros dialog box)			

Microsoft Word 2013 Quick Reference Summary *(continued)*

Task	Page Number	Ribbon	Other On-Screen Element	Shortcut Menu	Keyboard Shortcut
Macro, Delete	WD 709	View Macros button (DEVELOPER tab | Code group), Delete button (Macros dialog box)			
Macro, Edit VBA Code	WD 715	View Macros button (DEVELOPER tab | Code group), select macro to be edited (Macros dialog box), Edit button			
Macro, Record	WD 707	Record Macro button (DEVELOPER tab | Code group)			ALT+F8, Create button (Macros dialog box)
Macro, Rename	WD 721	View Macros button (DEVELOPER tab | Code group or VIEW tab | Macros group), Organizer button (Macros dialog box), select macro, Rename button (Organizer dialog box)			
Macro, Run	WD 709	View Macros button (DEVELOPER tab | Code group or VIEW tab | Macros group), select macro name (Macros dialog box), tap or click Run button			Press assigned shortcut key; or press ALT+F8, select macro name (Macros dialog box), tap or click Run button
Macro-Enabled Document, Create	WD 677	FILE tab | Save tab, 'Save as type' arrow (Save As dialog box), 'Word Macro-Enabled Document'			
Macro-Enabled Template, Save	WD 677	FILE tab | Save As tab, 'Save as type' arrow (Save As dialog box), 'Word Macro-Enabled Template'			
Macro Settings, Specify	WD 679	Macro Security button (DEVELOPER tab | Code group), select 'Disable all macros with notification' option button (Trust Center dialog box)			
Mailing Label, Print	WD 187	Create Labels button (MAILINGS tab | Create group)			
Mailing Labels, Print	WD 379	'Start Mail Merge' button (MAILINGS tab | Start Mail Merge group), 'Step-by-Step Mail Merge Wizard' on Start Mail Merge Menu, Labels in Mail Merge task pane			
Main Document, Identify for Form Letter	WD 341	'Start Mail Merge button (MAILINGS tab | Start Mail Merge group)			
Margin Settings, Change	WD 140	Adjust Margins button (PAGE LAYOUT tab | Page Setup group)	Drag margin boundary on ruler		
Margins, Custom	WD 280	Adjust Margins button (PAGE LAYOUT tab | Page Setup group), Custom Margins	Drag margin boundaries on ruler		

Microsoft Word 2013 Quick Reference Summary *(continued)*					
Task	**Page Number**	**Ribbon**	**Other On-Screen Element**	**Shortcut Menu**	**Keyboard Shortcut**
Mark as Final	WD 492	Protect Document button (FILE tab | Info tab), 'Mark as Final'			
Markups, Print	WD 487	FILE tab | Print tab, Settings area			
Markups, Show All	WD 487	'Display for Review' arrow (REVIEW tab | Tracking group), All Markup			
Markups and Comments, Change Display	WD 484	Show Markup button (REVIEW tab | Tracking group), Balloons			
Master Document, Expand	WD 566	Expand Subdocuments button (OUTLINING tab | Master Document group)			
Merge, Select Records	WD 374	'Edit Recipient List' button (MAILINGS tab | Start Mail Merge group)			
Merge Condition, Remove	WD 376	'Edit Recipient List' button (MAILINGS tab | Start Mail Merge group), Filter link (Mail Merge Recipients dialog box), Clear All button (Filter and Sort dialog box)			
Merge Field, Insert	WD 363	'Insert Merge Field' arrow (MAILINGS tab | Write & Insert Fields group)			
Merge Fields, Highlight	WD 367	'Highlight Merge Fields' button (MAILINGS tab | Write & Insert group)			
Merge Form Letters to New Document	WD 371	'Finish & Merge' button (MAILINGS tab | Finish group), 'Edit Individual Documents'	'Merge to new document' link in Mail Merge task pane		
Merge Form Letters to Printer	WD 373	'Finish & Merge' button (MAILINGS tab | Finish group), Print Documents	'Merge to printer' link in Mail Merge task pane		
Merge to Directory	WD 387	'Start Mail Merge' button (MAILINGS tab | Start Mail Merge group), Directory			
Merged Data, View in Main Document	WD 361	'View Merged Data' button (MAILINGS tab | Preview Results group)			
Merged Letters, Check for Errors	WD 371	'Auto Check for Errors' button (MAILINGS tab | Preview Results group)			ALT+SHIFT+K
Merged Letters, Preview	WD 370		'Next wizard step' link in Mail Merge task pane		
Metadata, Remove	WD 722	'Check for Issues' button (FILE tab | Info tab), Inspect Document, Remove All button			
Microsoft Account, Sign Out Of	WD 45	Sign out link (FILE tab | Account tab)			

Microsoft Word 2013 Quick Reference Summary *(continued)*

Task	Page Number	Ribbon	Other On-Screen Element	Shortcut Menu	Keyboard Shortcut
Microsoft Graph	WD 517	Object button (INSERT tab | Text group), Create New tab (Object dialog box), 'Microsoft Graph Chart'			
Modify Style Using Styles Dialog Box	WD 299	Styles Dialog Box Launcher (HOME tab | Styles group), Modify	Press and hold or right-click style name in Styles gallery, Modify		
Move Text	WD 49	Cut button (HOME tab | Clipboard group); Paste button (HOME tab | Clipboard group)	Drag and drop selected text	Cut, Paste	CTRL+X, CTRL+V
Multilevel Numbered List	WD 236	Multilevel List button (HOME tab | Paragraph group)			Type `1.`, SPACEBAR
Native Format, Open Files	WD 718	Browse button (FILE tab | Open tab), file type arrow (Open dialog box)			
New Document, Create from Online Template	WD 276	New (FILE tab), type file name in 'Search for online templates' box, Start searching button, select template, Create button			
Nonbreaking Hyphen, Insert	WD 173				CTRL+SHIFT+HYPHEN
Nonbreaking Space, Insert	WD 172	'Insert a Symbol' button (INSERT tab | Symbols group), More Symbols, Special Characters tab (Symbol dialog box)			CTRL+SHIFT+SPACEBAR
Normal Style, Apply	WD 165	No Spacing (HOME tab | Styles group)			CTRL+SHIFT+S
Normal Style, Modify	WD 70	Styles Dialog Box Launcher (HOME tab | Styles group), style arrow, Modify		Press and hold or right-click style (HOME tab | Styles group), Modify	
Object, Change Position	WD 144	Position Object button (DRAWING TOOLS FORMAT tab | Arrange group)	Layout Options button attached to graphic, See more link in Layout Options gallery		
On-Screen Keyboard, Display	WD 6		Touch mode: Touch Keyboard button on Windows taskbar		
Open a Document	WD 47	Open (FILE tab)			CTRL+O
Open Document Created from Template	WD 278	Open (FILE tab), select location, select file, Open button			
Outline View	WD 562	Outline View button (VIEW tab | Views group)			
Outline View, Add Entries	WD 562	'Demote to Body Text' button (OUTLINING tab | Outline Tools group) or 'Promote to Heading 1' button (OUTLINING tab | Outline Tools group)			
Outline View, Exit	WD 567	'Close Outline View' button (OUTLINING tab | Close group)			

Microsoft Word 2013 Quick Reference Summary *(continued)*					
Task	**Page Number**	**Ribbon**	**Other On-Screen Element**	**Shortcut Menu**	**Keyboard Shortcut**
Outline View, Show First Line Only	WD 564	'Show First Line Only' check box (OUTLINING tab | Outline Tools group)			
Page Border, Add	WD 41	'Borders and Shading' button (DESIGN tab | Page Background group)			
Page Break, Delete	WD 226	Select notation, Cut button (HOME tab | Clipboard group)	Touch Mode: Select notation, Cut button on mini toolbar	Cut	Select notation, DELETE or BACKSPACE
Page Break, Insert	WD 105	'Insert a Page Break' button (INSERT tab | Pages group)			CTRL+ENTER
Page Color	WD 618	Page Color button (DESIGN tab | Page Background group)			
Page Color, Add Pattern Fill Effect	WD 619	Page Color button (DESIGN tab | Page Background group), Fill Effects			
Page Color, Fill Effect	WD 693	Page Color button (DESIGN tab | Page Background group), Fill Effects, Texture tab (Fill Effects dialog box)			
Page Color, Remove	WD 694	Page Color button (DESIGN tab | Page Background group), No Color			
Page Number, Insert	WD 76	'Add Page Numbers' button (HEADER & FOOTER TOOLS DESIGN tab | Header & Footer group)			
Page Numbers, Start at Different	WD 230	'Add Page Numbers' button (HEADER & FOOTER TOOLS DESIGN tab | Header & Footer group), 'Format Page Numbers', Start at (Page Number Format dialog box)			
Page Orientation, Change	WD 387	'Change Page Orientation' button (PAGE LAYOUT tab | Page Setup group)			
Paper Size, Change	WD 615	'Choose Page Size' button (PAGE LAYOUT tab | Page Setup group)			
Paragraph Indent, Decrease	WD 80				CTRL+SHIFT+M
Paragraph Spacing, Change in Document	WD 551	Paragraph Spacing button (DESIGN tab | Document Formatting group)			
Password-Protect Document	WD 657	Restrict Editing button (DEVELOPER tab | Protect group), 'Yes, Start Enforcing Protection' button in Restrict Editing task pane, type password (Start Enforcing Protection dialog box)			

Microsoft Word 2013 Quick Reference Summary *(continued)*

Task	Page Number	Ribbon	Other On-Screen Element	Shortcut Menu	Keyboard Shortcut
Paste	WD 112	Paste arrow (HOME tab | Clipboard group)	Paste Options button by moved/copied text	Paste	CTRL+V
Paste Options	WD 156	Paste arrow (HOME tab | Clipboard group)	Paste Options button by moved/copied text		
Paste Options Menu, Display	WD 113		Paste Options button by moved/copied text		
PDF Document, Create	WD 302	'Create PDF/XPS Document' (FILE tab | Export tab)			
PDF Document, Open from Word	WD 304	FILE tab | Open tab, navigate to file location, File Types arrow, PDF Files in File Types list			F12
Picture, Insert	WD 34	From File button (INSERT tab | Illustrations group)			
Picture, Save in Other Format	WD 558			'Save as Picture', 'Save as type' arrow (File Save dialog box)	
Picture Effects, Apply	WD 39	Picture Effects button (PICTURE TOOLS FORMAT tab | Picture Styles gallery)		Format Picture or Format Object Touch mode: 'Show Context Menu' button on mini toolbar, Format Object or Format Picture on shortcut menu	
Picture Style, Apply	WD 38	More button in Picture Styles gallery (PICTURE TOOLS FORMAT tab | Picture Styles group)		'Picture Quick Styles'	
Placeholder Text, Replace	WD 284		Select content control, type new text		
Post Document to Social Network	WD 313	'Post to Social Networks' (FILE tab | Share tab)			
Print Document	WD 51	Print button (FILE tab | Print tab)			CTRL+P
Print Layout View	WD 53	Print Layout button (VIEW tab | Views group)	Print Layout button on status bar		
Print Scaling	WD 593	FILE tab | Print tab, Settings area in Print gallery, 'Scale to Paper Size'			
Print Specific Pages	WD 225	FILE tab | Print tab, type page numbers in Pages text box			
Protect Form	WD 655	Restrict Editing button (DEVELOPER tab | Protect group), select 'Allow only this type of editing in the document' check box, 'Yes Start Enforcing Protection' button in Restrict Editing task pane			

Microsoft Word 2013 Quick Reference Summary *(continued)*

Task	Page Number	Ribbon	Other On-Screen Element	Shortcut Menu	Keyboard Shortcut
Protected View	WD 541	FILE tab | Options, Trust Center (Word Options dialog box), 'Trust Center Settings' button, Protected View			
Quick Access Toolbar, Add Command/ Macro	WD 710	'Customize Quick Access Toolbar' button on Quick Access Toolbar, More commands, select command (Word Options dialog box), Add button		'Customize Quick Access Toolbar', More commands, select command (Word Options dialog box), Add button	
Quick Access Toolbar, Delete Buttons	WD 712			Right-click button, 'Remove from Quick Access Toolbar' Touch mode: Press and hold button, 'Remove from Quick Access Toolbar'	
Quick Table	WD 523	'Add a Table' button (INSERT tab | Tables group), Quick Tables			
Read Mode	WD 52	Read Mode button (VIEW tab | Views group)	Read Mode button on status bar		
Read Mode, Change Color	WD 121	Page Color on View menu	Read Mode button on status bar, Page Color on View menu		
Readability Statistics	WD 118	FILE tab | Print tab, Proofing (Word Options dialog box)			
Record, Display Specific	WD 378	First, Last, Next, or Previous buttons or 'Go to Record' text box (MAILINGS tab | Preview Results group)			
Recover Unsaved (Draft Version) Documents	WD 560	FILE tab | Open tab, 'Recover Unsaved Documents' button in Recent Documents list			
Redo	WD 24		Redo button on Quick Access Toolbar		CTRL+Y
Remove Character Formatting	WD 80				CTRL+SPACEBAR
Remove Paragraph Formatting	WD 80				CTRL+Q
Remove Space after Paragraph	WD 80	'Line and Paragraph Spacing' button (HOME tab | Paragraph group)		Paragraph, Indents and Spacing tab (Paragraph dialog box)	CTRL+0 (zero)
Replace Formats	WD 578	Replace button (HOME tab | Editing group), Format button (Find and Replace dialog box)			
Replace Text	WD 114	Replace button (HOME tab | Editing group)			CTRL+H
Research Task Pane, Look Up Information	WD 119		ALT+click desired word		ALT+SHIFT+F7

Microsoft Word 2013 Quick Reference Summary *(continued)*

Task	Page Number	Ribbon	Other On-Screen Element	Shortcut Menu	Keyboard Shortcut
Restrict Editing to Tracked Changes or Comments or No Edits	WD 656	Restrict Editing button (DEVELOPER tab | Protect group), select 'Allow only this type of editing in the document' check box in Restrict Editing task pane, 'Yes, Start Enforcing Protection' button			
Restrict Formatting	WD 656	Restrict Editing button (DEVELOPER tab | Protect group), select 'Limit formatting to a selection of styles' check box in Restrict Editing task pane, Settings link (Formatting Restrictions dialog box), 'Yes, Start Enforcing Protection' button			
Reveal Formatting	WD 298				SHIFT+F1
Reviewer Information, Change	WD 480	Change Tracking Options Dialog Box Launcher (REVIEW tab | Tracking group), 'Change User Name' button (Track Changes dialog box)			
Reviewing Task Pane	WD 484	Reviewing Pane arrow (REVIEW tab | Tracking group)			
Ribbon, Collapse	WD 616	'Collapse the Ribbon' button (HOME tab)			
Ribbon, Expand	WD 616	'Pin the ribbon' button (HOME tab)			
Right-Align	WD 75	Align Right button (HOME tab | Paragraph group)		Paragraph, Indents and Spacing tab (Paragraph dialog box) Touch mode: 'Show Context Menu' button on mini toolbar, Paragraph, Indents and Spacing tab (Paragraph dialog box)	CTRL+R
Rulers, Display	WD 82	View Ruler check box (VIEW tab | Show group)			
Save	WD 12	Save (FILE tab | Save tab)	Save button on Quick Access Toolbar		
Save as Template	WD 613	'Change File Type' (FILE tab | Export tab), Template			F12, Word Template
Save Document, Same File Name	WD 33	Save (FILE tab | Save tab)	Save button on Quick Access toolbar		
Save Location, Set Default	WD 319	Options (FILE tab), Save (Word Options dialog box)			
Save Word 2013 Document in Earlier Word Format	WD 307	'Change File Type' (FILE tab | Export tab), select new file format			F12

Microsoft Word 2013 Quick Reference Summary *(continued)*

Task	Page Number	Ribbon	Other On-Screen Element	Shortcut Menu	Keyboard Shortcut
Save Word Document as Different File Type	WD 309	'Change File Type' (FILE tab | Export tab), select new file type			
Schema, Attach	WD 727	Document Template button (DEVELOPER tab | Templates group), XML Schema tab (Templates and Add-ins dialog box), Add Schema button, select schema, Open button (Add Schema dialog box)			
Schema, Delete	WD 727	Document Template button (DEVELOPER tab | Templates group), XML Schema tab (Templates and Add-ins dialog box), Schema Library button, select schema, Delete Schema button (Schema Library dialog box)			
Screenshot, Insert	WD 542	'Take a Screenshot' button (INSERT tab | Illustrations group)			
Scroll, Up/Down One Line	WD 12		Tap or click scroll arrow at top/bottom of vertical scroll bar		
Scroll, Up/Down One Screen	WD 12		Tap or click above/ below scroll box on vertical scroll bar		
Scroll Documents Side by Side	WD 518	'View Side by Side' button (VIEW tab | Window group)			
Section Break, Continuous	WD 432	'Insert Page and Section Breaks' button (PAGE LAYOUT tab | Page Setup group), Continuous			
Section Break, Delete	WD 223			Select break notation, Cut	Select break notation, DELETE or BACKSPACE
Section Break, Next Page	WD 222	'Insert Page and Section Breaks' button (PAGE LAYOUT tab | Page Setup group), Next Page			
Select Block of Text	WD 32		Click beginning, SHIFT+click end Touch mode: Drag selection handle(s)		
Select Character(s)	WD 32		Drag pointer through characters Touch mode: Drag selection handle(s)		SHIFT+RIGHT ARROW or SHIFT+LEFT ARROW
Select Entire Document	WD 32	Select button arrow (HOME tab | Editing group)	In left margin, triple-click		CTRL+A
Select Graphic	WD 32		Tap or click graphic		
Select Group of Words	WD 28		Drag pointer through words Touch mode: Drag selection handle(s)		CTRL+SHIFT+RIGHT ARROW or CTRL+SHIFT+LEFT ARROW repeatedly

Microsoft Word 2013 Quick Reference Summary *(continued)*

Task	Page Number	Ribbon	Other On-Screen Element	Shortcut Menu	Keyboard Shortcut
Select Line	WD 16		Click in left margin Touch mode: Double-tap to left of line		SHIFT+DOWN ARROW
Select Multiple Lines	WD 32		Drag pointer in left margin Touch mode: Drag selection handle(s)		HOME, then SHIFT+DOWN ARROW; or END, then SHIFT+UP ARROW
Select Multiple Paragraphs	WD 32		Drag pointer in left margin Touch mode: Drag selection handle(s)		SHIFT+DOWN ARROW
Select Nonadjacent Items	WD 32		Select first item, hold down CTRL key while selecting item(s)		
Select Nonadjacent Items	WD 244				CTRL+select
Select Paragraph	WD 32		Triple-click paragraph		CTRL+SHIFT+DOWN ARROW or CTRL+SHIFT+UP ARROW
Select Sentence	WD 32		CTRL-click		
Select Word	WD 32		Double-tap or double-click word		CTRL+SHIFT+RIGHT ARROW or CTRL+SHIFT+LEFT ARROW
Select Words	WD 32		Drag pointer through words Touch mode: Drag selection handle(s)		CTRL+SHIFT+RIGHT ARROW or CTRL+SHIFT+LEFT ARROW repeatedly
Selection Pane	WD 428	'Display the Selection Pane' button (PICTURE TOOLS FORMAT tab | Arrange group)			
Shade Paragraph	WD 21	Shading arrow (HOME tab | Paragraph group)			
Shadow, Add to Shape	WD 652	Shape Effects button (DRAWING TOOLS FORMAT tab | Shape Styles group), Shadow			
Shadow, Change Color	WD 652	Shape Effects button (DRAWING TOOLS FORMAT tab | Shape Styles group), Shadow, Shadow Options			
Shadow Shape Effect, Apply	WD 696	Shape Effects button (DRAWING TOOLS FORMAT tab | Shape Styles group), Shadow, Shadow Options			
Shape, Add Text	WD 146			Add Text Edit Text button on mini toolbar	
Shape, Apply Style	WD 145	More button in Shape Styles gallery (DRAWING TOOLS FORMAT tab | Shape Styles group)	'Shape Quick Styles' on mini toolbar		

Microsoft Word 2013 Quick Reference Summary *(continued)*

Task	Page Number	Ribbon	Other On-Screen Element	Shortcut Menu	Keyboard Shortcut
Shape, Change	WD 694	Edit Shape button (DRAWING TOOLS FORMAT tab | Insert Shapes group), Change Shape			
Shape, Fill with Picture	WD 697	Shape Fill arrow (DRAWING TOOLS FORMAT tab | Shape Styles group), Picture			
Shape, Format	WD 651	Shape Fill arrow, Shape Outline arrow, or Shape Effects arrow (DRAWING TOOLS FORMAT tab | Shape Styles group)			
Shape, Insert	WD 142	'Draw a Shape' button (INSERT tab | Illustrations group)			
Sharing Link, Get	WD 312	'Get a Sharing Link' (FILE tab | Share tab)			
Shortcut Key, Assign to a Style	WD 689	Styles Dialog Box Launcher (HOME tab | Styles group), tap or click style arrow, Modify, Format button (Modify Style dialog box), Shortcut key		Press and hold or right-click style name in Styles gallery, tap or click style arrow, Modify, Format button (Modify Style dialog box), Shortcut key	
Signature Line	WD 719	'Add a Signature Line' button (INSERT tab | Text group)			
Single-Space Lines	WD 80	'Line and Paragraph Spacing' button (HOME tab | Paragraph group)		Paragraph, Indents and Spacing tab (Paragraph dialog box)	CTRL+1
Small Caps	WD 80	Font Dialog Box Launcher HOME Tab | Font group), Font tab (Font dialog box)			CTRL+SHIFT+K
SmartArt Graphic, Add Shapes To	WD 215	Add Shape button (SMARTART TOOLS DESIGN tab | Create Graphic group) Touch Mode: Add Shape button (SMARTART TOOLS DESIGN tab | Create Graphic group), 'Add Shape After'		Add Shape	
SmartArt Graphic, Add Text through Text Pane	WD 457		Text Pane control on left side of graphic		
SmartArt Graphic, Add Text To	WD 214		Select shape, type text	Edit Text	
SmartArt Graphic, Change Colors	WD 216	Change Colors button (SMARTART TOOLS DESIGN tab | SmartArt Styles group)			
SmartArt Graphic, Change Layout	WD 456	SMARTART TOOLS DESIGN tab, Layouts gallery			

Microsoft Word 2013 Quick Reference Summary *(continued)*

Task	Page Number	Ribbon	Other On-Screen Element	Shortcut Menu	Keyboard Shortcut
SmartArt Graphic, Copy Using Office Clipboard	WD 459	Clipboard Dialog Box Launcher (HOME tab | Clipboard group), Copy button (HOME tab | Clipboard group)		Copy	CTRL+C
SmartArt Graphic, Delete Shapes From	WD 214	Select shape, Cut button (HOME tab | Clipboard group)			
SmartArt Graphic, Insert	WD 212	'Insert a SmartArt Graphic' button (INSERT tab | Illustrations group)			
SmartArt Graphic, Layer in Front of Text	WD 461	Bring Forward arrow (SMARTART TOOLS FORMAT tab | Arrange group), 'Bring in Front on Text'			
SmartArt Graphic, Paste Using Office Clipboard	WD 459	Clipboard Dialog Box Launcher (HOME tab | Clipboard group), Paste graphic from Office Clipboard		Paste	CTRL+V
SmartArt Style, Apply	WD 217	More button (SMARTART TOOLS DESIGN tab | SmartArt Styles group)			
Sort Paragraphs	WD 232	Sort button (HOME tab | Paragraph group)			
Source, Edit	WD 96		Tap or click citation, Citation Options arrow, Edit Source		
Source, Modify	WD 109	Manage Sources button (REFERENCES tab | Citations & Bibliography group), Edit button			
Space after Paragraph, Remove	WD 80	'Line and Paragraph Spacing' button (HOME tab | Paragraph group)		Paragraph Touch mode: 'Show Context Menu' on mini toolbar, Paragraph	
Spelling, Check as You Type	WD 10		Tap or click word, 'Spelling and Grammar Check' icon on status bar	Press and hold or right-click error, tap or click correct word on shortcut menu	
Spelling and Grammar, Check at Once	WD 116	'Spelling & Grammar' button (REVIEW tab | Proofing group)	'Spelling and Grammar Check' icon on status bar, Spelling	Spelling	F7
Split Window	WD 445	Split Window button (VIEW tab | Windows group)			CTRL+ALT+S, ENTER
Style, Apply	WD 105	Style name in Quick Styles gallery (HOME tab | Styles group)			CTRL+SHIFT+S, Style Name arrow
Style, Copy from One Template or Document to Another	WD 719	Styles Dialog Box Launcher (HOME tab | Styles group), Manage Styles button in Styles task pane, Import/Export button (Manage Styles dialog box)			

Microsoft Word 2013 Quick Reference Summary *(continued)*

Task	Page Number	Ribbon	Other On-Screen Element	Shortcut Menu	Keyboard Shortcut
Style, Create	WD 297	More button (HOME tab | Styles group), 'Create a Style' (Styles gallery)			
Style, Delete	WD 720	Styles Dialog Box Launcher (HOME tab | Styles group), Manage Styles button in Styles task pane, Import/Export button (Manage Styles dialog box), select style, Delete button			
Style, Display Hidden	WD 688	Styles Dialog Box Launcher (HOME tab | Styles group), Manage Styles button in Styles task pane, Edit tab (Manage Styles dialog box)			
Style, Modify	WD 70	Styles Dialog Box Launcher (HOME tab | Styles group), select [style name], Modify		Modify	ALT+CTRL+SHIFT+S
Style, Modify Using Styles Task Pane	WD 687	Styles Dialog Box Launcher (HOME tab | Styles group), select style in Styles task pane, Modify			
Style, Rename	WD 720	Styles Dialog Box Launcher (HOME tab | Styles group), Manage Styles button in Styles task pane, Import/Export button (Manage Styles dialog box), select style, Rename button			
Style, Update to Match Selection	WD 73	Styles Dialog Box Launcher (HOME tab | Styles group), 'Update Normal to Match Selection'		'Update Normal to Match Selection'	ALT+CTRL+SHIFT+S
Style Set, Change	WD 321	More button (DESIGN tab | Document Formatting group)			
Subdocument, Convert to Part of Master Document	WD 566	Remove Subdocument button (OUTLINING tab | Master Document group)			
Subdocument, Insert	WD 564	Insert Subdocument button (OUTLINING tab | Master Document group)			
Subscript	WD 80	Subscript button (HOME tab | Font group)		Font, Font tab (Font dialog box)	CTRL+EQUAL SIGN
Superscript	WD 80	Superscript button (HOME tab | Font group)		Font, Font tab (Font dialog box)	CTRL+SHIFT+PLUS SIGN
Switch between Open Documents	WD 459	Switch Windows button (VIEW tab | Window group)	Tap or click app button on taskbar		ALT+TAB
Symbol, Insert	WD 158	'Insert a Symbol' button (INSERT tab | Symbols group)			
Synonym, Find and Insert	WD 116	Thesaurus button (REVIEW tab | Proofing group)		Tap or click desired synonym on Synonym submenu Touch Mode: 'Show Context Menu' button on mini toolbar, Synonyms on shortcut menu	SHIFT+F7

Microsoft Word 2013 Quick Reference Summary *(continued)*

Task	Page Number	Ribbon	Other On-Screen Element	Shortcut Menu	Keyboard Shortcut
Tab Stops, Set Custom	WD 167	Paragraph Dialog Box Launcher (HOME tab | Paragraph group), Tabs button (Paragraph dialog box)	Click desired tab stop on ruler	Paragraph, Tabs button (Paragraph dialog box)	
Table, Add Title	WD 723	Table Properties button (TABLE TOOLS LAYOUT tab | Table group), Alt Text tab (Table Properties dialog box)		Table Properties, Alt Text tab (Table Properties dialog box)	
Table, Align Data in Cells	WD 80	Align [location] button (TABLE TOOLS LAYOUT tab | Alignment group)			
Table, Apply Style	WD 177	More button in Table Styles gallery (TABLE TOOLS DESIGN tab | Table Styles group)			
Table, Border	WD 255	Borders arrow (TABLE TOOLS LAYOUT tab | Table Styles group), 'Borders and Shading' in Borders gallery			
Table, Center	WD 180	Select table, Center button (HOME tab | Font group)	Select table, Center button on mini toolbar		
Table, Change Cell Spacing	WD 245	Cell Margins button (TABLE TOOLS LAYOUT tab | Alignment group)		Table Properties	
Table, Change Column Width	WD 240	'Table Column Width' box (TABLE TOOLS LAYOUT tab | Cell Size group) Touch Mode: AutoFit button (TABLE TOOLS LAYOUT tab | Cell Size group), Autofit Contents	Drag column boundary in table or 'Move Table Column' marker on horizontal ruler		
Table, Change Row Height	WD 241	'Table Row Height' box (TABLE TOOLS LAYOUT tab | Cell Size group)	Drag row boundary in table or 'Adjust Table Row' marker on vertical ruler	Table Properties, Row tab (Table Properties dialog box)	
Table, Control Layout	WD 623	'Add a Table' button (INSERT tab | Tables group)			
Table, Convert to Text	WD 682	'Convert to Text' button (TABLE TOOLS LAYOUT tab | Data group)			
Table, Delete Cell Contents	WD 184	Cut button (HOME tab | Clipboard group)			Select cell contents, DELETE or BACKSPACE
Table, Delete Column/Row	WD 247	Delete Table button (TABLE TOOLS LAYOUT tab | Rows & Columns group)	Touch Mode: Delete Table on mini toolbar	Select column/row, Delete Columns or Delete Rows	
Table, Delete Entire	WD 184	Delete Table button (TABLE TOOLS LAYOUT tab | Rows & Columns group)			
Table, Delete Row or Column	WD 184	Delete Table button (TABLE TOOLS LAYOUT tab | Rows & Columns group)		Select row/column, Delete Rows or Delete Columns	

Microsoft Word 2013 Quick Reference Summary *(continued)*

Task	Page Number	Ribbon	Other On-Screen Element	Shortcut Menu	Keyboard Shortcut
Table, Distribute Columns	WD 251	Distribute Columns button (TABLE TOOLS LAYOUT tab | Cell Size group)		'Distribute Columns Evenly'	
Table, Distribute Rows	WD 252	Distribute Rows button (TABLE TOOLS LAYOUT tab | Cell Size group)		'Distribute Rows Evenly'	
Table, Insert	WD 174	'Add a Table' button (INSERT tab | Tables group)			
Table, Insert Column	WD 182	'Insert Columns to the Left/ Right' button (TABLE TOOLS LAYOUT tab | Rows & Columns group)		Insert	
Table, Insert Row	WD 181	'Insert Rows Above/Below' button (TABLE TOOLS LAYOUT Tab | Rows & Columns group)	Tap or click desired Insert Control	Insert	
Table, Merge Cells	WD 182	Merge Cells button (TABLE TOOLS LAYOUT tab | Merge group)		Merge Cells	
Table, Move Cell Boundary	WD 250	Table Properties button (TABLE TOOLS LAYOUT tab | Table group), Cell tab (Table Properties dialog box)	Drag cell boundary or 'Move Table Column' marker on horizontal ruler		
Table, Move Row	WD 286	Cut button (HOME tab | Clipboard group); Paste button (HOME tab | Clipboard group)	Drag selected row to new location Touch Mode: Use stylus to select and drag row to new location	Cut; Paste	CTRL+X; CTRL+V
Table, Remove Shading from Cell	WD 244	Shading arrow (TABLE TOOLS DESIGN tab | Table Styles group), No Color in Shading gallery			
Table, Repeat Header Rows	WD 392	'Repeat Header Rows' button (TABLE TOOLS LAYOUT tab | Data group)			
Table, Resize	WD 182	'Table Column Width' or 'Table Row Height' boxes (TABLE TOOLS LAYOUT tab | Cell Size group)	ALT-drag markers on ruler		
Table, Select Cell	WD 179	Select Table button (TABLE TOOLS LAYOUT tab | Table group)	Tap or click left edge of cell		
Table, Select Column	WD 178	Select Table button (TABLE TOOLS LAYOUT tab | Table group)	Click top border of column		
Table, Select Entire	WD 179	Select Table button (TABLE TOOLS LAYOUT tab | Table group)	Tap or click table move handle		
Table, Select Multiple Cells, Rows, or Columns, Adjacent	WD 179		Drag through cells, rows, or columns		

Microsoft Word 2013 Quick Reference Summary *(continued)*

Task	Page Number	Ribbon	Other On-Screen Element	Shortcut Menu	Keyboard Shortcut
Table, Select Next Cell	WD 179				TAB
Table, Select Previous Cell	WD 179				SHIFT+TAB
Table, Select Row	WD 179	Select button (TABLE TOOLS LAYOUT tab | Table group)	Tap or click to left of row		
Table, Shade Cell	WD 243	Shading arrow (TABLE TOOLS DESIGN tab | Table Styles group)			
Table, Sort	WD 248	Sort button (TABLE TOOLS LAYOUT tab | Data group)			
Table, Sort by Multiple Columns	WD 392	Sort button (TABLE TOOLS LAYOUT tab | Data group), Sort by arrow (Sort dialog box), Then by arrow (Sort dialog box)			
Table, Split	WD 183	Split Table button (TABLE TOOLS LAYOUT tab | Merge group)			
Table, Split Cells	WD 183	Split Cells button (TABLE TOOLS LAYOUT tab | Merge group)		Split Cells	
Table, Sum Columns/Rows	WD 256	Formula button (TABLE TOOLS LAYOUT tab | Data group)			
Table Columns, Resize to Fit Table Contents	WD 178	AutoFit button (TABLE TOOLS LAYOUT tab | Cell Size group)	Double-click column boundary	AutoFit	
Table Gridlines, Show/Hide	WD 239	'View Table Gridlines' button (TABLE TOOLS LAYOUT tab | Table group)			
Table Item, Copy and Paste	WD 294	Copy button (HOME tab | Clipboard group), display new location, Paste arrow (HOME tab | Clipboard group), Merge Table button (Paste gallery)		Copy, Paste Options	CTRL+C; CTRL+V
Table of Authorities, Build	WD 725	'Insert Table of Authorities' button (REFERENCES tab | Table of Authorities group)			
Table of Authorities, Change Format	WD 726	'Insert Table of Authorities' button (REFERENCES tab | Table of Authorities group), change desired settings/formats (Table of Authorities dialog box)			
Table of Authorities, Update	WD 725	Update Table of Authorities' button (REFERENCES tab | Table of Authorities group)			F9
Table of Contents, Change Format	WD 580	'Table of Contents' button (REFERENCES tab | Table of Contents group), 'Custom Table of Contents'			

Microsoft Word 2013 Quick Reference Summary *(continued)*

Task	Page Number	Ribbon	Other On-Screen Element	Shortcut Menu	Keyboard Shortcut
Table of Contents, Change Style Formatting	WD 583	'Table of Contents' button (REFERENCES tab | Table of Contents group), Modify button			
Table of Contents, Change Style Level	WD 583	'Table of Contents' button (REFERENCES tab | Table of Contents group), Options button			
Table of Contents, Create	WD 573	'Table of Contents' button (REFERENCES tab | Table of Contents group)			
Table of Contents, Delete	WD 573	'Table of Contents' button (REFERENCES tab | Table of Contents group), 'Remove Table of Contents'			
Table of Contents, Retain Formatting when Adding Text	WD 578	Add Text button (REFERENCES tab | Table of Contents group), select level on Add Text menu			
Table of Contents, Update Entire	WD 579	Update Table button (REFERENCES tab | Table of Contents group)	Update Table button attached to table, 'Update entire table' (Update Table of Contents dialog box)		F9
Table of Contents, Update Page Numbers	WD 575	Update Table button (REFERENCES tab | Table of Contents group)	Update Table button attached to table, OK button (Update Table of Contents dialog box)		F9
Table of Figures, Change Format	WD 583	'Table of Figures Dialog' button (REFERENCES tab | Captions group)			
Table of Figures, Create	WD 582	'Table of Figures Dialog' button (REFERENCES tab | Captions group)			
Table of Figures, Update	WD 583	'Update Table of Figures' button (REFERENCES tab | Captions group), 'Update entire table' (Update Table of Figures dialog box)			F9
Text Box, 3-D Effect	WD 704	Shape Effects button (DRAWING TOOLS FORMAT tab | Shape Styles group), '3-D Rotation'		Format Shape, TEXT OPTIONS tab (Format Shape task pane), Text Effects button	
Text Box, Change Shape Outline	WD 704	Shape Styles gallery (DRAWING TOOLS FORMAT tab | Shape Styles group)		Format Shape, LINE tab (Format Shape task pane)	
Text Box, Draw	WD 701	'Choose a Text Box' button (INSERT tab | Text group), 'Draw Text Box'			
Text Box, Insert	WD 444	'Choose a Text Box' button (INSERT tab | Text group)			

Microsoft Word 2013 Quick Reference Summary *(continued)*

Task	Page Number	Ribbon	Other On-Screen Element	Shortcut Menu	Keyboard Shortcut
Text Box, Insert Sidebar	WD 552	'Choose a Text Box' button (INSERT tab | Text group)			
Text Box, Link	WD 556	Create Link button (DRAWING TOOLS FORMAT tab | Text group)			
Text Box, Position	WD 449		Drag text box		
Text Direction, Change	WD 702	Text Direction button (DRAWING TOOLS FORMAT tab | Text group)		Format Shape, TEXT OPTIONS tab (Format Shape task pane)	
Text Effect, Apply	WD 20	'Text Effects and Typography' button (HOME tab | Font group)		Font Touch mode: 'Show Context Menu' on mini toolbar, Font on shortcut menu	
Text Wrapping, Change	WD 145	Wrap Text button (DRAWING TOOLS FORMAT tab | Arrange group)	Tap or click Layout Options button on graphic	Wrap Text	
Theme, Reset	WD 680	Themes button (DESIGN tab | Themes group), 'Reset to Theme from Template' in Themes gallery			
Theme, Save	WD 680	Themes button (DESIGN tab | Themes group), 'Save Current Theme' in Themes gallery			
Theme, Set as Default	WD 618	'Set as Default' button (DESIGN tab | Document Formatting group)			
Theme Color, Customize	WD 653	Theme Colors button (DESIGN tab | Document Formatting group), Customize Colors			
Theme Colors, Change	WD 31	Theme Colors button (DESIGN tab | Document Formatting group)			
Theme Effects, Modify	WD 458	Theme Effects button (DESIGN tab | Document Formatting group)			
Theme Fonts, Change	WD 259	Theme Fonts button (DESIGN tab | Document Formatting group)			
Theme Fonts, Customize	WD 296	Theme Fonts button (DESIGN tab | Document Formatting group), Customize Fonts			
Track Changes, Enable/Disable	WD 483	Track Changes button (REVIEW tab | Tracking group)	Track Changes indicator on status bar		CTRL+SHIFT+E
Tracked Changes, Accept/Reject All	WD 491	'Accept and Move to Next' arrow (REVIEW tab | Changes group), 'Accept All Changes' or 'Reject and Move to Next' arrow, 'Reject All Changes'			

Microsoft Word 2013 Quick Reference Summary *(continued)*

Task	Page Number	Ribbon	Other On-Screen Element	Shortcut Menu	Keyboard Shortcut
Tracked Changes, Review	WD 489	Next Change button (REVIEW tab | Changes group)		Tap or click desired command on shortcut menu Touch mode: 'Show Context Menu' button on mini toolbar tap or click desired command on shortcut	
Tracked Changes, Show Single Reviewer	WD 497	Show Markup button (REVIEW tab | Tracking group), Specific People			
Tracked Changes, Simple Markup	WD 486	'Display for Review' arrow (REVIEW tab | Tracking group), Simple Markup			
Tracking Options, Change	WD 491	Change Tracking Options Dialog Box Launcher (REVIEW tab | Tracking group), Advanced Options button (Track Changes Options dialog box)			
Underline	WD 29	Underline button (HOME tab | Font group)	Underline button on mini toolbar	Font, Font tab (Font dialog box) Touch mode: 'Show Context Menu' button on mini toolbar, Font on shortcut menu, Font tab (Font dialog box)	CTRL+U
Underline Words, Not Spaces	WD 80	Font Dialog Box Launcher (HOME tab | Font group), Font tab (Font dialog box), Underline style arrow			CTRL+SHIFT+W
Undo	WD 24		Undo button on Quick Access Toolbar		CTRL+Z
Ungroup Objects	WD 706	Select objects, Group Objects button (DRAWING TOOLS FORMAT tab | Arrange group), Ungroup			
Unprotect Document	WD 678	Restrict Editing button (DEVELOPER tab | Protect group), Stop Protection button in Restrict Editing task pane			
User Name and Initials, Change	WD 334	Options (FILE tab), General (Word Options dialog box)			
Vertical Alignment	WD 571	Page Setup Dialog Box Launcher (PAGE LAYOUT tab | Page Setup group), Vertical alignment arrow (Page Setup dialog box)			
Vertical Rule between Columns	WD 436	'Add or Remove Columns' button (PAGE LAYOUT tab | Page Setup group), More Columns in Add or Remove Columns gallery, Line between check box (Columns dialog box)			

Microsoft Word 2013 Quick Reference Summary *(continued)*

Task	Page Number	Ribbon	Other On-Screen Element	Shortcut Menu	Keyboard Shortcut
Vertically, Display Text	WD 253	Text Direction button (TABLE TOOLS LAYOUT tab | Alignment group)			
Watermark, Create	WD 258	Watermark button (DESIGN tab | Page Background group)			
Webpage, Save Word Document As	WD 317	'Change File Type' (FILE tab | Export tab), 'Single File Web Page'			
Wildcards, Replace Text or Formatting Using	WD 578	Replace button (HOME tab | Styles group), More button			
WordArt, Change Fill Color	WD 416	Text Fill arrow (DRAWING TOOLS FORMAT tab | WordArt Styles group)			
WordArt, Change Shape	WD 420	Text Effects button (DRAWING TOOLS FORMAT tab | WordArt Styles group)			
WordArt, Insert	WD 141	Insert WordArt button (INSERT tab | Text group)			
XML Format, Save Document In	WD 726	FILE tab | Save As, 'Save as type' arrow (Save as dialog box), 'Word XML Document'			
XPS Document, Create	WD 305	'Create PDF/XPS Document' (FILE tab | Export tab)			
Zoom 100%	WD 37	100% button (VIEW tab | Zoom group)			
Zoom Document	WD 35	Zoom button (VIEW tab | Zoom group)	Zoom Out or Zoom In button or Zoom level button on status bar Touch mode: Pinch or stretch		
Zoom Multiple Pages	WD 120	Multiple Pages button (VIEW tab | Zoom group)			
Zoom One Page	WD 30	One Page button (VIEW tab | Zoom group)			
Zoom Page Width	WD 7	Page Width button (VIEW tab | Zoom group)